2014 Getting Financial Aid

2014

Getting Financial Aid

Eighth Edition

The College Board, New York

About the College Board

The College Board is a mission-driven not-for-profit organization that connects students to college success and opportunity. Founded in 1900, the College Board was created to expand access to higher education. Today, the membership association is made up of over 6,000 of the world's leading educational institutions and is dedicated to promoting excellence and equity in education. Each year, the College Board helps more than seven million students prepare for a successful transition to college through programs and services in college readiness and college success — including the SAT® and the Advanced Placement Program®. The organization also serves the education community through research and advocacy on behalf of students, educators and schools.

For further information, visit www.collegeboard.org.

Editorial inquiries concerning this book should be directed to Guidance Publications, College Board, 45 Columbus Avenue, New York, NY 10023-6992.

Copies of this book are available from your local bookseller or may be ordered from College Board Publications, P.O. Box 4699, Mount Vernon, IL 62864. The book may also be ordered online through the College Board Store at www.collegeboard.org. The price is $22.99.

Distributed by Macmillan. For information on bulk purchases please contact Macmillan Corporate and Premium Sales Department at (800) 221-7945 x5442.

ISBN: 978-1-4573-0019-6

Printed in the United States of America

The College Board is committed to publishing in a manner that both respects the environment and helps preserve the Earth's resources. We seek to achieve this through eco-friendly practices, including the use of FSC and recycled paper and biodegradable materials. When you see this symbol, be assured that we are working to reduce our ecological footprint. The interior of this book is made of 100% recycled/40% PCW paper.

Contents

Preface ... vii

How to Use This Book ... ix

Part I: Financial Aid Step by Step

Yes, You Can Afford College ... 3

Step 1: Let's Go Over the Basics ... 9

Step 2: Estimate How Financial Aid Will Work for *You* ... 15

Step 3: Choosing Colleges, Thinking Costs ... 23

Step 4: Get Ready for the Forms ... 35

Step 5: Fill Out the FAFSA ... 43

Step 6: Fill Out the PROFILE (If Required) ... 57

Step 7: Fill Out Any Other Required Forms ... 69

Step 8: Make Your Special Circumstances Known ... 75

Step 9: Look for Scholarships ... 83

Step 10: Weigh the Offers ... 91

Step 11: Consider Your Out-of-Pocket Options ... 99

Once You're In College ... 115

Part II: Tables and Worksheets

Worksheet 1: Meet Your Application Deadlines ... 123

Worksheet 2: Scholarship Application Planner ... 124

Worksheet 3: Compare Your Awards ... 125

Sample Financial Aid Award Letters ... 126

Estimate Your EFC Under Federal Methodology ... 128

Contact Information for State Aid Programs ... 133

Part III: Financial Aid College by College

State-by-state descriptions of colleges ... 137

Part IV: Scholarship Lists

Academic scholarships ... 905

Art scholarships ... 913

Athletic scholarships ... 917

Music/drama scholarships ... 956

ROTC scholarships ... 961

Glossary ... 971

Alphabetical Index of Colleges ... 983

List of Figures

Fig. 1. Total Tuition, Fees, Room and Board Charges 2012–2013 4
Fig. 2. Median Annual Earnings by Education Level 5
Fig. 3. Estimated Cumulative Earnings Minus College Costs 6
Fig. 4. Undergraduate Student Aid (in billions) by Source, 2011–2012 13
Fig. 5. Distribution of Full-Time Undergraduates at Four-Year Institutions by Tuition and Fee Charges 26
Fig. 6. FAFSA PIN Site 40
Fig. 7. FAFSA on the Web 45
Fig. 8. Finding a College's Federal Code 48
Fig. 9. Finding a College's CSS Code 61
Fig. 10. Sample Financial Aid Award Letter 1 126
Fig. 11. Sample Financial Aid Award Letter 2 127

List of Tables

Table 1. Average Estimated Undergraduate Budgets, 2012–2013 28
Table 2. State Aid Deadlines 72
Table 3. Comparison of Education Savings Options 102
Table 4. Calculating Your Monthly Loan Payment 106
Table 5. Effects of Letting Interest Accrue While You're in College 107
Table 6. Comparison of Education Loan Options 108
Table 7. Federal Income Tax Benefits for Higher Education 112
Table 8. 2013–2014 Federal EFC Allowances for State Taxes 130
Table 9. Federal EFC Allowances for FICA and Employment 131
Table 10. Federal EFC Income Protection Allowance for Parents 131
Table 11. Federal EFC Adjusted Net Worth of a Business or Farm 131
Table 12. Federal EFC Education Savings and Asset Protection Allowance for Parents 132
Table 13. Federal EFC Parents' Contribution from Adjusted Available Income (AAI) 132

List of Worksheets

Worksheet 1. Meet Your Application Deadlines 123
Worksheet 2. Scholarship Application Planner 124
Worksheet 3. Compare Your Awards 125
Worksheet 4A. Estimate a Dependent Student's Expected Contribution 128
Worksheet 4B. Estimate the Parents' Expected Contribution 129

Preface

Financial aid is a great equalizer. In 2012, over $236 billion in aid was awarded from government and private sources. Coupled with the wide range of lower-cost college options available, financial aid should make a college education affordable for just about everyone.

Yet, according to the American Council on Education, each year almost *two million* students who are eligible for this boon don't even apply for it. We assume these students are either unaware of the possibility of aid, or mistakenly believe financial aid is not for them.

And many parents and students who apply for financial aid find the process to be confusing, even intimidating. Like the tax code, the forms and guidelines appear to be full of exceptions, convolutions and incomprehensible terms.

But it doesn't have to be that way. A central aim of this book is to take the confusion and intimidation out of the process by giving clear and direct explanations of what financial aid is all about and simple, step-by-step directions for how to get it. By combining these explanations and directions with costs and financial aid facts for every accredited college that reports this data, we hope this book will achieve our ultimate goal of connecting students to colleges that match both their needs and their means.

Acknowledgments

We gratefully acknowledge the contributions of the many individuals who originally helped bring the first edition of this book into being. George Ochoa, our writer for Part I of this book, "Financial Aid, Step by Step," transformed a complicated and intricate subject into clear and simple prose. Renée Gernand provided leadership and editorial guidance throughout the project. Kathie Little and Jack Joyce, our resident experts on financial aid, reviewed the content and kept our course true, as did Sandy Baum, Cindy Bailey, Myra Baas Smith and Linda Peckham.

While we had the advantage of many "in-house" resources, we also relied upon the knowledge and advice of seven financial aid officers who took time from their busy schedules to give us interviews: Vincent Amoroso of the University of North Carolina at Chapel Hill (now at Johns Hopkins University), Bonnie Lee Behm of Villanova University, Elizabeth Bickford of the University of Oregon (retired), Joe Paul Case of Amherst College, Mary San Agustin of Palomar College, Mike Scott of Texas Christian University and Forrest Stuart of Rhodes College (now at Furman University). We hope you will find their insight and advice, quoted throughout Part I, as illuminating as we did.

For the current edition, we relied on our resident experts Ami Boshardt and Andrea Mravlja for help with updating the information in Parts I and II. The descriptions of colleges presented in Part III, "Financial Aid, College by College," were compiled from the College Board's Annual Survey of Colleges in the spring of 2013. The college data were collected, edited and verified by a team of editors led by Connie Betterton and Stan Bernstein, with the assistance of Cathy Serico, Andrew Costello, Roger Harris and Doris Chow. Susan Bailey, Mary Anne Blazier, May Cooper, Diana McDermott, Marci Harman, Randy Peery, Leah Swaggerty and Jenny Xie compiled, edited and verified the data. Technical support was provided by Joe Antonellis, Sherry Chen, Linda DelaRosa, Robert Hargrove, Ajay Kumar, Wayne Lau, Janis Linkov-Johnson, Elizabeth Shroyer and Ant Zucaro. Finally, we would like to thank the team of programmers and composers at DataStream Content Solutions, Inc., who converted the database into readable pages.

Tom Vanderberg, Senior Editor
Guidance Publications

How to Use This Book

Part I: Financial Aid, Step by Step

The first chapter, "Yes, You Can Afford College," establishes our central point: a college can be found to fit any budget. If you are skeptical about that, please start here — we think we make a strong case.

Steps 1 through 11 provide easy-to-follow directions on how to get financial aid, including what you need to know, what you need to do and when you need to do it.

These "steps" are presented in a logical sequence. But depending upon your own circumstances — where you are in the college application process, your family's finances, what kinds of colleges you're applying to, and the policies of those individual colleges — you may need to take the steps in a slightly different order, skip some steps or do some steps simultaneously. To keep track of what should be done when, consult the planning calendar on the inside front cover.

Financial aid officers and the forms you need to fill out often use jargon that can at times seem vague or confusing. Terms like "need" and "cost of attendance" have specific meanings that might not be the same as what you would assume. Throughout Part I, you'll find key terms defined in "Know the Lingo" sidebars (you'll also find a detailed, comprehensive glossary at the end of this book). Other sidebars emphasize or illustrate the main points of each step.

Throughout Part I, you'll find graphs and charts that also illustrate key points, and tables that summarize information and let you compare different financial aid options. You'll also find checklists and prefilled sample worksheets that will help you plan and keep track of your applications. Blank copies of those worksheets for you to fill in are in Part II.

Part II: Tables and Worksheets

One of the worksheets that you'll find in Part II will help you compare the financial aid award letters that you'll receive from colleges. To drive home the point that no two award letters are alike, we've included two samples in Part II, immediately after the comparison worksheet. These are actual award letters that were sent to the same aid applicant by two different universities, the names of which we've changed.

Part II also includes a series of worksheets that you can use to estimate how much the federal government will say you should pay for college out of pocket — that's your "expected family contribution" (EFC) used by colleges to award financial aid. (You'll learn more about the EFC and how it's calculated in Part I.) These worksheets are designed for dependent students and their parents. If you are an independent student, you can do the same thing with the online tools at the collegeboard.org website. Finally, in Part II you'll find lists of state aid programs, state-sponsored 529 college savings plans and other useful places to find more information.

Part III: Financial Aid College by College

This is where we help you get the "financial aid picture" at specific colleges, including scholarships the colleges offer to entering students, and required forms and deadlines. To place this picture in context, we give you brief facts about the kind of college it is, and its basic costs. This information can help you compare the colleges you are considering and find colleges that look affordable. But keep in mind that the financial aid figures are mostly based on averages, meaning many students will be above or below these benchmarks.

The college descriptions in Part III are arranged alphabetically by state or territory. Running headers at the top of each page will help you orient yourself and find schools quickly. An alphabetical index of all the colleges in the book appears in Part IV.

Every college described in this book is accredited by an agency recognized by the U.S. Department of Education. Accreditation is a process in which an outside agency ensures that a college meets certain basic standards — it's a stamp of approval on the college's teaching, facilities and administration. For financial aid purposes, accreditation by a federally recognized agency means that federal student aid dollars can be used to attend the institution.

The College Board College Handbook also includes full descriptions of the colleges in this book, going beyond the cost and financial aid details presented here to include information about admission requirements, academics, housing, student life, athletics and more.

Where the College Information Comes From

The information in the college descriptions comes from the College Board's most recent Annual Survey of Colleges, which was conducted in the spring of 2013. Every college reported its own cost and financial aid information to us. Where possible, our staff of editors verified the information by consulting third-party sources, including public university system or district offices, state education departments and the federal government's Integrated Postsecondary Educational Database System. The information presented was current at the time this book went to press in May 2013 — but be warned that it may have changed by the time you're reading this. Once you have narrowed down a list of colleges that you're interested in, you should confirm critical information, such as financial aid application deadlines and requirements, by visiting the colleges' websites or contacting their financial aid offices.

What's in the College Descriptions

Each college description begins with a shaded box that contains the name of the college, the city or town where it's located, and its website address. For every college, its six-digit "federal code" — the code you will need in order to have your FAFSA information sent to the college — appears in this box. If a college requires the College Board's CSS/Financial Aid PROFILE®, its four-digit CSS code also appears in this box. (The CSS code is the same code you use to send SAT® and SAT Subject Tests™ scores and AP® Exam scores to a college; the federal code is only used for the FAFSA.)

Below the college name box you'll find a brief summary of what type of college it is — whether it's a four-year private university, a two-year community college or a four-year culinary school run on a for-profit basis. (Definitions of all the different types of schools you might find here are in the glossary.) You'll also find information about the number of students who were enrolled in the 2012–13 school year, and the relative difficulty of obtaining admission to the college.

BASIC COSTS

"Basic Costs" lists the tuition, fees, room and board charged by the college. The date indicates the school year for which these numbers apply — if the college was unable to report final or projected figures for the upcoming school year, last year's figures are given. If the college combines tuition, fees, and room and board expenses, that single figure is given as a comprehensive fee.

It's important to note that these figures do not include other out-of-pocket costs, such as books, supplies, transportation and personal expenses. These costs can be substantial, depending upon where and how you live, and what you study. But since these costs vary widely from student to student, we felt it would be misleading to display average amounts.

FINANCIAL AID PICTURE

The core of each college's description is the information about the financial aid it offers. Again, the date indicates the school year for which the college reported numbers — either the current year or the prior year. Depending on the aid programs offered by the college and the figures they reported, you may see one or several of these elements of the financial aid picture:

- **Students with Need.** This shows how financial aid was given to students who could not afford the full cost of attending the college on their own (a full explanation of how "need" is determined is found in Part I, Step 1). The focus is on the entering freshman class but, if a college was unable to provide that breakdown, the numbers are for all undergraduates. Most colleges disclosed the average percentage of need met by financial aid packages, and the relative proportion of aid given as scholarships and grants as opposed to loans or work-study jobs. Use this data to get a sense of how likely a college is to meet your full need, and how much aid will probably come in the form of loans.
- **Students Without Need.** Even though a student does not need financial aid, it's still possible that a college will provide aid based on merit or other criteria, such as alumni affiliation or minority status. That's what is shown here. If a college has a policy of only awarding aid to students who have need, this is also stated here.
- **Scholarships Offered.** This gives details on merit scholarships offered by the college and their criteria for being awarded. Here you can get a sense of whether your GPA or SAT scores put you in the right ballpark for a merit-based grant. You'll also find information about the number of student-athletes who were given a scholarship by the college, and the average award.
- **Cumulative Student Debt.** This tells you how many students borrowed money to pay for college and how much they owed, on average, when they graduated. This is another way for you to measure how much of a college's aid will be loan based. The numbers here only include student loans taken out through the college — not PLUS loans, private education loans or other borrowing done through a third-party lender.

FINANCIAL AID PROCEDURES

The financial aid application forms required by the college, and the priority date and/or deadlines that the financial aid office has set, appear here. This section also includes information about notification — that is, when you can expect to hear back from the financial aid office after applying, and by when they will need your final answer about whether you'll be attending. Unless otherwise noted, all dates given in this section are for applicants who intend to enroll in the fall of 2014. If you plan to apply for admission to the spring 2015 term, contact the college's financial aid office to find out about their policies and deadlines.

CONTACT

The final section of each college description lists the mailing address of the school's financial aid office.

Part IV: Scholarship Lists

If you want to zero in on colleges that offer scholarships for your particular talents and interests, the lists in Part IV will help you do that. Arranged alphabetically by state, these lists will point you to colleges that offer scholarships for a variety of achievements. Please note that, in many cases, merit is not the only criterion used by the college when awarding aid: It may require recipients to also demonstrate financial need by submitting the FAFSA or another financial aid form.

At some colleges, every applicant is automatically considered for merit scholarships. At others, you have to specifically apply for a given scholarship. And in some cases, a scholarship is only open to you if you've been recommended by your principal, school counselor or teacher.

What's in the Scholarship Lists

Each list points to colleges that offer aid for a specific talent or area of interest.

Academics. This list names colleges that offer merit aid for academic achievement. Typical criteria include the classes you've taken, your GPA and your standardized test scores.

Art. This list includes colleges that offer merit aid for artistic ability, as reflected by grades in art classes, teacher recommendations and/or a portfolio you submit to the college.

Athletics. If a college offers scholarships for a certain sport, it will be listed here. The letters "M" and "W" indicate whether the scholarship is available to men, women or both. Please note that, at most colleges, only a very few athletes receive significant scholarships. No one should rely on athletic achievements alone to get into college or to pay for it. Instead, make sure your academic record is solid, and be sure to apply for need-based financial aid by submitting the FAFSA and any other required forms.

Music/Drama. This list includes colleges and conservatories that offer merit aid for talent in the performing arts, as reflected by grades in music, dance or drama classes; teacher recommendations; and/or an audition or a submitted tape.

ROTC. Three lists are included here, one each for the Air Force, Army and Naval Reserve Officers' Training Corps. (Marine Corps ROTC is included in Naval ROTC; the Coast Guard and Merchant Marine do not have ROTC programs.) The schools listed may not necessarily have all their ROTC programs on campus; they may have a sponsorship agreement with a neighboring college or university instead. If you enroll in ROTC, you will need to apply separately for the actual ROTC scholarship from the service branch you've chosen — the money doesn't come automatically. (For information on how much money is awarded and how to apply, consult *The College Board Scholarship Handbook*, or visit your local recruiting station.) Some colleges offer additional institutional scholarships for ROTC candidates from their own funds, beyond what's awarded by the Department of Defense.

Part I

Financial Aid Step by Step

Yes, You Can Afford College

Yes, you can afford college. How do we know? Because most colleges are not as expensive as you think. Because if a college wants you as a student, it will try to help you with financial aid. Because most students get financial aid. And because there are ways to reduce the amount you have to pay now, including working part-time and taking out loans.

This is not what everyone will tell you. You may hear discouraging words like, "Most colleges are expensive" and "You won't qualify for financial aid." People may hint that college is not worth all the trouble. The financial aid forms may look complicated and confusing.

We will show you how to get past these doubts. You *can* afford college, and we will show you how. College is worth the expense; you should apply for financial aid. With our step-by-step guide through the process, you'll sidestep confusion and be able to focus on the important decisions in front of you.

This book will help you if you have already saved some money for college — and also if you have not. It will help if you are a student, or a parent of a student. It will help if you have already decided what colleges to apply to, and also if you are not sure where you'd like to go. You may be the first in your family to consider college, or the latest in a family tradition. You might think your family doesn't make enough money to afford college, or that it makes too much to be awarded financial aid. You may have an expensive "dream college" you hope to attend, or you may be looking only for the best buy. You may plan to work or not to work, commute or live on campus, rely on your parents' money or pay your own way. No matter what your situation, you can afford college and we will help you do it.

Why You Can Afford College

Despite media hype about pricey colleges and the soaring cost of higher education, most colleges are not as expensive as you might think. In addition, the published prices of many colleges, though high, are not the whole story. If a college wants you as a student, and if you and your parents don't have enough money, the college will usually offer help so you can attend. That help is financial aid — and because of it, **a college's published tuition and fees are not what most people pay**.

Financial aid is a great equalizer, and most students benefit from it. More than two-thirds of all full-time college students receive grants or scholarships to help them foot the bill. Those grants come either from the government, the college or both, and do not have to be paid back. Many students also receive other forms of help, including federal tax credits and deductions that allow their families to keep more of their money at tax time. Thanks to all this assistance, full-time college students pay, on average, much less than the advertised price of their education. In 2012-13, for example, students at four-year private colleges paid an average net price of $13,390 in tuition and fees instead of the published price of $29,056. Students at four-year public universities received a proportionally similar discount.

Even expensive colleges are less costly than you might think because they offer more financial aid. Since a high-priced college often awards more assistance than a low-priced one, a particular student might end up paying the same out-of-pocket cost at both, or even less at the college with a higher sticker price. **That's why you shouldn't rule out your "dream college" as too expensive until you find out if it wants you and what kind of financial aid package it will give you.**

MYTH/FACT

Myth: Most colleges are expensive.

Fact: The most expensive colleges get the most media attention, which creates the illusion that all colleges are expensive. The truth is that colleges vary greatly in price, and most are much more affordable than people think, especially once financial aid is factored in.

That said, there are great deals to be found. At a public college — one supported by a state or local government — the average tuition and fees in 2012-13 were $8,655 a year. That's a 70 percent saving over the $29,056 a year charged by private colleges. Another way to save money is to spend your first two years at a community college, which is a public college that specializes in two-year education programs. Published tuition and fees at community colleges averaged just over $3,200 a year — a 63 percent saving over the average at a public four-year college.

Here's one last reason you can afford college: you don't have to pay every penny up front. You can borrow money at a low interest rate and pay it back after your studies are over. There are also ways to reduce the amount you have to pay right now. (*See Step 11 for more on these "out-of-pocket" options.*)

Figure 1:
Total Tuition, Fees, Room and Board Charges, 2012-13

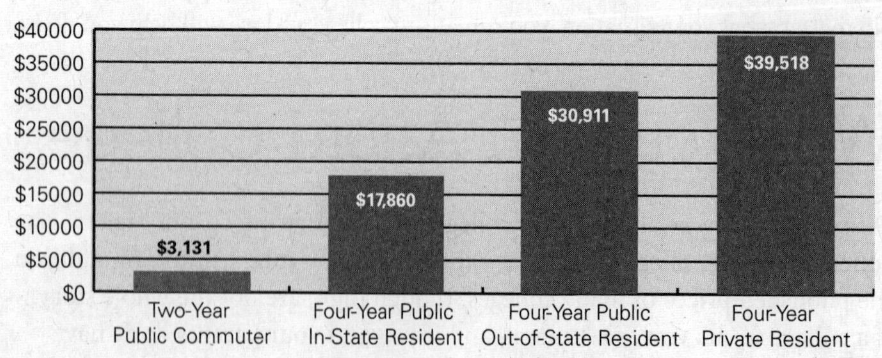

See Step 3 for more about the components of college costs.

Is College Worth It?

Even if you can afford college, is it a good idea? No matter how much financial aid you get, college will still require a sacrifice of money, time, and effort. Kids who go straight to work after high school have more spending money sooner. Does college give enough bang for the buck?

The answer is yes for many reasons including money, job insurance and personal growth.

In terms of money, college clearly pays. The difference in earnings between college graduates and high school graduates has increased sharply over the past three decades. The typical male college graduate now earns 74 percent more than the typical male high school graduate; for women, the difference is 79 percent. **College graduates earn almost twice as much over their careers than high school graduates**. Even if you borrow to pay for part of your education, it's still worth it. Provided you borrow intelligently, your increased earnings will help you pay back the loan. (*See Step 11 for more about loans.*)

You might think that the increased earnings from your college education won't make up for the total costs and the years that you won't be in the work force. But Figure 3 on the next page shows otherwise. The grey line shows the cumulative earnings at each age for the average high school graduate

Figure 2:

Median Annual Earnings by Education Level

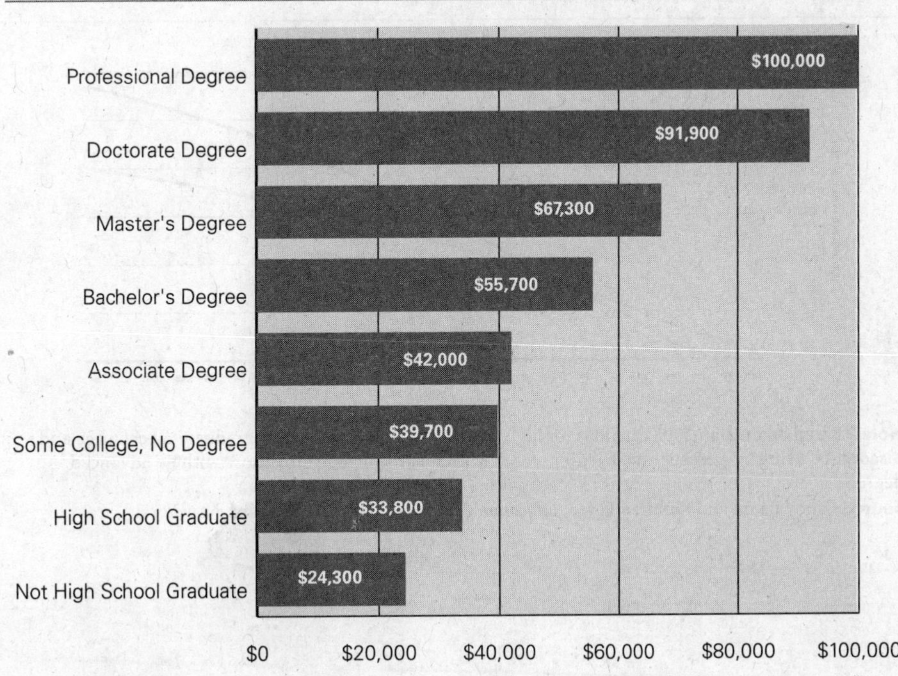

Note: Includes full-time, year-round workers age 25 and older.
Sources: U.S. Census Bureau, 2009; Internal Revenue Service, 2008; Davis, et al., 2009; calculations by the authors.

who enters the workforce full time at the age of 18. The black line shows the cumulative earnings at each age for the average four-year college graduate who enters the workforce at age 22, after subtracting average tuition and fees paid over four years at a public college or university. As you can see, by age 32 the lines intersect. From that point on, the investment in college pays off.

College also provides job insurance in a world whose economy is constantly changing. As new industries develop and many jobs are outsourced to foreign countries, you can compete better with a college degree. A college degree teaches you how to acquire knowledge and put it to use no matter what the circumstances. In fact, some higher-education credential — at least an associate degree — is a minimum to stay employed in the "knowledge economy" of the 21st century. **A mere high school diploma is obsolete; college helps to ensure employment.**

But the value of college can't be reduced to dollars alone. It involves intangibles, things you can't touch directly: how you value yourself, your dreams and your ambitions. If you are an artist, a musician, a writer, a builder, a scientist or a thinker, college will help you cultivate those talents. If you are hoping to find yourself, meet people who are more like you, and meet people who are different and interesting, college can contribute to that search too. College provides rich ground for personal growth.

On every front, as a matter of value for dollars, college is a good buy. You can afford college — and it is worth the price.

Figure 3:
Estimated Cumulative Earnings Minus College Costs

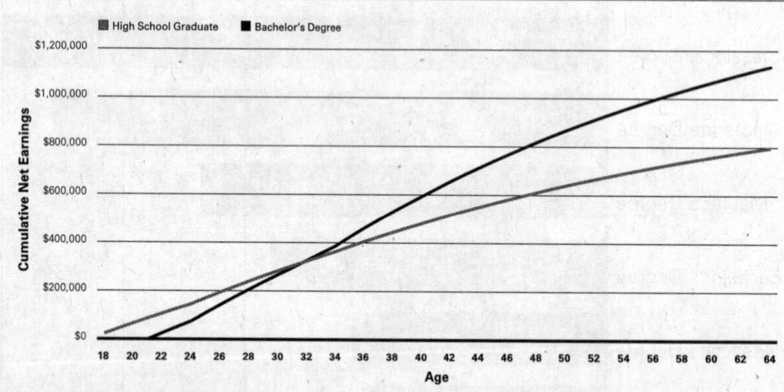

Notes: Based on median 2008 earnings for high school graduates and college graduates at each age and discounted using a 3 percent rate. Earnings for B.A. recipients include only those with no advanced degree.
Source: Sandy Baum and Kathleen Payea, *Education Pays 2010*, The College Board, New York.

How This Book Will Help You

KEEP IN MIND

Don't approach the chronology of this book too rigidly — **not all steps have to come in this order.** For example, Step 9, "Look for Other Sources of Money," can be done at any time. Since outside scholarships aren't tied to a particular college, you can start researching and applying for them before you've even made a short list of schools. In fact, this is a good idea because the application deadline for these scholarships may be as early as Nov. 1,, before most college admissions applications are due.

Through this book, you will learn how to make college affordable for you. You'll find out exactly what you need to know so you can apply for financial aid, choose an affordable college and control costs while at college. In Part I, we will walk you step-by-step through the process. There are 11 steps in all:

- **Step 1:** You'll find out the key facts about financial aid.
- **Step 2:** You'll get an idea of how much financial aid you can get.
- **Step 3:** You'll see how and why college costs vary.
- **Step 4:** You'll figure out which forms you need to fill out, and when.
- **Step 5:** You'll learn how to fill out the Free Application for Federal Student Aid (FAFSA).
- **Step 6:** You'll find out how to complete the CSS/Financial Aid PROFILE® application (called the PROFILE for short), if your colleges require it.
- **Step 7:** You'll learn how to fill out any other forms a particular college might require.
- **Step 8:** If your family has special circumstances, you'll find out the best way to explain them to colleges.
- **Step 9:** You'll learn about scholarships and other aid you can get from sources outside of a college.
- **Step 10:** You'll learn how to compare award letters from colleges and decide which offer is best for you.
- **Step 11:** You'll learn how to pay your share of the cost of college through work, loans and other means.

In Part II of the book, tables and worksheets will help you make informed decisions and stay in control of the financial aid process. Part III will paint a clear picture of the financial facts about each college you might want to investigate. That includes its costs and its approach to financial aid.

No one will tell you that paying for college is fun. But what you're getting — a college education — is worth it and is within reach. College is a big-ticket purchase that requires careful thought and preparation, like a house or a car. And it shouldn't be done in the dark. This book will guide you into one of the most important purchases you'll ever make — with your eyes wide open.

Step 1: Let's Go Over the Basics

QUICK OVERVIEW

The first step to getting financial aid is to understand the basic facts about it. In this step we will explain what financial aid is (money to help you pay for college), what types there are (the kind that comes free and the kind that doesn't), who gets it and where it comes from.

The most important point: almost everyone qualifies for at least one form of financial aid. As long as you apply, the chances are excellent that you will get some.

Just What Is Financial Aid?

KNOW THE LINGO

Grant — Money that is given away for free, usually on the basis of who needs it

Merit scholarship — Money that is given away for free on the basis of academic qualifications or special talents

Subsidized loan — Money that you have to pay back with interest; however, the federal government pays the interest for you while you are in college

Work-study — A program in which you take a part-time job to earn money for your education; the federal government pays part of your salary

Financial aid package — What a college offers to an accepted student who has applied for aid. Usually a mix of grants, loans and/or work-study.

Financial aid is money given or loaned to you to help you pay for college. Different forms have different rules. The vast majority of aid comes from the federal government, and most of it consists of loans that you must pay back. However, some aid does not require repayment — which makes it the best kind of aid to get.

If you qualify for financial aid, your college will put together an aid "package," usually with different types of aid bundled together. You and your parents will almost certainly still have to pay something, but the aid package will help. Most students qualify for some form of financial aid, so it makes sense to apply for it.

You'll apply for financial aid either at the same time or soon after you apply for admission. You may have to fill out more than one application. At the very least you will fill out the FAFSA, the federal government form. You may also fill out another form, the PROFILE, which many colleges require. And some colleges and state aid agencies require their own financial aid forms, too. The colleges to which you apply will use the forms to figure out what your family can afford to pay and what your "need" is — that is, the difference between what you can pay and what the college actually costs. If the school wants you as a student but sees that you can't handle the whole bill, it will make you a financial aid offer to help you meet your need. If you accept, that financial aid package is your award.

You will need to apply for financial aid every year that you are in college, mainly because your family's financial situation changes yearly. As a result, your financial aid package will probably be somewhat different from year to year.

Financial aid is a helping hand, not a free pass. In the United States, everyone has a right to a free public school education, but not to a free college education. The federal government and most colleges agree that students and their parents are the ones most responsible for paying for college. "The primary responsibility of paying for the student's education lies with the student and his or her parents," says Forrest M. Stuart, the director of financial aid at Furman University in Greenville, S.C. "Financial aid comes in to fill that gap, if you will, between what they can afford and what the college costs." Even so, financial aid can be the deciding factor in whether or not a student attends college.

Types of Aid

Financial aid may come in many forms. However, all forms can be grouped into two major categories: gift aid and self-help aid.

GIFT AID

Gift aid is free money, money that you don't have to pay back or work for. Naturally, this is the kind of aid most people want. It can take the form of grants or scholarships.

The terms "grant" and "scholarship" are often used interchangeably to mean free money. But here's the difference. A grant is usually given only on the basis of need, or your family's inability to pay the full cost of college. Scholarships are usually awarded only to those who have "merit," such as proven ability in academics, the arts or athletics. Once you're in college, you may have to maintain a minimum GPA or take certain courses to continue receiving a scholarship.

SELF-HELP AID

Self-help aid is money that requires a contribution from you. That can mean paying back the money (if the aid is a loan) or working for the money (if the aid is a work-study job).

The most common form of self-help aid is also the most common of any form of financial aid: the loan. A loan is money that you have to pay back with interest. In light of that, you might not consider this aid at all. But it is — a loan means you don't have to pay the full price of college all at once: You can stretch the payments over time, as you would when buying a house or a car. Furthermore, some student loans are subsidized by the federal government. With these loans, you don't have to pay the interest that comes due while you're in college. The federal government subsidizes, or helps to pay, the loan by paying that interest while you're enrolled and for the first few months after you graduate.

EXPERT ADVICE

"One of the **most important things for students** to understand is what loans are about, and what indebtedness means, so that they don't stumble through four years of college having signed promissory notes blindly, and then come to the end of their senior year and say, I really owe that much money? They should know that they have to pay loans back, and they should **think about their total indebtedness** in relation to what their prospective income is and how it might affect some life choices."

— Joe Paul Case, dean and director of financial aid, Amherst College, Amherst, Mass.

Subsidized loans, which are awarded based on need and administered by the college, are the best kind. But you can also take out unsubsidized student loans and parent loans, which are not packaged by most colleges. However, be careful not to take on more debt than necessary. No matter what kind of loan you take out, you will have to pay it back.

Another form of self-help is work-study. This is financial aid in the form of a job. Since you earn the money through your work, this too may not seem like aid. But it is, because the federal work-study program pays most of your wages. And work-study jobs are usually available right on campus, with limits on your hours so that you won't be unduly distracted from studying.

Aid can also come in the form of tax cuts — income tax deductions and credits for education. But colleges don't award this variety, and you don't apply for it in the same way as you would loans or grants, so we will discuss it separately, in Step 11.

Who Gets Aid?

Grants and loans are not just for the poorest of the poor, nor are scholarships only for the smartest of the smart. The truth about who gets financial aid is somewhat different from what many people think.

Those Who Need It

Most financial aid is based on need, not merit. There is money for merit, but since the 1950s most colleges in the United States have focused their financial aid packages on meeting financial need.

However, there is a lot of confusion about what need means. Many people think it means a state of dire poverty, so that no working-class or middle-class student need apply. "A lot of people think that they either have to be on welfare or Social Security — really poor — to get financial aid, and that's not correct," says Mary San Agustin, director of financial aid and scholarships at Palomar College in San Marcos, Calif. On the other hand, some rich families mistakenly think they are needy because their high living expenses leave them little money for college. "It's this expectation of, I pay my taxes, so my kid should be entitled to some federal financial aid regardless of how much money I make," says Ms. San Agustin.

Need simply means that your family can't afford to pay the full cost of a particular college. The *amount* of your need will vary from college to college, because it depends on the cost of attending an individual college. Whether your family has need is determined not by whether you think you are rich or poor, but by the financial aid forms you fill out.

Just fill out the forms. If you do have need, you will be considered for financial aid.

Those Who Don't

Despite the overall emphasis on need, many colleges do give away money on the basis of merit. They do this to attract the students they want most, and they may award this money even if it is more than the student needs. However, in many cases, the student both needs the money and has earned it on the basis of merit.

Don't think that only geniuses get merit aid. At many colleges a "B"-average GPA can put you in the running for merit money. Sometimes a separate application for merit aid is required to put you into consideration; sometimes your application for admission is enough. In either case, don't count yourself out by not applying; apply and let the college decide.

Grants are sometimes awarded based on neither need nor merit. For example, you may get a grant if you are in a certain field of study, are a resident of the state or are a student from the same town as the college. (*See Step 9 for more about grants and scholarships.*)

Part-Time Students

Some kinds of aid are only available to students enrolled in college full time — usually 12 or more credit hours of courses per semester. But part-time students are eligible for some financial aid. For example, federal programs such as the Stafford loan require only that students be enrolled at least half-time, whereas others, like the Pell Grant, are available to students enrolled less than half-time. Also, some employers offer tuition reimbursement benefits to students who work full time and go to college part time.

KNOW THE LINGO

Merit aid — Aid awarded on the basis of academics, character or talent

Need-based aid — Aid awarded on the basis of a family's inability to pay the cost of attending a particular college

Non-need-based aid — Aid awarded on some basis other than need or merit, such as grants with eligibility requirements related to field of study or state residence

Where the Money Comes From

Financial aid comes from three basic sources: governments (both federal and state), colleges and outside benefactors.

From the Government

The lion's share of total financial aid awarded in this country comes from the federal government. Fully 74 percent of all student aid is sent from Washington. For undergraduates, the largest chunk of that consists of federal loans, which total $70 billion a year and represent 38 percent of all student aid. The loans take multiple shapes. Perkins and Stafford loans are for students, while parents may take out a PLUS loan to help pay for their children's educations.

The federal government also funds several grants, including the Pell Grant, the Supplemental Educational Opportunity Grant (SEOG), the Academic Competitiveness Grant and the SMART Grant. The Pell and SEOG are strictly needbased, while the last two are based on both need and academic criteria. The government also funds the federal work-study program.

A much smaller piece of the financial aid pie (5 percent) comes from individual state governments. Most of this aid is for use only at colleges within the state, though a few states offer "portable" aid, which state residents can take with them to a college in another state.

From the College

A great deal of financial aid comes from individual colleges, using their own "institutional" funds. In fact, colleges award nearly half of all grants. Many, though not all, award merit scholarships as well as need-based grants. They may also offer on-campus job opportunities and loans.

Private colleges give more financial aid than public ones, but their tuition is usually higher as well. Public colleges award less aid, but taxpayer support keeps their tuition lower.

Outside Grants and Scholarships

Outside grants and scholarships come from sources other than the government or the college. These sources may include corporations like Coca-Cola or community groups like the Elks Club. Some are well known, such as the National Merit Scholarship, but altogether they are the smallest piece of the financial aid pie: **only 4 percent of all student aid comes from this source.** Pursue them, but don't expect them to outweigh the other aid you will get.

Bear in mind also that your outside scholarship is unlikely to expand the total aid you receive. Most colleges will use an outside scholarship to substitute for some other piece of aid rather than increase the total aid package. Think of your financial aid package as a barrel: when the barrel is full, no more can be added unless something is taken away. The last thing colleges will take away is whatever sum of money your family is expected to contribute. However, at many colleges, the first thing taken away is self-help aid such as loans. Since that could reduce the total amount you will have to

Figure 4:
Undergraduate Student Aid (in billions) by Source, 2011-12

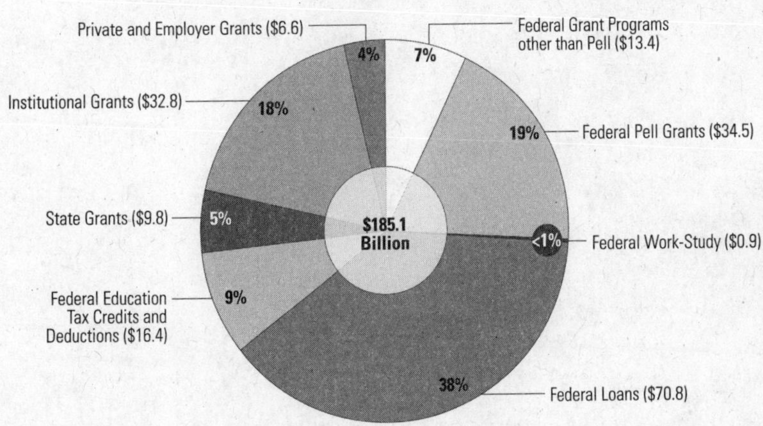

pay back later, it is worth applying for outside scholarships. (*See Step 9 for more on these sources of aid.*)

QUICK RECAP

There is a lot of financial aid out there, in many forms. Apply for it — there is a good chance you will get some. These are the main things to know about financial aid:

- It is money to help you pay for college.
- It may come in the form of a gift (grants and scholarships) or in the form of self-help (loans and work-study).
- Most people get it because they need it, though some get it solely because of merit.
- The federal government funds most of it, but states, colleges and outside sources also help.

Step 2: Estimate How Financial Aid Will Work for *You*

QUICK OVERVIEW

Only rarely does a student get a "free ride" scholarship. You and your parents will have to contribute some money to your education — the precise amount will be determined by the college's analysis of financial aid forms you'll fill out. But even before you fill out the forms, you can estimate your share of the cost and begin planning for how to pay it.

Don't Count Yourself Out

Most college students get some financial aid, but few receive exactly the same financial aid package. Financial aid packages are as individual as the financial circumstances of the students who apply. One family makes $50,000 a year and has two children, a house and a savings account; another makes $50,000 a year but has only one child, a rented apartment and no savings. What financial aid package will each family receive? The answer: It depends on several factors. Families must first submit their applications for consideration by the colleges.

"Probably the question I'm most often asked is, 'Is there a cutoff?'" says Joe Paul Case, the dean and director of financial aid at Amherst College in Amherst, Mass. Financial aid officers agree that there is no single salary cutoff for financial aid — no one income figure that will definitely exclude a student from receiving financial aid. Income is only one criterion for giving out aid: Colleges also consider such factors as family size, number of children in college, and savings. Many students who would be eligible for financial aid fail to apply because they don't realize this.

EXPERT ADVICE

"We always encourage students to **go ahead and apply** for financial aid even though you may not qualify for anything but a student loan. **At least get the paperwork in**, because if something happens in the middle of the year, we already have the financial aid data we need to make adjustments."

— Forrest M. Stuart, director of financial aid, Furman University, Greenville, S.C.

"I always tell families, don't cut yourself off from the application process," says Bonnie Lee Behm, the director of financial assistance at Villanova University in Villanova, Pa. "Apply and let it work through the system."

Even if you feel absolutely sure that your family doesn't qualify for financial aid, fill out the forms. Your family circumstances might change suddenly — a lost job, health problems, a new child. Then you may need financial aid, and it will help to be in the system already. A college can assist you faster if your financial aid application is on file.

What "Expected Family Contribution" Means

Even though you probably will qualify for financial aid, it's unlikely that you will get the fabled "full ride." Colleges do sometimes award full tuition — or even full room and board — to a student they greatly want to attract, but that is rare. Almost always, the family is expected to contribute some money. The exact dollar amount will be based on the family's ability to pay. That dollar amount is the expected family contribution, or EFC.

The EFC is carefully calculated to determine what you can afford to pay based on your financial circumstances — no more and no less. The formulas that the federal government and colleges use to calculate EFC are also calibrated to take into account varying costs of living across the country.

In some ways, the concept of EFC works in your favor. No matter what a college costs, so long as it awards you the full financial aid you need you won't have to pay more than your EFC — the amount your family is able to pay. Say your EFC is $8,000. At a college with a total cost of attendance of $11,000, you could get up to $3,000 in financial aid. At a college where the total cost is $25,000, you could get up to $17,000 in aid. **Because of financial aid, any college is at least worth considering; no college should be ruled out in advance as too expensive.**

On the other hand, even though the expected family contribution is based on ability to pay, that does not simply mean how much the family would like to pay. For any purchase, most people would *like* to pay zero dollars. But what they are *able* to pay is how much money they have minus how much they need to keep for other things, such as food, rent, heat and retirement. When colleges award financial aid, they calculate your ability to pay by looking at your income and financial assets as you lay them out in your financial aid application. Using what are called need-analysis formulas, they analyze your data to see how much of the college costs you are able to pay (your EFC) and how much you are unable to pay (your need). How much you would like to pay is not part of the calculation.

Costs – EFC = Need

Your expected family contribution is your family's share of college costs. Any cost greater than that is your need. Need varies from college to college because it depends on the cost of the individual college. **It's simple arithmetic: College costs minus your EFC equals the amount of aid you need.** At colleges that award enough financial aid to meet your need, the aid package will equal the amount of your need. Costs minus aid equals what you pay.

KEEP IN MIND

If a college offers you a financial aid award that doesn't meet your full need, you may be able to fill the "gap" in your package with an **outside scholarship**. For more on outside scholarships, see Step 9.

Unmet Need (a.k.a. "Gap")

Unfortunately, not all colleges will award enough aid to meet your full need. Some colleges may "gap" your package — that is, not meet your full need. Economics plays a part here. While some colleges may have enough aid dollars available to meet every student's full need, some colleges lack such funds. If your college cannot meet your full need, costs minus aid will still equal what you pay. But what you pay will be more than your EFC. (*See Step 11 for more information on loans* and other ways to help fill such a gap.)

If you do encounter a "gap" in your award, compare the package with the ones you've gotten from other schools, and consider your priorities. Do you want to go to that college, no matter the cost? Or does cost matter more? (*For more on this topic, see Step 10.*)

It Depends on the College

The amount of aid you get — along with the kind of aid you get, whether gift or self-help — ultimately depends on the college. Formulas and forms are important, but so is the professional judgment of the financial aid officer. And so is the desire of the college to attract you to its campus.

How Colleges Calculate Your Need

As you saw in Step 1, financial aid comes from two main sources: government money (usually in the form of loans and work-study), and the college's own "institutional" money — usually in the form of grants and scholarships. Your financial aid package will probably contain money from both sources.

Just as there are two main sources of aid, there are two main formulas that colleges use to figure out how much aid you should get. One is called the "Federal Methodology," used for aid coming from government money. Most colleges use it to award their own institutional funds as well. The Federal Methodology is based on the FAFSA, the federal financial aid form.

For aid coming out of their own money, some colleges and scholarship programs use a different formula called the "Institutional Methodology." This is based on the PROFILE (more formally known as the College Board's CSS/Financial Aid PROFILE application) and/or the college's own financial aid application form. (*For more about these forms, see Steps 6 and 7.*) Colleges that use the Institutional Methodology do so because they think it presents a fuller picture of your family's financial situation. "I just think it does a much better job of measuring ability to pay," says Forrest M. Stuart, whose institution, Furman University, requires the PROFILE.

So what does all this mean to you? The differences between the two formulas make it possible that your expected family contribution will be lower under one or the other; it all depends on your individual family circumstances, and the individual college(s) you are applying to. You don't have to know how these formulas work or remember what they are called. The thing to remember is that if you apply to several colleges, because of these different formulas you might end up with a different EFC for one college than you do for another.

KNOW THE LINGO

EFC (Expected Family Contribution) — How much money a family is expected to pay for college.

Need — The difference between your EFC and the cost of attending a particular college you've chosen. Financial aid is designed to meet your need, not your EFC.

Unmet need — The difference (if any) between the your need and the financial aid offered by a particular college. Informally, unmet need is also called a **gap**.

Asset protection allowance — The amount of money considered reasonable to set aside for educational savings and emergencies, and is therefore not part of your EFC.

Will College Savings Count Against You?

While some families save diligently for their children's college educations, others think this is a mistake. They worry that having a lot of savings will keep colleges from awarding financial aid. **But savings help you more than they hurt you**, and here is why.

When calculating your EFC, colleges subtract what they call an "asset protection allowance" from the amount you have saved. This "allowance" is the amount of money considered reasonable to set aside for educational savings and family emergencies. These "free" savings are not assessed at all. In Federal Methodology, the allowance varies based on the age of the oldest parent, and it can be several tens of thousands of dollars for a married couple in their 40s or 50s. These savings are clearly worth having, since they aren't included when calculating your EFC. (See Table 12 on page 136 to get an estimate of what your parents' asset protection allowance may be.)

Even if your family saves more than the asset protection allowance, those savings will be assessed at a maximum rate of only 5.6 percent. So even if 5.6 percent of your excess savings count "against" you when it comes to federal need determination, 94.4 percent count "for" you. You can use them to meet your expected contribution, whatever it turns out to be. That's good news, because your family will be expected to pay much more out of income than out of savings. Most colleges will expect your parents to contribute between 22 and 47 percent of their income toward your EFC.

Essentially, your family will be expected to pay some part of your college costs out of pocket, and if you have savings, you have a pot to draw from. The alternatives are to pay it out of your monthly income or to borrow it — both of which are less appealing choices than using savings. "If I were preparing to send a son or daughter off to school, I would want to have as much savings available to me as I realistically could," says Vincent Amoroso, director of the Office of Student Financial Services at Johns Hopkins University. "The reason is because, just like in other situations, having money on hand makes it easier for me to make choices that are good for myself and my child."

To be sure, there are other factors your family should consider before saving for college, such as whether they have enough money to save for retirement. But if they can put away any money for college, they should do so without hesitating. (*See Step 11 for information on tax-free college savings plans.*)

Responsibilities Within the Family

Who should pay for college? Is it entirely the parents' duty, or should the student be responsible? If both, which combination of both? There is no single right answer to questions like these. But families need to discuss the topic, and the sooner the better. Your college will expect someone in the family to make a contribution, and you and your parents should figure out who that is before the bill comes due.

"Families should discuss college costs, family budget, financial aid and financing options at the beginning of the college application process, not at the end," says Carlene Riccelli, a college adviser at Amherst Regional High School in Amherst, Mass. Try to reach decisions that are as specific as possible, so that you each know what's expected of you. Try to make the decisions fair, so that no one feels used. What portion of your summer job income should go toward college? If your family takes out loans, should they be in your name your parents' name or both? Don't forget to discuss ways of keeping costs down, such as living at home and taking community college courses.

If your family is nontraditional, the discussion should include all adults involved in your care. When considering the financial need of students with divorced parents, for example, some colleges that use the Institutional Methodology will assess the income and assets of both natural parents. It will be up to the family to decide how to pay the expected family contribution, but part of that contribution will be based on the income and assets of the parent without custody. (*See Step 8 for more about parental custody and financial aid.*)

While it's important to talk about money, your family also needs to talk about other aspects of choosing a college, such as its academic and social environment. Some of the discussion will have nothing to do with money, but others will have financial aspects: for example, going away to an expensive college versus staying home and commuting to a cheaper one. Step 3 will further explore how to think about these issues. But the important thing is to start having the discussions — financial and otherwise — as early as possible.

Crunch Some Numbers

If you want a sneak peek at what your expected family contribution will be, crunch some numbers. Part II contains worksheets and tables that you can use to calculate the EFC of a "typical" family under the Federal Methodology. Use the worksheets to add up your income, then subtract deductions and allowances. Total up your assets, too. Apply the formulas in the worksheets to calculate the contribution that is expected from you as a student. Then use the next set of worksheets and tables to calculate your parents' expected contribution. When you're finished, you will have your estimated EFC.

The figure you come up with will only be an estimate. Your actual EFC may be higher or lower, depending on the exact data you ultimately submit and the particular college's financial aid policies. But at least this exercise will give you a ballpark figure for what you can expect to pay.

Online Calculators

If you'd prefer to estimate your EFC online, there are several websites with special calculators. They include:

- **collegeboard.org** — Our Net Price Calculator lets you "Do the Math" on EFC and to compare your out-of-pocket expenses from one college to another.
- **College and university websites** — These sites also include calculators geared to their individual financial aid policies.

Your Unique Situation Counts Too

Colleges expect families to contribute some money toward students' education, and the amount they expect is your EFC. But colleges are not just faceless buildings of stone, and your EFC is not fixed in cement. The financial aid officer in charge of distributing a college's financial aid is a human being, and he or she does have some room to adjust how the EFC calculations are made based on your individual circumstances.

Step 8 will go into greater detail on how to notify your college about changes in your family's financial situation, such as a lost job. And Step 10 will discuss how to appeal if you think the college hasn't taken all your circumstances into account. Generally, financial aid officers are sympathetic if you are struggling with problems such as caring for an elderly parent or a lost job. They will be less sympathetic if it seems that you've chosen your financial problems — such as buying a new motorcycle with money that could have gone to pay your college bill. Still, financial aid officers are not heartless, and they will try to help when there is genuine distress.

QUICK RECAP

The American education system expects families to bear as much responsibility for the costs of higher education as they can, but not more. Your family will have to contribute to your college costs, but will also receive help.

- Your family will be required to pay an expected family contribution, or EFC.
- The costs of the college you attend minus the financial aid you receive equals what you pay.
- College savings will not be held against you.

Step 3: Choosing Colleges, Thinking Costs

QUICK OVERVIEW

This step shows you how to think about cost when choosing a college. You'll see why you shouldn't exclude any college from consideration just because of its price. You'll learn what your different college expenses will be, from tuition to pizza money; how costs can vary from college to college; and how to factor in the financial aid package the college is likely to give.

How to Think About College Costs

When you're thinking about where to apply for college, its "list price" should not be the main consideration. Because financial aid will probably be available to help meet your need, even a college that appears exorbitant may in fact be within reach. A college's published costs are only one part of the equation when it comes to what you'll actually pay. **Until you've applied for and received an offer of financial aid, you won't know the real cost to your family.**

Remember that financial aid works like this: Total cost of attendance *minus* your family's expected family contribution (EFC) *equals* your financial need. As long as the college meets your need, the amount you pay stays the same whatever the price of the college. "I don't think college cost really should be a factor in where students apply for admission," says Vincent Amoroso of Johns Hopkins University. "I say that because your family contribution, in theory, is the same whether you apply to a school that costs $4,000 or to a school that costs $40,000."

In practice, your expected family contribution may actually vary somewhat from college to college. As noted in Step 2, a college using the Federal Methodology to assess your ability to pay might calculate a higher or lower EFC than a college that uses the Institutional Methodology. Even two institutions using the same methodology might calculate slightly different EFCs, depending on how they have treated any special circumstances that may apply to your family. (*See Step 8 for more on special circumstances.*) But

KNOW THE LINGO

Total cost of attendance — Not just tuition, but also all fees, room and board, transportation, books and supplies, and personal expenses.

Public college — A college or university that is subsidized by taxes and other public revenues and governed by a county, state or federal government agency.

Community college — A two-year public college subsidized by a local government, such as a county or city.

Out-of-state tuition — What public colleges charge students from other states; often more than double the rate for in-state residents.

Reciprocity agreement — A deal between neighboring states that allows residents to attend a public college in either state at the in-state tuition rate.

in general, the principle holds that your EFC will be constant from college to college, while your need will vary depending on the price of each college.

The main thing to consider when applying for college is whether you and that school will be a good fit. Look for the academic and social aspects that are likely to make you happy and successful there. Are you artistic? Are you mathematical? Do you love to learn for learning's sake? Do you have strong career ambitions in a particular field? Do you long to get away and see the world? Or does it matter more to stay near your family and the place where you grew up? "Students should not just look at a school because it's affordable," says Bonnie Lee Behm of Villanova University. "They should look at a school because it's the right fit for them academically, socially, spiritually and physically. Is cost an important part? Yes. It's a consideration, but only one among many." **And remember — you can find a good fit at more than one college.**

To discover what specific colleges have to offer, research them. You can find a lot of information about majors offered, the composition of the student body, academic policies, and extracurricular and athletic offerings in *The College Board College Handbook*. You can also learn more on the College Search engine on collegeboard.org, and from college guidebooks and websites. If you know people who have gone to the colleges you're considering, talk to them and get their opinions.

So, when deciding which colleges to apply to, don't focus too much on cost. But do be aware of what the costs are; cost may become a factor depending on what financial aid packages you are ultimately offered. Even though your EFC should in principle be the same at all colleges, not all schools always meet full need. And even those that do may meet it with different packages — some with more loans, others with more grants. It makes sense to know what kinds of packages a particular school is likely to give.

By using Part III of this book as a guide, and also by contacting the admissions and financial aid offices of the colleges you're considering, gather as much information as you can about the costs of the school and the type of aid they offer. The rest of Step 3 suggests the kinds of information you should be seeking from each school.

Choosing Colleges

Both you and your parents should be involved in the discussion about where to apply for college. You will share the responsibility for paying for college, so you should all have a voice. Furthermore, your parents can give you good advice about what colleges to consider based on their life experiences, their knowledge of you, and their understanding of the family finances — even if they themselves have never been to college. The deciding vote, however, should be yours. You are the one who will have to start and finish college, and you are more likely to do so successfully if you have chosen the college yourself. "Only the student knows the fit that he or she will have at a particular institution academically, socially and financially as well," says Forrest Stuart of Furman University.

When you begin choosing where to apply, don't exclude any college. Let every college be on the table, even if it seems too difficult academically or financially. Aim high. Shop around. The best colleges for you may not be the ones that occur to you first.

If a college is a good fit for you, there is probably a way to make it work financially. "Apply to those colleges that you think, okay, maybe we could afford these, but also apply above that level, because some schools may be much more manageable than you expect," says Bonnie Lee Behm of Villanova University.

Do Consider a "Financial Safety"

KNOW THE LINGO

Need-blind admission — If a college has a "need-blind admission" policy, this means that it will admit a student solely on the basis of his or her academic merit or other characteristics, regardless of their ability to pay. However, it does not mean the college guarantees to meet full need. You may be admitted, but the college may be unable to offer a financial aid package equal to your need.

Even though all colleges should be on the drawing board, you should also consider applying to a financial "safety" school — one that is a good academic fit and that you feel fairly confident you can afford. Your financial safety school is one you would be happy attending and that has either low published costs or will almost certainly offer enough grant money to make attendance affordable. A public university in your state, a local community college or a private university where you are highly likely to win a merit scholarship might all be financial safeties.

A financial safety is a good idea because your top choices may not give you as much financial aid as you want. "We know students who are really strong academically, but they're not at the top of their class, and they apply to the college of their dreams," says Elizabeth Bickford, director of the Office of Student Financial Aid and Scholarships at the University of Oregon in Eugene. Despite their hopes for a full merit scholarship, such students may find that they can enroll only if they are willing to take out a large amount in unsubsidized loans — something their family may not be willing to do.

In these and other situations, a financial safety is a good backup. For example, if you accept admission to a far-off university, but find that you can't get used to it and want to come back to the financial safety school near home, it will be easier to transfer if you've already applied and been admitted. Still, Elizabeth Bickford says she encourages students to "dream large, because it's your one opportunity. When you go from high school to that first year in college, that's where most of the scholarships are — for entering freshmen. It's your opportunity to make that big step away from home."

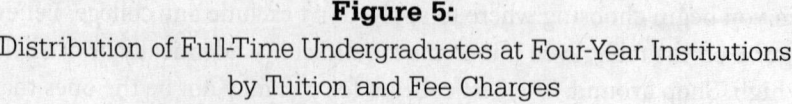

Figure 5:
Distribution of Full-Time Undergraduates at Four-Year Institutions by Tuition and Fee Charges

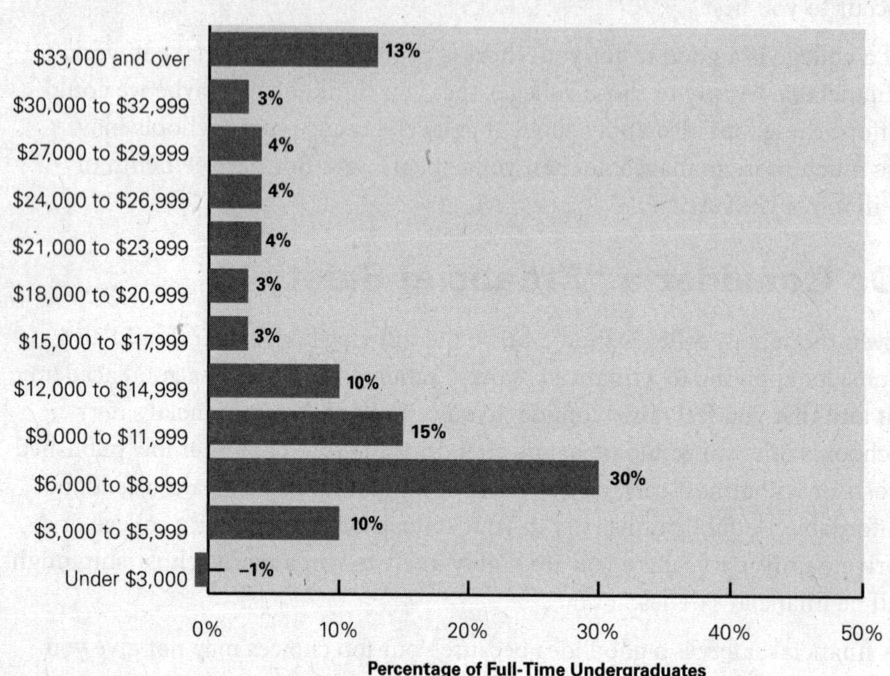

Forty-one percent of full-time undergraduates attend colleges with published tuition and fee charges of under $9,000. After financial aid, many of those students pay an even lower "net price" for tuition.

Source: *Annual Survey of Colleges*, The College Board, New York

Components of College Costs

The price of a college education has several parts. The most obvious is tuition, the cost of taking courses. Tuition varies depending on how many courses you take, but full time students pay a flat rate for a full schedule of courses. If you attend part time, you will likely pay by credit hours, a measure of how long each class is. Most courses are three credit hours apiece, which usually translates to three one-hour classes each week. Most full-time students take an average of four or five courses per semester, for a total of 12 to 15 credit hours per semester for a full load.

Fees are another component of college costs. Fees are usually billed to all students as funding for the college's general expenses, such as the library or student activities. But there may be additional special fees for students enrolled in certain classes or activities. A chemistry student may pay lab fees, for example.

Tuition and fees are just one part of what you'll pay for college, and often not even half. Another large component is room and board. "Room" is the cost of housing you, and "board" is the cost of food. You may live in a dorm on campus, or off campus — in an apartment or a house with other students or at home with your parents. You may be on a meal plan where all your meals are prepared for you for one price, or you may fend for yourself, buying groceries and cooking meals. Either way, these basic living expenses are your room and board.

Taken together, tuition, fees, room and board are the largest chunk of college costs. On average, at four-year public colleges across the nation, these elements together make up 80 percent of what students pay for college — tuition and fees 39 percent, room and board 41 percent. Yet there is still another 20 percent of costs to be accounted for. These include:

- Books and supplies — class expenses that are not covered by tuition and will vary depending on the courses you take.
- Transportation expenses — for on-campus students, this is the cost of trips home during holidays; for commuters, this is the cost of either mass transit or a car. Car costs include parking, gas, insurance and maintenance.
- Computer equipment costs — if required by the college. Some colleges may insist that you buy a certain model of computer, or bring your own computer but have special hardware and software installed to make it work on the campus network.
- Personal expenses — everything from snacks outside the meal plan to newspaper subscriptions to haircuts and toothpaste to membership fees for student groups.

How Costs Can Vary

Each college has different price tags for each of the cost components. For example, books and supplies might cost $1,200 for a typical student at a state university, but $2,500 or more at an art school. Table 1 on page 28 shows national averages for cost components.

To get specifics for a particular college that you're considering, check its website and look for the school's published estimate of what the average student spends on the different expense categories. The college will use these averages as part of the calculation of your "total cost of attendance," which will partly determine how much aid you're awarded. You can also consult Part III of this book for a school-by-school summary of costs.

However, remember that these average costs are only averages. You are an individual, and you may pay more or less than average, depending on your individual circumstances. For example, if you attend college in California but your family lives in New York, you will pay more for traveling to and from home than if your family is also in California.

Textbook and supply costs can also vary widely depending on your major. If you are an architecture or drafting student, you might have to buy an expensive computer-aided design program that your English major friends won't need. Science students might need to buy a statistical-modeling software package; studio artists a graphic-design suite. At least software like this only has to be bought once and is then used to do work for several classes; furthermore, educational discounts may be available for such purchases. In some programs, students might have to buy supplies that frequently get used up and must be replenished, such as brushes and paints for art students.

Rooming costs will vary a little between different dorm complexes on campus — for example, newer dorms may cost more, and a single room is always more expensive than one shared with a roommate. There will also be differences between various off-campus rooming locations.

Finally, your personal expenses may be higher or lower than average depending on lifestyle factors — but they will almost always be higher than you think. As James Schembari wrote in the *New York Times*, there is always a need for "pizza money" — money to buy pizza, go on a road trip, or hang out at the student union. Books, supplies, travel and everyday expenses "can add $3,000 or more a year, depending on parents' generosity and where their child goes to college," wrote Mr. Schembari.

Table 1:

Average Estimated Undergraduate Budgets, 2012-13

SECTOR	TUITION AND FEES	BOOKS AND SUPPLIES	ROOM AND BOARD	TRANSPOR-TATION	OTHER EXPENSES	TOTAL EXPENSES*
Public Two-Year						
Resident	$3,131	$1,229	$7,419	—	$2,157	$14,701
Commuter	$3,131	$1,229	—	$1,648	$2,157	$8,165
Public Four-Year						
Resident	$8,655	$1,200	$9,205	$1,110	$2,091	$22,261
Commuter	$8,655	$1,200	—	$1,110	$2,157	$13,122
Out-of-State	$21,706	$1,200	$9,205	$1,110	$2,091	$35,312
Private Four-Year						
Resident	$29,056	$1,244	$10,462	$957	$1,570	$43,289
Commuter	$29,056	$1,244	—	$1,648	$2,157	$34,105

Note: Estimates of individual budget items are based on reporting by institutional financial aid offices.
Source: *Annual Survey of Colleges*, The College Board, New York, N.Y.

Ways to Reduce Costs

There are a few time-tested ways of saving money on some of the major cost components of college. To save money on tuition and fees, many students have attended public colleges and community colleges. To save money on room and board, many have commuted rather than roomed on campus. Here are the pros and cons for these money-saving techniques.

Public vs. Private, In-State vs. Out-of-State

GOOD TO KNOW

This section discusses ways to **find inexpensive colleges** during your college search. For tips on how to cut costs once you've enrolled, see Step 11.

Attending a public college in your own state is an excellent way to save money on tuition and fees. Public colleges are subsidized by state taxes, so their tuition and fees for state residents are usually much less than at private colleges — 70 percent less, on average. Depending on the school, the quality of education may be as good or even better than what you would get at a private college.

On the other hand, the true cost picture is more complicated than it looks. Even though private colleges charge more for tuition and fees, most of them also give more scholarships and grants than public colleges do, which helps to even out the costs. "There's an adage that the more expensive the school, the more money they give away," says Mike Scott of Texas Christian University, a private institution.

Cost isn't everything. If a particular private school has some valuable characteristic that you want — smaller classes, professors with whom you want to study — it may be worth the extra tuition money. But cost is a factor to consider. If a certain state school can give you all that you want from college, why not go there and save some money?

If you would like to study at a public college or university in another state, be aware that most public schools charge higher tuition to students from out of state than they do to in-state students. Public colleges currently charge an average of $8,655 in tuition and fees to a state resident, but $21,706 to an out-of-state student. The in- and out-of-state rates for specific public colleges and universities are listed in Part III.

PAYING IN-STATE RATES IN ANOTHER STATE

It is sometimes possible to get the in-state tuition rate, or at least a lowered tuition rate, even if you are an out-of-state student. For example, some state universities have "reciprocity agreements" with neighboring states. South Dakota residents pay tuition rates comparable to state residents at the University of Minnesota and vice versa. There are also discipline-based "consortiums" of public colleges that let you get the in-state tuition rate at another state's public college if your desired major is not available at any public college in your own state.

Your school counselor and state board of education website can give you more information about programs for paying in-state rates in another state.

Community Colleges

Community colleges are another great way of saving money on tuition and fees. A community college is a two-year school subsidized by a state, county or city. Its cost for tuition and fees is usually much lower than that of a four-year institution — 64 percent lower, on average, than a public four-year college. Community colleges often charge tuition in three tiers — in district, in state and out of state — with the lowest price for those who live in the local district. Though most community colleges do not offer a four-year bachelor's degree (though the number that do are on the rise), they do provide courses whose credits can be transferred toward a bachelor's degree at another college. Because those courses cost much less, this can be a way to save money in your first two years of college — money you can use to help pay for the last two years. Four out of 10 college-bound high school graduates start their college education this way.

There are other reasons to attend a community college besides saving money. If you aren't sure whether you want to go to a four-year college, a community college will give you a sense of what the college experience is like. If you don't know what kind of program you want to pursue — science, art, business or something else — you can explore different subject areas at a community college before committing to a program. And if you need to be able to work, perhaps to support a family, you can work out a more flexible schedule at a community college, where many students work full time and attend classes at night and on weekends.

A community college is also a golden opportunity for students who didn't do well enough in high school to win admission to the college of their choice. Community colleges are open to everyone, and some have agreements with four-year colleges that guarantee admission in the third year for students who have maintained good grades. This is the case in California, according to Mary San Agustin of Palomar College, a community college. If students, she says, "have their heart set in going, let's say, to Stanford or U.C. Berkeley, we have an excellent articulation program that allows them to take the two-year required courses and get guaranteed admissions in their junior year at those schools that they prefer to go to." In this way, **a community college can open the door to a four-year college for you.**

Of course, there are advantages to entering a four-year college as a freshman rather than two years later as a transfer from a community college. Socially and academically, you may enjoy a fuller college experience. "It's all the things that you can't quite name," says Elizabeth Bickford of the University of Oregon. "There is something that you do lose in that transition as an 18- or 19-year-old." But those factors have to be balanced against financial realities, as Ms. Bickford found when she was making her own college decisions. "I'm a community college transfer to a four-year myself. So is my husband. We wouldn't have financially been able to make it if we hadn't done it that way. I think it's a good way to make it if all the support isn't there."

Living at Home

An obvious way to save money on room and board is to stay home and commute to a college close by. Instead of paying for campus housing and meals — an average cost of $10,462 a year for private colleges — your housing and meal costs remain what they are.

However, commuting has hidden costs. You will have transportation expenses that you wouldn't have if you lived on campus. If you can use mass transit, these costs will probably be low enough to make economic sense. But if you have to buy a car and pay for gas and insurance, your transportation costs might end up being close to the costs of on-campus room and board. And if you're thinking of relying on family and friends for rides to and from campus, remember that their schedules may not overlap with yours. Your own schedule may change day to day and semester to semester, depending on your classes and activities. You probably will need your own car if mass transit isn't available.

Also, don't forget that you cost money at home, too. You're still eating and using utilities at home, and you'll inevitably add pick-up meals on campus to those costs. Financial aid packages usually offer help in paying for room and board as well as tuition and fees, so your actual cost for living on campus would probably not be as high as the published price.

We're not saying that commuting isn't a bargain — it usually is. (There are other good reasons to live at home, too.) But if you are thinking of commuting just to save money, don't commit to it until you weigh all the costs and assess the financial aid offers from any "live away" colleges to which you may apply.

Living Off-Campus

If you don't want to commute but still want to save money on room and board, you might want to consider living off-campus. By residing near campus in an apartment that you share with classmates, you may be able to live more cheaply than you could in the dorms. **But be sure to check the college's policies** — many do not allow freshmen to live off campus if they're under 21 and not living with their parents.

How to Factor in Financial Aid

Every college publishes an average price for the various cost components, but that published price is probably not the price you will end up paying. Your financial aid package will reduce your actual costs. Yet financial aid packages vary from college to college as much as costs do. In thinking about where you will apply, you need to find out some financial aid basics about each college on your short list. How great a percentage of need does it usually meet? How much aid does it award in grants and how much in loans? Does the college offer any merit scholarships or other forms of aid not based on need?

KEEP IN MIND

The **college profiles in Part III** of this book give the "financial aid picture" for each college, based on averages. Use these profiles to **compare colleges only**; the aid you would get at any college is based on your own individual circumstances, so the amount might be higher or lower than the average for that college.

Part III of this book, "Financial Aid College by College," gives you these financial aid basics, along with a number of other essential facts. These include:

- the school's Web address
- what type of school it is, such as public or private
- how many students are enrolled
- how selective the school is
- basic costs, including tuition, fees, room and board
- financial aid application procedures, including deadlines and required forms
- contact information for the financial aid office

In addition, the "Financial Aid Picture" section of each college's profile tells you how much aid is being distributed to how many students and in what form. This information is useful, but note that it only shows averages. Since few families are "average," the numbers in the financial aid profile shouldn't be considered a guarantee of what you'll get or how much you'll have to pay. For example, in-state students at public colleges usually borrow much less than the average debt per student listed in the profiles, while out-of-state students usually borrow more. You can, however, use the profiles to compare colleges: This college meets a greater percentage of need than most; this college awards a relatively large portion of aid in grants.

Check with the Financial Aid Office Before You Apply

Before you apply for financial aid, check with the financial aid offices of the colleges to which you're planning to apply for admission — by simply visiting their website, or by talking to them on the phone or in person. Confirm which forms you need to complete and the deadlines. Better to get these details right before you get started than to find out after the fact that you filed too late or didn't file the proper form.

Bear in mind also that each college has its own financial aid policies, such as how outside scholarships are treated and whether or not aid awards can be appealed. When you contact the office, whether long distance or in a campus visit, find out as much as you can about these policies, along with facts about costs and the financial aid process. If possible, schedule an interview with a member of the financial aid staff. They'll give you a lot of information, but don't expect them to offer you aid until they've seen your forms.

Questions to Ask Colleges

Here are some questions worth asking the aid office:

✔ What are your average costs for the first year for:
- tuition and fees
- room and board
- books and supplies
- transportation
- other personal expenses

✔ What is the range of costs for:
- rooms (single, double)
- board (different meal plans)
- tuition rates (flat rate, per credit, etc.)

✔ By how much will total costs increase each year?

✔ How much have tuition and fees and room and board increased over the past three to five years?

✔ Does financial need have an impact on admission decisions?

✔ Does the school offer both need-based and merit-based financial aid?

✔ Do I need to file a separate application for merit-based scholarships?

✔ If the financial aid package isn't enough, under what conditions, if any, will the aid office reconsider the offer?

✔ How will the aid package change from year to year?

✔ What will happen if my family's financial situation changes?

✔ What are the terms and conditions of your aid programs? For example, what are the academic requirements or other conditions for renewing financial aid from year to year?

✔ When can we expect to receive bills from the college? Is there an option to spread the yearly payment over equal monthly installments?

QUICK RECAP

When deciding where to apply to college, cost is a factor, but not the most important factor. Don't exclude any college from consideration because of its "sticker price" — what you will actually pay might be much less. Remember:

- Each school has different costs and financial aid policies.
- When choosing colleges to apply to, consider a "financial safety."
- Your costs might vary from the published averages.
- You might be able to save money at a public college or community college or by commuting — but there are pros and cons to all those strategies.
- Research the colleges you're considering and contact their financial aid offices early.

Step 4: Get Ready for the Forms

QUICK OVERVIEW

Depending on where you'll apply, you may need to file up to three kinds of application forms to get financial aid: the FAFSA, the CSS/Financial Aid PROFILE and forms for individual colleges or states. Step 4 gets you ready for those forms. There are two main things to remember. First, file before the deadlines. The early bird — or at least the timely bird — gets the worm. Second, don't be intimidated. The forms are easier to fill out than they look.

Forms You'll Fill Out

Applying for financial aid is basically a matter of filling out a few financial aid forms on time. The forms may appear complicated, but they are simpler than they look, and millions of people fill them out every year. We will guide you through them so they make sense.

The three steps that follow this one walk you through the application forms you may need to complete: the FAFSA (Step 5), the PROFILE (Step 6) and whatever forms your individual colleges may require (Step 7). This step will help you create a timeline of which colleges require which forms when.

You may not need to fill out all the forms we describe. Most colleges require only one form, the FAFSA. If you do need to fill out more than one form, take heart. Most of the other forms ask for information similar to what the FAFSA requests. Repeating that information may be annoying, but it isn't hard.

KEEP IN MIND

Even though this book presents the financial aid forms in order of FAFSA, PROFILE and institutional forms, **you may need to submit these forms in a different order** depending on the financial aid deadlines of your colleges. In some cases, you may have to file PROFILE a few weeks before FAFSA, or the institutional form on the same day as FAFSA.

FAFSA: The Federal Form

This is the big one. The FAFSA, or Free Application for Federal Student Aid, must be completed by everyone who wants federal government aid. Just about every college financial aid program requires it, even if they also require other forms. Most schools and states use nothing but the FAFSA to determine eligibility for aid.

There is no charge for completing the FAFSA, and it's easy to do. **Don't pay someone to fill it out for you.**

FILING THE FAFSA

The FAFSA can be filled out and submittted online at www.fafsa.ed.gov (FAFSA on the Web). The FAFSA website gives lots of help in completing the form. You don't have to stress about making mistakes because the site checks your information as you go along, and it will find any errors for you to correct before submitting. You can also return to your FAFSA online to update or correct information as needed after you have submitted the form.

You cannot file the FAFSA before Jan. 1 of the year for which you're seeking aid. For example, if you will start college in September 2013, you cannot file the FAFSA before Jan. 1, 2013. If you want a head start, visit the FAFSA website earlier so you can familiarize yourself with the form and start working on your application as soon after Jan. 1 as possible.

Once it's Jan. 1, however, you should aim to file your FAFSA as soon as possible. Don't be fooled by the federal filing deadline (June 30). **Many college deadlines for financial aid are in February or March,** and they need your FAFSA information by then. So, come January, the earlier that you start working on the FAFSA, the better.

Since the FAFSA asks for information from income tax returns, you and your parents should plan to get an early start on those returns as well. If an early college deadline means you must file the FAFSA before you can complete your tax returns, you can file your FAFSA using estimated tax information. Check with your college(s) to determine how to best update your FAFSA information once your tax returns have been filed.

IF YOU NEED TO USE A PAPER FAFSA

If you are unable to file the FAFSA online, you can request a paper FAFSA by calling 1-800-433-3243. If you are hearing impaired, contact the TTY line at 1-800-730-8913.

On the paper FAFSA you can only list four colleges to receive your information. You can add up to six more later, but you'll have to wait until your FAFSA is processed and you've received your Student Aid Report.

You'll have to allow at least four weeks for mailing and processing before your earliest deadline. Be sure to make a photocopy for your records before mailing.

KEEP IN MIND

File your FAFSA as early as you can. When it comes to financial aid, time really is money. **Those who apply late usually get less** than they are entitled to, because there is less money available in the pool.

PROFILE

In addition to the FAFSA, some colleges and scholarship programs also require that you fill out the CSS/Financial Aid PROFILE to award their own nonfederal funds. They believe this form gives a more complete picture of students' financial circumstances, allowing them to allocate money as fairly as possible. The PROFILE service is administered by the College Board, though the College Board itself does not give out any need-based scholarships.

A few colleges require PROFILE only if you're applying for early decision or early action. Others require it for all applicants. If your college requires it and you're applying early, it is often the first form to fill out — ahead of even

KNOW THE LINGO

FAFSA (Free Application for Federal Student Aid) — The form that must be completed by everyone applying for federal government aid.

PROFILE (CSS/Financial Aid PROFILE) — A Web-based form offered by the College Board and used by some colleges and scholarship programs to award their own financial aid.

PIN (Personal Identification Number) — A number that serves as your electronic signature for filing the FAFSA on the Web.

SAR (Student Aid Report) — A report based on the information you provided in your FAFSA that reports your federally calculated EFC. The SAR is sent to every student who files a FAFSA.

Priority date — The date by which applications for financial aid must be received in order to be offered the best possible package. After the priority date, applicants are considered on a first-come, first-served basis, and are offered grants, scholarships and work-study only if the college still has money remaining.

FAFSA. To find out if your colleges require PROFILE, look them up in Part III of this book or refer to the college's websites.

PROFILE is online only; there are no paper forms. If you don't have a computer at home, use a computer at your school's guidance office or the library. After you register for the PROFILE, you can print a customized preapplication worksheet to help you gather the information you'll need, then complete the application online.

You can register for PROFILE at www.collegeboard.org beginning Oct. 1 of the year before you intend to start college. Once you register, you can either complete your application then and there or return to it at a later time. It's best if you submit it at least one week before your earliest college financial aid deadline. You can use the same application for multiple colleges, and you'll receive an online acknowledgment confirming the schools to which you're sending the information. There is a $25 fee to send your PROFILE to one college, plus a fee of $16 for each additional institution. However, depending on the information you submit, you may qualify for a fee waiver. Automatically awarded to low-income, first-time applicants, the fee waiver covers the costs of the PROFILE registration and up to six school reports.

College Forms

Some colleges — most of them private — require you to complete their own financial aid form as well as the FAFSA. Usually the forms are not complicated, and filling them out is not a big deal. Mike Scott of Texas Christian University says, "We have a very simple online form, where we just ask a couple of extra questions." Some of the questions are about projected enrollment: "Are they going to be full time or part time? When do they think they're going to graduate?" Others are aimed at matching students to outside sources of aid.

Find out if your colleges require you to file their own form, and if they do, file them on time.

State Forms

Most states offer need-based financial aid to their residents, and most colleges will require you to apply for it. Ask your school counselor for information on what form you need to complete to apply for state scholarship or grant programs. In many states, the FAFSA alone is enough to establish eligibility for state aid — but some states require their own form. If your state does, find out the deadline and add it to your master timeline for applying for aid. (*A table showing the deadlines for state aid, and which forms each state requires, appears on page 72 of this book.*)

Know the Deadlines!

Deadlines count. If you're on time, the colleges to which you've applied will have more money to give you; if you're late, they will have less money — or even none. **Late means less money, so be on time!** That means knowing and keeping track of all the financial aid deadlines you have to meet.

This can be tricky, because the deadlines are not all the same. Many schools and states may require you to fill out their own financial aid forms, and those forms may have deadlines that differ from those of the FAFSA or PROFILE. And **keep in mind that a college's due date for financial aid applications is typically different from its due date for admissions applications.**

Many colleges have no firm deadline or closing date for applying for financial aid; rather, they have a "priority" date. Often falling in February or March, the priority date is the date by which the school needs to receive your application to make its most attractive aid offer. After that date, funds may be limited or used up, and you may not get as much aid as you need. "I urge my students to apply for aid by the priority date," says Lauri Benton, a counselor at Columbia High School in Decatur, Ga. "They are more likely to get the aid they need early in the process, when the colleges have ample money to award."

Some colleges accept financial aid applications on a "rolling" basis. This means that applications are reviewed as they come in on a first-come, first-reviewed basis. Applicants are notified — that is, sent a financial aid award letter — a few weeks after they submit their forms. Most colleges that have a priority date will review late applications on a rolling basis. If you're applying to a rolling-applications college that doesn't have any set deadlines or priority dates, you're best off applying by mid-February or early March, when they will probably still have enough money available to meet your need.

Part III of this book, "Financial Aid College by College," lists deadlines and priority dates for colleges, along with their required forms. But it is worth confirming this information with the schools to which you're applying — at least by visiting their websites in November or December. Remember: Time is money. To get the most aid available, apply by the priority date. (*See also "Do You Get More Money If You Apply Early?" on page 40.*)

EXPERT ADVICE

"If you **meet our priority date**, we're going to guarantee you a full package here. You'll get 100 percent of need if you meet that priority deadline. If you don't, then it's what's left over, if we have money left over. And we typically do — but we don't have enough to meet 100 percent of the need of every late applicant."

— Vincent Amoroso, director, Student Financial Services, Johns Hopkins University

Creating a Timeline for Aid Applications

There are a lot of dates to remember as you apply for financial aid, but they don't have to be overwhelming. You can stay on top of them by making a timeline.

When you've found out the priority dates of the colleges and scholarship programs to which you're applying, as well as those of your state financial aid agency, list them in chronological order. Make that list part of a month-by-month timeline. Don't worry about the past; start the timeline with whatever month you're in now. The chart on the opposite page is an example of the sort of timeline you might construct. (*A blank copy of this chart for you to fill in appears in Part II on page 123.*)

SAMPLE WORKSHEET 1:

Meet Your Application Deadlines

		COLLEGE 1:	COLLEGE 2:	COLLEGE 3:
	College Name	*1st Choice Univ.*	*Private Univ.*	*Financial Safety*
FORMS REQUIRED	FAFSA	*Yes*	*Yes*	*Yes*
	PROFILE	*For ED (by 11/1)*	*Yes*	*No*
	State form	*Yes*	*No*	*Yes*
	Institutional form	*No*	*Laptop loaner*	*Yes*
	Tax returns	*Verification only*	*Verification only*	*Yes*
	Other			
SCHOOL CODES	Federal code	*999999*	*888888*	*777777*
	CSS code	*999Z*	*999X*	
PRIORITY DATE		*3/1 (FAFSA, State Form)*	*2/1*	*3/15*
CLOSING DATE		*None*	*2/15*	*None*
AFTER APPLYING	Need to send letter?			
	Documentation required?			
COMPARE AWARDS	Notification date	*12/15*	*4/1*	*2 weeks after applying*
	Reply-by date	*Immediately (if accepted ED)*	*5/1*	*4 weeks after notification*

For a blank version of this worksheet that you can photocopy for your own use, see page 123.

Throughout the period that you're applying for aid, keep your timeline where you can see it, check off what you've done, and remind yourself of what to do next. This will put the deadlines in your control. (*See the inside front cover of this book for a calendar of important dates and reminders.*)

Do You Get More Money If You Apply Early?

No. If you apply for financial aid Tuesday and another student applies Wednesday, you don't get more money than that student — so long as both of you apply by the deadline (or the priority date). However, when it comes to the college's own funds, and certain "campus-based" federal student aid programs (such as federal work-study), aid is distributed first-come, first-served once that date has passed. If you apply for aid after the college's deadline or priority date, the pool of funds may be used up. So always apply on time.

WHAT ABOUT EARLY DECISION?

Many schools allow students to apply for admission under early-decision or early-action programs. Whether early acceptance to a school affects the student's financial aid package varies from school to school. Depending on the college, the student accepted early may get more financial aid, less, or the same.

If you are considering early-decision programs, ask each school's financial aid officer: How is financial aid affected if I apply early decision? You may not know exactly what aid you'll get until after you accept. Don't panic: The rules of early decision allow you to turn down the college's acceptance offer if it doesn't offer you enough aid. Just don't put all your eggs into one basket — be sure to apply to a "financial safety school" as well.

Figure 6:
FAFSA PIN Site

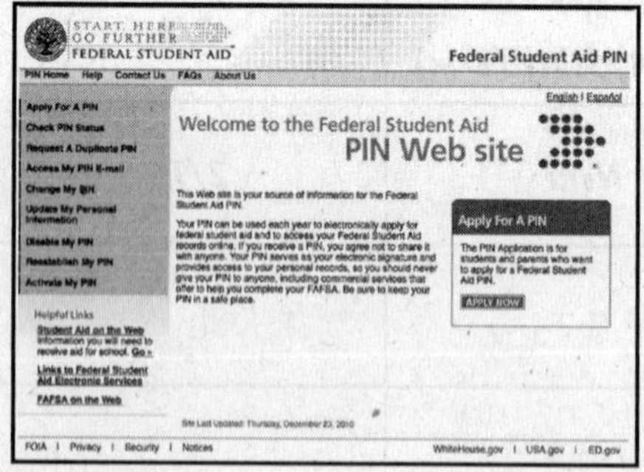

KEEP IN MIND

When you fill out the FAFSA, both you and one of your parents need a **Personal Identification Number**. This is important: the PIN will allow you to sign your FAFSA electronically, which will cut down your processing time. **You and one of your parents must each request a PIN** at **www.pin.ed.gov**. You should register for your PINs **before you fill out the FAFSA**. A good time to ask for your PINs is November of your senior year. **Remember your PIN and write it down in a safe place:** If you forget it, the government can't "remind" you of it later on.

Get Your Stuff Together

EXPERT ADVICE

If, like many students, you've never filed a tax return, you'll probably find it helpful to **get a blank copy of IRS Form 1040EZ** and the instructions that come with it. This is the simplest tax return form there is, and most high school and college students use it to report their summer and after-school job earnings. If your parents have filed for you in past years, **ask them to walk you through your return** for the last year.

For maximum efficiency, gather all the records you need to complete the forms before you sit down to work on them. That will save you a lot of time getting up, hunting around and forgetting where you left off. For both you and your parents, you'll probably need tax returns and related documents (such as W-2 forms) for the year that just ended, as well as end-of-year pay stubs, bank statements and other financial records. If you're filling out the PROFILE, you will also need tax documents from the previous year. If your parents own their home, you will need current value and mortgage information to fill out the PROFILE.

The FAFSA and PROFILE websites provide preapplication worksheets that you can print out as a way to help you gather your information before filling out the actual application. Use them that way. Add a list of all the records you need to assemble. It should be comprehensive and indicate which records are for all forms and which are for PROFILE only.

Establish Eligibility

To be eligible for federal financial aid, among other requirements, you'll have to:

- be a U.S. citizen or eligible noncitizen
- have a valid Social Security number
- not have been convicted of sale or possession of drugs
- if male and at least 18 years old, be registered with the Selective Service (in most cases)

Most of these requirements will not require extra work for most students. But two of them may. If you don't have a Social Security number, get one as soon as possible (go to www.ssa.gov to learn how), and certainly before you file your FAFSA. And if you are male, you can register for the Selective Service through the FAFSA application if you haven't already. If you do have a drug conviction, you may still be able to establish eligibility by completing a treatment program.

Income Tax Returns

PROFILE asks you for last year's tax information as well as for this year's. For this year, it asks you whether the figures are estimated or final. It also asks for estimated income for next year, which you can base on this year's information.

Income tax returns are due on April 15, but most colleges want your financial aid forms much sooner. **Don't wait until your taxes are done to file your financial aid forms if your college(s) have early deadlines.** Even if you or your parents haven't received your W-2s yet, you can still file the FAFSA with estimated tax information based on last year's returns and current-year pay stubs. Then file your tax return as soon as possible afterward, and go back to your FAFSA online to replace the estimated tax information with actual figures. But check first with your colleges to find out how they prefer you to provide updated tax information on the FAFSA. Some might want you to wait until the IRS Data Retrieval tool is available.

IRS Data Retrieval Tool

Accessible right from your FAFSA online, this tool allows you or your parents to access the IRS tax return information needed to complete the FAFSA and to transfer the data directly onto your FAFSA form. However, it takes a fair amount of time for your tax return information to become available for transfer from the IRS; up to three weeks if you filed your returns electronically and up to eight weeks if you filed by mail. So if you need to submit your FAFSA sooner than that, you might need to either enter your tax return information manually or return to the FAFSA at a later date to use the data retrieval tool.

For many colleges, the IRS Data Retrieval process is the preferred means of completing your FAFSA. If you cannot use this process at the time you initially complete your FAFSA, check with your college(s) to determine how best to update your FAFSA information once your tax returns have been filed.

QUICK RECAP

You'll have to file some forms to get financial aid, but they aren't as difficult as they might look. The main forms are FAFSA and PROFILE, plus whatever other forms your colleges or state may require.

- File on time — filing late can cost you money.
- File your FAFSA online. Get a PIN for yourself and for one of your parents early — and don't lose them.
- Make a timeline to keep track of your deadlines, including college priority dates.
- As early as possible, check with your colleges to be sure you know what forms they each require and how they want you to provide tax information.
- Gather together the records you need to fill out the forms.
- If you don't have one already, get a Social Security number.

Step 5: Fill Out the FAFSA

QUICK OVERVIEW

The FAFSA may look intimidating, but it's actually pretty easy to fill out. The questions mainly concern your income and assets and those of your parents, but they also touch on other matters, such as your citizenship status and the schools to which you want the FAFSA to be sent. We'll walk you through it, and give you tips about how to avoid delays. Above all: File on time!

General Advice

Nobody likes to fill out forms. And no one enjoys having to share information about family finances. But the potential result — money to help you pay for college — is well worth it. And you will see in this step that the FAFSA is really pretty simple. While the form has six sections, only one requires financial information, and another is, essentially, "sign here." The online FAFSA also has "skip logic" so you don't have to see questions that don't pertain to you.

Again, remember that you don't have to do the steps in this book in exactly the order presented. If the colleges require you to submit the PROFILE before the FAFSA, then do the PROFILE first, even though we present the FAFSA first. Since the PROFILE requires much of the same information needed to fill out the FAFSA, doing the PROFILE first will make this step much easier.

Help is available by phone and online if you have questions about FAFSA (see the "Good to Know" sidebar on page 45). And don't be afraid to call the financial aid offices of the colleges to which you're applying. If you're confused about this or any other aspect of the financial aid process, these offices can help. "People look at the FAFSA and they find it a bit overwhelming initially," says Vincent Amoroso of Johns Hopkins University. "They come to us seeking guidance and reassurance on how to get through the application process. We show them that it's not as complicated as it looks."

EXPERT ADVICE

"Our job is to get students through this maze. You'd call a mechanic if your car is broken. Well, why not call us if you have a question about financial aid applications? That's our job — to get you through the process."

— *Bonnie Lee Behm, director of financial assistance, Villanova University*

Apply on Time

You can't file your FAFSA before Jan. 1 of the year you're applying for aid. Most college deadlines for financial aid are in March, and some fall as early as February, so the window for filing is narrow. You have to leave time for your FAFSA to be processed. Be sure to file your online form at least one week before the earliest deadline.

Don't wait until the April 15 tax deadline to file your FAFSA. Most priority dates will be long over by then. If your earliest deadline doesn't fall until March, you can wait for W-2s, 1099s and other official tax documents to arrive from employers and banks and then complete draft income tax returns.

If your earliest deadline falls in February, check with the college to see how they want you to provide tax return data. You can usually use end-of-year pay stubs, quarterly bank statements and similar records to estimate your and your parents' income. You can also use tax returns from the previous year as a frame of reference, but don't just plug in the information from last year's returns into the FAFSA — you really do need to estimate the current information, not duplicate old information.

No matter how you derive the numbers, remember this above all: Get the FAFSA in on time.

Read Instructions Carefully; Fill Out the Form Accurately

With the FAFSA as with all financial aid forms, accuracy is vital. Read the directions. Understand the terms that are being used. Many terms, such as "date of birth," are straightforward, but others, such as "investments," require you to read the instructions carefully so you know what they mean in this context. Even the term "parent," as discussed below, has a special meaning on the FAFSA.

Be as complete and accurate as you can about your financial circumstances. If you submit incorrect data, you might create delays that could endanger your aid. By avoiding errors, you will increase your chances of getting all the aid for which you are eligible.

Keep Track of Your Pin and Password

You don't have to complete the FAFSA on the Web in one sitting. At the start, you'll supply a password that will allow you to leave the application before completing it and to return later, so long as you come back within 45 days.

Get PINs ahead of time for both yourself and for one of your parents so you can sign the form electronically. The PINs can be obtained at www.pin.ed.gov. If you forget your PIN number, don't worry. A "Forgot your PIN?" link is provided in the online FAFSA, so you can easily access the PIN website and retrieve it.

KNOW THE LINGO

If you've never filed an income tax return before — or if your parents file for you — you may not be familiar with these IRS forms:

1040 — The main form of your tax return, this is a summary of all the taxable income you or your parents made last year, possible deductions from that income, the tax owed on that income, and credits that give some of that tax back.

W-2 — A tax form prepared by the employer stating how much taxable income they paid you last year, as well as untaxed benefits you or your parents received from them. Information on this form is used on both the 1040 and the FAFSA.

1099 — A form similar to the W-2 that shows income you received from anyone other than an employer. For example, if one of your parents is an independent contractor, he or she may receive a 1099-MISC showing the nonemployee compensation a client paid them.

1098 — A tax form showing payments for which you can take a deduction or credit. For example, if you take out a student loan, once you begin repaying it you will receive a 1098-E from your lender every year showing how much interest you paid on the loan.

GOOD TO KNOW

Detailed information on how to complete the paper FAFSA is available on the Web at **www.studentaid.ed.gov/completefafsa.** If you're filing the FAFSA online at **www.fafsa.ed.gov**, that same site offers help screens for each question and live, one-on-one online help with a customer service representative. Click the "help" icon to access that feature. For help over the phone with either the paper or online FAFSA, call **1-800-4-FED-AID (1-800-433-3243)**.

Avoid any website that offers to help you file the FAFSA for a fee. The federal government offers its help for free and does not endorse any site that charges money for assistance.

Figure 7:
FAFSA on the Web

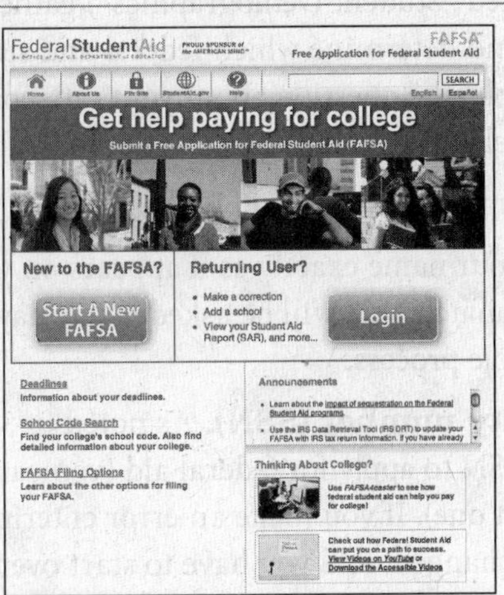

Let's Walk Through It

The FAFSA has five sections that ask questions, each with a common theme. The exact order or wording of these questions may change from year to year (last year's preapplication worksheet is in Part II), but the substance remains more or less the same. And the purpose never changes: to provide information about yourself and your family that colleges will use to figure out how much federal student aid you qualify for.

There are a few general tips to keep in mind while filling out the FAFSA:

- The word "you" always means you, the student.
- The word "college" means a college, university, community college or any other school beyond high school.
- The phrase "net worth" means the current value of an asset (such as a business) minus the amount of debt owed on it.
- Questions about income are for the previous year; questions about assets ask for their value as of the day you fill out the form.
- When entering dollar figures, round to the nearest dollar and don't use commas or decimal points.
- If you have special financial circumstances that you need to explain, you can't do it on the FAFSA. Instead, write to your colleges directly. (*See Step 8 of this book, "Make Your Special Circumstances Known."*)

Here is a step-by-step walk-through of the key questions on the FAFSA. Since the online form is interactive, it will automatically skip over some questions or sections depending on how you answer. For example, if you say that you're not married, you won't be asked questions about your spouse. For that reason, you might not see all the questions described here.

Step One: Questions About Yourself

These questions (labeled "Student Demographics") gather basic information used to identify you and determine which federal and state programs you may qualify for. For example, the question about your citizenship is there because only U.S. citizens (or eligible noncitizens) can get federal student aid.

Here's the main information this section will ask for:

Your name. Enter your name exactly as it appears on your Social Security card. If the two don't match, you will be asked a few days later to fix it, slowing down the whole process.

Your Social Security number (SSN). As noted in Step 4 of this book, you need to have an SSN to apply for federal aid (you can't even open the online FAFSA without one). If you make an error entering this number on the login page, you can't change it and you have to start over. More delay.

Whether you're male or female. If you are male between the ages of 18 and 25, you must be registered with the Selective Service (the draft) in order to be eligible for federal aid. If you're not registered, you can do it now on the FAFSA.

Where you live. Use a permanent home mailing address here, not a school or office address.

The state in which you legally reside. You will be asked this question if you have lived in your state for less than five years. Your answer will determine whether you're eligible for scholarships and grants from your state. In some cases, your state of legal residence might be different from the state where you're actually living at the time you fill out the FAFSA. This might be the case if you've recently moved or one of your parents is in the military.

You don't need to request that your information be sent to a state agency; the government will automatically send your processed information to the agency of your state government that administers financial aid programs for state residents, whether scholarships, grants or loans. Do be aware, however, that some states require an additional financial aid form, as discussed in Step 7 of this book.

Your permanent telephone number. Use a permanent home or cell phone number, not a school or office number.

Your e-mail address. This is optional, but if you provide it, the government can send your Student Aid Report (SAR) by e-mail instead of snail mail, so it will reach you faster. Supply an e-mail address you check regularly.

Your marital status as of today. That means the day you submit your FAFSA. If your marital status changes later, you cannot update it on your FAFSA. In that instance, contact the financial aid office at the colleges you want to attend.

Whether you are a citizen or an eligible noncitizen. You are a citizen if you were born in this country or became a citizen through the naturalization process. An eligible noncitizen is someone such as a U.S. permanent resident holding a green card (Permanent Resident Card), or someone who has refugee status who is allowed to live permanently in the United States. It is not someone visiting on a student visa. If you're an eligible noncitizen, you'll have to fill in your Alien Registration Number. If you're neither a citizen nor an eligible noncitizen, you can't get federal aid, but you may be eligible for state or college aid — so you should still fill out the FAFSA, unless you don't have a Social Security number. In that case, call your colleges.

Whether you've ever been convicted of possessing or selling illegal drugs. Say "yes" only if the offense occurred while you were receiving federal student aid (unlikely if this is your first FAFSA, in which case you won't even see this question online), it's still on your record, and you were tried as an adult.

Your high school completion status next year. Before you can get federal financial aid, you must have completed high school or its equivalent. Select "High school diploma" if you will graduate from a public or private high school this year; "General Educational Development (GED) if you have the GED diploma or expect to pass the GED exam; or "Home schooled" if you will satisfy your state's requirements for successfully completing home schooling at the high school level. If you must select "None of the above," contact the financial aid office at the colleges you want to attend.

Name, city and state of your high school: The online FAFSA provides a search tool to find your high school and auto-fill. This info will enable your high school to be notified of the status of your application.

What year of college you'll be in next year. Your answer determines the aid programs for which you qualify.

What degree will you be working on in the next school year. Some aid programs are not available for graduate study, a second bachelor's degree or nondegree study. If you are undecided about what type of degree you will be pursuing (for example, if you're applying to both two-year and four-year colleges), check "undecided," but be sure to follow up with each college you're applying to after you've submitted the FAFSA.

The highest level of education completed by your father and mother. This won't affect your federal aid, but some states use this information to award scholarships to students who are the first in their family to attend college.

Whether you're interested in work-study: The best answer is "yes." Preserve your options. You're not committing to anything, and your answer won't affect the amount of grant money you might get.

Step Two: School Selection

This is where you indicate which colleges should receive your FAFSA information. You list the colleges, and the government will send the processed information to them for free.

You can list up to 10 colleges online; but if you are using the paper FAFSA, you can only list four. In either case you can add additional schools later, when you get your Student Aid Report (SAR).

Identify each college by its name or federal school code. You can find the federal school code in Part III of this book (see Figure 8 below). You can also search for it on the FAFSA Web page.

Housing Plans. For each college, you have to say whether you plan to live on campus, off campus or with your parents. Your answer will affect the housing costs that the school will estimate for you, and therefore your financial need. If you haven't made a decision yet, assume you'll live on campus.

Figure 8:
Finding a College's Federal Code

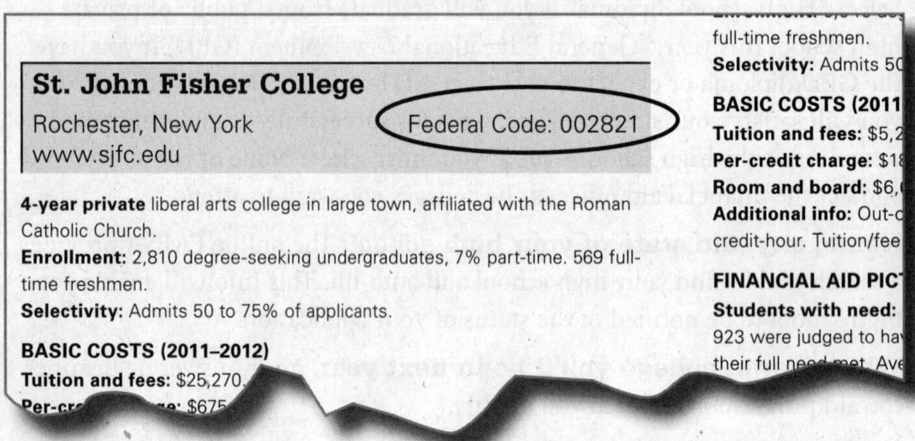
St. John Fisher College
Rochester, New York
www.sjfc.edu
Federal Code: 002821

4-year private liberal arts college in large town, affiliated with the Roman Catholic Church.
Enrollment: 2,810 degree-seeking undergraduates, 7% part-time. 569 full-time freshmen.
Selectivity: Admits 50 to 75% of applicants.

BASIC COSTS (2011–2012)
Tuition and fees: $25,270.
Per-cr... ge: $675

full-time freshmen.
Selectivity: Admits 50
BASIC COSTS (2011
Tuition and fees: $5,2
Per-credit charge: $18
Room and board: $6,
Additional info: Out-
credit-hour. Tuition/fee
FINANCIAL AID PIC
Students with need:
923 were judged to hav
their full need met. Ave

The Federal Code for each college in Part III of this book can be found in its college description.

Step Three: Are You Independent?

The questions in this step determine whether or not you're an independent student. To be considered independent for the purpose of federal student aid eligibility, it doesn't matter if you feel independent, have a job or even live on your own. It also has nothing to do with whether your parents claim you as a dependent on their tax return. But if you can truthfully answer "yes" to at least one of the questions in this step, you will be considered independent.

The things that would classify you as independent are:

- You turn age 24 or older in the year you start college.

- You'll be enrolled in a graduate degree program in the year for which you're seeking aid.
- You're married.
- You have children who get more than half of their support from you.
- You have dependents other than your children or spouse who live with you and get more than half their support from you.
- You're an orphan, or you've been a ward/dependent of the court.
- You're currently serving in, or are a veteran of, the active-duty U.S. armed forces. (If you served only as a reservist and were never activated for reasons other than training, answer "no.")
- You are a homeless, unaccompanied youth (or at risk of being such).

If you are independent, then you can skip the section about your parents' income and assets. But there are certain cases where a college financial aid office will want to know about your parents' finances even if you are an independent. If you do meet one of the criteria on the list above, it's a good idea to ask the colleges to which you're applying whether they'll consider you fully independent for the purpose of awarding their own institutional funds. If one or more of them won't, you should fill out the parent section. The online application will ask you whether you want to fill it out or skip it.

Are you unable to obtain information about your parents? Even if it is determined that you are a dependent, you might be able to show special circumstances that will allow you to submit your FAFSA without parental information. Follow the instructions on the FAFSA carefully, and then follow up immediately with the financial aid office at each college you want to attend.

Step Four: Questions About Your Parents

If you're a dependent student, you have to answer these questions (labeled "Parent Demographics") even if you don't live with your parents. When you're ready to submit the application, you will also need one of your parents to sign it, either on the paper form or by using a PIN on the electronic version.

Modern family life can make the definition of "parent" complicated. But the FAFSA definitions are fairly clear:

- If both your parents are living and married to each other, answer the questions about both of them.
- If only one of your parents is living, answer the questions about him or her.
- If your widowed parent remarried, answer the questions about your stepparent too.
- If you were raised by a single parent, answer the questions about him or her.
- If your parents are divorced or separated, answer the questions about the parent you lived with the most during the past 12 months.
- If that parent remarried, answer the questions about your stepparent, too.

- Don't provide information about grandparents, legal guardians or foster parents. FAFSA doesn't consider them your parents unless they have legally adopted you.

Here's a run-down of the important questions:

Marital status: Indicate the status as it is at the time you submit the form.

Their Social Security numbers: Unlike you, your parents are not required to have Social Security numbers in order for you to file the FAFSA (but in that case you have to enter zeroes). But if they do have Social Security numbers, they must provide them.

Their names: Again, if they have social security cards, their names must exactly match.

The number of people in your parents' household: These include you and your parents. The number who will be in college during the next year is also asked for: that also includes you (but not your parents). These questions affect how much money your parents will be expected to contribute to your education.

EXPERT ADVICE

"**Some people overthink the FAFSA** questions. They'll get to what we would see as straightforward questions: 'How many are in your household?' And then 'How many in your household go to college?' Well, some families will list every person who's ever lived in the household and then every member who has ever attended college. And actually **what we want to know** is, how many are living in your household now, and how many of them are in college now."

— Elizabeth Bickford, director, Office of Student Financial Aid and Scholarships, University of Oregon, Eugene

Step Five: Your Parents' Financial Information

OK, this is usually the most complicated part of the FAFSA. But this section has been greatly simplified. For the most part, it asks for the same information that your parents must provide on their federal income tax form, and even points out exactly where they can find that information. The main questions are:

Whether they've completed a tax return for the past year. This means the return that is due the coming April 15.

If either of your parents is a "dislocated worker." Answer "yes" if one (or both) of your parents has been laid off or has lost their business and is still unemployed. "Dislocated worker" also includes a stay-at-home mom or dad who no longer receives support from a spouse and can't find a job. If you answer "yes" to this question, you should also contact the financial aid office at each college you are applying to. *(See Step 8, "Make Your Special Circumstances Known.")*

Whether anyone in the household received certain federal benefits. A "yes" answer to any of the listed programs, such as free or reduced-price lunch or supplemental nutrition assistance (food stamps), will likely result in a determination that your family should not be expected to contribute any money toward your education.

Whether they're eligible to file the 1040A or 1040EZ tax form. It's to your advantage if they can answer yes, they're eligible to file this form. If they would normally file the 1040A but filed the full 1040 only to take advantage of an education tax benefit relating to a child already in college, they can still check this box.

GOOD TO KNOW

The FAFSA asks both you and your parents to report the amount of income tax you will have to pay on last year's income. The **amount they want here is only the federal income tax amount** — don't include Social Security, Medicare, or any of the taxes that are reported in the "other taxes" section of Form 1040. If you or one of your parents is self-employed or has to self-report tip income from a restaurant job, you should keep this in mind.

Their income tax information: These questions are easy to answer if they've already completed their tax return. But if they haven't, ask them to give estimates, using W-2s or pay stubs, bank statements, and last year's return. **Don't miss any college deadlines or priority dates because your parents haven't done their taxes yet.** After you submit your FAFSA, you'll be able to go back later and replace the estimated figures with the actual numbers. The IRS Data Retrieval Process is the preferred means of completing the FAFSA (see description on the next page). Check with your college(s) to determine how best to update your FAFSA information once your tax returns have been filed.

What their untaxed income and benefits are. These include items like earned income credits, welfare benefits, Social Security benefits, child support and other money that didn't get taxed. It also includes any contributions your parents made for the last tax year to deductible Individual Retirement Accounts (IRAs) or employer-sponsored retirement plans such as 401(k)s or 403(b)s. Add this up on worksheets and fill in the totals on the FAFSA. If you're filling out the worksheets online, the information will appear on the confirmation page you'll see after submitting, which you should print out and keep on file in case a financial aid administrator asks about them later.

What their assets are. These include cash, savings and the value of investments, such as stocks and bonds. The amounts to put down are "as of" the day you fill out the FAFSA. Often that is just a best guess, using the most recent bank statements. (Keep in mind that the amount of aid you are entitled to is based much more on family income than on assets.) They do *not* include the home where your parents primarily live (a summer cottage would be included), a family-owned business of less than 100 employees, or a family farm that they live on and operate. However, if your parents own more than one home — a summer cottage, for example, or an investment property — they also should report their equity in that home on the "investments" line. If they own a farm that they don't live on, they also should report the value of that farm as a business. Another thing your parents do not need to include here is any money they have in tax-advantaged retirement accounts, such as IRAs, 401(k)s, 403(b)s and the like.

The IRS Data Retrieval Tool

The IRS Data Retrieval Tool allows students and parents to access the IRS tax return information needed to complete the FAFSA, and transfer the data directly into their FAFSA from the IRS website.

You can use the IRS retrieval tool to transfer your tax return information if:

- You have filed your tax returns
- You have not filed an amended tax return
- Your marital status has not changed since you filed your tax returns
- You are not filing your tax returns as married, filing separately
- You did not file a Puerto Rican or foreign tax return

You might not be able to use the IRS retrieval tool to transfer your tax return information if you **very recently** filed your tax return.

- If you filed your taxes electronically, allow three weeks for the tool to be available.
- If you filed your taxes by mail, allow eight weeks for the tool to be available.

The IRS Retrieval Tool is the preferred means of completing your FAFSA. If you cannot use this process at the time you initially complete your FAFSA, check with your college(s) to determine how best to update your FAFSA information once your tax returns have been filed.

Follow the online instructions to have the IRS data fill in your income data. **Do not change any data once it is transferred to your FAFSA.** Changing any piece of tax data may require follow-up and verification by your college's financial aid office.

Step Six: Your Own Financial Information

These questions ask about *your* income and assets — whether or not you are independent. Income is how much money you made last year; assets are what you own and the savings you have. If you are married, they also want to know about your spouse's income and assets.

These are the main things that this section asks for:

Whether you've completed a tax return for the past year. This means the return that is due the coming April 15, not the one you filed a year ago. If you have filed a return or plan to file one, they will ask what form you're using, for example, the 1040 or 1040A. If you're not going to file any tax return, they will still ask how much you (and, if you have one, your spouse) earned from working.

Whether you're eligible to file the 1040A or 1040EZ tax form. The instructions on the FAFSA explain who can file these forms. Most students can. If you can, say yes.

GOOD TO KNOW

Most students are eligible to file IRS Form 1040EZ or 1040A as their tax return. Some parents can, too. (The rules determining whether you can are explained in the FAFSA instructions.) **If both you and your parents are eligible to file the 1040A or 1040EZ**, you may qualify for a "simplified needs analysis," wherein only your income (not your assets) will be assessed when calculating your expected family contribution.

What income and tax information you and your spouse will report on your tax returns. Again, these questions are easy to answer if you've already completed your tax return, and if the IRS Data Retrieval tool is available to you. If you haven't completed your tax return yet, check with your colleges to determine how best to update your FAFSA information once your tax returns have been filed. Just don't put off filing the FAFSA because you haven't done your taxes yet.

The number of people in your household: This question refers to the number of people in *your* household, if you have one — not your parents'.

What your untaxed income and benefits are. Once again, these include items like earned income credits, welfare benefits, Social Security benefits, child support and other money that came to you without being taxed. You will be asked about these in a series of questions on screen. (If you are filling out the paper FAFSA, you should use the worksheets that come with the form to add them all up, then fill in the totals on your FAFSA. Don't submit the worksheets, but keep copies of them on file. A financial aid office may want those details later.)

What your assets are. This question is meant to provide a snapshot of your assets, the money or property you currently own. Using current banking statements and investment records, say how much cash and savings you have, as well the total value of any stocks, other investments or investment properties that you might own. If you're still in high school, chances are that you only have a small savings or checking account, which you should report on the line asking for "cash, savings accounts and checking accounts." You may also have some government savings bonds, certificates of deposit (CDs) or a few shares of stock; those should be reported on the line asking about "investments."

Don't include any college savings accounts in this step unless you are independent (you answered "yes" to any question in FAFSA Step Three) and they are owned by you in your own name.

Step Seven: Review Your Answers, Then Sign and Submit

This is easy, but it's still an important step. Take the time to carefully review all your answers for accuracy and spelling — even your name. Be sure to print out your FAFSA if you're filling it out online.

Preparer's information. If you or your family paid a fee to someone to fill out your FAFSA, or to advise you on how to fill it out, that person must provide his or her Social Security number or Employment Identification Number (EIN), and must also sign and date the form. This requirement does not apply to school counselors, financial aid administrators, friends or mentors who helped but did not charge a fee.

Pay heed to this warning from the FAFSA website: "Be wary of organizations that charge a fee to submit your application, or to find you money for school.

Some are legitimate and some are scams. Generally, **any help that you pay for can be received free** from your school or Federal Student Aid."

Terms to read before signing. You'll see a list of terms you must agree to by signing. There is nothing onerous here, but there is a scary-sounding penalty for giving "false or misleading information." This does *not* mean honest mistakes or estimates that turn out to be way off; they're talking about intentional fraud.

If your parents provided financial information, one of them also needs to sign. Use your PINs to sign electronically — don't use the "print signature page and mail" option. It just wastes time.

Be sure to keep clicking on "next" until you get to the confirmation page! Your FAFSA is not truly submitted until then.

FAFSA Step Eight: Confirmation

You're done! Be sure to print the confirmation page, and save it to your hard drive as well. If you don't have a printer, write down the confirmation number, date and time. This is your proof that your FAFSA was received.

If you file using the paper form, make a photocopy of it before mailing it, and keep that photocopy together with the worksheets you filled out and all the records you used.

KEEP IN MIND

You have to leave time for your FAFSA to be processed. If you're filing on paper, allow at least four weeks before your earliest college or state deadline. If you're filing online, leave at least one week before the earliest deadline.

Check Your Student Aid Report!

After you submit your FAFSA, you'll receive your Student Aid Report, or SAR. How long it will take for you to receive it, and in what form, will depend on how you filed the FAFSA. If you filed FAFSA on the Web and signed it with your PIN, you should recieve it immediately, or at most within one to three days. If you filed a paper FAFSA and did not provide an e-mail address, you'll receive a paper SAR within about four weeks.

In whatever form the SAR reaches you, check it over carefully. It will include a summary detailing the information you supplied on the FAFSA. Make sure this information is correct. If not, then you must make corrections. It's easy to do — just go back to www.fafsa.ed.gov, log in and click on "Make FAFSA Corrections." You can also add or remove colleges this way.

Make corrections only if the data on the SAR doesn't accurately represent your family's financial situation at the time the FAFSA was originally filed. For example, if you estimated the previous year's income but have since filed a tax return with exact figures, substitute those figures now. Or if you mistyped a number, or if the federal data-entry clerk misread your handwriting, correct that. But **don't make changes that reflect changes to your income or assets since you filed the FAFSA**. If important changes of that sort have happened —

KEEP IN MIND

Eligibility for **federal student aid does not automatically continue** from one year to the next. You have to reapply every year that you're in college. Do that by filling out a **Renewal FAFSA**. This is a partially preformatted version of the FAFSA that you can use so long as you applied for federal aid the previous year.

such as a lost job — inform your colleges individually rather than through the FAFSA. (*See Step 8, "Make Your Special Circumstances Known."*)

At the top of the SAR, you should also see an estimate of your EFC: the amount of money your family is expected to contribute toward college costs. You might not see an EFC if there is incorrect or missing information that made it impossible to process your data. If that happens to you, submit the necessary corrections and you'll get your EFC estimate. **The actual EFC calculated by a given college may be different than what you'll see here,** especially if that college uses a different formula, or if its financial aid office has adjusted your EFC based on special circumstances that you brought to the college's attention.

The colleges you requested to receive your FAFSA information will automatically get your SAR. At the corrections stage, you'll have an opportunity to add more colleges to receive your FAFSA information. You can also give a school permission to add itself to the list. Just provide the college with the Data Release Number (DRN) that will be provided on your SAR. The school will use your DRN to access your application record.

The SAR gives you an estimate of how much money your family is expected to pay for college, but not how much financial aid you'll receive. You'll find that out when your individual colleges send you their award letters. Even so, by filing your FAFSA, you've taken a big step toward getting those letters.

If the expected family contribution (EFC) indicated on the SAR looks too high for your family to afford, you should talk to your parents and discuss other financing options with them. (*See Step 11, "Consider Your Out-of-Pocket Options."*) It could also mean that you need to explain some special financial circumstances to the colleges to which you've applied (see Step 8).

QUICK RECAP

The FAFSA is easier than it looks. Most of it is about your income and assets, and that of your parents. Remember:

- File on time. Submit your FAFSA as soon as possible, beginning Jan. 1 of the year you'll start college.
- It helps to have your tax return finished first, but don't let that delay you if your colleges have early financial aid deadlines or priority dates. You can estimate your figures and correct them later.
- Read instructions.
- Be accurate.
- Reapply every year.

Step 6: Fill Out the PROFILE (If Required)

QUICK OVERVIEW

Whether you have to fill out the CSS/Financial Aid PROFILE depends on the colleges to which you're applying. If you do, you'll find it mainly asks for "more of the same" — information about your family's income, expenses and assets — rather than something completely new. The online form is customized to your situation, so you won't be presented with too many questions that don't apply to you. However, the application does take time to fill out, so leave yourself plenty of time to submit it before your colleges' deadlines.

General Advice

Step 6 is to fill out the CSS/Financial Aid PROFILE® — but only if you need to. If the schools to which you're applying don't require this financial aid form, you don't have to complete it. Find out if they require it by checking Part III of this book or the colleges' websites.

The PROFILE is administered by the College Board, a not-for-profit association of schools and colleges (and the publisher of this book). It is available online only: You can't file on paper. The upside of this is that PROFILE is available 24 hours a day, seven days a week. Furthermore, its system of online edits alerts you to missing or incorrect information before you submit the application, eliminating a potential source of delays. Firewall protection and data encryption protect the information you submit about your family and their finances. The downside is that if you don't have a computer with Internet access at home, you will have to use one at your school, a library or a parent's workplace.

The PROFILE doesn't replace the FAFSA: You still need to complete that, too, because that's the form required for federal student aid, which any college will expect you to seek before they give away their own institutional funds. The schools that require the PROFILE do so because they believe it gives a more complete account of your financial situation to guide them in awarding their own funds. The College Board provides the colleges with your PROFILE information, and the colleges use it to calculate your expected family contribution and your need.

Since it's designed to give a more complete picture of your finances, it is not surprising that the PROFILE is longer than the FAFSA. It's the same general concept, but you'll need to gather more records to answer all the questions, and it will take more time to fill out.

Register and File Early

Because the PROFILE form is more involved, and because colleges may ask for additional information even after the form is filed, register well before your colleges' deadlines and leave yourself lots of time to fill out the application. The College Board usually processes your PROFILE information overnight, but delays can happen — especially in late January and early February. Also, don't assume it can all be completed in one session; you may need to return to the form if a college asks for supplemental information. Fortunately, you can go back and forth to your application online, rather than having to finish it in one sitting.

It's best to submit the PROFILE at least one week before your earliest financial aid priority date. Remember, colleges use PROFILE information to determine who gets their limited grant dollars. If you file late, you will have to make do with whatever funds, if any, are left over.

You may need to submit the PROFILE ahead of the FAFSA, depending on the deadlines your colleges set. In fact, some of the colleges that require the PROFILE will ask you to submit it before you submit your FAFSA. This is especially likely if you're applying early decision or early action for admission to the college. If a college requires the PROFILE before Jan. 1, you can submit a PROFILE with estimated income figures for this year based on your year-to-date pay stubs and your previous year's tax return, then send corrections to the college later if necessary.

Preparing for the PROFILE

You can get ready to complete the PROFILE with the Pre-Application Worksheet, available from the PROFILE site at collegeboard.org. (The worksheet is customized for you after you have registered.) You can also download and print out the PROFILE Student Guide and Application Instructions from the same site.

The Pre-Application Worksheet can save you a lot of time by helping you gather all your necessary family financial information before starting the application. Filling it out on paper can also speed your way if you have to file the application on a computer where your login time is limited, such as at school or a library.

Whether you're filling out the Pre-Application Worksheet or the PROFILE itself, you'll need to gather more records to fill out the PROFILE than you will for the FAFSA. For example, in addition to asking about your parents' income for the year before you plan to enter college, the PROFILE asks about their income the year before that, as well as their projected income in the

EXPERT ADVICE

Most schools that require the PROFILE use it when they're investing a lot of their own institutional dollars into need-based programs. We use it because **the PROFILE gives us an added, more in-depth look** at a family's financial strength. Our ultimate goal is to give the right dollars to the right students at the right time, and this PROFILE application helps us do that."

— Vincent Amoroso, director, Office of Student Financial Services, Johns Hopkins University

GOOD TO KNOW

Help is available to get you through the PROFILE application. If you're not sure about how to answer any question, **check the online Help Desk** that's built into the online application. If you can't find an answer to your question there, contact the PROFILE help line, either by e-mail (**help@cssprofile.org**) or by phone (**305-829-9793**). From January to April, PROFILE customer service hours are Monday through Friday, 8 a.m. to 10 p.m. Eastern Time.

You can also contact the financial aid office at the college to which you're applying. In addition, your high school counselor may be able to answer your questions.

year to come. There are also questions about your projected summer and school-year earnings during your first year in college. The purpose of this is to give financial aid officers a better idea of whether last year's income was typical or unusually low or high. But it also means that you must collect more documents, such as tax returns for the prior year, and you'll need to estimate future income.

Documents You'll Need Before You Fill Out Your PROFILE

It's a good idea to gather the necessary records before you start and have them handy as you work on the PROFILE. You'll need records for both yourself and your parents.

- ✔ Federal income tax return for the year before you start college, if completed, or pay stubs and other income-related records for estimates
- ✔ Federal income tax return for the year before that
- ✔ W-2 forms and other records of money earned the year before you start college
- ✔ Records of untaxed income for those two years
- ✔ Current bank statements and mortgage information
- ✔ Records of stocks, bonds, trusts and other investments

As with the FAFSA, it's easiest if you've already completed your tax return for the most recent tax year before you start filling out the PROFILE. But don't let that hold you up. Estimate your tax return information if you haven't completed your return by the time you need to file the PROFILE. (There are tools on the PROFILE site to help you and your parents estimate this information.) You can correct PROFILE information, if necessary, directly with the colleges after filing your return.

How to Register/File on the Web

Just like registering ahead of time for a FAFSA PIN, **it's best to register for the PROFILE well before the first college's deadline.** Since the PROFILE is entirely Web based, you do this online at www.collegeboard.org. You'll need to create a collegeboard.org account (with a username and password) before you can file; setting up the account is free. (If you previously registered online for the SAT, you already have this account: It's the same one you used then.) If you don't have Internet access at home, ask your school counselor or librarian if you can use one of the school's computers.

It's smart to register for PROFILE as soon as you're sure about where you'll be applying for aid, but in any case at least one week before the earliest financial aid filing date you need to meet. Registrations are accepted beginning Oct. 1 of the year before you intend to start college. Once you register, you can either complete your application then and there or return to it at a later time. Your PROFILE application will be customized to your circumstances based on the information you give when you register.

Most families will have to pay a fee of $25 to have their PROFILE sent to one college, plus $16 for each additional college. The fee can be paid with most major credit cards or bank debit cards. Low-income families applying for the first time may qualify for a fee waiver (see sidebar).

Registration will involve providing some preliminary information such as your date of birth; mailing address; the year in school for which you're seeking aid; whether you are a U.S. citizen, a veteran or an orphan; whether you have dependents or have separated or divorced parents; and whether your parents own a home, or all or part of a business or farm. The questions usually won't involve looking up documents; just answer them straightforwardly. Some of them (such as the questions about date of birth and being a veteran) are intended to clarify whether you're a dependent or an independent student.

GOOD TO KNOW

If your family's income and assets are very low, and you are applying for financial aid for the first time, **you may be eligible for a fee waiver** covering registration costs and up to six school reports. Whether you qualify will be determined based on the information that you provide in the PROFILE form itself. **You will automatically get the fee waiver if you qualify** — you don't have to apply for it separately.

Figure 9:
Finding a College's CSS code

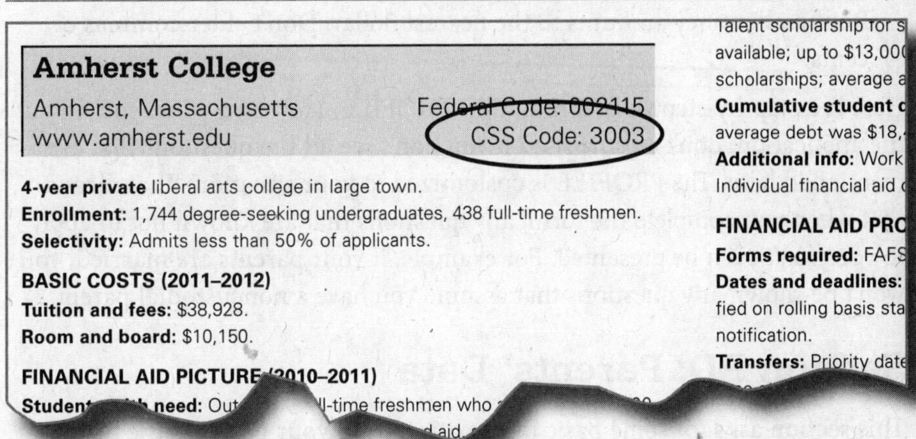

Amherst College

Amherst, Massachusetts — Federal Code: 002115
www.amherst.edu — CSS Code: 3003

4-year private liberal arts college in large town.
Enrollment: 1,744 degree-seeking undergraduates, 438 full-time freshmen.
Selectivity: Admits less than 50% of applicants.

BASIC COSTS (2011–2012)
Tuition and fees: $38,928.
Room and board: $10,150.

FINANCIAL AID PICTURE (2010–2011)
Student... need: Out... ll-time freshmen who ... aid.

Talent scholarship for s...
available; up to $13,00...
scholarships; average a...
Cumulative student c...
average debt was $18,...
Additional info: Work...
Individual financial aid ...

FINANCIAL AID PRO...
Forms required: FAFS...
Dates and deadlines: ...
fied on rolling basis sta...
notification.
Transfers: Priority date...

The College Scholarship Service (CSS) Code for each college in Part III of this book can be found in its college description.

During registration you will also be asked a few very basic questions about your family's finances; these determine whether you will be asked certain questions that usually don't apply to low-income families. For example, if your parents rent their house, they won't be asked about home equity in the Parents' Assets section.

You will also have to select the colleges or scholarship programs to which you would like to have your PROFILE report sent. Colleges and programs can be selected on collegeboard.org by name, code or state. You can add more colleges or programs to this list after you register, or even after filing your application. (See "After Submitting Your PROFILE" on page 67.)

Let's Walk Through It

Your PROFILE application may contain up to 18 sections, depending on your family's situation. The application includes questions about you and your finances and questions about your parents and their finances. There is a place for you to explain in your own words any special financial circumstances (section ES) and a place for any additional questions that may be required by one or more of the schools to which you're applying (section SQ). In addition, if your parents are divorced or separated, your noncustodial parent might need to complete an online Noncustodial PROFILE.

To help you fill out the PROFILE, there are instructions online that you can follow, along with other avenues for help (see sidebar on page 59). A few general points to keep in mind:

- If a financial question (such as one about income or assets) doesn't apply to you, enter a zero (0).

- If a nonfinancial question (such as a year or a name) doesn't apply to you, leave it blank.
- Round all money amounts to the nearest dollar. Don't enter commas or cents.

Here is a step-by-step walk through the PROFILE. However, when you fill out the application, don't be surprised if you don't see all the questions that are mentioned here. The PROFILE is customized to your situation. That means that when you complete the form, any questions that are known not to apply to you won't even be presented. For example, if your parents are married, you won't be shown any questions that assume you have a noncustodial parent.

Section PD: Parents' Data

This section asks for some basic information from your parents. The term "parents" as PROFILE understands it might need some defining. It basically means your custodial parents, the people with whom you live. If both your parents are living, married to each other and have custody of you, answer the questions about both of them. But if that isn't the case, follow these rules:

- If your birth or adoptive parents are divorced, separated or were never married, then you only need to provide information about the parent with whom you live. If you lived with both equally in the past 12 months, answer the questions about the parent who provided most of your financial support.
- If you have a widowed or single parent or a legal guardian, answer the questions only about that person.
- If your parent (as defined above) has married or remarried, include information about your stepparent too.

Your parents should use this section to provide information about themselves, including name, date of birth, employment status, and whether they themselves are in college or graduate school. Some of these questions have to do with clarifying financial strength — for example, the question about what kind of retirement plans your parents have. Some are just matters of housekeeping, such as their preferred daytime telephone number in case they need to be contacted.

Section PH: Parents' Household Information

Here your parents give basic information about their household, such as how many members are in their household and how many of them will be in college. The more dependents your parents have, and the more college educations they have to pay for, the less they will be expected to contribute to your own college education.

Section PI: Parents' Income and Benefits for the Previous Year

In this section, your parents report their income and benefits for the year before you intend to start college. Information in this section is important in establishing the resources they have available to pay for college.

If your parents have a completed tax return, filling in this section is mostly a matter of copying from the right lines. If they haven't filed a return but will do so later, they'll need to estimate the amounts. If they don't plan to file a return, they still have to report income. They will also have to report untaxed income and benefits, such as Social Security benefits or child support.

Section PP: Parents' Income and Benefits for the Year Before Last

Here your parents are asked to give information about income and benefits not for the year before you intend to start college, but the year before that year. Together with sections PI and PF, this is meant to give the PROFILE colleges a long-term view of your family's finances in order to clarify whether or not last year was typical. This section is fairly easy to fill out: for most of the questions — e.g., adjusted gross income, income taxes and itemized deductions — your family has only to look up their tax return for that year. You also have to calculate any untaxed income and benefits, using a worksheet that's provided.

Section PF: Parents' Expected Income and Benefits for This Year

Here your parents have to estimate how much they expect to receive in income and benefits during the year in which you start college. Again, the idea is to establish as clear a picture as possible about your family's finances in the long term, and to show whether the year before you started college was typical or not. Your parents will have to estimate work income, other taxable income, and untaxed income and benefits. In Section ES, explain any unusual increases or decreases in income and benefits (10 percent or more) from last year.

Section PA: Parents' Assets

This section asks about your parents' assets because these are resources that can help them finance college. There are questions about cash and savings and checking accounts (with their value as of the day you fill out the form). If they own their home, there are questions to determine home equity, the difference between the current market value of their home and the outstanding mortgage debt.

There are also questions about the current market value of any other assets they own, including investments and other real estate. They also need to include educational savings accounts, such as 529 prepaid tuition or college savings plans or Coverdell savings accounts that they've opened for you or your siblings.

Sections BA and FA: Business Assets and Farm Assets

These sections will only appear if your parents indicated ownership in a business or farm. There will be questions about value, debt, number of employees, tax form filed and if you live on the farm.

Section PE: Parents' Expenses

This section asks about certain special expenses your parents might have. These are not just any expenses, such as grocery bills or vacation airfare, but specific costs that might legitimately affect their ability to pay for college. Included here are child support payments, certain educational costs, and medical and dental expenses not covered by insurance.

Section NP: Information About a Noncustodial Parent

If your parents are divorced or separated, this section asks for information about the parent who doesn't have custody of you. But it should be filled out by your custodial parent. If for any reason you can't get sufficient information about the noncustodial parent, explain why in Section ES. Many colleges want this information because they believe it is the responsibility of both your biological or adoptive parents to pay for your college costs, even if they no longer live together, and even if the parent who does have custody of you has remarried. That's why, after you've filled out this section and submitted your PROFILE, they may request that your noncustodial parent fill out a supplemental form, the Noncustodial PROFILE. (See "After Submitting Your PROFILE" on page 67.) The section you're filling out here is not that supplemental form; your noncustodial parent will fill out that form if it's required.

Section SD: Student's Data

This is the beginning of the part of PROFILE that focuses on you, the student applying for aid. In Section SD, you provide some basic information about yourself. Much like on the FAFSA, you'll be asked to name your current legal state of residence, which may not be the same as the state you're actually living in now (see page 46).

Section SI: Student's Income and Benefits for the Previous Year

This section asks about your income and benefits in the year before you intend to start college.

If you have a completed tax return for that year, this section is mostly a matter of copying the amounts from the correct lines, such as the adjusted gross income and income tax paid. If you haven't filed a return but plan to do so later, you'll have to fill in estimates. If you don't plan to file a return but you did make some money last year, you'll have to report it. Untaxed income also goes in this section. A worksheet is available for you to tally it up.

Section SR: Student's Expected Summer/ School-Year Resources for the Coming School Year

Here you're asked to state your expected resources for this coming summer and this coming school year. You're also asked about scholarships you expect to get from sources other than the colleges to which you're applying and how much money your parents think they'll be able to pay for your college expenses.

This may seem like a strange series of questions, especially if you don't know yet where you'll be going to college next year, or where (even if) you'll be working. But colleges that use the PROFILE want to have as clear a picture as possible of your future resources, not just your past ones. For example, if you currently have an after-school job but will leave that job when you graduate, the financial aid offices need to know that the income from that job won't be available to you anymore once you've started college.

Do the best you can to estimate these figures. If you're not sure how to answer in your particular case, check the PROFILE help online or contact the financial aid office at the college to which you're applying.

Section SA: Student's Assets

This section asks about your assets — the money or property you, the student, currently own. These too affect your ability to pay for college. You need to list any cash you have and any checking or savings accounts in your name. Give their value as of the day you're filling out the application. You should also include any investments, such as certificates of deposit, savings bonds, stocks or real estate that you own. If you have any Individual Retirement Accounts (IRAs) or other tax-advantaged retirement accounts, you should also list them here.

If you're an independent student, then any money you have in 529 prepaid tuition or college savings plans or Coverdell savings accounts should be included here. If you're a dependent, those will be considered your parents' assets, and the information about them should go in Section PA.

This section will also ask you to answer questions about any trust accounts your parents or other relatives may have established for you. A trust account is money that is held for you by somebody else until you reach a certain age, at which point it becomes yours. Colleges want to know about this because if you have a trust, that money will eventually reach your hands, lowering your ultimate financial need. If you have any trust accounts, list their value here and answer the questions about them. But don't include money in Section 529 plans; those aren't the same as trusts.

Section SE: Student's Expenses for the Previous Year

You'll only see these questions if you're an independent student. If you are, you'll be asked about any child support you or your spouse paid to a former spouse and any medical and dental expenses you had last year that weren't covered by insurance. Most colleges will consider these expenses in determining your financial need.

Section FM: Family Member Listing

These sections ask questions about other dependent members of your household. If you are a dependent student, you will be shown the Parents' Household version. If you are an independent student, you will be asked questions about your household in the Student's Household version, and if required by your school, your parents' household in the Parents' Household section.yy

The questions in Section FM ask for more information about these household members: their names, how they're related to you, their ages, and to what extent you or your parents are required to pay for their school or college education last year and next year. The reason for these questions is that if household members other than you are enrolled in college, and your family is paying heavily to fund those educations, the colleges may take this into account when they determine the expected family contribution (EFC) to your own education. If there are younger children in the family, the colleges will assume that a certain portion of the household's income and assets need to be saved for their college educations, which will also affect your EFC.

Section ES: Explanations/ Special Circumstances

This is the one free-form part of the PROFILE, where you use your own words rather than fill in boxes. This section gives you a chance to explain anything unusual in your application or any special circumstances that affect your family's ability to pay for college. You can mention, for example, reasons for unusually high medical or dental expenses, steep rises or falls in income from year to year, or loss of employment. You should also give information about any outside scholarships you've been awarded. This allows the PROFILE colleges to better understand your financial picture.

In addition to telling the colleges about anything you think it's important that they know about, you should also use this section to expand on your answers to certain questions in previous sections, per the instructions that you'll find on the PROFILE website. For example, you can provide details about tuition benefits, gifts from relatives, etc.

You're limited to 2,000 characters in this section. If you need more space, send the information on paper directly to your colleges, including your name and Social Security number on all correspondence. (**See Step 8 for tips on how to let your college know about your special circumstances.**)

Section SQ: Supplemental Information

Section SQ may not be included in your application. You will only see it if one or more of the colleges to which you're applying requires more information. In that case, you'll see additional questions here. Your answers to these questions will be used only by the colleges that ask for them. Some of the questions colleges ask here are used to determine your eligibility for purely need-based financial aid; others are used to determine if you're eligible for scholarships that have non-need-based criteria.

Here are some examples of the types of questions you might see:

- What is the year, make and model of the family's primary car?
- Do you or either of your parents receive free food or housing as a job benefit?
- What is your family's religious denomination? (This information will be used to determine scholarship eligibility.)
- In what field of study do you plan to major?

After Submitting Your PROFILE

After you complete your PROFILE, you'll receive an online PROFILE acknowledgment that confirms the colleges to which you're sending the information and gives you the opportunity to correct any data you submitted. You should print the acknowledgment, which includes the list of colleges and the data you entered on the form. Once you submit your PROFILE, you can't revise your information online for the colleges you selected. Use the printed acknowledgment to make changes, if necessary, to the PROFILE information, and send those corrections directly to your colleges.

The College Board analyzes your data and reports it to the colleges to which you're applying. The schools then apply their own institutional policies to figure out your expected family contribution (EFC). From this analysis, they determine how great your need is and how much institutional financial aid to give you.

GOOD TO KNOW

If only one of your birth parents has custody of you, your college may still require information from both parents. If that happens, the main PROFILE application collects information from one parent, and the **Noncustodial PROFILE** collects information from the other. After the information is processed, the college will complete the EFC calculation. How to divide up payment of the EFC among you and your parents is a family decision.

SENDING YOUR PROFILE TO ADDITIONAL COLLEGES

You can delete colleges from your list of schools only before you submit the application. After that, all the listed colleges will get your information. But you can add colleges whenever you want, even after you submit the application. Just go to the PROFILE website and click on "Add Colleges to

Submitted Application." The fee is $16 for each additional college or program to which you want your information sent.

When you add additional colleges, you will also be given the opportunity to update or correct any of the information on your original application. Please note, however, that this new information will only be sent to the colleges you're adding. You should directly contact the colleges to which you submitted your original application to update your information with them.

SUPPLEMENTAL PROFILE FORMS

Some colleges require supplemental information that's not on the PROFILE application. For example, a college may require a Noncustodial PROFILE if you don't live with both of your birth parents. When you register for the PROFILE and indicate that your biological or adoptive parents are not married, you will receive an e-mail with instructions, a temporary password and a link to an application that you should forward to your noncustodial parent to complete. This form can be completed only by the noncustodial parent.

Be aware that these follow-ups take additional time. All the more reason to leave yourself plenty of time to file the PROFILE before your college financial aid deadlines.

QUICK RECAP

Since the PROFILE form is customized, the application may not necessarily be the same length as the FAFSA. In some cases the PROFILE will contain more questions than the FAFSA and in some cases it will contain fewer. The main difference is that it tries to get a more complete picture of your family's finances. A few points to keep in mind:

- File early.
- The PROFILE is online only, so you have to submit it on a computer.
- Prepare by using the Pre-Application Worksheet.
- There are fees, but students from low-income families may qualify for a fee waiver.
- After you submit your PROFILE, you'll get an online acknowledgment confirming that you submitted it. To make corrections to your information, you should write your colleges directly.
- Depending on your circumstances, you or one of your parents may have to submit supplemental information to one or more of your colleges.

Step 7: Fill Out Any Other Required Forms

QUICK OVERVIEW

The FAFSA and PROFILE are the big ones, but don't forget to file any other forms that may be required by your state or by the colleges to which you're applying. You don't want to have your application for financial aid marked "incomplete" because you didn't file a one-page form. These forms can vary widely from college to college, and from state to state.

Some Colleges Have Their Own Financial Aid Application

Some colleges have their own forms that you have to submit in addition to the FAFSA and the PROFILE. A purpose of the form may be to get more information about your finances, or to find out if you're a member of a particular group that is eligible for a special scholarship or grant. If a college requires such a form from all first-time applicants, its description in Part III of the book will say "institutional form required" under the "application procedures" section. Contact the financial aid office at your colleges to find out more.

The good news is that these forms are generally not long or complicated — they are usually just a page or two in length. They manage to stay short because they are intended not to duplicate the FAFSA or PROFILE forms but to supplement them and help the financial aid office keep track of applications. Such a "one pager" might, for example, ask for basic identifying information, some demographic facts and whether you are interested in loans and work-study. This kind of form is typical at community colleges and most four-year public colleges. "It's almost like an update form," Mary San Agustin says of the institutional form currently in use at her institution, Palomar College. "It's basically just a supplemental form in case any changes occurred since the time the student applied for admission or completed the FAFSA."

Sometimes a college might require a longer form that asks questions about your finances that are about as broad and deep as the FAFSA or PROFILE. Usually this only happens with colleges that use their own formulas to calculate need, but choose not to use the PROFILE to help them with it.

Another reason a college might require its own financial aid form is if it requires every student to have a computer on campus. Such schools sometimes have a supplemental form that qualifies needy applicants for a stipend to buy a computer, or places them in a "loaner" program so they can borrow one. The University of Virginia has two forms that deal with computers. One form is for its "laptop loaner" program, and a different form is for a "one-time computer expense" that allows students who want to buy a laptop to add the purchase price to their cost of attendance; that way their aid package may cover the cost.

Still another kind of institutional form is one for early decision applicants. Such a form works as a sort of "pre-read" meant to help students get an early estimate of their expected family contribution and the financial aid package they will receive if they accept an early-decision offer. (The rules of early decision require them to accept the offer if the college offers enough financial aid for them to attend.) Some schools offer a similar pre-read form for student athletes who are being recruited by a coach.

Scholarship and Grant Forms

Some colleges require a separate form for students applying for merit scholarships. This isn't always the case: At many schools, every student who applies for admission is automatically considered for merit scholarships. But at some schools, you must file a separate application for merit scholarships. The rules may even differ from department to department, depending on your major. "Theater majors may have to audition," says Bonnie Lee Behm of Villanova University. "Or a film major may need to send in a tape." Contact the financial aid office at your colleges for more details, and check with the department in which you're interested in majoring.

Some institutional forms ask questions to find out if you qualify for financial aid funds set aside for students with particular characteristics. For example, the college might offer grants that are only available to children of alumni or descendants of the town's founding families. At most colleges, these grants are part of the need-based aid program, so you have to demonstrate need through the FAFSA along with proving you have the right qualifications for the grant.

Verification of Your Tax Return

Some colleges require you to provide your family's federal or state tax returns for verification. **"Verification" doesn't mean that you did something wrong.** It's not like an IRS audit, where only suspicious tax returns are selected for special scrutiny. Since colleges disburse federal money — in the form of grants, work-study and loans — they are required by law to check the information that a certain percentage of financial aid applicants have submitted.

Not all colleges ask for this information the same way. Some will require you to use the IRS Data Retrieval process; some might require official tax transcripts; others might just want photocopies of the returns. Check directly with the college to verify how you should submit the returns, and if they also require any attached schedules or the W-2s or 1099s you received from employers and banks. Usually you'll also have to fill out a form that allows colleges to confirm details, like how many of your siblings are enrolled in college. The college may ask you to send your documents directly to the financial aid office, or it might ask you to send them to the College Board's Institutional Documentation (IDOC) service.

Some colleges will request verification if the data you submitted on the FAFSA looks unusual. As an extreme example, people who reported that they had no income last year may be asked how they supported themselves.

State Forms

Most states rely on the FAFSA to award their need-based grants and loans to students. But a few states have their own financial aid forms. For example, New York State has an application for its Tuition Assistance Program (TAP) that is sent to eligible students who submit a FAFSA.

Even though the thought of filling out yet another form may seem burdensome, and you feel sure that you won't qualify for the state aid program, fill it out. If you don't, your application might be marked "incomplete" at your colleges. These state forms are usually short and don't take long to fill out, especially once you do the prep work of filling out the FAFSA. **When you file the FAFSA online, you'll be automatically directed to your state's form.** (If you file the FAFSA paper form, you'll usually have to send away for a paper copy of your state form.)

Table 2:
State Aid Deadlines

STATE	FORM(S) REQUIRED	DEADLINE	NOTES
Alaska	FAFSA	6/30	
Arkansas	FAFSA	6/1	Higher Education Opportunity Grant Academic Challenge awards
California	FAFSA, state form	3/2 9/2	Initial awards Additional community college awards
Connecticut	FAFSA, state form	2/15	
Delaware	FAFSA	4/15	
District of Columbia	FAFSA, DC form	4/30	Priority date
Florida	FAFSA	5/15	
Idaho	FAFSA, state form	3/1	
Illinois	FAFSA	1/1	Priority date
Indiana	FAFSA	3/10	
Iowa	FAFSA	7/1	
Kansas	FAFSA, state form	4/1	
Kentucky	FAFSA	As soon as possible after 1/1	
Louisiana	FAFSA	6/30	
Maine	FAFSA	5/1	
Maryland	FAFSA	3/1	
Massachusetts	FAFSA	5/1	
Michigan	FAFSA	3/1	
Minnesota	FAFSA	30 days after start of term	
Missouri	FAFSA	4/1	
Montana	FAFSA	3/1	
Mississippi	FAFSA	3/31 9/15	HELP Scholarship MTAG and MESG Grants
New Jersey	FAFSA	6/1 10/1 3/1	Tuition Aid Grant applicants All other applicants Spring-term applicants only
New York	FAFSA, state form	6/30	
North Carolina		As soon as possible after 1/1	
North Dakota	FAFSA	4/15	
Ohio	FAFSA	10/1	
Oklahoma	FAFSA	3/1	
Oregon	FAFSA	2/1 3/1	Opportunity Grant OSAC Private Scholarships
Pennsylvania	FAFSA, state form	5/1 8/1	4-year degree candidates Other applicants

STATE	FORM(S) REQUIRED	DEADLINE	NOTES
Rhode Island	FAFSA	3/1	
South Carolina	FAFSA	As soon as possible after 1/1 6/30	SC Commission on Higher Education Grants Tuition Grants
Tennessee	FAFSA	As soon as possible after 1/1	
Vermont		As soon as possible after 1/1	
Washington	FAFSA	As soon as possible after 1/1	
West Virginia	FAFSA, state form	3/1 4/15	Promise Scholarship Higher Education Grant

Residents of states not listed in this table should contact their state aid office directly. See page 137 for a list of addresses, phone numbers and websites for each state's aid office.

QUICK RECAP

In addition to the FAFSA and PROFILE, some states and colleges have financial aid forms of their own. Here's what to know about them:

- They're usually short.
- Their questions vary from school to school and from state to state.
- They may determine if you're eligible for special grants.
- They may help verify your financial information, perhaps through questions about your tax returns.
- If state aid is available, apply for it, or your colleges might consider your financial aid application incomplete.
- If one of your colleges requires an institutional application, fill it out, or you'll disqualify yourself from financial aid.

Step 8: Make Your Special Circumstances Known

QUICK OVERVIEW

If something in your family's financial life can't be explained on the financial aid forms, make sure your colleges know about it. These "special circumstances" may include a lost job, high medical expenses or supporting an extended family. Colleges are willing to listen and, if you make your case, may be able to improve your financial aid package by taking those circumstances into account. This step is about how to prepare your case.

Be a Person, Not Just a Form

Sometimes the financial aid forms you fill out don't tell the whole story. They may not show that your family sends money every month to support relatives in another country. Since the forms are based on last year's tax forms, they may not reveal this year's events: how one of your parents just lost a job, or will be shifting from full-time to half-time work. When the forms don't adequately report a special circumstance that affects your family's ability to pay for college, let your college know — it may change how much financial aid you get!

Even if you're not sure your circumstance qualifies as special, speak up. The financial aid office will let you know whether it qualifies. Don't think you're limited to communicating with your college only through the financial aid forms. If there's any doubt in your mind about whether those forms give a true picture of your family's situation, feel free to go beyond the form and contact the financial aid office. **Be a person, not just a form.** There are two reasons to do this: It guarantees that the college knows how much you are able to pay, and it shows that you're interested in the college — which may affect the lengths to which they'll go to help you.

Using the Financial Aid Forms

In some cases, you can inform your colleges of special circumstances through the financial aid forms themselves — the FAFSA, PROFILE and institutional forms (Steps 5, 6 and 7, respectively, of this book). If you're supporting children, if you've been in the military, or if your parents are divorced, your FAFSA will make that clear. For colleges requiring PROFILE, you can use Section ES of that form to describe special financial circumstances. Elsewhere on the PROFILE form, you can list special family expenses, such as your family's medical and dental expenses, or any private school tuition that your parents might pay for your younger siblings. While forms may serve well enough, it may still be a good idea to write a letter or schedule a visit. If there's any doubt in your mind about whether forms convey your situation, definitely contact the college.

Going Beyond the Forms

You may have special circumstances that aren't covered by the forms. Or financially significant events may happen after you submit the forms — events that may be too complicated to explain in a simple correction. If that happens, communicate with the aid office as soon as possible after you realize you have special circumstances or after any financial hardships arise. The sooner you act, the sooner the college can adjust your award — and the more likely they are to still have the funds available to do so.

Even after you start college, if a financial emergency occurs, let the school know. The financial aid director can often help needy students with unusual expenses, such as medical costs, emergency trips home or funding to allow them to take an unpaid internship in the summer instead of working for money.

How to Contact the College

A letter to the financial aid office explaining your circumstances is often the best way to state your case. Some schools have a form specifically for explaining special circumstances; it's worth asking your colleges what they prefer. The more closely you follow their procedures, the more likely you are to be heard.

No matter how you communicate with your college, be polite, clear and specific. There's no need for a despairing or bullying tone. **Remember, you're trying to put a face to the form, so make it a friendly one**. You'll get further by calmly presenting your situation and giving as many relevant specifics as possible. A school will want to know not only that a parent got laid off, but what the prospects for reemployment might be, whether the parent has filed for unemployment benefits and, if so, the amount of the benefit payments awarded to the parent. Don't be surprised or offended if the college responds to you with a request for documentation, such as a copy of your tax return or a recent pay stub.

The Special Circumstances Form

Some colleges have a form through which you can let them know about special circumstances. At Furman University, it's called the Special Financial Circumstances Form, and it is available on the school's website. "The purpose of the form is not to make everybody jump through a hoop," says Forrest

Stuart, the director of financial aid at Furman. "It's to help the parents and the student put on paper all the information we need to help them out."

The form asks the student for the specific data — such as about changes in income and expenses — that the financial aid office will need to reach a decision about their case. It helps the school treat students equally, and it prevents the vagueness that might be found in a letter. "A lot of time we'll just get letters — I've lost my job, I need more aid," says Stuart. "Well, that doesn't tell me a whole lot. But if I can see some concrete information, then that gives me an idea of how I can help this student."

Communicating by Letter

With many schools, the best way to contact the aid office is in a letter. Often, it can strengthen your case to enclose photocopies of supporting documentation with the letter — for example, a paper showing your parent was laid off. The aid officer may also ask you for specific documentation.

EXPERT ADVICE

"**We must have documentation**, and what we really like too is a nice **letter explaining the situation**. But on top of that, we also like to have a phone call or, if the student's already on campus, to have them come in and talk to us. That way, we can have a **dialogue about the situation** and give them some direction on what to provide to us and how to provide it."

— Vincent Amoroso, director, Office of Student Financial Services, Johns Hopkins University

After sending your letter, follow up with the financial aid office a week or two later to make sure they received it and to see if they have any questions. You can do this by e-mail or telephone. If you live close by, or have scheduled a campus visit, you should also visit the aid office, but call first to make an appointment.

E-Mail

Some colleges prefer to have you contact them by e-mail. At the University of Oregon, applicants can communicate their special financial circumstances through the school's website, where they can find an e-mail address for the financial aid office. "That way, they can do it whenever they think about it," says Elizabeth Bickford, the financial aid director.

Examples of Special Situations

Many circumstances can affect your family's ability to pay for college. They may include a change in your financial situation from what was reported in the financial aid forms, such as a lost job, emergency expenses, health problems or even a windfall that misrepresents your usual level of income.

Family ties can also have financial implications, such as supporting an extended family or going through a divorce. And if you've served in the military, there are some special instructions you need to follow on the financial aid forms.

Change in Financial Situation

Financial aid officers want to know not only that your financial aid situation changed, but why it changed. Certain types of changes are more likely than others to persuade them to give you more financial aid. Generally, aid officers will look more kindly on circumstances that are beyond your control, rather than the result of poor planning. For example, if your father gets laid off because his company has fallen on hard times, that is more likely to get attention than if he retires early to spend more time golfing. And the college is more likely to turn a sympathetic eye to necessary roof repairs than a loan to install a backyard Jacuzzi.

GOOD TO KNOW

If you're explaining your special financial circumstances by letter, it's best to send it to the financial aid office via mail or fax, so that it can be **easily incorporated into your file**. Write and format it as a standard business letter. **Put your name and Social Security Number** in the first paragraph, so the financial aid office won't have trouble matching the letter to your file.

LOST JOB OR LOST INCOME

If you or your parents had a job when you filled out the FAFSA, and now don't, that will clearly affect your ability to pay. Even if you receive a severance package or collect unemployment benefits, your long-term ability to pay will still be reduced. This is information your financial aid office needs to know. For Palomar College, you would fill out a form that allows the financial aid office to override the FAFSA data with the new data. "You have to still report the prior year's income," according to Palomar's Mary San Agustin, "but we override it with the current-year income."

The FAFSA form for 2012-13 asks if you or a parent is a "dislocated worker." But don't think answering "yes" to that question is sufficient to alert colleges to the problem. They will want to know more, and the more information you give them, the more likely they can help you. And given the large number of job losses caused by the current recession, you should try to give them this information as soon as possible. Remember, there is a limit to the amount of financial aid funds available.

Equally important are unusual changes in other sources of income besides wages and salaries. For example, suppose a student's mother becomes disabled in August and has to stop working, and her employer's disability insurance plan gives her a large percentage of her salary for the first six months (through February), but a much lower percentage afterward. The FAFSA will show a larger income than she will be receiving once the student arrives in college. This change in disability benefits, like a lost job, needs to be explained to the college.

EMERGENCY SAVINGS DRAWDOWN

An emergency may force your family to spend some of the savings that you reported on the financial aid forms. For example, suppose your house is damaged by a fire the day after you submit the FAFSA. Your family needs to spend a large amount of money to pay for the repairs. Depending on where the money comes from — regular savings, a retirement account, borrowing through a home-equity loan — this will have different effects on your need calculation. But no matter what the emergency or the source of the money you wind up spending is, you should tell the aid office.

Sometimes one crisis will have several different effects. Hurricane Irene in 2011 might not only have destroyed an applicant's home in Vermont, but put the family breadwinners temporarily out of work. In such a case, make sure the aid office knows about all the different effects on your financial situation.

HEALTH PROBLEMS

A serious health problem in your family can have financial as well as medical effects. It may involve both an emergency savings drawdown to pay for medical expenses, and loss of income if the patient is too sick to work. If someone in your family has recently become disabled, developed a chronic illness or had major surgery, this has a clear impact on your family's ability to pay for college. Your college's financial aid office should be able to help.

A letter, or the school's own "special circumstances" form (if they have one), is a good way to let a college know about your family's medical problem. But the financial aid forms provide some paths as well. The PROFILE form allows you to list medical expenses that weren't covered by insurance last year, and estimate the same for this year. You can also explain high medical expenses in the "Explanations/Special Circumstances" box (Section ES). The FAFSA, on the other hand, doesn't ask specifically about medical expenses. If your college only uses the FAFSA, and you have unusually high medical expenses, a letter to the college makes sense.

WINDFALL

In financial terms, a windfall is a sum of money you didn't expect to get, which is normally a good thing — but even a windfall can have its downside. On your financial aid forms, if you received a windfall last year, that makes your annual income look higher than it normally is, which will tend to raise your expected family contribution (EFC).

Some windfalls are better than others. A windfall is usually understood as a genuine, one-time boost to your finances. It might be an inheritance from an aunt you never knew or an unusually high year-end bonus from your job. If you get such a windfall, inform the aid office that your income was higher than usual last year, and that they shouldn't expect a repeat performance next year.

But some windfalls not only make your annual income look bigger than it is, but represent an overall loss to your financial position. Examples include a severance package on losing your job, or an early withdrawal from a retirement plan, such as an IRA, to cover an emergency. In both situations, your records for that year show a boost in income, but that apparent good news conceals bad financial news — that you lost your job in one case, and suffered a massive hit to your retirement savings in the other. If you experience this kind of windfall, explain the reality to your aid office.

Family Ties

Not every family has two parents married to each other. And some families have stronger ties to grandparents, uncles, aunts and cousins than others. Different families live in different ways. The way your family lives may have financial implications that your financial aid office should recognize.

SUPPORTING EXTENDED FAMILY

The financial aid forms tell the colleges about how many people live in your household, including you, your parents and your siblings. But many families give financial support to an extended family of relatives who live outside the household. Immigrant families, for example, often send money regularly to grandparents, aunts or uncles in another country. Since that decreases the amount you have available to pay for college, make sure the financial aid office knows about it.

DIVORCED OR SEPARATED PARENTS

If your parents have divorced or separated, make sure the colleges know how that has affected your ability to pay. To do this, follow the rules on the financial aid forms. For the FAFSA, provide only the information about the parent you lived with more during the past 12 months (your custodial parent) — and, if that parent has remarried, your stepparent. For the PROFILE, provide not only that data but also information on your other parent, the one who does not have custody of you — your noncustodial parent. That information goes in Section NP of the PROFILE.

Some colleges that use PROFILE will also want your noncustodial parent to submit information separately on the Noncustodial PROFILE. That information will be confidential; you and your custodial parent won't be able to see the data the other parent provides, nor will that parent see yours. However, the information submitted by your noncustodial parent will affect the college's calculation of your total expected family contribution (EFC). If you don't think it will be possible to get your noncustodial parent to fill out the form, let the college know. However, the school isn't likely to waive its requirement for the form for anything less than a significant reason.

In the parent-income section of either the FAFSA or PROFILE, a custodial parent who is receiving alimony or child support payments should report only what he or she received, not what he or she was supposed to receive. In certain circumstances, documented evidence that your noncustodial parent is behind in payments could help support your case if you appeal your award.

Military Service

If you're currently serving in the active-duty military or the reserves, or if you are a veteran, don't assume that your military benefits alone will meet your full financial need. At most institutions, they no longer will. Benefits or not, you should apply for financial aid by submitting the FAFSA and any other required forms.

When filling out these forms, there are a few points to remember. Read the instructions carefully to make sure you qualify as a veteran for purposes of federal student aid. You should report housing allowances, subsistence allowances and untaxed combat pay as income. But don't include veterans' education benefits or ROTC scholarships when answering the questions about your untaxed income. The colleges consider them outside resources to be reported separately. (*See Step 9 for more information on outside resources.*)

Veterans are as liable as anyone to the special situations discussed earlier, from lost jobs to medical crises. That includes windfalls. For example, if you received a lot of combat pay last year but have now been discharged and won't receive it again, you should explain that to the colleges.

For more information on the intricacies of how veterans' benefits affect the FAFSA, see www.gibill.va.gov.

QUICK RECAP

If there are special circumstances that affect your ability to pay for college, let your college know.

- Tell the college financial aid office as soon as you know about your special circumstances — either before you get your award or afterward.
- If you have to go beyond the forms, write a letter, e-mail, call or visit.
- Explain your situation clearly, documenting it where appropriate.
- The situations that may affect your ability to pay range from a lost job or high medical bills to status as a veteran or an undocumented immigrant.

Step 9: Look for Scholarships

QUICK OVERVIEW

It's worth it to look for financial aid beyond what you'll get from colleges and federal student aid programs. This "outside money" probably won't amount to a "full ride," but it can help. Begin your search for outside scholarships around the time you start looking for a college because many scholarships have early deadlines.

Scholarships Colleges Give You vs. Scholarships You Get on Your Own

KNOW THE LINGO

Outside money — Grants and scholarships that come from sources other than colleges or the federal government, such as states and private organizations.

Portable money — Grants and scholarships that you can take with you to whichever college you attend.

College-offered money — Grants and scholarships that colleges award from their own funds.

Financial aid doesn't come only from the government and colleges. It also comes in the form of scholarships from outside sources, including states and private donors. This money doesn't come looking for you: You have to find the programs that fit you and apply. You will have to qualify for the scholarship in some way, whether through academic merit, artistic talent or fitting some set of criteria, such as being a person of Japanese descent living in either Connecticut, New York or New Jersey. **Very few outside scholarships offer anything close to full tuition, fees, room and board.** But they're worth the search because every little bit helps.

The scholarships you can get from outside sources are not exactly like the scholarships you might get from your college. These are the basic facts to know about each type.

College-Offered Scholarships

In most cases, you don't have to apply separately for the scholarships that colleges award. You're automatically considered for them when you apply to the school. If you qualify, the college will include the scholarship in your financial aid package as they see fit. However, some colleges have merit-based scholarships for which you must apply separately.

To find out what the rules are for scholarship aid at your colleges, contact the schools or look at their websites, which usually describe the process for applying for scholarships under "admission" and then under "financial aid." Be sure to do this research *before* you submit your application for admission. At some colleges, you have to indicate on your admissions application that you are applying for a special scholarship; for example, this is true of Boston University's Trustee Scholar Program. At others, you don't have to apply for special scholarships until after you've submitted your application for admission.

Many college merit scholarships have to be renewed from year to year. To make sure yours is renewed, know the school's criteria for keeping it — for example, maintaining a certain GPA. Different scholarships will have different criteria at each college.

Outside Scholarships: State Sources

Almost every state offers scholarships to their residents. These scholarships are usually available only for state residents attending colleges within the state, though a few states offer "portable" aid that a state resident can take to a college in another state.

Take the time to research scholarships and grants in your state. Almost every state has a department of education website that describes state scholarships and how to apply for them. These are usually separate from the state-sponsored, need-based financial aid programs for which you apply through the FAFSA or the state's own financial aid form, such as the Tuition Assistance Program (TAP) in New York State. An example of a state-sponsored, merit-based scholarship program with a separate application process is Florida's Merit Scholars Award, for which applicants must show high academic achievement.

Outside Scholarships: Private Sources

Private scholarships are offered by many sources, including foundations, corporations, civic groups, religious organizations, veterans' associations and the military. The Society of Women Engineers offers the Bechtel Corporation Scholarship to high-achieving female students of engineering. United Methodist Scholarships are available to students who belong to that Christian denomination. The Senator George J. Mitchell Scholarship Research Institute offers awards to Maine residents studying in state.

Don't assume you have to be a genius to get a private scholarship. Although many scholarship programs consider academic merit, a range of conditions may qualify you for a scholarship, including interests, ethnic background and community work. The Los Padres Foundation grants scholarships to low-income Latino students. California students pursuing a career in agriculture are eligible for a California Farm Bureau Scholarship.

Most scholarships come with limits. Though a few programs will pay full tuition, the amount of most awards is much smaller, as little as $500 or $1,000.

MYTH/FACT

Myth: "Untold millions" of scholarship dollars are available for use every year.

Fact: Private scholarships are only a small segment of the overall money available for college — **just 4 percent** of all aid to undergraduates. True, that share amounts to $6.6 billion a year, but that's dwarfed by the $185 billion paid out by other sources. Money from federal, college-granted and state funds, in that order, are likely to be much more important in your overall financial aid package. It's worth looking for private scholarships, but don't count on them as your sole source of funding.

Many awards are limited to the freshman year of study. Fortunately, other scholarships are only for later years. The Bechtel Corporation Scholarship, for example, is just for women in their sophomore, junior or senior year of study. And once you've declared a major you may find yourself eligible for a scholarship that is aimed only at students in your academic discipline.

Searching for Scholarships

Searching for private scholarships takes effort. But there are a number of Web-based scholarship search engines, like the ones on collegeboard.org and fastweb.com, that can help you zero in on scholarships for which you may qualify. If you like using this book, you might prefer to search for scholarships using the *College Board Scholarship Handbook*. It describes more than 2,100 outside scholarships, internships and loan programs, and is indexed by eligibility requirements — such as minority status, religious affiliation and state of residence — to help you match yourself to the programs.

Beware of commercial scholarship search companies that offer to help you find scholarships for a fee. Some do a responsible job, but many charge exorbitant fees and make fraudulent claims. For example, if they "guarantee" you a scholarship or promise to "do all the work for you," they are probably lying. Getting a scholarship is never guaranteed and, no matter what, you are going to have to do some work to apply.

Your school counselor may be of more help. Many private scholarships send application forms directly to school counselors. Tell your counselor in your junior year or early in your senior year that you are interested in applying for private scholarships.

Start researching options as soon as possible. You'll need time to learn about scholarships, request information and application materials, and complete your application. So look for scholarships as soon as you can — in the summer before your senior year, or by October or November of that year.

Look Locally

The national and state programs that you'll find on Web-based scholarship search engines and in print directories are good sources of scholarship aid. But don't forget to look even closer to home: your own county, city, town, employer or church. When looking for scholarships, it pays to look locally.

The fact is, you are more likely to obtain a scholarship from a local organization than from a state or national one. On the local level, you will be competing with a smaller pool of applicants and are more likely to have characteristics that interest the donors. Again, your school counselor can help. The counseling office will have a file of local scholarships — from banks, the Kiwanis, the local garden club and other groups. Let your counselor know you are looking for scholarships; stop by the counseling office regularly to read the scholarship files or check the scholarship bulletin board. The office may also use Internet announcements, e-mail postings or newsletters to spread the word about scholarship programs to interested students.

Employers can also be a source of scholarship money. If you have a part-time job after school or a summer job, check to see if the company that employs you has a scholarship program or offers tuition assistance. For example, Chick-fil-A has a well-known scholarship program for its restaurant employees. Some companies provide their employees with a dependent tuition-assistance benefit. That means one of your parents might be able to get his or her employer to pay some of your tuition.

Military Scholarships and Education Benefits

In return for military service, the armed forces offer a variety of college scholarships and education-assistance plans. For example, in the Reserve Officer Training Corps (ROTC) program offered by the Army, Navy and Air Force, you get scholarship assistance for college while being trained as a military officer. When you graduate, you are commissioned as an officer in the reserves and begin your term of military service.

Educational assistance for veterans is available in most states. If you're a veteran, contact your state veterans' administration for complete information and application forms.

Applying for Scholarships

Once you find the programs for which you qualify, you have to apply. This may mean not only another form to fill out, but compiling supporting documents, such as transcripts, recommendations and an essay. Depending on the program, you may have to provide evidence of leadership, patriotism, depth of character, desire to serve or financial need. Get to know the requirements of each scholarship as early as possible, so you can do any necessary extra work on time.

A few pointers to remember:

Apply early! Apply as early as possible to scholarship programs. If you can, do it in the fall of your senior year, even if the deadlines aren't until February or March. Very often, scholarship programs will have awarded all their funds for the year on a first-come, first-served basis before their stated deadline.

Follow directions. Read instructions carefully and do what they say. Scholarship programs receive hundreds and even thousands of applications. Don't lose out because of failure to submit a typewritten essay versus a handwritten one if required, or to provide appropriate recommendations. If you have a question about your eligibility for a particular scholarship or how to complete the application, contact the scholarship sponsors.

Be organized. It's a good idea to create a separate file for each scholarship and sort them by their due dates. Track application deadlines and requirements using Worksheet 2 (**a blank copy of this worksheet appears on page 124**). In one place, store the different supporting documents you may need, such as transcripts, standardized test scores and letters of recommendation.

Check your work. Proofread your applications for spelling or grammatical errors, fill in all blanks, and make sure your handwriting is legible.

Keep copies of everything. If application materials get lost, having copies on file will make it easier to resend the application quickly.

Reapply. Some programs only offer money for the first year of college, but others can be renewed each subsequent year. If your program is one of them, it pays to reapply once you're in college.

SAMPLE WORKSHEET 2:
Scholarship Application Planner

	PROGRAM 1	PROGRAM 2	PROGRAM 3
PROGRAM/SPONSOR	Wyzant College Scholarship	Young Epidemiology Scholars	First Bank
ELIGIBILITY REQUIREMENTS	Competition/talent	Competition/talent	Need, local residency
TYPE OF AWARD	Scholarship	Scholarship	Internship
AMOUNT OF AWARD	$1,000 or more	$1,000 or more	$2,500
CAN BE USED FOR	Tuition/fees	Any expense	Any expense
CAN BE USED AT	Any college	Any college	In-state colleges
DEADLINE	April 1	Feb. 1	April 1
FORMS REQUIRED	Application and essay	Web form	Application (includes need analysis)
TEST SCORES REQUIRED	None	None	SAT
ESSAY OR ACADEMIC SAMPLE	Essay	Essay, research project	None required
RECOMMENDATIONS	None	None	One teacher (Mr. Filmer), Local branch manager
NOTIFICATION BEGINS	Not sure	Not sure	May 15
REQUIREMENTS TO KEEP AFTER FRESHMAN YEAR	One-time payment only	One-time payment only	Based on performance during internship

For a blank version of this worksheet that you can photocopy for your own use, see the next page.

How a Scholarship Can Affect Your Financial Aid Package

SCHOLARSHIP PROFILE

The **Coca-Cola Scholars Program** is one example of the many sources of private scholarship aid. Run by the Coca-Cola Scholars Foundation, this annual program issues 50 national awards of $20,000 each, and 200 regional awards of $10,000 each. To be eligible, you must be a high school senior with a minimum 3.00 GPA at the end of junior year, and demonstrate high academic achievement, leadership and service orientation. Finalists attend an interview.

If a college to which you're applying hasn't met your full need — that is, if there's a "gap" in your financial aid award — outside scholarships can be used to fill that gap. That will make the college much more affordable and give you more choices when it comes time to decide which college you want to attend.

If, on the other hand, a college is already meeting your full need, it works a little differently. It would be nice if your outside scholarship were added on top of all your other financial aid to make your total aid package even bigger. But it probably won't be. Following federal policy, your college will most likely count any outside scholarship or tuition assistance you receive as an "outside resource" that decreases your aid package dollar for dollar. So the total amount of your financial aid package will be exactly the same.

You might think this is unfair: This is money you found and, in the case of employer tuition assistance and veteran's benefits, money you earned. On the other hand, it is money that's available to pay for your education without your having to dip into your income and assets. The philosophy behind financial aid is that everyone should pay what they can out of income and assets (your expected family contribution, or EFC), and then financial aid, including any outside resources, makes up the difference. The only way you can pay less than your EFC is if you get so many outside scholarships that they exceed your financial need. This is highly unlikely.

However, **it is still worth getting outside scholarships**. For one thing, it increases your freedom to choose a college regardless of cost. "If I'm a student, the more money that I can bring to the table for myself, the better position I'm going to be in to exercise choices that I might want to make," says Vincent Amoroso of Johns Hopkins University. For another thing, many colleges will use your outside scholarship money to reduce the self-help part of your aid package first — loans and work-study. This can significantly reduce the amount of money you'll owe after college or the time you'll need to spend working during college.

At some colleges, your outside scholarships will not be used to reduce your gift aid (grants and scholarships) unless the amount exceeds your self-help aid. Others use a formula in which at least a portion of your outside money will be used to decrease loans. For example, the first $500 in outside scholarships might be used to reduce your loans, then any funds remaining would be split 50/50 between reducing loans and cutting grants. Colleges that don't meet your full financial need may first apply outside scholarships toward filling the gap. Most colleges decide these issues on a case-by-case basis, but a few have stated policies that they publish on their financial aid Web page or will share with you if asked.

No matter what their policies, colleges welcome outside scholarships because they may reduce the amounts of college funds that have to be spent. Indeed, some schools encourage students to look for outside scholarships. According to Vincent Amoroso, the institutional financial aid form at his college asks students for data related to outside sources of financial aid, including global foundations, to "help us know [if] the student might match up to one of these other foundations that's awarding money."

In making admission decisions, admission offices are likely to look on outside scholarships favorably. Students who have searched for and found outside scholarships on their own will probably be seen as students with initiative and a sense of responsibility. That makes the student a stronger candidate for admission.

If you win a scholarship after you've already submitted your FAFSA and/or PROFILE, tell the colleges to which you've applied. Many schools have a special form specifically designed for you to submit this information. If you don't tell the colleges about a scholarship, it could jeopardize your eligibility for federal aid.

Tax Effects

Your outside scholarship may be taxed as income — this depends on the use for which it's designated by the program that awards the scholarship. Generally, scholarship dollars used for costs that are purely educational, such as tuition and fees, will be tax free. But money used for living expenses, transportation or books will be taxed as unearned income. The scholarship program will let you know how much (if any) of your award is taxable, and will send you a copy of the IRS's Form 1098 at the end of each tax year.

If your employer gives you tuition assistance, it's tax free up to $5,250 a year. After that amount, it's taxable. If you get tuition assistance from your parent's employer, the entire amount will be added to your parents' taxable income, but they might be able to deduct some of that amount (see Table 7 on page 112 for more info.)

QUICK RECAP

It takes work to hunt down and apply for outside scholarships, but it's worth it. Just remember:

- Outside scholarships will probably provide only a small part of the money you need for college, but every little bit helps.
- There are national and statewide scholarships programs, but look locally too.
- Websites, books and your school counselor can help you match outside scholarships to your qualifications.
- Search and apply early, and follow instructions.
- Your outside scholarship may affect the financial aid package awarded by your college, and it may be taxable as income.

Step 10: Weigh the Offers

QUICK OVERVIEW

After you've submitted all the financial aid forms, you'll receive offers of financial aid from the colleges that have accepted you. This step will help you weigh these award letters and make an informed decision based on an "apples to apples" comparison of the packages. If an award leaves you with a larger out-of-pocket share than you think your family can handle, you can appeal.

Comparing Award Letters from Colleges

Sometime after a college accepts you for admission, it will send you a financial aid award letter. The letter will detail your award — the financial aid package the college is offering you. It will contain an outline of the expected costs you will incur during a year at the college, your expected family contribution (EFC) toward those costs, and the types and amounts of financial aid the college is offering to make up the difference between the costs and the EFC.

The letter will also contain instructions on how to accept the aid package and how to contact the aid office if you have any questions or want to appeal the award.

It's best to wait until you have the award letters from all the different colleges that have accepted you before deciding which one to accept. If you have questions, wait until you've gotten answers from all the financial aid offices involved before you decide.

The offers in your award letters will differ. The amount and type of aid given will vary, and the letters may also differ in format, especially in how they itemize costs. Since most offers will only describe aid for your first year, an important question to ask is what you should expect to receive after that. Offers that look very similar for year one can be very different for subsequent years.

KNOW THE LINGO

Aid package — The total amount of all financial aid being offered to a student by a college.

Award letter — A document that a college sends to a student detailing the financial aid package. It indicates the type and amount of each scholarship, grant, loan or work-study opportunity being offered.

Appeal — A request that a college reconsider its financial aid package.

SAMPLE WORKSHEET 3:

Compare Your Awards

	COLLEGE 1	COLLEGE 2	COLLEGE 3
Step 1. List the name of each college you want to consider attending, the award deadline, and the total cost of attendance. This figure should be in your award letter. If not, refer to the college catalog or contact the college financial aid office.			
Name of college	*Private Univ.*	*Small College*	*Regional State*
Award deadline date	*5/1*	*5/1*	*4 weeks*
Total cost of attendance	*$31,825*	*$33,410*	*$15,566*
Step 2. List the financial aid awards each school is offering. Don't forget that grants, scholarships and work-study do not have to be repaid, while all loans must be repaid.			
Grants and scholarships			
• Pell Grant (federal)			
• SEOG (federal)			
• State	*can't use*	*$2,000*	*$2,000*
• College	*$12,700*	*$13,785*	*$941*
• Other			
Total grants/scholarships	*$12,700*	*$15,785*	*$2,941*
Percentage of package that is grant/scholarship	*60%*	*74%*	*53%*
Work-study opportunities	*$2,000*	*$1,000*	
Loans			
• Stafford-Direct (federal)	*$2,625*	*$2,625*	*$2,625*
• Perkins (federal)	*$4,000*	*$2,000*	
• Other			
Total loans	*$6,625*	*$4,625*	*$2,625*
Percentage of package that is work or loans	*40%*	*26%*	*47%*
Total financial aid award	*$21,325*	*$21,410*	*$5,566*
Grants and scholarships + work-study + loans			
Step 3. Calculate what it will cost you to attend each college you are considering. For each college, enter the total cost of attendance. Then, subtract the total financial aid award from the total cost of attendance. That number is the net cost, or what it will cost you to attend that college.			
a) Total cost of attendance	*$31,825*	*$33,410*	*$15,566*
b) Total financial aid award	*$21,325*	*$21,410*	*$5,566*
c) Net cost to attend (a minus b)	*$10,500*	*$12,000*	*$10,000*

For a blank version of this worksheet that you can photocopy for your own use, see page 125.

EXPERT ADVICE

"It's **not simply the dollar amount of the grant or scholarship** that families should focus on. They need to **lay out, side by side, the full picture**. What's the cost of attendance, including out-of-pocket expenses? What's the family contribution? What are the elements of aid? What's going to happen with loans, with work?"

— Joe Paul Case, dean and director of financial aid, Amherst College, Amherst, Mass.

In weighing the offers, the important thing is to compare apples to apples and not apples to oranges. For example, just because School A offers $10,000 in financial aid while School B only offers $8,000 doesn't necessarily mean School A has the better deal. If School A's aid package has $3,000 in grants and $7,000 in loans, but School B has $6,000 in grants and $2,000 in loans, School B is offering you more free money (grants) than School A.

There is another reason why a financial aid package may not be as big as it seems: higher costs. If one school's costs are higher than another's, you may be left with a higher out-of-pocket expense even after subtracting a "bigger" aid package. **Don't be dazzled by a large award. Instead, look for the bottom line: your net cost to attend the school.**

Here's a true story to illustrate this further. **Two sample award letters appear in Part II** (see pages 126, 127). These were taken from actual letters received by a student. Only the names of the colleges involved have been changed, to "Blue University" and "Green University." The student's first-choice college was Blue U, which cost about $2,000 more than Green U. When she first compared the letters, she was very upset because it looked like Green U was giving her a much bigger scholarship, and much more total aid.

But her school counselor showed her that Blue U was actually offering the better deal. First of all, the grants and scholarship from Green U only looked bigger because they were presented as a total. Secondly, the student loans offered by Blue U (Stafford and Perkins) were subsidized, while the Stafford loan offered by Green U was not. That meant at Green U she would have to pay interest on the loan while she was in college. And third, the $14,810 Green U was "offering" as a parent PLUS loan wasn't really aid at all, but just an option for how her family could pay for their contribution. Bottom line, the true cost to her would be about the same at both colleges, even though Blue U is more expensive.

Collegeboard.org has an online "Compare Your Aid Awards" tool that lets you do this kind of side-by-side comparison of your awards. You can also use Worksheet 3 to break out the different components of costs and aid packages and compare them side by side (a blank copy of this worksheet appears on page 125). When doing this analysis, keep an eye out for both quantity and quality. On the quantity side, for example, the "Family Share of Costs" figure tells you the amount of money your family will be expected to contribute. Your family will need to decide whether this amount is affordable. Look especially for evidence of "gapping," the practice of leaving a gap between the cost of attendance and the money accounted for by aid and EFC. You will be expected to fill that gap — in effect increasing your EFC.

On the quality side, consider the figures for "% of Award That Is Gift Aid" and "% of Award That Is Loan." The higher the proportion of gift aid (grant or scholarships) to loans, the better the award.

Loans vs. Grants

All other things being equal, it's better to receive a grant or scholarship than a loan. For that reason, a financial aid package with a high percentage of gift aid is more attractive, on the face of it, than one with a high percentage of loans. But there are circumstances where you might take the award that offers more loans and less gift aid: For example, if that college is a better fit for you overall.

In any event, don't be surprised if your award includes loans. Most aid packages contain them. Loans are optional; you don't have to take them out. But if offered as part of a need-based aid package, they can be an excellent way to help finance your education. The alternative — taking only grant aid and trying to pay the costs that the loans would cover out of pocket — could put your family under much more financial stress than the loan would.

It's usually in your best interest to accept subsidized Stafford and Perkins loans that are part of the aid package: The repayment terms are good and the government pays the interest while you're in school. Unsubsidized loans — such as unsubsidized Stafford, PLUS loan and private loans from a bank — should be studied more carefully to make sure the terms are acceptable. You should understand the specific terms of each loan, including its interest rate, the origination fee, the term of the loan and the grace period before repayment begins. You should also realize that unsubsidized loans are not need based and are typically used to help your families pay their EFC. If a college offers them as part of your aid package, consider them as an option, but don't weigh them equally with subsidized loans in the package.

Work-study jobs are also optional, but if you're offered one and you can manage the time, take it. Having a job on campus brings in income, expands your social networks, allows you to make contacts with professors and administrators, and gives you experience that can improve your résumé.

KEEP IN MIND

Just because you're awarded a loan to pay part of your college costs **doesn't mean you have to accept it**. If your family has funds available in savings or current income, you can use these funds if you prefer. The downside is that you'll have less money available now, which could put your family under financial stress. The upside is that you won't have to pay the money back later with interest.

Appealing Your Award

Even though your award letters are printed in black and white, they aren't necessarily the last word. It is possible to appeal the awards: to ask the colleges to reconsider their aid packages. There is no guarantee that they will grant your request, but there are circumstances where it's worth trying.

One reason you might appeal a package is if it has a lot of unsubsidized loans. However, bear in the mind that the college probably offered those loans because there wasn't enough gift aid to go around. Another reason to appeal is if you don't think you can afford the expected family contribution. You will need to have evidence to make that case. The college based its calculation of your EFC on the financial information you submitted. If you think this calculation was wrong, ask the financial aid office how it was made and see if you can find out if a mistake occurred. It will help if you have special circumstances that weren't communicated in your financial aid forms, such as a recent layoff; situations like this will clearly demonstrate why your

KNOW THE LINGO

There are three types of federal loans for educational expenses:

Stafford — Loan to students. May be subsidized (if student demonstrates need) or unsubsidized. If subsidized, the government pays the interest on the loan while the student is in college.

PLUS — A federal loan for parents to cover college costs not met by financial aid. Not subsidized.

Perkins — Subsidized loan to students with exceptional need. Perkins-loan debt may be forgiven if the borrower enters a career in the public service.

Questions to Ask About Your Award

These are some questions to ask your college financial aid office if you're awarded gift aid:

- ✔ What do I have to do to keep my scholarship — do I have to do anything more than maintain satisfactory academic progress?
- ✔ Is there a minimum GPA or other condition?
- ✔ Is the scholarship renewable in subsequent years?
- ✔ If I win an outside scholarship, what happens to my aid?

Questions to ask if you're awarded a loan:

- ✔ What are the terms of my loan?
- ✔ What is the interest rate, and when do I start repayment?
- ✔ How much will I owe by the time I graduate?
- ✔ What will my monthly repayment be?
- ✔ By how much will my loan increase after my first year?

Questions to ask if you're awarded work-study:

- ✔ Do I have a "guaranteed" job, or will I have to find one?
- ✔ How are jobs assigned?
- ✔ How many hours per week will I be expected to work?
- ✔ What is the hourly wage?
- ✔ How often will I be paid?
- ✔ Will I be paid directly, or will my student account get credited?

family would have difficulty paying its EFC. (*See Step 8, "Make Your Special Circumstances Known."*)

"I've changed financial aid packages on appeal if somebody can demonstrate why they can't afford it," says Forrest Stuart of Furman University. "It may be the need analysis just didn't take some things into account. If they can show me where there's a real problem, even to the point where they show me their monthly budget, I might say, 'Man, you are right. You've got these medical expenses or you've got this and that. Let me see if I can help you.' I am not perfect, and the need analysis is not perfect, and we'll sometimes overlook something."

Still another reason for appealing an award is if you have better offers from other colleges, and would like to see if this college can match them. Some aid offices will consider matching a better offer from another college. But most will only hear an appeal that's based on your family's financial circumstances. "We don't bargain," says Mike Scott of Texas Christian University. "We just don't want to play that game of, 'Well, we'll give you more money simply because another school gave you more money.'"

You might see the entire appeal process as essentially negotiation or bargaining — trying to get as much as possible from the school you'd like to attend. However, most financial aid officers loathe the term "negotiate." Your appeal will have a better chance of success if it appears not a matter of haggling but of providing information not previously available to the financial aid office.

It will also help your cause if you are obviously doing your part to fund your education. A student who accepts the self-help components of a school's financial aid package will be more likely to get extra help than one who declined them. "If the student is not willing to somehow contribute, either by working or taking out a student loan, then we are very unlikely to give them any extra money," says Mike Scott.

EXPERT ADVICE

"I tell families **not to use the word 'negotiate.'** If an aid package is much lower than what's being offered by similar institutions, families should call and ask if there is additional information that may make a difference."

— *Carlene Riccelli, college adviser, Amherst Regional High School, Amherst, Mass.*

A phone call is a good way to start the appeal process, even though most colleges will want you to put your reasons for an appeal in writing. Some have a specific form for appeals; others would like for you to state your case in a letter. Find out the college's preferred procedure by calling or checking their website. No matter how you file your appeal, your case will be stronger if you can provide data to back it up. A few days after filing your appeal, follow up with a phone call or, if possible, by visiting the aid office. Within a short time, the college will let you know its decision.

If you receive a revised award, take the new award letter and compare it to your other aid packages. **It's best not to decide where to enroll until you've received the final offer from each college.** But keep in mind the deadline set by each college for acceptance of its award. If you miss the deadline, you could lose the package. If you do need more time, try asking the college for an extension.

Follow Up: Accepting an Award

Once you've compared all the awards and any appeals have been ruled upon, you and your family will have to decide on a college. Many factors, including costs and financial aid, will be in play. If your first-choice college has accepted you but not given as much aid as you'd hoped, the choice may be difficult. Do you go to your first-choice college even though it's a financial risk for your family, or to a second-choice college your family can safely afford? In the end, your own preferences should have the greatest weight. Most of the loan debt, payable after graduation, will be on your shoulders. And your personal happiness at the school will have a major influence on whether you graduate successfully. If your family can put together a sensible financial plan to pay the costs, the best choice is the one that fits you best academically and personally.

Follow whatever instructions came in the award packet. If you're being asked for more information, send it. Complete any forms that came with the award letter. Sign the letter and return it by the due date.

QUICK RECAP

When you receive your award letters from colleges, you'll have to decide which offer to accept.

- Compare apples to apples, analyzing the awards to see what the real costs and financial aid elements are.
- Just because loans are offered, you don't have to accept them. But they're worth considering, especially if they're subsidized loans.
- If you appeal an award, you'll be on stronger ground if you can demonstrate circumstances that weren't previously made clear to the school.
- Your decision about which offer to accept should be based not just on cost but on how well the college fits you academically, socially and personally.

Step 11: Consider Your Out-of-Pocket Options

QUICK OVERVIEW

Financial aid is intended to cover the difference between your expected family contribution (EFC) and the total cost of college. However, you still have to pay your EFC and whatever gap there might be between the aid you received and your financial need. This step is about ways to meet those out-of-pocket costs.

Making Up the Difference

For almost every family, college is going to cost money. Even a generous financial aid package will usually leave you with some bills to pay. Some packages will meet less than your full need and leave you spending more than your EFC. You can afford to make up this difference between the total cost of attendance and the aid you're receiving if you take advantage of the various resources available to you. Most families use a combination of savings, current income and loans to pay their out-of-pocket costs. You'll have to decide how to do that in a way that fits your own particular situation. But you'll have help, because there are a number of programs and strategies that can help you save, pay or borrow for college.

KNOW THE LINGO

EFC (Expected Family Contribution) — How much money a family is expected to pay for college out of pocket, based on the family's ability to pay.

Need — The difference between your EFC and the cost of attending a particular college you've chosen. Financial aid is designed to meet your need, not your EFC.

Unmet need — The difference (if any) between your need and the financial aid offered by a particular college. Informally, unmet need is also called a **gap**.

Save for It

You shouldn't spend your entire family savings on college: You need to leave some for other uses, such as retirement and emergency medical costs. But it makes sense to use some of your savings for college.

Don't worry if your family doesn't already have a huge sum of money saved for college. **Every little bit helps, and it's never too late to start saving.** Even while you're applying to college, your family can start saving. Try to save as much as you can from summer and after-school jobs, and encourage your parents to set aside some money from every paycheck. Talk with your parents about how much money you and they already have saved for your college costs, and discuss how your family can afford the rest of the bill.

Don't believe anyone who says you shouldn't save for college because it will reduce your chances of getting financial aid. As noted in Step 2, savings are worth having so you can pay out-of-pocket costs without having to borrow. Very little, if any, of your parents' savings are counted against you when your financial need is determined. "Parents should not avoid saving because, frankly, a family that has saved has a resource to draw on, whereas a family that hasn't is totally dependent on current income and loans," says Joe Paul Case, dean and director of financial aid at Amherst College in Amherst, Mass.

There are a number of places families can put their savings. The most traditional is a regular bank savings account, which pays a little interest and offers freedom to withdraw and deposit money at any time. A certificate of deposit (CD) has stricter rules about when you can withdraw money, but it usually pays higher interest than a savings account. Both of these options are good for short-term, flexible savings. But neither has any tax incentives — tax breaks that make them especially attractive for college savings.

The following savings vehicles do come with tax breaks. For more details, see Table 3 on page 102:

529 college savings plan. Also known as the QTP (Qualified Tuition Program), these are tax-advantaged accounts sponsored by the various states. Interest earned in these plans is not taxed as income, and some states also offer a state income-tax deduction for contributions their residents make to the state's plan. There are no income restrictions, and contribution limits are high. Grandparents, uncles and aunts are also allowed to contribute to the plan, even if they don't live in the same state as you and your parents — in fact, you don't have to be a resident of a state to contribute to its plan, and you can withdraw funds from a state's plan to pay for expenses at a college in another state. Most plans offer a few different investment types, such as a fund that invests in stocks or one that invests in bonds.

Coverdell Education Savings Account. These tax-free trust or custodial accounts are similar to 529s, but they're sponsored by banks and brokerage houses instead of states, and therefore offer a greater range of investment choices. They can be used to pay private elementary and high school costs as well as college costs, unlike 529s, which can only be used for college costs. Total contributions for the student can't be more than $2,000 in a given year, and your family income has to be less than $110,000 (for single filers) or $220,000 (for joint filers). You can contribute to both a 529 and a Coverdell in the same year for the same student.

529 prepaid tuition plan. Like the 529 college savings plans, these are sponsored by the states, but they work differently. A 529 prepaid tuition plan lets a family make advance tuition payments years before their children will enter college. That allows them to "lock in" today's tuition rates instead of paying the higher rates likely to prevail years from now. Provided the student is admitted, the plans are guaranteed to be honored by public universities and some private colleges in the state that sponsors the plan. However, these plans have drawbacks. They can only be used for tuition and fees, not for room, board or other supplemental costs. When that's combined with the fact that the tuition rates are only locked in for in-state colleges, most parents prefer the more flexible 529 savings plans.

Independent 529 prepaid tuition plan. This is a special 529 prepaid tuition plan sponsored by a group of private colleges and universities and administered by TIAA-CREF. For more information, visit www.independent529plan.org.

U.S. savings bonds. If your parents pay for some of your college costs by cashing in U.S. government savings bonds, the interest that has accumulated on the bond may be tax exempt. That means the interest won't be taxed as income and your tax bill will be smaller. There's a penalty if you cash in the bonds less than five years after the date of issue, and there are some restrictions on the tax exemption. The bond must be issued after 1989 and your parent must have been age 24 or older when the bond was issued. This deduction can't overlap with any other education tax break. You can't use two different tax breaks to pay for the same expense. The family income must be less than $87,850 (for single filers) or $139,250 (for joint filers).

Uniform Gifts to Minors Act (UGMA) or Uniform Transfers to Minors Act (UTMA) account. These accounts allow parents to put money in the child's name so it will receive preferential tax treatment. Much of the earnings are taxed at the child's rate rather than the parent's rate. Such accounts were popular in the 1980s, but the advent of tax-free 529s and Coverdells has made them nearly obsolete as a college-savings vehicle.

Individual Retirement Account (IRA). Generally, it's not a good idea to raid the family retirement funds, such as IRAs, to pay for college. "We tell parents all the time, you can borrow money to pay for your kid's education. You cannot borrow money to retire with," says Mike Scott of Texas Christian University. It's usually better to take out a PLUS loan than to diminish retirement assets. Still, if your family does need to go into an IRA to pay college expenses, the government doesn't charge the 10 percent additional tax you would ordinarily have to pay for breaking open an IRA before age 59½.

Table 3:
Comparison of Education Savings Options

	COVERDELL EDUCATION SAVINGS ACCOUNT	529 COLLEGE SAVINGS PLAN (QUALIFIED TUITION PROGRAM)	529 PREPAID TUITION PLAN	U.S. GOVERNMENT SAVINGS BONDS	UNIFORM GIFTS TO MINORS ACT ACCOUNT	INDIVIDUAL RETIREMENT ACCOUNT
Tax advantages	Earnings in account not taxed as income	Earnings in account not taxed as income Some states allow residents to deduct contributions for state income tax purposes	Earnings in account not taxed as income Some states allow residents to deduct contributions for state income tax purposes	Interest earned is not taxed if used for qualified expenses	Interest earned is taxed at child's rate	Exception to the 10% early withdrawal penalty rule
Expenses that qualify	• Tuition & fees • Books & supplies • Room & board (if at least half-time) • Expenses for special needs services • K-12 education expenses	• Tuition & fees • Books & supplies • Room & board (if at least half-time) • Computer • Special needs services	Tuition & fees	• Tuition & fees • Contributions to a Coverdell or 529	Any expense (not limited to education)	• Tuition & fees • Books & supplies • Room & board (if at least half-time) • Special needs services
Contribution limits	$2,000 per year	None	None	None	None	$5,500 per year ($6,500 if over 50)
Income phaseout for benefits	$95,000–$110,000 (single filers) $190,000–$220,000 (joint filers)	None	None	$72,850–$87,850 (single filers) $109,250–$139,250 (joint filers)	None	Varies by type of account
Other limitations	Assets must be distributed by age 30 Must pay 10% penalty if distributions not used for qualified expenses	Must pay 10% penalty if distributions not used for qualified expenses	Benefits may only be used at colleges that participate in the plan Must pay 10% penalty if distributions not used for qualified expenses	Applies only to Series EE or Series I bonds issued after 1989 and purchased after owner turned 24	Counted as student asset for financial aid purposes	Interest earned will still be taxed at your regular rate

Work for It

Besides a summer job, you might also want to consider working during the school year to help meet expenses. There are two basic approaches. You can go to college full time while working part time, or you can hold a full-time job while attending college part time.

Full-Time Student, Part-Time Job

EXPERT ADVICE

"**Work gives students structure.** First, they have to be somewhere. They have to be doing something at certain times of the week, which helps them manage their time. Second, if the job is on campus, they get involved with an office or a department or a faculty member, and that helps to **strengthen that student's connection with that school**, which always enhances the academic experience."

— Vincent Amoroso, director, Office of Student Financial Services, Johns Hopkins University

If you're offered a work-study job as part of your financial aid package, the earnings from that job will go toward your college costs. Even if you're not offered work-study, you may still be able to find a part-time job on or near campus. You can also work during the summer to make money to put toward college.

Work has benefits beyond the extra income it generates. It can help you structure your time, which can make you a more disciplined student. Studies have shown that students who work part time get better grades and are more likely to finish college than those who don't work at all. If the job is on campus, it enhances the college experience by connecting students more closely with the school and giving them a chance to meet people they wouldn't meet in classes.

On the other hand, don't work so many hours that you jeopardize your ability to get through college. **If you're going to college full time, the recommended workload is about 10 to 15 hours a week.** If you work more than 20 hours a week, you're likely to get overloaded and put yourself at risk of dropping out. If you take fewer courses to make time for work, you may drop below full-time status, which could make you ineligible for many grants and scholarships. If your financial situation makes you feel that you have to work more hours, it might be better to borrow more money so you don't have to work so much.

Part-Time Student, Full-Time Job

A different (and much more difficult) way of approaching work is to be a full-time worker who goes to college part time. This is possible as long as you don't take too many credits in one semester. If you try for more than six to eight credits (two courses) while working full time, you'll probably have trouble getting everything done. On the other hand, if you take fewer than six credits a semester, you won't be eligible for need-based subsidized Stafford or Perkins loans or a Pell Grant.

Working full time while going to school part time is an especially attractive way to pay for an associate degree or a vocational certificate. Most community colleges cater to working students and offer classes at night to meet their needs. If you take six credits per semester, you can probably earn an associate degree in four or five years.

If you're planning on earning a bachelor's degree, however, you should strongly consider attending college full time and borrowing money to replace the income that you won't be earning through a job. Why? If you take only six credits a semester, it will take 10 years to earn a bachelor's! You will probably earn more money in the long run if you get that bachelor's in the usual four or five years, and concentrate on your career after you've earned that degree.

Some employers offer tuition assistance or scholarship money to employees who are attending college. Check to see if your employer is one of them. For a typical educational assistance program, up to $5,250 of those benefits will be tax free each year.

KEEP IN MIND

As noted in Step 2, you will be **expected to contribute** a larger percentage of your **work income to college costs** than your parents will. This is because it is expected that you have fewer financial responsibilities and will benefit more from college than your parents will. In general, you will be expected to pay about 50 percent of your earnings toward the EFC.

Co-op and Internship Programs

Many colleges sponsor internships or "co-op" (cooperative) programs with local employers. Some interns and almost all co-op participants receive payment from their employers along with academic credit. In co-op programs, you may be able to alternate periods of full-time work and full-time study. Often the business at which you intern hires you after graduation, or at least recommends you to others. Internship and co-op programs can help you make money, get academic credit, gain job experience and make contacts with potential employers.

Promising to Work Later

Holding a job during college is not the only way of using work to pay your college costs. There are several programs that allow you to commit to work in public service after graduation in exchange for either a non-need-based scholarship while in college or a stipend that can be used to repay student loans after college. The ROTC program is an example of the former, and AmeriCorps is an example of the latter.

ROTC

In return for military service, the armed forces offer career training and a number of educational benefits to help pay for college, including full college scholarships and education assistance plans. If you're interested in training to be a military officer during college in return for educational benefits, check with the Reserve Officers' Training Corps (ROTC) office at your high school or on your college campus. Each branch of the military offers ROTC training. Part IV of this book contains lists of colleges that offer ROTC programs for each service branch.

OTHER SERVICE PROGRAMS

AmeriCorps is a network of national service programs for which you can work as a volunteer, full or part time, for up to a year. After completing a term of service with AmeriCorps, you're eligible for an education award, which can be used either to repay student loans or to pay for college tuition. The amount of the award depends on how long you worked for the program, and for how many hours each week. (Currently, completion of one year's full-time service earns an award of $5,550.) For more information, go to www.americorps.org.

Another type of program is one that hinges on your financial aid package and the profession you choose after college. If you received a Perkins loan as part of your package, the loan may be forgiven if you enter certain professions serving the public, such as teaching, nursing or law enforcement.

Borrow It

To borrow money is to spend today what you'll earn in the future. You will have to pay the loan back, with interest, when you start earning money after college. A loan can be intimidating because it assumes you'll have the money for repayment, and you may not feel sure of that. But rest assured that college will increase your earning power, which will make it possible to repay your loans.

There are many forms of "bad debt" in our society, such as credit card debt, where you borrow money on unfavorable terms to buy consumer goods that will have little or no value in a year. By comparison, an education loan is a "good debt." You are borrowing money on favorable terms to achieve an outcome — higher lifetime earnings — that will more than pay back the loan.

Subsidized Stafford loans, Perkins loans and need-based state loans all have excellent terms that make them worth considering. Some institutions also offer their own need-based loans to qualified students. However, these loans are intended as financial aid to cover your need. In general, you won't be able to use them towards your expected family contribution.

However, loans are available that are not based on need and that your family can use to borrow money to meet their EFC. The terms are not as favorable as the need-based loans, but the loans may be helpful just the same. The most common types are the unsubsidized Stafford and the PLUS loan, both of which are guaranteed by the federal government, but there are also state and private sources.

How Much Should You Borrow?

If your family decides to borrow money to pay for college, they should consider the total debt that you will carry after graduation. That total debt includes any subsidized, need-meeting loans that you accept as part of the college's aid package as well as any non-need-based loans your family takes out to meet the EFC. When you pay back that debt, you'll do so in the form of monthly payments, and those payments should be reasonable ones that you can afford to pay from the income you're likely to have. The total monthly payment will usually be similar to a car payment — $200 to $300 a month. But the amount will vary with the amount borrowed and interest rate offered. See Table 4 on the next page for help in determining what your monthly payment will be. It shows monthly repayment over 10 years for a loan of $10,000 at various interest rates. To calculate a monthly payment for a loan amount not listed on the table, multiply the amount borrowed by the repayment factor for your interest rate. For example, if you borrowed $12,500 at 7.5 percent, your monthly payment would be $148.46 ($12,500 × .0118770).

KNOW THE LINGO

Principal — The portion of debt that is left over from the amount you originally borrowed.

Interest — The portion of debt that has been charged to you by the lender as a fee for loaning you the principal.

There are some ways to make your repayment burden lighter after college. Many lenders will offer to cut your interest rate a bit if you make your first 12 monthly payments on time. If you borrow from multiple federal loan programs, such as the Perkins, subsidized Stafford and unsubsidized Stafford, you can consolidate these loans after graduation, which will simplify things by allowing you to make only one payment a month. Consolidation also gives you the option of "re-amortizing" your loans — that means stretching your payments over a longer period of time than you would normally have left to repay the debt. If you re-amortize when you consolidate, you will usually have a lower monthly payment, but will pay more interest over the total life of all the loans.

Table 4:
Calculating Your Monthly Loan Payment

AMOUNT OF LOAN	INTEREST RATE	REPAYMENT FACTOR	MONTHLY PAYMENT
$10,000	4.00%	.010125	$101.25
	4.50%	.010364	$103.64
	5.00%	.010607	$106.07
	5.50%	.010853	$108.53
	6.00%	.011102	$111.02
	6.50%	.011355	$113.55
	7.00%	.011611	$116.11
	7.50%	.011870	$118.70
	8.00%	.012133	$121.33
	8.50%	.012399	$123.99
	9.00%	.012668	$126.68

GOOD TO KNOW

When you start paying back your educational loan, remember that the **interest may be tax deductible**. To a maximum of $2,500 per year, you can deduct the interest you pay from your income, which will lower your tax bite. In effect, the government will be subsidizing your loan. This is true for every kind of education loan, including PLUS loans.

Types of Non-Need-Based Loans

There are three basic types of loans you can use to pay your out-of-pocket costs: federal, state and private.

FEDERAL LOANS

Federal loans have relatively low interest rates and are guaranteed by the federal government. This means that if you don't pay your loan back to the lender (though, of course, you should), the federal government will. That encourages lenders to lend you money even if you're a student with no credit history and little employment record.

Two basic kinds of federal loans are used for paying an EFC, one for students, one for parents:

- **Student Loans (Direct Unsubsidized Stafford).** With an unsubsidized Stafford loan, you borrow money directly from the federal government, but the loan is provided through your college. You'll be charged only interest while you're in school, and can either pay it while you're in school or let it accrue (accumulate) for payment after school. If you let the interest accrue, the bank will "capitalize" it into the principal of the loan when you start sending them payments after graduation. Table 5 shows the effects of interest accrual. The calculations on the table are for example only — they assume that you borrow $3,500 at the beginning of your freshman year and don't borrow any more to fund subsequent years of education. With this amount and the interest rate shown, letting the interest accrue saves you a $20 monthly payment while you're in college, but it ends up costing you about $407 more over the life of the loan. Whether or not you let interest accrue, six months after leaving school (your grace period), you have to begin paying back both the principal and the interest. To apply for an unsubsidized Stafford loan, ask your college financial aid office; they will refer you to lenders.

Table 5:
Effects of Letting Interest Accrue While You're in College

	INTEREST RATE IN COLLEGE	MONTHLY PAYMENT IN COLLEGE	DEBT REMAINING AFTER COLLEGE	INTEREST RATE AFTER COLLEGE	MONTHLY PAYMENT AFTER COLLEGE	TOTAL INTEREST PAID OVER LIFE OF THE LOAN
Subsidized Stafford	0%	$0	$3,500.00	6.8%*	$40.28	$1,333.28
Unsubsidized Stafford (no interest accrual)	6.8%	$19.83	$3,500.00	6.8%	$40.28	$2,404.60
Unsubsidized Stafford (interest accrual option)	6.8%	$0	$4,571.00	6.8%	$52.60	$2,812.00

*After July 1, 2013, unless 3.4% rate extended by Congress.

- **Direct PLUS Loans for parents.** With a PLUS loan, your parents borrow money to pay for your education directly from the federal government (but through your college). They can borrow any amount up to the student's total cost of attendance minus the financial aid you receive. To get a PLUS loan, your parents have to fill out an application and pass a credit review. They will have to start making payments on the entire debt — both the principal and the interest — as soon as the loan money is disbursed to the school.

If you take out a federal loan, you'll receive a loan repayment schedule that spells out when your first payment is due and the number, frequency and amounts of the payments. You'll have to pay back the loan on schedule or go into default, an official state of failure to repay a loan. That would hurt your credit rating — your ability to borrow more money later.

Under certain circumstances, such as economic hardship, you can postpone repayment of a federal student loan by applying for a deferment (during which no interest accumulates) or forbearance (during which it does). Under exceptional circumstances, such as total disability or teaching in a designated low-income school, some borrowers get a loan discharge, or cancellation of the debt. These rules apply to all federal student loans, but not to PLUS loans.

STATE LOANS

Some states sponsor loan programs for students and parents in their state. These loans are usually neither subsidized nor based on need. Check with your state financial aid agency to find out more.

PRIVATE LOANS

Federal student loans are no longer available from private lenders. Under the new Direct Loan Program, Stafford student loans and PLUS parent loans now come directly from the U.S. Department of Education, and loan funds are provided through the college. If you have previously received a federal student or parent loan from a private lender, you will need to transfer the loan to the Direct Loan Program. Check with the financial aid office at your college for specific instructions.

HOME-EQUITY LOANS

Many parents consider taking out a loan against their home equity to pay for their children's higher education. While this may be an attractive option for your family, you should keep in mind that, unlike PLUS loans and other education loans, home-equity loans do come with the condition that if you can't pay back the loan, the bank can foreclose on your house.

Table 6:

Comparison of Education Loan Options

	DIRECT SUBSIDIZED STAFFORD	PERKINS	DIRECT UNSUBSIDIZED STAFFORD	DIRECT PLUS	PRIVATE/ ALTERNATIVE EDUCATION LOAN	HOME EQUITY LOAN OR LINE OF CREDIT
BORROWING LIMIT	$3,500 first year $4,500 second year $5,500 third and fourth years Higher limits for independent students and for graduate study	$5,500/year $27,500 undergraduate maximum	$5,500 first year $6,500 second year $7,500 third and fourth years Higher limits if parents were denied a PLUS loan	Maximum is difference between total cost of attendance and financial aid awarded	Depends on lender and credit check	Depends on credit check and home equity
INTEREST RATES FOR 2013-14	In school: 0% In repayment: 6.8% (fixed)	In school: 0% In repayment: 5% (fixed)	In school: 6.8% (fixed) In repayment: 6.8% (fixed)	7.9% (fixed)	Depends on lender and credit check; may be fixed or variable	Depends on lender and credit check; may be fixed or variable
PROS	Interest that accumulates while you're in college paid by federal government	No origination fee Interest that accumulates while you're in college paid by federal government Debt may be forgiven if you enter a career in the public service	Option of not making payments during college and "capitalizing" accrued interest into the loan upon graduation Same deferment, and forbearance rules as subsidized loans	No collateral required	Available for nondegree programs and adult continuing education	Can use money for noneducational purposes Repayment term may be longer than for federal loans
CONS	Only available to students with financial need 1% loan fee	Only available to students with financial need Amount of loan you're offered subject to college financial aid office's discretion	1% loan fee	Parents must pass credit check to take out loan Parents must begin paying interest immediately 4% origination fee	Student must pass credit check Parents may have to cosign promissory note May have high origination fees	Home used as collateral for loan Can take several months to secure loan; may need to have house appraised

KNOW THE LINGO

Advanced placement — Admission into an advanced-level course in a certain subject on the basis of an exam or other evidence that the student has already completed the equivalent of the introductory course in that subject.

Credit by examination — College credit earned by achieving a qualifying score on a standardized examination, such as an AP Exam or CLEP exam.

Accelerated program — A program of study completed in fewer semesters than normal, usually by taking extra courses and attending classes over the summer.

Cut It

In addition to spending past, present and future resources to pay your college bill, you can also take steps to make that bill smaller. This is an especially smart move if it looks like college won't be affordable otherwise, even when you contribute all you can from savings, current income and loans. But some strategies to cut college costs are worth using even if your family is financially comfortable.

Tuition "On the Cheap"

Tuition, the cost of taking classes, is usually high at four-year colleges. But you can get a reduced rate on those classes by taking them ahead of time at your own high school or a community college. By doing this, you may also be able to reduce the number of semesters you have to spend in college, which will cut not only your tuition costs but all other costs, such as room and board. Some colleges offer accelerated programs that will help you do that.

AP®/CLEP®

The Advanced Placement Program® (AP®) and the College-Level Examination Program® (CLEP®), which are sponsored by the College Board, help you earn college credit. The programs differ in various ways. For example, students take AP courses as part of their high school curriculum, but they can prepare to take the CLEP examinations by any number of means — in school, on the job or by just reading books in their spare time. These programs are similar, however, in that you earn credit by taking an examination and receiving a score that your college accepts.

Colleges differ as to which programs, courses and scores they accept and how much credit they grant. But every credit you receive means a credit you don't have to pay for in college. Depending on your exam scores and your college's policies, you may be able to graduate a semester or even a year early if you've taken enough CLEP or AP Exams.

CLEP exams help you earn college credit for what you already know at a fraction of a college course. Exams are offered in 33 subjects.

Find out if your institution grants credit for CLEP, then visit one of the 1,700 test centers that administer the exam. Study resources are also available. Visit www.collegeboard.org/clep. To find out about your college's policy on AP credit, go to the AP Credit Policy Info tool at collegeboard.org/apcreditpolicy.

TAKE COMMUNITY COLLEGE CLASSES OVER THE SUMMER

Courses at a community college usually cost much less than at a four-year college. Find out if there are courses you can take at a local community college in the summers and transfer to your four-year college. For example, if you don't have the knowledge of a certain subject that you need to pass a CLEP exam, you may still be able to take that course at a community college over the summer and transfer the credit to your four-year college.

OTHER ACCELERATED PROGRAMS

Some colleges offer an "accelerated program" designed for students who want to graduate in three years. These programs require a lot of work and dedication, but they will cut your college costs substantially by eliminating an entire year of expenses. It's possible to get through these programs if you're determined.

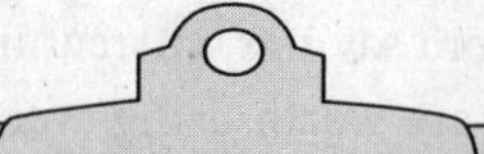

Cutting Other Expenses

Tuition is not the only college cost you can cut. Room, board, books, supplies, transportation — all of these add substantially to your total college bill. (Most people are shocked at what college textbooks cost these days.) Here are some suggestions to reduce these expenses:

BOOKS

- ✔ Buy used textbooks instead of new ones.
- ✔ Comparison shop for textbooks online.
- ✔ Sell your textbooks at the end of the semester.

ROOM AND BOARD

- ✔ Live off campus in a house or apartment that you share with classmates. That can be cheaper than a college dorm. (But check the policy at the college you want to attend — many require freshmen to live on campus.)
- ✔ If you plan to live in a dorm in your sophomore year and beyond, try to get a position as a resident adviser and the free room and board that comes with it.

TRANSPORTATION

- ✔ If you're commuting to school, carpool with a classmate from your area.

Education Tax Breaks

Federal student aid isn't the only way that Uncle Sam can help you pay for college. There are also tax breaks available for higher-education costs. By reducing the amount your family has to pay the government at tax time, these programs amount to federal subsidies for out-of-pocket costs. Some of them take the form of tax credits, which cut your taxes dollar for dollar: That is, a $1 tax credit would make your tax bill $1 smaller. Others take the form of tax deductions, which lower the amount of your income that is subject to tax, indirectly lowering your tax bill.

GOOD TO KNOW

The information about higher-education tax breaks printed here is current as of early 2013. **To make sure you qualify for a deduction or credit** before you file, download IRS Publication 970, "Tax Benefits for Education," from www.irs.gov.

There are two federal income tax credits for college expenses: the **American Opportunity credit** and the **Lifetime Learning credit**. These tax credits let your family reduce the taxes they pay dollar-for dollar, but each credit is for a different amount and has different requirements. And for any one student, a family can only elect to use only one of these credits on the same tax return.

The American Opportunity credit is worth up to $2,500 per year for each eligible student in the family. (This credit replaces the former Hope education credit.) Unlike the Lifetime Learning credit, if the amount of the American Opportunity credit is more than the amount of tax owed, all or a portion of the excess may be received as a refund. This credit is available for the *first four years* of college. To be eligible, a student must be enrolled at least half-time; and the credit can only be claimed for four tax years for each student in the family. If a family has more than one student in college, it can claim the American Opportunity credit for one student and the Lifetime Learning credit for another student in the same tax year.

The Lifetime Learning credit is worth up to $2,000 per year ($4,000 for students attending college in the Midwestern disaster area) for each eligible student in the family. There is *no limit on the number of years* this credit can be claimed for each student. If a family has more than one student in college, it can claim an education tax credit on a per-student, per-year basis. In other words, it can claim the American Opportunity credit for one student, and the Lifetime Learning credit for another student in the same year.

For each of these tax credits, the amount of the credit depends on your family's income. The American Opportunity credit is gradually reduced if your family's adjusted gross income is between $160,000 and $180,000 if you have two parents filing a joint return and between $80,000 and $90,000 for a parent filing singly. The Lifetime Learning credit phases out between $104,000 and $122,000 for joint returns and $51,000 and $62,000 for single returns.

If your family's income is too high to qualify for either of these tax credits, there's also a tax deduction that may help. With the tuition and fees deduction, you can deduct up to $4,000 of college tuition and fees if your family income isn't more than $65,000 (for single filers) or $130,000 (for joint filers); the deduction is up to $2,000 if your family income is higher than that. If you claim this deduction, you can't claim the American Opportunity or Lifetime Learning credits for the same student that year.

Interest paid on student loans is tax deductible to a maximum of $2,500 per year. This benefit applies to all loans used to pay for college, including PLUS loans. To be eligible for this deduction, your income has to be lower than $75,000 (for single filers) or $155,000 (for joint filers). The tax break is only for the amount of interest you paid, not the amount you borrowed. If you take out a student loan, the lender will send a 1098 form to you at the end of each tax year telling you how much of your payments were for interest that year.

Some states also allow you to take tax credits or deductions from your state income taxes. Find out about yours from your state government.

Table 7:
Federal Income Tax Benefits for Higher Education

	AMERICAN OPPORTUNITY CREDIT	LIFETIME LEARNING CREDIT	TUITION AND FEES DEDUCTION	STUDENT LOAN INTEREST DEDUCTION
AVAILABLE FOR	Tuition, fees, books, supplies and equipment 1st four years of undergraduate study only Associate and bachelor's degree programs only	Tuition and fees only All years of study Any degree program, also nondegree courses to acquire job skills	Tuition and fees only All years of study Attendance at any postsecondary institution participating in a federal student aid program	Any higher education cost All years of study Any degree program
MAXIMUM VALUE	$2,500 credit per student	$2,000 credit per family	Up to $4,000 deduction taken as an adjustment to gross income	$2,500 deduction from taxable income
MAXIMUM INCOME FOR ELIGIBILITY	$80,000–$90,000 (single filers) $160,000–$180,000 (joint filers)	$51,000–$61,000 (single filers) $102,000–$122,000 (joint filers)	$80,000 (single filers) $160,000 (joint filers)	$60,000–$75,000 (single filers) $120,000–$155,000 (joint filers)
CONDITIONS	Student must be enrolled at least half-time Cannot claim the Lifetime Learning credit for the same student in the same year	Cannot claim the American Opportunity credit for the same student in the same year	Cannot claim either the American Opportunity credit or the Lifetime Learning credit for the same student in the same year	Student must have been enrolled at least half-time

QUICK RECAP

To deal with out-of-pocket college costs, you have several options. You can draw on savings or current income to pay, or you can borrow some portion of the total bill. And you can cut the costs.

- Several savings options, including U.S. savings bonds, 529s and Coverdell accounts, have tax benefits that can also help.
- You can work during college or promise to work later through programs like ROTC or AmeriCorps.
- You can borrow through student or parent loans.
- You can reduce your costs by such means as taking college-level courses for credit before you enter college.
- Tax breaks can help you meet college costs.

Once You're in College

QUICK OVERVIEW

Once you're in college, you shouldn't be preoccupied with paying for it. Academics, extracurricular activities and making friends are more important. But there are some things you need to do to stay on target financially. This chapter will tell you what they are.

Reapply for Aid Each Year!

Don't forget to reapply to renew your aid package every year! Check at your financial aid office to make sure you have the right forms and know what the deadlines are. Most colleges have a renewal deadline for financial aid that's a week or two later than the deadline for new applicants.

When you renew, don't expect your aid package to stay exactly the same. It may become more loan heavy each year, with more money in subsidized loans. The borrowing limits on the subsidized Stafford loan are higher for sophomores than for freshmen, and even higher for juniors and seniors. Also, keep in mind that some scholarships and grants are for freshmen only.

While you're reapplying for the financial aid you already have, keep an eye out for new opportunities. As you move on to higher grades and declare a major, you may become eligible for outside scholarships that weren't open to you in the past. Follow the guidelines in Step 9 to look for outside sources of money.

EXPERT ADVICE

"There are students who tell me that the reason they didn't pass their class was they're **too busy working**, because they need the money to support themselves. And I tell them, you need to determine your priorities. There's a limit of how much financial aid I can give you to help offset that."

— Mary San Agustin, director of financial aid and scholarships, Palomar College, San Marcos, Calif.

Stay on Track

The next thing to keep in mind is that you have to maintain eligibility for financial aid. For federal student aid, stay in school at least half-time, and avoid illegal drugs. A drug-related conviction can lead to suspension or revocation of your federal-aid eligibility.

You don't have to maintain a particular GPA to maintain federal eligibility (though you do have to meet your individual school's standards for "satisfactory academic progress"). But the financial aid your college gives you, such as scholarships, may have specific academic requirements. Do your best in all your classes and stay on track academically, not only because it will help you get the most out of college but because it will help you keep your financial aid. To maintain or establish eligibility for academic scholarships, an on-campus job such as a teaching or research assistant, or a "co-op" program between your department and a local employer, you'll need to be in good academic standing.

MYTH/FACT

Myth: Only certain majors will lead to high earnings after graduation.

Fact: Don't be fooled. If you're not drawn to the major, you probably won't like the work and will leave that field before you ever reach the high earnings. Instead, **choose a major based on your interests and talents**, not on someone else's predictions of industrial trends. And remember that many of today's highest paying fields — such as marketing and software engineering — require critical thinking skills that you will acquire in courses like anthropology and philosophy. To learn more about specific academic fields and what it's like to major in them, read the College Board's *Book of Majors*.

Maintain Grades

To keep up your grades, you'll have to make decisions about how to spend your time. It's important to build social relationships, pursue extracurricular activities, and earn money through work, but balance those against the need to maintain a good academic record. If you have a job, don't work so hard at it that you jeopardize your aid eligibility. (See "Expert Advice" sidebar on page 11.)

Don't Stay Too Long (Pick a Major, Any Major)

Did you know that only about one-third of all students who enter a four-year college graduate in four years? Most take six or more years to earn a bachelor's degree. Obviously, the longer you stay in college, the more it's going to cost you — not only in tuition, fees, room, board and other expenses, but also in lost earnings from a delayed career.

Make it a goal to graduate on time. Make sure you are on track to complete your college's core requirements, as well as the core requirements for your major.

Speaking of majors, don't feel that you need to rush into choosing one. Except for some very specialized career and technical institutes, most colleges and universities allow you to take time during your first two years to take classes in different fields and make sure you know enough to choose a major that fits your interests and abilities. On the other hand, don't wait so long that you neglect to take the courses that are requirements for a major. You don't want to have to pay for an extra semester to get your biology degree because you didn't take that required organic chemistry course your sophomore year.

Transferring from a Community College

If you're going to a community college, and plan to transfer to a four-year college, **make sure you know all the transfer requirements** — including whatever courses are needed for the major you intend to declare. It helps if your community college has an articulation agreement with the four-year college specifying exactly what courses are required for transfer. Almost all community colleges have a transfer adviser on staff who can help you make sure you're on track. Get to know your adviser and check in with him or her regularly.

Watch Your Personal Expenses

The purpose of financial aid is to give you the money you need to pay for college costs. But that aid can quickly become too little if you spend too much. To avoid overspending, live within your means and don't run up frivolous debt. That means sticking to a budget and avoiding credit cards.

Student Budgeting

To live within your means, all you have to do is not spend more than you receive in income. The best way to do that is to create a budget at the beginning of each semester and stick to it. Your budget should list the funds you will receive (such as money from parents, savings, work, grants and loans), subtract how much money you plan to spend on given items (such as tuition, fees, room, board, books, clothes and recreation) and calculate the difference — the bottom line. If the bottom line is a negative number — that is, if your expenses exceed your income — you're overspending. Once you have a budget where your income is equal to or greater than your expenses, follow it, and you'll be living within your means.

To create a budget, first examine what you have actually been spending, then **set priorities if you're spending too much**. That alone can help you to spend less, as you realize you can make do with one latte a day instead of two. "You start making conscious decisions about what it is that you want to do," says Elizabeth Bickford of the University of Oregon at Eugene. "You're actually just taking control over your financial spending."

By all means have fun, but don't spend too much money on nonessential items like DVDs, high-end clothes or trips to the beach. Some of your friends at college may have more money than you, but don't let social pressure push you into trying to spend like they do. Learn to suggest ordering pizza from the local hangout instead of driving to an expensive restaurant.

Save money wherever you can — for example, limit your cell phone use to free times. Comparison shop for groceries and supplies. And don't visit the ATM too often: It's too easy to withdraw money and overspend. See collegeboard.org for more advice on budgeting and financial planning.

Credit Card Debt

Be especially careful with your credit cards. They can be convenient for paying for big-ticket items like textbooks and airplane tickets, if you use them sparingly and pay off the entire amount when you get the bill. But if you abuse them, they can land you in a world of trouble.

A credit card is essentially a high-interest loan. Pulling it out at a cash register to make an impulse purchase may give you a feeling of freedom, but you won't feel free once you get the bill — especially when you're still paying interest on that impulse purchase months or years later. If you let the debt accumulate, it may swell so much that you won't be able to pay down the debt. This can affect your future academic career. If you miss payments on your credit cards, or if your credit card debt is high, you can hurt your credit rating. A bad credit rating can harm your chances of getting student loans to pay for graduate school, or a car loan when you start working. It can even prevent you from getting a job with certain security-conscious employers, such as banks or government agencies.

Use credit cards only when you know you can repay the debt promptly. Save them for emergencies. (A spring-break vacation is not an emergency.) Think through each credit card purchase before you spend. If you do get in over your head with credit card use, cut your expenses and talk to your family and financial aid administrator for more guidance.

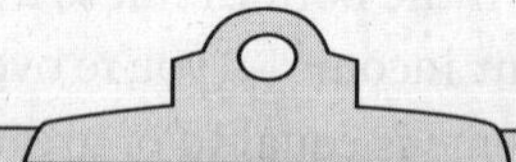

Saving for Future Needs

While you're trying to live within your means, it's also wise to save for the future. Savings will give you greater freedom to cope with college and personal costs to come. If at all possible, make sure your budget includes money set aside for future needs. Your parents, of course, should do the same.

Try to save what you can from the jobs you have during the school year and in the summer. Think about the following as goals for your savings:

Students should think about ...

- ✔ Next year's college expenses
- ✔ Application fees and tuition for graduate school
- ✔ A vacation with friends after you graduate
- ✔ Moving to another city after you graduate
- ✔ The unexpected (such as traveling to a friend's wedding or a family funeral)

Parents should think about ...

- ✔ Next year's college expenses
- ✔ College expenses for younger children (if any)
- ✔ Retirement
- ✔ The unexpected (such as making it through a layoff or paying for a child's wedding)

Final Thoughts

Once you're in college, you may sometimes wonder if it's worth it. Can your family afford the expense? Will you be able to repay your student loans? If you've made reasonable choices along the way, the answer is yes. If you ever have doubts, visit your school's career center and do some research into the fields of work you might enter. Find out how much money you're likely to be earning when you first graduate, and how much five years later. A light might go on for you, as Elizabeth Bickford has often observed with other students. "When they see that relationship, many students say, 'Oh, wait a second, I can do that.'"

You will be able to pay back your student loans. College is a sound investment. You can afford college!

QUICK RECAP

Once you're in college, make sure you stay on track financially.

- Reapply for aid every year.
- Maintain your federal eligibility by staying in school the right number of hours and avoiding illegal drugs.
- Keep up your grades. Don't let them get derailed by too much time spent on work or other nonacademic activities.
- Declare a major at a suitable time.
- Make a budget and stick to it.
- Be wary of credit cards.
- Save for future expenses.
- Keep an eye out for new sources of outside scholarships.
- Remember that college is worth it!

Part II

Tables and Worksheets

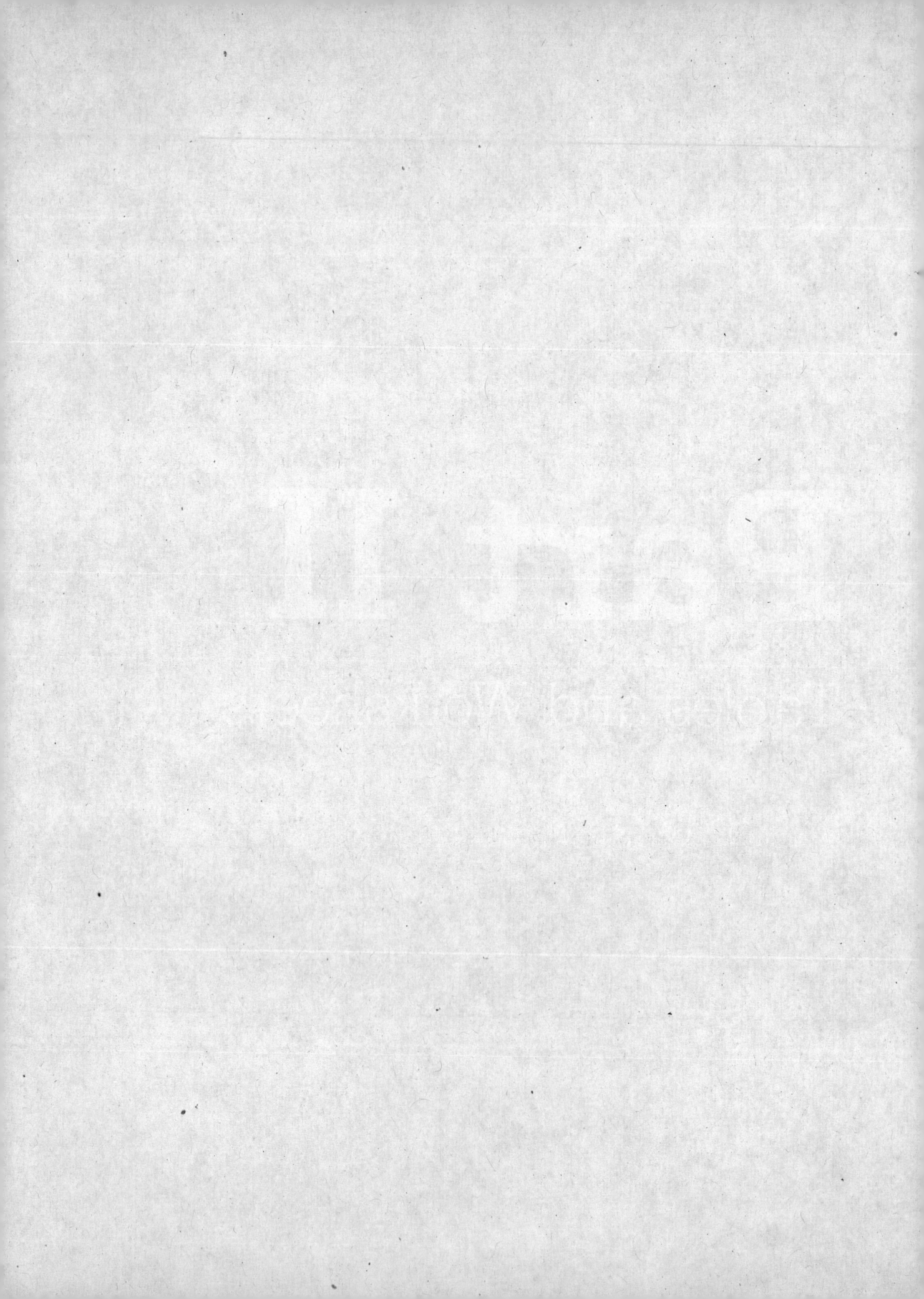

WORKSHEET 1:
Meet Your Application Deadlines

		COLLEGE 1:	COLLEGE 2:	COLLEGE 3:
	College Name	*1st Choice Univ.*	*Private Univ.*	*Financial Safety*
FORMS REQUIRED	FAFSA			
	PROFILE			
	State form			
	Institutional form			
	Tax returns			
	Other			
SCHOOL CODES	Federal code			
	CSS code			
PRIORITY DATE				
CLOSING DATE				
AFTER APPLYING	Need to send letter?			
	Documentation required?			
COMPARE AWARDS	Notification date			
	Reply-by date			

WORKSHEET 2:
Scholarship Application Planner

	PROGRAM 1	PROGRAM 2	PROGRAM 3
PROGRAM/SPONSOR			
ELIGIBILITY REQUIREMENTS			
TYPE OF AWARD			
AMOUNT OF AWARD			
CAN BE USED FOR			
CAN BE USED AT			
DEADLINE			
FORMS REQUIRED			
TEST SCORES REQUIRED			
ESSAY OR ACADEMIC SAMPLE			
RECOMMENDATIONS			
NOTIFICATION BEGINS			
REQUIREMENTS TO KEEP AFTER FRESHMAN YEAR			

WORKSHEET 3:
Compare Your Awards

	COLLEGE 1	COLLEGE 2	COLLEGE 3
Step 1. List the name of each college you want to consider attending, the award deadline and the total cost of attendance. This figure should be in your award letter. If not, refer to the college catalog or contact the college financial aid office.			
Name of college			
Award deadline date			
Total cost of attendance			
Step 2. List the financial aid awards each school is offering. Don't forget that grants, scholarships and work-study do not have to be repaid, while all loans must be repaid.			
Grants and scholarships			
• Pell Grant (federal)			
• SEOG (federal)			
• State			
• College			
• Other			
Total grants/scholarships			
Percentage of package that is grant/scholarship			
Work-study opportunities			
Loans			
• Stafford-Direct (federal)			
• Perkins (federal)			
• Other			
Total loans			
Percentage of package that is work or loans			
Total financial aid award			
Grants and scholarships + work-study + loans			
Step 3. Calculate what it will cost you to attend each college you are considering. For each college, enter the total cost of attendance. Then, subtract the total financial aid award from the total cost of attendance. That number is the net cost, or what it will cost you to attend that college.			
a) Total cost of attendance			
b) Total financial aid award			
c) Net cost to attend (a minus b)			

Figure 10:
Sample Financial Aid Award Letter 1

Blue University Cost of Attendance: $ 28,706.00

CLASS: 17

March 22, 2014

TENTATIVE
FINANCIAL AWARD NOTIFICATION FOR 2014-2015

Base Based on the information that you submitted on your FAFSA and to our office, **Blue** **Blue University** can offer you the following TENTATIVE awards.

This This package is based on an award period from 09/10/14 to 06/06/15.

AID AWARD	ACCEPT AWARD Yes	NO	OFFERED AMOUNT
FEDERAL PERKINS LOAN	______	______	$1,143
STATE WORK-STUDY	______	______	$2,400
BLUE EDUCATIONAL GRANT	______	______	$3,538
UNIVERSITY SCHOLARSHIP	______	______	$2,000
RESIDENCE HALL GRANT	______	______	$2,000
FEDERAL STAFFORD LOAN – SUB.	______	______	$2,625

Finalize your financial aid award as soon as possible by forwarding to our office the forms listed on the Missing Documents Form included with this letter.

Please read the important information pamphlet! Indicate your intent by checking whether or not you accept each aid award, then sign and return this letter in order to reserve your award(s).

Please refer to the Cost Worksheet to help determine your expenses for the academic year.

If direct loan amounts desired are less than above, please indicate below:

Requested Federal Stafford Loan (Sub.) $ ____________
Requested Federal Perkins Loan $ ____________

I acknowledge that I have read and will comply with all the supporting information in the Important Information Pamphlet. Furthermore, if I receive any financial assistance not included in this award letter, including tuition waivers or employer reimbursement, I will notify your office immediately.

Signature ______________________ Date ____________________1

Figure 11:
Sample Financial Aid Award Letter 2

Green University | Office of Student Financial Planning

Cost of Attendance: $ 26,005.00

March 1, 2014

Step 1. Circle A for Accept or D for Decline for each individual award where indicated below:

	Fall 2014	Spring 2015	Total	A / D
Presidential Freshman Scholarship	$3,250	$3,250	$6,500	A / D
Green University Grant	$705	$705	$1,410	A / D
Total Grants and Scholarships			**$7,910**	
Federal Unsubsidized Stafford Loan	$1,313	$1,312	$2,625	A / D
Total Student Loans			**$2,625**	
Federal College Work-Study	$330	$330	$660	A / D
Federal PLUS Loan and/or Green Partnership Loan	$7,405	$7,405	$14,810	

Step 2. Please note the following:

Your awards are based on full-time enrollment for the fall and spring terms and residence hall occupancy for the fall and spring terms (for financial aid purposes, full-time is defined as 12 credits or more per term).

You have been offered loan(s) that require separate loan materials.

The amount of your Green University Grant was based upon residence hall occupancy for the fall and spring terms. A change in housing status may result in a reduction of this award.

Step 3. Please list other financial assistance, scholarships, or loans you will receive not indicated above. List the scholarship/donor name and the expected amount (example: Elks Club $100).

Name	Amount

Step 4. Attention: Your awards are not final until you complete the items on the ACTION REQUESTED page.

PART II: TABLES AND WORKSHEETS

Estimate Your EFC Under Federal Methodology

WORKSHEET 4A:

Estimate a Dependent Student's Expected Contribution

STUDENT'S INCOME	
1. Taxable income ("adjusted gross income" from IRS Form 1040)	$
2. Untaxed income/benefits	+
3. Taxable student aid	-
4. Total student's income (sum of lines 1 and 2, minus line 3)	=
Allowances	
5. U.S. income tax paid (from IRS Form 1040)	
6. State and other taxes paid (% from Table 8 x line 4)	+
7. F.I.C.A. (Table 9)	+
8. Income protection allowance	$6,000
9. Parents' negative available income offset (line 20 of parents' worksheet, if negative)	+
10. Total allowances (sum of lines 5-9)	=
11. Available income (line 4 minus line 10)	=
12. Available income assessment rate	x 0.50
13. Contribution from income (line 11 x line 12; if negative, enter $0)	=
Student's Assets*	
14. Cash, savings and checking accounts	
15. Other real estate/investment equity	+
16. Business/nonfamily farm equity	+
17. Net worth (sum of lines 14-16)	=
18. Asset assessment rate	x 0.20
19. Contribution from assets (line 17 x line 18; if simple needs test or negative, enter $0)	=
Contribution**	
20. Total Student Contribution (sum of lines 13 and 19)	=

* If you are eligible to file an IRS 1040A or 1040EZ form, or you are not required to file a tax return, and your parents' taxable income is less than $50,000, no assets are included in the methodology.

** If your parents' adjusted gross income is $24,000 or less, and they file or are eligible to file an IRS 1040A or 1040EZ form, no contribution is expected.

WORKSHEET 4B:

Estimate the Parents' Expected Contribution

Parents' Income	
1. Taxable income ("adjusted gross income" from IRS Form 1040)	$
2. Untaxed income/benefits	+
3. Income exclusions (child support paid + education tax credits + taxable combat pay)	-
4. Total parents' income (sum of lines 1 and 2, minus line 3)	=
Allowances	
5. U.S. income tax paid (from IRS Form 1040)	
6. State and other taxes paid (% from Table 8 x line 4)	+
7. F.I.C.A. paid (Table 9)	+
8. Employment allowance (Table 9)	+
9. Income protection allowance (Table 10)	+
10. Total allowances (sum of lines 5-9)	=
11. Available income (line 4 minus line 10; may be negative)	=
Parents' Assets*	
12. Cash, savings and checking accounts	
13. Other real estate/investment equity	+
14. Adjusted business/nonfamily farm equity (Table 11)	+
15. Net worth (sum of lines 12-14)	=
16. Education Savings and Asset protection allowance (Table 12)	-
17. Discretionary net worth (line 15 minus line 16)	=
18. Conversion percentage	x 12%
19. Contribution from assets (line 17 x line 18; if simple needs test or negative, enter $0)	=
20. Adjusted available income (sum of line 11 and line 19; may be negative)	=
Contribution**	
21. Total contribution (calculate using line 20 and Table 13)	=
22. Number of dependent children in college at least half time	÷
23. Parents' contribution for student (line 21 divided by line 22; if negative, enter $0)	=

* If your parents are eligible to file an IRS 1040A or 1040EZ form, or are not required to file a tax return and their taxable income is less than $50,000, no assets are included in the methodology.

** If your parents' adjusted gross income is $24,000 or less, and they are eligible to file an IRS 1040A or 1040EZ form, or are not required to file a tax return, no contribution is expected.

TABLE 8: 2013–2014 Federal EFC Allowances for State Taxes

	Parents		Student
	TOTAL INCOME		TOTAL INCOME
	$ 0-14,999	$15,000 or more	Any amount
Alabama (AL)	3%	2%	2%
Alaska (AK)	2	1	0
American Samoa (AS)	2	1	2
Arizona (AZ)	4	3	2
Arkansas (AR)	4	3	3
California (CA)	8	7	5
Canada (CN)	2	1	2
Colorado (CO)	5	4	3
Connecticut (CT)	8	7	5
Delaware (DE)	5	4	3
District of Columbia (DC)	7	6	5
Federated States of Micronesia (FM)	2	1	2
Florida (FL)	3	2	1
Georgia (GA)	6	5	3
Guam (GU)	2	1	2
Hawaii (HI)	4	3	3
Idaho (ID)	5	4	3
Illinois (IL)	5	4	2
Indiana (IN)	4	3	3
Iowa (IA)	5	4	3
Kansas (KS)	5	4	3
Kentucky (KY)	5	4	4
Louisiana (LA)	3	2	2
Maine (ME)	6	5	4
Marshall Islands (MH)	2	1	2
Maryland (MD)	8	7	6
Massachusetts (MA)	7	6	4
Mexico (MX)	2	1	2
Michigan (MI)	5	4	3
Minnesota (MN)	6	5	4
Mississippi	3	2	3
Missouri (MO)	5	4	3
Montana (MT)	5	4	3
Nebraska (NE)	5	4	3
Nevada (NV)	3	2	1
New Hampshire (NH)	5	4	1
New Jersey (NJ)	9	8	4
New Mexico (NM)	3	2	2
New York (NY)	9	8	6
North Carolina (NC)	6	5	4

	Parents		Student
	TOTAL INCOME		TOTAL INCOME
	$ 0-14,999	$15,000 or more	Any amount
North Dakota (ND)	3%	2%	1%
Northern Mariana Islands (MP)	2	1	2
Ohio (OH)	6	5	3
Oklahoma (OK)	4	3	3
Oregon (OR)	7	6	5
Palau (PW)	2	1	2
Pennsylvania (PA)	5	4	3
Puerto Rico (PR)	2	1	2
Rhode Island (RI)	7	6	4
South Carolina (SC)	5	4	3
South Dakota (SD)	2	1	1
Tennessee (TN)	2	1	1
Texas (TX)	3	2	1
Utah (UT)	5	4	3
Vermont (VT)	6	5	3
Virgin Islands (VI)	2	1	2
Virginia (VA)	6	5	4
Washington (WA)	4	3	1
West Virginia (WV)	3	2	2
Wisconsin (WI)	7	6	4
Wyoming (WY)	2	1	1
Not Reported (NR)	2	1	2

TABLE 9: Federal EFC Allowances for FICA and Employment

FICA: WAGES	
$1 to $110,100	7.65% of income earned by each wage earner (maximum $8,422.65 per person)
$110,101 or more	$8,422.65 + 1.45% of income earned above $110,100 by each wage earner
EMPLOYMENT ALLOWANCE	35% of lesser earned income to a maximum $3,900 (single parent: 35% of earned income to a maximum of $3,900)

TABLE 10: Federal EFC Income Protection Allowance for Parents

Family Size (including student)	Number in College 1	2	3	4	5
2	$ 17,100	$ 14,170			
3	21,290	18,380	$ 15,450		
4	26,290	23,370	20,460	$ 17,530	
5	31,020	28,100	25,190	22,260	$ 19,350
6	36,290	33,360	30,450	27,530	24,620

For each additional family member, add $4,100.
For each additional college student, subtract $2,910.

TABLE 11: Federal EFC Adjusted Net Worth of a Business or Farm

NET WORTH	ADJUSTED NET WORTH			
Less than $1	$	0		
$1 to 120,000	$	0	+	40% of net worth
$120,001 to 365,000	$	48,000	+	50% of net worth over $120,000
$365,001 to 610,000	$	170,500	+	60% of net worth over $365,000
$610,001 or more	$	317,500	+	100% of net worth over $610,000

TABLE 12: Federal EFC Education Savings and Asset Protection Allowance for Parents

AGE OF OLDER PARENT OR STUDENT	COUPLE/ MARRIED	UNMARRIED/ SINGLE
25 or under	$ 0	$ 0
26	2,100	600
27	4,300	1,300
28	6,400	1,900
29	8,600	2,500
30	10,700	3,200
31	12,800	3,800
32	15,000	4,400
33	17,100	5,100
34	19,300	5,700
35	21,400	6,300
36	23,500	7,000
37	25,700	7,600
38	27,800	8,200
39	30,000	8,900
40	32,100	9,500
41	32,900	9,700
42	33,700	9,900
43	34,500	10,100
44	35,400	10,300
45	36,200	10,600
46	37,100	10,800
47	38,000	11,100
48	39,000	11,300
49	39,900	11,600
50	40,900	11,900
51	42,100	12,200
52	43,100	12,500
53	44,200	12,800
54	45,500	13,100
55	46,800	13,400
56	47,900	13,700
57	49,300	14,100
58	50,800	14,400
59	52,200	14,800
60	53,500	15,100
61	55,000	15,600
62	56,900	16,000
63	58,500	16,400
64	60,100	16,900
65 or over	61,800	17,400

TABLE 13: Federal EFC Parents' Contribution from Adjusted Available Income (AAI)

ADJUSTED AVAILABLE INCOME (AAI)	TOTAL CONTRIBUTIONS FROM INCOME
Less than $ -3,409 (3,409)	$ -750
$(3,409) to 15,300	22% of AI
$ 15,301 to 19,200	$ 3,366 + 25% of AAI over $ 15,300
$ 19,201 to 23,100	$ 4,341 + 29% of AAI over $ 19,200
$ 23,101 to 27,000	$ 5,472 + 34% of AAI over $ 23,100
$ 27,001 to 30,900	$ 6,798 + 40% of AAI over $ 27,000
$ 30,901 or more	$ 8,358 + 47% of AAI over $ 30,900

PART II: TABLES AND WORKSHEETS

Contact Information for State Aid Programs

ALABAMA
Alabama Commission on
Higher Education
P.O. Box 302000
Montgomery, AL 36130-2000
334-242-1998
www.ache.state.al.us

ALASKA
Alaska Commission on Postsecondary Education
P.O. Box 110510
Juneau, AK 99811-0510
800-441-2962
www.acpe.alaska.gov/

ARIZONA
Arizona Department of Education
1535 West Jefferson Street
Phoenix, AZ 85007
800-352-4558
www.azed.gov/

ARKANSAS
Arkansas Department of Higher Education
23 Main Street, Suite 400
Little Rock, AR 72201
501-371-2050
www.adhe.edu

CALIFORNIA
California Student Aid Commission
P.O. Box 419026
Rancho Cordova, CA 95741-9026
888-224-7268
www.csac.ca.gov

COLORADO
Colorado Department of Education
201 East Colfax Avenue
Denver, CO 80203-1799
303-866-6600
www.cde.state.co.us

CONNECTICUT
Connecticut Office of Higher Education
61 Woodland Street
Hartford, CT 06105-2326
860-947-1800
www.ctohe.org

DELAWARE
Delaware Higher Education Office
John G. Townsend Building
401 Federal Street, Suite 2
Dover, DE 19901
800-292-7935
www.doe.k12.de.us/dheo

DISTRICT OF COLUMBIA
Office of the State Superintendent
of Education
810 First Street, NE, 9th Floor
Washington, DC 20002
202-727-6436
www.seo.dc.gov

FLORIDA
Florida Department of Education
Office of Student Financial Assistance
325 W. Gaines Street, Suite 1314
Tallahassee, FL 32399-0400
888-827-2004
www.floridastudentfinancialaid.org

GEORGIA
Georgia Student Finance Commission
2082 East Exchange Place
Tucker, GA 30084
800-505-4732
www.gsfc.org

HAWAII
Hawaii State Department
of Education
P.O. Box 2360
Honolulu, HI 96804
808-586-3230
www.doe.k12.hi.us

IDAHO
Idaho State Department of Education
650 West State Street
P.O. Box 83720
Boise, ID 83720-0027
800-432-4601
www.sde.idaho.gov

ILLINOIS
Illinois Student Assistance Commission
1755 Lake Cook Road
Deerfield, IL 60015-5209
800-899-4722
www.isac.org

INDIANA
State Student Assistance Commission of Indiana
W462 Indiana Government
Center South
402 West Washington Street
Indianapolis, IN 46204
888-528-4719
www.in.gov/ssaci

IOWA
Iowa College Student
Aid Commission
603 E. 12th Street, 5th FL
Des Moines, IA 50319
877-272-4456
www.iowacollegeaid.gov

KANSAS
Kansas Board of Regents
1000 SW Jackson Street, Suite 520
Topeka, KS 66612-1368
785-296-3421
www.kansasregents.org

KENTUCKY
KHEAA Student Aid Branch
100 Airport Road
Frankfort, KY 40602
800-928-8926
www.kheaa.com

LOUISIANA
Louisiana Office of Student
Financial Assistance
602 North 5th Street
Baton Rouge, LA 70802
800-259-5626
www.osfa.la.gov

MAINE
Finance Authority of Maine
Education Assistance Division
P.O. Box 949
5 Community Drive
Augusta, ME 04332-0949
800-228-3734
www.famemaine.com

MARYLAND
Maryland Higher Education Commission
Office of Student Financial Assistance
6 N. Liberty St.
Baltimore, MD 21201
800-974-0203
www.mhec.state.md.us

MASSACHUSETTS
Massachusetts Department of Higher Education
Office of Student Financial Assistance
454 Broadway, Suite 200
Revere, MA 02151-3034
617-727-9420
www.osfa.mass.edu

MICHIGAN
Michigan Higher Education Assistance Authority
Office of Scholarships and Grants
P.O. Box 30462
Lansing, MI 48909-7962
888-447-2687
www.michigan.gov/mistudentaid

MINNESOTA
Minnesota Office of Higher Education
1450 Energy Park Drive, Suite 350
St. Paul, MN 55108-5227
800-657-3866
www.ohe.state.mn.us

MISSISSIPPI
Mississippi Office of Student Financial Aid
3825 Ridgewood Road
Jackson, MS 39211-6453
800-327-2980
www.mississippi.edu/riseupms/

MISSOURI
Missouri Department of
Higher Education
205 Jefferson Street
P.O. Box 1469
Jefferson City, MO 65102-1469
800-473-6757
www.dhe.mo.gov

MONTANA
Montana Board of Regents
P.O. Box 203201
2500 Broadway Street
Helena, MT 59620-3201
406-444-6570
http://mus.edu/board/

NEBRASKA
Coordinating Commission for Postsecondary Education
P.O. Box 95005
Lincoln, NE 68509-5005
402-471-2847
www.ccpe.state.ne.us

NEVADA
Nevada Department of Education
700 East Fifth Street
Carson City, NV 89701
775-687-9220
www.doe.nv.gov

NEW HAMPSHIRE
New Hampshire Postsecondary Education Commission
101 Pleasant Street
Concord, NH 03301-3494
888-747-2382, ext. 119
www.education.nh.gov/highered/

NEW JERSEY
HESAA Grants & Scholarships
P.O. Box 540
Trenton, NJ 08625-0540
800-792-8670
www.hesaa.org

NEW MEXICO
New Mexico Higher Education Department
2048 Galisteo Street
Santa Fe, NM 87505
505-476-8400
www.hed.state.nm.us

NEW YORK
New York State Higher Education Services Corporation
99 Washington Avenue
Albany, NY 12255
888-697-4372
www.hesc.ny.gov

NORTH CAROLINA
North Carolina State Education Assistance Authority
P.O. Box 14103
Research Triangle Park, NC 27709
919-549-8614
www.ncseaa.edu

NORTH DAKOTA
North Dakota University System
10th Floor, State Capitol
600 East Boulevard Ave, Dept. 215
Bismarck, ND 58505-0230
701-328-2960
www.ndus.edu

OHIO
Ohio Board of Regents
25 South Front Street
Columbus, OH 43215
614-466-6000
www.ohiohighered.org/

OKLAHOMA
Oklahoma State Regents for
Higher Education
Tuition Aid Grant Program
655 Research Parkway, Suite 200
Oklahoma City, OK 73104
405-225-9100
www.okhighered.org

OREGON
Oregon Student Assistance Commission
1500 Valley River Drive, Suite 100
Eugene, OR 97401
800-452-8807
www.oregonstudentaid.gov

PENNSYLVANIA
Pennsylvania Higher Education Assistance Agency
1200 North Seventh Street
Harrisburg, PA 17102-1444
800-233-0557
www.pheaa.org

PUERTO RICO
Departmento de Educacion
P.O. Box 190759
San Juan, PR 00919-0759
787-773-3475
www.de.gobierno.pr

RHODE ISLAND
Rhode Island Higher Education Assistance Authority
560 Jefferson Boulevard, Suite 100
Warwick, RI 02886-1304
800-922-9855
www.riheaa.org

SOUTH CAROLINA
South Carolina Commission on Higher Education
1122 Lady Street, Suite 300
Columbia, SC 29201
803-737-2260
www.che.sc.gov

SOUTH DAKOTA
South Dakota Department
of Education
Office of Finance and Management
800 Governors Drive
Pierre, SD 57501
605-773-3134
www.doe.sd.gov/

TENNESSEE
Tennessee Student Assistance Corporation
404 James Robertson Parkway,
Suite 1510, Parkway Towers
Nashville, TN 37243-0820
800-342-1663
www.state.tn.us/tsac

TEXAS
Texas Higher Education Coordinating Board
Student Loan Programs
P.O. Box 12788-2788
Austin, TX 78711
800-242-3062
www.hhloans.com

UTAH
Utah Higher Education
Assistance Authority
P.O. Box 145110
Salt Lake City, UT 84114-5112
877-336-7378
www.uheaa.org

VERMONT
Vermont Student Assistance Corporation
P.O. Box 999
Winooski, VT 05404
800-798-8722
www.vsac.org

VIRGINIA
State Council of Higher Education
for Virginia
James Monroe Building
101 North 14th Street, 10th Fl.
Richmond, VA 23219
804-225-2600
www.schev.edu

WASHINGTON
Washington Higher Education Coordinating Board
P.O. Box 43430
Olympia, WA 98504-3430
360-753-7800
www.hecb.wa.gov

WEST VIRGINIA
West Virginia Higher Education Policy Commission
Central Office, Higher Education Grant Program
1018 Kanawha Boulevard East, Suite 700
Charleston, WV 25301-2800
304-558-4614
wvhepcnew.wvnet.edu/

WISCONSIN
Wisconsin Higher Educational
Aids Board
P. O. Box 7885
Madison, WI 53707-7885
608-267-2206
www.heab.state.wi.us

WYOMING
Wyoming Department of Education
2300 Capitol Avenue
Hathaway Building, Second Floor
Cheyenne, WY 82002-0050
307-777-7690
www.k12.wy.us

GUAM
University of Guam
Student Financial Aid Office
UOG Station
Mangilao, GU 96923
www.uog.edu

VIRGIN ISLANDS
Financial Aid Office, Virgin Islands Board of Education
P.O. Box 11900
St. Thomas, VI 00801
340-774-4546
www.myviboe.com

Part III

Financial Aid College by College

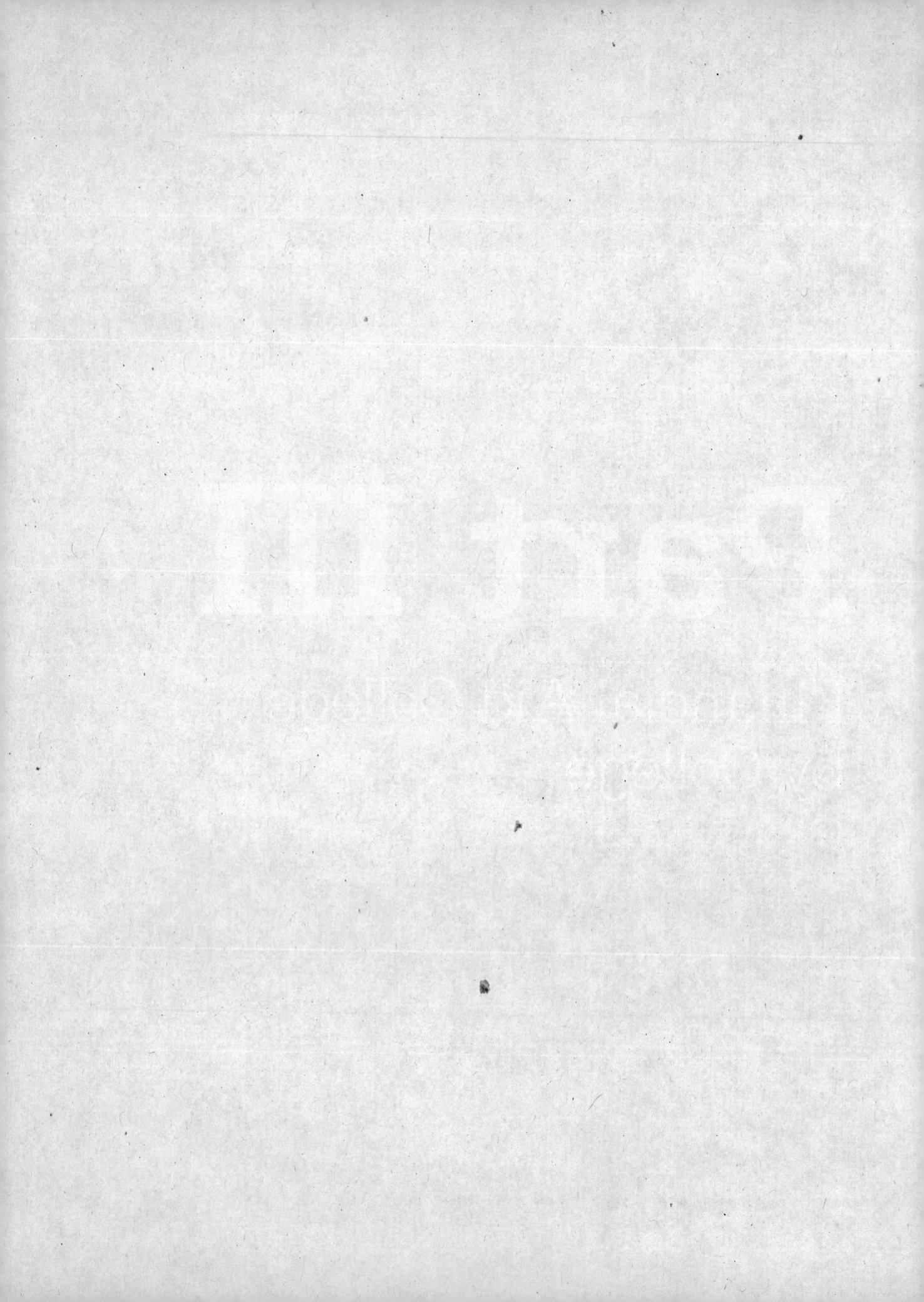

Alabama

Alabama Agricultural and Mechanical University

Huntsville, Alabama
www.aamu.edu Federal Code: 001002

4-year public university and agricultural college in large city.
Enrollment: 4,169 undergrads, 8% part-time. 1,023 full-time freshmen.
Selectivity: Admits 50 to 75% of applicants.

BASIC COSTS (2012-2013)

Tuition and fees: $7,785; out-of-state residents $14,775.
Room and board: $7,370.
Additional info: Tuition/fee waivers available for minority students.

FINANCIAL AID PICTURE (2012-2013)

Students with need: Average financial aid package met 66% of need; average scholarship/grant was $6,568; average loan was $3,516. For part-time students, average financial aid package was $6,119.
Students without need: No-need awards available for athletics, minority status.
Scholarships offered: Presidential Scholarship; full tuition, course fees, room and board, $1,000 for books and supplies per semester; for students with 3.5 GPA or higher. Provost Scholarship; full tuition, course fees, room and board, $800 for books and supplies per semester; for students with 3.4 GPA or higher. Dean's Scholarship; full tuition, course fees, room and board, $500 for books and supplies per semester; for students with 3.3 GPA or higher.
Cumulative student debt: 83% of graduating class had student loans; average debt was $33,133.

FINANCIAL AID PROCEDURES

Forms required: FAFSA, institutional form.
Dates and Deadlines: Closing date 3/1. Applicants notified on a rolling basis starting 4/15; must reply within 2 week(s) of notification.

CONTACT

Darryl Jackson, Director of Financial Aid
Box 908, Normal, AL 35762
(256) 372-5400

Alabama State University

Montgomery, Alabama
www.alasu.edu Federal Code: 001005

4-year public university in small city.
Enrollment: 5,125 undergrads, 9% part-time. 1,378 full-time freshmen.
Selectivity: Admits 50 to 75% of applicants.

BASIC COSTS (2012-2013)

Tuition and fees: $7,932; out-of-state residents $14,244.
Per-credit charge: $263; out-of-state residents $526.
Room and board: $5,366.

FINANCIAL AID PICTURE (2012-2013)

Students with need: Average financial aid package met 78% of need; average scholarship/grant was $5,382; average loan was $3,425. For part-time students, average financial aid package was $9,691.
Students without need: No-need awards available for academics, alumni affiliation, art, athletics, leadership, music/drama, religious affiliation, ROTC.

FINANCIAL AID PROCEDURES

Forms required: FAFSA.
Dates and Deadlines: Priority date 4/1; no closing date. Applicants notified on a rolling basis starting 5/1.
Transfers: Applicants notified on a rolling basis starting 5/1.

CONTACT

Dorenda Adams, Director of Financial Aid
PO Box 271, Montgomery, AL 36101-0271
(334) 229-4323

Amridge University

Montgomery, Alabama
www.amridgeuniversity.edu Federal Code: 016885

4-year private virtual university in small city, affiliated with Church of Christ.
Enrollment: 337 undergrads, 38% part-time. 10 full-time freshmen.
Selectivity: Open admission; but selective for some programs.

BASIC COSTS (2013-2014)

Additional info: Full-time incoming freshmen who remain in good academic standing are guaranteed the rate of $250 per semester hour through the Summer 2016 semester. Part-time students who remain in good academic standing are guaranteed the rate of $330 per semester hour through the Summer 2016 semester. Required fees $435 per term.

FINANCIAL AID PICTURE (2012-2013)

Students with need: 29% of average financial aid package awarded as scholarships/grants, 71% awarded as loans/jobs. Need-based aid available for part-time students.
Students without need: No-need awards available for academics, leadership.

FINANCIAL AID PROCEDURES

Forms required: FAFSA, institutional form.
Dates and Deadlines: Priority date 5/1; closing date 6/30. Must reply by 8/15 or within 2 week(s) of notification.
Transfers: No deadline.

CONTACT

Starr Fain, Financial Aid Director
PO Box 240240, Montgomery, AL 36124-0240
(800) 351-4040 ext. 7525

Athens State University

Athens, Alabama
www.athens.edu Federal Code: 001008

Upper-division public liberal arts and teachers college in large town.
Enrollment: 3,268 undergrads, 53% part-time.

BASIC COSTS (2012-2013)

Tuition and fees: $5,340; out-of-state residents $9,930.
Per-credit charge: $153; out-of-state residents $306.

FINANCIAL AID PICTURE (2012-2013)

Students with need: 50% of average financial aid package awarded as scholarships/grants, 50% awarded as loans/jobs. Need-based aid available for part-time students. Work study available nights, weekends, and for part-time students.
Students without need: No-need awards available for academics, alumni affiliation, art, athletics, leadership, minority status.

FINANCIAL AID PROCEDURES

Forms required: FAFSA.
Dates and Deadlines: Applicants notified on a rolling basis starting 6/1; must reply within 3 week(s) of notification.

CONTACT
Renee Stanford, Director, Student Financial Services
300 North Beaty Street, Athens, AL 35611
(256) 233-8170

Auburn University

Auburn, Alabama
www.auburn.edu Federal Code: 001009

4-year public university in large town.
Enrollment: 20,137 undergrads, 9% part-time. 4,202 full-time freshmen.
Selectivity: Admits over 75% of applicants.

BASIC COSTS (2012-2013)
Tuition and fees: $9,446; out-of-state residents $25,190.
Per-credit charge: $328; out-of-state residents $984.
Room and board: $10,606.

FINANCIAL AID PICTURE (2011-2012)
Students with need: Out of 2,606 full-time freshmen who applied for aid, 1,581 were judged to have need. Of these, 1,581 received aid, and 413 had their full need met. Average financial aid package met 59% of need; average scholarship/grant was $7,881; average loan was $3,503. For part-time students, average financial aid package was $5,995.
Students without need: 640 full-time freshmen who did not demonstrate need for aid received scholarships/grants; average award was $2,885.
Scholarships offered: ***Merit:*** Freshmen and General Scholarships; up to full-tuition; require 28 ACT/1240 SAT and 3.25 GPA. National Merit and National Achievement Finalists; full-tuition plus additional benefits. ***Athletic:*** 79 full-time freshmen received athletic scholarships; average amount $28,643.
Cumulative student debt: 45% of graduating class had student loans; average debt was $24,903.
Additional info: State of Alabama has pre-paid college tuition plan for residents.

FINANCIAL AID PROCEDURES
Forms required: FAFSA.
Dates and Deadlines: Priority date 3/1; no closing date. Applicants notified on a rolling basis starting 10/2.
Transfers: No deadline. Applicants notified on a rolling basis; must reply within 2 week(s) of notification.

CONTACT
Mike Reynolds, Director, Student Financial Services
Quad Center, Auburn, AL 36849-5111
(334) 844-4080

Auburn University at Montgomery

Montgomery, Alabama
www.aum.edu Federal Code: 008310

4-year public university in small city.
Enrollment: 4,155 undergrads, 30% part-time. 702 full-time freshmen.
Selectivity: Admits 50 to 75% of applicants.

BASIC COSTS (2013-2014)
Tuition and fees: $8,750; out-of-state residents $24,950.
Per-credit charge: $270; out-of-state residents $810.
Additional info: Board plan not available. Cost of room only $4,750.

FINANCIAL AID PICTURE
Students with need: Need-based aid available for full-time and part-time students. Work study available nights, weekends, and for part-time students.
Students without need: No-need awards available for academics, alumni affiliation, art, athletics, job skills, leadership, minority status, music/drama, religious affiliation, ROTC.

FINANCIAL AID PROCEDURES
Forms required: FAFSA.
Dates and Deadlines: Priority date 3/1; no closing date. Applicants notified on a rolling basis starting 6/1; must reply within 2 week(s) of notification.
Transfers: Aid awarded based on need and the availability of funds.

CONTACT
Anthony Richey, Director of Financial Aid
7400 East Drive, Room 139 Taylor Center, Montgomery, AL 36124-4023
(334) 244-3571

Bevill State Community College

Jasper, Alabama
www.bscc.edu Federal Code: 005733

2-year public community college in small town.
Enrollment: 3,739 undergrads.
Selectivity: Open admission; but selective for some programs.

BASIC COSTS (2012-2013)
Tuition and fees: $4,140; out-of-state residents $7,410.
Per-credit charge: $109; out-of-state residents $218.
Additional info: Board plan not available. Cost of room only, $1,650. Tuition/fee waivers available for unemployed or children of unemployed.

FINANCIAL AID PICTURE
Students with need: Need-based aid available for full-time and part-time students.
Students without need: No-need awards available for academics, leadership, music/drama.

FINANCIAL AID PROCEDURES
Forms required: FAFSA.
Dates and Deadlines: Priority date 5/1; no closing date. Applicants notified on a rolling basis starting 7/1.

CONTACT
Melissa Stowe, Assistan Dean for Admissions, Financial Aid, & Student Records
1411 Indiana Avenue, Jasper, AL 35501
(205) 387-0511 ext. 5814

Birmingham-Southern College

Birmingham, Alabama
www.bsc.edu Federal Code: 001012

4-year private liberal arts college in very large city, affiliated with United Methodist Church.
Enrollment: 1,226 undergrads, 2% part-time. 327 full-time freshmen.
Selectivity: Admits 50 to 75% of applicants.

BASIC COSTS (2013-2014)
Tuition and fees: $30,700.
Room and board: $10,700.

FINANCIAL AID PICTURE (2012-2013)
Students with need: Out of 265 full-time freshmen who applied for aid, 205 were judged to have need. Of these, 205 received aid, and 71 had their full need met. Average financial aid package met 96% of need; average scholarship/grant was $7,770; average loan was $3,157. For part-time students, average financial aid package was $19,995.
Students without need: 115 full-time freshmen who did not demonstrate need for aid received scholarships/grants; average award was $17,390. No-need awards available for academics, alumni affiliation, art, leadership, music/drama, religious affiliation, state/district residency.
Scholarships offered: Neal and Anne Berte Scholarship; full tuition; based on academic achievement; 1 awarded. Blount-Monaghan/Vulcan Materials

Company Scholarship; full tuition; based on academic achievement; 1 awarded. William Jones and Elizabeth Perry Rushton Scholarship; full tuition, room and board, fees, books, $2,000 travel stipend; based on academic achievement; 1 awarded. Phi Beta Kappa; full tuition; based on academic achievement. United Methodist Scholarship; $1,000-$2,500; awarded to United Methodist with recommendation from senior United Methodist Minister.

Cumulative student debt: 50% of graduating class had student loans; average debt was $27,629.

Additional info: Auditions required for music, theatre, dance applicants seeking scholarships. Portfolios required for art applicants seeking scholarships, and essays recommended for all applicants seeking scholarships.

FINANCIAL AID PROCEDURES

Forms required: FAFSA, state aid form.

Dates and Deadlines: Priority date 3/1; no closing date. Applicants notified on a rolling basis starting 3/1.

Transfers: No deadline. Applicants notified on a rolling basis starting 3/1; must reply within 2 week(s) of notification.

CONTACT

Brian Quisenberry, Director of Financial Aid Services
900 Arkadelphia Road, Birmingham, AL 35254
(205) 226-4688

Central Alabama Community College

Alexander City, Alabama
www.cacc.cc.al.us Federal Code: 001007

2-year public community college in large town.
Enrollment: 1,913 undergrads.
Selectivity: Open admission; but selective for some programs.

BASIC COSTS (2012-2013)

Tuition and fees: $4,140; out-of-state residents $7,410.

FINANCIAL AID PICTURE (2011-2012)

Students with need: 69% of average financial aid package awarded as scholarships/grants, 31% awarded as loans/jobs.

Students without need: No-need awards available for academics, athletics, state/district residency.

FINANCIAL AID PROCEDURES

Forms required: FAFSA, institutional form.

Dates and Deadlines: Priority date 7/15; no closing date. Applicants notified on a rolling basis.

CONTACT

Cindy Entrekin, Financial Aid Officer
1675 Cherokee Road, Alexander City, AL 35010
(256) 234-6346 ext. 4251

Chattahoochee Valley Community College

Phenix City, Alabama
www.cv.edu Federal Code: 012182

2-year public community college in small city.
Enrollment: 1,500 undergrads.
Selectivity: Open admission; but selective for some programs.

BASIC COSTS (2012-2013)

Tuition and fees: $4,200; out-of-state residents $7,470.
Per-credit charge: $109; out-of-state residents $218.

FINANCIAL AID PICTURE

Students with need: Need-based aid available for full-time and part-time students. Work study available nights, weekends, and for part-time students.

Students without need: No-need awards available for academics, art, athletics, leadership, music/drama.

FINANCIAL AID PROCEDURES

Forms required: FAFSA.

Dates and Deadlines: Priority date 7/1; no closing date. Applicants notified on a rolling basis; must reply within 1 week(s) of notification.

CONTACT

Joan Waters, Director of Financial Aid
2602 College Drive, Phenix City, AL 36869
(334) 291-4915

Enterprise State Community College

Enterprise, Alabama
www.escc.edu Federal Code: 001015

2-year public community college in large town.
Enrollment: 2,430 undergrads.
Selectivity: Open admission.

BASIC COSTS (2012-2013)

Tuition and fees: $3,990; out-of-state residents $7,260.
Per-credit charge: $109; out-of-state residents $218.

FINANCIAL AID PICTURE (2011-2012)

Students with need: 73% of average financial aid package awarded as scholarships/grants, 27% awarded as loans/jobs.

Students without need: No-need awards available for academics, art, athletics, leadership, music/drama, state/district residency.

FINANCIAL AID PROCEDURES

Forms required: FAFSA, institutional form.

Dates and Deadlines: Priority date 6/15; no closing date. Applicants notified on a rolling basis starting 7/1; must reply within 2 week(s) of notification.

CONTACT

Henry Quisenberry, Director of Financial Aid
Box 1300, Enterprise, AL 36331
(334) 347-2623 ext. 2214

Faulkner State Community College

Bay Minette, Alabama
www.faulknerstate.edu Federal Code: 001060

2-year public community college in large town.
Enrollment: 4,212 undergrads, 41% part-time. 971 full-time freshmen.
Selectivity: Open admission; but selective for some programs.

BASIC COSTS (2012-2013)

Tuition and fees: $4,140; out-of-state residents $7,410.
Per-credit charge: $109; out-of-state residents $218.
Room and board: $5,400.

FINANCIAL AID PICTURE (2012-2013)

Students with need: 59% of average financial aid package awarded as scholarships/grants, 41% awarded as loans/jobs.

Students without need: No-need awards available for academics, art, athletics, leadership, music/drama.

FINANCIAL AID PROCEDURES

Forms required: FAFSA, institutional form.

Dates and Deadlines: Priority date 7/1; no closing date. Applicants notified on a rolling basis starting 8/1.

CONTACT
Jim Theeuwes, Director of Financial Aid
1900 Highway 31 South, Bay Minette, AL 36507
(251) 580-2151

Faulkner University
Montgomery, Alabama
www.faulkner.edu Federal Code: 001003

4-year private university and liberal arts college in large city, affiliated with Church of Christ.
Enrollment: 2,763 undergrads, 28% part-time. 310 full-time freshmen.
Selectivity: Admits 50 to 75% of applicants.

BASIC COSTS (2013-2014)
Tuition and fees: $18,230.
Per-credit charge: $560.
Room and board: $6,780.
Additional info: Cost of $250 per semester for iPad and software required. Tuition/fee waivers available for adults, minority students, unemployed or children of unemployed.

FINANCIAL AID PICTURE (2011-2012)
Students with need: Out of 256 full-time freshmen who applied for aid, 218 were judged to have need. Of these, 201 received aid, and 74 had their full need met. Average financial aid package met 32% of need; average scholarship/grant was $4,000; average loan was $2,700. For part-time students, average financial aid package was $3,400.
Students without need: 45 full-time freshmen who did not demonstrate need for aid received scholarships/grants; average award was $1,500. No-need awards available for academics, alumni affiliation, athletics, music/drama, religious affiliation, state/district residency.
Scholarships offered: 75 full-time freshmen received athletic scholarships; average amount $450.
Cumulative student debt: 85% of graduating class had student loans; average debt was $9,500.

FINANCIAL AID PROCEDURES
Forms required: FAFSA, state aid form, institutional form.
Dates and Deadlines: Priority date 3/1; no closing date. Applicants notified on a rolling basis starting 6/1.
Transfers: No deadline. Applicants notified on a rolling basis; must reply within 3 week(s) of notification.

CONTACT
William Jackson, Director of Financial Aid
5345 Atlanta Highway, Montgomery, AL 36109-3398
(334) 386-7195

Gadsden State Community College
Gadsden, Alabama
www.gadsdenstate.edu Federal Code: 001017

2-year public community and technical college in small city.
Enrollment: 5,638 undergrads, 44% part-time. 1,380 full-time freshmen.
Selectivity: Open admission; but selective for some programs.

BASIC COSTS (2012-2013)
Tuition and fees: $3,840; out-of-state residents $7,110.
Per-credit charge: $109; out-of-state residents $218.
Room and board: $3,200.
Additional info: Tuition/fee waivers available for minority students, unemployed or children of unemployed.

FINANCIAL AID PICTURE (2011-2012)
Students with need: 96% of average financial aid package awarded as scholarships/grants, 4% awarded as loans/jobs. Need-based aid available for part-time students.
Students without need: No-need awards available for academics, alumni affiliation, art, athletics, job skills, leadership, minority status, music/drama, state/district residency.

FINANCIAL AID PROCEDURES
Forms required: FAFSA, institutional form.
Dates and Deadlines: Priority date 4/15; no closing date. Applicants notified on a rolling basis starting 6/10.

CONTACT
Jacqueline Clark, Director of Financial Services
1001 George Wallace Drive, Gadsden, AL 35902-0227
(256) 549-8267

Heritage Christian University
Florence, Alabama
www.hcu.edu Federal Code: 015370

4-year private Bible college in large town, affiliated with Church of Christ.
Enrollment: 88 undergrads.

BASIC COSTS (2012-2013)
Tuition and fees: $11,670.
Per-credit charge: $373.
Room and board: $3,850.
Additional info: Meal plan covers 10 meals per week.

FINANCIAL AID PICTURE
Students with need: Need-based aid available for full-time and part-time students.

FINANCIAL AID PROCEDURES
Forms required: FAFSA.
Dates and Deadlines: Priority date 6/1; no closing date. Applicants notified on a rolling basis starting 6/1; must reply by 7/28 or within 2 week(s) of notification.
Transfers: No deadline. Applicants notified on a rolling basis; must reply by 7/28 or within 3 week(s) of notification.

CONTACT
Mechelle Thompson, Financial Aid Director
3625 Helton Drive, Florence, AL 35630
(256) 766-6610 ext. 224

Herzing University: Birmingham
Birmingham, Alabama
www.herzing.edu Federal Code: 010193

4-year for-profit business and technical college in very large city.
Enrollment: 295 undergrads.

FINANCIAL AID PICTURE
Students with need: Need-based aid available for full-time students.
Students without need: This college awards aid only to students with need.

FINANCIAL AID PROCEDURES
Forms required: FAFSA.

CONTACT
Kentray Sims, Director of Financial Services
280 West Valley Avenue, Birmingham, AL 35209
(205) 916-2800

Huntingdon College

Montgomery, Alabama
www.huntingdon.edu Federal Code: 001019

4-year private liberal arts college in small city, affiliated with United Methodist Church.
Enrollment: 1,103 undergrads, 19% part-time. 276 full-time freshmen.
Selectivity: Admits 50 to 75% of applicants.

BASIC COSTS (2012-2013)
Tuition and fees: $22,500.
Per-credit charge: $900.
Room and board: $8,250.
Additional info: Full-time students in the traditional program are provided a laptop computer for use during all four years of study and is theirs to keep. The cost of the laptop is included in the Annual Student Fee. Tuition at time of enrollment locked for 4 years; tuition/fee waivers available for adults.

FINANCIAL AID PICTURE (2012-2013)
Students with need: Out of 255 full-time freshmen who applied for aid, 232 were judged to have need. Of these, 232 received aid, and 39 had their full need met. Average financial aid package met 66% of need; average scholarship/grant was $14,195; average loan was $3,359. For part-time students, average financial aid package was $6,398.
Students without need: 40 full-time freshmen who did not demonstrate need for aid received scholarships/grants; average award was $10,148. No-need awards available for academics, alumni affiliation, music/drama, religious affiliation, ROTC, state/district residency.
Cumulative student debt: 69% of graduating class had student loans; average debt was $21,034.

FINANCIAL AID PROCEDURES
Forms required: FAFSA, state aid form, institutional form.
Dates and Deadlines: Priority date 3/1; no closing date. Applicants notified on a rolling basis starting 3/1; must reply by 5/1 or within 2 week(s) of notification.
Transfers: No deadline. Applicants notified on a rolling basis starting 3/1; must reply by 5/1 or within 2 week(s) of notification. Transfer student should be in good academic standing at previous institution and cannot be in default on any previous student loans. While Academic Transfer scholarships are merit-based according to GPA, need-based aid (i.e. FAFSA) contingent upon eligibility and good-standing within Title IV.

CONTACT
Belinda Duett, Director of Financial Aid
1500 East Fairview Avenue, Montgomery, AL 36106-2148
(334) 833-4428

Jacksonville State University

Jacksonville, Alabama
www.jsu.edu Federal Code: 001020

4-year public university in small town.
Enrollment: 7,654 undergrads, 22% part-time. 1,302 full-time freshmen.
Selectivity: Admits over 75% of applicants.

BASIC COSTS (2012-2013)
Tuition and fees: $7,950; out-of-state residents $15,900.
Per-credit charge: $265; out-of-state residents $530.
Room and board: $6,432.

FINANCIAL AID PICTURE (2012-2013)
Students with need: For part-time students, average financial aid package was $7,740.
Students without need: No-need awards available for academics, alumni affiliation, art, athletics, music/drama, ROTC.
Scholarships offered: 4-year tuition scholarship; for entering freshmen from Alabama with 28 ACT or 1230 SAT.

FINANCIAL AID PROCEDURES
Forms required: FAFSA, institutional form.
Dates and Deadlines: Priority date 3/15; no closing date. Applicants notified on a rolling basis starting 4/16; must reply within 2 week(s) of notification.

CONTACT
Vickie Adams, Director of Financial Aid
700 Pelham Road North, Jacksonville, AL 36265-1602
(256) 782-5006

Jefferson Davis Community College

Brewton, Alabama
www.jdcc.edu Federal Code: 001021

2-year public nursing and community college in small town.
Enrollment: 1,034 undergrads, 41% part-time. 274 full-time freshmen.
Selectivity: Open admission; but selective for some programs.

BASIC COSTS (2012-2013)
Tuition and fees: $3,840; out-of-state residents $7,110.
Per-credit charge: $109; out-of-state residents $218.
Additional info: Board plan not available. Cost of room only, $3,000.

FINANCIAL AID PICTURE (2012-2013)
Students with need: Average financial aid package met 56% of need; average scholarship/grant was $5,050. For part-time students, average financial aid package was $6,638.
Students without need: No-need awards available for academics, athletics, leadership.

FINANCIAL AID PROCEDURES
Forms required: FAFSA.
Dates and Deadlines: Applicants notified on a rolling basis; must reply within 2 week(s) of notification.
Transfers: Must reply within 2 week(s) of notification.

CONTACT
Vanessa Kyles, Director of Financial Aid
PO Box 958, Brewton, AL 36427
(251) 809-1516

Jefferson State Community College

Birmingham, Alabama
www.jeffstateonline.com Federal Code: 001022

2-year public community college in large city.
Enrollment: 7,862 undergrads, 61% part-time. 1,062 full-time freshmen.
Selectivity: Open admission; but selective for some programs.

BASIC COSTS (2012-2013)
Tuition and fees: $4,200; out-of-state residents $7,470.
Per-credit charge: $109; out-of-state residents $218.

FINANCIAL AID PICTURE
Students with need: Need-based aid available for full-time and part-time students. Work study available nights.
Students without need: No-need awards available for academics, art, leadership, music/drama.
Additional info: Any Alabama resident over age 60 may attend classes tuition free, on a space available basis.

FINANCIAL AID PROCEDURES
Forms required: FAFSA, institutional form.
Dates and Deadlines: Closing date 5/1. Applicants notified on a rolling basis starting 6/1.

Transfers: Transfer students not eligible for academic scholarships until 12 hours have been completed on campus.

CONTACT

Tracy Adams, Financial Aid Director
2601 Carson Road, Birmingham, AL 35215-3098
(205) 856-8509

Judson College

Marion, Alabama
www.judson.edu Federal Code: 001023

4-year private liberal arts college for women in small town, affiliated with Baptist faith.
Enrollment: 346 undergrads, 15% part-time. 78 full-time freshmen.
Selectivity: Admits over 75% of applicants.

BASIC COSTS (2012-2013)
Tuition and fees: $15,100.
Per-credit charge: $480.
Room and board: $8,800.

FINANCIAL AID PICTURE (2012-2013)
Students with need: Average financial aid package met 82% of need; average scholarship/grant was $11,645; average loan was $8,043. For part-time students, average financial aid package was $13,490.
Students without need: No-need awards available for academics, art, athletics, leadership, music/drama, religious affiliation, ROTC, state/district residency.
Scholarships offered: Full Tuition Scholarship; given to National Merit Finalists or students with 29 ACT and 3.5 GPA; up to 5 awarded. Honor Scholarships; 1 for full-tuition, 2 for $2,500, 3 for $2,000; awarded based on exam scores. Music scholarships; variable amounts awarded based on audition.
Cumulative student debt: 76% of graduating class had student loans; average debt was $25,427.

FINANCIAL AID PROCEDURES
Forms required: FAFSA, state aid form, institutional form.
Dates and Deadlines: Priority date 3/1; no closing date. Applicants notified on a rolling basis starting 10/1; must reply within 2 week(s) of notification.
Transfers: No deadline. Applicants notified on a rolling basis starting 10/1; must reply within 2 week(s) of notification.

CONTACT

Ashley Clemons, Director of Financial Aid
302 Bibb Street, Marion, AL 36756
(334) 683-5157

Lawson State Community College

Birmingham, Alabama
www.lawsonstate.edu Federal Code: 001059

2-year public community college in small city.
Enrollment: 3,209 undergrads, 38% part-time. 632 full-time freshmen.
Selectivity: Open admission; but selective for some programs.

BASIC COSTS (2012-2013)
Tuition and fees: $4,170; out-of-state residents $7,470.
Per-credit charge: $110; out-of-state residents $220.
Room and board: $4,000.

FINANCIAL AID PICTURE (2012-2013)
Students with need: 98% of average financial aid package awarded as scholarships/grants, 2% awarded as loans/jobs. Need-based aid available for part-time students. Work study available nights.
Students without need: This college awards aid only to students with need.

FINANCIAL AID PROCEDURES
Forms required: FAFSA.
Dates and Deadlines: Closing date 6/1. Applicants notified on a rolling basis starting 8/1; must reply within 2 week(s) of notification.

CONTACT

Cassandra Byrd, Director of Student Financial Services
3060 Wilson Road SW, Birmingham, AL 35221-1717
(205) 929-6380

Lurleen B. Wallace Community College

Andalusia, Alabama
www.lbwcc.edu Federal Code: 008988

2-year public community college in small town.
Enrollment: 1,440 undergrads, 31% part-time. 349 full-time freshmen.
Selectivity: Open admission.

BASIC COSTS (2012-2013)
Tuition and fees: $3,960; out-of-state residents $7,230.
Per-credit charge: $109; out-of-state residents $218.

FINANCIAL AID PICTURE (2011-2012)
Students with need: 98% of average financial aid package awarded as scholarships/grants, 2% awarded as loans/jobs.

FINANCIAL AID PROCEDURES
Dates and Deadlines: Applicants notified on a rolling basis.

CONTACT

Donna Bass, Director of Financial Aid, Andalusia Campus
Box 1418, Andalusia, AL 36420-1418
(334) 881-2272

Marion Military Institute

Marion, Alabama
www.marionmilitary.edu Federal Code: 001026

2-year public junior and military college in small town.
Enrollment: 378 undergrads. 244 full-time freshmen.
Selectivity: Admits 50 to 75% of applicants.

BASIC COSTS (2012-2013)
Tuition and fees: $8,570; out-of-state residents $14,570.
Per-credit charge: $200; out-of-state residents $400.
Room and board: $3,950.
Additional info: Required fees include one-time uniform fee of $1,850 and accident insurance of $150 per academic year.

FINANCIAL AID PICTURE
Students with need: Need-based aid available for full-time and part-time students. Work study available nights, weekends, and for part-time students.

FINANCIAL AID PROCEDURES
Forms required: FAFSA.
Dates and Deadlines: Applicants notified on a rolling basis starting 6/15; must reply within 6 week(s) of notification.

CONTACT

Jackie Wilson, Director of Financial Aid
1101 Washington Street, Marion, AL 36756-0420
(334) 683-2309

Miles College

Birmingham, Alabama
www.miles.edu Federal Code: 001028

4-year private liberal arts college in very large city, affiliated with Christian Methodist Episcopal Church.
Enrollment: 1,650 undergrads.
Selectivity: Open admission; but selective for some programs.

BASIC COSTS (2012-2013)
Tuition and fees: $11,014.
Per-credit charge: $431.
Room and board: $6,812.

FINANCIAL AID PICTURE
Students with need: Need-based aid available for full-time and part-time students.
Students without need: This college awards aid only to students with need.

FINANCIAL AID PROCEDURES
Forms required: FAFSA, state aid form.
Dates and Deadlines: Priority date 4/15; no closing date. Applicants notified on a rolling basis starting 7/15; must reply within 2 week(s) of notification.

CONTACT
Percy Lanier, Director of Financial Aid
5500 Myron-Massey Boulevard, Fairfield, AL 35064
(205) 929-1665

Northeast Alabama Community College

Rainsville, Alabama
www.nacc.edu Federal Code: 001031

2-year public community college in rural community.
Enrollment: 2,751 undergrads.
Selectivity: Open admission.

BASIC COSTS (2012-2013)
Tuition and fees: $4,140; out-of-state residents $7,410.
Per-credit charge: $109; out-of-state residents $218.

FINANCIAL AID PICTURE
Students with need: Need-based aid available for full-time and part-time students.
Students without need: No-need awards available for academics, art, leadership, minority status, music/drama.

FINANCIAL AID PROCEDURES
Forms required: FAFSA.
Dates and Deadlines: Applicants notified on a rolling basis.

CONTACT
Nixon Willmon, Director of Financial Aid
Admissions Office, NACC, Rainsville, AL 35986-0159
(256) 228-6001 ext. 327

Northwest-Shoals Community College

Muscle Shoals, Alabama
www.nwscc.edu Federal Code: 005697

2-year public community and technical college in large town.
Enrollment: 3,231 undergrads, 41% part-time. 721 full-time freshmen.
Selectivity: Open admission; but selective for some programs.

BASIC COSTS (2012-2013)
Tuition and fees: $4,080; out-of-state residents $7,350.
Per-credit charge: $109; out-of-state residents $218.
Additional info: Tuition/fee waivers available for minority students, unemployed or children of unemployed.

FINANCIAL AID PICTURE (2011-2012)
Students with need: 63% of average financial aid package awarded as scholarships/grants, 37% awarded as loans/jobs. Need-based aid available for part-time students. Work study available nights.
Students without need: No-need awards available for academics, art, leadership, minority status, music/drama.

FINANCIAL AID PROCEDURES
Forms required: FAFSA, institutional form.
Dates and Deadlines: Priority date 4/1; closing date 8/1. Applicants notified on a rolling basis; must reply within 2 week(s) of notification.
Transfers: No deadline. Applicants notified on a rolling basis; must reply within 2 week(s) of notification. Students without 1-year Alabama residency before fall term ineligible for state grant.

CONTACT
Shauna James, Assistant Director of Student Financial Aid Services
PO Box 2545, Muscle Shoals, AL 35662
(256) 331-5368

Oakwood University

Huntsville, Alabama
www.oakwood.edu Federal Code: 001033

4-year private liberal arts college in small city, affiliated with Seventh-day Adventists.
Enrollment: 1,966 undergrads.
Selectivity: Admits less than 50% of applicants.

BASIC COSTS (2012-2013)
Tuition and fees: $15,414.
Room and board: $9,650.

FINANCIAL AID PICTURE
Students with need: Need-based aid available for full-time students.
Students without need: No-need awards available for academics, leadership, religious affiliation, state/district residency.

FINANCIAL AID PROCEDURES
Forms required: FAFSA, state aid form.
Dates and Deadlines: Closing date 4/15. Applicants notified on a rolling basis starting 4/1.

CONTACT
Joylin Trotman, Director of Financial Aid
7000 Adventist Boulevard, NW, Huntsville, AL 35896
(256) 726-7208

Prince Institute of Professional Studies

Montgomery, Alabama
www.princeinstitute.edu Federal Code: 022960

2-year for-profit technical and career college in large city.
Enrollment: 122 undergrads. 2 full-time freshmen.
Selectivity: Open admission.

BASIC COSTS (2012-2013)
Tuition and fees: $8,695.
Per-credit charge: $234.

FINANCIAL AID PICTURE
Students with need: Need-based aid available for full-time and part-time students.

Students without need: This college awards aid only to students with need.

FINANCIAL AID PROCEDURES

Forms required: FAFSA.

CONTACT

Emily Lee, Director of Financial Aid
7735 Atlanta Highway, Montgomery, AL 36117-4231
(334) 271-1670

Remington College: Mobile

Mobile, Alabama
www.remingtoncollege.edu Federal Code: 026055

2-year private career college in large city.
Enrollment: 623 undergrads.
Selectivity: Open admission.

FINANCIAL AID PICTURE

Students with need: Need-based aid available for full-time students. Work study available nights.

Students without need: This college awards aid only to students with need.

FINANCIAL AID PROCEDURES

Forms required: FAFSA.

CONTACT

James Dunn, National Director of Financial Aid
828 Downtowner Loop West, Mobile, AL 36609-5404
(251) 343-8200

Samford University

Birmingham, Alabama
www.samford.edu Federal Code: 001036

4-year private university in small city, affiliated with Southern Baptist Convention.
Enrollment: 2,948 undergrads, 6% part-time. 684 full-time freshmen.
Selectivity: Admits over 75% of applicants.

BASIC COSTS (2012-2013)

Tuition and fees: $25,150.
Per-credit charge: $821.
Room and board: $8,250.
Additional info: Tuition/fee waivers available for minority students.

FINANCIAL AID PICTURE (2011-2012)

Students with need: Out of 478 full-time freshmen who applied for aid, 310 were judged to have need. Of these, 310 received aid, and 72 had their full need met. Average financial aid package met 74% of need; average scholarship/grant was $13,739; average loan was $3,057. For part-time students, average financial aid package was $7,128.

Students without need: 335 full-time freshmen who did not demonstrate need for aid received scholarships/grants; average award was $8,668. No-need awards available for academics, alumni affiliation, art, athletics, leadership, minority status, music/drama, religious affiliation, ROTC, state/district residency.

Scholarships offered: 29 full-time freshmen received athletic scholarships; average amount $25,232.

Cumulative student debt: 52% of graduating class had student loans; average debt was $25,252.

FINANCIAL AID PROCEDURES

Forms required: FAFSA, state aid form.

Dates and Deadlines: Priority date 3/1; no closing date. Applicants notified on a rolling basis starting 3/1.

Transfers: Applicants notified on a rolling basis. Student must be fully admitted and all transcripts must be received by admissions office.

CONTACT

Lane Smith, Director of Financial Aid
800 Lakeshore Drive, Birmingham, AL 35229
(205) 726-2905

Selma University

Selma, Alabama
www.selmauniversity.org Federal Code: 040673

4-year private university in large town, affiliated with Baptist faith.
Enrollment: 378 full-time undergrads.
Selectivity: Open admission.

BASIC COSTS (2012-2013)

Additional info: Tuition/fee waivers available for minority students.

FINANCIAL AID PICTURE

Students with need: Need-based aid available for full-time and part-time students.

Students without need: This college awards aid only to students with need.

FINANCIAL AID PROCEDURES

Forms required: FAFSA, state aid form, institutional form.

Dates and Deadlines: Priority date 5/1; closing date 6/30. Applicants notified on a rolling basis starting 8/23; must reply within 2 week(s) of notification.

Transfers: Closing date 5/1. Applicants notified on a rolling basis; must reply within 2 week(s) of notification.

CONTACT

Nerieko Stephens, Director of Financial Aid
1501 Lapsley Street, Selma, AL 36701

Shelton State Community College

Tuscaloosa, Alabama
www.sheltonstate.edu Federal Code: 005691

2-year public community and technical college in small city.
Enrollment: 5,214 undergrads, 47% part-time. 913 full-time freshmen.
Selectivity: Open admission.

BASIC COSTS (2012-2013)

Tuition and fees: $4,140; out-of-state residents $7,410.
Per-credit charge: $109; out-of-state residents $218.

FINANCIAL AID PICTURE

Students with need: Need-based aid available for full-time and part-time students. Work study available nights.

Students without need: This college awards aid only to students with need.

FINANCIAL AID PROCEDURES

Forms required: FAFSA.

Dates and Deadlines: Priority date 6/30; no closing date. Applicants notified on a rolling basis starting 7/30.

CONTACT

Amanda Harbison, Financial Aid Director
9500 Old Greensboro Road, Tuscaloosa, AL 35405-8522
(205) 391-2376

Snead State Community College

Boaz, Alabama
www.snead.edu Federal Code: 001038

2-year public community college in small town.
Enrollment: 2,436 undergrads.
Selectivity: Open admission.

BASIC COSTS (2012-2013)
Tuition and fees: $4,200; out-of-state residents $7,470.
Per-credit charge: $109; out-of-state residents $218.
Room and board: $3,390.

FINANCIAL AID PICTURE
Students with need: Need-based aid available for full-time and part-time students. Work study available nights.
Students without need: No-need awards available for academics, alumni affiliation, art, athletics, leadership, music/drama.

FINANCIAL AID PROCEDURES
Forms required: FAFSA.
Dates and Deadlines: Applicants notified on a rolling basis starting 4/15.

CONTACT
Amanda Childress, Financial Aid Director
PO Box 734, Boaz, AL 35957-0734
(256) 840-4127

South University: Montgomery

Montgomery, Alabama
www.southuniversity.edu Federal Code: 004463

4-year for-profit university in small city.
Enrollment: 712 undergrads.

BASIC COSTS (2012-2013)
Tuition and fees: $16,185.
Additional info: Average cost of required fees, $400. Tuition and required fees for undergraduate nursing students, $23,160.

FINANCIAL AID PICTURE
Students with need: Need-based aid available for full-time and part-time students.
Students without need: This college awards aid only to students with need.

FINANCIAL AID PROCEDURES
Forms required: FAFSA.
Dates and Deadlines: Applicants notified on a rolling basis starting 6/1.
Transfers: No deadline. Applicants notified on a rolling basis.

CONTACT
Yvonne Miller, Director of Financial Aid
5355 Vaughn Road, Montgomery, AL 36116-1120
(334) 395-8800

Southeastern Bible College

Birmingham, Alabama
www.sebc.edu Federal Code: 013857

4-year private Bible college in very large city, affiliated with nondenominational tradition.
Enrollment: 178 undergrads, 18% part-time. 15 full-time freshmen.
Selectivity: Admits over 75% of applicants.

BASIC COSTS (2012-2013)
Tuition and fees: $12,080.
Per-credit charge: $390.
Additional info: Board plan not available. Cost of room only, $2,550.

FINANCIAL AID PICTURE
Students with need: Need-based aid available for full-time and part-time students.
Students without need: No-need awards available for academics, leadership.

FINANCIAL AID PROCEDURES
Forms required: FAFSA, institutional form.
Dates and Deadlines: Priority date 4/1; no closing date. Applicants notified on a rolling basis starting 1/1.
Transfers: No deadline. Applicants notified on a rolling basis.

CONTACT
Jay Powell, Director of Financial Aid
2545 Valleydale Road, Birmingham, AL 35244-2083
(205) 970-9215

Southern Union State Community College

Wadley, Alabama
www.suscc.edu Federal Code: 001040

2-year public community and technical college in small city.
Enrollment: 4,987 undergrads.
Selectivity: Open admission; but selective for some programs.

BASIC COSTS (2012-2013)
Tuition and fees: $3,840; out-of-state residents $7,110.
Per-credit charge: $109; out-of-state residents $218.
Room and board: $3,200.

FINANCIAL AID PICTURE
Students with need: Need-based aid available for full-time and part-time students.

FINANCIAL AID PROCEDURES
Forms required: FAFSA.
Dates and Deadlines: Priority date 4/1; no closing date. Applicants notified on a rolling basis.

CONTACT
Pam Jones, Director of Financial Aid
750 Roberts Street, Wadley, AL 36276
(256) 395-2215

Spring Hill College

Mobile, Alabama
www.shc.edu Federal Code: 001041

4-year private liberal arts college in large city, affiliated with Roman Catholic Church.
Enrollment: 1,187 undergrads, 6% part-time. 298 full-time freshmen.
Selectivity: Admits less than 50% of applicants.

BASIC COSTS (2013-2014)
Tuition and fees: $30,924.
Per-credit charge: $975.
Room and board: $11,296.

FINANCIAL AID PICTURE (2012-2013)
Students with need: Out of 262 full-time freshmen who applied for aid, 222 were judged to have need. Of these, 222 received aid, and 44 had their full need met. Average financial aid package met 90% of need; average

scholarship/grant was $9,864; average loan was $4,666. For part-time students, average financial aid package was $12,465.
Students without need: 71 full-time freshmen who did not demonstrate need for aid received scholarships/grants; average award was $16,574. No-need awards available for academics, alumni affiliation, art, athletics, job skills, leadership, minority status, ROTC, state/district residency.
Scholarships offered: 35 full-time freshmen received athletic scholarships; average amount $6,739.
Cumulative student debt: 71% of graduating class had student loans; average debt was $30,356.

FINANCIAL AID PROCEDURES
Forms required: FAFSA, state aid form.
Dates and Deadlines: Priority date 3/1; no closing date. Applicants notified on a rolling basis starting 2/15; must reply by 5/1 or within 2 week(s) of notification.
Transfers: No deadline. Applicants notified on a rolling basis starting 3/1; must reply within 2 week(s) of notification.

CONTACT
Ellen Foster, Director of Financial Aid
4000 Dauphin Street, Mobile, AL 36608-1791
(800) 548-7886

Stillman College
Tuscaloosa, Alabama
www.stillman.edu Federal Code: 001044

4-year private liberal arts college in small city, affiliated with Presbyterian Church (USA).
Enrollment: 1,080 undergrads.
Selectivity: Admits less than 50% of applicants.

BASIC COSTS (2012-2013)
Tuition and fees: $15,665.
Per-credit charge: $534.
Room and board: $7,056.

FINANCIAL AID PICTURE
Students with need: Need-based aid available for full-time and part-time students. Work study available nights, weekends, and for part-time students.
Students without need: This college awards aid only to students with need.

FINANCIAL AID PROCEDURES
Forms required: FAFSA, institutional form.
Dates and Deadlines: Priority date 4/15; no closing date. Applicants notified on a rolling basis; must reply within 4 week(s) of notification.
Transfers: Priority date 3/15; no deadline. Applicants notified by 11/15.

CONTACT
Jacqueline Morris, Director of Financial Aid
3600 Stillman Boulevard, Tuscaloosa, AL 35403
(205) 366-8950

Talladega College
Talladega, Alabama
www.talladega.edu Federal Code: 001046

4-year private liberal arts college in large town, affiliated with United Church of Christ.
Enrollment: 700 undergrads.
Selectivity: Open admission; but selective for some programs.

BASIC COSTS (2013-2014)
Tuition and fees: $11,492.
Room and board: $5,885.

FINANCIAL AID PICTURE (2011-2012)
Students with need: 68% of average financial aid package awarded as scholarships/grants, 32% awarded as loans/jobs. Need-based aid available for part-time students.
Students without need: This college awards aid only to students with need.

FINANCIAL AID PROCEDURES
Forms required: FAFSA, state aid form, institutional form.
Dates and Deadlines: Closing date 3/1. Applicants notified on a rolling basis starting 2/1; must reply within 2 week(s) of notification.
Transfers: Priority date 3/1; no deadline. Applicants notified on a rolling basis; must reply within 2 week(s) of notification.

CONTACT
Russelle Keese, Director of Financial Aid
627 West Battle Street, Talladega, AL 35160
(256) 761-6256

Troy University
Troy, Alabama
www.troy.edu Federal Code: 001047

4-year public university in large town.
Enrollment: 17,768 undergrads, 46% part-time. 1,444 full-time freshmen.
Selectivity: Admits 50 to 75% of applicants.

BASIC COSTS (2012-2013)
Tuition and fees: $9,070; out-of-state residents $16,540.
Per-credit charge: $249; out-of-state residents $498.
Room and board: $7,071.

FINANCIAL AID PICTURE (2012-2013)
Students with need: Out of 1,119 full-time freshmen who applied for aid, 1,118 were judged to have need. Of these, 1,118 received aid. For part-time students, average financial aid package was $4,841.
Students without need: 350 full-time freshmen who did not demonstrate need for aid received scholarships/grants; average award was $4,445. No-need awards available for academics, alumni affiliation, art, athletics, leadership, minority status, music/drama, ROTC.
Scholarships offered: 53 full-time freshmen received athletic scholarships; average amount $7,538.

FINANCIAL AID PROCEDURES
Forms required: FAFSA, institutional form.
Dates and Deadlines: Closing date 5/1. Applicants notified on a rolling basis starting 5/1; must reply within 2 week(s) of notification.

CONTACT
Carol Ballard, Director, Financial Aid
University Avenue, Adams Administration 111, Troy, AL 36082
(334) 670-3186

Tuskegee University
Tuskegee, Alabama
www.tuskegee.edu Federal Code: 001050

4-year private university in small town.
Enrollment: 2,598 undergrads, 3% part-time. 649 full-time freshmen.
Selectivity: Admits less than 50% of applicants.

BASIC COSTS (2013-2014)
Tuition and fees: $19,555.
Per-credit charge: $750.
Room and board: $8,450.

FINANCIAL AID PICTURE
Students with need: Need-based aid available for full-time and part-time students.
Students without need: No-need awards available for academics, athletics, ROTC, state/district residency.

FINANCIAL AID PROCEDURES
Forms required: FAFSA, institutional form.
Dates and Deadlines: Closing date 3/31. Applicants notified on a rolling basis starting 5/15; must reply within 2 week(s) of notification.

CONTACT
Advergus James, Director of Financial Aid Services
1200 Old Montgomery Road, Tuskegee, AL 36088
(334) 724-4733

University of Alabama
Tuscaloosa, Alabama
www.ua.edu Federal Code: 001051

4-year public university in small city.
Enrollment: 27,364 undergrads, 8% part-time. 5,703 full-time freshmen.
Selectivity: Admits 50 to 75% of applicants.

BASIC COSTS (2012-2013)
Tuition and fees: $9,200; out-of-state residents $22,950.
Room and board: $8,650.

FINANCIAL AID PICTURE (2011-2012)
Students with need: Out of 3,561 full-time freshmen who applied for aid, 2,533 were judged to have need. Of these, 2,454 received aid, and 516 had their full need met. Average financial aid package met 55% of need; average scholarship/grant was $9,420; average loan was $3,486. For part-time students, average financial aid package was $6,194.
Students without need: 1,472 full-time freshmen who did not demonstrate need for aid received scholarships/grants; average award was $10,365. No-need awards available for academics, alumni affiliation, art, athletics, leadership, minority status, music/drama, ROTC, state/district residency.
Scholarships offered: 80 full-time freshmen received athletic scholarships; average amount $23,225.
Cumulative student debt: 43% of graduating class had student loans; average debt was $27,639.

FINANCIAL AID PROCEDURES
Forms required: FAFSA.
Dates and Deadlines: Priority date 3/1; no closing date. Applicants notified on a rolling basis starting 4/1; must reply within 3 week(s) of notification.
Transfers: No deadline. Applicants notified on a rolling basis starting 3/1. Scholarship opportunities for transfer students.

CONTACT
Jeanetta Allen, Director, Student Financial Aid
Box 870132, Tuscaloosa, AL 35487-0132
(205) 348-6756

University of Alabama at Birmingham
Birmingham, Alabama
www.uab.edu Federal Code: 001052

4-year public university in very large city.
Enrollment: 11,014 undergrads, 25% part-time. 1,578 full-time freshmen.
Selectivity: Admits 50 to 75% of applicants.

BASIC COSTS (2012-2013)
Tuition and fees: $8,400; out-of-state residents $19,230.
Per-credit charge: $267; out-of-state residents $628.
Room and board: $9,294.

FINANCIAL AID PICTURE (2011-2012)
Students with need: Out of 1,221 full-time freshmen who applied for aid, 932 were judged to have need. Of these, 920 received aid, and 151 had their full need met. Average financial aid package met 44% of need; average scholarship/grant was $5,005; average loan was $4,023. For part-time students, average financial aid package was $6,424.
Students without need: 399 full-time freshmen who did not demonstrate need for aid received scholarships/grants; average award was $5,905. No-need awards available for academics, alumni affiliation, art, athletics, leadership, minority status, music/drama, ROTC.
Scholarships offered: ***Merit:*** Presidential Scholarships, Presidential Recognition Awards, and Endowed Scholarships; $7,500 to $18,900 per year; for in-state students with 33-36 ACT and 3.0 GPA. Golden Excellence Scholarship; $7,000 per year; for in-state students with 28-32 ACT and 3.3 GPA. Collegiate Honors Scholarship; $4,000 per year; for in-state students with 25-27 ACT and 3.5 GPA. Breakthrough Scholarship; $2,500 per year; for in-state students with 24 ACT and 3.5 GPA. Academic Achievement Scholarship; $1,000 per year; for in-state students with 24-27 ACT and 3.0-3.49 GPA or 28-32 ACT and 3.0-3.29 GPA. Blazer Elite Scholarship; $15,000 per year; for out-of-state students with 28-36 ACT and 3.0 GPA. Blazer Gold Scholarship; $10,000 per year; for out-of-state students with 26-27 ACT and 3.0 GPA. Blazer Pride Scholarship; $5,000 per year; for out-of-state students with 24-25 ACT and 3.0 GPA. National Merit Finalist/National Achievement Finalist/ National Hispanic Recognition Program Scholar Awards; full tuition and required fees for 4 years (up to 15 credit hours per semester for fall and spring only), annual on-campus housing allotment (up to $5,400), and a one-time $2,500 stipend to be used for experiential learning (study away, internships, co-ops, etc.) if students name UAB as first choice with NMSC. ***Athletic:*** 58 full-time freshmen received athletic scholarships; average amount $20,455.
Cumulative student debt: 48% of graduating class had student loans; average debt was $21,503.

FINANCIAL AID PROCEDURES
Forms required: FAFSA.
Dates and Deadlines: Priority date 3/1; no closing date. Applicants notified on a rolling basis starting 4/1; must reply within 4 week(s) of notification.
Transfers: Must reply within 4 week(s) of notification.

CONTACT
Janet May, Director of Financial Aid
HUC 260, 1530 Third Avenue South, Birmingham, AL 35294-1150
(205) 934-8223

University of Alabama in Huntsville
Huntsville, Alabama
www.uah.edu Federal Code: 001055

4-year public university in small city.
Enrollment: 5,703 undergrads, 23% part-time. 615 full-time freshmen.
Selectivity: Admits over 75% of applicants.

BASIC COSTS (2012-2013)
Tuition and fees: $8,794; out-of-state residents $21,108.
Per-credit charge: $331; out-of-state residents $794.
Room and board: $8,070.
Additional info: Each college has required course fees which vary by college. The average of all colleges' course fees at 15 hours per semester for 2 semesters is $741.

FINANCIAL AID PICTURE (2012-2013)
Students with need: Out of 561 full-time freshmen who applied for aid, 337 were judged to have need. Of these, 332 received aid, and 56 had their full need met. Average financial aid package met 61% of need; average scholarship/grant was $8,042; average loan was $6,055. For part-time students, average financial aid package was $6,311.

Students without need: 166 full-time freshmen who did not demonstrate need for aid received scholarships/grants; average award was $9,540. No-need awards available for academics, art, athletics, leadership, minority status, music/drama, ROTC.

Scholarships offered: ***Merit:*** Application deadline for institutional scholarships is December 1st. ***Athletic:*** 32 full-time freshmen received athletic scholarships; average amount $9,394.

Cumulative student debt: 53% of graduating class had student loans; average debt was $25,437.

FINANCIAL AID PROCEDURES

Forms required: FAFSA.

Dates and Deadlines: Priority date 4/1; closing date 7/31. Applicants notified on a rolling basis starting 4/1; must reply within 2 week(s) of notification.

Transfers: First-time regularly admitted transfer students who have earned transfer credits from an accredited 2-year institution of higher learning considered for one-time transfer scholarship award. Super Scholar Transfer Scholarship requires 3.75 college GPA and is currently valued at $2,000 plus a $500 textbook scholarship, renewable for an additional year. UAH Transfer Merit Scholarship requires 3.25 college GPA and is currently valued at $1,000 plus a $500 textbook scholarship, renewable for an additional year. Eligible students should submit the UAH Scholarship Application to apply.

CONTACT

Andy Weaver, Director of Student Financial Services
UAH Office of Undergraduate Admissions, Huntsville, AL 35899
(256) 824-6241

University of Mobile

Mobile, Alabama
www.umobile.edu Federal Code: 001029

4-year private university and liberal arts college in small city, affiliated with Baptist faith.

Enrollment: 1,550 undergrads, 18% part-time. 230 full-time freshmen.

Selectivity: Admits over 75% of applicants.

BASIC COSTS (2013-2014)

Tuition and fees: $18,540.

Per-credit charge: $640.

Room and board: $9,330.

FINANCIAL AID PICTURE (2012-2013)

Students with need: Out of 196 full-time freshmen who applied for aid, 170 were judged to have need. Of these, 170 received aid, and 33 had their full need met. Average financial aid package met 75% of need; average scholarship/grant was $4,791; average loan was $3,542. For part-time students, average financial aid package was $7,929.

Students without need: 26 full-time freshmen who did not demonstrate need for aid received scholarships/grants; average award was $5,900. No-need awards available for academics, alumni affiliation, athletics, music/drama, religious affiliation.

Scholarships offered: 5 full-time freshmen received athletic scholarships; average amount $4,200.

Cumulative student debt: 91% of graduating class had student loans; average debt was $29,474.

FINANCIAL AID PROCEDURES

Forms required: FAFSA, state aid form, institutional form.

Dates and Deadlines: Applicants notified on a rolling basis starting 2/1; must reply within 2 week(s) of notification.

CONTACT

Marie Batson, Associate Vice President for Enrollment Management
5735 College Parkway, Mobile, AL 36613-2842
(251) 442-2252

University of Montevallo

Montevallo, Alabama
www.montevallo.edu Federal Code: 001004

4-year public university and liberal arts college in small town.

Enrollment: 2,589 undergrads, 11% part-time. 539 full-time freshmen.

Selectivity: Admits over 75% of applicants.

BASIC COSTS (2012-2013)

Tuition and fees: $9,280; out-of-state residents $18,070.

Per-credit charge: $293; out-of-state residents $586.

Room and board: $5,522.

FINANCIAL AID PICTURE

Students with need: Need-based aid available for full-time and part-time students.

Students without need: No-need awards available for academics, art, athletics, job skills, leadership, minority status, music/drama, religious affiliation, ROTC.

FINANCIAL AID PROCEDURES

Forms required: FAFSA.

Dates and Deadlines: Priority date 4/1; no closing date. Applicants notified on a rolling basis starting 4/20; must reply within 2 week(s) of notification.

CONTACT

Maria Parker, Director of Financial Aid
Palmer Hall, Station 6030, Montevallo, AL 35115-6000
(205) 665-6050

University of North Alabama

Florence, Alabama
www.una.edu Federal Code: 001016

4-year public university in large town.

Enrollment: 5,681 undergrads, 14% part-time. 1,057 full-time freshmen.

Selectivity: Admits over 75% of applicants.

BASIC COSTS (2012-2013)

Tuition and fees: $8,148; out-of-state residents $14,808.

Per-credit charge: $222; out-of-state residents $444.

Room and board: $5,768.

FINANCIAL AID PICTURE (2011-2012)

Students with need: Average financial aid package met 65% of need; average scholarship/grant was $4,472; average loan was $3,224. For part-time students, average financial aid package was $7,345.

Students without need: No-need awards available for academics, alumni affiliation, art, athletics, job skills, leadership, minority status, music/drama, religious affiliation, ROTC, state/district residency.

Cumulative student debt: 72% of graduating class had student loans; average debt was $32,640.

FINANCIAL AID PROCEDURES

Forms required: FAFSA.

Dates and Deadlines: Priority date 6/1; no closing date. Applicants notified on a rolling basis starting 3/30.

CONTACT

Ben Baker, Director of Student Financial Services
One Harrison Plaza, UNA Box 5011, Florence, AL 35632-0001
(256) 765-4278

University of South Alabama

Mobile, Alabama
www.southalabama.edu Federal Code: 001057

4-year public university in small city.
Enrollment: 11,054 undergrads, 21% part-time. 1,826 full-time freshmen.
Selectivity: Admits over 75% of applicants.

BASIC COSTS (2012-2013)

Tuition and fees: $7,950; out-of-state residents $15,900.
Per-credit charge: $265; out-of-state residents $530.
Room and board: $6,770.
Additional info: Tuition/fee waivers available for minority students.

FINANCIAL AID PICTURE (2011-2012)

Students with need: Out of 1,588 full-time freshmen who applied for aid, 1,220 were judged to have need. Of these, 1,220 received aid, and 173 had their full need met. Average financial aid package met 61% of need; average scholarship/grant was $6,508; average loan was $3,404. For part-time students, average financial aid package was $7,351.
Students without need: 317 full-time freshmen who did not demonstrate need for aid received scholarships/grants; average award was $4,642. No-need awards available for academics, alumni affiliation, art, athletics, job skills, leadership, minority status, music/drama, ROTC, state/district residency.
Scholarships offered: 66 full-time freshmen received athletic scholarships; average amount $13,716.

FINANCIAL AID PROCEDURES

Forms required: FAFSA, institutional form.
Dates and Deadlines: Priority date 5/1; no closing date. Applicants notified on a rolling basis starting 5/15.

CONTACT

Emily Johnston, Director of Financial Aid
Meisler Hall, Suite 2500, Mobile, AL 36688-0002
(251) 460-6231

University of West Alabama

Livingston, Alabama
www.uwa.edu Federal Code: 001024

4-year public university in small town.
Enrollment: 2,100 undergrads, 15% part-time. 204 full-time freshmen.
Selectivity: Admits over 75% of applicants.

BASIC COSTS (2012-2013)

Tuition and fees: $7,320; out-of-state residents $13,490.
Per-credit charge: $263; out-of-state residents $526.
Room and board: $6,920.

FINANCIAL AID PICTURE (2012-2013)

Students with need: Average financial aid package met 30% of need; average scholarship/grant was $4,980. For part-time students, average financial aid package was $6,279.
Students without need: No-need awards available for academics, alumni affiliation, art, athletics, leadership, music/drama, state/district residency.

FINANCIAL AID PROCEDURES

Forms required: FAFSA.
Dates and Deadlines: Priority date 3/1; no closing date. Applicants notified on a rolling basis starting 4/15; must reply within 2 week(s) of notification.
Transfers: Priority date 2/12; no deadline. Applicants notified on a rolling basis.

CONTACT

Don Rainer, Director of Financial Aid
Station 4, Livingston, AL 35470
(205) 652-3576

Virginia College in Huntsville

Huntsville, Alabama
www.vc.edu Federal Code: 030106

4-year for-profit business and technical college in small city.
Enrollment: 668 undergrads.
Selectivity: Open admission.

FINANCIAL AID PICTURE

Students with need: Need-based aid available for full-time and part-time students. Work study available nights, weekends, and for part-time students.

FINANCIAL AID PROCEDURES

Forms required: FAFSA, institutional form.
Dates and Deadlines: Applicants notified on a rolling basis.

CONTACT

Samantha Williams, Director of Financial Aid
2800 Bob Wallace Avenue, Huntsville, AL 35805
(256) 533-7387

Wallace State Community College at Hanceville

Hanceville, Alabama
www.wallacestate.edu Federal Code: 007871

2-year public health science and community college in small town.
Enrollment: 5,075 undergrads. 1,023 full-time freshmen.
Selectivity: Open admission; but selective for some programs.

BASIC COSTS (2012-2013)

Tuition and fees: $4,140; out-of-state residents $7,410.
Per-credit charge: $109; out-of-state residents $218.
Additional info: Board plan not available. Cost of room only, $1,800.

FINANCIAL AID PICTURE

Students with need: Need-based aid available for full-time and part-time students. Work study available nights.
Students without need: This college awards aid only to students with need.

FINANCIAL AID PROCEDURES

Forms required: FAFSA.
Dates and Deadlines: Priority date 5/1; no closing date. Applicants notified on a rolling basis starting 7/15; must reply within 2 week(s) of notification.
Transfers: No deadline.

CONTACT

Becky Graves, Director of Student Financial Aid
PO Box 2000, Hanceville, AL 35077-2000
(256) 352-8182

Alaska

Alaska Bible College

Glennallen, Alaska
www.akbible.edu Federal Code: 014325

4-year private Bible college in rural community, affiliated with nondenominational tradition.
Enrollment: 19 undergrads, 16% part-time. 14 full-time freshmen.
Selectivity: Open admission; but selective for some programs.

BASIC COSTS (2013-2014)
Tuition and fees: $9,290.
Per-credit charge: $375.
Room and board: $5,400.

FINANCIAL AID PICTURE (2011-2012)
Students with need: Out of 9 full-time freshmen who applied for aid, 7 were judged to have need. Of these, 7 received aid, and 6 had their full need met. Average financial aid package met 74% of need; average scholarship/grant was $4,843; average loan was $3,358. For part-time students, average financial aid package was $4,480.
Students without need: 1 full-time freshmen who did not demonstrate need for aid received scholarships/grants; average award was $1,000. No-need awards available for academics.
Cumulative student debt: 15% of graduating class had student loans; average debt was $3,295.

FINANCIAL AID PROCEDURES
Forms required: FAFSA, institutional form.
Dates and Deadlines: Priority date 5/30; no closing date. Must reply within 2 week(s) of notification.
Transfers: Closing date 7/31. Applicants notified by 8/31; must reply within 2 week(s) of notification.

CONTACT
Jared Palmer, Business Manager
PO Box 289, Glennallen, AK 99588-0289
(907) 822-3201 ext. 225

Alaska Pacific University
Anchorage, Alaska
www.alaskapacific.edu Federal Code: 001061

4-year private university and liberal arts college in large city, affiliated with United Methodist Church.
Enrollment: 355 undergrads, 43% part-time. 35 full-time freshmen.
Selectivity: Admits 50 to 75% of applicants.

BASIC COSTS (2013-2014)
Tuition and fees: $30,180.
Room and board: $8,500.

FINANCIAL AID PICTURE (2012-2013)
Students with need: 49% of average financial aid package awarded as scholarships/grants, 51% awarded as loans/jobs. Need-based aid available for part-time students. Work study available nights, weekends, and for part-time students.
Students without need: No-need awards available for academics, alumni affiliation, art, leadership, music/drama, religious affiliation, state/district residency.

FINANCIAL AID PROCEDURES
Forms required: FAFSA.
Dates and Deadlines: Priority date 4/15; no closing date. Applicants notified on a rolling basis starting 2/1; must reply within 4 week(s) of notification.
Transfers: Priority date 6/1; no deadline. Applicants notified on a rolling basis starting 2/1; must reply within 2 week(s) of notification.

CONTACT
Phong Moua, Director, Student Financial Services
4101 University Drive, Anchorage, AK 99508-3051
(907) 564-8341

Ilisagvik College
Barrow, Alaska
www.ilisagvik.edu Federal Code: 034613

2-year public Tribal community college in rural community.
Enrollment: 121 undergrads, 62% part-time. 11 full-time freshmen.
Selectivity: Open admission.

BASIC COSTS (2013-2014)
Tuition and fees: $2,740; out-of-state residents $3,940.
Per-credit charge: $100; out-of-state residents $150.
Room and board: $10,600.

FINANCIAL AID PICTURE (2011-2012)
Students with need: 84% of average financial aid package awarded as scholarships/grants, 16% awarded as loans/jobs. Need-based aid available for part-time students. Work study available nights, weekends, and for part-time students.
Students without need: This college awards aid only to students with need.

FINANCIAL AID PROCEDURES
Forms required: FAFSA.
Dates and Deadlines: Closing date 4/15. Applicants notified by 4/15; must reply by 4/15.

CONTACT
Fred Miller, Director of Financial Aid
100 Stevenson Road, Barrow, AK 99723
(907) 852-1708

Prince William Sound Community College
Valdez, Alaska
www.pwscc.edu Federal Code: 011462

2-year public community college in small town.
Enrollment: 283 undergrads.
Selectivity: Open admission.

BASIC COSTS (2012-2013)
Tuition and fees: $4,670; out-of-state residents $4,670.
Per-credit charge: $142.
Additional info: Board plan not available. Cost of room only, $5,210.

FINANCIAL AID PICTURE
Students with need: Need-based aid available for full-time and part-time students.
Students without need: No-need awards available for state/district residency.

FINANCIAL AID PROCEDURES
Forms required: FAFSA.
Dates and Deadlines: Applicants notified on a rolling basis.
Transfers: Priority date 4/1; closing date 5/1.

CONTACT
Kate Amerelle, Financial Aid Director
Box 97, Valdez, AK 99686
(907) 834-1645

University of Alaska Anchorage
Anchorage, Alaska
www.uaa.alaska.edu Federal Code: 011462

4-year public university in large city.
Enrollment: 13,390 undergrads, 45% part-time. 1,412 full-time freshmen.

Selectivity: Admits over 75% of applicants.

BASIC COSTS (2012-2013)
Tuition and fees: $5,726; out-of-state residents $18,176.
Per-credit charge: $165; out-of-state residents $580.
Room and board: $9,580.

FINANCIAL AID PICTURE (2011-2012)
Students with need: Out of 1,211 full-time freshmen who applied for aid, 770 were judged to have need. Of these, 737 received aid, and 298 had their full need met. Average financial aid package met 78% of need; average scholarship/grant was $2,818; average loan was $3,216. For part-time students, average financial aid package was $6,714.
Students without need: 115 full-time freshmen who did not demonstrate need for aid received scholarships/grants; average award was $2,755. No-need awards available for academics, athletics.
Scholarships offered: 22 full-time freshmen received athletic scholarships; average amount $2,613.
Cumulative student debt: 49% of graduating class had student loans; average debt was $30,363.

FINANCIAL AID PROCEDURES
Forms required: FAFSA, institutional form.
Dates and Deadlines: Priority date 4/1; closing date 8/1. Applicants notified on a rolling basis starting 3/15; must reply within 4 week(s) of notification.
Transfers: Closing date 4/15.

CONTACT
Sonya Fisher, Student Financial Assistance
P0 Box 141629, Anchorage, AK 99514-1629
(907) 786-1480

University of Alaska Fairbanks
Fairbanks, Alaska
www.uaf.edu Federal Code: 001063

4-year public university in small city.
Enrollment: 5,769 undergrads, 37% part-time. 845 full-time freshmen.
Selectivity: Admits over 75% of applicants. GED not accepted.

BASIC COSTS (2013-2014)
Tuition and fees: $5,999; out-of-state residents $18,739.
Per-credit charge: $168; out-of-state residents $591.
Room and board: $7,200.

FINANCIAL AID PICTURE (2011-2012)
Students with need: Out of 755 full-time freshmen who applied for aid, 472 were judged to have need. Of these, 456 received aid, and 137 had their full need met. Average financial aid package met 66% of need; average scholarship/grant was $6,315; average loan was $6,081. For part-time students, average financial aid package was $6,373.
Students without need: 145 full-time freshmen who did not demonstrate need for aid received scholarships/grants; average award was $3,497. No-need awards available for academics, art, athletics, music/drama, state/district residency.
Scholarships offered: 22 full-time freshmen received athletic scholarships; average amount $5,283.
Cumulative student debt: 44% of graduating class had student loans; average debt was $29,762.

FINANCIAL AID PROCEDURES
Forms required: FAFSA.
Dates and Deadlines: Priority date 2/15; closing date 7/1. Applicants notified on a rolling basis starting 3/1; must reply within 2 week(s) of notification.
Transfers: Applicants notified on a rolling basis starting 3/1; must reply within 2 week(s) of notification.

CONTACT
Deanna Dieringer, Director of Financial Aid
PO Box 757480, Fairbanks, AK 99775-7480
(888) 474-7256

University of Alaska Southeast
Juneau, Alaska
www.uas.alaska.edu Federal Code: 001065

4-year public university and liberal arts college in large town.
Enrollment: 1,671 undergrads, 52% part-time. 194 full-time freshmen.
Selectivity: Admits over 75% of applicants.

BASIC COSTS (2012-2013)
Tuition and fees: $5,819; out-of-state residents $18,269.
Per-credit charge: $165; out-of-state residents $580.
Room and board: $9,550.

FINANCIAL AID PICTURE (2011-2012)
Students with need: Out of 164 full-time freshmen who applied for aid, 112 were judged to have need. Of these, 108 received aid, and 13 had their full need met. Average financial aid package met 49% of need; average scholarship/grant was $5,267; average loan was $3,206. For part-time students, average financial aid package was $3,525.
Students without need: 25 full-time freshmen who did not demonstrate need for aid received scholarships/grants; average award was $3,328. No-need awards available for academics, job skills, leadership, music/drama, state/district residency.
Cumulative student debt: 61% of graduating class had student loans; average debt was $19,436.
Additional info: Transfer, continuing, and freshman scholarship deadline March 1.

FINANCIAL AID PROCEDURES
Forms required: FAFSA.
Dates and Deadlines: Priority date 4/15; no closing date. Applicants notified on a rolling basis starting 3/1; must reply within 3 week(s) of notification.

CONTACT
Corinne Soltis, Director of Financial Aid
11120 Glacier Highway, Juneau, AK 99801-8681
(907) 796-6255

Arizona

Anthem College: Phoenix
Phoenix, Arizona
www.anthem.edu Federal Code: 022631

2-year for-profit technical college in very large city.
Enrollment: 2,663 undergrads.
Selectivity: Open admission.

BASIC COSTS (2012-2013)
Additional info: Estimated program costs as of July 2012: associate degrees,$24,280- $25,136; diplomas, $14,990- $22,000. Includes tuition, books, uniforms, supplies and testing fees, when applicable.

FINANCIAL AID PICTURE
Students with need: Need-based aid available for full-time students.
Students without need: This college awards aid only to students with need.

CONTACT
Holly Somers, Financial Aid Director
1515 East Indian School Road, Phoenix, AZ 85014-4901
(602) 279-9700

Arizona Christian University
Phoenix, Arizona
www.arizonachristian.edu Federal Code: 007113

4-year private university and liberal arts college in very large city, affiliated with nondenominational tradition.
Enrollment: 548 undergrads, 8% part-time. 95 full-time freshmen.
Selectivity: Admits 50 to 75% of applicants.

BASIC COSTS (2013-2014)
Tuition and fees: $21,936.
Per-credit charge: $873.
Room and board: $9,600.

FINANCIAL AID PICTURE
Students with need: Need-based aid available for full-time and part-time students.
Students without need: No-need awards available for academics, athletics, leadership, music/drama, religious affiliation.
Cumulative student debt: 58% of graduating class had student loans; average debt was $23,497.

FINANCIAL AID PROCEDURES
Forms required: FAFSA, institutional form.
Dates and Deadlines: Priority date 4/1; no closing date. Applicants notified on a rolling basis.
Transfers: Applicants notified on a rolling basis.

CONTACT
Michelle Elizer, Director of Financial Aid
2625 East Cactus Road, Phoenix, AZ 85032-7042
(602) 386-4106

Arizona State University
Tempe, Arizona
www.asu.edu Federal Code: 001081

4-year public university in very large city.
Enrollment: 59,183 undergrads, 16% part-time. 9,082 full-time freshmen.
Selectivity: Admits over 75% of applicants.

BASIC COSTS (2012-2013)
Tuition and fees: $9,724; out-of-state residents $22,977.
Per-credit charge: $658; out-of-state residents $936.
Room and board: $9,094.

FINANCIAL AID PICTURE (2011-2012)
Students with need: Out of 7,312 full-time freshmen who applied for aid, 5,864 were judged to have need. Of these, 5,864 received aid, and 1,017 had their full need met. Average financial aid package met 59% of need; average scholarship/grant was $9,323; average loan was $3,125. For part-time students, average financial aid package was $7,022.
Students without need: 1,797 full-time freshmen who did not demonstrate need for aid received scholarships/grants; average award was $7,505. No-need awards available for academics, art, athletics, leadership, music/drama, ROTC.
Scholarships offered: 44 full-time freshmen received athletic scholarships; average amount $18,509.
Cumulative student debt: 55% of graduating class had student loans; average debt was $18,615.

FINANCIAL AID PROCEDURES
Forms required: FAFSA.
Dates and Deadlines: Priority date 3/1; no closing date. Applicants notified on a rolling basis starting 3/1.

CONTACT
Melissa Pizzo, Executive Director Student Financial Assistance
PO Box 870112, Tempe, AZ 85287-0112
(480) 965-3355

Arizona Western College
Yuma, Arizona
www.azwestern.edu Federal Code: 001071

2-year public community college in small city.
Enrollment: 6,690 undergrads, 63% part-time. 840 full-time freshmen.
Selectivity: Open admission; but selective for some programs.

BASIC COSTS (2013-2014)
Tuition and fees: $2,430; out-of-state residents $7,917.
Per-credit charge: $74; out-of-state residents $255.
Room and board: $6,003.

FINANCIAL AID PICTURE
Students with need: Need-based aid available for full-time and part-time students. Work study available nights, weekends, and for part-time students.
Students without need: No-need awards available for academics, art, athletics, leadership, minority status, music/drama.

FINANCIAL AID PROCEDURES
Forms required: FAFSA, institutional form.
Dates and Deadlines: Priority date 4/1; no closing date. Applicants notified on a rolling basis starting 5/1.

CONTACT
Lisa Seale, Director of Financial Aid
PO Box 929, Yuma, AZ 85366-0929
(928) 344-7634

Art Institute of Phoenix
Phoenix, Arizona
www.artinstitutes.edu/phoenix Federal Code: 040513

3-year for-profit culinary school and visual arts college in very large city.
Enrollment: 1,190 undergrads.

FINANCIAL AID PICTURE
Students with need: Need-based aid available for full-time and part-time students.

FINANCIAL AID PROCEDURES
Forms required: FAFSA.

CONTACT
Abigail Garcia, Director of Administrative and Financial Services
2233 West Dunlap Avenue, Phoenix, AZ 85021-2859

Brookline College: Phoenix
Phoenix, Arizona
www.brooklinecollege.edu Federal Code: 022188

2-year for-profit career college in very large city.
Enrollment: 1,585 undergrads.
Selectivity: Open admission.

BASIC COSTS (2012-2013)
Additional info: As of April 2012, estimated annual tuition and fees for associate degree programs in accounting, business, criminal justice, paralegal studies: $13,500.

FINANCIAL AID PICTURE
Students with need: Need-based aid available for full-time students.
Students without need: This college awards aid only to students with need.

FINANCIAL AID PROCEDURES
Forms required: FAFSA, institutional form.

CONTACT
Genna Gillary, Corporate Manager of Financial Aid
2445 West Dunlap Avenue, Suite 100, Phoenix, AZ 85021-5820
(602) 644-7110

Brookline College: Tempe
Tempe, Arizona
www.brooklinecollege.edu Federal Code: 022188

2-year for-profit branch campus and career college in very large city.
Enrollment: 583 undergrads.
Selectivity: Open admission; but selective for some programs.

BASIC COSTS (2012-2013)
Additional info: As of April 2012, estimated annual tuition and fees for associate degree programs in accounting, business, criminal justice, paralegal studies: $13,500.

FINANCIAL AID PICTURE
Students with need: Need-based aid available for full-time students.
Students without need: This college awards aid only to students with need.

FINANCIAL AID PROCEDURES
Forms required: FAFSA, institutional form.

CONTACT
Genna Gillary, Corporate Manager of Financial Aid
1140-1150 South Priest Drive, Tempe, AZ 85281-5240
(480) 545-8755

Brookline College: Tucson
Tucson, Arizona
www.brooklinecollege.edu Federal Code: 022188

2-year for-profit branch campus and career college in very large city.
Enrollment: 849 undergrads.
Selectivity: Open admission.

BASIC COSTS (2012-2013)
Additional info: As of April 2012, estimated annual tuition and fees for associate degree programs in accounting, business, criminal justice, paralegal studies: $13,500.

FINANCIAL AID PICTURE
Students with need: Need-based aid available for full-time and part-time students.
Students without need: This college awards aid only to students with need.

FINANCIAL AID PROCEDURES
Forms required: FAFSA, institutional form.

CONTACT
Genna Gillary, Corporate Manager of Financial Aid
5441 East 22nd Street, Suite 125, Tucson, AZ 85711-5444
(602) 644-7090

Central Arizona College
Coolidge, Arizona
www.centralaz.edu Federal Code: 007283

2-year public community college in large town.
Enrollment: 5,833 undergrads, 62% part-time. 590 full-time freshmen.
Selectivity: Open admission; but selective for some programs.

BASIC COSTS (2012-2013)
Tuition and fees: $2,160; out-of-state residents $9,600.
Per-credit charge: $72; out-of-state residents $144.
Room and board: $5,080.

FINANCIAL AID PICTURE
Students with need: Need-based aid available for full-time and part-time students. Work study available nights, weekends, and for part-time students.

FINANCIAL AID PROCEDURES
Forms required: FAFSA.
Dates and Deadlines: Priority date 5/1; closing date 7/15. Must reply within 3 week(s) of notification.

CONTACT
Elisa Juarez, Director of Financial Aid
Admissions Office, Coolidge, AZ 85128-9030
(520) 494-5425

Chandler-Gilbert Community College
Chandler, Arizona
www.cgc.maricopa.edu Federal Code: 030722

2-year public community college in small city.
Enrollment: 10,894 undergrads, 64% part-time. 825 full-time freshmen.
Selectivity: Open admission; but selective for some programs.

BASIC COSTS (2012-2013)
Tuition and fees: $2,310; out-of-state residents $9,540.
Per-credit charge: $76; out-of-state residents $317.

FINANCIAL AID PICTURE (2011-2012)
Students with need: 64% of average financial aid package awarded as scholarships/grants, 36% awarded as loans/jobs. Work study available nights, weekends, and for part-time students.

CONTACT
Donna Pisano, Director of Financial Aid
2626 East Pecos Road, Chandler, AZ 85225
(480) 732-7311

Cochise College
Douglas, Arizona
www.cochise.edu Federal Code: 001072

2-year public community college in large town.
Enrollment: 3,775 undergrads, 63% part-time. 447 full-time freshmen.
Selectivity: Open admission; but selective for some programs.

BASIC COSTS (2012-2013)
Tuition and fees: $2,100; out-of-state residents $8,700.
Per-credit charge: $70; out-of-state residents $290.
Room and board: $5,600.

FINANCIAL AID PICTURE (2011-2012)
Students with need: Out of 376 full-time freshmen who applied for aid, 339 were judged to have need. Of these, 335 received aid. For part-time students, average financial aid package was $3,226.

Students without need: 8 full-time freshmen who did not demonstrate need for aid received scholarships/grants; average award was $795.
Scholarships offered: 39 full-time freshmen received athletic scholarships; average amount $4,342.

FINANCIAL AID PROCEDURES
Forms required: FAFSA.
Dates and Deadlines: Priority date 4/1; closing date 6/15. Applicants notified on a rolling basis starting 6/1.
Transfers: Applicants notified on a rolling basis starting 6/1. Official college or university transcripts for all institutions previously attended required.

CONTACT
Karen Bennett, Director of Financial Aid
901 North Colombo Avenue, Sierra Vista, AZ 85635
(520) 515-5417

DeVry University: Phoenix

Phoenix, Arizona
www.devry.edu Federal Code: 008322

4-year for-profit university in large city.
Enrollment: 1,111 undergrads, 53% part-time. 51 full-time freshmen.

BASIC COSTS (2012-2013)
Tuition and fees: $16,076.
Per-credit charge: $609.

FINANCIAL AID PICTURE
Students with need: Need-based aid available for full-time and part-time students.
Students without need: This college awards aid only to students with need.

FINANCIAL AID PROCEDURES
Forms required: FAFSA.
Dates and Deadlines: Applicants notified on a rolling basis.

CONTACT
Kathy Wyse, Dean of Student Finances
2149 West Dunlap Avenue, Phoenix, AZ 85021-2995
(602) 870-9229

Dine College

Tsaile, Arizona
www.dinecollege.edu Federal Code: 008246

2-year public community college in rural community.
Enrollment: 1,907 undergrads, 40% part-time. 500 full-time freshmen.
Selectivity: Open admission.

BASIC COSTS (2012-2013)
Tuition and fees: $850; out-of-state residents $850.
Per-credit charge: $720.
Room and board: $3,720.

FINANCIAL AID PICTURE (2011-2012)
Students with need: Out of 492 full-time freshmen who applied for aid, 491 were judged to have need. Of these, 486 received aid, and 2 had their full need met. Average financial aid package met 47% of need. For part-time students, average financial aid package was $3,057.
Students without need: This college awards aid only to students with need.

FINANCIAL AID PROCEDURES
Forms required: FAFSA, institutional form.
Dates and Deadlines: Priority date 4/15; no closing date. Applicants notified on a rolling basis starting 5/1; must reply within 4 week(s) of notification.
Transfers: Priority date 3/1; no deadline. Applicants notified on a rolling basis starting 1/1; must reply within 6 week(s) of notification.

CONTACT
Gary Segay, Financial Aid Officer
Box 67, Tsaile, AZ 86556
(928) 724-6738

Eastern Arizona College

Thatcher, Arizona
www.eac.edu Federal Code: 001073

2-year public community college in large town.
Enrollment: 5,071 undergrads, 56% part-time. 24,597 full-time freshmen.
Selectivity: Open admission; but selective for some programs.

BASIC COSTS (2012-2013)
Tuition and fees: $1,760; out-of-state residents $8,360.
Per-credit charge: $80; out-of-state residents $155.
Room and board: $5,390.

FINANCIAL AID PICTURE (2011-2012)
Students with need: Out of 19,158 full-time freshmen who applied for aid, 16,109 were judged to have need. Of these, 12,447 received aid, and 573 had their full need met. Average financial aid package met 37% of need; average scholarship/grant was $3,621; average loan was $4. For part-time students, average financial aid package was $2,549.
Students without need: 3,350 full-time freshmen who did not demonstrate need for aid received scholarships/grants; average award was $2,027. No-need awards available for academics, art, athletics, leadership, music/drama, state/district residency.
Scholarships offered: ***Merit:*** Departmental Scholarships; in-state tuition; based on 2.5 GPA. Academic Scholarships; in-state tuition; based on 3.0 GPA. Performing Arts Scholarships; amounts vary; based on 2.5 GPA and audition. ***Athletic:*** 865 full-time freshmen received athletic scholarships; average amount $3,587.
Additional info: Limited number of tuition waivers for New Mexico residents. Unlimited number of waivers for those meeting WUE requirements.

FINANCIAL AID PROCEDURES
Forms required: FAFSA, institutional form.
Dates and Deadlines: Priority date 3/1; no closing date. Applicants notified on a rolling basis starting 3/15.
Transfers: No deadline. Applicants notified on a rolling basis starting 3/15.

CONTACT
Sharon Montoya, Director of Financial Aid
615 North Stadium Avenue, Thatcher, AZ 85552-0769
(928) 428-8287

Embry-Riddle Aeronautical University: Prescott Campus

Prescott, Arizona
www.embryriddle.edu Federal Code: 014797

4-year private university in large town.
Enrollment: 1,669 undergrads, 6% part-time. 374 full-time freshmen.

BASIC COSTS (2013-2014)
Tuition and fees: $31,020.
Per-credit charge: $1,255.
Room and board: $9,340.

FINANCIAL AID PICTURE (2012-2013)
Students with need: Need-based aid available for full-time and part-time students.

Students without need: No-need awards available for academics, alumni affiliation, athletics, leadership, ROTC.

FINANCIAL AID PROCEDURES

Forms required: FAFSA.

Dates and Deadlines: Applicants notified on a rolling basis starting 3/1; must reply within 4 week(s) of notification.

CONTACT

Barbara Dryden, Director of Financial Aid
3700 Willow Creek Road, Prescott, AZ 86301-3720
(928) 777-3765

Estrella Mountain Community College

Avondale, Arizona
www.estrellamountain.edu Federal Code: 031563

2-year public community college in small city.
Enrollment: 2,471 full-time undergrads.
Selectivity: Open admission.

BASIC COSTS (2012-2013)

Tuition and fees: $2,295; out-of-state residents $9,525.
Per-credit charge: $76; out-of-state residents $317.

FINANCIAL AID PICTURE

Students with need: Need-based aid available for full-time and part-time students. Work study available nights.
Students without need: No-need awards available for leadership.

FINANCIAL AID PROCEDURES

Dates and Deadlines: Priority date 4/1; no closing date. Applicants notified on a rolling basis starting 4/15.

CONTACT

Rosanna Short, Director, Financial Aid
3000 North Dysart Road, Avondale, AZ 85392
(623) 935-8930

GateWay Community College

Phoenix, Arizona
www.gatewaycc.edu Federal Code: 008303

2-year public community and technical college in very large city.
Enrollment: 6,530 undergrads.
Selectivity: Open admission; but selective for some programs.

BASIC COSTS (2013-2014)

Tuition and fees: $2,295; out-of-state residents $9,525.
Per-credit charge: $76; out-of-state residents $317.

FINANCIAL AID PICTURE (2011-2012)

Students with need: 94% of average financial aid package awarded as scholarships/grants, 6% awarded as loans/jobs. Need-based aid available for part-time students. Work study available nights, weekends, and for part-time students.
Students without need: No-need awards available for athletics.

FINANCIAL AID PROCEDURES

Forms required: FAFSA, institutional form.
Dates and Deadlines: Priority date 4/15; no closing date. Applicants notified on a rolling basis; must reply within 4 week(s) of notification.

CONTACT

Suzanne Ringle, Director of Financial Aid
108 North 40th Street, Phoenix, AZ 85034
(602) 286-8115

Glendale Community College

Glendale, Arizona
www.gccaz.edu Federal Code: 001076

2-year public community college in small city.
Enrollment: 21,356 undergrads.
Selectivity: Open admission; but selective for some programs.

BASIC COSTS (2012-2013)

Tuition and fees: $2,310; out-of-state residents $9,540.
Per-credit charge: $76; out-of-state residents $317.

FINANCIAL AID PICTURE

Students with need: Need-based aid available for full-time and part-time students. Work study available nights, weekends, and for part-time students.
Students without need: No-need awards available for art, athletics, music/drama.

FINANCIAL AID PROCEDURES

Forms required: FAFSA.
Dates and Deadlines: Priority date 4/30; no closing date. Applicants notified on a rolling basis starting 5/1.
Transfers: No deadline. Applicants notified on a rolling basis.

CONTACT

Ellen Neel, Director of Financial Aid
6000 West Olive Avenue, Glendale, AZ 85302
(623) 845-3366

Grand Canyon University

Phoenix, Arizona
www.gcu.edu/clgbrd Federal Code: 001074

4-year for-profit university in very large city.
Enrollment: 30,241 undergrads.

BASIC COSTS (2012-2013)

Tuition and fees: $16,900.
Per-credit charge: $687.
Room and board: $12,400.

FINANCIAL AID PICTURE

Students with need: Need-based aid available for full-time and part-time students. Work study available nights, weekends, and for part-time students.
Students without need: No-need awards available for academics, alumni affiliation, art, athletics, leadership, minority status, music/drama, religious affiliation, ROTC, state/district residency.

FINANCIAL AID PROCEDURES

Forms required: FAFSA.
Dates and Deadlines: Applicants notified on a rolling basis.
Transfers: No deadline. Applicants notified on a rolling basis.

CONTACT

Chris Linderson, Vice President of Financial Aid
3300 West Camelback Road, Phoenix, AZ 85017-8562
(800) 800-9776

Mesa Community College

Mesa, Arizona
www.mesacc.edu Federal Code: 001077

2-year public community college in very large city.
Enrollment: 21,143 undergrads.
Selectivity: Open admission; but selective for some programs.

BASIC COSTS (2012-2013)
Tuition and fees: $2,295; out-of-state residents $9,525.
Per-credit charge: $76; out-of-state residents $317.

FINANCIAL AID PICTURE
Students with need: Need-based aid available for full-time and part-time students.
Students without need: No-need awards available for academics, athletics.
Additional info: Awards available for Maricopa County residents.

FINANCIAL AID PROCEDURES
Forms required: FAFSA, institutional form.
Dates and Deadlines: Priority date 5/1; no closing date. Applicants notified on a rolling basis starting 7/1.

CONTACT
Patricia Peppin, Financial Aid
1833 West Southern Avenue, Mesa, AZ 85202
(480) 471-7400

Mohave Community College
Kingman, Arizona
www.mohave.edu Federal Code: 011864

2-year public community college in small city.
Enrollment: 6,100 undergrads.
Selectivity: Open admission; but selective for some programs.

BASIC COSTS (2012-2013)
Tuition and fees: $2,520; out-of-state residents $9,360.
Per-credit charge: $74; out-of-state residents $304.

FINANCIAL AID PICTURE (2011-2012)
Students with need: 70% of average financial aid package awarded as scholarships/grants, 30% awarded as loans/jobs. Need-based aid available for part-time students. Work study available nights.
Students without need: This college awards aid only to students with need.

FINANCIAL AID PROCEDURES
Forms required: FAFSA, institutional form.
Dates and Deadlines: Priority date 4/15; closing date 7/15. Applicants notified on a rolling basis starting 5/1; must reply within 2 week(s) of notification.

CONTACT
Shannon Sheaff, Director of Financial Aid
1971 Jagerson Avenue, Kingman, AZ 86409
(866) 664-2832

Northcentral University
Prescott Valley, Arizona
www.ncu.edu Federal Code: 038133

Upper-division for-profit virtual university in large town.
Enrollment: 329 undergrads, 76% part-time.

BASIC COSTS (2013-2014)
Tuition and fees: $12,500.
Per-credit charge: $417.

FINANCIAL AID PICTURE
Students with need: Need-based aid available for full-time and part-time students.

FINANCIAL AID PROCEDURES
Dates and Deadlines: Applicants notified on a rolling basis; must reply within 4 week(s) of notification.
Transfers: No deadline. Applicants notified on a rolling basis.

CONTACT
Valerie Steinbock, Director, Learner Financial Services
8667 East Hartford Drive, Scottsdale, AZ 85255
(928) 541-7777 ext. 8080

Northern Arizona University
Flagstaff, Arizona
www.nau.edu Federal Code: 001082

4-year public university in small city.
Enrollment: 21,609 undergrads, 15% part-time. 3,226 full-time freshmen.
Selectivity: Admits over 75% of applicants.

BASIC COSTS (2012-2013)
Tuition and fees: $9,271; out-of-state residents $21,626.
Room and board: $8,784.
Additional info: Tuition at time of enrollment locked for 4 years.

FINANCIAL AID PICTURE (2011-2012)
Students with need: Out of 2,769 full-time freshmen who applied for aid, 2,103 were judged to have need. Of these, 2,037 received aid, and 242 had their full need met. Average financial aid package met 60% of need; average scholarship/grant was $6,306; average loan was $3,300. For part-time students, average financial aid package was $6,429.
Students without need: 460 full-time freshmen who did not demonstrate need for aid received scholarships/grants; average award was $5,098. No-need awards available for academics, alumni affiliation, art, athletics, leadership, minority status, music/drama, ROTC, state/district residency.
Scholarships offered: 58 full-time freshmen received athletic scholarships; average amount $12,942.
Cumulative student debt: 58% of graduating class had student loans; average debt was $22,621.
Additional info: Guaranteed fixed tuition for 4 years and guaranteed gift aid for 4 years.

FINANCIAL AID PROCEDURES
Forms required: FAFSA.
Dates and Deadlines: Priority date 2/14; no closing date. Applicants notified on a rolling basis starting 3/15.
Transfers: No deadline. Applicants notified on a rolling basis.

CONTACT
Andrew Griffin, Director of Financial Aid
PO Box 4084, Flagstaff, AZ 86011-4084
(928) 523-4951

Northland Pioneer College
Holbrook, Arizona
www.npc.edu Federal Code: 011862

2-year public community and technical college in small town.
Enrollment: 3,917 undergrads.
Selectivity: Open admission; but selective for some programs.

BASIC COSTS (2012-2013)
Tuition and fees: $1,930; out-of-state residents $9,220.
Per-credit charge: $62; out-of-state residents $305.

FINANCIAL AID PICTURE
Students with need: Need-based aid available for full-time and part-time students. Work study available nights, weekends, and for part-time students.
Students without need: No-need awards available for academics, art, job skills, leadership, minority status, music/drama, state/district residency.

FINANCIAL AID PROCEDURES
Forms required: FAFSA, institutional form.
Dates and Deadlines: Priority date 6/1; no closing date. Applicants notified on a rolling basis starting 5/15; must reply within 2 week(s) of notification.
Transfers: No deadline. Applicants notified on a rolling basis.

CONTACT
Beaulah Bob-Pennypacker, Financial Aid Coordinator
PO Box 610, Holbrook, AZ 86025-0610
(928) 524-7626

Paradise Valley Community College

Phoenix, Arizona
www.pvc.maricopa.edu Federal Code: 026236

2-year public community college in very large city.
Enrollment: 9,874 undergrads.
Selectivity: Open admission.

BASIC COSTS (2012-2013)
Tuition and fees: $2,310; out-of-state residents $9,540.
Per-credit charge: $76; out-of-state residents $317.

FINANCIAL AID PICTURE
Students with need: Need-based aid available for full-time and part-time students.

FINANCIAL AID PROCEDURES
Forms required: FAFSA.
Dates and Deadlines: Applicants notified on a rolling basis starting 6/1.

CONTACT
Ken Clarke, Director of Financial Aid
18401 North 32nd Street, Phoenix, AZ 85032
(602) 787-7100

Phoenix College

Phoenix, Arizona
www.phoenixcollege.edu Federal Code: 001078

2-year public community college in very large city.
Enrollment: 9,649 undergrads, 69% part-time. 708 full-time freshmen.
Selectivity: Open admission; but selective for some programs.

BASIC COSTS (2012-2013)
Tuition and fees: $2,310; out-of-state residents $9,570.
Per-credit charge: $76; out-of-state residents $317.

FINANCIAL AID PICTURE (2012-2013)
Students with need: 50% of average financial aid package awarded as scholarships/grants, 50% awarded as loans/jobs. Work study available weekends and for part-time students.

FINANCIAL AID PROCEDURES
Forms required: FAFSA.
Dates and Deadlines: Priority date 6/30; no closing date. Applicants notified on a rolling basis.

CONTACT
Chris Haines, Dean
1202 West Thomas Road, Phoenix, AZ 85013
(602) 285-7856

Pima Community College

Tucson, Arizona
www.pima.edu Federal Code: 007266

2-year public community and technical college in very large city.
Enrollment: 29,300 undergrads, 60% part-time. 2,746 full-time freshmen.
Selectivity: Open admission; but selective for some programs.

BASIC COSTS (2012-2013)
Tuition and fees: $2,060; out-of-state residents $9,725.
Per-credit charge: $64; out-of-state residents $106.

FINANCIAL AID PICTURE
Students with need: Need-based aid available for full-time and part-time students.
Students without need: No-need awards available for academics, alumni affiliation, art, athletics, minority status, music/drama.

FINANCIAL AID PROCEDURES
Forms required: FAFSA.
Dates and Deadlines: Priority date 4/4; no closing date. Applicants notified on a rolling basis starting 5/1; must reply within 2 week(s) of notification.

CONTACT
Anna Reese, Executive Director of Financial Aid
4905B East Broadway, Tucson, AZ 85709-1120
(520) 206-4950

Prescott College

Prescott, Arizona
www.prescott.edu Federal Code: 013659

4-year private liberal arts college in small city.
Enrollment: 671 undergrads, 20% part-time. 64 full-time freshmen.
Selectivity: Admits 50 to 75% of applicants.

BASIC COSTS (2012-2013)
Tuition and fees: $28,820.
Additional info: Health insurance is required; cost of school's health insurance is $871 for fall term and $1,208 for spring term. Board plan not available. Cost of room only: $4500.

FINANCIAL AID PICTURE (2012-2013)
Students with need: Out of 51 full-time freshmen who applied for aid, 50 were judged to have need. Of these, 50 received aid, and 5 had their full need met. Average financial aid package met 69% of need; average scholarship/grant was $18,100; average loan was $3,895. For part-time students, average financial aid package was $11,021.
Students without need: 9 full-time freshmen who did not demonstrate need for aid received scholarships/grants; average award was $8,777. No-need awards available for academics, leadership.
Scholarships offered: President's Excellence in Achievement Scholarship; $15,000 per year; 2200 SAT/33 ACT. President's Distinguished Scholarship; $10,000-$12,000 per year; 1800 SAT/27 ACT. Dean's Distinguished Scholar Award; $10,000 per year; for applicants without SAT/ACT but with 3.33 GPA, proof of volunteering/community involvement, superior application rating. Merit Scholarship; $8,000 per year; 1550 SAT/23 ACT, 3.0 GPA, proof of volunteering/community involvement, superior application rating. National Merit Finalist Recognition; $2,000 per year; in addition to student's other scholarships.
Cumulative student debt: 68% of graduating class had student loans; average debt was $23,476.

FINANCIAL AID PROCEDURES
Forms required: FAFSA.
Dates and Deadlines: Priority date 3/1; no closing date. Applicants notified on a rolling basis starting 3/15; must reply within 12 week(s) of notification.

Transfers: No deadline. Applicants notified on a rolling basis starting 3/15; must reply within 4 week(s) of notification. Dean's 21st Century Global Leader Scholarship; $10,000 per year; 2200 SAT/33 ACT or 3.25 college GPA, proof of volunteering, superior application rating. Merit Scholarship; $8,000 per year; 1550 SAT/23 ACT or 3.0 GPA, proof of volunteering, superior application rating. Phi Theta Kappa Scholarship; $2,000 per year.

CONTACT
Mary Frances Causey, Director of Financial Aid
220 Grove Avenue, Prescott, AZ 86301
(928) 350-2100

Rio Salado College

Tempe, Arizona
www.riosalado.edu Federal Code: 014483

2-year public community college in very large city.
Enrollment: 10,723 undergrads.
Selectivity: Open admission; but selective for some programs.

FINANCIAL AID PICTURE
Students with need: Need-based aid available for full-time and part-time students.
Students without need: This college awards aid only to students with need.

FINANCIAL AID PROCEDURES
Forms required: FAFSA, institutional form.
Dates and Deadlines: Priority date 6/30; no closing date. Applicants notified on a rolling basis starting 6/30.

CONTACT
Nanci Regehr, Director of Financial Aid
2323 West 14th Street, Tempe, AZ 85281
(480) 517-8310

Scottsdale Community College

Scottsdale, Arizona
www.scottsdalecc.edu Federal Code: 008304

2-year public community college in small city.
Enrollment: 4,510 undergrads, 74% part-time.
Selectivity: Open admission.

BASIC COSTS (2012-2013)
Tuition and fees: $2,310; out-of-state residents $9,540.
Per-credit charge: $76; out-of-state residents $317.

FINANCIAL AID PICTURE
Students with need: Need-based aid available for full-time and part-time students.
Students without need: No-need awards available for academics, athletics.

FINANCIAL AID PROCEDURES
Forms required: FAFSA.
Dates and Deadlines: Priority date 6/1; no closing date. Applicants notified on a rolling basis starting 7/1; must reply by 7/15 or within 3 week(s) of notification.
Transfers: No deadline. Applicants notified on a rolling basis starting 7/1; must reply by 6/1.

CONTACT
Stacie Beck, Director of Financial Aid
9000 East Chaparral Road, Scottsdale, AZ 85256-2626
(480) 423-6549

South Mountain Community College

Phoenix, Arizona
www.southmountaincc.edu Federal Code: 015001

2-year public community college in very large city.
Enrollment: 4,738 undergrads.
Selectivity: Open admission.

BASIC COSTS (2012-2013)
Tuition and fees: $2,310; out-of-state residents $9,540.
Per-credit charge: $76; out-of-state residents $317.

FINANCIAL AID PICTURE
Students with need: Need-based aid available for full-time and part-time students. Work study available nights, weekends, and for part-time students.
Students without need: No-need awards available for academics, athletics, minority status, music/drama.

FINANCIAL AID PROCEDURES
Forms required: FAFSA.
Dates and Deadlines: Priority date 5/1; no closing date. Applicants notified on a rolling basis starting 5/15; must reply within 3 week(s) of notification.

CONTACT
Inez Moreno-Weinert, Director of Financial Aid and Placement
7050 South 24th Street, Phoenix, AZ 85042
(602) 243-8300

Southwest University of Visual Arts

Tucson, Arizona
www.suva.edu Federal Code: 024915

4-year for-profit visual arts college in very large city.
Enrollment: 221 undergrads.

BASIC COSTS (2012-2013)
Tuition and fees: $18,360.
Per-credit charge: $765.

FINANCIAL AID PICTURE
Students with need: Need-based aid available for full-time and part-time students. Work study available nights, weekends, and for part-time students.
Students without need: This college awards aid only to students with need.
Scholarships offered: Board of Trustees Scholarship; Transfer Student Scholarship; Scholarship for Continuing Students.

FINANCIAL AID PROCEDURES
Forms required: FAFSA.
Transfers: No deadline. Applicants notified on a rolling basis.

CONTACT
Stephanie Dietzman, Manager of Office of Institutional Effectiveness
2525 North Country Club Road, Tucson, AZ 85716
(520) 325-0123

Tohono O'odham Community College

Sells, Arizona
www.tocc.edu Federal Code: 037844

2-year public community college in rural community.
Enrollment: 179 undergrads, 64% part-time. 25 full-time freshmen.
Selectivity: Open admission.

BASIC COSTS (2012-2013)
Tuition and fees: $1,680; out-of-state residents $4,740.

FINANCIAL AID PICTURE

Students with need: Need-based aid available for full-time and part-time students.

Students without need: This college awards aid only to students with need.

FINANCIAL AID PROCEDURES

Forms required: FAFSA, institutional form.

Dates and Deadlines: Applicants notified on a rolling basis.

CONTACT

Alvaro Rivera, Financial Aid Director
PO Box 3129, Sells, AZ 85634-3129
(520) 383-8401 ext. 41

University of Advancing Technology

Tempe, Arizona
www.uat.edu Federal Code: 017188

4-year for-profit university in small city.
Enrollment: 908 undergrads. 129 full-time freshmen.
Selectivity: Admits over 75% of applicants.

BASIC COSTS (2012-2013)

Tuition and fees: $20,100.
Room and board: $11,016.

FINANCIAL AID PICTURE (2011-2012)

Students with need: Out of 103 full-time freshmen who applied for aid, 100 were judged to have need. Of these, 98 received aid.

Students without need: No-need awards available for academics, art, leadership.

FINANCIAL AID PROCEDURES

Forms required: FAFSA.

Dates and Deadlines: Priority date 4/15; no closing date. Applicants notified on a rolling basis; must reply within 2 week(s) of notification.

Transfers: No deadline. Must reply within 2 week(s) of notification. Loan periods may not overlap.

CONTACT

Diana Mateer, Manager of Financial Aid
2625 West Baseline Road, Tempe, AZ 85283-1056
(602) 383-8217

University of Arizona

Tucson, Arizona Federal Code: 001083
www.arizona.edu CSS Code: 4832

4-year public university in very large city.
Enrollment: 31,217 undergrads, 10% part-time. 6,874 full-time freshmen.
Selectivity: Admits over 75% of applicants.

BASIC COSTS (2012-2013)

Tuition and fees: $10,035; out-of-state residents $26,231.
Per-credit charge: $651; out-of-state residents $1,055.
Room and board: $9,714.
Additional info: Tuition/fee waivers available for minority students.

FINANCIAL AID PICTURE (2011-2012)

Students with need: Out of 5,018 full-time freshmen who applied for aid, 3,774 were judged to have need. Of these, 3,672 received aid, and 487 had their full need met. Average financial aid package met 64% of need; average scholarship/grant was $10,795; average loan was $3,256. For part-time students, average financial aid package was $8,633.

Students without need: 1,770 full-time freshmen who did not demonstrate need for aid received scholarships/grants; average award was $7,643. No-need awards available for academics, art, music/drama.

Scholarships offered: ***Merit:*** Various merit scholarships available. National Merit scholarship; $6,000-$10,000 a year. ***Athletic:*** 74 full-time freshmen received athletic scholarships; average amount $19,299.

Cumulative student debt: 49% of graduating class had student loans; average debt was $22,269.

Additional info: Arizona Assurance Program; provides housing, books, and tuition for all new, incoming resident freshmen; must be Pell-eligible with combined family income less than $42,500; funding provided as grants, scholarships, and federal work-study.

FINANCIAL AID PROCEDURES

Forms required: FAFSA. CSS PROFILE required for some; subset of applicants asked to comply based on FAFSA information.

Dates and Deadlines: Priority date 3/1; no closing date. Applicants notified on a rolling basis starting 4/1; must reply within 3 week(s) of notification.

Transfers: Awards based on academic factors for both residents and non-residents and vary in amount each year.

CONTACT

John Nametz, Director of Student Financial Aid
1428 East University Boulevard, Tucson, AZ 85721-0073
(520) 621-1858

University of Phoenix: Phoenix-Hohokam

Tempe, Arizona
www.phoenix.edu Federal Code: 014593

4-year for-profit university in small city.
Enrollment: 3,704 undergrads.
Selectivity: Open admission; but selective for some programs.

BASIC COSTS (2012-2013)

Additional info: Estimated costs as of July 2012: per-credit-hour charge, $420 to $435, depending upon level and course of study; electronic course materials fee, $95, if applicable. Book and material charges may vary by course and program. All fees are subject to change.

FINANCIAL AID PICTURE

Students with need: Need-based aid available for full-time students.

FINANCIAL AID PROCEDURES

Forms required: FAFSA, institutional form.

Dates and Deadlines: Applicants notified on a rolling basis.

CONTACT

Kristen Vedder, Vice President, Student Administrative Services
1625 West Fountainhead Parkway, Tempe, AZ 85282-2371
(480) 804-7600

Western International University

Phoenix, Arizona
www.west.edu Federal Code: 014970

4-year for-profit university and business college in very large city.
Enrollment: 2,086 undergrads.
Selectivity: Open admission.

BASIC COSTS (2012-2013)

Tuition and fees: $13,800.
Per-credit charge: $460.

FINANCIAL AID PICTURE

Students with need: Need-based aid available for full-time students.

Students without need: This college awards aid only to students with need.

FINANCIAL AID PROCEDURES

Forms required: FAFSA, institutional form.

Dates and Deadlines: Applicants notified on a rolling basis.

Transfers: No deadline. Applicants notified on a rolling basis.

CONTACT

Beth Carlisle, Director of Finance
9215 North Black Canyon Highway, Phoenix, AZ 85021-2718
(602) 943-2311

Yavapai College

Prescott, Arizona
www.yc.edu Federal Code: 001079

2-year public community college in large town.

Enrollment: 7,837 undergrads.

Selectivity: Open admission; but selective for some programs.

BASIC COSTS (2012-2013)

Tuition and fees: $2,100; out-of-state residents $9,708.

Per-credit charge: $70; out-of-state residents $387.

Room and board: $6,694.

FINANCIAL AID PICTURE

Students with need: Need-based aid available for full-time and part-time students.

Students without need: No-need awards available for academics, athletics.

FINANCIAL AID PROCEDURES

Forms required: FAFSA.

Dates and Deadlines: Priority date 4/1; no closing date. Applicants notified on a rolling basis.

CONTACT

Terri Eckel, Financial Aid Operations
1100 East Sheldon Street, Prescott, AZ 86301
(928) 776-2152

Arkansas

Arkansas Northeastern College

Blytheville, Arkansas
www.anc.edu Federal Code: 012860

2-year public community college in small town.

Enrollment: 1,432 undergrads, 45% part-time. 234 full-time freshmen.

Selectivity: Open admission; but selective for some programs.

BASIC COSTS (2012-2013)

Tuition and fees: $2,000; out-of-district residents $2,300; out-of-state residents $3,500.

Per-credit charge: $59; out-of-district residents $69; out-of-state residents $109.

FINANCIAL AID PICTURE (2011-2012)

Students with need: Need-based aid available for part-time students.

Students without need: No-need awards available for academics, art, minority status, music/drama, state/district residency.

FINANCIAL AID PROCEDURES

Forms required: FAFSA, institutional form.

Dates and Deadlines: Priority date 4/15; no closing date. Applicants notified on a rolling basis starting 3/1; must reply within 2 week(s) of notification.

CONTACT

Laura Yarbrough, Director of Financial Aid
PO Box 1109, Blytheville, AR 72316-1109
(870) 762-1020 ext. 1160

Arkansas State University

State University, Arkansas
www.astate.edu Federal Code: 001090

4-year public university in small city.

Enrollment: 9,496 undergrads, 19% part-time. 1,633 full-time freshmen.

Selectivity: Admits 50 to 75% of applicants.

BASIC COSTS (2012-2013)

Tuition and fees: $7,180; out-of-state residents $12,610.

Per-credit charge: $181; out-of-state residents $362.

Room and board: $7,150.

FINANCIAL AID PICTURE (2012-2013)

Students with need: Out of 1,549 full-time freshmen who applied for aid, 1,498 were judged to have need. Of these, 1,497 received aid, and 519 had their full need met. Average financial aid package met 62% of need; average scholarship/grant was $9,900; average loan was $5,800. Need-based aid available for part-time students.

Students without need: 215 full-time freshmen who did not demonstrate need for aid received scholarships/grants; average award was $5,000. No-need awards available for academics, alumni affiliation, art, athletics, leadership, minority status, music/drama, ROTC, state/district residency.

Scholarships offered: 77 full-time freshmen received athletic scholarships; average amount $13,200.

Cumulative student debt: 68% of graduating class had student loans; average debt was $21,000.

FINANCIAL AID PROCEDURES

Forms required: FAFSA, institutional form.

Dates and Deadlines: Priority date 2/15; closing date 7/1. Applicants notified on a rolling basis starting 6/1; must reply within 2 week(s) of notification.

Transfers: Applicants notified on a rolling basis starting 6/1; must reply within 2 week(s) of notification.

CONTACT

Terry Finney, Director of Financial Aid and Scholarships
PO Box 1800, State University, AR 72467-1800
(870) 972-2310

Arkansas State University: Beebe

Beebe, Arkansas
www.asub.edu Federal Code: 001090

2-year public community college in small town.

Enrollment: 3,566 undergrads, 34% part-time. 884 full-time freshmen.

Selectivity: Open admission; but selective for some programs.

BASIC COSTS (2012-2013)

Tuition and fees: $2,970; out-of-state residents $4,830.

Per-credit charge: $85; out-of-state residents $147.

Room and board: $4,620.

FINANCIAL AID PICTURE

Students with need: Need-based aid available for full-time and part-time students. Work study available nights, weekends, and for part-time students.

Students without need: No-need awards available for academics, leadership, music/drama.

FINANCIAL AID PROCEDURES
Forms required: FAFSA, institutional form.
Dates and Deadlines: Priority date 6/1; no closing date. Applicants notified on a rolling basis starting 6/1; must reply within 2 week(s) of notification.
Transfers: No deadline. Applicants notified on a rolling basis.

CONTACT
Louise Driver, Director of Financial Aid
PO Box 1000, Beebe, AR 72012-1000
(501) 882-8245

Arkansas State University: Mountain Home

Mountain Home, Arkansas
www.asumh.edu Federal Code: 901090

2-year public community and technical college in large town.
Enrollment: 1,370 undergrads, 33% part-time. 252 full-time freshmen.
Selectivity: Open admission; but selective for some programs.

BASIC COSTS (2012-2013)
Tuition and fees: $3,090; out-of-state residents $4,890.
Per-credit charge: $86; out-of-state residents $146.

FINANCIAL AID PICTURE (2012-2013)
Students with need: 54% of average financial aid package awarded as scholarships/grants, 46% awarded as loans/jobs. Need-based aid available for part-time students.
Students without need: No-need awards available for academics, alumni affiliation, leadership, state/district residency.
Scholarships offered: Academic Distinction Scholarship; full tuition; for qualified Arkansas residents.
Additional info: Satisfactory academic progress policy for Title IV aid.

FINANCIAL AID PROCEDURES
Forms required: FAFSA, institutional form.
Dates and Deadlines: Priority date 6/1; no closing date. Applicants notified on a rolling basis starting 5/1; must reply within 2 week(s) of notification.
Transfers: No deadline. Applicants notified on a rolling basis starting 7/1; must reply within 2 week(s) of notification. All final academic transcripts required prior to awarding Title IV aid.

CONTACT
John Davidson, Vice Chancellor Administrative Affairs
1600 South College Street, Mountain Home, AR 72653
(870) 508-6100 ext. 195

Arkansas Tech University

Russellville, Arkansas
www.atu.edu Federal Code: 001089

4-year public university and liberal arts college in large town.
Enrollment: 8,643 undergrads, 18% part-time. 1,755 full-time freshmen.
Selectivity: Admits over 75% of applicants.

BASIC COSTS (2012-2013)
Tuition and fees: $6,798; out-of-state residents $12,408.
Per-credit charge: $187; out-of-state residents $374.
Room and board: $5,954.

FINANCIAL AID PICTURE (2011-2012)
Students with need: Out of 1,720 full-time freshmen who applied for aid, 1,153 were judged to have need. Of these, 1,132 received aid, and 95 had their full need met. Average financial aid package met 66% of need; average scholarship/grant was $4,115; average loan was $2,839. For part-time students, average financial aid package was $5,771.
Students without need: 349 full-time freshmen who did not demonstrate need for aid received scholarships/grants; average award was $5,853. No-need awards available for academics, athletics, leadership, music/drama, ROTC, state/district residency.
Scholarships offered: 53 full-time freshmen received athletic scholarships; average amount $3,561.
Cumulative student debt: 57% of graduating class had student loans; average debt was $22,649.

FINANCIAL AID PROCEDURES
Forms required: FAFSA, institutional form.
Dates and Deadlines: Priority date 4/15; no closing date. Applicants notified on a rolling basis starting 5/1; must reply within 2 week(s) of notification.
Transfers: No deadline. Applicants notified on a rolling basis starting 5/1; must reply within 2 week(s) of notification.

CONTACT
Shirley Goines, Director of Student Financial Aid
1605 Coliseum Drive, Suite 141, Russellville, AR 72801-2222
(479) 968-0399

Black River Technical College

Pocahontas, Arkansas
www.blackrivertech.edu Federal Code: 011948

2-year public technical college in small town.
Enrollment: 2,219 undergrads.
Selectivity: Open admission; but selective for some programs.

BASIC COSTS (2013-2014)
Tuition and fees: $2,850; out-of-state residents $6,210.
Per-credit charge: $78; out-of-state residents $190.

FINANCIAL AID PICTURE
Students with need: Need-based aid available for full-time and part-time students.
Students without need: No-need awards available for academics, leadership, minority status, music/drama, state/district residency.

FINANCIAL AID PROCEDURES
Forms required: FAFSA, institutional form.
Dates and Deadlines: Priority date 4/1; closing date 6/30. Applicants notified on a rolling basis starting 4/1.
Transfers: No deadline.

CONTACT
Brandi Chester, Financial Aid Director
Highway 304 East, Pocahontas, AR 72455
(870) 248-4000 ext. 4020

Central Baptist College

Conway, Arkansas
www.cbc.edu Federal Code: 001093

4-year private Bible college in large town, affiliated with Baptist faith.
Enrollment: 770 undergrads, 14% part-time. 102 full-time freshmen.
Selectivity: Admits less than 50% of applicants.

BASIC COSTS (2012-2013)
Tuition and fees: $12,530.
Per-credit charge: $375.
Room and board: $6,300.

FINANCIAL AID PICTURE
Students with need: Need-based aid available for full-time and part-time students.

Students without need: No-need awards available for academics, athletics, music/drama, religious affiliation.

FINANCIAL AID PROCEDURES
Forms required: FAFSA.
Dates and Deadlines: Priority date 7/1; closing date 8/1. Applicants notified on a rolling basis starting 4/1.
Transfers: No deadline.

CONTACT
Tonya Hammontree, Director of Financial Aid
1501 College Avenue, Conway, AR 72034
(501) 329-6872

College of the Ouachitas
Malvern, Arkansas
www.coto.edu Federal Code: 009976

2-year public community and technical college in small town.
Enrollment: 772 undergrads, 32% part-time. 120 full-time freshmen.
Selectivity: Open admission; but selective for some programs.

BASIC COSTS (2012-2013)
Tuition and fees: $2,715; out-of-state residents $4,665.
Per-credit charge: $65; out-of-state residents $130.

FINANCIAL AID PICTURE
Students with need: Need-based aid available for full-time and part-time students. Work study available nights.

FINANCIAL AID PROCEDURES
Forms required: FAFSA.
Dates and Deadlines: Applicants notified on a rolling basis starting 7/1; must reply within 6 week(s) of notification.

CONTACT
Teresa Avery, Director of Financial Aid
One College Circle, Malvern, AR 72104
(501) 337-5000 ext. 1122

Cossatot Community College of the University of Arkansas
De Queen, Arkansas
www.cccua.edu Federal Code: 012432

2-year public community college in small town.
Enrollment: 644 full-time undergrads.
Selectivity: Open admission; but selective for some programs.

BASIC COSTS (2012-2013)
Tuition and fees: $2,104; out-of-district residents $2,404; out-of-state residents $4,954.
Per-credit charge: $55; out-of-district residents $65; out-of-state residents $150.

FINANCIAL AID PICTURE
Students with need: Need-based aid available for full-time and part-time students. Work study available nights.
Additional info: Active or honorably discharged military and their dependents receive tuition discounts.

FINANCIAL AID PROCEDURES
Forms required: FAFSA, institutional form.
Dates and Deadlines: Priority date 5/1; no closing date. Applicants notified on a rolling basis starting 3/1.
Transfers: Applicants notified on a rolling basis starting 3/1.

CONTACT
Denise Hammond, Director of Financial Aid
183 Highway 399, De Queen, AR 71832
(870) 584-4471

Crowley's Ridge College
Paragould, Arkansas
www.crc.edu Federal Code: 001095

2-year private junior college in large town, affiliated with Church of Christ.
Enrollment: 154 undergrads, 3% part-time. 85 full-time freshmen.
Selectivity: Open admission.

BASIC COSTS (2012-2013)
Tuition and fees: $10,450.
Per-credit charge: $310.
Room and board: $6,100.

FINANCIAL AID PICTURE
Students with need: Work study available nights, weekends, and for part-time students.
Students without need: No-need awards available for academics, athletics, leadership, music/drama.

FINANCIAL AID PROCEDURES
Forms required: FAFSA.

CONTACT
David Goff, Director of Financial Aid
100 College Drive, Paragould, AR 72450
(870) 236-6901

East Arkansas Community College
Forrest City, Arkansas
www.eacc.edu Federal Code: 012260

2-year public community college in large town.
Enrollment: 1,302 undergrads.
Selectivity: Open admission; but selective for some programs.

BASIC COSTS (2012-2013)
Tuition and fees: $2,340; out-of-district residents $2,610; out-of-state residents $3,060.
Per-credit charge: $69; out-of-district residents $78; out-of-state residents $93.

FINANCIAL AID PICTURE
Students with need: Need-based aid available for full-time and part-time students.
Students without need: This college awards aid only to students with need.

FINANCIAL AID PROCEDURES
Forms required: FAFSA.
Dates and Deadlines: Priority date 3/1; closing date 7/1. Applicants notified on a rolling basis starting 5/15; must reply within 2 week(s) of notification.

CONTACT
Alvin Coleman, Director of Financial Aid
1700 Newcastle Road, Forrest City, AR 72335-2204
(870) 633-4480 ext. 225

Ecclesia College

Springdale, Arkansas
www.ecollege.edu Federal Code: 038553

4-year private Bible and liberal arts college in large town, affiliated with interdenominational tradition.
Enrollment: 150 undergrads.
Selectivity: Admits less than 50% of applicants.

BASIC COSTS (2013-2014)
Tuition and fees: $15,140.
Per-credit charge: $475.
Room and board: $5,010.
Additional info: Tuition/fee waivers available for adults.

FINANCIAL AID PICTURE
Students with need: Need-based aid available for full-time and part-time students. Work study available nights, weekends, and for part-time students.
Students without need: No-need awards available for academics, athletics, leadership, music/drama.

FINANCIAL AID PROCEDURES
Forms required: FAFSA.
Dates and Deadlines: Applicants notified on a rolling basis starting 7/1.
Transfers: No deadline. Applicants notified on a rolling basis; must reply within 4 week(s) of notification.

CONTACT
Lindsay Luecht, Director of Financial Aid
9653 Nations Drive, Springdale, AR 72762
(479) 248-7236 ext. 204

Harding University

Searcy, Arkansas
www.harding.edu Federal Code: 001097

4-year private university in large town, affiliated with Church of Christ.
Enrollment: 4,241 undergrads, 6% part-time. 1,013 full-time freshmen.
Selectivity: Admits 50 to 75% of applicants.

BASIC COSTS (2012-2013)
Tuition and fees: $15,210.
Per-credit charge: $492.
Room and board: $6,192.

FINANCIAL AID PICTURE (2011-2012)
Students with need: Out of 884 full-time freshmen who applied for aid, 629 were judged to have need. Of these, 627 received aid, and 183 had their full need met. Average financial aid package met 77% of need; average scholarship/grant was $9,151; average loan was $4,393. For part-time students, average financial aid package was $7,729.
Students without need: 233 full-time freshmen who did not demonstrate need for aid received scholarships/grants; average award was $6,076. No-need awards available for academics, alumni affiliation, art, athletics, leadership, music/drama, religious affiliation, ROTC, state/district residency.
Scholarships offered: 48 full-time freshmen received athletic scholarships; average amount $6,196.
Cumulative student debt: 63% of graduating class had student loans; average debt was $32,752.

FINANCIAL AID PROCEDURES
Forms required: FAFSA.
Dates and Deadlines: Priority date 4/15; no closing date. Applicants notified on a rolling basis starting 2/15; must reply within 2 week(s) of notification.
Transfers: No deadline.

CONTACT
Jon Roberts, Director of Student Financial Services
915 East Market Avenue, Searcy, AR 72149-2255
(501) 279-4257

Henderson State University

Arkadelphia, Arkansas
www.hsu.edu Federal Code: 001098

4-year public university and liberal arts college in large town.
Enrollment: 3,354 undergrads, 10% part-time. 818 full-time freshmen.
Selectivity: Admits 50 to 75% of applicants.

BASIC COSTS (2012-2013)
Tuition and fees: $6,984; out-of-state residents $12,864.
Per-credit charge: $196; out-of-state residents $392.
Room and board: $5,332.

FINANCIAL AID PICTURE (2011-2012)
Students with need: Out of 804 full-time freshmen who applied for aid, 707 were judged to have need. Of these, 707 received aid, and 43 had their full need met. Average financial aid package met 81% of need; average scholarship/grant was $6,548; average loan was $3,225. For part-time students, average financial aid package was $6,582.
Students without need: 62 full-time freshmen who did not demonstrate need for aid received scholarships/grants; average award was $7,931. No-need awards available for academics, alumni affiliation, art, athletics, job skills, leadership, minority status, music/drama, ROTC, state/district residency.
Scholarships offered: 59 full-time freshmen received athletic scholarships; average amount $4,280.

FINANCIAL AID PROCEDURES
Dates and Deadlines: Priority date 4/15; no closing date. Applicants notified on a rolling basis starting 3/1; must reply within 2 week(s) of notification.
Transfers: No deadline. Applicants notified on a rolling basis starting 3/1; must reply within 2 week(s) of notification.

CONTACT
Vicki Taylor, Director of Financial Aid
1100 Henderson Street, Arkadelphia, AR 71999-0001
(870) 230-5094

Hendrix College

Conway, Arkansas
www.hendrix.edu Federal Code: 001099

4-year private liberal arts college in small city, affiliated with United Methodist Church.
Enrollment: 1,365 undergrads, 1% part-time. 369 full-time freshmen.
Selectivity: Admits over 75% of applicants.

BASIC COSTS (2013-2014)
Tuition and fees: $37,816.
Per-credit charge: $1,173.
Room and board: $10,620.

FINANCIAL AID PICTURE (2012-2013)
Students with need: Out of 315 full-time freshmen who applied for aid, 245 were judged to have need. Of these, 245 received aid, and 102 had their full need met. Average financial aid package met 85% of need; average scholarship/grant was $26,065; average loan was $3,692. For part-time students, average financial aid package was $8,480.
Students without need: 114 full-time freshmen who did not demonstrate need for aid received scholarships/grants; average award was $22,394. No-need awards available for academics, art, leadership, music/drama.

Cumulative student debt: 52% of graduating class had student loans; average debt was $24,492.

FINANCIAL AID PROCEDURES

Forms required: FAFSA.

Dates and Deadlines: Priority date 3/1; no closing date. Applicants notified on a rolling basis starting 3/1; must reply by 5/1 or within 4 week(s) of notification.

Transfers: Applicants notified on a rolling basis starting 3/1; must reply by 5/1.

CONTACT

Kristina Burford, Director of Financial Aid
1600 Washington Avenue, Conway, AR 72032-3080
(501) 450-1368

John Brown University

Siloam Springs, Arkansas
www.jbu.edu Federal Code: 001100

4-year private university and liberal arts college in large town, affiliated with interdenominational tradition.

Enrollment: 1,305 undergrads.

Selectivity: Admits 50 to 75% of applicants.

BASIC COSTS (2013-2014)

Tuition and fees: $22,734.

Per-credit charge: $694.

Room and board: $8,262.

Additional info: Tuition/fee waivers available for adults.

FINANCIAL AID PICTURE (2012-2013)

Students with need: Average financial aid package met 76% of need; average scholarship/grant was $16,350; average loan was $3,301. For part-time students, average financial aid package was $3,357.

Students without need: No-need awards available for academics, alumni affiliation, art, athletics, leadership, music/drama, ROTC.

Cumulative student debt: 57% of graduating class had student loans; average debt was $24,160.

FINANCIAL AID PROCEDURES

Forms required: FAFSA, state aid form.

Dates and Deadlines: Priority date 3/1; no closing date. Applicants notified on a rolling basis starting 3/1; must reply by 5/1 or within 4 week(s) of notification.

Transfers: No deadline. Applicants notified on a rolling basis starting 3/1; must reply by 5/1 or within 4 week(s) of notification.

CONTACT

Kim Eldridge, Director of Financial Aid
2000 West University Street, Siloam Springs, AR 72761-2121
(877) 528-4636

Lyon College

Batesville, Arkansas
www.lyon.edu Federal Code: 001088

4-year private liberal arts college in small town, affiliated with Presbyterian Church (USA).

Enrollment: 582 undergrads, 2% part-time. 157 full-time freshmen.

Selectivity: Admits 50 to 75% of applicants.

BASIC COSTS (2013-2014)

Tuition and fees: $23,594.

Per-credit charge: $760.

Room and board: $7,560.

FINANCIAL AID PICTURE (2012-2013)

Students with need: Out of 142 full-time freshmen who applied for aid, 127 were judged to have need. Of these, 127 received aid, and 39 had their full need met. Average financial aid package met 86% of need; average scholarship/grant was $19,909; average loan was $3,279. For part-time students, average financial aid package was $8,624.

Students without need: 14 full-time freshmen who did not demonstrate need for aid received scholarships/grants; average award was $13,416. No-need awards available for academics, art, athletics, leadership, minority status, music/drama, religious affiliation, state/district residency.

Scholarships offered: ***Merit:*** Brown Scholarship; tuition, room, board, and mandatory fees; based on high school record, standardized test scores; 4 awarded. Anderson Scholarship; tuition and mandatory fees; based on high school record, test scores; 4 awarded. ***Athletic:*** 29 full-time freshmen received athletic scholarships; average amount $11,347.

Cumulative student debt: 72% of graduating class had student loans; average debt was $17,179.

FINANCIAL AID PROCEDURES

Forms required: FAFSA.

Dates and Deadlines: Priority date 3/15; no closing date. Applicants notified on a rolling basis starting 3/1; must reply by 8/15.

Transfers: No deadline. Applicants notified on a rolling basis starting 3/1; must reply within 2 week(s) of notification.

CONTACT

Tommy Tucker, Director of Student Financial Assistance
PO Box 2317, Batesville, AR 72503-2317
(870) 307-7257

Mid-South Community College

West Memphis, Arkansas
www.midsouthcc.edu Federal Code: 015862

2-year public community and junior college in large town.

Enrollment: 2,168 undergrads.

Selectivity: Open admission.

BASIC COSTS (2012-2013)

Tuition and fees: $2,760; out-of-district residents $3,300; out-of-state residents $5,520.

Per-credit charge: $80; out-of-district residents $98; out-of-state residents $172.

FINANCIAL AID PICTURE

Students with need: Need-based aid available for full-time and part-time students. Work study available nights.

Students without need: No-need awards available for academics, state/district residency.

FINANCIAL AID PROCEDURES

Forms required: FAFSA, institutional form.

Dates and Deadlines: Priority date 4/30; no closing date. Applicants notified on a rolling basis starting 6/1; must reply within 2 week(s) of notification.

CONTACT

LeChelle Davenport, Director of FInancial Aid
2000 West Broadway, West Memphis, AR 72301
(870) 733-6741

National Park Community College

Hot Springs, Arkansas
www.npcc.edu Federal Code: 012105

2-year public liberal arts and technical college in large town.

Enrollment: 4,268 undergrads.

Selectivity: Open admission; but selective for some programs.

BASIC COSTS (2012-2013)

Tuition and fees: $2,750; out-of-district residents $3,050; out-of-state residents $4,370.

Per-credit charge: $80; out-of-district residents $90; out-of-state residents $134.

FINANCIAL AID PICTURE

Students with need: Need-based aid available for full-time and part-time students. Work study available nights, weekends, and for part-time students.

Students without need: No-need awards available for academics, minority status, music/drama, state/district residency.

FINANCIAL AID PROCEDURES

Forms required: FAFSA, institutional form.

Dates and Deadlines: Priority date 7/1; no closing date. Applicants notified on a rolling basis.

Transfers: Transfer applicants must furnish evidence of good standing at previous institution to qualify for financial aid.

CONTACT

Lisa Hopper, Director, Financial Aid
101 College Drive, Hot Springs, AR 71913
(501) 760-4235

North Arkansas College

Harrison, Arkansas
www.northark.edu Federal Code: 012261

2-year public community and technical college in large town.

Enrollment: 2,307 undergrads.

Selectivity: Open admission; but selective for some programs.

BASIC COSTS (2012-2013)

Tuition and fees: $2,190; out-of-district residents $2,910; out-of-state residents $5,040.

FINANCIAL AID PICTURE

Students with need: Need-based aid available for full-time and part-time students. Work study available nights.

Students without need: No-need awards available for academics, athletics, state/district residency.

FINANCIAL AID PROCEDURES

Forms required: FAFSA, institutional form.

Dates and Deadlines: Priority date 5/1; no closing date. Applicants notified on a rolling basis starting 5/1.

Transfers: No deadline. Applicants notified on a rolling basis starting 5/1.

CONTACT

Jennifer Haddock, Director of Financial Aid
1515 Pioneer Drive, Harrison, AR 72601
(870) 391-3266

Northwest Arkansas Community College

Bentonville, Arkansas
www.nwacc.edu Federal Code: 030633

2-year public community college in small city.

Enrollment: 8,341 undergrads.

Selectivity: Open admission; but selective for some programs.

BASIC COSTS (2013-2014)

Tuition and fees: $3,025; out-of-district residents $4,450; out-of-state residents $6,025.

Per-credit charge: $75; out-of-district residents $123; out-of-state residents $175.

FINANCIAL AID PICTURE

Students with need: Need-based aid available for full-time and part-time students. Work study available nights, weekends, and for part-time students.

Students without need: No-need awards available for academics, leadership, music/drama, state/district residency.

FINANCIAL AID PROCEDURES

Forms required: FAFSA, institutional form.

Dates and Deadlines: Priority date 4/1; no closing date. Applicants notified on a rolling basis starting 4/1; must reply within 2 week(s) of notification.

CONTACT

Michelle Cordell, Director of Financial Aid
One College Drive, Bentonville, AR 72712
(479) 619-4329

Ouachita Baptist University

Arkadelphia, Arkansas
www.obu.edu Federal Code: 001102

4-year private liberal arts college in large town, affiliated with Arkansas Baptist State Convention.

Enrollment: 1,503 undergrads, 1% part-time. 363 full-time freshmen.

Selectivity: Admits 50 to 75% of applicants.

BASIC COSTS (2013-2014)

Tuition and fees: $22,340.

Per-credit charge: $605.

Room and board: $6,640.

FINANCIAL AID PICTURE (2012-2013)

Students with need: Out of 337 full-time freshmen who applied for aid, 262 were judged to have need. Of these, 262 received aid, and 79 had their full need met. Average financial aid package met 82% of need; average scholarship/grant was $13,758; average loan was $3,322. For part-time students, average financial aid package was $11,230.

Students without need: 101 full-time freshmen who did not demonstrate need for aid received scholarships/grants; average award was $9,338. No-need awards available for academics, alumni affiliation, art, athletics, job skills, leadership, minority status, music/drama, religious affiliation, ROTC, state/district residency.

Scholarships offered: 17 full-time freshmen received athletic scholarships; average amount $7,922.

Cumulative student debt: 46% of graduating class had student loans; average debt was $24,367.

FINANCIAL AID PROCEDURES

Forms required: FAFSA, state aid form.

Dates and Deadlines: Priority date 1/15; closing date 6/1. Applicants notified on a rolling basis starting 11/1; must reply by 6/1.

CONTACT

Susan Hurst, Director of Student Financial Services
OBU Box 3776, Arkadelphia, AR 71998-0001
(870) 245-5570

Ozarka College

Melbourne, Arkansas
www.ozarka.edu Federal Code: 013217

2-year public community and technical college in rural community.

Enrollment: 1,476 undergrads.

Selectivity: Open admission; but selective for some programs.

BASIC COSTS (2013-2014)

Tuition and fees: $2,810; out-of-state residents $5,600.

Per-credit charge: $75; out-of-state residents $168.

FINANCIAL AID PICTURE
Students with need: Need-based aid available for full-time and part-time students.

FINANCIAL AID PROCEDURES
Forms required: FAFSA.
Dates and Deadlines: Applicants notified on a rolling basis; must reply within 2 week(s) of notification.

CONTACT
Laura Lawrence, Financial Aid Director
218 College Drive, Melbourne, AR 72556-0010
(870) 368-7371 ext. 2010

Philander Smith College
Little Rock, Arkansas
www.philander.edu Federal Code: 001103

4-year private liberal arts college in small city, affiliated with United Methodist Church.
Enrollment: 607 full-time undergrads.

BASIC COSTS (2012-2013)
Tuition and fees: $12,464.
Per-credit charge: $495.
Room and board: $8,304.
Additional info: Tuition only for incoming freshman is $11,804. Returning undergraduates pay $9,880 for full-time tuition; all other fees are the same for all students.

FINANCIAL AID PICTURE
Students with need: Need-based aid available for full-time and part-time students.
Students without need: This college awards aid only to students with need.

FINANCIAL AID PROCEDURES
Forms required: FAFSA.
Dates and Deadlines: Priority date 3/1; no closing date. Applicants notified on a rolling basis starting 3/1; must reply within 2 week(s) of notification.
Transfers: Closing date 6/30.

CONTACT
David Page, Director of Financial Aid
900 Daisy Bates Drive, Little Rock, AR 72202-3718
(501) 370-5350

Phillips Community College of the University of Arkansas
Helena, Arkansas
www.pccua.edu Federal Code: 001104

2-year public community college in large town.
Enrollment: 1,038 undergrads.
Selectivity: Open admission; but selective for some programs.

BASIC COSTS (2012-2013)
Tuition and fees: $2,375; out-of-district residents $2,735; out-of-state residents $4,055.
Per-credit charge: $62; out-of-district residents $74; out-of-state residents $118.

FINANCIAL AID PICTURE (2011-2012)
Students with need: Need-based aid available for part-time students. Work study available nights.
Students without need: This college awards aid only to students with need.
Additional info: Tuition waivers given to firefighters and law enforcement officers.

FINANCIAL AID PROCEDURES
Forms required: FAFSA.
Dates and Deadlines: Priority date 4/12; closing date 6/12. Applicants notified on a rolling basis starting 4/12; must reply within 2 week(s) of notification.

CONTACT
Barbra Stevenson, Director of Financial Aid
1000 Campus Drive, Helena, AR 72342
(870) 338-6474 ext. 1160

Pulaski Technical College
North Little Rock, Arkansas
www.pulaskitech.edu Federal Code: 014167

2-year public community and technical college in small city.
Enrollment: 10,729 undergrads.
Selectivity: Open admission; but selective for some programs.

BASIC COSTS (2012-2013)
Tuition and fees: $3,183; out-of-state residents $4,923.
Per-credit charge: $90; out-of-state residents $148.

FINANCIAL AID PICTURE
Students with need: Need-based aid available for full-time and part-time students.

FINANCIAL AID PROCEDURES
Forms required: FAFSA, institutional form.
Dates and Deadlines: Closing date 5/15. Applicants notified on a rolling basis starting 5/1; must reply within 2 week(s) of notification.

CONTACT
Lavonne Juhl, Director Financial Aid
3000 West Scenic Drive, North Little Rock, AR 72118-3347
(501) 812-2289

Rich Mountain Community College
Mena, Arkansas
www.rmcc.edu Federal Code: 012435

2-year public community college in small town.
Enrollment: 632 undergrads, 31% part-time. 148 full-time freshmen.
Selectivity: Open admission; but selective for some programs.

BASIC COSTS (2012-2013)
Tuition and fees: $2,310; out-of-district residents $2,730; out-of-state residents $5,850.
Per-credit charge: $62; out-of-district residents $76; out-of-state residents $180.

FINANCIAL AID PICTURE (2011-2012)
Students with need: 99% of average financial aid package awarded as scholarships/grants, 1% awarded as loans/jobs. Need-based aid available for part-time students.
Students without need: No-need awards available for academics.

FINANCIAL AID PROCEDURES
Forms required: FAFSA, institutional form.
Dates and Deadlines: Priority date 7/1; no closing date. Applicants notified on a rolling basis starting 6/1; must reply within 2 week(s) of notification.

CONTACT
Mary Standerfer, Director of Financial Aid
1100 College Drive, Mena, AR 71953
(479) 394-7622 ext. 1420

South Arkansas Community College

El Dorado, Arkansas
www.southark.edu Federal Code: 013858

2-year public community and junior college in large town.
Enrollment: 1,757 undergrads.
Selectivity: Open admission; but selective for some programs.

BASIC COSTS (2012-2013)
Tuition and fees: $2,552; out-of-district residents $2,912; out-of-state residents $5,072.
Per-credit charge: $76; out-of-district residents $88; out-of-state residents $160.

FINANCIAL AID PICTURE
Students with need: Need-based aid available for full-time and part-time students.

FINANCIAL AID PROCEDURES
Forms required: FAFSA, institutional form.
Dates and Deadlines: Closing date 7/1. Applicants notified on a rolling basis starting 7/1; must reply within 2 week(s) of notification.

CONTACT
Veronda Tatum, Director of Financial Aid
Box 7010, El Dorado, AR 71731-7010
(870) 864-7133

Southeast Arkansas College

Pine Bluff, Arkansas
www.seark.edu Federal Code: 005707

2-year public community college in small city.
Enrollment: 1,488 undergrads, 41% part-time. 217 full-time freshmen.
Selectivity: Open admission; but selective for some programs.

BASIC COSTS (2012-2013)
Tuition and fees: $2,980; out-of-state residents $5,380.

FINANCIAL AID PICTURE (2012-2013)
Students with need: Out of 190 full-time freshmen who applied for aid, 186 were judged to have need. Of these, 186 received aid, and 73 had their full need met. Average financial aid package met 87% of need; average scholarship/grant was $2,159; average loan was $1,621. For part-time students, average financial aid package was $8,624.
Students without need: 69 full-time freshmen who did not demonstrate need for aid received scholarships/grants; average award was $955. No-need awards available for academics, leadership, state/district residency.
Scholarships offered: 79 full-time freshmen received athletic scholarships; average amount $1,010.

FINANCIAL AID PROCEDURES
Forms required: FAFSA.
Dates and Deadlines: Priority date 6/1; no closing date. Applicants notified on a rolling basis starting 5/1; must reply within 2 week(s) of notification.

CONTACT
Donna Cox, Director of Financial Aid
1900 Hazel Street, Pine Bluff, AR 71603
(870) 543-5909

Southern Arkansas University

Magnolia, Arkansas
www.saumag.edu Federal Code: 001107

4-year public university in large town.
Enrollment: 2,653 undergrads, 10% part-time. 642 full-time freshmen.
Selectivity: Admits 50 to 75% of applicants.

BASIC COSTS (2012-2013)
Tuition and fees: $7,346; out-of-state residents $10,376.
Per-credit charge: $196; out-of-state residents $297.
Room and board: $4,870.

FINANCIAL AID PICTURE (2011-2012)
Students with need: Out of 609 full-time freshmen who applied for aid, 538 were judged to have need. Of these, 536 received aid, and 215 had their full need met. Average financial aid package met 75% of need; average scholarship/grant was $4,515; average loan was $2,747. For part-time students, average financial aid package was $5,480.
Students without need: 80 full-time freshmen who did not demonstrate need for aid received scholarships/grants; average award was $8,342. No-need awards available for academics, alumni affiliation, art, athletics, leadership, minority status, music/drama, state/district residency.
Scholarships offered: 17 full-time freshmen received athletic scholarships; average amount $5,346.
Cumulative student debt: 58% of graduating class had student loans; average debt was $21,861.

FINANCIAL AID PROCEDURES
Forms required: FAFSA.
Dates and Deadlines: Priority date 7/1; no closing date. Applicants notified on a rolling basis starting 4/15; must reply within 2 week(s) of notification.

CONTACT
Bronwyn Sneed, Director of Financial Aid
Box 9382, Magnolia, AR 71754-9382
(870) 235-4023

Southern Arkansas University Tech

Camden, Arkansas
www.sautech.edu Federal Code: 007738

2-year public community and technical college in large town.
Enrollment: 906 undergrads, 32% part-time. 209 full-time freshmen.
Selectivity: Open admission; but selective for some programs.

BASIC COSTS (2012-2013)
Tuition and fees: $3,670; out-of-state residents $4,990.
Per-credit charge: $98; out-of-state residents $142.

FINANCIAL AID PICTURE
Students with need: Need-based aid available for full-time and part-time students. Work study available nights, weekends, and for part-time students.
Students without need: No-need awards available for academics, state/district residency.

FINANCIAL AID PROCEDURES
Forms required: FAFSA.
Dates and Deadlines: Priority date 6/1; no closing date. Applicants notified on a rolling basis starting 5/1.
Transfers: Priority date 4/15; closing date 6/1. Applicants notified on a rolling basis starting 5/1.

CONTACT
John Jefferson, Director of Financial Aid
PO Box 3499, Camden, AR 71711-1599
(870) 574-4511

University of Arkansas

Fayetteville, Arkansas
www.uark.edu Federal Code: 001108

4-year public university in small city.
Enrollment: 19,978 undergrads, 11% part-time. 4,414 full-time freshmen.

Selectivity: Admits 50 to 75% of applicants.

BASIC COSTS (2012-2013)
Tuition and fees: $7,553; out-of-state residents $18,434.
Per-credit charge: $205; out-of-state residents $567.
Room and board: $8,555.

FINANCIAL AID PICTURE (2011-2012)
Students with need: Out of 3,596 full-time freshmen who applied for aid, 2,195 were judged to have need. Of these, 2,158 received aid, and 557 had their full need met. Average financial aid package met 68% of need; average scholarship/grant was $7,286; average loan was $3,383. For part-time students, average financial aid package was $5,885.
Students without need: 587 full-time freshmen who did not demonstrate need for aid received scholarships/grants; average award was $4,830. No-need awards available for academics, alumni affiliation, art, athletics, leadership, minority status, music/drama, ROTC, state/district residency.
Scholarships offered: 97 full-time freshmen received athletic scholarships; average amount $7,512.

FINANCIAL AID PROCEDURES
Forms required: FAFSA.
Dates and Deadlines: Priority date 3/15; no closing date. Applicants notified on a rolling basis starting 4/1; must reply within 4 week(s) of notification.

CONTACT
Kattie Wing, Director of Student Financial Services
232 Silas Hunt Hall, Fayetteville, AR 72701
(479) 575-3806

University of Arkansas at Fort Smith
Fort Smith, Arkansas
www.uafs.edu Federal Code: 001110

4-year public university in small city.
Enrollment: 6,677 undergrads, 23% part-time. 1,296 full-time freshmen.
Selectivity: Open admission; but selective for some programs.

BASIC COSTS (2012-2013)
Tuition and fees: $5,436; out-of-state residents $12,186.
Per-credit charge: $130; out-of-state residents $355.
Room and board: $7,398.

FINANCIAL AID PICTURE (2012-2013)
Students with need: Out of 1,237 full-time freshmen who applied for aid, 1,034 were judged to have need. Of these, 1,024 received aid, and 229 had their full need met. Average financial aid package met 70% of need; average scholarship/grant was $4,938; average loan was $3,154. For part-time students, average financial aid package was $6,827.
Students without need: 143 full-time freshmen who did not demonstrate need for aid received scholarships/grants; average award was $4,288. No-need awards available for academics, athletics, job skills, leadership, music/drama.
Scholarships offered: 17 full-time freshmen received athletic scholarships; average amount $4,248.
Cumulative student debt: 64% of graduating class had student loans; average debt was $16,905.

FINANCIAL AID PROCEDURES
Forms required: FAFSA.
Dates and Deadlines: Priority date 6/15; no closing date. Applicants notified on a rolling basis starting 3/1; must reply within 4 week(s) of notification.
Transfers: No deadline. Applicants notified on a rolling basis starting 3/1; must reply within 4 week(s) of notification.

CONTACT
Alan Pixley, Director of Financial Aid
PO Box 3649, Fort Smith, AR 72913-3649
(479) 788-7090

University of Arkansas at Little Rock
Little Rock, Arkansas
www.ualr.edu Federal Code: 001161

4-year public university in small city.
Enrollment: 9,049 undergrads, 39% part-time. 807 full-time freshmen.
Selectivity: Admits over 75% of applicants.

BASIC COSTS (2012-2013)
Tuition and fees: $7,344; out-of-state residents $17,214.
Per-credit charge: $191; out-of-state residents $520.
Room and board: $8,989.

FINANCIAL AID PICTURE
Students with need: Need-based aid available for full-time and part-time students. Work study available weekends and for part-time students.
Students without need: No-need awards available for academics, art, athletics, leadership, music/drama.

FINANCIAL AID PROCEDURES
Forms required: FAFSA, state aid form.
Dates and Deadlines: Priority date 3/1; closing date 11/1. Applicants notified on a rolling basis starting 5/1.

CONTACT
Tammy Harrison, Director of Admissions and Financial Aid
2801 South University Avenue, Little Rock, AR 72204-1099
(501) 569-3035

University of Arkansas at Monticello
Monticello, Arkansas
www.uamont.edu Federal Code: 001085

4-year public university and technical college in large town.
Enrollment: 3,186 undergrads, 18% part-time. 726 full-time freshmen.
Selectivity: Open admission; but selective for some programs.

BASIC COSTS (2012-2013)
Tuition and fees: $5,560; out-of-state residents $11,050.
Per-credit charge: $132; out-of-state residents $315.
Room and board: $4,880.

FINANCIAL AID PICTURE (2011-2012)
Students with need: 67% of average financial aid package awarded as scholarships/grants, 33% awarded as loans/jobs. Need-based aid available for part-time students. Work study available nights, weekends, and for part-time students.
Students without need: No-need awards available for academics, athletics, job skills, leadership, music/drama, ROTC, state/district residency.

FINANCIAL AID PROCEDURES
Forms required: FAFSA.
Dates and Deadlines: Priority date 5/1; no closing date. Applicants notified on a rolling basis starting 5/1; must reply within 2 week(s) of notification.

CONTACT
Susan Brewer, Director of Financial Aid
Box 3600, Monticello, AR 71656
(870) 460-1050

University of Arkansas at Pine Bluff
Pine Bluff, Arkansas
www.uapb.edu Federal Code: 001086

4-year public university in small city.
Enrollment: 2,707 undergrads, 9% part-time. 564 full-time freshmen.

Selectivity: Admits less than 50% of applicants.

BASIC COSTS (2012-2013)
Tuition and fees: $5,517; out-of-state residents $10,947.
Per-credit charge: $137; out-of-state residents $318.
Room and board: $7,180.
Additional info: Tuition/fee waivers available for minority students.

FINANCIAL AID PICTURE
Students with need: Need-based aid available for full-time and part-time students. Work study available weekends and for part-time students.
Students without need: No-need awards available for academics, alumni affiliation, art, athletics, leadership, minority status, music/drama, religious affiliation, ROTC, state/district residency.

FINANCIAL AID PROCEDURES
Forms required: FAFSA.
Dates and Deadlines: Priority date 4/15; no closing date. Applicants notified on a rolling basis starting 3/1.
Transfers: Must supply financial aid transcript from prior college or university.

CONTACT
Kala Smith, Director Student Financial Aid
1200 North University Drive, Mail Slot 4981, Pine Bluff, AR 71601-2799
(870) 575-8302

University of Arkansas for Medical Sciences

Little Rock, Arkansas
www.uams.edu Federal Code: 001109

4-year public university and health science college in large city.
Enrollment: 780 undergrads, 26% part-time.

BASIC COSTS (2012-2013)
Additional info: In-state students pay $245 per-credit-hour for the following programs: dental hygiene, diagnostic medical sonography, nuclear medicine imaging sciences and radiologic technology. In-state students pay $231 per-credit-hour for the following programs: cytotechnology, health information management, medical dosimetry, medical technology, ophthalmic medical technology, radiation therapy, respiratory care, surgical technology and genetic counseling. All out-of-state students pay tuition of $561 per-credit-hour for programs. Emergency medical sciences/paramedic students pay according to program: 4-semester program, $1,163 tuition per semester; 5-semester program, $930 tuition per semester. Additional required fees vary by program. Tuition/fee waivers available for minority students.

FINANCIAL AID PICTURE
Students with need: Need-based aid available for full-time and part-time students.

FINANCIAL AID PROCEDURES
Forms required: FAFSA.
Dates and Deadlines: Applicants notified on a rolling basis starting 5/1; must reply within 2 week(s) of notification.

CONTACT
Gloria Kemp, Director of Student Financial Services
4301 West Markham Street, Little Rock, AR 72205
(501) 686-6128

University of Arkansas: Community College at Batesville

Batesville, Arkansas
www.uaccb.edu Federal Code: 020735

2-year public community college in small town.
Enrollment: 1,223 undergrads.
Selectivity: Open admission; but selective for some programs.

BASIC COSTS (2012-2013)
Tuition and fees: $2,540; out-of-district residents $2,900; out-of-state residents $4,850.
Per-credit charge: $63; out-of-district residents $75; out-of-state residents $140.

FINANCIAL AID PICTURE
Students with need: Need-based aid available for full-time students. Work study available nights, weekends, and for part-time students.
Students without need: This college awards aid only to students with need.

FINANCIAL AID PROCEDURES
Forms required: FAFSA.
Dates and Deadlines: Applicants notified on a rolling basis starting 3/1; must reply within 2 week(s) of notification.

CONTACT
Kristen Cross, Vice Chancellor for Finance and Administration
Box 3350, Batesville, AR 72503
(870) 612-2036

University of Arkansas: Community College at Hope

Hope, Arkansas
www.uacch.edu Federal Code: 005732

2-year public community and technical college in small town.
Enrollment: 1,513 undergrads.
Selectivity: Open admission; but selective for some programs.

BASIC COSTS (2012-2013)
Tuition and fees: $2,190; out-of-district residents $2,340; out-of-state residents $4,200.
Per-credit charge: $59; out-of-district residents $64; out-of-state residents $126.

FINANCIAL AID PICTURE
Students with need: Need-based aid available for full-time and part-time students. Work study available nights.
Students without need: No-need awards available for academics.

FINANCIAL AID PROCEDURES
Forms required: FAFSA, institutional form.
Dates and Deadlines: Closing date 7/6. Applicants notified on a rolling basis starting 1/1; must reply within 4 week(s) of notification.

CONTACT
Becky Wilson, Director of Financial Aid
2500 South Main, Hope, AR 71802-0140
(870) 722-8264

University of Arkansas: Community College at Morrilton

Morrilton, Arkansas
www.uaccm.edu Federal Code: 005245

2-year public community college in small town.
Enrollment: 2,054 undergrads, 38% part-time. 414 full-time freshmen.
Selectivity: Open admission.

BASIC COSTS (2012-2013)

Tuition and fees: $3,150; out-of-district residents $3,360; out-of-state residents $4,470.
Per-credit charge: $78; out-of-district residents $85; out-of-state residents $122.

FINANCIAL AID PICTURE (2012-2013)

Students with need: Average financial aid package met 49% of need; average scholarship/grant was $2,760; average loan was $1,621. For part-time students, average financial aid package was $5,458.
Students without need: No-need awards available for academics, leadership, state/district residency.

FINANCIAL AID PROCEDURES

Forms required: FAFSA, institutional form.
Dates and Deadlines: Priority date 7/1; no closing date.
Transfers: Applicants notified on a rolling basis starting 5/1.

CONTACT

Teresa Cash, Director of Financial Aid
1537 University Boulevard, Morrilton, AR 72110
(501) 977-2055

University of Central Arkansas

Conway, Arkansas
www.uca.edu Federal Code: 001092

4-year public university in small city.
Enrollment: 9,028 undergrads, 11% part-time. 2,130 full-time freshmen.
Selectivity: Admits over 75% of applicants.

BASIC COSTS (2012-2013)

Tuition and fees: $7,333; out-of-state residents $12,830.
Per-credit charge: $183; out-of-state residents $367.
Room and board: $5,270.

FINANCIAL AID PICTURE

Students with need: Need-based aid available for full-time students. Work study available nights, weekends, and for part-time students.
Students without need: No-need awards available for academics, art, athletics, leadership, minority status, music/drama, ROTC, state/district residency.
Additional info: Room and board may be paid monthly.

FINANCIAL AID PROCEDURES

Forms required: FAFSA.
Dates and Deadlines: Priority date 4/15; closing date 7/1. Applicants notified on a rolling basis starting 5/4.

CONTACT

Cheryl Lyons, Director of Financial Aid
201 Donaghey Avenue, Conway, AR 72035
(501) 450-3140

University of the Ozarks

Clarksville, Arkansas
www.ozarks.edu Federal Code: 001094

4-year private university and liberal arts college in small town, affiliated with Presbyterian Church (USA).
Enrollment: 558 undergrads.

BASIC COSTS (2012-2013)

Tuition and fees: $23,340.
Per-credit charge: $950.
Room and board: $6,700.
Additional info: Tuition/fee waivers available for minority students.

FINANCIAL AID PICTURE

Students with need: Need-based aid available for full-time and part-time students. Work study available nights, weekends, and for part-time students.
Students without need: No-need awards available for academics, alumni affiliation, art, leadership, minority status, music/drama, religious affiliation, state/district residency.
Additional info: Walton International Scholarship Program provides full scholarships to selected Central American and Mexican residents.

FINANCIAL AID PROCEDURES

Forms required: FAFSA.
Dates and Deadlines: Priority date 2/15; no closing date. Applicants notified on a rolling basis starting 3/1; must reply within 2 week(s) of notification.

CONTACT

Jana Hart, Dean of Admissions and Financial Aid
415 North College Avenue, Clarksville, AR 72830-2880
(479) 979-1221

Williams Baptist College

Walnut Ridge, Arkansas
www.wbcoll.edu Federal Code: 001106

4-year private liberal arts college in small town, affiliated with Southern Baptist Convention.
Enrollment: 509 undergrads, 3% part-time. 140 full-time freshmen.
Selectivity: Admits 50 to 75% of applicants.

BASIC COSTS (2013-2014)

Tuition and fees: $13,750.
Per-credit charge: $540.
Room and board: $6,200.

FINANCIAL AID PICTURE (2011-2012)

Students with need: Out of 120 full-time freshmen who applied for aid, 99 were judged to have need. Of these, 99 received aid. For part-time students, average financial aid package was $8,872.
Students without need: No-need awards available for academics, art, athletics, leadership, minority status, music/drama, religious affiliation, state/district residency.
Scholarships offered: Trustee's Scholarship; up to full tuition, room and board; based on 30 ACT and 3.5 GPA; 1 awarded; renewable for 4 years with 3.25 GPA with at least 15 credit hours per semester.
Cumulative student debt: 79% of graduating class had student loans; average debt was $18,720.
Additional info: Art scholarship applicants must submit portfolio.

FINANCIAL AID PROCEDURES

Forms required: FAFSA.
Dates and Deadlines: Priority date 5/1; no closing date. Applicants notified on a rolling basis starting 4/1; must reply within 2 week(s) of notification.
Transfers: Priority date 4/1; no deadline. Applicants notified on a rolling basis starting 4/1; must reply within 2 week(s) of notification.

CONTACT

Barbara Turner, Director of Financial Aid
PO Box 3665, Walnut Ridge, AR 72476
(870) 759-4112

California

Academy of Art University

San Francisco, California
www.academyart.edu Federal Code: 007531

4-year for-profit university and visual arts college in very large city.
Enrollment: 11,710 undergrads, 44% part-time. 1,029 full-time freshmen.
Selectivity: Open admission.

BASIC COSTS (2013-2014)
Tuition and fees: $23,840.
Per-credit charge: $785.
Room and board: $13,400.

FINANCIAL AID PICTURE (2011-2012)
Students with need: Out of 636 full-time freshmen who applied for aid, 586 were judged to have need. Of these, 576 received aid, and 1 had their full need met. Average financial aid package met 30% of need; average scholarship/grant was $5,379; average loan was $3,231. For part-time students, average financial aid package was $5,374.
Students without need: 1 full-time freshmen who did not demonstrate need for aid received scholarships/grants; average award was $1,110. No-need awards available for academics, art, athletics.
Scholarships offered: 28 full-time freshmen received athletic scholarships; average amount $23,339.
Cumulative student debt: 61% of graduating class had student loans; average debt was $46,726.
Additional info: Numerous summer grant programs available.

FINANCIAL AID PROCEDURES
Forms required: FAFSA, institutional form.
Dates and Deadlines: Priority date 7/10; no closing date. Applicants notified on a rolling basis.
Transfers: Priority date 3/1; no deadline. Applicants notified on a rolling basis.

CONTACT
Joe Vollaro, Executive Vice President for Financial Aid/Compliance
79 New Montgomery Street, San Francisco, CA 94105-3410
(415) 618-6273

Academy of Couture Art

Beverly Hills, California
www.academyofcoutureart.edu Federal Code: 041855

4-year private Institute of Couture Fashion Design in very large city.
Selectivity: Open admission; but selective for some programs.

BASIC COSTS (2013-2014)
Tuition and fees: $22,338.
Per-credit charge: $556.
Additional info: Tuition at time of enrollment locked for 4 years.

FINANCIAL AID PICTURE (2012-2013)
Students with need: 30% of average financial aid package awarded as scholarships/grants, 70% awarded as loans/jobs. Need-based aid available for part-time students.
Students without need: This college awards aid only to students with need.

FINANCIAL AID PROCEDURES
Forms required: FAFSA, state aid form, institutional form.
Dates and Deadlines: Priority date 3/2; no closing date. Applicants notified on a rolling basis starting 3/2.
Transfers: No deadline. Applicants notified on a rolling basis. Maximum college transfer credits cannot exceed 45% of the entire quarter credits hours needed for graduation from Academy if Couture Art.

CONTACT
Robert RICE, Director of Financial Aid
8484 Wilshire Boulevard, Beverly Hills, CA 90211
(310) 360-8888 ext. 110

Allan Hancock College

Santa Maria, California
www.hancockcollege.edu Federal Code: 001111

2-year public community college in small city.
Enrollment: 8,169 undergrads.
Selectivity: Open admission; but selective for some programs.

BASIC COSTS (2012-2013)
Tuition and fees: $1,428; out-of-state residents $7,128.
Per-credit charge: $46; out-of-state residents $236.

FINANCIAL AID PICTURE
Students with need: Need-based aid available for full-time and part-time students.
Students without need: This college awards aid only to students with need.

FINANCIAL AID PROCEDURES
Forms required: FAFSA.
Dates and Deadlines: Priority date 5/1; no closing date. Applicants notified on a rolling basis starting 6/1.

CONTACT
Robert Parisi, Dean, Student Services
800 South College Drive, Santa Maria, CA 93454-6399
(805) 922-6966 ext. 3200

Alliant International University

San Diego, California
www.alliant.edu Federal Code: 011117

Upper-division private university in very large city.
Enrollment: 320 undergrads.
Selectivity: Open admission; but selective for some programs.

BASIC COSTS (2012-2013)
Per-credit charge: $620.
Additional info: Tuition $620/unit. Required fees for full-time students: $190. Cost of room only, $7,340. Tuition/fee waivers available for minority students.

FINANCIAL AID PICTURE (2011-2012)
Students with need: 65% of average financial aid package awarded as scholarships/grants, 35% awarded as loans/jobs. Need-based aid available for part-time students. Work study available nights, weekends, and for part-time students.
Students without need: No-need awards available for academics, alumni affiliation, athletics, leadership.
Scholarships offered: Grants and scholarships available based on GPA and SAT/ACT scores.

FINANCIAL AID PROCEDURES
Forms required: FAFSA.
Dates and Deadlines: Closing date 3/2. Applicants notified on a rolling basis starting 2/1; must reply within 3 week(s) of notification.

CONTACT
Deborah Spindler, Director of Financial Aid
10455 Pomerado Road, San Diego, CA 92131-1799
(858) 635-4559

American Jewish University
Los Angeles, California
www.ajula.edu Federal Code: 002741

4-year private university and liberal arts college in very large city, affiliated with Jewish faith.
Enrollment: 120 undergrads, 5% part-time. 13 full-time freshmen.
Selectivity: Admits over 75% of applicants.

BASIC COSTS (2013-2014)
Tuition and fees: $28,496.
Per-credit charge: $1,116.
Room and board: $14,544.

FINANCIAL AID PICTURE (2012-2013)
Students with need: Out of 13 full-time freshmen who applied for aid, 12 were judged to have need. Of these, 11 received aid. Average financial aid package met 95% of need; average scholarship/grant was $5,500; average loan was $3,500. Need-based aid available for part-time students.
Students without need: 9 full-time freshmen who did not demonstrate need for aid received scholarships/grants; average award was $8,950. No-need awards available for leadership, minority status, music/drama, state/district residency.
Cumulative student debt: 100% of graduating class had student loans; average debt was $10,000.

FINANCIAL AID PROCEDURES
Forms required: FAFSA, institutional form.
Dates and Deadlines: Priority date 3/2; no closing date. Applicants notified on a rolling basis starting 1/1; must reply by 6/30.
Transfers: Priority date 7/1; no deadline. Applicants notified on a rolling basis; must reply within 3 week(s) of notification.

CONTACT
Larisa Zadoyen, Director of Financial Aid
Office of Undergraduate Admissions, Bel Air, CA 90077
(310) 476-9777 ext. 222

American River College
Sacramento, California
www.arc.losrios.edu Federal Code: 001232

2-year public community college in large city.
Enrollment: 20,481 undergrads.
Selectivity: Open admission; but selective for some programs.

BASIC COSTS (2012-2013)
Tuition and fees: $1,415; out-of-state residents $7,655.
Per-credit charge: $46; out-of-state residents $254.
Additional info: Tuition/fee waivers available for minority students.

FINANCIAL AID PICTURE
Students with need: Need-based aid available for full-time and part-time students.
Students without need: This college awards aid only to students with need.

FINANCIAL AID PROCEDURES
Forms required: FAFSA.
Dates and Deadlines: Priority date 3/2; closing date 6/30. Applicants notified on a rolling basis starting 7/1; must reply within 2 week(s) of notification.

CONTACT
Chad Funk, Financial Aid Supervisor
4700 College Oak Drive, Sacramento, CA 95841
(916) 484-8437

Antelope Valley College
Lancaster, California
www.avc.edu Federal Code: 001113

2-year public liberal arts and technical college in large city.
Enrollment: 10,420 undergrads.
Selectivity: Open admission; but selective for some programs.

BASIC COSTS (2012-2013)
Tuition and fees: $1,382; out-of-state residents $6,962.
Per-credit charge: $46; out-of-state residents $232.

FINANCIAL AID PICTURE
Students with need: Need-based aid available for full-time and part-time students.

FINANCIAL AID PROCEDURES
Forms required: FAFSA, state aid form, institutional form.
Dates and Deadlines: Applicants notified on a rolling basis starting 7/15; must reply within 2 week(s) of notification.

CONTACT
Sherrie Padilla, Director of Financial Aid
3041 West Avenue K, Lancaster, CA 93536-5426
(661) 722-6336

Antioch University Santa Barbara
Santa Barbara, California
www.antiochsb.edu Federal Code: 003010

Upper-division private university and liberal arts college in small city.
Enrollment: 145 undergrads, 55% part-time.

BASIC COSTS (2013-2014)
Tuition and fees: $21,945.
Per-credit charge: $481.

FINANCIAL AID PICTURE
Students with need: Need-based aid available for full-time and part-time students. Work study available nights, weekends, and for part-time students.

FINANCIAL AID PROCEDURES
Forms required: FAFSA, institutional form.
Dates and Deadlines: Priority date 4/15; no closing date. Applicants notified on a rolling basis; must reply within 4 week(s) of notification.
Transfers: Priority date 4/1; no deadline.

CONTACT
Steve Weir, Director of Communications & Enrollment
602 Anacapa Street, Santa Barbara, CA 93101
(805) 962-8179 ext. 5131

Art Center College of Design
Pasadena, California
www.artcenter.edu Federal Code: 001116

4-year private visual arts college in small city.
Enrollment: 1,647 undergrads, 13% part-time. 159 full-time freshmen.
Selectivity: Admits over 75% of applicants.

BASIC COSTS (2012-2013)
Tuition and fees: $35,552.
Per-credit charge: $1,198.

FINANCIAL AID PICTURE
Students with need: Need-based aid available for full-time and part-time students.
Additional info: Students may apply for scholarships after they enroll while progressing through the program.

FINANCIAL AID PROCEDURES
Forms required: FAFSA.
Dates and Deadlines: Priority date 3/1; no closing date. Applicants notified on a rolling basis starting 5/15.
Transfers: Applicants notified on a rolling basis starting 1/1.

CONTACT
Brenda Nieves, Director of Financial Aid
1700 Lida Street, Pasadena, CA 91103
(626) 396-2215

Art Institute of California: Hollywood

North Hollywood, California
www.artinstitutes.edu/hollywood Federal Code: 031254

4-year for-profit culinary school and visual arts college in very large city.
Enrollment: 1,788 undergrads.
Selectivity: Admits 50 to 75% of applicants.

BASIC COSTS (2012-2013)
Tuition and fees: $23,610.
Per-credit charge: $518.
Room and board: $11,190.

FINANCIAL AID PICTURE
Students with need: Need-based aid available for full-time and part-time students.

CONTACT
Adis Ceballos, Director of Student Financial Services
5250 Lankershim Boulevard, North Hollywood, CA 91601
(818) 299-5151

Art Institute of California: Los Angeles

Santa Monica, California
www.artinstitutes.edu/losangeles Federal Code: 007470

2-year for-profit visual arts and career college in large city.
Enrollment: 2,175 undergrads.
Selectivity: Admits less than 50% of applicants.

BASIC COSTS (2012-2013)
Tuition and fees: $23,310.
Per-credit charge: $518.
Additional info: Board plan not available. Cost of room only, $8,982.

FINANCIAL AID PICTURE
Students with need: Need-based aid available for full-time and part-time students. Work study available nights, weekends, and for part-time students.
Students without need: No-need awards available for academics.

FINANCIAL AID PROCEDURES
Forms required: FAFSA.
Dates and Deadlines: Applicants notified on a rolling basis.

CONTACT
Cynthia Galarza, Director of Student Financial Services
2900 31st Street, Santa Monica, CA 90405-3035
(310) 752-4700

Art Institute of California: Orange County

Santa Ana, California
www.artinstitutes.edu/orangecounty
Federal Code: 007236

3-year for-profit culinary school and visual arts college in very large city.
Enrollment: 2,230 undergrads.
Selectivity: Open admission.

BASIC COSTS (2012-2013)
Tuition and fees: $23,310.
Per-credit charge: $518.
Additional info: Board plan not available. Cost of room only, $8,991.

FINANCIAL AID PICTURE
Students with need: Need-based aid available for full-time and part-time students. Work study available nights, weekends, and for part-time students.
Students without need: No-need awards available for academics, art, minority status.

FINANCIAL AID PROCEDURES
Forms required: FAFSA, state aid form.
Dates and Deadlines: Applicants notified on a rolling basis; must reply within 2 week(s) of notification.

CONTACT
Silvia Dimas, Director of Student Financial Services
3601 West Sunflower Avenue, Santa Ana, CA 92704-7931
(714) 830-0202

Art Institute of California: San Diego

San Diego, California
www.artinstitutes.edu/sandiego Federal Code: 016471

3-year for-profit visual arts college in very large city.
Enrollment: 2,019 undergrads.
Selectivity: Admits over 75% of applicants.

BASIC COSTS (2012-2013)
Tuition and fees: $23,310.
Per-credit charge: $518.
Room and board: $12,576.

FINANCIAL AID PICTURE
Students with need: Need-based aid available for full-time students.

FINANCIAL AID PROCEDURES
Forms required: FAFSA.

CONTACT
Laverne Arberry-Lamb, Director of Student Financial Services
7650 Mission Valley Road, San Diego, CA 92108-4423

Azusa Pacific University

Azusa, California
www.apu.edu Federal Code: 001117

4-year private university in small city, affiliated with interdenominational tradition.
Enrollment: 6,224 undergrads, 13% part-time. 1,175 full-time freshmen.
Selectivity: Admits over 75% of applicants.

BASIC COSTS (2013-2014)
Tuition and fees: $32,256.
Per-credit charge: $1,309.
Room and board: $8,852.

Additional info: Tuition/fee waivers available for minority students.

FINANCIAL AID PICTURE (2011-2012)

Students with need: Out of 989 full-time freshmen who applied for aid, 904 were judged to have need. Of these, 904 received aid, and 24 had their full need met. Average financial aid package met 65% of need; average scholarship/grant was $9,705; average loan was $3,585. For part-time students, average financial aid package was $8,042.

Students without need: 199 full-time freshmen who did not demonstrate need for aid received scholarships/grants; average award was $7,680. No-need awards available for academics, athletics, leadership, minority status, music/drama, religious affiliation, ROTC.

Scholarships offered: 46 full-time freshmen received athletic scholarships; average amount $8,810.

Cumulative student debt: 78% of graduating class had student loans; average debt was $23,070.

FINANCIAL AID PROCEDURES

Forms required: FAFSA, institutional form.

Dates and Deadlines: Priority date 3/2; closing date 7/1. Applicants notified on a rolling basis starting 3/1; must reply within 3 week(s) of notification.

Transfers: Cal Grants not available to first time applicants who are seniors.

CONTACT

Todd Ross, Director of Student Financial Services
901 East Alosta Avenue, Azusa, CA 91702-7000
(626) 812-3009

Barstow Community College

Barstow, California
www.barstow.edu Federal Code: 001119

2-year public community college in large town.
Enrollment: 3,278 undergrads.
Selectivity: Open admission.

BASIC COSTS (2012-2013)

Tuition and fees: $1,380; out-of-state residents $6,750.
Per-credit charge: $46; out-of-state residents $225.

FINANCIAL AID PICTURE (2011-2012)

Students with need: 97% of average financial aid package awarded as scholarships/grants, 3% awarded as loans/jobs. Need-based aid available for part-time students.

Students without need: This college awards aid only to students with need.

FINANCIAL AID PROCEDURES

Forms required: FAFSA.

Dates and Deadlines: Closing date 6/17. Applicants notified on a rolling basis starting 7/1.

CONTACT

Danielle Cordova, Financial Aid Officer
2700 Barstow Road, Barstow, CA 92311-9984
(760) 252-2411 ext. 7205

Berkeley City College

Berkeley, California
www.berkeleycitycollege.edu Federal Code: 014311

2-year public community college in small city.
Enrollment: 7,300 undergrads.
Selectivity: Open admission.

BASIC COSTS (2012-2013)

Tuition and fees: $1,420; out-of-state residents $7,120.
Per-credit charge: $46; out-of-state residents $236.
Additional info: Tuition/fee waivers available for adults, minority students, unemployed or children of unemployed.

FINANCIAL AID PICTURE

Students with need: Need-based aid available for full-time and part-time students.

Students without need: This college awards aid only to students with need.

FINANCIAL AID PROCEDURES

Dates and Deadlines: Applicants notified on a rolling basis.

CONTACT

Loan Nguyen, Financial Aid Supervisor
2050 Center Street, Berkeley, CA 94704
(510) 981-2878

Bethesda University of California

Anaheim, California
www.buc.edu Federal Code: 032663

4-year private university in large city, affiliated with Christian Church.
Enrollment: 223 undergrads, 17% part-time. 55 full-time freshmen.
Selectivity: Admits over 75% of applicants. GED not accepted.

BASIC COSTS (2012-2013)

Tuition and fees: $7,160.
Per-credit charge: $231.
Room and board: $3,200.

FINANCIAL AID PICTURE (2011-2012)

Students with need: 99% of average financial aid package awarded as scholarships/grants, 1% awarded as loans/jobs. Need-based aid available for part-time students.

Students without need: This college awards aid only to students with need.

FINANCIAL AID PROCEDURES

Forms required: FAFSA, institutional form.

Dates and Deadlines: Applicants notified on a rolling basis starting 6/30.

Transfers: No deadline.

CONTACT

Grace Choi, Director of Financial Aid
730 North Euclid Street, Anaheim, CA 92801
(714) 517-1945

Biola University

La Mirada, California
www.biola.edu Federal Code: 001122

4-year private university and Bible college in large town, affiliated with interdenominational tradition.
Enrollment: 4,337 undergrads, 4% part-time. 913 full-time freshmen.
Selectivity: Admits 50 to 75% of applicants.

BASIC COSTS (2013-2014)

Tuition and fees: $32,142.
Per-credit charge: $1,340.
Room and board: $9,596.
Additional info: Tuition/fee waivers available for minority students.

FINANCIAL AID PICTURE (2011-2012)

Students with need: Out of 803 full-time freshmen who applied for aid, 640 were judged to have need. Of these, 632 received aid, and 36 had their full need met. Average financial aid package met 50% of need; average

scholarship/grant was $12,990; average loan was $2,752. For part-time students, average financial aid package was $9,963.
Students without need: 204 full-time freshmen who did not demonstrate need for aid received scholarships/grants; average award was $6,523. No-need awards available for academics, alumni affiliation, art, athletics, leadership, minority status, music/drama.
Scholarships offered: ***Merit:*** Scholarships for Underrepresented Groups of Ethnicity: up to $6,500; based on GPA and ethnicity. Community Service Scholarship: $2,700; based on demonstration of outstanding spiritual leadership. Alumni Dependent Scholarship: $500; given to students whose parents completed 30 units of coursework at Biola University. ***Athletic:*** 16 full-time freshmen received athletic scholarships; average amount $11,165.

FINANCIAL AID PROCEDURES
Forms required: FAFSA, state aid form.
Dates and Deadlines: Priority date 3/1; no closing date. Applicants notified on a rolling basis starting 3/1.
Transfers: No deadline. Applicants notified on a rolling basis starting 3/1.

CONTACT
Jonathan Choy, Director of Financial Aid
13800 Biola Avenue, La Mirada, CA 90639-0001
(562) 903-4742

Brooks Institute

Santa Barbara, California
www.brooks.edu Federal Code: 001123

3-year for-profit visual arts college in small city.
Enrollment: 750 undergrads.
Selectivity: Admits over 75% of applicants.

BASIC COSTS (2012-2013)
Tuition and fees: $19,600.
Additional info: Costs of books and supplies vary by program.

FINANCIAL AID PICTURE
Students with need: Need-based aid available for full-time and part-time students. Work study available nights, weekends, and for part-time students.

FINANCIAL AID PROCEDURES
Forms required: FAFSA, institutional form.
Dates and Deadlines: Priority date 3/2; no closing date. Applicants notified on a rolling basis starting 5/1.
Transfers: No deadline. Applicants notified on a rolling basis.

CONTACT
Stacey Eymann, Director of Student Finance
27 East Cota Street, Santa Barbara, CA 93101
(805) 966-3888

Cabrillo College

Aptos, California
www.cabrillo.edu Federal Code: 001124

2-year public community college in large town.
Enrollment: 8,752 undergrads.
Selectivity: Open admission; but selective for some programs.

BASIC COSTS (2012-2013)
Tuition and fees: $1,428; out-of-state residents $7,428.
Per-credit charge: $46; out-of-state residents $246.

FINANCIAL AID PICTURE (2011-2012)
Students with need: Need-based aid available for part-time students.

FINANCIAL AID PROCEDURES
Forms required: FAFSA, institutional form.
Dates and Deadlines: Applicants notified on a rolling basis starting 7/31; must reply within 3 week(s) of notification.
Transfers: Academic transcript required.

CONTACT
Tama Bolton, Director of Enrollment Services
6500 Soquel Drive, Aptos, CA 95003
(831) 479-6415

California Baptist University

Riverside, California
www.calbaptist.edu Federal Code: 001125

4-year private university in large city, affiliated with Southern Baptist Convention.
Enrollment: 4,923 undergrads, 12% part-time. 860 full-time freshmen.
Selectivity: Admits 50 to 75% of applicants.

BASIC COSTS (2012-2013)
Tuition and fees: $26,900.
Per-credit charge: $965.
Room and board: $8,990.

FINANCIAL AID PICTURE (2012-2013)
Students with need: Out of 697 full-time freshmen who applied for aid, 560 were judged to have need. Of these, 560 received aid, and 52 had their full need met. Average financial aid package met 55% of need; average scholarship/grant was $13,871; average loan was $3,475. For part-time students, average financial aid package was $7,520.
Students without need: 42 full-time freshmen who did not demonstrate need for aid received scholarships/grants; average award was $6,437. No-need awards available for academics, art, athletics, music/drama, religious affiliation, ROTC.
Scholarships offered: ***Merit:*** Matching room and board scholarship for recipients of the ROTC scholarships. Yellow Ribbon Scholarship for qualified veterans. ***Athletic:*** 6 full-time freshmen received athletic scholarships; average amount $14,726.
Cumulative student debt: 82% of graduating class had student loans; average debt was $33,807.

FINANCIAL AID PROCEDURES
Forms required: FAFSA, state aid form.
Dates and Deadlines: Priority date 3/2; no closing date. Applicants notified on a rolling basis starting 3/2; must reply by 6/1.
Transfers: No deadline. Applicants notified on a rolling basis starting 12/15; must reply by 6/1.

CONTACT
Rebecca Sanchez, Director of Financial Aid
8432 Magnolia Avenue, Riverside, CA 92504-3297
(951) 343-4236

California Christian College

Fresno, California
www.calchristiancollege.edu

4-year private Bible college in large city, affiliated with Free Will Baptists.
Enrollment: 24 undergrads, 12% part-time. 6 full-time freshmen.
Selectivity: Open admission.

BASIC COSTS (2013-2014)
Tuition and fees: $10,150.
Per-credit charge: $320.
Room and board: $4,400.

FINANCIAL AID PICTURE (2011-2012)
Students with need: 49% of average financial aid package awarded as scholarships/grants, 51% awarded as loans/jobs.

FINANCIAL AID PROCEDURES
Forms required: FAFSA, institutional form.

CONTACT
Melinda Scroggins, Financial Aid Coordinator
4881 East University Avenue, Fresno, CA 93703-3599

California College of the Arts
San Francisco, California
www.cca.edu Federal Code: 001127

4-year private visual arts college in very large city.
Enrollment: 1,450 undergrads, 6% part-time. 232 full-time freshmen.
Selectivity: Admits over 75% of applicants.

BASIC COSTS (2013-2014)
Tuition and fees: $40,334.
Per-credit charge: $1,666.
Additional info: Board plan not available. Cost of room only, $8,000. Estimated cost for Food is $2850.

FINANCIAL AID PICTURE (2011-2012)
Students with need: Out of 152 full-time freshmen who applied for aid, 141 were judged to have need. Of these, 141 received aid, and 5 had their full need met. Average financial aid package met 62% of need; average scholarship/grant was $24,319; average loan was $3,598. For part-time students, average financial aid package was $11,902.
Students without need: 48 full-time freshmen who did not demonstrate need for aid received scholarships/grants; average award was $8,875. No-need awards available for academics, art.
Scholarships offered: Creative Achievement Scholarship: up to $20,000 annually; renewable; based on academic achievement and strength of admissions portfolios.
Cumulative student debt: 57% of graduating class had student loans; average debt was $36,690.
Additional info: Application deadline for merit scholarships February 1.

FINANCIAL AID PROCEDURES
Forms required: FAFSA.
Dates and Deadlines: Priority date 3/1; no closing date. Applicants notified on a rolling basis starting 3/15; must reply by 5/1 or within 3 week(s) of notification.
Transfers: No deadline. Applicants notified on a rolling basis starting 3/15; must reply by 5/1 or within 3 week(s) of notification. Scholarships available for community college transfer students.

CONTACT
Silvia Marquez, Director of Financial Aid
1111 Eighth Street, San Francisco, CA 94107-2247
(415) 703-9528

California College San Diego
San Diego, California
www.cc-sd.edu

4-year for-profit business and health science college in very large city.
Enrollment: 832 undergrads.
Selectivity: Open admission.

BASIC COSTS (2012-2013)
Additional info: Associate programs: Business Management & Accounting $41,395; Computer Programming $41,395; Computer Networking & Technology $41,395; Medical Specialties $41,395; Respiratory Therapy $43,850. Bachelor programs: Accounting $72,960; Business Administration $72,960; Computer Science $72,960; Health Information Management $72,960; Healthcare Administration $72,960; Nursing Administration $30,910; Respiratory Therapy $80,020; Web Design and Development $72,960. Cost of books included.

FINANCIAL AID PICTURE (2011-2012)
Students with need: Need-based aid available for full-time and part-time students.

FINANCIAL AID PROCEDURES
Forms required: FAFSA, state aid form, institutional form.

CONTACT
Raul Rivera, Financial Aid Officer
6602 Convoy Court, Suite 100, San Diego, CA 92111
(619) 680-4430

California Culinary Academy
San Francisco, California
www.chefs.edu/San-Francisco Federal Code: 015698

2-year for-profit culinary school and career college in very large city.
Enrollment: 749 undergrads.

BASIC COSTS (2012-2013)
Additional info: Certificate in Le Cordon Bleu Culinary Arts; Tuition $19,200, Fees $325.50, STRF $47.50, Application Fee $50, Total Cost $19,623. Certificate in Le Cordon Bleu Pâtisserie and Baking: Tuition $19,200, Fees $325.50, STRF $47.50, Application Fee $50, Total Cost $19,623. Associate of Occupational Studies in Le Cordon Bleu Culinary Arts: Tuition $36,200, Fees $876, STRF $87.50, Application Fee $50, Total Cost $37,213.50. Associate of Occupational Studies (AOS) Degree in Le Cordon Bleu Culinary Arts Program (Non-Resident International Students): Tuition $39,200, Fees $876, STRF 97.50, Application Fee $50, Total Cost $40,223.50.

FINANCIAL AID PICTURE
Students with need: Need-based aid available for full-time students.

FINANCIAL AID PROCEDURES
Forms required: FAFSA, state aid form.
Dates and Deadlines: Applicants notified on a rolling basis; must reply within 1 week(s) of notification.

CONTACT
Director of Financial Aid
350 Rhode Island Street, San Francisco, CA 94103
(415) 771-3500

California Institute of Integral Studies
San Francisco, California
www.ciis.edu Federal Code: 012154

Upper-division private liberal arts college in very large city.
Enrollment: 93 undergrads, 9% part-time.

BASIC COSTS (2013-2014)
Tuition and fees: $17,476.
Per-credit charge: $666.

FINANCIAL AID PICTURE (2011-2012)
Students with need: 25% of average financial aid package awarded as scholarships/grants, 75% awarded as loans/jobs. Need-based aid available for part-time students. Work study available nights, weekends, and for part-time students.
Students without need: No-need awards available for academics, alumni affiliation, art, job skills, leadership, minority status, music/drama, ROTC, state/district residency.

FINANCIAL AID PROCEDURES

Dates and Deadlines: Closing date 4/15.
Transfers: Priority date 4/15; no deadline.

CONTACT

Marisol Mendoza, Financial Aid Director
1453 Mission Street, San Francisco, CA 94103
(415) 575-6156

California Institute of Technology

Pasadena, California Federal Code: 001131
www.caltech.edu/ CSS Code: 4034

4-year private university in small city.
Enrollment: 997 undergrads. 264 full-time freshmen.
Selectivity: Admits less than 50% of applicants.

BASIC COSTS (2013-2014)

Tuition and fees: $41,538.
Per-credit charge: $1,111.
Room and board: $12,507.

FINANCIAL AID PICTURE (2012-2013)

Students with need: Out of 216 full-time freshmen who applied for aid, 163 were judged to have need. Of these, 163 received aid, and 163 had their full need met. Average financial aid package met 100% of need; average scholarship/grant was $34,931; average loan was $4,147.
Cumulative student debt: 44% of graduating class had student loans; average debt was $15,090.

FINANCIAL AID PROCEDURES

Forms required: FAFSA, CSS PROFILE, institutional form.
Dates and Deadlines: Priority date 3/2; no closing date. Applicants notified on a rolling basis starting 4/15; must reply by 5/1 or within 2 week(s) of notification.
Transfers: Priority date 3/1; no deadline.

CONTACT

Don Crewell, Director of Financial Aid
383 South Hill Avenue, Mail Code 10-90, Pasadena, CA 91125
(626) 395-6280

California Institute of the Arts

Valencia, California Federal Code: 001132
www.calarts.edu CSS Code: 4049

4-year private visual arts and performing arts college in small city.
Enrollment: 938 undergrads, 1% part-time. 180 full-time freshmen.
Selectivity: Admits less than 50% of applicants.

BASIC COSTS (2013-2014)

Tuition and fees: $40,552.
Room and board: $10,188.

FINANCIAL AID PICTURE (2012-2013)

Students with need: Out of 135 full-time freshmen who applied for aid, 120 were judged to have need. Of these, 115 received aid, and 4 had their full need met. Average financial aid package met 78% of need; average scholarship/grant was $14,290; average loan was $7,054. Need-based aid available for part-time students.
Students without need: 9 full-time freshmen who did not demonstrate need for aid received scholarships/grants; average award was $4,167. No-need awards available for academics, art, minority status, music/drama.
Cumulative student debt: 75% of graduating class had student loans; average debt was $42,509.

FINANCIAL AID PROCEDURES

Forms required: FAFSA, CSS PROFILE.
Dates and Deadlines: Priority date 2/15; no closing date. Applicants notified on a rolling basis starting 4/1; must reply by 5/1 or within 3 week(s) of notification.
Transfers: Applicants notified by 4/1; must reply by 5/1 or within 3 week(s) of notification.

CONTACT

Robin Bailey-Chen, Director of Financial Aid
24700 McBean Parkway, Valencia, CA 91355
(661) 253-7869

California Lutheran University

Thousand Oaks, California
www.callutheran.edu Federal Code: 001133

4-year private university and liberal arts college in small city, affiliated with Evangelical Lutheran Church in America.
Enrollment: 2,788 undergrads, 7% part-time. 558 full-time freshmen.
Selectivity: Admits less than 50% of applicants.

BASIC COSTS (2013-2014)

Tuition and fees: $35,720.
Per-credit charge: $1,135.
Room and board: $11,920.

FINANCIAL AID PICTURE (2012-2013)

Students with need: Out of 463 full-time freshmen who applied for aid, 388 were judged to have need. Of these, 388 received aid, and 66 had their full need met. Average financial aid package met 70% of need; average scholarship/grant was $20,870; average loan was $3,500. For part-time students, average financial aid package was $7,000.
Students without need: 159 full-time freshmen who did not demonstrate need for aid received scholarships/grants; average award was $14,400. No-need awards available for academics, alumni affiliation, art, leadership, minority status, music/drama, religious affiliation, state/district residency.
Scholarships offered: Academic Scholarships: range from $3,000 up to $15,000 per year; based on GPA, test scores, and class rank at time of Admission. Presidential Scholarship Program: $17,000 up to full tuition; additional application required. Visual and Performing Arts Scholarships: $1,000-$6,000; application deadline of February 1 and audition with department deadline of February 22.
Cumulative student debt: 76% of graduating class had student loans; average debt was $26,610.

FINANCIAL AID PROCEDURES

Forms required: FAFSA.
Dates and Deadlines: Closing date 3/1. Applicants notified on a rolling basis starting 3/15; must reply within 2 week(s) of notification.
Transfers: No deadline. Applicants notified on a rolling basis starting 3/15; must reply within 2 week(s) of notification.

CONTACT

Susan Arias, Director of Financial Aid
60 West Olsen Road #1350, Thousand Oaks, CA 91360-2787
(805) 493-3115

California Maritime Academy

Vallejo, California
www.csum.edu Federal Code: 001134

4-year public university and maritime college in small city.
Enrollment: 973 undergrads.
Selectivity: Admits over 75% of applicants.

BASIC COSTS (2012-2013)
Tuition and fees: $7,034; out-of-state residents $18,194.
Room and board: $10,544.

FINANCIAL AID PICTURE (2012-2013)
Students with need: 51% of average financial aid package awarded as scholarships/grants, 49% awarded as loans/jobs. Need-based aid available for part-time students.
Students without need: This college awards aid only to students with need.
Additional info: US Maritime Administration provides annual incentive payment of $3,000 per student, with certain conditions. Tuition waiver for children of deceased or disabled California veterans.

FINANCIAL AID PROCEDURES
Forms required: FAFSA.
Dates and Deadlines: Closing date 3/2. Applicants notified on a rolling basis starting 4/1.

CONTACT
Nicole Hill, Director of Financial Aid
200 Maritime Academy Drive, Vallejo, CA 94590
(707) 654-1275

California Polytechnic State University: San Luis Obispo

San Luis Obispo, California
www.calpoly.edu Federal Code: 001143

4-year public university in large town.
Enrollment: 17,599 undergrads, 4% part-time. 4,305 full-time freshmen.
Selectivity: Admits less than 50% of applicants.

BASIC COSTS (2012-2013)
Tuition and fees: $8,958; out-of-state residents $20,181.
Room and board: $10,679.

FINANCIAL AID PICTURE (2011-2012)
Students with need: Out of 3,418 full-time freshmen who applied for aid, 1,865 were judged to have need. Of these, 1,657 received aid, and 102 had their full need met. Average financial aid package met 58% of need; average scholarship/grant was $3,370; average loan was $3,188. For part-time students, average financial aid package was $7,370.
Students without need: 373 full-time freshmen who did not demonstrate need for aid received scholarships/grants; average award was $1,948. No-need awards available for academics, alumni affiliation, art, athletics, job skills, leadership, music/drama, ROTC, state/district residency.
Scholarships offered: 80 full-time freshmen received athletic scholarships; average amount $2,837.
Additional info: College-administered financial aid is not available for undergraduate international students.

FINANCIAL AID PROCEDURES
Forms required: FAFSA.
Dates and Deadlines: Priority date 3/2; no closing date. Applicants notified on a rolling basis starting 4/1.

CONTACT
Lois Kelly, Director, Financial Aid
Admissions Office, Cal Poly, San Luis Obispo, CA 93407-0031
(805) 756-2927

California State Polytechnic University: Pomona

Pomona, California
www.csupomona.edu Federal Code: 001144

4-year public university in small city.
Enrollment: 20,461 undergrads, 13% part-time. 3,022 full-time freshmen.
Selectivity: Admits 50 to 75% of applicants.

BASIC COSTS (2012-2013)
Tuition and fees: $6,624; out-of-state residents $17,784.
Room and board: $11,616.

FINANCIAL AID PICTURE (2012-2013)
Students with need: Out of 2,611 full-time freshmen who applied for aid, 2,031 were judged to have need. Of these, 1,947 received aid, and 101 had their full need met. Average financial aid package met 62% of need; average scholarship/grant was $8,875; average loan was $3,491. For part-time students, average financial aid package was $9,749.
Students without need: 2 full-time freshmen who did not demonstrate need for aid received scholarships/grants; average award was $2,000. No-need awards available for academics, alumni affiliation, athletics, leadership, state/district residency.
Scholarships offered: 8 full-time freshmen received athletic scholarships; average amount $2,111.
Cumulative student debt: 45% of graduating class had student loans; average debt was $18,659.

FINANCIAL AID PROCEDURES
Forms required: FAFSA.
Dates and Deadlines: Priority date 3/2; no closing date. Applicants notified on a rolling basis starting 4/1; must reply within 2 week(s) of notification.

CONTACT
Diana Minor, Director of Financial Aid
3801 West Temple Avenue, Pomona, CA 91768-4019
(909) 869-3700

California State University: Bakersfield

Bakersfield, California
www.csub.edu Federal Code: 007993

4-year public university and liberal arts college in small city.
Enrollment: 7,086 undergrads, 11% part-time. 2,262 full-time freshmen.
Selectivity: Admits 50 to 75% of applicants. GED not accepted.

BASIC COSTS (2012-2013)
Tuition and fees: $7,207; out-of-state residents $18,367.
Room and board: $8,787.

FINANCIAL AID PICTURE (2011-2012)
Students with need: Out of 1,340 full-time freshmen who applied for aid, 1,014 were judged to have need. Of these, 630 received aid, and 23 had their full need met. Average financial aid package met 72% of need; average scholarship/grant was $8,322; average loan was $1,114. For part-time students, average financial aid package was $2,571.
Students without need: This college awards aid only to students with need.
Scholarships offered: 14 full-time freshmen received athletic scholarships; average amount $2,547.
Cumulative student debt: 86% of graduating class had student loans; average debt was $10,101.

FINANCIAL AID PROCEDURES
Forms required: FAFSA, state aid form.
Dates and Deadlines: Priority date 3/2; no closing date. Applicants notified on a rolling basis starting 4/15; must reply within 3 week(s) of notification.

CONTACT
Ron Radney, Director of Financial Aid & Scholarships
9001 Stockdale Highway, Bakersfield, CA 93311-1099
(661) 664-2011

California State University: Channel Islands

Camarillo, California
www.csuci.edu Federal Code: 039803

4-year public university in small city.
Enrollment: 4,908 undergrads, 18% part-time. 613 full-time freshmen.
Selectivity: Admits 50 to 75% of applicants.

BASIC COSTS (2012-2013)
Tuition and fees: $6,814; out-of-state residents $17,974.
Room and board: $12,650.

FINANCIAL AID PICTURE (2011-2012)
Students with need: Out of 417 full-time freshmen who applied for aid, 417 were judged to have need. Of these, 417 received aid, and 9 had their full need met. Average financial aid package met 100% of need; average scholarship/grant was $4,012. For part-time students, average financial aid package was $3,275.
Students without need: No-need awards available for academics, leadership, state/district residency.
Cumulative student debt: 50% of graduating class had student loans; average debt was $4,337.

FINANCIAL AID PROCEDURES
Forms required: FAFSA.
Dates and Deadlines: Priority date 3/2; no closing date. Applicants notified by 4/7.

CONTACT
Sunshine Garcia, Director of Financial Aid
One University Drive, Camarillo, CA 93012
(805) 437-8530

California State University: Chico

Chico, California
www.csuchico.edu Federal Code: 001146

4-year public university and liberal arts college in small city.
Enrollment: 15,316 undergrads, 8% part-time. 2,428 full-time freshmen.
Selectivity: Admits over 75% of applicants.

BASIC COSTS (2012-2013)
Tuition and fees: $7,438; out-of-state residents $18,598.
Room and board: $11,208.

FINANCIAL AID PICTURE (2011-2012)
Students with need: Out of 1,984 full-time freshmen who applied for aid, 1,480 were judged to have need. Of these, 1,382 received aid, and 185 had their full need met. Average financial aid package met 80% of need; average scholarship/grant was $10,449; average loan was $3,510. For part-time students, average financial aid package was $9,527.
Students without need: 58 full-time freshmen who did not demonstrate need for aid received scholarships/grants; average award was $211. No-need awards available for academics, art, athletics, leadership, minority status, music/drama, religious affiliation.
Scholarships offered: ***Merit:*** President's Scholar Award: 10 awards at $12,000 each; 12 awards at $1,000 each. ***Athletic:*** 20 full-time freshmen received athletic scholarships; average amount $4,400.

FINANCIAL AID PROCEDURES
Forms required: FAFSA.
Dates and Deadlines: Priority date 3/2; no closing date. Applicants notified on a rolling basis starting 3/2.

CONTACT
Dan Reed, Director of Financial Aid
400 West First Street, Chico, CA 95929-0722
(530) 898-6451

California State University: Dominguez Hills

Carson, California
www.csudh.edu Federal Code: 001141

4-year public university in small city.
Enrollment: 10,865 undergrads, 28% part-time. 1,100 full-time freshmen.
Selectivity: Admits over 75% of applicants.

BASIC COSTS (2012-2013)
Tuition and fees: $6,095; out-of-state residents $17,255.
Room and board: $10,733.
Additional info: Tuition/fee waivers available for adults.

FINANCIAL AID PICTURE (2011-2012)
Students with need: Out of 1,049 full-time freshmen who applied for aid, 984 were judged to have need. Of these, 978 received aid, and 21 had their full need met. Average financial aid package met 39% of need; average scholarship/grant was $6,108; average loan was $1,672. For part-time students, average financial aid package was $6,278.
Students without need: 35 full-time freshmen who did not demonstrate need for aid received scholarships/grants; average award was $4,518. No-need awards available for academics, alumni affiliation, art, athletics, leadership, music/drama.
Scholarships offered: 2 full-time freshmen received athletic scholarships; average amount $4,551.
Cumulative student debt: 54% of graduating class had student loans; average debt was $11,783.

FINANCIAL AID PROCEDURES
Forms required: FAFSA.
Dates and Deadlines: Priority date 3/2; no closing date. Applicants notified on a rolling basis starting 2/28; must reply within 4 week(s) of notification.
Transfers: Applicants notified on a rolling basis starting 2/28; must reply within 3 week(s) of notification.

CONTACT
Delores Lee, Director of Financial Aid
1000 East Victoria Street, Carson, CA 90747
(310) 243-3696

California State University: East Bay

Hayward, California
www.csueastbay.edu Federal Code: 001138

4-year public university in small city.
Enrollment: 10,529 undergrads, 13% part-time. 1,549 full-time freshmen.
Selectivity: Admits 50 to 75% of applicants.

BASIC COSTS (2012-2013)
Tuition and fees: $6,927; out-of-state residents $18,087.
Room and board: $11,352.

FINANCIAL AID PICTURE
Students with need: Need-based aid available for full-time and part-time students.

Students without need: No-need awards available for academics, athletics, music/drama.

FINANCIAL AID PROCEDURES
Forms required: FAFSA.
Dates and Deadlines: Priority date 3/2; no closing date. Applicants notified on a rolling basis starting 3/30; must reply within 3 week(s) of notification.

CONTACT
Rhonda Johnson, Director of Financial Aid
25800 Carlos Bee Boulevard, Hayward, CA 94542-3095
(510) 885-3018

California State University: Fresno

Fresno, California
www.csufresno.edu Federal Code: 001147

4-year public university in very large city.
Enrollment: 19,371 undergrads, 12% part-time. 3,036 full-time freshmen.
Selectivity: Admits 50 to 75% of applicants.

BASIC COSTS (2012-2013)
Tuition and fees: $6,762; out-of-state residents $17,922.
Room and board: $10,192.
Additional info: Tuition/fee waivers available for adults, minority students, unemployed or children of unemployed.

FINANCIAL AID PICTURE (2012-2013)
Students with need: Out of 2,656 full-time freshmen who applied for aid, 2,372 were judged to have need. Of these, 2,307 received aid, and 293 had their full need met. Average financial aid package met 69% of need; average scholarship/grant was $1,024; average loan was $3,114. For part-time students, average financial aid package was $9,042.
Students without need: 56 full-time freshmen who did not demonstrate need for aid received scholarships/grants; average award was $3,421. No-need awards available for academics, art, athletics, leadership, music/drama, ROTC, state/district residency.
Scholarships offered: 60 full-time freshmen received athletic scholarships; average amount $14,322.
Cumulative student debt: 71% of graduating class had student loans; average debt was $16,100.

FINANCIAL AID PROCEDURES
Forms required: FAFSA.
Dates and Deadlines: Closing date 3/3. Applicants notified on a rolling basis starting 4/1; must reply within 3 week(s) of notification.
Transfers: No deadline. Applicants notified on a rolling basis starting 4/1; must reply within 3 week(s) of notification.

CONTACT
Bernie Ogden, Director of Financial Aid
5150 North Maple Avenue, M/S JA 57, Fresno, CA 93740-8026
(559) 278-2182

California State University: Fullerton

Fullerton, California
www.fullerton.edu Federal Code: 001137

4-year public university in small city.
Enrollment: 32,278 undergrads, 19% part-time. 4,091 full-time freshmen.
Selectivity: Admits less than 50% of applicants.

BASIC COSTS (2012-2013)
Tuition and fees: $6,626; out-of-state residents $17,786.
Room and board: $12,097.

FINANCIAL AID PICTURE (2011-2012)
Students with need: Out of 3,507 full-time freshmen who applied for aid, 2,568 were judged to have need. Of these, 2,438 received aid, and 1,737 had their full need met. Average financial aid package met 84% of need; average scholarship/grant was $9,808; average loan was $1,917. For part-time students, average financial aid package was $10,871.
Students without need: 47 full-time freshmen who did not demonstrate need for aid received scholarships/grants; average award was $1,248. No-need awards available for academics.
Scholarships offered: 46 full-time freshmen received athletic scholarships; average amount $5,177.
Cumulative student debt: 40% of graduating class had student loans; average debt was $14,904.
Additional info: Fee waiver for children of veterans killed in action or with service-connected disability whose annual income is $5,000 or less.

FINANCIAL AID PROCEDURES
Forms required: FAFSA.
Dates and Deadlines: Priority date 3/2; closing date 7/7. Applicants notified on a rolling basis starting 4/22; must reply within 4 week(s) of notification.
Transfers: No deadline. Applicants notified on a rolling basis starting 4/22; must reply within 4 week(s) of notification.

CONTACT
Cecilia Schouwe, Director of Financial Aid
800 North State College Boulevard, Langsdorf Hall-114, Fullerton, CA 92831-6900
(657) 278-3125

California State University: Long Beach

Long Beach, California
www.csulb.edu Federal Code: 001139

4-year public university in large city.
Enrollment: 30,931 undergrads, 16% part-time. 4,097 full-time freshmen.
Selectivity: Admits less than 50% of applicants.

BASIC COSTS (2012-2013)
Tuition and fees: $6,738; out-of-state residents $17,898.
Room and board: $11,300.

FINANCIAL AID PICTURE (2012-2013)
Students with need: Out of 3,559 full-time freshmen who applied for aid, 2,987 were judged to have need. Of these, 2,710 received aid, and 2,045 had their full need met. Average financial aid package met 81% of need; average scholarship/grant was $7,982; average loan was $2,918. For part-time students, average financial aid package was $10,914.
Students without need: No-need awards available for academics, art, athletics, leadership, music/drama, state/district residency.
Scholarships offered: President's Scholar Award: full tuition and fees, campus housing, books.

FINANCIAL AID PROCEDURES
Forms required: FAFSA.
Dates and Deadlines: Priority date 3/2; no closing date. Applicants notified on a rolling basis starting 4/1; must reply within 4 week(s) of notification.
Transfers: Community college EOP students may be eligible for grant.

CONTACT
Nicholas Valdivia, Director of Financial Aid
1250 Bellflower Boulevard, Long Beach, CA 90840-0106
(562) 985-4641

California State University: Los Angeles

Los Angeles, California
www.calstatela.edu Federal Code: 001140

4-year public university in very large city.
Enrollment: 18,074 undergrads, 17% part-time. 2,368 full-time freshmen.
Selectivity: Admits 50 to 75% of applicants.

BASIC COSTS (2012-2013)
Tuition and fees: $6,839; out-of-state residents $17,999.
Room and board: $9,728.

FINANCIAL AID PICTURE (2011-2012)
Students with need: Out of 1,893 full-time freshmen who applied for aid, 1,776 were judged to have need. Of these, 1,741 received aid, and 169 had their full need met. Average financial aid package met 77% of need; average scholarship/grant was $14,748; average loan was $4,012. For part-time students, average financial aid package was $11,563.
Students without need: 10 full-time freshmen who did not demonstrate need for aid received scholarships/grants; average award was $1,932.
Scholarships offered: 3 full-time freshmen received athletic scholarships; average amount $7,871.

FINANCIAL AID PROCEDURES
Forms required: FAFSA.
Dates and Deadlines: Priority date 3/2; no closing date. Applicants notified on a rolling basis starting 4/1; must reply within 3 week(s) of notification.

CONTACT
Tamie Nguyen, Director of Center for Student Financial Aid
5151 State University Drive SA101, Los Angeles, CA 90032
(323) 343-6260

California State University: Monterey Bay

Seaside, California
www.csumb.edu Federal Code: 032603

4-year public liberal arts and teachers college in large town.
Enrollment: 5,194 undergrads, 6% part-time. 900 full-time freshmen.
Selectivity: Admits less than 50% of applicants.

BASIC COSTS (2012-2013)
Tuition and fees: $6,461; out-of-state residents $17,621.
Room and board: $9,498.

FINANCIAL AID PICTURE (2012-2013)
Students with need: Out of 806 full-time freshmen who applied for aid, 639 were judged to have need. Of these, 610 received aid, and 175 had their full need met. Average financial aid package met 78% of need; average scholarship/grant was $10,385; average loan was $3,316. For part-time students, average financial aid package was $5,988.
Students without need: 10 full-time freshmen who did not demonstrate need for aid received scholarships/grants; average award was $6,285. No-need awards available for academics, athletics, state/district residency.
Scholarships offered: 30 full-time freshmen received athletic scholarships; average amount $3,958.
Cumulative student debt: 78% of graduating class had student loans; average debt was $18,349.

FINANCIAL AID PROCEDURES
Forms required: FAFSA, state aid form.
Dates and Deadlines: Priority date 3/2; closing date 6/1. Applicants notified on a rolling basis starting 4/1.

CONTACT
Angeles Fuentes, Director of Financial Aid Services
100 Campus Center, Student Services Building, Seaside, CA 93955-8001
(831) 582-5100

California State University: Northridge

Northridge, California
www.csun.edu Federal Code: 001153

4-year public university in very large city.
Enrollment: 31,119 undergrads, 18% part-time. 5,162 full-time freshmen.
Selectivity: Admits less than 50% of applicants.

BASIC COSTS (2012-2013)
Tuition and fees: $7,002; out-of-state residents $18,162.
Room and board: $12,404.

FINANCIAL AID PICTURE (2011-2012)
Students with need: Out of 4,372 full-time freshmen who applied for aid, 3,994 were judged to have need. Of these, 3,994 received aid. For part-time students, average financial aid package was $14,004.
Students without need: 121 full-time freshmen who did not demonstrate need for aid received scholarships/grants; average award was $1,509. No-need awards available for academics, athletics, state/district residency.
Scholarships offered: 49 full-time freshmen received athletic scholarships; average amount $8,046.
Cumulative student debt: 46% of graduating class had student loans; average debt was $17,198.

FINANCIAL AID PROCEDURES
Forms required: FAFSA.
Dates and Deadlines: Priority date 3/2; no closing date. Applicants notified on a rolling basis starting 4/1.

CONTACT
Lili Vidal, Director of Financial Aid
18111 Nordhoff Street, Northridge, CA 91330-8207
(818) 677-4085

California State University: Sacramento

Sacramento, California
www.csus.edu Federal Code: 001233

4-year public university in very large city.
Enrollment: 25,457 undergrads, 19% part-time. 2,800 full-time freshmen.
Selectivity: Admits 50 to 75% of applicants.

BASIC COSTS (2012-2013)
Tuition and fees: $7,100; out-of-state residents $18,260.
Room and board: $11,724.

FINANCIAL AID PICTURE (2011-2012)
Students with need: Out of 2,500 full-time freshmen who applied for aid, 2,150 were judged to have need. Of these, 1,977 received aid, and 99 had their full need met. Average financial aid package met 60% of need; average scholarship/grant was $10,504; average loan was $3,367. For part-time students, average financial aid package was $7,502.
Students without need: 1 full-time freshmen who did not demonstrate need for aid received scholarships/grants; average award was $500.
Cumulative student debt: 43% of graduating class had student loans; average debt was $4,456.

FINANCIAL AID PROCEDURES
Forms required: FAFSA.
Dates and Deadlines: Applicants notified on a rolling basis starting 4/23; must reply within 4 week(s) of notification.

CONTACT
Craig Yamamoto, Financial Aid Director
6000 J Street, Sacramento, CA 95819-6048
(916) 278-6554

California State University: San Bernardino

San Bernardino, California
www.csusb.edu Federal Code: 001142

4-year public university and liberal arts college in small city.
Enrollment: 15,885 undergrads, 11% part-time. 2,391 full-time freshmen.
Selectivity: Admits 50 to 75% of applicants.

BASIC COSTS (2012-2013)

Tuition and fees: $7,047; out-of-state residents $18,207.
Room and board: $9,972.

FINANCIAL AID PICTURE (2012-2013)

Students with need: Out of 1,850 full-time freshmen who applied for aid, 1,689 were judged to have need. Of these, 1,646 received aid, and 89 had their full need met. Average financial aid package met 66% of need; average scholarship/grant was $9,764; average loan was $3,459. For part-time students, average financial aid package was $7,877.
Students without need: 4 full-time freshmen who did not demonstrate need for aid received scholarships/grants; average award was $4,713.
Scholarships offered: 17 full-time freshmen received athletic scholarships; average amount $18,699.
Cumulative student debt: 61% of graduating class had student loans; average debt was $22,691.

FINANCIAL AID PROCEDURES

Forms required: FAFSA, state aid form.
Dates and Deadlines: Priority date 3/2; no closing date. Applicants notified on a rolling basis starting 4/1.

CONTACT

Roseanna Ruiz, Director of Financial Aid
5500 University Parkway, San Bernardino, CA 92407-2397
(909) 537-7800

California State University: Stanislaus

Turlock, California
www.csustan.edu Federal Code: 001157

4-year public business and liberal arts college in small city.
Enrollment: 7,619 undergrads, 17% part-time. 1,082 full-time freshmen.
Selectivity: Admits 50 to 75% of applicants.

BASIC COSTS (2012-2013)

Tuition and fees: $7,080; out-of-state residents $18,240.
Room and board: $9,056.
Additional info: Tuition/fee waivers available for adults.

FINANCIAL AID PICTURE

Students with need: Need-based aid available for full-time and part-time students. Work study available nights, weekends, and for part-time students.
Students without need: No-need awards available for academics, alumni affiliation, art, athletics, leadership, minority status, music/drama, state/district residency.

FINANCIAL AID PROCEDURES

Forms required: FAFSA, state aid form.
Dates and Deadlines: Priority date 3/2; no closing date. Applicants notified on a rolling basis starting 3/15; must reply within 3 week(s) of notification.
Transfers: No deadline. Applicants notified on a rolling basis starting 3/15; must reply within 3 week(s) of notification.

CONTACT

Noelia Gonzales, Director of Financial Aid and Scholarships
One University Circle, Turlock, CA 95382-0256
(209) 667-3336

California University of Management and Sciences

Anaheim, California
www.calums.edu Federal Code: 041331

4-year private university and business college in very large city.
Enrollment: 43 undergrads.
Selectivity: Admits over 75% of applicants. GED not accepted.

BASIC COSTS (2013-2014)

Tuition and fees: $8,120.

FINANCIAL AID PICTURE (2012-2013)

Students with need: Need-based aid available for full-time students.
Students without need: This college awards aid only to students with need.

FINANCIAL AID PROCEDURES

Forms required: FAFSA, institutional form.
Dates and Deadlines: Applicants notified on a rolling basis; must reply within 2 week(s) of notification.
Transfers: No deadline. Applicants notified on a rolling basis; must reply within 2 week(s) of notification.

CONTACT

Jeffrey Beasca, Director of Administration
721 North Euclid Streeet, Anaheim, CA 92801-4116
(714) 533-3946

Carrington College California: Emeryville

Emeryville, California
www.carrington.edu

2-year for-profit technical college in small town.
Enrollment: 148 undergrads.

BASIC COSTS (2012-2013)

Additional info: Program cost $17,236 (36 weeks). Costs are provided for the largest program (Medical Assisting). Other programs may vary.

FINANCIAL AID PICTURE

Students with need: Need-based aid available for full-time students.

FINANCIAL AID PROCEDURES

Forms required: FAFSA.
Dates and Deadlines: Applicants notified on a rolling basis.

CONTACT

6001 Shellmound Street, #145, Emeryville, CA 94608
(510) 601-0133

Cerro Coso Community College

Ridgecrest, California
www.cerrocoso.edu Federal Code: 010111

2-year public community college in large town.
Enrollment: 2,490 undergrads.
Selectivity: Open admission.

BASIC COSTS (2012-2013)

Tuition and fees: $1,380; out-of-state residents $7,080.
Per-credit charge: $46; out-of-state residents $236.

FINANCIAL AID PICTURE

Students with need: Need-based aid available for full-time and part-time students. Work study available nights.

FINANCIAL AID PROCEDURES
Forms required: FAFSA.
Dates and Deadlines: Priority date 5/15; no closing date. Applicants notified on a rolling basis starting 6/1; must reply within 2 week(s) of notification.

CONTACT
JoAnn Spiller, Director of Financial Aid and Scholarships
3000 College Heights Boulevard, Ridgecrest, CA 93555-7777
(760) 384-6221

Chabot College
Hayward, California
www.chabotcollege.edu Federal Code: 001162

2-year public community college in large city.
Enrollment: 8,929 undergrads.
Selectivity: Open admission; but selective for some programs.

BASIC COSTS (2012-2013)
Tuition and fees: $1,414; out-of-state residents $8,194.
Per-credit charge: $46; out-of-state residents $272.

FINANCIAL AID PICTURE
Students with need: Work study available nights, weekends, and for part-time students.
Additional info: Tuition and/or fee waivers for low-income students.

FINANCIAL AID PROCEDURES
Forms required: FAFSA, institutional form.
Dates and Deadlines: Priority date 8/1; no closing date. Applicants notified on a rolling basis.

CONTACT
Kathryn Linzmeyer, Director of Financial Aid
25555 Hesperian Boulevard, Hayward, CA 94545
(510) 723-6746

Chaffey College
Rancho Cucamonga, California
www.chaffey.edu Federal Code: 001163

2-year public community college in small city.
Enrollment: 12,978 undergrads.
Selectivity: Open admission.

BASIC COSTS (2012-2013)
Tuition and fees: $1,414; out-of-state residents $6,784.
Per-credit charge: $46; out-of-state residents $225.
Additional info: Tuition/fee waivers available for adults.

FINANCIAL AID PICTURE
Students with need: Need-based aid available for full-time and part-time students.
Students without need: No-need awards available for academics.
Additional info: State of California Board of Governors fee waivers to qualified state residents. Criteria for eligibility: households which receive public assistance, meet state's low income guidelines, and demonstrate need as defined by Title IV programs.

FINANCIAL AID PROCEDURES
Forms required: FAFSA.
Dates and Deadlines: Applicants notified on a rolling basis starting 7/15; must reply within 2 week(s) of notification.

CONTACT
Karen Sanders, Financial Aid Supervisor
5885 Haven Avenue, Rancho Cucamonga, CA 91701-3002
(909) 652-6006

Chapman University
Orange, California
www.chapman.edu Federal Code: 001164

4-year private university and liberal arts college in very large city, affiliated with Christian Church (Disciples of Christ).
Enrollment: 5,645 undergrads, 4% part-time. 1,273 full-time freshmen.
Selectivity: Admits less than 50% of applicants.

BASIC COSTS (2013-2014)
Tuition and fees: $43,573.
Per-credit charge: $1,330.
Room and board: $12,446.

FINANCIAL AID PICTURE
Students with need: Need-based aid available for full-time and part-time students. Work study available nights, weekends, and for part-time students.
Students without need: No-need awards available for academics, alumni affiliation, art, music/drama, religious affiliation, ROTC.

FINANCIAL AID PROCEDURES
Forms required: FAFSA, state aid form.
Dates and Deadlines: Priority date 3/2; no closing date. Applicants notified on a rolling basis starting 3/15; must reply within 3 week(s) of notification.
Transfers: No deadline. Applicants notified on a rolling basis starting 3/15; must reply within 3 week(s) of notification.

CONTACT
Jim Whitaker, Associate Vice Chancellor of Enrollment Management and Chief Financial Aid Officer
Admission Office, Orange, CA 92866
(714) 997-6741

Charles Drew University of Medicine and Science
Los Angeles, California
www.cdrewu.edu Federal Code: 013653

4-year private university and health science college in very large city.
Enrollment: 98 undergrads, 70% part-time. 1 full-time freshmen.
Selectivity: Admits over 75% of applicants.

BASIC COSTS (2013-2014)
Tuition and fees: $14,701.
Per-credit charge: $487.
Additional info: Tuition charges are per unit, and vary by degree level. Additional fees are required for some academic programs.

FINANCIAL AID PICTURE (2012-2013)
Students with need: Average financial aid package for all full-time undergraduates was $10,309; for part-time $7,416. 61% awarded as scholarships/grants, 39% awarded as loans/jobs. Work study available nights, weekends, and for part-time students.

FINANCIAL AID PROCEDURES
Forms required: FAFSA.
Dates and Deadlines: Applicants notified on a rolling basis.
Transfers: No deadline. Applicants notified on a rolling basis.

CONTACT
Pierre Flood, Director of Financial Aid
1731 East 120th Street, Los Angeles, CA 90059
(323) 563-4824

Citrus College
Glendora, California
www.citruscollege.edu Federal Code: 001166

2-year public community college in large town.
Enrollment: 8,342 undergrads.
Selectivity: Open admission.

BASIC COSTS (2012-2013)
Tuition and fees: $1,448; out-of-state residents $7,958.
Per-credit charge: $46; out-of-state residents $263.

FINANCIAL AID PICTURE (2011-2012)
Students with need: 87% of average financial aid package awarded as scholarships/grants, 13% awarded as loans/jobs. Need-based aid available for part-time students. Work study available nights, weekends, and for part-time students.

FINANCIAL AID PROCEDURES
Forms required: FAFSA.
Dates and Deadlines: Closing date 3/1. Applicants notified on a rolling basis; must reply within 2 week(s) of notification.

CONTACT
Carol Thomas, Director of Financial Aid
1000 West Foothill Boulevard, Glendora, CA 91741-1899
(626) 914-8592

City College of San Francisco
San Francisco, California
www.ccsf.edu Federal Code: 012874

2-year public community college in very large city.
Enrollment: 19,480 undergrads.
Selectivity: Open admission; but selective for some programs.

BASIC COSTS (2012-2013)
Tuition and fees: $1,414; out-of-state residents $7,024.
Per-credit charge: $46; out-of-state residents $233.
Additional info: Tuition/fee waivers available for unemployed or children of unemployed.

FINANCIAL AID PICTURE
Students with need: Work study available nights, weekends, and for part-time students.
Additional info: Board of Governor fee waiver for low income students.

FINANCIAL AID PROCEDURES
Forms required: FAFSA.
Dates and Deadlines: Priority date 3/1; no closing date. Applicants notified on a rolling basis starting 7/1.

CONTACT
Jorge Bell, Dean, Financial Aid
Office of Admissions and Records E-107, San Francisco, CA 94112
(415) 239-3576

Claremont McKenna College
Claremont, California Federal Code: 001170
www.cmc.edu CSS Code: 4054

4-year private liberal arts college in large town.
Enrollment: 1,254 undergrads. 291 full-time freshmen.
Selectivity: Admits less than 50% of applicants.

BASIC COSTS (2013-2014)
Tuition and fees: $45,625.
Room and board: $14,385.

FINANCIAL AID PICTURE (2012-2013)
Students with need: Out of 158 full-time freshmen who applied for aid, 133 were judged to have need. Of these, 133 received aid, and 133 had their full need met. Average financial aid package met 100% of need; average scholarship/grant was $38,393. Need-based aid available for part-time students.
Students without need: 11 full-time freshmen who did not demonstrate need for aid received scholarships/grants; average award was $20,395. No-need awards available for academics, leadership.
Scholarships offered: McKenna Achievement Award: $10,000 for 4 years; based on strong academic record and outstanding leadership and involvement. Seaver Leadership Scholarship: full tuition for 4 years; awarded to students who demonstrate exceptional promise to become leaders intent on making a positive impact in the world. Interdisciplinary Science Scholarship: full tuition for 4 years; awarded to students who want to major in a science and a non-science and have financial need.
Cumulative student debt: 31% of graduating class had student loans; average debt was $23,179.

FINANCIAL AID PROCEDURES
Forms required: FAFSA, CSS PROFILE, state aid form.
Dates and Deadlines: Closing date 2/1. Applicants notified by 4/1; must reply by 5/1.
Transfers: Closing date 4/1. Applicants notified by 5/1; must reply by 6/1.

CONTACT
Georgette DeVeres, Associate Vice President and Dean of Admission and Financial Aid
888 Columbia Avenue, Claremont, CA 91711
(909) 621-8356

Coastline Community College
Fountain Valley, California
www.coastline.edu Federal Code: 013536

2-year public community college in small city.
Enrollment: 4,096 undergrads.
Selectivity: Open admission.

BASIC COSTS (2012-2013)
Tuition and fees: $1,414; out-of-state residents $7,834.
Per-credit charge: $46; out-of-state residents $260.
Additional info: Tuition/fee waivers available for unemployed or children of unemployed.

FINANCIAL AID PICTURE
Students with need: Need-based aid available for full-time and part-time students.
Students without need: This college awards aid only to students with need.
Additional info: Board of Governor's Grant: statewide fee waiver program for students or dependents receiving HFOL/TANF, SSI, General Relief, or whose income meets set standards or who are considered eligible through Federal needs analysis.

FINANCIAL AID PROCEDURES
Forms required: FAFSA, institutional form.
Dates and Deadlines: Priority date 3/2; no closing date. Applicants notified on a rolling basis starting 8/1; must reply within 2 week(s) of notification.

CONTACT
Cynthia Pienkowski, Director of Financial Aid
11460 Warner Avenue, Fountain Valley, CA 92708
(714) 241-6239

Cogswell Polytechnical College

Sunnyvale, California
www.cogswell.edu Federal Code: 001177

4-year for-profit visual arts and engineering college in small city.
Enrollment: 388 undergrads, 36% part-time. 52 full-time freshmen.
Selectivity: Admits less than 50% of applicants.

BASIC COSTS (2013-2014)
Tuition and fees: $24,540.
Per-credit charge: $812.
Room only: $6,000.

FINANCIAL AID PICTURE (2012-2013)
Students with need: 57% of average financial aid package awarded as scholarships/grants, 43% awarded as loans/jobs. Need-based aid available for part-time students.
Students without need: No-need awards available for academics.

FINANCIAL AID PROCEDURES
Forms required: FAFSA.
Dates and Deadlines: Priority date 3/8; no closing date. Applicants notified on a rolling basis starting 4/30; must reply within 4 week(s) of notification.
Transfers: No deadline. Applicants notified by 4/1; must reply within 4 week(s) of notification.

CONTACT
Lisa Mandy, Director of Financial Aid
1175 Bordeaux Drive, Sunnyvale, CA 94089-1299
(800) 264-7955

Coleman University

San Diego, California
www.coleman.edu Federal Code: 009273

4-year private technical college in very large city.
Enrollment: 608 undergrads, 26% part-time. 64 full-time freshmen.
Selectivity: Open admission; but selective for some programs.

BASIC COSTS (2013-2014)
Tuition and fees: $19,600.
Per-credit charge: $325.
Additional info: Tuition quoted is one year cost for undergraduate study. Associate's: $35,000. Bachelor's: $58,500. Master's: $23,100, for full programs.

FINANCIAL AID PICTURE (2011-2012)
Students with need: Out of 46 full-time freshmen who applied for aid, 46 were judged to have need. Of these, 46 received aid, and 46 had their full need met. Average financial aid package met 84% of need; average scholarship/grant was $3,464; average loan was $3,119. For part-time students, average financial aid package was $6,793.
Students without need: This college awards aid only to students with need.
Cumulative student debt: 54% of graduating class had student loans; average debt was $4,679.

FINANCIAL AID PROCEDURES
Forms required: FAFSA, institutional form.
Dates and Deadlines: Applicants notified on a rolling basis starting 1/2; must reply within 1 week(s) of notification.
Transfers: No deadline. Applicants notified on a rolling basis starting 1/2; must reply within 1 week(s) of notification.

CONTACT
Christina Miller, Director of Financial Aid
8888 Balboa Avenue, San Diego, CA 92123
(858) 499-0202

Coleman University: San Marcos

San Marcos, California
www.coleman.edu Federal Code: 009273

2-year for-profit technical college in small city.
Enrollment: 99 undergrads, 39% part-time.
Selectivity: Open admission; but selective for some programs.

BASIC COSTS (2013-2014)
Tuition and fees: $19,600.
Per-credit charge: $325.
Additional info: Tuition quoted is one year cost for undergraduate study. Associate's: $35,000. Bachelor's: $58,500. Master's: $23,100, for full programs.

FINANCIAL AID PICTURE (2012-2013)
Students with need: Need-based aid available for full-time and part-time students. Work study available nights.
Students without need: This college awards aid only to students with need.
Cumulative student debt: 54% of graduating class had student loans; average debt was $4,679.

FINANCIAL AID PROCEDURES
Forms required: FAFSA, institutional form.
Dates and Deadlines: Applicants notified on a rolling basis starting 1/2; must reply within 1 week(s) of notification.
Transfers: No deadline. Applicants notified on a rolling basis starting 1/2; must reply within 1 week(s) of notification.

CONTACT
Christina Miller, Director of Financial Services
1284 West San Marcos Boulevard, San Marcos, CA 92069
(858) 499-0202

College of Marin

Kentfield, California
www.marin.edu Federal Code: 001178

2-year public community college in small town.
Enrollment: 3,360 undergrads.
Selectivity: Open admission; but selective for some programs.

BASIC COSTS (2012-2013)
Tuition and fees: $1,414; out-of-state residents $7,474.
Per-credit charge: $46; out-of-state residents $248.

FINANCIAL AID PICTURE
Students with need: Need-based aid available for full-time and part-time students.
Students without need: This college awards aid only to students with need.

FINANCIAL AID PROCEDURES
Forms required: FAFSA.
Dates and Deadlines: Priority date 3/2; no closing date. Applicants notified on a rolling basis starting 5/15.

CONTACT
David Cook, Director of Financial Aid
835 College Avenue, Kentfield, CA 94904
(415) 457-8811 ext. 7405

College of San Mateo
San Mateo, California
www.collegeofsanmateo.edu Federal Code: 001181

2-year public community college in small city.
Enrollment: 5,125 undergrads.
Selectivity: Open admission; but selective for some programs.

BASIC COSTS (2012-2013)
Tuition and fees: $1,418; out-of-state residents $7,778.
Per-credit charge: $46; out-of-state residents $258.

FINANCIAL AID PICTURE (2012-2013)
Students with need: 92% of average financial aid package awarded as scholarships/grants, 8% awarded as loans/jobs. Need-based aid available for part-time students.
Students without need: This college awards aid only to students with need.

FINANCIAL AID PROCEDURES
Forms required: FAFSA.
Dates and Deadlines: Applicants notified on a rolling basis starting 6/15.
Transfers: No deadline. Applicants notified on a rolling basis.

CONTACT
Claudia Menjivar, Director of Financial Aid
1700 West Hillsdale Boulevard, San Mateo, CA 94402-3784
(650) 574-6147

College of the Canyons
Santa Clarita, California
www.canyons.edu Federal Code: 008903

2-year public community college in large city.
Enrollment: 9,720 undergrads. 1,055 full-time freshmen.
Selectivity: Open admission; but selective for some programs.

BASIC COSTS (2012-2013)
Tuition and fees: $1,430; out-of-state residents $6,530.
Per-credit charge: $46; out-of-state residents $216.

FINANCIAL AID PICTURE (2011-2012)
Students with need: 64% of average financial aid package awarded as scholarships/grants, 36% awarded as loans/jobs. Need-based aid available for part-time students. Work study available nights, weekends, and for part-time students.
Students without need: No-need awards available for academics, alumni affiliation, art, athletics, job skills, leadership, minority status, music/drama, religious affiliation, ROTC, state/district residency.

FINANCIAL AID PROCEDURES
Forms required: FAFSA, state aid form, institutional form.
Dates and Deadlines: Closing date 3/2. Applicants notified on a rolling basis starting 6/1; must reply within 4 week(s) of notification.
Transfers: No deadline.

CONTACT
Thomas Bilbruck, Director, Financial Aid and Scholarships
26455 Rockwell Canyon Road, Santa Clarita, CA 91355
(661) 362-3242

College of the Desert
Palm Desert, California
www.collegeofthedesert.edu Federal Code: 001182

2-year public community college in small city.
Enrollment: 6,680 undergrads.
Selectivity: Open admission; but selective for some programs.

BASIC COSTS (2012-2013)
Tuition and fees: $1,417; out-of-state residents $6,997.
Per-credit charge: $46; out-of-state residents $232.
Additional info: Tuition/fee waivers available for adults, minority students, unemployed or children of unemployed.

FINANCIAL AID PICTURE
Students with need: Need-based aid available for full-time and part-time students. Work study available nights, weekends, and for part-time students.
Students without need: No-need awards available for academics, art, minority status, music/drama.

FINANCIAL AID PROCEDURES
Forms required: FAFSA.
Dates and Deadlines: Priority date 3/2; no closing date. Applicants notified on a rolling basis starting 7/1.
Transfers: No deadline. Applicants notified on a rolling basis starting 7/1.

CONTACT
Ken Lira, Director of Financial Aid
43500 Monterey Avenue, Palm Desert, CA 92260
(760) 773-2532

College of the Redwoods
Eureka, California
www.redwoods.edu Federal Code: 001185

2-year public community college in large town.
Enrollment: 6,874 undergrads.
Selectivity: Open admission; but selective for some programs.

BASIC COSTS (2012-2013)
Tuition and fees: $1,404; out-of-state residents $8,274.
Per-credit charge: $46; out-of-state residents $275.
Room and board: $7,298.

FINANCIAL AID PICTURE
Students with need: Need-based aid available for full-time and part-time students.

FINANCIAL AID PROCEDURES
Forms required: FAFSA, institutional form.
Dates and Deadlines: Priority date 4/15; no closing date. Applicants notified on a rolling basis starting 5/1; must reply within 6 week(s) of notification.

CONTACT
Lynn Thiesen, Director of Financial Aid
7351 Tompkins Hill Road, Eureka, CA 95501-9300
(707) 476-4182

College of the Siskiyous
Weed, California
www.siskiyous.edu Federal Code: 001187

2-year public community and junior college in small town.
Enrollment: 1,220 undergrads.
Selectivity: Open admission; but selective for some programs.

BASIC COSTS (2012-2013)
Tuition and fees: $1,410; out-of-state residents $8,070.
Per-credit charge: $46; out-of-state residents $268.
Room and board: $8,725.

FINANCIAL AID PICTURE
Students with need: Need-based aid available for full-time and part-time students. Work study available nights, weekends, and for part-time students.

Students without need: This college awards aid only to students with need.

FINANCIAL AID PROCEDURES
Forms required: FAFSA.
Dates and Deadlines: Priority date 4/30; no closing date. Applicants notified on a rolling basis starting 6/1; must reply within 2 week(s) of notification.
Transfers: No deadline. Applicants notified on a rolling basis. Academic transcripts required.

CONTACT
Andrea Castro, Assistant Director of Financial Aid
800 College Avenue, Weed, CA 96094-2899
(530) 938-5209

Columbia College
Sonora, California
www.gocolumbia.edu Federal Code: 007707

2-year public community college in small town.
Enrollment: 579 undergrads, 56% part-time. 257 full-time freshmen.
Selectivity: Open admission.

BASIC COSTS (2012-2013)
Tuition and fees: $1,408; out-of-state residents $7,528.
Per-credit charge: $46; out-of-state residents $250.

FINANCIAL AID PICTURE (2011-2012)
Students with need: Need-based aid available for full-time and part-time students.
Students without need: No-need awards available for academics.

FINANCIAL AID PROCEDURES
Forms required: FAFSA, state aid form, institutional form.
Dates and Deadlines: Priority date 3/2; closing date 6/1. Applicants notified on a rolling basis starting 6/15; must reply within 2 week(s) of notification.

CONTACT
Marnie Shively, Director of Student Financial Services
11600 Columbia College Drive, Sonora, CA 95370
(209) 588-5105

Concordia University
Irvine, California
www.cui.edu Federal Code: 013885

4-year private university and liberal arts college in small city, affiliated with Lutheran Church - Missouri Synod.
Enrollment: 1,729 undergrads, 8% part-time. 300 full-time freshmen.
Selectivity: Admits 50 to 75% of applicants.

BASIC COSTS (2012-2013)
Tuition and fees: $28,500.
Per-credit charge: $870.
Room and board: $8,760.

FINANCIAL AID PICTURE (2012-2013)
Students with need: Out of 278 full-time freshmen who applied for aid, 226 were judged to have need. Of these, 226 received aid, and 33 had their full need met. Average financial aid package met 68% of need; average scholarship/grant was $15,415; average loan was $3,414. For part-time students, average financial aid package was $6,388.
Students without need: 52 full-time freshmen who did not demonstrate need for aid received scholarships/grants; average award was $7,673. No-need awards available for academics, athletics, music/drama, religious affiliation.
Scholarships offered: ***Merit:*** Presidential Honors: up to full tuition; based on 3.9 - 4.0 GPA and 1300 SAT or 29 ACT. Regent: up to $12,500; based on 3.8 - 4.0 GPA. Provost: up to $10,000; based on 3.4 - 3.79 GPA. Dean's: up to $7,500; based on 3.0 - 3.39 GPA. Phi Theta Kappa: up to $5,000; based on 2.50-4.00 GPA. ***Athletic:*** 21 full-time freshmen received athletic scholarships.
Cumulative student debt: 67% of graduating class had student loans; average debt was $29,091.

FINANCIAL AID PROCEDURES
Forms required: FAFSA, state aid form.
Dates and Deadlines: Closing date 3/2. Applicants notified on a rolling basis starting 3/15; must reply within 4 week(s) of notification.
Transfers: Applicants notified on a rolling basis starting 3/15; must reply within 4 week(s) of notification.

CONTACT
Lori McDonald, Director of Financial Aid
1530 Concordia West, Irvine, CA 92612-3203
(949) 214-3066

Copper Mountain College
Joshua Tree, California
www.cmccd.edu Federal Code: 035424

2-year public community college in small town.
Enrollment: 1,120 undergrads.
Selectivity: Open admission; but selective for some programs.

BASIC COSTS (2012-2013)
Tuition and fees: $1,382; out-of-state residents $7,082.
Per-credit charge: $46; out-of-state residents $236.

FINANCIAL AID PICTURE (2011-2012)
Students with need: Need-based aid available for full-time and part-time students.

FINANCIAL AID PROCEDURES
Forms required: FAFSA.
Dates and Deadlines: Priority date 3/2; no closing date.

CONTACT
Brian Heinemann, Director of Financial Aid
6162 Rotary Way, Joshua Tree, CA 92252
(866) 366-3791 ext. 4235

Crafton Hills College
Yucaipa, California
www.craftonhills.edu Federal Code: 009272

2-year public community college in small city.
Enrollment: 3,430 undergrads.
Selectivity: Open admission.

BASIC COSTS (2012-2013)
Tuition and fees: $1,408; out-of-state residents $6,268.
Per-credit charge: $46; out-of-state residents $208.
Additional info: Tuition/fee waivers available for adults, minority students, unemployed or children of unemployed.

FINANCIAL AID PICTURE (2012-2013)
Students with need: Need-based aid available for full-time and part-time students. Work study available nights.
Students without need: This college awards aid only to students with need.

FINANCIAL AID PROCEDURES
Forms required: FAFSA, institutional form.

Dates and Deadlines: Priority date 4/15; closing date 6/2. Applicants notified on a rolling basis starting 7/31; must reply within 2 week(s) of notification.
Transfers: Priority date 1/2; closing date 3/2.

CONTACT
John Muskavitch, Director of Financial Aid
11711 Sand Canyon Road, Yucaipa, CA 92399-1799
(909) 794-2161 ext. 3242

Cuyamaca College
El Cajon, California
www.cuyamaca.edu Federal Code: 014435

2-year public community college in small city.
Enrollment: 5,203 undergrads.
Selectivity: Open admission.

BASIC COSTS (2012-2013)
Tuition and fees: $1,420; out-of-state residents $7,120.
Per-credit charge: $46; out-of-state residents $236.

FINANCIAL AID PICTURE
Students with need: Work study available nights, weekends, and for part-time students.

FINANCIAL AID PROCEDURES
Forms required: FAFSA.
Dates and Deadlines: Priority date 3/2; no closing date. Applicants notified on a rolling basis; must reply within 2 week(s) of notification.

CONTACT
Ray Reyes, Financial Aid Director
900 Rancho San Diego Parkway, El Cajon, CA 92019-4304
(619) 660-4201

Cypress College
Cypress, California
www.cypresscollege.edu Federal Code: 001193

2-year public community college in small city.
Enrollment: 12,265 undergrads. 709 full-time freshmen.
Selectivity: Open admission.

BASIC COSTS (2012-2013)
Tuition and fees: $1,412; out-of-state residents $7,472.
Per-credit charge: $46; out-of-state residents $248.

FINANCIAL AID PICTURE (2011-2012)
Students with need: 88% of average financial aid package awarded as scholarships/grants, 12% awarded as loans/jobs. Need-based aid available for part-time students.

FINANCIAL AID PROCEDURES
Forms required: FAFSA.

CONTACT
Keith Cobb, Director of Financial Aid
9200 Valley View Street, Cypress, CA 90630
(714) 484-7114

De Anza College
Cupertino, California
www.deanza.edu Federal Code: 004480

2-year public community college in large town.
Enrollment: 17,254 undergrads.
Selectivity: Open admission; but selective for some programs.

BASIC COSTS (2012-2013)
Tuition and fees: $1,495; out-of-state residents $7,705.
Per-credit charge: $31; out-of-state residents $169.

FINANCIAL AID PICTURE (2011-2012)
Students with need: 70% of average financial aid package awarded as scholarships/grants, 30% awarded as loans/jobs. Need-based aid available for part-time students.
Students without need: This college awards aid only to students with need.

FINANCIAL AID PROCEDURES
Forms required: FAFSA.
Dates and Deadlines: Applicants notified on a rolling basis starting 5/15; must reply within 2 week(s) of notification.

CONTACT
Rob Mieso, Director of Financial Aid
21250 Stevens Creek Boulevard, Cupertino, CA 95014
(408) 864-8718

Deep Springs College
Dyer, Nevada
www.deepsprings.edu Federal Code: 015483

2-year private liberal arts college for men in rural community.
Enrollment: 25 undergrads. 13 full-time freshmen.
Selectivity: Admits less than 50% of applicants.

BASIC COSTS (2013-2014)
Additional info: Deep Springs does not charge tuition, room or board. There are no student fees. A damage deposit of $500 is required of each student. All students receive full scholarship covering tuition, room, and board valued at $56,000.

FINANCIAL AID PICTURE
Students with need: Work study available nights, weekends, and for part-time students.
Students without need: No-need awards available for academics.

CONTACT
David Neidorf, President
Applications Committee, Dyer, NV 89010-9803
(760) 872-2000 ext. 45

DeVry University: Pomona
Pomona, California
www.devry.edu Federal Code: 023329

4-year for-profit university in small city.
Enrollment: 2,225 undergrads, 64% part-time. 67 full-time freshmen.

BASIC COSTS (2012-2013)
Tuition and fees: $16,076.
Per-credit charge: $609.

FINANCIAL AID PICTURE
Students with need: Need-based aid available for full-time and part-time students.
Students without need: This college awards aid only to students with need.

FINANCIAL AID PROCEDURES
Forms required: FAFSA.
Dates and Deadlines: Applicants notified on a rolling basis.

CONTACT
Kathy Odom, Director of Financial Aid
901 Corporate Center Drive, Pomona, CA 91768-2642

Diablo Valley College
Pleasant Hill, California
www.dvc.edu Federal Code: 001191

2-year public community college in large town.
Enrollment: 10,205 undergrads. 572 full-time freshmen.
Selectivity: Open admission.

BASIC COSTS (2012-2013)
Tuition and fees: $1,380; out-of-state residents $7,230.
Per-credit charge: $46; out-of-state residents $241.

FINANCIAL AID PICTURE
Students with need: Need-based aid available for full-time and part-time students.

FINANCIAL AID PROCEDURES
Forms required: FAFSA, state aid form, institutional form.
Dates and Deadlines: Priority date 3/2; closing date 5/1. Applicants notified on a rolling basis starting 6/1; must reply within 2 week(s) of notification.

CONTACT
Emily Stone, Dean, CalWORKS, EOPS/CARE, Financial Aid and Scholarship
321 Golf Club Road, Pleasant Hill, CA 94523-1529
(925) 696-2009

Dominican University of California
San Rafael, California
www.dominican.edu Federal Code: 001196

4-year private university in small city.
Enrollment: 1,600 undergrads, 18% part-time. 279 full-time freshmen.
Selectivity: Admits 50 to 75% of applicants.

BASIC COSTS (2013-2014)
Tuition and fees: $40,600.
Per-credit charge: $1,695.
Room and board: $13,940.

FINANCIAL AID PICTURE (2011-2012)
Students with need: Out of 249 full-time freshmen who applied for aid, 228 were judged to have need. Of these, 228 received aid, and 18 had their full need met. Average financial aid package met 62% of need; average scholarship/grant was $24,659; average loan was $3,853. For part-time students, average financial aid package was $9,905.
Students without need: 42 full-time freshmen who did not demonstrate need for aid received scholarships/grants; average award was $13,354. No-need awards available for academics, alumni affiliation, athletics, leadership, minority status, music/drama.
Scholarships offered: 7 full-time freshmen received athletic scholarships; average amount $4,036.
Cumulative student debt: 89% of graduating class had student loans; average debt was $39,125.
Additional info: 4-year guarantee program.

FINANCIAL AID PROCEDURES
Forms required: FAFSA, institutional form.
Dates and Deadlines: Priority date 3/2; no closing date. Applicants notified on a rolling basis starting 3/15; must reply within 2 week(s) of notification.
Transfers: Must reply within 2 week(s) of notification.

CONTACT
Shanon Little, Director of Financial Aid
50 Acacia Avenue, San Rafael, CA 94901-2298
(415) 257-1350

East Los Angeles College
Monterey Park, California
www.elac.edu Federal Code: 001222

2-year public community college in very large city.
Enrollment: 16,040 undergrads.
Selectivity: Open admission; but selective for some programs.

BASIC COSTS (2012-2013)
Tuition and fees: $1,402; out-of-state residents $7,102.
Per-credit charge: $46; out-of-state residents $236.
Additional info: Tuition/fee waivers available for unemployed or children of unemployed.

FINANCIAL AID PICTURE
Students with need: Need-based aid available for full-time and part-time students. Work study available nights, weekends, and for part-time students.
Students without need: This college awards aid only to students with need.
Additional info: Need-based enrollment fee waivers available through a state aid program.

FINANCIAL AID PROCEDURES
Forms required: FAFSA, institutional form.
Dates and Deadlines: Priority date 4/30; no closing date. Applicants notified on a rolling basis; must reply within 4.3 week(s) of notification.
Transfers: No deadline.

CONTACT
Lindy Fong, Financial Aid Manager
1301 Avenida Cesar Chavez, Monterey Park, CA 91754-6099
(323) 265-8738

El Camino College
Torrance, California
www.elcamino.edu Federal Code: 001197

2-year public community and junior college in very large city.
Enrollment: 11,769 undergrads.
Selectivity: Open admission; but selective for some programs.

BASIC COSTS (2012-2013)
Tuition and fees: $1,415; out-of-state residents $6,785.
Per-credit charge: $46; out-of-state residents $225.
Additional info: Tuition/fee waivers available for adults.

FINANCIAL AID PICTURE
Students with need: Need-based aid available for full-time and part-time students.
Students without need: No-need awards available for academics, art, athletics, leadership, music/drama.
Additional info: Students may apply for Pell grants until June 30.

FINANCIAL AID PROCEDURES
Forms required: FAFSA, institutional form.
Dates and Deadlines: Priority date 3/2; closing date 6/30. Applicants notified on a rolling basis starting 7/15.
Transfers: Outside scholarships must be reported to financial aid office.

CONTACT
Hortense Cooper, Director of Financial Aid
16007 Crenshaw Boulevard, Torrance, CA 90506
(310) 660-3593 ext. 3493

Empire College

Santa Rosa, California
www.empcol.edu Federal Code: 009032

2-year for-profit business college in small city.
Enrollment: 306 undergrads.
Selectivity: Open admission; but selective for some programs.

BASIC COSTS (2012-2013)

Tuition and fees: $10,125.
Additional info: On-campus room and board rage: $539 per month.

FINANCIAL AID PICTURE

Students with need: Need-based aid available for full-time students.
Students without need: This college awards aid only to students with need.
Scholarships offered: Dean's Scholarship for high school seniors: 10 awarded; $250-$1,500. Dean's Scholarships for Empire College students: 7 awarded; $250-$1,000. Based on academic achievement, letter of intent, extracurricular activities and letter of recommendation.

FINANCIAL AID PROCEDURES

Forms required: FAFSA.
Dates and Deadlines: Applicants notified on a rolling basis.

CONTACT

Mary O'Brien, Financial Aid Officer
3035 Cleveland Avenue, Santa Rosa, CA 95403-2100
(707) 546-4000

Feather River College

Quincy, California
www.frc.edu Federal Code: 008597

2-year public community and liberal arts college in small town.
Enrollment: 874 undergrads, 32% part-time. 392 full-time freshmen.
Selectivity: Open admission.

BASIC COSTS (2012-2013)

Tuition and fees: $1,446; out-of-state residents $6,846.
Per-credit charge: $46; out-of-state residents $226.
Additional info: Board plan not available. Cost of room only, $4,950. Tuition/fee waivers available for adults, unemployed or children of unemployed.

FINANCIAL AID PICTURE

Students with need: Need-based aid available for full-time and part-time students. Work study available nights, weekends, and for part-time students.
Students without need: This college awards aid only to students with need.

FINANCIAL AID PROCEDURES

Forms required: FAFSA.
Dates and Deadlines: Priority date 3/2; no closing date. Applicants notified on a rolling basis starting 4/1; must reply within 3 week(s) of notification.

CONTACT

Barbara Cormack, Financial Aid Director
570 Golden Eagle Avenue, Quincy, CA 95971
(530) 283-0202 ext. 283

Foothill College

Los Altos Hills, California
www.foothill.edu Federal Code: 001199

2-year public community college in large town.
Enrollment: 8,815 undergrads.
Selectivity: Open admission; but selective for some programs.

BASIC COSTS (2012-2013)

Tuition and fees: $1,441; out-of-state residents $7,651.
Per-credit charge: $31; out-of-state residents $169.

FINANCIAL AID PICTURE (2011-2012)

Students with need: 49% of average financial aid package awarded as scholarships/grants, 51% awarded as loans/jobs. Need-based aid available for part-time students. Work study available nights, weekends, and for part-time students.
Scholarships offered: Chancellor's Scholarship: for first-time freshmen who graduate with a 3.5 GPA from Santa Clara or San Mateo County as Chancellor's Scholar; $2,000.

FINANCIAL AID PROCEDURES

Forms required: FAFSA, institutional form.
Dates and Deadlines: Priority date 3/30; no closing date. Applicants notified on a rolling basis starting 5/1; must reply within 3 week(s) of notification.

CONTACT

Kevin Harral, Director, Financial Aid
12345 El Monte Road, Los Altos Hills, CA 94022
(650) 949-7245

Fremont College: Cerritos

Los Angeles, California
www.fremont.edu Federal Code: 030399

2-year for-profit branch campus and career college in very large city.
Enrollment: 308 undergrads.
Selectivity: Open admission; but selective for some programs and for out-of-state students.

BASIC COSTS (2012-2013)

Additional info: Total program charges: BA in Design Entrepreneurship $70,360; BA in Business Leadership $66,350; AA in Design Interpretation $35,273; AA in Business Administration $33,268; AA in Paralegal Studies $33,268; AS in Sports & Rehabilitation Therapy $32,265; Diploma in Massage Therapy $21,571. Tuition/fee waivers available for unemployed or children of unemployed.

FINANCIAL AID PICTURE

Students with need: Need-based aid available for full-time students.
Students without need: This college awards aid only to students with need.

FINANCIAL AID PROCEDURES

Forms required: FAFSA, institutional form.

CONTACT

Lori Prince, Director of Finance
3440 Wilshire Boulevard, 10th floor, Los Angeles, CA 90010
(562) 809-5100

Fresno City College

Fresno, California
www.fresnocitycollege.edu Federal Code: 001307

2-year public community and liberal arts college in very large city.
Enrollment: 14,067 undergrads.
Selectivity: Open admission; but selective for some programs.

BASIC COSTS (2012-2013)

Tuition and fees: $1,416; out-of-state residents $8,076.
Per-credit charge: $46; out-of-state residents $268.
Additional info: Tuition/fee waivers available for adults, minority students, unemployed or children of unemployed.

FINANCIAL AID PICTURE
Students with need: Need-based aid available for full-time and part-time students.
Students without need: This college awards aid only to students with need.
Additional info: Board of Governors Grant Program to offset enrollment fees based on untaxed income, low income, or calculated need. Students qualifying for program also automatically exempt from health fees. March 2 application deadline for California grants.

FINANCIAL AID PROCEDURES
Forms required: FAFSA, state aid form.
Dates and Deadlines: Priority date 4/15; closing date 6/30. Applicants notified on a rolling basis starting 4/1.

CONTACT
Frank Ramon, Financial Aid Director
1101 East University Avenue, Fresno, CA 93741
(559) 442-8279

Fresno Pacific University

Fresno, California
www.fresno.edu Federal Code: 001253

4-year private university and liberal arts college in large city, affiliated with Mennonite Brethren Church.
Enrollment: 2,465 undergrads, 13% part-time. 227 full-time freshmen.

BASIC COSTS (2013-2014)
Tuition and fees: $25,716.
Room and board: $7,288.

FINANCIAL AID PICTURE (2011-2012)
Students with need: Out of 213 full-time freshmen who applied for aid, 188 were judged to have need. Of these, 188 received aid, and 39 had their full need met. Average financial aid package met 73% of need; average scholarship/grant was $10,567; average loan was $3,334. For part-time students, average financial aid package was $3,505.
Students without need: 25 full-time freshmen who did not demonstrate need for aid received scholarships/grants; average award was $8,601. No-need awards available for academics, athletics, leadership, music/drama, religious affiliation.
Scholarships offered: 41 full-time freshmen received athletic scholarships; average amount $9,092.
Cumulative student debt: 73% of graduating class had student loans; average debt was $19,711.

FINANCIAL AID PROCEDURES
Forms required: FAFSA.
Dates and Deadlines: Closing date 3/2. Applicants notified on a rolling basis starting 3/2; must reply by 7/30 or within 3 week(s) of notification.
Transfers: No deadline.

CONTACT
April Powell, Director of Student Financial Services
1717 South Chestnut Avenue, Fresno, CA 93702-4709
(559) 453-2041

Fullerton College

Fullerton, California
www.fullcoll.edu Federal Code: 001201

2-year public community and technical college in small city.
Enrollment: 11,254 undergrads, 73% part-time. 599 full-time freshmen.
Selectivity: Open admission.

BASIC COSTS (2012-2013)
Tuition and fees: $1,414; out-of-state residents $6,784.
Per-credit charge: $46; out-of-state residents $225.
Additional info: Tuition/fee waivers available for adults, minority students, unemployed or children of unemployed.

FINANCIAL AID PICTURE (2011-2012)
Students with need: 92% of average financial aid package awarded as scholarships/grants, 8% awarded as loans/jobs. Need-based aid available for part-time students.

FINANCIAL AID PROCEDURES
Forms required: FAFSA.
Dates and Deadlines: Applicants notified on a rolling basis.

CONTACT
Greg Ryan, Director of Financial Aid & Veterans Services
321 East Chapman Avenue, Fullerton, CA 92832-2095
(714) 992-7050

Glendale Community College

Glendale, California
www.glendale.edu Federal Code: 001203

2-year public community college in small city.
Enrollment: 10,965 undergrads, 62% part-time. 615 full-time freshmen.
Selectivity: Open admission; but selective for some programs.

BASIC COSTS (2012-2013)
Tuition and fees: $1,439; out-of-state residents $7,139.
Per-credit charge: $46; out-of-state residents $236.

FINANCIAL AID PICTURE
Students with need: Need-based aid available for full-time and part-time students. Work study available nights, weekends, and for part-time students.
Students without need: This college awards aid only to students with need.

FINANCIAL AID PROCEDURES
Forms required: FAFSA, institutional form.
Dates and Deadlines: Priority date 4/15; no closing date. Applicants notified on a rolling basis starting 6/15; must reply within 2 week(s) of notification.
Transfers: No deadline.

CONTACT
Patricia Hurley, Director of Financial Aid
1500 North Verdugo Road, Glendale, CA 91208-2809
(818) 240-1000 ext. 5916

Golden Gate University

San Francisco, California
www.ggu.edu Federal Code: 001205

4-year private university in very large city.
Enrollment: 442 undergrads.

BASIC COSTS (2013-2014)
Tuition and fees: $18,000.
Per-credit charge: $600.

FINANCIAL AID PICTURE
Students with need: Need-based aid available for full-time and part-time students. Work study available nights.
Students without need: This college awards aid only to students with need.

FINANCIAL AID PROCEDURES
Forms required: FAFSA, institutional form.

Dates and Deadlines: Priority date 1/2; no closing date. Applicants notified on a rolling basis; must reply within 3 week(s) of notification.
Transfers: Priority date 6/14; no deadline. Applicants notified on a rolling basis starting 1/2; must reply within 3 week(s) of notification.

CONTACT
Louis Riccardi
536 Mission Street, San Francisco, CA 94105-2968
(415) 442-7270

Grossmont College

El Cajon, California
www.grossmont.edu Federal Code: 001208

2-year public nursing and community college in small city.
Enrollment: 10,039 undergrads.
Selectivity: Open admission; but selective for some programs.

BASIC COSTS (2012-2013)
Tuition and fees: $1,410; out-of-state residents $7,110.
Per-credit charge: $46; out-of-state residents $236.

FINANCIAL AID PICTURE
Students with need: Need-based aid available for full-time and part-time students. Work study available nights, weekends, and for part-time students.
Students without need: This college awards aid only to students with need.

FINANCIAL AID PROCEDURES
Forms required: FAFSA.
Dates and Deadlines: Priority date 3/2; closing date 6/30. Applicants notified on a rolling basis starting 7/15; must reply within 2 week(s) of notification.

CONTACT
Michael Copenhaver, Director of Financial Aid
8800 Grossmont College Drive, El Cajon, CA 92020
(619) 644-7129

Harvey Mudd College

Claremont, California Federal Code: 001171
www.hmc.edu/admission CSS Code: 4341

4-year private engineering and liberal arts college in small city.
Enrollment: 779 undergrads. 194 full-time freshmen.
Selectivity: Admits less than 50% of applicants.

BASIC COSTS (2013-2014)
Tuition and fees: $46,509.
Per-credit charge: $1,445.
Room and board: $15,151.

FINANCIAL AID PICTURE (2011-2012)
Students with need: Out of 125 full-time freshmen who applied for aid, 92 were judged to have need. Of these, 92 received aid, and 92 had their full need met. Average financial aid package met 100% of need; average scholarship/grant was $33,945; average loan was $4,407. Need-based aid available for part-time students.
Students without need: 32 full-time freshmen who did not demonstrate need for aid received scholarships/grants; average award was $11,236. No-need awards available for academics.
Scholarships offered: Harvey S. Mudd Merit Award: for first-time first-year students in science and technology programs; $10,000 annually for 4 years; must maintain minimum 2.75 GPA. Harvey Mudd College-sponsored National Merit Scholarships: from $1,000 to $2,000; based on need.
Cumulative student debt: 48% of graduating class had student loans; average debt was $24,194.

Additional info: Students can use 100% of their outside awards toward first reducing the need-based portion of their student loans and/or Federal Work Study award. Once need-based student loans and/or Federal Work Study award have been completely eliminated, any additional outside scholarships may reduce need-based Harvey Mudd Scholarship only. However, to maximize financial aid eligibility, students may retain need-based student loans and/or Federal Work Study award up to their federal need.

FINANCIAL AID PROCEDURES
Forms required: FAFSA, CSS PROFILE, state aid form.
Dates and Deadlines: Closing date 2/1. Applicants notified by 4/1; must reply by 5/1 or within 2 week(s) of notification.
Transfers: Closing date 3/2. Applicants notified by 5/15; must reply by 6/10 or within 2 week(s) of notification.

CONTACT
Gilma Lopez, Director of Financial Aid
301 Platt Boulevard, Claremont, CA 91711-5901
(909) 621-8055

Heald College: Concord

Concord, California
www.heald.edu Federal Code: 030693

2-year for-profit business and technical college in small city.
Enrollment: 1,772 undergrads.
Selectivity: Open admission; but selective for some programs.

BASIC COSTS (2012-2013)
Additional info: Estimated tuition and fees for entire associate programs as of July 2012: $8,680. Books and supplies: $1,000. All costs subject to change at any time.

FINANCIAL AID PICTURE
Students with need: Need-based aid available for full-time and part-time students. Work study available nights, weekends, and for part-time students.
Students without need: This college awards aid only to students with need.

FINANCIAL AID PROCEDURES
Forms required: FAFSA.
Dates and Deadlines: Applicants notified on a rolling basis.

CONTACT
Maria Duenas, Director of Financial Aid
5130 Commercial Circle, Concord, CA 94520
(925) 288-5800

Heald College: Hayward

Hayward, California
www.heald.edu Federal Code: 008532

2-year for-profit technical and career college in small city.
Enrollment: 1,848 undergrads.
Selectivity: Open admission.

BASIC COSTS (2012-2013)
Additional info: Estimated tuition and fees for entire associate programs as of July 2012: $8,680. Books and supplies: $1,000. All costs subject to change at any time.

FINANCIAL AID PICTURE
Students with need: Need-based aid available for full-time and part-time students. Work study available nights, weekends, and for part-time students.
Students without need: This college awards aid only to students with need.

FINANCIAL AID PROCEDURES
Forms required: FAFSA.

CONTACT
Wylodin Banez, Director of Financial Aid
25500 Industrial Boulevard, Hayward, CA 94545
(510) 783-2100

Heald College: Rancho Cordova

Rancho Cordova, California
www.heald.edu Federal Code: 025931

2-year for-profit technical college in large city.
Enrollment: 1,448 undergrads.
Selectivity: Admits over 75% of applicants.

BASIC COSTS (2012-2013)
Additional info: Estimated tuition and fees for entire associate programs as of July 2012: $8,680 - $13,020. Books and supplies: $1,000. All costs subject to change at any time.

FINANCIAL AID PICTURE
Students with need: Need-based aid available for full-time and part-time students. Work study available nights, weekends, and for part-time students.
Students without need: This college awards aid only to students with need.

FINANCIAL AID PROCEDURES
Forms required: FAFSA.

CONTACT
James Wilson, Director of Financial Aid
2910 Prospect Park Drive, Rancho Cordova, CA 95670
(916) 414-2700

Heald College: Roseville

Roseville, California
www.heald.edu

2-year for-profit career college in small city.
Enrollment: 1,551 undergrads.
Selectivity: Open admission.

BASIC COSTS (2012-2013)
Additional info: Estimated tuition and fees for entire associate programs as of July 2012: $8,680. Books and supplies: $1,000. All costs subject to change at any time.

FINANCIAL AID PICTURE
Students with need: Need-based aid available for full-time and part-time students. Work study available nights, weekends, and for part-time students.
Students without need: This college awards aid only to students with need.

FINANCIAL AID PROCEDURES
Forms required: FAFSA.

CONTACT
Rhonda Shaw, Director of Financial Aid
7 Sierra Gate Plaza, Roseville, CA 95678
(916) 789-8600

Heald College: Salinas

Salinas, California
www.heald.edu Federal Code: 030340

2-year for-profit business college in small city.
Enrollment: 1,490 undergrads.
Selectivity: Admits 50 to 75% of applicants.

BASIC COSTS (2012-2013)
Additional info: Estimated tuition and fees for entire associate programs as of July 2012: $13,020. Books and supplies: $1,500. All costs subject to change at any time.

FINANCIAL AID PICTURE
Students with need: Need-based aid available for full-time and part-time students. Work study available nights, weekends, and for part-time students.
Students without need: This college awards aid only to students with need.

FINANCIAL AID PROCEDURES
Forms required: FAFSA.

CONTACT
Heloise Mata, Director of Financial Aid
1450 North Main Street, Salinas, CA 93906
(831) 443-1700

Heald College: San Francisco

San Francisco, California
www.heald.edu Federal Code: 007234

2-year for-profit business college in very large city.
Enrollment: 1,507 undergrads.
Selectivity: Admits over 75% of applicants.

BASIC COSTS (2012-2013)
Additional info: Estimated tuition and fees for entire associate programs as of July 2012: $8,680. Books and supplies: $1,000. All costs subject to change at any time.

FINANCIAL AID PICTURE
Students with need: Need-based aid available for full-time and part-time students. Work study available nights, weekends, and for part-time students.
Students without need: This college awards aid only to students with need.

FINANCIAL AID PROCEDURES
Forms required: FAFSA.

CONTACT
Judy Bacchus, Director of Financial Aid
875 Howard Street, San Francisco, CA 94103
(415) 808-3000

Heald College: San Jose

Milpitas, California
www.heald.edu Federal Code: 025932

2-year for-profit business college in very large city.
Enrollment: 1,719 undergrads.
Selectivity: Admits over 75% of applicants.

BASIC COSTS (2012-2013)
Additional info: Estimated tuition and fees for entire associate programs as of July 2012: $8,680 - $13,020. Books and supplies: $1,000. All costs subject to change at any time.

FINANCIAL AID PICTURE
Students with need: Need-based aid available for full-time and part-time students. Work study available nights, weekends, and for part-time students.
Students without need: This college awards aid only to students with need.

FINANCIAL AID PROCEDURES
Forms required: FAFSA.

Dates and Deadlines: Applicants notified on a rolling basis starting 6/15; must reply within 2 week(s) of notification.

CONTACT

Lidia Hurtado, Director of Financial Aid
341 Great Mall Parkway, Milpitas, CA 95035
(408) 934-4900

Heald College: Stockton

Stockton, California
www.heald.edu
Federal Code: 025933

2-year for-profit career college in large city.
Enrollment: 1,945 undergrads.
Selectivity: Open admission.

BASIC COSTS (2012-2013)

Additional info: Estimated tuition and fees for entire associate programs as of July 2012: $8,680 - $13,020. Books and supplies: $1,000. All costs subject to change at any time.

FINANCIAL AID PICTURE

Students with need: Need-based aid available for full-time students.

FINANCIAL AID PROCEDURES

Forms required: FAFSA.

CONTACT

Valerie Edwards-Bendy, Director of Financial Aid
1605 East March Lane, Stockton, CA 95210
(209) 473-5200

Holy Names University

Oakland, California
www.hnu.edu
Federal Code: 001183

4-year private university in large city, affiliated with Roman Catholic Church.
Enrollment: 806 undergrads, 23% part-time. 132 full-time freshmen.
Selectivity: Admits 50 to 75% of applicants.

BASIC COSTS (2012-2013)

Tuition and fees: $31,640.
Per-credit charge: $1,050.
Room and board: $10,680.

FINANCIAL AID PICTURE

Students with need: Need-based aid available for full-time and part-time students.
Students without need: No-need awards available for academics, athletics, leadership, music/drama, religious affiliation.
Scholarships offered: Aspiring Leadership Grant: $5,500 annually; based on 2.70-2.99 GPA. Honors Scholarship: $8,500 annually; based on 3.00-3.29 GPA. Dean's Scholarship: $9,500 annually; based on 3.30-3.49 GPA. President's Scholarship: $11,000 annually; based on 3.50-3.74 GPA. Regent's Scholarship: $12,000 annually; based on 3.75+ GPA. Durocher Scholarship: full tuition; campus residency required; based on evidence of leadership, contributions to school and/or community and academic achievement, minimum GPA 3.75, minimum SAT 1100 (exclusive of Writing); 1 awarded per year.

FINANCIAL AID PROCEDURES

Forms required: FAFSA, state aid form.
Dates and Deadlines: Priority date 3/2; no closing date. Applicants notified on a rolling basis starting 9/1; must reply by 5/1 or within 2 week(s) of notification.
Transfers: Applicants notified on a rolling basis starting 9/1; must reply by 5/1 or within 2 week(s) of notification.

CONTACT

Jeff Hardie, Director of Financial Aid
3500 Mountain Boulevard, Oakland, CA 94619-1699
(510) 436-1327

Hope International University

Fullerton, California
www.hiu.edu
Federal Code: 001252

4-year private university and liberal arts college in small city, affiliated with Christian Church.
Enrollment: 1,167 undergrads, 32% part-time. 213 full-time freshmen.
Selectivity: Admits 50 to 75% of applicants.

BASIC COSTS (2012-2013)

Tuition and fees: $25,264.
Per-credit charge: $1,050.
Room and board: $8,600.

FINANCIAL AID PICTURE

Students with need: Need-based aid available for full-time and part-time students. Work study available nights, weekends, and for part-time students.
Students without need: No-need awards available for academics, job skills, leadership, music/drama, state/district residency.

FINANCIAL AID PROCEDURES

Forms required: FAFSA, institutional form.
Dates and Deadlines: Closing date 3/2. Applicants notified on a rolling basis starting 3/15; must reply within 2 week(s) of notification.
Transfers: Priority date 3/2; no deadline. Applicants notified on a rolling basis starting 4/1; must reply within 2 week(s) of notification.

CONTACT

Shannon O'Shields, Director of Student Financial Aid
2500 East Nutwood Avenue, Fullerton, CA 92831-3199
(714) 879-3901 ext. 2232

Humboldt State University

Arcata, California
www.humboldt.edu
Federal Code: 001149

4-year public university and liberal arts college in large town.
Enrollment: 7,562 undergrads, 7% part-time. 1,245 full-time freshmen.
Selectivity: Admits over 75% of applicants.

BASIC COSTS (2012-2013)

Tuition and fees: $7,084; out-of-state residents $18,244.
Room and board: $10,948.

FINANCIAL AID PICTURE (2011-2012)

Students with need: Out of 1,086 full-time freshmen who applied for aid, 954 were judged to have need. Of these, 866 received aid, and 73 had their full need met. Average financial aid package met 67% of need; average scholarship/grant was $8,330; average loan was $5,608. For part-time students, average financial aid package was $10,045.
Students without need: 44 full-time freshmen who did not demonstrate need for aid received scholarships/grants; average award was $525. No-need awards available for academics, athletics.
Scholarships offered: 26 full-time freshmen received athletic scholarships; average amount $3,721.
Cumulative student debt: 81% of graduating class had student loans; average debt was $20,273.

FINANCIAL AID PROCEDURES

Forms required: FAFSA.
Dates and Deadlines: Priority date 3/2; no closing date. Applicants notified on a rolling basis starting 4/15; must reply within 6 week(s) of notification.

Transfers: Need is most salient factor for some programs.

CONTACT

Scott Hagg, Director of Financial Aid
One Harpst Street, Arcata, CA 95521-8299
(707) 826-4321

Humphreys College

Stockton, California
www.humphreys.edu Federal Code: 001212

4-year private business and liberal arts college in large city.
Enrollment: 882 undergrads.

BASIC COSTS (2012-2013)
Tuition and fees: $11,160.
Per-credit charge: $310.

FINANCIAL AID PICTURE
Students with need: Need-based aid available for full-time and part-time students. Work study available nights, weekends, and for part-time students.
Students without need: No-need awards available for academics.

FINANCIAL AID PROCEDURES
Forms required: FAFSA.
Dates and Deadlines: Applicants notified on a rolling basis starting 8/15; must reply within 2 week(s) of notification.

CONTACT

Rita Franco, Financial Aid Director
6650 Inglewood Avenue, Stockton, CA 95207-3896
(209) 478-0800 ext. 3

Imperial Valley College

Imperial, California
www.imperial.edu Federal Code: 001214

2-year public nursing and community college in large town.
Enrollment: 5,664 undergrads. 906 full-time freshmen.
Selectivity: Open admission; but selective for some programs.

BASIC COSTS (2012-2013)
Tuition and fees: $1,458; out-of-state residents $7,908.
Per-credit charge: $46; out-of-state residents $246.
Additional info: Tuition/fee waivers available for adults.

FINANCIAL AID PICTURE (2011-2012)
Students with need: 84% of average financial aid package awarded as scholarships/grants, 16% awarded as loans/jobs. Need-based aid available for part-time students. Work study available nights, weekends, and for part-time students.
Students without need: This college awards aid only to students with need.

FINANCIAL AID PROCEDURES
Forms required: FAFSA.
Dates and Deadlines: Priority date 3/2; closing date 6/30. Applicants notified on a rolling basis starting 5/1.
Transfers: No deadline. Applicants notified on a rolling basis.

CONTACT

Lisa Seals, Director of Financial Aid
Box 158, Imperial, CA 92251-0158
(760) 355-6266

Irvine Valley College

Irvine, California
www.ivc.edu Federal Code: 025395

2-year public community college in small city.
Enrollment: 8,860 undergrads.
Selectivity: Open admission.

BASIC COSTS (2012-2013)
Tuition and fees: $1,414; out-of-state residents $6,784.
Per-credit charge: $46; out-of-state residents $225.
Additional info: Tuition/fee waivers available for minority students.

FINANCIAL AID PICTURE
Students with need: Need-based aid available for full-time and part-time students. Work study available nights.
Students without need: This college awards aid only to students with need.

FINANCIAL AID PROCEDURES
Forms required: FAFSA, state aid form, institutional form.
Dates and Deadlines: Applicants notified on a rolling basis starting 4/30.

CONTACT

Darryl Cox, Director of Financial Aid
5500 Irvine Center Drive, Irvine, CA 92618-4399
(949) 451-5287

Kaplan College: Riverside

Riverside, California
www.riverside.kaplancollege.com/ Federal Code: 030445

2-year for-profit junior and technical college in very large city.
Enrollment: 293 undergrads.
Selectivity: Open admission.

BASIC COSTS (2012-2013)
Additional info: Associate program: Criminal Justice $29,364.50; Health Information Technology $29,112.50. Diploma program: Dental Assistant $17,162.50; Massage Therapy $15,341.50; Medical Assistant $15,341.50; Medical Billing and Coding Specialist $15,341.50.

FINANCIAL AID PICTURE
Students with need: Need-based aid available for full-time students. Work study available nights.
Students without need: This college awards aid only to students with need.

FINANCIAL AID PROCEDURES
Forms required: FAFSA, institutional form.
Transfers: No deadline.

CONTACT

Cynthia Arevalo
4040 Vine Street, Riverside, CA 92507
(818) 672-3000

The King's University

Los Angeles, California
www.kingsuniversity.edu Federal Code: 035163

4-year private Bible and seminary college in very large city, affiliated with nondenominational tradition.
Enrollment: 315 undergrads.

BASIC COSTS (2013-2014)
Tuition and fees: $11,205.

Per-credit charge: $240.
Additional info: Tuition/fee waivers available for adults.

FINANCIAL AID PICTURE
Students with need: Need-based aid available for full-time and part-time students. Work study available nights, weekends, and for part-time students.
Additional info: Specific scholarships may require specific essays.

FINANCIAL AID PROCEDURES
Forms required: FAFSA.
Dates and Deadlines: Applicants notified on a rolling basis; must reply within 4 week(s) of notification.

CONTACT
Norman Stoppenbrink, Financial Aid Director
14800 Sherman Way, Los Angeles, CA 91405-2233
(818) 779-8271

La Sierra University
Riverside, California
www.lasierra.edu Federal Code: 001215

4-year private university and liberal arts college in large city, affiliated with Seventh-day Adventists.
Enrollment: 2,023 undergrads, 7% part-time. 499 full-time freshmen.
Selectivity: Admits less than 50% of applicants.

BASIC COSTS (2013-2014)
Tuition and fees: $29,103.
Per-credit charge: $777.
Room and board: $7,500.

FINANCIAL AID PICTURE
Students with need: Need-based aid available for full-time and part-time students. Work study available nights, weekends, and for part-time students.
Students without need: No-need awards available for academics, art, athletics, leadership, music/drama, religious affiliation.
Scholarships offered: Sports and Honors Scholarship available for qualified students.

FINANCIAL AID PROCEDURES
Forms required: FAFSA, state aid form.
Dates and Deadlines: Priority date 3/2; closing date 9/15. Applicants notified by 8/15; must reply by 9/1.
Transfers: Closing date 7/1. Applicants notified by 8/15; must reply by 9/1 or within 15 week(s) of notification. Every student whose balance is not completely covered by financial aid must make a payment of at least one-third of the balance due by the published deadline before each quarter. There will continue to be three standard payment options available. Year-in-Advance: Pay the full year's charges—minus confirmed aid—by the published deadline for Fall and receive a 7% discount. Quarter-in-Advance: Pay each quarter's charges—minus confirmed aid—by the published deadline for that quarter and receive a 2% discount. Monthly Payment: Pay in three monthly installments for each quarter, with the first payment due by that quarter's published deadline. A $30 fee applies for each quarter that this option is chosen.

CONTACT
Esther Kinzer, Director of Student Financial Services
4500 Riverwalk Parkway, Riverside, CA 92515-8247
(951) 785-2175

Laguna College of Art and Design
Laguna Beach, California
www.lcad.edu Federal Code: 016517

4-year private visual arts college in large town.
Enrollment: 484 undergrads.
Selectivity: Admits less than 50% of applicants.

BASIC COSTS (2013-2014)
Tuition and fees: $26,500.
Per-credit charge: $1,104.
Room only: $8,400.

FINANCIAL AID PICTURE (2011-2012)
Students with need: 57% of average financial aid package awarded as scholarships/grants, 43% awarded as loans/jobs. Need-based aid available for part-time students. Work study available nights, weekends, and for part-time students.
Additional info: Need- and merit-based scholarship deadline June 1st.

FINANCIAL AID PROCEDURES
Forms required: FAFSA, institutional form.
Dates and Deadlines: Applicants notified on a rolling basis; must reply within 2 week(s) of notification.
Transfers: No deadline. Applicants notified on a rolling basis.

CONTACT
Christopher Brown, Director of Admission and Financial Aid
2222 Laguna Canyon Road, Laguna Beach, CA 92651-1136
(949) 376-6000 ext. 223

Lake Tahoe Community College
South Lake Tahoe, California
www.ltcc.edu Federal Code: 012907

2-year public community college in large town.
Enrollment: 3,000 undergrads.
Selectivity: Open admission.

BASIC COSTS (2012-2013)
Tuition and fees: $1,407; out-of-state residents $7,662.
Per-credit charge: $31; out-of-state residents $170.

FINANCIAL AID PICTURE
Students with need: Need-based aid available for full-time and part-time students. Work study available nights.

FINANCIAL AID PROCEDURES
Forms required: FAFSA.
Dates and Deadlines: Priority date 5/1; no closing date. Applicants notified on a rolling basis starting 7/1; must reply within 2 week(s) of notification.

CONTACT
Julie Cathie, Director of Financial Aid
One College Drive, South Lake Tahoe, CA 96150-4524
(530) 541-4660 ext. 236

Las Positas College
Livermore, California
www.laspositascollege.edu Federal Code: 030357

2-year public community college in small city.
Enrollment: 5,893 undergrads.
Selectivity: Open admission.

BASIC COSTS (2012-2013)
Tuition and fees: $1,408; out-of-state residents $8,188.
Per-credit charge: $46; out-of-state residents $272.
Additional info: Tuition/fee waivers available for unemployed or children of unemployed.

FINANCIAL AID PICTURE
Students with need: Need-based aid available for full-time students.

FINANCIAL AID PROCEDURES
Forms required: institutional form.
Dates and Deadlines: Priority date 5/1; no closing date. Applicants notified on a rolling basis starting 7/1; must reply within 2 week(s) of notification.

CONTACT
Andi Schreibman, Financial Aid Officer
3033 Collier Canyon Road, Livermore, CA 94551
(925) 424-1580

Lassen Community College
Susanville, California
www.lassencollege.edu Federal Code: 001217

2-year public community college in small town.
Enrollment: 961 undergrads.
Selectivity: Open admission; but selective for some programs.

BASIC COSTS (2012-2013)
Tuition and fees: $1,403; out-of-state residents $7,373.
Per-credit charge: $46; out-of-state residents $245.
Additional info: Board plan not available. Cost of room only, $5,000.

FINANCIAL AID PICTURE
Students with need: Need-based aid available for full-time students.
Students without need: This college awards aid only to students with need.
Additional info: Board of Governors Grant: low-income California residents can have registration fees waived.

FINANCIAL AID PROCEDURES
Forms required: FAFSA.
Dates and Deadlines: Priority date 7/1; no closing date. Applicants notified on a rolling basis starting 7/1; must reply within 2 week(s) of notification.

CONTACT
Matt Levine, Director of Financial Aid
Box 3000, Susanville, CA 96130
(530) 257-6181 ext. 8649

Le Cordon Bleu College of Culinary Arts: Los Angeles
Pasadena, California
www.chefs.edu/los-angeles Federal Code: 032103

2-year for-profit culinary school in very large city.
Enrollment: 1,832 undergrads.
Selectivity: Open admission.

BASIC COSTS (2012-2013)
Additional info: Diploma programs: Culinary Arts $19,200, books and supplies $326.25. Baking and Pastry Arts $19,200, books and supplies $326.25. Associate programs: Culinary Arts $36,200 (nonresident international $39,200), books and supplies $870. Baking and Pastry Arts $36,200 (nonresident international $39,200), books and supplies $870.

FINANCIAL AID PICTURE
Students with need: Need-based aid available for full-time and part-time students. Work study available nights, weekends, and for part-time students.

FINANCIAL AID PROCEDURES
Forms required: FAFSA.
Dates and Deadlines: Applicants notified on a rolling basis.
Transfers: No deadline.

CONTACT
Gabriela Arzate, Director of Student Finance
530 East Colorado Boulevard, Pasadena, CA 91101
(626) 229-1300

Life Pacific College
San Dimas, California
www.lifepacific.edu Federal Code: 016029

4-year private Bible college in large town, affiliated with Christian - The Foursquare Church.
Enrollment: 458 undergrads.
Selectivity: Admits 50 to 75% of applicants.

BASIC COSTS (2013-2014)
Tuition and fees: $12,500.
Per-credit charge: $500.
Room and board: $6,600.

FINANCIAL AID PICTURE
Students with need: Need-based aid available for full-time and part-time students.
Students without need: No-need awards available for academics, alumni affiliation.

FINANCIAL AID PROCEDURES
Forms required: FAFSA.
Dates and Deadlines: Applicants notified on a rolling basis starting 6/1.

CONTACT
Becky Huyck, Director of Financial Aid
Attn: Admissions, San Dimas, CA 91773
(909) 599-5433 ext. 325

Lincoln University
Oakland, California
www.lincolnuca.edu Federal Code: 006975

4-year private university and business college in very large city.
Enrollment: 99 undergrads.
Selectivity: Admits 50 to 75% of applicants.

BASIC COSTS (2012-2013)
Tuition and fees: $9,480.
Per-credit charge: $380.
Additional info: Tuition for Intensive Academic English Preparation is $3,000 per 16 weeks.

FINANCIAL AID PICTURE
Students with need: Need-based aid available for full-time and part-time students.
Students without need: This college awards aid only to students with need.

FINANCIAL AID PROCEDURES
Forms required: FAFSA.
Dates and Deadlines: Priority date 3/22; closing date 8/22. Applicants notified by 12/1; must reply by 1/2.
Transfers: Applicants notified by 12/1; must reply by 1/1.

CONTACT
James Peterson, Chief Financial Aid Director
401 15th Street, Oakland, CA 94612
(510) 628-8023

Loma Linda University

Loma Linda, California
www.llu.edu Federal Code: 001218

3-year private university and health science college in large town, affiliated with Seventh-day Adventists.
Enrollment: 1,183 undergrads.

BASIC COSTS (2012-2013)
Tuition and fees: $27,996.
Per-credit charge: $575.
Additional info: Tuition quoted is for nursing program. Board plan not available. Cost of room only, $2,790.

FINANCIAL AID PICTURE
Students with need: Need-based aid available for full-time and part-time students.

FINANCIAL AID PROCEDURES
Forms required: FAFSA.
Transfers: Priority date 3/2; no deadline. Applicants notified on a rolling basis starting 4/1; must reply within 4 week(s) of notification.

CONTACT
Verdell Schaefer, Director of Financial Aid
Admissions Processing, Loma Linda, CA 92350
(909) 558-4509

Long Beach City College

Long Beach, California
www.lbcc.edu Federal Code: 001219

2-year public community college in large city.
Enrollment: 15,701 undergrads.
Selectivity: Open admission.

BASIC COSTS (2012-2013)
Tuition and fees: $1,418; out-of-state residents $7,688.
Per-credit charge: $46; out-of-state residents $255.

FINANCIAL AID PICTURE
Students with need: Need-based aid available for full-time and part-time students.
Students without need: This college awards aid only to students with need.

FINANCIAL AID PROCEDURES
Forms required: FAFSA, institutional form.
Dates and Deadlines: Priority date 5/6; no closing date. Applicants notified on a rolling basis starting 7/6; must reply within 2 week(s) of notification.

CONTACT
Mike MacCallum, Director of Financial Aid and Veterans Affairs
4901 East Carson Street, Long Beach, CA 90808
(562) 938-4257

Los Angeles City College

Los Angeles, California
www.lacitycollege.edu Federal Code: 001223

2-year public community college in very large city.
Enrollment: 10,090 undergrads.
Selectivity: Open admission.

BASIC COSTS (2012-2013)
Tuition and fees: $1,402; out-of-state residents $7,102.
Per-credit charge: $46; out-of-state residents $236.

FINANCIAL AID PICTURE
Students with need: Need-based aid available for full-time and part-time students.
Students without need: This college awards aid only to students with need.
Additional info: Fee waivers available for public assistance and Social Security insurance recipients; fee credits available for low income families.

FINANCIAL AID PROCEDURES
Forms required: FAFSA.
Dates and Deadlines: Priority date 3/2; no closing date. Applicants notified on a rolling basis starting 7/6; must reply within 2 week(s) of notification.
Transfers: No deadline. Applicants notified by 7/1.

CONTACT
Jeremy Villar, Dean of Student Services
855 North Vermont Avenue, Los Angeles, CA 90029-3589
(323) 953-4000 ext. 2025

Los Angeles Harbor College

Wilmington, California
www.lahc.edu Federal Code: 001224

2-year public community college in small city.
Enrollment: 6,395 undergrads.
Selectivity: Open admission.

BASIC COSTS (2012-2013)
Tuition and fees: $1,402; out-of-state residents $7,102.
Per-credit charge: $46; out-of-state residents $236.

FINANCIAL AID PICTURE
Students with need: Need-based aid available for full-time and part-time students. Work study available nights, weekends, and for part-time students.
Students without need: This college awards aid only to students with need.

FINANCIAL AID PROCEDURES
Forms required: FAFSA, institutional form.
Dates and Deadlines: Priority date 3/2; no closing date. Applicants notified on a rolling basis; must reply within 2 week(s) of notification.
Transfers: Closing date 5/15.

CONTACT
Sheila Millman, Financial Aid Manager
1111 Figueroa Place, Wilmington, CA 90744-2397
(310) 233-4320

Los Angeles Mission College

Sylmar, California
www.lamission.edu Federal Code: 012550

2-year public community college in large town.
Enrollment: 9,956 undergrads.
Selectivity: Open admission.

BASIC COSTS (2012-2013)
Tuition and fees: $1,402; out-of-state residents $7,102.
Per-credit charge: $46; out-of-state residents $236.

FINANCIAL AID PICTURE (2011-2012)
Students with need: 90% of average financial aid package awarded as scholarships/grants, 10% awarded as loans/jobs. Need-based aid available for part-time students.
Additional info: Board of Governors Grant available to those in receipt of TANF (CalWORKS), Social Security Insurance (SSI), or General Relief. If not a receipt of these programs, may qualify based on income.

FINANCIAL AID PROCEDURES

Forms required: FAFSA.

Dates and Deadlines: Priority date 8/1; no closing date. Applicants notified on a rolling basis starting 5/1.

CONTACT

Dennis Schroeder, Financial Aid Director
13356 Eldridge Avenue, Sylmar, CA 91342-3245
(818) 364-7648

Los Angeles Pierce College

Woodland Hills, California
www.piercecollege.edu Federal Code: 001226

2-year public community college in very large city.
Enrollment: 13,240 undergrads.
Selectivity: Open admission; but selective for some programs.

BASIC COSTS (2012-2013)

Tuition and fees: $1,402; out-of-state residents $7,102.
Per-credit charge: $46; out-of-state residents $236.

FINANCIAL AID PICTURE

Students with need: Need-based aid available for full-time and part-time students. Work study available nights, weekends, and for part-time students.

Students without need: This college awards aid only to students with need.

FINANCIAL AID PROCEDURES

Forms required: FAFSA, institutional form.

Dates and Deadlines: Priority date 3/2; no closing date. Applicants notified on a rolling basis starting 8/1.

CONTACT

Anafe Robinson, Director of Financial Aid, Scholarships & Veterans
6201 Winnetka Avenue, Woodland Hills, CA 91371
(818) 719-6428

Los Angeles Southwest College

Los Angeles, California
www.lasc.edu Federal Code: 007047

2-year public community college in very large city.
Enrollment: 3,980 undergrads.
Selectivity: Open admission; but selective for some programs.

BASIC COSTS (2012-2013)

Tuition and fees: $1,402; out-of-state residents $7,102.
Per-credit charge: $46; out-of-state residents $236.

FINANCIAL AID PICTURE

Students with need: Need-based aid available for full-time and part-time students.

Additional info: Board of Governors Enrollment Fee Waiver available to students receiving AFDC, SSI/SSP, or General Assistance. May also qualify on basis of income.

FINANCIAL AID PROCEDURES

Forms required: FAFSA.

Dates and Deadlines: Applicants notified on a rolling basis; must reply within 2 week(s) of notification.

CONTACT

Kathaleen Stiger, Financial Aid Director
1600 West Imperial Highway, Los Angeles, CA 90047-4899
(323) 241-5328

Los Angeles Trade and Technical College

Los Angeles, California
www.lattc.edu Federal Code: 001227

2-year public community and technical college in very large city.
Enrollment: 12,935 undergrads.
Selectivity: Open admission; but selective for some programs.

BASIC COSTS (2012-2013)

Tuition and fees: $1,402; out-of-state residents $7,102.
Per-credit charge: $46; out-of-state residents $236.

FINANCIAL AID PICTURE

Students with need: Need-based aid available for full-time and part-time students. Work study available nights, weekends, and for part-time students.

Students without need: This college awards aid only to students with need.

FINANCIAL AID PROCEDURES

Forms required: FAFSA.

Dates and Deadlines: Priority date 5/1; closing date 6/30. Applicants notified on a rolling basis.

Transfers: No deadline.

CONTACT

Cecilia Kwan, Financial Aid Manager
400 West Washington Boulevard, Los Angeles, CA 90015-4181
(213) 744-9016

Los Angeles Valley College

Valley Glen, California
www.lavc.edu Federal Code: 001228

2-year public community college in very large city.
Enrollment: 10,710 undergrads.
Selectivity: Open admission; but selective for some programs.

BASIC COSTS (2012-2013)

Tuition and fees: $1,402; out-of-state residents $7,102.
Per-credit charge: $46; out-of-state residents $236.

FINANCIAL AID PICTURE

Students with need: Need-based aid available for full-time and part-time students.

Students without need: This college awards aid only to students with need.

FINANCIAL AID PROCEDURES

Forms required: FAFSA.

Dates and Deadlines: Priority date 5/1; no closing date. Applicants notified on a rolling basis.

CONTACT

Vernon Bridges, Financial Aid Manager
5800 Fulton Avenue, Valley Glen, CA 91401-4096
(818) 947-2412

Los Medanos College

Pittsburg, California
www.losmedanos.edu Federal Code: 010340

2-year public community college in small city.
Enrollment: 3,889 undergrads. 356 full-time freshmen.
Selectivity: Open admission.

BASIC COSTS (2012-2013)

Tuition and fees: $1,390; out-of-state residents $7,420.

Per-credit charge: $46; out-of-state residents $247.

FINANCIAL AID PICTURE

Students with need: Need-based aid available for full-time and part-time students.

Students without need: This college awards aid only to students with need.

FINANCIAL AID PROCEDURES

Forms required: FAFSA, state aid form.

Dates and Deadlines: Priority date 3/2; no closing date. Applicants notified on a rolling basis starting 6/1; must reply within 2 week(s) of notification.

Transfers: No deadline. Applicants notified by 6/1.

CONTACT

Loretta Canto-Williams, Director of Financial Aid
2700 East Leland Road, Pittsburg, CA 94565
(925) 439-2181 ext. 3139

Loyola Marymount University

Los Angeles, California
www.lmu.edu Federal Code: 001234

4-year private university in very large city, affiliated with Roman Catholic Church.

Enrollment: 5,962 undergrads, 2% part-time. 1,288 full-time freshmen.

Selectivity: Admits 50 to 75% of applicants.

BASIC COSTS (2013-2014)

Tuition and fees: $40,265.

Per-credit charge: $1,641.

Room and board: $13,550.

Additional info: Freshmen generally stay in the less expensive dorms.

FINANCIAL AID PICTURE (2011-2012)

Students with need: Out of 1,016 full-time freshmen who applied for aid, 761 were judged to have need. Of these, 748 received aid, and 115 had their full need met. Average financial aid package met 63% of need; average scholarship/grant was $18,065; average loan was $4,252. For part-time students, average financial aid package was $10,785.

Students without need: 30 full-time freshmen who did not demonstrate need for aid received scholarships/grants; average award was $8,178. No-need awards available for academics, alumni affiliation, art, athletics, music/drama, religious affiliation, ROTC.

Scholarships offered: ***Merit:*** Merit-based awards for entering freshmen: range from $1,000 to $15,000. Arrupe Scholarship program for high-achieving incoming freshmen; award lasts all four years and pays for substantial portion of tuition and fees. ***Athletic:*** 30 full-time freshmen received athletic scholarships; average amount $22,186.

Cumulative student debt: 57% of graduating class had student loans; average debt was $34,629.

FINANCIAL AID PROCEDURES

Forms required: FAFSA.

Dates and Deadlines: Priority date 2/1; closing date 5/15. Applicants notified on a rolling basis starting 3/15; must reply by 5/1 or within 4 week(s) of notification.

CONTACT

Catherine Graham, Director of Financial Aid
Office of Undergraduate Admission, Los Angeles, CA 90045-8350
(310) 338-2753

Marymount California University

Rancho Palos Verdes, California
www.marymountpv.edu Federal Code: 010474

2-year private junior and liberal arts college in large town, affiliated with Roman Catholic Church.

Enrollment: 1,001 undergrads, 4% part-time. 408 full-time freshmen.

Selectivity: Admits 50 to 75% of applicants.

BASIC COSTS (2013-2014)

Tuition and fees: $30,694.

Per-credit charge: $1,300.

Room and board: $12,750.

FINANCIAL AID PICTURE (2012-2013)

Students with need: Out of 342 full-time freshmen who applied for aid, 274 were judged to have need. Of these, 274 received aid, and 56 had their full need met. Average financial aid package met 83% of need; average scholarship/grant was $21,569. For part-time students, average financial aid package was $14,167.

Students without need: 261 full-time freshmen who did not demonstrate need for aid received scholarships/grants; average award was $11,126. No-need awards available for art, athletics, music/drama.

Scholarships offered: President's Scholarship: $8,000; Academic GPA: 3.30 and above; SAT 1530 or ACT 22. Dean's Scholarship: $6,000; Academic GPA 3.00-3.29; SAT 1410 or ACT 20. Achievement Scholarship: $4,500; Academic GPA 2.80-2.99; SAT 1210 or ACT 17. Deadline May 1. All admitted students considered. Renewable for one additional consecutive year.

Cumulative student debt: 68% of graduating class had student loans; average debt was $3,663.

FINANCIAL AID PROCEDURES

Forms required: FAFSA.

Dates and Deadlines: Priority date 3/2; no closing date. Applicants notified on a rolling basis starting 3/1; must reply by 5/1.

CONTACT

Barbara Layne, Director of Financial Aid
30800 Palos Verdes Drive East, Rancho Palos Verdes, CA 90275-6299
(310) 303-7282

The Master's College

Santa Clarita, California
www.masters.edu Federal Code: 001220

4-year private liberal arts and seminary college in small city, affiliated with Conservative Evangelical Christian Church.

Enrollment: 1,134 undergrads, 12% part-time. 254 full-time freshmen.

Selectivity: Admits 50 to 75% of applicants.

BASIC COSTS (2013-2014)

Tuition and fees: $28,930.

Per-credit charge: $1,190.

Room and board: $9,360.

FINANCIAL AID PICTURE (2011-2012)

Students with need: Out of 209 full-time freshmen who applied for aid, 178 were judged to have need. Of these, 176 received aid, and 21 had their full need met. Average financial aid package met 71% of need; average scholarship/grant was $17,722; average loan was $3,794. For part-time students, average financial aid package was $8,013.

Students without need: 44 full-time freshmen who did not demonstrate need for aid received scholarships/grants; average award was $9,237. No-need awards available for academics, alumni affiliation, art, athletics, leadership, music/drama.

Scholarships offered: 11 full-time freshmen received athletic scholarships; average amount $20,271.

Cumulative student debt: 43% of graduating class had student loans; average debt was $16,828.

FINANCIAL AID PROCEDURES

Forms required: FAFSA, state aid form, institutional form.

Dates and Deadlines: Priority date 3/2; no closing date. Applicants notified on a rolling basis starting 2/18; must reply by 5/1 or within 2 week(s) of notification.

Transfers: Closing date 3/2.

CONTACT

Gary Edwards, Director of Financial Aid
21726 Placerita Canyon Road, Santa Clarita, CA 91321-1200
(661) 259-3540 ext. 2291

Mendocino College

Ukiah, California
www.mendocino.edu Federal Code: 011672

2-year public community college in large town.
Enrollment: 2,232 undergrads, 53% part-time. 273 full-time freshmen.
Selectivity: Open admission.

BASIC COSTS (2012-2013)

Tuition and fees: $1,400; out-of-state residents $7,400.
Per-credit charge: $46; out-of-state residents $246.
Additional info: Tuition/fee waivers available for unemployed or children of unemployed.

FINANCIAL AID PICTURE (2012-2013)

Students with need: Out of 230 full-time freshmen who applied for aid, 204 were judged to have need. Of these, 204 received aid, and 18 had their full need met. Average financial aid package met 42% of need; average scholarship/grant was $4,298; average loan was $200. For part-time students, average financial aid package was $4,843.

Students without need: 7 full-time freshmen who did not demonstrate need for aid received scholarships/grants; average award was $1,178. No-need awards available for academics, leadership, music/drama, state/district residency.

Cumulative student debt: 10% of graduating class had student loans; average debt was $3,594.

FINANCIAL AID PROCEDURES

Forms required: FAFSA.

Dates and Deadlines: Priority date 5/31; no closing date. Applicants notified on a rolling basis starting 7/1; must reply within 2 week(s) of notification.

Transfers: No deadline. Applicants notified on a rolling basis.

CONTACT

Jacqueline Bradley, Director of Financial Aid
1000 Hensley Creek/Box 3000, Ukiah, CA 95482
(707) 468-3110

Menlo College

Atherton, California
www.menlo.edu Federal Code: 001236

4-year private business and liberal arts college in small city.
Enrollment: 681 undergrads, 2% part-time. 178 full-time freshmen.
Selectivity: Admits over 75% of applicants.

BASIC COSTS (2013-2014)

Tuition and fees: $37,100.
Per-credit charge: $1,521.
Room and board: $11,902.
Additional info: Student loan fees $126.

FINANCIAL AID PICTURE (2012-2013)

Students with need: Out of 126 full-time freshmen who applied for aid, 114 were judged to have need. Of these, 114 received aid, and 13 had their full need met. Average financial aid package met 71% of need; average scholarship/grant was $25,859; average loan was $3,090. For part-time students, average financial aid package was $14,503.

Students without need: 76 full-time freshmen who did not demonstrate need for aid received scholarships/grants; average award was $12,986. No-need awards available for academics, athletics.

Scholarships offered: 24 full-time freshmen received athletic scholarships; average amount $7,735.

Cumulative student debt: 43% of graduating class had student loans; average debt was $25,753.

FINANCIAL AID PROCEDURES

Forms required: FAFSA.

Dates and Deadlines: Priority date 3/2; closing date 8/1. Applicants notified on a rolling basis starting 12/15; must reply by 5/1 or within 2 week(s) of notification.

Transfers: No deadline. Applicants notified on a rolling basis starting 12/1; must reply by 5/1 or within 2 week(s) of notification.

CONTACT

Anne Heaton-Dunlap, Director, Office of Financial Aid
1000 El Camino Real, Atherton, CA 94027
(650) 543-3880

Merritt College

Oakland, California
www.merritt.edu Federal Code: 001267

2-year public community college in large city.
Enrollment: 2,720 undergrads.
Selectivity: Open admission.

BASIC COSTS (2012-2013)

Tuition and fees: $1,380; out-of-state residents $7,080.
Per-credit charge: $46; out-of-state residents $236.
Additional info: Tuition/fee waivers available for unemployed or children of unemployed.

FINANCIAL AID PICTURE

Students with need: Need-based aid available for full-time and part-time students.

FINANCIAL AID PROCEDURES

Forms required: FAFSA, institutional form.

Dates and Deadlines: Priority date 4/1; closing date 6/30. Applicants notified on a rolling basis starting 6/1.

CONTACT

Alice Freeman, Financial Aid Coordinator
12500 Campus Drive, Oakland, CA 94619
(510) 436-2465

Mills College

Oakland, California
www.mills.edu Federal Code: 001238

4-year private liberal arts college for women in large city.
Enrollment: 933 undergrads, 4% part-time. 207 full-time freshmen.
Selectivity: Admits 50 to 75% of applicants.

BASIC COSTS (2012-2013)

Tuition and fees: $40,080.
Room and board: $11,580.

FINANCIAL AID PICTURE (2012-2013)
Students with need: Out of 189 full-time freshmen who applied for aid, 175 were judged to have need. Of these, 175 received aid, and 35 had their full need met. Average financial aid package met 87% of need; average scholarship/grant was $22,402; average loan was $5,859. For part-time students, average financial aid package was $27,754.
Students without need: 32 full-time freshmen who did not demonstrate need for aid received scholarships/grants; average award was $15,101. No-need awards available for academics, music/drama.
Cumulative student debt: 77% of graduating class had student loans; average debt was $27,021.

FINANCIAL AID PROCEDURES
Forms required: FAFSA, state aid form, institutional form.
Dates and Deadlines: Priority date 2/1; closing date 2/15. Applicants notified on a rolling basis starting 3/1; must reply by 5/1 or within 2 week(s) of notification.
Transfers: Priority date 3/2; closing date 7/15. Applicants notified on a rolling basis starting 4/15; must reply by 5/1 or within 2 week(s) of notification.

CONTACT
Shari Keller, Associate Vice President for Student Finance and Administration Services
5000 MacArthur Boulevard, Oakland, CA 94613
(510) 430-2000

MiraCosta College
Oceanside, California
www.miracosta.edu Federal Code: 001239

2-year public community and junior college in large city.
Enrollment: 11,129 undergrads. 1,130 full-time freshmen.
Selectivity: Open admission; but selective for some programs.

BASIC COSTS (2012-2013)
Tuition and fees: $1,424; out-of-state residents $6,974.
Per-credit charge: $46; out-of-state residents $231.

FINANCIAL AID PICTURE (2011-2012)
Students with need: 89% of average financial aid package awarded as scholarships/grants, 11% awarded as loans/jobs. Need-based aid available for part-time students. Work study available nights.
Additional info: Waiver of in-state fees for eligible low-income students.

FINANCIAL AID PROCEDURES
Forms required: FAFSA, state aid form, institutional form.
Dates and Deadlines: Priority date 4/12; no closing date. Applicants notified on a rolling basis; must reply within 1 week(s) of notification.

CONTACT
Michael Dear, Director, Financial Aid and Scholarships
One Barnard Drive, Oceanside, CA 92056-3899
(760) 795-6711

Modesto Junior College
Modesto, California
www.mjc.edu Federal Code: 001240

2-year public community college in small city.
Enrollment: 14,380 undergrads.
Selectivity: Open admission; but selective for some programs.

BASIC COSTS (2012-2013)
Tuition and fees: $1,426; out-of-state residents $7,546.
Per-credit charge: $46; out-of-state residents $250.

FINANCIAL AID PICTURE
Students with need: Need-based aid available for full-time and part-time students. Work study available nights, weekends, and for part-time students.
Students without need: This college awards aid only to students with need.
Additional info: Modesto Junior College scholarship priority deadline 12/15.

FINANCIAL AID PROCEDURES
Forms required: FAFSA, state aid form, institutional form.
Dates and Deadlines: Priority date 3/2; no closing date. Applicants notified on a rolling basis starting 5/1; must reply within 2 week(s) of notification.

CONTACT
Myra Rush, Director of Financial Aid and Scholarships
435 College Avenue, Modesto, CA 95350-5800
(209) 575-6023

Monterey Peninsula College
Monterey, California
www.mpc.edu Federal Code: 001242

2-year public community college in large town.
Enrollment: 4,587 undergrads.
Selectivity: Open admission; but selective for some programs.

BASIC COSTS (2012-2013)
Tuition and fees: $1,446; out-of-state residents $6,816.
Per-credit charge: $46; out-of-state residents $225.
Additional info: Tuition/fee waivers available for adults, minority students, unemployed or children of unemployed.

FINANCIAL AID PICTURE
Students with need: Need-based aid available for full-time and part-time students.

FINANCIAL AID PROCEDURES
Forms required: FAFSA, institutional form.
Dates and Deadlines: Closing date 6/30. Applicants notified on a rolling basis starting 6/1.

CONTACT
Danielle Hodgkins, Student Financial Services Coordinator
980 Fremont Street, Monterey, CA 93940-4799
(831) 646-4000

Mount St. Mary's College
Los Angeles, California
www.msmc.la.edu Federal Code: 001243

4-year private liberal arts college for women in very large city, affiliated with Roman Catholic Church.
Enrollment: 2,445 undergrads, 22% part-time. 535 full-time freshmen.
Selectivity: Admits 50 to 75% of applicants.

BASIC COSTS (2013-2014)
Tuition and fees: $33,852.
Per-credit charge: $1,370.
Room and board: $10,530.

FINANCIAL AID PICTURE (2012-2013)
Students with need: Out of 519 full-time freshmen who applied for aid, 506 were judged to have need. Of these, 505 received aid, and 49 had their full need met. Average financial aid package met 67% of need; average scholarship/grant was $14,109; average loan was $3,121. For part-time students, average financial aid package was $10,000.

Students without need: 25 full-time freshmen who did not demonstrate need for aid received scholarships/grants; average award was $13,600. No-need awards available for academics, alumni affiliation, music/drama.
Cumulative student debt: 83% of graduating class had student loans; average debt was $34,998.

FINANCIAL AID PROCEDURES
Forms required: FAFSA.
Dates and Deadlines: Closing date 3/2. Applicants notified on a rolling basis starting 3/1; must reply by 5/1.
Transfers: No deadline. Applicants notified on a rolling basis starting 3/1; must reply by 5/1 or within 3 week(s) of notification.

CONTACT
La Royce Housely, Director of Student Financing
12001 Chalon Road, Los Angeles, CA 90049
(310) 954-4195

Mount San Antonio College

Walnut, California
www.mtsac.edu Federal Code: 001245

2-year public community college in small city.
Enrollment: 25,454 undergrads. 2,227 full-time freshmen.
Selectivity: Open admission.

BASIC COSTS (2012-2013)
Tuition and fees: $1,403; out-of-state residents $7,913.
Per-credit charge: $46; out-of-state residents $263.

FINANCIAL AID PICTURE (2011-2012)
Students with need: 95% of average financial aid package awarded as scholarships/grants, 5% awarded as loans/jobs. Need-based aid available for part-time students.
Students without need: This college awards aid only to students with need.

FINANCIAL AID PROCEDURES
Forms required: FAFSA.
Dates and Deadlines: Priority date 4/15; no closing date. Applicants notified on a rolling basis starting 7/1.

CONTACT
Chau Dao, Director Financial Aid
1100 North Grand Avenue, Walnut, CA 91789
(909) 274-4450

Mount San Jacinto College

San Jacinto, California
www.msjc.edu Federal Code: 001246

2-year public community college in small city.
Enrollment: 7,165 undergrads.
Selectivity: Open admission; but selective for some programs.

BASIC COSTS (2012-2013)
Tuition and fees: $1,380; out-of-state residents $6,750.
Per-credit charge: $46; out-of-state residents $225.

FINANCIAL AID PICTURE
Students with need: Need-based aid available for full-time and part-time students. Work study available nights.
Students without need: No-need awards available for academics, music/drama.
Additional info: Board of Governors Grant Program for state residents to defray cost of enrollment fees.

FINANCIAL AID PROCEDURES
Forms required: FAFSA, institutional form.
Dates and Deadlines: Priority date 3/2; no closing date. Applicants notified on a rolling basis starting 5/1; must reply within 3 week(s) of notification.
Transfers: No deadline.

CONTACT
Leisa Navarro, Financial Aid Supervisor
1499 North State Street, San Jacinto, CA 92583
(951) 487-3245

Mt. Sierra College

Monrovia, California
www.mtsierra.edu Federal Code: 031287

3-year for-profit visual arts and business college in large city.
Enrollment: 548 undergrads.
Selectivity: Admits over 75% of applicants.

BASIC COSTS (2012-2013)
Tuition and fees: $15,715.
Per-credit charge: $347.
Additional info: Mandatory STRF fee between $197.50 and $217.50 depending upon program and due upon enrollment; laptop expenses between $600 - $1,600 depending upon program. Books and supplies: $5,544 - $6,648 depending upon program.

FINANCIAL AID PICTURE
Students with need: Need-based aid available for full-time and part-time students.

FINANCIAL AID PROCEDURES
Forms required: FAFSA.

CONTACT
Lida Castillo, Financial Aid Director
101 East Huntington Drive, Monrovia, CA 91016
(626) 873-2100

MTI College

Sacramento, California
www.mticollege.edu Federal Code: 012912

2-year for-profit business and technical college in large city.
Enrollment: 635 undergrads.

BASIC COSTS (2012-2013)
Tuition and fees: $13,577.

FINANCIAL AID PICTURE
Students with need: Need-based aid available for full-time students. Work study available nights.

CONTACT
Paula Perez, Director of Financial Aid
5221 Madison Avenue, Sacramento, CA 95841
(916) 339-1500

National University

La Jolla, California
www.nu.edu Federal Code: 011460

4-year private university in very large city.
Enrollment: 13,868 undergrads, 66% part-time. 97 full-time freshmen.
Selectivity: Open admission; but selective for some programs.

BASIC COSTS (2013-2014)
Tuition and fees: $11,796.
Per-credit charge: $326.

FINANCIAL AID PICTURE
Students with need: Need-based aid available for full-time and part-time students.

FINANCIAL AID PROCEDURES
Forms required: FAFSA, state aid form, institutional form.
Dates and Deadlines: Applicants notified on a rolling basis.
Transfers: No deadline.

CONTACT
Valerie Ryan, Director of Financial Aid
11255 North Torrey Pines Road, La Jolla, CA 92037-1011
(858) 642-8500

Notre Dame de Namur University
Belmont, California
www.ndnu.edu — Federal Code: 001179

4-year private university and liberal arts college in large town, affiliated with Roman Catholic Church.
Enrollment: 1,180 undergrads, 32% part-time. 182 full-time freshmen.
Selectivity: Admits 50 to 75% of applicants.

BASIC COSTS (2013-2014)
Tuition and fees: $31,206.
Per-credit charge: $994.
Room and board: $12,280.

FINANCIAL AID PICTURE (2012-2013)
Students with need: Out of 179 full-time freshmen who applied for aid, 167 were judged to have need. Of these, 167 received aid, and 6 had their full need met. Average financial aid package met 61% of need; average scholarship/grant was $21,682; average loan was $3,487. For part-time students, average financial aid package was $8,571.
Students without need: 11 full-time freshmen who did not demonstrate need for aid received scholarships/grants; average award was $9,682. No-need awards available for academics, alumni affiliation, art, athletics, leadership, music/drama, religious affiliation.
Scholarships offered: ***Merit:*** Presidential Scholarships: up to $26,000 per year; based on academic merit and leadership. Emerging Artist Scholarship: up to $9,500 annually; based on demonstrated talent in the performing and fine arts. Belmont Scholarships: up to $9,000 annually; based on merit. Bay Area Catholic High School: up to $7,500 per year to one student from each of Bay Area Catholic high schools. ***Athletic:*** 3 full-time freshmen received athletic scholarships; average amount $5,333.
Cumulative student debt: 73% of graduating class had student loans; average debt was $31,915.

FINANCIAL AID PROCEDURES
Forms required: FAFSA. CSS PROFILE accepted but not required.
Dates and Deadlines: Priority date 3/2; no closing date. Applicants notified on a rolling basis starting 1/15.

CONTACT
Wilbert Lleses, Director of Financial Aid
1500 Ralston Avenue, Belmont, CA 94002-1908
(650) 508-3600

Occidental College
Los Angeles, California — Federal Code: 001249
www.oxy.edu — CSS Code: 4581

4-year private liberal arts college in very large city, affiliated with nondenominational tradition.
Enrollment: 2,172 undergrads, 1% part-time. 539 full-time freshmen.
Selectivity: Admits less than 50% of applicants.

BASIC COSTS (2012-2013)
Tuition and fees: $44,540.
Room and board: $12,458.

FINANCIAL AID PICTURE (2011-2012)
Students with need: Out of 379 full-time freshmen who applied for aid, 302 were judged to have need. Of these, 301 received aid, and 301 had their full need met. Average financial aid package met 100% of need; average scholarship/grant was $32,282; average loan was $4,637. For part-time students, average financial aid package was $27,213.
Students without need: 78 full-time freshmen who did not demonstrate need for aid received scholarships/grants; average award was $11,369. No-need awards available for academics, leadership, music/drama, state/district residency.
Scholarships offered: Margaret Bundy Scott Scholarship: $20,000. President's Scholarship: $15,000; awarded to top 10-15% of incoming class based on academic achievement, leadership, and citizenship.
Cumulative student debt: 51% of graduating class had student loans; average debt was $23,703.
Additional info: Work-study programs are available during the day when students are not in class.

FINANCIAL AID PROCEDURES
Forms required: FAFSA, CSS PROFILE, state aid form.
Dates and Deadlines: Closing date 2/1. Applicants notified by 4/1; must reply by 5/1.
Transfers: Closing date 3/15. Applicants notified on a rolling basis; must reply within 2 week(s) of notification. California residents must apply for Cal Grant by completing FAFSA and CSAC's GPA verification form by March 2.

CONTACT
Maureen McRae, Director of Financial Aid
1600 Campus Road, Los Angeles, CA 90041
(323) 259-2548

Ohlone College
Fremont, California
www.ohlone.edu — Federal Code: 004481

2-year public community college in large city.
Enrollment: 4,412 undergrads.
Selectivity: Open admission; but selective for some programs.

BASIC COSTS (2012-2013)
Tuition and fees: $1,428; out-of-state residents $7,968.
Per-credit charge: $46; out-of-state residents $264.
Additional info: Tuition/fee waivers available for adults, minority students, unemployed or children of unemployed.

FINANCIAL AID PICTURE (2011-2012)
Students with need: 83% of average financial aid package awarded as scholarships/grants, 17% awarded as loans/jobs. Need-based aid available for part-time students.
Students without need: No-need awards available for academics.

FINANCIAL AID PROCEDURES
Forms required: FAFSA, state aid form, institutional form.
Dates and Deadlines: Priority date 7/1; no closing date. Applicants notified on a rolling basis starting 7/30; must reply within 2 week(s) of notification.

CONTACT
Deborah Griffin, Financial Aid Director
43600 Mission Boulevard, Fremont, CA 94539-0390
(510) 659-6150

Orange Coast College

Costa Mesa, California
www.orangecoastcollege.edu Federal Code: 001250

2-year public community college in small city.
Enrollment: 16,345 undergrads. 1,192 full-time freshmen.
Selectivity: Open admission.

BASIC COSTS (2012-2013)
Tuition and fees: $1,418; out-of-state residents $7,838.
Per-credit charge: $46; out-of-state residents $260.
Additional info: Computer - $900. Tuition/fee waivers available for adults, minority students, unemployed or children of unemployed.

FINANCIAL AID PICTURE (2011-2012)
Students with need: Out of 1,192 full-time freshmen who applied for aid, 1,182 were judged to have need. Of these, 1,181 received aid. Average financial aid package met 29% of need; average scholarship/grant was $4,775; average loan was $2,300. For part-time students, average financial aid package was $4,053.

FINANCIAL AID PROCEDURES
Forms required: FAFSA.
Dates and Deadlines: Priority date 3/2; closing date 5/25. Applicants notified by 2/15; must reply within 2 week(s) of notification.

CONTACT
Melissa Moser, Financial Aid Director
2701 Fairview Road, Costa Mesa, CA 92628-5005
(714) 432-5508

Otis College of Art and Design

Los Angeles, California
www.otis.edu Federal Code: 001251

4-year private visual arts college in very large city.
Enrollment: 1,100 undergrads, 2% part-time. 183 full-time freshmen.
Selectivity: Admits 50 to 75% of applicants.

BASIC COSTS (2013-2014)
Tuition and fees: $38,300.
Per-credit charge: $1,219.

FINANCIAL AID PICTURE (2012-2013)
Students with need: Out of 140 full-time freshmen who applied for aid, 131 were judged to have need. Of these, 131 received aid, and 9 had their full need met. Average financial aid package met 58% of need; average scholarship/grant was $19,134; average loan was $3,475. For part-time students, average financial aid package was $5,535.
Students without need: 34 full-time freshmen who did not demonstrate need for aid received scholarships/grants; average award was $12,174. No-need awards available for academics, art.

FINANCIAL AID PROCEDURES
Forms required: FAFSA, state aid form.
Dates and Deadlines: Priority date 2/15; no closing date. Applicants notified on a rolling basis starting 3/1; must reply within 2 week(s) of notification.

CONTACT
Jessika Vasquez-Huerta, Director of Financial Aid
9045 Lincoln Boulevard, Los Angeles, CA 90045-9785
(310) 665-6880

Oxnard College

Oxnard, California
www.oxnardcollege.edu Federal Code: 016391

2-year public community college in small city.
Enrollment: 3,616 undergrads. 406 full-time freshmen.
Selectivity: Open admission.

BASIC COSTS (2012-2013)
Tuition and fees: $1,428; out-of-state residents $9,348.
Per-credit charge: $46; out-of-state residents $310.
Additional info: Tuition/fee waivers available for adults, minority students, unemployed or children of unemployed.

FINANCIAL AID PICTURE (2011-2012)
Students with need: 98% of average financial aid package awarded as scholarships/grants, 2% awarded as loans/jobs.

FINANCIAL AID PROCEDURES
Forms required: FAFSA.
Dates and Deadlines: Closing date 6/30. Applicants notified on a rolling basis; must reply within 2 week(s) of notification.

CONTACT
Linda Robison, Director of Financial Aid
4000 South Rose Avenue, Oxnard, CA 93033
(805) 986-5828

Pacific Oaks College

Pasadena, California
www.pacificoaks.edu Federal Code: 001255

Upper-division private teachers college in small city.
Enrollment: 180 undergrads.

BASIC COSTS (2012-2013)
Tuition and fees: $22,080.
Per-credit charge: $736.

FINANCIAL AID PICTURE
Students with need: Need-based aid available for full-time and part-time students. Work study available nights, weekends, and for part-time students.
Students without need: This college awards aid only to students with need.

FINANCIAL AID PROCEDURES
Dates and Deadlines: Priority date 4/15; no closing date. Applicants notified on a rolling basis starting 5/1; must reply by 5/15 or within 4 week(s) of notification.

CONTACT
Seph Rodriguez, Director of Financial Aid
55 Eureka Street, Pasadena, CA 91103
(626) 397-1350

Pacific States University

Los Angeles, California
www.psuca.edu Federal Code: 031633

4-year private university in very large city.
Enrollment: 19 undergrads.
Selectivity: Open admission; but selective for some programs.

BASIC COSTS (2013-2014)
Tuition and fees: $14,655.
Per-credit charge: $315.

Additional info: On-campus room-only expenses for academic year: $7,200. Tuition at time of enrollment locked for 4 years.

FINANCIAL AID PICTURE

Students with need: Need-based aid available for full-time and part-time students.

Students without need: No-need awards available for academics.

FINANCIAL AID PROCEDURES

Forms required: FAFSA, institutional form.

CONTACT

Min Kim, Financial Aid Officer
3450 Wilshire Boulevard, Suite 500, Los Angeles, CA 90010
(323) 731-2383 ext. 14

Pacific Union College

Angwin, California
www.puc.edu Federal Code: 001258

4-year private liberal arts college in small town, affiliated with Seventh-day Adventists.

Enrollment: 1,524 undergrads, 10% part-time. 291 full-time freshmen.

Selectivity: Admits less than 50% of applicants.

BASIC COSTS (2013-2014)

Tuition and fees: $26,850.

Room and board: $7,485.

Additional info: Health Insurance $630/year.

FINANCIAL AID PICTURE (2012-2013)

Students with need: Out of 291 full-time freshmen who applied for aid, 250 were judged to have need. Of these, 250 received aid, and 6 had their full need met. Average financial aid package met 73% of need; average scholarship/grant was $20,222; average loan was $3,180. Need-based aid available for part-time students.

Students without need: 41 full-time freshmen who did not demonstrate need for aid received scholarships/grants; average award was $9,886. No-need awards available for academics, art, athletics, leadership, music/drama, religious affiliation.

Scholarships offered: 6 full-time freshmen received athletic scholarships; average amount $2,833.

Cumulative student debt: 76% of graduating class had student loans; average debt was $33,662.

FINANCIAL AID PROCEDURES

Forms required: FAFSA, institutional form.

Dates and Deadlines: Priority date 3/2; no closing date. Applicants notified on a rolling basis starting 4/1; must reply within 3 week(s) of notification.

Transfers: No deadline. Applicants notified on a rolling basis starting 4/1; must reply within 3 week(s) of notification.

CONTACT

Laurie Wheeler, Director of Student Financial Services
One Angwin Avenue, Angwin, CA 94508-9707
(707) 965-7200

Palo Verde College

Blythe, California
www.paloverde.edu Federal Code: 001259

2-year public community college in large town.

Enrollment: 960 undergrads.

Selectivity: Open admission; but selective for some programs.

BASIC COSTS (2012-2013)

Tuition and fees: $1,380; out-of-state residents $6,750.

Per-credit charge: $46; out-of-state residents $225.

FINANCIAL AID PICTURE

Students with need: Need-based aid available for full-time and part-time students. Work study available nights.

Students without need: This college awards aid only to students with need.

FINANCIAL AID PROCEDURES

Forms required: FAFSA, state aid form, institutional form.

Dates and Deadlines: Applicants notified on a rolling basis starting 7/1; must reply within 4 week(s) of notification.

CONTACT

Linda Pratt, Financial Aid Officer
One College Drive, Blythe, CA 92225
(760) 921-5410

Palomar College

San Marcos, California
www.palomar.edu Federal Code: 001260

2-year public community college in large town.

Enrollment: 12,399 undergrads.

Selectivity: Open admission; but selective for some programs.

BASIC COSTS (2012-2013)

Tuition and fees: $1,428; out-of-state residents $6,828.

Per-credit charge: $46; out-of-state residents $226.

FINANCIAL AID PICTURE

Students with need: Need-based aid available for full-time and part-time students. Work study available nights.

Students without need: This college awards aid only to students with need.

FINANCIAL AID PROCEDURES

Forms required: FAFSA, institutional form.

Dates and Deadlines: Priority date 4/1; no closing date. Applicants notified on a rolling basis starting 6/1.

Transfers: No deadline.

CONTACT

Mary San Agustin, Director Financial Aid & Veterans Services
1140 West Mission Road, San Marcos, CA 92069-1487
(760) 744-1150 ext. 2373

Patten University

Oakland, California
www.patten.edu Federal Code: 004490

4-year private university and liberal arts college in large city, affiliated with interdenominational tradition.

Enrollment: 418 undergrads.

Selectivity: Open admission; but selective for some programs.

BASIC COSTS (2012-2013)

Tuition and fees: $13,440.

Per-credit charge: $560.

Room and board: $7,090.

FINANCIAL AID PICTURE

Students with need: Need-based aid available for full-time and part-time students.

Students without need: No-need awards available for academics, athletics, state/district residency.

FINANCIAL AID PROCEDURES
Forms required: FAFSA, institutional form.
Dates and Deadlines: Priority date 3/31; no closing date. Applicants notified on a rolling basis starting 5/31.
Transfers: No deadline.

CONTACT
Dennis Clark, Financial Aid Director
2433 Coolidge Avenue, Oakland, CA 94601-2699
(510) 261-8500 ext. 7747

Pepperdine University
Malibu, California
www.pepperdine.edu Federal Code: 001264

4-year private university and liberal arts college in small city, affiliated with Church of Christ.
Enrollment: 3,480 undergrads, 11% part-time. 678 full-time freshmen.
Selectivity: Admits less than 50% of applicants.

BASIC COSTS (2013-2014)
Tuition and fees: $44,902.
Per-credit charge: $1,395.
Room and board: $12,890.

FINANCIAL AID PICTURE (2011-2012)
Students with need: Out of 555 full-time freshmen who applied for aid, 407 were judged to have need. Of these, 402 received aid, and 100 had their full need met. Average financial aid package met 81% of need; average scholarship/grant was $37,504; average loan was $3,897. For part-time students, average financial aid package was $17,628.
Students without need: 80 full-time freshmen who did not demonstrate need for aid received scholarships/grants; average award was $16,690. No-need awards available for academics, art, athletics, leadership, music/drama, religious affiliation.
Scholarships offered: 22 full-time freshmen received athletic scholarships; average amount $40,512.
Cumulative student debt: 55% of graduating class had student loans; average debt was $32,238.

FINANCIAL AID PROCEDURES
Forms required: FAFSA.
Dates and Deadlines: Closing date 2/15. Applicants notified by 4/15; must reply by 5/1.

CONTACT
Janet Lockhart, Director of Financial Assistance
24255 Pacific Coast Highway, Malibu, CA 90263-4392
(310) 506-4301

Pitzer College
Claremont, California Federal Code: 001172
www.pitzer.edu CSS Code: 4619

4-year private liberal arts college in large town.
Enrollment: 1,084 undergrads, 4% part-time. 261 full-time freshmen.
Selectivity: Admits less than 50% of applicants.

BASIC COSTS (2012-2013)
Tuition and fees: $43,402.
Room and board: $13,864.

FINANCIAL AID PICTURE (2012-2013)
Students with need: Out of 120 full-time freshmen who applied for aid, 93 were judged to have need. Of these, 90 received aid, and 90 had their full need met. Average financial aid package met 100% of need; average scholarship/grant was $38,953; average loan was $2,748. For part-time students, average financial aid package was $22,683.
Students without need: 1 full-time freshmen who did not demonstrate need for aid received scholarships/grants; average award was $5,000. No-need awards available for academics, leadership.
Scholarships offered: Trustee Community Scholar Award: $5,000 per year; based on extraordinary academic achievement, outstanding leadership or exceptional community service.
Cumulative student debt: 47% of graduating class had student loans; average debt was $20,900.

FINANCIAL AID PROCEDURES
Forms required: FAFSA, CSS PROFILE, state aid form.
Dates and Deadlines: Closing date 2/1. Applicants notified by 4/1; must reply by 5/1.
Transfers: Closing date 3/1. Applicants notified by 5/15; must reply by 6/15.

CONTACT
Margaret Carothers, Director of Financial Aid
1050 North Mills Avenue, Claremont, CA 91711-6101
(909) 621-8208

Platt College: Los Angeles
Alhambra, California
www.plattcollege.edu Federal Code: 030627

2-year for-profit visual arts and technical college in very large city.
Enrollment: 426 undergrads.

FINANCIAL AID PICTURE
Students with need: Need-based aid available for full-time and part-time students. Work study available nights.

FINANCIAL AID PROCEDURES
Forms required: FAFSA, institutional form.
Dates and Deadlines: Priority date 3/2; no closing date. Applicants notified on a rolling basis starting 1/1.

CONTACT
Nina Martinez, Financial Aid Director
1000 South Fremont Avenue A9W, Alhambra, CA 91803
(626) 300-5444 ext. 230

Platt College: Ontario
Ontario, California
www.plattcollege.edu Federal Code: 030627

4-year for-profit branch campus and technical college in small city.
Enrollment: 472 undergrads.

FINANCIAL AID PICTURE
Students with need: Need-based aid available for full-time and part-time students. Work study available nights.
Scholarships offered: Presidential Scholarship, CAPPS Scholarship, Imagine America Scholarship: $1,000 each; based on application and essay; approximately 100 plus available per calendar year.

FINANCIAL AID PROCEDURES
Forms required: FAFSA, institutional form.
Dates and Deadlines: Priority date 3/2; no closing date. Applicants notified on a rolling basis starting 1/1.
Transfers: No deadline.

CONTACT
Rosemarie Young, Regional Director of Compliance and Civil Rights
3700 Inland Empire Boulevard, Ontario, CA 91764
(909) 941-9410

Platt College: San Diego

San Diego, California
www.platt.edu Federal Code: 023043

4-year for-profit visual arts and technical college in very large city.
Enrollment: 418 undergrads. 62 full-time freshmen.
Selectivity: Open admission; but selective for some programs and for out-of-state students.

BASIC COSTS (2012-2013)
Tuition and fees: $15,310.
Per-credit charge: $507.
Additional info: Total costs range from $17,910 to $36,310, depending on program.

FINANCIAL AID PICTURE
Students with need: Need-based aid available for full-time and part-time students.

FINANCIAL AID PROCEDURES
Forms required: FAFSA, state aid form, institutional form.
Dates and Deadlines: Closing date 3/2. Applicants notified on a rolling basis; must reply within 1 week(s) of notification.

CONTACT
Opel Oliver, Director of Financial Aid
6250 El Cajon Boulevard, San Diego, CA 92115
(619) 265-0107

Point Loma Nazarene University

San Diego, California
www.pointloma.edu Federal Code: 001262

4-year private university and liberal arts college in very large city, affiliated with Church of the Nazarene.
Enrollment: 2,410 undergrads, 3% part-time. 600 full-time freshmen.
Selectivity: Admits 50 to 75% of applicants.

BASIC COSTS (2013-2014)
Tuition and fees: $30,360.
Per-credit charge: $1,240.
Room and board: $9,810.

FINANCIAL AID PICTURE (2012-2013)
Students with need: Out of 499 full-time freshmen who applied for aid, 413 were judged to have need. Of these, 413 received aid, and 71 had their full need met. Average financial aid package met 65% of need; average scholarship/grant was $15,899; average loan was $3,444. For part-time students, average financial aid package was $10,199.
Students without need: 70 full-time freshmen who did not demonstrate need for aid received scholarships/grants; average award was $8,959. No-need awards available for academics, art, athletics, music/drama, religious affiliation, ROTC.
Scholarships offered: 12 full-time freshmen received athletic scholarships; average amount $7,082.
Cumulative student debt: 59% of graduating class had student loans; average debt was $31,851.

FINANCIAL AID PROCEDURES
Forms required: FAFSA.
Dates and Deadlines: Priority date 3/2; no closing date. Applicants notified on a rolling basis starting 12/15; must reply by 5/15.

CONTACT
Pam Macias, Director of Financial Aid
3900 Lomaland Drive, San Diego, CA 92106-2899
(619) 849-2068

Pomona College

Claremont, California Federal Code: 001173
www.pomona.edu CSS Code: 4607

4-year private liberal arts college in large town.
Enrollment: 1,585 undergrads. 394 full-time freshmen.
Selectivity: Admits less than 50% of applicants.

BASIC COSTS (2013-2014)
Tuition and fees: $43,580.
Room and board: $14,100.

FINANCIAL AID PICTURE (2011-2012)
Students with need: Out of 269 full-time freshmen who applied for aid, 216 were judged to have need. Of these, 216 received aid, and 216 had their full need met. Average financial aid package met 100% of need; average scholarship/grant was $38,475. For part-time students, average financial aid package was $49,334.
Students without need: This college awards aid only to students with need.
Cumulative student debt: 32% of graduating class had student loans; average debt was $15,714.
Additional info: Financial aid awards loan-free for all eligible students.

FINANCIAL AID PROCEDURES
Forms required: FAFSA, CSS PROFILE.
Dates and Deadlines: Closing date 2/15. Applicants notified by 4/1; must reply by 5/1.
Transfers: Closing date 3/1. Candidates required to submit financial aid transcript from previous institution directly to the college.

CONTACT
Mary Booker, Director of Financial Aid
333 North College Way, Claremont, CA 91711-6312
(909) 621-8205

Professional Golfers Career College

Temecula, California
www.golfcollege.edu Federal Code: 033673

2-year for-profit golf academy in small city.
Enrollment: 456 undergrads.

BASIC COSTS (2012-2013)
Tuition and fees: $14,400.

FINANCIAL AID PICTURE
Students with need: Need-based aid available for full-time students.

FINANCIAL AID PROCEDURES
Transfers: No deadline.

CONTACT
Ann Martin, Financial Aid Director
26109 Ynez Road, Temecula, CA 92591
(800) 877-4380

Reedley College

Reedley, California
www.reedleycollege.edu Federal Code: 001308

2-year public community college in large town.
Enrollment: 9,366 undergrads.
Selectivity: Open admission.

BASIC COSTS (2012-2013)
Tuition and fees: $1,416; out-of-state residents $8,466.

Per-credit charge: $46; out-of-state residents $281.
Room and board: $5,200.
Additional info: Tuition/fee waivers available for adults, minority students, unemployed or children of unemployed.

FINANCIAL AID PICTURE
Students with need: Need-based aid available for full-time and part-time students.
Students without need: This college awards aid only to students with need.
Additional info: Board of Governors fee waiver available for low-income students. Book voucher available for EOPS students.

FINANCIAL AID PROCEDURES
Forms required: FAFSA, state aid form.
Dates and Deadlines: Priority date 3/2; no closing date. Applicants notified on a rolling basis starting 3/2; must reply within 3 week(s) of notification.
Transfers: Priority date 4/15. March 2 deadline for California grants.

CONTACT
Chris Cortes, Director of Financial Aid
995 North Reed Avenue, Reedley, CA 93654
(559) 638-3641

Rio Hondo College

Whittier, California
www.riohondo.edu Federal Code: 001269

2-year public community college in small city.
Enrollment: 17,862 undergrads. 1,082 full-time freshmen.
Selectivity: Open admission; but selective for some programs.

BASIC COSTS (2012-2013)
Tuition and fees: $1,437; out-of-state residents $7,137.
Per-credit charge: $46; out-of-state residents $236.

FINANCIAL AID PICTURE (2011-2012)
Students with need: 93% of average financial aid package awarded as scholarships/grants, 7% awarded as loans/jobs. Need-based aid available for part-time students.

FINANCIAL AID PROCEDURES
Forms required: FAFSA.
Dates and Deadlines: Priority date 7/15; no closing date. Applicants notified on a rolling basis.

CONTACT
Elizabeth Coria, Director Financial Aid
3600 Workman Mill Road, Whittier, CA 90601-1699
(562) 908-3411

Riverside Community College

Riverside, California
www.rcc.edu Federal Code: 001270

2-year public community college in large city.
Enrollment: 11,983 undergrads.
Selectivity: Open admission; but selective for some programs.

BASIC COSTS (2012-2013)
Tuition and fees: $1,408; out-of-state residents $6,808.
Per-credit charge: $46; out-of-state residents $226.
Additional info: Tuition/fee waivers available for adults, unemployed or children of unemployed.

FINANCIAL AID PICTURE
Students with need: Need-based aid available for full-time and part-time students. Work study available nights, weekends, and for part-time students.
Students without need: No-need awards available for academics, alumni affiliation, art, leadership, minority status, music/drama, state/district residency.

FINANCIAL AID PROCEDURES
Forms required: FAFSA, institutional form.
Dates and Deadlines: Priority date 3/1; no closing date. Applicants notified on a rolling basis starting 7/1.
Transfers: Students who received financial aid at another institution and earned less than 2.0 GPA ineligible for aid during first semester. Students must complete 6 units and earn 2.0 GPA to be eligible.

CONTACT
Elizabeth Hilton, Director of Student Financial Services
4800 Magnolia Avenue, Riverside, CA 92506
(951) 222-8710

Sacramento City College

Sacramento, California
www.scc.losrios.edu Federal Code: 001233

2-year public community college in large city.
Enrollment: 16,304 undergrads.
Selectivity: Open admission.

BASIC COSTS (2012-2013)
Tuition and fees: $1,415; out-of-state residents $7,655.
Per-credit charge: $46; out-of-state residents $254.

FINANCIAL AID PICTURE
Students with need: Need-based aid available for full-time and part-time students. Work study available nights, weekends, and for part-time students.

FINANCIAL AID PROCEDURES
Forms required: FAFSA, state aid form.
Dates and Deadlines: Priority date 3/2; no closing date. Applicants notified on a rolling basis starting 7/1; must reply within 2 week(s) of notification.
Transfers: Priority date 5/30.

CONTACT
Kimberly Cortijo, Financial Aid Supervisor
3835 Freeport Boulevard, Sacramento, CA 95822
(916) 558-2546

Saddleback College

Mission Viejo, California
www.saddleback.edu Federal Code: 008918

2-year public community college in small city.
Enrollment: 14,160 undergrads.
Selectivity: Open admission; but selective for some programs.

BASIC COSTS (2012-2013)
Tuition and fees: $1,414; out-of-state residents $6,784.
Per-credit charge: $46; out-of-state residents $225.

FINANCIAL AID PICTURE
Students with need: Need-based aid available for full-time and part-time students.
Students without need: This college awards aid only to students with need.

FINANCIAL AID PROCEDURES
Forms required: FAFSA.
Dates and Deadlines: Closing date 6/30. Applicants notified on a rolling basis starting 4/1.

CONTACT
Mary Hall, Director, Financial Aid
28000 Marguerite Parkway, Mission Viejo, CA 92692
(949) 582-4860

St. Mary's College of California

Moraga, California
www.stmarys-ca.edu Federal Code: 001302

4-year private liberal arts college in large town, affiliated with Roman Catholic Church.
Enrollment: 3,017 undergrads, 8% part-time. 623 full-time freshmen.
Selectivity: Admits 50 to 75% of applicants.

BASIC COSTS (2013-2014)
Tuition and fees: $39,890.
Per-credit charge: $1,421.
Room and board: $13,660.

FINANCIAL AID PICTURE (2012-2013)
Students with need: Out of 537 full-time freshmen who applied for aid, 481 were judged to have need. Of these, 478 received aid, and 39 had their full need met. Average financial aid package met 62% of need; average scholarship/grant was $23,519; average loan was $3,700. For part-time students, average financial aid package was $15,447.
Students without need: 61 full-time freshmen who did not demonstrate need for aid received scholarships/grants; average award was $13,984. No-need awards available for academics, art, athletics, leadership, music/drama, religious affiliation.
Scholarships offered: ***Merit:*** Honors at Entrance Scholarship: $13,000 annually based on 3.7 GPA and 1200 SAT/27 ACT (SAT score exclusive of Writing). Presidential Scholars Scholarships: $11,000 annually based on 3.8 GPA and 1350 SAT (exclusive of writing) - recipients also receive Honors at Entrance Scholarship for total of $24,000 annually. Lasallian Scholarship: $11,000 annually based on attendance at a U.S. Lasallian high school. Gael Scholarships: $11,000 annually based on students noteworthy extracurricular involvement and demanding college preparatory schedules that include rigorous senior schedules with a GPA above 3.26. All scholarships are for fall term applicants admitted by March 1. ***Athletic:*** 20 full-time freshmen received athletic scholarships; average amount $33,748.
Cumulative student debt: 77% of graduating class had student loans; average debt was $31,828.

FINANCIAL AID PROCEDURES
Forms required: FAFSA, state aid form.
Dates and Deadlines: Priority date 2/15; no closing date. Applicants notified on a rolling basis starting 3/15; must reply by 5/1 or within 2 week(s) of notification.
Transfers: Closing date 2/15. Applicants notified on a rolling basis starting 3/20; must reply by 5/1. To receive consideration for all types of financial aid, transfer students must be admitted by March 1 prior to fall term. Honors at Entrance Scholarship; $13,000 annually; based on 3.5 GPA with 30 transferable credits.

CONTACT
Priscilla Muha, Director of Financial Aid
Box 4800, Moraga, CA 94575-4800
(925) 631-4370

Samuel Merritt University

Oakland, California
www.samuelmerritt.edu Federal Code: 007012

Upper-division private health science and nursing college in large city.
Enrollment: 521 undergrads.
Selectivity: GED not accepted.

BASIC COSTS (2012-2013)
Tuition and fees: $39,456.
Per-credit charge: $1,663.

FINANCIAL AID PICTURE
Students with need: Need-based aid available for full-time and part-time students. Work study available nights, weekends, and for part-time students.
Students without need: No-need awards available for academics, leadership, minority status.
Additional info: Ongoing private scholarships available. Students eligible to work in Medical Center (associated with college).

FINANCIAL AID PROCEDURES
Transfers: Priority date 3/2; no deadline. Applicants notified on a rolling basis; must reply within 3 week(s) of notification.

CONTACT
Mary Robinson, Director of Financial Aid
370 Hawthorne Avenue, Oakland, CA 94609-9954
(510) 869-1550

San Diego Christian College

El Cajon, California
www.sdcc.edu Federal Code: 012031

4-year private liberal arts college in small city, affiliated with nondenominational tradition.
Enrollment: 738 undergrads, 12% part-time. 95 full-time freshmen.
Selectivity: Admits less than 50% of applicants.

BASIC COSTS (2012-2013)
Tuition and fees: $25,208.
Per-credit charge: $964.
Room and board: $8,740.

FINANCIAL AID PICTURE (2012-2013)
Students with need: Out of 88 full-time freshmen who applied for aid, 88 were judged to have need. Of these, 88 received aid, and 2 had their full need met. Average financial aid package met 55% of need; average scholarship/grant was $4,300; average loan was $3,400. For part-time students, average financial aid package was $6,900.
Students without need: No-need awards available for academics, alumni affiliation, athletics, leadership, music/drama, state/district residency.
Scholarships offered: ***Merit:*** Early Acceptance Award: $1000; available to applicants who have turned in all admission materials by January 15th. ***Athletic:*** 1 full-time freshmen received athletic scholarships; average amount $23,324.
Cumulative student debt: 72% of graduating class had student loans; average debt was $23,868.

FINANCIAL AID PROCEDURES
Forms required: FAFSA, state aid form, institutional form.
Dates and Deadlines: Priority date 3/2; closing date 7/15. Applicants notified on a rolling basis starting 4/1; must reply by 5/1 or within 4 week(s) of notification.
Transfers: Applicants notified on a rolling basis starting 4/1; must reply by 5/1 or within 4 week(s) of notification. Transfer students with at least 30 units earned at one institution fall under a different Academic Scholarship awarding grid than first time freshman.

CONTACT
Susie Parks, Director of Enrollment Services
2100 Greenfield Drive, El Cajon, CA 92019-1157
(619) 201-8730

San Diego City College

San Diego, California
www.sdcity.edu Federal Code: 001273

2-year public community and junior college in very large city.
Enrollment: 9,889 undergrads.
Selectivity: Open admission.

BASIC COSTS (2012-2013)
Tuition and fees: $1,416; out-of-state residents $6,906.
Per-credit charge: $46; out-of-state residents $229.
Additional info: Tuition/fee waivers available for unemployed or children of unemployed.

FINANCIAL AID PICTURE
Students with need: Need-based aid available for full-time and part-time students.
Students without need: This college awards aid only to students with need.

FINANCIAL AID PROCEDURES
Forms required: FAFSA.
Dates and Deadlines: Priority date 4/15; no closing date. Applicants notified on a rolling basis starting 7/1; must reply within 4 week(s) of notification.
Transfers: No deadline. Applicants notified on a rolling basis starting 7/1. Aid is limited to remaining eligibility based on receipt of aid from previous college.

CONTACT
Greg Sanchez, Director of Financial Aid
1313 Park Boulevard, San Diego, CA 92101-4787
(619) 388-3501

San Diego Miramar College

San Diego, California
www.sdmiramar.edu Federal Code: 014172

2-year public community college in very large city.
Enrollment: 6,044 undergrads.
Selectivity: Open admission.

BASIC COSTS (2012-2013)
Tuition and fees: $1,416; out-of-state residents $6,906.
Per-credit charge: $46; out-of-state residents $229.
Additional info: Tuition/fee waivers available for unemployed or children of unemployed.

FINANCIAL AID PICTURE
Students with need: Need-based aid available for full-time and part-time students.
Additional info: Private scholarships available.

FINANCIAL AID PROCEDURES
Forms required: FAFSA.
Dates and Deadlines: Priority date 3/2; closing date 6/30. Applicants notified on a rolling basis; must reply within 3 week(s) of notification.
Transfers: No deadline. Transfers advised to apply early.

CONTACT
Teresa Vilaboy, Financial Aid Officer
10440 Black Mountain Road, San Diego, CA 92126-2999
(619) 388-7864

San Diego State University

San Diego, California
www.sdsu.edu Federal Code: 001151

4-year public university in very large city.
Enrollment: 26,624 undergrads, 12% part-time. 3,829 full-time freshmen.
Selectivity: Admits less than 50% of applicants.

BASIC COSTS (2012-2013)
Tuition and fees: $7,076; out-of-state residents $18,236.
Room and board: $11,549.

FINANCIAL AID PICTURE (2012-2013)
Students with need: Out of 3,160 full-time freshmen who applied for aid, 2,300 were judged to have need. Of these, 2,200 received aid, and 200 had their full need met. Average financial aid package met 69% of need; average scholarship/grant was $11,000; average loan was $3,100. For part-time students, average financial aid package was $7,800.
Students without need: 100 full-time freshmen who did not demonstrate need for aid received scholarships/grants; average award was $3,600. No-need awards available for academics, alumni affiliation, art, athletics, leadership, music/drama, ROTC, state/district residency.
Scholarships offered: ***Merit:*** Various departmental scholarships are open to first time freshman with declared majors. Brian Schultz Memorial Scholarship, amount varies (1 awarded); recipient must be a cancer survivor or have been affected by cancer. ***Athletic:*** 120 full-time freshmen received athletic scholarships; average amount $11,700.
Cumulative student debt: 44% of graduating class had student loans; average debt was $17,600.

FINANCIAL AID PROCEDURES
Forms required: FAFSA, state aid form.
Dates and Deadlines: Priority date 4/1; closing date 3/2. Applicants notified on a rolling basis starting 2/14.
Transfers: No deadline. Applicants notified on a rolling basis.

CONTACT
Chrys Dutton, Director of Financial Aid
5500 Campanile Drive, San Diego, CA 92182-7455
(619) 594-6323

San Francisco Art Institute

San Francisco, California
www.sfai.edu Federal Code: 003948

4-year private visual arts college in very large city.
Enrollment: 442 undergrads, 7% part-time. 87 full-time freshmen.
Selectivity: Admits 50 to 75% of applicants.

BASIC COSTS (2013-2014)
Tuition and fees: $38,406.
Per-credit charge: $1,644.
Room and board: $14,086.

FINANCIAL AID PICTURE (2011-2012)
Students with need: Out of 55 full-time freshmen who applied for aid, 40 were judged to have need. Of these, 40 received aid. Average financial aid package met 49% of need; average scholarship/grant was $6,420; average loan was $3,156. Need-based aid available for part-time students.
Students without need: 15 full-time freshmen who did not demonstrate need for aid received scholarships/grants; average award was $7,533. No-need awards available for academics, art.
Scholarships offered: Several awards based on portfolio reviews during application for admissions process.
Cumulative student debt: 53% of graduating class had student loans; average debt was $29,541.

FINANCIAL AID PROCEDURES
Forms required: FAFSA.
Dates and Deadlines: Priority date 3/1; closing date 5/31. Applicants notified on a rolling basis starting 4/15; must reply within 3 week(s) of notification.
Transfers: Priority date 3/2; no deadline. Applicants notified on a rolling basis starting 4/1; must reply within 3 week(s) of notification.

CONTACT
Larry Blair, Director of Financial Aid
SFAI - Admissions Office, San Francisco, CA 94133
(415) 749-4520

San Francisco Conservatory of Music
San Francisco, California
www.sfcm.edu Federal Code: 001278

4-year private music college in very large city.
Enrollment: 184 undergrads, 1% part-time. 38 full-time freshmen.
Selectivity: Admits less than 50% of applicants.

BASIC COSTS (2013-2014)
Tuition and fees: $39,580.
Per-credit charge: $1,716.
Room and board: $12,000.

FINANCIAL AID PICTURE (2012-2013)
Students with need: Out of 33 full-time freshmen who applied for aid, 23 were judged to have need. Of these, 23 received aid, and 5 had their full need met. Average financial aid package met 39% of need; average scholarship/grant was $17,174; average loan was $3,500. Need-based aid available for part-time students.
Students without need: 7 full-time freshmen who did not demonstrate need for aid received scholarships/grants; average award was $11,000. No-need awards available for music/drama.
Cumulative student debt: 68% of graduating class had student loans; average debt was $16,000.

FINANCIAL AID PROCEDURES
Forms required: FAFSA, institutional form.
Dates and Deadlines: Priority date 3/1; no closing date. Applicants notified on a rolling basis starting 3/15; must reply by 5/1 or within 2 week(s) of notification.
Transfers: Priority date 2/1; closing date 4/1. Applicants notified on a rolling basis starting 4/1; must reply by 5/1 or within 2 week(s) of notification.

CONTACT
Doris Howard, Financial Aid Officer
50 Oak Street, San Francisco, CA 94102
(415) 503-6235

San Francisco State University
San Francisco, California
www.sfsu.edu Federal Code: 001154

4-year public university in very large city.
Enrollment: 26,065 undergrads, 14% part-time. 3,710 full-time freshmen.
Selectivity: Admits 50 to 75% of applicants.

BASIC COSTS (2012-2013)
Tuition and fees: $6,774; out-of-state residents $17,934.
Room and board: $12,414.

FINANCIAL AID PICTURE (2012-2013)
Students with need: Out of 3,205 full-time freshmen who applied for aid, 2,667 were judged to have need. Of these, 2,558 received aid, and 184 had their full need met. Average financial aid package met 64% of need; average scholarship/grant was $10,404; average loan was $2,433. For part-time students, average financial aid package was $8,319.
Students without need: This college awards aid only to students with need.
Scholarships offered: ***Merit:*** Presidential Scholarship: 3.8 GPA and California residency required. ***Athletic:*** 15 full-time freshmen received athletic scholarships; average amount $3,449.
Cumulative student debt: 43% of graduating class had student loans; average debt was $20,493.

FINANCIAL AID PROCEDURES
Forms required: FAFSA.
Dates and Deadlines: Priority date 3/2; no closing date. Applicants notified on a rolling basis starting 3/30; must reply within 2 week(s) of notification.

CONTACT
Barbara Hubler, Director of Financial Aid
1600 Holloway Avenue, San Francisco, CA 94132
(415) 338-7000

San Joaquin Delta College
Stockton, California
www.deltacollege.edu Federal Code: 001280

2-year public community college in large city.
Enrollment: 11,605 undergrads. 9,156 full-time freshmen.
Selectivity: Open admission; but selective for some programs.

BASIC COSTS (2012-2013)
Tuition and fees: $1,382; out-of-state residents $7,082.
Per-credit charge: $46; out-of-state residents $236.

FINANCIAL AID PICTURE (2011-2012)
Students with need: Out of 9,155 full-time freshmen who applied for aid, 7,661 were judged to have need. Of these, 6,447 received aid, and 19 had their full need met. Average financial aid package met 31.54% of need; average scholarship/grant was $4,621; average loan was $2,787. For part-time students, average financial aid package was $4,386.
Students without need: No-need awards available for academics, athletics.
Cumulative student debt: 77% of graduating class had student loans; average debt was $12,637.
Additional info: Enrollment fee waivers available for low-income California residents.

FINANCIAL AID PROCEDURES
Forms required: FAFSA, institutional form.
Dates and Deadlines: Closing date 6/30. Applicants notified on a rolling basis starting 5/1; must reply within 3 week(s) of notification.
Transfers: No deadline.

CONTACT
Denise Donn, Director of Financial Aid
5151 Pacific Avenue, Stockton, CA 95207-6370
(209) 954-5115

San Joaquin Valley College
Visalia, California
www.sjvc.edu Federal Code: 021207

2-year for-profit junior college in small city.
Enrollment: 1,679 undergrads.
Selectivity: Open admission; but selective for some programs.

BASIC COSTS (2012-2013)
Tuition and fees: $15,500.

Additional info: Tuition quoted is for certificate program. Degree program costs vary ranging from $28,500 to $58,970.

FINANCIAL AID PICTURE

Students with need: Need-based aid available for full-time students.

FINANCIAL AID PROCEDURES

Forms required: FAFSA, state aid form, institutional form.

CONTACT

Kevin Robinson, Vice President of Student Financial Services
8400 West Mineral King Avenue, Visalia, CA 93291-9283
(559) 651-2500

San Jose City College

San Jose, California
www.sjcc.edu Federal Code: 001282

2-year public community college in very large city.
Enrollment: 8,515 undergrads.
Selectivity: Open admission.

BASIC COSTS (2012-2013)

Tuition and fees: $1,416; out-of-state residents $7,386.
Per-credit charge: $46; out-of-state residents $245.

FINANCIAL AID PICTURE

Students with need: Need-based aid available for full-time and part-time students.
Students without need: This college awards aid only to students with need.
Additional info: Board of Governors Grant (fee waivers) available to all qualified applicants.

FINANCIAL AID PROCEDURES

Forms required: FAFSA.
Dates and Deadlines: Applicants notified on a rolling basis; must reply within 4 week(s) of notification.

CONTACT

Takeo Kubo, Dean of Enrollment Services
2100 Moorpark Avenue, San Jose, CA 95128-2798
(408) 288-3741

San Jose State University

San Jose, California
www.sjsu.edu Federal Code: 001155

4-year public university and liberal arts college in very large city.
Enrollment: 25,157 undergrads, 19% part-time. 3,300 full-time freshmen.
Selectivity: Admits 50 to 75% of applicants.

BASIC COSTS (2012-2013)

Tuition and fees: $7,427; out-of-state residents $18,587.
Room and board: $11,730.

FINANCIAL AID PICTURE (2011-2012)

Students with need: Need-based aid available for full-time and part-time students. Work study available nights, weekends, and for part-time students.
Students without need: This college awards aid only to students with need.

FINANCIAL AID PROCEDURES

Dates and Deadlines: Priority date 3/2; closing date 6/15. Applicants notified on a rolling basis starting 4/1.

CONTACT

Coleetta Mcelroy, Director of Financial Aid & Scholarships
One Washington Square, San Jose, CA 95192-0011
(408) 283-7500

Santa Barbara City College

Santa Barbara, California
www.sbcc.edu Federal Code: 001285

2-year public community college in small city.
Enrollment: 12,610 undergrads.
Selectivity: Open admission; but selective for some programs.

BASIC COSTS (2012-2013)

Tuition and fees: $1,414; out-of-state residents $7,774.
Per-credit charge: $46; out-of-state residents $258.
Additional info: Tuition/fee waivers available for unemployed or children of unemployed.

FINANCIAL AID PICTURE

Students with need: Need-based aid available for full-time and part-time students.
Additional info: California residents may qualify for Board of Governor's Financial Assistance Program, which will allow institutions to waive enrollment fee.

FINANCIAL AID PROCEDURES

Forms required: FAFSA.
Dates and Deadlines: Applicants notified on a rolling basis starting 5/1; must reply within 2 week(s) of notification.

CONTACT

Brad Hardison, Director of Financial Aid
721 Cliff Drive, Santa Barbara, CA 93109-2394
(805) 965-0581 ext. 2716

Santa Clara University

Santa Clara, California Federal Code: 001326
www.scu.edu CSS Code: 4851

4-year private university in small city, affiliated with Roman Catholic Church.
Enrollment: 5,205 undergrads, 2% part-time. 1,276 full-time freshmen.
Selectivity: Admits 50 to 75% of applicants.

BASIC COSTS (2013-2014)

Tuition and fees: $42,156.
Room and board: $12,546.

FINANCIAL AID PICTURE (2012-2013)

Students with need: Out of 896 full-time freshmen who applied for aid, 634 were judged to have need. Of these, 627 received aid, and 241 had their full need met. Average financial aid package met 73% of need; average scholarship/grant was $19,450; average loan was $3,459. Need-based aid available for part-time students.
Students without need: 354 full-time freshmen who did not demonstrate need for aid received scholarships/grants; average award was $10,357. No-need awards available for academics, athletics, music/drama, ROTC.
Scholarships offered: 49 full-time freshmen received athletic scholarships; average amount $25,924.
Cumulative student debt: 46% of graduating class had student loans; average debt was $28,672.

FINANCIAL AID PROCEDURES

Forms required: FAFSA, CSS PROFILE.
Dates and Deadlines: Priority date 2/1; no closing date. Applicants notified by 4/1; must reply by 5/1 or within 2 week(s) of notification.
Transfers: No deadline. Applicants notified on a rolling basis starting 4/1; must reply by 5/1 or within 2 week(s) of notification.

CONTACT

Richard Toomey, Dean of Financial Services
500 El Camino Real, Santa Clara, CA 95053
(408) 554-4505

Santa Monica College

Santa Monica, California
www.smc.edu
Federal Code: 001286

2-year public community college in small city.
Enrollment: 24,467 undergrads. 2,787 full-time freshmen.
Selectivity: Open admission; but selective for some programs.

BASIC COSTS (2012-2013)
Tuition and fees: $1,416; out-of-state residents $8,886.
Per-credit charge: $46; out-of-state residents $295.

FINANCIAL AID PICTURE
Students with need: Need-based aid available for full-time and part-time students.

FINANCIAL AID PROCEDURES
Forms required: FAFSA, institutional form.
Dates and Deadlines: Applicants notified on a rolling basis starting 7/1; must reply within 2 week(s) of notification.
Transfers: No deadline.

CONTACT
Steve Myrow, Director of Financial Aid
1900 Pico Boulevard, Santa Monica, CA 90405-1628
(310) 434-4343

Santa Rosa Junior College

Santa Rosa, California
www.santarosa.edu
Federal Code: 001287

2-year public community college in small city.
Enrollment: 22,215 undergrads.
Selectivity: Open admission; but selective for some programs.

BASIC COSTS (2012-2013)
Tuition and fees: $1,418; out-of-state residents $7,388.
Per-credit charge: $46; out-of-state residents $245.

FINANCIAL AID PICTURE
Students with need: Need-based aid available for full-time and part-time students. Work study available nights.
Students without need: No-need awards available for academics, art, leadership, music/drama, state/district residency.
Additional info: California's Board of Governors Program provides fee waivers for applicants with need.

FINANCIAL AID PROCEDURES
Forms required: FAFSA.
Dates and Deadlines: Priority date 3/1; no closing date. Applicants notified on a rolling basis starting 4/15.

CONTACT
Kristin Shear, Director of Financial Services
1501 Mendocino Avenue, Santa Rosa, CA 95401-4395
(707) 527-4471

Santiago Canyon College

Orange, California
www.sccollege.edu

2-year public community college in small city.
Enrollment: 6,650 undergrads.
Selectivity: Open admission.

BASIC COSTS (2012-2013)
Tuition and fees: $1,418; out-of-state residents $7,508.
Per-credit charge: $46; out-of-state residents $249.
Additional info: Tuition/fee waivers available for adults, minority students, unemployed or children of unemployed.

FINANCIAL AID PICTURE
Students with need: Need-based aid available for full-time and part-time students.
Students without need: This college awards aid only to students with need.

FINANCIAL AID PROCEDURES
Forms required: FAFSA, state aid form, institutional form.
Dates and Deadlines: Priority date 7/1; no closing date. Applicants notified on a rolling basis starting 6/1.
Transfers: No deadline. Applicants notified by 6/1.

CONTACT
Syed Rizvi, Associate Dean of Student Support Services
8045 East Chapman Avenue, Orange, CA 92869
(714) 628-4876

School of Urban Missions: Oakland

Oakland, California
www.sum.edu
Federal Code: 037524

4-year private Bible and seminary college in very large city, affiliated with Assemblies of God.
Enrollment: 315 undergrads.
Selectivity: Open admission; but selective for some programs.

BASIC COSTS (2012-2013)
Tuition and fees: $8,200.
Per-credit charge: $260.
Additional info: Additional $520 charge for those required to attend the Mardi Gras practicum. Board plan not available. Cost of room only, $2,400.

FINANCIAL AID PICTURE
Students with need: Need-based aid available for full-time and part-time students.
Students without need: No-need awards available for academics, leadership, religious affiliation.

FINANCIAL AID PROCEDURES
Forms required: FAFSA.
Transfers: No deadline. Applicants notified on a rolling basis.

CONTACT
Kathryn Mangan, Financial Aid Director
735 105th Avenue, Oakland, CA 94603
(510) 567-6174

Scripps College

Claremont, California
www.scrippscollege.edu
Federal Code: 001174
CSS Code: 4693

4-year private liberal arts college for women in large town.
Enrollment: 935 undergrads. 235 full-time freshmen.
Selectivity: Admits less than 50% of applicants.

BASIC COSTS (2012-2013)
Tuition and fees: $43,620.
Per-credit charge: $1,357.
Room and board: $13,468.

FINANCIAL AID PICTURE
Students with need: Need-based aid available for full-time and part-time students. Work study available nights, weekends, and for part-time students.

Students without need: No-need awards available for academics, leadership.

Scholarships offered: James E. Scripps Scholarship; variable amount up to half-tuition; renewable; for distinguished young women whose intellectual and personal promise can be developed with a Scripps education.

FINANCIAL AID PROCEDURES

Forms required: FAFSA, CSS PROFILE, state aid form.

Dates and Deadlines: Closing date 2/1. Applicants notified by 4/1; must reply by 5/1.

Transfers: Priority date 4/1; closing date 4/1. Applicants notified by 5/1; must reply by 6/1 or within 2 week(s) of notification. Students applying for admission as a transfer student should be aware that financial aid may be limited or unavailable.

CONTACT

Victoria Romero, Vice President, Enrollment Management
1030 Columbia Avenue, Claremont, CA 91711-3905
(909) 621-8275

Shasta Bible College and Graduate School

Redding, California
www.shasta.edu Federal Code: 016802

4-year private Bible and seminary college in small city, affiliated with Baptist faith.

Enrollment: 59 undergrads.

Selectivity: Admits over 75% of applicants.

BASIC COSTS (2012-2013)

Tuition and fees: $9,680.

Per-credit charge: $300.

Additional info: Board plan not available. Cost of room only, $2,800.

FINANCIAL AID PICTURE

Students with need: Need-based aid available for full-time and part-time students.

Students without need: No-need awards available for music/drama.

FINANCIAL AID PROCEDURES

Forms required: FAFSA.

Dates and Deadlines: Closing date 8/1. Applicants notified on a rolling basis.

CONTACT

Linda Iles, Financial Aid Director
2951 Goodwater Avenue, Redding, CA 96002
(530) 221-4275 ext. 32

Shasta College

Redding, California
www.shastacollege.edu Federal Code: 001289

2-year public community and junior college in small city.

Enrollment: 4,684 undergrads.

Selectivity: Open admission; but selective for some programs.

BASIC COSTS (2012-2013)

Tuition and fees: $1,418; out-of-state residents $7,718.

Per-credit charge: $46; out-of-state residents $256.

Additional info: Board plan not available. Cost of room only: $3823.

FINANCIAL AID PICTURE

Students with need: Need-based aid available for full-time and part-time students.

Students without need: This college awards aid only to students with need.

FINANCIAL AID PROCEDURES

Forms required: FAFSA, institutional form.

Dates and Deadlines: Priority date 3/2; no closing date. Applicants notified on a rolling basis starting 7/1.

CONTACT

Benna Starrett, Director of Financial Aid
Box 496006, Redding, CA 96049-6006
(530) 225-4735

Sierra College

Rocklin, California
www.sierracollege.edu Federal Code: 001290

2-year public community college in small city.

Enrollment: 12,887 undergrads.

Selectivity: Open admission; but selective for some programs.

BASIC COSTS (2012-2013)

Tuition and fees: $1,428; out-of-state residents $7,128.

Per-credit charge: $46; out-of-state residents $236.

Room and board: $6,824.

FINANCIAL AID PICTURE

Students with need: Need-based aid available for full-time and part-time students. Work study available nights, weekends, and for part-time students.

FINANCIAL AID PROCEDURES

Forms required: FAFSA.

Dates and Deadlines: Priority date 3/2; no closing date. Applicants notified on a rolling basis starting 5/15.

Transfers: No deadline.

CONTACT

Linda Williams, Financial Aid Program Manager
5000 Rocklin Road, Rocklin, CA 95677-3397
(916) 660-7310

Simpson University

Redding, California
www.simpsonu.edu Federal Code: 001291

4-year private university in small city, affiliated with Christian and Missionary Alliance.

Enrollment: 1,033 undergrads, 3% part-time. 147 full-time freshmen.

Selectivity: Admits 50 to 75% of applicants.

BASIC COSTS (2013-2014)

Tuition and fees: $23,300.

Per-credit charge: $975.

Room only: $4,200.

Additional info: Tuition/fee waivers available for minority students.

FINANCIAL AID PICTURE (2012-2013)

Students with need: Out of 144 full-time freshmen who applied for aid, 136 were judged to have need. Of these, 136 received aid, and 7 had their full need met. Average financial aid package met 71% of need; average scholarship/grant was $13,660; average loan was $3,508. For part-time students, average financial aid package was $8,691.

Students without need: 6 full-time freshmen who did not demonstrate need for aid received scholarships/grants; average award was $9,667. No-need awards available for academics, alumni affiliation, athletics, leadership, minority status, music/drama, religious affiliation.

Scholarships offered: ***Merit:*** Academic awards; up to full tuition for 4.0 GPA and 1200 minimum SAT (exclusive of Writing). ***Athletic:*** 5 full-time freshmen received athletic scholarships; average amount $8,220.
Cumulative student debt: 70% of graduating class had student loans; average debt was $31,236.
Additional info: Work-study programs available.

FINANCIAL AID PROCEDURES
Forms required: FAFSA, state aid form, institutional form.
Dates and Deadlines: Priority date 3/2; no closing date. Applicants notified on a rolling basis starting 3/15; must reply within 4 week(s) of notification.
Transfers: No deadline. Applicants notified on a rolling basis starting 3/1; must reply within 4 week(s) of notification.

CONTACT
Melissa Hudson, Director of Financial Aid
2211 College View Drive, Redding, CA 96003-8606
(530) 226-4111

Skyline College
San Bruno, California
www.skylinecollege.edu Federal Code: 007713

2-year public community college in small city.
Enrollment: 5,356 undergrads.
Selectivity: Open admission; but selective for some programs.

BASIC COSTS (2012-2013)
Tuition and fees: $1,446; out-of-state residents $7,806.
Per-credit charge: $46; out-of-state residents $258.

FINANCIAL AID PICTURE
Students with need: Need-based aid available for full-time and part-time students.

FINANCIAL AID PROCEDURES
Forms required: FAFSA, institutional form.
Dates and Deadlines: Priority date 5/2; no closing date. Applicants notified on a rolling basis starting 5/1; must reply within 2 week(s) of notification.

CONTACT
Regina Morrison, Director of Financial Aid
3300 College Drive, San Bruno, CA 94066-1662
(650) 738-4484

Soka University of America
Aliso Viejo, California
www.soka.edu Federal Code: 038144

4-year private university and liberal arts college in large town.
Enrollment: 436 undergrads. 103 full-time freshmen.
Selectivity: Admits less than 50% of applicants.

BASIC COSTS (2013-2014)
Tuition and fees: $27,950.
Per-credit charge: $1,164.
Room and board: $10,916.

FINANCIAL AID PICTURE (2012-2013)
Students with need: Out of 102 full-time freshmen who applied for aid, 92 were judged to have need. Of these, 92 received aid, and 91 had their full need met. Average financial aid package met 80% of need; average scholarship/grant was $21,658; average loan was $5,676. Need-based aid available for part-time students.
Students without need: 11 full-time freshmen who did not demonstrate need for aid received scholarships/grants; average award was $19,924. No-need awards available for academics, athletics, leadership, minority status.
Scholarships offered: 19 full-time freshmen received athletic scholarships; average amount $9,796.
Cumulative student debt: 48% of graduating class had student loans; average debt was $22,506.
Additional info: All admitted students whose annual family income is $60,000 or less qualify for Soka Opportunity Scholarships which covers full tuition. All admitted students to the BA in Liberal Arts program will be considered for additional scholarship opportunities for higher income levels. The scholarship is awarded based on family income.

FINANCIAL AID PROCEDURES
Forms required: FAFSA, institutional form.
Dates and Deadlines: Priority date 2/15; closing date 3/2. Applicants notified on a rolling basis starting 3/15; must reply within 4 week(s) of notification.

CONTACT
Caterina D'Adamo, Manager of Financial Aid
One University Drive, Aliso Viejo, CA 92656-8081
(949) 480-4150

Sonoma State University
Rohnert Park, California
www.sonoma.edu Federal Code: 001156

4-year public university and liberal arts college in large town.
Enrollment: 8,058 undergrads, 10% part-time. 1,749 full-time freshmen.
Selectivity: Admits over 75% of applicants.

BASIC COSTS (2012-2013)
Tuition and fees: $7,546; out-of-state residents $18,706.
Room and board: $11,241.

FINANCIAL AID PICTURE (2011-2012)
Students with need: Out of 1,034 full-time freshmen who applied for aid, 732 were judged to have need. Of these, 699 received aid, and 198 had their full need met. Average financial aid package met 90% of need; average scholarship/grant was $10,295; average loan was $3,354. For part-time students, average financial aid package was $9,181.
Students without need: 8 full-time freshmen who did not demonstrate need for aid received scholarships/grants; average award was $1,156. No-need awards available for academics, alumni affiliation, art, athletics, leadership, minority status, music/drama.
Scholarships offered: 26 full-time freshmen received athletic scholarships; average amount $1,596.
Cumulative student debt: 63% of graduating class had student loans; average debt was $13,125.

FINANCIAL AID PROCEDURES
Forms required: FAFSA.
Dates and Deadlines: Priority date 1/31; no closing date. Applicants notified on a rolling basis starting 3/25; must reply within 2 week(s) of notification.

CONTACT
Susan Gutierrez, Director, Financial Aid
1801 East Cotati Avenue, Rohnert Park, CA 94928-3609
(707) 664-2389

Southern California Institute of Architecture
Los Angeles, California
www.sciarc.edu Federal Code: 014073

5-year private visual arts college in very large city.
Enrollment: 272 undergrads, 6% part-time. 2 full-time freshmen.
Selectivity: Admits over 75% of applicants.

BASIC COSTS (2012-2013)
Tuition and fees: $33,976.

FINANCIAL AID PICTURE (2011-2012)
Students with need: Out of 2 full-time freshmen who applied for aid, 2 were judged to have need. Of these, 2 received aid. Average financial aid package met 100% of need; average scholarship/grant was $5,400; average loan was $5,500. Need-based aid available for part-time students.
Students without need: No-need awards available for academics, state/district residency.

FINANCIAL AID PROCEDURES
Forms required: FAFSA, institutional form.
Dates and Deadlines: Closing date 3/2. Applicants notified on a rolling basis starting 3/15; must reply within 3 week(s) of notification.
Transfers: Applicants notified on a rolling basis starting 3/15; must reply within 3 week(s) of notification.

CONTACT
Helen Lara, Financial Aid Director
960 E 3rd Street, Los Angeles, CA 90013
(213) 356-5376

Southwestern College
Chula Vista, California
www.swccd.edu Federal Code: 001294

2-year public community college in small city.
Enrollment: 19,992 undergrads.
Selectivity: Open admission; but selective for some programs.

BASIC COSTS (2013-2014)
Tuition and fees: $1,426; out-of-state residents $7,126.
Per-credit charge: $46; out-of-state residents $236.

FINANCIAL AID PICTURE
Students with need: Need-based aid available for full-time and part-time students. Work study available nights, weekends, and for part-time students.

FINANCIAL AID PROCEDURES
Forms required: FAFSA.
Dates and Deadlines: Applicants notified on a rolling basis starting 7/1.

CONTACT
Patti Larkin, Director of Financial Aid
900 Otay Lakes Road, Chula Vista, CA 91910-7297
(619) 482-6357

Stanford University
Stanford, California Federal Code: 001305
www.stanford.edu CSS Code: 4704

4-year private university and liberal arts college in small city.
Enrollment: 6,999 undergrads. 1,707 full-time freshmen.
Selectivity: Admits less than 50% of applicants.

BASIC COSTS (2013-2014)
Tuition and fees: $42,690.
Room and board: $13,166.

FINANCIAL AID PICTURE (2011-2012)
Students with need: Out of 1,080 full-time freshmen who applied for aid, 895 were judged to have need. Of these, 879 received aid, and 755 had their full need met. Average financial aid package met 100% of need; average scholarship/grant was $39,933; average loan was $2,743. Need-based aid available for part-time students.
Students without need: This college awards aid only to students with need.
Scholarships offered: 119 full-time freshmen received athletic scholarships; average amount $28,679.
Cumulative student debt: 25% of graduating class had student loans; average debt was $18,833.
Additional info: For parents with total annual income below $60,000 and typical assets for this income range, parent contribution toward educational costs not expected. Students will still be expected to contribute from their income and savings. For parents with total annual income below $100,000 and typical assets for this income range, the expected parent contribution will be low enough to ensure that all tuition charges are covered with need-based scholarship, federal and state grants, and/or outside scholarship funds. Families with incomes at higher levels (typically up to $200,000) may also qualify for assistance, especially if more than one family member is enrolled in college.

FINANCIAL AID PROCEDURES
Forms required: FAFSA, CSS PROFILE.
Dates and Deadlines: Priority date 2/15; no closing date. Applicants notified on a rolling basis starting 4/1; must reply by 5/1.
Transfers: Priority date 3/15.

CONTACT
Karen Cooper, Director, Financial Aid
Montag Hall, Stanford, CA 94305-6106
(650) 723-3058

Taft College
Taft, California
www.taftcollege.edu Federal Code: 001309

2-year public community college in small town.
Enrollment: 4,165 undergrads.
Selectivity: Open admission.

BASIC COSTS (2012-2013)
Tuition and fees: $1,380; out-of-state residents $6,750.
Per-credit charge: $46; out-of-state residents $225.
Room and board: $4,172.

FINANCIAL AID PICTURE
Students with need: Need-based aid available for full-time and part-time students. Work study available nights.
Students without need: No-need awards available for academics.
Scholarships offered: Taft College Merit Awards: $250; for students from local high schools; available for 2 years; based on GPA of 3.0 or higher. Taft College High School Merit Award: $600; for students from local high schools. Taft College Nonresident Awards: $4,230; applied to nonresident tuition; available for 1 year; based on GPA of 3.0 or higher.

FINANCIAL AID PROCEDURES
Forms required: FAFSA, institutional form.
Dates and Deadlines: Applicants notified on a rolling basis; must reply within 4 week(s) of notification.
Transfers: No deadline.

CONTACT
Barbara Amerio, Director of Financial Aid
29 Emmons Park Drive, Taft, CA 93268
(661) 763-7762

Thomas Aquinas College
Santa Paula, California
www.thomasaquinas.edu Federal Code: 023580

4-year private liberal arts college in rural community, affiliated with Roman Catholic Church.

Enrollment: 370 undergrads. 84 full-time freshmen.
Selectivity: Admits over 75% of applicants.

BASIC COSTS (2013-2014)
Tuition and fees: $24,500.
Per-credit charge: $681.
Room and board: $7,950.

FINANCIAL AID PICTURE (2012-2013)
Students with need: Out of 81 full-time freshmen who applied for aid, 79 were judged to have need. Of these, 79 received aid, and 79 had their full need met. Average financial aid package met 100% of need; average scholarship/grant was $16,123; average loan was $3,221.
Students without need: This college awards aid only to students with need.
Cumulative student debt: 63% of graduating class had student loans; average debt was $17,820.

FINANCIAL AID PROCEDURES
Forms required: FAFSA, state aid form, institutional form.
Dates and Deadlines: Applicants notified on a rolling basis starting 2/1; must reply by 5/1 or within 2 week(s) of notification.

CONTACT
Gregory Becher, Director of Financial Aid
10000 Ojai Road, Santa Paula, CA 93060-9621
(800) 634-9797

Trident University International

Cypress, California
www.trident.edu Federal Code: 041279

4-year for-profit virtual university in very large city.
Enrollment: 3,273 undergrads, 41% part-time. 37 full-time freshmen.
Selectivity: Open admission.

BASIC COSTS (2013-2014)
Tuition and fees: $7,080.
Per-credit charge: $255.

FINANCIAL AID PICTURE (2011-2012)
Students with need: Out of 6 full-time freshmen who applied for aid, 6 were judged to have need. Of these, 6 received aid. Need-based aid available for part-time students.

FINANCIAL AID PROCEDURES
Forms required: FAFSA, institutional form.
Transfers: No deadline.

CONTACT
Taisha Wright, Director of Financial Aid
Attn: Office of the Registrar, Cypress, CA 90630
(714) 816-0366 ext. 1061

University of California: Berkeley

Berkeley, California
www.berkeley.edu Federal Code: 001312

4-year public university in small city.
Enrollment: 25,774 undergrads.
Selectivity: Admits less than 50% of applicants.

BASIC COSTS (2012-2013)
Tuition and fees: $12,874; out-of-state residents $35,752.
Room and board: $15,000.

FINANCIAL AID PICTURE
Students with need: Need-based aid available for full-time and part-time students.
Students without need: No-need awards available for academics.
Scholarships offered: University Scholarship, President's Undergraduate Fellowships, Regents and Chancellor's Scholarships, Alumni Scholarships.

FINANCIAL AID PROCEDURES
Forms required: FAFSA.
Dates and Deadlines: Closing date 3/2. Applicants notified by 4/15.
Transfers: Applicants notified by 4/15.

CONTACT
Rachelle Feldman, Director of Financial Aid
110 Sproul Hall, #5800, Berkeley, CA 94720-5800
(510) 642-6000

University of California: Davis

Davis, California
www.ucdavis.edu Federal Code: 001313

4-year public university in small city.
Enrollment: 25,588 undergrads, 1% part-time. 5,207 full-time freshmen.
Selectivity: Admits less than 50% of applicants.

BASIC COSTS (2012-2013)
Tuition and fees: $13,877; out-of-state residents $36,755.
Room and board: $13,503.
Additional info: Estimated personal expenses include $1,380 for our student health insurance plan. Although this is a mandatory fee, if a student is covered through private insurance, he or she can waive out.

FINANCIAL AID PICTURE
Students with need: Need-based aid available for full-time and part-time students. Work study available nights, weekends, and for part-time students.
Students without need: This college awards aid only to students with need.

FINANCIAL AID PROCEDURES
Forms required: FAFSA, state aid form.
Dates and Deadlines: Priority date 3/2; no closing date. Applicants notified on a rolling basis starting 3/16.

CONTACT
Kathryn Maloney, Director of Financial Aid
178 Mrak Hall, One Shields Ave, Davis, CA 95616
(530) 752-2390

University of California: Irvine

Irvine, California
www.uci.edu Federal Code: 001314

4-year public university in small city.
Enrollment: 22,216 undergrads, 2% part-time. 5,104 full-time freshmen.
Selectivity: Admits less than 50% of applicants.

BASIC COSTS (2012-2013)
Tuition and fees: $13,302; out-of-state residents $36,180.
Room and board: $11,706.
Additional info: Additional student health fee of $924; mandatory, unless student is covered through private health insurance.

FINANCIAL AID PICTURE (2011-2012)
Students with need: Out of 4,489 full-time freshmen who applied for aid, 3,653 were judged to have need. Of these, 3,538 received aid, and 1,337 had their full need met. Average financial aid package met 88% of need; average scholarship/grant was $16,424; average loan was $6,148. For part-time students, average financial aid package was $14,314.
Students without need: 70 full-time freshmen who did not demonstrate need for aid received scholarships/grants; average award was $11,171.

Scholarships offered: 31 full-time freshmen received athletic scholarships; average amount $15,081.
Cumulative student debt: 49% of graduating class had student loans; average debt was $18,719.
Additional info: Blue and Gold Opportunity Plan guarantees needy in-state students from families earning less than $80,000/yr that their system-wide tuition and fees will be paid through scholarships and grants.

FINANCIAL AID PROCEDURES
Forms required: FAFSA, state aid form.
Dates and Deadlines: Priority date 3/2; closing date 5/2. Applicants notified on a rolling basis starting 4/1.

CONTACT
Christopher Shultz, Director, Financial Aid & Scholarships
260 Aldrich Hall, Irvine, CA 92697-1075
(949) 824-8262

University of California: Los Angeles

Los Angeles, California
www.ucla.edu Federal Code: 001315

4-year public university in very large city.
Enrollment: 27,933 undergrads, 2% part-time. 5,609 full-time freshmen.
Selectivity: Admits less than 50% of applicants.

BASIC COSTS (2012-2013)
Tuition and fees: $12,692; out-of-state residents $35,570.
Room and board: $14,232.
Additional info: Estimated personal expenses include $1,318 for our student health insurance plan. Although this is a mandatory fee, if a student is covered through private insurance, he or she can waive out.

FINANCIAL AID PICTURE
Students with need: Need-based aid available for full-time and part-time students.
Students without need: No-need awards available for academics, alumni affiliation, athletics, ROTC.

FINANCIAL AID PROCEDURES
Forms required: FAFSA.
Dates and Deadlines: Priority date 3/2; no closing date. Applicants notified on a rolling basis starting 3/15; must reply within 3 week(s) of notification.

CONTACT
Ronald Johnson, Director, Financial Aid Office
1147 Murphy Hall, Los Angeles, CA 90095-1436
(310) 206-0400

University of California: Merced

Merced, California
www.ucmerced.edu Federal Code: 041271

4-year public university in small city.
Enrollment: 5,397 undergrads, 1% part-time. 1,490 full-time freshmen.
Selectivity: Admits over 75% of applicants.

BASIC COSTS (2012-2013)
Tuition and fees: $13,070; out-of-state residents $35,948.
Room and board: $14,272.
Additional info: Estimated personal expenses include $1,383 for our student health insurance plan. Although this is a mandatory fee, if a student is covered through private insurance, he or she can waive out.

FINANCIAL AID PICTURE (2011-2012)
Students with need: 78% of average financial aid package awarded as scholarships/grants, 22% awarded as loans/jobs. Need-based aid available for part-time students. Work study available nights, weekends, and for part-time students.
Students without need: No-need awards available for academics, leadership.
Scholarships offered: Regents' Scholarships: based on strength and breadth of academic program, grades, personal statement, extracurricular activities, community activities, first-generation status, other indicators of academic excellence and promise.

FINANCIAL AID PROCEDURES
Forms required: FAFSA.
Dates and Deadlines: Priority date 3/2; no closing date. Applicants notified on a rolling basis starting 3/2.
Transfers: Applicants notified on a rolling basis starting 3/2.

CONTACT
Diana Ralls, Director, Financial Aid & Scholarships
5200 North Lake Road, Merced, CA 95343-5603
(209) 228-4243

University of California: Riverside

Riverside, California
www.ucr.edu/ Federal Code: 001316

4-year public university in large city.
Enrollment: 18,537 undergrads, 3% part-time. 4,001 full-time freshmen.
Selectivity: Admits 50 to 75% of applicants.

BASIC COSTS (2012-2013)
Tuition and fees: $12,923; out-of-state residents $35,801.
Room and board: $13,200.

FINANCIAL AID PICTURE (2012-2013)
Students with need: Out of 3,617 full-time freshmen who applied for aid, 3,175 were judged to have need. Of these, 3,131 received aid, and 777 had their full need met. Average financial aid package met 91% of need; average scholarship/grant was $19,930; average loan was $5,094. For part-time students, average financial aid package was $16,421.
Students without need: 98 full-time freshmen who did not demonstrate need for aid received scholarships/grants; average award was $4,183. No-need awards available for academics, alumni affiliation, art, athletics, leadership, music/drama, state/district residency.
Scholarships offered: 17 full-time freshmen received athletic scholarships; average amount $19,738.
Cumulative student debt: 73% of graduating class had student loans; average debt was $21,373.

FINANCIAL AID PROCEDURES
Forms required: FAFSA, state aid form.
Dates and Deadlines: Priority date 3/2; closing date 5/1. Applicants notified on a rolling basis starting 3/1; must reply by 5/1 or within 3 week(s) of notification.
Transfers: Closing date 6/1. Applicants notified on a rolling basis starting 3/1; must reply by 6/1 or within 3 week(s) of notification.

CONTACT
Jose Aguilar, Director of Financial Aid
Admissions Office, Riverside, CA 92521
(951) 827-3878

University of California: San Diego

La Jolla, California
www.ucsd.edu Federal Code: 001317

4-year public university in large town.
Enrollment: 22,676 undergrads.

Selectivity: Admits less than 50% of applicants.

BASIC COSTS (2012-2013)
Tuition and fees: $13,234; out-of-state residents $36,112.
Room and board: $11,924.
Additional info: Estimated personal expenses include $1,156 for our student health insurance plan. Although this is a mandatory fee, if a student is covered through private insurance, he or she can waive out.

FINANCIAL AID PICTURE
Students with need: Need-based aid available for full-time and part-time students. Work study available nights, weekends, and for part-time students.
Students without need: No-need awards available for academics, art, athletics, leadership, minority status, music/drama.

FINANCIAL AID PROCEDURES
Forms required: FAFSA, state aid form.
Dates and Deadlines: Priority date 3/2; closing date 6/1. Applicants notified on a rolling basis starting 3/15; must reply within 3 week(s) of notification.
Transfers: Applicants notified on a rolling basis; must reply within 3 week(s) of notification.

CONTACT
Ann Klein, Director of Financial Aid
9500 Gilman Drive, 0021, La Jolla, CA 92093-0021
(858) 534-4480

University of California: Santa Barbara

Santa Barbara, California
www.ucsb.edu Federal Code: 001320

4-year public university in small city.
Enrollment: 18,974 undergrads, 1% part-time. 4,084 full-time freshmen.
Selectivity: Admits less than 50% of applicants.

BASIC COSTS (2012-2013)
Tuition and fees: $13,671; out-of-state residents $36,549.
Room and board: $13,275.

FINANCIAL AID PICTURE (2011-2012)
Students with need: Out of 3,398 full-time freshmen who applied for aid, 2,688 were judged to have need. Of these, 2,540 received aid, and 1,186 had their full need met. Average financial aid package met 25% of need; average scholarship/grant was $18,939; average loan was $6,651. For part-time students, average financial aid package was $16,895.
Students without need: 38 full-time freshmen who did not demonstrate need for aid received scholarships/grants; average award was $9,825. No-need awards available for academics, athletics.
Scholarships offered: 38 full-time freshmen received athletic scholarships; average amount $12,952.
Cumulative student debt: 49% of graduating class had student loans; average debt was $18,627.

FINANCIAL AID PROCEDURES
Forms required: FAFSA.
Dates and Deadlines: Priority date 3/2; closing date 5/31. Must reply within 2 week(s) of notification.
Transfers: California residents must apply for a CAL grant from the California Student Aid Commission; must complete and submit FAFSA by March 2.

CONTACT
Mike Miller, Director of Financial Aid
1210 Cheadle Hall, Santa Barbara, CA 93106-2014
(805) 893-2432

University of California: Santa Cruz

Santa Cruz, California
www.ucsc.edu Federal Code: 001321

4-year public university in small city.
Enrollment: 15,978 undergrads, 2% part-time. 3,827 full-time freshmen.
Selectivity: Admits 50 to 75% of applicants.

BASIC COSTS (2012-2013)
Tuition and fees: $13,417; out-of-state residents $36,295.
Room and board: $14,856.
Additional info: Estimated personal expenses include $1,563 for our student health insurance plan. Although this is a mandatory fee, if a student is covered through private insurance, he or she can waive out. Tuition/fee waivers available for unemployed or children of unemployed.

FINANCIAL AID PICTURE
Students with need: Need-based aid available for full-time and part-time students. Work study available nights, weekends, and for part-time students.
Students without need: No-need awards available for academics, alumni affiliation, art, leadership, music/drama.
Scholarships offered: Regents Scholarships; $4,000-$6,000 per year for 4 years; for outstanding academic achievement.
Additional info: Blue and Gold Opportunity Plan covers the educational and student services fees for CA residents whose family earns less than $80,000 a year. Blue and Gold students with sufficient financial need can qualify for more grant aid to reduce the cost of attendance.

FINANCIAL AID PROCEDURES
Forms required: FAFSA, state aid form.
Dates and Deadlines: Closing date 3/2. Applicants notified on a rolling basis starting 4/1; must reply within 4 week(s) of notification.
Transfers: The Karl S. Pister Leadership Opportunity Awards Program established by a former chancellor increases opportunities for talented community college students who want to transfer to UCSC. Candidates, nominated by the regional community college presidents, must have overcome adverse socioeconomic circumstances, have a demonstrated commitment to assisting and improving the lives of others and have financial aid eligibility. One recipient is named from each of 13 regional community colleges. Awards are $10,000 per year for 2 years.

CONTACT
Michelle Whittingham, Associate Vice Chancellor, Enrollment Management
Cook House, 1156 High Street, Santa Cruz, CA 95064
(831) 459-2963

University of La Verne

La Verne, California
www.laverne.edu Federal Code: 001216

4-year private university in large town.
Enrollment: 2,487 undergrads, 3% part-time. 619 full-time freshmen.
Selectivity: Admits less than 50% of applicants.

BASIC COSTS (2012-2013)
Tuition and fees: $33,350.
Per-credit charge: $890.
Room and board: $11,660.

FINANCIAL AID PICTURE (2012-2013)
Students with need: Out of 577 full-time freshmen who applied for aid, 544 were judged to have need. Of these, 544 received aid, and 81 had their full need met. Average financial aid package met 39% of need; average scholarship/grant was $8,622; average loan was $3,767. For part-time students, average financial aid package was $23,788.

Students without need: 60 full-time freshmen who did not demonstrate need for aid received scholarships/grants; average award was $21,205. No-need awards available for academics, alumni affiliation, art, leadership, minority status, music/drama.
Cumulative student debt: 78% of graduating class had student loans; average debt was $30,566.

FINANCIAL AID PROCEDURES
Forms required: FAFSA, state aid form.
Dates and Deadlines: Priority date 3/2; no closing date. Applicants notified on a rolling basis starting 4/1; must reply within 2 week(s) of notification.
Transfers: No deadline.

CONTACT
Jason Neal, Associate Director, Financial Aid Office
1950 Third Street, La Verne, CA 91750
(800) 649-0160

University of Redlands
Redlands, California
www.redlands.edu Federal Code: 001322

4-year private university and liberal arts college in small city.
Enrollment: 3,346 undergrads, 22% part-time. 724 full-time freshmen.
Selectivity: Admits 50 to 75% of applicants.

BASIC COSTS (2013-2014)
Tuition and fees: $41,290.
Per-credit charge: $1,281.
Room and board: $12,314.

FINANCIAL AID PICTURE (2012-2013)
Students with need: Out of 681 full-time freshmen who applied for aid, 596 were judged to have need. Of these, 596 received aid, and 289 had their full need met. Average financial aid package met 89% of need; average scholarship/grant was $28,446; average loan was $4,268. For part-time students, average financial aid package was $15,069.
Students without need: 85 full-time freshmen who did not demonstrate need for aid received scholarships/grants; average award was $15,260. No-need awards available for academics, art, music/drama.
Cumulative student debt: 68% of graduating class had student loans; average debt was $32,035.

FINANCIAL AID PROCEDURES
Forms required: FAFSA, state aid form.
Dates and Deadlines: Priority date 2/15; no closing date. Applicants notified on a rolling basis starting 2/28; must reply by 5/1.
Transfers: No deadline.

CONTACT
Alisha Aguilar, Director of Financial Aid
1200 East Colton Avenue, Redlands, CA 92373-0999
(909) 748-8047

University of San Diego
San Diego, California
www.sandiego.edu Federal Code: 010395

4-year private university in very large city, affiliated with Roman Catholic Church.
Enrollment: 5,368 undergrads, 3% part-time. 1,142 full-time freshmen.
Selectivity: Admits less than 50% of applicants.

BASIC COSTS (2012-2013)
Tuition and fees: $39,970.
Per-credit charge: $1,360.
Room and board: $11,910.

FINANCIAL AID PICTURE (2011-2012)
Students with need: Out of 819 full-time freshmen who applied for aid, 650 were judged to have need. Of these, 641 received aid, and 85 had their full need met. Average financial aid package met 73% of need; average scholarship/grant was $23,756; average loan was $6,398. For part-time students, average financial aid package was $12,085.
Students without need: 231 full-time freshmen who did not demonstrate need for aid received scholarships/grants; average award was $12,914. No-need awards available for academics, athletics, leadership, music/drama, religious affiliation, ROTC.
Scholarships offered: 24 full-time freshmen received athletic scholarships; average amount $33,243.
Cumulative student debt: 47% of graduating class had student loans; average debt was $29,874.

FINANCIAL AID PROCEDURES
Forms required: FAFSA.
Dates and Deadlines: Priority date 3/2; no closing date. Applicants notified on a rolling basis starting 3/1; must reply by 5/1 or within 3 week(s) of notification.
Transfers: Entering transfer students are not eligible for institutional merit-based scholarships.

CONTACT
Judith Lewis Logue, Director of Financial Aid Services
5998 Alcala Park, San Diego, CA 92110-2492
(619) 260-4720

University of San Francisco
San Francisco, California
www.usfca.edu Federal Code: 001325

4-year private university in very large city, affiliated with Roman Catholic Church.
Enrollment: 6,246 undergrads, 3% part-time. 1,348 full-time freshmen.
Selectivity: Admits 50 to 75% of applicants.

BASIC COSTS (2013-2014)
Tuition and fees: $40,294.
Per-credit charge: $1,415.
Room and board: $12,990.

FINANCIAL AID PICTURE
Students with need: Need-based aid available for full-time and part-time students.
Students without need: No-need awards available for academics, athletics, ROTC.
Scholarships offered: University Scholars Program: up to $20,000 per year for 8 UG Semesters; must have 3.8 weighted GPA as calculated by USF admissions and combined SAT of 1320 on Critical Reading and Math sections or minimum ACT composite test score of 30. Applicants must apply for admission no later than November 15 under the Early Action Plan for the following year. Renewal automatic as long as 3.25 GPA achieved each semester.
Additional info: Most aid to international students is for athletics.

FINANCIAL AID PROCEDURES
Forms required: FAFSA.
Dates and Deadlines: Priority date 2/1; no closing date. Applicants notified on a rolling basis starting 4/1; must reply within 4 week(s) of notification.
Transfers: Must reply within 4 week(s) of notification.

CONTACT
Susan Murphy, Senior Associate Dean, Director, Enrollment and Financial Services
2130 Fulton Street, San Francisco, CA 94117-1046
(415) 422-6303

University of Southern California

Los Angeles, California Federal Code: 001328
www.usc.edu CSS Code: 4852

4-year private university in very large city.
Enrollment: 17,994 undergrads, 3% part-time. 2,929 full-time freshmen.
Selectivity: Admits less than 50% of applicants. GED not accepted.

BASIC COSTS (2012-2013)

Tuition and fees: $44,463.
Room and board: $12,440.

FINANCIAL AID PICTURE (2011-2012)

Students with need: Out of 1,840 full-time freshmen who applied for aid, 1,208 were judged to have need. Of these, 1,208 received aid, and 1,181 had their full need met. Average financial aid package met 100% of need; average scholarship/grant was $28,937; average loan was $4,429. For part-time students, average financial aid package was $18,379.
Students without need: 579 full-time freshmen who did not demonstrate need for aid received scholarships/grants; average award was $20,165. No-need awards available for academics, alumni affiliation, art, athletics, leadership, music/drama, ROTC.
Scholarships offered: ***Merit:*** Trustee Scholarship: full tuition; approximately 100 awards annually; finalists invited to mandatory interview. Presidential Scholarship: one-half tuition; approximately 200 awarded annually; finalists invited to a mandatory interview. National Merit Presidential Scholarship: one-half tuition; number of awards varies; admitted Freshmen who are National Merit Finalists and who designate USC as their first-choice college. Deans Scholarship: one-quarter tuition; approximately 50 awards annually; Mork Family Scholarship: full tuition plus $5,000 living stipend; 10 awards annually; Leadership Scholarship: full tuition plus $5,000 enrichment fund (research, overseas study, etc.); 10 awards annually. ***Athletic:*** 91 full-time freshmen received athletic scholarships; average amount $40,660.
Cumulative student debt: 45% of graduating class had student loans; average debt was $28,575.

FINANCIAL AID PROCEDURES

Forms required: FAFSA. Student/parent tax information form, supplemental documents along with CSS PROFILE.
Dates and Deadlines: Priority date 2/1; no closing date. Applicants notified by 4/1; must reply by 5/1.
Transfers: Applicants notified by 5/1.

CONTACT

Thomas McWhorter, Dean of Financial Aid
Office of Admission, Los Angeles, CA 90089-0911
(213) 740-4444

University of the Pacific

Stockton, California
www.pacific.edu Federal Code: 001329

4-year private university in large city.
Enrollment: 3,854 undergrads, 3% part-time. 851 full-time freshmen.
Selectivity: Admits less than 50% of applicants.

BASIC COSTS (2012-2013)

Tuition and fees: $38,320.
Per-credit charge: $1,303.
Room and board: $12,038.

FINANCIAL AID PICTURE (2012-2013)

Students with need: Out of 697 full-time freshmen who applied for aid, 594 were judged to have need. Of these, 593 received aid, and 58 had their full need met. For part-time students, average financial aid package was $20,717.
Students without need: 154 full-time freshmen who did not demonstrate need for aid received scholarships/grants; average award was $8,773. No-need awards available for academics, athletics, leadership, music/drama, religious affiliation.
Scholarships offered: 33 full-time freshmen received athletic scholarships; average amount $24,551.

FINANCIAL AID PROCEDURES

Forms required: FAFSA.
Dates and Deadlines: Priority date 2/15; no closing date. Applicants notified on a rolling basis starting 4/1.

CONTACT

Lynn Fox, Director of Financial Aid
3601 Pacific Avenue, Stockton, CA 95211-0197
(209) 946-2011

University of the West

Rosemead, California
www.uwest.edu Federal Code: 036963

4-year private business and liberal arts college in small city, affiliated with Buddhist faith.
Enrollment: 75 undergrads, 16% part-time. 30 full-time freshmen.

BASIC COSTS (2013-2014)

Tuition and fees: $11,670.
Per-credit charge: $364.
Room and board: $4,270.

FINANCIAL AID PICTURE

Students with need: Need-based aid available for full-time and part-time students. Work study available nights, weekends, and for part-time students.
Students without need: No-need awards available for academics, leadership.
Scholarships offered: President's Fellowship: full-tuition award. Dean's Fellowship: half-tuition award. Campus Life Leadership Fellowship: full tuition and room and board award plus $1,000 scholarship. Campus Life Assistance Fellowship: full room and board award plus $1,000 scholarship. UWest Scholarship: $1,000 to $2,000 per academic year. Drs. Allen and Lily Huang Student Leadership Award: $2,000, one award each year. Lotus Scholarships: $10,000 or $5,000 per year.

FINANCIAL AID PROCEDURES

Forms required: FAFSA, institutional form.
Transfers: No deadline.

CONTACT

Lezli Fang, Financial Aid Officer
1409 North Walnut Grove Avenue, Rosemead, CA 91770
(626) 571-8811

Vanguard University of Southern California

Costa Mesa, California
www.vanguard.edu Federal Code: 001293

4-year private university and liberal arts college in small city, affiliated with Assemblies of God.
Enrollment: 1,945 undergrads.
Selectivity: Admits 50 to 75% of applicants.

BASIC COSTS (2013-2014)

Tuition and fees: $29,250.
Per-credit charge: $1,219.
Room and board: $8,880.

FINANCIAL AID PICTURE
Students with need: Need-based aid available for full-time students.
Students without need: No-need awards available for academics, athletics, music/drama, religious affiliation.

FINANCIAL AID PROCEDURES
Forms required: FAFSA, state aid form.
Dates and Deadlines: Closing date 3/2. Applicants notified on a rolling basis starting 4/1; must reply within 3 week(s) of notification.
Transfers: Applicants notified on a rolling basis.

CONTACT
Robyn Fournier, Director of Financial Aid
55 Fair Drive, Costa Mesa, CA 92626-9601
(714) 556-3610 ext. 4250

Ventura College
Ventura, California
www.venturacollege.edu Federal Code: 001334

2-year public community college in small city.
Enrollment: 6,877 undergrads.
Selectivity: Open admission; but selective for some programs.

BASIC COSTS (2012-2013)
Tuition and fees: $1,422; out-of-state residents $8,922.
Per-credit charge: $46; out-of-state residents $296.

FINANCIAL AID PICTURE
Students with need: Need-based aid available for full-time and part-time students.

FINANCIAL AID PROCEDURES
Forms required: FAFSA, state aid form.
Dates and Deadlines: Priority date 3/2; no closing date. Applicants notified on a rolling basis.

CONTACT
Alma Rodriguez, Director, Financial Aid
4667 Telegraph Road, Ventura, CA 93003
(805) 654-6369

Victor Valley College
Victorville, California
www.vvc.edu Federal Code: 001335

2-year public community college in small city.
Enrollment: 5,466 undergrads.
Selectivity: Open admission.

BASIC COSTS (2012-2013)
Tuition and fees: $1,392; out-of-state residents $6,672.
Per-credit charge: $46; out-of-state residents $222.

FINANCIAL AID PICTURE
Students with need: Need-based aid available for full-time and part-time students.
Additional info: Board of Governors grant pays enrollment fee in full for low-income students.

FINANCIAL AID PROCEDURES
Forms required: FAFSA, state aid form, institutional form.
Dates and Deadlines: Priority date 3/2; no closing date. Applicants notified on a rolling basis starting 8/1; must reply within 4 week(s) of notification.

CONTACT
Arthur Lopez, Associate Director, Office of Financial Aid
18422 Bear Valley Road, Victorville, CA 92392-5850
(760) 245-4271 ext. 2377

West Coast University: Los Angeles
North Hollywood, California
www.westcoastuniversity.edu Federal Code: 036983

4-year for-profit health science and nursing college in very large city.
Enrollment: 1,336 undergrads, 20% part-time. 2 full-time freshmen.
Selectivity: Admits over 75% of applicants.

BASIC COSTS (2012-2013)
Tuition and fees: $31,833.
Per-credit charge: $1,740.

FINANCIAL AID PICTURE (2012-2013)
Students with need: 15% of average financial aid package awarded as scholarships/grants, 85% awarded as loans/jobs. Need-based aid available for part-time students. Work study available nights, weekends, and for part-time students.
Students without need: No-need awards available for academics.

FINANCIAL AID PROCEDURES
Forms required: FAFSA, state aid form, institutional form.
Dates and Deadlines: Closing date 6/30. Applicants notified on a rolling basis.

CONTACT
Tracy Cabuco, Senior Director of Financial Aid
12215 Victory Boulevard, North Hollywood, CA 91606
(818) 299-5500

West Coast University: Ontario
Ontario, California
www.westcoastuniversity.edu Federal Code: 036983

2-year for-profit branch campus and nursing college in small city.
Enrollment: 1,090 undergrads, 19% part-time. 13 full-time freshmen.
Selectivity: Open admission; but selective for some programs.

BASIC COSTS (2012-2013)
Tuition and fees: $31,833.
Per-credit charge: $1,740.

FINANCIAL AID PICTURE (2012-2013)
Students with need: 18% of average financial aid package awarded as scholarships/grants, 82% awarded as loans/jobs. Need-based aid available for part-time students. Work study available nights, weekends, and for part-time students.
Students without need: No-need awards available for academics.

FINANCIAL AID PROCEDURES
Forms required: FAFSA, state aid form, institutional form.
Dates and Deadlines: Closing date 6/30. Applicants notified on a rolling basis.

CONTACT
Becky Verduzco, Director of Financial Aid
2855 East Guasti Road, Ontario, CA 91761
(909) 467-6100

West Coast University: Orange County
Anaheim, California
www.westcoastuniversity.edu Federal Code: 036983

2-year for-profit branch campus and nursing college in large city.
Enrollment: 1,508 undergrads, 19% part-time. 6 full-time freshmen.
Selectivity: Open admission; but selective for some programs.

BASIC COSTS (2012-2013)
Tuition and fees: $32,878.
Per-credit charge: $1,795.

FINANCIAL AID PICTURE (2012-2013)
Students with need: 12% of average financial aid package awarded as scholarships/grants, 88% awarded as loans/jobs. Need-based aid available for part-time students. Work study available nights, weekends, and for part-time students.
Students without need: No-need awards available for academics.

FINANCIAL AID PROCEDURES
Forms required: FAFSA, state aid form, institutional form.
Dates and Deadlines: Closing date 6/30. Applicants notified on a rolling basis.

CONTACT
Larissa Gomez Luna, Director of Financial Aid
1477 South Manchester Avenue, Anaheim, CA 92802
(714) 782-1700

West Hills College: Coalinga

Coalinga, California
www.westhillscollege.com Federal Code: 001176

2-year public community college in small town.
Enrollment: 1,742 undergrads.
Selectivity: Open admission.

BASIC COSTS (2012-2013)
Tuition and fees: $1,380; out-of-state residents $9,000.
Per-credit charge: $46; out-of-state residents $300.
Room and board: $7,977.
Additional info: Tuition/fee waivers available for unemployed or children of unemployed.

FINANCIAL AID PICTURE
Students with need: Need-based aid available for full-time and part-time students.

FINANCIAL AID PROCEDURES
Forms required: FAFSA.
Dates and Deadlines: Priority date 3/2; no closing date. Applicants notified on a rolling basis starting 6/1.

CONTACT
Marlon Hall, Vice President
300 Cherry Lane, Coalinga, CA 93210
(559) 934-2310

West Los Angeles College

Culver City, California
www.wlac.edu Federal Code: 008596

2-year public community college in large town.
Enrollment: 6,300 undergrads.
Selectivity: Open admission.

BASIC COSTS (2012-2013)
Tuition and fees: $1,404; out-of-state residents $7,104.
Per-credit charge: $46; out-of-state residents $236.
Additional info: Tuition/fee waivers available for unemployed or children of unemployed.

FINANCIAL AID PICTURE
Students with need: Need-based aid available for full-time and part-time students.
Students without need: This college awards aid only to students with need.
Additional info: California residents may qualify for Board of Governors Grant Program.

FINANCIAL AID PROCEDURES
Forms required: FAFSA.
Dates and Deadlines: Applicants notified on a rolling basis; must reply within 4 week(s) of notification.
Transfers: No deadline.

CONTACT
Glenn Schenk, Financial Aid Director
9000 Overland Avenue, Culver City, CA 90230
(310) 287-4533

West Valley College

Saratoga, California
www.westvalley.edu Federal Code: 001338

2-year public community college in large town.
Enrollment: 4,628 undergrads.
Selectivity: Open admission.

BASIC COSTS (2012-2013)
Tuition and fees: $1,466; out-of-state residents $7,586.
Per-credit charge: $46; out-of-state residents $250.
Additional info: Tuition/fee waivers available for unemployed or children of unemployed.

FINANCIAL AID PICTURE
Students with need: Need-based aid available for full-time and part-time students.
Students without need: This college awards aid only to students with need.

FINANCIAL AID PROCEDURES
Forms required: FAFSA.
Dates and Deadlines: Priority date 5/31; no closing date. Applicants notified on a rolling basis starting 7/1.

CONTACT
Maritza Cantarero, Director of Financial Aid
14000 Fruitvale Avenue, Saratoga, CA 95070-5698
(408) 867-2200

Westmont College

Santa Barbara, California
www.westmont.edu Federal Code: 001341

4-year private liberal arts college in small city, affiliated with nondenominational tradition.
Enrollment: 1,340 undergrads. 337 full-time freshmen.
Selectivity: Admits 50 to 75% of applicants.

BASIC COSTS (2013-2014)
Tuition and fees: $38,510.
Room and board: $12,160.

FINANCIAL AID PICTURE (2012-2013)
Students with need: Out of 265 full-time freshmen who applied for aid, 213 were judged to have need. Of these, 213 received aid, and 45 had their full need met. Average financial aid package met 78% of need; average scholarship/grant was $21,831; average loan was $3,901.
Students without need: 82 full-time freshmen who did not demonstrate need for aid received scholarships/grants; average award was $11,627. No-need awards available for academics, art, athletics, music/drama.

Scholarships offered: ***Merit:*** Scholarships automatically awarded to entering students based on GPA and SAT or ACT scores (first-year students) or college academic GPA (transfers): renewable annually; unlimited number awarded until class is full. First-year scholarships: Presidential, $14,000, must maintain 3.25 GPA; Provost, $12,000, must maintain 3.0 GPA; Dean's, $10,000, must maintain 2.75 GPA. ***Athletic:*** 16 full-time freshmen received athletic scholarships; average amount $8,996.
Cumulative student debt: 64% of graduating class had student loans; average debt was $31,277.

FINANCIAL AID PROCEDURES

Forms required: FAFSA, institutional form.
Dates and Deadlines: Priority date 3/1; no closing date. Applicants notified on a rolling basis starting 4/1; must reply by 5/1 or within 2 week(s) of notification.
Transfers: No deadline. Applicants notified on a rolling basis starting 4/1; must reply by 5/1 or within 2 week(s) of notification. Transfer students may qualify for academic merit scholarships.

CONTACT

Sean Smith, Director of Financial Aid
955 La Paz Road, Santa Barbara, CA 93108-1089
(888) 963-4624

Whittier College

Whittier, California
www.whittier.edu Federal Code: 001342

4-year private liberal arts college in small city.
Enrollment: 1,655 undergrads, 2% part-time. 408 full-time freshmen.
Selectivity: Admits 50 to 75% of applicants.

BASIC COSTS (2012-2013)

Tuition and fees: $38,640.
Per-credit charge: $1,540.
Room and board: $10,948.

FINANCIAL AID PICTURE (2012-2013)

Students with need: Out of 354 full-time freshmen who applied for aid, 330 were judged to have need. Of these, 330 received aid, and 40 had their full need met. Average financial aid package met 72% of need; average scholarship/grant was $29,652; average loan was $4,586. For part-time students, average financial aid package was $20,690.
Students without need: 63 full-time freshmen who did not demonstrate need for aid received scholarships/grants; average award was $17,849. No-need awards available for academics, alumni affiliation, art, minority status, music/drama.
Cumulative student debt: 73% of graduating class had student loans; average debt was $25,212.
Additional info: Auditions required for talent scholarship applicants in art, music, and theater.

FINANCIAL AID PROCEDURES

Forms required: FAFSA.
Dates and Deadlines: Priority date 3/1; closing date 6/30. Applicants notified on a rolling basis starting 2/15; must reply within 2 week(s) of notification.
Transfers: Priority date 2/1. Applicants notified on a rolling basis starting 3/1; must reply by 6/1 or within 2 week(s) of notification.

CONTACT

David Carnevale, Director of Financial Aid
13406 East Philadelphia Street, Whittier, CA 90608-0634
(562) 907-4285

William Jessup University

Rocklin, California
www.jessup.edu Federal Code: 001281

4-year private Bible and liberal arts college in small city, affiliated with nondenominational tradition.
Enrollment: 976 undergrads, 19% part-time. 135 full-time freshmen.
Selectivity: Admits 50 to 75% of applicants.

BASIC COSTS (2013-2014)

Tuition and fees: $24,040.
Per-credit charge: $1,020.
Room and board: $9,520.

FINANCIAL AID PICTURE (2012-2013)

Students with need: Out of 129 full-time freshmen who applied for aid, 117 were judged to have need. Of these, 117 received aid, and 15 had their full need met. Average financial aid package met 73% of need; average scholarship/grant was $17,433; average loan was $3,371. For part-time students, average financial aid package was $9,564.
Students without need: 15 full-time freshmen who did not demonstrate need for aid received scholarships/grants; average award was $4,503. No-need awards available for academics, art, athletics, leadership, minority status, music/drama, religious affiliation, state/district residency.
Scholarships offered: 12 full-time freshmen received athletic scholarships; average amount $6,910.
Cumulative student debt: 70% of graduating class had student loans; average debt was $21,057.

FINANCIAL AID PROCEDURES

Forms required: FAFSA.
Dates and Deadlines: Priority date 3/2; no closing date. Applicants notified on a rolling basis starting 3/2; must reply within 3 week(s) of notification.

CONTACT

Korey Compaan, Director of Financial Aid
333 Sunset Boulevard, Rocklin, CA 95765
(916) 577-2233

Woodbury University

Burbank, California
www.woodbury.edu Federal Code: 001343

4-year private university in very large city.
Enrollment: 1,424 undergrads, 13% part-time. 203 full-time freshmen.

BASIC COSTS (2013-2014)

Tuition and fees: $33,150.
Per-credit charge: $1,067.
Room and board: $10,372.

FINANCIAL AID PICTURE (2012-2013)

Students with need: Out of 139 full-time freshmen who applied for aid, 128 were judged to have need. Of these, 127 received aid, and 7 had their full need met. Average financial aid package met 58% of need; average scholarship/grant was $19,267; average loan was $3,432. For part-time students, average financial aid package was $11,841.
Students without need: 22 full-time freshmen who did not demonstrate need for aid received scholarships/grants; average award was $10,586. No-need awards available for academics.
Cumulative student debt: 88% of graduating class had student loans; average debt was $38,931.

FINANCIAL AID PROCEDURES

Forms required: FAFSA, state aid form, institutional form.
Dates and Deadlines: Priority date 3/1; no closing date. Applicants notified on a rolling basis starting 4/1; must reply within 2 week(s) of notification.

Transfers: No deadline. Applicants notified on a rolling basis starting 4/1; must reply by 5/1 or within 2 week(s) of notification.

CONTACT
Celeastia Williams, Director
7500 Glenoaks Boulevard, Burbank, CA 91510-7846
(818) 767-0888 ext. 273

Yeshiva Ohr Elchonon Chabad/West Coast Talmudical Seminary

Los Angeles, California
Federal Code: 015975

4-year private rabbinical college for men in very large city, affiliated with Jewish faith.
Enrollment: 152 undergrads.

BASIC COSTS (2012-2013)
Tuition and fees: $12,400.
Room and board: $7,450.
Additional info: Tuition/fee waivers available for minority students.

FINANCIAL AID PICTURE
Students with need: Need-based aid available for full-time students.
Students without need: This college awards aid only to students with need.

FINANCIAL AID PROCEDURES
Forms required: FAFSA, state aid form, institutional form.
Dates and Deadlines: Priority date 1/15; closing date 6/30. Applicants notified by 5/1; must reply by 7/1.

CONTACT
Hendy Tauber, Financial Aid Administrator
7215 Waring Avenue, Los Angeles, CA 90046
(323) 937-3763 ext. 112

Yuba Community College District

Marysville, California
http://yc.yccd.edu
Federal Code: 001344

2-year public community college in small city.
Enrollment: 8,123 undergrads.
Selectivity: Open admission; but selective for some programs.

BASIC COSTS (2012-2013)
Tuition and fees: $1,400; out-of-state residents $7,700.
Per-credit charge: $46; out-of-state residents $256.
Additional info: Tuition/fee waivers available for adults.

FINANCIAL AID PICTURE
Students with need: Need-based aid available for full-time and part-time students.
Students without need: No-need awards available for academics, athletics, job skills, minority status, music/drama.
Additional info: Tuition fee waiver based on Board of Governors Grant.

FINANCIAL AID PROCEDURES
Forms required: FAFSA.
Dates and Deadlines: Closing date 3/1. Applicants notified on a rolling basis starting 4/1.

CONTACT
Marisela Arce, Dean for EOP&S and Financial Aid
2088 North Beale Road, Marysville, CA 95901
(530) 741-6781

PART III: FINANCIAL AID COLLEGE BY COLLEGE

Colorado

Adams State College

Alamosa, Colorado
www.adams.edu
Federal Code: 001345

4-year public liberal arts college in small town.
Enrollment: 2,334 undergrads, 18% part-time. 517 full-time freshmen.
Selectivity: Admits 50 to 75% of applicants.

BASIC COSTS (2012-2013)
Tuition and fees: $6,448; out-of-state residents $17,416.
Per-credit charge: $159; out-of-state residents $616.
Room and board: $7,300.

FINANCIAL AID PICTURE
Students with need: Need-based aid available for full-time and part-time students. Work study available nights, weekends, and for part-time students.
Students without need: No-need awards available for academics, alumni affiliation, art, athletics, leadership, minority status, music/drama, state/district residency.

FINANCIAL AID PROCEDURES
Forms required: FAFSA.
Dates and Deadlines: Priority date 3/1; closing date 4/15. Applicants notified on a rolling basis starting 4/30; must reply within 4 week(s) of notification.
Transfers: No deadline. Applicants notified on a rolling basis starting 4/30; must reply within 4 week(s) of notification.

CONTACT
Philip Schroeder, Director of Financial Aid
208 Edgemont Boulevard, Alamosa, CO 81101
(719) 587-7306

Aims Community College

Greeley, Colorado
www.aims.edu
Federal Code: 007582

2-year public community college in small city.
Enrollment: 4,159 undergrads, 47% part-time. 554 full-time freshmen.
Selectivity: Open admission; but selective for some programs.

BASIC COSTS (2012-2013)
Tuition and fees: $2,621; out-of-district residents $3,772; out-of-state residents $13,358.
Per-credit charge: $67; out-of-district residents $106; out-of-state residents $425.
Additional info: Tuition/fee waivers available for adults.

FINANCIAL AID PICTURE
Students with need: Need-based aid available for full-time students.

FINANCIAL AID PROCEDURES
Forms required: FAFSA.
Dates and Deadlines: Priority date 4/15; no closing date. Applicants notified on a rolling basis starting 6/1.

CONTACT
Nancy Gray, Director of Student Financial Assistance
5401 West 20th Street, Greeley, CO 80632
(970) 339-6548

Anthem College: Aurora

Aurora, Colorado
www.anthem.edu Federal Code: 021829

2-year for-profit technical college in small city.
Enrollment: 302 undergrads.
Selectivity: Open admission.

FINANCIAL AID PICTURE
Students with need: Need-based aid available for full-time students.
Students without need: This college awards aid only to students with need.

FINANCIAL AID PROCEDURES
Forms required: FAFSA, institutional form.
Dates and Deadlines: Applicants notified on a rolling basis.

CONTACT
Suzanne Evans, Director of Financial Aid
350 Blackhawk Street, Aurora, CO 80011
(720) 859-7900

Arapahoe Community College

Littleton, Colorado
www.arapahoe.edu Federal Code: 001346

2-year public community college in large town.
Enrollment: 7,952 undergrads, 71% part-time. 509 full-time freshmen.
Selectivity: Open admission; but selective for some programs.

BASIC COSTS (2012-2013)
Tuition and fees: $3,575; out-of-state residents $14,069.
Per-credit charge: $113; out-of-state residents $463.
Additional info: In-state tuition based upon assumption of Colorado Opportunity Fund waiver of $62 per-credit-hour.

FINANCIAL AID PICTURE
Students with need: Need-based aid available for full-time and part-time students. Work study available nights, weekends, and for part-time students.
Students without need: No-need awards available for academics, leadership, state/district residency.
Scholarships offered: President's Scholarship; based on 3.0 GPA, references. College Bound Scholarship; based on high GED score. All awards $750 for full-time students, $375 for half-time, $563 for three-quarters time. Awards made on first-come first-served basis.

FINANCIAL AID PROCEDURES
Forms required: FAFSA, institutional form.
Dates and Deadlines: Priority date 5/1; no closing date. Applicants notified on a rolling basis starting 5/1; must reply within 3 week(s) of notification.
Transfers: No deadline. Applicants notified on a rolling basis starting 5/1.

CONTACT
Tyler Pruett, Director of Financial Aid
PO Box 9002, Littleton, CO 80160-9002
(303) 797-5661

Art Institute of Colorado

Denver, Colorado
www.artinstitutes.edu/denver Federal Code: 013961

4-year for-profit culinary school and visual arts college in very large city.
Enrollment: 2,050 undergrads.

BASIC COSTS (2012-2013)
Tuition and fees: $22,065.
Additional info: Depending on program, supply kit may cost up to $775.

FINANCIAL AID PICTURE
Students with need: Need-based aid available for full-time and part-time students.

FINANCIAL AID PROCEDURES
Forms required: FAFSA, institutional form.
Dates and Deadlines: Applicants notified on a rolling basis.
Transfers: No deadline.

CONTACT
Wendy Butler, Director of Student Financial Services
1200 Lincoln Street, Denver, CO 80203-2172
(303) 824-4889

Bel-Rea Institute of Animal Technology

Denver, Colorado
www.bel-rea.com Federal Code: 012670

2-year for-profit technical college in very large city.
Enrollment: 650 undergrads. 650 full-time freshmen.

BASIC COSTS (2012-2013)
Tuition and fees: $10,425.
Additional info: Tuition for full associate program is $27,900.

FINANCIAL AID PICTURE
Students with need: Need-based aid available for full-time students.
Students without need: This college awards aid only to students with need.

FINANCIAL AID PROCEDURES
Forms required: FAFSA.
Dates and Deadlines: Priority date 8/31; no closing date. Applicants notified on a rolling basis starting 8/15.
Transfers: No deadline.

CONTACT
Stasi Botinelli, Financial Aid Director
1681 South Dayton Street, Denver, CO 80247
(303) 751-8700

Boulder College of Massage Therapy

Boulder, Colorado
www.bcmt.org Federal Code: 030131

2-year private health science college in small city.
Enrollment: 115 undergrads.
Selectivity: Open admission; but selective for some programs.

FINANCIAL AID PICTURE
Students with need: Need-based aid available for full-time and part-time students.
Students without need: This college awards aid only to students with need.

FINANCIAL AID PROCEDURES
Forms required: FAFSA.

CONTACT
Debbie Clarke, Director of Financial Aid
6255 Longbow Drive, Boulder, CO 80301
(303) 530-2100 ext. 106

CollegeAmerica: Denver

Denver, Colorado
www.collegeamerica.com Federal Code: 025943

2-year for-profit technical college in very large city.
Enrollment: 502 undergrads.
Selectivity: Open admission.

BASIC COSTS (2012-2013)
Additional info: Tuition ranges from $324 to $511 per quarter credit depending on program.

FINANCIAL AID PICTURE
Students with need: Need-based aid available for full-time students.
Students without need: This college awards aid only to students with need.
Scholarships offered: High School Academic Scholarship.

FINANCIAL AID PROCEDURES
Forms required: FAFSA, institutional form.
Dates and Deadlines: Applicants notified on a rolling basis; must reply within 4 week(s) of notification.
Transfers: No deadline. Applicants notified on a rolling basis.

CONTACT
Sonia Martinez, Regional Director of Central Financial Aid
1385 South Colorado Boulevard, 5th Floor, Denver, CO 80222-1912
(303) 300-8740

Colorado Christian University

Lakewood, Colorado
www.ccu.edu Federal Code: 009401

4-year private university and liberal arts college in large city, affiliated with nondenominational tradition.
Enrollment: 3,145 undergrads, 57% part-time. 302 full-time freshmen.
Selectivity: Admits over 75% of applicants.

BASIC COSTS (2012-2013)
Tuition and fees: $23,870.
Room and board: $9,640.

FINANCIAL AID PICTURE
Students with need: Need-based aid available for full-time and part-time students. Work study available nights, weekends, and for part-time students.
Students without need: No-need awards available for academics, athletics, leadership, music/drama.

FINANCIAL AID PROCEDURES
Forms required: FAFSA.
Dates and Deadlines: Priority date 3/15; no closing date. Applicants notified on a rolling basis starting 4/1; must reply by 5/1 or within 4 week(s) of notification.
Transfers: Priority date 3/1; no deadline. Applicants notified by 3/10; must reply within 4 week(s) of notification.

CONTACT
Steve Woodburn, Director of Student Financial Aid
8787 West Alameda Avenue, Lakewood, CO 80226
(303) 963-3230

Colorado College

Colorado Springs, Colorado Federal Code: 001347
www.coloradocollege.edu CSS Code: 4072

4-year private liberal arts college in large city.
Enrollment: 1,983 undergrads. 510 full-time freshmen.
Selectivity: Admits less than 50% of applicants.

BASIC COSTS (2013-2014)
Tuition and fees: $44,222.
Additional info: Declining balance meal plans available. Cost of room only, $5,826.

FINANCIAL AID PICTURE (2012-2013)
Students with need: Need-based aid available for full-time and part-time students. Work study available nights, weekends, and for part-time students.
Students without need: No-need awards available for academics, athletics.

FINANCIAL AID PROCEDURES
Forms required: FAFSA, CSS PROFILE.
Dates and Deadlines: Closing date 2/15. Applicants notified by 3/15; must reply by 5/1.
Transfers: Must reply by 5/10.

CONTACT
James Swanson, Director of Financial Aid
14 East Cache La Poudre Street, Colorado Springs, CO 80903-9854
(800) 260-6458

Colorado Heights University

Denver, Colorado
www.chu.edu Federal Code: 032893

4-year private business and liberal arts college in very large city.
Enrollment: 89 undergrads.

BASIC COSTS (2012-2013)
Tuition and fees: $6,250.
Per-credit charge: $199.
Room and board: $6,592.

FINANCIAL AID PICTURE
Students with need: Need-based aid available for full-time and part-time students.
Students without need: This college awards aid only to students with need.

FINANCIAL AID PROCEDURES
Forms required: FAFSA.
Dates and Deadlines: Applicants notified on a rolling basis.
Transfers: No deadline. Applicants notified on a rolling basis.

CONTACT
Beba Predie, Director of Finance
3001 South Federal Boulevard, Denver, CO 80236
(303) 937-4538

Colorado Mesa University

Grand Junction, Colorado
www.coloradomesa.edu Federal Code: 001358

4-year public community and liberal arts college in small city.
Enrollment: 8,506 undergrads, 18% part-time. 2,001 full-time freshmen.
Selectivity: Admits over 75% of applicants.

BASIC COSTS (2012-2013)
Tuition and fees: $6,870; out-of-state residents $17,049.
Per-credit charge: $203; out-of-state residents $543.
Room and board: $9,103.

FINANCIAL AID PICTURE (2011-2012)
Students with need: Out of 1,787 full-time freshmen who applied for aid, 1,442 were judged to have need. Of these, 1,426 received aid, and 190 had their full need met. Average financial aid package met 56% of need; average

scholarship/grant was $4,943; average loan was $3,142. For part-time students, average financial aid package was $5,812.
Students without need: 121 full-time freshmen who did not demonstrate need for aid received scholarships/grants; average award was $2,595. No-need awards available for academics, art, athletics, leadership, music/drama.
Scholarships offered: 22 full-time freshmen received athletic scholarships; average amount $1,801.
Cumulative student debt: 69% of graduating class had student loans; average debt was $24,714.

FINANCIAL AID PROCEDURES
Forms required: FAFSA.
Dates and Deadlines: Priority date 3/1; no closing date. Applicants notified on a rolling basis starting 4/1; must reply within 2 week(s) of notification.

CONTACT
Curt Martin, Director of Financial Aid
1100 North Avenue, Grand Junction, CO 81501
(970) 248-1396

Colorado Mountain College

Glenwood Springs, Colorado
www.coloradomtn.edu Federal Code: 004506

2-year public community and liberal arts college in small town.
Enrollment: 3,467 undergrads.
Selectivity: Open admission; but selective for some programs.

BASIC COSTS (2012-2013)
Tuition and fees: $1,980; out-of-district residents $3,150; out-of-state residents $9,270.
Per-credit charge: $56; out-of-district residents $95; out-of-state residents $299.
Room and board: $9,000.

FINANCIAL AID PICTURE
Students with need: Need-based aid available for full-time and part-time students. Work study available nights, weekends, and for part-time students.
Students without need: This college awards aid only to students with need.

FINANCIAL AID PROCEDURES
Forms required: FAFSA.
Dates and Deadlines: Priority date 3/31; no closing date. Applicants notified on a rolling basis; must reply within 4 week(s) of notification.
Transfers: Transfer scholarships available for Colorado residents with 3.0 GPA and minimum 20 credit hours from previous schools.

CONTACT
Rita Bayless, Director of Student Financial Aid
802 Grand Avenue, Glenwood Springs, CO 81601
(970) 947-8277

Colorado Northwestern Community College

Rangely, Colorado
www.cncc.edu Federal Code: 001359

2-year public community college in rural community.
Enrollment: 711 undergrads, 39% part-time. 140 full-time freshmen.
Selectivity: Open admission; but selective for some programs.

BASIC COSTS (2012-2013)
Tuition and fees: $3,662; out-of-state residents $6,983.
Per-credit charge: $113; out-of-state residents $224.
Room and board: $6,136.
Additional info: In-state tuition based upon assumption of Colorado Opportunity Fund waiver of $62 per-credit-hour.

FINANCIAL AID PICTURE (2012-2013)
Students with need: 57% of average financial aid package awarded as scholarships/grants, 43% awarded as loans/jobs. Need-based aid available for part-time students. Work study available nights, weekends, and for part-time students.
Students without need: No-need awards available for academics, athletics, leadership, state/district residency.
Scholarships offered: Academic Scholarships; $200-$1,000; for Colorado residents based on grades, specific talent, area of study; requires application, essay, informal interview, 2.5 GPA.

FINANCIAL AID PROCEDURES
Forms required: FAFSA, institutional form.
Dates and Deadlines: Priority date 5/1; no closing date. Applicants notified on a rolling basis starting 5/15; must reply within 4 week(s) of notification.
Transfers: No deadline.

CONTACT
Tresa England, Director, Financial Aid
500 Kennedy Drive, Rangely, CO 81648
(970) 675-3204

Colorado School of Healing Arts

Lakewood, Colorado
www.csha.net Federal Code: 035844

2-year for-profit career college in small city.
Enrollment: 189 undergrads, 38% part-time. 39 full-time freshmen.
Selectivity: Open admission.

BASIC COSTS (2012-2013)
Tuition and fees: $14,621.
Per-credit charge: $197.
Additional info: Books, massage table package, materials fees, state registration fees and 1st year insurance included in required fees.

FINANCIAL AID PICTURE
Students with need: Need-based aid available for full-time and part-time students.
Students without need: This college awards aid only to students with need.

FINANCIAL AID PROCEDURES
Forms required: FAFSA.

CONTACT
Andrea Niece, Financial Aid Administrator
7655 West Mississippi Avenue, Suite 100, Lakewood, CO 80226
(303) 986-2320 ext. 26

Colorado School of Mines

Golden, Colorado
www.mines.edu Federal Code: 001348

4-year public university and engineering college in large town.
Enrollment: 4,075 undergrads, 4% part-time. 879 full-time freshmen.
Selectivity: Admits less than 50% of applicants.

BASIC COSTS (2012-2013)
Tuition and fees: $15,654; out-of-state residents $30,684.
Per-credit charge: $453; out-of-state residents $954.
Room and board: $9,922.

FINANCIAL AID PICTURE (2011-2012)
Students with need: Out of 742 full-time freshmen who applied for aid, 494 were judged to have need. Of these, 494 received aid, and 110 had their full need met. Average financial aid package met 62% of need; average scholarship/grant was $4,495; average loan was $3,411. For part-time students, average financial aid package was $8,674.
Students without need: 216 full-time freshmen who did not demonstrate need for aid received scholarships/grants; average award was $8,112. No-need awards available for academics, athletics, music/drama, ROTC.
Scholarships offered: 33 full-time freshmen received athletic scholarships; average amount $4,905.
Cumulative student debt: 51% of graduating class had student loans; average debt was $33,209.

FINANCIAL AID PROCEDURES
Forms required: FAFSA.
Dates and Deadlines: Priority date 2/14; closing date 4/1. Applicants notified on a rolling basis starting 3/1.
Transfers: No deadline. Applicants notified on a rolling basis starting 3/15. Federal aid only (Pell grant and Stafford loan). No aid available for second undergraduate degree candidates.

CONTACT
Jill Robertson, Director of Financial Aid
Undergraduate Admissions, Golden, CO 80401-6114
(303) 273-3220

Colorado School of Trades

Lakewood, Colorado
www.schooloftrades.edu Federal Code: 013513

2-year for-profit technical college in small city.
Enrollment: 162 undergrads.
Selectivity: Open admission.

BASIC COSTS (2012-2013)
Additional info: For gunsmithing program: tuition, $18,900 (fall 2012), $19,800 beginning January 2013; tools $3,500; miscellaneous $161.

FINANCIAL AID PICTURE
Students with need: Need-based aid available for full-time students.

FINANCIAL AID PROCEDURES
Forms required: FAFSA, institutional form.

CONTACT
Robert Martin, President
1575 Hoyt Street, Lakewood, CO 80215-2945
(303) 233-4697 ext. 14

Colorado State University

Fort Collins, Colorado
www.colostate.edu Federal Code: 001350

4-year public university in small city.
Enrollment: 22,412 undergrads, 7% part-time. 4,464 full-time freshmen.
Selectivity: Admits 50 to 75% of applicants.

BASIC COSTS (2012-2013)
Tuition and fees: $8,649; out-of-state residents $24,441.
Per-credit charge: $312; out-of-state residents $1,133.
Room and board: $10,278.

FINANCIAL AID PICTURE (2011-2012)
Students with need: Out of 3,636 full-time freshmen who applied for aid, 2,426 were judged to have need. Of these, 2,426 received aid, and 865 had their full need met. Average financial aid package met 71% of need; average scholarship/grant was $12,167; average loan was $5,246. For part-time students, average financial aid package was $6,828.
Students without need: 564 full-time freshmen who did not demonstrate need for aid received scholarships/grants; average award was $3,918. No-need awards available for academics, art, athletics, leadership, music/drama, state/district residency.
Scholarships offered: 24 full-time freshmen received athletic scholarships; average amount $15,516.
Cumulative student debt: 63% of graduating class had student loans; average debt was $22,039.

FINANCIAL AID PROCEDURES
Forms required: FAFSA.
Dates and Deadlines: Priority date 3/1; no closing date. Applicants notified on a rolling basis starting 3/1.

CONTACT
Tom Biedscheid, Director of Student Financial Aid
Office of Admissions/Colorado State University, Fort Collins, CO 80523-1062
(970) 491-6321

Colorado State University: Pueblo

Pueblo, Colorado
www.colostate-pueblo.edu Federal Code: 001365

4-year public university in small city.
Enrollment: 4,625 undergrads, 16% part-time. 868 full-time freshmen.
Selectivity: Admits over 75% of applicants.

BASIC COSTS (2012-2013)
Tuition and fees: $7,327; out-of-state residents $17,649.
Room and board: $8,970.

FINANCIAL AID PICTURE (2012-2013)
Students with need: Need-based aid available for full-time and part-time students. Work study available nights, weekends, and for part-time students.
Students without need: No-need awards available for academics, alumni affiliation, art, athletics, job skills, leadership, minority status, music/drama, ROTC, state/district residency.
Scholarships offered: Centennial Scholarship; $2,000; based on scholarship application and 3.5 GPA; must maintain 3.25 college GPA; over 100 awarded.
Additional info: Resident undergraduates with a family adjusted gross income of $50,000 or less and who receive a Pell grant will have tuition or mandatory fess covered by grant and institutional aid.

FINANCIAL AID PROCEDURES
Forms required: FAFSA, institutional form.
Dates and Deadlines: Closing date 3/1. Applicants notified on a rolling basis starting 3/13; must reply within 3 week(s) of notification.

CONTACT
Sean McGivney, Director of Financial Aid
2200 Bonforte Boulevard, Pueblo, CO 81001-4901
(719) 549-2753

Colorado Technical University

Colorado Springs, Colorado
www.coloradotech.edu Federal Code: 010148

4-year for-profit university and technical college in large city.
Enrollment: 2,052 undergrads.
Selectivity: Open admission; but selective for some programs.

BASIC COSTS (2012-2013)
Additional info: Cost of associate and bachelor's program, $305 per credit hour.

FINANCIAL AID PICTURE
Students with need: Need-based aid available for full-time and part-time students. Work study available nights, weekends, and for part-time students.
Students without need: No-need awards available for academics, ROTC.

FINANCIAL AID PROCEDURES
Forms required: FAFSA.
Dates and Deadlines: Applicants notified on a rolling basis starting 6/30.
Transfers: No deadline.

CONTACT
Cindy Rubek, Director of Student Financial Services
4435 North Chestnut Street, Colorado Springs, CO 80907
(719) 598-0200

Community College of Aurora
Aurora, Colorado
www.ccaurora.edu Federal Code: 016058

2-year public community college in large city.
Enrollment: 7,824 undergrads.
Selectivity: Open admission.

BASIC COSTS (2012-2013)
Tuition and fees: $3,568; out-of-state residents $14,062.
Per-credit charge: $113; out-of-state residents $463.
Additional info: In-state tuition based upon assumption of Colorado Opportunity Fund waiver of $62 per-credit-hour.

FINANCIAL AID PICTURE
Students with need: Need-based aid available for full-time and part-time students.
Students without need: No-need awards available for academics, minority status, music/drama, state/district residency.

FINANCIAL AID PROCEDURES
Forms required: FAFSA.
Dates and Deadlines: Priority date 6/1; no closing date. Applicants notified on a rolling basis starting 7/15.

CONTACT
John Young, Executive Director, Financial Aid
16000 East CentreTech Parkway, Aurora, CO 80011-9036
(303) 360-4709

Community College of Denver
Denver, Colorado
www.ccd.edu Federal Code: 009542

2-year public community college in very large city.
Enrollment: 9,720 undergrads, 71% part-time. 591 full-time freshmen.
Selectivity: Open admission; but selective for some programs.

BASIC COSTS (2012-2013)
Tuition and fees: $4,227; out-of-state residents $14,721.
Per-credit charge: $113; out-of-state residents $463.
Additional info: In-state tuition based upon assumption of Colorado Opportunity Fund waiver of $62 per-credit-hour.

FINANCIAL AID PICTURE (2011-2012)
Students with need: 61% of average financial aid package awarded as scholarships/grants, 39% awarded as loans/jobs. Need-based aid available for part-time students.
Students without need: No-need awards available for academics, leadership, state/district residency.

FINANCIAL AID PROCEDURES
Forms required: FAFSA, institutional form.
Dates and Deadlines: Priority date 4/15; no closing date. Applicants notified on a rolling basis.

CONTACT
Karla Nash, Director of Financial Aid
Campus Box 201, PO Box 173363, Denver, CO 80217-3363
(303) 556-2420

Denver School of Nursing
Denver, Colorado
www.denverschoolofnursing.edu

4-year for-profit nursing college in very large city.
Enrollment: 638 undergrads.

FINANCIAL AID PICTURE
Students with need: Need-based aid available for full-time and part-time students.
Students without need: This college awards aid only to students with need.

FINANCIAL AID PROCEDURES
Forms required: FAFSA.

CONTACT
Geri Reichmuth, Director of Financial Aid
1401 19th Street, Denver, CO 80202

DeVry University: Westminster
Westminster, Colorado
www.devry.edu Federal Code: 014831

4-year for-profit university in very large city.
Enrollment: 609 undergrads, 69% part-time. 19 full-time freshmen.

BASIC COSTS (2012-2013)
Tuition and fees: $16,076.
Per-credit charge: $609.

FINANCIAL AID PICTURE
Students with need: Need-based aid available for full-time and part-time students.
Students without need: This college awards aid only to students with need.

FINANCIAL AID PROCEDURES
Forms required: FAFSA.
Dates and Deadlines: Applicants notified on a rolling basis.

CONTACT
Terry Bargas, Director of Financial Aid
1870 West 122 Avenue, Westminster, CO 80234-2010
(303) 329-3340

Everest College: Aurora
Aurora, Colorado
www.cci.edu Federal Code: 004507

2-year for-profit branch campus and technical college in large city.
Enrollment: 485 undergrads.
Selectivity: Open admission.

BASIC COSTS (2012-2013)
Additional info: Costs reported are a representative estimate of annual tuition and fees. Estimated tuition and fees ranges for entire programs as of

July 2012: diploma programs, $16,160 to $18,728; associate degree programs, $41,760; does not include books and supplies, which vary by program. All costs subject to change at any time.

FINANCIAL AID PICTURE

Students with need: Need-based aid available for full-time and part-time students. Work study available nights.

Students without need: This college awards aid only to students with need.

FINANCIAL AID PROCEDURES

Forms required: FAFSA, state aid form, institutional form.

Dates and Deadlines: Applicants notified on a rolling basis; must reply within 4 week(s) of notification.

Transfers: $4,500 limitation on Colorado State Grant per award year.

CONTACT

Myra Dollar, Director of Student Finance
14280 East Jewell Suite 100, Aurora, CO 80012
(303) 745-624

Everest College: Colorado Springs

Colorado Springs, Colorado
www.cci.edu Federal Code: 004503

2-year for-profit business and junior college in large city.
Enrollment: 498 undergrads.
Selectivity: Open admission.

BASIC COSTS (2012-2013)

Additional info: Costs reported are a representative estimate of annual tuition and fees. Estimated tuition and fees ranges for entire programs as of July 2012: diploma programs, $13,816 to $18,720; associate degree programs, $37,440; does not include books and supplies, which vary by program. All costs subject to change at any time.

FINANCIAL AID PICTURE

Students with need: Need-based aid available for full-time and part-time students. Work study available nights.

FINANCIAL AID PROCEDURES

Forms required: FAFSA, institutional form.

Dates and Deadlines: Applicants notified on a rolling basis starting 7/1.

Transfers: No deadline.

CONTACT

Meng Johnson, Financial Aid Director
1815 Jet Wing Drive, Colorado Springs, CO 80916
(719) 638-6580 ext. 103

Fort Lewis College

Durango, Colorado
www.fortlewis.edu Federal Code: 001353

4-year public liberal arts college in large town.
Enrollment: 3,754 undergrads, 7% part-time. 760 full-time freshmen.
Selectivity: Admits over 75% of applicants.

BASIC COSTS (2013-2014)

Tuition and fees: $6,923; out-of-state residents $17,763.
Per-credit charge: $218; out-of-state residents $670.
Room and board: $8,590.
Additional info: Tuition/fee waivers available for minority students.

FINANCIAL AID PICTURE (2011-2012)

Students with need: Out of 610 full-time freshmen who applied for aid, 481 were judged to have need. Of these, 479 received aid, and 24 had their full need met. Average financial aid package met 98% of need; average scholarship/grant was $4,469; average loan was $303. For part-time students, average financial aid package was $8,116.

Students without need: 187 full-time freshmen who did not demonstrate need for aid received scholarships/grants; average award was $2,822. No-need awards available for academics, alumni affiliation, art, athletics, leadership, music/drama, state/district residency.

Scholarships offered: ***Merit:*** Presidential Scholarship; $8,000 out-of-state, $2,000 in-state; 121 admission index required. Provost Scholarship; $7,000 out-of-state, $1,500 in-state; 110-120 admission index required. Dean's Scholarship; $6,000 out-of-state, $1,000 in-state; 101-109 admission index required. Academic Promise Scholarship; $4,000 out-of-state, $750 in-state; 92-100 admission index required. New Mexico Reciprocal Scholarship; New Mexico residents are given in-state tuition rates; based on 3.5 GPA; number of awards limited. ***Athletic:*** 24 full-time freshmen received athletic scholarships; average amount $5,826.

Cumulative student debt: 57% of graduating class had student loans; average debt was $19,811.

Additional info: Tuition waived for Native Americans of federally recognized tribes; census number and Certificate of Indian Blood must accompany application.

FINANCIAL AID PROCEDURES

Forms required: FAFSA.

Dates and Deadlines: Priority date 2/15; no closing date. Applicants notified on a rolling basis starting 3/1.

Transfers: No deadline. Applicants notified on a rolling basis.

CONTACT

Jerry Martinez, Director of Financial Aid
1000 Rim Drive, Durango, CO 81301-3999
(970) 247-7142

Front Range Community College

Westminster, Colorado
www.frontrange.edu Federal Code: 007933

2-year public community college in large city.
Enrollment: 17,874 undergrads, 65% part-time. 1,362 full-time freshmen.
Selectivity: Open admission.

BASIC COSTS (2012-2013)

Tuition and fees: $3,647; out-of-state residents $14,141.
Per-credit charge: $113; out-of-state residents $463.
Additional info: In-state tuition based upon assumption of Colorado Opportunity Fund waiver of $62 per-credit-hour.

FINANCIAL AID PICTURE (2012-2013)

Students with need: 56% of average financial aid package awarded as scholarships/grants, 44% awarded as loans/jobs. Need-based aid available for part-time students. Work study available nights, weekends, and for part-time students.

Students without need: No-need awards available for academics, job skills, leadership, state/district residency.

FINANCIAL AID PROCEDURES

Forms required: FAFSA, institutional form.

Dates and Deadlines: Priority date 5/1; no closing date. Applicants notified on a rolling basis starting 4/15; must reply within 3 week(s) of notification.

CONTACT

Carolee Goldsmith, Director of Financial Aid
3645 West 112th Avenue, Westminster, CO 80031
(303) 439-9454

IntelliTec College

Colorado Springs, Colorado
www.intelliteccollege.com Federal Code: 008635

2-year for-profit technical college in large city.
Enrollment: 605 undergrads.
Selectivity: Open admission.

BASIC COSTS (2012-2013)
Additional info: Tuition as of April 2012: HVAC - Refrigeration Technician, $26,400; Computer and Network Systems, $26,880; Automotive Technician, $26,880; Mechanical Drafting, $24,480.

FINANCIAL AID PICTURE
Students with need: Need-based aid available for full-time and part-time students. Work study available nights.
Students without need: This college awards aid only to students with need.

FINANCIAL AID PROCEDURES
Forms required: FAFSA, state aid form, institutional form.
Dates and Deadlines: Applicants notified on a rolling basis.
Transfers: No deadline.

CONTACT
Kristy Sanchez, Lead Financial Services Representative
2315 East Pikes Peak Avenue, Colorado Springs, CO 80909
(719) 632-7626

IntelliTec College: Grand Junction

Grand Junction, Colorado
www.intelliteccollege.edu Federal Code: 030669

2-year for-profit technical college in small city.
Enrollment: 512 undergrads.
Selectivity: Open admission.

BASIC COSTS (2013-2014)
Additional info: Total costs include: Medical Assistant, $25,775; Automotive Technician, $27,2017; Administrative Professional, $27,271; Health Information Technician, $27,226. Total cost of certificate programs: Massage Therapist, $16,073; Dental Assistant, $18,041.

FINANCIAL AID PICTURE
Students with need: Need-based aid available for full-time students.
Students without need: This college awards aid only to students with need.

FINANCIAL AID PROCEDURES
Forms required: FAFSA.
Dates and Deadlines: Applicants notified on a rolling basis.
Transfers: No deadline.

CONTACT
Toni Garmong, Director of Financial Sevices
772 Horizon Drive, Grand Junction, CO 81506
(970) 245-8101

Johnson & Wales University: Denver

Denver, Colorado
www.jwu.edu Federal Code: 003404

4-year private university in large city.
Enrollment: 1,618 undergrads, 8% part-time. 362 full-time freshmen.
Selectivity: Admits 50 to 75% of applicants.

BASIC COSTS (2012-2013)
Tuition and fees: $26,112.
Room and board: $9,750.

FINANCIAL AID PICTURE
Students with need: Need-based aid available for full-time and part-time students.
Students without need: No-need awards available for academics, alumni affiliation, job skills, leadership, state/district residency.

FINANCIAL AID PROCEDURES
Forms required: FAFSA.
Dates and Deadlines: Applicants notified on a rolling basis starting 3/1; must reply within 2 week(s) of notification.

CONTACT
Lynn Robinson, Chief Financial Aid Officer
7150 Montview Boulevard, Denver, CO 80220
(800) 342-5598 ext. 4648

Jones International University

Centennial, Colorado
www.jiu.edu Federal Code: 035343

4-year for-profit virtual college in large city.
Enrollment: 1,688 undergrads, 57% part-time. 210 full-time freshmen.

BASIC COSTS (2013-2014)
Tuition and fees: $12,720.
Per-credit charge: $530.
Additional info: Tuition is $1,590 per course for bachelor's degrees. Average cost of books per course, $170.

FINANCIAL AID PICTURE
Students with need: Need-based aid available for full-time and part-time students.
Students without need: This college awards aid only to students with need.
Additional info: Many students have costs reimbursed by employers. GI Bill and VA benefits accepted.

FINANCIAL AID PROCEDURES
Forms required: FAFSA, institutional form.
Dates and Deadlines: Applicants notified on a rolling basis; must reply within 8 week(s) of notification.
Transfers: No deadline. Applicants notified on a rolling basis; must reply within 8 week(s) of notification.

CONTACT
Tim Lehmann, Director of Financial Aid
9697 East Mineral Avenue, Centennial, CO 80112
(800) 811-5663 ext. 3

Lamar Community College

Lamar, Colorado
www.lamarcc.edu Federal Code: 001355

2-year public community college in small town.
Enrollment: 561 undergrads, 25% part-time. 151 full-time freshmen.
Selectivity: Open admission; but selective for some programs.

BASIC COSTS (2012-2013)
Tuition and fees: $3,785; out-of-state residents $7,106.
Per-credit charge: $113; out-of-state residents $224.
Room and board: $5,606.
Additional info: In-state tuition based upon assumption of Colorado Opportunity Fund waiver of $62 per-credit-hour.

FINANCIAL AID PICTURE
Students with need: Need-based aid available for full-time and part-time students.

FINANCIAL AID PROCEDURES
Forms required: FAFSA, institutional form.
Dates and Deadlines: Priority date 4/1; no closing date. Applicants notified on a rolling basis starting 7/1.
Transfers: No deadline.

CONTACT
Teale Hemphill, Director of Financial Aid
2401 South Main Street, Lamar, CO 81052-3999

Metropolitan State University of Denver
Denver, Colorado
www.mscd.edu Federal Code: 001360

4-year public liberal arts college in very large city.
Enrollment: 22,373 undergrads, 41% part-time. 1,868 full-time freshmen.
Selectivity: Admits 50 to 75% of applicants.

BASIC COSTS (2012-2013)
Tuition and fees: $5,341; out-of-state residents $17,022.
Per-credit charge: $179; out-of-state residents $666.

FINANCIAL AID PICTURE (2011-2012)
Students with need: Out of 1,540 full-time freshmen who applied for aid, 1,192 were judged to have need. Of these, 1,085 received aid, and 15 had their full need met. Average financial aid package met 52% of need; average scholarship/grant was $4,776; average loan was $2,965. Need-based aid available for part-time students.
Students without need: 285 full-time freshmen who did not demonstrate need for aid received scholarships/grants; average award was $1,447.
Cumulative student debt: 60% of graduating class had student loans; average debt was $31,427.

FINANCIAL AID PROCEDURES
Forms required: FAFSA.
Dates and Deadlines: Applicants notified on a rolling basis starting 3/15.
Transfers: No deadline.

CONTACT
Cindy Hejl, Director of Financial Aid
Campus Box 16, Denver, CO 80217

Morgan Community College
Fort Morgan, Colorado
www.morgancc.edu Federal Code: 009981

2-year public community college in large town.
Enrollment: 1,062 undergrads, 65% part-time. 63 full-time freshmen.
Selectivity: Open admission; but selective for some programs.

BASIC COSTS (2012-2013)
Tuition and fees: $3,558; out-of-state residents $14,052.
Per-credit charge: $113; out-of-state residents $463.
Additional info: In-state tuition based upon assumption of Colorado Opportunity Fund waiver of $62 per-credit-hour.

FINANCIAL AID PICTURE (2011-2012)
Students with need: 65% of average financial aid package awarded as scholarships/grants, 35% awarded as loans/jobs. Need-based aid available for part-time students. Work study available nights, weekends, and for part-time students.

FINANCIAL AID PROCEDURES
Forms required: FAFSA.
Dates and Deadlines: Closing date 4/2. Applicants notified on a rolling basis.

CONTACT
Sally Nestor, Director of Financial Aid
920 Barlow Road, Fort Morgan, CO 80701
(970) 542-3100

Naropa University
Boulder, Colorado
www.naropa.edu Federal Code: 014652

4-year private university and liberal arts college in small city.
Enrollment: 384 undergrads, 7% part-time. 24 full-time freshmen.
Selectivity: Admits over 75% of applicants.

BASIC COSTS (2013-2014)
Tuition and fees: $28,780.
Per-credit charge: $936.

FINANCIAL AID PICTURE (2012-2013)
Students with need: Average financial aid package met 82% of need; average scholarship/grant was $23,254; average loan was $7,353. For part-time students, average financial aid package was $14,447.
Students without need: This college awards aid only to students with need.
Cumulative student debt: 70% of graduating class had student loans; average debt was $26,511.

FINANCIAL AID PROCEDURES
Forms required: FAFSA.
Dates and Deadlines: Priority date 3/1; no closing date. Applicants notified on a rolling basis starting 3/1; must reply within 4 week(s) of notification.
Transfers: No deadline. Applicants notified on a rolling basis starting 1/15; must reply within 4 week(s) of notification.

CONTACT
Nancy Morrell; Director of Student Financial Aid
2130 Arapahoe Avenue, Boulder, CO 80302-6697
(303) 546-3534

Nazarene Bible College
Colorado Springs, Colorado
www.nbc.edu Federal Code: 013007

4-year private Bible college in very large city, affiliated with Church of the Nazarene.
Enrollment: 1,006 undergrads, 88% part-time. 1 full-time freshmen.
Selectivity: Open admission.

BASIC COSTS (2013-2014)
Tuition and fees: $12,750.
Per-credit charge: $400.

FINANCIAL AID PICTURE
Students with need: Need-based aid available for full-time and part-time students. Work study available nights, weekends, and for part-time students.
Students without need: No-need awards available for academics, religious affiliation.
Additional info: Tuition waiver available to students serving as student body officers.

FINANCIAL AID PROCEDURES
Forms required: FAFSA.
Dates and Deadlines: Priority date 6/1; no closing date. Applicants notified on a rolling basis starting 6/15; must reply within 2 week(s) of notification.
Transfers: No deadline. Applicants notified on a rolling basis.

CONTACT
Mal Britton, Director of Financial Aid
1111 Academy Park Loop, Colorado Springs, CO 80910-3704
(719) 884-5050

Northeastern Junior College
Sterling, Colorado
www.njc.edu Federal Code: 001361

2-year public community and junior college in large town.
Enrollment: 1,306 undergrads, 28% part-time. 332 full-time freshmen.
Selectivity: Open admission; but selective for some programs.

BASIC COSTS (2012-2013)
Tuition and fees: $3,979; out-of-state residents $11,695.
Per-credit charge: $113; out-of-state residents $370.
Room and board: $6,190.
Additional info: In-state tuition based upon assumption of Colorado Opportunity Fund waiver of $62 per-credit-hour. Tuition/fee waivers available for adults, minority students.

FINANCIAL AID PICTURE (2011-2012)
Students with need: 57% of average financial aid package awarded as scholarships/grants, 43% awarded as loans/jobs. Need-based aid available for part-time students. Work study available nights, weekends, and for part-time students.
Students without need: No-need awards available for academics, alumni affiliation, art, athletics, job skills, leadership, music/drama, state/district residency.
Additional info: Need-based financial aid available to part-time students taking 6 credits or more per semester.

FINANCIAL AID PROCEDURES
Forms required: FAFSA, institutional form.
Dates and Deadlines: Priority date 3/1; no closing date. Applicants notified on a rolling basis starting 4/15; must reply within 3 week(s) of notification.
Transfers: No deadline. Applicants notified on a rolling basis starting 4/15; must reply within 3 week(s) of notification.

CONTACT
Alice Weingardt, Financial Aid Director
100 College Avenue, Sterling, CO 80751-2399
(970) 521-6800

Otero Junior College
La Junta, Colorado
www.ojc.edu Federal Code: 001362

2-year public community and junior college in small town.
Enrollment: 1,545 undergrads.
Selectivity: Open admission; but selective for some programs.

BASIC COSTS (2012-2013)
Tuition and fees: $3,658; out-of-state residents $6,979.
Per-credit charge: $113; out-of-state residents $224.
Room and board: $5,736.
Additional info: In-state tuition based upon assumption of Colorado Opportunity Fund waiver of $62 per-credit-hour.

FINANCIAL AID PICTURE
Students with need: Need-based aid available for full-time and part-time students. Work study available nights, weekends, and for part-time students.
Students without need: No-need awards available for academics, athletics, state/district residency.

FINANCIAL AID PROCEDURES
Forms required: FAFSA.
Dates and Deadlines: Priority date 4/15; no closing date. Applicants notified on a rolling basis starting 4/15; must reply within 2 week(s) of notification.
Transfers: No deadline. Applicants notified on a rolling basis starting 4/15; must reply within 2 week(s) of notification.

CONTACT
Angela Benfatti, Financial Aid Director
1802 Colorado Avenue, La Junta, CO 81050
(719) 384-6834

Pikes Peak Community College
Colorado Springs, Colorado
www.ppcc.edu Federal Code: 008896

2-year public community college in large city.
Enrollment: 14,114 undergrads, 59% part-time. 1,426 full-time freshmen.
Selectivity: Open admission.

BASIC COSTS (2012-2013)
Tuition and fees: $3,666; out-of-state residents $14,160.
Per-credit charge: $113; out-of-state residents $463.
Additional info: In-state tuition based upon assumption of Colorado Opportunity Fund waiver of $62 per-credit-hour.

FINANCIAL AID PICTURE
Students with need: Need-based aid available for full-time and part-time students. Work study available nights.

FINANCIAL AID PROCEDURES
Forms required: FAFSA.
Dates and Deadlines: Closing date 7/1. Applicants notified on a rolling basis; must reply within 2 week(s) of notification.

CONTACT
Sherri McCullough, Director of Financial Aid
5675 South Academy Boulevard, Colorado Springs, CO 80906-5498
(719) 502-3000

Platt College: Aurora
Aurora, Colorado
www.plattcolorado.edu Federal Code: 030149

4-year for-profit visual arts and nursing college in very large city.
Enrollment: 193 undergrads.
Selectivity: Open admission; but selective for some programs.

FINANCIAL AID PICTURE
Students with need: Need-based aid available for full-time students.
Students without need: This college awards aid only to students with need.

FINANCIAL AID PROCEDURES
Forms required: FAFSA, institutional form.
Dates and Deadlines: Applicants notified on a rolling basis.

CONTACT
Margie Rose, Director of Financial Aid
3100 South Parker Road, Aurora, CO 80014-3141
(303) 369-5151

Pueblo Community College
Pueblo, Colorado
www.pueblocc.edu Federal Code: 014829

2-year public community college in small city.
Enrollment: 5,661 undergrads, 59% part-time. 557 full-time freshmen.

Selectivity: Open admission; but selective for some programs.

BASIC COSTS (2012-2013)
Tuition and fees: $3,912; out-of-state residents $14,406.
Per-credit charge: $113; out-of-state residents $463.
Additional info: In-state tuition based upon assumption of Colorado Opportunity Fund waiver of $62 per-credit-hour.

FINANCIAL AID PICTURE (2011-2012)
Students with need: Out of 501 full-time freshmen who applied for aid, 475 were judged to have need. Of these, 465 received aid, and 25 had their full need met. Average financial aid package met 50% of need; average scholarship/grant was $3,500; average loan was $2,000. For part-time students, average financial aid package was $3,250.
Students without need: 20 full-time freshmen who did not demonstrate need for aid received scholarships/grants; average award was $300. No-need awards available for academics, art, job skills, leadership, music/drama.
Cumulative student debt: 65% of graduating class had student loans; average debt was $12,500.

FINANCIAL AID PROCEDURES
Forms required: FAFSA.
Dates and Deadlines: Priority date 3/15; no closing date. Applicants notified on a rolling basis starting 4/1.
Transfers: No deadline. Applicants notified on a rolling basis starting 4/1.

CONTACT
Ron Swartwood, Director of Financial Aid
900 West Orman Avenue, Pueblo, CO 81004-1499
(719) 549-3020

Red Rocks Community College
Lakewood, Colorado
www.rrcc.edu Federal Code: 009543

2-year public community and career college in small city.
Enrollment: 8,058 undergrads, 66% part-time. 490 full-time freshmen.
Selectivity: Open admission.

BASIC COSTS (2012-2013)
Tuition and fees: $3,668; out-of-state residents $14,162.
Per-credit charge: $113; out-of-state residents $463.
Additional info: In-state tuition based upon assumption of Colorado Opportunity Fund waiver of $62 per-credit-hour.

FINANCIAL AID PICTURE (2011-2012)
Students with need: 59% of average financial aid package awarded as scholarships/grants, 41% awarded as loans/jobs. Need-based aid available for part-time students.
Students without need: No-need awards available for academics, leadership, minority status, state/district residency.

FINANCIAL AID PROCEDURES
Forms required: FAFSA.
Dates and Deadlines: Priority date 4/1; no closing date. Applicants notified on a rolling basis starting 5/1.

CONTACT
Linda Crook, Director of Financial Aid
13300 West Sixth Avenue, Lakewood, CO 80228-1255
(303) 914-6256

Redstone College
Broomfield, Colorado
www.redstone.edu Federal Code: 007297

2-year for-profit technical college in small city.
Enrollment: 831 undergrads.
Selectivity: Open admission.

BASIC COSTS (2012-2013)
Additional info: Tuition and fees for entire Associate degree program $32,239 to $41,191 depending on program.

FINANCIAL AID PICTURE
Students with need: Need-based aid available for full-time students.
Students without need: This college awards aid only to students with need.

FINANCIAL AID PROCEDURES
Forms required: FAFSA, state aid form.
Dates and Deadlines: Applicants notified on a rolling basis; must reply within 2 week(s) of notification.

CONTACT
Alicia Harbin, Financial Aid Director
10851 West 120th Avenue, Broomfield, CO 80021-3401

Regis University
Denver, Colorado
www.regis.edu Federal Code: 001363

4-year private university and liberal arts college in very large city, affiliated with Roman Catholic Church.
Enrollment: 5,428 undergrads, 53% part-time. 509 full-time freshmen.
Selectivity: Admits over 75% of applicants.

BASIC COSTS (2013-2014)
Tuition and fees: $32,424.
Per-credit charge: $995.
Room and board: $9,380.

FINANCIAL AID PICTURE (2011-2012)
Students with need: Out of 430 full-time freshmen who applied for aid, 365 were judged to have need. Of these, 365 received aid, and 158 had their full need met. Average financial aid package met 75% of need; average scholarship/grant was $19,759; average loan was $2,339. For part-time students, average financial aid package was $6,220.
Students without need: 134 full-time freshmen who did not demonstrate need for aid received scholarships/grants; average award was $11,897. No-need awards available for academics, athletics, leadership, music/drama, religious affiliation, ROTC, state/district residency.
Scholarships offered: 21 full-time freshmen received athletic scholarships; average amount $10,605.

FINANCIAL AID PROCEDURES
Forms required: FAFSA.
Dates and Deadlines: Priority date 5/31; no closing date. Applicants notified on a rolling basis starting 3/15.

CONTACT
Ellie Miller, Director of Financial Aid
3333 Regis Boulevard, Mail Code B20, Denver, CO 80221-1099
(800) 388-2366 ext. 4126

Remington College: Colorado Springs
Colorado Springs, Colorado
www.remingtoncollege.edu/coloradosprings
Federal Code: 030121

2-year private technical college in very large city.
Enrollment: 149 undergrads.
Selectivity: Open admission; but selective for some programs.

PART III: FINANCIAL AID COLLEGE BY COLLEGE

BASIC COSTS (2012-2013)
Additional info: Cost of entire associate degree program in Criminal Justice, $30,900. Cost of diploma programs in Medical Assisting, Medical Billing and Coding, and Pharmacy Technician, $14,695. Includes all required textbooks and course/lab materials.

FINANCIAL AID PICTURE
Students with need: Need-based aid available for full-time and part-time students.
Students without need: This college awards aid only to students with need.

FINANCIAL AID PROCEDURES
Forms required: FAFSA.
Dates and Deadlines: Applicants notified on a rolling basis; must reply within 3 week(s) of notification.
Transfers: No deadline. Applicants notified on a rolling basis.

CONTACT
James Dunn, National Director of Financial Aid
6050 Erin Park Drive, Colorado Springs, CO 80918

Rocky Mountain College of Art & Design
Denver, Colorado
www.rmcad.edu Federal Code: 013991

4-year for-profit visual arts college in very large city.
Enrollment: 605 undergrads, 7% part-time. 105 full-time freshmen.
Selectivity: Open admission.

BASIC COSTS (2012-2013)
Tuition and fees: $27,648.
Per-credit charge: $1,152.
Additional info: Flat fee of $13,824 per term for students taking 12 to 18 credits.

FINANCIAL AID PICTURE (2012-2013)
Students with need: Out of 99 full-time freshmen who applied for aid, 87 were judged to have need. Of these, 87 received aid, and 11 had their full need met. Average financial aid package met 74% of need; average scholarship/grant was $5,252; average loan was $3,417. For part-time students, average financial aid package was $13,028.
Students without need: 18 full-time freshmen who did not demonstrate need for aid received scholarships/grants; average award was $9,647. No-need awards available for academics, art, state/district residency.
Cumulative student debt: 7% of graduating class had student loans; average debt was $30,067.

FINANCIAL AID PROCEDURES
Forms required: FAFSA.
Dates and Deadlines: Priority date 3/15; no closing date. Applicants notified on a rolling basis starting 4/1; must reply within 2 week(s) of notification.
Transfers: Must reply within 2 week(s) of notification.

CONTACT
Tammy Dybdahl, Director of Financial Aid
1600 Pierce Street, Denver, CO 80214
(303) 753-6046

Trinidad State Junior College
Trinidad, Colorado
www.trinidadstate.edu Federal Code: 001368

2-year public community and junior college in small town.
Enrollment: 1,839 undergrads.
Selectivity: Open admission; but selective for some programs.

BASIC COSTS (2012-2013)
Tuition and fees: $3,941; out-of-state residents $7,262.
Per-credit charge: $113; out-of-state residents $224.
Room and board: $5,480.
Additional info: In-state tuition based upon assumption of Colorado Opportunity Fund waiver of $62 per-credit-hour. Tuition at time of enrollment locked for 2 years.

FINANCIAL AID PICTURE
Students with need: Need-based aid available for full-time and part-time students. Work study available nights.
Students without need: No-need awards available for academics, athletics, state/district residency.

FINANCIAL AID PROCEDURES
Forms required: FAFSA, institutional form.
Dates and Deadlines: Priority date 5/1; no closing date. Applicants notified on a rolling basis starting 6/15.

CONTACT
Wilma Atencio, Financial Aid Director
600 Prospect Street, Trinidad, CO 81082
(719) 846-5553

United States Air Force Academy
USAF Academy, Colorado
www.academyadmissions.com Federal Code: 001369

4-year public liberal arts and military college in large city.
Enrollment: 4,120 undergrads. 981 full-time freshmen.
Selectivity: Admits less than 50% of applicants.

BASIC COSTS (2012-2013)
Additional info: Tuition, room, board, medical and dental care paid by U.S. Government. Each cadet receives monthly salary to pay for uniforms, supplies and personal expenses. A government loan is advanced to each member of the freshman class.

CONTACT
HQ USAFA/RR, 2304 Cadet Drive, Suite 2400, USAF Academy, CO 80840-5025

University of Colorado Boulder
Boulder, Colorado
www.colorado.edu Federal Code: 001370

4-year public university in small city.
Enrollment: 25,239 undergrads, 7% part-time. 5,436 full-time freshmen.
Selectivity: Admits over 75% of applicants.

BASIC COSTS (2012-2013)
Tuition and fees: $9,482; out-of-state residents $31,378.
Room and board: $11,730.

FINANCIAL AID PICTURE (2012-2013)
Students with need: Out of 3,671 full-time freshmen who applied for aid, 2,465 were judged to have need. Of these, 2,388 received aid, and 1,474 had their full need met. Average financial aid package met 87% of need; average scholarship/grant was $7,968; average loan was $5,337. For part-time students, average financial aid package was $12,497.
Students without need: 1,424 full-time freshmen who did not demonstrate need for aid received scholarships/grants; average award was $7,512. No-need awards available for academics, alumni affiliation, art, athletics, leadership, music/drama, ROTC, state/district residency.
Scholarships offered: ***Merit:*** Presidential Scholars Program; $15,000 per year during freshman and sophomore years, $12,500 per year during junior

and senior years; for out-of-state freshmen in top 1-3% of admitted out-of-state freshman class, based on GPA, class rank, and test scores; renewable based on minimum GPA. Chancellor's Achievement Scholarship; $5,000 per year; for top 25% of out-of-state admitted students, based on GPA, class rank, and test scores; renewable based on minimum GPA. Norlin Scholars Program; $4,000; based on excellent academic or creative ability; 20-30 annual awards; renewable for 2 or 4 years contingent upon academic progress. President Joseph A. Sewall Award; $5,000 per year; for Colorado residents; based on GPA and SAT/ACT. President Horace M. Hale Award; $3,500 per year; for Colorado residents; based on GPA and SAT/ACT. President James H. Baker Award; $2,500 per year; for Colorado residents; based on GPA and SAT/ACT. ***Athletic:*** 53 full-time freshmen received athletic scholarships; average amount $30,922.
Cumulative student debt: 45% of graduating class had student loans; average debt was $23,413.

FINANCIAL AID PROCEDURES
Forms required: FAFSA.
Dates and Deadlines: Priority date 4/1; no closing date. Applicants notified on a rolling basis starting 3/1; must reply within 3 week(s) of notification.
Transfers: Some financial aid programs available exclusively to transfer students.

CONTACT
Gwen Pomper, Director of Financial Aid
552 UCB, Boulder, CO 80309-0552
(303) 492-5091

University of Colorado Colorado Springs

Colorado Springs, Colorado
www.uccs.edu Federal Code: 004509

4-year public university in large city.
Enrollment: 8,111 undergrads, 21% part-time. 1,159 full-time freshmen.
Selectivity: Admits over 75% of applicants.

BASIC COSTS (2012-2013)
Tuition and fees: $8,239; out-of-state residents $17,909.
Room and board: $8,300.
Additional info: Tuition varies by program and Colorado Opportunity Fund eligibility.

FINANCIAL AID PICTURE (2011-2012)
Students with need: Out of 1,018 full-time freshmen who applied for aid, 726 were judged to have need. Of these, 665 received aid, and 397 had their full need met. Average financial aid package met 57% of need; average scholarship/grant was $5,096; average loan was $6,421. For part-time students, average financial aid package was $8,185.
Students without need: 96 full-time freshmen who did not demonstrate need for aid received scholarships/grants; average award was $2,166. No-need awards available for academics, alumni affiliation, athletics, ROTC.
Scholarships offered: 20 full-time freshmen received athletic scholarships; average amount $3,298.

FINANCIAL AID PROCEDURES
Forms required: FAFSA.
Dates and Deadlines: Priority date 3/1; no closing date. Applicants notified on a rolling basis starting 4/15.

CONTACT
Jevita Rogers, Director of Financial Aid
1420 Austin Bluffs Parkway, Colorado Springs, CO 80918
(719) 255-3460

University of Colorado Denver

Denver, Colorado
www.ucdenver.edu Federal Code: 006740

4-year public university in very large city.
Enrollment: 10,375 undergrads, 28% part-time. 947 full-time freshmen.
Selectivity: Admits 50 to 75% of applicants.

BASIC COSTS (2012-2013)
Tuition and fees: $8,741; out-of-state residents $23,419.
Room and board: $10,410.
Additional info: Tuition varies by level and program.

FINANCIAL AID PICTURE (2011-2012)
Students with need: Out of 739 full-time freshmen who applied for aid, 603 were judged to have need. Of these, 571 received aid, and 29 had their full need met. Average financial aid package met 45% of need; average scholarship/grant was $7,500; average loan was $3,125. For part-time students, average financial aid package was $6,128.
Students without need: 76 full-time freshmen who did not demonstrate need for aid received scholarships/grants; average award was $2,289. No-need awards available for academics, leadership, music/drama, state/district residency.
Cumulative student debt: 54% of graduating class had student loans; average debt was $21,285.

FINANCIAL AID PROCEDURES
Forms required: FAFSA.
Dates and Deadlines: Priority date 4/1; no closing date. Applicants notified on a rolling basis starting 5/1.
Transfers: No deadline. Applicants notified on a rolling basis.

CONTACT
James Broscheit, Director of Financial Aid
Box 173364, Campus Box 167, Denver, CO 80217-3364
(303) 556-2886

University of Denver

Denver, Colorado Federal Code: 001371
www.du.edu CSS Code: 4842

4-year private university in very large city.
Enrollment: 5,379 undergrads, 8% part-time. 1,203 full-time freshmen.
Selectivity: Admits 50 to 75% of applicants.

BASIC COSTS (2013-2014)
Tuition and fees: $40,707.
Per-credit charge: $1,104.
Room and board: $11,080.

FINANCIAL AID PICTURE (2012-2013)
Students with need: Out of 803 full-time freshmen who applied for aid, 589 were judged to have need. Of these, 587 received aid, and 186 had their full need met. Average financial aid package met 83% of need; average scholarship/grant was $25,916; average loan was $3,385. For part-time students, average financial aid package was $24,514.
Students without need: 388 full-time freshmen who did not demonstrate need for aid received scholarships/grants; average award was $15,347. No-need awards available for academics, art, athletics, leadership, music/drama.
Scholarships offered: 37 full-time freshmen received athletic scholarships; average amount $35,064.
Cumulative student debt: 43% of graduating class had student loans; average debt was $30,268.

FINANCIAL AID PROCEDURES
Forms required: FAFSA, CSS PROFILE.
Dates and Deadlines: Priority date 2/15; closing date 5/1. Applicants notified by 3/22; must reply by 5/1 or within 4 week(s) of notification.

CONTACT
Chris George, Director, Financial Aid
2197 South University Boulevard, Denver, CO 80208
(303) 871-2341

University of Northern Colorado

Greeley, Colorado
www.unco.edu Federal Code: 001349

4-year public university in small city.
Enrollment: 9,948 undergrads, 9% part-time. 2,193 full-time freshmen.
Selectivity: Admits over 75% of applicants.

BASIC COSTS (2012-2013)
Tuition and fees: $6,836; out-of-state residents $18,360.
Per-credit charge: $217; out-of-state residents $687.
Room and board: $10,044.
Additional info: Costs reflect student share of tuition after the Colorado College Opportunity Fund.

FINANCIAL AID PICTURE (2011-2012)
Students with need: Need-based aid available for full-time and part-time students. Work study available nights, weekends, and for part-time students.
Students without need: No-need awards available for academics, art, athletics.

FINANCIAL AID PROCEDURES
Forms required: FAFSA.
Dates and Deadlines: Priority date 3/1; no closing date. Applicants notified on a rolling basis starting 4/15; must reply within 4 week(s) of notification.

CONTACT
Marty Somero, Director of Financial Aid
501 20th Street, Campus Box 10, Greeley, CO 80639
(970) 351-2502

Western State Colorado University

Gunnison, Colorado
www.western.edu Federal Code: 001372

4-year public university and liberal arts college in small town.
Enrollment: 1,949 undergrads, 6% part-time. 449 full-time freshmen.
Selectivity: Admits over 75% of applicants.

BASIC COSTS (2012-2013)
Tuition and fees: $6,449; out-of-state residents $16,318.
Per-credit charge: $193; out-of-state residents $604.
Room and board: $8,688.
Additional info: In-state tuition based upon assumption of Colorado Opportunity Fund waiver. Tuition/fee waivers available for unemployed or children of unemployed.

FINANCIAL AID PICTURE (2011-2012)
Students with need: Out of 378 full-time freshmen who applied for aid, 284 were judged to have need. Of these, 262 received aid, and 54 had their full need met. Average financial aid package met 69% of need; average scholarship/grant was $5,480; average loan was $3,463. For part-time students, average financial aid package was $5,108.
Students without need: No-need awards available for academics, alumni affiliation, art, athletics, leadership, music/drama.
Scholarships offered: Academic Excellence Award; $1,000; based on 3.5 GPA and 22 ACT/1010 SAT. Non-resident Leadership Award; $2,500; based on 3.2 GPA, 990 SAT, leadership activities. SAT scores exclusive of Writing.
Cumulative student debt: 62% of graduating class had student loans; average debt was $18,558.

FINANCIAL AID PROCEDURES
Forms required: FAFSA.
Dates and Deadlines: Priority date 4/1; no closing date. Applicants notified on a rolling basis starting 4/1; must reply by 5/1 or within 4 week(s) of notification.

CONTACT
Jerry Martinez, Director of Financial Aid
600 North Adams Street, Gunnison, CO 81231
(970) 943-3085

Westwood College: Denver North

Denver, Colorado
www.westwood.edu/locations/colorado/denver-north-campus Federal Code: 007548

4-year for-profit technical college in very large city.
Enrollment: 550 undergrads.

BASIC COSTS (2012-2013)
Tuition and fees: $15,020.

FINANCIAL AID PICTURE
Students with need: Need-based aid available for full-time and part-time students. Work study available nights.
Students without need: No-need awards available for academics, state/district residency.

FINANCIAL AID PROCEDURES
Forms required: FAFSA, state aid form, institutional form.
Dates and Deadlines: Applicants notified on a rolling basis starting 1/1; must reply within 2 week(s) of notification.
Transfers: No deadline.

CONTACT
Armando Guardiola, Director, Financial Aid
7350 North Broadway, Denver, CO 80221
(303) 426-7000

Westwood College: Denver South

Denver, Colorado
www.westwood.edu/locations/colorado/denver-south-campus Federal Code: 007548

4-year for-profit technical and career college in very large city.
Enrollment: 333 undergrads.

BASIC COSTS (2012-2013)
Tuition and fees: $15,020.

FINANCIAL AID PICTURE
Students with need: Need-based aid available for full-time and part-time students. Work study available nights.

FINANCIAL AID PROCEDURES
Forms required: FAFSA, state aid form, institutional form.
Dates and Deadlines: Applicants notified on a rolling basis; must reply within 2 week(s) of notification.

CONTACT
Maureen Wallace, Director of Campus Operations
3150 South Sheridan Boulevard, Denver, CO 80227-5507
(303) 934-1122

Connecticut

Albertus Magnus College
New Haven, Connecticut
www.albertus.edu Federal Code: 001374

4-year private liberal arts college in small city, affiliated with Roman Catholic Church.
Enrollment: 1,572 undergrads.
Selectivity: Admits 50 to 75% of applicants.

BASIC COSTS (2012-2013)
Tuition and fees: $28,358.
Per-credit charge: $1,162.
Room and board: $11,754.

FINANCIAL AID PICTURE
Students with need: Need-based aid available for full-time and part-time students. Work study available nights, weekends, and for part-time students.
Students without need: No-need awards available for academics, art, job skills, leadership, music/drama, religious affiliation.

FINANCIAL AID PROCEDURES
Forms required: FAFSA.
Dates and Deadlines: Priority date 2/28; no closing date. Applicants notified on a rolling basis starting 3/1; must reply within 2 week(s) of notification.
Transfers: No deadline. Must reply within 2 week(s) of notification.

CONTACT
Andrew Foster, Director of Financial Aid
700 Prospect Street, New Haven, CT 06511-1189
(203) 773-8508

Asnuntuck Community College
Enfield, Connecticut
www.acc.commnet.edu Federal Code: 011150

2-year public community and technical college in large town.
Enrollment: 1,344 undergrads.
Selectivity: Open admission.

BASIC COSTS (2012-2013)
Tuition and fees: $3,598; out-of-state residents $10,754.
Per-credit charge: $133; out-of-state residents $399.

FINANCIAL AID PICTURE
Students with need: Need-based aid available for full-time and part-time students. Work study available nights, weekends, and for part-time students.

FINANCIAL AID PROCEDURES
Forms required: FAFSA, institutional form.
Dates and Deadlines: Closing date 6/1. Applicants notified on a rolling basis starting 7/1; must reply within 2 week(s) of notification.
Transfers: Financial aid transcript required.

CONTACT
Donna Jones-Searle, Director of Financial Aid
170 Elm Street, Enfield, CT 06082
(860) 253-3000 ext. 3030

Capital Community College
Hartford, Connecticut
www.ccc.commnet.edu Federal Code: 007635

2-year public community and technical college in small city.
Enrollment: 3,876 undergrads, 73% part-time. 300 full-time freshmen.
Selectivity: Open admission; but selective for some programs.

BASIC COSTS (2012-2013)
Tuition and fees: $3,598; out-of-state residents $10,754.
Per-credit charge: $133; out-of-state residents $399.
Additional info: Tuition/fee waivers available for minority students.

FINANCIAL AID PICTURE
Students with need: Need-based aid available for full-time and part-time students. Work study available nights, weekends, and for part-time students.
Students without need: This college awards aid only to students with need.

FINANCIAL AID PROCEDURES
Forms required: FAFSA.
Dates and Deadlines: Closing date 7/15. Applicants notified on a rolling basis starting 7/15; must reply within 2 week(s) of notification.
Transfers: Closing date 7/1.

CONTACT
Margaret Malaspina, Director of Financial Aid
950 Main Street, Hartford, CT 06103-1207
(860) 906-5127

Central Connecticut State University
New Britain, Connecticut
www.ccsu.edu Federal Code: 001378

4-year public university in small city.
Enrollment: 9,630 undergrads, 20% part-time. 1,340 full-time freshmen.
Selectivity: Admits 50 to 75% of applicants.

BASIC COSTS (2012-2013)
Tuition and fees: $8,321; out-of-state residents $19,353.
Room and board: $10,056.

FINANCIAL AID PICTURE (2012-2013)
Students with need: Out of 1,174 full-time freshmen who applied for aid, 896 were judged to have need. Of these, 878 received aid, and 18 had their full need met. Average financial aid package met 71% of need; average scholarship/grant was $4,574; average loan was $3,634. For part-time students, average financial aid package was $5,640.
Students without need: 42 full-time freshmen who did not demonstrate need for aid received scholarships/grants; average award was $3,144. No-need awards available for academics, athletics, minority status.
Scholarships offered: 13 full-time freshmen received athletic scholarships; average amount $5,322.
Cumulative student debt: 54% of graduating class had student loans; average debt was $22,171.

FINANCIAL AID PROCEDURES
Forms required: FAFSA.
Dates and Deadlines: Priority date 3/1; closing date 9/15. Applicants notified on a rolling basis starting 4/1; must reply within 2 week(s) of notification.
Transfers: Priority date 4/15. Applicants notified on a rolling basis.

CONTACT
Richard Bishop, Director of Financial Aid
1615 Stanley Street, New Britain, CT 06050
(860) 832-2200

Charter Oak State College
New Britain, Connecticut
www.charteroak.edu Federal Code: 032343

4-year public virtual liberal arts college in small city.
Enrollment: 1,477 undergrads, 82% part-time.

BASIC COSTS (2012-2013)
Per-credit charge: $245; out-of-state residents $322.
Additional info: Per-credit-hour charge, in-state: $245; out-of-state, $322. College Fee: In-state associate degree or bachelor's degree, $171per semester; out-of-state $228 per semester. Cost of education varies due to students having option to take courses at other institutions.

FINANCIAL AID PICTURE
Students with need: Need-based aid available for full-time and part-time students.
Students without need: This college awards aid only to students with need.

FINANCIAL AID PROCEDURES
Forms required: FAFSA, institutional form.
Dates and Deadlines: Closing date 7/15. Applicants notified on a rolling basis starting 8/23.

CONTACT
Deborah Flinn, Director of Financial Aid
55 Paul Manafort Drive, New Britain, CT 06053-2150
(860) 832-3872

Connecticut College
New London, Connecticut Federal Code: 001379
www.connecticutcollege.edu CSS Code: 3284

4-year private liberal arts college in large town.
Enrollment: 1,816 undergrads. 503 full-time freshmen.
Selectivity: Admits less than 50% of applicants.

BASIC COSTS (2012-2013)
Tuition and fees: $44,890.
Per-credit charge: $1,318.
Room and board: $11,900.

FINANCIAL AID PICTURE (2012-2013)
Students with need: Out of 293 full-time freshmen who applied for aid, 244 were judged to have need. Of these, 244 received aid, and 244 had their full need met. Average financial aid package met 100% of need; average scholarship/grant was $33,702; average loan was $3,369. Need-based aid available for part-time students.
Students without need: This college awards aid only to students with need.
Cumulative student debt: 50% of graduating class had student loans; average debt was $23,558.

FINANCIAL AID PROCEDURES
Forms required: FAFSA, CSS PROFILE.
Dates and Deadlines: Priority date 2/1; no closing date.
Transfers: Closing date 4/1.

CONTACT
Elaine Solinga, Director of Financial Aid
270 Mohegan Avenue, New London, CT 06320-4196
(860) 439-2058

Eastern Connecticut State University
Willimantic, Connecticut
www.easternct.edu Federal Code: 001425

4-year public university and liberal arts college in large town.
Enrollment: 4,990 undergrads, 11% part-time. 979 full-time freshmen.
Selectivity: Admits 50 to 75% of applicants.

BASIC COSTS (2012-2013)
Tuition and fees: $8,911; out-of-state residents $19,943.
Room and board: $10,674.

FINANCIAL AID PICTURE
Students with need: Need-based aid available for full-time and part-time students. Work study available nights, weekends, and for part-time students.
Students without need: No-need awards available for academics.
Additional info: Tuition waiver for veterans and members of National Guard.

FINANCIAL AID PROCEDURES
Forms required: FAFSA.
Dates and Deadlines: Priority date 3/15; no closing date. Applicants notified on a rolling basis starting 2/15; must reply within 2 week(s) of notification.
Transfers: Must reply within 2 week(s) of notification.

CONTACT
Mona Lucas, Director of Financial Aid
83 Windham Street, Willimantic, CT 06226-2295
(860) 465-5286

Fairfield University
Fairfield, Connecticut Federal Code: 001385
www.fairfield.edu CSS Code: 3390

4-year private university in small city, affiliated with Roman Catholic Church.
Enrollment: 3,696 undergrads, 6% part-time. 990 full-time freshmen.
Selectivity: Admits 50 to 75% of applicants. GED not accepted.

BASIC COSTS (2012-2013)
Tuition and fees: $41,690.
Room and board: $13,590.
Additional info: 12- and 14-meal plans available. Proof of health insurance required in order to waive health insurance fee.

FINANCIAL AID PICTURE (2012-2013)
Students with need: Out of 766 full-time freshmen who applied for aid, 534 were judged to have need. Of these, 534 received aid, and 65 had their full need met. Average financial aid package met 88% of need; average scholarship/grant was $15,122; average loan was $4,179. For part-time students, average financial aid package was $9,750.
Students without need: 315 full-time freshmen who did not demonstrate need for aid received scholarships/grants; average award was $13,148. No-need awards available for academics, alumni affiliation, art, athletics, leadership, music/drama.
Scholarships offered: ***Merit:*** Academic scholarship: $6,000-$22,000; based on high school academic achievement and leadership; renewable for four years; 450-500 awards per year. ***Athletic:*** 64 full-time freshmen received athletic scholarships; average amount $20,119.
Cumulative student debt: 67% of graduating class had student loans; average debt was $28,507.
Additional info: Veteran's Pride Program provides tuition discounts for children of qualified veterans. Bridgeport Tuition Program provides free tuition to qualified students from City of Bridgeport with family income under $50,000.

FINANCIAL AID PROCEDURES
Forms required: FAFSA, CSS PROFILE.
Dates and Deadlines: Closing date 2/15. Applicants notified by 4/1; must reply by 5/1.
Transfers: Closing date 5/1. Applicants notified on a rolling basis starting 5/1; must reply within 3 week(s) of notification.

CONTACT
Diana DeVellis, Senior Associate Director, Financial Aid
1073 North Benson Road, Fairfield, CT 06824-5195
(203) 254-4125

Gateway Community College

New Haven, Connecticut
www.gatewayct.edu/ Federal Code: 008303

2-year public community college in small city.
Enrollment: 7,261 undergrads.
Selectivity: Open admission; but selective for some programs.

BASIC COSTS (2012-2013)
Tuition and fees: $3,598; out-of-state residents $10,754.
Per-credit charge: $133; out-of-state residents $399.

FINANCIAL AID PICTURE
Students with need: Need-based aid available for full-time and part-time students. Work study available nights, weekends, and for part-time students.
Students without need: This college awards aid only to students with need.

FINANCIAL AID PROCEDURES
Forms required: FAFSA, institutional form.
Dates and Deadlines: Applicants notified on a rolling basis; must reply within 2 week(s) of notification.

CONTACT
Raymond Zeek, Director of Financial Aid
60 Sargent Drive, New Haven, CT 06511-5970
(203) 285-2013

Goodwin College

East Hartford, Connecticut
www.goodwin.edu Federal Code: 015833

2-year private health science and career college in small city.
Enrollment: 3,173 undergrads, 84% part-time. 168 full-time freshmen.
Selectivity: Open admission; but selective for some programs.

BASIC COSTS (2012-2013)
Tuition and fees: $19,400.
Per-credit charge: $590.

FINANCIAL AID PICTURE
Students with need: Need-based aid available for full-time and part-time students. Work study available nights.
Students without need: This college awards aid only to students with need.

FINANCIAL AID PROCEDURES
Forms required: FAFSA.
Dates and Deadlines: Applicants notified on a rolling basis starting 7/1.
Transfers: No deadline. Applicants notified on a rolling basis starting 8/1.

CONTACT
William Mangini, Director of Financial Aid
One Riverside Drive, East Hartford, CT 06118-9980
(860) 727-6723

Holy Apostles College and Seminary

Cromwell, Connecticut
www.holyapostles.edu Federal Code: 001389

4-year private liberal arts and seminary college in large town, affiliated with Roman Catholic Church.
Enrollment: 27 full-time undergrads.

BASIC COSTS (2012-2013)
Tuition and fees: $10,080.
Per-credit charge: $420.

FINANCIAL AID PICTURE
Students with need: Need-based aid available for full-time and part-time students.
Students without need: No-need awards available for religious affiliation.

FINANCIAL AID PROCEDURES
Forms required: FAFSA, institutional form.
Dates and Deadlines: Priority date 6/1; no closing date. Applicants notified on a rolling basis starting 8/25; must reply within 2 week(s) of notification.
Transfers: No deadline. Applicants notified on a rolling basis; must reply within 2 week(s) of notification.

CONTACT
Henry Miller, Financial Aid Director
33 Prospect Hill Road, Cromwell, CT 06416-2005
(860) 632-8120

Housatonic Community College

Bridgeport, Connecticut
www.hcc.commnet.edu Federal Code: 004513

2-year public community college in small city.
Enrollment: 5,454 undergrads.
Selectivity: Open admission; but selective for some programs.

BASIC COSTS (2012-2013)
Tuition and fees: $3,598; out-of-state residents $10,754.
Per-credit charge: $133; out-of-state residents $399.

FINANCIAL AID PICTURE
Students with need: Need-based aid available for full-time and part-time students.
Students without need: This college awards aid only to students with need.

FINANCIAL AID PROCEDURES
Forms required: FAFSA.
Dates and Deadlines: Priority date 11/1; closing date 5/1. Applicants notified on a rolling basis starting 6/1.

CONTACT
Barbara Surowiec, Director of Financial Aid
900 Lafayette Boulevard, Bridgeport, CT 06604-4704
(203) 332-5047

Lincoln College of New England

Southington, Connecticut
www.lincolncollegene.edu

2-year for-profit culinary school and business college in small town.
Enrollment: 1,174 undergrads.
Selectivity: Open admission.

BASIC COSTS (2012-2013)
Tuition and fees: $19,420.
Room and board: $8,600.

FINANCIAL AID PICTURE
Students with need: Need-based aid available for full-time and part-time students. Work study available nights, weekends, and for part-time students.
Students without need: No-need awards available for academics.

FINANCIAL AID PROCEDURES
Dates and Deadlines: Applicants notified on a rolling basis starting 1/1.

CONTACT
Rachel Bourjolly, Regional Director of Financial Aid
2279 Mount Vernon Road, Southington, CT 06489-1057
(860) 668-3515

Lyme Academy College of Fine Arts

Old Lyme, Connecticut
www.lymeacademy.edu Federal Code: 030794

4-year private visual arts college in small town.
Enrollment: 73 undergrads.

BASIC COSTS (2012-2013)
Tuition and fees: $28,536.
Per-credit charge: $1,121.

FINANCIAL AID PICTURE
Students with need: Need-based aid available for full-time and part-time students. Work study available nights, weekends, and for part-time students.
Students without need: No-need awards available for academics, art, leadership.

FINANCIAL AID PROCEDURES
Forms required: FAFSA.
Dates and Deadlines: Priority date 2/15; closing date 4/15. Applicants notified on a rolling basis starting 3/1; must reply by 5/1 or within 2 week(s) of notification.
Transfers: Closing date 7/31. Applicants notified on a rolling basis starting 2/15; must reply by 5/1 or within 2 week(s) of notification.

CONTACT
Jim Falconer, Director of Financial Aid
84 Lyme Street, Old Lyme, CT 06371
(860) 434-3571 ext. 114

Manchester Community College

Manchester, Connecticut
www.mcc.commnet.edu Federal Code: 001392

2-year public community college in small city.
Enrollment: 6,935 undergrads, 62% part-time. 920 full-time freshmen.
Selectivity: Open admission; but selective for some programs.

BASIC COSTS (2012-2013)
Tuition and fees: $3,598; out-of-state residents $10,754.
Per-credit charge: $133; out-of-state residents $399.

FINANCIAL AID PICTURE (2011-2012)
Students with need: 96% of average financial aid package awarded as scholarships/grants, 4% awarded as loans/jobs. Need-based aid available for part-time students.

FINANCIAL AID PROCEDURES
Forms required: FAFSA.
Dates and Deadlines: Priority date 5/15; closing date 8/13. Applicants notified on a rolling basis starting 5/1; must reply within 2 week(s) of notification.

CONTACT
Ivette Rivera-Dreyer, Director of Financial Aid
Great Path PO Box 1046, MS 12, Manchester, CT 06040-1046
(860) 512-3380

Middlesex Community College

Middletown, Connecticut
www.mxcc.commnet.edu Federal Code: 008038

2-year public community college in large town.
Enrollment: 2,335 undergrads, 56% part-time. 356 full-time freshmen.
Selectivity: Open admission; but selective for some programs.

BASIC COSTS (2012-2013)
Tuition and fees: $3,598; out-of-state residents $10,754.
Per-credit charge: $133; out-of-state residents $399.

FINANCIAL AID PICTURE
Students with need: Need-based aid available for full-time and part-time students.
Students without need: This college awards aid only to students with need.
Additional info: Tuition and/or fee waiver for veterans.

FINANCIAL AID PROCEDURES
Forms required: FAFSA, institutional form.
Dates and Deadlines: Priority date 6/1; no closing date. Applicants notified on a rolling basis starting 7/1; must reply within 2 week(s) of notification.
Transfers: Closing date 9/1.

CONTACT
Irene Martin, Director of Financial Aid
100 Training Hill Road, Middletown, CT 06457-4889
(860) 343-5741

Mitchell College

New London, Connecticut
www.mitchell.edu Federal Code: 001393

4-year private liberal arts college in small city.
Enrollment: 785 undergrads, 7% part-time. 145 full-time freshmen.
Selectivity: Admits 50 to 75% of applicants.

BASIC COSTS (2013-2014)
Tuition and fees: $29,458.
Room and board: $12,492.

FINANCIAL AID PICTURE (2012-2013)
Students with need: Out of 131 full-time freshmen who applied for aid, 120 were judged to have need. Of these, 120 received aid, and 7 had their full need met. Average financial aid package met 57% of need; average scholarship/grant was $16,739; average loan was $3,535. For part-time students, average financial aid package was $6,306.
Students without need: 22 full-time freshmen who did not demonstrate need for aid received scholarships/grants; average award was $7,636. No-need awards available for academics, alumni affiliation, art, leadership.

FINANCIAL AID PROCEDURES
Forms required: FAFSA.
Dates and Deadlines: Priority date 3/1; no closing date. Applicants notified on a rolling basis starting 2/15; must reply within 3 week(s) of notification.

CONTACT
Jacklyn Stoltz, Director of Financial Aid
437 Pequot Avenue, New London, CT 06320-4498
(860) 701-5040

Naugatuck Valley Community College

Waterbury, Connecticut
www.nvcc.commnet.edu Federal Code: 006982

2-year public community and technical college in small city.
Enrollment: 6,762 undergrads, 61% part-time. 861 full-time freshmen.
Selectivity: Open admission; but selective for some programs.

BASIC COSTS (2012-2013)
Tuition and fees: $3,598; out-of-state residents $10,754.
Per-credit charge: $133; out-of-state residents $399.

FINANCIAL AID PICTURE (2012-2013)
Students with need: Need-based aid available for full-time and part-time students.
Students without need: This college awards aid only to students with need.

FINANCIAL AID PROCEDURES
Forms required: FAFSA.
Dates and Deadlines: Priority date 4/1; no closing date. Applicants notified on a rolling basis starting 6/1.
Transfers: Financial aid transcripts required from all previous schools attended.

CONTACT
Catherine Hardy, Director of Financial Aid Services
750 Chase Parkway, Waterbury, CT 06708-3089
(203) 575-8006

Norwalk Community College
Norwalk, Connecticut
www.ncc.commnet.edu Federal Code: 001399

2-year public community and technical college in small city.
Enrollment: 5,241 undergrads, 61% part-time. 693 full-time freshmen.
Selectivity: Open admission; but selective for some programs.

BASIC COSTS (2012-2013)
Tuition and fees: $3,598; out-of-state residents $10,754.
Per-credit charge: $133; out-of-state residents $399.

FINANCIAL AID PICTURE
Students with need: Need-based aid available for full-time and part-time students.
Students without need: No-need awards available for academics, alumni affiliation.

FINANCIAL AID PROCEDURES
Forms required: FAFSA, institutional form.
Dates and Deadlines: Priority date 7/1; no closing date. Applicants notified on a rolling basis starting 7/1; must reply within 2 week(s) of notification.

CONTACT
Norma McNerney, Director of Financial Aid
188 Richards Avenue, Norwalk, CT 06854-1655
(203) 857-7023

Paier College of Art
Hamden, Connecticut
www.paiercollegeofart.edu Federal Code: 007459

4-year for-profit visual arts college in small city.
Enrollment: 164 undergrads, 23% part-time. 18 full-time freshmen.
Selectivity: Admits 50 to 75% of applicants.

BASIC COSTS (2013-2014)
Tuition and fees: $12,960.
Per-credit charge: $400.

FINANCIAL AID PICTURE (2011-2012)
Students with need: Out of 13 full-time freshmen who applied for aid, 10 were judged to have need. Of these, 10 received aid. Average financial aid package met 37% of need; average scholarship/grant was $2,072; average loan was $3,336. For part-time students, average financial aid package was $5,530.
Cumulative student debt: 61% of graduating class had student loans; average debt was $21,610.

FINANCIAL AID PROCEDURES
Forms required: FAFSA.
Dates and Deadlines: Priority date 4/15; closing date 8/1. Applicants notified on a rolling basis starting 6/1; must reply within 3 week(s) of notification.
Transfers: Applicants notified on a rolling basis starting 6/1; must reply within 3 week(s) of notification.

CONTACT
John DeRose, Director of Financial Aid
20 Gorham Avenue, Hamden, CT 06514-3902
(203) 287-3034

Post University
Waterbury, Connecticut
www.post.edu Federal Code: 001401

4-year for-profit university and business college in small city.
Enrollment: 715 undergrads, 3% part-time. 208 full-time freshmen.
Selectivity: Admits 50 to 75% of applicants.

BASIC COSTS (2012-2013)
Tuition and fees: $27,350.
Per-credit charge: $875.
Room and board: $10,430.

FINANCIAL AID PICTURE (2012-2013)
Students with need: Out of 190 full-time freshmen who applied for aid, 176 were judged to have need. Of these, 176 received aid, and 26 had their full need met. Average financial aid package met 55% of need; average scholarship/grant was $16,562; average loan was $3,456. For part-time students, average financial aid package was $7,893.
Students without need: 5 full-time freshmen who did not demonstrate need for aid received scholarships/grants; average award was $10,400.
Scholarships offered: 34 full-time freshmen received athletic scholarships; average amount $12,908.
Cumulative student debt: 90% of graduating class had student loans; average debt was $16,499.
Additional info: Academic merit scholarships available based on GPA and test scores. Renewable contingent upon maintaining specific GPA.

FINANCIAL AID PROCEDURES
Forms required: FAFSA.
Dates and Deadlines: Priority date 3/15; no closing date. Applicants notified on a rolling basis starting 4/15; must reply by 5/1 or within 3 week(s) of notification.
Transfers: No deadline. Applicants notified on a rolling basis starting 4/15; must reply within 1 week(s) of notification.

CONTACT
Gina Faulds, Director of Office of Student Finance
800 Country Club Road, Waterbury, CT 06723-2540
(203) 596-4571

Quinebaug Valley Community College
Danielson, Connecticut
www.qvcc.commnet.edu Federal Code: 010530

2-year public community and technical college in large town.
Enrollment: 1,895 undergrads.
Selectivity: Open admission.

BASIC COSTS (2012-2013)
Tuition and fees: $3,598; out-of-state residents $10,754.
Per-credit charge: $133; out-of-state residents $399.

FINANCIAL AID PICTURE
Students with need: Need-based aid available for full-time and part-time students. Work study available nights.
Students without need: This college awards aid only to students with need.

FINANCIAL AID PROCEDURES
Forms required: FAFSA.
Dates and Deadlines: Applicants notified on a rolling basis starting 5/1.

CONTACT
Kim Rich, Financial Aid Director
742 Upper Maple Street, Danielson, CT 06239-1440
(860) 412-7208

Quinnipiac University

Hamden, Connecticut — Federal Code: 001402
www.quinnipiac.edu — CSS Code: 3712

4-year private university in small city.
Enrollment: 6,366 undergrads, 2% part-time. 1,780 full-time freshmen.
Selectivity: Admits 50 to 75% of applicants.

BASIC COSTS (2013-2014)
Tuition and fees: $39,330.
Per-credit charge: $900.
Room and board: $14,250.

FINANCIAL AID PICTURE (2012-2013)
Students with need: Out of 1,450 full-time freshmen who applied for aid, 1,189 were judged to have need. Of these, 1,180 received aid, and 144 had their full need met. Average financial aid package met 66% of need; average scholarship/grant was $18,911; average loan was $3,582. For part-time students, average financial aid package was $6,915.
Students without need: 329 full-time freshmen who did not demonstrate need for aid received scholarships/grants; average award was $13,059. No-need awards available for academics, athletics.
Scholarships offered: ***Merit:*** Academic scholarships; $9,000-$20,000 per year; based on class rank and SAT/ACT scores; renewable with full-time status and 3.0 GPA. ***Athletic:*** 77 full-time freshmen received athletic scholarships; average amount $27,237.
Cumulative student debt: 67% of graduating class had student loans; average debt was $42,730.

FINANCIAL AID PROCEDURES
Forms required: FAFSA, CSS PROFILE.
Dates and Deadlines: Priority date 3/1; no closing date. Applicants notified on a rolling basis starting 2/15; must reply by 5/1 or within 2 week(s) of notification.
Transfers: No deadline. Applicants notified on a rolling basis starting 3/1; must reply by 5/1 or within 2 week(s) of notification. Students transferring with 2 years of full-time college work and 3.5 GPA may be eligible for transfer scholarship.

CONTACT
Dominic Yoia, Associate Vice President and University Director of Financial Aid
275 Mount Carmel Avenue, Hamden, CT 06518-1908
(800) 462-1944

Sacred Heart University

Fairfield, Connecticut — Federal Code: 001403
www.sacredheart.edu — CSS Code: 3780

4-year private university and liberal arts college in large town, affiliated with Roman Catholic Church.
Enrollment: 3,996 undergrads, 15% part-time. 980 full-time freshmen.
Selectivity: Admits over 75% of applicants.

BASIC COSTS (2012-2013)
Tuition and fees: $34,030.
Per-credit charge: $515.
Room and board: $13,230.
Additional info: Tuition/fee waivers available for adults, minority students.

FINANCIAL AID PICTURE (2011-2012)
Students with need: Out of 916 full-time freshmen who applied for aid, 744 were judged to have need. Of these, 743 received aid, and 86 had their full need met. Average financial aid package met 56% of need; average scholarship/grant was $13,596; average loan was $5,019. For part-time students, average financial aid package was $5,412.
Students without need: 188 full-time freshmen who did not demonstrate need for aid received scholarships/grants; average award was $6,271. No-need awards available for academics, alumni affiliation, art, athletics, leadership, music/drama, religious affiliation, state/district residency.
Scholarships offered: 39 full-time freshmen received athletic scholarships; average amount $16,434.
Cumulative student debt: 74% of graduating class had student loans; average debt was $42,779.

FINANCIAL AID PROCEDURES
Forms required: FAFSA, CSS PROFILE.
Dates and Deadlines: Priority date 2/15; no closing date. Applicants notified on a rolling basis starting 3/1; must reply within 2 week(s) of notification.
Transfers: Priority date 5/1; no deadline. Applicants notified on a rolling basis.

CONTACT
Julie Savino, Dean of University Financial Assistance
5151 Park Avenue, Fairfield, CT 06825
(203) 371-7980

Southern Connecticut State University

New Haven, Connecticut
www.southernct.edu — Federal Code: 001406

4-year public university in small city.
Enrollment: 8,525 undergrads, 14% part-time. 1,360 full-time freshmen.
Selectivity: Admits over 75% of applicants.

BASIC COSTS (2012-2013)
Tuition and fees: $8,541; out-of-state residents $19,573.
Room and board: $10,687.

FINANCIAL AID PICTURE (2012-2013)
Students with need: Out of 1,251 full-time freshmen who applied for aid, 994 were judged to have need. Of these, 929 received aid, and 230 had their full need met. Average financial aid package met 69% of need; average scholarship/grant was $5,795; average loan was $5,578. For part-time students, average financial aid package was $9,832.
Students without need: 54 full-time freshmen who did not demonstrate need for aid received scholarships/grants; average award was $4,263. No-need awards available for academics, alumni affiliation, athletics, job skills, ROTC, state/district residency.
Scholarships offered: ***Merit:*** General Academic Achievement Awards; 90 awarded. Presidential Scholarships, Trustees Scholarships available. ***Athletic:*** 15 full-time freshmen received athletic scholarships; average amount $9,267.
Cumulative student debt: 48% of graduating class had student loans; average debt was $23,663.

FINANCIAL AID PROCEDURES
Forms required: FAFSA.
Dates and Deadlines: Priority date 3/5; closing date 3/9. Applicants notified on a rolling basis starting 4/11; must reply within 2 week(s) of notification.

Transfers: Applicants notified on a rolling basis starting 6/15; must reply within 2 week(s) of notification.

CONTACT

Gloria Lee, Director of Financial Aid & Scholarships
131 Farnham Avenue, New Haven, CT 06515-1202
(203) 392-5222

Three Rivers Community College

Norwich, Connecticut
www.trcc.commnet.edu Federal Code: 009765

2-year public community and technical college in large town.
Enrollment: 5,154 undergrads.
Selectivity: Open admission; but selective for some programs.

BASIC COSTS (2012-2013)

Tuition and fees: $3,598; out-of-state residents $10,754.
Per-credit charge: $133; out-of-state residents $399.

FINANCIAL AID PICTURE

Students with need: Need-based aid available for full-time and part-time students. Work study available nights, weekends, and for part-time students.
Students without need: This college awards aid only to students with need.
Scholarships offered: Various scholarships; $75 to $500.

FINANCIAL AID PROCEDURES

Forms required: FAFSA.
Dates and Deadlines: Priority date 5/1; no closing date. Applicants notified on a rolling basis; must reply within 2 week(s) of notification.
Transfers: No deadline.

CONTACT

Hong-Yu Kovic, Financial Aid Counselor
574 New London Turnpike, Norwich, CT 06360-6598
(860) 823-2870

Trinity College

Hartford, Connecticut Federal Code: 001414
www.trincoll.edu CSS Code: 3899

4-year private liberal arts college in large city.
Enrollment: 2,223 undergrads, 2% part-time. 591 full-time freshmen.
Selectivity: Admits less than 50% of applicants.

BASIC COSTS (2012-2013)

Tuition and fees: $45,730.
Room and board: $11,800.
Additional info: One-time $25 transcript fee for new students only. Tuition/fee waivers available for adults.

FINANCIAL AID PICTURE (2012-2013)

Students with need: Out of 262 full-time freshmen who applied for aid, 230 were judged to have need. Of these, 230 received aid, and 230 had their full need met. Average financial aid package met 100% of need; average scholarship/grant was $39,009; average loan was $3,595. Need-based aid available for part-time students.
Students without need: 10 full-time freshmen who did not demonstrate need for aid received scholarships/grants; average award was $26,785. No-need awards available for academics, leadership.
Cumulative student debt: 41% of graduating class had student loans; average debt was $18,868.

FINANCIAL AID PROCEDURES

Forms required: FAFSA, CSS PROFILE.
Dates and Deadlines: Priority date 2/1; closing date 3/1. Applicants notified by 4/1; must reply by 5/1 or within 2 week(s) of notification.
Transfers: Closing date 4/1. Applicants notified on a rolling basis starting 5/15; must reply within 2 week(s) of notification.

CONTACT

Kelly O'Brien, Director of Financial Aid
300 Summit Street, Hartford, CT 06106
(860) 297-2046

Tunxis Community College

Farmington, Connecticut
www.tunxis.edu Federal Code: 009764

2-year public community college in large town.
Enrollment: 3,934 undergrads, 56% part-time. 584 full-time freshmen.
Selectivity: Open admission; but selective for some programs.

BASIC COSTS (2012-2013)

Tuition and fees: $3,598; out-of-state residents $10,754.
Per-credit charge: $133; out-of-state residents $399.

FINANCIAL AID PICTURE (2012-2013)

Students with need: 87% of average financial aid package awarded as scholarships/grants, 13% awarded as loans/jobs. Need-based aid available for part-time students. Work study available nights, weekends, and for part-time students.
Students without need: No-need awards available for academics.
Additional info: Financial aid available to all students showing need. Part-time students encouraged to apply.

FINANCIAL AID PROCEDURES

Forms required: FAFSA.
Dates and Deadlines: Priority date 6/1; no closing date. Applicants notified on a rolling basis starting 3/1.

CONTACT

David Welsh, Director of Financial Aid
271 Scott Swamp Road, Farmington, CT 06032-3187
(860) 255-3555

United States Coast Guard Academy

New London, Connecticut
www.uscga.edu Federal Code: 001415

4-year public engineering and military college in small city.
Enrollment: 967 undergrads. 225 full-time freshmen.
Selectivity: Admits less than 50% of applicants.

BASIC COSTS (2013-2014)

Additional info: For U.S. citizens, tuition, room and board are paid for by the government. All U.S. cadets receive pay totaling $11,150 per year. Cadet pay is furnished by the government for uniforms, equipment, textbooks and other expenses incidental to training. Before an international cadet is enrolled at the Academy, the sponsoring country must agree to reimburse the U.S. Coast Guard for the cost of instruction, $71,349 per year. Countries not listed on World Bank List would be eligible for partial tuition costs of $16,300 annually.

CONTACT

Noel Filipinas, Cadet Finance Manager
31 Mohegan Avenue, New London, CT 06320
(860) 444-8309

University of Bridgeport
Bridgeport, Connecticut
www.bridgeport.edu Federal Code: 001416

4-year private university in small city.
Enrollment: 2,688 undergrads, 31% part-time. 591 full-time freshmen.
Selectivity: Admits 50 to 75% of applicants.

BASIC COSTS (2012-2013)
Tuition and fees: $28,140.
Per-credit charge: $865.
Room and board: $12,050.

FINANCIAL AID PICTURE
Students with need: Need-based aid available for full-time and part-time students. Work study available nights, weekends, and for part-time students.
Students without need: No-need awards available for academics, art, athletics, leadership, music/drama, state/district residency.
Scholarships offered: Academic Excellence and Leadership Scholarship; up to full tuition, room, and board; for students ranking in the top quarter of high school class with 1200 SAT. Academic Scholarship; up to full tuition; for students in the top quarter of class and 1100 SAT. Academic Grant; up to half-tuition; for students in top half of class and 1100 SAT. Challenge Grant; $3,000; for students in the top half of class and 1000 SAT. All SAT scores exclusive of Writing.

FINANCIAL AID PROCEDURES
Forms required: FAFSA.
Dates and Deadlines: Priority date 4/1; no closing date. Applicants notified on a rolling basis starting 4/1; must reply within 4 week(s) of notification.
Transfers: No deadline. Applicants notified on a rolling basis starting 4/1; must reply by 5/1 or within 2 week(s) of notification.

CONTACT
Ciara Negron, Director of Student Financial Services
126 Park Avenue, Bridgeport, CT 06604
(203) 576-4568

University of Connecticut
Storrs, Connecticut
www.uconn.edu Federal Code: 007997

4-year public university in large town.
Enrollment: 17,170 undergrads, 3% part-time. 3,107 full-time freshmen.
Selectivity: Admits less than 50% of applicants.

BASIC COSTS (2013-2014)
Tuition and fees: $12,022; out-of-state residents $30,970.
Per-credit charge: $386; out-of-state residents $1,175.
Room and board: $11,722.

FINANCIAL AID PICTURE (2012-2013)
Students with need: Out of 2,539 full-time freshmen who applied for aid, 1,698 were judged to have need. Of these, 1,661 received aid, and 161 had their full need met. Average financial aid package met 61% of need; average scholarship/grant was $7,299; average loan was $3,566. For part-time students, average financial aid package was $6,784.
Students without need: 412 full-time freshmen who did not demonstrate need for aid received scholarships/grants; average award was $6,737. No-need awards available for academics, art, athletics, leadership, minority status, music/drama.
Scholarships offered: 101 full-time freshmen received athletic scholarships; average amount $26,398.
Cumulative student debt: 62% of graduating class had student loans; average debt was $24,373.
Additional info: Institution offers variety of need-based financial aid programs. Financial assistance packages may include grants, loans and work-study awards.

FINANCIAL AID PROCEDURES
Forms required: FAFSA.
Dates and Deadlines: Priority date 3/1; no closing date. Applicants notified on a rolling basis starting 3/1; must reply within 4 week(s) of notification.

CONTACT
Mona Lucas, Director of Student Financial Aid Services
2131 Hillside Road, Unit 3088, Storrs, CT 06269-3088
(860) 486-2819

University of Hartford
West Hartford, Connecticut
www.hartford.edu Federal Code: 001422

4-year private university in small city.
Enrollment: 5,067 undergrads, 11% part-time. 1,320 full-time freshmen.
Selectivity: Admits 50 to 75% of applicants.

BASIC COSTS (2013-2014)
Tuition and fees: $33,358.
Per-credit charge: $480.
Room and board: $12,248.
Additional info: Tuition/fee waivers available for minority students.

FINANCIAL AID PICTURE (2011-2012)
Students with need: Out of 1,320 full-time freshmen who applied for aid, 1,190 were judged to have need. Of these, 1,187 received aid, and 352 had their full need met. Average financial aid package met 92% of need; average scholarship/grant was $14,834; average loan was $3,038. Need-based aid available for part-time students.
Students without need: 112 full-time freshmen who did not demonstrate need for aid received scholarships/grants; average award was $14,101. No-need awards available for academics, art, athletics, music/drama.
Scholarships offered: 15 full-time freshmen received athletic scholarships; average amount $44,877.
Cumulative student debt: 77% of graduating class had student loans; average debt was $26,652.

FINANCIAL AID PROCEDURES
Forms required: FAFSA, institutional form.
Dates and Deadlines: Priority date 2/1; no closing date. Applicants notified on a rolling basis starting 3/1; must reply by 5/1.
Transfers: Closing date 3/1.

CONTACT
Jennifer Fuhrmann, Director of Student Financial Assistance
Bates House, West Hartford, CT 06117-1599
(860) 768-4296

University of New Haven
West Haven, Connecticut
www.newhaven.edu Federal Code: 001397

4-year private university in small city.
Enrollment: 4,635 undergrads, 8% part-time. 1,119 full-time freshmen.
Selectivity: Admits 50 to 75% of applicants.

BASIC COSTS (2012-2013)
Tuition and fees: $32,750.
Per-credit charge: $1,050.
Room and board: $13,600.

FINANCIAL AID PICTURE
Students with need: Need-based aid available for full-time and part-time students.

FINANCIAL AID PROCEDURES
Forms required: FAFSA.
Dates and Deadlines: Priority date 3/1; no closing date. Applicants notified on a rolling basis starting 3/1; must reply by 5/1 or within 2 week(s) of notification.

CONTACT
Karen Flynn, Director of Financial Aid
300 Boston Post Road, West Haven, CT 06516
(203) 932-7315

University of Saint Joseph
West Hartford, Connecticut
www.usj.edu Federal Code: 001409

4-year private liberal arts college for women in small city, affiliated with Roman Catholic Church.
Enrollment: 998 undergrads, 17% part-time. 161 full-time freshmen.
Selectivity: Admits over 75% of applicants.

BASIC COSTS (2013-2014)
Tuition and fees: $33,417.
Per-credit charge: $722.
Room and board: $11,884.

FINANCIAL AID PICTURE (2011-2012)
Students with need: Out of 151 full-time freshmen who applied for aid, 144 were judged to have need. Of these, 144 received aid, and 14 had their full need met. Average financial aid package met 69% of need; average scholarship/grant was $18,209; average loan was $3,755. For part-time students, average financial aid package was $6,393.
Students without need: 16 full-time freshmen who did not demonstrate need for aid received scholarships/grants; average award was $10,062. No-need awards available for academics.
Cumulative student debt: 95% of graduating class had student loans; average debt was $18,559.

FINANCIAL AID PROCEDURES
Forms required: FAFSA.
Dates and Deadlines: Priority date 2/15; no closing date. Applicants notified on a rolling basis starting 2/15.
Transfers: No deadline. Applicants notified on a rolling basis starting 2/15.

CONTACT
Gary Sherman, Vice President Enrollment Management
1678 Asylum Avenue, West Hartford, CT 06117
(866) 442-8752

Wesleyan University
Middletown, Connecticut
www.wesleyan.edu CSS Code: 3959

4-year private university and liberal arts college in large town.
Enrollment: 2,924 undergrads. 752 full-time freshmen.
Selectivity: Admits less than 50% of applicants.

BASIC COSTS (2012-2013)
Tuition and fees: $45,928.
Room and board: $12,574.

FINANCIAL AID PICTURE (2012-2013)
Students with need: Out of 402 full-time freshmen who applied for aid, 356 were judged to have need. Of these, 356 received aid, and 356 had their full need met. Average financial aid package met 100% of need; average scholarship/grant was $39,761; average loan was $3,280.
Students without need: This college awards aid only to students with need.
Scholarships offered: Freeman Asian Scholars; for international first-year applicants from select East and Southeast Asian countries; 22 awarded.
Cumulative student debt: 45% of graduating class had student loans; average debt was $20,966.
Additional info: Most families whose income is below $40,000 will not be packaged with loans; grant aid will replace the standard loan in the package. Other students demonstrating significant need will graduate with 4-year packaged loan debt of $10,000 or $14,000 depending on need level. All other students will have their 4-year packaged loan debt reduced by about 30%.

FINANCIAL AID PROCEDURES
Forms required: FAFSA, CSS PROFILE.
Dates and Deadlines: Closing date 2/15. Applicants notified by 4/1; must reply by 5/1.
Transfers: Priority date 2/15; closing date 3/15. Applicants notified by 5/15; must reply by 6/1 or within 2 week(s) of notification. No financial aid available for international transfer candidates.

CONTACT
Jennifer Lawton, Director of Financial Aid
70 Wyllys Avenue, Middletown, CT 06459-0260
(860) 685-2800

Western Connecticut State University
Danbury, Connecticut
www.wcsu.edu Federal Code: 001380

4-year public university in small city.
Enrollment: 5,278 undergrads, 15% part-time. 870 full-time freshmen.
Selectivity: Admits 50 to 75% of applicants.

BASIC COSTS (2012-2013)
Tuition and fees: $8,440; out-of-state residents $19,472.
Room and board: $10,630.

FINANCIAL AID PICTURE (2011-2012)
Students with need: Out of 777 full-time freshmen who applied for aid, 628 were judged to have need. Of these, 608 received aid, and 20 had their full need met. Average financial aid package met 67% of need; average scholarship/grant was $5,560; average loan was $3,363. For part-time students, average financial aid package was $5,076.
Students without need: 3 full-time freshmen who did not demonstrate need for aid received scholarships/grants; average award was $8,104. No-need awards available for academics.
Cumulative student debt: 88% of graduating class had student loans; average debt was $33,095.

FINANCIAL AID PROCEDURES
Forms required: FAFSA, institutional form.
Dates and Deadlines: Priority date 3/15; no closing date. Applicants notified on a rolling basis starting 4/15; must reply by 5/1 or within 2 week(s) of notification.

CONTACT
Nancy Barton, Director, Financial Aid/Veterans Affairs
181 White Street, Danbury, CT 06810-6826
(203) 837-8580

Yale University
New Haven, Connecticut Federal Code: 001426
www.yale.edu CSS Code: 3987

4-year private university in small city.
Enrollment: 5,397 undergrads. 1,349 full-time freshmen.
Selectivity: Admits less than 50% of applicants.

BASIC COSTS (2012-2013)
Tuition and fees: $42,300.
Room and board: $13,000.

FINANCIAL AID PICTURE (2011-2012)
Students with need: Out of 884 full-time freshmen who applied for aid, 729 were judged to have need. Of these, 729 received aid, and 729 had their full need met. Average financial aid package met 100% of need; average scholarship/grant was $41,877; average loan was $2,226. Need-based aid available for part-time students.
Students without need: This college awards aid only to students with need.
Cumulative student debt: 23% of graduating class had student loans; average debt was $8,940.
Additional info: All scholarships based on demonstrated need.

FINANCIAL AID PROCEDURES
Forms required: FAFSA, CSS PROFILE.
Dates and Deadlines: Closing date 3/1. Applicants notified by 4/1; must reply by 5/1 or within 1 week(s) of notification.

CONTACT
Caesar Storlazzi, Director of University Financial Aid
Box 208234, New Haven, CT 06520-8234
(203) 432-2700

Delaware

Delaware College of Art and Design
Wilmington, Delaware
www.dcad.edu Federal Code: 041398

2-year private visual arts college in large city.
Enrollment: 211 undergrads, 9% part-time. 143 full-time freshmen.
Selectivity: Admits 50 to 75% of applicants.

BASIC COSTS (2013-2014)
Tuition and fees: $22,390.
Per-credit charge: $915.
Room and board: $11,250.

FINANCIAL AID PICTURE (2011-2012)
Students with need: Out of 137 full-time freshmen who applied for aid, 118 were judged to have need. Of these, 118 received aid. Average financial aid package met 52% of need; average scholarship/grant was $2,369; average loan was $3,344. For part-time students, average financial aid package was $10,766.
Students without need: 11 full-time freshmen who did not demonstrate need for aid received scholarships/grants; average award was $2,000. No-need awards available for academics, art.

FINANCIAL AID PROCEDURES
Forms required: FAFSA.
Dates and Deadlines: Priority date 4/1; no closing date. Applicants notified on a rolling basis; must reply within 2 week(s) of notification.
Transfers: No deadline. Applicants notified on a rolling basis; must reply within 2 week(s) of notification.

CONTACT
Teresa Haman, Director of Financial Aid
600 North Market Street, Wilmington, DE 19801

Delaware State University
Dover, Delaware
www.desu.edu Federal Code: 001428

4-year public university in large town.
Enrollment: 3,955 undergrads, 13% part-time. 1,023 full-time freshmen.
Selectivity: Admits less than 50% of applicants.

BASIC COSTS (2012-2013)
Tuition and fees: $7,336; out-of-state residents $15,692.
Per-credit charge: $272; out-of-state residents $620.
Room and board: $10,708.

FINANCIAL AID PICTURE
Students with need: Need-based aid available for full-time and part-time students.
Students without need: This college awards aid only to students with need.
Additional info: Students must file FAFSA by March 15 every year.

FINANCIAL AID PROCEDURES
Forms required: FAFSA.
Dates and Deadlines: Priority date 3/1; closing date 7/1. Applicants notified on a rolling basis starting 4/1; must reply by 8/20.
Transfers: Closing date 2/15.

CONTACT
Lynn Iocono, Executive Director of Student Financial Services
1200 North DuPont Highway, Dover, DE 19901
(302) 857-6250

Delaware Technical and Community College: Dover
Dover, Delaware
www.dtcc.edu Federal Code: 011727

2-year public community and technical college in large town.
Enrollment: 2,936 undergrads, 52% part-time. 501 full-time freshmen.
Selectivity: Open admission; but selective for some programs.

BASIC COSTS (2012-2013)
Tuition and fees: $3,113; out-of-state residents $7,433.
Per-credit charge: $120; out-of-state residents $300.

FINANCIAL AID PICTURE
Students with need: Need-based aid available for full-time and part-time students.
Students without need: This college awards aid only to students with need.

FINANCIAL AID PROCEDURES
Forms required: FAFSA.
Dates and Deadlines: Priority date 6/15; no closing date. Applicants notified on a rolling basis starting 7/1; must reply within 2 week(s) of notification.

CONTACT
Jennifer Grunden, Financial Aid Director
100 Campus Drive, Dover, DE 19901
(302) 857-1040

Delaware Technical and Community College: Owens
Georgetown, Delaware
www.dtcc.edu Federal Code: 007053

2-year public community and technical college in small town.
Enrollment: 4,100 undergrads, 52% part-time. 719 full-time freshmen.

Selectivity: Open admission; but selective for some programs.

BASIC COSTS (2012-2013)
Tuition and fees: $3,113; out-of-state residents $7,433.
Per-credit charge: $120; out-of-state residents $300.

FINANCIAL AID PICTURE
Students with need: Need-based aid available for full-time and part-time students.
Students without need: This college awards aid only to students with need.

FINANCIAL AID PROCEDURES
Forms required: FAFSA.
Dates and Deadlines: Priority date 6/15; no closing date. Applicants notified on a rolling basis; must reply within 2 week(s) of notification.

CONTACT
Veronica Oney, Financial Aid Officer
PO Box 610, Georgetown, DE 19947
(302) 855-5692

Delaware Technical and Community College: Stanton/Wilmington

Newark, Delaware
www.dtcc.edu Federal Code: 021449

2-year public community and technical college in small city.
Enrollment: 6,552 undergrads, 62% part-time. 847 full-time freshmen.
Selectivity: Open admission; but selective for some programs.

BASIC COSTS (2012-2013)
Tuition and fees: $3,112; out-of-state residents $7,432.
Per-credit charge: $120; out-of-state residents $300.

FINANCIAL AID PICTURE
Students with need: Need-based aid available for full-time and part-time students.
Students without need: This college awards aid only to students with need.

FINANCIAL AID PROCEDURES
Forms required: FAFSA.
Dates and Deadlines: Priority date 6/15; no closing date. Applicants notified on a rolling basis; must reply within 2 week(s) of notification.

CONTACT
Debra Troxler, Student Financial Aid Officer
400 Stanton-Christiana Road, Newark, DE 19713
(302) 571-5380

Goldey-Beacom College

Wilmington, Delaware
www.gbc.edu Federal Code: 001429

4-year private business college in small city.
Enrollment: 617 undergrads, 25% part-time. 91 full-time freshmen.
Selectivity: Admits 50 to 75% of applicants.

BASIC COSTS (2013-2014)
Tuition and fees: $22,440.
Per-credit charge: $738.
Room only: $5,353.

FINANCIAL AID PICTURE
Students with need: Need-based aid available for full-time and part-time students. Work study available nights, weekends, and for part-time students.
Students without need: No-need awards available for academics, athletics.

FINANCIAL AID PROCEDURES
Forms required: FAFSA.
Dates and Deadlines: Priority date 4/15; closing date 7/15. Applicants notified on a rolling basis starting 3/1; must reply within 2 week(s) of notification.
Transfers: Applicants notified on a rolling basis starting 3/1; must reply within 2 week(s) of notification.

CONTACT
Jane Lysle, Dean of Enrollment Management
4701 Limestone Road, Wilmington, DE 19808
(302) 225-6265

University of Delaware

Newark, Delaware
www.udel.edu Federal Code: 001431

4-year public university in large town.
Enrollment: 16,709 undergrads, 5% part-time. 3,806 full-time freshmen.
Selectivity: Admits 50 to 75% of applicants.

BASIC COSTS (2012-2013)
Tuition and fees: $11,682; out-of-state residents $28,772.
Room and board: $11,046.

FINANCIAL AID PICTURE (2012-2013)
Students with need: Out of 3,503 full-time freshmen who applied for aid, 2,194 were judged to have need. Of these, 2,150 received aid, and 1,040 had their full need met. Average financial aid package met 75% of need; average scholarship/grant was $8,756; average loan was $6,569. For part-time students, average financial aid package was $9,501.
Students without need: This college awards aid only to students with need.
Scholarships offered: ***Merit:*** All freshman applicants evaluated for a wide range of merit scholarships ranging from $1,000 to full cost of education. ***Athletic:*** 99 full-time freshmen received athletic scholarships; average amount $15,631.
Cumulative student debt: 56% of graduating class had student loans; average debt was $33,649.
Additional info: December 15 application deadline to receive scholarship consideration. Sibling/parent tuition credit plan. Senior citizen tuition credit for state residents over 60.

FINANCIAL AID PROCEDURES
Forms required: FAFSA.
Dates and Deadlines: Priority date 2/1; closing date 3/15. Applicants notified on a rolling basis starting 3/15; must reply by 5/1 or within 3 week(s) of notification.
Transfers: No deadline. Aid usually limited to federal and state programs.

CONTACT
Melissa Stone, Director of Student Financial Services
210 South College Avenue, Newark, DE 19716
(302) 831-2126

Wesley College

Dover, Delaware
www.wesley.edu Federal Code: 001433

4-year private liberal arts college in large town, affiliated with United Methodist Church.
Enrollment: 1,574 undergrads, 15% part-time. 462 full-time freshmen.
Selectivity: Admits 50 to 75% of applicants.

BASIC COSTS (2013-2014)
Tuition and fees: $23,540.

Room and board: $10,440.

FINANCIAL AID PICTURE

Students with need: Need-based aid available for full-time and part-time students. Work study available nights, weekends, and for part-time students.

Students without need: This college awards aid only to students with need.

FINANCIAL AID PROCEDURES

Forms required: FAFSA, institutional form.

Dates and Deadlines: Priority date 2/1; no closing date. Applicants notified on a rolling basis starting 1/1; must reply within 2 week(s) of notification.

Transfers: No deadline. Applicants notified on a rolling basis; must reply within 2 week(s) of notification.

CONTACT

Michael Hall, Director of Student Financial Planning
120 North State Street, Dover, DE 19901-3875
(302) 736-2494

Wilmington University

New Castle, Delaware
www.wilmu.edu Federal Code: 007948

4-year private liberal arts college in large town.

Enrollment: 8,226 undergrads, 56% part-time. 306 full-time freshmen.

Selectivity: Open admission.

BASIC COSTS (2013-2014)

Tuition and fees: $9,950.

Per-credit charge: $330.

FINANCIAL AID PICTURE (2011-2012)

Students with need: 43% of average financial aid package awarded as scholarships/grants, 57% awarded as loans/jobs. Need-based aid available for part-time students. Work study available nights, weekends, and for part-time students.

Students without need: No-need awards available for academics, athletics.

FINANCIAL AID PROCEDURES

Forms required: FAFSA.

Dates and Deadlines: Priority date 4/30; no closing date. Applicants notified on a rolling basis starting 8/5; must reply within 2 week(s) of notification.

CONTACT

Nicole McDaniel-Smith, Director of Financial Aid
320 Dupont Highway, New Castle, DE 19720
(302) 328-9401 ext. 107

District of Columbia

American University

Washington, District of Columbia Federal Code: 001434
www.american.edu CSS Code: 5007

4-year private university in very large city, affiliated with United Methodist Church.

Enrollment: 6,784 undergrads, 3% part-time. 1,594 full-time freshmen.

Selectivity: Admits less than 50% of applicants.

BASIC COSTS (2013-2014)

Tuition and fees: $40,649.

Per-credit charge: $1,337.

Room and board: $14,180.

FINANCIAL AID PICTURE (2012-2013)

Students with need: Out of 1,141 full-time freshmen who applied for aid, 857 were judged to have need. Of these, 850 received aid, and 327 had their full need met. Average financial aid package met 85% of need; average scholarship/grant was $21,739; average loan was $4,313. For part-time students, average financial aid package was $9,128.

Students without need: This college awards aid only to students with need.

Scholarships offered: ***Merit:*** United Methodist scholarship; supplemental application required. ***Athletic:*** 69 full-time freshmen received athletic scholarships; average amount $16,188.

Additional info: Early decision applicants must submit estimated AU institutional financial aid application by 11/15 and a FASFA as soon as possible after Jan 1.

FINANCIAL AID PROCEDURES

Forms required: FAFSA. CSS Profile and FAFSA must be completed by freshmen who are seeking need-based aid.

Dates and Deadlines: Closing date 2/15. Applicants notified by 4/1; must reply by 5/1 or within 4 week(s) of notification.

Transfers: Priority date 3/1. Phi Theta Kappa scholarship available.

CONTACT

Brian Lee Sang, Director of Financial Aid
4400 Massachusetts Avenue NW, Washington, DC 20016-8001
(202) 885-6100

Catholic University of America

Washington, District of Columbia
www.cua.edu Federal Code: 001437

4-year private university in very large city, affiliated with Roman Catholic Church.

Enrollment: 3,629 undergrads, 6% part-time. 880 full-time freshmen.

Selectivity: Admits 50 to 75% of applicants.

BASIC COSTS (2013-2014)

Tuition and fees: $38,526.

Per-credit charge: $1,490.

Room and board: $14,326.

FINANCIAL AID PICTURE (2012-2013)

Students with need: Out of 699 full-time freshmen who applied for aid, 573 were judged to have need. Of these, 573 received aid, and 250 had their full need met. Average financial aid package met 81% of need; average scholarship/grant was $21,661; average loan was $3,887. For part-time students, average financial aid package was $5,914.

Students without need: 246 full-time freshmen who did not demonstrate need for aid received scholarships/grants; average award was $14,057. No-need awards available for academics, alumni affiliation, music/drama, religious affiliation.

FINANCIAL AID PROCEDURES

Forms required: FAFSA.

Dates and Deadlines: Priority date 2/15; closing date 4/10. Applicants notified on a rolling basis starting 4/1; must reply by 5/1 or within 2 week(s) of notification.

Transfers: Priority date 2/25. Applicants notified on a rolling basis starting 4/1; must reply by 5/1 or within 2 week(s) of notification.

CONTACT

Joe Dobrota, Director of Financial Aid
102 McMahon Hall, Washington, DC 20064
(202) 319-5307

Gallaudet University
Washington, District of Columbia
www.gallaudet.edu Federal Code: 001443

4-year private university and liberal arts college in very large city.
Enrollment: 1,097 undergrads, 5% part-time. 171 full-time freshmen.
Selectivity: Admits 50 to 75% of applicants.

BASIC COSTS (2013-2014)
Tuition and fees: $13,800.
Per-credit charge: $672.
Room and board: $11,580.

FINANCIAL AID PICTURE (2011-2012)
Students with need: Out of 158 full-time freshmen who applied for aid, 137 were judged to have need. Of these, 137 received aid, and 54 had their full need met. Average financial aid package met 80% of need; average scholarship/grant was $17,643; average loan was $2,962. Need-based aid available for part-time students.
Students without need: 33 full-time freshmen who did not demonstrate need for aid received scholarships/grants; average award was $7,319. No-need awards available for academics, alumni affiliation, art, leadership, minority status, music/drama, religious affiliation, state/district residency.
Cumulative student debt: 58% of graduating class had student loans; average debt was $13,767.
Additional info: Institution receives substantial aid from state vocational rehabilitation agencies, supplemented by institutional grants when needed.

FINANCIAL AID PROCEDURES
Forms required: FAFSA, institutional form.
Dates and Deadlines: Priority date 7/1; no closing date. Applicants notified on a rolling basis starting 3/1; must reply within 4 week(s) of notification.

CONTACT
Janel Grossinger, Director of Financial Aid
800 Florida Avenue, NE, Washington, DC 20002
(202) 651-5290

George Washington University
Washington, District of Columbia Federal Code: 001444
www.gwu.edu/explore CSS Code: 5246

4-year private university in very large city.
Enrollment: 10,240 undergrads, 5% part-time. 2,230 full-time freshmen.
Selectivity: Admits less than 50% of applicants. GED not accepted.

BASIC COSTS (2013-2014)
Tuition and fees: $47,335.
Per-credit charge: $1,315.
Room and board: $11,378.
Additional info: Tuition at time of enrollment locked for 4 years.

FINANCIAL AID PICTURE (2011-2012)
Students with need: Out of 1,422 full-time freshmen who applied for aid, 1,111 were judged to have need. Of these, 1,062 received aid, and 613 had their full need met. Average financial aid package met 90% of need; average scholarship/grant was $25,532; average loan was $4,854. For part-time students, average financial aid package was $11,317.
Students without need: 431 full-time freshmen who did not demonstrate need for aid received scholarships/grants; average award was $17,407. No-need awards available for academics, art, athletics, music/drama, ROTC.
Scholarships offered: 38 full-time freshmen received athletic scholarships; average amount $33,905.
Cumulative student debt: 47% of graduating class had student loans; average debt was $33,398.
Additional info: Auditions required for performing arts scholarships.

FINANCIAL AID PROCEDURES
Forms required: FAFSA, CSS PROFILE.
Dates and Deadlines: Closing date 2/1. Applicants notified on a rolling basis starting 3/24; must reply by 5/1.
Transfers: Closing date 5/1.

CONTACT
Daniel Small, Director of Student Financial Assistance
2121 I Street NW, Suite 201, Washington, DC 20052
(202) 994-6620

Georgetown University
Washington, District of Columbia Federal Code: 001445
www.georgetown.edu CSS Code: 5244

4-year private university in very large city, affiliated with Roman Catholic Church.
Enrollment: 7,201 undergrads, 3% part-time. 1,606 full-time freshmen.
Selectivity: Admits less than 50% of applicants.

BASIC COSTS (2012-2013)
Tuition and fees: $42,870.
Per-credit charge: $1,765.
Room and board: $13,836.

FINANCIAL AID PICTURE (2011-2012)
Students with need: Out of 1,056 full-time freshmen who applied for aid, 698 were judged to have need. Of these, 698 received aid, and 698 had their full need met. Average financial aid package met 100% of need; average scholarship/grant was $32,019; average loan was $3,109. Need-based aid available for part-time students.
Students without need: No-need awards available for athletics.
Cumulative student debt: 39% of graduating class had student loans; average debt was $28,035.

FINANCIAL AID PROCEDURES
Forms required: FAFSA, CSS PROFILE.
Dates and Deadlines: Closing date 2/1. Applicants notified by 4/1; must reply by 5/1 or within 2 week(s) of notification.
Transfers: Priority date 3/1. Applicants notified by 5/15; must reply by 5/30 or within 2 week(s) of notification.

CONTACT
Patricia McWade, Dean of Student Financial Services
103 White-Gravenor, Washington, DC 20057-1002
(202) 687-4547

Howard University
Washington, District of Columbia
www.howard.edu Federal Code: 001448

4-year private university in very large city.
Enrollment: 6,652 undergrads.

BASIC COSTS (2012-2013)
Tuition and fees: $22,683.
Room and board: $9,783.

FINANCIAL AID PICTURE (2011-2012)
Students with need: 58% of average financial aid package awarded as scholarships/grants, 42% awarded as loans/jobs. Need-based aid available for part-time students. Work study available nights, weekends, and for part-time students.
Students without need: No-need awards available for academics, alumni affiliation, art, athletics, leadership, music/drama, religious affiliation, ROTC.

FINANCIAL AID PROCEDURES
Forms required: FAFSA.
Dates and Deadlines: Closing date 2/1. Applicants notified on a rolling basis starting 3/30; must reply by 5/1 or within 4 week(s) of notification.
Transfers: Closing date 5/17. Applicants notified by 6/1; must reply within 3 week(s) of notification.

CONTACT
Derek Kindle, Associate Director, Office of Financial Aid, Scholarships, and Student Employment
2400 Sixth Street NW, Washington, DC 20059
(202) 806-2820

Potomac College
Washington, District of Columbia
www.potomac.edu Federal Code: 032183

3-year for-profit business college in very large city.
Enrollment: 290 undergrads, 11% part-time. 57 full-time freshmen.
Selectivity: Open admission.

BASIC COSTS (2012-2013)
Tuition and fees: $15,150.

FINANCIAL AID PICTURE
Students with need: Need-based aid available for full-time and part-time students.

FINANCIAL AID PROCEDURES
Forms required: FAFSA, institutional form.
Dates and Deadlines: Applicants notified on a rolling basis; must reply within 4 week(s) of notification.

CONTACT
David Wilhelmi, Director of Financial Aid
4000 Chesapeake Street NW, Washington, DC 20016
(602) 734-4372

Trinity Washington University
Washington, District of Columbia
www.trinitydc.edu Federal Code: 001460

4-year private liberal arts college in very large city, affiliated with Roman Catholic Church.
Enrollment: 1,856 undergrads, 36% part-time. 252 full-time freshmen.
Selectivity: Admits over 75% of applicants.

BASIC COSTS (2012-2013)
Tuition and fees: $20,710.
Per-credit charge: $655.
Room and board: $9,432.

FINANCIAL AID PICTURE (2011-2012)
Students with need: Need-based aid available for full-time and part-time students.
Students without need: No-need awards available for academics, alumni affiliation, leadership.

FINANCIAL AID PROCEDURES
Forms required: FAFSA.
Dates and Deadlines: Priority date 3/1; closing date 4/1. Applicants notified on a rolling basis starting 2/1; must reply within 2 week(s) of notification.

CONTACT
Meghan Howard, Director of Financial Aid
125 Michigan Avenue, NE, Washington, DC 20017
(202) 884-9530

University of the District of Columbia
Washington, District of Columbia
www.udc.edu Federal Code: 007015

4-year public university and liberal arts college in very large city.
Enrollment: 4,857 undergrads.

BASIC COSTS (2012-2013)
Tuition and fees: $7,244; out-of-state residents $14,540.
Per-credit charge: $276; out-of-state residents $580.

FINANCIAL AID PICTURE
Students with need: Need-based aid available for full-time and part-time students. Work study available nights, weekends, and for part-time students.
Students without need: This college awards aid only to students with need.

FINANCIAL AID PROCEDURES
Forms required: FAFSA.
Dates and Deadlines: Priority date 3/15; no closing date. Applicants notified on a rolling basis starting 5/1; must reply within 2 week(s) of notification.

CONTACT
James Contreras, Director, Financial Aid Office
4200 Connecticut Avenue NW, Washington, DC 20008
(202) 274-5060

Florida

Adventist University of Health Sciences
Orlando, Florida
www.adu.edu Federal Code: 031155

4-year private health science and nursing college in large city, affiliated with Seventh-day Adventists.
Enrollment: 2,515 undergrads. 88 full-time freshmen.

BASIC COSTS (2012-2013)
Tuition and fees: $10,780.
Per-credit charge: $340.
Room and board: $3,500.

FINANCIAL AID PICTURE (2011-2012)
Students with need: Out of 84 full-time freshmen who applied for aid, 80 were judged to have need. Of these, 74 received aid, and 1 had their full need met. Average financial aid package met 27.22% of need; average scholarship/grant was $5,111; average loan was $3,020. For part-time students, average financial aid package was $4,757.
Students without need: 3 full-time freshmen who did not demonstrate need for aid received scholarships/grants; average award was $5,646. No-need awards available for state/district residency.
Cumulative student debt: 68% of graduating class had student loans; average debt was $25,362.23.

FINANCIAL AID PROCEDURES
Forms required: FAFSA, institutional form.
Dates and Deadlines: Priority date 4/12; no closing date. Applicants notified on a rolling basis starting 3/1.

CONTACT
Starr Bender, Director of Financial Aid
671 Winyah Drive, Orlando, FL 32803
(407) 303-6963

Ave Maria University

Ave Maria, Florida
www.avemaria.edu Federal Code: 039413

4-year private university and liberal arts college in small town, affiliated with Roman Catholic Church.
Enrollment: 872 undergrads.

BASIC COSTS (2012-2013)

Tuition and fees: $21,496.
Room and board: $8,841.

FINANCIAL AID PICTURE

Students with need: Need-based aid available for full-time and part-time students. Work study available nights, weekends, and for part-time students.
Students without need: No-need awards available for academics, athletics, leadership, music/drama, religious affiliation, state/district residency.

FINANCIAL AID PROCEDURES

Forms required: FAFSA, state aid form.
Dates and Deadlines: Priority date 4/1; no closing date. Applicants notified on a rolling basis starting 10/1.

CONTACT

Anne Hart, Director of Financial Aid
5050 Ave Maria Boulevard, Ave Maria, FL 34142-9505

Baptist College of Florida

Graceville, Florida
www.baptistcollege.edu Federal Code: 013001

4-year private Bible and teachers college in small town, affiliated with Southern Baptist Convention.
Enrollment: 534 undergrads, 24% part-time. 187 full-time freshmen.
Selectivity: Admits less than 50% of applicants.

BASIC COSTS (2012-2013)

Tuition and fees: $9,350.
Per-credit charge: $300.
Room and board: $4,888.

FINANCIAL AID PICTURE (2011-2012)

Students with need: Out of 179 full-time freshmen who applied for aid, 164 were judged to have need. Of these, 77 received aid, and 3 had their full need met. Average financial aid package met 26% of need; average scholarship/grant was $5,283; average loan was $2,447. For part-time students, average financial aid package was $4,094.
Students without need: 1 full-time freshmen who did not demonstrate need for aid received scholarships/grants; average award was $2,000. No-need awards available for academics, minority status, music/drama, religious affiliation.

FINANCIAL AID PROCEDURES

Forms required: FAFSA, state aid form, institutional form.
Dates and Deadlines: Priority date 4/1; closing date 4/15. Applicants notified on a rolling basis starting 6/15; must reply within 4 week(s) of notification.
Transfers: No deadline.

CONTACT

Stephanie Powell, Director of Financial Aid
5400 College Drive, Graceville, FL 32440-3306
(850) 263-3261 ext. 461

Barry University

Miami Shores, Florida
www.barry.edu Federal Code: 001466

4-year private university in large town, affiliated with Roman Catholic Church.
Enrollment: 4,551 undergrads, 16% part-time. 622 full-time freshmen.
Selectivity: Admits 50 to 75% of applicants.

BASIC COSTS (2012-2013)

Tuition and fees: $28,160.
Per-credit charge: $845.
Room and board: $9,440.

FINANCIAL AID PICTURE

Students with need: Need-based aid available for full-time and part-time students. Work study available nights, weekends, and for part-time students.
Students without need: No-need awards available for academics, art, athletics, music/drama.

FINANCIAL AID PROCEDURES

Forms required: FAFSA.
Dates and Deadlines: Applicants notified on a rolling basis starting 1/25.

CONTACT

H. Dart Humeston, Director of Financial Aid
11300 NE Second Avenue, Miami Shores, FL 33161-6695
(305) 899-3673

Beacon College

Leesburg, Florida
www.beaconcollege.edu Federal Code: 033733

4-year private liberal arts college in large town.
Enrollment: 184 undergrads, 1% part-time. 39 full-time freshmen.
Selectivity: Admits less than 50% of applicants.

BASIC COSTS (2013-2014)

Tuition and fees: $31,496.
Room and board: $8,862.

FINANCIAL AID PICTURE (2012-2013)

Students with need: Need-based aid available for part-time students.
Students without need: This college awards aid only to students with need.
Cumulative student debt: 42% of graduating class had student loans; average debt was $15,000.
Additional info: Work-study programs offered based on financial need.

FINANCIAL AID PROCEDURES

Forms required: FAFSA, state aid form.
Dates and Deadlines: Priority date 4/1; no closing date. Applicants notified on a rolling basis starting 5/1; must reply within 2 week(s) of notification.
Transfers: No deadline. Applicants notified on a rolling basis starting 5/1; must reply within 2 week(s) of notification.

CONTACT

Shawna Wells-Booth, Financial Aid Director
105 East Main Street, Leesburg, FL 34748
(352) 638-9733

Bethune-Cookman University

Daytona Beach, Florida
www.cookman.edu Federal Code: 001467

4-year private liberal arts college in small city, affiliated with United Methodist Church.

Enrollment: 3,095 undergrads, 3% part-time. 876 full-time freshmen.
Selectivity: Admits 50 to 75% of applicants.

BASIC COSTS (2012-2013)
Tuition and fees: $14,410.
Per-credit charge: $600.
Room and board: $8,548.
Additional info: The Lee Rhyant Residential Center costs an additional $708 per year. Tuition at time of enrollment locked for 4 years.

FINANCIAL AID PICTURE (2012-2013)
Students with need: 51% of average financial aid package awarded as scholarships/grants, 49% awarded as loans/jobs. Need-based aid available for part-time students. Work study available nights, weekends, and for part-time students.
Students without need: This college awards aid only to students with need.

FINANCIAL AID PROCEDURES
Forms required: FAFSA.
Dates and Deadlines: Priority date 4/1; no closing date. Applicants notified on a rolling basis starting 4/1; must reply within 3 week(s) of notification.

CONTACT
Joseph Coleman, Director of Financial Aid
Dr. Mary McLeod Bethune Boulevard, Daytona Beach, FL 32114-3099
(800) 553-9369

Brevard Community College
Cocoa, Florida
www.brevardcc.edu Federal Code: 001470

2-year public community college in large town.
Enrollment: 12,994 undergrads, 56% part-time. 1,706 full-time freshmen.
Selectivity: Open admission; but selective for some programs.

BASIC COSTS (2012-2013)
Tuition and fees: $3,060; out-of-state residents $11,220.

FINANCIAL AID PICTURE
Students with need: Need-based aid available for full-time and part-time students.
Students without need: No-need awards available for academics, athletics.

FINANCIAL AID PROCEDURES
Forms required: FAFSA.
Dates and Deadlines: Priority date 4/15; closing date 6/30. Applicants notified on a rolling basis starting 6/1; must reply within 2 week(s) of notification.
Transfers: Transfer students must complete at least 15 credit hours with 3.5 GPA to be considered for merit scholarship.

CONTACT
Indira Dzadovsky, Director of Financial Aid/ Veteran Affairs
1519 Clearlake Road, Cocoa, FL 32922-9987
(321) 433-5530

Broward College
Fort Lauderdale, Florida
www.broward.edu Federal Code: 001500

2-year public community college in small city.
Enrollment: 37,622 undergrads, 68% part-time. 2,687 full-time freshmen.
Selectivity: Open admission; but selective for some programs.

BASIC COSTS (2012-2013)
Tuition and fees: $2,997; out-of-state residents $10,650.
Additional info: Reported tuition and fees for baccalaureate degree programs are slightly higher. Tuition/fee waivers available for adults, minority students.

FINANCIAL AID PICTURE (2011-2012)
Students with need: 75% of average financial aid package awarded as scholarships/grants, 25% awarded as loans/jobs. Need-based aid available for part-time students. Work study available nights, weekends, and for part-time students.
Students without need: No-need awards available for academics, athletics, leadership, state/district residency.

FINANCIAL AID PROCEDURES
Forms required: FAFSA, institutional form.
Dates and Deadlines: Priority date 4/15; no closing date. Applicants notified on a rolling basis starting 6/1.
Transfers: No deadline.

CONTACT
Robert Robbins, Associate Vice President of Student Affairs
225 East Las Olas Boulevard, Fort Lauderdale, FL 33301

Brown Mackie College: Miami
Miami, Florida
www.brownmackie.edu Federal Code: 005127

2-year for-profit business and career college in very large city.
Enrollment: 875 undergrads. 300 full-time freshmen.
Selectivity: Open admission.

BASIC COSTS (2012-2013)
Tuition and fees: $17,895.
Per-credit charge: $390.
Additional info: Tuition varies according to area of study, is $390 per credit hour for most programs leading to a degree.

FINANCIAL AID PICTURE (2011-2012)
Students with need: Out of 280 full-time freshmen who applied for aid, 280 were judged to have need. Of these, 280 received aid, and 9 had their full need met. Average financial aid package met 80% of need; average scholarship/grant was $500.
Students without need: No-need awards available for academics, state/district residency.

CONTACT
Ingrid Ayala, Director of Financial Aid
One Herald Plaza, Miami, FL 33132
(305) 341-6600

Carlos Albizu University
Miami, Florida
www.albizu.edu Federal Code: 010724

4-year private university in very large city.
Enrollment: 307 undergrads.

BASIC COSTS (2012-2013)
Tuition and fees: $14,874.
Additional info: Reported tuition and fees are for bachelor's degree program in business. Other programs individually priced.

FINANCIAL AID PICTURE
Students with need: Need-based aid available for full-time and part-time students. Work study available nights.
Students without need: This college awards aid only to students with need.

FINANCIAL AID PROCEDURES

Forms required: FAFSA, institutional form.

Dates and Deadlines: Priority date 6/1; no closing date. Applicants notified on a rolling basis starting 2/1.

Transfers: No deadline. Applicants notified on a rolling basis.

CONTACT

Ramona Morales, Financial Aid Director
2173 NW 99th Avenue, Miami, FL 33172
(305) 593-1223 ext. 153

Chipola College

Marianna, Florida
www.chipola.edu Federal Code: 001472

2-year public community college in small town.

Enrollment: 1,479 undergrads, 48% part-time. 193 full-time freshmen.

Selectivity: Open admission; but selective for some programs.

BASIC COSTS (2012-2013)

Tuition and fees: $3,060; out-of-state residents $8,891.

Additional info: Tuition and fees for baccalaureate degree programs are slightly higher.

FINANCIAL AID PICTURE (2011-2012)

Students with need: 88% of average financial aid package awarded as scholarships/grants, 12% awarded as loans/jobs. Need-based aid available for part-time students. Work study available nights.

Students without need: No-need awards available for academics, alumni affiliation, art, athletics, job skills, leadership, minority status, music/drama.

FINANCIAL AID PROCEDURES

Forms required: FAFSA, institutional form.

Dates and Deadlines: Priority date 5/1; no closing date. Applicants notified on a rolling basis starting 1/2; must reply within 2 week(s) of notification.

CONTACT

Sybil Cloud, Director of Financial Aid
3094 Indian Circle, Marianna, FL 32446
(850) 718-2223

Clearwater Christian College

Clearwater, Florida
www.clearwater.edu Federal Code: 015025

4-year private liberal arts college in small city, affiliated with nondenominational tradition.

Enrollment: 479 undergrads, 2% part-time. 95 full-time freshmen.

Selectivity: Admits 50 to 75% of applicants.

BASIC COSTS (2013-2014)

Tuition and fees: $17,125.

Room and board: $8,300.

Additional info: Tuition at time of enrollment locked for 4 years; tuition/fee waivers available for adults.

FINANCIAL AID PICTURE (2011-2012)

Students with need: Out of 82 full-time freshmen who applied for aid, 74 were judged to have need. Of these, 74 received aid, and 3 had their full need met. Average financial aid package met 53% of need; average scholarship/grant was $10,037; average loan was $4,081. For part-time students, average financial aid package was $9,671.

Students without need: 17 full-time freshmen who did not demonstrate need for aid received scholarships/grants; average award was $4,536. No-need awards available for academics, alumni affiliation, leadership, music/drama, religious affiliation, ROTC.

Cumulative student debt: 67% of graduating class had student loans; average debt was $21,983.

Additional info: Special consideration given to children of Christian service workers; need-based scholarships available to first-generation students; scholarships up to $3,000 available to dual-enrolled students.

FINANCIAL AID PROCEDURES

Forms required: FAFSA, state aid form, institutional form.

Dates and Deadlines: Priority date 3/1; no closing date. Applicants notified on a rolling basis starting 3/15; must reply within 2 week(s) of notification.

Transfers: No deadline. Applicants notified on a rolling basis starting 3/1.

CONTACT

Ryan McNamara, Director of Financial Aid
3400 Gulf-to-Bay Boulevard, Clearwater, FL 33759-4595
(727) 726-1153 ext. 214

College of Business and Technology: Cutler Bay

Cutler Bay, Florida
www.cbt.edu Federal Code: 030716

2-year for-profit technical and career college in very large city.

Enrollment: 233 undergrads.

Selectivity: Open admission.

BASIC COSTS (2012-2013)

Additional info: Tuition per semester credit $455.00; additional required fees vary by program.

FINANCIAL AID PICTURE (2011-2012)

Students with need: 39% of average financial aid package awarded as scholarships/grants, 61% awarded as loans/jobs. Need-based aid available for part-time students.

Students without need: This college awards aid only to students with need.

FINANCIAL AID PROCEDURES

Forms required: FAFSA.

CONTACT

Yazmin Palma, Director of Financial Aid
19151 South Dixie Highway, #203, Cutler Bay, FL 33157

College of Business and Technology: Flagler

Miami, Florida
www.cbt.edu Federal Code: 030716

2-year for-profit technical and career college in very large city.

Enrollment: 246 undergrads.

Selectivity: Open admission.

BASIC COSTS (2012-2013)

Additional info: Tuition per semester credit $455.00; additional required fees vary by program.

FINANCIAL AID PICTURE (2011-2012)

Students with need: 47% of average financial aid package awarded as scholarships/grants, 53% awarded as loans/jobs. Need-based aid available for part-time students. Work study available nights.

Students without need: This college awards aid only to students with need.

FINANCIAL AID PROCEDURES

Forms required: FAFSA.

CONTACT
Yazmin Palma, Financial Aid Director
8230 West Flagler Street, Miami, FL 33144

College of Business and Technology: Hialeah

Hialeah, Florida
www.cbt.edu Federal Code: 030716

2-year for-profit business and technical college in large city.
Enrollment: 262 undergrads.
Selectivity: Open admission.

BASIC COSTS (2012-2013)
Additional info: Tuition per semester credit $455.00; additional required fees vary by program.

FINANCIAL AID PICTURE (2012-2013)
Students with need: 45% of average financial aid package awarded as scholarships/grants, 55% awarded as loans/jobs. Need-based aid available for part-time students.
Students without need: This college awards aid only to students with need.

FINANCIAL AID PROCEDURES
Forms required: FAFSA.

CONTACT
Yazmin Palma, Financial Aid Director
935 West 49th Street Suite 203, Hialeah, FL 33012-3436

College of Business and Technology: Kendall

Miami, Florida
www.cbt.edu Federal Code: 030716

2-year for-profit junior and technical college in very large city.
Enrollment: 190 undergrads.
Selectivity: Open admission.

BASIC COSTS (2012-2013)
Additional info: Tuition per semester credit $455.00; additional required fees vary by program.

FINANCIAL AID PICTURE (2011-2012)
Students with need: 45% of average financial aid package awarded as scholarships/grants, 55% awarded as loans/jobs. Need-based aid available for part-time students.
Students without need: This college awards aid only to students with need.

FINANCIAL AID PROCEDURES
Forms required: FAFSA.

CONTACT
Yazmin Palma, Financial Aid Director
8991 SW 107 Avenue, Miami, FL 33176

College of Central Florida

Ocala, Florida
www.cf.edu Federal Code: 001471

2-year public community college in small city.
Enrollment: 7,378 undergrads, 58% part-time. 655 full-time freshmen.
Selectivity: Open admission; but selective for some programs.

BASIC COSTS (2012-2013)
Tuition and fees: $3,147; out-of-state residents $12,656.
Additional info: Reported tuition and fees for baccalaureate degree programs are slightly higher. Tuition/fee waivers available for minority students.

FINANCIAL AID PICTURE (2011-2012)
Students with need: 50% of average financial aid package awarded as scholarships/grants, 50% awarded as loans/jobs. Need-based aid available for part-time students.
Students without need: No-need awards available for academics, athletics, minority status, music/drama, state/district residency.

FINANCIAL AID PROCEDURES
Forms required: FAFSA.

CONTACT
Judy Menadier, Director, Financial Aid
3001 SW College Road, Ocala, FL 34474-4415
(352) 873-5803 ext. 1340

Daytona State College

Daytona Beach, Florida
www.daytonastate.edu Federal Code: 001475

2-year public community and technical college in large city.
Enrollment: 12,545 undergrads, 58% part-time. 1,072 full-time freshmen.
Selectivity: Open admission; but selective for some programs.

BASIC COSTS (2012-2013)
Tuition and fees: $3,134; out-of-state residents $12,204.
Additional info: Reported tuition and fees for baccalaureate degree programs are slightly higher.

FINANCIAL AID PICTURE (2011-2012)
Students with need: Need-based aid available for part-time students.
Students without need: No-need awards available for academics, athletics, leadership, music/drama, state/district residency.

FINANCIAL AID PROCEDURES
Forms required: FAFSA.
Dates and Deadlines: Priority date 5/15; no closing date. Applicants notified on a rolling basis starting 3/15.

CONTACT
Kevin McCrary, Director of Financial Aid
Daytona State College Admissions Office, Daytona Beach, FL 32120-2811
(386) 506-3000 ext. 3015

DeVry University: Miramar

Miramar, Florida
www.devry.edu

4-year for-profit university in large town.
Enrollment: 709 undergrads, 58% part-time. 28 full-time freshmen.

BASIC COSTS (2012-2013)
Tuition and fees: $16,076.

FINANCIAL AID PICTURE
Students with need: Need-based aid available for full-time and part-time students.
Students without need: This college awards aid only to students with need.

FINANCIAL AID PROCEDURES
Forms required: FAFSA.
Dates and Deadlines: Applicants notified on a rolling basis.

CONTACT
Scott Howard, Assistant Director of Student Finance
2300 SW 145th Avenue, Miramar, FL 33027
(954) 499-9700

DeVry University: Orlando
Orlando, Florida
www.devry.edu Federal Code: 022966

4-year for-profit university in very large city.
Enrollment: 1,327 undergrads, 59% part-time. 40 full-time freshmen.

BASIC COSTS (2012-2013)
Tuition and fees: $16,076.

FINANCIAL AID PICTURE
Students with need: Need-based aid available for full-time and part-time students.
Students without need: This college awards aid only to students with need.

FINANCIAL AID PROCEDURES
Forms required: FAFSA.
Dates and Deadlines: Applicants notified on a rolling basis.

CONTACT
Estrella Velasquez Domenech, Director of Student Finance
4000 Millennia Boulevard, Orlando, FL 32839-2426
(407) 345-2800

Digital Media Arts College
Boca Raton, Florida
www.dmac.edu

3-year for-profit visual arts college in large city.
Enrollment: 278 undergrads, 38% part-time. 50 full-time freshmen.
Selectivity: Open admission.

FINANCIAL AID PICTURE
Students with need: Need-based aid available for full-time and part-time students.
Students without need: No-need awards available for art.

FINANCIAL AID PROCEDURES
Forms required: FAFSA.
Dates and Deadlines: Applicants notified on a rolling basis starting 1/1; must reply within 4 week(s) of notification.
Transfers: No deadline. Applicants notified on a rolling basis starting 1/1.

CONTACT
Sharon Scheible, Director of Financial Aid
5400 Broken Sound Boulevard, Boca Raton, FL 33487

Eckerd College
St. Petersburg, Florida
www.eckerd.edu Federal Code: 001487

4-year private liberal arts college in large city, affiliated with Presbyterian Church (USA).
Enrollment: 1,866 undergrads, 2% part-time. 530 full-time freshmen.
Selectivity: Admits 50 to 75% of applicants.

BASIC COSTS (2013-2014)
Tuition and fees: $37,362.
Per-credit charge: $1,246.
Room and board: $10,144.

FINANCIAL AID PICTURE
Students with need: Need-based aid available for full-time and part-time students. Work study available nights, weekends, and for part-time students.
Students without need: No-need awards available for academics, art, athletics, music/drama, state/district residency.
Scholarships offered: Academic scholarships: ranging from $10,000 to $16,000 per year; available to entering freshmen regardless of financial need are awarded to outstanding incoming freshmen with strong scholastic records. Transfer scholarships are also available and range from $6,000-11,000. Limited number of Artistic Achievement Awards in music, theater, visual art and creative writing also available through separate application process. Freshman Research Associateships are also available.

FINANCIAL AID PROCEDURES
Forms required: FAFSA.
Dates and Deadlines: Priority date 3/1; no closing date. Applicants notified on a rolling basis starting 2/20.

CONTACT
Patricia Watkins, Director of Financial Aid
4200 54th Avenue South, St. Petersburg, FL 33711
(727) 864-8334

Edison State College
Fort Myers, Florida
www.edison.edu Federal Code: 001477

2-year public liberal arts college in very large city.
Enrollment: 12,456 undergrads.
Selectivity: Open admission; but selective for some programs.

BASIC COSTS (2012-2013)
Tuition and fees: $3,074; out-of-state residents $11,595.
Additional info: Reported tuition and fees for baccalaureate degree programs are slightly higher.

FINANCIAL AID PICTURE
Students with need: Need-based aid available for full-time and part-time students. Work study available nights, weekends, and for part-time students.
Students without need: No-need awards available for art, music/drama.

FINANCIAL AID PROCEDURES
Forms required: FAFSA.
Dates and Deadlines: Priority date 5/1; no closing date. Applicants notified on a rolling basis starting 6/1; must reply within 2 week(s) of notification.

CONTACT
Barry Paine, District Director of Financial Aid
Box 60210, Fort Myers, FL 33906-6210
(239) 489-9346

Edward Waters College
Jacksonville, Florida
www.ewc.edu Federal Code: 001478

4-year private liberal arts college in very large city, affiliated with African Methodist Episcopal Church.
Enrollment: 925 undergrads.

BASIC COSTS (2012-2013)
Tuition and fees: $11,158.
Per-credit charge: $465.
Room and board: $7,230.

FINANCIAL AID PICTURE

Students with need: Need-based aid available for full-time and part-time students. Work study available nights, weekends, and for part-time students.

FINANCIAL AID PROCEDURES

Forms required: FAFSA.

Dates and Deadlines: Closing date 4/15. Applicants notified on a rolling basis starting 5/1; must reply within 2 week(s) of notification.

CONTACT

Janice Nowak, Director of Financial Aid
1658 Kings Road, Jacksonville, FL 32209
(904) 470-8190

Embry-Riddle Aeronautical University

Daytona Beach, Florida
www.embryriddle.edu Federal Code: 001479

4-year private university in small city.
Enrollment: 4,499 undergrads, 6% part-time. 935 full-time freshmen.

BASIC COSTS (2013-2014)

Tuition and fees: $31,340.
Per-credit charge: $1,255.
Room and board: $10,310.

FINANCIAL AID PICTURE

Students with need: Need-based aid available for full-time and part-time students.

Students without need: No-need awards available for academics, alumni affiliation, athletics, leadership, ROTC.

FINANCIAL AID PROCEDURES

Forms required: FAFSA.

Dates and Deadlines: Applicants notified on a rolling basis starting 3/1; must reply within 4 week(s) of notification.

CONTACT

Barbara Dryden, Director of Financial Aid
600 South Clyde Morris Boulevard, Daytona Beach, FL 32114-3900
(386) 226-6300

Embry-Riddle Aeronautical University: Worldwide Campus

Daytona Beach, Florida
www.embryriddle.edu Federal Code: 001479

4-year private university in small city.
Enrollment: 10,861 undergrads, 74% part-time. 47 full-time freshmen.

BASIC COSTS (2012-2013)

Additional info: Per credit hour charges for undergraduates range from $250 - $350. Per credit hour charges for graduates range from $420 - $575.

FINANCIAL AID PICTURE

Students with need: Need-based aid available for full-time and part-time students.

Students without need: No-need awards available for academics.

FINANCIAL AID PROCEDURES

Forms required: FAFSA.

Dates and Deadlines: Priority date 4/15; no closing date. Applicants notified on a rolling basis starting 3/1; must reply within 4 week(s) of notification.

CONTACT

Barbara Dryden, Director of Financial Aid
600 South Clyde Morris Boulevard, Daytona Beach, FL 32114-3900
(866) 567-7202

Flagler College

Saint Augustine, Florida
www.flagler.edu Federal Code: 007893

4-year private liberal arts college in large town.
Enrollment: 2,848 undergrads, 3% part-time. 646 full-time freshmen.
Selectivity: Admits less than 50% of applicants.

BASIC COSTS (2012-2013)

Tuition and fees: $15,340.
Per-credit charge: $510.
Room and board: $8,350.

FINANCIAL AID PICTURE

Students with need: Need-based aid available for full-time and part-time students. Work study available nights, weekends, and for part-time students.

Students without need: No-need awards available for academics, art, athletics, job skills, leadership, minority status, music/drama, state/district residency.

FINANCIAL AID PROCEDURES

Forms required: FAFSA, state aid form, institutional form.

Dates and Deadlines: Priority date 4/1; no closing date. Applicants notified on a rolling basis starting 4/1; must reply within 2 week(s) of notification.

Transfers: No deadline. Applicants notified on a rolling basis starting 3/1; must reply within 2 week(s) of notification. Transfer students receiving Florida-sponsored aid must notify Florida Office of Student Financial Assistance of their transfer.

CONTACT

Christopher Haffner, Director of Financial Aid
74 King Street, St. Augustine, FL 32084
(800) 304-4208

Florida Agricultural and Mechanical University

Tallahassee, Florida
www.famu.edu Federal Code: 001480

4-year public university in small city.
Enrollment: 9,941 undergrads, 9% part-time. 1,497 full-time freshmen.
Selectivity: Admits less than 50% of applicants.

BASIC COSTS (2012-2013)

Tuition and fees: $5,785; out-of-state residents $17,726.
Room and board: $9,150.

FINANCIAL AID PICTURE (2011-2012)

Students with need: 61% of average financial aid package awarded as scholarships/grants, 39% awarded as loans/jobs. Need-based aid available for part-time students.

Students without need: No-need awards available for academics, art, athletics, leadership, music/drama, ROTC.

Cumulative student debt: 85% of graduating class had student loans; average debt was $29,702.

FINANCIAL AID PROCEDURES

Forms required: FAFSA.

Dates and Deadlines: Priority date 3/1; no closing date. Applicants notified on a rolling basis starting 4/15.

Transfers: No deadline. Applicants notified on a rolling basis starting 4/15.

CONTACT

Lisa Stewart, Director of Financial Aid
Foote-Hilyer Adminstration Center, G-9, Tallahassee, FL 32307-3200
(850) 599-3730

Florida Atlantic University

Boca Raton, Florida
www.fau.edu Federal Code: 001481

4-year public university in small city.
Enrollment: 24,057 undergrads, 36% part-time. 3,208 full-time freshmen.
Selectivity: Admits less than 50% of applicants.

BASIC COSTS (2012-2013)
Tuition and fees: $5,986; out-of-state residents $21,543.
Room and board: $11,353.

FINANCIAL AID PICTURE (2011-2012)
Students with need: Out of 2,940 full-time freshmen who applied for aid, 2,101 were judged to have need. Of these, 2,085 received aid, and 278 had their full need met. Average financial aid package met 65% of need; average scholarship/grant was $6,138; average loan was $5,025. For part-time students, average financial aid package was $9,469.
Students without need: 78 full-time freshmen who did not demonstrate need for aid received scholarships/grants; average award was $2,942. No-need awards available for academics, athletics, music/drama, state/district residency.
Scholarships offered: 42 full-time freshmen received athletic scholarships; average amount $9,017.

FINANCIAL AID PROCEDURES
Forms required: FAFSA.
Dates and Deadlines: Priority date 3/1; no closing date. Applicants notified on a rolling basis starting 4/1; must reply within 3 week(s) of notification.

CONTACT
Tracy Boulukos, Director of Financial Aid
777 Glades Road, Boca Raton, FL 33431
(561) 297-2738

Florida Christian College

Kissimmee, Florida
www.fcc.edu Federal Code: 015192

4-year private Bible and teachers college in small city, affiliated with Christian Churches/Churches of Christ.
Enrollment: 369 undergrads, 22% part-time. 79 full-time freshmen.
Selectivity: Admits less than 50% of applicants.

BASIC COSTS (2013-2014)
Tuition and fees: $15,320.
Per-credit charge: $475.
Room only: $3,200.

FINANCIAL AID PICTURE
Students with need: Need-based aid available for full-time and part-time students. Work study available nights, weekends, and for part-time students.
Students without need: No-need awards available for academics, alumni affiliation, leadership, music/drama, religious affiliation, state/district residency.

FINANCIAL AID PROCEDURES
Forms required: FAFSA, institutional form.
Dates and Deadlines: Priority date 5/1; closing date 7/15. Applicants notified on a rolling basis starting 3/1.
Transfers: Available only if funding remains.

CONTACT
Bryce Foulke, Director of Student Financial Aid
1011 Bill Beck Boulevard, Kissimmee, FL 34744-4402
(407) 569-1365

Florida College

Temple Terrace, Florida
www.floridacollege.edu Federal Code: 001482

4-year private liberal arts college in large town.
Enrollment: 532 undergrads, 5% part-time. 169 full-time freshmen.
Selectivity: Admits 50 to 75% of applicants.

BASIC COSTS (2013-2014)
Tuition and fees: $14,490.
Per-credit charge: $540.
Room and board: $7,438.

FINANCIAL AID PICTURE (2011-2012)
Students with need: Out of 151 full-time freshmen who applied for aid, 123 were judged to have need. Of these, 123 received aid, and 15 had their full need met. Average financial aid package met 42% of need; average scholarship/grant was $3,911; average loan was $2,569. For part-time students, average financial aid package was $3,850.
Students without need: 31 full-time freshmen who did not demonstrate need for aid received scholarships/grants; average award was $2,525. No-need awards available for academics, athletics, music/drama, state/district residency.
Scholarships offered: 20 full-time freshmen received athletic scholarships; average amount $2,818.

FINANCIAL AID PROCEDURES
Forms required: FAFSA, state aid form.
Dates and Deadlines: Closing date 9/30. Applicants notified on a rolling basis starting 9/30; must reply within 2 week(s) of notification.
Transfers: No deadline. Must reply within 2 week(s) of notification.

CONTACT
Stephen Blaylock, Financial Aid Director
119 North Glen Arven Avenue, Temple Terrace, FL 33617
(813) 988-5131 ext. 131

Florida College of Natural Health: Bradenton

Bradenton, Florida
www.fcnh.com

2-year for-profit health science and career college in small city.
Enrollment: 52 undergrads.
Selectivity: Open admission; but selective for some programs.

BASIC COSTS (2012-2013)
Additional info: Tuition for diploma programs range from $5,166 to $17,480 and programs leading to an associate degree range from $21,600-$22,986. $50 registration fee, books and supplies are not included.

FINANCIAL AID PICTURE
Students with need: Need-based aid available for full-time students.
Students without need: This college awards aid only to students with need.

FINANCIAL AID PROCEDURES
Forms required: FAFSA.
Dates and Deadlines: Applicants notified on a rolling basis.

CONTACT
Jason Sibley, Director
616 67th Street Circle East, Bradenton, FL 34208

Florida College of Natural Health: Maitland

Maitland, Florida
www.fcnh.com Federal Code: 030086

2-year for-profit health science and junior college in large town.
Enrollment: 646 undergrads.

BASIC COSTS (2012-2013)
Additional info: Tuition for diploma programs range from $5,166 to $17,480 and programs leading to an associate degree range from $21,600-$22,986. $50 registration fee, books and supplies are not included.

FINANCIAL AID PICTURE
Students with need: Need-based aid available for full-time students.
Students without need: This college awards aid only to students with need.

FINANCIAL AID PROCEDURES
Forms required: FAFSA.
Dates and Deadlines: Applicants notified on a rolling basis.

CONTACT
Lavern Walden, Director of Financial Aid
2600 Lake Lucien Drive; Suite 240, Maitland, FL 32751
(954) 975-6400

Florida Gateway College

Lake City, Florida
www.fgc.edu Federal Code: 001501

2-year public community college in large town.
Enrollment: 2,154 undergrads, 60% part-time. 165 full-time freshmen.
Selectivity: Open admission; but selective for some programs.

BASIC COSTS (2012-2013)
Tuition and fees: $3,069; out-of-state residents $11,717.
Additional info: Reported tuition and fees for baccalaureate degree programs are slightly higher. Tuition/fee waivers available for minority students.

FINANCIAL AID PICTURE
Students with need: Need-based aid available for full-time and part-time students.
Students without need: No-need awards available for academics, leadership, minority status, music/drama, state/district residency.
Scholarships offered: Top 20% Scholarship: $1000/yr.; top 20% of graduating class; complete 70% of all attempted classes and maintain cumulative GPA of 2.0. Florida Bright Futures Scholarship: must submit a completed (error-free) Florida Financial Aid Application during his/her last year in high school (after December 1 and prior to graduation).

FINANCIAL AID PROCEDURES
Forms required: FAFSA, institutional form.
Dates and Deadlines: Priority date 6/1; no closing date. Applicants notified on a rolling basis starting 6/1; must reply within 2 week(s) of notification.

CONTACT
Debberin Tunsil, Director of Financial Aid
149 SE College Place, Lake City, FL 32025-2007
(386) 754-4282

Florida Gulf Coast University

Ft. Myers, Florida
www.fgcu.edu Federal Code: 032553

4-year public university in small city.
Enrollment: 12,057 undergrads, 20% part-time. 2,534 full-time freshmen.
Selectivity: Admits 50 to 75% of applicants.

BASIC COSTS (2012-2013)
Tuition and fees: $6,068; out-of-state residents $25,112.
Room and board: $8,330.

FINANCIAL AID PICTURE (2011-2012)
Students with need: Out of 2,167 full-time freshmen who applied for aid, 1,382 were judged to have need. Of these, 1,382 received aid, and 130 had their full need met. Average financial aid package met 18% of need; average scholarship/grant was $4,998; average loan was $6,573. For part-time students, average financial aid package was $6,944.
Students without need: 100 full-time freshmen who did not demonstrate need for aid received scholarships/grants; average award was $3,427. No-need awards available for academics, alumni affiliation, athletics, leadership, minority status, music/drama, religious affiliation, state/district residency.
Scholarships offered: 17 full-time freshmen received athletic scholarships; average amount $6,301.
Cumulative student debt: 42% of graduating class had student loans; average debt was $27,308.

FINANCIAL AID PROCEDURES
Forms required: FAFSA, state aid form, institutional form.
Dates and Deadlines: Priority date 3/1; closing date 6/30. Applicants notified on a rolling basis starting 2/15.
Transfers: Applicants notified on a rolling basis.

CONTACT
Jorge Lopez-Rosado, Director of Student Financial Services
10501 FGCU Boulevard South, Ft. Myers, FL 33965-6565
(239) 590-7920

Florida Institute of Technology

Melbourne, Florida
www.fit.edu Federal Code: 001469

4-year private university in small city.
Enrollment: 2,887 undergrads, 4% part-time. 755 full-time freshmen.
Selectivity: Admits 50 to 75% of applicants.

BASIC COSTS (2012-2013)
Tuition and fees: $36,020.
Per-credit charge: $1,025.
Room and board: $12,270.

FINANCIAL AID PICTURE (2012-2013)
Students with need: Out of 544 full-time freshmen who applied for aid, 476 were judged to have need. Of these, 476 received aid, and 189 had their full need met. Average financial aid package met 86% of need; average scholarship/grant was $21,560; average loan was $3,488. For part-time students, average financial aid package was $14,185.
Students without need: 201 full-time freshmen who did not demonstrate need for aid received scholarships/grants; average award was $13,696. No-need awards available for academics, alumni affiliation, athletics, music/drama, ROTC, state/district residency.
Scholarships offered: 26 full-time freshmen received athletic scholarships; average amount $16,636.
Cumulative student debt: 61% of graduating class had student loans; average debt was $38,953.

FINANCIAL AID PROCEDURES
Forms required: FAFSA, state aid form.
Dates and Deadlines: Priority date 3/1; no closing date. Applicants notified on a rolling basis starting 2/15; must reply by 5/1 or within 4 week(s) of notification.
Transfers: No deadline. Applicants notified on a rolling basis starting 2/15; must reply by 5/1 or within 4 week(s) of notification.

CONTACT
Jay Lally, Director of Financial Aid
150 West University Boulevard, Melbourne, FL 32901-6975
(321) 674-8070

Florida International University

Miami, Florida
www.fiu.edu Federal Code: 009635

4-year public university in very large city.
Enrollment: 36,253 undergrads, 35% part-time. 4,113 full-time freshmen.
Selectivity: Admits less than 50% of applicants.

BASIC COSTS (2012-2013)
Tuition and fees: $6,418; out-of-state residents $18,816.
Room and board: $11,330.

FINANCIAL AID PICTURE
Students with need: Need-based aid available for full-time and part-time students. Work study available nights, weekends, and for part-time students.
Students without need: No-need awards available for academics, art, athletics, minority status, music/drama, state/district residency.

FINANCIAL AID PROCEDURES
Forms required: FAFSA.
Dates and Deadlines: Priority date 3/1; closing date 5/15. Applicants notified on a rolling basis; must reply by 5/1 or within 4 week(s) of notification.

CONTACT
Francisco Valines, Director of Financial Aid
Modesto Maidique Campus, PC 140, Miami, FL 33199
(305) 348-7272

Florida Keys Community College

Key West, Florida
www.fkcc.edu Federal Code: 001485

2-year public community college in large town.
Enrollment: 1,673 undergrads.
Selectivity: Open admission; but selective for some programs.

BASIC COSTS (2012-2013)
Tuition and fees: $3,276; out-of-state residents $13,161.

FINANCIAL AID PICTURE
Students with need: Need-based aid available for full-time and part-time students.
Students without need: No-need awards available for academics, art, leadership, minority status.

FINANCIAL AID PROCEDURES
Forms required: FAFSA, institutional form.
Dates and Deadlines: Priority date 5/1; no closing date. Applicants notified on a rolling basis starting 6/15; must reply within 2 week(s) of notification.
Transfers: Closing date 5/1. Florida Student Assistance Grant available to students paying Florida resident tuition.

CONTACT
Susan Urban, Director of Financial Aid
5901 College Road, Key West, FL 33040
(305) 809-3523

Florida National University

Hialeah, Florida
www.fnu.edu Federal Code: 017069

2-year for-profit junior college in very large city.
Enrollment: 2,392 undergrads, 24% part-time. 540 full-time freshmen.
Selectivity: Open admission; but selective for some programs.

BASIC COSTS (2012-2013)
Tuition and fees: $17,100.
Per-credit charge: $525.
Additional info: Tuition at time of enrollment locked for 2 years.

FINANCIAL AID PICTURE (2011-2012)
Students with need: Need-based aid available for part-time students.
Students without need: This college awards aid only to students with need.

FINANCIAL AID PROCEDURES
Forms required: FAFSA, institutional form.
Dates and Deadlines: Applicants notified on a rolling basis.

CONTACT
Omar Sanchez, Vice President of Assessment and Reasearch/Director of Financial Aid
4425 West Jose Regueiro (20th) Avenue, Hialeah, FL 33012
(305) 821-3333 ext. 1003

Florida Southern College

Lakeland, Florida
www.flsouthern.edu Federal Code: 001488

4-year private liberal arts college in small city, affiliated with United Methodist Church.
Enrollment: 2,021 undergrads, 2% part-time. 536 full-time freshmen.
Selectivity: Admits 50 to 75% of applicants.

BASIC COSTS (2012-2013)
Tuition and fees: $27,200.
Per-credit charge: $780.
Room and board: $9,100.

FINANCIAL AID PICTURE
Students with need: Need-based aid available for full-time and part-time students. Work study available nights, weekends, and for part-time students.
Students without need: No-need awards available for academics, alumni affiliation, art, athletics, job skills, leadership, minority status, music/drama, religious affiliation, ROTC, state/district residency.
Scholarships offered: McClug Scholarship: awarded annually to three first-time students; minimum SAT score of 1300 (exclusive of Writing) or ACT of 29; be in the top 5% of class. The Hollingsworth Scholarship: up to $10,000 towards tuition and fees; must have a minimum 1270 SAT (exclusive of Writing) or 28 ACT and minimum high school GPA of 3.5. The Alderman Scholarship: up to $9,000 towards tuition and fees ; based on high school GPA and SAT/ACT test scores.

FINANCIAL AID PROCEDURES
Forms required: FAFSA, institutional form.
Dates and Deadlines: Priority date 3/1; closing date 7/1. Applicants notified on a rolling basis starting 3/1; must reply within 3 week(s) of notification.
Transfers: No deadline. Applicants notified on a rolling basis; must reply within 2 week(s) of notification.

CONTACT
William Healy, Director of Financial Aid
111 Lake Hollingsworth Drive, Lakeland, FL 33801-5698
(863) 680-4140

Florida State College at Jacksonville
Jacksonville, Florida
www.fscj.edu Federal Code: 001484

2-year public community and junior college in very large city.
Enrollment: 26,634 undergrads, 66% part-time. 1,986 full-time freshmen.
Selectivity: Open admission; but selective for some programs.

BASIC COSTS (2012-2013)
Tuition and fees: $3,079; out-of-state residents $11,971.
Additional info: Bachelor's degree program costs are slightly higher than reported tuition and fees.

FINANCIAL AID PICTURE
Students with need: Need-based aid available for full-time and part-time students. Work study available nights, weekends, and for part-time students.
Students without need: No-need awards available for academics, alumni affiliation, art, athletics, job skills, leadership, minority status, music/drama.

FINANCIAL AID PROCEDURES
Forms required: FAFSA, institutional form.
Dates and Deadlines: Priority date 8/1; no closing date.

CONTACT
Peter Biegel, Director of Financial Aid
501 West State Street, Jacksonville, FL 32202
(904) 632-3154

Florida State University
Tallahassee, Florida
www.fsu.edu Federal Code: 001489

4-year public university in small city.
Enrollment: 31,652 undergrads, 10% part-time. 5,683 full-time freshmen.
Selectivity: Admits 50 to 75% of applicants.

BASIC COSTS (2012-2013)
Tuition and fees: $6,402; out-of-state residents $21,569.
Room and board: $9,626.

FINANCIAL AID PICTURE
Students with need: Need-based aid available for full-time and part-time students.
Students without need: No-need awards available for academics, athletics, state/district residency.

FINANCIAL AID PROCEDURES
Forms required: FAFSA.
Dates and Deadlines: Applicants notified on a rolling basis starting 3/15.

CONTACT
Darryl Marshall, Director of Financial Aid
PO Box 3062400, Tallahassee, FL 32306-2400
(850) 644-0539

Full Sail University
Winter Park, Florida
www.fullsail.edu Federal Code: 016812

4-year for-profit visual arts and music college in very large city.
Enrollment: 15,128 undergrads.
Selectivity: Open admission; but selective for some programs.

BASIC COSTS (2012-2013)
Additional info: Tuition ranges from $31,000-$80,500 for the entire degree program, including all books, lab fees, and other educational charges.

FINANCIAL AID PICTURE
Students with need: Need-based aid available for full-time students. Work study available nights, weekends, and for part-time students.

FINANCIAL AID PROCEDURES
Forms required: FAFSA.
Dates and Deadlines: Applicants notified on a rolling basis; must reply within 2 week(s) of notification.

CONTACT
3300 University Boulevard, Winter Park, FL 32792-7429
(407) 679-0100 ext. 2300

Gulf Coast State College
Panama City, Florida
www.gulfcoast.edu Federal Code: 001490

2-year public community college in small city.
Enrollment: 3,411 undergrads, 57% part-time. 382 full-time freshmen.
Selectivity: Open admission; but selective for some programs.

BASIC COSTS (2012-2013)
Tuition and fees: $2,844; out-of-state residents $10,691.
Additional info: Reported tuition and fees for baccalaureate degree programs are slightly higher.

FINANCIAL AID PICTURE (2011-2012)
Students with need: 73% of average financial aid package awarded as scholarships/grants, 27% awarded as loans/jobs. Need-based aid available for part-time students. Work study available nights, weekends, and for part-time students.
Students without need: No-need awards available for academics, athletics, job skills, leadership, minority status, music/drama, state/district residency.

FINANCIAL AID PROCEDURES
Forms required: FAFSA.
Dates and Deadlines: Priority date 5/15; closing date 7/1. Applicants notified on a rolling basis starting 7/1.
Transfers: Priority date 11/1; no deadline.

CONTACT
Chris Westlake, Director of Financial Aid
5230 West US Highway 98, Panama City, FL 32401-1041
(850) 872-3845

Hillsborough Community College
Tampa, Florida
www.hccfl.edu Federal Code: 007870

2-year public community college in large city.
Enrollment: 25,301 undergrads, 53% part-time. 3,450 full-time freshmen.
Selectivity: Open admission; but selective for some programs.

BASIC COSTS (2012-2013)
Tuition and fees: $3,116; out-of-state residents $11,372.

FINANCIAL AID PICTURE (2011-2012)
Students with need: 98% of average financial aid package awarded as scholarships/grants, 2% awarded as loans/jobs. Need-based aid available for part-time students. Work study available nights, weekends, and for part-time students.
Students without need: No-need awards available for academics, art, athletics, minority status, music/drama.

FINANCIAL AID PROCEDURES
Forms required: FAFSA, institutional form.
Dates and Deadlines: Priority date 7/13; closing date 8/10. Applicants notified on a rolling basis.

CONTACT
Tierra Smith, Director of Financial Aid
Box 31127, Tampa, FL 33631-3127
(877) 736-2575

Hobe Sound Bible College

Hobe Sound, Florida
www.hsbc.edu Federal Code: 015463

4-year private Bible college in small town, affiliated with interdenominational tradition.
Enrollment: 259 undergrads.

BASIC COSTS (2012-2013)
Tuition and fees: $5,440.
Per-credit charge: $215.
Room and board: $4,915.

FINANCIAL AID PICTURE
Students with need: Need-based aid available for full-time and part-time students.
Students without need: No-need awards available for academics, leadership.

FINANCIAL AID PROCEDURES
Forms required: FAFSA.
Dates and Deadlines: Closing date 8/1.

CONTACT
Joanna Wetherald, Director of Financial Aid
Box 1065, Hobe Sound, FL 33475
(772) 546-5534 ext. 1003

Hodges University

Naples, Florida
www.hodges.edu Federal Code: 030375

4-year private university in small city.
Enrollment: 2,058 undergrads, 32% part-time. 165 full-time freshmen.
Selectivity: Admits over 75% of applicants.

BASIC COSTS (2012-2013)
Tuition and fees: $15,200.
Per-credit charge: $490.

FINANCIAL AID PICTURE
Students with need: Need-based aid available for full-time and part-time students. Work study available nights, weekends, and for part-time students.
Students without need: No-need awards available for academics.

FINANCIAL AID PROCEDURES
Forms required: FAFSA.
Dates and Deadlines: Priority date 8/15; no closing date. Applicants notified on a rolling basis starting 7/7.
Transfers: No deadline. Applicants notified on a rolling basis.

CONTACT
Joe Gilchrist, Vice President of Student Financial Assistance
2655 Northbrooke Drive, Naples, FL 34119
(239) 513-1122

Indian River State College

Fort Pierce, Florida
www.irsc.edu Federal Code: 001493

2-year public community college in small city.
Enrollment: 14,177 undergrads, 62% part-time. 1,111 full-time freshmen.
Selectivity: Open admission; but selective for some programs.

BASIC COSTS (2012-2013)
Tuition and fees: $3,315; out-of-state residents $11,715.
Additional info: Reported tuition and fees for baccalaureate degree programs are slightly higher.

FINANCIAL AID PICTURE (2011-2012)
Students with need: Need-based aid available for full-time and part-time students.
Students without need: No-need awards available for academics, athletics, minority status, music/drama, state/district residency.

FINANCIAL AID PROCEDURES
Forms required: FAFSA, institutional form.
Dates and Deadlines: Priority date 7/18; no closing date. Applicants notified on a rolling basis starting 5/15.

CONTACT
Mary Lewis, Director of Financial Aid
3209 Virginia Avenue, Fort Pierce, FL 34981-5596
(772) 462-7450

International Academy of Design and Technology: Tampa

Tampa, Florida
www.academy.edu Federal Code: 030314

4-year for-profit visual arts and technical college in very large city.
Selectivity: Open admission.

BASIC COSTS (2012-2013)
Additional info: Effective May 2012: estimated total tuition for associate degree programs, $32,800; bachelor's degree programs, $64,800.

FINANCIAL AID PICTURE
Students with need: Need-based aid available for full-time and part-time students. Work study available nights, weekends, and for part-time students.
Students without need: No-need awards available for academics.

FINANCIAL AID PROCEDURES
Forms required: FAFSA.

CONTACT
Tim Coppola, Vice President of Finance
5104 Eisenhower Boulevard, Tampa, FL 33634
(813) 880-8056

Jacksonville University

Jacksonville, Florida
www.ju.edu Federal Code: 001495

4-year private university and liberal arts college in very large city.
Enrollment: 2,153 full-time undergrads.
Selectivity: Admits over 75% of applicants.

BASIC COSTS (2012-2013)
Tuition and fees: $29,100.
Per-credit charge: $966.
Room and board: $9,770.

FINANCIAL AID PICTURE
Students with need: Need-based aid available for full-time and part-time students. Work study available nights, weekends, and for part-time students.
Students without need: No-need awards available for academics, art, athletics, job skills, leadership, music/drama, ROTC, state/district residency.

FINANCIAL AID PROCEDURES
Forms required: FAFSA, state aid form, institutional form.

Dates and Deadlines: Priority date 3/15; no closing date. Applicants notified on a rolling basis starting 2/15.
Transfers: No deadline. Applicants notified on a rolling basis.

CONTACT
Catherine Huntress, Financial Aid Director
2800 University Boulevard North, Jacksonville, FL 32211-3394
(904) 256-7060

Johnson & Wales University: North Miami
North Miami, Florida
www.jwu.edu Federal Code: 003404

4-year private university in large city.
Enrollment: 1,990 undergrads, 3% part-time. 492 full-time freshmen.
Selectivity: Admits 50 to 75% of applicants.

BASIC COSTS (2013-2014)
Tuition and fees: $27,156.
Room and board: $10,140.

FINANCIAL AID PICTURE
Students with need: Need-based aid available for full-time and part-time students.
Students without need: No-need awards available for academics, alumni affiliation, leadership, state/district residency.

FINANCIAL AID PROCEDURES
Forms required: FAFSA.
Dates and Deadlines: Applicants notified on a rolling basis starting 3/1; must reply within 2 week(s) of notification.

CONTACT
Lynn Robinson, Director, Financial Aid
1701 Northeast 127th Street, North Miami, FL 33181
(800) 342-5598

Jones College
Jacksonville, Florida
www.jones.edu Federal Code: 001497

4-year private business college in very large city.
Enrollment: 489 undergrads, 87% part-time. 2 full-time freshmen.
Selectivity: Open admission.

BASIC COSTS (2012-2013)
Tuition and fees: $9,240.
Per-credit charge: $305.

FINANCIAL AID PICTURE
Students with need: Need-based aid available for full-time and part-time students. Work study available nights.
Students without need: This college awards aid only to students with need.

FINANCIAL AID PROCEDURES
Forms required: FAFSA.
Dates and Deadlines: Applicants notified on a rolling basis.

CONTACT
Becky Davis, Financial Assistant Director
5353 Arlington Expressway, Jacksonville, FL 32211
(904) 743-1122 ext. 100

Jose Maria Vargas University
Pembroke Pines, Florida
www.jmvu.edu Federal Code: 141620

4-year for-profit university in small city.
Enrollment: 33 undergrads, 64% part-time.
Selectivity: Open admission.

BASIC COSTS (2013-2014)
Tuition and fees: $6,320.
Per-credit charge: $240.

FINANCIAL AID PICTURE
Students with need: Need-based aid available for full-time and part-time students.
Students without need: No-need awards available for academics.

FINANCIAL AID PROCEDURES
Forms required: FAFSA, state aid form, institutional form.
Dates and Deadlines: Applicants notified on a rolling basis; must reply within 2 week(s) of notification.
Transfers: No deadline. Applicants notified on a rolling basis; must reply within 2 week(s) of notification.

CONTACT
Diane Castro, Director of Financial Aid
8300 South Palm Drive, Pembroke Pines, FL 33025
(954) 322-4460

Keiser University
Fort Lauderdale, Florida
www.keiseruniversity.edu Federal Code: 015159

2-year private health science and career college in large city.
Enrollment: 16,382 undergrads.

FINANCIAL AID PICTURE
Students with need: Need-based aid available for full-time and part-time students.

FINANCIAL AID PROCEDURES
Forms required: FAFSA.

CONTACT
1500 Northwest 49th Street, Fort Lauderdale, FL 33309
(954) 776-4456

Key College
Dania Beach, Florida
www.keycollege.edu Federal Code: 015191

2-year for-profit business and technical college in very large city.
Enrollment: 82 undergrads.

BASIC COSTS (2012-2013)
Tuition and fees: $11,085.
Additional info: Tuition at time of enrollment locked for 2 years.

FINANCIAL AID PICTURE
Students with need: Need-based aid available for full-time and part-time students.
Students without need: This college awards aid only to students with need.
Scholarships offered: Key College Scholarships and Employers Scholarships: merit based; approximately 10 scholarships of $1,000.00 each, awarded during the academic year.

Additional info: Federal Supplemental Educational Opportunities Grant (FSEOG), PELL grant, ACG, FFEL (federal loan program) available; direct loans offered.

FINANCIAL AID PROCEDURES

Forms required: FAFSA, institutional form.

CONTACT

Amber Young, Director of Financial Services
225 East Dania Beach Boulevard, Dania Beach, FL 33004-3046
(954) 923-4440

Lake-Sumter Community College

Leesburg, Florida
www.lscc.edu Federal Code: 001502

2-year public community college in small city.
Enrollment: 3,883 undergrads.
Selectivity: Open admission; but selective for some programs.

BASIC COSTS (2012-2013)

Tuition and fees: $3,142; out-of-state residents $13,246.

FINANCIAL AID PICTURE

Students with need: Need-based aid available for full-time and part-time students. Work study available nights.
Students without need: No-need awards available for academics, athletics, minority status, state/district residency.

FINANCIAL AID PROCEDURES

Forms required: FAFSA, institutional form.
Dates and Deadlines: Priority date 5/29; no closing date. Applicants notified on a rolling basis.
Transfers: No deadline. Applicants notified on a rolling basis.

CONTACT

Audrey Williams, Financial Aid Director
9501 U.S. Highway 441, Leesburg, FL 34788-8751
(352) 365-3512

Lynn University

Boca Raton, Florida
www.lynn.edu Federal Code: 001505

4-year private university in small city.
Enrollment: 1,626 undergrads, 8% part-time. 407 full-time freshmen.
Selectivity: Admits over 75% of applicants.

BASIC COSTS (2013-2014)

Tuition and fees: $33,400.
Room and board: $10,900.

FINANCIAL AID PICTURE (2012-2013)

Students with need: Average financial aid package met 50% of need; average scholarship/grant was $10,108; average loan was $4,012. For part-time students, average financial aid package was $7,055.
Students without need: No-need awards available for academics, alumni affiliation, athletics, leadership, music/drama.
Cumulative student debt: 35% of graduating class had student loans; average debt was $33,472.

FINANCIAL AID PROCEDURES

Forms required: FAFSA.
Dates and Deadlines: Priority date 3/1; no closing date. Applicants notified on a rolling basis starting 2/1; must reply within 2 week(s) of notification.

CONTACT

Chan Park, Director of Student Financial Assistance
3601 North Military Trail, Boca Raton, FL 33431-5598
(561) 237-7185

Miami Dade College

Miami, Florida
www.mdc.edu/main Federal Code: 001506

2-year public community college in very large city.
Enrollment: 62,050 undergrads, 59% part-time. 8,365 full-time freshmen.
Selectivity: Open admission; but selective for some programs.

BASIC COSTS (2012-2013)

Tuition and fees: $3,276; out-of-state residents $11,805.
Additional info: Reported tuition and fees for baccalaureate degree programs are slightly higher.

FINANCIAL AID PICTURE (2011-2012)

Students with need: Need-based aid available for full-time and part-time students. Work study available nights, weekends, and for part-time students.
Students without need: No-need awards available for academics, art, athletics, music/drama, state/district residency.

FINANCIAL AID PROCEDURES

Forms required: FAFSA.
Dates and Deadlines: Priority date 3/15; closing date 6/30. Applicants notified on a rolling basis starting 5/15.
Transfers: No deadline. Applicants notified on a rolling basis.

CONTACT

Mercedes Amaya, Collegewide Director of Financial Aid
11011 SW 104th Street, Miami, FL 33176-3393
(305) 237-0382

New College of Florida

Sarasota, Florida
www.ncf.edu Federal Code: 039574

4-year public liberal arts college in small city.
Enrollment: 832 undergrads. 223 full-time freshmen.
Selectivity: Admits 50 to 75% of applicants.

BASIC COSTS (2012-2013)

Tuition and fees: $6,783; out-of-state residents $29,812.
Room and board: $8,598.

FINANCIAL AID PICTURE (2012-2013)

Students with need: 66% of average financial aid package awarded as scholarships/grants, 34% awarded as loans/jobs. Work study available nights, weekends, and for part-time students.
Students without need: No-need awards available for academics, state/district residency.

FINANCIAL AID PROCEDURES

Forms required: FAFSA.
Dates and Deadlines: Priority date 2/15; no closing date. Applicants notified on a rolling basis starting 10/1; must reply by 5/1 or within 4 week(s) of notification.
Transfers: No deadline. Applicants notified on a rolling basis starting 10/1; must reply by 5/1 or within 4 week(s) of notification.

CONTACT

Tara Karas, Director of Financial Aid
5800 Bay Shore Road, Sarasota, FL 34243-2109
(941) 487-5000

North Florida Community College

Madison, Florida
www.nfcc.edu Federal Code: 001508

2-year public community college in rural community.
Enrollment: 1,302 undergrads.
Selectivity: Open admission; but selective for some programs.

BASIC COSTS (2012-2013)
Tuition and fees: $2,994; out-of-state residents $11,889.

FINANCIAL AID PICTURE
Students with need: Need-based aid available for full-time and part-time students. Work study available nights, weekends, and for part-time students.
Students without need: This college awards aid only to students with need.

FINANCIAL AID PROCEDURES
Forms required: FAFSA.
Dates and Deadlines: Priority date 5/15; no closing date. Applicants notified on a rolling basis starting 6/20; must reply within 2 week(s) of notification.

CONTACT
Amelia Mulkey, Director of Financial Aid
325 NW Turner Davis Drive, Madison, FL 32340
(850) 973-1621

Northwest Florida State College

Niceville, Florida
www.nwfsc.edu Federal Code: 001510

2-year public community and technical college in large town.
Enrollment: 5,931 undergrads, 56% part-time. 495 full-time freshmen.
Selectivity: Open admission.

BASIC COSTS (2012-2013)
Tuition and fees: $3,004; out-of-state residents $11,314.
Additional info: Reported tuition and fees for baccalaureate degree programs are slightly higher. Tuition/fee waivers available for minority students.

FINANCIAL AID PICTURE (2011-2012)
Students with need: 86% of average financial aid package awarded as scholarships/grants, 14% awarded as loans/jobs. Need-based aid available for part-time students.
Students without need: No-need awards available for academics, leadership, minority status, ROTC, state/district residency.

FINANCIAL AID PROCEDURES
Forms required: FAFSA, institutional form.
Dates and Deadlines: Priority date 4/1; no closing date. Applicants notified on a rolling basis starting 2/1; must reply within 2 week(s) of notification.
Transfers: Academic transcript evaluated to determine student eligibility for financial aid.

CONTACT
Pat Bennett, Director of Financial Aid
100 College Boulevard, Niceville, FL 32578-1347
(850) 729-5370

Northwood University: Florida

West Palm Beach, Florida
www.northwood.edu Federal Code: 013040

4-year private university and business college in small city.
Enrollment: 490 undergrads, 2% part-time. 103 full-time freshmen.
Selectivity: Admits 50 to 75% of applicants.

BASIC COSTS (2012-2013)
Tuition and fees: $20,996.
Per-credit charge: $776.
Room and board: $9,750.

FINANCIAL AID PICTURE (2012-2013)
Students with need: Out of 69 full-time freshmen who applied for aid, 63 were judged to have need. Of these, 63 received aid, and 16 had their full need met. Average financial aid package met 66% of need; average scholarship/grant was $7,779; average loan was $3,382. For part-time students, average financial aid package was $11,678.
Students without need: 18 full-time freshmen who did not demonstrate need for aid received scholarships/grants; average award was $10,567. No-need awards available for academics, athletics, leadership, minority status.
Scholarships offered: 21 full-time freshmen received athletic scholarships; average amount $6,069.
Cumulative student debt: 61% of graduating class had student loans; average debt was $27,505.

FINANCIAL AID PROCEDURES
Forms required: FAFSA, state aid form.
Dates and Deadlines: Priority date 2/1; no closing date.
Transfers: No deadline. Applicants notified on a rolling basis starting 3/1.

CONTACT
Hollie Crotts, Assistant Director
2600 North Military Trail, West Palm Beach, FL 33409-2911
(561) 478-5590

Nova Southeastern University

Fort Lauderdale, Florida
www.nova.edu Federal Code: 001509

4-year private university in small city.
Enrollment: 5,680 undergrads, 37% part-time. 610 full-time freshmen.
Selectivity: Admits 50 to 75% of applicants.

BASIC COSTS (2012-2013)
Tuition and fees: $24,500.
Per-credit charge: $795.
Room and board: $9,516.

FINANCIAL AID PICTURE
Students with need: Need-based aid available for full-time and part-time students. Work study available nights, weekends, and for part-time students.
Students without need: No-need awards available for academics, athletics, leadership, music/drama.

FINANCIAL AID PROCEDURES
Forms required: FAFSA, state aid form.
Dates and Deadlines: Priority date 4/15; no closing date. Applicants notified on a rolling basis starting 3/15.

CONTACT
Stephanie Brown, Associate Vice President, Enrollment and Student Services
3301 College Avenue, Fort Lauderdale, FL 33314
(954) 262-3380

Palm Beach Atlantic University

West Palm Beach, Florida
www.pba.edu Federal Code: 008849

4-year private university and liberal arts college in small city, affiliated with nondenominational tradition.
Enrollment: 2,334 undergrads, 6% part-time. 445 full-time freshmen.
Selectivity: Admits over 75% of applicants.

BASIC COSTS (2013-2014)
Tuition and fees: $25,532.
Room and board: $8,350.

FINANCIAL AID PICTURE (2012-2013)
Students with need: Out of 408 full-time freshmen who applied for aid, 329 were judged to have need. Of these, 329 received aid, and 44 had their full need met. Average financial aid package met 62.6% of need; average scholarship/grant was $15,229; average loan was $3,337. For part-time students, average financial aid package was $6,662.
Students without need: 114 full-time freshmen who did not demonstrate need for aid received scholarships/grants; average award was $8,285. No-need awards available for academics, art, athletics, leadership, music/drama, ROTC, state/district residency.
Scholarships offered: 21 full-time freshmen received athletic scholarships; average amount $12,541.
Cumulative student debt: 67% of graduating class had student loans; average debt was $24,750.

FINANCIAL AID PROCEDURES
Forms required: FAFSA, state aid form.
Dates and Deadlines: Priority date 5/1; no closing date. Applicants notified on a rolling basis starting 3/1; must reply by 5/1.
Transfers: Applicants notified on a rolling basis starting 3/1; must reply within 3 week(s) of notification. Florida residential undergraduate students eligible for grant from state if enrolled on full-time basis.

CONTACT
Todd Martin, Director, Student Financial Planning
PO Box 24708, West Palm Beach, FL 33416-4708
(561) 803-2126

Palm Beach State College
Lake Worth, Florida
www.palmbeachstate.edu Federal Code: 001512

2-year public community college in large town.
Enrollment: 26,520 undergrads, 63% part-time. 2,089 full-time freshmen.
Selectivity: Open admission; but selective for some programs.

BASIC COSTS (2012-2013)
Tuition and fees: $2,948; out-of-state residents $10,740.
Additional info: Reported tuition and fees for baccalaureate degree programs are slightly higher.

FINANCIAL AID PICTURE (2012-2013)
Students with need: 98% of average financial aid package awarded as scholarships/grants, 2% awarded as loans/jobs. Work study available nights, weekends, and for part-time students.
Students without need: No-need awards available for academics, alumni affiliation, athletics, leadership, state/district residency.

FINANCIAL AID PROCEDURES
Forms required: FAFSA, institutional form.
Dates and Deadlines: Priority date 7/1; no closing date. Applicants notified on a rolling basis; must reply within 2 week(s) of notification.

CONTACT
Susan Kadir, Director of Student Financial Aid
4200 Congress Avenue, Lake Worth, FL 33461
(561) 868-3330

Pasco-Hernando Community College
New Port Richey, Florida
www.phcc.edu Federal Code: 010652

2-year public community college in large town.
Enrollment: 10,795 undergrads.
Selectivity: Open admission; but selective for some programs.

BASIC COSTS (2012-2013)
Tuition and fees: $3,035; out-of-state residents $11,553.

FINANCIAL AID PICTURE (2012-2013)
Students with need: 79% of average financial aid package awarded as scholarships/grants, 21% awarded as loans/jobs. Need-based aid available for part-time students. Work study available nights, weekends, and for part-time students.
Students without need: No-need awards available for academics, athletics, minority status.
Additional info: Childcare assistance grants available to eligible students.

FINANCIAL AID PROCEDURES
Forms required: FAFSA.
Dates and Deadlines: Applicants notified on a rolling basis.

CONTACT
Rebecca Shanafelt, Director of Financial Aid/Veterans Services
10230 Ridge Road, New Port Richey, FL 34654-5199
(727) 816-3463

Pensacola State College
Pensacola, Florida
www.pensacolastate.edu Federal Code: 001513

2-year public community college in small city.
Enrollment: 9,502 undergrads, 54% part-time. 1,265 full-time freshmen.
Selectivity: Open admission; but selective for some programs.

BASIC COSTS (2012-2013)
Tuition and fees: $3,137; out-of-state residents $12,592.
Additional info: Bachelor's degree program costs are higher than reported tuition and fees.

FINANCIAL AID PICTURE
Students with need: Need-based aid available for full-time and part-time students.
Students without need: No-need awards available for academics, athletics, state/district residency.

FINANCIAL AID PROCEDURES
Forms required: FAFSA, institutional form.
Dates and Deadlines: Priority date 4/1; no closing date. Applicants notified on a rolling basis starting 7/1; must reply within 2 week(s) of notification.

CONTACT
Karen Kessler, Director of Financial Aid
1000 College Boulevard, Pensacola, FL 32504-8998
(850) 484-1680

Polk State College
Winter Haven, Florida
www.polk.edu Federal Code: 001514

2-year public community college in large town.
Enrollment: 9,413 undergrads, 62% part-time. 714 full-time freshmen.
Selectivity: Open admission; but selective for some programs.

BASIC COSTS (2012-2013)
Tuition and fees: $3,306; out-of-state residents $12,211.
Additional info: Reported tuition and fees for baccalaureate degree programs are slightly higher.

FINANCIAL AID PICTURE
Students with need: Need-based aid available for full-time and part-time students. Work study available nights, weekends, and for part-time students.

Students without need: No-need awards available for academics, athletics, leadership, state/district residency.

FINANCIAL AID PROCEDURES

Forms required: FAFSA.

Dates and Deadlines: Priority date 5/15; no closing date. Applicants notified on a rolling basis.

CONTACT

Marcia Conliffe, Director of Student Financial Services
999 Avenue H NE, Winter Haven, FL 33881-4299
(863) 298-6850

Rasmussen College: Fort Myers

Fort Myers, Florida
www.rasmussen.edu

4-year for-profit technical college in small city.
Enrollment: 765 undergrads.
Selectivity: Open admission; but selective for some programs.

BASIC COSTS (2012-2013)

Tuition and fees: $15,750.
Per-credit charge: $350.
Additional info: Full-time tuition varies according to program of study. Examples of per-credit-hour charges include Early Childhood Education or Medical Assisting ($310). Criminal Justice, Information Systems Mgmt, Multimedia Technician ($350). Professional Nursing ($395). Accounting, Marketing, Paralegal ($350).

FINANCIAL AID PICTURE

Students with need: Need-based aid available for full-time and part-time students.

FINANCIAL AID PROCEDURES

Forms required: FAFSA, institutional form.
Dates and Deadlines: Applicants notified on a rolling basis.

CONTACT

Debora Murray, Director of Financial Aid
9160 Forum Corporate Parkway, Suite 100, Fort Myers, FL 33905-7805

Rasmussen College: New Port Richey

New Port Richey, Florida
www.rasmussen.edu Federal Code: 008501

4-year for-profit career college in small city.
Enrollment: 874 undergrads.
Selectivity: Open admission; but selective for some programs.

BASIC COSTS (2012-2013)

Tuition and fees: $15,750.
Per-credit charge: $350.
Additional info: Full-time tuition varies according to program of study. Examples of per-credit-hour charges include Early Childhood Education or Medical Assisting ($310), Criminal Justice, Information Systems Mgmt, Multimedia Technician ($350). Accounting, Marketing, Paralegal ($350).

FINANCIAL AID PICTURE

Students with need: Need-based aid available for full-time and part-time students.

FINANCIAL AID PROCEDURES

Forms required: FAFSA, institutional form.
Dates and Deadlines: Applicants notified on a rolling basis.

CONTACT

Debora Murray, Director of Student Financial Services
8661 Citizens Drive, New Port Richey, FL 34654
(727) 942-0069

Rasmussen College: Ocala

Ocala, Florida
www.rasmussen.edu Federal Code: 008501

4-year for-profit career college in small city.
Enrollment: 3,715 undergrads.
Selectivity: Open admission; but selective for some programs.

BASIC COSTS (2012-2013)

Tuition and fees: $15,750.
Per-credit charge: $350.
Additional info: Full-time tuition varies according to program of study. Examples of per-credit-hour charges include Early Childhood Education or Medical Assisting ($310), Criminal Justice, Information Systems Mgmt, Multimedia Technician ($350). Professional Nursing ($395). Accounting, Marketing, Paralegal ($350).

FINANCIAL AID PICTURE

Students with need: Need-based aid available for full-time and part-time students.

FINANCIAL AID PROCEDURES

Forms required: FAFSA, institutional form.
Dates and Deadlines: Applicants notified on a rolling basis.

CONTACT

Debora Murray, Director of Financial Aid
2221 Southwest 46th Court, Ocala, FL 34474
(352) 629-1941 ext. 130

Rasmussen College: Tampa/Brandon

Tampa, Florida
www.rasmussen.edu

4-year for-profit branch campus and career college in large city.
Enrollment: 293 undergrads.
Selectivity: Open admission; but selective for some programs.

BASIC COSTS (2012-2013)

Tuition and fees: $15,750.
Per-credit charge: $350.
Additional info: Full-time tuition varies according to program of study. Examples of per-credit-hour charges include Early Childhood Education or Medical Assisting ($310), Criminal Justice, Information Systems Mgmt, Multimedia Technician ($350). Accounting, Marketing, Paralegal ($350).

FINANCIAL AID PICTURE

Students with need: Need-based aid available for full-time and part-time students.

FINANCIAL AID PROCEDURES

Forms required: FAFSA, institutional form.
Dates and Deadlines: Applicants notified on a rolling basis.

CONTACT

Debora Murray, Financial Aid Director
4042 Park Oak Boulevard, Tampa, FL 33610

Ringling College of Art and Design

Sarasota, Florida
www.ringling.edu
Federal Code: 012574

4-year private visual arts college in small city.
Enrollment: 1,364 undergrads, 4% part-time. 312 full-time freshmen.
Selectivity: Admits 50 to 75% of applicants.

BASIC COSTS (2012-2013)
Tuition and fees: $36,680.
Per-credit charge: $1,583.
Room and board: $12,670.

FINANCIAL AID PICTURE (2012-2013)
Students with need: Average financial aid package met 37% of need; average scholarship/grant was $9,762; average loan was $6,709. For part-time students, average financial aid package was $17,616.
Students without need: No-need awards available for academics, art.
Cumulative student debt: 73% of graduating class had student loans; average debt was $48,515.

FINANCIAL AID PROCEDURES
Forms required: FAFSA.
Dates and Deadlines: Priority date 3/1; no closing date. Applicants notified on a rolling basis starting 4/1; must reply within 2 week(s) of notification.
Transfers: No deadline. Applicants notified on a rolling basis starting 3/1; must reply within 2 week(s) of notification.

CONTACT
Kurt Wolf, Director of Financial Aid
2700 North Tamiami Trail, Sarasota, FL 34234-5895
(941) 359-7534

Rollins College

Winter Park, Florida
www.rollins.edu
Federal Code: 001515

4-year private business and liberal arts college in large town.
Enrollment: 1,884 undergrads. 518 full-time freshmen.
Selectivity: Admits 50 to 75% of applicants.

BASIC COSTS (2013-2014)
Tuition and fees: $41,460.
Room and board: $12,960.

FINANCIAL AID PICTURE (2012-2013)
Students with need: Out of 357 full-time freshmen who applied for aid, 276 were judged to have need. Of these, 276 received aid, and 171 had their full need met. Average financial aid package met 82% of need; average scholarship/grant was $29,818; average loan was $4,045. Need-based aid available for part-time students.
Students without need: 153 full-time freshmen who did not demonstrate need for aid received scholarships/grants; average award was $19,727. No-need awards available for academics, art, athletics, leadership, music/drama, state/district residency.
Scholarships offered: ***Merit:*** Presidential, Alonzo Rollins: $4,000-$15,000 per year; based on academic record; 130 available per year. Donald Cram: $3,000-$5,000 per year; based on academic record, science major; 10 available per year. ***Athletic:*** 39 full-time freshmen received athletic scholarships; average amount $17,541.
Cumulative student debt: 46% of graduating class had student loans; average debt was $24,096.
Additional info: Audition required for theater arts and music scholarship applicants. Portfolio required for art scholarships.

FINANCIAL AID PROCEDURES
Forms required: FAFSA.
Dates and Deadlines: Priority date 3/1; no closing date. Applicants notified on a rolling basis starting 3/1.
Transfers: Priority date 4/15; no deadline.

CONTACT
Steve Booker, Director of Financial Aid
1000 Holt Avenue, Campus Box 2720, Winter Park, FL 32789
(407) 646-2395

Saint Johns River State College

Palatka, Florida
www.sjrstate.edu
Federal Code: 001523

2-year public community college in large town.
Enrollment: 5,247 undergrads, 59% part-time. 739 full-time freshmen.
Selectivity: Open admission; but selective for some programs.

BASIC COSTS (2012-2013)
Tuition and fees: $3,120; out-of-state residents $11,608.
Additional info: Baccalaureate programs tuition and fees are slightly higher.

FINANCIAL AID PICTURE
Students with need: Need-based aid available for full-time and part-time students.

FINANCIAL AID PROCEDURES
Forms required: FAFSA.
Dates and Deadlines: Priority date 7/1; no closing date. Applicants notified on a rolling basis.

CONTACT
Wayne Bodiford, Director of Financial Aid/Veteran Affairs
5001 St. Johns Avenue, Palatka, FL 32177-3897
(386) 312-4040

Saint Leo University

Saint Leo, Florida
www.saintleo.edu
Federal Code: 001526

4-year private university in rural community, affiliated with Roman Catholic Church.
Enrollment: 2,162 undergrads, 3% part-time. 634 full-time freshmen.
Selectivity: Admits over 75% of applicants.

BASIC COSTS (2012-2013)
Tuition and fees: $19,070.
Room and board: $9,394.

FINANCIAL AID PICTURE (2012-2013)
Students with need: Out of 536 full-time freshmen who applied for aid, 459 were judged to have need. Of these, 458 received aid, and 80 had their full need met. Average financial aid package met 71% of need; average scholarship/grant was $14,342; average loan was $3,328. For part-time students, average financial aid package was $11,904.
Students without need: 132 full-time freshmen who did not demonstrate need for aid received scholarships/grants; average award was $6,328. No-need awards available for academics, alumni affiliation, athletics, leadership, minority status, religious affiliation, state/district residency.
Scholarships offered: 22 full-time freshmen received athletic scholarships; average amount $14,115.
Cumulative student debt: 72% of graduating class had student loans; average debt was $27,324.

FINANCIAL AID PROCEDURES
Forms required: FAFSA.
Dates and Deadlines: Priority date 3/1; no closing date. Applicants notified on a rolling basis starting 1/31.

CONTACT

Brenda Wright, Chief Operating Officer, University Financial Aid Solutions
Box 6665 MC2008, Saint Leo, FL 33574-6665
(800) 240-7658

St. Petersburg College

Saint Petersburg, Florida
www.spcollege.edu Federal Code: 001528

2-year public community college in large city.
Enrollment: 28,371 undergrads.
Selectivity: Open admission; but selective for some programs.

BASIC COSTS (2012-2013)

Tuition and fees: $3,172; out-of-state residents $11,427.
Additional info: Tuition and fees for baccalaureate degree programs are slightly higher.

FINANCIAL AID PICTURE

Students with need: Need-based aid available for full-time and part-time students. Work study available nights, weekends, and for part-time students.
Students without need: No-need awards available for academics, art, athletics, minority status, music/drama.

FINANCIAL AID PROCEDURES

Forms required: FAFSA, state aid form.
Dates and Deadlines: Priority date 4/15; no closing date. Applicants notified on a rolling basis starting 5/15; must reply within 2 week(s) of notification.

CONTACT

Michael Bennett, Associate Vice-President Financial Aid Services
Box 13489, St. Petersburg, FL 33733-3489
(727) 791-2485

Santa Fe College

Gainesville, Florida
www.sfcollege.edu Federal Code: 001519

2-year public community college in small city.
Enrollment: 14,093 undergrads.
Selectivity: Open admission; but selective for some programs.

BASIC COSTS (2012-2013)

Tuition and fees: $2,951; out-of-state residents $11,202.
Additional info: Reported tuition and fees for baccalaureate degree programs are slightly higher. Tuition/fee waivers available for minority students.

FINANCIAL AID PICTURE

Students with need: Need-based aid available for full-time and part-time students.
Students without need: No-need awards available for academics, art, athletics, leadership, minority status, music/drama, state/district residency.

FINANCIAL AID PROCEDURES

Forms required: FAFSA.
Dates and Deadlines: Priority date 3/15; closing date 6/30. Applicants notified by 8/1.
Transfers: Must have minimum 2.0 GPA to be eligible for financial aid.

CONTACT

Maureen McFarlane, Director of Financial Aid
3000 NW 83rd Street, R-112, Gainesville, FL 32606-6210
(352) 395-5480

Schiller International University

Largo, Florida
www.schiller.edu Federal Code: 023141

4-year for-profit university in small city.
Enrollment: 101 undergrads.
Selectivity: Open admission.

FINANCIAL AID PICTURE (2011-2012)

Students with need: Need-based aid available for full-time and part-time students. Work study available nights.
Students without need: No-need awards available for academics, alumni affiliation, leadership, minority status, state/district residency.
Scholarships offered: One-fourth tuition awards available to students possessing an outstanding academic record and who exhibit excellent potential for academic achievement; 50 available for one or two semesters. Knowledge Tuition Awards; one-fourth tuition; available to students with good academic records and financial need; 20 available for one or two semesters.
Additional info: Special scholarship program for US students studying abroad at European campuses of Schiller. Work-study available to students taking 2 or more courses.

FINANCIAL AID PROCEDURES

Forms required: FAFSA, state aid form, institutional form.
Dates and Deadlines: Closing date 4/1. Applicants notified on a rolling basis starting 5/1; must reply within 3 week(s) of notification.
Transfers: No deadline. Applicants notified on a rolling basis.

CONTACT

Andre Sergeyev, Financial Aid Advisor
8560 Ulmerton Road, Largo, FL 33771
(727) 736-5082 ext. 253

Seminole State College of Florida

Sanford, Florida
www.seminolestate.edu Federal Code: 001520

2-year public community college in large town.
Enrollment: 17,810 undergrads, 58% part-time. 1,780 full-time freshmen.
Selectivity: Open admission; but selective for some programs.

BASIC COSTS (2012-2013)

Tuition and fees: $3,074; out-of-state residents $11,399.
Additional info: Reported tuition and fees for baccalaureate degree programs are slightly higher.

FINANCIAL AID PICTURE (2011-2012)

Students with need: 47% of average financial aid package awarded as scholarships/grants, 53% awarded as loans/jobs. Need-based aid available for part-time students.
Students without need: No-need awards available for academics, art, athletics, leadership, minority status, music/drama, state/district residency.

FINANCIAL AID PROCEDURES

Forms required: FAFSA.
Dates and Deadlines: Priority date 7/1; no closing date. Applicants notified on a rolling basis starting 4/1.
Transfers: Priority date 5/31. Applicants notified on a rolling basis starting 4/1.

CONTACT

Carmen Afghani, Director of Financial Aid
100 Weldon Boulevard, Sanford, FL 32773-6199
(407) 708-4722 ext. 3422

South Florida Community College

Avon Park, Florida
www.southflorida.edu Federal Code: 001522

2-year public community and technical college in small town.
Enrollment: 2,057 undergrads, 54% part-time. 226 full-time freshmen.
Selectivity: Open admission; but selective for some programs.

BASIC COSTS (2012-2013)
Tuition and fees: $3,135; out-of-state residents $11,829.
Additional info: Tuition/fee waivers available for minority students.

FINANCIAL AID PICTURE (2011-2012)
Students with need: 92% of average financial aid package awarded as scholarships/grants, 8% awarded as loans/jobs. Need-based aid available for part-time students.
Students without need: No-need awards available for academics, athletics, leadership, minority status, music/drama, state/district residency.

FINANCIAL AID PROCEDURES
Forms required: FAFSA.
Dates and Deadlines: Priority date 4/15; no closing date. Applicants notified on a rolling basis starting 4/1.
Transfers: Students must maintain satisfactory academic progress.

CONTACT
Susie Johnson, Director of Financial Aid
600 West College Drive, Avon Park, FL 33825
(863) 453-6661 ext. 7254

South University: West Palm Beach

Royal Palm Beach, Florida
www.southuniversity.edu

4-year for-profit university in large city.
Enrollment: 895 undergrads.

BASIC COSTS (2012-2013)
Tuition and fees: $16,585.
Additional info: Tuition and fees are representative of most campus degree programs.

FINANCIAL AID PICTURE
Students with need: Need-based aid available for full-time and part-time students. Work study available nights.

FINANCIAL AID PROCEDURES
Forms required: FAFSA.
Dates and Deadlines: Applicants notified on a rolling basis; must reply within 2 week(s) of notification.

CONTACT
Kacey Atkinson, Director of Student Financial Services
9801 Belvedere Road, Royal Palm Beach, FL 33411

Southeastern University

Lakeland, Florida
www.seu.edu Federal Code: 001521

4-year private liberal arts and teachers college in small city, affiliated with Assemblies of God.
Enrollment: 2,266 undergrads, 7% part-time. 562 full-time freshmen.
Selectivity: Admits less than 50% of applicants.

BASIC COSTS (2013-2014)
Tuition and fees: $19,986.
Room and board: $8,648.

FINANCIAL AID PICTURE (2011-2012)
Students with need: Out of 497 full-time freshmen who applied for aid, 431 were judged to have need. Of these, 429 received aid, and 56 had their full need met. Average financial aid package met 64% of need; average scholarship/grant was $12,629; average loan was $3,350. For part-time students, average financial aid package was $5,839.
Students without need: 79 full-time freshmen who did not demonstrate need for aid received scholarships/grants; average award was $5,796. No-need awards available for academics, athletics, leadership, music/drama, ROTC.
Scholarships offered: 16 full-time freshmen received athletic scholarships; average amount $7,007.
Cumulative student debt: 79% of graduating class had student loans; average debt was $35,594.

FINANCIAL AID PROCEDURES
Forms required: FAFSA, state aid form, institutional form.
Dates and Deadlines: Priority date 4/15; no closing date. Applicants notified on a rolling basis starting 1/1; must reply within 6 week(s) of notification.
Transfers: Must reply within 6 week(s) of notification.

CONTACT
Rebekah Burdick, Director of Student Financial Services
1000 Longfellow Boulevard, Lakeland, FL 33801-6034
(863) 667-5024

Southwest Florida College

Fort Myers, Florida
www.swfc.edu Federal Code: 016068

2-year private career college in large city.
Enrollment: 1,284 undergrads.
Selectivity: Open admission; but selective for some programs.

BASIC COSTS (2012-2013)
Tuition and fees: $16,875.
Per-credit charge: $350.

FINANCIAL AID PICTURE
Students with need: Need-based aid available for full-time and part-time students. Work study available nights, weekends, and for part-time students.

FINANCIAL AID PROCEDURES
Forms required: FAFSA.
Dates and Deadlines: Applicants notified on a rolling basis.
Transfers: No deadline. Applicants notified on a rolling basis.

CONTACT
Laura Selvey, Director of Financial Aid
1685 Medical Lane, Ft. Myers, FL 33907-1108
(813) 630-4401

State College of Florida, Manatee-Sarasota

Bradenton, Florida
www.scf.edu Federal Code: 001504

2-year public nursing and community college in small city.
Enrollment: 9,719 undergrads, 56% part-time. 886 full-time freshmen.
Selectivity: Open admission; but selective for some programs.

BASIC COSTS (2012-2013)
Tuition and fees: $3,074; out-of-state residents $11,595.
Additional info: Slightly higher tuition and fees for baccalaureate degree programs.

FINANCIAL AID PICTURE

Students with need: Need-based aid available for full-time and part-time students. Work study available nights, weekends, and for part-time students.

Students without need: No-need awards available for academics, art, athletics, music/drama, state/district residency.

FINANCIAL AID PROCEDURES

Forms required: FAFSA.

Dates and Deadlines: Priority date 6/1; closing date 7/28. Applicants notified on a rolling basis starting 3/15.

CONTACT

Jack Toney, Director of Financial Aid
Box 1849, Bradenton, FL 34206-1849

Stetson University

DeLand, Florida
www.stetson.edu Federal Code: 001531

4-year private university in large town.
Enrollment: 2,508 undergrads, 2% part-time. 817 full-time freshmen.
Selectivity: Admits 50 to 75% of applicants.

BASIC COSTS (2012-2013)

Tuition and fees: $36,644.
Per-credit charge: $946.
Room and board: $10,688.

FINANCIAL AID PICTURE

Students with need: Need-based aid available for full-time and part-time students.

Students without need: No-need awards available for academics, alumni affiliation, art, athletics, leadership, minority status, music/drama, religious affiliation, ROTC, state/district residency.

FINANCIAL AID PROCEDURES

Forms required: FAFSA, institutional form.

Dates and Deadlines: Priority date 3/15; no closing date. Applicants notified on a rolling basis starting 2/15; must reply within 2 week(s) of notification.

CONTACT

Tara Jones, Director of Financial Aid
Campus Box 8378, DeLand, FL 32723
(386) 822-7120

Tallahassee Community College

Tallahassee, Florida
www.tcc.fl.edu Federal Code: 001533

2-year public community college in small city.
Enrollment: 12,952 undergrads, 48% part-time. 1,543 full-time freshmen.
Selectivity: Open admission; but selective for some programs.

BASIC COSTS (2012-2013)

Tuition and fees: $2,965; out-of-state residents $11,280.

FINANCIAL AID PICTURE (2011-2012)

Students with need: 49% of average financial aid package awarded as scholarships/grants, 51% awarded as loans/jobs. Need-based aid available for part-time students. Work study available nights.

Students without need: No-need awards available for academics, art, athletics, leadership, music/drama, state/district residency.

FINANCIAL AID PROCEDURES

Forms required: FAFSA, institutional form.

Dates and Deadlines: Priority date 5/1; no closing date. Applicants notified on a rolling basis starting 5/15.

CONTACT

William Spiers, Director of Financial Aid
444 Appleyard Drive, Tallahassee, FL 32304
(850) 201-8399

Trinity College of Florida

Trinity, Florida
www.trinitycollege.edu

4-year private Bible college in small city, affiliated with interdenominational tradition.
Enrollment: 212 undergrads, 11% part-time. 27 full-time freshmen.
Selectivity: Admits less than 50% of applicants.

BASIC COSTS (2013-2014)

Tuition and fees: $13,320.
Per-credit charge: $522.
Room and board: $7,066.

FINANCIAL AID PICTURE (2012-2013)

Students with need: Out of 25 full-time freshmen who applied for aid, 23 were judged to have need. Of these, 23 received aid. Average financial aid package met 48% of need; average scholarship/grant was $6,674; average loan was $3,495. For part-time students, average financial aid package was $5,612.

Students without need: 1 full-time freshmen who did not demonstrate need for aid received scholarships/grants; average award was $300. No-need awards available for academics.

Cumulative student debt: 25% of graduating class had student loans; average debt was $5,500.

FINANCIAL AID PROCEDURES

Forms required: FAFSA, institutional form.

Dates and Deadlines: Priority date 3/15; closing date 9/15. Applicants notified on a rolling basis starting 1/5; must reply within 2 week(s) of notification.

Transfers: No deadline. Applicants notified on a rolling basis starting 1/5; must reply within 2 week(s) of notification.

CONTACT

Sue Wayne, Financial Aid Director
2430 Welbilt Boulevard, Trinity, FL 34655-4401
(727) 376-6911 ext. 310

University of Central Florida

Orlando, Florida
www.ucf.edu Federal Code: 003954

4-year public university in very large city.
Enrollment: 50,722 undergrads, 28% part-time. 6,144 full-time freshmen.
Selectivity: Admits less than 50% of applicants.

BASIC COSTS (2012-2013)

Tuition and fees: $6,246; out-of-state residents $22,345.
Room and board: $9,357.

FINANCIAL AID PICTURE (2011-2012)

Students with need: Out of 6,025 full-time freshmen who applied for aid, 4,876 were judged to have need. Of these, 4,830 received aid, and 812 had their full need met. Average financial aid package met 58% of need; average scholarship/grant was $4,788; average loan was $3,419. For part-time students, average financial aid package was $5,374.

Students without need: 277 full-time freshmen who did not demonstrate need for aid received scholarships/grants; average award was $2,945. No-need awards available for academics, alumni affiliation, athletics, leadership, ROTC, state/district residency.

Scholarships offered: ***Merit:*** Academic scholarships: $2,000-$24,000 over 4-year period, freshmen automatically considered. ***Athletic:*** 60 full-time freshmen received athletic scholarships; average amount $9,915.
Cumulative student debt: 46% of graduating class had student loans; average debt was $20,086.

FINANCIAL AID PROCEDURES

Forms required: FAFSA.
Dates and Deadlines: Priority date 3/1; closing date 6/30. Applicants notified on a rolling basis starting 3/15; must reply within 3 week(s) of notification.

CONTACT

Mary McKinney, Executive Director of Financial Aid
Box 160111, Orlando, FL 32816-0111
(407) 823-2827

University of Florida

Gainesville, Florida
www.ufl.edu Federal Code: 001535

4-year public university in small city.
Enrollment: 32,023 undergrads, 6% part-time. 6,396 full-time freshmen.
Selectivity: Admits less than 50% of applicants.

BASIC COSTS (2012-2013)

Tuition and fees: $6,143; out-of-state residents $28,420.
Room and board: $9,370.

FINANCIAL AID PICTURE (2011-2012)

Students with need: Out of 6,198 full-time freshmen who applied for aid, 3,791 were judged to have need. Of these, 3,786 received aid, and 881 had their full need met. Average financial aid package met 74% of need; average scholarship/grant was $6,298; average loan was $3,737. Need-based aid available for part-time students.
Students without need: 366 full-time freshmen who did not demonstrate need for aid received scholarships/grants; average award was $2,923. No-need awards available for academics, alumni affiliation, art, athletics, leadership, minority status, music/drama, ROTC, state/district residency.
Scholarships offered: 105 full-time freshmen received athletic scholarships; average amount $13,056.
Cumulative student debt: 41% of graduating class had student loans; average debt was $19,636.

FINANCIAL AID PROCEDURES

Forms required: FAFSA.
Dates and Deadlines: Priority date 3/15; no closing date. Applicants notified on a rolling basis starting 4/1.
Transfers: Closing date 3/15. Applicants notified on a rolling basis starting 4/1.

CONTACT

Richard Wilder, Director of Student Financial Aid
201 Criser Hall-PO Box 114000, Gainesville, FL 32611-4000
(352) 392-1275

University of Miami

Coral Gables, Florida
www.miami.edu Federal Code: 001536

4-year private university in large town.
Enrollment: 10,237 undergrads, 5% part-time. 1,987 full-time freshmen.
Selectivity: Admits less than 50% of applicants.

BASIC COSTS (2013-2014)

Tuition and fees: $42,852.
Per-credit charge: $1,730.
Room and board: $12,314.

FINANCIAL AID PICTURE (2012-2013)

Students with need: Out of 1,371 full-time freshmen who applied for aid, 950 were judged to have need. Of these, 950 received aid, and 431 had their full need met. Average financial aid package met 83% of need; average scholarship/grant was $25,561; average loan was $4,479. For part-time students, average financial aid package was $20,510.
Students without need: 422 full-time freshmen who did not demonstrate need for aid received scholarships/grants; average award was $19,874. No-need awards available for academics, athletics, leadership, music/drama.
Scholarships offered: 48 full-time freshmen received athletic scholarships; average amount $26,823.
Cumulative student debt: 45% of graduating class had student loans; average debt was $26,786.

FINANCIAL AID PROCEDURES

Forms required: FAFSA.
Dates and Deadlines: Priority date 2/1; no closing date. Applicants notified on a rolling basis starting 3/15.
Transfers: Priority date 3/1. Applicants notified by 4/1.

CONTACT

James Bauer, Executive Director, Office of Financial Assistance Services
PO Box 248025, Coral Gables, FL 33124-4616
(305) 284-5212

University of North Florida

Jacksonville, Florida
www.unf.edu Federal Code: 009841

4-year public university in very large city.
Enrollment: 14,124 undergrads, 28% part-time. 1,584 full-time freshmen.
Selectivity: Admits 50 to 75% of applicants.

BASIC COSTS (2012-2013)

Tuition and fees: $6,235; out-of-state residents $20,005.
Room and board: $8,592.

FINANCIAL AID PICTURE (2012-2013)

Students with need: Out of 1,495 full-time freshmen who applied for aid, 977 were judged to have need. Of these, 962 received aid, and 158 had their full need met. Average financial aid package met 91% of need; average scholarship/grant was $6,748; average loan was $3,272. For part-time students, average financial aid package was $6,455.
Students without need: 115 full-time freshmen who did not demonstrate need for aid received scholarships/grants; average award was $2,791. No-need awards available for academics, athletics, leadership, minority status, music/drama, state/district residency.
Scholarships offered: 48 full-time freshmen received athletic scholarships; average amount $7,288.
Cumulative student debt: 42% of graduating class had student loans; average debt was $17,000.

FINANCIAL AID PROCEDURES

Forms required: FAFSA.
Dates and Deadlines: Closing date 4/1. Applicants notified on a rolling basis starting 3/15; must reply within 2 week(s) of notification.
Transfers: Priority date 4/1; no deadline. Applicants notified on a rolling basis; must reply within 2 week(s) of notification. Students must submit financial aid transcripts from previous institutions attended.

CONTACT

Anissa Agne, Director of Financial Aid
1 UNF Drive, Jacksonville, FL 32224-7699
(904) 620-2604

University of South Florida

Tampa, Florida
www.usf.edu Federal Code: 001537

4-year public university in very large city.
Enrollment: 29,636 undergrads, 22% part-time. 3,423 full-time freshmen.
Selectivity: Admits less than 50% of applicants.

BASIC COSTS (2012-2013)
Tuition and fees: $6,334; out-of-state residents $16,257.
Room and board: $8,960.
Additional info: Tuition/fee waivers available for unemployed or children of unemployed.

FINANCIAL AID PICTURE (2011-2012)
Students with need: Out of 3,308 full-time freshmen who applied for aid, 2,624 were judged to have need. Of these, 2,601 received aid, and 148 had their full need met. Average financial aid package met 47% of need; average scholarship/grant was $7,841; average loan was $3,253. For part-time students, average financial aid package was $5,225.
Students without need: 1,179 full-time freshmen who did not demonstrate need for aid received scholarships/grants; average award was $3,508. No-need awards available for academics, alumni affiliation, art, athletics, job skills, leadership, minority status, music/drama, religious affiliation, ROTC, state/district residency.
Scholarships offered: 70 full-time freshmen received athletic scholarships; average amount $5,429.
Cumulative student debt: 57% of graduating class had student loans; average debt was $22,623.
Additional info: Deferred tuition payment plan available for late financial aid recipients.

FINANCIAL AID PROCEDURES
Forms required: FAFSA.
Dates and Deadlines: Priority date 3/1; no closing date. Applicants notified on a rolling basis starting 3/15.

CONTACT
Billie Hamilton, Director of Financial Aid
4202 East Fowler Avenue, SVC 1036, Tampa, FL 33620-9951
(813) 974-4700

University of Tampa

Tampa, Florida
www.ut.edu Federal Code: 001538

4-year private university and liberal arts college in large city.
Enrollment: 6,123 undergrads, 5% part-time. 1,623 full-time freshmen.
Selectivity: Admits less than 50% of applicants.

BASIC COSTS (2013-2014)
Tuition and fees: $25,222.
Per-credit charge: $500.
Room and board: $9,116.

FINANCIAL AID PICTURE (2011-2012)
Students with need: Out of 1,347 full-time freshmen who applied for aid, 1,094 were judged to have need. Of these, 1,059 received aid, and 125 had their full need met. Average financial aid package met 65% of need; average scholarship/grant was $13,196; average loan was $3,225. For part-time students, average financial aid package was $5,306.
Students without need: 241 full-time freshmen who did not demonstrate need for aid received scholarships/grants; average award was $7,318. No-need awards available for academics, art, athletics, leadership, music/drama, state/district residency.
Scholarships offered: ***Merit:*** Presidential Scholarships: up to $9,000; 3.5 GPA. Dean's Scholarships: up to $8,000; 3.2 GPA. Departmental scholarships also awarded. ***Athletic:*** 54 full-time freshmen received athletic scholarships; average amount $7,010.
Cumulative student debt: 56% of graduating class had student loans; average debt was $30,338.
Additional info: Early aid estimator service.

FINANCIAL AID PROCEDURES
Forms required: state aid form.
Dates and Deadlines: Applicants notified on a rolling basis starting 3/1; must reply by 5/1 or within 3 week(s) of notification.
Transfers: No deadline. Applicants notified on a rolling basis starting 3/1; must reply within 3 week(s) of notification. Transfer scholarships available; Phi Theta Kappa Scholarships.

CONTACT
Jacqueline LaTorella, Director of Financial Aid
401 West Kennedy Boulevard, Tampa, FL 33606-1490
(813) 253-6239

University of West Florida

Pensacola, Florida
www.uwf.edu Federal Code: 003955

4-year public university in small city.
Enrollment: 9,948 undergrads, 25% part-time. 1,331 full-time freshmen.
Selectivity: Admits 50 to 75% of applicants.

BASIC COSTS (2012-2013)
Tuition and fees: $6,238; out-of-state residents $19,120.
Room and board: $9,210.

FINANCIAL AID PICTURE
Students with need: Need-based aid available for full-time and part-time students. Work study available nights, weekends, and for part-time students.
Students without need: No-need awards available for academics, alumni affiliation, art, athletics, minority status, music/drama, ROTC.
Scholarships offered: John C. Pace Scholars: $16,000; based on high school record and leadership; 8 awards. John C. Pace Honors and Presidential Scholarships: $4,000; based on high school record. Both available to Florida residents only. Non-Florida tuition reduction scholarships available to nonresidents.

FINANCIAL AID PROCEDURES
Forms required: FAFSA, institutional form.
Dates and Deadlines: Priority date 3/1; no closing date. Applicants notified on a rolling basis starting 2/1.

CONTACT
Janice Bass, Director of Financial Aid
11000 University Parkway, Pensacola, FL 32514-5750
(850) 474-2400

Valencia College

Orlando, Florida
www.valenciacollege.edu Federal Code: 006750

2-year public community college in very large city.
Enrollment: 35,728 undergrads, 56% part-time. 5,405 full-time freshmen.
Selectivity: Open admission; but selective for some programs.

BASIC COSTS (2012-2013)
Tuition and fees: $3,032; out-of-state residents $11,377.

FINANCIAL AID PICTURE
Students with need: Need-based aid available for full-time and part-time students. Work study available nights.

FINANCIAL AID PROCEDURES
Forms required: FAFSA.
Dates and Deadlines: Closing date 3/15. Applicants notified on a rolling basis starting 4/2; must reply within 2 week(s) of notification.
Transfers: No deadline.

CONTACT
Christen Christensen, Director, Financial Aid
PO Box 3028, Orlando, FL 32802-3028
(407) 299-5000

Warner University
Lake Wales, Florida
www.warner.edu Federal Code: 008848

4-year private liberal arts college in large town, affiliated with Church of God.
Enrollment: 984 undergrads.

BASIC COSTS (2012-2013)
Tuition and fees: $17,480.
Room and board: $7,420.

FINANCIAL AID PICTURE
Students with need: Need-based aid available for full-time and part-time students.
Students without need: No-need awards available for academics, alumni affiliation, art, athletics, leadership, music/drama, religious affiliation, state/district residency.

FINANCIAL AID PROCEDURES
Forms required: FAFSA, state aid form.
Dates and Deadlines: Priority date 5/1; no closing date. Applicants notified on a rolling basis starting 3/15; must reply within 2 week(s) of notification.
Transfers: Priority date 10/1; closing date 5/15. Applicants notified on a rolling basis; must reply within 2 week(s) of notification.

CONTACT
Lorrie Steedley, Financial Aid Director
13895 Highway 27, Lake Wales, FL 33859
(863) 638-7202

Webber International University
Babson Park, Florida
www.webber.edu Federal Code: 001540

4-year private university and business college in rural community.
Enrollment: 654 undergrads, 4% part-time. 175 full-time freshmen.
Selectivity: Admits 50 to 75% of applicants.

BASIC COSTS (2012-2013)
Tuition and fees: $20,418.
Per-credit charge: $294.
Room and board: $7,900.
Additional info: Tuition/fee waivers available for adults.

FINANCIAL AID PICTURE (2012-2013)
Students with need: Out of 142 full-time freshmen who applied for aid, 136 were judged to have need. Of these, 136 received aid, and 8 had their full need met. Average financial aid package met 62% of need; average scholarship/grant was $15,812; average loan was $3,189. For part-time students, average financial aid package was $4,632.
Students without need: 39 full-time freshmen who did not demonstrate need for aid received scholarships/grants; average award was $12,973. No-need awards available for academics, alumni affiliation, athletics, leadership, minority status, state/district residency.
Scholarships offered: 39 full-time freshmen received athletic scholarships; average amount $3,755.

FINANCIAL AID PROCEDURES
Forms required: FAFSA, state aid form.
Dates and Deadlines: Priority date 5/1; closing date 8/1. Applicants notified on a rolling basis starting 4/1; must reply within 4 week(s) of notification.
Transfers: Eligibility for academic scholarships predicated on 12 hours of transferable credit.

CONTACT
Kathleen Wilson, Registrar
1201 North Scenic Highway, Babson Park, FL 33827-0096
(863) 638-2930

Georgia

Agnes Scott College
Decatur, Georgia
www.agnesscott.edu Federal Code: 001542

4-year private liberal arts college for women in very large city, affiliated with Presbyterian Church (USA).
Enrollment: 831 undergrads. 232 full-time freshmen.
Selectivity: Admits 50 to 75% of applicants.

BASIC COSTS (2012-2013)
Tuition and fees: $33,461.
Per-credit charge: $1,385.
Room and board: $10,230.

FINANCIAL AID PICTURE (2012-2013)
Students with need: Out of 213 full-time freshmen who applied for aid, 198 were judged to have need. Of these, 195 received aid, and 35 had their full need met. Average financial aid package met 86% of need; average scholarship/grant was $27,143; average loan was $3,455. For part-time students, average financial aid package was $26,119.
Students without need: 34 full-time freshmen who did not demonstrate need for aid received scholarships/grants; average award was $16,951. No-need awards available for academics, leadership, minority status, music/drama, religious affiliation.
Scholarships offered: Presidential and Honor Scholarships; $8,750 to full tuition, room and board. Agnes Solution; $15,000 each year for four years to GA students who qualify for the GA HOPE Scholarship, or to other domestic students with 3.6 high school GPA and 1300 SAT (exclusive of Writing) or a 29 on the ACT. In addition, they receive $3,000 for internship, study abroad, or mentored research experience after sophomore year. Leadership and community service awards also available.
Cumulative student debt: 77% of graduating class had student loans; average debt was $27,462.
Additional info: Middle Income Assistance Grants available. Auditions required for music scholarship applicants.

FINANCIAL AID PROCEDURES
Forms required: FAFSA.
Dates and Deadlines: Priority date 2/15; closing date 5/1. Applicants notified on a rolling basis starting 3/1; must reply within 3 week(s) of notification.
Transfers: Must reply by 5/1 or within 2 week(s) of notification. Merit scholarships available.

CONTACT
Patrick Bonones, Director of Financial Aid
141 East College Avenue, Decatur, GA 30030-3797
(404) 471-6395

Albany State University

Albany, Georgia
www.asurams.edu Federal Code: 001544

4-year public university in small city.
Enrollment: 3,803 undergrads.

BASIC COSTS (2012-2013)
Tuition and fees: $5,912; out-of-state residents $17,816.
Per-credit charge: $150; out-of-state residents $547.
Room and board: $6,118.

FINANCIAL AID PICTURE
Students with need: Need-based aid available for full-time and part-time students. Work study available nights, weekends, and for part-time students.
Students without need: No-need awards available for academics, alumni affiliation, art, athletics, music/drama, ROTC.

FINANCIAL AID PROCEDURES
Forms required: FAFSA, state aid form.
Dates and Deadlines: Priority date 4/15; closing date 6/1. Applicants notified on a rolling basis starting 1/7; must reply within 2 week(s) of notification.
Transfers: Must reply within 2 week(s) of notification.

CONTACT
Thomas Harris, Director of Financial Aid
504 College Drive, Albany, GA 31705-2796
(229) 430-4650

Albany Technical College

Albany, Georgia
www.albanytech.edu Federal Code: 005601

2-year public technical college in small city.
Enrollment: 3,827 undergrads, 43% part-time. 379 full-time freshmen.
Selectivity: Open admission; but selective for some programs.

BASIC COSTS (2012-2013)
Tuition and fees: $2,544; out-of-state residents $4,794.
Per-credit charge: $75; out-of-state residents $150.

FINANCIAL AID PICTURE
Students with need: Need-based aid available for full-time and part-time students. Work study available nights,
Students without need: No-need awards available for academics, state/district residency.

FINANCIAL AID PROCEDURES
Forms required: FAFSA, state aid form.
Dates and Deadlines: Applicants notified on a rolling basis starting 5/1.

CONTACT
Helen Catt, Financial Aid Director
1704 South Slappy Boulevard, Albany, GA 31701-3514
(229) 430-3506

Andrew College

Cuthbert, Georgia
www.andrewcollege.edu Federal Code: 001545

2-year private junior and liberal arts college in small town, affiliated with United Methodist Church.
Enrollment: 290 undergrads. 289 full-time freshmen.
Selectivity: Admits less than 50% of applicants.

BASIC COSTS (2012-2013)
Tuition and fees: $12,474.
Room and board: $7,834.

FINANCIAL AID PICTURE
Students with need: Need-based aid available for full-time and part-time students.
Students without need: No-need awards available for academics, art, athletics, leadership, music/drama, religious affiliation, state/district residency.

FINANCIAL AID PROCEDURES
Forms required: FAFSA, state aid form, institutional form.
Dates and Deadlines: Priority date 4/1; closing date 8/1. Applicants notified on a rolling basis starting 4/15.

CONTACT
Amy Thompson, Financial Aid Administrator
501 College Street, Cuthbert, GA 39840-1395
(229) 732-5938

Armstrong Atlantic State University

Savannah, Georgia
www.armstrong.edu Federal Code: 001546

4-year public university in small city.
Enrollment: 6,731 undergrads, 28% part-time. 1,067 full-time freshmen.
Selectivity: Admits 50 to 75% of applicants.

BASIC COSTS (2012-2013)
Tuition and fees: $5,844; out-of-state residents $17,748.
Per-credit charge: $150; out-of-state residents $547.
Room and board: $9,966.

FINANCIAL AID PICTURE (2011-2012)
Students with need: Out of 1,054 full-time freshmen who applied for aid, 666 were judged to have need. Of these, 666 received aid, and 21 had their full need met. Average financial aid package met 78% of need; average scholarship/grant was $3,500; average loan was $3,500. For part-time students, average financial aid package was $7,500.
Students without need: 248 full-time freshmen who did not demonstrate need for aid received scholarships/grants; average award was $1,000. No-need awards available for academics, alumni affiliation, art, athletics, job skills, leadership, minority status, music/drama, ROTC, state/district residency.
Scholarships offered: 19 full-time freshmen received athletic scholarships; average amount $7,442.
Cumulative student debt: 54% of graduating class had student loans; average debt was $25,000.

FINANCIAL AID PROCEDURES
Forms required: FAFSA.
Dates and Deadlines: Priority date 3/15; no closing date. Applicants notified on a rolling basis starting 4/15; must reply by 4/15 or within 2 week(s) of notification.

CONTACT
LeeAnn Kirkland, Financial Aid Director
11935 Abercorn Street, Savannah, GA 31419-1997
(912) 344-3266

Athens Technical College

Athens, Georgia
www.athenstech.edu Federal Code: 005600

2-year public technical college in small city.
Enrollment: 4,479 undergrads, 71% part-time. 323 full-time freshmen.
Selectivity: Open admission; but selective for some programs.

BASIC COSTS (2012-2013)
Tuition and fees: $2,510; out-of-state residents $4,760.
Per-credit charge: $75; out-of-state residents $150.

FINANCIAL AID PICTURE
Students with need: Need-based aid available for full-time and part-time students.
Students without need: No-need awards available for academics, leadership.

FINANCIAL AID PROCEDURES
Forms required: FAFSA.
Dates and Deadlines: Applicants notified on a rolling basis starting 6/15; must reply within 2 week(s) of notification.

CONTACT
Wanda Hicks, Director of Financial Aid
800 US Highway 29 North, Athens, GA 30601-1500
(706) 355-5009

Atlanta Metropolitan College
Atlanta, Georgia
www.atlm.edu Federal Code: 012165

2-year public junior college in very large city.
Enrollment: 2,664 undergrads.

BASIC COSTS (2012-2013)
Tuition and fees: $3,462; out-of-state residents $10,512.
Per-credit charge: $84; out-of-state residents $319.

FINANCIAL AID PICTURE
Students with need: Need-based aid available for full-time and part-time students. Work study available nights, weekends, and for part-time students.
Students without need: This college awards aid only to students with need.

FINANCIAL AID PROCEDURES
Forms required: FAFSA, state aid form.
Dates and Deadlines: Closing date 6/1. Applicants notified on a rolling basis; must reply by 6/30.
Transfers: Priority date 6/1; closing date 6/30. Applicants notified on a rolling basis; must reply by 6/30.

CONTACT
Alicia Scott, Director
1630 Metropolitan Parkway, SW, Atlanta, GA 30310-4498
(404) 756-4002

Atlanta Technical College
Atlanta, Georgia
www.atlantatech.edu Federal Code: 008543

2-year public community and technical college in very large city.
Enrollment: 4,577 undergrads, 62% part-time. 403 full-time freshmen.
Selectivity: Open admission; but selective for some programs.

BASIC COSTS (2012-2013)
Tuition and fees: $2,522; out-of-state residents $4,772.
Per-credit charge: $75; out-of-state residents $150.

FINANCIAL AID PICTURE
Students with need: Need-based aid available for full-time and part-time students. Work study available nights.

FINANCIAL AID PROCEDURES
Forms required: state aid form.
Dates and Deadlines: Priority date 3/1; no closing date. Applicants notified on a rolling basis starting 4/15.

CONTACT
Deborah Clark, Director of Financial Aid
1560 Metropolitan Parkway, SW, Atlanta, GA 30310-4446
(404) 225-4716

Bainbridge College
Bainbridge, Georgia
www.bainbridge.edu Federal Code: 011074

2-year public health science and community college in large town.
Enrollment: 2,905 undergrads, 49% part-time. 544 full-time freshmen.

BASIC COSTS (2012-2013)
Tuition and fees: $3,420; out-of-state residents $10,470.
Per-credit charge: $84; out-of-state residents $319.

FINANCIAL AID PICTURE (2011-2012)
Students with need: Need-based aid available for full-time and part-time students.
Students without need: This college awards aid only to students with need.

FINANCIAL AID PROCEDURES
Forms required: FAFSA, institutional form.
Dates and Deadlines: Priority date 6/1; closing date 8/1. Applicants notified on a rolling basis starting 6/1; must reply within 2 week(s) of notification.
Transfers: Priority date 6/11.

CONTACT
Helen Catt, Director of Financial Aid
2500 East Shotwell Street, Bainbridge, GA 39818-0990
(229) 248-2505

Berry College
Mount Berry, Georgia
www.berry.edu Federal Code: 001554

4-year private liberal arts college in large town.
Enrollment: 2,018 undergrads, 1% part-time. 618 full-time freshmen.
Selectivity: Admits 50 to 75% of applicants.

BASIC COSTS (2013-2014)
Tuition and fees: $29,090.
Per-credit charge: $963.
Room and board: $10,164.

FINANCIAL AID PICTURE (2012-2013)
Students with need: Out of 578 full-time freshmen who applied for aid, 478 were judged to have need. Of these, 478 received aid, and 114 had their full need met. Average financial aid package met 84% of need; average scholarship/grant was $19,759; average loan was $4,269. For part-time students, average financial aid package was $5,445.
Students without need: 140 full-time freshmen who did not demonstrate need for aid received scholarships/grants; average award was $10,392. No-need awards available for academics, art, leadership, minority status, music/drama.
Scholarships offered: Georgia Tuition Equalization Grant (GTEG): $700; for Georgia residents who attend in-state private institutions. HOPE Scholarship: $3,600 annually; for Georgia residents from eligible high schools with at least B average in college prep coursework.
Cumulative student debt: 76% of graduating class had student loans; average debt was $20,611.21.
Additional info: All students are encouraged to work on-campus up to 16 hours per week.

FINANCIAL AID PROCEDURES
Forms required: FAFSA, state aid form.

Dates and Deadlines: Priority date 3/1; no closing date. Applicants notified on a rolling basis starting 2/15; must reply by 3/1.
Transfers: No deadline. Applicants notified on a rolling basis starting 11/15.

CONTACT
Marcia McConnell, Director of Financial Aid
PO Box 490159, Mount Berry, GA 30149-0159
(706) 236-1714

Beulah Heights University
Atlanta, Georgia
www.beulah.org Federal Code: 030763

5-year private university and Bible college in very large city, affiliated with interdenominational tradition.
Enrollment: 535 undergrads.
Selectivity: Open admission.

BASIC COSTS (2013-2014)
Tuition and fees: $7,500.
Per-credit charge: $240.

FINANCIAL AID PICTURE
Students with need: Need-based aid available for full-time and part-time students.

FINANCIAL AID PROCEDURES
Forms required: FAFSA.
Dates and Deadlines: Priority date 2/1; no closing date. Applicants notified on a rolling basis.
Transfers: No deadline. Applicants notified on a rolling basis; must reply within 1 week(s) of notification.

CONTACT
Patricia Banks, Director of Financial Aid
892 Berne Street SE, Atlanta, GA 30316
(404) 627-2681 ext. 124

Brenau University
Gainesville, Georgia
www.brenau.edu Federal Code: 001556

4-year private university and liberal arts college for women in small city.
Enrollment: 770 undergrads, 9% part-time. 170 full-time freshmen.
Selectivity: Admits less than 50% of applicants.

BASIC COSTS (2012-2013)
Tuition and fees: $22,238.
Per-credit charge: $730.
Room and board: $10,884.

FINANCIAL AID PICTURE (2012-2013)
Students with need: Out of 158 full-time freshmen who applied for aid, 142 were judged to have need. Of these, 142 received aid, and 19 had their full need met. Average financial aid package met 75% of need; average scholarship/grant was $18,435; average loan was $3,639. For part-time students, average financial aid package was $8,776.
Students without need: 14 full-time freshmen who did not demonstrate need for aid received scholarships/grants; average award was $13,376. No-need awards available for academics, art, athletics, leadership, music/drama.
Scholarships offered: 9 full-time freshmen received athletic scholarships; average amount $25,115.
Cumulative student debt: 89% of graduating class had student loans; average debt was $23,317.

FINANCIAL AID PROCEDURES
Forms required: FAFSA, state aid form.
Dates and Deadlines: Priority date 4/1; no closing date. Applicants notified on a rolling basis starting 3/1.

CONTACT
Pam Barrett, Director of Financial Aid
500 Washington Street SE, Gainesville, GA 30501
(770) 534-6152

Brewton-Parker College
Mount Vernon, Georgia
www.bpc.edu Federal Code: 001557

4-year private liberal arts college in small town, affiliated with Southern Baptist Convention.
Enrollment: 522 undergrads, 11% part-time. 264 full-time freshmen.
Selectivity: Admits over 75% of applicants.

BASIC COSTS (2012-2013)
Tuition and fees: $13,300.
Per-credit charge: $360.
Room and board: $6,926.

FINANCIAL AID PICTURE (2011-2012)
Students with need: Out of 93 full-time freshmen who applied for aid, 87 were judged to have need. Of these, 87 received aid, and 16 had their full need met. Average financial aid package met 70% of need; average scholarship/grant was $10,839; average loan was $3,090. For part-time students, average financial aid package was $7,080.
Students without need: 5 full-time freshmen who did not demonstrate need for aid received scholarships/grants; average award was $3,974. No-need awards available for academics, athletics, leadership, religious affiliation, state/district residency.
Scholarships offered: ***Merit:*** Scholarships available for academic achievement and SAT scores for incoming freshman transfer students, ranging from $1,500-$3,000 per academic year, available for four years. ***Athletic:*** 23 full-time freshmen received athletic scholarships; average amount $8,043.

FINANCIAL AID PROCEDURES
Forms required: FAFSA, state aid form.
Dates and Deadlines: Priority date 3/15; closing date 7/1. Applicants notified on a rolling basis starting 3/15; must reply within 2 week(s) of notification.

CONTACT
Rick Woolverton, Director of Financial Aid
Brewton-Parker College # 2011, Mount Vernon, GA 30445
(912) 583-2241 ext. 209

Carver Bible College
Atlanta, Georgia
www.carver.edu

4-year private Bible college in very large city.
Enrollment: 124 undergrads, 29% part-time. 30 full-time freshmen.

BASIC COSTS (2012-2013)
Tuition and fees: $9,950.
Per-credit charge: $315.

FINANCIAL AID PICTURE
Students with need: Need-based aid available for full-time students.
Students without need: This college awards aid only to students with need.

FINANCIAL AID PROCEDURES
Forms required: FAFSA, institutional form.

CONTACT
Ray Vaughan, Financial Aid Officer
3870 Cascade Road, SW, Atlanta, GA 30331
(404) 527-4520

Central Georgia Technical College
Macon, Georgia
www.centralgatech.edu Federal Code: 005763

2-year public community and technical college in small city.
Enrollment: 4,631 undergrads.
Selectivity: Open admission; but selective for some programs.

BASIC COSTS (2012-2013)
Tuition and fees: $2,530; out-of-state residents $4,780.
Per-credit charge: $75; out-of-state residents $150.

FINANCIAL AID PICTURE
Students with need: Need-based aid available for full-time and part-time students.

FINANCIAL AID PROCEDURES
Forms required: FAFSA, state aid form, institutional form.
Dates and Deadlines: Closing date 7/14.

CONTACT
Jackie White, Director, Financial Aid
3300 Macon Tech Drive, Macon, GA 31206
(478) 757-3422

Chattahoochee Technical College
Marietta, Georgia
www.chattahoocheetech.edu Federal Code: 005620

2-year public community and technical college in large city.
Enrollment: 11,235 undergrads.
Selectivity: Open admission; but selective for some programs.

BASIC COSTS (2012-2013)
Tuition and fees: $2,572; out-of-state residents $4,822.
Per-credit charge: $75; out-of-state residents $150.

FINANCIAL AID PICTURE
Students with need: Need-based aid available for full-time and part-time students. Work study available nights, weekends, and for part-time students.

FINANCIAL AID PROCEDURES
Forms required: FAFSA.
Dates and Deadlines: Applicants notified on a rolling basis.

CONTACT
Kristie Teasley, Director of Financial Aid
980 South Cobb Drive, SE, Marietta, GA 30060-3300
(770) 528-4531

Clark Atlanta University
Atlanta, Georgia
www.cau.edu Federal Code: 001559

4-year private university in very large city, affiliated with United Methodist Church.
Enrollment: 2,632 undergrads, 6% part-time. 624 full-time freshmen.
Selectivity: Admits 50 to 75% of applicants.

BASIC COSTS (2013-2014)
Tuition and fees: $21,100.
Per-credit charge: $812.
Room and board: $8,956.

FINANCIAL AID PICTURE
Students with need: Need-based aid available for full-time and part-time students.
Students without need: No-need awards available for academics, art, athletics, leadership, minority status, music/drama, religious affiliation, ROTC, state/district residency.

FINANCIAL AID PROCEDURES
Forms required: FAFSA, state aid form.
Dates and Deadlines: Priority date 3/1; no closing date. Applicants notified on a rolling basis starting 4/1.

CONTACT
Nigel Edwards, Director of Financial Aid
223 James P. Brawley Drive, SW, Atlanta, GA 30314-4391
(404) 880-6018

Clayton State University
Morrow, Georgia
www.clayton.edu Federal Code: 008976

4-year public liberal arts and technical college in small city.
Enrollment: 6,808 undergrads, 42% part-time. 498 full-time freshmen.
Selectivity: Admits less than 50% of applicants.

BASIC COSTS (2012-2013)
Tuition and fees: $5,916; out-of-state residents $17,820.
Per-credit charge: $150; out-of-state residents $547.
Room and board: $9,180.

FINANCIAL AID PICTURE
Students with need: Need-based aid available for full-time and part-time students.
Students without need: No-need awards available for academics, athletics, music/drama.

FINANCIAL AID PROCEDURES
Forms required: FAFSA, state aid form.
Dates and Deadlines: Priority date 7/1; no closing date. Applicants notified on a rolling basis.

CONTACT
Patricia Barton, Director of Financial Aid
2000 Clayton State Boulevard, Morrow, GA 30260-0285
(678) 466-4185

College of Coastal Georgia
Brunswick, Georgia
www.ccga.edu Federal Code: 001558

2-year public liberal arts college in large town.
Enrollment: 2,995 undergrads, 41% part-time. 645 full-time freshmen.
Selectivity: Admits over 75% of applicants.

BASIC COSTS (2012-2013)
Tuition and fees: $4,106; out-of-state residents $11,774.
Per-credit charge: $95; out-of-state residents $350.
Room and board: $8,126.

FINANCIAL AID PICTURE (2011-2012)
Students with need: Out of 589 full-time freshmen who applied for aid, 506 were judged to have need. Of these, 498 received aid, and 11 had their full need met. Average financial aid package met 69% of need; average scholarship/grant was $3,947; average loan was $2,752. For part-time students, average financial aid package was $3,394.

Students without need: 14 full-time freshmen who did not demonstrate need for aid received scholarships/grants; average award was $1,675. No-need awards available for academics, athletics, leadership, state/district residency.
Scholarships offered: 21 full-time freshmen received athletic scholarships; average amount $3,840.
Cumulative student debt: 58% of graduating class had student loans; average debt was $19,138.

FINANCIAL AID PROCEDURES
Forms required: FAFSA, state aid form.
Dates and Deadlines: Priority date 5/1; no closing date. Applicants notified on a rolling basis starting 5/1.
Transfers: No deadline. Applicants notified on a rolling basis.

CONTACT
Terral Harris, Director of Financial Aid
One College Drive, Brunswick, GA 31520
(912) 279-5722

Columbus State University
Columbus, Georgia
www.columbusstate.edu Federal Code: 001561

4-year public university and liberal arts college in small city.
Enrollment: 6,834 undergrads, 28% part-time. 1,052 full-time freshmen.
Selectivity: Admits 50 to 75% of applicants. GED not accepted.

BASIC COSTS (2012-2013)
Tuition and fees: $6,592; out-of-state residents $18,868.
Per-credit charge: $162; out-of-state residents $571.
Room and board: $8,542.

FINANCIAL AID PICTURE (2012-2013)
Students with need: Out of 982 full-time freshmen who applied for aid, 796 were judged to have need. Of these, 794 received aid, and 137 had their full need met. Average financial aid package met 71% of need; average scholarship/grant was $4,803; average loan was $3,319. For part-time students, average financial aid package was $7,288.
Students without need: 65 full-time freshmen who did not demonstrate need for aid received scholarships/grants; average award was $2,098. No-need awards available for academics, alumni affiliation, art, athletics, job skills, leadership, minority status, music/drama, ROTC.
Scholarships offered: 47 full-time freshmen received athletic scholarships; average amount $3,507.

FINANCIAL AID PROCEDURES
Forms required: FAFSA.
Dates and Deadlines: Priority date 5/1; no closing date. Applicants notified on a rolling basis starting 5/15; must reply within 4 week(s) of notification.

CONTACT
Janis Bowles, Director of Financial Aid
4225 University Avenue, Columbus, GA 31907-5645
(706) 507-8800

Columbus Technical College
Columbus, Georgia
www.columbustech.edu Federal Code: 005624

2-year public technical college in small city.
Enrollment: 4,136 undergrads, 65% part-time. 347 full-time freshmen.
Selectivity: Open admission; but selective for some programs.

BASIC COSTS (2012-2013)
Tuition and fees: $2,510; out-of-state residents $4,760.
Per-credit charge: $75; out-of-state residents $150.

FINANCIAL AID PICTURE
Students with need: Need-based aid available for full-time and part-time students.

FINANCIAL AID PROCEDURES
Forms required: FAFSA.
Dates and Deadlines: Applicants notified on a rolling basis.

CONTACT
Debbie Henshaw, Director of Financial Aid
928 Manchester Expressway, Columbus, GA 31904-6572
(706) 649-1859

Covenant College
Lookout Mountain, Georgia
www.covenant.edu Federal Code: 003484

4-year private liberal arts college in small city, affiliated with Presbyterian Church in America (PCA).
Enrollment: 1,027 undergrads, 2% part-time. 286 full-time freshmen.
Selectivity: Admits 50 to 75% of applicants.

BASIC COSTS (2012-2013)
Tuition and fees: $28,270.
Per-credit charge: $1,150.
Room and board: $8,040.

FINANCIAL AID PICTURE (2011-2012)
Students with need: Out of 234 full-time freshmen who applied for aid, 192 were judged to have need. Of these, 192 received aid, and 72 had their full need met. Average financial aid package met 85% of need; average scholarship/grant was $16,347; average loan was $5,484. For part-time students, average financial aid package was $1,833.
Students without need: 72 full-time freshmen who did not demonstrate need for aid received scholarships/grants; average award was $11,230. No-need awards available for academics, alumni affiliation, art, job skills, leadership, minority status, music/drama, religious affiliation, state/district residency.
Scholarships offered: Maclellan Scholars Program; minimum SAT 1200 (exclusive of Writing) or ACT 27, high school GPA 3.3. Presidential Scholarship; based on GPA, leadership, Christian commitment, extracurricular activities, work experience, references.
Cumulative student debt: 66% of graduating class had student loans; average debt was $22,861.

FINANCIAL AID PROCEDURES
Forms required: FAFSA, state aid form.
Dates and Deadlines: Applicants notified on a rolling basis starting 2/1; must reply within 3 week(s) of notification.
Transfers: Some scholarships may be depleted for mid-semester transfers, such as athletic, diversity or music.

CONTACT
Brenda Rapier, Director of Financial Aid
14049 Scenic Highway, Lookout Mountain, GA 30750
(706) 419-1126

Dalton State College
Dalton, Georgia
www.daltonstate.edu Federal Code: 003956

4-year public liberal arts and teachers college in large town.
Enrollment: 5,047 undergrads, 41% part-time. 1,030 full-time freshmen.
Selectivity: Admits less than 50% of applicants.

BASIC COSTS (2012-2013)
Tuition and fees: $3,732; out-of-state residents $11,400.
Per-credit charge: $95; out-of-state residents $350.
Additional info: Board plan not available. Cost of room only: $4170.

FINANCIAL AID PICTURE (2011-2012)
Students with need: Out of 946 full-time freshmen who applied for aid, 788 were judged to have need. Of these, 786 received aid, and 91 had their full need met. Average financial aid package met 67% of need; average scholarship/grant was $3,442; average loan was $2,778. For part-time students, average financial aid package was $5,331.
Students without need: 4 full-time freshmen who did not demonstrate need for aid received scholarships/grants; average award was $1,125. No-need awards available for academics, leadership, minority status, state/district residency.
Cumulative student debt: 33% of graduating class had student loans; average debt was $4,100.

FINANCIAL AID PROCEDURES
Forms required: FAFSA.
Dates and Deadlines: Applicants notified on a rolling basis starting 4/1.
Transfers: No deadline. Applicants notified on a rolling basis.

CONTACT
Holli Woods, Director of Student Financial Aid
650 College Drive, Dalton, GA 30720
(706) 272-4545

Darton College
Albany, Georgia
www.darton.edu Federal Code: 001543

2-year public community college in small city.
Enrollment: 6,226 undergrads, 50% part-time. 1,023 full-time freshmen.
Selectivity: Open admission; but selective for some programs.

BASIC COSTS (2012-2013)
Tuition and fees: $3,676; out-of-state residents $10,726.
Per-credit charge: $84; out-of-state residents $319.
Room and board: $8,760.

FINANCIAL AID PICTURE (2011-2012)
Students with need: Need-based aid available for full-time and part-time students. Work study available nights, weekends, and for part-time students.
Students without need: No-need awards available for academics, alumni affiliation, art, athletics, music/drama, state/district residency.
Additional info: Auditions, portfolios, essays, extracurricular activities impact scholarship decisions.

FINANCIAL AID PROCEDURES
Forms required: FAFSA, state aid form, institutional form.
Dates and Deadlines: Applicants notified on a rolling basis; must reply within 3 week(s) of notification.

CONTACT
Haley Hooks, Director of Financial Aid
2400 Gillionville Road, Albany, GA 31707-3098
(229) 317-6746

DeVry University: Decatur
Decatur, Georgia
www.devry.edu Federal Code: 009224

4-year for-profit university in large town.
Enrollment: 2,216 undergrads, 69% part-time. 37 full-time freshmen.

BASIC COSTS (2012-2013)
Tuition and fees: $16,076.
Per-credit charge: $609.

FINANCIAL AID PICTURE
Students with need: Need-based aid available for full-time and part-time students.
Students without need: This college awards aid only to students with need.

FINANCIAL AID PROCEDURES
Forms required: FAFSA.
Dates and Deadlines: Applicants notified on a rolling basis.

CONTACT
Robin Winston, Director of Financial Aid
One West Court Square, Suite 100, Decatur, GA 30030-2556
(404) 292-7900

East Georgia College
Swainsboro, Georgia
www.ega.edu Federal Code: 010997

2-year public community and junior college in small town.
Enrollment: 2,904 undergrads.
Selectivity: Admits 50 to 75% of applicants.

BASIC COSTS (2012-2013)
Tuition and fees: $3,368; out-of-state residents $10,418.
Per-credit charge: $84; out-of-state residents $319.
Room and board: $7,232.

FINANCIAL AID PICTURE (2012-2013)
Students with need: Average financial aid package met 61% of need; average scholarship/grant was $5,011; average loan was $5,478. For part-time students, average financial aid package was $4,195.
Students without need: No-need awards available for academics, leadership, state/district residency.
Cumulative student debt: 70% of graduating class had student loans; average debt was $4,653.

FINANCIAL AID PROCEDURES
Forms required: FAFSA, state aid form, institutional form.
Dates and Deadlines: Priority date 6/1; no closing date. Applicants notified on a rolling basis starting 6/1; must reply within 2 week(s) of notification.

CONTACT
Karen Jones, Director of Financial Aid
131 College Circle, Swainsboro, GA 30401-2699
(478) 289-2012

Emmanuel College
Franklin Springs, Georgia
www.ec.edu Federal Code: 001563

4-year private liberal arts and teachers college in rural community, affiliated with Pentecostal Holiness Church.
Enrollment: 723 undergrads, 3% part-time. 174 full-time freshmen.
Selectivity: Admits 50 to 75% of applicants.

BASIC COSTS (2013-2014)
Tuition and fees: $16,800.
Per-credit charge: $670.
Room and board: $6,900.

FINANCIAL AID PICTURE (2011-2012)
Students with need: Out of 154 full-time freshmen who applied for aid, 132 were judged to have need. Of these, 132 received aid, and 25 had their

full need met. Average financial aid package met 76% of need; average scholarship/grant was $10,700; average loan was $2,734. For part-time students, average financial aid package was $5,661.
Students without need: 36 full-time freshmen who did not demonstrate need for aid received scholarships/grants; average award was $4,432. No-need awards available for academics, art, athletics, job skills, leadership, music/drama, religious affiliation, state/district residency.
Scholarships offered: 40 full-time freshmen received athletic scholarships; average amount $6,966.
Cumulative student debt: 83% of graduating class had student loans; average debt was $24,268.

FINANCIAL AID PROCEDURES
Forms required: FAFSA, state aid form, institutional form.
Dates and Deadlines: Priority date 5/1; closing date 6/15. Applicants notified on a rolling basis starting 3/1; must reply within 2 week(s) of notification.
Transfers: Applicants notified on a rolling basis starting 3/1; must reply within 2 week(s) of notification.

CONTACT
Niki Stinson, Director of Financial Aid
181 Spring Street, Franklin Springs, GA 30639-0129
(706) 245-2843

Emory University
Atlanta, Georgia — Federal Code: 001564
www.emory.edu — CSS Code: 5187

4-year private university in very large city, affiliated with United Methodist Church.
Enrollment: 5,648 undergrads.
Selectivity: Admits less than 50% of applicants. GED not accepted.

BASIC COSTS (2012-2013)
Tuition and fees: $42,980.
Per-credit charge: $1,767.
Room and board: $12,000.

FINANCIAL AID PICTURE
Students with need: Need-based aid available for full-time and part-time students. Work study available nights, weekends, and for part-time students.
Students without need: No-need awards available for academics, art, leadership, music/drama, religious affiliation, state/district residency.
Scholarships offered: Emory and Goizueta Scholars programs: two-thirds tuition to full cost; based on academic merit of incoming first-year students, requires nomination by appropriate high school official by November 1 of senior year; renewable for four years of undergraduate study.
Additional info: Loan replacement grant and loan cap program available to students from families with total annual incomes of $100,000 or less who demonstrate need for financial aid.

FINANCIAL AID PROCEDURES
Forms required: FAFSA, CSS PROFILE.
Dates and Deadlines: Priority date 2/15; closing date 3/1. Applicants notified by 4/1; must reply by 5/1 or within 4 week(s) of notification.
Transfers: No deadline. Applicants notified on a rolling basis. Limitations on aid available to transfer students. Financial aid filing deadline for transfers is 30 days following transfer student admission date.

CONTACT
Dean Bentley, Director of Financial Aid
1390 Oxford Road NE, 3rd Floor, Atlanta, GA 30322
(800) 727-6039

Fort Valley State University
Fort Valley, Georgia
www.fvsu.edu — Federal Code: 001566

4-year public liberal arts and teachers college in small town.
Enrollment: 3,250 undergrads.

BASIC COSTS (2012-2013)
Tuition and fees: $6,080; out-of-state residents $17,984.
Per-credit charge: $150; out-of-state residents $547.
Room and board: $7,162.

FINANCIAL AID PICTURE
Students with need: Need-based aid available for full-time and part-time students.
Students without need: No-need awards available for academics, athletics, music/drama.
Additional info: Financial aid transcripts must be received from former institutions before application for aid will be considered complete and reviewed for awards.

FINANCIAL AID PROCEDURES
Forms required: FAFSA.
Dates and Deadlines: Priority date 3/1; no closing date. Applicants notified on a rolling basis starting 3/15; must reply within 1 week(s) of notification.

CONTACT
Eula Solomon, Director of Financial Aid
1005 State University Drive, Fort Valley, GA 31030-4313
(478) 825-6351

Georgia College and State University
Milledgeville, Georgia
www.gcsu.edu — Federal Code: 001602

4-year public university and liberal arts college in large town.
Enrollment: 5,487 undergrads, 7% part-time. 1,067 full-time freshmen.

BASIC COSTS (2012-2013)
Tuition and fees: $8,618; out-of-state residents $26,082.
Room and board: $9,268.

FINANCIAL AID PICTURE (2011-2012)
Students with need: Out of 1,028 full-time freshmen who applied for aid, 575 were judged to have need. Of these, 565 received aid. For part-time students, average financial aid package was $5,823.
Students without need: 9 full-time freshmen who did not demonstrate need for aid received scholarships/grants; average award was $1,973. No-need awards available for academics, alumni affiliation, art, athletics, job skills, leadership, minority status, music/drama, religious affiliation, ROTC, state/district residency.
Scholarships offered: ***Merit:*** Trustee Scholarships: $6,000 per year for four years. Presidential Scholarships: $4,000 per year for four years; both offered to freshman with superior academic accomplishments; include stipends to be used toward study abroad programs. ***Athletic:*** 52 full-time freshmen received athletic scholarships; average amount $2,834.

FINANCIAL AID PROCEDURES
Forms required: FAFSA, institutional form.
Dates and Deadlines: Priority date 3/1; no closing date. Applicants notified on a rolling basis starting 3/1; must reply within 2 week(s) of notification.
Transfers: No deadline. Applicants notified on a rolling basis starting 3/1; must reply within 2 week(s) of notification.

CONTACT
Cathy Crawley, Director of Financial Aid
Campus Box 23, Milledgeville, GA 31061-0490
(478) 445-5149

Georgia Gwinnett College

Lawrenceville, Georgia
www.ggc.edu

4-year public liberal arts college in large town.
Enrollment: 9,046 undergrads, 28% part-time. 1,996 full-time freshmen.
Selectivity: Admits over 75% of applicants.

BASIC COSTS (2012-2013)
Tuition and fees: $4,982; out-of-state residents $14,208.
Per-credit charge: $113; out-of-state residents $420.
Room and board: $10,558.

FINANCIAL AID PICTURE (2011-2012)
Students with need: Out of 1,754 full-time freshmen who applied for aid, 1,552 were judged to have need. Of these, 1,505 received aid, and 22 had their full need met. Average financial aid package met 40% of need; average scholarship/grant was $4,563. For part-time students, average financial aid package was $5,714.
Students without need: 67 full-time freshmen who did not demonstrate need for aid received scholarships/grants; average award was $2,365.

FINANCIAL AID PROCEDURES
Forms required: FAFSA, state aid form.
Dates and Deadlines: Priority date 7/1; no closing date. Applicants notified on a rolling basis starting 6/1.

CONTACT
Laurel Starling-McIntosh, Assistant Director of Financial Aid
1000 University Center Lane, Lawrenceville, GA 30043
(678) 407-5701

Georgia Highlands College

Rome, Georgia
www.highlands.edu Federal Code: 009507

2-year public community and liberal arts college in very large city.
Enrollment: 5,532 undergrads, 50% part-time. 830 full-time freshmen.

BASIC COSTS (2012-2013)
Tuition and fees: $3,466; out-of-state residents $10,516.
Per-credit charge: $84; out-of-state residents $319.

FINANCIAL AID PICTURE (2011-2012)
Students with need: 66% of average financial aid package awarded as scholarships/grants, 34% awarded as loans/jobs. Need-based aid available for part-time students. Work study available nights.
Students without need: No-need awards available for academics, art.
Scholarships offered: HOPE Scholarship and the Zell Miller Scholarship are opportunities that GA high school graduates must qualify for upon HS graduation. Eligibility is determined by Georgia Student Finance Commission based on transcripts and SAT/ACT scores submitted to GSFC. Zell Miller pays 100% of in-state tuition. HOPE Scholarship currently pays $71.94 a credit hour (excluding Learning Support classes). Several Foundation Scholarships are available, amounts and availability may vary.
Additional info: All Federal Work Study students must be Pell eligible and taking a minimum of 6 credit hours.

FINANCIAL AID PROCEDURES
Forms required: FAFSA.
Dates and Deadlines: Priority date 7/1; closing date 4/1. Applicants notified on a rolling basis starting 4/1; must reply within 2 week(s) of notification.
Transfers: Priority date 7/1; no deadline. Applicants notified on a rolling basis starting 5/1; must reply within 2 week(s) of notification. Transfer students are only eligible for aid not used at previous institution in the same aid year and/or the maximum eligibility allowed for a given term. Transfer students cannot receive Federal Aid at two institutions during the same term.

CONTACT
Megan Simpson, Director of Financial Aid
3175 Cedartown Highway, Rome, GA 30161
(706) 295-6311

Georgia Institute of Technology

Atlanta, Georgia
www.gatech.edu Federal Code: 001569

4-year public university in large city.
Enrollment: 13,954 undergrads, 5% part-time. 2,695 full-time freshmen.
Selectivity: Admits 50 to 75% of applicants.

BASIC COSTS (2012-2013)
Tuition and fees: $10,098; out-of-state residents $29,402.
Per-credit charge: $2,293; out-of-state residents $8,017.
Room and board: $9,236.

FINANCIAL AID PICTURE (2011-2012)
Students with need: Out of 2,169 full-time freshmen who applied for aid, 1,236 were judged to have need. Of these, 1,191 received aid, and 409 had their full need met. Average financial aid package met 65% of need; average scholarship/grant was $10,437; average loan was $3,835. For part-time students, average financial aid package was $12,847.
Students without need: 224 full-time freshmen who did not demonstrate need for aid received scholarships/grants; average award was $4,372. No-need awards available for academics, athletics, leadership, music/drama, ROTC, state/district residency.
Scholarships offered: ***Merit:*** President's Scholarship Program; 4-year awards range from half to full tuition; for freshmen with outstanding academic/leadership qualities. ***Athletic:*** 92 full-time freshmen received athletic scholarships; average amount $15,171.
Cumulative student debt: 44% of graduating class had student loans; average debt was $26,412.

FINANCIAL AID PROCEDURES
Forms required: FAFSA, institutional form.
Dates and Deadlines: Closing date 2/15. Applicants notified by 4/1; must reply by 5/1.
Transfers: Priority date 5/1; closing date 5/1. Applicants notified on a rolling basis starting 6/1; must reply by 8/1. Student must be officially admitted, all final transcripts must be received, and transcripts must be articulated.

CONTACT
Marie Mons, Director of Student Financial Planning and Services
Office of Undergraduate Admissions, Atlanta, GA 30332-0320
(404) 894-4160

Georgia Military College

Milledgeville, Georgia
www.gmc.cc.ga.us Federal Code: 001571

2-year public community and military college in large town.
Enrollment: 8,101 undergrads.
Selectivity: Open admission; but selective for some programs.

BASIC COSTS (2012-2013)
Tuition and fees: $6,274; out-of-state residents $6,274.
Per-credit charge: $118.

FINANCIAL AID PICTURE
Students with need: Need-based aid available for full-time and part-time students. Work study available nights.
Students without need: No-need awards available for athletics, leadership, ROTC, state/district residency.

Additional info: Institutional aid offered to those enrolled in Cadet Corps who reside on campus.

FINANCIAL AID PROCEDURES

Forms required: FAFSA, state aid form.

Dates and Deadlines: Applicants notified on a rolling basis starting 3/1.

Transfers: No deadline. Applicants notified on a rolling basis. Transfer students must submit financial aid transcript from any prior post-secondary institutions.

CONTACT

Alisa Stephens, Director of Financial Aid
201 East Greene Street, Milledgeville, GA 31061
(478) 387-4842

Georgia Perimeter College

Clarkston, Georgia
www.gpc.edu Federal Code: 001562

2-year public junior and liberal arts college in very large city.
Enrollment: 21,662 undergrads, 57% part-time. 1,718 full-time freshmen.

BASIC COSTS (2012-2013)

Tuition and fees: $3,502; out-of-state residents $10,552.
Per-credit charge: $84; out-of-state residents $319.

FINANCIAL AID PICTURE (2011-2012)

Students with need: Need-based aid available for full-time and part-time students. Work study available nights, weekends, and for part-time students.

FINANCIAL AID PROCEDURES

Forms required: FAFSA.

Dates and Deadlines: Closing date 6/1. Applicants notified on a rolling basis; must reply within 3 week(s) of notification.

Transfers: Priority date 6/1; no deadline.

CONTACT

Ron Stark, Vice President
555 North Indian Creek Drive, Clarkston, GA 30021-2361
(678) 891-3535

Georgia Piedmont Technical College

Clarkston, Georgia
www.dekalbtech.edu Federal Code: 016582

2-year public technical college in large city.
Enrollment: 3,884 undergrads, 69% part-time. 228 full-time freshmen.
Selectivity: Open admission; but selective for some programs.

BASIC COSTS (2012-2013)

Tuition and fees: $2,558; out-of-state residents $4,808.
Per-credit charge: $75; out-of-state residents $150.

FINANCIAL AID PICTURE

Students with need: Need-based aid available for full-time and part-time students. Work study available nights, weekends, and for part-time students.

FINANCIAL AID PROCEDURES

Forms required: FAFSA.

Dates and Deadlines: Closing date 8/20. Applicants notified on a rolling basis.

Transfers: No deadline.

CONTACT

John Gottardy, Director of Financial Aid
495 North Indian Creek Drive, Clarkston, GA 30021-2397
(404) 297-9522 ext. 1166

Georgia Regents University

Augusta, Georgia
www.gru.edu Federal Code: 001579

4-year public university in large city.
Enrollment: 6,245 undergrads.

BASIC COSTS (2012-2013)

Tuition and fees: $9,110; out-of-state residents $27,776.
Per-credit charge: $249; out-of-state residents $871.
Additional info: Board plan not available. Cost of room only: $3705.

FINANCIAL AID PICTURE

Students with need: Need-based aid available for full-time and part-time students. Work study available nights, weekends, and for part-time students.

Students without need: No-need awards available for academics, athletics, state/district residency.

Additional info: State Hope scholarships only available to Georgia residents.

FINANCIAL AID PROCEDURES

Forms required: FAFSA, state aid form, institutional form.

Dates and Deadlines: Must reply within 2 week(s) of notification.

CONTACT

Cynthia Parker, Director of Financial Aid
2500 Walton Way, Augusta, GA 30904
(706) 721-4901

Georgia Southern University

Statesboro, Georgia
www.georgiasouthern.edu Federal Code: 001572

4-year public university in large town.
Enrollment: 17,139 undergrads, 8% part-time. 3,518 full-time freshmen.
Selectivity: Admits 50 to 75% of applicants. GED not accepted.

BASIC COSTS (2012-2013)

Tuition and fees: $6,724; out-of-state residents $19,000.
Per-credit charge: $162; out-of-state residents $570.
Room and board: $9,290.

FINANCIAL AID PICTURE (2011-2012)

Students with need: Out of 3,295 full-time freshmen who applied for aid, 2,319 were judged to have need. Of these, 2,282 received aid, and 243 had their full need met. Average financial aid package met 53% of need; average scholarship/grant was $6,410; average loan was $3,428. For part-time students, average financial aid package was $6,284.

Students without need: 81 full-time freshmen who did not demonstrate need for aid received scholarships/grants; average award was $2,095. No-need awards available for academics, alumni affiliation, art, athletics, leadership, minority status, music/drama, ROTC, state/district residency.

Scholarships offered: ***Merit:*** 1906 Scholars; tuition for 4 years; 10 awards annually. UHP Scholarships; $1,500 for 4 years; 10 awards annually. Foundation Scholars; $1,500 for 4 years; 10 awards annually. Miscellaneous renewable and non-renewable awards; ranging from $500-$5,000. ***Athletic:*** 44 full-time freshmen received athletic scholarships; average amount $6,584.

Cumulative student debt: 68% of graduating class had student loans; average debt was $21,562.

Additional info: Majority of available scholarships are need-blind.

FINANCIAL AID PROCEDURES

Forms required: FAFSA.

Dates and Deadlines: Priority date 4/20; no closing date. Applicants notified on a rolling basis starting 4/20.

Transfers: No deadline. Applicants notified on a rolling basis starting 4/20.

CONTACT
Connie Murphey, Director of Financial Aid
PO Box 8024, Statesboro, GA 30458
(912) 478-5413

Georgia Southwestern State University

Americus, Georgia
www.gsw.edu Federal Code: 001573

4-year public university and liberal arts college in large town.
Enrollment: 2,694 undergrads, 27% part-time. 374 full-time freshmen.
Selectivity: Admits 50 to 75% of applicants.

BASIC COSTS (2012-2013)
Tuition and fees: $5,816; out-of-state residents $17,720.
Per-credit charge: $150; out-of-state residents $547.
Room and board: $6,420.

FINANCIAL AID PICTURE
Students with need: Need-based aid available for full-time and part-time students.
Students without need: No-need awards available for academics, athletics, leadership.
Scholarships offered: Wheatley Scholarship: $2,000-2,500; 3.0 in college preparatory course and either 1100 SAT (exclusive of Writing) or 24 ACT.

FINANCIAL AID PROCEDURES
Forms required: FAFSA, institutional form.
Dates and Deadlines: Priority date 4/1; closing date 6/1. Applicants notified on a rolling basis starting 3/1.

CONTACT
Angela Bryant, Director of Financial Aid
800 Georgia Southwestern State University Drive, Americus, GA 31709-9957
(229) 928-1378

Georgia State University

Atlanta, Georgia
www.gsu.edu Federal Code: 001574

4-year public university in very large city.
Enrollment: 23,964 undergrads, 25% part-time. 2,700 full-time freshmen.
Selectivity: Admits 50 to 75% of applicants. GED not accepted.

BASIC COSTS (2012-2013)
Tuition and fees: $9,664; out-of-state residents $27,874.
Per-credit charge: $251; out-of-state residents $858.
Room and board: $9,506.

FINANCIAL AID PICTURE (2011-2012)
Students with need: Out of 2,552 full-time freshmen who applied for aid, 2,121 were judged to have need. Of these, 2,086 received aid, and 84 had their full need met. Average financial aid package met 70% of need; average scholarship/grant was $4,779; average loan was $3,405. For part-time students, average financial aid package was $6,149.
Students without need: 363 full-time freshmen who did not demonstrate need for aid received scholarships/grants; average award was $757. No-need awards available for academics, alumni affiliation, art, athletics, job skills, leadership, minority status, music/drama, religious affiliation, ROTC, state/district residency.
Scholarships offered: 59 full-time freshmen received athletic scholarships; average amount $20,681.
Cumulative student debt: 70% of graduating class had student loans; average debt was $21,817.

FINANCIAL AID PROCEDURES
Forms required: FAFSA.
Dates and Deadlines: Closing date 4/1. Applicants notified on a rolling basis starting 3/1.
Transfers: Applicants notified on a rolling basis starting 3/1; must reply by 11/1.

CONTACT
Louis Scott, Director of Student Financial Aid
Box 4009, Atlanta, GA 30302-4009
(404) 413-2400

Gordon College

Barnesville, Georgia
www.gdn.edu Federal Code: 001575

2-year public junior and teachers college in small town.
Enrollment: 4,171 undergrads.
Selectivity: Admits less than 50% of applicants.

BASIC COSTS (2012-2013)
Tuition and fees: $3,642; out-of-state residents $11,310.
Per-credit charge: $95; out-of-state residents $350.
Room and board: $5,760.

FINANCIAL AID PICTURE (2012-2013)
Students with need: 44% of average financial aid package awarded as scholarships/grants, 56% awarded as loans/jobs. Need-based aid available for part-time students. Work study available nights, weekends, and for part-time students.
Students without need: No-need awards available for academics, athletics, music/drama, state/district residency.

FINANCIAL AID PROCEDURES
Forms required: FAFSA, state aid form.
Dates and Deadlines: Priority date 5/1; closing date 6/1. Applicants notified on a rolling basis starting 4/1.

CONTACT
Larry Mitcham, Director of Financial Aid
419 College Drive, Barnesville, GA 30204
(678) 359-5990

Gupton Jones College of Funeral Service

Decatur, Georgia
www.gupton-jones.edu Federal Code: 010771

2-year private technical college in very large city.
Enrollment: 185 undergrads.
Selectivity: Open admission.

BASIC COSTS (2012-2013)
Tuition and fees: $9,000.
Per-credit charge: $200.
Additional info: Tuition costs include all textbooks and supplies needed.

FINANCIAL AID PICTURE
Students with need: Need-based aid available for full-time and part-time students.
Students without need: This college awards aid only to students with need.

FINANCIAL AID PROCEDURES
Forms required: FAFSA.
Dates and Deadlines: Applicants notified on a rolling basis.

CONTACT
James Hinz, Dean
5141 Snapfinger Woods Drive, Decatur, GA 30035
(770) 593-2257

Gwinnett College

Lilburn, Georgia
www.gwinnettcollege.edu Federal Code: 025830

2-year for-profit junior and career college in large city.
Enrollment: 350 full-time undergrads.
Selectivity: Open admission; but selective for some programs.

BASIC COSTS (2013-2014)
Tuition and fees: $9,850.

FINANCIAL AID PICTURE
Students with need: Need-based aid available for full-time and part-time students.

FINANCIAL AID PROCEDURES
Forms required: FAFSA.
Dates and Deadlines: Applicants notified on a rolling basis.

CONTACT
James Davidson, Director of Financial Aid
4230 Highway 29, Lilburn, GA 30047
(770) 381-7200

Gwinnett Technical College

Lawrenceville, Georgia

2-year public technical college in large town.
Enrollment: 6,478 undergrads, 66% part-time. 391 full-time freshmen.
Selectivity: Open admission; but selective for some programs.

BASIC COSTS (2012-2013)
Tuition and fees: $2,564; out-of-state residents $4,814.
Per-credit charge: $75; out-of-state residents $150.

FINANCIAL AID PICTURE
Students with need: Need-based aid available for full-time and part-time students.

FINANCIAL AID PROCEDURES
Forms required: FAFSA.
Transfers: No deadline.

CONTACT
5150 Sugarloaf Parkway, Lawrenceville, GA 30043-5702

Herzing University: Atlanta

Atlanta, Georgia
www.herzing.edu Federal Code: 014030

3-year for-profit business and technical college in very large city.
Enrollment: 436 undergrads.

FINANCIAL AID PICTURE
Students with need: Need-based aid available for full-time and part-time students. Work study available nights.
Students without need: No-need awards available for academics.

FINANCIAL AID PROCEDURES
Forms required: FAFSA, institutional form.
Dates and Deadlines: Applicants notified on a rolling basis.

CONTACT
Stephanie Gunby, Director of Financial Aid
3393 Peachtree Road NE, Suite 1003, Atlanta, GA 30326
(404) 816-4533

Kennesaw State University

Kennesaw, Georgia
www.kennesaw.edu Federal Code: 001577

4-year public university in large town.
Enrollment: 22,574 undergrads, 25% part-time. 3,012 full-time freshmen.
Selectivity: Admits 50 to 75% of applicants. GED not accepted.

BASIC COSTS (2012-2013)
Tuition and fees: $6,486; out-of-state residents $18,762.
Per-credit charge: $162; out-of-state residents $571.
Room and board: $7,951.

FINANCIAL AID PICTURE
Students with need: Need-based aid available for full-time and part-time students.
Students without need: No-need awards available for academics, alumni affiliation, art, athletics, job skills, leadership, minority status, music/drama, ROTC, state/district residency.

FINANCIAL AID PROCEDURES
Dates and Deadlines: Priority date 7/1; no closing date. Applicants notified on a rolling basis starting 7/1.
Transfers: No deadline. Applicants notified on a rolling basis starting 7/1.

CONTACT
Ron Day, Director of Financial Aid
1000 Chastain Road, Kennesaw, GA 30144-5591
(770) 423-6074

LaGrange College

LaGrange, Georgia
www.lagrange.edu Federal Code: 001578

4-year private liberal arts college in large town, affiliated with United Methodist Church.
Enrollment: 833 undergrads, 1% part-time. 198 full-time freshmen.
Selectivity: Admits less than 50% of applicants.

BASIC COSTS (2012-2013)
Tuition and fees: $24,302.
Per-credit charge: $1,000.
Room and board: $9,930.

FINANCIAL AID PICTURE
Students with need: Need-based aid available for full-time and part-time students. Work study available nights, weekends, and for part-time students.
Students without need: No-need awards available for academics, art, leadership, music/drama, religious affiliation, state/district residency.
Scholarships offered: Presidential: tuition, room and board; competitive. Fellows: $12,500 per year; competitive. Founders: $10,000 per year; competitive. Hilltop: $7,500 per year. Gateway: $ 5,500 per year.

FINANCIAL AID PROCEDURES
Forms required: FAFSA, state aid form.
Dates and Deadlines: Priority date 3/1; no closing date. Applicants notified on a rolling basis starting 3/15; must reply by 8/15 or within 2 week(s) of notification.
Transfers: Priority date 4/1; no deadline. Applicants notified on a rolling basis starting 3/1; must reply within 3 week(s) of notification.

CONTACT
Sylvia Smith, Director of Financial Aid
601 Broad Street, LaGrange, GA 30240-2999
(706) 880-8241

Life University
Marietta, Georgia
www.life.edu
Federal Code: 014170

4-year private university in very large city.
Enrollment: 843 undergrads, 29% part-time. 154 full-time freshmen.
Selectivity: Admits 50 to 75% of applicants.

BASIC COSTS (2012-2013)
Tuition and fees: $9,342.
Per-credit charge: $191.

FINANCIAL AID PICTURE (2012-2013)
Students with need: 56% of average financial aid package awarded as scholarships/grants, 44% awarded as loans/jobs.
Students without need: No-need awards available for academics.

FINANCIAL AID PROCEDURES
Forms required: FAFSA.
Dates and Deadlines: Applicants notified on a rolling basis starting 5/1.

CONTACT
Kay Freeland, Director of Student Administrative Services
1269 Barclay Circle, Marietta, GA 30060
(770) 426-2944

Luther Rice University
Lithonia, Georgia
www.lru.edu
Federal Code: 031009

4-year private university and seminary college in very large city.
Enrollment: 504 undergrads. 2 full-time freshmen.
Selectivity: Open admission.

BASIC COSTS (2013-2014)
Tuition and fees: $7,140.
Per-credit charge: $223.

FINANCIAL AID PICTURE (2012-2013)
Students with need: Out of 2 full-time freshmen who applied for aid, 2 were judged to have need. Of these, 2 received aid. For part-time students, average financial aid package was $4,271.
Students without need: No-need awards available for alumni affiliation.
Additional info: Financial aid department monitors satisfactory academic progress very closely. Must have financial aid applications submitted 45 days prior to start of semester.

FINANCIAL AID PROCEDURES
Forms required: FAFSA, institutional form.
Dates and Deadlines: Closing date 7/20. Applicants notified on a rolling basis starting 7/27; must reply within 2 week(s) of notification.
Transfers: Letter required from previous school showing last day of attendance and cancellation of all financial aid.

CONTACT
Gary Cook, Director of Financial Aid
3038 Evans Mill Road, Lithonia, GA 30038

Mercer University
Macon, Georgia
www.mercer.edu
Federal Code: 001580

4-year private university in small city, affiliated with Baptist faith.
Enrollment: 2,363 undergrads, 2% part-time. 645 full-time freshmen.
Selectivity: Admits 50 to 75% of applicants.

BASIC COSTS (2012-2013)
Tuition and fees: $32,466.
Per-credit charge: $1,072.
Room and board: $10,697.

FINANCIAL AID PICTURE (2012-2013)
Students with need: Out of 645 full-time freshmen who applied for aid, 512 were judged to have need. Of these, 512 received aid, and 139 had their full need met. Average financial aid package met 83% of need; average scholarship/grant was $24,913; average loan was $5,624. For part-time students, average financial aid package was $9,191.
Students without need: 127 full-time freshmen who did not demonstrate need for aid received scholarships/grants; average award was $19,370. No-need awards available for academics, art, athletics, job skills, leadership, music/drama, religious affiliation, ROTC, state/district residency.
Scholarships offered: ***Merit:*** Various scholarships: primarily based on high school GPA, SAT/ACT scores, and personal interview; early applications given highest consideration. National Merit finalists and semi-finalists guaranteed full-tuition scholarships. ***Athletic:*** 22 full-time freshmen received athletic scholarships; average amount $17,450.
Cumulative student debt: 69% of graduating class had student loans; average debt was $31,488.

FINANCIAL AID PROCEDURES
Forms required: FAFSA, state aid form, institutional form.
Dates and Deadlines: Priority date 4/1; no closing date. Applicants notified on a rolling basis starting 3/15; must reply within 2 week(s) of notification.
Transfers: No deadline. Applicants notified on a rolling basis starting 3/15; must reply within 2 week(s) of notification.

CONTACT
Carol Williams, Associate Vice President, Student Financial Planning
1400 Coleman Avenue, Macon, GA 31207-0001
(478) 301-2670

Middle Georgia State College
Macon, Georgia
www.mga.edu
Federal Code: 001581

4-year public liberal arts college in small city.
Enrollment: 8,884 undergrads.

BASIC COSTS (2012-2013)
Tuition and fees: $3,692; out-of-state residents $11,360.
Per-credit charge: $95; out-of-state residents $350.
Room and board: $7,514.

FINANCIAL AID PICTURE
Students with need: Need-based aid available for full-time and part-time students. Work study available nights, weekends, and for part-time students.
Students without need: No-need awards available for academics, alumni affiliation, art, athletics, job skills, leadership, minority status, music/drama, state/district residency.

FINANCIAL AID PROCEDURES
Forms required: FAFSA.
Dates and Deadlines: Closing date 7/1. Applicants notified on a rolling basis starting 5/1.

CONTACT
Patricia Simmons, Director of Financial Aid
100 College Station Drive, Macon, GA 31206
(478) 471-2800

Morehouse College

Atlanta, Georgia
www.morehouse.edu Federal Code: 001582

4-year private liberal arts college for men in very large city.
Enrollment: 2,359 undergrads, 6% part-time. 566 full-time freshmen.
Selectivity: Admits 50 to 75% of applicants.

BASIC COSTS (2012-2013)
Tuition and fees: $24,744.
Per-credit charge: $937.
Room and board: $12,672.

FINANCIAL AID PICTURE (2012-2013)
Students with need: Out of 566 full-time freshmen who applied for aid, 566 were judged to have need. Of these, 546 received aid, and 10 had their full need met. Average financial aid package met 55% of need; average scholarship/grant was $19,118; average loan was $4,604. For part-time students, average financial aid package was $9,278.
Students without need: This college awards aid only to students with need.
Cumulative student debt: 80% of graduating class had student loans; average debt was $39,364.

FINANCIAL AID PROCEDURES
Forms required: FAFSA, state aid form, institutional form.
Dates and Deadlines: Priority date 2/15; closing date 4/1. Applicants notified on a rolling basis starting 11/15; must reply by 5/1 or within 4 week(s) of notification.
Transfers: Applicants notified by 4/1; must reply by 5/1.

CONTACT
James Stotts, Associate Vice President for Student Financial Aid
830 Westview Drive SW, Atlanta, GA 30314
(404) 215-2638

North Georgia Technical College

Clarkesville, Georgia
www.northgatech.edu Federal Code: 005619

2-year public community and technical college in small town.
Enrollment: 2,302 undergrads, 53% part-time. 362 full-time freshmen.
Selectivity: Open admission; but selective for some programs.

BASIC COSTS (2012-2013)
Tuition and fees: $2,580; out-of-state residents $4,830.
Per-credit charge: $75; out-of-state residents $150.
Additional info: Tuition/fee waivers available for unemployed or children of unemployed.

FINANCIAL AID PICTURE
Students with need: Need-based aid available for full-time and part-time students. Work study available nights, weekends, and for part-time students.

CONTACT
Kim Kelley, Director of Financial Aid
1500 Highway 197 North, Clarkesville, GA 30523
(706) 754-7727

Oglethorpe University

Atlanta, Georgia
www.oglethorpe.edu Federal Code: 001586

4-year private liberal arts college in very large city.
Enrollment: 1,023 undergrads, 7% part-time. 277 full-time freshmen.
Selectivity: Admits over 75% of applicants.

BASIC COSTS (2013-2014)
Tuition and fees: $31,280.
Room and board: $11,300.

FINANCIAL AID PICTURE
Students with need: Need-based aid available for full-time students.
Students without need: No-need awards available for academics, music/drama.

FINANCIAL AID PROCEDURES
Forms required: FAFSA, institutional form.
Dates and Deadlines: Applicants notified on a rolling basis starting 3/1; must reply by 5/1 or within 3 week(s) of notification.
Transfers: Priority date 2/1; no deadline.

CONTACT
Meg McGinness, Director of Financial Aid
4484 Peachtree Road NE, Atlanta, GA 30319-2797
(404) 364-8356

Oxford College of Emory University

Oxford, Georgia Federal Code: 001565
www.oxford.emory.edu CSS Code: 5186

2-year private branch campus and liberal arts college in large town, affiliated with United Methodist Church.
Enrollment: 909 undergrads. 460 full-time freshmen.
Selectivity: Admits less than 50% of applicants. GED not accepted.

BASIC COSTS (2013-2014)
Tuition and fees: $38,328.
Room and board: $10,784.

FINANCIAL AID PICTURE (2011-2012)
Students with need: Out of 266 full-time freshmen who applied for aid, 266 were judged to have need. Of these, 266 received aid, and 266 had their full need met. Average financial aid package met 100% of need; average scholarship/grant was $23,663; average loan was $3,500. Need-based aid available for part-time students.
Students without need: 30 full-time freshmen who did not demonstrate need for aid received scholarships/grants; average award was $20,440. No-need awards available for academics, leadership, religious affiliation, state/district residency.
Scholarships offered: Woodruff Scholarships; full tuition, room and board for 4 years. Dean's Scholarship; full tuition for 4 years. Faculty Scholarships; half tuition for 4 years. 2-year scholarships; range from $8,000-$10,000 a year.
Cumulative student debt: 41% of graduating class had student loans; average debt was $10,066.
Additional info: Loan reduction program for families with annual assessed incomes of $100,000 or less who demonstrate need.

FINANCIAL AID PROCEDURES
Forms required: FAFSA, CSS PROFILE, state aid form.
Dates and Deadlines: Priority date 2/15; closing date 3/1. Applicants notified on a rolling basis starting 4/2; must reply by 5/1.

CONTACT
Jennifer Patil, Associate Dean for Financial Aid and Enrollment
100 Hamill Street, Oxford, GA 30054-1418
(770) 784-8303

Paine College

Augusta, Georgia
www.paine.edu Federal Code: 001587

4-year private liberal arts college in large city, affiliated with Christian Methodist Episcopal Church.

Enrollment: 825 undergrads, 8% part-time. 173 full-time freshmen.

BASIC COSTS (2012-2013)
Tuition and fees: $12,502.
Per-credit charge: $481.
Room and board: $6,094.

FINANCIAL AID PICTURE
Students with need: Need-based aid available for full-time and part-time students. Work study available nights, weekends, and for part-time students.
Students without need: No-need awards available for academics, alumni affiliation, athletics, music/drama, religious affiliation, ROTC.

FINANCIAL AID PROCEDURES
Forms required: FAFSA, state aid form.
Dates and Deadlines: Priority date 3/1; no closing date. Applicants notified on a rolling basis starting 5/1; must reply within 2 week(s) of notification.

CONTACT
Gerri Bogan, Director of Financial Aid
1235 15th Street, Augusta, GA 30901-3182
(706) 821-8262

Piedmont College
Demorest, Georgia
www.piedmont.edu Federal Code: 001588

4-year private liberal arts and teachers college in rural community, affiliated with United Church of Christ.
Enrollment: 1,244 undergrads, 9% part-time. 208 full-time freshmen.
Selectivity: Admits 50 to 75% of applicants.

BASIC COSTS (2013-2014)
Tuition and fees: $20,730.
Per-credit charge: $864.
Room and board: $8,530.
Additional info: Tuition/fee waivers available for adults.

FINANCIAL AID PICTURE (2012-2013)
Students with need: Out of 173 full-time freshmen who applied for aid, 152 were judged to have need. Of these, 150 received aid, and 35 had their full need met. Average financial aid package met 74% of need; average scholarship/grant was $15,616; average loan was $3,394. For part-time students, average financial aid package was $8,742.
Students without need: 37 full-time freshmen who did not demonstrate need for aid received scholarships/grants; average award was $11,962. No-need awards available for academics, alumni affiliation, art, leadership, music/drama, religious affiliation, state/district residency.
Scholarships offered: The highest academic scholarships are awarded to high school seniors superior in academics, leadership, and extracurricular activities.
Cumulative student debt: 78% of graduating class had student loans; average debt was $24,651.

FINANCIAL AID PROCEDURES
Forms required: FAFSA, state aid form, institutional form.
Dates and Deadlines: Priority date 5/1; no closing date. Applicants notified on a rolling basis; must reply within 2 week(s) of notification.
Transfers: No deadline. Applicants notified on a rolling basis; must reply within 2 week(s) of notification.

CONTACT
David McMillion, Director of Financial Aid
165 Central Avenue, Demorest, GA 30535-0010
(706) 776-0114

Point University
West Point, Georgia
www.point.edu Federal Code: 001547

4-year private Bible and liberal arts college in small town, affiliated with Christian Church.
Enrollment: 1,439 undergrads, 9% part-time. 253 full-time freshmen.
Selectivity: Admits 50 to 75% of applicants.

BASIC COSTS (2012-2013)
Tuition and fees: $17,400.
Room and board: $6,200.
Additional info: Board plan covers 17 meals per week.

FINANCIAL AID PICTURE
Students with need: Need-based aid available for full-time and part-time students. Work study available nights.
Students without need: No-need awards available for academics, athletics, leadership.

FINANCIAL AID PROCEDURES
Forms required: FAFSA, state aid form.
Dates and Deadlines: Priority date 6/1; closing date 8/1. Applicants notified on a rolling basis starting 3/1; must reply within 3 week(s) of notification.
Transfers: Priority date 3/25; no deadline. Applicants notified on a rolling basis starting 3/1.

CONTACT
Karen Bailey, Director of Financial Aid
507 West 10th Street, West Point, GA 31833
(404) 460-2462

Reinhardt University
Waleska, Georgia
www.reinhardt.edu Federal Code: 001589

4-year private liberal arts and teachers college in rural community, affiliated with United Methodist Church.
Enrollment: 1,170 undergrads.
Selectivity: Admits 50 to 75% of applicants.

BASIC COSTS (2012-2013)
Tuition and fees: $18,120.
Per-credit charge: $598.
Room and board: $6,958.

FINANCIAL AID PICTURE
Students with need: Need-based aid available for full-time and part-time students.
Students without need: No-need awards available for academics, art, athletics, leadership, music/drama, religious affiliation, state/district residency.

FINANCIAL AID PROCEDURES
Forms required: FAFSA, state aid form.
Dates and Deadlines: Priority date 5/1; no closing date. Applicants notified on a rolling basis starting 2/1; must reply within 2 week(s) of notification.
Transfers: No deadline.

CONTACT
Angela Harlow, Director of Financial Aid
7300 Reinhardt Circle, Waleska, GA 30183-2981
(770) 720-5667

Savannah College of Art and Design

Savannah, Georgia
www.scad.edu Federal Code: 015022

4-year private visual arts and performing arts college in small city.
Enrollment: 9,036 undergrads, 15% part-time. 1,761 full-time freshmen.
Selectivity: Admits 50 to 75% of applicants.

BASIC COSTS (2012-2013)
Tuition and fees: $31,905.
Per-credit charge: $709.
Room and board: $12,945.
Additional info: A one-time matriculation fee of $500 is required of all students.

FINANCIAL AID PICTURE (2012-2013)
Students with need: Out of 1,256 full-time freshmen who applied for aid, 1,070 were judged to have need. Of these, 1,069 received aid, and 129 had their full need met. Average financial aid package met 16% of need; average scholarship/grant was $5,556; average loan was $2,852. For part-time students, average financial aid package was $20,325.
Students without need: 639 full-time freshmen who did not demonstrate need for aid received scholarships/grants; average award was $10,278. No-need awards available for academics, alumni affiliation, art, athletics, music/drama, ROTC.
Scholarships offered: 19 full-time freshmen received athletic scholarships; average amount $27,003.
Cumulative student debt: 62% of graduating class had student loans; average debt was $37,776.
Additional info: Degree-seeking students awarded maximum of one scholarship from college, but may receive additional scholarships from other sources, as well as additional forms of financial aid. Scholarships based on academic achievement awarded through admission office.

FINANCIAL AID PROCEDURES
Forms required: FAFSA, state aid form.
Dates and Deadlines: Applicants notified on a rolling basis starting 3/15; must reply within 4 week(s) of notification.
Transfers: No deadline. Applicants notified on a rolling basis. Transfer students eligible to apply for academic and portfolio scholarships.

CONTACT
Brenda Clark, Director of Financial Aid
PO Box 2072, Savannah, GA 31402-2072
(912) 525-5000

Savannah Technical College

Savannah, Georgia
www.savannahtech.edu Federal Code: 005618

2-year public technical college in large city.
Enrollment: 4,547 undergrads, 62% part-time. 384 full-time freshmen.
Selectivity: Open admission; but selective for some programs.

BASIC COSTS (2012-2013)
Tuition and fees: $2,522; out-of-state residents $4,772.
Per-credit charge: $75; out-of-state residents $150.

FINANCIAL AID PICTURE
Students with need: Need-based aid available for full-time and part-time students.
Students without need: No-need awards available for academics, leadership, minority status, state/district residency.

FINANCIAL AID PROCEDURES
Forms required: FAFSA.
Dates and Deadlines: Applicants notified on a rolling basis.

CONTACT
Faith Anderson, Financial Aid Director
5717 White Bluff Road, Savannah, GA 31401-5521
(912) 443-5776

Shorter University

Rome, Georgia
www.shorter.edu Federal Code: 001591

4-year private liberal arts college in large town, affiliated with Southern Baptist Convention.
Enrollment: 1,323 full-time undergrads.
Selectivity: Admits 50 to 75% of applicants.

BASIC COSTS (2012-2013)
Tuition and fees: $18,770.
Per-credit charge: $275.
Room and board: $9,000.

FINANCIAL AID PICTURE
Students with need: Need-based aid available for full-time and part-time students. Work study available nights.
Students without need: No-need awards available for academics, art, athletics, music/drama, religious affiliation, state/district residency.
Additional info: Cost is reduced for all in-state students by state tuition equalization grant program. College matches for out-of-state full-time students.

FINANCIAL AID PROCEDURES
Forms required: FAFSA, state aid form, institutional form.
Dates and Deadlines: Priority date 4/1; no closing date. Applicants notified on a rolling basis starting 3/1; must reply within 2 week(s) of notification.
Transfers: Priority date 4/15; no deadline. Applicants notified on a rolling basis starting 3/31; must reply within 2 week(s) of notification.

CONTACT
Colleen Lassiter, Financial Aid Director
315 Shorter Avenue, Rome, GA 30165
(706) 233-7227

South Georgia State College

Douglas, Georgia
www.sgc.edu Federal Code: 001592

4-year public liberal arts college in large town.
Enrollment: 2,783 undergrads, 25% part-time. 965 full-time freshmen.

BASIC COSTS (2012-2013)
Tuition and fees: $3,562; out-of-state residents $10,612.
Per-credit charge: $84; out-of-state residents $319.
Room and board: $7,750.

FINANCIAL AID PICTURE
Students with need: Need-based aid available for full-time and part-time students.
Students without need: No-need awards available for academics.

FINANCIAL AID PROCEDURES
Forms required: FAFSA, institutional form.
Dates and Deadlines: Priority date 6/1; no closing date. Applicants notified on a rolling basis starting 7/6; must reply within 2 week(s) of notification.
Transfers: No deadline.

CONTACT
Becky Rumker, Director of Financial Aid
100 West College Park Drive, Douglas, GA 31533-5098
(912) 260-4282

South University: Savannah

Savannah, Georgia
www.southuniversity.edu Federal Code: 013039

4-year for-profit university in small city.
Enrollment: 816 undergrads.

BASIC COSTS (2012-2013)

Tuition and fees: $16,585.
Additional info: Annual tuition for BSN program is $23,160 plus $600 required fees.

FINANCIAL AID PICTURE

Students with need: Need-based aid available for full-time students.

FINANCIAL AID PROCEDURES

Forms required: FAFSA, state aid form.
Dates and Deadlines: Applicants notified on a rolling basis starting 9/1.

CONTACT

Tressa Brush, Director of Financial Aid
709 Mall Boulevard, Savannah, GA 31406
(912) 201-8000

Southeastern Technical College

Vidalia, Georgia
www.southeasterntech.edu Federal Code: 030665

2-year public technical college in large town.
Enrollment: 1,526 undergrads, 69% part-time. 88 full-time freshmen.
Selectivity: Open admission; but selective for some programs.

BASIC COSTS (2012-2013)

Tuition and fees: $2,542; out-of-state residents $4,792.
Per-credit charge: $75; out-of-state residents $150.

FINANCIAL AID PICTURE (2011-2012)

Students with need: 69% of average financial aid package awarded as scholarships/grants, 31% awarded as loans/jobs. Need-based aid available for part-time students. Work study available nights.
Students without need: No-need awards available for state/district residency.

FINANCIAL AID PROCEDURES

Forms required: FAFSA, state aid form.
Dates and Deadlines: Applicants notified on a rolling basis starting 4/6.

CONTACT

Mitchell Fagler, Executive Director of Student Affairs/Financial Aid
3001 East First Street, Vidalia, GA 30474
(478) 289-2268

Southern Polytechnic State University

Marietta, Georgia
www.spsu.edu Federal Code: 001570

4-year public university in small city.
Enrollment: 5,324 undergrads, 28% part-time. 548 full-time freshmen.
Selectivity: Admits over 75% of applicants. GED not accepted.

BASIC COSTS (2012-2013)

Tuition and fees: $6,678; out-of-state residents $20,126.
Per-credit charge: $175; out-of-state residents $623.
Room and board: $7,280.

FINANCIAL AID PICTURE (2011-2012)

Students with need: Out of 500 full-time freshmen who applied for aid, 500 were judged to have need. Of these, 485 received aid, and 136 had their full need met. Average financial aid package met 71% of need; average scholarship/grant was $2,775; average loan was $1,854. For part-time students, average financial aid package was $2,121.
Students without need: No-need awards available for academics, athletics, minority status.
Scholarships offered: 7 full-time freshmen received athletic scholarships; average amount $3,649.
Cumulative student debt: 61% of graduating class had student loans; average debt was $6,850.

FINANCIAL AID PROCEDURES

Forms required: FAFSA.
Dates and Deadlines: Priority date 3/1; no closing date. Applicants notified on a rolling basis starting 5/1.
Transfers: No deadline. Applicants notified on a rolling basis starting 5/1.

CONTACT

Gary Mann, Director of Financial Aid
1100 South Marietta Parkway, Marietta, GA 30060-2896
(678) 915-7290

Southwest Georgia Technical College

Thomasville, Georgia
www.southwestgatech.edu Federal Code: 005615

2-year public technical college in large town.
Enrollment: 1,381 undergrads, 69% part-time. 85 full-time freshmen.
Selectivity: Open admission; but selective for some programs.

BASIC COSTS (2012-2013)

Tuition and fees: $2,498; out-of-state residents $4,748.
Per-credit charge: $75; out-of-state residents $150.

FINANCIAL AID PICTURE

Students with need: Need-based aid available for full-time and part-time students. Work study available nights.
Students without need: No-need awards available for state/district residency.

FINANCIAL AID PROCEDURES

Forms required: FAFSA.
Dates and Deadlines: Applicants notified on a rolling basis starting 7/1.

CONTACT

Amy Scoggins, Director of Financial Aid
15689 US Highway 19N, Thomasville, GA 31792
(229) 227-2687

Spelman College

Atlanta, Georgia
www.spelman.edu Federal Code: 001594

4-year private liberal arts college for women in very large city.
Enrollment: 2,145 undergrads, 3% part-time. 520 full-time freshmen.
Selectivity: Admits less than 50% of applicants.

BASIC COSTS (2012-2013)

Tuition and fees: $23,794.
Room and board: $11,541.

FINANCIAL AID PICTURE (2011-2012)

Students with need: Out of 495 full-time freshmen who applied for aid, 475 were judged to have need. Of these, 449 received aid, and 70 had their full need met. Average financial aid package met 53% of need; average scholarship/grant was $12,202; average loan was $3,324. For part-time students, average financial aid package was $7,828.

Students without need: No-need awards available for academics, alumni affiliation, leadership, music/drama, state/district residency.
Cumulative student debt: 74% of graduating class had student loans; average debt was $33,898.

FINANCIAL AID PROCEDURES
Forms required: FAFSA, institutional form.
Dates and Deadlines: Priority date 2/1; no closing date. Applicants notified on a rolling basis starting 2/15; must reply within 2 week(s) of notification.
Transfers: Closing date 10/1. No special aid for transfer students for the first year.

CONTACT
Lenora Jackson, Associate Vice President, Enrollment Management
350 Spelman Lane SW, Campus Box 277, Atlanta, GA 30314-4399
(404) 270-5212

Thomas University
Thomasville, Georgia
www.thomasu.edu Federal Code: 001555

4-year private university and liberal arts college in large town.
Enrollment: 819 undergrads, 40% part-time. 111 full-time freshmen.
Selectivity: Open admission; but selective for some programs.

BASIC COSTS (2013-2014)
Tuition and fees: $14,080.
Per-credit charge: $525.
Room only: $4,200.

FINANCIAL AID PICTURE (2012-2013)
Students with need: Average financial aid package for all full-time undergraduates was $10,055; for part-time $13,506.
Students without need: No-need awards available for academics, athletics, leadership, state/district residency.

FINANCIAL AID PROCEDURES
Forms required: FAFSA, state aid form.
Dates and Deadlines: Priority date 5/1; no closing date. Applicants notified on a rolling basis.
Transfers: Student must submit official academic transcripts from all colleges attended. Financial aid received during current academic year from previous school will be verified through the National Student Loan Data System (NSLDS).

CONTACT
Michael Rayburn, Director of Financial Aid
1501 Millpond Road, Thomasville, GA 31792-7499
(229) 227-6931

Toccoa Falls College
Toccoa Falls, Georgia
www.tfc.edu Federal Code: 001596

4-year private Bible and liberal arts college in large town, affiliated with Christian and Missionary Alliance.
Enrollment: 803 undergrads, 7% part-time. 165 full-time freshmen.
Selectivity: Admits less than 50% of applicants.

BASIC COSTS (2013-2014)
Tuition and fees: $19,000.
Per-credit charge: $750.
Room and board: $6,780.

FINANCIAL AID PICTURE (2012-2013)
Students with need: Out of 161 full-time freshmen who applied for aid, 152 were judged to have need. Of these, 152 received aid, and 10 had their full need met. Average financial aid package met 69% of need; average scholarship/grant was $13,262; average loan was $3,437. For part-time students, average financial aid package was $6,039.
Students without need: 10 full-time freshmen who did not demonstrate need for aid received scholarships/grants; average award was $8,200. No-need awards available for academics, alumni affiliation, leadership, music/drama, religious affiliation, state/district residency.
Cumulative student debt: 74% of graduating class had student loans; average debt was $24,502.

FINANCIAL AID PROCEDURES
Forms required: FAFSA, institutional form.
Dates and Deadlines: Priority date 5/1; closing date 8/1. Applicants notified on a rolling basis starting 3/1; must reply within 2 week(s) of notification.
Transfers: Priority date 12/15; no deadline. Applicants notified on a rolling basis starting 10/1; must reply within 2 week(s) of notification.

CONTACT
Truitt Franklin, Director of Financial Aid
PO Box 800899, Toccoa Falls, GA 30598
(706) 886-6831 ext. 5435

Truett-McConnell College
Cleveland, Georgia
www.truett.edu Federal Code: 001597

4-year private liberal arts college in small town, affiliated with Southern Baptist Convention.
Enrollment: 637 undergrads, 7% part-time. 189 full-time freshmen.
Selectivity: Admits over 75% of applicants.

BASIC COSTS (2012-2013)
Tuition and fees: $15,650.
Per-credit charge: $503.
Room and board: $6,700.

FINANCIAL AID PICTURE
Students with need: Need-based aid available for full-time and part-time students.
Students without need: No-need awards available for academics, alumni affiliation, athletics, leadership, music/drama, religious affiliation, state/district residency.

FINANCIAL AID PROCEDURES
Forms required: FAFSA, state aid form, institutional form.
Dates and Deadlines: Priority date 4/1; no closing date. Applicants notified on a rolling basis starting 3/15; must reply within 2 week(s) of notification.

CONTACT
Becky Moore, Director of Financial Aid
100 Alumni Drive, Cleveland, GA 30528
(800) 226-8621

University of Georgia
Athens, Georgia
www.uga.edu Federal Code: 001598

4-year public university in small city.
Enrollment: 26,060 undergrads, 6% part-time. 4,920 full-time freshmen.
Selectivity: Admits 50 to 75% of applicants.

BASIC COSTS (2012-2013)
Tuition and fees: $9,842; out-of-state residents $28,052.
Room and board: $8,758.

FINANCIAL AID PICTURE (2012-2013)
Students with need: Out of 4,077 full-time freshmen who applied for aid, 1,894 were judged to have need. Of these, 1,891 received aid, and 451 had

their full need met. Average financial aid package met 72% of need; average scholarship/grant was $10,061; average loan was $3,305. For part-time students, average financial aid package was $7,123.
Students without need: 316 full-time freshmen who did not demonstrate need for aid received scholarships/grants; average award was $2,340. No-need awards available for academics, athletics, ROTC, state/district residency.
Scholarships offered: 98 full-time freshmen received athletic scholarships; average amount $1,333.
Cumulative student debt: 44% of graduating class had student loans; average debt was $19,621.

FINANCIAL AID PROCEDURES
Forms required: FAFSA.
Dates and Deadlines: Priority date 3/1; no closing date. Applicants notified on a rolling basis starting 5/15; must reply within 2 week(s) of notification.

CONTACT
Bonnie Joerschke, Director of Student Financial Aid
Terrell Hall, Athens, GA 30602-1633
(706) 542-6147

University of North Georgia
Dahlonega, Georgia
www.ung.edu Federal Code: 001585

4-year public university and liberal arts college in small town.
Enrollment: . 1,114 full-time freshmen.
Selectivity: Admits 50 to 75% of applicants. GED not accepted.

BASIC COSTS (2012-2013)
Tuition and fees: $6,570; out-of-state residents $18,846.
Per-credit charge: $162; out-of-state residents $571.
Room and board: $6,772.

FINANCIAL AID PICTURE (2012-2013)
Students with need: Out of 977 full-time freshmen who applied for aid, 622 were judged to have need. Of these, 620 received aid, and 172 had their full need met. Average financial aid package met 65% of need; average scholarship/grant was $4,100; average loan was $3,772. For part-time students, average financial aid package was $6,010.
Students without need: 20 full-time freshmen who did not demonstrate need for aid received scholarships/grants; average award was $1,172. No-need awards available for academics, alumni affiliation, art, athletics, job skills, leadership, music/drama, religious affiliation, ROTC, state/district residency.
Scholarships offered: 44 full-time freshmen received athletic scholarships; average amount $4,454.
Cumulative student debt: 57% of graduating class had student loans; average debt was $12,166.

FINANCIAL AID PROCEDURES
Forms required: FAFSA.
Dates and Deadlines: Priority date 3/17; no closing date. Applicants notified on a rolling basis starting 3/1; must reply within 4 week(s) of notification.

CONTACT
Jill Rayner, Director of Financial Aid
82 College Circle, Dahlonega, GA 30597
(706) 864-1412

University of West Georgia
Carrollton, Georgia
www.westga.edu Federal Code: 001601

4-year public university in large town.
Enrollment: 9,963 undergrads, 18% part-time. 2,070 full-time freshmen.
Selectivity: Admits 50 to 75% of applicants. GED not accepted.

BASIC COSTS (2012-2013)
Tuition and fees: $6,710; out-of-state residents $18,986.
Per-credit charge: $162; out-of-state residents $571.
Room and board: $7,482.
Additional info: Tuition/fee waivers available for adults, minority students.

FINANCIAL AID PICTURE (2012-2013)
Students with need: Out of 1,626 full-time freshmen who applied for aid, 1,341 were judged to have need. Of these, 1,326 received aid, and 307 had their full need met. Average financial aid package met 55% of need; average scholarship/grant was $6,445; average loan was $3,417. For part-time students, average financial aid package was $7,785.
Students without need: 62 full-time freshmen who did not demonstrate need for aid received scholarships/grants; average award was $1,745. No-need awards available for academics, alumni affiliation, art, athletics, leadership, minority status, music/drama, religious affiliation, state/district residency.
Scholarships offered: 56 full-time freshmen received athletic scholarships; average amount $5,001.
Cumulative student debt: 65% of graduating class had student loans; average debt was $18,539.

FINANCIAL AID PROCEDURES
Forms required: FAFSA.
Dates and Deadlines: Closing date 4/1. Applicants notified by 5/1.
Transfers: Applicants notified on a rolling basis starting 5/15.

CONTACT
Kimberly Jordan, Director of Financial Aid
1601 Maple Street, Carrollton, GA 30118
(678) 839-6421

Valdosta State University
Valdosta, Georgia
www.valdosta.edu Federal Code: 001599

4-year public university in small city.
Enrollment: 10,213 undergrads, 13% part-time. 2,204 full-time freshmen.
Selectivity: Admits 50 to 75% of applicants. GED not accepted.

BASIC COSTS (2012-2013)
Tuition and fees: $6,762; out-of-state residents $19,038.
Per-credit charge: $162; out-of-state residents $571.
Room and board: $7,070.

FINANCIAL AID PICTURE (2011-2012)
Students with need: Out of 2,124 full-time freshmen who applied for aid, 1,720 were judged to have need. Of these, 1,714 received aid, and 392 had their full need met. Average financial aid package met 89% of need; average scholarship/grant was $6,586; average loan was $3,351. For part-time students, average financial aid package was $13,555.
Students without need: 18 full-time freshmen who did not demonstrate need for aid received scholarships/grants; average award was $1,925. No-need awards available for academics, art, athletics, minority status, music/drama, ROTC, state/district residency.
Scholarships offered: 21 full-time freshmen received athletic scholarships; average amount $3,885.
Cumulative student debt: 70% of graduating class had student loans; average debt was $23,847.

FINANCIAL AID PROCEDURES
Forms required: FAFSA.
Dates and Deadlines: Priority date 4/1; no closing date. Applicants notified on a rolling basis starting 4/15.
Transfers: Applicants notified on a rolling basis starting 4/15.

CONTACT
Doug Tanner, Director of Financial Aid
1500 North Patterson Street, Valdosta, GA 31698-0170
(229) 333-5935

Wesleyan College
Macon, Georgia
www.wesleyancollege.edu Federal Code: 001600

4-year private liberal arts college for women in small city, affiliated with United Methodist Church.
Enrollment: 648 undergrads, 32% part-time. 118 full-time freshmen.
Selectivity: Admits 50 to 75% of applicants.

BASIC COSTS (2012-2013)
Tuition and fees: $19,000.
Per-credit charge: $445.
Room and board: $8,400.
Additional info: Tuition/fee waivers available for adults.

FINANCIAL AID PICTURE (2012-2013)
Students with need: Average financial aid package met 73% of need; average scholarship/grant was $15,511; average loan was $3,453. For part-time students, average financial aid package was $6,242.
Students without need: No-need awards available for academics, alumni affiliation, art, job skills, leadership, minority status, music/drama, religious affiliation, state/district residency.
Scholarships offered: Academic Scholarships: $1,000 up to tuition and standard room/board; based on minimum 1100 SAT (exclusive of Writing) or 25 ACT and 3.75 GPA, or 1200 SAT (exclusive of Writing) or 27 ACT and 3.5 GPA. Leadership Awards and scholarships for music, art, and theater: range from $1,000-$18,500.
Cumulative student debt: 65% of graduating class had student loans; average debt was $14,729.

FINANCIAL AID PROCEDURES
Forms required: FAFSA, state aid form, institutional form.
Dates and Deadlines: Closing date 4/15. Applicants notified on a rolling basis starting 3/1; must reply by 5/1 or within 3 week(s) of notification.
Transfers: Priority date 7/15; no deadline. Applicants notified on a rolling basis starting 3/15; must reply within 3 week(s) of notification. Scholarships available based on number of hours and GPA transferred in, with minimum 30 semester or 45 quarter hours and 3.0 GPA required.

CONTACT
Danielle Lodge, Financial Aid Director
4760 Forsyth Road, Macon, GA 31210-4462
(478) 757-3902

West Georgia Technical College
Waco, Georgia
www.westgatech.edu Federal Code: 005614

2-year public technical college in small city.
Enrollment: 6,646 undergrads.
Selectivity: Open admission; but selective for some programs.

BASIC COSTS (2012-2013)
Tuition and fees: $2,522; out-of-state residents $4,772.
Per-credit charge: $75; out-of-state residents $150.

FINANCIAL AID PICTURE
Students with need: Need-based aid available for full-time and part-time students. Work study available nights.
Students without need: No-need awards available for state/district residency.

FINANCIAL AID PROCEDURES
Forms required: FAFSA, state aid form, institutional form.
Dates and Deadlines: Applicants notified on a rolling basis; must reply within 1 week(s) of notification.
Transfers: Aid must be in order or cash paid at registration for classes.

CONTACT
Anna English, Executive Director of Financial Aid
176 Murphy Campus Boulevard, Waco, GA 30182
(706) 845-4323

Wiregrass Georgia Technical College
Valdosta, Georgia
www.wiregrass.edu Federal Code: 005256

2-year public technical college in small city.
Enrollment: 3,836 undergrads, 60% part-time. 335 full-time freshmen.
Selectivity: Open admission; but selective for some programs.

BASIC COSTS (2012-2013)
Tuition and fees: $2,552; out-of-state residents $4,802.
Per-credit charge: $75; out-of-state residents $150.

FINANCIAL AID PICTURE (2011-2012)
Students with need: Need-based aid available for full-time and part-time students. Work study available nights.
Students without need: No-need awards available for academics, job skills, state/district residency.

FINANCIAL AID PROCEDURES
Forms required: FAFSA, institutional form.
Dates and Deadlines: Applicants notified on a rolling basis starting 6/1.

CONTACT
Shelia Thomas, Financial Aid Director
4089 Val Tech Road, Valdosta, GA 31602
(229) 333-2107

Young Harris College
Young Harris, Georgia
www.yhc.edu Federal Code: 001604

2-year private liberal arts college in rural community, affiliated with United Methodist Church.
Enrollment: 1,013 undergrads, 1% part-time. 491 full-time freshmen.
Selectivity: Admits less than 50% of applicants.

BASIC COSTS (2013-2014)
Tuition and fees: $25,280.
Per-credit charge: $675.
Room and board: $9,660.

FINANCIAL AID PICTURE (2011-2012)
Students with need: Out of 398 full-time freshmen who applied for aid, 342 were judged to have need. Of these, 342 received aid, and 76 had their full need met. Average financial aid package met 81% of need; average scholarship/grant was $16,998; average loan was $3,376. For part-time students, average financial aid package was $8,766.
Students without need: 146 full-time freshmen who did not demonstrate need for aid received scholarships/grants; average award was $14,928. No-need awards available for academics, art, athletics, job skills, leadership, music/drama, state/district residency.
Scholarships offered: Academic Scholarships; $11,000-$14,000; based on index including GPA and SAT/ACT. Additional awards to a percentage of recipients range from $1,000 to full tuition, room and board.

FINANCIAL AID PROCEDURES
Forms required: FAFSA, state aid form, institutional form.
Dates and Deadlines: Priority date 5/1; no closing date. Applicants notified on a rolling basis starting 2/15; must reply within 2 week(s) of notification.

CONTACT
Linda Adams, Financial Aid Director
PO Box 116, Young Harris, GA 30582-0116
(706) 379-3111

Hawaii

Brigham Young University-Hawaii

Laie, Hawaii
www.byuh.edu Federal Code: 001606

4-year private university and liberal arts college in small town, affiliated with Church of Jesus Christ of Latter-day Saints.
Enrollment: 2,766 undergrads.
Selectivity: GED not accepted.

BASIC COSTS (2012-2013)
Tuition and fees: $4,630.
Room and board: $5,048.
Additional info: 100% higher tuition and per-credit-hour charges for students who are not members of The Church of Jesus Christ of Latter-day Saints.

FINANCIAL AID PICTURE
Students with need: Need-based aid available for full-time and part-time students.
Students without need: No-need awards available for academics, art, athletics, leadership, music/drama, state/district residency.

FINANCIAL AID PROCEDURES
Forms required: FAFSA.
Dates and Deadlines: Closing date 3/15. Applicants notified by 5/1; must reply by 8/31.
Transfers: Closing date 3/15.

CONTACT
Michael Tegada, Financial Aid and Student Accounts Manager
55-220 Kulanui Street, #1973, Laie, HI 96762-1294
(808) 675-3539

Chaminade University of Honolulu

Honolulu, Hawaii
www.chaminade.edu Federal Code: 001605

4-year private university in large city, affiliated with Roman Catholic Church.
Enrollment: 1,258 undergrads.
Selectivity: Admits over 75% of applicants.

BASIC COSTS (2013-2014)
Tuition and fees: $20,090..
Per-credit charge: $665.
Room and board: $11,360.

FINANCIAL AID PICTURE
Students with need: Need-based aid available for full-time and part-time students.
Students without need: No-need awards available for academics, art, athletics, leadership, religious affiliation, ROTC, state/district residency.

Additional info: For students whose eligibility for federal and institutional aid does not meet entire costs, alternative student loans may be secured for eligible applicants.

FINANCIAL AID PROCEDURES
Forms required: FAFSA.
Dates and Deadlines: Priority date 2/15; no closing date. Applicants notified on a rolling basis starting 2/15; must reply within 4 week(s) of notification.

CONTACT
Amy Takiguchi, Director of Financial Aid
3140 Waialae Avenue, Honolulu, HI 96816
(808) 735-4780

Hawaii Pacific University

Honolulu, Hawaii
www.hpu.edu Federal Code: 007279

4-year private university and liberal arts college in large city.
Enrollment: 5,680 undergrads, 36% part-time. 464 full-time freshmen.
Selectivity: Admits 50 to 75% of applicants.

BASIC COSTS (2013-2014)
Tuition and fees: $20,080.
Per-credit charge: $665.
Room and board: $12,550.

FINANCIAL AID PICTURE (2012-2013)
Students with need: Out of 437 full-time freshmen who applied for aid, 322 were judged to have need. Of these, 321 received aid, and 61 had their full need met. Average financial aid package met 78% of need; average scholarship/grant was $1,964; average loan was $5,096. For part-time students, average financial aid package was $11,021.
Students without need: 29 full-time freshmen who did not demonstrate need for aid received scholarships/grants. No-need awards available for academics, alumni affiliation, athletics, leadership, music/drama, ROTC.

FINANCIAL AID PROCEDURES
Forms required: FAFSA.
Dates and Deadlines: Priority date 3/1; no closing date. Applicants notified on a rolling basis starting 4/1; must reply within 3 week(s) of notification.
Transfers: No deadline.

CONTACT
Adam Hatch, Director of Financial Aid
1164 Bishop Street, Suite 1100, Honolulu, HI 96813
(808) 544-0253

Heald College: Honolulu

Honolulu, Hawaii
www.heald.edu Federal Code: E00886

2-year for-profit technical and career college in very large city.
Enrollment: 1,951 undergrads.
Selectivity: Open admission.

BASIC COSTS (2012-2013)
Additional info: Estimated tuition and fees ranges for entire programs as of July 2012: diploma programs, $19,975-$21,205; associate degree programs, $7,475-$33,360; does not include books and supplies, which vary by program. All costs subject to change at any time.

FINANCIAL AID PICTURE
Students with need: Need-based aid available for full-time and part-time students. Work study available nights, weekends, and for part-time students.
Students without need: This college awards aid only to students with need.

FINANCIAL AID PROCEDURES
Forms required: FAFSA.

CONTACT
Candice Wong, Director of Financial Aid
1500 Kapiolani Boulevard, Honolulu, HI 96814-3715
(808) 955-1500 ext. 504

University of Hawaii at Hilo
Hilo, Hawaii
www.uhh.hawaii.edu Federal Code: 001611

4-year public university and liberal arts college in large town.
Enrollment: 3,404 undergrads, 18% part-time. 439 full-time freshmen.
Selectivity: Admits over 75% of applicants.

BASIC COSTS (2012-2013)
Tuition and fees: $6,184; out-of-state residents $17,776.
Per-credit charge: $245; out-of-state residents $728.
Room and board: $7,338.

FINANCIAL AID PICTURE
Students with need: Need-based aid available for full-time and part-time students. Work study available nights, weekends, and for part-time students.
Additional info: Hawaii student incentive grants and tuition waivers (merit and need-based) available to Hawaii residents at participating institutions.

FINANCIAL AID PROCEDURES
Forms required: FAFSA.
Dates and Deadlines: Priority date 3/1; no closing date. Applicants notified on a rolling basis starting 4/15; must reply within 2 week(s) of notification.

CONTACT
Jeff Scofield, Financial Aid Director
200 West Kawili Street, Hilo, HI 96720-4091
(808) 974-7324

University of Hawaii at Manoa
Honolulu, Hawaii
www.manoa.hawaii.edu Federal Code: 001610

4-year public university in very large city.
Enrollment: 14,279 undergrads, 18% part-time. 1,781 full-time freshmen.
Selectivity: Admits over 75% of applicants.

BASIC COSTS (2012-2013)
Tuition and fees: $9,404; out-of-state residents $25,652.
Per-credit charge: $361; out-of-state residents $1,038.
Room and board: $10,029.
Additional info: Tuition/fee waivers available for minority students.

FINANCIAL AID PICTURE (2011-2012)
Students with need: Out of 1,558 full-time freshmen who applied for aid, 1,049 were judged to have need. Of these, 1,041 received aid, and 359 had their full need met. Average financial aid package met 78% of need; average scholarship/grant was $8,545; average loan was $3,626. For part-time students, average financial aid package was $7,785.
Students without need: 407 full-time freshmen who did not demonstrate need for aid received scholarships/grants; average award was $8,291. No-need awards available for academics, alumni affiliation, art, athletics, leadership, music/drama, ROTC.
Scholarships offered: 48 full-time freshmen received athletic scholarships; average amount $11,943.
Cumulative student debt: 41% of graduating class had student loans; average debt was $20,655.
Additional info: Hawaii student incentive grants and tuition waivers (merit and need-based) available to Hawaii residents at participating institutions.

FINANCIAL AID PROCEDURES
Forms required: FAFSA.
Dates and Deadlines: Priority date 3/1; no closing date. Applicants notified on a rolling basis starting 4/1; must reply by 5/1 or within 4 week(s) of notification.
Transfers: No deadline. Applicants notified on a rolling basis starting 3/15; must reply within 4 week(s) of notification.

CONTACT
Jodie Kuba, Director of Financial Aid
2600 Campus Road, QLC Rm 001, Honolulu, HI 96822
(808) 956-7251

University of Hawaii: Hawaii Community College
Hilo, Hawaii
www.hawcc.hawaii.edu Federal Code: 005258

2-year public community college in small city.
Enrollment: 3,663 undergrads.
Selectivity: Open admission.

BASIC COSTS (2012-2013)
Tuition and fees: $3,164; out-of-state residents $9,014.
Per-credit charge: $101; out-of-state residents $296.

FINANCIAL AID PICTURE
Students with need: Need-based aid available for full-time and part-time students.
Students without need: This college awards aid only to students with need.
Additional info: Hawaii student incentive grants and tuition waivers (merit and need-based) available to Hawaii residents.

FINANCIAL AID PROCEDURES
Forms required: FAFSA.
Dates and Deadlines: Priority date 4/1; no closing date. Applicants notified on a rolling basis starting 2/1; must reply within 2 week(s) of notification.
Transfers: Applicants notified by 2/1; must reply within 2 week(s) of notification. Residents of Guam, Federated States of Micronesia, Palau, Marianas Islands and certain other island nations considered residents for tuition purpose.

CONTACT
Sheryl Lundberg-Spregue, Financial Aid Officer
200 West Kawili Street, Hilo, HI 96720-4091
(808) 974-7663

University of Hawaii: Honolulu Community College
Honolulu, Hawaii
www2.honolulu.hawaii.edu Federal Code: 001612

2-year public community and technical college in very large city.
Enrollment: 3,512 undergrads.
Selectivity: Open admission; but selective for out-of-state students.

BASIC COSTS (2012-2013)
Tuition and fees: $3,040; out-of-state residents $8,910.
Per-credit charge: $101; out-of-state residents $296.

FINANCIAL AID PICTURE
Students with need: Need-based aid available for full-time and part-time students.
Students without need: No-need awards available for academics, state/district residency.

Additional info: Hawaii student incentive grants and tuition waivers (merit and need-based) available to Hawaii residents at participating institutions.

FINANCIAL AID PROCEDURES

Forms required: FAFSA.

Dates and Deadlines: Priority date 4/1; no closing date. Applicants notified on a rolling basis starting 7/1; must reply within 3 week(s) of notification.

CONTACT

Jannine Oyama, Financial Aid Officer
874 Dillingham Boulevard, Honolulu, HI 96817
(808) 845-9116

University of Hawaii: Kapiolani Community College

Honolulu, Hawaii
www.kcc.hawaii.edu Federal Code: 001613

2-year public community college in very large city.
Enrollment: 8,892 undergrads.
Selectivity: Open admission; but selective for some programs.

BASIC COSTS (2012-2013)

Tuition and fees: $3,090; out-of-state residents $8,940.
Per-credit charge: $101; out-of-state residents $296.

FINANCIAL AID PICTURE

Students with need: Need-based aid available for full-time and part-time students.
Students without need: This college awards aid only to students with need.
Additional info: Hawaii student incentive grants and tuition waivers (merit and need-based) available to Hawaii residents.

FINANCIAL AID PROCEDURES

Forms required: FAFSA.
Dates and Deadlines: Priority date 4/1; no closing date. Applicants notified on a rolling basis; must reply within 2 week(s) of notification.

CONTACT

Jennifer Bradley, Financial Aid Manager
4303 Diamond Head Road, Honolulu, HI 96816-4421
(808) 734-9555

University of Hawaii: Kauai Community College

Lihue, Hawaii
www.kauai.hawaii.edu Federal Code: 001614

2-year public community college in small city.
Enrollment: 1,495 undergrads.
Selectivity: Open admission; but selective for out-of-state students.

BASIC COSTS (2012-2013)

Tuition and fees: $3,090; out-of-state residents $8,940.
Per-credit charge: $101; out-of-state residents $296.

FINANCIAL AID PICTURE

Students with need: Work study available nights.
Additional info: Hawaii student incentive grants and tuition waivers (merit and need-based) available to Hawaii residents.

FINANCIAL AID PROCEDURES

Forms required: FAFSA, institutional form.
Dates and Deadlines: Priority date 3/1; closing date 5/1. Applicants notified on a rolling basis starting 5/1.

Transfers: Academic transcript evaluation by end of first semester is required.

CONTACT

Rebecca Thompson, Financial Aid Officer
3-1901 Kaumualii Highway, Lihue, HI 96766-9500
(808) 245-8360

University of Hawaii: Leeward Community College

Pearl City, Hawaii
www.lcc.hawaii.edu Federal Code: 004549

2-year public community college in large town.
Enrollment: 5,997 undergrads.
Selectivity: Open admission.

BASIC COSTS (2012-2013)

Tuition and fees: $3,075; out-of-state residents $8,925.
Per-credit charge: $101; out-of-state residents $296.

FINANCIAL AID PICTURE (2011-2012)

Students with need: 91% of average financial aid package awarded as scholarships/grants, 9% awarded as loans/jobs. Need-based aid available for part-time students.
Additional info: Leveraging Educational Assistance Partnership (LEAP) funds or tuition waivers available to students with financial need.

FINANCIAL AID PROCEDURES

Forms required: FAFSA.
Dates and Deadlines: Priority date 4/15; no closing date. Applicants notified on a rolling basis starting 6/1; must reply within 2 week(s) of notification.

CONTACT

Aileen Lum-Akana, Financial Aid Director
96-045 Ala Ike, Pearl City, HI 96782
(808) 455-0606

University of Hawaii: Maui College

Kahului, Hawaii
www.maui.hawaii.edu

2-year public community college in small city.
Enrollment: 4,056 undergrads, 61% part-time. 446 full-time freshmen.
Selectivity: Open admission; but selective for some programs.

BASIC COSTS (2012-2013)

Tuition and fees: $3,156; out-of-state residents $12,126.
Per-credit charge: $101; out-of-state residents $400.
Additional info: Tuition/fee waivers available for minority students.

FINANCIAL AID PICTURE

Students with need: Need-based aid available for full-time and part-time students. Work study available nights.

FINANCIAL AID PROCEDURES

Forms required: FAFSA, institutional form.
Dates and Deadlines: Priority date 4/1; no closing date. Applicants notified on a rolling basis starting 6/1; must reply within 4 week(s) of notification.

CONTACT

Cathy Bio, Financial Aid Officer
310 West Kaahumanu Avenue, Kahului, HI 96732-1617
(808) 984-3277

University of Hawaii: West Oahu

Kapolei, Hawaii
www.uhwo.hawaii.edu Federal Code: 014315

4-year public liberal arts and teachers college in large town.
Enrollment: 1,950 undergrads, 58% part-time. 15 full-time freshmen.
Selectivity: Admits 50 to 75% of applicants.

BASIC COSTS (2012-2013)
Tuition and fees: $5,632; out-of-state residents $16,696.
Per-credit charge: $223; out-of-state residents $694.

FINANCIAL AID PICTURE (2011-2012)
Students with need: Out of 10 full-time freshmen who applied for aid, 10 were judged to have need. Of these, 10 received aid. Average financial aid package met 50% of need; average scholarship/grant was $7,884; average loan was $3,484. For part-time students, average financial aid package was $6,795.
Students without need: No-need awards available for academics.

FINANCIAL AID PROCEDURES
Forms required: FAFSA.
Dates and Deadlines: Priority date 5/1; no closing date. Applicants notified on a rolling basis starting 4/15.
Transfers: No deadline. Applicants notified by 7/1.

CONTACT
Lester Ishimoto, Financial Aid Officer
91-1001 Farrington Highway, Kapolei, HI 96707
(808) 454-4700

University of Hawaii: Windward Community College

Kaneohe, Hawaii
www.wcc.hawaii.edu Federal Code: 010390

2-year public community college in small city.
Enrollment: 2,741 undergrads.
Selectivity: Open admission.

BASIC COSTS (2012-2013)
Tuition and fees: $3,070; out-of-state residents $8,920.
Per-credit charge: $101; out-of-state residents $296.
Additional info: Tuition/fee waivers available for minority students.

FINANCIAL AID PICTURE
Students with need: Need-based aid available for full-time and part-time students.
Students without need: No-need awards available for academics.
Additional info: Hawaii student incentive grants and tuition waivers (merit and need-based) available to Hawaii residents.

FINANCIAL AID PROCEDURES
Forms required: FAFSA.
Dates and Deadlines: Priority date 4/1; no closing date. Applicants notified on a rolling basis starting 3/15; must reply within 2 week(s) of notification.

CONTACT
Steven Chigawa, Financial Aid Officer
45-720 Kea'ahala Road, Kaneohe, HI 96744
(808) 235-7449

Idaho

Boise Bible College

Boise, Idaho
www.boisebible.edu Federal Code: 015783

4-year private Bible college in small city, affiliated with nondenominational tradition.
Enrollment: 192 undergrads.

BASIC COSTS (2012-2013)
Tuition and fees: $10,425.
Room and board: $6,590.
Additional info: $200 additional laundry facility fee required for all resident students.

FINANCIAL AID PICTURE
Students with need: Need-based aid available for full-time and part-time students.
Students without need: No-need awards available for academics, leadership, music/drama, religious affiliation.

FINANCIAL AID PROCEDURES
Forms required: FAFSA, institutional form.
Dates and Deadlines: Priority date 5/1; no closing date. Applicants notified on a rolling basis starting 5/2; must reply by 8/1 or within 2 week(s) of notification.
Transfers: Financial aid and academic transcripts must be on file before federal aid is awarded.

CONTACT
Joyce Anderson, Financial Aid Officer
8695 West Marigold Street, Boise, ID 83714-1220
(800) 893-7755

Boise State University

Boise, Idaho
www.boisestate.edu Federal Code: 001616

4-year public university in small city.
Enrollment: 17,069 undergrads, 25% part-time. 2,216 full-time freshmen.
Selectivity: Admits over 75% of applicants.

BASIC COSTS (2012-2013)
Tuition and fees: $5,884; out-of-state residents $17,324.
Per-credit charge: $252; out-of-state residents $353.
Room and board: $6,240.

FINANCIAL AID PICTURE (2012-2013)
Students with need: Out of 1,515 full-time freshmen who applied for aid, 1,475 were judged to have need. Of these, 1,475 received aid, and 538 had their full need met. Average financial aid package met 18% of need; average scholarship/grant was $2,247; average loan was $5,262. For part-time students, average financial aid package was $4,824.
Students without need: 406 full-time freshmen who did not demonstrate need for aid received scholarships/grants; average award was $1,184. No-need awards available for academics, athletics, music/drama, ROTC, state/district residency.
Scholarships offered: 7 full-time freshmen received athletic scholarships; average amount $3,323.
Cumulative student debt: 64% of graduating class had student loans; average debt was $27,369.

FINANCIAL AID PROCEDURES
Forms required: FAFSA.

Dates and Deadlines: Priority date 4/1; no closing date. Applicants notified on a rolling basis starting 6/1; must reply within 2 week(s) of notification.
Transfers: No deadline. Applicants notified on a rolling basis; must reply within 2 week(s) of notification. Financial aid transcripts required from all postsecondary schools attended whether or not financial aid was received.

CONTACT
Diana Fairchild, Director of Financial Aid
1910 University Drive, Boise, ID 83725
(208) 426-1664

Brigham Young University-Idaho
Rexburg, Idaho
www.byui.edu Federal Code: 001625

4-year private university in large town, affiliated with Church of Jesus Christ of Latter-day Saints.
Enrollment: 16,690 undergrads.

BASIC COSTS (2012-2013)
Tuition and fees: $3,870.
Per-credit charge: $149.
Room and board: $7,590.
Additional info: Tuition for students who are not members of The Church of Jesus Christ of Latter-day Saints is $7,140 for academic year.

FINANCIAL AID PICTURE
Students with need: Need-based aid available for full-time and part-time students.
Students without need: No-need awards available for academics, alumni affiliation, art, leadership, music/drama.
Additional info: Application deadline for merit scholarships 3/1.

FINANCIAL AID PROCEDURES
Forms required: FAFSA.
Dates and Deadlines: Priority date 5/1; no closing date. Applicants notified on a rolling basis starting 2/1.

CONTACT
Aaron Sanns, Financial Aid and Scholarship Director
120 Kimball Building, Rexburg, ID 83460-1615
(208) 496-1600

Broadview University: Boise
Meridian, Idaho
www.broadviewuniversity.edu Federal Code: 011166

2-year for-profit career college in large town.
Enrollment: 125 undergrads.
Selectivity: Open admission.

BASIC COSTS (2012-2013)
Tuition and fees: $18,000.
Per-credit charge: $435.

FINANCIAL AID PICTURE
Students with need: Need-based aid available for full-time and part-time students.

FINANCIAL AID PROCEDURES
Forms required: FAFSA, institutional form.
Dates and Deadlines: Applicants notified on a rolling basis starting 7/1; must reply within 2 week(s) of notification.

CONTACT
Cynthianna Hamrick, Director of Financial Aid
2750 East Gala Court, Meridian, ID 83642
(208) 577-2900

College of Idaho
Caldwell, Idaho
www.collegeofidaho.edu Federal Code: 001617

4-year private liberal arts college in large town.
Enrollment: 1,030 undergrads, 3% part-time. 287 full-time freshmen.
Selectivity: Admits 50 to 75% of applicants.

BASIC COSTS (2013-2014)
Tuition and fees: $24,055.
Per-credit charge: $970.
Room and board: $8,600.
Additional info: Tuition/fee waivers available for adults.

FINANCIAL AID PICTURE (2012-2013)
Students with need: Out of 212 full-time freshmen who applied for aid, 212 were judged to have need. Of these, 212 received aid, and 35 had their full need met. Average financial aid package met 94% of need; average scholarship/grant was $7,630; average loan was $3,831. For part-time students, average financial aid package was $9,423.
Students without need: 51 full-time freshmen who did not demonstrate need for aid received scholarships/grants; average award was $13,304. No-need awards available for academics, alumni affiliation, art, athletics, leadership, minority status, music/drama, religious affiliation, ROTC.
Scholarships offered: 59 full-time freshmen received athletic scholarships; average amount $3,676.
Cumulative student debt: 55% of graduating class had student loans; average debt was $27,008.

FINANCIAL AID PROCEDURES
Forms required: FAFSA, institutional form.
Dates and Deadlines: Priority date 2/15; no closing date. Applicants notified on a rolling basis starting 2/1; must reply within 3 week(s) of notification.
Transfers: No deadline. Applicants notified on a rolling basis starting 1/31; must reply within 3 week(s) of notification.

CONTACT
Juanitta Pearson, Director of Student Financial Aid Services
2112 Cleveland Boulevard, Caldwell, ID 83605-4432
(208) 459-5307

College of Southern Idaho
Twin Falls, Idaho
www.csi.edu Federal Code: 001619

2-year public community and junior college in large town.
Enrollment: 9,085 undergrads.
Selectivity: Open admission; but selective for some programs.

BASIC COSTS (2012-2013)
Tuition and fees: $2,640; out-of-state residents $6,720.
Per-credit charge: $110; out-of-state residents $280.
Room and board: $5,230.

FINANCIAL AID PICTURE
Students with need: Need-based aid available for full-time and part-time students.
Additional info: Out-of-state tuition waivers based on GPA and activities.

FINANCIAL AID PROCEDURES
Forms required: FAFSA.
Dates and Deadlines: Priority date 3/1; no closing date. Applicants notified on a rolling basis starting 4/30; must reply within 3 week(s) of notification.

CONTACT
Jennifer Zimmers, Director of Student Financial Aid
Box 1238, Twin Falls, ID 83303-1238
(208) 732-6273

College of Western Idaho

Nampa, Idaho
www.cwidaho.cc Federal Code: 042118

2-year public community and technical college in large city.
Enrollment: 8,757 undergrads, 53% part-time. 1,555 full-time freshmen.
Selectivity: Open admission; but selective for some programs.

BASIC COSTS (2013-2014)
Tuition and fees: $3,264; out-of-district residents $4,264; out-of-state residents $7,200.
Per-credit charge: $136; out-of-state residents $300.

FINANCIAL AID PICTURE (2011-2012)
Students with need: Out of 1,499 full-time freshmen who applied for aid, 1,365 were judged to have need. Of these, 1,347 received aid, and 254 had their full need met. Average financial aid package met 64% of need; average scholarship/grant was $3,153; average loan was $2,737. For part-time students, average financial aid package was $4,712.
Students without need: 39 full-time freshmen who did not demonstrate need for aid received scholarships/grants; average award was $356. No-need awards available for academics, leadership, minority status.
Cumulative student debt: 67% of graduating class had student loans; average debt was $12,743.

FINANCIAL AID PROCEDURES
Forms required: FAFSA.
Dates and Deadlines: Priority date 7/15; no closing date. Applicants notified on a rolling basis starting 3/1; must reply within 4 week(s) of notification.
Transfers: No deadline. Applicants notified on a rolling basis starting 3/1; must reply within 4 week(s) of notification.

CONTACT
Kevin Jensen, Director of Financial Aid
Mail Stop 1000, PO Box 3010, Nampa, ID 83653
(208) 562-3000

Eastern Idaho Technical College

Idaho Falls, Idaho
www.eitc.edu Federal Code: 011133

2-year public technical college in small city.
Enrollment: 586 undergrads, 50% part-time. 143 full-time freshmen.
Selectivity: Open admission; but selective for some programs.

BASIC COSTS (2012-2013)
Tuition and fees: $2,022; out-of-state residents $7,168.
Per-credit charge: $92; out-of-state residents $182.

FINANCIAL AID PICTURE (2011-2012)
Students with need: 46% of average financial aid package awarded as scholarships/grants, 54% awarded as loans/jobs. Need-based aid available for part-time students.
Students without need: No-need awards available for academics, job skills, state/district residency.

FINANCIAL AID PROCEDURES
Forms required: FAFSA, institutional form.
Dates and Deadlines: Priority date 6/1; no closing date. Applicants notified on a rolling basis starting 6/6.

CONTACT
Shayna Sharp, Director of Financial Aid
1600 South 25th East, Idaho Falls, ID 83404-5788
(208) 524-3000 ext. 3389

Idaho State University

Pocatello, Idaho
www.isu.edu Federal Code: 001620

4-year public university in small city.
Enrollment: 11,831 undergrads, 37% part-time. 1,551 full-time freshmen.
Selectivity: Admits over 75% of applicants.

BASIC COSTS (2012-2013)
Tuition and fees: $6,070; out-of-state residents $17,870.
Per-credit charge: $304; out-of-state residents $494.
Room and board: $5,838.

FINANCIAL AID PICTURE (2011-2012)
Students with need: Out of 1,316 full-time freshmen who applied for aid, 1,101 were judged to have need. Of these, 1,096 received aid, and 76 had their full need met. Average financial aid package met 50% of need; average scholarship/grant was $4,559; average loan was $3,100. For part-time students, average financial aid package was $5,945.
Students without need: 112 full-time freshmen who did not demonstrate need for aid received scholarships/grants; average award was $2,586. No-need awards available for academics, alumni affiliation, art, athletics, leadership, minority status, music/drama, ROTC, state/district residency.
Scholarships offered: 51 full-time freshmen received athletic scholarships; average amount $8,144.
Cumulative student debt: 64% of graduating class had student loans; average debt was $24,602.

FINANCIAL AID PROCEDURES
Forms required: FAFSA.
Dates and Deadlines: Priority date 3/1; no closing date. Applicants notified on a rolling basis starting 4/1.
Transfers: Closing date 3/1. Applicants notified on a rolling basis starting 3/1.

CONTACT
Kent Larson, Director of Financial Aid
921 South 8th Stop 8270, Pocatello, ID 83209-8270
(208) 282-2756

Lewis-Clark State College

Lewiston, Idaho
www.lcsc.edu Federal Code: 001621

4-year public liberal arts and technical college in large town.
Enrollment: 3,266 undergrads, 24% part-time. 577 full-time freshmen.
Selectivity: Admits over 75% of applicants.

BASIC COSTS (2012-2013)
Tuition and fees: $5,562; out-of-state residents $15,476.
Per-credit charge: $285.
Room and board: $6,100.

FINANCIAL AID PICTURE (2011-2012)
Students with need: Out of 540 full-time freshmen who applied for aid, 461 were judged to have need. Of these, 448 received aid, and 34 had their full need met. Average financial aid package met 8% of need; average scholarship/grant was $3,978; average loan was $2,886. For part-time students, average financial aid package was $6,069.
Students without need: 64 full-time freshmen who did not demonstrate need for aid received scholarships/grants; average award was $1,398. No-need awards available for academics, alumni affiliation, art, athletics, leadership, minority status, music/drama.
Scholarships offered: 28 full-time freshmen received athletic scholarships; average amount $10,462.

FINANCIAL AID PROCEDURES
Forms required: FAFSA.

Dates and Deadlines: Closing date 3/1. Applicants notified on a rolling basis starting 4/15; must reply within 2 week(s) of notification.

CONTACT
Laura Hughes, Director of Financial Aid
500 Eighth Avenue, Lewiston, ID 83501-2698
(208) 792-2224

New Saint Andrews College

Moscow, Idaho
www.nsa.edu

4-year private liberal arts college in large town, affiliated with Christian Church.
Enrollment: 139 undergrads, 9% part-time. 46 full-time freshmen.
Selectivity: Admits over 75% of applicants.

BASIC COSTS (2013-2014)
Tuition and fees: $11,200.
Per-credit charge: $200.

FINANCIAL AID PICTURE (2012-2013)
Students with need: Out of 19 full-time freshmen who applied for aid, 19 were judged to have need. Of these, 19 received aid.

FINANCIAL AID PROCEDURES
Forms required: institutional form.
Dates and Deadlines: Priority date 2/15; no closing date.

CONTACT
Brenda Schlect, Bursar
PO Box 9025, Moscow, ID 83843
(208) 882-1566 ext. 113

North Idaho College

Coeur d'Alene, Idaho
www.nic.edu Federal Code: 001623

2-year public community college in large town.
Enrollment: 5,653 undergrads, 40% part-time. 343 full-time freshmen.
Selectivity: Admits 50 to 75% of applicants.

BASIC COSTS (2012-2013)
Tuition and fees: $2,846; out-of-district residents $3,846; out-of-state residents $7,534.
Room and board: $6,600.
Additional info: Tuition/fee waivers available for minority students.

FINANCIAL AID PICTURE (2011-2012)
Students with need: Out of 324 full-time freshmen who applied for aid, 324 were judged to have need. Of these, 324 received aid, and 61 had their full need met. Average financial aid package met 71% of need; average scholarship/grant was $5,136; average loan was $3,175. For part-time students, average financial aid package was $8,240.
Students without need: 18 full-time freshmen who did not demonstrate need for aid received scholarships/grants; average award was $16,978. No-need awards available for academics, art, athletics, leadership, minority status, music/drama, state/district residency.
Scholarships offered: 11 full-time freshmen received athletic scholarships; average amount $47,320.

FINANCIAL AID PROCEDURES
Forms required: FAFSA.
Dates and Deadlines: Priority date 3/15; no closing date. Applicants notified on a rolling basis starting 4/1; must reply within 2 week(s) of notification.

CONTACT
Joe Bekken, Director of Financial Aid
1000 West Garden Avenue, Coeur d'Alene, ID 83814-2199
(208) 769-3368

Northwest Nazarene University

Nampa, Idaho
www.nnu.edu Federal Code: 001624

4-year private university in small city, affiliated with Church of the Nazarene.
Enrollment: 1,263 undergrads, 9% part-time. 242 full-time freshmen.
Selectivity: Admits 50 to 75% of applicants.

BASIC COSTS (2012-2013)
Tuition and fees: $25,190.
Per-credit charge: $1,074.
Room and board: $6,400.

FINANCIAL AID PICTURE
Students with need: Need-based aid available for full-time and part-time students. Work study available nights, weekends, and for part-time students.
Students without need: No-need awards available for academics, alumni affiliation, art, athletics, leadership, minority status, music/drama, religious affiliation, ROTC.
Scholarships offered: Merit scholarships for freshmen based primarily on cumulative high school GPA and ACT test scores.

FINANCIAL AID PROCEDURES
Forms required: FAFSA, institutional form.
Dates and Deadlines: Priority date 3/1; no closing date. Applicants notified on a rolling basis starting 3/1; must reply within 3 week(s) of notification.

CONTACT
David Klaffke, Director of Financial Aid
623 S. University Boulevard, Nampa, ID 83686-5897
(208) 467-8422

Stevens-Henager College: Boise

Boise, Idaho
www.stevenshenager.edu Federal Code: 003674

2-year for-profit technical and career college in small city.
Enrollment: 512 undergrads.
Selectivity: Open admission; but selective for some programs.

BASIC COSTS (2012-2013)
Tuition and fees: $16,558.
Additional info: Cost shown is for associate degree program. Academic year cost of bachelor's degree program is $16,214. All costs inclusive of books, fees, and supplies.

FINANCIAL AID PICTURE
Students with need: Need-based aid available for full-time students.
Students without need: This college awards aid only to students with need.

FINANCIAL AID PROCEDURES
Forms required: FAFSA.

CONTACT
Ali Earle, Business Officer
1444 S Entertainment Avenue, Boise, ID 83709
(208) 383-4540 ext. 1804

University of Idaho

Moscow, Idaho
www.uidaho.edu Federal Code: 001626

4-year public university in large town.
Enrollment: 8,785 undergrads, 8% part-time. 1,603 full-time freshmen.
Selectivity: Admits 50 to 75% of applicants.

BASIC COSTS (2012-2013)
Tuition and fees: $6,212; out-of-state residents $19,000.
Per-credit charge: $311; out-of-state residents $950.
Room and board: $7,682.
Additional info: Tuition/fee waivers available for minority students.

FINANCIAL AID PICTURE (2011-2012)
Students with need: Out of 1,400 full-time freshmen who applied for aid, 1,121 were judged to have need. Of these, 1,110 received aid, and 398 had their full need met. Average financial aid package met 79% of need; average scholarship/grant was $4,681; average loan was $5,573. For part-time students, average financial aid package was $9,583.
Students without need: 307 full-time freshmen who did not demonstrate need for aid received scholarships/grants; average award was $4,420. No-need awards available for academics, alumni affiliation, art, athletics, leadership, minority status, music/drama, state/district residency.
Scholarships offered: 37 full-time freshmen received athletic scholarships; average amount $22,074.
Cumulative student debt: 66% of graduating class had student loans; average debt was $26,809.

FINANCIAL AID PROCEDURES
Forms required: FAFSA.
Dates and Deadlines: Priority date 2/15; no closing date. Applicants notified on a rolling basis starting 3/30; must reply within 4 week(s) of notification.
Transfers: No deadline. Applicants notified on a rolling basis starting 3/30; must reply within 4 week(s) of notification.

CONTACT
Daniel Davenport, Director Student Financial Aid
875 Perimeter Drive MS 4264, Moscow, ID 83844-4264
(208) 885-6312

Illinois

American Academy of Art

Chicago, Illinois
www.aaart.edu Federal Code: 001628

4-year for-profit visual arts college in very large city.
Enrollment: 432 undergrads.
Selectivity: Open admission.

BASIC COSTS (2012-2013)
Tuition and fees: $27,770.

FINANCIAL AID PICTURE
Students with need: Work study available nights.
Students without need: No-need awards available for art.

FINANCIAL AID PROCEDURES
Forms required: FAFSA, institutional form.
Dates and Deadlines: Applicants notified on a rolling basis.
Transfers: Financial aid transcript from previously attended college required.

CONTACT
Ione Fitzgerald, Financial Aid Director
332 South Michigan Avenue, Suite 300, Chicago, IL 60604-4302
(312) 461-0600

Augustana College

Rock Island, Illinois
www.augustana.edu Federal Code: 001633

4-year private liberal arts college in large city, affiliated with Evangelical Lutheran Church in America.
Enrollment: 2,531 undergrads, 1% part-time. 708 full-time freshmen.
Selectivity: Admits 50 to 75% of applicants.

BASIC COSTS (2012-2013)
Tuition and fees: $34,614.
Per-credit charge: $1,450.
Room and board: $8,784.

FINANCIAL AID PICTURE (2011-2012)
Students with need: Out of 677 full-time freshmen who applied for aid, 568 were judged to have need. Of these, 568 received aid, and 115 had their full need met. Average financial aid package met 86% of need; average scholarship/grant was $19,871; average loan was $4,031.
Students without need: 135 full-time freshmen who did not demonstrate need for aid received scholarships/grants; average award was $15,705. No-need awards available for academics, alumni affiliation, art, leadership, music/drama, religious affiliation.
Scholarships offered: Presidential Scholarship: $17,000 to full tuition; 28 ACT or 1260 SAT (exclusive of Writing) and rank in the top ten percent of high school class. Dean's Scholarship: $14,500-$16,000; 25 ACT or 1140 SAT (exclusive of Writing) and rank in the top 20 percent of high school class. Founders Scholarship: $10,500-$14,000; must plan to enroll full-time. Transfer Scholarship: $8,500-$12,500; demonstrated outstanding academic performance in previous college studies.
Cumulative student debt: 71% of graduating class had student loans; average debt was $34,120.

FINANCIAL AID PROCEDURES
Forms required: FAFSA, institutional form.
Dates and Deadlines: Priority date 3/1; no closing date. Applicants notified on a rolling basis starting 3/1; must reply by 5/1.
Transfers: Priority date 5/1. Financial aid transcripts from previous institutions required.

CONTACT
Sue Standley, Director of Financial Assistance
639 38th Street, Rock Island, IL 61201-2296
(309) 794-7207

Aurora University

Aurora, Illinois
www.aurora.edu Federal Code: 001634

4-year private university in small city.
Enrollment: 3,002 undergrads, 12% part-time. 525 full-time freshmen.
Selectivity: Admits 50 to 75% of applicants.

BASIC COSTS (2013-2014)
Tuition and fees: $20,470.
Per-credit charge: $590.
Room and board: $9,542.

FINANCIAL AID PICTURE (2012-2013)
Students with need: Out of 507 full-time freshmen who applied for aid, 449 were judged to have need. Of these, 449 received aid, and 80 had their full need met. Average financial aid package met 84% of need; average scholarship/grant was $7,803; average loan was $3,310. For part-time students, average financial aid package was $7,345.
Students without need: 76 full-time freshmen who did not demonstrate need for aid received scholarships/grants; average award was $9,070. No-need awards available for academics, alumni affiliation, art, music/drama, religious affiliation, ROTC, state/district residency.

Scholarships offered: T.P. Stephens Scholarship: $12,500; Board of Trustees scholarships: $10,000. James E. Crimi Presidential Scholarships: $9,500. Dean's Scholarships: $8,500. Aurora University Opportunity Grants: $7,000. AU Promise Grant: $2,000.
Cumulative student debt: 82% of graduating class had student loans; average debt was $25,484.

FINANCIAL AID PROCEDURES
Forms required: FAFSA.
Dates and Deadlines: Priority date 2/15; no closing date. Applicants notified on a rolling basis starting 3/1; must reply by 5/1 or within 3 week(s) of notification.

CONTACT
Heather McKane, Dean of Student Financial Services
347 South Gladstone Avenue, Aurora, IL 60506-4892
(630) 844-6190

Benedictine University
Lisle, Illinois
www.ben.edu Federal Code: 001767

4-year private university and liberal arts college in large town, affiliated with Roman Catholic Church.
Enrollment: 3,659 undergrads, 21% part-time. 594 full-time freshmen.
Selectivity: Admits over 75% of applicants.

BASIC COSTS (2013-2014)
Tuition and fees: $27,100.
Room and board: $11,250.
Additional info: Tuition/fee waivers available for adults, unemployed or children of unemployed.

FINANCIAL AID PICTURE (2012-2013)
Students with need: Out of 539 full-time freshmen who applied for aid, 493 were judged to have need. Of these, 491 received aid. For part-time students, average financial aid package was $8,532.
Students without need: 54 full-time freshmen who did not demonstrate need for aid received scholarships/grants; average award was $10,696. No-need awards available for academics, alumni affiliation, athletics, leadership, music/drama, ROTC, state/district residency.
Scholarships offered: 3 full-time freshmen received athletic scholarships; average amount $3,267.
Cumulative student debt: 77.2% of graduating class had student loans; average debt was $19,560.

FINANCIAL AID PROCEDURES
Forms required: FAFSA.
Dates and Deadlines: Priority date 3/1; no closing date. Applicants notified on a rolling basis starting 2/15; must reply within 2 week(s) of notification.
Transfers: No deadline. Applicants notified on a rolling basis starting 3/15; must reply within 2 week(s) of notification.

CONTACT
Diane Battistella, Senior Associate Dean
5700 College Road, Lisle, IL 60532
(630) 829-6100

Black Hawk College
Moline, Illinois
www.bhc.edu Federal Code: 001638

2-year public community college in large town.
Enrollment: 4,252 undergrads, 45% part-time. 661 full-time freshmen.
Selectivity: Open admission; but selective for some programs.

BASIC COSTS (2012-2013)
Tuition and fees: $3,225; out-of-district residents $6,495; out-of-state residents $6,495.
Per-credit charge: $95; out-of-district residents $204; out-of-state residents $204.
Additional info: Agreement with 5 contiguous Iowa counties for special tuition rate of $129 per credit plus required fees. Online courses (tuition only) are $109 per credit hour in-state; $129, out-of-state.

FINANCIAL AID PICTURE (2011-2012)
Students with need: Out of 661 full-time freshmen who applied for aid, 448 were judged to have need. Of these, 406 received aid, and 75 had their full need met. Average financial aid package met 79% of need; average scholarship/grant was $2,334; average loan was $1,571. For part-time students, average financial aid package was $1,733.
Students without need: 38 full-time freshmen who did not demonstrate need for aid received scholarships/grants; average award was $1,597. No-need awards available for academics, art, athletics, leadership, music/drama, state/district residency.
Scholarships offered: ***Merit:*** Scholarship program; based on need and/or merit. Tuition awards; awarded to students who graduate in the top 10% of their class. ***Athletic:*** 50 full-time freshmen received athletic scholarships; average amount $2,173.
Cumulative student debt: 26% of graduating class had student loans; average debt was $5,435.
Additional info: 5/15 deadline for scholarships.

FINANCIAL AID PROCEDURES
Forms required: FAFSA.
Dates and Deadlines: Priority date 5/15; no closing date. Applicants notified on a rolling basis starting 5/1.
Transfers: No deadline. Applicants notified on a rolling basis.

CONTACT
Joanna Dye, Director, Financial Aid
6600-34th Avenue, Moline, IL 61265-5899
(309) 796-5400

Blackburn College
Carlinville, Illinois
www.blackburn.edu Federal Code: 001639

4-year private liberal arts college in small town, affiliated with Presbyterian Church (USA).
Enrollment: 541 undergrads, 2% part-time. 135 full-time freshmen.
Selectivity: Admits 50 to 75% of applicants.

BASIC COSTS (2012-2013)
Tuition and fees: $17,502.
Per-credit charge: $576.
Room and board: $5,432.
Additional info: All on-campus students participate in a work program which reduces net tuition costs.

FINANCIAL AID PICTURE (2011-2012)
Students with need: Need-based aid available for full-time and part-time students. Work study available nights, weekends, and for part-time students.
Students without need: No-need awards available for academics, state/district residency.
Additional info: Each resident student works 160 hours per semester.

FINANCIAL AID PROCEDURES
Forms required: FAFSA.
Dates and Deadlines: Priority date 3/1; no closing date. Applicants notified on a rolling basis starting 3/1; must reply within 4 week(s) of notification.
Transfers: No deadline. Applicants notified on a rolling basis; must reply within 4 week(s) of notification.

CONTACT
Jane Kelsey, Director of Financial Aid
700 College Avenue, Carlinville, IL 62626
(217) 854-3231 ext. 4283

Blessing-Rieman College of Nursing
Quincy, Illinois
www.brcn.edu Federal Code: 006214

4-year private nursing college in small city.
Enrollment: 282 undergrads.
Selectivity: Admits over 75% of applicants.

BASIC COSTS (2012-2013)
Tuition and fees: $23,865.
Per-credit charge: $550.
Room and board: $8,700.
Additional info: Tuition and fees are average costs charged to freshman. Partnered with Quincy University and Culver-Stockton College. Freshmen and sophomores pay partnering school's tuition rate.

FINANCIAL AID PICTURE
Students with need: Need-based aid available for full-time and part-time students.
Students without need: No-need awards available for academics, alumni affiliation, leadership, state/district residency.
Additional info: Financial aid for freshmen and sophomores administered by Culver-Stockton College and Quincy University. B-RCN does not have first time, full-time students, only junior and senior students.

FINANCIAL AID PROCEDURES
Forms required: FAFSA.
Dates and Deadlines: Priority date 3/1; closing date 9/1.
Transfers: Applicants notified on a rolling basis starting 12/15.

CONTACT
Kevin Turnbull, Financial Aid Coordinator
PO Box 7005, Quincy, IL 62305-7005
(217) 228-5520 ext. 6993

Bradley University
Peoria, Illinois
www.bradley.edu Federal Code: 001641

4-year private university in large city.
Enrollment: 4,866 undergrads, 5% part-time. 1,016 full-time freshmen.
Selectivity: Admits 50 to 75% of applicants.

BASIC COSTS (2012-2013)
Tuition and fees: $28,264.
Per-credit charge: $740.
Room and board: $8,700.

FINANCIAL AID PICTURE (2011-2012)
Students with need: Out of 985 full-time freshmen who applied for aid, 901 were judged to have need. Of these, 882 received aid, and 119 had their full need met. Average financial aid package met 67% of need; average scholarship/grant was $14,747; average loan was $4,359. Need-based aid available for part-time students.
Students without need: 157 full-time freshmen who did not demonstrate need for aid received scholarships/grants; average award was $8,749. No-need awards available for academics, alumni affiliation, art, athletics, leadership, minority status, music/drama.
Scholarships offered: 36 full-time freshmen received athletic scholarships; average amount $17,166.

FINANCIAL AID PROCEDURES
Forms required: FAFSA.
Dates and Deadlines: Priority date 3/1; no closing date. Applicants notified on a rolling basis starting 3/1.
Transfers: No deadline. Applicants notified by 3/1; must reply by 5/1 or within 2 week(s) of notification.

CONTACT
Dave Pardieck, Financial Assistance Director
1501 West Bradley Avenue, Peoria, IL 61625
(309) 677-3089

Carl Sandburg College
Galesburg, Illinois
www.sandburg.edu Federal Code: 007265

2-year public community college in large town.
Enrollment: 1,939 undergrads.
Selectivity: Open admission; but selective for some programs.

BASIC COSTS (2012-2013)
Tuition and fees: $4,290; out-of-district residents $5,880; out-of-state residents $7,080.
Per-credit charge: $138; out-of-district residents $191; out-of-state residents $231.

FINANCIAL AID PICTURE
Students with need: Need-based aid available for full-time students.
Students without need: No-need awards available for academics, art, athletics, music/drama.

FINANCIAL AID PROCEDURES
Forms required: FAFSA, institutional form.
Dates and Deadlines: Priority date 5/1; no closing date. Applicants notified on a rolling basis starting 5/1; must reply by 8/25 or within 2 week(s) of notification.
Transfers: Must reply by 8/25. Tuition guarantee provides no increase in tuition up to three years as long as enrolled full-time.

CONTACT
Lisa Hanson, Director of Financial Aid
2400 Tom L. Wilson Boulevard, Galesburg, IL 61401
(309) 341-5283

Chicago State University
Chicago, Illinois
www.csu.edu Federal Code: 001694

4-year public university in very large city.
Enrollment: 4,593 undergrads, 35% part-time. 423 full-time freshmen.
Selectivity: Admits less than 50% of applicants.

BASIC COSTS (2012-2013)
Tuition and fees: $9,966; out-of-state residents $18,426.
Per-credit charge: $285; out-of-state residents $567.
Room and board: $8,222.

FINANCIAL AID PICTURE (2011-2012)
Students with need: Out of 409 full-time freshmen who applied for aid, 409 were judged to have need. Of these, 409 received aid, and 3 had their full need met. Average financial aid package met 58% of need; average scholarship/grant was $7,222; average loan was $2,992. For part-time students, average financial aid package was $6,702.
Students without need: 3 full-time freshmen who did not demonstrate need for aid received scholarships/grants; average award was $3,955. No-need awards available for academics, athletics, ROTC, state/district residency.

Scholarships offered: 3 full-time freshmen received athletic scholarships; average amount $3,955.
Additional info: Freshmen of outstanding academic ability and talent eligible for Scholars Program full-tuition scholarship.

FINANCIAL AID PROCEDURES
Forms required: FAFSA, institutional form.
Dates and Deadlines: Priority date 3/1; no closing date.
Transfers: Priority date 3/31. Must have valid financial aid transcripts from previous institutions whether or not aid was received.

CONTACT
Brenda Hooker, Director
9501 South King Drive, Chicago, IL 60628
(773) 995-2304

City Colleges of Chicago: Harold Washington College

Chicago, Illinois
www.ccc.edu

2-year public community college in very large city.
Enrollment: 8,775 undergrads.
Selectivity: Open admission; but selective for some programs.

BASIC COSTS (2012-2013)
Tuition and fees: $3,070; out-of-district residents $5,961; out-of-state residents $7,498.
Per-credit charge: $89; out-of-district residents $185; out-of-state residents $237.

FINANCIAL AID PICTURE
Students with need: Need-based aid available for full-time and part-time students. Work study available nights.
Students without need: This college awards aid only to students with need.

FINANCIAL AID PROCEDURES
Forms required: FAFSA.
Dates and Deadlines: Applicants notified on a rolling basis.

CONTACT
Pedro Ladino, Financial Aid Director
30 East Lake Street, Chicago, IL 60601
(312) 553-6041

City Colleges of Chicago: Harry S. Truman College

Chicago, Illinois
www.ccc.edu

2-year public community college in very large city.
Enrollment: 6,660 undergrads.
Selectivity: Open admission; but selective for some programs.

BASIC COSTS (2012-2013)
Tuition and fees: $3,070; out-of-district residents $5,961; out-of-state residents $7,498.
Per-credit charge: $89; out-of-district residents $185; out-of-state residents $237.
Additional info: Some courses have specific fees.

FINANCIAL AID PICTURE
Students with need: Need-based aid available for full-time and part-time students. Work study available nights, weekends, and for part-time students.
Students without need: This college awards aid only to students with need.

FINANCIAL AID PROCEDURES
Forms required: FAFSA.
Dates and Deadlines: Applicants notified on a rolling basis.

CONTACT
Robert Evans, Financial Aid Director
1145 West Wilson Avenue, Chicago, IL 60640
(773) 907-4810

City Colleges of Chicago: Kennedy-King College

Chicago, Illinois
www.ccc.edu

2-year public community college in very large city.
Enrollment: 4,615 undergrads.
Selectivity: Open admission.

BASIC COSTS (2012-2013)
Tuition and fees: $3,070; out-of-district residents $5,961; out-of-state residents $7,498.
Per-credit charge: $89; out-of-district residents $185; out-of-state residents $237.
Additional info: Some courses have specific fees.

FINANCIAL AID PICTURE
Students with need: Need-based aid available for full-time and part-time students.
Students without need: This college awards aid only to students with need.

FINANCIAL AID PROCEDURES
Forms required: FAFSA.
Dates and Deadlines: Applicants notified on a rolling basis; must reply within 2 week(s) of notification.

CONTACT
Tabitha O'Neil, Financial Aid Director
6301 South Halsted Street, Chicago, IL 60621
(773) 602-5133

City Colleges of Chicago: Malcolm X College

Chicago, Illinois
www.ccc.edu

2-year public community college in very large city.
Enrollment: 4,917 undergrads.
Selectivity: Open admission; but selective for some programs.

BASIC COSTS (2012-2013)
Tuition and fees: $3,070; out-of-district residents $5,961; out-of-state residents $7,498.
Per-credit charge: $89; out-of-district residents $185; out-of-state residents $237.
Additional info: Some courses have specific fees.

FINANCIAL AID PICTURE
Students with need: Need-based aid available for full-time and part-time students.
Students without need: This college awards aid only to students with need.

FINANCIAL AID PROCEDURES

Forms required: FAFSA, institutional form.

Dates and Deadlines: Applicants notified on a rolling basis; must reply within 2 week(s) of notification.

CONTACT

Marco Sepulveda, Financial Aid Director
1900 West Van Buren Street, Chicago, IL 60612

City Colleges of Chicago: Olive-Harvey College

Chicago, Illinois
www.ccc.edu

2-year public community college in very large city.

Enrollment: 3,744 undergrads.

Selectivity: Open admission; but selective for some programs.

BASIC COSTS (2012-2013)

Tuition and fees: $3,070; out-of-district residents $5,961; out-of-state residents $7,498.

Per-credit charge: $89; out-of-district residents $185; out-of-state residents $237.

Additional info: Some courses have specific fees.

FINANCIAL AID PICTURE

Students with need: Need-based aid available for full-time and part-time students.

FINANCIAL AID PROCEDURES

Forms required: FAFSA.

Dates and Deadlines: Applicants notified on a rolling basis.

CONTACT

Stacey Robbins, Financial Aid Director
10001 South Woodlawn Avenue, Chicago, IL 60628
(773) 291-6391

City Colleges of Chicago: Richard J. Daley College

Chicago, Illinois
www.ccc.edu

2-year public community college in very large city.

Enrollment: 4,920 undergrads.

Selectivity: Open admission; but selective for some programs.

BASIC COSTS (2012-2013)

Tuition and fees: $3,070; out-of-district residents $5,961; out-of-state residents $7,498.

Per-credit charge: $89; out-of-district residents $185; out-of-state residents $237.

Additional info: Some courses have specific fees.

FINANCIAL AID PICTURE

Students with need: Need-based aid available for full-time students.

FINANCIAL AID PROCEDURES

Forms required: FAFSA.

Dates and Deadlines: Applicants notified on a rolling basis.

Transfers: College workstudy jobs and Federal Supplemental Educational Opportunity Grant (SEOG) may not be available to transfers.

CONTACT

James Loague, Financial Aid Director
7500 South Pulaski Road, Chicago, IL 60652
(773) 838-7581

City Colleges of Chicago: Wilbur Wright College

Chicago, Illinois
www.ccc.edu

2-year public community college in very large city.

Enrollment: 9,209 undergrads.

Selectivity: Open admission.

BASIC COSTS (2012-2013)

Tuition and fees: $3,070; out-of-district residents $5,961; out-of-state residents $7,498.

Per-credit charge: $89; out-of-district residents $185; out-of-state residents $237.

Additional info: Some courses have specific fees.

FINANCIAL AID PICTURE

Students with need: Need-based aid available for full-time and part-time students.

FINANCIAL AID PROCEDURES

Forms required: FAFSA, institutional form.

Dates and Deadlines: Applicants notified on a rolling basis.

CONTACT

Ronda Rocquemore, Financial Aid Director
4300 North Narragansett Avenue, Chicago, IL 60634-4276
(773) 481-8100

College of DuPage

Glen Ellyn, Illinois
www.cod.edu
Federal Code: 006656

2-year public community college in large town.

Enrollment: 19,400 undergrads, 57% part-time. 2,721 full-time freshmen.

Selectivity: Open admission; but selective for some programs.

BASIC COSTS (2012-2013)

Tuition and fees: $4,080; out-of-district residents $9,690; out-of-state residents $11,790.

Per-credit charge: $136; out-of-district residents $323; out-of-state residents $393.

FINANCIAL AID PICTURE (2011-2012)

Students with need: Out of 1,745 full-time freshmen who applied for aid, 1,042 were judged to have need. Of these, 974 received aid. For part-time students, average financial aid package was $4,231.

Students without need: 51 full-time freshmen who did not demonstrate need for aid received scholarships/grants; average award was $3,488. No-need awards available for academics, art, leadership, minority status, music/drama, state/district residency.

FINANCIAL AID PROCEDURES

Forms required: FAFSA.

Dates and Deadlines: Priority date 4/30; no closing date. Applicants notified on a rolling basis starting 6/1; must reply within 2 week(s) of notification.

Transfers: No deadline. Applicants notified on a rolling basis; must reply within 2 week(s) of notification. Must have financial aid application on file indicating previous institutions attended.

CONTACT

Earl Dowling, Associate Vice President Enrollment Management
425 Fawell Boulevard, Glen Ellyn, IL 60137-6599
(630) 942-2380

College of Lake County

Grayslake, Illinois
www.clcillinois.edu Federal Code: 007694

2-year public community college in large town.
Enrollment: 13,236 undergrads, 68% part-time. 1,073 full-time freshmen.
Selectivity: Open admission; but selective for some programs.

BASIC COSTS (2012-2013)
Tuition and fees: $3,360; out-of-district residents $7,770; out-of-state residents $10,275.
Per-credit charge: $93; out-of-district residents $240; out-of-state residents $324.
Additional info: Tuition/fee waivers available for minority students.

FINANCIAL AID PICTURE
Students with need: Need-based aid available for full-time and part-time students. Work study available nights.
Students without need: No-need awards available for academics, alumni affiliation, art, athletics, leadership, minority status, music/drama.
Scholarships offered: Academic Achievement Scholarship: based on GPA and student essay; tuition and fees.

FINANCIAL AID PROCEDURES
Forms required: FAFSA.
Dates and Deadlines: Priority date 6/3; no closing date. Applicants notified on a rolling basis starting 6/15; must reply within 2 week(s) of notification.

CONTACT
Erin Fowles, Director, Financial Aid
19351 West Washington Street, Grayslake, IL 60030-1198
(847) 543-2062

College of Office Technology

Chicago, Illinois
www.cot.edu Federal Code: 017378

2-year for-profit career college in very large city.
Enrollment: 115 undergrads.
Selectivity: Open admission.

BASIC COSTS (2012-2013)
Tuition and fees: $11,995.
Additional info: Costs vary by program.

FINANCIAL AID PICTURE
Students with need: Need-based aid available for full-time and part-time students.
Students without need: This college awards aid only to students with need.

FINANCIAL AID PROCEDURES
Forms required: FAFSA.
Dates and Deadlines: Applicants notified on a rolling basis.

CONTACT
Merysol Perez, Financial Aid Director
1520 West Division Street, Chicago, IL 60642-3312
(773) 278-0042

Columbia College Chicago

Chicago, Illinois
www.colum.edu Federal Code: 001665

4-year private visual arts and liberal arts college in very large city.
Enrollment: 10,208 undergrads, 10% part-time. 2,093 full-time freshmen.
Selectivity: Admits over 75% of applicants.

BASIC COSTS (2012-2013)
Tuition and fees: $22,390.
Per-credit charge: $732.
Room and board: $11,796.

FINANCIAL AID PICTURE (2011-2012)
Students with need: Out of 1,800 full-time freshmen who applied for aid, 1,625 were judged to have need. Of these, 1,533 received aid, and 59 had their full need met. Need-based aid available for part-time students.
Students without need: No-need awards available for academics, art, leadership, music/drama, state/district residency.

FINANCIAL AID PROCEDURES
Forms required: FAFSA, institutional form.
Dates and Deadlines: Priority date 5/1; no closing date. Applicants notified on a rolling basis.

CONTACT
Jennifer Waters, Executive Director of Student Financial Services
600 South Michigan Avenue, Chicago, IL 60605-1996
(866) 705-0200

Concordia University Chicago

River Forest, Illinois
www.cuchicago.edu Federal Code: 001666

4-year private university and liberal arts college in large town, affiliated with Lutheran Church - Missouri Synod.
Enrollment: 1,461 undergrads, 4% part-time. 318 full-time freshmen.
Selectivity: Admits 50 to 75% of applicants.

BASIC COSTS (2012-2013)
Tuition and fees: $26,656.
Per-credit charge: $810.
Room and board: $8,580.

FINANCIAL AID PICTURE
Students with need: Need-based aid available for full-time and part-time students. Work study available nights.
Students without need: No-need awards available for academics, alumni affiliation, music/drama, religious affiliation, state/district residency.
Scholarships offered: Presidential Honors: full tuition; selection by essay; 5 per year. Presidential Scholarships: up to $12,000; selection by ACT and GPA. Community Awards: up to $7,000; selection by ACT and GPA. Transfer Honors: up to $10,000; selection by GPA. Music Scholarships: amount varies; selection by audition.

FINANCIAL AID PROCEDURES
Forms required: FAFSA.
Dates and Deadlines: Priority date 3/1; no closing date. Applicants notified on a rolling basis starting 3/1; must reply within 4 week(s) of notification.
Transfers: No deadline. Applicants notified on a rolling basis; must reply within 4 week(s) of notification.

CONTACT
Aida Asencio-Pinto, Director of Student Financial Planning
7400 Augusta Street, River Forest, IL 60305-1499
(708) 209-3113

Danville Area Community College

Danville, Illinois
www.dacc.edu Federal Code: 001669

2-year public community college in large town.
Enrollment: 2,508 undergrads.

Selectivity: Open admission.

BASIC COSTS (2012-2013)
Tuition and fees: $3,525; out-of-district residents $6,285; out-of-state residents $6,285.
Per-credit charge: $98; out-of-district residents $190; out-of-state residents $190.

FINANCIAL AID PICTURE (2011-2012)
Students with need: 81% of average financial aid package awarded as scholarships/grants, 19% awarded as loans/jobs. Need-based aid available for part-time students. Work study available nights, weekends, and for part-time students.
Students without need: No-need awards available for academics, art, athletics, leadership, minority status, music/drama, state/district residency.

FINANCIAL AID PROCEDURES
Forms required: FAFSA, institutional form.
Dates and Deadlines: Priority date 7/1; no closing date. Applicants notified on a rolling basis starting 4/1.
Transfers: NSLDS reviewed before aid disbursed.

CONTACT
Janet Ingargiola, Director of Financial Aid
2000 East Main Street, Danville, IL 61832
(217) 443-8891

DePaul University

Chicago, Illinois
www.depaul.edu Federal Code: 001671

4-year private university in very large city, affiliated with Roman Catholic Church.
Enrollment: 16,153 undergrads, 16% part-time. 2,455 full-time freshmen.
Selectivity: Admits 50 to 75% of applicants.

BASIC COSTS (2012-2013)
Tuition and fees: $32,295.
Per-credit charge: $530.
Room and board: $11,717.

FINANCIAL AID PICTURE (2011-2012)
Students with need: Out of 2,085 full-time freshmen who applied for aid, 1,790 were judged to have need. Of these, 1,778 received aid, and 170 had their full need met. Average financial aid package met 66% of need; average scholarship/grant was $12,012; average loan was $3,466. For part-time students, average financial aid package was $8,198.
Students without need: 521 full-time freshmen who did not demonstrate need for aid received scholarships/grants; average award was $9,370. No-need awards available for academics, art, athletics, leadership, music/drama, ROTC, state/district residency.
Scholarships offered: ***Merit:*** Various scholarships; based on top 10% of class, 1100 SAT (exclusive of Writing) or 26 ACT, and active in student/community organizations. ***Athletic:*** 58 full-time freshmen received athletic scholarships; average amount $25,207.
Cumulative student debt: 63% of graduating class had student loans; average debt was $28,284.

FINANCIAL AID PROCEDURES
Forms required: FAFSA.
Dates and Deadlines: Priority date 3/1; no closing date. Applicants notified on a rolling basis starting 3/15.
Transfers: Priority date 4/1; no deadline. Applicants notified on a rolling basis starting 5/1; must reply by 8/1. 5 different scholarships awarded to fall incoming transfer students who have been admitted and have submitted scholarship application by April 1. Scholarships range from $2,000-$7,000, and vary based on competitiveness of pool and student's qualifications.

CONTACT
Paula Luff, Director of Financial Aid
One East Jackson Boulevard, Chicago, IL 60604-2287
(312) 362-8610

DeVry University: Chicago

Chicago, Illinois
www.devry.edu Federal Code: 010727

4-year for-profit university in very large city.
Enrollment: 1,535 undergrads, 47% part-time. 87 full-time freshmen.

BASIC COSTS (2012-2013)
Tuition and fees: $16,076.
Per-credit charge: $609.

FINANCIAL AID PICTURE
Students with need: Need-based aid available for full-time and part-time students.
Students without need: This college awards aid only to students with need.

FINANCIAL AID PROCEDURES
Forms required: FAFSA.
Dates and Deadlines: Applicants notified on a rolling basis.

CONTACT
Milena Dobrina, Director of Financial Aid
3300 North Campbell Avenue, Chicago, IL 60618-5994
(773) 929-8509

Dominican University

River Forest, Illinois
www.dom.edu Federal Code: 001750

4-year private university and liberal arts college in large town, affiliated with Roman Catholic Church.
Enrollment: 1,920 undergrads, 8% part-time. 404 full-time freshmen.
Selectivity: Admits 50 to 75% of applicants.

BASIC COSTS (2012-2013)
Tuition and fees: $27,730.
Per-credit charge: $916.
Room and board: $8,520.

FINANCIAL AID PICTURE (2012-2013)
Students with need: Out of 388 full-time freshmen who applied for aid, 371 were judged to have need. Of these, 371 received aid, and 49 had their full need met. Average financial aid package met 78% of need; average scholarship/grant was $20,637; average loan was $3,232. For part-time students, average financial aid package was $5,870.
Students without need: 28 full-time freshmen who did not demonstrate need for aid received scholarships/grants; average award was $8,750. No-need awards available for academics, alumni affiliation, art.
Scholarships offered: Presidential Scholarships: $15,300-$17,500. Dean's Scholarships: $13,300-$14,700. University Honor Scholarships: $10,000-$12,200. Achievement Scholarships: $7,000-$9,900. Merit Scholarships: $7,500-$15,000. All based on ACT/SAT scores and GPA. Ida Brechtel Scholarships: $7,500; for students majoring in chemistry or biology/chemistry. Alice Welsh Skilling Scholarship: $7,500; for students majoring in the visual arts.
Cumulative student debt: 84% of graduating class had student loans; average debt was $28,281.

FINANCIAL AID PROCEDURES
Forms required: FAFSA.
Dates and Deadlines: Priority date 3/1; no closing date. Applicants notified on a rolling basis starting 2/15; must reply within 2 week(s) of notification.

Transfers: No deadline. Applicants notified on a rolling basis starting 3/15; must reply within 3 week(s) of notification. Merit scholarships available to full-time students with GPA of 3.3 from previous institution. Phi Theta Kappa scholarships available to PTK members.

CONTACT

Marie von Ebers, Director of Financial Aid
7900 West Division Street, River Forest, IL 60305-1099
(708) 524-6809

East-West University

Chicago, Illinois
www.eastwest.edu Federal Code: 015310

4-year private university in very large city.
Enrollment: 830 undergrads, 1% part-time. 224 full-time freshmen.
Selectivity: Open admission; but selective for some programs.

BASIC COSTS (2012-2013)

Tuition and fees: $17,595.

FINANCIAL AID PICTURE

Students with need: Need-based aid available for full-time and part-time students.
Students without need: No-need awards available for academics.
Additional info: Foreign students eligible for institutional scholarship.

FINANCIAL AID PROCEDURES

Forms required: FAFSA.
Dates and Deadlines: Closing date 3/31. Applicants notified on a rolling basis starting 1/4; must reply within 4 week(s) of notification.
Transfers: Closing date 4/1.

CONTACT

Cesar Campos, Director of Financial Aid
816 South Michigan Avenue, Chicago, IL 60605-2185
(312) 939-0111

Eastern Illinois University

Charleston, Illinois
www.eiu.edu Federal Code: 001674

4-year public university and teachers college in large town.
Enrollment: 8,861 undergrads, 11% part-time. 1,231 full-time freshmen.
Selectivity: Admits 50 to 75% of applicants.

BASIC COSTS (2012-2013)

Tuition and fees: $10,930; out-of-state residents $27,670.
Per-credit charge: $279; out-of-state residents $837.
Room and board: $9,174.
Additional info: New undergraduate students from bordering states of Indiana, Iowa, Kentucky, Missouri and Wisconsin will be billed at in-state tuition rate. Tuition at time of enrollment locked for 4 years.

FINANCIAL AID PICTURE (2012-2013)

Students with need: Out of 1,183 full-time freshmen who applied for aid, 906 were judged to have need. Of these, 896 received aid, and 85 had their full need met. Average financial aid package met 66% of need; average scholarship/grant was $3,479; average loan was $3,045. For part-time students, average financial aid package was $6,225.
Students without need: 161 full-time freshmen who did not demonstrate need for aid received scholarships/grants; average award was $3,083. No-need awards available for academics, art, athletics, leadership, music/drama, ROTC.
Scholarships offered: ***Merit:*** Commitment to Excellence Scholarship: for entering freshmen students who demonstrated high academic achievement based on high school GPA and ACT score; to include three tiers for new freshmen and two tiers for new transfer students; renewable, based on maintaining basic requirements. ***Athletic:*** 30 full-time freshmen received athletic scholarships; average amount $7,977.
Cumulative student debt: 72% of graduating class had student loans; average debt was $28,575.

FINANCIAL AID PROCEDURES

Forms required: FAFSA.
Dates and Deadlines: Priority date 3/1; no closing date. Applicants notified on a rolling basis starting 3/1; must reply within 2 week(s) of notification.

CONTACT

Jerry Donna, Director of Financial Aid
600 Lincoln Avenue, Charleston, IL 61920-3011
(217) 581-3713

Elgin Community College

Elgin, Illinois
www.elgin.edu Federal Code: 001675

2-year public community college in small city.
Enrollment: 8,731 undergrads, 58% part-time. 906 full-time freshmen.
Selectivity: Open admission; but selective for some programs.

BASIC COSTS (2012-2013)

Tuition and fees: $3,160; out-of-district residents $10,856; out-of-state residents $14,186.
Per-credit charge: $105; out-of-district residents $362; out-of-state residents $473.

FINANCIAL AID PICTURE

Students with need: Need-based aid available for full-time and part-time students. Work study available nights, weekends, and for part-time students.
Students without need: No-need awards available for academics, alumni affiliation, art, athletics, job skills, leadership, minority status, music/drama, religious affiliation, ROTC, state/district residency.

FINANCIAL AID PROCEDURES

Forms required: FAFSA, institutional form.
Dates and Deadlines: Priority date 6/1; no closing date. Applicants notified on a rolling basis starting 4/6; must reply within 3 week(s) of notification.

CONTACT

Amy Perrin, Director of Student Financial Assistance
1700 Spartan Drive, Elgin, IL 60123-7193
(847) 214-7520

Elmhurst College

Elmhurst, Illinois
www.elmhurst.edu Federal Code: 001676

4-year private liberal arts college in large town, affiliated with United Church of Christ.
Enrollment: 2,955 undergrads.
Selectivity: Admits 50 to 75% of applicants.

BASIC COSTS (2012-2013)

Tuition and fees: $31,750.
Per-credit charge: $896.
Room and board: $9,960.

FINANCIAL AID PICTURE

Students with need: Need-based aid available for full-time and part-time students. Work study available nights, weekends, and for part-time students.

Students without need: No-need awards available for academics, alumni affiliation, art, minority status, music/drama, religious affiliation, ROTC, state/district residency.
Scholarships offered: Presidential Scholarship: $18,000-$22,000, Dean's Scholarship: $13,000-$17,000, Founder's Scholarship: $7,000-$12,000. Combination of class rank, test scores, and GPA considered.
Additional info: Must apply for admission by 1/15 for priority consideration for scholarships.

FINANCIAL AID PROCEDURES
Forms required: FAFSA.
Dates and Deadlines: Priority date 3/1; no closing date. Applicants notified on a rolling basis starting 2/20; must reply within 3 week(s) of notification.

CONTACT
Ruth Pusich, Director of Financial Aid
190 South Prospect Avenue, Elmhurst, IL 60126-3296
(630) 617-3075

Eureka College
Eureka, Illinois
www.eureka.edu Federal Code: 001678

4-year private liberal arts college in small town, affiliated with Christian Church (Disciples of Christ).
Enrollment: 754 undergrads.

BASIC COSTS (2012-2013)
Tuition and fees: $19,480.
Per-credit charge: $535.
Room and board: $8,600.

FINANCIAL AID PICTURE
Students with need: Need-based aid available for full-time and part-time students. Work study available nights, weekends, and for part-time students.
Students without need: No-need awards available for academics, alumni affiliation, art, leadership, music/drama, religious affiliation.
Scholarships offered: Reagan Fellows Program: full tuition; 5 awarded, Sandifer Mentorships: fully paid mentorship anywhere in the world at end of sophomore year; all freshmen eligible. Eureka College Ministry Fellowship: full tuition scholarships; 2 available each year.

FINANCIAL AID PROCEDURES
Forms required: FAFSA.
Dates and Deadlines: Priority date 4/15; no closing date. Applicants notified on a rolling basis starting 2/15; must reply by 5/1 or within 3 week(s) of notification.
Transfers: No deadline. Applicants notified on a rolling basis; must reply within 2 week(s) of notification.

CONTACT
Ellen Rigsby, Director of Financial Aid
300 East College Avenue, Eureka, IL 61530-1500
(309) 467-6311

Governors State University
University Park, Illinois
www.govst.edu Federal Code: 009145

Upper-division public university in large town.
Enrollment: 3,103 undergrads, 59% part-time.
Selectivity: Open admission; but selective for some programs.

BASIC COSTS (2012-2013)
Tuition and fees: $9,116; out-of-state residents $16,586.
Additional info: Tuition/fee waivers available for minority students.

FINANCIAL AID PICTURE
Students with need: Need-based aid available for full-time and part-time students. Work study available nights, weekends, and for part-time students.
Students without need: No-need awards available for academics.

FINANCIAL AID PROCEDURES
Dates and Deadlines: Priority date 5/1; closing date 10/1. Applicants notified on a rolling basis.

CONTACT
Freda Whisenton-Comer, Office of Financial Aid
One University Parkway, University Park, IL 60484
(708) 534-4480

Greenville College
Greenville, Illinois
www.greenville.edu Federal Code: 001684

4-year private liberal arts college in small town, affiliated with Free Methodist Church of North America.
Enrollment: 1,157 undergrads, 3% part-time. 264 full-time freshmen.
Selectivity: Admits 50 to 75% of applicants.

BASIC COSTS (2012-2013)
Tuition and fees: $22,920.
Per-credit charge: $482.
Room and board: $7,576.

FINANCIAL AID PICTURE (2011-2012)
Students with need: Out of 252 full-time freshmen who applied for aid, 230 were judged to have need. Of these, 230 received aid, and 19 had their full need met. Average financial aid package met 75% of need; average scholarship/grant was $15,171; average loan was $3,427. For part-time students, average financial aid package was $7,869.
Students without need: 34 full-time freshmen who did not demonstrate need for aid received scholarships/grants; average award was $6,060. No-need awards available for academics, alumni affiliation, art, minority status, religious affiliation.
Scholarships offered: McAllaster Honors Scholarship: $12,000; 3.5 GPA and 27 ACT/1210 SAT. President's Scholarships: $9,000; 3.0 GPA, 27 ACT/1210 SAT, and leadership qualities. Dean's Scholarship: $8,000; 3.0 GPA, 22 ACT/1020 SAT and leadership qualities. Character & Service Scholarship: $500-$5,000, 2.5 GPA.

FINANCIAL AID PROCEDURES
Forms required: FAFSA.
Dates and Deadlines: Priority date 3/1; no closing date. Applicants notified on a rolling basis starting 3/31.
Transfers: No deadline. Applicants notified on a rolling basis; must reply within 3 week(s) of notification.

CONTACT
Marilae Latham, Director of Financial Aid
315 East College Avenue, Greenville, IL 62246
(618) 664-7111

Harper College
Palatine, Illinois
www.harpercollege.edu Federal Code: 003961

2-year public community college in small city.
Enrollment: 6,926 undergrads, 49% part-time. 1,197 full-time freshmen.
Selectivity: Open admission; but selective for some programs.

BASIC COSTS (2012-2013)
Tuition and fees: $3,789; out-of-district residents $11,499; out-of-state residents $13,764.

Per-credit charge: $107; out-of-district residents $364; out-of-state residents $439.

FINANCIAL AID PICTURE (2011-2012)

Students with need: Average financial aid package met 52% of need; average scholarship/grant was $4,798; average loan was $2,920. For part-time students, average financial aid package was $3,475.

Students without need: No-need awards available for academics, art, leadership, minority status, music/drama, state/district residency.

Scholarships offered: Distinguished Scholar Award: full tuition and fees, renewable for second year; minimum 27 ACT composite score; minimum of 23 in math, 20 in reading, and 19 in English OR minimum of 3.5/4.0 or 4.5/5.0 GPA. The Trustee Scholarship: minimum of 2.5/4.0 or 3.5/4.0 GPA and high school's recommendation.

FINANCIAL AID PROCEDURES

Forms required: FAFSA.

Dates and Deadlines: Closing date 3/1. Applicants notified on a rolling basis starting 3/1; must reply within 2 week(s) of notification.

Transfers: No deadline. Applicants notified on a rolling basis starting 3/1; must reply within 2 week(s) of notification.

CONTACT

Laura McGee, Director, Scholarships and Financial Assistance
1200 West Algonquin Road, Palatine, IL 60067-7398
(847) 925-6248

Harrington College of Design

Chicago, Illinois
www.harrington.edu Federal Code: 013601

4-year for-profit visual arts college in very large city.
Enrollment: 196 full-time undergrads.
Selectivity: Open admission; but selective for some programs.

BASIC COSTS (2012-2013)

Additional info: Program tuition and fees for associate degree in commercial photography: $38,100, interior design: $35,100; bachelor's degree in design and visual communications: $70,200, interior design: $79,000; master's degree in interior design, $51,000.

FINANCIAL AID PICTURE

Students with need: Need-based aid available for full-time and part-time students.

Students without need: No-need awards available for academics, leadership.

FINANCIAL AID PROCEDURES

Forms required: FAFSA.

Dates and Deadlines: Priority date 3/1; closing date 6/30. Applicants notified on a rolling basis; must reply within 2 week(s) of notification.

Transfers: Must reply within 2 week(s) of notification.

CONTACT

Ryan Froehle, Student Finance Manager
200 West Madison Avenue, Chicago, IL 60606-3433
(855) 777-7221

Heartland Community College

Normal, Illinois
www.heartland.edu Federal Code: 030838

2-year public community college in small city.
Enrollment: 5,456 undergrads.
Selectivity: Open admission; but selective for some programs.

BASIC COSTS (2012-2013)

Tuition and fees: $4,080; out-of-district residents $7,890; out-of-state residents $11,700.

Per-credit charge: $127; out-of-district residents $254; out-of-state residents $381.

FINANCIAL AID PICTURE

Students with need: Need-based aid available for full-time and part-time students. Work study available nights, weekends, and for part-time students.

Students without need: No-need awards available for academics, alumni affiliation, athletics, job skills, leadership, minority status, state/district residency.

FINANCIAL AID PROCEDURES

Forms required: FAFSA, institutional form.

Dates and Deadlines: Priority date 4/1; no closing date. Applicants notified on a rolling basis starting 5/15; must reply within 2 week(s) of notification.

CONTACT

Cheryl Schaffer, Director of Financial Aid
1500 West Raab Road, Normal, IL 61761
(309) 268-8020

Highland Community College

Freeport, Illinois
www.highland.edu Federal Code: 001681

2-year public community college in large town.
Enrollment: 1,749 undergrads, 42% part-time. 353 full-time freshmen.
Selectivity: Open admission; but selective for some programs.

BASIC COSTS (2012-2013)

Tuition and fees: $3,420; out-of-district residents $4,800; out-of-state residents $5,520.

Per-credit charge: $105; out-of-district residents $151; out-of-state residents $175.

FINANCIAL AID PICTURE (2011-2012)

Students with need: Out of 302 full-time freshmen who applied for aid, 263 were judged to have need. Of these, 257 received aid, and 1 had their full need met. Average financial aid package met 37% of need; average scholarship/grant was $5,020; average loan was $2,868. For part-time students, average financial aid package was $3,351.

Students without need: 5 full-time freshmen who did not demonstrate need for aid received scholarships/grants; average award was $4,489. No-need awards available for academics, athletics.

FINANCIAL AID PROCEDURES

Forms required: FAFSA, institutional form.

Dates and Deadlines: Applicants notified on a rolling basis starting 8/1; must reply within 2 week(s) of notification.

Transfers: No deadline. Applicants notified on a rolling basis starting 4/1.

CONTACT

Kathy Bangasser, Director of Financial Aid
2998 West Pearl City Road, Freeport, IL 61032-9341
(815) 599-3559

Illinois Central College

East Peoria, Illinois
www.icc.edu Federal Code: 006753

2-year public community college in large town.
Enrollment: 8,703 undergrads.
Selectivity: Open admission; but selective for some programs.

BASIC COSTS (2012-2013)
Tuition and fees: $3,195; out-of-district residents $7,050; out-of-state residents $7,050.
Per-credit charge: $107; out-of-district residents $235; out-of-state residents $235.

FINANCIAL AID PICTURE
Students with need: Need-based aid available for full-time and part-time students.
Students without need: No-need awards available for academics, athletics, minority status, music/drama, state/district residency.

FINANCIAL AID PROCEDURES
Forms required: FAFSA.
Dates and Deadlines: Priority date 6/1; no closing date. Applicants notified on a rolling basis starting 5/1; must reply within 2 week(s) of notification.

CONTACT
Beth McClain, Director of Financial Assistance
One College Drive, East Peoria, IL 61635-0001
(309) 694-5311

Illinois College
Jacksonville, Illinois
www.ic.edu Federal Code: 001688

4-year private liberal arts college in large town, affiliated with Presbyterian Church (USA) and United Church of Christ.
Enrollment: 965 undergrads, 1% part-time. 285 full-time freshmen.
Selectivity: Admits 50 to 75% of applicants.

BASIC COSTS (2012-2013)
Tuition and fees: $26,500.
Per-credit charge: $800.
Room and board: $8,500.

FINANCIAL AID PICTURE (2012-2013)
Students with need: Out of 252 full-time freshmen who applied for aid, 231 were judged to have need. Of these, 231 received aid, and 55 had their full need met. Average financial aid package met 87% of need; average scholarship/grant was $18,932; average loan was $4,271.
Students without need: 38 full-time freshmen who did not demonstrate need for aid received scholarships/grants; average award was $16,231. No-need awards available for academics, art, minority status, music/drama.
Scholarships offered: College transfer scholarship; available with 12 transferable credit hours and minimum 3.0 GPA.
Cumulative student debt: 79% of graduating class had student loans; average debt was $25,758.

FINANCIAL AID PROCEDURES
Forms required: FAFSA.
Dates and Deadlines: Priority date 3/1; no closing date. Applicants notified on a rolling basis starting 3/1; must reply within 2 week(s) of notification.
Transfers: No deadline. Applicants notified on a rolling basis starting 6/1; must reply within 2 week(s) of notification.

CONTACT
Katherine Taylor, Director of Financial Aid
1101 West College Avenue, Jacksonville, IL 62650
(217) 245-3035

Illinois Eastern Community Colleges: Frontier Community College
Fairfield, Illinois
www.iecc.edu/fcc Federal Code: 014090

2-year public community college in small town.
Enrollment: 543 undergrads, 58% part-time. 83 full-time freshmen.
Selectivity: Open admission; but selective for some programs.

BASIC COSTS (2013-2014)
Tuition and fees: $2,770; out-of-district residents $7,839; out-of-state residents $9,762.
Per-credit charge: $77; out-of-district residents $245; out-of-state residents $310.

FINANCIAL AID PICTURE
Students with need: Need-based aid available for full-time and part-time students.
Students without need: No-need awards available for academics, state/district residency.

FINANCIAL AID PROCEDURES
Forms required: FAFSA, institutional form.
Dates and Deadlines: Applicants notified on a rolling basis starting 8/1; must reply within 2 week(s) of notification.

CONTACT
Adam Bowles, Financial Aid Coordinator
Two Frontier Drive, Fairfield, IL 62837-9801
(618) 842-3711

Illinois Eastern Community Colleges: Lincoln Trail College
Robinson, Illinois
www.iecc.edu/ltc Federal Code: 009786

2-year public community college in small town.
Enrollment: 564 undergrads, 26% part-time. 128 full-time freshmen.
Selectivity: Open admission; but selective for some programs.

BASIC COSTS (2013-2014)
Tuition and fees: $2,770; out-of-district residents $7,839; out-of-state residents $9,762.
Per-credit charge: $77; out-of-district residents $245; out-of-state residents $310.

FINANCIAL AID PICTURE
Students with need: Need-based aid available for full-time and part-time students.
Students without need: No-need awards available for academics, athletics, state/district residency.

FINANCIAL AID PROCEDURES
Forms required: FAFSA, institutional form.
Dates and Deadlines: Applicants notified on a rolling basis starting 8/1; must reply within 2 week(s) of notification.

CONTACT
Jennifer Barthelemy, Coordinator of Financial Aid
11220 State Highway 1, Robinson, IL 62454-5707
(618) 544-8657

Illinois Eastern Community Colleges: Olney Central College
Olney, Illinois
www.iecc.edu/occ Federal Code: 001742

2-year public community college in small town.
Enrollment: 919 undergrads, 26% part-time. 257 full-time freshmen.
Selectivity: Open admission; but selective for some programs.

BASIC COSTS (2013-2014)
Tuition and fees: $2,770; out-of-district residents $7,839; out-of-state residents $9,762.

Per-credit charge: $77; out-of-district residents $245; out-of-state residents $310.

FINANCIAL AID PICTURE

Students with need: Need-based aid available for full-time and part-time students.

Students without need: No-need awards available for academics, athletics, state/district residency.

FINANCIAL AID PROCEDURES

Forms required: FAFSA, institutional form.

Dates and Deadlines: Applicants notified on a rolling basis starting 8/1; must reply within 2 week(s) of notification.

CONTACT

Vicki Stuckey, Financial Aid Coordinator
305 North West Street, Olney, IL 62450
(618) 395-7777

Illinois Eastern Community Colleges: Wabash Valley College

Mount Carmel, Illinois
www.iecc.edu/wvc Federal Code: 001779

2-year public community college in small town.

Enrollment: 969 undergrads, 43% part-time. 214 full-time freshmen.

Selectivity: Open admission; but selective for some programs.

BASIC COSTS (2013-2014)

Tuition and fees: $2,770; out-of-district residents $7,839; out-of-state residents $9,762.

Per-credit charge: $77; out-of-district residents $245; out-of-state residents $310.

FINANCIAL AID PICTURE

Students with need: Need-based aid available for full-time and part-time students.

Students without need: No-need awards available for academics, athletics, state/district residency.

FINANCIAL AID PROCEDURES

Forms required: FAFSA, institutional form.

Dates and Deadlines: Applicants notified on a rolling basis starting 8/1; must reply within 2 week(s) of notification.

CONTACT

Mary Johnson, Financial Aid Coordinator
2200 College Drive, Mount Carmel, IL 62863-2657
(618) 262-8641

Illinois Institute of Art: Chicago

Chicago, Illinois
www.ilic.artinstitutes.edu Federal Code: 012584

4-year for-profit visual arts college in very large city.

Enrollment: 2,860 undergrads.

BASIC COSTS (2012-2013)

Tuition and fees: $23,184.

Per-credit charge: $483.

Room and board: $10,197.

FINANCIAL AID PICTURE

Students with need: Need-based aid available for full-time and part-time students.

FINANCIAL AID PROCEDURES

Forms required: FAFSA.

Dates and Deadlines: Priority date 5/1; no closing date. Applicants notified on a rolling basis.

CONTACT

350 North Orleans Street, Chicago, IL 60654

Illinois Institute of Technology

Chicago, Illinois
www.iit.edu Federal Code: 001691

4-year private university and engineering college in very large city.

Enrollment: 2,731 undergrads, 4% part-time. 408 full-time freshmen.

Selectivity: Admits 50 to 75% of applicants.

BASIC COSTS (2012-2013)

Tuition and fees: $37,914.

Per-credit charge: $1,119.

Room and board: $10,626.

FINANCIAL AID PICTURE

Students with need: Need-based aid available for full-time and part-time students. Work study available nights, weekends, and for part-time students.

Students without need: No-need awards available for academics, alumni affiliation, leadership, ROTC.

Scholarships offered: Heald Academic Scholarships; $12,000- $25,000. Camras Scholar Program; full tuition and advanced access to research and leadership development; top 5% of applicant pool. Crown Scholarship; full tuition for five years; first-year full-time architecture student; one offered.

FINANCIAL AID PROCEDURES

Forms required: FAFSA.

Dates and Deadlines: Priority date 3/1; no closing date. Applicants notified on a rolling basis starting 3/5.

Transfers: No deadline. Applicants notified on a rolling basis starting 3/15.

CONTACT

Abigail McGrath, Director of Financial Aid
10 West 33rd Street, Chicago, IL 60616-3793
(312) 567-7219

Illinois State University

Normal, Illinois
www.ilstu.edu Federal Code: 001692

4-year public university in small city.

Enrollment: 18,179 undergrads, 6% part-time. 3,076 full-time freshmen.

Selectivity: Admits 50 to 75% of applicants.

BASIC COSTS (2012-2013)

Tuition and fees: $12,318; out-of-state residents $19,608.

Per-credit charge: $335; out-of-state residents $578.

Room and board: $9,575.

Additional info: Tuition at time of enrollment locked for 4 years.

FINANCIAL AID PICTURE (2011-2012)

Students with need: Out of 2,680 full-time freshmen who applied for aid, 2,077 were judged to have need. Of these, 2,077 received aid, and 92 had their full need met. Average financial aid package met 48% of need; average scholarship/grant was $3,164; average loan was $3,329. For part-time students, average financial aid package was $5,299.

Students without need: 31 full-time freshmen who did not demonstrate need for aid received scholarships/grants; average award was $1,779. No-need awards available for academics, art, athletics, music/drama.

Scholarships offered: ***Merit:*** Various non-need based merit scholarships available, including Presidential Scholars' Program, Provost's Scholarship, and

Dean's Scholarship. ***Athletic:*** 20 full-time freshmen received athletic scholarships; average amount $5,860.
Cumulative student debt: 67% of graduating class had student loans; average debt was $27,910.

FINANCIAL AID PROCEDURES
Forms required: FAFSA.
Dates and Deadlines: Priority date 3/1; no closing date. Applicants notified on a rolling basis starting 4/1; must reply within 2 week(s) of notification.

CONTACT
Jana Albrecht, Director of Financial Aid
Campus Box 2200, Normal, IL 61790-2200
(309) 438-2231

Illinois Valley Community College

Oglesby, Illinois
www.ivcc.edu Federal Code: 001705

2-year public community college in small town.
Enrollment: 2,563 undergrads, 44% part-time. 239 full-time freshmen.
Selectivity: Open admission; but selective for some programs.

BASIC COSTS (2012-2013)
Tuition and fees: $2,753; out-of-district residents $7,228; out-of-state residents $7,986.
Per-credit charge: $84; out-of-district residents $234; out-of-state residents $259.

FINANCIAL AID PICTURE (2011-2012)
Students with need: 74% of average financial aid package awarded as scholarships/grants, 26% awarded as loans/jobs. Need-based aid available for part-time students. Work study available nights.
Students without need: No-need awards available for academics, art, athletics, leadership, music/drama.
Scholarships offered: Foundation scholarships available.

FINANCIAL AID PROCEDURES
Forms required: FAFSA.
Dates and Deadlines: Priority date 3/1; no closing date. Applicants notified on a rolling basis starting 3/1.

CONTACT
Patty Williamson, Director, Financial Aid
815 North Orlando Smith Avenue, Oglesby, IL 61348-9693
(815) 224-0438

Illinois Wesleyan University

Bloomington, Illinois
www.iwu.edu Federal Code: 001696

4-year private university and liberal arts college in small city.
Enrollment: 2,007 undergrads. 490 full-time freshmen.
Selectivity: Admits 50 to 75% of applicants.

BASIC COSTS (2012-2013)
Tuition and fees: $37,954.
Per-credit charge: $1,180.
Room and board: $8,838.

FINANCIAL AID PICTURE (2012-2013)
Students with need: Out of 442 full-time freshmen who applied for aid, 350 were judged to have need. Of these, 350 received aid, and 119 had their full need met. Average financial aid package met 86% of need; average scholarship/grant was $22,782; average loan was $4,292.
Students without need: 133 full-time freshmen who did not demonstrate need for aid received scholarships/grants; average award was $15,192. No-need awards available for academics, art, music/drama.
Scholarships offered: Academic scholarships based on high school academic performance, recommendations, testing. Talent awards available in music, art, theater, and musical theater. Limited number of full-tuition awards in music.
Cumulative student debt: 70% of graduating class had student loans; average debt was $32,964.

FINANCIAL AID PROCEDURES
Forms required: FAFSA, institutional form.
Dates and Deadlines: Priority date 3/1; no closing date. Applicants notified on a rolling basis starting 3/1; must reply by 5/1.
Transfers: No deadline. Applicants notified on a rolling basis; must reply by 5/1 or within 3 week(s) of notification.

CONTACT
Scott Seibring, Director of Financial Aid
PO Box 2900, Bloomington, IL 61702-2900
(309) 556-3096

John A. Logan College

Carterville, Illinois
www.jalc.edu Federal Code: 008076

2-year public community college in small town.
Enrollment: 2,586 undergrads.
Selectivity: Open admission; but selective for some programs.

BASIC COSTS (2012-2013)
Tuition and fees: $2,760; out-of-district residents $6,492; out-of-state residents $8,337.
Per-credit charge: $92; out-of-district residents $216; out-of-state residents $278.

FINANCIAL AID PICTURE
Students with need: Need-based aid available for full-time and part-time students.
Students without need: This college awards aid only to students with need.

FINANCIAL AID PROCEDURES
Forms required: FAFSA, institutional form.
Dates and Deadlines: Priority date 5/1; no closing date. Applicants notified on a rolling basis starting 5/1.

CONTACT
Sherry Summary, Director for Student Financial Assistance
700 Logan College Road, Carterville, IL 62918
(618) 985-3741 ext. 8308

John Wood Community College

Quincy, Illinois
www.jwcc.edu Federal Code: 012813

2-year public community college in large town.
Enrollment: 1,887 undergrads.
Selectivity: Open admission; but selective for some programs.

BASIC COSTS (2012-2013)
Tuition and fees: $3,990; out-of-state residents $7,290.
Per-credit charge: $123; out-of-state residents $233.

FINANCIAL AID PICTURE
Students with need: Need-based aid available for full-time and part-time students. Work study available nights, weekends, and for part-time students.

Scholarships offered: Non-need based scholarships and awards are available, Interested students must apply and be selected. Area organizations also have scholarships and awards available.

FINANCIAL AID PROCEDURES

Forms required: FAFSA.

Dates and Deadlines: Applicants notified on a rolling basis starting 3/1.

CONTACT

Melanie Lechtenberg, Director of Financial Aid
1301 South 48th Street, Quincy, IL 62305-8736
(217) 641-4336

Joliet Junior College

Joliet, Illinois
www.jjc.edu Federal Code: 001699

2-year public community and junior college in small city.
Enrollment: 15,589 undergrads.
Selectivity: Open admission; but selective for some programs and for out-of-state students.

BASIC COSTS (2012-2013)

Tuition and fees: $3,210; out-of-district residents $7,860; out-of-state residents $8,550.
Per-credit charge: $80; out-of-district residents $235; out-of-state residents $258.
Additional info: Additional course fees may apply.

FINANCIAL AID PICTURE

Students with need: Need-based aid available for full-time and part-time students. Work study available nights, weekends, and for part-time students.
Students without need: No-need awards available for academics.

FINANCIAL AID PROCEDURES

Forms required: FAFSA, institutional form.
Dates and Deadlines: Closing date 5/1. Applicants notified on a rolling basis starting 5/15.

CONTACT

David Seward, Director of Financial Aid
1215 Houbolt Road, Joliet, IL 60431-8938
(815) 729-9020 ext. 2701

Judson University

Elgin, Illinois
www.judsonu.edu Federal Code: 001700

4-year private university and liberal arts college in small city, affiliated with American Baptist Churches in the USA.
Enrollment: 971 undergrads.
Selectivity: Open admission; but selective for some programs.

BASIC COSTS (2012-2013)

Tuition and fees: $27,000.
Room and board: $8,990.

FINANCIAL AID PICTURE

Students with need: Need-based aid available for full-time students. Work study available nights, weekends, and for part-time students.
Students without need: No-need awards available for academics, alumni affiliation, art, athletics, music/drama.
Scholarships offered: President's Scholarship; $12,000; based on ACT/SAT and GPA. Dean's Scholarship; $10,000; based on ACT/SAT and GPA. Faculty Scholarship; $8,000; based on ACT/SAT and GPA. University Scholarship; $6,000; based on ACT/SAT and GPA.

FINANCIAL AID PROCEDURES

Forms required: FAFSA.
Dates and Deadlines: Priority date 3/1; closing date 5/1. Applicants notified on a rolling basis starting 3/15; must reply by 5/1 or within 4 week(s) of notification.
Transfers: Must reply by 5/1 or within 4 week(s) of notification.

CONTACT

Roberto Santizo, Director of Financial Aid
1151 North State Street, Elgin, IL 60123-1404
(800) 879-5376

Kankakee Community College

Kankakee, Illinois
www.kcc.edu Federal Code: 007690

2-year public community college in large town.
Enrollment: 3,291 undergrads, 54% part-time. 263 full-time freshmen.
Selectivity: Open admission; but selective for some programs.

BASIC COSTS (2013-2014)

Tuition and fees: $3,390; out-of-district residents $6,071; out-of-state residents $13,990.
Per-credit charge: $100; out-of-district residents $189; out-of-state residents $453.

FINANCIAL AID PICTURE

Students with need: Need-based aid available for full-time and part-time students. Work study available nights.
Students without need: No-need awards available for athletics.

FINANCIAL AID PROCEDURES

Forms required: FAFSA.
Dates and Deadlines: Closing date 7/13. Applicants notified on a rolling basis; must reply within 4 week(s) of notification.
Transfers: Applicants notified on a rolling basis.

CONTACT

John Perry, Director of Financial Aid
100 College Drive, Kankakee, IL 60901-6505
(815) 802-8550

Kaskaskia College

Centralia, Illinois
www.kaskaskia.edu Federal Code: 001701

2-year public community college in large town.
Enrollment: 3,340 undergrads, 42% part-time. 284 full-time freshmen.
Selectivity: Open admission; but selective for some programs.

BASIC COSTS (2012-2013)

Tuition and fees: $3,120; out-of-district residents $5,730; out-of-state residents $12,060.
Per-credit charge: $92; out-of-district residents $179; out-of-state residents $390.

FINANCIAL AID PICTURE (2012-2013)

Students with need: Out of 212 full-time freshmen who applied for aid, 212 were judged to have need. Of these, 197 received aid. Average financial aid package met 63% of need; average scholarship/grant was $1,873; average loan was $1,620. For part-time students, average financial aid package was $1,543.
Students without need: No-need awards available for academics, athletics, state/district residency.

FINANCIAL AID PROCEDURES

Forms required: FAFSA.

Dates and Deadlines: Priority date 5/15; no closing date. Applicants notified on a rolling basis starting 4/1; must reply within 2 week(s) of notification.
Transfers: No deadline. Applicants notified on a rolling basis.

CONTACT

Lisa Collier, Director of Financial Aid
27210 College Road, Centralia, IL 62801
(618) 545-3080

Kendall College

Chicago, Illinois
www.kendall.edu Federal Code: 001703

4-year for-profit culinary school and teachers college in very large city.
Enrollment: 1,715 undergrads, 38% part-time. 91 full-time freshmen.
Selectivity: Admits over 75% of applicants.

BASIC COSTS (2012-2013)

Tuition and fees: $24,246.
Room and board: $10,995.
Additional info: Quoted cost is for culinary arts program. Board plan provides 15 meals per week.

FINANCIAL AID PICTURE

Students with need: Need-based aid available for full-time and part-time students. Work study available nights, weekends, and for part-time students.
Students without need: No-need awards available for academics, alumni affiliation, job skills.

FINANCIAL AID PROCEDURES

Forms required: FAFSA.
Dates and Deadlines: Priority date 4/15; no closing date. Applicants notified on a rolling basis starting 1/1; must reply within 2 week(s) of notification.
Transfers: No deadline. Applicants notified on a rolling basis; must reply within 2 week(s) of notification.

CONTACT

Frank Arce, Director of Financial Aid
900 N. North Branch Street, Chicago, IL 60642-4278
(312) 752-2070

Kishwaukee College

Malta, Illinois
www.kishwaukeecollege.edu Federal Code: 007684

2-year public community college in rural community.
Enrollment: 4,921 undergrads.
Selectivity: Open admission; but selective for some programs.

BASIC COSTS (2012-2013)

Tuition and fees: $3,060; out-of-district residents $7,740; out-of-state residents $11,490.
Per-credit charge: $89; out-of-district residents $245; out-of-state residents $370.

FINANCIAL AID PICTURE

Students with need: Need-based aid available for full-time and part-time students. Work study available nights, weekends, and for part-time students.
Students without need: No-need awards available for academics, athletics, leadership, music/drama, state/district residency.

FINANCIAL AID PROCEDURES

Forms required: FAFSA, institutional form.
Dates and Deadlines: Priority date 5/1; no closing date. Applicants notified on a rolling basis starting 5/1; must reply within 2 week(s) of notification.
Transfers: Must reply within 2 week(s) of notification. Some state programs not available to sophomore status students.

CONTACT

Pamela Wagener, Director, Financial Aid/Veterans Affairs
21193 Malta Road, Malta, IL 60150-9699
(815) 825-2086 ext. 2240

Knox College

Galesburg, Illinois
www.knox.edu Federal Code: 001704

4-year private liberal arts college in large town.
Enrollment: 1,394 undergrads. 377 full-time freshmen.
Selectivity: Admits over 75% of applicants.

BASIC COSTS (2013-2014)

Tuition and fees: $38,652.
Room and board: $8,400.

FINANCIAL AID PICTURE (2012-2013)

Students with need: Out of 353 full-time freshmen who applied for aid, 304 were judged to have need. Of these, 303 received aid, and 107 had their full need met. Average financial aid package met 90% of need; average scholarship/grant was $24,762; average loan was $2,978. Need-based aid available for part-time students.
Students without need: 73 full-time freshmen who did not demonstrate need for aid received scholarships/grants; average award was $14,942. No-need awards available for academics, art, leadership, music/drama.
Scholarships offered: Scholarships are awarded based on academic achievement, visual and performing arts, writing, service and leadership, and math.
Cumulative student debt: 64% of graduating class had student loans; average debt was $27,542.

FINANCIAL AID PROCEDURES

Forms required: FAFSA, institutional form.
Dates and Deadlines: Priority date 2/15; no closing date. Applicants notified on a rolling basis starting 3/1; must reply by 5/1.
Transfers: Applicants notified on a rolling basis starting 3/15; must reply by 6/1.

CONTACT

Ann Brill, Director of Financial Aid
2 East South Street, Galesburg, IL 61401
(309) 341-7149

Lake Forest College

Lake Forest, Illinois
www.lakeforest.edu Federal Code: 001706

4-year private liberal arts college in large town.
Enrollment: 1,534 undergrads. 416 full-time freshmen.
Selectivity: Admits 50 to 75% of applicants.

BASIC COSTS (2012-2013)

Tuition and fees: $38,300.
Room and board: $9,050.

FINANCIAL AID PICTURE (2012-2013)

Students with need: Out of 352 full-time freshmen who applied for aid, 314 were judged to have need. Of these, 314 received aid, and 51 had their full need met. Average financial aid package met 84% of need; average scholarship/grant was $28,175; average loan was $3,989. For part-time students, average financial aid package was $15,000.
Students without need: 94 full-time freshmen who did not demonstrate need for aid received scholarships/grants; average award was $17,043. No-need awards available for academics, alumni affiliation, art, leadership, music/drama, state/district residency.

Scholarships offered: Illinois students (graduated from an Illinois high school) receive a $12,000 In-state scholarship.
Cumulative student debt: 66% of graduating class had student loans; average debt was $30,801.

FINANCIAL AID PROCEDURES
Forms required: FAFSA, institutional form.
Dates and Deadlines: Priority date 3/1; closing date 5/1. Applicants notified on a rolling basis starting 3/1; must reply by 5/1.

CONTACT
Gerard Cebrzynski, Financial Aid Director
555 North Sheridan Road, Lake Forest, IL 60045-2338
(847) 735-5015

Lake Land College
Mattoon, Illinois
www.lakelandcollege.edu Federal Code: 007644

2-year public community college in large town.
Enrollment: 4,081 undergrads.
Selectivity: Open admission; but selective for some programs.

BASIC COSTS (2012-2013)
Tuition and fees: $3,024; out-of-district residents $6,444; out-of-state residents $11,701.
Per-credit charge: $81; out-of-district residents $195; out-of-state residents $370.

FINANCIAL AID PICTURE
Students with need: Need-based aid available for full-time and part-time students. Work study available nights, weekends, and for part-time students.
Students without need: No-need awards available for academics, athletics.

FINANCIAL AID PROCEDURES
Forms required: FAFSA.
Dates and Deadlines: Priority date 5/1; no closing date. Applicants notified on a rolling basis starting 6/1.
Transfers: No deadline.

CONTACT
Paula Carpenter, Director of Financial Aid and Veteran Services
5001 Lake Land Boulevard, Mattoon, IL 61938-9366
(217) 234-5231

Lakeview College of Nursing
Danville, Illinois
www.lakeviewcol.edu Federal Code: 010501

Upper-division private nursing college in large town.
Enrollment: 289 full-time undergrads.

BASIC COSTS (2013-2014)
Tuition and fees: $13,800.
Per-credit charge: $460.

FINANCIAL AID PICTURE (2012-2013)
Students with need: Need-based aid available for full-time and part-time students.
Students without need: This college awards aid only to students with need.

FINANCIAL AID PROCEDURES
Forms required: FAFSA, institutional form.
Transfers: Priority date 4/15; no deadline.

CONTACT
Janet Ingargiola, Director of Financial Aid
903 North Logan Avenue, Danville, IL 61832
(217) 554-6887

Le Cordon Bleu College of Culinary Arts: Chicago
Chicago, Illinois
www.chefs.edu/Chicago Federal Code: 016758

2-year for-profit culinary school in very large city.
Enrollment: 1,153 undergrads.
Selectivity: Open admission.

BASIC COSTS (2012-2013)
Additional info: Le Cordon Bleu patisserie and baking associate degree program : $39,200; Le Cordon Bleu culinary arts associate degree program: $36,200; Le Cordon Bleu culinary arts certificate program: $19,200. Additional charges for books and supplies.

FINANCIAL AID PICTURE
Students with need: Need-based aid available for full-time and part-time students. Work study available nights.

FINANCIAL AID PROCEDURES
Forms required: FAFSA, institutional form.
Dates and Deadlines: Applicants notified on a rolling basis.
Transfers: No deadline. Applicants notified on a rolling basis.

CONTACT
Nathan Nimrick, Director of Student Finance
361 West Chestnut, Chicago, IL 60610-3050
(312) 944-0882

Lewis and Clark Community College
Godfrey, Illinois
www.lc.edu Federal Code: 010020

2-year public community college in large town.
Enrollment: 4,734 undergrads.
Selectivity: Open admission; but selective for some programs.

BASIC COSTS (2012-2013)
Tuition and fees: $3,420; out-of-district residents $9,240; out-of-state residents $12,150.
Per-credit charge: $97; out-of-district residents $291; out-of-state residents $388.

FINANCIAL AID PICTURE
Students with need: Need-based aid available for full-time and part-time students.

FINANCIAL AID PROCEDURES
Forms required: FAFSA.
Dates and Deadlines: Priority date 6/1; no closing date. Applicants notified on a rolling basis starting 8/1; must reply within 3 week(s) of notification.
Transfers: No deadline. Applicants notified on a rolling basis.

CONTACT
Angela Weaver, Director, Financial Aid
5800 Godfrey Road, Godfrey, IL 62035-2466
(618) 468-2223

Lewis University

Romeoville, Illinois
www.lewisu.edu Federal Code: 001707

4-year private university in large town, affiliated with Roman Catholic Church.
Enrollment: 4,452 undergrads, 19% part-time. 673 full-time freshmen.
Selectivity: Admits 50 to 75% of applicants.

BASIC COSTS (2012-2013)
Tuition and fees: $25,770.
Per-credit charge: $760.
Room and board: $9,200.
Additional info: Tuition/fee waivers available for adults.

FINANCIAL AID PICTURE (2012-2013)
Students with need: Need-based aid available for full-time and part-time students. Work study available nights, weekends, and for part-time students.
Students without need: No-need awards available for academics, alumni affiliation, art, athletics, music/drama, religious affiliation, ROTC.

FINANCIAL AID PROCEDURES
Forms required: FAFSA.
Dates and Deadlines: Closing date 5/1. Applicants notified on a rolling basis starting 2/1; must reply by 5/1 or within 2 week(s) of notification.
Transfers: Priority date 5/1. Applicants notified on a rolling basis starting 2/1; must reply by 8/1 or within 2 week(s) of notification.

CONTACT
Janeen Decharinte, Director of Financial Aid
Unit #297, Romeoville, IL 60446-2200
(815) 836-5263

Lexington College

Chicago, Illinois
www.lexingtoncollege.edu Federal Code: 016942

4-year private culinary school and business college for women in very large city, affiliated with Roman Catholic Church.
Enrollment: 75 undergrads. 63 full-time freshmen.
Selectivity: Admits less than 50% of applicants.

BASIC COSTS (2013-2014)
Tuition and fees: $25,500.

FINANCIAL AID PICTURE
Students with need: Need-based aid available for full-time and part-time students.
Students without need: This college awards aid only to students with need.
Additional info: Work-study is available.

FINANCIAL AID PROCEDURES
Forms required: FAFSA.
Dates and Deadlines: Closing date 5/15. Applicants notified on a rolling basis starting 7/1; must reply within 2 week(s) of notification.
Transfers: Students who enroll and then transfer to another college within a given term can only receive Illinois state aid at one institution per academic year.

CONTACT
Maria LeBron, Director of Financial Aid
310 South Peoria Street, Chicago, IL 60607-3534
(312) 226-6294 ext. 227

Lincoln Christian University

Lincoln, Illinois
www.lincolnchristian.edu Federal Code: 001708

4-year private university and Bible college in large town, affiliated with Christian Church.
Enrollment: 675 undergrads, 14% part-time. 233 full-time freshmen.
Selectivity: Admits 50 to 75% of applicants.

BASIC COSTS (2012-2013)
Tuition and fees: $15,300.
Per-credit charge: $502.
Room and board: $7,080.

FINANCIAL AID PICTURE (2011-2012)
Students with need: Out of 212 full-time freshmen who applied for aid, 195 were judged to have need. Of these, 190 received aid, and 11 had their full need met. Average financial aid package met 48% of need; average scholarship/grant was $5,230; average loan was $3,086. Need-based aid available for part-time students.
Students without need: 22 full-time freshmen who did not demonstrate need for aid received scholarships/grants; average award was $5,074. No-need awards available for academics.
Cumulative student debt: 76% of graduating class had student loans; average debt was $18,452.

FINANCIAL AID PROCEDURES
Forms required: FAFSA.
Dates and Deadlines: Priority date 3/1; no closing date. Applicants notified on a rolling basis starting 2/1; must reply within 4 week(s) of notification.

CONTACT
Nancy Siddens, Director of Student Financial Aid
100 Campus View Drive, Lincoln, IL 62656-2111
(217) 732-3168 ext. 2304

Lincoln College

Lincoln, Illinois
www.lincolncollege.edu Federal Code: 001709

2-year private junior and liberal arts college in large town.
Enrollment: 1,170 undergrads, 31% part-time. 358 full-time freshmen.

BASIC COSTS (2012-2013)
Tuition and fees: $17,500.
Per-credit charge: $260.
Room and board: $7,000.

FINANCIAL AID PICTURE
Students with need: Need-based aid available for full-time and part-time students. Work study available nights, weekends, and for part-time students.
Students without need: No-need awards available for academics, alumni affiliation, art, athletics, leadership, music/drama.
Additional info: Auditions recommended for music, speech, theater, broadcasting, and dance scholarship candidates, portfolios recommended for art and technical theater scholarship candidates.

FINANCIAL AID PROCEDURES
Forms required: FAFSA.
Dates and Deadlines: Priority date 4/1; closing date 6/1. Applicants notified on a rolling basis starting 6/1; must reply within 3 week(s) of notification.
Transfers: No deadline. Applicants notified on a rolling basis.

CONTACT
Chris Steckmann, Director of Financial Aid
300 Keokuk Street, Lincoln, IL 62656
(217) 732-3155 ext. 231

Lincoln Land Community College

Springfield, Illinois
www.llcc.edu Federal Code: 007170

2-year public community and junior college in small city.
Enrollment: 7,193 undergrads.
Selectivity: Open admission; but selective for some programs.

BASIC COSTS (2012-2013)

Tuition and fees: $3,210; out-of-district residents $6,090; out-of-state residents $8,970.
Per-credit charge: $96; out-of-district residents $192; out-of-state residents $288.
Additional info: Tuition/fee waivers available for minority students.

FINANCIAL AID PICTURE

Students with need: Need-based aid available for full-time and part-time students. Work study available nights.
Students without need: No-need awards available for academics, athletics, minority status, state/district residency.

FINANCIAL AID PROCEDURES

Forms required: FAFSA, institutional form.
Dates and Deadlines: Priority date 5/1; no closing date. Applicants notified on a rolling basis starting 4/15; must reply within 2 week(s) of notification.

CONTACT

Lee Bursi, Associate Vice President, Financial Aid
5250 Shepherd Road, Springfield, IL 62794-9256
(217) 786-2237

Loyola University Chicago

Chicago, Illinois
www.luc.edu Federal Code: 001710

4-year private university in very large city, affiliated with Roman Catholic Church.
Enrollment: 9,465 undergrads, 7% part-time. 2,001 full-time freshmen.
Selectivity: Admits 50 to 75% of applicants.

BASIC COSTS (2013-2014)

Tuition and fees: $36,660.
Per-credit charge: $690.
Room and board: $12,900.

FINANCIAL AID PICTURE (2012-2013)

Students with need: Out of 1,752 full-time freshmen who applied for aid, 1,486 were judged to have need. Of these, 1,483 received aid, and 183 had their full need met. Average financial aid package met 82% of need; average scholarship/grant was $20,193; average loan was $3,824. For part-time students, average financial aid package was $17,273.
Students without need: 436 full-time freshmen who did not demonstrate need for aid received scholarships/grants; average award was $12,355. No-need awards available for academics, athletics, leadership, music/drama, religious affiliation.
Scholarships offered: 14 full-time freshmen received athletic scholarships; average amount $26,815.
Cumulative student debt: 72% of graduating class had student loans; average debt was $36,328.

FINANCIAL AID PROCEDURES

Forms required: FAFSA.
Dates and Deadlines: Priority date 3/1; no closing date. Applicants notified on a rolling basis starting 2/15; must reply within 3 week(s) of notification.
Transfers: FAFSA must be filed by July 1 to receive Illinois map grant.

CONTACT

1032 West Sheridan Road., Chicago, IL 60660
(773) 508-3155

MacMurray College

Jacksonville, Illinois
www.mac.edu Federal Code: 001717

4-year private liberal arts college in large town, affiliated with United Methodist Church.
Enrollment: 610 undergrads.

BASIC COSTS (2012-2013)

Tuition and fees: $21,400.
Per-credit charge: $693.
Room and board: $7,650.
Additional info: Tuition/fee waivers available for adults.

FINANCIAL AID PICTURE

Students with need: Need-based aid available for full-time and part-time students. Work study available nights, weekends, and for part-time students.
Students without need: No-need awards available for academics, alumni affiliation, leadership, religious affiliation.
Scholarships offered: Academic scholarships: $5,000-full tuition; based on merit. Transfer scholarships: to $8,000; based on academic merit. Leadership scholarship to one incoming female freshman annually: available based on committee selection. Religious scholarship matching up to $1500 per year.
Additional info: Merit scholarships for accepted, enrolled freshman based on academic record and notified upon admission.

FINANCIAL AID PROCEDURES

Forms required: FAFSA.
Dates and Deadlines: Priority date 3/1; no closing date. Applicants notified on a rolling basis starting 2/15; must reply within 2 week(s) of notification.
Transfers: Priority date 3/1; no deadline. Applicants notified on a rolling basis starting 2/15; must reply within 2 week(s) of notification. Phi Theta Kappa members may receive $2,500 per year.

CONTACT

Laci Engelbrecht, Director of Financial Aid
447 East College Avenue, Jacksonville, IL 62650-2590
(217) 479-7007

McHenry County College

Crystal Lake, Illinois
www.mchenry.edu Federal Code: 007691

2-year public community college in large town.
Enrollment: 5,017 undergrads.
Selectivity: Open admission; but selective for some programs.

BASIC COSTS (2013-2014)

Tuition and fees: $2,984; out-of-district residents $9,324; out-of-state residents $11,420.
Per-credit charge: $90; out-of-district residents $301; out-of-state residents $371.

FINANCIAL AID PICTURE (2011-2012)

Students with need: 73% of average financial aid package awarded as scholarships/grants, 27% awarded as loans/jobs. Need-based aid available for part-time students. Work study available nights, weekends, and for part-time students.
Students without need: No-need awards available for academics, athletics, leadership, music/drama, state/district residency.
Scholarships offered: President's Scholarship: full tuition for two years; based on talent in academic areas; students must complete portfolio and have 3.0 GPA. Founding Faculty Scholarship: full tuition for 2 years; based on GPA and essay.
Additional info: Students can apply throughout the award year for federal and state aid. Students with physical handicaps or learning disabilities may apply for special needs scholarship.

FINANCIAL AID PROCEDURES
Forms required: FAFSA, institutional form.
Dates and Deadlines: Priority date 6/1; no closing date. Applicants notified on a rolling basis starting 5/1.

CONTACT
Dane Klee, Director, Office of Financial Aid and Veteran Services
8900 US Highway 14, Crystal Lake, IL 60012-2738
(815) 455-8761

McKendree University
Lebanon, Illinois
www.mckendree.edu Federal Code: 001722

4-year private university and liberal arts college in small town, affiliated with United Methodist Church.
Enrollment: 2,193 undergrads, 28% part-time. 305 full-time freshmen.
Selectivity: Admits 50 to 75% of applicants.

BASIC COSTS (2012-2013)
Tuition and fees: $25,340.
Per-credit charge: $810.
Room and board: $9,010.

FINANCIAL AID PICTURE (2012-2013)
Students with need: Out of 268 full-time freshmen who applied for aid, 230 were judged to have need. Of these, 230 received aid, and 46 had their full need met. Average financial aid package met 78% of need; average scholarship/grant was $18,192; average loan was $3,153. For part-time students, average financial aid package was $5,453.
Students without need: 62 full-time freshmen who did not demonstrate need for aid received scholarships/grants; average award was $12,429. No-need awards available for academics, alumni affiliation, art, athletics, leadership, minority status, music/drama, religious affiliation.
Scholarships offered: ***Merit:*** Dean's Scholarships: $6,500 annually; awarded to students that have either 3.0 GPA or composite ACT score of 22. Presidential Scholarships: $8,000 annually; awarded to students with both 3.0 GPA and composite ACT score of 22 or higher. Honor's Scholarships: $12,000 annually; awarded to students with both 3.6 GPA and composite ACT score of 27 or higher. Leadership Scholarship: maximum value of $5,000 annually; available to students that have been awarded a McKendree University Presidential or Honor's Scholarship and attend the Leadership Scholarship Event, during which they complete two personal interviews and submit an essay. ***Athletic:*** 37 full-time freshmen received athletic scholarships; average amount $14,420.
Cumulative student debt: 76% of graduating class had student loans; average debt was $26,657.

FINANCIAL AID PROCEDURES
Forms required: FAFSA.
Dates and Deadlines: Priority date 5/31; no closing date. Applicants notified on a rolling basis starting 3/1; must reply within 4 week(s) of notification.
Transfers: No deadline. Applicants notified on a rolling basis starting 3/1; must reply within 4 week(s) of notification.

CONTACT
Elizabeth Juehne, Director of FInancial Aid
701 College Road, Lebanon, IL 62254-1299
(618) 537-6828

Midstate College
Peoria, Illinois
www.midstate.edu Federal Code: 004568

4-year for-profit business college in small city.
Enrollment: 584 undergrads.
Selectivity: Open admission; but selective for some programs and for out-of-state students.

BASIC COSTS (2012-2013)
Tuition and fees: $15,225.
Per-credit charge: $358.

FINANCIAL AID PICTURE
Students with need: Work study available nights, weekends, and for part-time students.

FINANCIAL AID PROCEDURES
Forms required: FAFSA, institutional form.
Dates and Deadlines: Applicants notified on a rolling basis; must reply within 4 week(s) of notification.

CONTACT
Irene Bimrose, Director of Financial Assistance
411 West Northmoor Road, Peoria, IL 61614-3558
(309) 692-4092

Millikin University
Decatur, Illinois
www.millikin.edu Federal Code: 001724

4-year private university in small city, affiliated with Presbyterian Church (USA).
Enrollment: 2,221 undergrads, 4% part-time. 432 full-time freshmen.
Selectivity: Admits 50 to 75% of applicants.

BASIC COSTS (2012-2013)
Tuition and fees: $28,644.
Per-credit charge: $931.
Room and board: $8,720.

FINANCIAL AID PICTURE (2011-2012)
Students with need: Out of 425 full-time freshmen who applied for aid, 379 were judged to have need. Of these, 379 received aid, and 110 had their full need met. Average financial aid package met 87% of need; average scholarship/grant was $10,832; average loan was $3,686. For part-time students, average financial aid package was $8,384.
Students without need: 46 full-time freshmen who did not demonstrate need for aid received scholarships/grants; average award was $10,898. No-need awards available for academics, alumni affiliation, art, leadership, minority status, music/drama.
Scholarships offered: Millikin University Merit Scholarships: for students who demonstrate significant potential for contributing to campus life; renewable for four years of attendance.
Cumulative student debt: 78% of graduating class had student loans; average debt was $29,777.

FINANCIAL AID PROCEDURES
Forms required: FAFSA.
Dates and Deadlines: Priority date 3/15; no closing date. Applicants notified on a rolling basis starting 3/15; must reply within 4 week(s) of notification.
Transfers: No deadline. Applicants notified on a rolling basis starting 3/15.

CONTACT
Cheryl Howerton, Director of Financial Aid
1184 West Main Street, Decatur, IL 62522-2084
(217) 424-6317

Monmouth College
Monmouth, Illinois
www.monmouthcollege.edu Federal Code: 001725

4-year private liberal arts college in small town, affiliated with Presbyterian Church (USA).

Enrollment: 1,236 undergrads. 344 full-time freshmen.
Selectivity: Admits 50 to 75% of applicants.

BASIC COSTS (2012-2013)
Tuition and fees: $30,450.
Room and board: $7,300.

FINANCIAL AID PICTURE (2012-2013)
Students with need: Out of 330 full-time freshmen who applied for aid, 303 were judged to have need. Of these, 303 received aid, and 49 had their full need met. Average financial aid package met 89% of need; average scholarship/grant was $25,651; average loan was $3,683. For part-time students, average financial aid package was $11,314.
Students without need: 41 full-time freshmen who did not demonstrate need for aid received scholarships/grants; average award was $16,210. No-need awards available for academics, art, leadership, music/drama, religious affiliation, ROTC.
Cumulative student debt: 82% of graduating class had student loans; average debt was $31,578.

FINANCIAL AID PROCEDURES
Forms required: FAFSA.
Dates and Deadlines: Priority date 3/1; no closing date. Applicants notified on a rolling basis starting 2/15; must reply by 5/1 or within 2 week(s) of notification.
Transfers: No deadline. Applicants notified on a rolling basis; must reply by 8/15.

CONTACT
Jayne Schreck, Director of Financial Aid
700 East Broadway, Monmouth, IL 61462-1998
(309) 457-2129

Moody Bible Institute
Chicago, Illinois
www.moody.edu Federal Code: 001727

4-year private Bible and seminary college in very large city, affiliated with interdenominational tradition.
Enrollment: 2,960 undergrads.

BASIC COSTS (2012-2013)
Tuition and fees: $10,954.
Per-credit charge: $275.
Room and board: $9,160.
Additional info: Chicago students receive a scholarship to cover all tuition expenses.

FINANCIAL AID PICTURE
Students with need: Need-based aid available for full-time and part-time students.
Students without need: This college awards aid only to students with need.
Additional info: Aid available to upperclassmen is based on private and not federal/state sources.

FINANCIAL AID PROCEDURES
Forms required: institutional form.
Dates and Deadlines: Applicants notified on a rolling basis; must reply by 7/1.
Transfers: No deadline. Applicants notified on a rolling basis; must reply by 7/1.

CONTACT
Dan Griffin, Director of Financial Aid
820 N LaSalle Boulevard, Chicago, IL 60610
(312) 329-4178

Moraine Valley Community College
Palos Hills, Illinois
www.morainevalley.edu Federal Code: 007692

2-year public community and junior college in large town.
Enrollment: 10,890 undergrads, 50% part-time. 1,120 full-time freshmen.
Selectivity: Open admission; but selective for some programs.

BASIC COSTS (2013-2014)
Tuition and fees: $3,636; out-of-district residents $8,256; out-of-state residents $9,576.
Per-credit charge: $121; out-of-district residents $275; out-of-state residents $319.

FINANCIAL AID PICTURE (2011-2012)
Students with need: 88% of average financial aid package awarded as scholarships/grants, 12% awarded as loans/jobs. Need-based aid available for part-time students. Work study available nights.
Students without need: No-need awards available for academics, alumni affiliation, art, athletics, leadership, minority status, music/drama, state/district residency.

FINANCIAL AID PROCEDURES
Forms required: FAFSA, institutional form.
Dates and Deadlines: Priority date 5/1; no closing date. Applicants notified on a rolling basis starting 6/15; must reply within 2 week(s) of notification.

CONTACT
Laurie Anema, Director of Financial Aid
9000 West College Parkway, Palos Hills, IL 60465-2478
(708) 974-5726

Morrison Institute of Technology
Morrison, Illinois
www.morrisontech.edu Federal Code: 008880

2-year private technical college in small town.
Enrollment: 82 full-time undergrads.
Selectivity: Open admission.

BASIC COSTS (2012-2013)
Tuition and fees: $15,100.
Per-credit charge: $579.
Additional info: Board plan not available. Cost of room only, $2,900.

FINANCIAL AID PICTURE
Students with need: Need-based aid available for full-time and part-time students. Work study available nights, weekends, and for part-time students.
Students without need: No-need awards available for academics.

FINANCIAL AID PROCEDURES
Forms required: FAFSA, institutional form.
Dates and Deadlines: Applicants notified on a rolling basis; must reply within 2 week(s) of notification.

CONTACT
Julie Damhoff, Financial Aid Officer
701 Portland Avenue, Morrison, IL 61270-2959
(815) 772-7218 ext. 203

Morton College
Cicero, Illinois
www.morton.edu Federal Code: 001728

2-year public community college in small city.
Enrollment: 4,785 undergrads.

Selectivity: Open admission; but selective for some programs and for out-of-state students.

BASIC COSTS (2012-2013)
Tuition and fees: $3,188; out-of-district residents $7,284; out-of-state residents $9,332.
Per-credit charge: $79; out-of-district residents $207; out-of-state residents $271.

FINANCIAL AID PICTURE
Students with need: Need-based aid available for full-time and part-time students. Work study available nights, weekends, and for part-time students.

FINANCIAL AID PROCEDURES
Forms required: FAFSA, institutional form.
Dates and Deadlines: Priority date 6/1; no closing date. Applicants notified on a rolling basis starting 8/3.

CONTACT
Robert Tebbe, Director of Financial Aid
3801 South Central Avenue, Cicero, IL 60804-4398
(708) 656-8000 ext. 428

National University of Health Sciences

Lombard, Illinois
www.nuhs.edu Federal Code: 001732

4-year private university and health science college in large town.
Enrollment: 52 full-time undergrads.

BASIC COSTS (2012-2013)
Tuition and fees: $9,511.
Per-credit charge: $312.
Additional info: Board plan not available. Cost of room only, $7,480.

FINANCIAL AID PICTURE
Students with need: Need-based aid available for full-time and part-time students.

FINANCIAL AID PROCEDURES
Transfers: No deadline.

CONTACT
Robert Dame, Director of Financial Aid
200 East Roosevelt Road, Lombard, IL 60148-4583
(630) 889-6700

North Central College

Naperville, Illinois
www.northcentralcollege.edu Federal Code: 001734

4-year private liberal arts college in small city, affiliated with United Methodist Church.
Enrollment: 2,662 undergrads, 4% part-time. 552 full-time freshmen.
Selectivity: Admits 50 to 75% of applicants.

BASIC COSTS (2012-2013)
Tuition and fees: $31,071.
Per-credit charge: $750.
Room and board: $8,883.

FINANCIAL AID PICTURE (2012-2013)
Students with need: Out of 517 full-time freshmen who applied for aid, 443 were judged to have need. Of these, 442 received aid, and 98 had their full need met. Average financial aid package met 78% of need; average scholarship/grant was $19,332; average loan was $3,675. For part-time students, average financial aid package was $13,699.
Students without need: 102 full-time freshmen who did not demonstrate need for aid received scholarships/grants; average award was $14,595. No-need awards available for academics, art, leadership, minority status, music/drama, religious affiliation, ROTC, state/district residency.
Scholarships offered: Numerous merit and talent scholarship opportunities available.
Cumulative student debt: 77% of graduating class had student loans; average debt was $33,304.

FINANCIAL AID PROCEDURES
Forms required: FAFSA, institutional form.
Dates and Deadlines: Applicants notified on a rolling basis starting 3/1; must reply within 4 week(s) of notification.
Transfers: No deadline. Applicants notified on a rolling basis starting 3/1; must reply within 4 week(s) of notification.

CONTACT
Marty Rossman, Director of Financial Aid
PO Box 3063, Naperville, IL 60566-7063
(630) 637-5600

North Park University

Chicago, Illinois
www.northpark.edu Federal Code: 001735

4-year private university and liberal arts college in very large city, affiliated with Evangelical Covenant Church of America.
Enrollment: 2,171 undergrads, 16% part-time. 333 full-time freshmen.
Selectivity: Admits less than 50% of applicants.

BASIC COSTS (2012-2013)
Tuition and fees: $22,090.
Per-credit charge: $730.
Room and board: $8,660.

FINANCIAL AID PICTURE (2012-2013)
Students with need: Out of 318 full-time freshmen who applied for aid, 246 were judged to have need. Of these, 246 received aid, and 10 had their full need met. Average financial aid package met 64% of need; average loan was $3,225.
Students without need: 36 full-time freshmen who did not demonstrate need for aid received scholarships/grants; average award was $5,576. No-need awards available for academics, art, music/drama, religious affiliation.
Cumulative student debt: 74% of graduating class had student loans; average debt was $27,306.

FINANCIAL AID PROCEDURES
Forms required: FAFSA.
Dates and Deadlines: Priority date 5/1; closing date 8/1. Applicants notified on a rolling basis starting 10/1; must reply by 5/1 or within 3 week(s) of notification.
Transfers: Priority date 6/1. Applicants notified on a rolling basis starting 10/1; must reply within 3 week(s) of notification.

CONTACT
Lucy Shaker, Director of Financial Aid
3225 West Foster Avenue Box 19, Chicago, IL 60625-4895
(773) 244-5506

Northeastern Illinois University

Chicago, Illinois
www.neiu.edu Federal Code: 001693

4-year public university in very large city.
Enrollment: 9,031 undergrads, 40% part-time. 886 full-time freshmen.
Selectivity: Admits 50 to 75% of applicants.

BASIC COSTS (2013-2014)
Tuition and fees: $9,542; out-of-state residents $15,878.
Additional info: Tuition at time of enrollment locked for 4 years.

FINANCIAL AID PICTURE (2011-2012)
Students with need: Out of 801 full-time freshmen who applied for aid, 704 were judged to have need. Of these, 638 received aid, and 5 had their full need met. Average financial aid package met 34% of need; average scholarship/grant was $7,392; average loan was $3,219. For part-time students, average financial aid package was $5,696.
Students without need: 9 full-time freshmen who did not demonstrate need for aid received scholarships/grants; average award was $795. No-need awards available for academics, art, leadership, music/drama.
Cumulative student debt: 14% of graduating class had student loans; average debt was $12,100.

FINANCIAL AID PROCEDURES
Forms required: FAFSA.
Dates and Deadlines: Priority date 2/15; no closing date. Applicants notified on a rolling basis starting 12/15; must reply within 2 week(s) of notification.

CONTACT
Maureen Amos, Director of Financial Aid
5500 North St. Louis Avenue, Chicago, IL 60625
(773) 442-5000

Northern Illinois University
DeKalb, Illinois
www.niu.edu Federal Code: 001737

4-year public university in large town.
Enrollment: 16,522 undergrads, 12% part-time. 2,599 full-time freshmen.
Selectivity: Admits 50 to 75% of applicants.

BASIC COSTS (2012-2013)
Tuition and fees: $11,484; out-of-state residents $20,377.
Per-credit charge: $330; out-of-state residents $659.
Room and board: $10,648.
Additional info: Tuition at time of enrollment locked for 4 years.

FINANCIAL AID PICTURE (2011-2012)
Students with need: Out of 2,322 full-time freshmen who applied for aid, 2,055 were judged to have need. Of these, 2,044 received aid, and 257 had their full need met. Average financial aid package met 69% of need; average scholarship/grant was $8,803; average loan was $3,399. For part-time students, average financial aid package was $6,974.
Students without need: No-need awards available for academics, alumni affiliation, art, athletics, leadership, music/drama, ROTC.
Scholarships offered: ***Merit:*** University Scholars: full tuition, fees, on-campus room and board; 33 ACT and either top 5% HS class or 3.75 GPA. NIU Scholars: $7,000; 27 ACT and either top 5% or 3.75 GPA. Northern Academic Scholarship: $4,000; 25-26 ACT and either top 10% or 3.0 GPA or 27 ACT and above; 6-10% of class or 3.0-3.74 GPA. Centennial Scholarship: $3,000; 22-24 ACT and either top 10% or 3.0 GPA. Red & Black Award: $3,000; 19-21 ACT and either top 10% or 3.0 GPA; or 22 ACT and above; 11-25% of class. Out-of-State Huskie Scholarship: $9,466; resident of Iowa, Indiana, Missouri, or Wisconsin; 19 ACT and either top 50% or 2.75 GPA. DeKalb County Scholarship: $4,000; DeKalb County public high school 2013 graduate with variable criteria (cannot be combined with other scholarships.) Pre-Law Scholarship: $2,000; for pre-law majors with 28 ACT and 3.5 GPA. Huskie Legacy Award: $1,000; incoming child of NIU alumnus/alumna. ***Athletic:*** 82 full-time freshmen received athletic scholarships; average amount $20,156.
Cumulative student debt: 72% of graduating class had student loans; average debt was $30,521.

FINANCIAL AID PROCEDURES
Forms required: FAFSA.
Dates and Deadlines: Priority date 3/1; no closing date. Applicants notified on a rolling basis starting 3/15.
Transfers: No deadline. Applicants notified on a rolling basis starting 3/15. Two year, $2,000/yr. transfer scholarship available with 3.5 cumulative transfer GPA and 30 transferable hours completed at time of admission.

CONTACT
Rebecca Babel, Director of Student Financial Aid DeKalb, IL 60115-2854
(815) 753-1395

Northwestern College
Chicago, Illinois
www.northwesterncollege.edu Federal Code: 012362

2-year for-profit technical and career college in very large city.
Enrollment: 1,357 undergrads, 62% part-time. 182 full-time freshmen.
Selectivity: Open admission; but selective for some programs.

BASIC COSTS (2013-2014)
Tuition and fees: $20,365.
Per-credit charge: $445.

FINANCIAL AID PICTURE (2012-2013)
Students with need: 76% of average financial aid package awarded as scholarships/grants, 24% awarded as loans/jobs. Need-based aid available for part-time students. Work study available nights.
Students without need: No-need awards available for academics.
Scholarships offered: Academic Scholarship: $600 per quarter up to six quarters. Board of Directors: $800 per quarter up to six quarters. Centennial: amount varies. Educational Achievement Scholarship: $600 per quarter up to six quarters. First Responders Scholarship: first responders $800 per quarter up to six quarters, dependents of first responders $600 per quarter up to six quarters. Military and Family Scholarship: military service member $800 per quarter up to six quarters, dependents of military service members: up to $600 per quarter up to six quarters. Community Scholarship: $800 per quarter up to six quarters. Early Incentive Scholarship: amount varies. Scholastic Scholarship: $667 per quarter up to six quarters. Presidential Scholarship: $800 per quarter up to six quarters. Excellence Scholarship: $1200 per quarter up to six quarters. Transfer Student Scholarship: $400 per quarter up four quarters.
Additional info: State grant programs for Illinois residents and alternative loans offered.

FINANCIAL AID PROCEDURES
Forms required: FAFSA, institutional form.
Dates and Deadlines: Priority date 6/30; no closing date. Applicants notified on a rolling basis starting 8/15; must reply within 4 week(s) of notification.

CONTACT
Ethel Arroyo, Director of Financial Aid
4829 North Lipps Ave, Chicago, IL 60630
(847) 233-7700 ext. 2126

Northwestern University
Evanston, Illinois Federal Code: 001739
www.northwestern.edu CSS Code: 1565

4-year private university in small city.
Enrollment: 8,343 undergrads, 1% part-time. 2,107 full-time freshmen.
Selectivity: Admits less than 50% of applicants.

BASIC COSTS (2012-2013)
Tuition and fees: $43,779.
Room and board: $13,329.

FINANCIAL AID PICTURE
Students with need: Need-based aid available for full-time students.
Students without need: No-need awards available for athletics, music/drama, ROTC.

FINANCIAL AID PROCEDURES
Forms required: FAFSA, CSS PROFILE.
Dates and Deadlines: Closing date 2/15. Applicants notified by 4/15; must reply by 5/1 or within 2 week(s) of notification.
Transfers: Closing date 6/1. Transfer student aid limited for first year.

CONTACT
Carolyn Lindley, Director of University Financial Aid
1801 Hinman Avenue, Evanston, IL 60204-3060
(847) 491-7400

Oakton Community College
Des Plaines, Illinois
www.oakton.edu Federal Code: 009896

2-year public community college in small city.
Enrollment: 3,124 full-time undergrads.
Selectivity: Open admission; but selective for some programs.

BASIC COSTS (2012-2013)
Tuition and fees: $2,897; out-of-district residents $8,720; out-of-state residents $10,528.
Per-credit charge: $94; out-of-district residents $288; out-of-state residents $348.

FINANCIAL AID PICTURE (2011-2012)
Students with need: 95% of average financial aid package awarded as scholarships/grants, 5% awarded as loans/jobs. Need-based aid available for part-time students. Work study available nights, weekends, and for part-time students.
Students without need: No-need awards available for academics, art, athletics, leadership, minority status, music/drama, state/district residency.
Scholarships offered: Oakton Merit Scholarship Program; tuition and related fees; first-time, in-district, freshmen in top 10% of high school class.

FINANCIAL AID PROCEDURES
Forms required: FAFSA, institutional form.
Dates and Deadlines: Priority date 3/1; no closing date. Applicants notified on a rolling basis starting 3/1; must reply within 2 week(s) of notification.
Transfers: Applicants notified on a rolling basis starting 5/1.

CONTACT
Jamie Petersen, Director of Financial Aid
Enrollment Center, Des Plaines, IL 60016
(847) 635-1708

Olivet Nazarene University
Bourbonnais, Illinois
www.olivet.edu Federal Code: 001741

4-year private university and liberal arts college in small city, affiliated with Church of the Nazarene.
Enrollment: 3,180 undergrads, 15% part-time. 697 full-time freshmen.
Selectivity: Admits over 75% of applicants.

BASIC COSTS (2013-2014)
Tuition and fees: $29,890.
Per-credit charge: $1,210.
Room and board: $7,900.

FINANCIAL AID PICTURE (2011-2012)
Students with need: Out of 660 full-time freshmen who applied for aid, 600 were judged to have need. Of these, 600 received aid, and 294 had their full need met. Average financial aid package met 83% of need; average scholarship/grant was $18,943; average loan was $3,435. Need-based aid available for part-time students.
Students without need: 92 full-time freshmen who did not demonstrate need for aid received scholarships/grants; average award was $13,224. No-need awards available for academics, alumni affiliation, art, athletics, leadership, music/drama, religious affiliation, ROTC, state/district residency.
Scholarships offered: 21 full-time freshmen received athletic scholarships; average amount $7,362.
Cumulative student debt: 74% of graduating class had student loans; average debt was $33,710.

FINANCIAL AID PROCEDURES
Dates and Deadlines: Priority date 3/1; no closing date. Applicants notified on a rolling basis starting 1/15; must reply within 2 week(s) of notification.
Transfers: No deadline. Applicants notified on a rolling basis starting 1/15; must reply within 2 week(s) of notification.

CONTACT
Greg Bruner, Director of Financial Aid
One University Avenue, Bourbonnais, IL 60914
(815) 939-5249

Parkland College
Champaign, Illinois
www.parkland.edu Federal Code: 007118

2-year public community college in small city.
Enrollment: 11,402 undergrads.
Selectivity: Open admission; but selective for some programs.

BASIC COSTS (2012-2013)
Tuition and fees: $3,360; out-of-district residents $7,815; out-of-state residents $13,305.
Per-credit charge: $112; out-of-district residents $261; out-of-state residents $444.

FINANCIAL AID PICTURE
Students with need: Need-based aid available for full-time students. Work study available nights.
Students without need: No-need awards available for academics, art, athletics, leadership, minority status, music/drama, state/district residency.

FINANCIAL AID PROCEDURES
Forms required: FAFSA, institutional form.
Dates and Deadlines: Closing date 3/1. Applicants notified on a rolling basis starting 6/1; must reply within 2 week(s) of notification.

CONTACT
Tim Wendt, Director of Financial Aid
2400 West Bradley Avenue, Champaign, IL 61821-1899
(217) 351-2276

Prairie State College
Chicago Heights, Illinois
www.prairiestate.edu Federal Code: 001640

2-year public community college in large town.
Enrollment: 5,416 undergrads.
Selectivity: Open admission; but selective for some programs.

BASIC COSTS (2012-2013)
Tuition and fees: $3,480; out-of-district residents $8,250; out-of-state residents $9,450.
Per-credit charge: $101; out-of-district residents $260; out-of-state residents $300.

FINANCIAL AID PICTURE

Students with need: Need-based aid available for full-time and part-time students. Work study available nights, weekends, and for part-time students.

FINANCIAL AID PROCEDURES

Forms required: FAFSA, institutional form.

Dates and Deadlines: Closing date 7/1. Applicants notified on a rolling basis; must reply within 2 week(s) of notification.

CONTACT

Alice Garcia, Director of Financial Aid
202 South Halsted Street, Chicago Heights, IL 60411
(708) 709-3523

Principia College

Elsah, Illinois — Federal Code: 001744
www.principiacollege.edu — CSS Code: 1630

4-year private liberal arts college in rural community, affiliated with First Church of Christ, Scientist (Christian Science).

Enrollment: 494 undergrads. 108 full-time freshmen.

Selectivity: Admits over 75% of applicants.

BASIC COSTS (2013-2014)

Tuition and fees: $25,980.

Per-credit charge: $850.

Room and board: $10,500.

FINANCIAL AID PICTURE (2011-2012)

Students with need: Out of 86 full-time freshmen who applied for aid, 77 were judged to have need. Of these, 77 received aid, and 28 had their full need met. Average financial aid package met 91% of need; average scholarship/grant was $23,168; average loan was $6,254. Need-based aid available for part-time students.

Students without need: 26 full-time freshmen who did not demonstrate need for aid received scholarships/grants; average award was $21,031. No-need awards available for academics, alumni affiliation, leadership.

Scholarships offered: Trustee Scholarship; full-tuition; based on GPA and SAT/ACT. Chairman's Scholarship; 3/4 tuition; based on GPA and SAT/ACT. President's Scholarship; 1/2 tuition; based on GPA and SAT/ACT. Dean's Scholarship; 1/4 tuition; based on GPA and SAT/ACT. Arthur Schulz, Jr. Alumni Scholarship; $4,500; based on GPA and SAT/ACT. Children and grandchildren of alumni scholarships; based on GPA. Founders' Scholarships; 1/4 to full-tuition; awarded to students who demonstrate deep commitment to Christian Science, character, and citizenship as evidenced by active participation in these areas.

Cumulative student debt: 49% of graduating class had student loans; average debt was $16,561.

FINANCIAL AID PROCEDURES

Forms required: CSS PROFILE, institutional form.

Dates and Deadlines: Closing date 3/1. Applicants notified by 4/1.

Transfers: Priority date 3/1. Dean's and Arthur Schulz Scholarships; $4,500 per year for 4 years; based on high school GPA, SAT/ACT, and 3.5 college GPA.

CONTACT

Tamara Gavaletz, Director of Financial Aid
One Maybeck Place, Elsah, IL 62028-9799
(800) 277-4648 ext. 2813

Quincy University

Quincy, Illinois
www.quincy.edu — Federal Code: 001745

4-year private university and liberal arts college in large town, affiliated with Roman Catholic Church.

Enrollment: 1,186 undergrads, 7% part-time. 262 full-time freshmen.

Selectivity: Admits over 75% of applicants.

BASIC COSTS (2012-2013)

Tuition and fees: $25,180.

Per-credit charge: $585.

Room and board: $9,800.

Additional info: Room and board charges vary according to board plan and housing facility selected.

FINANCIAL AID PICTURE (2012-2013)

Students with need: Out of 255 full-time freshmen who applied for aid, 240 were judged to have need. Of these, 240 received aid, and 45 had their full need met. Average financial aid package met 79% of need; average scholarship/grant was $21,038; average loan was $3,295. For part-time students, average financial aid package was $7,090.

Students without need: 11 full-time freshmen who did not demonstrate need for aid received scholarships/grants; average award was $12,818. No-need awards available for academics, alumni affiliation, art, athletics, leadership, music/drama.

Scholarships offered: ***Merit:*** Academic scholarships: $8,000-$15,000 per year; based on ACT and high school GPA; unlimited number awarded. ***Athletic:*** 4 full-time freshmen received athletic scholarships; average amount $4,125.

Cumulative student debt: 82% of graduating class had student loans; average debt was $26,080.

FINANCIAL AID PROCEDURES

Forms required: FAFSA.

Dates and Deadlines: Priority date 3/1; no closing date. Applicants notified on a rolling basis starting 3/1; must reply by 5/1 or within 2 week(s) of notification.

CONTACT

Lisa Flack, Director of Financial Aid
1800 College Avenue, Quincy, IL 62301-2699
(217) 228-5260

Rasmussen College: Aurora

Aurora, Illinois
www.rasmussen.edu

2-year for-profit technical college in small city.

Enrollment: 350 undergrads.

Selectivity: Open admission; but selective for some programs.

BASIC COSTS (2012-2013)

Tuition and fees: $15,750.

Per-credit charge: $350.

Additional info: Full-time tuition varies according to program of study. Examples of per-credit-hour charges include Early Childhood Education or Medical Assisting ($310), Criminal Justice, Information Systems Management, Multimedia Technician ($350). Accounting, Marketing, Paralegal ($350).

FINANCIAL AID PICTURE

Students with need: Need-based aid available for full-time and part-time students.

FINANCIAL AID PROCEDURES

Forms required: FAFSA, institutional form.

Dates and Deadlines: Applicants notified on a rolling basis.

CONTACT

Debora Murray, Director of Financial Services
2363 Sequoia Drive, Suite 131, Aurora, IL 60506

Rasmussen College: Mokena/Tinley Park

Mokena, Illinois
www.rasmussen.edu

4-year for-profit teachers and technical college in small town.
Enrollment: 236 undergrads.

BASIC COSTS (2012-2013)
Tuition and fees: $15,750.
Per-credit charge: $350.
Additional info: Full-time tuition varies according to program of study. Examples of per-credit-hour charges include Early Childhood Education or Medical Assisting ($310), Criminal Justice, Information Systems Management, Multimedia Technician ($350). Accounting, Marketing, Paralegal ($350).

FINANCIAL AID PICTURE
Students with need: Need-based aid available for full-time and part-time students.

FINANCIAL AID PROCEDURES
Forms required: FAFSA, institutional form.
Dates and Deadlines: Applicants notified on a rolling basis.

CONTACT
Debora Murray, Director of Financial Services
8650 West Spring Lake Road, Mokena, IL 60448

Rasmussen College: Rockford

Rockford, Illinois
www.rasmussen.edu

2-year for-profit technical college in small city.
Enrollment: 679 undergrads.
Selectivity: Open admission; but selective for some programs.

BASIC COSTS (2012-2013)
Tuition and fees: $15,750.
Per-credit charge: $350.
Additional info: Full-time tuition varies according to program of study. Examples of per-credit-hour charges include Early Childhood Education or Medical Assisting ($310), Criminal Justice, Information Systems Management, Multimedia Technician ($350). Accounting, Marketing, Paralegal ($350).

FINANCIAL AID PICTURE
Students with need: Need-based aid available for full-time and part-time students.

FINANCIAL AID PROCEDURES
Forms required: FAFSA, institutional form.
Dates and Deadlines: Applicants notified on a rolling basis.

CONTACT
Debora Murray, Director of Financial Services
6000 East State Street, Fourth Floor, Rockford, IL 61108-2513

Rasmussen College: Romeoville/Joliet

Romeoville, Illinois
www.rasmussen.edu

2-year for-profit career college in large town.
Enrollment: 456 undergrads.
Selectivity: Open admission; but selective for some programs.

BASIC COSTS (2012-2013)
Tuition and fees: $15,750.
Per-credit charge: $350.
Additional info: Full-time tuition varies according to program of study. Examples of per-credit-hour charges include Early Childhood Education or Medical Assisting ($310), Criminal Justice, Information Systems Management, Multimedia Technician ($350). Accounting, Marketing, Paralegal ($350).

FINANCIAL AID PICTURE
Students with need: Need-based aid available for full-time and part-time students.

FINANCIAL AID PROCEDURES
Forms required: FAFSA, institutional form.
Dates and Deadlines: Applicants notified on a rolling basis.

CONTACT
Debora Murray, Director of Financial Services
400 West Normantown Road, Romeoville, IL 60446

Rend Lake College

Ina, Illinois
www.rlc.edu Federal Code: 007119

2-year public community college in rural community.
Enrollment: 5,284 undergrads.
Selectivity: Open admission; but selective for some programs.

BASIC COSTS (2012-2013)
Tuition and fees: $2,880; out-of-district residents $4,360; out-of-state residents $4,590.
Per-credit charge: $93; out-of-district residents $143; out-of-state residents $150.

FINANCIAL AID PICTURE
Students with need: Need-based aid available for full-time and part-time students.
Students without need: No-need awards available for academics, art, athletics, leadership, music/drama, state/district residency.

FINANCIAL AID PROCEDURES
Forms required: FAFSA.
Dates and Deadlines: Applicants notified on a rolling basis starting 3/15; must reply within 4 week(s) of notification.

CONTACT
Cheri Rushing, Director of Financial Aid
468 North Ken Gray Parkway, Ina, IL 62846
(618) 437-5321 ext. 1385

Resurrection University

Oak Park, Illinois
www.wscn.edu Federal Code: 022141

Upper-division private nursing college in very large city, affiliated with Roman Catholic Church.
Enrollment: 361 undergrads.

BASIC COSTS (2012-2013)
Tuition and fees: $23,278.
Per-credit charge: $769.

FINANCIAL AID PICTURE
Students with need: Need-based aid available for full-time and part-time students. Work study available nights, weekends, and for part-time students.
Students without need: No-need awards available for academics, alumni affiliation.

FINANCIAL AID PROCEDURES
Forms required: FAFSA.
Dates and Deadlines: Closing date 6/30.

Transfers: Priority date 4/1; no deadline. Applicants notified on a rolling basis starting 4/1; must reply within 3 week(s) of notification.

CONTACT

Shirley Howell, Financial Aid Officer
Three Erie Court, Oak Park, IL 60302
(708) 763-1426

Richland Community College

Decatur, Illinois
www.richland.edu Federal Code: 010879

2-year public community college in small city.
Enrollment: 3,272 undergrads, 70% part-time. 258 full-time freshmen.
Selectivity: Open admission; but selective for some programs.

BASIC COSTS (2012-2013)

Tuition and fees: $3,030; out-of-district residents $7,080; out-of-state residents $11,040.
Per-credit charge: $96; out-of-district residents $231; out-of-state residents $363.

FINANCIAL AID PICTURE

Students with need: Need-based aid available for full-time and part-time students. Work study available nights.
Students without need: No-need awards available for academics, art, leadership, music/drama.

FINANCIAL AID PROCEDURES

Forms required: FAFSA.
Dates and Deadlines: Closing date 6/30. Applicants notified on a rolling basis starting 3/20.
Transfers: No deadline. Applicants notified on a rolling basis.

CONTACT

Carmin Ross, Director of Financial Aid
One College Park, Decatur, IL 62521
(217) 875-7200 ext. 271

Robert Morris University: Chicago

Chicago, Illinois
www.robertmorris.edu Federal Code: 001746

4-year private university in very large city.
Enrollment: 3,196 undergrads, 4% part-time. 1,147 full-time freshmen.
Selectivity: Admits less than 50% of applicants.

BASIC COSTS (2013-2014)

Tuition and fees: $22,800.
Per-credit charge: $633.
Room and board: $11,754.

FINANCIAL AID PICTURE (2011-2012)

Students with need: Out of 1,135 full-time freshmen who applied for aid, 1,090 were judged to have need. Of these, 1,053 received aid, and 37 had their full need met. Average financial aid package met 48% of need; average scholarship/grant was $10,355; average loan was $4,464. For part-time students, average financial aid package was $7,768.
Students without need: 19 full-time freshmen who did not demonstrate need for aid received scholarships/grants; average award was $5,472. No-need awards available for academics, art, athletics, leadership, music/drama, ROTC, state/district residency.
Scholarships offered: 189 full-time freshmen received athletic scholarships; average amount $9,602.
Cumulative student debt: 96% of graduating class had student loans; average debt was $29,771.

FINANCIAL AID PROCEDURES

Forms required: FAFSA.
Dates and Deadlines: Applicants notified on a rolling basis.
Transfers: No deadline. Applicants notified on a rolling basis.

CONTACT

Leigh Brinson, Vice President of Financial Services
401South State Street, Chicago, IL 60605
(312) 935-4077

Rock Valley College

Rockford, Illinois
www.rockvalleycollege.edu

2-year public community college in small city.
Enrollment: 7,493 undergrads, 53% part-time. 905 full-time freshmen.
Selectivity: Open admission; but selective for some programs.

BASIC COSTS (2012-2013)

Tuition and fees: $2,804; out-of-district residents $8,234; out-of-state residents $13,994.

FINANCIAL AID PICTURE

Students with need: Need-based aid available for full-time and part-time students. Work study available nights.
Students without need: No-need awards available for academics, ROTC.

FINANCIAL AID PROCEDURES

Forms required: FAFSA.
Dates and Deadlines: Closing date 5/1. Applicants notified on a rolling basis starting 4/1; must reply within 4 week(s) of notification.

CONTACT

Cyndi Stonesifer, Director of Financial Aid
3301 North Mulford Road, Rockford, IL 61114-5699
(815) 921-4150

Rockford Career College

Rockford, Illinois
www.rockfordcareercollege.edu Federal Code: 008545

2-year for-profit career college in small city.
Enrollment: 670 undergrads.
Selectivity: Open admission.

BASIC COSTS (2012-2013)

Tuition and fees: $9,432.
Per-credit charge: $262.

FINANCIAL AID PICTURE

Students with need: Need-based aid available for full-time and part-time students. Work study available nights.
Students without need: This college awards aid only to students with need.

FINANCIAL AID PROCEDURES

Forms required: FAFSA.
Dates and Deadlines: Applicants notified on a rolling basis.

CONTACT

Lisa Ruch, Director of Financial Aid
1130 South Alpine Road, Rockford, IL 61108
(815) 967-7314

Rockford College
Rockford, Illinois
www.rockford.edu Federal Code: 001748

4-year private liberal arts college in small city.
Enrollment: 998 undergrads, 12% part-time. 153 full-time freshmen.
Selectivity: Admits less than 50% of applicants.

BASIC COSTS (2012-2013)
Tuition and fees: $26,310.
Per-credit charge: $715.
Room and board: $7,320.

FINANCIAL AID PICTURE (2011-2012)
Students with need: Out of 125 full-time freshmen who applied for aid, 120 were judged to have need. Of these, 120 received aid, and 11 had their full need met. Average financial aid package met 68% of need; average scholarship/grant was $14,276; average loan was $3,252. For part-time students, average financial aid package was $8,044.
Students without need: 9 full-time freshmen who did not demonstrate need for aid received scholarships/grants; average award was $9,290. No-need awards available for academics, alumni affiliation, leadership, minority status, music/drama, state/district residency.
Cumulative student debt: 75% of graduating class had student loans; average debt was $39,897.

FINANCIAL AID PROCEDURES
Forms required: FAFSA.
Dates and Deadlines: Priority date 3/1; no closing date. Applicants notified on a rolling basis starting 3/1; must reply within 4 week(s) of notification.

CONTACT
Todd Fischer-Free, Assistant Vice President of Student Administrative Services
5050 East State Street, Rockford, IL 61108-2311
(815) 226-3383

Roosevelt University
Chicago, Illinois
www.roosevelt.edu Federal Code: 001749

4-year private university in very large city.
Enrollment: 3,728 undergrads, 26% part-time. 535 full-time freshmen.
Selectivity: Admits over 75% of applicants.

BASIC COSTS (2012-2013)
Tuition and fees: $25,950.
Per-credit charge: $699.
Room and board: $12,880.
Additional info: Tuition for College of Performing Arts is $32,950 per year; per-credit -hour, $1372.

FINANCIAL AID PICTURE (2011-2012)
Students with need: Need-based aid available for full-time and part-time students. Work study available nights, weekends, and for part-time students.
Students without need: No-need awards available for academics, music/drama.

FINANCIAL AID PROCEDURES
Forms required: FAFSA, institutional form.
Dates and Deadlines: Priority date 3/1; no closing date. Applicants notified on a rolling basis starting 2/1; must reply within 3 week(s) of notification.
Transfers: Applicants notified on a rolling basis starting 3/1; must reply within 2 week(s) of notification.

CONTACT
Grace McGinnis, Director, Financial Aid
430 South Michigan Avenue, Chicago, IL 60605-1394
(866) 421-0935

Rush University
Chicago, Illinois
www.rushu.rush.edu Federal Code: 009800

Upper-division private health science and nursing college in very large city.
Enrollment: 106 undergrads, 29% part-time.

BASIC COSTS (2012-2013)
Tuition and fees: $26,370.
Additional info: Tuition costs vary by program. Room charge of $9,360 based on 9 months occupancy of one-bedroom apartment. Board plan not available. Tuition/fee waivers available for minority students.

FINANCIAL AID PICTURE (2011-2012)
Students with need: Average financial aid package for all full-time undergraduates was $12,254; for part-time $6,113. 25% awarded as scholarships/grants, 75% awarded as loans/jobs.
Students without need: No-need awards available for academics, minority status.

FINANCIAL AID PROCEDURES
Transfers: Priority date 5/1; no deadline. Applicants notified on a rolling basis starting 3/7.

CONTACT
Michael Frechette, Director of Student Financial Aid
College Admissions, Chicago, IL 60612
(312) 942-6256

St. Francis Medical Center College of Nursing
Peoria, Illinois
www.sfmccon.edu Federal Code: 006240

Upper-division private nursing college in small city, affiliated with Roman Catholic Church.
Enrollment: 402 undergrads, 27% part-time.

BASIC COSTS (2013-2014)
Tuition and fees: $16,964.
Per-credit charge: $528.
Room only: $3,200.

FINANCIAL AID PICTURE (2011-2012)
Students with need: Average financial aid package for all full-time undergraduates was $10,453; for part-time $7,772. 38% awarded as scholarships/grants, 62% awarded as loans/jobs.
Students without need: No-need awards available for academics, alumni affiliation.
Additional info: OSF Saint Francis Medical Center Education student loan available to full-time students on a limited basis. Tuition waiver program for hospital employees available.

FINANCIAL AID PROCEDURES
Forms required: FAFSA, institutional form.
Dates and Deadlines: Priority date 6/1; no closing date. Must reply within 4 week(s) of notification.
Transfers: No deadline. Applicants notified on a rolling basis starting 5/15; must reply within 4 week(s) of notification.

CONTACT
Nancy Perryman, Coordinator of Student Finance, Financial Assistance
511 NE Greenleaf Street, Peoria, IL 61603-3783
(309) 655-4119

St. John's College
Springfield, Illinois
www.stjohnscollegespringfield.edu Federal Code: 030980

Upper-division private nursing college in small city, affiliated with Roman Catholic Church.
Enrollment: 55 undergrads.
Selectivity: Open admission; but selective for some programs.

BASIC COSTS (2012-2013)
Tuition and fees: $15,710.
Per-credit charge: $626.

FINANCIAL AID PICTURE
Students with need: Work study available nights.

CONTACT
Mary Brown, Financial Aid Officer
729 East Carpenter Street, Springfield, IL 62702
(217) 544-6464 ext. 44705

Saint Xavier University
Chicago, Illinois
www.sxu.edu Federal Code: 001768

4-year private university in very large city, affiliated with Roman Catholic Church.
Enrollment: 2,827 undergrads.
Selectivity: Open admission; but selective for some programs.

BASIC COSTS (2012-2013)
Tuition and fees: $28,110.
Per-credit charge: $650.
Room and board: $9,490.

FINANCIAL AID PICTURE
Students with need: Need-based aid available for full-time and part-time students.
Students without need: No-need awards available for academics, athletics, music/drama.

FINANCIAL AID PROCEDURES
Forms required: FAFSA.
Dates and Deadlines: Priority date 3/1; no closing date. Applicants notified on a rolling basis starting 2/1; must reply by 5/1 or within 2 week(s) of notification.
Transfers: Applicants notified on a rolling basis starting 2/15; must reply by 5/1 or within 2 week(s) of notification.

CONTACT
Susan Swisher, Director of Financial aid
3700 West 103rd Street, Chicago, IL 60655
(773) 298-3073

Sauk Valley Community College
Dixon, Illinois
www.svcc.edu Federal Code: 001752

2-year public community college in large town.
Enrollment: 1,929 undergrads, 46% part-time. 234 full-time freshmen.
Selectivity: Open admission; but selective for some programs.

BASIC COSTS (2012-2013)
Tuition and fees: $3,030; out-of-district residents $7,740; out-of-state residents $8,580.
Per-credit charge: $101; out-of-district residents $258; out-of-state residents $286.

FINANCIAL AID PICTURE (2011-2012)
Students with need: Out of 100 full-time freshmen who applied for aid, 87 were judged to have need. Of these, 81 received aid, and 2 had their full need met. Average financial aid package met 23% of need; average scholarship/grant was $4,565; average loan was $2,136. For part-time students, average financial aid package was $2,257.
Students without need: 6 full-time freshmen who did not demonstrate need for aid received scholarships/grants; average award was $3,284. No-need awards available for academics, athletics, minority status, state/district residency.
Scholarships offered: 6 full-time freshmen received athletic scholarships; average amount $3,120.

FINANCIAL AID PROCEDURES
Forms required: FAFSA, institutional form.
Dates and Deadlines: Priority date 3/1; no closing date. Applicants notified on a rolling basis starting 5/1; must reply within 4 week(s) of notification.
Transfers: Priority date 3/9; no deadline. Applicants notified on a rolling basis starting 3/1; must reply within 4 week(s) of notification.

CONTACT
Debra Stiefel, Coordinator of Financial Aid
173 Illinois Route 2, Dixon, IL 61021-9112
(815) 288-5511 ext. 339

School of the Art Institute of Chicago
Chicago, Illinois
www.saic.edu Federal Code: 001753

4-year private visual arts college in very large city.
Enrollment: 2,549 undergrads, 6% part-time. 561 full-time freshmen.
Selectivity: Admits over 75% of applicants.

BASIC COSTS (2012-2013)
Tuition and fees: $39,020.
Per-credit charge: $1,278.
Room and board: $13,810.

FINANCIAL AID PICTURE (2011-2012)
Students with need: 61% of average financial aid package awarded as scholarships/grants, 39% awarded as loans/jobs. Need-based aid available for part-time students. Work study available nights, weekends, and for part-time students.
Students without need: No-need awards available for academics, art.
Scholarships offered: Merit scholarships; $2,000 to full tuition; renewable.

FINANCIAL AID PROCEDURES
Forms required: FAFSA.
Dates and Deadlines: Priority date 3/15; no closing date. Applicants notified on a rolling basis starting 3/1.

CONTACT
Patrick James, Director of Financial Aid
36 South Wabash Avenue, Chicago, IL 60603
(312) 629-6600

Shawnee Community College
Ullin, Illinois
www.shawneecc.edu Federal Code: 007693

2-year public community college in rural community.
Enrollment: 2,070 undergrads.
Selectivity: Open admission; but selective for some programs.

BASIC COSTS (2012-2013)
Tuition and fees: $2,760; out-of-district residents $4,140; out-of-state residents $4,620.

Per-credit charge: $92; out-of-district residents $138; out-of-state residents $154.

FINANCIAL AID PICTURE

Students with need: Need-based aid available for full-time and part-time students.

Students without need: This college awards aid only to students with need.

FINANCIAL AID PROCEDURES

Forms required: FAFSA.

Dates and Deadlines: Priority date 9/1; no closing date. Applicants notified on a rolling basis; must reply within 2 week(s) of notification.

CONTACT

Tammy Capps, Director of Financial Aid
8364 Shawnee College Road, Ullin, IL 62992
(618) 634-3280 ext. 3280

Shimer College

Chicago, Illinois
www.shimer.edu Federal Code: 001756

4-year private liberal arts college in very large city.

Enrollment: 125 undergrads, 16% part-time. 19 full-time freshmen.

Selectivity: Admits 50 to 75% of applicants.

BASIC COSTS (2013-2014)

Tuition and fees: $31,230.

Room and board: $10,626.

Additional info: Required fees for the Shimer-in-Oxford Program are $11,400. One time graduation fee of $300 charged in final semester. Tuition/fee waivers available for adults.

FINANCIAL AID PICTURE (2011-2012)

Students with need: Out of 19 full-time freshmen who applied for aid, 14 were judged to have need. Of these, 14 received aid. Average financial aid package met 61% of need; average scholarship/grant was $9,399; average loan was $3,071. For part-time students, average financial aid package was $12,021.

Students without need: 6 full-time freshmen who did not demonstrate need for aid received scholarships/grants; average award was $9,566. No-need awards available for academics, alumni affiliation.

Scholarships offered: Michel de Montaigne Scholarship: half or full tuition; awarded to new students on the basis of merit in writing and discussion; 2 full and 2 half tuition scholarships awarded each year.

Cumulative student debt: 100% of graduating class had student loans; average debt was $30,000.

FINANCIAL AID PROCEDURES

Forms required: FAFSA.

Dates and Deadlines: Applicants notified on a rolling basis starting 3/15.

Transfers: Closing date 8/1. Applicants notified on a rolling basis; must reply by 5/1 or within 3 week(s) of notification.

CONTACT

Janet Henthorn, Financial Aid Officer
3424 South State Street, Chicago, IL 60616
(312) 235-3507

South Suburban College of Cook County

South Holland, Illinois
www.ssc.edu Federal Code: 001769

2-year public community college in large town.

Enrollment: 2,662 undergrads. 241 full-time freshmen.

Selectivity: Open admission; but selective for some programs.

BASIC COSTS (2013-2014)

Tuition and fees: $3,773; out-of-district residents $9,113; out-of-state residents $10,763.

Per-credit charge: $110; out-of-district residents $288; out-of-state residents $343.

Additional info: Tuition/fee waivers available for adults.

FINANCIAL AID PICTURE (2011-2012)

Students with need: Out of 162 full-time freshmen who applied for aid, 160 were judged to have need. Of these, 160 received aid. Average financial aid package met 70% of need; average scholarship/grant was $4,893. Need-based aid available for part-time students.

Students without need: No-need awards available for academics, art, athletics, music/drama, state/district residency.

Scholarships offered: 14 full-time freshmen received athletic scholarships; average amount $2,380.

FINANCIAL AID PROCEDURES

Forms required: FAFSA.

Dates and Deadlines: Priority date 6/30; no closing date. Applicants notified on a rolling basis starting 5/1.

Transfers: No deadline. Applicants notified on a rolling basis starting 5/11; must reply by 7/15 or within 2 week(s) of notification.

CONTACT

John Semple, Director of Financial Aid
15800 South State Street, South Holland, IL 60473
(708) 596-2000 ext. 2438

Southeastern Illinois College

Harrisburg, Illinois
www.sic.edu Federal Code: 001757

2-year public community college in small town.

Enrollment: 2,087 undergrads.

Selectivity: Open admission; but selective for some programs.

BASIC COSTS (2012-2013)

Tuition and fees: $2,760; out-of-district residents $4,290; out-of-state residents $4,530.

Per-credit charge: $88; out-of-district residents $139; out-of-state residents $147.

FINANCIAL AID PICTURE

Students with need: Need-based aid available for full-time and part-time students.

Students without need: No-need awards available for academics, alumni affiliation, art, athletics, music/drama.

FINANCIAL AID PROCEDURES

Forms required: FAFSA.

Dates and Deadlines: Applicants notified on a rolling basis starting 4/15; must reply within 2 week(s) of notification.

CONTACT

Emily Henson, Director of Financial Aid
3575 College Road, Harrisburg, IL 62946
(618) 252-5400 ext. 2450

Southern Illinois University Carbondale

Carbondale, Illinois
www.siuc.edu Federal Code: 001758

4-year public university in large town.

Enrollment: 14,077 undergrads, 12% part-time. 2,267 full-time freshmen.

Selectivity: Admits 50 to 75% of applicants.

BASIC COSTS (2012-2013)
Tuition and fees: $11,528; out-of-state residents $23,781.
Per-credit charge: $272; out-of-state residents $681.
Room and board: $9,126.
Additional info: Students living in Arkansas, Indiana, Kentucky, Missouri, and Tennessee pay in-state tuition rate. All newly entering freshmen and transfer undergraduate students who have parent(s), stepparent(s) or legal guardian(s) who are graduates of SIU-Carbondale receive 20% reduction in tuition. Tuition at time of enrollment locked for 4 years.

FINANCIAL AID PICTURE (2012-2013)
Students with need: Out of 2,064 full-time freshmen who applied for aid, 1,796 were judged to have need. Of these, 1,739 received aid, and 89 had their full need met. Average financial aid package met 38% of need; average scholarship/grant was $2,846; average loan was $3,414. For part-time students, average financial aid package was $9,212.
Students without need: 51 full-time freshmen who did not demonstrate need for aid received scholarships/grants; average award was $7,858. No-need awards available for academics, alumni affiliation, art, athletics, leadership, minority status, music/drama, ROTC, state/district residency.
Scholarships offered: 52 full-time freshmen received athletic scholarships; average amount $17,794.
Cumulative student debt: 68% of graduating class had student loans; average debt was $32,652.
Additional info: Need-based financial aid available to part-time students enrolled in minimum of 6 semester hours.

FINANCIAL AID PROCEDURES
Forms required: FAFSA.
Dates and Deadlines: Priority date 3/1; no closing date. Applicants notified on a rolling basis starting 3/15.
Transfers: Must reply within 4 week(s) of notification.

CONTACT
Terri Harfst, Director
425 Clocktower Drive, Carbondale, IL 62901
(618) 453-4334

Southern Illinois University Edwardsville
Edwardsville, Illinois
www.siue.edu Federal Code: 001759

4-year public university in very large city.
Enrollment: 11,290 undergrads, 15% part-time. 2,013 full-time freshmen.
Selectivity: Admits over 75% of applicants.

BASIC COSTS (2012-2013)
Tuition and fees: $9,251; out-of-state residents $19,673.
Per-credit charge: $232; out-of-state residents $579.
Room and board: $8,281.
Additional info: Required fees include book rental. Tuition at time of enrollment locked for 4 years.

FINANCIAL AID PICTURE (2011-2012)
Students with need: Out of 1,841 full-time freshmen who applied for aid, 1,562 were judged to have need. Of these, 1,507 received aid, and 438 had their full need met. Average financial aid package met 58% of need; average scholarship/grant was $8,827; average loan was $3,558. For part-time students, average financial aid package was $10,320.
Students without need: This college awards aid only to students with need.
Scholarships offered: 21 full-time freshmen received athletic scholarships; average amount $16,596.

FINANCIAL AID PROCEDURES
Forms required: FAFSA.
Dates and Deadlines: Priority date 3/1; closing date 6/1. Applicants notified on a rolling basis starting 3/15; must reply within 4 week(s) of notification.

CONTACT
Sharon Berry, Director of Student Financial Aid
Rendleman Hall, Rm 2120, Edwardsville, IL 62026-1600
(618) 650-3880

Southwestern Illinois College
Belleville, Illinois
www.swic.edu Federal Code: 001636

2-year public community college in small city.
Enrollment: 11,938 undergrads.
Selectivity: Open admission; but selective for some programs.

BASIC COSTS (2012-2013)
Tuition and fees: $3,120; out-of-district residents $7,440; out-of-state residents $11,100.
Per-credit charge: $99; out-of-district residents $243; out-of-state residents $365.

FINANCIAL AID PICTURE
Students with need: Need-based aid available for full-time and part-time students.
Students without need: No-need awards available for academics, athletics.

FINANCIAL AID PROCEDURES
Forms required: FAFSA, institutional form.
Dates and Deadlines: Closing date 5/31. Applicants notified on a rolling basis starting 7/1; must reply within 2 week(s) of notification.

CONTACT
Robert Tebbe, Director of Financial Aid
2500 Carlyle Avenue, Belleville, IL 62221-5899
(618) 235-2700 ext. 5288

Spoon River College
Canton, Illinois
www.src.edu Federal Code: 001643

2-year public community college in large town.
Enrollment: 1,712 undergrads.
Selectivity: Open admission; but selective for some programs.

BASIC COSTS (2012-2013)
Tuition and fees: $3,390; out-of-district residents $7,470; out-of-state residents $8,550.
Per-credit charge: $98; out-of-district residents $234; out-of-state residents $270.

FINANCIAL AID PICTURE
Students with need: Need-based aid available for full-time and part-time students. Work study available nights.
Students without need: No-need awards available for academics, art, athletics, music/drama, state/district residency.
Scholarships offered: SRC's Foundation offers many scholarships. The application deadline is March 15. Students are required to complete an application and a FAFSA for the upcoming year.
Additional info: Students who have submitted all required forms by the processing deadline are guaranteed to have aid eligibility established by the tuition deadline. All forms submitted after the processing deadline are processed in the order received on a continuing basis.

FINANCIAL AID PROCEDURES
Forms required: FAFSA.
Dates and Deadlines: Closing date 7/1. Applicants notified on a rolling basis starting 5/15.

CONTACT
Jo Branson, Director of Financial Aid
23235 North County Road 22, Canton, IL 61520
(309) 649-7030

Taylor Business Institute
Chicago, Illinois
www.tbiil.edu Federal Code: 011810

2-year for-profit business college in very large city.
Enrollment: 322 undergrads.

BASIC COSTS (2012-2013)
Tuition and fees: $13,500.

FINANCIAL AID PICTURE
Students with need: Need-based aid available for full-time students. Work study available nights.

FINANCIAL AID PROCEDURES
Forms required: FAFSA, state aid form, institutional form.

CONTACT
Florence Davis, Financial Aid Director
318 West Adams Street, 5th Floor, Chicago, IL 60606
(312) 658-5100

Trinity Christian College
Palos Heights, Illinois
www.trnty.edu Federal Code: 001771

4-year private liberal arts college in very large city, affiliated with Reformed (unaffiliated) Church.
Enrollment: 1,215 undergrads, 16% part-time. 187 full-time freshmen.
Selectivity: Admits over 75% of applicants.

BASIC COSTS (2012-2013)
Tuition and fees: $23,513.
Per-credit charge: $772.
Room and board: $8,442.
Additional info: Tuition/fee waivers available for adults, unemployed or children of unemployed.

FINANCIAL AID PICTURE (2012-2013)
Students with need: Out of 167 full-time freshmen who applied for aid, 146 were judged to have need. Of these, 146 received aid, and 17 had their full need met. Average financial aid package met 71% of need; average scholarship/grant was $14,193; average loan was $3,820. For part-time students, average financial aid package was $6,706.
Students without need: 28 full-time freshmen who did not demonstrate need for aid received scholarships/grants; average award was $6,384. No-need awards available for academics, alumni affiliation, athletics, leadership, minority status, music/drama, religious affiliation.
Scholarships offered: 9 full-time freshmen received athletic scholarships; average amount $11,972.
Cumulative student debt: 79% of graduating class had student loans; average debt was $28,124.
Additional info: High school transcripts and ACT or SAT scores required for merit scholarships.

FINANCIAL AID PROCEDURES
Forms required: FAFSA.
Dates and Deadlines: Priority date 2/15; no closing date. Applicants notified on a rolling basis starting 3/1; must reply by 5/1 or within 2 week(s) of notification.
Transfers: Applicants notified on a rolling basis starting 3/1; must reply by 5/1 or within 2 week(s) of notification.

CONTACT
Ryan Zantingh, Director of Financial Aid
6601 West College Drive, Palos Heights, IL 60463
(708) 239-4706

Trinity College of Nursing & Health Sciences
Rock Island, Illinois
www.trinitycollegeqc.edu Federal Code: 006225

4-year private health science and nursing college in large city.
Enrollment: 185 undergrads, 36% part-time.

BASIC COSTS (2012-2013)
Tuition and fees: $20,524.
Per-credit charge: $648.
Additional info: Tuition and fees vary by program. Listed cost is for bachelor's of science in nursing-basic program. Associate degree programs: $497 per-credit-hour.

FINANCIAL AID PICTURE (2011-2012)
Students with need: Average financial aid package for all full-time undergraduates was $3,856; for part-time $3,714. 47% awarded as scholarships/grants, 53% awarded as loans/jobs.
Students without need: This college awards aid only to students with need.

FINANCIAL AID PROCEDURES
Forms required: FAFSA, institutional form.

CONTACT
Christine Christopherson, Financial Aid Specialist
2122 25th Avenue, Rock Island, IL 61201-5317
(309) 779-7740

Trinity International University
Deerfield, Illinois
www.tiu.edu Federal Code: 001772

4-year private university and liberal arts college in large town, affiliated with Evangelical Free Church of America.
Enrollment: 986 undergrads.
Selectivity: Admits 50 to 75% of applicants.

BASIC COSTS (2012-2013)
Tuition and fees: $25,840.
Per-credit charge: $1,058.
Room and board: $8,530.
Additional info: Tuition/fee waivers available for minority students.

FINANCIAL AID PICTURE
Students with need: Need-based aid available for full-time and part-time students. Work study available nights, weekends, and for part-time students.
Students without need: No-need awards available for academics, alumni affiliation, athletics, minority status, music/drama, religious affiliation.

FINANCIAL AID PROCEDURES
Forms required: FAFSA.
Dates and Deadlines: Priority date 4/1; no closing date. Applicants notified on a rolling basis starting 2/15; must reply within 4 week(s) of notification.

Transfers: No deadline. Applicants notified on a rolling basis; must reply within 4 week(s) of notification.

CONTACT

Patricia Coles, Director of Financial Aid
2065 Half Day Road, Deerfield, IL 60015
(847) 317-8060

Triton College

River Grove, Illinois
www.triton.edu Federal Code: 001773

2-year public community and junior college in large town.
Enrollment: 9,678 undergrads.
Selectivity: Open admission; but selective for some programs.

BASIC COSTS (2012-2013)

Tuition and fees: $3,302; out-of-district residents $8,042; out-of-state residents $9,994.
Per-credit charge: $98; out-of-district residents $256; out-of-state residents $321.

FINANCIAL AID PICTURE

Students with need: Need-based aid available for full-time and part-time students. Work study available nights, weekends, and for part-time students.
Students without need: No-need awards available for academics, athletics.
Scholarships offered: Board of Trustees Honor Scholarship; covers tuition and fees; for in-district high school students in top 10% of graduating class.

FINANCIAL AID PROCEDURES

Forms required: FAFSA, institutional form.
Dates and Deadlines: Priority date 4/15; no closing date. Applicants notified on a rolling basis starting 4/1; must reply within 2 week(s) of notification.

CONTACT

Patricia Zinga, Director of Financial Aid
2000 North Fifth Avenue, River Grove, IL 60171
(708) 456-0300 ext. 3441

University of Chicago

Chicago, Illinois Federal Code: 001774
www.uchicago.edu/ CSS Code: 1832

4-year private university and liberal arts college in very large city.
Enrollment: 5,587 undergrads, 1% part-time. 1,527 full-time freshmen.
Selectivity: Admits less than 50% of applicants.

BASIC COSTS (2012-2013)

Tuition and fees: $44,574.
Room and board: $13,137.

FINANCIAL AID PICTURE (2012-2013)

Students with need: Out of 952 full-time freshmen who applied for aid, 683 were judged to have need. Of these, 683 received aid, and 683 had their full need met. Average financial aid package met 100% of need; average scholarship/grant was $39,904; average loan was $2,982.
Students without need: 282 full-time freshmen who did not demonstrate need for aid received scholarships/grants; average award was $11,707. No-need awards available for academics, leadership.
Cumulative student debt: 43% of graduating class had student loans; average debt was $23,930.
Additional info: Odyssey Scholarship program eliminates or reduces indebtedness of needy full-time undergraduates from low to moderate income families. A freshman student whose parental income is less than $75,000 is not expected to borrow. A student whose parental income is between $75,000 & $90,000 is expected to borrow half of the sum a typical needy freshman student is expected to borrow.

FINANCIAL AID PROCEDURES

Forms required: FAFSA, CSS PROFILE.
Dates and Deadlines: Closing date 2/1. Applicants notified by 4/16; must reply by 5/1.
Transfers: Closing date 4/15. Applicants notified on a rolling basis starting 5/1; must reply by 6/1.

CONTACT

Alicia Reyes, Director of College Aid
1101 East 58th Street, Chicago, IL 60637
(773) 702-8655

University of Illinois at Chicago

Chicago, Illinois
www.uic.edu Federal Code: 001776

4-year public university in very large city.
Enrollment: 16,593 undergrads, 8% part-time. 3,073 full-time freshmen.
Selectivity: Admits 50 to 75% of applicants.

BASIC COSTS (2012-2013)

Tuition and fees: $13,130; out-of-state residents $25,520.
Room and board: $10,399.
Additional info: Health Insurance: $802; refundable fees: $6. Tuition at time of enrollment locked for 4 years; tuition/fee waivers available for minority students.

FINANCIAL AID PICTURE (2011-2012)

Students with need: Out of 2,772 full-time freshmen who applied for aid, 2,468 were judged to have need. Of these, 2,330 received aid, and 285 had their full need met. Average financial aid package met 61% of need; average scholarship/grant was $13,019; average loan was $3,400. For part-time students, average financial aid package was $9,992.
Students without need: 80 full-time freshmen who did not demonstrate need for aid received scholarships/grants; average award was $2,436. No-need awards available for academics, art, athletics, music/drama, ROTC.
Scholarships offered: 29 full-time freshmen received athletic scholarships; average amount $15,712.
Cumulative student debt: 64% of graduating class had student loans; average debt was $22,256.

FINANCIAL AID PROCEDURES

Forms required: FAFSA.
Dates and Deadlines: Priority date 3/1; no closing date. Applicants notified on a rolling basis starting 3/15; must reply by 5/1.

CONTACT

Timothy Opgenorth, Director of the Office of Student Financial Aid
PO Box 5220, Chicago, IL 60680-5220
(312) 996-3126

University of Illinois at Urbana-Champaign

Champaign, Illinois
www.illinois.edu Federal Code: 001775

4-year public university in small city.
Enrollment: 31,260 undergrads, 2% part-time. 7,249 full-time freshmen.
Selectivity: Admits 50 to 75% of applicants.

BASIC COSTS (2012-2013)

Tuition and fees: $14,522; out-of-state residents $28,664.
Room and board: $10,666.

Additional info: Health Insurance $438. Tuition at time of enrollment locked for 4 years.

FINANCIAL AID PICTURE (2011-2012)

Students with need: Out of 5,173 full-time freshmen who applied for aid, 3,727 were judged to have need. Of these, 3,525 received aid, and 1,149 had their full need met. Average financial aid package met 66% of need; average scholarship/grant was $12,549; average loan was $4,169. For part-time students, average financial aid package was $8,227.

Students without need: 850 full-time freshmen who did not demonstrate need for aid received scholarships/grants; average award was $3,980. No-need awards available for academics, alumni affiliation, art, athletics, leadership, minority status, music/drama, ROTC, state/district residency.

Scholarships offered: ***Merit:*** President's Award Program: $1,000 - $4,000 for 4 years; for members of historically underrepresented group, with ACT score of 22-23 and in the top quarter of their class, or who have an ACT score of 24 or higher and are in the top half of their class. University Achievement Scholarship: $8,000; criteria set by each college, renewable with 3.0 GPA; 50 available. Matthews Scholars: $2,000 per year, renewable for 4 years if GPA of 3.3 is maintained; criteria includes academic achievement, leadership skills, commitment to campus and community efforts, good sponsor relations, diversity of college gender and ethnicity; approximately 150 available. FMC Award of Excellence: $1,000 a year, non-renewable; criteria set by individual colleges; 20 available. Provost Scholarship: full tuition, renewable with 3.0 GPA; National Achievement, National Hispanic Scholar finalists, or National Merit finalists who have indicated the University of Illinois at Urbana-Champaign as their top choice. Campus Merit: $3,000; students in historically under-represented groups who are in the top 10 percent of their graduating class. National Merit: $500; National Merit finalists who indicated the University of Illinois as their top choice, renewable with 3.0 GPA. James Hunter Anthony and Gerald Blackshear Scholarship: 1 year of tuition and fees, renewable with 3.0 GPA; incoming freshmen who are graduates of an Illinois high school, with superior academic and leadership qualities; need may be considered. ***Athletic:*** 53 full-time freshmen received athletic scholarships; average amount $30,578.

Cumulative student debt: 52% of graduating class had student loans; average debt was $24,657.

FINANCIAL AID PROCEDURES

Forms required: FAFSA.

Dates and Deadlines: Priority date 3/15; no closing date. Applicants notified on a rolling basis starting 3/15; must reply by 5/1 or within 3 week(s) of notification.

CONTACT

Daniel Mann, Director of Student Financial Aid
901 West Illinois, Urbana, IL 61801-3028
(217) 333-0100

University of Illinois: Springfield

Springfield, Illinois
www.uis.edu Federal Code: 009333

4-year public university and liberal arts college in small city.
Enrollment: 2,976 undergrads, 35% part-time. 239 full-time freshmen.
Selectivity: Admits 50 to 75% of applicants.

BASIC COSTS (2012-2013)

Tuition and fees: $10,865; out-of-state residents $20,015.
Per-credit charge: $303; out-of-state residents $608.
Room and board: $9,870.
Additional info: Health Insurance: $540; refundable fees: $8. Tuition at time of enrollment locked for 4 years.

FINANCIAL AID PICTURE (2011-2012)

Students with need: Out of 220 full-time freshmen who applied for aid, 179 were judged to have need. Of these, 179 received aid, and 30 had their full need met. Average financial aid package met 73% of need; average scholarship/grant was $9,873; average loan was $3,192. For part-time students, average financial aid package was $7,199.

Students without need: 48 full-time freshmen who did not demonstrate need for aid received scholarships/grants; average award was $4,152. No-need awards available for academics, alumni affiliation, art, athletics, job skills, leadership, minority status, music/drama, state/district residency.

Scholarships offered: 6 full-time freshmen received athletic scholarships; average amount $2,662.

Cumulative student debt: 67% of graduating class had student loans; average debt was $21,057.

FINANCIAL AID PROCEDURES

Forms required: FAFSA.

Dates and Deadlines: Priority date 3/1; closing date 11/15. Applicants notified on a rolling basis starting 1/1; must reply within 3 week(s) of notification.

Transfers: No deadline. Applicants notified on a rolling basis.

CONTACT

Gerard Joseph, Director of Financial Aid
One University Plaza, MS UHB 1080, Springfield, IL 62703
(217) 206-6724

University of St. Francis

Joliet, Illinois
www.stfrancis.edu Federal Code: 001664

4-year private university and liberal arts college in small city, affiliated with Roman Catholic Church.
Enrollment: 1,408 undergrads, 3% part-time. 220 full-time freshmen.
Selectivity: Admits 50 to 75% of applicants.

BASIC COSTS (2013-2014)

Tuition and fees: $27,950.
Per-credit charge: $825.
Room and board: $8,860.

FINANCIAL AID PICTURE (2012-2013)

Students with need: Out of 207 full-time freshmen who applied for aid, 197 were judged to have need. Of these, 197 received aid, and 148 had their full need met. Average financial aid package met 81% of need; average scholarship/grant was $8,937; average loan was $3,656. For part-time students, average financial aid package was $9,895.

Students without need: 23 full-time freshmen who did not demonstrate need for aid received scholarships/grants; average award was $11,921. No-need awards available for academics, alumni affiliation, art, athletics, leadership, music/drama, religious affiliation, state/district residency.

Scholarships offered: 10 full-time freshmen received athletic scholarships; average amount $9,222.

Cumulative student debt: 91% of graduating class had student loans; average debt was $28,267.

FINANCIAL AID PROCEDURES

Forms required: FAFSA, institutional form.

Dates and Deadlines: Priority date 3/1; no closing date. Applicants notified on a rolling basis starting 2/15.

Transfers: No deadline. Applicants notified on a rolling basis.

CONTACT

Bruce Foote, Executive Director Financial Aid Services
500 Wilcox Street, Joliet, IL 60435
(866) 890-8331

VanderCook College of Music

Chicago, Illinois
www.vandercook.edu Federal Code: 177800

4-year private music and teachers college in very large city.
Enrollment: 110 undergrads, 2% part-time. 21 full-time freshmen.
Selectivity: Admits 50 to 75% of applicants.

BASIC COSTS (2012-2013)
Tuition and fees: $24,116.
Per-credit charge: $950.
Room and board: $10,626.

FINANCIAL AID PICTURE (2011-2012)
Students with need: Out of 19 full-time freshmen who applied for aid, 17 were judged to have need. Of these, 17 received aid. For part-time students, average financial aid package was $10,855.
Students without need: 4 full-time freshmen who did not demonstrate need for aid received scholarships/grants; average award was $2,350. No-need awards available for academics, music/drama.
Cumulative student debt: 86% of graduating class had student loans; average debt was $31,553.
Additional info: Musical talent considered for partial tuition waiver.

FINANCIAL AID PROCEDURES
Forms required: FAFSA.
Dates and Deadlines: Priority date 4/1; no closing date. Applicants notified on a rolling basis starting 5/1; must reply within 2 week(s) of notification.
Transfers: Priority date 4/1. Must reply by 5/1.

CONTACT
Sirena Covington, Director of Financial Aid
3140 South Federal Street, Chicago, IL 60616-3731
(312) 225-6288 ext. 253

Waubonsee Community College

Sugar Grove, Illinois
www.waubonsee.edu Federal Code: 006931

2-year public community and junior college in small town.
Enrollment: 8,403 undergrads, 57% part-time. 911 full-time freshmen.
Selectivity: Open admission; but selective for some programs.

BASIC COSTS (2012-2013)
Tuition and fees: $3,060; out-of-district residents $8,412; out-of-state residents $9,110.
Per-credit charge: $97; out-of-district residents $276; out-of-state residents $299.

FINANCIAL AID PICTURE (2011-2012)
Students with need: 75% of average financial aid package awarded as scholarships/grants, 25% awarded as loans/jobs. Need-based aid available for part-time students. Work study available nights.
Students without need: No-need awards available for academics, art, athletics, leadership, minority status, music/drama, state/district residency.
Scholarships offered: Gustafson Scholarship; provides tuition for 64 semester hours; selected graduates from each in-district school.

FINANCIAL AID PROCEDURES
Forms required: FAFSA.
Dates and Deadlines: Priority date 3/1; no closing date. Applicants notified on a rolling basis starting 4/1.
Transfers: Priority date 3/13; no deadline. Applicants notified on a rolling basis starting 4/13.

CONTACT
Charles Boudreau, Director of Student Financial Aid Services
Route 47 at Waubonsee Drive, Sugar Grove, IL 60554-9454
(630) 466-7900 ext. 5774

Western Illinois University

Macomb, Illinois
www.wiu.edu Federal Code: 001780

4-year public university in large town.
Enrollment: 10,263 undergrads, 11% part-time. 1,732 full-time freshmen.
Selectivity: Admits 50 to 75% of applicants.

BASIC COSTS (2012-2013)
Tuition and fees: $10,444; out-of-state residents $14,450.
Per-credit charge: $267; out-of-state residents $401.
Room and board: $8,820.
Additional info: Tuition at time of enrollment locked for 4 years.

FINANCIAL AID PICTURE (2012-2013)
Students with need: Out of 1,534 full-time freshmen who applied for aid, 1,314 were judged to have need. Of these, 1,274 received aid, and 317 had their full need met. Average financial aid package met 52% of need; average scholarship/grant was $8,269; average loan was $3,483. For part-time students, average financial aid package was $6,748.
Students without need: 30 full-time freshmen who did not demonstrate need for aid received scholarships/grants; average award was $3,290. No-need awards available for academics, alumni affiliation, art, athletics, leadership, minority status, music/drama, ROTC.
Scholarships offered: 60 full-time freshmen received athletic scholarships; average amount $950.
Cumulative student debt: 73% of graduating class had student loans; average debt was $24,993.

FINANCIAL AID PROCEDURES
Forms required: FAFSA.
Dates and Deadlines: Applicants notified on a rolling basis starting 1/15.
Transfers: No deadline. Applicants notified on a rolling basis.

CONTACT
Robert Andersen, Director of Financial Aid
One University Circle, Macomb, IL 61455-1390
(309) 298-2446

Wheaton College

Wheaton, Illinois
www.wheaton.edu Federal Code: 001781

4-year private liberal arts college in small city, affiliated with nondenominational tradition.
Enrollment: 2,477 undergrads, 2% part-time. 569 full-time freshmen.
Selectivity: Admits 50 to 75% of applicants.

BASIC COSTS (2012-2013)
Tuition and fees: $30,120.
Per-credit charge: $1,255.
Room and board: $8,560.

FINANCIAL AID PICTURE (2011-2012)
Students with need: Out of 447 full-time freshmen who applied for aid, 331 were judged to have need. Of these, 331 received aid, and 51 had their full need met. Average financial aid package met 88% of need; average scholarship/grant was $18,569; average loan was $4,840. For part-time students, average financial aid package was $6,835.
Students without need: 91 full-time freshmen who did not demonstrate need for aid received scholarships/grants; average award was $5,464. No-need awards available for academics, alumni affiliation, art, minority status, music/drama.
Scholarships offered: President's Award; $3,500 per year for 4 years; U.S. citizens with 3.6 GPA on 4.0 scale, plus minimum 1400 SAT or 32 ACT; unlimited number.

Cumulative student debt: 59% of graduating class had student loans; average debt was $24,067.
Additional info: First $500 to $2,000 of need awarded as grant instead of loan.

FINANCIAL AID PROCEDURES
Forms required: FAFSA, institutional form.
Dates and Deadlines: Priority date 2/15; no closing date. Applicants notified on a rolling basis starting 3/10.
Transfers: Priority date 3/1; no deadline. Applicants notified on a rolling basis starting 3/10.

CONTACT
Karen Belling, Director of Financial Aid
501 College Avenue, Wheaton, IL 60187-5593
(630) 752-5021

Indiana

Ancilla College
Donaldson, Indiana
www.ancilla.edu Federal Code: 001784

2-year private junior and liberal arts college in rural community, affiliated with Roman Catholic Church.
Enrollment: 423 undergrads, 28% part-time. 115 full-time freshmen.
Selectivity: Open admission; but selective for some programs.

BASIC COSTS (2012-2013)
Tuition and fees: $13,880.
Per-credit charge: $455.

FINANCIAL AID PICTURE (2012-2013)
Students with need: 56% of average financial aid package awarded as scholarships/grants, 44% awarded as loans/jobs. Need-based aid available for part-time students.
Students without need: No-need awards available for academics, athletics, job skills, leadership.

FINANCIAL AID PROCEDURES
Forms required: FAFSA, institutional form.
Dates and Deadlines: Closing date 3/1. Applicants notified on a rolling basis starting 3/1; must reply within 2 week(s) of notification.

CONTACT
Katherine Mills, Director of Financial Aid
9001 Union Road, Donaldson, IN 46513
(574) 936-8898 ext. 349

Anderson University
Anderson, Indiana
www.anderson.edu Federal Code: 001785

4-year private liberal arts college in small city, affiliated with Church of God.
Enrollment: 2,019 undergrads, 8% part-time. 515 full-time freshmen.
Selectivity: Admits 50 to 75% of applicants.

BASIC COSTS (2012-2013)
Tuition and fees: $25,480.
Per-credit charge: $1,059.
Room and board: $8,860.
Additional info: Tuition/fee waivers available for adults.

FINANCIAL AID PICTURE
Students with need: Need-based aid available for full-time and part-time students. Work study available nights, weekends, and for part-time students.
Students without need: No-need awards available for academics, alumni affiliation, art, leadership, minority status, music/drama, religious affiliation.

FINANCIAL AID PROCEDURES
Forms required: FAFSA.
Dates and Deadlines: Priority date 3/1; no closing date. Applicants notified on a rolling basis starting 3/1.
Transfers: No deadline. Applicants notified on a rolling basis.

CONTACT
Kenneth Nieman, Director of Student Financial Services
1100 East Fifth Street, Anderson, IN 46012-3495
(765) 641-4182

Ball State University
Muncie, Indiana
www.bsu.edu Federal Code: 001786

4-year public university in small city.
Enrollment: 16,323 undergrads, 6% part-time. 3,543 full-time freshmen.
Selectivity: Admits 50 to 75% of applicants.

BASIC COSTS (2012-2013)
Tuition and fees: $8,980; out-of-state residents $23,650.
Room and board: $8,714.

FINANCIAL AID PICTURE (2012-2013)
Students with need: Average financial aid package met 65% of need; average scholarship/grant was $5,638; average loan was $3,526. For part-time students, average financial aid package was $7,459.
Students without need: No-need awards available for academics, athletics, leadership, minority status, music/drama, ROTC, state/district residency.

FINANCIAL AID PROCEDURES
Forms required: FAFSA.
Dates and Deadlines: Priority date 3/10; no closing date. Applicants notified on a rolling basis starting 4/1.
Transfers: No deadline. Applicants notified on a rolling basis starting 6/1.

CONTACT
John McPherson, Director of Scholarships/Financial Aid
Office of Admissions, Ball State University, Muncie, IN 47306-0855
(765) 285-5600

Bethel College
Mishawaka, Indiana
www.BethelCollege.edu Federal Code: 001787

4-year private liberal arts college in small city, affiliated with Missionary Church.
Enrollment: 1,733 undergrads, 18% part-time. 226 full-time freshmen.
Selectivity: Admits 50 to 75% of applicants.

BASIC COSTS (2013-2014)
Tuition and fees: $24,970.
Room and board: $7,460.
Additional info: Tuition/fee waivers available for adults, minority students.

FINANCIAL AID PICTURE (2012-2013)
Students with need: Out of 221 full-time freshmen who applied for aid, 200 were judged to have need. Of these, 200 received aid, and 29 had their full need met. Average financial aid package met 71% of need; average scholarship/grant was $8,680; average loan was $3,626. For part-time students, average financial aid package was $6,875.

Students without need: 25 full-time freshmen who did not demonstrate need for aid received scholarships/grants; average award was $8,338. No-need awards available for academics, alumni affiliation, art, athletics, job skills, leadership, minority status, music/drama, religious affiliation, ROTC.
Scholarships offered: 51 full-time freshmen received athletic scholarships; average amount $7,630.
Cumulative student debt: 82% of graduating class had student loans; average debt was $24,207.

FINANCIAL AID PROCEDURES
Forms required: FAFSA, institutional form.
Dates and Deadlines: Priority date 3/1; closing date 3/10. Applicants notified on a rolling basis starting 4/1.
Transfers: Applicants notified on a rolling basis starting 4/1.

CONTACT
Guy Fisher, Director of Financial Aid
1001 Bethel Circle, Mishawaka, IN 46545-5591
(574) 807-7415

Butler University
Indianapolis, Indiana
www.butler.edu Federal Code: 001788

4-year private university in very large city.
Enrollment: 3,970 undergrads, 1% part-time. 1,101 full-time freshmen.
Selectivity: Admits 50 to 75% of applicants.

BASIC COSTS (2012-2013)
Tuition and fees: $33,138.
Per-credit charge: $1,360.
Room and board: $11,110.

FINANCIAL AID PICTURE (2012-2013)
Students with need: Out of 1,059 full-time freshmen who applied for aid, 748 were judged to have need. Of these, 748 received aid, and 110 had their full need met. Average financial aid package met 74% of need; average scholarship/grant was $19,179; average loan was $4,076. For part-time students, average financial aid package was $6,077.
Students without need: 283 full-time freshmen who did not demonstrate need for aid received scholarships/grants; average award was $11,666. No-need awards available for academics, athletics, music/drama.
Scholarships offered: 19 full-time freshmen received athletic scholarships; average amount $25,922.
Cumulative student debt: 64% of graduating class had student loans; average debt was $35,210.

FINANCIAL AID PROCEDURES
Forms required: FAFSA.
Dates and Deadlines: Closing date 3/1. Applicants notified on a rolling basis starting 3/15; must reply within 3 week(s) of notification.
Transfers: Priority date 3/15.

CONTACT
Melissa Smurdon, Director of Financial Aid
4600 Sunset Avenue, Indianapolis, IN 46208
(317) 940-8200

Calumet College of St. Joseph
Whiting, Indiana
www.ccsj.edu Federal Code: 001834

4-year private liberal arts college in small city, affiliated with Roman Catholic Church.
Enrollment: 852 undergrads, 45% part-time. 107 full-time freshmen.
Selectivity: Admits less than 50% of applicants.

BASIC COSTS (2013-2014)
Tuition and fees: $15,520.
Per-credit charge: $490.

FINANCIAL AID PICTURE (2011-2012)
Students with need: Out of 105 full-time freshmen who applied for aid, 97 were judged to have need. Of these, 95 received aid, and 13 had their full need met. Average financial aid package met 66% of need; average scholarship/grant was $8,458; average loan was $1,627. For part-time students, average financial aid package was $7,884.
Students without need: 3 full-time freshmen who did not demonstrate need for aid received scholarships/grants; average award was $4,667. No-need awards available for academics, alumni affiliation, athletics, religious affiliation.
Scholarships offered: 47 full-time freshmen received athletic scholarships; average amount $5,249.
Cumulative student debt: 64% of graduating class had student loans; average debt was $23,000.
Additional info: Immediate computerized estimate of financial aid eligibility available to students applying in person.

FINANCIAL AID PROCEDURES
Forms required: FAFSA.
Dates and Deadlines: Priority date 3/1; no closing date. Applicants notified on a rolling basis starting 4/30; must reply within 2 week(s) of notification.

CONTACT
Gina Pirtle, Director of Financial Aid & Business Operations
2400 New York Avenue, Whiting, IN 46394-2195
(219) 473-4296

DePauw University
Greencastle, Indiana Federal Code: 001792
www.depauw.edu CSS Code: 1166

4-year private music and liberal arts college in small town, affiliated with United Methodist Church.
Enrollment: 2,298 undergrads. 578 full-time freshmen.
Selectivity: Admits 50 to 75% of applicants.

BASIC COSTS (2012-2013)
Tuition and fees: $38,750.
Room and board: $10,200.
Additional info: Incoming freshman students pay additional fee for mandatory purchase of laptop computer.

FINANCIAL AID PICTURE
Students with need: Need-based aid available for full-time and part-time students. Work study available nights, weekends, and for part-time students.
Students without need: No-need awards available for academics, alumni affiliation, leadership, music/drama.
Scholarships offered: Holton Scholarships; $1,000 to full tuition; based on exceptional leadership and/or service; 50 awarded.

FINANCIAL AID PROCEDURES
Forms required: FAFSA, CSS PROFILE.
Dates and Deadlines: Priority date 2/15; closing date 3/1. Applicants notified on a rolling basis starting 3/15; must reply by 5/1.
Transfers: Applicants notified by 3/27; must reply by 5/1.

CONTACT
Craig Slaughter, Director of Financial Aid
101 East Seminary Street, Greencastle, IN 46135-1611
(765) 658-4030

Earlham College

Richmond, Indiana
www.earlham.edu Federal Code: 001793

4-year private liberal arts and seminary college in large town, affiliated with Society of Friends (Quaker).
Enrollment: 1,020 undergrads, 1% part-time. 234 full-time freshmen.
Selectivity: Admits 50 to 75% of applicants.

BASIC COSTS (2012-2013)
Tuition and fees: $40,020.
Per-credit charge: $1,307.
Room and board: $7,910.

FINANCIAL AID PICTURE (2011-2012)
Students with need: Out of 162 full-time freshmen who applied for aid, 144 were judged to have need. Of these, 144 received aid, and 63 had their full need met. Average financial aid package met 96% of need; average scholarship/grant was $22,882; average loan was $4,170. Need-based aid available for part-time students.
Students without need: 30 full-time freshmen who did not demonstrate need for aid received scholarships/grants; average award was $9,214. No-need awards available for academics, religious affiliation.
Scholarships offered: Presidential Honors Scholarship; $9,000 per year; based on combination of grades and test scores; unlimited number. Cunningham Scholarship; $9,000 per year; based on combination of grades and test scores; unlimited number. C.B. Edwards Scholarship; up to $12,500 per year; for chemistry majors; 1-3 awarded per year. Wilkinson Award; $3,000 per year; must be Quaker; unlimited number awarded.
Cumulative student debt: 59% of graduating class had student loans; average debt was $25,577.

FINANCIAL AID PROCEDURES
Forms required: FAFSA.
Dates and Deadlines: Closing date 3/1. Applicants notified on a rolling basis starting 3/1; must reply by 5/1.
Transfers: Priority date 3/1; no deadline. Applicants notified on a rolling basis starting 3/1; must reply by 5/1 or within 3 week(s) of notification. Deadline for State of Indiana Grants, 3/1 (FAFSA date).

CONTACT
Robert Arnold, Director of Financial Aid
801 National Road West, Richmond, IN 47374-4095
(765) 983-1217

Franklin College

Franklin, Indiana
www.franklincollege.edu Federal Code: 001798

4-year private liberal arts college in large town, affiliated with American Baptist Churches in the USA.
Enrollment: 1,053 undergrads, 4% part-time. 276 full-time freshmen.
Selectivity: Admits 50 to 75% of applicants.

BASIC COSTS (2012-2013)
Tuition and fees: $26,895.
Room and board: $8,290.

FINANCIAL AID PICTURE (2011-2012)
Students with need: Out of 264 full-time freshmen who applied for aid, 237 were judged to have need. Of these, 237 received aid, and 25 had their full need met. Average financial aid package met 70% of need; average scholarship/grant was $15,521; average loan was $3,148. For part-time students, average financial aid package was $7,497.
Students without need: 38 full-time freshmen who did not demonstrate need for aid received scholarships/grants; average award was $10,090. No-need awards available for academics, alumni affiliation, art, leadership, minority status, music/drama, religious affiliation, state/district residency.
Cumulative student debt: 92% of graduating class had student loans; average debt was $34,160.

FINANCIAL AID PROCEDURES
Forms required: FAFSA, institutional form.
Dates and Deadlines: Closing date 3/10. Applicants notified on a rolling basis starting 3/1; must reply by 5/1 or within 4 week(s) of notification.
Transfers: Must reply by 5/1 or within 2 week(s) of notification.

CONTACT
Elizabeth Sappenfield, Director of Financial Aid
101 Branigin Boulevard, Franklin, IN 46131-2623
(317) 738-8075

Goshen College

Goshen, Indiana
www.goshen.edu Federal Code: 001799

4-year private nursing and liberal arts college in large town, affiliated with Mennonite Church.
Enrollment: 860 undergrads, 7% part-time. 164 full-time freshmen.
Selectivity: Admits 50 to 75% of applicants.

BASIC COSTS (2012-2013)
Tuition and fees: $26,900.
Per-credit charge: $1,120.
Room and board: $9,000.

FINANCIAL AID PICTURE (2011-2012)
Students with need: Out of 138 full-time freshmen who applied for aid, 123 were judged to have need. Of these, 123 received aid, and 24 had their full need met. Average financial aid package met 83% of need; average scholarship/grant was $19,226; average loan was $4,612. For part-time students, average financial aid package was $10,214.
Students without need: No-need awards available for academics, art, athletics, leadership, minority status, music/drama.
Scholarships offered: President's Leadership Award; $18,000; must meet 2 of the following criteria: 3.8 GPA, 1270 SAT (exclusive of Writing) or 29 ACT, top 5% of class, National Merit semifinalist; 15 awards offered each year, renews annually with 3.20 GPA. Menno Simons Scholarships; $9,000; 3.75 GPA and 1200 SAT (exclusive of Writing) or 26 ACT required. Wens Honors Scholarship; $7,000; 3.50 GPA and 1100 SAT (exclusive of Writing) or ACT of 25. Yoder Honors Scholarship; $6,000; 3.30 GPA and 1050 SAT or 22 ACT. Kratz Honors Scholarship; $3,000; 3.0 GPA required.
Cumulative student debt: 72% of graduating class had student loans; average debt was $21,953.

FINANCIAL AID PROCEDURES
Forms required: FAFSA.
Dates and Deadlines: Priority date 2/1; no closing date. Applicants notified on a rolling basis starting 3/1; must reply by 5/1 or within 2 week(s) of notification.
Transfers: Priority date 3/10; no deadline. Applicants notified on a rolling basis starting 3/1; must reply by 5/1 or within 2 week(s) of notification.

CONTACT
James Histand, Vice President for Finance
1700 South Main Street, Goshen, IN 46526-4724
(574) 535-7522

Grace College

Winona Lake, Indiana
www.grace.edu Federal Code: 001800

4-year private liberal arts college in small town, affiliated with Brethren Church.

Enrollment: 1,278 undergrads, 5% part-time. 344 full-time freshmen.
Selectivity: Admits over 75% of applicants.

BASIC COSTS (2012-2013)
Tuition and fees: $23,290.
Per-credit charge: $775.
Room and board: $7,454.
Additional info: Tuition/fee waivers available for minority students.

FINANCIAL AID PICTURE
Students with need: Need-based aid available for full-time and part-time students. Work study available nights, weekends, and for part-time students.
Students without need: No-need awards available for academics, art, athletics, leadership, minority status, music/drama, religious affiliation, state/district residency.

FINANCIAL AID PROCEDURES
Forms required: FAFSA.
Dates and Deadlines: Closing date 3/1. Applicants notified on a rolling basis starting 3/1; must reply by 5/1.
Transfers: Applicants notified by 3/15; must reply by 5/1. Applicants who miss dates for admission and financial aid are notified on rolling basis until class is full.

CONTACT
Charlette Sauders, Director of Financial Aid Services
200 Seminary Drive, Winona Lake, IN 46590
(574) 372-5100 ext. 6162

Hanover College
Hanover, Indiana
www.hanover.edu Federal Code: 001801

4-year private liberal arts college in rural community, affiliated with Presbyterian Church (USA).
Enrollment: 1,121 undergrads. 311 full-time freshmen.
Selectivity: Admits 50 to 75% of applicants. GED not accepted.

BASIC COSTS (2013-2014)
Tuition and fees: $31,760.
Per-credit charge: $866.
Room and board: $9,690.

FINANCIAL AID PICTURE (2011-2012)
Students with need: Out of 282 full-time freshmen who applied for aid, 203 were judged to have need. Of these, 203 received aid, and 65 had their full need met. Average financial aid package met 85% of need; average scholarship/grant was $20,376; average loan was $4,213. For part-time students, average financial aid package was $17,478.
Students without need: 59 full-time freshmen who did not demonstrate need for aid received scholarships/grants; average award was $14,636. No-need awards available for academics, alumni affiliation, art, leadership, minority status, music/drama, religious affiliation, state/district residency.
Cumulative student debt: 74% of graduating class had student loans; average debt was $27,992.
Additional info: Academic Honors Diploma Scholarship is a grant program committed to meeting 100% of Indiana student's demonstrated need. Available to Indiana students who graduate with an Academic Honors Diploma (AHD), have completed their application for admission by January 15, and file a complete and valid FAFSA by March 10.

FINANCIAL AID PROCEDURES
Forms required: FAFSA.
Dates and Deadlines: Priority date 3/1; no closing date. Applicants notified on a rolling basis starting 3/1; must reply by 5/1 or within 2 week(s) of notification.
Transfers: No deadline. Applicants notified on a rolling basis starting 3/1; must reply by 5/1 or within 2 week(s) of notification.

CONTACT
Richard Nash, Director of Financial Assistance
PO Box 108, Hanover, IN 47243-0108
(812) 866-7029

Harrison College: Indianapolis
Indianapolis, Indiana
www.harrison.edu Federal Code: 075218

2-year for-profit business and health science college in very large city.
Enrollment: 4,546 undergrads, 43% part-time. 172 full-time freshmen.
Selectivity: Open admission; but selective for some programs.

BASIC COSTS (2012-2013)
Additional info: Tuition varies by program. Leadership program, $200 per-credit hour. Other per-credit hour charges range from $341 to $385 depending on program. Additional required fees vary by program and range from $675 to $2,550 per academic year.

FINANCIAL AID PICTURE
Students with need: Need-based aid available for full-time and part-time students.
Additional info: Work-study programs available.

FINANCIAL AID PROCEDURES
Forms required: FAFSA.
Dates and Deadlines: Applicants notified on a rolling basis.

CONTACT
550 East Washington Street, Indianapolis, IN 46204
(800) 422-4723

Holy Cross College
Notre Dame, Indiana
www.hcc-nd.edu Federal Code: 007263

4-year private liberal arts college in small city, affiliated with Roman Catholic Church.
Enrollment: 433 undergrads, 3% part-time. 116 full-time freshmen.
Selectivity: Admits over 75% of applicants.

BASIC COSTS (2013-2014)
Tuition and fees: $25,450.
Room and board: $8,895.
Additional info: All entering new and transfer students pay the same tuition rate for all 4 years provided the student is enrolled consecutively. Tuition at time of enrollment locked for 4 years.

FINANCIAL AID PICTURE
Students with need: Need-based aid available for full-time and part-time students. Work study available nights, weekends, and for part-time students.
Students without need: No-need awards available for academics, athletics, leadership.
Scholarships offered: Community Service Scholarship; $500 - $2000; based on community service involvement and experience; renewable up to 8 consecutive semesters of full-time attendance; must maintain 2.5 GPA to renew. Leadership Scholarship; $500 - $2000; based on exceptional leadership experience; renewable up to 8 consecutive semesters of full-time attendance; must maintain 2.5 GPA.

FINANCIAL AID PROCEDURES
Forms required: FAFSA.
Dates and Deadlines: Priority date 3/1; no closing date. Applicants notified on a rolling basis starting 5/1; must reply within 2 week(s) of notification.
Transfers: No deadline. Applicants notified on a rolling basis starting 9/1; must reply within 3 week(s) of notification. Merit-based transfer scholarships available.

CONTACT
Shelly Barnes, Director of Financial Aid
54515 State Road 933 North, Notre Dame, IN 46556-0308
(574) 239-8400

Huntington University

Huntington, Indiana
www.huntington.edu Federal Code: 001803

4-year private liberal arts college in large town, affiliated with United Brethren in Christ.
Enrollment: 1,103 undergrads, 6% part-time. 236 full-time freshmen.
Selectivity: Admits over 75% of applicants.

BASIC COSTS (2013-2014)
Tuition and fees: $24,040.
Room and board: $8,180.
Additional info: Tuition/fee waivers available for minority students.

FINANCIAL AID PICTURE (2012-2013)
Students with need: Out of 217 full-time freshmen who applied for aid, 201 were judged to have need. Of these, 200 received aid, and 17 had their full need met. Average financial aid package met 75% of need; average scholarship/grant was $17,131; average loan was $3,727. For part-time students, average financial aid package was $5,266.
Students without need: 27 full-time freshmen who did not demonstrate need for aid received scholarships/grants; average award was $11,042. No-need awards available for academics, alumni affiliation, art, athletics, leadership, minority status, music/drama, religious affiliation.
Scholarships offered: ***Merit:*** Horizon Leader Scholarship: covers all fees associated with tuition and housing costs for up to 10 semesters. ***Athletic:*** 12 full-time freshmen received athletic scholarships; average amount $8,004.
Cumulative student debt: 66% of graduating class had student loans; average debt was $31,149.
Additional info: Loan repayment program offered to qualifying students. This program helps students payback their loans after graduation based on their income.

FINANCIAL AID PROCEDURES
Forms required: FAFSA.
Dates and Deadlines: Priority date 3/1; no closing date. Applicants notified on a rolling basis starting 2/1; must reply by 5/1 or within 2 week(s) of notification.
Transfers: No deadline. Applicants notified on a rolling basis; must reply by 5/1 or within 2 week(s) of notification.

CONTACT
Jeff Berggren, Acting Director of Financial Aid
2303 College Avenue, Huntington, IN 46750-1237
(260) 359-4015

Indiana Institute of Technology

Fort Wayne, Indiana
www.indianatech.edu Federal Code: 001805

4-year private business and engineering college in large city.
Enrollment: 5,195 undergrads, 33% part-time. 579 full-time freshmen.
Selectivity: Admits 50 to 75% of applicants.

BASIC COSTS (2013-2014)
Tuition and fees: $24,860.
Per-credit charge: $480.
Room and board: $9,380.
Additional info: Books are included in the cost of tuition. Tuition/fee waivers available for adults.

FINANCIAL AID PICTURE (2012-2013)
Students with need: 38% of average financial aid package awarded as scholarships/grants, 62% awarded as loans/jobs. Need-based aid available for part-time students. Work study available nights, weekends, and for part-time students.
Students without need: No-need awards available for academics, alumni affiliation, athletics, leadership, minority status, music/drama, state/district residency.

FINANCIAL AID PROCEDURES
Forms required: FAFSA, institutional form.
Dates and Deadlines: Applicants notified on a rolling basis starting 2/2; must reply within 2 week(s) of notification.
Transfers: Priority date 3/10; no deadline. Applicants notified on a rolling basis starting 2/2; must reply within 2 week(s) of notification.

CONTACT
Scott Thum, Director of Financial Aid
1600 East Washington Boulevard, Fort Wayne, IN 46803-1297
(260) 422-5561 ext. 2208

Indiana State University

Terre Haute, Indiana
www.indstate.edu Federal Code: 001807

4-year public university in small city.
Enrollment: 9,816 undergrads, 12% part-time. 2,512 full-time freshmen.
Selectivity: Admits over 75% of applicants.

BASIC COSTS (2012-2013)
Tuition and fees: $8,098; out-of-state residents $17,644.
Per-credit charge: $286; out-of-state residents $617.
Room and board: $8,262.

FINANCIAL AID PICTURE (2011-2012)
Students with need: Out of 2,364 full-time freshmen who applied for aid, 2,015 were judged to have need. Of these, 1,982 received aid, and 241 had their full need met. Average financial aid package met 82% of need; average scholarship/grant was $6,237; average loan was $3,242. For part-time students, average financial aid package was $5,408.
Students without need: This college awards aid only to students with need.
Scholarships offered: 76 full-time freshmen received athletic scholarships; average amount $12,631.
Cumulative student debt: 71% of graduating class had student loans; average debt was $24,484.
Additional info: Financial aid application deadline March 1 for Indiana residents applying for state grant.

FINANCIAL AID PROCEDURES
Forms required: FAFSA.
Dates and Deadlines: Priority date 3/1; no closing date. Applicants notified on a rolling basis starting 4/1.

CONTACT
Kim Donat, Director of Student Financial Aid
Office of Admissions, Erickson 114, Terre Haute, IN 47809-9989
(800) 841-4744

Indiana University Bloomington

Bloomington, Indiana
www.iub.edu Federal Code: 001809

4-year public university in small city.
Enrollment: 31,927 undergrads, 3% part-time. 7,383 full-time freshmen.
Selectivity: Admits 50 to 75% of applicants.

BASIC COSTS (2012-2013)
Tuition and fees: $10,033; out-of-state residents $31,483.
Per-credit charge: $273; out-of-state residents $944.
Room and board: $8,854.

FINANCIAL AID PICTURE (2011-2012)
Students with need: Out of 5,158 full-time freshmen who applied for aid, 3,481 were judged to have need. Of these, 3,319 received aid, and 525 had their full need met. Average financial aid package met 88% of need; average scholarship/grant was $10,920; average loan was $3,200. For part-time students, average financial aid package was $6,536.
Students without need: 1,232 full-time freshmen who did not demonstrate need for aid received scholarships/grants; average award was $8,074. No-need awards available for academics, art, athletics, leadership, minority status, music/drama, religious affiliation, ROTC.
Scholarships offered: ***Merit:*** Wells Scholarship; all costs for 4 years; individual schools nominate students; 25 students selected each year. Honors College Scholarship; $1,000-$6,000; 1300 SAT (30 ACT), top 10% class rank. Hudson & Holland; $6,000; 1100 SAT (23 ACT), top 20% class rank, 3.2 GPA, based on African, Hispanic, Native American ethnicity. Kelley Scholars Program; tuition, room and board, books (overseas study funding, if requested); business major, 1350 SAT (32 ACT), 3.8 GPA, top 10% class rank. School of Music Dean's Award; amounts vary; exceptional talent displayed in audition. Valedictorian Award; $1,000; for valedictorians from Indiana schools. 21st Century Scholars Award; in-state instructional fees; Indiana residence, fulfilled terms pledged in eighth grade, filed FAFSA before March 1 of senior year. Army and Air Force ROTC Scholarships; tuition, fees, books, $300 monthly stipend. All SAT scores listed exclusive of the writing portion. ***Athletic:*** 56 full-time freshmen received athletic scholarships; average amount $24,444.
Cumulative student debt: 52% of graduating class had student loans; average debt was $28,769.
Additional info: Majority of institutional gift aid merit-based. Some need-based grants go to merit winners with financial need.

FINANCIAL AID PROCEDURES
Forms required: FAFSA.
Dates and Deadlines: Priority date 3/10; no closing date. Applicants notified on a rolling basis starting 4/1.

CONTACT
300 North Jordan Avenue, Bloomington, IN 47405-1106
(812) 855-0321

Indiana University East
Richmond, Indiana
www.iue.edu Federal Code: 001811

4-year public university in large town.
Enrollment: 2,986 undergrads, 34% part-time. 392 full-time freshmen.
Selectivity: Admits 50 to 75% of applicants.

BASIC COSTS (2012-2013)
Tuition and fees: $6,496; out-of-state residents $17,426.
Per-credit charge: $199; out-of-state residents $563.

FINANCIAL AID PICTURE (2011-2012)
Students with need: Out of 379 full-time freshmen who applied for aid, 320 were judged to have need. Of these, 312 received aid, and 44 had their full need met. Average financial aid package met 97% of need; average scholarship/grant was $6,689; average loan was $2,811. For part-time students, average financial aid package was $5,588.
Students without need: 18 full-time freshmen who did not demonstrate need for aid received scholarships/grants; average award was $2,146. No-need awards available for academics, alumni affiliation, leadership.
Scholarships offered: 17 full-time freshmen received athletic scholarships; average amount $1,066.
Cumulative student debt: 81% of graduating class had student loans; average debt was $30,632.

FINANCIAL AID PROCEDURES
Forms required: FAFSA, institutional form.
Dates and Deadlines: Priority date 3/10; no closing date. Applicants notified on a rolling basis starting 5/1; must reply within 2 week(s) of notification.

CONTACT
Sarah Soper, Director, Financial Aid & Scholarships
2325 Chester Boulevard, Richmond, IN 47374-1289
(765) 973-8206

Indiana University Kokomo
Kokomo, Indiana
www.iuk.edu Federal Code: 001814

4-year public university in large town.
Enrollment: 2,654 undergrads, 30% part-time. 388 full-time freshmen.
Selectivity: Admits 50 to 75% of applicants.

BASIC COSTS (2012-2013)
Tuition and fees: $6,541; out-of-state residents $17,486.
Per-credit charge: $198; out-of-state residents $563.

FINANCIAL AID PICTURE (2011-2012)
Students with need: Out of 355 full-time freshmen who applied for aid, 288 were judged to have need. Of these, 282 received aid, and 10 had their full need met. Average financial aid package met 92% of need; average scholarship/grant was $5,913; average loan was $2,784. For part-time students, average financial aid package was $5,593.
Students without need: 25 full-time freshmen who did not demonstrate need for aid received scholarships/grants; average award was $1,467. No-need awards available for academics, athletics, leadership.
Cumulative student debt: 73% of graduating class had student loans; average debt was $26,217.

FINANCIAL AID PROCEDURES
Forms required: FAFSA.
Dates and Deadlines: Priority date 3/10; no closing date. Applicants notified on a rolling basis starting 3/25; must reply within 4 week(s) of notification.

CONTACT
John Delaney, Assistant Director of Financial Aid/Veterans Representative
Kelley Student Center, Room 230, Kokomo, IN 46904-9003
(765) 455-9216

Indiana University Northwest
Gary, Indiana
www.iun.edu Federal Code: 001815

4-year public university in small city.
Enrollment: 4,817 undergrads, 33% part-time. 754 full-time freshmen.
Selectivity: Admits 50 to 75% of applicants.

BASIC COSTS (2012-2013)
Tuition and fees: $6,626; out-of-state residents $17,477.
Per-credit charge: $201; out-of-state residents $563.

FINANCIAL AID PICTURE (2011-2012)
Students with need: Out of 659 full-time freshmen who applied for aid, 601 were judged to have need. Of these, 573 received aid, and 6 had their full need met. Average financial aid package met 91% of need; average scholarship/grant was $6,007; average loan was $3,130. For part-time students, average financial aid package was $5,518.

Students without need: 29 full-time freshmen who did not demonstrate need for aid received scholarships/grants; average award was $3,754. No-need awards available for academics, athletics.
Scholarships offered: 3 full-time freshmen received athletic scholarships; average amount $967.
Cumulative student debt: 73% of graduating class had student loans; average debt was $30,369.

FINANCIAL AID PROCEDURES
Forms required: FAFSA.
Dates and Deadlines: Priority date 3/10; no closing date. Applicants notified on a rolling basis starting 4/15.

CONTACT
Harold Burtley, Director, Scholarships and Financial Aid
3400 Broadway, Gary, IN 46408
(219) 980-6778

Indiana University South Bend
South Bend, Indiana
www.iusb.edu Federal Code: 001816

4-year public university in small city.
Enrollment: 5,945 undergrads, 31% part-time. 876 full-time freshmen.
Selectivity: Admits 50 to 75% of applicants.

BASIC COSTS (2012-2013)
Tuition and fees: $6,728; out-of-state residents $17,484.
Per-credit charge: $205; out-of-state residents $563.
Additional info: Board plan not available. Cost of room only, $6,838.

FINANCIAL AID PICTURE (2011-2012)
Students with need: Out of 800 full-time freshmen who applied for aid, 695 were judged to have need. Of these, 675 received aid, and 23 had their full need met. Average financial aid package met 92% of need; average scholarship/grant was $5,901; average loan was $2,946. For part-time students, average financial aid package was $5,592.
Students without need: 6 full-time freshmen who did not demonstrate need for aid received scholarships/grants; average award was $7,382. No-need awards available for academics, athletics.
Scholarships offered: ***Merit:*** Honors Scholarship; $1,500 per academic year (full-time); based on 1100 SAT (exclusive of Writing) or ACT equivalent, rank in top 10%, and 3.5 GPA. ***Athletic:*** 26 full-time freshmen received athletic scholarships; average amount $423.
Cumulative student debt: 75% of graduating class had student loans; average debt was $27,417.

FINANCIAL AID PROCEDURES
Forms required: FAFSA, institutional form.
Dates and Deadlines: Priority date 3/10; no closing date. Applicants notified on a rolling basis starting 5/1.
Transfers: No deadline.

CONTACT
Cathy Buckman, Assistant Vice Chancellor for Enrollment Services and Interim Director of Financial Aid
1700 Mishawaka Avenue, South Bend, IN 46634-7111
(574) 520-4357

Indiana University Southeast
New Albany, Indiana
www.ius.edu Federal Code: 001817

4-year public university in large town.
Enrollment: 5,746 undergrads, 35% part-time. 896 full-time freshmen.
Selectivity: Admits over 75% of applicants.

BASIC COSTS (2012-2013)
Tuition and fees: $6,576; out-of-state residents $17,510.
Per-credit charge: $199; out-of-state residents $563.
Room and board: $6,095.

FINANCIAL AID PICTURE (2011-2012)
Students with need: Out of 801 full-time freshmen who applied for aid, 629 were judged to have need. Of these, 609 received aid, and 28 had their full need met. Average financial aid package met 92% of need; average scholarship/grant was $6,203; average loan was $2,969. For part-time students, average financial aid package was $4,855.
Students without need: 59 full-time freshmen who did not demonstrate need for aid received scholarships/grants; average award was $1,380. No-need awards available for academics, art, athletics, leadership, minority status, music/drama.
Scholarships offered: 15 full-time freshmen received athletic scholarships; average amount $981.
Cumulative student debt: 63% of graduating class had student loans; average debt was $24,609.

FINANCIAL AID PROCEDURES
Forms required: FAFSA.
Dates and Deadlines: Closing date 3/10. Applicants notified on a rolling basis starting 5/1; must reply within 3 week(s) of notification.

CONTACT
Brittany Hubbard, Director of Financial Aid
4201 Grant Line Road, New Albany, IN 47150-6405
(812) 941-2246

Indiana University-Purdue University Fort Wayne
Fort Wayne, Indiana
www.ipfw.edu Federal Code: 001828

4-year public university and branch campus college in large city.
Enrollment: 10,601 undergrads, 26% part-time. 1,854 full-time freshmen.
Selectivity: Admits over 75% of applicants.

BASIC COSTS (2012-2013)
Tuition and fees: $7,640; out-of-state residents $18,350.
Per-credit charge: $222; out-of-state residents $579.
Additional info: Board plan not available. Cost of room only, $5,967.

FINANCIAL AID PICTURE (2011-2012)
Students with need: Out of 1,704 full-time freshmen who applied for aid, 1,461 were judged to have need. Of these, 1,382 received aid, and 48 had their full need met. Average financial aid package met 45% of need; average scholarship/grant was $5,601; average loan was $3,154. For part-time students, average financial aid package was $5,835.
Students without need: 10 full-time freshmen who did not demonstrate need for aid received scholarships/grants; average award was $4,001. No-need awards available for academics, alumni affiliation, art, athletics, leadership, minority status, music/drama, ROTC, state/district residency.
Scholarships offered: 21 full-time freshmen received athletic scholarships; average amount $12,779.
Cumulative student debt: 17% of graduating class had student loans; average debt was $26,498.

FINANCIAL AID PROCEDURES
Forms required: FAFSA.
Dates and Deadlines: Priority date 3/10; no closing date. Applicants notified on a rolling basis starting 4/1; must reply within 3 week(s) of notification.

CONTACT
Gerald Curd, Director of Financial Aid
2101 East Coliseum Boulevard, Fort Wayne, IN 46805-1499
(260) 481-6820

Indiana University-Purdue University Indianapolis

Indianapolis, Indiana
www.iupui.edu Federal Code: 001813

4-year public university in very large city.
Enrollment: 21,379 undergrads, 25% part-time. 2,809 full-time freshmen.
Selectivity: Admits 50 to 75% of applicants.

BASIC COSTS (2012-2013)
Tuition and fees: $8,605; out-of-state residents $29,062.
Per-credit charge: $254; out-of-state residents $936.
Additional info: Board plan not available. Cost of room only: $3906.

FINANCIAL AID PICTURE (2011-2012)
Students with need: Out of 2,518 full-time freshmen who applied for aid, 2,096 were judged to have need. Of these, 2,033 received aid, and 110 had their full need met. Average financial aid package met 90% of need; average scholarship/grant was $8,193; average loan was $3,409. For part-time students, average financial aid package was $5,715.
Students without need: 204 full-time freshmen who did not demonstrate need for aid received scholarships/grants; average award was $6,060. No-need awards available for academics, ROTC.
Scholarships offered: 23 full-time freshmen received athletic scholarships; average amount $11,258.
Cumulative student debt: 74% of graduating class had student loans; average debt was $30,752.

FINANCIAL AID PROCEDURES
Forms required: FAFSA.
Dates and Deadlines: Priority date 3/10; no closing date. Applicants notified on a rolling basis starting 4/1.

CONTACT
Marvin Smith, Director of Student Financial Services
420 University Boulevard, Campus Center Room 255, Indianapolis, IN 46202-5143
(317) 274-4162

Indiana Wesleyan University

Marion, Indiana
www.indwes.edu Federal Code: 001822

4-year private university and liberal arts college in large town, affiliated with Wesleyan Church.
Enrollment: 2,852 undergrads, 2% part-time. 753 full-time freshmen.
Selectivity: Admits 50 to 75% of applicants.

BASIC COSTS (2013-2014)
Tuition and fees: $23,628.
Room and board: $7,560.

FINANCIAL AID PICTURE (2011-2012)
Students with need: Out of 744 full-time freshmen who applied for aid, 632 were judged to have need. Of these, 632 received aid, and 196 had their full need met. Average financial aid package met 83% of need; average scholarship/grant was $13,192; average loan was $5,082. For part-time students, average financial aid package was $11,466.
Students without need: 98 full-time freshmen who did not demonstrate need for aid received scholarships/grants; average award was $4,617. No-need awards available for academics, alumni affiliation, art, athletics, music/drama, ROTC.
Scholarships offered: ***Merit:*** Academic Scholarships; $750-$6,000; 3.2 GPA and 1050 SAT (exclusive of Writing) or 23 ACT required. ***Athletic:*** 52 full-time freshmen received athletic scholarships; average amount $3,832.
Cumulative student debt: 78% of graduating class had student loans; average debt was $22,940.

FINANCIAL AID PROCEDURES
Forms required: FAFSA.
Dates and Deadlines: Closing date 3/10. Applicants notified on a rolling basis starting 3/10.
Transfers: Applicants notified on a rolling basis.

CONTACT
Gaytha Holloway, Director of Financial Aid
4201 South Washington Street, Marion, IN 46953-4999
(765) 677-2116

Ivy Tech Community College: Bloomington

Bloomington, Indiana
www.ivytech.edu Federal Code: 035213

2-year public community college in small city.
Enrollment: 5,073 undergrads.
Selectivity: Open admission; but selective for some programs.

BASIC COSTS (2012-2013)
Tuition and fees: $3,455; out-of-state residents $7,302.
Per-credit charge: $111; out-of-state residents $239.

FINANCIAL AID PICTURE
Students with need: Need-based aid available for full-time and part-time students. Work study available nights.

FINANCIAL AID PROCEDURES
Forms required: FAFSA.
Dates and Deadlines: Closing date 3/1. Applicants notified on a rolling basis starting 7/1.
Transfers: Closing date 3/1.

CONTACT
Patt McCafferty, Director of Financial Aid
200 Daniels Way, Bloomington, IN 47404-1511
(812) 332-1559

Ivy Tech Community College: Central Indiana

Indianapolis, Indiana
www.ivytech.edu Federal Code: 009917

2-year public community college in very large city.
Enrollment: 20,525 undergrads.
Selectivity: Open admission; but selective for some programs.

BASIC COSTS (2012-2013)
Tuition and fees: $3,455; out-of-state residents $7,302.
Per-credit charge: $111; out-of-state residents $239.

FINANCIAL AID PICTURE
Students with need: Need-based aid available for full-time and part-time students. Work study available nights.

FINANCIAL AID PROCEDURES
Forms required: FAFSA.
Dates and Deadlines: Closing date 3/1. Applicants notified on a rolling basis starting 7/1.

CONTACT
Lori Handy, Director of Financial Aid
50 West Fall Creek Parkway North Drive, Indianapolis, IN 46208-5752
(317) 921-4882

Ivy Tech Community College: Columbus

Columbus, Indiana
www.ivytech.edu Federal Code: 010038

2-year public community college in large town.
Enrollment: 3,615 undergrads.
Selectivity: Open admission; but selective for some programs.

BASIC COSTS (2012-2013)
Tuition and fees: $3,455; out-of-state residents $7,302.
Per-credit charge: $111; out-of-state residents $239.

FINANCIAL AID PICTURE
Students with need: Need-based aid available for full-time and part-time students. Work study available nights.

FINANCIAL AID PROCEDURES
Forms required: FAFSA.
Dates and Deadlines: Closing date 3/1. Applicants notified on a rolling basis starting 7/1.

CONTACT
Paul Johnston, Director of Financial Aid
4475 Central Avenue, Columbus, IN 47203-1868
(812) 372-9925

Ivy Tech Community College: East Central

Muncie, Indiana
www.ivytech.edu/eastcentral Federal Code: 009924

2-year public community college in small city.
Enrollment: 7,061 undergrads.
Selectivity: Open admission; but selective for some programs.

BASIC COSTS (2012-2013)
Tuition and fees: $3,455; out-of-state residents $7,302.
Per-credit charge: $111; out-of-state residents $239.

FINANCIAL AID PICTURE
Students with need: Need-based aid available for full-time and part-time students. Work study available nights.
Additional info: Higher Education Aid (HEA), Child of Disabled/Deceased Veterans (CDV), Ivy Tech Scholarships (IVTC) and grants, vocational rehabilitation and veteran's assistance available. None require repayment.

FINANCIAL AID PROCEDURES
Forms required: FAFSA.
Dates and Deadlines: Closing date 3/1. Applicants notified on a rolling basis starting 7/1.

CONTACT
Tammy Tomfohrde, Director of Financial Aid
4301 South Cowan Road, Muncie, IN 47302-9448
(765) 289-2291 ext. 1222

Ivy Tech Community College: Kokomo

Kokomo, Indiana
www.ivytech.edu Federal Code: 010041

2-year public community college in large town.
Enrollment: 4,307 undergrads.
Selectivity: Open admission; but selective for some programs.

BASIC COSTS (2012-2013)
Tuition and fees: $3,455; out-of-state residents $7,302.
Per-credit charge: $111; out-of-state residents $239.

FINANCIAL AID PICTURE
Students with need: Need-based aid available for full-time and part-time students. Work study available nights.

FINANCIAL AID PROCEDURES
Forms required: FAFSA.
Dates and Deadlines: Closing date 3/1. Applicants notified on a rolling basis starting 7/1.
Transfers: Applicants notified on a rolling basis starting 7/1.

CONTACT
Anjanetta Polk, Director of Financial Aid
1815 East Morgan Street, Kokomo, IN 46903-1373
(765) 459-0561

Ivy Tech Community College: Lafayette

Lafayette, Indiana
www.ivytech.edu Federal Code: 010039

2-year public community college in large town.
Enrollment: 5,454 undergrads.
Selectivity: Open admission; but selective for some programs.

BASIC COSTS (2012-2013)
Tuition and fees: $3,455; out-of-state residents $7,302.
Per-credit charge: $111; out-of-state residents $239.

FINANCIAL AID PICTURE
Students with need: Need-based aid available for full-time and part-time students. Work study available nights.

FINANCIAL AID PROCEDURES
Forms required: FAFSA.
Dates and Deadlines: Closing date 3/1. Applicants notified on a rolling basis starting 7/1.

CONTACT
Beverly Cooper, Director of Financial Aid
3101 South Creasy Lane, Lafayette, IN 47905-6299
(765) 772-9100

Ivy Tech Community College: North Central

South Bend, Indiana
www.ivytech.edu Federal Code: 008423

2-year public community college in small city.
Enrollment: 7,621 undergrads.
Selectivity: Open admission; but selective for some programs.

BASIC COSTS (2012-2013)
Tuition and fees: $3,455; out-of-state residents $7,302.
Per-credit charge: $111; out-of-state residents $239.

FINANCIAL AID PICTURE
Students with need: Need-based aid available for full-time and part-time students. Work study available nights.

FINANCIAL AID PROCEDURES
Forms required: FAFSA.
Dates and Deadlines: Closing date 3/1. Applicants notified on a rolling basis starting 7/1.

CONTACT
Jeff Fisher, Director of Financial Aid
220 Dean Johnson Boulevard, South Bend, IN 46601-3415
(219) 289-7001

Ivy Tech Community College: Northeast

Fort Wayne, Indiana
www.ivytech.edu Federal Code: 009926

2-year public community college in small city.
Enrollment: 9,186 undergrads.
Selectivity: Open admission; but selective for some programs.

BASIC COSTS (2012-2013)

Tuition and fees: $3,455; out-of-state residents $7,302.
Per-credit charge: $111; out-of-state residents $239.

FINANCIAL AID PICTURE

Students with need: Need-based aid available for full-time and part-time students. Work study available nights.

FINANCIAL AID PROCEDURES

Forms required: FAFSA.
Dates and Deadlines: Closing date 3/1. Applicants notified on a rolling basis starting 7/1.

CONTACT

Norman Newman, Director of Financial Aid
3800 North Anthony Boulevard, Fort Wayne, IN 46805-1489
(260) 482-9171

Ivy Tech Community College: Northwest

Gary, Indiana
www.ivytech.edu Federal Code: 010040

2-year public community college in small city.
Enrollment: 9,529 undergrads.
Selectivity: Open admission; but selective for some programs.

BASIC COSTS (2012-2013)

Tuition and fees: $3,455; out-of-state residents $7,302.
Per-credit charge: $111; out-of-state residents $239.

FINANCIAL AID PICTURE

Students with need: Need-based aid available for full-time and part-time students. Work study available nights.

FINANCIAL AID PROCEDURES

Forms required: FAFSA.
Dates and Deadlines: Closing date 3/1. Applicants notified on a rolling basis starting 7/1.

CONTACT

Barb Jerzyk, Director of Financial Aid
1440 East 35th Avenue, Gary, IN 46409-1499
(219) 981-1111

Ivy Tech Community College: Richmond

Richmond, Indiana
www.ivytech.edu Federal Code: 010037

2-year public community college in large town.
Enrollment: 2,936 undergrads.
Selectivity: Open admission; but selective for some programs.

BASIC COSTS (2012-2013)

Tuition and fees: $3,455; out-of-state residents $7,302.
Per-credit charge: $111; out-of-state residents $239.

FINANCIAL AID PICTURE

Students with need: Need-based aid available for full-time and part-time students. Work study available nights.

FINANCIAL AID PROCEDURES

Forms required: FAFSA.
Dates and Deadlines: Closing date 3/1. Applicants notified on a rolling basis starting 7/1.

CONTACT

Ann Franzen-Roha, Director of Financial Aid
2357 Chester Boulevard, Richmond, IN 47374-1298
(765) 966-2656

Ivy Tech Community College: South Central

Sellersburg, Indiana
www.ivytech.edu Federal Code: 010109

2-year public community college in small town.
Enrollment: 4,810 undergrads.
Selectivity: Open admission; but selective for some programs.

BASIC COSTS (2012-2013)

Tuition and fees: $3,455; out-of-state residents $7,302.
Per-credit charge: $111; out-of-state residents $239.

FINANCIAL AID PICTURE

Students with need: Need-based aid available for full-time and part-time students. Work study available nights.

FINANCIAL AID PROCEDURES

Forms required: FAFSA.
Dates and Deadlines: Closing date 3/1. Applicants notified on a rolling basis starting 7/1.

CONTACT

Gary Cottrill, Director of Financial Aid
8204 Highway 311, Sellersburg, IN 47172-1897
(812) 246-3301

Ivy Tech Community College: Southeast

Madison, Indiana
www.ivytech.edu Federal Code: 009923

2-year public community college in large town.
Enrollment: 2,491 undergrads.
Selectivity: Open admission; but selective for some programs.

BASIC COSTS (2012-2013)

Tuition and fees: $3,455; out-of-state residents $7,302.
Per-credit charge: $111; out-of-state residents $239.

FINANCIAL AID PICTURE

Students with need: Need-based aid available for full-time and part-time students. Work study available nights.

FINANCIAL AID PROCEDURES

Forms required: FAFSA.
Dates and Deadlines: Closing date 3/1. Applicants notified on a rolling basis starting 7/1.

CONTACT

Richard Hill, Director of Financial Aid
590 Ivy Tech Drive, Madison, IN 47250-1881
(812) 265-2580 ext. 4148

Ivy Tech Community College: Southwest

Evansville, Indiana
www.ivytech.edu Federal Code: 009925

2-year public community college in small city.
Enrollment: 5,401 undergrads.
Selectivity: Open admission; but selective for some programs.

BASIC COSTS (2012-2013)
Tuition and fees: $3,455; out-of-state residents $7,302.
Per-credit charge: $111; out-of-state residents $239.

FINANCIAL AID PICTURE
Students with need: Need-based aid available for full-time and part-time students. Work study available nights.

FINANCIAL AID PROCEDURES
Forms required: FAFSA.
Dates and Deadlines: Closing date 3/1. Applicants notified on a rolling basis starting 7/1.

CONTACT
Kristi Eidson, Director of Financial Aid
3501 First Avenue, Evansville, IN 47710-3398
(812) 426-2865

Ivy Tech Community College: Wabash Valley

Terre Haute, Indiana
www.ivytech.edu Federal Code: 008547

2-year public community college in small city.
Enrollment: 4,692 undergrads.
Selectivity: Open admission; but selective for some programs.

BASIC COSTS (2012-2013)
Tuition and fees: $3,455; out-of-state residents $7,302.
Per-credit charge: $111; out-of-state residents $239.

FINANCIAL AID PICTURE
Students with need: Need-based aid available for full-time and part-time students. Work study available nights.

FINANCIAL AID PROCEDURES
Forms required: FAFSA.
Dates and Deadlines: Closing date 3/1. Applicants notified on a rolling basis starting 7/1.
Transfers: Applicants notified on a rolling basis starting 7/1.

CONTACT
Julie Wonderlin, Director of Financial Aid
8000 South Education Drive, Terre Haute, IN 47802-4898
(812) 299-1121

Kaplan College: Indianapolis

Indianapolis, Indiana
www.kaplancollege.com Federal Code: 009777

2-year for-profit health science and nursing college in very large city.
Enrollment: 418 undergrads.
Selectivity: Open admission; but selective for some programs.

BASIC COSTS (2012-2013)
Additional info: Associate degree program: Medical practice management $29,345. Diploma programs range from $16,450 to $23,430. Fees, books and supplies included.

FINANCIAL AID PICTURE
Students with need: Need-based aid available for full-time students.
Students without need: This college awards aid only to students with need.

CONTACT
Vincent O'Neal, Financial Aid Director
7302 Woodland Drive, Indianapolis, IN 46278-1736
(317) 293-6503

Kaplan College: Merrillville

Merrillville, Indiana
www.sawyercollege.edu Federal Code: 022018

2-year for-profit technical college in large town.
Enrollment: 112 undergrads.
Selectivity: Open admission.

BASIC COSTS (2012-2013)
Additional info: Associate programs: Medical assisting $27,905; medical office administration $29,760; therapeutic massage and bodywork $29,875. Diploma programs: Clinical massage therapy $16,297; medical assistant $16,105; medical coding and billing $29,875. Fees, books and supplies included.

FINANCIAL AID PICTURE
Students with need: Need-based aid available for full-time and part-time students.

FINANCIAL AID PROCEDURES
Forms required: FAFSA.
Dates and Deadlines: Applicants notified on a rolling basis.

CONTACT
Lisa Coff, Director of Financial Aid
3803 East Lincoln Highway, Merrillville, IN 46410
(219) 947-8400 ext. 8409

Manchester University

North Manchester, Indiana
www.manchester.edu Federal Code: 001820

4-year private pharmacy and liberal arts college in small town, affiliated with Church of the Brethren.
Enrollment: 1,241 undergrads, 1% part-time. 372 full-time freshmen.
Selectivity: Admits 50 to 75% of applicants.

BASIC COSTS (2013-2014)
Tuition and fees: $27,920.
Per-credit charge: $700.
Room and board: $9,250.

FINANCIAL AID PICTURE (2012-2013)
Students with need: Out of 359 full-time freshmen who applied for aid, 338 were judged to have need. Of these, 338 received aid, and 87 had their full need met. Need-based aid available for part-time students.
Students without need: 27 full-time freshmen who did not demonstrate need for aid received scholarships/grants; average award was $15,158. No-need awards available for academics.
Scholarships offered: Honors Fellowship; full tuition; based on academics; 2 awarded. Presidential Leadership Award; $2,500 travel grant; 3 awarded. Trustee Scholarships; $12,000; based on merit; 40 awarded to each incoming class. Presidential Scholarships; $9,000; based on merit. Arts, service, modern language scholarships; $9,000; based on merit/ability.
Cumulative student debt: 85% of graduating class had student loans; average debt was $29,039.

Additional info: Students automatically considered for all scholarship programs.

FINANCIAL AID PROCEDURES

Forms required: FAFSA.

Dates and Deadlines: Priority date 3/1; no closing date. Applicants notified on a rolling basis starting 3/15.

Transfers: Aid eligibility remaining determined by reviewing total credit hours transferred and financial aid transcripts.

CONTACT

Sherri Shockey, Director of Student Financial Services
604 East College Avenue, North Manchester, IN 46962-0365
(260) 982-5066

Marian University

Indianapolis, Indiana
www.marian.edu Federal Code: 001821

4-year private liberal arts college in very large city, affiliated with Roman Catholic Church.

Enrollment: 1,698 full-time undergrads.

Selectivity: Admits 50 to 75% of applicants.

BASIC COSTS (2012-2013)

Tuition and fees: $27,300.

Per-credit charge: $1,200.

Room and board: $8,460.

FINANCIAL AID PICTURE

Students with need: Need-based aid available for full-time and part-time students. Work study available nights, weekends, and for part-time students.

Students without need: No-need awards available for academics, alumni affiliation, art, athletics, leadership, music/drama, religious affiliation.

FINANCIAL AID PROCEDURES

Forms required: FAFSA, institutional form.

Dates and Deadlines: Closing date 3/15. Applicants notified on a rolling basis starting 3/15; must reply within 2 week(s) of notification.

Transfers: No deadline. Applicants notified on a rolling basis starting 3/15; must reply within 2 week(s) of notification.

CONTACT

Chad Bir, Director of Financial Aid
3200 Cold Spring Road, Indianapolis, IN 46222-1997
(317) 955-6040

Oakland City University

Oakland City, Indiana
www.oak.edu Federal Code: 001824

4-year private university and liberal arts college in small town, affiliated with Baptist General Conference.

Enrollment: 569 undergrads, 16% part-time. 102 full-time freshmen.

Selectivity: Admits less than 50% of applicants.

BASIC COSTS (2013-2014)

Tuition and fees: $18,600.

Per-credit charge: $620.

Room and board: $8,100.

Additional info: Tuition/fee waivers available for minority students, unemployed or children of unemployed.

FINANCIAL AID PICTURE

Students with need: Need-based aid available for full-time and part-time students. Work study available nights, weekends, and for part-time students.

Students without need: No-need awards available for academics, alumni affiliation, art, athletics, minority status, music/drama, religious affiliation.

FINANCIAL AID PROCEDURES

Forms required: FAFSA.

Dates and Deadlines: Closing date 3/1. Applicants notified on a rolling basis starting 5/1.

CONTACT

Cassie Scraper, Director of Financial Aid
138 North Lucretia Street, Oakland City, IN 47660
(812) 749-1224

Purdue University

West Lafayette, Indiana
www.purdue.edu Federal Code: 001825

4-year public university in small city.

Enrollment: 29,945 undergrads, 4% part-time. 6,443 full-time freshmen.

Selectivity: Admits 50 to 75% of applicants.

BASIC COSTS (2012-2013)

Tuition and fees: $9,900; out-of-state residents $28,702.

Per-credit charge: $329; out-of-state residents $930.

Room and board: $10,378.

Additional info: Differential general service fees: Engineering undergraduate students pay an additional $1,550 per academic year. Management undergraduate students pay an additional $1,436 per academic year. School of Technology undergraduate students pay an additional $572 per academic year.

FINANCIAL AID PICTURE (2012-2013)

Students with need: Out of 4,539 full-time freshmen who applied for aid, 3,352 were judged to have need. Of these, 3,352 received aid, and 1,491 had their full need met. Average financial aid package met 84% of need; average scholarship/grant was $12,486; average loan was $3,847. For part-time students, average financial aid package was $7,365.

Students without need: 610 full-time freshmen who did not demonstrate need for aid received scholarships/grants; average award was $7,531. No-need awards available for academics, athletics, leadership, music/drama, ROTC, state/district residency.

Scholarships offered: ***Merit:*** Trustees Scholarship; $12,000-$16,000 per year to non-Indiana residents; $10,000 per year to Indiana residents; renewable for up to 4 years of continuous full-time enrollment; for exceptional academic achievement, leadership and service. Presidential Scholarship; $6,000-$10,000 per year to non-Indiana residents; $4,000-$8,000 per year to Indiana residents; renewable for up to four years of continuous full-time enrollment; exceptional academic achievement in leadership and service. ***Athletic:*** 40 full-time freshmen received athletic scholarships; average amount $23,106.

Cumulative student debt: 54% of graduating class had student loans; average debt was $27,798.

Additional info: Cooperative work for credit available in many programs. Purdue Promise replaces need based loans with institutional funds after and in conjunction with federal and state eligibility for high-need students.

FINANCIAL AID PROCEDURES

Forms required: FAFSA.

Dates and Deadlines: Priority date 3/1; no closing date.

CONTACT

Theodore Malone, Executive Director of Financial Aid
475 Stadium Mall Drive, West Lafayette, IN 47907-2050
(765) 494-0998

Purdue University Calumet

Hammond, Indiana
www.purduecal.edu Federal Code: 001827

4-year public university and branch campus college in small city.
Enrollment: 8,084 undergrads, 37% part-time. 950 full-time freshmen.
Selectivity: Admits 50 to 75% of applicants.

BASIC COSTS (2012-2013)

Tuition and fees: $6,959; out-of-state residents $15,720.
Per-credit charge: $209; out-of-state residents $501.
Additional info: Board plan not available. Cost of room only, $5,170.

FINANCIAL AID PICTURE (2011-2012)

Students with need: Out of 782 full-time freshmen who applied for aid, 658 were judged to have need. Of these, 615 received aid, and 80 had their full need met. Average financial aid package met 11% of need; average scholarship/grant was $3,130; average loan was $1,847. For part-time students, average financial aid package was $4,043.
Students without need: 35 full-time freshmen who did not demonstrate need for aid received scholarships/grants; average award was $2,392. No-need awards available for academics, athletics, minority status, state/district residency.
Scholarships offered: 4 full-time freshmen received athletic scholarships; average amount $1,148.
Cumulative student debt: 58% of graduating class had student loans; average debt was $26,273.

FINANCIAL AID PROCEDURES

Forms required: FAFSA.
Dates and Deadlines: Priority date 3/10; closing date 6/30. Applicants notified on a rolling basis starting 4/15; must reply within 2 week(s) of notification.

CONTACT

Beatriz Contreras, Director of Student Financial Services
2200 169th Street, Hammond, IN 46323-2094
(219) 989-2301

Purdue University North Central

Westville, Indiana
www.pnc.edu Federal Code: 001826

4-year public university in rural community.
Enrollment: 3,492 undergrads, 26% part-time. 611 full-time freshmen.
Selectivity: Admits 50 to 75% of applicants.

BASIC COSTS (2012-2013)

Tuition and fees: $7,045; out-of-state residents $16,769.
Per-credit charge: $215; out-of-state residents $539.

FINANCIAL AID PICTURE

Students with need: Need-based aid available for full-time and part-time students.
Students without need: No-need awards available for academics, athletics, leadership.

FINANCIAL AID PROCEDURES

Forms required: FAFSA.
Dates and Deadlines: Priority date 3/10; closing date 6/30. Applicants notified on a rolling basis starting 4/1; must reply by 8/1 or within 2 week(s) of notification.
Transfers: Priority date 3/1; no deadline.

CONTACT

Brad Remmenga, Director, Financial Aid and Compliance
1401 South US Highway 421, Westville, IN 46391-9542
(219) 785-55460

Rose-Hulman Institute of Technology

Terre Haute, Indiana
www.rose-hulman.edu Federal Code: 001830

4-year private engineering college in small city.
Enrollment: 2,097 undergrads. 621 full-time freshmen.
Selectivity: Admits 50 to 75% of applicants. GED not accepted.

BASIC COSTS (2013-2014)

Tuition and fees: $42,654.
Per-credit charge: $1,152.
Room and board: $11,484.
Additional info: Required fees for incoming freshman students include mandatory purchase of laptop computer, which is a $2,400 expense, activity fees, health services fee, technology fee, and Residence Hall Association fee.

FINANCIAL AID PICTURE (2012-2013)

Students with need: Out of 516 full-time freshmen who applied for aid, 444 were judged to have need. Of these, 444 received aid, and 68 had their full need met. Average financial aid package met 76% of need; average scholarship/grant was $23,657; average loan was $4,696. For part-time students, average financial aid package was $19,569.
Students without need: 175 full-time freshmen who did not demonstrate need for aid received scholarships/grants; average award was $10,527. No-need awards available for academics, minority status, ROTC.
Cumulative student debt: 71% of graduating class had student loans; average debt was $44,965.

FINANCIAL AID PROCEDURES

Forms required: FAFSA.
Dates and Deadlines: Priority date 3/1; no closing date. Applicants notified on a rolling basis starting 3/10; must reply by 5/1.
Transfers: No deadline. Applicants notified on a rolling basis; must reply by 6/1.

CONTACT

Melinda Middleton, Director of Financial Aid
Office of Admissions, Terre Haute, IN 47803-3999
(800) 248-7448

Saint Joseph's College

Rensselaer, Indiana
www.saintjoe.edu Federal Code: 001833

4-year private liberal arts college in small town, affiliated with Roman Catholic Church.
Enrollment: 1,068 undergrads, 8% part-time. 263 full-time freshmen.
Selectivity: Admits 50 to 75% of applicants.

BASIC COSTS (2013-2014)

Tuition and fees: $27,350.
Per-credit charge: $910.
Room and board: $8,440.

FINANCIAL AID PICTURE (2011-2012)

Students with need: Out of 263 full-time freshmen who applied for aid, 245 were judged to have need. Of these, 245 received aid, and 57 had their full need met. Average financial aid package met 79% of need; average scholarship/grant was $18,439; average loan was $3,846. For part-time students, average financial aid package was $6,167.
Students without need: 17 full-time freshmen who did not demonstrate need for aid received scholarships/grants; average award was $16,824. No-need awards available for academics, alumni affiliation, athletics, minority status, music/drama.
Scholarships offered: 9 full-time freshmen received athletic scholarships; average amount $12,513.

Cumulative student debt: 81% of graduating class had student loans; average debt was $30,963.

FINANCIAL AID PROCEDURES

Forms required: FAFSA.

Dates and Deadlines: Priority date 3/1; no closing date. Applicants notified on a rolling basis starting 3/1; must reply by 5/1 or within 2 week(s) of notification.

Transfers: No deadline. Applicants notified on a rolling basis starting 9/1; must reply by 5/1 or within 2 week(s) of notification.

CONTACT

Debra Sizemore, Director of Student Financial Services
Box 890, Rensselaer, IN 47978-0890
(219) 866-6163

St. Mary-of-the-Woods College

St. Mary-of-the-Woods, Indiana
www.smwc.edu Federal Code: 001835

4-year private liberal arts college for women in rural community, affiliated with Roman Catholic Church.

Enrollment: 756 undergrads, 43% part-time. 69 full-time freshmen.

Selectivity: Admits 50 to 75% of applicants.

BASIC COSTS (2013-2014)

Tuition and fees: $27,672.

Per-credit charge: $482.

Room and board: $10,050.

Additional info: Freshman students enter at 4-year locked tuition rate of $27,672. Tuition at time of enrollment locked for 4 years; tuition/fee waivers available for minority students.

FINANCIAL AID PICTURE

Students with need: Need-based aid available for full-time and part-time students. Work study available nights, weekends, and for part-time students.

Students without need: No-need awards available for academics, alumni affiliation, art, athletics, leadership, minority status, music/drama, state/district residency.

Scholarships offered: Saint Mother Theodore Guerin Scholarships; 2 per year at $20,000 a year for 4 years, 8 per year at $13,000 a year for 4 years; based on academics, service and leadership. Top Ten on 10 Scholarships; 2 per year at $20,000 a year for 4 years, 8 per year at $13,000 a year for four years; for local students based on academics, service and leadership. Trustees Scholarships; up to $11,000 a year for 4 years; based on academics. Presidential Scholarships; up to $9,000 a year for 4 years; based on academics. Dean's Scholarships; up to $6,000 a year for 4 years; based on academics. Woods Scholarships; up to $4,000 per year for 4 years; based on academics.

Additional info: Portfolio or audition required of applicants who wish to be considered for Creative Arts Scholarship.

FINANCIAL AID PROCEDURES

Forms required: FAFSA.

Dates and Deadlines: Priority date 3/1; no closing date. Applicants notified on a rolling basis starting 12/1; must reply within 6 week(s) of notification.

Transfers: Priority date 7/1; no deadline. Applicants notified on a rolling basis; must reply within 8 week(s) of notification. Transfer grants available for students graduating or transferring from Ivy Tech Community College.

CONTACT

Darla Hopper, Director of Financial Aid
Rooney Library, SMWC, St. Mary of the Woods, IN 47876
(812) 535-5110

Saint Mary's College

Notre Dame, Indiana Federal Code: 001836
www.saintmarys.edu CSS Code: 1702

4-year private liberal arts college for women in small city, affiliated with Roman Catholic Church.

Enrollment: 1,454 undergrads. 417 full-time freshmen.

Selectivity: Admits over 75% of applicants.

BASIC COSTS (2013-2014)

Tuition and fees: $34,600.

Per-credit charge: $1,340.

Room and board: $10,560.

FINANCIAL AID PICTURE (2012-2013)

Students with need: Out of 349 full-time freshmen who applied for aid, 275 were judged to have need. Of these, 275 received aid, and 76 had their full need met. Average financial aid package met 85% of need; average scholarship/grant was $23,149; average loan was $3,895. Need-based aid available for part-time students.

Students without need: 137 full-time freshmen who did not demonstrate need for aid received scholarships/grants; average award was $13,532. No-need awards available for academics, art, music/drama.

Scholarships offered: Credentials of all admitted candidates automatically reviewed for merit scholarship consideration. Amounts vary depending on academic qualifications, renewable provided minimum GPA requirements are maintained. Grant for the cost of a double room on-campus awarded to any admitted student with a full tuition ROTC scholarship.

Cumulative student debt: 68% of graduating class had student loans; average debt was $31,891.

Additional info: Saint Mary's also accepts veteran benefits and participates in the Yellow Ribbon Program, through which 100% of a student's tuition and fees can be paid.

FINANCIAL AID PROCEDURES

Forms required: FAFSA, CSS PROFILE.

Dates and Deadlines: Closing date 3/1. Applicants notified on a rolling basis starting 12/15.

Transfers: Priority date 5/15; no deadline. Applicants notified on a rolling basis. To meet Indiana grant deadlines, Indiana residents must submit FAFSA by March 1.

CONTACT

Kathleen Brown, Director of Financial Aid
122 Le Mans Hall, Notre Dame, IN 46556-5001
(574) 284-4557

Taylor University

Upland, Indiana
www.taylor.edu Federal Code: 001838

4-year private university and liberal arts college in small town, affiliated with interdenominational tradition.

Enrollment: 1,887 undergrads, 3% part-time. 498 full-time freshmen.

Selectivity: Admits over 75% of applicants.

BASIC COSTS (2013-2014)

Tuition and fees: $28,753.

Room and board: $7,989.

Additional info: Per-credit hour charge for 1 to 6 hours, $798; for 7 to 11 hours $1,005.

FINANCIAL AID PICTURE (2012-2013)

Students with need: Out of 415 full-time freshmen who applied for aid, 349 were judged to have need. Of these, 349 received aid, and 77 had their full need met. Average financial aid package met 73% of need; average

scholarship/grant was $15,069; average loan was $4,653. For part-time students, average financial aid package was $11,818.
Students without need: 111 full-time freshmen who did not demonstrate need for aid received scholarships/grants; average award was $9,829. No-need awards available for academics, alumni affiliation, art, athletics, leadership, minority status, music/drama, religious affiliation, state/district residency.
Scholarships offered: 22 full-time freshmen received athletic scholarships; average amount $5,723.
Cumulative student debt: 60% of graduating class had student loans; average debt was $26,003.

FINANCIAL AID PROCEDURES

Forms required: FAFSA.
Dates and Deadlines: Closing date 3/10. Applicants notified on a rolling basis starting 3/1; must reply by 5/1.
Transfers: Applicants notified on a rolling basis starting 3/1; must reply by 5/1.

CONTACT

Tim Nace, Associate Dean, Enrollment Management and Director of Financial Aid
236 West Reade Avenue, Upland, IN 46989-1001
(765) 998-5358

Trine University

Angola, Indiana
www.trine.edu Federal Code: 001839

4-year private university and engineering college in small town.
Enrollment: 1,525 undergrads, 3% part-time. 421 full-time freshmen.

BASIC COSTS (2013-2014)

Tuition and fees: $28,850.
Per-credit charge: $890.
Room and board: $9,500.
Additional info: Tuition for freshmen, sophomore, and junior engineering students $31,000.

FINANCIAL AID PICTURE (2012-2013)

Students with need: Average financial aid package met 84% of need; average scholarship/grant was $4,308; average loan was $3,331.
Students without need: No-need awards available for academics, alumni affiliation, minority status, music/drama, ROTC.
Cumulative student debt: 88% of graduating class had student loans; average debt was $32,662.

FINANCIAL AID PROCEDURES

Forms required: FAFSA.
Dates and Deadlines: Priority date 3/1; no closing date. Applicants notified on a rolling basis starting 3/15; must reply by 5/1 or within 2 week(s) of notification.
Transfers: Applicants notified on a rolling basis starting 3/1; must reply by 5/1 or within 2 week(s) of notification.

CONTACT

Kim Bennett, Executive Director of Admission and Financial Aid
One University Avenue, Angola, IN 46703
(260) 665-4158

University of Evansville

Evansville, Indiana
www.evansville.edu Federal Code: 001795

4-year private university and liberal arts college in small city, affiliated with United Methodist Church.
Enrollment: 2,498 undergrads, 3% part-time. 518 full-time freshmen.
Selectivity: Admits over 75% of applicants.

BASIC COSTS (2013-2014)

Tuition and fees: $30,596.
Per-credit charge: $830.
Room and board: $10,460.
Additional info: Tuition at time of enrollment locked for 4 years.

FINANCIAL AID PICTURE (2012-2013)

Students with need: Out of 448 full-time freshmen who applied for aid, 401 were judged to have need. Of these, 396 received aid, and 126 had their full need met. Average financial aid package met 88% of need; average scholarship/grant was $23,488; average loan was $4,049. For part-time students, average financial aid package was $8,670.
Students without need: 84 full-time freshmen who did not demonstrate need for aid received scholarships/grants; average award was $16,707. No-need awards available for academics, alumni affiliation, art, athletics, minority status, music/drama, religious affiliation, ROTC.
Scholarships offered: 18 full-time freshmen received athletic scholarships; average amount $27,226.
Cumulative student debt: 73% of graduating class had student loans; average debt was $27,679.

FINANCIAL AID PROCEDURES

Forms required: FAFSA.
Dates and Deadlines: Priority date 3/10; no closing date. Applicants notified on a rolling basis starting 3/20; must reply by 5/1.
Transfers: Applicants notified on a rolling basis starting 4/1; must reply by 6/1. Indiana state aid is available for a total of 8 semesters.

CONTACT

JoAnn Laugel, Director of Financial Aid
1800 Lincoln Avenue, Evansville, IN 47722
(812) 488-2364

University of Indianapolis

Indianapolis, Indiana
www.uindy.edu Federal Code: 001804

4-year private university and liberal arts college in very large city, affiliated with United Methodist Church.
Enrollment: 4,216 undergrads, 26% part-time. 826 full-time freshmen.
Selectivity: Admits over 75% of applicants.

BASIC COSTS (2013-2014)

Tuition and fees: $24,660.
Per-credit charge: $1,018.
Room and board: $9,320.

FINANCIAL AID PICTURE

Students with need: Need-based aid available for full-time and part-time students. Work study available nights, weekends, and for part-time students.
Students without need: No-need awards available for academics, alumni affiliation, art, athletics, music/drama, religious affiliation, state/district residency.
Scholarships offered: Presidential Scholarship; full tuition; upper 5% of class, 1270 SAT/29 ACT, strong college prep required. Dean's Scholarship; 50% tuition; upper 7% of class, 1270 SAT/29 ACT, demonstrated leadership, strong college prep required. Alumni Scholarship; 30% tuition; upper 15% of class, 1100 SAT/24 ACT, alumnus connection to school required. Service Award; $2,500; based on demonstrated commitment to community volunteerism. United Methodist Award; $2,500; based on demonstrated commitment to church, activities. SAT scores listed are exclusive of writing portion.

FINANCIAL AID PROCEDURES

Forms required: FAFSA, institutional form.

Dates and Deadlines: Closing date 3/10. Applicants notified on a rolling basis starting 3/1; must reply within 3 week(s) of notification.
Transfers: No deadline. Applicants notified on a rolling basis starting 3/1.

CONTACT
Linda Handy, Director of Financial Aid
1400 East Hanna Avenue, Indianapolis, IN 46227-3697
(317) 788-3217

University of Notre Dame

Notre Dame, Indiana Federal Code: 001840
www.nd.edu CSS Code: 1841

4-year private university in small city, affiliated with Roman Catholic Church.
Enrollment: 8,466 undergrads. 2,066 full-time freshmen.
Selectivity: Admits less than 50% of applicants. GED not accepted.

BASIC COSTS (2013-2014)
Tuition and fees: $44,605.
Per-credit charge: $1,837.
Room and board: $12,512.

FINANCIAL AID PICTURE (2011-2012)
Students with need: Out of 1,457 full-time freshmen who applied for aid, 1,080 were judged to have need. Of these, 1,080 received aid, and 1,057 had their full need met. Average financial aid package met 99% of need; average scholarship/grant was $28,953; average loan was $3,290. Need-based aid available for part-time students.
Students without need: 47 full-time freshmen who did not demonstrate need for aid received scholarships/grants; average award was $13,617. No-need awards available for athletics, ROTC.
Scholarships offered: 114 full-time freshmen received athletic scholarships; average amount $29,834.
Cumulative student debt: 56% of graduating class had student loans; average debt was $30,341.

FINANCIAL AID PROCEDURES
Forms required: FAFSA, CSS PROFILE.
Dates and Deadlines: Closing date 2/15. Applicants notified by 4/1; must reply by 5/1.
Transfers: Closing date 3/31. Applicants notified on a rolling basis; must reply within 2 week(s) of notification. Require signed and completed federal tax returns, including all schedules and W-2 forms from both the applicant and the parents of the applicant.

CONTACT
Mary Nucciarone, Associate Director of Financial Aid
220 Main Building, Notre Dame, IN 46556
(574) 631-6436

University of St. Francis

Fort Wayne, Indiana
www.sf.edu Federal Code: 001832

4-year private university and liberal arts college in small city, affiliated with Roman Catholic Church.
Enrollment: 1,847 undergrads, 14% part-time. 361 full-time freshmen.
Selectivity: Admits 50 to 75% of applicants.

BASIC COSTS (2012-2013)
Tuition and fees: $24,440.
Per-credit charge: $745.
Room and board: $7,976.
Additional info: Tuition/fee waivers available for adults.

FINANCIAL AID PICTURE (2011-2012)
Students with need: Out of 348 full-time freshmen who applied for aid, 330 were judged to have need. Of these, 330 received aid, and 55 had their full need met. Average financial aid package met 76% of need; average scholarship/grant was $15,088; average loan was $3,359. For part-time students, average financial aid package was $7,486.
Students without need: 27 full-time freshmen who did not demonstrate need for aid received scholarships/grants; average award was $5,407. No-need awards available for academics, alumni affiliation, art, athletics, music/drama.
Scholarships offered: 34 full-time freshmen received athletic scholarships; average amount $4,129.
Cumulative student debt: 90% of graduating class had student loans; average debt was $29,770.

FINANCIAL AID PROCEDURES
Forms required: FAFSA.
Dates and Deadlines: Priority date 3/10; no closing date. Applicants notified on a rolling basis starting 3/1.
Transfers: Closing date 3/10. Applicants notified on a rolling basis.

CONTACT
Michelle Nisun, Director of Financial Aid
2701 Spring Street, Fort Wayne, IN 46808
(260) 399-8003

University of Southern Indiana

Evansville, Indiana
www.usi.edu Federal Code: 001808

4-year public university and liberal arts college in small city.
Enrollment: 9,322 undergrads, 16% part-time. 1,852 full-time freshmen.
Selectivity: Admits 50 to 75% of applicants.

BASIC COSTS (2012-2013)
Tuition and fees: $6,325; out-of-state residents $14,725.
Per-credit charge: $203; out-of-state residents $483.
Room and board: $7,498.

FINANCIAL AID PICTURE (2012-2013)
Students with need: Out of 1,814 full-time freshmen who applied for aid, 1,249 were judged to have need. Of these, 1,227 received aid, and 95 had their full need met. Average financial aid package met 61% of need; average scholarship/grant was $5,404; average loan was $3,578. For part-time students, average financial aid package was $8,233.
Students without need: 170 full-time freshmen who did not demonstrate need for aid received scholarships/grants; average award was $2,906. No-need awards available for academics, art, athletics, leadership, music/drama, state/district residency.
Scholarships offered: 17 full-time freshmen received athletic scholarships; average amount $5,293.

FINANCIAL AID PROCEDURES
Forms required: FAFSA, institutional form.
Dates and Deadlines: Closing date 3/1. Applicants notified on a rolling basis starting 4/1.

CONTACT
Mary Harper, Director of Student Financial Assistance
8600 University Boulevard, Evansville, IN 47712
(812) 464-1767

Valparaiso University

Valparaiso, Indiana
www.valpo.edu Federal Code: 001842

4-year private university in large town, affiliated with Lutheran Church.
Enrollment: 2,930 undergrads, 3% part-time. 698 full-time freshmen.

Selectivity: Admits over 75% of applicants.

BASIC COSTS (2013-2014)
Tuition and fees: $33,480.
Per-credit charge: $1,455.
Room and board: $9,560.

FINANCIAL AID PICTURE (2011-2012)
Students with need: Out of 632 full-time freshmen who applied for aid, 570 were judged to have need. Of these, 569 received aid, and 150 had their full need met. Average financial aid package met 80% of need; average scholarship/grant was $21,795; average loan was $4,587. For part-time students, average financial aid package was $8,861.
Students without need: 115 full-time freshmen who did not demonstrate need for aid received scholarships/grants; average award was $15,226. No-need awards available for academics, alumni affiliation, art, athletics, leadership, music/drama, religious affiliation, ROTC, state/district residency.
Scholarships offered: ***Merit:*** Academic Scholarships; $9,000-full tuition. Departmental and Lutheran Scholarships; amounts vary. ***Athletic:*** 18 full-time freshmen received athletic scholarships; average amount $20,875.
Cumulative student debt: 72% of graduating class had student loans; average debt was $31,957.
Additional info: Financial assistance based on need, academic record, talent available through university.

FINANCIAL AID PROCEDURES
Forms required: FAFSA.
Dates and Deadlines: Priority date 3/1; no closing date. Applicants notified on a rolling basis starting 3/1.
Transfers: Transfer students eligible for scholarships based on previous college work. Scholarship amounts vary depending on the GPA at previous institutions.

CONTACT
David Fevig, Executive Director of Financial Aid and Enrollment Planning
Kretzmann Hall, 1700 Chapel Drive, Valparaiso, IN 46383-6493
(219) 464-5015

Vincennes University
Vincennes, Indiana
www.vinu.edu Federal Code: 001843

2-year public junior college in large town.
Enrollment: 17,530 undergrads. 1,986 full-time freshmen.
Selectivity: Open admission; but selective for some programs.

BASIC COSTS (2012-2013)
Tuition and fees: $4,882; out-of-state residents $11,542.
Per-credit charge: $155; out-of-state residents $377.
Room and board: $8,152.
Additional info: Tuition for students from Crawford, Richland, Lawrence and Wabash counties in Illinois is $240 per-credit hour (including capital improvement and technology fees, not including student activity fee).

FINANCIAL AID PICTURE (2011-2012)
Students with need: 64% of average financial aid package awarded as scholarships/grants, 36% awarded as loans/jobs. Need-based aid available for part-time students. Work study available nights, weekends, and for part-time students.
Students without need: No-need awards available for academics, art, athletics, leadership, music/drama, state/district residency.
Scholarships offered: Presidential Scholarship; $2,500 per year for 4 semesters; 1650 SAT and rank in upper 10% of class; limited in number. Blue & Gold Scholarship; $1,750 per year for 4 semesters; 1515 SAT and rank in upper 50% of class; limited number of awards. Indiana Academic Honors/Technical Honors Diploma; $1,250 per year for 4 semesters. Walters Scholarship; tuition, room and board; for candidates in good standing. Education Scholarship; for education majors, based on SAT scores and rank in upper 10% of class; 1 awarded. Valedictorian/Salutatorian scholarship; covers full costs.

FINANCIAL AID PROCEDURES
Forms required: FAFSA.
Dates and Deadlines: Priority date 3/1; no closing date. Applicants notified on a rolling basis starting 5/1; must reply by 8/24.
Transfers: No deadline. Applicants notified on a rolling basis starting 4/1. Transfer students must notify the State Student Assistance Commission within 30 days of start of term.

CONTACT
Stanley Werne, Director of Financial Aid
1002 North First Street, Vincennes, IN 47591
(812) 888-4361

Wabash College
Crawfordsville, Indiana Federal Code: 001844
www.wabash.edu CSS Code: 1895

4-year private liberal arts college for men in large town.
Enrollment: 901 undergrads. 252 full-time freshmen.
Selectivity: Admits 50 to 75% of applicants.

BASIC COSTS (2013-2014)
Tuition and fees: $35,650.
Room and board: $8,910.

FINANCIAL AID PICTURE (2012-2013)
Students with need: Out of 242 full-time freshmen who applied for aid, 210 were judged to have need. Of these, 210 received aid, and 154 had their full need met. Average financial aid package met 98% of need; average scholarship/grant was $20,169; average loan was $5,274. For part-time students, average financial aid package was $4,510.
Students without need: 26 full-time freshmen who did not demonstrate need for aid received scholarships/grants; average award was $14,804. No-need awards available for academics, art, leadership, music/drama, state/district residency.
Scholarships offered: Lilly Awards Program; full tuition, room, board, fees, and travel stipend; recognizes outstanding personal achievement and potential for leadership. Fine Arts Fellows; up to $15,000; based on creativity/ability; approximately 16 awarded. Honor Scholarships; up to $15,000; based on competitive exams; approximately 40 awarded. President's Scholarships; based on class rank, SAT scores; unlimited number awarded. Top-10 Scholarships; up to $17,500 per year; unlimited number awarded.
Cumulative student debt: 76% of graduating class had student loans; average debt was $28,919.

FINANCIAL AID PROCEDURES
Forms required: FAFSA, CSS PROFILE.
Dates and Deadlines: Priority date 2/15; closing date 3/1. Applicants notified by 3/31; must reply by 5/1 or within 2 week(s) of notification.
Transfers: Applicants notified by 4/1; must reply by 5/1 or within 2 week(s) of notification.

CONTACT
R. Clinton Gasaway, Director of Financial Aid
PO Box 352, Crawfordsville, IN 47933
(800) 718-9746

Iowa

AIB College of Business

Des Moines, Iowa
www.aib.edu Federal Code: 003963

2-year private business college in large city.
Enrollment: 888 undergrads, 32% part-time. 112 full-time freshmen.
Selectivity: Admits 50 to 75% of applicants.

BASIC COSTS (2013-2014)
Tuition and fees: $14,850.
Per-credit charge: $269.
Room only: $3,984.
Additional info: Tuition is frozen for any student who maintains continuous full-time enrollment. Tuition at time of enrollment locked for 2 years; tuition/fee waivers available for minority students, unemployed or children of unemployed.

FINANCIAL AID PICTURE (2011-2012)
Students with need: Out of 109 full-time freshmen who applied for aid, 97 were judged to have need. Of these, 90 received aid, and 43 had their full need met. Average financial aid package met 85% of need; average scholarship/grant was $11,443; average loan was $3,039. For part-time students, average financial aid package was $7,263.
Students without need: 13 full-time freshmen who did not demonstrate need for aid received scholarships/grants; average award was $5,662. No-need awards available for academics, alumni affiliation, athletics, leadership, minority status.
Scholarships offered: Founder's Scholarship; full tuition; 3.75 GPA and essay required; up to 20 awards per year. Honors Scholarship; $1,500 per term; 3.5 GPA. Eagles Scholarship; $1,000 per term; 3.0 GPA. AIB Scholarship; $750 per term; 2.5 GPA.
Cumulative student debt: 91% of graduating class had student loans; average debt was $28,373.

FINANCIAL AID PROCEDURES
Forms required: FAFSA, institutional form.
Dates and Deadlines: Priority date 4/1; no closing date. Applicants notified on a rolling basis starting 3/1; must reply within 2 week(s) of notification.
Transfers: No deadline. Applicants notified on a rolling basis starting 3/1; must reply within 2 week(s) of notification. Prior aid from previous institutions considered.

CONTACT
Laurie Sanders, Director of Financial Services
2500 Fleur Drive, Des Moines, IA 50321-1799
(515) 697-5907

PART III: FINANCIAL AID COLLEGE BY COLLEGE

Allen College

Waterloo, Iowa
www.allencollege.edu Federal Code: 030691

4-year private health science and nursing college in small city.
Enrollment: 385 undergrads, 36% part-time.

BASIC COSTS (2012-2013)
Tuition and fees: $18,103.
Room and board: $7,281.

FINANCIAL AID PICTURE (2011-2012)
Students with need: 44% of average financial aid package awarded as scholarships/grants, 56% awarded as loans/jobs. Need-based aid available for part-time students.
Students without need: No-need awards available for academics, leadership, minority status, ROTC.

FINANCIAL AID PROCEDURES
Forms required: FAFSA, institutional form.
Dates and Deadlines: Applicants notified on a rolling basis starting 6/1; must reply within 2 week(s) of notification.
Transfers: No deadline. Applicants notified on a rolling basis starting 4/1; must reply within 2 week(s) of notification.

CONTACT
Kathie Aswegan, Financial Aid Coordinator
1825 Logan Avenue, Waterloo, IA 50703
(319) 226-2003

Ashford University

Clinton, Iowa
www.ashford.edu Federal Code: 001881

4-year for-profit university in large town.
Enrollment: 68,874 undergrads. 2,547 full-time freshmen.
Selectivity: Admits over 75% of applicants.

BASIC COSTS (2012-2013)
Tuition and fees: $16,270.
Per-credit charge: $458.
Room and board: $6,000.
Additional info: Tuition/fee waivers available for minority students, unemployed or children of unemployed.

FINANCIAL AID PICTURE
Students with need: Need-based aid available for full-time and part-time students. Work study available nights, weekends, and for part-time students.
Students without need: No-need awards available for academics, art, athletics, music/drama.
Scholarships offered: Divisional Award; up to full tuition; based on 3.50 GPA/ 23-26 ACT. President's Scholarships; $1,500-$5,000; based on rank in top 20% of class, or 26 ACT, or 3.20 GPA. Departmental Awards; maximum $1,500; based on competitive exams in various departments. Leadership Awards; maximum $1,000; based on extracurricular activities and 2.3 GPA. Counselor's Choice Awards; $500; based on recommendation from guidance counselor, 2.5-3.19 GPA, 19-25 ACT, and at least one extracurricular activity. All awards for on-campus students.
Additional info: Work study only available to students at traditional campus in Clinton.

FINANCIAL AID PROCEDURES
Forms required: FAFSA, institutional form.
Dates and Deadlines: Priority date 3/1; no closing date. Applicants notified on a rolling basis starting 2/15; must reply within 2 week(s) of notification.
Transfers: Students with 3.50 GPA eligible for President's Scholarship, 3.25-3.49, eligible for Provost's Scholarship and 3.00-3.24, eligible for Dean's Scholarship.

CONTACT
Matthew Vallejo, Vice President of Financial Aid and Services
400 North Bluff Boulevard, Clinton, IA 52733-2967
(866) 711-1700

Briar Cliff University

Sioux City, Iowa
www.briarcliff.edu Federal Code: 001846

4-year private university and liberal arts college in small city, affiliated with Roman Catholic Church.
Enrollment: 982 undergrads, 13% part-time. 237 full-time freshmen.

Selectivity: Admits 50 to 75% of applicants.

BASIC COSTS (2013-2014)
Tuition and fees: $26,650.
Per-credit charge: $840.
Room and board: $7,660.

FINANCIAL AID PICTURE (2011-2012)
Students with need: Out of 227 full-time freshmen who applied for aid, 213 were judged to have need. Of these, 213 received aid, and 183 had their full need met. Average financial aid package met 86% of need; average scholarship/grant was $7,240; average loan was $3,940. For part-time students, average financial aid package was $5,120.
Students without need: 27 full-time freshmen who did not demonstrate need for aid received scholarships/grants; average award was $6,400. No-need awards available for academics, alumni affiliation, art, athletics, job skills, leadership, music/drama, religious affiliation.
Scholarships offered: ***Merit:*** Presidential Scholarships; awarded each year for achievement and demonstrated leadership, based on application and on-campus interview; 2-5 awarded. ***Athletic:*** 27 full-time freshmen received athletic scholarships; average amount $7,100.

FINANCIAL AID PROCEDURES
Forms required: FAFSA.
Dates and Deadlines: Priority date 3/15; no closing date. Applicants notified on a rolling basis starting 3/15; must reply by 5/1 or within 4 week(s) of notification.
Transfers: Closing date 3/15.

CONTACT
Brian Eben, Assistant Vice President for Enrollment Management
3303 Rebecca Street, Sioux City, IA 51104-2324
(712) 279-5200

Buena Vista University

Storm Lake, Iowa
www.bvu.edu Federal Code: 001847

4-year private liberal arts college in large town, affiliated with Presbyterian Church (USA).
Enrollment: 886 undergrads, 1% part-time. 228 full-time freshmen.
Selectivity: Admits 50 to 75% of applicants.

BASIC COSTS (2012-2013)
Tuition and fees: $28,314.
Per-credit charge: $952.
Room and board: $8,180.

FINANCIAL AID PICTURE (2012-2013)
Students with need: Out of 217 full-time freshmen who applied for aid, 197 were judged to have need. Of these, 197 received aid, and 94 had their full need met. Average financial aid package met 86% of need; average scholarship/grant was $20,131; average loan was $5,187. For part-time students, average financial aid package was $13,038.
Students without need: 7 full-time freshmen who did not demonstrate need for aid received scholarships/grants; average award was $16,907. No-need awards available for academics, art, minority status, music/drama.
Additional info: Portfolio required of art scholarship applicants, audition required of music and drama scholarship applicants.

FINANCIAL AID PROCEDURES
Forms required: FAFSA.
Dates and Deadlines: Priority date 6/1; no closing date. Applicants notified on a rolling basis starting 2/15.

CONTACT
Leanne Valentine, Director of Financial Assistance
610 West Fourth Street, Storm Lake, IA 50588
(714) 749-2164

Central College

Pella, Iowa
www.central.edu Federal Code: 001850

4-year private liberal arts college in large town, affiliated with Reformed Church in America.
Enrollment: 1,417 undergrads, 1% part-time. 320 full-time freshmen.
Selectivity: Admits 50 to 75% of applicants.

BASIC COSTS (2012-2013)
Tuition and fees: $29,540.
Per-credit charge: $1,210.
Room and board: $9,594.

FINANCIAL AID PICTURE (2012-2013)
Students with need: Out of 308 full-time freshmen who applied for aid, 285 were judged to have need. Of these, 285 received aid, and 54 had their full need met. Average financial aid package met 81% of need; average scholarship/grant was $22,609; average loan was $2,704. For part-time students, average financial aid package was $17,170.
Students without need: 35 full-time freshmen who did not demonstrate need for aid received scholarships/grants; average award was $15,409. No-need awards available for academics, alumni affiliation, art, minority status, music/drama, religious affiliation, state/district residency.
Scholarships offered: Students may qualify for academic scholarships up to and including three full-tuition scholarships. Funds are also awarded to students who demonstrate skills and talents in a variety of academic areas.
Cumulative student debt: 85% of graduating class had student loans; average debt was $27,990.
Additional info: Funds are awarded to students who qualify as National Merit Finalists.

FINANCIAL AID PROCEDURES
Forms required: FAFSA.
Dates and Deadlines: Priority date 3/15; no closing date. Applicants notified on a rolling basis starting 3/15; must reply by 5/1 or within 2 week(s) of notification.
Transfers: No deadline. Applicants notified on a rolling basis starting 3/15; must reply by 5/1 or within 2 week(s) of notification. Transfers only eligible for total of 4 years of state funds.

CONTACT
Wayne Dille, Director of Financial Aid
812 University Street, Pella, IA 50219-1999
(641) 628-5336

Clarke University

Dubuque, Iowa
www.clarke.edu Federal Code: 001852

4-year private university and liberal arts college in small city, affiliated with Roman Catholic Church.
Enrollment: 958 undergrads, 14% part-time. 157 full-time freshmen.
Selectivity: Admits 50 to 75% of applicants.

BASIC COSTS (2012-2013)
Tuition and fees: $26,620.
Per-credit charge: $660.
Room and board: $8,140.

FINANCIAL AID PICTURE (2012-2013)
Students with need: Out of 152 full-time freshmen who applied for aid, 137 were judged to have need. Of these, 137 received aid, and 36 had their full need met. Average financial aid package met 74% of need; average scholarship/grant was $19,704; average loan was $3,279. For part-time students, average financial aid package was $8,303.

Students without need: 19 full-time freshmen who did not demonstrate need for aid received scholarships/grants; average award was $15,089. No-need awards available for academics, alumni affiliation, art, athletics, leadership, music/drama, religious affiliation, state/district residency.
Scholarships offered: 52 full-time freshmen received athletic scholarships; average amount $5,406.
Cumulative student debt: 88% of graduating class had student loans; average debt was $30,793.
Additional info: Reduced tuition for family members of BVMs.

FINANCIAL AID PROCEDURES
Dates and Deadlines: Priority date 4/15; no closing date. Applicants notified on a rolling basis starting 3/12; must reply by 5/1 or within 2 week(s) of notification.
Transfers: Applicants notified on a rolling basis starting 3/12; must reply by 5/1 or within 2 week(s) of notification.

CONTACT
Amy Norton, Director of Financial Aid
1550 Clarke Drive, Dubuque, IA 52001-3198
(563) 588-6327

Coe College
Cedar Rapids, Iowa
www.coe.edu Federal Code: 001854

4-year private nursing and liberal arts college in small city, affiliated with Presbyterian Church (USA).
Enrollment: 1,320 undergrads, 2% part-time. 364 full-time freshmen.
Selectivity: Admits 50 to 75% of applicants.

BASIC COSTS (2012-2013)
Tuition and fees: $34,220.
Room and board: $7,700.
Additional info: Tuition/fee waivers available for adults.

FINANCIAL AID PICTURE (2012-2013)
Students with need: Out of 334 full-time freshmen who applied for aid, 313 were judged to have need. Of these, 313 received aid, and 46 had their full need met. Average financial aid package met 84% of need; average scholarship/grant was $24,234; average loan was $4,785. For part-time students, average financial aid package was $12,212.
Students without need: 40 full-time freshmen who did not demonstrate need for aid received scholarships/grants; average award was $18,514. No-need awards available for academics, alumni affiliation, art, leadership, minority status, music/drama, ROTC.
Scholarships offered: Scholarships for business/economics, music, art, theater, writing, foreign language, science; based on portfolio or audition; available for non-majors except in science and business/economics. Academic Awards; $6,000-$19,000; based on high school achievement.
Cumulative student debt: 80% of graduating class had student loans; average debt was $29,500.

FINANCIAL AID PROCEDURES
Forms required: FAFSA.
Dates and Deadlines: Priority date 3/1; no closing date. Applicants notified on a rolling basis starting 3/15; must reply by 5/1 or within 2 week(s) of notification.

CONTACT
Barb Hoffman, Director of Financial Aid
1220 First Avenue NE, Cedar Rapids, IA 52402
(319) 399-8540

Cornell College
Mount Vernon, Iowa
www.cornellcollege.edu Federal Code: 001856

4-year private liberal arts college in small town, affiliated with United Methodist Church.
Enrollment: 1,174 undergrads, 1% part-time. 340 full-time freshmen.
Selectivity: Admits 50 to 75% of applicants.

BASIC COSTS (2012-2013)
Tuition and fees: $34,705.
Room and board: $7,900.

FINANCIAL AID PICTURE (2011-2012)
Students with need: Out of 291 full-time freshmen who applied for aid, 259 were judged to have need. Of these, 259 received aid, and 73 had their full need met. Average financial aid package met 92% of need; average scholarship/grant was $26,365; average loan was $4,017. For part-time students, average financial aid package was $11,575.
Students without need: 38 full-time freshmen who did not demonstrate need for aid received scholarships/grants; average award was $11,732. No-need awards available for academics, art, leadership, minority status, music/drama, religious affiliation, state/district residency.
Cumulative student debt: 82% of graduating class had student loans; average debt was $27,227.

FINANCIAL AID PROCEDURES
Forms required: FAFSA.
Dates and Deadlines: Priority date 3/1; no closing date. Applicants notified on a rolling basis starting 3/1; must reply by 5/1 or within 2 week(s) of notification.
Transfers: No deadline. Applicants notified on a rolling basis starting 3/1; must reply by 5/1 or within 2 week(s) of notification.

CONTACT
Cindi Reints, Director of Financial Assistance
600 First Street SW, Mount Vernon, IA 52314-1098
(319) 895-4216

Des Moines Area Community College
Ankeny, Iowa
www.dmacc.edu Federal Code: 004589

2-year public community college in large town.
Enrollment: 15,784 undergrads.
Selectivity: Open admission; but selective for some programs.

BASIC COSTS (2012-2013)
Tuition and fees: $3,990; out-of-state residents $7,980.
Per-credit charge: $133; out-of-state residents $266.

FINANCIAL AID PICTURE
Students with need: Need-based aid available for full-time and part-time students. Work study available nights, weekends, and for part-time students.
Students without need: No-need awards available for academics, athletics, state/district residency.
Scholarships offered: Foundation Freshmen Scholar Award; full tuition, fees and books for maximum of 15 credit hours per semester based on available funds; open to all high school seniors in top 10% of graduating class.

FINANCIAL AID PROCEDURES
Forms required: FAFSA.
Dates and Deadlines: Priority date 4/1; no closing date. Applicants notified on a rolling basis starting 4/1; must reply within 2 week(s) of notification.

CONTACT
DeLores Hawkins, Director of Financial Aid
2006 South Ankeny Boulevard, Ankeny, IA 50023-3993
(515) 964-6282

Dordt College
Sioux Center, Iowa
www.dordt.edu Federal Code: 001859

4-year private liberal arts college in small town, affiliated with Christian Reformed Church.
Enrollment: 1,322 undergrads, 1% part-time. 341 full-time freshmen.
Selectivity: Admits over 75% of applicants.

BASIC COSTS (2012-2013)
Tuition and fees: $25,520.
Per-credit charge: $1,050.
Room and board: $7,230.
Additional info: Tuition/fee waivers available for adults.

FINANCIAL AID PICTURE (2012-2013)
Students with need: Out of 297 full-time freshmen who applied for aid, 251 were judged to have need. Of these, 251 received aid, and 78 had their full need met. Average financial aid package met 80% of need; average scholarship/grant was $15,042; average loan was $5,260. For part-time students, average financial aid package was $3,710.
Students without need: 69 full-time freshmen who did not demonstrate need for aid received scholarships/grants; average award was $17,434. No-need awards available for academics, alumni affiliation, art, athletics, job skills, leadership, minority status, music/drama, religious affiliation, state/district residency.
Scholarships offered: 29 full-time freshmen received athletic scholarships; average amount $1,880.
Cumulative student debt: 81% of graduating class had student loans; average debt was $21,859.

FINANCIAL AID PROCEDURES
Forms required: FAFSA, institutional form.
Dates and Deadlines: Priority date 4/1; no closing date. Applicants notified on a rolling basis starting 3/1; must reply within 3 week(s) of notification.
Transfers: Closing date 6/1. Applicants notified on a rolling basis starting 10/1.

CONTACT
Michael Epema, Director of Financial Aid
498 Fourth Avenue, NE, Sioux Center, IA 51250
(712) 722-6087

Drake University
Des Moines, Iowa
www.drake.edu Federal Code: 001860

4-year private university in large city.
Enrollment: 3,310 undergrads, 4% part-time. 848 full-time freshmen.
Selectivity: Admits 50 to 75% of applicants.

BASIC COSTS (2013-2014)
Tuition and fees: $30,880.
Room and board: $9,000.

FINANCIAL AID PICTURE
Students with need: Need-based aid available for full-time and part-time students. Work study available nights, weekends, and for part-time students.
Students without need: No-need awards available for academics, alumni affiliation, art, athletics, music/drama, ROTC, state/district residency.
Scholarships offered: Drake University Presidential Scholarship; $7,000-$12,000; based on academic merit and awards; unlimited available. National Alumni Scholarship Competition; 6 full-time tuition with room and board and 10 full-time tuition; available to top students.

FINANCIAL AID PROCEDURES
Forms required: FAFSA.
Dates and Deadlines: Applicants notified on a rolling basis starting 3/1; must reply by 5/1 or within 3 week(s) of notification.
Transfers: No deadline. Applicants notified on a rolling basis starting 3/1; must reply by 5/1 or within 2 week(s) of notification. FAFSA must be filed by July 1 for Iowa Tuition Grant deadline.

CONTACT
Susan Ladd, Director of Student Financial Planning
2507 University Avenue, Des Moines, IA 50311-4505
(515) 271-2905

Ellsworth Community College
Iowa Falls, Iowa
www.iavalley.cc.ia.us/ecc Federal Code: 001862

2-year public community college in small town.
Enrollment: 1,046 undergrads.
Selectivity: Open admission; but selective for some programs.

BASIC COSTS (2012-2013)
Tuition and fees: $5,100; out-of-state residents $6,060.
Per-credit charge: $144; out-of-state residents $176.
Room and board: $5,136.
Additional info: Tuition/fee waivers available for adults.

FINANCIAL AID PICTURE
Students with need: Need-based aid available for full-time and part-time students. Work study available nights, weekends, and for part-time students.
Students without need: No-need awards available for academics, art, athletics, leadership, minority status, music/drama.
Scholarships offered: Academic scholarships; $500-$1,800; based on ACT and GPA; unlimited number offered. Directors Scholarship; $2,300; for those who are 1st or 2nd in class; unlimited number offered.

FINANCIAL AID PROCEDURES
Forms required: FAFSA, institutional form.
Dates and Deadlines: Closing date 4/1. Applicants notified on a rolling basis starting 2/15; must reply within 4 week(s) of notification.
Transfers: Priority date 4/15.

CONTACT
Tara Miller, Financial Aid Administrator
1100 College Avenue, Iowa Falls, IA 50126
(641) 648-4611 ext. 432

Emmaus Bible College
Dubuque, Iowa
www.emmaus.edu Federal Code: 016487

4-year private Bible college in small city, affiliated with Brethren Church.
Enrollment: 206 undergrads.
Selectivity: Admits 50 to 75% of applicants.

BASIC COSTS (2012-2013)
Tuition and fees: $14,500.
Per-credit charge: $573.
Room and board: $6,200.

FINANCIAL AID PICTURE
Students with need: Need-based aid available for full-time and part-time students.
Students without need: No-need awards available for academics, leadership, minority status, music/drama.

FINANCIAL AID PROCEDURES
Forms required: FAFSA.

Dates and Deadlines: Applicants notified on a rolling basis starting 3/1; must reply within 2 week(s) of notification.

CONTACT

Steve Seeman, Financial Aid Director
2570 Asbury Road, Dubuque, IA 52001
(563) 588-8000 ext. 1309

Faith Baptist Bible College and Theological Seminary

Ankeny, Iowa
www.faith.edu Federal Code: 007121

4-year private Bible and seminary college in large town, affiliated with General Association of Regular Baptist Churches.
Enrollment: 253 undergrads, 8% part-time. 69 full-time freshmen.
Selectivity: Admits 50 to 75% of applicants.

BASIC COSTS (2012-2013)

Tuition and fees: $15,020.
Per-credit charge: $532.
Room and board: $5,988.

FINANCIAL AID PICTURE

Students with need: Need-based aid available for full-time and part-time students.
Students without need: No-need awards available for academics, leadership, music/drama.

FINANCIAL AID PROCEDURES

Forms required: FAFSA.
Dates and Deadlines: Priority date 4/1; no closing date. Applicants notified on a rolling basis starting 3/15.

CONTACT

Breck Appell, Financial Assistance Director
1900 NW Fourth Street, Ankeny, IA 50023
(515) 964-0601 ext. 216

Graceland University

Lamoni, Iowa
www.graceland.edu Federal Code: 001866

4-year private university and liberal arts college in rural community, affiliated with Community of Christ.
Enrollment: 1,347 undergrads, 12% part-time. 231 full-time freshmen.
Selectivity: Admits less than 50% of applicants.

BASIC COSTS (2012-2013)

Tuition and fees: $22,680.
Per-credit charge: $675.
Room and board: $7,580.

FINANCIAL AID PICTURE (2012-2013)

Students with need: 58% of average financial aid package awarded as scholarships/grants, 42% awarded as loans/jobs. Need-based aid available for part-time students. Work study available nights, weekends, and for part-time students.
Students without need: No-need awards available for academics, alumni affiliation, art, athletics, job skills, leadership, music/drama, religious affiliation.
Scholarships offered: Study and Faith Scholarship; 50% tuition; for Community of Christ members. Congregational Matching Grants; up to $500 for other faiths. Merit scholarships; up to $10,000; for incoming freshmen based on GPA and ACT/SAT. Fine Arts, Athletic and Computer Science scholarships available.
Additional info: Founders Scholarship will supplement other gift aid until percentage of calculated need has been met.

FINANCIAL AID PROCEDURES

Forms required: FAFSA.
Dates and Deadlines: Applicants notified on a rolling basis starting 2/1; must reply within 2 week(s) of notification.
Transfers: No deadline. Applicants notified on a rolling basis; must reply within 2 week(s) of notification.

CONTACT

James Wesenberg, Director of Student Finance
One University Place, Lamoni, IA 50140
(641) 784-5140

Grand View University

Des Moines, Iowa
www.admissions.grandview.edu Federal Code: 001867

4-year private university and liberal arts college in large city, affiliated with Evangelical Lutheran Church in America.
Enrollment: 2,162 undergrads, 18% part-time. 292 full-time freshmen.
Selectivity: Admits over 75% of applicants.

BASIC COSTS (2012-2013)

Tuition and fees: $21,896.
Per-credit charge: $534.
Room and board: $7,596.

FINANCIAL AID PICTURE (2012-2013)

Students with need: Out of 281 full-time freshmen who applied for aid, 250 were judged to have need. Of these, 250 received aid, and 87 had their full need met. Average financial aid package met 90% of need; average scholarship/grant was $16,335; average loan was $3,222. For part-time students, average financial aid package was $7,499.
Students without need: 40 full-time freshmen who did not demonstrate need for aid received scholarships/grants; average award was $8,442. No-need awards available for academics, alumni affiliation, art, athletics, leadership, music/drama, religious affiliation.
Scholarships offered: ***Merit:*** Presidential Scholarship; $10,000. Dean's Scholarship; $9,000. Director's Award; $8,000. ***Athletic:*** 145 full-time freshmen received athletic scholarships; average amount $4,518.
Cumulative student debt: 90% of graduating class had student loans; average debt was $33,464.

FINANCIAL AID PROCEDURES

Forms required: FAFSA.
Dates and Deadlines: Priority date 3/1; no closing date. Applicants notified on a rolling basis starting 3/1; must reply by 5/1 or within 4 week(s) of notification.

CONTACT

Michele Dunne, Director of Financial Aid
1200 Grandview Avenue, Des Moines, IA 50316-1599
(515) 263-2963

Grinnell College

Grinnell, Iowa
www.grinnell.edu Federal Code: 001868

4-year private liberal arts college in small town.
Enrollment: 1,611 undergrads. 444 full-time freshmen.
Selectivity: Admits less than 50% of applicants.

BASIC COSTS (2012-2013)

Tuition and fees: $41,004.

Per-credit charge: $1,270.
Room and board: $9,614.

FINANCIAL AID PICTURE (2012-2013)

Students with need: Out of 377 full-time freshmen who applied for aid, 331 were judged to have need. Of these, 331 received aid, and 331 had their full need met. Average financial aid package met 100% of need; average scholarship/grant was $32,267; average loan was $4,008. For part-time students, average financial aid package was $9,671.
Students without need: 57 full-time freshmen who did not demonstrate need for aid received scholarships/grants; average award was $15,791. No-need awards available for academics.
Cumulative student debt: 55% of graduating class had student loans; average debt was $16,226.
Additional info: Need-blind admission policy, 100% of demonstrated institutional need met for all domestic students, with loan cap programs. Students may apply financial aid to off-campus study programs.

FINANCIAL AID PROCEDURES

Forms required: FAFSA, institutional form.
Dates and Deadlines: Closing date 2/1. Applicants notified by 4/1; must reply by 5/1.
Transfers: Closing date 4/1. Applicants notified by 5/20; must reply by 6/1.

CONTACT

Arnold Woods, Director of Student Financial Aid
1103 Park Street, 2nd Floor, Grinnell, IA 50112-1690
(641) 269-3250

Hawkeye Community College

Waterloo, Iowa
www.hawkeyecollege.edu Federal Code: 004595

2-year public community and technical college in small city.
Enrollment: 4,261 undergrads, 33% part-time. 874 full-time freshmen.
Selectivity: Open admission; but selective for some programs.

BASIC COSTS (2012-2013)

Tuition and fees: $4,290; out-of-state residents $5,040.
Per-credit charge: $137; out-of-state residents $162.

FINANCIAL AID PICTURE

Students with need: Need-based aid available for full-time students. Work study available nights, weekends, and for part-time students.
Students without need: No-need awards available for academics, state/district residency.

FINANCIAL AID PROCEDURES

Forms required: FAFSA.
Dates and Deadlines: Priority date 7/1; no closing date. Applicants notified on a rolling basis starting 5/1; must reply within 2 week(s) of notification.

CONTACT

Gisella Baker, Director of Financial Aid
Box 8015, Waterloo, IA 50704-8015
(319) 296-4020

Iowa Central Community College

Fort Dodge, Iowa
www.iowacentral.edu Federal Code: 004597

2-year public community college in large town.
Enrollment: 6,216 undergrads.
Selectivity: Open admission.

BASIC COSTS (2012-2013)

Tuition and fees: $4,380; out-of-state residents $6,360.
Per-credit charge: $132; out-of-state residents $198.
Room and board: $5,650.

FINANCIAL AID PICTURE

Students with need: Need-based aid available for full-time and part-time students. Work study available nights, weekends, and for part-time students.
Students without need: No-need awards available for academics, art, athletics, leadership, music/drama.

FINANCIAL AID PROCEDURES

Forms required: FAFSA.
Dates and Deadlines: Priority date 3/8; no closing date. Applicants notified on a rolling basis starting 4/15; must reply within 2 week(s) of notification.

CONTACT

Darci Bangert, Director of Financial Aid
One Triton Circle, Fort Dodge, IA 50501

Iowa Lakes Community College

Estherville, Iowa
www.iowalakes.edu Federal Code: 001864

2-year public community college in small town.
Enrollment: 2,060 undergrads, 26% part-time. 425 full-time freshmen.
Selectivity: Open admission; but selective for some programs.

BASIC COSTS (2013-2014)

Tuition and fees: $5,210; out-of-state residents $5,274.
Per-credit charge: $146; out-of-state residents $148.
Room and board: $5,500.

FINANCIAL AID PICTURE (2012-2013)

Students with need: 37% of average financial aid package awarded as scholarships/grants, 63% awarded as loans/jobs. Need-based aid available for part-time students.
Students without need: This college awards aid only to students with need.

FINANCIAL AID PROCEDURES

Forms required: FAFSA, institutional form.
Dates and Deadlines: Priority date 4/22; no closing date. Applicants notified on a rolling basis starting 4/15.

CONTACT

Steve Pelzer, Director of Financial Aid
300 South 18th Street, Estherville, IA 51334-2725
(712) 362-7917

Iowa State University

Ames, Iowa
www.iastate.edu Federal Code: 001869

4-year public university in small city.
Enrollment: 25,058 undergrads, 4% part-time. 5,028 full-time freshmen.
Selectivity: Admits over 75% of applicants.

BASIC COSTS (2012-2013)

Tuition and fees: $7,726; out-of-state residents $19,838.
Per-credit charge: $277; out-of-state residents $782.
Room and board: $8,082.
Additional info: Differential tuition for upper division business; upper division engineering majors; architecture.

FINANCIAL AID PICTURE (2011-2012)

Students with need: Out of 4,280 full-time freshmen who applied for aid, 2,894 were judged to have need. Of these, 2,861 received aid, and 1,051 had their full need met. Average financial aid package met 84% of need;

average scholarship/grant was $7,846; average loan was $3,349. For part-time students, average financial aid package was $8,526.
Students without need: 1,579 full-time freshmen who did not demonstrate need for aid received scholarships/grants; average award was $3,112. No-need awards available for academics, alumni affiliation, art, athletics, leadership, minority status, music/drama, ROTC, state/district residency.
Scholarships offered: 70 full-time freshmen received athletic scholarships; average amount $18,091.
Cumulative student debt: 65% of graduating class had student loans; average debt was $30,374.
Additional info: Short-term loan program available to meet unplanned needs. Financial counseling clinic provides budget and credit education assistance.

FINANCIAL AID PROCEDURES
Forms required: FAFSA.
Dates and Deadlines: Priority date 3/1; no closing date. Applicants notified on a rolling basis starting 4/1; must reply by 5/1.
Transfers: Priority date 2/15.

CONTACT
Roberta Johnson, Director of Student Financial Aid
100 Enrollment Services Center, Ames, IA 50011-2011
(515) 294-0066

Iowa Wesleyan College

Mount Pleasant, Iowa
www.iwc.edu Federal Code: 001871

4-year private liberal arts college in small town, affiliated with United Methodist Church.
Enrollment: 650 undergrads, 18% part-time. 110 full-time freshmen.
Selectivity: Admits 50 to 75% of applicants.

BASIC COSTS (2012-2013)
Tuition and fees: $24,300.
Per-credit charge: $610.
Room and board: $8,220.

FINANCIAL AID PICTURE (2012-2013)
Students with need: Out of 110 full-time freshmen who applied for aid, 110 were judged to have need. Of these, 110 received aid.
Students without need: No-need awards available for academics, alumni affiliation, art, music/drama.
Scholarships offered: Unlimited merit based scholarships; based on ACT/SAT and GPA.

FINANCIAL AID PROCEDURES
Forms required: FAFSA.
Dates and Deadlines: Priority date 4/1; no closing date. Applicants notified on a rolling basis starting 1/1; must reply within 2 week(s) of notification.
Transfers: Applicants notified on a rolling basis.

CONTACT
Phyllis Whitney, Chief Financial Officer
601 North Main Street, Mount Pleasant, IA 52641-1398
(319) 385-6242

Iowa Western Community College

Council Bluffs, Iowa
www.iwcc.edu Federal Code: 004598

2-year public community and technical college in small city.
Enrollment: 3,978 full-time undergrads.
Selectivity: Open admission; but selective for some programs.

BASIC COSTS (2012-2013)
Tuition and fees: $4,270; out-of-state residents $4,410.
Per-credit charge: $129; out-of-state residents $134.
Room and board: $7,520.

FINANCIAL AID PICTURE
Students with need: Need-based aid available for full-time and part-time students.
Students without need: No-need awards available for athletics, music/drama.

FINANCIAL AID PROCEDURES
Forms required: FAFSA.
Dates and Deadlines: Applicants notified on a rolling basis starting 3/1; must reply within 3 week(s) of notification.

CONTACT
James Wesenberg, Coordinator of Financial Aid
2700 College Road, Council Bluffs, IA 51502-3004
(800) 432-5852 ext. 3277

Kaplan University: Cedar Falls

Cedar Falls, Iowa
www.kaplanuniversity.edu/cedar-falls-iowa.aspx?
Federal Code: 004586

4-year for-profit university and branch campus college in small city.
Enrollment: 374 undergrads.
Selectivity: Open admission; but selective for some programs.

BASIC COSTS (2012-2013)
Additional info: Cost of diploma program in practical nursing: $23,410; associate degree program in medical assisting: $32,025; cost of bachelor's degree program in information technology: $66,417; does not include books and supplies; costs vary by program, and are subject to change.

FINANCIAL AID PICTURE
Students with need: Need-based aid available for full-time and part-time students. Work study available nights, weekends, and for part-time students.
Students without need: This college awards aid only to students with need.

FINANCIAL AID PROCEDURES
Forms required: FAFSA, institutional form.
Dates and Deadlines: Applicants notified on a rolling basis.
Transfers: No deadline. Applicants notified on a rolling basis.

CONTACT
Amy Kramer, Director of Financial Aid
7009 Nordic Drive, Cedar Falls, IA 50613

Kaplan University: Cedar Rapids

Cedar Rapids, Iowa
www.kaplanuniversity.edu/cedar-rapids-iowa.aspx?
Federal Code: 004220

2-year for-profit liberal arts college in small city.
Enrollment: 423 undergrads.
Selectivity: Open admission; but selective for some programs.

BASIC COSTS (2012-2013)
Additional info: Cost of associate degree program in accounting: $30,654; cost of bachelor's degree program in accounting: $66,417; does not include books and supplies; costs vary by program, and are subject to change.

FINANCIAL AID PICTURE
Students with need: Need-based aid available for full-time and part-time students. Work study available nights, weekends, and for part-time students.

Students without need: No-need awards available for academics.

FINANCIAL AID PROCEDURES

Forms required: FAFSA, institutional form.

Dates and Deadlines: Priority date 6/30; no closing date. Applicants notified on a rolling basis.

Transfers: Priority date of 07/08 for filing Iowa Tuition Grant application.

CONTACT

Robert Brooks, Director of Financial Aid Operations
3165 Edgewood Parkway, SW, Cedar Rapids, IA 52404

Kaplan University: Davenport

Davenport, Iowa
www.kaplanuniversity.edu/davenport-iowa.aspx
Federal Code: 004586

4-year for-profit university in large city.
Enrollment: 464 undergrads.
Selectivity: Open admission; but selective for some programs.

BASIC COSTS (2012-2013)

Additional info: Cost of associate degree program in business administration: $30,654; cost of bachelor's degree program in accounting: $66,417; does not include books and supplies; costs vary by program, and are subject to change.

FINANCIAL AID PICTURE

Students with need: Need-based aid available for full-time and part-time students. Work study available nights.

Students without need: No-need awards available for academics.

FINANCIAL AID PROCEDURES

Forms required: FAFSA, institutional form.

Dates and Deadlines: Applicants notified on a rolling basis starting 3/4; must reply by 6/15 or within 2 week(s) of notification.

CONTACT

Chris Christopherson, Director of Financial Aid
1801 East Kimberly Road, Suite 1, Davenport, IA 52807-2095

Kaplan University: Des Moines

Urbandale, Iowa
www.kaplanuniversity.edu/des-moines-iowa.aspx?
Federal Code: 004220

4-year for-profit university in large city.
Enrollment: 582 undergrads.
Selectivity: Open admission; but selective for some programs.

BASIC COSTS (2012-2013)

Additional info: Cost of associate degree program in paralegal studies: $30,654; cost of bachelor's degree program in criminal justice: $66,417; does not include books and supplies; costs vary by program, and are subject to change.

FINANCIAL AID PICTURE

Students with need: Need-based aid available for full-time and part-time students. Work study available nights, weekends, and for part-time students.

Students without need: This college awards aid only to students with need.

FINANCIAL AID PROCEDURES

Forms required: FAFSA, institutional form.

Dates and Deadlines: Priority date 6/30; no closing date.

CONTACT

Summer Vaselaar, Director of Financial Aid
4655 121st Street, Urbandale, IA 50323
(515) 727-2100

Kirkwood Community College

Cedar Rapids, Iowa
www.kirkwood.edu
Federal Code: 004076

2-year public community college in small city.
Enrollment: 12,622 undergrads, 38% part-time. 1,835 full-time freshmen.
Selectivity: Open admission; but selective for some programs.

BASIC COSTS (2012-2013)

Tuition and fees: $3,990; out-of-state residents $4,740.
Per-credit charge: $133; out-of-state residents $158.

FINANCIAL AID PICTURE (2011-2012)

Students with need: Need-based aid available for full-time and part-time students. Work study available nights, weekends, and for part-time students.

Students without need: No-need awards available for art, athletics, leadership, music/drama.

FINANCIAL AID PROCEDURES

Forms required: FAFSA.

Dates and Deadlines: Closing date 6/30. Applicants notified on a rolling basis starting 4/1.

CONTACT

Peg Julius, Director of Financial Aid
6301 Kirkwood Boulevard SW, Cedar Rapids, IA 52406
(319) 398-1274

Loras College

Dubuque, Iowa
www.loras.edu
Federal Code: 001873

4-year private liberal arts college in small city, affiliated with Roman Catholic Church.
Enrollment: 1,537 undergrads.
Selectivity: Admits 50 to 75% of applicants.

BASIC COSTS (2012-2013)

Tuition and fees: $27,888.
Per-credit charge: $559.
Room and board: $7,650.
Additional info: Tuition/fee waivers available for minority students.

FINANCIAL AID PICTURE

Students with need: Need-based aid available for full-time and part-time students. Work study available nights, weekends, and for part-time students.

Students without need: No-need awards available for academics, alumni affiliation, music/drama.

Additional info: Audition or portfolio recommended for music and art financial aid applicants.

FINANCIAL AID PROCEDURES

Forms required: FAFSA.

Dates and Deadlines: Priority date 4/15; no closing date. Applicants notified on a rolling basis starting 3/1; must reply within 2 week(s) of notification.

CONTACT

Julie Dunn, Director of Financial Planning
1450 Alta Vista Street, Dubuque, IA 52004-0178
(563) 588-7136

Luther College

Decorah, Iowa
www.luther.edu Federal Code: 001874

4-year private liberal arts college in small town, affiliated with Evangelical Lutheran Church in America.
Enrollment: 2,402 undergrads, 1% part-time. 644 full-time freshmen.
Selectivity: Admits 50 to 75% of applicants.

BASIC COSTS (2012-2013)

Tuition and fees: $36,100.
Per-credit charge: $1,284.
Room and board: $6,450.

FINANCIAL AID PICTURE (2012-2013)

Students with need: Out of 545 full-time freshmen who applied for aid, 463 were judged to have need. Of these, 463 received aid, and 171 had their full need met. Average financial aid package met 90% of need; average scholarship/grant was $22,284; average loan was $4,799. For part-time students, average financial aid package was $9,073.
Students without need: 82 full-time freshmen who did not demonstrate need for aid received scholarships/grants; average award was $17,406. No-need awards available for academics, alumni affiliation, art, minority status, music/drama.
Scholarships offered: Academic scholarship; $14,000-$18,000; based on class rank and SAT/ACT. National Merit Scholarship; $1,000-$2,000. Diversity Enrichment Scholarship; $2,500; awarded to students with broadly diverse and distinctive backgrounds. Church Matching Scholarship; up to $750; for students from member churches. Music scholarship; $2,000-$4,000; plus one scholarship that covers one credit hour of lessons. Legacy Award; $1,000; for children of Luther College alumni. Competitive Nursing scholarship; $1,000; determined by nursing faculty and strength of admission file. Art scholarship; $150-$500; determined by evaluation of portfolio.
Cumulative student debt: 78% of graduating class had student loans; average debt was $35,619.

FINANCIAL AID PROCEDURES

Forms required: FAFSA, institutional form.
Dates and Deadlines: Priority date 3/1; no closing date. Applicants notified on a rolling basis starting 3/15; must reply by 5/1 or within 4 week(s) of notification.

CONTACT

Janice Cordell, Director of Student Financial Planning
700 College Drive, Decorah, IA 52101-1042
(563) 387-1018

Maharishi University of Management

Fairfield, Iowa
www.mum.edu Federal Code: 011113

4-year private university and liberal arts college in small town.
Enrollment: 350 undergrads, 4% part-time. 34 full-time freshmen.
Selectivity: Admits 50 to 75% of applicants.

BASIC COSTS (2012-2013)

Tuition and fees: $26,430.
Per-credit charge: $350.
Room and board: $7,400.

FINANCIAL AID PICTURE

Students with need: Need-based aid available for full-time and part-time students. Work study available nights, weekends, and for part-time students.
Scholarships offered: Shelley Hoffman Scholarship; $500-$900; applicant must have cerebral palsy, with preference given to students majoring in creative writing; 7 awarded. National Merit Scholarship; full tuition; for NMS finalists; 4 awarded. Ray Prat Scholarship; $500-$1,750; for musically-talented undergraduates; 4 awarded. Girl Scout Gold Award Scholarship; $1,500 renewable; for GS Gold Award recipients; 5 awarded. DeRoy D. Thomas Scholarship; $3,000 each; open to outstanding African American; 1 awarded.
Additional info: Students may earn scholarships through volunteer staff program.

FINANCIAL AID PROCEDURES

Forms required: FAFSA.
Dates and Deadlines: Priority date 7/15; closing date 7/30. Applicants notified on a rolling basis starting 3/1; must reply within 4 week(s) of notification.
Transfers: No deadline. Applicants notified on a rolling basis starting 3/15; must reply within 4 week(s) of notification.

CONTACT

Bill Christensen, Director of Financial Aid
Office of Admissions, Fairfield, IA 52557
(641) 472-1156

Mercy College of Health Sciences

Des Moines, Iowa
www.mchs.edu Federal Code: 006273

4-year private health science college in large city, affiliated with Roman Catholic Church.
Enrollment: 831 undergrads, 53% part-time. 34 full-time freshmen.
Selectivity: Admits over 75% of applicants.

BASIC COSTS (2012-2013)

Tuition and fees: $14,460.
Per-credit charge: $800.

FINANCIAL AID PICTURE

Students with need: Need-based aid available for full-time and part-time students. Work study available nights, weekends, and for part-time students.
Students without need: No-need awards available for academics, minority status.

FINANCIAL AID PROCEDURES

Forms required: FAFSA.
Dates and Deadlines: Closing date 7/1. Applicants notified on a rolling basis starting 3/1; must reply by 8/1 or within 3 week(s) of notification.
Transfers: Students must submit information by 7/1 to be eligible for Iowa Tuition Grant.

CONTACT

Lisa Croat, Financial Aid Director
921 Sixth Avenue, Des Moines, IA 50309-1200
(515) 643-6720

Morningside College

Sioux City, Iowa
www.morningside.edu Federal Code: 001879

4-year private liberal arts college in small city, affiliated with United Methodist Church.
Enrollment: 1,211 undergrads, 2% part-time. 273 full-time freshmen.
Selectivity: Admits 50 to 75% of applicants.

BASIC COSTS (2012-2013)

Tuition and fees: $25,000.
Per-credit charge: $730.
Room and board: $7,620.
Additional info: Required fees cover cost of new computer every two years as well as general and course-specific software. Tuition/fee waivers available for adults.

FINANCIAL AID PICTURE

Students with need: Need-based aid available for full-time and part-time students. Work study available nights, weekends, and for part-time students.

Students without need: No-need awards available for academics, alumni affiliation, art, athletics, job skills, leadership, music/drama, religious affiliation, ROTC, state/district residency.

Scholarships offered: President's Scholarship; $7,500 to $12,500; based on 27 ACT and top 10% of class or 3.9 high school GPA. Dean's Scholarship; $3,000 to $7,500; based on 23 ACT or top 20% of class. Mustang Co-Curricular Award; up to $3,000; based on leadership and involvement. National Merit; full tuition. Talent Awards; up to $4,000; based on talents in the areas of art, creative writing, computer technology, mass communications, mock trial, music, and/or theater.

FINANCIAL AID PROCEDURES

Forms required: FAFSA.

Dates and Deadlines: Priority date 3/1; no closing date. Applicants notified on a rolling basis starting 3/1.

Transfers: No deadline. Applicants notified by 3/1.

CONTACT

Karen Gagnon, Director Student Financial Planning
1501 Morningside Avenue, Sioux City, IA 51106
(712) 274-5159

Mount Mercy University

Cedar Rapids, Iowa
www.mtmercy.edu Federal Code: 001880

4-year private liberal arts college in small city, affiliated with Roman Catholic Church.

Enrollment: 1,482 undergrads, 38% part-time. 160 full-time freshmen.

Selectivity: Admits 50 to 75% of applicants.

BASIC COSTS (2013-2014)

Tuition and fees: $26,310.

Per-credit charge: $710.

Room and board: $8,070.

FINANCIAL AID PICTURE (2011-2012)

Students with need: Out of 149 full-time freshmen who applied for aid, 136 were judged to have need. Of these, 132 received aid, and 26 had their full need met. Average financial aid package met 74% of need; average scholarship/grant was $15,433; average loan was $3,427. For part-time students, average financial aid package was $8,298.

Students without need: 19 full-time freshmen who did not demonstrate need for aid received scholarships/grants; average award was $10,493. No-need awards available for academics, alumni affiliation, art, athletics, leadership, music/drama, religious affiliation.

Scholarships offered: 14 full-time freshmen received athletic scholarships; average amount $4,730.

Cumulative student debt: 100% of graduating class had student loans; average debt was $28,890.

FINANCIAL AID PROCEDURES

Forms required: FAFSA.

Dates and Deadlines: Priority date 3/1; no closing date. Applicants notified on a rolling basis starting 3/15; must reply by 5/1 or within 3 week(s) of notification.

Transfers: No deadline. Applicants notified on a rolling basis starting 3/1; must reply within 3 week(s) of notification.

CONTACT

Bethany Rinderknecht, Director of Financial Aid
1330 Elmhurst Drive NE, Cedar Rapids, IA 52402-4797
(319) 368-6467

North Iowa Area Community College

Mason City, Iowa
www.niacc.edu Federal Code: 001877

2-year public community college in large town.

Enrollment: 2,302 undergrads. 705 full-time freshmen.

Selectivity: Open admission; but selective for some programs.

BASIC COSTS (2012-2013)

Tuition and fees: $4,153; out-of-state residents $6,032.

Per-credit charge: $125; out-of-state residents $188.

Room and board: $5,350.

FINANCIAL AID PICTURE (2011-2012)

Students with need: Out of 591 full-time freshmen who applied for aid, 503 were judged to have need. Of these, 488 received aid, and 127 had their full need met. Average financial aid package met 26% of need; average scholarship/grant was $3,869; average loan was $2,916. For part-time students, average financial aid package was $4,402.

Students without need: No-need awards available for academics, art, athletics, leadership.

FINANCIAL AID PROCEDURES

Forms required: FAFSA, institutional form.

Dates and Deadlines: Priority date 3/1; no closing date. Applicants notified on a rolling basis starting 4/1; must reply within 2 week(s) of notification.

CONTACT

Mary Bloomingdale, Director of Financial Aid
500 College Drive, Mason City, IA 50401
(641) 422-4351

Northeast Iowa Community College

Calmar, Iowa
www.nicc.edu Federal Code: 004587

2-year public community college in rural community.

Enrollment: 3,168 undergrads, 37% part-time. 597 full-time freshmen.

Selectivity: Open admission; but selective for some programs.

BASIC COSTS (2012-2013)

Tuition and fees: $4,890; out-of-state residents $4,890.

Per-credit charge: $50.

FINANCIAL AID PICTURE

Students with need: Need-based aid available for full-time and part-time students. Work study available nights, weekends, and for part-time students.

Students without need: No-need awards available for academics, leadership, state/district residency.

FINANCIAL AID PROCEDURES

Forms required: FAFSA.

Dates and Deadlines: Priority date 7/1; no closing date. Applicants notified on a rolling basis starting 5/1.

Transfers: No deadline. Applicants notified on a rolling basis; must reply within 2 week(s) of notification.

CONTACT

Jeff Murphy, Director of Financial Aid
PO Box 400, Calmar, IA 52132
(563) 526-3263 ext. 447

Northwest Iowa Community College

Sheldon, Iowa
www.nwicc.edu Federal Code: 004600

2-year public community college in small town.

Enrollment: 892 undergrads, 25% part-time. 250 full-time freshmen.

Selectivity: Open admission; but selective for some programs.

BASIC COSTS (2012-2013)

Tuition and fees: $4,980; out-of-state residents $5,460.

Room and board: $4,340.

FINANCIAL AID PICTURE

Students with need: Need-based aid available for full-time and part-time students.

FINANCIAL AID PROCEDURES

Forms required: FAFSA, institutional form.

Dates and Deadlines: Priority date 4/1; no closing date. Applicants notified on a rolling basis starting 5/1.

CONTACT

Karna Hofmeyer, Financial Aid Director
603 West Park Street, Sheldon, IA 51201
(712) 324-5061 ext. 138

Northwestern College

Orange City, Iowa
www.nwciowa.edu Federal Code: 001883

4-year private liberal arts college in small town, affiliated with Reformed Church in America.

Enrollment: 1,195 undergrads, 3% part-time. 324 full-time freshmen.

Selectivity: Admits 50 to 75% of applicants.

BASIC COSTS (2012-2013)

Tuition and fees: $25,740.

Room and board: $7,770.

Additional info: Tuition/fee waivers available for adults.

FINANCIAL AID PICTURE (2011-2012)

Students with need: Out of 299 full-time freshmen who applied for aid, 273 were judged to have need. Of these, 273 received aid, and 226 had their full need met. Average financial aid package met 91% of need; average scholarship/grant was $7,443; average loan was $3,607. For part-time students, average financial aid package was $13,875.

Students without need: 43 full-time freshmen who did not demonstrate need for aid received scholarships/grants; average award was $7,949. No-need awards available for academics, alumni affiliation, art, athletics, music/drama, religious affiliation, state/district residency.

Scholarships offered: 154 full-time freshmen received athletic scholarships; average amount $4,986.

Cumulative student debt: 82% of graduating class had student loans; average debt was $30,589.

FINANCIAL AID PROCEDURES

Forms required: FAFSA.

Dates and Deadlines: Priority date 4/1; closing date 6/30. Applicants notified on a rolling basis starting 3/15; must reply within 3 week(s) of notification.

Transfers: No deadline. Financial aid transcript required for aid.

CONTACT

Eric Anderson, Director of Financial Aid
101 Seventh Street SW, Orange City, IA 51041
(712) 707-7131

St. Ambrose University

Davenport, Iowa
www.sau.edu Federal Code: 001889

4-year private university and liberal arts college in small city, affiliated with Roman Catholic Church.

Enrollment: 2,734 undergrads, 12% part-time. 581 full-time freshmen.

Selectivity: Admits 50 to 75% of applicants.

BASIC COSTS (2012-2013)

Tuition and fees: $25,970.

Per-credit charge: $798.

Room and board: $9,195.

Additional info: Tuition/fee waivers available for adults.

FINANCIAL AID PICTURE (2012-2013)

Students with need: Need-based aid available for full-time and part-time students. Work study available nights, weekends, and for part-time students.

Students without need: No-need awards available for academics, alumni affiliation, art, athletics, minority status, music/drama.

Scholarships offered: Ambrose Scholarship; 4.0 GPA and 30 ACT or 1320 SAT required. Presidential Scholarship; 3.8 GPA and ACT 26-29 or SAT 1170-1319 required. SAT scores listed are exclusive of Writing.

Additional info: Iowa applicants must apply for financial aid by July 1. Audition required for music, drama scholarship applicants.

FINANCIAL AID PROCEDURES

Forms required: FAFSA.

Dates and Deadlines: Priority date 3/15; no closing date. Applicants notified on a rolling basis starting 2/1; must reply within 2 week(s) of notification.

Transfers: No deadline. Must reply within 2 week(s) of notification.

CONTACT

Julie Haack, Director of Financial Aid
518 West Locust Street, Davenport, IA 52803-2898
(563) 333-6314

St. Luke's College

Sioux City, Iowa
www.stlukescollege.edu Federal Code: 007291

2-year private health science college in small city.

Enrollment: 194 undergrads, 24% part-time. 3 full-time freshmen.

Selectivity: Admits less than 50% of applicants.

BASIC COSTS (2013-2014)

Tuition and fees: $18,015.

Per-credit charge: $465.

FINANCIAL AID PICTURE (2011-2012)

Students with need: 44% of average financial aid package awarded as scholarships/grants, 56% awarded as loans/jobs. Need-based aid available for part-time students. Work study available nights, weekends, and for part-time students.

Students without need: No-need awards available for academics, job skills, leadership.

FINANCIAL AID PROCEDURES

Forms required: FAFSA.

Dates and Deadlines: Priority date 3/1; no closing date. Applicants notified on a rolling basis starting 4/1; must reply within 2 week(s) of notification.

CONTACT

Danelle Johannsen, Department Chair, Student and Administrative Services
2720 Stone Park Boulevard, Sioux City, IA 51104
(712) 279-3377

Simpson College

Indianola, Iowa
www.simpson.edu Federal Code: 001887

4-year private liberal arts college in large town, affiliated with United Methodist Church.

Enrollment: 1,844 undergrads, 23% part-time. 408 full-time freshmen.

Selectivity: Admits over 75% of applicants.

BASIC COSTS (2012-2013)
Tuition and fees: $29,529.
Per-credit charge: $333.
Room and board: $7,963.
Additional info: Tuition/fee waivers available for adults, minority students.

FINANCIAL AID PICTURE (2012-2013)
Students with need: Out of 408 full-time freshmen who applied for aid, 353 were judged to have need. Of these, 353 received aid, and 98 had their full need met. Average financial aid package met 91% of need; average scholarship/grant was $20,792; average loan was $3,529. For part-time students, average financial aid package was $10,297.
Students without need: 55 full-time freshmen who did not demonstrate need for aid received scholarships/grants; average award was $18,715. No-need awards available for academics, alumni affiliation, art, leadership, minority status, music/drama, religious affiliation.
Scholarships offered: United Methodist Service to Community Grant; $12,000 to $15,000 per year; awarded to United Methodist students who have excellent record of community service or have expressed desire to serve; number of awards varies. Wesley Service Scholarship; $500 per year; students commit to serve 80 hours of community service a year, keep service journal, read assigned readings, and attend monthly service reflection meetings; number of awards varies. George Washington Carver Scholarship; $11,000 to $15,000 per year; for outstanding freshmen from distinctive and broadly diverse backgrounds who bring in a multicultural perspective; number of awards varies. George Washington Carver Fellowship; 3/4 to full tuition; awarded to outstanding freshmen from distinctive and broadly diverse backgrounds who exhibit potential for leadership and service. John C. Culver Fellowship; minimum of $12,500, awarded to students who show interest in politics, history, or public service; up to 5 awarded. Great Ape Trust Scholarship; $15,000 renewable; for students who are interested in intelligence and conservation of great apes; two awarded.
Cumulative student debt: 89% of graduating class had student loans; average debt was $35,228.
Additional info: Music and theater scholarships based on audition. Art scholarships based on portfolio.

FINANCIAL AID PROCEDURES
Forms required: FAFSA.
Dates and Deadlines: Priority date 4/1; no closing date. Applicants notified on a rolling basis starting 3/15; must reply by 5/1 or within 3 week(s) of notification.
Transfers: No deadline.

CONTACT
Tracie Pavon, Assistant Vice President for Enrollment and Financial Assistance
701 North C Street, Indianola, IA 50125
(515) 961-1630

Southeastern Community College
West Burlington, Iowa
www.scciowa.edu Federal Code: 004603

2-year public community and junior college in large town.
Enrollment: 2,121 undergrads, 31% part-time. 263 full-time freshmen.
Selectivity: Open admission; but selective for some programs.

BASIC COSTS (2012-2013)
Tuition and fees: $4,260; out-of-state residents $4,410.
Per-credit charge: $142; out-of-state residents $147.
Room and board: $5,190.

FINANCIAL AID PICTURE (2011-2012)
Students with need: Out of 261 full-time freshmen who applied for aid, 226 were judged to have need. Of these, 226 received aid. For part-time students, average financial aid package was $4,819.
Students without need: 7 full-time freshmen who did not demonstrate need for aid received scholarships/grants; average award was $2,350. No-need awards available for academics, art, athletics, minority status.
Scholarships offered: 35 full-time freshmen received athletic scholarships; average amount $2,727.

FINANCIAL AID PROCEDURES
Forms required: FAFSA.
Dates and Deadlines: Applicants notified on a rolling basis starting 3/1; must reply within 4 week(s) of notification.

CONTACT
Gwen Scholer, Financial Aid Director
1500 West Agency Road, West Burlington, IA 52655-0605
(319) 752-2731 ext. 5014

Southwestern Community College
Creston, Iowa
www.swcciowa.edu Federal Code: 001857

2-year public community college in small town.
Enrollment: 1,666 undergrads.
Selectivity: Open admission; but selective for some programs.

BASIC COSTS (2012-2013)
Tuition and fees: $4,440; out-of-state residents $4,635.
Per-credit charge: $136; out-of-state residents $142.
Room and board: $5,650.
Additional info: Online tuition: $152 per credit hour, inclusive of required fees.

FINANCIAL AID PICTURE
Students with need: Need-based aid available for full-time and part-time students. Work study available nights, weekends, and for part-time students.
Students without need: No-need awards available for academics, athletics, leadership, music/drama, state/district residency.

FINANCIAL AID PROCEDURES
Forms required: FAFSA.
Dates and Deadlines: Closing date 7/1. Applicants notified on a rolling basis starting 6/1; must reply within 2 week(s) of notification.

CONTACT
Tracy Davis, Financial Aid Officer
1501 West Townline Street, Creston, IA 50801
(641) 782-1333

University of Dubuque
Dubuque, Iowa
www.dbq.edu Federal Code: 001891

4-year private university and seminary college in small city, affiliated with Presbyterian Church (USA).
Enrollment: 1,657 undergrads, 9% part-time. 428 full-time freshmen.
Selectivity: Admits over 75% of applicants.

BASIC COSTS (2012-2013)
Tuition and fees: $24,530.
Room and board: $7,880.

FINANCIAL AID PICTURE (2012-2013)
Students with need: Need-based aid available for full-time and part-time students. Work study available nights, weekends, and for part-time students.
Students without need: No-need awards available for academics, alumni affiliation, leadership, music/drama, religious affiliation, ROTC.

FINANCIAL AID PROCEDURES
Forms required: FAFSA.

Dates and Deadlines: Priority date 4/1; no closing date. Applicants notified on a rolling basis starting 3/1; must reply within 3 week(s) of notification.
Transfers: No deadline. Applicants notified on a rolling basis starting 3/1; must reply within 3 week(s) of notification. Iowa Tuition Grant available to Iowa residents.

CONTACT
Timothy Kremer, Dean of Student Financial Planning and Scholarships
2000 University Avenue, Dubuque, IA 52001-5099
(563) 589-3396

University of Iowa
Iowa City, Iowa
www.uiowa.edu Federal Code: 001892

4-year public university in small city.
Enrollment: 21,320 undergrads, 9% part-time. 4,565 full-time freshmen.
Selectivity: Admits over 75% of applicants.

BASIC COSTS (2012-2013)
Tuition and fees: $8,057; out-of-state residents $26,279.
Per-credit charge: $279; out-of-state residents $1,038.
Room and board: $8,343.

FINANCIAL AID PICTURE (2011-2012)
Students with need: Out of 3,355 full-time freshmen who applied for aid, 2,163 were judged to have need. Of these, 2,109 received aid, and 620 had their full need met. Average financial aid package met 63% of need; average scholarship/grant was $6,824; average loan was $4,805. For part-time students, average financial aid package was $5,827.
Students without need: 1,070 full-time freshmen who did not demonstrate need for aid received scholarships/grants; average award was $4,388. No-need awards available for academics, alumni affiliation, art, athletics, leadership, music/drama, ROTC, state/district residency.
Scholarships offered: ***Merit:*** Presidential Scholarship; $13,000 per year for 4 years; based on ACT/SAT, GPA, essay; 20 awarded each year. Old Gold Scholarship; $3,000 per year for 4 years; 30 ACT (or a combined SAT critical reading and math score of 1330) and a 3.80 grade-point average (GPA) on a 4.00 scale. National Scholars Award; $4,490 per year for 4 years; for nonresidents who are U.S residents or permanent residents with a Regent Admission Index score of 290. Iowa Scholars Award; $1,000 one-time award; for first-year Iowa residents with 27 ACT/1210 SAT and 3.8 GPA or 30 ACT/1330 SAT and 3.7 GPA. Iowa Heritage Award; $1,500 per year for up to four years; for nonresident students who have a parent, step-parent, legal guardian, or grandparent who graduated from UI. Advantage Iowa Award; from $2,000 to full resident tuition; for first-year students who are U.S. citizens or permanent residents whose enrollment will contribute to a diverse learning environment; eligibility criteria vary, but may include race/ethnicity, socioeconomic factors, first-generation college student, participation in federal Upward Bound program. ***Athletic:*** 109 full-time freshmen received athletic scholarships; average amount $20,455.
Cumulative student debt: 55% of graduating class had student loans; average debt was $28,554.

FINANCIAL AID PROCEDURES
Forms required: FAFSA, institutional form.
Dates and Deadlines: Applicants notified on a rolling basis starting 3/15; must reply by 5/1 or within 2 week(s) of notification.
Transfers: No deadline. Applicants notified on a rolling basis starting 3/15; must reply by 5/1 or within 2 week(s) of notification.

CONTACT
Mark Warner, Director of Student Financial Aid
107 Calvin Hall, Iowa City, IA 52242-1396
(319) 335-1450

University of Northern Iowa
Cedar Falls, Iowa
www.uni.edu Federal Code: 001890

4-year public university in small city.
Enrollment: 10,513 undergrads, 8% part-time. 1,678 full-time freshmen.
Selectivity: Admits over 75% of applicants.

BASIC COSTS (2012-2013)
Tuition and fees: $7,635; out-of-state residents $16,721.
Per-credit charge: $277; out-of-state residents $656.
Room and board: $7,597.
Additional info: Differential tuition for upper division business majors.

FINANCIAL AID PICTURE (2011-2012)
Students with need: Out of 1,645 full-time freshmen who applied for aid, 1,189 were judged to have need. Of these, 1,150 received aid, and 213 had their full need met. Average financial aid package met 69% of need; average scholarship/grant was $4,749; average loan was $2,839. For part-time students, average financial aid package was $7,389.
Students without need: 332 full-time freshmen who did not demonstrate need for aid received scholarships/grants; average award was $3,616. No-need awards available for academics, alumni affiliation, art, athletics, leadership, minority status, music/drama, ROTC, state/district residency.
Scholarships offered: ***Merit:*** Presidential Scholarship Award; $8,000/year for up to 4 years; must be in upper 10% of high school class with 29 ACT or Regent Admission Index of 335 and involved in leadership and service activities; 20 available. Distinguished Scholar Award for Iowans; $1,000-$2,500/year, renewable for a 2nd year; for Iowa residents with 28 ACT or Regent Admission Index of 300. ***Athletic:*** 49 full-time freshmen received athletic scholarships; average amount $8,922.
Cumulative student debt: 77% of graduating class had student loans; average debt was $23,575.

FINANCIAL AID PROCEDURES
Forms required: FAFSA.
Dates and Deadlines: Applicants notified on a rolling basis starting 3/1.

CONTACT
Joyce Morrow, Director Financial Aid and Student Employment
1227 West 27th Street, Cedar Falls, IA 50614-0018
(319) 273-2700

Upper Iowa University
Fayette, Iowa
www.uiu.edu Federal Code: 001893

4-year private university and liberal arts college in rural community.
Enrollment: 4,531 undergrads, 34% part-time. 230 full-time freshmen.
Selectivity: Admits 50 to 75% of applicants.

BASIC COSTS (2012-2013)
Tuition and fees: $24,400.
Per-credit charge: $850.
Room and board: $7,290.

FINANCIAL AID PICTURE (2012-2013)
Students with need: Out of 195 full-time freshmen who applied for aid, 195 were judged to have need. Of these, 195 received aid. Average financial aid package met 37% of need; average scholarship/grant was $6,260; average loan was $2,851. For part-time students, average financial aid package was $6,357.
Students without need: 57 full-time freshmen who did not demonstrate need for aid received scholarships/grants; average award was $7,900. No-need awards available for academics, alumni affiliation, athletics.
Scholarships offered: 40 full-time freshmen received athletic scholarships; average amount $10,218.

Cumulative student debt: 91% of graduating class had student loans; average debt was $27,361.

FINANCIAL AID PROCEDURES

Forms required: FAFSA.

Dates and Deadlines: Priority date 3/1; no closing date. Applicants notified on a rolling basis starting 3/1; must reply within 9 week(s) of notification.

Transfers: No deadline. Applicants notified on a rolling basis starting 7/1; must reply within 8 week(s) of notification.

CONTACT

Jobyna Johnston, Vice President for Admissions and Financial Aid
Parker Fox Hall, Fayette, IA 52142
(800) 553-4150 ext. 3

Vatterott College: Des Moines

Des Moines, Iowa
www.vatterott-college.edu Federal Code: 026092

2-year for-profit health science and technical college in large city.
Enrollment: 208 undergrads.
Selectivity: Open admission.

BASIC COSTS (2012-2013)

Additional info: Estimated program costs as of June 2012: diploma (40 weeks) $18,100 - $18,900, (60 weeks) $24,500 - $27,300; associate degree (70 weeks) $30,350 - $38,350, (90 weeks) $39,750. All costs, which include tuition, fees, books and supplies, and taxes, are subject to change.

FINANCIAL AID PICTURE

Students with need: Need-based aid available for full-time students.

Students without need: This college awards aid only to students with need.

Scholarships offered: Make the Grade Scholarship; up to $1,000; based on final semester grades; available for 1 year after high school graduation.

FINANCIAL AID PROCEDURES

Forms required: FAFSA.

Dates and Deadlines: Applicants notified on a rolling basis.

CONTACT

Afton Erdmann, Financial Aid Administrator
7000 Fleur Drive, Des Moines, IA 50321
(515) 309-9000

Waldorf College

Forest City, Iowa
www.waldorf.edu Federal Code: 001895

4-year private liberal arts college in small town, affiliated with Evangelical Lutheran Church in America.
Enrollment: 839 undergrads, 12% part-time. 171 full-time freshmen.
Selectivity: Admits 50 to 75% of applicants.

BASIC COSTS (2012-2013)

Tuition and fees: $19,820.
Per-credit charge: $512.
Room and board: $6,688.

FINANCIAL AID PICTURE (2011-2012)

Students with need: Out of 162 full-time freshmen who applied for aid, 148 were judged to have need. Of these, 148 received aid, and 17 had their full need met. Average financial aid package met 71% of need; average scholarship/grant was $9,744; average loan was $3,298. For part-time students, average financial aid package was $4,579.

Students without need: 20 full-time freshmen who did not demonstrate need for aid received scholarships/grants; average award was $5,210. No-need awards available for academics, alumni affiliation, athletics, job skills, leadership, music/drama, religious affiliation, state/district residency.

Scholarships offered: 24 full-time freshmen received athletic scholarships; average amount $3,882.

Cumulative student debt: 96% of graduating class had student loans; average debt was $29,812.

FINANCIAL AID PROCEDURES

Forms required: FAFSA, institutional form.

Dates and Deadlines: Priority date 3/1; no closing date. Applicants notified on a rolling basis starting 3/1; must reply within 2 week(s) of notification.

Transfers: Applicants notified on a rolling basis starting 3/1; must reply within 2 week(s) of notification.

CONTACT

Duane Polsdofer, Director of Student Financial Aid
106 South Sixth Street, Forest City, IA 50436-1713
(641) 585-8120

Wartburg College

Waverly, Iowa
www.wartburg.edu Federal Code: 001896

4-year private liberal arts college in small town, affiliated with Evangelical Lutheran Church in America.
Enrollment: 1,701 undergrads, 2% part-time. 482 full-time freshmen.
Selectivity: Admits 50 to 75% of applicants.

BASIC COSTS (2013-2014)

Tuition and fees: $34,250.
Room and board: $8,655.

FINANCIAL AID PICTURE (2012-2013)

Students with need: Out of 418 full-time freshmen who applied for aid, 361 were judged to have need. Of these, 361 received aid, and 56 had their full need met. Average financial aid package met 82% of need; average scholarship/grant was $21,689; average loan was $3,767. For part-time students, average financial aid package was $7,018.

Students without need: 118 full-time freshmen who did not demonstrate need for aid received scholarships/grants; average award was $18,266. No-need awards available for academics, alumni affiliation, leadership, music/drama, religious affiliation.

Scholarships offered: Regents scholarship; up to full tuition, fees, room and board; based on 28 ACT (1240 SAT, exclusive of Writing) or rank in top 10% of class; renewable for 4 years with 3.0 GPA. Presidential Scholarship; up to $6,000 per year; based on 25 ACT (1140 SAT, exclusive of Writing) or rank in top 20% of class or 3.5 GPA; renewable for 4 years with 2.7 GPA. Students who participate in Regents Scholarship competition not eligible for Presidential Scholarship.

FINANCIAL AID PROCEDURES

Forms required: FAFSA.

Dates and Deadlines: Priority date 3/1; no closing date. Applicants notified on a rolling basis starting 3/1; must reply within 2 week(s) of notification.

CONTACT

Jennifer Sassman, Director of Financial Aid
100 Wartburg Boulevard, PO Box 1003, Waverly, IA 50677-0903
(319) 352-8262

Western Iowa Tech Community College

Sioux City, Iowa
www.witcc.com Federal Code: 004590

2-year public community college in small city.
Enrollment: 3,745 undergrads, 36% part-time. 582 full-time freshmen.

Selectivity: Open admission; but selective for some programs.

BASIC COSTS (2012-2013)
Tuition and fees: $4,305; out-of-state residents $4,455.
Per-credit charge: $128; out-of-state residents $133.
Room and board: $4,550.

FINANCIAL AID PICTURE
Students with need: Need-based aid available for full-time and part-time students. Work study available nights, weekends, and for part-time students.
Students without need: No-need awards available for academics, leadership, music/drama.

FINANCIAL AID PROCEDURES
Forms required: FAFSA.
Dates and Deadlines: Applicants notified on a rolling basis starting 4/1.

CONTACT
Donald Duzik, Director of Financial Aid
Box 5199, Sioux City, IA 51102-5199
(712) 274-6402

William Penn University
Oskaloosa, Iowa
www.wmpenn.edu Federal Code: 001900

4-year private university and liberal arts college in large town, affiliated with Society of Friends (Quaker).
Enrollment: 1,545 undergrads.
Selectivity: Admits 50 to 75% of applicants.

BASIC COSTS (2012-2013)
Tuition and fees: $23,210.
Per-credit charge: $450.
Room and board: $5,475.

FINANCIAL AID PICTURE
Students with need: Need-based aid available for full-time and part-time students. Work study available nights, weekends, and for part-time students.
Students without need: No-need awards available for academics, alumni affiliation, athletics, leadership, music/drama, religious affiliation.
Scholarships offered: Participation awards for music, drama, media, cheerleading, dance, religious leadership. Academic scholarships; based on high school GPA and ACT/SAT.

FINANCIAL AID PROCEDURES
Forms required: FAFSA.
Dates and Deadlines: Priority date 4/15; no closing date. Applicants notified on a rolling basis starting 1/1; must reply within 3 week(s) of notification.
Transfers: No deadline. Applicants notified on a rolling basis starting 1/1.

CONTACT
Cyndi Peiffer, Director of Financial Aid
201 Trueblood Avenue, Oskaloosa, IA 52577
(641) 673-1060

Kansas

Allen County Community College
Iola, Kansas
www.allencc.edu Federal Code: 001901

2-year public community college in small town.
Enrollment: 3,148 undergrads.
Selectivity: Open admission.

BASIC COSTS (2012-2013)
Tuition and fees: $2,040; out-of-district residents $2,040; out-of-state residents $2,040.
Per-credit charge: $50; out-of-district residents $50; out-of-state residents $50.
Room and board: $4,375.

FINANCIAL AID PICTURE
Students with need: Need-based aid available for full-time and part-time students. Work study available nights, weekends, and for part-time students.
Students without need: No-need awards available for academics, art, athletics, music/drama, state/district residency.
Additional info: Scholarships for livestock judging, cheerleading, choir, dance, drama, art, academic challenge, and student ambassadors.

FINANCIAL AID PROCEDURES
Forms required: FAFSA.
Dates and Deadlines: Closing date 6/1. Applicants notified on a rolling basis starting 6/1; must reply within 2 week(s) of notification.

CONTACT
Vicki Curry, Director of Financial Aid
1801 North Cottonwood, Iola, KS 66749
(620) 365-5116 ext. 221

Baker University
Baldwin City, Kansas
www.bakeru.edu Federal Code: 001903

4-year private liberal arts and teachers college in small town, affiliated with United Methodist Church.
Enrollment: 824 undergrads, 1% part-time. 202 full-time freshmen.
Selectivity: Admits over 75% of applicants.

BASIC COSTS (2012-2013)
Tuition and fees: $24,550.
Per-credit charge: $740.
Room and board: $7,660.
Additional info: Tuition/fee waivers available for minority students.

FINANCIAL AID PICTURE
Students with need: Need-based aid available for full-time and part-time students. Work study available nights, weekends, and for part-time students.
Students without need: No-need awards available for academics, alumni affiliation, art, athletics, music/drama, religious affiliation.

FINANCIAL AID PROCEDURES
Forms required: FAFSA, institutional form.
Dates and Deadlines: Priority date 3/1; no closing date. Applicants notified on a rolling basis starting 3/1; must reply by 5/1 or within 6 week(s) of notification.
Transfers: No deadline. Applicants notified on a rolling basis starting 3/1; must reply within 6 week(s) of notification.

CONTACT
Jeanne Mott, Director of Financial Aid
618 Eighth Street, Baldwin City, KS 66006-0065
(785) 594-4595

Barclay College
Haviland, Kansas
www.barclaycollege.edu Federal Code: 001917

4-year private Bible college in rural community, affiliated with Society of Friends (Quaker).

Enrollment: 236 undergrads, 8% part-time. 40 full-time freshmen.

BASIC COSTS (2012-2013)
Tuition and fees: $14,590.
Room and board: $7,000.

FINANCIAL AID PICTURE
Students with need: Need-based aid available for full-time and part-time students. Work study available nights, weekends, and for part-time students.
Students without need: No-need awards available for academics, alumni affiliation, leadership, music/drama, state/district residency.

FINANCIAL AID PROCEDURES
Forms required: FAFSA, institutional form.
Dates and Deadlines: Priority date 5/31; closing date 7/15. Applicants notified on a rolling basis starting 1/1; must reply within 4 week(s) of notification.

CONTACT
Ryan Haase, Director of Student Financial Services
607 North Kingman, Haviland, KS 67059
(620) 862-5252 ext. 41

Barton County Community College
Great Bend, Kansas
www.bartonccc.edu Federal Code: 004608

2-year public community college in large town.
Enrollment: 4,909 undergrads.
Selectivity: Open admission; but selective for some programs.

BASIC COSTS (2012-2013)
Tuition and fees: $2,620; out-of-state residents $3,540.
Per-credit charge: $57; out-of-state residents $88.
Room and board: $4,880.

FINANCIAL AID PICTURE
Students with need: Need-based aid available for full-time and part-time students.
Students without need: No-need awards available for academics, athletics.

FINANCIAL AID PROCEDURES
Forms required: FAFSA, state aid form.
Dates and Deadlines: Priority date 3/1; no closing date. Applicants notified on a rolling basis starting 6/1; must reply within 4 week(s) of notification.

CONTACT
Myrna Perkins, Assistant Dean of Student Services/Director of Financial Aid
245 North East 30th Road, Great Bend, KS 67530-9283
(620) 792-2701

Benedictine College
Atchison, Kansas
www.benedictine.edu Federal Code: 010256

4-year private liberal arts college in large town, affiliated with Roman Catholic Church.
Enrollment: 1,729 undergrads, 1% part-time. 488 full-time freshmen.
Selectivity: Admits 50 to 75% of applicants.

BASIC COSTS (2012-2013)
Tuition and fees: $22,800.
Per-credit charge: $665.
Room and board: $7,895.

FINANCIAL AID PICTURE (2012-2013)
Students with need: Out of 429 full-time freshmen who applied for aid, 371 were judged to have need. Of these, 371 received aid, and 90 had their full need met. Average financial aid package met 75% of need; average scholarship/grant was $15,283; average loan was $3,724. For part-time students, average financial aid package was $11,568.
Students without need: 87 full-time freshmen who did not demonstrate need for aid received scholarships/grants; average award was $10,012. No-need awards available for academics, alumni affiliation, art, athletics, job skills, leadership, minority status, music/drama, religious affiliation, ROTC.
Scholarships offered: ***Merit:*** Presidential Scholarship: full tuition; maintain 3.5 GPA; 5 awarded. Dean's Scholarship: partial tuition; maintain 3.5 GPA; 5 awarded. ***Athletic:*** 29 full-time freshmen received athletic scholarships; average amount $14,771.
Cumulative student debt: 79% of graduating class had student loans; average debt was $26,980.

FINANCIAL AID PROCEDURES
Forms required: FAFSA.
Dates and Deadlines: Applicants notified on a rolling basis starting 2/1; must reply within 2 week(s) of notification.
Transfers: No deadline. Applicants notified on a rolling basis. Scholarship available for students transferring 2.0 cumulative GPA.

CONTACT
Tony Tanking, Director Financial Aid
1020 North Second Street, Atchison, KS 66002-1499
(913) 360-7484

Bethel College
North Newton, Kansas
www.bethelks.edu Federal Code: 001905

4-year private liberal arts college in large town, affiliated with Mennonite Church.
Enrollment: 472 undergrads, 4% part-time. 126 full-time freshmen.
Selectivity: Admits 50 to 75% of applicants.

BASIC COSTS (2013-2014)
Tuition and fees: $23,500.
Per-credit charge: $840.
Room and board: $7,980.

FINANCIAL AID PICTURE (2011-2012)
Students with need: Out of 121 full-time freshmen who applied for aid, 119 were judged to have need. Of these, 119 received aid, and 49 had their full need met. Average financial aid package met 90% of need; average scholarship/grant was $4,275; average loan was $7,082. For part-time students, average financial aid package was $10,981.
Students without need: 5 full-time freshmen who did not demonstrate need for aid received scholarships/grants; average award was $10,093. No-need awards available for academics, alumni affiliation, art, athletics, minority status, music/drama, religious affiliation.
Scholarships offered: ***Merit:*** Scholarships for academically talented students, ranging from 16% to 50% of tuition. ***Athletic:*** 79 full-time freshmen received athletic scholarships; average amount $4,403.
Cumulative student debt: 78% of graduating class had student loans; average debt was $20,356.

FINANCIAL AID PROCEDURES
Forms required: FAFSA.
Dates and Deadlines: Priority date 4/1; no closing date. Applicants notified on a rolling basis starting 2/15; must reply within 2 week(s) of notification.
Transfers: No deadline. Applicants notified on a rolling basis starting 2/1; must reply within 2 week(s) of notification.

CONTACT
Tony Graber, Director of Financial Aid
300 E 27th Street, North Newton, KS 67117-8061
(800) 522-1887 ext. 232

Butler Community College
El Dorado, Kansas
www.butlercc.edu Federal Code: 001906

2-year public community college in large town.
Enrollment: 9,258 undergrads.
Selectivity: Open admission; but selective for some programs.

BASIC COSTS (2012-2013)
Tuition and fees: $2,700; out-of-district residents $2,700; out-of-state residents $4,380.
Per-credit charge: $74; out-of-district residents $74; out-of-state residents $130.
Room and board: $5,350.
Additional info: Tuition/fee waivers available for unemployed or children of unemployed.

FINANCIAL AID PICTURE
Students with need: Need-based aid available for full-time and part-time students. Work study available nights, weekends, and for part-time students.
Students without need: No-need awards available for academics, art, athletics, music/drama.

FINANCIAL AID PROCEDURES
Forms required: FAFSA, institutional form.
Dates and Deadlines: Priority date 4/1; no closing date. Applicants notified on a rolling basis starting 5/1; must reply within 2 week(s) of notification.
Transfers: Students with 90 hours or more must have classes validated by degree-granting 4-year institution.

CONTACT
Susie Edwards, Director of Financial Aid
901 South Haverhill Road, El Dorado, KS 67042-3280
(316) 322-3121

Central Christian College of Kansas
McPherson, Kansas
www.centralchristian.edu Federal Code: 001908

4-year private liberal arts college in large town, affiliated with Free Methodist Church of North America.
Enrollment: 535 undergrads, 1% part-time. 114 full-time freshmen.
Selectivity: Admits less than 50% of applicants.

BASIC COSTS (2012-2013)
Tuition and fees: $19,050.
Per-credit charge: $525.
Room and board: $6,300.

FINANCIAL AID PICTURE
Students with need: Need-based aid available for full-time and part-time students. Work study available nights, weekends, and for part-time students.
Students without need: No-need awards available for academics, alumni affiliation, athletics, leadership, music/drama, religious affiliation.

FINANCIAL AID PROCEDURES
Forms required: FAFSA.
Dates and Deadlines: Priority date 3/1; no closing date. Applicants notified on a rolling basis starting 3/1; must reply within 4 week(s) of notification.
Transfers: Must reply within 4 week(s) of notification.

CONTACT
Mike Reimer, Director of Financial Aid
1200 South Main, McPherson, KS 67460-5740
(620) 241-0723 ext. 333

Cloud County Community College
Concordia, Kansas
www.cloud.edu Federal Code: 001909

2-year public community college in small town.
Enrollment: 1,105 undergrads, 27% part-time. 276 full-time freshmen.
Selectivity: Open admission.

BASIC COSTS (2012-2013)
Tuition and fees: $2,700; out-of-state residents $2,910.
Per-credit charge: $71; out-of-state residents $133.
Room and board: $5,540.

FINANCIAL AID PICTURE (2012-2013)
Students with need: Average financial aid package met 55% of need; average scholarship/grant was $4,541; average loan was $2,555. For part-time students, average financial aid package was $4,612.
Cumulative student debt: 50% of graduating class had student loans; average debt was $4,138.

FINANCIAL AID PROCEDURES
Forms required: FAFSA.
Dates and Deadlines: Priority date 4/1; no closing date. Applicants notified on a rolling basis starting 5/1; must reply within 4 week(s) of notification.

CONTACT
Suzi Knoettgen, Director of Student Financial Aid
2221 Campus Drive, Concordia, KS 66901-1002
(785) 243-1435 ext. 280

Coffeyville Community College
Coffeyville, Kansas
www.coffeyville.edu Federal Code: 001910

2-year public community and technical college in large town.
Enrollment: 1,792 undergrads.
Selectivity: Open admission.

BASIC COSTS (2012-2013)
Tuition and fees: $1,950; out-of-state residents $3,420.
Per-credit charge: $30; out-of-state residents $79.
Room and board: $5,100.

FINANCIAL AID PICTURE
Students with need: Need-based aid available for full-time and part-time students. Work study available nights, weekends, and for part-time students.
Students without need: No-need awards available for academics, alumni affiliation, art, athletics, leadership, music/drama, state/district residency.

FINANCIAL AID PROCEDURES
Forms required: FAFSA.
Dates and Deadlines: Priority date 8/1; no closing date. Applicants notified on a rolling basis starting 6/20.

CONTACT
Pam Feerer, Director of Financial Aid
400 West 11th Street, Coffeyville, KS 67337-5064
(620) 252-7357

Colby Community College
Colby, Kansas
www.colbycc.edu Federal Code: 001911

2-year public community college in small town.
Enrollment: 1,354 undergrads.
Selectivity: Open admission; but selective for some programs.

BASIC COSTS (2012-2013)
Tuition and fees: $2,850; out-of-state residents $4,410.
Per-credit charge: $57; out-of-state residents $109.
Room and board: $5,110.
Additional info: Nebraska, Colorado, Oklahoma, Texas and Missouri pay a reduced border rate of $76 per credit hour for tuition.

FINANCIAL AID PICTURE
Students with need: Need-based aid available for full-time and part-time students. Work study available nights, weekends, and for part-time students.
Students without need: No-need awards available for academics, athletics, leadership, music/drama.

FINANCIAL AID PROCEDURES
Forms required: FAFSA, state aid form.
Dates and Deadlines: Priority date 6/1; no closing date. Applicants notified on a rolling basis starting 5/1.

CONTACT
Paula Halvorson, Director of Financial Aid
1255 South Range Avenue, Colby, KS 67701
(785) 460-4695

Cowley County Community College
Arkansas City, Kansas
www.cowley.edu Federal Code: 001902

2-year public community and technical college in large town.
Enrollment: 3,888 undergrads, 41% part-time. 801 full-time freshmen.
Selectivity: Open admission; but selective for some programs.

BASIC COSTS (2012-2013)
Tuition and fees: $2,280; out-of-district residents $2,580; out-of-state residents $3,990.
Per-credit charge: $49; out-of-district residents $59; out-of-state residents $106.
Room and board: $4,475.

FINANCIAL AID PICTURE (2012-2013)
Students with need: For part-time students, average financial aid package was $3,330.
Students without need: No-need awards available for academics, alumni affiliation, art, athletics, leadership, music/drama, state/district residency.

FINANCIAL AID PROCEDURES
Forms required: FAFSA.
Dates and Deadlines: Priority date 4/15; no closing date. Applicants notified on a rolling basis starting 1/15; must reply within 2 week(s) of notification.

CONTACT
Sally Palmer, Director of Financial Aid
PO Box 1147, Arkansas City, KS 67005-1147
(620) 442-0430

Dodge City Community College
Dodge City, Kansas
www.dc3.edu Federal Code: 001913

2-year public community and technical college in large town.
Enrollment: 1,865 undergrads.
Selectivity: Open admission; but selective for some programs.

BASIC COSTS (2012-2013)
Tuition and fees: $2,400; out-of-state residents $2,700.
Per-credit charge: $35; out-of-district residents $35; out-of-state residents $45.
Room and board: $4,760.

FINANCIAL AID PICTURE
Students with need: Need-based aid available for full-time and part-time students. Work study available nights, weekends, and for part-time students.
Students without need: No-need awards available for academics, athletics, music/drama, state/district residency.

FINANCIAL AID PROCEDURES
Forms required: FAFSA, institutional form.
Dates and Deadlines: Priority date 3/15; no closing date. Applicants notified on a rolling basis; must reply within 2 week(s) of notification.

CONTACT
Russ McBee, Director of Financial Aid
2501 North 14th Avenue, Dodge City, KS 67801-2399
(620) 227-9336

Donnelly College
Kansas City, Kansas
www.donnelly.edu Federal Code: 001914

2-year private junior and liberal arts college in large city, affiliated with Roman Catholic Church.
Enrollment: 441 undergrads, 42% part-time. 78 full-time freshmen.
Selectivity: Open admission.

BASIC COSTS (2012-2013)
Tuition and fees: $6,552.
Per-credit charge: $234.
Room and board: $6,224.

FINANCIAL AID PICTURE
Students with need: Need-based aid available for full-time and part-time students.
Students without need: No-need awards available for academics, religious affiliation.

FINANCIAL AID PROCEDURES
Forms required: FAFSA, institutional form.
Dates and Deadlines: Priority date 4/1; no closing date. Applicants notified on a rolling basis starting 7/1.
Transfers: Applicants notified on a rolling basis starting 7/1.

CONTACT
Belinda Ogan, Director of Financial Aid
608 North 18th Street, Kansas City, KS 66102-4210
(913) 621-8740

Emporia State University
Emporia, Kansas
www.emporia.edu Federal Code: 001927

4-year public university in large town.
Enrollment: 3,653 undergrads, 10% part-time. 575 full-time freshmen.
Selectivity: Admits 50 to 75% of applicants.

BASIC COSTS (2012-2013)
Tuition and fees: $5,272; out-of-state residents $16,326.
Per-credit charge: $137; out-of-state residents $505.
Room and board: $6,628.

FINANCIAL AID PICTURE (2011-2012)
Students with need: Out of 507 full-time freshmen who applied for aid, 383 were judged to have need. Of these, 383 received aid, and 53 had their full need met. Average financial aid package met 65% of need; average scholarship/grant was $2,628; average loan was $5,026. For part-time students, average financial aid package was $3,135.

Students without need: 128 full-time freshmen who did not demonstrate need for aid received scholarships/grants; average award was $1,688. No-need awards available for academics, alumni affiliation, art, athletics, job skills, leadership, minority status, music/drama, religious affiliation, state/district residency.
Scholarships offered: ***Merit:*** Presidential Academic Awards; $1,000 to $1,200 (unlimited number) based on ACT. Challenge Awards; $500 (unlimited number) based on ACT/GPA. Transfer President's Academic Award; $500 to $1,000; based on cumulative GPA or Phi Theta Kappa membership. Guaranteed GPA Scholarship; $500 to $1,200; based on GPA for continuing full-time undergraduates. ***Athletic:*** 45 full-time freshmen received athletic scholarships; average amount $3,118.
Cumulative student debt: 74% of graduating class had student loans; average debt was $23,215.
Additional info: Institution's own payment plan is available.

FINANCIAL AID PROCEDURES
Forms required: FAFSA, state aid form.
Dates and Deadlines: Priority date 3/15; no closing date. Applicants notified on a rolling basis starting 2/2; must reply within 2 week(s) of notification.
Transfers: No deadline. Applicants notified on a rolling basis; must reply within 2 week(s) of notification.

CONTACT
M Henrie, Director of Financial Aid
1200 Commercial, Campus Box 4034, Emporia, KS 66801-5087
(620) 341-5457

Fort Hays State University
Hays, Kansas
www.fhsu.edu Federal Code: 001915

4-year public university in large town.
Enrollment: 5,934 undergrads.

BASIC COSTS (2012-2013)
Tuition and fees: $4,233; out-of-state residents $12,416.
Per-credit charge: $108; out-of-state residents $381.
Room and board: $7,003.

FINANCIAL AID PICTURE
Students with need: Need-based aid available for full-time and part-time students. Work study available nights, weekends, and for part-time students.
Students without need: No-need awards available for academics, art, athletics, leadership, minority status, music/drama.

FINANCIAL AID PROCEDURES
Forms required: FAFSA.
Dates and Deadlines: Priority date 3/15; no closing date. Applicants notified on a rolling basis starting 3/15; must reply within 2 week(s) of notification.
Transfers: No deadline. Applicants notified on a rolling basis starting 3/15; must reply within 3 week(s) of notification.

CONTACT
Craig Karlin, Director of Student Financial Aid
600 Park Street, Hays, KS 67601
(785) 628-4494

Friends University
Wichita, Kansas
www.friends.edu Federal Code: 001918

4-year private university and liberal arts college in large city, affiliated with nondenominational tradition.
Enrollment: 1,737 undergrads, 18% part-time. 240 full-time freshmen.
Selectivity: Admits 50 to 75% of applicants.

BASIC COSTS (2013-2014)
Tuition and fees: $23,430.
Per-credit charge: $775.
Room and board: $6,800.

FINANCIAL AID PICTURE (2011-2012)
Students with need: Out of 232 full-time freshmen who applied for aid, 209 were judged to have need. Of these, 209 received aid, and 61 had their full need met. Average financial aid package met 90% of need; average scholarship/grant was $12,444; average loan was $3,929. For part-time students, average financial aid package was $1,906.
Students without need: 22 full-time freshmen who did not demonstrate need for aid received scholarships/grants; average award was $5,776. No-need awards available for academics, alumni affiliation, art, athletics, leadership, music/drama, religious affiliation.
Scholarships offered: 50 full-time freshmen received athletic scholarships; average amount $2,832.
Cumulative student debt: 86% of graduating class had student loans; average debt was $18,750.

FINANCIAL AID PROCEDURES
Forms required: FAFSA.
Dates and Deadlines: Priority date 3/15; no closing date. Applicants notified on a rolling basis starting 3/1; must reply within 3 week(s) of notification.
Transfers: No deadline. Applicants notified on a rolling basis starting 3/1; must reply within 3 week(s) of notification.

CONTACT
Brandon Pierce, Director of Financial Aid
2100 West University Avenue, Wichita, KS 67213
(800) 794-6945

Garden City Community College
Garden City, Kansas
www.gcccks.edu Federal Code: 001919

2-year public community college in large town.
Enrollment: 1,414 undergrads, 30% part-time. 429 full-time freshmen.
Selectivity: Open admission; but selective for some programs.

BASIC COSTS (2012-2013)
Tuition and fees: $2,310; out-of-state residents $2,910.
Per-credit charge: $50; out-of-state residents $70.
Room and board: $4,700.

FINANCIAL AID PICTURE (2012-2013)
Students with need: 75% of average financial aid package awarded as scholarships/grants, 25% awarded as loans/jobs. Need-based aid available for part-time students. Work study available nights, weekends, and for part-time students.
Students without need: No-need awards available for academics, art, athletics, job skills, leadership, minority status, music/drama, state/district residency.

FINANCIAL AID PROCEDURES
Forms required: FAFSA, institutional form.
Dates and Deadlines: Priority date 3/1; no closing date. Applicants notified on a rolling basis starting 4/15; must reply within 2 week(s) of notification.

CONTACT
Kathleen Blau, Director of Financial Aid
801 Campus Drive, Garden City, KS 67846-6333
(620) 276-9519

Haskell Indian Nations University

Lawrence, Kansas
www.haskell.edu Federal Code: 010438

4-year public university in small city.
Enrollment: 842 undergrads.

BASIC COSTS (2012-2013)
Additional info: Haskell does not charge tuition. On-campus students pay $430 (includes room/board and required fees) for academic year; off-campus students pay $220 (required fees) for academic year.

FINANCIAL AID PICTURE
Students with need: Need-based aid available for full-time and part-time students. Work study available nights, weekends, and for part-time students.
Additional info: Some personal expenses may be offset by Bureau of Indian Affairs grants. Most students qualify for only minimum Pell grant.

FINANCIAL AID PROCEDURES
Forms required: FAFSA.
Dates and Deadlines: Priority date 5/15; no closing date. Applicants notified on a rolling basis starting 3/15; must reply within 9 week(s) of notification.
Transfers: Priority date 11/8; closing date 4/15.

CONTACT
Reta Beaver, Financial Aid Officer
155 Indian Avenue #5031, Lawrence, KS 66046-4800
(785) 830-2718

Hesston College

Hesston, Kansas
www.hesston.edu Federal Code: 001920

2-year private junior and liberal arts college in small town, affiliated with Mennonite Church.
Enrollment: 457 undergrads.
Selectivity: Open admission; but selective for some programs.

BASIC COSTS (2012-2013)
Tuition and fees: $22,622.
Room and board: $7,492.

FINANCIAL AID PICTURE
Students with need: Need-based aid available for full-time and part-time students. Work study available nights, weekends, and for part-time students.
Students without need: No-need awards available for academics, alumni affiliation, art, athletics, job skills, music/drama.

FINANCIAL AID PROCEDURES
Forms required: FAFSA.
Dates and Deadlines: Closing date 4/1. Applicants notified on a rolling basis starting 2/1; must reply within 4 week(s) of notification.
Transfers: No deadline. Applicants notified on a rolling basis starting 2/1.

CONTACT
Marcia Mendez, Financial Aid Director
Box 3000, Hesston, KS 67062-2093
(800) 995-2757

Highland Community College

Highland, Kansas
www.highlandcc.edu Federal Code: 001921

2-year public community college in rural community.
Enrollment: 2,054 undergrads, 48% part-time. 487 full-time freshmen.
Selectivity: Open admission; but selective for out-of-state students.

BASIC COSTS (2012-2013)
Tuition and fees: $2,790; out-of-district residents $3,180; out-of-state residents $4,710.
Per-credit charge: $47; out-of-district residents $60; out-of-state residents $111.
Room and board: $5,120.
Additional info: Out-of-state within 150 miles: $73 per-credit-hour.

FINANCIAL AID PICTURE (2011-2012)
Students with need: 99% of average financial aid package awarded as scholarships/grants, 1% awarded as loans/jobs. Need-based aid available for part-time students. Work study available nights, weekends, and for part-time students.
Students without need: No-need awards available for academics, alumni affiliation, art, athletics, job skills, leadership, music/drama.
Additional info: Auditions and portfolios important for certain scholarship candidates.

FINANCIAL AID PROCEDURES
Forms required: FAFSA.
Dates and Deadlines: Priority date 4/1; no closing date. Applicants notified on a rolling basis starting 4/15; must reply within 4 week(s) of notification.
Transfers: No deadline. Applicants notified on a rolling basis starting 4/1; must reply within 4 week(s) of notification.

CONTACT
Christi Waggoner, Director of Student Financial Aid
606 West Main Street, Highland, KS 66035
(785) 442-6023

Hutchinson Community College

Hutchinson, Kansas
www.hutchcc.edu Federal Code: 001923

2-year public community college in large town.
Enrollment: 4,430 undergrads, 43% part-time. 833 full-time freshmen.
Selectivity: Open admission; but selective for some programs.

BASIC COSTS (2012-2013)
Tuition and fees: $2,520; out-of-state residents $3,450.
Per-credit charge: $67; out-of-state residents $98.
Room and board: $5,150.

FINANCIAL AID PICTURE
Students with need: Need-based aid available for full-time and part-time students.
Students without need: No-need awards available for academics, athletics, minority status, state/district residency.

FINANCIAL AID PROCEDURES
Forms required: FAFSA, institutional form.
Dates and Deadlines: Priority date 2/1; no closing date. Applicants notified on a rolling basis starting 4/1; must reply within 2 week(s) of notification.

CONTACT
Jean Kibbe, Financial Aid Director
1300 North Plum, Hutchinson, KS 67501
(620) 665-3568

Independence Community College

Independence, Kansas
www.indycc.edu Federal Code: 001924

2-year public community and junior college in large town.
Enrollment: 1,166 undergrads.
Selectivity: Open admission.

BASIC COSTS (2012-2013)
Tuition and fees: $2,220; out-of-district residents $2,310; out-of-state residents $3,510.
Per-credit charge: $36; out-of-district residents $39; out-of-state residents $79.
Room and board: $4,700.
Additional info: NE, CO, OK, AR, MO resident: $46.00 per credit hour.

FINANCIAL AID PICTURE
Students with need: Need-based aid available for full-time and part-time students.
Students without need: No-need awards available for academics, athletics.

FINANCIAL AID PROCEDURES
Forms required: FAFSA.
Dates and Deadlines: Priority date 4/1; no closing date. Applicants notified on a rolling basis.

CONTACT
Sheila Smither, Director of Financial Aid
1057 West College Avenue, Independence, KS 67301

Johnson County Community College
Overland Park, Kansas
www.jccc.edu Federal Code: 008244

2-year public community college in very large city.
Enrollment: 20,443 undergrads.
Selectivity: Open admission; but selective for some programs.

BASIC COSTS (2012-2013)
Tuition and fees: $2,520; out-of-district residents $2,970; out-of-state residents $5,910.
Per-credit charge: $84; out-of-district residents $99; out-of-state residents $197.

FINANCIAL AID PICTURE (2012-2013)
Students with need: Need-based aid available for full-time and part-time students.
Students without need: No-need awards available for academics.

FINANCIAL AID PROCEDURES
Forms required: FAFSA, state aid form.
Dates and Deadlines: Priority date 4/1; no closing date. Applicants notified on a rolling basis starting 4/15; must reply within 2 week(s) of notification.

CONTACT
Christal Williams, Program Director for Student Financial Aid
12345 College Boulevard, Overland Park, KS 66210-1299
(913) 469-3840

Kansas City Kansas Community College
Kansas City, Kansas
www.kckcc.edu Federal Code: 001925

2-year public community and career college in very large city.
Enrollment: 6,338 undergrads, 61% part-time. 639 full-time freshmen.
Selectivity: Open admission; but selective for some programs.

BASIC COSTS (2012-2013)
Tuition and fees: $2,250; out-of-state residents $5,610.
Per-credit charge: $62; out-of-state residents $174.

FINANCIAL AID PICTURE (2011-2012)
Students with need: 70% of average financial aid package awarded as scholarships/grants, 30% awarded as loans/jobs. Need-based aid available for part-time students. Work study available nights, weekends, and for part-time students.
Students without need: No-need awards available for academics, art, athletics, music/drama.

FINANCIAL AID PROCEDURES
Forms required: FAFSA.
Dates and Deadlines: Applicants notified on a rolling basis starting 5/1; must reply within 4 week(s) of notification.

CONTACT
Mary Dorr, Director of Financial Aid
7250 State Avenue, Kansas City, KS 66112
(913) 288-7697

Kansas State University
Manhattan, Kansas
www.k-state.edu Federal Code: 001928

4-year public university in small city.
Enrollment: 19,376 undergrads, 9% part-time. 3,540 full-time freshmen.
Selectivity: Admits over 75% of applicants.

BASIC COSTS (2012-2013)
Tuition and fees: $8,047; out-of-state residents $20,146.
Per-credit charge: $244; out-of-state residents $647.
Room and board: $7,450.

FINANCIAL AID PICTURE (2011-2012)
Students with need: Out of 2,720 full-time freshmen who applied for aid, 1,902 were judged to have need. Of these, 1,871 received aid, and 379 had their full need met. Average financial aid package met 81% of need; average scholarship/grant was $4,433; average loan was $3,293. For part-time students, average financial aid package was $9,156.
Students without need: 515 full-time freshmen who did not demonstrate need for aid received scholarships/grants; average award was $4,017. No-need awards available for academics, alumni affiliation, art, athletics, leadership, music/drama, ROTC, state/district residency.
Scholarships offered: 9 full-time freshmen received athletic scholarships; average amount $2,488.
Cumulative student debt: 61% of graduating class had student loans; average debt was $25,147.

FINANCIAL AID PROCEDURES
Forms required: FAFSA.
Dates and Deadlines: Priority date 3/1; no closing date. Applicants notified on a rolling basis starting 4/1; must reply within 2 week(s) of notification.

CONTACT
Larry Moeder, Assistant Vice President for Student Financial Assistance and Admissions
119 Anderson Hall, Manhattan, KS 66506
(785) 532-6420

Kansas Wesleyan University
Salina, Kansas
www.kwu.edu Federal Code: 001929

4-year private university and liberal arts college in small city, affiliated with United Methodist Church.
Enrollment: 683 undergrads, 7% part-time. 139 full-time freshmen.
Selectivity: Admits less than 50% of applicants.

BASIC COSTS (2012-2013)
Tuition and fees: $22,600.
Per-credit charge: $240.
Room and board: $7,400.
Additional info: Tuition/fee waivers available for adults.

FINANCIAL AID PICTURE

Students with need: Need-based aid available for full-time and part-time students.

Students without need: No-need awards available for academics, alumni affiliation, art, athletics, music/drama, state/district residency.

Additional info: Awards available for residence hall students: minimum $7,000 for 3.0 GPA plus ACT score of 22 or SAT of 950 (exclusive of Writing); minimum $8,000 for 3.5 GPA plus ACT score of 22 or SAT score of 1030 (exclusive of Writing); minimum $9,000 for 3.75 GPA plus ACT score of 25 or SAT score of 1140 (exclusive of Writing). Application deadline March 15.

FINANCIAL AID PROCEDURES

Forms required: FAFSA.

Dates and Deadlines: Closing date 3/15. Applicants notified on a rolling basis starting 1/1; must reply by 8/1 or within 3 week(s) of notification.

Transfers: Academic scholarships based upon cumulative GPA of transferring credit hours.

CONTACT

Michelle Jensen, Associate Director of Financial Services
100 East Claflin Avenue, Salina, KS 67401-6196
(785) 827-5541 ext. 1260

Labette Community College

Parsons, Kansas
www.labette.edu Federal Code: 001930

2-year public community college in large town.

Enrollment: 1,746 undergrads.

Selectivity: Open admission; but selective for some programs.

BASIC COSTS (2012-2013)

Tuition and fees: $2,460; out-of-state residents $3,210.

Per-credit charge: $46; out-of-state residents $71.

Additional info: Tuition/fee waivers available for adults, minority students, unemployed or children of unemployed.

FINANCIAL AID PICTURE

Students with need: Need-based aid available for full-time and part-time students. Work study available nights.

Students without need: No-need awards available for academics, leadership.

Scholarships offered: Foundation Scholarships.

FINANCIAL AID PROCEDURES

Forms required: FAFSA.

Dates and Deadlines: Applicants notified on a rolling basis starting 4/4; must reply within 2 week(s) of notification.

CONTACT

Kathy Johnston, Director of Financial Aid
200 South 14th Street, Parsons, KS 67357
(620) 820-1219

Manhattan Area Technical College

Manhattan, Kansas
www.matc.net Federal Code: 005500

2-year public technical college in large town.

Enrollment: 737 undergrads.

Selectivity: Open admission; but selective for some programs.

BASIC COSTS (2012-2013)

Tuition and fees: $3,180; out-of-state residents $3,180.

Per-credit charge: $90; out-of-state residents $90.

FINANCIAL AID PICTURE

Students with need: Need-based aid available for full-time and part-time students.

Students without need: No-need awards available for academics, leadership.

FINANCIAL AID PROCEDURES

Forms required: FAFSA, institutional form.

Dates and Deadlines: Applicants notified on a rolling basis.

CONTACT

Sarah Saueressig, Director of Financial
3136 Dickens Avenue, Manhattan, KS 66503-2499
(785) 587-2800 ext. 105

Manhattan Christian College

Manhattan, Kansas
www.mccks.edu Federal Code: 001931

4-year private Bible college in large town, affiliated with Christian Church.

Enrollment: 317 undergrads.

BASIC COSTS (2012-2013)

Tuition and fees: $12,769.

Per-credit charge: $532.

Room and board: $7,268.

FINANCIAL AID PICTURE

Students with need: Need-based aid available for full-time and part-time students.

Students without need: No-need awards available for academics, leadership.

FINANCIAL AID PROCEDURES

Forms required: FAFSA, state aid form.

Dates and Deadlines: Priority date 4/1; no closing date. Applicants notified on a rolling basis starting 4/1; must reply within 2 week(s) of notification.

Transfers: No deadline. Applicants notified on a rolling basis; must reply within 2 week(s) of notification.

CONTACT

1415 Anderson Avenue, Manhattan, KS 66502

McPherson College

McPherson, Kansas
www.mcpherson.edu Federal Code: 001933

4-year private liberal arts college in large town, affiliated with Church of the Brethren.

Enrollment: 622 undergrads.

BASIC COSTS (2012-2013)

Tuition and fees: $21,216.

Room and board: $7,764.

FINANCIAL AID PICTURE

Students with need: Need-based aid available for full-time and part-time students. Work study available nights, weekends, and for part-time students.

Students without need: No-need awards available for academics, alumni affiliation, art, athletics, music/drama, religious affiliation, state/district residency.

Scholarships offered: Presidential Scholarship; $10,000 each year of attendance for four years; competition in fall and spring; 10 awards given per year.

FINANCIAL AID PROCEDURES

Forms required: FAFSA.

Dates and Deadlines: Priority date 3/1; no closing date. Applicants notified on a rolling basis starting 3/1; must reply within 3 week(s) of notification.
Transfers: No deadline. Applicants notified on a rolling basis; must reply within 3 week(s) of notification.

CONTACT
Brenda Krehbiel, Director of Financial Aid
1600 East Euclid Street, McPherson, KS 67460-1402
(620) 242-0400

MidAmerica Nazarene University
Olathe, Kansas
www.mnu.edu Federal Code: 007032

4-year private university and liberal arts college in small city, affiliated with Church of the Nazarene.
Enrollment: 1,474 undergrads, 21% part-time. 208 full-time freshmen.
Selectivity: Admits 50 to 75% of applicants.

BASIC COSTS (2013-2014)
Tuition and fees: $22,255.
Per-credit charge: $725.
Room and board: $7,200.

FINANCIAL AID PICTURE
Students with need: Need-based aid available for full-time and part-time students.
Students without need: No-need awards available for academics, athletics, music/drama, religious affiliation, ROTC.

FINANCIAL AID PROCEDURES
Forms required: FAFSA.
Dates and Deadlines: Priority date 3/1; no closing date. Applicants notified on a rolling basis starting 1/30; must reply within 2 week(s) of notification.

CONTACT
Perry Diehm, Director of Student Financial Services
2030 East College Way, Olathe, KS 66062-1899
(913) 917-3298

Neosho County Community College
Chanute, Kansas
www.neosho.edu Federal Code: 001936

2-year public community college in small town.
Enrollment: 2,602 undergrads.
Selectivity: Open admission; but selective for some programs.

BASIC COSTS (2012-2013)
Tuition and fees: $2,464; out-of-district residents $2,848; out-of-state residents $3,552.
Room and board: $5,200.

FINANCIAL AID PICTURE (2011-2012)
Students with need: 60% of average financial aid package awarded as scholarships/grants, 40% awarded as loans/jobs. Need-based aid available for part-time students. Work study available nights, weekends, and for part-time students.
Students without need: No-need awards available for academics, art, athletics, job skills, leadership, music/drama, state/district residency.
Scholarships offered: Visual and performing arts, Academic Challenge stipends, industrial engineering and business scholarship.

FINANCIAL AID PROCEDURES
Forms required: FAFSA.
Dates and Deadlines: Priority date 4/1; no closing date. Applicants notified on a rolling basis; must reply within 6 week(s) of notification.
Transfers: All academic transcripts and financial aid transcripts must be on file before aid will be awarded.

CONTACT
Kara Hale, Director of Financial Aid
800 West 14th Street, Chanute, KS 66720
(620) 431-2820 ext. 278

Newman University
Wichita, Kansas
www.newmanu.edu Federal Code: 001939

4-year private university and liberal arts college in large city, affiliated with Roman Catholic Church.
Enrollment: 1,317 undergrads, 13% part-time. 150 full-time freshmen.
Selectivity: Admits less than 50% of applicants.

BASIC COSTS (2012-2013)
Tuition and fees: $22,188.
Per-credit charge: $713.
Room and board: $6,390.
Additional info: Tuition/fee waivers available for adults, unemployed or children of unemployed.

FINANCIAL AID PICTURE (2011-2012)
Students with need: Out of 150 full-time freshmen who applied for aid, 125 were judged to have need. Of these, 125 received aid, and 31 had their full need met. Average financial aid package met 76% of need; average scholarship/grant was $4,894; average loan was $3,105. For part-time students, average financial aid package was $5,395.
Students without need: 10 full-time freshmen who did not demonstrate need for aid received scholarships/grants; average award was $7,400. No-need awards available for academics, alumni affiliation, art, athletics, leadership, music/drama.
Scholarships offered: 44 full-time freshmen received athletic scholarships; average amount $4,994.
Cumulative student debt: 71% of graduating class had student loans; average debt was $32,395.

FINANCIAL AID PROCEDURES
Forms required: FAFSA.
Dates and Deadlines: Priority date 3/1; no closing date. Applicants notified on a rolling basis starting 2/1.

CONTACT
Charly Smith, Director of Financial Aid
3100 McCormick, Wichita, KS 67213-2097
(316) 942-4291 ext. 2103

North Central Kansas Technical College
Beloit, Kansas
www.ncktc.edu Federal Code: 005265

2-year public technical college in small town.
Enrollment: 709 undergrads.
Selectivity: Open admission.

FINANCIAL AID PICTURE
Students with need: Need-based aid available for full-time and part-time students. Work study available nights.
Students without need: This college awards aid only to students with need.

FINANCIAL AID PROCEDURES
Forms required: FAFSA, state aid form.

CONTACT
Gary Odle, Financial Aid Director
PO Box 507, Beloit, KS 67420
(800) 658-4655

Ottawa University

Ottawa, Kansas
www.ottawa.edu Federal Code: 001937

4-year private university and liberal arts college in large town, affiliated with American Baptist Churches in the USA.
Enrollment: 593 undergrads.

BASIC COSTS (2012-2013)
Tuition and fees: $23,000.
Per-credit charge: $933.
Room and board: $6,500.

FINANCIAL AID PICTURE
Students with need: Need-based aid available for full-time and part-time students. Work study available nights, weekends, and for part-time students.
Students without need: No-need awards available for academics, alumni affiliation, athletics, music/drama, religious affiliation.

FINANCIAL AID PROCEDURES
Forms required: FAFSA.
Dates and Deadlines: Priority date 3/15; no closing date. Applicants notified on a rolling basis starting 2/1; must reply within 4 week(s) of notification.
Transfers: No deadline. Applicants notified on a rolling basis starting 2/1; must reply within 4 week(s) of notification.

CONTACT
Gary Bateman, Financial Aid Director
1001 South Cedar Street, #17, Ottawa, KS 66067-3399
(785) 242-5200 ext. 5571

Pittsburg State University

Pittsburg, Kansas
www.pittstate.edu Federal Code: 001926

4-year public university and business college in large town.
Enrollment: 5,780 undergrads, 9% part-time. 1,036 full-time freshmen.
Selectivity: Admits over 75% of applicants.

BASIC COSTS (2012-2013)
Tuition and fees: $5,494; out-of-state residents $15,050.
Per-credit charge: $147; out-of-state residents $465.
Room and board: $6,538.

FINANCIAL AID PICTURE
Students with need: Need-based aid available for full-time and part-time students. Work study available nights, weekends, and for part-time students.
Students without need: No-need awards available for academics, alumni affiliation, art, athletics, leadership, music/drama, ROTC.

FINANCIAL AID PROCEDURES
Forms required: FAFSA, state aid form.
Dates and Deadlines: Priority date 3/1; no closing date. Applicants notified on a rolling basis; must reply within 2 week(s) of notification.
Transfers: No deadline. Applicants notified on a rolling basis. Transfer student scholarships available.

CONTACT
Tammy Higgins, Director of Student Financial Assistance
1701 South Broadway, Pittsburg, KS 66762
(620) 235-4240

Pratt Community College

Pratt, Kansas
www.prattcc.edu Federal Code: 001938

2-year public community and technical college in small town.
Enrollment: 684 full-time undergrads.
Selectivity: Open admission; but selective for some programs.

BASIC COSTS (2012-2013)
Tuition and fees: $2,730; out-of-state residents $2,910.
Per-credit charge: $54; out-of-state residents $60.
Room and board: $5,159.

FINANCIAL AID PICTURE
Students with need: Need-based aid available for full-time and part-time students.
Students without need: No-need awards available for academics, art, athletics, leadership, minority status, music/drama, state/district residency.

FINANCIAL AID PROCEDURES
Forms required: FAFSA, institutional form.
Dates and Deadlines: Priority date 5/1; closing date 8/1. Applicants notified on a rolling basis starting 2/1; must reply within 2 week(s) of notification.

CONTACT
Nikki Powell, Director of Financial Aid
348 Northeast State Route 61, Pratt, KS 67124-8317
(620) 450-2248

Seward County Community College

Liberal, Kansas
www.sccc.edu Federal Code: 008228

2-year public community college in large town.
Enrollment: 1,297 undergrads.
Selectivity: Open admission.

BASIC COSTS (2012-2013)
Tuition and fees: $2,160; out-of-state residents $3,150.
Per-credit charge: $42; out-of-state residents $75.
Room and board: $4,320.

FINANCIAL AID PICTURE
Students with need: Need-based aid available for full-time and part-time students.
Students without need: No-need awards available for academics, athletics.

FINANCIAL AID PROCEDURES
Forms required: FAFSA, institutional form.
Dates and Deadlines: Priority date 4/1; no closing date. Applicants notified on a rolling basis starting 6/15; must reply within 4 week(s) of notification.

CONTACT
Donna Fisher, Financial Aid Director
1801 North Kansas Avenue, Liberal, KS 67905-1137
(620) 417-1110

Southwestern College

Winfield, Kansas
www.sckans.edu Federal Code: 001940

4-year private liberal arts college in large town, affiliated with United Methodist Church.
Enrollment: 1,252 undergrads, 58% part-time. 160 full-time freshmen.
Selectivity: Admits over 75% of applicants.

BASIC COSTS (2012-2013)
Tuition and fees: $22,756.
Per-credit charge: $942.
Room and board: $6,514.

FINANCIAL AID PICTURE (2011-2012)
Students with need: Out of 146 full-time freshmen who applied for aid, 131 were judged to have need. Of these, 131 received aid, and 16 had their full need met. Average financial aid package met 72% of need; average scholarship/grant was $14,578; average loan was $4,372. For part-time students, average financial aid package was $6,356.
Students without need: 29 full-time freshmen who did not demonstrate need for aid received scholarships/grants; average award was $7,231. No-need awards available for academics, athletics, leadership, minority status, music/drama.
Scholarships offered: ***Merit:*** Presidential Scholarship; based on GPA, SAT/ACT, essay, resume, leadership, community service. Scholarships for major; based on GPA, SAT, essay, interview; 3 awarded. ***Athletic:*** 18 full-time freshmen received athletic scholarships; average amount $3,639.
Cumulative student debt: 81% of graduating class had student loans; average debt was $34,056.

FINANCIAL AID PROCEDURES
Forms required: FAFSA, institutional form.
Dates and Deadlines: Priority date 4/1; closing date 8/15. Applicants notified on a rolling basis starting 2/1; must reply within 2 week(s) of notification.
Transfers: Applicants notified on a rolling basis starting 2/1; must reply within 2 week(s) of notification. Activity grants and scholarships, except for presidential scholarship and premier scholarships, available to transfer students. Phi Theta Kappa scholarship available for transfer students who are members.

CONTACT
Brenda Hicks, Director of Financial Aid
100 College Street, Winfield, KS 67156
(620) 229-6215

Sterling College
Sterling, Kansas
www.sterling.edu Federal Code: 001945

4-year private liberal arts college in small town, affiliated with Presbyterian Church (USA).
Enrollment: 617 undergrads, 7% part-time. 139 full-time freshmen.
Selectivity: Admits 50 to 75% of applicants.

BASIC COSTS (2012-2013)
Tuition and fees: $21,075.
Room and board: $7,172.

FINANCIAL AID PICTURE (2012-2013)
Students with need: Average financial aid package met 92% of need; average scholarship/grant was $11,677; average loan was $4,382. For part-time students, average financial aid package was $11,028.
Students without need: No-need awards available for academics, alumni affiliation, art, athletics, leadership, music/drama.
Cumulative student debt: 87% of graduating class had student loans; average debt was $30,251.

FINANCIAL AID PROCEDURES
Forms required: FAFSA.
Dates and Deadlines: Priority date 3/15; no closing date. Applicants notified on a rolling basis starting 2/1; must reply within 3 week(s) of notification.
Transfers: No deadline. Applicants notified on a rolling basis; must reply within 2 week(s) of notification.

CONTACT
Mitzi Suhler, Financial Aid Coordinator
125 West Cooper, Sterling, KS 67579
(620) 278-4207

Tabor College
Hillsboro, Kansas
www.tabor.edu Federal Code: 001946

4-year private liberal arts college in small town, affiliated with Mennonite Brethren Church.
Enrollment: 743 undergrads, 22% part-time. 140 full-time freshmen.
Selectivity: Admits over 75% of applicants.

BASIC COSTS (2012-2013)
Tuition and fees: $21,740.
Per-credit charge: $880.
Room and board: $8,120.
Additional info: Tuition/fee waivers available for adults.

FINANCIAL AID PICTURE (2012-2013)
Students with need: Out of 140 full-time freshmen who applied for aid, 129 were judged to have need. Of these, 129 received aid, and 37 had their full need met. Average financial aid package met 88% of need; average scholarship/grant was $4,550; average loan was $9,062. For part-time students, average financial aid package was $10,489.
Students without need: 11 full-time freshmen who did not demonstrate need for aid received scholarships/grants; average award was $9,815. No-need awards available for academics, alumni affiliation, athletics, leadership, music/drama, religious affiliation, state/district residency.
Scholarships offered: 92 full-time freshmen received athletic scholarships; average amount $4,564.
Cumulative student debt: 82% of graduating class had student loans; average debt was $26,129.

FINANCIAL AID PROCEDURES
Forms required: FAFSA.
Dates and Deadlines: Priority date 3/1; no closing date. Applicants notified on a rolling basis starting 2/15; must reply within 4 week(s) of notification.
Transfers: No deadline. Applicants notified on a rolling basis starting 2/20; must reply within 4 week(s) of notification. Transfer students with over 20 transferable credit hours not eligible for Presidential, National Merit or Dean's scholarships.

CONTACT
Scott Franz, Director of Student Financial Assistance
400 South Jefferson, Hillsboro, KS 67063-7135
(620) 947-3121 ext. 1726

University of Kansas
Lawrence, Kansas
www.ku.edu Federal Code: 001948

4-year public university in small city.
Enrollment: 18,381 undergrads, 10% part-time. 3,495 full-time freshmen.
Selectivity: Admits over 75% of applicants.

BASIC COSTS (2012-2013)
Tuition and fees: $9,678; out-of-state residents $23,748.
Per-credit charge: $293; out-of-state residents $762.
Room and board: $7,258.
Additional info: Tuition at time of enrollment locked for 4 years.

FINANCIAL AID PICTURE (2011-2012)
Students with need: Out of 2,697 full-time freshmen who applied for aid, 1,771 were judged to have need. Of these, 1,683 received aid, and 240 had

their full need met. Average financial aid package met 54% of need; average scholarship/grant was $5,106; average loan was $3,394. For part-time students, average financial aid package was $5,726.
Students without need: 542 full-time freshmen who did not demonstrate need for aid received scholarships/grants; average award was $3,470. No-need awards available for academics, alumni affiliation, art, athletics, leadership, minority status, music/drama, ROTC, state/district residency.
Scholarships offered: 99 full-time freshmen received athletic scholarships; average amount $21,769.
Cumulative student debt: 51% of graduating class had student loans; average debt was $23,506.

FINANCIAL AID PROCEDURES

Forms required: FAFSA.
Dates and Deadlines: Priority date 3/1; no closing date. Applicants notified on a rolling basis starting 4/1; must reply within 4 week(s) of notification.

CONTACT

Brenda Maigaard, Assistant Vice Provost
1502 Iowa Street, Lawrence, KS 66045-7576
(785) 864-4700

University of Kansas Medical Center

Kansas City, Kansas
www.kumc.edu Federal Code: 001948

Upper-division public university and health science college in very large city.
Enrollment: 427 undergrads, 17% part-time.

BASIC COSTS (2012-2013)

Tuition and fees: $8,317; out-of-state residents $21,039.
Per-credit charge: $261; out-of-state residents $685.
Additional info: Tuition at time of enrollment locked for 2 years.

FINANCIAL AID PICTURE (2011-2012)

Students with need: Average financial aid package for all full-time undergraduates was $14,927; for part-time $9,171. 32% awarded as scholarships/grants, 68% awarded as loans/jobs. Work study available nights, weekends, and for part-time students.
Students without need: No-need awards available for academics, leadership, state/district residency.

CONTACT

Sara Honeck, Director of Student Financial Aid
Office of the Registrar, Mail Stop 4029, Kansas City, KS 66160-7116
(913) 588-5170

University of St. Mary

Leavenworth, Kansas
www.stmary.edu Federal Code: 001943

4-year private university in large town, affiliated with Roman Catholic Church.
Enrollment: 787 undergrads, 26% part-time. 116 full-time freshmen.
Selectivity: Admits less than 50% of applicants.

BASIC COSTS (2013-2014)

Tuition and fees: $23,170.
Per-credit charge: $735.
Room and board: $7,050.

FINANCIAL AID PICTURE (2011-2012)

Students with need: Out of 94 full-time freshmen who applied for aid, 91 were judged to have need. Of these, 87 received aid, and 16 had their full need met. Average financial aid package met 41% of need; average scholarship/grant was $7,632; average loan was $2,267. For part-time students, average financial aid package was $7,136.
Students without need: 16 full-time freshmen who did not demonstrate need for aid received scholarships/grants; average award was $8,712. No-need awards available for academics, art, athletics, leadership, music/drama.
Scholarships offered: ***Merit:*** Essays may be required for scholarship applicants. Auditions recommended for music and drama scholarship applicants. Portfolio reviews for art award applicants. ***Athletic:*** 71 full-time freshmen received athletic scholarships; average amount $1,363.
Cumulative student debt: 96% of graduating class had student loans; average debt was $22,914.

FINANCIAL AID PROCEDURES

Forms required: FAFSA.
Dates and Deadlines: Priority date 4/1; no closing date. Applicants notified on a rolling basis starting 2/1; must reply within 2 week(s) of notification.
Transfers: No deadline. Applicants notified on a rolling basis starting 2/1; must reply within 2 week(s) of notification.

CONTACT

Annissa Epperson, Director of Financial Aid
4100 South Fourth Street Trafficway, Leavenworth, KS 66048
(913) 758-6172

Washburn University

Topeka, Kansas
www.washburn.edu Federal Code: 001949

4-year public university in small city.
Enrollment: 5,626 undergrads, 27% part-time. 803 full-time freshmen.
Selectivity: Open admission; but selective for some programs.

BASIC COSTS (2012-2013)

Tuition and fees: $6,836; out-of-state residents $15,356.
Per-credit charge: $225; out-of-state residents $509.
Room and board: $6,216.

FINANCIAL AID PICTURE (2012-2013)

Students with need: Out of 743 full-time freshmen who applied for aid, 506 were judged to have need. Of these, 506 received aid, and 79 had their full need met. Average financial aid package met 42% of need; average scholarship/grant was $5,022; average loan was $3,490. For part-time students, average financial aid package was $8,263.
Students without need: 169 full-time freshmen who did not demonstrate need for aid received scholarships/grants; average award was $2,589. No-need awards available for academics, alumni affiliation, art, athletics, job skills, leadership, minority status, music/drama, religious affiliation, ROTC, state/district residency.
Scholarships offered: 39 full-time freshmen received athletic scholarships; average amount $5,357.
Cumulative student debt: 61% of graduating class had student loans; average debt was $17,995.

FINANCIAL AID PROCEDURES

Forms required: FAFSA.
Dates and Deadlines: Priority date 2/15; no closing date. Applicants notified on a rolling basis starting 4/1; must reply within 4 week(s) of notification.
Transfers: No deadline. Applicants notified on a rolling basis starting 4/1; must reply within 4 week(s) of notification.

CONTACT

Gail Palmer, Director of Financial Aid
1700 SW College Avenue, Morgan 114, Topeka, KS 66621
(785) 670-1151

Wichita State University

Wichita, Kansas
www.wichita.edu Federal Code: 001950

4-year public university in large city.
Enrollment: 11,149 undergrads, 24% part-time. 1,146 full-time freshmen.
Selectivity: Admits over 75% of applicants.

BASIC COSTS (2012-2013)
Tuition and fees: $6,442; out-of-state residents $14,476.
Per-credit charge: $174; out-of-state residents $441.
Room and board: $6,460.

FINANCIAL AID PICTURE (2011-2012)
Students with need: Out of 1,079 full-time freshmen who applied for aid, 522 were judged to have need. Of these, 512 received aid, and 371 had their full need met. Average financial aid package met 65% of need; average scholarship/grant was $3,947; average loan was $3,203. For part-time students, average financial aid package was $5,950.
Students without need: 412 full-time freshmen who did not demonstrate need for aid received scholarships/grants; average award was $2,842. No-need awards available for academics, alumni affiliation, art, athletics, leadership, music/drama.
Scholarships offered: 45 full-time freshmen received athletic scholarships; average amount $7,804.
Cumulative student debt: 53% of graduating class had student loans; average debt was $21,068.

FINANCIAL AID PROCEDURES
Forms required: FAFSA.
Dates and Deadlines: Priority date 3/1; no closing date. Applicants notified on a rolling basis starting 3/15; must reply within 2 week(s) of notification.

CONTACT
Deborah Byers, Director of Financial Aid
1845 Fairmount, Box 124, Wichita, KS 67260-0124
(316) 978-3430

Kentucky

Alice Lloyd College

Pippa Passes, Kentucky
www.alc.edu Federal Code: 001951

4-year private liberal arts college in rural community.
Enrollment: 594 undergrads, 2% part-time.
Selectivity: Admits less than 50% of applicants.

BASIC COSTS (2012-2013)
Tuition and fees: $10,100.
Per-credit charge: $212.
Room and board: $5,140.
Additional info: Guaranteed tuition for students from 108-county central Appalachian service area in Kentucky, West Virginia, Virginia, Tennessee, and Ohio. Tuition/fee waivers available for minority students.

FINANCIAL AID PICTURE
Students with need: Need-based aid available for full-time and part-time students. Work study available nights, weekends, and for part-time students.
Students without need: No-need awards available for athletics, minority status, state/district residency.
Scholarships offered: Alice Lloyd Scholars Program; tuition, room, board, fees, and books; awarded to up to 3 freshmen a year.
Additional info: All students receive financial aid through student work program. No student denied admission because of inability to pay. All full-time students required to work minimum of 10 hours per week.

FINANCIAL AID PROCEDURES
Forms required: FAFSA.
Dates and Deadlines: Priority date 3/15; no closing date. Applicants notified on a rolling basis starting 4/1; must reply within 6 week(s) of notification.
Transfers: Closing date 3/15. Tuition guarantee only for total of 10 semesters of course work from all schools attended.

CONTACT
Jacqueline Stewart, Director of Financial Aid
100 Purpose Road, Pippa Passes, KY 41844
(606) 368-6058

Asbury University

Wilmore, Kentucky
www.asbury.edu Federal Code: 001952

4-year private university and liberal arts college in small town, affiliated with interdenominational tradition.
Enrollment: 1,382 undergrads, 4% part-time. 82 full-time freshmen.
Selectivity: Admits 50 to 75% of applicants.

BASIC COSTS (2013-2014)
Tuition and fees: $26,076.
Per-credit charge: $996.
Room and board: $5,962.

FINANCIAL AID PICTURE (2011-2012)
Students with need: Out of 80 full-time freshmen who applied for aid, 63 were judged to have need. Of these, 63 received aid, and 7 had their full need met. Average financial aid package met 69% of need; average scholarship/grant was $13,073; average loan was $2,924. For part-time students, average financial aid package was $5,649.
Students without need: 17 full-time freshmen who did not demonstrate need for aid received scholarships/grants; average award was $7,997. No-need awards available for academics, alumni affiliation, art, athletics, leadership, minority status, music/drama, religious affiliation, ROTC.
Scholarships offered: 7 full-time freshmen received athletic scholarships; average amount $2,414.
Cumulative student debt: 70% of graduating class had student loans; average debt was $28,871.

FINANCIAL AID PROCEDURES
Dates and Deadlines: Priority date 3/1; no closing date. Applicants notified on a rolling basis starting 1/31; must reply within 4 week(s) of notification.

CONTACT
Ronald Anderson, Director of Financial Aid
One Macklem Drive, Wilmore, KY 40390-1198
(859) 858-3511 ext. 2195

Beckfield College

Florence, Kentucky
www.beckfield.edu Federal Code: 016726

4-year for-profit nursing and career college in large town.
Enrollment: 727 undergrads.
Selectivity: Open admission; but selective for some programs.

BASIC COSTS (2012-2013)
Tuition and fees: $14,481.
Per-credit charge: $311.

FINANCIAL AID PICTURE

Students with need: Need-based aid available for full-time and part-time students.

Students without need: This college awards aid only to students with need.

Scholarships offered: High School scholarship; tuition for one course per quarter for maximum of 8 quarters; must achieve and maintain 3.0 GPA, be enrolled full-time, and enter college in July or October following graduation from high school. Merit scholarship; $100 per quarter; must maintain 4.0 GPA, perfect attendance, and carry at least 8 quarter credit hours.

Additional info: Deadline for filing of financial aid forms is end of first week of classes.

FINANCIAL AID PROCEDURES

Forms required: FAFSA.

Dates and Deadlines: Applicants notified on a rolling basis.

CONTACT

Patricia Nettleton, Corporate Director of Student Financial
16 Spiral Drive, Florence, KY 41042
(859) 371-9393 ext. 1121

Bellarmine University

Louisville, Kentucky
www.bellarmine.edu Federal Code: 001954

4-year private university and liberal arts college in very large city, affiliated with Roman Catholic Church.

Enrollment: 2,440 undergrads, 5% part-time. 606 full-time freshmen.

Selectivity: Admits over 75% of applicants.

BASIC COSTS (2013-2014)

Tuition and fees: $33,180.

Per-credit charge: $755.

Room and board: $9,770.

FINANCIAL AID PICTURE (2012-2013)

Students with need: Out of 569 full-time freshmen who applied for aid, 507 were judged to have need. Of these, 507 received aid, and 104 had their full need met. Average financial aid package met 76% of need; average scholarship/grant was $20,704; average loan was $3,391. For part-time students, average financial aid package was $10,555.

Students without need: 99 full-time freshmen who did not demonstrate need for aid received scholarships/grants; average award was $20,404. No-need awards available for academics, alumni affiliation, art, athletics, leadership, minority status, music/drama, religious affiliation, ROTC, state/district residency.

Scholarships offered: ***Merit:*** Academic awards range from $7,000 to full tuition. ***Athletic:*** 40 full-time freshmen received athletic scholarships; average amount $6,000.

Cumulative student debt: 69% of graduating class had student loans; average debt was $28,722.

FINANCIAL AID PROCEDURES

Forms required: FAFSA.

Dates and Deadlines: Priority date 3/1; no closing date. Applicants notified on a rolling basis starting 3/15; must reply by 5/1.

Transfers: Applicants notified on a rolling basis starting 4/15; must reply within 3 week(s) of notification.

CONTACT

Heather Boutell, Director of Financial Aid
2001 Newburg Road, Louisville, KY 40205
(502) 272-8124

Berea College

Berea, Kentucky
www.berea.edu Federal Code: 001955

4-year private liberal arts college in small town.

Enrollment: 1,604 undergrads. 391 full-time freshmen.

Selectivity: Admits less than 50% of applicants.

BASIC COSTS (2013-2014)

Additional info: Only those with financial need admitted. All students awarded 4-year tuition scholarship. Amount of scholarship varies depending on financial need and presence of any additional outside scholarships. Resources cover entire cost of tuition, which totals $22,100. Financial aid and scholarships available for meeting additional costs of room/board ($6,150) and fees ($1,070), depending on financial need. Every student is provided a personal notebook computer by the college.

FINANCIAL AID PICTURE (2012-2013)

Students with need: Out of 391 full-time freshmen who applied for aid, 391 were judged to have need. Of these, 391 received aid. Average financial aid package met 100% of need; average scholarship/grant was $28,163; average loan was $748. Need-based aid available for part-time students.

Students without need: This college awards aid only to students with need.

Cumulative student debt: 74% of graduating class had student loans; average debt was $7,224.

FINANCIAL AID PROCEDURES

Forms required: FAFSA.

Dates and Deadlines: Priority date 2/1; closing date 5/1. Applicants notified on a rolling basis starting 3/1; must reply by 5/1.

Transfers: Financial aid transcript from previous school(s) must be received before awarding aid.

CONTACT

Nancy Melton, Director of Student Financial Aid Services
CPO 2220, Berea, KY 40404
(859) 985-3310

Big Sandy Community and Technical College

Prestonsburg, Kentucky
www.bigsandy.kctcs.edu Federal Code: 001996

2-year public community and technical college in small town.

Enrollment: 3,517 undergrads.

Selectivity: Open admission; but selective for some programs.

BASIC COSTS (2012-2013)

Tuition and fees: $4,200; out-of-state residents $14,700.

Per-credit charge: $140; out-of-state residents $490.

FINANCIAL AID PICTURE

Students with need: Need-based aid available for full-time and part-time students.

Students without need: No-need awards available for academics.

FINANCIAL AID PROCEDURES

Forms required: FAFSA.

Dates and Deadlines: Priority date 4/1; no closing date. Applicants notified on a rolling basis; must reply within 2 week(s) of notification.

Transfers: Kentucky State Grant must be transferred by August 1 for fall semester, December 1 for spring semester.

CONTACT

Denise Trusty, Director of Financial Aid
One Bert T. Combs Drive, Prestonsburg, KY 41653
(606) 886-3863 ext. 67255

Bluegrass Community and Technical College

Lexington, Kentucky
www.bluegrass.kctcs.edu Federal Code: 009707

2-year public community and technical college in large city.
Enrollment: 11,631 undergrads.
Selectivity: Open admission; but selective for some programs.

BASIC COSTS (2012-2013)

Tuition and fees: $4,200; out-of-state residents $14,700.
Per-credit charge: $140; out-of-state residents $490.
Room and board: $6,976.
Additional info: Non-Kentucky students from counties which border Kentucky: $280 per credit hour.

FINANCIAL AID PICTURE

Students with need: Need-based aid available for full-time and part-time students. Work study available nights, weekends, and for part-time students.
Students without need: No-need awards available for academics, minority status, state/district residency.

FINANCIAL AID PROCEDURES

Forms required: FAFSA, institutional form.
Dates and Deadlines: Priority date 4/15; no closing date. Applicants notified on a rolling basis starting 6/5; must reply within 3 week(s) of notification.
Transfers: No deadline. Applicants notified on a rolling basis.

CONTACT

Runan Pendergrast, Director of Financial Aid
200 Oswald Building, Cooper Drive, Lexington, KY 40506-0235
(859) 246-6216

Brescia University

Owensboro, Kentucky
www.brescia.edu Federal Code: 001958

4-year private university and liberal arts college in small city, affiliated with Roman Catholic Church.
Enrollment: 798 undergrads, 20% part-time. 163 full-time freshmen.
Selectivity: Admits less than 50% of applicants.

BASIC COSTS (2013-2014)

Tuition and fees: $19,440.
Per-credit charge: $550.
Room and board: $8,250.

FINANCIAL AID PICTURE

Students with need: Need-based aid available for full-time and part-time students. Work study available nights, weekends, and for part-time students.
Students without need: No-need awards available for academics, alumni affiliation, art, athletics, minority status, music/drama, religious affiliation, state/district residency.

FINANCIAL AID PROCEDURES

Forms required: FAFSA.
Dates and Deadlines: Priority date 8/1; closing date 8/23. Applicants notified on a rolling basis starting 3/1; must reply within 3 week(s) of notification.

CONTACT

Marcie Tillett, Director of Financial Aid
717 Frederica Street, Owensboro, KY 42301-3023
(270) 685-3131 ext. 4216

Campbellsville University

Campbellsville, Kentucky
www.campbellsville.edu Federal Code: 001959

4-year private university in large town, affiliated with Baptist faith.
Enrollment: 2,250 undergrads, 13% part-time. 570 full-time freshmen.
Selectivity: Admits 50 to 75% of applicants.

BASIC COSTS (2013-2014)

Tuition and fees: $22,196.
Per-credit charge: $904.
Room and board: $8,200.
Additional info: Tuition/fee waivers available for adults, minority students, unemployed or children of unemployed.

FINANCIAL AID PICTURE

Students with need: Need-based aid available for full-time and part-time students. Work study available nights, weekends, and for part-time students.
Students without need: No-need awards available for academics, art, athletics, leadership, minority status, music/drama, religious affiliation, ROTC, state/district residency.
Additional info: Matching scholarships available for students whose church contributes $200 annually. Performance grants available to members of marching band.

FINANCIAL AID PROCEDURES

Forms required: FAFSA.
Dates and Deadlines: Priority date 4/1; no closing date. Applicants notified on a rolling basis starting 5/15.

CONTACT

Chris Tolson, Director of Financial Aid
One University Drive, Campbellsville, KY 42718-2799
(270) 789-5013

Centre College

Danville, Kentucky
www.centre.edu Federal Code: 001961

4-year private liberal arts college in large town, affiliated with Presbyterian Church (USA).
Enrollment: 1,337 undergrads. 351 full-time freshmen.
Selectivity: Admits 50 to 75% of applicants.

BASIC COSTS (2012-2013)

Comprehensive fee: $43,800.

FINANCIAL AID PICTURE (2012-2013)

Students with need: Out of 284 full-time freshmen who applied for aid, 223 were judged to have need. Of these, 223 received aid, and 75 had their full need met. Average financial aid package met 86% of need; average scholarship/grant was $24,790; average loan was $3,479.
Students without need: 114 full-time freshmen who did not demonstrate need for aid received scholarships/grants; average award was $16,036. No-need awards available for academics, alumni affiliation, music/drama, ROTC.
Scholarships offered: Institutional Merit Award: $9,500 to full tuition; applications must be on file by February 1; renewable. Music and Drama Scholarships: up to $7,500. Guaranteed minimum award available to admitted Centre Fellows and Kentucky Governor's Scholars.
Cumulative student debt: 53% of graduating class had student loans; average debt was $25,700.

FINANCIAL AID PROCEDURES

Forms required: FAFSA, institutional form.
Dates and Deadlines: Priority date 1/31; closing date 3/1. Applicants notified by 4/1; must reply by 5/1 or within 2 week(s) of notification.
Transfers: No deadline. Applicants notified on a rolling basis starting 3/1; must reply within 2 week(s) of notification. Financial aid transcript required.

PART III: FINANCIAL AID COLLEGE BY COLLEGE

CONTACT
Elaine Larson, Director of Student Financial Planning
600 West Walnut Street, Danville, KY 40422-1394
(859) 238-5365

Clear Creek Baptist Bible College

Pineville, Kentucky
www.ccbbc.edu Federal Code: 017044

4-year private Bible college in small town, affiliated with Southern Baptist Convention.
Enrollment: 160 undergrads, 29% part-time. 13 full-time freshmen.
Selectivity: Open admission; but selective for some programs.

BASIC COSTS (2013-2014)
Tuition and fees: $7,520.
Per-credit charge: $239.
Room and board: $3,570.
Additional info: Tuition will be calculated on a per hour basis without a block rate as in previous year's.

FINANCIAL AID PICTURE (2011-2012)
Students with need: Out of 12 full-time freshmen who applied for aid, 9 were judged to have need. Of these, 9 received aid, and 1 had their full need met. Average financial aid package met 82% of need; average scholarship/grant was $293. For part-time students, average financial aid package was $2,089.
Students without need: 1 full-time freshmen who did not demonstrate need for aid received scholarships/grants; average award was $400. No-need awards available for academics.

FINANCIAL AID PROCEDURES
Forms required: FAFSA, institutional form.
Dates and Deadlines: Priority date 6/30; no closing date. Applicants notified on a rolling basis.
Transfers: Priority date 5/5; no deadline. Applicants notified on a rolling basis starting 5/5; must reply by 8/1.

CONTACT
Sam Risner, Director of Financial Aid
300 Clear Creek Road, Pineville, KY 40977-9754
(606) 337-3196 ext. 142

Daymar College: Bowling Green

Bowling Green, Kentucky
www.daymarcollege.edu Federal Code: 004934

2-year for-profit branch campus and career college in small city.
Enrollment: 228 undergrads.
Selectivity: Open admission.

BASIC COSTS (2012-2013)
Tuition and fees: $18,000.
Additional info: Program inclusive pricing, including tuition, books, and all fees. Tuition/fee waivers available for adults.

FINANCIAL AID PICTURE
Students with need: Need-based aid available for full-time and part-time students. Work study available nights.
Students without need: This college awards aid only to students with need.

FINANCIAL AID PROCEDURES
Forms required: FAFSA.

CONTACT
Janice Cutliff, Director of Financial Services
2421 Fitzgerald Industrial Drive, Bowling Green, KY 42101
(270) 843-6750

Daymar College: Owensboro

Owensboro, Kentucky
www.daymarcollege.edu Federal Code: 009313

2-year for-profit business and junior college in small city.
Enrollment: 324 undergrads.
Selectivity: Open admission.

BASIC COSTS (2012-2013)
Tuition and fees: $18,000.
Additional info: Program inclusive pricing, including tuition, books, and all fees.

FINANCIAL AID PICTURE
Students with need: Need-based aid available for full-time and part-time students.
Students without need: This college awards aid only to students with need.

FINANCIAL AID PROCEDURES
Forms required: FAFSA.
Dates and Deadlines: Applicants notified on a rolling basis.

CONTACT
Denise Jernigan, Director of Financial Services
3361 Buckland Square, Owensboro, KY 42301
(270) 926-4040

Daymar College: Paducah

Paducah, Kentucky Federal Code: 013661
www.daymarcollege.edu CSS Code: 0669

2-year for-profit technical college in small city.
Enrollment: 220 undergrads.
Selectivity: Open admission.

BASIC COSTS (2012-2013)
Tuition and fees: $18,000.
Additional info: Program inclusive pricing, including tuition, books, and all fees.

FINANCIAL AID PICTURE
Students with need: Need-based aid available for full-time students.

FINANCIAL AID PROCEDURES
Forms required: FAFSA, CSS PROFILE.
Dates and Deadlines: Applicants notified on a rolling basis; must reply within 3 week(s) of notification.

CONTACT
JoAnn Price, Financial Aid Officer
509 South 30th Street, Paducah, KY 42001

Eastern Kentucky University

Richmond, Kentucky
www.eku.edu Federal Code: 001963

4-year public university in large town.
Enrollment: 13,376 undergrads, 16% part-time. 2,274 full-time freshmen.
Selectivity: Admits 50 to 75% of applicants.

BASIC COSTS (2012-2013)
Tuition and fees: $7,320; out-of-state residents $16,464.
Per-credit charge: $305; out-of-state residents $686.
Room and board: $7,316.

FINANCIAL AID PICTURE
Students with need: Need-based aid available for full-time and part-time students. Work study available nights, weekends, and for part-time students.
Students without need: No-need awards available for academics, alumni affiliation, art, athletics, job skills, leadership, minority status, music/drama, ROTC, state/district residency.

FINANCIAL AID PROCEDURES
Forms required: FAFSA.
Dates and Deadlines: Applicants notified on a rolling basis starting 4/1.

CONTACT
Shelley Park, Director of Student Financial Assistance, Scholarship and Veteran Affairs
SSB CPO 54, 521 Lancaster Avenue, Richmond, KY 40475-3102

Elizabethtown Community and Technical College
Elizabethtown, Kentucky
www.elizabethtown.kctcs.edu Federal Code: 001991

2-year public community and technical college in large town.
Enrollment: 5,567 undergrads.
Selectivity: Open admission; but selective for some programs.

BASIC COSTS (2012-2013)
Tuition and fees: $4,200; out-of-state residents $14,700.
Per-credit charge: $140; out-of-state residents $490.

FINANCIAL AID PICTURE
Students with need: Need-based aid available for full-time and part-time students. Work study available nights, weekends, and for part-time students.
Students without need: This college awards aid only to students with need.

FINANCIAL AID PROCEDURES
Forms required: FAFSA.
Dates and Deadlines: Priority date 8/1; no closing date. Applicants notified on a rolling basis starting 6/1; must reply within 2 week(s) of notification.
Transfers: Priority date 7/11; no deadline. Applicants notified on a rolling basis; must reply within 2 week(s) of notification.

CONTACT
Michael Barlow, Director of Financial Aid
600 College Street Road, Elizabethtown, KY 42701
(270) 769-2371 ext. 68614

Georgetown College
Georgetown, Kentucky
www.georgetowncollege.edu Federal Code: 001964

4-year private liberal arts college in large town, affiliated with Baptist faith.
Enrollment: 1,103 undergrads, 1% part-time. 238 full-time freshmen.
Selectivity: Admits over 75% of applicants.

BASIC COSTS (2013-2014)
Tuition and fees: $32,310.
Per-credit charge: $1,330.
Room and board: $8,230.

FINANCIAL AID PICTURE (2012-2013)
Students with need: Need-based aid available for full-time students.
Students without need: No-need awards available for academics, alumni affiliation, art, athletics, leadership, minority status, music/drama, religious affiliation, ROTC, state/district residency.

FINANCIAL AID PROCEDURES
Forms required: FAFSA.
Dates and Deadlines: Priority date 2/1; closing date 3/15. Applicants notified on a rolling basis starting 3/1; must reply by 5/1.

CONTACT
Tiffany Hornberger, Director of Student Financial Planning
400 East College Street, Georgetown, KY 40324-1696
(502) 863-8027

Hazard Community and Technical College
Hazard, Kentucky
www.hazard.kctcs.edu Federal Code: 006962

2-year public community and technical college in small town.
Enrollment: 2,572 undergrads.
Selectivity: Open admission; but selective for some programs and for out-of-state students.

BASIC COSTS (2012-2013)
Tuition and fees: $4,200; out-of-state residents $14,700.
Per-credit charge: $140; out-of-state residents $490.

FINANCIAL AID PICTURE
Students with need: Need-based aid available for full-time and part-time students.
Students without need: This college awards aid only to students with need.

FINANCIAL AID PROCEDURES
Forms required: FAFSA.
Dates and Deadlines: Priority date 4/1; no closing date. Applicants notified on a rolling basis starting 6/15; must reply within 2 week(s) of notification.

CONTACT
Chuck Anderson, Financial Aid Director
One Community College Drive, Hazard, KY 41701
(606) 487-3061

Hopkinsville Community College
Hopkinsville, Kentucky
www.hopkinsville.kctcs.edu Federal Code: 001994

2-year public community college in small city.
Enrollment: 4,450 undergrads.
Selectivity: Open admission; but selective for some programs.

BASIC COSTS (2012-2013)
Tuition and fees: $4,200; out-of-state residents $14,700.
Per-credit charge: $140; out-of-state residents $490.

FINANCIAL AID PICTURE
Students with need: Need-based aid available for full-time and part-time students. Work study available nights.
Students without need: No-need awards available for academics, leadership, minority status, state/district residency.
Scholarships offered: The Rotary Scholars Program: two years of full-time study; any graduate of a Christian County high school (beginning with the Class of 2012); 2.5 high school GPA and 95% attendance required.
Additional info: ACT required for academic scholarships.

FINANCIAL AID PROCEDURES
Forms required: FAFSA.
Dates and Deadlines: Priority date 7/15; no closing date. Applicants notified on a rolling basis starting 7/1.
Transfers: No deadline. Applicants notified on a rolling basis.

CONTACT
Janet Gunther, Director, Financial Aid
PO Box 2100, Hopkinsville, KY 42241-2100
(270) 707-3830

Kentucky Christian University

Grayson, Kentucky
www.kcu.edu Federal Code: 001965

4-year private university and Bible college in small town, affiliated with Church of Christ.
Enrollment: 574 undergrads, 5% part-time. 189 full-time freshmen.
Selectivity: Admits 50 to 75% of applicants.

BASIC COSTS (2013-2014)
Tuition and fees: $16,350.
Per-credit charge: $534.
Room and board: $6,900.

FINANCIAL AID PICTURE (2011-2012)
Students with need: Out of 185 full-time freshmen who applied for aid, 173 were judged to have need. Of these, 173 received aid, and 18 had their full need met. Average financial aid package met 64% of need; average scholarship/grant was $4,939; average loan was $3,261. For part-time students, average financial aid package was $1,198.
Students without need: No-need awards available for academics, alumni affiliation, leadership, minority status, music/drama, religious affiliation.
Scholarships offered: 4 full-time freshmen received athletic scholarships; average amount $2,875.
Cumulative student debt: 87% of graduating class had student loans; average debt was $31,005.

FINANCIAL AID PROCEDURES
Forms required: FAFSA.
Dates and Deadlines: Priority date 3/1; no closing date. Applicants notified on a rolling basis starting 3/15; must reply within 2 week(s) of notification.

CONTACT
Jennie Bender, Director of Financial Aid
100 Academic Parkway, Grayson, KY 41143-2205
(606) 474-3226

Kentucky Mountain Bible College

Jackson, Kentucky
www.kmbc.edu Federal Code: 030021

4-year private Bible college in rural community, affiliated with Kentucky Mountain Holiness Association.
Enrollment: 74 undergrads, 7% part-time. 20 full-time freshmen.
Selectivity: Admits 50 to 75% of applicants.

BASIC COSTS (2012-2013)
Tuition and fees: $6,990.
Per-credit charge: $210.
Room and board: $4,360.

FINANCIAL AID PICTURE
Students with need: Need-based aid available for full-time and part-time students. Work study available nights, weekends, and for part-time students.
Students without need: No-need awards available for academics, job skills, leadership, music/drama.

FINANCIAL AID PROCEDURES
Forms required: FAFSA, institutional form.
Dates and Deadlines: Priority date 4/1; closing date 6/30. Applicants notified on a rolling basis starting 3/15.
Transfers: No deadline. Applicants notified on a rolling basis starting 8/30; must reply within 6 week(s) of notification.

CONTACT
Rosita Marshall, Director of Financial Aid
855 Highway 541, Jackson, KY 41339
(606) 693-5000 ext. 175

Kentucky State University

Frankfort, Kentucky
www.kysu.edu Federal Code: 001968

4-year public university in large town.
Enrollment: 2,084 undergrads, 15% part-time. 321 full-time freshmen.
Selectivity: Admits less than 50% of applicants.

BASIC COSTS (2012-2013)
Tuition and fees: $6,858; out-of-state residents $16,458.
Per-credit charge: $254; out-of-state residents $610.
Room and board: $6,580.
Additional info: Per-credit-hour charges include $25 required fees.

FINANCIAL AID PICTURE (2012-2013)
Students with need: Out of 314 full-time freshmen who applied for aid, 314 were judged to have need. Of these, 290 received aid, and 4 had their full need met. Average financial aid package met 43% of need; average scholarship/grant was $6,866; average loan was $3,466. For part-time students, average financial aid package was $6,791.
Students without need: No-need awards available for academics, alumni affiliation, art, athletics, minority status, music/drama, state/district residency.
Cumulative student debt: 26% of graduating class had student loans; average debt was $39,623.

FINANCIAL AID PROCEDURES
Forms required: FAFSA.
Dates and Deadlines: Priority date 4/15; no closing date. Applicants notified on a rolling basis starting 3/15; must reply within 2 week(s) of notification.
Transfers: No deadline. Applicants notified on a rolling basis; must reply within 2 week(s) of notification.

CONTACT
Victoria Owens, Director of Financial Aid
400 East Main Street, ASB 312, Frankfort, KY 40601
(502) 597-5960

Kentucky Wesleyan College

Owensboro, Kentucky
www.kwc.edu Federal Code: 001969

4-year private liberal arts college in small city, affiliated with United Methodist Church.
Enrollment: 665 undergrads, 4% part-time. 194 full-time freshmen.
Selectivity: Admits less than 50% of applicants.

BASIC COSTS (2013-2014)
Tuition and fees: $21,200.
Per-credit charge: $585.
Room and board: $7,500.

FINANCIAL AID PICTURE (2011-2012)
Students with need: Out of 188 full-time freshmen who applied for aid, 174 were judged to have need. Of these, 172 received aid, and 19 had their full need met. Average financial aid package met 63% of need; average

scholarship/grant was $12,408; average loan was $3,230. For part-time students, average financial aid package was $4,755.
Students without need: 17 full-time freshmen who did not demonstrate need for aid received scholarships/grants; average award was $9,804. No-need awards available for academics, alumni affiliation, art, athletics, leadership, music/drama, religious affiliation, state/district residency.
Scholarships offered: Scholarships range from $1,000 to full tuition. Students compete in on-campus scholarship competitions.

FINANCIAL AID PROCEDURES
Forms required: FAFSA.
Dates and Deadlines: Closing date 3/15. Applicants notified on a rolling basis starting 2/15; must reply within 2 week(s) of notification.

CONTACT
Samantha Hayes, Director of Financial Aid
3000 Frederica Street, Owensboro, KY 42301
(270) 852-3130

Lincoln College of Technology: Florence

Florence, Kentucky
www.swcollege.net Federal Code: 012128

2-year for-profit health science and career college in small city.
Enrollment: 314 undergrads.
Selectivity: Open admission.

BASIC COSTS (2012-2013)
Tuition and fees: $14,840.
Additional info: Total program costs range from $9,935 up to $32,008 depending on program. Cost of books and materials included in tuition.

FINANCIAL AID PICTURE
Students with need: Need-based aid available for full-time and part-time students.
Students without need: This college awards aid only to students with need.

FINANCIAL AID PROCEDURES
Forms required: FAFSA.
Dates and Deadlines: Applicants notified on a rolling basis.
Transfers: No deadline. Applicants notified on a rolling basis.

CONTACT
Victoria Hubbard, Director of Financial Aid
8095 Connector Drive, Florence, KY 41042
(859) 282-9999

Lindsey Wilson College

Columbia, Kentucky
www.lindsey.edu Federal Code: 001972

4-year private liberal arts college in small town, affiliated with United Methodist Church.
Enrollment: 2,176 undergrads, 4% part-time. 523 full-time freshmen.
Selectivity: Open admission; but selective for some programs.

BASIC COSTS (2013-2014)
Tuition and fees: $22,070.
Per-credit charge: $910.
Room and board: $8,400.

FINANCIAL AID PICTURE
Students with need: Need-based aid available for full-time and part-time students. Work study available nights, weekends, and for part-time students.
Students without need: This college awards aid only to students with need.

FINANCIAL AID PROCEDURES
Forms required: FAFSA, institutional form.
Dates and Deadlines: Priority date 3/1; no closing date. Applicants notified on a rolling basis starting 5/1; must reply within 2 week(s) of notification.
Transfers: Applicants notified on a rolling basis.

CONTACT
Marilyn Radford, Director of Financial Aid
210 Lindsey Wilson Street, Columbia, KY 42728
(270) 384-8022

Madisonville Community College

Madisonville, Kentucky
www.madisonville.kctcs.edu Federal Code: 009010

2-year public community college in large town.
Enrollment: 3,200 undergrads.
Selectivity: Open admission; but selective for some programs.

BASIC COSTS (2012-2013)
Tuition and fees: $4,200; out-of-state residents $14,700.
Per-credit charge: $140; out-of-state residents $490.
Additional info: Tuition/fee waivers available for minority students, unemployed or children of unemployed.

FINANCIAL AID PICTURE
Students with need: Need-based aid available for full-time and part-time students. Work study available nights, weekends, and for part-time students.
Students without need: No-need awards available for minority status.

FINANCIAL AID PROCEDURES
Forms required: FAFSA, institutional form.
Dates and Deadlines: Priority date 3/15; no closing date. Applicants notified on a rolling basis; must reply within 3 week(s) of notification.

CONTACT
Martha Phelps, Director of Financial Aid
2000 College Drive, Madisonville, KY 42431
(270) 824-8693

Maysville Community and Technical College

Maysville, Kentucky
www.maysville.kctcs.edu Federal Code: 006960

2-year public community and technical college in small town.
Enrollment: 3,652 undergrads.
Selectivity: Open admission; but selective for some programs.

BASIC COSTS (2012-2013)
Tuition and fees: $4,200; out-of-state residents $14,700.
Per-credit charge: $140; out-of-state residents $490.

FINANCIAL AID PICTURE
Students with need: Need-based aid available for full-time and part-time students. Work study available nights.
Students without need: No-need awards available for academics.

FINANCIAL AID PROCEDURES
Forms required: FAFSA, institutional form.
Dates and Deadlines: Priority date 4/1; no closing date. Applicants notified on a rolling basis starting 3/1; must reply within 3 week(s) of notification.

CONTACT
Karen Overkey, Financial Aid Director
1755 US HIghway 68, Maysville, KY 41056
(606) 759-7141 ext. 66207

Mid-Continent University

Mayfield, Kentucky
www.midcontinent.edu Federal Code: 025762

4-year private Bible and liberal arts college in large town, affiliated with Southern Baptist Convention.
Enrollment: 2,171 undergrads, 20% part-time. 206 full-time freshmen.
Selectivity: Admits over 75% of applicants.

BASIC COSTS (2012-2013)

Tuition and fees: $13,350.
Per-credit charge: $403.
Room and board: $6,900.

FINANCIAL AID PICTURE (2011-2012)

Students with need: Out of 196 full-time freshmen who applied for aid, 190 were judged to have need. Of these, 190 received aid, and 12 had their full need met. Average financial aid package met 40% of need; average scholarship/grant was $15,180; average loan was $5,412. For part-time students, average financial aid package was $11,080.
Students without need: 14 full-time freshmen who did not demonstrate need for aid received scholarships/grants; average award was $4,471. No-need awards available for academics.
Cumulative student debt: 77% of graduating class had student loans; average debt was $13,812.

FINANCIAL AID PROCEDURES

Forms required: FAFSA, institutional form.
Dates and Deadlines: Priority date 3/15; closing date 5/30. Applicants notified on a rolling basis starting 4/1; must reply within 2 week(s) of notification.
Transfers: No deadline. Must reply within 2 week(s) of notification.

CONTACT

Paula Clendenen, Executive Director of Financial Aid
99 Powell Road East, Mayfield, KY 42066-9007
(270) 247-8521 ext. 340

Midway College

Midway, Kentucky
www.midway.edu Federal Code: 001975

4-year private liberal arts college for women in small town, affiliated with Christian Church (Disciples of Christ).
Enrollment: 1,423 undergrads, 40% part-time. 95 full-time freshmen.
Selectivity: Admits 50 to 75% of applicants.

BASIC COSTS (2012-2013)

Tuition and fees: $20,700.
Per-credit charge: $690.
Room and board: $8,000.

FINANCIAL AID PICTURE

Students with need: Need-based aid available for full-time and part-time students.
Students without need: No-need awards available for academics, alumni affiliation, art, athletics, leadership, minority status, religious affiliation.
Additional info: Audition required of applicants for music scholarships. Portfolio required for art scholarships.

FINANCIAL AID PROCEDURES

Forms required: FAFSA, institutional form.
Dates and Deadlines: Applicants notified on a rolling basis; must reply within 4 week(s) of notification.

CONTACT

Katie Conrad, Director of Financial Aid
512 East Stephens Street, Midway, KY 40347-1120
(859) 846-5410

Morehead State University

Morehead, Kentucky
www.moreheadstate.edu Federal Code: 001976

4-year public university in large town.
Enrollment: 7,152 undergrads.
Selectivity: Admits over 75% of applicants.

BASIC COSTS (2012-2013)

Tuition and fees: $7,284; out-of-state residents $18,030.
Per-credit charge: $276; out-of-state residents $683.
Room and board: $7,475.
Additional info: Tuition/fee waivers available for minority students.

FINANCIAL AID PICTURE

Students with need: Need-based aid available for full-time students. Work study available nights, weekends, and for part-time students.
Students without need: No-need awards available for academics, alumni affiliation, art, athletics, leadership, minority status, music/drama, ROTC, state/district residency.

FINANCIAL AID PROCEDURES

Forms required: FAFSA, institutional form.
Dates and Deadlines: Priority date 3/15; no closing date. Applicants notified on a rolling basis.
Transfers: No deadline. Applicants notified on a rolling basis. Transfer scholarships available.

CONTACT

Donna King, Director of Financial Aid
100 Admissions Center, Morehead, KY 40351
(606) 783-2000

Murray State University

Murray, Kentucky
www.murraystate.edu Federal Code: 001977

4-year public university in large town.
Enrollment: 7,849 undergrads, 11% part-time. 1,603 full-time freshmen.
Selectivity: Admits over 75% of applicants.

BASIC COSTS (2012-2013)

Tuition and fees: $6,840; out-of-state residents $18,600.
Per-credit charge: $285; out-of-state residents $755.
Room and board: $7,638.
Additional info: Students from Illinois, Indiana, Missouri, Ohio and Tennessee receive a reduced non-resident rate on tuition. Tuition/fee waivers available for minority students.

FINANCIAL AID PICTURE (2012-2013)

Students with need: For part-time students, average financial aid package was $7,386.
Students without need: No-need awards available for academics, alumni affiliation, art, athletics, job skills, leadership, minority status, music/drama, ROTC, state/district residency.
Cumulative student debt: 47% of graduating class had student loans; average debt was $20,644.

FINANCIAL AID PROCEDURES

Forms required: FAFSA, institutional form.
Dates and Deadlines: Priority date 2/1; closing date 9/1. Applicants notified on a rolling basis starting 3/15; must reply by 5/1.
Transfers: No deadline. Applicants notified on a rolling basis starting 5/15; must reply by 5/1. Transfer Scholarship.

CONTACT

Lori Mitchum, Director of Financial Aid
102 Curris Center Murray State University, Murray, KY 42071
(270) 809-2546

National College: Danville

Danville, Kentucky
www.national-college.edu Federal Code: 010489

2-year for-profit business college in large town.
Enrollment: 125 undergrads.
Selectivity: Open admission.

BASIC COSTS (2012-2013)
Tuition and fees: $14,310.
Per-credit charge: $317.

FINANCIAL AID PICTURE
Students with need: Need-based aid available for full-time and part-time students.
Students without need: This college awards aid only to students with need.

FINANCIAL AID PROCEDURES
Forms required: FAFSA.
Dates and Deadlines: Applicants notified on a rolling basis.

CONTACT
Pam Cotton, Director of Financial Aid and Auditing
115 East Lexington Avenue, Danville, KY 40422
(540) 986-1800

National College: Florence

Florence, Kentucky
www.national-college.edu Federal Code: 010489

2-year for-profit business college in large town.
Enrollment: 93 undergrads.
Selectivity: Open admission.

BASIC COSTS (2012-2013)
Tuition and fees: $14,310.
Per-credit charge: $317.

FINANCIAL AID PICTURE
Students with need: Need-based aid available for full-time and part-time students.
Students without need: This college awards aid only to students with need.

FINANCIAL AID PROCEDURES
Forms required: FAFSA.
Dates and Deadlines: Applicants notified on a rolling basis.

CONTACT
Pam Cotton, Director of Financial Aid and Auditing
7627 Ewing Boulevard, Florence, KY 41042
(540) 986-1800

National College: Lexington

Lexington, Kentucky
www.national-college.edu Federal Code: 010489

2-year for-profit business and junior college in small city.
Enrollment: 274 undergrads.
Selectivity: Open admission; but selective for some programs.

BASIC COSTS (2012-2013)
Tuition and fees: $14,310.
Per-credit charge: $317.

FINANCIAL AID PICTURE
Students with need: Need-based aid available for full-time and part-time students.
Students without need: This college awards aid only to students with need.

FINANCIAL AID PROCEDURES
Forms required: FAFSA.
Dates and Deadlines: Applicants notified on a rolling basis.

CONTACT
Pam Cotton, Director of Financial Aid and Auditing
2376 Sir Barton Way, Lexington, KY 40509
(859) 255-0621

National College: Louisville

Louisville, Kentucky
www.ncbt.edu Federal Code: 010489

2-year for-profit business college in large city.
Enrollment: 284 undergrads.
Selectivity: Open admission; but selective for some programs.

BASIC COSTS (2012-2013)
Tuition and fees: $14,310.
Per-credit charge: $317.

FINANCIAL AID PICTURE
Students with need: Need-based aid available for full-time and part-time students.
Students without need: This college awards aid only to students with need.

FINANCIAL AID PROCEDURES
Forms required: FAFSA.
Dates and Deadlines: Applicants notified on a rolling basis.

CONTACT
Pamela Cotton, Director of Financial Aid and Compliance Officer
4205 Dixie Highway, Louisville, KY 40216
(540) 986-1800

National College: Pikeville

Pikeville, Kentucky
www.national-college.edu Federal Code: 010489

2-year for-profit business college in large town.
Enrollment: 165 undergrads.
Selectivity: Open admission; but selective for some programs.

BASIC COSTS (2012-2013)
Tuition and fees: $14,310.
Per-credit charge: $317.

FINANCIAL AID PICTURE
Students with need: Need-based aid available for full-time and part-time students.
Students without need: This college awards aid only to students with need.

FINANCIAL AID PROCEDURES
Forms required: FAFSA.

CONTACT
Pam Cotton, Director of Financial Aid and Auditing
50 National Collge Boulevard, Pikeville, KY 41501
(540) 986-1800

National College: Richmond
Richmond, Kentucky
www.national-college.edu Federal Code: 010489

2-year for-profit business college in large town.
Enrollment: 154 undergrads.
Selectivity: Open admission.

BASIC COSTS (2012-2013)
Tuition and fees: $14,310.
Per-credit charge: $317.

FINANCIAL AID PICTURE
Students with need: Need-based aid available for full-time and part-time students.
Students without need: This college awards aid only to students with need.

FINANCIAL AID PROCEDURES
Forms required: FAFSA.
Dates and Deadlines: Applicants notified on a rolling basis.

CONTACT
Pam Cotton, Director of Financial Aid and Auditing
125 South Killarney Lane, Richmond, KY 40475
(540) 986-1800

Northern Kentucky University
Highland Heights, Kentucky
www.nku.edu Federal Code: 009275

4-year public university in small town.
Enrollment: 12,531 undergrads, 20% part-time. 2,039 full-time freshmen.
Selectivity: Admits less than 50% of applicants.

BASIC COSTS (2012-2013)
Tuition and fees: $8,064; out-of-state residents $15,936.
Per-credit charge: $328; out-of-state residents $656.
Room and board: $7,430.
Additional info: $8 per credit hour campus recreation fee; maximum fee is $96 per semester.

FINANCIAL AID PICTURE (2011-2012)
Students with need: Average financial aid package met 60% of need; average scholarship/grant was $5,682; average loan was $2,834. For part-time students, average financial aid package was $6,417.
Students without need: No-need awards available for academics, alumni affiliation, art, athletics, leadership, music/drama, ROTC, state/district residency.
Cumulative student debt: 73% of graduating class had student loans; average debt was $13,432.

FINANCIAL AID PROCEDURES
Forms required: FAFSA.
Dates and Deadlines: Priority date 3/1; no closing date. Applicants notified on a rolling basis starting 4/1.
Transfers: Applicants notified by 5/30.

CONTACT
Leah Stewart, Director of Financial Assistance
Administrative Center 401, Northern Kentucky University, Highland Heights, KY 41099
(859) 572-5143

Owensboro Community and Technical College
Owensboro, Kentucky
www.owensboro.kctcs.edu Federal Code: 030345

2-year public community and technical college in small city.
Enrollment: 3,463 undergrads.
Selectivity: Open admission; but selective for some programs.

BASIC COSTS (2012-2013)
Tuition and fees: $4,200; out-of-state residents $14,700.
Per-credit charge: $140; out-of-state residents $490.

FINANCIAL AID PICTURE
Students with need: Need-based aid available for full-time and part-time students.
Students without need: No-need awards available for academics, state/district residency.

FINANCIAL AID PROCEDURES
Forms required: FAFSA.
Dates and Deadlines: Priority date 3/16; no closing date. Must reply within 2 week(s) of notification.
Transfers: Must have financial aid transcripts from previous institutions.

CONTACT
Bernice Ayer, Financial Aid Officer
4800 New Hartford Road, Owensboro, KY 42303-1899
(270) 686-4655

St. Catharine College
St. Catharine, Kentucky
www.sccky.edu Federal Code: 001983

4-year private health science and liberal arts college in small town, affiliated with Roman Catholic Church.
Enrollment: 655 undergrads, 10% part-time. 153 full-time freshmen.
Selectivity: Open admission.

BASIC COSTS (2013-2014)
Tuition and fees: $18,076.
Per-credit charge: $600.
Room and board: $8,210.

FINANCIAL AID PICTURE
Students with need: Need-based aid available for full-time and part-time students.
Students without need: This college awards aid only to students with need.

FINANCIAL AID PROCEDURES
Forms required: FAFSA, institutional form.
Dates and Deadlines: Priority date 3/15; no closing date. Applicants notified on a rolling basis.
Transfers: Priority date 2/1; no deadline. Applicants notified on a rolling basis.

CONTACT
Melinda Lynch, Financial Aid Director
2735 Bardstown Road, St. Catharine, KY 40061
(859) 336-5082 ext. 1216

Somerset Community College
Somerset, Kentucky
www.somerset.kctcs.edu Federal Code: 001997

2-year public community and technical college in large town.
Enrollment: 6,353 undergrads.

Selectivity: Open admission; but selective for some programs.

BASIC COSTS (2012-2013)
Tuition and fees: $4,200; out-of-state residents $14,700.
Per-credit charge: $140; out-of-state residents $490.

FINANCIAL AID PICTURE
Students with need: Need-based aid available for full-time and part-time students.
Students without need: This college awards aid only to students with need.

FINANCIAL AID PROCEDURES
Forms required: FAFSA.
Dates and Deadlines: Priority date 3/1; no closing date. Applicants notified on a rolling basis starting 5/1; must reply within 2 week(s) of notification.
Transfers: Priority date 3/15; closing date 8/15. Applicants notified on a rolling basis starting 5/1; must reply within 2 week(s) of notification.

CONTACT
Emily Phillips, Director of Financial Aid
808 Monticello Street, Somerset, KY 42501
(606) 679-8501 ext. 16640

Southeast Kentucky Community and Technical College

Cumberland, Kentucky
www.southeast.kctcs.edu Federal Code: 001998

2-year public community and technical college in small town.
Enrollment: 2,461 undergrads, 43% part-time. 360 full-time freshmen.
Selectivity: Open admission; but selective for some programs.

BASIC COSTS (2012-2013)
Tuition and fees: $4,200; out-of-state residents $14,700.
Per-credit charge: $140; out-of-state residents $490.

FINANCIAL AID PICTURE (2011-2012)
Students with need: Need-based aid available for full-time and part-time students.
Students without need: This college awards aid only to students with need.
Additional info: March 15 deadline for state financial aid.

FINANCIAL AID PROCEDURES
Forms required: FAFSA.
Dates and Deadlines: Priority date 3/15; no closing date. Must reply within 2 week(s) of notification.

CONTACT
Rebecca Parrott, Vice President for Student Affairs
700 College Road, Cumberland, KY 40823
(606) 589-2145

Spalding University

Louisville, Kentucky
www.spalding.edu Federal Code: 001960

4-year private university in very large city, affiliated with Roman Catholic Church.
Enrollment: 1,317 undergrads.
Selectivity: Admits less than 50% of applicants.

BASIC COSTS (2013-2014)
Tuition and fees: $21,450.
Per-credit charge: $715.
Room and board: $10,400.
Additional info: Tuition/fee waivers available for unemployed or children of unemployed.

FINANCIAL AID PICTURE
Students with need: Need-based aid available for full-time and part-time students.
Students without need: No-need awards available for academics, religious affiliation.
Scholarships offered: Egan Service Learning Program, covers the cost of a double room on campus, awarded to students who demonstrate leadership in campus activities and agree to complete service hours within the community. Catherine Spalding Grant is a need based award with a maximum dollar amount of $6,500, opportunity for renewal for eight semesters, and requires a minimum GPA of 2.0 and completion of FAFSA.

FINANCIAL AID PROCEDURES
Forms required: FAFSA.
Dates and Deadlines: Priority date 1/1; no closing date. Applicants notified on a rolling basis starting 3/31.
Transfers: No deadline. Applicants notified on a rolling basis; must reply within 2 week(s) of notification.

CONTACT
Gina Kuzuoka, Director of Financial Aid
845 S Third Street, Louisville, KY 40203
(502) 588-9911 ext. 4335

Spencerian College

Louisville, Kentucky
www.spencerian.edu Federal Code: 004618

2-year for-profit career college in large city.
Enrollment: 686 undergrads, 37% part-time. 102 full-time freshmen.
Selectivity: Open admission; but selective for some programs.

BASIC COSTS (2012-2013)
Tuition and fees: $16,860.
Per-credit charge: $272.
Room and board: $7,965.

FINANCIAL AID PICTURE
Students with need: Need-based aid available for full-time and part-time students.
Students without need: No-need awards available for academics.

FINANCIAL AID PROCEDURES
Forms required: FAFSA, institutional form.

CONTACT
Jill Schuler, Director of Financial Aid
4627 Dixie Highway, Louisville, KY 40216

Spencerian College: Lexington

Lexington, Kentucky
spencerian.edu Federal Code: 004618

2-year for-profit branch campus and technical college in small city.
Enrollment: 614 undergrads.
Selectivity: Open admission; but selective for some programs.

BASIC COSTS (2012-2013)
Tuition and fees: $14,839.
Per-credit charge: $360.
Room and board: $5,535.

FINANCIAL AID PICTURE
Students with need: Need-based aid available for full-time and part-time students.

Students without need: This college awards aid only to students with need.

FINANCIAL AID PROCEDURES

Forms required: FAFSA, state aid form, institutional form.

Dates and Deadlines: Applicants notified on a rolling basis starting 1/1.

Transfers: No deadline. Applicants notified on a rolling basis.

CONTACT

Brian Highley, Director of Financial Aid/Compliance Officer
1575 Winchester Road, Lexington, KY 40505
(859) 223-9608 ext. 5441

Sullivan College of Technology and Design

Louisville, Kentucky
www.sctd.edu Federal Code: 012088

2-year for-profit technical and career college in very large city.
Enrollment: 456 undergrads, 31% part-time. 89 full-time freshmen.
Selectivity: Admits 50 to 75% of applicants.

BASIC COSTS (2012-2013)

Room and board: $8,820.

Additional info: Full-program tuition for the academic year ranges from $17,340 to $20,230 depending on the program of study. The per-credit-hour tuition rate ranges from $410 to $480 also depending on the program of study. The approximate cost of books and supplies per academic year ranges by program of study from $1,500 to $2,600. Required fees are a $540 general fee plus a fee of $200 for online courses. Rent for a semi-private room is $615 per month or $5,535 for the academic year (9 months/3 quarters). The required meal plan for all housing students includes three meals a day Mon-Fri and brunch and dinner on Sat-Sun (19 meals) and costs $3,285 per academic year. Total room and board for an academic year is $8,820. Tuition at time of enrollment locked for 2 years; tuition/fee waivers available for unemployed or children of unemployed.

FINANCIAL AID PICTURE (2011-2012)

Students with need: Out of 89 full-time freshmen who applied for aid, 89 were judged to have need. Of these, 89 received aid. For part-time students, average financial aid package was $3,312.

Students without need: No-need awards available for academics, art, job skills.

Scholarships offered: Academic Scholarships; up to $3,000; based on class rank, GPA, essay. Scholarship Day Competition; up to $1,500 based upon testing scores. Scholarship Fair Competition; up to $3,000; based upon open competition in electronics, drafting, interior design, computer networking and art skills. Kentucky Skills USA Scholarships; up to $1,500; based upon state championship competitions in such fields as drafting, electronics, etc.

Cumulative student debt: 100% of graduating class had student loans; average debt was $21,170.

FINANCIAL AID PROCEDURES

Forms required: FAFSA.

Dates and Deadlines: Applicants notified on a rolling basis; must reply within 2 week(s) of notification.

Transfers: No deadline. Applicants notified on a rolling basis.

CONTACT

Andre Downing, Financial Planning Director
3901 Atkinson Square Drive, Louisville, KY 40218-4524
(502) 456-6509 ext. 8240

Sullivan University

Louisville, Kentucky
www.sullivan.edu Federal Code: 004619

4-year for-profit university in large city.
Enrollment: 4,100 undergrads.

BASIC COSTS (2012-2013)

Additional info: Tuition, fees and per-credit-hour charges vary by program. Per-credit-hour charges range from $135 to $570. Enrollment fee $100, general fee $50 per class, online class fee $50 per-credit-hour. Board plan not available. Cost of room only, $5,535.

FINANCIAL AID PICTURE

Students with need: Need-based aid available for full-time and part-time students. Work study available nights.

Students without need: This college awards aid only to students with need.

FINANCIAL AID PROCEDURES

Forms required: FAFSA.

Dates and Deadlines: Applicants notified on a rolling basis starting 1/2.

CONTACT

Rene Kutz, Financial Planning Director
3101 Bardstown Road, Louisville, KY 40205
(502) 456-6771

Thomas More College

Crestview Hills, Kentucky
www.thomasmore.edu Federal Code: 002001

4-year private liberal arts college in small town, affiliated with Roman Catholic Church.
Enrollment: 1,319 undergrads, 5% part-time. 263 full-time freshmen.
Selectivity: Admits over 75% of applicants.

BASIC COSTS (2012-2013)

Tuition and fees: $26,470.
Per-credit charge: $575.
Room and board: $7,280.

FINANCIAL AID PICTURE (2012-2013)

Students with need: Need-based aid available for full-time and part-time students. Work study available nights, weekends, and for part-time students.

Students without need: No-need awards available for academics, alumni affiliation, art, job skills, leadership, minority status, music/drama, religious affiliation, ROTC, state/district residency.

FINANCIAL AID PROCEDURES

Forms required: FAFSA.

Dates and Deadlines: Closing date 3/15. Applicants notified on a rolling basis starting 3/1; must reply by 5/1.

Transfers: No deadline. Applicants notified on a rolling basis; must reply by 5/1.

CONTACT

Mary Givhan, Director of Financial Aid
333 Thomas More Parkway, Crestview Hills, KY 41017-3495
(859) 344-4043

Transylvania University

Lexington, Kentucky
www.transy.edu Federal Code: 001987

4-year private liberal arts college in large city, affiliated with Christian Church (Disciples of Christ).

Enrollment: 1,070 undergrads, 1% part-time. 333 full-time freshmen.
Selectivity: Admits over 75% of applicants.

BASIC COSTS (2013-2014)
Tuition and fees: $31,560.
Room and board: $8,975.

FINANCIAL AID PICTURE (2012-2013)
Students with need: Out of 288 full-time freshmen who applied for aid, 248 were judged to have need. Of these, 248 received aid, and 54 had their full need met. Average financial aid package met 84% of need; average scholarship/grant was $20,791; average loan was $3,887. For part-time students, average financial aid package was $3,339.
Students without need: 80 full-time freshmen who did not demonstrate need for aid received scholarships/grants; average award was $13,767. No-need awards available for academics, art, leadership, minority status, music/drama, religious affiliation, state/district residency.
Scholarships offered: William T. Young Merit Scholarships: 20 awarded; tuition and fees.
Cumulative student debt: 66% of graduating class had student loans; average debt was $26,604.
Additional info: Auditions and portfolios required for music and art scholarships respectively. Essays required for other scholarship programs. Applications for William T. Young scholarships must be received by December 1.

FINANCIAL AID PROCEDURES
Forms required: FAFSA.
Dates and Deadlines: Priority date 1/15; no closing date. Applicants notified on a rolling basis starting 3/15; must reply by 5/1 or within 2 week(s) of notification.
Transfers: No deadline. Applicants notified on a rolling basis starting 3/15; must reply by 8/6.

CONTACT
David Cecil, Director of Financial Aid
300 North Broadway, Lexington, KY 40508-1797
(859) 233-8239

Union College
Barbourville, Kentucky
www.unionky.edu Federal Code: 001988

4-year private liberal arts and teachers college in small town, affiliated with United Methodist Church.
Enrollment: 771 undergrads, 7% part-time. 212 full-time freshmen.
Selectivity: Admits over 75% of applicants.

BASIC COSTS (2013-2014)
Tuition and fees: $22,100.
Per-credit charge: $330.
Room and board: $6,700.

FINANCIAL AID PICTURE (2012-2013)
Students with need: Out of 200 full-time freshmen who applied for aid, 189 were judged to have need. Of these, 188 received aid, and 21 had their full need met. Average financial aid package met 67.8% of need; average scholarship/grant was $15,186; average loan was $3,518. For part-time students, average financial aid package was $4,544.
Students without need: 21 full-time freshmen who did not demonstrate need for aid received scholarships/grants; average award was $11,234. No-need awards available for academics, alumni affiliation, athletics, leadership, music/drama, religious affiliation.
Cumulative student debt: 83% of graduating class had student loans; average debt was $18,843.

FINANCIAL AID PROCEDURES
Forms required: FAFSA.
Dates and Deadlines: Priority date 3/15; no closing date. Applicants notified on a rolling basis starting 3/1; must reply within 2 week(s) of notification.

CONTACT
Jessica Cook, Associate Dean for Financial Aid
310 College Street, Box 005, Barbourville, KY 40906
(606) 546-1618

University of Kentucky
Lexington, Kentucky
www.uky.edu Federal Code: 001989

4-year public university in large city.
Enrollment: 20,436 undergrads, 6% part-time. 4,588 full-time freshmen.
Selectivity: Admits 50 to 75% of applicants.

BASIC COSTS (2012-2013)
Tuition and fees: $9,676; out-of-state residents $19,864.
Per-credit charge: $389; out-of-state residents $813.
Room and board: $10,192.
Additional info: Tuition/fee waivers available for adults, minority students.

FINANCIAL AID PICTURE
Students with need: Need-based aid available for full-time and part-time students. Work study available weekends and for part-time students.
Students without need: No-need awards available for academics, alumni affiliation, art, athletics, job skills, leadership, minority status, music/drama, ROTC, state/district residency.

FINANCIAL AID PROCEDURES
Forms required: FAFSA.
Dates and Deadlines: Closing date 2/15. Applicants notified on a rolling basis starting 4/1; must reply within 3 week(s) of notification.
Transfers: Priority date 4/1.

CONTACT
Lynda George, Director of Student Financial Aid
100 W.D. Funkhouser Building, Lexington, KY 40506-0054
(859) 257-3172

University of Louisville
Louisville, Kentucky
www.louisville.edu Federal Code: 001999

4-year public university in very large city.
Enrollment: 14,854 undergrads, 19% part-time. 2,647 full-time freshmen.
Selectivity: Admits over 75% of applicants.

BASIC COSTS (2012-2013)
Tuition and fees: $9,662; out-of-state residents $23,146.
Per-credit charge: $403; out-of-state residents $965.
Room and board: $8,278.

FINANCIAL AID PICTURE (2011-2012)
Students with need: Need-based aid available for full-time and part-time students. Work study available nights, weekends, and for part-time students.
Students without need: No-need awards available for academics, art, athletics, leadership, minority status, music/drama, ROTC, state/district residency.

FINANCIAL AID PROCEDURES
Forms required: FAFSA.
Dates and Deadlines: Priority date 2/15; no closing date. Applicants notified on a rolling basis starting 4/1.
Transfers: Priority date 3/1.

CONTACT
Patricia Arauz, Director of Student Financial Aid
2211 South Brook Street, Louisville, KY 40292
(502) 852-5511

University of Pikeville
Pikeville, Kentucky
www.upike.edu Federal Code: 001980

4-year private liberal arts college in small town, affiliated with Presbyterian Church (USA).
Enrollment: 1,245 undergrads, 2% part-time. 368 full-time freshmen.
Selectivity: Open admission; but selective for some programs.

BASIC COSTS (2013-2014)
Tuition and fees: $17,750.
Per-credit charge: $740.
Room and board: $7,000.

FINANCIAL AID PICTURE (2012-2013)
Students with need: Out of 363 full-time freshmen who applied for aid, 362 were judged to have need. Of these, 362 received aid, and 125 had their full need met. Average financial aid package met 82% of need; average scholarship/grant was $14,107; average loan was $3,400. For part-time students, average financial aid package was $9,271.
Students without need: This college awards aid only to students with need.
Scholarships offered: University of Pikeville Promise; full-tuition, four-year scholarship that places emphasis on academics and financial need; applicants must submit ACT and GPA, file FAFSA by February 15 of senior year, be a Kentucky resident, display full eligibility for Pell Grant and receive CAP and KTG state grants.
Cumulative student debt: 75% of graduating class had student loans; average debt was $24,954.

FINANCIAL AID PROCEDURES
Forms required: FAFSA.
Dates and Deadlines: Priority date 3/15; no closing date. Applicants notified on a rolling basis starting 2/1; must reply by 5/1 or within 2 week(s) of notification.
Transfers: No deadline. Must reply by 5/1 or within 2 week(s) of notification.

CONTACT
Judy Bradley, Financial Aid Director
147 Sycamore Street, Pikeville, KY 41501-1194
(606) 218-5251

University of the Cumberlands
Williamsburg, Kentucky
www.ucumberlands.edu Federal Code: 001962

4-year private university and liberal arts college in small town, affiliated with Baptist faith.
Enrollment: 1,527 undergrads, 3% part-time. 456 full-time freshmen.
Selectivity: Admits 50 to 75% of applicants.

BASIC COSTS (2013-2014)
Tuition and fees: $20,000.
Per-credit charge: $590.
Room and board: $7,500.

FINANCIAL AID PICTURE (2012-2013)
Students with need: Out of 423 full-time freshmen who applied for aid, 406 were judged to have need. Of these, 406 received aid, and 50 had their full need met. Average financial aid package met 77% of need; average scholarship/grant was $15,106; average loan was $3,276. For part-time students, average financial aid package was $8,596.
Students without need: 47 full-time freshmen who did not demonstrate need for aid received scholarships/grants; average award was $7,105. No-need awards available for academics, athletics, job skills, leadership, music/drama, religious affiliation.
Scholarships offered: ***Merit:*** Trustee, full-tuition, room and board, based on outstanding academic credentials, 5 per year; Presidential, up to $20,000, based on outstanding academic credentials, no limit; Dean's, up to $15,000, based on ACT/SAT score and high school GPA, no limit; Kentucky Rogers Scholar, up to full-tuition; Rogers Scholar Graduate, based on ACT/SAT score and GPA, up to 3 per year; Kentucky Governor's Scholar, up to $15,000, GSP graduate, no limit; Christian Leadership $1,000-$5,000, based on involvement/leadership in church or other religious organizations, no limit. ***Athletic:*** 41 full-time freshmen received athletic scholarships; average amount $6,006.
Cumulative student debt: 76% of graduating class had student loans; average debt was $20,090.

FINANCIAL AID PROCEDURES
Forms required: FAFSA.
Dates and Deadlines: Priority date 2/1; no closing date. Applicants notified on a rolling basis starting 3/1; must reply within 2 week(s) of notification.
Transfers: Applicants notified on a rolling basis starting 3/1; must reply within 2 week(s) of notification.

CONTACT
Steve Allen, Director of Financial Planning
6178 College Station Drive, Williamsburg, KY 40769
(800) 343-1609

West Kentucky Community and Technical College
Paducah, Kentucky
www.westkentucky.kctcs.edu Federal Code: 001979

2-year public community and technical college in large town.
Enrollment: 4,677 undergrads.
Selectivity: Open admission; but selective for some programs.

BASIC COSTS (2012-2013)
Tuition and fees: $4,200; out-of-state residents $14,700.
Per-credit charge: $140; out-of-state residents $490.

FINANCIAL AID PICTURE
Students with need: Need-based aid available for full-time and part-time students.

FINANCIAL AID PROCEDURES
Forms required: FAFSA.
Dates and Deadlines: Priority date 4/1; closing date 7/15. Applicants notified on a rolling basis starting 7/15; must reply within 4 week(s) of notification.

CONTACT
Nate Slaton, Director of Financial Aid
4810 Alben Barkley Drive, Paducah, KY 42002-7380
(270) 534-3248

Western Kentucky University
Bowling Green, Kentucky
www.wku.edu Federal Code: 002002

4-year public university in small city.
Enrollment: 16,351 undergrads, 16% part-time. 3,287 full-time freshmen.
Selectivity: Admits over 75% of applicants.

BASIC COSTS (2012-2013)
Tuition and fees: $8,472; out-of-state residents $21,000.
Per-credit charge: $353; out-of-state residents $875.
Room and board: $7,320.

FINANCIAL AID PICTURE (2011-2012)
Students with need: Out of 2,881 full-time freshmen who applied for aid, 2,305 were judged to have need. Of these, 2,286 received aid, and 691 had their full need met. Average financial aid package met 30% of need; average scholarship/grant was $5,109; average loan was $3,035. For part-time students, average financial aid package was $9,923.
Students without need: 295 full-time freshmen who did not demonstrate need for aid received scholarships/grants; average award was $5,422. No-need awards available for academics, alumni affiliation, art, athletics, job skills, leadership, minority status, music/drama, religious affiliation, ROTC, state/district residency.
Scholarships offered: ***Merit:*** Academic scholarships; $200 to full tuition; number awarded varies. ***Athletic:*** 96 full-time freshmen received athletic scholarships; average amount $13,495.
Cumulative student debt: 59% of graduating class had student loans; average debt was $26,110.

FINANCIAL AID PROCEDURES
Forms required: FAFSA.
Dates and Deadlines: Priority date 2/15; no closing date. Applicants notified on a rolling basis starting 3/1.
Transfers: Transfer students receiving CAP Grant must notify the state agency by December 1 of each year.

CONTACT
Cynthia Burnette, Director of Financial Assistance
1906 College Heights Boulevard, Bowling Green, KY 42101
(270) 745-2755

Louisiana

Baton Rouge Community College
Baton Rouge, Louisiana
www.mybrcc.edu Federal Code: 037303

2-year public community college in large city.
Enrollment: 8,289 undergrads, 45% part-time. 1,600 full-time freshmen.
Selectivity: Open admission.

BASIC COSTS (2012-2013)
Tuition and fees: $3,091; out-of-state residents $6,643.

FINANCIAL AID PICTURE
Students with need: Need-based aid available for full-time and part-time students. Work study available weekends and for part-time students.
Students without need: No-need awards available for academics, athletics, leadership, minority status, state/district residency.

FINANCIAL AID PROCEDURES
Forms required: FAFSA, institutional form.
Dates and Deadlines: Priority date 4/15; closing date 6/30. Applicants notified on a rolling basis.
Transfers: No deadline. Applicants notified on a rolling basis.

CONTACT
Rosey Toney, Director of Financial Aid
201 Community College Drive, Baton Rouge, LA 70806
(225) 216-8640

Bossier Parish Community College
Bossier City, Louisiana
www.bpcc.edu Federal Code: 012033

2-year public community college in small city.
Enrollment: 7,184 undergrads. 1,509 full-time freshmen.
Selectivity: Open admission; but selective for out-of-state students.

BASIC COSTS (2012-2013)
Tuition and fees: $2,911; out-of-state residents $6,137.

FINANCIAL AID PICTURE (2011-2012)
Students with need: Out of 1,359 full-time freshmen who applied for aid, 1,243 were judged to have need. Of these, 1,116 received aid, and 21 had their full need met. Average financial aid package met 30% of need; average scholarship/grant was $2,533; average loan was $2,880. For part-time students, average financial aid package was $11,253.
Students without need: 1 full-time freshmen who did not demonstrate need for aid received scholarships/grants; average award was $500. No-need awards available for academics, alumni affiliation, athletics, minority status, music/drama.
Scholarships offered: 10 full-time freshmen received athletic scholarships; average amount $1,741.

FINANCIAL AID PROCEDURES
Forms required: FAFSA, institutional form.
Dates and Deadlines: Priority date 6/1; no closing date. Applicants notified on a rolling basis starting 6/1.
Transfers: No deadline.

CONTACT
Vickie Temple, Financial Aid Director
6220 East Texas Street, Bossier City, LA 71111-6922
(318) 678-6026

Centenary College of Louisiana
Shreveport, Louisiana
www.centenary.edu Federal Code: 002003

4-year private liberal arts college in large city, affiliated with United Methodist Church.
Enrollment: 689 undergrads, 2% part-time. 158 full-time freshmen.
Selectivity: Admits 50 to 75% of applicants.

BASIC COSTS (2012-2013)
Tuition and fees: $29,500.
Per-credit charge: $880.
Room and board: $9,320.

FINANCIAL AID PICTURE (2012-2013)
Students with need: Out of 151 full-time freshmen who applied for aid, 119 were judged to have need. Of these, 119 received aid, and 34 had their full need met. Average financial aid package met 77% of need; average scholarship/grant was $20,939; average loan was $3,418. For part-time students, average financial aid package was $8,835.
Students without need: 39 full-time freshmen who did not demonstrate need for aid received scholarships/grants; average award was $13,437. No-need awards available for academics, alumni affiliation, art, music/drama, religious affiliation, state/district residency.
Cumulative student debt: 50% of graduating class had student loans; average debt was $21,820.

FINANCIAL AID PROCEDURES
Forms required: FAFSA.
Dates and Deadlines: Priority date 2/15; no closing date. Applicants notified on a rolling basis starting 3/15; must reply by 5/1.
Transfers: No deadline. Applicants notified on a rolling basis starting 2/15; must reply within 4 week(s) of notification.

CONTACT
Lynette Viskozki, Director of Financial Aid
Box 41188, Shreveport, LA 71134-1188
(318) 869-5137

Delgado Community College

New Orleans, Louisiana
www.dcc.edu Federal Code: 004625

2-year public community college in very large city.
Enrollment: 14,708 undergrads, 55% part-time. 1,639 full-time freshmen.
Selectivity: Open admission; but selective for some programs.

BASIC COSTS (2012-2013)
Tuition and fees: $3,061; out-of-state residents $6,410.

FINANCIAL AID PICTURE
Students with need: Need-based aid available for full-time and part-time students. Work study available nights.
Students without need: No-need awards available for academics, athletics, leadership, music/drama, state/district residency.

FINANCIAL AID PROCEDURES
Forms required: FAFSA, institutional form.
Dates and Deadlines: Priority date 5/1; closing date 7/15. Applicants notified on a rolling basis starting 4/1; must reply within 2 week(s) of notification.

CONTACT
Barrye Bailey, Director of Student Financial Assistance
615 City Park Avenue, New Orleans, LA 70119
(504) 671-5037

Dillard University

New Orleans, Louisiana
www.dillard.edu Federal Code: 002004

4-year private university and liberal arts college in large city, affiliated with United Church of Christ and United Methodist Church.
Enrollment: 1,307 undergrads.

BASIC COSTS (2012-2013)
Tuition and fees: $14,850.
Room and board: $8,868.

FINANCIAL AID PICTURE
Students with need: Need-based aid available for full-time and part-time students. Work study available nights, weekends, and for part-time students.
Students without need: This college awards aid only to students with need.

FINANCIAL AID PROCEDURES
Forms required: FAFSA, institutional form.
Dates and Deadlines: Priority date 12/1; closing date 3/1. Applicants notified on a rolling basis starting 3/1; must reply by 5/1 or within 2 week(s) of notification.

CONTACT
Theodis Wright, Director of Financial Aid
2601 Gentilly Boulevard, New Orleans, LA 70122-3097
(800) 216-8094

Grambling State University

Grambling, Louisiana
www.gram.edu Federal Code: 002006

4-year public university in small town.
Enrollment: 4,429 undergrads, 8% part-time. 746 full-time freshmen.
Selectivity: Admits less than 50% of applicants.

BASIC COSTS (2012-2013)
Tuition and fees: $5,240; out-of-state residents $13,610.
Per-credit charge: $164; out-of-state residents $349.
Room and board: $9,674.

FINANCIAL AID PICTURE
Students with need: Need-based aid available for full-time and part-time students. Work study available nights, weekends, and for part-time students.
Students without need: No-need awards available for academics, alumni affiliation, art, athletics, job skills, leadership, minority status, music/drama, religious affiliation, ROTC, state/district residency.

FINANCIAL AID PROCEDURES
Forms required: FAFSA.
Dates and Deadlines: Priority date 4/1; closing date 6/1. Applicants notified on a rolling basis starting 3/1; must reply within 2 week(s) of notification.
Transfers: Applicants notified on a rolling basis starting 3/1; must reply within 2 week(s) of notification.

CONTACT
Albert Tezno, Director of Student Financial Aid
403 Main Street, GSU Box 4200, Grambling, LA 71245
(318) 274-6190

Herzing University: Kenner

Kenner, Louisiana
www.herzing.edu Federal Code: 020897

4-year for-profit branch campus and technical college in very large city.
Enrollment: 286 undergrads.

FINANCIAL AID PICTURE
Students with need: Work study available nights, weekends, and for part-time students.

CONTACT
Ava Gomez, Financial Aid Director
2500 Williams Boulevard, Kenner, LA 70062

ITI Technical College

Baton Rouge, Louisiana
www.iticollege.edu Federal Code: 015270

2-year for-profit technical and career college in large city.
Enrollment: 597 undergrads.
Selectivity: Open admission; but selective for some programs.

BASIC COSTS (2012-2013)
Additional info: Full-time tuition varies by program from $9,500 - $26,500. Registration fee $150. Estimated average total books and supplies from $1,385 - $3,355.

FINANCIAL AID PICTURE
Students with need: Need-based aid available for full-time students.
Students without need: This college awards aid only to students with need.

FINANCIAL AID PROCEDURES
Forms required: FAFSA.

CONTACT
Connie Roubique, Financial Aid Director
13944 Airline Highway, Baton Rouge, LA 70817
(225) 752-4233

Louisiana College

Pineville, Louisiana
www.lacollege.edu Federal Code: 002007

4-year private liberal arts college in small city, affiliated with Southern Baptist Convention.
Enrollment: 1,069 full-time undergrads.

BASIC COSTS (2012-2013)
Tuition and fees: $13,780.
Per-credit charge: $405.
Room and board: $4,960.

FINANCIAL AID PICTURE
Students with need: Need-based aid available for full-time and part-time students. Work study available nights, weekends, and for part-time students.
Students without need: No-need awards available for academics, art, leadership, music/drama, ROTC.

FINANCIAL AID PROCEDURES
Forms required: FAFSA, institutional form.
Dates and Deadlines: Priority date 3/31; no closing date. Applicants notified on a rolling basis starting 3/1; must reply by 5/1 or within 2 week(s) of notification.
Transfers: Scholarships available.

CONTACT
Eric Gossett, Director of Financial Aid
LC Box 566, Pineville, LA 71359
(318) 487-7386

Louisiana State University and Agricultural and Mechanical College

Baton Rouge, Louisiana
www.lsu.edu Federal Code: 002010

4-year public university and agricultural college in large city.
Enrollment: 23,872 undergrads, 5% part-time. 5,283 full-time freshmen.
Selectivity: Admits over 75% of applicants.

BASIC COSTS (2012-2013)
Tuition and fees: $6,989; out-of-state residents $22,265.
Room and board: $10,218.

FINANCIAL AID PICTURE (2011-2012)
Students with need: Out of 3,437 full-time freshmen who applied for aid, 2,346 were judged to have need. Of these, 2,345 received aid, and 643 had their full need met. Average financial aid package met 72% of need; average scholarship/grant was $8,782; average loan was $4,715. For part-time students, average financial aid package was $9,343.
Students without need: 830 full-time freshmen who did not demonstrate need for aid received scholarships/grants; average award was $3,073. No-need awards available for academics, athletics, music/drama, ROTC.
Scholarships offered: 87 full-time freshmen received athletic scholarships; average amount $20,736.
Cumulative student debt: 39% of graduating class had student loans; average debt was $20,125.

FINANCIAL AID PROCEDURES
Forms required: FAFSA, institutional form.
Dates and Deadlines: Priority date 4/1; no closing date. Applicants notified on a rolling basis starting 12/15; must reply by 5/1 or within 3 week(s) of notification.
Transfers: No deadline. Applicants notified on a rolling basis starting 12/15; must reply by 5/1 or within 3 week(s) of notification.

CONTACT
Amy Marix
1146 Pleasant Hall, Baton Rouge, LA 70803-2750
(225) 578-3103

Louisiana State University at Alexandria

Alexandria, Louisiana
www.lsua.edu Federal Code: 002011

4-year public university in small city.
Enrollment: 2,063 undergrads.

BASIC COSTS (2012-2013)
Tuition and fees: $4,617; out-of-state residents $9,400.
Additional info: Cost of room only, $6,950.

FINANCIAL AID PICTURE
Students with need: Need-based aid available for full-time and part-time students. Work study available nights.
Students without need: No-need awards available for academics, state/district residency.

FINANCIAL AID PROCEDURES
Forms required: FAFSA, institutional form.
Dates and Deadlines: Priority date 4/1; no closing date. Applicants notified on a rolling basis starting 4/20; must reply within 3 week(s) of notification.

CONTACT
Paul Monteleone, Director of Financial Aid & Scholarships
8100 Highway 71 South, Alexandria, LA 71302-9121
(318) 473-6423

Louisiana State University at Eunice

Eunice, Louisiana
www.lsue.edu Federal Code: 002012

2-year public nursing and junior college in large town.
Enrollment: 2,663 undergrads, 48% part-time. 568 full-time freshmen.
Selectivity: Open admission; but selective for some programs.

BASIC COSTS (2012-2013)
Tuition and fees: $2,835; out-of-state residents $8,007.
Room and board: $8,642.

FINANCIAL AID PICTURE
Students with need: Need-based aid available for full-time and part-time students.

FINANCIAL AID PROCEDURES
Forms required: FAFSA, institutional form.
Dates and Deadlines: Priority date 6/1; no closing date. Applicants notified on a rolling basis starting 4/1; must reply within 2 week(s) of notification.

CONTACT
Jacqueline LaChapelle, Director of Financial Aid
Box 1129, Eunice, LA 70535
(337) 550-1282

Louisiana State University Health Sciences Center

New Orleans, Louisiana
www.lsuhsc.edu Federal Code: 002014

Upper-division public health science and nursing college in large city.
Enrollment: 882 undergrads.

BASIC COSTS (2012-2013)

Tuition and fees: $5,932; out-of-state residents $10,436.

Additional info: Tuition and fees quoted are for Allied Health program. Nursing: $5,608 residents, $9,519 non-residents. Dental Hygiene: $4,429 residents, $7,109 non-residents. Dental Laboratory Technology: $4,060 residents, $6,542 non-residents. Allied Health Shreveport campus: $7,414.50 residents, $13,044.50 non-residents. Board plan not available. Cost of room only, $2,520.

FINANCIAL AID PICTURE

Students with need: Need-based aid available for full-time and part-time students. Work study available nights, weekends, and for part-time students.

Students without need: No-need awards available for academics.

FINANCIAL AID PROCEDURES

Forms required: FAFSA, institutional form.

Dates and Deadlines: Priority date 4/15; no closing date. Applicants notified on a rolling basis starting 7/1.

CONTACT

Patrick Gorman, Director of Financial Aid
433 Bolivar Street, New Orleans, LA 70112-2223
(504) 568-4820

Louisiana State University in Shreveport

Shreveport, Louisiana
www.lsus.edu Federal Code: 002013

4-year public university and teachers college in large city.

Enrollment: 2,949 undergrads, 24% part-time. 364 full-time freshmen.

Selectivity: Admits over 75% of applicants.

BASIC COSTS (2012-2013)

Tuition and fees: $5,123; out-of-state residents $11,859.

FINANCIAL AID PICTURE

Students with need: Need-based aid available for full-time and part-time students. Work study available nights, weekends, and for part-time students.

FINANCIAL AID PROCEDURES

Dates and Deadlines: Applicants notified on a rolling basis.

CONTACT

Betty McCrary, Director of Student Financial Aid
One University Place, Shreveport, LA 71115-2399
(318) 797-5363

Louisiana Tech University

Ruston, Louisiana
www.latech.edu Federal Code: 002008

4-year public university in large town.

Enrollment: 6,990 undergrads, 10% part-time. 1,269 full-time freshmen.

Selectivity: Admits 50 to 75% of applicants. GED not accepted.

BASIC COSTS (2012-2013)

Tuition and fees: $6,543; out-of-state residents $14,403.

Room and board: $5,385.

FINANCIAL AID PICTURE (2012-2013)

Students with need: Out of 805 full-time freshmen who applied for aid, 560 were judged to have need. Of these, 546 received aid, and 109 had their full need met. Average financial aid package met 26% of need; average scholarship/grant was $7,537; average loan was $2,735. For part-time students, average financial aid package was $5,140.

Students without need: 781 full-time freshmen who did not demonstrate need for aid received scholarships/grants; average award was $1,436. No-need awards available for academics, alumni affiliation, art, athletics, job skills, leadership, music/drama, ROTC, state/district residency.

Scholarships offered: 14 full-time freshmen received athletic scholarships; average amount $9,446.

Cumulative student debt: 55% of graduating class had student loans; average debt was $18,555.

FINANCIAL AID PROCEDURES

Forms required: FAFSA, institutional form.

Dates and Deadlines: Priority date 4/15; no closing date. Applicants notified on a rolling basis starting 4/1; must reply within 3 week(s) of notification.

Transfers: Priority date 8/1; no deadline. Applicants notified on a rolling basis starting 8/20; must reply within 2 week(s) of notification.

CONTACT

Roger Vick, Director of Student Financial Aid
Box 3178, Ruston, LA 71272
(318) 257-2641

Loyola University New Orleans

New Orleans, Louisiana
www.loyno.edu/ Federal Code: 002016

4-year private university and liberal arts college in large city, affiliated with Roman Catholic Church.

Enrollment: 3,135 undergrads, 6% part-time. 843 full-time freshmen.

Selectivity: Admits 50 to 75% of applicants.

BASIC COSTS (2013-2014)

Tuition and fees: $36,610.

Per-credit charge: $1,012.

Room and board: $12,185.

FINANCIAL AID PICTURE (2012-2013)

Students with need: Out of 739 full-time freshmen who applied for aid, 638 were judged to have need. Of these, 638 received aid, and 94 had their full need met. Average financial aid package met 79% of need; average scholarship/grant was $26,199; average loan was $3,303. For part-time students, average financial aid package was $8,340.

Students without need: 198 full-time freshmen who did not demonstrate need for aid received scholarships/grants; average award was $14,633. No-need awards available for academics, alumni affiliation, art, leadership, ROTC.

Scholarships offered: 14 full-time freshmen received athletic scholarships; average amount $11,094.

Cumulative student debt: 66% of graduating class had student loans; average debt was $23,178.

FINANCIAL AID PROCEDURES

Forms required: FAFSA.

Dates and Deadlines: Priority date 2/15; closing date 6/1. Applicants notified on a rolling basis starting 3/1; must reply by 5/1 or within 2 week(s) of notification.

Transfers: Priority date 3/1; closing date 5/1. Applicants notified by 3/1; must reply by 5/1. Transfer scholarship deadline June 1.

CONTACT

Catherine Simoneaux, Director of Scholarships and Financial Aid
6363 St. Charles Avenue, New Orleans, LA 70118-6195
(504) 865-3231

McNeese State University

Lake Charles, Louisiana
www.mcneese.edu Federal Code: 002017

4-year public university in small city.

Enrollment: 6,975 undergrads, 13% part-time. 1,299 full-time freshmen.

Selectivity: Admits 50 to 75% of applicants.

BASIC COSTS (2012-2013)
Tuition and fees: $5,104; out-of-state residents $15,186.
Room and board: $5,968.

FINANCIAL AID PICTURE
Students with need: Need-based aid available for full-time and part-time students. Work study available nights, weekends, and for part-time students.
Students without need: No-need awards available for academics, alumni affiliation, art, athletics, leadership, minority status, music/drama, state/district residency.
Additional info: Books may be charged and paid in 2 installments during semester.

FINANCIAL AID PROCEDURES
Forms required: FAFSA, institutional form.
Dates and Deadlines: Priority date 5/1; no closing date. Applicants notified on a rolling basis starting 4/15; must reply within 2 week(s) of notification.
Transfers: Transfer students must exhibit satisfactory academic progress at school most recently attended to be eligible for financial aid.

CONTACT
Taina Savoit, Director of Financial Aid
MSU Box 91740, Lake Charles, LA 70609-1740
(337) 475-5065

Nicholls State University
Thibodaux, Louisiana
www.nicholls.edu Federal Code: 002005

4-year public university in large town.
Enrollment: 5,788 undergrads, 18% part-time. 1,035 full-time freshmen.
Selectivity: Admits over 75% of applicants.

BASIC COSTS (2012-2013)
Tuition and fees: $5,679; out-of-state residents $14,529.
Room and board: $8,560.

FINANCIAL AID PICTURE (2011-2012)
Students with need: Need-based aid available for full-time and part-time students. Work study available nights, weekends, and for part-time students.
Students without need: No-need awards available for academics, athletics, state/district residency.

FINANCIAL AID PROCEDURES
Forms required: FAFSA, state aid form, institutional form.
Dates and Deadlines: Closing date 4/15. Applicants notified on a rolling basis; must reply within 2 week(s) of notification.
Transfers: Priority date 5/1; no deadline. Applicants notified on a rolling basis.

CONTACT
Casie Triche, Director of Financial Aid
PO Box 2004-NSU, Thibodaux, LA 70310
(985) 448-4048

Northwestern State University
Natchitoches, Louisiana
www.nsula.edu Federal Code: 002021

4-year public university in large town.
Enrollment: 7,584 undergrads, 30% part-time. 1,288 full-time freshmen.
Selectivity: Admits over 75% of applicants.

BASIC COSTS (2012-2013)
Tuition and fees: $5,480; out-of-state residents $14,846.
Room and board: $7,826.

FINANCIAL AID PICTURE
Students with need: Need-based aid available for full-time and part-time students. Work study available nights, weekends, and for part-time students.
Students without need: No-need awards available for academics, alumni affiliation, art, athletics, job skills, leadership, minority status, music/drama, religious affiliation, ROTC, state/district residency.

FINANCIAL AID PROCEDURES
Forms required: FAFSA, institutional form.
Dates and Deadlines: Priority date 5/1; no closing date. Applicants notified on a rolling basis starting 5/1; must reply within 4 week(s) of notification.
Transfers: No deadline. Applicants notified on a rolling basis starting 5/1; must reply within 4 week(s) of notification.

CONTACT
Greg Ross, Director of Financial Aid
175 Sam Sibley Drive, Student Services Center, Suite 235, Natchitoches, LA 71497
(800) 823-3008

Nunez Community College
Chalmette, Louisiana
www.nunez.edu Federal Code: 015130

2-year public community and technical college in large town.
Enrollment: 1,521 undergrads, 49% part-time. 133 full-time freshmen.
Selectivity: Open admission; but selective for some programs.

BASIC COSTS (2012-2013)
Tuition and fees: $2,539; out-of-state residents $5,610.
Additional info: Tuition/fee waivers available for minority students.

FINANCIAL AID PICTURE (2012-2013)
Students with need: 71% of average financial aid package awarded as scholarships/grants, 29% awarded as loans/jobs. Need-based aid available for part-time students. Work study available nights.
Additional info: Pell Grants, Stafford Loans, campus work-study, and tuition waiver scholarships available. Louisiana National Guard tuition exemption, teacher tuition exemption, dependents of injured fire-police tuition waivers available.

FINANCIAL AID PROCEDURES
Forms required: FAFSA.
Dates and Deadlines: Priority date 6/1; closing date 8/1.
Transfers: Applicant must supply academic transcripts from every post-secondary school attended before aid is awarded.

CONTACT
Glenda Despenza, Financial Aid Officer
3710 Paris Road, Chalmette, LA 70043
(504) 278-6487

Our Lady of Holy Cross College
New Orleans, Louisiana
www.olhcc.edu Federal Code: 002023

4-year private liberal arts college in very large city, affiliated with Roman Catholic Church.
Enrollment: 940 undergrads.

BASIC COSTS (2012-2013)
Tuition and fees: $11,822.
Per-credit charge: $355.

FINANCIAL AID PICTURE
Students with need: Need-based aid available for full-time and part-time students. Work study available nights, weekends, and for part-time students.

Students without need: No-need awards available for academics, state/district residency.

FINANCIAL AID PROCEDURES
Forms required: FAFSA.
Dates and Deadlines: Priority date 7/1; no closing date. Applicants notified on a rolling basis starting 5/15; must reply within 4 week(s) of notification.
Transfers: Must reply within 2 week(s) of notification.

CONTACT
Anna Vaughan, Financial Aid Coordinator
4123 Woodland Drive, New Orleans, LA 70131-7399
(504) 394-7744

Our Lady of the Lake College

Baton Rouge, Louisiana
www.ololcollege.edu Federal Code: 031062

4-year private health science and nursing college in large city, affiliated with Roman Catholic Church.
Enrollment: 1,578 undergrads.

BASIC COSTS (2013-2014)
Tuition and fees: $13,037.
Per-credit charge: $402.

FINANCIAL AID PICTURE
Students with need: Need-based aid available for full-time students.

FINANCIAL AID PROCEDURES
Forms required: FAFSA.
Dates and Deadlines: Priority date 3/1; no closing date.

CONTACT
Tiffany MaGee, Director of Financial Aid
7434 Perkins Road, Baton Rouge, LA 70808
(225) 768-1714

Remington College: Baton Rouge

Baton Rouge, Louisiana
www.remingtoncollege.edu/batonrouge/
Federal Code: E00907

2-year private technical college in large city.
Enrollment: 409 undergrads.
Selectivity: Open admission; but selective for some programs.

BASIC COSTS (2012-2013)
Additional info: Diploma program costs range from $14,700 to $22,600.

FINANCIAL AID PICTURE
Students with need: Need-based aid available for full-time students. Work study available nights.
Students without need: This college awards aid only to students with need.

FINANCIAL AID PROCEDURES
Forms required: FAFSA.
Dates and Deadlines: Applicants notified on a rolling basis; must reply within 1 week(s) of notification.

CONTACT
James Dunn, National Director of Financial Aid
10551 Coursey Boulevard, Baton Rouge, LA 70816
(225) 236-3200

Remington College: Lafayette

Lafayette, Louisiana
www.remingtoncollege.edu/lafayette/
Federal Code: 005203

2-year private junior college in small city.
Enrollment: 420 undergrads.
Selectivity: Open admission; but selective for some programs.

BASIC COSTS (2012-2013)
Additional info: Diploma program costs range from $14,700 to $22,600.

FINANCIAL AID PICTURE
Students with need: Need-based aid available for full-time students. Work study available nights.
Students without need: This college awards aid only to students with need.

FINANCIAL AID PROCEDURES
Forms required: FAFSA, institutional form.

CONTACT
James Dunn, National Director of Financial Aid
303 Rue Louis XIV, Lafayette, LA 70508

St. Joseph Seminary College

St. Benedict, Louisiana
www.sjasc.edu Federal Code: 002027

4-year private seminary college for men in rural community, affiliated with Roman Catholic Church.
Enrollment: 104 undergrads. 11 full-time freshmen.
Selectivity: Admits over 75% of applicants.

BASIC COSTS (2013-2014)
Tuition and fees: $15,330.
Per-credit charge: $225.
Room and board: $13,040.

FINANCIAL AID PICTURE (2011-2012)
Students with need: Need-based aid available for part-time students.
Students without need: No-need awards available for academics, leadership.

FINANCIAL AID PROCEDURES
Forms required: FAFSA.
Dates and Deadlines: Priority date 3/15; no closing date. Applicants notified on a rolling basis starting 7/1; must reply within 4 week(s) of notification.
Transfers: Closing date 5/1. Applicants notified on a rolling basis starting 7/1; must reply within 4 week(s) of notification.

CONTACT
George Binder, Director of Student Financial Aid
75376 River Road, St. Benedict, LA 70457-9990
(985) 867-2248

South Louisiana Community College

Lafayette, Louisiana
www.southlouisiana.edu Federal Code: 039563

2-year public community college in small city.
Enrollment: 3,898 undergrads.
Selectivity: Open admission; but selective for some programs.

BASIC COSTS (2012-2013)
Tuition and fees: $2,881; out-of-state residents $5,562.

FINANCIAL AID PICTURE
Students with need: Need-based aid available for full-time and part-time students.
Students without need: No-need awards available for academics, leadership, state/district residency.

FINANCIAL AID PROCEDURES
Forms required: FAFSA, institutional form.
Dates and Deadlines: Priority date 5/15; no closing date.

CONTACT
Shonda Rosinski, Director of Financial Aid
320 Devalcourt, Lafayette, LA 70506-4124
(337) 521-8910

Southeastern Louisiana University

Hammond, Louisiana
www.selu.edu Federal Code: 002024

4-year public university in large town.
Enrollment: 12,295 undergrads, 15% part-time. 2,294 full-time freshmen.
Selectivity: Admits over 75% of applicants.

BASIC COSTS (2012-2013)
Tuition and fees: $5,242; out-of-state residents $16,101.
Room and board: $6,800.

FINANCIAL AID PICTURE (2011-2012)
Students with need: Out of 2,051 full-time freshmen who applied for aid, 1,409 were judged to have need. Of these, 1,398 received aid, and 455 had their full need met. For part-time students, average financial aid package was $5,079.
Students without need: 237 full-time freshmen who did not demonstrate need for aid received scholarships/grants; average award was $3,476. No-need awards available for academics, athletics, job skills, leadership, music/drama, state/district residency.
Scholarships offered: ***Merit:*** Various scholarships; $1,000-$3,500; any student admitted with 24 ACT and 3.0 GPA on a seven-semester transcript qualifies for scholarship. On-campus housing scholarships; range from half-room award to full-room award; based on ACT and GPA. Presidential Honors Scholarship; $2,500-$3,500 plus on-campus housing and meals; based on 30 ACT, 3.0 GPA. ***Athletic:*** 62 full-time freshmen received athletic scholarships; average amount $6,790.
Cumulative student debt: 60% of graduating class had student loans; average debt was $19,661.

FINANCIAL AID PROCEDURES
Forms required: FAFSA, institutional form.
Dates and Deadlines: Priority date 5/1; no closing date. Applicants notified on a rolling basis starting 4/1; must reply within 2 week(s) of notification.
Transfers: Applicants notified on a rolling basis starting 3/1; must reply within 2 week(s) of notification. Financial aid is available for transfer students, including those admitted on probation.

CONTACT
Mary Lacour, Director of Financial Aid
SLU 10752, Hammond, LA 70402
(985) 549-2244

Southern University and Agricultural and Mechanical College

Baton Rouge, Louisiana
www.subr.edu Federal Code: 002025

4-year public university in large city.
Enrollment: 5,287 undergrads, 16% part-time. 742 full-time freshmen.

BASIC COSTS (2012-2013)
Tuition and fees: $5,126; out-of-state residents $11,664.
Room and board: $5,616.

FINANCIAL AID PICTURE
Students with need: Need-based aid available for full-time students.
Students without need: No-need awards available for academics, athletics, ROTC, state/district residency.
Scholarships offered: College of Education Scholarship; full-tuition; based on 22 ACT (or comparable SAT), 3.2 GPA, evidence of community involvement/extracurricular activities, two letters of recommendation. College of Education Scholarship; tuition only; based on 20 ACT (or comparable SAT), 3.0 GPA, evidence of community involvement/extracurricular activities, two letters of recommendation.

FINANCIAL AID PROCEDURES
Forms required: FAFSA.
Dates and Deadlines: Priority date 1/31; closing date 3/30. Applicants notified on a rolling basis starting 5/1; must reply within 3 week(s) of notification.
Transfers: Closing date 5/31. Applicants notified on a rolling basis starting 5/31; must reply within 3 week(s) of notification.

CONTACT
Ursula Shorty, Director of Financial Aid
T.H. Harris Hall, Baton Rouge, LA 70813
(225) 771-2790

Southern University at New Orleans

New Orleans, Louisiana
www.suno.edu Federal Code: 002026

4-year public university in large city.
Enrollment: 2,805 undergrads.

BASIC COSTS (2012-2013)
Tuition and fees: $4,338; out-of-state residents $9,630.
Room and board: $7,680.

FINANCIAL AID PICTURE
Students with need: Need-based aid available for full-time and part-time students.
Students without need: This college awards aid only to students with need.

FINANCIAL AID PROCEDURES
Forms required: FAFSA.
Dates and Deadlines: Closing date 4/15. Applicants notified by 5/15; must reply within 1 week(s) of notification.

CONTACT
Leatrice Latimore, Director of Financial Aid
6801 Press Drive, New Orleans, LA 70126
(504) 286-5263

Tulane University

New Orleans, Louisiana Federal Code: 002029
www.tulane.edu CSS Code: 6832

4-year private university in very large city.
Enrollment: 8,357 undergrads, 23% part-time. 1,641 full-time freshmen.
Selectivity: Admits less than 50% of applicants.

BASIC COSTS (2012-2013)
Tuition and fees: $45,240.
Per-credit charge: $1,729.
Room and board: $11,540.

FINANCIAL AID PICTURE (2011-2012)
Students with need: Out of 1,046 full-time freshmen who applied for aid, 660 were judged to have need. Of these, 654 received aid, and 502 had their full need met. Average financial aid package met 95% of need; average scholarship/grant was $26,426; average loan was $6,211. For part-time students, average financial aid package was $10,015.
Students without need: 566 full-time freshmen who did not demonstrate need for aid received scholarships/grants; average award was $19,847. No-need awards available for academics, athletics, leadership, music/drama, ROTC, state/district residency.
Scholarships offered: ***Merit:*** Dean's Honor Scholarship; full-tuition. Distinguished Scholars Award; partial tuition. Founders Scholarship; partial tuition. Urban Scholars Award; full-tuition. ***Athletic:*** 42 full-time freshmen received athletic scholarships; average amount $35,726.
Cumulative student debt: 41% of graduating class had student loans; average debt was $35,100.
Additional info: Application deadline for merit scholarships December 1. Full time freshmen entering in the fall and showing parental adjusted gross income (AGI on the custodial parents' current year federal tax return) being equal to or less than $75,000 will be reviewed for Tulane's No Loan Assistance (NOLA) if the aid application (including both the FAFSA and CSS Profile) are submitted to be processed by 2/15. Tulane's NOLA scholarship will be added if gift aid plus Tulane's Institutional Methodology Expected Family Contribution (IM EFC) does not total at least the tuition, fee and transportation components of the student's standard Cost of Attendance (COA), in an amount to make up the difference; however, final determination of eligibility for Tulane's NOLA program will adhere to the same merit threshold established for need-based Tulane Scholarship.

FINANCIAL AID PROCEDURES
Forms required: FAFSA, CSS PROFILE.
Dates and Deadlines: Priority date 2/15; no closing date. Applicants notified on a rolling basis starting 3/15; must reply within 2 week(s) of notification.
Transfers: Applicants notified on a rolling basis starting 2/1; must reply by 5/1 or within 2 week(s) of notification.

CONTACT
Michael Goodman, Associate Vice President for Financial Aid
6823 St. Charles Avenue, New Orleans, LA 70118-5680
(504) 865-5723

University of Louisiana at Lafayette
Lafayette, Louisiana
www.louisiana.edu Federal Code: 002031

4-year public university in small city.
Enrollment: 14,390 undergrads, 13% part-time. 2,929 full-time freshmen.
Selectivity: Admits 50 to 75% of applicants.

BASIC COSTS (2012-2013)
Tuition and fees: $5,404; out-of-state residents $14,374.
Room and board: $6,684.

FINANCIAL AID PICTURE (2011-2012)
Students with need: Out of 2,720 full-time freshmen who applied for aid, 1,774 were judged to have need. Of these, 1,736 received aid, and 212 had their full need met. Average financial aid package met 62% of need; average scholarship/grant was $6,560; average loan was $3,143. For part-time students, average financial aid package was $4,439.
Students without need: This college awards aid only to students with need.
Scholarships offered: 71 full-time freshmen received athletic scholarships; average amount $8,496.

FINANCIAL AID PROCEDURES
Forms required: FAFSA.
Dates and Deadlines: Priority date 5/1; no closing date. Applicants notified on a rolling basis starting 4/1; must reply within 2 week(s) of notification.

CONTACT
Cindy Perez, Director, Student Financial Aid
Box 41210, Lafayette, LA 70504-1210
(337) 482-6506

University of Louisiana at Monroe
Monroe, Louisiana
www.ulm.edu Federal Code: 002020

4-year public university in small city.
Enrollment: 5,786 undergrads, 13% part-time. 1,158 full-time freshmen.
Selectivity: Admits over 75% of applicants.

BASIC COSTS (2012-2013)
Tuition and fees: $5,443; out-of-state residents $14,263.
Room and board: $6,486.

FINANCIAL AID PICTURE
Students with need: Need-based aid available for full-time and part-time students.
Students without need: No-need awards available for academics, alumni affiliation, art, athletics, job skills, leadership, minority status, music/drama, religious affiliation, ROTC, state/district residency.

FINANCIAL AID PROCEDURES
Forms required: FAFSA.
Dates and Deadlines: Priority date 4/1; no closing date. Applicants notified on a rolling basis starting 6/1; must reply within 2 week(s) of notification.

CONTACT
Cori Smith, Director of Financial Aid
700 University Avenue, Monroe, LA 71209-1160
(318) 342-5320

University of New Orleans
New Orleans, Louisiana
www.uno.edu Federal Code: 002015

4-year public university in very large city.
Enrollment: 7,364 undergrads, 22% part-time. 858 full-time freshmen.
Selectivity: Admits less than 50% of applicants.

BASIC COSTS (2012-2013)
Tuition and fees: $5,922; out-of-state residents $17,934.
Per-credit charge: $172; out-of-state residents $572.
Room and board: $8,310.

FINANCIAL AID PICTURE (2012-2013)
Students with need: Out of 803 full-time freshmen who applied for aid, 679 were judged to have need. Of these, 656 received aid, and 80 had their full need met. Average financial aid package met 56% of need; average scholarship/grant was $6,081; average loan was $3,141. For part-time students, average financial aid package was $4,825.
Students without need: 1 full-time freshmen who did not demonstrate need for aid received scholarships/grants; average award was $1,000. No-need awards available for academics, athletics, music/drama.
Scholarships offered: 21 full-time freshmen received athletic scholarships; average amount $4,360.
Cumulative student debt: 18% of graduating class had student loans; average debt was $18,271.
Additional info: Students in good academic and financial standing eligible to participate in Extended Payment Plan option.

FINANCIAL AID PROCEDURES
Forms required: FAFSA.
Dates and Deadlines: Priority date 3/15; no closing date. Applicants notified on a rolling basis starting 4/20; must reply within 4 week(s) of notification.
Transfers: Mid-year transfers must submit financial aid transcript from all post-secondary schools attended. Others submit NSLDS.

CONTACT
Denise Spellman, Director of Student Financial Aid
Administration Building, Room 103, New Orleans, LA 70148
(504) 280-6603

Xavier University of Louisiana

New Orleans, Louisiana
www.xula.edu Federal Code: 002032

4-year private university in very large city, affiliated with Roman Catholic Church.
Enrollment: 2,496 undergrads, 4% part-time. 659 full-time freshmen.
Selectivity: Admits 50 to 75% of applicants.

BASIC COSTS (2012-2013)
Tuition and fees: $18,700.
Per-credit charge: $775.
Room and board: $7,600.

FINANCIAL AID PICTURE (2012-2013)
Students with need: Out of 635 full-time freshmen who applied for aid, 561 were judged to have need. Of these, 560 received aid, and 1 had their full need met. Average financial aid package met 14% of need; average scholarship/grant was $5,745; average loan was $3,707. For part-time students, average financial aid package was $9,888.
Students without need: 45 full-time freshmen who did not demonstrate need for aid received scholarships/grants; average award was $1,293.
Scholarships offered: 24 full-time freshmen received athletic scholarships; average amount $16,172.

FINANCIAL AID PROCEDURES
Forms required: FAFSA.
Dates and Deadlines: Priority date 1/1; no closing date. Applicants notified on a rolling basis starting 4/1; must reply within 2 week(s) of notification.

CONTACT
Mildred Higgins, Director of Financial Aid
One Drexel Drive, New Orleans, LA 70125-1098
(504) 520-7517

Maine

Bates College

Lewiston, Maine
www.bates.edu Federal Code: 002036
CSS Code: 3076

4-year private liberal arts college in small city.
Enrollment: 1,753 undergrads. 503 full-time freshmen.
Selectivity: Admits less than 50% of applicants. GED not accepted.

BASIC COSTS (2013-2014)
Comprehensive fee: $58,950.

FINANCIAL AID PICTURE (2012-2013)
Students with need: Out of 258 full-time freshmen who applied for aid, 224 were judged to have need. Of these, 209 received aid, and 202 had their full need met. Average financial aid package met 100% of need; average scholarship/grant was $36,387; average loan was $3,446.
Students without need: This college awards aid only to students with need.
Cumulative student debt: 40% of graduating class had student loans; average debt was $24,515.
Additional info: Priority date for filing required financial aid forms for early decision students is 11/15.

FINANCIAL AID PROCEDURES
Forms required: FAFSA, CSS PROFILE.
Dates and Deadlines: Closing date 2/15. Applicants notified by 4/1; must reply by 5/1.
Transfers: Closing date 1/1. Applicants notified by 6/1; must reply by 6/15.

CONTACT
Wendy Glass, Director of Student Financial Services
23 Campus Avenue, Lindholm House, Lewiston, ME 04240-9917
(207) 786-6096

Bowdoin College

Brunswick, Maine Federal Code: 002038
www.bowdoin.edu CSS Code: 3089

4-year private liberal arts college in large town.
Enrollment: 1,831 undergrads. 483 full-time freshmen.
Selectivity: Admits less than 50% of applicants. GED not accepted.

BASIC COSTS (2012-2013)
Tuition and fees: $44,118.
Per-credit charge: $854.
Room and board: $12,010.

FINANCIAL AID PICTURE (2011-2012)
Students with need: Out of 284 full-time freshmen who applied for aid, 215 were judged to have need. Of these, 215 received aid, and 215 had their full need met. Average financial aid package met 100% of need; average scholarship/grant was $35,427.
Students without need: 17 full-time freshmen who did not demonstrate need for aid received scholarships/grants; average award was $1,000. No-need awards available for academics, leadership.
Cumulative student debt: 33% of graduating class had student loans; average debt was $23,092.
Additional info: Regardless of financial circumstances, students admitted will receive money they need to attend. International students for regular admission must submit their financial aid applications by January 1st.

FINANCIAL AID PROCEDURES
Forms required: FAFSA, CSS PROFILE.
Dates and Deadlines: Closing date 2/15. Applicants notified by 4/5; must reply by 5/1 or within 1 week(s) of notification.
Transfers: Closing date 3/1. Applicants notified by 5/1; must reply by 6/1 or within 1 week(s) of notification. Financial aid usually not available for transfer students. Early Decision applicants must submit financial aid applications by November 15 (ED I) and January 1 (ED II).

CONTACT
Stephen Joyce, Director of Student Aid
5000 College Station, Brunswick, ME 04011-8441
(207) 725-3273

Central Maine Community College

Auburn, Maine
www.cmcc.edu Federal Code: 005276

2-year public community and technical college in small city.
Enrollment: 2,490 undergrads.

Selectivity: Open admission; but selective for some programs.

BASIC COSTS (2012-2013)
Tuition and fees: $3,324; out-of-state residents $5,904.
Per-credit charge: $86; out-of-state residents $172.
Room and board: $7,976.
Additional info: Additional lab and technology fees may apply to specific programs and courses. Tuition/fee waivers available for minority students.

FINANCIAL AID PICTURE
Students with need: Need-based aid available for full-time and part-time students. Work study available nights, weekends, and for part-time students.
Students without need: This college awards aid only to students with need.
Additional info: Tuition and/or fee waivers may be available to orphans, Native Americans, fire fighters, police, disabled veterans, dependents or survivors of veterans killed in line of duty.

FINANCIAL AID PROCEDURES
Forms required: FAFSA, institutional form.
Dates and Deadlines: Priority date 5/8; no closing date. Applicants notified on a rolling basis starting 3/15; must reply within 2 week(s) of notification.
Transfers: Priority date 8/1; no deadline. Applicants notified on a rolling basis starting 1/15; must reply within 2 week(s) of notification.

CONTACT
Trisha Mallow, Director of Financial Aid
1250 Turner Street, Auburn, ME 04210
(207) 755-5269

Central Maine Medical Center College of Nursing and Health Professions

Lewiston, Maine
www.cmmccollege.edu Federal Code: 006305

2-year private health science and nursing college in large town.
Enrollment: 216 undergrads, 69% part-time. 2 full-time freshmen.
Selectivity: Admits less than 50% of applicants.

BASIC COSTS (2013-2014)
Tuition and fees: $9,550.
Per-credit charge: $230.
Room only: $1,960.

FINANCIAL AID PICTURE
Students with need: Need-based aid available for full-time and part-time students.
Students without need: This college awards aid only to students with need.

FINANCIAL AID PROCEDURES
Forms required: FAFSA, institutional form.
Dates and Deadlines: Closing date 7/1. Applicants notified on a rolling basis starting 4/1; must reply within 2 week(s) of notification.

CONTACT
Jenna Rocque, Financial Aid Specialist
70 Middle Street, Lewiston, ME 04240
(207) 795-2270

Colby College

Waterville, Maine Federal Code: 002039
www.colby.edu CSS Code: 3280

4-year private liberal arts college in large town.
Enrollment: 1,863 undergrads. 493 full-time freshmen.
Selectivity: Admits less than 50% of applicants.

BASIC COSTS (2012-2013)
Comprehensive fee: $55,700.

FINANCIAL AID PICTURE
Students with need: Need-based aid available for full-time students. Work study available nights, weekends, and for part-time students.
Students without need: No-need awards available for academics.
Additional info: Institutional loans have been replaced with institutional grants.

FINANCIAL AID PROCEDURES
Forms required: FAFSA, CSS PROFILE.
Dates and Deadlines: Closing date 2/1. Applicants notified by 4/1; must reply by 5/1.
Transfers: Priority date 2/1. Applicants notified by 5/15; must reply within 2 week(s) of notification. Students admitted as other than first semester freshmen are eligible for Colby aid for the number of semesters required for graduation as determined by the College at the time of entry.

CONTACT
Melissa Rose, Director of Financial Aid
4800 Mayflower Hill, Waterville, ME 04901-8848
(800) 723-3032

College of the Atlantic

Bar Harbor, Maine
www.coa.edu Federal Code: 011385

4-year private liberal arts college in small town.
Enrollment: 321 undergrads, 4% part-time. 73 full-time freshmen.
Selectivity: Admits 50 to 75% of applicants.

BASIC COSTS (2013-2014)
Tuition and fees: $38,951.
Per-credit charge: $1,280.
Room and board: $9,252.

FINANCIAL AID PICTURE (2012-2013)
Students with need: Out of 67 full-time freshmen who applied for aid, 66 were judged to have need. Of these, 66 received aid, and 31 had their full need met. Average financial aid package met 94% of need; average scholarship/grant was $28,542; average loan was $4,048. For part-time students, average financial aid package was $34,597.
Students without need: 5 full-time freshmen who did not demonstrate need for aid received scholarships/grants; average award was $6,800.
Scholarships offered: Students from selected secondary schools, special programs such as robotics, selected summer programs, may receive $10,000 a year in scholarships; graduates of community colleges with a 3.0 average may be eligible for $15,000 per year scholarship.
Cumulative student debt: 56% of graduating class had student loans; average debt was $22,473.
Additional info: Low-cost classes available for local residents; some business courses covered by grant to the college.

FINANCIAL AID PROCEDURES
Forms required: FAFSA, institutional form.
Dates and Deadlines: Closing date 2/15. Applicants notified by 4/1; must reply by 5/1.
Transfers: Priority date 2/15. Applicants notified by 4/1; must reply by 5/1. FAFSA must be filed by 5/1 for Maine residents to be eligible for Maine state grant.

CONTACT
Bruce Hazam, Director of Financial Aid
105 Eden Street, Bar Harbor, ME 04609
(207) 288-5015

Eastern Maine Community College

Bangor, Maine
www.emcc.edu Federal Code: 005277

2-year public community and technical college in large town.
Enrollment: 2,052 undergrads.
Selectivity: Open admission; but selective for some programs.

BASIC COSTS (2012-2013)
Tuition and fees: $3,519; out-of-state residents $6,099.
Per-credit charge: $86; out-of-state residents $172.
Room and board: $6,880.
Additional info: Additional lab and technology fees may apply to specific programs and courses. Tuition/fee waivers available for minority students.

FINANCIAL AID PICTURE
Students with need: Need-based aid available for full-time and part-time students. Work study available nights, weekends, and for part-time students.
Students without need: This college awards aid only to students with need.

FINANCIAL AID PROCEDURES
Forms required: FAFSA, institutional form.
Dates and Deadlines: Priority date 5/1; no closing date. Applicants notified on a rolling basis starting 5/1; must reply within 3 week(s) of notification.

CONTACT
Candace Ward, Registrar/Financial Aid Director
354 Hogan Road, Bangor, ME 04401
(207) 974-4625

Husson University

Bangor, Maine
www.husson.edu Federal Code: 002043

4-year private business and health science college in large town.
Enrollment: 2,384 undergrads, 17% part-time. 383 full-time freshmen.
Selectivity: Admits over 75% of applicants.

BASIC COSTS (2012-2013)
Tuition and fees: $14,540.
Per-credit charge: $473.
Room and board: $7,900.

FINANCIAL AID PICTURE (2012-2013)
Students with need: Out of 364 full-time freshmen who applied for aid, 323 were judged to have need. Of these, 318 received aid, and 14 had their full need met. Average financial aid package met 58% of need; average scholarship/grant was $9,716; average loan was $3,186. For part-time students, average financial aid package was $6,042.
Students without need: 40 full-time freshmen who did not demonstrate need for aid received scholarships/grants; average award was $2,777. No-need awards available for academics, leadership.
Cumulative student debt: 98% of graduating class had student loans; average debt was $25,724.

FINANCIAL AID PROCEDURES
Forms required: FAFSA.
Dates and Deadlines: Priority date 4/15; no closing date. Applicants notified on a rolling basis starting 4/1; must reply by 5/1 or within 2 week(s) of notification.
Transfers: No deadline. Applicants notified on a rolling basis starting 2/20; must reply within 2 week(s) of notification.

CONTACT
Linda Hill, Director of Financial Aid
1 College Circle, Bangor, ME 04401-2999
(207) 941-7156

Kennebec Valley Community College

Fairfield, Maine
www.kvcc.me.edu Federal Code: 009826

2-year public community and technical college in small town.
Enrollment: 1,767 undergrads, 60% part-time. 366 full-time freshmen.
Selectivity: Open admission; but selective for some programs.

BASIC COSTS (2012-2013)
Tuition and fees: $3,186; out-of-state residents $5,766.
Per-credit charge: $86; out-of-state residents $172.
Additional info: Additional lab and technology fees apply to specific programs and courses.

FINANCIAL AID PICTURE (2011-2012)
Students with need: Out of 334 full-time freshmen who applied for aid, 305 were judged to have need. Of these, 294 received aid, and 26 had their full need met. Average financial aid package met 59% of need; average loan was $2,806. For part-time students, average financial aid package was $4,946.
Students without need: This college awards aid only to students with need.

FINANCIAL AID PROCEDURES
Forms required: FAFSA, institutional form.
Dates and Deadlines: Priority date 4/1; no closing date. Applicants notified on a rolling basis starting 5/1.
Transfers: No deadline. Applicants notified on a rolling basis.

CONTACT
Anne Connors, Director of Financial Aid
92 Western Avenue, Fairfield, ME 04937-1367
(207) 453-5121

Landing School of Boatbuilding and Design

Arundel, Maine
www.landingschool.edu

2-year private career college in small town.
Enrollment: 68 undergrads. 12 full-time freshmen.
Selectivity: Open admission; but selective for some programs.

BASIC COSTS (2012-2013)
Tuition and fees: $18,500.
Additional info: Fees vary by program $525 - $1,860.

FINANCIAL AID PICTURE (2011-2012)
Students with need: Need-based aid available for full-time students.
Students without need: This college awards aid only to students with need.

FINANCIAL AID PROCEDURES
Forms required: FAFSA.
Dates and Deadlines: Priority date 4/1; no closing date. Applicants notified on a rolling basis starting 3/1; must reply within 3 week(s) of notification.

CONTACT
Susan Gross, Director of Student Services
286 River Road, Arundel, ME 04046
(207) 985-7976

Maine College of Art

Portland, Maine
www.meca.edu Federal Code: 011673

4-year private visual arts college in small city.
Enrollment: 365 undergrads.

Selectivity: Admits over 75% of applicants.

BASIC COSTS (2012-2013)
Tuition and fees: $30,110.
Per-credit charge: $1,224.
Room and board: $10,000.

FINANCIAL AID PICTURE
Students with need: Need-based aid available for full-time and part-time students. Work study available nights, weekends, and for part-time students.
Students without need: No-need awards available for academics, art.

FINANCIAL AID PROCEDURES
Forms required: FAFSA.
Dates and Deadlines: Priority date 3/1; no closing date. Applicants notified on a rolling basis starting 2/15; must reply within 2 week(s) of notification.
Transfers: Closing date 4/15. Applicants notified on a rolling basis starting 2/15; must reply within 2 week(s) of notification.

CONTACT
Adrienne Amari, Director of Financial Aid
522 Congress Street, Portland, ME 04101
(207) 699-5073

Maine Maritime Academy
Castine, Maine
www.mainemaritime.edu Federal Code: 002044

4-year public maritime college in rural community.
Enrollment: 993 undergrads. 320 full-time freshmen.

BASIC COSTS (2012-2013)
Tuition and fees: $11,525; out-of-district residents $15,925; out-of-state residents $21,525.
Per-credit charge: $334; out-of-district residents $501; out-of-state residents $645.
Room and board: $9,548.

FINANCIAL AID PICTURE
Students with need: Need-based aid available for full-time and part-time students. Work study available nights, weekends, and for part-time students.
Students without need: No-need awards available for academics, leadership, state/district residency.

FINANCIAL AID PROCEDURES
Forms required: FAFSA.
Dates and Deadlines: Closing date 4/15. Applicants notified on a rolling basis starting 4/1; must reply within 4 week(s) of notification.

CONTACT
Kathy Heath, Director of Financial Aid
Pleasant Street, Castine, ME 04420
(207) 326-2339

New England School of Communications
Bangor, Maine
www.nescom.edu Federal Code: 023471

4-year private college of communications in small city.
Enrollment: 499 undergrads, 7% part-time. 107 full-time freshmen.
Selectivity: Admits 50 to 75% of applicants.

BASIC COSTS (2013-2014)
Tuition and fees: $13,404.
Room and board: $8,256.

FINANCIAL AID PICTURE (2012-2013)
Students with need: Out of 103 full-time freshmen who applied for aid, 103 were judged to have need. Of these, 84 received aid. For part-time students, average financial aid package was $8,078.
Students without need: No-need awards available for academics, leadership.
Cumulative student debt: 89% of graduating class had student loans; average debt was $30,422.

FINANCIAL AID PROCEDURES
Forms required: FAFSA, institutional form.
Dates and Deadlines: Priority date 4/15; no closing date. Applicants notified on a rolling basis starting 2/1; must reply by 8/12.
Transfers: No deadline. Applicants notified on a rolling basis starting 2/15; must reply within 4 week(s) of notification.

CONTACT
Nicole Vachon, Director of Financial Aid
One College Circle, Bangor, ME 04401
(207) 941-7176

Northern Maine Community College
Presque Isle, Maine
www.nmcc.edu Federal Code: 005760

2-year public community and technical college in small town.
Enrollment: 976 undergrads.

BASIC COSTS (2012-2013)
Tuition and fees: $3,268; out-of-state residents $5,848.
Per-credit charge: $86; out-of-state residents $172.
Room and board: $6,460.
Additional info: Additional lab and technology fees may apply to specific programs and courses. Tuition/fee waivers available for minority students.

FINANCIAL AID PICTURE
Students with need: Need-based aid available for full-time and part-time students.

FINANCIAL AID PROCEDURES
Forms required: FAFSA, institutional form.
Dates and Deadlines: Applicants notified on a rolling basis starting 4/15; must reply within 2 week(s) of notification.

CONTACT
Norma Smith, Financial Aid Coordinator
33 Edgemont Drive, Presque Isle, ME 04769
(207) 768-2790

Saint Joseph's College of Maine
Standish, Maine
www.sjcme.edu Federal Code: 002051

4-year private liberal arts college in small town, affiliated with Roman Catholic Church.
Enrollment: 945 undergrads, 3% part-time. 257 full-time freshmen.
Selectivity: Admits over 75% of applicants.

BASIC COSTS (2013-2014)
Tuition and fees: $30,090.
Per-credit charge: $970.
Room and board: $11,900.

FINANCIAL AID PICTURE
Students with need: Need-based aid available for full-time and part-time students. Work study available nights, weekends, and for part-time students.

Students without need: No-need awards available for academics, alumni affiliation, leadership.

FINANCIAL AID PROCEDURES

Forms required: FAFSA, institutional form.

Dates and Deadlines: Priority date 3/1; no closing date. Applicants notified on a rolling basis starting 3/1; must reply within 3 week(s) of notification.

CONTACT

Andrea Cross, Associate Dean for Financial Aid
278 Whites Bridge Road, Standish, ME 04084-5236
(800) 752-1266

Southern Maine Community College

South Portland, Maine
www.smccme.edu Federal Code: 005525

2-year public community and technical college in large town.
Enrollment: 6,072 undergrads, 50% part-time. 1,010 full-time freshmen.
Selectivity: Open admission; but selective for some programs.

BASIC COSTS (2012-2013)

Tuition and fees: $3,341; out-of-state residents $5,921.
Per-credit charge: $86; out-of-state residents $172.
Room and board: $8,280.
Additional info: Additional lab and technology fees may apply to specific programs and courses.

FINANCIAL AID PICTURE

Students with need: Need-based aid available for full-time and part-time students. Work study available nights, weekends, and for part-time students.
Students without need: This college awards aid only to students with need.

FINANCIAL AID PROCEDURES

Forms required: FAFSA.
Dates and Deadlines: Priority date 5/1; no closing date. Applicants notified on a rolling basis.

CONTACT

Shaun Gray, Director of Financial Services
2 Fort Road, South Portland, ME 04106
(207) 741-5518

Thomas College

Waterville, Maine
www.thomas.edu Federal Code: 002052

4-year private business and liberal arts college in large town.
Enrollment: 808 undergrads, 10% part-time. 247 full-time freshmen.
Selectivity: Admits 50 to 75% of applicants.

BASIC COSTS (2012-2013)

Tuition and fees: $22,770.
Per-credit charge: $924.
Room and board: $9,540.

FINANCIAL AID PICTURE (2012-2013)

Students with need: Out of 226 full-time freshmen who applied for aid, 210 were judged to have need. Of these, 210 received aid, and 13 had their full need met. Average financial aid package met 85% of need; average scholarship/grant was $16,298; average loan was $3,995. For part-time students, average financial aid package was $7,818.
Students without need: 27 full-time freshmen who did not demonstrate need for aid received scholarships/grants; average award was $8,056. No-need awards available for academics, leadership, state/district residency.

Cumulative student debt: 95% of graduating class had student loans; average debt was $34,613.

FINANCIAL AID PROCEDURES

Forms required: FAFSA.
Dates and Deadlines: Priority date 2/15; no closing date. Applicants notified on a rolling basis starting 3/15; must reply within 2 week(s) of notification.

CONTACT

Jeannine Bosse, Director of Student Financial Services
180 West River Road, Waterville, ME 04901
(207) 859-1105

Unity College

Unity, Maine
www.unity.edu Federal Code: 006858

4-year private liberal arts college in rural community.
Enrollment: 537 undergrads, 1% part-time. 120 full-time freshmen.
Selectivity: Admits over 75% of applicants.

BASIC COSTS (2012-2013)

Tuition and fees: $24,000.
Room and board: $8,714.
Additional info: Tuition/fee waivers available for minority students.

FINANCIAL AID PICTURE (2012-2013)

Students with need: Out of 118 full-time freshmen who applied for aid, 102 were judged to have need. Of these, 102 received aid, and 10 had their full need met. Average financial aid package met 71% of need; average scholarship/grant was $13,411; average loan was $4,400. For part-time students, average financial aid package was $6,340.
Students without need: 17 full-time freshmen who did not demonstrate need for aid received scholarships/grants; average award was $3,352. No-need awards available for academics, leadership, minority status.

FINANCIAL AID PROCEDURES

Forms required: FAFSA.
Dates and Deadlines: Priority date 3/1; no closing date. Applicants notified on a rolling basis starting 3/10; must reply within 2 week(s) of notification.
Transfers: Priority date 3/10. Applicants notified on a rolling basis starting 3/10; must reply within 2 week(s) of notification.

CONTACT

Rand Newell, Director of Financial Aid
P.O. 532, Unity, ME 04988-0532
(207) 948-9235

University of Maine

Orono, Maine
www.umaine.edu Federal Code: 002053

4-year public university in large town.
Enrollment: 8,228 undergrads, 9% part-time. 1,949 full-time freshmen.
Selectivity: Admits over 75% of applicants.

BASIC COSTS (2012-2013)

Tuition and fees: $10,594; out-of-state residents $27,454.
Per-credit charge: $279; out-of-state residents $841.
Room and board: $9,148.
Additional info: New England Regional Student Program tuition is $12,570.

FINANCIAL AID PICTURE (2012-2013)

Students with need: Need-based aid available for full-time and part-time students. Work study available nights, weekends, and for part-time students.

Students without need: No-need awards available for academics, alumni affiliation, art, athletics, job skills, leadership, minority status, music/drama, ROTC, state/district residency.
Scholarships offered: Academic merit scholarships range in value from $1,000 to full tuition. All awards are renewable for up to eight (8) consecutive semesters, based upon academic performance. Top Scholar Awards and Tuition Scholarships pay full resident tuition or full nonresident differential per semester each academic year.
Additional info: Financial aid is available for students entering in the spring.

FINANCIAL AID PROCEDURES
Forms required: FAFSA.
Dates and Deadlines: Priority date 3/1; closing date 5/1. Applicants notified on a rolling basis starting 3/15; must reply by 5/1 or within 2 week(s) of notification.

CONTACT
Gianna Marrs, Director of Student Financial Aid
5713 Chadbourne Hall, Orono, ME 04469-5713
(207) 581-1324

University of Maine at Augusta

Augusta, Maine
www.uma.edu Federal Code: 006760

4-year public university in large town.
Enrollment: 4,523 undergrads, 58% part-time. 324 full-time freshmen.
Selectivity: Open admission; but selective for some programs.

BASIC COSTS (2012-2013)
Tuition and fees: $7,448; out-of-state residents $16,688.
Per-credit charge: $217; out-of-state residents $525.
Additional info: New England Regional Student Program tuition is $9,750.

FINANCIAL AID PICTURE (2012-2013)
Students with need: Out of 301 full-time freshmen who applied for aid, 273 were judged to have need. Of these, 268 received aid, and 9 had their full need met. Average financial aid package met 59% of need; average scholarship/grant was $5,816; average loan was $6,156. For part-time students, average financial aid package was $6,752.
Students without need: No-need awards available for academics, athletics, leadership, music/drama, state/district residency.
Scholarships offered: 1 full-time freshmen received athletic scholarships; average amount $2,850.
Cumulative student debt: 76% of graduating class had student loans; average debt was $24,353.

FINANCIAL AID PROCEDURES
Forms required: FAFSA.
Dates and Deadlines: Priority date 3/1; no closing date. Applicants notified on a rolling basis starting 3/15; must reply within 2 week(s) of notification.

CONTACT
Sherry McCollett, Director of Financial Aid
46 University Drive, Augusta, ME 04330
(207) 621-3455

University of Maine at Farmington

Farmington, Maine
www.farmington.edu Federal Code: 002040

4-year public liberal arts and teachers college in small town.
Enrollment: 1,972 undergrads, 8% part-time. 458 full-time freshmen.
Selectivity: Admits over 75% of applicants.

BASIC COSTS (2012-2013)
Tuition and fees: $9,137; out-of-state residents $18,225.
Per-credit charge: $261; out-of-state residents $545.
Room and board: $8,454.
Additional info: New England Regional Student Program tuition and fees: $12,544. Tuition/fee waivers available for minority students.

FINANCIAL AID PICTURE (2011-2012)
Students with need: Out of 452 full-time freshmen who applied for aid, 408 were judged to have need. Of these, 408 received aid, and 30 had their full need met. Average financial aid package met 65% of need; average scholarship/grant was $7,806; average loan was $5,835. For part-time students, average financial aid package was $6,550.
Students without need: 27 full-time freshmen who did not demonstrate need for aid received scholarships/grants; average award was $2,284. No-need awards available for academics, leadership, minority status, state/district residency.
Scholarships offered: Presidential Scholarships; $2,000 renewable annually; for non-residents graduating in top half of high school class.
Cumulative student debt: 87% of graduating class had student loans; average debt was $29,251.
Additional info: Federal processor must receive FAFSA by 3/1.

FINANCIAL AID PROCEDURES
Forms required: FAFSA.
Dates and Deadlines: Closing date 3/1. Applicants notified on a rolling basis starting 3/15; must reply within 2 week(s) of notification.

CONTACT
Ronald Milliken, Director of Financial Aid
246 Main Street, Farmington, ME 04938
(207) 778-7100

University of Maine at Fort Kent

Fort Kent, Maine
www.umfk.maine.edu Federal Code: 002041

4-year public university and branch campus college in small town.
Enrollment: 836 undergrads, 27% part-time. 175 full-time freshmen.
Selectivity: Admits 50 to 75% of applicants.

BASIC COSTS (2012-2013)
Tuition and fees: $7,575; out-of-state residents $17,535.
Per-credit charge: $220; out-of-state residents $552.
Room and board: $7,550.
Additional info: New England Regional Student Program tuition is $9,900.

FINANCIAL AID PICTURE (2012-2013)
Students with need: Out of 140 full-time freshmen who applied for aid, 125 were judged to have need. Of these, 125 received aid, and 24 had their full need met. Average financial aid package met 69% of need; average scholarship/grant was $6,142; average loan was $4,621. For part-time students, average financial aid package was $7,133.
Students without need: 1 full-time freshmen who did not demonstrate need for aid received scholarships/grants; average award was $3,000. No-need awards available for academics, leadership.
Cumulative student debt: 65% of graduating class had student loans; average debt was $9,506.

FINANCIAL AID PROCEDURES
Forms required: FAFSA, state aid form, institutional form.
Dates and Deadlines: Priority date 3/1; no closing date. Applicants notified on a rolling basis starting 3/15.

CONTACT
Michael Huddy, Director of Financial Aid
23 University Drive, Fort Kent, ME 04743
(207) 834-7607

University of Maine at Machias

Machias, Maine
www.umm.maine.edu Federal Code: 002055

4-year public university and liberal arts college in rural community.
Enrollment: 627 undergrads, 25% part-time. 126 full-time freshmen.
Selectivity: Admits over 75% of applicants.

BASIC COSTS (2012-2013)
Tuition and fees: $7,480; out-of-state residents $19,300.
Per-credit charge: $222; out-of-state residents $616.
Room and board: $7,900.
Additional info: New England Regional Student Program tuition is $9,990.

FINANCIAL AID PICTURE
Students with need: Need-based aid available for full-time and part-time students.
Students without need: No-need awards available for academics, alumni affiliation, art, athletics.

FINANCIAL AID PROCEDURES
Forms required: FAFSA.
Dates and Deadlines: Priority date 3/1; no closing date. Applicants notified on a rolling basis starting 3/1.
Transfers: Applicants notified on a rolling basis starting 3/1.

CONTACT
Stephanie Larrabee, Director of Financial Aid
116 O'Brien Avenue, Machias, ME 04654-1397
(207) 255-1203

University of Maine at Presque Isle

Presque Isle, Maine
www.umpi.edu Federal Code: 002033

4-year public university in small town.
Enrollment: 1,022 undergrads, 22% part-time. 170 full-time freshmen.
Selectivity: Admits over 75% of applicants.

BASIC COSTS (2012-2013)
Tuition and fees: $7,300; out-of-state residents $17,260.
Per-credit charge: $220; out-of-state residents $552.
Room and board: $7,422.
Additional info: New England Regional Student Program tuition is $9,900. Tuition/fee waivers available for minority students.

FINANCIAL AID PICTURE (2012-2013)
Students with need: Out of 164 full-time freshmen who applied for aid, 146 were judged to have need. Of these, 146 received aid, and 49 had their full need met. Average financial aid package met 83% of need; average scholarship/grant was $7,559; average loan was $4,674. For part-time students, average financial aid package was $6,638.
Students without need: 11 full-time freshmen who did not demonstrate need for aid received scholarships/grants; average award was $2,709. No-need awards available for academics, alumni affiliation, art, job skills, leadership, minority status, music/drama, state/district residency.
Cumulative student debt: 75% of graduating class had student loans; average debt was $18,052.

FINANCIAL AID PROCEDURES
Forms required: FAFSA.
Dates and Deadlines: Priority date 4/1; no closing date. Applicants notified on a rolling basis starting 3/1; must reply within 2 week(s) of notification.

CONTACT
Christopher Bell, Director of Financial Aid
181 Main Street, Presque Isle, ME 04769
(207) 768-9510

University of New England

Biddeford, Maine
www.une.edu Federal Code: 002050

4-year private university in small city.
Enrollment: 2,173 undergrads, 1% part-time. 632 full-time freshmen.
Selectivity: Admits over 75% of applicants.

BASIC COSTS (2012-2013)
Tuition and fees: $31,870.
Per-credit charge: $1,090.
Room and board: $12,500.

FINANCIAL AID PICTURE (2011-2012)
Students with need: Need-based aid available for full-time and part-time students. Work study available nights, weekends, and for part-time students.
Scholarships offered: UNE Scholarships and UNE Departmental Award: non-need; based on academic qualifications as determined from GPA and SAT/ACT scores; must be a full-time undergraduate student and maintain a 2.5 GPA.

FINANCIAL AID PROCEDURES
Forms required: FAFSA.
Dates and Deadlines: Priority date 5/1; no closing date. Applicants notified on a rolling basis starting 2/1.

CONTACT
Paul Henderson, Director of Financial Aid
Hills Beach Road, Biddeford, ME 04005
(207) 602-2404

University of Southern Maine

Portland, Maine
www.usm.maine.edu Federal Code: 009762

4-year public university and liberal arts college in small city.
Enrollment: 6,461 undergrads, 30% part-time. 823 full-time freshmen.
Selectivity: Admits over 75% of applicants.

BASIC COSTS (2012-2013)
Tuition and fees: $8,920; out-of-state residents $21,280.
Per-credit charge: $253; out-of-state residents $665.
Room and board: $9,130.

FINANCIAL AID PICTURE
Students with need: Need-based aid available for full-time and part-time students. Work study available nights, weekends, and for part-time students.
Students without need: No-need awards available for academics, alumni affiliation, music/drama, state/district residency.

FINANCIAL AID PROCEDURES
Forms required: FAFSA.
Dates and Deadlines: Priority date 2/15; no closing date. Applicants notified on a rolling basis starting 3/15; must reply by 5/1 or within 2 week(s) of notification.
Transfers: Applicants notified on a rolling basis; must reply by 5/1 or within 2 week(s) of notification.

CONTACT
Keith Dubois, Director of Financial Aid Office
PO Box 9300, Portland, ME 04104
(207) 780-5250

Washington County Community College

Calais, Maine
www.wccc.me.edu Federal Code: 009231

2-year public community and technical college in small town.
Enrollment: 370 undergrads.
Selectivity: Open admission; but selective for some programs.

BASIC COSTS (2012-2013)
Tuition and fees: $3,206; out-of-state residents $5,786.
Per-credit charge: $86; out-of-state residents $172.
Room and board: $4,890.
Additional info: Additional lab and technology fees may apply to specific programs and courses.

FINANCIAL AID PICTURE
Students with need: Need-based aid available for full-time and part-time students.
Students without need: No-need awards available for academics.

FINANCIAL AID PROCEDURES
Forms required: FAFSA, institutional form.
Dates and Deadlines: Priority date 4/1; no closing date. Applicants notified on a rolling basis starting 6/1; must reply within 2 week(s) of notification.

CONTACT
William O'Shea, Financial Aid Director
One College Drive, Calais, ME 04619
(207) 454-1033

York County Community College

Wells, Maine
www.yccc.edu Federal Code: 031229

2-year public community and technical college in small town.
Enrollment: 1,281 undergrads, 59% part-time. 146 full-time freshmen.
Selectivity: Open admission.

BASIC COSTS (2012-2013)
Tuition and fees: $3,186; out-of-state residents $5,766.
Per-credit charge: $86; out-of-state residents $172.
Additional info: Additional lab and technology fees may apply to specific programs and courses. Tuition/fee waivers available for minority students.

FINANCIAL AID PICTURE (2011-2012)
Students with need: Out of 146 full-time freshmen who applied for aid, 129 were judged to have need. Of these, 125 received aid, and 6 had their full need met. Average financial aid package met 53% of need; average scholarship/grant was $4,797; average loan was $2,890. For part-time students, average financial aid package was $3,550.
Students without need: 3 full-time freshmen who did not demonstrate need for aid received scholarships/grants; average award was $647. No-need awards available for academics, art, leadership.
Cumulative student debt: 73% of graduating class had student loans; average debt was $11,536.

FINANCIAL AID PROCEDURES
Forms required: FAFSA.
Dates and Deadlines: Priority date 5/1; no closing date. Must reply within 2 week(s) of notification.

CONTACT
David Daigle, Director of Financial Aid
112 College Drive, Wells, ME 04090
(207) 216-4410

Maryland

Allegany College of Maryland

Cumberland, Maryland
www.allegany.edu Federal Code: 002057

2-year public community college in large town.
Enrollment: 3,065 undergrads.
Selectivity: Open admission; but selective for some programs.

BASIC COSTS (2012-2013)
Tuition and fees: $3,390; out-of-district residents $6,120; out-of-state residents $7,290.
Per-credit charge: $105; out-of-district residents $196; out-of-state residents $235.

FINANCIAL AID PICTURE
Students with need: Need-based aid available for full-time and part-time students. Work study available nights.
Students without need: No-need awards available for academics, athletics, leadership, state/district residency.

FINANCIAL AID PROCEDURES
Forms required: FAFSA, institutional form.
Dates and Deadlines: Priority date 3/1; no closing date. Applicants notified on a rolling basis starting 4/15; must reply within 2 week(s) of notification.

CONTACT
Vicki Smith, Director of Financial Aid
12401 Willowbrook Road, SE, Cumberland, MD 21502
(301) 784-5213

Anne Arundel Community College

Arnold, Maryland
www.aacc.edu Federal Code: 002058

2-year public community college in large town.
Enrollment: 15,147 undergrads, 67% part-time. 1,701 full-time freshmen.
Selectivity: Open admission; but selective for some programs.

BASIC COSTS (2012-2013)
Tuition and fees: $3,600; out-of-district residents $6,270; out-of-state residents $10,590.
Per-credit charge: $97; out-of-district residents $186; out-of-state residents $330.

FINANCIAL AID PICTURE (2011-2012)
Students with need: 66% of average financial aid package awarded as scholarships/grants, 34% awarded as loans/jobs. Need-based aid available for part-time students. Work study available nights, weekends, and for part-time students.

FINANCIAL AID PROCEDURES
Forms required: FAFSA, institutional form.
Dates and Deadlines: Priority date 5/15; no closing date. Applicants notified on a rolling basis starting 7/1; must reply within 2 week(s) of notification.

CONTACT
Richard Heath, Director of Student Financial Services
101 College Parkway, Arnold, MD 21012-1895
(410) 777-2203

Baltimore City Community College

Baltimore, Maryland
www.bccc.edu Federal Code: 002061

2-year public community college in very large city.
Enrollment: 7,085 undergrads.
Selectivity: Open admission; but selective for some programs.

BASIC COSTS (2012-2013)
Tuition and fees: $3,062; out-of-state residents $6,722.

FINANCIAL AID PICTURE
Students with need: Need-based aid available for full-time and part-time students. Work study available nights, weekends, and for part-time students.
Students without need: This college awards aid only to students with need.

FINANCIAL AID PROCEDURES
Forms required: FAFSA, state aid form, institutional form.
Dates and Deadlines: Priority date 6/1; no closing date. Applicants notified on a rolling basis starting 7/1; must reply within 2 week(s) of notification.

CONTACT
Vera Brooks, Director of Financial Aid
2901 Liberty Heights Avenue, Baltimore, MD 21215-7893
(410) 462-8348

Bowie State University

Bowie, Maryland
www.bowiestate.edu Federal Code: 002062

4-year public university in small city.
Enrollment: 4,247 undergrads, 18% part-time. 477 full-time freshmen.
Selectivity: Admits less than 50% of applicants.

BASIC COSTS (2012-2013)
Tuition and fees: $6,639; out-of-state residents $17,195.
Per-credit charge: $207; out-of-state residents $641.
Room and board: $8,912.

FINANCIAL AID PICTURE
Students with need: Need-based aid available for full-time and part-time students. Work study available weekends and for part-time students.
Students without need: No-need awards available for academics, alumni affiliation, art, athletics, leadership, music/drama, ROTC, state/district residency.

FINANCIAL AID PROCEDURES
Forms required: FAFSA.
Dates and Deadlines: Closing date 3/1. Applicants notified on a rolling basis starting 4/1; must reply within 2 week(s) of notification.
Transfers: Applicants notified on a rolling basis starting 4/1; must reply within 2 week(s) of notification.

CONTACT
Deborah Stanley, Director of Financial Aid
14000 Jericho Park Road, Bowie, MD 20715
(301) 860-3540

Carroll Community College

Westminster, Maryland
www.carrollcc.edu Federal Code: 031007

2-year public community college in large town.
Enrollment: 3,925 undergrads, 59% part-time. 575 full-time freshmen.
Selectivity: Open admission; but selective for some programs.

BASIC COSTS (2012-2013)
Tuition and fees: $3,900; out-of-district residents $5,670; out-of-state residents $7,950.
Per-credit charge: $130; out-of-district residents $189; out-of-state residents $265.

FINANCIAL AID PICTURE (2011-2012)
Students with need: 98% of average financial aid package awarded as scholarships/grants, 2% awarded as loans/jobs. Need-based aid available for part-time students. Work study available nights, weekends, and for part-time students.
Students without need: No-need awards available for academics, art, job skills, leadership, state/district residency.

FINANCIAL AID PROCEDURES
Forms required: FAFSA.
Dates and Deadlines: Priority date 3/1; no closing date. Applicants notified by 6/1; must reply within 2 week(s) of notification.

CONTACT
John Gay, Director of Financial Aid
1601 Washington Road, Westminster, MD 21157
(410) 386-8437

Cecil College

North East, Maryland
www.my.cecil.edu Federal Code: 008308

2-year public community college in small town.
Enrollment: 2,591 undergrads, 66% part-time. 280 full-time freshmen.
Selectivity: Open admission; but selective for some programs.

BASIC COSTS (2012-2013)
Tuition and fees: $3,235; out-of-district residents $5,935; out-of-state residents $7,285.
Per-credit charge: $95; out-of-district residents $185; out-of-state residents $230.
Additional info: Tuition at time of enrollment locked for 2 years.

FINANCIAL AID PICTURE (2011-2012)
Students with need: 79% of average financial aid package awarded as scholarships/grants, 21% awarded as loans/jobs. Work study available nights, weekends, and for part-time students.
Students without need: No-need awards available for academics, alumni affiliation, athletics, job skills, state/district residency.

FINANCIAL AID PROCEDURES
Forms required: FAFSA.
Dates and Deadlines: Priority date 8/1; no closing date. Applicants notified on a rolling basis; must reply within 2 week(s) of notification.

CONTACT
Stephen Ampersand, Director of Financial Aid
One Seahawk Drive, North East, MD 21901
(410) 287-1003

Chesapeake College

Wye Mills, Maryland
www.chesapeake.edu Federal Code: 004650

2-year public community college in rural community.
Enrollment: 2,341 undergrads, 61% part-time. 348 full-time freshmen.
Selectivity: Open admission; but selective for some programs.

BASIC COSTS (2012-2013)
Tuition and fees: $3,950; out-of-district residents $6,020; out-of-state residents $8,330.

Per-credit charge: $104; out-of-district residents $172; out-of-state residents $249.

FINANCIAL AID PICTURE (2011-2012)

Students with need: Average financial aid package met 33% of need. For part-time students, average financial aid package was $2,439.

Students without need: No-need awards available for academics, art, athletics, state/district residency.

FINANCIAL AID PROCEDURES

Forms required: FAFSA, institutional form.

Dates and Deadlines: Priority date 5/1; no closing date. Applicants notified on a rolling basis starting 5/5; must reply within 2 week(s) of notification.

CONTACT

Mindy Schaffer, Director of Financial Aid
Box 8, Wye Mills, MD 21679-0008
(410) 822-5400 ext. 252

College of Southern Maryland

La Plata, Maryland
www.csmd.edu Federal Code: 002064

2-year public community college in large town.

Enrollment: 8,216 undergrads.

Selectivity: Open admission; but selective for some programs.

BASIC COSTS (2012-2013)

Tuition and fees: $4,096; out-of-district residents $6,526; out-of-state residents $8,206.

Per-credit charge: $111; out-of-district residents $192; out-of-state residents $248.

FINANCIAL AID PICTURE

Students with need: Need-based aid available for full-time and part-time students. Work study available nights, weekends, and for part-time students.

Students without need: No-need awards available for academics, athletics, state/district residency.

FINANCIAL AID PROCEDURES

Forms required: FAFSA.

Dates and Deadlines: Priority date 3/1; no closing date. Applicants notified on a rolling basis starting 5/15; must reply within 2 week(s) of notification.

CONTACT

Christian Zimmermann, Director of Financial Assistance
College of Southern Maryland-AOD, La Plata, MD 20646-0910
(301) 934-7531

Community College of Baltimore County

Baltimore, Maryland
www.ccbcmd.edu Federal Code: 002063

2-year public community college in very large city.

Enrollment: 23,529 undergrads, 65% part-time. 2,535 full-time freshmen.

Selectivity: Open admission; but selective for some programs.

BASIC COSTS (2012-2013)

Tuition and fees: $3,922; out-of-district residents $6,802; out-of-state residents $9,832.

Per-credit charge: $106; out-of-district residents $202; out-of-state residents $303.

FINANCIAL AID PICTURE

Students with need: Need-based aid available for full-time and part-time students. Work study available nights, weekends, and for part-time students.

Students without need: No-need awards available for academics, athletics, state/district residency.

Additional info: On-campus employment typically available.

FINANCIAL AID PROCEDURES

Forms required: FAFSA.

Dates and Deadlines: Priority date 1/2; no closing date. Applicants notified on a rolling basis; must reply within 2 week(s) of notification.

CONTACT

Virginia Zawodny, Interium Director of Financial Aid
800 South Rolling Road, Baltimore, MD 21228
(443) 840-5046

Coppin State University

Baltimore, Maryland
www.coppin.edu Federal Code: 002068

4-year public liberal arts college in very large city.

Enrollment: 3,067 undergrads, 20% part-time. 429 full-time freshmen.

BASIC COSTS (2012-2013)

Tuition and fees: $5,720; out-of-state residents $10,511.

Per-credit charge: $165; out-of-state residents $482.

Room and board: $7,199.

Additional info: Out of state room and board is $9,595.

FINANCIAL AID PICTURE

Students with need: Need-based aid available for full-time and part-time students.

Students without need: No-need awards available for academics, alumni affiliation, athletics, ROTC, state/district residency.

Scholarships offered: Gold Freshman Merit Award: $2,000 per year; awarded to freshmen with 950 combined SAT and 2.5 high school GPA. Gold Transfer Merit Award: $1,500 per year; awarded to Maryland Community College transfer students with 2.8 GPA and successful completion of 56 credits. Blue Freshman Merit Award: $1,000 per year; awarded to freshman with 900 combined SAT and 2.5 GPA. Blue Transfer Merit Award: $800 per year; awarded to Maryland Community College transfer students with 2.5 GPA and successful completion of 25 credits. SAT scores exclusive of Writing.

Additional info: Funds allocated by State of Maryland for minority students enrolled for at least 6 credits who are Maryland residents and US citizens (Minority Grant).

FINANCIAL AID PROCEDURES

Forms required: FAFSA.

Dates and Deadlines: Priority date 3/1; no closing date. Applicants notified on a rolling basis starting 4/15; must reply within 2 week(s) of notification.

CONTACT

Mose Cartier, Director of Financial Aid
2500 West North Avenue, Baltimore, MD 21216
(410) 951-3636

Frederick Community College

Frederick, Maryland
www.frederick.edu Federal Code: 002071

2-year public community college in small city.

Enrollment: 5,101 undergrads, 59% part-time. 846 full-time freshmen.

Selectivity: Open admission; but selective for some programs.

BASIC COSTS (2012-2013)

Tuition and fees: $3,934; out-of-district residents $7,774; out-of-state residents $10,294.

Per-credit charge: $109; out-of-district residents $237; out-of-state residents $321.

FINANCIAL AID PICTURE

Students with need: Need-based aid available for full-time and part-time students.

Students without need: No-need awards available for academics, athletics, state/district residency.

Scholarships offered: Scholarships available for Frederick County Public Schools students with high GPA to participate in student ambassador program; other general scholarships available for prospective students.

FINANCIAL AID PROCEDURES

Forms required: FAFSA, institutional form.

Dates and Deadlines: Priority date 6/1; no closing date. Applicants notified on a rolling basis starting 5/15; must reply within 2 week(s) of notification.

Transfers: Applicants notified on a rolling basis starting 6/1. Financial aid transcripts from prior institutions must be submitted before awards are made.

CONTACT

Brenda Dayhoff, Executive Director, Financial Aid
7932 Opossumtown Pike, Frederick, MD 21702
(301) 846-2480

Frostburg State University

Frostburg, Maryland
www.frostburg.edu Federal Code: 002072

4-year public university and teachers college in small town.
Enrollment: 4,522 undergrads, 7% part-time. 813 full-time freshmen.
Selectivity: Admits 50 to 75% of applicants.

BASIC COSTS (2012-2013)

Tuition and fees: $7,436; out-of-state residents $17,624.
Per-credit charge: $226; out-of-state residents $440.
Room and board: $7,796.

FINANCIAL AID PICTURE

Students with need: Need-based aid available for full-time and part-time students.

Students without need: No-need awards available for academics, leadership, minority status.

FINANCIAL AID PROCEDURES

Forms required: FAFSA.

Dates and Deadlines: Priority date 3/1; no closing date. Applicants notified on a rolling basis starting 3/15; must reply within 3 week(s) of notification.

CONTACT

Angela Hovatter, Director of Financial Aid
101 Braddock Road, Frostburg, MD 21532-1099
(301) 687-4201

Garrett College

McHenry, Maryland
www.garrettcollege.edu Federal Code: 010014

2-year public community college in rural community.
Enrollment: 659 undergrads, 15% part-time. 221 full-time freshmen.
Selectivity: Open admission.

BASIC COSTS (2012-2013)

Tuition and fees: $3,450; out-of-district residents $7,230; out-of-state residents $8,400.
Per-credit charge: $90; out-of-district residents $216; out-of-state residents $255.
Room and board: $5,770.

FINANCIAL AID PICTURE

Students with need: Need-based aid available for full-time and part-time students. Work study available nights, weekends, and for part-time students.

Students without need: No-need awards available for academics, athletics, leadership.

Additional info: Many local scholarships both merit and need based.

FINANCIAL AID PROCEDURES

Forms required: FAFSA.

Dates and Deadlines: Priority date 3/1; no closing date. Applicants notified on a rolling basis starting 6/1; must reply within 2 week(s) of notification.

CONTACT

Cissy Vansickle, Director of Financial Aid
687 Mosser Road, McHenry, MD 21541
(301) 387-3012

Goucher College

Baltimore, Maryland Federal Code: 002073
www.goucher.edu CSS Code: 5257

4-year private liberal arts college in very large city.
Enrollment: 1,469 undergrads, 2% part-time. 410 full-time freshmen.
Selectivity: Admits 50 to 75% of applicants.

BASIC COSTS (2013-2014)

Tuition and fees: $39,084.
Per-credit charge: $1,282.
Room and board: $1,282.

FINANCIAL AID PICTURE (2012-2013)

Students with need: Out of 341 full-time freshmen who applied for aid, 290 were judged to have need. Of these, 290 received aid, and 39 had their full need met. Average financial aid package met 81% of need; average scholarship/grant was $27,204; average loan was $3,237. For part-time students, average financial aid package was $7,991.

Students without need: 76 full-time freshmen who did not demonstrate need for aid received scholarships/grants; average award was $13,867. No-need awards available for academics, art, music/drama.

Cumulative student debt: 43% of graduating class had student loans; average debt was $29,135.

FINANCIAL AID PROCEDURES

Forms required: FAFSA, CSS PROFILE.

Dates and Deadlines: Closing date 2/1. Applicants notified on a rolling basis starting 3/1; must reply by 5/1.

Transfers: Must reply within 2 week(s) of notification.

CONTACT

Stephanie Bender, Director of Financial Aid
1021 Dulaney Valley Road, Baltimore, MD 21204-2753
(410) 337-6141

Hagerstown Community College

Hagerstown, Maryland
www.hagerstowncc.edu Federal Code: 002074

2-year public community college in small city.
Enrollment: 4,211 undergrads, 68% part-time. 445 full-time freshmen.
Selectivity: Open admission; but selective for some programs.

BASIC COSTS (2012-2013)

Tuition and fees: $3,610; out-of-district residents $5,410; out-of-state residents $6,970.
Per-credit charge: $106; out-of-district residents $166; out-of-state residents $218.

FINANCIAL AID PICTURE

Students with need: Need-based aid available for full-time and part-time students. Work study available nights, weekends, and for part-time students.

Students without need: This college awards aid only to students with need.

FINANCIAL AID PROCEDURES

Forms required: FAFSA.

Dates and Deadlines: Priority date 3/1; no closing date. Applicants notified on a rolling basis starting 5/1.

Transfers: No deadline.

CONTACT

Carolyn Cox, Director of Financial Aid
11400 Robinwood Drive, Hagerstown, MD 21742-6514
(240) 500-2473

Harford Community College

Bel Air, Maryland
www.harford.edu Federal Code: 002075

2-year public community college in small city.
Enrollment: 6,139 undergrads, 58% part-time. 1,032 full-time freshmen.
Selectivity: Open admission; but selective for some programs.

BASIC COSTS (2012-2013)

Tuition and fees: $2,925; out-of-district residents $5,535; out-of-state residents $8,145.

Per-credit charge: $87; out-of-district residents $174; out-of-state residents $261.

FINANCIAL AID PICTURE (2011-2012)

Students with need: Out of 666 full-time freshmen who applied for aid, 481 were judged to have need. Of these, 415 received aid. Need-based aid available for part-time students.

Scholarships offered: Alfred C. O'Connell Homes Scholarship; full tuition & fees for 2 years, grade point average of 3.25 and above; 25 awards.

FINANCIAL AID PROCEDURES

Forms required: FAFSA, institutional form.

Dates and Deadlines: Priority date 3/15; no closing date. Applicants notified on a rolling basis starting 4/1; must reply within 2 week(s) of notification.

CONTACT

Lynn Lee, Director of Financial Aid
401 Thomas Run Road, Bel Air, MD 21015
(443) 443-2257

Hood College

Frederick, Maryland
www.hood.edu Federal Code: 002076

4-year private liberal arts college in small city.
Enrollment: 1,383 undergrads, 8% part-time. 270 full-time freshmen.
Selectivity: Admits over 75% of applicants.

BASIC COSTS (2012-2013)

Tuition and fees: $32,300.
Per-credit charge: $920.
Room and board: $10,910.

FINANCIAL AID PICTURE (2012-2013)

Students with need: Out of 240 full-time freshmen who applied for aid, 210 were judged to have need. Of these, 210 received aid, and 45 had their full need met. Average financial aid package met 75% of need; average scholarship/grant was $21,590; average loan was $3,151. For part-time students, average financial aid package was $9,059.

Students without need: 53 full-time freshmen who did not demonstrate need for aid received scholarships/grants; average award was $16,542. No-need awards available for academics, alumni affiliation, minority status, music/drama, ROTC.

Scholarships offered: Hood Trust Academic Scholarship: amount varies. Hodson Scholarship: amount varies. Project Excellence Scholarship: up to full tuition. Presidential Scholarship: $10,000-$14,000. Trustee Scholarship: $8,000-$10,000.

Cumulative student debt: 33% of graduating class had student loans; average debt was $18,250.

FINANCIAL AID PROCEDURES

Forms required: FAFSA, institutional form.

Dates and Deadlines: Priority date 2/15; no closing date. Applicants notified on a rolling basis starting 3/1; must reply by 5/1 or within .3 week(s) of notification.

CONTACT

Carol Schroyer, Director of Financial Aid
401 Rosemont Avenue, Frederick, MD 21701-8575
(301) 696-3411

Howard Community College

Columbia, Maryland
www.howardcc.edu Federal Code: 008175

2-year public community college in small city.
Enrollment: 9,242 undergrads, 62% part-time. 985 full-time freshmen.
Selectivity: Open admission; but selective for some programs.

BASIC COSTS (2013-2014)

Tuition and fees: $4,318; out-of-district residents $6,808; out-of-state residents $8,158.

Per-credit charge: $124; out-of-district residents $207; out-of-state residents $252.

FINANCIAL AID PICTURE (2011-2012)

Students with need: 74% of average financial aid package awarded as scholarships/grants, 26% awarded as loans/jobs. Need-based aid available for part-time students. Work study available nights, weekends, and for part-time students.

FINANCIAL AID PROCEDURES

Forms required: FAFSA.

Dates and Deadlines: Priority date 3/1; no closing date. Applicants notified on a rolling basis starting 5/1.

CONTACT

Stephanie Bender, Director of Financial Aid Services
10901 Little Patuxent Parkway, Columbia, MD 21044-3197
(443) 518-1260

Johns Hopkins University

Baltimore, Maryland Federal Code: 002077
www.jhu.edu CSS Code: 5332

4-year private university in very large city.
Enrollment: 5,165 undergrads. 1,330 full-time freshmen.
Selectivity: Admits less than 50% of applicants.

BASIC COSTS (2013-2014)

Tuition and fees: $45,970.
Per-credit charge: $1,515.
Room and board: $13,832.

FINANCIAL AID PICTURE

Students with need: Need-based aid available for full-time students. Work study available nights, weekends, and for part-time students.

Students without need: No-need awards available for academics, athletics, leadership, ROTC, state/district residency.

...ered: Hodson Trust Scholarship; $28,500 annually for 4 ...wards. Westgate Scholarship for engineering freshmen; tuition ...1,000 for 4 years: academic excellence, leadership, demonstrated research experience required, 2 offered per year per class. Wilson Research grants; $10,000. Baltimore Scholars Program; full tuition scholarship for US citizens or permanent residents who have attended a Baltimore City public school for at least 10th, 11th, and 12th grades and meet a residency requirement.

Additional info: Selected students receive aid packages without loan expectation, grants to full need. Private merit aid does not reduce Hopkins grant.

FINANCIAL AID PROCEDURES

Forms required: FAFSA, CSS PROFILE.

Dates and Deadlines: Closing date 3/1. Applicants notified by 4/1; must reply by 5/1 or within 2 week(s) of notification.

Transfers: Closing date 3/15. Must reply within 2 week(s) of notification. Aid on funds-available basis.

CONTACT

Tom McDermott, Director of Student Financial Services
3400 North Charles Street, Mason Hall, Baltimore, MD 21218
(410) 516-8028

Johns Hopkins University: Peabody Conservatory of Music

Baltimore, Maryland
www.peabody.jhu.edu Federal Code: E00233

4-year private music college in very large city.

Enrollment: 309 undergrads, 3% part-time. 79 full-time freshmen.

Selectivity: Admits less than 50% of applicants.

BASIC COSTS (2013-2014)

Tuition and fees: $40,986.

Per-credit charge: $1,135.

Room and board: $13,126.

FINANCIAL AID PICTURE (2011-2012)

Students with need: Out of 70 full-time freshmen who applied for aid, 61 were judged to have need. Of these, 57 received aid, and 9 had their full need met. Average financial aid package met 76% of need; average scholarship/grant was $17,877; average loan was $4,377. Need-based aid available for part-time students.

Students without need: 8 full-time freshmen who did not demonstrate need for aid received scholarships/grants; average award was $14,688. No-need awards available for academics, music/drama.

Cumulative student debt: 47% of graduating class had student loans; average debt was $33,888.

FINANCIAL AID PROCEDURES

Forms required: FAFSA, institutional form.

Dates and Deadlines: Closing date 2/1. Applicants notified by 4/1; must reply by 5/1.

Transfers: Applicants notified by 4/1; must reply by 5/1.

CONTACT

Rebecca Polgar, Director Financial Aid
One East Mount Vernon Place, Baltimore, MD 21202
(410) 234-4900

Kaplan University: Hagerstown

Hagerstown, Maryland
www.Hagerstown.KaplanUniversity.edu
Federal Code: 007946

2-year for-profit business and junior college in large town.

Enrollment: 657 undergrads.

Selectivity: Open admission; but selective for some programs.

BASIC COSTS (2012-2013)

Additional info: Estimated tuition and fees ranges for entire programs as of February 2012: diploma programs, $16,695 -$23,373; associate degree programs, $33,390; bachelor's degree programs, $66,780; does not include books and supplies, which vary by program. All costs subject to change at any time.

FINANCIAL AID PICTURE

Students with need: Need-based aid available for full-time and part-time students.

FINANCIAL AID PROCEDURES

Forms required: FAFSA, institutional form.

Dates and Deadlines: Applicants notified on a rolling basis starting 6/1; must reply within 2 week(s) of notification.

CONTACT

Kristen Brezler, Director of Financial Aid
18618 Crestwood Drive, Hagerstown, MD 21742
(301) 739-2670

Loyola University Maryland

Baltimore, Maryland Federal Code: 002078
www.loyola.edu CSS Code: 5370

4-year private university in very large city, affiliated with Roman Catholic Church.

Enrollment: 3,898 undergrads, 1% part-time. 1,070 full-time freshmen.

Selectivity: Admits 50 to 75% of applicants.

BASIC COSTS (2013-2014)

Tuition and fees: $43,250.

Per-credit charge: $678.

Room and board: $12,300.

FINANCIAL AID PICTURE (2011-2012)

Students with need: Out of 838 full-time freshmen who applied for aid, 671 were judged to have need. Of these, 671 received aid, and 669 had their full need met. Average financial aid package met 100% of need; average scholarship/grant was $20,680; average loan was $4,425. For part-time students, average financial aid package was $5,500.

Students without need: 71 full-time freshmen who did not demonstrate need for aid received scholarships/grants; average award was $15,320. No-need awards available for academics, athletics, ROTC.

Scholarships offered: 24 full-time freshmen received athletic scholarships; average amount $26,110.

Cumulative student debt: 63% of graduating class had student loans; average debt was $32,392.

FINANCIAL AID PROCEDURES

Forms required: FAFSA, CSS PROFILE.

Dates and Deadlines: Closing date 2/15. Applicants notified by 3/15; must reply by 5/1.

Transfers: No deadline. Applicants notified on a rolling basis starting 5/1; must reply by 7/1. Transfer students are not eligible to be considered for merit (non-need-based) scholarships.

CONTACT

Mark Lindenmeyer, Director of Financial Aid / Assistant Vice President for Enrollment
4501 North Charles Street, Baltimore, MD 21210-2699
(410) 617-2576

Maryland Institute College of Art

Baltimore, Maryland
www.mica.edu Federal Code: 002080

4-year private visual arts college in very large city.
Enrollment: 1,821 undergrads, 1% part-time. 413 full-time freshmen.
Selectivity: Admits 50 to 75% of applicants.

BASIC COSTS (2013-2014)
Tuition and fees: $40,890.
Per-credit charge: $1,640.
Room and board: $11,260.

FINANCIAL AID PICTURE
Students with need: Need-based aid available for full-time and part-time students. Work study available nights, weekends, and for part-time students.
Students without need: No-need awards available for academics, art.

FINANCIAL AID PROCEDURES
Forms required: FAFSA, institutional form.
Dates and Deadlines: Closing date 2/15. Applicants notified by 4/8; must reply by 5/1.
Transfers: Priority date 3/1. Applicants notified by 4/24; must reply by 5/21.

CONTACT
Diane Prengaman, Associate Vice President for Financial Aid
1300 Mount Royal Avenue, Baltimore, MD 21217-4134
(410) 225-2285

McDaniel College

Westminster, Maryland
www.mcdaniel.edu Federal Code: 002109

4-year private liberal arts college in large town.
Enrollment: 1,614 undergrads, 1% part-time. 437 full-time freshmen.
Selectivity: Admits 50 to 75% of applicants.

BASIC COSTS (2012-2013)
Tuition and fees: $35,800.
Per-credit charge: $1,119.
Room and board: $7,740.

FINANCIAL AID PICTURE (2012-2013)
Students with need: Out of 400 full-time freshmen who applied for aid, 360 were judged to have need. Of these, 360 received aid, and 91 had their full need met. Average financial aid package met 85% of need; average scholarship/grant was $25,674; average loan was $4,340. For part-time students, average financial aid package was $10,724.
Students without need: 71 full-time freshmen who did not demonstrate need for aid received scholarships/grants; average award was $17,312. No-need awards available for academics, ROTC, state/district residency.
Cumulative student debt: 64% of graduating class had student loans; average debt was $31,919.

FINANCIAL AID PROCEDURES
Forms required: FAFSA, institutional form.
Dates and Deadlines: Priority date 3/1; no closing date. Applicants notified on a rolling basis starting 2/15; must reply by 5/1 or within 2 week(s) of notification.
Transfers: No deadline. Applicants notified on a rolling basis starting 2/15; must reply by 8/1 or within 2 week(s) of notification.

CONTACT
Patricia Williams, Director of Financial Aid
Two College Hill, Westminster, MD 21157-4390
(410) 857-2233

Montgomery College

Rockville, Maryland
www.montgomerycollege.edu Federal Code: 006911

2-year public community college in very large city.
Enrollment: 26,996 undergrads.
Selectivity: Open admission; but selective for some programs.

BASIC COSTS (2012-2013)
Tuition and fees: $4,452; out-of-district residents $8,664; out-of-state residents $11,724.

FINANCIAL AID PICTURE
Students with need: Need-based aid available for full-time and part-time students. Work study available nights, weekends, and for part-time students.
Students without need: No-need awards available for academics, alumni affiliation, art, athletics, leadership, minority status, music/drama, state/district residency.
Scholarships offered: Board of Trustees Academic Potential Scholarship; first year of tuition; based on GPA and high school nominations; 125 awards available.

FINANCIAL AID PROCEDURES
Forms required: FAFSA, institutional form.
Dates and Deadlines: Priority date 5/15; no closing date. Applicants notified on a rolling basis starting 5/30.
Transfers: No deadline. Applicants notified on a rolling basis starting 1/1; must reply within 4 week(s) of notification.

CONTACT
Melissa Gregory, Director of Financial Aid
51 Mannakee Street, Rockville, MD 20850
(240) 567-5100

Morgan State University

Baltimore, Maryland
www.morgan.edu Federal Code: 002083

4-year public university and liberal arts college in large city.
Enrollment: 6,567 undergrads, 12% part-time. 1,014 full-time freshmen.
Selectivity: Admits 50 to 75% of applicants.

BASIC COSTS (2012-2013)
Tuition and fees: $7,012; out-of-state residents $16,356.
Per-credit charge: $212; out-of-state residents $552.
Room and board: $8,878.
Additional info: Tuition/fee waivers available for minority students.

FINANCIAL AID PICTURE
Students with need: Need-based aid available for full-time and part-time students.

FINANCIAL AID PROCEDURES
Forms required: FAFSA.
Dates and Deadlines: Priority date 4/1; no closing date. Applicants notified on a rolling basis starting 6/1; must reply within 2 week(s) of notification.

CONTACT
Tanya Wilkerson, Director of Financial Aid
1700 East Cold Spring Lane, Baltimore, MD 21251
(443) 885-3170

Mount St. Mary's University

Emmitsburg, Maryland
www.msmary.edu Federal Code: 002086

4-year private university and liberal arts college in rural community, affiliated with Roman Catholic Church.

Enrollment: 1,831 undergrads, 4% part-time. 447 full-time freshmen.
Selectivity: Admits 50 to 75% of applicants.

BASIC COSTS (2013-2014)
Tuition and fees: $34,644.
Per-credit charge: $1,122.
Room and board: $11,514.
Additional info: Tuition/fee waivers available for minority students.

FINANCIAL AID PICTURE (2012-2013)
Students with need: Out of 385 full-time freshmen who applied for aid, 331 were judged to have need. Of these, 331 received aid, and 92 had their full need met. Average financial aid package met 78% of need; average scholarship/grant was $19,453; average loan was $4,202. For part-time students, average financial aid package was $5,019.
Students without need: 112 full-time freshmen who did not demonstrate need for aid received scholarships/grants; average award was $15,073. No-need awards available for academics, art, athletics, leadership, minority status, music/drama, ROTC.
Scholarships offered: ***Merit:*** Founder's Scholarship: full-tuition scholarship based on on-campus written examination, 3.5 GPA, and SAT scores of 1150 or higher (exclusive of writing) or ACT score of 25 or higher; 2 awards. ***Athletic:*** 23 full-time freshmen received athletic scholarships; average amount $11,938.
Cumulative student debt: 70% of graduating class had student loans; average debt was $32,311.

FINANCIAL AID PROCEDURES
Forms required: FAFSA.
Dates and Deadlines: Closing date 3/1. Applicants notified on a rolling basis starting 2/15; must reply by 5/1.
Transfers: Scholarships available based on GPA at previous institution.

CONTACT
David Reeder, Director of Financial Aid
16300 Old Emmitsburg Road, Emmitsburg, MD 21727
(800) 448-4347

Notre Dame of Maryland University
Baltimore, Maryland
www.ndm.edu
Federal Code: 002065

4-year private liberal arts college for women in very large city, affiliated with Roman Catholic Church.
Enrollment: 530 full-time undergrads.
Selectivity: Admits 50 to 75% of applicants.

BASIC COSTS (2012-2013)
Tuition and fees: $30,850.
Room and board: $10,150.

FINANCIAL AID PICTURE
Students with need: Need-based aid available for full-time and part-time students.
Students without need: No-need awards available for academics, alumni affiliation, art, leadership, music/drama, ROTC.
Scholarships offered: Academic/achievement awards; $6,000 to full tuition. Endowed scholarships; $1,000 to $8,000; variable criteria; usually 20-35 awards.
Additional info: Maximum consideration for financial aid if application received by February 15. Auditions and portfolios in areas of art, music and writing considered for scholarships.

FINANCIAL AID PROCEDURES
Forms required: FAFSA.
Dates and Deadlines: Priority date 2/15; no closing date. Applicants notified on a rolling basis starting 3/15; must reply by 5/1 or within 2 week(s) of notification.
Transfers: Applicants notified by 3/15; must reply by 5/1 or within 2 week(s) of notification. Specific non-need based merit scholarships available for transfer students. Transfer scholarships; range from $7000 to full tuition.

CONTACT
Zhana Goltser, Director of Financial Aid
4701 North Charles Street, Baltimore, MD 21210
(410) 532-5369

Prince George's Community College
Largo, Maryland
www.pgcc.edu
Federal Code: 002089

2-year public community college in very large city.
Enrollment: 12,875 undergrads.
Selectivity: Open admission; but selective for some programs.

BASIC COSTS (2012-2013)
Tuition and fees: $4,200; out-of-district residents $6,420; out-of-state residents $9,210.
Per-credit charge: $98; out-of-district residents $172; out-of-state residents $265.

FINANCIAL AID PICTURE
Students with need: Need-based aid available for full-time and part-time students.
Students without need: This college awards aid only to students with need.

FINANCIAL AID PROCEDURES
Forms required: FAFSA, institutional form.
Dates and Deadlines: Priority date 6/1; no closing date. Applicants notified on a rolling basis starting 6/1; must reply within 2 week(s) of notification.

CONTACT
Sharon Hasson, Director of Financial Aid
301 Largo Road, Largo, MD 20774
(301) 322-0866

St. John's College
Annapolis, Maryland
www.stjohnscollege.edu
Federal Code: 002092
CSS Code: 5598

4-year private liberal arts college in large town.
Enrollment: 449 undergrads. 118 full-time freshmen.
Selectivity: Admits over 75% of applicants.

BASIC COSTS (2012-2013)
Tuition and fees: $44,954.
Room and board: $10,644.

FINANCIAL AID PICTURE (2012-2013)
Students with need: Out of 108 full-time freshmen who applied for aid, 97 were judged to have need. Of these, 97 received aid, and 13 had their full need met. Need-based aid available for part-time students.
Students without need: 7 full-time freshmen who did not demonstrate need for aid received scholarships/grants; average award was $17,804. No-need awards available for academics.
Cumulative student debt: 69% of graduating class had student loans; average debt was $13,357.

FINANCIAL AID PROCEDURES
Forms required: FAFSA, CSS PROFILE, state aid form.
Dates and Deadlines: Applicants notified on a rolling basis starting 1/15; must reply by 5/1 or within 2 week(s) of notification.

CONTACT
Dana Kennedy, Director of Financial Aid
PO Box 2800, Annapolis, MD 21404
(410) 626-2502

St. Mary's College of Maryland
St. Mary's City, Maryland
www.smcm.edu Federal Code: 002095

4-year public liberal arts college in small town.
Enrollment: 1,863 undergrads, 2% part-time. 446 full-time freshmen.
Selectivity: Admits 50 to 75% of applicants.

BASIC COSTS (2012-2013)
Tuition and fees: $14,773; out-of-state residents $27,573.
Per-credit charge: $185.
Room and board: $11,305.

FINANCIAL AID PICTURE (2011-2012)
Students with need: Out of 368 full-time freshmen who applied for aid, 220 were judged to have need. Of these, 208 received aid, and 21 had their full need met. Average financial aid package met 68% of need; average scholarship/grant was $12,071; average loan was $3,161. For part-time students, average financial aid package was $5,717.
Students without need: 93 full-time freshmen who did not demonstrate need for aid received scholarships/grants; average award was $3,898. No-need awards available for academics, leadership.
Cumulative student debt: 54% of graduating class had student loans; average debt was $23,834.

FINANCIAL AID PROCEDURES
Forms required: FAFSA.
Dates and Deadlines: Closing date 2/28. Applicants notified by 4/1; must reply by 5/1.
Transfers: Priority date 2/28. Applicants notified by 5/15; must reply by 5/1 or within 2 week(s) of notification. All financial aid recipients must have GED or high school diploma. Financial aid transcript required from previous colleges attended.

CONTACT
Caroline Bright, Director of Financial Aid
18952 East Fisher Road, St. Mary's City, MD 20686-3001
(240) 895-3000

Salisbury University
Salisbury, Maryland
www.salisbury.edu Federal Code: 002091

4-year public university and liberal arts college in large town.
Enrollment: 7,714 undergrads, 5% part-time. 1,246 full-time freshmen.
Selectivity: Admits 50 to 75% of applicants.

BASIC COSTS (2012-2013)
Tuition and fees: $7,700; out-of-state residents $16,046.
Per-credit charge: $231; out-of-state residents $578.
Room and board: $9,120.

FINANCIAL AID PICTURE (2011-2012)
Students with need: Out of 1,052 full-time freshmen who applied for aid, 601 were judged to have need. Of these, 588 received aid, and 97 had their full need met. Average financial aid package met 52% of need; average scholarship/grant was $5,644; average loan was $3,164. For part-time students, average financial aid package was $4,442.
Students without need: 337 full-time freshmen who did not demonstrate need for aid received scholarships/grants; average award was $2,514. No-need awards available for academics, alumni affiliation, art, leadership, music/drama, ROTC, state/district residency.
Cumulative student debt: 59% of graduating class had student loans; average debt was $23,159.

FINANCIAL AID PROCEDURES
Forms required: FAFSA.
Dates and Deadlines: Priority date 3/1; closing date 12/31. Applicants notified on a rolling basis starting 3/15; must reply by 5/1.
Transfers: No deadline. Financial aid transcripts from previous schools required.

CONTACT
Elizabeth Zimmerman, Director of Financial Aid
1200 Camden Avenue, Salisbury, MD 21801
(410) 543-6165

Sojourner-Douglass College
Baltimore, Maryland
www.sdc.edu Federal Code: 021279

4-year private liberal arts college in very large city.
Enrollment: 1,237 undergrads.
Selectivity: Open admission.

BASIC COSTS (2012-2013)
Tuition and fees: $8,850.
Per-credit charge: $519.

FINANCIAL AID PICTURE
Students with need: Need-based aid available for full-time and part-time students.

FINANCIAL AID PROCEDURES
Forms required: FAFSA, institutional form.
Dates and Deadlines: Priority date 3/1; no closing date. Applicants notified on a rolling basis; must reply within 2 week(s) of notification.

CONTACT
Rebecca Chalk, Financial Aid Administrator
500 North Caroline Street, Baltimore, MD 21205
(410) 276-0306 ext. 260

Stevenson University
Stevenson, Maryland
www.stevenson.edu Federal Code: 002107

4-year private university in very large city.
Enrollment: 3,855 undergrads, 16% part-time. 866 full-time freshmen.
Selectivity: Admits 50 to 75% of applicants.

BASIC COSTS (2012-2013)
Tuition and fees: $25,310.
Per-credit charge: $596.
Room and board: $12,310.
Additional info: Room and board fees includes laundry.

FINANCIAL AID PICTURE (2011-2012)
Students with need: Out of 816 full-time freshmen who applied for aid, 726 were judged to have need. Of these, 723 received aid, and 71 had their full need met. Average financial aid package met 59% of need; average scholarship/grant was $13,707; average loan was $3,262. For part-time students, average financial aid package was $5,050.
Students without need: 135 full-time freshmen who did not demonstrate need for aid received scholarships/grants; average award was $6,868. No-need awards available for academics, art, leadership, music/drama, ROTC.
Cumulative student debt: 69% of graduating class had student loans; average debt was $28,032.

Additional info: Cooperative Education Program allows students to work in their field of study with area corporations.

FINANCIAL AID PROCEDURES

Forms required: FAFSA.

Dates and Deadlines: Priority date 2/15; no closing date. Applicants notified on a rolling basis starting 3/15; must reply by 5/1 or within 2 week(s) of notification.

CONTACT

Barbara Miller, Director of Financial Aid
1525 Greenspring Valley Road, Stevenson, MD 21153-0641
(443) 334-3500

Towson University

Towson, Maryland
www.towson.edu Federal Code: 002099

4-year public university in large city.
Enrollment: 17,503 undergrads, 10% part-time. 2,463 full-time freshmen.
Selectivity: Admits 50 to 75% of applicants.

BASIC COSTS (2012-2013)

Tuition and fees: $8,132; out-of-state residents $19,754.
Per-credit charge: $246; out-of-state residents $723.
Room and board: $10,338.

FINANCIAL AID PICTURE (2012-2013)

Students with need: Out of 2,072 full-time freshmen who applied for aid, 1,402 were judged to have need. Of these, 1,279 received aid, and 163 had their full need met. Average financial aid package met 57% of need; average scholarship/grant was $8,668; average loan was $3,250. For part-time students, average financial aid package was $5,962.

Students without need: 171 full-time freshmen who did not demonstrate need for aid received scholarships/grants; average award was $4,935. No-need awards available for academics, alumni affiliation, art, athletics, leadership, music/drama, ROTC.

Scholarships offered: ***Merit:*** Provost Scholarship; $3,000-$6,000 in-state, $10,000-$14,000 out-of-state. Honors College Scholarship; $1,000-$3,000; based on GPA and SAT. ***Athletic:*** 68 full-time freshmen received athletic scholarships; average amount $8,050.

Cumulative student debt: 60% of graduating class had student loans; average debt was $23,812.

FINANCIAL AID PROCEDURES

Forms required: FAFSA.

Dates and Deadlines: Closing date 2/15. Applicants notified on a rolling basis starting 3/21; must reply within 2 week(s) of notification.

Transfers: Priority date 2/15. Applicants notified on a rolling basis starting 3/21; must reply within 2 week(s) of notification.

CONTACT

David Horne, Director of Financial Aid
8000 York Road, Towson, MD 21252-0001
(410) 704-4236

United States Naval Academy

Annapolis, Maryland
www.usna.edu

4-year public military college in large town.
Enrollment: 4,536 undergrads. 1,186 full-time freshmen.
Selectivity: Admits less than 50% of applicants.

BASIC COSTS (2013-2014)

Additional info: The Naval Academy does not charge tuition, room, board or any other fees. Medical and dental care are provided by the United States Government. Each midshipman receives a monthly salary to cover costs of books, supplies, uniforms, laundry, and equipment including a computer and printer.

CONTACT

117 Decatur Road, Annapolis, MD 21402-5018

University of Baltimore

Baltimore, Maryland
www.ubalt.edu Federal Code: 002102

4-year public university and liberal arts college in very large city.
Enrollment: 3,399 undergrads, 41% part-time. 215 full-time freshmen.

BASIC COSTS (2012-2013)

Tuition and fees: $7,664; out-of-state residents $17,914.
Per-credit charge: $266; out-of-state residents $839.

FINANCIAL AID PICTURE

Students with need: Need-based aid available for full-time and part-time students.

FINANCIAL AID PROCEDURES

Forms required: FAFSA, institutional form.

Dates and Deadlines: Applicants notified on a rolling basis.

Transfers: Closing date 5/1. Applicants notified on a rolling basis; must reply within 2 week(s) of notification. Scholarship application deadline, March 1.

CONTACT

Anne Hamill, Director, Financial Aid
1420 North Charles Street, Baltimore, MD 21201-5779
(410) 837-4763

University of Maryland: Baltimore

Baltimore, Maryland
www.umaryland.edu Federal Code: 002104

Upper-division public university and health science college in very large city.
Enrollment: 722 undergrads, 23% part-time.

BASIC COSTS (2012-2013)

Tuition and fees: $9,173; out-of-state residents $28,687.
Per-credit charge: $328; out-of-state residents $697.

FINANCIAL AID PICTURE

Students with need: Need-based aid available for full-time and part-time students. Work study available nights, weekends, and for part-time students.

Additional info: Maryland state deadline 3/1.

FINANCIAL AID PROCEDURES

Forms required: FAFSA, state aid form.

Dates and Deadlines: Priority date 3/15; no closing date. Applicants notified on a rolling basis starting 4/15; must reply within 2 week(s) of notification.

CONTACT

Patricia Scott, Associate Director of Financial Aid
620 West Lexington Street, Baltimore, MD 21201
(410) 706-7347

University of Maryland: Baltimore County

Baltimore, Maryland
www.umbc.edu Federal Code: 002105

4-year public university in large city.
Enrollment: 10,838 undergrads, 14% part-time. 1,415 full-time freshmen.

Selectivity: Admits 50 to 75% of applicants.

BASIC COSTS (2012-2013)
Tuition and fees: $9,764; out-of-state residents $20,825.
Per-credit charge: $295; out-of-state residents $754.
Room and board: $10,492.

FINANCIAL AID PICTURE (2011-2012)
Students with need: Out of 1,027 full-time freshmen who applied for aid, 700 were judged to have need. Of these, 634 received aid, and 124 had their full need met. Average financial aid package met 59% of need; average scholarship/grant was $8,059; average loan was $3,349. For part-time students, average financial aid package was $5,848.
Students without need: 225 full-time freshmen who did not demonstrate need for aid received scholarships/grants; average award was $8,128. No-need awards available for academics, alumni affiliation, art, athletics, music/drama.
Scholarships offered: ***Merit:*** UMBC General Merit Awards, range from $500-$22,000 per year. Scholars Programs, awards range from $5,000-$22,000 per year. These programs include Center for Women and Information Technology Scholars Program, Humanities Scholars Program, Linehan Artist Scholars Program, Meyerhoff Scholars Program (Sciences and Engineering), and Sondheim Public Affairs Scholars Program Scholars Programs; tuition, fees, room and board. ***Athletic:*** 41 full-time freshmen received athletic scholarships; average amount $9,708.
Cumulative student debt: 53% of graduating class had student loans; average debt was $22,600.

FINANCIAL AID PROCEDURES
Forms required: FAFSA.
Dates and Deadlines: Priority date 2/14; no closing date. Applicants notified on a rolling basis starting 3/26; must reply within 2 week(s) of notification.
Transfers: 2-year merit scholarships available for transfer students from community colleges.

CONTACT
Stephanie Johnson, Director of Financial Aid
1000 Hilltop Circle, Baltimore, MD 21250
(410) 455-2387

University of Maryland: College Park
College Park, Maryland
www.maryland.edu Federal Code: 002103

4-year public university in large town.
Enrollment: 25,831 undergrads, 6% part-time. 3,893 full-time freshmen.
Selectivity: Admits less than 50% of applicants.

BASIC COSTS (2012-2013)
Tuition and fees: $8,908; out-of-state residents $27,287.
Per-credit charge: $299; out-of-state residents $1,065.
Room and board: $10,093.

FINANCIAL AID PICTURE (2011-2012)
Students with need: Need-based aid available for full-time and part-time students. Work study available nights, weekends, and for part-time students.
Students without need: No-need awards available for academics, art, athletics, state/district residency.
Additional info: Prepaid tuition plans available through state. University of Maryland has created a financial assistance program called "Maryland Pathways." This three-tiered program reduces the debt component and increases the grant component of the student's financial aid package.

FINANCIAL AID PROCEDURES
Forms required: FAFSA.
Dates and Deadlines: Priority date 2/15; no closing date. Applicants notified on a rolling basis starting 4/1; must reply by 5/1.

CONTACT
Sarah Bauder, Director of Enrollment Services and Student Financial Aid
College Park, MD 20742-5235
(301) 314-9000

University of Maryland: Eastern Shore
Princess Anne, Maryland
www.umes.edu Federal Code: 002106

4-year public university in rural community.
Enrollment: 3,681 undergrads, 6% part-time. 748 full-time freshmen.
Selectivity: Admits 50 to 75% of applicants.

BASIC COSTS (2013-2014)
Tuition and fees: $6,998; out-of-state residents $15,504.
Room and board: $8,374.

FINANCIAL AID PICTURE (2011-2012)
Students with need: Out of 730 full-time freshmen who applied for aid, 646 were judged to have need. Of these, 636 received aid. Average financial aid package met 48% of need; average scholarship/grant was $7,368; average loan was $3,325. For part-time students, average financial aid package was $5,063.
Students without need: 20 full-time freshmen who did not demonstrate need for aid received scholarships/grants; average award was $5,163. No-need awards available for academics, alumni affiliation, art, athletics, leadership, music/drama, ROTC, state/district residency.
Scholarships offered: 11 full-time freshmen received athletic scholarships; average amount $17,351.
Cumulative student debt: 82% of graduating class had student loans; average debt was $27,215.

FINANCIAL AID PROCEDURES
Forms required: FAFSA.
Dates and Deadlines: Priority date 3/1; closing date 4/1. Applicants notified on a rolling basis starting 4/15.
Transfers: No deadline. Applicants notified on a rolling basis starting 6/15.

CONTACT
James Kellam, Director of Financial Aid
Student Development Center, Suite 1140, Princess Anne, MD 21853
(410) 651-6172

University of Maryland: University College
Adelphi, Maryland
www.umuc.edu Federal Code: 011644

4-year public university in large town.
Enrollment: 27,462 undergrads, 78% part-time. 159 full-time freshmen.
Selectivity: Open admission.

BASIC COSTS (2012-2013)
Tuition and fees: $6,474; out-of-state residents $12,426.
Per-credit charge: $251; out-of-state residents $499.

FINANCIAL AID PICTURE (2011-2012)
Students with need: Out of 135 full-time freshmen who applied for aid, 132 were judged to have need. Of these, 123 received aid, and 4 had their full need met. Average financial aid package met 26% of need; average scholarship/grant was $3,248; average loan was $3,115. For part-time students, average financial aid package was $4,780.
Students without need: No-need awards available for academics, leadership.

FINANCIAL AID PROCEDURES
Forms required: FAFSA.
Dates and Deadlines: Priority date 6/1; no closing date. Applicants notified on a rolling basis starting 5/1; must reply within 2 week(s) of notification.

CONTACT
1616 McCormick Drive, Largo, MD 20774
(301) 985-7510

Washington Adventist University
Takoma Park, Maryland
www.cuc.edu Federal Code: 002067

4-year private liberal arts college in large town, affiliated with Seventh-day Adventists.
Enrollment: 1,111 undergrads, 15% part-time. 134 full-time freshmen.
Selectivity: Admits less than 50% of applicants.

BASIC COSTS (2012-2013)
Tuition and fees: $20,220.
Per-credit charge: $760.
Room and board: $7,600.

FINANCIAL AID PICTURE (2011-2012)
Students with need: 52% of average financial aid package awarded as scholarships/grants, 48% awarded as loans/jobs. Need-based aid available for part-time students.
Students without need: No-need awards available for academics, alumni affiliation, athletics, religious affiliation.

FINANCIAL AID PROCEDURES
Forms required: FAFSA.
Dates and Deadlines: Closing date 3/31. Applicants notified on a rolling basis starting 5/31; must reply within 4 week(s) of notification.

CONTACT
Sharon Conway, Director of Financial Aid
7600 Flower Avenue, Takoma Park, MD 20912
(301) 891-4005

Washington College
Chestertown, Maryland
www.washcoll.edu Federal Code: 002108

4-year private liberal arts college in small town.
Enrollment: 1,458 undergrads, 1% part-time. 397 full-time freshmen.
Selectivity: Admits 50 to 75% of applicants.

BASIC COSTS (2012-2013)
Tuition and fees: $39,944.
Room and board: $8,824.

FINANCIAL AID PICTURE (2012-2013)
Students with need: Out of 295 full-time freshmen who applied for aid, 249 were judged to have need. Of these, 249 received aid, and 164 had their full need met. Average financial aid package met 95% of need; average scholarship/grant was $25,047; average loan was $3,413. For part-time students, average financial aid package was $28,911.
Students without need: 116 full-time freshmen who did not demonstrate need for aid received scholarships/grants; average award was $15,782. No-need awards available for academics.
Scholarships offered: National Honor Society Scholarship; $50,000 over 4 years; applicant must be member of the National Honor Society, the National Society of High School Scholars, or the Cum Laude Society.
Cumulative student debt: 66% of graduating class had student loans; average debt was $34,208.

FINANCIAL AID PROCEDURES
Forms required: FAFSA, institutional form.
Dates and Deadlines: Priority date 3/1; no closing date. Applicants notified on a rolling basis starting 2/15; must reply by 5/1.

CONTACT
Jean Narcum, Director of Financial Aid
300 Washington Avenue, Chestertown, MD 21620-1197
(410) 778-7214

Wor-Wic Community College
Salisbury, Maryland
www.worwic.edu Federal Code: 013842

2-year public community college in large town.
Enrollment: 3,420 undergrads, 66% part-time. 427 full-time freshmen.
Selectivity: Open admission; but selective for some programs.

BASIC COSTS (2013-2014)
Tuition and fees: $3,090; out-of-district residents $6,652; out-of-state residents $8,160.
Per-credit charge: $96; out-of-district residents $215; out-of-state residents $265.

FINANCIAL AID PICTURE
Students with need: Need-based aid available for full-time and part-time students. Work study available nights, weekends, and for part-time students.
Students without need: No-need awards available for academics, state/district residency.

FINANCIAL AID PROCEDURES
Forms required: FAFSA, institutional form.
Dates and Deadlines: Priority date 6/1; no closing date. Applicants notified on a rolling basis starting 4/1.

CONTACT
Deborah Jenkins, Director of Financial Aid
32000 Campus Drive, Salisbury, MD 21804
(410) 334-2905

Massachusetts

American International College
Springfield, Massachusetts
www.aic.edu Federal Code: 002114

4-year private liberal arts college in small city.
Enrollment: 1,492 undergrads, 9% part-time. 265 full-time freshmen.
Selectivity: Admits 50 to 75% of applicants.

BASIC COSTS (2012-2013)
Tuition and fees: $29,158.
Per-credit charge: $601.
Room and board: $11,710.

FINANCIAL AID PICTURE (2011-2012)
Students with need: Out of 239 full-time freshmen who applied for aid, 223 were judged to have need. Of these, 223 received aid, and 31 had their full need met. Average financial aid package met 69% of need; average scholarship/grant was $19,768; average loan was $2,960. For part-time students, average financial aid package was $8,040.
Students without need: 39 full-time freshmen who did not demonstrate need for aid received scholarships/grants; average award was $12,467. No-need awards available for academics, athletics.

Scholarships offered: ***Merit:*** Presidential, Provost, Opportunity Scholarships; $5,000 to $11,000; based on class rank, SAT, GPA. ***Athletic:*** 31 full-time freshmen received athletic scholarships; average amount $15,639.
Cumulative student debt: 86% of graduating class had student loans; average debt was $33,170.

FINANCIAL AID PROCEDURES
Forms required: FAFSA, state aid form.
Dates and Deadlines: Priority date 5/1; no closing date. Applicants notified on a rolling basis starting 2/15.

CONTACT
Douglas Fish, Director of Financial Aid
1000 State Street, Springfield, MA 01109
(413) 205-3259

Amherst College
Amherst, Massachusetts
www.amherst.edu
Federal Code: 002115
CSS Code: 3003

4-year private liberal arts college in large town.
Enrollment: 1,817 undergrads. 469 full-time freshmen.
Selectivity: Admits less than 50% of applicants.

BASIC COSTS (2012-2013)
Tuition and fees: $44,610.
Room and board: $11,650.

FINANCIAL AID PICTURE (2011-2012)
Students with need: Out of 309 full-time freshmen who applied for aid, 264 were judged to have need. Of these, 264 received aid, and 264 had their full need met. Average financial aid package met 100% of need; average scholarship/grant was $43,576; average loan was $2,131.
Students without need: This college awards aid only to students with need.
Cumulative student debt: 30% of graduating class had student loans; average debt was $14,566.

FINANCIAL AID PROCEDURES
Forms required: FAFSA, CSS PROFILE.
Dates and Deadlines: Priority date 2/15; no closing date.

CONTACT
Joe Case, Dean of Financial Aid
PO Box 5000, Amherst, MA 01002-5000
(413) 542-2296

Anna Maria College
Paxton, Massachusetts
www.annamaria.edu
Federal Code: 002117

4-year private liberal arts college in small town, affiliated with Roman Catholic Church.
Enrollment: 1,030 undergrads, 22% part-time. 246 full-time freshmen.
Selectivity: Admits 50 to 75% of applicants.

BASIC COSTS (2012-2013)
Tuition and fees: $30,676.
Per-credit charge: $1,198.
Room and board: $11,450.

FINANCIAL AID PICTURE
Students with need: Need-based aid available for full-time and part-time students. Work study available nights, weekends, and for part-time students.
Students without need: No-need awards available for academics, alumni affiliation, music/drama, religious affiliation, state/district residency.

FINANCIAL AID PROCEDURES
Forms required: FAFSA, state aid form.
Dates and Deadlines: Priority date 3/1; no closing date. Applicants notified on a rolling basis starting 4/1; must reply within 4 week(s) of notification.
Transfers: No deadline. Applicants notified on a rolling basis starting 4/1; must reply within 4 week(s) of notification. Deadline May 1 for state aid.

CONTACT
Sandra Pereira, Director of Financial Aid
50 Sunset Lane, Box O, Paxton, MA 01612-1198
(508) 849-3363

Assumption College
Worcester, Massachusetts
www.assumption.edu
Federal Code: 002118

4-year private liberal arts college in small city, affiliated with Roman Catholic Church.
Enrollment: 2,037 undergrads. 559 full-time freshmen.
Selectivity: Admits over 75% of applicants.

BASIC COSTS (2012-2013)
Tuition and fees: $34,070.
Per-credit charge: $1,113.
Room and board: $10,590.

FINANCIAL AID PICTURE (2012-2013)
Students with need: Out of 516 full-time freshmen who applied for aid, 462 were judged to have need. Of these, 462 received aid, and 83 had their full need met. Average financial aid package met 76% of need; average scholarship/grant was $20,746; average loan was $3,916. Need-based aid available for part-time students.
Students without need: 83 full-time freshmen who did not demonstrate need for aid received scholarships/grants; average award was $11,424. No-need awards available for academics, athletics.
Scholarships offered: ***Merit:*** Academic scholarships; $2,500-$20,000 per year; based on academic achievement and leadership talents. ***Athletic:*** 9 full-time freshmen received athletic scholarships; average amount $19,272.
Cumulative student debt: 81% of graduating class had student loans; average debt was $34,579.

FINANCIAL AID PROCEDURES
Forms required: FAFSA.
Dates and Deadlines: Closing date 2/15. Applicants notified on a rolling basis starting 2/16; must reply by 5/1.
Transfers: Closing date 3/31. Applicants notified on a rolling basis starting 3/15.

CONTACT
William Smith, Director of Financial Aid
500 Salisbury Street, Worcester, MA 01609-1296
(508) 767-7158

Babson College
Babson Park, Massachusetts
www.babson.edu
Federal Code: 002121
CSS Code: 3075

4-year private business college in large town.
Enrollment: 2,015 undergrads. 470 full-time freshmen.
Selectivity: Admits less than 50% of applicants.

BASIC COSTS (2012-2013)
Tuition and fees: $41,888.
Per-credit charge: $1,309.
Room and board: $13,730.

FINANCIAL AID PICTURE (2012-2013)
Students with need: Out of 260 full-time freshmen who applied for aid, 203 were judged to have need. Of these, 203 received aid, and 138 had their full need met. Average financial aid package met 96% of need; average scholarship/grant was $32,063; average loan was $3,445.
Students without need: This college awards aid only to students with need.
Scholarships offered: Presidential Scholarship; half tuition; based on high school record, co-curricular achievements, demonstrated leadership, writing skills, standardized test scores; approximately 40 awarded each year. Woman's Leadership Award; one quarter tuition; based on demonstrated leadership experience, future leadership potential, and academic achievement. Diversity Leadership Award; either full or half tuition; awarded to students with the greatest potential for leadership in creating a diverse Babson community. Weissmann Scholarship; full tuition.
Cumulative student debt: 48% of graduating class had student loans; average debt was $31,918.

FINANCIAL AID PROCEDURES
Forms required: FAFSA, CSS PROFILE.
Dates and Deadlines: Closing date 2/15. Applicants notified by 4/1; must reply by 5/1.
Transfers: Priority date 2/15; closing date 4/15. Applicants notified by 5/1; must reply by 6/1.

CONTACT
Melissa Shaak, Director, Student Financial Services
231 Forest Street, Babson Park, MA 02457-0310
(781) 239-4219

Bard College at Simon's Rock

Great Barrington, Massachusetts Federal Code: 009645
www.simons-rock.edu CSS Code: 3795

4-year private liberal arts college in small town.
Enrollment: 343 undergrads, 1% part-time. 146 full-time freshmen.
Selectivity: Admits over 75% of applicants.

BASIC COSTS (2012-2013)
Tuition and fees: $44,075.
Room and board: $12,260.

FINANCIAL AID PICTURE
Students with need: Need-based aid available for full-time students. Work study available nights, weekends, and for part-time students.
Students without need: No-need awards available for academics, alumni affiliation, minority status.
Scholarships offered: Acceleration to Excellence Program; up to full-tuition; for outstanding students who apply during 10th or 11th grade; based on academic excellence, extracurricular distinction, personal motivation, and character.

FINANCIAL AID PROCEDURES
Forms required: FAFSA, CSS PROFILE.
Dates and Deadlines: Priority date 2/15; no closing date. Applicants notified on a rolling basis starting 3/15; must reply within 2 week(s) of notification.

CONTACT
Director of Financial Aid
Office of Admission, Great Barrington, MA 01230-1990
(413) 528-7297

Bay Path College

Longmeadow, Massachusetts
www.baypath.edu Federal Code: 002122

4-year private liberal arts college for women in large town.
Enrollment: 1,556 undergrads, 19% part-time. 155 full-time freshmen.
Selectivity: Admits 50 to 75% of applicants.

BASIC COSTS (2012-2013)
Tuition and fees: $28,532.
Per-credit charge: $480.
Room and board: $12,440.

FINANCIAL AID PICTURE (2012-2013)
Students with need: Out of 149 full-time freshmen who applied for aid, 146 were judged to have need. Of these, 146 received aid, and 17 had their full need met. Average financial aid package met 79% of need; average scholarship/grant was $20,473; average loan was $5,396. For part-time students, average financial aid package was $3,984.
Students without need: 8 full-time freshmen who did not demonstrate need for aid received scholarships/grants; average award was $14,653. No-need awards available for academics.
Scholarships offered: 1897 Founders Scholarship; $15,000/year for residents, $12,000/year for commuters. Provost's Scholarship; $14,000/year for residents, $11,000/year for commuters. Dean's Scholarship; $13,000/year for residents, $10,000/year for commuters. Seize the Day Award; $8,000/year for residents, $7,000/year for commuters. Pathways Award; $5,000/year for residents, $5,000/year for commuters.
Cumulative student debt: 91% of graduating class had student loans; average debt was $31,456.

FINANCIAL AID PROCEDURES
Forms required: FAFSA.
Dates and Deadlines: Priority date 3/1; no closing date. Applicants notified on a rolling basis starting 3/1; must reply within 2 week(s) of notification.

CONTACT
Stephanie King, Director of Student Financial Services
588 Longmeadow Street, Longmeadow, MA 01106
(413) 565-1000 ext. 1345

Bay State College

Boston, Massachusetts
www.baystate.edu Federal Code: 003965

2-year for-profit career college in very large city.
Enrollment: 1,219 undergrads, 40% part-time. 187 full-time freshmen.
Selectivity: Admits 50 to 75% of applicants.

BASIC COSTS (2013-2014)
Tuition and fees: $24,510.
Per-credit charge: $802.
Room and board: $11,800.
Additional info: Tuition varies by program; evening and on-line classes offered at much lower rate.

FINANCIAL AID PICTURE (2011-2012)
Students with need: 42% of average financial aid package awarded as scholarships/grants, 58% awarded as loans/jobs. Need-based aid available for part-time students. Work study available nights, weekends, and for part-time students.
Students without need: No-need awards available for academics, art, job skills, leadership.
Scholarships offered: Community Service Scholarship; $1,000-$2,500; based on essay and community service involvement. Presidential and Honors Scholarship; $1,500-$2,500; based on essay and academic achievement.

FINANCIAL AID PROCEDURES
Forms required: FAFSA.
Dates and Deadlines: Priority date 3/15; closing date 6/30. Applicants notified on a rolling basis starting 3/1.

CONTACT
Jeanne Devani, Director of Student Financial Services
122 Commonwealth Avenue, Boston, MA 02116
(617) 217-9066

Becker College

Worcester, Massachusetts
www.becker.edu Federal Code: 002123

4-year private liberal arts college in small city.
Enrollment: 1,826 undergrads. 381 full-time freshmen.
Selectivity: Admits 50 to 75% of applicants.

BASIC COSTS (2012-2013)
Tuition and fees: $30,340.
Per-credit charge: $1,200.
Room and board: $11,050.

FINANCIAL AID PICTURE
Students with need: Need-based aid available for full-time and part-time students. Work study available nights, weekends, and for part-time students.
Students without need: No-need awards available for academics.

FINANCIAL AID PROCEDURES
Forms required: FAFSA.
Dates and Deadlines: Priority date 3/1; no closing date. Applicants notified on a rolling basis starting 2/1; must reply within 2 week(s) of notification.

CONTACT
Heather Ruland, Director of Finacial Aid
61 Sever Street, Worcester, MA 01609
(508) 373-9433

Benjamin Franklin Institute of Technology

Boston, Massachusetts
www.bfit.edu Federal Code: 002151

2-year private technical college in very large city.
Enrollment: 445 undergrads.

BASIC COSTS (2012-2013)
Tuition and fees: $16,950.
Per-credit charge: $707.
Room and board: $10,200.
Additional info: Cost shown is for Associate and Certificate programs. Bachelor degree tuition is $18,190 for the third and fourth year courses.

FINANCIAL AID PICTURE
Students with need: Need-based aid available for full-time and part-time students.
Students without need: No-need awards available for academics, leadership.

FINANCIAL AID PROCEDURES
Forms required: FAFSA.
Dates and Deadlines: Priority date 4/1; no closing date. Applicants notified on a rolling basis starting 3/1; must reply within 4 week(s) of notification.

CONTACT
Tatjana Haskaj, Director of Financial Aid
41 Berkeley Street, Boston, MA 02116
(617) 423-4630 ext. 120

Bentley University

Waltham, Massachusetts Federal Code: 002124
www.bentley.edu CSS Code: 3096

4-year private university and business college in small city.
Enrollment: 4,176 undergrads, 3% part-time. 911 full-time freshmen.
Selectivity: Admits less than 50% of applicants.

BASIC COSTS (2012-2013)
Tuition and fees: $39,628.
Room and board: $12,960.
Additional info: Required fees include cost of laptop computer.

FINANCIAL AID PICTURE (2011-2012)
Students with need: Out of 617 full-time freshmen who applied for aid, 423 were judged to have need. Of these, 419 received aid, and 185 had their full need met. Average financial aid package met 96% of need; average scholarship/grant was $23,988; average loan was $3,833. For part-time students, average financial aid package was $5,183.
Students without need: 176 full-time freshmen who did not demonstrate need for aid received scholarships/grants; average award was $16,709. No-need awards available for academics, athletics, leadership, minority status.
Scholarships offered: ***Merit:*** Various scholarships; full-tuition to one-third tuition; based on superior academic accomplishment. ***Athletic:*** 12 full-time freshmen received athletic scholarships; average amount $23,595.
Cumulative student debt: 59% of graduating class had student loans; average debt was $30,560.

FINANCIAL AID PROCEDURES
Forms required: FAFSA. CSS PROFILE required if applying for institutional grants. Deadlines for receipt of CSS Profile: Early Decision, 12/1; Early Action and Regular Decision, 2/1.
Dates and Deadlines: Closing date 2/1. Applicants notified by 3/25.
Transfers: Closing date 4/15. Applicants notified on a rolling basis starting 4/15.

CONTACT
Donna Kendall, Executive Director of Financial Assistance and Enrollment Management
175 Forest Street, Waltham, MA 02452-4705
(781) 891-3441

Berklee College of Music

Boston, Massachusetts
www.berklee.edu Federal Code: 002126

4-year private music college in very large city.
Enrollment: 3,846 undergrads, 8% part-time. 778 full-time freshmen.
Selectivity: Admits less than 50% of applicants.

BASIC COSTS (2012-2013)
Tuition and fees: $36,490.
Per-credit charge: $1,255.
Room and board: $16,950.

FINANCIAL AID PICTURE
Students with need: Need-based aid available for full-time and part-time students. Work study available nights, weekends, and for part-time students.
Students without need: No-need awards available for academics, music/drama.

FINANCIAL AID PROCEDURES
Forms required: FAFSA.
Dates and Deadlines: Priority date 3/1; closing date 5/7. Applicants notified on a rolling basis starting 1/31; must reply within 2 week(s) of notification.

CONTACT
Frank Mullen, Director of Financial Aid
1140 Boylston Street, Boston, MA 02215
(800) 538-3844

Berkshire Community College

Pittsfield, Massachusetts
www.berkshirecc.edu Federal Code: 002167

2-year public community college in large town.
Enrollment: 2,120 undergrads, 57% part-time. 289 full-time freshmen.
Selectivity: Open admission; but selective for some programs.

BASIC COSTS (2012-2013)

Tuition and fees: $5,760; out-of-state residents $12,780.
Per-credit charge: $26; out-of-state residents $260.

FINANCIAL AID PICTURE (2011-2012)

Students with need: Need-based aid available for full-time and part-time students. Work study available nights, weekends, and for part-time students.
Students without need: No-need awards available for academics, job skills, leadership, state/district residency.
Additional info: "Free College" Financial aid pledge to cover 100% of tuition and fees up to 12 credits/semester for students who file FAFSA by May 1 each year and who become eligible for Federal Pell grant.

FINANCIAL AID PROCEDURES

Forms required: FAFSA.
Dates and Deadlines: Priority date 5/1; no closing date. Applicants notified on a rolling basis starting 5/10.
Transfers: No deadline. Applicants notified on a rolling basis.

CONTACT

Anne Moore, Director of Financial Aid
1350 West Street, Pittsfield, MA 01201-5786
(413) 236-1644

Boston Architectural College

Boston, Massachusetts
www.the-bac.edu Federal Code: 003966

6-year private architecture and design college in very large city.
Enrollment: 466 undergrads, 2% part-time. 20 full-time freshmen.
Selectivity: Open admission; but selective for some programs.

BASIC COSTS (2012-2013)

Tuition and fees: $17,330.
Per-credit charge: $1,440.
Additional info: Academic Only program tuition is $22,980 plus $50 required fee.

FINANCIAL AID PICTURE (2011-2012)

Students with need: Average financial aid package met 9% of need; average scholarship/grant was $6,479; average loan was $5,656. For part-time students, average financial aid package was $8,992.
Students without need: No-need awards available for academics, art, leadership.
Cumulative student debt: 90% of graduating class had student loans; average debt was $43,446.

FINANCIAL AID PROCEDURES

Forms required: FAFSA.
Dates and Deadlines: Priority date 4/15; no closing date. Applicants notified on a rolling basis starting 3/30; must reply within 2 week(s) of notification.
Transfers: No deadline. Applicants notified on a rolling basis starting 3/1; must reply within 2 week(s) of notification.

CONTACT

James Ryan, Director of Financial Aid Operations
Boston Architectural College, Boston, MA 02115-2795
(617) 585-0125

Boston College

Chestnut Hill, Massachusetts Federal Code: 002128
www.bc.edu CSS Code: 3083

4-year private university in small city, affiliated with Roman Catholic Church.
Enrollment: 9,110 undergrads. 2,113 full-time freshmen.
Selectivity: Admits less than 50% of applicants.

BASIC COSTS (2012-2013)

Tuition and fees: $43,878.
Room and board: $12,608.

FINANCIAL AID PICTURE (2011-2012)

Students with need: Out of 1,098 full-time freshmen who applied for aid, 895 were judged to have need. Of these, 895 received aid, and 895 had their full need met. Average financial aid package met 100% of need; average scholarship/grant was $29,414; average loan was $4,364. Need-based aid available for part-time students.
Students without need: 23 full-time freshmen who did not demonstrate need for aid received scholarships/grants; average award was $19,490. No-need awards available for academics, athletics, leadership, ROTC.
Scholarships offered: 68 full-time freshmen received athletic scholarships; average amount $43,462.
Cumulative student debt: 52% of graduating class had student loans; average debt was $20,975.

FINANCIAL AID PROCEDURES

Forms required: FAFSA, CSS PROFILE.
Dates and Deadlines: Priority date 2/1; no closing date. Applicants notified on a rolling basis starting 4/1.
Transfers: Priority date 3/15. Must reply within 2 week(s) of notification.

CONTACT

Mary McGranahan, Director of Financial Aid
140 Commonwealth Avenue, Devlin Hall 208, Chestnut Hill, MA 02467-3809
(617) 552-3300

Boston Conservatory

Boston, Massachusetts
www.bostonconservatory.edu Federal Code: 002129

4-year private music and performing arts college in very large city.
Enrollment: 535 undergrads.

BASIC COSTS (2012-2013)

Tuition and fees: $39,300.
Per-credit charge: $1,500.
Room and board: $17,080.

FINANCIAL AID PICTURE

Students with need: Need-based aid available for full-time and part-time students. Work study available nights, weekends, and for part-time students.
Students without need: No-need awards available for music/drama.

FINANCIAL AID PROCEDURES

Forms required: FAFSA.
Dates and Deadlines: Priority date 3/1; no closing date. Applicants notified on a rolling basis.
Transfers: Applicants notified on a rolling basis starting 4/1; must reply within 4 week(s) of notification.

CONTACT

Nicole Brennan, Director of Financial Aid
8 The Fenway, Boston, MA 02215

Boston University

Boston, Massachusetts Federal Code: 002130
www.bu.edu CSS Code: 3087

4-year private university in very large city.
Enrollment: 16,466 undergrads, 3% part-time. 3,877 full-time freshmen.
Selectivity: Admits less than 50% of applicants.

BASIC COSTS (2012-2013)
Tuition and fees: $42,994.
Per-credit charge: $1,325.
Room and board: $13,190.

FINANCIAL AID PICTURE
Students with need: Need-based aid available for full-time and part-time students. Work study available nights, weekends, and for part-time students.
Students without need: No-need awards available for academics, alumni affiliation, art, athletics, leadership, music/drama, religious affiliation, ROTC, state/district residency.
Scholarships offered: Trustee Scholar Program; full-tuition and fees (renewable); candidates nominated by high school principals, headmasters, or students. Presidential Scholarship; $20,000 (renewable); based on exceptionally strong high school academic record. Dean's Scholarships; $10,000 (renewable); based on strong academic credentials; for students who have applied for need-based financial aid but have financial resources that exceed cost of attendance.
Additional info: Financial aid deadline for early decision applicants: 11/1; graduates of Boston's public high schools who complete financial aid application and demonstrate need will be awarded financial aid packages that contain no loans and meet full demonstrated need.

FINANCIAL AID PROCEDURES
Forms required: FAFSA, CSS PROFILE, state aid form.
Dates and Deadlines: Closing date 2/15. Applicants notified on a rolling basis starting 4/1; must reply by 5/1 or within 2 week(s) of notification.
Transfers: Priority date 4/1. Applicants notified on a rolling basis. Transfer students cannot receive duplicate disbursements simultaneously from different institutions.

CONTACT
Christine McGuire, Associate Vice President & Executive Director of Financial Assistance
121 Bay State Road, Boston, MA 02215
(617) 353-2965

Brandeis University

Waltham, Massachusetts Federal Code: 002133
www.brandeis.edu CSS Code: 3092

4-year private university in small city.
Enrollment: 3,570 undergrads. 878 full-time freshmen.
Selectivity: Admits less than 50% of applicants.

BASIC COSTS (2012-2013)
Tuition and fees: $44,294.
Room and board: $12,422.

FINANCIAL AID PICTURE
Students with need: Need-based aid available for full-time and part-time students.
Students without need: This college awards aid only to students with need.
Scholarships offered: Justice Brandeis Scholarships; full tuition. Martin Luther King scholarships; tuition and room and board. Presidential scholarships; $25,000. Dean's Awards; $15,000. Waltham High School scholarships; full tuition.

FINANCIAL AID PROCEDURES
Forms required: CSS PROFILE.
Dates and Deadlines: Closing date 2/1. Applicants notified by 4/1; must reply by 5/1.
Transfers: Priority date 4/1. International transfer students seeking scholarship or need-based financial assistance must apply by 2/1.

CONTACT
Peter Giumette, Dean of Student Financial Services
415 South Street, MS003, Waltham, MA 02453
(781) 736-3700

Bridgewater State University

Bridgewater, Massachusetts
www.bridgew.edu Federal Code: 002183

4-year public university in large town.
Enrollment: 9,551 undergrads, 16% part-time. 1,451 full-time freshmen.
Selectivity: Admits 50 to 75% of applicants.

BASIC COSTS (2012-2013)
Tuition and fees: $8,052; out-of-state residents $14,192.
Per-credit charge: $38; out-of-state residents $294.
Room and board: $10,593.
Additional info: Tuition/fee waivers available for minority students, unemployed or children of unemployed.

FINANCIAL AID PICTURE (2011-2012)
Students with need: Out of 1,421 full-time freshmen who applied for aid, 1,058 were judged to have need. Of these, 1,047 received aid, and 55 had their full need met. For part-time students, average financial aid package was $6,629.
Students without need: 8 full-time freshmen who did not demonstrate need for aid received scholarships/grants; average award was $6,915. No-need awards available for academics, minority status, state/district residency.
Cumulative student debt: 85% of graduating class had student loans; average debt was $30,189.
Additional info: Tuition and/or fee waivers for Native Americans. Work-study programs available to half-time and full-time students.

FINANCIAL AID PROCEDURES
Forms required: FAFSA.
Dates and Deadlines: Priority date 5/1; no closing date. Applicants notified on a rolling basis starting 3/30.

CONTACT
Janet Gumbris, Director of Financial Aid
Office of Admission-Gates House, Bridgewater, MA 02325
(508) 531-1341

Bristol Community College

Fall River, Massachusetts
www.bristolcc.edu Federal Code: 002176

2-year public community college in small city.
Enrollment: 9,022 undergrads.
Selectivity: Open admission; but selective for some programs.

BASIC COSTS (2012-2013)
Tuition and fees: $5,130; out-of-state residents $11,310.
Per-credit charge: $24; out-of-state residents $230.
Additional info: Tuition/fee waivers available for unemployed or children of unemployed.

FINANCIAL AID PICTURE
Students with need: Need-based aid available for full-time and part-time students. Work study available nights, weekends, and for part-time students.

Students without need: No-need awards available for academics, art, leadership, minority status, music/drama.

FINANCIAL AID PROCEDURES

Forms required: FAFSA, institutional form.

Dates and Deadlines: Priority date 5/1; no closing date. Applicants notified on a rolling basis starting 5/1; must reply within 2 week(s) of notification.

Transfers: No deadline. Applicants notified on a rolling basis starting 3/1.

CONTACT

David Allen, Director of Financial Aid
777 Elsbree Street, Fall River, MA 02720-7395
(508) 678-2811 ext. 2513

Bunker Hill Community College

Boston, Massachusetts
www.bhcc.mass.edu Federal Code: 011210

2-year public community college in very large city.

Enrollment: 11,889 undergrads.

Selectivity: Open admission; but selective for some programs.

BASIC COSTS (2012-2013)

Tuition and fees: $4,230; out-of-state residents $10,410.

Additional info: New England Regional Tuition: $153 per-credit-hour. Tuition/fee waivers available for minority students.

FINANCIAL AID PICTURE

Students with need: Need-based aid available for full-time and part-time students.

Students without need: No-need awards available for academics.

FINANCIAL AID PROCEDURES

Forms required: FAFSA.

Dates and Deadlines: Priority date 5/1; no closing date. Applicants notified on a rolling basis starting 6/1; must reply within 2 week(s) of notification.

Transfers: No deadline. Applicants notified on a rolling basis; must reply within 2 week(s) of notification.

CONTACT

Melissa Holster, Director of Financial Aid
250 New Rutherford Avenue, Boston, MA 02129-2925
(617) 228-2275

Cambridge College

Cambridge, Massachusetts
www.cambridgecollege.edu Federal Code: 021829

4-year private liberal arts and teachers college in small city.

Enrollment: 872 undergrads, 69% part-time. 27 full-time freshmen.

Selectivity: Open admission.

BASIC COSTS (2012-2013)

Additional info: Cost of 3-semester academic year tuition and fees: $13,240; for 2-semester, $10,950.

FINANCIAL AID PICTURE (2011-2012)

Students with need: Out of 3 full-time freshmen who applied for aid, 1 were judged to have need. Of these, 1 received aid. For part-time students, average financial aid package was $10,716.

Students without need: This college awards aid only to students with need.

FINANCIAL AID PROCEDURES

Forms required: FAFSA, institutional form.

Dates and Deadlines: Priority date 9/1; no closing date. Applicants notified on a rolling basis starting 6/1.

Transfers: No deadline. Applicants notified on a rolling basis.

CONTACT

Francis Lauder, Director of Financial Aid
1000 Massachusetts Avenue, Cambridge, MA 02138-5304
(800) 877-4723 ext. 1440

Cape Cod Community College

West Barnstable, Massachusetts
www.capecod.edu Federal Code: 002168

2-year public community college in small town.

Enrollment: 3,602 undergrads, 63% part-time. 486 full-time freshmen.

Selectivity: Open admission; but selective for some programs.

BASIC COSTS (2012-2013)

Tuition and fees: $4,830; out-of-state residents $11,010.

Per-credit charge: $24; out-of-state residents $230.

Additional info: Tuition/fee waivers available for minority students.

FINANCIAL AID PICTURE

Students with need: Need-based aid available for full-time and part-time students.

Students without need: No-need awards available for academics, art, job skills, leadership, music/drama, state/district residency.

FINANCIAL AID PROCEDURES

Forms required: FAFSA.

Dates and Deadlines: Priority date 5/1; no closing date. Applicants notified on a rolling basis starting 5/1.

Transfers: No deadline. Applicants notified on a rolling basis starting 6/1.

CONTACT

Sherry Andersen, Director of Financial Aid
2240 Iyannough Road, West Barnstable, MA 02668-1599
(508) 362-2131 ext. 4393

Clark University

Worcester, Massachusetts Federal Code: 002139
www.clarku.edu CSS Code: 3279

4-year private university and liberal arts college in small city.

Enrollment: 2,276 undergrads, 2% part-time. 587 full-time freshmen.

Selectivity: Admits 50 to 75% of applicants.

BASIC COSTS (2013-2014)

Tuition and fees: $39,550.

Per-credit charge: $1,225.

Room and board: $7,470.

FINANCIAL AID PICTURE (2012-2013)

Students with need: Out of 424 full-time freshmen who applied for aid, 339 were judged to have need. Of these, 337 received aid, and 229 had their full need met. Average financial aid package met 95% of need; average scholarship/grant was $25,010; average loan was $3,778. Need-based aid available for part-time students.

Students without need: 175 full-time freshmen who did not demonstrate need for aid received scholarships/grants; average award was $15,601. No-need awards available for academics, leadership.

Scholarships offered: Scholarships; $12,000-$18,000 per year; based on superior academic achievement or community service involvement.

FINANCIAL AID PROCEDURES

Forms required: FAFSA, CSS PROFILE.

Dates and Deadlines: Closing date 2/1. Applicants notified by 3/31; must reply by 5/1.

Transfers: Closing date 4/1. Applicants notified on a rolling basis. Financial aid transcript from previous institution(s) attended required.

CONTACT

Mary Ellen Severance, Director of Financial Aid and Student Employment
950 Main Street, Worcester, MA 01610-1477
(508) 793-7478

College of the Holy Cross

Worcester, Massachusetts Federal Code: 002141
www.holycross.edu CSS Code: 3282

4-year private liberal arts college in small city, affiliated with Roman Catholic Church.
Enrollment: 2,891 undergrads. 763 full-time freshmen.
Selectivity: Admits less than 50% of applicants.

BASIC COSTS (2013-2014)
Tuition and fees: $44,272.
Room and board: $11,960.

FINANCIAL AID PICTURE (2012-2013)
Students with need: Out of 574 full-time freshmen who applied for aid, 501 were judged to have need. Of these, 471 received aid, and 471 had their full need met. Average financial aid package met 100% of need; average scholarship/grant was $30,733; average loan was $5,138.
Students without need: 5 full-time freshmen who did not demonstrate need for aid received scholarships/grants; average award was $16,560. No-need awards available for academics, athletics, music/drama.
Scholarships offered: 12 full-time freshmen received athletic scholarships; average amount $47,240.
Cumulative student debt: 55% of graduating class had student loans; average debt was $26,567.
Additional info: Cost of tuition above amount of Pell Grant waived for Worcester residents whose families earn less than $50,000.

FINANCIAL AID PROCEDURES
Forms required: FAFSA. CSS PROFILE required of all students applying for institutional aid.
Dates and Deadlines: Closing date 2/1. Applicants notified by 4/1; must reply by 5/1.
Transfers: Financial aid generally not available to transfer students.

CONTACT

Lynne Myers, Director of Financial Aid
One College Street, Worcester, MA 01610-2395
(508) 793-2265

Curry College

Milton, Massachusetts
www.curry.edu Federal Code: 002143

4-year private nursing and liberal arts college in large town.
Enrollment: 2,716 undergrads, 27% part-time. 579 full-time freshmen.
Selectivity: Admits over 75% of applicants.

BASIC COSTS (2013-2014)
Tuition and fees: $34,415.
Room and board: $13,130.

FINANCIAL AID PICTURE (2012-2013)
Students with need: Out of 457 full-time freshmen who applied for aid, 457 were judged to have need. Of these, 457 received aid, and 27 had their full need met. Average financial aid package met 67% of need; average scholarship/grant was $15,108; average loan was $3,599. For part-time students, average financial aid package was $6,126.
Students without need: 78 full-time freshmen who did not demonstrate need for aid received scholarships/grants; average award was $5,416. No-need awards available for academics, leadership.
Scholarships offered: Curry College Trustees Scholarship; $12,000. Academic Achievement Scholarship; $6,500. Excellence in Education Scholarship; $3,000. All based on past academic achievement, promising academic ability, demonstrated leadership skills, character and citizenship, community service and talent.
Cumulative student debt: 79% of graduating class had student loans; average debt was $41,876.

FINANCIAL AID PROCEDURES
Forms required: FAFSA.
Dates and Deadlines: Priority date 3/1; no closing date. Applicants notified on a rolling basis starting 3/1; must reply by 5/1 or within 2 week(s) of notification.
Transfers: No deadline. Applicants notified on a rolling basis starting 3/1; must reply by 5/1 or within 2 week(s) of notification.

CONTACT

Stephanny Elias, Director, Student Financial Services
1071 Blue Hill Avenue, Milton, MA 02186-9984
(617) 333-2354

Dean College

Franklin, Massachusetts
www.dean.edu Federal Code: 002144

2-year private liberal arts college in large town.
Enrollment: 1,235 undergrads, 14% part-time. 528 full-time freshmen.
Selectivity: Admits 50 to 75% of applicants.

BASIC COSTS (2013-2014)
Tuition and fees: $33,480.
Room and board: $14,260.

FINANCIAL AID PICTURE (2012-2013)
Students with need: Out of 417 full-time freshmen who applied for aid, 380 were judged to have need. Of these, 380 received aid, and 64 had their full need met. Average financial aid package met 33% of need; average scholarship/grant was $5,768; average loan was $3,446. For part-time students, average financial aid package was $3,757.
Students without need: 145 full-time freshmen who did not demonstrate need for aid received scholarships/grants; average award was $13,321. No-need awards available for academics, alumni affiliation, art, athletics, leadership, music/drama.
Scholarships offered: ***Merit:*** Trustee's Scholarship; $10,000 - $12,000 per year; based on outstanding academic accomplishments or potential. President's Leadership Scholarship; $8,000 - $12,000 per year; given to students with leadership positions during their high school careers. Performing Arts Scholarship; $5,000 - $11,000 per year; based on achievement in dance or theater. ***Athletic:*** 9 full-time freshmen received athletic scholarships; average amount $2,856.
Cumulative student debt: 82% of graduating class had student loans; average debt was $8,375,136.

FINANCIAL AID PROCEDURES
Forms required: FAFSA.
Dates and Deadlines: Priority date 3/15; no closing date. Applicants notified on a rolling basis starting 2/25; must reply by 5/1 or within 2 week(s) of notification.
Transfers: No deadline. Applicants notified on a rolling basis starting 3/1.

CONTACT

Jenny Aguiar, Director of Financial Aid
99 Main Street, Franklin, MA 02038-1994
(508) 541-1518

Eastern Nazarene College

Quincy, Massachusetts
www.enc.edu
Federal Code: 002145

4-year private liberal arts college in small city, affiliated with Church of the Nazarene.
Enrollment: 910 undergrads.

BASIC COSTS (2013-2014)
Tuition and fees: $27,922.
Room and board: $8,700.
Additional info: Tuition/fee waivers available for minority students.

FINANCIAL AID PICTURE
Students with need: Need-based aid available for full-time and part-time students. Work study available nights, weekends, and for part-time students.
Students without need: No-need awards available for academics, alumni affiliation, leadership, religious affiliation, ROTC.
Scholarships offered: Academic scholarships; amounts vary based on test scores; minimum 1500 SAT or 21 ACT. Honors Scholar; based on 1800 SAT or 27 ACT. Dean's Scholar; based on 2100 SAT or 32 ACT. Munro Scholar; full-tuition; based on interview and 2100 SAT or 32 ACT. President's Scholar; full-tuition plus room and board; based on interview and 2250 SAT or 34 ACT.
Additional info: Participant in Massachusetts University pre-payment plan.

FINANCIAL AID PROCEDURES
Forms required: FAFSA, institutional form.
Dates and Deadlines: Priority date 3/1; closing date 8/1. Applicants notified on a rolling basis starting 3/14; must reply by 8/1 or within 2 week(s) of notification.

CONTACT
Lerick Fanfanx, Director of Financial Aid
23 East Elm Avenue, Quincy, MA 02170
(617) 745-3712

Elms College

Chicopee, Massachusetts
www.elms.edu
Federal Code: 002140

4-year private liberal arts college in small city, affiliated with Roman Catholic Church.
Enrollment: 1,194 undergrads, 22% part-time. 194 full-time freshmen.
Selectivity: Admits over 75% of applicants.

BASIC COSTS (2013-2014)
Tuition and fees: $30,132.
Room and board: $10,930.

FINANCIAL AID PICTURE (2012-2013)
Students with need: Out of 191 full-time freshmen who applied for aid, 159 were judged to have need. Of these, 159 received aid. For part-time students, average financial aid package was $8,362.
Students without need: 32 full-time freshmen who did not demonstrate need for aid received scholarships/grants; average award was $11,431. No-need awards available for academics, alumni affiliation, leadership, religious affiliation, state/district residency.
Scholarships offered: Elms Presidential Scholar Award; $12,000-$14,000 per year. Elms Distinguished Scholar Award; $10,000-12,000 per year. Elms Scholar Award; $8,000-10,000 per year. All based on GPA and SAT/ACT.

FINANCIAL AID PROCEDURES
Forms required: FAFSA.
Dates and Deadlines: Priority date 3/1; no closing date. Applicants notified on a rolling basis starting 3/10; must reply by 5/1 or within 2 week(s) of notification.
Transfers: No deadline. Applicants notified on a rolling basis starting 3/15.

CONTACT
Kristin Hmieleski, Director of Financial Aid
291 Springfield Street, Chicopee, MA 01013-2839
(413) 265-2249

Emerson College

Boston, Massachusetts
www.emerson.edu
Federal Code: 002146
CSS Code: 3367

4-year private college of communication and the arts in very large city.
Enrollment: 3,660 undergrads, 2% part-time. 866 full-time freshmen.
Selectivity: Admits less than 50% of applicants.

BASIC COSTS (2012-2013)
Tuition and fees: $34,198.
Per-credit charge: $1,049.
Room and board: $13,958.

FINANCIAL AID PICTURE (2011-2012)
Students with need: Out of 671 full-time freshmen who applied for aid, 565 were judged to have need. Of these, 564 received aid, and 65 had their full need met. Average financial aid package met 75% of need; average scholarship/grant was $17,589; average loan was $3,736. For part-time students, average financial aid package was $6,384.
Students without need: 28 full-time freshmen who did not demonstrate need for aid received scholarships/grants; average award was $13,627. No-need awards available for academics, leadership, music/drama, state/district residency.
Scholarships offered: Trustees Scholarships; half-tuition; honors program students may apply. Dean's Scholarships; $14,000. Emerson Stage Scholarships; amounts vary; based on performing arts audition and academic merit.
Cumulative student debt: 64% of graduating class had student loans; average debt was $33,572.
Additional info: Massachusetts Loan Plan available for parents of dependent undergraduates.

FINANCIAL AID PROCEDURES
Forms required: FAFSA, CSS PROFILE.
Dates and Deadlines: Priority date 3/1; no closing date. Must reply by 5/1 or within 3 week(s) of notification.
Transfers: Priority date 4/1.

CONTACT
Ruthanne Madsen, Associate Vice President for Enrollment, Student Financial Services
120 Boylston Street, Boston, MA 02116-4624
(617) 824-8655

Emmanuel College

Boston, Massachusetts
www.emmanuel.edu
Federal Code: 002147

4-year private liberal arts college in very large city, affiliated with Roman Catholic Church.
Enrollment: 2,056 undergrads, 11% part-time. 553 full-time freshmen.
Selectivity: Admits 50 to 75% of applicants.

BASIC COSTS (2012-2013)
Tuition and fees: $33,650.
Room and board: $12,990.

FINANCIAL AID PICTURE (2012-2013)
Students with need: Out of 517 full-time freshmen who applied for aid, 476 were judged to have need. Of these, 476 received aid, and 233 had their full need met. Average financial aid package met 78% of need; average

scholarship/grant was $19,694; average loan was $3,677. For part-time students, average financial aid package was $7,995.

Students without need: 71 full-time freshmen who did not demonstrate need for aid received scholarships/grants; average award was $10,074. No-need awards available for academics, alumni affiliation, leadership.

Cumulative student debt: 74% of graduating class had student loans; average debt was $33,452.

FINANCIAL AID PROCEDURES

Forms required: FAFSA, institutional form.

Dates and Deadlines: Priority date 2/15; no closing date. Applicants notified on a rolling basis starting 3/1.

CONTACT

Jennifer Porter, Associate Vice President for Student Financial Services
400 The Fenway, Boston, MA 02115
(617) 735-9938

Endicott College

Beverly, Massachusetts
www.endicott.edu Federal Code: 002148

4-year private liberal arts college in large town.
Enrollment: 2,565 undergrads, 7% part-time. 643 full-time freshmen.
Selectivity: Admits 50 to 75% of applicants.

BASIC COSTS (2012-2013)

Tuition and fees: $28,166.
Per-credit charge: $850.
Room and board: $13,200.

FINANCIAL AID PICTURE (2012-2013)

Students with need: Average financial aid package met 61% of need; average scholarship/grant was $10,534; average loan was $3,685. For part-time students, average financial aid package was $7,733.

Students without need: No-need awards available for academics, alumni affiliation, art, job skills, leadership, music/drama, religious affiliation, ROTC, state/district residency.

Cumulative student debt: 73% of graduating class had student loans; average debt was $36,198.

FINANCIAL AID PROCEDURES

Forms required: FAFSA, institutional form.

Dates and Deadlines: Priority date 3/15; no closing date. Applicants notified on a rolling basis starting 3/15; must reply within 2 week(s) of notification.

CONTACT

Marcia Toomey, Director of Financial Aid
376 Hale Street, Beverly, MA 01915-9985
(978) 232-2060

Fisher College

Boston, Massachusetts
www.fisher.edu Federal Code: 002150

2-year private business and liberal arts college in very large city.
Enrollment: 1,776 undergrads, 30% part-time. 354 full-time freshmen.
Selectivity: Admits 50 to 75% of applicants.

BASIC COSTS (2012-2013)

Tuition and fees: $26,775.
Per-credit charge: $825.
Room and board: $13,924.

FINANCIAL AID PICTURE (2012-2013)

Students with need: 82% of average financial aid package awarded as scholarships/grants, 18% awarded as loans/jobs. Need-based aid available for part-time students. Work study available nights, weekends, and for part-time students.

Students without need: No-need awards available for academics.

Scholarships offered: Fisher Honor Scholarship; $5,000; based on outstanding academic and personal achievement, contribution to school and community; renewable with 3.0 GPA. Presidential Scholarship; $8,000. Achievement Scholarship; $6,000. Opportunity Award; $5,000. Charles River Award; $3,000.

FINANCIAL AID PROCEDURES

Forms required: FAFSA.

Dates and Deadlines: Priority date 5/1; no closing date. Applicants notified on a rolling basis starting 3/1.

Transfers: Transfer Student Scholarship; $2,500.

CONTACT

Anne Sylvain, Director of Financial Aid
Office of Admissions, Boston, MA 02116
(617) 236-8821

Fitchburg State University

Fitchburg, Massachusetts
www.fitchburgstate.edu Federal Code: 002184

4-year public liberal arts and teachers college in small city.
Enrollment: 3,944 undergrads, 16% part-time. 739 full-time freshmen.
Selectivity: Admits 50 to 75% of applicants.

BASIC COSTS (2012-2013)

Tuition and fees: $8,710; out-of-state residents $14,790.
Per-credit charge: $40; out-of-state residents $294.
Room and board: $8,602.

FINANCIAL AID PICTURE

Students with need: Need-based aid available for full-time and part-time students. Work study available nights, weekends, and for part-time students.

Students without need: No-need awards available for academics, alumni affiliation, leadership, ROTC, state/district residency.

FINANCIAL AID PROCEDURES

Forms required: FAFSA.

Dates and Deadlines: Priority date 3/1; no closing date. Applicants notified on a rolling basis starting 3/15.

CONTACT

Pamela McCafferty, Dean of Enrollment Management
160 Pearl Street, Fitchburg, MA 01420-2697
(978) 665-3156

Framingham State University

Framingham, Massachusetts
www.framingham.edu Federal Code: 002185

4-year public liberal arts and teachers college in small city.
Enrollment: 4,147 undergrads, 10% part-time. 821 full-time freshmen.
Selectivity: Admits 50 to 75% of applicants.

BASIC COSTS (2012-2013)

Tuition and fees: $8,080; out-of-state residents $14,160.
Per-credit charge: $40; out-of-state residents $294.
Room and board: $9,540.

FINANCIAL AID PICTURE

Students with need: Need-based aid available for full-time and part-time students. Work study available nights, weekends, and for part-time students.

Students without need: No-need awards available for academics, state/district residency.

Scholarships offered: Senator Paul E. Tsongas Scholarship; full-tuition and fees; available to Massachusetts residents based on 3.75 GPA and test scores; 5 awarded. Merit scholarships; available to students majoring in education, natural or physical sciences based on GPA and test scores.

FINANCIAL AID PROCEDURES

Forms required: FAFSA.

Dates and Deadlines: Priority date 3/1; no closing date. Applicants notified on a rolling basis starting 3/15; must reply by 5/1 or within 2 week(s) of notification.

Transfers: Priority date 11/1; no deadline. Applicants notified on a rolling basis starting 11/1; must reply within 2 week(s) of notification.

CONTACT

Susan Lanzillo, Director of Financial Aid
PO Box 9101, Framingham, MA 01701-9101
(508) 626-4534

Franklin W. Olin College of Engineering

Needham, Massachusetts
www.olin.edu Federal Code: 039463

4-year private engineering college in large town.
Enrollment: 342 undergrads. 81 full-time freshmen.
Selectivity: Admits less than 50% of applicants.

BASIC COSTS (2012-2013)

Tuition and fees: $40,475.
Per-credit charge: $1,333.
Room and board: $14,500.
Additional info: All admitted students receive a half-tuition scholarship; Additional need-based aid available to cover other costs. Cost of mandatory laptop purchase for freshmen, $2500.

FINANCIAL AID PICTURE

Students with need: Need-based aid available for full-time students.
Students without need: No-need awards available for academics, leadership.
Scholarships offered: Olin Scholarship; 50% of tuition; awarded to all students.
Additional info: Financial aid forms not needed for one-half tuition scholarship which all students receive; FAFSA forms required for need-based aid considerations.

FINANCIAL AID PROCEDURES

Forms required: FAFSA.
Dates and Deadlines: Closing date 2/15. Applicants notified on a rolling basis starting 4/1; must reply by 5/1.

CONTACT

Jean Ricker, Manager, Financial Aid
Olin Way, Needham, MA 02492
(781) 292-2343

Gordon College

Wenham, Massachusetts
www.gordon.edu Federal Code: 002153

4-year private liberal arts college in small town, affiliated with nondenominational tradition.
Enrollment: 1,563 undergrads, 2% part-time. 478 full-time freshmen.
Selectivity: Admits less than 50% of applicants.

BASIC COSTS (2012-2013)

Tuition and fees: $32,100.
Room and board: $8,840.

FINANCIAL AID PICTURE (2012-2013)

Students with need: Out of 412 full-time freshmen who applied for aid, 356 were judged to have need. Of these, 356 received aid, and 58 had their full need met. Average financial aid package met 68% of need; average scholarship/grant was $17,158; average loan was $3,749. For part-time students, average financial aid package was $13,188.
Students without need: 109 full-time freshmen who did not demonstrate need for aid received scholarships/grants; average award was $11,657. No-need awards available for academics, alumni affiliation, art, leadership, minority status, music/drama, ROTC, state/district residency.
Scholarships offered: A.J. Gordon Scholarship; $15,000; based on academic achievement and leadership. Presidential Scholarships; $12,000 - $13,000; based on academic record. Provost's Scholarships; $9,000 - $11,000; based on academic record. Dean's Scholarships; $7,000; based on academic record. Choral Scholars Program; $5,000; for students with excellent ability/academic performance seeking career in vocal music field. National Merit Finalists and National Achievement Finalist Scholars; 75% of tuition. All scholarships renewable annually.
Cumulative student debt: 82% of graduating class had student loans; average debt was $37,534.

FINANCIAL AID PROCEDURES

Forms required: FAFSA.
Dates and Deadlines: Priority date 3/1; no closing date. Applicants notified on a rolling basis starting 2/15; must reply by 5/1 or within 2 week(s) of notification.
Transfers: Applicants notified on a rolling basis starting 2/15; must reply by 5/1 or within 2 week(s) of notification.

CONTACT

Daniel O'Connell, Director of Student Financial Services
255 Grapevine Road, Wenham, MA 01984-0198
(800) 343-1379

Greenfield Community College

Greenfield, Massachusetts
www.gcc.mass.edu Federal Code: 002169

2-year public community college in large town.
Enrollment: 2,275 undergrads, 61% part-time. 211 full-time freshmen.
Selectivity: Open admission; but selective for some programs.

BASIC COSTS (2012-2013)

Tuition and fees: $6,017; out-of-state residents $13,667.
Per-credit charge: $26; out-of-state residents $281.
Additional info: Tuition/fee waivers available for adults.

FINANCIAL AID PICTURE

Students with need: Need-based aid available for full-time and part-time students. Work study available nights, weekends, and for part-time students.
Students without need: This college awards aid only to students with need.

FINANCIAL AID PROCEDURES

Forms required: FAFSA, institutional form.
Dates and Deadlines: Priority date 4/15; no closing date. Applicants notified on a rolling basis starting 5/1; must reply within 2 week(s) of notification.

CONTACT

Linda Dejardins, Director of Financial Aid
One College Drive, Greenfield, MA 01301
(413) 775-1109

Hampshire College

Amherst, Massachusetts Federal Code: 004661
www.hampshire.edu CSS Code: 3447

4-year private liberal arts college in large town.
Enrollment: 1,438 undergrads. 350 full-time freshmen.
Selectivity: Admits 50 to 75% of applicants.

BASIC COSTS (2013-2014)
Tuition and fees: $46,625.
Room and board: $12,030.

FINANCIAL AID PICTURE (2012-2013)
Students with need: Out of 275 full-time freshmen who applied for aid, 192 were judged to have need. Of these, 192 received aid, and 43 had their full need met. Average financial aid package met 87% of need; average scholarship/grant was $29,118; average loan was $2,671.
Students without need: 121 full-time freshmen who did not demonstrate need for aid received scholarships/grants; average award was $9,649. No-need awards available for academics, leadership.
Cumulative student debt: 55% of graduating class had student loans; average debt was $22,550.

FINANCIAL AID PROCEDURES
Forms required: FAFSA, CSS PROFILE.
Dates and Deadlines: Closing date 2/1. Applicants notified by 4/1; must reply by 5/1 or within 2 week(s) of notification.
Transfers: Applicants notified by 4/1; must reply by 5/1.

CONTACT
Jennifer Lawton, Director of Financial Aid
893 West Street, Amherst, MA 01002-9988
(413) 559-5484

Harvard College

Cambridge, Massachusetts Federal Code: 002155
www.college.harvard.edu CSS Code: 3434

4-year private university and liberal arts college in small city.
Enrollment: 6,610 undergrads. 1,670 full-time freshmen.
Selectivity: Admits less than 50% of applicants.

BASIC COSTS (2012-2013)
Tuition and fees: $40,866.
Room and board: $13,630.

FINANCIAL AID PICTURE (2011-2012)
Students with need: Out of 1,178 full-time freshmen who applied for aid, 1,017 were judged to have need. Of these, 1,017 received aid, and 1,017 had their full need met. Average financial aid package met 100% of need; average scholarship/grant was $44,326; average loan was $3,211. Need-based aid available for part-time students.
Students without need: This college awards aid only to students with need.
Additional info: Loans not included in aid packages. Families with incomes below $65,000 have a zero expected parent contribution and families with incomes between $65,000 and $150,000 and standard asset worth have reduced parent expectation, on average 0-10% of income.

FINANCIAL AID PROCEDURES
Forms required: FAFSA, CSS PROFILE.
Dates and Deadlines: Closing date 2/1. Applicants notified by 4/1; must reply by 5/1 or within 2 week(s) of notification.
Transfers: Closing date 2/15. Applicants notified by 5/30; must reply within 2 week(s) of notification.

CONTACT
Sarah Donahue, Director of Financial Aid
86 Brattle Street, Cambridge, MA 02138
(617) 495-1581

Hellenic College/Holy Cross

Brookline, Massachusetts
www.hchc.edu Federal Code: 002154

4-year private liberal arts and seminary college in large town, affiliated with Eastern Orthodox Church.
Enrollment: 84 undergrads.
Selectivity: Admits 50 to 75% of applicants.

FINANCIAL AID PICTURE
Students with need: Need-based aid available for full-time students. Work study available nights, weekends, and for part-time students.
Students without need: This college awards aid only to students with need.

FINANCIAL AID PROCEDURES
Forms required: FAFSA, institutional form.
Dates and Deadlines: Closing date 4/1. Applicants notified by 4/1; must reply within 2 week(s) of notification.
Transfers: No deadline. Applicants notified on a rolling basis; must reply within 2 week(s) of notification.

CONTACT
Christine Burke, Director of Financial Aid
50 Goddard Avenue, Brookline, MA 02445
(617) 850-1216

Holyoke Community College

Holyoke, Massachusetts
www.hcc.edu Federal Code: 002170

2-year public community college in large town.
Enrollment: 6,809 undergrads, 49% part-time. 1,162 full-time freshmen.
Selectivity: Open admission; but selective for some programs.

BASIC COSTS (2012-2013)
Tuition and fees: $4,420; out-of-state residents $10,600.
Per-credit charge: $24; out-of-state residents $230.

FINANCIAL AID PICTURE (2011-2012)
Students with need: 74% of average financial aid package awarded as scholarships/grants, 26% awarded as loans/jobs. Need-based aid available for part-time students. Work study available nights.
Students without need: No-need awards available for academics, art, leadership, music/drama.

FINANCIAL AID PROCEDURES
Forms required: FAFSA.
Dates and Deadlines: Priority date 5/1; no closing date. Applicants notified on a rolling basis starting 5/1; must reply within 2 week(s) of notification.

CONTACT
Karen Derouin, Director of Financial Aid
303 Homestead Avenue, Holyoke, MA 01040
(413) 552-2150

Laboure College

Dorchester, Massachusetts
www.laboure.edu Federal Code: 006324

2-year private health science college in very large city, affiliated with Roman Catholic Church.

Enrollment: 737 undergrads, 90% part-time. 1 full-time freshmen.
Selectivity: Admits less than 50% of applicants.

BASIC COSTS (2012-2013)
Tuition and fees: $25,320.
Per-credit charge: $820.

FINANCIAL AID PICTURE (2012-2013)
Students with need: Average financial aid package met 1% of need; average scholarship/grant was $5,700; average loan was $4,000. For part-time students, average financial aid package was $3,100.
Students without need: No-need awards available for academics, alumni affiliation, leadership, religious affiliation.
Scholarships offered: Steward Health Care Employee; 25% of tuition for all professional courses for those who work 16 plus hours per week, 10% for all professional courses for those who work 10-15 hours a week. Nursing scholarship; 25% of cost of nursing courses for students with LPN credential. First year scholarship; 50% of tuition; for graduates of Catholic high schools; 2 awarded annually.
Cumulative student debt: 85% of graduating class had student loans; average debt was $34,500.

FINANCIAL AID PROCEDURES
Forms required: FAFSA.
Dates and Deadlines: Priority date 4/1; no closing date. Applicants notified on a rolling basis starting 6/15; must reply within 2 week(s) of notification.
Transfers: Priority date 12/1. Applicants notified on a rolling basis starting 12/1; must reply within 2 week(s) of notification.

CONTACT
Erin Hanlon, Director of Financial Aid
2120 Dorchester Avenue, Dorchester, MA 02124-5698
(617) 296-8300 ext. 4054

Lasell College

Newton, Massachusetts
www.lasell.edu Federal Code: 002158

4-year private business and liberal arts college in small city.
Enrollment: 1,645 undergrads, 1% part-time. 375 full-time freshmen.
Selectivity: Admits 50 to 75% of applicants.

BASIC COSTS (2012-2013)
Tuition and fees: $29,000.
Per-credit charge: $940.
Room and board: $12,300.

FINANCIAL AID PICTURE (2011-2012)
Students with need: Out of 342 full-time freshmen who applied for aid, 311 were judged to have need. Of these, 310 received aid, and 65 had their full need met. Average financial aid package met 65% of need; average scholarship/grant was $18,390; average loan was $3,400. For part-time students, average financial aid package was $9,500.
Students without need: 55 full-time freshmen who did not demonstrate need for aid received scholarships/grants; average award was $9,684. No-need awards available for academics, alumni affiliation.
Cumulative student debt: 85% of graduating class had student loans; average debt was $39,559.

FINANCIAL AID PROCEDURES
Forms required: FAFSA, institutional form.
Dates and Deadlines: Priority date 3/1; no closing date. Applicants notified on a rolling basis starting 2/15; must reply by 5/1 or within 2 week(s) of notification.
Transfers: No deadline. Applicants notified on a rolling basis starting 2/15.

CONTACT
Michele Kosboth, Director of Student Financial Planning
1844 Commonwealth Avenue, Newton, MA 02466-2709
(617) 243-2227

Lesley University

Cambridge, Massachusetts
www.lesley.edu Federal Code: 002160

4-year private liberal arts and teachers college in very large city.
Enrollment: 1,550 undergrads, 6% part-time. 364 full-time freshmen.
Selectivity: Admits 50 to 75% of applicants.

BASIC COSTS (2012-2013)
Tuition and fees: $32,310.
Per-credit charge: $510.
Room and board: $14,250.

FINANCIAL AID PICTURE (2011-2012)
Students with need: Out of 318 full-time freshmen who applied for aid, 289 were judged to have need. Of these, 288 received aid, and 83 had their full need met. Average financial aid package met 72% of need; average scholarship/grant was $13,000; average loan was $3,698. For part-time students, average financial aid package was $15,025.
Students without need: 65 full-time freshmen who did not demonstrate need for aid received scholarships/grants; average award was $12,520. No-need awards available for academics, art, leadership, minority status, state/district residency.
Scholarships offered: Freshmen scholarships; $5,000-full tuition; for students with strong academic backgrounds who have shown a commitment to community service and making a difference in the lives of others.
Cumulative student debt: 90% of graduating class had student loans; average debt was $23,000.

FINANCIAL AID PROCEDURES
Forms required: FAFSA.
Dates and Deadlines: Priority date 2/15; no closing date. Applicants notified on a rolling basis starting 2/1.
Transfers: Priority date 3/15.

CONTACT
Scott Jewell, Director of Financial Aid
29 Everett Street, Cambridge, MA 02140-2790
(617) 349-8667

Marian Court College

Swampscott, Massachusetts
www.mariancourt.edu Federal Code: 006873

2-year private business and liberal arts college in large town, affiliated with Roman Catholic Church.
Enrollment: 200 full-time undergrads.

BASIC COSTS (2012-2013)
Tuition and fees: $16,200.
Additional info: Evening degree program: $800 per 3-credit course.

FINANCIAL AID PICTURE (2011-2012)
Students with need: 64% of average financial aid package awarded as scholarships/grants, 36% awarded as loans/jobs. Need-based aid available for part-time students.
Students without need: No-need awards available for academics.
Scholarships offered: Academic Scholarships; $2,000-$5,000; based on GPA.

FINANCIAL AID PROCEDURES
Forms required: FAFSA, institutional form.
Dates and Deadlines: Priority date 5/1; no closing date. Applicants notified on a rolling basis starting 1/15.
Transfers: No deadline.

CONTACT
Stacy Bonsang, Director of Financial Aid
35 Little's Point Road, Swampscott, MA 01907-2896
(781) 309-5200

Massachusetts Bay Community College

Wellesley Hills, Massachusetts
www.massbay.edu Federal Code: 002171

2-year public community college in large town.
Enrollment: 4,623 undergrads, 58% part-time. 708 full-time freshmen.
Selectivity: Open admission; but selective for some programs.

BASIC COSTS (2012-2013)
Tuition and fees: $5,220; out-of-state residents $11,400.
Per-credit charge: $24; out-of-state residents $230.
Additional info: Tuition/fee waivers available for unemployed or children of unemployed.

FINANCIAL AID PICTURE
Students with need: Need-based aid available for full-time and part-time students.

FINANCIAL AID PROCEDURES
Forms required: FAFSA.
Dates and Deadlines: Priority date 5/1; no closing date. Applicants notified on a rolling basis starting 7/1.
Transfers: No deadline. Applicants notified on a rolling basis.

CONTACT
Elizabeth Enos, Director of Financial Aid
50 Oakland Street, Wellesley Hills, MA 02481
(781) 239-2600

Massachusetts College of Art and Design

Boston, Massachusetts
www.massart.edu Federal Code: 002180

4-year public visual arts college in very large city.
Enrollment: 1,824 undergrads, 10% part-time. 312 full-time freshmen.
Selectivity: Admits 50 to 75% of applicants.

BASIC COSTS (2012-2013)
Tuition and fees: $10,400; out-of-state residents $27,500.
Room and board: $12,150.
Additional info: Tuition for New England resident students $17,600. Tuition/fee waivers available for unemployed or children of unemployed.

FINANCIAL AID PICTURE (2011-2012)
Students with need: Out of 246 full-time freshmen who applied for aid, 197 were judged to have need. Of these, 197 received aid. For part-time students, average financial aid package was $6,566.
Students without need: 17 full-time freshmen who did not demonstrate need for aid received scholarships/grants; average award was $5,766. No-need awards available for academics, art, leadership, state/district residency.
Cumulative student debt: 73% of graduating class had student loans; average debt was $25,875.
Additional info: Tuition waiver available to Vietnam veterans.

FINANCIAL AID PROCEDURES
Forms required: FAFSA.
Dates and Deadlines: Priority date 3/1; no closing date. Applicants notified on a rolling basis starting 3/15; must reply within 3 week(s) of notification.
Transfers: Financial aid transcripts required.

CONTACT
Aurelio Ramirez, Director of Financial Aid
621 Huntington Avenue, Boston, MA 02115-5882
(617) 879-7850

Massachusetts College of Liberal Arts

North Adams, Massachusetts
www.mcla.edu Federal Code: 002187

4-year public liberal arts college in large town.
Enrollment: 1,553 undergrads, 10% part-time. 308 full-time freshmen.
Selectivity: Admits 50 to 75% of applicants.

BASIC COSTS (2012-2013)
Tuition and fees: $8,700; out-of-state residents $17,645.
Per-credit charge: $43; out-of-state residents $416.
Room and board: $9,102.
Additional info: Tuition/fee waivers available for unemployed or children of unemployed.

FINANCIAL AID PICTURE (2012-2013)
Students with need: Out of 297 full-time freshmen who applied for aid, 251 were judged to have need. Of these, 249 received aid, and 183 had their full need met. Average financial aid package met 80% of need; average scholarship/grant was $6,832; average loan was $3,450. For part-time students, average financial aid package was $9,878.
Students without need: 21 full-time freshmen who did not demonstrate need for aid received scholarships/grants; average award was $4,424. No-need awards available for academics, art, leadership, minority status, music/drama.
Cumulative student debt: 69% of graduating class had student loans; average debt was $29,534.

FINANCIAL AID PROCEDURES
Forms required: FAFSA, institutional form.
Dates and Deadlines: Priority date 3/1; no closing date. Applicants notified on a rolling basis starting 3/1; must reply by 5/1 or within 2 week(s) of notification.

CONTACT
Elizabeth Petri, Director of Financial Aid
375 Church Street, North Adams, MA 01247
(413) 662-5219

Massachusetts College of Pharmacy and Health Sciences

Boston, Massachusetts
www.mcphs.edu Federal Code: 002165

4-year private health science and pharmacy college in very large city.
Enrollment: 3,627 undergrads.

BASIC COSTS (2012-2013)
Tuition and fees: $27,440.
Per-credit charge: $980.
Room and board: $13,580.

FINANCIAL AID PICTURE
Students with need: Need-based aid available for full-time and part-time students. Work study available weekends and for part-time students.
Students without need: No-need awards available for academics.

FINANCIAL AID PROCEDURES
Forms required: FAFSA.
Dates and Deadlines: Priority date 3/15; no closing date. Applicants notified on a rolling basis.

Transfers: Massachusetts State Grant deadline May 1.

CONTACT

Kevin Piotrowski, Executive Director of Enrollment Services
179 Longwood Avenue, Boston, MA 02115-5896
(617) 732-2864

Massachusetts Institute of Technology

Cambridge, Massachusetts Federal Code: 002178
www.web.mit.edu CSS Code: 3514

4-year private university in small city.
Enrollment: 4,477 undergrads. 1,128 full-time freshmen.
Selectivity: Admits less than 50% of applicants.

BASIC COSTS (2013-2014)
Tuition and fees: $43,498.
Room and board: $12,744.

FINANCIAL AID PICTURE (2011-2012)
Students with need: Out of 887 full-time freshmen who applied for aid, 699 were judged to have need. Of these, 699 received aid, and 699 had their full need met. Average financial aid package met 100% of need; average scholarship/grant was $35,719; average loan was $3,159. For part-time students, average financial aid package was $24,162.
Students without need: This college awards aid only to students with need.
Cumulative student debt: 41% of graduating class had student loans; average debt was $20,794.
Additional info: Filing deadline 2/15 for CSS PROFILE.

FINANCIAL AID PROCEDURES
Forms required: FAFSA, CSS PROFILE.
Dates and Deadlines: Closing date 2/15. Applicants notified by 4/1; must reply by 5/1.
Transfers: Closing date 3/1. Applicants notified by 4/15; must reply by 5/1. Access to MIT funds may be limited to fewer than 8 terms.

CONTACT

Elizabeth Hicks, Executive Director of Student Financial Services
77 Massachusetts Avenue, Room 3-108, Cambridge, MA 02139-4307
(617) 258-8600

Massachusetts Maritime Academy

Buzzards Bay, Massachusetts
www.maritime.edu Federal Code: 002181

4-year public engineering and maritime college in large town.
Enrollment: 1,309 undergrads.

BASIC COSTS (2012-2013)
Tuition and fees: $7,045; out-of-state residents $21,951.
Room and board: $10,068.
Additional info: Additional cost for uniform/seabag of $2,300 required of all first year students.

FINANCIAL AID PICTURE
Students with need: Need-based aid available for full-time and part-time students. Work study available nights, weekends, and for part-time students.
Students without need: No-need awards available for academics, leadership, music/drama.

FINANCIAL AID PROCEDURES
Forms required: FAFSA, institutional form.
Dates and Deadlines: Closing date 5/1. Applicants notified on a rolling basis starting 3/1.

CONTACT

Catherine Kedski, Financial Aid Director
101 Academy Drive, Buzzards Bay, MA 02532-1803
(508) 830-5086

Massasoit Community College

Brockton, Massachusetts
www.massasoit.mass.edu Federal Code: 002177

2-year public community college in small city.
Enrollment: 6,645 undergrads, 49% part-time. 1,287 full-time freshmen.
Selectivity: Open admission; but selective for some programs.

BASIC COSTS (2012-2013)
Tuition and fees: $5,070; out-of-state residents $11,250.
Per-credit charge: $24; out-of-state residents $230.
Additional info: Tuition/fee waivers available for unemployed or children of unemployed.

FINANCIAL AID PICTURE
Students with need: Need-based aid available for full-time and part-time students.
Students without need: This college awards aid only to students with need.

FINANCIAL AID PROCEDURES
Forms required: FAFSA.
Dates and Deadlines: Priority date 4/15; no closing date. Applicants notified on a rolling basis starting 6/1.

CONTACT

MaryBeth Courtright, Director of Financial Aid
One Massasoit Boulevard, Brockton, MA 02302-3996
(508) 588-9100 ext. 1479

Merrimack College

North Andover, Massachusetts
www.merrimack.edu Federal Code: 002120

4-year private business and liberal arts college in large town, affiliated with Roman Catholic Church.
Enrollment: 2,408 undergrads, 4% part-time. 698 full-time freshmen.
Selectivity: Admits over 75% of applicants.

BASIC COSTS (2012-2013)
Tuition and fees: $33,920.
Room and board: $11,690.

FINANCIAL AID PICTURE (2012-2013)
Students with need: Need-based aid available for full-time students. Work study available nights, weekends, and for part-time students.
Students without need: No-need awards available for academics, athletics, leadership, minority status, religious affiliation.

FINANCIAL AID PROCEDURES
Forms required: FAFSA.
Dates and Deadlines: Closing date 2/15. Applicants notified by 3/15; must reply by 5/1 or within 2 week(s) of notification.
Transfers: Must reply within 2 week(s) of notification.

CONTACT

Adrienne Montgomery, Director of Financial Aid
315 Turnpike Street, North Andover, MA 01845
(978) 837-5186

Middlesex Community College
Bedford, Massachusetts
www.middlesex.mass.edu Federal Code: 009936

2-year public community college in small city.
Enrollment: 8,849 undergrads, 58% part-time. 1,535 full-time freshmen.
Selectivity: Open admission; but selective for some programs.

BASIC COSTS (2012-2013)
Tuition and fees: $5,280; out-of-state residents $11,460.
Per-credit charge: $176; out-of-state residents $382.
Additional info: Tuition/fee waivers available for adults.

FINANCIAL AID PICTURE
Students with need: Need-based aid available for full-time and part-time students.
Students without need: This college awards aid only to students with need.
Additional info: Application priority date 5/1 for Massachusetts state funds.

FINANCIAL AID PROCEDURES
Forms required: FAFSA, institutional form.
Dates and Deadlines: Priority date 5/1; no closing date. Applicants notified on a rolling basis starting 6/1; must reply within 2 week(s) of notification.

CONTACT
Robert Baumel, Financial Aid Director
33 Kearney Square, Lowell, MA 01852-1987
(978) 656-3242

Montserrat College of Art
Beverly, Massachusetts
www.montserrat.edu Federal Code: 013774

4-year private visual arts college in large town.
Enrollment: 384 undergrads, 1% part-time. 97 full-time freshmen.
Selectivity: Admits over 75% of applicants.

BASIC COSTS (2012-2013)
Tuition and fees: $26,650.
Per-credit charge: $1,065.
Room and board: $7,300.

FINANCIAL AID PICTURE
Students with need: Need-based aid available for full-time and part-time students. Work study available nights, weekends, and for part-time students.
Students without need: No-need awards available for academics, art.
Scholarships offered: Talent Awards; $5,000-$10,000; based on artistic and academic ability.

FINANCIAL AID PROCEDURES
Forms required: FAFSA, institutional form.
Dates and Deadlines: Priority date 3/1; no closing date. Applicants notified on a rolling basis starting 3/1; must reply by 5/1 or within 2 week(s) of notification.
Transfers: No deadline. Applicants notified on a rolling basis starting 12/20; must reply within 2 week(s) of notification.

CONTACT
Anne McDermott, Director of Financial Aid
23 Essex Street, Beverly, MA 01915
(978) 921-4242 ext. 1155

Mount Holyoke College
South Hadley, Massachusetts Federal Code: 002192
www.mtholyoke.edu CSS Code: 3529

4-year private liberal arts college for women in large town.
Enrollment: 2,291 undergrads, 1% part-time. 497 full-time freshmen.
Selectivity: Admits less than 50% of applicants.

BASIC COSTS (2013-2014)
Tuition and fees: $41,456.
Room and board: $12,140.

FINANCIAL AID PICTURE (2012-2013)
Students with need: Out of 362 full-time freshmen who applied for aid, 300 were judged to have need. Of these, 300 received aid, and 300 had their full need met. Average financial aid package met 100% of need; average scholarship/grant was $28,248; average loan was $3,580. For part-time students, average financial aid package was $23,159.
Students without need: 81 full-time freshmen who did not demonstrate need for aid received scholarships/grants; average award was $15,756. No-need awards available for academics, leadership.
Scholarships offered: Academic scholarships; awarded competitively to first-year candidates who have outstanding record of scholarship and co-curricular achievement in high school and who demonstrate noteworthy leadership skills; renewable for up to 8 semesters with full-time status and good academic standing. Not transferrable. Number awarded each year varies; approximately 25% of entering class awarded merit-based awards.
Cumulative student debt: 65% of graduating class had student loans; average debt was $22,691.

FINANCIAL AID PROCEDURES
Forms required: FAFSA, CSS PROFILE.
Dates and Deadlines: Priority date 2/12; closing date 3/1. Applicants notified by 4/1; must reply by 5/1.
Transfers: Closing date 5/15. Applicants notified on a rolling basis; must reply within 4 week(s) of notification.

CONTACT
Kathy Blaisdell, Director of Student Financial Services
Newhall Center, South Hadley, MA 01075-1488
(413) 538-2291

Mount Ida College
Newton, Massachusetts
www.mountida.edu Federal Code: 002193

4-year private business and liberal arts college in small city.
Enrollment: 1,370 undergrads, 6% part-time. 329 full-time freshmen.
Selectivity: Admits 50 to 75% of applicants.

BASIC COSTS (2012-2013)
Tuition and fees: $26,928.
Per-credit charge: $705.
Room and board: $12,500.

FINANCIAL AID PICTURE
Students with need: Need-based aid available for full-time and part-time students. Work study available nights.

FINANCIAL AID PROCEDURES
Forms required: FAFSA, institutional form.
Dates and Deadlines: Priority date 4/15; no closing date. Applicants notified on a rolling basis starting 3/1; must reply within 3 week(s) of notification.

CONTACT
Dyan Teehan, Director of Financial Aid
777 Dedham Street, Newton, MA 02459
(617) 928-4785

Mount Wachusett Community College

Gardner, Massachusetts
www.mwcc.edu Federal Code: 002172

2-year public community college in large town.
Enrollment: 4,283 undergrads.
Selectivity: Open admission; but selective for some programs.

BASIC COSTS (2012-2013)
Tuition and fees: $6,040; out-of-state residents $12,190.
Per-credit charge: $25; out-of-state residents $230.
Additional info: New England resident tuition is $1,125.

FINANCIAL AID PICTURE
Students with need: Need-based aid available for full-time and part-time students. Work study available nights.
Students without need: This college awards aid only to students with need.

FINANCIAL AID PROCEDURES
Forms required: FAFSA, institutional form.
Dates and Deadlines: Priority date 4/15; no closing date. Applicants notified on a rolling basis starting 5/1.

CONTACT
Kelly Morrissey, Director, Student Records and Financial Management
444 Green Street, Gardner, MA 01440-1000
(978) 632-6600 ext. 524

New England Conservatory of Music

Boston, Massachusetts
www.necmusic.edu Federal Code: 002194

4-year private music college in very large city.
Enrollment: 418 undergrads, 4% part-time. 99 full-time freshmen.
Selectivity: Admits less than 50% of applicants.

BASIC COSTS (2012-2013)
Tuition and fees: $38,455.
Per-credit charge: $1,210.
Room and board: $12,350.

FINANCIAL AID PICTURE (2012-2013)
Students with need: Out of 64 full-time freshmen who applied for aid, 53 were judged to have need. Of these, 53 received aid, and 5 had their full need met. Average financial aid package met 56% of need; average scholarship/grant was $17,098; average loan was $4,939. Need-based aid available for part-time students.
Students without need: 52 full-time freshmen who did not demonstrate need for aid received scholarships/grants; average award was $15,423. No-need awards available for academics, music/drama.
Cumulative student debt: 49% of graduating class had student loans; average debt was $25,189.

FINANCIAL AID PROCEDURES
Forms required: FAFSA, institutional form.
Dates and Deadlines: Closing date 12/1. Applicants notified by 4/1; must reply by 5/1 or within 2 week(s) of notification.

CONTACT
Lauren Urbanek, Director of Financial Aid
290 Huntington Avenue, Boston, MA 02115-5018
(617) 585-1110

New England Institute of Art

Brookline, Massachusetts
www.artinstitutes.edu/boston Federal Code: 007486

4-year for-profit visual arts and technical college in very large city.
Enrollment: 1,052 undergrads.

FINANCIAL AID PICTURE
Students with need: Need-based aid available for full-time and part-time students. Work study available nights, weekends, and for part-time students.
Students without need: No-need awards available for academics.

FINANCIAL AID PROCEDURES
Forms required: FAFSA, institutional form.
Dates and Deadlines: Priority date 5/1; no closing date. Applicants notified on a rolling basis starting 3/1.

CONTACT
Leanne DiLeo, Director of Student Financial Services
10 Brookline Place West, Brookline, MA 02445-7295
(617) 739-1700

Newbury College

Brookline, Massachusetts
www.newbury.edu Federal Code: 007484

4-year private business and liberal arts college in large city.
Enrollment: 1,004 undergrads, 12% part-time. 297 full-time freshmen.
Selectivity: Admits 50 to 75% of applicants.

BASIC COSTS (2012-2013)
Tuition and fees: $27,850.
Room and board: $12,520.

FINANCIAL AID PICTURE (2011-2012)
Students with need: Out of 286 full-time freshmen who applied for aid, 277 were judged to have need. Of these, 277 received aid, and 3 had their full need met. Average financial aid package met 55% of need; average scholarship/grant was $11,414; average loan was $3,500. Need-based aid available for part-time students.
Students without need: This college awards aid only to students with need.
Cumulative student debt: 90% of graduating class had student loans; average debt was $40,000.

FINANCIAL AID PROCEDURES
Forms required: FAFSA.
Dates and Deadlines: Priority date 3/1; closing date 5/1. Applicants notified on a rolling basis starting 3/1; must reply by 5/1 or within 2 week(s) of notification.
Transfers: No deadline. Applicants notified on a rolling basis starting 3/1; must reply by 5/1 or within 2 week(s) of notification.

CONTACT
Joseph Chillo, Executive Vice President
129 Fisher Avenue, Brookline, MA 02445
(617) 730-7100

Nichols College

Dudley, Massachusetts
www.nichols.edu Federal Code: 002197

4-year private business and liberal arts college in rural community.
Enrollment: 1,220 undergrads, 16% part-time. 334 full-time freshmen.
Selectivity: Admits 50 to 75% of applicants.

BASIC COSTS (2013-2014)
Tuition and fees: $32,740.
Room and board: $11,700.

FINANCIAL AID PICTURE
Students with need: Need-based aid available for full-time and part-time students. Work study available nights, weekends, and for part-time students.
Students without need: No-need awards available for academics, alumni affiliation, leadership, ROTC.

FINANCIAL AID PROCEDURES
Forms required: FAFSA.
Dates and Deadlines: Priority date 3/1; closing date 6/1. Applicants notified on a rolling basis starting 2/26; must reply within 4 week(s) of notification.
Transfers: Applicants notified by 3/1; must reply within 4 week(s) of notification.

CONTACT
Denise Brindle, Director of Financial Aid
PO Box 5000, Dudley, MA 01571-5000
(508) 213-2372

North Shore Community College
Danvers, Massachusetts
www.northshore.edu Federal Code: 002173

2-year public community college in small city.
Enrollment: 7,240 undergrads, 58% part-time. 950 full-time freshmen.
Selectivity: Open admission; but selective for some programs.

BASIC COSTS (2012-2013)
Tuition and fees: $5,070; out-of-state residents $12,030.
Per-credit charge: $25; out-of-state residents $257.
Additional info: New England Regional Tuition: $181.50 per credit.

FINANCIAL AID PICTURE
Students with need: Need-based aid available for full-time and part-time students.
Students without need: This college awards aid only to students with need.

FINANCIAL AID PROCEDURES
Forms required: FAFSA.
Dates and Deadlines: Priority date 4/15; no closing date. Applicants notified on a rolling basis starting 4/1; must reply within 2 week(s) of notification.

CONTACT
Stephen Creamer, Dean of Student Financial Services
One Ferncroft Road, Danvers, MA 01923-0840
(978) 762-4000

Northeastern University
Boston, Massachusetts Federal Code: 002199
www.northeastern.edu CSS Code: 3667

4-year private university in very large city.
Enrollment: 16,685 undergrads. 2,664 full-time freshmen.
Selectivity: Admits less than 50% of applicants.

BASIC COSTS (2012-2013)
Tuition and fees: $39,736.
Room and board: $13,620.

FINANCIAL AID PICTURE (2012-2013)
Students with need: Out of 1,866 full-time freshmen who applied for aid, 1,305 were judged to have need. Of these, 1,305 received aid, and 476 had their full need met. Average financial aid package met 89% of need; average scholarship/grant was $24,949; average loan was $4,556. For part-time students, average financial aid package was $6,669.
Students without need: 603 full-time freshmen who did not demonstrate need for aid received scholarships/grants; average award was $18,338. No-need awards available for academics, athletics, leadership, ROTC.
Scholarships offered: 47 full-time freshmen received athletic scholarships; average amount $32,738.

FINANCIAL AID PROCEDURES
Forms required: FAFSA, CSS PROFILE.
Dates and Deadlines: Priority date 2/15; no closing date.
Transfers: Priority date 5/1; no deadline. Applicants notified on a rolling basis.

CONTACT
Anthony Erwin, Dean of Student Financial Services
360 Huntington Avenue, 150 Richards Hall, Boston, MA 02115
(617) 373-3190

Northern Essex Community College
Haverhill, Massachusetts
www.necc.mass.edu Federal Code: 002174

2-year public community and junior college in small city.
Enrollment: 6,780 undergrads, 62% part-time. 835 full-time freshmen.
Selectivity: Open admission; but selective for some programs.

BASIC COSTS (2012-2013)
Tuition and fees: $4,710; out-of-state residents $11,940.
Per-credit charge: $25; out-of-state residents $266.
Additional info: New England residents pay $170 per credit hour.

FINANCIAL AID PICTURE
Students with need: Need-based aid available for full-time and part-time students.
Students without need: No-need awards available for academics.

FINANCIAL AID PROCEDURES
Forms required: FAFSA, institutional form.
Dates and Deadlines: Priority date 5/1; no closing date. Must reply within 2 week(s) of notification.

CONTACT
Alexis Fishbone, Director of Financial Aid
100 Elliott Street, Haverhill, MA 01830-2399
(978) 556-3600

Northpoint Bible College
Haverhill, Massachusetts
www.northpoint.edu Federal Code: 035705

4-year private Bible college in small city, affiliated with Assemblies of God.
Enrollment: 336 undergrads, 14% part-time. 52 full-time freshmen.
Selectivity: Admits over 75% of applicants.

BASIC COSTS (2013-2014)
Tuition and fees: $10,430.
Room and board: $7,850.

FINANCIAL AID PICTURE (2011-2012)
Students with need: Out of 44 full-time freshmen who applied for aid, 40 were judged to have need. Of these, 38 received aid, and 2 had their full need met. Average financial aid package met 68% of need; average scholarship/grant was $4,374; average loan was $3,641. For part-time students, average financial aid package was $3,881.

Students without need: 8 full-time freshmen who did not demonstrate need for aid received scholarships/grants; average award was $9,876. No-need awards available for academics, leadership, minority status, music/drama, state/district residency.

FINANCIAL AID PROCEDURES

Forms required: FAFSA.

Dates and Deadlines: Priority date 6/1; no closing date. Applicants notified on a rolling basis; must reply within 4 week(s) of notification.

CONTACT

Patricia Stauffer, Financial Aid Director
320 South Main Street, Haverhill, MA 01835

Pine Manor College

Chestnut Hill, Massachusetts
www.pmc.edu Federal Code: 002201

4-year private liberal arts college in very large city.
Enrollment: 317 undergrads, 3% part-time. 103 full-time freshmen.
Selectivity: Admits 50 to 75% of applicants.

BASIC COSTS (2013-2014)

Tuition and fees: $24,930.
Room and board: $12,690.

FINANCIAL AID PICTURE (2012-2013)

Students with need: Out of 59 full-time freshmen who applied for aid, 58 were judged to have need. Of these, 58 received aid, and 1 had their full need met. Average financial aid package met 76% of need; average scholarship/grant was $22,500; average loan was $3,350. For part-time students, average financial aid package was $3,500.

Students without need: 18 full-time freshmen who did not demonstrate need for aid received scholarships/grants; average award was $12,750. No-need awards available for academics, alumni affiliation, leadership.

Cumulative student debt: 89% of graduating class had student loans; average debt was $30,808.

FINANCIAL AID PROCEDURES

Forms required: FAFSA.

Dates and Deadlines: Priority date 5/1; no closing date. Applicants notified on a rolling basis starting 3/1; must reply by 5/1 or within 2 week(s) of notification.

Transfers: No deadline. Applicants notified on a rolling basis starting 3/1; must reply by 5/1 or within 2 week(s) of notification.

CONTACT

Elizabeth Gorra
400 Heath Street, Chestnut Hill, MA 02467
(617) 731-7000

Quinsigamond Community College

Worcester, Massachusetts
www.qcc.edu Federal Code: 002175

2-year public community college in small city.
Enrollment: 7,881 undergrads, 54% part-time. 1,215 full-time freshmen.
Selectivity: Open admission; but selective for some programs.

BASIC COSTS (2012-2013)

Tuition and fees: $6,140; out-of-state residents $12,320.
Per-credit charge: $24; out-of-state residents $230.

FINANCIAL AID PICTURE (2011-2012)

Students with need: 73% of average financial aid package awarded as scholarships/grants, 27% awarded as loans/jobs. Need-based aid available for part-time students. Work study available nights, weekends, and for part-time students.

Students without need: No-need awards available for academics, leadership, minority status.

Additional info: All Pell Grant eligible students applying by May 1 will receive enough grant aid to cover tuition, fees and books.

FINANCIAL AID PROCEDURES

Forms required: FAFSA.

Dates and Deadlines: Priority date 4/1; no closing date. Applicants notified on a rolling basis starting 4/1.

CONTACT

Paula Ogden, Director of Financial Aid
670 West Boylston Street, Worcester, MA 01606
(508) 854-4261

Regis College

Weston, Massachusetts
www.regiscollege.edu Federal Code: 002206

4-year private health science and liberal arts college in large town, affiliated with Roman Catholic Church.
Enrollment: 1,149 undergrads, 21% part-time. 278 full-time freshmen.
Selectivity: Admits 50 to 75% of applicants.

BASIC COSTS (2012-2013)

Tuition and fees: $33,060.
Room and board: $12,800.
Additional info: Tuition/fee waivers available for adults.

FINANCIAL AID PICTURE (2012-2013)

Students with need: Out of 267 full-time freshmen who applied for aid, 251 were judged to have need. Of these, 251 received aid, and 44 had their full need met. Average financial aid package met 48% of need; average scholarship/grant was $14,755; average loan was $3,462. For part-time students, average financial aid package was $6,445.

Students without need: 25 full-time freshmen who did not demonstrate need for aid received scholarships/grants; average award was $17,738. No-need awards available for academics, alumni affiliation, leadership, religious affiliation, ROTC.

Cumulative student debt: 92% of graduating class had student loans; average debt was $32,643.

Additional info: Family tuition discount scholarship; offered during any semester in which 2 or more unmarried, dependent siblings attend full-time.

FINANCIAL AID PROCEDURES

Forms required: FAFSA, institutional form.

Dates and Deadlines: Priority date 2/15; no closing date. Applicants notified on a rolling basis starting 3/15; must reply by 5/1 or within 2 week(s) of notification.

Transfers: No deadline. Applicants notified on a rolling basis.

CONTACT

Bonnie Quinn, Director of Financial Aid
235 Wellesley Street, Weston, MA 02493-1571
(781) 768-7180

Roxbury Community College

Roxbury Crossing, Massachusetts
www.rcc.mass.edu Federal Code: 011930

2-year public community college in very large city.
Enrollment: 2,511 undergrads, 63% part-time. 275 full-time freshmen.
Selectivity: Open admission; but selective for some programs.

BASIC COSTS (2012-2013)
Tuition and fees: $4,800; out-of-state residents $12,450.
Per-credit charge: $26; out-of-state residents $247.

FINANCIAL AID PICTURE
Students with need: Need-based aid available for full-time and part-time students.
Students without need: This college awards aid only to students with need.

FINANCIAL AID PROCEDURES
Forms required: FAFSA, institutional form.
Dates and Deadlines: Closing date 5/1. Applicants notified on a rolling basis starting 6/15; must reply within 2 week(s) of notification.

CONTACT
Ray O'Rourke, Director of Financial Aid
1234 Columbus Avenue, Roxbury Crossing, MA 02120-3400
(617) 541-5322

Salem State University
Salem, Massachusetts
www.salemstate.edu/ Federal Code: 002188

4-year public university in large town.
Enrollment: 7,143 undergrads, 19% part-time. 1,086 full-time freshmen.
Selectivity: Admits 50 to 75% of applicants.

BASIC COSTS (2012-2013)
Tuition and fees: $7,730; out-of-state residents $13,870.
Per-credit charge: $38; out-of-state residents $294.
Room and board: $11,050.

FINANCIAL AID PICTURE
Students with need: Need-based aid available for full-time and part-time students. Work study available nights, weekends, and for part-time students.
Students without need: No-need awards available for academics.

FINANCIAL AID PROCEDURES
Forms required: FAFSA.
Dates and Deadlines: Priority date 3/1; closing date 9/1. Applicants notified on a rolling basis starting 3/15; must reply within 2 week(s) of notification.

CONTACT
Judy Cramer, Director of Financial Aid
352 Lafayette Street, Salem, MA 01970-5353
(978) 542-6112

School of the Museum of Fine Arts
Boston, Massachusetts
www.smfa.edu Federal Code: 004667

4-year private visual arts college in very large city.
Enrollment: 426 undergrads, 6% part-time. 94 full-time freshmen.
Selectivity: Admits over 75% of applicants.

BASIC COSTS (2012-2013)
Tuition and fees: $38,028.
Additional info: Board plan not available. Cost of room only, $13,590.

FINANCIAL AID PICTURE
Students with need: Need-based aid available for full-time and part-time students. Work study available nights, weekends, and for part-time students.
Students without need: No-need awards available for art.

FINANCIAL AID PROCEDURES
Forms required: FAFSA, institutional form.
Dates and Deadlines: Closing date 3/15. Applicants notified by 4/15; must reply by 5/1 or within 2 week(s) of notification.
Transfers: Priority date 4/1; no deadline. Applicants notified on a rolling basis starting 4/15; must reply by 5/1 or within 2 week(s) of notification.

CONTACT
Elizabeth Goreham, Director of Financial Aid
230 The Fenway, Boston, MA 02115
(800) 776-0135

Simmons College
Boston, Massachusetts
www.simmons.edu Federal Code: 002208

4-year private health science and liberal arts college for women in very large city.
Enrollment: 1,772 undergrads.
Selectivity: Admits less than 50% of applicants.

BASIC COSTS (2012-2013)
Tuition and fees: $34,350.
Room and board: $13,140.

FINANCIAL AID PICTURE
Students with need: Need-based aid available for full-time and part-time students.
Students without need: No-need awards available for academics, alumni affiliation.

FINANCIAL AID PROCEDURES
Forms required: FAFSA, institutional form.
Dates and Deadlines: Priority date 3/1; no closing date. Applicants notified on a rolling basis starting 3/15; must reply by 5/1.

CONTACT
Daniel Forster, Director of Student Financial Services
300 The Fenway, Boston, MA 02115-5898
(617) 521-2001

Smith College
Northampton, Massachusetts Federal Code: 002209
www.smith.edu CSS Code: 3762

4-year private liberal arts college for women in large town.
Enrollment: 2,664 undergrads, 1% part-time. 651 full-time freshmen.
Selectivity: Admits less than 50% of applicants.

BASIC COSTS (2012-2013)
Tuition and fees: $41,460.
Per-credit charge: $1,290.
Room and board: $13,860.

FINANCIAL AID PICTURE (2012-2013)
Students with need: Out of 513 full-time freshmen who applied for aid, 422 were judged to have need. Of these, 422 received aid, and 422 had their full need met. Average financial aid package met 100% of need; average scholarship/grant was $36,172; average loan was $3,247. For part-time students, average financial aid package was $25,038.
Students without need: 17 full-time freshmen who did not demonstrate need for aid received scholarships/grants; average award was $16,176. No-need awards available for academics, state/district residency.
Scholarships offered: Zollman Scholarships; $20,000; for academic excellence; about 15 awarded. STRIDE scholarship; $15,000; about 50 awarded. Springfield/Holyoke Partnership; full-tuition; for academic excellence in Springfield or Holyoke public high schools; up to 4 awarded.
Cumulative student debt: 67% of graduating class had student loans; average debt was $23,071.

Additional info: Financial aid policy guarantees to meet full financial need, as calculated by college, of all admitted students who have met application deadlines.

FINANCIAL AID PROCEDURES

Forms required: FAFSA, CSS PROFILE, institutional form.

Dates and Deadlines: Closing date 2/15. Applicants notified by 4/1; must reply by 5/1.

Transfers: Priority date 2/15; closing date 4/1. Applicants notified by 4/1; must reply by 5/1. Applicants who apply after admission decision is made cannot receive college aid until they complete at least 32 credits at Smith.

CONTACT

David Belanger, Director of Student Financial Services
7 College Lane, Northampton, MA 01063
(413) 585-2530

Springfield College

Springfield, Massachusetts
www.springfieldcollege.edu Federal Code: 002211

4-year private health science and liberal arts college in small city.
Enrollment: 2,222 undergrads, 2% part-time. 541 full-time freshmen.
Selectivity: Admits 50 to 75% of applicants.

BASIC COSTS (2012-2013)

Tuition and fees: $31,690.
Per-credit charge: $940.
Room and board: $11,390.

FINANCIAL AID PICTURE

Students with need: Need-based aid available for full-time students. Work study available nights, weekends, and for part-time students.
Students without need: No-need awards available for academics.

FINANCIAL AID PROCEDURES

Forms required: FAFSA, institutional form.

Dates and Deadlines: Priority date 3/15; no closing date. Applicants notified on a rolling basis starting 3/15; must reply by 5/1 or within 2 week(s) of notification.

Transfers: Priority date 5/1. Applicants notified on a rolling basis starting 5/1; must reply by 6/1 or within 2 week(s) of notification.

CONTACT

Edward Ciosek, Director of Financial Aid
263 Alden Street, Springfield, MA 01109
(413) 748-3108

Springfield Technical Community College

Springfield, Massachusetts
www.stcc.edu Federal Code: 005549

2-year public community and technical college in small city.
Enrollment: 6,259 undergrads, 51% part-time. 961 full-time freshmen.
Selectivity: Open admission; but selective for some programs.

BASIC COSTS (2012-2013)

Tuition and fees: $5,106; out-of-state residents $11,616.
Per-credit charge: $25; out-of-state residents $242.
Additional info: New England reciprocal rate $284 per credit hour, including fees.

FINANCIAL AID PICTURE (2011-2012)

Students with need: 73% of average financial aid package awarded as scholarships/grants, 27% awarded as loans/jobs. Need-based aid available for part-time students.

FINANCIAL AID PROCEDURES

Forms required: FAFSA.

Dates and Deadlines: Priority date 5/1; no closing date. Applicants notified on a rolling basis starting 7/1.

CONTACT

Jeremy Greenhouse, Director of Financial Aid
One Armory Square, Springfield, MA 01102-9000
(413) 755-4214

Stonehill College

Easton, Massachusetts Federal Code: 002217
www.stonehill.edu CSS Code: 3770

4-year private liberal arts college in large town, affiliated with Roman Catholic Church.
Enrollment: 2,599 undergrads. 815 full-time freshmen.
Selectivity: Admits over 75% of applicants.

BASIC COSTS (2012-2013)

Tuition and fees: $35,110.
Per-credit charge: $1,170.
Room and board: $13,310.
Additional info: Tuition/fee waivers available for minority students, unemployed or children of unemployed.

FINANCIAL AID PICTURE (2012-2013)

Students with need: Out of 691 full-time freshmen who applied for aid, 496 were judged to have need. Of these, 495 received aid, and 238 had their full need met. Average financial aid package met 90% of need; average scholarship/grant was $22,796; average loan was $4,359. Need-based aid available for part-time students.

Students without need: 221 full-time freshmen who did not demonstrate need for aid received scholarships/grants; average award was $12,762. No-need awards available for academics, athletics, leadership, ROTC.

Scholarships offered: ***Merit:*** Moreau Honors Scholarship; $10,000-$22,000; awarded to incoming students in the Moreau Honors Program in recognition of strong academic achievement, test scores, rank in class, and competitive curriculum at the high school level. Shields Merit Scholars Program; $8,000-$10,000; awarded to incoming students of the highest caliber and promise in the Moreau Honors Program, in recognition of outstanding academic achievement. Novak/Sakmar/Templeton Scholarship; $2,500-$10,000; awarded to incoming students, typically valedictorians, in recognition of outstanding academic achievement and co-curricular contributions. Presidential Scholarship; $16,000-$19,000; awarded to incoming students in recognition of strong academic achievement, test scores, and competitive curriculum at the high school level. Dean's Scholarship; $10,000-$14,000; awarded to entering students in recognition of strong academic credentials and co-curricular contributions at the high school level. ***Athletic:*** 21 full-time freshmen received athletic scholarships; average amount $15,051.

Cumulative student debt: 73% of graduating class had student loans; average debt was $27,794.

FINANCIAL AID PROCEDURES

Forms required: FAFSA, CSS PROFILE.

Dates and Deadlines: Closing date 2/1. Applicants notified by 4/1; must reply by 5/1.

Transfers: Closing date 4/1. Applicants notified by 5/25. For transfer students who qualify, merit scholarships and need based aid are provided as aid availability allows.

CONTACT

Eileen O'Leary, Assistant Vice President for Finance/Director of Student Aid and Finance
320 Washington Street, Easton, MA 02357-0100
(508) 565-1088

Suffolk University
Boston, Massachusetts
www.suffolk.edu Federal Code: 002218

4-year private university in very large city.
Enrollment: 5,646 undergrads, 5% part-time. 1,239 full-time freshmen.
Selectivity: Admits over 75% of applicants.

BASIC COSTS (2012-2013)
Tuition and fees: $30,792.
Per-credit charge: $752.
Room and board: $14,730.

FINANCIAL AID PICTURE (2012-2013)
Students with need: Out of 952 full-time freshmen who applied for aid, 874 were judged to have need. Of these, 871 received aid, and 51 had their full need met. Average financial aid package met 66% of need; average scholarship/grant was $15,882; average loan was $3,887. For part-time students, average financial aid package was $10,100.
Students without need: 85 full-time freshmen who did not demonstrate need for aid received scholarships/grants; average award was $10,522. No-need awards available for academics, alumni affiliation.
Scholarships offered: Various scholarships; amounts vary; based on academic achievement, talent, and contribution to applicant's school and community.
Cumulative student debt: 77% of graduating class had student loans; average debt was $33,823.
Additional info: Foreign students may apply for institutional employment awards.

FINANCIAL AID PROCEDURES
Forms required: FAFSA, institutional form.
Dates and Deadlines: Closing date 2/15. Applicants notified on a rolling basis starting 2/5; must reply by 5/1 or within 2 week(s) of notification.

CONTACT
Christine Perry, Director of Financial Aid
8 Ashburton Place, Boston, MA 02108
(617) 573-8470

Tufts University
Medford, Massachusetts Federal Code: 002219
www.tufts.edu CSS Code: 3901

4-year private university in small city.
Enrollment: 5,186 undergrads, 1% part-time. 1,309 full-time freshmen.
Selectivity: Admits less than 50% of applicants.

BASIC COSTS (2012-2013)
Tuition and fees: $44,776.
Room and board: $11,880.

FINANCIAL AID PICTURE (2012-2013)
Students with need: Out of 667 full-time freshmen who applied for aid, 519 were judged to have need. Of these, 519 received aid, and 519 had their full need met. Average financial aid package met 100% of need; average scholarship/grant was $33,208; average loan was $2,964. For part-time students, average financial aid package was $20,491.
Students without need: This college awards aid only to students with need.
Scholarships offered: National Merit Scholarships; $500 for non-need; $2,000 for need.
Cumulative student debt: 37% of graduating class had student loans; average debt was $23,068.
Additional info: Students from families with incomes less than $40,000 receive aid awards in which student loans are replaced by grants.

FINANCIAL AID PROCEDURES
Forms required: FAFSA, CSS PROFILE.
Dates and Deadlines: Closing date 2/15. Applicants notified by 4/1; must reply by 5/1.
Transfers: Closing date 3/1. Applicants notified by 5/1.

CONTACT
Patricia Reilly, Director of Financial Aid
Bendetson Hall, Medford, MA 02155
(617) 627-2000

University of Massachusetts Amherst
Amherst, Massachusetts
www.umass.edu Federal Code: 002221

4-year public university in large town.
Enrollment: 21,448 undergrads, 6% part-time. 4,679 full-time freshmen.
Selectivity: Admits 50 to 75% of applicants.

BASIC COSTS (2012-2013)
Tuition and fees: $13,230; out-of-state residents $26,645.
Room and board: $10,767.

FINANCIAL AID PICTURE (2011-2012)
Students with need: Out of 4,244 full-time freshmen who applied for aid, 2,878 were judged to have need. Of these, 2,793 received aid, and 364 had their full need met. Average financial aid package met 80% of need; average scholarship/grant was $8,520; average loan was $3,698. For part-time students, average financial aid package was $11,218.
Students without need: 536 full-time freshmen who did not demonstrate need for aid received scholarships/grants; average award was $4,146. No-need awards available for academics, art, athletics, music/drama, state/district residency.
Scholarships offered: ***Merit:*** Merit scholarships; all applicants automatically considered. ***Athletic:*** 48 full-time freshmen received athletic scholarships; average amount $19,794.
Cumulative student debt: 71% of graduating class had student loans; average debt was $27,945.

FINANCIAL AID PROCEDURES
Forms required: FAFSA.
Dates and Deadlines: Priority date 3/1; no closing date. Applicants notified on a rolling basis starting 4/1; must reply by 5/1 or within 2 week(s) of notification.

CONTACT
Suzanne Peters, Director of Financial Aid
University Admissions Center, Amherst, MA 01003-9291
(413) 545-0801

University of Massachusetts Boston
Boston, Massachusetts
www.umb.edu Federal Code: 002222

4-year public university in very large city.
Enrollment: 11,457 undergrads, 28% part-time. 1,172 full-time freshmen.
Selectivity: Admits 50 to 75% of applicants.

BASIC COSTS (2012-2013)
Tuition and fees: $11,966; out-of-state residents $26,150.

FINANCIAL AID PICTURE
Students with need: Need-based aid available for full-time and part-time students.
Students without need: No-need awards available for academics, leadership.

Additional info: Some Massachusetts state employees and Massachusetts Vietnam veterans eligible for tuition waiver. Some waivers available based on talent and academic excellence.

FINANCIAL AID PROCEDURES

Forms required: FAFSA.

Dates and Deadlines: Priority date 3/1; no closing date. Applicants notified on a rolling basis starting 3/22.

CONTACT

Judy Keyes, Director of Financial Aid Services
100 Morrissey Boulevard, Boston, MA 02125-3393
(617) 287-6300

University of Massachusetts Dartmouth

North Dartmouth, Massachusetts
www.umassd.edu Federal Code: 002210

4-year public university in large town.
Enrollment: 7,326 undergrads, 11% part-time. 1,561 full-time freshmen.
Selectivity: Admits 50 to 75% of applicants.

BASIC COSTS (2012-2013)

Tuition and fees: $11,681; out-of-state residents $23,028.
Room and board: $10,235.

FINANCIAL AID PICTURE

Students with need: Need-based aid available for full-time and part-time students. Work study available nights, weekends, and for part-time students.
Students without need: No-need awards available for academics, alumni affiliation, leadership, minority status, ROTC, state/district residency.
Scholarships offered: Chancellor's Merit Scholarship; approximately $2,000; for Massachusetts high school seniors with 1250 SAT (exclusive of Writing) and in top 25% of class; 50 awarded. Solveig E.J. Balestracci Scholarship; $1,000; for academic achievement in marine-related area for residents of New Bedford, Dartmouth, Acushnet, Westport, Mattapoisett, Marion, Rochester or Lakeville; 1 awarded. Boivon Scholarship; $1,000; based on academic involvement in French language and culture. A.J. Carvalho Memorial Scholarship; approximately $5,000; for New Bedford graduates of Portuguese descent with 3.0 GPA. Cranston Foundation Scholarship; $500; for students in the Textile Science Department.

FINANCIAL AID PROCEDURES

Forms required: FAFSA.
Dates and Deadlines: Priority date 3/1; no closing date. Applicants notified on a rolling basis starting 3/25; must reply within 3 week(s) of notification.

CONTACT

Bruce Palmer, Director of Financial Aid
285 Old Westport Road, North Dartmouth, MA 02747-2300
(508) 999-8632

University of Massachusetts Lowell

Lowell, Massachusetts
www.uml.edu Federal Code: 002161

4-year public university in small city.
Enrollment: 11,470 undergrads, 25% part-time. 1,427 full-time freshmen.
Selectivity: Admits 50 to 75% of applicants.

BASIC COSTS (2012-2013)

Tuition and fees: $11,852; out-of-state residents $18,965.
Per-credit charge: $61; out-of-state residents $357.
Room and board: $10,282.

FINANCIAL AID PICTURE (2011-2012)

Students with need: Out of 1,269 full-time freshmen who applied for aid, 976 were judged to have need. Of these, 976 received aid, and 576 had their full need met. Average financial aid package met 93% of need; average scholarship/grant was $8,320; average loan was $5,673. For part-time students, average financial aid package was $9,339.
Students without need: 194 full-time freshmen who did not demonstrate need for aid received scholarships/grants; average award was $4,405. No-need awards available for academics, alumni affiliation, art, athletics, job skills, leadership, minority status, music/drama, ROTC, state/district residency.
Scholarships offered: 30 full-time freshmen received athletic scholarships; average amount $6,485.
Cumulative student debt: 77% of graduating class had student loans; average debt was $29,212.

FINANCIAL AID PROCEDURES

Forms required: FAFSA.
Dates and Deadlines: Priority date 3/1; no closing date. Applicants notified on a rolling basis starting 3/22.
Transfers: Closing date 3/1. Applicants notified on a rolling basis starting 3/22.

CONTACT

Joyce McLaughlin, Director of Financial Aid
883 Broadway Street, Room 110, Lowell, MA 01854-5104
(978) 934-4220

Urban College of Boston

Boston, Massachusetts
www.urbancollege.edu Federal Code: 031305

2-year private community college in very large city.
Enrollment: 562 undergrads.
Selectivity: Open admission.

BASIC COSTS (2012-2013)

Tuition and fees: $8,900.
Per-credit charge: $296.

FINANCIAL AID PICTURE

Students with need: Need-based aid available for full-time and part-time students.
Students without need: This college awards aid only to students with need.

FINANCIAL AID PROCEDURES

Forms required: FAFSA.
Dates and Deadlines: Priority date 12/10; no closing date. Applicants notified on a rolling basis starting 4/15.

CONTACT

Mia Taylor, Director of Financial Aid
178 Tremont Street, Seventh Floor, Boston, MA 02111
(617) 348-6220

Wellesley College

Wellesley, Massachusetts Federal Code: 002224
www.wellesley.edu CSS Code: 3957

4-year private liberal arts college for women in large town.
Enrollment: 2,364 undergrads, 1% part-time. 585 full-time freshmen.
Selectivity: Admits less than 50% of applicants.

BASIC COSTS (2012-2013)

Tuition and fees: $42,082.
Room and board: $13,032.

FINANCIAL AID PICTURE (2012-2013)

Students with need: Out of 493 full-time freshmen who applied for aid, 359 were judged to have need. Of these, 359 received aid, and 359 had

their full need met. Average financial aid package met 100% of need; average scholarship/grant was $39,528; average loan was $2,505. Need-based aid available for part-time students.
Students without need: This college awards aid only to students with need.
Cumulative student debt: 54% of graduating class had student loans; average debt was $14,189.
Additional info: No student will graduate with more than $12,825 in packaged student loans. Students from families with a calculated income between $60,000 and $100,000 will graduate with no more than $8,600 in packaged student loans. Students from families with the greatest need ($60,000 income or less) will graduate with $0 in packaged student loans; their packages will consist of scholarship and work-study money.

FINANCIAL AID PROCEDURES
Forms required: FAFSA, CSS PROFILE.
Dates and Deadlines: Priority date 1/15; no closing date. Applicants notified by 4/1; must reply by 5/1.
Transfers: Closing date 3/1.

CONTACT
Scott Juedes, Director of Student Financial Services
106 Central Street, Wellesley, MA 02481
(781) 283-2360

Wentworth Institute of Technology
Boston, Massachusetts
www.wit.edu Federal Code: 002225

4-year private engineering and technical college in very large city.
Enrollment: 3,972 undergrads, 10% part-time. 1,026 full-time freshmen.
Selectivity: Admits 50 to 75% of applicants.

BASIC COSTS (2012-2013)
Tuition and fees: $25,900.
Room and board: $11,900.
Additional info: Tuition includes cost of laptop computer.

FINANCIAL AID PICTURE (2012-2013)
Students with need: Out of 929 full-time freshmen who applied for aid, 844 were judged to have need. Of these, 844 received aid, and 53 had their full need met. For part-time students, average financial aid package was $5,359.
Students without need: 84 full-time freshmen who did not demonstrate need for aid received scholarships/grants; average award was $8,984. No-need awards available for academics, leadership, ROTC, state/district residency.
Scholarships offered: Applicants for admission automatically considered for merit scholarships.
Cumulative student debt: 82% of graduating class had student loans; average debt was $33,968.

FINANCIAL AID PROCEDURES
Forms required: FAFSA.
Dates and Deadlines: Priority date 3/1; no closing date. Applicants notified on a rolling basis starting 3/15; must reply within 2 week(s) of notification.
Transfers: Review of NSLDS history within 30 days of beginning of enrollment required.

CONTACT
Anne-Marie Caruso, Director of Financial Aid
550 Huntington Avenue, Boston, MA 02115
(617) 989-4020

Western New England University
Springfield, Massachusetts
www.wne.edu Federal Code: 002226

4-year private university in small city.
Enrollment: 2,671 undergrads, 6% part-time. 795 full-time freshmen.
Selectivity: Admits over 75% of applicants.

BASIC COSTS (2012-2013)
Tuition and fees: $31,912.
Per-credit charge: $560.
Room and board: $12,144.

FINANCIAL AID PICTURE (2012-2013)
Students with need: Out of 731 full-time freshmen who applied for aid, 660 were judged to have need. Of these, 660 received aid, and 68 had their full need met. Average financial aid package met 72% of need; average scholarship/grant was $18,651; average loan was $3,480. For part-time students, average financial aid package was $6,885.
Students without need: 109 full-time freshmen who did not demonstrate need for aid received scholarships/grants; average award was $11,466. No-need awards available for academics, music/drama, ROTC.

FINANCIAL AID PROCEDURES
Forms required: FAFSA.
Dates and Deadlines: Applicants notified on a rolling basis starting 2/15; must reply by 5/1 or within 2 week(s) of notification.
Transfers: No deadline. Applicants notified on a rolling basis starting 3/1.

CONTACT
Kathy Chambers
1215 Wilbraham Road, Springfield, MA 01119-2684
(800) 325-1122 ext. 2080

Westfield State University
Westfield, Massachusetts
www.westfield.ma.edu Federal Code: 002189

4-year public university in large town.
Enrollment: 5,191 undergrads, 10% part-time. 1,132 full-time freshmen.
Selectivity: Admits 50 to 75% of applicants.

BASIC COSTS (2012-2013)
Tuition and fees: $8,297; out-of-state residents $14,377.
Room and board: $9,233.

FINANCIAL AID PICTURE (2011-2012)
Students with need: Out of 1,067 full-time freshmen who applied for aid, 745 were judged to have need. Of these, 725 received aid, and 63 had their full need met. Average financial aid package met 65% of need; average scholarship/grant was $5,808; average loan was $3,256. Need-based aid available for part-time students.
Students without need: 14 full-time freshmen who did not demonstrate need for aid received scholarships/grants; average award was $4,190.
Cumulative student debt: 76% of graduating class had student loans; average debt was $24,825.

FINANCIAL AID PROCEDURES
Forms required: FAFSA.
Dates and Deadlines: Priority date 3/1; no closing date. Applicants notified on a rolling basis starting 4/1.
Transfers: Applicants notified on a rolling basis starting 4/1.

CONTACT
Catherine Ryan, Director of Financial Aid
577 Western Avenue, Westfield, MA 01086-1630
(413) 572-5218

Wheaton College

Norton, Massachusetts Federal Code: 002227
www.wheatoncollege.edu CSS Code: 3963

4-year private liberal arts college in large town.
Enrollment: 1,616 undergrads. 466 full-time freshmen.
Selectivity: Admits 50 to 75% of applicants.

BASIC COSTS (2012-2013)
Tuition and fees: $43,774.
Room and board: $11,160.

FINANCIAL AID PICTURE (2012-2013)
Students with need: Out of 365 full-time freshmen who applied for aid, 323 were judged to have need. Of these, 323 received aid, and 167 had their full need met. Average financial aid package met 94% of need; average scholarship/grant was $27,905; average loan was $3,562. For part-time students, average financial aid package was $23,900.
Students without need: 118 full-time freshmen who did not demonstrate need for aid received scholarships/grants; average award was $11,008. No-need awards available for academics.
Scholarships offered: Balfour Scholarship; $17,500 annually plus $3,000 total in research/internship/community service stipends. Trustee Scholarship; $15,000 annually plus $3,000 total in research/internship/community service stipends. Community Scholarship; $12,500 annually plus $3,000 total in research/internship/community service stipends. All selected from top 30% of applicant pool.
Cumulative student debt: 61% of graduating class had student loans; average debt was $27,520.

FINANCIAL AID PROCEDURES
Forms required: FAFSA, CSS PROFILE.
Dates and Deadlines: Closing date 2/1. Applicants notified by 4/1; must reply by 5/1.
Transfers: Closing date 3/1. Applicants notified on a rolling basis; must reply by 6/1. Limited funds available for transfer applicants.

CONTACT
Robin Randall, Assistant Vice President for Enrollment and Student Financial Services
26 East Main Street, Norton, MA 02766
(508) 286-8232

Wheelock College

Boston, Massachusetts
www.wheelock.edu Federal Code: 002228

4-year private liberal arts and teachers college in very large city.
Enrollment: 866 undergrads, 5% part-time. 202 full-time freshmen.
Selectivity: Admits 50 to 75% of applicants.

BASIC COSTS (2012-2013)
Tuition and fees: $30,955.
Per-credit charge: $935.
Room and board: $12,800.

FINANCIAL AID PICTURE (2012-2013)
Students with need: Out of 189 full-time freshmen who applied for aid, 174 were judged to have need. Of these, 173 received aid, and 29 had their full need met. Average financial aid package met 64% of need; average scholarship/grant was $17,447; average loan was $3,292. For part-time students, average financial aid package was $10,211.
Students without need: 27 full-time freshmen who did not demonstrate need for aid received scholarships/grants; average award was $13,592. No-need awards available for academics, leadership, state/district residency.
Scholarships offered: Wheelock College Grant; $12,000-$17,000; granted to all new incoming first year students; amount based on GPA and SAT.
Cumulative student debt: 82% of graduating class had student loans; average debt was $49,439.

FINANCIAL AID PROCEDURES
Forms required: FAFSA.
Dates and Deadlines: Priority date 2/15; no closing date. Applicants notified on a rolling basis starting 3/1; must reply by 5/1 or within 2 week(s) of notification.
Transfers: Priority date 4/15. Applicants notified on a rolling basis starting 4/1.

CONTACT
Roxanne Dumas, Director of Financial Aid
200 The Riverway, Boston, MA 02215-4176
(617) 879-2443

Williams College

Williamstown, Massachusetts Federal Code: 002229
www.williams.edu CSS Code: 3965

4-year private liberal arts college in small town.
Enrollment: 2,011 undergrads. 547 full-time freshmen.
Selectivity: Admits less than 50% of applicants.

BASIC COSTS (2012-2013)
Tuition and fees: $44,920.
Room and board: $11,850.

FINANCIAL AID PICTURE (2012-2013)
Students with need: Out of 358 full-time freshmen who applied for aid, 289 were judged to have need. Of these, 289 received aid, and 289 had their full need met. Average financial aid package met 100% of need; average scholarship/grant was $36,679; average loan was $2,678.
Cumulative student debt: 31% of graduating class had student loans; average debt was $12,749.

FINANCIAL AID PROCEDURES
Forms required: FAFSA, CSS PROFILE.
Dates and Deadlines: Priority date 2/1; closing date 4/15. Must reply by 5/1.
Transfers: Closing date 4/1. Applicants notified by 5/15; must reply within 2 week(s) of notification.

CONTACT
Paul Boyer, Director of Financial Aid
33 Stetson Court, Williamstown, MA 01267
(413) 597-3131

Worcester Polytechnic Institute

Worcester, Massachusetts Federal Code: 002233
www.wpi.edu CSS Code: 3969

4-year private university in small city.
Enrollment: 3,841 undergrads, 3% part-time. 1,005 full-time freshmen.
Selectivity: Admits 50 to 75% of applicants.

BASIC COSTS (2012-2013)
Tuition and fees: $41,380.
Per-credit charge: $1,133.
Room and board: $12,650.

FINANCIAL AID PICTURE (2011-2012)
Students with need: Out of 879 full-time freshmen who applied for aid, 730 were judged to have need. Of these, 729 received aid, and 333 had their full need met. Average financial aid package met 71% of need; average scholarship/grant was $20,547; average loan was $2,712. For part-time students, average financial aid package was $17,717.

Students without need: 244 full-time freshmen who did not demonstrate need for aid received scholarships/grants; average award was $12,858. No-need awards available for academics, leadership, minority status, ROTC.
Scholarships offered: Merit scholarships; typically $10,000-$25,000; renewable for 4 years.

FINANCIAL AID PROCEDURES
Forms required: FAFSA, CSS PROFILE.
Dates and Deadlines: Priority date 2/1; no closing date. Applicants notified on a rolling basis starting 4/1; must reply by 5/1 or within 2 week(s) of notification.
Transfers: Closing date 3/1. Applicants notified by 4/15; must reply by 5/1.

CONTACT
Monica Blondin, Director, Financial Aid
100 Institute Road, Worcester, MA 01609-2280
(508) 831-5469

Worcester State University
Worcester, Massachusetts
www.worcester.edu Federal Code: 002190

4-year public liberal arts and teachers college in small city.
Enrollment: 4,808 undergrads, 18% part-time. 790 full-time freshmen.
Selectivity: Admits 50 to 75% of applicants.

BASIC COSTS (2012-2013)
Tuition and fees: $8,157; out-of-state residents $14,237.
Per-credit charge: $40; out-of-state residents $294.
Room and board: $10,500.

FINANCIAL AID PICTURE (2011-2012)
Students with need: Out of 733 full-time freshmen who applied for aid, 510 were judged to have need. Of these, 501 received aid, and 208 had their full need met. Average financial aid package met 82% of need; average scholarship/grant was $4,759; average loan was $2,732. For part-time students, average financial aid package was $6,697.
Students without need: 17 full-time freshmen who did not demonstrate need for aid received scholarships/grants; average award was $1,760. No-need awards available for academics, ROTC.
Scholarships offered: Presidential Scholarship; full in-state tuition and fees; 3.5 GPA and 1150 SAT required; 15 awarded. Tsongas Scholarship; full in-state tuition and fees to Massachusetts residents; 3.75 GPA and 1200 SAT required; 5 awarded. Access Scholarship; $1,000 per year; for underserved groups with 2.5 GPA and 920 SAT; 15 awarded. Teacher Education Scholarship; full in-state tuition and fees; for future teachers with 3.2 GPA and 1100 SAT; 15 awarded. Honors Scholarship; $1,500 per year; 3.2 GPA and 1100 SAT required; 25 awarded. All SAT scores exclusive of writing.
Cumulative student debt: 74% of graduating class had student loans; average debt was $20,449.
Additional info: Veterans, Native Americans and those certified by Massachusetts Rehabilitation Commission and Massachusetts Commission for the Blind considered for tuition waivers while funds available. Tuition also waived for needy Massachusetts residents and in-state National Guard members.

FINANCIAL AID PROCEDURES
Forms required: FAFSA.
Dates and Deadlines: Priority date 3/1; closing date 5/1. Applicants notified on a rolling basis starting 3/1; must reply within 2 week(s) of notification.

CONTACT
Jayne McGinn, Director of Financial Aid
Office of Undergraduate Admission, Worcester, MA 01602-2597
(508) 929-8056

Michigan

Adrian College
Adrian, Michigan
www.adrian.edu Federal Code: 002234

4-year private liberal arts college in large town, affiliated with United Methodist Church.
Enrollment: 1,709 undergrads.
Selectivity: Admits 50 to 75% of applicants.

BASIC COSTS (2012-2013)
Tuition and fees: $29,156.
Room and board: $8,796.

FINANCIAL AID PICTURE
Students with need: Need-based aid available for full-time and part-time students. Work study available nights, weekends, and for part-time students.
Students without need: No-need awards available for academics, alumni affiliation, art, leadership, music/drama, religious affiliation, state/district residency.
Scholarships offered: Academic scholarships; based on ACT score of 20 and GPA of 3.0.

FINANCIAL AID PROCEDURES
Forms required: FAFSA.
Dates and Deadlines: Priority date 3/1; no closing date. Applicants notified on a rolling basis starting 3/15; must reply by 5/1 or within 2 week(s) of notification.

CONTACT
Andrew Spohn, Director of Financial Aid
110 South Madison Street, Adrian, MI 49221-2575
(517) 265-5161 ext. 4306

Albion College
Albion, Michigan
www.albion.edu Federal Code: 002235

4-year private liberal arts college in small town, affiliated with United Methodist Church.
Enrollment: 1,355 undergrads, 1% part-time. 360 full-time freshmen.
Selectivity: Admits 50 to 75% of applicants.

BASIC COSTS (2012-2013)
Tuition and fees: $34,194.
Per-credit charge: $1,430.
Room and board: $9,690.

FINANCIAL AID PICTURE (2012-2013)
Students with need: Out of 310 full-time freshmen who applied for aid, 268 were judged to have need. Of these, 268 received aid, and 52 had their full need met. Average financial aid package met 81% of need; average scholarship/grant was $21,465; average loan was $5,392.
Students without need: 86 full-time freshmen who did not demonstrate need for aid received scholarships/grants; average award was $16,731. No-need awards available for academics, alumni affiliation, art, leadership, music/drama.
Scholarships offered: Academic scholarships, range from $16,000 -$19,000 per year ($64,000 to $76,000 over four years), renewable each year subject to satisfactory progress, awarded to students with outstanding academic records or unique skills, talents, or abilities.
Cumulative student debt: 62% of graduating class had student loans; average debt was $36,029.

FINANCIAL AID PROCEDURES
Forms required: FAFSA.
Dates and Deadlines: Priority date 2/1; no closing date. Applicants notified on a rolling basis starting 3/15.
Transfers: Applicants notified on a rolling basis.

CONTACT
Ann Whitmer, Director of Financial Aid
611 East Porter Street, Albion, MI 49224-1831
(517) 629-0440

Alma College
Alma, Michigan
www.alma.edu Federal Code: 002236

4-year private liberal arts college in small town, affiliated with Presbyterian Church (USA).
Enrollment: 1,430 undergrads, 1% part-time. 427 full-time freshmen.
Selectivity: Admits 50 to 75% of applicants.

BASIC COSTS (2013-2014)
Tuition and fees: $33,135.
Per-credit charge: $1,050.
Room and board: $9,265.

FINANCIAL AID PICTURE (2012-2013)
Students with need: Out of 425 full-time freshmen who applied for aid, 389 were judged to have need. Of these, 389 received aid, and 50 had their full need met. Average financial aid package met 91% of need; average scholarship/grant was $22,204; average loan was $3,813. For part-time students, average financial aid package was $6,680.
Students without need: 53 full-time freshmen who did not demonstrate need for aid received scholarships/grants; average award was $13,279. No-need awards available for academics, alumni affiliation, art, minority status, music/drama, religious affiliation, state/district residency.
Scholarships offered: Distinguished Scholar Award; up to full tuition; awarded to designated National Merit Scholarship Finalist. Trustee Honors Scholarship; $14,000; awarded on basis of superior academic achievement, national test scores. Presidential Scholarships; $13,000; awarded on basis of outstanding scholarship and high national test scores. Dean's Scholarship; $12,000; awarded on basis on academic achievement and high national test scores. Tartan Scholars Award ($10,000) and Achievement Awards ($8,000); both awards based on academic achievement or high national test scores. Performance Scholarships; up to $1,000; awarded to students with a demonstrated high level of accomplishment in the fine or performing arts.
Cumulative student debt: 77% of graduating class had student loans; average debt was $31,297.
Additional info: Auditions required for music, drama, dance scholarship candidates. Portfolios required for art scholarship candidates.

FINANCIAL AID PROCEDURES
Forms required: FAFSA.
Dates and Deadlines: Priority date 3/1; no closing date. Applicants notified on a rolling basis starting 3/1; must reply within 3 week(s) of notification.
Transfers: No deadline. Applicants notified on a rolling basis starting 3/1; must reply within 3 week(s) of notification.

CONTACT
Michelle McNier, Director of Financial Assistance
614 West Superior Street, Alma, MI 48801-1599
(989) 463-7347

Alpena Community College
Alpena, Michigan
www.alpenacc.edu Federal Code: 002237

2-year public community college in large town.
Enrollment: 2,150 undergrads.
Selectivity: Open admission; but selective for some programs.

BASIC COSTS (2012-2013)
Tuition and fees: $3,720; out-of-district residents $5,520; out-of-state residents $5,520.
Per-credit charge: $106; out-of-district residents $166; out-of-state residents $166.
Additional info: Tuition and fees are per contact hour.

FINANCIAL AID PICTURE
Students with need: Need-based aid available for full-time and part-time students.
Students without need: No-need awards available for academics, art, athletics, job skills, leadership, music/drama.

FINANCIAL AID PROCEDURES
Forms required: FAFSA.
Dates and Deadlines: Priority date 8/1; no closing date. Applicants notified on a rolling basis starting 5/15; must reply within 3 week(s) of notification.

CONTACT
Rob Roose, Dean of Students
665 Johnson Street, Alpena, MI 49707
(989) 358-7205

Andrews University
Berrien Springs, Michigan
www.andrews.edu Federal Code: 002238

4-year private university in small town, affiliated with Seventh-day Adventists.
Enrollment: 1,826 undergrads, 8% part-time. 385 full-time freshmen.
Selectivity: Admits less than 50% of applicants.

BASIC COSTS (2013-2014)
Tuition and fees: $25,530.
Per-credit charge: $1,020.
Room and board: $7,968.

FINANCIAL AID PICTURE
Students with need: Need-based aid available for full-time and part-time students. Work study available nights, weekends, and for part-time students.
Students without need: No-need awards available for academics, alumni affiliation, job skills, leadership, music/drama, religious affiliation.

FINANCIAL AID PROCEDURES
Forms required: FAFSA, institutional form.
Dates and Deadlines: Priority date 3/31; no closing date. Applicants notified on a rolling basis starting 3/15.

CONTACT
Elynda Bedney, Director of Student Financial Services
100 US Highway 31, Berrien Springs, MI 49104

Aquinas College
Grand Rapids, Michigan
www.aquinas.edu Federal Code: 002239

4-year private liberal arts college in small city, affiliated with Roman Catholic Church.

Enrollment: 1,922 undergrads, 12% part-time. 452 full-time freshmen.
Selectivity: Admits 50 to 75% of applicants. GED not accepted.

BASIC COSTS (2013-2014)
Tuition and fees: $26,460.
Per-credit charge: $498.
Room and board: $7,810.
Additional info: Tuition/fee waivers available for adults.

FINANCIAL AID PICTURE (2012-2013)
Students with need: Out of 430 full-time freshmen who applied for aid, 382 were judged to have need. Of these, 382 received aid, and 151 had their full need met. Average financial aid package met 85% of need; average scholarship/grant was $18,711; average loan was $3,200. For part-time students, average financial aid package was $9,509.
Students without need: 72 full-time freshmen who did not demonstrate need for aid received scholarships/grants; average award was $12,033. No-need awards available for academics, alumni affiliation, art, athletics, leadership, music/drama.
Scholarships offered: ***Merit:*** Spectrum Scholarship; $3,000 to full tuition; awarded to students who have excelled in academics, leadership or community service; renewable. ***Athletic:*** 33 full-time freshmen received athletic scholarships; average amount $3,212.
Cumulative student debt: 78% of graduating class had student loans; average debt was $20,694.

FINANCIAL AID PROCEDURES
Forms required: FAFSA.
Dates and Deadlines: Priority date 3/1; no closing date. Applicants notified on a rolling basis starting 2/15; must reply within 2 week(s) of notification.
Transfers: Priority date 4/15; closing date 7/1. Must reply within 2 week(s) of notification.

CONTACT
David Steffee, Director of Financial Aid
1607 Robinson Road Southeast, Grand Rapids, MI 49506-1799
(616) 632-2893

Baker College of Auburn Hills

Auburn Hills, Michigan
www.baker.edu Federal Code: E00466

4-year private business and technical college in small city.
Enrollment: 3,433 undergrads.
Selectivity: Open admission; but selective for some programs.

BASIC COSTS (2012-2013)
Tuition and fees: $9,675.
Per-credit charge: $215.

FINANCIAL AID PICTURE
Students with need: Work study available nights, weekends, and for part-time students.
Students without need: No-need awards available for academics, alumni affiliation.

FINANCIAL AID PROCEDURES
Forms required: FAFSA, institutional form.
Dates and Deadlines: Priority date 2/21; closing date 9/1. Applicants notified on a rolling basis starting 4/1.
Transfers: Must have been deemed financial aid-eligible at previous school.

CONTACT
Greg Little, Financial Aid Director
1500 University Drive, Auburn Hills, MI 48326
(248) 340-0600

Baker College of Cadillac

Cadillac, Michigan
www.baker.edu Federal Code: E00461

4-year private business and health science college in large town.
Enrollment: 1,718 undergrads.
Selectivity: Open admission.

BASIC COSTS (2012-2013)
Tuition and fees: $9,675.
Per-credit charge: $215.

FINANCIAL AID PICTURE
Students with need: Need-based aid available for full-time and part-time students. Work study available nights, weekends, and for part-time students.
Students without need: No-need awards available for academics.
Scholarships offered: Baker College Career Scholarships; $400 per term for 4 years; based on 2.5 GPA after junior year of high school. Board of Regents Scholarships; half tuition for 4 years; based on 3.5 GPA through grade 11.

FINANCIAL AID PROCEDURES
Forms required: FAFSA, institutional form.
Dates and Deadlines: Priority date 2/21; no closing date. Applicants notified on a rolling basis starting 5/1.
Transfers: Priority date 3/20; closing date 9/1.

CONTACT
Kristin Bonney, Financial Aid Officer
9600 East 13th Street, Cadillac, MI 49601
(231) 876-3118

Baker College of Clinton Township

Clinton Township, Michigan
www.baker.edu Federal Code: E00462

4-year private business and technical college in very large city.
Enrollment: 5,138 undergrads.
Selectivity: Open admission; but selective for some programs.

BASIC COSTS (2012-2013)
Tuition and fees: $9,675.
Per-credit charge: $215.

FINANCIAL AID PICTURE
Students with need: Need-based aid available for full-time and part-time students. Work study available nights, weekends, and for part-time students.
Students without need: No-need awards available for academics, minority status.

FINANCIAL AID PROCEDURES
Forms required: FAFSA, institutional form.
Dates and Deadlines: Priority date 2/21; closing date 9/1. Applicants notified on a rolling basis starting 4/1.

CONTACT
Lisa Harvener, Vice President of Student Services
34950 Little Mack Avenue, Clinton Township, MI 48035
(586) 790-9589

Baker College of Muskegon

Muskegon, Michigan
www.baker.edu Federal Code: E00463

4-year private business and technical college in small city.
Enrollment: 4,990 undergrads.
Selectivity: Open admission; but selective for some programs.

BASIC COSTS (2012-2013)
Tuition and fees: $9,675.
Per-credit charge: $215.
Additional info: Board plan not available. Cost of room only, $3,000.

FINANCIAL AID PICTURE
Students with need: Need-based aid available for full-time and part-time students. Work study available nights, weekends, and for part-time students.
Students without need: No-need awards available for academics, minority status.
Scholarships offered: Career Scholarship; $4,800 over 4 years; based on GPA over 3.0. Board Regents Scholarship; one-half tuition for 4 years; based on GPA over 3.5. Alternative Scholarship; one-half tuition for 2 years; based on academic success in alternative high school education program.

FINANCIAL AID PROCEDURES
Forms required: FAFSA, institutional form.
Dates and Deadlines: Priority date 2/21; no closing date. Applicants notified on a rolling basis starting 4/1.
Transfers: Priority date 3/21.

CONTACT
Jody Zerlant, Director of Financial Aid
1903 Marquette Avenue, Muskegon, MI 49442
(231) 777-5231

Baker College of Owosso

Owosso, Michigan
www.baker.edu Federal Code: E00464

4-year private business and technical college in large town.
Enrollment: 2,853 undergrads.
Selectivity: Open admission; but selective for some programs.

BASIC COSTS (2012-2013)
Tuition and fees: $9,675.
Per-credit charge: $215.
Additional info: Board plan not available. Cost of room only, $3,000.

FINANCIAL AID PICTURE
Students with need: Need-based aid available for full-time and part-time students. Work study available nights, weekends, and for part-time students.
Students without need: No-need awards available for academics, minority status.

FINANCIAL AID PROCEDURES
Forms required: FAFSA, institutional form.
Dates and Deadlines: Priority date 2/21; closing date 9/1. Applicants notified on a rolling basis starting 4/1.
Transfers: Priority date 3/21.

CONTACT
Nicole Patterson, Financial Aid Director
1020 South Washington Street, Owosso, MI 48867
(989) 720-3430

Baker College of Port Huron

Port Huron, Michigan
www.baker.edu Federal Code: E00465

4-year private business and technical college in large town.
Enrollment: 1,171 undergrads.
Selectivity: Open admission; but selective for some programs.

BASIC COSTS (2012-2013)
Tuition and fees: $9,675.
Per-credit charge: $215.

FINANCIAL AID PICTURE
Students with need: Need-based aid available for full-time and part-time students. Work study available nights.
Students without need: This college awards aid only to students with need.

FINANCIAL AID PROCEDURES
Forms required: FAFSA, institutional form.
Dates and Deadlines: Priority date 2/21; no closing date. Applicants notified on a rolling basis starting 4/1.
Transfers: Priority date 3/21; closing date 9/1.

CONTACT
Barbara Fosgard, Financial Aid Director
3403 Lapeer Road, Port Huron, MI 48060-2597
(810) 985-7000

Bay de Noc Community College

Escanaba, Michigan
www.baycollege.edu Federal Code: 002240

2-year public community college in large town.
Enrollment: 2,252 undergrads, 40% part-time. 413 full-time freshmen.
Selectivity: Open admission; but selective for some programs.

BASIC COSTS (2012-2013)
Tuition and fees: $3,468; out-of-district residents $5,808; out-of-state residents $9,408.
Per-credit charge: $99; out-of-district residents $177; out-of-state residents $297.
Additional info: Tuition and instructional fees based on contact hours. Board plan not available. Cost of room only, $3,000.

FINANCIAL AID PICTURE
Students with need: Need-based aid available for full-time and part-time students. Work study available nights, weekends, and for part-time students.
Students without need: No-need awards available for academics.

FINANCIAL AID PROCEDURES
Forms required: FAFSA.
Dates and Deadlines: Priority date 4/1; no closing date. Applicants notified on a rolling basis starting 2/1; must reply within 2 week(s) of notification.

CONTACT
Laurie Spangenberg, Financial Aid Director
2001 North Lincoln Road, Escanaba, MI 49829-2511
(906) 217-4032

Bay Mills Community College

Brimley, Michigan
www.bmcc.edu Federal Code: 030666

2-year public community college in rural community.
Enrollment: 570 undergrads.
Selectivity: Open admission.

BASIC COSTS (2012-2013)
Tuition and fees: $3,230; out-of-state residents $3,230.
Per-credit charge: $95; out-of-state residents $95.

FINANCIAL AID PICTURE
Students with need: Work study available nights.

FINANCIAL AID PROCEDURES
Forms required: FAFSA.
Dates and Deadlines: Priority date 6/30; no closing date.

CONTACT
Tina Miller, Financial Aid Director
12214 West Lakeshore Drive, Brimley, MI 49715
(906) 248-3354 ext. 8437

Calvin College
Grand Rapids, Michigan
www.calvin.edu Federal Code: 002241

4-year private liberal arts college in large city, affiliated with Christian Reformed Church.
Enrollment: 3,838 undergrads, 2% part-time. 977 full-time freshmen.
Selectivity: Admits over 75% of applicants.

BASIC COSTS (2012-2013)
Tuition and fees: $26,705.
Per-credit charge: $630.
Room and board: $9,110.

FINANCIAL AID PICTURE (2012-2013)
Students with need: Out of 861 full-time freshmen who applied for aid, 638 were judged to have need. Of these, 638 received aid, and 117 had their full need met. Average financial aid package met 74% of need; average scholarship/grant was $14,671; average loan was $4,900. For part-time students, average financial aid package was $11,403.
Students without need: 314 full-time freshmen who did not demonstrate need for aid received scholarships/grants; average award was $8,354. No-need awards available for academics, alumni affiliation, art, leadership, minority status, music/drama, religious affiliation, state/district residency.
Cumulative student debt: 63% of graduating class had student loans; average debt was $32,957.

FINANCIAL AID PROCEDURES
Forms required: FAFSA.
Dates and Deadlines: Priority date 2/15; no closing date. Applicants notified on a rolling basis starting 3/15.
Transfers: Priority date 3/15; closing date 8/15. Applicants notified on a rolling basis starting 3/15.

CONTACT
Paul Witte, Director of Financial Aid
3201 Burton Street Southeast, Grand Rapids, MI 49546
(616) 526-6134

Central Michigan University
Mount Pleasant, Michigan
www.cmich.edu Federal Code: 002243

4-year public university in large town.
Enrollment: 20,849 undergrads, 12% part-time. 3,831 full-time freshmen.

BASIC COSTS (2012-2013)
Tuition and fees: $10,950; out-of-state residents $23,670.
Per-credit charge: $365; out-of-state residents $789.
Room and board: $8,376.

FINANCIAL AID PICTURE (2011-2012)
Students with need: Out of 3,399 full-time freshmen who applied for aid, 2,570 were judged to have need. Of these, 2,472 received aid, and 1,497 had their full need met. Average financial aid package met 85.9% of need; average scholarship/grant was $8,013; average loan was $5,565. For part-time students, average financial aid package was $8,953.
Students without need: 478 full-time freshmen who did not demonstrate need for aid received scholarships/grants; average award was $4,759.
Scholarships offered: 37 full-time freshmen received athletic scholarships; average amount $15,177.
Cumulative student debt: 75% of graduating class had student loans; average debt was $31,520.
Additional info: Tuition waiver for Native American students qualifying under state program criteria.

FINANCIAL AID PROCEDURES
Forms required: FAFSA.
Dates and Deadlines: Closing date 3/1. Applicants notified on a rolling basis starting 4/1.

CONTACT
Kirk Yats, Director, Scholarships and Financial Aid
Admissions Office, Mount Pleasant, MI 48859
(989) 774-3674

Cleary University
Howell, Michigan
www.cleary.edu Federal Code: 002246

4-year private university and business college in small city.
Enrollment: 470 undergrads, 43% part-time. 42 full-time freshmen.
Selectivity: Open admission; but selective for some programs.

BASIC COSTS (2012-2013)
Tuition and fees: $18,480.
Per-credit charge: $385.
Additional info: Tuition at time of enrollment locked for 4 years.

FINANCIAL AID PICTURE (2011-2012)
Students with need: Out of 32 full-time freshmen who applied for aid, 32 were judged to have need. Of these, 32 received aid, and 2 had their full need met. Average financial aid package met 42% of need; average scholarship/grant was $1,107; average loan was $1,309. For part-time students, average financial aid package was $11,878.
Students without need: This college awards aid only to students with need.
Scholarships offered: Oren Beutler Endowed Scholarship: $750; new or continuing full-time student maintaining 3.0 GPA, demonstrated leadership and service to community; one awarded annually, renewable for 4 years. Scholarship for veteran/military students (honorable discharge only).
Cumulative student debt: 81% of graduating class had student loans; average debt was $32,259.
Additional info: Filing electronically preferred; paper applications available. Tuition guarantee based on continuous enrollment. Essay and recommendations required for scholarship consideration.

FINANCIAL AID PROCEDURES
Forms required: FAFSA.
Dates and Deadlines: Priority date 3/1; no closing date. Applicants notified on a rolling basis starting 3/1; must reply within 2 week(s) of notification.
Transfers: No deadline. Applicants notified on a rolling basis starting 4/1; must reply within 2 week(s) of notification. Aid eligibility for transfer students is determined using aid already received from the other school.

CONTACT
Vesta Smith-Campbell, Director of Financial Aid
3750 Cleary Drive, Howell, MI 48843
(517) 338-3015

College for Creative Studies
Detroit, Michigan
www.collegeforcreativestudies.edu Federal Code: 006771

4-year private visual arts college in very large city.
Enrollment: 1,379 undergrads, 20% part-time. 248 full-time freshmen.
Selectivity: Admits less than 50% of applicants.

BASIC COSTS (2013-2014)
Tuition and fees: $35,710.
Per-credit charge: $1,144.
Room and board: $8,600.

FINANCIAL AID PICTURE
Students with need: Need-based aid available for full-time and part-time students. Work study available nights, weekends, and for part-time students.
Students without need: No-need awards available for academics, art.

FINANCIAL AID PROCEDURES
Forms required: FAFSA.
Dates and Deadlines: Priority date 7/1; no closing date. Applicants notified on a rolling basis starting 3/15; must reply within 3 week(s) of notification.
Transfers: Priority date 3/21.

CONTACT
Kristin Moskovitz, Director of Financial Aid
201 East Kirby, Detroit, MI 48202-4034
(313) 664-7495

Concordia University
Ann Arbor, Michigan
www.cuaa.edu Federal Code: 002247

4-year private liberal arts and teachers college in small city, affiliated with Lutheran Church - Missouri Synod.
Enrollment: 490 undergrads.
Selectivity: Admits over 75% of applicants.

BASIC COSTS (2012-2013)
Tuition and fees: $22,464.
Per-credit charge: $936.
Room and board: $8,298.

FINANCIAL AID PICTURE
Students with need: Need-based aid available for full-time and part-time students. Work study available nights, weekends, and for part-time students.
Students without need: No-need awards available for academics, alumni affiliation, art, athletics, leadership, music/drama, religious affiliation.

FINANCIAL AID PROCEDURES
Forms required: FAFSA.
Dates and Deadlines: Closing date 3/1. Applicants notified on a rolling basis starting 3/1; must reply within 3 week(s) of notification.
Transfers: Priority date 5/1. Applicants notified on a rolling basis; must reply within 3 week(s) of notification.

CONTACT
Steven Taylor, Director of Financial Aid
4090 Geddes Road, Ann Arbor, MI 48105
(734) 995-7408

Cornerstone University
Grand Rapids, Michigan
www.cornerstone.edu Federal Code: 002266

4-year private university and liberal arts college in small city, affiliated with interdenominational tradition.
Enrollment: 372 undergrads.
Selectivity: Admits 50 to 75% of applicants.

BASIC COSTS (2012-2013)
Tuition and fees: $23,260.
Per-credit charge: $870.
Room and board: $7,606.
Additional info: Tuition includes laptop computer.

FINANCIAL AID PICTURE
Students with need: Need-based aid available for full-time and part-time students. Work study available nights, weekends, and for part-time students.
Students without need: No-need awards available for academics, athletics, leadership, music/drama, state/district residency.
Scholarships offered: Academic scholarships; based on high school GPA and ACT scores.
Additional info: Audition required for music scholarship applicants.

FINANCIAL AID PROCEDURES
Forms required: FAFSA.
Dates and Deadlines: Priority date 3/1; no closing date. Applicants notified on a rolling basis starting 3/15; must reply within 2 week(s) of notification.
Transfers: No deadline.

CONTACT
Carol Carpenter, Student Financial Services
1001 East Beltline NE, Grand Rapids, MI 49525-5897
(616) 222-1424

Davenport University
Grand Rapids, Michigan
www.davenport.edu Federal Code: 015260

4-year private university and business college in small city.
Enrollment: 7,843 undergrads, 66% part-time. 414 full-time freshmen.
Selectivity: Admits over 75% of applicants.

BASIC COSTS (2013-2014)
Tuition and fees: $17,240.
Per-credit charge: $564.
Room and board: $8,692.

FINANCIAL AID PICTURE
Students with need: Need-based aid available for full-time and part-time students. Work study available nights, weekends, and for part-time students.
Students without need: No-need awards available for academics, alumni affiliation, athletics, leadership.

FINANCIAL AID PROCEDURES
Forms required: FAFSA.
Dates and Deadlines: Priority date 3/1; no closing date. Applicants notified on a rolling basis starting 3/1; must reply within 2 week(s) of notification.
Transfers: No deadline. Applicants notified on a rolling basis.

CONTACT
David De Boer, Executive Director of Financial Aid
6191 Kraft Avenue SE, Grand Rapids, MI 49512-9396
(866) 925-3884

Delta College
University Center, Michigan
www.delta.edu Federal Code: 002251

2-year public community college in small city.
Enrollment: 9,697 undergrads.
Selectivity: Open admission.

BASIC COSTS (2012-2013)
Tuition and fees: $3,180; out-of-district residents $4,650; out-of-state residents $6,600.

FINANCIAL AID PICTURE
Students with need: Need-based aid available for full-time and part-time students. Work study available nights.
Students without need: No-need awards available for academics, athletics.

FINANCIAL AID PROCEDURES
Forms required: FAFSA.
Dates and Deadlines: Applicants notified on a rolling basis; must reply within 2 week(s) of notification.
Transfers: No deadline. Applicants notified on a rolling basis.

CONTACT
David Urbaniak, Financial Aid Director
1961 Delta Road D101, University Center, MI 48710
(989) 686-9080

Eastern Michigan University
Ypsilanti, Michigan
www.emich.edu Federal Code: 002259

4-year public university in small city.
Enrollment: 18,403 undergrads, 29% part-time. 2,119 full-time freshmen.
Selectivity: Admits 50 to 75% of applicants.

BASIC COSTS (2012-2013)
Tuition and fees: $9,026; out-of-state residents $24,008.
Per-credit charge: $257; out-of-state residents $756.
Room and board: $8,287.

FINANCIAL AID PICTURE (2011-2012)
Students with need: Out of 1,895 full-time freshmen who applied for aid, 1,593 were judged to have need. Of these, 1,569 received aid, and 22 had their full need met. Average financial aid package met 70% of need; average scholarship/grant was $4,399; average loan was $3,220. For part-time students, average financial aid package was $5,601.
Students without need: 381 full-time freshmen who did not demonstrate need for aid received scholarships/grants; average award was $4,524. No-need awards available for academics, alumni affiliation, art, athletics, leadership, minority status, music/drama, ROTC, state/district residency.
Scholarships offered: 87 full-time freshmen received athletic scholarships; average amount $14,930.
Cumulative student debt: 68% of graduating class had student loans; average debt was $25,133.

FINANCIAL AID PROCEDURES
Forms required: FAFSA.
Dates and Deadlines: Priority date 3/15; no closing date. Applicants notified on a rolling basis starting 3/1.
Transfers: No deadline. Applicants notified on a rolling basis.

CONTACT
Bernice Lindke, Vice President
400 Pierce Hall, Ypsilanti, MI 48197
(734) 487-0455

Ferris State University
Big Rapids, Michigan
www.ferris.edu Federal Code: 002260

4-year public university in large town.
Enrollment: 12,694 undergrads, 27% part-time. 2,084 full-time freshmen.
Selectivity: Admits 50 to 75% of applicants.

BASIC COSTS (2012-2013)
Tuition and fees: $10,710; out-of-state residents $16,080.
Per-credit charge: $357; out-of-state residents $536.
Room and board: $9,344.

FINANCIAL AID PICTURE (2012-2013)
Students with need: Out of 1,953 full-time freshmen who applied for aid, 1,635 were judged to have need. Of these, 1,624 received aid, and 286 had their full need met. Average financial aid package met 67% of need; average scholarship/grant was $4,555; average loan was $3,730. For part-time students, average financial aid package was $7,185.
Students without need: 294 full-time freshmen who did not demonstrate need for aid received scholarships/grants; average award was $4,660. No-need awards available for academics, alumni affiliation, art, athletics, leadership, minority status, music/drama, ROTC, state/district residency.
Scholarships offered: 12 full-time freshmen received athletic scholarships; average amount $7,880.
Cumulative student debt: 81% of graduating class had student loans; average debt was $37,055.

FINANCIAL AID PROCEDURES
Forms required: FAFSA.
Dates and Deadlines: Priority date 2/1; no closing date. Applicants notified on a rolling basis starting 3/15; must reply within 3 week(s) of notification.
Transfers: Applicants notified on a rolling basis.

CONTACT
Sara Dew, Director of Financial Aid
1201 South State Street, CSS 201, Big Rapids, MI 49307-2714
(231) 591-2110

Finlandia University
Hancock, Michigan
www.finlandia.edu Federal Code: 002322

4-year private university and liberal arts college in small town, affiliated with Evangelical Lutheran Church in America.
Enrollment: 534 undergrads.
Selectivity: Open admission; but selective for some programs.

BASIC COSTS (2012-2013)
Tuition and fees: $20,480.
Per-credit charge: $665.
Room and board: $6,900.

FINANCIAL AID PICTURE
Students with need: Need-based aid available for full-time and part-time students. Work study available nights, weekends, and for part-time students.
Students without need: No-need awards available for academics, leadership, religious affiliation, state/district residency.
Additional info: Work/study program; up to $2,800 per year.

FINANCIAL AID PROCEDURES
Forms required: FAFSA, institutional form.
Dates and Deadlines: Priority date 3/1; no closing date. Applicants notified on a rolling basis starting 3/1; must reply within 2 week(s) of notification.
Transfers: Priority date 3/10; no deadline. Applicants notified on a rolling basis starting 2/1; must reply within 2 week(s) of notification.

CONTACT
Sandra Turnquist, Director of Financial Aid
601 Quincy Street, Hancock, MI 49930-1882
(906) 487-7261

Glen Oaks Community College
Centreville, Michigan
www.glenoaks.edu Federal Code: 002263

2-year public community college in rural community.
Enrollment: 1,334 undergrads.
Selectivity: Open admission; but selective for some programs.

BASIC COSTS (2012-2013)
Tuition and fees: $3,324; out-of-district residents $4,764; out-of-state residents $5,904.

Per-credit charge: $90; out-of-district residents $138; out-of-state residents $176.

FINANCIAL AID PICTURE

Students with need: Need-based aid available for full-time and part-time students. Work study available nights.

Students without need: No-need awards available for academics, art, athletics, leadership.

FINANCIAL AID PROCEDURES

Forms required: FAFSA, institutional form.

Dates and Deadlines: Applicants notified on a rolling basis.

CONTACT

Jean Zimmerman, Director of Financial Aid and Scholarship
62249 Shimmel Road, Centreville, MI 49032-9719
(269) 467-9945 ext. 260

Gogebic Community College

Ironwood, Michigan
www.gogebic.edu Federal Code: 002264

2-year public community college in small town.
Enrollment: 960 undergrads, 31% part-time. 215 full-time freshmen.
Selectivity: Open admission; but selective for some programs.

BASIC COSTS (2012-2013)

Tuition and fees: $3,904; out-of-district residents $4,954; out-of-state residents $5,884.

Per-credit charge: $99; out-of-district residents $134; out-of-state residents $165.

Additional info: Board plan not available. Cost of room only: $4004.

FINANCIAL AID PICTURE (2011-2012)

Students with need: 80% of average financial aid package awarded as scholarships/grants, 20% awarded as loans/jobs. Need-based aid available for part-time students. Work study available nights, weekends, and for part-time students.

Students without need: No-need awards available for academics, art, athletics, job skills, leadership, music/drama, state/district residency.

FINANCIAL AID PROCEDURES

Forms required: FAFSA.

Dates and Deadlines: Priority date 5/1; no closing date. Applicants notified on a rolling basis starting 3/15; must reply within 2 week(s) of notification.

CONTACT

Sue Forbes, Director of Financial Aid
E4946 Jackson Road, Ironwood, MI 49938
(906) 932-4231 ext. 206

Grand Rapids Community College

Grand Rapids, Michigan
www.grcc.edu Federal Code: 002267

2-year public community college in small city.
Enrollment: 16,679 undergrads, 63% part-time. 1,971 full-time freshmen.
Selectivity: Open admission; but selective for some programs.

BASIC COSTS (2012-2013)

Tuition and fees: $3,399; out-of-district residents $6,909; out-of-state residents $10,119.

Per-credit charge: $98; out-of-district residents $215; out-of-state residents $322.

FINANCIAL AID PICTURE

Students with need: Need-based aid available for full-time and part-time students. Work study available nights, weekends, and for part-time students.

Students without need: No-need awards available for academics.

Scholarships offered: Michigan Merit Award; $2,500; based on Michigan Educational Assessment Program scores.

Additional info: Tuition reimbursement and/or child-care services for single parents and displaced homemakers who meet Perkins guidelines.

FINANCIAL AID PROCEDURES

Forms required: FAFSA.

Dates and Deadlines: Priority date 4/1; no closing date. Applicants notified on a rolling basis starting 5/1; must reply within 3 week(s) of notification.

CONTACT

Ken Fridsma, Interim Director of Financial Aid
143 Bostwick Avenue NE, Grand Rapids, MI 49503-3295
(616) 234-4030

Grand Valley State University

Allendale, Michigan
www.gvsu.edu Federal Code: 002268

4-year public university in large town.
Enrollment: 21,227 undergrads, 12% part-time. 3,940 full-time freshmen.
Selectivity: Admits over 75% of applicants.

BASIC COSTS (2012-2013)

Tuition and fees: $10,078; out-of-state residents $14,568.

Per-credit charge: $420; out-of-state residents $607.

Room and board: $7,920.

FINANCIAL AID PICTURE (2012-2013)

Students with need: Out of 3,581 full-time freshmen who applied for aid, 2,672 were judged to have need. Of these, 2,650 received aid, and 322 had their full need met. Average financial aid package met 72% of need; average scholarship/grant was $77,469; average loan was $3,867. For part-time students, average financial aid package was $5,996.

Students without need: 555 full-time freshmen who did not demonstrate need for aid received scholarships/grants; average award was $2,362. No-need awards available for academics, alumni affiliation, art, athletics, music/drama, state/district residency.

Scholarships offered: 30 full-time freshmen received athletic scholarships; average amount $6,075.

Cumulative student debt: 72% of graduating class had student loans; average debt was $28,728.

FINANCIAL AID PROCEDURES

Forms required: FAFSA.

Dates and Deadlines: Priority date 3/1; no closing date. Applicants notified on a rolling basis starting 3/10; must reply by 5/1 or within 4 week(s) of notification.

Transfers: No deadline. Applicants notified on a rolling basis starting 3/20; must reply within 4 week(s) of notification.

CONTACT

Michelle Rhodes, Director of Financial Aid
1 Campus Drive, Allendale, MI 49401-9403
(616) 331-3234

Great Lakes Christian College

Lansing, Michigan
www.glcc.edu Federal Code: 002269

4-year private Bible college in small city, affiliated with Christian Churches/Churches of Christ.
Enrollment: 207 undergrads.

BASIC COSTS (2013-2014)
Tuition and fees: $14,500.
Per-credit charge: $424.
Room and board: $8,500.

FINANCIAL AID PICTURE
Students with need: Need-based aid available for full-time and part-time students. Work study available nights, weekends, and for part-time students.
Students without need: No-need awards available for academics, alumni affiliation, music/drama.

FINANCIAL AID PROCEDURES
Forms required: FAFSA, state aid form, institutional form.
Dates and Deadlines: Closing date 8/1. Applicants notified on a rolling basis starting 5/1; must reply within 3 week(s) of notification.
Transfers: Priority date 3/31; closing date 8/31. Applicants notified on a rolling basis; must reply within 3 week(s) of notification. FAFSA due by 6/30.

CONTACT
Tedd Kees, Financial Aid Director
6211 West Willow Highway, Lansing, MI 48917-1231
(517) 321-0242 ext. 227

Henry Ford Community College

Dearborn, Michigan
www.hfcc.edu

2-year public community college in small city.
Enrollment: 17,650 undergrads.
Selectivity: Open admission; but selective for some programs.

BASIC COSTS (2012-2013)
Tuition and fees: $2,792; out-of-district residents $4,592; out-of-state residents $4,742.
Per-credit charge: $75; out-of-district residents $135; out-of-state residents $140.

FINANCIAL AID PICTURE
Students with need: Work study available nights, weekends, and for part-time students.

FINANCIAL AID PROCEDURES
Forms required: FAFSA.
Dates and Deadlines: Priority date 4/1; no closing date. Applicants notified on a rolling basis starting 3/1.

CONTACT
Kevin Culler, Director, Financial Aid
5101 Evergreen Road, Dearborn, MI 48128
(313) 845-9616

Hillsdale College

Hillsdale, Michigan
www.hillsdale.edu Federal Code: 002272

4-year private liberal arts college in large town.
Enrollment: 1,434 undergrads, 2% part-time. 363 full-time freshmen.
Selectivity: Admits less than 50% of applicants.

BASIC COSTS (2013-2014)
Tuition and fees: $22,890.
Per-credit charge: $880.
Room and board: $9,000.

FINANCIAL AID PICTURE (2011-2012)
Students with need: Out of 204 full-time freshmen who applied for aid, 183 were judged to have need. Of these, 157 received aid, and 61 had their full need met. Average financial aid package met 60% of need; average scholarship/grant was $2,200; average loan was $5,100. For part-time students, average financial aid package was $3,500.
Students without need: 175 full-time freshmen who did not demonstrate need for aid received scholarships/grants; average award was $8,900. No-need awards available for academics, alumni affiliation, art, athletics, leadership, music/drama, state/district residency.
Scholarships offered: ***Merit:*** Distinct Honor Scholarship, full tuition, 5 awarded; Presidential Scholarship, half tuition, 30 awarded; Trustee Scholarship, up to $10,000, 35 awarded. ***Athletic:*** 57 full-time freshmen received athletic scholarships; average amount $9,400.
Cumulative student debt: 55% of graduating class had student loans; average debt was $17,000.
Additional info: Campus employment available to all students.

FINANCIAL AID PROCEDURES
Forms required: institutional form. CSS PROFILE required for returning students only.
Dates and Deadlines: Priority date 2/1; closing date 3/15. Applicants notified on a rolling basis starting 2/1; must reply by 5/1 or within 4 week(s) of notification.
Transfers: Applicants notified on a rolling basis starting 2/1; must reply by 5/1 or within 4 week(s) of notification.

CONTACT
Richard Moeggenberg, Director of Financial Aid
33 East College Street, Hillsdale, MI 49242
(517) 607-2350

Hope College

Holland, Michigan
www.hope.edu Federal Code: 002273

4-year private liberal arts college in small city, affiliated with Reformed Church in America.
Enrollment: 3,251 undergrads, 2% part-time. 901 full-time freshmen.
Selectivity: Admits over 75% of applicants.

BASIC COSTS (2013-2014)
Tuition and fees: $28,720.
Room and board: $8,810.
Additional info: Tuition/fee waivers available for minority students.

FINANCIAL AID PICTURE (2012-2013)
Students with need: Out of 772 full-time freshmen who applied for aid, 613 were judged to have need. Of these, 612 received aid, and 163 had their full need met. Average financial aid package met 79% of need; average scholarship/grant was $18,259; average loan was $3,940. For part-time students, average financial aid package was $8,883.
Students without need: 213 full-time freshmen who did not demonstrate need for aid received scholarships/grants; average award was $8,287. No-need awards available for academics, art, minority status, music/drama, religious affiliation.
Scholarships offered: Merit Scholarships: $3,000-$17,000 per year. Talent Awards: $2,500; for music, art, theater, creative writing.
Cumulative student debt: 65% of graduating class had student loans; average debt was $37,010.

FINANCIAL AID PROCEDURES
Forms required: FAFSA, institutional form.
Dates and Deadlines: Priority date 3/1; no closing date. Applicants notified on a rolling basis starting 3/15.
Transfers: No deadline. Applicants notified on a rolling basis starting 3/25.

CONTACT
Jill Nutt, Director of Financial Aid
69 East 10th Street, Holland, MI 49422-9000
(888) 439-8907

Jackson Community College
Jackson, Michigan
www.jccmi.edu Federal Code: 002274

2-year public community college in small city.
Enrollment: 5,805 undergrads, 56% part-time. 770 full-time freshmen.
Selectivity: Open admission; but selective for some programs.

BASIC COSTS (2012-2013)
Tuition and fees: $4,140; out-of-district residents $5,730; out-of-state residents $7,320.
Per-credit charge: $106; out-of-district residents $159; out-of-state residents $212.

FINANCIAL AID PICTURE
Students with need: Need-based aid available for full-time and part-time students. Work study available nights, weekends, and for part-time students.
Students without need: No-need awards available for academics, art, leadership, music/drama, state/district residency.

FINANCIAL AID PROCEDURES
Forms required: FAFSA, institutional form.
Dates and Deadlines: Priority date 6/15; no closing date. Applicants notified on a rolling basis starting 3/1.

CONTACT
Jennifer Dorer
2111 Emmons Road, Jackson, MI 49201-8399
(517) 796-8436

Kalamazoo College
Kalamazoo, Michigan
www.kzoo.edu Federal Code: 002275

4-year private liberal arts college in small city.
Enrollment: 1,349 undergrads, 1% part-time. 335 full-time freshmen.
Selectivity: Admits 50 to 75% of applicants.

BASIC COSTS (2013-2014)
Tuition and fees: $39,350.
Room and board: $8,475.

FINANCIAL AID PICTURE (2012-2013)
Students with need: Out of 260 full-time freshmen who applied for aid, 218 were judged to have need. Of these, 218 received aid, and 101 had their full need met. Average financial aid package met 92% of need; average scholarship/grant was $25,717; average loan was $3,991.
Students without need: 101 full-time freshmen who did not demonstrate need for aid received scholarships/grants; average award was $16,483. No-need awards available for academics, alumni affiliation, art, leadership, minority status, music/drama.
Scholarships offered: Honors Scholarship: $10,000-24,000 annually; based on academic and co-curricular record and accomplishments; varied number awarded. Enlightened Leadership Awards: $5,000; based on written application and/or creative expression portfolio.
Cumulative student debt: 53% of graduating class had student loans; average debt was $27,845.
Additional info: Paid career development internship and senior project experiences available on campus.

FINANCIAL AID PROCEDURES
Forms required: FAFSA, institutional form.
Dates and Deadlines: Closing date 2/15. Applicants notified on a rolling basis starting 3/21; must reply by 5/1.
Transfers: Closing date 3/1. Must reply by 5/1.

CONTACT
Marian Stowers, Director of Financial Aid
1200 Academy Street, Kalamazoo, MI 49006
(269) 337-7192

Kalamazoo Valley Community College
Kalamazoo, Michigan
www.kvcc.edu Federal Code: 006949

2-year public community college in small city.
Enrollment: 10,318 undergrads.
Selectivity: Open admission.

BASIC COSTS (2012-2013)
Tuition and fees: $2,505; out-of-district residents $4,080; out-of-state residents $5,520.
Per-credit charge: $84; out-of-district residents $136; out-of-state residents $184.

FINANCIAL AID PICTURE
Students with need: Need-based aid available for full-time and part-time students. Work study available nights, weekends, and for part-time students.
Students without need: No-need awards available for academics, athletics.

FINANCIAL AID PROCEDURES
Forms required: FAFSA, institutional form.
Dates and Deadlines: Priority date 6/1; no closing date. Applicants notified on a rolling basis starting 5/1; must reply within 2 week(s) of notification.

CONTACT
Roger Miller, Director of Financial Aid
6767 West O Avenue, Kalamazoo, MI 49003-4070
(269) 488-4340

Kellogg Community College
Battle Creek, Michigan
www.kellogg.edu Federal Code: 002276

2-year public community college in small city.
Enrollment: 6,000 undergrads.
Selectivity: Open admission; but selective for some programs.

BASIC COSTS (2012-2013)
Tuition and fees: $2,935; out-of-district residents $4,350; out-of-state residents $6,015.
Per-credit charge: $88; out-of-district residents $137; out-of-state residents $193.

FINANCIAL AID PICTURE
Students with need: Need-based aid available for full-time and part-time students. Work study available nights.
Students without need: No-need awards available for academics, art, athletics, music/drama, state/district residency.

FINANCIAL AID PROCEDURES
Forms required: FAFSA, institutional form.
Dates and Deadlines: Priority date 4/1; no closing date. Applicants notified on a rolling basis starting 3/13.
Transfers: No deadline. Applicants notified on a rolling basis.

CONTACT
Nikki Jewell, Director, Financial Aid
450 North Avenue, Battle Creek, MI 49017-3397
(269) 965-4123

Kettering University
Flint, Michigan
www.kettering.edu Federal Code: 002262

4-year private university and engineering college in small city.
Enrollment: 1,658 undergrads, 4% part-time. 372 full-time freshmen.
Selectivity: Admits 50 to 75% of applicants.

BASIC COSTS (2012-2013)
Tuition and fees: $33,946.
Per-credit charge: $1,132.
Room and board: $6,660.
Additional info: Fixed-tuition guarantee for all undergraduate students beginning in 2012-13.

FINANCIAL AID PICTURE (2012-2013)
Students with need: Out of 372 full-time freshmen who applied for aid, 354 were judged to have need. Of these, 354 received aid, and 43 had their full need met. Average financial aid package met 65% of need; average scholarship/grant was $17,421; average loan was $3,442. Need-based aid available for part-time students.
Students without need: 69 full-time freshmen who did not demonstrate need for aid received scholarships/grants; average award was $14,893. No-need awards available for academics, leadership, minority status.
Scholarships offered: Various scholarships; $20,000-$40,000 for 4 years; based on merit. Renewable scholarships; $250-$5,000 per year.

FINANCIAL AID PROCEDURES
Forms required: FAFSA.
Dates and Deadlines: Applicants notified on a rolling basis starting 1/31.
Transfers: No deadline. Applicants notified on a rolling basis starting 1/31.

CONTACT
Diane Bice, Director of Financial Aid
1700 University Avenue, Flint, MI 48504-6214
(810) 762-7859

Kirtland Community College
Roscommon, Michigan
www.kirtland.edu Federal Code: 007171

2-year public community college in rural community.
Enrollment: 1,647 undergrads, 58% part-time. 359 full-time freshmen.
Selectivity: Open admission; but selective for some programs.

BASIC COSTS (2012-2013)
Tuition and fees: $3,235; out-of-district residents $4,045; out-of-state residents $6,835.
Additional info: Tuition/fee waivers available for minority students.

FINANCIAL AID PICTURE (2011-2012)
Students with need: Out of 329 full-time freshmen who applied for aid, 307 were judged to have need. Of these, 291 received aid, and 5 had their full need met. Average financial aid package met 32% of need; average scholarship/grant was $3,391; average loan was $2,144. For part-time students, average financial aid package was $3,490.
Students without need: 8 full-time freshmen who did not demonstrate need for aid received scholarships/grants; average award was $1,980. No-need awards available for academics, athletics, minority status.
Scholarships offered: 9 full-time freshmen received athletic scholarships; average amount $3,825.
Additional info: Federal and institutional work-study programs available.

FINANCIAL AID PROCEDURES
Forms required: FAFSA.
Dates and Deadlines: Priority date 5/1; no closing date. Applicants notified on a rolling basis.
Transfers: No deadline.

CONTACT
Christin Horndt, Director of Financial Aid
10775 North Saint Helen Road, Roscommon, MI 48653
(989) 275-5000 ext. 310

Kuyper College
Grand Rapids, Michigan
www.kuyper.edu Federal Code: 002311

4-year private liberal arts college in large city, affiliated with Christian Reformed Church.
Enrollment: 300 undergrads.
Selectivity: Admits 50 to 75% of applicants.

BASIC COSTS (2012-2013)
Tuition and fees: $17,950.
Room and board: $6,720.

FINANCIAL AID PICTURE
Students with need: Need-based aid available for full-time and part-time students. Work study available nights, weekends, and for part-time students.
Students without need: No-need awards available for academics, leadership, minority status.
Scholarships offered: Kuyper Achievement Awards: $1,000-$6,000; GPA of 3.0-4.0, ACT of 21 and above. Christian Leadership Scholarship: $1,500 renewable annually; based on Christian service activities, 3.2 cumulative GPA. Christian Ministry Scholarship: up to $2,000; renewable annually; based on family's primary source of income. Multicultural Scholarships: $500-$5,000; based on academic record, leadership involvement, essays, cross-cultural experiences, and student's ethnic, cultural and socioeconomic background; 2.5 cumulative GPA.

FINANCIAL AID PROCEDURES
Forms required: FAFSA.
Dates and Deadlines: Priority date 3/1; no closing date. Applicants notified on a rolling basis starting 3/15; must reply within 2 week(s) of notification.
Transfers: No deadline. Applicants notified on a rolling basis; must reply within 2 week(s) of notification.

CONTACT
Agnes Russell, Director of Financial Aid
3333 East Beltline Avenue Northeast, Grand Rapids, MI 49525-9749
(616) 988-3656

Lake Michigan College
Benton Harbor, Michigan
www.lakemichigancollege.edu Federal Code: 002277

2-year public community college in large town.
Enrollment: 3,967 undergrads, 64% part-time. 492 full-time freshmen.
Selectivity: Open admission; but selective for some programs.

BASIC COSTS (2012-2013)
Tuition and fees: $3,660; out-of-district residents $5,010; out-of-state residents $6,240.
Per-credit charge: $83; out-of-district residents $128; out-of-state residents $169.
Additional info: Tuition/fee waivers available for adults.

FINANCIAL AID PICTURE (2011-2012)
Students with need: Out of 445 full-time freshmen who applied for aid, 382 were judged to have need. Of these, 366 received aid, and 27 had their full need met. Average financial aid package met 60% of need. For part-time students, average financial aid package was $6,726.
Students without need: 33 full-time freshmen who did not demonstrate need for aid received scholarships/grants; average award was $1,637.

Scholarships offered: ***Merit:*** Presidential Scholarship, full tuition and fees. At least 10 scholarships available to new high school graduates each year. ***Athletic:*** 9 full-time freshmen received athletic scholarships; average amount $1,442.

FINANCIAL AID PROCEDURES
Forms required: FAFSA.
Dates and Deadlines: Priority date 3/1; no closing date. Applicants notified on a rolling basis starting 4/1; must reply within 2 week(s) of notification.
Transfers: No deadline. Must reply within 2 week(s) of notification.

CONTACT
Anne Tews, Director of Financial Aid
2755 East Napier Avenue, Benton Harbor, MI 49022-1899
(269) 927-8100 ext. 5200

Lake Superior State University

Sault Ste. Marie, Michigan
www.lssu.edu Federal Code: 002293

4-year public university and engineering college in large town.
Enrollment: 2,440 undergrads, 14% part-time. 489 full-time freshmen.
Selectivity: Admits over 75% of applicants.

BASIC COSTS (2012-2013)
Tuition and fees: $9,540; out-of-state residents $14,310.
Per-credit charge: $398; out-of-state residents $596.
Room and board: $8,481.
Additional info: Residents of Ontario pay in-state tuition.

FINANCIAL AID PICTURE (2011-2012)
Students with need: Out of 412 full-time freshmen who applied for aid, 359 were judged to have need. Of these, 359 received aid, and 113 had their full need met. Average financial aid package met 67% of need; average scholarship/grant was $6,771; average loan was $3,188. For part-time students, average financial aid package was $5,855.
Students without need: 77 full-time freshmen who did not demonstrate need for aid received scholarships/grants; average award was $4,231. No-need awards available for academics, athletics, state/district residency.
Scholarships offered: 51 full-time freshmen received athletic scholarships; average amount $5,375.
Cumulative student debt: 71% of graduating class had student loans; average debt was $29,108.

FINANCIAL AID PROCEDURES
Forms required: FAFSA.
Dates and Deadlines: Priority date 3/1; no closing date. Applicants notified on a rolling basis starting 10/1; must reply by 5/1 or within 3 week(s) of notification.
Transfers: Closing date 3/1. Applicants notified on a rolling basis starting 3/1.

CONTACT
Deborah Faust, Director of Financial Aid
650 West Easterday Avenue, Sault Ste. Marie, MI 49783-1699
(906) 635-2678

Lansing Community College

Lansing, Michigan
www.lcc.edu Federal Code: 002278

2-year public community college in small city.
Enrollment: 18,746 undergrads, 62% part-time. 2,263 full-time freshmen.
Selectivity: Open admission; but selective for some programs.

BASIC COSTS (2013-2014)
Tuition and fees: $2,630; out-of-district residents $5,060; out-of-state residents $7,490.
Per-credit charge: $81; out-of-district residents $162; out-of-state residents $243.

FINANCIAL AID PICTURE (2011-2012)
Students with need: 38% of average financial aid package awarded as scholarships/grants, 62% awarded as loans/jobs. Need-based aid available for part-time students. Work study available nights, weekends, and for part-time students.
Students without need: No-need awards available for academics, athletics.

FINANCIAL AID PROCEDURES
Forms required: FAFSA.
Dates and Deadlines: Closing date 7/18. Applicants notified on a rolling basis starting 4/3.
Transfers: Closing date 7/1. Applicants notified on a rolling basis starting 4/3.

CONTACT
Stephanie Bogard Trapp, Director of Financial Aid
1121 Enrollment Services, Lansing, MI 48901-7210
(517) 483-1200

Lawrence Technological University

Southfield, Michigan
www.ltu.edu Federal Code: 002279

4-year private university in small city.
Enrollment: 1,909 undergrads, 29% part-time. 252 full-time freshmen.
Selectivity: Admits less than 50% of applicants.

BASIC COSTS (2012-2013)
Tuition and fees: $28,440.
Room and board: $8,987.
Additional info: Tuition/fee waivers available for unemployed or children of unemployed.

FINANCIAL AID PICTURE (2011-2012)
Students with need: Out of 234 full-time freshmen who applied for aid, 190 were judged to have need. Of these, 190 received aid, and 49 had their full need met. Average financial aid package met 72% of need; average scholarship/grant was $14,050; average loan was $6,079. For part-time students, average financial aid package was $14,296.
Students without need: 35 full-time freshmen who did not demonstrate need for aid received scholarships/grants; average award was $12,596. No-need awards available for academics, alumni affiliation, art, job skills, leadership, minority status, ROTC, state/district residency.
Scholarships offered: 13 full-time freshmen received athletic scholarships; average amount $2,148.
Cumulative student debt: 75% of graduating class had student loans; average debt was $41,529.
Additional info: March 1 state deadline for Michigan Competitive Scholarship and Michigan Tuition Grant.

FINANCIAL AID PROCEDURES
Forms required: FAFSA.
Dates and Deadlines: Priority date 4/1; no closing date. Applicants notified on a rolling basis starting 3/1; must reply within 2 week(s) of notification.
Transfers: Applicants notified on a rolling basis starting 4/1; must reply within 2 week(s) of notification.

CONTACT
Dee King, Director of Student Financial Aid
21000 West Ten Mile Road, Southfield, MI 48075-1058
(248) 204-2121

Macomb Community College

Warren, Michigan
www.macomb.edu Federal Code: 008906

2-year public community college in small city.
Enrollment: 14,056 undergrads, 67% part-time. 628 full-time freshmen.
Selectivity: Open admission; but selective for some programs.

BASIC COSTS (2012-2013)
Tuition and fees: $2,680; out-of-district residents $4,030; out-of-state residents $5,200.
Per-credit charge: $86; out-of-district residents $131; out-of-state residents $170.

FINANCIAL AID PICTURE
Students with need: Need-based aid available for full-time and part-time students. Work study available nights, weekends, and for part-time students.
Students without need: No-need awards available for academics, athletics, leadership, music/drama, state/district residency.

FINANCIAL AID PROCEDURES
Forms required: FAFSA, institutional form.
Dates and Deadlines: Priority date 4/15; no closing date. Applicants notified on a rolling basis starting 5/15; must reply within 2 week(s) of notification.
Transfers: Must submit financial aid transcripts from all institutions attended.

CONTACT
Doug Levy, Director of Financial Aid
14500 East Twelve Mile Road, Warren, MI 48088-3896
(586) 445-7228

Madonna University

Livonia, Michigan
www.madonna.edu Federal Code: 002282

4-year private university and liberal arts college in small city, affiliated with Roman Catholic Church.
Enrollment: 3,037 undergrads, 47% part-time. 174 full-time freshmen.
Selectivity: Admits 50 to 75% of applicants.

BASIC COSTS (2012-2013)
Tuition and fees: $15,300.
Per-credit charge: $506.
Room and board: $7,694.

FINANCIAL AID PICTURE (2011-2012)
Students with need: Out of 142 full-time freshmen who applied for aid, 123 were judged to have need. Of these, 120 received aid, and 22 had their full need met. Average financial aid package met 61% of need; average scholarship/grant was $7,890; average loan was $3,146. For part-time students, average financial aid package was $6,098.
Students without need: 27 full-time freshmen who did not demonstrate need for aid received scholarships/grants; average award was $4,376. No-need awards available for academics, alumni affiliation, art, athletics, leadership, minority status, music/drama, religious affiliation, state/district residency.
Scholarships offered: 9 full-time freshmen received athletic scholarships; average amount $4,471.
Cumulative student debt: 63% of graduating class had student loans; average debt was $23,614.

FINANCIAL AID PROCEDURES
Forms required: FAFSA.
Dates and Deadlines: Priority date 3/1; no closing date. Applicants notified on a rolling basis starting 3/15; must reply by 9/1 or within 2 week(s) of notification.
Transfers: No deadline. Applicants notified on a rolling basis starting 4/15; must reply by 9/1 or within 2 week(s) of notification. Deadline for state aid is March 1st.

CONTACT
Chris Ziegler, Director of Financial Aid
36600 Schoolcraft Road, Livonia, MI 48150-1176
(734) 432-5664

Marygrove College

Detroit, Michigan
www.marygrove.edu Federal Code: 002284

4-year private liberal arts college in very large city, affiliated with Roman Catholic Church.
Enrollment: 950 undergrads.
Selectivity: Admits 50 to 75% of applicants.

BASIC COSTS (2013-2014)
Tuition and fees: $19,850.
Per-credit charge: $690.
Room and board: $7,600.

FINANCIAL AID PICTURE
Students with need: Need-based aid available for full-time and part-time students.
Students without need: This college awards aid only to students with need.

FINANCIAL AID PROCEDURES
Forms required: FAFSA, institutional form.
Dates and Deadlines: Priority date 3/15; no closing date. Applicants notified on a rolling basis starting 5/15; must reply within 2 week(s) of notification.

CONTACT
Patricia Chaplin, Director of Financial Aid
8425 West McNichols Road, Detroit, MI 48221
(313) 927-1245

Michigan State University

East Lansing, Michigan
www.msu.edu Federal Code: 002290

4-year public university in small city.
Enrollment: 37,076 undergrads, 8% part-time. 8,218 full-time freshmen.
Selectivity: Admits 50 to 75% of applicants.

BASIC COSTS (2012-2013)
Tuition and fees: $12,623; out-of-state residents $32,580.
Per-credit charge: $421; out-of-state residents $1,086.
Room and board: $8,476.

FINANCIAL AID PICTURE (2012-2013)
Students with need: Out of 5,608 full-time freshmen who applied for aid, 3,938 were judged to have need. Of these, 3,849 received aid, and 804 had their full need met. Average financial aid package met 63% of need; average scholarship/grant was $9,685; average loan was $3,393. For part-time students, average financial aid package was $8,917.
Students without need: 459 full-time freshmen who did not demonstrate need for aid received scholarships/grants; average award was $7,417. No-need awards available for academics, alumni affiliation, art, athletics, leadership, music/drama, ROTC, state/district residency.
Scholarships offered: 70 full-time freshmen received athletic scholarships; average amount $23,907.
Cumulative student debt: 46% of graduating class had student loans; average debt was $24,987.

FINANCIAL AID PROCEDURES
Forms required: FAFSA.
Dates and Deadlines: Applicants notified on a rolling basis starting 3/15; must reply within 4 week(s) of notification.

CONTACT
Richard Shipman, Director of Financial Aid
250 Administration Building, East Lansing, MI 48824
(517) 353-5940

Michigan Technological University
Houghton, Michigan
www.mtu.edu Federal Code: 002292

4-year public university in small town.
Enrollment: 5,532 undergrads, 6% part-time. 1,151 full-time freshmen.
Selectivity: Admits over 75% of applicants.

BASIC COSTS (2012-2013)
Tuition and fees: $13,353; out-of-state residents $27,258.
Per-credit charge: $437; out-of-state residents $900.
Room and board: $8,865.

FINANCIAL AID PICTURE (2012-2013)
Students with need: Out of 1,019 full-time freshmen who applied for aid, 808 were judged to have need. Of these, 807 received aid, and 173 had their full need met. Average financial aid package met 78% of need; average scholarship/grant was $7,897; average loan was $3,532. For part-time students, average financial aid package was $6,824.
Students without need: 277 full-time freshmen who did not demonstrate need for aid received scholarships/grants; average award was $5,594. No-need awards available for academics, alumni affiliation, art, athletics, job skills, leadership, music/drama, ROTC, state/district residency.
Scholarships offered: 54 full-time freshmen received athletic scholarships; average amount $7,914.
Cumulative student debt: 72% of graduating class had student loans; average debt was $34,938.

FINANCIAL AID PROCEDURES
Forms required: FAFSA.
Dates and Deadlines: Applicants notified on a rolling basis starting 3/15; must reply by 5/1.

CONTACT
Bill Roberts, Director of Financial Aid
1400 Townsend Drive, Houghton, MI 49931-1295
(906) 487-2622

Mid Michigan Community College
Harrison, Michigan
www.midmich.edu Federal Code: 006768

2-year public community college in small town.
Enrollment: 4,694 undergrads.
Selectivity: Open admission; but selective for some programs.

BASIC COSTS (2012-2013)
Tuition and fees: $3,215; out-of-district residents $5,600; out-of-state residents $10,160.
Per-credit charge: $92; out-of-district residents $172; out-of-state residents $324.
Additional info: Tuition and fees reported are for contact hours. Tuition/fee waivers available for adults.

FINANCIAL AID PICTURE
Students with need: Need-based aid available for full-time and part-time students. Work study available nights.
Students without need: No-need awards available for academics, art.

FINANCIAL AID PROCEDURES
Forms required: FAFSA, institutional form.
Dates and Deadlines: Priority date 5/1; no closing date. Applicants notified on a rolling basis starting 4/1; must reply within 2 week(s) of notification.

CONTACT
Gale Crandell, Financial Aid Director
1375 South Clare Avenue, Harrison, MI 48625-9442
(989) 386-6622

Monroe County Community College
Monroe, Michigan
www.monroeccc.edu Federal Code: 002294

2-year public community college in large town.
Enrollment: 4,085 undergrads.
Selectivity: Open admission; but selective for some programs.

BASIC COSTS (2012-2013)
Tuition and fees: $2,855; out-of-district residents $4,655; out-of-state residents $5,135.
Per-credit charge: $94; out-of-district residents $154; out-of-state residents $170.
Additional info: Tuition and fees reported are for 30 contact hours. Tuition/fee waivers available for minority students.

FINANCIAL AID PICTURE
Students with need: Need-based aid available for full-time and part-time students. Work study available nights, weekends, and for part-time students.
Students without need: No-need awards available for academics, alumni affiliation, art, leadership, music/drama, state/district residency.

FINANCIAL AID PROCEDURES
Forms required: FAFSA, institutional form.
Dates and Deadlines: Priority date 4/1; no closing date. Applicants notified on a rolling basis starting 4/1; must reply within 2 week(s) of notification.

CONTACT
Valerie Culler, Director of Financial Aid/Placement
1555 South Raisinville Road, Monroe, MI 48161-9746
(734) 384-4135

Montcalm Community College
Sidney, Michigan
www.montcalm.edu Federal Code: 002295

2-year public community and liberal arts college in rural community.
Enrollment: 1,669 undergrads, 60% part-time. 126 full-time freshmen.
Selectivity: Open admission; but selective for some programs.

BASIC COSTS (2012-2013)
Tuition and fees: $3,030; out-of-district residents $5,340; out-of-state residents $7,740.
Per-credit charge: $87; out-of-district residents $164; out-of-state residents $244.

FINANCIAL AID PICTURE (2012-2013)
Students with need: Out of 116 full-time freshmen who applied for aid, 106 were judged to have need. Of these, 100 received aid, and 12 had their full need met. Average financial aid package met 65% of need; average scholarship/grant was $500; average loan was $5,500. Need-based aid available for part-time students.
Students without need: 3 full-time freshmen who did not demonstrate need for aid received scholarships/grants; average award was $500. No-need awards available for academics, state/district residency.

Cumulative student debt: 29% of graduating class had student loans; average debt was $2,600.

FINANCIAL AID PROCEDURES

Forms required: FAFSA, institutional form.
Dates and Deadlines: Priority date 2/15; no closing date. Applicants notified on a rolling basis starting 4/15; must reply within 2 week(s) of notification.
Transfers: Priority date 3/1; no deadline. Applicants notified on a rolling basis starting 4/15.

CONTACT

Traci Nichols, Director of Financial Aid
2800 College Drive, Sidney, MI 48885
(989) 328-1285

Mott Community College

Flint, Michigan
www.mcc.edu Federal Code: 002261

2-year public community college in small city.
Enrollment: 8,263 undergrads, 67% part-time. 279 full-time freshmen.
Selectivity: Open admission; but selective for some programs.

BASIC COSTS (2013-2014)

Tuition and fees: $3,953; out-of-district residents $5,564; out-of-state residents $7,726.
Per-credit charge: $117; out-of-district residents $171; out-of-state residents $243.
Additional info: Tuition and fees are based on 30 contact hours.

FINANCIAL AID PICTURE (2011-2012)

Students with need: 55% of average financial aid package awarded as scholarships/grants, 45% awarded as loans/jobs. Need-based aid available for part-time students. Work study available nights.
Students without need: No-need awards available for academics, alumni affiliation, art, athletics, leadership, minority status, music/drama, state/district residency.

FINANCIAL AID PROCEDURES

Forms required: FAFSA.
Dates and Deadlines: Priority date 6/1; no closing date. Applicants notified on a rolling basis starting 5/1.
Transfers: Pell Grants adjusted for amount used at another institution.

CONTACT

Jennifer Dow-McDonald, Executive Director of Student Financial Services
1401 East Court Street, Flint, MI 48503-2089
(810) 762-0144

Muskegon Community College

Muskegon, Michigan
www.muskegoncc.edu Federal Code: 002297

2-year public community college in small city.
Enrollment: 3,100 undergrads, 62% part-time. 364 full-time freshmen.
Selectivity: Open admission; but selective for some programs.

BASIC COSTS (2012-2013)

Tuition and fees: $3,006; out-of-district residents $4,931; out-of-state residents $6,755.
Per-credit charge: $86; out-of-district residents $153; out-of-state residents $210.
Additional info: Students also assessed contact hour fees, which vary according to residency status, and course fees, which vary.

FINANCIAL AID PICTURE

Students with need: Need-based aid available for full-time and part-time students. Work study available nights, weekends, and for part-time students.

FINANCIAL AID PROCEDURES

Forms required: FAFSA, institutional form.
Dates and Deadlines: Priority date 5/1; no closing date. Applicants notified on a rolling basis starting 6/1; must reply within 2 week(s) of notification.

CONTACT

Bruce Wierda, Director of Financial Aid
221 South Quarterline Road, Muskegon, MI 49442
(231) 777-0221

North Central Michigan College

Petoskey, Michigan
www.ncmich.edu Federal Code: 002299

2-year public community college in small town.
Enrollment: 2,600 undergrads.
Selectivity: Open admission; but selective for some programs.

BASIC COSTS (2012-2013)

Tuition and fees: $2,880; out-of-district residents $4,395; out-of-state residents $5,513.
Per-credit charge: $78; out-of-district residents $128; out-of-state residents $165.
Room and board: $6,300.
Additional info: Tuition is based on contact hours and may vary by program.

FINANCIAL AID PICTURE

Students with need: Need-based aid available for full-time and part-time students. Work study available nights, weekends, and for part-time students.

FINANCIAL AID PROCEDURES

Forms required: FAFSA, institutional form.
Dates and Deadlines: Closing date 4/1. Applicants notified on a rolling basis starting 4/30.

CONTACT

Virginia Panoff, Director of Financial Aid
1515 Howard Street, Petoskey, MI 49770
(231) 348-6627

Northern Michigan University

Marquette, Michigan
www.nmu.edu Federal Code: 002301

4-year public university in large town.
Enrollment: 7,977 undergrads, 7% part-time. 1,748 full-time freshmen.
Selectivity: Admits 50 to 75% of applicants.

BASIC COSTS (2012-2013)

Tuition and fees: $8,709; out-of-state residents $13,605.
Per-credit charge: $336; out-of-state residents $540.
Room and board: $8,404.
Additional info: Art and design students pay $250/semester MacBook fee, nursing students pay $75 per semester program fee, lab fees are charged for chemistry ($40) and biology ($25) courses. Excludes one-time $225 athletic fee for first time freshmen. Tuition/fee waivers available for minority students.

FINANCIAL AID PICTURE (2011-2012)

Students with need: Out of 1,717 full-time freshmen who applied for aid, 1,219 were judged to have need. Of these, 1,188 received aid, and 158 had their full need met. Average financial aid package met 57% of need; average scholarship/grant was $5,147; average loan was $3,222. For part-time students, average financial aid package was $6,837.

Students without need: 145 full-time freshmen who did not demonstrate need for aid received scholarships/grants; average award was $3,686. No-need awards available for academics, art, athletics, leadership, music/drama, ROTC, state/district residency.
Scholarships offered: ***Merit:*** Talent recognition awards: available in art and design, music, theater. Freshman Fellowship: $1,000 in student employment; 3.5+ GPA and ACT 24+. Dr. Edgar L. Harden Scholarship: "full ride"; 3.5+ GPA and ACT 24+. National Academic Award: $3,500; minimum 3.0+ GPA and ACT 19+; awarded to non-Michigan residents. NMU Merit Excellence Award: $2,750-$3,500; based on 3.0+ GPA and 33+ ACT. NMU Merit Award: $2,250-$3,000; 3.0+ GPA and 30-32 ACT. NMU Scholars Award: $1,250-$2,000; 3.0+ GPA and ACT 27-29. NMU Outstanding Achievement: $750-$1,500; 3.0+ GPA and 25-26 ACT. ***Athletic:*** 13 full-time freshmen received athletic scholarships; average amount $7,785.
Cumulative student debt: 68% of graduating class had student loans; average debt was $29,371.
Additional info: Audition or portfolio required for music, drama, and art scholarship applicants. Alumni Dependent Tuition Program gives resident tuition rates to nonresident dependents of NMU alumni who received master's, baccalaureate, or associate degree; renewable.

FINANCIAL AID PROCEDURES
Forms required: FAFSA.
Dates and Deadlines: Priority date 3/1; no closing date. Applicants notified on a rolling basis starting 4/1; must reply within 2 week(s) of notification.
Transfers: No deadline. Applicants notified on a rolling basis starting 4/1; must reply within 2 week(s) of notification. Merit-based transfer scholarships available.

CONTACT
Michael Rotundo, Director of Financial Aid
1401 Presque Isle Avenue, Marquette, MI 49855
(906) 227-2327

Northwestern Michigan College
Traverse City, Michigan
www.nmc.edu Federal Code: 002302

2-year public community and maritime college in large town.
Enrollment: 4,844 undergrads.
Selectivity: Open admission; but selective for some programs.

BASIC COSTS (2012-2013)
Tuition and fees: $3,276; out-of-district residents $5,715; out-of-state residents $7,112.
Per-credit charge: $85; out-of-district residents $166; out-of-state residents $212.
Room and board: $8,700.
Additional info: Tuition and fees reported are based on contact hours. Tuition/fee waivers available for adults, minority students, unemployed or children of unemployed.

FINANCIAL AID PICTURE
Students with need: Need-based aid available for full-time and part-time students. Work study available nights, weekends, and for part-time students.
Students without need: No-need awards available for academics, art, job skills, leadership, minority status, music/drama, ROTC, state/district residency.

FINANCIAL AID PROCEDURES
Forms required: FAFSA.
Dates and Deadlines: Priority date 4/1; no closing date. Applicants notified on a rolling basis starting 5/1; must reply within 2 week(s) of notification.

CONTACT
Pam Palermo, Director for Financial Aid
1701 East Front Street, Traverse City, MI 49686
(231) 995-1035

Northwood University: Michigan
Midland, Michigan
www.northwood.edu Federal Code: 004072

4-year private university and business college in large town.
Enrollment: 1,530 undergrads, 5% part-time. 323 full-time freshmen.
Selectivity: Admits 50 to 75% of applicants.

BASIC COSTS (2012-2013)
Tuition and fees: $20,996.
Per-credit charge: $776.
Room and board: $8,770.

FINANCIAL AID PICTURE (2012-2013)
Students with need: Average financial aid package met 65% of need; average scholarship/grant was $6,289; average loan was $3,302. For part-time students, average financial aid package was $9,271.
Students without need: No-need awards available for academics, alumni affiliation, athletics, leadership, minority status, state/district residency.
Scholarships offered: Academic scholarships based on test scores and GPA; unlimited number awarded.
Cumulative student debt: 74% of graduating class had student loans; average debt was $32,457.

FINANCIAL AID PROCEDURES
Forms required: FAFSA, state aid form.
Dates and Deadlines: Priority date 2/1; no closing date. Applicants notified on a rolling basis starting 3/1.
Transfers: No deadline. Applicants notified on a rolling basis.

CONTACT
Theresa Mieler, Financial Aid Director
4000 Whiting Drive, Midland, MI 48640
(989) 837-4230

Oakland Community College
Bloomfield Hills, Michigan
www.oaklandcc.edu Federal Code: 002303

2-year public community college in very large city.
Enrollment: 15,754 undergrads, 68% part-time. 1,294 full-time freshmen.
Selectivity: Open admission.

BASIC COSTS (2012-2013)
Tuition and fees: $2,212; out-of-district residents $3,830; out-of-state residents $5,414.
Per-credit charge: $71; out-of-district residents $125; out-of-state residents $176.

FINANCIAL AID PICTURE (2012-2013)
Students with need: Average financial aid package met 43% of need; average scholarship/grant was $4,956; average loan was $40. For part-time students, average financial aid package was $4,404.
Students without need: No-need awards available for academics, athletics, job skills.

FINANCIAL AID PROCEDURES
Forms required: FAFSA.
Dates and Deadlines: Priority date 4/15; no closing date. Applicants notified on a rolling basis starting 4/15.
Transfers: Closing date 6/30. Applicants notified on a rolling basis starting 6/30. Michigan residency required for aid to transfer students.

CONTACT
Wilma Porter, Director of Financial Assistance and Scholarships
2480 Opdyke Road, Bloomfield Hills, MI 48304-2266
(248) 341-2000

Oakland University

Rochester, Michigan
www.oakland.edu Federal Code: 002307

4-year public university in small city.
Enrollment: 15,727 undergrads, 25% part-time. 2,361 full-time freshmen.
Selectivity: Admits 50 to 75% of applicants.

BASIC COSTS (2012-2013)
Tuition and fees: $10,230; out-of-state residents $23,873.
Room and board: $8,208.

FINANCIAL AID PICTURE
Students with need: Need-based aid available for full-time and part-time students.
Students without need: No-need awards available for academics, art, athletics, leadership, music/drama, state/district residency.
Scholarships offered: Wide range of scholarships awarded on the basis of accomplishment.

FINANCIAL AID PROCEDURES
Forms required: FAFSA.
Dates and Deadlines: Priority date 2/15; no closing date. Applicants notified on a rolling basis starting 3/15.

CONTACT
Cindy Hermsen, Director of Financial Aid
101 North Foundation Hall, Rochester, MI 48309-4401
(248) 370-2550

Olivet College

Olivet, Michigan
www.olivetcollege.edu Federal Code: 002308

4-year private liberal arts college in rural community, affiliated with United Church of Christ.
Enrollment: 1,069 undergrads.
Selectivity: Admits 50 to 75% of applicants. GED not accepted.

BASIC COSTS (2013-2014)
Tuition and fees: $23,021.
Room and board: $7,400.

FINANCIAL AID PICTURE
Students with need: Need-based aid available for full-time and part-time students.
Students without need: This college awards aid only to students with need.
Scholarships offered: Scholarships: up to $2,000; for students who demonstrate history of community service and civic responsibility during high school or college. Academic merit scholarships: up to full tuition. All scholarships renewable for 4 years.

FINANCIAL AID PROCEDURES
Forms required: FAFSA.
Dates and Deadlines: Applicants notified on a rolling basis starting 2/1; must reply within 3 week(s) of notification.

CONTACT
Libby Jean, Director of Student Services
320 South Main Street, Olivet, MI 49076
(269) 749-7645

Robert B. Miller College

Battle Creek, Michigan
www.millercollege.edu Federal Code: 040943

4-year private liberal arts college in small city.
Enrollment: 365 undergrads, 78% part-time.

BASIC COSTS (2012-2013)
Tuition and fees: $10,590.
Per-credit charge: $353.

FINANCIAL AID PICTURE (2012-2013)
Students with need: 46% of average financial aid package awarded as scholarships/grants, 54% awarded as loans/jobs. Need-based aid available for part-time students.
Students without need: No-need awards available for academics, leadership.

FINANCIAL AID PROCEDURES
Transfers: No deadline. Applicants notified on a rolling basis starting 4/1.

CONTACT
Kim Cvitkovic, Director of Financial Aid
450 North Avenue, Battle Creek, MI 49017
(269) 660-8021 ext. 2720

Rochester College

Rochester Hills, Michigan
www.rc.edu Federal Code: 002288

4-year private liberal arts college in small city, affiliated with Church of Christ.
Enrollment: 1,183 undergrads.
Selectivity: Admits over 75% of applicants.

BASIC COSTS (2012-2013)
Tuition and fees: $19,760.
Room and board: $6,304.
Additional info: Tuition/fee waivers available for minority students.

FINANCIAL AID PICTURE
Students with need: Need-based aid available for full-time and part-time students. Work study available nights, weekends, and for part-time students.
Students without need: No-need awards available for academics, alumni affiliation, athletics, leadership, music/drama, state/district residency.

FINANCIAL AID PROCEDURES
Forms required: FAFSA.
Dates and Deadlines: Priority date 8/1; no closing date. Applicants notified on a rolling basis starting 6/1; must reply within 2 week(s) of notification.

CONTACT
Jessica Bristow, Director of Financial Aid
800 West Avon Road, Rochester Hills, MI 48307
(248) 218-2029

Sacred Heart Major Seminary

Detroit, Michigan
www.shms.edu Federal Code: 002313

4-year private seminary college in very large city, affiliated with Roman Catholic Church.
Enrollment: 100 undergrads.
Selectivity: Admits over 75% of applicants.

BASIC COSTS (2012-2013)
Tuition and fees: $16,505.

Per-credit charge: $385.
Room and board: $8,940.
Additional info: Tuition/fee waivers available for adults.

FINANCIAL AID PICTURE

Students with need: Work study available nights, weekends, and for part-time students.
Students without need: No-need awards available for academics, religious affiliation.

FINANCIAL AID PROCEDURES

Forms required: FAFSA, institutional form.
Dates and Deadlines: Applicants notified on a rolling basis; must reply within 2 week(s) of notification.
Transfers: No deadline. Applicants notified on a rolling basis. Must submit certified high school transcript, copy of high school diploma, copy of GED certificate showing passing score, or college transcript showing associate degree as certification of eligibility; must submit financial aid transcripts from all previous post-secondary institutions attended.

CONTACT

Jeannette Murrell, Director of Financial Aid
2701 Chicago Boulevard, Detroit, MI 48206-1799
(313) 883-8781

Saginaw Valley State University

University Center, Michigan
www.svsu.edu Federal Code: 002314

4-year public university in small city.
Enrollment: 9,035 undergrads, 14% part-time. 1,635 full-time freshmen.
Selectivity: Admits over 75% of applicants.

BASIC COSTS (2012-2013)

Tuition and fees: $8,120; out-of-state residents $19,063.
Per-credit charge: $256; out-of-state residents $621.
Room and board: $8,220.

FINANCIAL AID PICTURE

Students with need: Need-based aid available for full-time and part-time students. Work study available nights, weekends, and for part-time students.
Students without need: No-need awards available for academics, art, athletics, leadership, minority status, music/drama.
Scholarships offered: Presidential Scholarships; tuition and selective fees up to 136 credit hours; granted to students who are first or second in high school class with minimum 24 ACT or 3.7 GPA and 28 ACT. Dean's Scholarship; $3,000 per year for four years; 3.0 GPA and 24 ACT. University Foundation Scholarship; tuition and selective fees for four courses and $1,000 to apply toward study abroad or a research project; 3.5 GPA and 24 ACT. University Scholarship; $1,000 per year for four years; 3.5 GPA. Various private scholarships also available.

FINANCIAL AID PROCEDURES

Forms required: FAFSA.
Dates and Deadlines: Priority date 2/14; no closing date. Applicants notified on a rolling basis starting 3/20; must reply within 10 week(s) of notification.
Transfers: No deadline. Applicants notified on a rolling basis; must reply within 10 week(s) of notification. Community college scholarship, private scholarships, and Transfer Dean's scholarships available.

CONTACT

Robert Lemuel, Director of Scholarships and Financial Aid
7400 Bay Road, University Center, MI 48710
(989) 964-4103

St. Clair County Community College

Port Huron, Michigan
www.sc4.edu Federal Code: 002310

2-year public community college in large town.
Enrollment: 3,879 undergrads, 53% part-time. 585 full-time freshmen.
Selectivity: Open admission; but selective for some programs.

BASIC COSTS (2012-2013)

Tuition and fees: $3,253; out-of-district residents $5,938; out-of-state residents $8,458.
Per-credit charge: $95; out-of-district residents $184; out-of-state residents $268.
Additional info: Residents of Lambton County, Canada pay in-state, out-of-district rate for tuition. Lambton County residents pay in-district tuition rate if enrolled in program of study not offered at Lambton College.

FINANCIAL AID PICTURE (2012-2013)

Students with need: Work study available nights.

FINANCIAL AID PROCEDURES

Forms required: FAFSA.
Dates and Deadlines: Priority date 6/1; no closing date. Applicants notified on a rolling basis starting 5/15; must reply within 2 week(s) of notification.
Transfers: No deadline. Applicants notified on a rolling basis.

CONTACT

Josephine Cassar, Executive Director, Financial Assistance
323 Erie Street, Port Huron, MI 48061-5015
(810) 989-5530

Schoolcraft College

Livonia, Michigan
www.schoolcraft.edu Federal Code: 002315

2-year public community college in small city.
Enrollment: 12,550 undergrads.
Selectivity: Open admission; but selective for some programs.

BASIC COSTS (2012-2013)

Tuition and fees: $2,760; out-of-district residents $3,960; out-of-state residents $5,790.
Per-credit charge: $87; out-of-district residents $127; out-of-state residents $188.

FINANCIAL AID PICTURE (2012-2013)

Students with need: Need-based aid available for full-time and part-time students. Work study available nights, weekends, and for part-time students.
Students without need: No-need awards available for academics, athletics, leadership, music/drama, state/district residency.
Scholarships offered: Trustee Scholarships; $1,000-$1,200; renewable for 2nd year; based on essay, placement test, trustee application, graduation from local high school; 80 awarded.

FINANCIAL AID PROCEDURES

Forms required: FAFSA.
Dates and Deadlines: Applicants notified on a rolling basis starting 6/1.
Transfers: No deadline.

CONTACT

Regina Mosley, Director of Financial Aid
18600 Haggerty Road, Livonia, MI 48152-2696
(734) 462-4433

Siena Heights University

Adrian, Michigan
Federal Code: 002316
www.sienaheights.edu
CSS Code: 1719

4-year private university and liberal arts college in large town, affiliated with Roman Catholic Church.
Enrollment: 2,277 undergrads, 48% part-time.
Selectivity: Admits 50 to 75% of applicants.

BASIC COSTS (2012-2013)
Tuition and fees: $21,152.
Room and board: $8,210.

FINANCIAL AID PICTURE
Students with need: Need-based aid available for full-time students. Work study available nights, weekends, and for part-time students.
Students without need: No-need awards available for academics, art, athletics, music/drama.
Scholarships offered: Scholarships from $2,000 to $12,000, for first time freshmen, based on GPA and ACT and housing status.
Additional info: All new incoming students are guaranteed a work study job, if they would like to have a job on campus.

FINANCIAL AID PROCEDURES
Forms required: FAFSA, CSS PROFILE, institutional form.
Dates and Deadlines: Priority date 3/15; closing date 8/15. Applicants notified on a rolling basis starting 2/15.
Transfers: Priority date 3/1; no deadline. Applicants notified on a rolling basis starting 3/1. Transfer scholarships available for students range from $2,200 to $9,500. Based on transfer GPA and housing status.

CONTACT
Lori Kosarue, Director of Financial Aid
1247 East Siena Heights Drive, Adrian, MI 49221-1796
(517) 264-7110

Southwestern Michigan College

Dowagiac, Michigan
www.swmich.edu
Federal Code: 002317

2-year public community college in small town.
Enrollment: 2,308 undergrads, 44% part-time. 511 full-time freshmen.
Selectivity: Open admission; but selective for some programs.

BASIC COSTS (2012-2013)
Tuition and fees: $4,321; out-of-district residents $5,236; out-of-state residents $5,596.
Per-credit charge: $104; out-of-district residents $135; out-of-state residents $147.

FINANCIAL AID PICTURE (2011-2012)
Students with need: Need-based aid available for full-time and part-time students. Work study available nights, weekends, and for part-time students.
Students without need: No-need awards available for academics, art, leadership, music/drama.

FINANCIAL AID PROCEDURES
Forms required: FAFSA, institutional form.
Dates and Deadlines: Priority date 7/1; no closing date. Applicants notified on a rolling basis starting 4/1; must reply within 2 week(s) of notification.

CONTACT
Christine Passer, Director of Financial Aid
58900 Cherry Grove Road, Dowagiac, MI 49047-9793
(800) 456-8675 ext. 1313

Spring Arbor University

Spring Arbor, Michigan
www.arbor.edu
Federal Code: 002318

4-year private university and liberal arts college in rural community, affiliated with Free Methodist Church of North America.
Enrollment: 2,937 undergrads, 27% part-time. 313 full-time freshmen.
Selectivity: Admits 50 to 75% of applicants.

BASIC COSTS (2013-2014)
Tuition and fees: $23,400.
Per-credit charge: $555.
Room and board: $8,170.

FINANCIAL AID PICTURE (2012-2013)
Students with need: Out of 300 full-time freshmen who applied for aid, 269 were judged to have need. Of these, 269 received aid, and 56 had their full need met. Average financial aid package met 85% of need; average scholarship/grant was $14,552; average loan was $4,445. For part-time students, average financial aid package was $6,809.
Students without need: No-need awards available for academics, art, athletics, minority status, music/drama, religious affiliation.
Scholarships offered: ***Merit:*** Trustee Scholarship: $12,000; President Scholarship: $10,000; Provost Scholarship: $7,500; Faculty Scholarship: $4,000; Partnership Scholarship: $1,000; based on GPA, rank in class, and ACT scores. National Merit Finalist/Semifinalist: 60% tuition. ***Athletic:*** 70 full-time freshmen received athletic scholarships; average amount $5,550.
Cumulative student debt: 87% of graduating class had student loans; average debt was $32,613.

FINANCIAL AID PROCEDURES
Forms required: FAFSA.
Dates and Deadlines: Priority date 3/1; no closing date. Applicants notified on a rolling basis starting 3/1; must reply within 2 week(s) of notification.
Transfers: No deadline. Applicants notified on a rolling basis starting 5/1; must reply within 2 week(s) of notification. A financial aid transcript is required from each college previously attended.

CONTACT
Geoff Marsh, Director of Financial Aid
106 East Main Street, Spring Arbor, MI 49283-9799
(517) 750-6468

University of Detroit Mercy

Detroit, Michigan
www.udmercy.edu
Federal Code: 002323

4-year private university in very large city, affiliated with Roman Catholic Church.
Enrollment: 2,808 undergrads, 20% part-time. 479 full-time freshmen.
Selectivity: Admits 50 to 75% of applicants.

BASIC COSTS (2012-2013)
Tuition and fees: $34,530.
Per-credit charge: $880.
Room and board: $9,680.
Additional info: Engineering and architecture students pay slightly higher tuition; $37,410.

FINANCIAL AID PICTURE
Students with need: Need-based aid available for full-time and part-time students.
Students without need: No-need awards available for academics, alumni affiliation, athletics, leadership, minority status, music/drama, religious affiliation.

FINANCIAL AID PROCEDURES
Forms required: FAFSA.

Dates and Deadlines: Closing date 3/1. Applicants notified on a rolling basis starting 3/1; must reply within 3 week(s) of notification.

CONTACT

Jenny McAlonan, Director of Scholarship and Financial Aid
4001 West McNichols Road, Detroit, MI 48221-3038
(313) 993-3350

University of Michigan

Ann Arbor, Michigan — Federal Code: 002325
www.umich.edu — CSS Code: 1839

4-year public university in small city.
Enrollment: 27,774 undergrads, 3% part-time. 6,211 full-time freshmen.
Selectivity: Admits less than 50% of applicants.

BASIC COSTS (2012-2013)

Tuition and fees: $12,994; out-of-state residents $39,122.
Room and board: $10,572.

FINANCIAL AID PICTURE (2011-2012)

Students with need: Out of 4,259 full-time freshmen who applied for aid, 2,669 were judged to have need. Of these, 2,540 received aid, and 1,022 had their full need met. Average financial aid package met 82% of need; average scholarship/grant was $13,107; average loan was $3,950. Need-based aid available for part-time students.
Students without need: 1,243 full-time freshmen who did not demonstrate need for aid received scholarships/grants; average award was $6,816. No-need awards available for academics, alumni affiliation, art, athletics, leadership, music/drama, religious affiliation, ROTC, state/district residency.
Scholarships offered: 99 full-time freshmen received athletic scholarships; average amount $31,701.
Cumulative student debt: 44% of graduating class had student loans; average debt was $27,815.

FINANCIAL AID PROCEDURES

Forms required: FAFSA, CSS PROFILE.
Dates and Deadlines: Priority date 4/30; closing date 5/31. Applicants notified on a rolling basis.
Transfers: Applicants notified on a rolling basis.

CONTACT

Pamela Fowler, Executive Director, Office of Financial Aid
1220 Student Activities Building, Ann Arbor, MI 48109-1316
(734) 763-6600

University of Michigan: Dearborn

Dearborn, Michigan
www.umd.umich.edu — Federal Code: 002326

4-year public university in small city.
Enrollment: 6,983 undergrads, 32% part-time. 913 full-time freshmen.
Selectivity: Admits 50 to 75% of applicants.

BASIC COSTS (2012-2013)

Tuition and fees: $10,482; out-of-state residents $22,896.
Per-credit charge: $391; out-of-state residents $887.

FINANCIAL AID PICTURE (2011-2012)

Students with need: Out of 804 full-time freshmen who applied for aid, 598 were judged to have need. Of these, 583 received aid, and 16 had their full need met. Average financial aid package met 76% of need; average scholarship/grant was $5,644; average loan was $3,368. Need-based aid available for part-time students.
Students without need: 159 full-time freshmen who did not demonstrate need for aid received scholarships/grants; average award was $4,350. No-need awards available for academics, alumni affiliation, athletics, leadership, minority status, ROTC, state/district residency.
Scholarships offered: 20 full-time freshmen received athletic scholarships; average amount $1,800.
Cumulative student debt: 55% of graduating class had student loans; average debt was $23,437.

FINANCIAL AID PROCEDURES

Forms required: FAFSA.
Dates and Deadlines: Priority date 2/15; no closing date. Applicants notified on a rolling basis starting 3/1; must reply within 3 week(s) of notification.
Transfers: Priority date 3/1; no deadline. Applicants notified on a rolling basis starting 4/1; must reply within 3 week(s) of notification.

CONTACT

Katherine Allen, Director of Financial Aid
4901 Evergreen Road, 1145 UC, Dearborn, MI 48128-1491
(313) 593-5000

University of Michigan: Flint

Flint, Michigan
www.umflint.edu — Federal Code: 002327

4-year public university and branch campus college in small city.
Enrollment: 6,677 undergrads, 35% part-time. 727 full-time freshmen.
Selectivity: Admits 50 to 75% of applicants.

BASIC COSTS (2012-2013)

Tuition and fees: $9,514; out-of-state residents $18,166.
Per-credit charge: $359; out-of-state residents $717.
Room and board: $7,506.

FINANCIAL AID PICTURE (2011-2012)

Students with need: Out of 638 full-time freshmen who applied for aid, 501 were judged to have need. Of these, 477 received aid, and 32 had their full need met. Average financial aid package met 73% of need; average scholarship/grant was $5,595; average loan was $3,287. For part-time students, average financial aid package was $9,571.
Students without need: 54 full-time freshmen who did not demonstrate need for aid received scholarships/grants; average award was $3,256. No-need awards available for academics, art, leadership, music/drama.
Cumulative student debt: 71% of graduating class had student loans; average debt was $26,899.
Additional info: SAT/ACT scores must be submitted for scholarship consideration.

FINANCIAL AID PROCEDURES

Forms required: FAFSA, institutional form.
Dates and Deadlines: Priority date 3/1; no closing date. Applicants notified on a rolling basis starting 3/15.
Transfers: Must not be in default or owe refunds for Title IV aid.

CONTACT

Lori Vedder, Financial Aid Director
303 East Kearsley Street, Flint, MI 48502-1950
(810) 762-3444

Walsh College of Accountancy and Business Administration

Troy, Michigan
www.walshcollege.edu — Federal Code: 004071

Upper-division private business college in large city.
Enrollment: 1,019 undergrads, 89% part-time.

BASIC COSTS (2012-2013)
Tuition and fees: $11,050.
Per-credit charge: $360.

FINANCIAL AID PICTURE (2011-2012)
Students with need: Average financial aid package for all full-time undergraduates was $8,473. Need-based aid available for part-time students.
Students without need: No-need awards available for academics.

FINANCIAL AID PROCEDURES
Forms required: FAFSA.
Dates and Deadlines: Priority date 3/23; no closing date.
Transfers: Priority date 3/1; no deadline. Applicants notified on a rolling basis.

CONTACT
Howard Thomas, Director, Financial Aid
PO Box 7006, Troy, MI 48007-7006
(248) 823-1285

Wayne County Community College
Detroit, Michigan
www.wcccd.edu Federal Code: 009230

2-year public community and liberal arts college in very large city.
Enrollment: 14,687 undergrads, 74% part-time. 1,236 full-time freshmen.
Selectivity: Open admission; but selective for some programs.

BASIC COSTS (2012-2013)
Tuition and fees: $3,340; out-of-district residents $3,670; out-of-state residents $4,570.
Per-credit charge: $99; out-of-district residents $110; out-of-state residents $140.

FINANCIAL AID PICTURE
Students with need: Need-based aid available for full-time and part-time students.
Additional info: High school diploma, GED, or passing grade on ABT required for financial aid.

FINANCIAL AID PROCEDURES
Forms required: FAFSA.
Dates and Deadlines: Priority date 5/1; no closing date. Applicants notified on a rolling basis starting 5/1.

CONTACT
Myra Hawkins, Executive District Director of Financial Aid
801 West Fort Street, Detroit, MI 48226
(313) 496-2614

Wayne State University
Detroit, Michigan
www.wayne.edu Federal Code: 002329

4-year public university in very large city.
Enrollment: 18,532 undergrads, 34% part-time. 2,173 full-time freshmen.
Selectivity: Admits over 75% of applicants.

BASIC COSTS (2012-2013)
Tuition and fees: $10,190; out-of-state residents $21,735.
Room and board: $8,048.

FINANCIAL AID PICTURE
Students with need: Need-based aid available for full-time and part-time students. Work study available nights, weekends, and for part-time students.
Students without need: No-need awards available for academics, art, athletics, leadership, music/drama.
Scholarships offered: Presidential Scholarships; full tuition and fees; offered to top academic students; more than 350 available.
Additional info: Need-based institutional grants cover tuition and fees with grants and EFC (no loans).

FINANCIAL AID PROCEDURES
Forms required: FAFSA.
Dates and Deadlines: Priority date 2/15; closing date 4/30. Applicants notified on a rolling basis starting 3/1; must reply within 2 week(s) of notification.
Transfers: No deadline. Applicants notified on a rolling basis starting 3/1; must reply within 2 week(s) of notification.

CONTACT
Al Hermsen, Sr. Director of Student Financial Aid
P.O. Box 02759, Detroit, MI 48202-0759
(313) 577-3378

West Shore Community College
Scottville, Michigan
www.westshore.edu Federal Code: 007950

2-year public community college in rural community.
Enrollment: 1,476 undergrads.
Selectivity: Open admission; but selective for some programs.

BASIC COSTS (2012-2013)
Tuition and fees: $2,772; out-of-district residents $4,782; out-of-state residents $6,282.
Per-credit charge: $83; out-of-district residents $150; out-of-state residents $200.

FINANCIAL AID PICTURE (2012-2013)
Students with need: For part-time students, average financial aid package was $453.
Cumulative student debt: 37% of graduating class had student loans; average debt was $6,479.

FINANCIAL AID PROCEDURES
Forms required: FAFSA, institutional form.
Dates and Deadlines: Priority date 6/1; no closing date. Applicants notified on a rolling basis starting 5/15; must reply within 2 week(s) of notification.

CONTACT
Juliann Murphy, Director of Financial Aid
3000 North Stiles Road, P.O. Box 277, Scottville, MI 49454-0277
(231) 845-5518

Western Michigan University
Kalamazoo, Michigan
www.wmich.edu Federal Code: 002330

4-year public university in small city.
Enrollment: 19,044 undergrads, 15% part-time. 3,301 full-time freshmen.
Selectivity: Admits over 75% of applicants.

BASIC COSTS (2012-2013)
Tuition and fees: $9,982; out-of-state residents $23,262.
Per-credit charge: $316; out-of-state residents $775.
Room and board: $8,414.

FINANCIAL AID PICTURE (2011-2012)
Students with need: Out of 2,690 full-time freshmen who applied for aid, 2,224 were judged to have need. Of these, 2,224 received aid, and 534 had their full need met. Average financial aid package met 80% of need; average scholarship/grant was $5,604; average loan was $2,727. Need-based aid available for part-time students.

Students without need: 253 full-time freshmen who did not demonstrate need for aid received scholarships/grants; average award was $4,278. No-need awards available for academics, alumni affiliation, art, athletics, minority status, music/drama, ROTC, state/district residency.

Scholarships offered: ***Merit:*** Medallion Scholarship, $50,000, may be renewed for up to eight consecutive semesters, based on high school performance (cumulative GPA of 3.7, ACT composite of 26 or higher or SAT combined score of 1170 or higher), minimum of 20 available; Dean's Scholarship (finalists of and not awarded Medallion), $6,000 over two years, recipients who live in the residence halls in both the 2013-14 and 2014-15 academic years will be awarded a $4,000 Residence Hall Award for the 2014-15 academic year, minimum of 20 available . ***Athletic:*** 75 full-time freshmen received athletic scholarships; average amount $20,764.

Cumulative student debt: 62% of graduating class had student loans; average debt was $30,867.

FINANCIAL AID PROCEDURES

Forms required: FAFSA.

Dates and Deadlines: Priority date 3/1; no closing date. Applicants notified on a rolling basis starting 3/15.

Transfers: No deadline. Applicants notified on a rolling basis starting 3/15.

CONTACT

Mark Delorey, Director of Financial Aid
1903 West Michigan Avenue, Kalamazoo, MI 49008-5211
(269) 387-6000

Minnesota

Academy College

Bloomington, Minnesota
www.academycollege.edu Federal Code: 013505

2-year for-profit junior and career college in large city.
Enrollment: 152 undergrads.
Selectivity: Open admission.

FINANCIAL AID PICTURE

Students with need: Need-based aid available for full-time and part-time students. Work study available nights, weekends, and for part-time students.

FINANCIAL AID PROCEDURES

Forms required: FAFSA, institutional form.

Dates and Deadlines: Applicants notified on a rolling basis.

CONTACT

Mary Erickson, Director of Administration
1101 East 78th Street, Bloomington, MN 55420
(952) 851-0066

Alexandria Technical and Community College

Alexandria, Minnesota
www.alextech.edu Federal Code: 005544

2-year public community and technical college in large town.
Enrollment: 1,910 undergrads.
Selectivity: Open admission; but selective for some programs.

BASIC COSTS (2012-2013)

Tuition and fees: $5,378; out-of-state residents $5,378.
Per-credit charge: $161.

Additional info: Tuition for online courses $199 per-credit hour, some high cost courses have a differentiated tuition. Laptop lease required for some programs-approximately $800 annually.

FINANCIAL AID PICTURE

Students with need: Need-based aid available for full-time and part-time students.

Students without need: This college awards aid only to students with need.

FINANCIAL AID PROCEDURES

Forms required: FAFSA, institutional form.

Dates and Deadlines: Priority date 5/1; no closing date. Applicants notified on a rolling basis starting 6/30; must reply within 2 week(s) of notification.

Transfers: No deadline. Applicants notified on a rolling basis; must reply within 2 week(s) of notification.

CONTACT

Steve Richards, Dean of Technology & Student Financial Services
1601 Jefferson Street, Alexandria, MN 56308-3799
(320) 762-4540

Anoka Technical College

Anoka, Minnesota
www.anokatech.edu Federal Code: 007350

2-year public technical college in large town.
Enrollment: 2,061 undergrads.
Selectivity: Open admission; but selective for some programs.

BASIC COSTS (2012-2013)

Tuition and fees: $5,589; out-of-state residents $5,589.
Per-credit charge: $167.

FINANCIAL AID PICTURE

Students with need: Need-based aid available for full-time and part-time students. Work study available nights.

Students without need: This college awards aid only to students with need.

FINANCIAL AID PROCEDURES

Forms required: FAFSA.

Dates and Deadlines: Applicants notified on a rolling basis starting 7/1.

CONTACT

Lucy Ross, Director of Financial Aid
1355 West Highway 10, Anoka, MN 55303
(763) 576-4700

Anoka-Ramsey Community College

Coon Rapids, Minnesota
www.anokaramsey.edu Federal Code: 002332

2-year public community college in small city.
Enrollment: 7,120 undergrads.
Selectivity: Open admission; but selective for some programs.

BASIC COSTS (2012-2013)

Tuition and fees: $4,916; out-of-state residents $4,916.
Per-credit charge: $145.

FINANCIAL AID PICTURE

Students with need: Need-based aid available for full-time and part-time students. Work study available nights, weekends, and for part-time students.

Students without need: This college awards aid only to students with need.

FINANCIAL AID PROCEDURES
Forms required: FAFSA, institutional form.
Dates and Deadlines: Priority date 4/1; no closing date. Applicants notified on a rolling basis; must reply within 2 week(s) of notification.

CONTACT
Karla Seymour, Financial Aid Officer
11200 Mississippi Boulevard NW, Coon Rapids, MN 55433
(763) 433-1500

Art Institutes International Minnesota
Minneapolis, Minnesota
www.artinstitutes.edu/minneapolis Federal Code: 010248

4-year for-profit culinary school and visual arts college in large city.
Enrollment: 1,423 undergrads.
Selectivity: Open admission.

BASIC COSTS (2012-2013)
Tuition and fees: $23,088.
Per-credit charge: $481.
Additional info: Typical full-time credit load 16 credits/quarter. Starter kits for most programs $350 to $1,005.

FINANCIAL AID PICTURE (2012-2013)
Students with need: Need-based aid available for full-time and part-time students.
Students without need: No-need awards available for academics.

FINANCIAL AID PROCEDURES
Forms required: FAFSA.

CONTACT
Dave Aune, Director of Administrative and Financial Services
15 South Ninth Street, Minneapolis, MN 55402
(612) 332-3361

Augsburg College
Minneapolis, Minnesota
www.augsburg.edu Federal Code: 002334

4-year private liberal arts college in large city, affiliated with Evangelical Lutheran Church in America.
Enrollment: 2,846 undergrads, 17% part-time. 381 full-time freshmen.
Selectivity: Admits 50 to 75% of applicants.

BASIC COSTS (2012-2013)
Tuition and fees: $31,937.
Room and board: $8,458.

FINANCIAL AID PICTURE
Students with need: Need-based aid available for full-time and part-time students.
Students without need: No-need awards available for academics, alumni affiliation, leadership, minority status, music/drama, religious affiliation.
Scholarships offered: President's Scholarships: up to full tuition annually; 3.7 GPA and ACT/SAT score 27 or higher; number awarded determined annually. Regents Scholarships: $4,000-$10,000; top 30% of class rank or test scores. Must apply before 5/1 for both scholarships.

FINANCIAL AID PROCEDURES
Forms required: FAFSA.
Dates and Deadlines: Priority date 4/15; closing date 8/1. Applicants notified on a rolling basis starting 3/1; must reply within 3 week(s) of notification.
Transfers: Priority date 7/1; closing date 8/15. Applicants notified on a rolling basis starting 3/1; must reply by 9/1.

CONTACT
Paul Terrio, Director of Enrollment Services
2211 Riverside Avenue, Minneapolis, MN 55454
(612) 330-1046

Bemidji State University
Bemidji, Minnesota
www.bemidjistate.edu Federal Code: 002336

4-year public university in large town.
Enrollment: 4,371 undergrads, 20% part-time. 709 full-time freshmen.
Selectivity: Admits less than 50% of applicants.

BASIC COSTS (2012-2013)
Tuition and fees: $8,105; out-of-state residents $8,105.
Per-credit charge: $250.
Room and board: $6,970.
Additional info: Tuition/fee waivers available for minority students.

FINANCIAL AID PICTURE (2011-2012)
Students with need: Out of 615 full-time freshmen who applied for aid, 440 were judged to have need. Of these, 438 received aid, and 104 had their full need met. Average financial aid package met 71% of need; average scholarship/grant was $6,030; average loan was $3,598. For part-time students, average financial aid package was $6,695.
Students without need: 163 full-time freshmen who did not demonstrate need for aid received scholarships/grants; average award was $9,967. No-need awards available for academics, alumni affiliation, art, athletics, job skills, leadership, minority status, music/drama, ROTC.
Scholarships offered: 87 full-time freshmen received athletic scholarships; average amount $4,080.

FINANCIAL AID PROCEDURES
Forms required: FAFSA, institutional form.
Dates and Deadlines: Closing date 3/31. Applicants notified on a rolling basis starting 3/24.

CONTACT
Paul Lindseth, Director of Financial Aid
102 Deputy Hall #13, Bemidji, MN 56601-2699
(218) 755-2034

Bethany Lutheran College
Mankato, Minnesota
www.blc.edu Federal Code: 002337

4-year private liberal arts college in small city, affiliated with Evangelical Lutheran Synod.
Enrollment: 575 undergrads, 3% part-time. 162 full-time freshmen.
Selectivity: Admits over 75% of applicants.

BASIC COSTS (2013-2014)
Tuition and fees: $23,950.
Per-credit charge: $990.
Room and board: $7,470.

FINANCIAL AID PICTURE (2011-2012)
Students with need: Out of 153 full-time freshmen who applied for aid, 134 were judged to have need. Of these, 134 received aid, and 19 had their full need met. Average financial aid package met 84% of need; average scholarship/grant was $15,084; average loan was $5,261. For part-time students, average financial aid package was $8,554.
Students without need: 22 full-time freshmen who did not demonstrate need for aid received scholarships/grants; average award was $7,461. No-need awards available for academics, art, music/drama.

Cumulative student debt: 94% of graduating class had student loans; average debt was $31,884.

FINANCIAL AID PROCEDURES

Forms required: FAFSA, institutional form.

Dates and Deadlines: Priority date 4/15; no closing date. Applicants notified on a rolling basis starting 3/1; must reply within 4 week(s) of notification.

Transfers: No deadline. Applicants notified on a rolling basis starting 3/1; must reply within 4 week(s) of notification.

CONTACT

Jeffrey Younge, Financial Aid Director
700 Luther Drive, Mankato, MN 56001-4490
(507) 344-7328

Bethel University

Saint Paul, Minnesota
www.bethel.edu
Federal Code: 002338

4-year private university and liberal arts college in large city, affiliated with Converge Worldwide.

Enrollment: 3,361 undergrads, 21% part-time. 674 full-time freshmen.

Selectivity: Admits 50 to 75% of applicants.

BASIC COSTS (2013-2014)

Tuition and fees: $31,760.
Per-credit charge: $1,320.
Room and board: $9,200.
Additional info: Housing rate frozen as long as student continues to reside in campus housing.

FINANCIAL AID PICTURE (2011-2012)

Students with need: Out of 632 full-time freshmen who applied for aid, 529 were judged to have need. Of these, 529 received aid, and 93 had their full need met. Average financial aid package met 76% of need; average scholarship/grant was $16,682; average loan was $3,811. For part-time students, average financial aid package was $12,180.

Students without need: 140 full-time freshmen who did not demonstrate need for aid received scholarships/grants; average award was $9,908. No-need awards available for academics, alumni affiliation, art, leadership, music/drama, state/district residency.

Scholarships offered: Academic and Achievement Scholarships ranging from $4,000 to $15,000 available to qualified students. Leadership scholarships available up to $4,000. Performance scholarships available for theatre, music, art, and forensics.

Cumulative student debt: 76% of graduating class had student loans; average debt was $32,483.

FINANCIAL AID PROCEDURES

Forms required: FAFSA, institutional form.

Dates and Deadlines: Priority date 4/15; no closing date. Applicants notified on a rolling basis starting 3/1.

Transfers: Phi Theta Kappa Scholarship ($1,000 per year) awarded to transfer students with a minimum cumulative college GPA of 3.00 and previous membership in Phi Theta Kappa academic honor society for at least one term.

CONTACT

Jeffrey Olson, Director of Financial Aid
3900 Bethel Dr., Saint Paul, MN 55112
(651) 638-6241

Capella University

Minneapolis, Minnesota
www.capella.edu
Federal Code: 032673

4-year for-profit virtual university in very large city.

Enrollment: 8,066 undergrads.

Selectivity: Open admission; but selective for some programs.

BASIC COSTS (2012-2013)

Tuition and fees: $15,750.
Per-credit charge: $350.

FINANCIAL AID PICTURE

Students with need: Need-based aid available for full-time and part-time students.

CONTACT

Tonia Teasley, VP Learner Services and Operations
225 South Sixth Street, Minneapolis, MN 55402
(888) 227-3552

Carleton College

Northfield, Minnesota
www.carleton.edu
Federal Code: 002340
CSS Code: 6081

4-year private liberal arts college in large town.

Enrollment: 2,035 undergrads. 528 full-time freshmen.

Selectivity: Admits less than 50% of applicants.

BASIC COSTS (2012-2013)

Tuition and fees: $44,445.
Room and board: $11,553.

FINANCIAL AID PICTURE (2011-2012)

Students with need: Out of 380 full-time freshmen who applied for aid, 294 were judged to have need. Of these, 294 received aid, and 294 had their full need met. Average financial aid package met 100% of need; average scholarship/grant was $31,445; average loan was $4,138.

Students without need: This college awards aid only to students with need.

Scholarships offered: National Merit, National Achievement, National Hispanic Scholars Awards: $2,000 per year; based on outstanding academic achievement and promise.

Cumulative student debt: 40% of graduating class had student loans; average debt was $17,289.

Additional info: Full financial need of all admitted applicants met through combination of work, loans, grants.

FINANCIAL AID PROCEDURES

Forms required: FAFSA, CSS PROFILE.

Dates and Deadlines: Closing date 2/15. Applicants notified by 4/1; must reply by 5/1 or within 2 week(s) of notification.

Transfers: Closing date 3/15. Applicants notified by 5/15; must reply by 6/1 or within 2 week(s) of notification.

CONTACT

Rodney Oto, Director of Student Financial Services
100 South College Street, Northfield, MN 55057
(507) 222-4138

Central Lakes College

Brainerd, Minnesota
www.clcmn.edu
Federal Code: 002339

2-year public community and technical college in large town.

Enrollment: 2,748 undergrads.

Selectivity: Open admission; but selective for some programs.

BASIC COSTS (2012-2013)

Tuition and fees: $5,393; out-of-state residents $5,393.
Per-credit charge: $159.

FINANCIAL AID PICTURE (2011-2012)
Students with need: 40% of average financial aid package awarded as scholarships/grants, 60% awarded as loans/jobs. Need-based aid available for part-time students.

FINANCIAL AID PROCEDURES
Forms required: FAFSA, institutional form.
Dates and Deadlines: Priority date 6/1; no closing date. Applicants notified on a rolling basis starting 6/10; must reply within 2 week(s) of notification.

CONTACT
Mike Barnaby, Director of Financial Aid
501 West College Drive, Brainerd, MN 56401
(218) 855-8025

Century College

White Bear Lake, Minnesota
www.century.edu Federal Code: 010546

2-year public community and technical college in large town.
Enrollment: 9,899 undergrads, 56% part-time. 933 full-time freshmen.
Selectivity: Open admission; but selective for some programs.

BASIC COSTS (2012-2013)
Tuition and fees: $5,357; out-of-state residents $5,357.
Per-credit charge: $161.

FINANCIAL AID PICTURE (2011-2012)
Students with need: Need-based aid available for full-time and part-time students.
Students without need: This college awards aid only to students with need.
Additional info: Minnesota resident out of high school or not enrolled in college for 7 years without bachelor's or other higher degree offered cost of tuition and books for 1 course in 1 semester up to maximum of 5 credits.

FINANCIAL AID PROCEDURES
Forms required: FAFSA.
Dates and Deadlines: Priority date 5/1; no closing date. Applicants notified on a rolling basis starting 5/15.
Transfers: Priority date 7/1; no deadline. Applicants notified on a rolling basis starting 5/15.

CONTACT
Pam Engebretson, Financial Aid Director
3300 Century Avenue North, White Bear Lake, MN 55110
(651) 779-3305

College of St. Benedict

St. Joseph, Minnesota
www.csbsju.edu Federal Code: 002341

4-year private liberal arts college for women in small town, affiliated with Roman Catholic Church.
Enrollment: 2,070 undergrads, 2% part-time. 490 full-time freshmen.
Selectivity: Admits over 75% of applicants.

BASIC COSTS (2013-2014)
Tuition and fees: $37,926.
Per-credit charge: $1,541.
Room and board: $9,644.
Additional info: Meal plan is flexible meal plan.

FINANCIAL AID PICTURE (2012-2013)
Students with need: Out of 415 full-time freshmen who applied for aid, 354 were judged to have need. Of these, 354 received aid, and 157 had their full need met. Average financial aid package met 90% of need; average scholarship/grant was $24,394; average loan was $4,289. For part-time students, average financial aid package was $11,700.
Students without need: 115 full-time freshmen who did not demonstrate need for aid received scholarships/grants; average award was $15,133. No-need awards available for academics, art, leadership, music/drama, ROTC.
Scholarships offered: Trustees' Scholarships: $18,000-$20,000; based on 3.6 GPA, 30 ACT/1980 SAT, demonstrated leadership and service, faculty interview. President's Scholarships: $13,000-$16,500; based on GPA, high school rank, ACT/SAT, leadership and service. Dean's Scholarships: $5,000-$12,000; based on GPA, high school rank, ACT/SAT, leadership and service. Art, music and theater scholarships: up to $4,000. Intercultural LEAD fellowship: up to $10,000; based on GPA, leadership, financial need, first generation college students, commitment to intercultural issues and action, diversity of high school. Army ROTC and ROTC Nursing Scholarships: based on demonstrated leadership potential, GPA, class standing, ACT/SAT, high achievement with broad interests and willingness to take on challenges. Catholic High School Scholarship: $3,000; for students attending Catholic high schools outside Minnesota. Saints Scholarship: $1,000-$3,000; for students attending public high schools outside Minnesota. FoCuS Scholarship: $20,000 renewable for students majoring in Chemistry; Bonner Leader Scholarship: $2,500 renewable for students with a strong interest in doing service at CSB/SJU and financial need.
Cumulative student debt: 74% of graduating class had student loans; average debt was $40,030.
Additional info: Scholarship letters will be mailed on a rolling basis approximately two weeks from the time the admission acceptance letter is sent.

FINANCIAL AID PROCEDURES
Forms required: FAFSA, institutional form.
Dates and Deadlines: Priority date 3/15; no closing date. Applicants notified on a rolling basis starting 3/15; must reply by 5/1.
Transfers: No deadline. Applicants notified on a rolling basis starting 3/15; must reply by 5/1. Phi Theta Kappa Scholarship; $1,500 renewable; for members of Phi Theta Kappa.

CONTACT
Stuart Perry, Executive Director of Financial Aid
College of Saint Benedict/Saint John's University, Collegeville, MN 56321-7155
(320) 363-5388

College of St. Scholastica

Duluth, Minnesota
www.css.edu Federal Code: 002343

4-year private liberal arts college in small city, affiliated with Roman Catholic Church.
Enrollment: 2,843 undergrads, 14% part-time. 477 full-time freshmen.
Selectivity: Admits over 75% of applicants.

BASIC COSTS (2013-2014)
Tuition and fees: $31,612.
Per-credit charge: $981.
Room and board: $8,348.
Additional info: Tuition/fee waivers available for minority students.

FINANCIAL AID PICTURE (2012-2013)
Students with need: Out of 434 full-time freshmen who applied for aid, 384 were judged to have need. Of these, 384 received aid, and 110 had their full need met. Average financial aid package met 75% of need; average scholarship/grant was $7,345; average loan was $3,435. For part-time students, average financial aid package was $6,736.
Students without need: 45 full-time freshmen who did not demonstrate need for aid received scholarships/grants; average award was $12,717. No-need awards available for academics, alumni affiliation, minority status, music/drama, religious affiliation, state/district residency.

Scholarships offered: Benedictine Scholarship: $5,000-$15,000 per year for up to 4 years. Access Scholarship: $8,500. Both based on GPA, SAT/ACT score; unlimited number awarded. Summit Scholarship: an additional $1,500 for those who qualify for the Benedictine Scholarship and who graduate at the top of their high school class or ACT score greater than 30. Divisional Merit Awards: $4,000; available to transfer students; based on major; unlimited number awarded.
Cumulative student debt: 75% of graduating class had student loans; average debt was $39,918.

FINANCIAL AID PROCEDURES
Forms required: FAFSA.
Dates and Deadlines: Priority date 3/1; no closing date. Applicants notified on a rolling basis starting 3/1; must reply by 5/1 or within 2 week(s) of notification.

CONTACT
Jon Erickson, Director of Financial Aid
1200 Kenwood Avenue, Duluth, MN 55811-4199
(218) 723-6570

College of Visual Arts
Saint Paul, Minnesota
www.cva.edu Federal Code: 007462

4-year private visual arts college in large city.
Enrollment: 177 undergrads, 4% part-time. 63 full-time freshmen.
Selectivity: Admits 50 to 75% of applicants.

BASIC COSTS (2012-2013)
Tuition and fees: $25,761.
Per-credit charge: $1,258.

FINANCIAL AID PICTURE (2011-2012)
Students with need: Average financial aid package met 60% of need; average scholarship/grant was $12,600; average loan was $3,400. Need-based aid available for part-time students.
Students without need: No-need awards available for academics, art.
Scholarships offered: Merit scholarship program provides annual awards ranging from $2,000 to $8,500; stipends are based on artistic and academic merit.
Cumulative student debt: 90% of graduating class had student loans; average debt was $43,000.

FINANCIAL AID PROCEDURES
Forms required: FAFSA, institutional form.
Dates and Deadlines: Priority date 3/1; no closing date. Applicants notified on a rolling basis starting 2/15; must reply within 2 week(s) of notification.
Transfers: Priority date 4/15. Applicants notified on a rolling basis starting 3/1; must reply within 2 week(s) of notification.

CONTACT
David Woodward, Director of Financial Aid
344 Summit Avenue, Saint Paul, MN 55102-2199
(651) 757-4000

Concordia College: Moorhead
Moorhead, Minnesota
www.ConcordiaCollege.edu Federal Code: 002346

4-year private liberal arts college in large town, affiliated with Evangelical Lutheran Church in America.
Enrollment: 2,521 undergrads, 1% part-time. 722 full-time freshmen.
Selectivity: Admits over 75% of applicants.

BASIC COSTS (2013-2014)
Tuition and fees: $32,814.
Per-credit charge: $1,280.
Room and board: $7,160.

FINANCIAL AID PICTURE (2011-2012)
Students with need: Out of 672 full-time freshmen who applied for aid, 576 were judged to have need. Of these, 576 received aid, and 123 had their full need met. Average financial aid package met 92% of need; average scholarship/grant was $18,449; average loan was $6,909. For part-time students, average financial aid package was $5,487.
Students without need: 136 full-time freshmen who did not demonstrate need for aid received scholarships/grants; average award was $11,914. No-need awards available for academics, art, leadership, minority status, music/drama.
Scholarships offered: Concordia College Regents Scholarship; tuition for 4 years; based on 3.9 GPA and 31 ACT/2060 SAT; 5 awarded annually. Presidential Distinction Scholarships; $17,000 per year up to 4 years; eligibility based on 3.8 GPA and 26 ACT/1770 SAT; approximately 80 awarded. Faculty Scholarships; $16,000 per year up to 4 years; eligibility based on 3.8 GPA and 26 ACT/1770 SAT; approximately 160 awarded. National Merit Scholars; National Merit finalists who name Concordia as their first choice receive minimum of $17,000 per year. Excellence Scholarships; $13,000 to $15,000 per year; based on academic achievement. Concordia College Scholarships; $7,000 to $11,000 per year; for students who show strong potential for success and contribution to the Concordia community. Performance Scholarships; $2,500 per year for up to 4 years; for excellence in music performance, theater performance, speech and debate, and visual arts.

FINANCIAL AID PROCEDURES
Forms required: FAFSA.
Dates and Deadlines: Applicants notified on a rolling basis starting 3/15.
Transfers: No deadline. Applicants notified on a rolling basis starting 4/1. Eligible transfer students are offered merit aid limited to the number of semesters needed to complete their degree as determined through the transfer credit evaluation.

CONTACT
Eric Addington, Director of Financial Aid
901 Eighth Street South, Moorhead, MN 56562
(218) 299-3010

Concordia University St. Paul
Saint Paul, Minnesota
www.csp.edu Federal Code: 002347

4-year private university in large city, affiliated with Lutheran Church - Missouri Synod.
Enrollment: 1,515 undergrads, 40% part-time. 181 full-time freshmen.
Selectivity: Admits 50 to 75% of applicants.

BASIC COSTS (2013-2014)
Tuition and fees: $19,700.
Per-credit charge: $635.
Room and board: $7,750.

FINANCIAL AID PICTURE (2012-2013)
Students with need: Out of 176 full-time freshmen who applied for aid, 162 were judged to have need. Of these, 162 received aid, and 25 had their full need met. Average financial aid package met 79% of need; average scholarship/grant was $21,183; average loan was $3,940. For part-time students, average financial aid package was $7,056.
Students without need: 8 full-time freshmen who did not demonstrate need for aid received scholarships/grants; average award was $13,100. No-need awards available for academics, art, athletics, minority status, music/drama, religious affiliation.

Cumulative student debt: 87% of graduating class had student loans; average debt was $42,020.
Additional info: Church districts and local congregations are major sources of aid for church-vocation students.

FINANCIAL AID PROCEDURES
Forms required: FAFSA, institutional form.
Dates and Deadlines: Priority date 5/1; no closing date. Applicants notified on a rolling basis starting 3/1.
Transfers: No deadline. Applicants notified on a rolling basis. Adult learners in degree completion programs typically not eligible for most types of institutional scholarships/grants because of discounted tuition rates.

CONTACT
Jeanie Peck, Director of Financial Aid
1282 Concordia Ave, St. Paul, MN 55104-5494
(651) 603-6300

Crossroads College
Rochester, Minnesota
www.crossroadscollege.edu Federal Code: 002366

4-year private Bible college in small city, affiliated with Christian Church.
Enrollment: 143 undergrads, 11% part-time. 26 full-time freshmen.
Selectivity: Admits over 75% of applicants.

BASIC COSTS (2012-2013)
Tuition and fees: $15,280.
Per-credit charge: $425.
Additional info: Board plan not available. Cost of room only: $4070.

FINANCIAL AID PICTURE
Students with need: Need-based aid available for full-time and part-time students. Work study available nights.
Students without need: No-need awards available for academics, leadership, music/drama, religious affiliation.
Scholarships offered: Home-Educated Grant: $500 per semester if home-schooled for two years during high school. Travel Grant: $500 per semester for student who resides in states other than Minnesota, Iowa, Wisconsin. Crossroads Matching Grant: church funds matched up to $500 per semester; awarded to first year students.

FINANCIAL AID PROCEDURES
Forms required: FAFSA, institutional form.
Dates and Deadlines: Priority date 4/1; no closing date. Applicants notified on a rolling basis starting 2/1; must reply within 4 week(s) of notification.
Transfers: Mid-year transfer students will have financial aid calculated with the prior school term award in mind.

CONTACT
Polly Kellogg-Bradley, Director of Financial Aid
920 Mayowood Road SW, Rochester, MN 55902
(507) 288-4563

Crown College
Saint Bonifacius, Minnesota
www.crown.edu Federal Code: 002383

4-year private liberal arts college in small town, affiliated with Christian and Missionary Alliance.
Enrollment: 885 full-time undergrads.

BASIC COSTS (2012-2013)
Tuition and fees: $22,100.
Per-credit charge: $920.
Room and board: $7,480.
Additional info: Tuition/fee waivers available for minority students.

FINANCIAL AID PICTURE
Students with need: Need-based aid available for full-time and part-time students. Work study available nights, weekends, and for part-time students.
Students without need: No-need awards available for academics, alumni affiliation, leadership, minority status, music/drama, religious affiliation.

FINANCIAL AID PROCEDURES
Forms required: FAFSA.
Dates and Deadlines: Priority date 4/1; no closing date. Applicants notified on a rolling basis starting 4/1; must reply within 3 week(s) of notification.
Transfers: No deadline. Applicants notified on a rolling basis; must reply within 3 week(s) of notification. Cannot have attended more than 4 years of college to receive state grant.

CONTACT
Shannon Schaaf, Director of Financial Aid
8700 College View Drive, St. Bonifacius, MN 55375-9001
(952) 446-4177

Dakota County Technical College
Rosemount, Minnesota
www.dctc.edu Federal Code: 010402

2-year public technical college in large town.
Enrollment: 2,866 undergrads, 42% part-time. 637 full-time freshmen.
Selectivity: Open admission; but selective for some programs.

BASIC COSTS (2012-2013)
Tuition and fees: $5,693; out-of-state residents $5,693.
Per-credit charge: $169.

FINANCIAL AID PICTURE (2011-2012)
Students with need: 49% of average financial aid package awarded as scholarships/grants, 51% awarded as loans/jobs. Need-based aid available for part-time students. Work study available nights.
Students without need: No-need awards available for academics, athletics, leadership.

FINANCIAL AID PROCEDURES
Forms required: FAFSA.
Dates and Deadlines: Applicants notified on a rolling basis starting 3/15.
Transfers: No deadline. FAFSA must be processed within 14 days of the first day of the semester to be considered for Minnesota State Grant for the semester.

CONTACT
Scott Roelke, Director of Scholarships and Financial Aid
1300 145th Street East, Rosemount, MN 55068
(651) 423-8299

Dunwoody College of Technology
Minneapolis, Minnesota
www.dunwoody.edu

2-year private technical college in very large city.
Enrollment: 1,052 undergrads, 21% part-time. 194 full-time freshmen.
Selectivity: Admits 50 to 75% of applicants.

BASIC COSTS (2013-2014)
Tuition and fees: $19,819.
Additional info: Cost of required laptop ranges from $144 to $379. Per-credit-hour charge varies per program.

FINANCIAL AID PICTURE
Students with need: Need-based aid available for full-time and part-time students.

Students without need: No-need awards available for academics.

FINANCIAL AID PROCEDURES

Forms required: FAFSA, state aid form.

Dates and Deadlines: Priority date 6/1; no closing date. Applicants notified on a rolling basis starting 2/1; must reply within 4 week(s) of notification.

Transfers: No deadline. Applicants notified on a rolling basis starting 7/1.

CONTACT

Barbara Charboneau, Director of Financial Aid
818 Dunwoody Boulevard, Minneapolis, MN 55403-1192
(612) 374-5800

Fond du Lac Tribal and Community College

Cloquet, Minnesota
www.fdltcc.edu Federal Code: E00482

2-year public community college in large town.
Enrollment: 2,319 undergrads.
Selectivity: Open admission.

BASIC COSTS (2012-2013)

Tuition and fees: $5,256; out-of-state residents $5,256.
Additional info: Board plan not available. Cost of room only: $3536.

FINANCIAL AID PICTURE

Students with need: Need-based aid available for full-time and part-time students.

Students without need: No-need awards available for academics.

FINANCIAL AID PROCEDURES

Forms required: FAFSA, institutional form.

Dates and Deadlines: Priority date 3/15; no closing date. Applicants notified on a rolling basis starting 4/15.

CONTACT

David Sutherland, Director of Financial Aid
2101 14th Street, Cloquet, MN 55720
(218) 879-0816

Globe University: Minneapolis

Minneapolis, Minnesota
www.globeuniversity.edu Federal Code: 004642

4-year for-profit university and career college in large city.
Enrollment: 167 undergrads.
Selectivity: Open admission; but selective for some programs.

BASIC COSTS (2012-2013)

Tuition and fees: $19,125.
Per-credit charge: $460.

FINANCIAL AID PICTURE

Students with need: Need-based aid available for full-time and part-time students.

FINANCIAL AID PROCEDURES

Forms required: FAFSA, state aid form, institutional form.

Dates and Deadlines: Applicants notified on a rolling basis starting 7/1; must reply within 2 week(s) of notification.

CONTACT

Katie Bergstrom, Director of Financial Aid
80 South 8th Street, Minneapolis, MN 55402
(612) 455-3000

Globe University: Woodbury

Woodbury, Minnesota
www.globeuniversity.edu Federal Code: 004642

4-year for-profit business and health science college in small city.
Enrollment: 983 undergrads.
Selectivity: Open admission; but selective for some programs.

BASIC COSTS (2012-2013)

Tuition and fees: $19,125.
Per-credit charge: $460.

FINANCIAL AID PICTURE

Students with need: Need-based aid available for full-time and part-time students.

FINANCIAL AID PROCEDURES

Forms required: FAFSA, state aid form, institutional form.

Dates and Deadlines: Applicants notified on a rolling basis starting 7/1; must reply within 2 week(s) of notification.

CONTACT

Jill Garcia, Director of Financial Aid
8089 Globe Drive, Woodbury, MN 55125
(651) 730-5100

Gustavus Adolphus College

St. Peter, Minnesota
www.gustavus.edu Federal Code: 002353

4-year private liberal arts college in large town, affiliated with Evangelical Lutheran Church in America.
Enrollment: 2,513 undergrads, 1% part-time. 733 full-time freshmen.
Selectivity: Admits 50 to 75% of applicants.

BASIC COSTS (2013-2014)

Tuition and fees: $39,120.
Room and board: $9,050.

FINANCIAL AID PICTURE (2011-2012)

Students with need: Out of 631 full-time freshmen who applied for aid, 570 were judged to have need. Of these, 562 received aid, and 168 had their full need met. Average financial aid package met 91% of need; average scholarship/grant was $26,577; average loan was $3,128.

Students without need: 171 full-time freshmen who did not demonstrate need for aid received scholarships/grants; average award was $14,912. No-need awards available for academics, alumni affiliation, art, music/drama, ROTC.

Scholarships offered: Presidential Scholarship: $10,000-$14,000. National Merit finalist: $7,500; academic. Legacy Scholarship: $2,500; academic for children or siblings of alumni. Jussi Bjorling Scholarship: $1,000-$4,000; for music; 40 awarded. Anderson Theatre and Dance Scholarship: $2,000; 15 awarded. Dean's Scholarship: $1,000-$10,000; Forensic $500 - $2,000.

Cumulative student debt: 71% of graduating class had student loans; average debt was $28,124.

FINANCIAL AID PROCEDURES

Forms required: FAFSA. CSS PROFILE required of students applying for need-based assistance.

Dates and Deadlines: Priority date 3/15; closing date 5/1. Applicants notified on a rolling basis starting 3/15; must reply by 5/1 or within 2 week(s) of notification.

Transfers: Applicants notified on a rolling basis starting 12/20; must reply by 5/1 or within 2 week(s) of notification.

CONTACT

Doug Minter, Director of Student Financial Assistance
800 West College Avenue, St. Peter, MN 56082
(507) 933-7527

Hamline University

St. Paul, Minnesota
www.hamline.edu Federal Code: 002354

4-year private university and liberal arts college in very large city, affiliated with United Methodist Church.
Enrollment: 2,007 undergrads, 2% part-time. 513 full-time freshmen.
Selectivity: Admits 50 to 75% of applicants.

BASIC COSTS (2013-2014)

Tuition and fees: $35,108.
Per-credit charge: $1,080.
Room and board: $9,090.

FINANCIAL AID PICTURE (2011-2012)

Students with need: Out of 510 full-time freshmen who applied for aid, 452 were judged to have need. Of these, 452 received aid, and 101 had their full need met. Average financial aid package met 86% of need; average scholarship/grant was $21,726; average loan was $3,930. For part-time students, average financial aid package was $6,433.
Students without need: 55 full-time freshmen who did not demonstrate need for aid received scholarships/grants; average award was $14,996. No-need awards available for academics, alumni affiliation, art, leadership, minority status, music/drama, religious affiliation.
Scholarships offered: Academic scholarships ranging from $7,500 to $18,000. Departmental scholarships in biology, chemistry, French, German, music, physics, theater, creative writing: $3,000-$5,000 depending on department. National Merit Finalist Scholarship: $20,000. Bishop Hamline Scholarship - Participation in College Preparedness Program: $6,000. Eagle Scout or Gold Award Scholarships: $3,000. Hamline Heritage Award (legacy scholarship): $2,000. All scholarships renewable for a total of four years.
Cumulative student debt: 77% of graduating class had student loans; average debt was $40,472.

FINANCIAL AID PROCEDURES

Forms required: FAFSA.
Dates and Deadlines: Priority date 3/15; no closing date. Applicants notified on a rolling basis starting 3/15; must reply by 5/1 or within 2 week(s) of notification.
Transfers: Priority date 4/1; no deadline. Applicants notified on a rolling basis starting 4/1; must reply within 2 week(s) of notification.

CONTACT

Lynette Wahl, Director of Financial Aid
1536 Hewitt Avenue, St. Paul, MN 55104-1284
(651) 523-3000

Institute of Production and Recording

Minneapolis, Minnesota
www.ipr.edu Federal Code: 041302

2-year for-profit career college in large city.
Enrollment: 286 undergrads.
Selectivity: Open admission.

BASIC COSTS (2012-2013)

Tuition and fees: $19,125.
Per-credit charge: $460.

FINANCIAL AID PICTURE

Students with need: Need-based aid available for full-time and part-time students.

FINANCIAL AID PROCEDURES

Forms required: FAFSA, state aid form, institutional form.
Dates and Deadlines: Applicants notified on a rolling basis starting 7/1; must reply within 2 week(s) of notification.

CONTACT

Andrea Howie, Director of Financial Aid
300 North 1st Avenue, Suite 500, Minneapolis, MN 55401
(612) 244-2800

Inver Hills Community College

Inver Grove Heights, Minnesota
www.inverhills.edu Federal Code: 006935

2-year public community college in large town.
Enrollment: 5,074 undergrads, 62% part-time. 451 full-time freshmen.
Selectivity: Open admission; but selective for some programs.

BASIC COSTS (2012-2013)

Tuition and fees: $5,542; out-of-state residents $5,542.
Per-credit charge: $168.

FINANCIAL AID PICTURE (2011-2012)

Students with need: 46% of average financial aid package awarded as scholarships/grants, 54% awarded as loans/jobs. Need-based aid available for part-time students. Work study available nights, weekends, and for part-time students.
Students without need: This college awards aid only to students with need.

FINANCIAL AID PROCEDURES

Forms required: FAFSA.
Dates and Deadlines: Applicants notified on a rolling basis starting 4/1.
Transfers: Priority date 4/1; no deadline. Applicants notified on a rolling basis.

CONTACT

Steve Yang, Director of Financial Aid
2500 80th Street East, Inver Grove Heights, MN 55076-3224
(651) 450-3495

Itasca Community College

Grand Rapids, Minnesota
www.itascacc.edu Federal Code: 002356

2-year public community college in large town.
Enrollment: 960 undergrads.
Selectivity: Open admission; but selective for some programs.

BASIC COSTS (2012-2013)

Tuition and fees: $5,301; out-of-state residents $6,483.
Per-credit charge: $158; out-of-state residents $197.
Room and board: $6,292.

FINANCIAL AID PICTURE

Students with need: Need-based aid available for full-time and part-time students. Work study available nights, weekends, and for part-time students.
Students without need: No-need awards available for academics, leadership, music/drama, state/district residency.

FINANCIAL AID PROCEDURES

Forms required: FAFSA.
Dates and Deadlines: Priority date 5/1; no closing date. Applicants notified on a rolling basis starting 4/20.
Transfers: No deadline. Applicants notified on a rolling basis starting 4/20.

CONTACT

Nathan Wright, Financial Aid Director
1851 Highway 169 East, Grand Rapids, MN 55744
(218) 322-2320

Lake Superior College

Duluth, Minnesota
www.lsc.edu
Federal Code: 005757

2-year public community and technical college in small city.
Enrollment: 3,949 undergrads, 48% part-time. 404 full-time freshmen.
Selectivity: Open admission; but selective for some programs.

BASIC COSTS (2012-2013)
Tuition and fees: $5,072; out-of-state residents $9,489.
Per-credit charge: $147; out-of-state residents $295.

FINANCIAL AID PICTURE (2011-2012)
Students with need: 32% of average financial aid package awarded as scholarships/grants, 68% awarded as loans/jobs. Need-based aid available for part-time students. Work study available nights, weekends, and for part-time students.
Students without need: No-need awards available for academics, leadership.

FINANCIAL AID PROCEDURES
Forms required: FAFSA.
Dates and Deadlines: Applicants notified on a rolling basis.
Transfers: No deadline.

CONTACT
LaNita Robinson, Director of Financial Aid
2101 Trinity Road, Duluth, MN 55811
(218) 733-7616

Leech Lake Tribal College

Cass Lake, Minnesota
www.lltc.edu
Federal Code: 030964

2-year public Tribal college grounded in Anishinaabe values. in small town.
Enrollment: 338 undergrads, 25% part-time. 97 full-time freshmen.
Selectivity: Open admission.

BASIC COSTS (2013-2014)
Tuition and fees: $4,432; out-of-state residents $4,432.
Per-credit charge: $140.

FINANCIAL AID PICTURE
Students with need: Need-based aid available for full-time and part-time students.

FINANCIAL AID PROCEDURES
Forms required: FAFSA, state aid form, institutional form.
Dates and Deadlines: Applicants notified on a rolling basis; must reply within 4 week(s) of notification.
Transfers: No deadline. Applicants notified on a rolling basis; must reply within 4 week(s) of notification.

CONTACT
Heather Broda, Director of Financial Aid
PO Box 180, Cass Lake, MN 56633
(218) 335-4270

Macalester College

St. Paul, Minnesota
www.macalester.edu
Federal Code: 002358
CSS Code: 6390

4-year private liberal arts college in very large city, affiliated with Presbyterian Church (USA).
Enrollment: 2,047 undergrads, 1% part-time. 534 full-time freshmen.
Selectivity: Admits less than 50% of applicants.

BASIC COSTS (2013-2014)
Tuition and fees: $45,388.
Per-credit charge: $1,411.
Room and board: $10,068.

FINANCIAL AID PICTURE (2012-2013)
Students with need: Out of 439 full-time freshmen who applied for aid, 395 were judged to have need. Of these, 395 received aid, and 395 had their full need met. Average financial aid package met 100% of need; average scholarship/grant was $33,450; average loan was $3,436. Need-based aid available for part-time students.
Students without need: 20 full-time freshmen who did not demonstrate need for aid received scholarships/grants; average award was $10,425. No-need awards available for academics, minority status.
Scholarships offered: Merit scholarship annual award amounts ranging from $1,000 to $22,000, renewable for four years. Recipients are selected on the basis of the admission application with no additional application required. Approximately 30% of U.S. first-year students were awarded a merit-based scholarship in 2012-2013.
Cumulative student debt: 60% of graduating class had student loans; average debt was $23,285.
Additional info: College constructs a financial aid package that meets full need for all admitted students.

FINANCIAL AID PROCEDURES
Forms required: FAFSA, CSS PROFILE.
Dates and Deadlines: Closing date 2/8. Applicants notified by 4/1; must reply by 5/1.
Transfers: Priority date 4/15; closing date 4/15. Applicants notified by 5/15; must reply within 2 week(s) of notification.

CONTACT
Brian Lindeman, Director of Financial Aid
1600 Grand Avenue, St. Paul, MN 55105-1899
(651) 696-6214

Martin Luther College

New Ulm, Minnesota
www.mlc-wels.edu
Federal Code: 002361

4-year private college of theology and education in large town, affiliated with Wisconsin Evangelical Lutheran Synod.
Enrollment: 720 undergrads, 4% part-time. 179 full-time freshmen.
Selectivity: Admits over 75% of applicants.

BASIC COSTS (2013-2014)
Tuition and fees: $12,300.
Room and board: $4,860.

FINANCIAL AID PICTURE (2011-2012)
Students with need: Out of 160 full-time freshmen who applied for aid, 130 were judged to have need. Of these, 130 received aid, and 16 had their full need met. Average financial aid package met 69% of need; average scholarship/grant was $6,752; average loan was $3,447. For part-time students, average financial aid package was $3,172.
Students without need: 61 full-time freshmen who did not demonstrate need for aid received scholarships/grants; average award was $3,027. No-need awards available for academics, music/drama.
Scholarships offered: Academic Scholarship: $500; 3.75 GPA after 6 semesters of high school or 27 ACT. Presidential Scholarship: $1,000; to student selected as high school valedictorian or ranked first in class after 7 semesters.
Cumulative student debt: 75% of graduating class had student loans; average debt was $12,780.

FINANCIAL AID PROCEDURES
Forms required: FAFSA, institutional form.

Dates and Deadlines: Closing date 4/15. Applicants notified on a rolling basis starting 4/15; must reply by 9/1.

CONTACT

Gene Slettedahl, Director of Financial Aid
1995 Luther Court, New Ulm, MN 56073-3965
(507) 354-8221

Mesabi Range Community and Technical College

Virginia, Minnesota
www.mesabirange.edu Federal Code: 004009

2-year public community and technical college in large town.
Enrollment: 1,538 undergrads.
Selectivity: Open admission.

BASIC COSTS (2012-2013)
Tuition and fees: $5,293; out-of-state residents $6,475.
Per-credit charge: $158; out-of-state residents $197.
Additional info: Board plan not available. Cost of room only: $3858.

FINANCIAL AID PICTURE
Students with need: Need-based aid available for full-time and part-time students. Work study available nights, weekends, and for part-time students.
Students without need: No-need awards available for state/district residency.

FINANCIAL AID PROCEDURES
Forms required: FAFSA, institutional form.
Dates and Deadlines: Priority date 4/22; no closing date. Applicants notified on a rolling basis starting 5/1; must reply within 2 week(s) of notification.

CONTACT

Jodi Pontinen, Director of Financial Aid
1001 Chestnut Street West, Virginia, MN 55792-3448
(218) 741-3095

Metropolitan State University

St. Paul, Minnesota
www.metrostate.edu Federal Code: 010374

4-year public university in very large city.
Enrollment: 7,320 undergrads, 62% part-time. 66 full-time freshmen.
Selectivity: Admits over 75% of applicants.

BASIC COSTS (2012-2013)
Tuition and fees: $6,642; out-of-state residents $13,227.
Per-credit charge: $211; out-of-state residents $430.

FINANCIAL AID PICTURE
Students with need: Need-based aid available for full-time and part-time students. Work study available nights, weekends, and for part-time students.
Students without need: No-need awards available for academics, leadership, minority status, state/district residency.

FINANCIAL AID PROCEDURES
Forms required: FAFSA.
Dates and Deadlines: Priority date 3/1; no closing date. Applicants notified on a rolling basis starting 5/1; must reply within 2 week(s) of notification.

CONTACT

Lois Larson, Director of Financial Aid
700 East Seventh Street, St. Paul, MN 55106-5000
(651) 793-1414

Minneapolis Business College

Roseville, Minnesota
www.minneapolisbusinesscollege.edu
Federal Code: 004645

2-year for-profit business and technical college in very large city.
Enrollment: 220 undergrads. 220 full-time freshmen.
Selectivity: Open admission.

BASIC COSTS (2012-2013)
Tuition and fees: $14,220.
Additional info: Board plan not available. Cost of room only, $6,860.

FINANCIAL AID PICTURE
Students with need: Need-based aid available for full-time students.
Students without need: This college awards aid only to students with need.
Cumulative student debt: 80% of graduating class had student loans; average debt was $10,240.
Additional info: Individual financial planning available for all students to meet the cost of education.

FINANCIAL AID PROCEDURES
Forms required: FAFSA.
Dates and Deadlines: Applicants notified on a rolling basis.

CONTACT

Marie Martin, Director of Student Services
1711 West County Road B, Roseville, MN 55113
(651) 636-7406

Minneapolis College of Art and Design

Minneapolis, Minnesota
www.mcad.edu Federal Code: 002365

4-year private visual arts college in very large city.
Enrollment: 613 undergrads, 3% part-time. 117 full-time freshmen.
Selectivity: Admits 50 to 75% of applicants.

BASIC COSTS (2013-2014)
Tuition and fees: $32,750.
Per-credit charge: $1,356.
Additional info: New undergraduate students only: required laptop computer purchase $1,400. Board plan not available. Cost of room only: $4770.

FINANCIAL AID PICTURE
Students with need: Need-based aid available for full-time and part-time students.
Students without need: No-need awards available for academics, alumni affiliation, art.
Scholarships offered: Admissions Merit Scholarships: $6,000-$15,000; based on admissions file. Students admitted to the college automatically entered into scholarship competition.

FINANCIAL AID PROCEDURES
Forms required: FAFSA.
Dates and Deadlines: Priority date 3/1; closing date 6/1. Applicants notified on a rolling basis starting 2/15; must reply by 5/1 or within 2 week(s) of notification.
Transfers: Priority date 4/1; closing date 7/1. Applicants notified on a rolling basis starting 2/15; must reply by 5/1 or within 2 week(s) of notification. Transfer students may apply for admission by the priority deadline of Feb. 15. Only students accepted will receive an award letter. Complete the FAFSA by March 1. Be sure to include MCAD on the list of schools to receive your FAFSA analysis.

CONTACT
Laura Link, Director of Financial Aid
2501 Stevens Avenue, Minneapolis, MN 55404
(612) 874-8782

Minneapolis Community and Technical College

Minneapolis, Minnesota
www.minneapolis.edu Federal Code: 002362

2-year public community and technical college in large city.
Enrollment: 9,405 undergrads, 62% part-time. 754 full-time freshmen.
Selectivity: Open admission; but selective for some programs.

BASIC COSTS (2012-2013)
Tuition and fees: $5,342; out-of-state residents $5,342.
Per-credit charge: $155.

FINANCIAL AID PICTURE
Students with need: Need-based aid available for full-time and part-time students. Work study available nights, weekends, and for part-time students.
Students without need: This college awards aid only to students with need.

FINANCIAL AID PROCEDURES
Forms required: FAFSA.
Dates and Deadlines: Priority date 7/20; no closing date. Applicants notified on a rolling basis starting 7/1.
Transfers: Priority date 7/22; no deadline. Applicants notified on a rolling basis starting 7/1.

CONTACT
Angela Christensen, Director of Financial Aid
1501 Hennepin Avenue, Minneapolis, MN 55403-1710
(612) 659-6240

Minnesota School of Business: Blaine

Blaine, Minnesota
www.msbcollege.edu Federal Code: 017145

4-year for-profit university and career college in small city.
Enrollment: 520 undergrads.
Selectivity: Open admission.

BASIC COSTS (2012-2013)
Tuition and fees: $19,125.
Per-credit charge: $460.

FINANCIAL AID PICTURE
Students with need: Need-based aid available for full-time and part-time students.

FINANCIAL AID PROCEDURES
Forms required: FAFSA, institutional form.
Dates and Deadlines: Applicants notified on a rolling basis starting 7/1; must reply within 2 week(s) of notification.

CONTACT
Laura Fourniea, Director of Financial Aid
3680 Pheasant Ridge Dr. NE, Blaine, MN 55449
(763) 225-8000

Minnesota School of Business: Brooklyn Center

Brooklyn Center, Minnesota
www.msbcollege.edu Federal Code: 017145

2-year for-profit career college in large town.
Enrollment: 255 undergrads.
Selectivity: Open admission.

BASIC COSTS (2012-2013)
Tuition and fees: $19,125.
Per-credit charge: $460.

FINANCIAL AID PICTURE
Students with need: Need-based aid available for full-time and part-time students.

FINANCIAL AID PROCEDURES
Forms required: FAFSA, institutional form.
Dates and Deadlines: Applicants notified on a rolling basis starting 7/1; must reply within 2 week(s) of notification.

CONTACT
Kari Martin, Director of Financial Aid
5910 Shingle Creek Parkway, Brooklyn Center, MN 55430
(763) 566-7777

Minnesota School of Business: Elk River

Elk River, Minnesota
www.msbcollege.edu Federal Code: 017145

4-year for-profit university and career college in large town.
Enrollment: 360 undergrads.
Selectivity: Open admission.

BASIC COSTS (2012-2013)
Tuition and fees: $19,125.
Per-credit charge: $460.

FINANCIAL AID PICTURE
Students with need: Need-based aid available for full-time and part-time students.

FINANCIAL AID PROCEDURES
Forms required: FAFSA, state aid form, institutional form.
Dates and Deadlines: Applicants notified on a rolling basis starting 7/1; must reply within 2 week(s) of notification.

CONTACT
Breanna Persons, Director of Financial Aid
11500 193rd Avenue NW, Elk River, MN 55330
(763) 367-7000

Minnesota School of Business: Lakeville

Lakeville, Minnesota
www.msbcollege.edu Federal Code: 017145

4-year for-profit university and career college in small city.
Enrollment: 233 undergrads.
Selectivity: Open admission.

BASIC COSTS (2012-2013)
Tuition and fees: $19,125.
Per-credit charge: $460.

FINANCIAL AID PICTURE
Students with need: Need-based aid available for full-time and part-time students.

FINANCIAL AID PROCEDURES
Forms required: FAFSA, state aid form, institutional form.
Dates and Deadlines: Applicants notified on a rolling basis starting 7/1; must reply within 2 week(s) of notification.

CONTACT
Tara Clinkscales, Director of Financial Aid
17685 Juniper Path, Lakeville, MN 55044
(952) 892-9000

Minnesota School of Business: Moorhead

Moorhead, Minnesota
www.msbcollege.edu Federal Code: 017145

4-year for-profit university and career college in large town.
Enrollment: 211 undergrads.
Selectivity: Open admission.

BASIC COSTS (2012-2013)
Tuition and fees: $19,125.
Per-credit charge: $460.

FINANCIAL AID PICTURE
Students with need: Need-based aid available for full-time and part-time students.

FINANCIAL AID PROCEDURES
Forms required: FAFSA, state aid form, institutional form.
Dates and Deadlines: Applicants notified on a rolling basis starting 7/1; must reply within 2 week(s) of notification.

CONTACT
Lisa Roesch, Director of Financial Aid
2777 34th Street South, Moorhead, MN 56560
(218) 422-1000

Minnesota School of Business: Plymouth

Plymouth, Minnesota
www.msbcollege.edu Federal Code: 017145

4-year for-profit university and career college in small city.
Enrollment: 265 undergrads.
Selectivity: Open admission.

BASIC COSTS (2012-2013)
Tuition and fees: $19,125.
Per-credit charge: $460.

FINANCIAL AID PICTURE
Students with need: Need-based aid available for full-time and part-time students.

FINANCIAL AID PROCEDURES
Forms required: FAFSA, state aid form, institutional form.
Dates and Deadlines: Applicants notified on a rolling basis starting 7/1; must reply within 2 week(s) of notification.

CONTACT
Erin Poster, Director of Financial Aid
1455 County Road 101 North, Plymouth, MN 55447
(763) 476-2000

Minnesota School of Business: Richfield

Richfield, Minnesota
www.msbcollege.edu Federal Code: 017145

4-year for-profit university and career college in large town.
Enrollment: 1,070 undergrads.
Selectivity: Open admission; but selective for some programs.

BASIC COSTS (2012-2013)
Tuition and fees: $19,125.
Per-credit charge: $460.
Additional info: Nursing program courses $650 per-credit hour.

FINANCIAL AID PICTURE
Students with need: Need-based aid available for full-time and part-time students.

FINANCIAL AID PROCEDURES
Forms required: FAFSA, state aid form, institutional form.
Dates and Deadlines: Applicants notified on a rolling basis starting 7/1; must reply within 2 week(s) of notification.

CONTACT
Kelly Running, Director of Financial Aid
1401 West 76 Street, Suite 500, Richfield, MN 55423
(612) 861-2000

Minnesota School of Business: Rochester

Rochester, Minnesota
www.msbcollege.edu Federal Code: 017145

4-year for-profit university and career college in small city.
Enrollment: 331 undergrads.
Selectivity: Open admission.

BASIC COSTS (2012-2013)
Tuition and fees: $19,125.
Per-credit charge: $460.

FINANCIAL AID PICTURE
Students with need: Need-based aid available for full-time and part-time students.

FINANCIAL AID PROCEDURES
Forms required: FAFSA, state aid form.
Dates and Deadlines: Applicants notified on a rolling basis starting 7/1; must reply within 2 week(s) of notification.

CONTACT
Laurie Dresow, Director of Financial Aid
2521 Pennington Drive NW, Rochester, MN 55901
(507) 536-9500

Minnesota School of Business: St. Cloud

Waite Park, Minnesota
www.msbcollege.edu Federal Code: 017145

4-year for-profit university and career college in small city.
Enrollment: 452 undergrads.
Selectivity: Open admission.

BASIC COSTS (2012-2013)
Tuition and fees: $19,125.
Per-credit charge: $460.

FINANCIAL AID PICTURE
Students with need: Need-based aid available for full-time and part-time students.

FINANCIAL AID PROCEDURES
Forms required: FAFSA, state aid form, institutional form.
Dates and Deadlines: Applicants notified on a rolling basis starting 7/1; must reply within 2 week(s) of notification.

CONTACT
Jennifer May, Director of Financial Aid
1201 Second Street South, Waite Park, MN 55387
(866) 403-3333

Minnesota School of Business: Shakopee

Shakopee, Minnesota
www.msbcollege.edu Federal Code: 017145

4-year for-profit university and career college in large town.
Enrollment: 185 undergrads.
Selectivity: Open admission.

BASIC COSTS (2012-2013)
Tuition and fees: $19,125.
Per-credit charge: $460.

FINANCIAL AID PICTURE
Students with need: Need-based aid available for full-time and part-time students.

FINANCIAL AID PROCEDURES
Forms required: FAFSA, state aid form, institutional form.
Dates and Deadlines: Applicants notified on a rolling basis starting 7/1; must reply within 2 week(s) of notification.

CONTACT
Karen Samstad, Director of Financial Aid
1200 Shakopee Town Square, Shakopee, MN 55379
(952) 345-1200

Minnesota State College - Southeast Technical

Winona, Minnesota
www.southeastmn.edu Federal Code: 002393

2-year public technical college in large town.
Enrollment: 2,066 undergrads, 42% part-time. 439 full-time freshmen.
Selectivity: Open admission; but selective for some programs.

BASIC COSTS (2012-2013)
Tuition and fees: $5,614; out-of-state residents $5,614.
Per-credit charge: $167.

FINANCIAL AID PICTURE
Students with need: Need-based aid available for full-time and part-time students.
Students without need: No-need awards available for academics, leadership.

FINANCIAL AID PROCEDURES
Forms required: FAFSA, state aid form, institutional form.
Dates and Deadlines: Priority date 5/15; closing date 6/30. Applicants notified on a rolling basis; must reply within 3 week(s) of notification.
Transfers: Applicants notified on a rolling basis; must reply within 3 week(s) of notification. Mid-year transfer application forms must be accompanied by financial aid transcript.

CONTACT
Anne Dahlen, Director of Financial Aid
1250 Homer Road, Winona, MN 55987-0409
(507) 453-2710

Minnesota State Community and Technical College

Fergus Falls, Minnesota
www.minnesota.edu Federal Code: 002352

2-year public community and technical college in large town.
Enrollment: 5,214 undergrads, 40% part-time. 767 full-time freshmen.
Selectivity: Open admission.

BASIC COSTS (2013-2014)
Tuition and fees: $5,400; out-of-state residents $5,400.
Room only: $3,900.

FINANCIAL AID PICTURE (2011-2012)
Students with need: 44% of average financial aid package awarded as scholarships/grants, 56% awarded as loans/jobs. Need-based aid available for part-time students. Work study available nights, weekends, and for part-time students.
Students without need: No-need awards available for academics, art, leadership, minority status, music/drama, state/district residency.
Scholarships offered: Academic and leadership scholarships: $400-$1,000 each; available to 1st and 2nd year students; over 150 awarded annually.

FINANCIAL AID PROCEDURES
Forms required: FAFSA.
Dates and Deadlines: Priority date 6/1; no closing date. Applicants notified on a rolling basis starting 7/1.
Transfers: Priority date 7/1; no deadline. Applicants notified on a rolling basis.

CONTACT
Anthony Schaffhauser, Director of Access
150 2nd St. SW, Suite B, Perham, MN 56573
(218) 736-1534

Minnesota State University Mankato

Mankato, Minnesota
www.mnsu.edu Federal Code: 002360

4-year public university in small city.
Enrollment: 12,810 undergrads. 2,523 full-time freshmen.
Selectivity: Admits 50 to 75% of applicants.

BASIC COSTS (2012-2013)
Tuition and fees: $7,532; out-of-state residents $15,010.
Per-credit charge: $262; out-of-state residents $564.
Room and board: $7,368.

FINANCIAL AID PICTURE (2011-2012)
Students with need: Out of 2,235 full-time freshmen who applied for aid, 1,586 were judged to have need. Of these, 1,569 received aid, and 380 had their full need met. Average financial aid package met 78% of need; average scholarship/grant was $5,096; average loan was $3,598. For part-time students, average financial aid package was $624.
Students without need: 228 full-time freshmen who did not demonstrate need for aid received scholarships/grants; average award was $2,372. No-need awards available for academics, art, athletics, leadership, minority status, music/drama.
Scholarships offered: 46 full-time freshmen received athletic scholarships; average amount $5,669.
Cumulative student debt: 75% of graduating class had student loans; average debt was $29,415.

FINANCIAL AID PROCEDURES
Forms required: FAFSA.
Dates and Deadlines: Priority date 3/15; no closing date. Applicants notified on a rolling basis starting 3/30; must reply within 2 week(s) of notification.

CONTACT
Sandra Loerts, Director of Financial Aid
122 Taylor Center, Mankato, MN 56001
(507) 389-1185

Minnesota State University Moorhead

Moorhead, Minnesota
www.mnstate.edu Federal Code: 002367

4-year public university in small city.
Enrollment: 6,071 undergrads, 14% part-time. 1,030 full-time freshmen.
Selectivity: Admits over 75% of applicants.

BASIC COSTS (2012-2013)
Tuition and fees: $7,790; out-of-state residents $14,688.
Per-credit charge: $222; out-of-state residents $460.
Room and board: $6,984.

FINANCIAL AID PICTURE (2011-2012)
Students with need: Out of 900 full-time freshmen who applied for aid, 665 were judged to have need. Of these, 665 received aid. Need-based aid available for part-time students.
Students without need: 48 full-time freshmen who did not demonstrate need for aid received scholarships/grants; average award was $2,547. No-need awards available for academics, art, athletics, leadership, music/drama, state/district residency.
Scholarships offered: 225 full-time freshmen received athletic scholarships; average amount $1,210.
Cumulative student debt: 57% of graduating class had student loans; average debt was $30,037.

FINANCIAL AID PROCEDURES
Forms required: FAFSA.
Dates and Deadlines: Priority date 2/15; no closing date. Applicants notified on a rolling basis starting 6/1; must reply within 2 week(s) of notification.

CONTACT
Carolyn Zehren, Director of Financial Aid and Scholarships
Owens Hall, Moorhead, MN 56563
(218) 236-2251

Minnesota West Community and Technical College

Pipestone, Minnesota
www.mnwest.edu Federal Code: 005263

2-year public community and technical college in large town.
Enrollment: 2,134 undergrads.
Selectivity: Open admission; but selective for some programs.

BASIC COSTS (2012-2013)
Tuition and fees: $5,657; out-of-state residents $5,657.
Per-credit charge: $172.
Additional info: Board plan not available. Cost of room only, $1,800.

FINANCIAL AID PICTURE
Students with need: Need-based aid available for full-time and part-time students. Work study available nights, weekends, and for part-time students.

FINANCIAL AID PROCEDURES
Forms required: FAFSA.
Dates and Deadlines: Priority date 6/9; no closing date. Applicants notified on a rolling basis starting 4/9; must reply within 2 week(s) of notification.

CONTACT
Jodi Landgaard, Financial Aid Director
1314 North Hiawatha Avenue, Pipestone, MN 56164
(507) 372-3403

Normandale Community College

Bloomington, Minnesota
www.normandale.edu Federal Code: 007954

2-year public community college in very large city.
Enrollment: 9,141 undergrads, 55% part-time. 1,322 full-time freshmen.
Selectivity: Open admission; but selective for some programs.

BASIC COSTS (2012-2013)
Tuition and fees: $5,694; out-of-state residents $5,694.
Per-credit charge: $162.
Additional info: Laptop lease required for some programs; approximately $800 annually.

FINANCIAL AID PICTURE (2011-2012)
Students with need: 36% of average financial aid package awarded as scholarships/grants, 64% awarded as loans/jobs. Need-based aid available for part-time students. Work study available nights, weekends, and for part-time students.
Students without need: No-need awards available for academics, art, leadership, music/drama, state/district residency.

FINANCIAL AID PROCEDURES
Forms required: FAFSA, state aid form.
Dates and Deadlines: Priority date 4/1; no closing date. Applicants notified on a rolling basis starting 4/15.

CONTACT
Susan Ant, Director, Financial Aid and Scholarships
9700 France Avenue South, Bloomington, MN 55431
(952) 358-8250

North Central University

Minneapolis, Minnesota
www.northcentral.edu Federal Code: 002369

Upper-division private university in large city, affiliated with Assemblies of God.
Enrollment: 1,309 undergrads.

BASIC COSTS (2012-2013)
Tuition and fees: $18,160.
Room and board: $5,650.

FINANCIAL AID PICTURE
Students with need: Need-based aid available for full-time and part-time students. Work study available nights, weekends, and for part-time students.
Students without need: No-need awards available for academics, leadership, music/drama.
Scholarships offered: President's Scholarship: $2,500 per year; renewable; based on academic performance. Dean's Scholarship: $1,500 per year; renewable; based on academic performance. First Choice Scholarship awarded to those who submit their application early and meet academic criteria.

FINANCIAL AID PROCEDURES
Forms required: FAFSA.
Dates and Deadlines: Applicants notified on a rolling basis starting 3/1; must reply within 2 week(s) of notification.
Transfers: Priority date 4/15; no deadline. Applicants notified on a rolling basis starting 3/1.

CONTACT
Donna Jager, Director of Financial Aid
910 Elliot Avenue, Minneapolis, MN 55404
(800) 289-4488 ext. 289

North Hennepin Community College
Brooklyn Park, Minnesota
www.nhcc.edu Federal Code: 002370

2-year public community college in small city.
Enrollment: 7,007 undergrads, 68% part-time. 553 full-time freshmen.
Selectivity: Open admission; but selective for some programs.

BASIC COSTS (2012-2013)
Tuition and fees: $5,447; out-of-state residents $5,447.
Per-credit charge: $165.

FINANCIAL AID PICTURE
Students with need: Need-based aid available for full-time and part-time students. Work study available nights, weekends, and for part-time students.
Students without need: No-need awards available for academics, art, leadership.
Additional info: Computerized financial aid application.

FINANCIAL AID PROCEDURES
Forms required: FAFSA.
Dates and Deadlines: Priority date 4/15; no closing date. Applicants notified on a rolling basis starting 6/1.
Transfers: No deadline. Applicants notified on a rolling basis.

CONTACT
Jackie Olsson, Director of Financial Aid
7411 85th Avenue North, Brooklyn Park, MN 55445
(763) 424-0702

Northland Community & Technical College
Thief River Falls, Minnesota
www.northlandcollege.edu Federal Code: 002385

2-year public community and technical college in small town.
Enrollment: 3,549 undergrads, 52% part-time. 874 full-time freshmen.
Selectivity: Open admission; but selective for some programs.

BASIC COSTS (2013-2014)
Tuition and fees: $5,700; out-of-state residents $5,700.
Per-credit charge: $165.

FINANCIAL AID PICTURE
Students with need: Need-based aid available for full-time and part-time students. Work study available nights.
Students without need: This college awards aid only to students with need.

FINANCIAL AID PROCEDURES
Forms required: FAFSA.
Dates and Deadlines: Priority date 5/1; no closing date. Applicants notified on a rolling basis starting 5/15.
Transfers: No deadline.

CONTACT
Gerald Schulte, Financial Aid Director
1101 Highway One East, Thief River Falls, MN 56701
(218) 683-8557

Northwest Technical College
Bemidji, Minnesota
www.ntcmn.edu Federal Code: 005759

2-year public technical college in large town.
Enrollment: 892 undergrads, 53% part-time. 85 full-time freshmen.
Selectivity: Open admission; but selective for some programs.

BASIC COSTS (2012-2013)
Tuition and fees: $5,482; out-of-state residents $5,482.
Per-credit charge: $173.
Room and board: $2,190.

FINANCIAL AID PICTURE (2011-2012)
Students with need: 60% of average financial aid package awarded as scholarships/grants, 40% awarded as loans/jobs. Need-based aid available for part-time students. Work study available nights.
Students without need: This college awards aid only to students with need.

FINANCIAL AID PROCEDURES
Forms required: FAFSA, institutional form.
Dates and Deadlines: Priority date 6/1; no closing date. Applicants notified on a rolling basis.

CONTACT
Paul Lindseth, Director of Financial Aid
905 Grant Avenue Southeast, Bemidji, MN 56601-4907
(218) 333-6648

Northwestern College
Saint Paul, Minnesota
www.nwc.edu Federal Code: 002371

4-year private university and liberal arts college in very large city, affiliated with nondenominational tradition.
Enrollment: 1,739 undergrads, 3% part-time. 449 full-time freshmen.
Selectivity: Admits 50 to 75% of applicants.

BASIC COSTS (2012-2013)
Tuition and fees: $26,960.
Per-credit charge: $1,140.
Room and board: $8,210.
Additional info: Tuition/fee waivers available for minority students.

FINANCIAL AID PICTURE (2011-2012)
Students with need: Out of 447 full-time freshmen who applied for aid, 379 were judged to have need. Of these, 379 received aid, and 24 had their full need met. Average financial aid package met 71% of need; average scholarship/grant was $15,938; average loan was $3,870. Need-based aid available for part-time students.
Students without need: 68 full-time freshmen who did not demonstrate need for aid received scholarships/grants; average award was $8,617. No-need awards available for academics, alumni affiliation, leadership, music/drama.
Scholarships offered: Eagle Scholars Program: $12,000-$15,000 per year; ACT score of 30 or SAT score of 1320; up to 15 awarded yearly to incoming freshmen; renewable annually with successful involvement in program, including a cumulative GPA of 3.65 or higher.
Additional info: Students enrolled at least half-time in the FOCUS or Distance Education degree programs may apply for financial aid from the same Federal and state sources as traditional undergraduates. However, their expense budgets and aid are less due to lower tuition.

FINANCIAL AID PROCEDURES
Forms required: FAFSA, institutional form.
Dates and Deadlines: Priority date 3/1; closing date 8/1. Applicants notified on a rolling basis starting 3/1; must reply within 2 week(s) of notification.

CONTACT
Richard Blatchley, Director of Financial Aid
3003 Snelling Avenue North, Saint Paul, MN 55113-1598
(651) 631-5212

Oak Hills Christian College

Bemidji, Minnesota
www.oakhills.edu Federal Code: 016116

4-year private Bible college in large town, affiliated with interdenominational tradition.
Enrollment: 199 undergrads.

BASIC COSTS (2012-2013)
Tuition and fees: $14,670.
Per-credit charge: $600.
Room and board: $5,340.

FINANCIAL AID PICTURE
Students with need: Need-based aid available for full-time and part-time students. Work study available nights, weekends, and for part-time students.
Students without need: No-need awards available for academics, alumni affiliation.

FINANCIAL AID PROCEDURES
Forms required: FAFSA, institutional form.
Dates and Deadlines: Applicants notified on a rolling basis starting 3/1.
Transfers: No deadline. Applicants notified on a rolling basis starting 3/1.

CONTACT
Dan Hovestol, Director of Financial Aid
1600 Oak Hills Road SW, Bemidji, MN 56601-8826
(218) 751-8671 ext. 1220

Pine Technical College

Pine City, Minnesota
www.pinetech.edu Federal Code: 005535

2-year public technical college in small town.
Enrollment: 758 undergrads.
Selectivity: Open admission; but selective for some programs.

BASIC COSTS (2012-2013)
Tuition and fees: $5,081; out-of-state residents $9,676.
Per-credit charge: $153; out-of-state residents $306.

FINANCIAL AID PICTURE
Students with need: Need-based aid available for full-time and part-time students.
Students without need: No-need awards available for academics, state/district residency.

FINANCIAL AID PROCEDURES
Forms required: FAFSA, institutional form.
Dates and Deadlines: Priority date 5/5; no closing date. Applicants notified on a rolling basis starting 6/5.

CONTACT
Shawn Reynolds, Financial Aid Director
900 Fourth Street SE, Pine City, MN 55063
(320) 629-5100 ext. 161

Rainy River Community College

International Falls, Minnesota
www.rrcc.mnscu.edu Federal Code: 006775

2-year public community and technical college in small town.
Enrollment: 334 undergrads, 14% part-time.
Selectivity: Open admission.

BASIC COSTS (2012-2013)
Tuition and fees: $5,323; out-of-state residents $6,505.
Per-credit charge: $158; out-of-state residents $197.
Room and board: $3,750.
Additional info: Tuition/fee waivers available for unemployed or children of unemployed.

FINANCIAL AID PICTURE (2011-2012)
Students with need: 71% of average financial aid package awarded as scholarships/grants, 29% awarded as loans/jobs. Need-based aid available for part-time students. Work study available nights, weekends, and for part-time students.
Students without need: No-need awards available for academics, alumni affiliation, leadership, minority status, state/district residency.
Additional info: Many scholarship and employment opportunities for applicants showing little or no need.

FINANCIAL AID PROCEDURES
Forms required: FAFSA, institutional form.
Dates and Deadlines: Priority date 6/1; no closing date. Applicants notified on a rolling basis starting 5/1; must reply within 3 week(s) of notification.

CONTACT
Scott Riley, Director of Financial Aid
1501 Highway 71, International Falls, MN 56649
(218) 285-7722

Rasmussen College: Blaine

Blaine, Minnesota
www.rasmussen.edu

4-year for-profit branch campus and career college in small city.
Enrollment: 426 undergrads.
Selectivity: Open admission; but selective for some programs.

BASIC COSTS (2012-2013)
Tuition and fees: $17,750.
Per-credit charge: $395.
Additional info: Full-time tuition varies according to program of study. Examples of per-credit-hour charges include Early Childhood Education or Medical Assisting ($310), Medical Lab Technician, Surgical Technician, Practical Nursing ($395), Professional Nursing, Information Systems Mgmt, Multimedia Technician ($395). Medical Administration ($350).

FINANCIAL AID PICTURE
Students with need: Need-based aid available for full-time and part-time students.

FINANCIAL AID PROCEDURES
Forms required: FAFSA, institutional form.
Dates and Deadlines: Applicants notified on a rolling basis.

CONTACT
Debora Murray, Director of Financial Services
3629 95th Avenue NE, Blaine, MN 55014

Rasmussen College: Bloomington

Bloomington, Minnesota
www.rasmussen.edu Federal Code: 011686

2-year for-profit career college in small city.
Enrollment: 525 undergrads.
Selectivity: Open admission; but selective for some programs.

BASIC COSTS (2012-2013)
Tuition and fees: $17,750.
Per-credit charge: $395.
Additional info: Full-time tuition varies according to program of study. Examples of per-credit-hour charges include Early Childhood Education or Medical

Assisting ($310), Medical Lab Technician, Surgical Technician, Practical Nursing ($395), Professional Nursing, Information Systems Mgmt, Multimedia Technician ($395). Medical Administration ($350).

FINANCIAL AID PICTURE

Students with need: Need-based aid available for full-time and part-time students.

FINANCIAL AID PROCEDURES

Forms required: FAFSA, institutional form.

Dates and Deadlines: Applicants notified on a rolling basis.

CONTACT

Debora Murray, Director of Financial Services
4400 West 78th Street, Eden Prairie, MN 55435
(952) 545-2000

Rasmussen College: Brooklyn Park

Brooklyn Park, Minnesota
www.rasmussen.edu

2-year for-profit career college in small city.
Enrollment: 876 undergrads.
Selectivity: Open admission; but selective for some programs.

BASIC COSTS (2012-2013)

Tuition and fees: $17,750.
Per-credit charge: $395.
Additional info: Full-time tuition varies according to program of study. Examples of per-credit-hour charges include Early Childhood Education or Medical Assisting ($310), Medical Lab Technician, Surgical Technician, Practical Nursing ($395), Professional Nursing, Information Systems Mgmt, Multimedia Technician ($395), Medical Administration ($350).

FINANCIAL AID PICTURE

Students with need: Need-based aid available for full-time and part-time students.

FINANCIAL AID PROCEDURES

Forms required: FAFSA, institutional form.

Dates and Deadlines: Applicants notified on a rolling basis.

CONTACT

Debora Murray, Director of Financial Services
8301 93rd Avenue North, Brooklyn Park, MN 55445

Rasmussen College: Eagan

Eagan, Minnesota
www.rasmussen.edu Federal Code: 004648

2-year for-profit career college in small city.
Enrollment: 853 undergrads.
Selectivity: Open admission; but selective for some programs.

BASIC COSTS (2012-2013)

Tuition and fees: $17,750.
Per-credit charge: $395.
Additional info: Full-time tuition varies according to program of study. Examples of per-credit-hour charges include Early Childhood Education or Medical Assisting ($310), Medical Lab Technician, Surgical Technician, Practical Nursing ($395), Professional Nursing, Information Systems Mgmt, Multimedia Technician ($395), Medical Administration ($350).

FINANCIAL AID PICTURE

Students with need: Need-based aid available for full-time and part-time students.

FINANCIAL AID PROCEDURES

Forms required: FAFSA, institutional form.

Dates and Deadlines: Applicants notified on a rolling basis.

CONTACT

Debora Murray, Director of Financial Services
3500 Federal Drive, Eagan, MN 55122
(651) 687-9000

Rasmussen College: Lake Elmo/ Woodbury

Lake Elmo, Minnesota
www.rasmussen.edu

4-year for-profit technical college in small city.
Enrollment: 656 undergrads.
Selectivity: Open admission; but selective for some programs.

BASIC COSTS (2012-2013)

Tuition and fees: $17,750.
Per-credit charge: $395.
Additional info: Full-time tuition varies according to program of study. Examples of per-credit-hour charges include Early Childhood Education or Medical Assisting ($310), Medical Lab Technician, Surgical Technician, Practical Nursing ($395), Professional Nursing, Information Systems Mgmt, Multimedia Technician ($395), Medical Administration ($350).

FINANCIAL AID PICTURE

Students with need: Need-based aid available for full-time and part-time students.

FINANCIAL AID PROCEDURES

Forms required: FAFSA, institutional form.

Dates and Deadlines: Applicants notified on a rolling basis.

CONTACT

Debora Murray, Director of Financial Services
8565 Eagle Point Circle, Lake Elmo, MN 55042-8637

Rasmussen College: Mankato

Mankato, Minnesota
www.rasmussen.edu Federal Code: 016845

2-year for-profit career college in large town.
Enrollment: 716 undergrads.
Selectivity: Open admission; but selective for some programs.

BASIC COSTS (2012-2013)

Tuition and fees: $17,750.
Per-credit charge: $395.
Additional info: Full-time tuition varies according to program of study. Examples of per-credit-hour charges include Early Childhood Education or Medical Assisting ($310), Medical Lab Technician, Surgical Technician, Practical Nursing ($395), Professional Nursing, Information Systems Mgmt, Multimedia Technician ($395), Medical Administration ($350).

FINANCIAL AID PICTURE

Students with need: Need-based aid available for full-time and part-time students.

FINANCIAL AID PROCEDURES

Forms required: FAFSA, institutional form.

Dates and Deadlines: Applicants notified on a rolling basis.

CONTACT

Debora Murray, Director of Financial Services
130 Saint Andrews Drive, Mankato, MN 56001
(507) 625-6556

Rasmussen College: Moorhead

Moorhead, Minnesota
www.rasmussen.edu

4-year for-profit branch campus and career college in small city.
Enrollment: 416 undergrads.
Selectivity: Open admission; but selective for some programs.

BASIC COSTS (2012-2013)
Tuition and fees: $17,750.
Per-credit charge: $395.
Additional info: Full-time tuition varies according to program of study. Examples of per-credit-hour charges include Early Childhood Education or Medical Assisting ($310), Medical Lab Technician, Surgical Technician, Practical Nursing ($395), Professional Nursing, Information Systems Mgmt, Multimedia Technician ($395). Medical Administration ($350).

FINANCIAL AID PICTURE
Students with need: Need-based aid available for full-time and part-time students.

FINANCIAL AID PROCEDURES
Forms required: FAFSA, institutional form.
Dates and Deadlines: Applicants notified on a rolling basis.

CONTACT
Debora Murray, Director of Financial Services
1250 29th Avenue South, Moorhead, MN 56560

Rasmussen College: St. Cloud

St. Cloud, Minnesota
www.rasmussen.edu Federal Code: 008694

2-year for-profit community and career college in small city.
Enrollment: 816 undergrads.
Selectivity: Open admission; but selective for some programs.

BASIC COSTS (2012-2013)
Tuition and fees: $17,750.
Per-credit charge: $395.
Additional info: Full-time tuition varies according to program of study. Examples of per-credit-hour charges include Early Childhood Education or Medical Assisting ($310), Medical Lab Technician, Surgical Technician, Practical Nursing ($395), Professional Nursing, Information Systems Mgmt, Multimedia Technician ($395), Medical Administration ($350).

FINANCIAL AID PICTURE
Students with need: Need-based aid available for full-time and part-time students.

FINANCIAL AID PROCEDURES
Forms required: FAFSA, institutional form.
Dates and Deadlines: Applicants notified on a rolling basis.

CONTACT
Debora Murray, Director of Financial Services
226 Park Avenue South, St. Cloud, MN 56301-3713
(320) 251-5600

Ridgewater College

Willmar, Minnesota
www.ridgewater.edu Federal Code: 005252

2-year public community and technical college in large town.
Enrollment: 3,717 undergrads.
Selectivity: Open admission; but selective for some programs.

BASIC COSTS (2012-2013)
Tuition and fees: $5,375; out-of-state residents $5,375.
Per-credit charge: $161.
Additional info: Tuition/fee waivers available for adults.

FINANCIAL AID PICTURE
Students with need: Need-based aid available for full-time and part-time students. Work study available nights, weekends, and for part-time students.
Additional info: Special funds are available for adult transfer students returning or continuing education after a 7-year absence from academic training. ALLISS grants provide reimbursement for one class, up to five credits for one semester.

FINANCIAL AID PROCEDURES
Forms required: FAFSA, institutional form.
Dates and Deadlines: Applicants notified on a rolling basis.

CONTACT
Jim Rice, Director of Financial Aid
2101 15th Avenue Northwest, Willmar, MN 56201
(320) 222-7474

Riverland Community College

Austin, Minnesota
www.riverland.edu Federal Code: 002335

2-year public community and technical college in large town.
Enrollment: 3,473 undergrads.
Selectivity: Open admission; but selective for some programs.

BASIC COSTS (2012-2013)
Tuition and fees: $5,510; out-of-state residents $5,510.
Per-credit charge: $165.
Additional info: $400 laptop charge for each term.

FINANCIAL AID PICTURE
Students with need: Need-based aid available for full-time and part-time students.
Students without need: No-need awards available for alumni affiliation, art, job skills, leadership, music/drama, state/district residency.
Additional info: One class tuition-free for Minnesota residents over 25 who have not attended college for at least 7 years.

FINANCIAL AID PROCEDURES
Forms required: FAFSA.
Dates and Deadlines: Priority date 5/15; no closing date. Applicants notified on a rolling basis; must reply within 5 week(s) of notification.
Transfers: No deadline. Applicants notified on a rolling basis.

CONTACT
Judy Robeck, Financial Aid Director
1900 Eighth Avenue, NW, Austin, MN 55912-1407
(507) 433-0511

Rochester Community and Technical College

Rochester, Minnesota
www.rctc.edu Federal Code: 002373

2-year public community and technical college in small city.
Enrollment: 6,055 undergrads.
Selectivity: Open admission; but selective for some programs.

BASIC COSTS (2012-2013)
Tuition and fees: $5,609; out-of-state residents $5,609.
Per-credit charge: $164.

Additional info: South Dakota residents pay $186.74 per-credit hour charges.

FINANCIAL AID PICTURE

Students with need: Need-based aid available for full-time and part-time students. Work study available nights, weekends, and for part-time students.

FINANCIAL AID PROCEDURES

Forms required: FAFSA.

Dates and Deadlines: Priority date 4/15; no closing date. Applicants notified on a rolling basis.

CONTACT

Beth Diekmann, Director of Financial Aid
851 30th Avenue SE, Rochester, MN 55904-4999
(507) 285-7271

St. Catherine University

Saint Paul, Minnesota
www.stkate.edu Federal Code: 002342

4-year private health science and liberal arts college for women in large city, affiliated with Roman Catholic Church.

Enrollment: 3,565 undergrads, 33% part-time. 446 full-time freshmen.

Selectivity: Admits 50 to 75% of applicants.

BASIC COSTS (2012-2013)

Tuition and fees: $31,220.

Per-credit charge: $1,028.

Room and board: $8,288.

FINANCIAL AID PICTURE

Students with need: Need-based aid available for full-time and part-time students. Work study available nights, weekends, and for part-time students.

Students without need: No-need awards available for academics, alumni affiliation, leadership, state/district residency.

Scholarships offered: St. Catherine of Alexandria Merit Scholarships: $2,000-$6,000; high school seniors in top 15% of class, evidence of academic preparation, outstanding leadership abilities, involvement in extracurricular activities and community service; renewable for 3 years.

Additional info: Audition required for music scholarships.

FINANCIAL AID PROCEDURES

Forms required: FAFSA, institutional form.

Dates and Deadlines: Priority date 4/15; no closing date. Applicants notified on a rolling basis starting 3/30; must reply within 2 week(s) of notification.

CONTACT

Elizabeth Stevens, Director of Financial Aid
2004 Randolph Avenue #F-02, St. Paul, MN 55105
(651) 690-6540

Saint Cloud State University

St. Cloud, Minnesota
www.stcloudstate.edu Federal Code: 002377

4-year public university in small city.

Enrollment: 12,292 undergrads, 17% part-time. 1,848 full-time freshmen.

Selectivity: Admits over 75% of applicants.

BASIC COSTS (2012-2013)

Tuition and fees: $7,472; out-of-state residents $15,114.

Per-credit charge: $219; out-of-state residents $474.

Room and board: $6,994.

FINANCIAL AID PICTURE

Students with need: Work study available nights, weekends, and for part-time students.

Students without need: No-need awards available for academics, art, athletics, leadership, music/drama.

FINANCIAL AID PROCEDURES

Forms required: FAFSA, institutional form.

Dates and Deadlines: Applicants notified on a rolling basis starting 6/15.

Transfers: No deadline. Applicants notified on a rolling basis starting 6/15.

CONTACT

Michael Uran, Financial Aid Director
720 Fourth Avenue South, AS 115, St. Cloud, MN 56301
(320) 308-2047

St. Cloud Technical and Community College

St Cloud, Minnesota
www.sctcc.edu Federal Code: 005534

2-year public community and technical college in small city.

Enrollment: 4,327 undergrads, 50% part-time. 762 full-time freshmen.

Selectivity: Open admission; but selective for some programs.

BASIC COSTS (2012-2013)

Tuition and fees: $5,293; out-of-state residents $5,293.

Per-credit charge: $159.

FINANCIAL AID PICTURE (2011-2012)

Students with need: 53% of average financial aid package awarded as scholarships/grants, 47% awarded as loans/jobs. Need-based aid available for part-time students. Work study available nights, weekends, and for part-time students.

Students without need: No-need awards available for academics, leadership, state/district residency.

FINANCIAL AID PROCEDURES

Forms required: FAFSA.

Dates and Deadlines: Applicants notified on a rolling basis starting 6/1.

CONTACT

Anita Baugh, Director of Financial Aid
1540 Northway Drive, St. Cloud, MN 56303
(320) 308-5961

St. John's University

Collegeville, Minnesota
www.csbsju.edu Federal Code: 002379

4-year private university and liberal arts college for men in rural community, affiliated with Roman Catholic Church.

Enrollment: 1,854 undergrads, 2% part-time. 449 full-time freshmen.

Selectivity: Admits 50 to 75% of applicants.

BASIC COSTS (2013-2014)

Tuition and fees: $37,162.

Per-credit charge: $1,521.

Room and board: $8,984.

Additional info: Meal plan is flexible meal plan.

FINANCIAL AID PICTURE (2012-2013)

Students with need: Out of 365 full-time freshmen who applied for aid, 314 were judged to have need. Of these, 314 received aid, and 133 had their full need met. Average financial aid package met 92% of need; average scholarship/grant was $23,415; average loan was $3,868. For part-time students, average financial aid package was $3,750.

Students without need: 108 full-time freshmen who did not demonstrate need for aid received scholarships/grants; average award was $14,539. No-need awards available for academics, art, leadership, music/drama, ROTC.

Scholarships offered: Trustees' Scholarships: $18,000-$20,000; based on 3.6 GPA, 30 ACT/1980 SAT, demonstrated leadership and service, faculty interview. President's Scholarships: $13,000-$16,500; based on GPA, high school rank, ACT/SAT, leadership and service. Dean's Scholarships: $5,000-$12,000; based on GPA, high school rank, ACT/SAT, leadership and service. Art, music and theater scholarships: up to $4,000. Intercultural LEAD fellowship: up to $10,000; based on GPA, leadership, financial need, first generation college students, commitment to intercultural issues and action, diversity of high school. Army ROTC and ROTC Nursing Scholarships: based on demonstrated leadership potential, GPA, class standing, ACT/SAT, high achievement with broad interests and willingness to take on challenges. Catholic High School Scholarship: $3,000; for students attending Catholic high schools outside Minnesota. Saints Scholarship: $1,000-$3,000; for students attending public high schools outside Minnesota. FoCuS Scholarship: $20,000 renewable for students majoring in Chemistry; Bonner Leader Scholarship: $2,500 renewable for students with a strong interest in doing service at CSB/SJU and financial need.
Cumulative student debt: 70% of graduating class had student loans; average debt was $34,889.
Additional info: Scholarship letters will be mailed on rolling basis approximately 2 weeks from the time admission acceptance letter is sent.

FINANCIAL AID PROCEDURES

Forms required: FAFSA, institutional form.
Dates and Deadlines: Priority date 3/15; no closing date. Applicants notified on a rolling basis starting 3/15; must reply by 5/1.
Transfers: Applicants notified on a rolling basis starting 3/15; must reply by 5/1. Phi Theta Kappa Scholarship; $1,500 renewable; for members of Phi Theta Kappa.

CONTACT

Robert Piechota, Director of Financial Aid
College of St Benedict/St John's University, Collegeville, MN 56321-7155
(320) 363-3664

St. Mary's University of Minnesota

Winona, Minnesota
www.smumn.edu Federal Code: 002380

4-year private university in large town, affiliated with Roman Catholic Church.
Enrollment: 1,935 undergrads, 32% part-time. 328 full-time freshmen.
Selectivity: Admits over 75% of applicants.

BASIC COSTS (2013-2014)

Tuition and fees: $29,315.
Per-credit charge: $960.
Room and board: $7,700.

FINANCIAL AID PICTURE (2012-2013)

Students with need: Out of 292 full-time freshmen who applied for aid, 271 were judged to have need. Of these, 271 received aid, and 50 had their full need met. Average financial aid package met 81% of need; average scholarship/grant was $19,358; average loan was $4,175. Need-based aid available for part-time students.
Students without need: 50 full-time freshmen who did not demonstrate need for aid received scholarships/grants; average award was $8,982. No-need awards available for academics, alumni affiliation, art, leadership, minority status, music/drama.
Cumulative student debt: 77% of graduating class had student loans; average debt was $35,134.

FINANCIAL AID PROCEDURES

Forms required: FAFSA.
Dates and Deadlines: Priority date 3/15; no closing date. Applicants notified on a rolling basis starting 2/1; must reply within 3 week(s) of notification.
Transfers: No deadline. Applicants notified on a rolling basis starting 2/1.

CONTACT

Jayne Wobig, Director of Financial Aid
700 Terrace Heights #2, Winona, MN 55987-1399
(507) 457-1437

St. Olaf College

Northfield, Minnesota Federal Code: 002382
www.stolaf.edu CSS Code: 6638

4-year private liberal arts college in large town, affiliated with Evangelical Lutheran Church in America.
Enrollment: 3,128 undergrads. 864 full-time freshmen.
Selectivity: Admits 50 to 75% of applicants.

BASIC COSTS (2013-2014)

Tuition and fees: $40,700.
Per-credit charge: $1,272.
Room and board: $9,260.

FINANCIAL AID PICTURE (2012-2013)

Students with need: Out of 718 full-time freshmen who applied for aid, 584 were judged to have need. Of these, 584 received aid, and 584 had their full need met. Average financial aid package met 100% of need; average scholarship/grant was $28,491; average loan was $3,346.
Students without need: 210 full-time freshmen who did not demonstrate need for aid received scholarships/grants; average award was $12,670. No-need awards available for academics, art, leadership, music/drama.
Scholarships offered: Buntrock Scholarship: $18,000. Presidential Scholarship: $13,000, St. Olaf Scholarship: $10,000. National Hispanic Scholar/National Achievement: $7,500. National Merit Scholarship: $7,500. Access Scholarships: $8,000. Fine Arts scholarships: $4,000 - $11,500. Service leadership awards: $8,000. All are 4-year renewable; number awarded varies yearly.
Cumulative student debt: 61% of graduating class had student loans; average debt was $27,637.
Additional info: Limited number of music lesson fee waivers available for music majors, awarded on audition basis only.

FINANCIAL AID PROCEDURES

Forms required: FAFSA. CSS PROFILE due February 1.
Dates and Deadlines: Priority date 2/1; closing date 3/1. Applicants notified by 3/22; must reply by 5/1 or within 2 week(s) of notification.
Transfers: Closing date 4/1. Applicants notified by 5/15; must reply within 2 week(s) of notification.

CONTACT

Sandy Sundstrom, Director of Student Financial Aid
1520 St. Olaf Avenue, Northfield, MN 55057
(507) 786-3019

St. Paul College

Saint Paul, Minnesota
www.saintpaul.edu Federal Code: 005533

2-year public community and technical college in large city.
Enrollment: 6,159 undergrads.
Selectivity: Open admission; but selective for some programs.

BASIC COSTS (2012-2013)

Tuition and fees: $5,198; out-of-state residents $5,198.
Per-credit charge: $162.

FINANCIAL AID PICTURE

Students with need: Need-based aid available for full-time and part-time students. Work study available nights.
Students without need: No-need awards available for leadership.

FINANCIAL AID PROCEDURES
Forms required: FAFSA.
Dates and Deadlines: Applicants notified on a rolling basis starting 6/1.
Transfers: Priority date 5/1; no deadline. Applicants notified on a rolling basis starting 6/1.

CONTACT
Susan Pixley, Financial Aid Director
235 Marshall Avenue, Saint Paul, MN 55102-1800
(651) 846-1386

South Central College
North Mankato, Minnesota
www.southcentral.edu Federal Code: 005537

2-year public community and technical college in large town.
Enrollment: 3,707 undergrads.
Selectivity: Open admission.

BASIC COSTS (2012-2013)
Tuition and fees: $5,355; out-of-state residents $5,355.
Per-credit charge: $161.

FINANCIAL AID PICTURE (2011-2012)
Students with need: 55% of average financial aid package awarded as scholarships/grants, 45% awarded as loans/jobs. Need-based aid available for part-time students. Work study available nights.

FINANCIAL AID PROCEDURES
Forms required: FAFSA.
Dates and Deadlines: Priority date 5/1; no closing date. Applicants notified on a rolling basis starting 6/1.
Transfers: No deadline. Applicants notified on a rolling basis starting 6/1.

CONTACT
Jayne Dinse, Financial Aid Director
1920 Lee Boulevard, North Mankato, MN 56003
(507) 389-7220

Southwest Minnesota State University
Marshall, Minnesota
www.smsu.edu Federal Code: 002375

4-year public university and liberal arts college in large town.
Enrollment: 2,489 undergrads, 16% part-time. 476 full-time freshmen.
Selectivity: Admits 50 to 75% of applicants.

BASIC COSTS (2013-2014)
Tuition and fees: $8,275; out-of-state residents $8,275.
Per-credit charge: $237.
Room and board: $7,586.

FINANCIAL AID PICTURE (2012-2013)
Students with need: Out of 443 full-time freshmen who applied for aid, 352 were judged to have need. Of these, 351 received aid, and 65 had their full need met. Average financial aid package met 54% of need; average scholarship/grant was $5,491; average loan was $3,445. For part-time students, average financial aid package was $6,313.
Students without need: 80 full-time freshmen who did not demonstrate need for aid received scholarships/grants; average award was $2,211. No-need awards available for academics, alumni affiliation, art, athletics, leadership, minority status, music/drama, state/district residency.
Scholarships offered: 73 full-time freshmen received athletic scholarships; average amount $2,598.
Cumulative student debt: 83% of graduating class had student loans; average debt was $18,521.

FINANCIAL AID PROCEDURES
Forms required: FAFSA, institutional form.
Dates and Deadlines: Priority date 3/1; no closing date. Applicants notified on a rolling basis starting 6/1.

CONTACT
David Vikander, Director of Financial Aid
1501 State Street, Marshall, MN 56258-1598
(507) 537-6281

University of Minnesota: Crookston
Crookston, Minnesota
www1.crk.umn.edu Federal Code: 004069

4-year public branch campus college in small town.
Enrollment: 1,802 undergrads, 26% part-time. 233 full-time freshmen.
Selectivity: Admits 50 to 75% of applicants.

BASIC COSTS (2012-2013)
Tuition and fees: $11,455; out-of-state residents $11,455.
Per-credit charge: $386.
Room and board: $6,978.

FINANCIAL AID PICTURE (2012-2013)
Students with need: Out of 212 full-time freshmen who applied for aid, 177 were judged to have need. Of these, 173 received aid, and 47 had their full need met. Average financial aid package met 75% of need; average scholarship/grant was $9,574; average loan was $4,404. For part-time students, average financial aid package was $6,261.
Students without need: 29 full-time freshmen who did not demonstrate need for aid received scholarships/grants; average award was $3,640. No-need awards available for academics, alumni affiliation, athletics, leadership, minority status, music/drama, ROTC, state/district residency.
Scholarships offered: Merit Scholarship: based on a minimum GPA of 3.25 and a minimum ACT score of 21. Presidential Scholarship: $20,000 total ($5,000 annually for four years); based on ACT score of 30 and GPA of 3.25. Chancellor Scholarship: $8,000 total ($4,000 annually for two years); based on ACT score of 27-29 and GPA of 3.25. Distinguished Scholarship: $6,000 total ($3,000 annually for two years); based on ACT score of 25-26 and 3.25 GPA. Merriam Legacy Scholarship: $4,000 total ($2,000 annually for two years); based on ACT score of 23-24 and a 3.25 GPA. Achievement Scholarship: $2,000; based on ACT score of 21-22 and 3.25 GPA. Students must have earned a cumulative GPA of 3.3 at the end of Spring Semester in order to renew for the following year.
Cumulative student debt: 73% of graduating class had student loans; average debt was $27,608.
Additional info: Under the University of Minnesota Promise Scholarship (U Promise), eligible new Minnesota resident undergraduates with a family income of up to $100,000 will be guaranteed a U Promise Scholarship. Eligible new freshman and transfer students enrolling for the first time will receive a guaranteed, multi-year, U Promise Scholarship. Eligible new freshmen will receive a guaranteed need-based scholarship, ranging from $500 to $3,500 each year, for four years. Eligible new transfer students will receive a guaranteed, need-based scholarship, ranging from $500 to $1,500 each year, for two years.

FINANCIAL AID PROCEDURES
Forms required: FAFSA.
Dates and Deadlines: Priority date 3/1; no closing date. Applicants notified on a rolling basis starting 3/1; must reply within 8 week(s) of notification.

CONTACT
Melissa Dingmann, Director of Financial Aid
2900 University Avenue, Crookston, MN 56716-5001
(218) 281-8563

University of Minnesota: Duluth

Duluth, Minnesota
www.d.umn.edu Federal Code: 002388

4-year public university in small city.
Enrollment: 9,452 undergrads, 4% part-time. 2,096 full-time freshmen.
Selectivity: Admits over 75% of applicants.

BASIC COSTS (2012-2013)
Tuition and fees: $12,785; out-of-state residents $15,450.
Per-credit charge: $451; out-of-state residents $553.
Room and board: $6,732.

FINANCIAL AID PICTURE (2011-2012)
Students with need: Out of 1,849 full-time freshmen who applied for aid, 1,322 were judged to have need. Of these, 1,290 received aid, and 278 had their full need met. Average financial aid package met 68% of need; average scholarship/grant was $7,667; average loan was $4,139. For part-time students, average financial aid package was $5,959.
Students without need: 273 full-time freshmen who did not demonstrate need for aid received scholarships/grants; average award was $3,118. No-need awards available for academics, alumni affiliation, art, athletics, music/drama, ROTC, state/district residency.
Scholarships offered: 35 full-time freshmen received athletic scholarships; average amount $3,854.
Cumulative student debt: 74% of graduating class had student loans; average debt was $31,711.

FINANCIAL AID PROCEDURES
Forms required: FAFSA.
Dates and Deadlines: Priority date 3/1; no closing date. Applicants notified on a rolling basis starting 3/1; must reply within 2 week(s) of notification.
Transfers: No deadline. Applicants notified on a rolling basis starting 4/1.

CONTACT
Brenda Herzig, Director of Financial Aid
25 Solon Campus Center, Duluth, MN 55812-3000
(218) 726-8000

University of Minnesota: Morris

Morris, Minnesota
www.morris.umn.edu Federal Code: 002389

4-year public university and liberal arts college in small town.
Enrollment: 1,788 undergrads, 3% part-time. 411 full-time freshmen.
Selectivity: Admits 50 to 75% of applicants.

BASIC COSTS (2012-2013)
Tuition and fees: $12,549; out-of-state residents $12,549.
Per-credit charge: $451.
Room and board: $7,324.

FINANCIAL AID PICTURE (2012-2013)
Students with need: Out of 376 full-time freshmen who applied for aid, 285 were judged to have need. Of these, 284 received aid, and 118 had their full need met. Average financial aid package met 80% of need; average scholarship/grant was $10,011; average loan was $7,969. For part-time students, average financial aid package was $9,639.
Students without need: 77 full-time freshmen who did not demonstrate need for aid received scholarships/grants; average award was $3,656. No-need awards available for academics.
Scholarships offered: Chancellor's Scholarship: $3,500/year for 4 years; top 5%. Dean's Scholarship: $2,500/year for 4 years; top 10%. Founder's Scholarship: $1,000/year for 4 years; top 20%. National Merit Scholarship: full tuition scholarship for 4 years. Prairie Scholars Award: full tuition/year for 4 years; Morris Scholars Award: $5,000/year for 4 years plus one-time $2,500 research or creative project stipend. President's Distinguished Scholar Award: $1,000 to $3,000/year for four years.
Cumulative student debt: 66% of graduating class had student loans; average debt was $25,124.
Additional info: Land-grant program waiving tuition for Native Americans.

FINANCIAL AID PROCEDURES
Forms required: FAFSA.
Dates and Deadlines: Applicants notified on a rolling basis starting 4/1.

CONTACT
Jill Beauregard, Director of Financial Aid
600 East 4th Street, Morris, MN 56267
(800) 992-8863

University of Minnesota: Rochester

Rochester, Minnesota
www.r.umn.edu

4-year public university and health science college in small city.
Enrollment: 375 undergrads, 3% part-time. 140 full-time freshmen.
Selectivity: Admits 50 to 75% of applicants.

BASIC COSTS (2012-2013)
Tuition and fees: $13,414; out-of-state residents $13,414.
Per-credit charge: $451.
Room and board: $8,000.
Additional info: Mandatory laptop expense ($400) included in required fees.

FINANCIAL AID PICTURE (2012-2013)
Students with need: Need-based aid available for part-time students.
Students without need: No-need awards available for academics, leadership, state/district residency.

FINANCIAL AID PROCEDURES
Forms required: FAFSA.
Dates and Deadlines: Priority date 3/1; no closing date. Applicants notified on a rolling basis starting 3/30.
Transfers: Applicants notified by 7/1.

CONTACT
Nathan Tesch, Assistant Director of Student Life and Registrar
111 South Broadway, Rochester, MN 55904
(507) 258-8457

University of Minnesota: Twin Cities

Minneapolis, Minnesota
www.umn.edu Federal Code: 003969

4-year public university in very large city.
Enrollment: 30,375 undergrads, 8% part-time. 5,501 full-time freshmen.
Selectivity: Admits less than 50% of applicants.

BASIC COSTS (2012-2013)
Tuition and fees: $13,459; out-of-state residents $18,709.
Per-credit charge: $464; out-of-state residents $666.
Room and board: $8,412.
Additional info: Carlson School of Management undergraduate students pay a $500 tuition surcharge.

FINANCIAL AID PICTURE (2012-2013)
Students with need: Out of 4,518 full-time freshmen who applied for aid, 2,942 were judged to have need. Of these, 2,902 received aid, and 875 had their full need met. Average financial aid package met 73% of need; average scholarship/grant was $9,279; average loan was $4,831. For part-time students, average financial aid package was $7,414.

Students without need: This college awards aid only to students with need.
Cumulative student debt: 63% of graduating class had student loans; average debt was $29,702.

FINANCIAL AID PROCEDURES
Forms required: FAFSA, institutional form.
Dates and Deadlines: Priority date 3/1; no closing date. Applicants notified on a rolling basis starting 2/15.

CONTACT
Kris Wright, Director of Financial Aid
240 Williamson Hall, Minneapolis, MN 55455-0213
(612) 624-1111

University of St. Thomas

Saint Paul, Minnesota
www.stthomas.edu Federal Code: 002345

4-year private university in very large city, affiliated with Roman Catholic Church.
Enrollment: 6,237 undergrads, 3% part-time. 1,447 full-time freshmen.
Selectivity: Admits over 75% of applicants.

BASIC COSTS (2013-2014)
Tuition and fees: $35,308.
Per-credit charge: $1,079.
Room and board: $8,986.

FINANCIAL AID PICTURE (2012-2013)
Students with need: Out of 1,163 full-time freshmen who applied for aid, 926 were judged to have need. Of these, 926 received aid, and 171 had their full need met. Average financial aid package met 84% of need; average scholarship/grant was $17,354; average loan was $7,279. For part-time students, average financial aid package was $11,310.
Students without need: 220 full-time freshmen who did not demonstrate need for aid received scholarships/grants; average award was $14,712. No-need awards available for academics, music/drama, ROTC.
Cumulative student debt: 69% of graduating class had student loans; average debt was $36,077.

FINANCIAL AID PROCEDURES
Forms required: FAFSA.
Dates and Deadlines: Priority date 4/1; no closing date. Applicants notified on a rolling basis starting 3/1; must reply within 3 week(s) of notification.

CONTACT
2115 Summit Avenue - 32F, Saint Paul, MN

Vermilion Community College

Ely, Minnesota
www.vcc.edu Federal Code: 002350

2-year public community and technical college in small town.
Enrollment: 781 undergrads.
Selectivity: Open admission.

BASIC COSTS (2012-2013)
Tuition and fees: $5,323; out-of-state residents $6,505.
Per-credit charge: $158; out-of-state residents $197.
Room and board: $5,190.

FINANCIAL AID PICTURE
Students with need: Need-based aid available for full-time and part-time students. Work study available nights, weekends, and for part-time students.

FINANCIAL AID PROCEDURES
Forms required: FAFSA, institutional form.
Dates and Deadlines: Priority date 4/15; no closing date. Applicants notified on a rolling basis starting 4/1.

CONTACT
Kristi L'Allier, Financial Aid Director
1900 East Camp Street, Ely, MN 55731-9989
(218) 235-2153

Walden University

Minneapolis, Minnesota
www.waldenu.edu Federal Code: 025402

4-year for-profit virtual university in large city.
Enrollment: 8,560 undergrads, 90% part-time.
Selectivity: Open admission; but selective for some programs.

BASIC COSTS (2012-2013)
Tuition and fees: $13,335.
Per-credit charge: $290.

FINANCIAL AID PICTURE
Students with need: Need-based aid available for full-time and part-time students.
Students without need: This college awards aid only to students with need.

FINANCIAL AID PROCEDURES
Forms required: FAFSA.
Dates and Deadlines: Applicants notified on a rolling basis.
Transfers: No deadline. Applicants notified on a rolling basis.

CONTACT
Teresa Drzewiecki, Senior Associate Director of Financial Aid
100 Washington Ave South, Suite 900, Minneapolis, MN 55401
(410) 843-8506

Winona State University

Winona, Minnesota
www.winona.edu Federal Code: 002394

4-year public university in large town.
Enrollment: 8,223 undergrads, 9% part-time. 1,782 full-time freshmen.
Selectivity: Admits 50 to 75% of applicants.

BASIC COSTS (2012-2013)
Tuition and fees: $8,710; out-of-state residents $14,310.
Per-credit charge: $227; out-of-state residents $412.
Room and board: $7,690.
Additional info: Fees include mandatory laptop lease for full-time students.

FINANCIAL AID PICTURE
Students with need: Need-based aid available for full-time and part-time students. Work study available nights, weekends, and for part-time students.
Students without need: No-need awards available for academics, alumni affiliation, art, athletics, leadership, minority status, music/drama, ROTC, state/district residency.
Scholarships offered: Outstanding Academics Honors Award: $2,500, renewable, top 5% of class, ACT 32 or above. WSU Foundation Board Scholarship: $2,000 renewable, top 15% of class, ACT 28-31, essay/interview. Presidential Honor Scholarships: $1,500 renewable; top 15% of class, ACT 28-31; $1,000, renewable, top 10% of class, ACT 27; $750, renewable, top 15% of class, ACT 26. Resident Tuition Scholarships: $3,400, renewable, to out-of-state students, top 15% of class or ACT 25.

FINANCIAL AID PROCEDURES
Forms required: FAFSA.

Dates and Deadlines: Applicants notified on a rolling basis starting 5/1; must reply within 3 week(s) of notification.

CONTACT

Greg Peterson, Director of Financial Aid
Office of Admissions, Winona, MN 55987
(800) 342-5978

Mississippi

Alcorn State University

Alcorn State, Mississippi
www.alcorn.edu Federal Code: 002396

4-year public university and agricultural college in rural community.
Enrollment: 3,208 undergrads, 12% part-time. 563 full-time freshmen.
Selectivity: Admits less than 50% of applicants.

BASIC COSTS (2012-2013)

Tuition and fees: $5,712; out-of-state residents $14,052.
Per-credit charge: $190; out-of-state residents $468.
Room and board: $8,000.

FINANCIAL AID PICTURE (2012-2013)

Students with need: Average financial aid package met 49% of need; average scholarship/grant was $5,629; average loan was $3,390. For part-time students, average financial aid package was $11,188.
Students without need: No-need awards available for academics, athletics, leadership, ROTC.
Cumulative student debt: 89% of graduating class had student loans; average debt was $29,001.

FINANCIAL AID PROCEDURES

Forms required: FAFSA, institutional form.
Dates and Deadlines: Priority date 3/15; no closing date. Applicants notified on a rolling basis starting 4/1; must reply within 4 week(s) of notification.

CONTACT

Juanita Russell, Director of Financial Aid
1000 ASU Drive #300, Alcorn State, MS 39096-7500
(601) 877-6190

Belhaven University

Jackson, Mississippi
www.belhaven.edu Federal Code: 002397

4-year private liberal arts college in large city, affiliated with Presbyterian Church (USA).
Enrollment: 2,518 undergrads, 52% part-time. 220 full-time freshmen.
Selectivity: Admits less than 50% of applicants.

BASIC COSTS (2013-2014)

Tuition and fees: $19,970.
Per-credit charge: $425.
Room and board: $7,200.

FINANCIAL AID PICTURE (2012-2013)

Students with need: Average financial aid package met 75% of need; average scholarship/grant was $4,150; average loan was $3,162. For part-time students, average financial aid package was $11,628.
Students without need: No-need awards available for academics, alumni affiliation, art, athletics, job skills, leadership, music/drama.
Cumulative student debt: 74% of graduating class had student loans; average debt was $28,952.

FINANCIAL AID PROCEDURES

Forms required: FAFSA.
Dates and Deadlines: Priority date 1/31; no closing date. Applicants notified on a rolling basis starting 2/1.
Transfers: No deadline. Applicants notified on a rolling basis.

CONTACT

Tawesia Colyer, Director of Student Financial Services
1500 Peachtree Street, Jackson, MS 39202
(601) 968-5933

Blue Mountain College

Blue Mountain, Mississippi
www.bmc.edu Federal Code: 002398

4-year private liberal arts college in rural community, affiliated with Southern Baptist Convention.
Enrollment: 494 undergrads, 7% part-time. 70 full-time freshmen.
Selectivity: Admits less than 50% of applicants.

BASIC COSTS (2012-2013)

Tuition and fees: $9,674.
Per-credit charge: $290.
Room and board: $4,000.

FINANCIAL AID PICTURE (2011-2012)

Students with need: Average financial aid package met 82% of need; average scholarship/grant was $2,815; average loan was $5,120. For part-time students, average financial aid package was $6,303.
Students without need: No-need awards available for academics, alumni affiliation, art, athletics, leadership, music/drama, religious affiliation, state/district residency.
Scholarships offered: ACT/SAT Scholarships: varies from $1,000 to $7,000 per year; based on ACT/SAT score; number varies depending on number of applicants. Valedictorian/Salutatorian Scholarships: $1,000 to $5,000 first year; based on rank in class; unlimited number available. Child of Alumnae/Alumni: $500 first year; must be dependent of graduate; unlimited number available.
Cumulative student debt: 80% of graduating class had student loans; average debt was $23,107.

FINANCIAL AID PROCEDURES

Forms required: FAFSA, institutional form.
Dates and Deadlines: Priority date 3/1; closing date 7/31. Applicants notified on a rolling basis starting 4/1; must reply within 4 week(s) of notification.
Transfers: No deadline.

CONTACT

Michelle Hall, Director of Financial Aid
201 West Main Street, PO Box 160, Blue Mountain, MS 38610-0160
(662) 685-4771 ext. 145

Coahoma Community College

Clarksdale, Mississippi
www.coahomacc.edu Federal Code: 002401

2-year public community college in large town.
Enrollment: 2,316 undergrads.
Selectivity: Open admission; but selective for some programs.

BASIC COSTS (2012-2013)

Tuition and fees: $1,840; out-of-state residents $2,900.
Room and board: $3,514.

FINANCIAL AID PICTURE

Students with need: Need-based aid available for full-time and part-time students.

Students without need: This college awards aid only to students with need.

FINANCIAL AID PROCEDURES

Forms required: FAFSA, institutional form.

Dates and Deadlines: Priority date 4/1; no closing date. Applicants notified on a rolling basis starting 7/1.

Transfers: Priority date 3/1.

CONTACT

Patricia Brooks, Director of Financial Aid
3240 Friars Point Road, Clarksdale, MS 38614-9799
(662) 627-2571

Copiah-Lincoln Community College

Wesson, Mississippi
www.colin.edu Federal Code: 002402

2-year public community college in small town.
Enrollment: 3,410 undergrads, 15% part-time. 171 full-time freshmen.
Selectivity: Open admission; but selective for some programs.

BASIC COSTS (2012-2013)

Tuition and fees: $2,100; out-of-state residents $3,900.
Per-credit charge: $108; out-of-state residents $183.
Room and board: $3,300.

FINANCIAL AID PICTURE (2011-2012)

Students with need: Need-based aid available for full-time and part-time students. Work study available nights, weekends, and for part-time students.

Students without need: No-need awards available for academics, art, athletics, job skills, leadership, music/drama, state/district residency.

FINANCIAL AID PROCEDURES

Forms required: FAFSA.

Dates and Deadlines: Closing date 4/1. Applicants notified on a rolling basis starting 4/1; must reply within 2 week(s) of notification.

CONTACT

Leslie Smith, Director of Financial Aid
PO Box 649, Wesson, MS 39191
(601) 643-8340

Delta State University

Cleveland, Mississippi
www.deltastate.edu Federal Code: 002403

4-year public university in large town.
Enrollment: 2,756 undergrads, 18% part-time. 382 full-time freshmen.
Selectivity: Admits over 75% of applicants.

BASIC COSTS (2012-2013)

Tuition and fees: $5,724; out-of-state residents $14,820.
Per-credit charge: $191; out-of-state residents $494.
Room and board: $5,993.

FINANCIAL AID PICTURE (2011-2012)

Students with need: 39% of average financial aid package awarded as scholarships/grants, 61% awarded as loans/jobs. Need-based aid available for part-time students. Work study available nights, weekends, and for part-time students.

Students without need: No-need awards available for academics, alumni affiliation, art, athletics, leadership, music/drama, state/district residency.

FINANCIAL AID PROCEDURES

Forms required: FAFSA, institutional form.

Dates and Deadlines: Priority date 3/1; no closing date. Applicants notified on a rolling basis starting 5/1.

CONTACT

Ann Mullins, Director of Student Financial Assistance
117 Kent Wyatt Hall, Cleveland, MS 38733
(662) 846-4670

East Mississippi Community College

Scooba, Mississippi
www.eastms.edu Federal Code: 002405

2-year public community college in rural community.
Enrollment: 4,698 undergrads.
Selectivity: Open admission; but selective for some programs.

BASIC COSTS (2012-2013)

Tuition and fees: $2,450; out-of-state residents $4,500.
Per-credit charge: $135; out-of-state residents $139.
Room and board: $3,670.
Additional info: Tuition at time of enrollment locked for 2 years.

FINANCIAL AID PICTURE (2012-2013)

Students with need: Need-based aid available for full-time and part-time students.

Students without need: No-need awards available for academics, art, athletics, leadership, music/drama, state/district residency.

FINANCIAL AID PROCEDURES

Forms required: FAFSA, state aid form, institutional form.

Dates and Deadlines: Priority date 4/1; no closing date. Applicants notified on a rolling basis starting 4/1; must reply within 2 week(s) of notification.

CONTACT

Jim Gibson, Vice President for Financial Aid
Admissions Office, Scooba, MS 39358
(662) 476-5079

Hinds Community College

Raymond, Mississippi
www.hindscc.edu Federal Code: 002407

2-year public branch campus and community college in small town.
Enrollment: 11,667 undergrads, 31% part-time. 2,801 full-time freshmen.
Selectivity: Open admission; but selective for some programs.

BASIC COSTS (2012-2013)

Tuition and fees: $2,060; out-of-state residents $4,660.
Per-credit charge: $100; out-of-state residents $200.
Room and board: $4,000.

FINANCIAL AID PICTURE (2012-2013)

Students with need: 74% of average financial aid package awarded as scholarships/grants, 26% awarded as loans/jobs. Need-based aid available for part-time students. Work study available nights, weekends, and for part-time students.

Students without need: No-need awards available for academics, art, athletics, job skills, leadership, minority status, music/drama, state/district residency.

FINANCIAL AID PROCEDURES

Forms required: FAFSA.

Dates and Deadlines: Priority date 4/1; no closing date. Applicants notified on a rolling basis starting 5/15; must reply within 2 week(s) of notification.

Transfers: Financial aid transcripts from all previous colleges must be on file prior to award letter being released.

CONTACT

Joy Willis, Director of Financial Aid
505 East Main Street, Raymond, MS 39154-1100
(601) 857-3223

Holmes Community College

Goodman, Mississippi
www.holmescc.edu Federal Code: 002408

2-year public community college in rural community.
Enrollment: 6,395 undergrads.
Selectivity: Open admission; but selective for some programs.

BASIC COSTS (2012-2013)
Tuition and fees: $2,210; out-of-state residents $4,790.
Per-credit charge: $102; out-of-state residents $212.
Room and board: $2,800.

FINANCIAL AID PICTURE (2011-2012)
Students with need: 77% of average financial aid package awarded as scholarships/grants, 23% awarded as loans/jobs.
Students without need: No-need awards available for academics, athletics.
Scholarships offered: President's Scholarship for full-time students provides full tuition, requires ACT of 20 or higher. Board of Trustees Scholarship for full-time students provides tuition, room and board, requires ACT of 28 or higher.

FINANCIAL AID PROCEDURES
Forms required: FAFSA, state aid form, institutional form.
Dates and Deadlines: Priority date 6/1; no closing date. Applicants notified on a rolling basis.

CONTACT
Gail Muse, Director of Financial Aid
Box 398, Goodman, MS 39079
(662) 472-9027

Itawamba Community College

Fulton, Mississippi
www.iccms.edu Federal Code: 002409

2-year public community and technical college in small town.
Enrollment: 5,991 undergrads.
Selectivity: Open admission; but selective for some programs.

BASIC COSTS (2012-2013)
Tuition and fees: $2,020; out-of-state residents $3,770.
Room and board: $3,330.

FINANCIAL AID PICTURE
Students with need: Need-based aid available for full-time and part-time students.
Students without need: No-need awards available for academics, art, athletics, leadership, music/drama, state/district residency.

FINANCIAL AID PROCEDURES
Forms required: FAFSA, institutional form.
Dates and Deadlines: Priority date 4/30; closing date 7/31. Applicants notified on a rolling basis starting 4/15.

CONTACT
Robert Walker, Director of Financial Aid
602 West Hill Street, Fulton, MS 38843-1099
(662) 862-8222

Jackson State University

Jackson, Mississippi
www.jsums.edu Federal Code: 002410

4-year public university in large city.
Enrollment: 6,675 undergrads, 18% part-time. 862 full-time freshmen.
Selectivity: Admits 50 to 75% of applicants.

BASIC COSTS (2012-2013)
Tuition and fees: $5,988; out-of-state residents $14,676.
Per-credit charge: $250; out-of-state residents $612.
Room and board: $6,996.

FINANCIAL AID PICTURE
Students with need: Need-based aid available for full-time and part-time students.
Students without need: This college awards aid only to students with need.

FINANCIAL AID PROCEDURES
Forms required: FAFSA.
Dates and Deadlines: Priority date 4/1; closing date 5/1. Applicants notified on a rolling basis starting 5/1.

CONTACT
Betty Moncure, Director, Financial Aid
1400 John R. Lynch Street, Jackson, MS 39217
(601) 979-2227

Meridian Community College

Meridian, Mississippi
www.meridiancc.edu Federal Code: 002413

2-year public community college in large town.
Enrollment: 3,831 full-time undergrads.
Selectivity: Open admission; but selective for some programs.

BASIC COSTS (2012-2013)
Tuition and fees: $2,230; out-of-state residents $3,630.
Per-credit charge: $100; out-of-state residents $157.
Room and board: $3,974.

FINANCIAL AID PICTURE (2012-2013)
Students with need: 85% of average financial aid package awarded as scholarships/grants, 15% awarded as loans/jobs. Need-based aid available for part-time students.
Students without need: No-need awards available for academics, art, athletics, leadership, music/drama, state/district residency.
Scholarships offered: Incoming freshmen graduating from a school in Lauderdale County can attend tuition-free.

FINANCIAL AID PROCEDURES
Forms required: FAFSA, institutional form.
Dates and Deadlines: Priority date 6/1; no closing date. Applicants notified on a rolling basis starting 5/15; must reply within 2 week(s) of notification.

CONTACT
Nedra Bradley, Director of Financial Aid
910 Highway 19 North, Meridian, MS 39307-5890
(601) 484-8628

Millsaps College

Jackson, Mississippi
www.millsaps.edu Federal Code: 002414

4-year private business and liberal arts college in large city, affiliated with United Methodist Church.
Enrollment: 837 undergrads, 1% part-time. 211 full-time freshmen.
Selectivity: Admits 50 to 75% of applicants.

BASIC COSTS (2012-2013)
Tuition and fees: $30,974.
Per-credit charge: $982.
Room and board: $10,826.

FINANCIAL AID PICTURE (2012-2013)

Students with need: Out of 170 full-time freshmen who applied for aid, 141 were judged to have need. Of these, 141 received aid, and 44 had their full need met. Average financial aid package met 80% of need; average scholarship/grant was $22,038; average loan was $3,518. For part-time students, average financial aid package was $4,555.

Students without need: 69 full-time freshmen who did not demonstrate need for aid received scholarships/grants; average award was $21,612. No-need awards available for academics, art, leadership, music/drama, religious affiliation.

Cumulative student debt: 56% of graduating class had student loans; average debt was $28,965.

FINANCIAL AID PROCEDURES

Forms required: FAFSA.

Dates and Deadlines: Priority date 3/1; no closing date. Applicants notified on a rolling basis starting 3/15; must reply by 5/1 or within 2 week(s) of notification.

Transfers: No deadline. Applicants notified on a rolling basis; must reply within 2 week(s) of notification.

CONTACT

Patrick James, Director of Financial Aid
1701 North State Street, Jackson, MS 39210-0001
(601) 974-1220

Mississippi College

Clinton, Mississippi
www.mc.edu Federal Code: 002415

4-year private university in large town, affiliated with Southern Baptist Convention.

Enrollment: 3,030 undergrads, 14% part-time. 461 full-time freshmen.

Selectivity: Admits 50 to 75% of applicants.

BASIC COSTS (2013-2014)

Tuition and fees: $14,868.

Per-credit charge: $442.

Room and board: $7,150.

FINANCIAL AID PICTURE (2012-2013)

Students with need: Out of 392 full-time freshmen who applied for aid, 187 were judged to have need. Of these, 187 received aid, and 1 had their full need met. Average financial aid package met 63% of need; average scholarship/grant was $5,305; average loan was $3,177. For part-time students, average financial aid package was $4,792.

Students without need: 257 full-time freshmen who did not demonstrate need for aid received scholarships/grants; average award was $8,032. No-need awards available for academics, alumni affiliation, art, leadership, music/drama, religious affiliation.

Scholarships offered: Scholarships up to $1,500 based on various criteria including leadership, academics, church and community involvement; extensive number awarded.

Cumulative student debt: 54% of graduating class had student loans; average debt was $26,578.

Additional info: Student reply date for institutional scholarships: May 1.

FINANCIAL AID PROCEDURES

Forms required: FAFSA, state aid form.

Dates and Deadlines: Priority date 3/1; no closing date. Applicants notified on a rolling basis starting 3/1; must reply by 5/1.

Transfers: No deadline. Applicants notified on a rolling basis starting 3/1; must reply by 5/1.

CONTACT

Karon McMillan, Director of Financial Aid
Box 4026, Clinton, MS 39058-0001
(601) 925-3212

Mississippi Delta Community College

Moorhead, Mississippi
www.msdelta.edu Federal Code: 002416

2-year public community college in rural community.

Enrollment: 3,364 undergrads.

Selectivity: Open admission; but selective for some programs.

BASIC COSTS (2012-2013)

Tuition and fees: $2,450; out-of-state residents $4,058.

Per-credit charge: $110.

Room and board: $2,740.

FINANCIAL AID PICTURE

Students with need: Need-based aid available for full-time students.

Students without need: No-need awards available for academics, athletics, state/district residency.

FINANCIAL AID PROCEDURES

Forms required: FAFSA, institutional form.

Dates and Deadlines: Closing date 8/1. Applicants notified on a rolling basis; must reply within 2 week(s) of notification.

CONTACT

Mary Rodgers, Director of Financial Aid
Box 668, Moorhead, MS 38761
(662) 246-6263

Mississippi Gulf Coast Community College

Perkinston, Mississippi
www.mgccc.edu Federal Code: 002419

2-year public community college in large city.

Enrollment: 10,055 undergrads.

Selectivity: Open admission; but selective for some programs.

BASIC COSTS (2012-2013)

Tuition and fees: $2,772; out-of-state residents $4,618.

Per-credit charge: $115; out-of-state residents $192.

Room and board: $3,810.

FINANCIAL AID PICTURE

Students with need: Need-based aid available for full-time students.

Students without need: This college awards aid only to students with need.

FINANCIAL AID PROCEDURES

Forms required: institutional form.

Dates and Deadlines: Priority date 6/1; no closing date. Applicants notified on a rolling basis starting 7/1.

CONTACT

LaShanda Chamberlain, Director of Financial Aid
PO Box 548, Perkinston, MS 39573
(228) 497-7687

Mississippi State University

Mississippi State, Mississippi
www.msstate.edu Federal Code: 002423

4-year public university and agricultural college in large town.

Enrollment: 15,585 undergrads, 8% part-time. 2,898 full-time freshmen.

Selectivity: Admits 50 to 75% of applicants.

BASIC COSTS (2012-2013)

Tuition and fees: $6,264; out-of-state residents $15,828.

Per-credit charge: $209; out-of-state residents $528.
Room and board: $7,074.
Additional info: Tuition/fee waivers available for minority students.

FINANCIAL AID PICTURE (2011-2012)

Students with need: Out of 2,390 full-time freshmen who applied for aid, 1,990 were judged to have need. Of these, 1,970 received aid, and 583 had their full need met. Average financial aid package met 63% of need; average scholarship/grant was $5,440; average loan was $3,253. For part-time students, average financial aid package was $9,333.
Students without need: 622 full-time freshmen who did not demonstrate need for aid received scholarships/grants; average award was $3,161. No-need awards available for academics, alumni affiliation, art, athletics, job skills, leadership, minority status, music/drama, ROTC, state/district residency.
Scholarships offered: 82 full-time freshmen received athletic scholarships; average amount $12,426.
Cumulative student debt: 49% of graduating class had student loans; average debt was $26,139.

FINANCIAL AID PROCEDURES

Forms required: FAFSA.
Dates and Deadlines: Priority date 4/1; no closing date. Applicants notified on a rolling basis starting 12/1; must reply by 5/1.
Transfers: No deadline. Applicants notified on a rolling basis.

CONTACT

Paul McKinney, Director
Box 6334, Mississippi State, MS 39762
(662) 325-2450

Mississippi University for Women

Columbus, Mississippi
www.muw.edu Federal Code: 002422

4-year public university and liberal arts college in large town.
Enrollment: 2,319 undergrads.

BASIC COSTS (2012-2013)

Tuition and fees: $5,316; out-of-state residents $14,484.
Per-credit charge: $222; out-of-state residents $604.
Room and board: $5,991.
Additional info: Tuition/fee waivers available for adults, minority students.

FINANCIAL AID PICTURE

Students with need: Need-based aid available for full-time and part-time students. Work study available nights, weekends, and for part-time students.
Students without need: No-need awards available for academics, alumni affiliation, leadership, minority status, music/drama, ROTC, state/district residency.

FINANCIAL AID PROCEDURES

Forms required: FAFSA, state aid form.
Dates and Deadlines: Priority date 3/1; no closing date. Applicants notified on a rolling basis starting 3/15; must reply within 2 week(s) of notification.
Transfers: Closing date 4/1.

CONTACT

Searcy Taylor, Director of Financial Aid
1100 College St. MUW-1613, Columbus, MS 39701
(662) 329-7114

Pearl River Community College

Poplarville, Mississippi
www.prcc.edu Federal Code: 002430

2-year public community college in small town.
Enrollment: 5,500 undergrads.
Selectivity: Open admission; but selective for some programs.

BASIC COSTS (2012-2013)

Tuition and fees: $2,380; out-of-state residents $4,778.
Per-credit charge: $115; out-of-state residents $215.
Room and board: $3,800.

FINANCIAL AID PICTURE

Students with need: Need-based aid available for full-time and part-time students.
Students without need: No-need awards available for academics, alumni affiliation, athletics, leadership, music/drama, state/district residency.

FINANCIAL AID PROCEDURES

Forms required: FAFSA, institutional form.
Dates and Deadlines: Priority date 4/17; no closing date. Applicants notified on a rolling basis.

CONTACT

Valerie Horne, Director of Financial Aid
101 Highway 11 North, Poplarville, MS 39470
(601) 403-1212

Rust College

Holly Springs, Mississippi
www.rustcollege.edu Federal Code: 002433

4-year private liberal arts and teachers college in small town, affiliated with United Methodist Church.
Enrollment: 934 undergrads, 8% part-time. 271 full-time freshmen.
Selectivity: Admits less than 50% of applicants.

BASIC COSTS (2013-2014)

Tuition and fees: $8,900.
Per-credit charge: $399.
Room and board: $4,000.
Additional info: Tuition at time of enrollment locked for 4 years.

FINANCIAL AID PICTURE

Students with need: Need-based aid available for full-time and part-time students.
Students without need: No-need awards available for academics, leadership, music/drama, religious affiliation, state/district residency.
Scholarships offered: Honor Track Scholarship: $11,800; minimum GPA 3.5, ACT 22, SAT 1530. Presidential Scholarship: $3,000; minimum GPA 3.25, ACT 19, SAT 1350. Academic Dean's Scholarship: $2500; minimum GPA 3.0, ACT 17, SAT 1230.

FINANCIAL AID PROCEDURES

Forms required: FAFSA, institutional form.
Dates and Deadlines: Priority date 3/15; closing date 6/30. Applicants notified on a rolling basis starting 4/1; must reply within 2 week(s) of notification.
Transfers: No deadline. Applicants notified on a rolling basis starting 4/1; must reply within 2 week(s) of notification.

CONTACT

Helen Street, Director of Financial Aid
150 Rust Avenue, Holly Springs, MS 38635-2328
(662) 252-8000 ext. 4062

Southwest Mississippi Community College

Summit, Mississippi
www.smcc.edu Federal Code: 002436

2-year public community college in rural community.
Enrollment: 1,977 undergrads, 9% part-time. 655 full-time freshmen.

Selectivity: Open admission; but selective for some programs.

BASIC COSTS (2012-2013)
Tuition and fees: $2,090; out-of-state residents $4,790.
Per-credit charge: $100; out-of-state residents $215.
Room and board: $2,880.

FINANCIAL AID PICTURE (2011-2012)
Students with need: 99% of average financial aid package awarded as scholarships/grants, 1% awarded as loans/jobs. Need-based aid available for part-time students.

FINANCIAL AID PROCEDURES
Forms required: FAFSA.
Dates and Deadlines: Applicants notified on a rolling basis.

CONTACT
Stacey Hodges, Director of Financial Aid
1156 College Drive, Summit, MS 39666
(601) 276-3708

Tougaloo College

Tougaloo, Mississippi
www.tougaloo.edu Federal Code: 002439

4-year private liberal arts college in large city, affiliated with United Christian Mission Society and United Church of Christ.
Enrollment: 962 undergrads, 3% part-time. 234 full-time freshmen.
Selectivity: Admits less than 50% of applicants.

BASIC COSTS (2012-2013)
Tuition and fees: $10,210.
Per-credit charge: $406.
Room and board: $6,572.
Additional info: Tuition/fee waivers available for adults.

FINANCIAL AID PICTURE (2011-2012)
Students with need: Out of 227 full-time freshmen who applied for aid, 226 were judged to have need. Of these, 226 received aid, and 45 had their full need met. Average financial aid package met 40% of need; average scholarship/grant was $2,700; average loan was $3,500. For part-time students, average financial aid package was $7,500.
Students without need: 21 full-time freshmen who did not demonstrate need for aid received scholarships/grants; average award was $15,121. No-need awards available for academics, art, athletics, leadership, music/drama.
Scholarships offered: 35 full-time freshmen received athletic scholarships; average amount $8,000.
Cumulative student debt: 80% of graduating class had student loans; average debt was $23,145.

FINANCIAL AID PROCEDURES
Forms required: FAFSA, state aid form, institutional form.
Dates and Deadlines: Priority date 4/15; no closing date. Applicants notified on a rolling basis starting 5/1; must reply within 2 week(s) of notification.
Transfers: No deadline. Applicants notified on a rolling basis starting 2/1; must reply within 2 week(s) of notification.

CONTACT
Maria Thomas, Director of Financial Aid
500 West County Line Road, Tougaloo, MS 39174
(601) 977-7766

University of Mississippi

University, Mississippi
www.olemiss.edu Federal Code: 002440

4-year public university in large town.
Enrollment: 15,791 undergrads, 7% part-time. 3,351 full-time freshmen.
Selectivity: Admits 50 to 75% of applicants.

BASIC COSTS (2012-2013)
Tuition and fees: $6,282; out-of-state residents $16,266.
Per-credit charge: $209; out-of-state residents $542.
Room and board: $6,850.
Additional info: Tuition/fee waivers available for minority students.

FINANCIAL AID PICTURE
Students with need: Need-based aid available for full-time and part-time students. Work study available nights, weekends, and for part-time students.
Students without need: No-need awards available for academics, alumni affiliation, art, athletics, leadership, minority status, music/drama, ROTC, state/district residency.

FINANCIAL AID PROCEDURES
Forms required: FAFSA.
Dates and Deadlines: Priority date 3/1; no closing date. Applicants notified on a rolling basis starting 4/1; must reply within 4 week(s) of notification.
Transfers: No deadline. Applicants notified on a rolling basis starting 4/1; must reply within 4 week(s) of notification.

CONTACT
Laura Diven-Brown, Director of Financial Aid
145 Martindale, University, MS 38677-1848
(800) 891-4596

University of Mississippi Medical Center

Jackson, Mississippi
www.umc.edu Federal Code: 004688

Upper-division public health science college in large city.
Enrollment: 633 undergrads.
Selectivity: Open admission; but selective for some programs. GED not accepted.

BASIC COSTS (2012-2013)
Tuition and fees: $6,282; out-of-state residents $16,266.
Per-credit charge: $209; out-of-state residents $542.

FINANCIAL AID PICTURE
Students with need: Need-based aid available for full-time and part-time students.
Students without need: This college awards aid only to students with need.

FINANCIAL AID PROCEDURES
Forms required: FAFSA, state aid form, institutional form.
Dates and Deadlines: Closing date 4/1. Applicants notified by 7/15; must reply within 2 week(s) of notification.

CONTACT
Stacey Mathews, Director of Student Financial Aid
2500 North State Street, Jackson, MS 39216
(601) 984-1117

University of Southern Mississippi

Hattiesburg, Mississippi
www.usm.edu Federal Code: 002441

4-year public university in small city.
Enrollment: 13,460 undergrads, 16% part-time. 1,916 full-time freshmen.
Selectivity: Admits 50 to 75% of applicants.

BASIC COSTS (2012-2013)
Tuition and fees: $6,336; out-of-state residents $14,448.
Per-credit charge: $264; out-of-state residents $602.
Room and board: $6,907.

FINANCIAL AID PICTURE (2011-2012)
Students with need: Average financial aid package met 75% of need; average scholarship/grant was $4,505; average loan was $3,552. For part-time students, average financial aid package was $5,776.

FINANCIAL AID PROCEDURES
Forms required: FAFSA, institutional form.
Dates and Deadlines: Priority date 3/15; no closing date.
Transfers: Merit scholarships available to community college transfer students based on college GPA.

CONTACT
David Williamson, Director of Financial Aid
118 College Drive #5166, Hattiesburg, MS 39406-0001
(601) 266-4774

Missouri

Avila University
Kansas City, Missouri
www.avila.edu Federal Code: 002449

4-year private university and liberal arts college in very large city, affiliated with Roman Catholic Church.
Enrollment: 1,268 undergrads, 18% part-time. 210 full-time freshmen.
Selectivity: Admits 50 to 75% of applicants.

BASIC COSTS (2013-2014)
Tuition and fees: $24,850.
Per-credit charge: $600.
Room and board: $6,800.
Additional info: Tuition/fee waivers available for adults.

FINANCIAL AID PICTURE (2012-2013)
Students with need: Out of 207 full-time freshmen who applied for aid, 188 were judged to have need. Of these, 187 received aid, and 34 had their full need met. Average financial aid package met 72.51% of need; average scholarship/grant was $16,261; average loan was $3,420. For part-time students, average financial aid package was $6,338.
Students without need: 49 full-time freshmen who did not demonstrate need for aid received scholarships/grants; average award was $10,634. No-need awards available for academics, alumni affiliation, art, athletics, music/drama, religious affiliation.
Scholarships offered: 40 full-time freshmen received athletic scholarships; average amount $4,007.
Cumulative student debt: 86% of graduating class had student loans; average debt was $30,322.
Additional info: Financial aid adjusted based on need for increases in tuition.

FINANCIAL AID PROCEDURES
Forms required: FAFSA, institutional form.
Dates and Deadlines: Closing date 4/1. Applicants notified on a rolling basis starting 2/1; must reply within 2 week(s) of notification.
Transfers: No deadline. Applicants notified on a rolling basis starting 2/1; must reply within 2 week(s) of notification. Non-need-based academic scholarship available for transfer students.

CONTACT
Crystal Bruntz, Director of Financial Aid
11901 Wornall Road, Kansas City, MO 64145-1007
(816) 501-3600

Bolivar Technical College
Bolivar, Missouri
www.bolivarcollege.org Federal Code: 035793

2-year private branch campus and technical college in small town.
Enrollment: 111 full-time undergrads.
Selectivity: Open admission; but selective for some programs.

BASIC COSTS (2012-2013)
Tuition and fees: $12,528.
Per-credit charge: $405.
Additional info: Tuition varies by program, $162-$405 per credit hour.

FINANCIAL AID PICTURE
Students with need: Need-based aid available for full-time and part-time students.
Students without need: This college awards aid only to students with need.

FINANCIAL AID PROCEDURES
Forms required: FAFSA, institutional form.
Dates and Deadlines: Priority date 4/1; no closing date.

CONTACT
Wendy McGowin, Financial Aid
PO Box 592, Bolivar, MO 65613

Calvary Bible College and Theological Seminary
Kansas City, Missouri
www.calvary.edu Federal Code: 002450

4-year private Bible and seminary college in large city, affiliated with nondenominational tradition.
Enrollment: 229 undergrads, 29% part-time. 32 full-time freshmen.
Selectivity: Admits over 75% of applicants.

BASIC COSTS (2013-2014)
Tuition and fees: $10,116.
Per-credit charge: $310.
Room and board: $5,000.
Additional info: Tuition/fee waivers available for minority students.

FINANCIAL AID PICTURE
Students with need: Need-based aid available for full-time and part-time students.
Students without need: No-need awards available for academics, alumni affiliation, job skills, music/drama, religious affiliation, ROTC.

FINANCIAL AID PROCEDURES
Forms required: FAFSA, institutional form.
Dates and Deadlines: Priority date 3/1; closing date 4/1. Applicants notified on a rolling basis starting 5/1.
Transfers: Applicants notified on a rolling basis.

CONTACT
Bob Crank, Financial Aid Director
15800 Calvary Road, Kansas City, MO 64147-1341
(816) 322-5152 ext. 1323

Central Methodist University
Fayette, Missouri
www.centralmethodist.edu Federal Code: E00605

4-year private university and liberal arts college in small town, affiliated with United Methodist Church.

Enrollment: 1,158 undergrads. 298 full-time freshmen.
Selectivity: Admits 50 to 75% of applicants.

BASIC COSTS (2013-2014)
Tuition and fees: $21,320.
Per-credit charge: $190.
Room and board: $6,920.

FINANCIAL AID PICTURE (2011-2012)
Students with need: Out of 273 full-time freshmen who applied for aid, 253 were judged to have need. Of these, 252 received aid, and 45 had their full need met. Average financial aid package met 27% of need; average scholarship/grant was $5,030; average loan was $3,467. For part-time students, average financial aid package was $9,844.
Students without need: 46 full-time freshmen who did not demonstrate need for aid received scholarships/grants; average award was $8,871. No-need awards available for academics, alumni affiliation, athletics, leadership, music/drama, religious affiliation, ROTC.
Scholarships offered: 30 full-time freshmen received athletic scholarships; average amount $4,725.
Cumulative student debt: 73% of graduating class had student loans; average debt was $6,909.

FINANCIAL AID PROCEDURES
Forms required: FAFSA.
Dates and Deadlines: Priority date 3/15; no closing date. Applicants notified on a rolling basis starting 1/1; must reply within 2 week(s) of notification.
Transfers: No deadline. Applicants notified on a rolling basis. Merit based institutional financial aid is determined by college transfer GPA.

CONTACT
Kristen Gibbs, Director of Financial Assistance
411 Central Methodist Square, Fayette, MO 65248-1198
(660) 248-6245

Chamberlain College of Nursing: St. Louis

St Louis, Missouri
www.chamberlain.edu Federal Code: 006385

4-year for-profit nursing college in very large city.
Enrollment: 536 undergrads, 31% part-time. 9 full-time freshmen.

BASIC COSTS (2012-2013)
Tuition and fees: $16,360.
Per-credit charge: $665.

FINANCIAL AID PICTURE
Students with need: Need-based aid available for full-time and part-time students.
Students without need: No-need awards available for academics.
Scholarships offered: Tenet Nurse Citizen Award: full tuition; based on application, essay, interview, renewable with 3.25 GPA, 1 awarded. Chancellor's Award: half tuition; for students with 24 ACT, 3.5 GPA; number awarded subject to fund availability. Merit Scholarships: up to $3,000; based on academic achievement; number awarded subject to fund availability.

FINANCIAL AID PROCEDURES
Forms required: FAFSA, institutional form.
Dates and Deadlines: Applicants notified on a rolling basis starting 4/1; must reply within 2 week(s) of notification.
Transfers: No deadline.

CONTACT
Michelle Mohn, Financial Counselor St. Louis, MO 63139
(314) 768-5604

College of the Ozarks

Point Lookout, Missouri
www.cofo.edu Federal Code: 002500

4-year private liberal arts college in small town, affiliated with interdenominational tradition.
Enrollment: 1,376 undergrads, 1% part-time. 389 full-time freshmen.
Selectivity: Admits less than 50% of applicants.

BASIC COSTS (2012-2013)
Tuition and fees: $18,330.
Room and board: $5,900.
Additional info: Students attend tuition-free. Each student participates in the mandatory on-campus Work Education Program 15 hours each week and two forty hour work weeks. Credit from participation in the Work Program, plus any federal and/or state aid for which student qualifies, plus an institutional scholarship combine to meet each student's full tuition charge.

FINANCIAL AID PICTURE (2011-2012)
Students with need: Out of 389 full-time freshmen who applied for aid, 382 were judged to have need. Of these, 382 received aid, and 81 had their full need met. Average financial aid package met 82% of need; average scholarship/grant was $11,978. For part-time students, average financial aid package was $6,950.
Students without need: 8 full-time freshmen who did not demonstrate need for aid received scholarships/grants; average award was $12,740. No-need awards available for academics, art, athletics, leadership, music/drama, ROTC, state/district residency.
Scholarships offered: 11 full-time freshmen received athletic scholarships; average amount $2,101.
Cumulative student debt: 11% of graduating class had student loans; average debt was $8,915.
Additional info: The College guarantees to meet total cost for each full-time student by using a combination of earnings from its endowment, mandatory student Work Education Program, as well as student aid grants, gifts, and other sources. As a result, each full-time student's cost of education is met 100%, without loans of any kind.

FINANCIAL AID PROCEDURES
Forms required: FAFSA.
Dates and Deadlines: Priority date 2/15; no closing date. Applicants notified on a rolling basis starting 7/1.
Transfers: Applicants notified by 7/1.

CONTACT
Kyla McCarty, Financial Aid Director
PO Box 17, Point Lookout, MO 65726-0017
(417) 690-3290

Columbia College

Columbia, Missouri
www.ccis.edu Federal Code: 002456

4-year private liberal arts college in small city, affiliated with Christian Church (Disciples of Christ).
Enrollment: 903 undergrads, 13% part-time. 116 full-time freshmen.
Selectivity: Admits 50 to 75% of applicants.

BASIC COSTS (2012-2013)
Tuition and fees: $17,950.
Per-credit charge: $354.
Room and board: $6,254.
Additional info: Tuition at time of enrollment locked for 4 years.

FINANCIAL AID PICTURE (2011-2012)
Students with need: Out of 98 full-time freshmen who applied for aid, 85 were judged to have need. Of these, 72 received aid, and 16 had their full

need met. Average financial aid package met 61% of need; average scholarship/grant was $3,712; average loan was $3,306. For part-time students, average financial aid package was $5,053.
Students without need: 11 full-time freshmen who did not demonstrate need for aid received scholarships/grants; average award was $7,774. No-need awards available for academics, alumni affiliation, art, athletics, job skills, leadership, music/drama, religious affiliation, ROTC, state/district residency.
Scholarships offered: ***Merit:*** Columbia College Scholarship: full tuition, room/board; requires 3.5 GPA, 26 ACT or SAT equivalent, campus visit, interview, essay, 2 letters of recommendation, resume; renewable with 30 semester hours and 3.6 GPA. Presidential Scholarship: full tuition; requires 3.5 GPA, 26 ACT/SAT equivalent, campus visit, interview, essay, 2 letters of recommendation, resume; renewable with 30 semester hours and 3.6 GPA. Capstone scholarship: 60% of tuition; 28 ACT and 3.6 GPA; renewable with 3.6 GPA and 27 Columbia College credits earned annually. Keystone Scholarship: 3.4 GPA or GED equivalent; 26 ACT/SAT equivalent; renewable with 27 semester hours per year and 3.4 GPA for up to 3 years. ***Athletic:*** 4 full-time freshmen received athletic scholarships; average amount $15,842.
Cumulative student debt: 53% of graduating class had student loans; average debt was $11,726.

FINANCIAL AID PROCEDURES

Forms required: FAFSA.
Dates and Deadlines: Priority date 3/1; no closing date. Applicants notified on a rolling basis starting 3/1.

CONTACT

Sharon Abernathy, Director of Financial Aid
1001 Rogers Street, Columbia, MO 65216
(573) 875-7390

Conception Seminary College

Conception, Missouri
www.conception.edu Federal Code: 002467

4-year private seminary college for men in rural community, affiliated with Roman Catholic Church.
Enrollment: 91 undergrads. 14 full-time freshmen.
Selectivity: Admits over 75% of applicants.

BASIC COSTS (2013-2014)

Tuition and fees: $18,436.
Room and board: $10,954.

FINANCIAL AID PICTURE

Students with need: Need-based aid available for full-time and part-time students. Work study available nights, weekends, and for part-time students.
Students without need: No-need awards available for academics.

FINANCIAL AID PROCEDURES

Forms required: FAFSA.
Dates and Deadlines: Applicants notified on a rolling basis starting 8/1; must reply by 8/20.

CONTACT

Justin Hernandez, Financial Aid Officer
Box 502, Conception, MO 64433-0502
(660) 944-2851

Cottey College

Nevada, Missouri
www.cottey.edu Federal Code: 002458

2-year private junior and liberal arts college for women in small town.
Enrollment: 292 undergrads.
Selectivity: Admits 50 to 75% of applicants.

BASIC COSTS (2012-2013)

Tuition and fees: $17,400.
Per-credit charge: $200.
Room and board: $6,400.

FINANCIAL AID PICTURE

Students with need: Need-based aid available for full-time and part-time students. Work study available nights, weekends, and for part-time students.
Students without need: No-need awards available for academics, alumni affiliation, art, athletics, leadership, music/drama.

FINANCIAL AID PROCEDURES

Forms required: FAFSA.
Dates and Deadlines: Priority date 3/1; no closing date. Applicants notified on a rolling basis starting 4/1; must reply within 2 week(s) of notification.
Transfers: Applicants notified on a rolling basis starting 4/1; must reply within 2 week(s) of notification.

CONTACT

Sherry Pennington, Coordinator of Financial Aid
1000 West Austin Boulevard, Nevada, MO 64772
(417) 667-8181 ext. 2190

Crowder College

Neosho, Missouri
www.crowder.edu Federal Code: 002459

2-year public community and liberal arts college in small town.
Enrollment: 4,232 undergrads, 41% part-time. 845 full-time freshmen.
Selectivity: Open admission; but selective for some programs.

BASIC COSTS (2012-2013)

Tuition and fees: $2,670; out-of-district residents $3,510; out-of-state residents $4,380.
Per-credit charge: $77; out-of-district residents $105; out-of-state residents $134.
Room and board: $4,000.

FINANCIAL AID PICTURE (2011-2012)

Students with need: 74% of average financial aid package awarded as scholarships/grants, 26% awarded as loans/jobs. Need-based aid available for part-time students. Work study available nights, weekends, and for part-time students.
Students without need: No-need awards available for academics, art, athletics, leadership, minority status, music/drama, state/district residency.
Cumulative student debt: 27% of graduating class had student loans; average debt was $3,400.

FINANCIAL AID PROCEDURES

Forms required: FAFSA, institutional form.
Dates and Deadlines: Priority date 7/1; no closing date. Applicants notified on a rolling basis starting 5/15; must reply within 4 week(s) of notification.

CONTACT

Michelle Paul, Director of Financial Aid
601 LaClede Avenue, Neosho, MO 64850
(417) 451-3223 ext. 5434

Culver-Stockton College

Canton, Missouri
www.culver.edu Federal Code: 002460

4-year private liberal arts college in small town, affiliated with Christian Church (Disciples of Christ).
Enrollment: 749 undergrads, 5% part-time. 217 full-time freshmen.

Selectivity: Admits 50 to 75% of applicants.

BASIC COSTS (2012-2013)
Tuition and fees: $22,550.
Per-credit charge: $515.
Room and board: $7,600.

FINANCIAL AID PICTURE (2012-2013)
Students with need: Out of 214 full-time freshmen who applied for aid, 202 were judged to have need. Of these, 202 received aid, and 45 had their full need met. Average financial aid package met 78% of need; average scholarship/grant was $18,126; average loan was $3,487. For part-time students, average financial aid package was $7,782.
Students without need: 15 full-time freshmen who did not demonstrate need for aid received scholarships/grants; average award was $7,433. No-need awards available for academics, alumni affiliation, art, athletics, leadership, music/drama, religious affiliation.
Scholarships offered: 29 full-time freshmen received athletic scholarships; average amount $6,834.
Cumulative student debt: 85% of graduating class had student loans; average debt was $24,859.

FINANCIAL AID PROCEDURES
Forms required: FAFSA.
Dates and Deadlines: Priority date 3/1; closing date 6/1. Applicants notified on a rolling basis starting 2/15; must reply within 2 week(s) of notification.
Transfers: Must reply within 2 week(s) of notification.

CONTACT
Tina Wiseman, Director of Financial Aid
One College Hill, Canton, MO 63435-1299
(573) 288-6307

DeVry University: Kansas City
Kansas City, Missouri
www.devry.edu

4-year for-profit university in large city.
Enrollment: 688 undergrads, 56% part-time. 28 full-time freshmen.

BASIC COSTS (2012-2013)
Tuition and fees: $16,076.
Per-credit charge: $609.

FINANCIAL AID PICTURE
Students with need: Need-based aid available for full-time and part-time students.
Students without need: This college awards aid only to students with need.

FINANCIAL AID PROCEDURES
Forms required: FAFSA.
Dates and Deadlines: Applicants notified on a rolling basis.

CONTACT
Maureen Kelly, Senior Associate Director of Financial Aid
11224 Holmes Street, Kansas City, MO 64131-3626
(816) 941-0439

Drury University
Springfield, Missouri
www.drury.edu Federal Code: 002461

4-year private university and liberal arts college in large city, affiliated with United Church of Christ.
Enrollment: 1,601 undergrads, 2% part-time. 364 full-time freshmen.
Selectivity: Admits over 75% of applicants.

BASIC COSTS (2013-2014)
Tuition and fees: $22,815.
Per-credit charge: $730.
Room and board: $7,960.

FINANCIAL AID PICTURE (2012-2013)
Students with need: Out of 346 full-time freshmen who applied for aid, 304 were judged to have need. Of these, 304 received aid, and 263 had their full need met. Average financial aid package met 81% of need; average scholarship/grant was $6,255; average loan was $4,500. Need-based aid available for part-time students.
Students without need: 14 full-time freshmen who did not demonstrate need for aid received scholarships/grants; average award was $4,075. No-need awards available for academics, alumni affiliation, art, athletics, job skills, leadership, minority status, music/drama, religious affiliation.
Scholarships offered: ***Merit:*** Phi Theta Kappa Scholarship; $1,000. ***Athletic:*** 2 full-time freshmen received athletic scholarships; average amount $20,500.
Cumulative student debt: 68% of graduating class had student loans; average debt was $21,550.

FINANCIAL AID PROCEDURES
Forms required: FAFSA, institutional form.
Dates and Deadlines: Priority date 2/15; closing date 3/1. Applicants notified on a rolling basis starting 3/30; must reply within 2 week(s) of notification.
Transfers: No deadline.

CONTACT
Annette Avery, Director of Financial Aid
900 North Benton Avenue, Springfield, MO 65802-3712
(417) 873-7312

East Central College
Union, Missouri
www.eastcentral.edu Federal Code: 008862

2-year public community college in large town.
Enrollment: 3,165 undergrads, 40% part-time. 631 full-time freshmen.
Selectivity: Open admission; but selective for some programs.

BASIC COSTS (2012-2013)
Tuition and fees: $2,430; out-of-district residents $3,330; out-of-state residents $4,860.
Per-credit charge: $71; out-of-district residents $101; out-of-state residents $152.

FINANCIAL AID PICTURE
Students with need: Need-based aid available for full-time and part-time students.
Students without need: No-need awards available for academics, alumni affiliation, art, athletics, music/drama, state/district residency.

FINANCIAL AID PROCEDURES
Forms required: FAFSA.
Dates and Deadlines: Priority date 3/15; no closing date. Applicants notified on a rolling basis starting 4/1.
Transfers: No deadline. Applicants notified on a rolling basis starting 4/1.

CONTACT
Karen Koenig-Griffin, Director of Financial Aid
1964 Prairie Dell Road, Union, MO 63084-0529
(636) 584-6588

Evangel University
Springfield, Missouri
www.evangel.edu Federal Code: 002463

4-year private liberal arts college in small city, affiliated with Assemblies of God.

Enrollment: 1,864 undergrads, 9% part-time. 409 full-time freshmen.
Selectivity: Admits 50 to 75% of applicants.

BASIC COSTS (2012-2013)
Tuition and fees: $18,930.
Room and board: $6,640.

FINANCIAL AID PICTURE (2011-2012)
Students with need: Out of 398 full-time freshmen who applied for aid, 365 were judged to have need. Of these, 365 received aid, and 27 had their full need met. Average financial aid package met 62% of need; average scholarship/grant was $10,468; average loan was $3,933. For part-time students, average financial aid package was $7,312.
Students without need: This college awards aid only to students with need.
Scholarships offered: 14 full-time freshmen received athletic scholarships; average amount $5,477.
Cumulative student debt: 79% of graduating class had student loans; average debt was $34,434.

FINANCIAL AID PROCEDURES
Forms required: FAFSA.
Dates and Deadlines: Priority date 3/1; closing date 7/1. Applicants notified on a rolling basis starting 3/15; must reply within 3 week(s) of notification.

CONTACT
Dorynda Carpenter, Director of Student Financial Services
1111 North Glenstone, Springfield, MO 65802
(417) 865-2811 ext. 7300

Fontbonne University
St. Louis, Missouri
www.fontbonne.edu Federal Code: 002464

4-year private university and liberal arts college in large city, affiliated with Roman Catholic Church.
Enrollment: 1,282 undergrads, 25% part-time. 136 full-time freshmen.
Selectivity: Admits 50 to 75% of applicants.

BASIC COSTS (2012-2013)
Tuition and fees: $22,054.
Room and board: $8,156.

FINANCIAL AID PICTURE
Students with need: Need-based aid available for full-time and part-time students. Work study available nights, weekends, and for part-time students.
Students without need: No-need awards available for academics, alumni affiliation, art, leadership, minority status, music/drama, religious affiliation, state/district residency.
Scholarships offered: Dean's Scholarship: $6,000-$8,000; GPA, ACT, rank criteria. Alumni Scholarship: $1,000-$6,000; GPA, ACT and class rank criteria. Presidential Scholarship: up to full tuition. Campus Service Scholarship: $500-$3,000; activities, leadership. Art, theater, English, writing and computer science scholarships also available.

FINANCIAL AID PROCEDURES
Forms required: FAFSA, institutional form.
Dates and Deadlines: Closing date 4/1. Applicants notified on a rolling basis starting 2/1; must reply within 2 week(s) of notification.
Transfers: Applicants notified on a rolling basis starting 2/1; must reply within 2 week(s) of notification.

CONTACT
K. Moore, Director of the Office of Student Financial Aid
6800 Wydown Boulevard, St. Louis, MO 63105-3098
(314) 889-1414

Goldfarb School of Nursing at Barnes-Jewish College
St. Louis, Missouri
www.barnesjewishcollege.edu Federal Code: 003689

Upper-division private nursing college in very large city.
Enrollment: 637 undergrads, 1% part-time.

BASIC COSTS (2013-2014)
Tuition and fees: $17,896.
Per-credit charge: $633.

FINANCIAL AID PICTURE
Students with need: Need-based aid available for full-time and part-time students.
Students without need: No-need awards available for academics, leadership, minority status.

FINANCIAL AID PROCEDURES
Forms required: FAFSA.
Dates and Deadlines: Priority date 4/1; no closing date. Applicants notified on a rolling basis.
Transfers: No deadline. Applicants notified on a rolling basis.

CONTACT
Jason Crowe, Financial Aid Director
4483 Duncan Avenue, St. Louis, MO 63110-1091
(314) 362-9250

Hannibal-LaGrange University
Hannibal, Missouri
www.hlg.edu Federal Code: 009089

4-year private university and liberal arts college in large town, affiliated with Southern Baptist Convention.
Enrollment: 1,028 undergrads.

BASIC COSTS (2013-2014)
Tuition and fees: $18,770.
Room and board: $6,840.

FINANCIAL AID PICTURE
Students with need: Need-based aid available for full-time and part-time students.
Students without need: No-need awards available for academics, art, athletics, music/drama, religious affiliation.
Additional info: Work-study opportunities vary according to on- and off-campus needs.

FINANCIAL AID PROCEDURES
Forms required: FAFSA, institutional form.
Dates and Deadlines: Applicants notified on a rolling basis; must reply by 8/31.
Transfers: No deadline.

CONTACT
Brice Baumgardner, Financial Aid Director
2800 Palmyra Road, Hannibal, MO 63401
(573) 629-3267

Harris-Stowe State University
St. Louis, Missouri
www.hssu.edu Federal Code: 002466

4-year public university in large city.
Enrollment: 1,462 undergrads, 25% part-time. 290 full-time freshmen.

Selectivity: Open admission.

BASIC COSTS (2012-2013)

Tuition and fees: $5,110; out-of-state residents $9,648.
Per-credit charge: $195; out-of-state residents $384.
Room and board: $8,700.

FINANCIAL AID PICTURE

Students with need: Need-based aid available for full-time and part-time students. Work study available nights, weekends, and for part-time students.
Students without need: No-need awards available for academics, alumni affiliation, art, athletics, leadership, music/drama, state/district residency.

FINANCIAL AID PROCEDURES

Forms required: FAFSA, institutional form.
Dates and Deadlines: Closing date 4/1. Applicants notified on a rolling basis starting 4/1; must reply within 3 week(s) of notification.
Transfers: Priority date 4/1. Applicants notified on a rolling basis starting 4/1.

CONTACT

Regina Blackshear, Director of Financial Assistance
3026 Laclede Avenue, St. Louis, MO 63103-2199
(314) 340-3500

Hickey College

St. Louis, Missouri
www.hickeycollege.edu Federal Code: 014209

4-year for-profit business and technical college in very large city.
Enrollment: 398 undergrads.
Selectivity: Open admission; but selective for some programs.

BASIC COSTS (2012-2013)

Tuition and fees: $13,560.
Additional info: Cost of room only, $5,840.

FINANCIAL AID PICTURE

Students with need: Need-based aid available for full-time students.

FINANCIAL AID PROCEDURES

Forms required: FAFSA.
Dates and Deadlines: Applicants notified on a rolling basis.

CONTACT

Deana Pecoroni, Director, Student Services
940 West Port Plaza, St. Louis, MO 63146
(314) 434-2212 ext. 128

Jefferson College

Hillsboro, Missouri
www.jeffco.edu Federal Code: 002468

2-year public community and technical college in rural community.
Enrollment: 5,494 undergrads, 46% part-time. 1,136 full-time freshmen.
Selectivity: Open admission; but selective for some programs.

BASIC COSTS (2013-2014)

Tuition and fees: $3,000; out-of-district residents $4,350; out-of-state residents $5,700.
Per-credit charge: $97; out-of-district residents $142; out-of-state residents $187.
Room and board: $5,121.

FINANCIAL AID PICTURE (2011-2012)

Students with need: Out of 1,071 full-time freshmen who applied for aid, 849 were judged to have need. Of these, 821 received aid, and 20 had their full need met. Average financial aid package met 52% of need; average scholarship/grant was $2,340; average loan was $2,534. For part-time students, average financial aid package was $3,270.
Students without need: 5 full-time freshmen who did not demonstrate need for aid received scholarships/grants; average award was $1,453. No-need awards available for academics, art, athletics, leadership, music/drama, state/district residency.
Scholarships offered: 48 full-time freshmen received athletic scholarships; average amount $5,745.

FINANCIAL AID PROCEDURES

Forms required: FAFSA.
Dates and Deadlines: Priority date 4/1; no closing date. Applicants notified on a rolling basis starting 4/15.

CONTACT

Sarah Bright, Director of Student Financial Services
1000 Viking Drive, Hillsboro, MO 63050-2441
(636) 797-3000 ext. 3212

Kansas City Art Institute

Kansas City, Missouri
www.kcai.edu Federal Code: 002473

4-year private visual arts college in large city.
Enrollment: 822 undergrads.

BASIC COSTS (2012-2013)

Tuition and fees: $31,992.
Per-credit charge: $1,330.
Room and board: $9,466.

FINANCIAL AID PICTURE

Students with need: Need-based aid available for full-time and part-time students. Work study available nights, weekends, and for part-time students.
Students without need: No-need awards available for academics, art.
Scholarships offered: February 1 and March 1 priority application dates for merit scholarships; deadline August 1.

FINANCIAL AID PROCEDURES

Forms required: FAFSA.
Dates and Deadlines: Priority date 3/15; closing date 4/1. Applicants notified on a rolling basis starting 4/1; must reply within 2 week(s) of notification.
Transfers: No deadline. Applicants notified on a rolling basis starting 4/1; must reply within 2 week(s) of notification.

CONTACT

Darci Webster, Director of Financial Aid
4415 Warwick Boulevard, Kansas City, MO 64111
(816) 802-3337

Lincoln University

Jefferson City, Missouri
www.lincolnu.edu Federal Code: 002479

4-year public university and liberal arts college in large town.
Enrollment: 2,394 undergrads, 21% part-time. 424 full-time freshmen.
Selectivity: Open admission; but selective for some programs and for out-of-state students.

BASIC COSTS (2012-2013)

Tuition and fees: $6,725; out-of-state residents $12,725.
Per-credit charge: $205; out-of-state residents $405.
Room and board: $5,271.
Additional info: Full-time students must pay $247.50 per semester for health insurance if proof of other coverage is not provided. Enrollment in the

student health insurance program is required for international students. Lab and/or course fees are charged, depending on program.

FINANCIAL AID PICTURE (2012-2013)

Students with need: Out of 409 full-time freshmen who applied for aid, 383 were judged to have need. Of these, 383 received aid, and 10 had their full need met. Average financial aid package met 59% of need; average scholarship/grant was $5,740; average loan was $3,409. For part-time students, average financial aid package was $6,661.

Students without need: 1 full-time freshmen who did not demonstrate need for aid received scholarships/grants; average award was $2,000. No-need awards available for academics, art, athletics, job skills, leadership, minority status, music/drama, ROTC, state/district residency.

Scholarships offered: 48 full-time freshmen received athletic scholarships; average amount $3,118.

Cumulative student debt: 70% of graduating class had student loans; average debt was $27,910.

FINANCIAL AID PROCEDURES

Forms required: FAFSA, institutional form.

Dates and Deadlines: Priority date 3/1; no closing date. Applicants notified on a rolling basis starting 3/15; must reply within 2 week(s) of notification.

Transfers: No deadline. Applicants notified on a rolling basis starting 3/15; must reply within 2 week(s) of notification.

CONTACT

Alfred Robinson, Director of Financial Aid and Student Employment
820 Chestnut Street, B7 Young Hall, Jefferson City, MO 65102-0029
(573) 681-6156

Lindenwood University

St. Charles, Missouri
www.lindenwood.edu/ Federal Code: 002480

4-year private university and liberal arts college in large city, affiliated with Presbyterian Church (USA).

Enrollment: 7,833 undergrads, 6% part-time. 1,285 full-time freshmen.

Selectivity: Admits 50 to 75% of applicants.

BASIC COSTS (2012-2013)

Tuition and fees: $14,960.

Per-credit charge: $412.

Room and board: $7,220.

FINANCIAL AID PICTURE (2012-2013)

Students with need: Out of 905 full-time freshmen who applied for aid, 726 were judged to have need. Of these, 726 received aid, and 649 had their full need met. Average financial aid package met 86% of need; average scholarship/grant was $7,010; average loan was $4,234. For part-time students, average financial aid package was $4,983.

Students without need: 553 full-time freshmen who did not demonstrate need for aid received scholarships/grants; average award was $3,498. No-need awards available for academics, alumni affiliation, art, athletics, job skills, music/drama, ROTC.

Scholarships offered: 126 full-time freshmen received athletic scholarships; average amount $13,822.

FINANCIAL AID PROCEDURES

Forms required: FAFSA.

Dates and Deadlines: Priority date 4/1; no closing date. Applicants notified on a rolling basis.

CONTACT

Lori Bode, Director of Financial Aid
209 South Kingshighway, St. Charles, MO 63301
(636) 949-4923

Linn State Technical College

Linn, Missouri
www.linnstate.edu Federal Code: 004711

2-year public community and technical college in rural community.

Enrollment: 1,153 undergrads, 9% part-time. 483 full-time freshmen.

Selectivity: Open admission; but selective for some programs.

BASIC COSTS (2012-2013)

Tuition and fees: $5,220; out-of-state residents $9,870.

Per-credit charge: $155; out-of-state residents $310.

Room and board: $5,020.

FINANCIAL AID PICTURE (2011-2012)

Students with need: Out of 479 full-time freshmen who applied for aid, 390 were judged to have need. Of these, 390 received aid, and 64 had their full need met. Average financial aid package met 19% of need; average scholarship/grant was $5,673; average loan was $2,127. Need-based aid available for part-time students.

Students without need: 3 full-time freshmen who did not demonstrate need for aid received scholarships/grants; average award was $944. No-need awards available for academics, alumni affiliation, state/district residency.

Scholarships offered: 36 full-time freshmen received athletic scholarships; average amount $1,625.

FINANCIAL AID PROCEDURES

Forms required: FAFSA.

Dates and Deadlines: Priority date 4/1; no closing date. Applicants notified on a rolling basis starting 4/1; must reply within 3 week(s) of notification.

CONTACT

Becky Whithaus, Director of Financial Aid
One Technology Drive, Linn, MO 65051
(573) 897-5143

Maryville University of Saint Louis

St. Louis, Missouri
www.maryville.edu Federal Code: 002482

4-year private university in very large city.

Enrollment: 2,911 undergrads, 41% part-time. 348 full-time freshmen.

Selectivity: Admits 50 to 75% of applicants.

BASIC COSTS (2013-2014)

Tuition and fees: $25,002.

Per-credit charge: $714.

Room and board: $9,918.

FINANCIAL AID PICTURE (2012-2013)

Students with need: Out of 271 full-time freshmen who applied for aid, 244 were judged to have need. Of these, 244 received aid, and 49 had their full need met. Average financial aid package met 69% of need; average scholarship/grant was $16,323; average loan was $6,685. For part-time students, average financial aid package was $5,294.

Students without need: 61 full-time freshmen who did not demonstrate need for aid received scholarships/grants; average award was $9,300. No-need awards available for academics, art, athletics, leadership, minority status, ROTC, state/district residency.

Scholarships offered: ***Merit:*** University Scholars Program: awarded to full-time freshmen with 28 ACT or 1170 SAT (exclusive of Writing), high school GPA 3.5-4.0; interview required. M-PACT Award: awarded to full-time freshmen based on campus activity and impact on student life. ***Athletic:*** 10 full-time freshmen received athletic scholarships; average amount $21,780.

Cumulative student debt: 76% of graduating class had student loans; average debt was $21,835.

FINANCIAL AID PROCEDURES

Forms required: FAFSA.

Dates and Deadlines: Priority date 3/1; no closing date. Applicants notified on a rolling basis starting 2/15; must reply by 5/1 or within 2 week(s) of notification.
Transfers: No deadline. Applicants notified on a rolling basis starting 2/1; must reply by 5/1 or within 2 week(s) of notification. Scholarships available for transfer students.

CONTACT
Martha Harbaugh, Director of Financial Aid
650 Maryville University Drive, St. Louis, MO 63141-7299
(314) 529-9361

Metro Business College: Jefferson City

Jefferson City, Missouri
www.metrobusinesscollege.edu Federal Code: 014710

2-year for-profit business and health science college in large town.
Enrollment: 102 undergrads, 20% part-time. 9 full-time freshmen.
Selectivity: Open admission; but selective for some programs.

BASIC COSTS (2012-2013)
Tuition and fees: $9,850.
Additional info: Cost may vary by program. Tuition at time of enrollment locked for 2 years.

FINANCIAL AID PICTURE
Students with need: Need-based aid available for full-time and part-time students.

FINANCIAL AID PROCEDURES
Forms required: FAFSA, institutional form.
Dates and Deadlines: Applicants notified on a rolling basis.

CONTACT
Debbie Jenkins, Financial Aid Coordinator
210 El Mercado Plaza, Jefferson City, MO 65109
(573) 635-6600

Metropolitan Community College - Kansas City

Kansas City, Missouri
www.mcckc.edu Federal Code: 002484

2-year public community college in large city.
Enrollment: 17,990 undergrads, 58% part-time. 2,548 full-time freshmen.
Selectivity: Open admission; but selective for some programs.

BASIC COSTS (2012-2013)
Tuition and fees: $2,780; out-of-district residents $4,850; out-of-state residents $6,470.
Per-credit charge: $87; out-of-district residents $156; out-of-state residents $210.

FINANCIAL AID PICTURE
Students with need: Need-based aid available for full-time students. Work study available nights.
Students without need: No-need awards available for academics, athletics, leadership.

FINANCIAL AID PROCEDURES
Forms required: FAFSA, institutional form.
Dates and Deadlines: Priority date 5/30; closing date 6/30. Applicants notified on a rolling basis starting 4/8.

CONTACT
Dena Norris, Director of Student Financial Aid Services
3201 Southwest Trafficway, Kansas City, MO 64111-2429
(816) 604-1527

Mineral Area College

Park Hills, Missouri
www.mineralarea.edu Federal Code: 002486

2-year public community college in small town.
Enrollment: 2,790 undergrads.
Selectivity: Open admission; but selective for some programs.

BASIC COSTS (2013-2014)
Tuition and fees: $2,760; out-of-district residents $3,660; out-of-state residents $4,650.
Per-credit charge: $92; out-of-district residents $122; out-of-state residents $155.
Room and board: $5,995.

FINANCIAL AID PICTURE (2011-2012)
Students with need: 74% of average financial aid package awarded as scholarships/grants, 26% awarded as loans/jobs. Need-based aid available for part-time students.
Students without need: No-need awards available for academics, alumni affiliation, art, athletics, leadership, music/drama, state/district residency.

FINANCIAL AID PROCEDURES
Forms required: FAFSA.
Dates and Deadlines: Closing date 4/1. Applicants notified on a rolling basis starting 2/15; must reply within 4 week(s) of notification.

CONTACT
Denise Sebastian, Financial Aid Director
PO Box 1000, Park Hills, MO 63601-1000
(573) 518-2133

Missouri Baptist University

St. Louis, Missouri
www.mobap.edu Federal Code: 007540

4-year private university and liberal arts college in very large city, affiliated with Baptist faith.
Enrollment: 1,701 undergrads, 18% part-time. 239 full-time freshmen.
Selectivity: Admits 50 to 75% of applicants.

BASIC COSTS (2012-2013)
Tuition and fees: $20,704.
Per-credit charge: $680.
Room and board: $8,230.

FINANCIAL AID PICTURE
Students with need: Need-based aid available for full-time and part-time students.
Students without need: No-need awards available for academics, alumni affiliation, athletics, leadership, music/drama, religious affiliation.

FINANCIAL AID PROCEDURES
Forms required: FAFSA, institutional form.
Dates and Deadlines: Priority date 4/1; no closing date. Applicants notified on a rolling basis starting 4/15; must reply within 2 week(s) of notification.
Transfers: Institutional academic scholarships available.

CONTACT
Terry Cruse, Director of Student Financial Services
One College Park Drive, St. Louis, MO 63141-8660
(314) 392-2366

Missouri Southern State University

Joplin, Missouri
www.mssu.edu Federal Code: 002488

4-year public university and liberal arts college in large town.
Enrollment: 4,976 undergrads, 20% part-time. 550 full-time freshmen.
Selectivity: Admits over 75% of applicants.

BASIC COSTS (2012-2013)
Tuition and fees: $5,386; out-of-state residents $10,276.
Per-credit charge: $163; out-of-state residents $326.
Room and board: $6,113.

FINANCIAL AID PICTURE (2011-2012)
Students with need: Out of 547 full-time freshmen who applied for aid, 425 were judged to have need. Of these, 423 received aid, and 33 had their full need met. Average financial aid package met 45% of need; average scholarship/grant was $3,971; average loan was $3,332. For part-time students, average financial aid package was $8,585.
Students without need: 103 full-time freshmen who did not demonstrate need for aid received scholarships/grants; average award was $2,841. No-need awards available for academics, alumni affiliation, art, athletics, minority status, music/drama, religious affiliation, state/district residency.
Scholarships offered: 76 full-time freshmen received athletic scholarships; average amount $3,917.
Cumulative student debt: 52% of graduating class had student loans; average debt was $20,005.

FINANCIAL AID PROCEDURES
Forms required: FAFSA.
Dates and Deadlines: Priority date 4/1; no closing date. Applicants notified on a rolling basis starting 3/15; must reply by 5/1.

CONTACT
Rebecca Diskin, Director of Student Financial Aid
3950 East Newman Road, Joplin, MO 64801-1595
(417) 625-9325

Missouri State University

Springfield, Missouri
www.missouristate.edu Federal Code: 002503

4-year public university in small city.
Enrollment: 15,343 undergrads, 13% part-time. 2,525 full-time freshmen.
Selectivity: Admits over 75% of applicants.

BASIC COSTS (2012-2013)
Tuition and fees: $6,882; out-of-state residents $13,138.
Per-credit charge: $200; out-of-state residents $412.
Room and board: $6,844.

FINANCIAL AID PICTURE (2012-2013)
Students with need: Out of 2,125 full-time freshmen who applied for aid, 1,600 were judged to have need. Of these, 1,600 received aid, and 220 had their full need met. Average financial aid package met 87% of need; average scholarship/grant was $5,897; average loan was $3,444. For part-time students, average financial aid package was $5,922.
Students without need: 102 full-time freshmen who did not demonstrate need for aid received scholarships/grants; average award was $3,948. No-need awards available for academics, alumni affiliation, art, athletics, job skills, leadership, minority status, music/drama, ROTC, state/district residency.
Scholarships offered: ***Merit:*** Presidential Scholarship: $12,500 per year plus a full waiver of non-resident fees for non-Missouri residents; based on 30 ACT and either top 10% class rank or 3.90 GPA; 30 awarded. Board of Governors Scholarship: $5,000 per year plus a full waiver of non-resident fees; based on 28 ACT and either top 10% class rank or 3.90 GPA; unlimited number of awards. Provost Scholarship: $2,500 per year plus a full waiver of non-resident fees; based on 26 ACT and either top 20% class rank or 3.70 GPA; unlimited number of awards. Multicultural Leadership Scholarship: $6,250 per year for students in top half of class or 3.00 GPA and who have demonstrated leadership in multicultural school or community activities; 50 awarded. Dean's Scholarship: $1,500 per year plus a full waiver of non-resident fees; based on 24 ACT and either top 10% class rank or 3.90 GPA; unlimited number of awards. ***Athletic:*** 40 full-time freshmen received athletic scholarships; average amount $11,563.
Cumulative student debt: 77% of graduating class had student loans; average debt was $20,545.
Additional info: Extensive scholarship program offered to freshmen and transfer students. Out-of-state fee stipends available. Student employment service available to assist students in securing employment on campus and in community.

FINANCIAL AID PROCEDURES
Forms required: FAFSA.
Dates and Deadlines: Priority date 3/31; no closing date. Applicants notified on a rolling basis starting 3/31; must reply within 4 week(s) of notification.
Transfers: No deadline. Applicants notified on a rolling basis.

CONTACT
Vicki Mattocks, Director of Financial Aid
901 South National Avenue, Springfield, MO 65897
(417) 836-5262

Missouri State University: West Plains

West Plains, Missouri
www.wp.missouristate.edu Federal Code: 031060

2-year public branch campus and liberal arts college in large town.
Enrollment: 1,633 undergrads, 25% part-time. 497 full-time freshmen.
Selectivity: Open admission; but selective for some programs.

BASIC COSTS (2013-2014)
Tuition and fees: $3,624; out-of-state residents $6,954.
Per-credit charge: $111; out-of-state residents $222.
Room and board: $5,300.

FINANCIAL AID PICTURE (2011-2012)
Students with need: 66% of average financial aid package awarded as scholarships/grants, 34% awarded as loans/jobs. Need-based aid available for part-time students. Work study available nights, weekends, and for part-time students.
Students without need: No-need awards available for academics, athletics, state/district residency.

FINANCIAL AID PROCEDURES
Forms required: FAFSA, institutional form.
Dates and Deadlines: Priority date 3/31; no closing date. Applicants notified on a rolling basis; must reply by 4/15.

CONTACT
Donna Bassham, Coordinator of Financial Aid
128 Garfield Avenue, West Plains, MO 65775-2715
(417) 255-7243

Missouri University of Science and Technology

Rolla, Missouri
www.mst.edu Federal Code: 002517

4-year public university in large town.
Enrollment: 5,752 undergrads, 9% part-time. 1,090 full-time freshmen.

Selectivity: Admits over 75% of applicants.

BASIC COSTS (2012-2013)

Tuition and fees: $9,350; out-of-state residents $23,666.
Per-credit charge: $269; out-of-state residents $747.
Room and board: $8,900.
Additional info: Tuition/fee waivers available for minority students.

FINANCIAL AID PICTURE (2011-2012)

Students with need: Out of 1,034 full-time freshmen who applied for aid, 685 were judged to have need. Of these, 685 received aid, and 425 had their full need met. Average financial aid package met 62% of need; average scholarship/grant was $7,408; average loan was $2,812. For part-time students, average financial aid package was $5,834.
Students without need: 215 full-time freshmen who did not demonstrate need for aid received scholarships/grants; average award was $5,858. No-need awards available for academics, alumni affiliation, athletics, job skills, leadership, minority status, music/drama, religious affiliation, ROTC, state/district residency.
Scholarships offered: 8 full-time freshmen received athletic scholarships; average amount $4,675.

FINANCIAL AID PROCEDURES

Forms required: FAFSA.
Dates and Deadlines: Priority date 3/1; no closing date. Applicants notified on a rolling basis starting 4/1; must reply within 3 week(s) of notification.
Transfers: Special scholarships available to transfer students.

CONTACT

Bridgette Betz, Director of Financial Assistance
106 Parker Hall, Rolla, MO 65409-1060
(573) 341-4282

Missouri Valley College

Marshall, Missouri
www.moval.edu Federal Code: 002489

4-year private liberal arts college in large town, affiliated with Presbyterian Church (USA).
Enrollment: 1,734 undergrads.
Selectivity: Admits 50 to 75% of applicants.

BASIC COSTS (2013-2014)

Tuition and fees: $18,800.
Room and board: $7,700.
Additional info: Includes books.

FINANCIAL AID PICTURE

Students with need: Need-based aid available for full-time and part-time students. Work study available nights, weekends, and for part-time students.
Students without need: No-need awards available for academics, state/district residency.
Scholarships offered: Talent scholarships: $1,000 to $13,000; 100 awarded for general achievement.

FINANCIAL AID PROCEDURES

Forms required: FAFSA, state aid form.
Dates and Deadlines: Priority date 3/1; no closing date. Applicants notified on a rolling basis starting 2/1; must reply within 6 week(s) of notification.
Transfers: Closing date 3/1.

CONTACT

Rachel Robinson, Director of Financial Aid
500 East College Street, Marshall, MO 65340
(660) 831-4176

Missouri Western State University

St. Joseph, Missouri
www.missouriwestern.edu Federal Code: 002490

4-year public business and liberal arts college in small city.
Enrollment: 4,077 full-time undergrads.
Selectivity: Open admission; but selective for some programs.

BASIC COSTS (2012-2013)

Tuition and fees: $6,243; out-of-state residents $11,746.
Per-credit charge: $189; out-of-state residents $372.
Room and board: $7,170.

FINANCIAL AID PICTURE

Students with need: Need-based aid available for full-time and part-time students.
Students without need: No-need awards available for academics, alumni affiliation, art, athletics, job skills, leadership, minority status, music/drama, state/district residency.
Scholarships offered: Golden Griffon Scholarship: up to $10,000 per year for 4 years; 27 ACT, top 10% of class or 3.5 GPA, evidence of involvement in extracurricular activities and community service; 2 essays and personal interview required; application deadline 2/1. President's Academic Scholarship: up to $4,000 per year; 25 ACT and either rank in the top 15% of class or 3.25 GPA required; application deadline 3/1.

FINANCIAL AID PROCEDURES

Forms required: FAFSA, institutional form.
Dates and Deadlines: Priority date 3/1; no closing date. Applicants notified on a rolling basis starting 4/5; must reply within 3 week(s) of notification.
Transfers: No deadline. Applicants notified on a rolling basis starting 4/15; must reply within 2 week(s) of notification.

CONTACT

Marilyn Baker, Director of Student Financial Aid
4525 Downs Drive, St. Joseph, MO 64507

Moberly Area Community College

Moberly, Missouri
www.macc.edu Federal Code: 002491

2-year public community college in large town.
Enrollment: 5,291 undergrads.
Selectivity: Open admission; but selective for some programs.

BASIC COSTS (2012-2013)

Tuition and fees: $2,640; out-of-district residents $3,660; out-of-state residents $5,220.
Per-credit charge: $75; out-of-district residents $109; out-of-state residents $161.
Room and board: $4,200.
Additional info: Board plan covers breakfast and lunch only, five-days-a-week.

FINANCIAL AID PICTURE

Students with need: Need-based aid available for full-time and part-time students. Work study available nights, weekends, and for part-time students.
Students without need: No-need awards available for academics, alumni affiliation, art, athletics, leadership, music/drama.

FINANCIAL AID PROCEDURES

Forms required: FAFSA.
Dates and Deadlines: Priority date 4/1; no closing date. Applicants notified on a rolling basis starting 4/1; must reply by 7/15 or within 2 week(s) of notification.

CONTACT
Amy Hager, Director of Financial Aid
101 College Avenue, Moberly, MO 65270-1304
(660) 263-4110 ext. 301

National American University: Kansas City
Independence, Missouri
www.national.edu

4-year for-profit university in large city.
Enrollment: 800 undergrads.
Selectivity: Open admission.

FINANCIAL AID PICTURE
Students with need: Need-based aid available for full-time and part-time students. Work study available nights, weekends, and for part-time students.
Students without need: This college awards aid only to students with need.

FINANCIAL AID PROCEDURES
Forms required: FAFSA, institutional form.
Dates and Deadlines: Applicants notified on a rolling basis starting 6/4.

CONTACT
Katie Williams, Financial Services Advisor
3620 Arrowhead Avenue, Independence, MO 64057
(816) 412-7736

North Central Missouri College
Trenton, Missouri
www.ncmissouri.edu Federal Code: 002514

2-year public community college in small town.
Enrollment: 1,235 undergrads, 26% part-time. 323 full-time freshmen.
Selectivity: Open admission; but selective for some programs.

BASIC COSTS (2012-2013)
Tuition and fees: $2,790; out-of-district residents $3,780; out-of-state residents $4,950.
Per-credit charge: $73; out-of-district residents $106; out-of-state residents $145.
Room and board: $5,323.

FINANCIAL AID PICTURE
Students with need: Need-based aid available for full-time and part-time students.
Students without need: No-need awards available for academics, athletics, leadership.

FINANCIAL AID PROCEDURES
Forms required: FAFSA, institutional form.
Dates and Deadlines: Priority date 7/1; no closing date. Applicants notified on a rolling basis starting 3/15.
Transfers: No deadline. Applicants notified on a rolling basis starting 4/1. Transfer students may not receive same awards after transferring since some funds campus-based.

CONTACT
Megan DeWitt, Financial Aid Director
1301 Main Street, Trenton, MO 64683
(660) 359-3948 ext. 1402

Northwest Missouri State University
Maryville, Missouri
www.nwmissouri.edu Federal Code: 002496

4-year public university in large town.
Enrollment: 5,648 undergrads, 6% part-time. 1,586 full-time freshmen.
Selectivity: Admits over 75% of applicants.

BASIC COSTS (2012-2013)
Tuition and fees: $7,719; out-of-state residents $13,828.
Per-credit charge: $257; out-of-state residents $461.
Room and board: $8,614.
Additional info: Tuition/fee waivers available for minority students.

FINANCIAL AID PICTURE (2011-2012)
Students with need: Out of 1,489 full-time freshmen who applied for aid, 1,148 were judged to have need. Of these, 1,143 received aid, and 534 had their full need met. Average financial aid package met 69% of need; average scholarship/grant was $6,587; average loan was $3,250. For part-time students, average financial aid package was $4,895.
Students without need: 227 full-time freshmen who did not demonstrate need for aid received scholarships/grants; average award was $2,275. No-need awards available for academics, alumni affiliation, art, athletics, job skills, leadership, minority status, music/drama, ROTC, state/district residency.
Scholarships offered: 15 full-time freshmen received athletic scholarships; average amount $3,623.

FINANCIAL AID PROCEDURES
Forms required: FAFSA.
Dates and Deadlines: Priority date 4/1; no closing date. Applicants notified on a rolling basis starting 3/15; must reply within 4 week(s) of notification.
Transfers: No deadline. Applicants notified on a rolling basis starting 5/10; must reply within 4 week(s) of notification. Transfer scholarship based on academic record.

CONTACT
Del Morley, Director of Financial Assistance
800 University Drive, Maryville, MO 64468-6001
(660) 562-1363

Ozark Christian College
Joplin, Missouri
www.occ.edu Federal Code: 015569

4-year private Bible college in small city, affiliated with nondenominational tradition.
Enrollment: 708 undergrads, 12% part-time. 181 full-time freshmen.
Selectivity: Open admission.

BASIC COSTS (2012-2013)
Tuition and fees: $9,800.
Per-credit charge: $310.
Room and board: $4,460.

FINANCIAL AID PICTURE (2011-2012)
Students with need: 49% of average financial aid package awarded as scholarships/grants, 51% awarded as loans/jobs. Need-based aid available for part-time students.
Students without need: No-need awards available for academics, leadership.

FINANCIAL AID PROCEDURES
Forms required: FAFSA.
Dates and Deadlines: Priority date 4/1; no closing date. Applicants notified on a rolling basis starting 4/15; must reply within 3 week(s) of notification.
Transfers: Academic transcripts required. ACT scores may qualify student for grants or scholarships.

CONTACT
Kim Balentine, Director of Financial Aid
1111 North Main Street, Joplin, MO 64801
(417) 624-2518

Ozarks Technical Community College
Springfield, Missouri
www.otc.edu Federal Code: 030830

2-year public community and technical college in small city.
Enrollment: 13,496 undergrads.
Selectivity: Open admission; but selective for some programs.

BASIC COSTS (2012-2013)
Tuition and fees: $3,300; out-of-district residents $4,365; out-of-state residents $5,580.
Per-credit charge: $91; out-of-district residents $129; out-of-state residents $169.

FINANCIAL AID PICTURE
Students with need: Need-based aid available for full-time and part-time students.
Students without need: This college awards aid only to students with need.

FINANCIAL AID PROCEDURES
Forms required: FAFSA, institutional form.
Dates and Deadlines: Closing date 3/31. Applicants notified on a rolling basis starting 5/16.

CONTACT
Jeff Ford, Director of Financial Aid
1001 East Chestnut Expressway, Springfield, MO 65802
(417) 447-6930

Park University
Parkville, Missouri
www.park.edu Federal Code: 002498

4-year private university in small town.
Enrollment: 1,672 undergrads, 28% part-time. 173 full-time freshmen.
Selectivity: Admits 50 to 75% of applicants.

BASIC COSTS (2012-2013)
Tuition and fees: $10,480.
Per-credit charge: $346.
Room and board: $7,045.

FINANCIAL AID PICTURE (2011-2012)
Students with need: Out of 140 full-time freshmen who applied for aid, 108 were judged to have need. Of these, 108 received aid, and 23 had their full need met. Average financial aid package met 70% of need; average scholarship/grant was $4,582; average loan was $2,933. For part-time students, average financial aid package was $7,115.
Students without need: 15 full-time freshmen who did not demonstrate need for aid received scholarships/grants; average award was $7,863. No-need awards available for academics, alumni affiliation, art, athletics, job skills, leadership, minority status, music/drama, religious affiliation, ROTC.
Scholarships offered: 29 full-time freshmen received athletic scholarships; average amount $6,164.
Cumulative student debt: 41% of graduating class had student loans; average debt was $22,210.

FINANCIAL AID PROCEDURES
Forms required: FAFSA, institutional form.
Dates and Deadlines: Priority date 3/15; closing date 8/1. Applicants notified on a rolling basis starting 2/15.
Transfers: No deadline. Applicants notified by 11/1.

CONTACT
Cathy Colapietro, Associate Director of Admissions and Student Financial Services
8700 NW River Park Drive, Parkville, MO 64152
(816) 584-6290

Ranken Technical College
St. Louis, Missouri
www.ranken.edu Federal Code: 012500

2-year private technical college in very large city.
Enrollment: 2,119 undergrads.
Selectivity: Open admission.

BASIC COSTS (2012-2013)
Tuition and fees: $14,219.
Per-credit charge: $581.
Room and board: $6,476.

FINANCIAL AID PICTURE
Students with need: Need-based aid available for full-time and part-time students. Work study available nights.

FINANCIAL AID PROCEDURES
Forms required: FAFSA, institutional form.
Dates and Deadlines: Applicants notified on a rolling basis starting 4/1.

CONTACT
Peter Murtaugh, Vice President for Finance and Administration
4431 Finney Avenue, St. Louis, MO 63113
(314) 286-4863

Research College of Nursing
Kansas City, Missouri
www.researchcollege.edu Federal Code: 006392

4-year for-profit nursing college in very large city.
Enrollment: 306 undergrads, 2% part-time. 82 full-time freshmen.
Selectivity: Admits 50 to 75% of applicants.

BASIC COSTS (2012-2013)
Tuition and fees: $29,840.
Room and board: $8,460.

FINANCIAL AID PICTURE (2011-2012)
Students with need: Average financial aid package for all full-time undergraduates was $31,000. 37% awarded as scholarships/grants, 63% awarded as loans/jobs. Need-based aid available for part-time students.
Students without need: No-need awards available for academics, alumni affiliation, leadership.
Cumulative student debt: 55% of graduating class had student loans; average debt was $14,000.
Additional info: Financial aid handled by Rockhurst University for freshmen and sophomores.

FINANCIAL AID PROCEDURES
Forms required: FAFSA, institutional form.
Dates and Deadlines: Priority date 3/15; no closing date. Applicants notified on a rolling basis starting 3/15.
Transfers: No deadline.

CONTACT
Maureen McKinnon, Interim Director of Financial Aid
2525 East Meyer Boulevard, Kansas City, MO 64132-1199
(816) 995-2814

Rockhurst University

Kansas City, Missouri
www.rockhurst.edu Federal Code: 002499

4-year private business and liberal arts college in very large city, affiliated with Roman Catholic Church.
Enrollment: 1,613 undergrads, 8% part-time. 446 full-time freshmen.
Selectivity: Admits over 75% of applicants.

BASIC COSTS (2012-2013)
Tuition and fees: $29,840.
Per-credit charge: $970.
Room and board: $8,060.

FINANCIAL AID PICTURE
Students with need: Need-based aid available for full-time and part-time students.
Students without need: No-need awards available for academics, alumni affiliation, athletics, leadership, music/drama.
Additional info: Auditions, portfolios required for some scholarships.

FINANCIAL AID PROCEDURES
Forms required: FAFSA.
Dates and Deadlines: Priority date 3/1; no closing date. Applicants notified on a rolling basis starting 3/1; must reply within 4 week(s) of notification.
Transfers: No deadline. Applicants notified on a rolling basis starting 1/30; must reply within 4 week(s) of notification. Scholarships awarded to qualified first-time transfers.

CONTACT
Angela Karlin, Director of Financial Aid
1100 Rockhurst Road, Kansas City, MO 64110-2561
(816) 405-4600

St. Charles Community College

Cottleville, Missouri
www.stchas.edu Federal Code: 017027

2-year public community college in small city.
Enrollment: 6,963 undergrads, 48% part-time. 1,181 full-time freshmen.
Selectivity: Open admission; but selective for some programs.

BASIC COSTS (2012-2013)
Tuition and fees: $2,770; out-of-district residents $4,050; out-of-state residents $6,090.
Per-credit charge: $90; out-of-district residents $135; out-of-state residents $203.

FINANCIAL AID PICTURE (2011-2012)
Students with need: 76% of average financial aid package awarded as scholarships/grants, 24% awarded as loans/jobs. Need-based aid available for part-time students.
Students without need: No-need awards available for academics, art, athletics, leadership, music/drama.

FINANCIAL AID PROCEDURES
Forms required: FAFSA, institutional form.
Dates and Deadlines: Priority date 6/1; no closing date. Applicants notified on a rolling basis starting 4/1; must reply by 8/1.
Transfers: Applicants notified on a rolling basis starting 4/1; must reply by 8/1.

CONTACT
Kathy Brockgreitens-Gober, Dean of Enrollment Services
4601 Mid Rivers Mall Drive, Cottleville, MO 63376
(636) 922-8270

St. Louis Christian College

Florissant, Missouri
www.slcconline.edu Federal Code: 012580

4-year private Bible college in small city, affiliated with Christian Church.
Enrollment: 228 undergrads, 16% part-time. 23 full-time freshmen.
Selectivity: Admits less than 50% of applicants.

BASIC COSTS (2012-2013)
Tuition and fees: $15,700.
Per-credit charge: $480.
Room and board: $9,000.

FINANCIAL AID PICTURE (2011-2012)
Students with need: 62% of average financial aid package awarded as scholarships/grants, 38% awarded as loans/jobs. Need-based aid available for part-time students.

FINANCIAL AID PROCEDURES
Forms required: FAFSA.
Dates and Deadlines: Closing date 8/1. Applicants notified on a rolling basis starting 7/20; must reply within 2 week(s) of notification.

CONTACT
Cathi Wilhoit, Financial Aid Director
1360 Grandview Drive, Florissant, MO 63033
(314) 837-6777 ext. 1101

Saint Louis University

Saint Louis, Missouri
www.slu.edu Federal Code: 002506

4-year private university in very large city, affiliated with Roman Catholic Church.
Enrollment: 8,566 undergrads, 10% part-time. 1,705 full-time freshmen.
Selectivity: Admits 50 to 75% of applicants.

BASIC COSTS (2012-2013)
Tuition and fees: $35,256.
Per-credit charge: $1,215.
Room and board: $9,612.
Additional info: Tuition/fee waivers available for unemployed or children of unemployed.

FINANCIAL AID PICTURE (2011-2012)
Students with need: Out of 1,427 full-time freshmen who applied for aid, 1,191 were judged to have need. Of these, 1,191 received aid, and 216 had their full need met. Average financial aid package met 71% of need; average scholarship/grant was $21,349; average loan was $3,820. For part-time students, average financial aid package was $11,211.
Students without need: 424 full-time freshmen who did not demonstrate need for aid received scholarships/grants; average award was $13,369. No-need awards available for academics, art, athletics, leadership, music/drama, religious affiliation, ROTC.
Scholarships offered: ***Merit:*** A number of merit based scholarships are available ranging from $3,000 to $16,000. Selection based on applicants' high school academic achievement, test scores, leadership, and community service. ***Athletic:*** 31 full-time freshmen received athletic scholarships; average amount $14,371.
Cumulative student debt: 63% of graduating class had student loans; average debt was $36,797.
Additional info: Emergency scholarship fund established to assist students and families with special circumstances, especially loss of job; new Institutional loan program instituted to assist some students who do not have other financing options.

FINANCIAL AID PROCEDURES
Forms required: FAFSA.

Dates and Deadlines: Priority date 3/1; no closing date. Applicants notified on a rolling basis starting 3/1; must reply by 5/1 or within 4 week(s) of notification.
Transfers: No deadline. Applicants notified on a rolling basis starting 3/1; must reply by 5/1 or within 4 week(s) of notification. Students should file FAFSA by March 1 for Missouri State Funds.

CONTACT

Cari Wickliffe, Assistant Vice President and Director of Student Financial Services
One Grand Boulevard, St. Louis, MO 63103
(314) 977-2350

St. Luke's College

Kansas City, Missouri
www.saintlukescollege.edu Federal Code: 009782

Upper-division private nursing college in large city, affiliated with Episcopal Church.
Enrollment: 263 full-time undergrads.

BASIC COSTS (2012-2013)

Tuition and fees: $13,620.
Per-credit charge: $406.

FINANCIAL AID PICTURE

Students with need: Need-based aid available for full-time and part-time students.

FINANCIAL AID PROCEDURES

Transfers: No deadline. Applicants notified on a rolling basis; must reply within 3 week(s) of notification.

CONTACT

Marcia Ladage, Executive Director, Business Operations and Student Services
624 Westport Road, Kansas City, MO 64111
(816) 932-6742

Southeast Missouri State University

Cape Girardeau, Missouri
www.semo.edu Federal Code: 002501

4-year public university in large town.
Enrollment: 9,510 undergrads, 16% part-time. 1,768 full-time freshmen.
Selectivity: Admits over 75% of applicants.

BASIC COSTS (2012-2013)

Tuition and fees: $6,750; out-of-state residents $11,985.
Per-credit charge: $194; out-of-state residents $368.
Room and board: $8,110.

FINANCIAL AID PICTURE (2011-2012)

Students with need: Out of 1,528 full-time freshmen who applied for aid, 1,166 were judged to have need. Of these, 1,156 received aid, and 184 had their full need met. Average financial aid package met 61% of need; average scholarship/grant was $5,794; average loan was $3,408. For part-time students, average financial aid package was $5,402.
Students without need: 351 full-time freshmen who did not demonstrate need for aid received scholarships/grants; average award was $3,790. No-need awards available for academics, alumni affiliation, art, athletics, job skills, leadership, minority status, music/drama, ROTC, state/district residency.
Scholarships offered: 30 full-time freshmen received athletic scholarships; average amount $10,132.

FINANCIAL AID PROCEDURES

Forms required: FAFSA.
Dates and Deadlines: Priority date 3/1; no closing date. Applicants notified on a rolling basis starting 4/1; must reply within 3 week(s) of notification.
Transfers: Must reply by 8/20 or within 3 week(s) of notification.

CONTACT

Karen Walker, Director of Financial Aid Services
One University Plaza, Cape Girardeau, MO 63701
(573) 651-2253

Southwest Baptist University

Bolivar, Missouri
www.sbuniv.edu Federal Code: 002502

4-year private university in large town, affiliated with Southern Baptist Convention.
Enrollment: 2,595 undergrads, 22% part-time. 403 full-time freshmen.
Selectivity: Admits 50 to 75% of applicants.

BASIC COSTS (2012-2013)

Tuition and fees: $19,150.
Room and board: $6,350.

FINANCIAL AID PICTURE (2011-2012)

Students with need: Out of 379 full-time freshmen who applied for aid, 333 were judged to have need. Of these, 333 received aid, and 71 had their full need met. Average financial aid package met 74% of need; average scholarship/grant was $5,093; average loan was $3,895. For part-time students, average financial aid package was $9,173.
Students without need: 66 full-time freshmen who did not demonstrate need for aid received scholarships/grants; average award was $9,311. No-need awards available for academics, alumni affiliation, art, athletics, minority status, music/drama, religious affiliation.
Scholarships offered: 64 full-time freshmen received athletic scholarships; average amount $8,119.
Cumulative student debt: 72% of graduating class had student loans; average debt was $25,430.

FINANCIAL AID PROCEDURES

Forms required: FAFSA.
Dates and Deadlines: Priority date 3/15; no closing date. Applicants notified on a rolling basis starting 3/1; must reply within 2 week(s) of notification.

CONTACT

Brad Gamble, Director of Financial Aid
1600 University Avenue, Bolivar, MO 65613-2597
(417) 328-1822

State Fair Community College

Sedalia, Missouri
www.sfccmo.edu Federal Code: 007628

2-year public community college in large town.
Enrollment: 4,473 undergrads.
Selectivity: Open admission; but selective for some programs.

BASIC COSTS (2012-2013)

Tuition and fees: $2,850; out-of-district residents $3,810; out-of-state residents $5,700.
Per-credit charge: $95; out-of-district residents $127; out-of-state residents $190.
Room and board: $6,158.

FINANCIAL AID PICTURE

Students with need: Need-based aid available for full-time and part-time students. Work study available nights, weekends, and for part-time students.

Students without need: No-need awards available for academics, art, athletics, music/drama, state/district residency.

FINANCIAL AID PROCEDURES

Forms required: FAFSA.
Dates and Deadlines: Priority date 7/1; no closing date. Applicants notified on a rolling basis starting 7/15; must reply within 3 week(s) of notification.
Transfers: No deadline. Applicants notified on a rolling basis starting 7/15; must reply within 3 week(s) of notification.

CONTACT

John Matthews, Director of Financial Aid
3201 West 16th Street, Sedalia, MO 65301-2199
(660) 596-7295

Stephens College

Columbia, Missouri
www.stephens.edu Federal Code: 002512

4-year private liberal arts and career college for women in small city.
Enrollment: 672 undergrads, 18% part-time. 154 full-time freshmen.
Selectivity: Admits 50 to 75% of applicants.

BASIC COSTS (2012-2013)

Tuition and fees: $27,310.
Per-credit charge: $715.
Room and board: $9,694.

FINANCIAL AID PICTURE (2011-2012)

Students with need: Out of 152 full-time freshmen who applied for aid, 125 were judged to have need. Of these, 125 received aid. Average financial aid package met 69% of need; average scholarship/grant was $2,228; average loan was $2,977. For part-time students, average financial aid package was $14,509.
Students without need: 16 full-time freshmen who did not demonstrate need for aid received scholarships/grants; average award was $7,281. No-need awards available for academics, alumni affiliation, athletics, leadership, music/drama, state/district residency.
Scholarships offered: ***Merit:*** Stephens Scholars: 75% to 100% tuition for 4 years; competitive for accepted students with 25 ACT or 1700 SAT and cumulative GPA of 3.5 through essays and on-campus interviews; 6 available. ***Athletic:*** 17 full-time freshmen received athletic scholarships; average amount $15,517.
Cumulative student debt: 83% of graduating class had student loans; average debt was $22,293.

FINANCIAL AID PROCEDURES

Forms required: FAFSA.
Dates and Deadlines: Priority date 3/15; no closing date. Applicants notified on a rolling basis starting 3/1.
Transfers: Phi Theta Kappa students transferring from 2-year institutions eligible for scholarship.

CONTACT

Paul Gordon, Director of Financial Aid
1200 East Broadway, Columbia, MO 65215
(800) 876-7106

Stevens Institute of Business & Arts

St. Louis, Missouri
www.siba.edu Federal Code: 008552

2-year for-profit business and liberal arts college in very large city.
Enrollment: 245 undergrads.
Selectivity: Open admission; but selective for some programs.

BASIC COSTS (2012-2013)

Tuition and fees: $10,125.
Per-credit charge: $225.

FINANCIAL AID PICTURE

Students with need: Need-based aid available for full-time and part-time students.
Students without need: This college awards aid only to students with need.

FINANCIAL AID PROCEDURES

Forms required: FAFSA.
Dates and Deadlines: Applicants notified on a rolling basis.

CONTACT

Greg Elsenrath, Financial Aid Director
1521 Washington Avenue, St. Louis, MO 63103
(314) 421-0949 ext. 1405

Texas County Technical Institute

Houston, Missouri
www.texascountytech.edu Federal Code: 035793

2-year private nursing and technical college in small town.
Enrollment: 62 undergrads. 55 full-time freshmen.
Selectivity: Open admission.

BASIC COSTS (2012-2013)

Tuition and fees: $12,528.
Per-credit charge: $405.

FINANCIAL AID PICTURE

Students with need: Need-based aid available for full-time and part-time students.
Students without need: This college awards aid only to students with need.

FINANCIAL AID PROCEDURES

Forms required: FAFSA, institutional form.
Transfers: No deadline.

CONTACT

Clarice Casebeer, Director of Financial Aid
6915 South Highway 63, Houston, MO 65483
(417) 967-5466

Three Rivers Community College

Poplar Bluff, Missouri
www.trcc.edu Federal Code: 004713

2-year public community college in large town.
Enrollment: 3,090 undergrads, 31% part-time. 836 full-time freshmen.
Selectivity: Open admission; but selective for some programs.

BASIC COSTS (2012-2013)

Tuition and fees: $2,790; out-of-district residents $4,140; out-of-state residents $4,860.
Per-credit charge: $75; out-of-district residents $120; out-of-state residents $150.
Additional info: Book rental: $30 per book. Board plan not available. Cost of room only, $3,324.

FINANCIAL AID PICTURE (2011-2012)

Students with need: 73% of average financial aid package awarded as scholarships/grants, 27% awarded as loans/jobs. Need-based aid available for part-time students.
Students without need: No-need awards available for academics, athletics, state/district residency.

FINANCIAL AID PROCEDURES
Forms required: FAFSA, institutional form.
Dates and Deadlines: Priority date 5/1; no closing date. Applicants notified on a rolling basis starting 6/1; must reply within 2 week(s) of notification.

CONTACT
Charlotte Eubank, Chief Financial Officer
2080 Three Rivers Boulevard, Poplar Bluff, MO 63901-1308
(573) 840-9607

Truman State University
Kirksville, Missouri
www.truman.edu Federal Code: 002495

4-year public university and liberal arts college in large town.
Enrollment: 5,452 undergrads, 3% part-time. 1,377 full-time freshmen.
Selectivity: Admits 50 to 75% of applicants.

BASIC COSTS (2012-2013)
Tuition and fees: $7,216; out-of-state residents $12,952.
Per-credit charge: $291; out-of-state residents $530.
Room and board: $7,504.
Additional info: Tuition/fee waivers available for adults.

FINANCIAL AID PICTURE (2011-2012)
Students with need: Out of 1,182 full-time freshmen who applied for aid, 791 were judged to have need. Of these, 791 received aid, and 299 had their full need met. Average financial aid package met 86% of need; average scholarship/grant was $7,282; average loan was $3,410. For part-time students, average financial aid package was $6,525.
Students without need: 550 full-time freshmen who did not demonstrate need for aid received scholarships/grants; average award was $4,714. No-need awards available for academics, alumni affiliation, art, athletics, leadership, minority status, music/drama, ROTC, state/district residency.
Scholarships offered: ***Merit:*** Pershing Scholarship; up to full-tuition, average room and board price, up to $4,000 for study-abroad; awarded to outstanding scholars and leaders; 12 awarded. Truman Leadership Award; up to full-tuition, average room and board price; awarded to Missouri residents for demonstrated leadership and academic achievement. International Baccalaureate Scholarship; $2,000 per academic year; awarded to students who complete the IB Diploma Program. President's Combined Ability; $2,000-$3,000; combined ability score of 170 or higher; calculated by adding high school rank percent or GPA percent (whichever is higher) to national percentile on ACT/SAT; unlimited number available. ***Athletic:*** 69 full-time freshmen received athletic scholarships; average amount $4,273.
Cumulative student debt: 52% of graduating class had student loans; average debt was $22,922.

FINANCIAL AID PROCEDURES
Forms required: FAFSA, institutional form.
Dates and Deadlines: Priority date 4/1; no closing date. Applicants notified on a rolling basis starting 3/1.
Transfers: Applicants notified on a rolling basis starting 3/1. Limited number of automatic and competitive awards offered to transfer students.

CONTACT
Kathy Elsea, Financial Aid Director
100 East Normal Avenue, Kirksville, MO 63501
(660) 785-4130

University of Central Missouri
Warrensburg, Missouri
www.ucmo.edu Federal Code: 02454

4-year public university in large town.
Enrollment: 9,077 undergrads, 11% part-time. 1,587 full-time freshmen.
Selectivity: Admits over 75% of applicants.

BASIC COSTS (2012-2013)
Tuition and fees: $7,147; out-of-state residents $13,435.
Per-credit charge: $210; out-of-state residents $419.
Room and board: $7,388.

FINANCIAL AID PICTURE (2011-2012)
Students with need: Out of 1,586 full-time freshmen who applied for aid, 1,045 were judged to have need. Of these, 1,041 received aid, and 167 had their full need met. Average financial aid package met 22% of need; average scholarship/grant was $4,042; average loan was $3,565. For part-time students, average financial aid package was $7,362.
Students without need: 330 full-time freshmen who did not demonstrate need for aid received scholarships/grants; average award was $5,213. No-need awards available for academics, alumni affiliation, art, athletics, leadership, minority status, music/drama, ROTC, state/district residency.
Scholarships offered: 82 full-time freshmen received athletic scholarships; average amount $4,744.

FINANCIAL AID PROCEDURES
Forms required: FAFSA.
Dates and Deadlines: Priority date 3/1; no closing date. Applicants notified on a rolling basis starting 3/1; must reply within 2 week(s) of notification.
Transfers: No deadline. Must reply within 2 week(s) of notification.

CONTACT
Angelina Karlin, Director of Student Financial Assistance
WDE 1400, Warrensburg, MO 64093
(660) 543-8080

University of Missouri: Columbia
Columbia, Missouri
www.missouri.edu Federal Code: 002516

4-year public university in small city.
Enrollment: 26,590 undergrads, 6% part-time. 6,004 full-time freshmen.
Selectivity: Admits over 75% of applicants.

BASIC COSTS (2012-2013)
Tuition and fees: $9,257; out-of-state residents $23,366.
Per-credit charge: $269; out-of-state residents $740.
Room and board: $8,944.

FINANCIAL AID PICTURE (2011-2012)
Students with need: Out of 4,698 full-time freshmen who applied for aid, 3,238 were judged to have need. Of these, 3,134 received aid, and 472 had their full need met. Average financial aid package met 84% of need; average scholarship/grant was $7,922; average loan was $3,600. For part-time students, average financial aid package was $10,676.
Students without need: 1,206 full-time freshmen who did not demonstrate need for aid received scholarships/grants; average award was $3,544. No-need awards available for academics, alumni affiliation, art, athletics, leadership, minority status, music/drama, ROTC, state/district residency.
Scholarships offered: 213 full-time freshmen received athletic scholarships; average amount $10,217.
Additional info: Scholarship available for international students based on success during 1st semester.

FINANCIAL AID PROCEDURES
Forms required: FAFSA.
Dates and Deadlines: Priority date 3/1; no closing date. Applicants notified on a rolling basis starting 4/1; must reply within 4 week(s) of notification.
Transfers: No deadline. Applicants notified on a rolling basis starting 4/1; must reply within 4 week(s) of notification.

CONTACT
Nicholas Prewett, Director of Student Financial Aid
230 Jesse Hall, Columbia, MO 65211
(573) 882-7506

University of Missouri: Kansas City

Kansas City, Missouri
www.umkc.edu Federal Code: 002518

4-year public university in large city.
Enrollment: 8,447 undergrads, 20% part-time. 1,101 full-time freshmen.
Selectivity: Admits 50 to 75% of applicants.

BASIC COSTS (2012-2013)
Tuition and fees: $9,299; out-of-state residents $21,833.
Per-credit charge: $266; out-of-state residents $683.
Room and board: $9,264.

FINANCIAL AID PICTURE (2012-2013)
Students with need: Out of 922 full-time freshmen who applied for aid, 773 were judged to have need. Of these, 761 received aid, and 68 had their full need met. Average financial aid package met 53% of need; average scholarship/grant was $7,401; average loan was $6,357. For part-time students, average financial aid package was $5,773.
Students without need: 202 full-time freshmen who did not demonstrate need for aid received scholarships/grants; average award was $4,306. No-need awards available for academics, alumni affiliation, art, athletics, leadership, minority status, music/drama, state/district residency.
Scholarships offered: ***Merit:*** Many automatic scholarships and non-resident fee waivers are available for students who apply for admission by February 1. Automatic awards range from $1000 to a complete non-resident fee differential. A competitive Trustees Scholarship is available that covers most educational expenses. ***Athletic:*** 26 full-time freshmen received athletic scholarships; average amount $14,282.

FINANCIAL AID PROCEDURES
Forms required: FAFSA.
Dates and Deadlines: Priority date 3/1; no closing date. Applicants notified on a rolling basis starting 4/15; must reply within 2 week(s) of notification.

CONTACT
Nancy Merz, Director of Student Financial Aid
5100 Rockhill Road, AC120, Kansas City, MO 64110-2499
(816) 235-1154

University of Missouri: St. Louis

St. Louis, Missouri
www.umsl.edu Federal Code: 002519

4-year public university in very large city.
Enrollment: 8,984 undergrads, 34% part-time. 533 full-time freshmen.
Selectivity: Admits 50 to 75% of applicants.

BASIC COSTS (2012-2013)
Tuition and fees: $9,314; out-of-state residents $22,883.
Per-credit charge: $266; out-of-state residents $718.
Room and board: $8,690.

FINANCIAL AID PICTURE
Students with need: Need-based aid available for full-time and part-time students. Work study available nights.
Students without need: No-need awards available for academics, alumni affiliation, art, athletics, music/drama, ROTC, state/district residency.
Scholarships offered: Curators' Scholarship: $7,000; 28 ACT, top 5% of high school class, Missouri resident. Chancellor's Scholarship: $5,000; 26 ACT, top 10% of high school class. Additional scholarships available based on test scores, high school academic achievement, leadership, and community service. Must be admitted by 3/1 for consideration.

FINANCIAL AID PROCEDURES
Forms required: FAFSA.
Dates and Deadlines: Priority date 4/1; no closing date. Applicants notified on a rolling basis starting 4/1; must reply within 2 week(s) of notification.
Transfers: Transfer scholarships awarded to new students entering in fall or spring semesters. Must transfer at least 45 credit hours. Students transferring from Missouri 2-year institution must have minimum cumulative GPA of 3.25 for consideration. Students transferring from non-Missouri 2-year institution or any 4-year institution must have minimum cumulative GPA of 3.5 for consideration. Students starting in fall must be admitted by March 15; spring students must be admitted by 10/15.

CONTACT
Anthony Georges, Director of Student Financial Aid
One University Boulevard, St. Louis, MO 63121-4400
(314) 516-5526

Vatterott College: St. Joseph

Saint Joseph, Missouri
www.vatterott-college.edu Federal Code: 026092

2-year for-profit branch campus and technical college in small city.
Enrollment: 341 undergrads.
Selectivity: Open admission.

BASIC COSTS (2012-2013)
Additional info: Estimated program costs as of June 2012: diploma (30 weeks) $13,350, (40 weeks) $19,800, (50 weeks) $20,300, (60 weeks) $20,550 - $24,500; associate degree (70 weeks) $31,050 - $33,000. All costs, which include tuition, fees, books and supplies, and taxes, are subject to change.

FINANCIAL AID PICTURE
Students with need: Need-based aid available for full-time and part-time students.
Scholarships offered: Make the Grade Scholarship; up to $1,000; based on high school grades.

FINANCIAL AID PROCEDURES
Forms required: FAFSA.

CONTACT
Marcia Hurley, Financial Aid Administrator
3131 Frederick Avenue, St. Joseph, MO 64506
(816) 364-5399

Washington University in St. Louis

Saint Louis, Missouri Federal Code: 002520
www.wustl.edu CSS Code: 6929

4-year private university in large city.
Enrollment: 6,702 undergrads, 5% part-time. 1,622 full-time freshmen.
Selectivity: Admits less than 50% of applicants.

BASIC COSTS (2013-2014)
Tuition and fees: $44,841.
Room and board: $13,977.

FINANCIAL AID PICTURE (2012-2013)
Students with need: Out of 1,059 full-time freshmen who applied for aid, 680 were judged to have need. Of these, 658 received aid, and 658 had their full need met. Average financial aid package met 100% of need; average scholarship/grant was $32,644; average loan was $5,458. Need-based aid available for part-time students.
Students without need: 229 full-time freshmen who did not demonstrate need for aid received scholarships/grants; average award was $10,143. No-need awards available for academics, leadership, ROTC.
Scholarships offered: Numerous merit scholarships available ranging up to full tuition plus stipend, renewable for 4 years, based upon academic merit.

Additional info: Offers program that seeks to eliminate need-based loans as part of its undergraduate financial assistance awards to students from low-to middle-income families. Students who receive financial assistance come from broad range of economic backgrounds.

FINANCIAL AID PROCEDURES
Forms required: CSS PROFILE.
Dates and Deadlines: Closing date 2/1. Applicants notified by 4/1; must reply by 5/1.

CONTACT
Michael Runiewicz, Director of Student Financial Services
Campus Box 1089, One Brookings Drive, St. Louis, MO 63130-4899
(314) 935-5900

Webster University
St. Louis, Missouri
www.webster.edu Federal Code: 002521

4-year private university in very large city.
Enrollment: 2,958 undergrads, 17% part-time. 415 full-time freshmen.
Selectivity: Admits 50 to 75% of applicants.

BASIC COSTS (2012-2013)
Tuition and fees: $23,010.
Per-credit charge: $590.
Room and board: $9,950.
Additional info: Tuition is $26,720 for theatre conservatory students.

FINANCIAL AID PICTURE (2012-2013)
Students with need: Out of 384 full-time freshmen who applied for aid, 326 were judged to have need. Of these, 326 received aid, and 3 had their full need met. Average financial aid package met 34% of need; average scholarship/grant was $4,030; average loan was $3,079. For part-time students, average financial aid package was $2,219.
Students without need: 51 full-time freshmen who did not demonstrate need for aid received scholarships/grants; average award was $4,591. No-need awards available for academics, art, leadership, music/drama, state/district residency.
Scholarships offered: Daniel Webster Scholarships: full tuition; 3.8 GPA, top 10% class rank, 29 ACT and interview; 5 awarded. Webster Academic Scholarships: from $2,000-$10,000; minimum 3.0 GPA and 23 ACT; unlimited awarded. Leadership Scholarships: $1,500; minimum 3.3 GPA and 24 ACT, resume of activities; 15 awarded.
Cumulative student debt: 51% of graduating class had student loans; average debt was $29,723.

FINANCIAL AID PROCEDURES
Forms required: FAFSA, institutional form.
Dates and Deadlines: Priority date 4/1; no closing date. Applicants notified on a rolling basis starting 2/1; must reply within 2 week(s) of notification.

CONTACT
James Myers, Director of Financial Aid
470 East Lockwood Avenue, St. Louis, MO 63119-3194
(314) 968-6992

Westminster College
Fulton, Missouri
www.westminster-mo.edu Federal Code: 002523

4-year private liberal arts college in large town, affiliated with Presbyterian Church (USA).
Enrollment: 1,080 undergrads, 1% part-time. 260 full-time freshmen.
Selectivity: Admits 50 to 75% of applicants.

BASIC COSTS (2013-2014)
Tuition and fees: $21,680.
Per-credit charge: $800.
Room and board: $8,810.
Additional info: Tuition/fee waivers available for minority students.

FINANCIAL AID PICTURE (2012-2013)
Students with need: Out of 200 full-time freshmen who applied for aid, 155 were judged to have need. Of these, 155 received aid, and 153 had their full need met. Average financial aid package met 82% of need; average scholarship/grant was $15,940; average loan was $3,286. For part-time students, average financial aid package was $13,602.
Students without need: 106 full-time freshmen who did not demonstrate need for aid received scholarships/grants; average award was $11,509. No-need awards available for academics, alumni affiliation, leadership, minority status, music/drama, religious affiliation, ROTC.
Cumulative student debt: 64% of graduating class had student loans; average debt was $26,723.

FINANCIAL AID PROCEDURES
Forms required: FAFSA.
Dates and Deadlines: Priority date 2/15; no closing date. Applicants notified on a rolling basis starting 3/15; must reply within 3 week(s) of notification.
Transfers: Applicants notified on a rolling basis starting 3/1; must reply within 3 week(s) of notification.

CONTACT
Aimee Bristow, Director of Financial Aid
501 Westminster Avenue, Fulton, MO 65251-1299
(573) 592-5365

William Jewell College
Liberty, Missouri
www.jewell.edu Federal Code: 002524

4-year private liberal arts college in large town.
Enrollment: 1,052 undergrads, 4% part-time. 305 full-time freshmen.
Selectivity: Admits 50 to 75% of applicants.

BASIC COSTS (2013-2014)
Tuition and fees: $30,800.
Per-credit charge: $890.
Room and board: $8,020.

FINANCIAL AID PICTURE (2012-2013)
Students with need: Out of 245 full-time freshmen who applied for aid, 245 were judged to have need. Of these, 245 received aid, and 44 had their full need met. Average financial aid package met 78% of need; average scholarship/grant was $22,300; average loan was $4,037. Need-based aid available for part-time students.
Students without need: 54 full-time freshmen who did not demonstrate need for aid received scholarships/grants; average award was $13,504. No-need awards available for academics, alumni affiliation, athletics, music/drama.
Scholarships offered: ***Merit:*** Academic scholarships; $10,000-$15,000 awarded at time of admittance; competitive academic scholarship program offered by invitation only to qualified high school seniors with $1,000-$9,000 increases over previous awards. National Merit Semifinalists will automatically qualify for academic scholarship of $24,000. IB Diploma Scholarship of $17,000 is awarded to eligible applicants. All academic scholarships are available for 8 consecutive semesters with a 2.5 cumulative GPA requirement. Limit of one academic scholarship per applicant. ***Athletic:*** 28 full-time freshmen received athletic scholarships; average amount $9,953.
Cumulative student debt: 70% of graduating class had student loans; average debt was $31,324.

FINANCIAL AID PROCEDURES
Forms required: FAFSA.

Dates and Deadlines: Priority date 3/1; no closing date. Applicants notified on a rolling basis starting 2/15; must reply within 2 week(s) of notification.
Transfers: Must reply within 2 week(s) of notification. Transfer students evaluated individually by financial aid staff to determine number of semesters of aid available.

CONTACT
Susan Karnes, Director, Financial Aid and Scholarship Services
500 College Hill, Liberty, MO 64068
(816) 415-5977

William Woods University
Fulton, Missouri
www.williamwoods.edu Federal Code: 002525

4-year private university and teachers college in large town, affiliated with Christian Church (Disciples of Christ).
Enrollment: 1,364 undergrads.
Selectivity: Admits over 75% of applicants.

BASIC COSTS (2012-2013)
Tuition and fees: $19,850.
Room and board: $7,900.

FINANCIAL AID PICTURE
Students with need: Need-based aid available for full-time and part-time students. Work study available nights, weekends, and for part-time students.
Students without need: No-need awards available for academics, alumni affiliation, art, athletics, leadership, music/drama, religious affiliation.
Scholarships offered: LEAD (Leading, Educating, Achieving and Developing) Award; $5,000 for campus residents, $2,500 for commuters; based on commitment to campus and community involvement; renewable each year if commitment has been met in previous year.

FINANCIAL AID PROCEDURES
Forms required: FAFSA, institutional form.
Dates and Deadlines: Priority date 3/1; no closing date. Applicants notified on a rolling basis starting 3/15; must reply within 2 week(s) of notification.
Transfers: No deadline. Applicants notified on a rolling basis; must reply within 2 week(s) of notification. Transfer students eligible for scholarship.

CONTACT
Deana Ready, Director of Financial Aid
One University Avenue, Fulton, MO 65251-2388
(573) 592-4232

Montana

Blackfeet Community College
Browning, Montana
http://bfcc.edu/ Federal Code: 014902

2-year public Tribal community college in small town.
Enrollment: 404 undergrads, 10% part-time. 94 full-time freshmen.
Selectivity: Open admission.

BASIC COSTS (2013-2014)
Tuition and fees: $2,900; out-of-state residents $2,900.
Per-credit charge: $85.

FINANCIAL AID PICTURE
Students with need: Need-based aid available for full-time and part-time students.

FINANCIAL AID PROCEDURES
Forms required: FAFSA, institutional form.

CONTACT
Gaylene DuCharme, Director of Financial Aid
504 SE Boundary, Browning, MT 59417
(406) 338-5421 ext. 2245

Carroll College
Helena, Montana
www.carroll.edu Federal Code: 002526

4-year private liberal arts college in large town, affiliated with Roman Catholic Church.
Enrollment: 1,406 undergrads, 3% part-time. 344 full-time freshmen.
Selectivity: Admits 50 to 75% of applicants.

BASIC COSTS (2013-2014)
Tuition and fees: $27,914.
Per-credit charge: $1,138.
Room and board: $8,668.

FINANCIAL AID PICTURE (2011-2012)
Students with need: Out of 286 full-time freshmen who applied for aid, 230 were judged to have need. Of these, 229 received aid, and 44 had their full need met. Average financial aid package met 75% of need; average scholarship/grant was $14,979; average loan was $3,166. For part-time students, average financial aid package was $10,446.
Students without need: 112 full-time freshmen who did not demonstrate need for aid received scholarships/grants; average award was $12,208. No-need awards available for academics, art, athletics, leadership, minority status, music/drama, religious affiliation, ROTC.
Scholarships offered: 69 full-time freshmen received athletic scholarships; average amount $7,169.
Cumulative student debt: 69% of graduating class had student loans; average debt was $28,005.

FINANCIAL AID PROCEDURES
Forms required: FAFSA.
Dates and Deadlines: Priority date 3/1; no closing date. Applicants notified on a rolling basis starting 3/1; must reply by 5/1 or within 2 week(s) of notification.

CONTACT
Janet Riis, Director of Financial Aid
1601 North Benton Avenue, Helena, MT 59625
(406) 447-5425

Chief Dull Knife College
Lame Deer, Montana
www.cdkc.edu Federal Code: 014878

2-year public junior college in rural community.
Enrollment: 374 undergrads.
Selectivity: Open admission.

BASIC COSTS (2012-2013)
Tuition and fees: $2,240; out-of-state residents $2,240.
Per-credit charge: $70.

FINANCIAL AID PICTURE
Students with need: Need-based aid available for full-time and part-time students. Work study available nights.
Students without need: No-need awards available for academics.

FINANCIAL AID PROCEDURES
Forms required: FAFSA, institutional form.

Dates and Deadlines: Priority date 3/1; no closing date. Applicants notified on a rolling basis; must reply within 2 week(s) of notification.
Transfers: No deadline. Applicants notified on a rolling basis; must reply within 2 week(s) of notification.

CONTACT
Devin Wertman, Director of Financial Aid
Box 98, Lame Deer, MT 59043
(406) 477-6215

Dawson Community College

Glendive, Montana
www.dawson.edu Federal Code: 002529

2-year public community college in small town.
Enrollment: 443 undergrads.
Selectivity: Open admission.

BASIC COSTS (2012-2013)
Tuition and fees: $3,083; out-of-district residents $4,245; out-of-state residents $9,135.
Per-credit charge: $55; out-of-district residents $94; out-of-state residents $257.
Room and board: $3,500.

FINANCIAL AID PICTURE
Students with need: Work study available nights, weekends, and for part-time students.
Students without need: No-need awards available for academics, art, athletics, music/drama.

FINANCIAL AID PROCEDURES
Forms required: FAFSA.
Dates and Deadlines: Priority date 3/1; no closing date. Applicants notified on a rolling basis starting 5/15; must reply within 2 week(s) of notification.

CONTACT
Jolene Myers, Director of Admissions
300 College Drive, Glendive, MT 59330
(406) 377-9410

Flathead Valley Community College

Kalispell, Montana
www.fvcc.edu Federal Code: 006777

2-year public community college in large town.
Enrollment: 1,969 undergrads, 42% part-time. 304 full-time freshmen.
Selectivity: Open admission; but selective for some programs.

BASIC COSTS (2012-2013)
Tuition and fees: $3,728; out-of-district residents $5,100; out-of-state residents $10,868.

FINANCIAL AID PICTURE
Students with need: Need-based aid available for full-time and part-time students.
Students without need: No-need awards available for academics, athletics.

FINANCIAL AID PROCEDURES
Forms required: FAFSA.
Dates and Deadlines: Priority date 3/1; no closing date. Applicants notified on a rolling basis starting 4/15; must reply within 2 week(s) of notification.

CONTACT
Cynthia Kiefer, Director of Financial Aid
777 Grandview Drive, Kalispell, MT 59901
(406) 756-3849

Fort Peck Community College

Poplar, Montana
www.fpcc.edu Federal Code: 016616

2-year public community college in rural community.
Enrollment: 311 undergrads, 23% part-time. 61 full-time freshmen.
Selectivity: Open admission.

BASIC COSTS (2012-2013)
Tuition and fees: $2,250; out-of-state residents $2,250.
Per-credit charge: $70.
Additional info: Tuition/fee waivers available for adults, minority students.

FINANCIAL AID PICTURE (2012-2013)
Students with need: Need-based aid available for part-time students.
Students without need: This college awards aid only to students with need.

FINANCIAL AID PROCEDURES
Forms required: FAFSA.
Dates and Deadlines: Applicants notified on a rolling basis; must reply within 2 week(s) of notification.
Transfers: No deadline. Applicants notified on a rolling basis; must reply within 2 week(s) of notification.

CONTACT
Lanette Clark, Financial Aid Director
Box 398, 605 Indian, Poplar, MT 59255-0398
(406) 768-6327

Great Falls College Montana State University

Great Falls, Montana
www.msugf.edu Federal Code: 009314

2-year public community college in small city.
Enrollment: 1,645 undergrads, 45% part-time. 203 full-time freshmen.
Selectivity: Open admission; but selective for some programs.

BASIC COSTS (2012-2013)
Tuition and fees: $3,077; out-of-state residents $9,329.
Per-credit charge: $104; out-of-state residents $634.
Additional info: Tuition/fee waivers available for minority students.

FINANCIAL AID PICTURE (2011-2012)
Students with need: Out of 189 full-time freshmen who applied for aid, 169 were judged to have need. Of these, 166 received aid, and 2 had their full need met. Average financial aid package met 58% of need; average scholarship/grant was $4,803; average loan was $2,814. For part-time students, average financial aid package was $6,071.
Students without need: No-need awards available for academics, leadership.
Cumulative student debt: 76% of graduating class had student loans; average debt was $16,557.

FINANCIAL AID PROCEDURES
Forms required: FAFSA, institutional form.
Dates and Deadlines: Priority date 3/1; no closing date. Applicants notified on a rolling basis starting 4/15.
Transfers: No deadline. Applicants notified on a rolling basis; must reply within 3 week(s) of notification.

CONTACT
Leah Habel, Director of Financial Aid
2100 16th Avenue South, Great Falls, MT 59405
(800) 446-2698 ext. 4334

Helena College University of Montana

Helena, Montana
www.umhelena.edu Federal Code: 007570

2-year public community and technical college in large town.
Enrollment: 1,258 undergrads, 37% part-time. 187 full-time freshmen.
Selectivity: Open admission.

BASIC COSTS (2012-2013)

Tuition and fees: $3,061; out-of-state residents $8,357.
Per-credit charge: $79; out-of-state residents $255.
Additional info: Tuition/fee waivers available for minority students.

FINANCIAL AID PICTURE

Students with need: Need-based aid available for full-time and part-time students.

FINANCIAL AID PROCEDURES

Forms required: FAFSA, institutional form.
Dates and Deadlines: Priority date 3/1; no closing date. Applicants notified on a rolling basis starting 5/1.
Transfers: Applicants notified on a rolling basis starting 5/1.

CONTACT

Valerie Curtin, Director of Financial Aid
1115 North Roberts Street, Helena, MT 59601-3098
(406) 447-6916

Little Big Horn College

Crow Agency, Montana
www.lbhc.edu Federal Code: 016135

2-year private community college in rural community.
Enrollment: 366 undergrads. 139 full-time freshmen.
Selectivity: Open admission.

BASIC COSTS (2012-2013)

Tuition and fees: $2,760.
Per-credit charge: $75.

FINANCIAL AID PICTURE (2011-2012)

Students with need: Out of 139 full-time freshmen who applied for aid, 139 were judged to have need. Of these, 111 received aid. Average financial aid package met 50% of need; average scholarship/grant was $1,620. For part-time students, average financial aid package was $2,081.
Students without need: This college awards aid only to students with need.

FINANCIAL AID PROCEDURES

Forms required: FAFSA, institutional form.
Dates and Deadlines: Applicants notified on a rolling basis.
Transfers: No deadline. Applicants notified on a rolling basis.

CONTACT

Beverly Snell, Financial Aid Director
Box 370, Crow Agency, MT 59022
(406) 638-3140

Miles Community College

Miles City, Montana
www.milescc.edu Federal Code: 002528

2-year public community college in small town.
Enrollment: 418 undergrads, 33% part-time. 98 full-time freshmen.
Selectivity: Open admission; but selective for some programs.

BASIC COSTS (2012-2013)

Tuition and fees: $3,720; out-of-district residents $4,710; out-of-state residents $7,500.
Per-credit charge: $79; out-of-district residents $112; out-of-state residents $205.
Room and board: $5,280.

FINANCIAL AID PICTURE

Students with need: Need-based aid available for full-time and part-time students. Work study available nights, weekends, and for part-time students.
Students without need: No-need awards available for academics, athletics, leadership.

FINANCIAL AID PROCEDURES

Forms required: FAFSA.
Dates and Deadlines: Priority date 3/1; no closing date. Applicants notified on a rolling basis starting 4/15; must reply within 4 week(s) of notification.

CONTACT

Loren Lancaster, Financial Aid Officer
2715 Dickinson Street, Miles City, MT 59301
(406) 874-6208

Montana State University

Bozeman, Montana
www.montana.edu Federal Code: 002532

4-year public university in large town.
Enrollment: 12,614 undergrads, 17% part-time. 1,974 full-time freshmen.
Selectivity: Admits 50 to 75% of applicants.

BASIC COSTS (2012-2013)

Tuition and fees: $6,749; out-of-state residents $20,018.
Per-credit charge: $222; out-of-state residents $775.
Room and board: $8,070.
Additional info: Tuition/fee waivers available for minority students.

FINANCIAL AID PICTURE (2011-2012)

Students with need: Out of 1,556 full-time freshmen who applied for aid, 1,158 were judged to have need. Of these, 1,120 received aid, and 68 had their full need met. Average financial aid package met 76% of need; average scholarship/grant was $4,957; average loan was $3,718. For part-time students, average financial aid package was $10,940.
Students without need: 73 full-time freshmen who did not demonstrate need for aid received scholarships/grants; average award was $1,084. No-need awards available for academics, alumni affiliation, art, athletics, job skills, leadership, minority status, music/drama, ROTC, state/district residency.
Scholarships offered: 11 full-time freshmen received athletic scholarships; average amount $5,197.
Cumulative student debt: 65% of graduating class had student loans; average debt was $27,320.
Additional info: Tuition waiver for honorably discharged veterans, children of members of the United States armed forces who, at the time of entry into service, had legal residence in Montana and who were killed in action or who died as a result of injury, disease, or other disability incurred while in the service.

FINANCIAL AID PROCEDURES

Forms required: FAFSA.
Dates and Deadlines: Priority date 3/1; no closing date. Applicants notified on a rolling basis starting 4/1; must reply within 3 week(s) of notification.
Transfers: Priority date 7/1; no deadline.

CONTACT

Brandi Payne, Director of Financial Aid Services
PO Box 172190, Bozeman, MT 59717-2190
(406) 994-2845

Montana State University: Billings

Billings, Montana
www.msubillings.edu Federal Code: 002530

4-year public university and technical college in small city.
Enrollment: 4,354 undergrads, 26% part-time. 754 full-time freshmen.
Selectivity: Admits over 75% of applicants.

BASIC COSTS (2012-2013)

Tuition and fees: $5,711; out-of-state residents $16,609.
Per-credit charge: $147; out-of-state residents $510.
Room and board: $6,320.

FINANCIAL AID PICTURE (2011-2012)

Students with need: Out of 636 full-time freshmen who applied for aid, 528 were judged to have need. Of these, 509 received aid, and 22 had their full need met. Average financial aid package met 65% of need; average scholarship/grant was $4,831; average loan was $2,794. For part-time students, average financial aid package was $7,463.
Students without need: 15 full-time freshmen who did not demonstrate need for aid received scholarships/grants; average award was $1,832. No-need awards available for academics, alumni affiliation, art, athletics, job skills, leadership, minority status, music/drama, ROTC, state/district residency.
Scholarships offered: 25 full-time freshmen received athletic scholarships; average amount $2,625.
Cumulative student debt: 73% of graduating class had student loans; average debt was $27,178.
Additional info: Veterans and honors fee waivers offered.

FINANCIAL AID PROCEDURES

Forms required: FAFSA.
Dates and Deadlines: Priority date 3/1; no closing date. Applicants notified on a rolling basis starting 4/1; must reply within 3 week(s) of notification.

CONTACT

Leslie Weldon, Director of Financial Aid
1500 University Drive, Billings, MT 59101-0298
(406) 657-2188

Montana State University: Northern

Havre, Montana
www.msun.edu Federal Code: 002533

4-year public university in large town.
Enrollment: 1,203 undergrads, 25% part-time. 179 full-time freshmen.

BASIC COSTS (2012-2013)

Tuition and fees: $4,817; out-of-state residents $16,554.
Per-credit charge: $117; out-of-state residents $508.
Room and board: $6,048.
Additional info: Tuition/fee waivers available for minority students.

FINANCIAL AID PICTURE

Students with need: Need-based aid available for full-time and part-time students. Work study available nights, weekends, and for part-time students.
Students without need: No-need awards available for academics, athletics.

FINANCIAL AID PROCEDURES

Forms required: FAFSA, institutional form.
Dates and Deadlines: Priority date 4/15; no closing date. Applicants notified on a rolling basis starting 5/1; must reply within 4 week(s) of notification.

CONTACT

Cindy Small, Director of Financial Aid
Box 7751, Havre, MT 59501
(406) 265-3700

Montana Tech of the University of Montana

Butte, Montana
www.mtech.edu Federal Code: 002531

4-year public engineering and technical college in large town.
Enrollment: 2,427 undergrads, 10% part-time. 466 full-time freshmen.
Selectivity: Admits over 75% of applicants.

BASIC COSTS (2012-2013)

Tuition and fees: $6,435; out-of-state residents $18,080.
Per-credit charge: $205; out-of-state residents $690.
Room and board: $7,626.

FINANCIAL AID PICTURE (2011-2012)

Students with need: Out of 399 full-time freshmen who applied for aid, 298 were judged to have need. Of these, 298 received aid, and 125 had their full need met. Average financial aid package met 80% of need; average scholarship/grant was $5,363; average loan was $3,071. For part-time students, average financial aid package was $8,497.
Students without need: 61 full-time freshmen who did not demonstrate need for aid received scholarships/grants; average award was $3,060. No-need awards available for academics, alumni affiliation, athletics, job skills, leadership, minority status, religious affiliation, ROTC, state/district residency.
Scholarships offered: 15 full-time freshmen received athletic scholarships; average amount $3,415.
Cumulative student debt: 55% of graduating class had student loans; average debt was $25,360.

FINANCIAL AID PROCEDURES

Forms required: FAFSA, institutional form.
Dates and Deadlines: Priority date 3/1; no closing date. Applicants notified on a rolling basis starting 3/15; must reply within 2 week(s) of notification.
Transfers: No deadline. Applicants notified on a rolling basis; must reply within 2 week(s) of notification.

CONTACT

Mike Richardson, Director of Financial Aid
1300 West Park Street, Butte, MT 59701-8997
(406) 496-4212

Rocky Mountain College

Billings, Montana
www.rocky.edu Federal Code: 002534

4-year private liberal arts college in small city, affiliated with Presbyterian Church (USA).
Enrollment: 984 undergrads, 2% part-time. 262 full-time freshmen.
Selectivity: Admits 50 to 75% of applicants.

BASIC COSTS (2013-2014)

Tuition and fees: $23,718.
Per-credit charge: $968.
Room and board: $7,430.

FINANCIAL AID PICTURE (2012-2013)

Students with need: Out of 232 full-time freshmen who applied for aid, 213 were judged to have need. Of these, 213 received aid, and 40 had their full need met. Average financial aid package met 95% of need; average scholarship/grant was $15,470; average loan was $3,494. For part-time students, average financial aid package was $8,308.
Students without need: 17 full-time freshmen who did not demonstrate need for aid received scholarships/grants; average award was $10,500. No-need awards available for academics, athletics.
Scholarships offered: 69 full-time freshmen received athletic scholarships; average amount $8,308.

Cumulative student debt: 77% of graduating class had student loans; average debt was $30,948.

FINANCIAL AID PROCEDURES

Forms required: FAFSA.

Dates and Deadlines: Priority date 3/1; no closing date. Applicants notified on a rolling basis starting 2/15; must reply within 4 week(s) of notification.

Transfers: No deadline. Applicants notified on a rolling basis.

CONTACT

Jessica Francischetti, Director of Financial Assistance
1511 Poly Drive, Billings, MT 59102-1796
(406) 657-1031

Salish Kootenai College

Pablo, Montana
www.skc.edu Federal Code: 015023

4-year private liberal arts college in rural community.

Enrollment: 905 undergrads.

Selectivity: Open admission; but selective for some programs.

BASIC COSTS (2012-2013)

Tuition and fees: $6,279; out-of-state residents $11,463.

Additional info: Full-time tuition and required fees for Native American students and students of Native American descent, $4,191. Tuition/fee waivers available for minority students.

FINANCIAL AID PICTURE

Students with need: Need-based aid available for full-time and part-time students. Work study available nights, weekends, and for part-time students.

FINANCIAL AID PROCEDURES

Forms required: FAFSA.

Dates and Deadlines: Priority date 3/31; no closing date. Applicants notified on a rolling basis starting 7/15; must reply within 6 week(s) of notification.

CONTACT

Jackie Swain, Financial Aid Director
PO Box 70, Pablo, MT 59855
(406) 275-4855

Stone Child College

Box Elder, Montana
www.stonechild.edu Federal Code: 026109

2-year public community and junior college in rural community.

Enrollment: 180 undergrads.

Selectivity: Open admission.

BASIC COSTS (2013-2014)

Tuition and fees: $2,505; out-of-state residents $2,505.

Additional info: Tuition/fee waivers available for unemployed or children of unemployed.

FINANCIAL AID PICTURE

Students with need: Need-based aid available for full-time and part-time students.

Students without need: No-need awards available for academics.

Additional info: Scholarships available to high school and GED graduates who apply for college admission during the first term after graduation.

FINANCIAL AID PROCEDURES

Forms required: FAFSA, institutional form.

Dates and Deadlines: Priority date 3/1; no closing date. Applicants notified on a rolling basis.

CONTACT

Tiffany Galbavy, Financial Aid Director
8294 Upper Box Elder Road, Box Elder, MT 59521
(406) 395-4313 ext. 220

University of Great Falls

Great Falls, Montana
www.ugf.edu Federal Code: 002527

4-year private university and liberal arts college in small city, affiliated with Roman Catholic Church.

Enrollment: 974 undergrads, 32% part-time. 136 full-time freshmen.

Selectivity: Admits over 75% of applicants.

BASIC COSTS (2013-2014)

Tuition and fees: $20,960.

Per-credit charge: $607.

Room and board: $7,163.

FINANCIAL AID PICTURE (2012-2013)

Students with need: Out of 125 full-time freshmen who applied for aid, 111 were judged to have need. Of these, 109 received aid, and 8 had their full need met. Average financial aid package met 72% of need; average scholarship/grant was $10,524; average loan was $3,392. For part-time students, average financial aid package was $8,430.

Students without need: 16 full-time freshmen who did not demonstrate need for aid received scholarships/grants; average award was $7,119. No-need awards available for academics, alumni affiliation, art, athletics, music/drama, religious affiliation, state/district residency.

Scholarships offered: ***Merit:*** Freshmen scholarships: $1,000-$6,000; based on high school GPA; renewable. ***Athletic:*** 26 full-time freshmen received athletic scholarships; average amount $9,364.

Cumulative student debt: 85% of graduating class had student loans; average debt was $25,690.

FINANCIAL AID PROCEDURES

Forms required: FAFSA.

Dates and Deadlines: Priority date 3/1; no closing date. Applicants notified on a rolling basis starting 3/1; must reply within 3 week(s) of notification.

Transfers: Transfer student scholarships; $2,500-$4,000; based on college GPA; renewable.

CONTACT

Sandra Bauman, Director of Financial Aid
1301 20th Street South, Great Falls, MT 59405
(406) 791-5235

University of Montana

Missoula, Montana
www.umt.edu Federal Code: 002536

4-year public university and liberal arts college in small city.

Enrollment: 12,443 undergrads, 21% part-time. 1,985 full-time freshmen.

Selectivity: Admits over 75% of applicants.

BASIC COSTS (2012-2013)

Tuition and fees: $5,985; out-of-state residents $21,077.

Per-credit charge: $146; out-of-state residents $646.

Room and board: $7,262.

Additional info: Out of state tuition total is $19,465 ($19,393 plus $72 nonresident building fee). Tuition/fee waivers available for minority students.

FINANCIAL AID PICTURE (2011-2012)

Students with need: Out of 1,634 full-time freshmen who applied for aid, 1,287 were judged to have need. Of these, 1,259 received aid, and 123 had their full need met. Average financial aid package met 58% of need; average

scholarship/grant was $4,769; average loan was $3,625. For part-time students, average financial aid package was $5,525.
Students without need: 283 full-time freshmen who did not demonstrate need for aid received scholarships/grants; average award was $3,327. No-need awards available for academics, alumni affiliation, athletics, leadership, music/drama, ROTC, state/district residency.
Scholarships offered: 50 full-time freshmen received athletic scholarships; average amount $2,588.
Cumulative student debt: 57% of graduating class had student loans; average debt was $20,532.

FINANCIAL AID PROCEDURES
Forms required: FAFSA.
Dates and Deadlines: Priority date 2/15; no closing date. Applicants notified on a rolling basis starting 4/1; must reply within 4 week(s) of notification.
Transfers: Applicants notified on a rolling basis starting 4/1.

CONTACT
Kent McGowan, Director of Financial Aid
Lommasson Center 103, Missoula, MT 59812
(406) 243-5373

University of Montana: Western
Dillon, Montana
www.umwestern.edu Federal Code: 002537

4-year public liberal arts and teachers college in small town.
Enrollment: 1,465 undergrads, 16% part-time. 278 full-time freshmen.
Selectivity: Open admission; but selective for some programs.

BASIC COSTS (2012-2013)
Tuition and fees: $4,109; out-of-state residents $14,357.
Per-credit charge: $103; out-of-state residents $455.
Room and board: $6,058.
Additional info: Tuition/fee waivers available for minority students.

FINANCIAL AID PICTURE (2011-2012)
Students with need: Average financial aid package met 28% of need; average scholarship/grant was $3,010; average loan was $3,110. For part-time students, average financial aid package was $3,288.
Students without need: No-need awards available for academics, alumni affiliation, art, athletics, leadership, minority status, music/drama, state/district residency.
Cumulative student debt: 71% of graduating class had student loans; average debt was $23,894.
Additional info: Tuition waivers available for veterans, Native Americans, senior citizens, and dependents of Montana University System employees.

FINANCIAL AID PROCEDURES
Forms required: FAFSA, institutional form.
Dates and Deadlines: Priority date 3/1; no closing date. Applicants notified on a rolling basis starting 4/1; must reply within 4 week(s) of notification.
Transfers: No deadline. Applicants notified on a rolling basis starting 4/1; must reply within 4 week(s) of notification. Transfer students must have a cumulative GPA of 2.0 or greater to enter in with good academic standing. Students with a transfer GPA below 2.0 must appeal to receive Financial Aid at Montana Western.

CONTACT
Erica Jones, Director of Financial Aid
710 South Atlantic Street, Dillon, MT 59725
(406) 683-7511

Nebraska

Bellevue University
Bellevue, Nebraska
www.bellevue.edu Federal Code: 002538

4-year private university and business college in large city.
Enrollment: 6,166 undergrads, 30% part-time. 2 full-time freshmen.
Selectivity: Open admission; but selective for some programs.

BASIC COSTS (2012-2013)
Tuition and fees: $7,800.
Per-credit charge: $250.
Additional info: Tuition costs may vary for online and cohort classes.

FINANCIAL AID PICTURE
Students with need: Need-based aid available for full-time and part-time students. Work study available nights, weekends, and for part-time students.
Students without need: No-need awards available for academics, athletics, leadership.

FINANCIAL AID PROCEDURES
Forms required: FAFSA, institutional form.
Dates and Deadlines: Priority date 4/15; no closing date. Applicants notified on a rolling basis starting 4/15; must reply within 2 week(s) of notification.
Transfers: No deadline. Applicants notified on a rolling basis starting 4/15; must reply within 2 week(s) of notification.

CONTACT
Jon Dotterer, Director of Financial Aid
1000 Galvin Road South, Bellevue, NE 68005-3098
(402) 557-7326

BryanLGH College of Health Sciences
Lincoln, Nebraska
www.bryanhealthcollege.edu Federal Code: 006399

4-year private health science college in large city, affiliated with United Methodist Church.
Enrollment: 582 undergrads.

BASIC COSTS (2012-2013)
Tuition and fees: $14,130.
Per-credit charge: $447.

FINANCIAL AID PICTURE
Students with need: Need-based aid available for full-time and part-time students.
Students without need: No-need awards available for academics, leadership.

FINANCIAL AID PROCEDURES
Forms required: FAFSA, institutional form.
Dates and Deadlines: Closing date 5/1. Applicants notified on a rolling basis starting 5/1; must reply within 3 week(s) of notification.

CONTACT
Deborah Wilke, Financial Aid Director
5035 Everett Street, Lincoln, NE 68506
(402) 481-8984

Central Community College

Grand Island, Nebraska
www.cccneb.edu Federal Code: 014468

2-year public community and technical college in large town.
Enrollment: 4,613 undergrads, 48% part-time. 740 full-time freshmen.
Selectivity: Open admission; but selective for some programs and for out-of-state students.

BASIC COSTS (2012-2013)
Tuition and fees: $2,640; out-of-state residents $3,840.
Per-credit charge: $80; out-of-state residents $120.
Room and board: $6,504.

FINANCIAL AID PICTURE
Students with need: Need-based aid available for full-time and part-time students. Work study available nights.
Students without need: No-need awards available for academics, art, athletics, job skills, leadership, music/drama.
Additional info: All students are eligible to apply for a Pell Grant. Students enrolled for at least six semester hours (half-time) are eligible to apply for grants, loans, work study, and scholarships. To be considered for full-time benefits, students must be enrolled for at least 12 credit hours during the semester.

FINANCIAL AID PROCEDURES
Forms required: FAFSA, institutional form.
Dates and Deadlines: Priority date 3/1; no closing date. Applicants notified on a rolling basis starting 2/1; must reply within 2 week(s) of notification.

CONTACT
Hylee Asche, Financial Aid Director
3134 West Highway 34, Grand Island, NE 68802-4903
(308) 398-7424

Chadron State College

Chadron, Nebraska
www.csc.edu Federal Code: 002539

4-year public business and liberal arts college in small town.
Enrollment: 2,365 undergrads.
Selectivity: Open admission; but selective for some programs.

BASIC COSTS (2012-2013)
Tuition and fees: $5,576; out-of-state residents $9,776.
Per-credit charge: $140; out-of-state residents $280.
Room and board: $5,520.

FINANCIAL AID PICTURE
Students with need: Need-based aid available for full-time and part-time students. Work study available nights, weekends, and for part-time students.
Students without need: No-need awards available for academics, alumni affiliation, art, athletics, leadership, minority status, music/drama, state/district residency.

FINANCIAL AID PROCEDURES
Forms required: FAFSA, institutional form.
Dates and Deadlines: Priority date 6/1; no closing date. Applicants notified on a rolling basis starting 4/1; must reply within 2 week(s) of notification.

CONTACT
Sherry Douglas, Director of Financial Aid
1000 Main Street, Chadron, NE 69337
(308) 432-6230

Clarkson College

Omaha, Nebraska
www.clarksoncollege.edu Federal Code: 009862

4-year private health science college in large city, affiliated with Episcopal Church.
Enrollment: 813 undergrads.
Selectivity: Open admission; but selective for some programs.

BASIC COSTS (2012-2013)
Tuition and fees: $14,585.
Per-credit charge: $437.
Room and board: $6,700.

FINANCIAL AID PICTURE
Students with need: Need-based aid available for full-time and part-time students. Work study available nights, weekends, and for part-time students.
Students without need: No-need awards available for academics, alumni affiliation, minority status, religious affiliation.

FINANCIAL AID PROCEDURES
Forms required: FAFSA, institutional form.
Dates and Deadlines: Priority date 4/1; no closing date. Applicants notified on a rolling basis starting 4/13; must reply within 3 week(s) of notification.
Transfers: Priority date 3/1; no deadline. Applicants notified on a rolling basis starting 3/30.

CONTACT
Margie Harris, Director of Student Financial Services
101 South 42nd Street, Omaha, NE 68131-2739
(402) 552-2749

College of Saint Mary

Omaha, Nebraska
www.csm.edu Federal Code: 002540

4-year private university and liberal arts college for women in large city, affiliated with Roman Catholic Church.
Enrollment: 697 undergrads, 10% part-time. 91 full-time freshmen.
Selectivity: Admits 50 to 75% of applicants.

BASIC COSTS (2013-2014)
Tuition and fees: $26,934.
Per-credit charge: $880.
Room and board: $6,800.

FINANCIAL AID PICTURE (2012-2013)
Students with need: Average financial aid package met 78% of need; average scholarship/grant was $17,064; average loan was $3,650. For part-time students, average financial aid package was $6,411.
Students without need: No-need awards available for academics, athletics.
Cumulative student debt: 77% of graduating class had student loans; average debt was $31,522.

FINANCIAL AID PROCEDURES
Forms required: FAFSA.
Dates and Deadlines: Priority date 3/15; no closing date. Applicants notified on a rolling basis starting 2/15; must reply within 2 week(s) of notification.
Transfers: No deadline. Applicants notified on a rolling basis starting 2/15; must reply within 2 week(s) of notification. Scholarships and need based grants available for full-time transfer students.

CONTACT
Beth Sisk, Director of Financial Aid
7000 Mercy Road, Omaha, NE 68106
(402) 399-2362

Concordia University

Seward, Nebraska
www.cune.edu Federal Code: 002541

4-year private university in small town, affiliated with Lutheran Church - Missouri Synod.
Enrollment: 1,193 undergrads, 3% part-time. 296 full-time freshmen.
Selectivity: Admits over 75% of applicants.

BASIC COSTS (2013-2014)

Tuition and fees: $24,750.
Per-credit charge: $765.
Room and board: $6,700.

FINANCIAL AID PICTURE (2012-2013)

Students with need: Out of 272 full-time freshmen who applied for aid, 243 were judged to have need. Of these, 243 received aid, and 67 had their full need met. Average financial aid package met 78% of need; average scholarship/grant was $15,144; average loan was $3,675. For part-time students, average financial aid package was $5,591.
Students without need: 17 full-time freshmen who did not demonstrate need for aid received scholarships/grants; average award was $9,580. No-need awards available for academics, alumni affiliation, art, athletics, leadership, music/drama, religious affiliation.
Scholarships offered: ***Merit:*** President's scholarship; $15,000 per year; based on academic achievement. Regent's scholarship; $9,000-$12,000 per year; based on GPA and SAT/ACT. Achievement award; $3,500-$8,000 per year; based on GPA and SAT/ACT. ***Athletic:*** 44 full-time freshmen received athletic scholarships; average amount $4,794.
Cumulative student debt: 78% of graduating class had student loans; average debt was $27,222.

FINANCIAL AID PROCEDURES

Forms required: FAFSA.
Dates and Deadlines: Priority date 3/1; no closing date. Applicants notified on a rolling basis starting 3/1; must reply within 4 week(s) of notification.
Transfers: Applicants notified on a rolling basis starting 3/1; must reply within 4 week(s) of notification.

CONTACT

Gloria Hennig, Director of Financial Aid
800 North Columbia Avenue, Seward, NE 68434-1556
(800) 535-5494 ext. 7270

Creative Center

Omaha, Nebraska
www.creativecenter.edu Federal Code: 031643

4-year for-profit visual arts and career college in large city.
Enrollment: 109 undergrads, 2% part-time. 32 full-time freshmen.
Selectivity: Admits over 75% of applicants.

BASIC COSTS (2012-2013)

Tuition and fees: $25,600.
Additional info: Tuition quoted is average one year cost. Three-year program total cost (including fees) $89,210: first year $30,900, second year $29,155, third year $29,155.

FINANCIAL AID PICTURE

Students with need: Need-based aid available for full-time and part-time students.
Students without need: No-need awards available for academics, art.
Scholarships offered: President's Award: $500. Founder's Award: $1,000. Both awards based on portfolio and high school academics. Andy Arrants Memorial Scholarship: supply kit (approx. $500); based on submitted artwork and essay.

FINANCIAL AID PROCEDURES

Forms required: FAFSA.
Dates and Deadlines: Closing date 7/15. Applicants notified on a rolling basis starting 2/1.
Transfers: No deadline. Applicants notified on a rolling basis starting 2/1.

CONTACT

Sandy LaRocca, Director of Financial Aid
10850 Emmet Street, Omaha, NE 68164-2911
(402) 898-1000 ext. 203

Creighton University

Omaha, Nebraska
www.creighton.edu Federal Code: 002542

4-year private university in very large city, affiliated with Roman Catholic Church.
Enrollment: 4,032 undergrads, 5% part-time. 942 full-time freshmen.
Selectivity: Admits over 75% of applicants.

BASIC COSTS (2012-2013)

Tuition and fees: $33,330.
Per-credit charge: $996.
Room and board: $9,446.
Additional info: Tuition/fee waivers available for adults, minority students.

FINANCIAL AID PICTURE (2012-2013)

Students with need: Out of 768 full-time freshmen who applied for aid, 593 were judged to have need. Of these, 593 received aid, and 183 had their full need met. Average financial aid package met 88% of need; average scholarship/grant was $22,896; average loan was $4,850. Need-based aid available for part-time students.
Students without need: 289 full-time freshmen who did not demonstrate need for aid received scholarships/grants; average award was $15,107. No-need awards available for academics, alumni affiliation, art, athletics, leadership, minority status, music/drama, ROTC.
Scholarships offered: ***Merit:*** William Jennings Bryan Debate and Speech Scholarship: $4,000. Diversity Scholarship & Native American Merit Scholarship: three-quarter tuition scholarships; awarded to students who show commitment to diversity; 3.3 GPA or higher on a 4.0 scale required; applicants evaluated on academic merit, community service, school activities, leadership, and financial need. First-generation college bound students and families that earn under $60,000 encouraged to apply. Ron Hansen Scholarship in Creative Writing: $4,000. Grace Keenan Scholarship for Excellence in the Arts: $3,000; awarded to students who intend to major in visual or performing arts. Christina M. Hixson Scholarship in Business Administration: $4,500; awarded to freshman business students from high schools in CO, IA, IL, KA, MN, MO, NE, ND, SD, WI or WY with a minimum of 3.0 GPA. College of Business Administration Ethics and Social Responsibility Scholarship: $4,500; awarded to students with exceptional service accomplishments and leadership potential; 3.8 GPA and a minimum 26 ACT or 1200 SAT. Presidential Scholarship: three-quarter tuition scholarship awarded to selected applicants in the top 10% of applicant pool, based upon academics. Scott Scholarship: full tuition scholarship in the College of Business Administration; awarded to selected students in the top 10% of applicant pool; based on academics. G. Robert Muchemore Foundation Undergraduate Scholarship: full tuition scholarship; awarded to graduates of Nebraska high schools entering as freshmen; based upon academics. ***Athletic:*** 52 full-time freshmen received athletic scholarships; average amount $18,878.
Cumulative student debt: 61% of graduating class had student loans; average debt was $36,333.

FINANCIAL AID PROCEDURES

Forms required: FAFSA, institutional form.
Dates and Deadlines: Priority date 3/1; no closing date. Applicants notified on a rolling basis starting 3/15; must reply by 5/1 or within 4 week(s) of notification.

Transfers: If transferring 24 or more hours of credit, student not eligible for academic, non-need scholarships.

CONTACT

Robert Walker, Director of Financial Aid
2500 California Plaza, Omaha, NE 68178-0001
(402) 280-2731

Doane College

Crete, Nebraska
www.doane.edu Federal Code: 002544

4-year private liberal arts college in small town, affiliated with United Church of Christ.
Enrollment: 1,148 undergrads, 1% part-time. 337 full-time freshmen.
Selectivity: Admits over 75% of applicants.

BASIC COSTS (2013-2014)
Tuition and fees: $26,180.
Per-credit charge: $850.
Room and board: $7,550.

FINANCIAL AID PICTURE (2012-2013)
Students with need: Out of 323 full-time freshmen who applied for aid, 280 were judged to have need. Of these, 280 received aid, and 84 had their full need met. Average financial aid package met 88% of need; average scholarship/grant was $15,982; average loan was $3,437. Need-based aid available for part-time students.
Students without need: 24 full-time freshmen who did not demonstrate need for aid received scholarships/grants; average award was $10,627. No-need awards available for academics, art, athletics, music/drama, religious affiliation.
Scholarships offered: 49 full-time freshmen received athletic scholarships; average amount $9,406.
Cumulative student debt: 80% of graduating class had student loans; average debt was $26,803.

FINANCIAL AID PROCEDURES
Forms required: FAFSA.
Dates and Deadlines: Priority date 3/1; no closing date. Applicants notified on a rolling basis starting 3/15; must reply within 2 week(s) of notification.

CONTACT

Peggy Tvrdy, Director of Financial Aid
1014 Boswell Avenue, Crete, NE 68333
(402) 826-8260

Grace University

Omaha, Nebraska
www.graceuniversity.edu Federal Code: 002547

4-year private university and Bible college in very large city, affiliated with interdenominational tradition.
Enrollment: 380 undergrads.
Selectivity: Admits 50 to 75% of applicants.

BASIC COSTS (2012-2013)
Tuition and fees: $17,366.
Per-credit charge: $473.
Room and board: $6,318.
Additional info: Tuition/fee waivers available for minority students.

FINANCIAL AID PICTURE
Students with need: Need-based aid available for full-time and part-time students.
Students without need: No-need awards available for academics, alumni affiliation, leadership, minority status, music/drama.

FINANCIAL AID PROCEDURES
Forms required: FAFSA.
Dates and Deadlines: Priority date 3/1; closing date 4/1. Applicants notified on a rolling basis starting 3/1; must reply within 3 week(s) of notification.
Transfers: No deadline. Applicants notified on a rolling basis starting 3/1; must reply within 3 week(s) of notification.

CONTACT

Mike James, Executive Vice President
1311 South Ninth Street, Omaha, NE 68108-3629
(402) 449-2810

Hastings College

Hastings, Nebraska
www.hastings.edu Federal Code: 002548

4-year private liberal arts college in large town, affiliated with Presbyterian Church (USA).
Enrollment: 1,039 undergrads, 1% part-time. 319 full-time freshmen.

BASIC COSTS (2012-2013)
Tuition and fees: $24,900.
Room and board: $7,100.
Additional info: Tuition/fee waivers available for adults.

FINANCIAL AID PICTURE (2011-2012)
Students with need: Out of 298 full-time freshmen who applied for aid, 246 were judged to have need. Of these, 246 received aid, and 65 had their full need met. Average financial aid package met 75% of need; average scholarship/grant was $14,650; average loan was $3,910. For part-time students, average financial aid package was $11,909.
Students without need: 70 full-time freshmen who did not demonstrate need for aid received scholarships/grants; average award was $11,461. No-need awards available for academics, alumni affiliation, art, athletics, leadership, music/drama.
Scholarships offered: ***Merit:*** Walter Scott Scholarship Competition: full-tuition, for freshman; 3 awarded. Trustees Scholarships: $14,000 per year. President's Scholarships: $13,000 per year. Dean Scholarships: $12,000 per year. Ambassador Scholarships: $10,000 per year. Ringland Scholarships: $8,000 per year. Pro Rege Scholarships: $7,000 per year. Kessler Scholarship: full tuition, for Christian Ministry students; 3 awarded. Christian Ministry scholarships: $5,000 per year; 3 awarded. ***Athletic:*** 55 full-time freshmen received athletic scholarships; average amount $4,040.
Cumulative student debt: 76% of graduating class had student loans; average debt was $26,669.

FINANCIAL AID PROCEDURES
Forms required: FAFSA, institutional form.
Dates and Deadlines: Closing date 5/1. Applicants notified on a rolling basis starting 2/15; must reply within 2 week(s) of notification.
Transfers: No deadline. Stafford loans based on number of transferable credits.

CONTACT

Terri Graham, Financial Aid Director
710 North Turner Avenue, Hastings, NE 68901-7621
(402) 461-7391

Kaplan University: Lincoln

Lincoln, Nebraska
www.kucampus.edu Federal Code: 004721

2-year for-profit branch campus college in small city.
Enrollment: 469 undergrads.

Selectivity: Open admission; but selective for some programs.

BASIC COSTS (2012-2013)
Tuition and fees: $15,352.
Per-credit charge: $405.
Additional info: Cost of books and supplies is included in tuition.

FINANCIAL AID PICTURE
Students with need: Need-based aid available for full-time and part-time students. Work study available nights, weekends, and for part-time students.
Students without need: This college awards aid only to students with need.

FINANCIAL AID PROCEDURES
Forms required: FAFSA, institutional form.
Dates and Deadlines: Applicants notified on a rolling basis starting 2/1.
Transfers: No deadline.

CONTACT
Corinne Combs, Director of Financial Aid
1821 K Street, Lincoln, NE 68508
(402) 474-5315

Kaplan University: Omaha

Omaha, Nebraska
www.omaha.kaplanuniversity.edu Federal Code: 008491

2-year for-profit career college in large city.
Enrollment: 700 undergrads.
Selectivity: Open admission; but selective for some programs.

BASIC COSTS (2012-2013)
Tuition and fees: $15,352.

FINANCIAL AID PICTURE
Students with need: Need-based aid available for full-time and part-time students. Work study available nights, weekends, and for part-time students.
Students without need: This college awards aid only to students with need.

FINANCIAL AID PROCEDURES
Forms required: FAFSA, institutional form.
Dates and Deadlines: Applicants notified on a rolling basis.

CONTACT
Crystal Faxon, Director Of Financial Aid
5425 North 103rd Street, Omaha, NE 68134
(402) 431-6100

Little Priest Tribal College

Winnebago, Nebraska
www.littlepriest.edu Federal Code: 033233

2-year private community college in rural community.
Enrollment: 172 undergrads.
Selectivity: Open admission.

BASIC COSTS (2012-2013)
Tuition and fees: $3,750.
Per-credit charge: $100.

FINANCIAL AID PICTURE
Students with need: Need-based aid available for full-time and part-time students.

FINANCIAL AID PROCEDURES
Forms required: FAFSA, institutional form.

CONTACT
Billie Kitcheyan, Director of Financial Aid
PO Box 270, Winnebago, NE 68071
(402) 878-2380 ext. 125

Metropolitan Community College

Omaha, Nebraska
www.mccneb.edu Federal Code: 004432

2-year public community and technical college in large city.
Enrollment: 18,518 undergrads.
Selectivity: Open admission; but selective for some programs.

BASIC COSTS (2012-2013)
Tuition and fees: $2,520; out-of-state residents $3,668.
Per-credit charge: $51; out-of-state residents $77.
Room and board: $3,555.

FINANCIAL AID PICTURE
Students with need: Need-based aid available for full-time and part-time students.
Students without need: No-need awards available for academics.

FINANCIAL AID PROCEDURES
Forms required: FAFSA, institutional form.
Dates and Deadlines: Priority date 3/15; no closing date. Applicants notified on a rolling basis starting 4/15.

CONTACT
Wilma Hjelum, Director of Financial Aid & Veteran Services
Box 3777, Omaha, NE 68103-0777
(402) 457-2330

Mid-Plains Community College

North Platte, Nebraska
www.mpcc.edu Federal Code: 002557

2-year public community and technical college in large town.
Enrollment: 1,473 undergrads, 35% part-time. 453 full-time freshmen.
Selectivity: Open admission; but selective for some programs.

BASIC COSTS (2013-2014)
Tuition and fees: $2,760; out-of-state residents $3,900.
Per-credit charge: $77; out-of-state residents $100.
Room and board: $5,460.
Additional info: Students from the following bordering states receive the same tuition rate as in state students: Kansas, Colorado, South Dakota, and Wyoming.

FINANCIAL AID PICTURE (2011-2012)
Students with need: 67% of average financial aid package awarded as scholarships/grants, 33% awarded as loans/jobs. Need-based aid available for part-time students. Work study available nights.
Students without need: No-need awards available for academics, art, athletics, music/drama.

FINANCIAL AID PROCEDURES
Forms required: FAFSA, institutional form.
Dates and Deadlines: Priority date 5/1; no closing date. Applicants notified on a rolling basis starting 5/1; must reply within 3 week(s) of notification.

CONTACT
Dale Brown, Director of Financial Aid
1101 Halligan Drive, North Platte, NE 69101
(800) 658-4348

Nebraska Christian College

Papillion, Nebraska
www.nechristian.edu Federal Code: 012976

4-year private Bible college in large town, affiliated with Christian Churches and Churches of Christ.
Enrollment: 127 full-time undergrads.

BASIC COSTS (2012-2013)

Tuition and fees: $10,900.
Per-credit charge: $425.
Room and board: $7,600.

FINANCIAL AID PICTURE

Students with need: Need-based aid available for full-time and part-time students. Work study available nights, weekends, and for part-time students.
Students without need: No-need awards available for academics, leadership, religious affiliation.

FINANCIAL AID PROCEDURES

Forms required: FAFSA, institutional form.
Dates and Deadlines: Priority date 6/1; no closing date. Applicants notified on a rolling basis starting 5/5.

CONTACT

Tina Larsen, Financial Aid Officer
12550 South 114th Street, Papillion, NE 68046

Nebraska College of Technical Agriculture

Curtis, Nebraska
www.ncta.unl.edu Federal Code: 007358

2-year public agricultural college in rural community.
Enrollment: 245 undergrads, 3% part-time. 96 full-time freshmen.
Selectivity: Open admission.

BASIC COSTS (2012-2013)

Tuition and fees: $4,264; out-of-state residents $7,744.
Per-credit charge: $116; out-of-state residents $232.
Room and board: $6,742.

FINANCIAL AID PICTURE (2012-2013)

Students with need: Out of 87 full-time freshmen who applied for aid, 80 were judged to have need. Of these, 78 received aid, and 22 had their full need met. Average financial aid package met 71% of need; average scholarship/grant was $4,923; average loan was $3,095. Need-based aid available for part-time students.
Students without need: 9 full-time freshmen who did not demonstrate need for aid received scholarships/grants; average award was $2,734.
Cumulative student debt: 69% of graduating class had student loans; average debt was $7,563.

FINANCIAL AID PROCEDURES

Forms required: FAFSA.
Dates and Deadlines: Priority date 4/1; no closing date. Applicants notified on a rolling basis starting 5/1; must reply within 2 week(s) of notification.
Transfers: Applicants notified on a rolling basis.

CONTACT

Jean Hinton, Financial Aid Specialist
404 East 7th Street, Curtis, NE 69025-0069
(308) 367-5207

Nebraska Indian Community College

Macy, Nebraska
www.thenicc.edu Federal Code: 015339

2-year public tribal college in rural community.
Enrollment: 172 undergrads.
Selectivity: Open admission.

BASIC COSTS (2012-2013)

Per-credit charge: $170.
Additional info: Tuition is a flat rate of $170 per credit hour, which includes books, tuition, and fees.

FINANCIAL AID PICTURE

Students with need: Need-based aid available for full-time and part-time students.
Students without need: This college awards aid only to students with need.

FINANCIAL AID PROCEDURES

Forms required: FAFSA, state aid form, institutional form.
Dates and Deadlines: Closing date 6/30. Applicants notified on a rolling basis starting 8/30; must reply within 2 week(s) of notification.
Transfers: No deadline. Applicants notified on a rolling basis; must reply within 2 week(s) of notification.

CONTACT

Cecilei Pappan, Financial Aid Director
PO Box 428, Macy, NE 68039
(402) 494-2311 ext. 2583

Nebraska Methodist College of Nursing and Allied Health

Omaha, Nebraska
www.methodistcollege.edu Federal Code: 009937

4-year private health science and nursing college in large city, affiliated with United Methodist Church.
Enrollment: 738 undergrads, 38% part-time. 27 full-time freshmen.
Selectivity: Admits 50 to 75% of applicants.

BASIC COSTS (2013-2014)

Tuition and fees: $16,470.
Per-credit charge: $528.
Additional info: Cost of room only: $6,460.

FINANCIAL AID PICTURE (2012-2013)

Students with need: Out of 26 full-time freshmen who applied for aid, 20 were judged to have need. Of these, 20 received aid, and 4 had their full need met. Average financial aid package met 52% of need; average scholarship/grant was $6,950; average loan was $3,193. For part-time students, average financial aid package was $7,140.
Students without need: 7 full-time freshmen who did not demonstrate need for aid received scholarships/grants; average award was $3,429. No-need awards available for academics, leadership, religious affiliation, ROTC.
Scholarships offered: Presidential Leadership Scholarship: $8,000 per year for 4 years; 4 awarded. Dean's Scholarship: $5,000 for 4 years; 3 awarded. Excellence in Allied Health Scholarship: $5,000 per year for 2 years; 3 awarded. Horizon Scholarship: $3,000 per year; based on academic and personal merit; 50 awarded.
Cumulative student debt: 84% of graduating class had student loans; average debt was $39,753.

FINANCIAL AID PROCEDURES

Forms required: FAFSA, institutional form.
Dates and Deadlines: Priority date 4/1; no closing date. Applicants notified on a rolling basis starting 3/15; must reply within 3 week(s) of notification.

CONTACT
Penny James, Director of Financial Aid
720 North 87th Street, Omaha, NE 68114-2852
(402) 354-7225

Nebraska Wesleyan University

Lincoln, Nebraska
www.nebrwesleyan.edu Federal Code: 002555

4-year private liberal arts college in small city, affiliated with United Methodist Church.
Enrollment: 1,778 undergrads, 15% part-time. 356 full-time freshmen.
Selectivity: Admits over 75% of applicants.

BASIC COSTS (2012-2013)
Tuition and fees: $25,918.
Per-credit charge: $958.
Room and board: $7,042.
Additional info: Tuition/fee waivers available for adults, minority students.

FINANCIAL AID PICTURE (2012-2013)
Students with need: Out of 310 full-time freshmen who applied for aid, 258 were judged to have need. Of these, 258 received aid, and 52 had their full need met. Average financial aid package met 71% of need; average scholarship/grant was $14,027; average loan was $4,370. For part-time students, average financial aid package was $3,824.
Students without need: 92 full-time freshmen who did not demonstrate need for aid received scholarships/grants; average award was $10,298. No-need awards available for academics, alumni affiliation, art, minority status, music/drama.
Scholarships offered: Huge-NWU Scholarship: tuition, books, fees, and room and board up to $27,000; competitive; 2 awards per year.
Cumulative student debt: 74% of graduating class had student loans; average debt was $28,077.

FINANCIAL AID PROCEDURES
Forms required: FAFSA.
Dates and Deadlines: Applicants notified on a rolling basis starting 2/1; must reply within 3 week(s) of notification.
Transfers: No deadline. Applicants notified on a rolling basis starting 2/1; must reply within 3 week(s) of notification.

CONTACT
Thomas Ochsner, Director of Scholarships and Financial Aid
5000 St. Paul Avenue, Lincoln, NE 68504
(402) 465-2212

Northeast Community College

Norfolk, Nebraska
www.northeast.edu Federal Code: 002556

2-year public community college in large town.
Enrollment: 2,800 undergrads.
Selectivity: Open admission; but selective for some programs.

BASIC COSTS (2012-2013)
Tuition and fees: $2,745; out-of-state residents $3,315.
Per-credit charge: $76; out-of-state residents $95.
Room and board: $6,043.

FINANCIAL AID PICTURE
Students with need: Need-based aid available for full-time and part-time students. Work study available nights, weekends, and for part-time students.
Students without need: No-need awards available for academics, athletics, music/drama.

FINANCIAL AID PROCEDURES
Forms required: FAFSA, institutional form.
Dates and Deadlines: Applicants notified on a rolling basis; must reply within 2 week(s) of notification.

CONTACT
Stacy Dieckman, Director of Financial Aid
801 East Benjamin Avenue, Norfolk, NE 68702-0469
(402) 844-7285

Peru State College

Peru, Nebraska
www.peru.edu Federal Code: 002559

4-year public liberal arts and teachers college in rural community.
Enrollment: 1,509 undergrads, 24% part-time. 145 full-time freshmen.
Selectivity: Open admission.

BASIC COSTS (2012-2013)
Tuition and fees: $5,588; out-of-state residents $5,618.
Per-credit charge: $140; out-of-state residents $141.
Room and board: $6,110.

FINANCIAL AID PICTURE (2012-2013)
Students with need: 45% of average financial aid package awarded as scholarships/grants, 55% awarded as loans/jobs. Need-based aid available for part-time students. Work study available nights.
Students without need: This college awards aid only to students with need.

FINANCIAL AID PROCEDURES
Forms required: FAFSA, institutional form.
Dates and Deadlines: Priority date 3/1; no closing date. Applicants notified on a rolling basis starting 3/1; must reply within 2 week(s) of notification.
Transfers: Must have financial aid transcripts from all previous schools sent to college.

CONTACT
Janice Volker, Director of Financial Aid
PO Box 10, Peru, NE 68421-0010
(402) 872-2228

Southeast Community College

Lincoln, Nebraska
www.southeast.edu Federal Code: 007591

2-year public community college in small city.
Enrollment: 10,168 undergrads.
Selectivity: Open admission.

BASIC COSTS (2012-2013)
Tuition and fees: $2,486; out-of-state residents $3,049.
Per-credit charge: $54; out-of-state residents $67.
Room and board: $4,356.

FINANCIAL AID PICTURE
Students with need: Need-based aid available for full-time and part-time students. Work study available nights, weekends, and for part-time students.
Students without need: No-need awards available for academics.

FINANCIAL AID PROCEDURES
Forms required: FAFSA, institutional form.
Dates and Deadlines: Applicants notified on a rolling basis; must reply within 2 week(s) of notification.

CONTACT
Dave Sonenberg, Director of Financial Aid/Dean of Student Services
8800 O Street, Lincoln, NE 68520
(402) 437-2619

Union College

Lincoln, Nebraska
www.ucollege.edu Federal Code: 002563

4-year private liberal arts college in large city, affiliated with Seventh-day Adventists.
Enrollment: 720 undergrads, 9% part-time. 147 full-time freshmen.
Selectivity: Admits less than 50% of applicants.

BASIC COSTS (2013-2014)
Tuition and fees: $20,470.
Per-credit charge: $815.
Room and board: $6,370.

FINANCIAL AID PICTURE
Students with need: Need-based aid available for full-time and part-time students.
Students without need: No-need awards available for academics.
Additional info: Special institutional grants offered to all freshmen and sophomores demonstrating exceptional financial need.

FINANCIAL AID PROCEDURES
Forms required: FAFSA.
Dates and Deadlines: Closing date 4/1. Applicants notified on a rolling basis starting 4/15; must reply by 5/1 or within 3 week(s) of notification.

CONTACT
Elina Bascom, Director of Financial Aid
3800 South 48th Street, Lincoln, NE 68506-4300
(402) 486-2505

University of Nebraska - Kearney

Kearney, Nebraska
www.unk.edu Federal Code: 002551

4-year public university in large town.
Enrollment: 5,384 undergrads, 9% part-time. 1,123 full-time freshmen.
Selectivity: Admits over 75% of applicants.

BASIC COSTS (2012-2013)
Tuition and fees: $6,506; out-of-state residents $12,011.
Per-credit charge: $175; out-of-state residents $358.
Room and board: $8,038.

FINANCIAL AID PICTURE (2012-2013)
Students with need: Out of 866 full-time freshmen who applied for aid, 719 were judged to have need. Of these, 718 received aid, and 336 had their full need met. Average financial aid package met 78% of need; average scholarship/grant was $6,981; average loan was $3,219. For part-time students, average financial aid package was $7,183.
Students without need: 80 full-time freshmen who did not demonstrate need for aid received scholarships/grants; average award was $2,373. No-need awards available for academics, alumni affiliation, art, athletics, leadership, minority status, music/drama, ROTC, state/district residency.
Scholarships offered: 20 full-time freshmen received athletic scholarships; average amount $2,345.

FINANCIAL AID PROCEDURES
Forms required: FAFSA, institutional form.
Dates and Deadlines: Priority date 4/1; no closing date. Applicants notified on a rolling basis starting 3/15; must reply within 2 week(s) of notification.
Transfers: No deadline. Applicants notified on a rolling basis starting 3/15.

CONTACT
Mary Sommers, Director of Financial Aid
905 West 25th, Kearney, NE 68849
(308) 865-8520

University of Nebraska - Lincoln

Lincoln, Nebraska
www.unl.edu Federal Code: 002565

4-year public university in large city.
Enrollment: 19,103 undergrads, 7% part-time. 4,056 full-time freshmen.
Selectivity: Admits 50 to 75% of applicants.

BASIC COSTS (2012-2013)
Tuition and fees: $7,897; out-of-state residents $20,647.
Per-credit charge: $216; out-of-state residents $641.
Room and board: $9,122.

FINANCIAL AID PICTURE (2011-2012)
Students with need: Out of 3,066 full-time freshmen who applied for aid, 2,207 were judged to have need. Of these, 2,160 received aid, and 413 had their full need met. Average financial aid package met 82% of need; average scholarship/grant was $6,834; average loan was $3,359. For part-time students, average financial aid package was $10,545.
Students without need: 465 full-time freshmen who did not demonstrate need for aid received scholarships/grants; average award was $4,822. No-need awards available for academics, alumni affiliation, art, athletics, leadership, minority status, music/drama, state/district residency.
Scholarships offered: 122 full-time freshmen received athletic scholarships; average amount $11,044.
Cumulative student debt: 60% of graduating class had student loans; average debt was $23,280.

FINANCIAL AID PROCEDURES
Forms required: FAFSA.
Dates and Deadlines: Priority date 4/15; no closing date. Applicants notified on a rolling basis starting 4/1.
Transfers: No deadline. Applicants notified on a rolling basis starting 4/1.

CONTACT
Craig Munier, Director of Scholarships and Financial Aid
1410 Q Street, Lincoln, NE 68588-0417
(402) 472-2030

University of Nebraska - Omaha

Omaha, Nebraska
www.unomaha.edu Federal Code: 002554

4-year public university in large city.
Enrollment: 11,871 undergrads, 24% part-time. 1,648 full-time freshmen.
Selectivity: Admits over 75% of applicants.

BASIC COSTS (2012-2013)
Tuition and fees: $7,173; out-of-state residents $18,685.
Per-credit charge: $197; out-of-state residents $581.
Room and board: $8,465.

FINANCIAL AID PICTURE (2011-2012)
Students with need: For part-time students, average financial aid package was $4,596.
Students without need: No-need awards available for academics, alumni affiliation, art, athletics, leadership, minority status, music/drama, ROTC, state/district residency.
Cumulative student debt: 56% of graduating class had student loans; average debt was $23,500.

FINANCIAL AID PROCEDURES
Forms required: FAFSA.
Dates and Deadlines: Priority date 3/1; no closing date. Applicants notified on a rolling basis starting 4/15; must reply within 2 week(s) of notification.

CONTACT

Randall Sell, Director of Financial Aid
6001 Dodge Street, Omaha, NE 68182-0005
(402) 554-2327

University of Nebraska Medical Center

Omaha, Nebraska
www.unmc.edu Federal Code: 006895

Upper-division public health science college in very large city.
Enrollment: 822 undergrads, 14% part-time.

BASIC COSTS (2012-2013)

Additional info: College of Medicine: resident $27,992; nonresident $65,634; required fees $575. College of Dentistry: resident $22,954; nonresident $53,090; required fees $1,180. College of Pharmacy: resident $18,328; nonresident $35,596; required fees $543. Tuition is assessed on per semester not credit hour basis. Tuition/fee waivers available for minority students.

FINANCIAL AID PICTURE

Students with need: Need-based aid available for full-time and part-time students. Work study available nights, weekends, and for part-time students.

FINANCIAL AID PROCEDURES

Forms required: FAFSA, institutional form.
Dates and Deadlines: Closing date 4/1. Applicants notified by 7/1; must reply by 7/30 or within 2 week(s) of notification.
Transfers: No deadline. Applicants notified on a rolling basis starting 5/1; must reply within 2 week(s) of notification.

CONTACT

Judith Walker, Director of Financial Aid
984230 Nebraska Medical Center, Omaha, NE 68198-4230
(402) 559-4199

Wayne State College

Wayne, Nebraska
www.wsc.edu Federal Code: 002566

4-year public liberal arts and teachers college in small town.
Enrollment: 2,967 undergrads, 6% part-time. 693 full-time freshmen.
Selectivity: Open admission.

BASIC COSTS (2012-2013)

Tuition and fees: $5,520; out-of-state residents $9,720.
Per-credit charge: $140; out-of-state residents $280.
Room and board: $5,960.
Additional info: Additional Special Rates apply for residents of qualifying states.

FINANCIAL AID PICTURE (2012-2013)

Students with need: Out of 617 full-time freshmen who applied for aid, 467 were judged to have need. Of these, 457 received aid, and 185 had their full need met. Average financial aid package met 54% of need; average scholarship/grant was $4,079; average loan was $3,149. For part-time students, average financial aid package was $2,231.
Students without need: 89 full-time freshmen who did not demonstrate need for aid received scholarships/grants; average award was $1,191. No-need awards available for academics, art, athletics, leadership, minority status, music/drama, religious affiliation, state/district residency.
Scholarships offered: 16 full-time freshmen received athletic scholarships; average amount $4,468.

FINANCIAL AID PROCEDURES

Forms required: FAFSA.
Dates and Deadlines: Priority date 4/1; no closing date. Applicants notified on a rolling basis starting 3/1; must reply within 4 week(s) of notification.

CONTACT

Kyle Rose, Director of Financial Aid
1111 Main Street, Wayne, NE 68787
(402) 375-7230

Western Nebraska Community College

Scottsbluff, Nebraska
www.wncc.edu Federal Code: 002560

2-year public community college in large town.
Enrollment: 1,655 undergrads, 41% part-time. 375 full-time freshmen.
Selectivity: Open admission; but selective for some programs.

BASIC COSTS (2012-2013)

Tuition and fees: $2,895; out-of-state residents $3,315.
Per-credit charge: $80; out-of-state residents $94.
Room and board: $6,510.
Additional info: Border states Colorado, Wyoming & South Dakota pay in-state, out-of district tuition.

FINANCIAL AID PICTURE (2012-2013)

Students with need: Out of 300 full-time freshmen who applied for aid, 258 were judged to have need. Of these, 254 received aid. Average financial aid package met 95% of need; average scholarship/grant was $4,789; average loan was $2,497. For part-time students, average financial aid package was $8,744.
Students without need: 54 full-time freshmen who did not demonstrate need for aid received scholarships/grants; average award was $806. No-need awards available for academics, art, athletics, leadership, music/drama, state/district residency.
Scholarships offered: 66 full-time freshmen received athletic scholarships; average amount $5,248.
Cumulative student debt: 26% of graduating class had student loans; average debt was $4,933.

FINANCIAL AID PROCEDURES

Forms required: FAFSA.
Dates and Deadlines: Priority date 3/1; no closing date. Applicants notified on a rolling basis starting 4/1.
Transfers: State of Nebraska limits the amount of Nebraska State Grant funds a student receives in any one year.

CONTACT

Sheila Johns, Director of Financial Aid
1601 East 27th Street, Scottsbluff, NE 69361
(308) 635-6011

York College

York, Nebraska
www.york.edu Federal Code: 002567

4-year private liberal arts and teachers college in small town, affiliated with Church of Christ.
Enrollment: 598 undergrads.

BASIC COSTS (2012-2013)

Tuition and fees: $15,600.
Room and board: $5,850.

FINANCIAL AID PICTURE

Students with need: Need-based aid available for full-time and part-time students. Work study available nights, weekends, and for part-time students.
Students without need: No-need awards available for academics, alumni affiliation, athletics, leadership, music/drama.

FINANCIAL AID PROCEDURES

Forms required: FAFSA.

Dates and Deadlines: Priority date 4/1; no closing date. Applicants notified on a rolling basis starting 3/1; must reply within 4 week(s) of notification.
Transfers: No deadline. Applicants notified on a rolling basis starting 3/1; must reply within 4 week(s) of notification.

CONTACT
Brien Alley, Director of Financial Aid
1125 East 8th Street, York, NE 68467
(402) 363-5624

Nevada

College of Southern Nevada

Las Vegas, Nevada
www.csn.edu Federal Code: 010362

2-year public community college in very large city.
Enrollment: 29,362 undergrads.
Selectivity: Open admission; but selective for some programs.

BASIC COSTS (2012-2013)
Tuition and fees: $2,700; out-of-state residents $9,345.
Per-credit charge: $76.

FINANCIAL AID PICTURE
Students with need: Work study available nights, weekends, and for part-time students.
Students without need: No-need awards available for state/district residency.

FINANCIAL AID PROCEDURES
Forms required: FAFSA.
Dates and Deadlines: Priority date 5/1; closing date 6/30. Applicants notified on a rolling basis starting 7/15; must reply within 2 week(s) of notification.

CONTACT
Director, Student Financial Services
6375 West Charleston Boulevard, Las Vegas, NV 89146-1164
(702) 651-4047

Everest College: Las Vegas

Henderson, Nevada
www.lasvegas-college.com Federal Code: 015804

2-year for-profit business and health science college in very large city.
Enrollment: 1,031 undergrads.
Selectivity: Open admission.

BASIC COSTS (2012-2013)
Additional info: Estimated program costs, which vary according to area of study, as of July 2012: diploma, $18,336 - $20,652; associate degree, $39,480- $41,725, does not include books and supplies, which vary by program. All figures are subject to change.

FINANCIAL AID PICTURE
Students with need: Need-based aid available for full-time and part-time students. Work study available nights, weekends, and for part-time students.
Students without need: This college awards aid only to students with need.

FINANCIAL AID PROCEDURES
Forms required: FAFSA.
Dates and Deadlines: Applicants notified on a rolling basis; must reply within 2 week(s) of notification.

CONTACT
RoseMarie Young, Director of Financial Aid
170 North Stephanie Street, Henderson, NV 89074

Great Basin College

Elko, Nevada
www.gbcnv.edu Federal Code: 006977

4-year public community and teachers college in large town.
Enrollment: 2,436 undergrads.
Selectivity: Open admission; but selective for some programs.

BASIC COSTS (2012-2013)
Tuition and fees: $2,700; out-of-state residents $9,345.
Per-credit charge: $76.
Additional info: Board plan not available. Cost of room only, $2,299.

FINANCIAL AID PICTURE
Students with need: Need-based aid available for full-time and part-time students. Work study available nights, weekends, and for part-time students.

FINANCIAL AID PROCEDURES
Forms required: FAFSA.
Dates and Deadlines: Priority date 6/1; no closing date. Applicants notified on a rolling basis starting 7/1.
Transfers: Priority date 4/1.

CONTACT
Scott Neilsen, Director of Financial Aid
1500 College Parkway, Elko, NV 89801
(775) 753-2267

Kaplan College: Las Vegas

Las Vegas, Nevada
www.kaplancollege.com Federal Code: 030432

2-year for-profit career college in very large city.
Enrollment: 765 undergrads.
Selectivity: Open admission; but selective for some programs.

BASIC COSTS (2012-2013)
Additional info: Diploma programs range from $15,658 to $29,726. Associate programs: range from 30,800 - 52,089. Fees, books and supplies included.

FINANCIAL AID PICTURE
Students with need: Need-based aid available for full-time and part-time students. Work study available nights.

FINANCIAL AID PROCEDURES
Forms required: FAFSA, institutional form.
Transfers: No deadline. Applicants notified on a rolling basis.

CONTACT
Carmen Torres, Director of Finance
3535 West Sahara Avenue, Las Vegas, NV 89102
(702) 368-2338

Morrison University

Reno, Nevada
www.morrisonuniversity.com Federal Code: 008441

4-year for-profit university and business college in small city.
Enrollment: 288 undergrads.
Selectivity: Open admission.

FINANCIAL AID PICTURE

Students with need: Need-based aid available for full-time students. Work study available nights.

FINANCIAL AID PROCEDURES

Forms required: FAFSA.

Dates and Deadlines: Applicants notified on a rolling basis starting 7/1.

CONTACT

Jim Hadwick, Director of Financial Aid
10315 Professional Circle, #201, Reno, NV 89521
(775) 850-0700 ext. 110

Nevada State College

Henderson, Nevada
www.nsc.nevada.edu Federal Code: 041143

4-year public liberal arts and teachers college in large city.

Enrollment: 2,841 undergrads, 61% part-time. 158 full-time freshmen.

Selectivity: Admits less than 50% of applicants.

BASIC COSTS (2012-2013)

Tuition and fees: $4,313; out-of-state residents $14,588.

Per-credit charge: $124.

FINANCIAL AID PICTURE

Students with need: Need-based aid available for full-time and part-time students.

FINANCIAL AID PROCEDURES

Forms required: FAFSA, institutional form.

Dates and Deadlines: Priority date 3/1; no closing date. Applicants notified on a rolling basis starting 5/1.

Transfers: Applicants notified on a rolling basis starting 5/1.

CONTACT

Anthony Morrone, Associate Director
1125 Nevada State Drive, Henderson, NV 89002
(702) 992-2150

Roseman University of Health Sciences

Henderson, Nevada
www.roseman.edu Federal Code: 040653

Upper-division private university in very large city.

Enrollment: 205 undergrads.

BASIC COSTS (2012-2013)

Tuition and fees: $32,510.

Per-credit charge: $561.

Additional info: Tuition and fees reported cover the first 12 months of study within an 18 month expedited BSN program.

FINANCIAL AID PICTURE (2012-2013)

Students with need: Average financial aid package for all full-time undergraduates was $8,453. 15% awarded as scholarships/grants, 85% awarded as loans/jobs. Work study available nights, weekends, and for part-time students.

Students without need: No-need awards available for academics.

Cumulative student debt: 100% of graduating class had student loans; average debt was $25,000.

FINANCIAL AID PROCEDURES

Forms required: FAFSA, institutional form.

Dates and Deadlines: Applicants notified on a rolling basis starting 8/6; must reply within 4 week(s) of notification.

Transfers: No deadline. Applicants notified on a rolling basis starting 7/1; must reply within 2 week(s) of notification.

CONTACT

Jesse Stasher, Director of Financial Aid
11 Sunset Way, Henderson, NV 89014-2333
(702) 968-1635

Sierra Nevada College

Incline Village, Nevada
www.sierranevada.edu Federal Code: 009192

4-year private liberal arts college in small town.

Enrollment: 529 undergrads, 3% part-time. 70 full-time freshmen.

Selectivity: Admits 50 to 75% of applicants.

BASIC COSTS (2012-2013)

Tuition and fees: $27,654.

Per-credit charge: $1,146.

Room and board: $11,492.

FINANCIAL AID PICTURE (2012-2013)

Students with need: Out of 48 full-time freshmen who applied for aid, 43 were judged to have need. Of these, 43 received aid, and 4 had their full need met. Average financial aid package met 55% of need; average scholarship/grant was $14,120; average loan was $4,750. Need-based aid available for part-time students.

Students without need: 27 full-time freshmen who did not demonstrate need for aid received scholarships/grants; average award was $6,500. No-need awards available for academics, alumni affiliation, athletics.

Scholarships offered: ***Merit:*** Academic scholarships; $2,000-$12,500 per year; renewable. ***Athletic:*** 18 full-time freshmen received athletic scholarships; average amount $7,783.

Cumulative student debt: 50% of graduating class had student loans; average debt was $27,000.

Additional info: SNC provides students with an institutional need based grant based on the remaining need after being awarded all scholarships and Federal Student Aid. First time Freshmen are awarded 50% of remaining need and 45% to continuing students.

FINANCIAL AID PROCEDURES

Forms required: FAFSA.

Dates and Deadlines: Priority date 1/1; no closing date. Applicants notified on a rolling basis starting 4/1; must reply by 8/20.

Transfers: Priority date 3/15.

CONTACT

Nicole Ferguson, Director of Financial Aid
999 Tahoe Boulevard, Incline Village, NV 89451-4269
(775) 831-1314 ext. 7440

Truckee Meadows Community College

Reno, Nevada
www.tmcc.edu Federal Code: 010363

2-year public community and technical college in large city.

Enrollment: 9,967 undergrads, 70% part-time. 806 full-time freshmen.

Selectivity: Open admission; but selective for some programs.

BASIC COSTS (2013-2014)

Tuition and fees: $2,880; out-of-state residents $9,525.

Additional info: Required fees included in in-state and out of state fees.

FINANCIAL AID PICTURE (2011-2012)

Students with need: 61% of average financial aid package awarded as scholarships/grants, 39% awarded as loans/jobs. Work study available nights, weekends, and for part-time students.

Students without need: No-need awards available for academics, art, leadership, minority status, music/drama, state/district residency.

Additional info: Institutional grants to state residents, short-term emergency loans available. Work-study applications must reply within 10 days of notification.

FINANCIAL AID PROCEDURES

Forms required: FAFSA, institutional form.

Dates and Deadlines: Priority date 1/15; no closing date.

Transfers: Priority date 3/9; no deadline. Must provide academic transcript from previous institution.

CONTACT

Sharon Wurm, Director of Financial Aid, Scholarships and Student Employment
7000 Dandini Boulevard, Reno, NV 89512
(775) 673-7072

University of Nevada: Las Vegas

Las Vegas, Nevada
www.unlv.edu Federal Code: 002569

4-year public university in very large city.

Enrollment: 22,038 undergrads, 28% part-time. 2,996 full-time freshmen.

Selectivity: Admits over 75% of applicants.

BASIC COSTS (2012-2013)

Tuition and fees: $6,585; out-of-state residents $20,495.

Per-credit charge: $192; out-of-state residents $398.

Room and board: $10,524.

FINANCIAL AID PICTURE

Students with need: Need-based aid available for full-time and part-time students.

Students without need: No-need awards available for academics, alumni affiliation, athletics, music/drama.

Additional info: Tuition reduction for state residents through consortium programs and for out-of-state students graduating from high schools in designated counties bordering Nevada, for military dependents residing in-state, and for dependents of children of alumni not residing in-state.

FINANCIAL AID PROCEDURES

Forms required: FAFSA.

Dates and Deadlines: Priority date 2/1; no closing date. Applicants notified on a rolling basis starting 3/20; must reply within 6 week(s) of notification.

CONTACT

Norm Bedford, Director of Financial Aid & Scholarships
4505 Maryland Parkway, Box 451021, Las Vegas, NV 89154-1021
(702) 895-3424

University of Nevada: Reno

Reno, Nevada
www.unr.edu Federal Code: 002568

4-year public university in small city.

Enrollment: 14,675 undergrads, 16% part-time. 2,840 full-time freshmen.

Selectivity: Admits over 75% of applicants. GED not accepted.

BASIC COSTS (2012-2013)

Tuition and fees: $6,603; out-of-state residents $20,513.

Per-credit charge: $171; out-of-state residents $359.

Room and board: $10,196.

FINANCIAL AID PICTURE (2011-2012)

Students with need: Out of 2,460 full-time freshmen who applied for aid, 1,900 were judged to have need. Of these, 1,575 received aid, and 179 had their full need met. Average financial aid package met 62% of need; average scholarship/grant was $5,440; average loan was $5,450. For part-time students, average financial aid package was $2,954.

Students without need: 585 full-time freshmen who did not demonstrate need for aid received scholarships/grants; average award was $1,890. No-need awards available for academics, alumni affiliation, art, athletics, leadership, music/drama, ROTC, state/district residency.

Scholarships offered: ***Merit:*** Presidential scholarship awards: $5,000 per year; must have 3.5 unweighted GPA and 1380 SAT (exclusive of writing) or 31 ACT; must be admitted by 2/1 of year prior to enrollment and meet Nevada residency requirements. Additional scholarships: ranging from $2,500 to $5,000; based on combination of test scores and unweighted GPA. ***Athletic:*** 73 full-time freshmen received athletic scholarships; average amount $12,000.

Cumulative student debt: 41% of graduating class had student loans; average debt was $19,500.

Additional info: Reduced out-of-state tuition available for participants in WUE program.

FINANCIAL AID PROCEDURES

Forms required: FAFSA.

Dates and Deadlines: Priority date 3/1; no closing date. Applicants notified on a rolling basis starting 4/1; must reply within 2 week(s) of notification.

Transfers: No deadline. Applicants notified on a rolling basis; must reply within 2 week(s) of notification. Transfer GPA must be 2.0 or higher to be eligible for aid.

CONTACT

Tim Wolfe, Director, Student Financial Services
Mail Stop 120, Reno, NV 89557
(775) 784-4666

Western Nevada College

Carson City, Nevada
www.wnc.edu Federal Code: 013896

2-year public community college in small city.

Enrollment: 3,650 undergrads, 65% part-time. 339 full-time freshmen.

Selectivity: Open admission; but selective for some programs.

BASIC COSTS (2012-2013)

Tuition and fees: $2,700; out-of-state residents $9,345.

Per-credit charge: $76.

FINANCIAL AID PICTURE (2012-2013)

Students with need: 71% of average financial aid package awarded as scholarships/grants, 29% awarded as loans/jobs. Need-based aid available for part-time students. Work study available nights.

Students without need: No-need awards available for academics, state/district residency.

FINANCIAL AID PROCEDURES

Forms required: FAFSA.

Dates and Deadlines: Priority date 4/1; no closing date. Applicants notified on a rolling basis; must reply within 3 week(s) of notification.

Transfers: No deadline. Applicants notified on a rolling basis; must reply within 3 week(s) of notification. Loans received at other schools counted toward limit.

CONTACT

George McNulty, Director of Financial Assistance
2201 West College Parkway, Carson City, NV 89703-7399
(775) 445-3264

New Hampshire

Colby-Sawyer College

New London, New Hampshire
www.colby-sawyer.edu Federal Code: 002572

4-year private liberal arts college in small town.
Enrollment: 1,400 undergrads, 2% part-time. 508 full-time freshmen.
Selectivity: Admits over 75% of applicants.

BASIC COSTS (2013-2014)

Tuition and fees: $37,300.
Room and board: $12,500.

FINANCIAL AID PICTURE (2012-2013)

Students with need: Average financial aid package met 74% of need; average scholarship/grant was $17,111; average loan was $3,553. For part-time students, average financial aid package was $27,751.
Students without need: No-need awards available for academics, alumni affiliation, art, leadership, minority status, music/drama.
Cumulative student debt: 82% of graduating class had student loans; average debt was $38,519.

FINANCIAL AID PROCEDURES

Forms required: FAFSA.
Dates and Deadlines: Priority date 2/15; closing date 3/1. Applicants notified on a rolling basis starting 2/1; must reply by 5/1.
Transfers: Priority date 3/1; closing date 4/15. Applicants notified on a rolling basis starting 12/15; must reply within 2 week(s) of notification.

CONTACT

Ted Craigie, Director of Financial Aid
541 Main Street, New London, NH 03257-7835
(603) 526-3717

College of St. Mary Magdalen

Warner, New Hampshire
www.magdalen.edu Federal Code: 022233

4-year private liberal arts college in small town, affiliated with Roman Catholic Church.
Enrollment: 60 undergrads.

BASIC COSTS (2012-2013)

Tuition and fees: $19,000.
Room and board: $7,500.

FINANCIAL AID PICTURE

Students with need: Need-based aid available for full-time and part-time students. Work study available nights, weekends, and for part-time students.
Students without need: This college awards aid only to students with need.
Scholarships offered: Presidential Scholarship: four year, full tuition scholarship (not including room and board costs); applicant must have 1800 cumulative SAT score or 26 ACT; 1 awarded annually to incoming freshman. St. Mary Magdalen Scholarship: amount varies; awarded to students who have demonstrated leadership or initiative in various ministry activities. Saint Cecilia Music: amount varies; awarded to students who have demonstrated talent, leadership and initiative in various musical activities including but not limited to choir, polyphony choir, vocal or instrumental performance. Saint Luke Scholarship: amount varies; awarded to students who have demonstrated achievement in art. T.S. Eliot award: amount varies; awarded to students whose quality of writing surpasses that of their peers and who have demonstrated an ongoing interest in writing. Achievement Awards: amounts vary; awarded to students who demonstrate a strong academic record, leadership skills, or outstanding community service.

FINANCIAL AID PROCEDURES

Forms required: institutional form.
Dates and Deadlines: Priority date 3/15; no closing date. Applicants notified on a rolling basis starting 3/15.
Transfers: No deadline. Applicants notified on a rolling basis; must reply within 4 week(s) of notification. Certain scholarships that are available to freshman are also available to new transfer students.

CONTACT

Marie Lasher, Director of Financial Aid
511 Kearsarge Mountain Road, Warner, NH 03278
(603) 456-2656

Daniel Webster College

Nashua, New Hampshire
www.dwc.edu Federal Code: 004731

4-year for-profit business and engineering college in small city.
Enrollment: 598 undergrads, 9% part-time. 143 full-time freshmen.
Selectivity: Admits 50 to 75% of applicants.

BASIC COSTS (2012-2013)

Tuition and fees: $15,090.
Room and board: $10,290.

FINANCIAL AID PICTURE (2012-2013)

Students with need: Out of 134 full-time freshmen who applied for aid, 113 were judged to have need. Of these, 109 received aid, and 6 had their full need met. Average financial aid package met 38% of need; average scholarship/grant was $3,183; average loan was $3,403. For part-time students, average financial aid package was $5,792.
Students without need: No-need awards available for academics.
Cumulative student debt: 84% of graduating class had student loans; average debt was $45,665.

FINANCIAL AID PROCEDURES

Forms required: FAFSA, institutional form.
Dates and Deadlines: Priority date 3/1; no closing date. Applicants notified on a rolling basis starting 3/15; must reply within 2 week(s) of notification.
Transfers: No deadline. Applicants notified on a rolling basis starting 3/15; must reply within 2 week(s) of notification.

CONTACT

Darla Ammidown, Director of Financial Operations
20 University Drive, Nashua, NH 03063
(603) 577-6533

Dartmouth College

Hanover, New Hampshire Federal Code: 002573
www.dartmouth.edu CSS Code: 3351

4-year private university and liberal arts college in large town.
Enrollment: 4,095 undergrads. 1,112 full-time freshmen.
Selectivity: Admits less than 50% of applicants.

BASIC COSTS (2013-2014)

Tuition and fees: $46,752.
Room and board: $13,446.

FINANCIAL AID PICTURE (2011-2012)

Students with need: Out of 589 full-time freshmen who applied for aid, 487 were judged to have need. Of these, 487 received aid, and 487 had

their full need met. Average financial aid package met 100% of need; average scholarship/grant was $38,753; average loan was $4,141. Need-based aid available for part-time students.
Students without need: This college awards aid only to students with need.
Cumulative student debt: 46% of graduating class had student loans; average debt was $17,825.

FINANCIAL AID PROCEDURES
Forms required: FAFSA, CSS PROFILE.
Dates and Deadlines: Closing date 2/1. Applicants notified by 4/10; must reply by 5/1.
Transfers: Closing date 3/15. Applicants notified by 4/2; must reply by 5/1. Grant budget for transfer students is limited. Some admitted transfer students may not have their full needs met.

CONTACT
Virginia Hazen, Director of Financial Aid
6016 McNutt Hall, Hanover, NH 03755
(603) 646-2451

Franklin Pierce University

Rindge, New Hampshire
www.franklinpierce.edu Federal Code: 002575

4-year private university and liberal arts college in small town.
Enrollment: 1,697 undergrads, 12% part-time. 538 full-time freshmen.
Selectivity: Admits over 75% of applicants.

BASIC COSTS (2012-2013)
Tuition and fees: $29,950.
Per-credit charge: $945.
Room and board: $11,260.

FINANCIAL AID PICTURE (2012-2013)
Students with need: Average financial aid package met 75% of need; average scholarship/grant was $19,782; average loan was $3,870. For part-time students, average financial aid package was $15,810.
Students without need: No-need awards available for academics, alumni affiliation, athletics, leadership, minority status, music/drama.
Scholarships offered: Trustee, Presidential, Provost, Deans, Transfer, Achieve, Success, Opportunity, Mascenic, Monadonock, International, Academic Ambition, Athletic, and Alumni scholarships range from $1,000 to $25,000. Marlin Fitzwater Mass Communication: $2,000; 6 awarded. Robert Alvin Performing Arts-Theater, Music, Dance; $2,000; 2 awarded in each category. Leadership Scholarship: $2,000; 10 awarded.
Cumulative student debt: 80% of graduating class had student loans; average debt was $35,511.

FINANCIAL AID PROCEDURES
Forms required: FAFSA.
Dates and Deadlines: Closing date 3/1. Applicants notified on a rolling basis starting 3/1; must reply within 2 week(s) of notification.
Transfers: No deadline. Applicants notified on a rolling basis starting 3/1; must reply within 2 week(s) of notification.

CONTACT
Ken Ferreira, Executive Director of Student Financial Services
40 University Drive, Rindge, NH 03461-0060
(603) 899-4180

Granite State College

Concord, New Hampshire
www.granite.edu Federal Code: 031013

4-year public liberal arts college in large town.
Enrollment: 1,657 undergrads, 47% part-time. 70 full-time freshmen.
Selectivity: Open admission; but selective for some programs.

BASIC COSTS (2012-2013)
Tuition and fees: $8,775; out-of-state residents $9,075.
Per-credit charge: $285; out-of-state residents $295.

FINANCIAL AID PICTURE
Students with need: Need-based aid available for full-time and part-time students. Work study available nights.
Students without need: This college awards aid only to students with need.

FINANCIAL AID PROCEDURES
Forms required: FAFSA, institutional form.
Dates and Deadlines: Applicants notified on a rolling basis starting 4/15.
Transfers: No deadline. Applicants notified on a rolling basis starting 4/15.

CONTACT
Barbara Layne, Executive Director of Financial Aid and Strategic Enrollment Planning
25 Hall Street, Concord, NH 03301-7317
(603) 228-3000 ext. 324

Great Bay Community College

Portsmouth, New Hampshire
www.greatbay.edu Federal Code: 002583

2-year public community and technical college in small town.
Enrollment: 1,941 undergrads.
Selectivity: Open admission; but selective for some programs.

BASIC COSTS (2012-2013)
Tuition and fees: $6,570; out-of-state residents $14,610.
Per-credit charge: $210; out-of-state residents $478.
Additional info: New England Regional tuition: $315 per credit hour.

FINANCIAL AID PICTURE
Students with need: Need-based aid available for full-time and part-time students. Work study available nights, weekends, and for part-time students.
Students without need: This college awards aid only to students with need.

FINANCIAL AID PROCEDURES
Forms required: FAFSA, institutional form.
Dates and Deadlines: Applicants notified on a rolling basis; must reply within 2 week(s) of notification.
Transfers: No deadline. Applicants notified on a rolling basis; must reply within 2 week(s) of notification.

CONTACT
Lauren Hughes, Director of Financial Aid
320 Corporate Drive, Portsmouth, NH 03801
(603) 772-1194

Hesser College

Manchester, New Hampshire
www.hesser.edu Federal Code: 004729

4-year for-profit business and junior college in small city.
Enrollment: 3,543 undergrads.
Selectivity: Open admission; but selective for some programs.

BASIC COSTS (2012-2013)
Additional info: Estimated program costs: Diploma programs range from $14,344 to $15,351; associate degree programs, $19,740 to $39,195; bachelor's degree programs, $39,480. All costs subject to change at any time.

FINANCIAL AID PICTURE

Students with need: Need-based aid available for full-time and part-time students. Work study available nights, weekends, and for part-time students.

Students without need: This college awards aid only to students with need.

Additional info: Two private loans available to assist students in paying their balance; Tree Loan, SLM Loan.

FINANCIAL AID PROCEDURES

Forms required: FAFSA, institutional form.

Dates and Deadlines: Priority date 5/1; no closing date. Applicants notified on a rolling basis starting 3/1; must reply within 3 week(s) of notification.

CONTACT

Shaman Quinn, Director of Financial Aid
3 Sundial Avenue, Manchester, NH 03103
(603) 668-6660 ext. 2210

Keene State College

Keene, New Hampshire
www.keene.edu Federal Code: 002590

4-year public liberal arts and teachers college in large town.
Enrollment: 4,787 undergrads, 3% part-time. 1,260 full-time freshmen.
Selectivity: Admits over 75% of applicants.

BASIC COSTS (2012-2013)

Tuition and fees: $12,776; out-of-state residents $19,676.
Per-credit charge: $440; out-of-state residents $720.
Room and board: $9,088.
Additional info: New England Regional Student Program tuition is 160% of in-state tuition.

FINANCIAL AID PICTURE (2011-2012)

Students with need: Out of 1,158 full-time freshmen who applied for aid, 867 were judged to have need. Of these, 850 received aid, and 85 had their full need met. Average financial aid package met 65% of need; average scholarship/grant was $6,682; average loan was $3,873. For part-time students, average financial aid package was $6,364.

Students without need: 112 full-time freshmen who did not demonstrate need for aid received scholarships/grants; average award was $2,091. No-need awards available for academics, alumni affiliation, art, music/drama.

Cumulative student debt: 80% of graduating class had student loans; average debt was $33,248.

FINANCIAL AID PROCEDURES

Forms required: FAFSA.

Dates and Deadlines: Closing date 3/1. Applicants notified on a rolling basis; must reply within 4 week(s) of notification.

Transfers: Applicants notified on a rolling basis; must reply within 4 week(s) of notification.

CONTACT

Patricia Blodgett, Director of Financial Aid
229 Main Street, Keene, NH 03435-2604
(603) 358-2280

Lakes Region Community College

Laconia, New Hampshire
www.lrcc.edu Federal Code: 007555

2-year public community and technical college in small city.
Enrollment: 1,045 undergrads.
Selectivity: Open admission; but selective for some programs.

BASIC COSTS (2012-2013)

Tuition and fees: $6,480; out-of-state residents $14,520.
Per-credit charge: $210; out-of-state residents $478.
Additional info: New England regional tuition: $315 per-credit-hour.

FINANCIAL AID PICTURE

Students with need: Need-based aid available for full-time and part-time students.

FINANCIAL AID PROCEDURES

Forms required: FAFSA, institutional form.

Dates and Deadlines: Priority date 5/1; no closing date.

CONTACT

Kristen Purrington, Financial Aid Officer
379 Belmont Road, Laconia, NH 03246-9204
(603) 524-3207

Lebanon College

Lebanon, New Hampshire
www.lebanoncollege.edu Federal Code: 007025

2-year private health science and community college in large town.
Enrollment: 95 undergrads, 43% part-time. 26 full-time freshmen.
Selectivity: Open admission; but selective for some programs.

BASIC COSTS (2013-2014)

Tuition and fees: $7,694.
Per-credit charge: $198.

FINANCIAL AID PICTURE (2012-2013)

Students with need: Average financial aid package met 50% of need; average scholarship/grant was $4,775; average loan was $3,500. For part-time students, average financial aid package was $8,413.

FINANCIAL AID PROCEDURES

Forms required: FAFSA, institutional form.

Dates and Deadlines: Applicants notified on a rolling basis.

Transfers: No deadline. Applicants notified on a rolling basis.

CONTACT

Tina Popielski, Director of Financial Aid
15 Hanover Street, Lebanon, NH 03766
(603) 448-2445 ext. 121

Manchester Community College

Manchester, New Hampshire
www.mccnh.edu Federal Code: 002582

2-year public community and technical college in small city.
Enrollment: 2,744 undergrads.
Selectivity: Open admission; but selective for some programs.

BASIC COSTS (2012-2013)

Tuition and fees: $6,720; out-of-state residents $14,760.
Per-credit charge: $210; out-of-state residents $478.
Additional info: New England Regional tuition: $315 per credit hour.

FINANCIAL AID PICTURE

Students with need: Need-based aid available for full-time and part-time students. Work study available nights, weekends, and for part-time students.

Students without need: This college awards aid only to students with need.

Scholarships offered: NH high school valedictorians receive 100% tuition scholarship.

FINANCIAL AID PROCEDURES

Forms required: FAFSA, institutional form.

Dates and Deadlines: Priority date 5/1; no closing date. Applicants notified on a rolling basis starting 4/15; must reply within 2 week(s) of notification.

CONTACT
Stephanie Weldon, Financial Aid Officer
1066 Front Street, Manchester, NH 03102-8518
(603) 668-6706 ext. 352

Nashua Community College
Nashua, New Hampshire
www.nashuacc.edu Federal Code: 009236

2-year public community and technical college in small city.
Enrollment: 2,312 undergrads.
Selectivity: Open admission; but selective for some programs.

BASIC COSTS (2012-2013)
Tuition and fees: $6,780; out-of-state residents $14,820.
Per-credit charge: $210; out-of-state residents $478.
Additional info: New England regional tuition: $315 per credit hour.

FINANCIAL AID PICTURE
Students with need: Need-based aid available for full-time and part-time students. Work study available nights.
Students without need: This college awards aid only to students with need.

FINANCIAL AID PROCEDURES
Forms required: FAFSA.
Dates and Deadlines: Priority date 5/1; no closing date. Applicants notified on a rolling basis starting 3/1; must reply within 2 week(s) of notification.

CONTACT
Lisbeth Gonzalez, Director of Financial Aid
505 Amherst Street, Nashua, NH 03063-1026
(603) 882-6923 ext. 1528

New England College
Henniker, New Hampshire
www.nec.edu Federal Code: 002579

4-year private liberal arts and teachers college in small town.
Enrollment: 1,096 undergrads, 5% part-time. 323 full-time freshmen.
Selectivity: Admits 50 to 75% of applicants.

BASIC COSTS (2012-2013)
Tuition and fees: $31,744.
Per-credit charge: $1,502.
Room and board: $12,434.
Additional info: Tuition/fee waivers available for adults.

FINANCIAL AID PICTURE (2012-2013)
Students with need: Out of 281 full-time freshmen who applied for aid, 267 were judged to have need. Of these, 267 received aid, and 35 had their full need met. Average financial aid package met 75% of need; average scholarship/grant was $13,229; average loan was $4,306. For part-time students, average financial aid package was $11,300..
Students without need: 38 full-time freshmen who did not demonstrate need for aid received scholarships/grants; average award was $12,541. No-need awards available for academics, alumni affiliation, art, job skills, leadership, music/drama, state/district residency.
Scholarships offered: Russell Durgin veteran scholarship, up to $16,000. Any veteran is eligible regardless of time of service.
Cumulative student debt: 72% of graduating class had student loans; average debt was $33,797.
Additional info: Significant scholarship programs for veterans including non-Post 911 eligible veterans.

FINANCIAL AID PROCEDURES
Forms required: FAFSA.
Dates and Deadlines: Priority date 4/1; no closing date. Applicants notified on a rolling basis starting 1/12; must reply within 2 week(s) of notification.
Transfers: No deadline. Applicants notified on a rolling basis starting 1/1; must reply within 2 week(s) of notification. May 1 deadline for state grant consideration.

CONTACT
Kristen Blase, Director of Student Financial Services
103 Bridge Street, Henniker, NH 03242
(603) 428-2226

NHTI-Concord's Community College
Concord, New Hampshire
www.nhti.edu Federal Code: 002581

2-year public community and technical college in large town.
Enrollment: 4,342 undergrads.
Selectivity: Open admission; but selective for some programs.

BASIC COSTS (2012-2013)
Tuition and fees: $6,900; out-of-state residents $14,940.
Per-credit charge: $210; out-of-state residents $478.
Room and board: $8,486.
Additional info: New England Regional tuition: $315 per credit hour.

FINANCIAL AID PICTURE
Students with need: Need-based aid available for full-time and part-time students. Work study available nights, weekends, and for part-time students.
Students without need: This college awards aid only to students with need.
Additional info: 60% of students who apply receive some form of financial aid. State school; all financial aid need-based, primarily from federal sources. No scholarships awarded.

FINANCIAL AID PROCEDURES
Forms required: FAFSA, institutional form.
Dates and Deadlines: Priority date 5/1; no closing date. Applicants notified on a rolling basis starting 6/1; must reply within 2 week(s) of notification.
Transfers: No deadline. Applicants notified on a rolling basis.

CONTACT
Sheri Gonthier, Financial Aid Director
31 College Drive, Concord, NH 03301
(603) 271-7136

Plymouth State University
Plymouth, New Hampshire
www.plymouth.edu Federal Code: 002591

4-year public university and teachers college in small town.
Enrollment: 4,128 undergrads, 5% part-time. 1,017 full-time freshmen.
Selectivity: Admits over 75% of applicants.

BASIC COSTS (2012-2013)
Tuition and fees: $12,560; out-of-state residents $19,460.
Per-credit charge: $435; out-of-state residents $720.
Room and board: $9,440.
Additional info: New England Regional Student Program tuition is 160% of in-state tuition.

FINANCIAL AID PICTURE (2011-2012)
Students with need: Out of 958 full-time freshmen who applied for aid, 760 were judged to have need. Of these, 755 received aid, and 93 had their full need met. Average financial aid package met 52% of need; average scholarship/grant was $6,604; average loan was $3,221. For part-time students, average financial aid package was $5,850.

Students without need: 51 full-time freshmen who did not demonstrate need for aid received scholarships/grants; average award was $4,059. No-need awards available for academics, alumni affiliation, art, leadership, music/drama.

Scholarships offered: Presidential Scholars; $5,000; based on outstanding academic performance and overall achievement. PSU Scholars; $6,000; based on overall merit and past achievement. New Hampshire Top Scholars; $3,500; for New Hampshire residents in top 25%. Music/Theater Talent Grants; $5,000; based on talent and audition.

Cumulative student debt: 83% of graduating class had student loans; average debt was $31,214.

FINANCIAL AID PROCEDURES

Forms required: FAFSA.

Dates and Deadlines: Priority date 3/1; no closing date. Applicants notified on a rolling basis starting 3/1.

Transfers: Applicants notified on a rolling basis starting 3/1.

CONTACT

June Schlabach, Director of Financial Aid
17 High Street MSC 52, Plymouth, NH 03264-1595
(603) 535-2338

River Valley Community College

Claremont, New Hampshire
www.rivervalley.edu Federal Code: 007560

2-year public community college in large town.

Enrollment: 814 undergrads.

Selectivity: Open admission; but selective for some programs.

BASIC COSTS (2012-2013)

Tuition and fees: $6,450; out-of-state residents $14,490.

Per-credit charge: $210; out-of-state residents $478.

Additional info: New England Regional tuition: $315 per credit hour.

FINANCIAL AID PICTURE

Students with need: Need-based aid available for full-time and part-time students.

Students without need: This college awards aid only to students with need.

FINANCIAL AID PROCEDURES

Forms required: FAFSA.

Dates and Deadlines: Closing date 4/1. Applicants notified on a rolling basis; must reply within 2 week(s) of notification.

CONTACT

Julia Dower, Director of Financial Aid
One College Drive, Claremont, NH 03743-9707
(603) 542-7744 ext. 5725

Rivier University

Nashua, New Hampshire
www.rivier.edu Federal Code: 002586

4-year private university and nursing college in small city, affiliated with Roman Catholic Church.

Enrollment: 1,460 undergrads, 38% part-time. 218 full-time freshmen.

Selectivity: Admits over 75% of applicants.

BASIC COSTS (2012-2013)

Tuition and fees: $27,030.

Per-credit charge: $881.

Room and board: $10,718.

Additional info: Tuition/fee waivers available for unemployed or children of unemployed.

FINANCIAL AID PICTURE

Students with need: Need-based aid available for full-time and part-time students. Work study available nights, weekends, and for part-time students.

Students without need: No-need awards available for academics, alumni affiliation.

Scholarships offered: Dean's Scholarship: $6,000 for residents, $5,000 for commuters; minimum 1000 SAT (exclusive of Writing); 3.0 GPA; renewable with minimum 2.67 GPA. Presidential Scholarship: $7,000 for residents, $6,000 for commuters; minimum 1150 SAT (exclusive of Writing); 3.4 GPA; renewable with minimum 3.0 GPA. Catholic High School Grant: $4,000 for residents, $3,000 for commuters; for students graduating from Catholic high school; renewable with 2.5 GPA. Honors Scholarship: for honors program participants; $10,000 for residents, $2,000 for commuters. Alumni Scholarship: $2,000; for children of Rivier alumni; renewable with minimum 2.0 GPA. Trustee Scholarship: $8,000 for residents, $7,000 for commuters; minimum 1200 SAT (exclusive of Writing); 3.4 GPA; renewable with minimum 3.0 GPA. Founders Scholarship for National Merit Finalists: full tuition; renewable with minimum 3.0 GPA.

FINANCIAL AID PROCEDURES

Forms required: FAFSA.

Dates and Deadlines: Priority date 3/1; no closing date. Applicants notified on a rolling basis starting 3/1; must reply by 5/1 or within 2 week(s) of notification.

Transfers: No deadline. Applicants notified on a rolling basis starting 3/1; must reply by 5/1 or within 2 week(s) of notification. Scholarship for transfer students with minimum 2.5 GPA and 12 transferable credits.

CONTACT

Valerie Patnaude, Director of Financial Aid
420 South Main Street, Nashua, NH 03060-5086
(603) 897-8510

Saint Anselm College

Manchester, New Hampshire Federal Code: 002587
www.anselm.edu CSS Code: 3748

4-year private nursing and liberal arts college in small city, affiliated with Roman Catholic Church.

Enrollment: 1,934 undergrads, 2% part-time. 527 full-time freshmen.

Selectivity: Admits 50 to 75% of applicants.

BASIC COSTS (2012-2013)

Tuition and fees: $34,205.

Room and board: $12,380.

Additional info: Tuition/fee waivers available for minority students.

FINANCIAL AID PICTURE (2012-2013)

Students with need: Out of 491 full-time freshmen who applied for aid, 408 were judged to have need. Of these, 408 received aid, and 92 had their full need met. Average financial aid package met 82% of need; average scholarship/grant was $19,744; average loan was $4,550. For part-time students, average financial aid package was $11,282.

Students without need: 102 full-time freshmen who did not demonstrate need for aid received scholarships/grants; average award was $10,208. No-need awards available for academics, alumni affiliation, athletics, leadership, music/drama, state/district residency.

Scholarships offered: ***Merit:*** Presidential Scholarships: $5,000 to $17,000; based on grades, class rank, SAT results and extracurricular experience. ***Athletic:*** 26 full-time freshmen received athletic scholarships; average amount $12,445.

Cumulative student debt: 79% of graduating class had student loans; average debt was $42,630.82.

FINANCIAL AID PROCEDURES
Forms required: FAFSA, CSS PROFILE.
Dates and Deadlines: Closing date 3/15. Applicants notified on a rolling basis starting 3/1; must reply by 5/1 or within 2 week(s) of notification.
Transfers: Merit scholarships are awarded to qualified transfer students.

CONTACT
Elizabeth Keuffel, Director of Financial Aid
100 Saint Anselm Drive, Manchester, NH 03102-1310
(603) 641-7110

Southern New Hampshire University

Manchester, New Hampshire
www.snhu.edu Federal Code: 002580

4-year private university and culinary school in small city.
Enrollment: 10,374 undergrads, 44% part-time. 770 full-time freshmen.
Selectivity: Admits over 75% of applicants.

BASIC COSTS (2013-2014)
Tuition and fees: $29,204.
Per-credit charge: $1,190.
Room and board: $11,620.

FINANCIAL AID PICTURE (2012-2013)
Students with need: Out of 711 full-time freshmen who applied for aid, 637 were judged to have need. Of these, 637 received aid, and 25 had their full need met. Average financial aid package met 74% of need; average scholarship/grant was $9,474; average loan was $4,032. For part-time students, average financial aid package was $14,320.
Students without need: 116 full-time freshmen who did not demonstrate need for aid received scholarships/grants; average award was $9,836. No-need awards available for academics, alumni affiliation, athletics, job skills, leadership, state/district residency.
Scholarships offered: ***Merit:*** Scholarships up to $20,000 are available to students based primarily on high school GPA. ***Athletic:*** 9 full-time freshmen received athletic scholarships; average amount $21,873.
Cumulative student debt: 67% of graduating class had student loans; average debt was $30,392.

FINANCIAL AID PROCEDURES
Forms required: FAFSA.
Dates and Deadlines: Priority date 3/15; no closing date. Applicants notified on a rolling basis starting 3/15; must reply within 3 week(s) of notification.

CONTACT
Beverly Cotton, Associate VP Enrolled Student Services
2500 North River Road, Manchester, NH 03106-1045
(603) 668-2211

Thomas More College of Liberal Arts

Merrimack, New Hampshire
www.thomasmorecollege.edu Federal Code: 030431

4-year private liberal arts college in large town, affiliated with Roman Catholic Church.
Enrollment: 96 undergrads.

BASIC COSTS (2012-2013)
Tuition and fees: $17,600.
Room and board: $9,100.

FINANCIAL AID PICTURE
Students with need: Need-based aid available for full-time and part-time students. Work study available nights, weekends, and for part-time students.
Students without need: No-need awards available for academics.
Scholarships offered: Thomas More Scholarship: full or partial tuition; based on superior academic achievement, exceptional promise or potential; several awarded. Commuter Grants: full-time students within commuting distance of the college. Faith and Reason Essay Contest: half tuition for 4 years; based on essay. Summer Program Scholarship: $1,000; for students who attended the Thomas More College Summer Program for high school students.

FINANCIAL AID PROCEDURES
Forms required: FAFSA.
Dates and Deadlines: Priority date 5/1; no closing date. Applicants notified on a rolling basis starting 5/15; must reply within 2 week(s) of notification.

CONTACT
Clint Hanson, Director of Financial Aid
Six Manchester Street, Merrimack, NH 03054-4818
(603) 880-8308 ext. 23

University of New Hampshire

Durham, New Hampshire
www.unh.edu/ Federal Code: 002589

4-year public university in small town.
Enrollment: 12,565 undergrads, 2% part-time. 2,779 full-time freshmen.
Selectivity: Admits over 75% of applicants.

BASIC COSTS (2012-2013)
Tuition and fees: $16,422; out-of-state residents $28,882.
Per-credit charge: $570; out-of-state residents $1,089.
Room and board: $9,764.
Additional info: Tuition/fee waivers available for minority students.

FINANCIAL AID PICTURE (2011-2012)
Students with need: Out of 2,455 full-time freshmen who applied for aid, 1,958 were judged to have need. Of these, 1,923 received aid, and 427 had their full need met. Average financial aid package met 80% of need; average scholarship/grant was $5,249; average loan was $2,670. For part-time students, average financial aid package was $12,264.
Students without need: 440 full-time freshmen who did not demonstrate need for aid received scholarships/grants; average award was $7,296. No-need awards available for academics, art, athletics, leadership, music/drama, religious affiliation, ROTC.
Scholarships offered: ***Merit:*** Presidential Scholarship: half tuition. Various other awards recognizing outstanding high school achievement determined during freshmen candidate application review process; no additional application materials required. ***Athletic:*** 39 full-time freshmen received athletic scholarships; average amount $28,887.

FINANCIAL AID PROCEDURES
Forms required: FAFSA.
Dates and Deadlines: Closing date 3/1. Applicants notified on a rolling basis starting 3/1; must reply by 5/1.
Transfers: Closing date 5/1. Applicants notified on a rolling basis starting 5/1.

CONTACT
Susan Allen, Director of Financial Aid
3 Garrison Avenue, Durham, NH 03824
(603) 862-3600

University of New Hampshire at Manchester

Manchester, New Hampshire
www.manchester.unh.edu Federal Code: 002589

4-year public university and liberal arts college in small city.
Enrollment: 776 undergrads, 25% part-time. 72 full-time freshmen.

Selectivity: Admits less than 50% of applicants.

BASIC COSTS (2012-2013)

Tuition and fees: $13,757; out-of-state residents $26,217.

Per-credit charge: $556; out-of-state residents $1,075.

Additional info: New England Regional Student Program tuition is 175% of in-state tuition.

FINANCIAL AID PICTURE

Students with need: Work study available nights, weekends, and for part-time students.

Students without need: No-need awards available for academics, state/district residency.

FINANCIAL AID PROCEDURES

Forms required: FAFSA.

Dates and Deadlines: Closing date 3/1. Applicants notified on a rolling basis starting 4/1; must reply within 2 week(s) of notification.

CONTACT

Jodi Abad, Director of Financial Aid
400 Commercial Street, Manchester, NH 03101-1113
(603) 641-4189

White Mountains Community College

Berlin, New Hampshire
www.wmcc.edu Federal Code: 005291

2-year public community college in large town.

Enrollment: 713 undergrads, 60% part-time. 97 full-time freshmen.

Selectivity: Open admission; but selective for some programs.

BASIC COSTS (2012-2013)

Tuition and fees: $6,840; out-of-state residents $14,880.

Per-credit charge: $210; out-of-state residents $478.

Additional info: New England Regional tuition: $315 per credit hour.

FINANCIAL AID PICTURE

Students with need: Need-based aid available for full-time and part-time students.

Students without need: This college awards aid only to students with need.

FINANCIAL AID PROCEDURES

Forms required: FAFSA, institutional form.

Dates and Deadlines: Priority date 5/1; no closing date. Applicants notified on a rolling basis starting 5/1; must reply within 2 week(s) of notification.

Transfers: No deadline. Applicants notified on a rolling basis.

CONTACT

Tyler Bergmeier, Director of Financial Aid
2020 Riverside Drive, Berlin, NH 03570
(603) 752-1113

New Jersey

Atlantic Cape Community College

Mays Landing, New Jersey
www.atlantic.edu Federal Code: 002596

2-year public culinary school and community college in small town.

Enrollment: 6,906 undergrads, 50% part-time. 1,144 full-time freshmen.

Selectivity: Open admission; but selective for some programs.

BASIC COSTS (2012-2013)

Tuition and fees: $3,735; out-of-district residents $5,295; out-of-state residents $6,795.

Per-credit charge: $102; out-of-district residents $154; out-of-state residents $204.

Additional info: Tuition/fee waivers available for unemployed or children of unemployed.

FINANCIAL AID PICTURE

Students with need: Need-based aid available for full-time and part-time students.

Additional info: Installment plan available for culinary arts majors. Employees of Atlantic City casinos may attend ACCC at in-county rates regardless of residence.

FINANCIAL AID PROCEDURES

Forms required: FAFSA, institutional form.

Dates and Deadlines: Priority date 5/1; no closing date. Applicants notified on a rolling basis starting 5/1.

CONTACT

Linda Desantis, Director of Financial Aid and Veterans' Affairs
5100 Black Horse Pike, Mays Landing, NJ 08330-2699
(609) 343-5082

Berkeley College

Woodland Park, New Jersey
www.berkeleycollege.edu Federal Code: 007502

4-year for-profit business and career college in large town.

Enrollment: 2,859 undergrads.

BASIC COSTS (2012-2013)

Tuition and fees: $22,500.

FINANCIAL AID PICTURE

Students with need: Need-based aid available for full-time students.

Students without need: No-need awards available for academics, alumni affiliation.

Additional info: Alumni scholarship examination given in November and December. Full and partial scholarships awarded.

FINANCIAL AID PROCEDURES

Forms required: FAFSA.

Dates and Deadlines: Applicants notified on a rolling basis starting 3/1; must reply within 6 week(s) of notification.

CONTACT

Howard Leslie, Vice President Financial Aid
44 Rifle Camp Road, Woodland Park, NJ 07424-0440
(973) 278-5400

Bloomfield College

Bloomfield, New Jersey
www.bloomfield.edu Federal Code: 002597

4-year private nursing and liberal arts college in large town, affiliated with Presbyterian Church (USA).

Enrollment: 2,029 undergrads, 11% part-time. 373 full-time freshmen.

Selectivity: Admits 50 to 75% of applicants.

BASIC COSTS (2013-2014)

Tuition and fees: $25,880.

Per-credit charge: $771.

Room and board: $10,900.

FINANCIAL AID PICTURE (2012-2013)

Students with need: Out of 368 full-time freshmen who applied for aid, 363 were judged to have need. Of these, 362 received aid, and 7 had their full need met. Average financial aid package met 56% of need; average scholarship/grant was $17,965; average loan was $3,460. For part-time students, average financial aid package was $12,090.

Students without need: 2 full-time freshmen who did not demonstrate need for aid received scholarships/grants; average award was $7,500. No-need awards available for academics, alumni affiliation, athletics, leadership.

Scholarships offered: ***Merit:*** Trustee Scholar Award; $8,000-full tuition; 3.6 GPA, 900 SAT required. Presidential Scholarship; $6,000-full tuition; 3.0 GPA and 900 SAT required. Community Service Scholarships; up to $5,000; for students with commitment to community service. ***Athletic:*** 1 full-time freshmen received athletic scholarships; average amount $35,750.

Cumulative student debt: 92% of graduating class had student loans; average debt was $20,467.

FINANCIAL AID PROCEDURES

Forms required: FAFSA.

Dates and Deadlines: Priority date 3/15; closing date 6/1. Applicants notified on a rolling basis starting 2/15; must reply within 2 week(s) of notification.

Transfers: Applicants notified on a rolling basis starting 2/15; must reply within 2 week(s) of notification. Transfer Scholarship; $5,000-full tuition; for transfer students from 2-year colleges with 3.0 GPA. Phi Theta Kappa Transfer Scholarships; up to full tuition; for day transfer students from 2-year colleges with 3.5 GPA with a completed AA/AS degree and are members of Phi Theta Kappa.

CONTACT

Stacy Salinas, Director of Financial Aid
One Park Place, Bloomfield, NJ 07003
(973) 748-9000 ext. 1212

Brookdale Community College

Lincroft, New Jersey
www.brookdalecc.edu Federal Code: 008404

2-year public community college in small city.
Enrollment: 12,835 undergrads, 40% part-time.
Selectivity: Open admission; but selective for some programs.

BASIC COSTS (2012-2013)

Tuition and fees: $4,297; out-of-district residents $7,362; out-of-state residents $8,512.

Per-credit charge: $116; out-of-district residents $231; out-of-state residents $256.

Additional info: Tuition/fee waivers available for unemployed or children of unemployed.

FINANCIAL AID PICTURE

Students with need: Need-based aid available for full-time and part-time students.

Students without need: No-need awards available for academics, athletics.

FINANCIAL AID PROCEDURES

Forms required: FAFSA, institutional form.

Dates and Deadlines: Priority date 5/1; no closing date. Applicants notified on a rolling basis starting 5/1; must reply within 2 week(s) of notification.

CONTACT

Stephanie Fitzsimmons, Director of Financial Aid
765 Newman Springs Road, Lincroft, NJ 07738
(732) 224-2362

Burlington County College

Pemberton, New Jersey
www.bcc.edu Federal Code: 007730

2-year public community college in small town.
Enrollment: 9,236 undergrads, 46% part-time. 1,832 full-time freshmen.
Selectivity: Open admission; but selective for some programs.

BASIC COSTS (2012-2013)

Tuition and fees: $3,615; out-of-district residents $4,095; out-of-state residents $6,045.

Per-credit charge: $92; out-of-district residents $108; out-of-state residents $173.

Additional info: Special rates for culinary courses. Tuition/fee waivers available for unemployed or children of unemployed.

FINANCIAL AID PICTURE (2011-2012)

Students with need: 66% of average financial aid package awarded as scholarships/grants, 34% awarded as loans/jobs. Need-based aid available for part-time students. Work study available nights, weekends, and for part-time students.

Students without need: This college awards aid only to students with need.

FINANCIAL AID PROCEDURES

Forms required: FAFSA.

Dates and Deadlines: Applicants notified on a rolling basis.

CONTACT

Ronald Brand, Vice President of Finance and Administration
601 Pemberton-Browns Mills Road, Pemberton, NJ 08068-1599
(609) 894-9311 ext. 1575

Caldwell College

Caldwell, New Jersey
www.caldwell.edu Federal Code: 002598

4-year private liberal arts college in large town, affiliated with Roman Catholic Church.
Enrollment: 1,572 undergrads, 20% part-time. 289 full-time freshmen.
Selectivity: Admits 50 to 75% of applicants.

BASIC COSTS (2013-2014)

Tuition and fees: $29,000.
Per-credit charge: $750.
Room and board: $10,198.
Additional info: Tuition/fee waivers available for adults.

FINANCIAL AID PICTURE (2012-2013)

Students with need: Out of 275 full-time freshmen who applied for aid, 275 were judged to have need. Of these, 268 received aid, and 28 had their full need met. Average financial aid package met 74% of need; average scholarship/grant was $17,882; average loan was $3,431. For part-time students, average financial aid package was $7,101.

Students without need: 14 full-time freshmen who did not demonstrate need for aid received scholarships/grants; average award was $12,585. No-need awards available for academics, alumni affiliation, art, athletics, leadership, music/drama, religious affiliation.

Scholarships offered: 3 full-time freshmen received athletic scholarships; average amount $5,333.

Cumulative student debt: 57% of graduating class had student loans; average debt was $21,209.

FINANCIAL AID PROCEDURES

Forms required: FAFSA, state aid form, institutional form.

Dates and Deadlines: Priority date 4/1; no closing date. Applicants notified on a rolling basis starting 3/1; must reply within 4 week(s) of notification.

Transfers: No deadline. Applicants notified on a rolling basis; must reply within 4 week(s) of notification. Students who have filed for aid through the state previously must file FAFSA by June 1 for succeeding year.

CONTACT

Hayto Suzuki, Financial Aid Director
120 Bloomfield Avenue, Caldwell, NJ 07006-6195
(973) 618-3221

Camden County College

Blackwood, New Jersey
www.camdencc.edu Federal Code: 006865

2-year public community college in large town.
Enrollment: 13,414 undergrads.
Selectivity: Open admission; but selective for some programs.

BASIC COSTS (2012-2013)

Tuition and fees: $3,990; out-of-district residents $4,110; out-of-state residents $6,060.
Per-credit charge: $101; out-of-district residents $105; out-of-state residents $170.
Additional info: Tuition/fee waivers available for unemployed or children of unemployed.

FINANCIAL AID PICTURE

Students with need: Need-based aid available for full-time and part-time students.

FINANCIAL AID PROCEDURES

Forms required: FAFSA, institutional form.
Dates and Deadlines: Priority date 5/1; closing date 7/1. Applicants notified on a rolling basis starting 7/1.
Transfers: Must submit financial aid transcripts from all previously attended institutions.

CONTACT

Felicia Bryant, Director of Financial Aid
Box 200, Blackwood, NJ 08012
(856) 227-7200

Centenary College

Hackettstown, New Jersey
www.centenarycollege.edu Federal Code: 002599

4-year private liberal arts college in large town, affiliated with United Methodist Church.
Enrollment: 1,891 undergrads.
Selectivity: Admits over 75% of applicants.

BASIC COSTS (2012-2013)

Tuition and fees: $29,630.
Per-credit charge: $550.
Room and board: $10,016.
Additional info: Additional fees required for equine majors and for comprehensive learning support program.

FINANCIAL AID PICTURE

Students with need: Need-based aid available for full-time students. Work study available nights, weekends, and for part-time students.
Students without need: No-need awards available for academics, alumni affiliation, art, leadership, minority status, music/drama, religious affiliation, state/district residency.
Scholarships offered: Academic awards; based on 2.5 GPA, 800 SAT (exclusive of Writing) or 16 ACT. Leadership awards; based on demonstrated leadership ability and potential. Equine Award. Centenary Resident Grant. Out-of-State Centenary Grant. Skylands Centenary Grant. Centenary United Methodist Scholarship.

FINANCIAL AID PROCEDURES

Forms required: FAFSA.
Dates and Deadlines: Priority date 4/1; closing date 6/1. Applicants notified on a rolling basis starting 3/1.
Transfers: Students from New Jersey colleges who have received tuition aid grants (TAG) must apply by state deadline. Students must submit financial aid transcripts from all previous institutions attended.

CONTACT

Glenna Warren, Dean of Admissions and Financial Aid
400 Jefferson Street, Hackettstown, NJ 07840-9989
(908) 852-1400 ext. 2350

The College of New Jersey

Ewing, New Jersey
www.tcnj.edu Federal Code: 002642

4-year public liberal arts college in large town.
Enrollment: 6,434 undergrads, 2% part-time. 1,370 full-time freshmen.
Selectivity: Admits less than 50% of applicants.

BASIC COSTS (2012-2013)

Tuition and fees: $14,378; out-of-state residents $24,530.
Per-credit charge: $358; out-of-state residents $717.
Room and board: $10,998.
Additional info: Tuition/fee waivers available for unemployed or children of unemployed.

FINANCIAL AID PICTURE (2011-2012)

Students with need: Out of 1,184 full-time freshmen who applied for aid, 775 were judged to have need. Of these, 758 received aid, and 95 had their full need met. Average financial aid package met 44% of need; average scholarship/grant was $12,565; average loan was $3,649. For part-time students, average financial aid package was $4,758.
Students without need: 178 full-time freshmen who did not demonstrate need for aid received scholarships/grants; average award was $4,850. No-need awards available for academics, art, music/drama.
Additional info: Merit scholarships available to New Jersey high school graduates based on academic distinction. Limited number of scholarships available to out-of-state students who demonstrate exceptional academic achievement in high school and on SAT. The EOF Promise Award meets the direct cost of attendance freshman and sophomore years, with merit scholarship awards available in junior and senior years.

FINANCIAL AID PROCEDURES

Forms required: FAFSA.
Dates and Deadlines: Priority date 3/1; closing date 10/1. Applicants notified on a rolling basis starting 6/1; must reply within 2 week(s) of notification.
Transfers: No deadline. Applicants notified on a rolling basis; must reply within 2 week(s) of notification.

CONTACT

Wilbert Casaine, Director of Financial Aid
2000 Pennington Road,Box 7718, Ewing, NJ 08628-0718
(609) 771-2211

College of St. Elizabeth

Morristown, New Jersey
www.cse.edu Federal Code: 002600

4-year private liberal arts college for women in large town, affiliated with Roman Catholic Church.

Enrollment: 1,034 undergrads, 44% part-time. 146 full-time freshmen.
Selectivity: Admits 50 to 75% of applicants.

BASIC COSTS (2012-2013)
Tuition and fees: $29,901.
Room and board: $12,254.
Additional info: Tuition/fee waivers available for adults.

FINANCIAL AID PICTURE (2011-2012)
Students with need: Need-based aid available for full-time and part-time students. Work study available nights, weekends, and for part-time students.
Students without need: No-need awards available for academics, alumni affiliation, art, leadership, state/district residency.
Scholarships offered: Presidential Scholarship for campus residents; full tuition. Elizabethan Scholarship; $8,000-$10,000. Seton Scholarship; $3,000-$7,000. Awards guaranteed to eligible students who apply by March 1 and enroll by May 1 for fall semester. International scholarships; tuition, room and board; awarded annually for fall semester only to first year students enrolled in Women's College; based on academic record, SAT scores (if submitted) and TOEFL score.

FINANCIAL AID PROCEDURES
Forms required: FAFSA.
Dates and Deadlines: Closing date 10/1. Applicants notified on a rolling basis starting 11/15; must reply by 5/1 or within 2 week(s) of notification.
Transfers: Priority date 4/15; closing date 8/20. Scholarships available for full-time students who enroll immediately following full-time enrollment at another college. Applicants must have completed 32 credits and have 3.0 GPA. Awards range from $3,500 to half tuition. Minimum of 5 awarded annually. Preference given to applications received by June 1 for fall semester and by December 1 for spring semester. Limited number of partial scholarships awarded to international students.

CONTACT
Debra Wulff, Director of Financial Aid
2 Convent Road, Morristown, NJ 07960-6989
(973) 290-4445

County College of Morris
Randolph, New Jersey
www.ccm.edu Federal Code: 007106

2-year public community college in small city.
Enrollment: 7,530 undergrads.
Selectivity: Open admission; but selective for some programs.

BASIC COSTS (2012-2013)
Tuition and fees: $4,155; out-of-district residents $7,615; out-of-state residents $10,575.
Per-credit charge: $116; out-of-district residents $232; out-of-state residents $330.
Additional info: Tuition/fee waivers available for unemployed or children of unemployed.

FINANCIAL AID PICTURE
Students with need: Need-based aid available for full-time and part-time students.
Students without need: No-need awards available for athletics.

FINANCIAL AID PROCEDURES
Forms required: FAFSA.
Dates and Deadlines: Priority date 3/1; no closing date. Applicants notified on a rolling basis starting 5/1.

CONTACT
Harvey Willis, Director, Financial Aid
214 Center Grove Road, Randolph, NJ 07869-2086
(973) 328-5230

Cumberland County College
Vineland, New Jersey
www.cccnj.edu Federal Code: 002601

2-year public community college in small city.
Enrollment: 3,944 undergrads.
Selectivity: Open admission; but selective for some programs.

BASIC COSTS (2012-2013)
Tuition and fees: $4,170; out-of-district residents $6,420; out-of-state residents $14,070.
Per-credit charge: $110; out-of-district residents $185; out-of-state residents $440.
Additional info: Students who provide proof of residence may get out-of-county per credit hour charge-back rate of $120. Tuition/fee waivers available for unemployed or children of unemployed.

FINANCIAL AID PICTURE (2011-2012)
Students with need: 98% of average financial aid package awarded as scholarships/grants, 2% awarded as loans/jobs. Need-based aid available for part-time students.
Students without need: No-need awards available for academics.

FINANCIAL AID PROCEDURES
Forms required: FAFSA.
Dates and Deadlines: Applicants notified on a rolling basis; must reply within 3 week(s) of notification.

CONTACT
Kimberly Mitchell, Director, Financial Aid
PO Box 1500, Vineland, NJ 08362-9912
(856) 691-8600

DeVry University: North Brunswick
North Brunswick, New Jersey
www.devry.edu Federal Code: 009228

4-year for-profit university in small city.
Enrollment: 1,193 undergrads, 53% part-time. 77 full-time freshmen.

BASIC COSTS (2012-2013)
Tuition and fees: $16,076.

FINANCIAL AID PICTURE
Students with need: Need-based aid available for full-time and part-time students.
Students without need: This college awards aid only to students with need.

FINANCIAL AID PROCEDURES
Forms required: FAFSA.
Dates and Deadlines: Applicants notified on a rolling basis.

CONTACT
Albert Cama, Director of Financial Aid
630 US Highway One, North Brunswick, NJ 08902-3362
(800) 333-3879

Drew University
Madison, New Jersey
www.drew.edu Federal Code: 002603

4-year private university and liberal arts college in large town, affiliated with United Methodist Church.
Enrollment: 1,582 undergrads, 1% part-time. 362 full-time freshmen.
Selectivity: Admits over 75% of applicants.

BASIC COSTS (2012-2013)
Tuition and fees: $42,620.
Per-credit charge: $1,736.
Room and board: $11,596.

FINANCIAL AID PICTURE (2011-2012)
Students with need: Average financial aid package for all full-time undergraduates was $30,732. 85% awarded as scholarships/grants, 15% awarded as loans/jobs. Work study available nights, weekends, and for part-time students.
Students without need: No-need awards available for academics, art, minority status, music/drama.
Cumulative student debt: 66% of graduating class had student loans; average debt was $24,470.

FINANCIAL AID PROCEDURES
Forms required: FAFSA.
Dates and Deadlines: Closing date 2/15. Must reply by 5/1.

CONTACT
Renee Volak, Vice President for Enrollment Management
36 Madison Avenue, Madison, NJ 07940-4063
(973) 408-3112

Essex County College
Newark, New Jersey
www.essex.edu Federal Code: 007107

2-year public community college in large city.
Enrollment: 11,076 undergrads, 42% part-time. 1,797 full-time freshmen.
Selectivity: Open admission; but selective for some programs.

BASIC COSTS (2012-2013)
Tuition and fees: $4,051; out-of-district residents $7,305; out-of-state residents $7,305.
Additional info: Tuition/fee waivers available for unemployed or children of unemployed.

FINANCIAL AID PICTURE
Students with need: Need-based aid available for full-time and part-time students.

FINANCIAL AID PROCEDURES
Forms required: FAFSA, institutional form.
Dates and Deadlines: Priority date 6/30; no closing date. Applicants notified on a rolling basis starting 6/15; must reply within 3 week(s) of notification.

CONTACT
Mildred Cofer, Director of Financial Aid
303 University Avenue, Newark, NJ 07102
(973) 877-3000

Felician College
Lodi, New Jersey
www.felician.edu Federal Code: 002610

4-year private liberal arts college in large town, affiliated with Roman Catholic Church.
Enrollment: 1,769 undergrads, 16% part-time. 341 full-time freshmen.
Selectivity: Admits over 75% of applicants.

BASIC COSTS (2013-2014)
Tuition and fees: $29,990.
Per-credit charge: $935.
Room and board: $11,650.
Additional info: Tuition/fee waivers available for adults.

FINANCIAL AID PICTURE (2011-2012)
Students with need: Out of 325 full-time freshmen who applied for aid, 308 were judged to have need. Of these, 307 received aid, and 49 had their full need met. Average financial aid package met 70% of need; average scholarship/grant was $11,515; average loan was $3,267. For part-time students, average financial aid package was $10,772.
Students without need: 31 full-time freshmen who did not demonstrate need for aid received scholarships/grants; average award was $13,958. No-need awards available for academics, alumni affiliation, athletics, religious affiliation.
Scholarships offered: 37 full-time freshmen received athletic scholarships; average amount $12,741.
Cumulative student debt: 73% of graduating class had student loans; average debt was $31,972.

FINANCIAL AID PROCEDURES
Forms required: FAFSA.
Dates and Deadlines: Priority date 6/1; no closing date. Applicants notified on a rolling basis starting 4/1; must reply within 2 week(s) of notification.

CONTACT
Janet Merli, Director of Financial Aid
262 South Main Street, Lodi, NJ 07644-2198
(201) 559-6000 ext. 6010

Georgian Court University
Lakewood, New Jersey
www.georgian.edu Federal Code: 002608

4-year private university and liberal arts college for women in large town, affiliated with Roman Catholic Church.
Enrollment: 1,432 undergrads, 13% part-time. 160 full-time freshmen.
Selectivity: Admits 50 to 75% of applicants.

BASIC COSTS (2012-2013)
Tuition and fees: $28,040.
Per-credit charge: $611.
Room and board: $10,560.

FINANCIAL AID PICTURE (2011-2012)
Students with need: Need-based aid available for full-time and part-time students. Work study available nights.
Students without need: No-need awards available for academics, alumni affiliation, art, athletics, leadership, music/drama, religious affiliation, state/district residency.

FINANCIAL AID PROCEDURES
Forms required: FAFSA, institutional form.
Dates and Deadlines: Priority date 4/15; closing date 8/20. Applicants notified on a rolling basis starting 2/1; must reply within 2 week(s) of notification.
Transfers: Transfer students who have outstanding financial obligations to previous college or who are in default are not admitted before being cleared by previous college or following federal guidelines concerning defaults.

CONTACT
Alice Eichhorn, Assistant Director of Financial Aid
900 Lakewood Avenue, Lakewood, NJ 08701-2697
(732) 987-2254

Gloucester County College
Sewell, New Jersey
www.gccnj.edu Federal Code: 006901

2-year public community and liberal arts college in large town.
Enrollment: 6,762 undergrads.

Selectivity: Open admission; but selective for some programs.

BASIC COSTS (2012-2013)

Tuition and fees: $3,570; out-of-district residents $4,020; out-of-state residents $7,170.

Per-credit charge: $90; out-of-district residents $105; out-of-state residents $210.

FINANCIAL AID PICTURE

Students with need: Need-based aid available for full-time and part-time students. Work study available nights.

FINANCIAL AID PROCEDURES

Forms required: FAFSA, institutional form.

Dates and Deadlines: Priority date 5/1; no closing date. Applicants notified on a rolling basis starting 3/20.

CONTACT

Michael Chando, Director Financial Aid/Vet Affairs
1400 Tanyard Road, Sewell, NJ 08080
(856) 415-2210

Hudson County Community College

Jersey City, New Jersey
www.hccc.edu Federal Code: 012954

2-year public community college in small city.

Enrollment: 9,056 undergrads, 35% part-time. 3,021 full-time freshmen.

Selectivity: Open admission.

BASIC COSTS (2013-2014)

Tuition and fees: $4,511; out-of-district residents $7,818; out-of-state residents $11,126.

Per-credit charge: $110; out-of-district residents $221; out-of-state residents $331.

FINANCIAL AID PICTURE (2011-2012)

Students with need: Out of 3,021 full-time freshmen who applied for aid, 3,021 were judged to have need. Of these, 2,490 received aid, and 20 had their full need met. For part-time students, average financial aid package was $281.

Students without need: This college awards aid only to students with need.

FINANCIAL AID PROCEDURES

Forms required: FAFSA.

Dates and Deadlines: Priority date 7/15; no closing date. Applicants notified on a rolling basis starting 6/1; must reply within 1 week(s) of notification.

Transfers: No deadline.

CONTACT

Pamela Littles, Associate Dean of Student Financial Assistance
70 Sip Avenue, 1st Floor, Jersey City, NJ 07306
(201) 360-4200

Kean University

Union, New Jersey
www.kean.edu Federal Code: 002622

4-year public university and liberal arts college in small city.

Enrollment: 12,543 undergrads, 22% part-time. 1,381 full-time freshmen.

Selectivity: Admits 50 to 75% of applicants.

BASIC COSTS (2012-2013)

Tuition and fees: $10,601; out-of-state residents $16,643.

Per-credit charge: $270; out-of-state residents $457.

Room and board: $13,934.

Additional info: Tuition/fee waivers available for unemployed or children of unemployed.

FINANCIAL AID PICTURE (2012-2013)

Students with need: Out of 1,188 full-time freshmen who applied for aid, 1,020 were judged to have need. Of these, 939 received aid, and 31 had their full need met. Average financial aid package met 79% of need; average scholarship/grant was $7,579; average loan was $3,515. For part-time students, average financial aid package was $6,315.

Students without need: 25 full-time freshmen who did not demonstrate need for aid received scholarships/grants; average award was $3,101. No-need awards available for academics, alumni affiliation, art, leadership, music/drama.

Scholarships offered: Freshman Merit Scholarships; renewable each year with 3.0 GPA. William Livingston Scholarship; full in-state tuition; 3.50 GPA and 1300 SAT or 29 ACT required. Kean Scholarship; $4,000; 3.50 GPA and 1250 SAT or 28 ACT required. Trustee Scholarship; $3,000; 3.00 GPA and 1200 SAT or 26 ACT required. Presidential Scholarship; $2,500; 3.00 GPA and 1150 SAT or 25 ACT required. Academic Merit Scholarship; $2,000; 3.0 GPA and 1100 SAT of 24 ACT required. SAT scores exclusive of writing/essay section.

Cumulative student debt: 71% of graduating class had student loans; average debt was $30,335.

FINANCIAL AID PROCEDURES

Forms required: FAFSA.

Dates and Deadlines: Closing date 4/17. Applicants notified on a rolling basis starting 3/1; must reply by 5/1.

Transfers: No deadline. Applicants notified on a rolling basis; must reply by 5/1.

CONTACT

Sherrell Watson-Hall, Associate Director Financial Aid
1000 Morris Avenue, Union, NJ 07083-0411
(908) 737-3220

Mercer County Community College

Trenton, New Jersey
www.mccc.edu Federal Code: 002641

2-year public community college in small city.

Enrollment: 8,121 undergrads, 58% part-time. 1,304 full-time freshmen.

Selectivity: Open admission.

BASIC COSTS (2012-2013)

Tuition and fees: $4,140; out-of-district residents $5,475; out-of-state residents $8,085.

Per-credit charge: $109; out-of-district residents $154; out-of-state residents $241.

Additional info: Tuition/fee waivers available for unemployed or children of unemployed.

FINANCIAL AID PICTURE

Students with need: Need-based aid available for full-time and part-time students. Work study available nights.

Students without need: No-need awards available for academics, athletics, state/district residency.

Scholarships offered: MCCC Foundation Scholarship; $2,500; top 25% of high school class; 15 total awards. NJ STARS program; for top 20% of high school class.

FINANCIAL AID PROCEDURES

Forms required: FAFSA.

Dates and Deadlines: Closing date 5/1. Applicants notified on a rolling basis.

CONTACT
Jason Taylor, Director of Financial Aid
Box B, Trenton, NJ 08690-1099
(609) 570-3210

Middlesex County College
Edison, New Jersey
www.middlesexcc.edu Federal Code: 002615

2-year public community college in small city.
Enrollment: 12,597 undergrads.
Selectivity: Open admission; but selective for some programs.

BASIC COSTS (2012-2013)
Tuition and fees: $4,095; out-of-state residents $7,155.
Per-credit charge: $102; out-of-state residents $204.
Additional info: Out-of-county and out-of-state students pay additional $1,035 in required fees, based on 30 credit hours.

FINANCIAL AID PICTURE
Students with need: Need-based aid available for full-time and part-time students.

FINANCIAL AID PROCEDURES
Forms required: FAFSA, institutional form.
Dates and Deadlines: Priority date 4/1; no closing date. Applicants notified on a rolling basis starting 5/4.

CONTACT
2600 Woodbridge Avenue, Edison, NJ 08818-3050
(732) 906-2520 ext. 4157

Monmouth University
West Long Branch, New Jersey
www.monmouth.edu Federal Code: 002616

4-year private university in small town.
Enrollment: 4,697 undergrads, 6% part-time. 1,006 full-time freshmen.
Selectivity: Admits 50 to 75% of applicants.

BASIC COSTS (2012-2013)
Tuition and fees: $29,711.
Per-credit charge: $842.
Room and board: $10,802.

FINANCIAL AID PICTURE (2012-2013)
Students with need: Out of 894 full-time freshmen who applied for aid, 728 were judged to have need. Of these, 728 received aid, and 131 had their full need met. Average financial aid package met 68% of need; average scholarship/grant was $12,995; average loan was $3,713. For part-time students, average financial aid package was $7,036.
Students without need: 271 full-time freshmen who did not demonstrate need for aid received scholarships/grants; average award was $8,704. No-need awards available for academics, alumni affiliation, art, athletics, leadership.
Scholarships offered: ***Merit:*** Academic Excellence Awards; $3,000-$16,000; based on SAT scores and high school GPA; renewable annually as long as required GPA is maintained. ***Athletic:*** 94 full-time freshmen received athletic scholarships; average amount $18,960.
Cumulative student debt: 73% of graduating class had student loans; average debt was $34,361.

FINANCIAL AID PROCEDURES
Forms required: FAFSA.
Dates and Deadlines: Priority date 2/15; no closing date. Applicants notified on a rolling basis starting 3/1; must reply within 2 week(s) of notification.
Transfers: No deadline. Applicants notified on a rolling basis; must reply within 2 week(s) of notification.

CONTACT
Claire Alasio, Associate Vice President for Enrollment Management
400 Cedar Avenue, West Long Branch, NJ 07764-1898
(732) 571-3463

Montclair State University
Montclair, New Jersey
www.montclair.edu Federal Code: 002617

4-year public university in large town.
Enrollment: 14,222 undergrads, 14% part-time. 2,200 full-time freshmen.
Selectivity: Admits 50 to 75% of applicants.

BASIC COSTS (2012-2013)
Tuition and fees: $11,058; out-of-state residents $20,136.
Per-credit charge: $266; out-of-state residents $569.
Room and board: $11,556.
Additional info: Tuition/fee waivers available for unemployed or children of unemployed.

FINANCIAL AID PICTURE
Students with need: Need-based aid available for full-time and part-time students. Work study available nights, weekends, and for part-time students.
Students without need: No-need awards available for academics, alumni affiliation, art, leadership, minority status, music/drama, ROTC, state/district residency.

FINANCIAL AID PROCEDURES
Forms required: FAFSA.
Dates and Deadlines: Priority date 3/1; no closing date. Applicants notified on a rolling basis starting 4/1; must reply within 2 week(s) of notification.
Transfers: Students will be eligible for financial aid beginning fall semester of the academic year for which they are admitted.

CONTACT
James Anderson, Director of Financial Aid
One Normal Avenue, Montclair, NJ 07042
(973) 655-4461

New Jersey City University
Jersey City, New Jersey
www.njcu.edu Federal Code: 002613

4-year public university in small city.
Enrollment: 6,550 undergrads, 26% part-time. 672 full-time freshmen.
Selectivity: Admits less than 50% of applicants.

BASIC COSTS (2012-2013)
Tuition and fees: $10,422; out-of-state residents $18,609.
Per-credit charge: $245; out-of-state residents $518.
Room and board: $10,128.

FINANCIAL AID PICTURE (2011-2012)
Students with need: Out of 634 full-time freshmen who applied for aid, 596 were judged to have need. Of these, 577 received aid, and 37 had their full need met. Average financial aid package met 59% of need; average scholarship/grant was $8,702; average loan was $9,654. For part-time students, average financial aid package was $16,797.
Students without need: 12 full-time freshmen who did not demonstrate need for aid received scholarships/grants; average award was $4,995.
Cumulative student debt: 65% of graduating class had student loans; average debt was $19,233.

FINANCIAL AID PROCEDURES
Forms required: FAFSA.
Dates and Deadlines: Priority date 4/15; no closing date.

CONTACT
Carmen Panlilio, Vice President for Admissions and Financial Aid
2039 Kennedy Boulevard, Jersey City, NJ 07305-1597
(201) 200-3173

New Jersey Institute of Technology
Newark, New Jersey
www.njit.edu Federal Code: 002621

4-year public university in large city.
Enrollment: 6,154 undergrads, 12% part-time. 939 full-time freshmen.
Selectivity: Admits 50 to 75% of applicants.

BASIC COSTS (2012-2013)
Tuition and fees: $14,740; out-of-state residents $27,140.
Per-credit charge: $472; out-of-state residents $1,060.
Room and board: $11,542.

FINANCIAL AID PICTURE
Students with need: Need-based aid available for full-time and part-time students. Work study available nights, weekends, and for part-time students.
Students without need: No-need awards available for academics, alumni affiliation, athletics, leadership, minority status, music/drama, religious affiliation, ROTC, state/district residency.
Additional info: Extensive co-op program for all majors.

FINANCIAL AID PROCEDURES
Forms required: FAFSA.
Dates and Deadlines: Priority date 3/15; no closing date. Applicants notified on a rolling basis starting 1/1; must reply by 5/1.
Transfers: No deadline. Applicants notified on a rolling basis starting 1/1; must reply within 2 week(s) of notification.

CONTACT
Ivon Nunez, Director of Financial Aid
University Heights, Newark, NJ 07102
(973) 596-3479

Ocean County College
Toms River, New Jersey
www.ocean.edu Federal Code: 002624

2-year public community college in small city.
Enrollment: 8,573 undergrads, 40% part-time. 1,826 full-time freshmen.
Selectivity: Open admission; but selective for some programs.

BASIC COSTS (2013-2014)
Tuition and fees: $3,900; out-of-district residents $4,860; out-of-state residents $7,410.
Per-credit charge: $98; out-of-district residents $130; out-of-state residents $215.
Additional info: Tuition/fee waivers available for unemployed or children of unemployed.

FINANCIAL AID PICTURE (2011-2012)
Students with need: 57% of average financial aid package awarded as scholarships/grants, 43% awarded as loans/jobs. Need-based aid available for part-time students. Work study available nights, weekends, and for part-time students.
Students without need: No-need awards available for academics, state/district residency.

FINANCIAL AID PROCEDURES
Forms required: FAFSA.
Dates and Deadlines: Priority date 5/31; no closing date. Applicants notified on a rolling basis starting 7/15; must reply within 1 week(s) of notification.

CONTACT
Norma Betz, Executive Director of Admissions and Financial Aid
College Drive, Toms River, NJ 08754-2001
(732) 255-0400 ext. 2020

Passaic County Community College
Paterson, New Jersey
www.pccc.edu Federal Code: 009994

2-year public community college in small city.
Enrollment: 9,382 undergrads, 63% part-time. 867 full-time freshmen.
Selectivity: Open admission; but selective for some programs.

BASIC COSTS (2012-2013)
Tuition and fees: $4,034; out-of-state residents $7,109.
Per-credit charge: $103; out-of-state residents $205.
Additional info: Tuition/fee waivers available for unemployed or children of unemployed.

FINANCIAL AID PICTURE
Students with need: Need-based aid available for full-time and part-time students.
Students without need: No-need awards available for academics.
Additional info: Limited scholarship funds available for low income students eligible for federal or state aid.

FINANCIAL AID PROCEDURES
Forms required: FAFSA.
Dates and Deadlines: Priority date 8/1; no closing date. Applicants notified on a rolling basis starting 8/1; must reply within 2 week(s) of notification.
Transfers: Priority date 5/15; closing date 6/30.

CONTACT
Linda Gayton, Director of Financial Aid
1 College Boulevard, Paterson, NJ 07505-1179
(973) 684-6100

Princeton University
Princeton, New Jersey
www.princeton.edu Federal Code: 002627

4-year private university in large town.
Enrollment: 5,255 undergrads. 1,357 full-time freshmen.
Selectivity: Admits less than 50% of applicants.

BASIC COSTS (2012-2013)
Tuition and fees: $38,650.
Room and board: $12,630.

FINANCIAL AID PICTURE
Students with need: Need-based aid available for full-time students.
Students without need: This college awards aid only to students with need.
Additional info: All aid need-based; all aid grant money (no loans); institution meets full demonstrated need.

FINANCIAL AID PROCEDURES
Forms required: FAFSA, institutional form.
Dates and Deadlines: Priority date 2/1; no closing date. Must reply by 5/1.

CONTACT
Robin Moscato, Director of Financial Aid
Box 430, Princeton, NJ 08542-0430
(609) 258-3330

Ramapo College of New Jersey

Mahwah, New Jersey
www.ramapo.edu Federal Code: 009344

4-year public liberal arts college in large town.
Enrollment: 5,390 undergrads, 7% part-time. 893 full-time freshmen.
Selectivity: Admits less than 50% of applicants.

BASIC COSTS (2012-2013)
Tuition and fees: $13,144; out-of-state residents $21,624.
Per-credit charge: $265; out-of-state residents $530.
Room and board: $11,370.
Additional info: Tuition/fee waivers available for unemployed or children of unemployed.

FINANCIAL AID PICTURE (2011-2012)
Students with need: Out of 753 full-time freshmen who applied for aid, 548 were judged to have need. Of these, 513 received aid, and 89 had their full need met. Average financial aid package met 71% of need; average scholarship/grant was $14,465; average loan was $3,303. For part-time students, average financial aid package was $3,978.
Students without need: 98 full-time freshmen who did not demonstrate need for aid received scholarships/grants; average award was $10,419. No-need awards available for academics, state/district residency.
Cumulative student debt: 67% of graduating class had student loans; average debt was $30,053.

FINANCIAL AID PROCEDURES
Forms required: FAFSA.
Dates and Deadlines: Priority date 3/1; no closing date. Applicants notified on a rolling basis starting 4/1; must reply by 5/1 or within 2 week(s) of notification.
Transfers: No deadline. Applicants notified on a rolling basis.

CONTACT
Mark Singer, Director of Financial Aid
505 Ramapo Valley Road, Mahwah, NJ 07430-1680
(201) 684-7549

Raritan Valley Community College

Branchburg, New Jersey
www.raritanval.edu Federal Code: 007731

2-year public community college in large town.
Enrollment: 7,219 undergrads, 50% part-time. 1,194 full-time freshmen.
Selectivity: Open admission; but selective for some programs.

BASIC COSTS (2012-2013)
Tuition and fees: $4,170; out-of-state residents $4,470.
Per-credit charge: $117; out-of-state residents $127.
Additional info: Tuition/fee waivers available for unemployed or children of unemployed.

FINANCIAL AID PICTURE
Students with need: Need-based aid available for full-time and part-time students.
Students without need: No-need awards available for academics.

FINANCIAL AID PROCEDURES
Forms required: FAFSA.
Dates and Deadlines: Applicants notified on a rolling basis starting 4/1.

CONTACT
Leonard Mesonas, Director of Financial Aid
118 Lamington Road, Branchburg, NJ 08876-1265
(908) 526-1200 ext. 8273

Richard Stockton College of New Jersey

Galloway, New Jersey
www.stockton.edu Federal Code: 009345

4-year public liberal arts college in large town.
Enrollment: 7,340 undergrads, 7% part-time. 1,001 full-time freshmen.
Selectivity: Admits 50 to 75% of applicants.

BASIC COSTS (2012-2013)
Tuition and fees: $12,322; out-of-state residents $18,715.
Per-credit charge: $306; out-of-state residents $552.
Room and board: $10,796.
Additional info: Tuition/fee waivers available for unemployed or children of unemployed.

FINANCIAL AID PICTURE (2012-2013)
Students with need: Out of 932 full-time freshmen who applied for aid, 766 were judged to have need. Of these, 738 received aid, and 214 had their full need met. Average financial aid package met 67% of need; average scholarship/grant was $8,939; average loan was $3,436. For part-time students, average financial aid package was $10,333.
Students without need: 64 full-time freshmen who did not demonstrate need for aid received scholarships/grants; average award was $6,567. No-need awards available for academics, art, leadership, minority status, music/drama, state/district residency.
Scholarships offered: Freshman Scholarship Program; $2,000-$18,000; based on class rank in top 15%, SAT scores (exclusive of Writing).
Cumulative student debt: 74% of graduating class had student loans; average debt was $34,287.
Additional info: Institutional grants are provided to the neediest incoming students.

FINANCIAL AID PROCEDURES
Forms required: FAFSA, state aid form.
Dates and Deadlines: Priority date 3/1; no closing date. Applicants notified on a rolling basis starting 4/1; must reply within 2 week(s) of notification.
Transfers: Applicants notified on a rolling basis starting 4/1; must reply within 2 week(s) of notification.

CONTACT
Jeanne Lewis, Director of Financial Aid
101 Vera King Farris Drive, Galloway, NJ 08205
(609) 652-4201

Rider University

Lawrenceville, New Jersey
www.rider.edu Federal Code: 002628

4-year private university in small town.
Enrollment: 4,409 undergrads, 11% part-time. 919 full-time freshmen.
Selectivity: Admits 50 to 75% of applicants.

BASIC COSTS (2012-2013)
Tuition and fees: $33,420.
Per-credit charge: $950.
Room and board: $12,340.

FINANCIAL AID PICTURE
Students with need: Need-based aid available for full-time and part-time students. Work study available nights, weekends, and for part-time students.
Students without need: No-need awards available for academics, alumni affiliation, athletics, leadership, minority status, music/drama.

FINANCIAL AID PROCEDURES
Forms required: FAFSA.
Dates and Deadlines: Priority date 3/1; no closing date. Applicants notified on a rolling basis starting 2/20.
Transfers: No deadline.

CONTACT

Dennis Levy, Director of Student Financial Services
2083 Lawrenceville Road, Lawrenceville, NJ 08648-3099
(609) 896-5360

Rowan University

Glassboro, New Jersey
www.rowan.edu Federal Code: 002609

4-year public university in large town.
Enrollment: 10,499 undergrads, 12% part-time. 1,574 full-time freshmen.
Selectivity: Admits 50 to 75% of applicants.

BASIC COSTS (2012-2013)

Tuition and fees: $12,380; out-of-state residents $20,186.
Per-credit charge: $342; out-of-state residents $644.
Room and board: $10,712.

FINANCIAL AID PICTURE (2011-2012)

Students with need: Out of 1,424 full-time freshmen who applied for aid, 1,047 were judged to have need. Of these, 963 received aid, and 107 had their full need met. Average financial aid package met 87% of need; average scholarship/grant was $9,814; average loan was $3,276. For part-time students, average financial aid package was $5,443.
Students without need: 174 full-time freshmen who did not demonstrate need for aid received scholarships/grants; average award was $5,475. No-need awards available for academics, art, music/drama.
Cumulative student debt: 74% of graduating class had student loans; average debt was $35,027.

FINANCIAL AID PROCEDURES

Forms required: FAFSA.
Dates and Deadlines: Priority date 3/16; no closing date. Applicants notified on a rolling basis starting 3/16.
Transfers: No deadline. Applicants notified on a rolling basis starting 3/1; must reply within 3 week(s) of notification.

CONTACT

Luis Taverez, Director of Financial Aid
Savitz Hall, 201 Mullica Hill Road, Glassboro, NJ 08028
(856) 256-4250

Rutgers, The State University of New Jersey: New Brunswick/Piscataway Campus

Piscataway, New Jersey
www.rutgers.edu Federal Code: 002629

4-year public university in large town.
Enrollment: 31,226 undergrads, 4% part-time. 6,166 full-time freshmen.
Selectivity: Admits 50 to 75% of applicants.

BASIC COSTS (2012-2013)

Tuition and fees: $13,073; out-of-state residents $26,393.
Per-credit charge: $333; out-of-state residents $768.
Room and board: $11,412.
Additional info: Tuition/fee waivers available for unemployed or children of unemployed.

FINANCIAL AID PICTURE

Students with need: Need-based aid available for full-time and part-time students.
Students without need: No-need awards available for academics, alumni affiliation, art, athletics, leadership, minority status, music/drama, state/district residency.
Scholarships offered: Outstanding Scholarship Recruitment Program; $2,500-$7,500; for selected in-state resident applicants based on SAT scores and class rank; 2,500 awarded. Carr Scholarship; $10,000; for selected minority applicants; 150 awarded. Class of 1941 Scholarship; $1,941; descendent of Class of 1941 alumni preferred; 1 awarded. National Merit Scholarship; $1,000-$2,000; for National Merit finalists; 15 or more awarded. National Achievement Scholarship; $1,000-$2,000; for National Achievement finalists; 2 awarded. Rockland County-Herman T. Hopper Scholarship; out-of-state tuition; for Rockland County, New York resident; 1 awarded. Rutgers University Academic Achievement Award; $1,000; 20 awarded; for in- and out-of-state minority students. Rutgers University Alumni Federation Scholarship; $1,000; for children of Rutgers University alumni; 20 awarded. Rutgers University National Scholarship; $5,000; for out-of-state students; about 100 awards university-wide.

FINANCIAL AID PROCEDURES

Forms required: FAFSA.
Dates and Deadlines: Priority date 3/15; no closing date. Applicants notified on a rolling basis starting 3/1; must reply within 2 week(s) of notification.

CONTACT

Jean McDonald-Rash, University Director of Financial Aid
65 Davidson Road, Room 202, Piscataway, NJ 08854-8097
(848) 932-7057

Rutgers, The State University of New Jersey: Newark Campus

Newark, New Jersey
www.newark.rutgers.edu Federal Code: 002629

4-year public university in large city.
Enrollment: 7,241 undergrads, 14% part-time. 1,051 full-time freshmen.
Selectivity: Admits 50 to 75% of applicants.

BASIC COSTS (2012-2013)

Tuition and fees: $12,590; out-of-state residents $25,910.
Per-credit charge: $333; out-of-state residents $768.
Room and board: $12,285.
Additional info: Tuition/fee waivers available for unemployed or children of unemployed.

FINANCIAL AID PICTURE

Students with need: Need-based aid available for full-time and part-time students.
Students without need: No-need awards available for academics, alumni affiliation, art, athletics, leadership, minority status, music/drama, religious affiliation.
Scholarships offered: Outstanding Scholarship Recruitment Program: $2,500-$7,500; for selected in-state resident applicants; based on SAT scores and class rank; 2,500 awarded. Carr Scholarship: $10,000; for selected minority applicants; 150 awarded. Class of 1941 Scholarship: $1,941; descendent of Class of 1941 alumni preferred; 1 awarded. National Merit Scholarship: $1,000-$2,000; for National Merit finalists; 15 or more awarded. National Achievement Scholarship: $1,000-$2,000; for National Achievement finalists; 2 awarded. Rockland County-Herman T. Hopper Scholarship: out-of-state tuition; for Rockland County, New York resident; 1 awarded. Rutgers University Academic Achievement Award: $1,000; for in- and out-of-state minority students; 20 awarded. Rutgers University Alumni Federation Scholarship: $1,000; for children of Rutgers University alumni; 20 awarded. James Bryan Scholarship; $400; for selected in-state freshmen; 3 awarded. Rutgers University National Scholarship: $5,000; for out-of-state students; about 100 awards university-wide.

FINANCIAL AID PROCEDURES

Forms required: FAFSA.
Dates and Deadlines: Priority date 3/15; no closing date. Applicants notified on a rolling basis starting 3/1; must reply within 2 week(s) of notification.

CONTACT
Melvin Brown, Manager, Financial Aid
249 University Avenue, Newark, NJ 07102-1896
(973) 353-5151

Saint Peter's University

Jersey City, New Jersey
www.spc.edu Federal Code: 002638

4-year private liberal arts college in small city, affiliated with Roman Catholic Church.
Enrollment: 2,199 undergrads, 14% part-time. 388 full-time freshmen.
Selectivity: Admits 50 to 75% of applicants.

BASIC COSTS (2012-2013)
Tuition and fees: $31,510.
Per-credit charge: $990.
Room and board: $13,020.

FINANCIAL AID PICTURE
Students with need: Need-based aid available for full-time students.
Students without need: No-need awards available for academics, athletics.
Scholarships offered: Academic Awards: full tuition; based on 1100 SAT (exclusive of Writing), 3.0 GPA, and top 20% of class; 50 awarded. Incentive Awards: $500-$4,000; for selected applicants with some qualities necessary for academic awards but who are otherwise ineligible. Residential Grants: $500-$2,500 toward housing; based on academics and extracurricular activities.
Additional info: Cooperative education internships available in all majors, with average salaries exceeding $5,200.

FINANCIAL AID PROCEDURES
Forms required: FAFSA.
Dates and Deadlines: Priority date 3/15; no closing date. Applicants notified on a rolling basis starting 2/15; must reply by 5/1 or within 2 week(s) of notification.
Transfers: Student and parents (if dependent students) must be New Jersey residents for at least 1 year prior to start date. Students must complete renewal application before June 1.

CONTACT
Jennifer Ragsdale, Director of Financial Aid
2641 Kennedy Boulevard, Jersey City, NJ 07306
(201) 761-6060

Salem Community College

Carneys Point, New Jersey
www.salemcc.edu Federal Code: 005461

2-year public community and junior college in small town.
Enrollment: 1,123 undergrads, 39% part-time. 204 full-time freshmen.
Selectivity: Open admission; but selective for some programs.

BASIC COSTS (2012-2013)
Tuition and fees: $4,104; out-of-state residents $4,794.
Per-credit charge: $102; out-of-state residents $125.
Additional info: Tuition/fee waivers available for unemployed or children of unemployed.

FINANCIAL AID PICTURE (2011-2012)
Students with need: Need-based aid available for full-time and part-time students.
Students without need: No-need awards available for academics, athletics, state/district residency.

FINANCIAL AID PROCEDURES
Forms required: FAFSA, institutional form.
Dates and Deadlines: Priority date 6/1; no closing date. Applicants notified on a rolling basis starting 4/1; must reply within 2 week(s) of notification.

CONTACT
Maurice Thomas, Director of Financial Aid
460 Hollywood Avenue, Carneys Point, NJ 08069-2799
(856) 351-2699

Seton Hall University

South Orange, New Jersey
www.shu.edu Federal Code: 002632

4-year private university in large town, affiliated with Roman Catholic Church.
Enrollment: 5,295 undergrads, 5% part-time. 1,455 full-time freshmen.
Selectivity: Admits over 75% of applicants.

BASIC COSTS (2012-2013)
Tuition and fees: $34,950.
Per-credit charge: $1,033.
Room and board: $12,952.
Additional info: Required fees include lease of laptop computer.

FINANCIAL AID PICTURE
Students with need: Need-based aid available for full-time and part-time students. Work study available nights, weekends, and for part-time students.
Students without need: No-need awards available for academics, alumni affiliation, athletics, leadership, music/drama, ROTC.

FINANCIAL AID PROCEDURES
Forms required: FAFSA.

CONTACT
Javonda Asante, Director of Financial Aid
400 South Orange Avenue, South Orange, NJ 07079-2680
(973) 761-9350

Somerset Christian College

Zarephath, New Jersey
www.somerset.edu Federal Code: 036663

4-year private Bible and liberal arts college in small town, affiliated with Pillar of Fire International.
Enrollment: 350 undergrads.

BASIC COSTS (2012-2013)
Tuition and fees: $16,162.
Per-credit charge: $663.

FINANCIAL AID PICTURE
Students with need: Need-based aid available for full-time and part-time students. Work study available nights.
Students without need: This college awards aid only to students with need.

FINANCIAL AID PROCEDURES
Forms required: FAFSA, state aid form.
Dates and Deadlines: Applicants notified on a rolling basis starting 1/31.

CONTACT
Marsha Griffin, Financial Aid Administrator
10 College Way, Zarephath, NJ 08890
(800) 234-9305 ext. 1101

Stevens Institute of Technology

Hoboken, New Jersey
www.stevens.edu Federal Code: 002639

4-year private university and engineering college in small city.
Enrollment: 2,548 undergrads.
Selectivity: Admits less than 50% of applicants. GED not accepted.

BASIC COSTS (2012-2013)

Tuition and fees: $43,656.
Per-credit charge: $1,390.
Room and board: $13,400.

FINANCIAL AID PICTURE

Students with need: Need-based aid available for full-time and part-time students. Work study available nights, weekends, and for part-time students.
Students without need: No-need awards available for academics, leadership, music/drama, ROTC.
Scholarships offered: Neupauer Scholarship; full tuition; for top candidates in freshman class. Edwin A. Stevens Scholarship; $3,000-$20,000; for top candidates in freshman class. Becton Dickinson Scholarship; full tuition; for top student pursuing engineering degree. DeBaun Performing Arts Scholarship; $1,000-$5,000.

FINANCIAL AID PROCEDURES

Forms required: FAFSA.
Dates and Deadlines: Priority date 2/15; no closing date. Applicants notified on a rolling basis starting 3/30; must reply by 5/1 or within 2 week(s) of notification.
Transfers: Transfer merit scholarships, Phi Theta Kappa awards.

CONTACT

Randy Greene, CFO Vice President for Finance and Treasurer
1 Castle Point on Hudson, Hoboken, NJ 07030-5991
(201) 216-5555

Sussex County Community College

Newton, New Jersey
www.sussex.edu Federal Code: 025688

2-year public community college in small town.
Enrollment: 3,404 undergrads.
Selectivity: Open admission; but selective for some programs.

BASIC COSTS (2012-2013)

Tuition and fees: $5,010; out-of-district residents $8,820; out-of-state residents $8,820.
Per-credit charge: $127; out-of-district residents $254; out-of-state residents $254.
Additional info: Residents of Wayne, Monroe and Pike County (PA): $190 per credit hour. Tuition/fee waivers available for unemployed or children of unemployed.

FINANCIAL AID PICTURE

Students with need: Need-based aid available for full-time and part-time students.
Students without need: This college awards aid only to students with need.

FINANCIAL AID PROCEDURES

Forms required: FAFSA, institutional form.
Dates and Deadlines: Closing date 6/1. Applicants notified on a rolling basis; must reply within 2 week(s) of notification.

CONTACT

Michael Corso, Director, Financial Aid
One College Hill Road, Newton, NJ 07860
(973) 300-2225

Thomas Edison State College

Trenton, New Jersey
www.tesc.edu Federal Code: 011648

4-year public liberal arts college in small city.
Enrollment: 19,404 undergrads, 100% part-time.
Selectivity: Open admission; but selective for some programs.

BASIC COSTS (2012-2013)

Tuition and fees: $5,508; out-of-state residents $8,111.

FINANCIAL AID PICTURE (2011-2012)

Students with need: 20% of average financial aid package awarded as scholarships/grants, 80% awarded as loans/jobs.
Students without need: This college awards aid only to students with need.
Additional info: Financial aid applications should be received two months before each new term begins.

FINANCIAL AID PROCEDURES

Forms required: FAFSA, institutional form.
Dates and Deadlines: Applicants notified on a rolling basis starting 3/1.
Transfers: No deadline. Applicants notified on a rolling basis; must reply within 4 week(s) of notification.

CONTACT

James Owens, Director of Financial Aid
101 West State Street, Trenton, NJ 08608-1176
(609) 633-9658

Union County College

Cranford, New Jersey
www.ucc.edu Federal Code: 002643

2-year public community college in large town.
Enrollment: 11,254 undergrads, 50% part-time. 892 full-time freshmen.
Selectivity: Open admission; but selective for some programs.

BASIC COSTS (2012-2013)

Tuition and fees: $4,508; out-of-state residents $7,868.
Per-credit charge: $112; out-of-state residents $224.
Additional info: Tuition/fee waivers available for unemployed or children of unemployed.

FINANCIAL AID PICTURE (2012-2013)

Students with need: Need-based aid available for full-time and part-time students. Work study available nights, weekends, and for part-time students.
Students without need: This college awards aid only to students with need.

FINANCIAL AID PROCEDURES

Forms required: FAFSA, institutional form.
Dates and Deadlines: Priority date 5/1; no closing date. Must reply within 2 week(s) of notification.

CONTACT

Rebecca Royal, Director of Financial Aid
1033 Springfield Avenue, Cranford, NJ 07016-1599
(908) 709-7018

University of Medicine and Dentistry of New Jersey: School of Health Related Professions

Newark, New Jersey
www.shrp.umdnj.edu

Upper-division public health science college in large city.
Enrollment: 657 undergrads.

BASIC COSTS (2012-2013)
Tuition and fees: $10,520; out-of-state residents $11,120.
Per-credit charge: $329; out-of-state residents $347.
Additional info: Costs may vary by program.

FINANCIAL AID PICTURE
Students with need: Need-based aid available for full-time and part-time students.

FINANCIAL AID PROCEDURES
Forms required: FAFSA, institutional form.

CONTACT
Cheryl White, Senior Financial Aid Analyst
65 Bergen Street, Newark, NJ 07101-1709
(973) 972-4376

University of Medicine and Dentistry of New Jersey: School of Nursing

Newark, New Jersey
www.sn.umdnj.edu

4-year public nursing college in large city.
Enrollment: 360 undergrads.

BASIC COSTS (2012-2013)
Additional info: Cost of accelerated BSN (bachelor of science in nursing) program, which is usually completed in 15 months and always by students who already have a bachelor's degree at time of entering BSN program: $29,815 (in-state), $39,549 (out-of-state). Students may also choose part-time study, which lasts for 30 months and costs the same as the 15-month (full-time) plan.

FINANCIAL AID PICTURE
Students with need: Need-based aid available for full-time and part-time students.

FINANCIAL AID PROCEDURES
Dates and Deadlines: Priority date 3/1; no closing date. Applicants notified on a rolling basis.

CONTACT
Elaine Varas, University Director of Financial Aid
65 Bergen Street, Room 149, Newark, NJ 07101-1709
(973) 972-4376

Warren County Community College

Washington, New Jersey
www.warren.edu Federal Code: 016857

2-year public community college in small town.
Enrollment: 2,266 undergrads, 59% part-time.
Selectivity: Open admission; but selective for some programs.

BASIC COSTS (2012-2013)
Tuition and fees: $3,991; out-of-district residents $4,291; out-of-state residents $4,891.
Per-credit charge: $109; out-of-district residents $119; out-of-state residents $139.
Additional info: Tuition/fee waivers available for unemployed or children of unemployed.

FINANCIAL AID PICTURE
Students with need: Need-based aid available for full-time and part-time students. Work study available nights, weekends, and for part-time students.
Students without need: This college awards aid only to students with need.

FINANCIAL AID PROCEDURES
Forms required: FAFSA, institutional form.
Dates and Deadlines: Closing date 7/1. Applicants notified on a rolling basis; must reply within 2 week(s) of notification.
Transfers: No deadline. Applicants notified on a rolling basis.

CONTACT
Jessica Leeper, Director of Financial Aid
Route 57 West, Washington, NJ 07882-4343
(908) 835-2309

William Paterson University of New Jersey

Wayne, New Jersey
www.wpunj.edu Federal Code: 002625

4-year public university and liberal arts college in large town.
Enrollment: 9,915 undergrads, 16% part-time. 1,232 full-time freshmen.
Selectivity: Admits 50 to 75% of applicants.

BASIC COSTS (2012-2013)
Tuition and fees: $11,694; out-of-state residents $19,094.
Room and board: $10,540.
Additional info: Tuition/fee waivers available for unemployed or children of unemployed.

FINANCIAL AID PICTURE (2012-2013)
Students with need: Out of 1,134 full-time freshmen who applied for aid, 914 were judged to have need. Of these, 892 received aid, and 359 had their full need met. For part-time students, average financial aid package was $6,045.
Students without need: 92 full-time freshmen who did not demonstrate need for aid received scholarships/grants; average award was $6,363. No-need awards available for academics, alumni affiliation, music/drama.
Scholarships offered: Trustee Scholarships; $2,000-$8,000; for full time freshmen. Honors College Scholarship; $2,000; for full time freshmen enrolled in program. Talent Awards for Music and Art Students; up to $9,000; based on audition.
Cumulative student debt: 75% of graduating class had student loans; average debt was $29,906.

FINANCIAL AID PROCEDURES
Forms required: FAFSA.
Dates and Deadlines: Priority date 4/1; no closing date. Applicants notified on a rolling basis starting 4/1.
Transfers: Must reply within 2 week(s) of notification.

CONTACT
Stella James, Associate Director of Financial Aid
300 Pompton Road, Wayne, NJ 07470
(973) 720-2202

New Mexico

Brookline College: Albuquerque

Albuquerque, New Mexico
www.brooklinecollege.edu Federal Code: 022188

2-year for-profit branch campus and career college in large city.
Enrollment: 707 undergrads.
Selectivity: Open admission.

BASIC COSTS (2012-2013)

Additional info: As of April 2012, estimated annual tuition and fees for associate degree programs in accounting, business, criminal justice, paralegal studies: $13,500. Tuition for Bachelor of Science - Criminal Justice is $14,445.

FINANCIAL AID PICTURE

Students with need: Need-based aid available for full-time students.

Students without need: This college awards aid only to students with need.

FINANCIAL AID PROCEDURES

Forms required: FAFSA, institutional form.

CONTACT

Genna Gillary, Corporate Manager of Financial Aid
4201 Central Avenue NW, Suite J, Albuquerque, NM 87105-1649
(505) 880-2877

Central New Mexico Community College

Albuquerque, New Mexico
www.cnm.edu Federal Code: 004742

2-year public community and technical college in very large city.
Enrollment: 26,712 undergrads, 65% part-time. 2,301 full-time freshmen.
Selectivity: Open admission.

BASIC COSTS (2012-2013)

Tuition and fees: $1,244; out-of-state residents $6,398.

Per-credit charge: $48; out-of-state residents $263.

Additional info: Cost provided is for academic transfer courses. Career technical courses available at much lower rate.

FINANCIAL AID PICTURE (2011-2012)

Students with need: 63% of average financial aid package awarded as scholarships/grants, 37% awarded as loans/jobs. Need-based aid available for part-time students.

Students without need: No-need awards available for academics, state/district residency.

FINANCIAL AID PROCEDURES

Forms required: FAFSA.

Dates and Deadlines: Priority date 5/1; no closing date. Applicants notified on a rolling basis starting 5/1.

CONTACT

Lee Carrillo, Director of Financial Aid
525 Buena Vista Drive, SE, Albuquerque, NM 87106
(505) 224-3090

Clovis Community College

Clovis, New Mexico
www.clovis.edu Federal Code: 004743

2-year public community and junior college in large town.
Enrollment: 2,062 undergrads, 57% part-time. 228 full-time freshmen.
Selectivity: Open admission; but selective for some programs.

BASIC COSTS (2013-2014)

Tuition and fees: $1,176; out-of-district residents $1,248; out-of-state residents $2,376.

Per-credit charge: $39; out-of-district residents $42; out-of-state residents $89.

FINANCIAL AID PICTURE

Students with need: Need-based aid available for full-time and part-time students. Work study available nights, weekends, and for part-time students.

Students without need: No-need awards available for academics, state/district residency.

Additional info: Endowment of over $1,000,000 to assist nursing students.

FINANCIAL AID PROCEDURES

Forms required: FAFSA.

Dates and Deadlines: Priority date 9/1; no closing date. Applicants notified on a rolling basis starting 4/15.

Transfers: No deadline. Applicants notified on a rolling basis.

CONTACT

April Chavez, Director of Financial Aid
417 Schepps Boulevard, Clovis, NM 88101-8381
(575) 769-4060

Dona Ana Community College of New Mexico State University

Las Cruces, New Mexico
www.dacc.nmsu.edu Federal Code: 002657

2-year public branch campus and community college in small city.
Enrollment: 9,270 undergrads.
Selectivity: Open admission; but selective for some programs.

BASIC COSTS (2012-2013)

Tuition and fees: $1,536; out-of-district residents $1,848; out-of-state residents $4,872.

Per-credit charge: $64; out-of-district residents $77; out-of-state residents $203.

Room and board: $7,182.

FINANCIAL AID PICTURE

Students with need: Need-based aid available for full-time and part-time students.

FINANCIAL AID PROCEDURES

Forms required: FAFSA.

Dates and Deadlines: Priority date 3/1; no closing date. Applicants notified on a rolling basis starting 5/1.

CONTACT

Gladys Chairez, Financial Aid Director
MSC-3DA, Las Cruces, NM 88003-8001
(505) 527-7510

Eastern New Mexico University

Portales, New Mexico
www.enmu.edu Federal Code: 002651

4-year public university in large town.
Enrollment: 3,918 undergrads, 28% part-time. 702 full-time freshmen.
Selectivity: Admits 50 to 75% of applicants.

BASIC COSTS (2012-2013)

Tuition and fees: $4,350; out-of-state residents $9,861.

Per-credit charge: $122; out-of-state residents $351.

Room and board: $6,090.

Additional info: Tuition at time of enrollment locked for 4 years.

FINANCIAL AID PICTURE (2012-2013)

Students with need: Out of 434 full-time freshmen who applied for aid, 433 were judged to have need. Of these, 433 received aid, and 433 had their full need met. Average financial aid package met 42% of need; average scholarship/grant was $4,736; average loan was $3,382. For part-time students, average financial aid package was $10,170.

Students without need: 126 full-time freshmen who did not demonstrate need for aid received scholarships/grants; average award was $3,539. No-need awards available for academics, alumni affiliation, art, athletics, leadership, music/drama, state/district residency.
Scholarships offered: ***Merit:*** Admissions scholarships are available based on SAT or ACT scores. ***Athletic:*** 78 full-time freshmen received athletic scholarships; average amount $2,905.
Cumulative student debt: 94% of graduating class had student loans; average debt was $14,821.

FINANCIAL AID PROCEDURES
Forms required: FAFSA.
Dates and Deadlines: Applicants notified on a rolling basis starting 5/1.
Transfers: No deadline. Applicants notified on a rolling basis starting 4/1; must reply by 8/31. Child care grants and non-need-based college work study limited to New Mexico residents.

CONTACT
Brent Small, Director of Financial Aid
1500 South Avenue K, Portales, NM 88130
(575) 562-2194

Eastern New Mexico University: Roswell
Roswell, New Mexico
www.roswell.enmu.edu Federal Code: 002651

2-year public branch campus and community college in large town.
Enrollment: 2,545 undergrads, 44% part-time. 453 full-time freshmen.
Selectivity: Open admission; but selective for some programs.

BASIC COSTS (2013-2014)
Tuition and fees: $1,541; out-of-district residents $1,613; out-of-state residents $3,941.
Per-credit charge: $58; out-of-district residents $61; out-of-state residents $158.
Room and board: $7,670.

FINANCIAL AID PICTURE (2012-2013)
Students with need: 85% of average financial aid package awarded as scholarships/grants, 15% awarded as loans/jobs. Need-based aid available for part-time students. Work study available nights, weekends, and for part-time students.
Scholarships offered: New Mexico Lottery Scholarship; tuition for New Mexico residents; must attend school full-time the semester following high school graduation or GED and maintain 12 credit hours and 2.5 GPA.

FINANCIAL AID PROCEDURES
Forms required: FAFSA.
Dates and Deadlines: Priority date 4/1; no closing date. Applicants notified on a rolling basis starting 7/1; must reply within 3 week(s) of notification.
Transfers: All students receiving state aid must be New Mexico residents and enrolled in at least 6 credit hours.

CONTACT
Jessie Sjue, Director of Financial Aid
Box 6000, Roswell, NM 88202-6000
(575) 624-7152

Institute of American Indian Arts
Santa Fe, New Mexico
www.iaia.edu Federal Code: 014152

4-year public visual arts and liberal arts college in small city.
Enrollment: 374 undergrads.

BASIC COSTS (2012-2013)
Tuition and fees: $4,170; out-of-state residents $4,170.
Per-credit charge: $130; out-of-state residents $130.
Room and board: $6,368.

FINANCIAL AID PICTURE
Students with need: Need-based aid available for full-time and part-time students. Work study available nights.
Students without need: No-need awards available for academics, art.
Scholarships offered: IAIA merit scholarships; $1,000 for all students with 3.0 GPA, $1,500 for 3.5 GPA, $2,000 for 4.0 GPA.
Additional info: For American Indian and Alaskan natives, financial aid available through Tribe or Native Corporation in which student is enrolled.

FINANCIAL AID PROCEDURES
Forms required: FAFSA, institutional form.
Dates and Deadlines: Priority date 3/15; no closing date. Applicants notified on a rolling basis starting 5/1.

CONTACT
LaLa Gallegos, Financial Aid Manager
83 Avan Nu Po Road, Santa Fe, NM 87508-1300
(505) 424-4500

Luna Community College
Las Vegas, New Mexico
www.luna.edu Federal Code: 009962

2-year public community and liberal arts college in large town.
Enrollment: 969 undergrads, 47% part-time. 106 full-time freshmen.
Selectivity: Open admission; but selective for some programs and for out-of-state students.

BASIC COSTS (2013-2014)
Tuition and fees: $932; out-of-district residents $1,244; out-of-state residents $2,276.

FINANCIAL AID PICTURE (2011-2012)
Students with need: 80% of average financial aid package awarded as scholarships/grants, 20% awarded as loans/jobs. Work study available nights.
Students without need: No-need awards available for academics, athletics, state/district residency.

CONTACT
Michael Montoya, Financial Aid Director
366 Luna Drive, Las Vegas, NM 87701
(505) 454-2500 ext. 2002

Mesalands Community College
Tucumcari, New Mexico
www.mesalands.edu Federal Code: 032063

2-year public community and technical college in small town.
Enrollment: 484 undergrads.
Selectivity: Open admission.

BASIC COSTS (2012-2013)
Tuition and fees: $1,805; out-of-state residents $2,789.
Per-credit charge: $48; out-of-state residents $86.

FINANCIAL AID PICTURE
Students with need: Need-based aid available for full-time and part-time students. Work study available nights.
Students without need: No-need awards available for academics, athletics, leadership, minority status, state/district residency.

FINANCIAL AID PROCEDURES
Forms required: FAFSA.

Dates and Deadlines: Priority date 3/31; no closing date. Applicants notified on a rolling basis starting 4/1; must reply within 3 week(s) of notification.

CONTACT

Amanda Hammer, Director of Financial Aid
911 South Tenth Street, Tucumcari, NM 88401
(575) 461-4413 ext. 136

Navajo Technical College

Crownpoint, New Mexico
www.navajotech.edu

2-year public community and technical college in rural community.
Enrollment: 1,511 undergrads, 26% part-time. 292 full-time freshmen.
Selectivity: Open admission.

BASIC COSTS (2013-2014)

Tuition and fees: $2,780; out-of-district residents $5,180.
Room and board: $2,280.
Additional info: Members of federally recognized tribes pay $50 per-credit for 100-200 level courses, $100 per-credit for 300-400 level courses. Non-tribal members pay $100 per-credit for 100-200 level courses and $200 per-credit for 300-400 level courses. Tuition at time of enrollment locked for 2 years.

FINANCIAL AID PICTURE (2012-2013)

Students with need: Need-based aid available for full-time and part-time students. Work study available nights, weekends, and for part-time students.
Students without need: No-need awards available for academics.

FINANCIAL AID PROCEDURES

Forms required: FAFSA, institutional form.
Dates and Deadlines: Closing date 6/25. Applicants notified on a rolling basis starting 8/5; must reply by 11/30 or within 4 week(s) of notification.
Transfers: Priority date 8/30; closing date 11/30. Applicants notified by 9/30; must reply within 4 week(s) of notification.

CONTACT

Tyrell Hardy, Financial Aid Officer
PO Box 849, Crownpoint, NM 87313
(505) 786-4309

New Mexico Highlands University

Las Vegas, New Mexico
www.nmhu.edu Federal Code: 002653

4-year public university in large town.
Enrollment: 2,298 undergrads, 26% part-time. 411 full-time freshmen.
Selectivity: Open admission.

BASIC COSTS (2012-2013)

Tuition and fees: $3,504; out-of-state residents $5,672.
Per-credit charge: $221; out-of-state residents $402.
Room and board: $5,920.

FINANCIAL AID PICTURE (2011-2012)

Students with need: Out of 364 full-time freshmen who applied for aid, 310 were judged to have need. Of these, 306 received aid, and 4 had their full need met. Need-based aid available for part-time students.
Students without need: No-need awards available for academics, alumni affiliation, art, athletics, music/drama, state/district residency.
Additional info: Work study funds available on no-need basis to state residents.

FINANCIAL AID PROCEDURES

Forms required: FAFSA.
Dates and Deadlines: Applicants notified on a rolling basis starting 3/15; must reply within 2 week(s) of notification.
Transfers: Closing date 6/30.

CONTACT

Eileen Sedillo, Director of Financial Aid
Box 9000, Las Vegas, NM 87701
(505) 454-3318

New Mexico Institute of Mining and Technology

Socorro, New Mexico
www.nmt.edu Federal Code: 002654

4-year public engineering and liberal arts college in small town.
Enrollment: 1,425 undergrads, 5% part-time. 346 full-time freshmen.
Selectivity: Admits less than 50% of applicants.

BASIC COSTS (2012-2013)

Tuition and fees: $5,496; out-of-state residents $16,367.
Per-credit charge: $201; out-of-state residents $654.
Room and board: $6,304.

FINANCIAL AID PICTURE (2012-2013)

Students with need: Average financial aid package met 84% of need; average scholarship/grant was $6,818; average loan was $2,862. For part-time students, average financial aid package was $9,145.
Students without need: No-need awards available for academics, alumni affiliation, minority status, state/district residency.
Cumulative student debt: 42% of graduating class had student loans; average debt was $18,834.
Additional info: Campus research projects offer student employment based on abilities, interest, and merit.

FINANCIAL AID PROCEDURES

Forms required: FAFSA, institutional form.
Dates and Deadlines: Priority date 5/1; no closing date. Applicants notified on a rolling basis starting 5/1; must reply within 2 week(s) of notification.
Transfers: Priority date 3/1; no deadline. Applicants notified on a rolling basis starting 4/1; must reply within 2 week(s) of notification. Financial aid transcripts required from all colleges attended.

CONTACT

Annette Kaus, Director of Financial Aid
801 Leroy Place, Socorro, NM 87801
(575) 835-5333

New Mexico Junior College

Hobbs, New Mexico
www.nmjc.edu Federal Code: 002655

2-year public community and technical college in large town.
Enrollment: 1,596 undergrads.
Selectivity: Open admission; but selective for some programs.

BASIC COSTS (2012-2013)

Tuition and fees: $1,272; out-of-district residents $1,728; out-of-state residents $1,920.
Per-credit charge: $33; out-of-district residents $52; out-of-state residents $60.
Room and board: $4,100.

FINANCIAL AID PICTURE

Students with need: Need-based aid available for full-time and part-time students. Work study available nights, weekends, and for part-time students.

Students without need: No-need awards available for academics, art, athletics, leadership, music/drama.

FINANCIAL AID PROCEDURES
Forms required: FAFSA.
Dates and Deadlines: Priority date 6/1; no closing date. Applicants notified on a rolling basis; must reply within 2 week(s) of notification.

CONTACT
Kerrie Mitchell, Director of Financial Aid
5317 Lovington Highway, Hobbs, NM 88240
(575) 392-4510

New Mexico Military Institute

Roswell, New Mexico
www.nmmi.edu Federal Code: 002656

2-year public junior and military college in large town.
Enrollment: 464 undergrads.

BASIC COSTS (2012-2013)
Tuition and fees: $6,151; out-of-state residents $10,670.
Room and board: $4,670.
Additional info: One time cost for uniforms: $2,100.

FINANCIAL AID PICTURE
Students with need: Need-based aid available for full-time students.
Students without need: No-need awards available for academics, alumni affiliation, athletics, leadership, minority status, ROTC, state/district residency.

FINANCIAL AID PROCEDURES
Forms required: FAFSA.
Dates and Deadlines: Priority date 4/1; no closing date. Applicants notified on a rolling basis starting 5/1; must reply within 3 week(s) of notification.
Transfers: New Mexico Scholars Program, New Mexico Success Scholarship programs available.

CONTACT
Sonya Rodriguez, Director of Admissions & Financial Aid
101 West College Boulevard, Roswell, NM 88201-5173
(575) 624-8066

New Mexico State University

Las Cruces, New Mexico
www.nmsu.edu Federal Code: 002657

4-year public university in small city.
Enrollment: 13,399 undergrads, 14% part-time. 2,258 full-time freshmen.
Selectivity: Admits over 75% of applicants.

BASIC COSTS (2013-2014)
Tuition and fees: $6,220; out-of-state residents $19,644.
Per-credit charge: $205; out-of-state residents $764.
Room and board: $7,292.

FINANCIAL AID PICTURE (2011-2012)
Students with need: Out of 1,991 full-time freshmen who applied for aid, 1,633 were judged to have need. Of these, 1,633 received aid, and 311 had their full need met. Average financial aid package met 66% of need; average scholarship/grant was $7,585; average loan was $2,941. For part-time students, average financial aid package was $9,415.
Students without need: 110 full-time freshmen who did not demonstrate need for aid received scholarships/grants; average award was $828. No-need awards available for academics, alumni affiliation, athletics, leadership, minority status, music/drama, ROTC, state/district residency.
Scholarships offered: 35 full-time freshmen received athletic scholarships; average amount $9,830.

FINANCIAL AID PROCEDURES
Forms required: FAFSA.
Dates and Deadlines: Priority date 1/1; no closing date.
Transfers: No deadline. Applicants notified on a rolling basis starting 4/9; must reply within 4 week(s) of notification.

CONTACT
Janie Merchant, Director of Financial Aid
Box 30001, MSC 3A, Las Cruces, NM 88003-8001
(575) 646-4105

New Mexico State University at Alamogordo

Alamogordo, New Mexico
www.nmsua.edu/ Federal Code: 002658

2-year public branch campus college in large town.
Enrollment: 3,173 undergrads.
Selectivity: Open admission; but selective for some programs.

BASIC COSTS (2012-2013)
Tuition and fees: $1,896; out-of-district residents $2,256; out-of-state residents $5,088.
Per-credit charge: $75; out-of-district residents $90; out-of-state residents $208.

FINANCIAL AID PICTURE
Students with need: Need-based aid available for full-time and part-time students.
Students without need: No-need awards available for academics, state/district residency.

FINANCIAL AID PROCEDURES
Forms required: FAFSA, institutional form.
Dates and Deadlines: Priority date 3/1; no closing date.

CONTACT
Darlene Duvall, Financial Aid Coordinator
2400 North Scenic Drive, Alamogordo, NM 88310
(575) 439-3600

New Mexico State University at Carlsbad

Carlsbad, New Mexico
www.cavern.nmsu.edu Federal Code: 002657

2-year public branch campus and community college in large town.
Enrollment: 1,409 undergrads, 65% part-time. 181 full-time freshmen.
Selectivity: Open admission; but selective for some programs.

BASIC COSTS (2013-2014)
Tuition and fees: $1,060; out-of-district residents $1,780; out-of-state residents $3,700.
Per-credit charge: $40; out-of-district residents $70; out-of-state residents $150.

FINANCIAL AID PICTURE
Students with need: Need-based aid available for full-time and part-time students. Work study available nights.
Students without need: No-need awards available for academics, state/district residency.

FINANCIAL AID PROCEDURES
Forms required: FAFSA.

Dates and Deadlines: Priority date 3/1; no closing date. Applicants notified on a rolling basis starting 5/1; must reply within 4 week(s) of notification.

CONTACT

Diana Campos, Financial Aid Coordinator
1500 University Drive, Carlsbad, NM 88220
(575) 234-9226

New Mexico State University at Grants

Grants, New Mexico
www.grants.nmsu.edu Federal Code: 008854

2-year public branch campus and community college in small town.
Enrollment: 1,141 undergrads.
Selectivity: Open admission.

BASIC COSTS (2012-2013)

Tuition and fees: $1,782; out-of-district residents $1,956; out-of-state residents $3,696.
Per-credit charge: $74; out-of-district residents $82; out-of-state residents $154.

FINANCIAL AID PICTURE

Students with need: Need-based aid available for full-time and part-time students. Work study available nights, weekends, and for part-time students.

FINANCIAL AID PROCEDURES

Forms required: FAFSA, institutional form.
Dates and Deadlines: Priority date 3/5; no closing date. Applicants notified on a rolling basis starting 6/15; must reply by 8/28.

CONTACT

Beth Armstead, Vice President for Student Services
1500 North Third Street, Grants, NM 87020
(505) 287-6678

Northern New Mexico College

Espanola, New Mexico
www.nnmc.edu Federal Code: 005286

2-year public business and nursing college in small town.
Enrollment: 1,714 undergrads.
Selectivity: Open admission; but selective for some programs and for out-of-state students.

BASIC COSTS (2012-2013)

Tuition and fees: $2,871; out-of-state residents $10,671.
Per-credit charge: $100; out-of-state residents $425.

FINANCIAL AID PICTURE

Students with need: Need-based aid available for full-time students.
Students without need: This college awards aid only to students with need.

FINANCIAL AID PROCEDURES

Forms required: FAFSA.
Dates and Deadlines: Priority date 3/1; no closing date. Applicants notified on a rolling basis starting 6/1; must reply within 2 week(s) of notification.

CONTACT

Alfredo Montoya, Director of Financial Aid
921 Paseo de Onate, Espanola, NM 87532
(505) 747-2128 ext. 128

St. John's College

Santa Fe, New Mexico Federal Code: 002093
www.sjcsf.edu CSS Code: 4737

4-year private liberal arts college in small city.
Enrollment: 349 undergrads, 1% part-time. 99 full-time freshmen.
Selectivity: Admits over 75% of applicants.

BASIC COSTS (2013-2014)

Tuition and fees: $46,296.
Room and board: $10,954.

FINANCIAL AID PICTURE

Students with need: Need-based aid available for full-time and part-time students. Work study available nights, weekends, and for part-time students.
Students without need: This college awards aid only to students with need.
Additional info: Families receive individual attention in determining need. Independent students must submit parental data. Financial aid information also required of noncustodial parent in cases of separation or divorce. Aid is awarded on a first-come, first-served basis until institutional money is exhausted. Apply by February 15; after April 1 aid is difficult to obtain.

FINANCIAL AID PROCEDURES

Forms required: FAFSA, CSS PROFILE.
Dates and Deadlines: Priority date 2/15; no closing date. Applicants notified on a rolling basis starting 12/1; must reply by 5/1 or within 3 week(s) of notification.
Transfers: Applicants notified on a rolling basis starting 3/15; must reply by 5/1.

CONTACT

Michael Rodriguez, Director of Financial Aid
1160 Camino Cruz Blanca, Santa Fe, NM 87505
(505) 984-6058

San Juan College

Farmington, New Mexico
www.sanjuancollege.edu Federal Code: 002660

2-year public community college in large town.
Enrollment: 6,283 undergrads, 59% part-time. 729 full-time freshmen.
Selectivity: Open admission.

BASIC COSTS (2013-2014)

Tuition and fees: $1,610; out-of-state residents $3,770.
Per-credit charge: $41; out-of-state residents $105.

FINANCIAL AID PICTURE (2011-2012)

Students with need: 70% of average financial aid package awarded as scholarships/grants, 30% awarded as loans/jobs. Need-based aid available for part-time students. Work study available nights, weekends, and for part-time students.
Students without need: No-need awards available for academics, state/district residency.

FINANCIAL AID PROCEDURES

Forms required: FAFSA.
Dates and Deadlines: Applicants notified on a rolling basis starting 7/1; must reply within 2 week(s) of notification.

CONTACT

Jerry McKeen, Director for Financial Aid
4601 College Boulevard, Farmington, NM 87402-4699
(505) 566-3323

Santa Fe Community College

Santa Fe, New Mexico
www.sfcc.edu Federal Code: 016065

2-year public community college in small city.
Enrollment: 4,893 undergrads.
Selectivity: Open admission; but selective for some programs.

BASIC COSTS (2012-2013)

Tuition and fees: $1,329; out-of-district residents $1,689; out-of-state residents $3,084.
Per-credit charge: $40; out-of-district residents $52; out-of-state residents $98.

FINANCIAL AID PICTURE

Students with need: Need-based aid available for full-time and part-time students. Work study available nights, weekends, and for part-time students.
Students without need: No-need awards available for academics, state/district residency.

FINANCIAL AID PROCEDURES

Forms required: FAFSA, institutional form.
Dates and Deadlines: Priority date 5/1; no closing date. Applicants notified on a rolling basis starting 6/1; must reply within 4 week(s) of notification.

CONTACT

Scott Whitaker, Financial Aid Director
6401 Richards Avenue, Santa Fe, NM 87508-4887
(505) 428-1268

Santa Fe University of Art and Design

Santa Fe, New Mexico
www.santafeuniversity.edu Federal Code: 002649

4-year for-profit visual arts and liberal arts college in small city.
Enrollment: 544 undergrads, 1% part-time. 173 full-time freshmen.
Selectivity: Admits over 75% of applicants.

BASIC COSTS (2012-2013)

Tuition and fees: $30,136.
Per-credit charge: $886.
Room and board: $8,984.

FINANCIAL AID PICTURE (2011-2012)

Students with need: Out of 158 full-time freshmen who applied for aid, 139 were judged to have need. Of these, 139 received aid, and 8 had their full need met. Average financial aid package met 60% of need; average scholarship/grant was $18,474; average loan was $3,613. For part-time students, average financial aid package was $12,071.
Students without need: 26 full-time freshmen who did not demonstrate need for aid received scholarships/grants; average award was $9,629. No-need awards available for academics, art, music/drama, state/district residency.

FINANCIAL AID PROCEDURES

Forms required: FAFSA.
Dates and Deadlines: Priority date 3/15; no closing date. Applicants notified on a rolling basis starting 3/1.
Transfers: No deadline. Applicants notified on a rolling basis starting 3/1. No financial aid credited to student accounts until all financial aid transcripts received.

CONTACT

Amy Kearns, Director of Financial Aid
1600 Saint Michael's Drive, Santa Fe, NM 87505-7634
(505) 473-6454

Southwest University of Visual Arts

Albuquerque, New Mexico
www.suva.edu Federal Code: 024915

4-year for-profit visual arts college in very large city.
Enrollment: 239 undergrads.

BASIC COSTS (2012-2013)

Tuition and fees: $21,000.
Additional info: Tuition at time of enrollment locked for 4 years.

FINANCIAL AID PICTURE

Students with need: Work study available nights, weekends, and for part-time students.
Students without need: No-need awards available for academics.
Scholarships offered: Board of Trustees Scholarship, Transfer Student Scholarship, Scholarship for Continuing Students.

FINANCIAL AID PROCEDURES

Forms required: FAFSA.
Transfers: No deadline. Applicants notified on a rolling basis.

CONTACT

Stephanie Dietzman, Registrar, Office of Institutional Effectiveness
5000 Marble Avenue NE, Albuquerque, NM 87119
(520) 325-0123

Southwestern Indian Polytechnic Institute

Albuquerque, New Mexico
www.sipi.edu Federal Code: 011185

2-year public community and technical college in large city.
Enrollment: 482 undergrads, 12% part-time. 165 full-time freshmen.
Selectivity: Open admission.

BASIC COSTS (2013-2014)

Additional info: Only accepts registered members of Federally-recognized tribes and is tuition free. Students are responsible for required fees: full-time Lodge student, $560; full-time commuter, $450; part-time, $300. Board plan not available. Cost of room only, $110. Comprehensive tuition and room/board fee: $840 for 3 trimesters. Tuition/fee waivers available for minority students.

FINANCIAL AID PICTURE

Students with need: Need-based aid available for full-time and part-time students. Work study available nights, weekends, and for part-time students.
Students without need: No-need awards available for academics, leadership, minority status.
Additional info: Students with valid membership in recognized Indian tribe attend tuition-free.

FINANCIAL AID PROCEDURES

Forms required: FAFSA, institutional form.
Dates and Deadlines: Closing date 3/1. Applicants notified on a rolling basis starting 9/30.
Transfers: Priority date 9/13; no deadline.

CONTACT

Joseph Carpio, Director Admissions & Financial aid
PO Box 10146, Albuquerque, NM 87184
(505) 346-2324

University of New Mexico

Albuquerque, New Mexico
www.unm.edu Federal Code: 002663

4-year public university in very large city.
Enrollment: 21,008 undergrads.
Selectivity: Admits 50 to 75% of applicants.

BASIC COSTS (2012-2013)

Tuition and fees: $6,049; out-of-state residents $20,688.
Per-credit charge: $201; out-of-state residents $811.
Room and board: $8,312.

FINANCIAL AID PICTURE

Students with need: Need-based aid available for full-time and part-time students. Work study available nights, weekends, and for part-time students.
Students without need: No-need awards available for academics, alumni affiliation, art, athletics, job skills, leadership, minority status, music/drama, religious affiliation, ROTC, state/district residency.
Scholarships offered: Bridge to Success Scholarship, for first semester only while awaiting other scholarship aid, requires New Mexico residency, full-time status in degree-granting program, and acceptable GED test score and/or requisite high school GPA per sponsor. NM Legislature Lottery Scholarship, for second and subsequent semesters, requires New Mexico residency, full-time status in degree-granting program, and acceptable GED test score and/or requisite high school GPA, and 12 or more credit hours with a 2.5 GPA in the first semester.

FINANCIAL AID PROCEDURES

Forms required: FAFSA.
Dates and Deadlines: Priority date 3/1; no closing date. Applicants notified on a rolling basis starting 3/31.

CONTACT

Brian Malone, Director of Student Financial Aid
Office of Admissions, Albuquerque, NM 87196-4895
(505) 277-8900

University of the Southwest

Hobbs, New Mexico
www.usw.edu Federal Code: 013935

4-year private liberal arts and teachers college in large town, affiliated with nondenominational tradition.
Enrollment: 325 undergrads, 24% part-time. 49 full-time freshmen.
Selectivity: Open admission; but selective for some programs.

BASIC COSTS (2012-2013)

Tuition and fees: $14,305.
Per-credit charge: $510.
Room and board: $6,640.

FINANCIAL AID PICTURE (2011-2012)

Students with need: Out of 49 full-time freshmen who applied for aid, 49 were judged to have need. Of these, 49 received aid. Average financial aid package met 61% of need; average scholarship/grant was $2,500; average loan was $3,500. For part-time students, average financial aid package was $4,500.
Students without need: No-need awards available for academics, athletics, leadership.
Scholarships offered: 49 full-time freshmen received athletic scholarships; average amount $5,000.
Cumulative student debt: 80% of graduating class had student loans; average debt was $27,679.

FINANCIAL AID PROCEDURES

Forms required: FAFSA.
Dates and Deadlines: Priority date 4/1; closing date 6/1. Applicants notified on a rolling basis starting 4/1; must reply within 2 week(s) of notification.
Transfers: Applicants notified on a rolling basis starting 4/1; must reply within 2 week(s) of notification.

CONTACT

Anne Gaglia, Director of Financial Aid
6610 North Lovington Highway, #506, Hobbs, NM 88240
(575) 492-2114

Western New Mexico University

Silver City, New Mexico
www.wnmu.edu Federal Code: 002664

4-year public university in large town.
Enrollment: 2,258 undergrads, 26% part-time. 336 full-time freshmen.
Selectivity: Open admission.

BASIC COSTS (2012-2013)

Tuition and fees: $4,525; out-of-state residents $12,724.
Room and board: $6,049.

FINANCIAL AID PICTURE (2011-2012)

Students with need: Average financial aid package met 50% of need; average scholarship/grant was $2,358; average loan was $1,677. For part-time students, average financial aid package was $4,846.
Students without need: 14 full-time freshmen who did not demonstrate need for aid received scholarships/grants; average award was $695. No-need awards available for academics, art, athletics, music/drama.
Scholarships offered: 51 full-time freshmen received athletic scholarships; average amount $1,626.
Cumulative student debt: 43% of graduating class had student loans; average debt was $12,640.

FINANCIAL AID PROCEDURES

Forms required: FAFSA, institutional form.
Dates and Deadlines: Priority date 3/1; no closing date. Applicants notified on a rolling basis starting 3/1; must reply within 2 week(s) of notification.

CONTACT

Charles Kelly, Director of Financial Aid
Castorena 106, Silver City, NM 88062
(505) 538-6173

New York

Adelphi University

Garden City, New York
www.adelphi.edu Federal Code: 002666

4-year private university in large town.
Enrollment: 5,053 undergrads, 10% part-time. 996 full-time freshmen.
Selectivity: Admits 50 to 75% of applicants.

BASIC COSTS (2012-2013)

Tuition and fees: $29,320.
Per-credit charge: $860.
Room and board: $11,900.

FINANCIAL AID PICTURE (2012-2013)

Students with need: Out of 880 full-time freshmen who applied for aid, 751 were judged to have need. Of these, 725 received aid, and 7 had their full need met. Average financial aid package met 34% of need; average

scholarship/grant was $6,837; average loan was $4,262. Need-based aid available for part-time students.
Students without need: 202 full-time freshmen who did not demonstrate need for aid received scholarships/grants; average award was $13,967. No-need awards available for academics, alumni affiliation, art, athletics, leadership, minority status, music/drama, religious affiliation.
Scholarships offered: ***Merit:*** Trustee Scholarships: for full-time freshmen with the most outstanding academic achievement and co-curricular activities, minimum 2020 score on SAT and rank in top 10% of high school class; 12 available. Presidential Scholarship: typically have minimum SAT of 1950 and rank in top 10% of high school class; $15,000-$16,000 depending upon the individual's academic profile; 25 available. Provost Scholarship: minimum SAT of 1800 and rank in the top 15% of high school class or have minimum transfer GPA of 3.5; $12,000 to $14,500; 55 available. Dean's Scholarship: for full-time freshmen with very good academic performances. Generally minimum SAT scores 1580 to 1790 and rank in top 25% of high school class. ***Athletic:*** 28 full-time freshmen received athletic scholarships; average amount $13,490.
Cumulative student debt: 72% of graduating class had student loans; average debt was $35,429.

FINANCIAL AID PROCEDURES
Forms required: FAFSA, state aid form.
Dates and Deadlines: Priority date 3/1; no closing date. Applicants notified on a rolling basis starting 3/1.
Transfers: No deadline. Applicants notified on a rolling basis.

CONTACT
Sheryl Mihopulos, Assistant Vice President
One South Avenue, Levermore 110, Garden City, NY 11530-0701
(516) 877-3080

Adirondack Community College
Queensbury, New York
www.sunyacc.edu Federal Code: 002860

2-year public community college in large town.
Enrollment: 3,326 undergrads, 33% part-time. 740 full-time freshmen.
Selectivity: Open admission; but selective for some programs.

BASIC COSTS (2012-2013)
Tuition and fees: $3,973; out-of-state residents $7,637.
Per-credit charge: $153; out-of-state residents $306.

FINANCIAL AID PICTURE
Students with need: Need-based aid available for full-time and part-time students.
Students without need: No-need awards available for academics, state/district residency.
Scholarships offered: Academic Excellence Scholarship: $750 per semester for up to 4 semesters; for local high school graduates who are 1st or 2nd in class, GPA 3.5. Hill Scholarship: $500 per semester for 4 semesters; for Fort Edward High School graduate.

FINANCIAL AID PROCEDURES
Forms required: FAFSA, state aid form, institutional form.
Dates and Deadlines: Priority date 4/15; no closing date. Applicants notified on a rolling basis starting 5/1.

CONTACT
Maureen Reilly, Director of Financial Aid
640 Bay Road, Queensbury, NY 12804
(518) 743-2223

Albany College of Pharmacy and Health Sciences
Albany, New York Federal Code: 002885
www.acphs.edu CSS Code: 2013

4-year private health science and pharmacy college in small city.
Enrollment: 1,069 undergrads, 1% part-time. 250 full-time freshmen.
Selectivity: Admits 50 to 75% of applicants.

BASIC COSTS (2012-2013)
Tuition and fees: $27,630.
Per-credit charge: $900.
Room and board: $9,760.

FINANCIAL AID PICTURE (2012-2013)
Students with need: Out of 238 full-time freshmen who applied for aid, 214 were judged to have need. Of these, 211 received aid, and 29 had their full need met. Average financial aid package met 55% of need; average scholarship/grant was $12,120; average loan was $3,826. For part-time students, average financial aid package was $2,750.
Students without need: 29 full-time freshmen who did not demonstrate need for aid received scholarships/grants; average award was $10,146. No-need awards available for academics.
Cumulative student debt: 61% of graduating class had student loans; average debt was $29,160.

FINANCIAL AID PROCEDURES
Forms required: FAFSA. CSS PROFILE priority date 11/15, filing deadline 12/15.
Dates and Deadlines: Priority date 2/1; closing date 5/1. Applicants notified by 3/25; must reply within 2 week(s) of notification.
Transfers: Applicants notified by 3/25; must reply within 2 week(s) of notification.

CONTACT
Kathleen Montague, Director of Financial Aid
106 New Scotland Avenue, Albany, NY 12208-3492
(518) 694-7256

Alfred University
Alfred, New York
www.alfred.edu Federal Code: 002668

4-year private university in rural community.
Enrollment: 1,903 undergrads, 1% part-time. 536 full-time freshmen.
Selectivity: Admits 50 to 75% of applicants.

BASIC COSTS (2013-2014)
Tuition and fees: $28,774.
Per-credit charge: $902.
Room and board: $11,618.
Additional info: Tuition figures provided are for the College of Liberal Arts & Sciences and Professional Studies. Tuition for the School of Art & Design and Biomaterials, Ceramic, and Glass Engineering is $22,524 for non-NYS residents and $16,368 for NYS residents. Tuition for Mechanical, Renewable, and Undecided Engineering is $22,524.

FINANCIAL AID PICTURE
Students with need: Need-based aid available for full-time students. Work study available nights, weekends, and for part-time students.
Students without need: No-need awards available for academics, art, leadership, music/drama.

FINANCIAL AID PROCEDURES
Forms required: FAFSA, state aid form, institutional form. CSS PROFILE accepted but not required.
Dates and Deadlines: Closing date 3/15. Applicants notified on a rolling basis starting 2/15; must reply by 5/1 or within 2 week(s) of notification.

Transfers: No deadline. Applicants notified on a rolling basis starting 2/15; must reply by 5/1 or within 2 week(s) of notification.

CONTACT
Earl Pierce, Director of Student Financial Aid
Alumni Hall, Alfred, NY 14802-1205
(607) 871-2159

American Academy McAllister Institute of Funeral Service

New York, New York
www.funeraleducation.org Federal Code: 010813

2-year private school of mortuary science in very large city.
Enrollment: 406 undergrads, 67% part-time. 132 full-time freshmen.
Selectivity: Admits 50 to 75% of applicants.

BASIC COSTS (2013-2014)
Tuition and fees: $12,580.

FINANCIAL AID PICTURE
Students with need: Need-based aid available for full-time students.
Students without need: This college awards aid only to students with need.

FINANCIAL AID PROCEDURES
Forms required: FAFSA, state aid form.
Dates and Deadlines: Applicants notified on a rolling basis starting 7/1; must reply by 9/1 or within 3 week(s) of notification.
Transfers: Priority date 6/1.

CONTACT
Jaway Tso, Financial Aid Administrator
619 West 54th Street, 2nd Floor, New York, NY 10019-3602
(212) 220-4275

American Academy of Dramatic Arts

New York, New York
www.aada.edu Federal Code: 007465

2-year private junior and performing arts college in very large city.
Enrollment: 219 undergrads. 61 full-time freshmen.
Selectivity: Admits 50 to 75% of applicants.

BASIC COSTS (2012-2013)
Tuition and fees: $30,650.

FINANCIAL AID PICTURE (2011-2012)
Students with need: Out of 54 full-time freshmen who applied for aid, 51 were judged to have need. Of these, 49 received aid, and 42 had their full need met. Average financial aid package met 82% of need; average scholarship/grant was $3,500; average loan was $9,500.
Students without need: This college awards aid only to students with need.
Scholarships offered: Merit awards of $1,000-$6,000 for first-year students. Scholarships of $500-$4,000 available for second year. Scholarships of $500-$6,000 available for post-degree third year.
Additional info: Need-based incentive grants of $200-$2,000 for first-year students.

FINANCIAL AID PROCEDURES
Forms required: FAFSA, institutional form.
Dates and Deadlines: Applicants notified on a rolling basis.

CONTACT
Roberto Lopez, Financial Aid Director
120 Madison Avenue, New York, NY 10016
(212) 686-9244 ext. 342

ASA Institute of Business and Computer Technology

Brooklyn, New York
www.asa.edu Federal Code: 030955

2-year for-profit technical and career college in very large city.
Enrollment: 4,688 undergrads, 7% part-time. 1,538 full-time freshmen.
Selectivity: Open admission.

BASIC COSTS (2012-2013)
Tuition and fees: $12,099.
Per-credit charge: $495.

FINANCIAL AID PICTURE (2011-2012)
Students with need: 67% of average financial aid package awarded as scholarships/grants, 33% awarded as loans/jobs. Need-based aid available for part-time students. Work study available nights, weekends, and for part-time students.
Students without need: No-need awards available for academics, alumni affiliation, athletics, leadership, state/district residency.

FINANCIAL AID PROCEDURES
Forms required: FAFSA, state aid form.
Dates and Deadlines: Applicants notified on a rolling basis starting 7/12; must reply by 10/12.
Transfers: No deadline. Applicants notified on a rolling basis starting 7/12; must reply by 10/12.

CONTACT
Victoria Shtamler, Vice President of Student Financial Services
81 Willoughby Street, Brooklyn, NY 11201
(718) 522-9073 ext. 2037

Bard College

Annandale-on-Hudson, New York Federal Code: 002671
www.bard.edu CSS Code: 2037

4-year private liberal arts college in small town, affiliated with Episcopal Church.
Enrollment: 1,971 undergrads, 2% part-time. 537 full-time freshmen.
Selectivity: Admits less than 50% of applicants.

BASIC COSTS (2013-2014)
Tuition and fees: $46,370.
Per-credit charge: $1,429.
Room and board: $13,502.

FINANCIAL AID PICTURE (2012-2013)
Students with need: Out of 394 full-time freshmen who applied for aid, 380 were judged to have need. Of these, 380 received aid, and 220 had their full need met. Average financial aid package met 88% of need; average scholarship/grant was $34,385; average loan was $5,253. For part-time students, average financial aid package was $13,319.
Students without need: 5 full-time freshmen who did not demonstrate need for aid received scholarships/grants; average award was $16,800. No-need awards available for academics.
Scholarships offered: Distinguished Scientist Scholarship: full tuition; for students intending to major in math or sciences; 10-20 awarded annually.
Cumulative student debt: 49% of graduating class had student loans; average debt was $24,913.
Additional info: Excellence and Equal Cost Program for students who graduate in top 10 of public high school class lowers fees to levels equivalent to those at home state university or college.

FINANCIAL AID PROCEDURES
Forms required: FAFSA, CSS PROFILE, state aid form.
Dates and Deadlines: Closing date 2/15. Applicants notified by 4/1; must reply by 5/1.

Transfers: Applicants notified by 4/1; must reply by 5/1.

CONTACT

Denise Ackerman, Director of Financial Aid
30 Campus Road, Annandale-on-Hudson, NY 12504-5000
(845) 758-7526

Barnard College

New York, New York
www.barnard.edu
Federal Code: 002708
CSS Code: 2038

4-year private liberal arts college for women in very large city.
Enrollment: 2,509 undergrads, 2% part-time. 599 full-time freshmen.
Selectivity: Admits less than 50% of applicants.

BASIC COSTS (2013-2014)
Tuition and fees: $44,790.
Per-credit charge: $1,440.
Room and board: $14,210.

FINANCIAL AID PICTURE (2012-2013)
Students with need: Out of 318 full-time freshmen who applied for aid, 239 were judged to have need. Of these, 239 received aid, and 239 had their full need met. Average financial aid package met 100% of need; average scholarship/grant was $42,306; average loan was $3,450.
Students without need: This college awards aid only to students with need.
Cumulative student debt: 46% of graduating class had student loans; average debt was $19,931.

FINANCIAL AID PROCEDURES
Forms required: FAFSA, state aid form. CSS Profile required for returning students, except those who had a parent contribution less than $2,000 in the prior academic year. Returning international students also not required to complete the CSS Profile.
Dates and Deadlines: Closing date 2/15. Applicants notified by 3/31; must reply by 5/1.
Transfers: Closing date 4/16. Transfers admitted in the spring are not eligible for institutional grant aid.

CONTACT

Nanette Dilauro, Director of Financial Aid
3009 Broadway, New York, NY 10027-6598
(212) 854-2154

Boricua College

New York, New York
www.boricuacollege.edu
Federal Code: 013029

4-year private liberal arts college in very large city.
Enrollment: 1,176 undergrads. 236 full-time freshmen.

BASIC COSTS (2013-2014)
Tuition and fees: $11,025.

FINANCIAL AID PICTURE
Students with need: Need-based aid available for full-time students.

FINANCIAL AID PROCEDURES
Forms required: FAFSA, state aid form.
Dates and Deadlines: Priority date 4/30; no closing date. Applicants notified on a rolling basis; must reply within 3 week(s) of notification.

CONTACT

Rosalia Cruz, Director of Financial Aid
3755 Broadway, New York, NY 10032
(212) 694-1000 ext. 611

Briarcliffe College

Bethpage, New York
www.briarcliffe.edu
Federal Code: 020757

4-year for-profit business and career college in large town.
Enrollment: 1,822 undergrads, 23% part-time. 222 full-time freshmen.
Selectivity: Admits over 75% of applicants.

BASIC COSTS (2012-2013)
Tuition and fees: $18,360.
Additional info: Reported tuition includes cost of books.

FINANCIAL AID PICTURE
Students with need: Need-based aid available for full-time and part-time students.
Students without need: No-need awards available for academics, alumni affiliation.

FINANCIAL AID PROCEDURES
Forms required: FAFSA, state aid form, institutional form.
Dates and Deadlines: Applicants notified on a rolling basis.

CONTACT

Cindy Roys, Director of Financial Aid
1055 Stewart Avenue, Bethpage, NY 11714
(516) 918-3600

Broome Community College

Binghamton, New York
www.sunybroome.edu
Federal Code: 002862

2-year public community college in small city.
Enrollment: 5,474 undergrads.
Selectivity: Open admission; but selective for some programs.

BASIC COSTS (2012-2013)
Tuition and fees: $4,258; out-of-state residents $8,078.
Per-credit charge: $159; out-of-state residents $318.

FINANCIAL AID PICTURE
Students with need: Need-based aid available for full-time and part-time students. Work study available nights.

FINANCIAL AID PROCEDURES
Forms required: FAFSA.
Dates and Deadlines: Priority date 3/1; no closing date. Applicants notified on a rolling basis starting 3/15; must reply within 2 week(s) of notification.

CONTACT

Doug Lukasik, Director of Financial Aid
Box 1017, Binghamton, NY 13902
(607) 778-5028

Bryant & Stratton College: Albany

Albany, New York
www.bryantstratton.edu
Federal Code: 004749

2-year for-profit business and career college in small city.
Enrollment: 706 undergrads, 38% part-time. 218 full-time freshmen.

BASIC COSTS (2012-2013)
Tuition and fees: $16,050.
Per-credit charge: $535.
Additional info: Tuition and fees may vary by program.

FINANCIAL AID PICTURE
Students with need: Need-based aid available for full-time and part-time students. Work study available nights, weekends, and for part-time students.

Students without need: This college awards aid only to students with need.

FINANCIAL AID PROCEDURES
Forms required: FAFSA, state aid form.
Dates and Deadlines: Closing date 9/22. Applicants notified on a rolling basis.

CONTACT
Jackie Rivers, FA Coordinator
1259 Central Avenue, Albany, NY 12205
(518) 437-1802

Bryant & Stratton College: Syracuse

Syracuse, New York
www.bryantstratton.edu Federal Code: 008276

2-year for-profit business and junior college in small city.
Enrollment: 702 undergrads.
Selectivity: Open admission.

BASIC COSTS (2012-2013)
Tuition and fees: $16,050.
Per-credit charge: $535.
Additional info: Tuition and fees may vary by program.

FINANCIAL AID PICTURE
Students with need: Work study available nights, weekends, and for part-time students.
Students without need: This college awards aid only to students with need.

FINANCIAL AID PROCEDURES
Forms required: FAFSA.
Dates and Deadlines: Closing date 9/22. Applicants notified on a rolling basis starting 10/1.
Transfers: Priority date 5/1.

CONTACT
Tami Eiklor, Financial Aid Supervisor
953 James Street, Syracuse, NY 13203
(315) 472-6603

Bryant & Stratton College: Syracuse North

Liverpool, New York
www.bryantstratton.edu

2-year for-profit career college in small city.
Enrollment: 478 undergrads.

BASIC COSTS (2012-2013)
Tuition and fees: $16,050.
Per-credit charge: $535.
Additional info: Tuition and fees may vary by program.

FINANCIAL AID PICTURE
Students with need: Need-based aid available for full-time and part-time students. Work study available nights.
Students without need: This college awards aid only to students with need.

FINANCIAL AID PROCEDURES
Forms required: FAFSA, state aid form, institutional form.
Dates and Deadlines: Closing date 9/22.
Transfers: No deadline.

CONTACT
Stacey McConnell, Financial Services Manager
8687 Carling Road, Liverpool, NY 13090
(315) 652-6500

Canisius College

Buffalo, New York
www.canisius.edu Federal Code: 002681

4-year private liberal arts and teachers college in large city, affiliated with Roman Catholic Church.
Enrollment: 2,992 undergrads, 2% part-time. 713 full-time freshmen.
Selectivity: Admits 50 to 75% of applicants.

BASIC COSTS (2013-2014)
Tuition and fees: $33,252.
Per-credit charge: $914.
Room and board: $12,270.
Additional info: Tuition/fee waivers available for minority students.

FINANCIAL AID PICTURE (2012-2013)
Students with need: Out of 660 full-time freshmen who applied for aid, 611 were judged to have need. Of these, 610 received aid, and 198 had their full need met. Average financial aid package met 85% of need; average scholarship/grant was $22,566; average loan was $3,682. Need-based aid available for part-time students.
Students without need: 97 full-time freshmen who did not demonstrate need for aid received scholarships/grants; average award was $15,448. No-need awards available for academics, alumni affiliation, art, athletics, job skills, music/drama, religious affiliation, ROTC.
Scholarships offered: ***Merit:*** Presidential Scholarship: full tuition; for four years of full-time study. Trustee's Scholarship: $16,000 to $17,000; based on GPA, test scores. Dean's Scholarship: $12,000 to $13,000; based on GPA, test scores. Benefactor's Scholarship: $9,000 to $10,000; based on GPA, test scores. International Scholarships: international students, including Canadian students, may be eligible for academic scholarships based on academic records. ***Athletic:*** 20 full-time freshmen received athletic scholarships; average amount $16,594.
Cumulative student debt: 72% of graduating class had student loans; average debt was $36,383.

FINANCIAL AID PROCEDURES
Forms required: FAFSA, state aid form.
Dates and Deadlines: Priority date 2/15; no closing date. Applicants notified on a rolling basis starting 3/1; must reply within 2 week(s) of notification.

CONTACT
Curtis Gaume, Director of Student Financial Aid
2001 Main Street, Buffalo, NY 14208-1098
(800) 541-6348

Cayuga Community College

Auburn, New York
www.cayuga-cc.edu Federal Code: 002861

2-year public community college in large town.
Enrollment: 3,058 undergrads, 27% part-time. 652 full-time freshmen.
Selectivity: Open admission; but selective for some programs.

BASIC COSTS (2012-2013)
Tuition and fees: $4,326; out-of-state residents $8,276.
Per-credit charge: $160; out-of-state residents $320.

FINANCIAL AID PICTURE (2011-2012)
Students with need: 52% of average financial aid package awarded as scholarships/grants, 48% awarded as loans/jobs. Need-based aid available

for part-time students. Work study available nights, weekends, and for part-time students.
Students without need: This college awards aid only to students with need.

FINANCIAL AID PROCEDURES
Forms required: FAFSA, state aid form.
Dates and Deadlines: Priority date 4/15; no closing date. Applicants notified on a rolling basis starting 3/15.

CONTACT
Judith Miladin, Director of Financial Aid
197 Franklin Street, Auburn, NY 13021-3099
(315) 255-1743 ext. 2470

Cazenovia College
Cazenovia, New York
www.cazenovia.edu Federal Code: 002685

4-year private liberal arts college in small town.
Enrollment: 980 undergrads, 10% part-time. 268 full-time freshmen.
Selectivity: Admits 50 to 75% of applicants.

BASIC COSTS (2012-2013)
Tuition and fees: $28,022.
Room and board: $11,398.

FINANCIAL AID PICTURE (2012-2013)
Students with need: Out of 261 full-time freshmen who applied for aid, 249 were judged to have need. Of these, 249 received aid, and 21 had their full need met. Average financial aid package met 79% of need; average scholarship/grant was $12,147; average loan was $3,452. For part-time students, average financial aid package was $9,100.
Students without need: 16 full-time freshmen who did not demonstrate need for aid received scholarships/grants; average award was $17,965. No-need awards available for academics, leadership.
Cumulative student debt: 82% of graduating class had student loans; average debt was $29,973.

FINANCIAL AID PROCEDURES
Forms required: FAFSA, state aid form.
Dates and Deadlines: Priority date 3/1; no closing date. Applicants notified on a rolling basis starting 3/1; must reply by 5/1 or within 2 week(s) of notification.
Transfers: No deadline. Applicants notified on a rolling basis starting 11/1; must reply by 5/1 or within 2 week(s) of notification.

CONTACT
Christine Mandel, Director of Financial Aid
3 Sullivan Street, Cazenovia, NY 13035
(315) 655-7887

City University of New York: Baruch College
New York, New York
www.baruch.cuny.edu Federal Code: 007273

4-year public business and liberal arts college in very large city.
Enrollment: 13,584 undergrads, 24% part-time. 1,171 full-time freshmen.
Selectivity: Admits less than 50% of applicants.

BASIC COSTS (2012-2013)
Tuition and fees: $5,910; out-of-state residents $15,030.
Per-credit charge: $230; out-of-state residents $485.

FINANCIAL AID PICTURE
Students with need: Need-based aid available for full-time and part-time students.
Students without need: No-need awards available for academics, state/district residency.
Scholarships offered: Honors college scholarships based on SAT scores and high school GPA.

FINANCIAL AID PROCEDURES
Forms required: FAFSA, state aid form.
Dates and Deadlines: Priority date 4/15; no closing date. Applicants notified on a rolling basis starting 4/15; must reply within 2 week(s) of notification.
Transfers: No deadline. Applicants notified on a rolling basis; must reply within 2 week(s) of notification.

CONTACT
Stephen O'Meara, Director of Financial Aid
One Bernard Baruch Way, Box H-0720, New York, NY 10010-5585
(646) 312-1360

City University of New York: Borough of Manhattan Community College
New York, New York
www.bmcc.cuny.edu Federal Code: 002691

2-year public community college in very large city.
Enrollment: 23,964 undergrads, 33% part-time. 4,843 full-time freshmen.
Selectivity: Open admission; but selective for some programs.

BASIC COSTS (2012-2013)
Tuition and fees: $4,218; out-of-state residents $8,118.
Per-credit charge: $165; out-of-state residents $260.
Additional info: Tuition/fee waivers available for unemployed or children of unemployed.

FINANCIAL AID PICTURE (2012-2013)
Students with need: Out of 4,517 full-time freshmen who applied for aid, 4,322 were judged to have need. Of these, 4,110 received aid. Need-based aid available for part-time students.
Students without need: This college awards aid only to students with need.
Cumulative student debt: 9% of graduating class had student loans; average debt was $3,000.

FINANCIAL AID PROCEDURES
Forms required: FAFSA, state aid form, institutional form.
Dates and Deadlines: Priority date 5/1; no closing date. Applicants notified on a rolling basis starting 4/15.
Transfers: No deadline. Applicants notified on a rolling basis starting 6/1; must reply within 2 week(s) of notification.

CONTACT
Howard Entin, Director of Financial Aid
199 Chambers Street, New York, NY 10007-1097
(212) 220-1430

City University of New York: Bronx Community College
Bronx, New York
www.bcc.cuny.edu/ Federal Code: 002692

2-year public community college in very large city.
Enrollment: 10,650 undergrads, 39% part-time. 1,544 full-time freshmen.
Selectivity: Open admission.

BASIC COSTS (2012-2013)
Tuition and fees: $4,254; out-of-state residents $8,154.
Per-credit charge: $165; out-of-state residents $260.

FINANCIAL AID PICTURE
Students with need: Need-based aid available for full-time and part-time students. Work study available nights, weekends, and for part-time students.
Students without need: This college awards aid only to students with need.

FINANCIAL AID PROCEDURES
Forms required: FAFSA.
Dates and Deadlines: Closing date 6/30. Applicants notified on a rolling basis starting 8/1.

CONTACT
Maria Barlaam, Financial Aid Officer
2155 University Avenue, Bronx, NY 10453
(718) 289-5608

City University of New York: Brooklyn College

Brooklyn, New York
www.brooklyn.cuny.edu Federal Code: 002687

4-year public liberal arts college in very large city.
Enrollment: 12,125 undergrads, 24% part-time. 1,140 full-time freshmen.
Selectivity: Admits less than 50% of applicants.

BASIC COSTS (2012-2013)
Tuition and fees: $5,884; out-of-state residents $15,004.
Per-credit charge: $230; out-of-state residents $485.

FINANCIAL AID PICTURE (2012-2013)
Students with need: Out of 1,013 full-time freshmen who applied for aid, 840 were judged to have need. Of these, 787 received aid, and 640 had their full need met. Average financial aid package met 94% of need; average scholarship/grant was $3,300; average loan was $3,200. For part-time students, average financial aid package was $3,700.
Students without need: 250 full-time freshmen who did not demonstrate need for aid received scholarships/grants; average award was $1,500. No-need awards available for academics, art, leadership, music/drama, state/district residency.
Scholarships offered: Presidential Scholarship Program: for 25 freshman students for 8 tuition payments totaling $13,000. Brooklyn College Freshman Scholarships: $1,000 per year of study. Many scholarships for freshman students based on degree of study, academic merit, and community service.
Cumulative student debt: 48% of graduating class had student loans; average debt was $12,200.

FINANCIAL AID PROCEDURES
Forms required: FAFSA, state aid form.
Dates and Deadlines: Priority date 4/11; no closing date. Applicants notified on a rolling basis starting 5/11.

CONTACT
Ahad Farhang, Director of Financial Aid
2900 Bedford Avenue, Brooklyn, NY 11210
(718) 951-5051

City University of New York: City College

New York, New York
www.ccny.cuny.edu Federal Code: 002688

4-year public university in very large city.
Enrollment: 12,276 undergrads, 23% part-time. 1,397 full-time freshmen.
Selectivity: Admits less than 50% of applicants.

BASIC COSTS (2012-2013)
Tuition and fees: $5,759; out-of-state residents $14,879.
Per-credit charge: $230; out-of-state residents $485.
Additional info: Board plan not available. Cost of room only, $12,570. Tuition/fee waivers available for minority students.

FINANCIAL AID PICTURE (2011-2012)
Students with need: Out of 1,218 full-time freshmen who applied for aid, 1,099 were judged to have need. Of these, 1,032 received aid, and 680 had their full need met. Average financial aid package met 83% of need; average scholarship/grant was $7,942; average loan was $2,002. For part-time students, average financial aid package was $9,102.
Students without need: 189 full-time freshmen who did not demonstrate need for aid received scholarships/grants; average award was $2,900. No-need awards available for academics, alumni affiliation, art, leadership, music/drama, state/district residency.
Cumulative student debt: 22% of graduating class had student loans; average debt was $16,944.

FINANCIAL AID PROCEDURES
Forms required: FAFSA, state aid form.
Dates and Deadlines: Priority date 3/15; no closing date. Applicants notified on a rolling basis starting 4/1.
Transfers: Priority date 3/31; no deadline. Applicants notified on a rolling basis starting 3/31.

CONTACT
Thelma Mason, Director of Financial Aid
160 Convent Avenue, A100, New York, NY 10031
(212) 650-7000

City University of New York: College of Staten Island

Staten Island, New York
www.csi.cuny.edu Federal Code: 002698

4-year public liberal arts college in very large city.
Enrollment: 12,977 undergrads, 24% part-time. 2,402 full-time freshmen.
Selectivity: Admits over 75% of applicants.

BASIC COSTS (2012-2013)
Tuition and fees: $5,858; out-of-state residents $14,978.
Per-credit charge: $230; out-of-state residents $485.

FINANCIAL AID PICTURE (2012-2013)
Students with need: Out of 2,098 full-time freshmen who applied for aid, 1,613 were judged to have need. Of these, 1,495 received aid, and 42 had their full need met. Average financial aid package met 58% of need; average scholarship/grant was $7,517; average loan was $2,823. For part-time students, average financial aid package was $5,103.
Students without need: 142 full-time freshmen who did not demonstrate need for aid received scholarships/grants; average award was $1,499. No-need awards available for academics, alumni affiliation, art, leadership, minority status, music/drama, state/district residency.

FINANCIAL AID PROCEDURES
Forms required: FAFSA, state aid form.
Dates and Deadlines: Priority date 3/30; no closing date. Applicants notified on a rolling basis starting 6/1.

CONTACT
Philippe Marius, Director of Financial Aid
2800 Victory Boulevard 2A-103, Staten Island, NY 10314
(718) 982-2030

City University of New York: CUNY Online

New York, New York
http://sps.cuny.edu/home Federal Code: 004765

4-year public virtual college in very large city.
Enrollment: 950 undergrads, 68% part-time.
Selectivity: Open admission; but selective for some programs.

BASIC COSTS (2012-2013)
Tuition and fees: $5,810; out-of-state residents $5,810.

FINANCIAL AID PICTURE (2011-2012)
Students with need: Average financial aid package for all full-time undergraduates was $16,000; for part-time $14,100. 44% awarded as scholarships/grants, 56% awarded as loans/jobs.
Students without need: This college awards aid only to students with need.

FINANCIAL AID PROCEDURES
Dates and Deadlines: Closing date 8/1.
Transfers: Closing date 4/15. Applicants notified on a rolling basis starting 6/1.

CONTACT
Felix Huertas, Coordinator of Financial Aid
101 West 31st Street, Room 905, New York, NY 10001-3507
(212) 652-2895

City University of New York: Hostos Community College

Bronx, New York
www.hostos.cuny.edu Federal Code: 008611

2-year public community college in very large city.
Enrollment: 5,790 undergrads, 39% part-time. 827 full-time freshmen.
Selectivity: Open admission; but selective for some programs.

BASIC COSTS (2012-2013)
Tuition and fees: $4,255; out-of-state residents $8,155.
Per-credit charge: $165; out-of-state residents $260.

FINANCIAL AID PICTURE
Students with need: Need-based aid available for full-time and part-time students.

FINANCIAL AID PROCEDURES
Forms required: FAFSA.
Dates and Deadlines: Priority date 7/1; no closing date. Applicants notified on a rolling basis; must reply within 3 week(s) of notification.

CONTACT
Joseph Alicea, Director of Financial Aid
500 Grand Concourse, Bronx, NY 10451
(718) 518-6555

City University of New York: Hunter College

New York, New York
www.hunter.cuny.edu/ Federal Code: 002689

4-year public liberal arts college in very large city.
Enrollment: 15,867 undergrads, 24% part-time. 2,130 full-time freshmen.
Selectivity: Admits less than 50% of applicants.

BASIC COSTS (2012-2013)
Tuition and fees: $5,829; out-of-state residents $14,949.
Per-credit charge: $230; out-of-state residents $485.
Additional info: Board plan not available. Cost of room only: $4200.

FINANCIAL AID PICTURE (2011-2012)
Students with need: Out of 1,809 full-time freshmen who applied for aid, 1,465 were judged to have need. Of these, 1,395 received aid, and 262 had their full need met. Average financial aid package met 78% of need; average scholarship/grant was $5,094; average loan was $4,177. For part-time students, average financial aid package was $4,656.
Students without need: 164 full-time freshmen who did not demonstrate need for aid received scholarships/grants; average award was $2,460. No-need awards available for academics.
Cumulative student debt: 62% of graduating class had student loans; average debt was $11,000.

FINANCIAL AID PROCEDURES
Forms required: FAFSA, state aid form.
Dates and Deadlines: Priority date 5/1; no closing date. Applicants notified on a rolling basis starting 5/15.

CONTACT
Aristalia Cortorreal Diaz, Director of Financial Aid
695 Park Avenue, New York, NY 10065
(212) 772-4820

City University of New York: John Jay College of Criminal Justice

New York, New York
www.jjay.cuny.edu/ Federal Code: 002693

4-year public College of criminal justice and public safety in very large city.
Enrollment: 13,030 undergrads, 20% part-time. 3,089 full-time freshmen.
Selectivity: Admits less than 50% of applicants.

BASIC COSTS (2012-2013)
Tuition and fees: $5,759; out-of-state residents $14,879.
Per-credit charge: $230; out-of-state residents $485.

FINANCIAL AID PICTURE (2011-2012)
Students with need: Out of 2,774 full-time freshmen who applied for aid, 2,459 were judged to have need. Of these, 2,144 received aid. Average financial aid package met 85% of need; average scholarship/grant was $3,175; average loan was $3,500. For part-time students, average financial aid package was $10,150.
Students without need: No-need awards available for academics, leadership, minority status, state/district residency.
Cumulative student debt: 20% of graduating class had student loans; average debt was $11,890.

FINANCIAL AID PROCEDURES
Forms required: FAFSA, state aid form.
Dates and Deadlines: Priority date 4/30; no closing date. Applicants notified on a rolling basis starting 4/1; must reply within 2 week(s) of notification.
Transfers: Closing date 4/30.

CONTACT
Sylvia Lopez-Crespo, Director of Financial Aid
445 West 59th Street, New York, NY 10019
(212) 237-8149

City University of New York: Kingsborough Community College

Brooklyn, New York
www.kbcc.cuny.edu Federal Code: 002694

2-year public community college in very large city.
Enrollment: 14,765 undergrads, 27% part-time. 2,520 full-time freshmen.
Selectivity: Open admission.

BASIC COSTS (2012-2013)
Tuition and fees: $4,250; out-of-state residents $8,150.
Per-credit charge: $165; out-of-state residents $260.

FINANCIAL AID PICTURE
Students with need: Need-based aid available for full-time and part-time students.
Students without need: This college awards aid only to students with need.

FINANCIAL AID PROCEDURES
Forms required: FAFSA.
Dates and Deadlines: Closing date 4/30. Applicants notified on a rolling basis; must reply within 2 week(s) of notification.

CONTACT
Wayne Harewood, Director of Financial Aid
2001 Oriental Boulevard, Brooklyn, NY 11235
(718) 368-4644

City University of New York: LaGuardia Community College

Long Island City, New York
www.lagcc.cuny.edu Federal Code: 010051

2-year public community college in very large city.
Enrollment: 16,613 undergrads, 42% part-time. 2,621 full-time freshmen.
Selectivity: Open admission.

BASIC COSTS (2012-2013)
Tuition and fees: $4,266; out-of-state residents $8,166.
Per-credit charge: $165; out-of-state residents $260.
Additional info: Tuition/fee waivers available for adults, minority students, unemployed or children of unemployed.

FINANCIAL AID PICTURE
Students with need: Need-based aid available for full-time and part-time students. Work study available nights, weekends, and for part-time students.
Students without need: This college awards aid only to students with need.

FINANCIAL AID PROCEDURES
Forms required: FAFSA, state aid form, institutional form.
Dates and Deadlines: Closing date 4/15. Applicants notified on a rolling basis starting 3/1; must reply within 4 week(s) of notification.
Transfers: No deadline. Applicants notified on a rolling basis.

CONTACT
Gail Baksh-Jarrett, Executive Director of Student Financial Services
31-10 Thomson Avenue, Long Island City, NY 11101
(718) 482-7218

City University of New York: Lehman College

Bronx, New York
www.lehman.edu Federal Code: 007022

4-year public liberal arts college in very large city.
Enrollment: 8,853 undergrads, 44% part-time. 535 full-time freshmen.
Selectivity: Admits less than 50% of applicants.

BASIC COSTS (2012-2013)
Tuition and fees: $5,808; out-of-state residents $14,928.
Per-credit charge: $230; out-of-state residents $485.

FINANCIAL AID PICTURE (2011-2012)
Students with need: 67% of average financial aid package awarded as scholarships/grants, 33% awarded as loans/jobs. Need-based aid available for part-time students. Work study available nights, weekends, and for part-time students.
Students without need: This college awards aid only to students with need.

FINANCIAL AID PROCEDURES
Forms required: FAFSA, state aid form.
Dates and Deadlines: Applicants notified on a rolling basis starting 3/1.
Transfers: No deadline. Applicants notified on a rolling basis starting 3/1.

CONTACT
David Martinez, Director of Financial Aid
250 Bedford Park Boulevard West, Bronx, NY 10468
(718) 960-8545

City University of New York: Medgar Evers College

Brooklyn, New York
www.mec.cuny.edu Federal Code: 010097

4-year public liberal arts college in very large city.
Enrollment: 6,219 undergrads, 33% part-time. 988 full-time freshmen.
Selectivity: Open admission; but selective for some programs.

BASIC COSTS (2012-2013)
Tuition and fees: $5,732; out-of-state residents $14,852.
Per-credit charge: $230; out-of-state residents $485.

FINANCIAL AID PICTURE
Students with need: Need-based aid available for full-time and part-time students. Work study available weekends and for part-time students.
Students without need: No-need awards available for academics, leadership.

FINANCIAL AID PROCEDURES
Forms required: FAFSA, state aid form.
Dates and Deadlines: Priority date 1/2; closing date 6/1. Applicants notified on a rolling basis; must reply within 3 week(s) of notification.
Transfers: Priority date 3/1. Must reply within 2 week(s) of notification.

CONTACT
Conley James, Director of Financial Aid
1665 Bedford Avenue, Brooklyn, NY 11225-2201
(718) 270-6194

City University of New York: New York City College of Technology

Brooklyn, New York
www.citytech.cuny.edu Federal Code: 002696

4-year public technical college in very large city.
Enrollment: 15,303 undergrads, 35% part-time. 2,747 full-time freshmen.
Selectivity: Open admission; but selective for some programs.

BASIC COSTS (2012-2013)
Tuition and fees: $5,769; out-of-state residents $14,889.
Per-credit charge: $230; out-of-state residents $485.

FINANCIAL AID PICTURE (2012-2013)
Students with need: Out of 2,566 full-time freshmen who applied for aid, 2,320 were judged to have need. Of these, 2,244 received aid, and 222 had their full need met. Average financial aid package met 64% of need; average scholarship/grant was $8,730; average loan was $3,297. For part-time students, average financial aid package was $5,528.
Students without need: 84 full-time freshmen who did not demonstrate need for aid received scholarships/grants; average award was $271. No-need awards available for state/district residency.
Additional info: Foreign students applying for aid must have resided in New York for at least 1 year.

FINANCIAL AID PROCEDURES
Forms required: FAFSA.
Dates and Deadlines: Priority date 3/31; no closing date.

CONTACT
Sandra Higgins, Director of Financial Aid
300 Jay Street Namm G17, Brooklyn, NY 11201
(718) 260-5700

City University of New York: Queens College

Flushing, New York
www.qc.cuny.edu Federal Code: 002690

4-year public liberal arts and teachers college in very large city.
Enrollment: 15,257 undergrads, 26% part-time. 1,419 full-time freshmen.
Selectivity: Admits less than 50% of applicants.

BASIC COSTS (2012-2013)
Tuition and fees: $5,907; out-of-state residents $15,027.
Per-credit charge: $230; out-of-state residents $485.
Additional info: Board plan not available. Room-only rates range from $9,950-$15,390 depending on room size and semester.

FINANCIAL AID PICTURE (2012-2013)
Students with need: Out of 1,307 full-time freshmen who applied for aid, 1,185 were judged to have need. Of these, 1,185 received aid, and 747 had their full need met. Need-based aid available for part-time students.
Students without need: No-need awards available for academics, athletics, minority status, music/drama, ROTC, state/district residency.
Scholarships offered: ***Merit:*** CUNY Honors College; full tuition. Regents Award for Deceased or Disabled Veterans; $450 per year. Vietnam Veteran Tuition Aid Program; cost of tuition per semester. Regents Award for children of deceased police officers, firefighters, or corrections officers; $450 per year. Paul Douglas Teacher Scholarship Program; up to $5,000 per year. State Aid to Native Americans; $1,100 per year. SEEK Presidential Scholarship; Beinstock Memorial Scholarship for students with disabilities; CMP Publications Scholarship in Journalism or English; Daly Scholarship in the Physical Sciences; Foster Scholarship for women and minorities; Kupferberg Memorial Scholarship; Linakis Scholarship; Mitsui USA Scholarships; Nagdimon Scholarship; Queens College Scholarships; Weprin Memorial Scholarship in the Public Interest. ***Athletic:*** 25 full-time freshmen received athletic scholarships; average amount $6,268.
Cumulative student debt: 45% of graduating class had student loans; average debt was $17,700.

FINANCIAL AID PROCEDURES
Forms required: FAFSA, state aid form, institutional form.
Dates and Deadlines: Priority date 2/15; no closing date. Applicants notified on a rolling basis starting 5/1; must reply within 3 week(s) of notification.
Transfers: Priority date 5/1; no deadline. Applicants notified on a rolling basis.

CONTACT
Rena Smith-Kiawu, Director of Financial Aid
6530 Kissena Boulevard, Jefferson 117, Flushing, NY 11367-1597
(718) 997-5123

City University of New York: Queensborough Community College

Bayside, New York
www.qcc.cuny.edu Federal Code: 002697

2-year public community college in very large city.
Enrollment: 14,092 undergrads, 34% part-time. 3,050 full-time freshmen.
Selectivity: Open admission.

BASIC COSTS (2012-2013)
Tuition and fees: $4,240; out-of-state residents $8,140.
Per-credit charge: $165; out-of-state residents $260.

FINANCIAL AID PICTURE
Students with need: Need-based aid available for full-time students.

FINANCIAL AID PROCEDURES
Forms required: FAFSA, institutional form.
Dates and Deadlines: Applicants notified on a rolling basis starting 7/15.

CONTACT
Veronica Lukas, Director of Enrollment Management and Student Financial Services
222-05 56th Avenue, Bayside, NY 11364-1497
(718) 631-6267

City University of New York: York College

Jamaica, New York
www.york.cuny.edu Federal Code: 004759

4-year public liberal arts college in very large city.
Enrollment: 7,568 undergrads, 30% part-time. 1,089 full-time freshmen.

BASIC COSTS (2012-2013)
Tuition and fees: $5,796; out-of-state residents $14,916.
Per-credit charge: $230; out-of-state residents $485.

FINANCIAL AID PICTURE (2012-2013)
Students with need: Out of 958 full-time freshmen who applied for aid, 761 were judged to have need. Of these, 756 received aid, and 13 had their full need met. Average financial aid package met 36% of need; average scholarship/grant was $2,103; average loan was $1,843. For part-time students, average financial aid package was $4,001.
Students without need: 6 full-time freshmen who did not demonstrate need for aid received scholarships/grants; average award was $583. No-need awards available for academics.

Cumulative student debt: 10% of graduating class had student loans; average debt was $7,531.

FINANCIAL AID PROCEDURES

Forms required: FAFSA, state aid form.

Dates and Deadlines: Priority date 4/1; closing date 6/1. Applicants notified on a rolling basis starting 2/15; must reply within 4 week(s) of notification.

Transfers: No deadline. Applicants notified on a rolling basis starting 3/1.

CONTACT

Cathy Michaels, Director of Financial Aid
94-20 Guy R. Brewer Boulevard, Jamaica, NY 11451-9989
(718) 262-2230

Clarkson University

Potsdam, New York
www.clarkson.edu Federal Code: 002699

4-year private university in small town.
Enrollment: 3,014 undergrads. 778 full-time freshmen.
Selectivity: Admits over 75% of applicants.

BASIC COSTS (2013-2014)

Tuition and fees: $40,610.
Per-credit charge: $1,324.
Room and board: $12,998.
Additional info: Tuition/fee waivers available for minority students.

FINANCIAL AID PICTURE (2012-2013)

Students with need: Out of 722 full-time freshmen who applied for aid, 680 were judged to have need. Of these, 680 received aid, and 105 had their full need met. Average financial aid package met 90% of need; average scholarship/grant was $29,869; average loan was $3,848. For part-time students, average financial aid package was $6,597.

Students without need: 90 full-time freshmen who did not demonstrate need for aid received scholarships/grants; average award was $18,807. No-need awards available for academics, alumni affiliation, leadership, minority status, ROTC.

Scholarships offered: 13 full-time freshmen received athletic scholarships; average amount $38,084.

Cumulative student debt: 80% of graduating class had student loans; average debt was $27,866.

FINANCIAL AID PROCEDURES

Forms required: FAFSA, state aid form.

Dates and Deadlines: Priority date 2/15; closing date 3/1. Applicants notified on a rolling basis starting 3/18; must reply by 5/1 or within 2 week(s) of notification.

Transfers: Closing date 4/15. Applicants notified on a rolling basis starting 3/1. Transfer Leadership & Achievement scholarships, Phi Theta Kappa scholarships and Alpha Beta Gamma awards available in addition to state and federal programs.

CONTACT

Kara Pitts, Associate Dean of New Student Financial Aid
Holcroft House, Potsdam, NY 13699
(800) 527-6577

Clinton Community College

Plattsburgh, New York
www.clinton.edu Federal Code: 006787

2-year public community college in large town.
Enrollment: 1,519 undergrads, 22% part-time. 310 full-time freshmen.
Selectivity: Admits 50 to 75% of applicants.

BASIC COSTS (2012-2013)

Tuition and fees: $4,308; out-of-state residents $8,988.
Per-credit charge: $159; out-of-state residents $350.

FINANCIAL AID PICTURE (2012-2013)

Students with need: Need-based aid available for full-time and part-time students.

Students without need: This college awards aid only to students with need.

FINANCIAL AID PROCEDURES

Forms required: FAFSA, state aid form.

Dates and Deadlines: Priority date 6/12; no closing date. Applicants notified on a rolling basis starting 4/12; must reply within 2 week(s) of notification.

CONTACT

Cheryl Seymour, Director of Financial Aid
136 Clinton Point Drive, Plattsburgh, NY 12901-4297
(518) 562-4125

Cochran School of Nursing

Yonkers, New York
www.cochranschoolofnursing.us Federal Code: 006443

2-year private nursing college in small city.
Enrollment: 88 undergrads.

BASIC COSTS (2012-2013)

Additional info: Tuition and required fees for full 2-year AAS program is $27,781.

FINANCIAL AID PICTURE

Students with need: Need-based aid available for full-time and part-time students.

Students without need: This college awards aid only to students with need.

FINANCIAL AID PROCEDURES

Forms required: FAFSA.

Dates and Deadlines: Closing date 4/30. Applicants notified on a rolling basis.

CONTACT

Maria Goncalves, Financial Aid Officer
967 North Broadway, Yonkers, NY 10701
(914) 964-4316

Colgate University

Hamilton, New York Federal Code: 002701
www.colgate.edu CSS Code: 2086

4-year private university and liberal arts college in small town.
Enrollment: 2,850 undergrads. 756 full-time freshmen.
Selectivity: Admits less than 50% of applicants.

BASIC COSTS (2012-2013)

Tuition and fees: $44,640.
Room and board: $11,075.

FINANCIAL AID PICTURE (2012-2013)

Students with need: Out of 312 full-time freshmen who applied for aid, 252 were judged to have need. Of these, 252 received aid, and 252 had their full need met. Average financial aid package met 100% of need; average scholarship/grant was $38,421; average loan was $1,802.

Students without need: No-need awards available for athletics.

Scholarships offered: 50 full-time freshmen received athletic scholarships; average amount $30,577.

Cumulative student debt: 34% of graduating class had student loans; average debt was $20,751.

FINANCIAL AID PROCEDURES

Forms required: CSS PROFILE.

Dates and Deadlines: Closing date 1/15. Applicants notified by 3/25; must reply by 5/1 or within 2 week(s) of notification.

Transfers: Closing date 3/15. Applicants notified by 4/15; must reply by 5/15 or within 2 week(s) of notification. Financial aid for transfer students extremely limited.

CONTACT

Marcelle Tyburski, Director of Financial Aid
13 Oak Drive, Hamilton, NY 13346-1383
(315) 228-7431

College of Mount St. Vincent

Riverdale, New York
www.mountsaintvincent.edu Federal Code: 002703

4-year private liberal arts college in very large city, affiliated with Roman Catholic Church.

Enrollment: 1,655 undergrads, 12% part-time. 486 full-time freshmen.

Selectivity: Admits over 75% of applicants.

BASIC COSTS (2012-2013)

Tuition and fees: $29,470.

Per-credit charge: $860.

Room and board: $11,650.

FINANCIAL AID PICTURE

Students with need: Need-based aid available for full-time students.

Students without need: No-need awards available for academics, alumni affiliation, leadership.

FINANCIAL AID PROCEDURES

Forms required: FAFSA, state aid form.

Dates and Deadlines: Priority date 3/1; no closing date. Applicants notified on a rolling basis starting 3/1; must reply by 5/1 or within 3 week(s) of notification.

Transfers: Priority date 5/15. Applicants notified on a rolling basis starting 3/1; must reply by 5/1 or within 3 week(s) of notification.

CONTACT

Monica Simotas, Director of Financial Aid
6301 Riverdale Avenue, Riverdale, NY 10471-1093
(718) 405-3289

College of New Rochelle

New Rochelle, New York
www.cnr.edu Federal Code: 002704

4-year private nursing and liberal arts college for women in small city, affiliated with Roman Catholic Church.

Enrollment: 861 undergrads, 37% part-time. 90 full-time freshmen.

Selectivity: Admits 50 to 75% of applicants.

BASIC COSTS (2013-2014)

Tuition and fees: $31,260.

Per-credit charge: $896.

Room and board: $11,690.

FINANCIAL AID PICTURE

Students with need: Need-based aid available for full-time and part-time students. Work study available nights, weekends, and for part-time students.

Students without need: No-need awards available for academics, art, leadership, music/drama.

FINANCIAL AID PROCEDURES

Forms required: FAFSA, institutional form.

Dates and Deadlines: Priority date 3/1; no closing date. Applicants notified on a rolling basis starting 1/1; must reply within 2 week(s) of notification.

CONTACT

Ann Pelak, Director of Financial Aid
29 Castle Place, New Rochelle, NY 10805-2339
(914) 654-5225

College of Saint Rose

Albany, New York
www.strose.edu Federal Code: 002705

4-year private liberal arts college in small city.

Enrollment: 2,835 undergrads, 4% part-time. 595 full-time freshmen.

Selectivity: Admits 50 to 75% of applicants.

BASIC COSTS (2012-2013)

Tuition and fees: $26,622.

Per-credit charge: $856.

Room and board: $10,870.

FINANCIAL AID PICTURE (2011-2012)

Students with need: Out of 579 full-time freshmen who applied for aid, 519 were judged to have need. Of these, 518 received aid, and 95 had their full need met. Average financial aid package met 79% of need; average scholarship/grant was $3,233; average loan was $3,229. For part-time students, average financial aid package was $6,920.

Students without need: 63 full-time freshmen who did not demonstrate need for aid received scholarships/grants; average award was $11,711. No-need awards available for academics, alumni affiliation, art, athletics, music/drama.

Scholarships offered: ***Merit:*** Academic, music, art, athletic awards based on talent. ***Athletic:*** 11 full-time freshmen received athletic scholarships; average amount $13,517.

Cumulative student debt: 85% of graduating class had student loans; average debt was $33,824.

FINANCIAL AID PROCEDURES

Forms required: FAFSA, state aid form.

Dates and Deadlines: Priority date 2/1; closing date 4/1. Applicants notified on a rolling basis starting 2/20; must reply by 5/1 or within 2 week(s) of notification.

Transfers: Applicants notified on a rolling basis starting 2/1; must reply by 5/1 or within 2 week(s) of notification.

CONTACT

Steve Dwire, Director of Financial Aid
432 Western Avenue, Albany, NY 12203
(518) 458-5424

College of Westchester

White Plains, New York
www.cw.edu Federal Code: 005208

2-year for-profit business and career college in small city.

Enrollment: 1,036 undergrads.

BASIC COSTS (2012-2013)

Tuition and fees: $22,900.

Per-credit charge: $730.

Additional info: Tuition/fee waivers available for unemployed or children of unemployed.

FINANCIAL AID PICTURE

Students with need: Need-based aid available for full-time and part-time students. Work study available nights, weekends, and for part-time students.

Students without need: No-need awards available for academics, alumni affiliation.

FINANCIAL AID PROCEDURES

Forms required: FAFSA, state aid form, institutional form.

Dates and Deadlines: Applicants notified on a rolling basis starting 2/7; must reply within 2 week(s) of notification.

CONTACT

Dianne Pepitone, Director, Student Financial Services
325 Central Park Avenue, White Plains, NY 10602
(914) 831-0473

Columbia University

New York, New York
www.columbia.edu
Federal Code: E00485
CSS Code: 2116

4-year private university in very large city.
Enrollment: 6,068 undergrads. 1,415 full-time freshmen.
Selectivity: Admits less than 50% of applicants.

BASIC COSTS (2012-2013)

Tuition and fees: $47,246.
Room and board: $11,496.

FINANCIAL AID PICTURE (2012-2013)

Students with need: Out of 882 full-time freshmen who applied for aid, 725 were judged to have need. Of these, 725 received aid, and 725 had their full need met. Average financial aid package met 100% of need; average scholarship/grant was $42,785; average loan was $2,346.

Students without need: This college awards aid only to students with need.

Additional info: We have eliminated student loans for those receiving Columbia need-based aid and replaced them with additional University grants, and significantly reduced the parent contribution for families making less than $100,000 per year.

FINANCIAL AID PROCEDURES

Forms required: FAFSA, CSS PROFILE.

Dates and Deadlines: Closing date 3/1. Applicants notified by 4/1; must reply by 5/1.

Transfers: Closing date 4/20. Must reply within 3 week(s) of notification.

CONTACT

Jessica Marinaccio, Dean of Undergraduate Admissions & Financial Aid
1130 Amsterdam Avenue, New York, NY 10027
(212) 854-3711

Columbia University: School of General Studies

New York, New York
www.gs.columbia.edu
Federal Code: E00487

4-year private university and liberal arts college in very large city.
Enrollment: 1,632 undergrads, 32% part-time. 108 full-time freshmen.
Selectivity: Admits less than 50% of applicants.

BASIC COSTS (2012-2013)

Tuition and fees: $45,699.
Per-credit charge: $1,454.
Room and board: $10,123.
Additional info: First-year students also pay a one-time transcript fee of $105.

FINANCIAL AID PICTURE (2011-2012)

Students with need: 49% of average financial aid package awarded as scholarships/grants, 51% awarded as loans/jobs. Need-based aid available for part-time students.

Students without need: This college awards aid only to students with need.

Scholarships offered: All applicants should submit General Studies Application for Financial Aid.

FINANCIAL AID PROCEDURES

Forms required: FAFSA, institutional form.

Dates and Deadlines: Closing date 6/1. Applicants notified on a rolling basis; must reply within 3 week(s) of notification.

Transfers: Applicants notified on a rolling basis starting 4/1; must reply within 2 week(s) of notification.

CONTACT

William Bailey, Director of Educational Financing
408 Lewisohn Hall, Mail Code 4101, New York, NY 10027
(212) 854-5410

Columbia-Greene Community College

Hudson, New York
www.sunycgcc.edu
Federal Code: 006789

2-year public community college in small town.
Enrollment: 1,596 undergrads, 36% part-time. 348 full-time freshmen.
Selectivity: Admits over 75% of applicants.

BASIC COSTS (2012-2013)

Tuition and fees: $4,122; out-of-state residents $7,914.
Per-credit charge: $158; out-of-state residents $316.

FINANCIAL AID PICTURE

Students with need: Need-based aid available for full-time and part-time students. Work study available nights, weekends, and for part-time students.

FINANCIAL AID PROCEDURES

Forms required: FAFSA, institutional form.

CONTACT

Richard Sabbia, Director of Financial Aid
4400 Route 23, Hudson, NY 12534

Concordia College

Bronxville, New York
www.concordia-ny.edu
Federal Code: 002709

4-year private liberal arts college in small town, affiliated with Lutheran Church - Missouri Synod.
Enrollment: 867 undergrads.
Selectivity: Admits 50 to 75% of applicants.

BASIC COSTS (2012-2013)

Tuition and fees: $27,520.
Room and board: $9,750.

FINANCIAL AID PICTURE

Students with need: Need-based aid available for full-time and part-time students. Work study available nights, weekends, and for part-time students.

Students without need: No-need awards available for academics, athletics, leadership, music/drama, religious affiliation.

Scholarships offered: Fellows Scholarship: $15,000 a year; for 1800 SAT (exclusive of Writing) and 3.5/4.0 GPA. Merit Scholarships: $6,000-$9,000 for 80 average and above. Athletic, Faith Based and Leadership Scholarships are also available.

FINANCIAL AID PROCEDURES
Forms required: FAFSA, state aid form.
Dates and Deadlines: Priority date 4/1; no closing date. Applicants notified on a rolling basis starting 2/15; must reply by 5/1 or within 3 week(s) of notification.
Transfers: Priority date 6/1; no deadline. Applicants notified on a rolling basis starting 4/1; must reply by 8/1 or within 3 week(s) of notification.

CONTACT
Kenneth Fick, Director of Financial Aid
171 White Plains Road, Bronxville, NY 10708-1923
(914) 337-9300 ext. 2146

Cooper Union for the Advancement of Science and Art
New York, New York — Federal Code: 002710
cooper.edu — CSS Code: 2097

4-year private visual arts and engineering college in very large city.
Enrollment: 855 undergrads, 1% part-time. 198 full-time freshmen.
Selectivity: Admits less than 50% of applicants.

BASIC COSTS (2013-2014)
Tuition and fees: $41,400.
Additional info: All students receive a full-tuition scholarship. Cost of room only $11,000. Board plan not available.

FINANCIAL AID PICTURE (2011-2012)
Students with need: Out of 120 full-time freshmen who applied for aid, 60 were judged to have need. Of these, 60 received aid, and 38 had their full need met. Average financial aid package met 92% of need; average scholarship/grant was $42,754; average loan was $3,291.
Students without need: 138 full-time freshmen who did not demonstrate need for aid received scholarships/grants; average award was $37,500. No-need awards available for academics.
Cumulative student debt: 23% of graduating class had student loans; average debt was $15,864.
Additional info: All undergraduate students receive full-tuition scholarships. Students able to document need receive financial aid package that may include combination of grants, loans, work-study, internships. Late financial aid applications processed on rolling basis.

FINANCIAL AID PROCEDURES
Forms required: FAFSA, CSS PROFILE.
Dates and Deadlines: Priority date 4/15; closing date 6/1. Applicants notified on a rolling basis starting 6/1; must reply by 6/30 or within 2 week(s) of notification.
Transfers: Priority date 4/1; closing date 5/1. Applicants notified by 6/1; must reply by 6/30 or within 2 week(s) of notification.

CONTACT
Mary Ruokonen, Director of Financial Aid
30 Cooper Square, Suite 300, New York, NY 10003-7183
(212) 353-4130

Cornell University
Ithaca, New York — Federal Code: 002711
www.cornell.edu — CSS Code: 2098

4-year private university in large town.
Enrollment: 14,186 undergrads. 3,217 full-time freshmen.
Selectivity: Admits less than 50% of applicants.

BASIC COSTS (2013-2014)
Tuition and fees: $45,359.
Room and board: $13,678.
Additional info: Tuition amounts listed are for Endowed/Private colleges only: Architecture, Art & Planning; Arts & Sciences; Engineering; Hotel Administration. Contract/State college tuition differs and varies by residency.

FINANCIAL AID PICTURE (2012-2013)
Students with need: Out of 1,907 full-time freshmen who applied for aid, 1,527 were judged to have need. Of these, 1,527 received aid, and 1,527 had their full need met. Average financial aid package met 100% of need; average scholarship/grant was $37,941; average loan was $2,757.
Students without need: This college awards aid only to students with need.
Cumulative student debt: 45% of graduating class had student loans; average debt was $20,490.

FINANCIAL AID PROCEDURES
Forms required: FAFSA, CSS PROFILE, institutional form.
Dates and Deadlines: Closing date 2/15. Applicants notified by 4/1; must reply by 5/1.
Transfers: Applicants notified on a rolling basis starting 4/1; must reply by 6/1. Submit Cornell aid application forms in addition to regular required forms.

CONTACT
Thomas Keane, Director, Financial Aid and Student Employment
410 Thurston Avenue, Ithaca, NY 14850-2488
(607) 255-2000

Corning Community College
Corning, New York
www.corning-cc.edu — Federal Code: 002863

2-year public community college in large town.
Enrollment: 3,226 undergrads, 33% part-time. 789 full-time freshmen.
Selectivity: Open admission; but selective for some programs.

BASIC COSTS (2012-2013)
Tuition and fees: $4,392; out-of-state residents $8,342.
Per-credit charge: $165; out-of-state residents $330.

FINANCIAL AID PICTURE (2011-2012)
Students with need: Need-based aid available for part-time students. Work study available weekends and for part-time students.
Students without need: This college awards aid only to students with need.

FINANCIAL AID PROCEDURES
Forms required: FAFSA, state aid form.
Dates and Deadlines: Priority date 4/1; no closing date. Applicants notified on a rolling basis starting 4/1; must reply within 4 week(s) of notification.

CONTACT
Barbara Snow, Director of Financial Aid
One Academic Drive, Corning, NY 14830
(607) 962-9011

Culinary Institute of America
Hyde Park, New York
www.ciachef.edu — Federal Code: 007304

4-year private culinary school in large town.
Enrollment: 2,765 undergrads. 532 full-time freshmen.
Selectivity: Admits over 75% of applicants.

BASIC COSTS (2013-2014)
Tuition and fees: $27,720.
Room and board: $8,830.

FINANCIAL AID PICTURE (2011-2012)
Students with need: Out of 495 full-time freshmen who applied for aid, 472 were judged to have need. Of these, 472 received aid, and 26 had their full need met. Average financial aid package met 45% of need; average scholarship/grant was $9,201; average loan was $3,307. Need-based aid available for part-time students.
Students without need: 134 full-time freshmen who did not demonstrate need for aid received scholarships/grants; average award was $3,393. No-need awards available for academics, alumni affiliation, job skills, leadership.
Cumulative student debt: 90% of graduating class had student loans; average debt was $34,802.

FINANCIAL AID PROCEDURES
Forms required: FAFSA.
Dates and Deadlines: Priority date 4/15; no closing date. Applicants notified on a rolling basis starting 3/5; must reply by 5/1 or within 4 week(s) of notification.

CONTACT
Kathleen Gailor, Director of Financial Aid
1946 Campus Drive, Hyde Park, NY 12538-1499
(845) 451-1243

Daemen College
Amherst, New York
www.daemen.edu Federal Code: 002808

4-year private liberal arts college in small city.
Enrollment: 2,190 undergrads.
Selectivity: Admits less than 50% of applicants.

BASIC COSTS (2012-2013)
Tuition and fees: $23,130.
Per-credit charge: $750.
Room and board: $10,700.

FINANCIAL AID PICTURE
Students with need: Need-based aid available for full-time and part-time students. Work study available nights, weekends, and for part-time students.
Students without need: No-need awards available for academics, art, athletics, leadership.
Scholarships offered: President's Scholarship, Dean's Scholarship, Alumni Grant: $2,500-$10,000; renewable awards to freshmen and transfers; based on high school GPA and SAT scores. Trustee Scholarship: $17,000 (2 awards) and $14,000 (4 awards). Renewable visual arts scholarships: $5,000; 2 awards.

FINANCIAL AID PROCEDURES
Forms required: FAFSA, state aid form.
Dates and Deadlines: Priority date 2/15; no closing date. Applicants notified on a rolling basis starting 2/1; must reply within 2 week(s) of notification.

CONTACT
Jeffrey Pagano, Director of Financial Aid
4380 Main Street, Amherst, NY 14226-3592
(716) 839-8254

Davis College
Johnson City, New York
www.davisny.edu Federal Code: 015291

4-year private Bible college in large town, affiliated with nondenominational tradition.
Enrollment: 351 undergrads.

BASIC COSTS (2012-2013)
Tuition and fees: $11,940.
Per-credit charge: $405.
Room and board: $6,000.
Additional info: Tuition at time of enrollment locked for 4 years.

FINANCIAL AID PICTURE
Students with need: Work study available nights, weekends, and for part-time students.
Students without need: No-need awards available for academics, alumni affiliation.

FINANCIAL AID PROCEDURES
Forms required: FAFSA, state aid form, institutional form.
Dates and Deadlines: Applicants notified on a rolling basis.
Transfers: No deadline. Applicants notified on a rolling basis.

CONTACT
Sandra Baker, Director of Financial Aid
400 Riverside Drive, Johnson City, NY 13790
(607) 729-1581 ext. 331

DeVry College of New York: Midtown Campus
New York, New York
www.devry.edu Federal Code: 003099

4-year for-profit business and technical college in very large city.
Enrollment: 1,238 undergrads, 43% part-time. 73 full-time freshmen.

BASIC COSTS (2012-2013)
Tuition and fees: $16,076.
Per-credit charge: $609.

FINANCIAL AID PICTURE
Students with need: Need-based aid available for full-time and part-time students.
Students without need: This college awards aid only to students with need.

CONTACT
Elvira Senese, Director, Student Finance
180 Madison Avenue, Suite 900, New York, NY 10016
(718) 472-2728

Dominican College of Blauvelt
Orangeburg, New York
www.dc.edu Federal Code: 002713

4-year private health science and liberal arts college in small town.
Enrollment: 1,559 undergrads, 13% part-time. 293 full-time freshmen.
Selectivity: Admits 50 to 75% of applicants.

BASIC COSTS (2013-2014)
Tuition and fees: $24,790.
Per-credit charge: $725.
Room and board: $11,650.

FINANCIAL AID PICTURE (2012-2013)
Students with need: Out of 289 full-time freshmen who applied for aid, 266 were judged to have need. Of these, 266 received aid, and 28 had their full need met. Average financial aid package met 61% of need; average scholarship/grant was $14,615; average loan was $3,259. For part-time students, average financial aid package was $5,885.
Students without need: 41 full-time freshmen who did not demonstrate need for aid received scholarships/grants; average award was $6,730. No-need awards available for academics, athletics.

Scholarships offered: ***Merit:*** All applicants considered for non-need based scholarships or grants based on high school GPA and SAT/ACT scores. ***Athletic:*** 18 full-time freshmen received athletic scholarships; average amount $1,472.
Cumulative student debt: 95% of graduating class had student loans; average debt was $17,930.
Additional info: Individual financial aid counseling available.

FINANCIAL AID PROCEDURES
Forms required: FAFSA, state aid form.
Dates and Deadlines: Priority date 2/15; no closing date. Applicants notified on a rolling basis starting 2/1; must reply within 2 week(s) of notification.

CONTACT
Daniel Shields, Director of Financial Aid
470 Western Highway, Orangeburg, NY 10962-1210
(845) 848-7821

Dowling College
Oakdale, New York
www.dowling.edu Federal Code: 002667

4-year private business and liberal arts college in large town.
Enrollment: 2,133 undergrads, 16% part-time. 345 full-time freshmen.
Selectivity: Admits over 75% of applicants.

BASIC COSTS (2012-2013)
Tuition and fees: $27,124.
Per-credit charge: $849.
Room and board: $10,590.

FINANCIAL AID PICTURE (2011-2012)
Students with need: Out of 330 full-time freshmen who applied for aid, 313 were judged to have need. Of these, 313 received aid, and 175 had their full need met. Average financial aid package met 96% of need; average scholarship/grant was $7,760; average loan was $3,021. For part-time students, average financial aid package was $8,351.
Students without need: 38 full-time freshmen who did not demonstrate need for aid received scholarships/grants; average award was $6,471. No-need awards available for academics, alumni affiliation, athletics.
Scholarships offered: 39 full-time freshmen received athletic scholarships; average amount $7,667.
Cumulative student debt: 78% of graduating class had student loans; average debt was $16,840.

FINANCIAL AID PROCEDURES
Forms required: FAFSA, state aid form.
Dates and Deadlines: Priority date 3/1; no closing date. Applicants notified on a rolling basis starting 3/15.
Transfers: No deadline. Applicants notified on a rolling basis. Academic scholarships available for transfers with 60 credits or the equivalent of an associate degree.

CONTACT
Carla Guevara, Director of Financial Aid
150 Idle Hour Boulevard, Oakdale, NY 11769-1999
(631) 244-3110

Dutchess Community College
Poughkeepsie, New York
www.sunydutchess.edu Federal Code: 002864

2-year public community college in large town.
Enrollment: 7,571 undergrads, 34% part-time. 2,043 full-time freshmen.
Selectivity: Open admission; but selective for some programs.

BASIC COSTS (2012-2013)
Tuition and fees: $3,520; out-of-state residents $6,620.
Per-credit charge: $129; out-of-state residents $258.
Room and board: $8,900.

FINANCIAL AID PICTURE (2011-2012)
Students with need: 74% of average financial aid package awarded as scholarships/grants, 26% awarded as loans/jobs. Need-based aid available for part-time students.
Students without need: No-need awards available for academics.
Scholarships offered: Dutchess County high school graduates in top 10% of their class: full tuition payment for 4 full-time consecutive semesters.

FINANCIAL AID PROCEDURES
Forms required: FAFSA, state aid form.
Dates and Deadlines: Priority date 5/1; no closing date. Applicants notified on a rolling basis starting 5/15; must reply within 2 week(s) of notification.

CONTACT
Susan Mead, Director of Financial Aid
53 Pendell Road, Poughkeepsie, NY 12601-1595
(845) 431-8030

D'Youville College
Buffalo, New York
www.dyc.edu

4-year private health science and liberal arts college in large city.
Enrollment: 1,982 undergrads, 14% part-time. 272 full-time freshmen.
Selectivity: Admits over 75% of applicants.

BASIC COSTS (2012-2013)
Tuition and fees: $22,240.
Per-credit charge: $680.
Room and board: $10,250.

FINANCIAL AID PICTURE (2012-2013)
Students with need: Out of 272 full-time freshmen who applied for aid, 243 were judged to have need. Of these, 242 received aid, and 60 had their full need met. Average financial aid package met 75.8% of need; average scholarship/grant was $14,667; average loan was $3,704. For part-time students, average financial aid package was $8,240.
Students without need: 21 full-time freshmen who did not demonstrate need for aid received scholarships/grants; average award was $8,482. No-need awards available for academics, leadership, religious affiliation, ROTC.
Scholarships offered: Presidential Honors Scholarship: for students with 1100 SAT (Math and Verbal) or 24 ACT Composite; covers 50% tuition and 25% of standard double room rate. Academic Initiative Scholarship: For students with 1000-1090 SAT (math & verbal scores only) or 21-23 ACT score and an 85 high school average. The award is for 25% of tuition and 50% of the standard double room rate in Marguerite Hall or 50% of the standard room rate in the apartments for full-time students. Achievement Scholarship: For students with 900-1090 SAT score or 19-23 ACT and an 80-84 high school average, demonstrated leadership and community service. The awards range from $1,000- $4,000. Transfer Achievement Scholarship: For students with a G.P.A. of 2.75-4.0 from previously attended institution(s). The award amounts range from $2,500-$5,000. All awards are renewable for the standard duration of the specific academic program and have GPA and other requirements.
Cumulative student debt: 94% of graduating class had student loans; average debt was $41,281.

FINANCIAL AID PROCEDURES
Forms required: FAFSA, state aid form.
Dates and Deadlines: Priority date 3/1; no closing date. Applicants notified on a rolling basis starting 4/1; must reply within 2 week(s) of notification.
Transfers: Applicants notified on a rolling basis starting 4/1; must reply within 2 week(s) of notification.

CONTACT
Lorraine Metz, Director of Financial Aid
320 Porter Avenue, Buffalo, NY 14201-1084

Eastman School of Music of the University of Rochester

Rochester, New York
www.esm.rochester.edu Federal Code: 008124

4-year private music and performing arts college in small city.
Enrollment: 521 undergrads. 122 full-time freshmen.
Selectivity: Admits less than 50% of applicants.

BASIC COSTS (2012-2013)
Tuition and fees: $43,924.
Per-credit charge: $1,275.
Room and board: $12,586.

FINANCIAL AID PICTURE
Students with need: Need-based aid available for full-time and part-time students.
Students without need: No-need awards available for academics, alumni affiliation, job skills, leadership, minority status, music/drama, state/district residency.
Scholarships offered: All merit scholarships awarded based on admission criteria, and do not require separate application, audition, or interview.

FINANCIAL AID PROCEDURES
Forms required: FAFSA, state aid form, institutional form.
Dates and Deadlines: Closing date 2/28. Applicants notified on a rolling basis starting 3/15; must reply by 5/1 or within 2 week(s) of notification.
Transfers: No deadline. Applicants notified on a rolling basis starting 3/15; must reply by 5/1 or within 2 week(s) of notification.

CONTACT
Mary Ellen Nugent, Director of Financial Aid
26 Gibbs Street, Rochester, NY 14604-2599
(585) 274-1070

Elmira Business Institute

Elmira, New York
www.ebi-college.com Federal Code: 009043

2-year for-profit business and technical college in large town.
Enrollment: 176 undergrads. 380 full-time freshmen.
Selectivity: Open admission.

BASIC COSTS (2013-2014)
Tuition and fees: $12,100.
Per-credit charge: $400.

FINANCIAL AID PICTURE (2011-2012)
Students with need: Out of 380 full-time freshmen who applied for aid, 380 were judged to have need. Of these, 369 received aid. Average financial aid package met 60% of need; average scholarship/grant was $4,412; average loan was $1,720. For part-time students, average financial aid package was $2,696.
Students without need: This college awards aid only to students with need.
Cumulative student debt: 97% of graduating class had student loans; average debt was $3,805.

FINANCIAL AID PROCEDURES
Forms required: FAFSA, state aid form, institutional form.
Dates and Deadlines: Closing date 5/1.

CONTACT
Sue Reinbold, Financial Aid Director
303 North Main Street, Elmira, NY 14901
(607) 729-8915

Elmira Business Institute: Vestal

Vestal, New York
www.elmirabusinessinstitute.edu Federal Code: 009043

2-year for-profit business and technical college in small city.
Enrollment: 165 undergrads. 380 full-time freshmen.
Selectivity: Open admission.

BASIC COSTS (2013-2014)
Tuition and fees: $12,100.
Per-credit charge: $400.

FINANCIAL AID PICTURE (2011-2012)
Students with need: Out of 380 full-time freshmen who applied for aid, 380 were judged to have need. Of these, 369 received aid. Average financial aid package met 60% of need; average scholarship/grant was $4,412; average loan was $1,720. For part-time students, average financial aid package was $2,696.
Students without need: This college awards aid only to students with need.
Cumulative student debt: 97% of graduating class had student loans; average debt was $3,805.

FINANCIAL AID PROCEDURES
Forms required: FAFSA, state aid form, institutional form.
Dates and Deadlines: Applicants notified on a rolling basis.

CONTACT
Susan Reinbold, Director of Finanical Services
4100 Vestal Road, Vestal, NY 13850
(607) 729-8915

Elmira College

Elmira, New York
www.elmira.edu Federal Code: 002718

4-year private liberal arts college in large town.
Enrollment: 1,333 undergrads, 14% part-time. 356 full-time freshmen.
Selectivity: Admits over 75% of applicants. GED not accepted.

BASIC COSTS (2012-2013)
Tuition and fees: $38,150.
Room and board: $11,800.

FINANCIAL AID PICTURE (2012-2013)
Students with need: Out of 322 full-time freshmen who applied for aid, 300 were judged to have need. Of these, 300 received aid, and 54 had their full need met. Average financial aid package met 77% of need; average scholarship/grant was $27,361; average loan was $3,529. Need-based aid available for part-time students.
Students without need: 53 full-time freshmen who did not demonstrate need for aid received scholarships/grants; average award was $26,083. No-need awards available for academics, leadership, ROTC, state/district residency.
Scholarships offered: Valedictorian and salutatorian awards: 30 anticipated awards; full-tuition; renewable for 3 years. Additional scholarships: $26,000, $23,000, $21,000, $16,000 or $13,000; based on GPA, test scores, class rank, leadership; renewable for 3 additional years.
Cumulative student debt: 80% of graduating class had student loans; average debt was $28,586.

Additional info: Sibling Scholarship program provides 50% discounts on second immediate family member's room and board, regardless of need.

FINANCIAL AID PROCEDURES

Forms required: FAFSA, state aid form.

Dates and Deadlines: Priority date 2/1; no closing date. Applicants notified on a rolling basis starting 2/1; must reply by 5/1 or within 2 week(s) of notification.

Transfers: No deadline. Applicants notified on a rolling basis starting 2/1; must reply by 5/1 or within 2 week(s) of notification. Award for enrolled U.S. citizens from outside New York State. New merit scholarship for transfer students.

CONTACT

Kathleen Cohen, Dean of Financial Aid
One Park Place, Elmira, NY 14901
(607) 735-1728

Erie Community College

Buffalo, New York
www.ecc.edu Federal Code: 010684

2-year public community college in large city.
Enrollment: 11,684 undergrads, 22% part-time. 2,566 full-time freshmen.
Selectivity: Open admission; but selective for some programs.

BASIC COSTS (2012-2013)

Tuition and fees: $4,400; out-of-state residents $8,300.
Per-credit charge: $163; out-of-state residents $326.

FINANCIAL AID PICTURE (2011-2012)

Students with need: 75% of average financial aid package awarded as scholarships/grants, 25% awarded as loans/jobs. Need-based aid available for part-time students. Work study available weekends and for part-time students.

Students without need: This college awards aid only to students with need.

FINANCIAL AID PROCEDURES

Forms required: FAFSA, state aid form.

Dates and Deadlines: Priority date 5/1; no closing date. Applicants notified on a rolling basis starting 4/1; must reply within 2 week(s) of notification.

CONTACT

Scott Weltjen, Director of Financial Aid
6205 Main Street, Williamsville, NY 14221-7095
(716) 851-1677

Eugene Lang College The New School for Liberal Arts

New York, New York
www.newschool.edu/lang/ Federal Code: 002780

4-year private liberal arts college in very large city.
Enrollment: 1,457 undergrads, 7% part-time. 263 full-time freshmen.
Selectivity: Admits 50 to 75% of applicants.

BASIC COSTS (2012-2013)

Tuition and fees: $38,570.
Per-credit charge: $1,280.
Room and board: $17,770.
Additional info: Reported room and board price is for double-occupancy open room and unlimited meal plan. Other options: declining value meal plan; apartment-style suites; singles with private bath.

FINANCIAL AID PICTURE (2011-2012)

Students with need: Out of 149 full-time freshmen who applied for aid, 130 were judged to have need. Of these, 123 received aid, and 13 had their full need met. Average financial aid package met 66% of need; average scholarship/grant was $22,285; average loan was $8,190. Need-based aid available for part-time students.

Students without need: 16 full-time freshmen who did not demonstrate need for aid received scholarships/grants; average award was $11,980. No-need awards available for academics, leadership, minority status, state/district residency.

Cumulative student debt: 44% of graduating class had student loans; average debt was $34,455.

FINANCIAL AID PROCEDURES

Forms required: FAFSA, state aid form.

Dates and Deadlines: Applicants notified on a rolling basis starting 4/1; must reply within 4 week(s) of notification.

Transfers: Must reply within 4 week(s) of notification.

CONTACT

Lisa Shaheen, Director of Student Financial Aid
72 Fifth Avenue, New York, NY 10011
(212) 229-8930

Excelsior College

Albany, New York
www.excelsior.edu Federal Code: 014251

4-year private virtual liberal arts college in small city.
Enrollment: 35,302 undergrads, 100% part-time.
Selectivity: Open admission; but selective for some programs.

BASIC COSTS (2012-2013)

Additional info: Students charged $1015 enrollment fee and $390 per credit hour. Because of nontraditional pricing, school does not charge set tuition based on 15 credit hours per semester.

FINANCIAL AID PICTURE (2011-2012)

Students with need: 29% of average financial aid package awarded as scholarships/grants, 71% awarded as loans/jobs.

Students without need: This college awards aid only to students with need.

Additional info: Excelsior College is Title IV eligible for its degree programs, except for associate degree in nursing; approved for all veterans' education benefit programs.

FINANCIAL AID PROCEDURES

Dates and Deadlines: Applicants notified on a rolling basis; must reply within 2 week(s) of notification.

CONTACT

Thomas Dalton, Assistant Vice President for Enrollment Management, Financial Aid
7 Columbia Circle, Albany, NY 12203
(518) 464-8500

Fashion Institute of Technology

New York, New York
www.fitnyc.edu Federal Code: 002866

4-year public visual arts and business college in very large city.
Enrollment: 8,012 undergrads, 12% part-time. 1,210 full-time freshmen.
Selectivity: Admits less than 50% of applicants.

BASIC COSTS (2012-2013)

Tuition and fees: $4,790; out-of-state residents $13,190.
Per-credit charge: $175; out-of-state residents $525.

Room and board: $12,598.

FINANCIAL AID PICTURE (2011-2012)
Students with need: 33% of average financial aid package awarded as scholarships/grants, 67% awarded as loans/jobs. Need-based aid available for part-time students. Work study available nights, weekends, and for part-time students.
Students without need: This college awards aid only to students with need.

FINANCIAL AID PROCEDURES
Forms required: FAFSA, state aid form.
Dates and Deadlines: Priority date 2/15; no closing date. Applicants notified on a rolling basis starting 4/15; must reply within 2 week(s) of notification.

CONTACT
Mina Friedmann, Director of Financial Aid
227 West 27th Street, New York, NY 10001-5992
(212) 217-3560

Finger Lakes Community College
Canandaigua, New York
www.flcc.edu Federal Code: 007532

2-year public community college in small town.
Enrollment: 4,640 undergrads, 23% part-time. 1,492 full-time freshmen.
Selectivity: Open admission; but selective for some programs.

BASIC COSTS (2012-2013)
Tuition and fees: $4,068; out-of-state residents $7,722.
Per-credit charge: $138; out-of-state residents $276.

FINANCIAL AID PICTURE (2011-2012)
Students with need: Out of 1,406 full-time freshmen who applied for aid, 1,194 were judged to have need. Of these, 1,182 received aid. Need-based aid available for part-time students.
Students without need: This college awards aid only to students with need.

FINANCIAL AID PROCEDURES
Forms required: FAFSA, state aid form.
Dates and Deadlines: Priority date 3/15; no closing date. Applicants notified on a rolling basis starting 3/1; must reply within 2 week(s) of notification.

CONTACT
Susan Romano, Director, Financial Aid
3325 Marvin Sands Drive, Canandaigua, NY 14424-8395
(585) 785-1275

Five Towns College
Dix Hills, New York
www.ftc.edu Federal Code: 012561

4-year for-profit liberal arts and performing arts college in large town.
Enrollment: 867 undergrads, 4% part-time. 177 full-time freshmen.
Selectivity: Admits less than 50% of applicants.

BASIC COSTS (2013-2014)
Tuition and fees: $20,170.
Per-credit charge: $825.
Room and board: $13,170.

FINANCIAL AID PICTURE (2011-2012)
Students with need: 49% of average financial aid package awarded as scholarships/grants, 51% awarded as loans/jobs. Need-based aid available for part-time students. Work study available nights, weekends, and for part-time students.
Students without need: No-need awards available for academics, music/drama.

FINANCIAL AID PROCEDURES
Forms required: FAFSA, state aid form, institutional form.
Dates and Deadlines: Priority date 3/31; no closing date. Applicants notified on a rolling basis; must reply within 4 week(s) of notification.
Transfers: No deadline. Applicants notified on a rolling basis starting 1/1; must reply within 4 week(s) of notification.

CONTACT
Christine DeSousa, Director of Financial Aid
305 North Service Road, Dix Hills, NY 11746-6055
(631) 656-2164

Fordham University
Bronx, New York Federal Code: 002722
www.fordham.edu CSS Code: 2259

4-year private university in very large city, affiliated with Roman Catholic Church.
Enrollment: 8,197 undergrads, 6% part-time. 1,943 full-time freshmen.
Selectivity: Admits less than 50% of applicants.

BASIC COSTS (2012-2013)
Tuition and fees: $41,732.
Room and board: $15,374.

FINANCIAL AID PICTURE (2011-2012)
Students with need: Out of 1,730 full-time freshmen who applied for aid, 1,249 were judged to have need. Of these, 1,246 received aid, and 368 had their full need met. Average financial aid package met 78% of need; average scholarship/grant was $19,867; average loan was $4,844. For part-time students, average financial aid package was $13,960.
Students without need: 470 full-time freshmen who did not demonstrate need for aid received scholarships/grants; average award was $11,737. No-need awards available for academics, athletics, ROTC.
Scholarships offered: 38 full-time freshmen received athletic scholarships; average amount $27,764.

FINANCIAL AID PROCEDURES
Forms required: FAFSA, CSS PROFILE.
Dates and Deadlines: Closing date 2/1. Applicants notified by 4/1; must reply by 5/1 or within 2 week(s) of notification.
Transfers: Priority date 2/1; closing date 5/1.

CONTACT
Angela Van Dekker, Assistant Vice President of Student Financial Services
Office of Undergraduate Admission, Fordham University, Bronx, NY 10458-9993
(718) 817-3800

Fulton-Montgomery Community College
Johnstown, New York
www.fmcc.suny.edu Federal Code: 002867

2-year public community college in large town.
Enrollment: 2,155 undergrads, 23% part-time. 682 full-time freshmen.
Selectivity: Open admission; but selective for some programs.

BASIC COSTS (2012-2013)
Tuition and fees: $4,024; out-of-state residents $7,468.
Per-credit charge: $143; out-of-state residents $286.

FINANCIAL AID PICTURE
Students with need: Need-based aid available for full-time and part-time students. Work study available nights, weekends, and for part-time students.

Students without need: No-need awards available for academics.

FINANCIAL AID PROCEDURES

Forms required: FAFSA, state aid form.

Dates and Deadlines: Priority date 6/1; no closing date. Applicants notified on a rolling basis starting 6/15; must reply within 2 week(s) of notification.

CONTACT

Rebecca Cozzocrea, Coordinator of Financial Aid
2805 State Highway 67, Johnstown, NY 12095
(518) 736-4651 ext. 8201

Genesee Community College

Batavia, New York
www.genesee.edu
Federal Code: 006782

2-year public community college in large town.
Enrollment: 4,321 undergrads, 25% part-time. 1,975 full-time freshmen.
Selectivity: Open admission; but selective for some programs.

BASIC COSTS (2012-2013)

Tuition and fees: $3,900; out-of-state residents $4,500.
Per-credit charge: $145; out-of-state residents $165.

FINANCIAL AID PICTURE (2011-2012)

Students with need: Out of 1,758 full-time freshmen who applied for aid, 1,319 were judged to have need. Of these, 1,319 received aid, and 923 had their full need met. Average financial aid package met 89% of need; average scholarship/grant was $4,320; average loan was $3,405. For part-time students, average financial aid package was $1,234.

Students without need: 41 full-time freshmen who did not demonstrate need for aid received scholarships/grants; average award was $1,150. No-need awards available for academics, alumni affiliation, athletics, leadership, state/district residency.

Scholarships offered: 15 full-time freshmen received athletic scholarships; average amount $2,500.

Cumulative student debt: 71% of graduating class had student loans; average debt was $9,725.

FINANCIAL AID PROCEDURES

Forms required: FAFSA, state aid form.

Dates and Deadlines: Priority date 3/1; closing date 5/1. Applicants notified on a rolling basis starting 4/15; must reply within 2 week(s) of notification.

Transfers: No deadline.

CONTACT

Joseph Bailey, Director of Student Financial Services/Assistant Dean for Enrollment Services
One College Road, Batavia, NY 14020-9704
(585) 345-6900

Globe Institute of Technology

New York, New York
www.globe.edu
Federal Code: 025408

4-year for-profit university and business college in very large city.
Enrollment: 752 undergrads.
Selectivity: Open admission; but selective for some programs.

BASIC COSTS (2012-2013)

Tuition and fees: $11,088.
Additional info: Tuition/fee waivers available for adults, minority students, unemployed or children of unemployed.

FINANCIAL AID PICTURE

Students with need: Need-based aid available for full-time and part-time students. Work study available nights, weekends, and for part-time students.

Students without need: No-need awards available for academics, athletics.

FINANCIAL AID PROCEDURES

Forms required: FAFSA, state aid form, institutional form.

Dates and Deadlines: Applicants notified on a rolling basis.

Transfers: No deadline. Applicants notified on a rolling basis.

CONTACT

Tatyana Nusenbaum, Director of Financial Aid
500 Seventh Avenue, 2nd Floor, New York, NY 10018
(212) 349-4330

Hamilton College

Clinton, New York
www.hamilton.edu
Federal Code: 002728
CSS Code: 2286

4-year private liberal arts college in rural community.
Enrollment: 1,867 undergrads. 481 full-time freshmen.
Selectivity: Admits less than 50% of applicants.

BASIC COSTS (2013-2014)

Tuition and fees: $46,080.
Room and board: $11,710.

FINANCIAL AID PICTURE (2011-2012)

Students with need: Out of 296 full-time freshmen who applied for aid, 228 were judged to have need. Of these, 228 received aid, and 228 had their full need met. Average financial aid package met 100% of need; average scholarship/grant was $33,576; average loan was $3,024.

Students without need: This college awards aid only to students with need.

Cumulative student debt: 39% of graduating class had student loans; average debt was $18,568.

FINANCIAL AID PROCEDURES

Forms required: FAFSA, CSS PROFILE, state aid form, institutional form.

Dates and Deadlines: Closing date 2/8. Applicants notified by 4/1; must reply by 5/1.

Transfers: Closing date 4/15. Applicants notified by 5/10; must reply by 5/23.

CONTACT

198 College Hill Road, Clinton, NY 13323-1293
(315) 859-4413

Hartwick College

Oneonta, New York
www.hartwick.edu
Federal Code: 002729

4-year private liberal arts college in large town.
Enrollment: 1,541 undergrads, 2% part-time. 446 full-time freshmen.
Selectivity: Admits over 75% of applicants.

BASIC COSTS (2013-2014)

Tuition and fees: $39,330.
Per-credit charge: $1,220.
Room and board: $10,485.
Additional info: Reported mandatory fees include $400 matriculation fee for new students.

FINANCIAL AID PICTURE

Students with need: Need-based aid available for full-time and part-time students. Work study available nights, weekends, and for part-time students.

Students without need: No-need awards available for academics, alumni affiliation, art, athletics, music/drama.

FINANCIAL AID PROCEDURES

Forms required: FAFSA.

Dates and Deadlines: Priority date 2/15; no closing date. Applicants notified on a rolling basis starting 1/15; must reply by 5/1 or within 2 week(s) of notification.
Transfers: Priority date 8/1; no deadline. Applicants notified on a rolling basis starting 3/15; must reply within 2 week(s) of notification.

CONTACT
Melissa Allen, Director of Financial Aid
Box 4022, Oneonta, NY 13820-4022
(607) 431-4130

Helene Fuld College of Nursing
New York, New York
www.helenefuld.edu Federal Code: 015395

2-year private nursing and junior college in very large city.
Enrollment: 317 undergrads.

BASIC COSTS (2012-2013)
Tuition and fees: $17,088.

FINANCIAL AID PICTURE
Students with need: Need-based aid available for full-time and part-time students.
Students without need: This college awards aid only to students with need.

FINANCIAL AID PROCEDURES
Forms required: FAFSA, state aid form.
Dates and Deadlines: Applicants notified on a rolling basis.

CONTACT
Andrine Thomas, Financial Aid Counselor and Loan Coordinator
24 East 120th Street, New York, NY 10035
(212) 616-7253

Herkimer County Community College
Herkimer, New York
www.herkimer.edu Federal Code: 004788

2-year public community college in small town.
Enrollment: 2,660 undergrads, 17% part-time. 825 full-time freshmen.
Selectivity: Open admission; but selective for some programs.

BASIC COSTS (2012-2013)
Tuition and fees: $4,200; out-of-state residents $6,360.
Per-credit charge: $129; out-of-state residents $233.
Additional info: Tuition/fee waivers available for unemployed or children of unemployed.

FINANCIAL AID PICTURE
Students with need: Need-based aid available for full-time and part-time students. Work study available nights, weekends, and for part-time students.

FINANCIAL AID PROCEDURES
Forms required: FAFSA, state aid form.
Dates and Deadlines: Closing date 4/1. Applicants notified on a rolling basis starting 4/1; must reply within 2 week(s) of notification.

CONTACT
Susan Tripp, Director of Financial Aid
100 Reservoir Road, Herkimer, NY 13350-1598
(315) 866-0300 ext. 8282

Hilbert College
Hamburg, New York
www.hilbert.edu Federal Code: 002735

4-year private liberal arts college in small city, affiliated with Roman Catholic Church.
Enrollment: 995 undergrads, 12% part-time. 180 full-time freshmen.
Selectivity: Admits over 75% of applicants.

BASIC COSTS (2012-2013)
Tuition and fees: $19,400.
Per-credit charge: $465.
Room and board: $8,418.
Additional info: Tuition/fee waivers available for adults, minority students.

FINANCIAL AID PICTURE (2011-2012)
Students with need: Need-based aid available for full-time and part-time students. Work study available nights, weekends, and for part-time students.
Students without need: No-need awards available for academics, alumni affiliation, leadership, minority status, state/district residency.

FINANCIAL AID PROCEDURES
Forms required: FAFSA, state aid form.
Dates and Deadlines: Priority date 3/1; no closing date. Applicants notified on a rolling basis starting 3/1; must reply within 2 week(s) of notification.
Transfers: No deadline. Applicants notified on a rolling basis; must reply within 2 week(s) of notification.

CONTACT
Beverly Chudy, Director of Student Financial Aid
5200 South Park Avenue, Hamburg, NY 14075-1597
(716) 649-7900

Hobart and William Smith Colleges
Geneva, New York Federal Code: 002731
www.hws.edu CSS Code: 2294

4-year private liberal arts college in large town.
Enrollment: 2,248 undergrads. 586 full-time freshmen.
Selectivity: Admits 50 to 75% of applicants.

BASIC COSTS (2013-2014)
Tuition and fees: $46,165.
Room and board: $11,685.

FINANCIAL AID PICTURE (2011-2012)
Students with need: Out of 502 full-time freshmen who applied for aid, 423 were judged to have need. Of these, 419 received aid, and 318 had their full need met. Average financial aid package met 79% of need; average scholarship/grant was $26,869; average loan was $3,448.
Students without need: 133 full-time freshmen who did not demonstrate need for aid received scholarships/grants; average award was $15,572. No-need awards available for academics, art, leadership, music/drama, religious affiliation.
Scholarships offered: Cornelius and Muriel P. Wood Scholarship: full tuition for 4 years. Richard Hersh Scholarship: full tuition and fees for 4 years. Trustee Scholarship for Academic Excellence: $20,000 annually, for 4 years; based on GPA, test scores, class standing. Faculty Scholarships: $17,000. Presidential Leaders and Service Scholarships: $15,000; based on academic excellence, leadership, service, personal qualities. Arts Scholarships: $3,000-$15,000; for special talent in studio art, creative writing, music and/or dance. Blackwell Medical Scholarships: full tuition for 4 years; MCAT score of 30 required and GPA requirements for guaranteed seat at Upstate Medical Center at Syracuse University.
Cumulative student debt: 53% of graduating class had student loans; average debt was $34,463.

FINANCIAL AID PROCEDURES
Forms required: FAFSA, CSS PROFILE, state aid form.
Dates and Deadlines: Closing date 2/15. Applicants notified by 4/1; must reply by 5/1 or within 2 week(s) of notification.
Transfers: No deadline. Applicants notified on a rolling basis; must reply within 2 week(s) of notification.

CONTACT
Beth Nepa, Director of Financial Aid Services
629 South Main Street, Geneva, NY 14456
(315) 781-3315

Hofstra University

Hempstead, New York
www.hofstra.edu Federal Code: 002732

4-year private university in large city.
Enrollment: 6,747 undergrads, 6% part-time. 1,672 full-time freshmen.
Selectivity: Admits 50 to 75% of applicants.

BASIC COSTS (2012-2013)
Tuition and fees: $35,950.
Per-credit charge: $1,100.
Room and board: $12,370.
Additional info: Tuition at time of enrollment locked for 4 years.

FINANCIAL AID PICTURE (2011-2012)
Students with need: Out of 1,463 full-time freshmen who applied for aid, 1,239 were judged to have need. Of these, 1,234 received aid, and 252 had their full need met. Average financial aid package met 67% of need; average scholarship/grant was $16,336; average loan was $3,661. For part-time students, average financial aid package was $9,458.
Students without need: 274 full-time freshmen who did not demonstrate need for aid received scholarships/grants; average award was $13,693. No-need awards available for academics, alumni affiliation, art, athletics, leadership, music/drama, ROTC, state/district residency.
Scholarships offered: ***Merit:*** Trustee Scholar: full-tuition; approximately 30 offered; based on holistic review of admission application; average SAT /ACT equivalent of 1500 on a 1600 scale; weighted GPA of 3.9; typically in top 10% of HS graduating class. Presidential Scholar: partial tuition; number awarded varies; for students with high academic achievement, usually top third of admitted students. Provost Scholar: partial tuition; number awarded varies; for students with high academic achievement; usually 20% of admitted students. ***Athletic:*** 13 full-time freshmen received athletic scholarships; average amount $24,713.

FINANCIAL AID PROCEDURES
Forms required: FAFSA, state aid form.
Dates and Deadlines: Priority date 2/15; no closing date. Applicants notified on a rolling basis starting 3/1; must reply by 5/1 or within 2 week(s) of notification.

CONTACT
Sandra Filbry, Director of Financial Aid
Admissions Center, 100 Hofstra University, Hempstead, NY 11549
(516) 463-8000

Houghton College

Houghton, New York
www.houghton.edu Federal Code: 002734

4-year private liberal arts college in rural community, affiliated with Wesleyan Church.
Enrollment: 1,113 undergrads, 3% part-time. 234 full-time freshmen.
Selectivity: Admits 50 to 75% of applicants.

BASIC COSTS (2013-2014)
Tuition and fees: $27,728.
Per-credit charge: $1,159.
Room and board: $8,012.
Additional info: Tuition/fee waivers available for minority students.

FINANCIAL AID PICTURE (2012-2013)
Students with need: Out of 213 full-time freshmen who applied for aid, 198 were judged to have need. Of these, 198 received aid, and 23 had their full need met. Average financial aid package met 80% of need; average scholarship/grant was $18,668; average loan was $4,831. For part-time students, average financial aid package was $8,591.
Students without need: 32 full-time freshmen who did not demonstrate need for aid received scholarships/grants; average award was $12,007. No-need awards available for academics, alumni affiliation, art, music/drama, religious affiliation, ROTC, state/district residency.
Scholarships offered: Academic Scholarships: $4,000-$10,000. Heritage Scholarships: $12,000. Phi Theta Kappa: $4,000. Art Scholarships: $1,000-$5,000 (based on art portfolio). Music Scholarships: $1,000-$12,500 (based on audition). Excellence Scholarships: $1,000-$4,000. James S. Luckey Scholarship: full tuition.
Cumulative student debt: 78% of graduating class had student loans; average debt was $25,049.

FINANCIAL AID PROCEDURES
Forms required: FAFSA, state aid form.
Dates and Deadlines: Priority date 3/1; no closing date. Applicants notified on a rolling basis starting 3/15; must reply by 5/1 or within 4 week(s) of notification.
Transfers: No deadline. Applicants notified on a rolling basis starting 3/15; must reply by 5/1 or within 4 week(s) of notification.

CONTACT
Marianne Loper, Director of Student Financial Services
1 Willard Avenue/PO Box 128, Houghton, NY 14744-0128
(585) 567-9328

Institute of Design and Construction

Brooklyn, New York
www.idc.edu Federal Code: 012107

2-year private junior and technical college in very large city.
Enrollment: 112 undergrads, 51% part-time. 17 full-time freshmen.
Selectivity: Open admission.

BASIC COSTS (2012-2013)
Tuition and fees: $9,890.
Per-credit charge: $325.

FINANCIAL AID PICTURE (2011-2012)
Students with need: 79% of average financial aid package awarded as scholarships/grants, 21% awarded as loans/jobs. Need-based aid available for part-time students.
Students without need: This college awards aid only to students with need.

FINANCIAL AID PROCEDURES
Forms required: FAFSA, state aid form, institutional form.
Dates and Deadlines: Applicants notified on a rolling basis starting 3/1; must reply within 4 week(s) of notification.
Transfers: Priority date 7/1; closing date 9/1. Applicants notified on a rolling basis; must reply within 4 week(s) of notification.

CONTACT
Giovanny Santana, Assistant Director of Financial Aid
141 Willoughby Street, Brooklyn, NY 11201-5380
(718) 855-3661 ext. 19

Iona College

New Rochelle, New York
www.iona.edu Federal Code: 002737

4-year private business and liberal arts college in small city, affiliated with Roman Catholic Church.
Enrollment: 2,988 undergrads, 2% part-time. 722 full-time freshmen.
Selectivity: Admits over 75% of applicants.

BASIC COSTS (2012-2013)
Tuition and fees: $31,490.
Per-credit charge: $980.
Room and board: $12,488.

FINANCIAL AID PICTURE (2012-2013)
Students with need: Out of 718 full-time freshmen who applied for aid, 609 were judged to have need. Of these, 608 received aid, and 102 had their full need met. Average financial aid package met 26% of need; average scholarship/grant was $6,659; average loan was $2,042. For part-time students, average financial aid package was $3,791.
Students without need: 105 full-time freshmen who did not demonstrate need for aid received scholarships/grants; average award was $15,776. No-need awards available for academics, alumni affiliation, athletics.
Scholarships offered: 49 full-time freshmen received athletic scholarships; average amount $17,688.
Cumulative student debt: 71% of graduating class had student loans; average debt was $31,960.

FINANCIAL AID PROCEDURES
Forms required: FAFSA, state aid form.
Dates and Deadlines: Priority date 4/15; no closing date. Applicants notified on a rolling basis starting 3/1; must reply by 5/1 or within 2 week(s) of notification.
Transfers: No deadline. Applicants notified on a rolling basis starting 3/1; must reply within 2 week(s) of notification.

CONTACT
Mary Grant, Director of Financial Aid
715 North Avenue, New Rochelle, NY 10801-1890
(914) 633-2497

Island Drafting and Technical Institute

Amityville, New York
www.idti.edu Federal Code: 007375

2-year for-profit technical and career college in large town.
Enrollment: 118 undergrads.
Selectivity: Open admission.

BASIC COSTS (2012-2013)
Tuition and fees: $15,700.
Per-credit charge: $510.

FINANCIAL AID PICTURE
Students with need: Need-based aid available for full-time students.
Students without need: This college awards aid only to students with need.

FINANCIAL AID PROCEDURES
Dates and Deadlines: Applicants notified on a rolling basis.

CONTACT
Daniel Greener, Financial Aid Office
128 Broadway, Amityville, NY 11701-2704
(631) 691-8733 ext. 115

Ithaca College

Ithaca, New York Federal Code: 002739
www.ithaca.edu CSS Code: 2325

4-year private health science and liberal arts college in large town.
Enrollment: 6,233 undergrads, 1% part-time. 1,580 full-time freshmen.
Selectivity: Admits 50 to 75% of applicants.

BASIC COSTS (2013-2014)
Tuition and fees: $38,400.
Per-credit charge: $1,280.
Room and board: $13,900.
Additional info: Tuition/fee waivers available for minority students.

FINANCIAL AID PICTURE (2012-2013)
Students with need: Out of 1,372 full-time freshmen who applied for aid, 1,134 were judged to have need. Of these, 1,134 received aid, and 642 had their full need met. Average financial aid package met 89% of need; average scholarship/grant was $22,576; average loan was $5,346. For part-time students, average financial aid package was $19,796.
Students without need: 285 full-time freshmen who did not demonstrate need for aid received scholarships/grants; average award was $10,967. No-need awards available for academics, alumni affiliation, leadership, minority status, music/drama, ROTC.
Scholarships offered: President's Scholarship: $18,000; approximately top 10% of applicants. Dean's Scholarship: $10,000-$15,000; approximately top 11% to 35% of applicants. ALANA Scholarship: $3,000-5,000; representatives of minority groups who show excellent academic achievement. Flora Brown Award: $7,000. MLK Scholarship: $25,000 to full tuition; academic excellence; community service involvement; approximately 15. Leadership Scholarship: $7,000; record of leadership and above average academic performance; approximately 120. Premier Talent Scholarship: maximum $18,000 for music and theater majors; approximately 35. Park Scholar Achievement award: full cost of attendance; outstanding achievement in communications; approximately 20. National Merit Recognition Award: $2,000 plus Ithaca College Merit Scholarship of $16,000 for students who designate Ithaca their first-choice institution to National Merit Scholarship Corporation.

FINANCIAL AID PROCEDURES
Forms required: FAFSA, CSS PROFILE.
Dates and Deadlines: Priority date 2/1; no closing date. Applicants notified on a rolling basis starting 2/15; must reply by 5/1.
Transfers: No deadline. Applicants notified on a rolling basis starting 2/15; must reply by 5/1. All need-based and merit awards available for freshmen are also available for transfers.

CONTACT
Lisa Hoskey, Director, Student Financial Services
953 Danby Road, Ithaca, NY 14850-7002
(607) 274-3131

Jamestown Business College

Jamestown, New York
www.jamestownbusinesscollege.edu
Federal Code: 008495

2-year for-profit business and junior college in large town.
Enrollment: 294 undergrads, 2% part-time. 70 full-time freshmen.
Selectivity: Admits over 75% of applicants.

BASIC COSTS (2013-2014)
Tuition and fees: $11,400.

FINANCIAL AID PICTURE (2012-2013)
Students with need: 63% of average financial aid package awarded as scholarships/grants, 37% awarded as loans/jobs. Need-based aid available for part-time students.

Students without need: No-need awards available for academics.

FINANCIAL AID PROCEDURES
Forms required: FAFSA, state aid form.
Dates and Deadlines: Applicants notified on a rolling basis starting 2/15.
Transfers: Priority date 3/1; no deadline. Applicants notified on a rolling basis starting 5/1.

CONTACT
Diane Sturzenbecker, Financial Aid Officer
7 Fairmount Avenue, Jamestown, NY 14701-0429
(716) 664-5100

Jamestown Community College
Jamestown, New York
www.sunyjcc.edu Federal Code: 002869

2-year public community college in large town.
Enrollment: 3,409 undergrads, 26% part-time. 938 full-time freshmen.
Selectivity: Open admission; but selective for some programs.

BASIC COSTS (2012-2013)
Tuition and fees: $4,495; out-of-state residents $8,545.
Per-credit charge: $170; out-of-state residents $305.
Room and board: $9,600.

FINANCIAL AID PICTURE
Students with need: Need-based aid available for full-time and part-time students. Work study available nights, weekends, and for part-time students.
Students without need: No-need awards available for academics, alumni affiliation, art, athletics, music/drama, state/district residency.
Scholarships offered: 100% resident tuition scholarship (less federal and state grants) for students who apply for admissions by 3/1 and are in the top 20% of their high school graduating class with Regents diploma if residents of Chautauqua, Cattaraugus, or Allegany counties. Guaranteed in-state tuition rate for students in Warren, Potter, McKean, Forest, Elk and Cameron counties in Pennsylvania, in top 20% of graduating class with an academic diploma.

FINANCIAL AID PROCEDURES
Forms required: FAFSA, state aid form.
Dates and Deadlines: Priority date 3/1; no closing date. Applicants notified on a rolling basis starting 4/15.

CONTACT
Laurie Vorp, Director of Financial Aid
525 Falconer Street, Jamestown, NY 14701-0020
(800) 388-8557

Jefferson Community College
Watertown, New York
www.sunyjefferson.edu Federal Code: 002870

2-year public community college in large town.
Enrollment: 3,042 undergrads, 29% part-time. 767 full-time freshmen.
Selectivity: Open admission; but selective for some programs.

BASIC COSTS (2012-2013)
Tuition and fees: $4,277; out-of-state residents $5,927.
Per-credit charge: $156; out-of-state residents $225.

FINANCIAL AID PICTURE
Students with need: Need-based aid available for full-time and part-time students.
Students without need: This college awards aid only to students with need.

FINANCIAL AID PROCEDURES
Forms required: FAFSA, state aid form, institutional form.
Dates and Deadlines: Priority date 4/1; closing date 8/15. Applicants notified on a rolling basis starting 4/15; must reply within 2 week(s) of notification.
Transfers: No deadline.

CONTACT
James Ambrose, Director of Financial Aid
1220 Coffeen Street, Watertown, NY 13601
(315) 786-2355

Jewish Theological Seminary of America
New York, New York
www.jtsa.edu CSS Code: 2339

4-year private liberal arts and rabbinical college in very large city, affiliated with Jewish faith.
Enrollment: 169 undergrads, 1% part-time. 39 full-time freshmen.
Selectivity: Admits 50 to 75% of applicants. GED not accepted.

BASIC COSTS (2013-2014)
Tuition and fees: $19,045.
Room only: $10,050.

FINANCIAL AID PICTURE
Students with need: Need-based aid available for full-time students.
Students without need: No-need awards available for academics, alumni affiliation, leadership.

FINANCIAL AID PROCEDURES
Forms required: FAFSA, CSS PROFILE, state aid form, institutional form.
Dates and Deadlines: Priority date 2/1; closing date 3/1. Applicants notified on a rolling basis starting 4/1; must reply within 4 week(s) of notification.

CONTACT
Linda Levine, Registrar/Director of Financial Aid
3080 Broadway, New York, NY 10027
(212) 678-8007

Juilliard School
New York, New York
www.juilliard.edu Federal Code: 002742

4-year private music and performing arts college in very large city.
Enrollment: 508 undergrads. 108 full-time freshmen.
Selectivity: Admits less than 50% of applicants.

BASIC COSTS (2012-2013)
Tuition and fees: $35,340.
Room and board: $13,280.

FINANCIAL AID PICTURE (2011-2012)
Students with need: Out of 103 full-time freshmen who applied for aid, 81 were judged to have need. Of these, 81 received aid, and 19 had their full need met. Average financial aid package met 78% of need; average scholarship/grant was $26,259; average loan was $3,456. Need-based aid available for part-time students.
Students without need: 7 full-time freshmen who did not demonstrate need for aid received scholarships/grants; average award was $10,285. No-need awards available for music/drama.
Cumulative student debt: 70% of graduating class had student loans; average debt was $24,117.

FINANCIAL AID PROCEDURES
Forms required: FAFSA, institutional form.
Dates and Deadlines: Closing date 3/1. Applicants notified by 4/1; must reply by 5/1.

Transfers: Applicants notified by 4/1; must reply by 5/1 or within 2 week(s) of notification.

CONTACT

Tina Gonzalez, Director of Financial Aid
60 Lincoln Center Plaza, New York, NY 10023-6588
(212) 799-5000 ext. 211

Keuka College

Keuka Park, New York
www.keuka.edu Federal Code: 002744

4-year private liberal arts college in rural community, affiliated with American Baptist Churches in the USA.
Enrollment: 1,874 undergrads, 17% part-time. 244 full-time freshmen.
Selectivity: Admits over 75% of applicants.

BASIC COSTS (2012-2013)

Tuition and fees: $26,330.
Per-credit charge: $850.
Room and board: $9,880.

FINANCIAL AID PICTURE

Students with need: Need-based aid available for full-time and part-time students. Work study available nights, weekends, and for part-time students.
Students without need: No-need awards available for academics, alumni affiliation, leadership, minority status, religious affiliation.

FINANCIAL AID PROCEDURES

Forms required: FAFSA.
Dates and Deadlines: Priority date 3/15; no closing date. Applicants notified on a rolling basis starting 3/1; must reply by 5/1 or within 2 week(s) of notification.

CONTACT

Jen Bates, Executive Director of Financial Aid
141 Central Avenue, Keuka Park, NY 14478-0098
(315) 279-5232

The King's College

New York, New York
www.tkc.edu Federal Code: 040953

4-year private liberal arts college in very large city, affiliated with nondenominational tradition.
Enrollment: 573 undergrads, 2% part-time. 162 full-time freshmen.

BASIC COSTS (2012-2013)

Tuition and fees: $29,240.
Per-credit charge: $1,204.
Additional info: The King's College does not offer a meal plan. Estimated food expenses for an on campus student are $1,800. Cost of room only, $11,600.

FINANCIAL AID PICTURE (2011-2012)

Students with need: Out of 147 full-time freshmen who applied for aid, 136 were judged to have need. Of these, 136 received aid, and 16 had their full need met. Average financial aid package met 62% of need; average scholarship/grant was $21,592; average loan was $4,017. For part-time students, average financial aid package was $13,149.
Students without need: 25 full-time freshmen who did not demonstrate need for aid received scholarships/grants; average award was $15,760. No-need awards available for academics.
Scholarships offered: Presidential Scholarships: unlimited number; based on composite SAT/ACT and high school GPA.

FINANCIAL AID PROCEDURES

Forms required: FAFSA.
Dates and Deadlines: Applicants notified on a rolling basis starting 2/15.

CONTACT

Anna Peters, Director of Financial Aid
52 Broadway, New York, NY 10004
(646) 237-8902

Le Moyne College

Syracuse, New York
www.lemoyne.edu Federal Code: 002748

4-year private liberal arts college in small city, affiliated with Roman Catholic Church.
Enrollment: 2,549 undergrads, 8% part-time. 636 full-time freshmen.
Selectivity: Admits 50 to 75% of applicants.

BASIC COSTS (2013-2014)

Tuition and fees: $30,460.
Per-credit charge: $618.
Room and board: $11,740.

FINANCIAL AID PICTURE (2011-2012)

Students with need: Out of 598 full-time freshmen who applied for aid, 553 were judged to have need. Of these, 553 received aid, and 139 had their full need met. Average financial aid package met 77% of need; average scholarship/grant was $18,064; average loan was $3,781. For part-time students, average financial aid package was $6,610.
Students without need: 70 full-time freshmen who did not demonstrate need for aid received scholarships/grants; average award was $6,003. No-need awards available for academics, alumni affiliation, athletics, leadership, minority status, ROTC.
Scholarships offered: ***Merit:*** Presidential Scholarship; $23,750 per year for 4 years; based on 95% GPA, 1300 SAT/29 ACT; must maintain 3.25 GPA. Dean Scholarship; $17,500 per year for 4 years; based on 92% GPA, 1200 SAT/27 ACT; must maintain 3.0 GPA. Ignatian Scholarship; $17,500 per year for 4 years; awarded to students from Jesuit high schools with superior academic records; must maintain 3.0 GPA. Leader Scholarship; $12,500 per year for 4 years; based on 85% GPA, 1050 SAT/22 ACT; must remain in good academic standing. Loyola Scholarship; $17,500 per year for 4 years; for multicultural students with demonstrated academic excellence; must maintain 3.0 GPA. Academic scholarships are based on review of the student's admission application. To be considered, students must file an admission application by February 1. ***Athletic:*** 48 full-time freshmen received athletic scholarships; average amount $6,968.
Cumulative student debt: 85% of graduating class had student loans; average debt was $34,532.
Additional info: Parent loan program at low interest, monthly payment plans and alternative loans for students.

FINANCIAL AID PROCEDURES

Forms required: FAFSA, state aid form, institutional form.
Dates and Deadlines: Priority date 2/1; closing date 3/1. Applicants notified by 3/15; must reply by 5/1 or within 2 week(s) of notification.
Transfers: Priority date 6/1; no deadline. Must reply by 5/1 or within 2 week(s) of notification.

CONTACT

William Cheetham, Director of Financial Aid
1419 Salt Springs Road, Syracuse, NY 13214-1301
(315) 445-4400

LIM College

New York, New York
www.limcollege.edu Federal Code: 007466

4-year for-profit college of fashion business in very large city.
Enrollment: 1,467 undergrads.
Selectivity: Admits 50 to 75% of applicants.

BASIC COSTS (2012-2013)

Tuition and fees: $22,995.
Per-credit charge: $745.
Room and board: $19,850.

FINANCIAL AID PICTURE

Students with need: Need-based aid available for full-time and part-time students.
Students without need: This college awards aid only to students with need.

FINANCIAL AID PROCEDURES

Forms required: FAFSA, state aid form, institutional form.
Dates and Deadlines: Priority date 4/1; no closing date. Applicants notified on a rolling basis starting 2/15; must reply within 2 week(s) of notification.

CONTACT

Christopher Barto, Dean of Student Financial Services
12 East 53rd Street, New York, NY 10022
(212) 752-1530

Long Island Business Institute

Flushing, New York
www.libi.edu

2-year for-profit business and career college in very large city.
Enrollment: 489 undergrads, 22% part-time. 103 full-time freshmen.
Selectivity: Admits less than 50% of applicants.

BASIC COSTS (2012-2013)

Tuition and fees: $13,899.

FINANCIAL AID PICTURE (2012-2013)

Students with need: Out of 101 full-time freshmen who applied for aid, 101 were judged to have need. Of these, 101 received aid. Average financial aid package met 85% of need; average scholarship/grant was $2,500; average loan was $1,300. For part-time students, average financial aid package was $2,200.
Students without need: No-need awards available for academics.
Cumulative student debt: 39% of graduating class had student loans; average debt was $2,300.

FINANCIAL AID PROCEDURES

Forms required: FAFSA, state aid form.
Dates and Deadlines: Closing date 5/1. Applicants notified by 1/1; must reply by 4/30.
Transfers: Applicants notified by 1/1; must reply by 4/30.

CONTACT

Nazaret Kiregian, Director of Financial Aid
136-18 39th Avenue, 5th Floor, Flushing, NY 11354
(631) 499-7100 ext. 13

Long Island University: Brooklyn Campus

Brooklyn, New York
http://liu.edu/Brooklyn Federal Code: 004779

4-year private university and liberal arts college in very large city.
Enrollment: 5,002 undergrads, 14% part-time. 905 full-time freshmen.
Selectivity: Admits over 75% of applicants.

BASIC COSTS (2012-2013)

Tuition and fees: $32,818.
Per-credit charge: $974.
Room and board: $11,700.

FINANCIAL AID PICTURE

Students with need: Need-based aid available for full-time and part-time students.
Students without need: No-need awards available for academics, alumni affiliation, art, athletics, leadership, music/drama.

FINANCIAL AID PROCEDURES

Forms required: FAFSA, state aid form.
Dates and Deadlines: Priority date 3/15; closing date 5/1. Applicants notified on a rolling basis starting 2/16; must reply within 4 week(s) of notification.
Transfers: No deadline. Applicants notified on a rolling basis.

CONTACT

Margaret Nelson, Associate Dean of Integrated Student Financial Services
1 University Plaza, Brooklyn, NY 11201-8423
(718) 488-1037

Long Island University: C. W. Post Campus

Brookville, New York
http://liu.edu/CWPost Federal Code: 002751

4-year private university and liberal arts college in small town.
Enrollment: 4,413 undergrads, 11% part-time. 959 full-time freshmen.
Selectivity: Admits over 75% of applicants.

BASIC COSTS (2012-2013)

Tuition and fees: $32,862.
Per-credit charge: $974.
Room and board: $12,240.

FINANCIAL AID PICTURE

Students with need: Need-based aid available for full-time and part-time students. Work study available nights, weekends, and for part-time students.
Students without need: No-need awards available for academics, alumni affiliation, art, athletics, leadership, music/drama.

FINANCIAL AID PROCEDURES

Forms required: FAFSA.
Dates and Deadlines: Priority date 3/1; no closing date. Applicants notified on a rolling basis starting 3/15; must reply by 5/1 or within 2 week(s) of notification.
Transfers: No deadline. Applicants notified on a rolling basis starting 3/1; must reply by 5/1.

CONTACT

Karen Urdahl, Director of Financial Assistance
720 Northern Boulevard, Brookville, NY 11548-1300
(516) 299-2338

Manhattan College

Riverdale, New York
www.manhattan.edu Federal Code: 002758

4-year private engineering and liberal arts college in very large city, affiliated with Roman Catholic Church.
Enrollment: 3,351 undergrads, 6% part-time. 843 full-time freshmen.
Selectivity: Admits 50 to 75% of applicants.

BASIC COSTS (2012-2013)
Tuition and fees: $32,735.
Room and board: $12,220.

FINANCIAL AID PICTURE (2012-2013)
Students with need: Out of 747 full-time freshmen who applied for aid, 637 were judged to have need. Of these, 633 received aid, and 72 had their full need met. Average financial aid package met 69% of need; average scholarship/grant was $14,551; average loan was $2,756.
Students without need: This college awards aid only to students with need.
Scholarships offered: 19 full-time freshmen received athletic scholarships; average amount $31,336.
Cumulative student debt: 73% of graduating class had student loans; average debt was $34,189.

FINANCIAL AID PROCEDURES
Forms required: FAFSA.
Dates and Deadlines: Priority date 3/1; closing date 4/15. Applicants notified on a rolling basis starting 2/15; must reply by 5/1.
Transfers: Priority date 4/1; no deadline.

CONTACT
Ed Keough, Director of Student Financial Services
4513 Manhattan College Parkway, Riverdale, NY 10471
(718) 862-7100

Manhattan School of Music

New York, New York Federal Code: 002759
www.msmnyc.edu CSS Code: 2396

4-year private music college in very large city.
Enrollment: 391 undergrads, 1% part-time. 101 full-time freshmen.

BASIC COSTS (2012-2013)
Tuition and fees: $35,140.
Per-credit charge: $1,400.
Room and board: $11,590.

FINANCIAL AID PICTURE (2011-2012)
Students with need: Out of 68 full-time freshmen who applied for aid, 24 were judged to have need. Of these, 24 received aid, and 5 had their full need met. Average financial aid package met 52% of need; average scholarship/grant was $18,614; average loan was $1,486. For part-time students, average financial aid package was $21,831.
Students without need: 11 full-time freshmen who did not demonstrate need for aid received scholarships/grants; average award was $15,557. No-need awards available for academics, alumni affiliation, leadership, music/drama.
Cumulative student debt: 61% of graduating class had student loans; average debt was $11,088.

FINANCIAL AID PROCEDURES
Forms required: FAFSA, CSS PROFILE, institutional form.
Dates and Deadlines: Closing date 3/1. Applicants notified by 4/1; must reply by 5/1 or within 2 week(s) of notification.
Transfers: Applicants notified by 4/1; must reply by 5/1 or within 2 week(s) of notification. CSS PROFILE required for transfer students.

CONTACT
Amy Anderson, Associate Dean for Enrollment Management
120 Claremont Avenue, New York, NY 10027-4698
(212) 749-2802 ext. 4463

Manhattanville College

Purchase, New York
www.manhattanville.edu Federal Code: 002760

4-year private liberal arts and teachers college in small town.
Enrollment: 1,711 undergrads, 3% part-time. 533 full-time freshmen.
Selectivity: Admits 50 to 75% of applicants.

BASIC COSTS (2012-2013)
Tuition and fees: $35,370.
Per-credit charge: $790.
Room and board: $14,340.

FINANCIAL AID PICTURE
Students with need: Need-based aid available for full-time and part-time students. Work study available nights, weekends, and for part-time students.
Students without need: No-need awards available for academics, alumni affiliation, art, leadership, music/drama.
Additional info: Upper level students may earn additional money and academic credit through internship program.

FINANCIAL AID PROCEDURES
Forms required: FAFSA, state aid form.
Dates and Deadlines: Closing date 3/1. Applicants notified on a rolling basis starting 2/1; must reply by 5/1 or within 2 week(s) of notification.
Transfers: No deadline.

CONTACT
Robert Gilmore, Director of Financial Aid
2900 Purchase Street, Purchase, NY 10577
(914) 323-5357

Mannes College The New School for Music

New York, New York
www.mannes.edu Federal Code: 002780

4-year private music college in very large city.
Enrollment: 198 undergrads, 9% part-time. 47 full-time freshmen.
Selectivity: Admits less than 50% of applicants.

BASIC COSTS (2012-2013)
Tuition and fees: $37,520.
Per-credit charge: $1,200.
Room and board: $17,770.
Additional info: Reported room and board price is for double-occupancy open room and unlimited meal plan. Other options: declining value meal plan; apartment-style suites; singles with private bath.

FINANCIAL AID PICTURE (2011-2012)
Students with need: Out of 12 full-time freshmen who applied for aid, 10 were judged to have need. Of these, 8 received aid, and 1 had their full need met. Average financial aid package met 60% of need; average scholarship/grant was $18,280; average loan was $7,945. Need-based aid available for part-time students.
Students without need: 1 full-time freshmen who did not demonstrate need for aid received scholarships/grants; average award was $13,480. No-need awards available for academics, leadership, minority status, music/drama, state/district residency.
Cumulative student debt: 42% of graduating class had student loans; average debt was $34,455.

FINANCIAL AID PROCEDURES
Forms required: FAFSA, state aid form.
Dates and Deadlines: Priority date 3/1; no closing date. Applicants notified on a rolling basis starting 4/1; must reply within 4 week(s) of notification.

CONTACT
Lisa Shaheen, Director of Student Financial Aid
150 West 85th Street, New York, NY 10024
(212) 229-8930

Maria College

Albany, New York
www.mariacollege.edu Federal Code: 002763

2-year private health science and liberal arts college in small city.
Enrollment: 872 undergrads, 77% part-time. 26 full-time freshmen.
Selectivity: Admits less than 50% of applicants.

BASIC COSTS (2012-2013)
Tuition and fees: $10,700.
Per-credit charge: $435.

FINANCIAL AID PICTURE
Students with need: Need-based aid available for full-time and part-time students. Work study available nights, weekends, and for part-time students.
Students without need: This college awards aid only to students with need.

FINANCIAL AID PROCEDURES
Forms required: FAFSA, state aid form.
Dates and Deadlines: Applicants notified on a rolling basis starting 2/1; must reply within 2 week(s) of notification.
Transfers: No deadline. Applicants notified on a rolling basis; must reply within 2 week(s) of notification.

CONTACT
Harleen Laramie, Director of Financial Aid
700 New Scotland Avenue, Albany, NY 12208
(518) 438-3111 ext. 229

Marist College

Poughkeepsie, New York
www.marist.edu/ Federal Code: 002765

4-year private liberal arts college in small city.
Enrollment: 5,137 undergrads, 7% part-time. 1,098 full-time freshmen.
Selectivity: Admits less than 50% of applicants.

BASIC COSTS (2012-2013)
Tuition and fees: $30,000.
Per-credit charge: $634.
Room and board: $12,600.
Additional info: Tuition/fee waivers available for minority students.

FINANCIAL AID PICTURE (2012-2013)
Students with need: Out of 911 full-time freshmen who applied for aid, 677 were judged to have need. Of these, 675 received aid, and 118 had their full need met. For part-time students, average financial aid package was $6,550.
Students without need: 270 full-time freshmen who did not demonstrate need for aid received scholarships/grants; average award was $7,698. No-need awards available for academics, athletics, music/drama, ROTC, state/district residency.
Scholarships offered: ***Merit:*** Awards vary, as much as $12,000 per recipient. ***Athletic:*** 63 full-time freshmen received athletic scholarships; average amount $14,148.
Cumulative student debt: 73% of graduating class had student loans; average debt was $33,707.

FINANCIAL AID PROCEDURES
Forms required: FAFSA, institutional form.
Dates and Deadlines: Priority date 2/15; closing date 5/1. Applicants notified on a rolling basis starting 4/1; must reply by 5/1 or within 2 week(s) of notification.
Transfers: No deadline. Applicants notified on a rolling basis. FAFSA should be filed as soon as possible after January 1.

CONTACT
Joseph Weglarz, Executive Director, Student Financial Services
3399 North Road, Poughkeepsie, NY 12601-1387
(845) 575-3230

Marymount Manhattan College

New York, New York
www.mmm.edu Federal Code: 002769

4-year private liberal arts college in very large city.
Enrollment: 1,876 undergrads, 17% part-time. 420 full-time freshmen.
Selectivity: Admits 50 to 75% of applicants.

BASIC COSTS (2012-2013)
Tuition and fees: $25,688.
Per-credit charge: $816.
Additional info: Board plan not available. Cost of room only, $12,228. Mandatory $2,000 charge for food debit card that students can draw against for meals.

FINANCIAL AID PICTURE (2011-2012)
Students with need: Out of 347 full-time freshmen who applied for aid, 305 were judged to have need. Of these, 305 received aid, and 10 had their full need met. Average financial aid package met 54% of need; average scholarship/grant was $10,521; average loan was $3,477. For part-time students, average financial aid package was $5,971.
Students without need: 8 full-time freshmen who did not demonstrate need for aid received scholarships/grants; average award was $714. No-need awards available for academics, art, leadership, state/district residency.
Cumulative student debt: 77% of graduating class had student loans; average debt was $15,206.
Additional info: Limited international scholarships for top applicants.

FINANCIAL AID PROCEDURES
Forms required: FAFSA.
Dates and Deadlines: Applicants notified on a rolling basis starting 3/15; must reply by 5/1 or within 2 week(s) of notification.
Transfers: Applicants notified by 3/1. Must submit academic and financial transcripts from previous institutions.

CONTACT
Paul Ciraulo, Executive VP for Administration and Finance
221 East 71st Street, New York, NY 10021-4597
(212) 517-0500

Medaille College

Buffalo, New York
www.medaille.edu Federal Code: 002777

4-year private liberal arts college in large city.
Enrollment: 1,835 undergrads, 10% part-time. 373 full-time freshmen.
Selectivity: Admits 50 to 75% of applicants.

BASIC COSTS (2012-2013)
Tuition and fees: $22,678.
Per-credit charge: $799.
Room and board: $10,760.
Additional info: Tuition/fee waivers available for adults.

FINANCIAL AID PICTURE (2011-2012)
Students with need: Out of 335 full-time freshmen who applied for aid, 324 were judged to have need. Of these, 324 received aid, and 66 had their full need met. Average financial aid package met 71% of need; average scholarship/grant was $16,066. Need-based aid available for part-time students.
Students without need: No-need awards available for academics, leadership.
Scholarships offered: Available from $1,000 to $10,500.

FINANCIAL AID PROCEDURES
Forms required: FAFSA, state aid form.
Dates and Deadlines: Priority date 3/1; no closing date. Applicants notified on a rolling basis starting 3/1; must reply within 2 week(s) of notification.
Transfers: Applicants notified on a rolling basis starting 3/1.

CONTACT
Catherine Buzanski, Director of Financial Aid
18 Agassiz Circle, Buffalo, NY 14214
(716) 880-2256

Medaille College: Amherst
Williamsville, New York
www.medaille.edu

4-year private liberal arts college in small town.
Enrollment: 304 undergrads, 22% part-time. 11 full-time freshmen.

BASIC COSTS (2012-2013)
Tuition and fees: $22,678.
Per-credit charge: $799.
Additional info: Tuition/fee waivers available for adults.

FINANCIAL AID PICTURE
Students with need: Work study available nights, weekends, and for part-time students.
Students without need: No-need awards available for academics, leadership.

FINANCIAL AID PROCEDURES
Transfers: Applicants notified on a rolling basis.

CONTACT
Phyllis Hart, Director of Financial Aid
30 Wilson Road, Williamsville, NY 14221

Mercy College
Dobbs Ferry, New York
www.mercy.edu Federal Code: 002772

4-year private liberal arts college in large town.
Enrollment: 6,970 undergrads, 22% part-time. 1,173 full-time freshmen.
Selectivity: Admits 50 to 75% of applicants.

BASIC COSTS (2012-2013)
Tuition and fees: $17,556.
Per-credit charge: $715.
Room and board: $11,996.

FINANCIAL AID PICTURE (2011-2012)
Students with need: Out of 1,140 full-time freshmen who applied for aid, 1,099 were judged to have need. Of these, 1,071 received aid, and 20 had their full need met. Average financial aid package met 58% of need; average scholarship/grant was $11,925; average loan was $3,228. For part-time students, average financial aid package was $5,107.
Students without need: 14 full-time freshmen who did not demonstrate need for aid received scholarships/grants; average award was $3,054. No-need awards available for academics, athletics.
Scholarships offered: 48 full-time freshmen received athletic scholarships; average amount $4,729.
Cumulative student debt: 71% of graduating class had student loans; average debt was $24,138.

FINANCIAL AID PROCEDURES
Forms required: FAFSA, state aid form.
Dates and Deadlines: Priority date 2/15; no closing date. Applicants notified on a rolling basis starting 2/20; must reply by 5/1 or within 2 week(s) of notification.
Transfers: No deadline. Applicants notified on a rolling basis starting 4/1; must reply within 2 week(s) of notification.

CONTACT
Margaret McGrail, Vice President for Student Services
555 Broadway, Dobbs Ferry, NY 10522
(888) 464-6737

Metropolitan College of New York
New York, New York
www.metropolitan.edu Federal Code: 009769

4-year private business and liberal arts college in very large city.
Enrollment: 910 undergrads, 6% part-time. 126 full-time freshmen.

BASIC COSTS (2012-2013)
Tuition and fees: $17,230.

FINANCIAL AID PICTURE
Students with need: Need-based aid available for full-time and part-time students.
Additional info: Limited merit scholarships.

FINANCIAL AID PROCEDURES
Forms required: FAFSA.

CONTACT
Andrea Damar, Director of Financial Aid
431 Canal Street, New York, NY 10013-1919
(212) 343-1234 ext. 3500

Mildred Elley
Albany, New York
www.mildred-elley.edu Federal Code: 022195

2-year for-profit junior and career college in very large city.
Enrollment: 420 undergrads, 2% part-time. 91 full-time freshmen.
Selectivity: Open admission; but selective for some programs.

BASIC COSTS (2013-2014)
Tuition and fees: $11,304.
Per-credit charge: $373.
Additional info: Tuition at time of enrollment locked for 2 years.

FINANCIAL AID PICTURE (2011-2012)
Students with need: Out of 89 full-time freshmen who applied for aid, 89 were judged to have need. Of these, 89 received aid, and 17 had their full need met. Average financial aid package met 75% of need; average scholarship/grant was $5,700; average loan was $3,300. For part-time students, average financial aid package was $5,200.
Students without need: This college awards aid only to students with need.

FINANCIAL AID PROCEDURES
Forms required: FAFSA, state aid form.

Dates and Deadlines: Applicants notified on a rolling basis; must reply within 2 week(s) of notification.
Transfers: No deadline. Applicants notified on a rolling basis; must reply within 2 week(s) of notification.

CONTACT
Mary Ellen Duffy, Vice President of Financial Aid & Compliance
855 Central Avenue, Albany, NY 12206-1513
(518) 786-0855

Mohawk Valley Community College
Utica, New York
www.mvcc.edu Federal Code: 002871

2-year public community college in small city.
Enrollment: 5,849 undergrads, 22% part-time. 1,508 full-time freshmen.
Selectivity: Open admission; but selective for some programs.

BASIC COSTS (2012-2013)
Tuition and fees: $4,130; out-of-state residents $7,710.
Per-credit charge: $130; out-of-state residents $260.
Room and board: $9,150.

FINANCIAL AID PICTURE (2012-2013)
Students with need: Out of 1,360 full-time freshmen who applied for aid, 1,052 were judged to have need. Of these, 1,028 received aid, and 821 had their full need met. Average financial aid package met 85% of need; average scholarship/grant was $5,871; average loan was $3,542. For part-time students, average financial aid package was $8,422.
Students without need: No-need awards available for academics, alumni affiliation, art, leadership, state/district residency.
Additional info: Students in families that are above the threshold of the federal and state allowances for full grant aid (and thus receive little or no grant funding) may be eligible to receive assistance with books, fees, or other expenses.

FINANCIAL AID PROCEDURES
Forms required: FAFSA, institutional form.
Dates and Deadlines: Priority date 4/15; no closing date. Applicants notified on a rolling basis starting 3/1; must reply within 2 week(s) of notification.
Transfers: No deadline. Applicants notified on a rolling basis.

CONTACT
Annette Broski, Director, Financial Aid
1101 Sherman Drive, Utica, NY 13501-5394
(315) 792-5415

Molloy College
Rockville Centre, New York
www.molloy.edu Federal Code: 002775

4-year private liberal arts college in large town, affiliated with Roman Catholic Church.
Enrollment: 3,371 undergrads, 22% part-time. 396 full-time freshmen.
Selectivity: Admits 50 to 75% of applicants.

BASIC COSTS (2012-2013)
Tuition and fees: $24,420.
Per-credit charge: $770.
Room and board: $12,480.
Additional info: Tuition/fee waivers available for unemployed or children of unemployed.

FINANCIAL AID PICTURE (2011-2012)
Students with need: Out of 379 full-time freshmen who applied for aid, 332 were judged to have need. Of these, 332 received aid, and 56 had their full need met. Average financial aid package met 61% of need; average scholarship/grant was $13,214; average loan was $3,651. For part-time students, average financial aid package was $7,481.
Students without need: 36 full-time freshmen who did not demonstrate need for aid received scholarships/grants; average award was $9,076. No-need awards available for academics, alumni affiliation, art, athletics, leadership, music/drama, religious affiliation.
Scholarships offered: ***Merit:*** Molloy Scholar Scholarship: full tuition; minimum 95 high school average and minimum 1250 SAT (exclusive of Writing) or 28 ACT; 10 awarded annually; renewable for 3.5 GPA. Dominican Academic Scholarship: $1,000 to $8,500; minimum 88 high school average and minimum 1000 SAT (exclusive of Writing); 50 awarded annually, renewable with 3.0 GPA. Community Service Awards: $1,000 to $3,000; awarded to incoming freshmen demonstrating commitment to community and school; 10 awarded annually; renewable for 2.5 GPA. ***Athletic:*** 14 full-time freshmen received athletic scholarships; average amount $9,250.
Cumulative student debt: 77% of graduating class had student loans; average debt was $29,823.

FINANCIAL AID PROCEDURES
Forms required: FAFSA, state aid form.
Dates and Deadlines: Priority date 4/15; closing date 5/1. Applicants notified on a rolling basis starting 2/1; must reply within 5 week(s) of notification.
Transfers: No deadline. All transfer applicants with a minimum of 30 credits and 3.0 GPA automatically considered for transfer scholarships ranging from $1,500-$3,000.

CONTACT
Ana Lockward, Director of Financial Aid
PO Box 5002, Rockville Centre, NY 11570
(516) 678-5000 ext. 6249

Monroe College
Bronx, New York
www.monroecollege.edu Federal Code: 004799

4-year for-profit business and health science college in very large city.
Enrollment: 6,470 undergrads.

BASIC COSTS (2012-2013)
Tuition and fees: $12,848.
Per-credit charge: $502.
Room and board: $8,700.

FINANCIAL AID PICTURE
Students with need: Need-based aid available for full-time and part-time students. Work study available nights, weekends, and for part-time students.
Students without need: This college awards aid only to students with need.

FINANCIAL AID PROCEDURES
Forms required: FAFSA.
Dates and Deadlines: Closing date 6/30. Applicants notified on a rolling basis starting 7/1.
Transfers: No deadline. Applicants notified on a rolling basis.

CONTACT
Daniel Sharon, Financial Aid Director
2501 Jerome Avenue, Bronx, NY 10468
(718) 933-6700

Monroe Community College
Rochester, New York
www.monroecc.edu Federal Code: 002872

2-year public community college in large city.
Enrollment: 15,800 undergrads, 33% part-time. 3,500 full-time freshmen.

Selectivity: Open admission; but selective for some programs.

BASIC COSTS (2012-2013)
Tuition and fees: $3,538; out-of-state residents $6,678.
Per-credit charge: $131; out-of-state residents $262.
Additional info: Cost of room only, $6,550.

FINANCIAL AID PICTURE
Students with need: Need-based aid available for full-time and part-time students. Work study available nights, weekends, and for part-time students.
Students without need: This college awards aid only to students with need.

FINANCIAL AID PROCEDURES
Forms required: FAFSA, state aid form.
Dates and Deadlines: Priority date 3/30; no closing date. Applicants notified on a rolling basis starting 3/15; must reply within 2 week(s) of notification.
Transfers: No deadline. Applicants notified on a rolling basis starting 3/15; must reply within 2 week(s) of notification.

CONTACT
Jerome St. Croix, Director of Financial Aid
Office of Admissions-Monroe Community College, Rochester, NY 14692-8908
(585) 292-2050

Mount Saint Mary College

Newburgh, New York
www.msmc.edu Federal Code: 002778

4-year private liberal arts college in large town, affiliated with Roman Catholic Church.
Enrollment: 2,261 undergrads, 18% part-time. 441 full-time freshmen.
Selectivity: Admits over 75% of applicants.

BASIC COSTS (2013-2014)
Tuition and fees: $26,250.
Per-credit charge: $843.
Room and board: $13,290.
Additional info: Tuition/fee waivers available for adults.

FINANCIAL AID PICTURE (2012-2013)
Students with need: Out of 430 full-time freshmen who applied for aid, 377 were judged to have need. Of these, 377 received aid, and 76 had their full need met. Average financial aid package met 64% of need; average scholarship/grant was $13,424; average loan was $3,193. For part-time students, average financial aid package was $7,408.
Students without need: 64 full-time freshmen who did not demonstrate need for aid received scholarships/grants; average award was $7,845. No-need awards available for academics, alumni affiliation, leadership, ROTC, state/district residency.
Scholarships offered: Presidential Scholarship: approximately 65% of tuition in the year of enrollment, renewable for three years with minimum 3.0 GPA. Merit Awards: $3,000-$7,500; renewable each year with 2.5 GPA. Based on combined SAT/ACT test scores, GPA, and class rank.
Cumulative student debt: 81% of graduating class had student loans; average debt was $28,716.

FINANCIAL AID PROCEDURES
Forms required: FAFSA.
Dates and Deadlines: Priority date 2/15; closing date 3/1. Applicants notified on a rolling basis starting 3/1; must reply by 5/1.
Transfers: Applicants notified on a rolling basis starting 3/15; must reply by 5/1.

CONTACT
Barbara Winchell, Director of Financial Aid
330 Powell Avenue, Newburgh, NY 12550
(845) 569-3194

Nassau Community College

Garden City, New York
www.ncc.edu Federal Code: 002873

2-year public community college in large town.
Enrollment: 21,407 undergrads, 34% part-time. 4,224 full-time freshmen.
Selectivity: Open admission; but selective for some programs.

BASIC COSTS (2012-2013)
Tuition and fees: $4,330; out-of-state residents $8,320.
Per-credit charge: $167; out-of-state residents $334.

FINANCIAL AID PICTURE
Students with need: Need-based aid available for full-time and part-time students. Work study available nights, weekends, and for part-time students.
Students without need: No-need awards available for academics, minority status.

FINANCIAL AID PROCEDURES
Forms required: FAFSA, state aid form.
Dates and Deadlines: Priority date 6/7; no closing date. Applicants notified on a rolling basis; must reply within 1 week(s) of notification.

CONTACT
Patricia Noren, Director, Financial Aid Office
One Education Drive, Garden City, NY 11530
(516) 572-7259

Nazareth College

Rochester, New York
www.naz.edu Federal Code: 002779

4-year private liberal arts college in large city.
Enrollment: 2,057 undergrads, 5% part-time. 472 full-time freshmen.
Selectivity: Admits 50 to 75% of applicants.

BASIC COSTS (2012-2013)
Tuition and fees: $28,330.
Per-credit charge: $646.
Room and board: $11,588.
Additional info: Tuition/fee waivers available for minority students.

FINANCIAL AID PICTURE (2012-2013)
Students with need: 60% of average financial aid package awarded as scholarships/grants, 40% awarded as loans/jobs. Need-based aid available for part-time students. Work study available nights, weekends, and for part-time students.
Students without need: No-need awards available for academics, alumni affiliation, art, leadership, minority status, music/drama, ROTC.
Scholarships offered: Presidential Scholarship: $10,500. Dean's Scholarship: $9,500. Founders Scholarship: $9,000. Trustee Scholarship: $8,500. Class of 1928 Scholarship: $7,500. Nazareth Grant: $5,500-$7,500. All linked with student's grade point average. Campus diversity, regional, art, music, and theater scholarships also available.

FINANCIAL AID PROCEDURES
Forms required: FAFSA, state aid form. CSS PROFILE required of early decision applicants only.
Dates and Deadlines: Closing date 2/15. Applicants notified on a rolling basis starting 2/1; must reply by 5/1.
Transfers: No deadline.

CONTACT
Samantha Veeder, Director of Financial Aid
4245 East Avenue, Rochester, NY 14618-3790
(585) 389-2310

New York Career Institute

New York, New York
www.nyci.edu Federal Code: 014576

2-year for-profit career college in very large city.
Enrollment: 705 undergrads.
Selectivity: Open admission.

BASIC COSTS (2012-2013)
Tuition and fees: $12,750.
Additional info: Tuition for paralegal and medical evening programs $400 per credit hour.

FINANCIAL AID PICTURE
Students with need: Need-based aid available for full-time and part-time students. Work study available nights.
Students without need: This college awards aid only to students with need.

FINANCIAL AID PROCEDURES
Dates and Deadlines: Applicants notified on a rolling basis.

CONTACT
Brenda Soriano, Director of Student Financial Services
11 Park Place, New York, NY 10007

New York Institute of Technology

Old Westbury, New York
www.nyit.edu Federal Code: 002782

4-year private university and health science college in large town.
Enrollment: 4,577 undergrads, 14% part-time. 850 full-time freshmen.
Selectivity: Admits 50 to 75% of applicants.

BASIC COSTS (2013-2014)
Tuition and fees: $30,780.
Per-credit charge: $1,005.
Additional info: Tuition/fee waivers available for unemployed or children of unemployed.

FINANCIAL AID PICTURE
Students with need: Need-based aid available for full-time and part-time students.
Students without need: No-need awards available for academics, athletics.

FINANCIAL AID PROCEDURES
Forms required: FAFSA.
Dates and Deadlines: Priority date 3/1; no closing date. Applicants notified on a rolling basis starting 3/15; must reply by 5/1 or within 2 week(s) of notification.

CONTACT
Rosemary Ferrucci, Associate Dean of Financial Aid
Box 8000, Old Westbury, NY 11568
(516) 686-3835

New York School of Interior Design

New York, New York
www.nysid.edu Federal Code: 013606

4-year private visual arts college in very large city.
Enrollment: 429 undergrads, 61% part-time. 24 full-time freshmen.
Selectivity: Admits less than 50% of applicants.

BASIC COSTS (2013-2014)
Tuition and fees: $28,983.
Per-credit charge: $861.

FINANCIAL AID PICTURE (2012-2013)
Students with need: Average financial aid package met 33% of need; average scholarship/grant was $6,485; average loan was $3,022. For part-time students, average financial aid package was $5,312.
Cumulative student debt: 67% of graduating class had student loans; average debt was $35,502.

FINANCIAL AID PROCEDURES
Forms required: FAFSA, state aid form.
Dates and Deadlines: Priority date 8/1; no closing date. Applicants notified on a rolling basis starting 4/1; must reply within 2 week(s) of notification.
Transfers: No deadline. Applicants notified on a rolling basis; must reply within 2 week(s) of notification.

CONTACT
Rashmi Wadhvani, Financial Aid Officer
170 East 70th Street, New York, NY 10021-5110
(212) 472-1500 ext. 212

New York University

New York, New York Federal Code: 002785
www.nyu.edu CSS Code: 2562

4-year private university in very large city.
Enrollment: 22,080 undergrads, 5% part-time. 4,855 full-time freshmen.
Selectivity: Admits less than 50% of applicants.

BASIC COSTS (2012-2013)
Tuition and fees: $43,204.
Per-credit charge: $1,204.
Room and board: $16,133.

FINANCIAL AID PICTURE (2011-2012)
Students with need: Out of 3,216 full-time freshmen who applied for aid, 2,711 were judged to have need. Of these, 2,653 received aid, and 87 had their full need met. Average financial aid package met 59% of need; average scholarship/grant was $20,882; average loan was $5,486. For part-time students, average financial aid package was $20,097.
Students without need: 102 full-time freshmen who did not demonstrate need for aid received scholarships/grants; average award was $7,371. No-need awards available for academics.
Cumulative student debt: 53% of graduating class had student loans; average debt was $35,104.

FINANCIAL AID PROCEDURES
Forms required: FAFSA, CSS PROFILE.
Dates and Deadlines: Closing date 2/15. Applicants notified by 4/1; must reply by 5/1.
Transfers: Priority date 2/15; no deadline.

CONTACT
Randall Deike, Vice President for Enrollment Management and University Institutional Research
665 Broadway, 11th floor, New York, NY 10012-2339
(212) 998-4444

Niagara County Community College

Sanborn, New York
www.niagaracc.suny.edu Federal Code: 002874

2-year public community college in rural community.
Enrollment: 5,332 undergrads, 22% part-time. 1,345 full-time freshmen.
Selectivity: Open admission; but selective for some programs.

BASIC COSTS (2012-2013)
Tuition and fees: $4,040; out-of-state residents $9,584.
Per-credit charge: $154; out-of-state residents $385.

FINANCIAL AID PICTURE (2011-2012)
Students with need: 61% of average financial aid package awarded as scholarships/grants, 39% awarded as loans/jobs. Need-based aid available for part-time students. Work study available nights.
Students without need: This college awards aid only to students with need.
Additional info: Assistance offered with placing students in part-time employment through the Job Locator office. Students can charge books and food coupons.

FINANCIAL AID PROCEDURES
Forms required: FAFSA, state aid form.
Dates and Deadlines: Priority date 4/1; no closing date. Applicants notified on a rolling basis starting 5/1; must reply within 2 week(s) of notification.
Transfers: Must file appropriate state and federal change forms at least 4 weeks before registration date.

CONTACT
James Trimboli, Director of Financial Aid
3111 Saunders Settlement Road, Sanborn, NY 14132-9460
(716) 614-6266

Niagara University

Niagara University, New York
www.niagara.edu Federal Code: 002788

4-year private university in small city, affiliated with Roman Catholic Church.
Enrollment: 3,138 undergrads, 11% part-time. 641 full-time freshmen.
Selectivity: Admits 50 to 75% of applicants.

BASIC COSTS (2013-2014)
Tuition and fees: $28,200.
Per-credit charge: $900.
Room and board: $11,600.
Additional info: Tuition at time of enrollment locked for 4 years.

FINANCIAL AID PICTURE (2012-2013)
Students with need: Out of 590 full-time freshmen who applied for aid, 590 were judged to have need. Of these, 540 received aid, and 268 had their full need met. Average financial aid package met 88% of need; average scholarship/grant was $20,935; average loan was $4,684. For part-time students, average financial aid package was $11,082.
Students without need: 86 full-time freshmen who did not demonstrate need for aid received scholarships/grants; average award was $13,011. No-need awards available for academics, athletics, music/drama, ROTC.
Scholarships offered: ***Merit:*** Trustee Scholarship: $15,000-$20,000; minimum 95 average, 1150 SAT or 26 ACT; or 91 average, 1210 SAT or 27 ACT; unlimited. Presidential Scholarship: $13,500, 90 average, 1050 SAT or 23 ACT; or 85 average, 1120 SAT or 24 ACT; unlimited. Achievement Grant: $12,000; mid to upper 80 average; 950-1050 SAT or 20-22 ACT; unlimited. Niagara University Grant: $8,000; mid 80 average; SAT above 950 or ACT above 20; unlimited. ***Athletic:*** 16 full-time freshmen received athletic scholarships; average amount $20,569.
Cumulative student debt: 79% of graduating class had student loans; average debt was $32,114.
Additional info: Opportunity program available for academically and economically disadvantaged students.

FINANCIAL AID PROCEDURES
Forms required: FAFSA, state aid form.
Dates and Deadlines: Priority date 2/15; no closing date. Applicants notified on a rolling basis starting 3/1; must reply within 3 week(s) of notification.
Transfers: Must reply within 3 week(s) of notification. Academic scholarship available: $12,000 per year, minimum 3.34 GPA from transfer institution; $11,000 per year for 3.0 to 3.33 GPA; $8,000 per year for 2.5 to 2.99 GPA.

CONTACT
Maureen Salfi, Director of Financial Aid Niagara University, NY 14109
(716) 286-8686

North Country Community College

Saranac Lake, New York
www.nccc.edu Federal Code: 007111

2-year public community college in small town.
Enrollment: 1,023 full-time undergrads.
Selectivity: Open admission; but selective for some programs.

BASIC COSTS (2012-2013)
Tuition and fees: $4,980; out-of-state residents $10,680.
Per-credit charge: $163; out-of-state residents $400.
Room and board: $9,700.
Additional info: Annual room rate based on single-occupancy bedroom within suite; no double-occupancy rooms available.

FINANCIAL AID PICTURE
Students with need: Need-based aid available for full-time and part-time students. Work study available nights, weekends, and for part-time students.
Students without need: This college awards aid only to students with need.

FINANCIAL AID PROCEDURES
Forms required: FAFSA, state aid form.
Dates and Deadlines: Priority date 4/1; no closing date. Applicants notified on a rolling basis starting 4/1; must reply within 3 week(s) of notification.

CONTACT
Edwin Trathen, Vice President for Enrollment and Student Services
23 Santanoni Avenue, Saranac Lake, NY 12983
(518) 891-2915 ext. 229

Nyack College

Nyack, New York
www.nyack.edu Federal Code: 002790

4-year private liberal arts and seminary college in large town, affiliated with Christian and Missionary Alliance.
Enrollment: 1,993 undergrads, 15% part-time. 295 full-time freshmen.

BASIC COSTS (2013-2014)
Tuition and fees: $23,250.
Per-credit charge: $960.
Room and board: $8,650.

FINANCIAL AID PICTURE (2011-2012)
Students with need: Out of 281 full-time freshmen who applied for aid, 267 were judged to have need. Of these, 267 received aid, and 46 had their full need met. Average financial aid package met 66% of need; average scholarship/grant was $15,158; average loan was $3,474. For part-time students, average financial aid package was $7,635.
Students without need: 26 full-time freshmen who did not demonstrate need for aid received scholarships/grants; average award was $8,115. No-need awards available for academics, alumni affiliation, athletics, leadership, music/drama, religious affiliation, state/district residency.
Scholarships offered: 17 full-time freshmen received athletic scholarships; average amount $10,063.
Cumulative student debt: 87% of graduating class had student loans; average debt was $32,003.

FINANCIAL AID PROCEDURES
Forms required: FAFSA.
Dates and Deadlines: Applicants notified on a rolling basis starting 3/1; must reply within 4 week(s) of notification.

CONTACT
Dona Schepens, Assistant Treasurer
1 South Boulevard, Nyack, NY 10960-3698
(845) 675-4737

Onondaga Community College
Syracuse, New York
www.sunyocc.edu Federal Code: 002875

2-year public community college in small city.
Enrollment: 8,880 undergrads, 26% part-time. 2,293 full-time freshmen.
Selectivity: Open admission; but selective for some programs.

BASIC COSTS (2012-2013)
Tuition and fees: $4,634; out-of-state residents $8,684.
Per-credit charge: $161; out-of-state residents $322.

FINANCIAL AID PICTURE (2011-2012)
Students with need: Out of 2,073 full-time freshmen who applied for aid, 1,839 were judged to have need. Of these, 1,727 received aid, and 54 had their full need met. Average financial aid package met 57% of need; average scholarship/grant was $5,405; average loan was $3,026. For part-time students, average financial aid package was $3,793.
Students without need: This college awards aid only to students with need.

FINANCIAL AID PROCEDURES
Forms required: FAFSA, state aid form.
Dates and Deadlines: Priority date 2/15; no closing date. Applicants notified on a rolling basis starting 4/15; must reply within 4 week(s) of notification.

CONTACT
Lorna Roberts, Director of Financial Aid
4585 West Seneca Turnpike, Syracuse, NY 13215-4585
(315) 498-2291

Orange County Community College
Middletown, New York
www.sunyorange.edu Federal Code: 002876

2-year public community college in large town.
Enrollment: 5,677 undergrads, 40% part-time. 1,235 full-time freshmen.
Selectivity: Open admission; but selective for some programs.

BASIC COSTS (2012-2013)
Tuition and fees: $4,548; out-of-state residents $8,648.
Per-credit charge: $170; out-of-state residents $340.
Additional info: Tuition/fee waivers available for unemployed or children of unemployed.

FINANCIAL AID PICTURE (2011-2012)
Students with need: 74% of average financial aid package awarded as scholarships/grants, 26% awarded as loans/jobs. Need-based aid available for part-time students. Work study available nights.

FINANCIAL AID PROCEDURES
Forms required: FAFSA, state aid form, institutional form.
Dates and Deadlines: Priority date 4/15; closing date 7/1. Applicants notified on a rolling basis starting 4/1; must reply within 4 week(s) of notification.

CONTACT
John Ivankovic, Director of Financial Aid
115 South Street, Middletown, NY 10940-0115
(845) 341-4190

Pace University
New York, New York
www.pace.edu Federal Code: 002791

4-year private university in very large city.
Enrollment: 7,867 undergrads, 10% part-time. 1,812 full-time freshmen.
Selectivity: Admits over 75% of applicants.

BASIC COSTS (2013-2014)
Tuition and fees: $38,019.
Per-credit charge: $1,054.
Room and board: $16,000.
Additional info: Fees vary depending on campus.

FINANCIAL AID PICTURE
Students with need: Need-based aid available for full-time and part-time students. Work study available nights, weekends, and for part-time students.
Students without need: No-need awards available for academics, alumni affiliation, athletics.

FINANCIAL AID PROCEDURES
Forms required: FAFSA.
Dates and Deadlines: Priority date 2/15; no closing date. Applicants notified on a rolling basis starting 3/1; must reply by 5/1 or within 2 week(s) of notification.

CONTACT
Mark Stephens, University Director, Financial Aid
1 Pace Plaza, New York, NY 10038-1598
(212) 346-1300

Parsons The New School for Design
New York, New York
www.parsons.edu Federal Code: 002780

4-year private visual arts college in very large city.
Enrollment: 4,260 undergrads, 10% part-time. 703 full-time freshmen.
Selectivity: Admits 50 to 75% of applicants.

BASIC COSTS (2012-2013)
Tuition and fees: $40,140.
Per-credit charge: $1,335.
Room and board: $17,770.
Additional info: Reported room and board price is for double-occupancy open room and unlimited meal plan. Other options: declining value meal plan; apartment-style suites; singles with private bath.

FINANCIAL AID PICTURE (2011-2012)
Students with need: Out of 395 full-time freshmen who applied for aid, 336 were judged to have need. Of these, 317 received aid, and 79 had their full need met. Average financial aid package met 65% of need; average scholarship/grant was $17,490; average loan was $9,495. Need-based aid available for part-time students.
Students without need: 53 full-time freshmen who did not demonstrate need for aid received scholarships/grants; average award was $9,315. No-need awards available for academics, art, leadership, minority status.
Cumulative student debt: 56% of graduating class had student loans; average debt was $32,715.

FINANCIAL AID PROCEDURES
Forms required: FAFSA, state aid form.
Dates and Deadlines: Priority date 3/1; no closing date. Applicants notified on a rolling basis starting 4/1; must reply within 4 week(s) of notification.

CONTACT
Lisa Shaheen, Director of Student Financial Aid
72 Fifth Avenue, New York, NY 10011
(212) 229-8930

Paul Smith's College
Paul Smiths, New York
www.paulsmiths.edu Federal Code: 002795

4-year private liberal arts college in rural community.
Enrollment: 1,064 undergrads, 1% part-time. 290 full-time freshmen.

Selectivity: Admits over 75% of applicants.

BASIC COSTS (2012-2013)
Tuition and fees: $22,152.
Per-credit charge: $597.
Room and board: $9,960.
Additional info: Program fees range from $700 to $2,256 depending on program.

FINANCIAL AID PICTURE (2012-2013)
Students with need: Out of 283 full-time freshmen who applied for aid, 267 were judged to have need. Of these, 267 received aid, and 35 had their full need met. Average financial aid package met 77% of need; average scholarship/grant was $16,441; average loan was $4,446. For part-time students, average financial aid package was $5,110.
Students without need: 21 full-time freshmen who did not demonstrate need for aid received scholarships/grants; average award was $9,078. No-need awards available for academics.
Cumulative student debt: 91% of graduating class had student loans; average debt was $16,175.
Additional info: Merit aid only for international students; no financial aid application required.

FINANCIAL AID PROCEDURES
Forms required: FAFSA.
Dates and Deadlines: Priority date 3/31; no closing date. Applicants notified on a rolling basis starting 3/5; must reply within 4 week(s) of notification.
Transfers: No deadline. Applicants notified by 2/5; must reply within 4 week(s) of notification.

CONTACT
Mary Ellen Chamberlain, Director of Financial Aid
PO Box 265, Routes 30 & 86, Paul Smiths, NY 12970-0265
(518) 327-6220

Phillips Beth Israel School of Nursing

New York, New York
www.futurenursebi.org Federal Code: 006438

2-year private nursing college in very large city.
Enrollment: 287 undergrads, 92% part-time. 1 full-time freshmen.
Selectivity: Admits less than 50% of applicants.

BASIC COSTS (2012-2013)
Tuition and fees: $20,590.
Per-credit charge: $420.

FINANCIAL AID PICTURE
Students with need: Need-based aid available for full-time and part-time students.
Scholarships offered: Hillman Scholarship Program: full tuition, books, and uniforms; variable number awarded each year; based on academic achievement. Karpas Scholarship Program: $3,000 a year awarded to senior students; 15 awarded; based on academic achievement.

FINANCIAL AID PROCEDURES
Forms required: FAFSA, state aid form, institutional form.
Dates and Deadlines: Closing date 6/1. Applicants notified by 8/1; must reply within 3 week(s) of notification.
Transfers: Applicants notified by 8/1; must reply within 3 week(s) of notification.

CONTACT
Wendy Chan, Financial Aid Director
776 Sixth Avenue, Fourth Floor, New York, NY 10001
(212) 614-6104

Polytechnic Institute of New York University

Brooklyn, New York Federal Code: 002796
www.poly.edu CSS Code: 2668

4-year private university in very large city.
Enrollment: 2,000 undergrads, 4% part-time. 416 full-time freshmen.
Selectivity: Admits 50 to 75% of applicants.

BASIC COSTS (2012-2013)
Tuition and fees: $39,564.
Per-credit charge: $1,218.
Room and board: $13,500.

FINANCIAL AID PICTURE (2011-2012)
Students with need: Out of 409 full-time freshmen who applied for aid, 309 were judged to have need. Of these, 303 received aid, and 130 had their full need met. Average financial aid package met 91% of need; average scholarship/grant was $13,421; average loan was $3,922. For part-time students, average financial aid package was $9,199.
Students without need: 98 full-time freshmen who did not demonstrate need for aid received scholarships/grants; average award was $14,888. No-need awards available for academics.
Scholarships offered: Board of Trustees Scholarships: full tuition, less any outside aid for which students are eligible; awarded to academically superior freshmen. Geiger/Fialkov Scholarships: full tuition less any outside aid for which students are eligible; awarded to superior freshmen majoring in engineering or computer science. High School Principal's Scholarship: $10,000 per year; for students nominated by high school principals in New York metropolitan region. Students must file FAFSA to be eligible for merit scholarships.
Cumulative student debt: 68% of graduating class had student loans; average debt was $30,560.

FINANCIAL AID PROCEDURES
Forms required: FAFSA, CSS PROFILE.
Dates and Deadlines: Priority date 3/1; no closing date. Applicants notified on a rolling basis starting 3/15; must reply within 2 week(s) of notification.
Transfers: Priority date 5/5; no deadline. Applicants notified on a rolling basis; must reply within 2 week(s) of notification.

CONTACT
Christine Falzerano, Director of Financial Aid
6 Metrotech Center, Brooklyn, NY 11201-2999
(718) 260-3300

Pratt Institute

Brooklyn, New York
www.pratt.edu Federal Code: 002798

4-year private university and visual arts college in very large city.
Enrollment: 3,054 undergrads, 4% part-time. 619 full-time freshmen.
Selectivity: Admits 50 to 75% of applicants.

BASIC COSTS (2012-2013)
Tuition and fees: $41,092.
Per-credit charge: $1,267.
Room and board: $10,506.

FINANCIAL AID PICTURE
Students with need: Need-based aid available for full-time and part-time students.
Students without need: No-need awards available for academics.

FINANCIAL AID PROCEDURES
Forms required: FAFSA, state aid form.
Dates and Deadlines: Closing date 2/1. Applicants notified on a rolling basis starting 3/10; must reply within 2 week(s) of notification.

Transfers: Must reply by 5/1 or within 2 week(s) of notification.

CONTACT
Fiona Approo, Director of Financial Aid
200 Willoughby Avenue, Brooklyn, NY 11205-3817
(718) 636-3519

Rensselaer Polytechnic Institute

Troy, New York
Federal Code: 002803
www.rpi.edu
CSS Code: 2757

4-year private university in small city.
Enrollment: 5,300 undergrads. 1,326 full-time freshmen.
Selectivity: Admits less than 50% of applicants.

BASIC COSTS (2013-2014)
Tuition and fees: $46,269.
Per-credit charge: $1,879.
Room and board: $12,960.
Additional info: Freshmen are required to have a laptop. Students may purchase a university-subsidized laptop costing approximately $1,500, or they may bring one with them but it must contain the software and capabilities required to complete the coursework.

FINANCIAL AID PICTURE
Students with need: Need-based aid available for full-time students. Work study available nights, weekends, and for part-time students.
Students without need: No-need awards available for academics, alumni affiliation, art, athletics, leadership, minority status, music/drama, ROTC.
Scholarships offered: Rensselaer Medals: $15,000; awarded by participating high schools for excellence in science and mathematics.

FINANCIAL AID PROCEDURES
Forms required: FAFSA, CSS PROFILE.
Dates and Deadlines: Closing date 2/1. Applicants notified by 3/12.
Transfers: No deadline. Applicants notified on a rolling basis starting 3/31. Entering transfer students must complete two applications to apply for institutional and federal need-based aid: FAFSA and Transfer Financial Aid Application/Verification Worksheet (available upon acceptance). A number of special transfer scholarships available each year.

CONTACT
Larry Chambers, Director of Financial Aid
110 Eighth Street, Troy, NY 12180-3590
(518) 276-6813

Roberts Wesleyan College

Rochester, New York
www.roberts.edu
Federal Code: 002805

4-year private liberal arts college in large city, affiliated with Free Methodist Church of North America.
Enrollment: 1,288 undergrads, 9% part-time. 211 full-time freshmen.
Selectivity: Admits less than 50% of applicants.

BASIC COSTS (2012-2013)
Tuition and fees: $26,699.
Room and board: $9,264.

FINANCIAL AID PICTURE (2012-2013)
Students with need: Out of 190 full-time freshmen who applied for aid, 185 were judged to have need. Of these, 185 received aid, and 30 had their full need met. Average financial aid package met 80% of need; average scholarship/grant was $18,934; average loan was $4,319. For part-time students, average financial aid package was $8,035.
Students without need: 24 full-time freshmen who did not demonstrate need for aid received scholarships/grants; average award was $11,385. No-need awards available for academics, alumni affiliation, art, athletics, music/drama, religious affiliation, ROTC.
Scholarships offered: 12 full-time freshmen received athletic scholarships; average amount $12,625.
Cumulative student debt: 90% of graduating class had student loans; average debt was $33,353.
Additional info: Dollars for Scholars offer matching grants of up to $750.

FINANCIAL AID PROCEDURES
Forms required: FAFSA, state aid form.
Dates and Deadlines: Priority date 3/15; no closing date. Applicants notified on a rolling basis starting 3/15; must reply by 5/1 or within 2 week(s) of notification.
Transfers: Applicants notified on a rolling basis starting 3/15.

CONTACT
Stephen Field, Director of Student Financial Services
2301 Westside Drive, Rochester, NY 14624-1997
(585) 594-6150

Rochester Institute of Technology

Rochester, New York
www.rit.edu
Federal Code: 002806

4-year private university in large city.
Enrollment: 13,005 undergrads, 5% part-time. 2,669 full-time freshmen.
Selectivity: Admits 50 to 75% of applicants.

BASIC COSTS (2013-2014)
Tuition and fees: $34,424.
Per-credit charge: $1,191.
Room and board: $11,178.
Additional info: Tuition/fee waivers available for unemployed or children of unemployed.

FINANCIAL AID PICTURE (2011-2012)
Students with need: Out of 2,362 full-time freshmen who applied for aid, 2,074 were judged to have need. Of these, 2,073 received aid, and 1,690 had their full need met. Average financial aid package met 87% of need; average scholarship/grant was $18,500; average loan was $3,500. For part-time students, average financial aid package was $9,000.
Students without need: 390 full-time freshmen who did not demonstrate need for aid received scholarships/grants; average award was $12,000. No-need awards available for academics, art, leadership, ROTC.
Scholarships offered: Presidential Scholarship: $10,000 to $15,000 per year; top 10% of high school class with 1860 SAT/27 ACT or top 20% of high school class with 1950 SAT/28 ACT. RIT Achievement Scholarships: $7,000 to $10,000 per year; qualifications vary by area of interest.
Additional info: Most juniors and seniors participate in cooperative education program, earning an average $4,500-$6,500 per 3-month employment period through paid employment in jobs related to major.

FINANCIAL AID PROCEDURES
Forms required: FAFSA, state aid form.
Dates and Deadlines: Priority date 3/1; no closing date. Applicants notified on a rolling basis starting 3/15; must reply by 5/1.
Transfers: Priority date 3/15. Applicants notified on a rolling basis starting 4/1; must reply by 5/1. Special merit scholarship programs available specifically for transfers with high GPA.

CONTACT
Verna Hazen, Assistant Vice President and Director of Financial Aid
60 Lomb Memorial Drive, Rochester, NY 14623-5604
(585) 475-2186

Rockland Community College

Suffern, New York
www.sunyrockland.edu Federal Code: 002877

2-year public community college in large town.
Enrollment: 6,773 undergrads, 31% part-time. 1,421 full-time freshmen.
Selectivity: Open admission.

BASIC COSTS (2012-2013)

Tuition and fees: $4,318; out-of-state residents $8,343.
Per-credit charge: $168; out-of-state residents $335.

FINANCIAL AID PICTURE (2011-2012)

Students with need: Need-based aid available for part-time students.
Scholarships offered: Jack Watson Scholarship: minimum 3.5 high school GPA or 94 average in Regents; 5 awarded; $1,163 per semester; renewable for 2nd year. Alumni Scholarship: for children of alumni; 75 average; varying amounts.

FINANCIAL AID PROCEDURES

Forms required: FAFSA, institutional form.
Dates and Deadlines: Priority date 5/31; no closing date. Applicants notified on a rolling basis starting 6/1.

CONTACT

Debra Bouabidi, Director of Financial Aid
145 College Road, Suffern, NY 10901-3699
(845) 574-4282

The Sage Colleges

Troy, New York
www.sage.edu Federal Code: 002810

4-year private university in small city.
Enrollment: 1,686 undergrads, 14% part-time. 282 full-time freshmen.
Selectivity: Admits 50 to 75% of applicants.

BASIC COSTS (2013-2014)

Tuition and fees: $28,000.
Per-credit charge: $900.
Room and board: $11,370.

FINANCIAL AID PICTURE (2012-2013)

Students with need: Out of 276 full-time freshmen who applied for aid, 266 were judged to have need. Of these, 266 received aid. Need-based aid available for part-time students.
Students without need: 9 full-time freshmen who did not demonstrate need for aid received scholarships/grants; average award was $8,222. No-need awards available for academics, alumni affiliation, leadership, music/drama.
Scholarships offered: Multiple awards to qualified students: Presidential and Dean's scholarship, Girl Scout scholarship, first-generation scholarship, valedictorian-salutatorian scholarship, student Sage scholarship, endowed scholarships for minority students and specific majors.
Cumulative student debt: 86% of graduating class had student loans; average debt was $31,896.

FINANCIAL AID PROCEDURES

Forms required: FAFSA, state aid form.
Dates and Deadlines: Priority date 3/1; no closing date. Applicants notified on a rolling basis starting 3/1; must reply by 5/1 or within 2 week(s) of notification.
Transfers: Phi Theta Kappa Transfer Scholarship available.

CONTACT

Kelley Robinson, Director of Financial Aid Operations
65 1st Street, Troy, NY 12180-4115
(518) 292-7701

Saint Bonaventure University

St. Bonaventure, New York
www.sbu.edu Federal Code: 002817

4-year private university in small city, affiliated with Roman Catholic Church.
Enrollment: 1,848 undergrads, 1% part-time. 489 full-time freshmen.
Selectivity: Admits over 75% of applicants.

BASIC COSTS (2012-2013)

Tuition and fees: $28,727.
Per-credit charge: $830.
Room and board: $10,404.
Additional info: Tuition/fee waivers available for minority students.

FINANCIAL AID PICTURE (2011-2012)

Students with need: Out of 449 full-time freshmen who applied for aid, 379 were judged to have need. Of these, 379 received aid, and 74 had their full need met. Average financial aid package met 74% of need; average scholarship/grant was $18,394; average loan was $3,899. For part-time students, average financial aid package was $10,748.
Students without need: 103 full-time freshmen who did not demonstrate need for aid received scholarships/grants; average award was $13,393. No-need awards available for academics, athletics, minority status, music/drama, religious affiliation, ROTC, state/district residency.
Scholarships offered: ***Merit:*** Buckeye Award: $2,000; for first-time freshmen who graduate from a high school in Ohio (except students receiving athletic awards); renewable. Geographic Diversity Award: $2,000; given to all out-of-state students except those who graduate from high schools in Ohio, who will receive Buckeye Award. ***Athletic:*** 56 full-time freshmen received athletic scholarships; average amount $9,471.
Additional info: Families experiencing financial difficulties not adequately reflected by the FAFSA should contact the Office of Financial Assistance. Outside scholarships do not reduce other financial aid unless, when added to total aid, the new total exceeds need. If it exceeds need, then loans and work are reduced first.

FINANCIAL AID PROCEDURES

Forms required: FAFSA, state aid form.
Dates and Deadlines: Priority date 2/15; no closing date. Applicants notified on a rolling basis starting 3/1; must reply by 5/1 or within 2 week(s) of notification.
Transfers: Priority date 3/1; no deadline. Applicants notified on a rolling basis starting 3/15; must reply by 5/1 or within 2 week(s) of notification.

CONTACT

Troy Martin, Director of Financial Aid
Route 417, St. Bonaventure, NY 14778-2284
(716) 375-2400

St. Elizabeth College of Nursing

Utica, New York
www.secon.edu Federal Code: 006461

2-year private nursing college in small city, affiliated with Roman Catholic Church.
Enrollment: 199 undergrads, 55% part-time. 6 full-time freshmen.
Selectivity: Admits less than 50% of applicants.

BASIC COSTS (2012-2013)

Tuition and fees: $14,000.
Per-credit charge: $375.

FINANCIAL AID PICTURE (2012-2013)

Students with need: Need-based aid available for full-time and part-time students.

FINANCIAL AID PROCEDURES

Forms required: FAFSA, state aid form.

Dates and Deadlines: Applicants notified on a rolling basis starting 1/1; must reply within 2 week(s) of notification.

CONTACT
Sherry Wojnas, Director, Financial Aid
2215 Genesee Street, Utica, NY 13501
(315) 798-8206

St. Francis College

Brooklyn Heights, New York
www.sfc.edu Federal Code: 002820

4-year private liberal arts college in very large city, affiliated with Roman Catholic Church.
Enrollment: 2,790 undergrads.
Selectivity: Admits 50 to 75% of applicants.

BASIC COSTS (2012-2013)
Tuition and fees: $19,200.

FINANCIAL AID PICTURE
Students with need: Need-based aid available for full-time and part-time students.
Students without need: No-need awards available for academics, athletics.

FINANCIAL AID PROCEDURES
Forms required: FAFSA, state aid form.
Dates and Deadlines: Priority date 2/15; no closing date. Applicants notified on a rolling basis starting 3/15; must reply within 2 week(s) of notification.
Transfers: No deadline. Applicants notified on a rolling basis.

CONTACT
Joseph Cummings, AVP Enrollment Services
180 Remsen Street, Brooklyn Heights, NY 11201-9902
(718) 489-5255

St. John Fisher College

Rochester, New York
www.sjfc.edu Federal Code: 002821

4-year private liberal arts college in large town, affiliated with Roman Catholic Church.
Enrollment: 2,937 undergrads, 6% part-time. 554 full-time freshmen.
Selectivity: Admits 50 to 75% of applicants. GED not accepted.

BASIC COSTS (2012-2013)
Tuition and fees: $27,370.
Per-credit charge: $730.
Room and board: $10,720.

FINANCIAL AID PICTURE (2011-2012)
Students with need: Out of 553 full-time freshmen who applied for aid, 452 were judged to have need. Of these, 452 received aid, and 201 had their full need met. Average financial aid package met 83% of need; average scholarship/grant was $15,390; average loan was $3,737.
Students without need: 102 full-time freshmen who did not demonstrate need for aid received scholarships/grants; average award was $10,095. No-need awards available for academics, leadership.
Scholarships offered: Scholarships range from $10,000 to $14,000. Honors and Science Scholars programs receive additional $3,000 annually. Fisher Service Scholars Program: one-half the total cost of education. First Generation Scholars Program: from $5,000 up to one-half of the total cost of education.
Cumulative student debt: 82% of graduating class had student loans; average debt was $32,157.

FINANCIAL AID PROCEDURES
Forms required: FAFSA, state aid form.
Dates and Deadlines: Priority date 2/15; no closing date. Applicants notified on a rolling basis starting 3/15; must reply by 5/1 or within 3 week(s) of notification.
Transfers: No deadline. Applicants notified on a rolling basis starting 3/15; must reply within 3 week(s) of notification.

CONTACT
Angela Monnat, Director of Financial Aid
3690 East Avenue, Rochester, NY 14618-3597
(585) 385-8042

St. John's University

Queens, New York
www.stjohns.edu Federal Code: 002823

4-year private university in very large city, affiliated with Roman Catholic Church.
Enrollment: 11,191 undergrads, 3% part-time. 2,761 full-time freshmen.
Selectivity: Admits 50 to 75% of applicants.

BASIC COSTS (2012-2013)
Tuition and fees: $35,520.
Per-credit charge: $1,158.
Room and board: $15,270.
Additional info: Tuition may vary by program and class year. A four-year fixed rate tuition plan is available for incoming freshmen. Full-time freshman or transfer students are provided with a laptop for their entire St. John's career. Tuition at time of enrollment locked for 4 years.

FINANCIAL AID PICTURE (2011-2012)
Students with need: Out of 2,505 full-time freshmen who applied for aid, 2,351 were judged to have need. Of these, 2,350 received aid, and 276 had their full need met. Average financial aid package met 86% of need; average scholarship/grant was $14,275; average loan was $3,621. For part-time students, average financial aid package was $14,679.
Students without need: 131 full-time freshmen who did not demonstrate need for aid received scholarships/grants; average award was $12,628. No-need awards available for academics, alumni affiliation, art, athletics, leadership, music/drama, religious affiliation, ROTC.
Scholarships offered: 38 full-time freshmen received athletic scholarships; average amount $29,152.
Cumulative student debt: 71% of graduating class had student loans; average debt was $29,199.

FINANCIAL AID PROCEDURES
Forms required: FAFSA.
Dates and Deadlines: Priority date 2/1; no closing date. Applicants notified on a rolling basis starting 3/15; must reply within 2 week(s) of notification.
Transfers: No deadline. Applicants notified by 3/15; must reply by 5/1 or within 2 week(s) of notification. Scholarships available if 12 credits college study completed with a minimum GPA of 3.0.

CONTACT
Jorge Rodriguez, Associate Vice President Student Financial Services
8000 Utopia Parkway, Queens, NY 11439
(718) 990-2000

St. Joseph's College New York: Suffolk Campus

Patchogue, New York
www.sjcny.edu Federal Code: 002825

4-year private branch campus and liberal arts college in large town.
Enrollment: 3,451 undergrads, 18% part-time. 439 full-time freshmen.
Selectivity: Admits 50 to 75% of applicants.

BASIC COSTS (2012-2013)
Tuition and fees: $20,125.
Per-credit charge: $635.

FINANCIAL AID PICTURE (2011-2012)
Students with need: Out of 433 full-time freshmen who applied for aid, 308 were judged to have need. Of these, 305 received aid, and 91 had their full need met. Average financial aid package met 72% of need; average scholarship/grant was $9,001; average loan was $3,106. For part-time students, average financial aid package was $5,970.
Students without need: 101 full-time freshmen who did not demonstrate need for aid received scholarships/grants; average award was $9,166. No-need awards available for academics, alumni affiliation, leadership.
Cumulative student debt: 71% of graduating class had student loans; average debt was $25,137.

FINANCIAL AID PROCEDURES
Forms required: FAFSA, state aid form.
Dates and Deadlines: Priority date 2/25; no closing date. Applicants notified on a rolling basis starting 3/15; must reply by 5/1 or within 2 week(s) of notification.
Transfers: Priority date 3/15; no deadline.

CONTACT
Amy Thompson, Director of Financial Aid
155 West Roe Boulevard, Patchogue, NY 11772-2325
(631) 687-2600

St. Joseph's College of Nursing
Syracuse, New York
www.sjhsyr.org/nursing Federal Code: 006467

2-year private nursing college in small city, affiliated with Roman Catholic Church.
Enrollment: 306 undergrads. 7 full-time freshmen.

BASIC COSTS (2012-2013)
Tuition and fees: $16,792.
Per-credit charge: $488.
Additional info: Board plan not available. Cost of room only: $4400.

FINANCIAL AID PICTURE
Students with need: Need-based aid available for full-time and part-time students.
Students without need: This college awards aid only to students with need.

FINANCIAL AID PROCEDURES
Forms required: FAFSA, state aid form.
Dates and Deadlines: Priority date 3/1; no closing date. Applicants notified on a rolling basis starting 6/15.

CONTACT
Theresa Moser, Coordinator for Financial Aid
206 Prospect Avenue, Syracuse, NY 13203
(315) 448-5040

St. Joseph's College, New York
Brooklyn, New York
www.sjcny.edu Federal Code: 002825

4-year private liberal arts and teachers college in very large city.
Enrollment: 1,260 undergrads, 24% part-time. 205 full-time freshmen.
Selectivity: Admits 50 to 75% of applicants.

BASIC COSTS (2012-2013)
Tuition and fees: $20,115.
Per-credit charge: $635.

FINANCIAL AID PICTURE (2011-2012)
Students with need: Out of 193 full-time freshmen who applied for aid, 151 were judged to have need. Of these, 151 received aid, and 24 had their full need met. Average financial aid package met 72% of need; average scholarship/grant was $12,431; average loan was $2,865. For part-time students, average financial aid package was $5,710.
Students without need: 46 full-time freshmen who did not demonstrate need for aid received scholarships/grants; average award was $10,180. No-need awards available for academics, alumni affiliation, leadership.
Cumulative student debt: 62% of graduating class had student loans; average debt was $25,836.

FINANCIAL AID PROCEDURES
Forms required: FAFSA, state aid form.
Dates and Deadlines: Priority date 2/25; no closing date. Applicants notified on a rolling basis starting 3/15; must reply by 5/1 or within 2 week(s) of notification.
Transfers: Priority date 3/15; no deadline.

CONTACT
Amy Thompson, Director of Financial Aid
245 Clinton Avenue, Brooklyn, NY 11205-3602
(631) 687-2600

St. Lawrence University
Canton, New York Federal Code: 002829
www.stlawu.edu CSS Code: 2805

4-year private liberal arts college in small town.
Enrollment: 2,374 undergrads. 644 full-time freshmen.
Selectivity: Admits less than 50% of applicants.

BASIC COSTS (2013-2014)
Tuition and fees: $46,030.
Room and board: $11,860.

FINANCIAL AID PICTURE (2012-2013)
Students with need: Out of 469 full-time freshmen who applied for aid, 413 were judged to have need. Of these, 412 received aid, and 136 had their full need met. Average financial aid package met 89% of need; average scholarship/grant was $31,089; average loan was $3,279.
Students without need: 195 full-time freshmen who did not demonstrate need for aid received scholarships/grants; average award was $17,957. No-need awards available for academics, alumni affiliation, athletics, leadership, minority status, ROTC, state/district residency.
Scholarships offered: ***Merit:*** Merit scholarships; $10,000 to $30,000 annually. Augsbury/North Country Scholarship; for students in some schools in northern New York and southern Ontario; nomination by counselor required. Community Service Scholarship; based on past and current service. Presidential Diversity Scholarship; for students of African American, Asian American, Hispanic American and Native American heritage and those who support multiculturalism. Sesquicentennial and University Scholarship; based on academic excellence, character and leadership. Vilas Scholarship; for students interested in business. Leadership Scholarship; based on evidence of leadership in schools and communities. ***Athletic:*** 6 full-time freshmen received athletic scholarships; average amount $55,835.
Cumulative student debt: 61% of graduating class had student loans; average debt was $25,058.

FINANCIAL AID PROCEDURES
Forms required: FAFSA, CSS PROFILE.
Dates and Deadlines: Closing date 2/1. Applicants notified by 3/31; must reply by 5/1 or within 2 week(s) of notification.
Transfers: Priority date 4/1; closing date 5/1. Applicants notified on a rolling basis starting 6/1; must reply within 2 week(s) of notification.

CONTACT
Patricia Farmer, Director of Financial Aid
Payson Hall, Canton, NY 13617
(315) 229-5265

St. Thomas Aquinas College

Sparkill, New York
www.stac.edu Federal Code: 002832

4-year private liberal arts college in large town.
Enrollment: 1,295 undergrads, 4% part-time. 270 full-time freshmen.
Selectivity: Admits over 75% of applicants.

BASIC COSTS (2013-2014)
Tuition and fees: $26,340.
Per-credit charge: $825.
Room and board: $11,280.

FINANCIAL AID PICTURE
Students with need: Need-based aid available for full-time and part-time students.
Students without need: No-need awards available for academics, athletics.

FINANCIAL AID PROCEDURES
Forms required: FAFSA, state aid form.
Dates and Deadlines: Priority date 2/15; no closing date. Applicants notified on a rolling basis starting 3/1; must reply by 5/1 or within 4 week(s) of notification.
Transfers: Closing date 5/1. Applicants notified on a rolling basis; must reply within 4 week(s) of notification.

CONTACT
Jean-Marie Mohr, Director of Financial Aid
125 Route 340, Sparkill, NY 10976-1050
(845) 398-4097

Sarah Lawrence College

Bronxville, New York Federal Code: 002813
www.slc.edu CSS Code: 2810

4-year private liberal arts college in small city.
Enrollment: 1,342 undergrads, 2% part-time. 344 full-time freshmen.
Selectivity: Admits 50 to 75% of applicants.

BASIC COSTS (2012-2013)
Tuition and fees: $46,924.
Per-credit charge: $1,530.
Room and board: $14,312.

FINANCIAL AID PICTURE (2012-2013)
Students with need: Out of 265 full-time freshmen who applied for aid, 221 were judged to have need. Of these, 218 received aid, and 115 had their full need met. Average financial aid package met 83% of need; average scholarship/grant was $29,670; average loan was $2,811. For part-time students, average financial aid package was $32,172.
Students without need: This college awards aid only to students with need.
Scholarships offered: Presidential and Dean Scholarships: available regardless of need to admitted students demonstrating substantial academic achievement, creativity and potential for leadership; available for up to four years of full-time study contingent on satisfactory academic progress.
Cumulative student debt: 61% of graduating class had student loans; average debt was $19,922.

FINANCIAL AID PROCEDURES
Forms required: FAFSA, CSS PROFILE, state aid form.
Dates and Deadlines: Closing date 2/1. Applicants notified by 4/1; must reply by 5/1.
Transfers: Closing date 3/15. Applicants notified by 5/15.

CONTACT
Heather McDonnell, Director of Financial Aid
1 Mead Way, Bronxville, NY 10708-5999
(914) 395-2570

Schenectady County Community College

Schenectady, New York
www.sunysccc.edu Federal Code: 006785

2-year public community college in small city.
Enrollment: 4,393 undergrads.
Selectivity: Open admission; but selective for some programs.

BASIC COSTS (2012-2013)
Tuition and fees: $3,745; out-of-state residents $7,129.

FINANCIAL AID PICTURE (2011-2012)
Students with need: Need-based aid available for full-time and part-time students.
Students without need: This college awards aid only to students with need.
Additional info: Federal Work Study for full time students.

FINANCIAL AID PROCEDURES
Forms required: FAFSA.
Dates and Deadlines: Priority date 5/1; no closing date. Applicants notified on a rolling basis starting 3/1; must reply by 8/31.

CONTACT
Brian McGarvey, Director of Financial Aid
78 Washington Avenue, Schenectady, NY 12305
(518) 381-1352

School of Visual Arts

New York, New York
www.sva.edu Federal Code: 007468

4-year for-profit visual arts college in very large city.
Enrollment: 3,493 undergrads. 615 full-time freshmen.

BASIC COSTS (2012-2013)
Tuition and fees: $31,030.
Additional info: Board plan not available. Cost of room only, $13,200. Additional fees vary by department.

FINANCIAL AID PICTURE (2012-2013)
Students with need: Out of 401 full-time freshmen who applied for aid, 349 were judged to have need. Of these, 333 received aid, and 6 had their full need met. Average financial aid package met 39% of need; average scholarship/grant was $11,295; average loan was $3,594. For part-time students, average financial aid package was $10,402.
Students without need: 31 full-time freshmen who did not demonstrate need for aid received scholarships/grants; average award was $8,653. No-need awards available for art.
Scholarships offered: SVA matching scholarship available to full- and part-time undergraduate and graduate students. SVA will match 25% of any outside scholarship, up to $2,500, that a student obtains.
Cumulative student debt: 63% of graduating class had student loans; average debt was $29,678.

FINANCIAL AID PROCEDURES
Forms required: FAFSA, state aid form.

Dates and Deadlines: Priority date 2/1; closing date 3/1. Applicants notified on a rolling basis starting 2/15; must reply within 4 week(s) of notification.
Transfers: No deadline. Applicants notified on a rolling basis; must reply within 4 week(s) of notification.

CONTACT

William Berrios, Director of Financial Aid
209 East 23rd Street, New York, NY 10010-3994
(212) 592-2030

Siena College

Loudonville, New York
www.siena.edu Federal Code: 002816

4-year private liberal arts college in large town, affiliated with Roman Catholic Church.
Enrollment: 3,149 undergrads, 4% part-time. 734 full-time freshmen.
Selectivity: Admits 50 to 75% of applicants.

BASIC COSTS (2013-2014)

Tuition and fees: $31,528.
Room and board: $12,495.

FINANCIAL AID PICTURE

Students with need: Need-based aid available for full-time and part-time students. Work study available nights, weekends, and for part-time students.
Students without need: No-need awards available for academics, athletics, leadership, minority status, ROTC, state/district residency.

FINANCIAL AID PROCEDURES

Forms required: FAFSA, state aid form.
Dates and Deadlines: Priority date 2/15; closing date 5/1. Applicants notified by 4/1; must reply by 5/1.
Transfers: Priority date 3/1.

CONTACT

Mary Lawyer, Associate Vice President for Enrollment Management
515 Loudon Road, Loudonville, NY 12211-1462
(518) 783-2427

Skidmore College

Saratoga Springs, New York Federal Code: 002814
www.skidmore.edu CSS Code: 2815

4-year private liberal arts college in large town.
Enrollment: 2,631 undergrads, 1% part-time. 647 full-time freshmen.
Selectivity: Admits less than 50% of applicants.

BASIC COSTS (2012-2013)

Tuition and fees: $44,020.
Per-credit charge: $1,438.
Room and board: $11,744.

FINANCIAL AID PICTURE (2012-2013)

Students with need: Out of 304 full-time freshmen who applied for aid, 297 were judged to have need. Of these, 297 received aid, and 297 had their full need met. Average financial aid package met 100% of need; average scholarship/grant was $35,770; average loan was $2,347.
Students without need: 4 full-time freshmen who did not demonstrate need for aid received scholarships/grants; average award was $12,500. No-need awards available for music/drama.
Scholarships offered: Porter Presidential Scholarships in Science and Mathematics: $15,000 annually; based on outstanding ability and achievement in math, science, or computer science. Filene Undergraduate Music Scholarships: $12,000 annually; based on music ability.
Cumulative student debt: 42% of graduating class had student loans; average debt was $22,753.

FINANCIAL AID PROCEDURES

Forms required: FAFSA, CSS PROFILE.
Dates and Deadlines: Closing date 2/1. Applicants notified by 4/1; must reply by 5/1.
Transfers: Priority date 4/1. Applicants notified on a rolling basis starting 4/15; must reply within 3 week(s) of notification. Some transfer students eligible for need-based grant assistance.

CONTACT

Beth Post-Lundquist, Director of Financial Aid
815 North Broadway, Saratoga Springs, NY 12866
(518) 580-5750

Suffolk County Community College

Selden, New York
www.sunysuffolk.edu Federal Code: 002878

2-year public community college in large town.
Enrollment: 26,219 undergrads.
Selectivity: Open admission; but selective for some programs.

BASIC COSTS (2012-2013)

Tuition and fees: $4,519; out-of-state residents $8,509.
Per-credit charge: $167; out-of-state residents $334.

FINANCIAL AID PICTURE

Students with need: Need-based aid available for full-time and part-time students. Work study available nights, weekends, and for part-time students.
Students without need: No-need awards available for academics, art, leadership, minority status, music/drama, state/district residency.

FINANCIAL AID PROCEDURES

Forms required: FAFSA, state aid form.
Dates and Deadlines: Priority date 4/15; closing date 6/1. Applicants notified on a rolling basis starting 4/15; must reply within 2 week(s) of notification.
Transfers: No deadline. Applicants notified on a rolling basis starting 4/15.

CONTACT

Nancy Dunnagan, Director of Financial Aid
533 College Road, Selden, NY 11784
(631) 451-4110

Sullivan County Community College

Loch Sheldrake, New York
www.sunysullivan.edu Federal Code: 002879

2-year public community college in small town.
Enrollment: 1,260 undergrads, 21% part-time. 375 full-time freshmen.
Selectivity: Open admission; but selective for some programs.

BASIC COSTS (2012-2013)

Tuition and fees: $5,116; out-of-state residents $9,590.
Per-credit charge: $174; out-of-state residents $230.

FINANCIAL AID PICTURE (2011-2012)

Students with need: 77% of average financial aid package awarded as scholarships/grants, 23% awarded as loans/jobs. Need-based aid available for part-time students.
Additional info: 60% of students hold part-time jobs locally.

FINANCIAL AID PROCEDURES

Forms required: FAFSA.
Dates and Deadlines: Priority date 4/15; no closing date. Applicants notified on a rolling basis starting 5/15; must reply within 2 week(s) of notification.

CONTACT
James Winderl, Director of Financial Aid
112 College Road, Loch Sheldrake, NY 12759-5151
(845) 434-5750

SUNY College at Brockport
Brockport, New York
www.brockport.edu Federal Code: 002841

4-year public liberal arts college in small town.
Enrollment: 7,043 undergrads, 9% part-time. 941 full-time freshmen.
Selectivity: Admits less than 50% of applicants.

BASIC COSTS (2012-2013)
Tuition and fees: $6,881; out-of-state residents $16,131.
Per-credit charge: $232; out-of-state residents $618.
Room and board: $10,940.

FINANCIAL AID PICTURE (2011-2012)
Students with need: Out of 886 full-time freshmen who applied for aid, 694 were judged to have need. Of these, 685 received aid, and 98 had their full need met. Average financial aid package met 71% of need; average scholarship/grant was $5,342; average loan was $4,383. For part-time students, average financial aid package was $5,240.
Students without need: 60 full-time freshmen who did not demonstrate need for aid received scholarships/grants; average award was $3,466. No-need awards available for academics, alumni affiliation, art, leadership, minority status, music/drama, ROTC.
Scholarships offered: Extraordinary Academic Scholarships: $2,250 to $5,270 per year; minimum qualifications include SAT scores of 1100 (24 ACT), rank in top 25% of class, 90 average or higher. SAT score exclusive of Writing portion.
Cumulative student debt: 82% of graduating class had student loans; average debt was $27,844.

FINANCIAL AID PROCEDURES
Forms required: FAFSA.
Dates and Deadlines: Priority date 3/15; no closing date. Applicants notified on a rolling basis starting 3/1; must reply by 5/1.

CONTACT
J. Atkinson, Director of Enrollment Services
350 New Campus Drive, Brockport, NY 14420-2915
(585) 395-2501

SUNY College at Buffalo
Buffalo, New York
www.buffalostate.edu Federal Code: 002842

4-year public liberal arts and teachers college in large city.
Enrollment: 9,731 undergrads.
Selectivity: Admits less than 50% of applicants.

BASIC COSTS (2012-2013)
Tuition and fees: $6,694; out-of-state residents $15,944.
Per-credit charge: $232; out-of-state residents $618.
Room and board: $11,192.
Additional info: Tuition/fee waivers available for minority students.

FINANCIAL AID PICTURE
Students with need: Need-based aid available for full-time and part-time students.
Students without need: This college awards aid only to students with need.
Scholarships offered: Empire Minority Scholarships; $1,000 annually for 4 years. Honors Program; $2,000 for 2 years and $1,000 for remaining 2 years.

FINANCIAL AID PROCEDURES
Forms required: FAFSA.
Dates and Deadlines: Priority date 3/15; closing date 5/1. Applicants notified on a rolling basis starting 5/1; must reply within 4 week(s) of notification.
Transfers: No deadline.

CONTACT
Connie Cooke, Director of Financial Aid
1300 Elmwood Avenue, Moot Hall, Buffalo, NY 14222-1095
(716) 878-4902

SUNY College at Cortland
Cortland, New York
www.cortland.edu Federal Code: 002843

4-year public liberal arts and teachers college in large town.
Enrollment: 6,328 undergrads, 2% part-time. 1,210 full-time freshmen.
Selectivity: Admits less than 50% of applicants.

BASIC COSTS (2012-2013)
Tuition and fees: $6,942; out-of-state residents $16,192.
Per-credit charge: $232; out-of-state residents $618.
Room and board: $11,430.

FINANCIAL AID PICTURE (2011-2012)
Students with need: Out of 1,115 full-time freshmen who applied for aid, 751 were judged to have need. Of these, 718 received aid, and 67 had their full need met. Average financial aid package met 70% of need; average scholarship/grant was $5,117; average loan was $3,528. For part-time students, average financial aid package was $8,486.
Students without need: 59 full-time freshmen who did not demonstrate need for aid received scholarships/grants; average award was $2,413. No-need awards available for academics, art, leadership, minority status, music/drama, state/district residency.
Cumulative student debt: 79% of graduating class had student loans; average debt was $27,534.

FINANCIAL AID PROCEDURES
Forms required: FAFSA, state aid form.
Dates and Deadlines: Priority date 3/1; no closing date. Applicants notified on a rolling basis starting 3/15; must reply by 5/1 or within 4 week(s) of notification.

CONTACT
Karen Gallagher, Director of Financial Aid
PO Box 2000, Cortland, NY 13045-0900
(607) 753-4717

SUNY College at Fredonia
Fredonia, New York
www.fredonia.edu Federal Code: 002844

4-year public liberal arts college in large town.
Enrollment: 5,171 undergrads, 2% part-time. 984 full-time freshmen.
Selectivity: Admits 50 to 75% of applicants.

BASIC COSTS (2012-2013)
Tuition and fees: $7,058; out-of-state residents $16,308.
Per-credit charge: $232; out-of-state residents $618.
Room and board: $10,740.

FINANCIAL AID PICTURE (2012-2013)
Students with need: Out of 900 full-time freshmen who applied for aid, 678 were judged to have need. Of these, 661 received aid, and 91 had their full need met. Average financial aid package met 63% of need; average scholarship/grant was $5,534; average loan was $5,317. For part-time students, average financial aid package was $7,617.

Students without need: 87 full-time freshmen who did not demonstrate need for aid received scholarships/grants; average award was $2,382. No-need awards available for academics, alumni affiliation, art, minority status, music/drama, state/district residency.
Cumulative student debt: 87% of graduating class had student loans; average debt was $27,354.

FINANCIAL AID PROCEDURES
Forms required: FAFSA, state aid form.
Dates and Deadlines: Applicants notified on a rolling basis starting 3/1; must reply by 5/1.
Transfers: Priority date 1/31; no deadline. Applicants notified on a rolling basis starting 10/15. Financial aid transcripts required from prior institutions attended.

CONTACT
Daniel Tramuta, Director of Financial Aid
178 Central Avenue, Fredonia, NY 14063-1136
(716) 673-3253

SUNY College at Geneseo
Geneseo, New York
www.geneseo.edu Federal Code: 002845

4-year public liberal arts college in small town.
Enrollment: 5,339 undergrads, 2% part-time. 1,008 full-time freshmen.
Selectivity: Admits less than 50% of applicants.

BASIC COSTS (2012-2013)
Tuition and fees: $7,093; out-of-state residents $16,343.
Per-credit charge: $232; out-of-state residents $618.
Room and board: $10,962.

FINANCIAL AID PICTURE (2011-2012)
Students with need: Out of 826 full-time freshmen who applied for aid, 418 were judged to have need. Of these, 382 received aid, and 237 had their full need met. Average financial aid package met 62% of need; average scholarship/grant was $3,821; average loan was $3,211. Need-based aid available for part-time students.
Students without need: 8 full-time freshmen who did not demonstrate need for aid received scholarships/grants; average award was $3,300. No-need awards available for academics, art, leadership, minority status, music/drama, religious affiliation, ROTC, state/district residency.
Cumulative student debt: 67% of graduating class had student loans; average debt was $21,000.

FINANCIAL AID PROCEDURES
Forms required: FAFSA, state aid form.
Dates and Deadlines: Closing date 2/15. Applicants notified on a rolling basis starting 3/15; must reply by 5/1.

CONTACT
Archie Cureton, Director of Financial Aid
1 College Circle, Geneseo, NY 14454-1401
(585) 245-5731

SUNY College at New Paltz
New Paltz, New York
www.newpaltz.edu Federal Code: 002846

4-year public liberal arts college in large town.
Enrollment: 6,439 undergrads, 6% part-time. 1,119 full-time freshmen.
Selectivity: Admits less than 50% of applicants.

BASIC COSTS (2012-2013)
Tuition and fees: $6,758; out-of-state residents $16,008.
Per-credit charge: $232; out-of-state residents $618.
Room and board: $10,084.

FINANCIAL AID PICTURE (2012-2013)
Students with need: Out of 999 full-time freshmen who applied for aid, 662 were judged to have need. Of these, 652 received aid, and 42 had their full need met. Average financial aid package met 54% of need; average scholarship/grant was $4,990; average loan was $3,464. For part-time students, average financial aid package was $5,155.
Students without need: This college awards aid only to students with need.
Cumulative student debt: 63% of graduating class had student loans; average debt was $24,857.

FINANCIAL AID PROCEDURES
Forms required: FAFSA, state aid form.
Dates and Deadlines: Priority date 3/15; no closing date. Applicants notified on a rolling basis starting 4/1; must reply within 6 week(s) of notification.
Transfers: No deadline. Applicants notified on a rolling basis starting 4/1; must reply within 4 week(s) of notification.

CONTACT
Daniel Sistarenik, Director of Financial Aid
100 Hawk Drive, New Paltz, NY 12561-2443
(845) 257-3250

SUNY College at Old Westbury
Old Westbury, New York
www.oldwestbury.edu Federal Code: 007109

4-year public business and liberal arts college in small city.
Enrollment: 4,077 undergrads, 12% part-time. 399 full-time freshmen.
Selectivity: Admits 50 to 75% of applicants.

BASIC COSTS (2012-2013)
Tuition and fees: $6,624; out-of-state residents $15,874.
Per-credit charge: $232; out-of-state residents $618.
Room and board: $9,700.

FINANCIAL AID PICTURE (2011-2012)
Students with need: Out of 366 full-time freshmen who applied for aid, 366 were judged to have need. Of these, 333 received aid, and 307 had their full need met. Average financial aid package met 59% of need; average scholarship/grant was $7,703; average loan was $4,043. For part-time students, average financial aid package was $4,670.
Students without need: No-need awards available for academics, alumni affiliation, state/district residency.
Cumulative student debt: 53% of graduating class had student loans; average debt was $17,395.

FINANCIAL AID PROCEDURES
Forms required: FAFSA, state aid form, institutional form.
Dates and Deadlines: Closing date 4/1. Applicants notified on a rolling basis starting 4/15; must reply within 2 week(s) of notification.
Transfers: No deadline. Applicants notified on a rolling basis starting 4/15; must reply within 2 week(s) of notification. Financial aid transcript required.

CONTACT
Mildred O'Keefe, Director of Financial Aid
Box 307, Old Westbury, NY 11568-0307
(516) 876-3222

SUNY College at Oneonta

Oneonta, New York
www.oneonta.edu/home/default.asp
Federal Code: 002847

4-year public liberal arts college in large town.
Enrollment: 5,804 undergrads, 2% part-time. 1,144 full-time freshmen.
Selectivity: Admits less than 50% of applicants.

BASIC COSTS (2012-2013)

Tuition and fees: $6,896; out-of-state residents $16,146.
Per-credit charge: $232; out-of-state residents $618.
Room and board: $10,540.

FINANCIAL AID PICTURE (2012-2013)

Students with need: Out of 900 full-time freshmen who applied for aid, 665 were judged to have need. Of these, 665 received aid, and 25 had their full need met. Average financial aid package met 81% of need; average scholarship/grant was $6,510; average loan was $3,850. For part-time students, average financial aid package was $3,956.
Students without need: 282 full-time freshmen who did not demonstrate need for aid received scholarships/grants; average award was $2,841. No-need awards available for academics, leadership, minority status, music/drama, state/district residency.
Scholarships offered: Presidential Scholarship: $5,870; awarded to students who have shown exceptional academic ability. Presidential Diversity Scholarship and Organization of Auxiliary Services Diversity Student Leadership Scholarship: $5,870; for students who will contribute to the diversity of the student body and who have shown exceptional academic ability and strong commitment to diversity through activities and leadership. Deans' Scholarship: $3,000; awarded based on academics. Oneonta Auxiliary Services Merit Scholarship: $2,000; awarded to applicants for academics, service, extracurricular activities. All scholarships are renewable.
Cumulative student debt: 66% of graduating class had student loans; average debt was $15,373.

FINANCIAL AID PROCEDURES

Forms required: FAFSA.
Dates and Deadlines: Priority date 3/1; no closing date. Applicants notified on a rolling basis starting 3/1.
Transfers: No deadline. Applicants notified on a rolling basis starting 3/1.

CONTACT

C. Goodhue, Director of Student Financial Aid
Admissions Office, 116 Alumni Hall, Oneonta, NY 13820-4016
(607) 436-2532

SUNY College at Oswego

Oswego, New York
www.oswego.edu
Federal Code: 002848

4-year public university in large town.
Enrollment: 7,113 undergrads, 4% part-time. 1,270 full-time freshmen.
Selectivity: Admits less than 50% of applicants.

BASIC COSTS (2012-2013)

Tuition and fees: $6,841; out-of-state residents $16,091.
Per-credit charge: $232; out-of-state residents $618.
Room and board: $12,510.

FINANCIAL AID PICTURE (2011-2012)

Students with need: Out of 1,229 full-time freshmen who applied for aid, 891 were judged to have need. Of these, 891 received aid, and 91 had their full need met. Average financial aid package met 77% of need; average scholarship/grant was $6,391; average loan was $3,728. For part-time students, average financial aid package was $5,970.
Students without need: 194 full-time freshmen who did not demonstrate need for aid received scholarships/grants; average award was $3,204. No-need awards available for academics, state/district residency.
Scholarships offered: Annual scholarships: $500 to $4,400; based on class rank in top 15%. Additional residential scholarships for out-of-state students: $4,490 annually; requires on-campus housing.
Cumulative student debt: 80% of graduating class had student loans; average debt was $26,611.

FINANCIAL AID PROCEDURES

Forms required: FAFSA.
Dates and Deadlines: Priority date 3/1; no closing date. Applicants notified on a rolling basis starting 3/1; must reply by 5/1 or within 3 week(s) of notification.
Transfers: No deadline. Applicants notified on a rolling basis starting 3/15; must reply by 5/1 or within 21 week(s) of notification.

CONTACT

Mark Humbert, Director of Financial Aid
229 Sheldon Hall, Oswego, NY 13126-3599
(315) 312-2248

SUNY College at Plattsburgh

Plattsburgh, New York
www.plattsburgh.edu
Federal Code: 002849

4-year public liberal arts and teachers college in large town.
Enrollment: 5,623 undergrads, 6% part-time. 961 full-time freshmen.
Selectivity: Admits less than 50% of applicants.

BASIC COSTS (2012-2013)

Tuition and fees: $6,808; out-of-state residents $16,058.
Per-credit charge: $232; out-of-state residents $618.
Room and board: $10,582.

FINANCIAL AID PICTURE (2011-2012)

Students with need: Out of 875 full-time freshmen who applied for aid, 642 were judged to have need. Of these, 640 received aid, and 120 had their full need met. Average financial aid package met 88% of need; average scholarship/grant was $6,635; average loan was $5,793. For part-time students, average financial aid package was $6,765.
Students without need: 273 full-time freshmen who did not demonstrate need for aid received scholarships/grants; average award was $5,753. No-need awards available for academics, alumni affiliation, art, leadership, minority status, music/drama, ROTC, state/district residency.
Cumulative student debt: 70% of graduating class had student loans; average debt was $25,268.

FINANCIAL AID PROCEDURES

Forms required: FAFSA, state aid form.
Dates and Deadlines: Priority date 2/15; no closing date. Applicants notified on a rolling basis starting 3/1; must reply by 5/1.
Transfers: No deadline. Applicants notified on a rolling basis.

CONTACT

Todd Moravec, Director of Student Financial Services
Kehoe Administration Building, Plattsburgh, NY 12901
(518) 564-4076

SUNY College at Potsdam

Potsdam, New York
www.potsdam.edu
Federal Code: 002850

4-year public liberal arts and teachers college in large town.
Enrollment: 3,850 undergrads, 2% part-time. 883 full-time freshmen.
Selectivity: Admits 50 to 75% of applicants.

BASIC COSTS (2012-2013)
Tuition and fees: $6,842; out-of-state residents $16,092.
Per-credit charge: $232; out-of-state residents $618.
Room and board: $10,620.

FINANCIAL AID PICTURE (2012-2013)
Students with need: Out of 845 full-time freshmen who applied for aid, 675 were judged to have need. Of these, 670 received aid, and 312 had their full need met. Average financial aid package met 88% of need; average scholarship/grant was $7,175; average loan was $3,946. For part-time students, average financial aid package was $8,449.
Students without need: 76 full-time freshmen who did not demonstrate need for aid received scholarships/grants; average award was $2,196. No-need awards available for academics, art, leadership, music/drama, ROTC.
Scholarships offered: Mt. Emmons Scholarship: covers balance of in-state tuition and mandatory fees after TAP awards; $500 book stipend; residence hall fee waiver and board; renewable with minimum 3.25 GPA; 5 awarded. Freshman Scholars Program: $1,000-$4,600; for students who show academic promise and potential for leadership; 1300 or higher SAT (exclusive of Writing), ACT composite of 24, or minimum 92 high school average and history of participation, leadership in extracurricular activities and community service.
Cumulative student debt: 78% of graduating class had student loans; average debt was $20,734.
Additional info: Apply early to access limited, need-based awards.

FINANCIAL AID PROCEDURES
Forms required: FAFSA, state aid form.
Dates and Deadlines: Priority date 3/1; closing date 5/1. Applicants notified on a rolling basis starting 2/1; must reply by 5/1 or within 4 week(s) of notification.
Transfers: Transfer Scholars Program for incoming transfer students based upon outstanding academic achievement as measured by previous college GPA. $1,000-$3,000 to students with minimum cumulative GPA of 3.25 and higher. Renewable for 1 year with cumulative 3.25 GPA.

CONTACT
Susan Aldrich, Director of Financial Aid
44 Pierrepont Avenue, Potsdam, NY 13676
(315) 267-2162

SUNY College at Purchase
Purchase, New York
www.purchase.edu Federal Code: 006791

4-year public university in large town.
Enrollment: 3,900 undergrads, 6% part-time. 693 full-time freshmen.
Selectivity: Admits less than 50% of applicants.

BASIC COSTS (2012-2013)
Tuition and fees: $7,230; out-of-state residents $16,480.
Per-credit charge: $232; out-of-state residents $618.
Room and board: $11,518.

FINANCIAL AID PICTURE (2012-2013)
Students with need: Out of 597 full-time freshmen who applied for aid, 445 were judged to have need. Of these, 444 received aid, and 14 had their full need met. Average financial aid package met 50% of need; average scholarship/grant was $6,413; average loan was $3,771. For part-time students, average financial aid package was $10,194.
Students without need: 29 full-time freshmen who did not demonstrate need for aid received scholarships/grants; average award was $2,844. No-need awards available for academics, art, minority status, music/drama.
Cumulative student debt: 60% of graduating class had student loans; average debt was $26,684.
Additional info: All applicants automatically considered for scholarship upon review of applications, essays, auditions, and/or portfolio.

FINANCIAL AID PROCEDURES
Forms required: FAFSA, state aid form.
Dates and Deadlines: Priority date 2/1; no closing date. Applicants notified on a rolling basis starting 3/1; must reply within 2 week(s) of notification.
Transfers: Financial aid transcripts required from all previously attended institutions.

CONTACT
Corey York, Director of Financial Aid
735 Anderson Hill Road, Purchase, NY 10577-1400
(914) 251-6350

SUNY College of Agriculture and Technology at Cobleskill
Cobleskill, New York
www.cobleskill.edu Federal Code: 002856

2-year public agricultural and technical college in small town.
Enrollment: 2,461 undergrads, 6% part-time. 986 full-time freshmen.
Selectivity: Admits 50 to 75% of applicants.

BASIC COSTS (2012-2013)
Tuition and fees: $6,819; out-of-state residents $10,989.
Per-credit charge: $232; out-of-state residents $406.
Room and board: $10,966.
Additional info: Out-of-state tuition for bachelor's program: $14,820; per-credit-hour $618.

FINANCIAL AID PICTURE (2011-2012)
Students with need: Out of 903 full-time freshmen who applied for aid, 797 were judged to have need. Of these, 795 received aid, and 14 had their full need met. Average financial aid package met 80% of need; average scholarship/grant was $5,354; average loan was $3,981. For part-time students, average financial aid package was $4,268.
Students without need: 106 full-time freshmen who did not demonstrate need for aid received scholarships/grants; average award was $383. No-need awards available for academics, alumni affiliation, leadership, minority status, state/district residency.
Cumulative student debt: 73% of graduating class had student loans; average debt was $21,195.
Additional info: Application deadline for scholarships March 15. Separate application required, available through admissions office.

FINANCIAL AID PROCEDURES
Forms required: FAFSA, state aid form.
Dates and Deadlines: Priority date 2/15; no closing date. Applicants notified on a rolling basis starting 3/15; must reply within 2 week(s) of notification.
Transfers: No deadline. Applicants notified on a rolling basis; must reply within 3 week(s) of notification.

CONTACT
Brian Smith, Director of Financial Aid
Knapp Hall, Cobleskill, NY 12043
(800) 295-8998

SUNY College of Agriculture and Technology at Morrisville
Morrisville, New York
www.morrisville.edu Federal Code: 002859

2-year public agricultural and technical college in rural community.
Enrollment: 3,095 undergrads, 13% part-time. 885 full-time freshmen.
Selectivity: Admits 50 to 75% of applicants.

BASIC COSTS (2012-2013)
Tuition and fees: $6,945; out-of-state residents $11,115.
Per-credit charge: $232; out-of-state residents $406.
Room and board: $10,720.
Additional info: Out-of-state tuition for bachelor's program: $14,820; per credit hour $618. Tuition/fee waivers available for unemployed or children of unemployed.

FINANCIAL AID PICTURE (2012-2013)
Students with need: Need-based aid available for full-time and part-time students. Work study available nights, weekends, and for part-time students.
Students without need: No-need awards available for academics, state/district residency.

FINANCIAL AID PROCEDURES
Forms required: FAFSA, state aid form.
Dates and Deadlines: Priority date 2/1; no closing date. Applicants notified on a rolling basis.
Transfers: No deadline. Applicants notified on a rolling basis.

CONTACT
Dacia Banks, Director of Financial Aid
PO Box 901, Morrisville, NY 13408-0901

SUNY College of Environmental Science and Forestry

Syracuse, New York
www.esf.edu Federal Code: 002851

4-year public university in small city.
Enrollment: 1,717 undergrads, 3% part-time. 325 full-time freshmen.
Selectivity: Admits 50 to 75% of applicants.

BASIC COSTS (2012-2013)
Tuition and fees: $6,593; out-of-state residents $15,843.
Per-credit charge: $238; out-of-state residents $618.
Room and board: $14,400.

FINANCIAL AID PICTURE (2012-2013)
Students with need: Out of 300 full-time freshmen who applied for aid, 207 were judged to have need. Of these, 207 received aid, and 180 had their full need met. Average financial aid package met 90% of need; average scholarship/grant was $3,500; average loan was $4,500. For part-time students, average financial aid package was $8,000.
Students without need: 42 full-time freshmen who did not demonstrate need for aid received scholarships/grants; average award was $3,874. No-need awards available for academics, alumni affiliation, leadership, minority status, ROTC, state/district residency.
Scholarships offered: Merit scholarships: up to 50% of undergraduate tuition; based on high school grades, class rank, and SAT or ACT scores.
Cumulative student debt: 80% of graduating class had student loans; average debt was $26,000.

FINANCIAL AID PROCEDURES
Forms required: FAFSA, state aid form.
Dates and Deadlines: Priority date 3/1; no closing date. Applicants notified on a rolling basis starting 3/15; must reply within 2 week(s) of notification.
Transfers: No deadline. Applicants notified on a rolling basis starting 3/15; must reply within 2 week(s) of notification.

CONTACT
John View, Director of Financial Aid
106 Bray Hall, Syracuse, NY 13210
(315) 470-6670

SUNY College of Technology at Alfred

Alfred, New York
www.alfredstate.edu Federal Code: 002854

2-year public liberal arts and technical college in rural community.
Enrollment: 3,461 undergrads, 7% part-time. 1,097 full-time freshmen.
Selectivity: Admits less than 50% of applicants.

BASIC COSTS (2012-2013)
Tuition and fees: $6,874; out-of-state residents $11,044.
Per-credit charge: $232; out-of-state residents $406.
Room and board: $11,160.
Additional info: Tuition for bachelor degree: full-time, out-of-state $14,820; per-credit-hour $618.

FINANCIAL AID PICTURE
Students with need: Need-based aid available for full-time and part-time students. Work study available nights, weekends, and for part-time students.
Students without need: No-need awards available for academics, alumni affiliation, job skills, minority status.

FINANCIAL AID PROCEDURES
Forms required: FAFSA, state aid form.
Dates and Deadlines: Applicants notified on a rolling basis starting 3/15; must reply by 3/15 or within 4 week(s) of notification.
Transfers: No deadline. Applicants notified on a rolling basis starting 3/15; must reply within 4 week(s) of notification.

CONTACT
Jane Gilliland, Senior Director Student Records and Financial Services
Huntington Administration Building, Alfred, NY 14802-1196
(607) 587-4253

SUNY College of Technology at Canton

Canton, New York
www.canton.edu Federal Code: 002855

2-year public technical college in small town.
Enrollment: 3,628 undergrads, 15% part-time. 945 full-time freshmen.
Selectivity: Admits 50 to 75% of applicants.

BASIC COSTS (2012-2013)
Tuition and fees: $6,909; out-of-state residents $11,079.
Per-credit charge: $232; out-of-state residents $406.
Room and board: $10,540.
Additional info: Laundry fee of $90 annually added to the bill for room and board. Out-of-state tuition for bachelor's degree program: $14,820; $610 per credit hour.

FINANCIAL AID PICTURE (2011-2012)
Students with need: Out of 917 full-time freshmen who applied for aid, 834 were judged to have need. Of these, 830 received aid, and 93 had their full need met. For part-time students, average financial aid package was $5,129.
Students without need: 21 full-time freshmen who did not demonstrate need for aid received scholarships/grants; average award was $1,573. No-need awards available for academics, alumni affiliation, leadership, minority status, state/district residency.
Cumulative student debt: 91% of graduating class had student loans; average debt was $28,378.
Additional info: Students can apply after the priority deadline has passed, but not all types of aid will be available.

FINANCIAL AID PROCEDURES
Forms required: FAFSA, state aid form.
Dates and Deadlines: Priority date 3/15; no closing date. Applicants notified on a rolling basis starting 2/15; must reply within 4 week(s) of notification.

Transfers: Financial aid transcripts required from all previously attended schools for mid-year transfers.

CONTACT

Kerrie Cooper, Director of Financial Aid
34 Cornell Drive, Canton, NY 13617-1098
(315) 386-7616

SUNY College of Technology at Delhi

Delhi, New York
www.delhi.edu Federal Code: 002857

2-year public liberal arts and technical college in rural community.
Enrollment: 3,151 undergrads.

BASIC COSTS (2012-2013)

Tuition and fees: $7,090; out-of-state residents $11,260.
Per-credit charge: $232; out-of-state residents $406.
Room and board: $10,346.
Additional info: Out-of-state tuition for bachelor's program: $14,820; per-credit-hour $618.

FINANCIAL AID PICTURE

Students with need: Need-based aid available for full-time and part-time students.

FINANCIAL AID PROCEDURES

Forms required: FAFSA, state aid form.
Dates and Deadlines: Priority date 2/15; no closing date. Applicants notified on a rolling basis starting 3/1; must reply within 2 week(s) of notification.
Transfers: No deadline.

CONTACT

Nancy Hughes, Financial Aid Director
2 Main Street, Delhi, NY 13753-1190
(607) 746-4000

SUNY Downstate Medical Center

Brooklyn, New York
www.downstate.edu Federal Code: 002839

Upper-division public health science and nursing college in very large city.
Enrollment: 335 undergrads.

BASIC COSTS (2012-2013)

Tuition and fees: $6,096; out-of-state residents $15,346.
Per-credit charge: $232; out-of-state residents $618.
Additional info: Board plan not available. Cost of room only, $4,750.

FINANCIAL AID PICTURE

Students with need: Need-based aid available for full-time and part-time students.

FINANCIAL AID PROCEDURES

Forms required: FAFSA.
Dates and Deadlines: Priority date 3/1; no closing date. Applicants notified on a rolling basis.

CONTACT

James Newell, Director of Financial Aid
450 Clarkson Avenue, Box 60, Brooklyn, NY 11203-2098
(718) 270-2488

SUNY Empire State College

Saratoga Springs, New York
www.esc.edu Federal Code: 010286

4-year public liberal arts college in large town.
Enrollment: 10,128 undergrads, 58% part-time. 241 full-time freshmen.
Selectivity: Admits over 75% of applicants.

BASIC COSTS (2012-2013)

Tuition and fees: $5,915; out-of-state residents $15,165.
Per-credit charge: $232; out-of-state residents $618.

FINANCIAL AID PICTURE

Students with need: Need-based aid available for full-time and part-time students.
Students without need: This college awards aid only to students with need.

FINANCIAL AID PROCEDURES

Forms required: FAFSA, state aid form.
Dates and Deadlines: Priority date 4/1; no closing date. Applicants notified on a rolling basis; must reply within 3 week(s) of notification.
Transfers: No deadline. Applicants notified on a rolling basis.

CONTACT

Kristina Delbridge, Director of Financial Aid
Two Union Avenue, Saratoga Springs, NY 12866
(518) 587-2100 ext. 2311

SUNY Farmingdale State College

Farmingdale, New York
www.farmingdale.edu Federal Code: 002858

4-year public technical college in large town.
Enrollment: 7,257 undergrads, 22% part-time. 1,162 full-time freshmen.
Selectivity: Admits 50 to 75% of applicants.

BASIC COSTS (2012-2013)

Tuition and fees: $6,793; out-of-state residents $16,043.
Per-credit charge: $232; out-of-state residents $618.
Room and board: $13,440.

FINANCIAL AID PICTURE (2012-2013)

Students with need: Out of 919 full-time freshmen who applied for aid, 649 were judged to have need. Of these, 649 received aid, and 103 had their full need met. Average financial aid package met 69% of need; average scholarship/grant was $6,827; average loan was $3,284. For part-time students, average financial aid package was $5,620.
Students without need: 4 full-time freshmen who did not demonstrate need for aid received scholarships/grants; average award was $1,450. No-need awards available for academics, leadership, minority status, state/district residency.
Scholarships offered: 1 full-time freshmen received athletic scholarships; average amount $1,500.
Cumulative student debt: 43% of graduating class had student loans; average debt was $18,867.

FINANCIAL AID PROCEDURES

Forms required: FAFSA, state aid form, institutional form.
Dates and Deadlines: Priority date 4/1; no closing date. Applicants notified on a rolling basis starting 4/1.

CONTACT

Diane Kazanecki-Kempter, Director of Financial Aid
2350 Broadhollow Road, Farmingdale, NY 11735-1021
(631) 420-2578

SUNY Institute of Technology at Utica/Rome

Utica, New York
www.sunyit.edu Federal Code: 011678

4-year public business and engineering college in small city.
Enrollment: 1,558 undergrads, 19% part-time. 198 full-time freshmen.
Selectivity: Admits less than 50% of applicants.

BASIC COSTS (2013-2014)
Tuition and fees: $6,840; out-of-state residents $16,090.
Per-credit charge: $232; out-of-state residents $618.
Room and board: $10,985.

FINANCIAL AID PICTURE (2011-2012)
Students with need: Out of 195 full-time freshmen who applied for aid, 163 were judged to have need. Of these, 159 received aid, and 1 had their full need met. Average financial aid package met 39% of need; average scholarship/grant was $3,414; average loan was $1,511. For part-time students, average financial aid package was $4,421.
Students without need: 48 full-time freshmen who did not demonstrate need for aid received scholarships/grants; average award was $1,151. No-need awards available for academics.
Cumulative student debt: 86% of graduating class had student loans; average debt was $25,480.

FINANCIAL AID PROCEDURES
Forms required: FAFSA, state aid form.
Dates and Deadlines: Priority date 3/1; no closing date. Applicants notified on a rolling basis starting 3/17; must reply within 2 week(s) of notification.
Transfers: No deadline. Applicants notified on a rolling basis starting 3/17; must reply within 2 week(s) of notification.

CONTACT
Kimberly Pfendler, Financial Aid Assistant
100 Seymour Road, Utica, NY 13502
(315) 792-7210

SUNY Maritime College

Throggs Neck, New York
www.sunymaritime.edu Federal Code: 002853

4-year public maritime college in very large city.
Enrollment: 1,578 undergrads, 2% part-time. 327 full-time freshmen.
Selectivity: Admits 50 to 75% of applicants.

BASIC COSTS (2012-2013)
Tuition and fees: $6,782; out-of-state residents $16,032.
Per-credit charge: $232; out-of-state residents $618.
Room and board: $10,444.
Additional info: Students from Alabama, Connecticut, Delaware, Florida, Georgia, Louisiana, Mississippi, Maryland, New Jersey, North Carolina, Pennsylvania, Rhode Island, South Carolina, Virginia, Washington DC pay in-state rates.

FINANCIAL AID PICTURE (2011-2012)
Students with need: 39% of average financial aid package awarded as scholarships/grants, 61% awarded as loans/jobs. Need-based aid available for part-time students. Work study available nights, weekends, and for part-time students.
Students without need: No-need awards available for academics, leadership, ROTC, state/district residency.
Scholarships offered: NROTC Scholarships: tuition and full room for 4 years.
Additional info: All cadets who are United States citizens, physically qualified for Merchant Marine license, and not yet 25 at time of enrollment eligible to apply for Student Incentive Payment (SIP) of $3,000 per year from Maritime Administration of the Department of Transportation. Out-of-state students who elect to participate in SIP pay in-state tuition fees.

FINANCIAL AID PROCEDURES
Forms required: FAFSA, institutional form.
Dates and Deadlines: Priority date 3/15; closing date 7/15. Applicants notified on a rolling basis starting 3/15.
Transfers: Must have minimum 2.0 cumulative GPA if degree has not yet been earned.

CONTACT
Paul Bamonte, Director of Financial Aid
6 Pennyfield Avenue, Throggs Neck, NY 10465
(718) 409-7267

SUNY University at Albany

Albany, New York
http://albany.edu Federal Code: 002835

4-year public university in small city.
Enrollment: 12,632 undergrads, 5% part-time. 2,562 full-time freshmen.
Selectivity: Admits 50 to 75% of applicants.

BASIC COSTS (2012-2013)
Tuition and fees: $7,525; out-of-state residents $18,145.
Per-credit charge: $232; out-of-state residents $675.
Room and board: $11,276.

FINANCIAL AID PICTURE (2012-2013)
Students with need: Out of 2,243 full-time freshmen who applied for aid, 1,637 were judged to have need. Of these, 1,590 received aid, and 117 had their full need met. Average financial aid package met 62% of need; average scholarship/grant was $6,988; average loan was $3,792. For part-time students, average financial aid package was $5,044.
Students without need: 185 full-time freshmen who did not demonstrate need for aid received scholarships/grants; average award was $3,097. No-need awards available for academics, athletics, state/district residency.
Scholarships offered: ***Merit:*** Presidential Scholarship: up to $4,000 per year for NY residents and $6,000 per year for out-of-state students; renewable; requires minimum 90 high school average and combined SAT Critical Reading and Math scores in the upper 1200s or higher. ***Athletic:*** 46 full-time freshmen received athletic scholarships; average amount $11,201.
Cumulative student debt: 68% of graduating class had student loans; average debt was $24,126.

FINANCIAL AID PROCEDURES
Forms required: FAFSA.
Dates and Deadlines: Priority date 3/15; no closing date. Applicants notified on a rolling basis starting 3/20.

CONTACT
Diane Corbett, Director of Financial Aid
Office of Undergraduate Admissions, University Hall, Albany, NY 12222
(518) 442-3202

SUNY University at Binghamton

Binghamton, New York
www.binghamton.edu Federal Code: 002836

4-year public university in small city.
Enrollment: 12,296 undergrads, 3% part-time. 2,569 full-time freshmen.
Selectivity: Admits less than 50% of applicants.

BASIC COSTS (2012-2013)
Tuition and fees: $7,645; out-of-state residents $16,795.
Per-credit charge: $232; out-of-state residents $613.

Room and board: $12,446.

FINANCIAL AID PICTURE (2012-2013)

Students with need: Out of 2,061 full-time freshmen who applied for aid, 1,183 were judged to have need. Of these, 1,183 received aid, and 143 had their full need met. Average financial aid package met 66% of need; average scholarship/grant was $7,706; average loan was $4,141. For part-time students, average financial aid package was $6,214.

Students without need: 36 full-time freshmen who did not demonstrate need for aid received scholarships/grants; average award was $3,439. No-need awards available for academics, art, athletics, leadership, minority status, music/drama, state/district residency.

Scholarships offered: 82 full-time freshmen received athletic scholarships; average amount $10,832.

Cumulative student debt: 53% of graduating class had student loans; average debt was $23,710.

Additional info: Most institutional aid awarded on a first-come first-served basis while considering student's ability to pay (determined by use of the FAFSA application) and the student's academic achievement.

FINANCIAL AID PROCEDURES

Forms required: FAFSA, state aid form.

Dates and Deadlines: Priority date 2/1; no closing date. Applicants notified on a rolling basis starting 3/4; must reply within 2 week(s) of notification.

Transfers: No deadline. Applicants notified on a rolling basis starting 3/7; must reply within 2 week(s) of notification. Awards based on self-reported grade level until an official transfer credit evaluation is completed.

CONTACT

Dennis Chavez, Director, Financial Aid and Student Records
Box 6001, Binghamton, NY 13902-6001
(607) 777-2428

SUNY University at Buffalo

Buffalo, New York
www.buffalo.edu Federal Code: 002837

4-year public university in large city.

Enrollment: 19,101 undergrads, 8% part-time. 3,231 full-time freshmen.

Selectivity: Admits 50 to 75% of applicants.

BASIC COSTS (2012-2013)

Tuition and fees: $7,989; out-of-state residents $18,609.

Per-credit charge: $232; out-of-state residents $675.

Room and board: $11,310.

Additional info: Tuition/fee waivers available for adults.

FINANCIAL AID PICTURE (2011-2012)

Students with need: Out of 2,728 full-time freshmen who applied for aid, 2,028 were judged to have need. Of these, 2,013 received aid, and 1,997 had their full need met. Average financial aid package met 66% of need; average scholarship/grant was $5,770; average loan was $3,544. For part-time students, average financial aid package was $5,695.

Students without need: 91 full-time freshmen who did not demonstrate need for aid received scholarships/grants; average award was $6,025. No-need awards available for academics, job skills, minority status, music/drama, state/district residency.

Scholarships offered: ***Merit:*** Presidential Scholarship; full cost of attendance; minimum 1470 SAT (Critical Reading and Math), or 33 ACT; unweighted high school average of 95 or better; 25 awards. Provost Scholarships; starts at $2,500; minimum high school average of 90; 1200 combined SAT (Critical Reading and Math) or ACT score of 27. Provost Scholarships for outstanding talent in the performing and creative arts; minimum unweighted high school average of 90; minimum 1230 combined SAT (Critical Reading and Math), or minimum 28 ACT. UB Buffalo Partnership Scholars Program (BPSP); full tuition and fees for up to four consecutive years, a yearly book stipend of $600, and a laptop computer; for students from the Buffalo Public Schools who excel both academically and civically through service to their respective communities. ***Athletic:*** 39 full-time freshmen received athletic scholarships; average amount $17,420.

Cumulative student debt: 45% of graduating class had student loans; average debt was $16,025.

FINANCIAL AID PROCEDURES

Forms required: FAFSA.

Dates and Deadlines: Priority date 3/1; no closing date. Applicants notified on a rolling basis starting 2/1; must reply by 5/1.

CONTACT

Jennifer Pollard, Director of Financial Aid
12 Capen Hall, Buffalo, NY 14260-1660
(716) 645-2450

SUNY University at Stony Brook

Stony Brook, New York
www.stonybrook.edu Federal Code: 002838

4-year public university in large town.

Enrollment: 15,618 undergrads, 8% part-time. 2,501 full-time freshmen.

Selectivity: Admits less than 50% of applicants.

BASIC COSTS (2012-2013)

Tuition and fees: $7,560; out-of-state residents $18,180.

Per-credit charge: $232; out-of-state residents $675.

Room and board: $10,934.

FINANCIAL AID PICTURE (2011-2012)

Students with need: Out of 2,038 full-time freshmen who applied for aid, 1,468 were judged to have need. Of these, 1,453 received aid, and 242 had their full need met. Average financial aid package met 70% of need; average scholarship/grant was $7,472; average loan was $3,584. For part-time students, average financial aid package was $6,532.

Students without need: 399 full-time freshmen who did not demonstrate need for aid received scholarships/grants; average award was $3,262. No-need awards available for academics, alumni affiliation, art, athletics, job skills, leadership, music/drama.

Scholarships offered: 27 full-time freshmen received athletic scholarships; average amount $15,685.

Cumulative student debt: 59% of graduating class had student loans; average debt was $20,933.

FINANCIAL AID PROCEDURES

Forms required: FAFSA.

Dates and Deadlines: Priority date 3/1; no closing date. Applicants notified on a rolling basis starting 3/15; must reply by 5/1 or within 2 week(s) of notification.

CONTACT

Jacqueline Pascariello, Director Financial Aid
118 Administration Building, Stony Brook, NY 11794-1901
(631) 632-6840

SUNY Upstate Medical University

Syracuse, New York
www.upstate.edu Federal Code: 002840

Upper-division public health science and nursing college in small city.

Enrollment: 211 full-time undergrads.

BASIC COSTS (2012-2013)

Tuition and fees: $6,220; out-of-state residents $15,470.

Additional info: Costs reported are for undergraduate Nursing program. Cost of room only, $6,525.

FINANCIAL AID PICTURE
Students with need: Need-based aid available for full-time and part-time students. Work study available nights, weekends, and for part-time students.
Students without need: This college awards aid only to students with need.

FINANCIAL AID PROCEDURES
Forms required: FAFSA.
Dates and Deadlines: Priority date 3/1; no closing date. Applicants notified on a rolling basis starting 4/1; must reply within 2 week(s) of notification.
Transfers: Applicants notified on a rolling basis starting 4/15; must reply within 2 week(s) of notification.

CONTACT
Mike Pede, Director of Financial Aid
766 Irving Avenue, Syracuse, NY 13210
(315) 464-4329

Swedish Institute
New York, New York
www.swedishinstitute.edu Federal Code: 021700

2-year for-profit health science college in very large city.
Enrollment: 480 undergrads.

BASIC COSTS (2012-2013)
Tuition and fees: $11,450.
Additional info: Students generally attend 3 semesters/year.

FINANCIAL AID PICTURE
Students with need: Need-based aid available for full-time and part-time students.
Students without need: This college awards aid only to students with need.

FINANCIAL AID PROCEDURES
Forms required: FAFSA, institutional form.

CONTACT
Martha Padilla, Financial Aid Director
226 West 26th Street, 5th Floor, New York, NY 10001-6700
(212) 924-5900 ext. 124

Syracuse University
Syracuse, New York Federal Code: 002882
http://syr.edu CSS Code: 2823

4-year private university in small city.
Enrollment: 14,429 undergrads, 3% part-time. 3,382 full-time freshmen.
Selectivity: Admits 50 to 75% of applicants.

BASIC COSTS (2012-2013)
Tuition and fees: $39,004.
Per-credit charge: $1,637.
Room and board: $13,692.

FINANCIAL AID PICTURE (2012-2013)
Students with need: Out of 2,517 full-time freshmen who applied for aid, 1,977 were judged to have need. Of these, 1,977 received aid, and 1,380 had their full need met. Average financial aid package met 96% of need; average scholarship/grant was $26,000; average loan was $6,500. Need-based aid available for part-time students.
Students without need: 350 full-time freshmen who did not demonstrate need for aid received scholarships/grants; average award was $9,010. No-need awards available for academics, art, athletics, music/drama, ROTC, state/district residency.
Scholarships offered: 74 full-time freshmen received athletic scholarships; average amount $46,590.
Cumulative student debt: 61% of graduating class had student loans; average debt was $33,504.

FINANCIAL AID PROCEDURES
Forms required: FAFSA, CSS PROFILE.
Dates and Deadlines: Closing date 2/1. Applicants notified by 3/15; must reply by 5/1.
Transfers: Applicants notified on a rolling basis starting 3/20; must reply by 5/1.

CONTACT
Patricia Johnson, Associate Director of Financial Aid
900 South Crouse Avenue, Syracuse, NY 13208
(315) 443-1513

Technical Career Institutes
New York, New York
www.tcicollege.edu Federal Code: 011031

2-year for-profit technical and career college in very large city.
Enrollment: 3,601 undergrads, 12% part-time. 533 full-time freshmen.
Selectivity: Open admission.

BASIC COSTS (2012-2013)
Tuition and fees: $13,075.
Per-credit charge: $529.
Additional info: Required fees $265/year for second-year students.

FINANCIAL AID PICTURE
Students with need: Need-based aid available for full-time and part-time students.
Students without need: No-need awards available for academics, alumni affiliation.

FINANCIAL AID PROCEDURES
Forms required: FAFSA, institutional form.
Dates and Deadlines: Applicants notified on a rolling basis.

CONTACT
Cynthia Fekaris, Vice President of Financial Aid
320 West 31st Street, New York, NY 10001
(212) 594-4000

Tompkins Cortland Community College
Dryden, New York
www.TC3.edu Federal Code: 006788

2-year public community college in small town.
Enrollment: 3,219 undergrads, 20% part-time. 952 full-time freshmen.
Selectivity: Open admission; but selective for some programs.

BASIC COSTS (2012-2013)
Tuition and fees: $4,871; out-of-state residents $9,321.
Per-credit charge: $147; out-of-state residents $304.

FINANCIAL AID PICTURE
Students with need: Need-based aid available for full-time and part-time students. Work study available nights, weekends, and for part-time students.
Students without need: No-need awards available for academics.

FINANCIAL AID PROCEDURES
Forms required: FAFSA, state aid form, institutional form.
Dates and Deadlines: Priority date 4/15; no closing date. Applicants notified on a rolling basis starting 3/15; must reply within 4 week(s) of notification.

CONTACT
Sharon Karwowski, Director of Financial Aid
170 North Street, Dryden, NY 13053-0139
(607) 844-6581

Trocaire College
Buffalo, New York
www.trocaire.edu Federal Code: 002812

2-year private health science and career college in large city, affiliated with Roman Catholic Church.
Enrollment: 1,406 undergrads, 51% part-time. 125 full-time freshmen.
Selectivity: Open admission; but selective for some programs.

BASIC COSTS (2012-2013)
Tuition and fees: $14,720.
Per-credit charge: $595.

FINANCIAL AID PICTURE
Students with need: Need-based aid available for full-time and part-time students.
Students without need: No-need awards available for academics, alumni affiliation.

FINANCIAL AID PROCEDURES
Forms required: FAFSA, state aid form.
Dates and Deadlines: Applicants notified on a rolling basis starting 3/1; must reply within 2 week(s) of notification.

CONTACT
Janet McGrath, Director of Financial Aid
360 Choate Avenue, Buffalo, NY 14220
(716) 826-1200

Ulster County Community College
Stone Ridge, New York
www.sunyulster.edu Federal Code: 002880

2-year public community college in small town.
Enrollment: 2,236 undergrads, 33% part-time. 561 full-time freshmen.
Selectivity: Open admission; but selective for some programs.

BASIC COSTS (2012-2013)
Tuition and fees: $4,800; out-of-state residents $8,930.
Per-credit charge: $149; out-of-state residents $298.

FINANCIAL AID PICTURE
Students with need: Need-based aid available for full-time and part-time students.

FINANCIAL AID PROCEDURES
Forms required: FAFSA.
Dates and Deadlines: Priority date 6/1; no closing date. Applicants notified on a rolling basis starting 6/1; must reply within 2 week(s) of notification.

CONTACT
Christopher Chang, Director of Financial Aid
Cottekill Road, Stone Ridge, NY 12484
(845) 687-5058

Union College
Schenectady, New York Federal Code: 002889
www.union.edu CSS Code: 2920

4-year private engineering and liberal arts college in small city.
Enrollment: 2,192 undergrads. 591 full-time freshmen.
Selectivity: Admits less than 50% of applicants. GED not accepted.

BASIC COSTS (2012-2013)
Tuition and fees: $45,219.
Room and board: $11,070.

FINANCIAL AID PICTURE (2012-2013)
Students with need: Out of 378 full-time freshmen who applied for aid, 293 were judged to have need. Of these, 293 received aid, and 290 had their full need met. Average financial aid package met 99% of need; average scholarship/grant was $32,307; average loan was $3,388. Need-based aid available for part-time students.
Students without need: 164 full-time freshmen who did not demonstrate need for aid received scholarships/grants; average award was $8,493. No-need awards available for academics, ROTC.
Cumulative student debt: 58% of graduating class had student loans; average debt was $27,336.

FINANCIAL AID PROCEDURES
Forms required: FAFSA, CSS PROFILE, state aid form.
Dates and Deadlines: Closing date 2/1. Applicants notified by 3/25; must reply by 5/1.
Transfers: No deadline. Applicants notified on a rolling basis; must reply within 2 week(s) of notification. Financial aid applicants must submit the CSS PROFILE form and FAFSA to their respective processing agencies at least two months prior to application deadline.

CONTACT
Linda Parker, Director of Financial Aid
Grant Hall, 807 Union Street, Schenectady, NY 12308-3107
(518) 388-6123

United States Merchant Marine Academy
Kings Point, New York
www.usmma.edu Federal Code: 002892

4-year public military and maritime college in large town.
Enrollment: 1,008 undergrads. 273 full-time freshmen.
Selectivity: Admits less than 50% of applicants.

BASIC COSTS (2012-2013)
Additional info: All midshipmen receive full tuition, room and board, books, and uniforms from the federal government. Total required freshmen fees ($846) include laundry, tailor, barber, etc. Supplemental medical coverage may be required if not under parent's (or other) plan. Freshmen must also procure a laptop computer that conforms to Academy/government requirements. International freshmen students pay required fees plus additional international student fee ($11,066 total), and are also required to obtain a laptop computer.

FINANCIAL AID PICTURE (2011-2012)
Students with need: 95% of average financial aid package awarded as scholarships/grants, 5% awarded as loans/jobs.
Additional info: Students paid by steamship companies while at sea.

FINANCIAL AID PROCEDURES
Forms required: FAFSA, institutional form.
Dates and Deadlines: Priority date 5/1; no closing date. Applicants notified on a rolling basis starting 1/31.

CONTACT
Robert Johnson, Director of Admissions and Financial Aid
300 Steamboat Road, Admissions Center, Kings Point, NY 11024-1699
(516) 726-5638

United States Military Academy

West Point, New York
www.westpoint.edu

4-year public military college in small town.
Enrollment: 4,592 undergrads. 1,164 full-time freshmen.
Selectivity: Admits less than 50% of applicants.

BASIC COSTS (2012-2013)
Additional info: Tuition covered by a full scholarship. Room and board, medical and dental care provided by the U.S. Army. All students are on Active Duty Status as members of the U.S. Army and receive an annual salary. A portion of the cadet pay is deposited to a "Cadet Account" to help pay for uniforms, books, a computer, activity fees, etc. Each cadet pays a standard amount for laundry, dry cleaning, haircuts, tailoring services and shoe repair. The only cost for students is a one-time deposit upon admission to defray the initial issue of uniforms, books, supplies, and equipment. If needed, loans of $100 to $2,000 are available for the deposit. Upon graduation, cadets are commissioned officers and incur a 5-year Active Duty service obligation and three years of reserve duty in the U.S. Army.

FINANCIAL AID PICTURE
Additional info: Cadets are permitted to receive scholarships, but since there are no tuition, room or board charges, scholarships stipulated for tuition, room or board that are based only on need rather than merit cannot be accepted. Scholarships may be used for textbooks, uniforms and other expenses, or used dollar for dollar to offset initial $2,000 deposit.

CONTACT
646 Swift Road, West Point, NY 10996-1905

Utica College

Utica, New York
www.utica.edu Federal Code: 002883

4-year private health science and liberal arts college in small city.
Enrollment: 2,750 undergrads.
Selectivity: Admits over 75% of applicants.

BASIC COSTS (2012-2013)
Tuition and fees: $31,410.
Per-credit charge: $1,030.
Room and board: $11,934.

FINANCIAL AID PICTURE (2012-2013)
Students with need: Average financial aid package met 76% of need; average scholarship/grant was $9,107; average loan was $3,419. For part-time students, average financial aid package was $5,913.
Students without need: No-need awards available for academics.
Cumulative student debt: 83% of graduating class had student loans; average debt was $42,303.

FINANCIAL AID PROCEDURES
Forms required: FAFSA, state aid form.
Dates and Deadlines: Priority date 2/15; no closing date. Applicants notified on a rolling basis starting 2/1; must reply by 5/1 or within 4 week(s) of notification.
Transfers: Applicants notified on a rolling basis.

CONTACT
Laura Bedford, Executive Director of Student Financial Services
1600 Burrstone Road, Utica, NY 13502-4892
(315) 792-3179

University of Rochester

Rochester, New York Federal Code: 002894
www.rochester.edu CSS Code: 2928

4-year private university in large city.
Enrollment: 5,606 undergrads, 2% part-time. 1,343 full-time freshmen.
Selectivity: Admits less than 50% of applicants.

BASIC COSTS (2013-2014)
Tuition and fees: $45,372.
Per-credit charge: $1,394.
Room and board: $13,128.

FINANCIAL AID PICTURE (2012-2013)
Students with need: Average financial aid package met 100% of need; average scholarship/grant was $34,472; average loan was $4,083. For part-time students, average financial aid package was $9,055.
Students without need: No-need awards available for academics, alumni affiliation, art, leadership, music/drama, ROTC.
Cumulative student debt: 53% of graduating class had student loans; average debt was $27,601.
Additional info: Alternative loans and financing information available.

FINANCIAL AID PROCEDURES
Forms required: FAFSA, CSS PROFILE, state aid form.
Dates and Deadlines: Closing date 2/15. Applicants notified by 4/1; must reply by 5/1.
Transfers: Priority date 2/1. Must reply by 8/1.

CONTACT
Charles Puls, Associate Dean and Director of Financial Aid
300 Wilson Boulevard, Rochester, NY 14627-0251
(585) 275-3226

Vassar College

Poughkeepsie, New York Federal Code: 002895
www.vassar.edu CSS Code: 2956

4-year private liberal arts college in small city.
Enrollment: 2,372 undergrads, 1% part-time. 660 full-time freshmen.
Selectivity: Admits less than 50% of applicants.

BASIC COSTS (2013-2014)
Tuition and fees: $47,890.
Per-credit charge: $1,600.
Room and board: $11,180.

FINANCIAL AID PICTURE (2012-2013)
Students with need: Out of 464 full-time freshmen who applied for aid, 390 were judged to have need. Of these, 390 received aid, and 390 had their full need met. Average financial aid package met 100% of need; average scholarship/grant was $42,101; average loan was $1,630.
Students without need: This college awards aid only to students with need.
Cumulative student debt: 48% of graduating class had student loans; average debt was $17,234.
Additional info: No loans in the initial financial aid packages for students from families with total income used in need analysis of $60,000 or less.

FINANCIAL AID PROCEDURES
Forms required: FAFSA, CSS PROFILE.
Dates and Deadlines: Closing date 2/15. Applicants notified by 3/30; must reply by 5/1.
Transfers: Closing date 3/15. Applicants notified by 5/1; must reply within 4 week(s) of notification. Limited number of need-based award packages offered to transfers.

CONTACT
Jessica Bernier, Director of Financial Aid
Box 10, 124 Raymond Avenue, Poughkeepsie, NY 12604-0077
(845) 437-5320

Vaughn College of Aeronautics and Technology
Flushing, New York
www.vaughn.edu Federal Code: 002665

4-year private engineering college in very large city.
Enrollment: 1,796 undergrads, 24% part-time. 299 full-time freshmen.
Selectivity: Admits over 75% of applicants.

BASIC COSTS (2013-2014)
Tuition and fees: $20,410.
Per-credit charge: $665.
Room and board: $11,880.

FINANCIAL AID PICTURE (2012-2013)
Students with need: Out of 263 full-time freshmen who applied for aid, 197 were judged to have need. Of these, 197 received aid, and 55 had their full need met. Average financial aid package met 90% of need; average scholarship/grant was $1,100; average loan was $1,750. For part-time students, average financial aid package was $7,100.
Students without need: 37 full-time freshmen who did not demonstrate need for aid received scholarships/grants; average award was $5,030. No-need awards available for academics, alumni affiliation, job skills, leadership, ROTC, state/district residency.
Cumulative student debt: 95% of graduating class had student loans; average debt was $32,500.

FINANCIAL AID PROCEDURES
Forms required: FAFSA, state aid form.
Dates and Deadlines: Priority date 3/1; no closing date. Applicants notified on a rolling basis starting 4/15; must reply within 2 week(s) of notification.
Transfers: No deadline. Applicants notified on a rolling basis; must reply within 2 week(s) of notification.

CONTACT
Dorothy Martin, Director of Financial Aid
86-01 23rd Avenue, Flushing, NY 11369
(718) 429-6600 ext. 100

Villa Maria College of Buffalo
Buffalo, New York
www.villa.edu Federal Code: 002896

2-year private visual arts and music college in large city, affiliated with Roman Catholic Church.
Enrollment: 408 undergrads, 22% part-time. 70 full-time freshmen.
Selectivity: Admits over 75% of applicants.

BASIC COSTS (2012-2013)
Tuition and fees: $17,150.
Per-credit charge: $560.
Additional info: Tuition/fee waivers available for unemployed or children of unemployed.

FINANCIAL AID PICTURE (2011-2012)
Students with need: Need-based aid available for full-time and part-time students.
Students without need: No-need awards available for academics, alumni affiliation, art, leadership, minority status, music/drama.

FINANCIAL AID PROCEDURES
Forms required: FAFSA.
Dates and Deadlines: Applicants notified on a rolling basis starting 2/15; must reply within 2 week(s) of notification.
Transfers: No deadline. Applicants notified on a rolling basis starting 2/15; must reply within 2 week(s) of notification.

CONTACT
Laura Fitzgerald, Director of Financial Aid
240 Pine Ridge Road, Buffalo, NY 14225-3999
(716) 896-0700 ext. 1850

Wagner College
Staten Island, New York
www.wagner.edu Federal Code: 002899

4-year private liberal arts college in very large city, affiliated with Lutheran Church in America.
Enrollment: 1,816 undergrads, 4% part-time. 426 full-time freshmen.
Selectivity: Admits 50 to 75% of applicants.

BASIC COSTS (2013-2014)
Tuition and fees: $39,220.
Room and board: $11,660.
Additional info: Tuition/fee waivers available for unemployed or children of unemployed.

FINANCIAL AID PICTURE (2012-2013)
Students with need: Out of 372 full-time freshmen who applied for aid, 323 were judged to have need. Of these, 323 received aid, and 81 had their full need met. Average financial aid package met 76% of need; average scholarship/grant was $16,613; average loan was $3,624.
Students without need: 67 full-time freshmen who did not demonstrate need for aid received scholarships/grants; average award was $15,507. No-need awards available for academics, athletics, music/drama.
Scholarships offered: 22 full-time freshmen received athletic scholarships; average amount $33,347.

FINANCIAL AID PROCEDURES
Forms required: FAFSA, state aid form.
Dates and Deadlines: Priority date 2/15; no closing date. Applicants notified on a rolling basis starting 3/1; must reply within 3 week(s) of notification.
Transfers: No deadline. Applicants notified on a rolling basis starting 3/1; must reply within 3 week(s) of notification.

CONTACT
Theresa Weimer, Director of Financial Aid
One Campus Road, Staten Island, NY 10301-4495
(718) 390-3183

Webb Institute
Glen Cove, New York
www.webb-institute.edu Federal Code: 002900

4-year private engineering college in large town.
Enrollment: 79 undergrads. 22 full-time freshmen.
Selectivity: Admits less than 50% of applicants. GED not accepted.

BASIC COSTS (2013-2014)
Room and board: $13,750.
Additional info: All students receive 4-year, full-tuition scholarships.

FINANCIAL AID PICTURE (2011-2012)
Students with need: Out of 6 full-time freshmen who applied for aid, 6 were judged to have need. Of these, 6 received aid.
Students without need: This college awards aid only to students with need.

Cumulative student debt: 33% of graduating class had student loans; average debt was $4,500.

FINANCIAL AID PROCEDURES

Forms required: FAFSA, institutional form.
Dates and Deadlines: Closing date 7/1. Applicants notified on a rolling basis; must reply within 2 week(s) of notification.

CONTACT

Lauri D'Ambra, Assistant Director of Financial Aid
298 Crescent Beach Road, Glen Cove, NY 11542-1398
(516) 671-2213 ext. 107

Wells College

Aurora, New York
www.wells.edu Federal Code: 002901

4-year private liberal arts college in rural community.
Enrollment: 530 undergrads, 1% part-time. 197 full-time freshmen.
Selectivity: Admits 50 to 75% of applicants.

BASIC COSTS (2012-2013)

Tuition and fees: $34,700.
Per-credit charge: $1,200.
Room and board: $11,900.

FINANCIAL AID PICTURE (2012-2013)

Students with need: Out of 191 full-time freshmen who applied for aid, 185 were judged to have need. Of these, 185 received aid, and 35 had their full need met. Average financial aid package met 84% of need; average scholarship/grant was $29,388; average loan was $3,246. Need-based aid available for part-time students.
Students without need: 10 full-time freshmen who did not demonstrate need for aid received scholarships/grants; average award was $21,550. No-need awards available for academics, alumni affiliation, leadership.
Scholarships offered: Henry Wells Scholarship: guaranteed first-year internship or related experience and paid $3,000 internship or experiential learning program in student's upper-class years; tuition-based scholarship valued at $18,000 a year for four years. Scholarship for Leaders: $8,000 to $60,000 over 4 years, based on academic and leadership abilities.
Cumulative student debt: 82% of graduating class had student loans; average debt was $30,933.

FINANCIAL AID PROCEDURES

Forms required: FAFSA. CSS PROFILE required of early decision candidates only.
Dates and Deadlines: Priority date 2/15; no closing date. Applicants notified on a rolling basis starting 3/1; must reply by 5/1.
Transfers: Priority date 3/1; no deadline. Applicants notified on a rolling basis starting 3/1; must reply by 8/1.

CONTACT

Cathleen Patella, Director of Financial Aid
170 Main Street, Aurora, NY 13026
(315) 364-3289

Westchester Community College

Valhalla, New York
www.sunywcc.edu Federal Code: 002881

2-year public community college in large town.
Enrollment: 12,290 undergrads, 40% part-time. 2,231 full-time freshmen.
Selectivity: Open admission; but selective for some programs.

BASIC COSTS (2012-2013)

Tuition and fees: $4,643; out-of-state residents $12,133.
Per-credit charge: $179; out-of-state residents $493.

FINANCIAL AID PICTURE (2011-2012)

Students with need: 91% of average financial aid package awarded as scholarships/grants, 9% awarded as loans/jobs. Need-based aid available for part-time students. Work study available nights, weekends, and for part-time students.
Students without need: No-need awards available for academics.
Cumulative student debt: 26% of graduating class had student loans; average debt was $10,328.

FINANCIAL AID PROCEDURES

Forms required: FAFSA, state aid form, institutional form.
Dates and Deadlines: Applicants notified on a rolling basis; must reply within 4 week(s) of notification.
Transfers: No deadline.

CONTACT

Alikhan Morgan, Director of Financial Aid
75 Grasslands Road, Valhalla, NY 10595
(914) 606-6773

Yeshivat Mikdash Melech

Brooklyn, New York
www.mikdashmelech.net Federal Code: 014615

5-year private rabbinical college for men in very large city, affiliated with Jewish faith.
Enrollment: 71 undergrads.
Selectivity: Open admission; but selective for some programs.

BASIC COSTS (2012-2013)

Tuition and fees: $7,500.
Room and board: $4,300.
Additional info: Tuition/fee waivers available for adults.

FINANCIAL AID PICTURE

Students with need: Need-based aid available for full-time and part-time students. Work study available nights.
Students without need: No-need awards available for academics, leadership, religious affiliation.

FINANCIAL AID PROCEDURES

Forms required: FAFSA, institutional form.
Dates and Deadlines: Applicants notified on a rolling basis starting 5/1.
Transfers: No deadline. Applicants notified on a rolling basis starting 5/1.

CONTACT

Amram Sananes, Financial Aid Administrator
1326 Ocean Parkway, Brooklyn, NY 11230
(718) 339-1090

North Carolina

Alamance Community College

Graham, North Carolina
www.alamancecc.edu Federal Code: 005463

2-year public community college in large town.
Enrollment: 4,237 undergrads, 45% part-time. 472 full-time freshmen.
Selectivity: Open admission; but selective for some programs.

BASIC COSTS (2012-2013)

Tuition and fees: $2,130; out-of-state residents $7,890.

Per-credit charge: $69; out-of-state residents $261.

FINANCIAL AID PICTURE

Students with need: Need-based aid available for full-time and part-time students. Work study available nights.

Students without need: No-need awards available for academics, state/district residency.

FINANCIAL AID PROCEDURES

Forms required: FAFSA.

Dates and Deadlines: Priority date 5/15; no closing date. Applicants notified on a rolling basis starting 3/15; must reply within 2 week(s) of notification.

Transfers: Supplemental educational opportunity grants limited.

CONTACT

Sabrina Degain, Director of Financial Aid
Box 8000, Graham, NC 27253
(336) 506-4109

Appalachian State University

Boone, North Carolina
www.appstate.edu Federal Code: 002906

4-year public university in large town.

Enrollment: 15,527 undergrads, 5% part-time. 2,971 full-time freshmen.

Selectivity: Admits 50 to 75% of applicants. GED not accepted.

BASIC COSTS (2012-2013)

Tuition and fees: $5,859; out-of-state residents $17,907.

Room and board: $7,060.

FINANCIAL AID PICTURE (2011-2012)

Students with need: Out of 1,460 full-time freshmen who applied for aid, 1,429 were judged to have need. Of these, 1,311 received aid, and 540 had their full need met. Average financial aid package met 72% of need; average scholarship/grant was $7,548; average loan was $3,339. For part-time students, average financial aid package was $6,027.

Students without need: 74 full-time freshmen who did not demonstrate need for aid received scholarships/grants; average award was $3,060. No-need awards available for academics, alumni affiliation, art, athletics, job skills, leadership, minority status, music/drama, religious affiliation, ROTC, state/district residency.

Scholarships offered: 32 full-time freshmen received athletic scholarships; average amount $6,978.

FINANCIAL AID PROCEDURES

Forms required: FAFSA.

Dates and Deadlines: Priority date 3/1; no closing date. Applicants notified on a rolling basis starting 4/1; must reply within 3 week(s) of notification.

Transfers: No deadline. Applicants notified on a rolling basis starting 4/1; must reply within 3 week(s) of notification.

CONTACT

Esther Manogin, Director of Financial Aid
ASU Box 32004, Boone, NC 28608
(828) 262-2190

Art Institute of Charlotte

Charlotte, North Carolina
www.artinstitutes.edu/charlotte Federal Code: 014578

4-year for-profit visual arts and career college in very large city.

Enrollment: 1,571 undergrads.

Selectivity: Open admission; but selective for some programs.

BASIC COSTS (2012-2013)

Tuition and fees: $21,285.

Per-credit charge: $473.

Additional info: Fees for culinary students $300; for all other students: enrollment fee $100. Kit pricing varies by major. Board plan not available. Board plan not available. Cost of room only, $5,250.

FINANCIAL AID PICTURE

Students with need: Need-based aid available for full-time and part-time students. Work study available nights, weekends, and for part-time students.

FINANCIAL AID PROCEDURES

Forms required: FAFSA.

Dates and Deadlines: Applicants notified on a rolling basis starting 7/1; must reply within 1 week(s) of notification.

Transfers: No deadline. Applicants notified on a rolling basis starting 7/1; must reply within 1 week(s) of notification.

CONTACT

Beth Mikel, Director of Student Financial Services
Three LakePointe Plaza, Charlotte, NC 28217-4536
(704) 357-8020 ext. 5893

Barton College

Wilson, North Carolina
www.barton.edu Federal Code: 002908

4-year private liberal arts college in large town, affiliated with Christian Church (Disciples of Christ).

Enrollment: 1,069 undergrads, 18% part-time. 201 full-time freshmen.

Selectivity: Admits less than 50% of applicants.

BASIC COSTS (2013-2014)

Tuition and fees: $25,396.

Per-credit charge: $986.

Room and board: $8,258.

Additional info: Tuition/fee waivers available for adults.

FINANCIAL AID PICTURE

Students with need: Need-based aid available for full-time and part-time students. Work study available nights, weekends, and for part-time students.

Students without need: No-need awards available for academics, alumni affiliation, art, athletics, leadership, minority status, music/drama, religious affiliation, state/district residency.

FINANCIAL AID PROCEDURES

Forms required: FAFSA.

Dates and Deadlines: Priority date 4/1; no closing date. Applicants notified on a rolling basis starting 5/1; must reply within 2 week(s) of notification.

CONTACT

Bridget Ellis, Director of Financial Aid
Box 5000, Wilson, NC 27893-7000
(252) 399-6323

Beaufort County Community College

Washington, North Carolina
www.beaufortccc.edu Federal Code: 008558

2-year public community college in small town.

Enrollment: 999 full-time undergrads.

Selectivity: Open admission; but selective for some programs.

BASIC COSTS (2012-2013)

Tuition and fees: $2,130; out-of-state residents $7,890.

Per-credit charge: $69; out-of-state residents $261.

FINANCIAL AID PICTURE

Students with need: Need-based aid available for full-time and part-time students.

Students without need: No-need awards available for academics.

FINANCIAL AID PROCEDURES

Forms required: FAFSA, institutional form.

Dates and Deadlines: Closing date 8/1. Applicants notified on a rolling basis starting 5/1; must reply within 2 week(s) of notification.

CONTACT

Harold Smith, Director of Student Financial Aid
Box 1069, Washington, NC 27889
(252) 940-6222

Belmont Abbey College

Belmont, North Carolina
www.belmontabbeycollege.edu Federal Code: 002910

4-year private liberal arts college in small town, affiliated with Roman Catholic Church.

Enrollment: 1,695 undergrads, 6% part-time. 269 full-time freshmen.

Selectivity: Admits 50 to 75% of applicants.

BASIC COSTS (2013-2014)

Tuition and fees: $18,500.

Per-credit charge: $617.

Room and board: $10,094.

FINANCIAL AID PICTURE (2011-2012)

Students with need: Out of 112 full-time freshmen who applied for aid, 94 were judged to have need. Of these, 94 received aid, and 10 had their full need met. Average financial aid package met 67% of need; average scholarship/grant was $17,418; average loan was $3,235. For part-time students, average financial aid package was $5,151.

Students without need: 18 full-time freshmen who did not demonstrate need for aid received scholarships/grants; average award was $13,542. No-need awards available for academics, athletics.

Scholarships offered: ***Merit:*** Many merit scholarships offered; ranging from $4,000 to $20,000; based solely on academic achievement. ***Athletic:*** 11 full-time freshmen received athletic scholarships; average amount $4,706.

Cumulative student debt: 62% of graduating class had student loans; average debt was $17,004.

FINANCIAL AID PROCEDURES

Forms required: FAFSA.

Dates and Deadlines: Priority date 4/1; no closing date. Applicants notified on a rolling basis starting 3/1; must reply within 2 week(s) of notification.

Transfers: Priority date 6/1; no deadline. Applicants notified on a rolling basis starting 3/1; must reply within 2 week(s) of notification.

CONTACT

Anne Stevens, Director of Financial Aid
100 Belmont - Mt. Holly Road, Belmont, NC 28012-2795
(704) 825-6665

Bennett College for Women

Greensboro, North Carolina
www.bennett.edu Federal Code: 002911

4-year private liberal arts college for women in large city, affiliated with United Methodist Church.

Enrollment: 651 undergrads, 1% part-time. 151 full-time freshmen.

Selectivity: Admits 50 to 75% of applicants.

BASIC COSTS (2012-2013)

Tuition and fees: $16,794.

Per-credit charge: $609.

Room and board: $7,428.

FINANCIAL AID PICTURE (2011-2012)

Students with need: Out of 151 full-time freshmen who applied for aid, 146 were judged to have need. Of these, 146 received aid, and 6 had their full need met. Average financial aid package met 45% of need; average scholarship/grant was $9,792; average loan was $3,417. For part-time students, average financial aid package was $6,957.

Students without need: 1 full-time freshmen who did not demonstrate need for aid received scholarships/grants; average award was $4,000. No-need awards available for state/district residency.

Cumulative student debt: 95% of graduating class had student loans; average debt was $27,489.

FINANCIAL AID PROCEDURES

Forms required: FAFSA, institutional form.

Dates and Deadlines: Closing date 4/15. Applicants notified by 7/15.

CONTACT

Keisha Ragsdale, Director of Financial Aid
900 East Washington Street, Greensboro, NC 27401-3239
(336) 517-2204

Bladen Community College

Dublin, North Carolina
www.bladencc.edu Federal Code: 007987

2-year public community college in rural community.

Enrollment: 1,393 undergrads.

Selectivity: Open admission; but selective for some programs.

BASIC COSTS (2012-2013)

Tuition and fees: $2,128; out-of-state residents $7,888.

Per-credit charge: $69; out-of-state residents $261.

FINANCIAL AID PICTURE

Students with need: Need-based aid available for full-time and part-time students. Work study available nights.

FINANCIAL AID PROCEDURES

Forms required: FAFSA.

Dates and Deadlines: Priority date 6/1; no closing date. Applicants notified on a rolling basis starting 8/1; must reply within 2 week(s) of notification.

CONTACT

Samantha Benson, Financial Aid Director
Post Office Box 266, Dublin, NC 28332-0266
(910) 879-5562

Blue Ridge Community College

Flat Rock, North Carolina
www.blueridge.edu Federal Code: 009684

2-year public community and technical college in large town.

Enrollment: 2,501 undergrads.

Selectivity: Open admission; but selective for some programs.

BASIC COSTS (2013-2014)

Tuition and fees: $1,146.3; out-of-district residents $1,146.3.

FINANCIAL AID PICTURE

Students with need: Need-based aid available for full-time and part-time students. Work study available nights.

Students without need: No-need awards available for academics, athletics, leadership, minority status, state/district residency.

FINANCIAL AID PROCEDURES

Forms required: FAFSA, institutional form.

Dates and Deadlines: Priority date 6/30; no closing date. Applicants notified on a rolling basis starting 2/1; must reply within 4 week(s) of notification.

CONTACT
Lisanne Masterson, Financial Aid Officer
180 West Campus Drive, Flat Rock, NC 28731-9624
(828) 694-1815

Brevard College
Brevard, North Carolina
www.brevard.edu Federal Code: 002912

4-year private liberal arts college in small town, affiliated with United Methodist Church.
Enrollment: 630 undergrads, 2% part-time. 190 full-time freshmen.
Selectivity: Admits 50 to 75% of applicants.

BASIC COSTS (2013-2014)
Tuition and fees: $25,200.
Per-credit charge: $485.
Room and board: $8,800.

FINANCIAL AID PICTURE (2011-2012)
Students with need: Out of 165 full-time freshmen who applied for aid, 149 were judged to have need. Of these, 149 received aid, and 21 had their full need met. Average financial aid package met 73% of need; average scholarship/grant was $16,655; average loan was $2,786. For part-time students, average financial aid package was $11,159.
Students without need: 40 full-time freshmen who did not demonstrate need for aid received scholarships/grants; average award was $6,379. No-need awards available for academics, art, athletics, leadership, music/drama, religious affiliation, state/district residency.
Scholarships offered: 18 full-time freshmen received athletic scholarships; average amount $8,533.
Cumulative student debt: 52% of graduating class had student loans; average debt was $29,002.

FINANCIAL AID PROCEDURES
Forms required: FAFSA.
Dates and Deadlines: Priority date 2/1; no closing date. Applicants notified on a rolling basis starting 2/1; must reply by 5/1 or within 4 week(s) of notification.
Transfers: No deadline. Applicants notified on a rolling basis; must reply within 4 week(s) of notification. Phi Theta Kappa Scholarship.

CONTACT
Beth Pocock, Director of Financial Aid
One Brevard College Drive, Brevard, NC 28712
(828) 884-8287

Brunswick Community College
Supply, North Carolina
www.brunswickcc.edu Federal Code: 015285

2-year public community college in small town.
Enrollment: 1,272 undergrads, 47% part-time. 186 full-time freshmen.
Selectivity: Open admission; but selective for some programs.

BASIC COSTS (2012-2013)
Tuition and fees: $2,170; out-of-state residents $7,930.
Per-credit charge: $69; out-of-state residents $261.

FINANCIAL AID PICTURE (2012-2013)
Students with need: 96% of average financial aid package awarded as scholarships/grants, 4% awarded as loans/jobs. Need-based aid available for part-time students.
Students without need: No-need awards available for academics, state/district residency.
Additional info: Attendance required at financial aid orientation session for those receiving federal student aid.

FINANCIAL AID PROCEDURES
Forms required: FAFSA, institutional form.
Dates and Deadlines: Priority date 6/1; closing date 6/15. Applicants notified on a rolling basis starting 3/1; must reply by 6/30 or within 2 week(s) of notification.
Transfers: Priority date 6/15; no deadline. Applicants notified on a rolling basis starting 3/1; must reply by 6/30 or within 2 week(s) of notification. Must submit all college transcripts. All transcripts must be evaluated prior to funds being applied to account.

CONTACT
Paula Almond, Coordinator of Financial Aid and Veterans Affairs
PO Box 30, Supply, NC 28462
(910) 755-7322

Caldwell Community College and Technical Institute
Hudson, North Carolina
www.cccti.edu Federal Code: 004835

2-year public community and technical college in small town.
Enrollment: 4,245 undergrads, 54% part-time. 582 full-time freshmen.
Selectivity: Open admission; but selective for some programs.

BASIC COSTS (2012-2013)
Tuition and fees: $2,126; out-of-state residents $7,886.
Per-credit charge: $69; out-of-state residents $261.

FINANCIAL AID PICTURE
Students with need: Need-based aid available for full-time and part-time students.
Students without need: This college awards aid only to students with need.

FINANCIAL AID PROCEDURES
Forms required: FAFSA.
Dates and Deadlines: Closing date 5/1. Applicants notified on a rolling basis starting 6/30.

CONTACT
Eva Rader-Harmon, Director of Financial Aid
2855 Hickory Boulevard, Hudson, NC 28638-2672
(828) 726-2713

Campbell University
Buies Creek, North Carolina
www.campbell.edu Federal Code: 002913

4-year private university and liberal arts college in rural community, affiliated with Baptist faith.
Enrollment: 4,589 undergrads, 26% part-time. 867 full-time freshmen.
Selectivity: Admits 50 to 75% of applicants.

BASIC COSTS (2013-2014)
Tuition and fees: $26,240.
Per-credit charge: $525.
Room and board: $9,300.

FINANCIAL AID PICTURE (2011-2012)
Students with need: Out of 820 full-time freshmen who applied for aid, 744 were judged to have need. Of these, 744 received aid, and 381 had their full need met. Average financial aid package met 80% of need; average scholarship/grant was $6,157; average loan was $3,314. For part-time students, average financial aid package was $18,204.

Students without need: 66 full-time freshmen who did not demonstrate need for aid received scholarships/grants; average award was $12,202. No-need awards available for academics, athletics, music/drama, religious affiliation, ROTC, state/district residency.
Scholarships offered: ***Merit:*** Presidential Scholarship: $13,000-$15,000. Campbell Scholarship: $7,000-$12,000. ***Athletic:*** 12 full-time freshmen received athletic scholarships; average amount $11,335.
Cumulative student debt: 75% of graduating class had student loans; average debt was $24,820.

FINANCIAL AID PROCEDURES
Forms required: FAFSA.
Dates and Deadlines: Priority date 2/15; no closing date. Applicants notified on a rolling basis starting 2/1; must reply within 2 week(s) of notification.
Transfers: Priority date 3/12. Applicants notified on a rolling basis; must reply within 2 week(s) of notification.

CONTACT
Michelle Day, Director of Financial Aid
PO Box 546, Buies Creek, NC 27506
(800) 334-4111 ext. 1310

Cape Fear Community College
Wilmington, North Carolina
www.cfcc.edu Federal Code: 005320

2-year public community college in small city.
Enrollment: 9,146 undergrads, 49% part-time. 1,235 full-time freshmen.
Selectivity: Open admission; but selective for some programs.

BASIC COSTS (2012-2013)
Tuition and fees: $2,205; out-of-state residents $7,965.
Per-credit charge: $69; out-of-state residents $261.

FINANCIAL AID PICTURE (2012-2013)
Students with need: 68% of average financial aid package awarded as scholarships/grants, 32% awarded as loans/jobs. Need-based aid available for part-time students. Work study available nights.
Students without need: No-need awards available for academics, athletics, leadership.

FINANCIAL AID PROCEDURES
Forms required: FAFSA.
Dates and Deadlines: Priority date 6/1; no closing date. Applicants notified on a rolling basis starting 4/1; must reply within 2 week(s) of notification.

CONTACT
Jo-Ann Craig, Director of Financial Aid
411 North Front Street, Wilmington, NC 28401-3910
(910) 362-7055

Carolina Christian College
Winston-Salem, North Carolina
www.carolina.edu

4-year private Bible college in large city, affiliated with nondenominational tradition.
Enrollment: 49 undergrads. 2 full-time freshmen.
Selectivity: Open admission.

BASIC COSTS (2012-2013)
Tuition and fees: $4,900.
Per-credit charge: $125.

FINANCIAL AID PICTURE (2012-2013)
Students with need: Out of 2 full-time freshmen who applied for aid, 2 were judged to have need. Of these, 2 received aid. Need-based aid available for part-time students.
Students without need: This college awards aid only to students with need.

FINANCIAL AID PROCEDURES
Forms required: FAFSA.
Dates and Deadlines: Applicants notified on a rolling basis.
Transfers: No deadline. Applicants notified on a rolling basis.

CONTACT
LaTanya Lucas, Director of Financial Aid
PO Box 777, Winston-Salem, NC 27102
(336) 744-0900 ext. 106

Carolinas College of Health Sciences
Charlotte, North Carolina
www.carolinascollege.edu Federal Code: 031042

2-year public health science and junior college in very large city.
Enrollment: 434 undergrads, 87% part-time. 2 full-time freshmen.
Selectivity: Open admission; but selective for some programs.

BASIC COSTS (2013-2014)
Tuition and fees: $9,271; out-of-state residents $9,271.
Per-credit charge: $308.

FINANCIAL AID PICTURE
Students with need: Need-based aid available for full-time and part-time students. Work study available nights, weekends, and for part-time students.
Students without need: No-need awards available for academics.
Additional info: The College offers the Carolinas HealthCare System Educational Forgiveness Loan that allows students in a 2-year program to borrow up to $10,000 and up to $5,000 in a 1-year program. The loan may be forgiven if the student obtains an eligible full-time position after graduation.

FINANCIAL AID PROCEDURES
Forms required: FAFSA.
Dates and Deadlines: Priority date 5/1; no closing date. Applicants notified on a rolling basis starting 5/1.

CONTACT
Jill Powell, Financial Aid Coordinator
PO Box 32861, Charlotte, NC 28232
(704) 355-8894

Carteret Community College
Morehead City, North Carolina
www.carteret.edu Federal Code: 008081

2-year public community and technical college in small town.
Enrollment: 1,604 undergrads.
Selectivity: Open admission; but selective for some programs.

BASIC COSTS (2012-2013)
Tuition and fees: $2,130; out-of-state residents $7,890.
Per-credit charge: $69; out-of-state residents $261.

FINANCIAL AID PICTURE
Students with need: Need-based aid available for full-time and part-time students.
Students without need: No-need awards available for academics, leadership, minority status, state/district residency.
Additional info: Institutional student loan program administered by college. Student may charge up to $600 for books, supplies and tuition per quarter. Repayment due by 11th week of semester.

FINANCIAL AID PROCEDURES
Forms required: FAFSA, institutional form.
Dates and Deadlines: Must reply within 2 week(s) of notification.

CONTACT
Brenda Long, Financial Aid Officer
3505 Arendell Street, Morehead City, NC 28557-2989
(252) 222-6297

Catawba College
Salisbury, North Carolina
www.catawba.edu Federal Code: 002914

4-year private liberal arts college in large town, affiliated with United Church of Christ.
Enrollment: 1,279 undergrads, 6% part-time. 306 full-time freshmen.
Selectivity: Admits less than 50% of applicants.

BASIC COSTS (2013-2014)
Tuition and fees: $26,820.
Per-credit charge: $680.
Room and board: $9,410.
Additional info: Tuition/fee waivers available for adults.

FINANCIAL AID PICTURE (2011-2012)
Students with need: Out of 286 full-time freshmen who applied for aid, 260 were judged to have need. Of these, 260 received aid, and 36 had their full need met. For part-time students, average financial aid package was $4,663.
Students without need: 40 full-time freshmen who did not demonstrate need for aid received scholarships/grants; average award was $8,327. No-need awards available for academics, athletics, leadership, music/drama, religious affiliation, state/district residency.
Scholarships offered: 70 full-time freshmen received athletic scholarships; average amount $9,809.
Cumulative student debt: 86% of graduating class had student loans; average debt was $31,966.

FINANCIAL AID PROCEDURES
Forms required: FAFSA, state aid form.
Dates and Deadlines: Priority date 3/15; no closing date. Applicants notified on a rolling basis starting 2/15; must reply within 2 week(s) of notification.

CONTACT
Dawn Snook, Director of Scholarships and Financial Assistance
2300 West Innes Street, Salisbury, NC 28144-2488
(704) 637-4416

Catawba Valley Community College
Hickory, North Carolina
www.cvcc.edu Federal Code: 005318

2-year public community college in large town.
Enrollment: 4,542 undergrads, 59% part-time. 505 full-time freshmen.
Selectivity: Open admission; but selective for some programs.

BASIC COSTS (2012-2013)
Tuition and fees: $2,157; out-of-state residents $7,917.
Per-credit charge: $69; out-of-state residents $261.
Additional info: Tuition/fee waivers available for unemployed or children of unemployed.

FINANCIAL AID PICTURE (2011-2012)
Students with need: Out of 425 full-time freshmen who applied for aid, 402 were judged to have need. Of these, 363 received aid. Need-based aid available for part-time students.
Students without need: No-need awards available for academics, athletics, leadership, music/drama.

FINANCIAL AID PROCEDURES
Forms required: FAFSA.
Dates and Deadlines: Closing date 3/15. Applicants notified on a rolling basis starting 5/15.

CONTACT
Debbie Barger, Director of Scholarships and Financial Aid
2550 Highway 70 SE, Hickory, NC 28602
(828) 327-7000 ext. 4214

Central Carolina Community College
Sanford, North Carolina
www.cccc.edu Federal Code: 005449

2-year public community college in large town.
Enrollment: 4,302 undergrads, 53% part-time. 489 full-time freshmen.
Selectivity: Open admission; but selective for some programs.

BASIC COSTS (2012-2013)
Tuition and fees: $2,158; out-of-state residents $7,918.
Per-credit charge: $69; out-of-state residents $261.

FINANCIAL AID PICTURE (2011-2012)
Students with need: 99% of average financial aid package awarded as scholarships/grants, 1% awarded as loans/jobs. Need-based aid available for part-time students. Work study available nights.
Students without need: No-need awards available for academics.

FINANCIAL AID PROCEDURES
Forms required: FAFSA.
Dates and Deadlines: Priority date 6/1; no closing date. Applicants notified on a rolling basis; must reply within 2 week(s) of notification.
Transfers: No deadline. Must reply within 2 week(s) of notification.

CONTACT
Heather Willett, Dean Of Student Services/FA
1105 Kelly Drive, Sanford, NC 27330
(919) 718-7229

Central Piedmont Community College
Charlotte, North Carolina
www.cpcc.edu Federal Code: 002915

2-year public community college in very large city.
Enrollment: 18,049 undergrads, 62% part-time. 1,157 full-time freshmen.
Selectivity: Open admission; but selective for some programs.

BASIC COSTS (2012-2013)
Tuition and fees: $2,156; out-of-state residents $7,916.
Per-credit charge: $69; out-of-state residents $261.

FINANCIAL AID PICTURE
Students with need: Need-based aid available for full-time and part-time students.
Students without need: No-need awards available for academics, minority status.

FINANCIAL AID PROCEDURES
Forms required: FAFSA.
Dates and Deadlines: Priority date 4/1; closing date 6/1. Applicants notified on a rolling basis.

CONTACT
Debbie Brooks, Director, Student Financial Aid
Box 35009, Charlotte, NC 28235-5009
(704) 330-6942

Chowan University

Murfreesboro, North Carolina
www.chowan.edu Federal Code: 002916

4-year private university and liberal arts college in rural community, affiliated with Southern Baptist Convention.
Enrollment: 1,308 undergrads.
Selectivity: Admits 50 to 75% of applicants.

BASIC COSTS (2012-2013)

Tuition and fees: $21,950.
Per-credit charge: $355.
Room and board: $7,680.

FINANCIAL AID PICTURE

Students with need: Need-based aid available for full-time and part-time students. Work study available nights, weekends, and for part-time students.
Students without need: No-need awards available for academics, athletics, leadership, music/drama, religious affiliation, state/district residency.
Scholarships offered: Scholarship program for students serving as student body president who qualify for admission; full tuition.

FINANCIAL AID PROCEDURES

Forms required: FAFSA.
Dates and Deadlines: Priority date 3/1; no closing date. Applicants notified on a rolling basis starting 3/1; must reply within 2 week(s) of notification.

CONTACT

Sharon Rose, Director of Financial Aid
One University Place, Murfreesboro, NC 27855-9901
(252) 398-1229

Cleveland Community College

Shelby, North Carolina
www.clevelandcc.edu Federal Code: 008082

2-year public community college in large town.
Enrollment: 3,216 undergrads, 46% part-time. 333 full-time freshmen.
Selectivity: Open admission; but selective for some programs.

BASIC COSTS (2012-2013)

Tuition and fees: $2,135; out-of-state residents $7,895.
Per-credit charge: $69; out-of-state residents $261.

FINANCIAL AID PICTURE

Students with need: Need-based aid available for full-time and part-time students. Work study available nights.

FINANCIAL AID PROCEDURES

Forms required: FAFSA.
Dates and Deadlines: Priority date 6/28; no closing date. Applicants notified on a rolling basis starting 5/1.

CONTACT

Emily Hurdt, Financial Aid Coordinator
137 South Post Road, Shelby, NC 28152-6224
(704) 669-4204

Coastal Carolina Community College

Jacksonville, North Carolina
www.coastalcarolina.edu Federal Code: 005316

2-year public community college in small city.
Enrollment: 3,715 undergrads, 58% part-time. 396 full-time freshmen.
Selectivity: Open admission; but selective for some programs.

BASIC COSTS (2012-2013)

Tuition and fees: $2,085; out-of-state residents $7,845.
Per-credit charge: $69; out-of-state residents $261.

FINANCIAL AID PICTURE (2011-2012)

Students with need: 95% of average financial aid package awarded as scholarships/grants, 5% awarded as loans/jobs. Need-based aid available for part-time students. Work study available nights, weekends, and for part-time students.
Students without need: No-need awards available for academics, state/district residency.

FINANCIAL AID PROCEDURES

Forms required: FAFSA, institutional form.
Dates and Deadlines: Priority date 5/15; no closing date. Applicants notified on a rolling basis starting 5/15; must reply within 2 week(s) of notification.

CONTACT

Lyon Tammy, Director for Financial Aid Services
444 Western Boulevard, Jacksonville, NC 28546-6816

College of the Albemarle

Elizabeth City, North Carolina
www.albemarle.edu Federal Code: 002917

2-year public branch campus and community college in large town.
Enrollment: 2,284 undergrads, 51% part-time. 353 full-time freshmen.
Selectivity: Open admission; but selective for some programs.

BASIC COSTS (2012-2013)

Tuition and fees: $2,167; out-of-state residents $7,927.
Per-credit charge: $69; out-of-state residents $261.

FINANCIAL AID PICTURE

Students with need: Need-based aid available for full-time and part-time students.
Students without need: No-need awards available for academics, art, leadership, minority status, music/drama, state/district residency.
Additional info: Separate application must be submitted for COA Private Scholarships.

FINANCIAL AID PROCEDURES

Forms required: FAFSA.
Dates and Deadlines: Priority date 3/15; closing date 6/1. Applicants notified on a rolling basis starting 5/1; must reply within 2 week(s) of notification.

CONTACT

Angie Dawson, Director of Scholarships and Student Aid
1208 North Road Street, Elizabeth City, NC 27906-2327
(252) 335-0821 ext. 2355

Davidson College

Davidson, North Carolina Federal Code: 002918
www.davidson.edu CSS Code: 5150

4-year private liberal arts college in small town, affiliated with Presbyterian Church (USA).
Enrollment: 1,785 undergrads. 490 full-time freshmen.
Selectivity: Admits less than 50% of applicants. GED not accepted.

BASIC COSTS (2012-2013)

Tuition and fees: $40,809.
Room and board: $11,346.

FINANCIAL AID PICTURE (2011-2012)

Students with need: Need-based aid available for full-time and part-time students.

Students without need: No-need awards available for academics, art, athletics, leadership, minority status, music/drama, ROTC.
Scholarships offered: Thompson S./Sarah S. Baker Scholarships: comprehensive fees; for first-time students with highest achievements; 3 awarded. John Montgomery Belk Scholarship: comprehensive fees; for Southeast applicants with highest achievements; 6 awarded. Amos Norris Scholarship: full cost; for first-time student athlete; 1 awarded. William Holt Terry Scholarships: full tuition; for first-year students with leadership skills and personal qualities, 2 awarded. John I. Smith Scholars Programs: full tuition; for first-year students with leadership, academic excellence, and commitment to community service; 2 awarded.
Additional info: The college has increased the money it provides for grants in financial aid packages and eliminated mandatory loans, allowing all students, regardless of socio-economic background, to graduate debt-free.

FINANCIAL AID PROCEDURES
Forms required: FAFSA, CSS PROFILE.
Dates and Deadlines: Priority date 2/15; closing date 3/15. Applicants notified by 4/7; must reply by 5/1.
Transfers: Applicants notified by 5/15.

CONTACT
David Gelinas, Director of Financial Aid
Box 7156, Davidson, NC 28035-7156
(704) 894-2232

Davidson County Community College
Lexington, North Carolina
www.davidsonccc.edu Federal Code: 002919

2-year public community college in large town.
Enrollment: 3,941 undergrads.
Selectivity: Open admission; but selective for some programs.

BASIC COSTS (2012-2013)
Tuition and fees: $2,167; out-of-state residents $7,927.
Per-credit charge: $69; out-of-state residents $261.

FINANCIAL AID PICTURE
Students with need: Need-based aid available for full-time and part-time students.
Students without need: No-need awards available for academics, leadership.

FINANCIAL AID PROCEDURES
Forms required: FAFSA, institutional form.
Dates and Deadlines: Priority date 6/30; no closing date. Applicants notified on a rolling basis starting 7/31; must reply within 2 week(s) of notification.

CONTACT
Lori Blevins, Director, Financial Aid
PO Box 1287, Lexington, NC 27293-1287
(336) 249-8186 ext. 237

Duke University
Durham, North Carolina Federal Code: 002920
www.duke.edu CSS Code: 5156

4-year private university in large city.
Enrollment: 6,493 undergrads. 1,718 full-time freshmen.
Selectivity: Admits less than 50% of applicants. GED not accepted.

BASIC COSTS (2013-2014)
Tuition and fees: $45,376.
Per-credit charge: $1,375.
Room and board: $12,902.

FINANCIAL AID PICTURE (2011-2012)
Students with need: Out of 985 full-time freshmen who applied for aid, 826 were judged to have need. Of these, 826 received aid, and 826 had their full need met. Average financial aid package met 100% of need; average scholarship/grant was $35,951; average loan was $3,119.
Students without need: 51 full-time freshmen who did not demonstrate need for aid received scholarships/grants; average award was $17,636. No-need awards available for alumni affiliation, athletics, leadership, minority status, state/district residency.
Cumulative student debt: 40% of graduating class had student loans; average debt was $21,713.

FINANCIAL AID PROCEDURES
Forms required: FAFSA, CSS PROFILE.
Dates and Deadlines: Priority date 3/1; no closing date. Applicants notified by 4/1; must reply by 5/1 or within 4 week(s) of notification.

CONTACT
Alison Rabil, Director of Financial Aid
2138 Campus Drive, Durham, NC 27708
(919) 684-6225

Durham Technical Community College
Durham, North Carolina
www.durhamtech.edu Federal Code: 005448

2-year public community and technical college in small city.
Enrollment: 5,119 undergrads.
Selectivity: Open admission; but selective for some programs.

BASIC COSTS (2012-2013)
Tuition and fees: $2,162; out-of-state residents $7,922.
Per-credit charge: $69; out-of-state residents $261.

FINANCIAL AID PICTURE
Students with need: Need-based aid available for full-time and part-time students. Work study available nights.
Students without need: No-need awards available for academics, minority status, state/district residency.
Additional info: Special funds available to single parents for tuition, fees, books, supplies and child care expenses.

FINANCIAL AID PROCEDURES
Forms required: FAFSA.
Dates and Deadlines: Applicants notified on a rolling basis starting 1/31; must reply within 3 week(s) of notification.

CONTACT
Everett Jeter, Director of Financial Aid
1637 Lawson Street, Durham, NC 27703
(919) 536-7209

East Carolina University
Greenville, North Carolina
www.ecu.edu Federal Code: 002923

4-year public university in small city.
Enrollment: 20,446 undergrads, 11% part-time. 3,955 full-time freshmen.
Selectivity: Admits 50 to 75% of applicants.

BASIC COSTS (2012-2013)
Tuition and fees: $5,869; out-of-state residents $19,683.
Room and board: $8,300.

FINANCIAL AID PICTURE (2012-2013)
Students with need: Out of 3,301 full-time freshmen who applied for aid, 2,485 were judged to have need. Of these, 2,389 received aid, and 209 had

their full need met. Average financial aid package met 66% of need; average scholarship/grant was $8,031; average loan was $3,452. For part-time students, average financial aid package was $7,316.
Students without need: 65 full-time freshmen who did not demonstrate need for aid received scholarships/grants; average award was $4,532. No-need awards available for academics, alumni affiliation, art, athletics, music/drama, ROTC.
Scholarships offered: 58 full-time freshmen received athletic scholarships; average amount $11,120.
Cumulative student debt: 65% of graduating class had student loans; average debt was $25,983.

FINANCIAL AID PROCEDURES
Forms required: FAFSA.
Dates and Deadlines: Priority date 3/1; no closing date. Applicants notified on a rolling basis starting 4/1; must reply within 3 week(s) of notification.

CONTACT
Julie Poorman, Director of Student Financial Aid
Office of Undergraduate Admissions, Greenville, NC 27858-4353
(252) 328-6610

Edgecombe Community College
Tarboro, North Carolina
www.edgecombe.edu Federal Code: 008855

2-year public community college in large town.
Enrollment: 3,049 undergrads.
Selectivity: Open admission; but selective for some programs.

BASIC COSTS (2012-2013)
Tuition and fees: $2,123; out-of-state residents $7,883.
Per-credit charge: $69; out-of-state residents $261.

FINANCIAL AID PICTURE
Students with need: Need-based aid available for full-time and part-time students.
Students without need: This college awards aid only to students with need.

FINANCIAL AID PROCEDURES
Forms required: FAFSA, institutional form.
Dates and Deadlines: Applicants notified on a rolling basis starting 8/15; must reply within 3 week(s) of notification.
Transfers: No deadline.

CONTACT
Henry Anderson, Director of Financial Aid
2009 West Wilson Street, Tarboro, NC 27886
(252) 823-5166 ext. 258

Elizabeth City State University
Elizabeth City, North Carolina
www.ecsu.edu Federal Code: 002926

4-year public liberal arts college in large town.
Enrollment: 2,529 undergrads, 7% part-time. 387 full-time freshmen.
Selectivity: Admits 50 to 75% of applicants.

BASIC COSTS (2012-2013)
Tuition and fees: $4,491; out-of-state residents $15,209.
Room and board: $6,659.

FINANCIAL AID PICTURE (2011-2012)
Students with need: Out of 369 full-time freshmen who applied for aid, 369 were judged to have need. Of these, 369 received aid.
Students without need: No-need awards available for academics, athletics, minority status, ROTC, state/district residency.

FINANCIAL AID PROCEDURES
Forms required: FAFSA.
Dates and Deadlines: Priority date 3/15; closing date 6/1. Applicants notified on a rolling basis starting 6/1; must reply by 6/30 or within 3 week(s) of notification.
Transfers: Closing date 3/15. Applicants notified on a rolling basis starting 6/30; must reply within 3 week(s) of notification.

CONTACT
Kenneth Wilson, Associate Director of Financial Aid
1704 Weeksville Road, Campus Box 901, Elizabeth City, NC 27909
(252) 335-3283

Elon University
Elon, North Carolina Federal Code: 002927
www.elon.edu CSS Code: 5183

4-year private university and liberal arts college in large town.
Enrollment: 5,357 undergrads, 3% part-time. 1,425 full-time freshmen.
Selectivity: Admits 50 to 75% of applicants.

BASIC COSTS (2013-2014)
Tuition and fees: $30,149.
Per-credit charge: $948.
Room and board: $9,897.

FINANCIAL AID PICTURE (2012-2013)
Students with need: Out of 839 full-time freshmen who applied for aid, 508 were judged to have need. Of these, 504 received aid. Average financial aid package met 62% of need; average scholarship/grant was $12,349; average loan was $3,380. Need-based aid available for part-time students.
Students without need: 316 full-time freshmen who did not demonstrate need for aid received scholarships/grants; average award was $6,114. No-need awards available for academics, art, athletics, leadership, music/drama, ROTC, state/district residency.
Scholarships offered: ***Merit:*** Presidential Scholarships: up to $4,500 annually; based on academic credentials. Fellows Programs (Honors, Business, Communications, Elon College Fellows, Isabella Cannon Leadership, Teaching, International): $3,500-$12,000 annually; based on merit. Elon Teaching Fellows: $4,500 annually. Engineering Scholarships: $7,000 annually. Performing Arts Scholarships: $500-$6,000; talent-based. Music Scholarships: $500-$5,000; talent and need-based. ***Athletic:*** 63 full-time freshmen received athletic scholarships; average amount $28,991.
Cumulative student debt: 44% of graduating class had student loans; average debt was $28,183.

FINANCIAL AID PROCEDURES
Forms required: FAFSA, CSS PROFILE, institutional form.
Dates and Deadlines: Priority date 2/15; no closing date. Applicants notified on a rolling basis starting 3/30.

CONTACT
Pat Murphy, Director of Financial Planning
2700 Campus Box, Elon, NC 27244-2010
(336) 278-7640

Fayetteville State University
Fayetteville, North Carolina
www.uncfsu.edu Federal Code: 002928

4-year public university in small city.
Enrollment: 5,012 undergrads, 23% part-time. 639 full-time freshmen.
Selectivity: Admits 50 to 75% of applicants.

BASIC COSTS (2012-2013)
Tuition and fees: $4,394; out-of-state residents $15,098.
Room and board: $6,092.

FINANCIAL AID PICTURE (2011-2012)
Students with need: Out of 631 full-time freshmen who applied for aid, 580 were judged to have need. Of these, 575 received aid, and 150 had their full need met. Average financial aid package met 88% of need; average scholarship/grant was $7,323; average loan was $5,341. For part-time students, average financial aid package was $7,494.
Students without need: 38 full-time freshmen who did not demonstrate need for aid received scholarships/grants; average award was $830. No-need awards available for academics, alumni affiliation, athletics, music/drama, ROTC, state/district residency.
Scholarships offered: 21 full-time freshmen received athletic scholarships; average amount $12,220.

FINANCIAL AID PROCEDURES
Forms required: FAFSA.
Dates and Deadlines: Closing date 3/1. Applicants notified on a rolling basis starting 4/15; must reply within 2 week(s) of notification.

CONTACT
Kamesia Ewing, Director of Financial Aid
1200 Murchison Road, Fayetteville, NC 28301-4298
(910) 672-1325

Fayetteville Technical Community College

Fayetteville, North Carolina
www.faytechcc.edu Federal Code: 007640

2-year public community and technical college in large city.
Enrollment: 10,385 undergrads, 51% part-time. 1,193 full-time freshmen.
Selectivity: Open admission; but selective for some programs.

BASIC COSTS (2012-2013)
Tuition and fees: $2,160; out-of-state residents $7,920.
Per-credit charge: $69; out-of-state residents $261.

FINANCIAL AID PICTURE (2011-2012)
Students with need: Out of 1,011 full-time freshmen who applied for aid, 957 were judged to have need. Of these, 911 received aid, and 897 had their full need met. Average financial aid package met 98% of need; average scholarship/grant was $1,200; average loan was $3,500. For part-time students, average financial aid package was $4,888.
Cumulative student debt: 90% of graduating class had student loans; average debt was $32,000.

FINANCIAL AID PROCEDURES
Forms required: FAFSA.
Dates and Deadlines: Priority date 6/1; closing date 7/15. Applicants notified on a rolling basis starting 4/1; must reply by 6/1.
Transfers: Priority date 3/1; closing date 6/1. Applicants notified by 1/1; must reply within 2 week(s) of notification.

CONTACT
Christine Porchia-Gaddy, Director of Student Financial Aid
PO Box 35236, Fayetteville, NC 28303-0236
(910) 678-8242

Forsyth Technical Community College

Winston-Salem, North Carolina
www.forsythtech.edu Federal Code: 005317

2-year public community and technical college in small city.
Enrollment: 9,349 undergrads, 58% part-time. 814 full-time freshmen.
Selectivity: Open admission; but selective for some programs.

BASIC COSTS (2012-2013)
Tuition and fees: $2,142; out-of-state residents $7,902.
Per-credit charge: $69; out-of-state residents $261.

FINANCIAL AID PICTURE (2011-2012)
Students with need: 91% of average financial aid package awarded as scholarships/grants, 9% awarded as loans/jobs. Need-based aid available for part-time students. Work study available nights.
Students without need: No-need awards available for academics, state/district residency.
Additional info: Apply for aid as close to January 1 as possible for best consideration.

FINANCIAL AID PROCEDURES
Forms required: FAFSA, institutional form.
Dates and Deadlines: Closing date 6/1. Applicants notified on a rolling basis starting 7/1; must reply within 2 week(s) of notification.
Transfers: No deadline. Mid-year transfer students must submit a financial aid transcript from previous college in order for financial aid office to award any Federal Pell Grant funds to eligible students.

CONTACT
Ricky Hodges, Director of Student Financial Services
2100 Silas Creek Parkway, Winston-Salem, NC 27103

Gardner-Webb University

Boiling Springs, North Carolina
www.gardner-webb.edu Federal Code: 002929

4-year private university and liberal arts college in small town, affiliated with Southern Baptist Convention.
Enrollment: 2,677 undergrads, 18% part-time. 453 full-time freshmen.
Selectivity: Admits 50 to 75% of applicants.

BASIC COSTS (2013-2014)
Tuition and fees: $25,905.
Per-credit charge: $406.
Room and board: $8,330.

FINANCIAL AID PICTURE (2011-2012)
Students with need: Out of 437 full-time freshmen who applied for aid, 383 were judged to have need. Of these, 383 received aid, and 61 had their full need met. Average financial aid package met 68% of need; average scholarship/grant was $7,764; average loan was $3,805.
Students without need: 56 full-time freshmen who did not demonstrate need for aid received scholarships/grants; average award was $7,601. No-need awards available for academics, athletics, leadership, music/drama, religious affiliation, ROTC, state/district residency.
Scholarships offered: ***Merit:*** Presidential Fellow: full tuition, room and board for four years; 5 awarded. Academic Fellow: full tuition for four years; 5 awarded. University Fellow: 80% tuition for four years; 2 awarded. Selection based on academic accomplishments and interview. ***Athletic:*** 17 full-time freshmen received athletic scholarships; average amount $14,091.

FINANCIAL AID PROCEDURES
Forms required: FAFSA, state aid form.
Dates and Deadlines: Priority date 3/1; no closing date. Applicants notified on a rolling basis starting 3/1; must reply within 2 week(s) of notification.
Transfers: No deadline. Applicants notified on a rolling basis starting 3/1; must reply within 2 week(s) of notification.

CONTACT
Summer Nance, Assistant Vice President for Financial Planning
PO Box 817, Boiling Springs, NC 28017
(704) 406-4243

Gaston College
Dallas, North Carolina
www.gaston.edu Federal Code: 002973

2-year public community college in small town.
Enrollment: 6,464 undergrads.
Selectivity: Open admission; but selective for some programs.

BASIC COSTS (2012-2013)
Tuition and fees: $2,130; out-of-state residents $7,890.
Per-credit charge: $69; out-of-state residents $261.

FINANCIAL AID PICTURE
Students with need: Need-based aid available for full-time students.
Students without need: No-need awards available for academics, state/district residency.
Scholarships offered: Academic Scholarship: over 30 available, $1,100, GPA of 3.0 or better. Careers Scholarship: 10 available, $1,100 each, must pursue career in specified engineering technologies or industrial technologies major and have GPA of 3.0 or better.
Additional info: Grants/scholarships available for women pursuing nontraditional roles.

FINANCIAL AID PROCEDURES
Forms required: FAFSA, institutional form.
Dates and Deadlines: Priority date 3/15; closing date 6/30. Applicants notified on a rolling basis.

CONTACT
Peggy Oates, Director of Financial Aid and Veterans Affairs
201 Highway 321 South, Dallas, NC 28034-1499
(704) 922-6227

Greensboro College
Greensboro, North Carolina
www.greensboro.edu Federal Code: 002930

4-year private liberal arts college in large city, affiliated with United Methodist Church.
Enrollment: 1,030 undergrads.
Selectivity: Admits less than 50% of applicants.

BASIC COSTS (2012-2013)
Tuition and fees: $25,600.
Room and board: $9,400.

FINANCIAL AID PICTURE
Students with need: Need-based aid available for full-time and part-time students. Work study available nights, weekends, and for part-time students.
Students without need: No-need awards available for academics, alumni affiliation, art, leadership, music/drama, religious affiliation, state/district residency.
Scholarships offered: Barrett Scholarships and Presidential Scholarships; full tuition; fees, room, and board; number of awards vary.

FINANCIAL AID PROCEDURES
Forms required: FAFSA, state aid form, institutional form.
Dates and Deadlines: Priority date 4/15; no closing date. Applicants notified on a rolling basis starting 2/1; must reply within 2 week(s) of notification.
Transfers: Closing date 4/15. Must reply within 4 week(s) of notification.

CONTACT
Ann Campbell, Executive Director of Financial Aid
815 West Market Street, Greensboro, NC 27401-1875
(336) 272-7102 ext. 217

Guilford College
Greensboro, North Carolina
www.guilford.edu Federal Code: 002931

4-year private liberal arts college in large town, affiliated with Society of Friends (Quaker).
Enrollment: 2,330 undergrads, 17% part-time. 303 full-time freshmen.
Selectivity: Admits over 75% of applicants.

BASIC COSTS (2013-2014)
Tuition and fees: $32,470.
Per-credit charge: $951.
Room and board: $8,800.

FINANCIAL AID PICTURE (2012-2013)
Students with need: Out of 225 full-time freshmen who applied for aid, 123 were judged to have need. Of these, 121 received aid, and 11 had their full need met. Average financial aid package met 77% of need; average scholarship/grant was $26,364; average loan was $7,851. For part-time students, average financial aid package was $3,461.
Students without need: 70 full-time freshmen who did not demonstrate need for aid received scholarships/grants; average award was $13,444. No-need awards available for academics.
Scholarships offered: Honors Scholarship: $7,500 to full tuition. Presidential Scholarship: $5,000. Incentive grants: $3,000; based on participation or leadership in school or community activities. Quaker Leadership Scholarships: $3,000; candidates must be active members of the Religious Society of Friends.
Cumulative student debt: 75% of graduating class had student loans; average debt was $25,025.

FINANCIAL AID PROCEDURES
Forms required: FAFSA.
Dates and Deadlines: Priority date 3/1; no closing date. Applicants notified on a rolling basis starting 2/15; must reply by 3/1.

CONTACT
Paul Coscia, Director of Student Financial Services
Admissions, New Garden Hall, Greensboro, NC 27410-4108
(336) 316-2354

Guilford Technical Community College
Jamestown, North Carolina
www.gtcc.edu Federal Code: 004838

2-year public community and technical college in large city.
Enrollment: 14,728 undergrads, 47% part-time. 808 full-time freshmen.
Selectivity: Open admission; but selective for some programs.

BASIC COSTS (2012-2013)
Tuition and fees: $2,154; out-of-state residents $7,914.
Per-credit charge: $69; out-of-state residents $261.
Additional info: Fees for 1-11 credit hours: $25 access and parking fees, $10 activity fee, $10 technology fee; Fees for 12+ credit hours: $50 access and parking fees, $17.50 activity fee, $16 technology fee. Other expenses include transportation.

FINANCIAL AID PICTURE (2011-2012)
Students with need: Out of 679 full-time freshmen who applied for aid, 646 were judged to have need. Of these, 645 received aid, and 4 had their full need met. Average financial aid package met 39% of need; average scholarship/grant was $5,098; average loan was $3,106. For part-time students, average financial aid package was $5,210.
Students without need: 13 full-time freshmen who did not demonstrate need for aid received scholarships/grants; average award was $1,904. No-need awards available for academics, athletics, leadership, minority status, state/district residency.

Scholarships offered: 1 full-time freshmen received athletic scholarships; average amount $8,310.

FINANCIAL AID PROCEDURES

Forms required: FAFSA.

Dates and Deadlines: Priority date 3/15; closing date 7/25. Applicants notified on a rolling basis starting 7/1; must reply within 2 week(s) of notification.

CONTACT

Lisa Koretoff, Director of Financial Aid
PO Box 309, Jamestown, NC 27282
(336) 334-4822 ext. 50317

Halifax Community College

Weldon, North Carolina
www.halifaxcc.edu Federal Code: 007986

2-year public community college in small town.
Enrollment: 1,556 undergrads.
Selectivity: Open admission; but selective for some programs.

BASIC COSTS (2012-2013)

Tuition and fees: $2,160; out-of-state residents $7,920.
Per-credit charge: $69; out-of-state residents $261.

FINANCIAL AID PICTURE (2011-2012)

Students with need: Need-based aid available for full-time students.

FINANCIAL AID PROCEDURES

Dates and Deadlines: Priority date 6/1; no closing date. Applicants notified on a rolling basis starting 8/1; must reply within 2 week(s) of notification.

CONTACT

Tara Keeter, Director, Financial Aid
100 College Drive, Drawer 809, Weldon, NC 27890
(252) 536-7223

Haywood Community College

Clyde, North Carolina
www.haywood.edu Federal Code: 008083

2-year public community and technical college in rural community.
Enrollment: 1,804 undergrads.
Selectivity: Open admission; but selective for some programs.

BASIC COSTS (2012-2013)

Tuition and fees: $2,123; out-of-state residents $7,883.
Per-credit charge: $69; out-of-state residents $261.

FINANCIAL AID PICTURE (2011-2012)

Students with need: 87% of average financial aid package awarded as scholarships/grants, 13% awarded as loans/jobs. Need-based aid available for part-time students.
Students without need: No-need awards available for academics.
Additional info: Complete FAFSA by priority filing date for consideration for institutional scholarships.

FINANCIAL AID PROCEDURES

Forms required: FAFSA, institutional form.

Dates and Deadlines: Priority date 4/1; no closing date. Applicants notified on a rolling basis starting 4/15; must reply within 2 week(s) of notification.

CONTACT

Sayward Cabe, Director of Financial Aid
185 Freelander Drive, Clyde, NC 28721-9454
(828) 627-4506

High Point University

High Point, North Carolina Federal Code: 002933
www.highpoint.edu CSS Code: 5293

4-year private university and liberal arts college in small city, affiliated with United Methodist Church.
Enrollment: 4,070 undergrads, 2% part-time. 1,257 full-time freshmen.
Selectivity: Admits 50 to 75% of applicants.

BASIC COSTS (2012-2013)

Per-credit charge: $800.
Comprehensive fee: $39,800.

FINANCIAL AID PICTURE (2011-2012)

Students with need: Need-based aid available for full-time and part-time students. Work study available nights, weekends, and for part-time students.
Students without need: No-need awards available for academics, alumni affiliation, art, athletics, leadership, music/drama, religious affiliation, state/district residency.
Scholarships offered: Awarded annually to qualified freshmen: Keller Scholarship: $24,000. University Fellowship: $20,000. Presidential Fellowship: $15,000. Presidential Scholarship: $9,000. Leadership Fellowship: $7,000. Leadership Scholarship: $5,000. All scholarships based on merit. Application and interview required.

FINANCIAL AID PROCEDURES

Forms required: FAFSA, CSS PROFILE, state aid form.

Dates and Deadlines: Priority date 3/1; no closing date. Applicants notified on a rolling basis starting 4/1; must reply within 3 week(s) of notification.

Transfers: No deadline. Applicants notified on a rolling basis starting 5/1; must reply within 3 week(s) of notification.

CONTACT

Ron Elmore, Director of Student Financial Services
833 Montlieu Avenue, High Point, NC 27262-3598
(336) 841-9128

Isothermal Community College

Spindale, North Carolina
www.isothermal.edu Federal Code: 002934

2-year public community college in small town.
Enrollment: 2,432 undergrads.
Selectivity: Open admission; but selective for some programs.

BASIC COSTS (2012-2013)

Tuition and fees: $2,124; out-of-state residents $7,884.
Per-credit charge: $69; out-of-state residents $261.

FINANCIAL AID PICTURE

Students with need: Need-based aid available for full-time and part-time students. Work study available nights.
Students without need: No-need awards available for academics, job skills, leadership, minority status, music/drama, state/district residency.

FINANCIAL AID PROCEDURES

Forms required: FAFSA, institutional form.

Dates and Deadlines: Priority date 5/31; closing date 7/1. Applicants notified on a rolling basis starting 4/30; must reply within 4 week(s) of notification.

CONTACT

Jeffery Boyle, Director of Financial Aid
PO Box 804, Spindale, NC 28160-0804
(828) 286-3636 ext. 468

James Sprunt Community College

Kenansville, North Carolina
www.jamessprunt.edu Federal Code: 007687

2-year public community college in rural community.
Enrollment: 1,489 undergrads, 42% part-time. 164 full-time freshmen.
Selectivity: Open admission; but selective for some programs.

BASIC COSTS (2012-2013)

Tuition and fees: $2,140; out-of-state residents $7,900.
Per-credit charge: $69; out-of-state residents $261.

FINANCIAL AID PICTURE (2011-2012)

Students with need: Out of 138 full-time freshmen who applied for aid, 131 were judged to have need. Of these, 131 received aid, and 101 had their full need met. Average financial aid package met 100% of need; average scholarship/grant was $5,775. For part-time students, average financial aid package was $2,987.
Students without need: 32 full-time freshmen who did not demonstrate need for aid received scholarships/grants; average award was $650. No-need awards available for academics, state/district residency.

FINANCIAL AID PROCEDURES

Forms required: FAFSA, state aid form, institutional form.
Dates and Deadlines: Closing date 7/1. Applicants notified on a rolling basis starting 5/15; must reply within 2 week(s) of notification.

CONTACT

Melissa Whitman, Interim Financial Aid Officer
PO Box 398, Kenansville, NC 28349-0398
(910) 296-2503

Johnson C. Smith University

Charlotte, North Carolina
www.jcsu.edu Federal Code: 002936

4-year private university and liberal arts college in very large city.
Enrollment: 1,665 undergrads, 4% part-time. 386 full-time freshmen.
Selectivity: Admits less than 50% of applicants.

BASIC COSTS (2012-2013)

Tuition and fees: $18,236.
Per-credit charge: $418.
Room and board: $7,100.
Additional info: Tuition/fee waivers available for adults.

FINANCIAL AID PICTURE (2012-2013)

Students with need: Out of 324 full-time freshmen who applied for aid, 317 were judged to have need. Of these, 317 received aid, and 16 had their full need met. Average financial aid package met 57% of need; average scholarship/grant was $13,324; average loan was $4,095. For part-time students, average financial aid package was $9,966.
Students without need: 55 full-time freshmen who did not demonstrate need for aid received scholarships/grants; average award was $16,441. No-need awards available for academics, athletics, ROTC, state/district residency.
Scholarships offered: 20 full-time freshmen received athletic scholarships; average amount $16,006.
Cumulative student debt: 93% of graduating class had student loans; average debt was $32,621.

FINANCIAL AID PROCEDURES

Forms required: FAFSA, state aid form.
Dates and Deadlines: Priority date 3/1; no closing date. Applicants notified on a rolling basis starting 3/1; must reply within 2 week(s) of notification.
Transfers: No deadline. Applicants notified on a rolling basis starting 4/1; must reply within 2 week(s) of notification.

CONTACT

Jacqueline Williams, Director of Financial Aid
100 Beatties Ford Road, Charlotte, NC 28216-5398
(704) 378-1035

Johnston Community College

Smithfield, North Carolina
www.johnstoncc.edu Federal Code: 009336

2-year public community and technical college in large town.
Enrollment: 3,925 undergrads, 49% part-time. 468 full-time freshmen.
Selectivity: Open admission; but selective for some programs.

BASIC COSTS (2012-2013)

Tuition and fees: $2,167; out-of-state residents $7,927.
Per-credit charge: $69; out-of-state residents $261.

FINANCIAL AID PICTURE

Students with need: Need-based aid available for full-time and part-time students.
Students without need: This college awards aid only to students with need.

FINANCIAL AID PROCEDURES

Forms required: FAFSA, institutional form.
Dates and Deadlines: Priority date 5/31; no closing date. Applicants notified on a rolling basis starting 6/1; must reply within 2 week(s) of notification.

CONTACT

Betty Woodall, Financial Aid Director
PO Box 2350, Smithfield, NC 27577
(919) 209-2036

Laurel University

High Point, North Carolina
www.laureluniversity.edu Federal Code: 013819

4-year private university and Bible college in small city, affiliated with interdenominational tradition.
Enrollment: 278 undergrads, 49% part-time. 7 full-time freshmen.
Selectivity: Admits less than 50% of applicants.

BASIC COSTS (2012-2013)

Tuition and fees: $10,930.
Per-credit charge: $340.
Additional info: Board plan not available. Cost of room only, $2,344.

FINANCIAL AID PICTURE

Students with need: Need-based aid available for full-time and part-time students. Work study available nights, weekends, and for part-time students.
Scholarships offered: Early Acceptance; $100. Academic Honor; 10% of tuition.
Additional info: Early Acceptance Scholarships, Academic Honor Scholarships, Married Student Credit and Minister/Missionary Dependent Scholarship available.

FINANCIAL AID PROCEDURES

Forms required: FAFSA.
Dates and Deadlines: Priority date 3/15; no closing date. Applicants notified on a rolling basis starting 6/1; must reply within 3 week(s) of notification.
Transfers: Closing date 3/15.

CONTACT

Shirley Carter, Director of Financial Aid
1215 Eastchester Drive, High Point, NC 27265-3115
(336) 887-3000 ext. 129

Lees-McRae College

Banner Elk, North Carolina
www.lmc.edu Federal Code: 002923

4-year private liberal arts college in rural community, affiliated with Presbyterian Church (USA).
Enrollment: 835 undergrads, 1% part-time. 182 full-time freshmen.
Selectivity: Admits 50 to 75% of applicants.

BASIC COSTS (2013-2014)
Tuition and fees: $24,150.
Per-credit charge: $650.
Room and board: $9,250.

FINANCIAL AID PICTURE (2012-2013)
Students with need: Out of 161 full-time freshmen who applied for aid, 141 were judged to have need. Of these, 141 received aid. Average financial aid package met 74% of need; average scholarship/grant was $8,700; average loan was $3,500. Need-based aid available for part-time students.
Students without need: 31 full-time freshmen who did not demonstrate need for aid received scholarships/grants; average award was $9,440. No-need awards available for academics, athletics, leadership, music/drama, religious affiliation, state/district residency.
Scholarships offered: 67 full-time freshmen received athletic scholarships; average amount $6,334.

FINANCIAL AID PROCEDURES
Forms required: FAFSA, state aid form.
Dates and Deadlines: Priority date 4/15; no closing date. Applicants notified on a rolling basis starting 3/1; must reply within 2 week(s) of notification.

CONTACT
Cathy Shell, Director of Financial Aid
Box 128, Banner Elk, NC 28604
(828) 898-8740

Lenoir Community College

Kinston, North Carolina
www.lenoircc.edu Federal Code: 002940

2-year public community college in large town.
Enrollment: 2,613 undergrads, 52% part-time. 1,206 full-time freshmen.
Selectivity: Open admission; but selective for some programs.

BASIC COSTS (2012-2013)
Tuition and fees: $2,166; out-of-state residents $7,926.
Per-credit charge: $69; out-of-state residents $261.

FINANCIAL AID PICTURE (2011-2012)
Students with need: Average financial aid package for all full-time undergraduates was $2,775. 97% awarded as scholarships/grants, 3% awarded as loans/jobs. Need-based aid available for part-time students. Work study available nights.
Students without need: No-need awards available for academics, athletics, leadership, state/district residency.

FINANCIAL AID PROCEDURES
Forms required: institutional form.
Dates and Deadlines: Priority date 7/1; closing date 8/15. Applicants notified on a rolling basis starting 8/1; must reply within 2 week(s) of notification.

CONTACT
Brandi Massey, Director of Student Financial Aid
PO Box 188, Kinston, NC 28502-0188
(252) 527-6223

Lenoir-Rhyne University

Hickory, North Carolina
www.lr.edu Federal Code: 002941

4-year private university and liberal arts college in large town, affiliated with Evangelical Lutheran Church in America.
Enrollment: 1,447 undergrads. 384 full-time freshmen.
Selectivity: Admits 50 to 75% of applicants.

BASIC COSTS (2013-2014)
Tuition and fees: $29,310.
Per-credit charge: $1,215.
Room and board: $10,040.
Additional info: Tuition/fee waivers available for minority students.

FINANCIAL AID PICTURE (2011-2012)
Students with need: Out of 380 full-time freshmen who applied for aid, 355 were judged to have need. Of these, 354 received aid, and 90 had their full need met. Average financial aid package met 79% of need; average scholarship/grant was $20,866; average loan was $2,903. For part-time students, average financial aid package was $9,794.
Students without need: 26 full-time freshmen who did not demonstrate need for aid received scholarships/grants; average award was $11,486. No-need awards available for academics, alumni affiliation, athletics, leadership, minority status, music/drama, religious affiliation, state/district residency.
Scholarships offered: 42 full-time freshmen received athletic scholarships; average amount $5,622.
Cumulative student debt: 84% of graduating class had student loans; average debt was $26,935.

FINANCIAL AID PROCEDURES
Forms required: FAFSA.
Dates and Deadlines: Priority date 3/1; no closing date. Applicants notified on a rolling basis starting 3/1; must reply by 5/1.

CONTACT
Nick, Director of Financial Aid
LR Box 7227, Hickory, NC 28603
(800) 277-5721

Livingstone College

Salisbury, North Carolina
www.livingstone.edu Federal Code: 002942

4-year private liberal arts college in large town, affiliated with African Methodist Episcopal Zion Church.
Enrollment: 1,150 undergrads.
Selectivity: Admits 50 to 75% of applicants.

BASIC COSTS (2012-2013)
Tuition and fees: $15,408.
Room and board: $6,342.

FINANCIAL AID PICTURE
Students with need: Need-based aid available for full-time and part-time students. Work study available nights, weekends, and for part-time students.
Students without need: No-need awards available for academics, alumni affiliation, athletics, leadership, music/drama, religious affiliation, ROTC, state/district residency.

FINANCIAL AID PROCEDURES
Forms required: FAFSA, state aid form.
Dates and Deadlines: Priority date 3/15; closing date 6/30. Applicants notified by 5/1; must reply within 4 week(s) of notification.

CONTACT
Sherri Jefferson, Director of Financial Aid
701 West Monroe Street, Salisbury, NC 28144-5213
(704) 216-6273

Louisburg College
Louisburg, North Carolina
www.louisburg.edu Federal Code: 002943

2-year private junior college in small town, affiliated with United Methodist Church.
Enrollment: 679 undergrads. 349 full-time freshmen.

BASIC COSTS (2012-2013)
Tuition and fees: $14,944.
Room and board: $9,452.

FINANCIAL AID PICTURE
Students with need: Need-based aid available for full-time students. Work study available nights, weekends, and for part-time students.
Students without need: No-need awards available for academics, art, athletics, leadership, minority status, music/drama, religious affiliation, ROTC, state/district residency.
Scholarships offered: Academic Merit Scholarships: $2,000-$6,000. Leadership Scholarship: $1,000. Robbins Scholarship: $1,000.
Additional info: Job location and development program helps students obtain work in the community.

FINANCIAL AID PROCEDURES
Forms required: FAFSA, state aid form.
Dates and Deadlines: Priority date 3/1; no closing date.

CONTACT
Mike Abernathy, Director of Financial Aid
501 North Main Street, Louisburg, NC 27549
(919) 497-3203

Mars Hill College
Mars Hill, North Carolina
www.mhc.edu Federal Code: 002944

4-year private liberal arts college in small town, affiliated with Baptist faith.
Enrollment: 1,323 undergrads, 6% part-time. 385 full-time freshmen.
Selectivity: Admits 50 to 75% of applicants.

BASIC COSTS (2012-2013)
Tuition and fees: $24,536.
Per-credit charge: $775.
Room and board: $8,290.

FINANCIAL AID PICTURE (2011-2012)
Students with need: Out of 369 full-time freshmen who applied for aid, 349 were judged to have need. Of these, 349 received aid, and 52 had their full need met. Average financial aid package met 58% of need; average scholarship/grant was $5,146; average loan was $3,086. For part-time students, average financial aid package was $5,254.
Students without need: 36 full-time freshmen who did not demonstrate need for aid received scholarships/grants; average award was $5,945. No-need awards available for academics, athletics, state/district residency.
Scholarships offered: 244 full-time freshmen received athletic scholarships; average amount $8,354.
Cumulative student debt: 82% of graduating class had student loans; average debt was $13,829.

FINANCIAL AID PROCEDURES
Forms required: FAFSA, state aid form.
Dates and Deadlines: Priority date 3/15; no closing date. Applicants notified on a rolling basis; must reply within 2 week(s) of notification.
Transfers: No deadline. Applicants notified on a rolling basis; must reply within 2 week(s) of notification.

CONTACT
Nichole Thomas, Director of Financial Aid
Mars Hill College Admissions Office, Mars Hill, NC 28754
(828) 689-1123

Martin Community College
Williamston, North Carolina
www.martincc.edu Federal Code: 007988

2-year public community and technical college in small town.
Enrollment: 719 undergrads, 45% part-time. 75 full-time freshmen.
Selectivity: Open admission; but selective for some programs.

BASIC COSTS (2012-2013)
Tuition and fees: $2,108; out-of-state residents $7,868.
Per-credit charge: $69; out-of-state residents $261.

FINANCIAL AID PICTURE (2011-2012)
Students with need: 98% of average financial aid package awarded as scholarships/grants, 2% awarded as loans/jobs. Need-based aid available for part-time students. Work study available nights.
Students without need: No-need awards available for academics.

FINANCIAL AID PROCEDURES
Forms required: FAFSA.
Dates and Deadlines: Applicants notified on a rolling basis starting 5/1.

CONTACT
Michelle Cobb, Director of Financial Aid
1161 Kehukee Park Road, Williamston, NC 27892-9988
(252) 792-1521 ext. 244

Mayland Community College
Spruce Pine, North Carolina
www.mayland.edu Federal Code: 011197

2-year public community college in rural community.
Enrollment: 1,328 undergrads, 63% part-time. 153 full-time freshmen.
Selectivity: Open admission; but selective for some programs.

BASIC COSTS (2012-2013)
Tuition and fees: $2,166; out-of-state residents $7,926.
Per-credit charge: $69; out-of-state residents $261.

FINANCIAL AID PICTURE (2011-2012)
Students with need: 82% of average financial aid package awarded as scholarships/grants, 18% awarded as loans/jobs. Need-based aid available for part-time students.

FINANCIAL AID PROCEDURES
Forms required: FAFSA, institutional form.
Dates and Deadlines: Priority date 3/15; closing date 6/30. Applicants notified on a rolling basis starting 6/15.

CONTACT
Cassie Forbes, Director, Financial Aid
PO Box 547, Spruce Pine, NC 28777
(828) 766-1234

McDowell Technical Community College
Marion, North Carolina
www.mcdowelltech.edu Federal Code: 008085

2-year public community and technical college in small town.
Enrollment: 1,291 undergrads, 57% part-time. 144 full-time freshmen.

Selectivity: Open admission; but selective for some programs.

BASIC COSTS (2012-2013)

Tuition and fees: $2,165; out-of-state residents $7,925.

Per-credit charge: $69; out-of-state residents $261.

FINANCIAL AID PICTURE (2011-2012)

Students with need: 72% of average financial aid package awarded as scholarships/grants, 28% awarded as loans/jobs. Need-based aid available for part-time students. Work study available nights.

Students without need: This college awards aid only to students with need.

FINANCIAL AID PROCEDURES

Forms required: FAFSA, institutional form.

Dates and Deadlines: Priority date 3/15; no closing date. Applicants notified on a rolling basis starting 7/1.

CONTACT

Kim Ledbetter, Director of Financial Aid
54 College Drive, Marion, NC 28752
(828) 652-0602

Meredith College

Raleigh, North Carolina
www.meredith.edu Federal Code: 002945

4-year private liberal arts college for women in large city.

Enrollment: 1,630 undergrads, 3% part-time. 407 full-time freshmen.

Selectivity: Admits 50 to 75% of applicants. GED not accepted.

BASIC COSTS (2012-2013)

Tuition and fees: $29,186.

Per-credit charge: $723.

Room and board: $8,348.

FINANCIAL AID PICTURE

Students with need: Need-based aid available for full-time and part-time students.

Students without need: No-need awards available for academics, art, leadership, minority status, music/drama, religious affiliation, state/district residency.

Scholarships offered: Presidential Scholarships: tuition plus a stipend for study abroad; based on superior academic ability and achievement; 3-5 awarded. Talent Scholarships: varying amounts; available for students planning to major in art, music, interior design and computer science/mathematics/pre-engineering and based on on-campus competition. Teaching Fellows Scholarship: $6,500 per year to match a similar stipend from the State; study abroad opportunity, based on state-wide competition; approximately 25 awarded.

FINANCIAL AID PROCEDURES

Forms required: FAFSA.

Dates and Deadlines: Priority date 2/15; no closing date. Applicants notified on a rolling basis starting 3/15; must reply by 5/1 or within 2 week(s) of notification.

CONTACT

Kevin Michaelsen, Director of Financial Assistance
3800 Hillsborough Street, Raleigh, NC 27607-5298
(919) 760-8565

Methodist University

Fayetteville, North Carolina
www.methodist.edu Federal Code: 002946

4-year private liberal arts college in small city, affiliated with United Methodist Church.

Enrollment: 2,104 undergrads.

Selectivity: Admits 50 to 75% of applicants.

BASIC COSTS (2012-2013)

Tuition and fees: $27,122.

Per-credit charge: $858.

Room and board: $10,063.

FINANCIAL AID PICTURE

Students with need: Need-based aid available for full-time and part-time students. Work study available nights, weekends, and for part-time students.

Students without need: No-need awards available for academics, alumni affiliation, leadership, music/drama, religious affiliation, ROTC, state/district residency.

Scholarships offered: Presidential Scholarship: $5,250-$17,000/yr; 3.1+ GPA, 1000+ SAT or 22+ ACT. Merit scholarship: $3,250-$4,250; residential freshmen; 2.9+ GPA, 900+ SAT or 19+ ACT; leadership. SAT scores exclusive of Writing.

FINANCIAL AID PROCEDURES

Forms required: FAFSA.

Dates and Deadlines: Priority date 5/1; no closing date. Applicants notified on a rolling basis starting 3/1; must reply within 2 week(s) of notification.

Transfers: No deadline. Applicants notified on a rolling basis; must reply within 2 week(s) of notification.

CONTACT

Bonnie Adamson, Director of Financial Aid
5400 Ramsey Street, Fayetteville, NC 28311-1498
(910) 630-7192

Mid-Atlantic Christian University

Elizabeth City, North Carolina
www.macuniversity.edu Federal Code: 014101

4-year private university and Bible college in large town, affiliated with Church of Christ.

Enrollment: 159 undergrads, 21% part-time. 30 full-time freshmen.

Selectivity: Admits less than 50% of applicants.

BASIC COSTS (2012-2013)

Tuition and fees: $10,950.

Per-credit charge: $365.

Room and board: $7,580.

FINANCIAL AID PICTURE (2011-2012)

Students with need: Out of 29 full-time freshmen who applied for aid, 29 were judged to have need. Of these, 29 received aid. Average financial aid package met 51% of need; average scholarship/grant was $5,644; average loan was $2,920. For part-time students, average financial aid package was $4,300.

Students without need: No-need awards available for academics, alumni affiliation, leadership, music/drama, religious affiliation.

Scholarships offered: Full tuition and half tuition available, based on demonstration of exceptional academic ability.

Cumulative student debt: 99% of graduating class had student loans; average debt was $32,434.

FINANCIAL AID PROCEDURES

Forms required: FAFSA, institutional form.

Dates and Deadlines: Closing date 2/1. Applicants notified on a rolling basis starting 5/1; must reply within 2 week(s) of notification.

Transfers: Priority date 3/1; no deadline. Must reply within 2 week(s) of notification.

CONTACT

Lisa Pipkin, Financial Aid Administrator
715 North Poindexter Street, Elizabeth City, NC 27909
(252) 334-2020

Miller-Motte College: Wilmington

Wilmington, North Carolina
www.miller-motte.edu Federal Code: E00896

4-year for-profit technical college in small city.
Enrollment: 2,436 undergrads.

FINANCIAL AID PICTURE
Students with need: Need-based aid available for full-time and part-time students. Work study available nights, weekends, and for part-time students.
Students without need: This college awards aid only to students with need.

FINANCIAL AID PROCEDURES
Forms required: FAFSA, institutional form.

CONTACT
Michele Carroll, Financial Services Manager
5000 Market Street, Wilmington, NC 28405
(910) 392-4660

Mitchell Community College

Statesville, North Carolina
www.mitchellcc.edu Federal Code: 002947

2-year public community college in large town.
Enrollment: 2,783 undergrads.
Selectivity: Open admission; but selective for some programs.

BASIC COSTS (2012-2013)
Tuition and fees: $2,141; out-of-state residents $7,901.
Per-credit charge: $69; out-of-state residents $261.
Additional info: Student activity fee: $1.50 per credit hour up to 8 hours, $19.00 for 9 or more hours. Computer/technology fee: $1.00 per credit hour. Student accident insurance: $1.25 per semester.

FINANCIAL AID PICTURE
Students with need: Need-based aid available for full-time and part-time students.

FINANCIAL AID PROCEDURES
Forms required: FAFSA, institutional form.
Dates and Deadlines: Applicants notified on a rolling basis starting 3/1; must reply within 2 week(s) of notification.
Transfers: Students are monitored through NSLDS's Transfer Monitoring List.

CONTACT
Candace Cooper, Director of Financial Aid
500 West Broad Street, Statesville, NC 28677
(704) 878-3256

Montgomery Community College

Troy, North Carolina
www.montgomery.edu Federal Code: 008087

2-year public community college in small town.
Enrollment: 756 undergrads, 50% part-time. 100 full-time freshmen.
Selectivity: Open admission; but selective for some programs.

BASIC COSTS (2012-2013)
Tuition and fees: $2,146; out-of-state residents $7,906.
Per-credit charge: $69; out-of-state residents $261.

FINANCIAL AID PICTURE (2011-2012)
Students with need: Need-based aid available for part-time students. Work study available nights.
Students without need: No-need awards available for academics, minority status, state/district residency.

FINANCIAL AID PROCEDURES
Forms required: FAFSA, institutional form.
Dates and Deadlines: Closing date 7/1. Applicants notified on a rolling basis starting 6/1.
Transfers: Applicants notified on a rolling basis starting 6/1.

CONTACT
Doni Cody, Director of Financial Aid
1011 Page Street, Troy, NC 27371-0787
(910) 576-6222 ext. 519

Montreat College

Montreat, North Carolina
www.montreat.edu Federal Code: 002948

4-year private liberal arts college in small town, affiliated with Presbyterian Church Reformed and Independent.
Enrollment: 636 undergrads, 34% part-time. 97 full-time freshmen.
Selectivity: Admits 50 to 75% of applicants.

BASIC COSTS (2013-2014)
Tuition and fees: $22,784.
Per-credit charge: $600.
Room and board: $7,494.

FINANCIAL AID PICTURE (2012-2013)
Students with need: Out of 92 full-time freshmen who applied for aid, 82 were judged to have need. Of these, 82 received aid, and 6 had their full need met. Average financial aid package met 81% of need; average scholarship/grant was $4,120; average loan was $3,820. For part-time students, average financial aid package was $4,466.
Students without need: 6 full-time freshmen who did not demonstrate need for aid received scholarships/grants; average award was $8,833. No-need awards available for academics, alumni affiliation, athletics, leadership, music/drama, religious affiliation.
Scholarships offered: 4 full-time freshmen received athletic scholarships; average amount $1,575.
Cumulative student debt: 91% of graduating class had student loans; average debt was $38,830.

FINANCIAL AID PROCEDURES
Forms required: FAFSA, state aid form.
Dates and Deadlines: Priority date 3/1; no closing date. Applicants notified on a rolling basis starting 3/1; must reply within 2 week(s) of notification.
Transfers: Priority date 4/1; no deadline. Applicants notified on a rolling basis starting 1/15; must reply within 2 week(s) of notification.

CONTACT
Beth Pocock, Director of Financial Aid
P.O. Box 1267, Montreat, NC 28757
(800) 545-4656

Mount Olive College

Mount Olive, North Carolina
www.moc.edu Federal Code: 002949

4-year private business and liberal arts college in small town, affiliated with Free Will Baptists.
Enrollment: 3,461 undergrads, 57% part-time. 241 full-time freshmen.
Selectivity: Admits less than 50% of applicants.

BASIC COSTS (2012-2013)
Tuition and fees: $16,800.

Per-credit charge: $405.
Room and board: $6,800.

FINANCIAL AID PICTURE (2011-2012)

Students with need: Out of 219 full-time freshmen who applied for aid, 197 were judged to have need. Of these, 197 received aid, and 28 had their full need met. Average financial aid package met 73% of need; average scholarship/grant was $11,963; average loan was $2,967. For part-time students, average financial aid package was $8,098.
Students without need: 4 full-time freshmen who did not demonstrate need for aid received scholarships/grants; average award was $2,448. No-need awards available for academics, art, athletics, leadership, music/drama, religious affiliation.
Scholarships offered: 11 full-time freshmen received athletic scholarships; average amount $4,767.
Cumulative student debt: 82% of graduating class had student loans; average debt was $28,201.

FINANCIAL AID PROCEDURES

Forms required: FAFSA, state aid form.
Dates and Deadlines: Applicants notified on a rolling basis starting 3/1; must reply within 2 week(s) of notification.
Transfers: Special scholarship program available for transfers from North Carolina community colleges.

CONTACT

Katrina Lee, Director of Financial Aid
634 Henderson Street, Mount Olive, NC 28365
(919) 658-7164

Nash Community College

Rocky Mount, North Carolina
www.nashcc.edu Federal Code: 008557

2-year public community college in small city.
Enrollment: 3,200 undergrads.
Selectivity: Open admission; but selective for some programs.

BASIC COSTS (2012-2013)

Tuition and fees: $2,165; out-of-state residents $7,925.
Per-credit charge: $69; out-of-state residents $261.

FINANCIAL AID PICTURE

Students with need: Need-based aid available for full-time and part-time students.
Students without need: No-need awards available for academics.

FINANCIAL AID PROCEDURES

Forms required: FAFSA, institutional form.
Dates and Deadlines: Priority date 6/30; no closing date. Applicants notified on a rolling basis starting 7/15.

CONTACT

Tammy Lester, Financial Aid Officer
Box 7488, Rocky Mount, NC 27804-0488
(252) 451-8371

North Carolina Agricultural and Technical State University

Greensboro, North Carolina
www.ncat.edu Federal Code: 002905

4-year public university in small city.
Enrollment: 8,932 undergrads.
Selectivity: Admits 50 to 75% of applicants.

BASIC COSTS (2012-2013)

Tuition and fees: $5,059; out-of-state residents $15,657.
Room and board: $7,350.

FINANCIAL AID PICTURE

Students with need: Need-based aid available for full-time and part-time students.
Students without need: No-need awards available for academics.

FINANCIAL AID PROCEDURES

Forms required: FAFSA.
Dates and Deadlines: Priority date 3/1; no closing date. Must reply within 2 week(s) of notification.

CONTACT

Sherri Avent, Director of Student Financial Aid
Webb Hall, Greensboro, NC 27411-0002
(336) 334-7973

North Carolina Central University

Durham, North Carolina
www.nccu.edu Federal Code: 002950

4-year public university in small city.
Enrollment: 6,276 undergrads, 12% part-time. 1,244 full-time freshmen.
Selectivity: Admits 50 to 75% of applicants.

BASIC COSTS (2012-2013)

Tuition and fees: $5,119; out-of-state residents $15,692.
Room and board: $7,618.

FINANCIAL AID PICTURE (2011-2012)

Students with need: Out of 1,230 full-time freshmen who applied for aid, 1,171 were judged to have need. Of these, 1,170 received aid, and 44 had their full need met. Average financial aid package met 64% of need; average scholarship/grant was $6,142; average loan was $3,318. For part-time students, average financial aid package was $7,363.
Students without need: 15 full-time freshmen who did not demonstrate need for aid received scholarships/grants; average award was $4,265. No-need awards available for academics, alumni affiliation, art, athletics, leadership, music/drama, ROTC.
Scholarships offered: 36 full-time freshmen received athletic scholarships; average amount $24,392.
Additional info: Departmental grants based on need plus other available criteria.

FINANCIAL AID PROCEDURES

Forms required: FAFSA.
Dates and Deadlines: Priority date 3/1; no closing date. Must reply within 2 week(s) of notification.

CONTACT

Sharon Oliver, Director of Student Financial Aid
PO Box 19717, Durham, NC 27707
(919) 530-6180

North Carolina State University

Raleigh, North Carolina
www.ncsu.edu Federal Code: 002972

4-year public university in large city.
Enrollment: 23,291 undergrads, 7% part-time. 4,389 full-time freshmen.
Selectivity: Admits less than 50% of applicants. GED not accepted.

BASIC COSTS (2012-2013)

Tuition and fees: $7,788; out-of-state residents $20,953.
Room and board: $8,414.

FINANCIAL AID PICTURE (2012-2013)

Students with need: Out of 3,287 full-time freshmen who applied for aid, 2,149 were judged to have need. Of these, 2,109 received aid, and 711 had their full need met. Average financial aid package met 86% of need; average scholarship/grant was $9,771; average loan was $3,196. For part-time students, average financial aid package was $7,427.

Students without need: 168 full-time freshmen who did not demonstrate need for aid received scholarships/grants; average award was $5,982. No-need awards available for academics, alumni affiliation, athletics, leadership, ROTC, state/district residency.

Scholarships offered: ***Merit:*** Park Scholarships: 4 year scholarship that covers almost all expenses; approximately 50 awarded each year. Caldwell scholarships: awarded at end of freshmen year for 3 years covering most expenses. ***Athletic:*** 70 full-time freshmen received athletic scholarships; average amount $11,238.

Cumulative student debt: 57% of graduating class had student loans; average debt was $22,626.

Additional info: Freshman Merit Scholarships; students submitting complete admissions application by the November 1 Early Action deadline automatically considered, additional information may be required after initial review.

FINANCIAL AID PROCEDURES

Forms required: FAFSA.

Dates and Deadlines: Priority date 3/1; no closing date. Applicants notified on a rolling basis starting 4/1.

CONTACT

Julia Mallette, Associate Vice Provost and Director of Scholarships and Financial Aid
Campus Box 7103, Raleigh, NC 27695-7103
(919) 515-2421

North Carolina Wesleyan College

Rocky Mount, North Carolina
www.ncwc.edu Federal Code: 002951

4-year private liberal arts college in small city, affiliated with United Methodist Church.

Enrollment: 1,520 undergrads, 23% part-time. 223 full-time freshmen.

Selectivity: Admits less than 50% of applicants.

BASIC COSTS (2013-2014)

Tuition and fees: $26,531.

Per-credit charge: $370.

Room and board: $8,679.

FINANCIAL AID PICTURE

Students with need: Need-based aid available for full-time and part-time students.

Students without need: This college awards aid only to students with need.

Additional info: Scholarships based on GPA. Various scholarship and leadership awards available.

FINANCIAL AID PROCEDURES

Forms required: FAFSA.

Dates and Deadlines: Priority date 3/1; no closing date. Applicants notified on a rolling basis starting 1/1; must reply within 2 week(s) of notification.

Transfers: No deadline. Applicants notified on a rolling basis; must reply within 2 week(s) of notification.

CONTACT

Leah Hill, Director of Financial Aid
3400 North Wesleyan Boulevard, Rocky Mount, NC 27804
(252) 985-5295

Pfeiffer University

Misenheimer, North Carolina
www.pfeiffer.edu Federal Code: 002955

4-year private university and liberal arts college in rural community, affiliated with United Methodist Church.

Enrollment: 975 undergrads, 9% part-time. 213 full-time freshmen.

Selectivity: Admits less than 50% of applicants.

BASIC COSTS (2013-2014)

Tuition and fees: $24,210.

Per-credit charge: $540.

Room and board: $9,230.

Additional info: Commuter transportation expenses estimated by 300 miles/wk @ 30 wks/yr @ 30 miles/gal @ $4/gal.

FINANCIAL AID PICTURE

Students with need: Need-based aid available for full-time students. Work study available nights, weekends, and for part-time students.

Students without need: No-need awards available for academics, alumni affiliation, athletics, leadership, music/drama, religious affiliation, state/district residency.

Scholarships offered: Honor, Presidential, University, and Legacy Scholarships - from $3,500 to full tuition per year.

FINANCIAL AID PROCEDURES

Forms required: FAFSA, state aid form.

Dates and Deadlines: Priority date 4/15; no closing date. Applicants notified on a rolling basis starting 3/1; must reply within 2 week(s) of notification.

Transfers: Priority date 3/15.

CONTACT

Amy Brown, Director of Financial Aid
PO Box 960, Misenheimer, NC 28109
(704) 463-1360 ext. 2074

Piedmont International University

Winston-Salem, North Carolina
www.piedmontu.edu Federal Code: 002956

4-year private university and seminary college in small city, affiliated with Baptist faith.

Enrollment: 240 undergrads, 29% part-time. 26 full-time freshmen.

Selectivity: Admits 50 to 75% of applicants.

BASIC COSTS (2012-2013)

Tuition and fees: $12,395.

Per-credit charge: $480.

Room and board: $6,410.

FINANCIAL AID PICTURE

Students with need: Need-based aid available for full-time and part-time students. Work study available nights, weekends, and for part-time students.

FINANCIAL AID PROCEDURES

Forms required: institutional form.

Dates and Deadlines: Applicants notified on a rolling basis starting 3/1.

CONTACT

Alan Cox, Executive Vice President of Operations
420 South Boad Street, Winston-Salem, NC 27101-5133
(336) 714-7933

Pitt Community College

Greenville, North Carolina
www.pittcc.edu Federal Code: 004062

2-year public community and technical college in small city.
Enrollment: 9,023 undergrads.
Selectivity: Open admission; but selective for some programs.

BASIC COSTS (2012-2013)

Tuition and fees: $2,144; out-of-state residents $7,904.
Per-credit charge: $69; out-of-state residents $261.

FINANCIAL AID PICTURE

Students with need: Need-based aid available for full-time and part-time students. Work study available nights.
Students without need: No-need awards available for academics, athletics, ROTC.

FINANCIAL AID PROCEDURES

Forms required: FAFSA.
Dates and Deadlines: Priority date 3/15; no closing date. Applicants notified on a rolling basis starting 2/1.

CONTACT

Lisa Reichstein, Financial Aid Director
PO Drawer 7007, Greenville, NC 27835-7007
(252) 493-7264

Queens University of Charlotte

Charlotte, North Carolina
www.queens.edu Federal Code: 002957

4-year private university in very large city, affiliated with Presbyterian Church (USA).
Enrollment: 1,821 undergrads, 21% part-time. 360 full-time freshmen.
Selectivity: Admits 50 to 75% of applicants.

BASIC COSTS (2012-2013)

Tuition and fees: $27,576.
Per-credit charge: $526.
Room and board: $10,152.

FINANCIAL AID PICTURE (2012-2013)

Students with need: Out of 281 full-time freshmen who applied for aid, 237 were judged to have need. Of these, 237 received aid, and 37 had their full need met. Average financial aid package met 69% of need; average scholarship/grant was $18,690; average loan was $3,418. For part-time students, average financial aid package was $6,610.
Students without need: 93 full-time freshmen who did not demonstrate need for aid received scholarships/grants; average award was $11,606. No-need awards available for academics, art, athletics, leadership, minority status, music/drama, religious affiliation.
Scholarships offered: ***Merit:*** Presidential Scholarships: full tuition; based on special application/recommendations; deadline 12/13; up to 10 awarded. University Scholars (Trustee, Deans' & Alumni): range from $9,000 - $15,000; based on admitted student's academic profile. ***Athletic:*** 38 full-time freshmen received athletic scholarships; average amount $9,325.
Cumulative student debt: 80% of graduating class had student loans; average debt was $28,168.

FINANCIAL AID PROCEDURES

Forms required: FAFSA, state aid form.
Dates and Deadlines: Priority date 3/1; no closing date. Applicants notified on a rolling basis starting 3/1; must reply by 5/1 or within 3 week(s) of notification.
Transfers: No deadline. Applicants notified on a rolling basis starting 3/15; must reply by 5/1 or within 3 week(s) of notification.

CONTACT

Christy Majors, Assistant Vice President of Student Financial Services
1900 Selwyn Avenue, Charlotte, NC 28274-0001
(704) 337-2225

Randolph Community College

Asheboro, North Carolina
www.randolph.edu Federal Code: 005447

2-year public community and technical college in large town.
Enrollment: 2,814 undergrads.
Selectivity: Open admission; but selective for some programs.

BASIC COSTS (2012-2013)

Tuition and fees: $2,153; out-of-state residents $7,913.
Per-credit charge: $69; out-of-state residents $261.

FINANCIAL AID PICTURE

Students with need: Need-based aid available for full-time and part-time students. Work study available nights.
Students without need: No-need awards available for academics, leadership, minority status, state/district residency.

FINANCIAL AID PROCEDURES

Forms required: FAFSA.
Dates and Deadlines: Applicants notified on a rolling basis starting 3/1.
Transfers: No deadline. Applicants notified on a rolling basis starting 3/1.

CONTACT

Chad Williams, Director of Financial Aid
629 Industrial Park Avenue, Asheboro, NC 27205
(336) 633-0223

Richmond Community College

Hamlet, North Carolina
www.richmondcc.edu Federal Code: 005464

2-year public community college in small town.
Enrollment: 2,064 undergrads, 41% part-time.
Selectivity: Open admission; but selective for some programs.

BASIC COSTS (2012-2013)

Tuition and fees: $2,126; out-of-state residents $7,886.
Per-credit charge: $69; out-of-state residents $261.

FINANCIAL AID PICTURE

Students with need: Need-based aid available for full-time and part-time students. Work study available nights.
Students without need: No-need awards available for academics, leadership.

FINANCIAL AID PROCEDURES

Forms required: FAFSA, institutional form.
Dates and Deadlines: Closing date 7/25. Applicants notified on a rolling basis starting 7/8; must reply within 2 week(s) of notification.

CONTACT

Bruce Blackmon, Director of Financial Aid
Box 1189, Hamlet, NC 28345
(910) 410-1726

Roanoke-Chowan Community College

Ahoskie, North Carolina
www.roanokechowan.edu Federal Code: 008613

2-year public community college in small town.
Enrollment: 870 undergrads, 48% part-time. 122 full-time freshmen.

Selectivity: Open admission; but selective for some programs.

BASIC COSTS (2012-2013)

Tuition and fees: $2,167; out-of-state residents $7,927.
Per-credit charge: $69; out-of-state residents $261.

FINANCIAL AID PICTURE

Students with need: Need-based aid available for full-time and part-time students.
Students without need: No-need awards available for academics.

FINANCIAL AID PROCEDURES

Forms required: FAFSA.
Dates and Deadlines: Priority date 3/15; no closing date. Applicants notified on a rolling basis starting 7/1.

CONTACT

Crystal Harris, Financial Aid Director
109 Community College Road, Ahoskie, NC 27910-9522
(252) 862-1320

Robeson Community College

Lumberton, North Carolina
www.robeson.edu Federal Code: 008612

2-year public community college in large town.
Enrollment: 2,566 undergrads.
Selectivity: Open admission; but selective for some programs.

BASIC COSTS (2012-2013)

Tuition and fees: $2,144; out-of-state residents $7,904.
Per-credit charge: $69; out-of-state residents $261.

FINANCIAL AID PICTURE

Students with need: Need-based aid available for full-time and part-time students.

FINANCIAL AID PROCEDURES

Forms required: FAFSA.
Dates and Deadlines: Priority date 5/15; no closing date. Applicants notified on a rolling basis starting 7/31.

CONTACT

Teresa Tubbs, Director of Financial Aid
PO Box 1420, Lumberton, NC 28359
(910) 272-3352

Rowan-Cabarrus Community College

Salisbury, North Carolina
www.rowancabarrus.edu Federal Code: 005754

2-year public community and technical college in large town.
Enrollment: 6,924 undergrads.
Selectivity: Open admission; but selective for some programs.

BASIC COSTS (2012-2013)

Tuition and fees: $2,152; out-of-state residents $7,912.
Per-credit charge: $69; out-of-state residents $261.

FINANCIAL AID PICTURE

Students with need: Need-based aid available for full-time and part-time students. Work study available nights.
Students without need: No-need awards available for academics, job skills, state/district residency.

FINANCIAL AID PROCEDURES

Forms required: FAFSA.
Dates and Deadlines: Priority date 3/15; no closing date. Applicants notified on a rolling basis starting 5/1; must reply within 3 week(s) of notification.
Transfers: No deadline.

CONTACT

Lisa Ledbetter, Director, Financial Aid
Box 1595, Salisbury, NC 28145
(704) 637-0760 ext. 273

St. Andrews University

Laurinburg, North Carolina
www.sapc.edu Federal Code: 002967

4-year private liberal arts college in large town, affiliated with Presbyterian Church (USA).
Enrollment: 448 undergrads, 3% part-time. 145 full-time freshmen.
Selectivity: Admits 50 to 75% of applicants.

BASIC COSTS (2013-2014)

Tuition and fees: $23,332.
Per-credit charge: $270.
Room and board: $9,658.

FINANCIAL AID PICTURE (2011-2012)

Students with need: Out of 122 full-time freshmen who applied for aid, 104 were judged to have need. Of these, 104 received aid, and 11 had their full need met. Average financial aid package met 69% of need; average scholarship/grant was $16,114; average loan was $3,254. For part-time students, average financial aid package was $3,546.
Students without need: 41 full-time freshmen who did not demonstrate need for aid received scholarships/grants; average award was $5,546. No-need awards available for academics, art, athletics, religious affiliation.
Scholarships offered: 29 full-time freshmen received athletic scholarships; average amount $3,743.
Cumulative student debt: 76% of graduating class had student loans; average debt was $31,944.

FINANCIAL AID PROCEDURES

Forms required: FAFSA, state aid form.
Dates and Deadlines: Priority date 5/1; no closing date. Applicants notified on a rolling basis starting 3/1; must reply within 2 week(s) of notification.
Transfers: No deadline. Applicants notified on a rolling basis starting 10/1; must reply within 2 week(s) of notification.

CONTACT

Kimberly Driggers, Director of Student Financial Planning
1700 Dogwood Mile, Laurinburg, NC 28352
(910) 277-5560

St. Augustine's University

Raleigh, North Carolina
www.st-aug.edu Federal Code: 002968

4-year private liberal arts college in large city, affiliated with Episcopal Church.
Enrollment: 1,442 undergrads, 6% part-time. 455 full-time freshmen.
Selectivity: Admits less than 50% of applicants.

BASIC COSTS (2013-2014)

Tuition and fees: $17,890.
Per-credit charge: $547.
Room and board: $7,692.

FINANCIAL AID PICTURE (2011-2012)

Students with need: Out of 440 full-time freshmen who applied for aid, 440 were judged to have need. Of these, 440 received aid. For part-time students, average financial aid package was $1,918.

Students without need: 2 full-time freshmen who did not demonstrate need for aid received scholarships/grants; average award was $12,390. No-need awards available for academics, art, athletics, leadership, minority status, music/drama, religious affiliation, ROTC, state/district residency.
Scholarships offered: ***Merit:*** Institutional Merit Scholarships based on high school record, evidence of leadership, and SAT score. ***Athletic:*** 1 full-time freshmen received athletic scholarships; average amount $7,750.
Cumulative student debt: 92% of graduating class had student loans; average debt was $31,267.

FINANCIAL AID PROCEDURES
Forms required: FAFSA, institutional form.
Dates and Deadlines: Closing date 3/15. Applicants notified on a rolling basis starting 5/1; must reply within 2 week(s) of notification.
Transfers: All transfer students must submit a financial aid transcript.

CONTACT
Nadine Ford, Director of Financial Aid
1315 Oakwood Avenue, Raleigh, NC 27610-2298
(919) 516-4131

Salem College
Winston-Salem, North Carolina
www.salem.edu Federal Code: 002960

4-year private liberal arts college for women in small city, affiliated with Moravian Church in America.
Enrollment: 911 undergrads.
Selectivity: Admits 50 to 75% of applicants.

BASIC COSTS (2012-2013)
Tuition and fees: $23,478.
Room and board: $11,764.
Additional info: Tuition for a Fleer Center student will be $1,328 per full-credit class. Tuition for a Fleer student who takes courses off campus is $1,448 per full-credit course for undergraduate students. Tuition/fee waivers available for adults.

FINANCIAL AID PICTURE
Students with need: Need-based aid available for full-time and part-time students. Work study available nights, weekends, and for part-time students.
Students without need: No-need awards available for academics, alumni affiliation, leadership, minority status, music/drama, state/district residency.

FINANCIAL AID PROCEDURES
Forms required: FAFSA.
Dates and Deadlines: Priority date 3/1; no closing date. Applicants notified on a rolling basis starting 3/1; must reply by 5/1 or within 2 week(s) of notification.

CONTACT
Lori Lewis, Director of Financial Aid
601 South Church Street, Winston-Salem, NC 27108
(336) 721-2808

Sampson Community College
Clinton, North Carolina
www.sampsoncc.edu Federal Code: 007892

2-year public community college in small town.
Enrollment: 1,574 undergrads.
Selectivity: Open admission; but selective for some programs.

BASIC COSTS (2012-2013)
Tuition and fees: $2,134; out-of-state residents $7,894.
Per-credit charge: $69; out-of-state residents $261.

FINANCIAL AID PICTURE
Students with need: Need-based aid available for full-time and part-time students.
Students without need: No-need awards available for academics, state/district residency.

FINANCIAL AID PROCEDURES
Forms required: FAFSA.
Dates and Deadlines: Priority date 7/1; no closing date. Applicants notified on a rolling basis starting 7/15; must reply within 2 week(s) of notification.

CONTACT
Judye Tart, Director of Financial Aid
PO Box 318, Clinton, NC 28329
(910) 592-8084 ext. 2024

Sandhills Community College
Pinehurst, North Carolina
www.sandhills.edu Federal Code: 002961

2-year public community college in large town.
Enrollment: 4,199 undergrads.
Selectivity: Open admission; but selective for some programs.

BASIC COSTS (2012-2013)
Tuition and fees: $2,167; out-of-state residents $7,927.
Per-credit charge: $69; out-of-state residents $261.

FINANCIAL AID PICTURE
Students with need: Need-based aid available for full-time and part-time students.
Students without need: No-need awards available for academics.

FINANCIAL AID PROCEDURES
Forms required: FAFSA.
Dates and Deadlines: Closing date 6/1. Applicants notified on a rolling basis starting 5/1; must reply by 8/1 or within 4 week(s) of notification.

CONTACT
Lindsey Farmer, Director of Financial Aid
3395 Airport Road, Pinehurst, NC 28374
(910) 695-3743

Shaw University
Raleigh, North Carolina
www.shawu.edu Federal Code: 002962

4-year private university and liberal arts college in large city, affiliated with Baptist faith.
Enrollment: 2,027 undergrads, 7% part-time. 495 full-time freshmen.
Selectivity: Admits 50 to 75% of applicants.

BASIC COSTS (2012-2013)
Tuition and fees: $14,124.
Per-credit charge: $465.
Room and board: $7,844.

FINANCIAL AID PICTURE
Students with need: Need-based aid available for full-time and part-time students. Work study available nights, weekends, and for part-time students.
Students without need: No-need awards available for academics, athletics, music/drama.
Scholarships offered: Presidential Scholarship, based on GPA and SAT.

FINANCIAL AID PROCEDURES
Forms required: FAFSA.
Dates and Deadlines: Priority date 3/1; closing date 6/30. Applicants notified on a rolling basis starting 3/15.

CONTACT
Rochelle King, Dean of Enrollment Management
118 East South Street, Raleigh, NC 27601
(919) 546-8240

South College
Asheville, North Carolina
www.southcollegenc.edu Federal Code: 010264

2-year for-profit health science and career college in small city.
Enrollment: 251 undergrads, 14% part-time. 38 full-time freshmen.
Selectivity: Open admission; but selective for some programs.

BASIC COSTS (2012-2013)
Additional info: Non-Specialized Degree - Not Living w/parent: $33,430. Non-Specialized Degree - Living w/parent: $24,255. Specialized Degree - Not Living w/parent: $34,330. Specialized Degree - Living w/parent: $25,155. RN-Degree - Not Living w/parent: $35230. RN-Degree - Living w/parent: $26,055. Bachelor programs: Legal Studies $71,600, Radiological Sciences $71,600. Associate programs: Accounting $40,000, Business Administration $40,000, Criminal Justice $40,000, Medical Assisting $40,000, Nursing $42,000, Paralegal Studies $40,000, Physical Therapist Assistant $42,400, Radiologic Technology $42,400. Certificate program: Surgical Technology $25,700. Tuition amounts include fees. Books and supplies costs vary by program.

FINANCIAL AID PICTURE (2011-2012)
Students with need: 24% of average financial aid package awarded as scholarships/grants, 76% awarded as loans/jobs. Need-based aid available for part-time students.
Cumulative student debt: 96% of graduating class had student loans; average debt was $16,759.

FINANCIAL AID PROCEDURES
Forms required: FAFSA, institutional form.
Dates and Deadlines: Applicants notified on a rolling basis; must reply within 4 week(s) of notification.

CONTACT
Ronda Blackman, Financial Aid Director
140 Sweeten Creek Road, Asheville, NC 28803
(828) 398-2500

South Piedmont Community College
Polkton, North Carolina
www.spcc.edu Federal Code: 007985

2-year public community college in small city.
Enrollment: 1,903 undergrads.
Selectivity: Open admission; but selective for some programs.

BASIC COSTS (2012-2013)
Tuition and fees: $2,218; out-of-state residents $7,978.
Per-credit charge: $69; out-of-state residents $261.

FINANCIAL AID PICTURE (2012-2013)
Students with need: 98% of average financial aid package awarded as scholarships/grants, 2% awarded as loans/jobs. Need-based aid available for part-time students. Work study available nights.
Additional info: Small amount of non-federal scholarship aid available. FAFSA applications received before June 1 will receive first priority.

FINANCIAL AID PROCEDURES
Forms required: FAFSA.
Dates and Deadlines: Priority date 6/1; no closing date. Applicants notified on a rolling basis.

CONTACT
John Ratliff, Director of Financial Aid
PO Box 126, Polkton, NC 28135
(704) 272-5325

Southeastern Community College
Whiteville, North Carolina
www.sccnc.edu Federal Code: 002964

2-year public community college in small town.
Enrollment: 1,610 undergrads.
Selectivity: Open admission; but selective for some programs.

BASIC COSTS (2012-2013)
Tuition and fees: $2,154; out-of-state residents $7,914.
Per-credit charge: $69; out-of-state residents $261.

FINANCIAL AID PICTURE
Students with need: Need-based aid available for full-time and part-time students.
Students without need: No-need awards available for academics, athletics, leadership, music/drama, state/district residency.

FINANCIAL AID PROCEDURES
Forms required: FAFSA.
Dates and Deadlines: Priority date 4/1; no closing date. Applicants notified on a rolling basis starting 6/1; must reply within 2 week(s) of notification.

CONTACT
Glenn Hanson, Director of Financial Aid
4564 Chadbourn Highway, Whiteville, NC 28472-0151
(910) 642-7141 ext. 214

Southwestern Community College
Sylva, North Carolina
www.southwesterncc.edu Federal Code: 008466

2-year public community college in rural community.
Enrollment: 2,501 undergrads.
Selectivity: Open admission; but selective for some programs.

BASIC COSTS (2012-2013)
Tuition and fees: $2,160; out-of-state residents $7,920.
Per-credit charge: $69; out-of-state residents $261.

FINANCIAL AID PICTURE
Students with need: Need-based aid available for full-time and part-time students.

FINANCIAL AID PROCEDURES
Forms required: FAFSA.
Dates and Deadlines: Closing date 6/30. Applicants notified on a rolling basis starting 5/1; must reply within 2 week(s) of notification.

CONTACT
Melody Lawrence, Director of Financial Aid
447 College Drive, Sylva, NC 28779
(828) 586-4091 ext. 224

Stanly Community College
Albemarle, North Carolina
www.stanly.edu Federal Code: 011194

2-year public community college in large town.
Enrollment: 2,321 undergrads.

Selectivity: Open admission; but selective for some programs.

BASIC COSTS (2012-2013)

Tuition and fees: $2,190; out-of-state residents $7,950.

Per-credit charge: $69; out-of-state residents $261.

FINANCIAL AID PICTURE

Students with need: Need-based aid available for full-time and part-time students.

Students without need: This college awards aid only to students with need.

FINANCIAL AID PROCEDURES

Forms required: FAFSA, institutional form.

Dates and Deadlines: Applicants notified on a rolling basis starting 6/1; must reply within 2 week(s) of notification.

Transfers: No deadline. Applicants notified on a rolling basis.

CONTACT

Petra Fields, Director of Financial Aid
141 College Drive, Albemarle, NC 28001
(704) 991-0231

Surry Community College

Dobson, North Carolina
www.surry.edu Federal Code: 002970

2-year public community college in rural community.

Enrollment: 3,179 undergrads.

Selectivity: Open admission; but selective for some programs.

BASIC COSTS (2012-2013)

Tuition and fees: $2,143; out-of-state residents $7,903.

Per-credit charge: $69; out-of-state residents $261.

FINANCIAL AID PICTURE

Students with need: Need-based aid available for full-time and part-time students. Work study available nights.

Students without need: No-need awards available for academics.

FINANCIAL AID PROCEDURES

Forms required: FAFSA, institutional form.

Dates and Deadlines: Closing date 5/1. Applicants notified on a rolling basis starting 6/1; must reply within 2 week(s) of notification.

Transfers: Priority date 6/1.

CONTACT

Andrea Simpson, Director of Financial Aid
ATTN: Admissions Offfice 630 South Main Street, Dobson, NC 27017
(336) 386-3263

Tri-County Community College

Murphy, North Carolina
www.tricountycc.edu Federal Code: 009430

2-year public community college in rural community.

Enrollment: 1,200 undergrads.

Selectivity: Open admission.

BASIC COSTS (2012-2013)

Tuition and fees: $2,118; out-of-state residents $7,878.

Per-credit charge: $69; out-of-state residents $261.

FINANCIAL AID PICTURE

Students with need: Need-based aid available for full-time and part-time students.

Students without need: This college awards aid only to students with need.

FINANCIAL AID PROCEDURES

Forms required: FAFSA.

Dates and Deadlines: Priority date 6/30; no closing date. Applicants notified on a rolling basis starting 6/1; must reply within 4 week(s) of notification.

CONTACT

Diane Owl, Financial Aid Officer
21 Campus Circle, Murphy, NC 28906
(828) 837-6810

University of North Carolina at Asheville

Asheville, North Carolina
www.unca.edu Federal Code: 002907

4-year public university and liberal arts college in small city.

Enrollment: 3,259 undergrads, 10% part-time. 538 full-time freshmen.

Selectivity: Admits 50 to 75% of applicants. GED not accepted.

BASIC COSTS (2012-2013)

Tuition and fees: $5,866; out-of-state residents $19,682.

Room and board: $7,584.

FINANCIAL AID PICTURE (2011-2012)

Students with need: Out of 438 full-time freshmen who applied for aid, 283 were judged to have need. Of these, 279 received aid, and 92 had their full need met. Average financial aid package met 82% of need; average scholarship/grant was $6,728; average loan was $3,663. For part-time students, average financial aid package was $7,545.

Students without need: 28 full-time freshmen who did not demonstrate need for aid received scholarships/grants; average award was $2,909. No-need awards available for academics, alumni affiliation, art, athletics, job skills, leadership, music/drama, state/district residency.

Scholarships offered: ***Merit:*** University Laurels Program: a variety of scholarships, ranging from approximately $1,000 per year to full tuition, fees, room and board, to entering freshman who demonstrate high academic achievements. Leadership Scholarship: $1,000, renewable; solid academic record and leadership ability. ***Athletic:*** 14 full-time freshmen received athletic scholarships; average amount $11,261.

Cumulative student debt: 58% of graduating class had student loans; average debt was $17,696.

FINANCIAL AID PROCEDURES

Forms required: FAFSA.

Dates and Deadlines: Priority date 3/1; no closing date. Applicants notified on a rolling basis starting 3/15.

CONTACT

Elizabeth Bartlett, Associate Director of Financial Aid
CPO#1320, UNCA, Asheville, NC 28804-8502
(828) 251-6535

University of North Carolina at Chapel Hill

Chapel Hill, North Carolina Federal Code: 002974
www.unc.edu CSS Code: 5816

4-year public university in large town.

Enrollment: 17,918 undergrads, 2% part-time. 4,025 full-time freshmen.

Selectivity: Admits less than 50% of applicants. GED not accepted.

BASIC COSTS (2012-2013)

Tuition and fees: $7,693; out-of-state residents $28,445.

Room and board: $9,734.

FINANCIAL AID PICTURE (2011-2012)

Students with need: Out of 2,954 full-time freshmen who applied for aid, 1,713 were judged to have need. Of these, 1,713 received aid, and 1,337

had their full need met. Average financial aid package met 100% of need; average scholarship/grant was $13,982; average loan was $3,449. For part-time students, average financial aid package was $8,332.
Students without need: 138 full-time freshmen who did not demonstrate need for aid received scholarships/grants; average award was $6,885. No-need awards available for academics, alumni affiliation, art, athletics, leadership, music/drama, religious affiliation, state/district residency.
Scholarships offered: ***Merit:*** Morehead-Cain Scholarships: full tuition and expenses; based on academic merit, leadership, athletics, moral character; approximately 50 awarded. Robertson Scholarships: full tuition and expenses; based on academic merit, leadership, community service; 15 to 18 awarded. Carolina Scholars: $9,000 for in-state residents; cost of tuition, fees, room and board for non-NC residents; based on academic merit, leadership, residency specifications; 25-30 awarded with majority going to in-state residents. Pogue Scholarships: $9,000 for NC residents; cost of tuition, fees, room and board for non-NC residents; based on academic merit, leadership, involvement and interest in issues of diversity; up to 10 in-state and 3 out-of-state awarded. Colonel Robinson Scholarships: $9,000 for in-state residents; cost of tuition, fees, room and board for non-NC residents; based on academic merit; approximately 15 awarded to NC residents and 10 to non-NC residents. Old Well, College Fellows, and Founders Awards: $2,500-$6,000; based on academic merit, leadership; North Carolina residency; 15-20 awarded. ***Athletic:*** 68 full-time freshmen received athletic scholarships; average amount $20,380.
Cumulative student debt: 35% of graduating class had student loans; average debt was $16,983.
Additional info: 100% of all need met for both resident and non-resident undergraduates who quality for need based aid, with a favorable mix of approximately 2/3 grants and scholarships and 1/3 loans and work study.

FINANCIAL AID PROCEDURES

Forms required: FAFSA, CSS PROFILE.
Dates and Deadlines: Priority date 3/1; no closing date. Applicants notified on a rolling basis starting 3/15; must reply by 5/1.

CONTACT

Shirley Ort, Associate Provost and Director of Scholarships and Student Aid
Jackson Hall, Chapel Hill, NC 27599-2200
(919) 962-8396

University of North Carolina at Charlotte

Charlotte, North Carolina
www.uncc.edu Federal Code: 002975

4-year public university in very large city.
Enrollment: 21,085 undergrads, 14% part-time. 2,898 full-time freshmen.
Selectivity: Admits 50 to 75% of applicants.

BASIC COSTS (2012-2013)

Tuition and fees: $5,873; out-of-state residents $18,402.
Room and board: $8,130.

FINANCIAL AID PICTURE (2011-2012)

Students with need: Out of 2,457 full-time freshmen who applied for aid, 1,871 were judged to have need. Of these, 1,834 received aid, and 212 had their full need met. Average financial aid package met 65% of need; average scholarship/grant was $5,840; average loan was $2,976. For part-time students, average financial aid package was $7,709.
Students without need: 27 full-time freshmen who did not demonstrate need for aid received scholarships/grants; average award was $7,434. No-need awards available for academics, athletics, music/drama, state/district residency.
Scholarships offered: 78 full-time freshmen received athletic scholarships; average amount $14,221.

FINANCIAL AID PROCEDURES

Forms required: FAFSA.
Dates and Deadlines: Applicants notified on a rolling basis; must reply within 3 week(s) of notification.

CONTACT

Anthony Carter, Director of Student Financial Aid
Undergraduate Admissions- Cato Hall, Charlotte, NC 28223-0001
(704) 687-2461

University of North Carolina at Greensboro

Greensboro, North Carolina
www.uncg.edu Federal Code: 002976

4-year public university in large city.
Enrollment: 14,591 undergrads, 12% part-time. 2,498 full-time freshmen.
Selectivity: Admits 50 to 75% of applicants. GED not accepted.

BASIC COSTS (2012-2013)

Tuition and fees: $6,086; out-of-state residents $19,884.
Per-credit charge: $472; out-of-state residents $2,197.
Room and board: $7,228.

FINANCIAL AID PICTURE (2012-2013)

Students with need: Need-based aid available for full-time and part-time students.
Students without need: No-need awards available for academics, alumni affiliation, art, athletics, leadership, music/drama, state/district residency.

FINANCIAL AID PROCEDURES

Forms required: FAFSA.
Dates and Deadlines: Priority date 3/1; no closing date. Applicants notified on a rolling basis starting 3/15; must reply within 3 week(s) of notification.

CONTACT

Deborah Tollefson, Director of Financial Aid
PO Box 26170, Greensboro, NC 27402-6170
(336) 334-5702

University of North Carolina at Pembroke

Pembroke, North Carolina
www.uncp.edu Federal Code: 002954

4-year public university and liberal arts college in small town.
Enrollment: 5,310 undergrads, 17% part-time. 1,012 full-time freshmen.
Selectivity: Admits 50 to 75% of applicants.

BASIC COSTS (2012-2013)

Tuition and fees: $4,867; out-of-state residents $14,074.
Room and board: $8,630.

FINANCIAL AID PICTURE

Students with need: Need-based aid available for full-time and part-time students.
Students without need: No-need awards available for academics, alumni affiliation, art, athletics, music/drama.
Scholarships offered: Academic Scholarships, Endowed Scholarship, University Incentive Scholarship, University Scholarships for Native Americans, Epsilon Sigma Alpha Scholarship.

FINANCIAL AID PROCEDURES

Forms required: FAFSA.
Dates and Deadlines: Priority date 3/15; no closing date. Applicants notified on a rolling basis starting 4/15; must reply within 2 week(s) of notification.
Transfers: No deadline.

CONTACT
Jenelle Handcox, Director of Financial Aid
Box 1510, Pembroke, NC 28372
(910) 521-6255

University of North Carolina at Wilmington

Wilmington, North Carolina
www.uncw.edu Federal Code: 002984

4-year public university in small city.
Enrollment: 12,060 undergrads, 7% part-time. 2,051 full-time freshmen.
Selectivity: Admits 50 to 75% of applicants.

BASIC COSTS (2012-2013)
Tuition and fees: $6,122; out-of-state residents $18,225.
Room and board: $8,338.

FINANCIAL AID PICTURE (2012-2013)
Students with need: Out of 1,762 full-time freshmen who applied for aid, 1,090 were judged to have need. Of these, 1,087 received aid, and 291 had their full need met. Average financial aid package met 62% of need; average scholarship/grant was $4,534; average loan was $3,332. For part-time students, average financial aid package was $8,959.
Students without need: 36 full-time freshmen who did not demonstrate need for aid received scholarships/grants; average award was $2,026. No-need awards available for academics, art, athletics, leadership, minority status, music/drama, state/district residency.
Scholarships offered: 47 full-time freshmen received athletic scholarships; average amount $8,025.
Cumulative student debt: 58% of graduating class had student loans; average debt was $25,821.

FINANCIAL AID PROCEDURES
Forms required: FAFSA.
Dates and Deadlines: Priority date 3/1; no closing date. Applicants notified on a rolling basis starting 3/15; must reply within 3 week(s) of notification.
Transfers: No deadline. Applicants notified by 3/15; must reply within 3 week(s) of notification.

CONTACT
Emily Bliss, Director of Financial Aid and Veteran Services
601 South College Road, Wilmington, NC 28403-5904
(910) 962-3177

University of North Carolina School of the Arts

Winston-Salem, North Carolina
www.uncsa.edu Federal Code: 003981

4-year public visual arts and performing arts college in small city.
Enrollment: 752 undergrads, 2% part-time. 172 full-time freshmen.
Selectivity: Admits less than 50% of applicants.

BASIC COSTS (2012-2013)
Tuition and fees: $7,558; out-of-state residents $20,703.
Room and board: $8,160.
Additional info: Health Insurance $1,418.

FINANCIAL AID PICTURE
Students with need: Need-based aid available for full-time and part-time students. Work study available nights, weekends, and for part-time students.
Students without need: No-need awards available for academics, art, leadership, music/drama, state/district residency.

FINANCIAL AID PROCEDURES
Forms required: FAFSA.
Dates and Deadlines: Priority date 3/1; no closing date. Applicants notified on a rolling basis starting 4/1; must reply within 2 week(s) of notification.

CONTACT
Jane Kamiab, Director of Financial Aid
1533 South Main Street, Winston-Salem, NC 27127-2188
(336) 770-3297

Vance-Granville Community College

Henderson, North Carolina
www.vgcc.edu Federal Code: 009903

2-year public community college in large town.
Enrollment: 3,974 undergrads.
Selectivity: Open admission; but selective for some programs.

BASIC COSTS (2012-2013)
Tuition and fees: $2,189; out-of-state residents $7,949.
Per-credit charge: $69; out-of-state residents $261.

FINANCIAL AID PICTURE
Students with need: Need-based aid available for full-time and part-time students.
Students without need: No-need awards available for academics.

FINANCIAL AID PROCEDURES
Forms required: FAFSA.
Dates and Deadlines: Closing date 3/15. Applicants notified on a rolling basis starting 5/1; must reply within 2 week(s) of notification.

CONTACT
Kali Brown, Assistant Director of Financial Aid
Box 917, Henderson, NC 27536
(252) 492-2061

Wake Forest University

Winston-Salem, North Carolina Federal Code: 002978
www.wfu.edu CSS Code: 5885

4-year private university in small city.
Enrollment: 4,801 undergrads, 1% part-time. 1,234 full-time freshmen.
Selectivity: Admits less than 50% of applicants.

BASIC COSTS (2013-2014)
Tuition and fees: $44,742.
Per-credit charge: $1,832.
Room and board: $12,000.

FINANCIAL AID PICTURE (2012-2013)
Students with need: Out of 556 full-time freshmen who applied for aid, 495 were judged to have need. Of these, 487 received aid, and 433 had their full need met. Average financial aid package met 100% of need; average scholarship/grant was $32,846; average loan was $5,629. For part-time students, average financial aid package was $29,538.
Students without need: 51 full-time freshmen who did not demonstrate need for aid received scholarships/grants; average award was $17,809. No-need awards available for academics, alumni affiliation, art, athletics, leadership, music/drama, religious affiliation, ROTC, state/district residency.
Scholarships offered: ***Merit:*** Reynolds Scholarship: full tuition, room and board, books, fees for 4 years, also provides for summer study; 6 awarded. Joseph G. Gordon Scholarship: full tuition for 4 years; for underrepresented students with exceptional promise and leadership; 7 awarded. Carswell Scholarship: based on intellect and leadership; between 3/4 and full tuition for 4 years, including summer grant for travel and study projects; 10-12

awarded. Presidential Scholarship: for students gifted in areas such as writing, studio art, music theater, debate, leadership, dance, entrepreneurship, and community service; 20 awarded. Poteat Scholarship: $12,100; for North Carolina residents who are active members of a Baptist Church in North Carolina, must make an active contribution to church and society; 18 awarded.
Athletic: 73 full-time freshmen received athletic scholarships; average amount $42,041.
Cumulative student debt: 38% of graduating class had student loans; average debt was $33,262.
Additional info: First-year students with an annual family income of less than $40,000 will have their student loans capped at $4,000 per year during their college years. Other financial aid to the students will come from grant and scholarship increases and work-study opportunities.

FINANCIAL AID PROCEDURES
Forms required: FAFSA, CSS PROFILE, state aid form.
Dates and Deadlines: Priority date 2/15; closing date 3/1. Applicants notified on a rolling basis starting 4/1; must reply by 5/1 or within 4 week(s) of notification.

CONTACT
William Wells, Director of Financial Aid
PO Box 7305, Winston-Salem, NC 27109-7305
(336) 758-5154

Wake Technical Community College

Raleigh, North Carolina
www.waketech.edu Federal Code: 004844

2-year public community and technical college in large city.
Enrollment: 20,139 undergrads, 57% part-time.
Selectivity: Open admission; but selective for some programs.

BASIC COSTS (2012-2013)
Tuition and fees: $2,240; out-of-state residents $8,000.
Per-credit charge: $69; out-of-state residents $261.

FINANCIAL AID PICTURE
Students with need: Need-based aid available for full-time and part-time students.
Students without need: No-need awards available for academics, job skills, leadership, ROTC, state/district residency.

FINANCIAL AID PROCEDURES
Forms required: FAFSA, institutional form.
Dates and Deadlines: Priority date 3/15; no closing date. Applicants notified on a rolling basis starting 4/1; must reply within 2 week(s) of notification.
Transfers: Child care grant and NCCCS Grant and Loan Program available.

CONTACT
Regina Huggins, Dean, Student Support Services
9101 Fayetteville Road, Raleigh, NC 27603
(919) 866-5410

Warren Wilson College

Asheville, North Carolina
www.warren-wilson.edu Federal Code: 002979

4-year private liberal arts college in small city, affiliated with Presbyterian Church (USA).
Enrollment: 846 undergrads, 1% part-time. 227 full-time freshmen.
Selectivity: Admits over 75% of applicants.

BASIC COSTS (2013-2014)
Tuition and fees: $30,200.
Room and board: $8,844.

Additional info: All resident students are required to work 15 hours per week in college's work program. $3,480 earnings are credited toward tuition costs.

FINANCIAL AID PICTURE (2011-2012)
Students with need: Out of 190 full-time freshmen who applied for aid, 159 were judged to have need. Of these, 159 received aid, and 44 had their full need met. Average financial aid package met 72% of need; average scholarship/grant was $16,219; average loan was $3,112. Need-based aid available for part-time students.
Students without need: 19 full-time freshmen who did not demonstrate need for aid received scholarships/grants; average award was $4,362. No-need awards available for academics, art, athletics, leadership, religious affiliation, state/district residency.
Scholarships offered: Wilson Honor; $8,000 annually; 1 awarded. Warner Honor; $7,000 annually; 2 awarded. Transfer Honor; varies annually; 4 awarded. Sutton Honor; $1,000 annually; 20 awarded. Work Scholarship; $2,000 annually; 20 awarded. Service Scholarship; $2,000 annually; 2 awarded. Sustainability Scholarship; $2,000 annually; 2 awarded. National Merit; $4,000 annually; unlimited numbers awarded. Valedictorian/Salutatorian Scholarship; $4,000 annually; 10 awarded. North Carolina Presidential Scholarship; $4,000 annually; 30 awarded. All renewable with satisfactory academic progress and successful completion of 12 credit hours each semester.
Cumulative student debt: 64% of graduating class had student loans; average debt was $22,629.

FINANCIAL AID PROCEDURES
Forms required: FAFSA, state aid form, institutional form.
Dates and Deadlines: Priority date 4/1; no closing date. Applicants notified on a rolling basis starting 3/2; must reply by 5/1 or within 3 week(s) of notification.
Transfers: No deadline. Applicants notified on a rolling basis starting 3/1; must reply within 3 week(s) of notification.

CONTACT
Kathy Pack, Director of Financial Aid
Office of Admission, Asheville, NC 28815-9000
(828) 771-2082

Wayne Community College

Goldsboro, North Carolina
www.waynecc.edu Federal Code: 008216

2-year public community college in large town.
Enrollment: 3,189 undergrads.
Selectivity: Open admission; but selective for some programs.

BASIC COSTS (2012-2013)
Tuition and fees: $2,130; out-of-state residents $7,890.
Per-credit charge: $69; out-of-state residents $261.

FINANCIAL AID PICTURE
Students with need: Need-based aid available for full-time and part-time students. Work study available nights.
Students without need: No-need awards available for academics, job skills.

FINANCIAL AID PROCEDURES
Forms required: FAFSA, institutional form.
Dates and Deadlines: Priority date 3/15; closing date 5/1. Applicants notified on a rolling basis starting 6/1; must reply within 2 week(s) of notification.

CONTACT
Brenda Mercer, Financial Aid Director
PO Box 8002, Goldsboro, NC 27533-8002
(919) 735-5151 ext. 6735

Western Carolina University

Cullowhee, North Carolina
www.wcu.edu Federal Code: 002981

4-year public university in small town.
Enrollment: 7,796 undergrads, 13% part-time. 1,552 full-time freshmen.
Selectivity: Admits less than 50% of applicants.

BASIC COSTS (2012-2013)
Tuition and fees: $6,139; out-of-state residents $15,736.
Room and board: $6,932.

FINANCIAL AID PICTURE (2011-2012)
Students with need: Out of 1,365 full-time freshmen who applied for aid, 1,040 were judged to have need. Of these, 1,028 received aid, and 148 had their full need met. Average financial aid package met 68% of need; average scholarship/grant was $6,214; average loan was $3,344. For part-time students, average financial aid package was $4,729.
Students without need: 36 full-time freshmen who did not demonstrate need for aid received scholarships/grants; average award was $3,071. No-need awards available for academics, art, athletics, leadership, music/drama, state/district residency.
Scholarships offered: ***Merit:*** WCU awards merit-based scholarships each year to students that demonstrate excellent academic, athletic, artistic, professional, cultural and/or civic achievement. The number and amount of awards vary. ***Athletic:*** 72 full-time freshmen received athletic scholarships; average amount $9,802.

FINANCIAL AID PROCEDURES
Forms required: FAFSA, institutional form.
Dates and Deadlines: Priority date 3/15; no closing date. Applicants notified on a rolling basis starting 4/1.

CONTACT
Trina Orr, Director of Student Financial Aid
102 Camp Building, Cullowhee, NC 28723
(828) 227-7290

Western Piedmont Community College

Morganton, North Carolina
www.wpcc.edu Federal Code: 002982

2-year public community college in large town.
Enrollment: 2,620 undergrads.
Selectivity: Open admission; but selective for some programs.

BASIC COSTS (2012-2013)
Tuition and fees: $2,130; out-of-state residents $7,890.
Per-credit charge: $69; out-of-state residents $261.

FINANCIAL AID PICTURE
Students with need: Need-based aid available for full-time and part-time students.
Students without need: No-need awards available for academics.

FINANCIAL AID PROCEDURES
Forms required: FAFSA.
Dates and Deadlines: Priority date 6/1; no closing date. Applicants notified on a rolling basis starting 6/15; must reply within 2 week(s) of notification.

CONTACT
Keith Conley, Director of Financial Aid
1001 Burkemont Avenue, Morganton, NC 28655-4504
(828) 448-6042

Wilkes Community College

Wilkesboro, North Carolina
www.wilkescc.edu Federal Code: 002983

2-year public community college in small town.
Enrollment: 2,519 undergrads.
Selectivity: Open admission; but selective for some programs.

BASIC COSTS (2012-2013)
Tuition and fees: $2,165; out-of-state residents $7,925.
Per-credit charge: $69; out-of-state residents $261.

FINANCIAL AID PICTURE
Students with need: Need-based aid available for full-time and part-time students. Work study available nights.
Students without need: No-need awards available for academics, art, job skills, leadership, minority status, music/drama, state/district residency.

FINANCIAL AID PROCEDURES
Forms required: FAFSA.
Dates and Deadlines: Closing date 5/15. Applicants notified on a rolling basis starting 4/1; must reply by 8/1.
Transfers: No deadline.

CONTACT
Vickie Call, Director of Financial Aid
1328 South Collegiate Drive, Wilkesboro, NC 28697-0120
(336) 838-6146

William Peace University

Raleigh, North Carolina
www.peace.edu Federal Code: 002953

4-year private liberal arts college in large city, affiliated with Presbyterian Church (USA).
Enrollment: 791 undergrads, 12% part-time. 231 full-time freshmen.
Selectivity: Admits 50 to 75% of applicants.

BASIC COSTS (2013-2014)
Tuition and fees: $24,025.
Room and board: $9,000.

FINANCIAL AID PICTURE (2012-2013)
Students with need: Out of 221 full-time freshmen who applied for aid, 210 were judged to have need. Of these, 210 received aid, and 14 had their full need met. Average financial aid package met 74% of need; average scholarship/grant was $20,850; average loan was $3,308. For part-time students, average financial aid package was $6,222.
Students without need: 24 full-time freshmen who did not demonstrate need for aid received scholarships/grants; average award was $6,666. No-need awards available for academics, leadership, music/drama.
Cumulative student debt: 71% of graduating class had student loans; average debt was $33,147.

FINANCIAL AID PROCEDURES
Forms required: FAFSA.
Dates and Deadlines: Priority date 3/15; no closing date. Applicants notified on a rolling basis starting 3/15; must reply within 4 week(s) of notification.
Transfers: Priority date 3/1; no deadline. Applicants notified on a rolling basis starting 2/28; must reply within 4 week(s) of notification. Transfer merit scholarships available.

CONTACT
Angela Kirkley, Director of Financial Aid
15 East Peace Street, Raleigh, NC 27604-1194
(919) 508-2249

Wilson Community College

Wilson, North Carolina
www.wilsoncc.edu Federal Code: 004845

2-year public community college in large town.
Enrollment: 1,504 undergrads, 42% part-time. 224 full-time freshmen.
Selectivity: Open admission; but selective for some programs.

BASIC COSTS (2012-2013)
Tuition and fees: $2,173; out-of-state residents $7,933.
Per-credit charge: $69; out-of-state residents $261.

FINANCIAL AID PICTURE
Students with need: Need-based aid available for full-time and part-time students. Work study available nights.
Students without need: No-need awards available for academics.

FINANCIAL AID PROCEDURES
Forms required: FAFSA, institutional form.
Dates and Deadlines: Priority date 3/15; no closing date. Applicants notified on a rolling basis.
Transfers: No deadline. Applicants notified on a rolling basis.

CONTACT
Lisa Shearin, Director of Financial Aid and Veterans Affairs
Box 4305, Wilson, NC 27893-0305
(252) 246-1274

Wingate University

Wingate, North Carolina
www.wingate.edu Federal Code: 002985

4-year private university in small town.
Enrollment: 1,767 undergrads, 3% part-time. 548 full-time freshmen.
Selectivity: Admits over 75% of applicants.

BASIC COSTS (2013-2014)
Tuition and fees: $25,040.
Room and board: $9,950.

FINANCIAL AID PICTURE (2012-2013)
Students with need: Out of 509 full-time freshmen who applied for aid, 440 were judged to have need. Of these, 431 received aid, and 91 had their full need met. Average financial aid package met 86% of need; average scholarship/grant was $19,076; average loan was $3,266. For part-time students, average financial aid package was $5,917.
Students without need: 237 full-time freshmen who did not demonstrate need for aid received scholarships/grants; average award was $12,250. No-need awards available for academics, alumni affiliation, art, athletics, music/drama, religious affiliation.
Scholarships offered: 103 full-time freshmen received athletic scholarships; average amount $8,428.
Cumulative student debt: 68% of graduating class had student loans; average debt was $28,484.
Additional info: Institutional aid may not be available after June 1.

FINANCIAL AID PROCEDURES
Forms required: FAFSA, state aid form.
Dates and Deadlines: Priority date 5/1; no closing date. Applicants notified on a rolling basis starting 3/15; must reply within 2 week(s) of notification.
Transfers: Priority date 3/1; no deadline. Applicants notified on a rolling basis; must reply within 2 week(s) of notification. Must submit financial aid transcripts from previous colleges attended.

CONTACT
Teresa Williams, Director of Financial Planning
Campus Box 3059, Wingate, NC 28174-0157
(704) 233-8209

Winston-Salem State University

Winston-Salem, North Carolina
www.wssu.edu Federal Code: 002986

4-year public university and health science college in small city.
Enrollment: 5,183 undergrads, 14% part-time. 680 full-time freshmen.
Selectivity: Admits 50 to 75% of applicants.

BASIC COSTS (2012-2013)
Tuition and fees: $4,960; out-of-state residents $14,110.
Room and board: $7,506.

FINANCIAL AID PICTURE
Students with need: Need-based aid available for full-time students.
Students without need: No-need awards available for academics, athletics, ROTC, state/district residency.

FINANCIAL AID PROCEDURES
Forms required: FAFSA.
Dates and Deadlines: Priority date 5/1; no closing date. Must reply within 2 week(s) of notification.
Transfers: Closing date 3/15. Applicants notified on a rolling basis.

CONTACT
Robert Muhammad, Director of Financial Aid
601 Martin Luther King Jr Drive, Winston-Salem, NC 27110
(336) 750-3280

North Dakota

Bismarck State College

Bismarck, North Dakota
www.bismarckstate.edu Federal Code: 002988

2-year public community college in small city.
Enrollment: 4,109 undergrads.
Selectivity: Open admission; but selective for some programs.

BASIC COSTS (2012-2013)
Tuition and fees: $4,007; out-of-state residents $9,625.
Per-credit charge: $112; out-of-state residents $299.
Room and board: $5,300.
Additional info: Full-time annual tuition for residents of South Dakota, Montana, Manitoba, Saskatchewan: $4,205. Tuition/fee waivers available for minority students.

FINANCIAL AID PICTURE
Students with need: Need-based aid available for full-time and part-time students. Work study available nights, weekends, and for part-time students.
Students without need: This college awards aid only to students with need.

FINANCIAL AID PROCEDURES
Forms required: FAFSA.
Dates and Deadlines: Priority date 3/15; no closing date. Applicants notified on a rolling basis starting 6/1; must reply within 3 week(s) of notification.
Transfers: Financial aid based on funds available.

CONTACT
Jeffrey Jacobs, Director of Financial Aid
PO Box 5587, Bismarck, ND 58506-5587
(701) 224-5494

Cankdeska Cikana Community College

Fort Totten, North Dakota
www.littlehoop.edu Federal Code: 015793

2-year public community college in rural community.
Enrollment: 219 undergrads.
Selectivity: Open admission.

BASIC COSTS (2012-2013)
Tuition and fees: $3,300; out-of-state residents $3,300.
Per-credit charge: $125.

FINANCIAL AID PICTURE
Students with need: Need-based aid available for full-time and part-time students.
Students without need: This college awards aid only to students with need.

FINANCIAL AID PROCEDURES
Forms required: FAFSA, institutional form.
Dates and Deadlines: Closing date 8/20. Applicants notified on a rolling basis.

CONTACT
Dixie Omen, Financial Aid Director
Box 269, Fort Totten, ND 58335
(701) 766-1374

Dakota College at Bottineau

Bottineau, North Dakota
www.dakotacollege.edu Federal Code: 002995

2-year public nursing and junior college in small town.
Enrollment: 774 undergrads.
Selectivity: Open admission.

BASIC COSTS (2012-2013)
Tuition and fees: $3,887; out-of-state residents $5,447.
Per-credit charge: $130; out-of-state residents $195.
Room and board: $5,219.
Additional info: Full-time annual tuition for residents of South Dakota, Montana $3,901; Manitoba, Saskatchewan $3,120. Tuition/fee waivers available for minority students.

FINANCIAL AID PICTURE
Students with need: Need-based aid available for full-time and part-time students. Work study available nights, weekends, and for part-time students.
Students without need: No-need awards available for academics, alumni affiliation, athletics, minority status, music/drama, state/district residency.

FINANCIAL AID PROCEDURES
Forms required: FAFSA.
Dates and Deadlines: Priority date 4/15; no closing date. Applicants notified on a rolling basis starting 6/1; must reply within 2 week(s) of notification.

CONTACT
Valerie Heilman, Financial Aid Officer
105 Simrall Boulevard, Bottineau, ND 58318-1198
(701) 228-5437

Dickinson State University

Dickinson, North Dakota
www.dickinsonstate.edu Federal Code: 002989

4-year public university in large town.
Enrollment: 1,548 undergrads, 21% part-time. 211 full-time freshmen.
Selectivity: Open admission; but selective for some programs.

BASIC COSTS (2012-2013)
Tuition and fees: $5,718; out-of-state residents $12,978.
Per-credit charge: $188; out-of-state residents $491.
Room and board: $5,197.
Additional info: Tuition for South Dakota, Montana, Manitoba, Saskatchewan residents: $5,655. Tuition/fee waivers available for minority students.

FINANCIAL AID PICTURE (2012-2013)
Students with need: Average financial aid package met 3% of need; average scholarship/grant was $4,353; average loan was $4,113. For part-time students, average financial aid package was $6,241.
Students without need: No-need awards available for academics, alumni affiliation, art, athletics, job skills, leadership, minority status, music/drama, religious affiliation, state/district residency.
Cumulative student debt: 66% of graduating class had student loans; average debt was $20,928.

FINANCIAL AID PROCEDURES
Forms required: FAFSA.
Dates and Deadlines: Priority date 4/15; no closing date. Applicants notified on a rolling basis starting 5/15; must reply within 2 week(s) of notification.
Transfers: No deadline. Applicants notified on a rolling basis starting 5/15; must reply within 2 week(s) of notification.

CONTACT
Sandy Klein, Director of Financial Aid
291 Campus Drive, Dickinson, ND 58601-4896
(701) 483-2371

Jamestown College

Jamestown, North Dakota
www.jc.edu Federal Code: 002990

4-year private liberal arts college in large town, affiliated with Presbyterian Church (USA).
Enrollment: 890 undergrads, 2% part-time. 221 full-time freshmen.
Selectivity: Admits 50 to 75% of applicants.

BASIC COSTS (2013-2014)
Tuition and fees: $18,424.
Per-credit charge: $435.
Room and board: $6,244.

FINANCIAL AID PICTURE (2012-2013)
Students with need: Out of 186 full-time freshmen who applied for aid, 155 were judged to have need. Of these, 155 received aid, and 29 had their full need met. Average financial aid package met 71% of need; average scholarship/grant was $11,352; average loan was $3,479. For part-time students, average financial aid package was $2,997.
Students without need: 69 full-time freshmen who did not demonstrate need for aid received scholarships/grants; average award was $6,766. No-need awards available for academics, alumni affiliation, art, athletics, job skills, leadership, music/drama, religious affiliation.
Scholarships offered: ***Merit:*** Wilson Scholarships: full tuition; for academic merit and leadership. Presidential Scholarships: $9,000 annually; Other academic scholarships: $3,000 - $9,000 annually. Arnold Chemistry Scholarships: $2,500 annually; for chemistry majors. ***Athletic:*** 62 full-time freshmen received athletic scholarships; average amount $4,207.
Cumulative student debt: 82% of graduating class had student loans; average debt was $31,342.
Additional info: FAFSA must be received by March 15th for residents to be considered for North Dakota state grants.

FINANCIAL AID PROCEDURES
Forms required: FAFSA.

Dates and Deadlines: Priority date 3/15; no closing date. Applicants notified on a rolling basis starting 2/1; must reply within 2 week(s) of notification.
Transfers: No deadline. Applicants notified on a rolling basis starting 2/1; must reply within 2 week(s) of notification.

CONTACT

Margery Michael, Director of Financial Aid
6081 College Lane, Jamestown, ND 58405
(701) 252-3467 ext. 5556

Lake Region State College

Devils Lake, North Dakota
www.lrsc.edu Federal Code: 002991

2-year public community and technical college in small town.
Enrollment: 762 undergrads, 33% part-time. 203 full-time freshmen.
Selectivity: Open admission; but selective for some programs.

BASIC COSTS (2012-2013)

Tuition and fees: $3,908; out-of-state residents $3,908.
Per-credit charge: $128; out-of-state residents $128.
Room and board: $5,316.
Additional info: Tuition/fee waivers available for minority students.

FINANCIAL AID PICTURE (2012-2013)

Students with need: Out of 165 full-time freshmen who applied for aid, 125 were judged to have need. Of these, 125 received aid, and 14 had their full need met. For part-time students, average financial aid package was $7,394.
Students without need: 57 full-time freshmen who did not demonstrate need for aid received scholarships/grants; average award was $626. No-need awards available for academics, athletics, leadership, minority status, music/drama.
Scholarships offered: 12 full-time freshmen received athletic scholarships; average amount $3,869.

FINANCIAL AID PROCEDURES

Forms required: FAFSA.
Dates and Deadlines: Priority date 4/15; no closing date. Applicants notified on a rolling basis starting 5/15; must reply within 4 week(s) of notification.
Transfers: No deadline. Applicants notified on a rolling basis starting 5/15; must reply within 4 week(s) of notification.

CONTACT

Katie Nettell, Director of Financial Aid
1801 College Drive North, Devils Lake, ND 58301-1598
(701) 662-1516

Mayville State University

Mayville, North Dakota
www.mayvillestate.edu Federal Code: 002993

4-year public business and teachers college in small town.
Enrollment: 990 undergrads, 38% part-time. 149 full-time freshmen.
Selectivity: Open admission; but selective for some programs.

BASIC COSTS (2012-2013)

Tuition and fees: $6,193; out-of-state residents $8,436.
Per-credit charge: $187; out-of-state residents $280.
Room and board: $4,854.
Additional info: Full time annual tuition for South Dakota, Montana, Kansas, Michigan, Missouri, Nebraska, Manitoba, Saskatchewan residents: $5,605. Tuition/fee waivers available for minority students.

FINANCIAL AID PICTURE (2012-2013)

Students with need: Out of 131 full-time freshmen who applied for aid, 102 were judged to have need. Of these, 102 received aid, and 17 had their full need met. For part-time students, average financial aid package was $7,280.
Students without need: 59 full-time freshmen who did not demonstrate need for aid received scholarships/grants; average award was $1,098. No-need awards available for academics, athletics, leadership, minority status, music/drama, state/district residency.
Scholarships offered: 38 full-time freshmen received athletic scholarships; average amount $1,173.
Cumulative student debt: 74% of graduating class had student loans; average debt was $30,351.

FINANCIAL AID PROCEDURES

Forms required: FAFSA.
Dates and Deadlines: Priority date 2/15; no closing date. Applicants notified on a rolling basis starting 5/1; must reply within 2 week(s) of notification.
Transfers: No deadline. Applicants notified on a rolling basis starting 5/1; must reply within 2 week(s) of notification.

CONTACT

Shirley Hanson, Director of Financial Aid
330 Third Street, NE, Mayville, ND 58257-1299
(701) 788-4767

Minot State University

Minot, North Dakota
www.minotstateu.edu Federal Code: 002994

4-year public university and liberal arts college in large town.
Enrollment: 3,298 undergrads, 34% part-time. 387 full-time freshmen.
Selectivity: Admits 50 to 75% of applicants.

BASIC COSTS (2012-2013)

Tuition and fees: $5,922; out-of-state residents $5,922.
Per-credit charge: $196; out-of-state residents $196.
Room and board: $5,168.
Additional info: Tuition/fee waivers available for minority students.

FINANCIAL AID PICTURE (2011-2012)

Students with need: Out of 278 full-time freshmen who applied for aid, 170 were judged to have need. Of these, 167 received aid, and 32 had their full need met. Average financial aid package met 2% of need; average scholarship/grant was $4,048; average loan was $3,184. For part-time students, average financial aid package was $601,746.
Students without need: 58 full-time freshmen who did not demonstrate need for aid received scholarships/grants; average award was $526. No-need awards available for academics, alumni affiliation, art, athletics, minority status, music/drama, state/district residency.
Scholarships offered: 28 full-time freshmen received athletic scholarships; average amount $2,161.
Cumulative student debt: 66% of graduating class had student loans; average debt was $25,117.
Additional info: Scholarship application deadline is 2/15.

FINANCIAL AID PROCEDURES

Forms required: FAFSA.
Dates and Deadlines: Priority date 3/15; no closing date. Applicants notified on a rolling basis starting 5/1; must reply within 2 week(s) of notification.
Transfers: No deadline. Applicants notified by 5/1; must reply within 2 week(s) of notification.

CONTACT

Dale Gehring, Director of Financial Aid
500 University Avenue West, Minot, ND 58707-5002
(701) 858-3375

North Dakota State College of Science

Wahpeton, North Dakota
www.ndscs.edu Federal Code: 002996

2-year public junior and technical college in small town.
Enrollment: 3,066 undergrads, 41% part-time. 631 full-time freshmen.
Selectivity: Open admission; but selective for some programs.

BASIC COSTS (2012-2013)
Tuition and fees: $3,953; out-of-state residents $9,576.
Per-credit charge: $112; out-of-state residents $300.
Room and board: $5,474.
Additional info: Full-time annual tuition for residents of South Dakota, Montana, Manitoba, Saskatchewan: $4,209. Tuition/fee waivers available for minority students.

FINANCIAL AID PICTURE (2011-2012)
Students with need: Out of 568 full-time freshmen who applied for aid, 567 were judged to have need. Of these, 546 received aid, and 31 had their full need met. Average financial aid package met 2% of need; average scholarship/grant was $4,246; average loan was $3,869. For part-time students, average financial aid package was $4,785.
Students without need: 88 full-time freshmen who did not demonstrate need for aid received scholarships/grants; average award was $689. No-need awards available for academics, alumni affiliation, athletics, leadership, minority status, music/drama, state/district residency.
Scholarships offered: 32 full-time freshmen received athletic scholarships; average amount $2,212.
Cumulative student debt: 80% of graduating class had student loans; average debt was $15,349.

FINANCIAL AID PROCEDURES
Forms required: FAFSA, institutional form.
Dates and Deadlines: Closing date 3/15. Applicants notified on a rolling basis starting 6/1; must reply within 2 week(s) of notification.
Transfers: No deadline. Must reply within 2 week(s) of notification.

CONTACT
Shelly Blome, Director of Financial Aid
800 North 6th Street, Wahpeton, ND 58076-0001
(701) 671-2207

North Dakota State University

Fargo, North Dakota
www.ndsu.edu Federal Code: 002997

4-year public university in small city.
Enrollment: 12,028 undergrads, 8% part-time. 2,222 full-time freshmen.
Selectivity: Admits over 75% of applicants.

BASIC COSTS (2012-2013)
Tuition and fees: $7,233; out-of-state residents $17,479.
Per-credit charge: $256; out-of-state residents $683.
Room and board: $7,284.
Additional info: Full-time annual tuition for residents of South Dakota, Montana, Manitoba, Saskatchewan: $9,203. Tuition/fee waivers available for minority students.

FINANCIAL AID PICTURE (2011-2012)
Students with need: Out of 1,887 full-time freshmen who applied for aid, 1,246 were judged to have need. Of these, 1,217 received aid, and 1,214 had their full need met. Average financial aid package met 65% of need; average scholarship/grant was $3,955; average loan was $4,642. For part-time students, average financial aid package was $5,773.
Students without need: 593 full-time freshmen who did not demonstrate need for aid received scholarships/grants; average award was $1,042. No-need awards available for academics, alumni affiliation, art, athletics, leadership, minority status, music/drama, ROTC, state/district residency.
Scholarships offered: ***Merit:*** New Student Scholarships: vary in amount awarded; based on 25 ACT or 1200 SAT (exclusive of writing) and 3.5 GPA. ***Athletic:*** 65 full-time freshmen received athletic scholarships; average amount $8,400.
Cumulative student debt: 85% of graduating class had student loans; average debt was $28,738.

FINANCIAL AID PROCEDURES
Forms required: FAFSA.
Dates and Deadlines: Closing date 3/15. Applicants notified on a rolling basis starting 4/20.

CONTACT
Jeanne Enebo, Director of Student Financial Services
Ceres Hall 114, Fargo, ND 58108-6050
(701) 231-7533

Rasmussen College: Bismarck

Bismarck, North Dakota
www.rasmussen.edu

2-year for-profit career college in small city.
Enrollment: 210 undergrads.
Selectivity: Open admission; but selective for some programs.

BASIC COSTS (2012-2013)
Tuition and fees: $15,750.
Additional info: Full-time tuition varies according to program of study. Examples of per-credit-hour charges include Early Childhood Education ($310), Criminal Justice, Information Systems Management, Multimedia Technician ($350).

FINANCIAL AID PICTURE
Students with need: Need-based aid available for full-time and part-time students.

FINANCIAL AID PROCEDURES
Forms required: FAFSA, institutional form.
Dates and Deadlines: Applicants notified on a rolling basis.

CONTACT
Debora Murray, Director of Financial Services
1701 East Century Avenue, Bismarck, ND 58503
(701) 530-9600

Rasmussen College: Fargo

Fargo, North Dakota
www.rasmussen.edu Federal Code: 004846

4-year for-profit career college in small city.
Enrollment: 386 undergrads.
Selectivity: Open admission; but selective for some programs.

BASIC COSTS (2012-2013)
Tuition and fees: $15,750.
Per-credit charge: $350.
Additional info: Full-time tuition varies according to program of study. Examples of per-credit-hour charges include Early Childhood Education ($310), Criminal Justice, Information Systems Mgmt, Multimedia Technician ($350).

FINANCIAL AID PICTURE
Students with need: Need-based aid available for full-time and part-time students.

FINANCIAL AID PROCEDURES
Forms required: FAFSA, institutional form.
Dates and Deadlines: Applicants notified on a rolling basis.

CONTACT
Debora Murray, Director of Financial Aid
4012 19th Avenue SW, Fargo, ND 58103
(701) 277-3889

Sanford College of Nursing

Bismarck, North Dakota
www.bismarck.sanfordhealth.org/collegeofnursing
Federal Code: 009354

Upper-division private nursing college in small city.
Enrollment: 109 undergrads.

BASIC COSTS (2012-2013)
Tuition and fees: $10,852.
Per-credit charge: $430.

FINANCIAL AID PICTURE (2011-2012)
Students with need: Average financial aid package for all full-time undergraduates was $13,706; for part-time $6,383. 30% awarded as scholarships/grants, 70% awarded as loans/jobs. Work study available weekends and for part-time students.

FINANCIAL AID PROCEDURES
Dates and Deadlines: Priority date 4/1; no closing date. Must reply within 2 week(s) of notification.
Transfers: No deadline. Applicants notified on a rolling basis starting 6/1; must reply within 2 week(s) of notification.

CONTACT
Janell Thomas, Financial Aid Director
512 North 7th Street, Bismarck, ND 58501-4425
(701) 323-6270

Sitting Bull College

Fort Yates, North Dakota
www.sittingbull.edu
Federal Code: 014993

2-year public community college in small town.
Enrollment: 313 undergrads.
Selectivity: Open admission.

BASIC COSTS (2012-2013)
Tuition and fees: $3,910; out-of-state residents $3,910.
Per-credit charge: $125.

FINANCIAL AID PICTURE
Students with need: Need-based aid available for full-time and part-time students.

FINANCIAL AID PROCEDURES
Forms required: FAFSA, institutional form.
Dates and Deadlines: Priority date 5/1; no closing date. Applicants notified on a rolling basis starting 7/15; must reply within 6 week(s) of notification.
Transfers: No deadline. Applicants notified on a rolling basis.

CONTACT
Donna Seaboy, Financial Aid Director
9299 Hwy 24, Fort Yates, ND 58538
(701) 854-8013

Trinity Bible College

Ellendale, North Dakota
www.trinitybiblecollege.edu
Federal Code: 012059

4-year private Bible college in rural community, affiliated with Assemblies of God.
Enrollment: 227 undergrads.

BASIC COSTS (2012-2013)
Tuition and fees: $13,440.
Per-credit charge: $397.
Room and board: $5,302.

FINANCIAL AID PICTURE
Students with need: Need-based aid available for full-time and part-time students. Work study available nights, weekends, and for part-time students.
Students without need: No-need awards available for academics, alumni affiliation, art, leadership, music/drama, religious affiliation.

FINANCIAL AID PROCEDURES
Forms required: FAFSA.
Dates and Deadlines: Priority date 3/1; closing date 9/1. Applicants notified on a rolling basis starting 3/1; must reply within 3 week(s) of notification.

CONTACT
Nicole McIntosh, Financial Aid Director
50 6th Avenue South, Ellendale, ND 58436-7150
(701) 349-5787

United Tribes Technical College

Bismarck, North Dakota
www.uttc.edu
Federal Code: 014470

2-year private technical college in small city.
Enrollment: 651 undergrads.
Selectivity: Open admission; but selective for some programs.

BASIC COSTS (2012-2013)
Tuition and fees: $5,210.
Additional info: Tuition/fee waivers available for adults, minority students.

FINANCIAL AID PICTURE
Students with need: Need-based aid available for full-time and part-time students. Work study available nights, weekends, and for part-time students.

FINANCIAL AID PROCEDURES
Forms required: FAFSA.
Dates and Deadlines: Priority date 5/29; closing date 6/30. Applicants notified on a rolling basis starting 5/29; must reply within 2 week(s) of notification.

CONTACT
Sheila Morin, Financial Aid Director
3315 University Drive, Bismarck, ND 58504
(701) 255-3285 ext. 1211

University of Mary

Bismarck, North Dakota
www.umary.edu
Federal Code: 002992

4-year private university in small city, affiliated with Roman Catholic Church.
Enrollment: 3,098 undergrads.

BASIC COSTS (2012-2013)
Tuition and fees: $14,000.
Per-credit charge: $450.
Room and board: $5,520.

FINANCIAL AID PICTURE
Students with need: Need-based aid available for full-time and part-time students. Work study available nights, weekends, and for part-time students.
Students without need: No-need awards available for academics, athletics, music/drama, religious affiliation, state/district residency.

FINANCIAL AID PROCEDURES

Forms required: FAFSA.

Dates and Deadlines: Priority date 3/1; no closing date. Applicants notified on a rolling basis starting 2/1; must reply within 2 week(s) of notification.

Transfers: No deadline. Applicants notified on a rolling basis starting 2/1; must reply within 2 week(s) of notification.

CONTACT

Brenda Zastoupil, Director of Student Financial Aid
7500 University Drive, Bismarck, ND 58504-9652
(701) 355-8244

University of North Dakota

Grand Forks, North Dakota
www.und.edu Federal Code: 003005

4-year public university in small city.
Enrollment: 11,953 undergrads, 19% part-time. 1,842 full-time freshmen.
Selectivity: Admits 50 to 75% of applicants.

BASIC COSTS (2012-2013)

Tuition and fees: $7,254; out-of-state residents $17,170.
Per-credit charge: $247; out-of-state residents $661.
Room and board: $6,332.
Additional info: Full-time annual tuition for residents of South Dakota, Montana, Manitoba, Saskatchewan: $8,907. Tuition/fee waivers available for minority students.

FINANCIAL AID PICTURE (2011-2012)

Students with need: Out of 1,493 full-time freshmen who applied for aid, 1,053 were judged to have need. Of these, 1,042 received aid, and 1,036 had their full need met. Average financial aid package met 46% of need; average scholarship/grant was $3,886; average loan was $4,754. For part-time students, average financial aid package was $6,947.

Students without need: 761 full-time freshmen who did not demonstrate need for aid received scholarships/grants; average award was $1,173. No-need awards available for academics, alumni affiliation, art, athletics, job skills, leadership, music/drama, religious affiliation, ROTC.

Scholarships offered: ***Merit:*** Presidential Scholarship; $2,500-$3,000; based on 29 ACT/1290 SAT (exclusive of Writing) and 3.65 GPA; approximately 180 awarded. Community of Learner's Scholarship; $1,000 per year for 4 years; based on 24 ACT/1090 SAT (exclusive of Writing) and 3.0 GPA; approximately 600 awarded. Presidential Scholarship; $5,000 per year for 4 years; for National Merit Finalists listing UND as their first choice. ***Athletic:*** 63 full-time freshmen received athletic scholarships; average amount $8,470.

FINANCIAL AID PROCEDURES

Forms required: FAFSA.

Dates and Deadlines: Priority date 3/15; no closing date. Applicants notified on a rolling basis starting 5/15; must reply within 4 week(s) of notification.

CONTACT

Janelle Kilgore, Director of Student Financial Aid
2901 University Avenue Stop 8264, Grand Forks, ND 58202-8264
(701) 777-3121

Valley City State University

Valley City, North Dakota
www.vcsu.edu Federal Code: 003008

4-year public liberal arts and teachers college in small town.
Enrollment: 957 undergrads, 24% part-time. 175 full-time freshmen.
Selectivity: Admits over 75% of applicants.

BASIC COSTS (2012-2013)

Tuition and fees: $6,334; out-of-state residents $14,111.
Per-credit charge: $155; out-of-state residents $414.
Room and board: $5,110.
Additional info: Full-time annual tuition for residents of South Dakota, Montana, Manitoba, Saskatchewan: $5,820. Tuition/fee waivers available for minority students.

FINANCIAL AID PICTURE (2012-2013)

Students with need: Out of 155 full-time freshmen who applied for aid, 155 were judged to have need. Of these, 155 received aid, and 29 had their full need met. Average financial aid package met 4% of need; average scholarship/grant was $4,359; average loan was $3,170. For part-time students, average financial aid package was $6,092.

Students without need: 93 full-time freshmen who did not demonstrate need for aid received scholarships/grants; average award was $1,686. No-need awards available for academics, athletics, minority status, music/drama.

Scholarships offered: ***Merit:*** Presidents Scholarship: $2,500 per year for 4 years. Meredith Scholarship: $3,000 per year for 4 years; science or math students only. McCready Scholarship: tuition and books for 4 years. ***Athletic:*** 37 full-time freshmen received athletic scholarships; average amount $996.

Cumulative student debt: 78% of graduating class had student loans; average debt was $27,884.

FINANCIAL AID PROCEDURES

Forms required: FAFSA.

Dates and Deadlines: Priority date 3/15; no closing date. Applicants notified on a rolling basis starting 2/15; must reply within 4 week(s) of notification.

CONTACT

Betty Schumacher, Director of Financial Aid
101 College Street SW, Valley City, ND 58072-4098
(701) 845-7412

Williston State College

Williston, North Dakota
www.willistonstate.edu Federal Code: 003007

2-year public community and junior college in large town.
Enrollment: 524 undergrads, 25% part-time. 146 full-time freshmen.
Selectivity: Open admission; but selective for some programs.

BASIC COSTS (2012-2013)

Tuition and fees: $4,181; out-of-state residents $4,181.
Per-credit charge: $101; out-of-state residents $101.
Room and board: $6,562.
Additional info: Tuition/fee waivers available for minority students.

FINANCIAL AID PICTURE

Students with need: Need-based aid available for full-time and part-time students. Work study available nights, weekends, and for part-time students.

Students without need: No-need awards available for academics, athletics, music/drama.

FINANCIAL AID PROCEDURES

Forms required: FAFSA.

Dates and Deadlines: Priority date 3/15; no closing date. Applicants notified on a rolling basis starting 5/15.

CONTACT

Erica Renville, Financial Aid Director
1410 University Avenue, Williston, ND 58801
(701) 774-4244

Ohio

Antioch University Midwest

Yellow Springs, Ohio
www.midwest.antioch.edu Federal Code: E00553

4-year private university and branch campus college in small town.
Enrollment: 116 undergrads, 53% part-time.

BASIC COSTS (2012-2013)

Tuition and fees: $16,410.
Per-credit charge: $527.

FINANCIAL AID PICTURE

Students with need: Need-based aid available for full-time and part-time students.

FINANCIAL AID PROCEDURES

Dates and Deadlines: Applicants notified on a rolling basis.

CONTACT

Kathy John, Director of Financial Aid
900 Dayton Street, Yellow Springs, OH 45387
(937) 769-1840

Art Institute of Cincinnati

Cincinnati, Ohio
www.aic-arts.edu Federal Code: 014804

2-year for-profit visual arts college in large city.
Enrollment: 26 undergrads. 13 full-time freshmen.
Selectivity: Admits 50 to 75% of applicants.

BASIC COSTS (2013-2014)

Tuition and fees: $23,951.
Additional info: Tuition at time of enrollment locked for 2 years.

FINANCIAL AID PICTURE (2011-2012)

Students with need: Out of 12 full-time freshmen who applied for aid, 12 were judged to have need. Of these, 12 received aid.
Students without need: No-need awards available for academics, art.
Cumulative student debt: 84% of graduating class had student loans; average debt was $22,487.

FINANCIAL AID PROCEDURES

Forms required: FAFSA, institutional form.
Dates and Deadlines: Applicants notified on a rolling basis starting 9/1; must reply within 1 week(s) of notification.
Transfers: No deadline. Applicants notified on a rolling basis; must reply within 4 week(s) of notification.

CONTACT

Rita Schrand, Financial Aid Director
1171 East Kemper Road, Cincinnati, OH 45246
(513) 751-1206

Ashland University

Ashland, Ohio
www.ashland.edu Federal Code: 003012

4-year private university and liberal arts college in large town, affiliated with Brethren Church.
Enrollment: 2,536 undergrads, 6% part-time. 546 full-time freshmen.
Selectivity: Admits 50 to 75% of applicants.

BASIC COSTS (2012-2013)

Tuition and fees: $28,858.
Room and board: $9,502.
Additional info: Tuition/fee waivers available for minority students, unemployed or children of unemployed.

FINANCIAL AID PICTURE (2012-2013)

Students with need: Out of 468 full-time freshmen who applied for aid, 468 were judged to have need. Of these, 468 received aid. For part-time students, average financial aid package was $13,882.
Students without need: 51 full-time freshmen who did not demonstrate need for aid received scholarships/grants; average award was $11,968. No-need awards available for academics, alumni affiliation, art, athletics, job skills, leadership, minority status, music/drama, religious affiliation, state/district residency.
Scholarships offered: 18 full-time freshmen received athletic scholarships; average amount $13,673.
Cumulative student debt: 87% of graduating class had student loans; average debt was $36,058.

FINANCIAL AID PROCEDURES

Forms required: FAFSA.
Dates and Deadlines: Priority date 3/1; no closing date. Applicants notified on a rolling basis starting 3/1.
Transfers: No deadline. Applicants notified on a rolling basis starting 3/15. Transfer scholarships based on college GPA: $10,000 per year based on 3.75 GPA; $9,000 per year based on 3.5 - 3.74 GPA; $8,000 per year based on 3.25 - 3.49 GPA; $7,000 per year based on 3.0 - 3.24 GPA.

CONTACT

Stephen Howell, Director of Financial Aid
401 College Avenue, Ashland, OH 44805-9981
(419) 289-5002

Aultman College of Nursing and Health Sciences

Canton, Ohio
www.aultmancollege.edu Federal Code: 006487

2-year private health science and nursing college in small city.
Enrollment: 337 undergrads, 85% part-time. 3 full-time freshmen.
Selectivity: Admits over 75% of applicants.

BASIC COSTS (2012-2013)

Tuition and fees: $14,745.
Per-credit charge: $484.

FINANCIAL AID PICTURE (2011-2012)

Students with need: 28% of average financial aid package awarded as scholarships/grants, 72% awarded as loans/jobs. Need-based aid available for part-time students.
Students without need: This college awards aid only to students with need.
Scholarships offered: 1892 Scholarship; two $1,000 awards; for incoming Fall or Spring freshman based on 3.0 GPA, 25 ACT (or equivalent SAT score); one page essay and 6 credit hours per semester required.

FINANCIAL AID PROCEDURES

Forms required: FAFSA, institutional form.
Dates and Deadlines: Priority date 3/1; closing date 10/1. Applicants notified on a rolling basis starting 6/15; must reply within 2 week(s) of notification.

CONTACT

Jennie Carlson, Financial Aid Administrator
2600 Sixth Street SW, Canton, OH 44710-1799
(330) 363-6479

Baldwin Wallace University

Berea, Ohio
www.bw.edu Federal Code: 003014

4-year private university in large town, affiliated with United Methodist Church.
Enrollment: 3,428 undergrads, 12% part-time. 712 full-time freshmen.
Selectivity: Admits 50 to 75% of applicants.

BASIC COSTS (2012-2013)
Tuition and fees: $27,060.
Per-credit charge: $840.
Room and board: $7,520.
Additional info: Tuition/fee waivers available for minority students.

FINANCIAL AID PICTURE (2012-2013)
Students with need: Out of 688 full-time freshmen who applied for aid, 604 were judged to have need. Of these, 604 received aid, and 198 had their full need met. Average financial aid package met 89% of need; average scholarship/grant was $18,455; average loan was $3,530. For part-time students, average financial aid package was $6,427.
Students without need: 105 full-time freshmen who did not demonstrate need for aid received scholarships/grants; average award was $11,215. No-need awards available for academics, alumni affiliation, art, minority status, music/drama, religious affiliation, state/district residency.
Scholarships offered: Presidential Scholarship: $13,000; ACT 28 or SAT 1260 and above.
Cumulative student debt: 83% of graduating class had student loans; average debt was $31,022.

FINANCIAL AID PROCEDURES
Forms required: FAFSA.
Dates and Deadlines: Priority date 5/1; closing date 9/1. Applicants notified on a rolling basis starting 2/14.

CONTACT
George Rolleston, Director of Financial Aid
275 Eastland Road, Berea, OH 44017-2088
(440) 826-2108

Belmont College

St Clairsville, Ohio
www.btc.edu Federal Code: 009941

2-year public community and technical college in small town.
Enrollment: 2,063 undergrads.
Selectivity: Open admission; but selective for some programs.

BASIC COSTS (2012-2013)
Tuition and fees: $4,290; out-of-state residents $7,320.
Per-credit charge: $102; out-of-state residents $203.
Additional info: Tuition/fee waivers available for unemployed or children of unemployed.

FINANCIAL AID PICTURE
Students with need: Need-based aid available for full-time and part-time students.
Students without need: No-need awards available for state/district residency.

FINANCIAL AID PROCEDURES
Forms required: FAFSA.
Dates and Deadlines: Applicants notified on a rolling basis starting 6/1; must reply within 2 week(s) of notification.

CONTACT
Jody Peeler, Associate Dean of Financial Aid
120 Fox Shannon Place, St. Clairsville, OH 43950
(740) 695-8510

Bluffton University

Bluffton, Ohio
www.bluffton.edu Federal Code: 003016

4-year private liberal arts college in small town, affiliated with Mennonite Church.
Enrollment: 940 undergrads, 12% part-time. 239 full-time freshmen.
Selectivity: Admits 50 to 75% of applicants.

BASIC COSTS (2012-2013)
Tuition and fees: $27,426.
Per-credit charge: $1,124.
Room and board: $9,010.

FINANCIAL AID PICTURE (2012-2013)
Students with need: Out of 233 full-time freshmen who applied for aid, 217 were judged to have need. Of these, 217 received aid, and 106 had their full need met. Average financial aid package met 92% of need; average scholarship/grant was $19,998; average loan was $4,369. For part-time students, average financial aid package was $13,808.
Students without need: 21 full-time freshmen who did not demonstrate need for aid received scholarships/grants; average award was $12,820. No-need awards available for academics, art, job skills, minority status, music/drama, religious affiliation, state/district residency.
Cumulative student debt: 85% of graduating class had student loans; average debt was $37,879.

FINANCIAL AID PROCEDURES
Forms required: FAFSA.
Dates and Deadlines: Priority date 5/1; closing date 10/1. Applicants notified on a rolling basis starting 3/1; must reply within 3 week(s) of notification.

CONTACT
Lawrence Matthews, Director of Financial Aid
1 University Drive, Bluffton, OH 45817-2104
(419) 358-3266

Bowling Green State University

Bowling Green, Ohio
www.bgsu.edu Federal Code: 003018

4-year public university in large town.
Enrollment: 14,514 undergrads, 6% part-time. 3,810 full-time freshmen.
Selectivity: Admits 50 to 75% of applicants.

BASIC COSTS (2012-2013)
Tuition and fees: $10,514; out-of-state residents $17,822.
Per-credit charge: $371; out-of-state residents $676.
Room and board: $8,064.

FINANCIAL AID PICTURE (2011-2012)
Students with need: Out of 3,419 full-time freshmen who applied for aid, 2,834 were judged to have need. Of these, 2,834 received aid, and 341 had their full need met. Average financial aid package met 78% of need; average scholarship/grant was $6,021; average loan was $6,245. For part-time students, average financial aid package was $10,160.
Students without need: 751 full-time freshmen who did not demonstrate need for aid received scholarships/grants; average award was $3,723. No-need awards available for academics, alumni affiliation, art, athletics, leadership, minority status, music/drama, ROTC, state/district residency.
Scholarships offered: 79 full-time freshmen received athletic scholarships; average amount $15,721.
Cumulative student debt: 80% of graduating class had student loans; average debt was $31,262.

FINANCIAL AID PROCEDURES
Forms required: FAFSA.

Dates and Deadlines: Applicants notified on a rolling basis starting 4/15; must reply within 3 week(s) of notification.

CONTACT

Laura Emch, Director, Financial Aid
110 McFall Center, Bowling Green, OH 43403-0085
(419) 372-2651

Bowling Green State University: Firelands College

Huron, Ohio
www.firelands.bgsu.edu Federal Code: 003018

2-year public branch campus college in small town.
Enrollment: 1,786 undergrads, 34% part-time. 324 full-time freshmen.
Selectivity: Open admission.

BASIC COSTS (2012-2013)

Tuition and fees: $4,850; out-of-state residents $12,158.
Per-credit charge: $192; out-of-state residents $506.

FINANCIAL AID PICTURE

Students with need: Need-based aid available for full-time and part-time students.
Students without need: This college awards aid only to students with need.
Scholarships offered: FOCUS Scholarship (Firelands Opportunities in College for Under-represented Students); full tuition; for historically under-represented students in all Firelands majors; 4-6 awards annually.
Additional info: Scholarship application deadline May 1. Technology computer loan program available. Based on need, students may receive computer on semester by semester loan basis.

FINANCIAL AID PROCEDURES

Forms required: FAFSA.
Dates and Deadlines: Priority date 3/1; no closing date. Applicants notified on a rolling basis starting 4/15; must reply within 2 week(s) of notification.

CONTACT

Debralee Divers, Director of Enrollment Mgmt & Student Retention Services
One University Drive, Huron, OH 44839-9719
(419) 433-5560

Brown Mackie College: Cincinnati

Cincinnati, Ohio
www.brownmackie.edu Federal Code: 005127

2-year for-profit business and nursing college in large city.
Enrollment: 1,522 undergrads.
Selectivity: Open admission; but selective for some programs.

BASIC COSTS (2012-2013)

Tuition and fees: $13,230.
Per-credit charge: $294.

FINANCIAL AID PICTURE

Students with need: Need-based aid available for full-time and part-time students.
Students without need: This college awards aid only to students with need.

FINANCIAL AID PROCEDURES

Forms required: FAFSA, state aid form, institutional form.
Dates and Deadlines: Priority date 3/15; no closing date. Applicants notified on a rolling basis.

CONTACT

Charlene Howard, Director of Financial Aid
1011 Glendale-Milford Road, Cincinnati, OH 45215
(513) 771-2424

Brown Mackie College: Findlay

Findlay, Ohio
www.brownmackie.edu Federal Code: 026162

2-year for-profit business and junior college in small city.
Enrollment: 742 undergrads.
Selectivity: Open admission.

BASIC COSTS (2012-2013)

Tuition and fees: $13,230.
Per-credit charge: $294.

FINANCIAL AID PICTURE

Students with need: Need-based aid available for full-time and part-time students. Work study available nights, weekends, and for part-time students.
Students without need: No-need awards available for academics, state/district residency.

FINANCIAL AID PROCEDURES

Forms required: FAFSA.
Transfers: No deadline.

CONTACT

Heidi Bright, Director of Financial Aid
1700 Fostoria Avenue, Suite 100, Findlay, OH 45840
(419) 423-2211

Brown Mackie College: North Canton

Canton, Ohio
www.brownmackie.edu Federal Code: 030778

2-year for-profit career college in small city.
Enrollment: 543 undergrads.
Selectivity: Open admission.

FINANCIAL AID PICTURE

Students with need: Work study available nights.

FINANCIAL AID PROCEDURES

Forms required: FAFSA.

CONTACT

Jessica Petitte, Director of Student Financial Services
4300 Munson Street Northwest, Canton, OH 44718-3674

Bryant & Stratton College: Cleveland

Cleveland, Ohio
www.bryantstratton.edu Federal Code: 022744

2-year for-profit technical and career college in very large city.
Enrollment: 739 undergrads.
Selectivity: Open admission; but selective for some programs.

BASIC COSTS (2012-2013)

Tuition and fees: $16,050.
Per-credit charge: $535.
Additional info: Tuition and fees may vary by program.

FINANCIAL AID PICTURE

Students with need: Need-based aid available for full-time and part-time students. Work study available nights.

Students without need: No-need awards available for academics.

FINANCIAL AID PROCEDURES

Forms required: FAFSA, institutional form.

Dates and Deadlines: Closing date 9/22. Applicants notified on a rolling basis starting 5/1; must reply within 2 week(s) of notification.

Transfers: No deadline. By state regulation, Ohio Institutional Grant can be awarded only 3 times a fiscal year.

CONTACT

Donna Logan, Financial Aid Manager
3121 Euclid Avenue, Cleveland, OH 44115
(216) 771-1700

Bryant & Stratton College: Eastlake

Eastlake, Ohio
www.bryantstratton.edu Federal Code: 022744

4-year for-profit business college in small town.
Enrollment: 731 undergrads.
Selectivity: Open admission.

BASIC COSTS (2012-2013)

Tuition and fees: $16,050.
Per-credit charge: $535.
Additional info: Tuition and fees may vary by program.

FINANCIAL AID PICTURE

Students with need: Need-based aid available for full-time and part-time students.

Students without need: No-need awards available for academics.

FINANCIAL AID PROCEDURES

Forms required: FAFSA.

Dates and Deadlines: Applicants notified on a rolling basis.

CONTACT

Lisa Wolf, Financial Aid Manager
35350 Curtis Boulevard, Eastlake, OH 44095
(440) 510-1112

Bryant & Stratton College: Parma

Parma, Ohio
www.bryantstratton.edu Federal Code: 015298

4-year for-profit nursing and junior college in small city.
Enrollment: 739 undergrads.
Selectivity: Open admission; but selective for some programs.

BASIC COSTS (2012-2013)

Tuition and fees: $16,050.
Per-credit charge: $535.
Additional info: Tuition and fees may vary by program.

FINANCIAL AID PICTURE

Students with need: Need-based aid available for full-time and part-time students. Work study available nights.

Students without need: This college awards aid only to students with need.

FINANCIAL AID PROCEDURES

Forms required: FAFSA.

Dates and Deadlines: Closing date 9/22. Applicants notified on a rolling basis starting 6/1.

Transfers: Transfer form must be completed for state grant.

CONTACT

Laura Shannon, Financial Services Manager
12955 Snow Road, Parma, OH 44130-1013
(216) 265-3151 ext. 231

Capital University

Columbus, Ohio
www.capital.edu Federal Code: 003023

4-year private university in very large city, affiliated with Evangelical Lutheran Church in America.
Enrollment: 2,606 undergrads, 8% part-time. 625 full-time freshmen.
Selectivity: Admits 50 to 75% of applicants.

BASIC COSTS (2012-2013)

Tuition and fees: $31,364.
Per-credit charge: $1,045.
Room and board: $8,460.

FINANCIAL AID PICTURE (2011-2012)

Students with need: Out of 600 full-time freshmen who applied for aid, 556 were judged to have need. Of these, 556 received aid, and 96 had their full need met. Average financial aid package met 76% of need; average scholarship/grant was $18,701; average loan was $3,753. For part-time students, average financial aid package was $6,773.

Students without need: 69 full-time freshmen who did not demonstrate need for aid received scholarships/grants; average award was $16,697. No-need awards available for academics, alumni affiliation, art, leadership, minority status, music/drama, religious affiliation, state/district residency.

Scholarships offered: Scholarships and grants; $1,000 to full tuition.

Cumulative student debt: 79% of graduating class had student loans; average debt was $33,200.

FINANCIAL AID PROCEDURES

Forms required: FAFSA.

Dates and Deadlines: Priority date 3/1; no closing date. Applicants notified on a rolling basis starting 3/25; must reply by 5/1.

Transfers: Priority date 7/15.

CONTACT

Susan Kannenwischer, Director of Financial Aid
1 College and Main, Columbus, OH 43209-2394
(614) 236-6511

Case Western Reserve University

Cleveland, Ohio Federal Code: E00077
www.case.edu CSS Code: 1105

4-year private university in very large city.
Enrollment: 4,278 undergrads, 1% part-time. 1,371 full-time freshmen.
Selectivity: Admits 50 to 75% of applicants.

BASIC COSTS (2012-2013)

Tuition and fees: $40,490.
Per-credit charge: $1,672.
Room and board: $12,436.

FINANCIAL AID PICTURE (2012-2013)

Students with need: Out of 1,080 full-time freshmen who applied for aid, 855 were judged to have need. Of these, 853 received aid. Average financial aid package met 88% of need; average scholarship/grant was $29,227; average loan was $3,889. For part-time students, average financial aid package was $18,564.

Students without need: 350 full-time freshmen who did not demonstrate need for aid received scholarships/grants; average award was $23,626. No-need awards available for academics, alumni affiliation, art, leadership, music/drama.

Cumulative student debt: 52% of graduating class had student loans; average debt was $39,886.

FINANCIAL AID PROCEDURES

Forms required: FAFSA, CSS PROFILE, institutional form.
Dates and Deadlines: Priority date 2/15; closing date 5/15. Applicants notified on a rolling basis starting 3/15; must reply within 2 week(s) of notification.
Transfers: Priority date 3/15.

CONTACT

Venus Puliafico, Director of University Financial Aid
Wolstein Hall, Cleveland, OH 44106-7055
(216) 368-4530

Cedarville University

Cedarville, Ohio
www.cedarville.edu Federal Code: 003025

4-year private university and liberal arts college in small town, affiliated with Baptist faith.
Enrollment: 3,102 undergrads, 2% part-time. 926 full-time freshmen.
Selectivity: Admits over 75% of applicants.

BASIC COSTS (2013-2014)

Tuition and fees: $26,320.
Room and board: $5,750.

FINANCIAL AID PICTURE (2011-2012)

Students with need: Out of 813 full-time freshmen who applied for aid, 666 were judged to have need. Of these, 666 received aid, and 120 had their full need met. Average financial aid package met 31% of need; average scholarship/grant was $3,684; average loan was $4,712. For part-time students, average financial aid package was $13,426.
Students without need: 175 full-time freshmen who did not demonstrate need for aid received scholarships/grants; average award was $18,636. No-need awards available for academics, alumni affiliation, athletics, leadership, minority status, music/drama, ROTC, state/district residency.
Scholarships offered: 48 full-time freshmen received athletic scholarships; average amount $6,047.
Cumulative student debt: 69% of graduating class had student loans; average debt was $28,251.

FINANCIAL AID PROCEDURES

Forms required: FAFSA.
Dates and Deadlines: Priority date 3/1; no closing date. Applicants notified on a rolling basis starting 3/1; must reply within 4 week(s) of notification.
Transfers: No deadline. Applicants notified on a rolling basis starting 2/1.

CONTACT

Fred Merritt, Director of Financial Aid
251 North Main Street, Cedarville, OH 45314-0601
(937) 766-4969

Central Ohio Technical College

Newark, Ohio
www.cotc.edu Federal Code: 011046

2-year public technical college in large town.
Enrollment: 3,513 undergrads, 68% part-time. 256 full-time freshmen.
Selectivity: Open admission; but selective for some programs.

BASIC COSTS (2012-2013)

Tuition and fees: $4,200; out-of-state residents $6,960.
Per-credit charge: $175; out-of-state residents $290.

FINANCIAL AID PICTURE (2011-2012)

Students with need: 3% of average financial aid package awarded as scholarships/grants, 97% awarded as loans/jobs. Need-based aid available for part-time students. Work study available nights, weekends, and for part-time students.
Students without need: No-need awards available for academics, state/district residency.
Scholarships offered: Presidential Achievement Award; $1,800 annually; based on 3.0 GPA; 5 awarded. Minority Achievement Award; $850 annually; based on 2.5 GPA; 2 awarded.

FINANCIAL AID PROCEDURES

Forms required: FAFSA.
Dates and Deadlines: Priority date 2/15; no closing date. Applicants notified on a rolling basis starting 5/1; must reply within 3 week(s) of notification.

CONTACT

Faith Phillips, Director of Financial Aid
1179 University Drive, Newark, OH 43055
(740) 366-9435

Central State University

Wilberforce, Ohio
www.centralstate.edu Federal Code: 003026

4-year public university and liberal arts college in rural community.
Enrollment: 2,090 undergrads, 10% part-time. 503 full-time freshmen.
Selectivity: Admits less than 50% of applicants.

BASIC COSTS (2012-2013)

Tuition and fees: $5,870; out-of-state residents $13,090.
Per-credit charge: $161; out-of-state residents $486.
Room and board: $8,782.
Additional info: Required fees include annual health fee $518.

FINANCIAL AID PICTURE (2012-2013)

Students with need: 29% of average financial aid package awarded as scholarships/grants, 71% awarded as loans/jobs. Need-based aid available for part-time students. Work study available nights, weekends, and for part-time students.
Students without need: No-need awards available for academics, alumni affiliation, art, athletics, leadership, music/drama, religious affiliation, ROTC.

FINANCIAL AID PROCEDURES

Forms required: FAFSA, institutional form.
Dates and Deadlines: Priority date 2/15; no closing date. Applicants notified on a rolling basis starting 5/1.
Transfers: No deadline.

CONTACT

Sonia Slomba, Director, Student Financial Aid Office
PO Box 1004, Wilberforce, OH 45384-1004
(937) 376-6519

Chatfield College

St. Martin, Ohio
www.chatfield.edu Federal Code: 010880

2-year private liberal arts college in rural community, affiliated with Roman Catholic Church.
Enrollment: 562 undergrads.
Selectivity: Open admission.

BASIC COSTS (2012-2013)

Tuition and fees: $10,456.
Per-credit charge: $335.

FINANCIAL AID PICTURE
Students with need: Need-based aid available for full-time and part-time students.
Students without need: No-need awards available for academics, leadership.
Additional info: Institutional grants/scholarships given primarily to first-year students to reduce debt load during initial year.

FINANCIAL AID PROCEDURES
Forms required: FAFSA, institutional form.
Dates and Deadlines: Priority date 5/1; closing date 8/3. Applicants notified on a rolling basis starting 4/1; must reply within 2 week(s) of notification.

CONTACT
Dawn Hundley
20918 State Route 251, St. Martin, OH 45118
(513) 875-3344

Cincinnati Christian University
Cincinnati, Ohio
www.ccuniversity.edu Federal Code: 003029

4-year private university in very large city, affiliated with Christian Church.
Enrollment: 678 undergrads.

BASIC COSTS (2012-2013)
Tuition and fees: $15,266.
Per-credit charge: $527.
Room and board: $6,560.

FINANCIAL AID PICTURE
Students with need: Need-based aid available for full-time and part-time students. Work study available nights, weekends, and for part-time students.
Students without need: No-need awards available for academics, alumni affiliation, athletics, leadership, music/drama, religious affiliation.

FINANCIAL AID PROCEDURES
Forms required: FAFSA.
Dates and Deadlines: Priority date 3/1; no closing date. Applicants notified on a rolling basis starting 4/1.
Transfers: No deadline.

CONTACT
Marcella Farmer, Financial Aid Director
2700 Glenway Avenue, Cincinnati, OH 45204-3200
(513) 244-8100 ext. 8450

Cincinnati College of Mortuary Science
Cincinnati, Ohio
www.ccms.edu Federal Code: 010906

2-year private school of mortuary science in large city.
Enrollment: 108 undergrads.

BASIC COSTS (2012-2013)
Per-credit charge: $225.
Additional info: Tuition for 4-quarter A.A.S. $16,875; 5-quarter B.M.S. $20,250. $100 lab fee per quarter.

FINANCIAL AID PICTURE
Students with need: Need-based aid available for full-time and part-time students.
Students without need: This college awards aid only to students with need.

FINANCIAL AID PROCEDURES
Forms required: FAFSA.
Transfers: No deadline.

CONTACT
Financial Aid Officer
645 West North Bend Road, Cincinnati, OH 45224-1428
(513) 761-2020

Cincinnati State Technical and Community College
Cincinnati, Ohio
www.cincinnatistate.edu Federal Code: 010345

2-year public community and technical college in large city.
Enrollment: 9,453 undergrads, 59% part-time. 862 full-time freshmen.
Selectivity: Open admission; but selective for some programs.

BASIC COSTS (2012-2013)
Tuition and fees: $4,523; out-of-state residents $8,788.

FINANCIAL AID PICTURE
Students with need: Need-based aid available for full-time and part-time students. Work study available nights, weekends, and for part-time students.
Students without need: No-need awards available for academics, athletics, state/district residency.

FINANCIAL AID PROCEDURES
Forms required: FAFSA.
Dates and Deadlines: Priority date 2/15; no closing date. Applicants notified on a rolling basis starting 3/15; must reply within 4 week(s) of notification.

CONTACT
LaSaundra Craig, Director of Student Financial Aid/Scholarships
3520 Central Parkway, Cincinnati, OH 45223-2690
(513) 569-1530

Clark State Community College
Springfield, Ohio
www.clarkstate.edu Federal Code: 004852

2-year public community college in small city.
Enrollment: 4,977 undergrads.
Selectivity: Open admission; but selective for some programs.

BASIC COSTS (2012-2013)
Tuition and fees: $3,983; out-of-state residents $7,425.
Per-credit charge: $115; out-of-state residents $230.

FINANCIAL AID PICTURE
Students with need: Work study available nights, weekends, and for part-time students.

FINANCIAL AID PROCEDURES
Forms required: FAFSA.
Dates and Deadlines: Priority date 6/15; no closing date. Applicants notified on a rolling basis.
Transfers: No deadline. Applicants notified on a rolling basis.

CONTACT
Kathy Klay, Director of Financial Aid
Box 570, Springfield, OH 45501-0570
(937) 328-6034

Cleveland Institute of Art
Cleveland, Ohio
www.cia.edu Federal Code: 003982

4-year private visual arts college in large city.
Enrollment: 549 undergrads, 1% part-time. 140 full-time freshmen.

Selectivity: Admits 50 to 75% of applicants.

BASIC COSTS (2013-2014)
Tuition and fees: $36,200.
Per-credit charge: $1,415.
Room and board: $12,250.

FINANCIAL AID PICTURE (2011-2012)
Students with need: Out of 123 full-time freshmen who applied for aid, 119 were judged to have need. Of these, 119 received aid, and 4 had their full need met. Average financial aid package met 60% of need; average scholarship/grant was $20,787; average loan was $4,597. For part-time students, average financial aid package was $9,400.
Students without need: 19 full-time freshmen who did not demonstrate need for aid received scholarships/grants; average award was $11,845. No-need awards available for academics, art.
Cumulative student debt: 86% of graduating class had student loans; average debt was $32,080.

FINANCIAL AID PROCEDURES
Forms required: FAFSA.
Dates and Deadlines: Closing date 3/15. Applicants notified on a rolling basis starting 3/16; must reply within 2 week(s) of notification.
Transfers: No deadline. Applicants notified on a rolling basis starting 4/1; must reply within 2 week(s) of notification.

CONTACT
Martin Carney, Director of Financial Aid
11141 East Boulevard, Cleveland, OH 44106-1710
(216) 421-7425

Cleveland Institute of Music
Cleveland, Ohio
www.cim.edu
Federal Code: 003031
CSS Code: 1124

4-year private music college in very large city.
Enrollment: 251 undergrads. 51 full-time freshmen.
Selectivity: Admits less than 50% of applicants.

BASIC COSTS (2012-2013)
Tuition and fees: $41,620.
Per-credit charge: $1,679.
Room and board: $12,198.

FINANCIAL AID PICTURE (2011-2012)
Students with need: Out of 49 full-time freshmen who applied for aid, 38 were judged to have need. Of these, 38 received aid, and 12 had their full need met. Average financial aid package met 68% of need; average scholarship/grant was $21,756; average loan was $4,250. For part-time students, average financial aid package was $23,411.
Students without need: 12 full-time freshmen who did not demonstrate need for aid received scholarships/grants; average award was $16,010. No-need awards available for academics, music/drama.

FINANCIAL AID PROCEDURES
Forms required: FAFSA. CSS Profile is now required for all applications.
Dates and Deadlines: Priority date 2/15; no closing date. Applicants notified on a rolling basis starting 4/1; must reply by 5/1 or within 2 week(s) of notification.
Transfers: Applicants notified on a rolling basis starting 4/1; must reply by 5/1 or within 2 week(s) of notification.

CONTACT
Kristie Gripp, Director of Financial Aid
11021 East Boulevard, Cleveland, OH 44106
(216) 795-3192

Cleveland State University
Cleveland, Ohio
www.csuohio.edu
Federal Code: 003032

4-year public university in large city.
Enrollment: 11,170 undergrads, 24% part-time. 1,531 full-time freshmen.
Selectivity: Admits 50 to 75% of applicants.

BASIC COSTS (2012-2013)
Tuition and fees: $9,314; out-of-state residents $12,436.
Per-credit charge: $386; out-of-state residents $516.
Room and board: $11,162.

FINANCIAL AID PICTURE (2012-2013)
Students with need: Out of 1,334 full-time freshmen who applied for aid, 1,207 were judged to have need. Of these, 1,197 received aid, and 79 had their full need met. Average financial aid package met 48% of need; average scholarship/grant was $6,853; average loan was $3,321. For part-time students, average financial aid package was $5,896.
Students without need: 81 full-time freshmen who did not demonstrate need for aid received scholarships/grants; average award was $5,298. No-need awards available for academics, alumni affiliation, art, athletics, leadership, minority status, music/drama, religious affiliation, ROTC.
Scholarships offered: 22 full-time freshmen received athletic scholarships; average amount $10,175.
Cumulative student debt: 57% of graduating class had student loans; average debt was $23,436.

FINANCIAL AID PROCEDURES
Forms required: FAFSA.
Dates and Deadlines: Priority date 2/15; no closing date. Applicants notified on a rolling basis starting 3/15; must reply within 4 week(s) of notification.

CONTACT
Rachel Schmidt, Director of Financial Aid
2121 Euclid Avenue, Cleveland, OH 44115-2214
(888) 278-6446

College of Mount St. Joseph
Cincinnati, Ohio
www.msj.edu
Federal Code: 003033

4-year private liberal arts college in very large city, affiliated with Roman Catholic Church.
Enrollment: 1,688 undergrads, 27% part-time. 274 full-time freshmen.
Selectivity: Admits 50 to 75% of applicants.

BASIC COSTS (2012-2013)
Tuition and fees: $25,100.
Per-credit charge: $495.
Room and board: $7,860.

FINANCIAL AID PICTURE (2012-2013)
Students with need: Average financial aid package met 54% of need; average scholarship/grant was $15,735; average loan was $4,042. Need-based aid available for part-time students.
Students without need: No-need awards available for academics, alumni affiliation, art, leadership, music/drama, ROTC, state/district residency.
Scholarships offered: Elizabeth Seton Scholarship; $13,000; 30-36 ACT 1330 SAT. Presidential Scholarship; $11,500; 26-36 ACT or 1170 SAT. Trustee Scholarship; $10,500; 24-25 ACT or 1090 SAT. Dean's Scholarship; $9,500; 22-23 ACT or 1020 SAT. Merit Award; $8,500; 20-21 ACT or 940 SAT.

FINANCIAL AID PROCEDURES
Forms required: FAFSA.
Dates and Deadlines: Priority date 3/1; no closing date. Applicants notified on a rolling basis starting 1/31; must reply by 5/1 or within 4 week(s) of notification.

Transfers: Applicants notified on a rolling basis starting 2/15; must reply within 4 week(s) of notification. Transfer Scholarship; $5,000; 3.0 college GPA with at least 24 hours earned.

CONTACT

Kathryn Kelly, Director of Student Administrative Services
5701 Delhi Road, Cincinnati, OH 45233-1670
(513) 244-4418

College of Wooster

Wooster, Ohio
www.wooster.edu
Federal Code: 003037
CSS Code: 1134

4-year private liberal arts college in large town.
Enrollment: 2,038 undergrads. 573 full-time freshmen.
Selectivity: Admits 50 to 75% of applicants.

BASIC COSTS (2012-2013)

Tuition and fees: $39,810.
Room and board: $9,590.

FINANCIAL AID PICTURE (2012-2013)

Students with need: Out of 435 full-time freshmen who applied for aid, 376 were judged to have need. Of these, 376 received aid, and 238 had their full need met. Average financial aid package met 95% of need; average scholarship/grant was $28,247; average loan was $5,072. Need-based aid available for part-time students.
Students without need: 190 full-time freshmen who did not demonstrate need for aid received scholarships/grants; average award was $17,410. No-need awards available for academics, minority status, music/drama, religious affiliation.
Cumulative student debt: 49% of graduating class had student loans; average debt was $26,750.

FINANCIAL AID PROCEDURES

Forms required: FAFSA, institutional form. Either CSS PROFILE or institution application from prospective students.
Dates and Deadlines: Priority date 2/15; no closing date. Applicants notified on a rolling basis starting 3/1; must reply by 5/1 or within 2 week(s) of notification.
Transfers: Priority date 4/1; no deadline. Applicants notified on a rolling basis.

CONTACT

Joseph Winge, Director of Financial Aid
Gault Admissions Center, Wooster, OH 44691-2363
(330) 263-2317

Columbus College of Art and Design

Columbus, Ohio
www.ccad.edu
Federal Code: 003039

4-year private visual arts college in very large city.
Enrollment: 1,317 undergrads, 4% part-time. 264 full-time freshmen.
Selectivity: Admits over 75% of applicants.

BASIC COSTS (2012-2013)

Tuition and fees: $27,504.
Per-credit charge: $1,146.
Room and board: $7,260.

FINANCIAL AID PICTURE (2012-2013)

Students with need: Out of 247 full-time freshmen who applied for aid, 232 were judged to have need. Of these, 223 received aid, and 12 had their full need met. Average financial aid package met 50% of need; average scholarship/grant was $15,283; average loan was $4,835. For part-time students, average financial aid package was $7,769.
Students without need: 38 full-time freshmen who did not demonstrate need for aid received scholarships/grants; average award was $11,105. No-need awards available for academics, art, ROTC, state/district residency.

FINANCIAL AID PROCEDURES

Forms required: FAFSA.
Dates and Deadlines: Closing date 3/1. Applicants notified on a rolling basis starting 3/15; must reply within 2 week(s) of notification.
Transfers: Closing date 3/15.

CONTACT

Anna Marie Schofield, Director of Financial Aid
60 Cleveland Avenue, Columbus, OH 43215-3875
(614) 222-3274

Columbus State Community College

Columbus, Ohio
www.cscc.edu
Federal Code: 006867

2-year public community and technical college in very large city.
Enrollment: 13,014 undergrads.
Selectivity: Open admission; but selective for some programs.

BASIC COSTS (2012-2013)

Tuition and fees: $3,729; out-of-state residents $8,195.
Per-credit charge: $123; out-of-state residents $272.

FINANCIAL AID PICTURE

Students with need: Need-based aid available for full-time and part-time students. Work study available nights, weekends, and for part-time students.
Students without need: No-need awards available for athletics, state/district residency.

FINANCIAL AID PROCEDURES

Forms required: FAFSA.
Dates and Deadlines: Priority date 7/15; no closing date. Applicants notified on a rolling basis starting 4/1.

CONTACT

David Metz, Director of Financial Aid
550 East Spring Street, Columbus, OH 43216-1609
(614) 287-2648

Cuyahoga Community College: Metropolitan

Cleveland, Ohio
www.tri-c.edu
Federal Code: 003040

2-year public community college in very large city.
Enrollment: 14,708 undergrads, 60% part-time. 1,605 full-time freshmen.
Selectivity: Open admission; but selective for some programs.

BASIC COSTS (2012-2013)

Tuition and fees: $2,936; out-of-district residents $3,753; out-of-state residents $7,268.

FINANCIAL AID PICTURE (2012-2013)

Students with need: Average financial aid package met 100% of need; average scholarship/grant was $5,038; average loan was $2,589. For part-time students, average financial aid package was $4,789.
Students without need: No-need awards available for academics, art, athletics, leadership, minority status, music/drama.
Cumulative student debt: 36% of graduating class had student loans; average debt was $6,861.

FINANCIAL AID PROCEDURES
Forms required: FAFSA, institutional form.
Dates and Deadlines: Applicants notified on a rolling basis starting 5/13.
Transfers: Priority date 5/13.

CONTACT
Angela Johnson, Director of Enrollment Management and Student Financial Services
2900 Community College Avenue, Cleveland, OH 44115-2878
(216) 987-4100

Davis College
Toledo, Ohio
www.daviscollege.edu
Federal Code: 004855

2-year for-profit junior college in large city.
Enrollment: 284 undergrads, 66% part-time. 9 full-time freshmen.
Selectivity: Admits over 75% of applicants.

BASIC COSTS (2012-2013)
Tuition and fees: $18,510.
Per-credit charge: $388.

FINANCIAL AID PICTURE
Students with need: Need-based aid available for full-time and part-time students. Work study available nights, weekends, and for part-time students.
Students without need: This college awards aid only to students with need.

FINANCIAL AID PROCEDURES
Forms required: FAFSA.
Dates and Deadlines: Applicants notified on a rolling basis.
Transfers: No deadline. Applicants notified on a rolling basis. Student completes a clearance withdrawal letter that is completed from the previous school's financial aid office.

CONTACT
Melissa Kosinski, Director of Financial Aid
4747 Monroe Street, Toledo, OH 43623
(419) 473-2700

Daymar College: Chillicothe
Chillicothe, Ohio
www.daymarcollege.edu/college/chillicothe
Federal Code: 020568

2-year for-profit business college in large town.
Enrollment: 269 undergrads.
Selectivity: Open admission.

BASIC COSTS (2012-2013)
Tuition and fees: $18,000.
Additional info: Program inclusive pricing, including tuition, books, and all fees.

FINANCIAL AID PICTURE
Students with need: Need-based aid available for full-time and part-time students.
Students without need: This college awards aid only to students with need.
Scholarships offered: Ohio Legislative Scholarship: administered by the Ohio Council of Private Colleges and Schools, for Ohio-resident high school seniors nominated by their state representative who reviews applications; 2-year tuition for associate degree valued at $11,500.

FINANCIAL AID PROCEDURES
Forms required: FAFSA, institutional form.
Transfers: No deadline.

CONTACT
Connie Pruitt, Financial Aid Coordinator
1410 Industrial Drive, Chillicothe, OH 45601
(740) 774-2063

Defiance College
Defiance, Ohio
www.defiance.edu
Federal Code: 003041

4-year private liberal arts college in large town, affiliated with United Church of Christ.
Enrollment: 917 undergrads.
Selectivity: Admits 50 to 75% of applicants.

BASIC COSTS (2012-2013)
Tuition and fees: $27,075.
Per-credit charge: $430.
Room and board: $8,850.

FINANCIAL AID PICTURE
Students with need: Need-based aid available for full-time and part-time students. Work study available nights, weekends, and for part-time students.
Students without need: No-need awards available for academics, leadership, minority status, music/drama.
Scholarships offered: Presidential Scholar Program; $12,000 to full tuition; based on 3.5 GPA, 27 ACT/1210 SAT, and interview. Pilgrim Scholar Program; $11,000-$16,000; based on 3.2 GPA, 24 ACT/1090 SAT, and interview. Achievement Scholar Program; $10,000-$14,000; based on 2.8 GPA, 21 ACT/980 SAT, and interview. Defiance College Scholarship; $5,000-$10,000; based on 2.5-4.0 GPA and 18-36 ACT/850-1600 SAT.

FINANCIAL AID PROCEDURES
Forms required: FAFSA.
Dates and Deadlines: Priority date 4/1; no closing date. Applicants notified on a rolling basis starting 2/15; must reply by 5/1 or within 2 week(s) of notification.

CONTACT
Amy Francis, Director of Financial Aid
701 North Clinton Street, Defiance, OH 43512-1695
(419) 782-458

Denison University
Granville, Ohio
www.denison.edu
Federal Code: 003042

4-year private liberal arts college in small town.
Enrollment: 2,304 undergrads. 629 full-time freshmen.
Selectivity: Admits less than 50% of applicants.

BASIC COSTS (2012-2013)
Tuition and fees: $42,280.
Per-credit charge: $1,293.
Room and board: $10,360.
Additional info: Tuition/fee waivers available for adults.

FINANCIAL AID PICTURE (2012-2013)
Students with need: Out of 436 full-time freshmen who applied for aid, 355 were judged to have need. Of these, 355 received aid, and 170 had their full need met. Average financial aid package met 97% of need; average scholarship/grant was $32,388; average loan was $3,748. Need-based aid available for part-time students.

Students without need: 253 full-time freshmen who did not demonstrate need for aid received scholarships/grants; average award was $18,421. No-need awards available for academics, alumni affiliation, art, leadership, minority status, music/drama, state/district residency.

FINANCIAL AID PROCEDURES

Forms required: FAFSA.

Dates and Deadlines: Priority date 3/15; no closing date. Applicants notified on a rolling basis starting 3/28.

CONTACT

Nancy Hoover, Director of Financial Aid and Student Employment
100 West College, Granville, OH 43023
(740) 587-6279

DeVry University: Columbus

Columbus, Ohio
www.devry.edu Federal Code: 003099

4-year for-profit university in very large city.
Enrollment: 2,142 undergrads, 64% part-time. 65 full-time freshmen.

BASIC COSTS (2012-2013)

Tuition and fees: $16,076.
Per-credit charge: $609.

FINANCIAL AID PICTURE

Students with need: Need-based aid available for full-time and part-time students.
Students without need: This college awards aid only to students with need.

FINANCIAL AID PROCEDURES

Forms required: FAFSA.
Dates and Deadlines: Applicants notified on a rolling basis.

CONTACT

Cynthia Price, Director of Financial Aid
1350 Alum Creek Drive, Columbus, OH 43209-2705
(614) 253-7291

Eastern Gateway Community College

Steubenville, Ohio
www.egcc.edu Federal Code: 007275

2-year public community college in large town.
Enrollment: 1,907 undergrads.
Selectivity: Open admission; but selective for some programs.

BASIC COSTS (2012-2013)

Tuition and fees: $3,280; out-of-district residents $3,460; out-of-state residents $4,300.
Per-credit charge: $105; out-of-district residents $111; out-of-state residents $139.
Additional info: Residents of 5 neighboring West Virginia counties eligible for in-state, out-of-district tuition rates.

FINANCIAL AID PICTURE

Students with need: Need-based aid available for full-time and part-time students. Work study available nights, weekends, and for part-time students.
Students without need: This college awards aid only to students with need.
Scholarships offered: Horizon Grant; two-year tuition scholarship; awarded to all students graduating from a Jefferson County high school with 2.5 GPA; student must enroll full-time for fall semester immediately following high school graduation.

FINANCIAL AID PROCEDURES

Forms required: FAFSA, institutional form.
Dates and Deadlines: Priority date 4/1; no closing date. Applicants notified on a rolling basis starting 6/15.

CONTACT

Kelly Wilson, Director of Financial Aid
Eastern Gateway Community College- Jefferson County Campus, Steubenville, OH 43952
(740) 264-5591 ext. 135

Edison State Community College

Piqua, Ohio
www.edisonohio.edu Federal Code: 012750

2-year public community college in large town.
Enrollment: 2,487 undergrads, 65% part-time. 282 full-time freshmen.
Selectivity: Open admission; but selective for some programs.

BASIC COSTS (2012-2013)

Tuition and fees: $4,019; out-of-state residents $7,429.
Per-credit charge: $134; out-of-state residents $248.

FINANCIAL AID PICTURE

Students with need: Need-based aid available for full-time and part-time students. Work study available nights, weekends, and for part-time students.
Students without need: No-need awards available for academics, alumni affiliation, art, athletics, job skills, leadership, minority status, state/district residency.

FINANCIAL AID PROCEDURES

Forms required: FAFSA, institutional form.
Dates and Deadlines: Priority date 5/2; no closing date. Applicants notified on a rolling basis starting 5/15.

CONTACT

Kathi Richards, Director of Student Financial Aid
1973 Edison Drive, Piqua, OH 45356-9253
(937) 778-7910

ETI Technical College of Niles

Niles, Ohio
www.eticollege.edu Federal Code: 030790

2-year for-profit technical college in large town.
Enrollment: 98 undergrads. 17 full-time freshmen.
Selectivity: Open admission; but selective for some programs.

BASIC COSTS (2013-2014)

Tuition and fees: $9,054.
Per-credit charge: $330.
Additional info: Tuition at time of enrollment locked for 2 years.

FINANCIAL AID PICTURE (2011-2012)

Students with need: Out of 17 full-time freshmen who applied for aid, 14 were judged to have need. Of these, 14 received aid. Average financial aid package met 100% of need; average scholarship/grant was $3,550; average loan was $3,500. Need-based aid available for part-time students.
Students without need: No-need awards available for academics.

FINANCIAL AID PROCEDURES

Forms required: FAFSA.
Dates and Deadlines: Applicants notified on a rolling basis; must reply within 4 week(s) of notification.
Transfers: No deadline. Applicants notified on a rolling basis; must reply within 4 week(s) of notification.

CONTACT

Kay Madigan, Financial Aid Director
2076 Youngstown Warren Road, Niles, OH 44446-4398
(330) 652-9919

Fortis College: Centerville

Centerville, Ohio
www.fortis.edu Federal Code: 012267

2-year for-profit junior and technical college in large town.
Enrollment: 887 undergrads.
Selectivity: Open admission.

FINANCIAL AID PICTURE

Students with need: Need-based aid available for full-time and part-time students.
Students without need: This college awards aid only to students with need.

FINANCIAL AID PROCEDURES

Forms required: FAFSA, institutional form.
Dates and Deadlines: Applicants notified on a rolling basis.

CONTACT

Lynda Linsey, Director of Financial Aid
555 East Alex Bell Road, Centerville, OH 45459-9627

Fortis College: Ravenna

Ravenna, Ohio
www.fortis.edu Federal Code: 016270

2-year for-profit business college in large town.
Enrollment: 442 undergrads.

FINANCIAL AID PICTURE

Students with need: Need-based aid available for full-time and part-time students.
Students without need: This college awards aid only to students with need.

FINANCIAL AID PROCEDURES

Forms required: FAFSA.
Dates and Deadlines: Applicants notified on a rolling basis.

CONTACT

Trudy Young, Financial Aid Director
653 Enterprise Parkway, Ravenna, OH 44266
(330) 297-7319

Franciscan University of Steubenville

Steubenville, Ohio
www.franciscan.edu Federal Code: 003036

4-year private university in large town, affiliated with Roman Catholic Church.
Enrollment: 2,038 undergrads, 4% part-time. 435 full-time freshmen.
Selectivity: Admits over 75% of applicants.

BASIC COSTS (2012-2013)

Tuition and fees: $22,180.
Per-credit charge: $725.
Room and board: $7,400.

FINANCIAL AID PICTURE (2012-2013)

Students with need: Out of 381 full-time freshmen who applied for aid, 307 were judged to have need. Of these, 306 received aid, and 53 had their full need met. Average financial aid package met 57% of need; average scholarship/grant was $9,328; average loan was $3,403. For part-time students, average financial aid package was $9,500.
Students without need: 100 full-time freshmen who did not demonstrate need for aid received scholarships/grants; average award was $5,408. No-need awards available for academics, alumni affiliation, leadership, religious affiliation.
Cumulative student debt: 76% of graduating class had student loans; average debt was $32,125.

FINANCIAL AID PROCEDURES

Forms required: FAFSA.
Dates and Deadlines: Priority date 4/1; no closing date. Applicants notified on a rolling basis starting 2/15; must reply within 3 week(s) of notification.
Transfers: Closing date 8/1. Applicants notified on a rolling basis starting 2/15; must reply within 3 week(s) of notification.

CONTACT

John Herrmann, Director of Student Financial Services
1235 University Boulevard, Steubenville, OH 43952-1763
(740) 283-6226

Franklin University

Columbus, Ohio
www.franklin.edu Federal Code: 003046

4-year private university and business college in very large city.
Enrollment: 5,769 undergrads.
Selectivity: Open admission; but selective for some programs.

BASIC COSTS (2012-2013)

Tuition and fees: $12,450.
Per-credit charge: $415.

FINANCIAL AID PICTURE (2012-2013)

Students with need: 22% of average financial aid package awarded as scholarships/grants, 78% awarded as loans/jobs. Need-based aid available for part-time students.
Students without need: No-need awards available for academics, leadership, minority status.

FINANCIAL AID PROCEDURES

Forms required: FAFSA.
Dates and Deadlines: Priority date 6/15; no closing date. Applicants notified on a rolling basis; must reply within 2 week(s) of notification.
Transfers: One scholarship specifically for transfer students: Transfer Achievement.

CONTACT

Goldie Langley, Director of Financial Aid
201 South Grant Avenue, Columbus, OH 43215-5399
(614) 797-4700

Gallipolis Career College

Gallipolis, Ohio
www.gallipoliscareercollege.com Federal Code: 030079

2-year for-profit business and technical college in small town.
Enrollment: 152 undergrads.
Selectivity: Open admission.

FINANCIAL AID PICTURE

Students with need: Need-based aid available for full-time and part-time students.

Students without need: This college awards aid only to students with need.

FINANCIAL AID PROCEDURES

Forms required: FAFSA, institutional form.

CONTACT

Jeanette Shirey, Financial Aid Administrator
1176 Jackson Pike, Suite 312, Gallipolis, OH 45631
(740) 446-4367

Heidelberg University

Tiffin, Ohio
www.heidelberg.edu Federal Code: 003048

4-year private liberal arts college in large town, affiliated with United Church of Christ.
Enrollment: 1,089 undergrads, 5% part-time. 345 full-time freshmen.
Selectivity: Admits 50 to 75% of applicants.

BASIC COSTS (2012-2013)

Tuition and fees: $24,590.
Room and board: $8,974.

FINANCIAL AID PICTURE (2012-2013)

Students with need: Out of 326 full-time freshmen who applied for aid, 307 were judged to have need. Of these, 307 received aid, and 45 had their full need met. Average financial aid package met 80% of need; average scholarship/grant was $16,642; average loan was $4,037. Need-based aid available for part-time students.
Students without need: 26 full-time freshmen who did not demonstrate need for aid received scholarships/grants; average award was $11,830. No-need awards available for art, athletics.
Cumulative student debt: 86% of graduating class had student loans; average debt was $35,470.

FINANCIAL AID PROCEDURES

Forms required: FAFSA.
Dates and Deadlines: Priority date 3/1; no closing date. Applicants notified on a rolling basis starting 3/1; must reply by 5/1 or within 2 week(s) of notification.
Transfers: No deadline. Applicants notified on a rolling basis starting 3/1; must reply by 5/1 or within 2 week(s) of notification.

CONTACT

Juli Weininger, Director of Financial Aid
310 East Market Street, Tiffin, OH 44883-2462
(419) 448-2293

Hiram College

Hiram, Ohio
www.hiram.edu Federal Code: 003049

4-year private liberal arts college in rural community, affiliated with Christian Church (Disciples of Christ).
Enrollment: 1,276 undergrads, 11% part-time. 304 full-time freshmen.
Selectivity: Admits 50 to 75% of applicants.

BASIC COSTS (2012-2013)

Tuition and fees: $30,040.
Room and board: $9,560.
Additional info: The Hiram College Tuition Guarantee ensures that the annual cost for tuition will not increase between the first year a student is enrolled at Hiram and the student's senior year.

FINANCIAL AID PICTURE

Students with need: Need-based aid available for full-time and part-time students. Work study available nights, weekends, and for part-time students.
Students without need: No-need awards available for academics, alumni affiliation, music/drama, religious affiliation, state/district residency.

FINANCIAL AID PROCEDURES

Forms required: FAFSA.
Dates and Deadlines: Priority date 2/15; no closing date. Applicants notified on a rolling basis starting 2/15; must reply by 5/1 or within 2 week(s) of notification.
Transfers: Transfer merit scholarships available. Phi Theta Kappa scholarships available.

CONTACT

Andrea Caputo, Director of Student Financial Aid
Teachout Price Hall, Hiram, OH 44234
(330) 569-5107

Hocking College

Nelsonville, Ohio
www.hocking.edu Federal Code: 007598

2-year public technical college in small town.
Enrollment: 3,447 undergrads.
Selectivity: Open admission; but selective for some programs.

BASIC COSTS (2012-2013)

Tuition and fees: $4,191; out-of-state residents $8,382.

FINANCIAL AID PICTURE

Students with need: Need-based aid available for full-time and part-time students. Work study available nights, weekends, and for part-time students.
Students without need: No-need awards available for academics, minority status, state/district residency.

FINANCIAL AID PROCEDURES

Forms required: FAFSA, institutional form.
Dates and Deadlines: Priority date 2/28; no closing date. Applicants notified on a rolling basis starting 4/15.
Transfers: No deadline. Applicants notified on a rolling basis. Non-entitlement aid awarded on first-come, first-served basis.

CONTACT

Roger Springer, Financial Services Director
3301 Hocking Parkway, Nelsonville, OH 45764-9704
(740) 753-7080

Hondros College

Westerville, Ohio
www.nursing.hondros.edu Federal Code: 040743

2-year for-profit nursing and career college in very large city.
Enrollment: 1,420 undergrads, 18% part-time. 50 full-time freshmen.
Selectivity: Admits 50 to 75% of applicants.

BASIC COSTS (2012-2013)

Per-credit charge: $230.
Additional info: LPN nursing program cost for 3 quarters $12,370. ADN nursing courses are 250 per credit hour.

FINANCIAL AID PICTURE (2011-2012)

Students with need: 24% of average financial aid package awarded as scholarships/grants, 76% awarded as loans/jobs. Need-based aid available for part-time students.

FINANCIAL AID PROCEDURES

Forms required: FAFSA.
Transfers: No deadline. Applicants notified on a rolling basis starting 2/1.

CONTACT
Ed Colestock, Director of Financial Aid
4140 Executive Parkway, Westerville, OH 43081-3855
(614) 508-7200

International College of Broadcasting
Dayton, Ohio
www.icbcollege.com Federal Code: 013132

2-year for-profit technical college in small city.
Enrollment: 63 undergrads.
Selectivity: Open admission.

FINANCIAL AID PICTURE
Students with need: Need-based aid available for full-time and part-time students.

FINANCIAL AID PROCEDURES
Forms required: FAFSA.
Dates and Deadlines: Applicants notified on a rolling basis starting 11/1.

CONTACT
Lizzie Miller, Financial Aid Director
6 South Smithville Road, Dayton, OH 45431
(937) 258-8251

James A. Rhodes State College
Lima, Ohio
www.rhodesstate.edu Federal Code: 010027

2-year public community and technical college in large town.
Enrollment: 3,345 undergrads, 54% part-time. 418 full-time freshmen.
Selectivity: Open admission; but selective for some programs.

BASIC COSTS (2012-2013)
Tuition and fees: $4,613; out-of-state residents $9,226.
Per-credit charge: $154; out-of-state residents $307.

FINANCIAL AID PICTURE
Students with need: Need-based aid available for full-time and part-time students. Work study available nights, weekends, and for part-time students.
Students without need: No-need awards available for academics.

FINANCIAL AID PROCEDURES
Forms required: FAFSA.
Dates and Deadlines: Priority date 2/15; no closing date. Applicants notified on a rolling basis starting 5/1; must reply within 2 week(s) of notification.

CONTACT
Cathy Kohli, Director of Financial Aid
4240 Campus Drive, PS 148, Lima, OH 45804-3597
(419) 995-8800

John Carroll University
University Heights, Ohio
www.jcu.edu Federal Code: 003050

4-year private university in large town, affiliated with Roman Catholic Church.
Enrollment: 2,914 undergrads, 2% part-time. 681 full-time freshmen.
Selectivity: Admits over 75% of applicants.

BASIC COSTS (2012-2013)
Tuition and fees: $33,180.
Per-credit charge: $980.
Room and board: $9,610.

FINANCIAL AID PICTURE (2012-2013)
Students with need: Out of 637 full-time freshmen who applied for aid, 519 were judged to have need. Of these, 517 received aid, and 88 had their full need met. Average financial aid package met 81% of need; average scholarship/grant was $23,065; average loan was $2,976. For part-time students, average financial aid package was $14,832.
Students without need: 154 full-time freshmen who did not demonstrate need for aid received scholarships/grants; average award was $15,167. No-need awards available for academics, alumni affiliation, leadership, minority status, ROTC, state/district residency.
Cumulative student debt: 77% of graduating class had student loans; average debt was $31,727.
Additional info: John Carroll grant combined with federal and state grant aid, and the Federal Stafford Loan program to meet the published flat, full-time tuition cost for Pell-eligible Ohio families.

FINANCIAL AID PROCEDURES
Forms required: FAFSA.
Dates and Deadlines: Priority date 2/15; closing date 3/15. Applicants notified on a rolling basis starting 2/15; must reply by 5/1 or within 4 week(s) of notification.
Transfers: Priority date 5/1; no deadline. Applicants notified on a rolling basis starting 4/1; must reply by 8/1 or within 3 week(s) of notification.

CONTACT
Claudia Wenzel, Director of Financial Assistance
Office of Admission, University Heights, OH 44118-4581
(216) 397-4294

Kaplan College: Columbus
Columbus, Ohio
www.kc-columbus.com Federal Code: 011005

2-year for-profit technical and career college in very large city.
Enrollment: 335 undergrads.
Selectivity: Open admission.

BASIC COSTS (2012-2013)
Additional info: Associate degree program: Criminal Justice $32,413. Diploma program: Computer Support Technician $17,066; Medical Assistant $15,925; Medical Billing and Coding Specialist $15,535.

FINANCIAL AID PICTURE
Students with need: Need-based aid available for full-time and part-time students. Work study available nights.
Students without need: This college awards aid only to students with need.

FINANCIAL AID PROCEDURES
Forms required: FAFSA, institutional form.
Dates and Deadlines: Applicants notified on a rolling basis.

CONTACT
Ashley South, Director of Financial Aid
2745 Winchester Pike, Columbus, OH 43232
(614) 456-4600

Kaplan College: Dayton
Dayton, Ohio
www.dayton.kaplancollege.com Federal Code: 020520

2-year for-profit technical college in very large city.
Enrollment: 523 undergrads.
Selectivity: Open admission; but selective for some programs.

BASIC COSTS (2012-2013)
Additional info: Associate degree program: Criminal Justice $32,413. Diploma program: Dental Assistant $16,814; Medical Assistant $15,925; Pharmacy Technician $15,954.

FINANCIAL AID PICTURE
Students with need: Need-based aid available for full-time and part-time students.

FINANCIAL AID PROCEDURES
Forms required: FAFSA, institutional form.
Dates and Deadlines: Applicants notified on a rolling basis starting 3/1.

CONTACT
Tiphany Pugh, Director of Operations
2800 East River Road, Dayton, OH 45439
(937) 294-6155

Kent State University

Kent, Ohio
www.kent.edu Federal Code: 003051

4-year public university in large town.
Enrollment: 21,588 undergrads, 12% part-time. 4,071 full-time freshmen.
Selectivity: Admits over 75% of applicants.

BASIC COSTS (2012-2013)
Tuition and fees: $9,672; out-of-state residents $17,632.
Per-credit charge: $440; out-of-state residents $802.
Room and board: $9,178.

FINANCIAL AID PICTURE (2012-2013)
Students with need: Out of 3,587 full-time freshmen who applied for aid, 2,995 were judged to have need. Of these, 2,990 received aid, and 1,172 had their full need met. Average financial aid package met 53% of need; average scholarship/grant was $6,217; average loan was $3,711. For part-time students, average financial aid package was $6,971.
Students without need: 646 full-time freshmen who did not demonstrate need for aid received scholarships/grants; average award was $4,295. No-need awards available for academics, alumni affiliation, art, athletics, leadership, minority status, music/drama, ROTC, state/district residency.
Scholarships offered: ***Merit:*** Trustee Scholarship; $1,000-$2,500 annually; based on 3.25 GPA, ACT scores, leadership activities; 500 available. ***Athletic:*** 31 full-time freshmen received athletic scholarships; average amount $17,074.
Cumulative student debt: 76% of graduating class had student loans; average debt was $31,954.
Additional info: Participant in US Department of Education's Quality Assurance Program and Experimental Sites Program.

FINANCIAL AID PROCEDURES
Forms required: FAFSA.
Dates and Deadlines: Priority date 3/1; no closing date. Applicants notified on a rolling basis starting 3/15; must reply within 2 week(s) of notification.

CONTACT
Mark Evans, Director of Student Financial Aid
PO Box 5190, Kent, OH 44242-0001
(330) 672-2972

Kent State University: Ashtabula

Ashtabula, Ohio
www.ashtabula.kent.edu Federal Code: 003051

2-year public branch campus college in large town.
Enrollment: 2,392 undergrads, 48% part-time. 236 full-time freshmen.
Selectivity: Open admission; but selective for some programs.

BASIC COSTS (2012-2013)
Tuition and fees: $5,472; out-of-state residents $13,432.
Per-credit charge: $249; out-of-state residents $611.

FINANCIAL AID PICTURE (2012-2013)
Students with need: Out of 222 full-time freshmen who applied for aid, 212 were judged to have need. Of these, 211 received aid, and 62 had their full need met. Average financial aid package met 45% of need; average scholarship/grant was $4,665; average loan was $3,347. For part-time students, average financial aid package was $6,257.
Students without need: No-need awards available for academics, alumni affiliation, art, athletics, leadership, minority status, music/drama, ROTC, state/district residency.

FINANCIAL AID PROCEDURES
Forms required: FAFSA.
Dates and Deadlines: Priority date 3/1; no closing date. Applicants notified on a rolling basis starting 3/15; must reply within 2 week(s) of notification.

CONTACT
Robyn Gifford, Student Financial Services Coordinator
3300 Lake Road West, Ashtabula, OH 44004
(440) 964-3322

Kent State University: East Liverpool

East Liverpool, Ohio
www.eliv.kent.edu Federal Code: 003051

2-year public branch campus college in large town.
Enrollment: 1,335 undergrads, 39% part-time. 115 full-time freshmen.
Selectivity: Open admission; but selective for some programs.

BASIC COSTS (2012-2013)
Tuition and fees: $5,472; out-of-state residents $13,432.
Per-credit charge: $249; out-of-state residents $611.

FINANCIAL AID PICTURE (2012-2013)
Students with need: Out of 108 full-time freshmen who applied for aid, 97 were judged to have need. Of these, 97 received aid, and 37 had their full need met. Average financial aid package met 48% of need; average scholarship/grant was $4,388; average loan was $3,464. For part-time students, average financial aid package was $6,489.
Students without need: 2 full-time freshmen who did not demonstrate need for aid received scholarships/grants; average award was $750. No-need awards available for academics, alumni affiliation, art, leadership, minority status, music/drama, ROTC, state/district residency.

FINANCIAL AID PROCEDURES
Forms required: FAFSA.
Dates and Deadlines: Priority date 3/1; no closing date. Applicants notified on a rolling basis starting 3/15; must reply within 2 week(s) of notification.

CONTACT
Beth Allison-Christy, Administrative Assistant
400 East Fourth Street, East Liverpool, OH 43920
(330) 385-3805

Kent State University: Geauga

Burton, Ohio
www.geauga.kent.edu Federal Code: 003059

2-year public branch campus college in rural community.
Enrollment: 2,351 undergrads, 38% part-time. 233 full-time freshmen.
Selectivity: Open admission; but selective for some programs.

BASIC COSTS (2012-2013)
Tuition and fees: $5,472; out-of-state residents $13,432.

Per-credit charge: $249; out-of-state residents $611.

FINANCIAL AID PICTURE (2012-2013)

Students with need: Out of 188 full-time freshmen who applied for aid, 164 were judged to have need. Of these, 162 received aid, and 69 had their full need met. Average financial aid package met 46% of need; average scholarship/grant was $4,321; average loan was $3,319. For part-time students, average financial aid package was $5,827.

Students without need: 4 full-time freshmen who did not demonstrate need for aid received scholarships/grants; average award was $505. No-need awards available for academics, alumni affiliation, art, leadership, minority status, music/drama, ROTC, state/district residency.

FINANCIAL AID PROCEDURES

Forms required: FAFSA.

Dates and Deadlines: Priority date 3/1; no closing date. Must reply within 2 week(s) of notification.

CONTACT

Donna Holcomb, Financial Aid Advisor
Office of Admissions, Burton, OH 44021
(440) 834-8846

Kent State University: Salem

Salem, Ohio
www.salem.kent.edu Federal Code: 003061

2-year public branch campus college in large town.
Enrollment: 1,699 undergrads, 29% part-time. 243 full-time freshmen.
Selectivity: Open admission; but selective for some programs.

BASIC COSTS (2012-2013)

Tuition and fees: $5,472; out-of-state residents $13,432.
Per-credit charge: $249; out-of-state residents $611.

FINANCIAL AID PICTURE (2012-2013)

Students with need: Out of 232 full-time freshmen who applied for aid, 204 were judged to have need. Of these, 202 received aid, and 92 had their full need met. Average financial aid package met 48% of need; average scholarship/grant was $4,228; average loan was $3,299. For part-time students, average financial aid package was $6,333.

Students without need: 3 full-time freshmen who did not demonstrate need for aid received scholarships/grants; average award was $1,833. No-need awards available for academics, alumni affiliation, art, athletics, leadership, minority status, music/drama, ROTC.

FINANCIAL AID PROCEDURES

Forms required: FAFSA.

Dates and Deadlines: Priority date 3/1; no closing date. Applicants notified on a rolling basis starting 3/15; must reply within 2 week(s) of notification.

Transfers: Priority date 2/15.

CONTACT

Ailishia Clemons, Administrative Clerk
2491 State Route 45 South, Salem, OH 44460

Kent State University: Stark

Canton, Ohio
www.stark.kent.edu Federal Code: 003054

2-year public branch campus college in small city.
Enrollment: 4,636 undergrads, 33% part-time. 584 full-time freshmen.
Selectivity: Open admission; but selective for some programs.

BASIC COSTS (2012-2013)

Tuition and fees: $5,472; out-of-state residents $13,432.
Per-credit charge: $249; out-of-state residents $611.

FINANCIAL AID PICTURE (2012-2013)

Students with need: Out of 518 full-time freshmen who applied for aid, 443 were judged to have need. Of these, 442 received aid, and 190 had their full need met. Average financial aid package met 51% of need; average scholarship/grant was $4,228; average loan was $3,362. For part-time students, average financial aid package was $6,080.

Students without need: 30 full-time freshmen who did not demonstrate need for aid received scholarships/grants; average award was $2,535. No-need awards available for academics, alumni affiliation, art, athletics, leadership, minority status, music/drama, ROTC, state/district residency.

FINANCIAL AID PROCEDURES

Forms required: FAFSA.

Dates and Deadlines: Priority date 3/1; no closing date. Applicants notified on a rolling basis starting 3/15; must reply within 2 week(s) of notification.

CONTACT

Nina Antram, Financial Aid Officer
6000 Frank Avenue NW, Canton, OH 44720-7599
(330) 535-3377

Kent State University: Trumbull

Warren, Ohio
www.trumbull.kent.edu Federal Code: 003051

2-year public branch campus college in small city.
Enrollment: 2,999 undergrads, 38% part-time. 306 full-time freshmen.
Selectivity: Open admission; but selective for some programs.

BASIC COSTS (2012-2013)

Tuition and fees: $5,472; out-of-state residents $13,432.
Per-credit charge: $249; out-of-state residents $611.

FINANCIAL AID PICTURE (2012-2013)

Students with need: Out of 279 full-time freshmen who applied for aid, 259 were judged to have need. Of these, 258 received aid, and 103 had their full need met. Average financial aid package met 45% of need; average scholarship/grant was $4,581; average loan was $3,341. For part-time students, average financial aid package was $6,260.

Students without need: 1 full-time freshmen who did not demonstrate need for aid received scholarships/grants; average award was $1,000. No-need awards available for academics, alumni affiliation, art, athletics, leadership, minority status, music/drama, ROTC, state/district residency.

FINANCIAL AID PROCEDURES

Forms required: FAFSA.

Dates and Deadlines: Priority date 3/1; no closing date. Applicants notified on a rolling basis starting 3/15; must reply within 2 week(s) of notification.

CONTACT

Sarah Helmick, Assistant Director, Enrollment Management
4314 Mahoning Avenue, NW, Warren, OH 44483-1998
(330) 847-0571

Kent State University: Tuscarawas

New Philadelphia, Ohio
www.tusc.kent.edu Federal Code: 003051

2-year public branch campus college in large town.
Enrollment: 2,284 undergrads, 38% part-time. 289 full-time freshmen.
Selectivity: Open admission; but selective for some programs and for out-of-state students.

BASIC COSTS (2012-2013)

Tuition and fees: $5,472; out-of-state residents $13,432.
Per-credit charge: $249; out-of-state residents $611.

FINANCIAL AID PICTURE (2012-2013)

Students with need: Out of 263 full-time freshmen who applied for aid, 241 were judged to have need. Of these, 241 received aid, and 92 had their full need met. Average financial aid package met 49% of need; average scholarship/grant was $4,502; average loan was $3,371. For part-time students, average financial aid package was $6,389.

Students without need: 5 full-time freshmen who did not demonstrate need for aid received scholarships/grants; average award was $1,200. No-need awards available for academics, alumni affiliation, art, athletics, leadership, minority status, music/drama, ROTC.

FINANCIAL AID PROCEDURES

Forms required: FAFSA.

Dates and Deadlines: Closing date 3/1. Applicants notified on a rolling basis starting 3/15; must reply within 2 week(s) of notification.

Transfers: Financial aid transcripts from all previous institutions required.

CONTACT

Dawn Plug, Financial Aid Coordinator
330 University Drive NE, New Philadelphia, OH 44663-9403
(330) 339-3391 ext. 47474

Kenyon College

Gambier, Ohio
www.kenyon.edu
Federal Code: 003065
CSS Code: 1370

4-year private liberal arts college in rural community, affiliated with nondenominational tradition.
Enrollment: 1,657 undergrads. 445 full-time freshmen.
Selectivity: Admits less than 50% of applicants.

BASIC COSTS (2013-2014)

Tuition and fees: $45,640.
Room and board: $11,170.

FINANCIAL AID PICTURE (2012-2013)

Students with need: Out of 257 full-time freshmen who applied for aid, 190 were judged to have need. Of these, 189 received aid, and 142 had their full need met. Average financial aid package met 96% of need; average scholarship/grant was $36,339; average loan was $2,911.

Students without need: 64 full-time freshmen who did not demonstrate need for aid received scholarships/grants; average award was $12,640. No-need awards available for academics, art, minority status, music/drama.

Scholarships offered: Honor Scholarships, Science Scholarships, Trustee Opportunity Scholarships; averages around $16,000 a year; competitively based on excellence in academic achievement, extracurricular leadership, and community involvement. Distinguished Academic Scholarships; $2,000-$10,000; based on academic accomplishment, standardized test results, and extracurricular achievement. Scholarships for National Merit finalists available.

Cumulative student debt: 41% of graduating class had student loans; average debt was $20,992.

Additional info: Financial aid incentive guarantees a loan-free education for 25 students with the greatest need who bring the qualities of creativity, community service, and leadership.

FINANCIAL AID PROCEDURES

Forms required: FAFSA, CSS PROFILE.

Dates and Deadlines: Closing date 2/15. Applicants notified by 4/1; must reply by 5/1.

Transfers: Closing date 4/15. Applicants notified by 5/15; must reply by 6/1.

CONTACT

Craig Daugherty, Director of Financial Aid
Ransom Hall-Admissions, Gambier, OH 43022-9623
(740) 427-5430

Kettering College

Kettering, Ohio
www.kc.edu
Federal Code: 007035

4-year private health science and nursing college in large city, affiliated with Seventh-day Adventists.
Enrollment: 901 undergrads.

BASIC COSTS (2012-2013)

Tuition and fees: $11,970.
Per-credit charge: $399.
Additional info: $200 program fee per semester for areas of study with clinical requirements. Board plan not available. Cost of room only, $3,500.

FINANCIAL AID PICTURE

Students with need: Need-based aid available for full-time and part-time students.

Students without need: No-need awards available for academics.

FINANCIAL AID PROCEDURES

Forms required: FAFSA, institutional form.

Dates and Deadlines: Priority date 3/31; no closing date. Applicants notified on a rolling basis starting 5/15; must reply within 3 week(s) of notification.

CONTACT

Kim Snell, Director of Student Finance
3737 Southern Boulevard, Kettering, OH 45429-1299
(937) 296-7210

Lake Erie College

Painesville, Ohio
www.lec.edu
Federal Code: 003066

4-year private liberal arts college in large town.
Enrollment: 934 undergrads, 3% part-time. 275 full-time freshmen.
Selectivity: Admits 50 to 75% of applicants.

BASIC COSTS (2012-2013)

Tuition and fees: $27,368.
Room and board: $8,336.
Additional info: Equestrian fee $1,075 per course.

FINANCIAL AID PICTURE (2012-2013)

Students with need: Out of 250 full-time freshmen who applied for aid, 229 were judged to have need. Of these, 229 received aid, and 37 had their full need met. Average financial aid package met 75% of need; average scholarship/grant was $19,076; average loan was $3,226. For part-time students, average financial aid package was $7,427.

Students without need: 1 full-time freshmen who did not demonstrate need for aid received scholarships/grants; average award was $2,000. No-need awards available for academics, art, leadership, music/drama, state/district residency.

Cumulative student debt: 90% of graduating class had student loans; average debt was $34,837.

Additional info: Twins' scholarship, sibling discount.

FINANCIAL AID PROCEDURES

Forms required: FAFSA.

Dates and Deadlines: Applicants notified on a rolling basis starting 2/15; must reply by 5/1 or within 4 week(s) of notification.

Transfers: No deadline.

CONTACT

Patricia Pangonis, Director of Financial Aid
391 West Washington Street, Painesville, OH 44077-3389
(440) 375-7100

Lakeland Community College

Kirtland, Ohio
www.lakelandcc.edu Federal Code: 006804

2-year public community and technical college in large town.
Enrollment: 9,307 undergrads.
Selectivity: Open admission; but selective for some programs.

BASIC COSTS (2012-2013)

Tuition and fees: $3,116; out-of-district residents $3,965; out-of-state residents $8,601.
Per-credit charge: $91; out-of-district residents $119; out-of-state residents $274.

FINANCIAL AID PICTURE

Students with need: Need-based aid available for full-time and part-time students. Work study available nights, weekends, and for part-time students.
Students without need: No-need awards available for academics, art, athletics, job skills, leadership, minority status, music/drama, state/district residency.
Additional info: Loans available for tuition and books.

FINANCIAL AID PROCEDURES

Forms required: FAFSA, institutional form.
Dates and Deadlines: Closing date 3/1. Applicants notified on a rolling basis starting 5/1.
Transfers: Ohio Instructional Grant Transfer Form.

CONTACT

Melissa Amspaugh, Director of Financial Aid
7700 Clocktower Drive, Kirtland, OH 44094-5198
(440) 525-7070

Lincoln College of Technology: Dayton

Dayton, Ohio
www.swcollege.net Federal Code: 030161

2-year for-profit business college in small city.
Enrollment: 343 undergrads.
Selectivity: Open admission.

BASIC COSTS (2012-2013)

Additional info: Total program costs range from $9,935 up to $32,008 depending on program. Cost of books and materials included in tuition.

FINANCIAL AID PICTURE

Students with need: Need-based aid available for full-time and part-time students.
Students without need: This college awards aid only to students with need.

FINANCIAL AID PROCEDURES

Forms required: FAFSA.

CONTACT

Jill Matosky, Director of Financial Aid
111 West 1st Street, Dayton, OH 45402

Lincoln College of Technology: Tri-County

Cincinnati, Ohio
www.lincolnedu.com/campus/cincinnati-tri-county-oh
Federal Code: 012128

2-year for-profit career college in large city.
Enrollment: 464 undergrads.
Selectivity: Open admission.

BASIC COSTS (2012-2013)

Additional info: Total program costs range from $9,935 up to $32,008 depending on program. Cost of books and materials included in tuition.

FINANCIAL AID PICTURE

Students with need: Need-based aid available for full-time students.
Students without need: This college awards aid only to students with need.

FINANCIAL AID PROCEDURES

Forms required: FAFSA, state aid form.

CONTACT

Jill Matosky, Director of Financial Aid
149 Northland Boulevard, Cincinnati, OH 45246
(513) 874-0432

Lorain County Community College

Elyria, Ohio
www.lorainccc.edu Federal Code: 003068

2-year public community college in small city.
Enrollment: 11,096 undergrads, 67% part-time. 1,224 full-time freshmen.
Selectivity: Open admission.

BASIC COSTS (2012-2013)

Tuition and fees: $2,878; out-of-district residents $3,439; out-of-state residents $6,822.
Per-credit charge: $100; out-of-district residents $122; out-of-state residents $252.

FINANCIAL AID PICTURE

Students with need: Need-based aid available for full-time and part-time students. Work study available nights, weekends, and for part-time students.
Students without need: No-need awards available for academics.
Scholarships offered: Presidential Scholarships and Trustee Scholarships available.

FINANCIAL AID PROCEDURES

Forms required: FAFSA.
Dates and Deadlines: Priority date 8/15; no closing date. Applicants notified on a rolling basis starting 7/1; must reply within 3 week(s) of notification.

CONTACT

Stephanie Sutton, Manager of Financial Aid
1005 Abbe Road North, Elyria, OH 44035-1691
(490) 366-4034

Lourdes University

Sylvania, Ohio
www.lourdes.edu Federal Code: 003069

4-year private university in large town, affiliated with Roman Catholic Church.
Enrollment: 1,962 undergrads, 35% part-time. 254 full-time freshmen.
Selectivity: Open admission.

BASIC COSTS (2012-2013)

Tuition and fees: $16,950.
Per-credit charge: $565.
Room and board: $8,000.

FINANCIAL AID PICTURE (2012-2013)

Students with need: Out of 253 full-time freshmen who applied for aid, 217 were judged to have need. Of these, 217 received aid. For part-time students, average financial aid package was $7,048.

Students without need: No-need awards available for academics, art, athletics, minority status, religious affiliation, ROTC, state/district residency.
Scholarships offered: 44 full-time freshmen received athletic scholarships; average amount $3,761.

FINANCIAL AID PROCEDURES
Forms required: FAFSA.
Dates and Deadlines: Priority date 3/1; no closing date. Applicants notified on a rolling basis starting 3/1; must reply within 4 week(s) of notification.
Transfers: Must reply within 4 week(s) of notification.

CONTACT
Denise McCluskey, Director of Financial Aid
6832 Convent Boulevard, Sylvania, OH 43560-2898
(419) 824-3732

Malone University
Canton, Ohio
www.malone.edu Federal Code: 003072

4-year private university in small city, affiliated with Evangelical Friends Church-Eastern Region.
Enrollment: 1,816 undergrads, 9% part-time. 352 full-time freshmen.
Selectivity: Admits 50 to 75% of applicants.

BASIC COSTS (2013-2014)
Tuition and fees: $25,678.
Per-credit charge: $445.
Room and board: $8,656.

FINANCIAL AID PICTURE (2012-2013)
Students with need: Out of 336 full-time freshmen who applied for aid, 323 were judged to have need. Of these, 323 received aid, and 57 had their full need met. Average financial aid package met 79% of need; average scholarship/grant was $18,204; average loan was $3,592. For part-time students, average financial aid package was $7,029.
Students without need: 30 full-time freshmen who did not demonstrate need for aid received scholarships/grants; average award was $9,394. No-need awards available for academics, athletics, leadership, music/drama, religious affiliation.
Scholarships offered: 27 full-time freshmen received athletic scholarships; average amount $7,223.
Cumulative student debt: 79% of graduating class had student loans; average debt was $33,263.
Additional info: Prepayment discounts and employer deferred payments available for students in adult degree-completion programs. Employer deferred payment plan is available for traditional undergraduate students.

FINANCIAL AID PROCEDURES
Forms required: FAFSA.
Dates and Deadlines: Priority date 3/1; closing date 7/31. Applicants notified on a rolling basis starting 3/1; must reply within 2 week(s) of notification.

CONTACT
Pamela Pustay, Director of Financial Aid
2600 Cleveland Avenue NW, Canton, OH 44709-3897
(330) 471-8100 ext. 8159

Marietta College
Marietta, Ohio
www.marietta.edu Federal Code: 003073

4-year private liberal arts college in large town.
Enrollment: 1,470 undergrads, 4% part-time. 393 full-time freshmen.
Selectivity: Admits 50 to 75% of applicants.

BASIC COSTS (2012-2013)
Tuition and fees: $30,950.
Room and board: $9,560.

FINANCIAL AID PICTURE
Students with need: Need-based aid available for full-time and part-time students. Work study available nights, weekends, and for part-time students.
Students without need: No-need awards available for academics, alumni affiliation, art, leadership, minority status, music/drama, state/district residency.
Scholarships offered: McCoy Scholarship; full tuition, room/board. Trustees' Scholarships; full tuition; up to 10 awarded. President's Scholarship; half tuition; up to 20 awarded. Dean's Awards; $6,000-$10,000. Rickey Physics Scholarships; $18,000. Charles Sumner Harrison Awards; $5,000; for multicultural students and leaders. Fine Arts Awards; $1,000-$3,000; audition/portfolio required. All scholarships renewable for four years.
Additional info: Auditions/portfolios for art, creative writing, music and theater required for competitive fine art scholarships.

FINANCIAL AID PROCEDURES
Forms required: FAFSA, institutional form.
Dates and Deadlines: Priority date 3/1; closing date 4/15. Applicants notified on a rolling basis starting 3/15; must reply by 5/1 or within 2 week(s) of notification.
Transfers: Priority date 4/15; closing date 6/15. Applicants notified on a rolling basis starting 4/1; must reply by 6/30 or within 2 week(s) of notification.

CONTACT
Kevin Lamb, Director of Student Financial Services
215 Fifth Street, Marietta, OH 45750-4005
(740) 376-4712

Marion Technical College
Marion, Ohio
www.mtc.edu Federal Code: 010736

2-year public community and technical college in large town.
Enrollment: 1,005 full-time undergrads.
Selectivity: Open admission; but selective for some programs.

BASIC COSTS (2012-2013)
Tuition and fees: $4,582; out-of-state residents $6,490.
Per-credit charge: $160; out-of-state residents $234.

FINANCIAL AID PICTURE
Students with need: Need-based aid available for full-time and part-time students.
Students without need: No-need awards available for academics, leadership, minority status.
Scholarships offered: Foundation Scholarship; first year full tuition; for applicants in top 5% of class. President's Scholarship; $1,500; for applicants in top 50% of class. Tech Prep Scholarship; $1,200; for graduates of Tech Prep program. All scholarships require 2.5 GPA and successful completion of proficiency exams.

FINANCIAL AID PROCEDURES
Forms required: FAFSA, institutional form.
Dates and Deadlines: Closing date 6/1. Applicants notified on a rolling basis.
Transfers: No deadline. Applicants notified on a rolling basis.

CONTACT
Deb Langdon, Coordinator of Financial Aid
1467 Mt. Vernon Avenue, Marion, OH 43302-5694
(740) 389-4636 ext. 334

Mercy College of Ohio

Toledo, Ohio
www.mercycollege.edu Federal Code: 030970

4-year private health science and nursing college in large city, affiliated with Roman Catholic Church.
Enrollment: 1,164 undergrads, 63% part-time. 32 full-time freshmen.
Selectivity: Admits 50 to 75% of applicants.

BASIC COSTS (2012-2013)
Tuition and fees: $10,920.
Per-credit charge: $342.

FINANCIAL AID PICTURE (2011-2012)
Students with need: Out of 31 full-time freshmen who applied for aid, 24 were judged to have need. Of these, 24 received aid. Average financial aid package met 40% of need; average scholarship/grant was $5,236; average loan was $3,417. For part-time students, average financial aid package was $6,549.
Students without need: 4 full-time freshmen who did not demonstrate need for aid received scholarships/grants; average award was $1,000. No-need awards available for academics, alumni affiliation, leadership, religious affiliation, state/district residency.
Cumulative student debt: 100% of graduating class had student loans; average debt was $24,127.

FINANCIAL AID PROCEDURES
Forms required: FAFSA.
Dates and Deadlines: Priority date 3/1; no closing date. Applicants notified on a rolling basis starting 3/1; must reply within 2 week(s) of notification.

CONTACT
Julie Leslie, Financial Aid Director
2221 Madison Avenue, Toledo, OH 43604
(419) 251-1219

Miami University: Hamilton

Hamilton, Ohio
www.ham.muohio.edu Federal Code: 003077

2-year public branch campus college in small city.
Enrollment: 3,536 undergrads.
Selectivity: Open admission; but selective for some programs.

BASIC COSTS (2012-2013)
Tuition and fees: $4,958; out-of-state residents $14,243.
Per-credit charge: $190; out-of-state residents $560.

FINANCIAL AID PICTURE
Students with need: Need-based aid available for full-time and part-time students. Work study available nights, weekends, and for part-time students.
Students without need: No-need awards available for academics, athletics, leadership, minority status, state/district residency.
Additional info: Special gift funds for needy, multicultural students who enter with appropriate academic record. Separate application required for scholarships; closing date January 31.

FINANCIAL AID PROCEDURES
Forms required: FAFSA.
Dates and Deadlines: Priority date 2/15; no closing date. Applicants notified on a rolling basis starting 4/1.
Transfers: Transfer students must complete one semester at Miami University to be considered for scholarships.

CONTACT
Archie Nelson
1601 University Boulevard, Hamilton, OH 45011-3399
(513) 785-3123

Miami University: Middletown

Middletown, Ohio
www.mid.muohio.edu Federal Code: 003077

2-year public branch campus and community college in large town.
Enrollment: 2,021 undergrads.
Selectivity: Open admission; but selective for some programs.

BASIC COSTS (2012-2013)
Tuition and fees: $4,958; out-of-state residents $14,243.
Per-credit charge: $190; out-of-state residents $560.

FINANCIAL AID PICTURE
Students with need: Need-based aid available for full-time and part-time students.
Students without need: This college awards aid only to students with need.

FINANCIAL AID PROCEDURES
Forms required: FAFSA.
Dates and Deadlines: Priority date 2/15; no closing date. Applicants notified on a rolling basis.
Transfers: Applicants must file by February 15 to be considered for campus-based aid or alumni scholarships.

CONTACT
Archie Nelson, Director of Admissions and Financial Aid
4200 East University Boulevard, Middletown, OH 45042
(513) 727-3346

Miami University: Oxford

Oxford, Ohio
www.miamioh.edu Federal Code: 003077

4-year public university in large town.
Enrollment: 14,984 undergrads, 3% part-time. 3,581 full-time freshmen.
Selectivity: Admits 50 to 75% of applicants.

BASIC COSTS (2012-2013)
Tuition and fees: $13,595; out-of-state residents $29,159.
Room and board: $10,640.

FINANCIAL AID PICTURE (2011-2012)
Students with need: Out of 2,579 full-time freshmen who applied for aid, 1,730 were judged to have need. Of these, 1,713 received aid, and 232 had their full need met. Average financial aid package met 53% of need; average scholarship/grant was $4,238; average loan was $3,636. For part-time students, average financial aid package was $9,831.
Students without need: 784 full-time freshmen who did not demonstrate need for aid received scholarships/grants; average award was $6,579. No-need awards available for academics, art, athletics, leadership, minority status, music/drama, ROTC, state/district residency.
Scholarships offered: 101 full-time freshmen received athletic scholarships; average amount $19,950.
Cumulative student debt: 54% of graduating class had student loans; average debt was $27,178.
Additional info: The Miami Access Initiative guarantees eligible students with scholarships and/or grants that meet or exceed the cost of tuition and academic fees. One of the eligibility requirements includes a total family income equal to or less than $35,000.

FINANCIAL AID PROCEDURES
Forms required: FAFSA.
Dates and Deadlines: Priority date 2/15; no closing date. Applicants notified on a rolling basis starting 3/20; must reply by 5/1 or within 3 week(s) of notification.

CONTACT
Brent Shock, Director of Student Financial Assistance
301 South Campus Avenue, Oxford, OH 45056
(513) 529-8734

Miami-Jacobs Career College: Columbus

Columbus, Ohio
www.miamijacobs.edu Federal Code: 021521

2-year for-profit junior college in very large city.
Enrollment: 331 undergrads.

BASIC COSTS (2012-2013)
Additional info: Tuition per-credit-hour charge $324. Program fees vary from $4 to $20 per-credit-hour.

FINANCIAL AID PICTURE
Students with need: Work study available nights.

FINANCIAL AID PROCEDURES
Forms required: FAFSA.

CONTACT
Lynn Mizanin, Director of Financial Aid
150 East Gay Street, 15th Floor, Columbus, OH 43215
(330) 867-4030

Miami-Jacobs Career College: Dayton

Dayton, Ohio
www.miamijacobs.edu Federal Code: 003076

2-year for-profit career college in small city.
Enrollment: 200 undergrads.

BASIC COSTS (2012-2013)
Additional info: Tuition per-credit-hour charge $324. Program fees vary from $4 to $20 per-credit-hour.

FINANCIAL AID PICTURE
Students with need: Need-based aid available for full-time and part-time students.
Students without need: This college awards aid only to students with need.

FINANCIAL AID PROCEDURES
Forms required: FAFSA, institutional form.
Dates and Deadlines: Applicants notified on a rolling basis.

CONTACT
Marcia Byrd, Director of Financial Aid
110 North Patterson Boulevard, Dayton, OH 45402
(937) 461-5174

Mount Carmel College of Nursing

Columbus, Ohio
www.mccn.edu Federal Code: 030719

4-year private nursing college in very large city, affiliated with Roman Catholic Church.
Enrollment: 886 undergrads, 28% part-time. 121 full-time freshmen.
Selectivity: Admits 50 to 75% of applicants.

BASIC COSTS (2012-2013)
Tuition and fees: $11,365.
Per-credit charge: $343.

FINANCIAL AID PICTURE (2011-2012)
Students with need: Out of 64 full-time freshmen who applied for aid, 64 were judged to have need. Of these, 64 received aid, and 5 had their full need met. Average financial aid package met 52% of need; average scholarship/grant was $1,200; average loan was $3,500.
Students without need: 9 full-time freshmen who did not demonstrate need for aid received scholarships/grants; average award was $1,844. No-need awards available for academics.
Cumulative student debt: 94% of graduating class had student loans; average debt was $20,500.

FINANCIAL AID PROCEDURES
Forms required: FAFSA.
Dates and Deadlines: Priority date 3/1; no closing date. Applicants notified on a rolling basis starting 9/1; must reply within 2 week(s) of notification.

CONTACT
Alyncia Bowen, Financial Aid Director
127 South Davis Avenue, Columbus, OH 43222-1589
(614) 234-5800

Mount Vernon Nazarene University

Mount Vernon, Ohio
www.mvnu.edu Federal Code: 007085

4-year private university in large town, affiliated with Church of the Nazarene.
Enrollment: 1,705 undergrads, 16% part-time. 290 full-time freshmen.
Selectivity: Admits 50 to 75% of applicants.

BASIC COSTS (2013-2014)
Tuition and fees: $23,690.
Per-credit charge: $658.
Room and board: $6,980.
Additional info: Tuition/fee waivers available for minority students.

FINANCIAL AID PICTURE (2012-2013)
Students with need: Out of 290 full-time freshmen who applied for aid, 269 were judged to have need. Of these, 269 received aid, and 42 had their full need met. Average financial aid package met 69% of need; average scholarship/grant was $13,023; average loan was $3,318. For part-time students, average financial aid package was $9,876.
Students without need: 10 full-time freshmen who did not demonstrate need for aid received scholarships/grants; average award was $8,225. No-need awards available for academics, athletics, minority status, music/drama, religious affiliation, state/district residency.
Scholarships offered: ***Merit:*** Academic scholarships; $5,000-$15,000; for first time students based on ACT/SAT and GPA. ***Athletic:*** 21 full-time freshmen received athletic scholarships; average amount $6,340.
Cumulative student debt: 85% of graduating class had student loans; average debt was $25,313.

FINANCIAL AID PROCEDURES
Forms required: FAFSA, institutional form.
Dates and Deadlines: Priority date 3/15; no closing date. Applicants notified on a rolling basis starting 3/15; must reply within 2 week(s) of notification.
Transfers: No deadline. Applicants notified on a rolling basis starting 3/15; must reply within 2 week(s) of notification. Filing deadline for Ohio financial aid is October 1st.

CONTACT
Mary Cannon, Director of Student Financial Services
800 Martinsburg Road, Mount Vernon, OH 43050
(740) 397-9000 ext. 4520

Muskingum University

New Concord, Ohio
www.muskingum.edu Federal Code: 003084

4-year private university and liberal arts college in small town, affiliated with Presbyterian Church (USA).
Enrollment: 1,681 undergrads, 13% part-time. 423 full-time freshmen.
Selectivity: Admits over 75% of applicants.

BASIC COSTS (2013-2014)
Tuition and fees: $24,036.
Per-credit charge: $500.
Room and board: $9,320.
Additional info: Tuition/fee waivers available for minority students.

FINANCIAL AID PICTURE (2011-2012)
Students with need: Out of 397 full-time freshmen who applied for aid, 375 were judged to have need. Of these, 375 received aid, and 112 had their full need met. Average financial aid package met 76% of need; average scholarship/grant was $15,480; average loan was $4,019. For part-time students, average financial aid package was $10,370.
Students without need: 41 full-time freshmen who did not demonstrate need for aid received scholarships/grants; average award was $9,748. No-need awards available for academics, alumni affiliation, art, leadership, minority status, music/drama, religious affiliation, state/district residency.
Cumulative student debt: 78% of graduating class had student loans; average debt was $31,513.
Additional info: Scholarship priority date February 1.

FINANCIAL AID PROCEDURES
Forms required: FAFSA.
Dates and Deadlines: Priority date 3/1; no closing date. Applicants notified on a rolling basis starting 3/1; must reply by 5/1 or within 2 week(s) of notification.
Transfers: No deadline. Applicants notified on a rolling basis starting 3/1; must reply by 8/15 or within 2 week(s) of notification.

CONTACT
Jeff Zellers, Vice President of Enrollment
163 Stormont Street, New Concord, OH 43762-1199
(740) 826-8139

North Central State College

Mansfield, Ohio
www.ncstatecollege.edu Federal Code: 005313

2-year public technical college in small city.
Enrollment: 2,461 undergrads, 69% part-time. 300 full-time freshmen.
Selectivity: Open admission; but selective for some programs.

BASIC COSTS (2012-2013)
Tuition and fees: $4,288; out-of-state residents $8,580.
Per-credit charge: $120; out-of-state residents $240.

FINANCIAL AID PICTURE
Students with need: Need-based aid available for full-time and part-time students.
Students without need: This college awards aid only to students with need.

FINANCIAL AID PROCEDURES
Forms required: FAFSA.
Dates and Deadlines: Priority date 4/1; no closing date. Applicants notified on a rolling basis starting 5/30; must reply within 1 week(s) of notification.

CONTACT
James Phinney, Assistant Dean of Financial Aid
2441 Kenwood Circle, PO Box 698, Mansfield, OH 44901-0698
(419) 755-4899

Northwest State Community College

Archbold, Ohio
www.northweststate.edu Federal Code: 008677

2-year public community and technical college in small town.
Enrollment: 2,461 undergrads, 72% part-time. 211 full-time freshmen.
Selectivity: Open admission; but selective for some programs.

BASIC COSTS (2012-2013)
Tuition and fees: $4,260; out-of-state residents $8,340.
Per-credit charge: $136; out-of-state residents $272.

FINANCIAL AID PICTURE (2011-2012)
Students with need: Need-based aid available for part-time students.
Students without need: No-need awards available for academics.

FINANCIAL AID PROCEDURES
Forms required: FAFSA, institutional form.
Dates and Deadlines: Priority date 6/1; no closing date. Applicants notified on a rolling basis starting 4/1.
Transfers: No deadline. Applicants notified on a rolling basis starting 2/1.

CONTACT
Charlotte Sorg, Director of Financial Aid
22600 State Route 34, Archbold, OH 43502-9517
(419) 267-1333

Notre Dame College

Cleveland, Ohio
www.notredamecollege.edu Federal Code: 003085

4-year private nursing and liberal arts college in large town, affiliated with Roman Catholic Church.
Enrollment: 1,714 undergrads.

BASIC COSTS (2012-2013)
Tuition and fees: $25,514.
Per-credit charge: $508.
Room and board: $8,296.

FINANCIAL AID PICTURE
Students with need: Need-based aid available for full-time students.
Students without need: No-need awards available for academics, athletics, state/district residency.
Scholarships offered: Merit Scholarships; $2,500-$7,500; based on GPA and ACT or SAT scores. Presidential Scholarships; $3,000 awarded in addition to Merit Scholarships; based on 3.9 GPA and 27 ACT or 1210 SAT (exclusive of Writing).

FINANCIAL AID PROCEDURES
Forms required: FAFSA.
Dates and Deadlines: Closing date 5/1. Applicants notified on a rolling basis starting 1/1; must reply within 2 week(s) of notification.
Transfers: No deadline. Applicants notified on a rolling basis.

CONTACT
Mary McCrystal, Director of Student Financial Assistance
4545 College Road, South Euclid, OH 44121-4293
(216) 373-5263

Oberlin College

Oberlin, Ohio Federal Code: 003086
www.oberlin.edu CSS Code: 1587

4-year private music and liberal arts college in small town.
Enrollment: 2,930 undergrads, 1% part-time. 759 full-time freshmen.

Selectivity: Admits less than 50% of applicants. GED not accepted.

BASIC COSTS (2012-2013)
Tuition and fees: $44,905.
Per-credit charge: $1,850.
Room and board: $12,120.

FINANCIAL AID PICTURE (2012-2013)
Students with need: Out of 510 full-time freshmen who applied for aid, 421 were judged to have need. Of these, 421 received aid, and 421 had their full need met. Average financial aid package met 100% of need; average scholarship/grant was $29,351; average loan was $4,533. For part-time students, average financial aid package was $27,196.
Students without need: 243 full-time freshmen who did not demonstrate need for aid received scholarships/grants; average award was $13,169. No-need awards available for academics, music/drama.
Scholarships offered: Bonner Scholarship; based on community service. John Frederick Oberlin Scholarship; based on academic merit. Stern Scholarship; based on excellence in sciences. Dean's Scholarship; available to Conservatory of Music students.

FINANCIAL AID PROCEDURES
Forms required: FAFSA, CSS PROFILE, state aid form, institutional form.
Dates and Deadlines: Priority date 1/15; closing date 2/1. Applicants notified by 4/1; must reply by 5/1 or within 2 week(s) of notification.
Transfers: Closing date 3/1. Applicants notified by 5/15; must reply within 2 week(s) of notification. Limited scholarship funding available for transfer students.

CONTACT
Robert Reddy, Director of Financial Aid
Carnegie Building, 101 North Professor Street, Oberlin, OH 44074-1075
(440) 775-8142

Ohio Business College: Sandusky

Sandusky, Ohio
www.ohiobusinesscollege.edu Federal Code: 021585

2-year for-profit business college in small city.
Enrollment: 387 undergrads.
Selectivity: Open admission.

BASIC COSTS (2012-2013)
Tuition and fees: $8,140.

FINANCIAL AID PICTURE
Students with need: Need-based aid available for full-time and part-time students.

FINANCIAL AID PROCEDURES
Forms required: FAFSA.

CONTACT
Gerilyn Wilson, Lead Financial Aid Administrator
5202 Timber Commons Drive, Sandusky, OH 44870
(419) 627-8345 ext. 14

Ohio Business College: Sheffield

Sheffield, Ohio
www.ohiobusinesscollege.edu Federal Code: 021585

2-year for-profit branch campus and business college in small city.
Enrollment: 395 undergrads.
Selectivity: Open admission.

BASIC COSTS (2012-2013)
Tuition and fees: $8,140.

FINANCIAL AID PICTURE
Students with need: Need-based aid available for full-time and part-time students.

FINANCIAL AID PROCEDURES
Forms required: FAFSA.
Dates and Deadlines: Applicants notified on a rolling basis.

CONTACT
Becky Booher, Director of Financial Aid
5095 Waterford Drive, Sheffield Village, OH 44055

Ohio Christian University

Circleville, Ohio
www.ohiochristian.edu Federal Code: 003030

4-year private university and Bible college in large town, affiliated with Churches of Christ in Christian Union.
Enrollment: 2,797 undergrads, 40% part-time. 413 full-time freshmen.
Selectivity: Admits 50 to 75% of applicants.

BASIC COSTS (2012-2013)
Tuition and fees: $17,750.
Per-credit charge: $690.
Room and board: $6,886.
Additional info: Tuition/fee waivers available for minority students.

FINANCIAL AID PICTURE (2012-2013)
Students with need: 50% of average financial aid package awarded as scholarships/grants, 50% awarded as loans/jobs. Need-based aid available for part-time students.
Students without need: No-need awards available for academics, alumni affiliation, religious affiliation, state/district residency.
Additional info: Religious affiliation tuition discount.

FINANCIAL AID PROCEDURES
Forms required: FAFSA, institutional form.
Dates and Deadlines: Closing date 5/7. Applicants notified on a rolling basis starting 5/1; must reply within 2 week(s) of notification.
Transfers: Closing date 3/1. Applicants notified on a rolling basis; must reply within 2 week(s) of notification.

CONTACT
Wes Brothers, Director of Financial Aid
1476 Lancaster Pike, Circleville, OH 43113
(470) 477-7757

Ohio Dominican University

Columbus, Ohio
www.ohiodominican.edu Federal Code: 003035

4-year private university and liberal arts college in very large city, affiliated with Roman Catholic Church.
Enrollment: 1,557 undergrads, 8% part-time. 266 full-time freshmen.
Selectivity: Admits 50 to 75% of applicants.

BASIC COSTS (2012-2013)
Tuition and fees: $28,104.
Per-credit charge: $558.
Room and board: $9,020.

FINANCIAL AID PICTURE
Students with need: Need-based aid available for full-time and part-time students. Work study available nights, weekends, and for part-time students.
Students without need: No-need awards available for academics, athletics, state/district residency.

FINANCIAL AID PROCEDURES
Forms required: FAFSA.
Dates and Deadlines: Priority date 4/1; no closing date. Applicants notified on a rolling basis starting 3/1; must reply within 2 week(s) of notification.

CONTACT
Laura Meek, Director of Financial Aid
1216 Sunbury Road, Columbus, OH 43219
(614) 251-4778

Ohio Northern University
Ada, Ohio
www.onu.edu Federal Code: 003089

4-year private university in small town, affiliated with United Methodist Church.
Enrollment: 2,273 undergrads, 3% part-time. 630 full-time freshmen.
Selectivity: Admits over 75% of applicants.

BASIC COSTS (2012-2013)
Tuition and fees: $35,678.
Room and board: $10,220.
Additional info: Tuition/fee waivers available for minority students.

FINANCIAL AID PICTURE
Students with need: Need-based aid available for full-time and part-time students. Work study available nights, weekends, and for part-time students.
Students without need: No-need awards available for academics, alumni affiliation, art, leadership, minority status, music/drama, ROTC, state/district residency.
Scholarships offered: Presidential Scholarship: $20,000-$22,000 renewable; based on 3.5 GPA, 30 ACT or 1330 SAT (Pharmacy - 3.8, 31 ACT or 1360 SAT). Trustees Scholarship: $17,000-$19,000 renewable; based on 3.5 GPA, 27 ACT or 1210 SAT (Pharmacy - 3.7 GPA, 29 ACT or 1290 SAT). Academic Achievement Award: $14,000-$16,000; based on 3.3 GPA, 24 ACT or 1090 SAT (Pharmacy - 3.5 GPA, 27 ACT or 1210 SAT). SAT scores exclusive of Writing.

FINANCIAL AID PROCEDURES
Forms required: FAFSA.

CONTACT
Melanie Weaver, Director of Financial Aid
525 South Main Street, Ada, OH 45810
(419) 772-2272

Ohio State University Agricultural Technical Institute
Wooster, Ohio
www.ati.osu.edu Federal Code: 003090

2-year public agricultural and branch campus college in large town.
Enrollment: 607 undergrads, 10% part-time. 304 full-time freshmen.
Selectivity: Open admission; but selective for out-of-state students.

BASIC COSTS (2012-2013)
Tuition and fees: $6,744; out-of-state residents $22,152.
Per-credit charge: $281; out-of-state residents $923.

FINANCIAL AID PICTURE (2012-2013)
Students with need: Out of 278 full-time freshmen who applied for aid, 226 were judged to have need. Of these, 225 received aid, and 17 had their full need met. Average financial aid package met 56% of need; average scholarship/grant was $4,441; average loan was $3,906. For part-time students, average financial aid package was $6,498.
Students without need: This college awards aid only to students with need.

FINANCIAL AID PROCEDURES
Forms required: FAFSA.
Dates and Deadlines: Priority date 2/15; no closing date. Must reply by 5/1 or within 4 week(s) of notification.
Transfers: Priority date 6/1. Applicants notified on a rolling basis starting 6/1; must reply within 4 week(s) of notification.

CONTACT
Barbara LaMoreaux, Coordinator, Financial Aid
1328 Dover Road, Wooster, OH 44691

Ohio State University: Columbus Campus
Columbus, Ohio
www.osu.edu Federal Code: 003090

4-year public university in very large city.
Enrollment: 41,877 undergrads, 8% part-time. 7,204 full-time freshmen.
Selectivity: Admits 50 to 75% of applicants.

BASIC COSTS (2012-2013)
Tuition and fees: $10,037; out-of-state residents $25,445.
Room and board: $9,495.

FINANCIAL AID PICTURE (2012-2013)
Students with need: Out of 5,787 full-time freshmen who applied for aid, 3,827 were judged to have need. Of these, 3,795 received aid, and 903 had their full need met. Average financial aid package met 69% of need; average scholarship/grant was $9,404; average loan was $3,599. For part-time students, average financial aid package was $8,838.
Students without need: 1,871 full-time freshmen who did not demonstrate need for aid received scholarships/grants; average award was $6,003. No-need awards available for academics, alumni affiliation, art, athletics, job skills, leadership, minority status, music/drama, ROTC, state/district residency.
Scholarships offered: 67 full-time freshmen received athletic scholarships; average amount $22,406.
Cumulative student debt: 59% of graduating class had student loans; average debt was $26,409.

FINANCIAL AID PROCEDURES
Forms required: FAFSA.
Dates and Deadlines: Priority date 2/15; no closing date. Must reply by 5/1 or within 4 week(s) of notification.
Transfers: Priority date 6/1. Applicants notified on a rolling basis starting 6/1; must reply within 4 week(s) of notification.

CONTACT
Director of Student Financial Aid
110 Enarson Hall, Columbus, OH 43210
(614) 292-0300

Ohio State University: Lima Campus
Lima, Ohio
www.lima.ohio-state.edu Federal Code: 003090

4-year public university and branch campus college in large town.
Enrollment: 1,021 undergrads, 12% part-time. 414 full-time freshmen.
Selectivity: Open admission; but selective for out-of-state students.

BASIC COSTS (2012-2013)
Tuition and fees: $6,564; out-of-state residents $21,972.
Per-credit charge: $274; out-of-state residents $916.

FINANCIAL AID PICTURE (2012-2013)
Students with need: Out of 390 full-time freshmen who applied for aid, 331 were judged to have need. Of these, 328 received aid, and 26 had their full need met. Average financial aid package met 54% of need; average scholarship/grant was $3,757; average loan was $3,678. For part-time students, average financial aid package was $7,508.
Students without need: 55 full-time freshmen who did not demonstrate need for aid received scholarships/grants; average award was $946. No-need awards available for academics, alumni affiliation, art, athletics, job skills, leadership, minority status, music/drama, ROTC, state/district residency.

FINANCIAL AID PROCEDURES
Forms required: FAFSA.
Dates and Deadlines: Priority date 2/15; no closing date. Must reply by 5/1 or within 4 week(s) of notification.
Transfers: Priority date 6/21. Applicants notified on a rolling basis starting 6/1; must reply within 4 week(s) of notification.

CONTACT
Bryan Albright, Coordinator, Financial Aid
4240 Campus Drive, Lima, OH 45804-3596
(419) 995-8147

Ohio State University: Mansfield Campus
Mansfield, Ohio
www.mansfield.ohio-state.edu Federal Code: 003090

4-year public university and branch campus college in large town.
Enrollment: 1,155 undergrads, 13% part-time. 470 full-time freshmen.
Selectivity: Open admission; but selective for out-of-state students.

BASIC COSTS (2012-2013)
Tuition and fees: $6,564; out-of-state residents $21,972.
Room and board: $5,205.

FINANCIAL AID PICTURE (2012-2013)
Students with need: Out of 425 full-time freshmen who applied for aid, 358 were judged to have need. Of these, 355 received aid, and 29 had their full need met. Average financial aid package met 52% of need; average scholarship/grant was $4,664; average loan was $3,577. For part-time students, average financial aid package was $7,665.
Students without need: 27 full-time freshmen who did not demonstrate need for aid received scholarships/grants; average award was $1,858. No-need awards available for academics, alumni affiliation, art, athletics, job skills, leadership, minority status, music/drama, ROTC, state/district residency.

FINANCIAL AID PROCEDURES
Forms required: FAFSA.
Dates and Deadlines: Priority date 2/15; no closing date. Must reply by 5/1 or within 4 week(s) of notification.
Transfers: Priority date 6/1. Applicants notified on a rolling basis starting 6/1; must reply within 4 week(s) of notification.

CONTACT
Ken Sigler, Director of Admissions & Financial Aid
1680 University Drive, Mansfield, OH 44906
(419) 755-4011

Ohio State University: Marion Campus
Marion, Ohio
www.osumarion.osu.edu Federal Code: 003090

4-year public university and branch campus college in large town.
Enrollment: 1,193 undergrads, 21% part-time. 353 full-time freshmen.
Selectivity: Open admission; but selective for out-of-state students.

BASIC COSTS (2012-2013)
Tuition and fees: $6,564; out-of-state residents $21,972.
Per-credit charge: $274; out-of-state residents $916.

FINANCIAL AID PICTURE (2012-2013)
Students with need: Out of 310 full-time freshmen who applied for aid, 239 were judged to have need. Of these, 238 received aid, and 27 had their full need met. Average financial aid package met 58% of need; average scholarship/grant was $4,550; average loan was $3,485. For part-time students, average financial aid package was $8,007.
Students without need: 79 full-time freshmen who did not demonstrate need for aid received scholarships/grants; average award was $1,451. No-need awards available for academics, alumni affiliation, art, athletics, job skills, leadership, minority status, music/drama, ROTC, state/district residency.

FINANCIAL AID PROCEDURES
Forms required: FAFSA.
Dates and Deadlines: Priority date 2/15; no closing date. Must reply by 5/1 or within 4 week(s) of notification.
Transfers: Priority date 6/1. Applicants notified on a rolling basis starting 6/1; must reply within 4 week(s) of notification.

CONTACT
Matt Moreau, Coordinator of Admissions
1465 Mount Vernon Avenue, Marion, OH 43302
(740) 389-6786 ext. 6273

Ohio State University: Newark Campus
Newark, Ohio
www.newark.osu.edu Federal Code: 003090

4-year public university and branch campus college in large town.
Enrollment: 2,230 undergrads, 14% part-time. 1,090 full-time freshmen.
Selectivity: Open admission; but selective for out-of-state students.

BASIC COSTS (2012-2013)
Tuition and fees: $6,564; out-of-state residents $21,972.
Additional info: Cost of room only, $7,185.

FINANCIAL AID PICTURE (2012-2013)
Students with need: Out of 955 full-time freshmen who applied for aid, 766 were judged to have need. Of these, 766 received aid, and 65 had their full need met. Average financial aid package met 55% of need; average scholarship/grant was $3,962; average loan was $3,484. For part-time students, average financial aid package was $7,286.
Students without need: 324 full-time freshmen who did not demonstrate need for aid received scholarships/grants; average award was $629. No-need awards available for academics, alumni affiliation, art, athletics, job skills, leadership, minority status, music/drama, ROTC, state/district residency.

FINANCIAL AID PROCEDURES
Forms required: FAFSA.
Dates and Deadlines: Priority date 2/15; no closing date. Must reply by 5/1 or within 4 week(s) of notification.
Transfers: Priority date 6/1. Applicants notified on a rolling basis starting 6/1; must reply within 4 week(s) of notification.

CONTACT
Faith Phillips, Director of Financial Aid
1179 University Drive, Newark, OH 43055
(740) 366-9435

Ohio University
Athens, Ohio
www.ohio.edu Federal Code: 003100

4-year public university in large town.
Enrollment: 22,573 undergrads, 25% part-time. 3,873 full-time freshmen.
Selectivity: Admits over 75% of applicants.

BASIC COSTS (2012-2013)
Tuition and fees: $10,282; out-of-state residents $19,246.
Per-credit charge: $487; out-of-state residents $929.
Room and board: $10,010.

FINANCIAL AID PICTURE (2012-2013)
Students with need: Out of 3,348 full-time freshmen who applied for aid, 2,390 were judged to have need. Of these, 2,390 received aid. For part-time students, average financial aid package was $6,820.
Students without need: 492 full-time freshmen who did not demonstrate need for aid received scholarships/grants. No-need awards available for academics, art, athletics, minority status, music/drama, religious affiliation, ROTC.
Scholarships offered: 72 full-time freshmen received athletic scholarships; average amount $16,283.
Cumulative student debt: 68% of graduating class had student loans; average debt was $27,079.

FINANCIAL AID PROCEDURES
Forms required: FAFSA.
Dates and Deadlines: Priority date 3/15; closing date 4/1. Applicants notified on a rolling basis starting 4/1; must reply within 3 week(s) of notification.
Transfers: Priority date 5/15; no deadline. Applicants notified on a rolling basis starting 5/15.

CONTACT
Valerie Miller, Director, Student Financial Aid and Scholarships
120 Chubb Hall, Athens, OH 45701-2979
(740) 593-4141

Ohio University: Chillicothe Campus
Chillicothe, Ohio
www.chillicothe.ohiou.edu Federal Code: 003102

4-year public branch campus college in large town.
Enrollment: 2,291 undergrads.
Selectivity: Open admission; but selective for some programs.

FINANCIAL AID PICTURE
Students with need: Need-based aid available for full-time and part-time students.

FINANCIAL AID PROCEDURES
Forms required: FAFSA.
Dates and Deadlines: Applicants notified on a rolling basis.

CONTACT
Dennis Bothel, Coordinator of Academic Advising
101 University Drive, Chillicothe, OH 45601
(740) 774-7228

Ohio University: Eastern Campus
St. Clairsville, Ohio
www.eastern.ohiou.edu Federal Code: 003101

4-year public branch campus college in small town.
Enrollment: 1,087 undergrads.
Selectivity: Open admission; but selective for some programs.

FINANCIAL AID PICTURE
Students with need: Need-based aid available for full-time and part-time students.
Students without need: No-need awards available for academics, alumni affiliation, minority status.

FINANCIAL AID PROCEDURES
Forms required: FAFSA.
Dates and Deadlines: Priority date 3/15; no closing date.
Transfers: Priority date 3/1; closing date 5/1.

CONTACT
Kevin Chenoweth, Student Services Manager
45425 National Road West, St. Clairsville, OH 43950-9724
(740) 695-1720 ext. 209

Ohio University: Lancaster Campus
Lancaster, Ohio
www.lancaster.ohiou.edu Federal Code: 003104

4-year public branch campus college in large town.
Enrollment: 2,575 undergrads.
Selectivity: Open admission; but selective for some programs.

BASIC COSTS (2012-2013)
Tuition and fees: $5,022; out-of-state residents $6,868.
Per-credit charge: $222; out-of-state residents $308.

FINANCIAL AID PICTURE
Students with need: Need-based aid available for full-time and part-time students.
Additional info: Scholarship application deadline April 1.

FINANCIAL AID PROCEDURES
Forms required: FAFSA.
Dates and Deadlines: Priority date 2/15; no closing date. Applicants notified on a rolling basis; must reply within 2 week(s) of notification.

CONTACT
Pat Fox, Coordinator of Financial Aid
1570 Granville Pike, Lancaster, OH 43130
(740) 654-6711 ext. 209

Ohio University: Southern Campus at Ironton
Ironton, Ohio
www.southern.ohiou.edu Federal Code: 003103

4-year public branch campus college in large town.
Enrollment: 2,100 undergrads.
Selectivity: Open admission.

FINANCIAL AID PICTURE
Students with need: Need-based aid available for full-time and part-time students.
Students without need: No-need awards available for academics, state/district residency.

FINANCIAL AID PROCEDURES
Forms required: FAFSA.
Dates and Deadlines: Priority date 3/15; no closing date. Applicants notified on a rolling basis starting 4/1.

CONTACT
Jacki Adkins, Coordinator of Financial Aid and Scholarships
1804 Liberty Avenue, Ironton, OH 45638
(740) 533-4600

Ohio Valley College of Technology

East Liverpool, Ohio
www.ovct.edu Federal Code: 016261

2-year for-profit junior and technical college in large town.
Enrollment: 213 undergrads.

BASIC COSTS (2012-2013)

Tuition and fees: $10,580.
Additional info: Tuition and fees include book rentals.

FINANCIAL AID PICTURE

Students with need: Need-based aid available for full-time and part-time students.
Students without need: This college awards aid only to students with need.

FINANCIAL AID PROCEDURES

Forms required: FAFSA.
Dates and Deadlines: Applicants notified on a rolling basis; must reply within 6 week(s) of notification.

CONTACT

Rebecca Steckman, Regional Financial Aid Director
15258 State Route 170, East Liverpool, OH 43920-9585
(330) 385-1070

Ohio Wesleyan University

Delaware, Ohio
www.owu.edu Federal Code: 003109

4-year private liberal arts college in large town, affiliated with United Methodist Church.
Enrollment: 1,812 undergrads. 483 full-time freshmen.
Selectivity: Admits 50 to 75% of applicants.

BASIC COSTS (2012-2013)

Tuition and fees: $39,150.
Room and board: $10,760.

FINANCIAL AID PICTURE (2011-2012)

Students with need: Out of 393 full-time freshmen who applied for aid, 341 were judged to have need. Of these, 341 received aid, and 106 had their full need met. Average financial aid package met 84% of need; average scholarship/grant was $25,446; average loan was $3,079.
Students without need: 126 full-time freshmen who did not demonstrate need for aid received scholarships/grants; average award was $20,485. No-need awards available for academics, alumni affiliation, art, leadership, minority status, music/drama, religious affiliation, state/district residency.
Scholarships offered: Presidential scholarships; full tuition; 25 awarded. Trustee scholarships; 75% of tuition; 40 awarded. Faculty scholarships; 50% of tuition; 140 awarded.
Cumulative student debt: 65% of graduating class had student loans; average debt was $30,900.

FINANCIAL AID PROCEDURES

Forms required: FAFSA.
Dates and Deadlines: Priority date 2/15; no closing date. Applicants notified on a rolling basis starting 2/15; must reply by 5/1 or within 2 week(s) of notification.
Transfers: Must reply within 2 week(s) of notification.

CONTACT

Lee Harrell, Assistant Vice President of Admission and Financial Aid
61 South Sandusky Street, Delaware, OH 43015-2398
(740) 368-3050

Otterbein University

Westerville, Ohio
www.otterbein.edu Federal Code: 003110

4-year private university and liberal arts college in large town, affiliated with United Methodist Church.
Enrollment: 2,457 undergrads.
Selectivity: Admits over 75% of applicants.

BASIC COSTS (2012-2013)

Tuition and fees: $30,658.
Room and board: $8,684.
Additional info: Tuition/fee waivers available for adults, minority students.

FINANCIAL AID PICTURE (2011-2012)

Students with need: Work study available nights, weekends, and for part-time students.
Students without need: No-need awards available for academics, alumni affiliation, art, leadership, minority status, music/drama, state/district residency.

FINANCIAL AID PROCEDURES

Forms required: FAFSA.
Dates and Deadlines: Priority date 4/1; no closing date. Applicants notified on a rolling basis starting 2/15.
Transfers: Transfer students must complete appropriate state grant transfer paperwork.

CONTACT

Thomas Yarnell, Director of Financial Aid
One Otterbein College, Westerville, OH 43081
(614) 823-1502

Owens Community College: Toledo

Toledo, Ohio
www.owens.edu Federal Code: 005753

2-year public community college in very large city.
Enrollment: 12,535 undergrads, 54% part-time. 1,538 full-time freshmen.
Selectivity: Open admission; but selective for some programs.

BASIC COSTS (2012-2013)

Tuition and fees: $4,047; out-of-state residents $8,136.
Per-credit charge: $131; out-of-state residents $277.

FINANCIAL AID PICTURE (2012-2013)

Students with need: Out of 1,399 full-time freshmen who applied for aid, 1,244 were judged to have need. Of these, 1,234 received aid, and 68 had their full need met. Average financial aid package met 62% of need; average scholarship/grant was $4,936; average loan was $7,745. For part-time students, average financial aid package was $6,405.
Students without need: 14 full-time freshmen who did not demonstrate need for aid received scholarships/grants; average award was $1,038. No-need awards available for academics, athletics, job skills, state/district residency.
Scholarships offered: 15 full-time freshmen received athletic scholarships; average amount $3,999.
Additional info: Other types of financial aid available: federal family education loan program, private foundation loan (SCHELL).

FINANCIAL AID PROCEDURES

Forms required: FAFSA.
Dates and Deadlines: Priority date 3/31; no closing date.

CONTACT

Betsy Johnson, Dean, Student Accounts
30335 Oregon Road, Toledo, OH 43699-1947
(567) 661-7343

Pontifical College Josephinum
Columbus, Ohio
www.pcj.edu Federal Code: 003113

4-year private liberal arts and seminary college for men in very large city, affiliated with Roman Catholic Church.
Enrollment: 104 undergrads.

BASIC COSTS (2013-2014)
Tuition and fees: $20,614.
Per-credit charge: $750.
Room and board: $8,984.

FINANCIAL AID PICTURE
Students with need: Need-based aid available for full-time and part-time students. Work study available nights, weekends, and for part-time students.
Students without need: This college awards aid only to students with need.

FINANCIAL AID PROCEDURES
Forms required: FAFSA, institutional form.
Dates and Deadlines: Priority date 9/2; no closing date. Applicants notified on a rolling basis starting 8/15; must reply within 2 week(s) of notification.

CONTACT
Marky Leichtnam, Director of Financial Aid
7625 North High Street, Columbus, OH 43235-1499
(614) 985-2212

Rosedale Bible College
Irwin, Ohio
www.rosedale.edu Federal Code: 034253

2-year private Bible and junior college in rural community, affiliated with Mennonite Church.
Enrollment: 56 undergrads.
Selectivity: Open admission.

BASIC COSTS (2013-2014)
Tuition and fees: $8,401.
Per-credit charge: $269.
Room and board: $5,650.

FINANCIAL AID PICTURE
Students with need: Need-based aid available for full-time and part-time students.
Students without need: No-need awards available for academics, leadership, religious affiliation.

FINANCIAL AID PROCEDURES
Forms required: FAFSA, institutional form.
Dates and Deadlines: Applicants notified on a rolling basis.
Transfers: Priority date 5/1. Applicants notified on a rolling basis.

CONTACT
Twila Weber
2270 Rosedale Road, Irwin, OH 43029
(740) 857-1311

School of Advertising Art
Kettering, Ohio
www.saa.edu Federal Code: 017160

2-year for-profit visual arts and technical college in small city.
Enrollment: 112 undergrads.

BASIC COSTS (2012-2013)
Tuition and fees: $23,724.
Per-credit charge: $375.
Additional info: Tuition/fee waivers available for minority students.

FINANCIAL AID PICTURE
Students with need: Need-based aid available for full-time students.
Students without need: No-need awards available for academics, art, leadership, minority status.

FINANCIAL AID PROCEDURES
Forms required: FAFSA.
Dates and Deadlines: Priority date 7/1; no closing date. Applicants notified on a rolling basis starting 4/1; must reply by 7/1 or within 1 week(s) of notification.
Transfers: No deadline. Applicants notified on a rolling basis starting 4/1; must reply by 7/1 or within 1 week(s) of notification.

CONTACT
Tracy Gardner, Financial Aid Director
1725 East David Road, Kettering, OH 45440-1612
(937) 294-0592 ext. 106

Shawnee State University
Portsmouth, Ohio
www.shawnee.edu Federal Code: 009942

4-year public university in large town.
Enrollment: 4,411 undergrads, 14% part-time. 1,115 full-time freshmen.
Selectivity: Open admission; but selective for some programs.

BASIC COSTS (2012-2013)
Tuition and fees: $6,988; out-of-state residents $11,963.
Per-credit charge: $247; out-of-state residents $454.
Room and board: $9,012.

FINANCIAL AID PICTURE
Students with need: Need-based aid available for full-time and part-time students.
Additional info: ACT recommended for scholarship applicants.

FINANCIAL AID PROCEDURES
Forms required: FAFSA.
Dates and Deadlines: Applicants notified on a rolling basis starting 3/15; must reply within 4 week(s) of notification.

CONTACT
Nicole Neal, Director Financial Aid
940 Second Street, Portsmouth, OH 45662
(740) 351-4243

Sinclair Community College
Dayton, Ohio
www.sinclair.edu Federal Code: 003119

2-year public community college in small city.
Enrollment: 20,932 undergrads, 64% part-time. 2,170 full-time freshmen.
Selectivity: Open admission; but selective for some programs.

BASIC COSTS (2012-2013)
Tuition and fees: $2,771; out-of-district residents $4,189; out-of-state residents $7,992.
Per-credit charge: $92; out-of-district residents $140; out-of-state residents $266.

FINANCIAL AID PICTURE
Students with need: Need-based aid available for full-time and part-time students. Work study available nights, weekends, and for part-time students.

Students without need: No-need awards available for academics, athletics.

FINANCIAL AID PROCEDURES

Forms required: FAFSA, institutional form.

Dates and Deadlines: Priority date 5/1; closing date 8/1. Applicants notified on a rolling basis.

Transfers: No deadline.

CONTACT

Annesa Cheek, Director of Financial Aid and Scholarships
444 West Third Street, Dayton, OH 45402-1460
(937) 512-2781

Southern State Community College

Hillsboro, Ohio
www.sscc.edu Federal Code: 012870

2-year public community college in small town.
Enrollment: 2,239 undergrads, 49% part-time. 192 full-time freshmen.
Selectivity: Open admission; but selective for some programs.

BASIC COSTS (2012-2013)

Tuition and fees: $4,505; out-of-state residents $8,035.
Per-credit charge: $139; out-of-state residents $276.

FINANCIAL AID PICTURE

Students with need: Need-based aid available for full-time and part-time students. Work study available nights.

Students without need: No-need awards available for academics, art, athletics, music/drama.

FINANCIAL AID PROCEDURES

Forms required: FAFSA, institutional form.

Dates and Deadlines: Priority date 7/1; closing date 9/1. Applicants notified by 4/15; must reply within 2 week(s) of notification.

Transfers: No deadline.

CONTACT

Janeen Deatley, Financial Aid Director
100 Hobart Drive, Hillsboro, OH 45133
(937) 393-3431 ext. 2610

Stark State College of Technology

North Canton, Ohio
www.starkstate.edu Federal Code: 011141

2-year public community college in small city.
Enrollment: 12,945 undergrads, 67% part-time. 1,431 full-time freshmen.
Selectivity: Open admission; but selective for some programs.

BASIC COSTS (2012-2013)

Tuition and fees: $4,410; out-of-state residents $7,140.
Per-credit charge: $147; out-of-state residents $238.

FINANCIAL AID PICTURE

Students with need: Need-based aid available for full-time and part-time students. Work study available nights, weekends, and for part-time students.

Students without need: This college awards aid only to students with need.

FINANCIAL AID PROCEDURES

Forms required: FAFSA, institutional form.

Dates and Deadlines: Priority date 5/1; no closing date. Applicants notified on a rolling basis starting 4/1; must reply within 4 week(s) of notification.

CONTACT

Amy Welty, Director of Financial Aid
6200 Frank Avenue NW, North Canton, OH 44720
(330) 494-6170

Stautzenberger College

Maumee, Ohio
www.sctoday.edu Federal Code: 004866

2-year for-profit technical and career college in large town.
Enrollment: 850 undergrads.
Selectivity: Open admission; but selective for some programs.

FINANCIAL AID PICTURE

Students with need: Need-based aid available for full-time and part-time students.

Students without need: This college awards aid only to students with need.

FINANCIAL AID PROCEDURES

Forms required: FAFSA.

Dates and Deadlines: Applicants notified on a rolling basis.

CONTACT

Mari Huffman, Financial Aid Director
1796 Indian Wood Circle, Maumee, OH 43537-4007
(419) 866-0261

Stautzenberger College: Brecksville

Brecksville, Ohio
www.LearnWhatYouLove.com

2-year for-profit career college in large town.
Enrollment: 294 undergrads, 74% part-time.
Selectivity: Open admission.

BASIC COSTS (2012-2013)

Additional info: Tuition ranges from $262 to $275 per credit hour; required fees, $270.

FINANCIAL AID PICTURE

Students with need: Need-based aid available for full-time and part-time students.

Students without need: This college awards aid only to students with need.

FINANCIAL AID PROCEDURES

Forms required: FAFSA.

Dates and Deadlines: Applicants notified on a rolling basis.

Transfers: No deadline. Applicants notified on a rolling basis.

CONTACT

Mari Huffman, Director of Financial Aid
8001 Katherine Boulevard, Brecksville, OH 44141

Terra State Community College

Fremont, Ohio
www.terra.edu Federal Code: 008278

2-year public community and technical college in large town.
Enrollment: 3,172 undergrads.
Selectivity: Open admission.

BASIC COSTS (2012-2013)

Tuition and fees: $4,244; out-of-state residents $6,663.
Per-credit charge: $127; out-of-state residents $208.

FINANCIAL AID PICTURE

Students with need: Need-based aid available for full-time and part-time students.

Students without need: No-need awards available for academics.

FINANCIAL AID PROCEDURES
Forms required: FAFSA, institutional form.
Dates and Deadlines: Priority date 5/1; no closing date. Applicants notified on a rolling basis starting 5/15.

CONTACT
Christina Bratton, Director of Financial Aid
2830 Napoleon Road, Fremont, OH 43420-9600
(419) 559-2387

Tiffin University
Tiffin, Ohio
www.tiffin.edu Federal Code: 003121

4-year private university and liberal arts college in large town.
Enrollment: 5,016 undergrads, 45% part-time. 701 full-time freshmen.
Selectivity: Admits less than 50% of applicants.

BASIC COSTS (2013-2014)
Tuition and fees: $20,700.
Per-credit charge: $690.
Room and board: $9,573.

FINANCIAL AID PICTURE (2012-2013)
Students with need: Out of 480 full-time freshmen who applied for aid, 458 were judged to have need. Of these, 458 received aid, and 46 had their full need met. Average financial aid package met 65% of need; average scholarship/grant was $11,966; average loan was $4,816. For part-time students, average financial aid package was $7,298.
Students without need: No-need awards available for academics, alumni affiliation, athletics, leadership, music/drama, state/district residency.
Scholarships offered: 25 full-time freshmen received athletic scholarships; average amount $9,676.
Cumulative student debt: 73% of graduating class had student loans; average debt was $30,119.

FINANCIAL AID PROCEDURES
Forms required: FAFSA.
Dates and Deadlines: Applicants notified on a rolling basis starting 1/15; must reply within 2 week(s) of notification.
Transfers: No deadline.

CONTACT
Cindy Little, Director of Financial Aid
155 Miami Street, Tiffin, OH 44883
(800) 968-6446 ext. 3415

Trumbull Business College
Warren, Ohio
www.trumbull.edu Federal Code: 013585

2-year for-profit business college in large town.
Enrollment: 233 undergrads.
Selectivity: Open admission.

BASIC COSTS (2012-2013)
Tuition and fees: $11,340.
Per-credit charge: $252.

FINANCIAL AID PICTURE
Students with need: Need-based aid available for full-time and part-time students.

FINANCIAL AID PROCEDURES
Forms required: FAFSA.

CONTACT
Florence Henning, Financial Assistance Director
3200 Ridge Road, Warren, OH 44484
(330) 369-3200 ext. 12

Union Institute & University
Cincinnati, Ohio
www.myunion.edu Federal Code: 010923

4-year private university in very large city.
Enrollment: 1,184 undergrads.

BASIC COSTS (2012-2013)
Tuition and fees: $14,550.
Per-credit charge: $481.

FINANCIAL AID PICTURE
Students with need: Need-based aid available for full-time and part-time students.
Students without need: No-need awards available for academics, state/district residency.

FINANCIAL AID PROCEDURES
Forms required: FAFSA.
Dates and Deadlines: Must reply within 4 week(s) of notification.

CONTACT
Edward Walton, Director of Financial Aid
440 East McMillan Street, Cincinnati, OH 45206
(800) 861-6400

University of Akron
Akron, Ohio
www.uakron.edu Federal Code: 003123

4-year public university in small city.
Enrollment: 20,716 undergrads, 20% part-time. 4,371 full-time freshmen.
Selectivity: Admits over 75% of applicants.

BASIC COSTS (2012-2013)
Tuition and fees: $9,863; out-of-state residents $18,063.
Per-credit charge: $345; out-of-state residents $686.
Room and board: $9,878.

FINANCIAL AID PICTURE (2011-2012)
Students with need: Out of 4,022 full-time freshmen who applied for aid, 3,452 were judged to have need. Of these, 3,452 received aid, and 259 had their full need met. Average financial aid package met 47% of need; average scholarship/grant was $4,574; average loan was $3,151. For part-time students, average financial aid package was $5,249.
Students without need: 431 full-time freshmen who did not demonstrate need for aid received scholarships/grants; average award was $3,886. No-need awards available for academics, art, athletics, leadership, music/drama, ROTC, state/district residency.
Scholarships offered: ***Merit:*** Scholarships for Excellence; $6,000 per year; based on 3.8 GPA, 30 ACT, 1320 SAT (exclusive of Writing); deadline February 1. Presidential Scholarships; $3,000 per year; based on 3.8 GPA, 27 ACT, 1200 SAT. Honors Scholarships; $1,500-$3,000 per year; based on top 10% of class, 3.5 GPA; deadline December 31. Jim and Vanita Oelschlager Leadership Award; $1,000-$17,000 per year; based on leadership and service. Academic Scholarship; $500-$1,500 per year; based on upper 30% of high school class, 21 ACT, 3.0 GPA. Akron Advantage Award; non-resident surcharge reduction of 60% or 100%; for students who meet academic criteria from 49 states outside of Ohio plus U.S. territories. ***Athletic:*** 26 full-time freshmen received athletic scholarships; average amount $10,186.

Cumulative student debt: 72% of graduating class had student loans; average debt was $23,392.

FINANCIAL AID PROCEDURES

Forms required: FAFSA, institutional form.

Dates and Deadlines: Priority date 2/1; no closing date. Applicants notified on a rolling basis starting 4/1; must reply within 2 week(s) of notification.

Transfers: Priority date 3/1; no deadline. Applicants notified on a rolling basis starting 6/15; must reply within 2 week(s) of notification.

CONTACT

Michelle Ellis, Director, Student Financial Aid
Simmons Hall, Akron, OH 44325-2001
(330) 972-7032

University of Akron: Wayne College

Orrville, Ohio
www.wayne.uakron.edu Federal Code: 003123

2-year public branch campus and junior college in small town.
Enrollment: 1,843 undergrads, 44% part-time. 298 full-time freshmen.
Selectivity: Open admission.

BASIC COSTS (2012-2013)

Tuition and fees: $6,116; out-of-state residents $14,457.
Per-credit charge: $248; out-of-state residents $526.

FINANCIAL AID PICTURE

Students with need: Need-based aid available for full-time and part-time students. Work study available nights, weekends, and for part-time students.

Students without need: No-need awards available for academics, art, athletics, leadership, minority status, music/drama, state/district residency.

Additional info: All financial aid processed through University of Akron.

FINANCIAL AID PROCEDURES

Forms required: FAFSA, institutional form.

Dates and Deadlines: Closing date 3/15. Applicants notified on a rolling basis starting 4/15.

CONTACT

Theresa Rabbitts, Financial Aid Counselor
1901 Smucker Road, Orrville, OH 44667-9758
(330) 684-8900

University of Cincinnati

Cincinnati, Ohio
www.uc.edu Federal Code: 003125

4-year public university in large city.
Enrollment: 22,698 undergrads, 14% part-time. 4,106 full-time freshmen.
Selectivity: Admits 50 to 75% of applicants.

BASIC COSTS (2012-2013)

Tuition and fees: $10,784; out-of-state residents $25,816.
Per-credit charge: $381; out-of-state residents $1,007.
Room and board: $10,170.

FINANCIAL AID PICTURE (2012-2013)

Students with need: Average financial aid package met 48% of need; average scholarship/grant was $6,292; average loan was $3,626. For part-time students, average financial aid package was $7,687.

Students without need: No-need awards available for academics, alumni affiliation, art, athletics, leadership, minority status, music/drama, ROTC, state/district residency.

Cumulative student debt: 69% of graduating class had student loans; average debt was $30,078.

FINANCIAL AID PROCEDURES

Forms required: FAFSA.

Dates and Deadlines: Applicants notified on a rolling basis starting 4/1; must reply within 2 week(s) of notification.

CONTACT

Connie Williams, Director, Financial Aid
PO Box 210091, Cincinnati, OH 45221-0091
(513) 556-6982

University of Cincinnati: Clermont College

Batavia, Ohio
www.ucclermont.edu Federal Code: 003125

2-year public branch campus college in small town.
Enrollment: 3,198 undergrads, 38% part-time. 622 full-time freshmen.
Selectivity: Open admission; but selective for some programs.

BASIC COSTS (2012-2013)

Tuition and fees: $5,210; out-of-state residents $12,302.
Per-credit charge: $218; out-of-state residents $513.

FINANCIAL AID PICTURE

Students with need: Need-based aid available for full-time and part-time students. Work study available nights, weekends, and for part-time students.

Students without need: No-need awards available for academics, leadership, minority status, state/district residency.

Additional info: All financial aid applications and awards administered through Uptown campus except in-house loans and scholarships.

FINANCIAL AID PROCEDURES

Forms required: FAFSA.

Dates and Deadlines: Applicants notified on a rolling basis.

Transfers: No deadline. Applicants notified on a rolling basis.

CONTACT

Jessica Max, University Services Associate
4200 Clermont College Drive, Batavia, OH 45103
(513) 732-5202

University of Cincinnati: Raymond Walters College

Cincinnati, Ohio
www.rwc.uc.edu Federal Code: 003125

2-year public branch campus college in large city.
Enrollment: 4,971 undergrads.
Selectivity: Open admission; but selective for some programs.

BASIC COSTS (2012-2013)

Tuition and fees: $5,890; out-of-state residents $14,516.

FINANCIAL AID PICTURE

Students with need: Need-based aid available for full-time and part-time students.

Students without need: This college awards aid only to students with need.

Scholarships offered: Dean's scholarships: $1,500; based on 2.5 GPA, tech prep program participation, 2-page essay; 10 available. Cincinnatus Scholarship Competition: $1,500 to full tuition, room, board and books; must have 26 ACT or be in top 5% of high school class to qualify.

Additional info: All financial aid applications and awards administered through main campus.

FINANCIAL AID PROCEDURES

Forms required: FAFSA.

Dates and Deadlines: Priority date 3/15; no closing date. Applicants notified on a rolling basis starting 3/15; must reply within 2 week(s) of notification.

CONTACT

Chris Powers, Director of Enrollment Management
9555 Plainfield Road, Cincinnati, OH 45236-1096
(513) 745-5740

University of Dayton

Dayton, Ohio
www.udayton.edu Federal Code: 003127

4-year private university in small city, affiliated with Roman Catholic Church.
Enrollment: 7,793 undergrads, 5% part-time. 2,043 full-time freshmen.
Selectivity: Admits 50 to 75% of applicants.

BASIC COSTS (2012-2013)

Tuition and fees: $33,400.
Room and board: $10,500.
Additional info: Tuition/fee waivers available for adults.

FINANCIAL AID PICTURE (2012-2013)

Students with need: Out of 1,747 full-time freshmen who applied for aid, 1,210 were judged to have need. Of these, 1,210 received aid, and 410 had their full need met. Average financial aid package met 80% of need; average scholarship/grant was $24,112; average loan was $3,377. For part-time students, average financial aid package was $8,332.

Students without need: 707 full-time freshmen who did not demonstrate need for aid received scholarships/grants; average award was $12,225. No-need awards available for academics, alumni affiliation, art, athletics, job skills, leadership, minority status, music/drama, religious affiliation, ROTC, state/district residency.

Scholarships offered: ***Merit:*** Merit Scholarships; $1,000 to full tuition; based on GPA, ACT/SAT, service and leadership. Visual arts awards; amounts vary; based on student portfolios. Chaminade Scholarships; $2,500; for students accepted to Chaminade Scholars Program. National Merit Scholarships; $1,000 to $2,000; available to all students who are selected by the National Merit Scholarship Corporation and select UD as their first choice. Army ROTC awards; supplements U.S. Army ROTC awards with scholarship incentives. ***Athletic:*** 45 full-time freshmen received athletic scholarships; average amount $17,638.

Cumulative student debt: 62% of graduating class had student loans; average debt was $40,628.

FINANCIAL AID PROCEDURES

Forms required: FAFSA.
Dates and Deadlines: Priority date 3/1; no closing date. Applicants notified on a rolling basis starting 3/25; must reply by 5/1 or within 2 week(s) of notification.
Transfers: Priority date 6/1; no deadline. Applicants notified on a rolling basis starting 3/15; must reply within 2 week(s) of notification. Students must submit FAFSA prior to October 1 each year for consideration for state funds.

CONTACT

Kathy McEuen Harmon, Dean of Admission and Financial Aid
300 College Park, Dayton, OH 45469-1300
(800) 427-5029

University of Findlay

Findlay, Ohio
www.findlay.edu Federal Code: 003045

4-year private university and health science college in small city, affiliated with Church of God.
Enrollment: 2,641 undergrads, 6% part-time. 592 full-time freshmen.
Selectivity: Admits 50 to 75% of applicants.

BASIC COSTS (2012-2013)

Tuition and fees: $28,914.
Per-credit charge: $623.
Room and board: $9,166.

FINANCIAL AID PICTURE (2011-2012)

Students with need: Out of 529 full-time freshmen who applied for aid, 467 were judged to have need. Of these, 467 received aid, and 79 had their full need met. Average financial aid package met 69% of need; average scholarship/grant was $18,403; average loan was $3,374.

Students without need: 125 full-time freshmen who did not demonstrate need for aid received scholarships/grants; average award was $12,924. No-need awards available for academics, alumni affiliation, athletics, music/drama, state/district residency.

Scholarships offered: ***Merit:*** Full tuition available to select valedictorian/salutatorians. Automatic academic awards available based on GPA, test scores. ***Athletic:*** 86 full-time freshmen received athletic scholarships; average amount $7,899.

Cumulative student debt: 75% of graduating class had student loans; average debt was $33,623.

FINANCIAL AID PROCEDURES

Forms required: FAFSA.
Dates and Deadlines: Priority date 8/1; closing date 9/1. Applicants notified on a rolling basis starting 3/1; must reply within 2 week(s) of notification.
Transfers: No deadline.

CONTACT

Edward Recker, Director of Financial Aid
1000 North Main Street, Findlay, OH 45840-3653
(419) 434-4791

University of Mount Union

Alliance, Ohio
www.mountunion.edu Federal Code: 003083

4-year private university in large town, affiliated with United Methodist Church.
Enrollment: 2,141 undergrads, 1% part-time. 662 full-time freshmen.
Selectivity: Admits 50 to 75% of applicants.

BASIC COSTS (2013-2014)

Tuition and fees: $27,380.
Per-credit charge: $1,140.
Room and board: $8,780.
Additional info: Tuition/fee waivers available for minority students.

FINANCIAL AID PICTURE (2011-2012)

Students with need: Out of 567 full-time freshmen who applied for aid, 529 were judged to have need. Of these, 529 received aid, and 35 had their full need met. Average financial aid package met 73% of need; average scholarship/grant was $14,651; average loan was $4,955. For part-time students, average financial aid package was $8,606.

Students without need: 90 full-time freshmen who did not demonstrate need for aid received scholarships/grants; average award was $9,883. No-need awards available for academics, alumni affiliation, art, job skills, leadership, minority status, music/drama, religious affiliation, ROTC, state/district residency.

Cumulative student debt: 93% of graduating class had student loans; average debt was $34,586.

FINANCIAL AID PROCEDURES

Forms required: FAFSA.
Dates and Deadlines: Applicants notified on a rolling basis starting 3/15; must reply within 4 week(s) of notification.

Transfers: No deadline. Applicants notified on a rolling basis; must reply within 4 week(s) of notification.

CONTACT

Emily Mattison, Director of Student Financial Services
1972 Clark Avenue, Alliance, OH 44601-3993
(330) 823-2674

University of Northwestern Ohio

Lima, Ohio
www.unoh.edu Federal Code: 004861

2-year private business and technical college in large town.
Enrollment: 4,167 undergrads.

BASIC COSTS (2012-2013)
Tuition and fees: $9,345.
Per-credit charge: $199.
Additional info: Board plan not available. Cost of room only, $2,700. Tuition/fee waivers available for minority students.

FINANCIAL AID PICTURE
Students with need: Need-based aid available for full-time and part-time students. Work study available nights.
Students without need: No-need awards available for academics, job skills, minority status.

FINANCIAL AID PROCEDURES
Forms required: FAFSA.
Dates and Deadlines: Priority date 4/1; no closing date. Applicants notified on a rolling basis starting 4/30; must reply within 2 week(s) of notification.
Transfers: No deadline. Applicants notified on a rolling basis.

CONTACT

Wendell Schick, Director of Financial Aid
1441 North Cable Road, Lima, OH 45805
(419) 227-3141

University of Rio Grande

Rio Grande, Ohio
www.rio.edu Federal Code: 003116

4-year private community and liberal arts college in rural community.
Enrollment: 1,451 undergrads, 19% part-time. 312 full-time freshmen.
Selectivity: Open admission; but selective for some programs.

BASIC COSTS (2012-2013)
Tuition and fees: $19,720.
Room and board: $8,639.
Additional info: Tuition reported is for private university sector of institution. Public community college in-state in-district tuition: $3,300 ($110 per credit hour); in-state out-of-district, $3,690 ($123 per credit hour). All public community college undergraduates pay $750 in required fees. Out-of-state community college students charged private tuition rate.

FINANCIAL AID PICTURE (2011-2012)
Students with need: Out of 300 full-time freshmen who applied for aid, 298 were judged to have need. Of these, 281 received aid, and 205 had their full need met. Average financial aid package met 44% of need; average scholarship/grant was $2,777; average loan was $3,632. For part-time students, average financial aid package was $4,782.
Students without need: 52 full-time freshmen who did not demonstrate need for aid received scholarships/grants; average award was $2,080. No-need awards available for academics, alumni affiliation, athletics, leadership, music/drama, state/district residency.
Scholarships offered: 31 full-time freshmen received athletic scholarships; average amount $2,252.
Cumulative student debt: 78% of graduating class had student loans; average debt was $22,633.

FINANCIAL AID PROCEDURES
Forms required: FAFSA, institutional form.
Dates and Deadlines: Priority date 3/15; no closing date. Applicants notified on a rolling basis starting 1/15; must reply within 3 week(s) of notification.

CONTACT

Zana Smith, Financial Aid Director
218 North College Avenue, Rio Grande, OH 45674
(740) 245-7218

University of Toledo

Toledo, Ohio
www.utoledo.edu Federal Code: 003131

4-year public university in large city.
Enrollment: 16,171 undergrads, 17% part-time. 3,346 full-time freshmen.
Selectivity: Open admission; but selective for some programs and for out-of-state students.

BASIC COSTS (2012-2013)
Tuition and fees: $9,192; out-of-state residents $18,312.
Room and board: $9,876.

FINANCIAL AID PICTURE
Students with need: Need-based aid available for full-time and part-time students.
Students without need: No-need awards available for academics, alumni affiliation, art, athletics, leadership, minority status, music/drama, ROTC.
Scholarships offered: Freshman merit scholarships; $100-$4,500; 400 awarded.
Additional info: March priority date for federal aid. Students encouraged to apply as early as December for priority consideration for institutional aid.

FINANCIAL AID PROCEDURES
Forms required: FAFSA.
Dates and Deadlines: Priority date 3/1; no closing date. Applicants notified on a rolling basis starting 3/1.

CONTACT

Carolyn Baumgartner, Director of Financial Aid
Rocket Hall, Suite 1300, MS 338, Toledo, OH 43606-3390
(419) 530-2800

Ursuline College

Pepper Pike, Ohio
www.ursuline.edu Federal Code: 003134

4-year private liberal arts college for women in small town, affiliated with Roman Catholic Church.
Enrollment: 863 undergrads, 34% part-time. 78 full-time freshmen.
Selectivity: Admits 50 to 75% of applicants.

BASIC COSTS (2012-2013)
Tuition and fees: $25,790.
Per-credit charge: $851.
Room and board: $8,578.

FINANCIAL AID PICTURE (2011-2012)
Students with need: Out of 75 full-time freshmen who applied for aid, 74 were judged to have need. Of these, 74 received aid, and 7 had their full

need met. Average financial aid package met 83% of need; average scholarship/grant was $19,330; average loan was $3,845. For part-time students, average financial aid package was $8,583.
Students without need: 1 full-time freshmen who did not demonstrate need for aid received scholarships/grants; average award was $15,000. No-need awards available for academics, alumni affiliation, art, athletics, minority status.
Scholarships offered: ***Merit:*** Ursuline Scholarship; $5,000 to $7,500. Ursuline Award; $1,500 to $4,500. Presidential Scholarship; $11,000. Dean's Scholarship; $9,500. Unlimited number available for each; all renewable. ***Athletic:*** 8 full-time freshmen received athletic scholarships; average amount $11,777.
Cumulative student debt: 89% of graduating class had student loans; average debt was $25,963.

FINANCIAL AID PROCEDURES

Forms required: FAFSA.
Dates and Deadlines: Priority date 2/15; no closing date. Applicants notified on a rolling basis starting 2/15; must reply within 3 week(s) of notification.
Transfers: No deadline. Applicants notified on a rolling basis; must reply within 4 week(s) of notification.

CONTACT

Mary Lynn Perri, Director of Financial Aid
2550 Lander Road, Pepper Pike, OH 44124-4398
(440) 684-6114

Virginia Marti College of Art and Design

Lakewood, Ohio
www.vmcad.edu Federal Code: 012896

2-year for-profit visual arts and business college in large city.
Enrollment: 187 undergrads.

FINANCIAL AID PICTURE

Students with need: Need-based aid available for full-time students.
Students without need: This college awards aid only to students with need.

FINANCIAL AID PROCEDURES

Forms required: FAFSA.
Dates and Deadlines: Applicants notified on a rolling basis.

CONTACT

Jennifer Minkiewicz, Financial Aid Officer
11724 Detroit Avenue, Lakewood, OH 44107

Walsh University

North Canton, Ohio
www.walsh.edu Federal Code: 003135

4-year private university and liberal arts college in small city, affiliated with Roman Catholic Church.
Enrollment: 2,292 undergrads, 16% part-time. 494 full-time freshmen.
Selectivity: Admits over 75% of applicants.

BASIC COSTS (2013-2014)

Tuition and fees: $25,840.
Per-credit charge: $820.
Room and board: $9,260.

FINANCIAL AID PICTURE (2012-2013)

Students with need: Out of 479 full-time freshmen who applied for aid, 419 were judged to have need. Of these, 419 received aid, and 276 had their full need met. Average financial aid package met 68% of need; average scholarship/grant was $7,166; average loan was $3,825. For part-time students, average financial aid package was $6,165.
Students without need: 67 full-time freshmen who did not demonstrate need for aid received scholarships/grants; average award was $7,929. No-need awards available for academics, alumni affiliation, athletics, music/drama, religious affiliation, state/district residency.
Scholarships offered: 81 full-time freshmen received athletic scholarships; average amount $6,034.
Cumulative student debt: 87% of graduating class had student loans; average debt was $23,895.

FINANCIAL AID PROCEDURES

Forms required: FAFSA.
Dates and Deadlines: Priority date 5/1; no closing date. Applicants notified on a rolling basis starting 2/15.
Transfers: No deadline. Applicants notified on a rolling basis starting 3/15.

CONTACT

Holly Van Gilder, Financial Aid Director
2020 East Maple Street, North Canton, OH 44720-3396
(330) 490-7146

Wilberforce University

Wilberforce, Ohio
www.wilberforce.edu/home/home.html
Federal Code: 003141

4-year private liberal arts college in rural community, affiliated with African Methodist Episcopal Church.
Enrollment: 534 undergrads.

BASIC COSTS (2012-2013)

Tuition and fees: $13,250.
Per-credit charge: $500.
Room and board: $6,100.

FINANCIAL AID PICTURE

Students with need: Need-based aid available for full-time and part-time students.

FINANCIAL AID PROCEDURES

Forms required: FAFSA, institutional form.
Dates and Deadlines: Priority date 3/15; closing date 6/30. Applicants notified on a rolling basis starting 3/15; must reply within 2 week(s) of notification.

CONTACT

Lloyd Dixon, Director for Financial Aid
1055 North Bickett Road, Wilberforce, OH 45384-1001
(937) 708-5727

Wilmington College

Wilmington, Ohio
www.wilmington.edu Federal Code: 003142

4-year private liberal arts college in large town, affiliated with Society of Friends (Quaker).
Enrollment: 1,274 full-time undergrads.

BASIC COSTS (2012-2013)

Tuition and fees: $27,970.
Room and board: $9,216.

FINANCIAL AID PICTURE

Students with need: Need-based aid available for full-time and part-time students.

Students without need: No-need awards available for academics, alumni affiliation, religious affiliation, state/district residency.

FINANCIAL AID PROCEDURES

Forms required: FAFSA.

Dates and Deadlines: Priority date 3/31; closing date 6/1. Applicants notified on a rolling basis starting 3/1; must reply by 5/1 or within 2 week(s) of notification.

CONTACT

Cheryl Louallen, Director of Financial Aid
Box 1325 Pyle Center, Wilmington, OH 45177
(937) 382-6661 ext. 249

Wittenberg University

Springfield, Ohio
www.wittenberg.edu Federal Code: 003143

4-year private liberal arts college in small city, affiliated with Evangelical Lutheran Church in America.

Enrollment: 1,720 undergrads. 489 full-time freshmen.

Selectivity: Admits over 75% of applicants.

BASIC COSTS (2013-2014)

Tuition and fees: $38,030.

Per-credit charge: $1,241.

Room and board: $9,736.

Additional info: Tuition/fee waivers available for adults.

FINANCIAL AID PICTURE (2012-2013)

Students with need: Out of 453 full-time freshmen who applied for aid, 405 were judged to have need. Of these, 405 received aid, and 4 had their full need met. Average financial aid package met 81% of need; average scholarship/grant was $26,028; average loan was $3,708. For part-time students, average financial aid package was $5,804.

Students without need: This college awards aid only to students with need.

Scholarships offered: Smith Family Scholar Award; full tuition; renewable; based on academic achievement and other qualities. University Scholar Award; half tuition; renewable; based on academic achievement and other qualities. Broadwell Chinn Scholarship; half tuition; renewable; based on minority status, academic achievement, and other qualities.

Cumulative student debt: 71% of graduating class had student loans; average debt was $31,712.

Additional info: Auditions required from applicants for music, theater, and dance scholarships. Portfolio required of applicants for art scholarships.

FINANCIAL AID PROCEDURES

Forms required: FAFSA.

Dates and Deadlines: Priority date 3/1; no closing date. Applicants notified on a rolling basis starting 3/1; must reply by 5/1 or within 2 week(s) of notification.

Transfers: Priority date 5/15; no deadline. Applicants notified on a rolling basis; must reply within 2 week(s) of notification.

CONTACT

Jonathan Green, Director of Financial Aid
Ward Street and North Wittenberg, Springfield, OH 45501-0720
(937) 327-7321

Wright State University

Dayton, Ohio
www.wright.edu Federal Code: 003078

4-year public university in small city.

Enrollment: 12,602 undergrads, 18% part-time. 2,270 full-time freshmen.

Selectivity: Admits 50 to 75% of applicants.

BASIC COSTS (2012-2013)

Tuition and fees: $8,354; out-of-state residents $16,182.

Room and board: $8,629.

FINANCIAL AID PICTURE (2012-2013)

Students with need: Out of 1,990 full-time freshmen who applied for aid, 1,638 were judged to have need. Of these, 1,622 received aid, and 199 had their full need met. Average financial aid package met 60% of need; average scholarship/grant was $5,937; average loan was $3,743. For part-time students, average financial aid package was $8,799.

Students without need: 225 full-time freshmen who did not demonstrate need for aid received scholarships/grants; average award was $3,132. No-need awards available for academics, alumni affiliation, art, athletics, leadership, minority status, music/drama, ROTC, state/district residency.

Scholarships offered: 32 full-time freshmen received athletic scholarships; average amount $10,010.

Cumulative student debt: 83% of graduating class had student loans; average debt was $28,349.

FINANCIAL AID PROCEDURES

Forms required: FAFSA.

Dates and Deadlines: Priority date 3/1; no closing date. Applicants notified on a rolling basis starting 3/15.

CONTACT

Amy Barnhart, Director of Financial Aid
3640 Colonel Glenn Highway, 108 SU, Dayton, OH 45435
(937) 775-4000

Wright State University: Lake Campus

Celina, Ohio
www.wright.edu/lake Federal Code: 003078

2-year public branch campus college in small town.

Enrollment: 838 undergrads, 22% part-time. 186 full-time freshmen.

Selectivity: Open admission; but selective for some programs.

BASIC COSTS (2012-2013)

Tuition and fees: $5,614; out-of-state residents $13,442.

FINANCIAL AID PICTURE (2012-2013)

Students with need: Out of 161 full-time freshmen who applied for aid, 135 were judged to have need. Of these, 133 received aid, and 26 had their full need met. Average financial aid package met 67% of need; average scholarship/grant was $6,011; average loan was $3,495. For part-time students, average financial aid package was $8,997.

Students without need: 27 full-time freshmen who did not demonstrate need for aid received scholarships/grants; average award was $3,389. No-need awards available for academics, alumni affiliation, art, athletics, leadership, minority status, music/drama, ROTC, state/district residency.

Cumulative student debt: 83% of graduating class had student loans; average debt was $28,349.

FINANCIAL AID PROCEDURES

Forms required: FAFSA.

Dates and Deadlines: Priority date 3/1; no closing date. Applicants notified on a rolling basis starting 3/15.

CONTACT

Amy Barnhart, Director of Financial Aid
7600 State Route 703, Celina, OH 45822-2952
(937) 775-4000

Xavier University

Cincinnati, Ohio
www.xavier.edu Federal Code: 003144

4-year private university in large city, affiliated with Roman Catholic Church.
Enrollment: 4,351 undergrads, 7% part-time. 1,061 full-time freshmen.
Selectivity: Admits 50 to 75% of applicants.

BASIC COSTS (2012-2013)
Tuition and fees: $32,070.
Per-credit charge: $605.
Room and board: $10,430.

FINANCIAL AID PICTURE
Students with need: Need-based aid available for full-time and part-time students. Work study available nights, weekends, and for part-time students.
Students without need: No-need awards available for academics, alumni affiliation, art, athletics, leadership, music/drama, religious affiliation.
Scholarships offered: Saint Francis Xavier Scholarship; full tuition; based on leadership, talent and highest academic achievement, competitive; 10 awarded. Community Engaged Fellowship; $22,000; 10 awarded. Chancellor Scholarship; $17,000; based on leadership, talent, and highest academic achievement; number of awards varies. Trustee Scholarship; $15,000; based on academic achievement; number of awards varies. Schawe Scholarship; $15,000; based on academic achievement; number of awards varies. Presidential Scholarship; $14,000; based on academic achievement; number of awards varies. Miguel Pro Scholarship; amount varies; awarded annually to students committed to promoting diversity and demonstrate leadership; number varies. Francis X. Weninger Scholarship; amount varies; awarded annually to students who promote diversity in our society and who demonstrate leadership; number varies.

FINANCIAL AID PROCEDURES
Forms required: FAFSA.
Dates and Deadlines: Priority date 2/15; no closing date. Applicants notified on a rolling basis starting 2/15; must reply by 5/1.
Transfers: No deadline. Applicants notified on a rolling basis starting 3/1.

CONTACT
Todd Everett, Director of Financial Aid
3800 Victory Parkway, Cincinnati, OH 45207-5311
(513) 745-3142

Youngstown State University

Youngstown, Ohio
www.ysu.edu Federal Code: 003145

4-year public university in small city.
Enrollment: 12,238 undergrads, 20% part-time. 2,366 full-time freshmen.
Selectivity: Open admission; but selective for some programs and for out-of-state students.

BASIC COSTS (2012-2013)
Tuition and fees: $7,712; out-of-state residents $13,668.
Room and board: $8,150.

FINANCIAL AID PICTURE (2011-2012)
Students with need: Out of 2,178 full-time freshmen who applied for aid, 1,941 were judged to have need. Of these, 1,940 received aid, and 183 had their full need met. Average financial aid package met 31% of need; average scholarship/grant was $5,143; average loan was $3,285. For part-time students, average financial aid package was $7,495.
Students without need: 162 full-time freshmen who did not demonstrate need for aid received scholarships/grants; average award was $3,151. No-need awards available for academics, alumni affiliation, athletics, ROTC, state/district residency.
Scholarships offered: 83 full-time freshmen received athletic scholarships; average amount $10,162.

FINANCIAL AID PROCEDURES
Forms required: FAFSA, institutional form.
Dates and Deadlines: Priority date 2/15; no closing date. Applicants notified on a rolling basis starting 5/30; must reply within 2 week(s) of notification.

CONTACT
Elaine Ruse, Director of Scholarships and Financial Aid
One University Plaza, Youngstown, OH 44555-0001
(330) 941-3505

Zane State College

Zanesville, Ohio
www.zanestate.edu Federal Code: 008133

2-year public technical college in large town.
Enrollment: 2,797 undergrads.
Selectivity: Open admission; but selective for some programs.

BASIC COSTS (2012-2013)
Tuition and fees: $4,380; out-of-state residents $8,760.

FINANCIAL AID PICTURE
Students with need: Need-based aid available for full-time and part-time students.

FINANCIAL AID PROCEDURES
Forms required: FAFSA.
Dates and Deadlines: Priority date 5/1; closing date 6/30. Must reply by 9/1.

CONTACT
Amanda Reisinger, Financial Aid Director
1555 Newark Road, Zanesville, OH 43701-2626
(740) 454-2501 ext. 1275

Oklahoma

Bacone College

Muskogee, Oklahoma
www.bacone.edu Federal Code: 003147

4-year private liberal arts college in large town, affiliated with American Baptist Churches in the USA.
Enrollment: 1,040 undergrads.

BASIC COSTS (2012-2013)
Tuition and fees: $13,510.
Per-credit charge: $495.
Room and board: $9,190.

FINANCIAL AID PICTURE
Students with need: Need-based aid available for full-time and part-time students. Work study available nights, weekends, and for part-time students.
Students without need: This college awards aid only to students with need.

FINANCIAL AID PROCEDURES
Forms required: FAFSA.
Dates and Deadlines: Priority date 3/31; no closing date. Applicants notified on a rolling basis starting 4/1; must reply within 2 week(s) of notification.
Transfers: No deadline. Applicants notified on a rolling basis.

CONTACT
Kathye Watson, Director of Financial Aid
2299 Old Bacone Road, Muskogee, OK 74403
(918) 781-7340

Cameron University
Lawton, Oklahoma
www.cameron.edu Federal Code: 003150

4-year public university in small city.
Enrollment: 5,258 undergrads, 29% part-time. 1,095 full-time freshmen.
Selectivity: Admits over 75% of applicants.

BASIC COSTS (2012-2013)
Tuition and fees: $4,770; out-of-state residents $11,745.
Per-credit charge: $108; out-of-state residents $340.
Room and board: $3,884.

FINANCIAL AID PICTURE (2011-2012)
Students with need: Out of 925 full-time freshmen who applied for aid, 768 were judged to have need. Of these, 696 received aid, and 34 had their full need met. Average financial aid package met 55% of need; average scholarship/grant was $5,571; average loan was $2,973. For part-time students, average financial aid package was $5,890.
Students without need: 48 full-time freshmen who did not demonstrate need for aid received scholarships/grants; average award was $1,043. No-need awards available for academics, alumni affiliation, art, athletics, leadership, minority status, music/drama, ROTC, state/district residency.
Scholarships offered: 23 full-time freshmen received athletic scholarships; average amount $3,310.
Cumulative student debt: 36% of graduating class had student loans; average debt was $15,020.

FINANCIAL AID PROCEDURES
Forms required: FAFSA.
Dates and Deadlines: Priority date 4/1; no closing date. Applicants notified on a rolling basis starting 4/1; must reply within 2 week(s) of notification.
Transfers: Priority date 6/1; no deadline. Applicants notified on a rolling basis starting 6/1. Academic transcripts required.

CONTACT
Donald Hall, Director of Financial Assistance
2800 West Gore Boulevard, Lawton, OK 73505-6377
(580) 581-2293

Carl Albert State College
Poteau, Oklahoma
www.carlalbert.edu Federal Code: 003176

2-year public community and junior college in large town.
Enrollment: 2,441 undergrads.
Selectivity: Open admission; but selective for some programs.

BASIC COSTS (2012-2013)
Tuition and fees: $2,664; out-of-state residents $5,664.
Per-credit charge: $59; out-of-state residents $159.
Room and board: $3,860.
Additional info: Tuition/fee waivers available for minority students.

FINANCIAL AID PICTURE
Students with need: Need-based aid available for full-time and part-time students. Work study available nights.
Students without need: This college awards aid only to students with need.

FINANCIAL AID PROCEDURES
Forms required: FAFSA, institutional form.
Dates and Deadlines: Applicants notified on a rolling basis.

CONTACT
Robin Benson, Director of Financial Aid
1507 South McKenna, Poteau, OK 74953-5208
(918) 647-1343

Connors State College
Warner, Oklahoma
www.connorsstate.edu Federal Code: 003153

2-year public community and junior college in rural community.
Enrollment: 2,563 undergrads.
Selectivity: Open admission; but selective for some programs.

BASIC COSTS (2012-2013)
Tuition and fees: $3,147; out-of-state residents $7,374.
Per-credit charge: $70; out-of-state residents $211.
Room and board: $5,050.

FINANCIAL AID PICTURE
Students with need: Need-based aid available for full-time and part-time students.
Students without need: No-need awards available for academics, alumni affiliation, athletics, leadership, state/district residency.

FINANCIAL AID PROCEDURES
Forms required: FAFSA, institutional form.
Dates and Deadlines: Closing date 3/1. Applicants notified on a rolling basis starting 4/1; must reply within 2 week(s) of notification.

CONTACT
Jennifer Watkins, Director of Financial Aid
RR 1, Box 1000, Warner, OK 74469-9700
(918) 463-6220 ext. 6220

East Central University
Ada, Oklahoma
www.ecok.edu Federal Code: 003154

4-year public university in large town.
Enrollment: 3,801 undergrads, 20% part-time. 603 full-time freshmen.
Selectivity: Admits over 75% of applicants.

BASIC COSTS (2012-2013)
Tuition and fees: $4,907; out-of-state residents $11,903.
Per-credit charge: $120; out-of-state residents $353.
Room and board: $4,824.

FINANCIAL AID PICTURE
Students with need: Need-based aid available for full-time and part-time students. Work study available nights, weekends, and for part-time students.
Students without need: No-need awards available for academics, athletics.

FINANCIAL AID PROCEDURES
Forms required: FAFSA.
Dates and Deadlines: Closing date 3/1. Applicants notified on a rolling basis starting 4/15; must reply within 2 week(s) of notification.

CONTACT
Becky Isaacs, Director of Financial Aid
PMBJ8, 1100 East 14th Street, Ada, OK 74820
(580) 559-5243

Eastern Oklahoma State College

Wilburton, Oklahoma
www.eosc.edu Federal Code: 003155

2-year public community college in small town.
Enrollment: 1,946 undergrads.
Selectivity: Open admission; but selective for some programs.

BASIC COSTS (2012-2013)
Tuition and fees: $3,360; out-of-state residents $6,977.
Per-credit charge: $82; out-of-state residents $202.
Room and board: $4,720.
Additional info: Tuition/fee waivers available for minority students, unemployed or children of unemployed.

FINANCIAL AID PICTURE
Students with need: Need-based aid available for full-time and part-time students.
Students without need: This college awards aid only to students with need.

FINANCIAL AID PROCEDURES
Forms required: FAFSA, institutional form.
Dates and Deadlines: Priority date 3/1; closing date 6/30. Applicants notified on a rolling basis starting 5/1; must reply within 2 week(s) of notification.
Transfers: Priority date 4/30.

CONTACT
Mimi Kelley, Director of Financial Aid
1301 West Main Street, Wilburton, OK 74578-4999
(918) 465-2361 ext. 207

Langston University

Langston, Oklahoma
www.lunet.edu Federal Code: 003157

4-year public university and liberal arts college in rural community.
Enrollment: 1,998 undergrads.

BASIC COSTS (2012-2013)
Tuition and fees: $4,328; out-of-state residents $10,788.
Per-credit charge: $102; out-of-state residents $317.
Room and board: $8,090.
Additional info: Apartment-style housing, includes 4 private bedrooms with shared living room and kitchen.

FINANCIAL AID PICTURE
Students with need: Need-based aid available for full-time and part-time students.
Students without need: This college awards aid only to students with need.

FINANCIAL AID PROCEDURES
Forms required: FAFSA, state aid form.
Dates and Deadlines: Priority date 3/1; closing date 5/1. Applicants notified on a rolling basis starting 7/15; must reply within 2 week(s) of notification.

CONTACT
Linda Morris, Financial Aid Director
Box 728, Langston, OK 73050

Mid-America Christian University

Oklahoma City, Oklahoma
www.macu.edu Federal Code: 006942

4-year private university and liberal arts college in very large city, affiliated with Church of God.
Enrollment: 1,984 undergrads.
Selectivity: Open admission.

BASIC COSTS (2012-2013)
Tuition and fees: $15,092.
Per-credit charge: $584.
Room and board: $6,134.

FINANCIAL AID PICTURE
Students with need: Need-based aid available for full-time and part-time students.
Students without need: No-need awards available for academics, athletics, leadership, minority status, music/drama, religious affiliation.

FINANCIAL AID PROCEDURES
Forms required: FAFSA.
Dates and Deadlines: Priority date 5/1; no closing date. Applicants notified on a rolling basis starting 5/1.

CONTACT
Christina Padilla, Director of Student Financial Services
3500 SW 119th Street, Oklahoma City, OK 73170
(405) 692-3182

Northeastern Oklahoma Agricultural and Mechanical College

Miami, Oklahoma
www.neo.edu Federal Code: 316000

2-year public community and junior college in large town.
Enrollment: 1,855 full-time undergrads.
Selectivity: Open admission.

BASIC COSTS (2012-2013)
Tuition and fees: $3,196; out-of-state residents $7,786.
Per-credit charge: $72; out-of-state residents $225.
Room and board: $5,128.

FINANCIAL AID PICTURE
Students with need: Need-based aid available for full-time and part-time students. Work study available nights, weekends, and for part-time students.
Students without need: No-need awards available for academics, athletics, leadership, music/drama, state/district residency.

FINANCIAL AID PROCEDURES
Forms required: FAFSA.
Dates and Deadlines: Priority date 4/1; no closing date. Applicants notified on a rolling basis starting 4/1; must reply by 8/30 or within 2 week(s) of notification.
Transfers: No deadline. Applicants notified on a rolling basis starting 4/1; must reply within 2 week(s) of notification.

CONTACT
David Fisher, Director of Financial Aid
200 I Street Northeast, Miami, OK 74354-6497
(918) 540-6235

Northeastern State University

Tahlequah, Oklahoma
www.nsuok.edu Federal Code: 003161

4-year public university in large town.
Enrollment: 7,517 undergrads, 29% part-time. 864 full-time freshmen.
Selectivity: Admits over 75% of applicants.

BASIC COSTS (2012-2013)
Tuition and fees: $4,882; out-of-state residents $11,632.

Per-credit charge: $125; out-of-state residents $350.
Room and board: $5,580.
Additional info: Tuition/fee waivers available for adults, minority students.

FINANCIAL AID PICTURE (2012-2013)
Students with need: Out of 765 full-time freshmen who applied for aid, 553 were judged to have need. Of these, 546 received aid, and 455 had their full need met. Average financial aid package met 100% of need; average scholarship/grant was $6,727; average loan was $4,489. For part-time students, average financial aid package was $9,739.
Students without need: 61 full-time freshmen who did not demonstrate need for aid received scholarships/grants; average award was $2,651. No-need awards available for academics, alumni affiliation, art, athletics, leadership, minority status, music/drama, religious affiliation, ROTC, state/district residency.
Scholarships offered: ***Merit:*** Academic scholarship; up to $8,348 a year for 4 years; based primarily on ACT and GPA. Leadership scholarship; up to $5,895 a year for 4 years. Legacies scholarship; up to $2,800 a year for 4 years. Valedictorians scholarship; up to $2,800 a year for 4 years. ***Athletic:*** 46 full-time freshmen received athletic scholarships; average amount $3,932.
Cumulative student debt: 60% of graduating class had student loans; average debt was $20,503.
Additional info: Participates in off-campus job location and development program to assist students with off-campus employers to earn money for college expenses.

FINANCIAL AID PROCEDURES
Forms required: FAFSA.
Dates and Deadlines: Priority date 3/1; no closing date. Applicants notified on a rolling basis starting 4/1.
Transfers: Priority date 12/15; no deadline. State grant deadline is April 15.

CONTACT
Teri Cochran, Director of Student Financial Services
600 North Grand Avenue, Tahlequah, OK 74464-2399
(918) 444-3456

Northern Oklahoma College
Tonkawa, Oklahoma
www.north-ok.edu Federal Code: 003162

2-year public community college in small town.
Enrollment: 5,210 undergrads.
Selectivity: Open admission; but selective for out-of-state students.

BASIC COSTS (2012-2013)
Tuition and fees: $2,749; out-of-state residents $6,938.
Per-credit charge: $66; out-of-state residents $205.
Room and board: $4,460.
Additional info: Tuition/fee waivers available for adults, minority students, unemployed or children of unemployed.

FINANCIAL AID PICTURE
Students with need: Need-based aid available for full-time and part-time students.

FINANCIAL AID PROCEDURES
Forms required: FAFSA, institutional form.
Dates and Deadlines: Priority date 6/1; no closing date. Applicants notified on a rolling basis starting 4/1.

CONTACT
Linda Brown, Director of Financial Aid
Box 310, Tonkawa, OK 74653-0310
(580) 628-6240

Northwestern Oklahoma State University
Alva, Oklahoma
www.nwosu.edu Federal Code: 003163

4-year public university and teachers college in small town.
Enrollment: 2,055 undergrads, 21% part-time. 359 full-time freshmen.
Selectivity: Admits 50 to 75% of applicants.

BASIC COSTS (2012-2013)
Tuition and fees: $4,906; out-of-state residents $10,838.
Per-credit charge: $142; out-of-state residents $340.
Room and board: $3,900.

FINANCIAL AID PICTURE (2011-2012)
Students with need: Out of 283 full-time freshmen who applied for aid, 216 were judged to have need. Of these, 214 received aid. Need-based aid available for part-time students.
Students without need: No-need awards available for academics, alumni affiliation, art, athletics, leadership, music/drama.
Cumulative student debt: 43% of graduating class had student loans; average debt was $14,975.

FINANCIAL AID PROCEDURES
Forms required: FAFSA.
Dates and Deadlines: Applicants notified on a rolling basis starting 5/1; must reply by 8/15.

CONTACT
Calleb Mosburg, Director of Financial Aid
709 Oklahoma Boulevard, Alva, OK 73717-2799
(580) 327-8542

Oklahoma Baptist University
Shawnee, Oklahoma
www.okbu.edu Federal Code: 003164

4-year private university and liberal arts college in large town, affiliated with Southern Baptist Convention.
Enrollment: 1,714 undergrads, 2% part-time. 323 full-time freshmen.
Selectivity: Admits 50 to 75% of applicants.

BASIC COSTS (2013-2014)
Tuition and fees: $21,842.
Room and board: $6,360.

FINANCIAL AID PICTURE (2011-2012)
Students with need: Out of 274 full-time freshmen who applied for aid, 221 were judged to have need. Of these, 221 received aid, and 128 had their full need met. Average financial aid package met 67% of need; average scholarship/grant was $3,980; average loan was $2,508. For part-time students, average financial aid package was $4,552.
Students without need: 102 full-time freshmen who did not demonstrate need for aid received scholarships/grants; average award was $1,417. No-need awards available for academics, alumni affiliation, art, athletics, job skills, leadership, minority status, music/drama, religious affiliation, ROTC, state/district residency.
Scholarships offered: ***Merit:*** Prichard Church Vocation Scholarship; $1,000; offered to students preparing for vocational ministry associated with Southern Baptist Convention and majoring in certain programs. Missionary Kid (MK) Scholarship; minimum 50% tuition per year; for children of Southern Baptist missionaries. OBU Bison Grants; amount varies; based on award package and need. ***Athletic:*** 84 full-time freshmen received athletic scholarships; average amount $6,351.
Cumulative student debt: 58% of graduating class had student loans; average debt was $17,008.

FINANCIAL AID PROCEDURES
Forms required: FAFSA.

Dates and Deadlines: Priority date 3/1; no closing date. Applicants notified on a rolling basis starting 2/1; must reply within 2 week(s) of notification.
Transfers: No deadline. Applicants notified on a rolling basis starting 2/1. Transfers receive 1 semester of financial aid on probationary basis. During probation semester, must complete 12 hours with at least 2.0 GPA in order to receive financial aid in subsequent semesters.

CONTACT

Jonna Raney, Director of Student Financial Services
500 West University, Shawnee, OK 74804
(405) 878-2016

Oklahoma Christian University

Oklahoma City, Oklahoma
www.oc.edu Federal Code: 003165

4-year private liberal arts college in very large city, affiliated with Church of Christ.
Enrollment: 1,858 undergrads, 1% part-time. 446 full-time freshmen.
Selectivity: Admits less than 50% of applicants.

BASIC COSTS (2012-2013)

Tuition and fees: $18,800.
Per-credit charge: $738.
Room and board: $6,775.

FINANCIAL AID PICTURE (2011-2012)

Students with need: Out of 383 full-time freshmen who applied for aid, 307 were judged to have need. Of these, 307 received aid, and 122 had their full need met. Average financial aid package met 73% of need; average scholarship/grant was $2,940; average loan was $2,474. For part-time students, average financial aid package was $15,243.
Students without need: 109 full-time freshmen who did not demonstrate need for aid received scholarships/grants; average award was $4,340. No-need awards available for academics, art, athletics, music/drama, religious affiliation, ROTC.
Scholarships offered: ***Merit:*** Academic merit scholarships available. ***Athletic:*** 39 full-time freshmen received athletic scholarships; average amount $8,634.
Cumulative student debt: 65% of graduating class had student loans; average debt was $29,389.

FINANCIAL AID PROCEDURES

Forms required: FAFSA.
Dates and Deadlines: Priority date 3/15; closing date 8/31. Applicants notified on a rolling basis starting 1/15; must reply within 4 week(s) of notification.
Transfers: Applicants notified on a rolling basis starting 1/15; must reply within 4 week(s) of notification. Will award based on unofficial transcript. Must have all official transcripts before awards will be disbursed.

CONTACT

Clint LaRue, Director, Student Financial Services
Box 11000, Oklahoma City, OK 73136-1100
(405) 425-5190

Oklahoma City Community College

Oklahoma City, Oklahoma
www.occc.edu Federal Code: 010391

2-year public community college in large city.
Enrollment: 13,202 undergrads, 64% part-time. 1,328 full-time freshmen.
Selectivity: Open admission; but selective for some programs.

BASIC COSTS (2012-2013)

Tuition and fees: $2,971; out-of-state residents $7,585.
Per-credit charge: $75; out-of-state residents $228.
Additional info: Tuition/fee waivers available for adults.

FINANCIAL AID PICTURE

Students with need: Need-based aid available for full-time and part-time students. Work study available nights, weekends, and for part-time students.
Students without need: No-need awards available for academics, alumni affiliation, art, leadership, music/drama, state/district residency.

FINANCIAL AID PROCEDURES

Forms required: FAFSA.
Dates and Deadlines: Priority date 4/15; no closing date. Applicants notified on a rolling basis starting 2/15.
Transfers: Applicants notified on a rolling basis starting 2/15. Those with previous degrees or over 90 credit hours attempted must appeal for eligibility for federally funded financial assistance.

CONTACT

Harold Case, Director of Financial Aid
7777 South May Avenue, Oklahoma City, OK 73159
(405) 682-7525

Oklahoma City University

Oklahoma City, Oklahoma
www.okcu.edu Federal Code: 003166

4-year private university and liberal arts college in very large city, affiliated with United Methodist Church.
Enrollment: 2,075 undergrads. 325 full-time freshmen.
Selectivity: Admits 50 to 75% of applicants.

BASIC COSTS (2012-2013)

Tuition and fees: $28,190.
Per-credit charge: $840.
Room and board: $7,880.
Additional info: Tuition/fee waivers available for adults.

FINANCIAL AID PICTURE

Students with need: Need-based aid available for full-time and part-time students. Work study available nights, weekends, and for part-time students.
Students without need: No-need awards available for academics, alumni affiliation, art, athletics, leadership, music/drama, religious affiliation, ROTC, state/district residency.
Additional info: Four year, fixed rate tuition plan available to any undergraduate student who elects to enroll in the plan prior to start of fall term. To be eligible, student must matriculate in or before Fall semester. Fixed rate applies to block of 12-16 hours for fall/spring and summer semesters. The required fees charged each semester are not fixed and subject to increases.

FINANCIAL AID PROCEDURES

Forms required: FAFSA, institutional form.
Dates and Deadlines: Priority date 3/1; closing date 6/3. Applicants notified on a rolling basis; must reply within 2 week(s) of notification.
Transfers: Applicants notified on a rolling basis; must reply within 2 week(s) of notification. Financial aid transcripts required from all previously attended institutions whether or not financial aid was received.

CONTACT

Denise Flis, Director of Financial Aid
2501 North Blackwelder Avenue, Oklahoma City, OK 73106-1493
(405) 208-5211

Oklahoma Panhandle State University

Goodwell, Oklahoma
www.opsu.edu Federal Code: 003174

4-year public university and liberal arts college in rural community.
Enrollment: 1,279 undergrads, 14% part-time. 281 full-time freshmen.

Selectivity: Admits 50 to 75% of applicants.

BASIC COSTS (2012-2013)
Tuition and fees: $6,519; out-of-state residents $12,078.
Per-credit charge: $116; out-of-state residents $301.
Room and board: $4,110.
Additional info: Tuition at time of enrollment locked for 4 years.

FINANCIAL AID PICTURE
Students with need: Need-based aid available for full-time and part-time students.
Students without need: This college awards aid only to students with need.

FINANCIAL AID PROCEDURES
Forms required: FAFSA, institutional form.
Dates and Deadlines: Priority date 3/15; no closing date.
Transfers: No deadline. Applicants notified on a rolling basis.

CONTACT
Lori Ferguson, Director of Financial Aid
OPSU Admissions, Goodwell, OK 73939-0430
(580) 349-1566

Oklahoma State University

Stillwater, Oklahoma
www.okstate.edu Federal Code: 003170

4-year public university in large town.
Enrollment: 19,912 undergrads, 12% part-time. 3,635 full-time freshmen.
Selectivity: Admits over 75% of applicants.

BASIC COSTS (2012-2013)
Tuition and fees: $7,622; out-of-state residents $19,637.
Per-credit charge: $148; out-of-state residents $548.
Room and board: $6,704.

FINANCIAL AID PICTURE (2011-2012)
Students with need: Out of 2,824 full-time freshmen who applied for aid, 2,016 were judged to have need. Of these, 1,961 received aid, and 329 had their full need met. Average financial aid package met 79% of need; average scholarship/grant was $6,584; average loan was $3,166. For part-time students, average financial aid package was $9,674.
Students without need: 1,039 full-time freshmen who did not demonstrate need for aid received scholarships/grants; average award was $6,126. No-need awards available for academics, alumni affiliation, art, athletics, leadership, minority status, music/drama, ROTC, state/district residency.
Scholarships offered: 68 full-time freshmen received athletic scholarships; average amount $11,131.
Cumulative student debt: 52% of graduating class had student loans; average debt was $22,736.
Additional info: Students benefiting from the state funded Oklahoma's Promise program do not have to pay out of pocket for tuition, mandatory fees, or books.

FINANCIAL AID PROCEDURES
Forms required: FAFSA.
Dates and Deadlines: Priority date 2/1; no closing date. Applicants notified on a rolling basis starting 4/1; must reply by 5/1 or within 2 week(s) of notification.

CONTACT
Charles Bruce, Senior Director of Scholarships & Financial Aid
219 Student Union, Stillwater, OK 74078
(405) 744-6604

Oklahoma State University Institute of Technology: Okmulgee

Okmulgee, Oklahoma
www.osuit.edu Federal Code: 003172

2-year public branch campus and technical college in large town.
Enrollment: 2,418 undergrads.
Selectivity: Open admission; but selective for some programs.

BASIC COSTS (2012-2013)
Tuition and fees: $4,215; out-of-state residents $9,525.
Per-credit charge: $106; out-of-state residents $283.
Room and board: $5,642.

FINANCIAL AID PICTURE
Students with need: Need-based aid available for full-time and part-time students. Work study available nights, weekends, and for part-time students.
Additional info: OSUIT Foundation Scholarship application due March 1.

FINANCIAL AID PROCEDURES
Forms required: FAFSA, institutional form.
Dates and Deadlines: Priority date 4/1; no closing date. Applicants notified on a rolling basis.
Transfers: Requirement of financial aid transcript from any institution(s) attended during transferring academic year.

CONTACT
Mary Bledsoe, Director of Student Financial Services
1801 East Fourth Street, Okmulgee, OK 74447-3901
(918) 293-5290

Oklahoma State University: Oklahoma City

Oklahoma City, Oklahoma
www.osuokc.edu Federal Code: 009647

2-year public branch campus and technical college in very large city.
Enrollment: 7,121 undergrads, 65% part-time. 562 full-time freshmen.
Selectivity: Open admission; but selective for some programs.

BASIC COSTS (2012-2013)
Tuition and fees: $3,310; out-of-state residents $9,013.
Per-credit charge: $88; out-of-state residents $278.
Additional info: Tuition/fee waivers available for adults, minority students.

FINANCIAL AID PICTURE
Students with need: Need-based aid available for full-time and part-time students.
Students without need: This college awards aid only to students with need.

FINANCIAL AID PROCEDURES
Forms required: FAFSA.
Dates and Deadlines: Priority date 7/19; no closing date. Applicants notified on a rolling basis starting 8/1; must reply within 2 week(s) of notification.

CONTACT
Bessie Carter, Director of Financial Aid & Scholarships
900 North Portland, Oklahoma City, OK 73107-6195
(405) 945-8646

Oklahoma Wesleyan University

Bartlesville, Oklahoma
www.okwu.edu Federal Code: 003151

4-year private university and liberal arts college in large town, affiliated with Wesleyan Church.

Enrollment: 1,028 undergrads, 42% part-time. 137 full-time freshmen.
Selectivity: Admits 50 to 75% of applicants.

BASIC COSTS (2013-2014)
Tuition and fees: $22,252.
Room and board: $7,343.

FINANCIAL AID PICTURE (2012-2013)
Students with need: Out of 111 full-time freshmen who applied for aid, 98 were judged to have need. Of these, 98 received aid, and 13 had their full need met. Average financial aid package met 63% of need; average scholarship/grant was $12,503; average loan was $4,274. For part-time students, average financial aid package was $5,832.
Students without need: 36 full-time freshmen who did not demonstrate need for aid received scholarships/grants; average award was $4,789. No-need awards available for academics, alumni affiliation, athletics, leadership, music/drama, religious affiliation, state/district residency.
Scholarships offered: 40 full-time freshmen received athletic scholarships; average amount $7,573.
Cumulative student debt: 76% of graduating class had student loans; average debt was $20,060.

FINANCIAL AID PROCEDURES
Forms required: FAFSA, institutional form.
Dates and Deadlines: Priority date 3/1; no closing date. Applicants notified on a rolling basis starting 3/1; must reply by 5/1 or within 2 week(s) of notification.
Transfers: Closing date 8/1. Applicants notified on a rolling basis; must reply within 2 week(s) of notification.

CONTACT
Kandi Molder, Director of Student Financial Services
2201 Silver Lake Road, Bartlesville, OK 74006
(918) 335-6282

Oral Roberts University
Tulsa, Oklahoma
www.oru.edu Federal Code: 003985

4-year private university and liberal arts college in large city, affiliated with nondenominational tradition.
Enrollment: 2,782 undergrads. 598 full-time freshmen.
Selectivity: Admits 50 to 75% of applicants.

BASIC COSTS (2013-2014)
Tuition and fees: $22,438.
Per-credit charge: $906.
Room and board: $9,296.

FINANCIAL AID PICTURE (2011-2012)
Students with need: Average financial aid package met 86% of need; average scholarship/grant was $9,759; average loan was $6,534. For part-time students, average financial aid package was $6,289.
Students without need: 152 full-time freshmen who did not demonstrate need for aid received scholarships/grants; average award was $6,871. No-need awards available for academics, alumni affiliation, art, athletics, leadership, music/drama, state/district residency.
Scholarships offered: 16 full-time freshmen received athletic scholarships; average amount $19,354.
Cumulative student debt: 67% of graduating class had student loans; average debt was $34,555.

FINANCIAL AID PROCEDURES
Forms required: FAFSA.
Dates and Deadlines: Priority date 3/15; closing date 4/19. Applicants notified on a rolling basis starting 3/15; must reply by 7/15.
Transfers: Priority date 3/30. Applicants notified on a rolling basis starting 4/1. Transfer applicants eligible for some scholarships.

CONTACT
William Womack, Director of Financial Aid
7777 South Lewis Avenue, Tulsa, OK 74171
(918) 495-6510

Platt College: Oklahoma City Central
Oklahoma City, Oklahoma
www.plattcollege.org Federal Code: 023068

2-year for-profit branch campus and career college in small city.
Enrollment: 209 undergrads.
Selectivity: Open admission; but selective for some programs.

BASIC COSTS (2012-2013)
Tuition and fees: $15,100.
Additional info: Costs vary by program.

FINANCIAL AID PICTURE
Students with need: Need-based aid available for full-time students.

FINANCIAL AID PROCEDURES
Forms required: FAFSA.

CONTACT
Amy Hocker, Financial Aid Director
309 South Ann Arbor, Oklahoma City, OK 73128
(405) 946-7799

Platt College: Tulsa
Tulsa, Oklahoma
www.plattcollege.org Federal Code: 016312

2-year for-profit culinary school and health science college in large city.
Enrollment: 536 undergrads.
Selectivity: Open admission; but selective for some programs.

BASIC COSTS (2012-2013)
Tuition and fees: $15,100.
Additional info: Costs vary by program.

FINANCIAL AID PICTURE
Students with need: Need-based aid available for full-time and part-time students.
Students without need: This college awards aid only to students with need.

FINANCIAL AID PROCEDURES
Forms required: FAFSA.

CONTACT
Linda Bates, Director of Compliance-Financial Services
3801 South Sheridan, Tulsa, OK 74145-1132
(918) 663-9000

Redlands Community College
El Reno, Oklahoma
www.redlandscc.edu Federal Code: 003156

2-year public community college in large town.
Enrollment: 1,737 undergrads, 60% part-time. 187 full-time freshmen.
Selectivity: Open admission; but selective for some programs.

BASIC COSTS (2012-2013)
Tuition and fees: $3,330; out-of-state residents $5,580.
Per-credit charge: $111; out-of-state residents $186.

Additional info: Board plan not available. Cost of room only, $4,986. Campus apartment includes all utilities and telecommunications. Tuition/fee waivers available for adults.

FINANCIAL AID PICTURE

Students with need: Need-based aid available for full-time and part-time students. Work study available nights, weekends, and for part-time students.
Students without need: No-need awards available for academics, athletics, leadership.

FINANCIAL AID PROCEDURES

Forms required: FAFSA.
Dates and Deadlines: Priority date 7/1; no closing date. Applicants notified on a rolling basis starting 6/1; must reply within 6 week(s) of notification.
Transfers: No deadline. Applicants notified on a rolling basis; must reply within 6 week(s) of notification.

CONTACT

Karen Jeffers, Director of Financial Aid
1300 South Country Club Road, El Reno, OK 73036
(866) 415-6367 ext. 1442

Rogers State University

Claremore, Oklahoma
www.rsu.edu Federal Code: 003168

4-year public university in large town.
Enrollment: 4,608 undergrads, 38% part-time. 681 full-time freshmen.
Selectivity: Admits 50 to 75% of applicants.

BASIC COSTS (2013-2014)

Tuition and fees: $5,047; out-of-state residents $11,572.
Per-credit charge: $109; out-of-state residents $326.
Room only: $6,225.
Additional info: Apartment-style housing. All residents required to purchase $750 per semester declining balance meal plan.

FINANCIAL AID PICTURE (2012-2013)

Students with need: Out of 608 full-time freshmen who applied for aid, 508 were judged to have need. Of these, 490 received aid, and 20 had their full need met. Average financial aid package met 42% of need; average scholarship/grant was $6,073; average loan was $3,449. For part-time students, average financial aid package was $5,949.
Students without need: 13 full-time freshmen who did not demonstrate need for aid received scholarships/grants; average award was $4,804. No-need awards available for academics, art, athletics, leadership, music/drama, state/district residency.
Scholarships offered: 9 full-time freshmen received athletic scholarships; average amount $4,291.
Cumulative student debt: 45% of graduating class had student loans; average debt was $19,019.

FINANCIAL AID PROCEDURES

Forms required: FAFSA, institutional form.
Dates and Deadlines: Priority date 6/1; no closing date. Applicants notified on a rolling basis starting 4/1; must reply within 1 week(s) of notification.
Transfers: No deadline. Applicants notified on a rolling basis starting 4/1; must reply within 3 week(s) of notification.

CONTACT

Kelly Hicks, Director, Financial Aid
1701 West Will Rogers Boulevard, Claremore, OK 74017
(918) 343-7553

Rose State College

Midwest City, Oklahoma
www.rose.edu Federal Code: 009185

2-year public community college in small city.
Enrollment: 7,576 undergrads, 61% part-time. 898 full-time freshmen.
Selectivity: Open admission; but selective for some programs.

BASIC COSTS (2012-2013)

Tuition and fees: $2,969; out-of-state residents $9,121.
Per-credit charge: $79; out-of-state residents $284.

FINANCIAL AID PICTURE (2012-2013)

Students with need: 52% of average financial aid package awarded as scholarships/grants, 48% awarded as loans/jobs. Need-based aid available for part-time students. Work study available nights, weekends, and for part-time students.
Students without need: No-need awards available for academics, athletics, leadership.
Additional info: Ticket to Rose grant available to students from Midwest City/Choctaw high schools to cover unmet need in tuition/fees.

FINANCIAL AID PROCEDURES

Forms required: FAFSA.
Dates and Deadlines: Priority date 6/1; no closing date. Applicants notified on a rolling basis starting 3/1; must reply within 4 week(s) of notification.

CONTACT

Steven Daffer, Director of Financial Aid
6420 SE 15th Street, Midwest City, OK 73110-2799
(405) 733-7424

St. Gregory's University

Shawnee, Oklahoma
www.stgregorys.edu Federal Code: 003183

4-year private university and liberal arts college in large town, affiliated with Roman Catholic Church.
Enrollment: 619 undergrads, 46% part-time. 86 full-time freshmen.
Selectivity: Admits less than 50% of applicants.

BASIC COSTS (2012-2013)

Tuition and fees: $20,195.
Per-credit charge: $623.
Room and board: $7,444.
Additional info: Tuition/fee waivers available for adults.

FINANCIAL AID PICTURE (2011-2012)

Students with need: 30% of average financial aid package awarded as scholarships/grants, 70% awarded as loans/jobs. Need-based aid available for part-time students. Work study available nights, weekends, and for part-time students.
Students without need: No-need awards available for academics, alumni affiliation, art, athletics, job skills, leadership, music/drama, religious affiliation.
Scholarships offered: Leadership Scholarship; $500-$2,000. Academic Scholarship; $500-$5,100. Need-based scholarship; $500-$1,500.

FINANCIAL AID PROCEDURES

Forms required: FAFSA, institutional form.
Dates and Deadlines: Priority date 4/1; no closing date. Applicants notified on a rolling basis starting 2/15; must reply within 3 week(s) of notification.
Transfers: No deadline. Applicants notified on a rolling basis.

CONTACT

Kelly Harjo-Cox, Director of Financial Aid
1900 West MacArthur Drive, Shawnee, OK 74804
(405) 878-5412

Seminole State College

Seminole, Oklahoma
www.sscok.edu Federal Code: 003178

2-year public community and junior college in small town.
Enrollment: 2,282 undergrads.
Selectivity: Open admission; but selective for some programs.

BASIC COSTS (2012-2013)

Tuition and fees: $3,331; out-of-state residents $7,861.
Per-credit charge: $72; out-of-state residents $223.
Room and board: $6,500.

FINANCIAL AID PICTURE (2011-2012)

Students with need: 67% of average financial aid package awarded as scholarships/grants, 33% awarded as loans/jobs. Need-based aid available for part-time students.
Students without need: No-need awards available for academics, athletics, leadership, music/drama, state/district residency.

FINANCIAL AID PROCEDURES

Forms required: FAFSA, institutional form.
Dates and Deadlines: Priority date 6/1; no closing date. Applicants notified on a rolling basis starting 3/1; must reply within 4 week(s) of notification.

CONTACT

Tammy Kasterke, Financial Aid Specialist
PO Box 351, Seminole, OK 74818
(405) 382-9247

Southeastern Oklahoma State University

Durant, Oklahoma
www.se.edu Federal Code: 003179

4-year public liberal arts and teachers college in large town.
Enrollment: 3,664 undergrads, 23% part-time. 536 full-time freshmen.
Selectivity: Admits 50 to 75% of applicants.

BASIC COSTS (2012-2013)

Tuition and fees: $5,160; out-of-state residents $12,895.
Per-credit charge: $148; out-of-state residents $405.
Room and board: $5,390.
Additional info: Tuition/fee waivers available for minority students.

FINANCIAL AID PICTURE (2011-2012)

Students with need: Out of 522 full-time freshmen who applied for aid, 462 were judged to have need. Of these, 454 received aid, and 85 had their full need met. Average financial aid package met 20% of need; average scholarship/grant was $1,764; average loan was $1,381. For part-time students, average financial aid package was $5,954.
Students without need: No-need awards available for academics, alumni affiliation, art, athletics, leadership, minority status, music/drama, state/district residency.
Scholarships offered: 62 full-time freshmen received athletic scholarships; average amount $2,218.
Cumulative student debt: 63% of graduating class had student loans; average debt was $15,605.

FINANCIAL AID PROCEDURES

Forms required: FAFSA, institutional form.
Dates and Deadlines: Priority date 3/1; no closing date. Applicants notified on a rolling basis starting 4/1.

CONTACT

Tony Lehrling, Director of Student Financial Aid
1405 North Fourth Avenue, PMB 4225, Durant, OK 74701-0607
(580) 745-2186

Southwestern Christian University

Bethany, Oklahoma
www.swcu.edu Federal Code: 003180

4-year private liberal arts college in large town, affiliated with Pentecostal Holiness Church.
Enrollment: 669 undergrads, 28% part-time. 111 full-time freshmen.

BASIC COSTS (2013-2014)

Tuition and fees: $14,775.
Per-credit charge: $425.
Room and board: $6,086.

FINANCIAL AID PICTURE

Students with need: Need-based aid available for full-time and part-time students. Work study available nights, weekends, and for part-time students.
Students without need: No-need awards available for academics, alumni affiliation, leadership, music/drama, religious affiliation.

FINANCIAL AID PROCEDURES

Forms required: FAFSA.
Dates and Deadlines: Priority date 8/1; no closing date. Applicants notified on a rolling basis starting 5/1; must reply within 2 week(s) of notification.

CONTACT

Kellye Johnson, Director of Financial Aid
Box 340, Bethany, OK 73008
(405) 789-7661 ext. 3456

Southwestern Oklahoma State University

Weatherford, Oklahoma
www.swosu.edu Federal Code: 003181

4-year public university in large town.
Enrollment: 4,297 undergrads.

BASIC COSTS (2012-2013)

Tuition and fees: $4,905; out-of-state residents $11,265.
Per-credit charge: $133; out-of-state residents $345.
Room and board: $4,600.

FINANCIAL AID PICTURE

Students with need: Need-based aid available for full-time and part-time students.
Students without need: No-need awards available for academics, alumni affiliation, art, athletics, leadership, music/drama, state/district residency.

FINANCIAL AID PROCEDURES

Forms required: FAFSA, institutional form.
Dates and Deadlines: Closing date 3/1. Applicants notified by 3/15.

CONTACT

Jerome Wichert, Director of Student Financial Services
100 Campus Drive, Weatherford, OK 73096
(508) 774-3786

Spartan College of Aeronautics and Technology

Tulsa, Oklahoma
www.spartan.edu

4-year for-profit technical college in large city.
Enrollment: 1,100 undergrads.

BASIC COSTS (2012-2013)

Tuition and fees: $15,450.

Additional info: Board plan not available. Cost of room only, $3,520. Tuition at time of enrollment locked for 4 years.

FINANCIAL AID PICTURE

Students with need: Need-based aid available for full-time and part-time students. Work study available nights, weekends, and for part-time students.

FINANCIAL AID PROCEDURES

Forms required: FAFSA, institutional form.
Dates and Deadlines: Applicants notified on a rolling basis starting 2/1; must reply within 2 week(s) of notification.
Transfers: No deadline. Applicants notified on a rolling basis starting 2/1; must reply within 2 week(s) of notification.

CONTACT

8820 East Pine Street, Tulsa, OK 74158-2833

Tulsa Community College

Tulsa, Oklahoma
www.tulsacc.edu Federal Code: 009763

2-year public community college in large city.
Enrollment: 15,571 undergrads, 58% part-time. 2,053 full-time freshmen.
Selectivity: Open admission; but selective for some programs.

BASIC COSTS (2012-2013)

Tuition and fees: $3,181; out-of-state residents $8,605.
Per-credit charge: $76; out-of-state residents $257.
Additional info: Tuition/fee waivers available for minority students.

FINANCIAL AID PICTURE (2012-2013)

Students with need: Average financial aid package met 31% of need; average scholarship/grant was $734; average loan was $741. For part-time students, average financial aid package was $1,768.
Students without need: 15 full-time freshmen who did not demonstrate need for aid received scholarships/grants; average award was $233. No-need awards available for academics, art, job skills, leadership, music/drama, state/district residency.

FINANCIAL AID PROCEDURES

Forms required: FAFSA.
Dates and Deadlines: Priority date 8/1; no closing date. Applicants notified on a rolling basis starting 3/1.

CONTACT

Karen Jeffers, Director of Financial Aid
6111 East Skelly Drive, Tulsa, OK 74135-6198
(918) 595-7155

Tulsa Welding School

Tulsa, Oklahoma
www.weldingschool.com Federal Code: 015733

2-year for-profit technical college in very large city.
Enrollment: 1,791 undergrads.
Selectivity: Open admission.

BASIC COSTS (2013-2014)

Additional info: Program tuition varies from $13,271 to $35,274.

FINANCIAL AID PICTURE (2011-2012)

Students with need: 39% of average financial aid package awarded as scholarships/grants, 61% awarded as loans/jobs.
Students without need: This college awards aid only to students with need.

FINANCIAL AID PROCEDURES

Forms required: FAFSA.

CONTACT

Teresa Franklin, Financial Aid Director
2545 East 11th Street, Tulsa, OK 74104-3909
(918) 587-6789

University of Central Oklahoma

Edmond, Oklahoma
www.uco.edu Federal Code: 003152

4-year public university in small city.
Enrollment: 15,176 undergrads, 28% part-time. 2,169 full-time freshmen.
Selectivity: Admits over 75% of applicants.

BASIC COSTS (2012-2013)

Tuition and fees: $5,092; out-of-state residents $12,767.
Per-credit charge: $149; out-of-state residents $405.
Room and board: $6,708.
Additional info: Tuition/fee waivers available for minority students.

FINANCIAL AID PICTURE

Students with need: Need-based aid available for full-time students.
Students without need: No-need awards available for academics, alumni affiliation, art, athletics, leadership, minority status, music/drama, ROTC, state/district residency.

FINANCIAL AID PROCEDURES

Forms required: FAFSA, institutional form.
Dates and Deadlines: Priority date 5/31; no closing date. Applicants notified on a rolling basis starting 5/1; must reply by 6/30 or within 4 week(s) of notification.
Transfers: No deadline. Applicants notified on a rolling basis starting 5/1; must reply by 6/30 or within 4 week(s) of notification.

CONTACT

Susan Prater, Director of Financial Aid
100 North University Drive, Edmond, OK 73034-0151
(405) 974-3334

University of Oklahoma

Norman, Oklahoma
www.ou.edu Federal Code: 003184

4-year public university in small city.
Enrollment: 21,572 undergrads, 13% part-time. 3,996 full-time freshmen.
Selectivity: Admits over 75% of applicants.

BASIC COSTS (2012-2013)

Tuition and fees: $8,706; out-of-state residents $20,343.
Per-credit charge: $132; out-of-state residents $520.
Room and board: $8,382.
Additional info: Tuition at time of enrollment locked for 4 years; tuition/fee waivers available for adults, minority students.

FINANCIAL AID PICTURE (2011-2012)

Students with need: Out of 2,960 full-time freshmen who applied for aid, 2,055 were judged to have need. Of these, 1,988 received aid, and 1,690 had their full need met. Average financial aid package met 85% of need; average scholarship/grant was $6,131; average loan was $3,534. For part-time students, average financial aid package was $8,524.
Students without need: 498 full-time freshmen who did not demonstrate need for aid received scholarships/grants; average award was $1,871. No-need awards available for academics, alumni affiliation, art, athletics, leadership, music/drama, religious affiliation, ROTC.
Scholarships offered: 48 full-time freshmen received athletic scholarships; average amount $13,874.

Cumulative student debt: 55% of graduating class had student loans; average debt was $26,574.

FINANCIAL AID PROCEDURES
Forms required: FAFSA.
Dates and Deadlines: Priority date 3/1; no closing date. Applicants notified on a rolling basis starting 3/15; must reply within 6 week(s) of notification.
Transfers: No deadline. Applicants notified on a rolling basis starting 4/1; must reply within 6 week(s) of notification.

CONTACT
Caryn Pacheco, Director of Financial Aid
1000 Asp Avenue, Room 127, Norman, OK 73019-4076
(405) 325-5505

University of Science and Arts of Oklahoma

Chickasha, Oklahoma
www.usao.edu Federal Code: 003167

4-year public university and liberal arts college in large town.
Enrollment: 946 undergrads, 9% part-time. 183 full-time freshmen.
Selectivity: Admits less than 50% of applicants.

BASIC COSTS (2012-2013)
Tuition and fees: $5,400; out-of-state residents $12,720.
Per-credit charge: $141; out-of-state residents $385.
Room and board: $5,310.
Additional info: Tuition at time of enrollment locked for 4 years.

FINANCIAL AID PICTURE (2012-2013)
Students with need: Out of 143 full-time freshmen who applied for aid, 129 were judged to have need. Of these, 125 received aid, and 14 had their full need met. Average financial aid package met 62% of need; average scholarship/grant was $7,452; average loan was $2,843. For part-time students, average financial aid package was $6,518.
Students without need: 8 full-time freshmen who did not demonstrate need for aid received scholarships/grants; average award was $1,943. No-need awards available for academics, art, athletics, leadership, music/drama, state/district residency.
Scholarships offered: 24 full-time freshmen received athletic scholarships; average amount $10,674.
Cumulative student debt: 58% of graduating class had student loans; average debt was $18,378.

FINANCIAL AID PROCEDURES
Forms required: FAFSA, institutional form.
Dates and Deadlines: Priority date 3/15; no closing date. Applicants notified on a rolling basis starting 3/15.
Transfers: No deadline. Applicants notified on a rolling basis starting 3/15; must reply within 4 week(s) of notification.

CONTACT
Nancy Moats, Director of Financial Aid
1727 West Alabama, Chickasha, OK 73018-5322
(405) 574-1240

University of Tulsa

Tulsa, Oklahoma
www.utulsa.edu Federal Code: 003185

4-year private university in large city, affiliated with Presbyterian Church (USA).
Enrollment: 3,117 undergrads, 4% part-time. 613 full-time freshmen.
Selectivity: Admits less than 50% of applicants.

BASIC COSTS (2013-2014)
Tuition and fees: $34,350.
Per-credit charge: $1,221.
Room and board: $10,426.

FINANCIAL AID PICTURE (2011-2012)
Students with need: Out of 554 full-time freshmen who applied for aid, 311 were judged to have need. Of these, 311 received aid, and 138 had their full need met. Average financial aid package met 82% of need; average scholarship/grant was $6,786; average loan was $4,345. For part-time students, average financial aid package was $16,821.
Students without need: 211 full-time freshmen who did not demonstrate need for aid received scholarships/grants; average award was $12,630. No-need awards available for academics, alumni affiliation, athletics, leadership, minority status, music/drama, religious affiliation, ROTC.
Scholarships offered: 67 full-time freshmen received athletic scholarships; average amount $28,836.

FINANCIAL AID PROCEDURES
Forms required: FAFSA.
Dates and Deadlines: Priority date 3/1; no closing date. Applicants notified on a rolling basis starting 3/1; must reply by 5/1 or within 2 week(s) of notification.
Transfers: Priority date 5/1; no deadline. Applicants notified on a rolling basis starting 3/1; must reply by 5/1 or within 2 week(s) of notification.

CONTACT
Vicki Hendrickson, Director of Student Financial Services
800 South Tucker Drive, Tulsa, OK 74104-3189
(918) 631-2526

Vatterott College: Oklahoma City

Oklahoma City, Oklahoma
www.vatterott.edu Federal Code: 020693

2-year for-profit technical and career college in very large city.
Enrollment: 371 undergrads.
Selectivity: Open admission.

BASIC COSTS (2012-2013)
Additional info: Estimated program costs as of April 2012: diploma (60 weeks) $25,200 - $26,800; associate degree (70 weeks) $28,075 - $37,450, (90 weeks) $37,800 - $40,150. All costs, which include tuition, fees, books and supplies, and taxes, are subject to change.

FINANCIAL AID PICTURE
Students with need: Need-based aid available for full-time students.
Students without need: This college awards aid only to students with need.

FINANCIAL AID PROCEDURES
Forms required: FAFSA.

CONTACT
Janice Stepp, Director of Financial Aid
5537 Northwest Expressway, Oklahoma City, OK 73132
(405) 945-0088

Western Oklahoma State College

Altus, Oklahoma
www.wosc.edu Federal Code: 003146

2-year public community college in large town.
Enrollment: 855 full-time undergrads.
Selectivity: Open admission; but selective for some programs.

BASIC COSTS (2012-2013)
Tuition and fees: $3,004; out-of-state residents $7,151.
Per-credit charge: $67; out-of-state residents $206.
Room and board: $3,750.

FINANCIAL AID PICTURE
Students with need: Need-based aid available for full-time and part-time students. Work study available nights, weekends, and for part-time students.
Students without need: No-need awards available for academics, alumni affiliation, art, athletics, leadership, music/drama, state/district residency.

FINANCIAL AID PROCEDURES
Forms required: FAFSA, institutional form.
Dates and Deadlines: Closing date 3/1. Applicants notified on a rolling basis; must reply within 3 week(s) of notification.

CONTACT
Myrna Cross, Director of Financial Aid/Veterans' Affairs
2801 North Main Street, Altus, OK 73521
(580) 477-7709

Oregon

Art Institute of Portland
Portland, Oregon
www.aipd.artinstitutes.edu Federal Code: 007819

4-year for-profit visual arts and liberal arts college in large city.
Enrollment: 1,509 undergrads.

BASIC COSTS (2012-2013)
Tuition and fees: $21,695.
Per-credit charge: $481.
Additional info: Board plan not available. Cost of room only, $9,711.

FINANCIAL AID PICTURE
Students with need: Need-based aid available for full-time and part-time students. Work study available nights, weekends, and for part-time students.
Students without need: No-need awards available for art.
Additional info: Applicants encouraged to apply early for financial aid. Scholarship deadlines range from January 1 to March 1.

FINANCIAL AID PROCEDURES
Forms required: FAFSA.
Dates and Deadlines: Priority date 3/1; no closing date. Applicants notified on a rolling basis starting 1/1; must reply within 5 week(s) of notification.
Transfers: No deadline. Applicants notified on a rolling basis starting 1/1.

CONTACT
Mickey Jacobson, Director of Student Financial Services
1122 Northwest Davis Street, Portland, OR 97209-2911
(503) 382-4784

Central Oregon Community College
Bend, Oregon
www.cocc.edu Federal Code: 003188

2-year public community college in small city.
Enrollment: 7,132 undergrads.
Selectivity: Open admission; but selective for some programs.

BASIC COSTS (2012-2013)
Tuition and fees: $3,978; out-of-district residents $5,148; out-of-state residents $10,188.
Per-credit charge: $82; out-of-district residents $108; out-of-state residents $220.
Room and board: $8,384.
Additional info: Residents of WA, ID, NV and CA pay the in-state, out-of-district tuition.

FINANCIAL AID PICTURE (2012-2013)
Students with need: Average financial aid package met 72% of need; average scholarship/grant was $5,560; average loan was $3,304. For part-time students, average financial aid package was $10,935.
Students without need: No-need awards available for academics, leadership, state/district residency.
Additional info: Institution-sponsored short-term loans. Extensive part-time student employment.

FINANCIAL AID PROCEDURES
Forms required: FAFSA.
Dates and Deadlines: Applicants notified on a rolling basis starting 4/1; must reply within 4 week(s) of notification.

CONTACT
Kevin Multop, Director of Financial Aid
2600 Northwest College Way, Bend, OR 97701-5998
(541) 383-7260

Chemeketa Community College
Salem, Oregon
www.chemeketa.edu Federal Code: 003218

2-year public community and junior college in small city.
Enrollment: 10,900 undergrads, 46% part-time. 825 full-time freshmen.
Selectivity: Open admission; but selective for some programs.

BASIC COSTS (2012-2013)
Tuition and fees: $4,050; out-of-state residents $11,340.
Per-credit charge: $80; out-of-state residents $242.
Additional info: International students have additional required fees. Individual courses may have extra fees.

FINANCIAL AID PICTURE
Students with need: Need-based aid available for full-time and part-time students. Work study available nights, weekends, and for part-time students.
Students without need: This college awards aid only to students with need.

FINANCIAL AID PROCEDURES
Forms required: FAFSA.
Dates and Deadlines: Priority date 4/1; no closing date. Applicants notified on a rolling basis starting 6/30; must reply within 2 week(s) of notification.
Transfers: Priority date 6/30; no deadline. Applicants notified on a rolling basis; must reply within 4 week(s) of notification.

CONTACT
Kathy Campbell, Financial Aid Director
Admissions Office, Salem, OR 97309-7070
(503) 399-5018

Clackamas Community College
Oregon City, Oregon
www.clackamas.edu Federal Code: 004878

2-year public community college in large town.
Enrollment: 7,630 undergrads.
Selectivity: Open admission; but selective for some programs.

BASIC COSTS (2012-2013)
Tuition and fees: $3,849; out-of-state residents $10,824.

Per-credit charge: $79; out-of-state residents $234.
Additional info: In-state tuition applies to residents of Oregon, Washington, Idaho, Nevada and California.

FINANCIAL AID PICTURE (2011-2012)
Students with need: 62% of average financial aid package awarded as scholarships/grants, 38% awarded as loans/jobs. Need-based aid available for part-time students. Work study available nights, weekends, and for part-time students.
Students without need: No-need awards available for academics, art, athletics, leadership, music/drama.
Additional info: Institutional tuition rebate guarantee. Frozen tuition rates for new fall students who graduate within 3 years. Any tuition increase levied by college during those 3 years will be refunded to student upon graduation.

FINANCIAL AID PROCEDURES
Forms required: FAFSA, institutional form.
Dates and Deadlines: Priority date 4/10; no closing date. Applicants notified on a rolling basis starting 3/15; must reply within 3 week(s) of notification.
Transfers: No deadline. Applicants notified on a rolling basis.

CONTACT
Chippi Bello, Financial Aid Director
19600 Molalla Avenue, Oregon City, OR 97045
(503) 594-6100

Clatsop Community College
Astoria, Oregon
www.clatsopcc.edu Federal Code: 003189

2-year public community and maritime college in large town.
Enrollment: 1,064 undergrads, 56% part-time.
Selectivity: Open admission; but selective for some programs.

BASIC COSTS (2012-2013)
Tuition and fees: $4,713; out-of-state residents $8,943.
Per-credit charge: $94; out-of-state residents $188.
Additional info: Residents of Washington, Nevada, California and Idaho charged border rates, $97 per credit hour.

FINANCIAL AID PICTURE
Students with need: Need-based aid available for full-time and part-time students.
Students without need: No-need awards available for academics, leadership.

FINANCIAL AID PROCEDURES
Forms required: FAFSA, institutional form.
Dates and Deadlines: Priority date 5/1; no closing date. Applicants notified on a rolling basis starting 2/1.
Transfers: Students who apply after July 1 may only be eligible for Pell Grants and loans depending on availability of funds. Reply deadline 1 week before start of classes.

CONTACT
Lloyd Mueller, Director of Financial Aid
1651 Lexington, Astoria, OR 97103
(503) 338-2412

Concordia University
Portland, Oregon
www.cu-portland.edu Federal Code: 003191

4-year private liberal arts and teachers college in very large city, affiliated with Lutheran Church - Missouri Synod.
Enrollment: 1,332 undergrads, 14% part-time. 246 full-time freshmen.
Selectivity: Admits 50 to 75% of applicants.

BASIC COSTS (2013-2014)
Tuition and fees: $27,420.
Per-credit charge: $850.
Room and board: $8,030.
Additional info: Tuition/fee waivers available for adults.

FINANCIAL AID PICTURE
Students with need: Need-based aid available for full-time and part-time students. Work study available nights, weekends, and for part-time students.
Students without need: No-need awards available for academics, athletics, leadership, music/drama, religious affiliation.
Scholarships offered: President's Scholarship; $8,000; based on academic index. Regent's Scholarship; $6,000; calculated from GPA and ACT/SAT score. University Award; $4,500; calculated from GPA and ACT/SAT score. Dean's Award; $5,000; based on academic index. Honors Scholarship; 50% tuition.

FINANCIAL AID PROCEDURES
Forms required: FAFSA.
Dates and Deadlines: Applicants notified on a rolling basis.
Transfers: No deadline. Applicants notified on a rolling basis.

CONTACT
Breana Sylwester, Financial Aid Director
2811 Northeast Holman Street, Portland, OR 97211-6099
(503) 280-8514

Corban University
Salem, Oregon
www.corban.edu Federal Code: 001339

4-year private liberal arts college in small city, affiliated with Baptist faith.
Enrollment: 913 undergrads, 5% part-time. 218 full-time freshmen.
Selectivity: Admits less than 50% of applicants.

BASIC COSTS (2012-2013)
Tuition and fees: $25,486.
Per-credit charge: $1,040.
Room and board: $8,590.

FINANCIAL AID PICTURE (2012-2013)
Students with need: Average financial aid package met 63% of need; average scholarship/grant was $16,774; average loan was $3,702. For part-time students, average financial aid package was $6,574.
Students without need: No-need awards available for academics, alumni affiliation, athletics, leadership, music/drama, ROTC.
Cumulative student debt: 80% of graduating class had student loans; average debt was $23,853.

FINANCIAL AID PROCEDURES
Forms required: FAFSA.
Dates and Deadlines: Priority date 2/15; no closing date. Applicants notified on a rolling basis starting 3/1.

CONTACT
Nathan Warthan, Director of Financial Aid
5000 Deer Park Drive SE, Salem, OR 97317-9392
(503) 375-7006

Eastern Oregon University
La Grande, Oregon
www.eou.edu Federal Code: 003193

4-year public university and liberal arts college in large town.
Enrollment: 3,596 undergrads, 34% part-time. 381 full-time freshmen.

Selectivity: Admits 50 to 75% of applicants.

BASIC COSTS (2012-2013)
Tuition and fees: $7,239; out-of-state residents $15,720.
Room and board: $7,550.

FINANCIAL AID PICTURE (2012-2013)
Students with need: Out of 348 full-time freshmen who applied for aid, 295 were judged to have need. Of these, 295 received aid, and 61 had their full need met. Average financial aid package met 45% of need; average scholarship/grant was $5,204; average loan was $3,332. For part-time students, average financial aid package was $7,983.
Students without need: 9 full-time freshmen who did not demonstrate need for aid received scholarships/grants; average award was $2,244. No-need awards available for academics, art, leadership, minority status, music/drama, state/district residency.
Scholarships offered: ***Merit:*** University Scholars Scholarships; full-tuition; based on personal essay, recommendations, GPA, activities and awards. ***Athletic:*** 51 full-time freshmen received athletic scholarships; average amount $4,258.

FINANCIAL AID PROCEDURES
Forms required: FAFSA.
Dates and Deadlines: Priority date 1/1; no closing date. Applicants notified on a rolling basis starting 4/1; must reply within 4 week(s) of notification.
Transfers: No deadline. Applicants notified on a rolling basis.

CONTACT
Lara Moore, Director of Financial Aid
One University Boulevard, La Grande, OR 97850
(541) 962-3550

George Fox University
Newberg, Oregon
www.georgefox.edu Federal Code: 003194

4-year private university and seminary college in large town, affiliated with Society of Friends (Quaker).
Enrollment: 2,165 undergrads, 11% part-time. 420 full-time freshmen.
Selectivity: Admits over 75% of applicants.

BASIC COSTS (2013-2014)
Tuition and fees: $31,120.
Per-credit charge: $930.
Room and board: $9,630.
Additional info: Tuition/fee waivers available for minority students.

FINANCIAL AID PICTURE (2012-2013)
Students with need: Out of 384 full-time freshmen who applied for aid, 342 were judged to have need. Of these, 342 received aid, and 119 had their full need met. Average financial aid package met 85% of need; average scholarship/grant was $10,116; average loan was $2,986. For part-time students, average financial aid package was $11,833.
Students without need: 35 full-time freshmen who did not demonstrate need for aid received scholarships/grants; average award was $10,329. No-need awards available for academics, alumni affiliation, art, job skills, leadership, minority status, music/drama, religious affiliation.
Scholarships offered: Academic merit awards; $2,500-$15,000 per year; based on GPA, SAT/ACT and rigor of high school curriculum; renewable based on academic performance.
Cumulative student debt: 79% of graduating class had student loans; average debt was $23,512.
Additional info: Audition required for music and drama scholarships.

FINANCIAL AID PROCEDURES
Forms required: FAFSA, state aid form.
Dates and Deadlines: Priority date 2/1; no closing date. Applicants notified on a rolling basis starting 3/1; must reply within 6 week(s) of notification.
Transfers: Priority date 3/1.

CONTACT
James Oshiro, Director of Financial Aid
414 North Meridian Street #6089, Newberg, OR 97132-2697
(503) 554-2290

Klamath Community College
Klamath Falls, Oregon
www.klamathcc.edu Federal Code: 034283

2-year public community college in large town.
Enrollment: 1,172 undergrads.
Selectivity: Open admission.

BASIC COSTS (2013-2014)
Tuition and fees: $4,290; out-of-state residents $7,800.
Per-credit charge: $83; out-of-state residents $161.

FINANCIAL AID PICTURE
Students with need: Need-based aid available for full-time and part-time students.

FINANCIAL AID PROCEDURES
Forms required: FAFSA.

CONTACT
Donna Fulton, Financial Aid Specialist
7390 South 6th Street, Klamath Falls, OR 97603
(541) 882-3521

Lane Community College
Eugene, Oregon
www.lanecc.edu Federal Code: 003196

2-year public community college in small city.
Enrollment: 14,486 undergrads.
Selectivity: Open admission; but selective for some programs.

BASIC COSTS (2012-2013)
Tuition and fees: $4,537; out-of-state residents $10,387.
Per-credit charge: $90; out-of-state residents $220.

FINANCIAL AID PICTURE
Students with need: Need-based aid available for full-time and part-time students. Work study available nights, weekends, and for part-time students.
Students without need: No-need awards available for art, athletics, minority status, music/drama.

FINANCIAL AID PROCEDURES
Forms required: FAFSA.
Dates and Deadlines: Closing date 2/15. Applicants notified on a rolling basis starting 6/1; must reply within 2 week(s) of notification.

CONTACT
Helen Faith, Director of Financial Aid
4000 East 30th Avenue, Eugene, OR 97405
(541) 463-3100

Lewis & Clark College
Portland, Oregon Federal Code: 003197
www.lclark.edu CSS Code: 4384

4-year private liberal arts college in very large city.
Enrollment: 2,031 undergrads, 1% part-time. 606 full-time freshmen.
Selectivity: Admits 50 to 75% of applicants.

BASIC COSTS (2012-2013)
Tuition and fees: $40,330.
Per-credit charge: $1,999.
Room and board: $10,358.

FINANCIAL AID PICTURE (2011-2012)
Students with need: 80% of average financial aid package awarded as scholarships/grants, 20% awarded as loans/jobs. Need-based aid available for part-time students. Work study available nights, weekends, and for part-time students.
Students without need: No-need awards available for academics.

FINANCIAL AID PROCEDURES
Forms required: FAFSA, CSS PROFILE.
Dates and Deadlines: Priority date 2/15; no closing date. Applicants notified on a rolling basis starting 3/1.
Transfers: Transfers eligible for merit-based Dean's scholarships of up to $10,000, not eligible for Neely or Trustee scholarships. Financial aid transcript form from previous institutions required.

CONTACT
Anastacia Dillon, Director of Student Financial Services
0615 SW Palatine Hill Road, Portland, OR 97219-7899
(503) 768-7090

Linfield College
McMinnville, Oregon
www.linfield.edu Federal Code: 003198

4-year private liberal arts college in large town, affiliated with American Baptist Churches in the USA.
Enrollment: 1,608 undergrads, 1% part-time. 443 full-time freshmen.
Selectivity: Admits over 75% of applicants.

BASIC COSTS (2012-2013)
Tuition and fees: $34,328.
Per-credit charge: $1,060.
Room and board: $9,400.

FINANCIAL AID PICTURE (2012-2013)
Students with need: Out of 399 full-time freshmen who applied for aid, 338 were judged to have need. Of these, 338 received aid, and 112 had their full need met. Average financial aid package met 86% of need; average scholarship/grant was $9,884; average loan was $3,848. For part-time students, average financial aid package was $16,747.
Students without need: 93 full-time freshmen who did not demonstrate need for aid received scholarships/grants; average award was $11,464. No-need awards available for academics, minority status, music/drama.
Scholarships offered: National Merit Scholarship; half- to full-tuition for National Merit Finalists who list Linfield as first choice. Trustee Scholarships; based on academic record and 3.75 GPA. Faculty Scholarships; based on academic record and 3.4 GPA. Linfield Competitive Scholarships; separate application required. Music Achievement Awards; audition or recorded performance required; must intend to major or minor in music. Leadership/ Service Scholarship; based on high levels of leadership, initiative, and service to others through student government, school activities, community organizations, and church or social service agencies; separate application required; up to 5 awarded. Academic All-Star Scholarships; supplements other competition-based scholarships.
Cumulative student debt: 72% of graduating class had student loans; average debt was $29,793.

FINANCIAL AID PROCEDURES
Forms required: FAFSA.
Dates and Deadlines: Priority date 2/1; no closing date.
Transfers: Priority date 2/15. Applicants notified by 5/15; must reply by 6/15. Transfer Scholarships for students who have attended 2- or 4-year accredited colleges full-time and have 3.25 GPA. Phi Theta Kappa Scholarships for members of Phi Theta Kappa, 3.25 GPA in transferable courses required, up to 10 awarded each year. Chemeketa Scholars at Linfield is a scholarship program for participants in the Chemeketa Scholars program at Chemeketa Community College (Oregon), up to 10 awarded each year.

CONTACT
Keri Burke, Director of Financial Aid
900 Southeast Baker Street, McMinnville, OR 97128-3725
(503) 883-2225

Linn-Benton Community College
Albany, Oregon
www.linnbenton.edu Federal Code: 006938

2-year public community college in large town.
Enrollment: 6,279 undergrads, 50% part-time. 1,366 full-time freshmen.
Selectivity: Open admission; but selective for some programs.

BASIC COSTS (2012-2013)
Tuition and fees: $4,320; out-of-state residents $9,261.
Per-credit charge: $91; out-of-state residents $201.
Additional info: Tuition/fee waivers available for unemployed or children of unemployed.

FINANCIAL AID PICTURE
Students with need: Need-based aid available for full-time and part-time students. Work study available nights, weekends, and for part-time students.
Students without need: No-need awards available for academics, alumni affiliation, art, athletics, leadership, music/drama.

FINANCIAL AID PROCEDURES
Forms required: FAFSA.
Dates and Deadlines: Priority date 4/1; no closing date. Applicants notified on a rolling basis starting 3/30; must reply within 4 week(s) of notification.

CONTACT
Bev Gerig
6500 SW Pacific Boulevard, Albany, OR 97321-3779
(541) 917-4850

Marylhurst University
Marylhurst, Oregon
www.marylhurst.edu Federal Code: 003199

4-year private university and liberal arts college in large town, affiliated with Roman Catholic Church.
Enrollment: 817 undergrads.

BASIC COSTS (2012-2013)
Tuition and fees: $18,945.
Per-credit charge: $421.

FINANCIAL AID PICTURE
Students with need: Need-based aid available for full-time and part-time students. Work study available weekends and for part-time students.
Students without need: No-need awards available for academics.

FINANCIAL AID PROCEDURES
Forms required: FAFSA, institutional form.
Dates and Deadlines: Priority date 3/1; no closing date. Applicants notified on a rolling basis starting 5/1.
Transfers: No deadline. Applicants notified on a rolling basis starting 5/1.

CONTACT
Tracy Reisinger, Director of Financial Aid
PO Box 261, Marylhurst, OR 97036-0261
(503) 699-6253

Mt. Hood Community College

Gresham, Oregon
www.mhcc.cc.or.us Federal Code: 003204

2-year public community college in small city.
Enrollment: 8,608 undergrads, 49% part-time. 1,462 full-time freshmen.
Selectivity: Open admission; but selective for some programs.

BASIC COSTS (2012-2013)
Tuition and fees: $4,579; out-of-state residents $9,979.
Per-credit charge: $89; out-of-state residents $209.

FINANCIAL AID PICTURE
Students with need: Need-based aid available for full-time and part-time students.
Students without need: No-need awards available for academics.

FINANCIAL AID PROCEDURES
Forms required: FAFSA, institutional form.
Dates and Deadlines: Closing date 4/1. Applicants notified on a rolling basis starting 4/1; must reply within 4 week(s) of notification.

CONTACT
Christi Hart, Financial Aid Director
26000 SE Stark Street, Gresham, OR 97030
(503) 491-7379

Multnomah University

Portland, Oregon
www.multnomah.edu Federal Code: 003206

4-year private Bible and seminary college in very large city, affiliated with interdenominational tradition.
Enrollment: 503 undergrads, 18% part-time. 59 full-time freshmen.
Selectivity: Admits 50 to 75% of applicants.

BASIC COSTS (2012-2013)
Tuition and fees: $21,240.
Per-credit charge: $655.
Room and board: $7,200.

FINANCIAL AID PICTURE (2011-2012)
Students with need: Out of 58 full-time freshmen who applied for aid, 52 were judged to have need. Of these, 52 received aid, and 4 had their full need met. Average financial aid package met 43% of need; average scholarship/grant was $6,570; average loan was $2,534. For part-time students, average financial aid package was $5,213.
Students without need: 5 full-time freshmen who did not demonstrate need for aid received scholarships/grants; average award was $2,460. No-need awards available for academics, alumni affiliation.

FINANCIAL AID PROCEDURES
Forms required: FAFSA.
Dates and Deadlines: Priority date 4/1; closing date 8/1. Applicants notified on a rolling basis starting 3/15; must reply within 2 week(s) of notification.
Transfers: Must reply within 2 week(s) of notification.

CONTACT
Mary McGlothlan, Director of Financial Aid
8435 Northeast Glisan Street, Portland, OR 97220-5898
(503) 251-5336

New Hope Christian College

Eugene, Oregon
www.newhope.edu Federal Code: 015167

4-year private Bible college in small city, affiliated with nondenominational tradition.
Enrollment: 200 undergrads.

BASIC COSTS (2012-2013)
Tuition and fees: $13,590.
Per-credit charge: $515.
Room and board: $6,510.

FINANCIAL AID PICTURE
Students with need: Need-based aid available for full-time and part-time students. Work study available nights, weekends, and for part-time students.
Students without need: No-need awards available for academics, art, athletics, job skills, leadership, music/drama, religious affiliation, state/district residency.
Scholarships offered: Honors award; $300; 3.7 GPA required.
Additional info: Some early acceptance awards possible for those admitted by May 15. Distance awards to those coming from over 1,000 miles away. Some awards for husbands and wives enrolled at same time.

FINANCIAL AID PROCEDURES
Forms required: FAFSA, institutional form.
Dates and Deadlines: Priority date 4/1; closing date 8/1. Applicants notified on a rolling basis starting 2/1; must reply within 4 week(s) of notification.
Transfers: No deadline.

CONTACT
Nathan Icenhowe, Director of Financial Aid
2155 Bailey Hill Road, Eugene, OR 97405
(800) 322-2638

Northwest Christian University

Eugene, Oregon
www.nwcu.edu Federal Code: 003208

4-year private university in small city, affiliated with Christian Church (Disciples of Christ).
Enrollment: 451 undergrads, 21% part-time. 68 full-time freshmen.
Selectivity: Admits 50 to 75% of applicants.

BASIC COSTS (2012-2013)
Tuition and fees: $24,880.
Per-credit charge: $826.
Room and board: $7,600.

FINANCIAL AID PICTURE (2012-2013)
Students with need: Average financial aid package met 72% of need; average scholarship/grant was $16,614; average loan was $2,950. For part-time students, average financial aid package was $6,487.
Students without need: No-need awards available for academics, athletics, leadership, music/drama, religious affiliation.
Scholarships offered: Academic scholarships; $3,000-$11,000; GPA/SAT or ACT scores; not limited. Leadership bonuses; $500-$1,000; school, community, church leadership roles; not limited.
Cumulative student debt: 68% of graduating class had student loans; average debt was $32,045.

FINANCIAL AID PROCEDURES
Forms required: FAFSA.
Dates and Deadlines: Priority date 3/1; no closing date. Applicants notified on a rolling basis starting 3/1; must reply within 2 week(s) of notification.
Transfers: No deadline. Applicants notified on a rolling basis starting 3/1.

CONTACT
Scott Palmer, Director of Financial Aid
828 E. 11th Avenue, Eugene, OR 97401-3745
(541) 684-7218

Oregon College of Art & Craft
Portland, Oregon
www.ocac.edu Federal Code: 030073

4-year private visual arts college in very large city.
Enrollment: 164 undergrads, 19% part-time. 18 full-time freshmen.
Selectivity: Admits over 75% of applicants.

BASIC COSTS (2012-2013)
Tuition and fees: $24,200.

FINANCIAL AID PICTURE (2012-2013)
Students with need: Average financial aid package met 68% of need; average scholarship/grant was $5,858; average loan was $3,250. For part-time students, average financial aid package was $17,905.
Students without need: No-need awards available for academics, art.
Cumulative student debt: 66% of graduating class had student loans; average debt was $22,500.

FINANCIAL AID PROCEDURES
Forms required: FAFSA.
Dates and Deadlines: Priority date 3/1; no closing date. Applicants notified on a rolling basis starting 3/1.

CONTACT
Linda Anderson, Financial Aid Director
8245 SW Barnes Road, Portland, OR 97225-6349
(971) 255-4224

Oregon Health & Science University
Portland, Oregon
www.ohsu.edu Federal Code: 004883

3-year public university and health science college in very large city.
Enrollment: 825 undergrads, 83% part-time.

BASIC COSTS (2012-2013)
Tuition and fees: $20,044; out-of-state residents $32,059.
Per-credit charge: $321; out-of-state residents $588.
Additional info: Tuition shown is for undergraduate nursing program; costs for other programs vary.

FINANCIAL AID PICTURE (2012-2013)
Students with need: Average financial aid package for all full-time undergraduates was $9,806; for part-time $6,887. 14% awarded as scholarships/grants, 86% awarded as loans/jobs. Work study available nights, weekends, and for part-time students.

FINANCIAL AID PROCEDURES
Transfers: Priority date 3/1. Applicants notified on a rolling basis starting 5/1; must reply within 4 week(s) of notification.

CONTACT
Rachel Durbin, Director of Financial Aid
3181 SW Sam Jackson Park Road, Portland, OR 97239-3098
(503) 494-7800

Oregon Institute of Technology
Klamath Falls, Oregon
www.oit.edu Federal Code: 003211

4-year public career college in small city.
Enrollment: 3,331 undergrads, 31% part-time. 331 full-time freshmen.
Selectivity: Admits over 75% of applicants.

BASIC COSTS (2012-2013)
Tuition and fees: $8,307; out-of-state residents $23,670.
Room and board: $8,635.
Additional info: Tuition/fee waivers available for minority students.

FINANCIAL AID PICTURE (2012-2013)
Students with need: 36% of average financial aid package awarded as scholarships/grants, 64% awarded as loans/jobs. Need-based aid available for part-time students. Work study available weekends and for part-time students.
Students without need: No-need awards available for academics, athletics, leadership, minority status.

FINANCIAL AID PROCEDURES
Forms required: FAFSA.
Dates and Deadlines: Priority date 2/1; no closing date. Applicants notified on a rolling basis starting 4/1; must reply within 3 week(s) of notification.
Transfers: Closing date 2/1.

CONTACT
Tracey Lehman, Director of Financial Aid
3201 Campus Drive, Klamath Falls, OR 97601
(541) 885-1280

Oregon State University
Corvallis, Oregon
www.oregonstate.edu Federal Code: 003210

4-year public university in small city.
Enrollment: 20,464 undergrads, 16% part-time. 3,134 full-time freshmen.
Selectivity: Admits over 75% of applicants.

BASIC COSTS (2012-2013)
Tuition and fees: $8,139; out-of-state residents $22,323.
Room and board: $10,563.

FINANCIAL AID PICTURE
Students with need: Need-based aid available for full-time students.
Students without need: No-need awards available for academics, athletics, job skills, leadership, minority status, ROTC, state/district residency.

FINANCIAL AID PROCEDURES
Forms required: FAFSA.
Dates and Deadlines: Closing date 2/1. Applicants notified on a rolling basis starting 4/1; must reply within 4 week(s) of notification.
Transfers: Priority date 2/1; no deadline.

CONTACT
Doug Severs, Director of Financial Aid & Scholarships
104 Kerr Administration Building, Corvallis, OR 97331-2130
(541) 731-2241

Pacific Northwest College of Art
Portland, Oregon
www.pnca.edu Federal Code: 003207

4-year private visual arts college in large city.
Enrollment: 446 undergrads, 12% part-time. 78 full-time freshmen.
Selectivity: Admits 50 to 75% of applicants.

BASIC COSTS (2012-2013)
Tuition and fees: $29,994.
Per-credit charge: $1,203.
Additional info: Off-campus housing available, approximately one mile from campus. Annual cost is $4,534 for shared bedroom.

FINANCIAL AID PICTURE (2011-2012)
Students with need: Out of 71 full-time freshmen who applied for aid, 64 were judged to have need. Of these, 64 received aid. Need-based aid available for part-time students.

Students without need: No-need awards available for academics, art.
Scholarships offered: Leta Kennedy Student Scholarships; $10,000; based on artistic merit. Dorothy Lemelson Scholarship; cost of attendance; based on artistic and academic merit; renewable up to 4 years; 1 awarded. Other renewable scholarships available.

FINANCIAL AID PROCEDURES
Forms required: FAFSA.
Dates and Deadlines: Priority date 3/1; no closing date. Applicants notified on a rolling basis starting 4/1; must reply by 5/1 or within 4 week(s) of notification.
Transfers: No deadline. Applicants notified on a rolling basis starting 4/1; must reply by 5/1 or within 4 week(s) of notification.

CONTACT
Heidi Locke, Director of Financial Aid
1241 NW Johnson Street, Portland, OR 97209
(503) 821-8972

Pacific University
Forest Grove, Oregon
www.pacificu.edu Federal Code: 003212

4-year private university in large town, affiliated with United Church of Christ.
Enrollment: 1,670 undergrads, 2% part-time. 450 full-time freshmen.
Selectivity: Admits over 75% of applicants.

BASIC COSTS (2012-2013)
Tuition and fees: $35,260.
Per-credit charge: $1,435.
Room and board: $9,992.

FINANCIAL AID PICTURE (2012-2013)
Students with need: Out of 435 full-time freshmen who applied for aid, 391 were judged to have need. Of these, 391 received aid, and 65 had their full need met. Average financial aid package met 85% of need; average scholarship/grant was $21,788; average loan was $5,671. For part-time students, average financial aid package was $18,495.
Students without need: 63 full-time freshmen who did not demonstrate need for aid received scholarships/grants; average award was $16,110. No-need awards available for academics, alumni affiliation, art, music/drama.
Scholarships offered: Founder's Scholarship; $15,000. Honors Scholarship; $12,000. Presidential Scholarship; $10,000. Trustee Scholarship; $8,500. University Scholarship; $7,500. Pacific Opportunity Award; $5,000. Pacesetters Scholarship; $1,000-$3,000. Music and Forensics Talent Awards; $1,000-$3,000. Number of awards vary.
Cumulative student debt: 74% of graduating class had student loans; average debt was $30,880.

FINANCIAL AID PROCEDURES
Forms required: FAFSA.
Dates and Deadlines: Priority date 3/1; no closing date. Applicants notified on a rolling basis starting 3/1.

CONTACT
Michael Johnson, Director of Financial Aid
2043 College Way, Forest Grove, OR 97116-1797
(503) 352-2222

Pioneer Pacific College
Wilsonville, Oregon
www.pioneerpacific.edu Federal Code: 016520

2-year for-profit career college in large town.
Enrollment: 1,063 full-time undergrads.
Selectivity: Open admission; but selective for some programs.

FINANCIAL AID PICTURE
Students with need: Need-based aid available for full-time and part-time students.
Students without need: This college awards aid only to students with need.
Scholarships offered: High school scholarship program and community scholarship program available.

FINANCIAL AID PROCEDURES
Forms required: FAFSA.
Dates and Deadlines: Applicants notified on a rolling basis starting 2/27.

CONTACT
Mark Johnson, Executive Director of Financial Aid
27501 Southwest Parkway Avenue, Wilsonville, OR 97070
(503) 654-8000

Portland Community College
Portland, Oregon
www.pcc.edu Federal Code: 003213

2-year public community college in very large city.
Enrollment: 30,089 undergrads, 53% part-time. 1,038 full-time freshmen.
Selectivity: Open admission; but selective for some programs.

BASIC COSTS (2013-2014)
Tuition and fees: $3,960; out-of-state residents $9,720.

FINANCIAL AID PICTURE
Students with need: Need-based aid available for full-time and part-time students. Work study available nights, weekends, and for part-time students.
Students without need: This college awards aid only to students with need.

FINANCIAL AID PROCEDURES
Forms required: FAFSA.
Dates and Deadlines: Priority date 3/1; no closing date. Applicants notified on a rolling basis starting 6/1; must reply within 3 week(s) of notification.

CONTACT
Bert Logan, Director of Financial Aid
Box 19000, Portland, OR 97280-0990
(503) 722-4934

Portland State University
Portland, Oregon
www.pdx.edu Federal Code: 003216

4-year public university in very large city.
Enrollment: 18,367 undergrads, 27% part-time. 1,301 full-time freshmen.
Selectivity: Admits 50 to 75% of applicants.

BASIC COSTS (2012-2013)
Tuition and fees: $7,653; out-of-state residents $22,863.
Room and board: $9,729.

FINANCIAL AID PICTURE
Students with need: Need-based aid available for full-time and part-time students. Work study available nights, weekends, and for part-time students.
Students without need: No-need awards available for academics, art, athletics, music/drama, state/district residency.

FINANCIAL AID PROCEDURES
Forms required: FAFSA.
Dates and Deadlines: Priority date 2/28; no closing date. Applicants notified on a rolling basis; must reply within 4 week(s) of notification.

Transfers: No deadline. Applicants notified on a rolling basis.

CONTACT
Phillip Rodgers, Director of Financial Aid
PO Box 751-ADM, Portland, OR 97207-0751
(800) 547-8887

Reed College

Portland, Oregon
www.reed.edu
Federal Code: 003217
CSS Code: 4654

4-year private liberal arts college in very large city.
Enrollment: 1,390 undergrads, 1% part-time. 320 full-time freshmen.
Selectivity: Admits less than 50% of applicants.

BASIC COSTS (2013-2014)
Tuition and fees: $46,010.
Per-credit charge: $1,943.
Room and board: $11,770.

FINANCIAL AID PICTURE (2012-2013)
Students with need: Out of 210 full-time freshmen who applied for aid, 179 were judged to have need. Of these, 179 received aid, and 179 had their full need met. Average financial aid package met 100% of need; average scholarship/grant was $38,917; average loan was $3,217.
Students without need: This college awards aid only to students with need.
Cumulative student debt: 57% of graduating class had student loans; average debt was $19,407.
Additional info: College meets demonstrated need of continuing students who have attended Reed minimum of 2 semesters, who file financial aid applications on time, and who maintain satisfactory academic progress. Institutional aid consideration is for total of 8 semesters.

FINANCIAL AID PROCEDURES
Forms required: FAFSA, CSS PROFILE.
Dates and Deadlines: Closing date 2/1. Applicants notified by 4/1; must reply by 5/1 or within 2 week(s) of notification.
Transfers: Closing date 3/1. Applicants notified by 5/15; must reply by 6/1 or within 2 week(s) of notification.

CONTACT
Leslie Limper, Director of Financial Aid
3203 SE Woodstock Boulevard, Portland, OR 97202-8199
(800) 547-4750

Rogue Community College

Grants Pass, Oregon
www.roguecc.edu
Federal Code: 010071

2-year public community college in large town.
Enrollment: 4,647 undergrads, 56% part-time. 389 full-time freshmen.
Selectivity: Open admission; but selective for some programs.

BASIC COSTS (2012-2013)
Tuition and fees: $4,500; out-of-state residents $5,400.
Per-credit charge: $87; out-of-state residents $107.
Additional info: Washington, Idaho, Nevada, and California residents pay in-state tuition. Tuition/fee waivers available for unemployed or children of unemployed.

FINANCIAL AID PICTURE (2012-2013)
Students with need: Out of 337 full-time freshmen who applied for aid, 284 were judged to have need. Of these, 283 received aid, and 72 had their full need met. Average financial aid package met 78% of need; average loan was $3,159. Need-based aid available for part-time students.
Students without need: 9 full-time freshmen who did not demonstrate need for aid received scholarships/grants; average award was $1,308.

FINANCIAL AID PROCEDURES
Forms required: FAFSA, institutional form.
Dates and Deadlines: Priority date 5/1; no closing date. Applicants notified on a rolling basis; must reply within 2 week(s) of notification.

CONTACT
Anna Manley, Director of Financial Aid
3345 Redwood Highway, Grants Pass, OR 97527
(541) 956-7501 ext. 1

Southern Oregon University

Ashland, Oregon
www.sou.edu
Federal Code: 003219

4-year public university and liberal arts college in large town.
Enrollment: 4,337 undergrads, 15% part-time. 676 full-time freshmen.
Selectivity: Admits over 75% of applicants.

BASIC COSTS (2012-2013)
Tuition and fees: $7,521; out-of-state residents $20,238.
Room and board: $10,332.
Additional info: Tuition/fee waivers available for minority students.

FINANCIAL AID PICTURE (2011-2012)
Students with need: Need-based aid available for full-time and part-time students. Work study available nights, weekends, and for part-time students.
Students without need: No-need awards available for academics, alumni affiliation, art, athletics, leadership, minority status, music/drama, state/district residency.

FINANCIAL AID PROCEDURES
Forms required: FAFSA.
Dates and Deadlines: Priority date 3/1; no closing date. Applicants notified on a rolling basis starting 3/2; must reply within 4 week(s) of notification.

CONTACT
Peggy Mezger, Director of Financial Aid
1250 Siskiyou Boulevard, Ashland, OR 97520-5032
(541) 552-6600

Southwestern Oregon Community College

Coos Bay, Oregon
www.socc.edu
Federal Code: 003220

2-year public culinary school and community college in large town.
Enrollment: 1,027 undergrads.
Selectivity: Open admission; but selective for some programs.

BASIC COSTS (2012-2013)
Tuition and fees: $4,770; out-of-state residents $4,770.
Room and board: $7,056.
Additional info: Tuition/fee waivers available for adults, unemployed or children of unemployed.

FINANCIAL AID PICTURE
Students with need: Need-based aid available for full-time and part-time students.
Students without need: No-need awards available for art, athletics, leadership, music/drama.

FINANCIAL AID PROCEDURES
Forms required: FAFSA.

Dates and Deadlines: Closing date 3/1. Applicants notified on a rolling basis starting 5/1; must reply within 3 week(s) of notification.

CONTACT

Avena Singh, Director of Financial Aid
1988 Newmark Avenue, Coos Bay, OR 97420-2956
(541) 888-7337

Treasure Valley Community College

Ontario, Oregon
www.tvcc.cc Federal Code: 003221

2-year public community college in small town.
Enrollment: 2,423 undergrads, 50% part-time. 384 full-time freshmen.
Selectivity: Open admission; but selective for some programs.

BASIC COSTS (2012-2013)

Tuition and fees: $4,680; out-of-state residents $5,130.
Room and board: $6,505.

FINANCIAL AID PICTURE (2012-2013)

Students with need: Average financial aid package met 42% of need; average scholarship/grant was $5,114; average loan was $2,793. For part-time students, average financial aid package was $7,319.
Students without need: No-need awards available for academics, athletics, leadership, music/drama, state/district residency.

FINANCIAL AID PROCEDURES

Forms required: FAFSA.
Dates and Deadlines: Priority date 4/1; no closing date. Applicants notified on a rolling basis starting 5/1.
Transfers: No deadline. Applicants notified on a rolling basis.

CONTACT

Keith Raab, Director of Financial Aid
650 College Boulevard, Ontario, OR 97914
(541) 881-5833

Umpqua Community College

Roseburg, Oregon
www.umpqua.edu Federal Code: 003222

2-year public community college in large town.
Enrollment: 1,681 undergrads, 47% part-time. 190 full-time freshmen.
Selectivity: Open admission; but selective for some programs.

BASIC COSTS (2012-2013)

Tuition and fees: $4,200; out-of-state residents $9,415.
Per-credit charge: $85; out-of-state residents $206.

FINANCIAL AID PICTURE (2011-2012)

Students with need: Out of 185 full-time freshmen who applied for aid, 104 were judged to have need. Of these, 101 received aid, and 67 had their full need met. Average financial aid package met 54% of need; average scholarship/grant was $4,977; average loan was $1,556. For part-time students, average financial aid package was $3,710.
Students without need: No-need awards available for academics, athletics.

FINANCIAL AID PROCEDURES

Forms required: FAFSA, institutional form.
Dates and Deadlines: Priority date 3/10; no closing date. Applicants notified on a rolling basis starting 2/9; must reply within 2 week(s) of notification.

CONTACT

Michelle Bergmann, Director of Financial Aid
1140 College Road, Roseburg, OR 97470-0226
(541) 440-4602

University of Oregon

Eugene, Oregon
www.uoregon.edu Federal Code: 003223

4-year public university in small city.
Enrollment: 20,464 undergrads, 8% part-time. 3,962 full-time freshmen.
Selectivity: Admits 50 to 75% of applicants.

BASIC COSTS (2012-2013)

Tuition and fees: $9,310; out-of-state residents $28,660.
Room and board: $10,580.

FINANCIAL AID PICTURE

Students with need: Need-based aid available for full-time and part-time students. Work study available nights, weekends, and for part-time students.
Students without need: No-need awards available for academics, athletics, leadership, minority status, music/drama, ROTC, state/district residency.
Scholarships offered: Presidential Scholarship; approximately $8,500 per year for up to 4 years, Oregon residency required. National Merit Scholarship; $2,000 per year for up to 4 years. Laurel Award; $1,500-$2,700 for one year only. General University Scholarship; $1,500-$2,700 for one year only. Dean's Scholarship; $1,000-$7,000 per year (depending on residency status) for up to 12 terms.

FINANCIAL AID PROCEDURES

Forms required: FAFSA.
Dates and Deadlines: Priority date 3/1; no closing date. Applicants notified on a rolling basis starting 4/15; must reply within 4 week(s) of notification.

CONTACT

James Brooks, Director, Financial Aid and Scholarship
1217 University of Oregon, Eugene, OR 97403-1217
(541) 346-3221

University of Portland

Portland, Oregon
www.up.edu Federal Code: 003224

4-year private university in large city, affiliated with Roman Catholic Church.
Enrollment: 3,374 undergrads, 2% part-time. 873 full-time freshmen.
Selectivity: Admits 50 to 75% of applicants.

BASIC COSTS (2013-2014)

Tuition and fees: $36,840.
Per-credit charge: $1,150.
Room and board: $11,004.

FINANCIAL AID PICTURE

Students with need: Need-based aid available for full-time and part-time students. Work study available nights, weekends, and for part-time students.
Students without need: No-need awards available for academics, athletics, music/drama, religious affiliation, ROTC.
Scholarships offered: President's Scholarship; up to $10,000; based on academic excellence, school and community involvement, and other factors. Holy Cross Scholarship; up to $6,000; based on academic excellence, school and community involvement, and other factors. Arthur A. Schulte Scholarship; up to $6,000.

FINANCIAL AID PROCEDURES

Forms required: FAFSA.
Dates and Deadlines: Priority date 3/1; no closing date. Applicants notified on a rolling basis starting 2/28; must reply within 3 week(s) of notification.
Transfers: No deadline. Applicants notified on a rolling basis; must reply within 4 week(s) of notification.

CONTACT

Janet Turner, Director of Financial Aid
5000 North Willamette Boulevard, Portland, OR 97203-5798
(503) 943-7311

Warner Pacific College

Portland, Oregon
www.warnerpacific.edu Federal Code: 003225

4-year private liberal arts college in very large city, affiliated with Church of God.
Enrollment: 551 undergrads, 5% part-time. 86 full-time freshmen.
Selectivity: Admits 50 to 75% of applicants.

BASIC COSTS (2012-2013)

Tuition and fees: $19,030.
Room and board: $7,690.

FINANCIAL AID PICTURE (2012-2013)

Students with need: Out of 85 full-time freshmen who applied for aid, 81 were judged to have need. Of these, 81 received aid, and 6 had their full need met. Average financial aid package met 64% of need; average scholarship/grant was $5,342; average loan was $3,775. For part-time students, average financial aid package was $11,903.
Students without need: 5 full-time freshmen who did not demonstrate need for aid received scholarships/grants; average award was $4,000. No-need awards available for academics, alumni affiliation, athletics, leadership, music/drama, religious affiliation, state/district residency.
Scholarships offered: 17 full-time freshmen received athletic scholarships; average amount $4,779.
Cumulative student debt: 91% of graduating class had student loans; average debt was $33,035.

FINANCIAL AID PROCEDURES

Forms required: FAFSA.
Dates and Deadlines: Priority date 3/1; closing date 8/1. Applicants notified on a rolling basis starting 3/1; must reply within 2 week(s) of notification.
Transfers: Applicants notified on a rolling basis starting 3/1; must reply within 2 week(s) of notification. Highest Academic Scholarships not available to transfer students. Phi Theta Kappa award available to transfers only.

CONTACT

Katrina Matano, Director of Student Financial Services and Financial Aid
2219 SE 68th Avenue, Portland, OR 97215-4026
(503) 517-1091

Western Oregon University

Monmouth, Oregon
www.wou.edu Federal Code: 003209

4-year public liberal arts and teachers college in small town.
Enrollment: 5,287 undergrads, 12% part-time. 817 full-time freshmen.
Selectivity: Admits over 75% of applicants.

BASIC COSTS (2012-2013)

Tuition and fees: $7,989; out-of-state residents $21,114.
Room and board: $8,870.
Additional info: Reported resident tuition reflects "Traditional" rate subject to annual adjustments. Resident students can also select a Tuition Promise base tuition rate that is not subject to annual adjustments for 4 years. Tuition at time of enrollment locked for 4 years; tuition/fee waivers available for minority students.

FINANCIAL AID PICTURE (2011-2012)

Students with need: Out of 796 full-time freshmen who applied for aid, 688 were judged to have need. Of these, 688 received aid, and 55 had their full need met. Average financial aid package met 56% of need; average scholarship/grant was $7,124; average loan was $3,522. For part-time students, average financial aid package was $6,294.
Students without need: 45 full-time freshmen who did not demonstrate need for aid received scholarships/grants; average award was $1,865. No-need awards available for academics, alumni affiliation, art, athletics, leadership, music/drama.
Scholarships offered: 11 full-time freshmen received athletic scholarships; average amount $4,037.

FINANCIAL AID PROCEDURES

Forms required: FAFSA.
Dates and Deadlines: Priority date 2/1; no closing date. Applicants notified on a rolling basis starting 2/28; must reply within 3 week(s) of notification.

CONTACT

Donna Fossum, Director of Financial Aid
345 North Monmouth Avenue, Monmouth, OR 97361
(503) 838-8475

Willamette University

Salem, Oregon
www.willamette.edu Federal Code: 003227

4-year private university and liberal arts college in small city, affiliated with United Methodist Church.
Enrollment: 1,966 undergrads, 1% part-time. 525 full-time freshmen.
Selectivity: Admits over 75% of applicants.

BASIC COSTS (2013-2014)

Tuition and fees: $42,305.
Room and board: $10,380.

FINANCIAL AID PICTURE (2012-2013)

Students with need: Out of 454 full-time freshmen who applied for aid, 366 were judged to have need. Of these, 366 received aid, and 160 had their full need met. Average financial aid package met 86% of need; average scholarship/grant was $23,699; average loan was $4,152. For part-time students, average financial aid package was $14,797.
Students without need: 155 full-time freshmen who did not demonstrate need for aid received scholarships/grants; average award was $16,032. No-need awards available for academics, alumni affiliation, leadership, minority status, music/drama, religious affiliation.
Scholarships offered: Academic merit awards; $5,000-$15,000; based on superior academic achievement and promise. Music, forensics, theater scholarships; average $3,000-$5,000; based on talent. Mark O. Hatfield Scholarship; full tuition; based on excellent academic record and demonstrated commitment to service leadership.
Cumulative student debt: 61% of graduating class had student loans; average debt was $26,740.

FINANCIAL AID PROCEDURES

Forms required: FAFSA. CSS PROFILE recommended of early action applicants.
Dates and Deadlines: Priority date 2/1; no closing date. Applicants notified on a rolling basis starting 4/1; must reply by 5/1 or within 2 week(s) of notification.
Transfers: Applicants notified on a rolling basis starting 4/1; must reply by 5/1 or within 2 week(s) of notification.

CONTACT

Patricia Hoban, Director of Financial Aid
900 State Street, Salem, OR 97301-3922
(503) 370-6273

Pennsylvania

Albright College

Reading, Pennsylvania
www.albright.edu
Federal Code: 003229
CSS Code: 2004

4-year private liberal arts college in small city, affiliated with United Methodist Church.
Enrollment: 2,172 undergrads. 410 full-time freshmen.
Selectivity: Admits less than 50% of applicants.

BASIC COSTS (2012-2013)

Tuition and fees: $35,320.
Per-credit charge: $1,079.
Room and board: $9,570.
Additional info: Tuition/fee waivers available for minority students.

FINANCIAL AID PICTURE (2012-2013)

Students with need: Need-based aid available for full-time and part-time students.
Students without need: No-need awards available for academics, alumni affiliation, art, leadership, minority status, music/drama, religious affiliation.

FINANCIAL AID PROCEDURES

Forms required: FAFSA, CSS PROFILE, state aid form.
Dates and Deadlines: Priority date 3/1; no closing date. Applicants notified on a rolling basis starting 2/15; must reply by 5/1 or within 2 week(s) of notification.
Transfers: Priority date 6/1; no deadline. Applicants notified on a rolling basis starting 2/15; must reply within 2 week(s) of notification.

CONTACT

Chris Hanlon, Director of Financial Aid
13th and Bern Streets, Reading, PA 19612-5234
(800) 252-1856

Allegheny College

Meadville, Pennsylvania
www.allegheny.edu
Federal Code: 003230

4-year private liberal arts college in large town, affiliated with United Methodist Church.
Enrollment: 2,112 undergrads, 1% part-time. 584 full-time freshmen.
Selectivity: Admits 50 to 75% of applicants.

BASIC COSTS (2013-2014)

Tuition and fees: $39,100.
Per-credit charge: $1,613.
Room and board: $9,920.

FINANCIAL AID PICTURE (2012-2013)

Students with need: Out of 514 full-time freshmen who applied for aid, 439 were judged to have need. Of these, 439 received aid, and 126 had their full need met. Average financial aid package met 89% of need; average scholarship/grant was $24,732; average loan was $4,450. For part-time students, average financial aid package was $14,225.
Students without need: 140 full-time freshmen who did not demonstrate need for aid received scholarships/grants; average award was $16,411. No-need awards available for academics, leadership, minority status, state/district residency.
Scholarships offered: Trustee Scholarships; up to $20,000 per year.
Additional info: Non need-based financial aid also determined by extracurricular and co-curricular involvement. Daytime work-study programs available.

FINANCIAL AID PROCEDURES

Forms required: FAFSA.
Dates and Deadlines: Priority date 2/15; no closing date. Applicants notified on a rolling basis starting 3/1; must reply by 5/1 or within 4 week(s) of notification.
Transfers: Priority date 6/1; no deadline. Applicants notified on a rolling basis; must reply within 3 week(s) of notification. Trustee Scholarships; up to $17,500; available for entering transfer students.

CONTACT

Jonathan Boleratz, Director of Financial Aid
Box 5, 520 North Main Street, Meadville, PA 16335
(800) 835-7780

Alvernia University

Reading, Pennsylvania
www.alvernia.edu
Federal Code: 003233

4-year private university and liberal arts college in small city, affiliated with Roman Catholic Church.
Enrollment: 2,123 undergrads, 20% part-time. 411 full-time freshmen.
Selectivity: Admits over 75% of applicants.

BASIC COSTS (2012-2013)

Tuition and fees: $27,950.
Per-credit charge: $750.
Room and board: $10,010.
Additional info: Tuition/fee waivers available for minority students.

FINANCIAL AID PICTURE

Students with need: Need-based aid available for full-time and part-time students. Work study available nights.
Students without need: No-need awards available for academics, ROTC.
Scholarships offered: Presidential Scholarship: $14,000; minimum 1130 SAT (or 25 ACT) and minimum 3.5 GPA. Trustee's Scholarship: $12,000; minimum 1050 SAT (or 23 ACT) and minimum 3.2 GPA. Veronica Founder's Scholarship: $10,000; minimum 980 SAT (or 21 ACT) and 3.0 GPA.

FINANCIAL AID PROCEDURES

Forms required: FAFSA, state aid form.
Dates and Deadlines: Priority date 5/1; no closing date. Applicants notified on a rolling basis starting 2/20; must reply within 2 week(s) of notification.
Transfers: Priority date 5/8; no deadline. Applicants notified on a rolling basis starting 2/20; must reply within 2 week(s) of notification.

CONTACT

Christine Saadi, Associate Director of Financial Aid
400 St. Bernardine Street, Reading, PA 19607-1799
(610) 796-8356

Antonelli Institute of Art and Photography

Erdenheim, Pennsylvania
www.antonelli.edu
Federal Code: 007430

2-year for-profit visual arts and junior college in large town.
Enrollment: 183 undergrads.

BASIC COSTS (2012-2013)

Tuition and fees: $20,880.

FINANCIAL AID PICTURE

Students with need: Need-based aid available for full-time and part-time students. Work study available nights.
Students without need: This college awards aid only to students with need.

FINANCIAL AID PROCEDURES

Forms required: FAFSA.

Dates and Deadlines: Applicants notified on a rolling basis; must reply within 2 week(s) of notification.

Transfers: Priority date 3/15; closing date 8/1. Applicants notified on a rolling basis.

CONTACT

Eugene Awot, Director of Financial Aid
300 Montgomery Avenue, Erdenheim, PA 19038-8242
(215) 836-2222

Arcadia University

Glenside, Pennsylvania
www.arcadia.edu Federal Code: 003235

4-year private university in large town, affiliated with Presbyterian Church (USA).

Enrollment: 2,288 undergrads, 6% part-time. 678 full-time freshmen.

Selectivity: Admits 50 to 75% of applicants.

BASIC COSTS (2012-2013)

Tuition and fees: $35,620.

Per-credit charge: $580.

Room and board: $12,150.

FINANCIAL AID PICTURE

Students with need: Need-based aid available for full-time and part-time students. Work study available nights, weekends, and for part-time students.

Students without need: No-need awards available for academics, alumni affiliation, art, leadership, music/drama.

Scholarships offered: Distinguished Scholarships: $15,000-$20,500; for full-time students based on grades, test scores, coursework taken, high school rank and involvement. Arcadia University Achievement Awards: $1,000-$14,500; for full-time students who have demonstrated outstanding leadership, exceptional community and/or volunteer service or special talents. President's Scholarship: full tuition; based on academic excellence, outstanding leadership, and community and volunteer service. Writing Achievement Awards: offered to those who score among the highest in the applicant pool annually on SAT or ACT writing sections.

Additional info: Automatic $1,000 renewable FAFSA Early Filer Grant for new incoming full-time undergraduates who file FAFSA by March 1, listing Arcadia as a recipient school on the form, and have a completed admissions application on file by March 1.

FINANCIAL AID PROCEDURES

Forms required: FAFSA, institutional form.

Dates and Deadlines: Priority date 3/1; no closing date. Applicants notified on a rolling basis starting 2/1; must reply by 5/1.

Transfers: No deadline. Applicants notified on a rolling basis starting 2/1.

CONTACT

Holly Kirkpatrick, Director of Enrollment Management and Director of Financial Aid
450 South Easton Road, Glenside, PA 19038-3295
(215) 572-2980

Art Institute of Pittsburgh

Pittsburgh, Pennsylvania
www.artinstitutes.edu/pittsburgh Federal Code: 007470

4-year for-profit culinary school and visual arts college in large city.

Enrollment: 1,904 undergrads.

BASIC COSTS (2012-2013)

Tuition and fees: $23,476.

Additional info: Board plan not available. Cost of room only, $7,410.

FINANCIAL AID PICTURE

Students with need: Need-based aid available for full-time and part-time students.

FINANCIAL AID PROCEDURES

Forms required: FAFSA, institutional form.

Dates and Deadlines: Applicants notified on a rolling basis starting 4/15.

CONTACT

Lara Hemwall, Director Student Financial Services
420 Boulevard of the Allies, Pittsburgh, PA 15219-1328
(412) 291-6200

Art Institute of York

York, Pennsylvania
www.artinstitutes.edu/york Federal Code: 017171

2-year for-profit visual arts and technical college in large town.

Enrollment: 581 undergrads.

BASIC COSTS (2012-2013)

Tuition and fees: $23,092.

FINANCIAL AID PICTURE

Students with need: Work study available nights.

Students without need: This college awards aid only to students with need.

FINANCIAL AID PROCEDURES

Forms required: FAFSA.

Dates and Deadlines: Priority date 8/1; no closing date. Applicants notified on a rolling basis starting 6/1.

CONTACT

Kirstin Zabierowsky, Director of Student Financial Services
1409 Williams Road, York, PA 17402
(717) 757-1202

Baptist Bible College of Pennsylvania

Clarks Summit, Pennsylvania
www.bbc.edu Federal Code: 002670

4-year private Bible and teachers college in small city, affiliated with Baptist faith.

Enrollment: 604 undergrads.

Selectivity: Admits less than 50% of applicants.

BASIC COSTS (2012-2013)

Tuition and fees: $19,030.

Per-credit charge: $634.

Room and board: $6,950.

FINANCIAL AID PICTURE

Students with need: Need-based aid available for full-time and part-time students. Work study available nights, weekends, and for part-time students.

Students without need: No-need awards available for academics, leadership, music/drama, religious affiliation.

FINANCIAL AID PROCEDURES

Forms required: FAFSA, institutional form.

Dates and Deadlines: Closing date 5/1. Applicants notified on a rolling basis starting 4/1.

CONTACT

Steve Brown, Director of Student Financial Services
538 Venard Road, Clarks Summit, PA 18411-1297
(570) 585-9215

Bloomsburg University of Pennsylvania

Bloomsburg, Pennsylvania
www.bloomu.edu Federal Code: 003315

4-year public university in large town.
Enrollment: 9,044 undergrads, 5% part-time. 1,910 full-time freshmen.
Selectivity: Admits 50 to 75% of applicants.

BASIC COSTS (2012-2013)
Tuition and fees: $8,343; out-of-state residents $17,985.
Room and board: $7,498.
Additional info: Tuition/fee waivers available for minority students.

FINANCIAL AID PICTURE
Students with need: Need-based aid available for full-time and part-time students. Work study available nights, weekends, and for part-time students.
Students without need: No-need awards available for academics, art, athletics, job skills, leadership, minority status, music/drama, ROTC, state/district residency.

FINANCIAL AID PROCEDURES
Forms required: FAFSA.
Dates and Deadlines: Priority date 3/15; no closing date. Applicants notified on a rolling basis starting 4/1.
Transfers: Evaluation of transfer credits must be completed before financial aid can be finalized.

CONTACT
John Bieryla, Director of Financial Aid
104 Student Service Center, Bloomsburg, PA 17815
(570) 389-4297

Bradford School: Pittsburgh

Pittsburgh, Pennsylvania
www.bradfordpittsburgh.edu Federal Code: 009721

2-year for-profit junior college in very large city.
Enrollment: 441 undergrads.

FINANCIAL AID PICTURE
Students with need: Need-based aid available for full-time students.

FINANCIAL AID PROCEDURES
Forms required: FAFSA.

CONTACT
Director of Financial Aid
125 West Station Square Drive, Pittsburgh, PA 15219
(412) 391-6710

Bryn Athyn College

Bryn Athyn, Pennsylvania
www.brynathyn.edu Federal Code: 003228

4-year private liberal arts college in small town, affiliated with Christian, General Church of the New Jerusalem.
Enrollment: 239 undergrads, 2% part-time. 54 full-time freshmen.
Selectivity: Admits less than 50% of applicants.

BASIC COSTS (2013-2014)
Tuition and fees: $17,722.
Per-credit charge: $635.
Room and board: $10,260.

FINANCIAL AID PICTURE (2012-2013)
Students with need: Out of 44 full-time freshmen who applied for aid, 40 were judged to have need. Of these, 40 received aid. Average financial aid package met 84% of need; average scholarship/grant was $10,374; average loan was $2,993. For part-time students, average financial aid package was $8,275.
Students without need: 16 full-time freshmen who did not demonstrate need for aid received scholarships/grants; average award was $5,104. No-need awards available for academics, religious affiliation.
Cumulative student debt: 45% of graduating class had student loans; average debt was $8,100.

FINANCIAL AID PROCEDURES
Forms required: FAFSA, state aid form.
Dates and Deadlines: Priority date 2/15; closing date 6/1. Applicants notified on a rolling basis starting 3/1; must reply within 3 week(s) of notification.
Transfers: No deadline. Applicants notified on a rolling basis starting 7/1; must reply within 6 week(s) of notification.

CONTACT
Eiben Carole, Financial Aid Director
PO Box 462, Bryn Athyn, PA 19009-0462
(267) 502-2493

Bryn Mawr College

Bryn Mawr, Pennsylvania Federal Code: 003237
www.brynmawr.edu CSS Code: 2049

4-year private liberal arts college for women in very large city.
Enrollment: 1,309 undergrads. 365 full-time freshmen.
Selectivity: Admits less than 50% of applicants.

BASIC COSTS (2013-2014)
Tuition and fees: $43,900.
Room and board: $13,860.

FINANCIAL AID PICTURE (2012-2013)
Students with need: Out of 235 full-time freshmen who applied for aid, 186 were judged to have need. Of these, 186 received aid, and 186 had their full need met. Average financial aid package met 100% of need; average scholarship/grant was $35,239; average loan was $4,828. For part-time students, average financial aid package was $46,083.
Students without need: This college awards aid only to students with need.
Cumulative student debt: 52% of graduating class had student loans; average debt was $23,579.

FINANCIAL AID PROCEDURES
Forms required: FAFSA, CSS PROFILE.
Dates and Deadlines: Priority date 2/5; closing date 3/1. Applicants notified by 3/23; must reply by 5/1.
Transfers: Closing date 3/15. Must reply by 5/1.

CONTACT
Ethel Desmarais, Director of Financial Aid
101 North Merion Avenue, Bryn Mawr, PA 19010-2899
(610) 526-5245

Bucknell University

Lewisburg, Pennsylvania Federal Code: 003238
www.bucknell.edu CSS Code: 2050

4-year private university in small town.
Enrollment: 3,502 undergrads. 918 full-time freshmen.
Selectivity: Admits less than 50% of applicants.

BASIC COSTS (2013-2014)
Tuition and fees: $46,902.
Room and board: $11,258.

FINANCIAL AID PICTURE (2012-2013)

Students with need: Out of 481 full-time freshmen who applied for aid, 402 were judged to have need. Of these, 402 received aid, and 382 had their full need met. Average financial aid package met 95% of need; average scholarship/grant was $24,649; average loan was $3,456.

Students without need: 53 full-time freshmen who did not demonstrate need for aid received scholarships/grants; average award was $14,855. No-need awards available for academics, art, athletics, leadership, music/drama, ROTC.

Scholarships offered: ***Merit:*** Scholarships available to a limited number of students who have demonstrated exceptional achievements in academics, art and performing arts, music, and athletics. ***Athletic:*** 24 full-time freshmen received athletic scholarships; average amount $9,259.

Cumulative student debt: 55% of graduating class had student loans; average debt was $21,163.

FINANCIAL AID PROCEDURES

Forms required: FAFSA, CSS PROFILE.

Dates and Deadlines: Closing date 1/15. Applicants notified by 4/1; must reply by 5/1.

Transfers: Closing date 3/15. Applicants notified by 5/1; must reply by 6/1. Aid restricted to 2-year college graduates.

CONTACT

Andrea Stauffer, Director of Financial Aid
Office of Admissions, Bucknell University, Lewisburg, PA 17837-9988
(570) 577-1331

Bucks County Community College

Newtown, Pennsylvania
www.bucks.edu Federal Code: 003239

2-year public community college in large town.
Enrollment: 10,069 undergrads, 60% part-time. 1,608 full-time freshmen.
Selectivity: Open admission; but selective for some programs.

BASIC COSTS (2013-2014)

Tuition and fees: $4,634; out-of-district residents $8,144; out-of-state residents $11,654.

Per-credit charge: $117; out-of-district residents $234; out-of-state residents $351.

Additional info: $1,124 required fees are for in-county students. Out-of-county students pay additional $300 capital fee; out-of-state students pay additional $600 capital fee.

FINANCIAL AID PICTURE (2011-2012)

Students with need: 70% of average financial aid package awarded as scholarships/grants, 30% awarded as loans/jobs. Need-based aid available for part-time students. Work study available nights, weekends, and for part-time students.

Students without need: No-need awards available for academics, art, music/drama.

Additional info: Files are processed in order of receipt and completion date.

FINANCIAL AID PROCEDURES

Forms required: FAFSA.

Dates and Deadlines: Closing date 5/1. Applicants notified on a rolling basis starting 6/1; must reply within 2 week(s) of notification.

Transfers: Applicants notified on a rolling basis starting 6/1; must reply within 2 week(s) of notification.

CONTACT

Donna Wilkoski, Director of Financial Aid
275 Swamp Road, Newtown, PA 18940
(215) 968-8200

Butler County Community College

Butler, Pennsylvania
www.bc3.edu Federal Code: 003240

2-year public community college in small city.
Enrollment: 3,813 undergrads.
Selectivity: Open admission; but selective for some programs.

BASIC COSTS (2012-2013)

Tuition and fees: $3,684; out-of-district residents $6,060; out-of-state residents $8,700.

Per-credit charge: $88; out-of-district residents $176; out-of-state residents $264.

FINANCIAL AID PICTURE

Students with need: Need-based aid available for full-time and part-time students.

Students without need: No-need awards available for academics, state/district residency.

FINANCIAL AID PROCEDURES

Forms required: FAFSA.

Dates and Deadlines: Priority date 4/15; no closing date. Applicants notified on a rolling basis starting 5/1; must reply within 2 week(s) of notification.

CONTACT

Julianne Louttit, Director of Financial Aid
PO Box 1203, Butler, PA 16003-1203
(724) 287-8711 ext. 8329

Cabrini College

Radnor, Pennsylvania
www.cabrini.edu Federal Code: 003241

4-year private liberal arts college in large town, affiliated with Roman Catholic Church.
Enrollment: 1,380 undergrads, 6% part-time. 384 full-time freshmen.
Selectivity: Admits 50 to 75% of applicants.

BASIC COSTS (2012-2013)

Tuition and fees: $29,000.
Room and board: $11,859.

FINANCIAL AID PICTURE

Students with need: Need-based aid available for full-time and part-time students. Work study available nights, weekends, and for part-time students.

Students without need: No-need awards available for academics, religious affiliation, state/district residency.

FINANCIAL AID PROCEDURES

Forms required: FAFSA.

Dates and Deadlines: Closing date 4/1. Applicants notified on a rolling basis starting 2/15.

Transfers: Achievement scholarships available.

CONTACT

Michelle Taylor, Director of Financial Aid
610 King of Prussia Road, Radnor, PA 19087-3698
(610) 902-8420

Cairn University

Langhorne, Pennsylvania
www.cairn.edu Federal Code: 003351

4-year private university and Bible college in small town, affiliated with Protestant Evangelical tradition.

Enrollment: 947 undergrads, 7% part-time. 172 full-time freshmen.
Selectivity: Admits 50 to 75% of applicants.

BASIC COSTS (2013-2014)
Tuition and fees: $22,455.
Room and board: $8,800.

FINANCIAL AID PICTURE (2012-2013)
Students with need: Out of 160 full-time freshmen who applied for aid, 144 were judged to have need. Of these, 144 received aid, and 25 had their full need met. Average financial aid package met 75% of need; average scholarship/grant was $13,969; average loan was $4,128. For part-time students, average financial aid package was $6,321.
Students without need: 26 full-time freshmen who did not demonstrate need for aid received scholarships/grants; average award was $8,933. No-need awards available for academics, leadership, music/drama.
Scholarships offered: Cairn U Merit Scholarship based on high school GPA, 668 awards.
Cumulative student debt: 82% of graduating class had student loans; average debt was $30,633.

FINANCIAL AID PROCEDURES
Forms required: FAFSA.
Dates and Deadlines: Priority date 3/1; no closing date. Applicants notified on a rolling basis starting 2/15; must reply within 2 week(s) of notification.
Transfers: No deadline. Applicants notified on a rolling basis.

CONTACT
Stephen Cassel, Director of Financial Aid
200 Manor Avenue, Langhorne, PA 19047-2990
(215) 702-4246

California University of Pennsylvania
California, Pennsylvania
www.calu.edu Federal Code: 003316

4-year public university in small town.
Enrollment: 6,625 undergrads, 12% part-time. 952 full-time freshmen.
Selectivity: Admits less than 50% of applicants.

BASIC COSTS (2012-2013)
Tuition and fees: $9,379; out-of-state residents $13,237.
Room and board: $10,170.
Additional info: Tuition/fee waivers available for adults, minority students.

FINANCIAL AID PICTURE (2012-2013)
Students with need: Average financial aid package met 56% of need; average scholarship/grant was $5,881; average loan was $3,206. For part-time students, average financial aid package was $7,732.
Students without need: No-need awards available for academics, athletics, leadership, minority status, music/drama, state/district residency.
Cumulative student debt: 77% of graduating class had student loans; average debt was $55,984.

FINANCIAL AID PROCEDURES
Forms required: FAFSA.
Dates and Deadlines: Priority date 3/1; no closing date. Applicants notified on a rolling basis starting 4/1; must reply within 2 week(s) of notification.

CONTACT
Jill Fernandes, Director of Financial Aid
250 University Avenue, California, PA 15419-1394
(724) 938-4415

Cambria-Rowe Business College
Johnstown, Pennsylvania
www.crbc.net

2-year for-profit business and career college in small city.
Enrollment: 133 undergrads.
Selectivity: Open admission.

BASIC COSTS (2012-2013)
Tuition and fees: $12,630.
Per-credit charge: $239.

FINANCIAL AID PICTURE
Students with need: Need-based aid available for full-time and part-time students.
Students without need: No-need awards available for academics, leadership.
Scholarships offered: Presidential Grant (3 awarded) 50% tuition; FBLA Scholarship (2 awarded) $3,000.

FINANCIAL AID PROCEDURES
Forms required: FAFSA, state aid form.
Dates and Deadlines: Applicants notified on a rolling basis.
Transfers: Closing date 5/1.

CONTACT
Linda Wess, Director of Financial Aid
221 Central Avenue, Johnstown, PA 15902

Cambria-Rowe Business College: Indiana
Indiana, Pennsylvania
www.crbc.net Federal Code: 004889

2-year for-profit business and career college in small town.
Enrollment: 91 undergrads.

BASIC COSTS (2012-2013)
Tuition and fees: $12,630.
Per-credit charge: $239.

FINANCIAL AID PICTURE
Students with need: Need-based aid available for full-time and part-time students.
Students without need: No-need awards available for academics, leadership.

FINANCIAL AID PROCEDURES
Forms required: FAFSA, state aid form.
Dates and Deadlines: Applicants notified on a rolling basis.
Transfers: Closing date 5/1.

CONTACT
Linda Wess, Director of Enrollment Services
422 South 13th Street, Indiana, PA 15701
(814) 536-5168

Career Training Academy
New Kensington, Pennsylvania
www.careerta.edu Federal Code: 026095

2-year for-profit career college in small town.
Enrollment: 56 undergrads.
Selectivity: Open admission; but selective for some programs.

BASIC COSTS (2012-2013)
Additional info: Tuition and fees for entire programs (diploma or associate degree) range from $8,400 to $21,790; programs vary from 8 to 18 months

in duration. Additional expenses include books, fees, insurance and supplies, which range from $1,707 to $4,625, depending upon program of study.

FINANCIAL AID PICTURE

Students with need: Need-based aid available for full-time students.

Students without need: This college awards aid only to students with need.

Additional info: Work study available after class day.

FINANCIAL AID PROCEDURES

Forms required: FAFSA, institutional form.

CONTACT

Amber Tate, Director of Financial Aid
950 Fifth Avenue, New Kensington, PA 15068

Career Training Academy: Monroeville

Monroeville, Pennsylvania
www.careerta.edu Federal Code: 026095

2-year for-profit branch campus college in small city.
Enrollment: 28 undergrads.
Selectivity: Open admission; but selective for some programs.

BASIC COSTS (2012-2013)

Additional info: Tuition and fees for entire programs (diploma or associate degree) range from $8,400 to $21,790; programs vary from 8 to 18 months in duration. Additional expenses include books, fees, insurance and supplies, which range from $1,707 to $4,625, depending upon program of study.

FINANCIAL AID PICTURE

Students with need: Need-based aid available for full-time and part-time students.

Students without need: This college awards aid only to students with need.

FINANCIAL AID PROCEDURES

Forms required: FAFSA, state aid form, institutional form.

CONTACT

Amber Tate, Director of Financial Aid
4314 Old William Penn Highway #103, Monroeville, PA 15146
(724) 337-1000

Carlow University

Pittsburgh, Pennsylvania
www.carlow.edu Federal Code: 003303

4-year private university and liberal arts college in large city, affiliated with Roman Catholic Church.
Enrollment: 1,373 undergrads, 25% part-time. 210 full-time freshmen.
Selectivity: Admits 50 to 75% of applicants.

BASIC COSTS (2013-2014)

Tuition and fees: $25,416.
Per-credit charge: $801.
Room and board: $10,014.
Additional info: Undergraduate adult students pay $608 per-credit-hour.

FINANCIAL AID PICTURE

Students with need: Need-based aid available for full-time and part-time students. Work study available nights, weekends, and for part-time students.

Scholarships offered: Full tuition scholarship: 3.75 GPA, 1300 SAT required. Half tuition scholarship: 3.5 GPA, 1200 SAT required. Presidential scholarship: $5,000 to $10,000; 3.25 GPA, 1000 SAT required. Valedictorian scholarship: $10,000. McAuley scholarship: $2,500; 3.25 GPA, 930 SAT required; one per Catholic high school in diocese of Pittsburgh, Johnston/Altoona and Greensburg. Legacy scholarship: $2,500; to children or grandchildren of alumnae. Dean's Recognition scholarship: $4,000; 3.00 GPA and 930 SAT required. Sister Maurice Whalen scholarship: to those who submit projects to Pittsburgh Regional Science and Engineering Fair, also requires 3.25 GPA and 1000 SAT. Rose Marie Beard Women of Spirit Honors Scholarship: $4,000 for first year; 3.5 GPA, 1100 SAT, rank in top 15% of high school class, evidence of significant leadership required. All SAT scores exclusive of Writing.

FINANCIAL AID PROCEDURES

Forms required: FAFSA.

Dates and Deadlines: Priority date 4/1; no closing date. Applicants notified on a rolling basis starting 2/15; must reply within 4 week(s) of notification.

Transfers: No deadline. Applicants notified on a rolling basis; must reply within 4 week(s) of notification.

CONTACT

Natalie Wilson, Director of Financial Aid
3333 Fifth Avenue, Pittsburgh, PA 15213-3165
(412) 578-6058

Carnegie Mellon University

Pittsburgh, Pennsylvania Federal Code: 003242
www.cmu.edu CSS Code: 2074

4-year private university in large city.
Enrollment: 6,203 undergrads, 2% part-time. 1,408 full-time freshmen.
Selectivity: Admits less than 50% of applicants.

BASIC COSTS (2013-2014)

Tuition and fees: $47,642.
Per-credit charge: $648.
Room and board: $11,990.

FINANCIAL AID PICTURE (2012-2013)

Students with need: Out of 984 full-time freshmen who applied for aid, 747 were judged to have need. Of these, 741 received aid, and 194 had their full need met. Average financial aid package met 83% of need; average scholarship/grant was $26,048; average loan was $4,842. For part-time students, average financial aid package was $13,859.

Students without need: 107 full-time freshmen who did not demonstrate need for aid received scholarships/grants; average award was $7,295. No-need awards available for academics, art, leadership, minority status, music/drama, state/district residency.

Cumulative student debt: 45% of graduating class had student loans; average debt was $31,747.

Additional info: Early need analysis offered; merit awards available. Students notified within week to 10 days of receipt of financial aid application.

FINANCIAL AID PROCEDURES

Forms required: FAFSA, CSS PROFILE, institutional form.

Dates and Deadlines: Priority date 2/15; closing date 5/1. Applicants notified by 3/15.

Transfers: Students applying for spring transfer must file FAFSA by 11/1 and are notified of award 12/15 or soon after. College of Fine Arts applicants applying for fall transfer must file FAFSA by 2/15 and are notified of award by 4/15. All other applicants for fall transfer must submit FAFSA by 5/1 and are notified of award during the month of June.

CONTACT

Mark Kamlet, Provost
5000 Forbes Avenue, Pittsburgh, PA 15213-3890
(412) 268-8186

Cedar Crest College
Allentown, Pennsylvania
www.cedarcrest.edu Federal Code: 003243

4-year private liberal arts college for women in small city.
Enrollment: 1,310 undergrads, 47% part-time. 145 full-time freshmen.
Selectivity: Admits 50 to 75% of applicants.

BASIC COSTS (2012-2013)
Tuition and fees: $31,596.
Room and board: $9,990.

FINANCIAL AID PICTURE (2012-2013)
Students with need: Out of 141 full-time freshmen who applied for aid, 134 were judged to have need. Of these, 134 received aid, and 13 had their full need met. Average financial aid package met 79% of need; average scholarship/grant was $23,477; average loan was $3,497. For part-time students, average financial aid package was $7,216.
Students without need: 11 full-time freshmen who did not demonstrate need for aid received scholarships/grants; average award was $13,545. No-need awards available for academics, alumni affiliation, art, leadership, music/drama.
Scholarships offered: Presidential Scholarship; up to half tuition; for freshmen with SAT scores over 1150 and in top 10% of class; renewable for four years with GPA of 3.0. 1867 Award; one-third of tuition; renewable for four years with GPA of 3.0; for freshmen with SAT of 1100 and in top 25% of class. Girl Scout Gold Awards; $1,000 per year; for recipients of the Girl Scout Gold Award. Art, Dance, and Performing Arts Scholarships; $1,500 per year; based on portfolio review, audition, and commitment to the creative process. Governor's School of Excellence Award; $1,000 per year; for graduates of Governor's Schools of Excellence. Hugh O'Brian Youth (HOBY) Awards; $1,000 per year; for freshmen who are HOBY alumnae. SAT scores exclusive of Writing portion.
Cumulative student debt: 92% of graduating class had student loans; average debt was $31,933.

FINANCIAL AID PROCEDURES
Forms required: FAFSA.
Dates and Deadlines: Priority date 5/1; no closing date. Applicants notified on a rolling basis starting 1/1; must reply within 2 week(s) of notification.
Transfers: Must reply by 5/15. Certain academic scholarships are available for transfers only, such as the Phi Theta Kappa Scholarship, Lifelong Learning Transfer Scholarship and Traditional Transfer Scholarship.

CONTACT
Valerie Kreiser, Director of Student Financial Services
100 College Drive, Allentown, PA 18104-6196
(610) 606-4653

Central Penn College
Summerdale, Pennsylvania
www.centralpenn.edu Federal Code: 004890

4-year for-profit technical and career college in rural community.
Enrollment: 1,462 undergrads, 50% part-time. 97 full-time freshmen.
Selectivity: Admits less than 50% of applicants.

BASIC COSTS (2012-2013)
Tuition and fees: $19,440.
Per-credit charge: $415.
Room and board: $6,835.

FINANCIAL AID PICTURE (2011-2012)
Students with need: Need-based aid available for full-time and part-time students.
Students without need: No-need awards available for academics, alumni affiliation, job skills, leadership, minority status, state/district residency.

FINANCIAL AID PROCEDURES
Forms required: FAFSA, state aid form, institutional form.
Dates and Deadlines: Priority date 3/15; no closing date. Applicants notified on a rolling basis starting 2/1; must reply within 2 week(s) of notification.

CONTACT
Kathy Shepard, Financial Aid Director
College Hill and Valley Roads, Summerdale, PA 17093-0309
(717) 728-2261

Chatham University
Pittsburgh, Pennsylvania
www.chatham.edu Federal Code: 003244

4-year private university and liberal arts college for women in large city.
Enrollment: 677 undergrads, 12% part-time. 117 full-time freshmen.
Selectivity: Admits 50 to 75% of applicants.

BASIC COSTS (2013-2014)
Tuition and fees: $32,454.
Per-credit charge: $759.
Room and board: $9,986.
Additional info: Required fees ($1,160) cover technology fee, which includes cost of a MacBook Pro (required for all first-time first-year students) and the campus fee.

FINANCIAL AID PICTURE (2012-2013)
Students with need: Average financial aid package met 71% of need; average scholarship/grant was $10,043; average loan was $3,794. For part-time students, average financial aid package was $3,358.
Students without need: No-need awards available for academics, alumni affiliation, art, leadership, music/drama.
Scholarships offered: Presidential Scholarship; up to $12,000. Trustee Scholarship; up to $9,000. Founders' Scholarship; up to $7,000. All based on academic excellence and renewable annually based on GPA of 2.8 or higher.
Cumulative student debt: 76% of graduating class had student loans; average debt was $40,297.

FINANCIAL AID PROCEDURES
Forms required: FAFSA.
Dates and Deadlines: Priority date 3/1; no closing date. Applicants notified on a rolling basis starting 3/1; must reply by 5/1 or within 4 week(s) of notification.
Transfers: Special scholarships are available for transfer students.

CONTACT
Jennifer Burns, Director of Financial Aid
Woodland Road, Pittsburgh, PA 15232
(412) 365-2781

Chestnut Hill College
Philadelphia, Pennsylvania
www.chc.edu Federal Code: 003245

4-year private liberal arts college in very large city, affiliated with Roman Catholic Church.
Enrollment: 1,556 undergrads, 20% part-time. 210 full-time freshmen.
Selectivity: Admits over 75% of applicants.

BASIC COSTS (2013-2014)
Tuition and fees: $31,170.
Per-credit charge: $665.
Room and board: $9,008.

FINANCIAL AID PICTURE (2012-2013)
Students with need: Out of 201 full-time freshmen who applied for aid, 188 were judged to have need. Of these, 184 received aid, and 19 had their

full need met. Average financial aid package met 64% of need; average scholarship/grant was $16,788; average loan was $3,343. For part-time students, average financial aid package was $6,634.

Students without need: 12 full-time freshmen who did not demonstrate need for aid received scholarships/grants; average award was $11,125. No-need awards available for academics, athletics.

Scholarships offered: ***Merit:*** Full-tuition and partial-tuition awards; based on academics. ***Athletic:*** 32 full-time freshmen received athletic scholarships; average amount $7,578.

FINANCIAL AID PROCEDURES

Forms required: FAFSA.

Dates and Deadlines: Priority date 4/1; no closing date. Applicants notified on a rolling basis starting 2/15.

Transfers: Priority date 4/15; no deadline. Applicants notified on a rolling basis starting 2/15.

CONTACT

Kristina Wilhelm-Nelson, Director of Financial Aid
9601 Germantown Avenue, Philadelphia, PA 19118-2693
(215) 248-7182

Cheyney University of Pennsylvania

Cheyney, Pennsylvania
www.cheyney.edu Federal Code: 003317

4-year public university in small town.
Enrollment: 1,210 undergrads, 5% part-time. 315 full-time freshmen.
Selectivity: Admits over 75% of applicants.

BASIC COSTS (2012-2013)

Tuition and fees: $8,602; out-of-state residents $12,782.
Room and board: $8,901.
Additional info: Tuition/fee waivers available for minority students.

FINANCIAL AID PICTURE

Students with need: Need-based aid available for full-time and part-time students.

Students without need: No-need awards available for academics, athletics.

FINANCIAL AID PROCEDURES

Forms required: FAFSA.

Dates and Deadlines: Priority date 3/15; no closing date. Applicants notified on a rolling basis starting 4/1; must reply within 2 week(s) of notification.

CONTACT

Michelle Burwell, Director of Financial Aid
1837 University Circle, Cheyney, PA 19319-0019
(610) 399-2302

Clarion University of Pennsylvania

Clarion, Pennsylvania
www.clarion.edu Federal Code: 003318

4-year public business and teachers college in small town.
Enrollment: 5,335 undergrads, 14% part-time. 1,199 full-time freshmen.
Selectivity: Admits over 75% of applicants.

BASIC COSTS (2012-2013)

Tuition and fees: $9,090; out-of-state residents $12,304.
Room and board: $7,186.

FINANCIAL AID PICTURE (2011-2012)

Students with need: Out of 1,145 full-time freshmen who applied for aid, 983 were judged to have need. Of these, 960 received aid, and 36 had their full need met. Average financial aid package met 53% of need; average scholarship/grant was $5,712; average loan was $3,195. For part-time students, average financial aid package was $4,585.

Students without need: 52 full-time freshmen who did not demonstrate need for aid received scholarships/grants; average award was $1,701. No-need awards available for academics, alumni affiliation, art, athletics, job skills, leadership, minority status, music/drama, state/district residency.

Scholarships offered: 17 full-time freshmen received athletic scholarships; average amount $2,980.

Cumulative student debt: 81% of graduating class had student loans; average debt was $29,410.

FINANCIAL AID PROCEDURES

Forms required: FAFSA, state aid form.

Dates and Deadlines: Priority date 5/1; no closing date. Applicants notified on a rolling basis starting 3/30.

CONTACT

Kenneth Grugel, Director of Financial Aid
840 Wood Street, Clarion, PA 16214
(814) 226-2315

Community College of Allegheny County

Pittsburgh, Pennsylvania
www.ccac.edu

2-year public community college in very large city.
Enrollment: 17,945 undergrads, 61% part-time. 2,395 full-time freshmen.
Selectivity: Open admission; but selective for some programs.

BASIC COSTS (2012-2013)

Tuition and fees: $3,312; out-of-district residents $6,176; out-of-state residents $9,042.

Per-credit charge: $96; out-of-district residents $191; out-of-state residents $287.

FINANCIAL AID PICTURE

Students with need: Need-based aid available for full-time and part-time students. Work study available nights, weekends, and for part-time students.

Students without need: No-need awards available for academics, minority status.

FINANCIAL AID PROCEDURES

Forms required: FAFSA.

Dates and Deadlines: Priority date 5/1; no closing date. Applicants notified on a rolling basis starting 5/1.

CONTACT

Margaret Barton, Director of Financial Aid
808 Ridge Avenue, Pittsburgh, PA 15212
(412) 323-2323

Community College of Beaver County

Monaca, Pennsylvania
www.ccbc.edu Federal Code: 006807

2-year public community college in small town.
Enrollment: 2,576 undergrads.
Selectivity: Open admission; but selective for some programs.

BASIC COSTS (2013-2014)

Tuition and fees: $4,380; out-of-district residents $8,430; out-of-state residents $12,480.

Per-credit charge: $115; out-of-district residents $230; out-of-state residents $345.

FINANCIAL AID PICTURE

Students with need: Need-based aid available for full-time and part-time students. Work study available nights, weekends, and for part-time students.

Students without need: No-need awards available for academics, athletics, state/district residency.
Scholarships offered: Academic Excellence Scholarship; full tuition.

FINANCIAL AID PROCEDURES

Forms required: FAFSA, state aid form, institutional form.
Dates and Deadlines: Priority date 5/1; closing date 7/1. Applicants notified on a rolling basis starting 8/5; must reply within 2 week(s) of notification.
Transfers: Priority date 5/6.

CONTACT

Janet Davidson, Director of Financial Aid
One Campus Drive, Monaca, PA 15061-2588
(724) 480-3501

Community College of Philadelphia

Philadelphia, Pennsylvania
www.ccp.edu Federal Code: 003249

2-year public community college in very large city.
Enrollment: 18,090 undergrads, 72% part-time. 1,126 full-time freshmen.
Selectivity: Open admission; but selective for some programs.

BASIC COSTS (2012-2013)

Tuition and fees: $5,400; out-of-district residents $9,840; out-of-state residents $14,280.
Per-credit charge: $148; out-of-district residents $296; out-of-state residents $444.
Additional info: Tuition/fee waivers available for unemployed or children of unemployed.

FINANCIAL AID PICTURE (2011-2012)

Students with need: Out of 930 full-time freshmen who applied for aid, 892 were judged to have need. Of these, 886 received aid, and 7 had their full need met. Average financial aid package met 23% of need; average scholarship/grant was $2,220. For part-time students, average financial aid package was $2,207.
Students without need: This college awards aid only to students with need.

FINANCIAL AID PROCEDURES

Forms required: FAFSA, institutional form.
Dates and Deadlines: Closing date 5/1. Applicants notified on a rolling basis.
Transfers: No deadline.

CONTACT

Gim Lim, Director of Financial Aid
1700 Spring Garden Street, Philadelphia, PA 19130-3991
(215) 751-8270

Consolidated School of Business: Lancaster

Lancaster, Pennsylvania
www.csb.edu Federal Code: 030299

2-year for-profit career college in small city.
Enrollment: 135 undergrads.
Selectivity: Open admission.

BASIC COSTS (2013-2014)

Tuition and fees: $14,150.
Additional info: Fees include laptop computer. Tuition at time of enrollment locked for 2 years; tuition/fee waivers available for unemployed or children of unemployed.

FINANCIAL AID PICTURE

Students with need: Need-based aid available for full-time and part-time students.
Students without need: No-need awards available for academics, leadership.

FINANCIAL AID PROCEDURES

Forms required: FAFSA, state aid form.
Dates and Deadlines: Applicants notified on a rolling basis.

CONTACT

Gail Dougherty, Director of Financial Aid
2124 Ambassador Circle, Lancaster, PA 17603
(717) 394-6211

Consolidated School of Business: York

York, Pennsylvania
www.csb.edu Federal Code: 022896

2-year for-profit career college in small city.
Enrollment: 143 undergrads.
Selectivity: Open admission.

BASIC COSTS (2013-2014)

Tuition and fees: $14,150.
Additional info: Fees include laptop computer. Tuition at time of enrollment locked for 2 years; tuition/fee waivers available for unemployed or children of unemployed.

FINANCIAL AID PICTURE

Students with need: Need-based aid available for full-time and part-time students.
Students without need: No-need awards available for academics.

FINANCIAL AID PROCEDURES

Forms required: FAFSA, state aid form.
Dates and Deadlines: Applicants notified on a rolling basis.

CONTACT

Gail Dougherty, Director of Financial Aid
York City Business and Industry Park, York, PA 17404
(717) 764-9550

Curtis Institute of Music

Philadelphia, Pennsylvania
www.curtis.edu Federal Code: 003251

4-year private music college in very large city.
Enrollment: 125 undergrads. 13 full-time freshmen.
Selectivity: Admits less than 50% of applicants.

BASIC COSTS (2013-2014)

Room and board: $14,000.
Additional info: Bachelor of Music students pay $2,350 in required fees. Students who do not have comprehensive health insurance are required to purchase insurance through Curtis; the approximate cost is $2,500 for 12 months of coverage.

FINANCIAL AID PICTURE (2012-2013)

Students with need: Out of 13 full-time freshmen who applied for aid, 7 were judged to have need. Of these, 7 received aid, and 1 had their full need met. Average financial aid package met 75% of need; average scholarship/grant was $9,633; average loan was $3,500. Need-based aid available for part-time students.
Students without need: This college awards aid only to students with need.

Cumulative student debt: 60% of graduating class had student loans; average debt was $17,167.

Additional info: All admitted students receive a full tuition scholarship. The estimated value of this scholarship is $36,500.

FINANCIAL AID PROCEDURES

Forms required: FAFSA, institutional form.

Dates and Deadlines: Priority date 3/1; no closing date. Applicants notified on a rolling basis starting 4/1; must reply by 5/1 or within 2 week(s) of notification.

Transfers: Must reply by 5/1 or within 2 week(s) of notification.

CONTACT

Veronica McAuley, Associate Director
1726 Locust Street, Philadelphia, PA 19103-6187
(215) 717-3188

Delaware County Community College

Media, Pennsylvania
www.dccc.edu

2-year public community college in large town.
Enrollment: 13,051 undergrads.
Selectivity: Open admission; but selective for some programs.

BASIC COSTS (2012-2013)

Tuition and fees: $4,660; out-of-district residents $7,870; out-of-state residents $11,080.

Per-credit charge: $104; out-of-district residents $208; out-of-state residents $312.

FINANCIAL AID PICTURE

Students with need: Need-based aid available for full-time and part-time students. Work study available nights, weekends, and for part-time students.

Students without need: No-need awards available for academics, job skills.

Additional info: DCCC provides federal, college-funded and international work study.

FINANCIAL AID PROCEDURES

Forms required: FAFSA, state aid form.

Dates and Deadlines: Closing date 7/1. Applicants notified on a rolling basis.

Transfers: No deadline. Applicants notified on a rolling basis.

CONTACT

Ray Toole, Director of Financial Aid
901 South Media Line Road, Media, PA 19063
(610) 359-5330

Delaware Valley College

Doylestown, Pennsylvania
www.delval.edu Federal Code: 003252

4-year private agricultural and liberal arts college in large town.
Enrollment: 1,894 undergrads, 9% part-time. 465 full-time freshmen.
Selectivity: Admits 50 to 75% of applicants.

BASIC COSTS (2012-2013)

Tuition and fees: $31,746.
Per-credit charge: $818.
Room and board: $11,262.
Additional info: Tuition/fee waivers available for adults.

FINANCIAL AID PICTURE

Students with need: Need-based aid available for full-time and part-time students. Work study available nights, weekends, and for part-time students.

Students without need: No-need awards available for academics, alumni affiliation, music/drama, state/district residency.

FINANCIAL AID PROCEDURES

Forms required: FAFSA, state aid form.

Dates and Deadlines: Priority date 4/15; no closing date. Applicants notified on a rolling basis starting 2/15; must reply by 5/1 or within 2 week(s) of notification.

Transfers: No deadline. Applicants notified on a rolling basis; must reply by 4/1.

CONTACT

Joan Hock, Director of Financial Aid
700 East Butler Avenue, Doylestown, PA 18901-2697
(215) 489-2272

DeSales University

Center Valley, Pennsylvania
www.desales.edu Federal Code: 003986

4-year private university in small town, affiliated with Roman Catholic Church.
Enrollment: 2,468 undergrads, 28% part-time. 389 full-time freshmen.
Selectivity: Admits 50 to 75% of applicants.

BASIC COSTS (2013-2014)

Tuition and fees: $31,250.
Per-credit charge: $1,250.
Room and board: $11,420.

FINANCIAL AID PICTURE (2012-2013)

Students with need: Out of 369 full-time freshmen who applied for aid, 325 were judged to have need. Of these, 325 received aid, and 65 had their full need met. Average financial aid package met 72% of need; average scholarship/grant was $18,552; average loan was $3,377. For part-time students, average financial aid package was $6,895.

Students without need: 61 full-time freshmen who did not demonstrate need for aid received scholarships/grants; average award was $10,436. No-need awards available for academics, alumni affiliation, art, leadership, music/drama, religious affiliation, ROTC.

Scholarships offered: Presidential Scholarships; $18,000 to full tuition; top 5% of class and 1300 SAT. Trustee Scholarships; $6,000 to $10,000; top 15% of class, minimum 1200 SAT. DeSales Scholarships; $4,000; top 25% of class, minimum 1100 SAT. SAT scores exclusive of Writing.

Cumulative student debt: 79% of graduating class had student loans; average debt was $28,875.

FINANCIAL AID PROCEDURES

Forms required: FAFSA, state aid form.

Dates and Deadlines: Priority date 2/1; closing date 5/1. Applicants notified on a rolling basis starting 2/15; must reply by 5/1 or within 2 week(s) of notification.

Transfers: No deadline. Applicants notified on a rolling basis. Merit scholarships automatically awarded for transfer students with a qualifying GPA. Award amounts are based on factors such as GPA, courses completed, and credits accumulated. Three levels of transfer scholarships: $3,500, $5,000, and $8,000 per year.

CONTACT

Joyce Farmer, Director of Financial Aid
2755 Station Avenue, Center Valley, PA 18034-9568
(610) 282-1100 ext. 1287

DeVry University: Fort Washington

Fort Washington, Pennsylvania
www.devry.edu

4-year for-profit university in large town.
Enrollment: 657 undergrads, 61% part-time. 37 full-time freshmen.

BASIC COSTS (2012-2013)

Tuition and fees: $16,156.
Per-credit charge: $609.

FINANCIAL AID PICTURE

Students with need: Need-based aid available for full-time and part-time students.
Students without need: This college awards aid only to students with need.

FINANCIAL AID PROCEDURES

Forms required: FAFSA.
Dates and Deadlines: Applicants notified on a rolling basis.

CONTACT

Citristal Claiborne, Director of Financial Aid
1140 Virginia Drive, Fort Washington, PA 19034-3204
(215) 591-5724

Dickinson College

Carlisle, Pennsylvania
www.dickinson.edu
Federal Code: 003253
CSS Code: 2186

4-year private liberal arts college in large town.
Enrollment: 2,340 undergrads, 1% part-time. 601 full-time freshmen.
Selectivity: Admits less than 50% of applicants.

BASIC COSTS (2012-2013)

Tuition and fees: $44,576.
Per-credit charge: $1,379.
Room and board: $11,178.

FINANCIAL AID PICTURE (2012-2013)

Students with need: Out of 417 full-time freshmen who applied for aid, 342 were judged to have need. Of these, 335 received aid, and 283 had their full need met. Average financial aid package met 99% of need; average scholarship/grant was $29,030; average loan was $4,634. For part-time students, average financial aid package was $30,940.
Students without need: 78 full-time freshmen who did not demonstrate need for aid received scholarships/grants; average award was $10,770. No-need awards available for academics, leadership, ROTC.
Scholarships offered: John Dickinson and Benjamin Rush Scholarships; awarded to most academically competitive students. Additional Engage the World Fellowship for selected John Dickinson Scholarship winners. John Montgomery Scholarship; awarded to first-year students who possess strong credentials, talent in the arts, or competency in 2 foreign languages in addition to English. Scholars must also demonstrate strong leadership in high school and community.
Cumulative student debt: 53% of graduating class had student loans; average debt was $25,574.

FINANCIAL AID PROCEDURES

Forms required: FAFSA, CSS PROFILE, state aid form.
Dates and Deadlines: Priority date 11/15; closing date 2/1. Applicants notified by 3/20; must reply by 5/1 or within 2 week(s) of notification.
Transfers: Closing date 4/1. Applicants notified by 5/1; must reply within 2 week(s) of notification.

CONTACT

Richard Heckman, Director of Financial Aid
PO Box 1773, Carlisle, PA 17013-2896
(717) 245-1308

Douglas Education Center

Monessen, Pennsylvania
www.dec.edu
Federal Code: 013957

2-year for-profit visual arts and business college in small town.
Enrollment: 250 undergrads.
Selectivity: Open admission.

FINANCIAL AID PICTURE

Students with need: Need-based aid available for full-time and part-time students.
Students without need: This college awards aid only to students with need.

FINANCIAL AID PROCEDURES

Forms required: FAFSA.
Dates and Deadlines: Applicants notified on a rolling basis.

CONTACT

Amanda Phillips, Director of Financial Aid
130 Seventh Street, Monessen, PA 15062
(724) 684-3684

Drexel University

Philadelphia, Pennsylvania
www.drexel.edu
Federal Code: 003256
CSS Code: 2194

5-year private university in very large city.
Enrollment: 15,593 undergrads, 16% part-time. 3,027 full-time freshmen.
Selectivity: Admits 50 to 75% of applicants.

BASIC COSTS (2012-2013)

Tuition and fees: $36,090.
Per-credit charge: $930.
Room and board: $14,175.

FINANCIAL AID PICTURE

Students with need: Need-based aid available for full-time students.
Students without need: No-need awards available for academics, alumni affiliation, art, athletics, leadership, music/drama, ROTC.

FINANCIAL AID PROCEDURES

Forms required: FAFSA. College of Engineering does not accept PROFILE from domestic applicants and they will accept International PROFILE or an institutional alternative for international students.
Dates and Deadlines: Closing date 2/15. Applicants notified on a rolling basis starting 2/15.
Transfers: Priority date 3/2. Scholarships available in amounts up to $8,000. 3.2 GPA and 30 credit hours at time of application required for eligibility.

CONTACT

Helen Gourousis, Director of Financial Aid
3141 Chestnut Street, Philadelphia, PA 19104-2876
(215) 895-2537

DuBois Business College

DuBois, Pennsylvania
www.dbcollege.edu
Federal Code: 004893

2-year for-profit business and technical college in large town.
Enrollment: 132 undergrads.
Selectivity: Open admission.

BASIC COSTS (2012-2013)

Additional info: Tuition for associate degree programs $20,100 to $23,450; individual programs vary from 9 to 21 months in duration. Tuition for diploma programs $10,050 to $13,400 and vary from 9 to 12 months in duration. Additional expenses include lab fees, which vary by program and range from $600 to $1,400. Cost of books and supplies range from $2,250 to $6,784.

FINANCIAL AID PICTURE

Students with need: Need-based aid available for full-time students.

FINANCIAL AID PROCEDURES

Forms required: FAFSA.

Dates and Deadlines: Closing date 8/1. Applicants notified on a rolling basis.

CONTACT

Karen Alderton, Financial Aid Director
One Beaver Drive, DuBois, PA 15801
(814) 371-6920

Duquesne University

Pittsburgh, Pennsylvania
www.duq.edu Federal Code: 003258

4-year private university in large city, affiliated with Roman Catholic Church.
Enrollment: 5,805 undergrads, 3% part-time. 1,331 full-time freshmen.
Selectivity: Admits 50 to 75% of applicants.

BASIC COSTS (2013-2014)

Tuition and fees: $31,385.
Per-credit charge: $943.
Room and board: $10,632.

FINANCIAL AID PICTURE (2011-2012)

Students with need: Out of 1,193 full-time freshmen who applied for aid, 989 were judged to have need. Of these, 989 received aid, and 224 had their full need met. Average financial aid package met 89% of need; average scholarship/grant was $16,383; average loan was $3,726. For part-time students, average financial aid package was $10,449.

Students without need: 323 full-time freshmen who did not demonstrate need for aid received scholarships/grants; average award was $10,216. No-need awards available for academics, alumni affiliation, athletics, music/drama, ROTC.

Scholarships offered: ***Merit:*** Competitive scholarships available for academically and/or artistically talented students. ***Athletic:*** 87 full-time freshmen received athletic scholarships; average amount $16,202.

Cumulative student debt: 80% of graduating class had student loans; average debt was $25,228.

FINANCIAL AID PROCEDURES

Forms required: FAFSA, institutional form.

Dates and Deadlines: Closing date 5/1. Applicants notified on a rolling basis starting 3/1; must reply by 5/1 or within 3 week(s) of notification.

Transfers: No deadline. Must reply within 3 week(s) of notification.

CONTACT

Richard Esposito, Director of Financial Aid
600 Forbes Avenue, Administration Building, Pittsburgh, PA 15282-0201
(412) 396-6607

East Stroudsburg University of Pennsylvania

East Stroudsburg, Pennsylvania
www4.esu.edu Federal Code: 003320

4-year public university in large town.
Enrollment: 6,289 undergrads, 9% part-time. 1,229 full-time freshmen.
Selectivity: Admits over 75% of applicants.

BASIC COSTS (2012-2013)

Tuition and fees: $8,758; out-of-state residents $18,400.
Per-credit charge: $268; out-of-state residents $670.
Room and board: $9,176.
Additional info: Tuition for incoming out-of-state residents who are high achieving science and technology majors (biology, chemistry, computer science, mathematics, and physics) is $9,642.

FINANCIAL AID PICTURE

Students with need: Need-based aid available for full-time and part-time students.

Students without need: No-need awards available for academics, alumni affiliation, art, athletics, leadership, minority status, music/drama, religious affiliation, state/district residency.

FINANCIAL AID PROCEDURES

Forms required: FAFSA.

Dates and Deadlines: Closing date 4/9. Must reply by 5/1.

Transfers: Applicants notified by 4/1; must reply by 5/1.

CONTACT

Phyllis Swinson, Associate Director of Financial Aid
200 Prospect Street, East Stroudsburg, PA 18301-2999
(570) 422-2800

Edinboro University of Pennsylvania

Edinboro, Pennsylvania
www.edinboro.edu Federal Code: 003321

4-year public university in small town.
Enrollment: 5,992 undergrads, 7% part-time. 1,482 full-time freshmen.
Selectivity: Admits over 75% of applicants.

BASIC COSTS (2012-2013)

Tuition and fees: $8,578; out-of-state residents $11,792.
Room and board: $8,168.

FINANCIAL AID PICTURE (2011-2012)

Students with need: Out of 1,402 full-time freshmen who applied for aid, 1,256 were judged to have need. Of these, 1,225 received aid, and 40 had their full need met. Average financial aid package met 47% of need; average scholarship/grant was $4,261; average loan was $3,063. For part-time students, average financial aid package was $5,209.

Students without need: 22 full-time freshmen who did not demonstrate need for aid received scholarships/grants; average award was $3,193. No-need awards available for academics, alumni affiliation, art, athletics, job skills, leadership, minority status, music/drama, religious affiliation, ROTC, state/district residency.

Scholarships offered: 55 full-time freshmen received athletic scholarships; average amount $4,401.

FINANCIAL AID PROCEDURES

Forms required: FAFSA.

Dates and Deadlines: Priority date 3/15; closing date 5/1. Applicants notified on a rolling basis starting 3/22; must reply within 2 week(s) of notification.

CONTACT

Dorothy Body, Assistant Vice President for Student Financial Support and Services
200 East Normal Street, Edinboro, PA 16444
(888) 611-2680

Elizabethtown College

Elizabethtown, Pennsylvania
www.etown.edu Federal Code: 003262

4-year private liberal arts college in large town.
Enrollment: 1,858 undergrads. 505 full-time freshmen.

Selectivity: Admits 50 to 75% of applicants.

BASIC COSTS (2013-2014)
Tuition and fees: $38,200.
Room and board: $9,400.

FINANCIAL AID PICTURE (2012-2013)
Students with need: Out of 441 full-time freshmen who applied for aid, 401 were judged to have need. Of these, 401 received aid, and 76 had their full need met. Average financial aid package met 81% of need; average scholarship/grant was $22,240; average loan was $3,533. Need-based aid available for part-time students.
Students without need: 89 full-time freshmen who did not demonstrate need for aid received scholarships/grants; average award was $18,537. No-need awards available for academics, art, music/drama, religious affiliation.
Scholarships offered: Presidential Scholarship; up to $22,000 annually; top percentages of class and minimum 1300 SAT score. Provost Scholarship; up to $19,000 annually; top 10% of class with minimum 1150 SAT; unlimited number awarded. Dean's Scholarship; up to $16,000 annually; for students with very strong academic achievement who do not qualify for other merit awards; unlimited number awarded. Music scholarships; $1,000-$4,000; based on audition. SAT scores exclusive of Writing portion. Stamps Scholarship; full tuition, $4,000 enrichment fund and personal mentor.
Cumulative student debt: 71% of graduating class had student loans; average debt was $27,587.

FINANCIAL AID PROCEDURES
Forms required: FAFSA, institutional form.
Dates and Deadlines: Priority date 3/15; no closing date. Applicants notified on a rolling basis starting 3/1; must reply by 5/1 or within 2 week(s) of notification.
Transfers: No deadline. Applicants notified on a rolling basis; must reply within 2 week(s) of notification.

CONTACT
Elizabeth McCloud, Director of Financial Aid
One Alpha Drive, Elizabethtown, PA 17022-2298
(717) 361-1404

Erie Business Center
Erie, Pennsylvania
www.eriebc.edu Federal Code: 004894

2-year for-profit business college in small city.
Enrollment: 218 undergrads.

FINANCIAL AID PICTURE
Students with need: Need-based aid available for full-time and part-time students.

FINANCIAL AID PROCEDURES
Forms required: FAFSA.
Transfers: Applicants notified on a rolling basis.

CONTACT
Jeff Lasky, Financial Aid Administrator
246 West Ninth Street, Erie, PA 16501
(814) 456-7504 ext. 115

Franklin & Marshall College
Lancaster, Pennsylvania Federal Code: 003265
www.fandm.edu CSS Code: 2261

4-year private liberal arts college in small city.
Enrollment: 2,314 undergrads, 1% part-time. 599 full-time freshmen.
Selectivity: Admits less than 50% of applicants.

BASIC COSTS (2013-2014)
Tuition and fees: $46,285.
Room and board: $12,010.

FINANCIAL AID PICTURE (2012-2013)
Students with need: 84% of average financial aid package awarded as scholarships/grants, 16% awarded as loans/jobs.
Students without need: No-need awards available for leadership, music/drama.
Cumulative student debt: 49% of graduating class had student loans; average debt was $33,200.

FINANCIAL AID PROCEDURES
Forms required: FAFSA, CSS PROFILE, state aid form.
Dates and Deadlines: Closing date 2/15. Applicants notified by 4/1; must reply by 5/1.
Transfers: Closing date 2/1.

CONTACT
Clarke Paine, Director of Student Aid
PO Box 3003, Lancaster, PA 17604-3003
(717) 291-3991

Gannon University
Erie, Pennsylvania
www.gannon.edu Federal Code: 003266

4-year private university in small city, affiliated with Roman Catholic Church.
Enrollment: 2,674 undergrads, 6% part-time. 618 full-time freshmen.
Selectivity: Admits over 75% of applicants.

BASIC COSTS (2013-2014)
Tuition and fees: $27,546.
Room and board: $10,940.
Additional info: Tuition/fee waivers available for adults, unemployed or children of unemployed.

FINANCIAL AID PICTURE (2012-2013)
Students with need: Out of 611 full-time freshmen who applied for aid, 519 were judged to have need. Of these, 519 received aid, and 90 had their full need met. Average financial aid package met 73% of need; average scholarship/grant was $18,390; average loan was $3,572. For part-time students, average financial aid package was $7,331.
Students without need: 83 full-time freshmen who did not demonstrate need for aid received scholarships/grants; average award was $12,543. No-need awards available for academics, athletics, leadership, music/drama, religious affiliation, ROTC.
Scholarships offered: ***Merit:*** Academic Awards; $1,000 to full tuition; based on high school rank, GPA, and test scores. Leadership Awards; $1,000-$1,500; based on leadership and activities. Diocesan Scholarship; $1,000 Parish Grant; for students that belong to a parish within the Diocese of Erie. Diocesan High School Grant; $1,500; for students who attended a Catholic high school within the Diocese of Erie. Catholic High School Grant; $1,000; for any student who attended a Catholic high school outside of the Diocese of Erie. Athletic scholarships; $1,000 to full tuition, room and board. ***Athletic:*** 17 full-time freshmen received athletic scholarships; average amount $9,466.

FINANCIAL AID PROCEDURES
Forms required: FAFSA.
Dates and Deadlines: Priority date 3/15; no closing date. Applicants notified on a rolling basis starting 11/1.
Transfers: No deadline. Applicants notified on a rolling basis starting 11/1; must reply by 5/1 or within 4 week(s) of notification.

CONTACT
Sharon Krahe, Director of Financial Aid
109 University Square, Erie, PA 16541-0001
(814) 871-7337

Geneva College

Beaver Falls, Pennsylvania
www.geneva.edu Federal Code: 003267

4-year private liberal arts college in large town, affiliated with Reformed Presbyterian Church of North America.
Enrollment: 1,329 undergrads, 2% part-time. 391 full-time freshmen.
Selectivity: Admits 50 to 75% of applicants.

BASIC COSTS (2012-2013)

Tuition and fees: $24,480.
Per-credit charge: $820.
Room and board: $8,980.
Additional info: Tuition/fee waivers available for minority students, unemployed or children of unemployed.

FINANCIAL AID PICTURE (2011-2012)

Students with need: Out of 381 full-time freshmen who applied for aid, 341 were judged to have need. Of these, 337 received aid, and 62 had their full need met. Average financial aid package met 67% of need; average scholarship/grant was $13,880; average loan was $3,317. For part-time students, average financial aid package was $6,766.
Students without need: 34 full-time freshmen who did not demonstrate need for aid received scholarships/grants; average award was $9,518. No-need awards available for academics, alumni affiliation, music/drama, religious affiliation.
Scholarships offered: Academic scholarships, scholarships for National Merit finalists and semifinalists, grants for members of controlling church and other denominations identified by the college.
Cumulative student debt: 83% of graduating class had student loans; average debt was $26,990.

FINANCIAL AID PROCEDURES

Forms required: FAFSA.
Dates and Deadlines: Priority date 3/15; no closing date. Applicants notified on a rolling basis starting 3/1; must reply by 5/1 or within 4 week(s) of notification.
Transfers: Applicants notified on a rolling basis starting 3/1; must reply within 4 week(s) of notification.

CONTACT

Steven Bell, Director of Financial Aid
3200 College Avenue, Beaver Falls, PA 15010
(724) 847-6530

Gettysburg College

Gettysburg, Pennsylvania Federal Code: 003268
www.gettysburg.edu CSS Code: 2275

4-year private liberal arts college in large town, affiliated with Evangelical Lutheran Church in America.
Enrollment: 2,585 undergrads. 769 full-time freshmen.
Selectivity: Admits less than 50% of applicants.

BASIC COSTS (2013-2014)

Tuition and fees: $45,870.
Room and board: $10,950.

FINANCIAL AID PICTURE (2012-2013)

Students with need: Out of 541 full-time freshmen who applied for aid, 438 were judged to have need. Of these, 426 received aid, and 390 had their full need met. Average financial aid package met 94% of need; average scholarship/grant was $29,881; average loan was $4,238.
Students without need: 99 full-time freshmen who did not demonstrate need for aid received scholarships/grants; average award was $13,222. No-need awards available for academics, religious affiliation.
Scholarships offered: Lincoln, Presidential, Dean's, and Founders Scholarships; based on high school GPA, class rank and standardized test scores; number awarded varies. Wagnild Scholarship and Sunderman Scholarships for music talent; audition required.
Cumulative student debt: 58% of graduating class had student loans; average debt was $25,530.

FINANCIAL AID PROCEDURES

Forms required: FAFSA, CSS PROFILE.
Dates and Deadlines: Closing date 2/15. Applicants notified by 3/26; must reply by 5/1.
Transfers: Priority date 4/15. Must reply within 2 week(s) of notification.

CONTACT

Christina Gormley, Director of Financial Aid
300 North Washington Street, Gettysburg, PA 17325-1400
(717) 337-6611

Grove City College

Grove City, Pennsylvania
www.gcc.edu Federal Code: G03269

4-year private liberal arts college in small town, affiliated with Presbyterian Church (USA).
Enrollment: 2,483 undergrads, 1% part-time. 670 full-time freshmen.
Selectivity: Admits over 75% of applicants.

BASIC COSTS (2013-2014)

Tuition and fees: $14,880.
Per-credit charge: $465.
Room and board: $8,108.

FINANCIAL AID PICTURE (2012-2013)

Students with need: Out of 419 full-time freshmen who applied for aid, 300 were judged to have need. Of these, 296 received aid, and 32 had their full need met. Average financial aid package met 51% of need; average scholarship/grant was $6,405.
Students without need: 40 full-time freshmen who did not demonstrate need for aid received scholarships/grants; average award was $2,941. No-need awards available for academics, leadership.
Scholarships offered: Trustee Scholarships; $5,000; issued to a select group of accepted students who meet academic requirements; 24 awarded. Presidential Scholarships; $500; for all valedictorians in class of 30 or more, salutatorians in class of 100 or more, and National Merit Finalists. Engineering Scholarships; $2,500; 4 awarded.
Cumulative student debt: 60% of graduating class had student loans; average debt was $28,767.
Additional info: Institutional aid applications required for institutional scholarships, loans, and student employment.

FINANCIAL AID PROCEDURES

Forms required: institutional form.
Dates and Deadlines: Closing date 4/15. Applicants notified on a rolling basis starting 3/15; must reply by 5/1.
Transfers: Closing date 8/15. Applicants notified on a rolling basis; must reply within 2 week(s) of notification. Financial aid form must be submitted with transfer enrollment application.

CONTACT

Thomas Ball, Director of Financial Aid
100 Campus Drive, Grove City, PA 16127-2104
(724) 458-3300

Gwynedd-Mercy College

Gwynedd Valley, Pennsylvania
www.gmc.edu Federal Code: 003270

4-year private nursing and liberal arts college in large town, affiliated with Roman Catholic Church.
Enrollment: 2,183 undergrads, 9% part-time. 261 full-time freshmen.
Selectivity: Admits 50 to 75% of applicants.

BASIC COSTS (2012-2013)
Tuition and fees: $29,690.
Room and board: $10,180.
Additional info: Cost reported is annual tuition for allied health and nursing programs; tuition for other programs, $27,740.

FINANCIAL AID PICTURE (2012-2013)
Students with need: Out of 238 full-time freshmen who applied for aid, 216 were judged to have need. Of these, 216 received aid, and 32 had their full need met. Average financial aid package met 70% of need; average scholarship/grant was $16,199; average loan was $3,365. For part-time students, average financial aid package was $6,515.
Students without need: 27 full-time freshmen who did not demonstrate need for aid received scholarships/grants; average award was $10,786. No-need awards available for academics, alumni affiliation, leadership, ROTC.
Scholarships offered: Presidential scholarship; $10,000; must have 1200 SAT and be in top 30% of class, essay required; 2/15 deadline. Connelly Scholarship; $6,000-$7,000; must have 1100 SAT and be in top 50% of class. Mother Mary Bernard Scholarship; $4,500-$5,000; must have 1000 SAT, be in top 50% of class, and have documented leadership experience. Yearly scholarship for Catholic school graduates; $2,000 (tuition incentive grant). All SAT scores exclusive of Writing.
Cumulative student debt: 91% of graduating class had student loans; average debt was $36,067.

FINANCIAL AID PROCEDURES
Forms required: FAFSA, institutional form.
Dates and Deadlines: Priority date 3/15; closing date 5/1. Applicants notified on a rolling basis starting 2/15; must reply by 5/1 or within 2 week(s) of notification.

CONTACT
Barbara Kaufmann, Director of Student Financial Aid
1325 Sumneytown Pike, Gwynedd Valley, PA 19437-0901
(215) 646-7300 ext. 483

Harcum College

Bryn Mawr, Pennsylvania
www.harcum.edu Federal Code: 003272

2-year private junior college in large town.
Enrollment: 1,516 undergrads.

BASIC COSTS (2013-2014)
Tuition and fees: $20,830.
Per-credit charge: $655.
Room and board: $8,780.

FINANCIAL AID PICTURE (2011-2012)
Students with need: 43% of average financial aid package awarded as scholarships/grants, 57% awarded as loans/jobs. Need-based aid available for part-time students. Work study available nights.
Students without need: No-need awards available for academics, alumni affiliation, athletics, leadership.
Scholarships offered: Scholarships available based on academic achievement.

FINANCIAL AID PROCEDURES
Forms required: FAFSA.
Dates and Deadlines: Priority date 4/15; closing date 5/1. Applicants notified on a rolling basis starting 3/1; must reply within 3 week(s) of notification.

CONTACT
Eli Moinester, Director of Financial Aid
750 Montgomery Avenue, Bryn Mawr, PA 19010-3476
(610) 526-6098

Harrisburg Area Community College

Harrisburg, Pennsylvania
www.hacc.edu Federal Code: 003273

2-year public community college in small city.
Enrollment: 13,698 undergrads, 71% part-time. 1,016 full-time freshmen.
Selectivity: Open admission; but selective for some programs.

BASIC COSTS (2012-2013)
Tuition and fees: $5,055; out-of-district residents $6,720; out-of-state residents $9,645.
Per-credit charge: $140; out-of-district residents $195; out-of-state residents $293.
Additional info: Additional fees of $150 for out-of-district students; of $300 for out-of-state.

FINANCIAL AID PICTURE (2012-2013)
Students with need: Need-based aid available for part-time students.
Students without need: No-need awards available for academics, art, leadership, music/drama, religious affiliation, state/district residency.
Additional info: Federal work study community service positions available.

FINANCIAL AID PROCEDURES
Forms required: FAFSA, institutional form.
Dates and Deadlines: Priority date 4/15; no closing date. Applicants notified on a rolling basis starting 4/15.
Transfers: PHEAA state grants require separate academic progress review by financial aid staff.

CONTACT
James Carideo, Director of Financial Aid
One HACC Drive, Cooper 206, Harrisburg, PA 17110-2999
(717) 780-2330

Harrisburg University of Science and Technology

Harrisburg, Pennsylvania
www.HarrisburgU.edu Federal Code: 039483

4-year private university in small city.
Enrollment: 272 undergrads, 5% part-time. 138 full-time freshmen.
Selectivity: Admits less than 50% of applicants.

BASIC COSTS (2013-2014)
Tuition and fees: $23,900.
Per-credit charge: $1,000.
Additional info: Cost of room only, $ 6,700.

FINANCIAL AID PICTURE (2012-2013)
Students with need: Out of 130 full-time freshmen who applied for aid, 125 were judged to have need. Of these, 125 received aid, and 10 had their full need met. Average financial aid package met 59% of need; average scholarship/grant was $14,499; average loan was $4,631. For part-time students, average financial aid package was $8,297.
Students without need: 5 full-time freshmen who did not demonstrate need for aid received scholarships/grants; average award was $15,840. No-need awards available for academics, leadership, state/district residency.

Scholarships offered: Various scholarships; $1,000-$18,000, depending on specific criteria.
Cumulative student debt: 80% of graduating class had student loans; average debt was $40,643.

FINANCIAL AID PROCEDURES
Forms required: FAFSA.
Dates and Deadlines: Applicants notified on a rolling basis; must reply within 2 week(s) of notification.
Transfers: Priority date 5/1; no deadline. Applicants notified on a rolling basis; must reply within 4 week(s) of notification.

CONTACT
Vincent Frank, Director of Financial Aid
326 Market Street, Harrisburg, PA 17101-2208
(717) 901-5115

Haverford College
Haverford, Pennsylvania
www.haverford.edu
Federal Code: 003274
CSS Code: 2289

4-year private liberal arts college in large town.
Enrollment: 1,205 undergrads. 323 full-time freshmen.
Selectivity: Admits less than 50% of applicants.

BASIC COSTS (2013-2014)
Tuition and fees: $45,636.
Room and board: $13,810.

FINANCIAL AID PICTURE (2012-2013)
Students with need: Out of 173 full-time freshmen who applied for aid, 166 were judged to have need. Of these, 166 received aid, and 166 had their full need met. Average financial aid package met 100% of need; average scholarship/grant was $39,317; average loan was $832.
Students without need: This college awards aid only to students with need.
Cumulative student debt: 33% of graduating class had student loans; average debt was $14,171.

FINANCIAL AID PROCEDURES
Forms required: FAFSA, CSS PROFILE.
Dates and Deadlines: Closing date 2/1. Applicants notified by 4/1; must reply by 5/1.
Transfers: Closing date 3/1.

CONTACT
David Hoy, Director of Financial Aid
370 Lancaster Avenue, Haverford, PA 19041-1392
(610) 896-1350

Holy Family University
Philadelphia, Pennsylvania
www.holyfamily.edu
Federal Code: 003275

4-year private university in very large city, affiliated with Roman Catholic Church.
Enrollment: 2,053 undergrads, 25% part-time. 308 full-time freshmen.
Selectivity: Admits 50 to 75% of applicants.

BASIC COSTS (2013-2014)
Tuition and fees: $27,100.
Per-credit charge: $560.
Room and board: $12,930.

FINANCIAL AID PICTURE (2012-2013)
Students with need: 55% of average financial aid package awarded as scholarships/grants, 45% awarded as loans/jobs. Need-based aid available for part-time students. Work study available nights, weekends, and for part-time students.
Students without need: No-need awards available for academics, alumni affiliation, athletics.

FINANCIAL AID PROCEDURES
Forms required: FAFSA, institutional form.
Dates and Deadlines: Closing date 2/15. Applicants notified on a rolling basis starting 3/15; must reply within 2 week(s) of notification.
Transfers: Priority date 4/1; closing date 5/1. Applicants notified on a rolling basis starting 5/1; must reply within 3 week(s) of notification.

CONTACT
Janice Hetrick, Director of Financial Aid
9801 Frankford Avenue, Philadelphia, PA 19114-2009
(215) 637-5538

Hussian School of Art
Philadelphia, Pennsylvania
www.hussianart.edu
Federal Code: 007469

2-year for-profit visual arts and technical college in very large city.
Enrollment: 98 undergrads, 100% part-time.
Selectivity: Admits over 75% of applicants.

BASIC COSTS (2012-2013)
Tuition and fees: $14,895.

FINANCIAL AID PICTURE
Students with need: Need-based aid available for full-time students.

FINANCIAL AID PROCEDURES
Forms required: FAFSA, state aid form, institutional form.
Dates and Deadlines: Applicants notified on a rolling basis starting 2/15; must reply within 3 week(s) of notification.
Transfers: Priority date 3/15; no deadline. Applicants notified on a rolling basis starting 4/1. August 1 deadline for PHEAA State Grant consideration.

CONTACT
Susan Cohen, Financial Aid Director
The Bourse, Suite 300, 111 South Independence Mall East, Philadelphia, PA 19106
(215) 574-9600 ext. 206

Immaculata University
Immaculata, Pennsylvania
www.immaculata.edu
Federal Code: 003276

4-year private university and liberal arts college in large town, affiliated with Roman Catholic Church.
Enrollment: 2,683 undergrads, 56% part-time. 243 full-time freshmen.
Selectivity: Admits over 75% of applicants.

BASIC COSTS (2013-2014)
Tuition and fees: $30,740.
Per-credit charge: $500.
Room and board: $12,260.
Additional info: Immaculata University has a fixed rate tuition plan. Students will pay the same rate for all four years of undergraduate study.

FINANCIAL AID PICTURE
Students with need: Need-based aid available for full-time and part-time students. Work study available nights, weekends, and for part-time students.
Students without need: No-need awards available for academics, alumni affiliation, art, job skills, leadership, minority status, music/drama, religious affiliation, state/district residency.

FINANCIAL AID PROCEDURES
Forms required: FAFSA.
Dates and Deadlines: Priority date 2/15; closing date 4/15. Applicants notified on a rolling basis starting 2/1; must reply within 2 week(s) of notification.
Transfers: No deadline. Applicants notified on a rolling basis starting 1/1; must reply within 2 week(s) of notification.

CONTACT
Robert Forest, Director of Financial Aid
1145 King Road, Immaculata, PA 19345
(610) 647-4400 ext. 3026

Indiana University of Pennsylvania
Indiana, Pennsylvania
www.iup.edu Federal Code: 003277

4-year public university in large town.
Enrollment: 12,690 undergrads, 5% part-time. 2,903 full-time freshmen.
Selectivity: Admits 50 to 75% of applicants.

BASIC COSTS (2012-2013)
Tuition and fees: $8,672; out-of-state residents $19,480.
Room and board: $10,466.
Additional info: Tuition for students in any of these categories: OH, VA, WV, IN and MI residents; branch campus students from any state; out-of-state students with high school GPA of at least 3.0; any transfer student with GPA of at least 3.0 is $10,928 plus required fees of $3,410.20 for a total of $14,338.20.

FINANCIAL AID PICTURE (2011-2012)
Students with need: Out of 2,683 full-time freshmen who applied for aid, 2,114 were judged to have need. Of these, 2,069 received aid, and 116 had their full need met. Average financial aid package met 60% of need; average scholarship/grant was $5,897; average loan was $3,545. For part-time students, average financial aid package was $6,715.
Students without need: 53 full-time freshmen who did not demonstrate need for aid received scholarships/grants; average award was $1,496. No-need awards available for academics, alumni affiliation, art, athletics, job skills, leadership, music/drama, ROTC, state/district residency.
Scholarships offered: 54 full-time freshmen received athletic scholarships; average amount $3,809.
Cumulative student debt: 83% of graduating class had student loans; average debt was $35,229.

FINANCIAL AID PROCEDURES
Forms required: FAFSA.
Dates and Deadlines: Priority date 4/25; no closing date. Applicants notified on a rolling basis starting 3/15.
Transfers: Must reply within 2 week(s) of notification.

CONTACT
Patricia McCarthy, Director of Financial Aid
117 John Sutton Hall, 1011 South Drive, Indiana, PA 15705-1088
(724) 357-2218

JNA Institute of Culinary Arts
Philadelphia, Pennsylvania
www.culinaryarts.edu Federal Code: 031033

2-year for-profit technical college in very large city.
Enrollment: 85 undergrads.
Selectivity: Open admission.

BASIC COSTS (2013-2014)
Tuition and fees: $11,075.
Additional info: Costs reported are for diploma program; associate degree program, $22,000.

FINANCIAL AID PICTURE
Students with need: Need-based aid available for full-time students.

FINANCIAL AID PROCEDURES
Forms required: FAFSA.

CONTACT
Joseph Digironimo, Financial Aid Director
1212 South Broad Street, Philadelphia, PA 19146
(215) 468-8800

Juniata College
Huntingdon, Pennsylvania
www.juniata.edu Federal Code: 003279

4-year private liberal arts college in small town.
Enrollment: 1,565 undergrads, 8% part-time. 413 full-time freshmen.
Selectivity: Admits 50 to 75% of applicants.

BASIC COSTS (2013-2014)
Tuition and fees: $37,170.
Room and board: $10,200.
Additional info: Tuition/fee waivers available for adults.

FINANCIAL AID PICTURE (2012-2013)
Students with need: Out of 350 full-time freshmen who applied for aid, 296 were judged to have need. Of these, 296 received aid, and 67 had their full need met. Average financial aid package met 86% of need; average scholarship/grant was $24,589; average loan was $4,093. Need-based aid available for part-time students.
Students without need: 113 full-time freshmen who did not demonstrate need for aid received scholarships/grants; average award was $16,401. No-need awards available for academics, alumni affiliation, art, minority status, music/drama.
Scholarships offered: Burkholder Scholarship; full tuition, room and board; 1 awarded. Friendship Scholarship; $2,000; awarded to international student, Ray Day Scholarship; up to $5,000; for a minority student. Eagles Abroad Scholarship; international experience plus $3,000; based on commitment to international experience in France, Germany, Mexico, Spain, or Russia.
Cumulative student debt: 72% of graduating class had student loans; average debt was $31,213.

FINANCIAL AID PROCEDURES
Forms required: FAFSA.
Dates and Deadlines: Closing date 3/1. Applicants notified on a rolling basis starting 3/1; must reply by 5/1.
Transfers: Applicants notified on a rolling basis starting 2/28; must reply by 5/1.

CONTACT
Shane Himes, Director of Student Financial Planning
1700 Moore Street, Huntingdon, PA 16652-2196
(814) 641-3142

Kaplan Career Institute: Harrisburg
Harrisburg, Pennsylvania
www.kaplancareerinstitute.com Federal Code: 004910

2-year for-profit health science and technical college in small city.
Enrollment: 439 undergrads.
Selectivity: Open admission; but selective for some programs.

BASIC COSTS (2012-2013)
Additional info: Associate degree programs: Business administration $30,965; computer networking technology $36,089; criminal justice $28,985.

Diploma programs: Medical assistant $15,365; medical billing and coding $15,315. Fees, books and supplies included.

FINANCIAL AID PICTURE

Students with need: Need-based aid available for full-time and part-time students. Work study available nights.

FINANCIAL AID PROCEDURES

Forms required: FAFSA, institutional form.

CONTACT

Sarah Brooker, Financial Aid Director
5650 Derry Street, Harrisburg, PA 17111-4112

Kaplan Career Institute: Pittsburgh

Pittsburgh, Pennsylvania
www.kaplancareerinstitute.com Federal Code: 007436

2-year for-profit business and health science college in large city.
Enrollment: 719 undergrads.

BASIC COSTS (2012-2013)

Additional info: Associate degree programs range from $31,770 to $34,904. Diploma programs range from $16,471 to $18,064. Books, fees and supplies included.

FINANCIAL AID PICTURE

Students with need: Need-based aid available for full-time and part-time students. Work study available nights.
Students without need: This college awards aid only to students with need.

FINANCIAL AID PROCEDURES

Forms required: FAFSA, state aid form, institutional form.
Dates and Deadlines: Closing date 4/30. Applicants notified on a rolling basis.

CONTACT

Chrissy Kapusniak, Director of Financial Aid
933 Penn Avenue, Pittsburgh, PA 15222
(412) 261-2647 ext. 265

Keystone College

La Plume, Pennsylvania
www.keystone.edu Federal Code: 003280

4-year private liberal arts college in rural community.
Enrollment: 1,651 undergrads, 16% part-time. 362 full-time freshmen.
Selectivity: Admits 50 to 75% of applicants.

BASIC COSTS (2013-2014)

Tuition and fees: $21,800.
Room and board: $9,800.

FINANCIAL AID PICTURE (2012-2013)

Students with need: Out of 346 full-time freshmen who applied for aid, 335 were judged to have need. Of these, 335 received aid, and 37 had their full need met. Average financial aid package met 76% of need; average scholarship/grant was $15,921; average loan was $3,258. For part-time students, average financial aid package was $1,827.
Students without need: 24 full-time freshmen who did not demonstrate need for aid received scholarships/grants; average award was $9,738. No-need awards available for academics, alumni affiliation, art.
Scholarships offered: Academic Excellence Scholarship: one-half up to full tuition; for full-time, first-time students in the top 5% of their class with SAT scores of 1100 or above (exclusive of Writing). Presidential Scholarship: up to $9,500 each year; based on class rank and SAT/ACT scores. Trustee Scholarship: up to $8,500 each year; based on class rank and SAT/ACT scores. Promise Award: up to $6,500 each year; for students demonstrating non-athletic leadership skills.
Cumulative student debt: 92% of graduating class had student loans; average debt was $8,675.

FINANCIAL AID PROCEDURES

Forms required: FAFSA, state aid form.
Dates and Deadlines: Priority date 4/1; closing date 5/1. Applicants notified on a rolling basis starting 2/1; must reply within 3 week(s) of notification.
Transfers: Must reply within 2 week(s) of notification.

CONTACT

Brian Weber, Director of Financial Assistance & Planning
One College Green, La Plume, PA 18440-1099
(570) 945-8134

Keystone Technical Institute

Harrisburg, Pennsylvania
www.kti.edu Federal Code: 022342

2-year for-profit culinary school and technical college in small city.
Enrollment: 335 undergrads.
Selectivity: Open admission.

FINANCIAL AID PICTURE

Students with need: Need-based aid available for full-time and part-time students. Work study available nights.
Students without need: This college awards aid only to students with need.
Scholarships offered: Half-tuition scholarships; 13 available to degree-seeking students.

FINANCIAL AID PROCEDURES

Forms required: FAFSA, state aid form.
Dates and Deadlines: Closing date 8/1. Applicants notified on a rolling basis.
Transfers: State grant deadline for first-time recipients August 1. Renewal application deadline May 1.

CONTACT

Tracy Stewart, Financial Aid Coordinator
2301 Academy Drive, Harrisburg, PA 17112-1012
(717) 545-4747

King's College

Wilkes-Barre, Pennsylvania
www.kings.edu Federal Code: 003282

4-year private business and liberal arts college in small city, affiliated with Roman Catholic Church.
Enrollment: 2,048 undergrads, 4% part-time. 514 full-time freshmen.
Selectivity: Admits 50 to 75% of applicants.

BASIC COSTS (2012-2013)

Tuition and fees: $29,174.
Per-credit charge: $540.
Room and board: $11,020.

FINANCIAL AID PICTURE (2012-2013)

Students with need: Average financial aid package met 71% of need; average scholarship/grant was $16,842; average loan was $3,720. For part-time students, average financial aid package was $7,234.
Students without need: No-need awards available for academics, leadership, ROTC.
Cumulative student debt: 82% of graduating class had student loans; average debt was $36,538.

Additional info: Any minority student with financial need may receive some aid in the form of a diversity scholarship.

FINANCIAL AID PROCEDURES
Forms required: FAFSA, institutional form.
Dates and Deadlines: Priority date 2/15; no closing date. Applicants notified on a rolling basis starting 3/1; must reply within 2 week(s) of notification.
Transfers: Priority date 2/1; no deadline. Applicants notified on a rolling basis; must reply by 5/1 or within 2 week(s) of notification.

CONTACT
Donna Cerza, Director of Financial Aid
133 North River Street, Wilkes-Barre, PA 18711
(570) 208-5868

Kutztown University of Pennsylvania
Kutztown, Pennsylvania
www.kutztown.edu Federal Code: 003322

4-year public university in small town.
Enrollment: 8,916 undergrads, 5% part-time. 2,030 full-time freshmen.
Selectivity: Admits 50 to 75% of applicants.

BASIC COSTS (2012-2013)
Tuition and fees: $8,596; out-of-state residents $18,238.
Room and board: $8,890.

FINANCIAL AID PICTURE (2011-2012)
Students with need: Out of 1,856 full-time freshmen who applied for aid, 1,483 were judged to have need. Of these, 1,440 received aid, and 90 had their full need met. Average financial aid package met 45% of need; average scholarship/grant was $5,453; average loan was $3,269. For part-time students, average financial aid package was $6,402.
Students without need: 13 full-time freshmen who did not demonstrate need for aid received scholarships/grants; average award was $793. No-need awards available for academics, art, athletics, leadership, minority status, music/drama.
Scholarships offered: 76 full-time freshmen received athletic scholarships; average amount $2,047.
Cumulative student debt: 81% of graduating class had student loans; average debt was $30,831.

FINANCIAL AID PROCEDURES
Forms required: FAFSA.
Dates and Deadlines: Priority date 3/1; no closing date. Applicants notified on a rolling basis starting 3/30; must reply by 5/1 or within 4 week(s) of notification.

CONTACT
Bernard McCree, Director of Financial Aid
Admissions Office, Kutztown, PA 19530-0730
(610) 683-4077

La Roche College
Pittsburgh, Pennsylvania
www.laroche.edu Federal Code: 003987

4-year private liberal arts college in large city, affiliated with Roman Catholic Church.
Enrollment: 1,323 undergrads, 17% part-time. 249 full-time freshmen.
Selectivity: Admits 50 to 75% of applicants.

BASIC COSTS (2012-2013)
Tuition and fees: $24,058.
Per-credit charge: $595.
Room and board: $9,732.

FINANCIAL AID PICTURE (2012-2013)
Students with need: Out of 207 full-time freshmen who applied for aid, 183 were judged to have need. Of these, 181 received aid, and 52 had their full need met. Average financial aid package met 92% of need; average scholarship/grant was $7,500; average loan was $3,464. For part-time students, average financial aid package was $12,084.
Students without need: 11 full-time freshmen who did not demonstrate need for aid received scholarships/grants; average award was $12,795. No-need awards available for academics.
Cumulative student debt: 78% of graduating class had student loans; average debt was $26,296.

FINANCIAL AID PROCEDURES
Forms required: FAFSA.
Dates and Deadlines: Priority date 5/1; no closing date. Applicants notified on a rolling basis starting 3/1; must reply within 2 week(s) of notification.

CONTACT
Sharon Platt, Director of Financial Aid
9000 Babcock Boulevard, Pittsburgh, PA 15237
(412) 536-1125

La Salle University
Philadelphia, Pennsylvania
www.lasalle.edu Federal Code: 003287

4-year private university and liberal arts college in very large city, affiliated with Roman Catholic Church.
Enrollment: 4,302 undergrads, 17% part-time. 954 full-time freshmen.
Selectivity: Admits 50 to 75% of applicants.

BASIC COSTS (2013-2014)
Tuition and fees: $38,200.
Room and board: $13,060.

FINANCIAL AID PICTURE (2011-2012)
Students with need: Out of 891 full-time freshmen who applied for aid, 835 were judged to have need. Of these, 835 received aid, and 111 had their full need met. Average financial aid package met 74% of need; average scholarship/grant was $21,359; average loan was $3,749. For part-time students, average financial aid package was $8,212.
Students without need: 113 full-time freshmen who did not demonstrate need for aid received scholarships/grants; average award was $15,114. No-need awards available for academics, athletics, ROTC.
Scholarships offered: ***Merit:*** Christian Brothers Scholarship; full tuition; based on academics and extracurricular leadership. Community Service Scholarship; half tuition; based on involvement in community service and academics. ***Athletic:*** 46 full-time freshmen received athletic scholarships; average amount $13,117.
Cumulative student debt: 77% of graduating class had student loans; average debt was $37,225.

FINANCIAL AID PROCEDURES
Forms required: FAFSA.
Dates and Deadlines: Priority date 2/15; no closing date. Applicants notified on a rolling basis starting 3/15; must reply by 5/1 or within 2 week(s) of notification.
Transfers: Applicants notified on a rolling basis starting 3/15; must reply by 5/1 or within 2 week(s) of notification.

CONTACT
Michael WIsniewski, Director of Student Financial Services
1900 West Olney Avenue, Philadelphia, PA 19141-1199
(215) 951-1070

Lackawanna College

Scranton, Pennsylvania
www.lackawanna.edu Federal Code: 003283

2-year private junior college in small city.
Enrollment: 1,361 undergrads, 26% part-time. 325 full-time freshmen.
Selectivity: Open admission.

BASIC COSTS (2012-2013)
Tuition and fees: $12,280.
Per-credit charge: $410.
Room and board: $7,700.

FINANCIAL AID PICTURE (2012-2013)
Students with need: Average financial aid package met 51% of need; average scholarship/grant was $7,022; average loan was $3,389. For part-time students, average financial aid package was $6,515.
Students without need: No-need awards available for academics, athletics.
Cumulative student debt: 98% of graduating class had student loans; average debt was $21,476.

FINANCIAL AID PROCEDURES
Forms required: FAFSA, state aid form, institutional form.
Dates and Deadlines: Priority date 5/1; no closing date. Applicants notified on a rolling basis starting 5/1.
Transfers: No deadline. Applicants notified on a rolling basis starting 5/1.

CONTACT
Barbara Hapeman, Director of Financial Aid
501 Vine Street, Scranton, PA 18509
(570) 961-7859

Lafayette College

Easton, Pennsylvania Federal Code: 003284
www.lafayette.edu CSS Code: 2361

4-year private engineering and liberal arts college in large town.
Enrollment: 2,454 undergrads, 1% part-time. 629 full-time freshmen.
Selectivity: Admits less than 50% of applicants.

BASIC COSTS (2013-2014)
Tuition and fees: $44,670.
Room and board: $13,080.
Additional info: Of the required fees, $700 is a one time Matriculation Fee charged only to new students: returning students pay only $390 in activity and technology fees.

FINANCIAL AID PICTURE (2012-2013)
Students with need: Out of 401 full-time freshmen who applied for aid, 262 were judged to have need. Of these, 261 received aid, and 212 had their full need met. Average financial aid package met 98% of need; average scholarship/grant was $33,213; average loan was $3,587. Need-based aid available for part-time students.
Students without need: 45 full-time freshmen who did not demonstrate need for aid received scholarships/grants; average award was $19,252. No-need awards available for academics, athletics, leadership, ROTC.
Scholarships offered: ***Merit:*** Marquis Scholarships; $20,000; based on academic merit, awarded to 10% of each entering class. ***Athletic:*** 16 full-time freshmen received athletic scholarships; average amount $38,454.
Cumulative student debt: 56% of graduating class had student loans; average debt was $26,717.
Additional info: Parent loans, up to $7,500 annually, available with college absorbing interest while student is enrolled. Family has 8 years after graduation to repay. Not limited to those demonstrating need.

FINANCIAL AID PROCEDURES
Forms required: FAFSA, CSS PROFILE.
Dates and Deadlines: Priority date 1/15; closing date 3/1. Applicants notified by 4/1; must reply by 5/1.
Transfers: Closing date 4/1. Applicants notified on a rolling basis starting 5/1; must reply within 2 week(s) of notification.

CONTACT
Arlina DeNardo, Director of Student Financial Aid
118 Markle Hall, Easton, PA 18042
(610) 330-5055

Lancaster Bible College

Lancaster, Pennsylvania
www.lbc.edu Federal Code: 003285

4-year private Bible college in small city, affiliated with nondenominational tradition.
Enrollment: 870 undergrads.

BASIC COSTS (2012-2013)
Tuition and fees: $17,740.
Per-credit charge: $575.
Room and board: $7,810.
Additional info: Students required to purchase Logos Bible Software; costs range from $325 to $510 depending on level.

FINANCIAL AID PICTURE
Students with need: Need-based aid available for full-time and part-time students. Work study available nights, weekends, and for part-time students.
Students without need: No-need awards available for academics, alumni affiliation, leadership, music/drama.

FINANCIAL AID PROCEDURES
Forms required: FAFSA, state aid form.
Dates and Deadlines: Priority date 5/1; no closing date. Applicants notified on a rolling basis starting 3/1; must reply within 3 week(s) of notification.

CONTACT
Karen Fox, Director of Financial Aid
901 Eden Road, Lancaster, PA 17601-5036
(717) 560-8254

Laurel Business Institute

Uniontown, Pennsylvania
www.laurel.edu Federal Code: 017118

2-year for-profit technical and career college in large town.
Enrollment: 185 undergrads.

FINANCIAL AID PICTURE
Students with need: Need-based aid available for full-time and part-time students.
Students without need: This college awards aid only to students with need.
Scholarships offered: One full tuition, several half tuition (including GED scholarships); based on high school transcripts or GED scores, letters of reference, and personal interview.

FINANCIAL AID PROCEDURES
Forms required: FAFSA, institutional form.
Dates and Deadlines: Applicants notified on a rolling basis; must reply within 4 week(s) of notification.
Transfers: No deadline. Must reply within 4 week(s) of notification.

CONTACT
Stephanie Migyanko, Director of Financial Aid
11 East Penn Street, Uniontown, PA 15401
(724) 439-4900

Lebanon Valley College

Annville, Pennsylvania
www.lvc.edu Federal Code: 003288

4-year private liberal arts college in small town, affiliated with United Methodist Church.
Enrollment: 1,678 undergrads, 4% part-time. 405 full-time freshmen.
Selectivity: Admits 50 to 75% of applicants.

BASIC COSTS (2012-2013)
Tuition and fees: $34,470.
Per-credit charge: $575.
Room and board: $9,180.
Additional info: Tuition/fee waivers available for minority students.

FINANCIAL AID PICTURE (2012-2013)
Students with need: Out of 381 full-time freshmen who applied for aid, 351 were judged to have need. Of these, 351 received aid, and 59 had their full need met. Average financial aid package met 75% of need; average scholarship/grant was $22,325; average loan was $3,715. For part-time students, average financial aid package was $5,223.
Students without need: 55 full-time freshmen who did not demonstrate need for aid received scholarships/grants; average award was $14,396. No-need awards available for academics, alumni affiliation, music/drama.
Scholarships offered: Vickroy Scholarship; half tuition; automatic for admitted applicants in top 10% of graduating class. Leadership scholarship; one-third tuition; automatic for admitted applicants in top 20% of graduating class. Achievement Scholarship; one-quarter tuition; automatic for admitted applicants in top 30% of graduating class.
Cumulative student debt: 84% of graduating class had student loans; average debt was $34,561.
Additional info: Students and families impacted by the struggling economy are encouraged to contact the Financial Aid Office.

FINANCIAL AID PROCEDURES
Forms required: FAFSA.
Dates and Deadlines: Priority date 3/1; no closing date. Applicants notified on a rolling basis starting 3/1; must reply by 5/1 or within 2 week(s) of notification.
Transfers: Must reply by 5/1 or within 2 week(s) of notification. Students transferring 15 or fewer credits are considered for scholarships on the same basis as high school seniors. Students transferring 16 or more credits are considered for scholarships based on their college academic performance and program.

CONTACT
Kendra Feigert, Director of Financial Aid
101 North College Avenue, Annville, PA 17003-1400
(717) 867-6181

Lehigh Carbon Community College

Schnecksville, Pennsylvania
www.lccc.edu Federal Code: 006810

2-year public community college in small town.
Enrollment: 6,193 undergrads, 56% part-time. 869 full-time freshmen.
Selectivity: Open admission; but selective for some programs.

BASIC COSTS (2013-2014)
Tuition and fees: $3,450; out-of-district residents $6,660; out-of-state residents $9,870.
Per-credit charge: $98; out-of-district residents $205; out-of-state residents $312.
Additional info: Tuition/fee waivers available for unemployed or children of unemployed.

FINANCIAL AID PICTURE (2011-2012)
Students with need: Out of 719 full-time freshmen who applied for aid, 606 were judged to have need. Of these, 606 received aid, and 606 had their full need met. Average financial aid package met 100% of need; average scholarship/grant was $4,087; average loan was $2,810. For part-time students, average financial aid package was $1,599.
Students without need: No-need awards available for academics, job skills.

FINANCIAL AID PROCEDURES
Forms required: FAFSA.
Dates and Deadlines: Priority date 5/1; no closing date. Applicants notified on a rolling basis starting 1/1; must reply within 2 week(s) of notification.
Transfers: No deadline. Applicants notified on a rolling basis.

CONTACT
Marian Snyder, Director of Financial Aid
4525 Education Park Drive, Schnecksville, PA 18078-2502
(610) 799-1133

Lehigh University

Bethlehem, Pennsylvania Federal Code: 003289
www.lehigh.edu CSS Code: 2365

4-year private university in small city.
Enrollment: 4,857 undergrads, 1% part-time. 1,217 full-time freshmen.
Selectivity: Admits less than 50% of applicants.

BASIC COSTS (2013-2014)
Tuition and fees: $43,520.
Per-credit charge: $1,805.
Room and board: $11,560.

FINANCIAL AID PICTURE (2012-2013)
Students with need: Out of 820 full-time freshmen who applied for aid, 537 were judged to have need. Of these, 537 received aid, and 260 had their full need met. Average financial aid package met 94% of need; average scholarship/grant was $31,494; average loan was $3,887. For part-time students, average financial aid package was $19,755.
Students without need: 80 full-time freshmen who did not demonstrate need for aid received scholarships/grants; average award was $11,550. No-need awards available for academics, art, athletics, leadership, music/drama, ROTC.
Scholarships offered: ***Merit:*** Dean's Scholarships; $10,000; for academic excellence and leadership skills. Baker Scholarship; $3,000; for excellence in music or theater and superior academic record. Choral Arts Scholarships; $2,500; for singing talent. Performing Arts Scholarship; $3,000; for those who display exceptional theatrical talent (including performance, design, technical, and playwriting). Snyder Family Marching 97 Scholarships; $1,000-$2,500; for those who demonstrate musical talent and leadership and who fully participate in the marching band. Athletic Awards/Scholarships. ***Athletic:*** 36 full-time freshmen received athletic scholarships; average amount $29,503.
Cumulative student debt: 54% of graduating class had student loans; average debt was $31,122.
Additional info: Loans eliminated in financial aid packages for students eligible for financial aid and whose calculated total family income is less than $50,000. Loans limited to $3,000 in financial aid packages for students eligible for financial aid and who have a calculated total family income between $50,000 and $75,000.

FINANCIAL AID PROCEDURES
Forms required: FAFSA, CSS PROFILE.
Dates and Deadlines: Closing date 2/15. Applicants notified by 3/30; must reply by 5/1 or within 3 week(s) of notification.
Transfers: Closing date 4/1. Applicants notified on a rolling basis starting 5/15; must reply within 3 week(s) of notification.

CONTACT
Jennifer Mertz, Director of Financial Aid
27 Memorial Drive West, Bethlehem, PA 18015
(610) 758-3181

Lincoln University
Lincoln University, Pennsylvania
www.lincoln.edu Federal Code: 003290

4-year public university and liberal arts college in small town.
Enrollment: 1,680 undergrads. 447 full-time freshmen.
Selectivity: Admits less than 50% of applicants.

BASIC COSTS (2012-2013)
Tuition and fees: $9,996; out-of-state residents $14,930.
Room and board: $8,536.

FINANCIAL AID PICTURE
Students with need: Need-based aid available for full-time and part-time students. Work study available nights, weekends, and for part-time students.
Students without need: No-need awards available for academics, alumni affiliation, leadership, music/drama.

FINANCIAL AID PROCEDURES
Forms required: FAFSA.
Dates and Deadlines: Closing date 5/1. Applicants notified on a rolling basis starting 4/1; must reply within 3 week(s) of notification.

CONTACT
Thelma Ross, Director of Financial Aid
1570 Baltimore Pike, Lincoln University, PA 19352-0999
(800) 561-2606

Lock Haven University of Pennsylvania
Lock Haven, Pennsylvania
www.lhup.edu Federal Code: 003323

4-year public university and liberal arts college in small town.
Enrollment: 4,877 undergrads, 6% part-time. 1,140 full-time freshmen.
Selectivity: Admits 50 to 75% of applicants.

BASIC COSTS (2012-2013)
Tuition and fees: $8,564; out-of-state residents $16,206.
Room and board: $7,816.
Additional info: Tuition/fee waivers available for minority students.

FINANCIAL AID PICTURE (2012-2013)
Students with need: Need-based aid available for full-time and part-time students.
Students without need: No-need awards available for academics, art, athletics, leadership, minority status, music/drama, ROTC, state/district residency.

FINANCIAL AID PROCEDURES
Forms required: FAFSA.
Dates and Deadlines: Closing date 3/15. Applicants notified on a rolling basis starting 4/1; must reply within 2 week(s) of notification.
Transfers: Priority date 4/1.

CONTACT
Heidi Hunter-Goldsworthy, Director of Student Financial Services
LHU Office of Admissions, Lock Haven, PA 17745
(877) 405-3057

Luzerne County Community College
Nanticoke, Pennsylvania
www.luzerne.edu Federal Code: 006811

2-year public community college in large town.
Enrollment: 6,284 undergrads, 47% part-time. 1,240 full-time freshmen.
Selectivity: Open admission; but selective for some programs.

BASIC COSTS (2012-2013)
Tuition and fees: $3,600; out-of-district residents $6,480; out-of-state residents $9,360.
Per-credit charge: $96; out-of-district residents $192; out-of-state residents $288.

FINANCIAL AID PICTURE
Students with need: Need-based aid available for full-time and part-time students.

FINANCIAL AID PROCEDURES
Forms required: FAFSA, institutional form.
Dates and Deadlines: Priority date 4/15; no closing date. Applicants notified on a rolling basis starting 7/1.

CONTACT
Mary Kosin, Director of Financial Aid
1333 South Prospect Street, Nanticoke, PA 18634-3899
(570) 740-0395

Lycoming College
Williamsport, Pennsylvania
www.lycoming.edu Federal Code: 003293

4-year private liberal arts college in small city, affiliated with United Methodist Church.
Enrollment: 1,343 undergrads. 321 full-time freshmen.
Selectivity: Admits 50 to 75% of applicants.

BASIC COSTS (2013-2014)
Tuition and fees: $33,756.
Per-credit charge: $1,033.
Room and board: $9,890.
Additional info: Tuition/fee waivers available for minority students.

FINANCIAL AID PICTURE (2012-2013)
Students with need: Out of 295 full-time freshmen who applied for aid, 264 were judged to have need. Of these, 264 received aid, and 57 had their full need met. Average financial aid package met 78% of need; average scholarship/grant was $22,426; average loan was $3,701. For part-time students, average financial aid package was $6,262.
Students without need: 56 full-time freshmen who did not demonstrate need for aid received scholarships/grants; average award was $16,263. No-need awards available for academics, art, minority status, music/drama, ROTC.
Cumulative student debt: 85% of graduating class had student loans; average debt was $35,990.

FINANCIAL AID PROCEDURES
Forms required: FAFSA, state aid form, institutional form.
Dates and Deadlines: Priority date 5/1; no closing date. Applicants notified on a rolling basis starting 3/1; must reply by 5/1.
Transfers: No deadline.

CONTACT
James Spencer, Vice President, Admissions and Financial Aid
700 College Place, Williamsport, PA 17701
(570) 321-4026

Manor College

Jenkintown, Pennsylvania
www.manor.edu Federal Code: 003294

2-year private junior college in small town, affiliated with Ukrainian Catholic Church.
Enrollment: 869 undergrads, 36% part-time. 209 full-time freshmen.
Selectivity: Admits less than 50% of applicants.

BASIC COSTS (2013-2014)
Tuition and fees: $15,250.
Per-credit charge: $365.
Room and board: $6,870.
Additional info: Tuition for Allied Health program $15,366; $449 per-credit hour. Tuition/fee waivers available for minority students, unemployed or children of unemployed.

FINANCIAL AID PICTURE (2012-2013)
Students with need: Average financial aid package met 33% of need; average scholarship/grant was $6,394; average loan was $4,691. For part-time students, average financial aid package was $7,677.
Students without need: This college awards aid only to students with need.
Scholarships offered: Basilian Scholarship; for every freshman with A or B high school average and minimum 900 SAT (exclusive of Writing).
Cumulative student debt: 97% of graduating class had student loans; average debt was $9,000.

FINANCIAL AID PROCEDURES
Forms required: FAFSA.
Dates and Deadlines: Priority date 3/15; no closing date. Applicants notified on a rolling basis starting 3/1; must reply within 2 week(s) of notification.
Transfers: No deadline. Applicants notified on a rolling basis starting 12/1; must reply within 2 week(s) of notification.

CONTACT
Chris Hartman, Director of Financial Aid
700 Fox Chase Road, Jenkintown, PA 19046-3319
(215) 884-6051

Mansfield University of Pennsylvania

Mansfield, Pennsylvania
www.mansfield.edu Federal Code: 003324

4-year public university in small town.
Enrollment: 2,743 undergrads, 7% part-time. 617 full-time freshmen.
Selectivity: Admits over 75% of applicants.

BASIC COSTS (2012-2013)
Tuition and fees: $8,926; out-of-state residents $18,568.
Room and board: $8,592.
Additional info: NJ and NY residents pay $10,608 in tuition.

FINANCIAL AID PICTURE (2011-2012)
Students with need: Average financial aid package met 46% of need; average scholarship/grant was $6,584; average loan was $3,722. For part-time students, average financial aid package was $5,805.
Students without need: 30 full-time freshmen who did not demonstrate need for aid received scholarships/grants; average award was $2,112. No-need awards available for academics, art, athletics, leadership, music/drama.
Scholarships offered: 23 full-time freshmen received athletic scholarships; average amount $3,142.
Cumulative student debt: 87% of graduating class had student loans; average debt was $34,174.

FINANCIAL AID PROCEDURES
Forms required: FAFSA.
Dates and Deadlines: Priority date 3/15; no closing date. Applicants notified on a rolling basis starting 3/15; must reply within 2 week(s) of notification.

CONTACT
Karen Price Scott, Director of Financial Aid
71 Academy Street, Mansfield, PA 16933
(570) 662-4129

Marywood University

Scranton, Pennsylvania
www.marywood.edu Federal Code: 003296

4-year private university in small city, affiliated with Roman Catholic Church.
Enrollment: 2,174 undergrads, 4% part-time. 452 full-time freshmen.
Selectivity: Admits 50 to 75% of applicants.

BASIC COSTS (2013-2014)
Tuition and fees: $30,690.
Room and board: $13,566.

FINANCIAL AID PICTURE (2012-2013)
Students with need: Out of 429 full-time freshmen who applied for aid, 394 were judged to have need. Of these, 361 received aid, and 6 had their full need met. Average financial aid package met 38% of need; average scholarship/grant was $8,439; average loan was $3,433. For part-time students, average financial aid package was $8,167.
Students without need: 55 full-time freshmen who did not demonstrate need for aid received scholarships/grants; average award was $14,609. No-need awards available for academics, art, leadership, music/drama, ROTC.
Cumulative student debt: 84% of graduating class had student loans; average debt was $41,198.

FINANCIAL AID PROCEDURES
Forms required: FAFSA.
Dates and Deadlines: Closing date 2/15. Applicants notified on a rolling basis starting 2/15; must reply by 5/1 or within 3 week(s) of notification.
Transfers: No deadline. Applicants notified on a rolling basis starting 3/1; must reply by 5/1 or within 3 week(s) of notification.

CONTACT
Stanley Skrutski, Director of Financial Aid
2300 Adams Avenue, Scranton, PA 18509-1598
(570) 348-6225

Mercyhurst University

Erie, Pennsylvania
www.mercyhurst.edu Federal Code: 003297

4-year private liberal arts college in small city, affiliated with Roman Catholic Church.
Enrollment: 2,764 undergrads, 6% part-time. 661 full-time freshmen.
Selectivity: Admits over 75% of applicants.

BASIC COSTS (2013-2014)
Tuition and fees: $30,300.
Per-credit charge: $947.
Room and board: $10,400.
Additional info: Tuition/fee waivers available for adults, minority students, unemployed or children of unemployed.

FINANCIAL AID PICTURE (2012-2013)
Students with need: Need-based aid available for full-time and part-time students. Work study available nights, weekends, and for part-time students.
Students without need: No-need awards available for academics, alumni affiliation, art, athletics, leadership, minority status, music/drama, religious affiliation, ROTC.

FINANCIAL AID PROCEDURES
Forms required: FAFSA.
Dates and Deadlines: Priority date 3/1; no closing date. Applicants notified on a rolling basis starting 2/15; must reply by 5/1 or within 2 week(s) of notification.
Transfers: No deadline. Applicants notified on a rolling basis; must reply within 2 week(s) of notification.

CONTACT
Carrie Newman, Director of Student Financial Services
501 East 38th Street, Erie, PA 16546-0001
(814) 824-2288

Messiah College
Mechanicsburg, Pennsylvania
www.messiah.edu Federal Code: 003298

4-year private liberal arts college in small town, affiliated with interdenominational tradition.
Enrollment: 2,754 undergrads, 2% part-time. 708 full-time freshmen.
Selectivity: Admits 50 to 75% of applicants.

BASIC COSTS (2013-2014)
Tuition and fees: $30,470.
Per-credit charge: $1,235.
Room and board: $9,070.
Additional info: Tuition/fee waivers available for adults.

FINANCIAL AID PICTURE (2012-2013)
Students with need: Out of 617 full-time freshmen who applied for aid, 545 were judged to have need. Of these, 545 received aid, and 94 had their full need met. Average financial aid package met 72% of need; average scholarship/grant was $16,835; average loan was $3,727. For part-time students, average financial aid package was $7,600.
Students without need: 160 full-time freshmen who did not demonstrate need for aid received scholarships/grants; average award was $12,886. No-need awards available for academics, art, leadership, music/drama, religious affiliation.
Cumulative student debt: 74% of graduating class had student loans; average debt was $35,306.

FINANCIAL AID PROCEDURES
Forms required: FAFSA.
Dates and Deadlines: Priority date 4/1; no closing date. Applicants notified on a rolling basis starting 3/15; must reply by 5/1 or within 4 week(s) of notification.

CONTACT
Greg Gearhart, Director of Financial Aid
One College Avenue Suite 3005, Mechanicsburg, PA 17055
(717) 691-6007

Metropolitan Career Center Computer Technology Institute
Philadelphia, Pennsylvania
www.careersinit.org

2-year private technical and career college in very large city.
Enrollment: 91 undergrads.

BASIC COSTS (2012-2013)
Per-credit charge: $387.
Additional info: Full program cost is $23,994; does not include all fees and supplies.

FINANCIAL AID PICTURE
Students with need: Need-based aid available for full-time and part-time students. Work study available nights.
Students without need: This college awards aid only to students with need.

FINANCIAL AID PROCEDURES
Forms required: FAFSA, state aid form.
Dates and Deadlines: Applicants notified on a rolling basis starting 1/1; must reply within 2 week(s) of notification.
Transfers: No deadline. Applicants notified on a rolling basis starting 1/1; must reply within 2 week(s) of notification. Because we offer transfer enrollment on a rolling basis, aid is process based on need and remaining eligibility at any given start date.

CONTACT
Madeline Sargent, Vice President of Finance
100 South Broad Street, Suite 830, Philadelphia, PA 19110

Millersville University of Pennsylvania
Millersville, Pennsylvania
www.millersville.edu Federal Code: 003325

4-year public university and liberal arts college in small town.
Enrollment: 7,325 undergrads, 9% part-time. 1,289 full-time freshmen.
Selectivity: Admits 50 to 75% of applicants.

BASIC COSTS (2012-2013)
Tuition and fees: $8,600; out-of-state residents $18,242.
Per-credit charge: $268; out-of-state residents $670.
Room and board: $8,834.
Additional info: Tuition for transfer students from five neighboring MD community colleges with dual admission agreements is $9,642. Tuition is $11,250 for high performing students who earn a 1,200 SAT or better, or graduate in the top 10% of their class (renewal is based upon performance); and to students who select a STEM or STEM Education major, as long as they stay in the selected major.

FINANCIAL AID PICTURE (2011-2012)
Students with need: Out of 1,175 full-time freshmen who applied for aid, 869 were judged to have need. Of these, 826 received aid, and 79 had their full need met. Average financial aid package met 67% of need; average scholarship/grant was $5,451; average loan was $3,237. For part-time students, average financial aid package was $6,606.
Students without need: 24 full-time freshmen who did not demonstrate need for aid received scholarships/grants; average award was $1,924. No-need awards available for academics, athletics, minority status.
Scholarships offered: 15 full-time freshmen received athletic scholarships; average amount $2,477.
Cumulative student debt: 67% of graduating class had student loans; average debt was $30,210.

FINANCIAL AID PROCEDURES
Forms required: FAFSA.
Dates and Deadlines: Priority date 3/15; no closing date. Applicants notified on a rolling basis starting 3/19; must reply within 2 week(s) of notification.
Transfers: No deadline. Applicants notified on a rolling basis.

CONTACT
Dwight Horsey, Assistant Vice President for Student Affairs and Director of Financial Aid
PO Box 1002, Millersville, PA 17551-0302
(717) 872-3026

Misericordia University

Dallas, Pennsylvania
www.misericordia.edu Federal Code: 003247

4-year private health science and liberal arts college in large town, affiliated with Roman Catholic Church.
Enrollment: 2,326 undergrads, 24% part-time. 511 full-time freshmen.
Selectivity: Admits 50 to 75% of applicants.

BASIC COSTS (2012-2013)
Tuition and fees: $27,230.
Per-credit charge: $495.
Room and board: $11,190.
Additional info: Tuition/fee waivers available for adults, minority students.

FINANCIAL AID PICTURE (2012-2013)
Students with need: Out of 499 full-time freshmen who applied for aid, 415 were judged to have need. Of these, 415 received aid, and 97 had their full need met. Average financial aid package met 78% of need; average scholarship/grant was $14,021; average loan was $7,741. For part-time students, average financial aid package was $5,296.
Students without need: 83 full-time freshmen who did not demonstrate need for aid received scholarships/grants; average award was $9,162. No-need awards available for academics, alumni affiliation, leadership, minority status, state/district residency.
Scholarships offered: McAuley Award; $1,000-$5,000 per year; based on out-of-classroom activities. Academic Scholarship; $2,000-$15,000 per year; based on academic abilities.

FINANCIAL AID PROCEDURES
Forms required: FAFSA, institutional form.
Dates and Deadlines: Priority date 3/1; closing date 5/1. Applicants notified on a rolling basis starting 3/15.
Transfers: No deadline. Applicants notified on a rolling basis starting 3/15.

CONTACT
Jane Dessoye, Executive Director of Enrollment Management
301 Lake Street, Dallas, PA 18612-1098
(570) 674-6280

Montgomery County Community College

Blue Bell, Pennsylvania
www.mc3.edu Federal Code: 004452

2-year public community college in large town.
Enrollment: 12,543 undergrads, 60% part-time. 1,984 full-time freshmen.
Selectivity: Open admission; but selective for some programs.

BASIC COSTS (2012-2013)
Tuition and fees: $4,050; out-of-district residents $7,710; out-of-state residents $11,370.
Per-credit charge: $112; out-of-district residents $224; out-of-state residents $336.

FINANCIAL AID PICTURE (2011-2012)
Students with need: Out of 1,342 full-time freshmen who applied for aid, 1,085 were judged to have need. Of these, 955 received aid, and 52 had their full need met. Average financial aid package met 22% of need; average scholarship/grant was $2,898; average loan was $1,650. For part-time students, average financial aid package was $2,899.
Students without need: 160 full-time freshmen who did not demonstrate need for aid received scholarships/grants; average award was $2,654. No-need awards available for academics.

FINANCIAL AID PROCEDURES
Forms required: FAFSA.
Dates and Deadlines: Priority date 5/1; no closing date. Applicants notified on a rolling basis starting 2/1.
Transfers: No deadline.

CONTACT
Tracey Richards, Director of Financial Aid
340 DeKalb Pike, Blue Bell, PA 19422
(215) 641-6566

Moore College of Art and Design

Philadelphia, Pennsylvania
www.moore.edu Federal Code: 003300

4-year private visual arts college for women in very large city.
Enrollment: 482 undergrads, 6% part-time. 104 full-time freshmen.
Selectivity: Admits 50 to 75% of applicants.

BASIC COSTS (2013-2014)
Tuition and fees: $34,047.
Room and board: $12,789.

FINANCIAL AID PICTURE
Students with need: Need-based aid available for full-time and part-time students.
Students without need: No-need awards available for academics, art, leadership.

FINANCIAL AID PROCEDURES
Forms required: FAFSA.
Dates and Deadlines: Priority date 3/1; closing date 5/1. Applicants notified on a rolling basis starting 2/15; must reply within 2 week(s) of notification.
Transfers: Priority date 5/1; no deadline.

CONTACT
Melissa Walsh, Director of Financial Aid
The Parkway at 20th Street, Philadelphia, PA 19103-1179
(215) 568-4515

Moravian College

Bethlehem, Pennsylvania
www.moravian.edu Federal Code: 003301

4-year private liberal arts college in small city, affiliated with Moravian Church in America.
Enrollment: 1,476 undergrads, 2% part-time. 378 full-time freshmen.
Selectivity: Admits over 75% of applicants.

BASIC COSTS (2012-2013)
Tuition and fees: $34,484.
Per-credit charge: $942.
Room and board: $10,146.

FINANCIAL AID PICTURE (2012-2013)
Students with need: Out of 362 full-time freshmen who applied for aid, 334 were judged to have need. Of these, 334 received aid, and 36 had their full need met. Average financial aid package met 77% of need; average scholarship/grant was $21,404; average loan was $3,814. For part-time students, average financial aid package was $5,366.
Students without need: 41 full-time freshmen who did not demonstrate need for aid received scholarships/grants; average award was $10,292. No-need awards available for academics, alumni affiliation, leadership, minority status, music/drama, religious affiliation, ROTC.
Scholarships offered: Comenius Scholarship; $10,000 to full tuition; top 10% of high school class and minimum 1850 SAT required. Founders Scholarship; $4,000-$8,000; for top 25% or 1700 SAT. Trustee Scholarship; $6,000-$10,000; must be National Honor Society member, in top 20% of class. All scholarships require at least 500 on each section of SAT. Other

scholarships available based on interest in the sciences, leadership and interest in promoting diversity and/or challenging circumstances in attending college.
Cumulative student debt: 79% of graduating class had student loans; average debt was $39,055.

FINANCIAL AID PROCEDURES
Forms required: FAFSA, institutional form. CSS PROFILE accepted but not required.
Dates and Deadlines: Priority date 2/15; closing date 3/15. Applicants notified by 3/15; must reply by 5/1 or within 2 week(s) of notification.
Transfers: Priority date 3/15; closing date 5/1. Applicants notified on a rolling basis starting 4/1.

CONTACT
Colby McCarthy, Director of Financial Aid
1200 Main Street, Bethlehem, PA 18018
(610) 861-1330

Mount Aloysius College
Cresson, Pennsylvania
www.mtaloy.edu Federal Code: 003302

4-year private liberal arts college in small town, affiliated with Roman Catholic Church.
Enrollment: 1,532 undergrads, 19% part-time. 372 full-time freshmen.
Selectivity: Admits 50 to 75% of applicants.

BASIC COSTS (2013-2014)
Tuition and fees: $20,268.
Per-credit charge: $650.
Room and board: $8,830.
Additional info: Tuition/fee waivers available for unemployed or children of unemployed.

FINANCIAL AID PICTURE (2012-2013)
Students with need: Out of 372 full-time freshmen who applied for aid, 334 were judged to have need. Of these, 334 received aid. Average financial aid package met 30% of need; average scholarship/grant was $4,840; average loan was $3,650. For part-time students, average financial aid package was $3,600.
Students without need: 38 full-time freshmen who did not demonstrate need for aid received scholarships/grants; average award was $4,860. No-need awards available for academics, art, leadership, music/drama, religious affiliation, state/district residency.

FINANCIAL AID PROCEDURES
Forms required: FAFSA.
Dates and Deadlines: Priority date 4/1; no closing date. Applicants notified on a rolling basis starting 3/15; must reply within 2 week(s) of notification.
Transfers: No deadline.

CONTACT
Stacy Schenk, Director of Financial Aid
7373 Admiral Peary Highway, Cresson, PA 16630
(814) 886-6357

Muhlenberg College
Allentown, Pennsylvania Federal Code: 003304
www.muhlenberg.edu CSS Code: 2424

4-year private liberal arts college in small city, affiliated with Evangelical Lutheran Church in America.
Enrollment: 2,332 undergrads, 3% part-time. 581 full-time freshmen.
Selectivity: Admits less than 50% of applicants.

BASIC COSTS (2013-2014)
Tuition and fees: $42,755.
Per-credit charge: $1,249.
Room and board: $10,080.

FINANCIAL AID PICTURE (2012-2013)
Students with need: Out of 417 full-time freshmen who applied for aid, 298 were judged to have need. Of these, 298 received aid, and 258 had their full need met. Average financial aid package met 92% of need; average scholarship/grant was $23,105; average loan was $3,694. For part-time students, average financial aid package was $5,896.
Students without need: 191 full-time freshmen who did not demonstrate need for aid received scholarships/grants; average award was $9,858. No-need awards available for academics, art, leadership, music/drama, ROTC.
Cumulative student debt: 65% of graduating class had student loans; average debt was $25,858.

FINANCIAL AID PROCEDURES
Forms required: FAFSA, CSS PROFILE, institutional form.
Dates and Deadlines: Closing date 2/15. Applicants notified by 3/20; must reply by 5/1.
Transfers: Closing date 4/15. Applicants notified by 6/1; must reply by 7/1. Transfers awarded aid on a funds-available basis after returning students and freshmen have been served.

CONTACT
Gregory Mitton, Director of Financial Aid
2400 Chew Street, Allentown, PA 18104
(484) 664-3175

Neumann University
Aston, Pennsylvania
www.neumann.edu Federal Code: 003988

4-year private university in large town, affiliated with Roman Catholic Church.
Enrollment: 2,578 undergrads, 17% part-time. 574 full-time freshmen.
Selectivity: Admits 50 to 75% of applicants.

BASIC COSTS (2013-2014)
Tuition and fees: $24,948.
Per-credit charge: $547.
Room and board: $11,512.

FINANCIAL AID PICTURE (2011-2012)
Students with need: Need-based aid available for full-time students.
Students without need: This college awards aid only to students with need.

FINANCIAL AID PROCEDURES
Forms required: FAFSA.
Dates and Deadlines: Applicants notified on a rolling basis; must reply within 2 week(s) of notification.
Transfers: Priority date 3/7; closing date 6/1. Must reply within 2 week(s) of notification.

CONTACT
Deborah Cawley, Director of Financial Aid
Office of Admissions, Aston, PA 19014-1298
(610) 558-5520

Newport Business Institute: Lower Burrell
Lower Burrell, Pennsylvania
www.nbi.edu Federal Code: 004901

2-year for-profit business college in small town.
Enrollment: 70 full-time undergrads.

Selectivity: Open admission.

BASIC COSTS (2012-2013)
Tuition and fees: $11,775.

FINANCIAL AID PICTURE
Students with need: Need-based aid available for full-time and part-time students.
Students without need: No-need awards available for academics, leadership.

FINANCIAL AID PROCEDURES
Forms required: FAFSA, state aid form.
Dates and Deadlines: Applicants notified on a rolling basis starting 5/1.

CONTACT
Rosemary Leipertz, Director of Financial Aid
945 Greensburg Road, Lower Burrell, PA 15068
(724) 339-7542

Northampton Community College

Bethlehem, Pennsylvania
www.northampton.edu Federal Code: 007191

2-year public community college in small city.
Enrollment: 10,549 undergrads, 56% part-time. 1,517 full-time freshmen.
Selectivity: Open admission; but selective for some programs.

BASIC COSTS (2012-2013)
Tuition and fees: $3,570; out-of-district residents $7,830; out-of-state residents $11,610.
Per-credit charge: $85; out-of-district residents $170; out-of-state residents $255.
Room and board: $7,676.
Additional info: Tuition/fee waivers available for unemployed or children of unemployed.

FINANCIAL AID PICTURE (2012-2013)
Students with need: 78% of average financial aid package awarded as scholarships/grants, 22% awarded as loans/jobs. Need-based aid available for part-time students. Work study available nights, weekends, and for part-time students.
Students without need: No-need awards available for academics, alumni affiliation, art, leadership, minority status, music/drama, state/district residency.

FINANCIAL AID PROCEDURES
Forms required: FAFSA, state aid form, institutional form.
Dates and Deadlines: Priority date 3/31; no closing date. Applicants notified on a rolling basis starting 5/1.

CONTACT
Cindy King, Director of Financial Aid
3835 Green Pond Road, Bethlehem, PA 18020-7599
(610) 861-5510

Oakbridge Academy of Arts

Lower Burrell, Pennsylvania
www.oaa.edu Federal Code: 015063

2-year for-profit visual arts college in large town.
Enrollment: 54 undergrads.
Selectivity: Open admission.

BASIC COSTS (2012-2013)
Tuition and fees: $12,225.

FINANCIAL AID PICTURE
Students with need: Need-based aid available for full-time and part-time students.
Students without need: This college awards aid only to students with need.
Scholarships offered: Jeanne H. Mullen art scholarship; half tuition; based on portfolio; 2 awarded per year.

FINANCIAL AID PROCEDURES
Forms required: FAFSA, state aid form.
Dates and Deadlines: Closing date 5/1. Applicants notified on a rolling basis.

CONTACT
Rosemary Leipertz, Financial Aid Director
1250 Greensburg Road, Lower Burrell, PA 15068
(724) 335-5336

Peirce College

Philadelphia, Pennsylvania
www.peirce.edu Federal Code: 003309

4-year private business and technical college in very large city.
Enrollment: 2,254 undergrads, 64% part-time. 37 full-time freshmen.
Selectivity: Open admission; but selective for some programs.

BASIC COSTS (2013-2014)
Tuition and fees: $17,040.
Per-credit charge: $533.

FINANCIAL AID PICTURE (2012-2013)
Students with need: Average financial aid package met 35% of need; average scholarship/grant was $3,997; average loan was $3,983. For part-time students, average financial aid package was $5,097.
Students without need: No-need awards available for academics, alumni affiliation, leadership, state/district residency.
Additional info: Tuition discounts available for US students serving in US military and in protect-and-serve fields.

FINANCIAL AID PROCEDURES
Forms required: FAFSA.
Dates and Deadlines: Priority date 5/1; no closing date. Applicants notified on a rolling basis starting 5/1.
Transfers: No deadline. Applicants notified on a rolling basis.

CONTACT
Chanel Greene, Manager, Financial Aid
1420 Pine Street, Philadelphia, PA 19102-4699
(888) 467-3472 ext. 9370

Penn Commercial Business and Technical School

Washington, Pennsylvania
www.penncommercial.edu Federal Code: 004902

2-year for-profit business and technical college in small city.
Enrollment: 164 undergrads, 2% part-time. 161 full-time freshmen.
Selectivity: Open admission; but selective for some programs.

BASIC COSTS (2013-2014)
Tuition and fees: $8,975.
Per-credit charge: $187.

FINANCIAL AID PICTURE (2011-2012)
Students with need: 37% of average financial aid package awarded as scholarships/grants, 63% awarded as loans/jobs.

FINANCIAL AID PROCEDURES
Dates and Deadlines: Closing date 5/15.

CONTACT
Timothy Shaffer, Director of Financial Aid
242 Oak Spring Road, Washington, PA 15301
(724) 222-5330 ext. 3

Penn State Abington

Abington, Pennsylvania
www.abington.psu.edu Federal Code: 003329

4-year public branch campus college in small city.
Enrollment: 3,078 undergrads, 14% part-time. 803 full-time freshmen.
Selectivity: Admits over 75% of applicants.

BASIC COSTS (2012-2013)
Tuition and fees: $13,356; out-of-state residents $19,912.
Per-credit charge: $504; out-of-state residents $793.

FINANCIAL AID PICTURE (2011-2012)
Students with need: Out of 734 full-time freshmen who applied for aid, 603 were judged to have need. Of these, 592 received aid, and 16 had their full need met. Average financial aid package met 61% of need; average scholarship/grant was $7,794; average loan was $3,257. For part-time students, average financial aid package was $6,904.
Students without need: 29 full-time freshmen who did not demonstrate need for aid received scholarships/grants; average award was $1,627. No-need awards available for academics, alumni affiliation, ROTC.
Cumulative student debt: 66% of graduating class had student loans; average debt was $35,100.

FINANCIAL AID PROCEDURES
Forms required: FAFSA.
Dates and Deadlines: Priority date 2/15; no closing date. Applicants notified on a rolling basis.
Transfers: Closing date 5/1. Schools required to obtain student aid information through National Student Loan Data System (NSLDS).

CONTACT
Anna Griswold, Assistant Vice Provost for Student Aid
106 Sutherland, Abingdon, PA 19001-3990
(814) 865-6301

Penn State Altoona

Altoona, Pennsylvania
www.altoona.psu.edu Federal Code: 003329

4-year public branch campus college in small city.
Enrollment: 3,788 undergrads, 5% part-time. 1,577 full-time freshmen.
Selectivity: Admits over 75% of applicants.

BASIC COSTS (2012-2013)
Tuition and fees: $13,900; out-of-state residents $20,794.
Per-credit charge: $542; out-of-state residents $830.
Room and board: $9,690.

FINANCIAL AID PICTURE (2011-2012)
Students with need: Out of 1,360 full-time freshmen who applied for aid, 1,090 were judged to have need. Of these, 1,054 received aid, and 54 had their full need met. Average financial aid package met 57% of need; average scholarship/grant was $6,044; average loan was $3,378. For part-time students, average financial aid package was $6,703.
Students without need: 44 full-time freshmen who did not demonstrate need for aid received scholarships/grants; average award was $926. No-need awards available for academics, alumni affiliation, ROTC.
Cumulative student debt: 66% of graduating class had student loans; average debt was $35,100.

FINANCIAL AID PROCEDURES
Forms required: FAFSA.
Dates and Deadlines: Priority date 2/15; no closing date. Applicants notified on a rolling basis.
Transfers: Closing date 5/1. Schools required to obtain student aid information through National Student Loan Data System (NSLDS).

CONTACT
Anna Griswold, Assistant Vice Provost for Student Aid
E108 Smith Building, Altoona, PA 16801-3760
(814) 865-6301

Penn State Beaver

Monaca, Pennsylvania
www.br.psu.edu Federal Code: 003329

4-year public branch campus college in small town.
Enrollment: 656 undergrads, 6% part-time. 250 full-time freshmen.
Selectivity: Admits over 75% of applicants.

BASIC COSTS (2012-2013)
Tuition and fees: $13,350; out-of-state residents $19,906.
Per-credit charge: $504; out-of-state residents $793.
Room and board: $9,690.

FINANCIAL AID PICTURE (2011-2012)
Students with need: Out of 234 full-time freshmen who applied for aid, 182 were judged to have need. Of these, 178 received aid, and 10 had their full need met. Average financial aid package met 68% of need; average scholarship/grant was $7,078; average loan was $3,451. For part-time students, average financial aid package was $5,900.
Students without need: 21 full-time freshmen who did not demonstrate need for aid received scholarships/grants; average award was $2,276. No-need awards available for academics, alumni affiliation, ROTC.
Cumulative student debt: 66% of graduating class had student loans; average debt was $35,100.

FINANCIAL AID PROCEDURES
Forms required: FAFSA.
Dates and Deadlines: Priority date 2/15; no closing date. Applicants notified on a rolling basis.
Transfers: Closing date 5/1. Schools required to obtain student aid information through National Student Loan Data System (NSLDS).

CONTACT
Anna Griswold, Assistant Vice Provost for Student Aid
100 University Drive, Monaca, PA 15061-2799
(814) 865-6301

Penn State Berks

Reading, Pennsylvania
www.bk.psu.edu Federal Code: 003329

4-year public branch campus college in small city.
Enrollment: 2,577 undergrads, 8% part-time. 849 full-time freshmen.
Selectivity: Admits over 75% of applicants.

BASIC COSTS (2012-2013)
Tuition and fees: $13,900; out-of-state residents $20,794.
Per-credit charge: $542; out-of-state residents $830.
Room and board: $10,560.

FINANCIAL AID PICTURE (2011-2012)
Students with need: Out of 750 full-time freshmen who applied for aid, 621 were judged to have need. Of these, 588 received aid, and 24 had their

full need met. Average financial aid package met 56% of need; average scholarship/grant was $6,489; average loan was $3,332. For part-time students, average financial aid package was $6,677.
Students without need: 15 full-time freshmen who did not demonstrate need for aid received scholarships/grants; average award was $1,839. No-need awards available for academics, alumni affiliation, ROTC.
Cumulative student debt: 66% of graduating class had student loans; average debt was $35,100.

FINANCIAL AID PROCEDURES
Forms required: FAFSA.
Dates and Deadlines: Priority date 2/15; no closing date. Applicants notified on a rolling basis.
Transfers: Closing date 5/1. Schools required to obtain student aid information through National Student Loan Data System (NSLDS).

CONTACT
Anna Griswold, Assistant Vice Provost for Student Aid
Tulpehocken Road, Reading, PA 19610-6009
(814) 865-6301

Penn State Brandywine
Media, Pennsylvania
www.brandywine.psu.edu Federal Code: 006922

4-year public branch campus college in small town.
Enrollment: 1,403 undergrads, 10% part-time. 394 full-time freshmen.
Selectivity: Admits over 75% of applicants.

BASIC COSTS (2012-2013)
Tuition and fees: $13,356; out-of-state residents $19,912.
Per-credit charge: $504; out-of-state residents $793.

FINANCIAL AID PICTURE (2011-2012)
Students with need: Out of 346 full-time freshmen who applied for aid, 254 were judged to have need. Of these, 248 received aid, and 5 had their full need met. Average financial aid package met 60% of need; average scholarship/grant was $6,184; average loan was $3,219. For part-time students, average financial aid package was $6,326.
Students without need: 45 full-time freshmen who did not demonstrate need for aid received scholarships/grants; average award was $2,183. No-need awards available for academics, alumni affiliation, ROTC.
Cumulative student debt: 66% of graduating class had student loans; average debt was $35,100.

FINANCIAL AID PROCEDURES
Forms required: FAFSA.
Dates and Deadlines: Priority date 2/15; no closing date. Applicants notified on a rolling basis.
Transfers: Closing date 5/1. Schools required to obtain student aid information through National Student Loan Data System (NSLDS).

CONTACT
Anna Griswold, Assistant Vice Provost for Student Aid
25 Yearsley Mill Road, Media, PA 19063-5596
(814) 865-6301

Penn State DuBois
DuBois, Pennsylvania
www.ds.psu.edu Federal Code: 003335

4-year public branch campus college in small town.
Enrollment: 580 undergrads, 12% part-time. 160 full-time freshmen.
Selectivity: Admits over 75% of applicants.

BASIC COSTS (2012-2013)
Tuition and fees: $13,244; out-of-state residents $19,800.
Per-credit charge: $504; out-of-state residents $793.

FINANCIAL AID PICTURE (2011-2012)
Students with need: Out of 153 full-time freshmen who applied for aid, 133 were judged to have need. Of these, 132 received aid, and 1 had their full need met. Average financial aid package met 60% of need; average scholarship/grant was $6,112; average loan was $3,278. For part-time students, average financial aid package was $7,341.
Students without need: 7 full-time freshmen who did not demonstrate need for aid received scholarships/grants; average award was $1,608. No-need awards available for academics, alumni affiliation, ROTC.
Cumulative student debt: 66% of graduating class had student loans; average debt was $35,100.

FINANCIAL AID PROCEDURES
Forms required: FAFSA.
Dates and Deadlines: Priority date 2/15; no closing date. Applicants notified on a rolling basis.
Transfers: Closing date 5/1. Schools required to obtain student aid information through National Student Loan Data System (NSLDS).

CONTACT
Anna Griswold, Assistant Vice Provost for Student Aid
Enrollment Services House, DuBois, PA 15801-3199
(814) 865-6301

Penn State Erie, The Behrend College
Erie, Pennsylvania
http://psbehrend.psu.edu Federal Code: 003329

4-year public branch campus college in small city.
Enrollment: 3,859 undergrads, 5% part-time. 1,077 full-time freshmen.
Selectivity: Admits over 75% of applicants.

BASIC COSTS (2012-2013)
Tuition and fees: $13,900; out-of-state residents $20,794.
Per-credit charge: $542; out-of-state residents $830.
Room and board: $9,690.

FINANCIAL AID PICTURE (2011-2012)
Students with need: Out of 981 full-time freshmen who applied for aid, 808 were judged to have need. Of these, 779 received aid, and 35 had their full need met. Average financial aid package met 61% of need; average scholarship/grant was $6,254; average loan was $3,384. For part-time students, average financial aid package was $6,400.
Students without need: 22 full-time freshmen who did not demonstrate need for aid received scholarships/grants; average award was $1,752. No-need awards available for academics, alumni affiliation, ROTC.
Cumulative student debt: 66% of graduating class had student loans; average debt was $35,100.

FINANCIAL AID PROCEDURES
Forms required: FAFSA.
Dates and Deadlines: Priority date 2/15; no closing date. Applicants notified on a rolling basis.
Transfers: Closing date 5/1. Schools required to obtain student aid information through National Student Loan Data System (NSLDS).

CONTACT
Anna Griswold, Assistant Vice Provost for Student Aid
4701 College Drive, Erie, PA 16563-0105
(814) 865-6301

Penn State Fayette, The Eberly Campus

Uniontown, Pennsylvania
www.fe.psu.edu Federal Code: 003329

4-year public branch campus college in large town.
Enrollment: 818 undergrads, 18% part-time. 230 full-time freshmen.
Selectivity: Admits over 75% of applicants.

BASIC COSTS (2012-2013)
Tuition and fees: $13,286; out-of-state residents $19,842.
Per-credit charge: $504; out-of-state residents $793.

FINANCIAL AID PICTURE (2011-2012)
Students with need: Out of 221 full-time freshmen who applied for aid, 197 were judged to have need. Of these, 195 received aid, and 8 had their full need met. Average financial aid package met 61% of need; average scholarship/grant was $6,122; average loan was $3,388. For part-time students, average financial aid package was $6,037.
Students without need: 14 full-time freshmen who did not demonstrate need for aid received scholarships/grants; average award was $3,041. No-need awards available for academics, alumni affiliation, ROTC.
Cumulative student debt: 66% of graduating class had student loans; average debt was $35,100.

FINANCIAL AID PROCEDURES
Forms required: FAFSA.
Dates and Deadlines: Priority date 2/15; no closing date. Applicants notified on a rolling basis.
Transfers: Closing date 5/1. Schools required to obtain student aid information through National Student Loan Data System (NSLDS).

CONTACT
Anna Griswold, Assistant Vice Provost for Student Aid
One University Drive, PO Box 519, Route 119 North, Uniontown, PA 15401-0519
(814) 865-6301

Penn State Greater Allegheny

McKeesport, Pennsylvania
www.ga.psu.edu Federal Code: 003329

4-year public branch campus college in large town.
Enrollment: 596 undergrads, 6% part-time. 230 full-time freshmen.
Selectivity: Admits over 75% of applicants.

BASIC COSTS (2012-2013)
Tuition and fees: $13,356; out-of-state residents $19,912.
Per-credit charge: $504; out-of-state residents $793.
Room and board: $9,690.

FINANCIAL AID PICTURE (2011-2012)
Students with need: Out of 213 full-time freshmen who applied for aid, 192 were judged to have need. Of these, 191 received aid, and 10 had their full need met. Average financial aid package met 70% of need; average scholarship/grant was $7,953; average loan was $3,393. For part-time students, average financial aid package was $7,402.
Students without need: 16 full-time freshmen who did not demonstrate need for aid received scholarships/grants; average award was $2,944. No-need awards available for academics, alumni affiliation, ROTC.
Cumulative student debt: 66% of graduating class had student loans; average debt was $35,100.

FINANCIAL AID PROCEDURES
Forms required: FAFSA.
Dates and Deadlines: Priority date 2/15; no closing date. Applicants notified on a rolling basis.
Transfers: Closing date 5/1. Schools required to obtain student aid information through National Student Loan Data System (NSLDS).

CONTACT
Anna Griswold, Assistant Vice Provost for Student Aid
101 Frable Building, McKeesport, PA 15132-7698
(814) 865-6301

Penn State Harrisburg

Middletown, Pennsylvania
www.hbg.psu.edu Federal Code: 003329

4-year public branch campus college in small town.
Enrollment: 3,255 undergrads, 12% part-time. 539 full-time freshmen.
Selectivity: Admits over 75% of applicants.

BASIC COSTS (2012-2013)
Tuition and fees: $13,900; out-of-state residents $20,794.
Per-credit charge: $542; out-of-state residents $830.
Room and board: $11,000.

FINANCIAL AID PICTURE (2011-2012)
Students with need: Out of 443 full-time freshmen who applied for aid, 369 were judged to have need. Of these, 357 received aid, and 24 had their full need met. Average financial aid package met 62% of need; average scholarship/grant was $6,820; average loan was $3,300. For part-time students, average financial aid package was $7,114.
Students without need: 11 full-time freshmen who did not demonstrate need for aid received scholarships/grants; average award was $1,864. No-need awards available for academics, alumni affiliation, ROTC.
Cumulative student debt: 66% of graduating class had student loans; average debt was $35,100.

FINANCIAL AID PROCEDURES
Forms required: FAFSA.
Dates and Deadlines: Priority date 2/15; no closing date. Applicants notified on a rolling basis.
Transfers: Closing date 5/1. Schools required to obtain student aid information through National Student Loan Data System (NSLDS).

CONTACT
Anna Griswold, Assistant Vice Provost for Student Aid
Swatara Building, Middletown, PA 17057-4898
(814) 865-6301

Penn State Hazleton

Hazleton, Pennsylvania
www.hn.psu.edu Federal Code: 003338

4-year public branch campus college in large town.
Enrollment: 1,037 undergrads, 5% part-time. 456 full-time freshmen.
Selectivity: Admits over 75% of applicants.

BASIC COSTS (2012-2013)
Tuition and fees: $13,300; out-of-state residents $19,856.
Per-credit charge: $504; out-of-state residents $793.
Room and board: $9,690.

FINANCIAL AID PICTURE (2011-2012)
Students with need: Out of 425 full-time freshmen who applied for aid, 365 were judged to have need. Of these, 358 received aid, and 6 had their full need met. Average financial aid package met 62% of need; average scholarship/grant was $6,804; average loan was $3,342. For part-time students, average financial aid package was $8,368.
Students without need: 29 full-time freshmen who did not demonstrate need for aid received scholarships/grants; average award was $2,530. No-need awards available for academics, alumni affiliation, ROTC.
Cumulative student debt: 66% of graduating class had student loans; average debt was $35,100.

FINANCIAL AID PROCEDURES
Forms required: FAFSA.
Dates and Deadlines: Priority date 2/15; no closing date. Applicants notified on a rolling basis.
Transfers: Closing date 5/1. Schools required to obtain student aid information through National Student Loan Data System (NSLDS).

CONTACT
Anna Griswold, Assistant Vice Provost for Student Aid
110 Administration Building, University Park, PA 18202-1291
(814) 865-6301

Penn State Lehigh Valley
Center Valley, Pennsylvania
www.lv.psu.edu Federal Code: 003329

4-year public branch campus college in rural community.
Enrollment: 787 undergrads, 11% part-time. 253 full-time freshmen.
Selectivity: Admits over 75% of applicants.

BASIC COSTS (2012-2013)
Tuition and fees: $13,342; out-of-state residents $19,898.
Per-credit charge: $504; out-of-state residents $793.

FINANCIAL AID PICTURE (2011-2012)
Students with need: Out of 225 full-time freshmen who applied for aid, 180 were judged to have need. Of these, 175 received aid, and 4 had their full need met. Average financial aid package met 58% of need; average scholarship/grant was $6,403; average loan was $3,426. For part-time students, average financial aid package was $6,563.
Students without need: 15 full-time freshmen who did not demonstrate need for aid received scholarships/grants; average award was $1,936. No-need awards available for academics, alumni affiliation, ROTC.
Cumulative student debt: 66% of graduating class had student loans; average debt was $35,100.

FINANCIAL AID PROCEDURES
Forms required: FAFSA.
Dates and Deadlines: Priority date 2/15; no closing date. Applicants notified on a rolling basis.
Transfers: Closing date 5/1. Schools required to obtain student aid information through National Student Loan Data System (NSLDS).

CONTACT
Anna Griswold, Assistant Vice Provost for Student Aid
2809 Saucon Valley Road, Center Vally, PA 18034-8447
(814) 865-6301

Penn State Mont Alto
Mont Alto, Pennsylvania
www.ma.psu.edu Federal Code: 003329

4-year public branch campus college in rural community.
Enrollment: 1,008 undergrads, 20% part-time. 384 full-time freshmen.
Selectivity: Admits over 75% of applicants.

BASIC COSTS (2012-2013)
Tuition and fees: $13,356; out-of-state residents $19,912.
Per-credit charge: $504; out-of-state residents $793.
Room and board: $9,690.

FINANCIAL AID PICTURE (2011-2012)
Students with need: Out of 360 full-time freshmen who applied for aid, 309 were judged to have need. Of these, 304 received aid, and 18 had their full need met. Average financial aid package met 64% of need; average scholarship/grant was $6,213; average loan was $3,357. For part-time students, average financial aid package was $6,612.
Students without need: 21 full-time freshmen who did not demonstrate need for aid received scholarships/grants; average award was $3,806. No-need awards available for academics, alumni affiliation, ROTC.
Cumulative student debt: 66% of graduating class had student loans; average debt was $35,100.

FINANCIAL AID PROCEDURES
Forms required: FAFSA.
Dates and Deadlines: Priority date 2/15; no closing date. Applicants notified on a rolling basis starting 3/1.
Transfers: Closing date 5/1. Schools required to obtain student aid information through National Student Loan Data System (NSLDS).

CONTACT
Anna Griswold, Assistant Vice Provost for Student Aid
1 Campus Drive, Mont Alto, PA 17237-9703
(814) 865-6301

Penn State New Kensington
New Kensington, Pennsylvania
www.nk.psu.edu Federal Code: 003329

4-year public branch campus college in large town.
Enrollment: 650 undergrads, 16% part-time. 187 full-time freshmen.
Selectivity: Admits 50 to 75% of applicants.

BASIC COSTS (2012-2013)
Tuition and fees: $13,300; out-of-state residents $19,856.
Per-credit charge: $504; out-of-state residents $793.

FINANCIAL AID PICTURE (2011-2012)
Students with need: Out of 176 full-time freshmen who applied for aid, 148 were judged to have need. Of these, 148 received aid, and 2 had their full need met. Average financial aid package met 65% of need; average scholarship/grant was $6,031; average loan was $3,193. For part-time students, average financial aid package was $5,377.
Students without need: 15 full-time freshmen who did not demonstrate need for aid received scholarships/grants; average award was $2,203. No-need awards available for academics, alumni affiliation, ROTC.
Cumulative student debt: 66% of graduating class had student loans; average debt was $35,100.

FINANCIAL AID PROCEDURES
Forms required: FAFSA.
Dates and Deadlines: Priority date 2/15; no closing date. Applicants notified on a rolling basis.
Transfers: Closing date 5/1. Schools required to obtain student aid information through National Student Loan Data System (NSLDS).

CONTACT
Anna Griswold, Assistant Vice Provost for Student Aid
3550 Seventh Street Road, Route 780, New Kensington, PA 15068-1765
(814) 865-6301

Penn State Schuylkill
Schuylkill Haven, Pennsylvania
www.sl.psu.edu Federal Code: 003329

4-year public branch campus college in small town.
Enrollment: 807 undergrads, 18% part-time. 325 full-time freshmen.
Selectivity: Admits over 75% of applicants.

BASIC COSTS (2012-2013)
Tuition and fees: $13,238; out-of-state residents $19,794.
Per-credit charge: $504; out-of-state residents $793.

FINANCIAL AID PICTURE (2011-2012)
Students with need: Out of 314 full-time freshmen who applied for aid, 285 were judged to have need. Of these, 285 received aid, and 10 had their full need met. Average financial aid package met 64% of need; average scholarship/grant was $7,206; average loan was $3,261. For part-time students, average financial aid package was $6,154.
Students without need: 10 full-time freshmen who did not demonstrate need for aid received scholarships/grants; average award was $2,445. No-need awards available for academics, alumni affiliation, ROTC.
Cumulative student debt: 66% of graduating class had student loans; average debt was $35,100.

FINANCIAL AID PROCEDURES
Forms required: FAFSA.
Dates and Deadlines: Priority date 2/15; no closing date. Applicants notified on a rolling basis.
Transfers: Closing date 5/1. Schools required to obtain student aid information through National Student Loan Data System (NSLDS).

CONTACT
Anna Griswold, Assistant Vice Provost for Student Aid
200 University Drive, Schuylkill Haven, PA 17972-2208
(814) 865-6301

Penn State Shenango
Sharon, Pennsylvania
www.shenango.psu.edu Federal Code: 003329

4-year public branch campus college in large town.
Enrollment: 484 undergrads, 36% part-time. 92 full-time freshmen.
Selectivity: Admits 50 to 75% of applicants.

BASIC COSTS (2012-2013)
Tuition and fees: $13,244; out-of-state residents $19,800.
Per-credit charge: $504; out-of-state residents $793.

FINANCIAL AID PICTURE (2011-2012)
Students with need: Out of 91 full-time freshmen who applied for aid, 87 were judged to have need. Of these, 86 received aid, and 1 had their full need met. Average financial aid package met 63% of need; average scholarship/grant was $6,643; average loan was $3,392. For part-time students, average financial aid package was $7,588.
Students without need: 3 full-time freshmen who did not demonstrate need for aid received scholarships/grants; average award was $1,740. No-need awards available for academics, alumni affiliation, ROTC.
Cumulative student debt: 66% of graduating class had student loans; average debt was $35,100.

FINANCIAL AID PROCEDURES
Forms required: FAFSA.
Dates and Deadlines: Priority date 2/15; no closing date. Applicants notified on a rolling basis.
Transfers: Closing date 5/1. Schools required to obtain student aid information through National Student Loan Data System (NSLDS).

CONTACT
Anna Griswold, Assistant Vice Provost for Student Aid
147 Shenango Avenue, Room 206, Sharon, PA 16146-1597
(814) 865-6301

Penn State University Park
University Park, Pennsylvania
www.psu.edu Federal Code: 003329

4-year public university in large town.
Enrollment: 38,548 undergrads, 2% part-time. 7,346 full-time freshmen.
Selectivity: Admits 50 to 75% of applicants.

BASIC COSTS (2012-2013)
Tuition and fees: $16,444; out-of-state residents $28,746.
Per-credit charge: $648; out-of-state residents $1,161.
Room and board: $9,690.

FINANCIAL AID PICTURE (2011-2012)
Students with need: Out of 5,374 full-time freshmen who applied for aid, 3,685 were judged to have need. Of these, 3,418 received aid, and 273 had their full need met. Average financial aid package met 59% of need; average scholarship/grant was $6,655; average loan was $3,380. For part-time students, average financial aid package was $8,018.
Students without need: 489 full-time freshmen who did not demonstrate need for aid received scholarships/grants; average award was $3,532. No-need awards available for academics, alumni affiliation, athletics, ROTC.
Scholarships offered: 119 full-time freshmen received athletic scholarships; average amount $21,953.
Cumulative student debt: 66% of graduating class had student loans; average debt was $35,100.

FINANCIAL AID PROCEDURES
Forms required: FAFSA.
Dates and Deadlines: Priority date 2/15; no closing date. Applicants notified on a rolling basis.
Transfers: Closing date 5/1. Schools required to obtain student aid information through National Student Loan Data System (NSLDS).

CONTACT
Anna Griswold, Assistant Vice Provost for Student Aid
201 Shields Building, University Park, PA 16804-3000
(814) 865-6301

Penn State Wilkes-Barre
Lehman, Pennsylvania
www.wb.psu.edu Federal Code: 003329

4-year public branch campus college in small city.
Enrollment: 561 undergrads, 5% part-time. 191 full-time freshmen.
Selectivity: Admits over 75% of applicants.

BASIC COSTS (2012-2013)
Tuition and fees: $13,238; out-of-state residents $19,794.
Per-credit charge: $504; out-of-state residents $793.

FINANCIAL AID PICTURE (2011-2012)
Students with need: Out of 180 full-time freshmen who applied for aid, 138 were judged to have need. Of these, 137 received aid, and 11 had their full need met. Average financial aid package met 66% of need; average scholarship/grant was $6,817; average loan was $3,162. For part-time students, average financial aid package was $4,343.
Students without need: 22 full-time freshmen who did not demonstrate need for aid received scholarships/grants; average award was $3,102. No-need awards available for academics, alumni affiliation, ROTC.
Cumulative student debt: 66% of graduating class had student loans; average debt was $35,100.

FINANCIAL AID PROCEDURES
Forms required: FAFSA.
Dates and Deadlines: Priority date 2/15; no closing date. Applicants notified on a rolling basis.
Transfers: Closing date 5/1. Schools required to obtain student aid information through National Student Loan Data System (NSLDS).

CONTACT
Anna Griswold, Assistant Vice Provost for Student Aid
Hayfield House 101, Lehman, PA 18627-0217
(814) 865-6301

Penn State Worthington Scranton

Dunmore, Pennsylvania
www.sn.psu.edu Federal Code: 003344

4-year public branch campus college in large town.
Enrollment: 1,130 undergrads, 16% part-time. 306 full-time freshmen.
Selectivity: Admits over 75% of applicants.

BASIC COSTS (2012-2013)
Tuition and fees: $13,230; out-of-state residents $19,786.
Per-credit charge: $504; out-of-state residents $793.

FINANCIAL AID PICTURE (2011-2012)
Students with need: Out of 285 full-time freshmen who applied for aid, 244 were judged to have need. Of these, 240 received aid, and 3 had their full need met. Average financial aid package met 61% of need; average scholarship/grant was $6,580; average loan was $3,373. For part-time students, average financial aid package was $6,836.
Students without need: 12 full-time freshmen who did not demonstrate need for aid received scholarships/grants; average award was $2,251. No-need awards available for academics, alumni affiliation, ROTC.
Cumulative student debt: 66% of graduating class had student loans; average debt was $35,100.

FINANCIAL AID PROCEDURES
Forms required: FAFSA.
Dates and Deadlines: Priority date 2/15; no closing date. Applicants notified on a rolling basis.
Transfers: Closing date 5/1. Schools required to obtain student aid information through National Student Loan Data System (NSLDS).

CONTACT
Anna Griswold, Assistant Vice Provost for Student Aid
120 Ridge View Drive, Dunmore, PA 18512-1602
(814) 865-6301

Penn State York

York, Pennsylvania
www.yk.psu.edu Federal Code: 003329

4-year public branch campus college in large town.
Enrollment: 976 undergrads, 18% part-time. 272 full-time freshmen.
Selectivity: Admits over 75% of applicants.

BASIC COSTS (2012-2013)
Tuition and fees: $13,238; out-of-state residents $19,794.
Per-credit charge: $504; out-of-state residents $793.

FINANCIAL AID PICTURE (2011-2012)
Students with need: Out of 240 full-time freshmen who applied for aid, 190 were judged to have need. Of these, 188 received aid, and 17 had their full need met. Average financial aid package met 60% of need; average scholarship/grant was $6,535; average loan was $3,281. For part-time students, average financial aid package was $6,391.
Students without need: 24 full-time freshmen who did not demonstrate need for aid received scholarships/grants; average award was $4,154. No-need awards available for academics, alumni affiliation, ROTC.
Cumulative student debt: 66% of graduating class had student loans; average debt was $35,100.

FINANCIAL AID PROCEDURES
Forms required: FAFSA.
Dates and Deadlines: Priority date 2/15; no closing date. Applicants notified on a rolling basis.
Transfers: Closing date 5/1. Schools required to obtain student aid information through National Student Loan Data System (NSLDS).

CONTACT
Anna Griswold, Assistant Vice Provost for Student Aid
1031 Edgecomb Avenue, York, PA 17403-3398
(814) 865-6301

Pennsylvania Academy of the Fine Arts

Philadelphia, Pennsylvania
www.pafa.edu Federal Code: 014653

4-year private visual arts college in very large city.
Enrollment: 220 undergrads, 4% part-time. 36 full-time freshmen.
Selectivity: Admits over 75% of applicants.

BASIC COSTS (2013-2014)
Tuition and fees: $29,990.
Per-credit charge: $964.

FINANCIAL AID PICTURE (2012-2013)
Students with need: 37% of average financial aid package awarded as scholarships/grants, 63% awarded as loans/jobs. Need-based aid available for part-time students.
Students without need: No-need awards available for academics, art.

FINANCIAL AID PROCEDURES
Forms required: FAFSA.
Dates and Deadlines: Closing date 3/1. Applicants notified on a rolling basis; must reply by 5/1 or within 14 week(s) of notification.
Transfers: Applicants notified on a rolling basis starting 1/31; must reply by 5/1 or within 4 week(s) of notification.

CONTACT
Dana Moore, Director of Financial Aid
128 North Broad Street, Philadelphia, PA 19102
(215) 972-2019

Pennsylvania College of Art and Design

Lancaster, Pennsylvania
www.pcad.edu Federal Code: 016021

4-year private visual arts college in small city.
Enrollment: 247 undergrads, 9% part-time. 62 full-time freshmen.
Selectivity: Admits less than 50% of applicants.

BASIC COSTS (2013-2014)
Tuition and fees: $20,680.
Per-credit charge: $821.

FINANCIAL AID PICTURE (2011-2012)
Students with need: 98% of average financial aid package awarded as scholarships/grants, 2% awarded as loans/jobs. Need-based aid available for part-time students.

FINANCIAL AID PROCEDURES
Forms required: FAFSA, state aid form.
Dates and Deadlines: Applicants notified on a rolling basis starting 4/15.

CONTACT
David Hershey, Director of Financial Aid
PO Box 59, Lancaster, PA 17608-0059

Pennsylvania College of Technology

Williamsport, Pennsylvania
www.pct.edu Federal Code: 003395

4-year public technical college in large town.
Enrollment: 5,599 undergrads, 15% part-time. 1,212 full-time freshmen.

Selectivity: Open admission; but selective for some programs.

BASIC COSTS (2012-2013)

Tuition and fees: $14,370; out-of-state residents $18,000.
Per-credit charge: $400; out-of-state residents $521.
Room and board: $10,500.

FINANCIAL AID PICTURE

Students with need: Need-based aid available for full-time and part-time students. Work study available nights, weekends, and for part-time students.
Students without need: No-need awards available for academics, alumni affiliation, leadership.

FINANCIAL AID PROCEDURES

Forms required: FAFSA, institutional form.
Dates and Deadlines: Priority date 4/15; no closing date. Applicants notified on a rolling basis starting 6/1; must reply by 7/1 or within 4 week(s) of notification.

CONTACT

Candace Baran, Director of Financial Aid
One College Avenue, Williamsport, PA 17701-5799
(570) 327-4766

Pennsylvania Highlands Community College

Johnstown, Pennsylvania
www.pennhighlands.edu Federal Code: 031804

2-year public community college in large town.
Enrollment: 3,015 undergrads.
Selectivity: Open admission.

BASIC COSTS (2012-2013)

Tuition and fees: $4,190; out-of-district residents $7,120; out-of-state residents $10,050.
Per-credit charge: $97; out-of-district residents $194; out-of-state residents $291.
Additional info: Students in Blair, Bedford, Fulton, Huntingdon, and Somerset counties pay a special regional tuition of $5,274.

FINANCIAL AID PICTURE

Students with need: Need-based aid available for full-time and part-time students. Work study available nights.
Students without need: No-need awards available for academics, state/district residency.

FINANCIAL AID PROCEDURES

Forms required: FAFSA.
Dates and Deadlines: Closing date 4/1. Applicants notified on a rolling basis; must reply by 8/1.

CONTACT

Brenda Coughenour, Director of Financial Aid
101 Community College Way, Johnstown, PA 15904
(814) 262-6454

Pennsylvania Institute of Technology

Media, Pennsylvania
www.pit.edu Federal Code: 010998

2-year private junior and technical college in small town.
Enrollment: 760 undergrads.
Selectivity: Open admission; but selective for some programs.

BASIC COSTS (2013-2014)

Tuition and fees: $12,750.
Per-credit charge: $425.
Additional info: Tuition will sometimes vary by program. School of Professional Programs Certificates Tuition is $14,300; Practical Nursing program tuition is $21,500.

FINANCIAL AID PICTURE

Students with need: Need-based aid available for full-time and part-time students.
Students without need: No-need awards available for academics, leadership.
Scholarships offered: Presidential Scholarship; half tuition; for current high school graduates; SAT scores required.
Additional info: Application deadline of May 1 for PHEAA and Philadelphia State Grant aid.

FINANCIAL AID PROCEDURES

Forms required: FAFSA, institutional form.
Dates and Deadlines: Applicants notified on a rolling basis starting 7/1.
Transfers: No deadline.

CONTACT

Kristina Fripps, Director of Financial Aid
800 Manchester Avenue, Media, PA 19063-4098
(610) 892-1536

Pennsylvania School of Business

Allentown, Pennsylvania
www.psb.edu Federal Code: 022552

2-year for-profit career college in small city.
Enrollment: 88 full-time undergrads.
Selectivity: Open admission; but selective for some programs.

BASIC COSTS (2012-2013)

Tuition and fees: $9,275.

FINANCIAL AID PICTURE

Students with need: Need-based aid available for full-time and part-time students.

FINANCIAL AID PROCEDURES

Forms required: FAFSA.
Dates and Deadlines: Applicants notified on a rolling basis.
Transfers: No deadline.

CONTACT

Megan Bauder, Director of Financial Aid
265 Lehigh Street, Allentown, PA 18102
(610) 841-3333

Philadelphia University

Philadelphia, Pennsylvania
www.PhilaU.edu Federal Code: 003354

4-year private university in very large city.
Enrollment: 2,883 undergrads, 7% part-time. 604 full-time freshmen.
Selectivity: Admits 50 to 75% of applicants.

BASIC COSTS (2013-2014)

Tuition and fees: $33,590.
Per-credit charge: $575.
Room and board: $10,660.

FINANCIAL AID PICTURE (2012-2013)

Students with need: Out of 529 full-time freshmen who applied for aid, 464 were judged to have need. Of these, 464 received aid, and 67 had their full need met. Average financial aid package met 74% of need; average

scholarship/grant was $20,708; average loan was $3,997. Need-based aid available for part-time students.
Students without need: 124 full-time freshmen who did not demonstrate need for aid received scholarships/grants; average award was $8,914. No-need awards available for academics, athletics.
Scholarships offered: 16 full-time freshmen received athletic scholarships; average amount $15,475.
Cumulative student debt: 79% of graduating class had student loans; average debt was $39,938.

FINANCIAL AID PROCEDURES
Forms required: FAFSA.
Dates and Deadlines: Closing date 4/15. Applicants notified on a rolling basis starting 2/10; must reply by 5/1.

CONTACT
Lisa Cooper, Director of Financial Aid
School House Lane and Henry Avenue, Philadelphia, PA 19144-5497
(215) 951-2940

Pittsburgh Institute of Aeronautics
Pittsburgh, Pennsylvania
www.pia.edu Federal Code: 005310

2-year private technical college in large city.
Enrollment: 183 undergrads. 58 full-time freshmen.
Selectivity: Open admission.

BASIC COSTS (2012-2013)
Tuition and fees: $14,715.

FINANCIAL AID PICTURE
Students with need: Need-based aid available for full-time students.

FINANCIAL AID PROCEDURES
Forms required: FAFSA.
Dates and Deadlines: Priority date 5/1; no closing date. Applicants notified on a rolling basis.
Transfers: No deadline. Applicants notified on a rolling basis.

CONTACT
Jonathan Vukmanic, Director of Financial Aid
Box 10897, Pittsburgh, PA 15236-0897
(412) 346-2100

Pittsburgh Institute of Mortuary Science
Pittsburgh, Pennsylvania
www.pims.edu Federal Code: 010814

2-year private technical college in large city.
Enrollment: 213 undergrads.

BASIC COSTS (2012-2013)
Tuition and fees: $17,900.
Per-credit charge: $260.

FINANCIAL AID PICTURE
Students with need: Need-based aid available for full-time and part-time students.

FINANCIAL AID PROCEDURES
Forms required: FAFSA.
Dates and Deadlines: Closing date 9/17. Applicants notified on a rolling basis.

CONTACT
Karen Rocco, Financial Aid Officer
5808 Baum Boulevard, Pittsburgh, PA 15206-3706
(412) 362-8500

Point Park University
Pittsburgh, Pennsylvania
www.pointpark.edu Federal Code: 003357

4-year private university in large city.
Enrollment: 3,167 undergrads, 20% part-time. 516 full-time freshmen.
Selectivity: Admits over 75% of applicants.

BASIC COSTS (2012-2013)
Tuition and fees: $25,190.
Per-credit charge: $682.
Room and board: $9,920.
Additional info: Students in Conservatory of Performing Arts (COPA) pay full-time tuition of $30,320 per year ($860 per-credit hour). Required fees, room and board are the same for COPA and non-COPA students.

FINANCIAL AID PICTURE (2012-2013)
Students with need: Average financial aid package met 73% of need; average scholarship/grant was $16,030; average loan was $4,311. For part-time students, average financial aid package was $8,442.
Students without need: No-need awards available for academics, athletics, music/drama.
Cumulative student debt: 79% of graduating class had student loans; average debt was $26,526.

FINANCIAL AID PROCEDURES
Forms required: FAFSA.
Dates and Deadlines: Closing date 12/1. Applicants notified by 2/15; must reply within 2 week(s) of notification.
Transfers: No deadline. Applicants notified on a rolling basis starting 2/15. Merit aid is awarded on GPA only.

CONTACT
Sheila Nelson-Hensley, Director of Financial Aid
201 Wood Street, Pittsburgh, PA 15222-1984
(412) 392-3930

Restaurant School at Walnut Hill College
Philadelphia, Pennsylvania
www.walnuthillcollege.edu Federal Code: 015499

4-year for-profit culinary school and business college in very large city.
Enrollment: 537 undergrads.

FINANCIAL AID PICTURE
Students with need: Need-based aid available for full-time students.
Students without need: No-need awards available for leadership.

FINANCIAL AID PROCEDURES
Forms required: FAFSA, state aid form, institutional form.

CONTACT
Rhonda Moore, Director of Financial Aid
4207 Walnut Street, Philadelphia, PA 19104
(267) 295-2311

Robert Morris University
Moon Township, Pennsylvania
www.rmu.edu Federal Code: 001746

4-year private university in large town.
Enrollment: 4,089 undergrads, 11% part-time. 848 full-time freshmen.
Selectivity: Admits over 75% of applicants.

BASIC COSTS (2013-2014)
Tuition and fees: $25,239.

Per-credit charge: $775.
Room and board: $11,585.

FINANCIAL AID PICTURE (2012-2013)
Students with need: Out of 756 full-time freshmen who applied for aid, 685 were judged to have need. Of these, 685 received aid, and 72 had their full need met. Average financial aid package met 77% of need; average scholarship/grant was $15,786; average loan was $4,398. For part-time students, average financial aid package was $5,714.
Students without need: 128 full-time freshmen who did not demonstrate need for aid received scholarships/grants; average award was $11,118. No-need awards available for academics, athletics, ROTC.
Scholarships offered: 27 full-time freshmen received athletic scholarships; average amount $17,937.
Cumulative student debt: 73% of graduating class had student loans; average debt was $41,093.

FINANCIAL AID PROCEDURES
Forms required: FAFSA.
Dates and Deadlines: Applicants notified on a rolling basis starting 3/1.

CONTACT
Stephanie Hendershot, Director of Financial Aid
6001 University Boulevard, Moon Township, PA 15108-1189
(412) 397-6250

Rosedale Technical Institute
Pittsburgh, Pennsylvania
www.rosedaletech.org Federal Code: 012050

2-year private technical and career college in large city.
Enrollment: 328 undergrads.
Selectivity: Open admission; but selective for some programs.

BASIC COSTS (2012-2013)
Tuition and fees: $12,770.
Additional info: Cost of total program: $25,280 for tuition plus books (vary based on program) and tools (vary based on program).

FINANCIAL AID PICTURE
Students with need: Need-based aid available for full-time students.

FINANCIAL AID PROCEDURES
Forms required: FAFSA.
Dates and Deadlines: Closing date 8/1.

CONTACT
Anna Bartolini, Director of Financial Aid
215 Beecham Drive, Pittsburgh, PA 15205-9791
(412) 521-6200

Rosemont College
Rosemont, Pennsylvania
www.rosemont.edu Federal Code: 003360

4-year private liberal arts college in small town, affiliated with Roman Catholic Church.
Enrollment: 524 undergrads, 19% part-time. 75 full-time freshmen.
Selectivity: Admits less than 50% of applicants.

BASIC COSTS (2012-2013)
Tuition and fees: $30,450.
Per-credit charge: $1,120.
Room and board: $11,900.
Additional info: Tuition/fee waivers available for adults, minority students, unemployed or children of unemployed.

FINANCIAL AID PICTURE
Students with need: Need-based aid available for full-time and part-time students. Work study available nights, weekends, and for part-time students.
Students without need: No-need awards available for academics, alumni affiliation, art, religious affiliation.
Scholarships offered: Kelly Award; for student intending to major in Studio Art. Cornelian Catholic High School Student scholarship; offers 2 full tuition scholarship per year.

FINANCIAL AID PROCEDURES
Forms required: FAFSA.
Dates and Deadlines: Priority date 2/15; no closing date. Applicants notified on a rolling basis starting 3/1; must reply within 4 week(s) of notification.
Transfers: No deadline. Applicants notified on a rolling basis starting 3/1.

CONTACT
LaVerne Glenn, Director of Financial Aid
1400 Montgomery Avenue, Rosemont, PA 19010-1699
(610) 527-0200 ext. 2236

St. Charles Borromeo Seminary - Overbrook
Wynnewood, Pennsylvania
www.scs.edu Federal Code: 016229

4-year private seminary college for men in large town, affiliated with Roman Catholic Church.
Enrollment: 47 undergrads. 7 full-time freshmen.
Selectivity: Admits over 75% of applicants.

BASIC COSTS (2013-2014)
Tuition and fees: $19,500.
Per-credit charge: $555.
Room and board: $12,300.

FINANCIAL AID PICTURE
Students with need: Need-based aid available for full-time students.
Students without need: No-need awards available for religious affiliation.

FINANCIAL AID PROCEDURES
Forms required: FAFSA, institutional form.
Dates and Deadlines: Closing date 4/15. Applicants notified on a rolling basis starting 6/1; must reply by 6/1 or within 4 week(s) of notification.

CONTACT
Nora Downey, Financial Aid Coordinator
100 East Wynnewood Road, Wynnewood, PA 19096
(610) 785-6582

St. Francis University
Loretto, Pennsylvania
www.francis.edu Federal Code: 003366

4-year private university and liberal arts college in rural community, affiliated with Roman Catholic Church.
Enrollment: 1,734 undergrads, 8% part-time. 444 full-time freshmen.
Selectivity: Admits 50 to 75% of applicants.

BASIC COSTS (2013-2014)
Tuition and fees: $29,992.
Per-credit charge: $909.
Room and board: $10,346.
Additional info: Tuition/fee waivers available for adults.

FINANCIAL AID PICTURE (2012-2013)
Students with need: Out of 435 full-time freshmen who applied for aid, 391 were judged to have need. Of these, 391 received aid, and 63 had their

full need met. Average financial aid package met 78% of need; average scholarship/grant was $5,552; average loan was $3,539. For part-time students, average financial aid package was $11,161.
Students without need: 39 full-time freshmen who did not demonstrate need for aid received scholarships/grants; average award was $12,214. No-need awards available for academics, alumni affiliation, athletics, music/drama, religious affiliation.
Scholarships offered: ***Merit:*** Red Flash Co-Curricular Award: $1,000-$6,000; 2.5 GPA minimum. Assisi Scholarship: $3,000-$7,000; 3.2 GPA,1020 SAT, 22 ACT minimum. Presidential Scholarship: $7,500-$10,000; 3.5 GPA, 1100 SAT, 24 ACT minimum. Founders Award: $10,500-$16,000; 3.7 GPA, 1250 SAT, 28 ACT minimum. Franciscan Scholarship: $2,000 over four years awarded to graduates of a Catholic high school. ***Athletic:*** 97 full-time freshmen received athletic scholarships; average amount $17,343.
Cumulative student debt: 78% of graduating class had student loans; average debt was $43,289.

FINANCIAL AID PROCEDURES

Forms required: FAFSA.
Dates and Deadlines: Priority date 5/1; no closing date. Applicants notified on a rolling basis starting 3/1.
Transfers: No deadline. Applicants notified on a rolling basis. Associate degree transfer scholarship based on academic achievement. Returning adult student scholarships available to qualifying transfers after one semester.

CONTACT

Jamie Kosh, Director of Financial Aid
Box 600, Loretto, PA 15940

Saint Joseph's University

Philadelphia, Pennsylvania
www.sju.edu Federal Code: 003367

4-year private university in very large city, affiliated with Roman Catholic Church.
Enrollment: 5,202 undergrads, 15% part-time. 1,229 full-time freshmen.
Selectivity: Admits over 75% of applicants.

BASIC COSTS (2012-2013)

Tuition and fees: $37,830.
Room and board: $12,800.
Additional info: Traditional undergraduate day students taking additional credits over 5 courses pay an additional per-credit-hour fee of $1,201. Part-time, adult undergraduate evening division per-credit-hour fee is $500 (non-traditional, adult continuing education). Business and Psychology majors required to have a laptop but are not required to purchase it from the University.

FINANCIAL AID PICTURE

Students with need: Need-based aid available for full-time and part-time students. Work study available nights, weekends, and for part-time students.
Students without need: No-need awards available for academics, alumni affiliation, art, athletics, minority status, music/drama, ROTC.

FINANCIAL AID PROCEDURES

Forms required: FAFSA.
Dates and Deadlines: Priority date 2/15; no closing date. Applicants notified on a rolling basis starting 3/31; must reply by 5/1.
Transfers: Financial aid for transfer students subject to availability of funds.

CONTACT

Eileen Tucker, Director of Financial Aid
5600 City Avenue, Philadelphia, PA 19131
(610) 660-1555

St. Vincent College

Latrobe, Pennsylvania
www.stvincent.edu Federal Code: 003368

4-year private liberal arts college in large town, affiliated with Roman Catholic Church.
Enrollment: 1,485 undergrads, 2% part-time. 339 full-time freshmen.
Selectivity: Admits 50 to 75% of applicants.

BASIC COSTS (2012-2013)

Tuition and fees: $29,312.
Per-credit charge: $892.
Room and board: $9,594.

FINANCIAL AID PICTURE

Students with need: Need-based aid available for full-time and part-time students. Work study available nights, weekends, and for part-time students.
Students without need: No-need awards available for academics, alumni affiliation, leadership, minority status, religious affiliation.
Scholarships offered: Academic Merit Scholarship: $5,000 to $14,000, based on high school GPA, class rank, and SAT scores. Leadership Merit Grant: $500 to $3,000, based on extracurricular activities and recommendations. Competitive scholarships from $4,000 to full tuition.

FINANCIAL AID PROCEDURES

Forms required: FAFSA, state aid form.
Dates and Deadlines: Priority date 3/1; no closing date. Applicants notified on a rolling basis starting 3/1; must reply within 2 week(s) of notification.
Transfers: Applicants notified on a rolling basis starting 3/1; must reply within 2 week(s) of notification.

CONTACT

George Santucci, Director of Financial Aid
300 Fraser Purchase Road, Latrobe, PA 15650-2690
(800) 782-5549

Sanford-Brown Institute: Monroeville

Pittsburgh, Pennsylvania
www.sanfordbrown.edu Federal Code: 022023

2-year for-profit health science and career college in large town.
Enrollment: 602 undergrads.
Selectivity: Open admission; but selective for some programs.

BASIC COSTS (2012-2013)

Additional info: Program tuition and fees for associate degrees vary from $23,253 to $41,472; diploma programs vary from $11,284 to $16,224.

FINANCIAL AID PICTURE

Students with need: Need-based aid available for full-time and part-time students.

FINANCIAL AID PROCEDURES

Dates and Deadlines: Applicants notified on a rolling basis.

CONTACT

Kim Dankis, Director of Financial Aid
777 Penn Center Boulevard, Pittsburgh, PA 15235
(412) 373-6400 ext. 12

Seton Hill University

Greensburg, Pennsylvania
www.setonhill.edu Federal Code: 003362

4-year private university and liberal arts college in large town, affiliated with Roman Catholic Church.

Enrollment: 1,576 undergrads, 8% part-time. 347 full-time freshmen.
Selectivity: Admits 50 to 75% of applicants.

BASIC COSTS (2013-2014)
Tuition and fees: $30,300.
Per-credit charge: $780.
Room and board: $10,100.
Additional info: Required fees vary according to what technology plan student chooses and by number of credits if part-time. Various options available for room and board. Tuition/fee waivers available for adults.

FINANCIAL AID PICTURE (2012-2013)
Students with need: Out of 337 full-time freshmen who applied for aid, 316 were judged to have need. Of these, 316 received aid, and 59 had their full need met. Average financial aid package met 76% of need; average scholarship/grant was $19,742; average loan was $5,069. For part-time students, average financial aid package was $6,557.
Students without need: 35 full-time freshmen who did not demonstrate need for aid received scholarships/grants; average award was $9,769. No-need awards available for academics, alumni affiliation, art, athletics, music/drama.
Scholarships offered: ***Merit:*** Presidential and Seton Scholarships; up to full tuition per academic year; given to top students. ***Athletic:*** 30 full-time freshmen received athletic scholarships; average amount $12,540.
Cumulative student debt: 90% of graduating class had student loans; average debt was $32,290.

FINANCIAL AID PROCEDURES
Forms required: FAFSA, state aid form, institutional form.
Dates and Deadlines: Closing date 5/1. Applicants notified on a rolling basis starting 11/30; must reply by 5/1.
Transfers: Priority date 8/1; closing date 8/15. Applicants notified on a rolling basis starting 1/1; must reply within 2 week(s) of notification. Scholarship available for full-time transfer students with 3.5 GPA.

CONTACT
Maryann Dudas, Director of Financial Aid
1 Seton Hill Drive, Greensburg, PA 15601
(724) 838-4293

Shippensburg University of Pennsylvania

Shippensburg, Pennsylvania
www.ship.edu Federal Code: 003326

4-year public university in small town.
Enrollment: 6,654 undergrads, 5% part-time. 1,480 full-time freshmen.
Selectivity: Admits over 75% of applicants.

BASIC COSTS (2012-2013)
Tuition and fees: $9,154; out-of-state residents $17,190.
Room and board: $7,910.
Additional info: Tuition is $9,642 per year for Dual Admit students and $11,250 for STEM and high-achieving out-of-state students.

FINANCIAL AID PICTURE (2012-2013)
Students with need: Average financial aid package met 56% of need; average scholarship/grant was $6,086; average loan was $3,339. For part-time students, average financial aid package was $6,562.
Students without need: No-need awards available for academics, athletics.
Cumulative student debt: 78% of graduating class had student loans; average debt was $27,661.

FINANCIAL AID PROCEDURES
Forms required: FAFSA.
Dates and Deadlines: Priority date 3/15; no closing date. Applicants notified on a rolling basis; must reply within 2 week(s) of notification.
Transfers: No deadline. Applicants notified on a rolling basis; must reply within 2 week(s) of notification.

CONTACT
Sandra Tarbox, Director of Financial Aid
1871 Old Main Drive, Shippensburg, PA 17257-2299
(717) 477-1131

Slippery Rock University of Pennsylvania

Slippery Rock, Pennsylvania
www.sru.edu Federal Code: 003327

4-year public university in small town.
Enrollment: 7,769 undergrads, 6% part-time. 1,544 full-time freshmen.
Selectivity: Admits 50 to 75% of applicants.

BASIC COSTS (2012-2013)
Tuition and fees: $8,747; out-of-state residents $11,961.
Room and board: $9,364.

FINANCIAL AID PICTURE (2012-2013)
Students with need: Out of 1,445 full-time freshmen who applied for aid, 1,118 were judged to have need. Of these, 1,113 received aid, and 141 had their full need met. Average financial aid package met 58% of need; average scholarship/grant was $5,608; average loan was $3,508. For part-time students, average financial aid package was $6,048.
Students without need: 109 full-time freshmen who did not demonstrate need for aid received scholarships/grants; average award was $2,177. No-need awards available for academics, alumni affiliation, art, athletics, job skills, leadership, minority status, music/drama, ROTC, state/district residency.
Scholarships offered: 78 full-time freshmen received athletic scholarships; average amount $3,188.
Cumulative student debt: 85% of graduating class had student loans; average debt was $28,959.
Additional info: May 1 closing date for Pennsylvania state grants.

FINANCIAL AID PROCEDURES
Forms required: FAFSA.
Dates and Deadlines: Priority date 5/1; no closing date. Applicants notified on a rolling basis starting 3/15.

CONTACT
Patricia Hladio, Director of Financial Aid
1 Morrow Way, Slippery Rock, PA 16057-1383
(724) 738-2044

Susquehanna University

Selinsgrove, Pennsylvania Federal Code: 003369
www.susqu.edu CSS Code: 2820

4-year private university and liberal arts college in small town, affiliated with Evangelical Lutheran Church in America.
Enrollment: 2,151 undergrads, 1% part-time. 631 full-time freshmen.
Selectivity: Admits over 75% of applicants.

BASIC COSTS (2013-2014)
Tuition and fees: $38,780.
Per-credit charge: $1,215.
Room and board: $10,390.

FINANCIAL AID PICTURE (2012-2013)
Students with need: Out of 548 full-time freshmen who applied for aid, 476 were judged to have need. Of these, 476 received aid, and 92 had their full need met. Average financial aid package met 82% of need; average

scholarship/grant was $24,649; average loan was $3,265. For part-time students, average financial aid package was $2,825.
Students without need: 146 full-time freshmen who did not demonstrate need for aid received scholarships/grants; average award was $13,726. No-need awards available for academics, alumni affiliation, leadership, minority status, music/drama, ROTC.
Scholarships offered: Academic scholarships; $1,000 to $16,000; renewable annually; based on outstanding academic achievement, personal accomplishment, and/or musical talent. Alumni scholarships; $2,500; for 5 new legacy students with best academic records. Annual scholarships; $2,500; to dependent children of ordained Lutheran clergy. Founder Scholarships; Full tuition; renewable annually; based on outstanding academic achievement and personal accomplishment. University Assistantships; beginning at $5,000 annually, includes professional work experience with a faculty or staff mentor.
Cumulative student debt: 76% of graduating class had student loans; average debt was $32,952.
Additional info: Graduated pay scale for federal work-study program. $1,000 Visit Grant awarded to enrolling students who make an official campus visit between March 1 of sophomore year and March 1 of senior year of high school.

FINANCIAL AID PROCEDURES

Forms required: FAFSA, CSS PROFILE.
Dates and Deadlines: Priority date 3/1; closing date 5/1. Applicants notified on a rolling basis starting 3/15; must reply by 5/1.
Transfers: Priority date 5/1; closing date 7/1. Applicants notified on a rolling basis. Transfer students eligible for financial aid and scholarship consideration.

CONTACT

Helen Nunn, Director of Financial Aid
514 University Avenue, Selinsgrove, PA 17870-1164
(570) 372-4450

Swarthmore College

Swarthmore, Pennsylvania — Federal Code: 003370
www.swarthmore.edu — CSS Code: 2821

4-year private liberal arts college in small town.
Enrollment: 1,532 undergrads. 378 full-time freshmen.
Selectivity: Admits less than 50% of applicants.

BASIC COSTS (2013-2014)

Tuition and fees: $44,718.
Room and board: $13,152.

FINANCIAL AID PICTURE (2012-2013)

Students with need: Out of 251 full-time freshmen who applied for aid, 184 were judged to have need. Of these, 184 received aid, and 184 had their full need met. Average financial aid package met 100% of need; average scholarship/grant was $37,775.
Students without need: 2 full-time freshmen who did not demonstrate need for aid received scholarships/grants; average award was $42,744. No-need awards available for academics, leadership, state/district residency.
Cumulative student debt: 34% of graduating class had student loans; average debt was $20,020.
Additional info: Swarthmore maintains a need-blind admissions policy for U.S. citizens and permanent residents, wherein admission and financial aid decisions are made independently. Financial aid is also available for some international students. All Swarthmore aid awards are loan-free and are packaged to meet the full demonstrated need for admitted students.

FINANCIAL AID PROCEDURES

Forms required: FAFSA, CSS PROFILE, state aid form, institutional form.
Dates and Deadlines: Closing date 2/15. Applicants notified by 4/1; must reply by 5/1.
Transfers: Closing date 4/1. Applicants notified by 5/15. No aid consideration for foreign national transfer applicants.

CONTACT

Laura Talbot, Director of Financial Aid
500 College Avenue, Swarthmore, PA 19081
(610) 328-8358

Talmudical Yeshiva of Philadelphia

Philadelphia, Pennsylvania — Federal Code: 012523

4-year private rabbinical college for men in very large city, affiliated with Jewish faith.
Enrollment: 120 undergrads. 34 full-time freshmen.
Selectivity: Admits over 75% of applicants.

BASIC COSTS (2013-2014)

Tuition and fees: $8,650.
Room and board: $7,000.

FINANCIAL AID PICTURE (2011-2012)

Students with need: 97% of average financial aid package awarded as scholarships/grants, 3% awarded as loans/jobs.
Students without need: This college awards aid only to students with need.

FINANCIAL AID PROCEDURES

Forms required: FAFSA, institutional form.
Dates and Deadlines: Priority date 8/1; closing date 5/1. Applicants notified on a rolling basis starting 3/15; must reply within 2 week(s) of notification.

CONTACT

Chaya Hoberman, Financial Aid Officer
6063 Drexel Road, Philadelphia, PA 19131
(215) 477-1000

Temple University

Philadelphia, Pennsylvania
www.temple.edu — Federal Code: 003371

4-year public university in very large city.
Enrollment: 26,981 undergrads, 10% part-time. 4,259 full-time freshmen.
Selectivity: Admits 50 to 75% of applicants.

BASIC COSTS (2012-2013)

Tuition and fees: $13,596; out-of-state residents $23,422.
Per-credit charge: $502; out-of-state residents $813.
Room and board: $10,276.

FINANCIAL AID PICTURE (2011-2012)

Students with need: Out of 3,730 full-time freshmen who applied for aid, 2,947 were judged to have need. Of these, 2,893 received aid, and 878 had their full need met. Average financial aid package met 70% of need; average scholarship/grant was $6,206; average loan was $3,594. For part-time students, average financial aid package was $10,390.
Students without need: 535 full-time freshmen who did not demonstrate need for aid received scholarships/grants; average award was $4,604. No-need awards available for academics, art, athletics, music/drama, ROTC.
Scholarships offered: 76 full-time freshmen received athletic scholarships; average amount $20,709.
Cumulative student debt: 76% of graduating class had student loans; average debt was $33,500.

FINANCIAL AID PROCEDURES

Forms required: FAFSA.
Dates and Deadlines: Closing date 3/1. Applicants notified on a rolling basis starting 2/15; must reply by 5/1 or within 3 week(s) of notification.

Transfers: Priority date 3/1; no deadline. Must reply within 2 week(s) of notification.

CONTACT

John Morris, Director, Student Financial Services
103 Conwell Hall, Philadelphia, PA 19122-6096
(215) 204-2244

Thaddeus Stevens College of Technology

Lancaster, Pennsylvania
www.stevenscollege.edu Federal Code: 007912

2-year public technical and career college in small city.
Enrollment: 790 undergrads. 486 full-time freshmen.
Selectivity: Admits less than 50% of applicants.

BASIC COSTS (2012-2013)

Tuition and fees: $7,030; out-of-state residents $7,030.
Room and board: $8,100.
Additional info: Tuition/fee waivers available for unemployed or children of unemployed.

FINANCIAL AID PICTURE (2012-2013)

Students with need: 89% of average financial aid package awarded as scholarships/grants, 11% awarded as loans/jobs.
Additional info: Tuition and room and board costs waived for students with adjusted family income of $18,500 or less. Tuition and other costs also waived for orphans.

FINANCIAL AID PROCEDURES

Dates and Deadlines: Priority date 3/15; no closing date. Applicants notified on a rolling basis starting 7/15.

CONTACT

Michael Degroft, Director of Financial Aid & Registrar
750 East King Street, Lancaster, PA 17602
(717) 299-7796

Thiel College

Greenville, Pennsylvania
www.thiel.edu Federal Code: 003376

4-year private liberal arts college in small town, affiliated with Evangelical Lutheran Church in America.
Enrollment: 1,023 undergrads, 1% part-time. 371 full-time freshmen.
Selectivity: Admits 50 to 75% of applicants.

BASIC COSTS (2013-2014)

Tuition and fees: $26,952.
Per-credit charge: $834.
Room and board: $10,476.
Additional info: Required fees Include technology fee of $950; student services fee of $630; health & wellness fee of $224; auto permit $150 (waived if no vehicle is brought to campus). Required laptop fee included in aforementioned $950 technology fee. Incoming freshman are charged an additional $300 First Year Experience fee.

FINANCIAL AID PICTURE (2011-2012)

Students with need: Out of 370 full-time freshmen who applied for aid, 268 were judged to have need. Of these, 268 received aid, and 37 had their full need met. Average financial aid package met 70% of need; average scholarship/grant was $16,810; average loan was $3,775. For part-time students, average financial aid package was $13,302.
Students without need: 21 full-time freshmen who did not demonstrate need for aid received scholarships/grants; average award was $10,636. No-need awards available for academics, alumni affiliation, leadership, music/drama, religious affiliation.
Cumulative student debt: 86% of graduating class had student loans; average debt was $31,077.

FINANCIAL AID PROCEDURES

Forms required: FAFSA, state aid form.
Dates and Deadlines: Priority date 3/15; no closing date. Applicants notified on a rolling basis starting 2/15; must reply within 2 week(s) of notification.
Transfers: Priority date 6/1; no deadline. Applicants notified on a rolling basis starting 2/15; must reply within 2 week(s) of notification.

CONTACT

Cynthia Farrell, Executive Director of Student Financial Services
75 College Avenue, Greenville, PA 16125-2181
(724) 589-2250

Thomas Jefferson University: College of Health Professions

Philadelphia, Pennsylvania
www.jefferson.edu Federal Code: 012393

Upper-division private health science and nursing college in very large city.
Enrollment: 902 undergrads.

BASIC COSTS (2013-2014)

Additional info: Costs vary according to program. Examples of full-time (academic year) tuition rates for bachelor's degree programs in radiologic sciences and bioscience technology, $29,337; bachelor's degree program in occupational therapy, $29,533. All full-time students pay an annual technology fee, $408, and library fee, $306. On-campus room and board, $10,215.

FINANCIAL AID PICTURE

Students with need: Need-based aid available for full-time students.
Students without need: No-need awards available for academics, leadership, state/district residency.
Scholarships offered: Range of merit-based scholarships available for selected applicants.

FINANCIAL AID PROCEDURES

Forms required: FAFSA, institutional form.
Dates and Deadlines: Closing date 4/1. Applicants notified on a rolling basis starting 4/1; must reply within 2 week(s) of notification.
Transfers: Applicants notified on a rolling basis starting 11/15; must reply within 2 week(s) of notification.

CONTACT

Susan McFadden, University Director of Financial Aid
130 South Ninth Street, Edison Building, Suite 100, Philadelphia, PA 19107
(215) 955-2867

Triangle Tech: Bethlehem

Bethlehem, Pennsylvania
www.triangle-tech.edu Federal Code: 014895

2-year for-profit branch campus and technical college in small city.
Enrollment: 130 undergrads. 99 full-time freshmen.
Selectivity: Open admission.

BASIC COSTS (2012-2013)

Tuition and fees: $16,292.

FINANCIAL AID PICTURE (2011-2012)

Students with need: Out of 96 full-time freshmen who applied for aid, 96 were judged to have need. Of these, 96 received aid. Average financial aid package met 74% of need; average scholarship/grant was $7,206; average loan was $4,172. Need-based aid available for part-time students.
Cumulative student debt: 86% of graduating class had student loans; average debt was $11,026.

FINANCIAL AID PROCEDURES
Forms required: FAFSA.
Dates and Deadlines: Applicants notified on a rolling basis.

CONTACT
Catherine Waxter, Director of Financial Aid
3184 Airport Road, Bethlehem, PA 18017
(610) 266-2910

Triangle Tech: DuBois

DuBois, Pennsylvania
www.triangle-tech.edu Federal Code: 021744

2-year for-profit technical college in large town.
Enrollment: 172 undergrads. 87 full-time freshmen.
Selectivity: Open admission.

BASIC COSTS (2012-2013)
Tuition and fees: $16,191.

FINANCIAL AID PICTURE (2011-2012)
Students with need: Out of 85 full-time freshmen who applied for aid, 81 were judged to have need. Of these, 81 received aid, and 20 had their full need met. Average financial aid package met 25% of need; average scholarship/grant was $4,763; average loan was $2,528. Need-based aid available for part-time students.
Students without need: This college awards aid only to students with need.

FINANCIAL AID PROCEDURES
Forms required: FAFSA, state aid form, institutional form.
Dates and Deadlines: Applicants notified on a rolling basis.

CONTACT
Catherine Waxter, Corporate Director of Financial Aid
PO Box 551, DuBois, PA 15801-0551
(724) 832-1050

Triangle Tech: Erie

Erie, Pennsylvania
www.triangle-tech.edu Federal Code: 014417

2-year for-profit technical and career college in small city.
Enrollment: 86 undergrads. 100 full-time freshmen.
Selectivity: Open admission.

BASIC COSTS (2012-2013)
Tuition and fees: $16,062.

FINANCIAL AID PICTURE (2011-2012)
Students with need: Out of 94 full-time freshmen who applied for aid, 92 were judged to have need. Of these, 92 received aid, and 70 had their full need met. Average financial aid package met 76% of need; average scholarship/grant was $6,704; average loan was $3,856. Need-based aid available for part-time students.
Students without need: This college awards aid only to students with need.

FINANCIAL AID PROCEDURES
Forms required: FAFSA.
Dates and Deadlines: Applicants notified on a rolling basis.

CONTACT
Cathy Waxter, Corporate Director of Financial Aid
2000 Liberty Street, Erie, PA 16502-2594
(724) 832-1050

Triangle Tech: Greensburg

Greensburg, Pennsylvania
www.triangle-tech.edu Federal Code: 014895

2-year for-profit technical college in large town.
Enrollment: 165 undergrads. 128 full-time freshmen.
Selectivity: Open admission.

BASIC COSTS (2012-2013)
Tuition and fees: $16,052.

FINANCIAL AID PICTURE (2011-2012)
Students with need: Out of 121 full-time freshmen who applied for aid, 112 were judged to have need. Of these, 112 received aid, and 20 had their full need met. Average financial aid package met 18% of need; average scholarship/grant was $7,354; average loan was $4,302. Need-based aid available for part-time students.
Cumulative student debt: 73% of graduating class had student loans; average debt was $7,951.

FINANCIAL AID PROCEDURES
Forms required: FAFSA, institutional form.
Dates and Deadlines: Applicants notified on a rolling basis starting 1/1.
Transfers: No deadline.

CONTACT
Catherine Waxter, Director of Financial Aid
222 East Pittsburgh Street, Suite A, Greensburg, PA 15601-3304
(724) 832-1050

Triangle Tech: Pittsburgh

Pittsburgh, Pennsylvania
www.triangle-tech.edu Federal Code: 007839

2-year for-profit technical college in large city.
Enrollment: 265 undergrads. 90 full-time freshmen.
Selectivity: Open admission; but selective for some programs.

BASIC COSTS (2012-2013)
Tuition and fees: $16,157.

FINANCIAL AID PICTURE
Students with need: Need-based aid available for full-time and part-time students. Work study available nights.
Students without need: No-need awards available for academics, state/district residency.

FINANCIAL AID PROCEDURES
Forms required: FAFSA, institutional form.
Dates and Deadlines: Applicants notified on a rolling basis.
Transfers: No deadline.

CONTACT
Cathy Waxter, Corporate Director of Financial Aid
1940 Perrysville Avenue, Pittsburgh, PA 15214-3897
(412) 359-1000

Triangle Tech: Sunbury

Sunbury, Pennsylvania
www.triangle-tech.edu

2-year for-profit technical college in large town.
Enrollment: 107 undergrads. 60 full-time freshmen.
Selectivity: Open admission.

BASIC COSTS (2013-2014)
Tuition and fees: $16,292.

FINANCIAL AID PICTURE (2011-2012)
Students with need: Out of 52 full-time freshmen who applied for aid, 46 were judged to have need. Of these, 46 received aid, and 44 had their full need met. Average financial aid package met 98% of need; average scholarship/grant was $6,658; average loan was $3,974. Need-based aid available for part-time students.
Students without need: 1 full-time freshmen who did not demonstrate need for aid received scholarships/grants; average award was $5,459.
Cumulative student debt: 82% of graduating class had student loans; average debt was $6,500.

FINANCIAL AID PROCEDURES
Forms required: FAFSA, institutional form.
Dates and Deadlines: Applicants notified on a rolling basis.
Transfers: No deadline.

CONTACT
Cathy Waxter, Director of Financial Aid
191 Performance Road, Sunbury, PA 17801

University of Pennsylvania

Philadelphia, Pennsylvania — Federal Code: 003378
www.upenn.edu — CSS Code: 2926

4-year private university in very large city.
Enrollment: 9,839 undergrads, 3% part-time. 2,467 full-time freshmen.
Selectivity: Admits less than 50% of applicants.

BASIC COSTS (2012-2013)
Tuition and fees: $43,566.
Per-credit charge: $1,247.
Room and board: $12,368.

FINANCIAL AID PICTURE (2011-2012)
Students with need: Out of 1,376 full-time freshmen who applied for aid, 1,170 were judged to have need. Of these, 1,170 received aid, and 1,170 had their full need met. Average financial aid package met 100% of need; average scholarship/grant was $38,414; average loan was $212. Need-based aid available for part-time students.
Students without need: This college awards aid only to students with need.
Cumulative student debt: 38% of graduating class had student loans; average debt was $21,190.
Additional info: All loans have been eliminated from need-based aid packages.

FINANCIAL AID PROCEDURES
Forms required: FAFSA, CSS PROFILE, institutional form.
Dates and Deadlines: Priority date 2/15; no closing date. Applicants notified on a rolling basis starting 4/1; must reply by 5/1.
Transfers: Priority date 3/15. Applicants notified on a rolling basis starting 5/15; must reply within 4 week(s) of notification.

CONTACT
Joel Carstens, Director of Financial Aid
1 College Hall, Philadelphia, PA 19104-6376
(215) 898-1988

University of Pittsburgh

Pittsburgh, Pennsylvania
www.pitt.edu — Federal Code: 008815

4-year public university in large city.
Enrollment: 18,105 undergrads, 5% part-time. 3,707 full-time freshmen.
Selectivity: Admits 50 to 75% of applicants. GED not accepted.

BASIC COSTS (2012-2013)
Tuition and fees: $16,590; out-of-state residents $26,280.
Per-credit charge: $655; out-of-state residents $1,059.
Room and board: $9,870.

FINANCIAL AID PICTURE (2011-2012)
Students with need: Out of 3,034 full-time freshmen who applied for aid, 2,129 were judged to have need. Of these, 2,051 received aid, and 269 had their full need met. Average financial aid package met 60% of need; average scholarship/grant was $8,653; average loan was $4,311. For part-time students, average financial aid package was $6,467.
Students without need: 203 full-time freshmen who did not demonstrate need for aid received scholarships/grants; average award was $11,177. No-need awards available for academics, athletics.
Scholarships offered: ***Merit:*** Academic Scholarships; $1,000 to full tuition, room and board; renewable up to 4 years with 3.0 GPA. ***Athletic:*** 68 full-time freshmen received athletic scholarships; average amount $14,673.
Cumulative student debt: 67% of graduating class had student loans; average debt was $33,662.

FINANCIAL AID PROCEDURES
Forms required: FAFSA.
Dates and Deadlines: Priority date 3/1; no closing date. Applicants notified on a rolling basis starting 3/15.
Transfers: Priority date 5/1; no deadline. Applicants notified on a rolling basis. Transfer students not eligible for freshman scholarships.

CONTACT
Marc Harding, Chief Enrollment Officer
4227 Fifth Avenue, 1st Floor, Alumni Hall, Pittsburgh, PA 15260
(412) 624-7488

University of Pittsburgh at Bradford

Bradford, Pennsylvania
www.upb.pitt.edu — Federal Code: 003380

4-year public university in large town.
Enrollment: 1,495 undergrads, 8% part-time. 363 full-time freshmen.
Selectivity: Admits over 75% of applicants.

BASIC COSTS (2012-2013)
Tuition and fees: $12,890; out-of-state residents $23,286.
Per-credit charge: $498; out-of-state residents $931.
Room and board: $7,960.

FINANCIAL AID PICTURE (2011-2012)
Students with need: Out of 347 full-time freshmen who applied for aid, 312 were judged to have need. Of these, 312 received aid, and 69 had their full need met. Average financial aid package met 66% of need; average scholarship/grant was $9,313; average loan was $3,464. For part-time students, average financial aid package was $6,472.
Students without need: 35 full-time freshmen who did not demonstrate need for aid received scholarships/grants; average award was $6,660. No-need awards available for academics, alumni affiliation, ROTC, state/district residency.
Scholarships offered: Panther Scholarship; for full-time on-campus residents or students who commute from Cameron, Elk, Forest, McKean, Potter, or Warren counties. Valedictorian/Salutatorian Scholarship; for Pennsylvania students. International Student Scholarship; for international students who plan to enroll full-time and reside on campus.
Cumulative student debt: 85% of graduating class had student loans; average debt was $30,415.

FINANCIAL AID PROCEDURES
Forms required: FAFSA.
Dates and Deadlines: Priority date 3/1; no closing date. Applicants notified on a rolling basis starting 4/1; must reply within 2 week(s) of notification.

Transfers: No deadline. Applicants notified on a rolling basis starting 4/1; must reply within 2 week(s) of notification. Transfers must meet academic policy guidelines.

CONTACT

Melissa Ibanez, Director of Financial Aid
300 Campus Drive, Bradford, PA 16701
(814) 362-7550

University of Pittsburgh at Greensburg

Greensburg, Pennsylvania
www.greensburg.pitt.edu Federal Code: 003381

4-year public branch campus and liberal arts college in large town.
Enrollment: 1,722 undergrads, 7% part-time. 415 full-time freshmen.
Selectivity: Admits over 75% of applicants.

BASIC COSTS (2012-2013)

Tuition and fees: $12,890; out-of-state residents $23,286.
Per-credit charge: $498; out-of-state residents $931.
Room and board: $9,030.

FINANCIAL AID PICTURE (2011-2012)

Students with need: Out of 391 full-time freshmen who applied for aid, 351 were judged to have need. Of these, 351 received aid, and 43 had their full need met. Average financial aid package met 46% of need; average scholarship/grant was $7,449; average loan was $3,409. For part-time students, average financial aid package was $5,311.
Students without need: 22 full-time freshmen who did not demonstrate need for aid received scholarships/grants; average award was $5,038. No-need awards available for academics, leadership, minority status, state/district residency.
Cumulative student debt: 83% of graduating class had student loans; average debt was $33,095.

FINANCIAL AID PROCEDURES

Forms required: FAFSA, state aid form.
Dates and Deadlines: Priority date 2/15; no closing date. Applicants notified on a rolling basis starting 3/15; must reply within 3 week(s) of notification.
Transfers: No deadline.

CONTACT

Brandi Darr, Director of Financial Aid
150 Finoli Drive, Greensburg, PA 15601
(724) 836-9881

University of Pittsburgh at Johnstown

Johnstown, Pennsylvania
www.upj.pitt.edu Federal Code: 008815

4-year public engineering and liberal arts college in small city.
Enrollment: 2,930 undergrads, 4% part-time. 732 full-time freshmen.
Selectivity: Admits over 75% of applicants.

BASIC COSTS (2012-2013)

Tuition and fees: $12,892; out-of-state residents $23,288.
Per-credit charge: $498; out-of-state residents $931.
Room and board: $8,230.

FINANCIAL AID PICTURE (2011-2012)

Students with need: Out of 663 full-time freshmen who applied for aid, 564 were judged to have need. Of these, 560 received aid, and 68 had their full need met. Average financial aid package met 54% of need; average scholarship/grant was $6,362; average loan was $3,833. For part-time students, average financial aid package was $5,662.
Students without need: 19 full-time freshmen who did not demonstrate need for aid received scholarships/grants; average award was $4,984. No-need awards available for academics, alumni affiliation, athletics, leadership, minority status, state/district residency.
Scholarships offered: ***Merit:*** President's Scholarships and Leadership Scholarships; $1,500 to full tuition yearly; renewable; 1220 SAT (exclusive of Writing), 3.8 GPA, and top 10% of graduating class required; priority given to those who apply by 12/1. ***Athletic:*** 42 full-time freshmen received athletic scholarships; average amount $4,863.
Cumulative student debt: 81% of graduating class had student loans; average debt was $30,058.

FINANCIAL AID PROCEDURES

Forms required: FAFSA, state aid form.
Dates and Deadlines: Priority date 4/1; no closing date. Applicants notified on a rolling basis starting 3/1; must reply within 2 week(s) of notification.

CONTACT

Jeanine Lawn, Director of Financial Aid
450 Schoolhouse Road, 157 Blackington Hall, Johnstown, PA 15904-1200
(800) 881-5544

University of Pittsburgh at Titusville

Titusville, Pennsylvania
www.upt.pitt.edu Federal Code: 008815

2-year public branch campus and liberal arts college in small town.
Enrollment: 386 undergrads, 19% part-time. 193 full-time freshmen.
Selectivity: Admits over 75% of applicants.

BASIC COSTS (2012-2013)

Tuition and fees: $11,324; out-of-state residents $20,698.
Per-credit charge: $439; out-of-state residents $829.
Room and board: $9,364.

FINANCIAL AID PICTURE (2011-2012)

Students with need: Out of 193 full-time freshmen who applied for aid, 182 were judged to have need. Of these, 182 received aid. Average financial aid package met 58% of need; average scholarship/grant was $1,899; average loan was $2,509. For part-time students, average financial aid package was $7,183.
Students without need: 10 full-time freshmen who did not demonstrate need for aid received scholarships/grants; average award was $3,040. No-need awards available for academics, athletics, state/district residency.
Scholarships offered: Rees scholarships; $2,000; awarded to top 5 students with science as a major; renewable with 3.0 GPA and continued science major. Presidential scholarships; $2,500; based on high school academic record; 10 awarded.

FINANCIAL AID PROCEDURES

Forms required: FAFSA.
Dates and Deadlines: Priority date 3/1; no closing date. Applicants notified on a rolling basis starting 4/1; must reply within 2 week(s) of notification.
Transfers: No deadline. Applicants notified on a rolling basis starting 4/1; must reply within 2 week(s) of notification. Pennsylvania residents must apply by 5/1 for PHEAA. Transfer students must have completed 24 credits to renew. Information retrieved from NSLDS is utilized to determine transfer student eligibility for financial aid.

CONTACT

Melissa Ibanez, Director of Financial Aid
UPT Admissions Office, Titusville, PA 16354-0287
(814) 827-4495

University of Scranton

Scranton, Pennsylvania
www.scranton.edu Federal Code: 003384

4-year private university and liberal arts college in small city, affiliated with Roman Catholic Church.
Enrollment: 3,927 undergrads, 3% part-time. 1,044 full-time freshmen.
Selectivity: Admits 50 to 75% of applicants.

BASIC COSTS (2012-2013)
Tuition and fees: $37,456.
Per-credit charge: $955.
Room and board: $12,804.

FINANCIAL AID PICTURE (2011-2012)
Students with need: Out of 945 full-time freshmen who applied for aid, 811 were judged to have need. Of these, 806 received aid, and 85 had their full need met. Average financial aid package met 66% of need; average scholarship/grant was $18,787; average loan was $6,786. For part-time students, average financial aid package was $8,615.
Students without need: 140 full-time freshmen who did not demonstrate need for aid received scholarships/grants; average award was $12,481. No-need awards available for academics, ROTC.
Cumulative student debt: 75% of graduating class had student loans; average debt was $34,260.

FINANCIAL AID PROCEDURES
Forms required: FAFSA.
Dates and Deadlines: Priority date 2/15; no closing date. Applicants notified on a rolling basis starting 3/15; must reply by 5/1 or within 2 week(s) of notification.
Transfers: Institutional grants available based on financial need.

CONTACT
William Burke, Director of Financial Aid
800 Linden Street, Scranton, PA 18510-4699
(570) 941-7700

University of the Arts

Philadelphia, Pennsylvania
www.uarts.edu Federal Code: 003350

4-year private visual arts and performing arts college in very large city.
Enrollment: 1,881 undergrads, 2% part-time. 414 full-time freshmen.
Selectivity: Admits 50 to 75% of applicants.

BASIC COSTS (2012-2013)
Tuition and fees: $34,840.
Per-credit charge: $1,452.
Room and board: $12,700.
Additional info: Students should set aside funds for a mandatory laptop.

FINANCIAL AID PICTURE
Students with need: Need-based aid available for full-time and part-time students. Work study available nights, weekends, and for part-time students.
Students without need: No-need awards available for academics, art, music/drama.
Scholarships offered: Merit awards; available to students who demonstrate exceptional talent and academic abilities.

FINANCIAL AID PROCEDURES
Forms required: FAFSA.
Dates and Deadlines: Priority date 3/1; no closing date. Applicants notified on a rolling basis starting 3/15; must reply within 2 week(s) of notification.
Transfers: Undergraduate transfers not eligible for federal, state, or university aid if 4-year degree previously conferred.

CONTACT
Chris Pesotski, Director, Financial Aid
320 South Broad Street, Philadelphia, PA 19102
(215) 717-6170

University of the Sciences in Philadelphia

Philadelphia, Pennsylvania
www.usciences.edu Federal Code: 003353

4-year private health science and pharmacy college in very large city.
Enrollment: 2,425 undergrads, 1% part-time. 483 full-time freshmen.
Selectivity: Admits 50 to 75% of applicants.

BASIC COSTS (2012-2013)
Tuition and fees: $33,406.
Per-credit charge: $1,324.
Room and board: $13,054.

FINANCIAL AID PICTURE (2011-2012)
Students with need: Out of 457 full-time freshmen who applied for aid, 419 were judged to have need. Of these, 419 received aid, and 141 had their full need met. Average financial aid package met 34% of need; average scholarship/grant was $12,678; average loan was $3,627. For part-time students, average financial aid package was $28,157.
Students without need: 54 full-time freshmen who did not demonstrate need for aid received scholarships/grants; average award was $10,505. No-need awards available for academics, athletics.
Scholarships offered: 8 full-time freshmen received athletic scholarships; average amount $8,742.

FINANCIAL AID PROCEDURES
Forms required: FAFSA.
Dates and Deadlines: Closing date 3/15. Applicants notified on a rolling basis starting 1/15; must reply by 5/1 or within 2 week(s) of notification.

CONTACT
Paula Lehrberger, Director of Financial Aid
600 South 43rd Street, Philadelphia, PA 19104-4495
(215) 596-8894

Ursinus College

Collegeville, Pennsylvania Federal Code: 003385
www.ursinus.edu CSS Code: 2931

4-year private liberal arts college in small town.
Enrollment: 1,650 undergrads. 456 full-time freshmen.
Selectivity: Admits 50 to 75% of applicants. GED not accepted.

BASIC COSTS (2013-2014)
Tuition and fees: $44,530.
Per-credit charge: $1,386.
Room and board: $11,100.

FINANCIAL AID PICTURE
Students with need: Need-based aid available for full-time students.
Students without need: No-need awards available for academics, alumni affiliation, art, leadership, music/drama.

FINANCIAL AID PROCEDURES
Forms required: FAFSA, CSS PROFILE, institutional form.
Dates and Deadlines: Priority date 2/15; closing date 5/1. Applicants notified by 4/1; must reply by 5/1 or within 2 week(s) of notification.
Transfers: Closing date 8/1.

CONTACT
Suzanne Sparrow, Director of Student Financial Services
PO Box 1000, Collegeville, PA 19426-1000
(610) 409-3600

Valley Forge Christian College

Phoenixville, Pennsylvania
www.vfcc.edu Federal Code: 003306

4-year private liberal arts college in large town, affiliated with Assemblies of God.
Enrollment: 805 undergrads, 12% part-time. 172 full-time freshmen.
Selectivity: Admits 50 to 75% of applicants.

BASIC COSTS (2013-2014)
Tuition and fees: $19,394.
Room and board: $7,794.
Additional info: Cost of $700 for mandatory laptop is included in the required fees.

FINANCIAL AID PICTURE (2012-2013)
Students with need: Out of 151 full-time freshmen who applied for aid, 135 were judged to have need. Of these, 134 received aid, and 10 had their full need met. Average financial aid package met 49% of need; average scholarship/grant was $8,534; average loan was $3,397. For part-time students, average financial aid package was $7,151.
Students without need: 34 full-time freshmen who did not demonstrate need for aid received scholarships/grants; average award was $6,423. No-need awards available for academics, leadership, music/drama, religious affiliation, state/district residency.
Scholarships offered: Trustee's Scholarship, President's Scholarship, Dean's Scholarship, Professor's Scholarship; ranging from full tuition (minimum 3.5 GPA, 1300 SAT or 29 ACT, and upper 10% class rank) to $1,000-$5,000 (minimum 3.3 GPA and 1030 SAT or 22 ACT); application required for awards; renewable with 3.5 GPA. SAT scores exclusive of Writing.
Cumulative student debt: 97% of graduating class had student loans; average debt was $36,199.

FINANCIAL AID PROCEDURES
Forms required: FAFSA.
Dates and Deadlines: Priority date 5/1; no closing date. Applicants notified on a rolling basis starting 3/15; must reply within 3 week(s) of notification.
Transfers: No deadline. Applicants notified on a rolling basis starting 3/15; must reply within 3 week(s) of notification.

CONTACT
Linda Stein, Director of Financial Aid
1401 Charlestown Road, Phoenixville, PA 19460-2373
(610) 917-1475

Valley Forge Military Academy and College

Wayne, Pennsylvania
www.vfmac.edu Federal Code: 003386

2-year private junior and military college in small city.
Enrollment: 209 undergrads. 137 full-time freshmen.
Selectivity: Admits over 75% of applicants.

BASIC COSTS (2013-2014)
Tuition and fees: $31,355.
Room and board: $11,145.

FINANCIAL AID PICTURE
Students with need: Need-based aid available for full-time students. Work study available nights, weekends, and for part-time students.
Students without need: No-need awards available for academics, alumni affiliation, athletics, music/drama, ROTC.
Additional info: Students enrolled in advanced military science program can receive up to $5,000 from the Army. In addition, competitively awarded ROTC scholarships pay average of another $14,100 per school year for direct educational expenses.

FINANCIAL AID PROCEDURES
Forms required: FAFSA.
Dates and Deadlines: Closing date 5/1. Applicants notified on a rolling basis starting 5/15; must reply within 2 week(s) of notification.
Transfers: No deadline. Applicants notified on a rolling basis. Must submit transcripts from all previously attended colleges, even if aid was not received.

CONTACT
Michelle Molina, Financial Aid Director
1001 Eagle Road, Wayne, PA 19087
(610) 989-1300 ext. 1306

Vet Tech Institute

Pittsburgh, Pennsylvania
www.vettechinstitute.edu Federal Code: 008568

2-year for-profit health science and technical college in large city.
Enrollment: 316 undergrads.

BASIC COSTS (2013-2014)
Tuition and fees: $14,520.

FINANCIAL AID PICTURE (2012-2013)
Students with need: Work study available nights.
Students without need: No-need awards available for academics.
Scholarships offered: $1,000 scholarships; 5 offered to commuters. $2,000 scholarships; 2 offered to students not living at home. Awarded based on results of examination given at school in November and March.

FINANCIAL AID PROCEDURES
Forms required: FAFSA, state aid form.
Dates and Deadlines: Applicants notified on a rolling basis.

CONTACT
Donna Durr, Financial Aid Director
125 Seventh Street, Pittsburgh, PA 15222-3400
(800) 570-0693

Villanova University

Villanova, Pennsylvania Federal Code: 003388
www.villanova.edu CSS Code: 2959

4-year private university in large town, affiliated with Roman Catholic Church.
Enrollment: 6,899 undergrads, 5% part-time. 1,642 full-time freshmen.
Selectivity: Admits less than 50% of applicants.

BASIC COSTS (2012-2013)
Tuition and fees: $42,890.
Per-credit charge: $1,760.
Room and board: $11,370.

FINANCIAL AID PICTURE (2012-2013)
Students with need: Out of 1,158 full-time freshmen who applied for aid, 846 were judged to have need. Of these, 834 received aid, and 143 had their full need met. Average financial aid package met 82% of need; average scholarship/grant was $27,851; average loan was $3,393. For part-time students, average financial aid package was $11,950.

Students without need: 91 full-time freshmen who did not demonstrate need for aid received scholarships/grants; average award was $13,622. No-need awards available for academics, alumni affiliation, athletics, leadership, minority status, religious affiliation, ROTC.
Scholarships offered: 38 full-time freshmen received athletic scholarships; average amount $37,800.
Cumulative student debt: 53% of graduating class had student loans; average debt was $35,297.

FINANCIAL AID PROCEDURES
Forms required: FAFSA, CSS PROFILE.
Dates and Deadlines: Closing date 2/7. Applicants notified by 4/1; must reply by 5/1 or within 2 week(s) of notification.
Transfers: Closing date 7/15. Applicants notified on a rolling basis starting 5/1; must reply within 2 week(s) of notification.

CONTACT
Bonnie Lee Behm, Director of Financial Assistance
Austin Hall, 800 Lancaster Avenue, Villanova, PA 19085-1672
(610) 519-4010

Washington & Jefferson College

Washington, Pennsylvania
www.washjeff.edu Federal Code: 003389

4-year private liberal arts college in large town.
Enrollment: 1,394 undergrads, 1% part-time. 376 full-time freshmen.
Selectivity: Admits less than 50% of applicants.

BASIC COSTS (2013-2014)
Tuition and fees: $39,710.
Per-credit charge: $988.
Room and board: $10,490.

FINANCIAL AID PICTURE (2012-2013)
Students with need: Out of 335 full-time freshmen who applied for aid, 298 were judged to have need. Of these, 298 received aid, and 52 had their full need met. Average financial aid package met 79% of need; average scholarship/grant was $11,116; average loan was $3,514. For part-time students, average financial aid package was $11,145.
Students without need: 77 full-time freshmen who did not demonstrate need for aid received scholarships/grants; average award was $13,327. No-need awards available for academics, alumni affiliation, leadership.
Scholarships offered: Presidential Scholarship; based on distinguished academic performance. Scholars Award; based on distinguished academic performance. Joseph Hardy Sr. Scholarship; for students in entrepreneurial studies program. Dean's Award; based on academic performance in high school, distinguished achievement outside the classroom, and good citizenship. Challenge Grant; for students who show academic promise. Alumni Scholarship; for students whose father and/or mother are alumni.

FINANCIAL AID PROCEDURES
Forms required: FAFSA.
Dates and Deadlines: Priority date 2/15; no closing date. Applicants notified on a rolling basis starting 3/1; must reply by 5/1.
Transfers: Must reply within 2 week(s) of notification. Students should complete the FAFSA as soon as possible. Financial aid awards will be made when FAFSA has been received and the student has been accepted for admission. For students selected for verification, these awards are estimated until the required tax documentation has been received and reviewed.

CONTACT
Michelle Anderson, Director of Financial Aid
60 South Lincoln Street, Washington, PA 15301
(724) 223-6019

Waynesburg University

Waynesburg, Pennsylvania
www.waynesburg.edu Federal Code: 003391

4-year private liberal arts college in small town, affiliated with Presbyterian Church (USA).
Enrollment: 1,501 undergrads, 4% part-time. 352 full-time freshmen.
Selectivity: Admits over 75% of applicants.

BASIC COSTS (2013-2014)
Tuition and fees: $20,540.
Per-credit charge: $840.
Room and board: $8,560.

FINANCIAL AID PICTURE (2012-2013)
Students with need: Average financial aid package met 78% of need; average scholarship/grant was $12,015; average loan was $3,877. For part-time students, average financial aid package was $4,156.
Students without need: No-need awards available for academics, alumni affiliation, job skills, leadership, religious affiliation, state/district residency.
Scholarships offered: A.B. Miller Scholarship; $8,000. Presidential Honor Scholarship; $6,000. Honor Scholarship; $4,000. College Leadership Program; $1,000-$1,900.
Cumulative student debt: 89% of graduating class had student loans; average debt was $27,625.

FINANCIAL AID PROCEDURES
Forms required: FAFSA, state aid form.
Dates and Deadlines: Priority date 3/15; no closing date. Applicants notified on a rolling basis starting 2/15; must reply within 2 week(s) of notification.
Transfers: No deadline. Applicants notified on a rolling basis; must reply within 2 week(s) of notification.

CONTACT
Matthew Stokan, Director of Financial Aid
51 West College Street, Waynesburg, PA 15370-1222
(724) 852-3269

West Chester University of Pennsylvania

West Chester, Pennsylvania
www.wcupa.edu Federal Code: 003328

4-year public university in large town.
Enrollment: 13,053 undergrads, 7% part-time. 2,326 full-time freshmen.
Selectivity: Admits less than 50% of applicants.

BASIC COSTS (2012-2013)
Tuition and fees: $8,620; out-of-state residents $18,262.
Room and board: $7,922.

FINANCIAL AID PICTURE
Students with need: Need-based aid available for full-time and part-time students. Work study available nights, weekends, and for part-time students.
Students without need: No-need awards available for academics, art, athletics, leadership, music/drama.

FINANCIAL AID PROCEDURES
Forms required: FAFSA.
Dates and Deadlines: Priority date 3/1; no closing date. Applicants notified on a rolling basis starting 4/1; must reply within 4 week(s) of notification.
Transfers: Must reply within 4 week(s) of notification.

CONTACT
Dana Parker, Director of Financial Aid
Emil H. Messikomer Hall, West Chester, PA 19383
(610) 436-2627

Westminster College

New Wilmington, Pennsylvania
www.westminster.edu Federal Code: 003392

4-year private liberal arts college in small town, affiliated with Presbyterian Church (USA).
Enrollment: 1,403 undergrads.
Selectivity: Admits 50 to 75% of applicants.

BASIC COSTS (2013-2014)
Tuition and fees: $32,445.
Room and board: $9,860.
Additional info: Tuition/fee waivers available for adults.

FINANCIAL AID PICTURE
Students with need: Need-based aid available for full-time and part-time students.
Students without need: No-need awards available for academics, alumni affiliation, leadership, religious affiliation, state/district residency.

FINANCIAL AID PROCEDURES
Forms required: FAFSA, institutional form.
Dates and Deadlines: Priority date 5/1; no closing date. Applicants notified on a rolling basis starting 3/1; must reply by 5/1 or within 3 week(s) of notification.

CONTACT
Cheryl Gerber, Director of Financial Aid
Admissions, Westminster College, New Wilmington, PA 16172-0001
(724) 946-7102

Westmoreland County Community College

Youngwood, Pennsylvania
www.wccc.edu Federal Code: 010176

2-year public community college in small town.
Enrollment: 5,941 undergrads, 52% part-time. 1,076 full-time freshmen.
Selectivity: Open admission; but selective for some programs.

BASIC COSTS (2012-2013)
Tuition and fees: $3,330; out-of-district residents $6,030; out-of-state residents $8,730.
Per-credit charge: $90; out-of-district residents $180; out-of-state residents $270.

FINANCIAL AID PICTURE
Students with need: Need-based aid available for full-time and part-time students. Work study available nights.
Students without need: No-need awards available for academics.

FINANCIAL AID PROCEDURES
Forms required: FAFSA, institutional form.
Dates and Deadlines: Applicants notified on a rolling basis starting 5/1.

CONTACT
Gary Means, Director of Financial Aid
145 Pavilion Lane, Youngwood, PA 15697
(724) 925-4063

Widener University

Chester, Pennsylvania
www.widener.edu Federal Code: 003313

4-year private university in large town.
Enrollment: 3,209 undergrads, 15% part-time. 710 full-time freshmen.
Selectivity: Admits 50 to 75% of applicants.

BASIC COSTS (2013-2014)
Tuition and fees: $38,028.
Per-credit charge: $1,244.
Room and board: $12,340.

FINANCIAL AID PICTURE (2012-2013)
Students with need: Out of 673 full-time freshmen who applied for aid, 624 were judged to have need. Of these, 623 received aid, and 126 had their full need met. Average financial aid package met 79% of need; average scholarship/grant was $8,920; average loan was $3,650. For part-time students, average financial aid package was $6,820.
Students without need: 44 full-time freshmen who did not demonstrate need for aid received scholarships/grants; average award was $19,150. No-need awards available for academics, leadership, music/drama, ROTC.
Scholarships offered: Academic Scholarships; $4,000 to full tuition; based on SAT and GPA; renewable. Music, leadership, and community service scholarships; based on performance evaluations.
Cumulative student debt: 88% of graduating class had student loans; average debt was $40,460.

FINANCIAL AID PROCEDURES
Forms required: FAFSA.
Dates and Deadlines: Priority date 2/15; no closing date. Applicants notified on a rolling basis starting 3/15; must reply within 4 week(s) of notification.
Transfers: Transfer scholarships; $2,500 to $10,000; based on GPA and minimum of 24 transferable credits.

CONTACT
Thomas Malloy, Director of Student Financial Services
One University Place, Chester, PA 19013
(610) 499-4174

Wilkes University

Wilkes-Barre, Pennsylvania
www.wilkes.edu Federal Code: 003394

4-year private university in small city.
Enrollment: 2,196 undergrads, 5% part-time. 589 full-time freshmen.
Selectivity: Admits over 75% of applicants.

BASIC COSTS (2013-2014)
Tuition and fees: $30,350.
Per-credit charge: $802.
Room and board: $12,436.

FINANCIAL AID PICTURE (2012-2013)
Students with need: Out of 553 full-time freshmen who applied for aid, 506 were judged to have need. Of these, 505 received aid, and 50 had their full need met. Average financial aid package met 69% of need; average scholarship/grant was $17,736; average loan was $3,445. For part-time students, average financial aid package was $9,302.
Students without need: 53 full-time freshmen who did not demonstrate need for aid received scholarships/grants; average award was $11,223. No-need awards available for academics, leadership, minority status, music/drama.
Cumulative student debt: 86% of graduating class had student loans; average debt was $38,442.

FINANCIAL AID PROCEDURES
Forms required: FAFSA.
Dates and Deadlines: Priority date 3/1; no closing date. Applicants notified on a rolling basis starting 3/1.

CONTACT
Melanie Wade, Vice President of Enrollment Services
84 West South Street, Wilkes-Barre, PA 18766
(570) 408-2000

Wilson College

Chambersburg, Pennsylvania
www.wilson.edu Federal Code: 003396

4-year private liberal arts college for women in large town, affiliated with Presbyterian Church (USA).
Enrollment: 499 undergrads.

BASIC COSTS (2012-2013)
Tuition and fees: $29,360.
Per-credit charge: $2,875.
Room and board: $10,148.

FINANCIAL AID PICTURE
Students with need: Need-based aid available for full-time and part-time students. Work study available nights, weekends, and for part-time students.
Students without need: No-need awards available for academics, alumni affiliation, religious affiliation, state/district residency.
Scholarships offered: Presidential Merit Scholarship: half tuition, cumulative GPA 3.75 or higher, top 15% of class. Dean's Merit Scholarship: 35% tuition, 3.40 to 3.74 cumulative GPA, top 25% of class. Faculty Merit Scholarship: 25% tuition, 3.0-3.39 cumulative GPA, rank top 50% of class. Scholarships for full-time students who are members of Presbyterian Church, USA. Curran Scholarships: awarded to incoming students with significant community service.

FINANCIAL AID PROCEDURES
Forms required: FAFSA, state aid form, institutional form.
Dates and Deadlines: Priority date 4/30; no closing date. Applicants notified on a rolling basis starting 2/15.
Transfers: Applicants notified on a rolling basis starting 2/15. Tuition scholarships available to transfer articulation students who hold associate degrees from Harrisburg Area Community College, Hagerstown Community College, Central Penn College, Luzerne County Community College, Lehigh Carbon Community College, Harcum College, Cottey College, Frederick Community College, Howard Community College; transfer merit scholarships for students with 3.0 GPA from 25% to 50% tuition, Phi Theta Kappa scholarship.

CONTACT
Linda Brittain, Dean of Financial Aid
1015 Philadelphia Avenue, Chambersburg, PA 17201-1285
(717) 262-2016

York College of Pennsylvania

York, Pennsylvania
www.ycp.edu Federal Code: 003399

4-year private liberal arts college in small city.
Enrollment: 5,011 undergrads, 8% part-time. 1,135 full-time freshmen.
Selectivity: Admits 50 to 75% of applicants.

BASIC COSTS (2013-2014)
Tuition and fees: $17,010.
Per-credit charge: $475.
Room and board: $9,580.

FINANCIAL AID PICTURE (2012-2013)
Students with need: Out of 1,063 full-time freshmen who applied for aid, 819 were judged to have need. Of these, 815 received aid, and 208 had their full need met. Average financial aid package met 64% of need; average scholarship/grant was $4,242; average loan was $5,183. For part-time students, average financial aid package was $6,776.
Students without need: 309 full-time freshmen who did not demonstrate need for aid received scholarships/grants; average award was $4,243. No-need awards available for academics, alumni affiliation, minority status, music/drama.
Scholarships offered: All accepted freshman applicants considered for merit scholarships, including Presidential and Dean's Scholarships, based on academic criteria (GPA, rank, test scores). Scholarship awards reduce tuition to approximately $7,000 - $11,500 annually for many students, not including additional eligibility for need-based financial aid.
Cumulative student debt: 77% of graduating class had student loans; average debt was $35,297.

FINANCIAL AID PROCEDURES
Forms required: FAFSA.
Dates and Deadlines: Applicants notified on a rolling basis starting 3/1; must reply within 4 week(s) of notification.
Transfers: No deadline. Applicants notified on a rolling basis starting 3/1; must reply within 4 week(s) of notification. Transfer Merit Scholarship; $2,000 ($1,000 per semester) for entering transfer students with minimum 3.3 GPA.

CONTACT
Calvin Williams, Director of Financial Aid
441 Country Club Road, York, PA 17403-3651
(717) 849-1682

Puerto Rico

Atlantic University College

Guaynabo, Puerto Rico
www.atlanticu.edu Federal Code: 016871

4-year private liberal arts college in small city.
Enrollment: 1,370 undergrads.
Selectivity: Open admission.

FINANCIAL AID PICTURE
Students with need: Need-based aid available for full-time and part-time students. Work study available nights.
Students without need: This college awards aid only to students with need.

FINANCIAL AID PROCEDURES
Forms required: FAFSA, institutional form.
Dates and Deadlines: Closing date 6/30. Applicants notified on a rolling basis starting 4/1; must reply within 2 week(s) of notification.
Transfers: Priority date 1/7; closing date 6/7.

CONTACT
Janice Rivera, Director of Financial Aid
PO Box 3918, Guaynabo, PR 00970
(787) 789-4251

Bayamon Central University

Bayamon, Puerto Rico
www.ucb.edu.pr Federal Code: 010015

4-year private university in large city, affiliated with Roman Catholic Church.
Enrollment: 1,691 undergrads, 28% part-time. 225 full-time freshmen.
Selectivity: Admits 50 to 75% of applicants.

BASIC COSTS (2012-2013)
Additional info: Tuition/fee waivers available for unemployed or children of unemployed.

FINANCIAL AID PICTURE (2011-2012)
Students with need: Need-based aid available for full-time and part-time students. Work study available nights.

Students without need: This college awards aid only to students with need.

FINANCIAL AID PROCEDURES

Forms required: FAFSA, institutional form.

Dates and Deadlines: Priority date 5/31; closing date 7/2. Applicants notified on a rolling basis starting 5/31; must reply within 6 week(s) of notification.

Transfers: No deadline. Applicants notified on a rolling basis starting 4/30.

CONTACT

Edna Ortiz, Director of Financial Aid Office
PO Box 1725, Bayamon, PR 00960-1725
(787) 786-3030 ext. 2116

Caribbean University

Bayamon, Puerto Rico
www.caribbean.edu Federal Code: 012525

4-year private university in large city.
Enrollment: 4,128 undergrads, 20% part-time. 702 full-time freshmen.
Selectivity: Open admission; but selective for some programs.

BASIC COSTS (2012-2013)

Tuition and fees: $5,870.
Per-credit charge: $170.

FINANCIAL AID PICTURE (2011-2012)

Students with need: Need-based aid available for full-time and part-time students. Work study available nights, weekends, and for part-time students.

Students without need: This college awards aid only to students with need.

FINANCIAL AID PROCEDURES

Forms required: FAFSA.

Dates and Deadlines: Priority date 5/30; no closing date. Applicants notified on a rolling basis starting 7/30; must reply within 2 week(s) of notification.

Transfers: Closing date 5/30. Applicants notified on a rolling basis.

CONTACT

Hector Gracia, Financial Aid Director
PO Box 493, Bayamon, PR 00960-0493
(787) 780-0070 ext. 1125

Columbia Centro Universitario: Caguas

Caguas, Puerto Rico
www.columbiaco.edu Federal Code: 013517

4-year for-profit branch campus and technical college in small city.
Enrollment: 1,637 undergrads, 59% part-time. 271 full-time freshmen.
Selectivity: Open admission; but selective for some programs.

FINANCIAL AID PICTURE (2011-2012)

Students with need: Out of 271 full-time freshmen who applied for aid, 235 were judged to have need. Of these, 235 received aid. For part-time students, average financial aid package was $6,050.

Students without need: This college awards aid only to students with need.

FINANCIAL AID PROCEDURES

Forms required: FAFSA, state aid form, institutional form.

CONTACT

Virginia Guang, Financial Aid Administrator
PO Box 8517, Caguas, PR 00726-8517
(787) 743-4041 ext. 223

Columbia Centro Universitario: Yauco

Yauco, Puerto Rico
www.columbiaco.edu Federal Code: 008902

2-year for-profit business and health science college in large town.
Enrollment: 324 undergrads, 43% part-time. 63 full-time freshmen.
Selectivity: Open admission; but selective for some programs.

FINANCIAL AID PICTURE (2011-2012)

Students with need: Out of 63 full-time freshmen who applied for aid, 63 were judged to have need. Of these, 56 received aid. Need-based aid available for part-time students.

Students without need: This college awards aid only to students with need.

FINANCIAL AID PROCEDURES

Forms required: FAFSA, state aid form, institutional form.

CONTACT

Virginia Guang, Director of Financial Aid
PO Box 3062, Yauco, PR 00698-3062
(787) 856-0845 ext. 112

Conservatory of Music of Puerto Rico

San Juan, Puerto Rico
www.cmpr.edu Federal Code: 010819

4-year public music college in large city.
Enrollment: 406 undergrads, 31% part-time. 28 full-time freshmen.
Selectivity: Admits 50 to 75% of applicants.

BASIC COSTS (2012-2013)

Tuition and fees: $3,010.
Per-credit charge: $90.
Additional info: Tuition at time of enrollment locked for 4 years.

FINANCIAL AID PICTURE (2012-2013)

Students with need: Average financial aid package met 38% of need; average scholarship/grant was $5,850; average loan was $3,500. Need-based aid available for part-time students.

Students without need: This college awards aid only to students with need.

FINANCIAL AID PROCEDURES

Forms required: FAFSA.

Dates and Deadlines: Priority date 12/15; no closing date. Applicants notified on a rolling basis starting 4/30.

Transfers: Closing date 4/15.

CONTACT

Mike Rajaballey, Financial Aid Officer
951 Ave. Ponce de Leon, San Juan, PR 00907-3373
(787) 751-0160 ext. 231

EDIC College

Caguas, Puerto Rico
www.ediccollege.com Federal Code: 030219

2-year for-profit health science and technical college in large city.
Enrollment: 870 full-time undergrads.
Selectivity: Open admission; but selective for some programs.

BASIC COSTS (2012-2013)

Tuition and fees: $6,525.
Per-credit charge: $265.

FINANCIAL AID PICTURE (2011-2012)
Students with need: 99% of average financial aid package awarded as scholarships/grants, 1% awarded as loans/jobs. Need-based aid available for part-time students. Work study available nights.
Students without need: This college awards aid only to students with need.

FINANCIAL AID PROCEDURES
Forms required: FAFSA, state aid form, institutional form.
Dates and Deadlines: Applicants notified on a rolling basis.
Transfers: No deadline. Applicants notified on a rolling basis.

CONTACT
Julio Melendez, Financial Aid Director
Box 9120, Caguas, PR 00726-9120
(787) 744-8519

EDP University of Puerto Rico: Hato Rey
Hato Rey, Puerto Rico
www.edpcollege.edu Federal Code: 021651

4-year for-profit business and technical college in very large city.
Enrollment: 1,139 undergrads.

FINANCIAL AID PICTURE
Students with need: Work study available nights.

FINANCIAL AID PROCEDURES
Forms required: FAFSA, state aid form.
Dates and Deadlines: Closing date 9/30. Applicants notified on a rolling basis starting 9/30; must reply within 2 week(s) of notification.

CONTACT
Yaitzaenid Gonzalez Melendez, Institutional Financial Aid Director
PO Box 1923, Hato Rey, PR 00919-2303
(787) 765-3560 ext. 222

EDP University of Puerto Rico: San Sebastian
San Sebastian, Puerto Rico
www.edpcollege.edu Federal Code: 021651

4-year for-profit business and health science college in small city.
Enrollment: 1,077 undergrads.

FINANCIAL AID PICTURE
Students with need: Need-based aid available for full-time and part-time students.
Students without need: This college awards aid only to students with need.

FINANCIAL AID PROCEDURES
Dates and Deadlines: Closing date 6/30.
Transfers: Must reply by 7/15.

CONTACT
Gloria Mirabal, Financial Aid Officer
PO Box 1674, San Sebastian, PR 00685
(787) 765-3560

Escuela de Artes Plasticas de Puerto Rico
San Juan, Puerto Rico
www.eap.edu Federal Code: 017345

4-year public visual arts college in large city.
Enrollment: 489 undergrads, 37% part-time. 68 full-time freshmen.
Selectivity: Admits 50 to 75% of applicants.

BASIC COSTS (2013-2014)
Tuition and fees: $3,921; out-of-state residents $6,621.
Per-credit charge: $90; out-of-state residents $180.

FINANCIAL AID PICTURE (2011-2012)
Students with need: 98% of average financial aid package awarded as scholarships/grants, 2% awarded as loans/jobs. Need-based aid available for part-time students. Work study available nights, weekends, and for part-time students.
Students without need: This college awards aid only to students with need.

FINANCIAL AID PROCEDURES
Forms required: FAFSA.
Dates and Deadlines: Priority date 4/25; closing date 5/18. Applicants notified by 7/11.

CONTACT
Alfred Diaz, Financial Aid Officer
PO Box 9021112, San Juan, PR 00902-1112

Huertas Junior College
Caguas, Puerto Rico
www.huertas.edu Federal Code: 014105

2-year for-profit junior and technical college in large city.
Enrollment: 1,493 undergrads, 23% part-time. 267 full-time freshmen.
Selectivity: Open admission.

FINANCIAL AID PICTURE (2012-2013)
Students with need: Out of 247 full-time freshmen who applied for aid, 247 were judged to have need. Of these, 247 received aid, and 247 had their full need met. For part-time students, average financial aid package was $4,462.
Students without need: This college awards aid only to students with need.

FINANCIAL AID PROCEDURES
Forms required: FAFSA, institutional form.
Dates and Deadlines: Applicants notified on a rolling basis.

CONTACT
Wanda Ortiz, Financial Aid Director
PO Box 8429, Caguas, PR 00726
(787) 746-1400

Humacao Community College
Humacao, Puerto Rico
www.hccpr.edu Federal Code: 014952

2-year private business and community college in small city.
Enrollment: 566 full-time undergrads.
Selectivity: Open admission.

BASIC COSTS (2013-2014)
Tuition and fees: $6,450.
Per-credit charge: $135.

FINANCIAL AID PICTURE
Students with need: Need-based aid available for full-time and part-time students. Work study available nights.
Students without need: This college awards aid only to students with need.

FINANCIAL AID PROCEDURES
Forms required: FAFSA, state aid form, institutional form.

Dates and Deadlines: Priority date 1/1; closing date 6/30. Applicants notified on a rolling basis starting 3/4.
Transfers: No deadline.

CONTACT
Cheryle Perez, Financial Aid Director
PO Box 9139, Humacao, PR 00792-9139
(787) 852-1430 ext. 234

Inter American University of Puerto Rico: Aguadilla Campus
Aguadilla, Puerto Rico
www.aguadilla.inter.edu Federal Code: 003939

4-year private university and liberal arts college in small city.
Enrollment: 4,267 undergrads, 15% part-time. 806 full-time freshmen.
Selectivity: Admits 50 to 75% of applicants.

BASIC COSTS (2012-2013)
Tuition and fees: $5,582.
Per-credit charge: $170.
Additional info: Tuition at time of enrollment locked for 4 years.

FINANCIAL AID PICTURE (2011-2012)
Students with need: 98% of average financial aid package awarded as scholarships/grants, 2% awarded as loans/jobs. Need-based aid available for part-time students. Work study available nights, weekends, and for part-time students.
Students without need: No-need awards available for academics.

FINANCIAL AID PROCEDURES
Forms required: FAFSA.
Dates and Deadlines: Closing date 4/30. Applicants notified by 6/15; must reply by 8/8.
Transfers: No deadline.

CONTACT
Gloria Cortes, Director of Financial Aid
Box 20000, Aguadilla, PR 00605
(787) 891-0925 ext. 2110

Inter American University of Puerto Rico: Arecibo Campus
Arecibo, Puerto Rico
www.arecibo.inter.edu Federal Code: 005026

4-year private liberal arts college in small city.
Enrollment: 4,481 undergrads.

BASIC COSTS (2012-2013)
Tuition and fees: $5,620.
Per-credit charge: $170.

FINANCIAL AID PICTURE
Students with need: Need-based aid available for full-time and part-time students. Work study available nights, weekends, and for part-time students.
Students without need: No-need awards available for academics, athletics.

FINANCIAL AID PROCEDURES
Forms required: FAFSA, institutional form.
Dates and Deadlines: Closing date 5/15. Applicants notified on a rolling basis.

CONTACT
Ramon de Jesus, Director of Financial Aid
PO Box 4050, Arecibo, PR 00614-4050
(787) 878-5475 ext. 2275

Inter American University of Puerto Rico: Barranquitas Campus
Barranquitas, Puerto Rico
www.br.inter.edu Federal Code: 005027

4-year private university and branch campus college in large town.
Enrollment: 2,318 undergrads.

BASIC COSTS (2012-2013)
Tuition and fees: $5,582.
Per-credit charge: $170.
Additional info: Tuition/fee waivers available for adults, minority students.

FINANCIAL AID PICTURE
Students with need: Need-based aid available for full-time and part-time students.
Students without need: This college awards aid only to students with need.

FINANCIAL AID PROCEDURES
Forms required: FAFSA.
Dates and Deadlines: Closing date 4/30. Applicants notified on a rolling basis; must reply within 2 week(s) of notification.

CONTACT
Eduardo Fontanez, Financial Aid Director
PO Box 517, Barranquitas, PR 00794
(787) 857-3600 ext. 2050

Inter American University of Puerto Rico: Bayamon Campus
Bayamon, Puerto Rico
www.bayamon.inter.edu Federal Code: 003938

4-year private university and engineering college in small city.
Enrollment: 4,765 undergrads, 13% part-time. 934 full-time freshmen.
Selectivity: Admits less than 50% of applicants.

BASIC COSTS (2012-2013)
Tuition and fees: $5,620.
Per-credit charge: $170.

FINANCIAL AID PICTURE (2012-2013)
Students with need: Average financial aid package met 1% of need; average scholarship/grant was $125; average loan was $94. For part-time students, average financial aid package was $149.
Students without need: This college awards aid only to students with need.

FINANCIAL AID PROCEDURES
Forms required: FAFSA.
Dates and Deadlines: Priority date 6/30; no closing date. Applicants notified on a rolling basis starting 5/10.

CONTACT
Hector Vargas, Director of Student Services
500 Dr. John Will Harris Road, Bayamon, PR 00957
(787) 279-1912 ext. 2025

Inter American University of Puerto Rico: Guayama Campus
Guayama, Puerto Rico
www.guayama.inter.edu Federal Code: 010764

4-year private university in large town.
Enrollment: 2,113 undergrads, 18% part-time. 182 full-time freshmen.

Selectivity: Admits 50 to 75% of applicants.

BASIC COSTS (2012-2013)
Tuition and fees: $5,582.
Per-credit charge: $170.

FINANCIAL AID PICTURE
Students with need: Need-based aid available for full-time and part-time students. Work study available nights, weekends, and for part-time students.
Students without need: This college awards aid only to students with need.

FINANCIAL AID PROCEDURES
Forms required: FAFSA, institutional form.
Dates and Deadlines: Closing date 4/29. Applicants notified by 6/15; must reply by 7/30.
Transfers: No deadline.

CONTACT
Jose Vechini-Rodriguez, Director of Financial Aid
PO Box 10004, Guayama, PR 00785
(787) 864-2222 ext. 2206

Inter American University of Puerto Rico: Metropolitan Campus

San Juan, Puerto Rico
www.metro.inter.edu Federal Code: 003938

4-year private branch campus college in large city.
Enrollment: 8,313 undergrads.

BASIC COSTS (2012-2013)
Tuition and fees: $5,620.
Per-credit charge: $170.

FINANCIAL AID PICTURE
Students with need: Need-based aid available for full-time and part-time students. Work study available nights, weekends, and for part-time students.

FINANCIAL AID PROCEDURES
Forms required: FAFSA.
Dates and Deadlines: Closing date 4/30. Applicants notified on a rolling basis.

CONTACT
Glenda Diaz, Director of Financial Aid
Box 191293, San Juan, PR 00919-1293
(787) 250-1912 ext. 2185

Inter American University of Puerto Rico: Ponce Campus

Mercedita, Puerto Rico
www.ponce.inter.edu Federal Code: 005029

4-year private university in large town.
Enrollment: 5,510 undergrads, 15% part-time. 1,290 full-time freshmen.
Selectivity: Admits less than 50% of applicants.

BASIC COSTS (2012-2013)
Tuition and fees: $5,620.
Per-credit charge: $170.

FINANCIAL AID PICTURE (2011-2012)
Students with need: Out of 1,285 full-time freshmen who applied for aid, 1,277 were judged to have need. Of these, 935 received aid. Average financial aid package met 2% of need; average scholarship/grant was $219; average loan was $194. For part-time students, average financial aid package was $191.
Students without need: This college awards aid only to students with need.
Scholarships offered: ***Merit:*** Scholarship program for first-time freshmen with a high school academic index of 3.0 or higher. ***Athletic:*** 30 full-time freshmen received athletic scholarships; average amount $253.

FINANCIAL AID PROCEDURES
Forms required: FAFSA.

CONTACT
Debra Martinez, Director of Financial Aid
104 Turpo Industrial Park Road #1, Mercedita, PR 00715-1602
(787) 284-1912 ext. 2018

Inter American University of Puerto Rico: San German Campus

San German, Puerto Rico
www.sg.inter.edu Federal Code: 00714

4-year private university in large town.
Enrollment: 4,494 undergrads, 10% part-time. 1,372 full-time freshmen.
Selectivity: Admits over 75% of applicants.

BASIC COSTS (2012-2013)
Tuition and fees: $5,620.
Per-credit charge: $170.
Room and board: $2,700.

FINANCIAL AID PICTURE (2011-2012)
Students with need: Out of 1,345 full-time freshmen who applied for aid, 1,325 were judged to have need. Of these, 749 received aid, and 5 had their full need met. Average financial aid package met 3% of need; average scholarship/grant was $291; average loan was $323. For part-time students, average financial aid package was $238.
Students without need: No-need awards available for academics, athletics.
Scholarships offered: 44 full-time freshmen received athletic scholarships; average amount $1,277.

FINANCIAL AID PROCEDURES
Forms required: FAFSA, institutional form.
Dates and Deadlines: Closing date 5/14. Applicants notified on a rolling basis; must reply by 8/1.

CONTACT
Maria Lugo, Director of Financial Aid
Box 5100, San German, PR 00683-9801
(787) 264-1912 ext. 7250

National University College: Arecibo

Arecibo, Puerto Rico
www.nuc.edu Federal Code: 015953

3-year for-profit career college in small city.
Enrollment: 1,656 undergrads, 32% part-time. 258 full-time freshmen.
Selectivity: Admits over 75% of applicants.

BASIC COSTS (2012-2013)
Tuition and fees: $6,930.
Additional info: Full-time online tuition, $9,900; required fees, $375.

FINANCIAL AID PICTURE
Students with need: Need-based aid available for full-time and part-time students. Work study available nights, weekends, and for part-time students.

FINANCIAL AID PROCEDURES
Forms required: FAFSA.

Dates and Deadlines: Priority date 12/31; closing date 4/30. Applicants notified on a rolling basis starting 5/2; must reply by 5/15 or within 2 week(s) of notification.
Transfers: No deadline.

CONTACT
Evelyn Quinones, Director of Financial Aid
PO Box 4035, MSC 452, Arecibo, PR 00614
(787) 780-5134 ext. 4020

National University College: Bayamon
Bayamon, Puerto Rico
www.nuc.edu Federal Code: 015953

3-year for-profit career college in large town.
Enrollment: 3,431 undergrads, 42% part-time. 571 full-time freshmen.
Selectivity: Admits less than 50% of applicants.

BASIC COSTS (2012-2013)
Tuition and fees: $6,930.

FINANCIAL AID PICTURE
Students with need: Need-based aid available for full-time and part-time students. Work study available nights, weekends, and for part-time students.
Students without need: This college awards aid only to students with need.

FINANCIAL AID PROCEDURES
Forms required: FAFSA.
Dates and Deadlines: Priority date 12/31; closing date 4/30. Applicants notified on a rolling basis starting 5/2; must reply by 5/15 or within 2 week(s) of notification.
Transfers: No deadline.

CONTACT
Elizabeth Cruz, Director of Financial Aid
PO Box 2036, Bayamon, PR 00960
(787) 780-5134 ext. 4020

National University College: Ponce
Coto Laurel, Puerto Rico
www.nuc.edu

3-year for-profit career college in large city.
Enrollment: 983 undergrads, 35% part-time. 129 full-time freshmen.
Selectivity: Admits over 75% of applicants.

BASIC COSTS (2012-2013)
Tuition and fees: $6,930.
Additional info: Full-time online tuition, $9,900; required fees, $375.

FINANCIAL AID PICTURE
Students with need: Need-based aid available for full-time and part-time students. Work study available nights, weekends, and for part-time students.
Students without need: This college awards aid only to students with need.

FINANCIAL AID PROCEDURES
Dates and Deadlines: Closing date 4/30.
Transfers: No deadline.

CONTACT
Lorraine Centeno, Director of Financial Aid
PO Box 801243, Coto Laurel, PR 00780-1243

National University College: Rio Grande
Rio Grande, Puerto Rico
www.nuc.edu Federal Code: E01213

3-year for-profit career college in small town.
Enrollment: 1,615 undergrads.
Selectivity: Admits over 75% of applicants.

BASIC COSTS (2012-2013)
Tuition and fees: $6,930.
Additional info: Full-time online tuition, $9,900; required fees, $375.

FINANCIAL AID PICTURE
Students with need: Need-based aid available for full-time and part-time students. Work study available nights, weekends, and for part-time students.
Students without need: This college awards aid only to students with need.

FINANCIAL AID PROCEDURES
Forms required: FAFSA.
Dates and Deadlines: Priority date 12/31; closing date 4/30. Must reply by 5/15 or within 2 week(s) of notification.
Transfers: No deadline.

CONTACT
Nelson Diaz, Director of Financial Aid
PO Box 3064, Rio Grande, PR 00745
(787) 780-5134 ext. 4120

Pontifical Catholic University of Puerto Rico
Ponce, Puerto Rico
www.pucpr.edu Federal Code: 003936

4-year private university in small city, affiliated with Roman Catholic Church.
Enrollment: 5,825 full-time undergrads.

BASIC COSTS (2012-2013)
Tuition and fees: $5,768.
Per-credit charge: $175.
Additional info: Board plan not available. Cost of room only, $1,353.

FINANCIAL AID PICTURE
Students with need: Need-based aid available for full-time and part-time students. Work study available nights, weekends, and for part-time students.
Students without need: No-need awards available for academics, athletics, music/drama.

FINANCIAL AID PROCEDURES
Forms required: FAFSA.
Dates and Deadlines: Closing date 5/15. Applicants notified by 6/15; must reply within 4 week(s) of notification.
Transfers: Priority date 5/11. Applicants notified by 6/15; must reply within 4 week(s) of notification. Distribution of awards based on availability of funds when application received.

CONTACT
Rosalia Martinez, Director of Financial Aid
2250 Las Americas Avenue, Suite 284, Ponce, PR 00717-9777
(787) 651-2041

Turabo University
Gurabo, Puerto Rico
www.suagm.edu/ut Federal Code: 011719

4-year private university in small city.
Enrollment: 14,333 undergrads, 23% part-time. 2,628 full-time freshmen.

Selectivity: Admits less than 50% of applicants.

BASIC COSTS (2012-2013)
Tuition and fees: $5,184.
Per-credit charge: $181.

FINANCIAL AID PICTURE (2011-2012)
Students with need: Need-based aid available for full-time and part-time students.
Students without need: This college awards aid only to students with need.

FINANCIAL AID PROCEDURES
Forms required: FAFSA.
Dates and Deadlines: Priority date 5/30; no closing date.

CONTACT
Carmen Rivera-Lopez, Admissions and Financial Aid Director
PO Box 3030, Gurabo, PR 00778
(787) 743-7979 ext. 4350

Universal Technology College of Puerto Rico

Aguadilla, Puerto Rico
www.unitecpr.edu/ Federal Code: 030297

2-year private health science and career college in small city.
Enrollment: 1,395 undergrads.
Selectivity: Open admission.

FINANCIAL AID PICTURE
Students with need: Need-based aid available for full-time and part-time students. Work study available nights, weekends, and for part-time students.
Students without need: This college awards aid only to students with need.

FINANCIAL AID PROCEDURES
Forms required: FAFSA, state aid form, institutional form.
Dates and Deadlines: Priority date 4/30; closing date 6/30. Applicants notified on a rolling basis starting 2/1; must reply by 6/30.
Transfers: No deadline.

CONTACT
Samuel Hernandez, Financial Aid Administrator
Apartado 1955, Victoria Station, Aguadilla, PR 00605
(787) 882-2065 ext. 313

Universidad Adventista de las Antillas

Mayaguez, Puerto Rico
www.uaa.edu Federal Code: 005019

4-year private university and liberal arts college in small city, affiliated with Seventh-day Adventists.
Enrollment: 373 undergrads, 12% part-time. 235 full-time freshmen.
Selectivity: Open admission; but selective for some programs.

BASIC COSTS (2013-2014)
Tuition and fees: $5,550.
Per-credit charge: $165.
Room and board: $2,900.

FINANCIAL AID PICTURE
Students with need: Need-based aid available for full-time and part-time students.

FINANCIAL AID PROCEDURES
Forms required: FAFSA, institutional form.
Dates and Deadlines: Applicants notified on a rolling basis starting 8/15; must reply within 3 week(s) of notification.
Transfers: No deadline. Applicants notified on a rolling basis.

CONTACT
Awilda Matos, Director of Financial Aid
PO Box 118, Mayaguez, PR 00681-0118
(787) 834-9595 ext. 2200

Universidad del Este

Carolina, Puerto Rico
www.suagm.edu/une Federal Code: 011718

4-year private university and liberal arts college in small city.
Enrollment: 12,489 undergrads, 26% part-time. 2,125 full-time freshmen.
Selectivity: Open admission; but selective for some programs.

BASIC COSTS (2012-2013)
Tuition and fees: $5,184.
Per-credit charge: $181.

FINANCIAL AID PICTURE (2011-2012)
Students with need: 92% of average financial aid package awarded as scholarships/grants, 8% awarded as loans/jobs. Need-based aid available for part-time students. Work study available nights, weekends, and for part-time students.
Students without need: This college awards aid only to students with need.

FINANCIAL AID PROCEDURES
Forms required: FAFSA, state aid form, institutional form.
Dates and Deadlines: Priority date 5/30; no closing date. Applicants notified by 7/30.

CONTACT
Norberto Pagán, Financial Aid Director
PO Box 2010, Carolina, PR 00984-2010
(787) 257-7373 ext. 3304

Universidad Metropolitana

Rio Piedras, Puerto Rico
www.suagm.edu/umet Federal Code: 025875

4-year private university and liberal arts college in large city.
Enrollment: 11,293 undergrads, 21% part-time. 2,092 full-time freshmen.
Selectivity: Admits less than 50% of applicants.

BASIC COSTS (2012-2013)
Tuition and fees: $5,194.
Per-credit charge: $181.

FINANCIAL AID PICTURE (2012-2013)
Students with need: Need-based aid available for full-time and part-time students. Work study available nights.
Students without need: This college awards aid only to students with need.

FINANCIAL AID PROCEDURES
Forms required: FAFSA.
Dates and Deadlines: Priority date 5/30; no closing date.

CONTACT
Julio Rodriguez, Financial Aid Director
Apartado 21150, San Juan, PR 00928
(787) 766-1717 ext. 6587

Universidad Pentecostal Mizpa

San Juan, Puerto Rico
www.mizpa.edu Federal Code: 035313

4-year private university and Bible college in very large city, affiliated with Pentecostal Holiness Church.
Enrollment: 329 undergrads, 60% part-time. 15 full-time freshmen.
Selectivity: Admits over 75% of applicants.

BASIC COSTS (2012-2013)
Tuition and fees: $4,150.
Per-credit charge: $125.
Additional info: Board plan not available. Cost of room only, $1,280.

FINANCIAL AID PICTURE (2012-2013)
Students with need: Out of 15 full-time freshmen who applied for aid, 15 were judged to have need. Of these, 15 received aid. Need-based aid available for part-time students.
Students without need: This college awards aid only to students with need.

FINANCIAL AID PROCEDURES
Forms required: FAFSA.

CONTACT
Elisamuel Rodriguez, Administrative Dean
PO Box 20966, San Juan, PR 00928-0966

Universidad Politecnica de Puerto Rico

Hato Rey, Puerto Rico
www.pupr.edu Federal Code: 014055

5-year private university and engineering college in large city.
Enrollment: 4,031 undergrads, 52% part-time. 383 full-time freshmen.
Selectivity: Admits over 75% of applicants.

BASIC COSTS (2012-2013)
Tuition and fees: $9,240.
Per-credit charge: $188.

FINANCIAL AID PICTURE
Students with need: Need-based aid available for full-time and part-time students.
Students without need: No-need awards available for academics, music/drama.

FINANCIAL AID PROCEDURES
Forms required: FAFSA.
Dates and Deadlines: Priority date 5/15; closing date 6/30. Applicants notified by 7/15.

CONTACT
Sergio Villoldo, Director of Financial Aid
PO Box 192017, San Juan, PR 00919-2017
(787) 622-8000 ext. 249

University College of San Juan

San Juan, Puerto Rico
www.cunisanjuan.edu Federal Code: 010567

4-year public university and community college in large city.
Enrollment: 1,570 undergrads, 13% part-time. 347 full-time freshmen.
Selectivity: Admits over 75% of applicants.

BASIC COSTS (2012-2013)
Tuition and fees: $3,150; out-of-state residents $3,150.
Per-credit charge: $85.

FINANCIAL AID PICTURE (2011-2012)
Students with need: 99% of average financial aid package awarded as scholarships/grants, 1% awarded as loans/jobs. Need-based aid available for part-time students.
Students without need: This college awards aid only to students with need.

FINANCIAL AID PROCEDURES
Forms required: FAFSA, institutional form.
Dates and Deadlines: Closing date 9/30. Applicants notified by 10/30.
Transfers: Financial aid transcripts.

CONTACT
Gloria Mirabal, Director of Financial Aid
180 Jose R. Oliver Avenue, San Juan, PR 00918
(787) 480-2400 ext. 2425

University of Puerto Rico: Aguadilla

Aguadilla, Puerto Rico
www.uprag.edu Federal Code: 012123

4-year public liberal arts and technical college in small city.
Enrollment: 2,837 undergrads, 6% part-time. 787 full-time freshmen.
Selectivity: Admits 50 to 75% of applicants.

BASIC COSTS (2012-2013)
Tuition and fees: $2,666.
Per-credit charge: $55.
Additional info: Nonresidents who are U.S. citizens will be charged amount that will be equal to the rate for nonresidents at a state university in their home state. In second year of residency in Puerto Rico, such students will be charged in-state rate.

FINANCIAL AID PICTURE (2011-2012)
Students with need: 98% of average financial aid package awarded as scholarships/grants, 2% awarded as loans/jobs. Need-based aid available for part-time students.
Students without need: This college awards aid only to students with need.

FINANCIAL AID PROCEDURES
Forms required: FAFSA, institutional form.
Dates and Deadlines: Closing date 5/6. Applicants notified on a rolling basis starting 4/1; must reply within 1 week(s) of notification.
Transfers: No deadline.

CONTACT
Carmen Santiago, Financial Aid Director
Box 6150, Aguadilla, PR 00604-6150
(787) 890-0109

University of Puerto Rico: Arecibo

Arecibo, Puerto Rico
www.upra.edu Federal Code: 007228

4-year public university in small city.
Enrollment: 3,693 undergrads, 7% part-time. 940 full-time freshmen.

BASIC COSTS (2012-2013)
Tuition and fees: $2,666.
Per-credit charge: $55.
Additional info: Nonresidents who are U.S. citizens will be charged amount that will be equal to the rate for nonresidents at a state university in their home state. In second year of residency in Puerto Rico, such students will be charged in-state rate.

FINANCIAL AID PICTURE
Students with need: Need-based aid available for full-time and part-time students.
Students without need: This college awards aid only to students with need.

FINANCIAL AID PROCEDURES
Forms required: FAFSA, institutional form.
Dates and Deadlines: Closing date 4/27.
Transfers: Closing date 5/25.

CONTACT
Myrta Ortiz, Financial Aid Officer
PO Box 4010, Arecibo, PR 00614-4010
(787) 815-0000 ext. 4501

University of Puerto Rico: Carolina Regional College

Carolina, Puerto Rico
www.uprc.edu Federal Code: 003942

4-year public university in small city.
Enrollment: 3,681 undergrads, 19% part-time. 946 full-time freshmen.
Selectivity: Admits over 75% of applicants.

BASIC COSTS (2012-2013)
Tuition and fees: $3,491.
Per-credit charge: $55.
Additional info: Nonresidents who are U.S. citizens will be charged amount that will be equal to the rate for nonresidents at a state university in their home state. In second year of residency in Puerto Rico, such students will be charged in-state rate.

FINANCIAL AID PICTURE (2012-2013)
Students with need: 91% of average financial aid package awarded as scholarships/grants, 9% awarded as loans/jobs. Need-based aid available for part-time students.
Students without need: This college awards aid only to students with need.

FINANCIAL AID PROCEDURES
Forms required: FAFSA, state aid form, institutional form.
Dates and Deadlines: Closing date 4/30. Applicants notified on a rolling basis starting 6/10.

CONTACT
Rafael Ruiz, Financial Aid Director
PO Box 4800, Carolina, PR 00984-4800
(787) 769-0188

University of Puerto Rico: Cayey University College

Cayey, Puerto Rico
www.cayey.upr.edu Federal Code: 007206

4-year public university and liberal arts college in large town.
Enrollment: 3,611 undergrads, 7% part-time. 889 full-time freshmen.
Selectivity: Admits over 75% of applicants.

BASIC COSTS (2012-2013)
Tuition and fees: $2,666.
Per-credit charge: $55.
Additional info: Nonresidents who are U.S. citizens will be charged amount that will be equal to the rate for nonresidents at a state university in their home state. In second year of residency in Puerto Rico, such students will be charged in-state rate. Tuition at time of enrollment locked for 4 years.

FINANCIAL AID PICTURE (2011-2012)
Students with need: Need-based aid available for part-time students. Work study available weekends and for part-time students.
Students without need: This college awards aid only to students with need.

FINANCIAL AID PROCEDURES
Forms required: FAFSA.
Dates and Deadlines: Closing date 6/30. Applicants notified by 7/30.
Transfers: Priority date 1/30; closing date 2/28.

CONTACT
Sonia Placeres, Director of Financial Aid
Oficina de Admisiones UPR- Cayey, Cayey, PR 00737-2230
(787) 738-2161 ext. 2061

University of Puerto Rico: Humacao

Humacao, Puerto Rico
www.uprh.edu Federal Code: 003942

4-year public university and liberal arts college in small city.
Enrollment: 3,603 undergrads.

BASIC COSTS (2012-2013)
Tuition and fees: $2,666.
Per-credit charge: $55.
Additional info: Nonresidents who are U.S. citizens will be charged amount that will be equal to the rate for nonresidents at a state university in their home state. In second year of residency in Puerto Rico, such students will be charged in-state rate.

FINANCIAL AID PICTURE
Students with need: Need-based aid available for full-time and part-time students.
Students without need: No-need awards available for academics, athletics, music/drama.

FINANCIAL AID PROCEDURES
Forms required: FAFSA.
Dates and Deadlines: Priority date 3/1; closing date 6/30. Applicants notified on a rolling basis starting 4/30; must reply by 7/31.

CONTACT
Larry Cruz, Director of Financial Aid
Call Box 860, Humacao, PR 00792
(787) 850-9342

University of Puerto Rico: Mayaguez

Mayaguez, Puerto Rico
www.uprm.edu Federal Code: 003944

5-year public university and engineering college in small city.
Enrollment: 10,832 undergrads, 5% part-time. 1,723 full-time freshmen.
Selectivity: Admits 50 to 75% of applicants.

BASIC COSTS (2012-2013)
Tuition and fees: $2,666.
Per-credit charge: $55.
Additional info: Nonresidents who are U.S. citizens will be charged amount that will be equal to the rate for nonresidents at a state university in their home state. In second year of residency in Puerto Rico, such students will be charged in-state rate.

FINANCIAL AID PICTURE (2011-2012)
Students with need: Out of 1,467 full-time freshmen who applied for aid, 1,253 were judged to have need. Of these, 1,198 received aid. Average financial aid package met 96% of need; average scholarship/grant was

$6,190; average loan was $2,394. For part-time students, average financial aid package was $2,137.
Students without need: This college awards aid only to students with need.

FINANCIAL AID PROCEDURES
Forms required: FAFSA, institutional form.
Dates and Deadlines: Priority date 1/30; closing date 6/30. Applicants notified on a rolling basis starting 6/30.
Transfers: Must reply by 6/30. Deadline according to admission date.

CONTACT
Lynette Feliciano, Director of Financial Aid
Admissions Office, Mayaguez, PR 00681-9000
(787) 265-1920

University of Puerto Rico: Medical Sciences
San Juan, Puerto Rico
www.rcm.upr.edu Federal Code: 003945

4-year public university in large city.
Enrollment: 476 undergrads, 8% part-time.

BASIC COSTS (2012-2013)
Tuition and fees: $2,666.
Per-credit charge: $55.
Additional info: Nonresidents who are U.S. citizens will be charged amount that will be equal to the rate for nonresidents at a state university in their home state. In second year of residency in Puerto Rico, such students will be charged in-state rate.

FINANCIAL AID PICTURE
Students with need: Need-based aid available for full-time and part-time students. Work study available nights, weekends, and for part-time students.
Students without need: This college awards aid only to students with need.

FINANCIAL AID PROCEDURES
Forms required: FAFSA, institutional form.
Dates and Deadlines: Priority date 4/30; closing date 6/15. Applicants notified on a rolling basis starting 8/1; must reply within 2 week(s) of notification.

CONTACT
Rafael Solis, Director of Financial Aid
PO Box 365067, San Juan, PR 00936-5067
(787) 758-2525 ext. 3205

University of Puerto Rico: Ponce
Ponce, Puerto Rico
www.uprp.edu Federal Code: 009652

4-year public university and branch campus college in small city.
Enrollment: 3,089 undergrads, 6% part-time. 766 full-time freshmen.
Selectivity: Admits over 75% of applicants.

BASIC COSTS (2012-2013)
Tuition and fees: $2,666.
Per-credit charge: $55.
Additional info: Nonresidents who are U.S. citizens will be charged amount that will be equal to the rate for nonresidents at a state university in their home state. In second year of residency in Puerto Rico, such students will be charged in-state rate. Tuition at time of enrollment locked for 4 years.

FINANCIAL AID PICTURE (2011-2012)
Students with need: 87% of average financial aid package awarded as scholarships/grants, 13% awarded as loans/jobs.
Students without need: This college awards aid only to students with need.

FINANCIAL AID PROCEDURES
Forms required: FAFSA, institutional form.
Dates and Deadlines: Closing date 5/30.

CONTACT
Ada Herencia, Financial Aid Officer
Box 7186, Ponce, PR 00732
(787) 844-8181 ext. 2555

University of Puerto Rico: Rio Piedras
San Juan, Puerto Rico
www.uprrp.edu Federal Code: 007108

4-year public university in very large city.
Enrollment: 11,739 undergrads, 9% part-time. 1,938 full-time freshmen.

BASIC COSTS (2012-2013)
Tuition and fees: $2,666.
Per-credit charge: $55.
Room and board: $8,280.
Additional info: Nonresidents who are U.S. citizens will be charged amount that will be equal to the rate for nonresidents at a state university in their home state. In second year of residency in Puerto Rico, such students will be charged in-state rate.

FINANCIAL AID PICTURE
Students with need: Need-based aid available for full-time and part-time students.
Students without need: This college awards aid only to students with need.
Additional info: Tuition waived for honor students, athletes, members of chorus, and others with special talents.

FINANCIAL AID PROCEDURES
Forms required: FAFSA.
Dates and Deadlines: Closing date 4/1.

CONTACT
Evaristo Marrero, Director of Financial Aid
Box 21907, San Juan, PR 00931-1907

University of Puerto Rico: Utuado
Utuado, Puerto Rico
www.web.uprutuado.edu/main/ Federal Code: 010922

4-year public agricultural college in large town.
Enrollment: 1,426 undergrads, 4% part-time. 636 full-time freshmen.
Selectivity: Admits 50 to 75% of applicants.

BASIC COSTS (2012-2013)
Tuition and fees: $2,666.
Per-credit charge: $55.
Additional info: Nonresidents who are U.S. citizens will be charged amount that will be equal to the rate for nonresidents at a state university in their home state. In second year of residency in Puerto Rico, such students will be charged in-state rate.

FINANCIAL AID PICTURE
Students with need: Need-based aid available for full-time and part-time students. Work study available nights.

Students without need: This college awards aid only to students with need.

FINANCIAL AID PROCEDURES
Forms required: FAFSA.
Dates and Deadlines: Priority date 5/31; no closing date. Applicants notified on a rolling basis starting 9/30; must reply within 4 week(s) of notification.
Transfers: Priority date 5/30; closing date 6/15. Closing date for Pell Grant applicants March 31.

CONTACT
Edymariel Cortes, Financial Aid Director
PO Box 2500, Utuado, PR 00641
(787) 894-2828 ext. 2603

University of the Sacred Heart
San Juan, Puerto Rico
www.sagrado.edu Federal Code: 003937

4-year private university and liberal arts college in large city, affiliated with Roman Catholic Church.
Enrollment: 5,443 undergrads, 13% part-time. 824 full-time freshmen.
Selectivity: Admits less than 50% of applicants.

BASIC COSTS (2012-2013)
Tuition and fees: $6,500.
Per-credit charge: $185.
Additional info: Board plan not available. Cost of room only, $2,800.

FINANCIAL AID PICTURE
Students with need: Need-based aid available for full-time and part-time students.
Students without need: No-need awards available for academics, athletics.

FINANCIAL AID PROCEDURES
Forms required: FAFSA, institutional form.
Dates and Deadlines: Priority date 4/30; closing date 5/30. Applicants notified on a rolling basis starting 6/15; must reply by 8/30.
Transfers: No deadline.

CONTACT
June Adrade, Director of Financial Aid
Universidad del Sagrado Corazon Oficina de Nuevo Ingreso, San Juan, PR 00914-0383

Rhode Island

Brown University
Providence, Rhode Island Federal Code: 003401
www.brown.edu CSS Code: 3094

4-year private university and liberal arts college in small city.
Enrollment: 6,133 undergrads. 1,536 full-time freshmen.
Selectivity: Admits less than 50% of applicants.

BASIC COSTS (2013-2014)
Tuition and fees: $45,612.
Room and board: $11,620.

FINANCIAL AID PICTURE
Students with need: Need-based aid available for full-time and part-time students.
Students without need: This college awards aid only to students with need.

FINANCIAL AID PROCEDURES
Forms required: FAFSA, CSS PROFILE.
Dates and Deadlines: Closing date 1/1. Applicants notified by 4/1; must reply by 5/1.
Transfers: Financial aid for transfer applicants is limited. Transfer admissions are not need-blind. If awarded financial aid, your demonstrated need will be met. In order for an applicant to be considered for available funds, each candidate for financial aid must check "yes" to the Financial Aid question on Form 1 of the admission application and complete the appropriate application forms by the requisite deadlines.

CONTACT
James Tilton, Director of Financial Aid
45 Prospect Street, Providence, RI 02912
(401) 863-2721

Bryant University
Smithfield, Rhode Island
www.bryant.edu Federal Code: 003402

4-year private business and liberal arts college in large town.
Enrollment: 3,157 undergrads, 3% part-time. 772 full-time freshmen.
Selectivity: Admits 50 to 75% of applicants.

BASIC COSTS (2013-2014)
Tuition and fees: $37,234.
Room and board: $13,664.

FINANCIAL AID PICTURE
Students with need: Need-based aid available for full-time and part-time students. Work study available nights, weekends, and for part-time students.
Students without need: No-need awards available for academics, athletics, minority status, ROTC, state/district residency.

FINANCIAL AID PROCEDURES
Forms required: FAFSA.
Dates and Deadlines: Closing date 2/15. Applicants notified by 3/24; must reply by 5/1.
Transfers: Closing date 4/1.

CONTACT
John Canning, Director of Financial Aid
1150 Douglas Pike, Smithfield, RI 02917-1291
(401) 232-6020

Community College of Rhode Island
Warwick, Rhode Island
www.ccri.edu Federal Code: 004916

2-year public community college in small city.
Enrollment: 16,944 undergrads, 66% part-time. 1,966 full-time freshmen.
Selectivity: Open admission; but selective for some programs.

BASIC COSTS (2012-2013)
Tuition and fees: $3,950; out-of-state residents $10,582.
Per-credit charge: $165; out-of-state residents $490.
Additional info: Fall 2012: Reduced fee (in-state plus 50%) for residents of MA and CT communities within a 50-mile radius of Providence AND/OR for New England residents whose home states do not offer a particular program/course. Beginning Spring 2013, same policy applies to all New England residents (no mileage limitation). Tuition/fee waivers available for unemployed or children of unemployed.

FINANCIAL AID PICTURE
Students with need: Need-based aid available for full-time and part-time students. Work study available nights, weekends, and for part-time students.
Students without need: No-need awards available for athletics.

FINANCIAL AID PROCEDURES
Forms required: FAFSA, institutional form.
Dates and Deadlines: Priority date 3/1; closing date 7/1. Applicants notified on a rolling basis starting 5/1; must reply within 2 week(s) of notification.

CONTACT
Joel Friedman, Director of Financial Aid
400 East Avenue, Warwick, RI 02886-1807
(401) 825-2003

Johnson & Wales University: Providence
Providence, Rhode Island
www.jwu.edu Federal Code: 003404

4-year private university in small city.
Enrollment: 9,525 undergrads, 7% part-time. 2,073 full-time freshmen.
Selectivity: Admits 50 to 75% of applicants.

BASIC COSTS (2012-2013)
Tuition and fees: $26,112.
Room and board: $10,728.

FINANCIAL AID PICTURE
Students with need: Need-based aid available for full-time and part-time students.
Students without need: No-need awards available for academics, alumni affiliation, leadership, state/district residency.

FINANCIAL AID PROCEDURES
Forms required: FAFSA.
Dates and Deadlines: Applicants notified on a rolling basis starting 3/1; must reply within 2 week(s) of notification.
Transfers: Transfer scholarships available.

CONTACT
Lynn Robinson, Director of Financial Aid
8 Abbott Park Place, Providence, RI 02903-3703
(800) 342-5598 ext. 4648

New England Institute of Technology
East Greenwich, Rhode Island
www.neit.edu Federal Code: 007845

4-year private technical college in small city.
Enrollment: 2,713 undergrads, 14% part-time. 444 full-time freshmen.
Selectivity: Open admission.

BASIC COSTS (2012-2013)
Tuition and fees: $20,841.

FINANCIAL AID PICTURE
Students with need: Need-based aid available for full-time and part-time students. Work study available nights, weekends, and for part-time students.
Students without need: No-need awards available for academics.
Additional info: Tuition at time of first enrollment guaranteed all students for 2 years.

FINANCIAL AID PROCEDURES
Forms required: FAFSA.
Dates and Deadlines: Applicants notified on a rolling basis.
Transfers: No deadline. Applicants notified on a rolling basis.

CONTACT
Anna Kelly, Director of Financial Aid
One New England Tech Blvd., East Greenwich, RI 02818
(401) 739-5000 ext. 3354

Providence College
Providence, Rhode Island Federal Code: 003406
www.providence.edu CSS Code: 3693

4-year private liberal arts college in small city, affiliated with Roman Catholic Church.
Enrollment: 3,804 undergrads. 998 full-time freshmen.
Selectivity: Admits 50 to 75% of applicants. GED not accepted.

BASIC COSTS (2013-2014)
Tuition and fees: $42,206.
Room and board: $12,440.
Additional info: Tuition/fee waivers available for minority students.

FINANCIAL AID PICTURE (2012-2013)
Students with need: Out of 728 full-time freshmen who applied for aid, 514 were judged to have need. Of these, 514 received aid, and 200 had their full need met. Average financial aid package met 87% of need; average scholarship/grant was $23,530; average loan was $4,890. For part-time students, average financial aid package was $6,078.
Students without need: 121 full-time freshmen who did not demonstrate need for aid received scholarships/grants; average award was $15,222. No-need awards available for academics, athletics, leadership, minority status, music/drama, ROTC.
Scholarships offered: 54 full-time freshmen received athletic scholarships; average amount $24,382.
Cumulative student debt: 70% of graduating class had student loans; average debt was $26,832.

FINANCIAL AID PROCEDURES
Forms required: FAFSA, CSS PROFILE.
Dates and Deadlines: Closing date 2/1. Applicants notified by 3/15; must reply by 5/1.
Transfers: Closing date 4/15. Applicants notified on a rolling basis starting 4/15; must reply within 2 week(s) of notification. Merit scholarships available to transfer students with superior academic performance in college course work completed prior to enrolling at Providence College.

CONTACT
Sandra Oliveira, Director of Financial Aid
Harkins Hall 103, One Cunningham Square, Providence, RI 02918-0001
(401) 865-2286

Rhode Island College
Providence, Rhode Island
www.ric.edu Federal Code: 003407

4-year public liberal arts college in small city.
Enrollment: 7,261 undergrads, 25% part-time. 1,038 full-time freshmen.
Selectivity: Admits 50 to 75% of applicants.

BASIC COSTS (2012-2013)
Tuition and fees: $7,598; out-of-state residents $18,296.
Per-credit charge: $272; out-of-state residents $670.
Room and board: $9,534.
Additional info: Reduced fee (in-state plus 50%) for residents of MA and CT communities within a 50-mile radius of Providence AND/OR for New England residents whose home states do not offer a particular program/course. Tuition/fee waivers available for unemployed or children of unemployed.

FINANCIAL AID PICTURE (2012-2013)
Students with need: Out of 950 full-time freshmen who applied for aid, 718 were judged to have need. Of these, 698 received aid, and 135 had their full need met. Average financial aid package met 73% of need; average scholarship/grant was $6,665; average loan was $3,351. For part-time students, average financial aid package was $6,382.

Students without need: 46 full-time freshmen who did not demonstrate need for aid received scholarships/grants; average award was $1,999. No-need awards available for academics, alumni affiliation, art, music/drama.

Scholarships offered: Presidential Scholarships: $2,000 per year; for entering freshmen in the top 30% of class; minimum combined SAT score of 1100 (exclusive of Writing); must apply for admission by Dec 15; approximately 100 awards.

Cumulative student debt: 79% of graduating class had student loans; average debt was $23,110.

Additional info: Metropolitan Tuition Policy (MTP) for Connecticut and Massachusetts students whose permanent address is within a 50-mile radius of the College allows students to pay the in-state tuition rate plus 50%. Using figures for 2012-2013, this is an annual savings of over $7,400 compared with the out-of-state rate.

FINANCIAL AID PROCEDURES

Forms required: FAFSA, institutional form.

Dates and Deadlines: Priority date 3/1; no closing date. Applicants notified on a rolling basis starting 3/15; must reply by 5/1 or within 3 week(s) of notification.

Transfers: Priority date 5/15. Applicants notified on a rolling basis starting 3/15; must reply by 5/1 or within 3 week(s) of notification.

CONTACT

James Hanbury, Director of Financial Aid
600 Mount Pleasant Avenue, Providence, RI 02908
(401) 456-8033

Rhode Island School of Design

Providence, Rhode Island — Federal Code: 003409
www.risd.edu — CSS Code: 3726

4-year private visual arts college in small city.

Enrollment: 1,971 undergrads. 452 full-time freshmen.

Selectivity: Admits less than 50% of applicants.

BASIC COSTS (2013-2014)

Tuition and fees: $42,932.

Room and board: $12,272.

FINANCIAL AID PICTURE (2011-2012)

Students with need: Out of 236 full-time freshmen who applied for aid, 189 were judged to have need. Of these, 189 received aid, and 8 had their full need met. Average financial aid package met 70% of need; average scholarship/grant was $20,929; average loan was $2,874.

Students without need: 5 full-time freshmen who did not demonstrate need for aid received scholarships/grants; average award was $10,000. No-need awards available for academics, art.

Cumulative student debt: 60% of graduating class had student loans; average debt was $32,207.

FINANCIAL AID PROCEDURES

Forms required: FAFSA, CSS PROFILE.

Dates and Deadlines: Closing date 2/15. Applicants notified by 4/1; must reply by 5/1.

Transfers: Closing date 3/15. Applicants notified by 4/25; must reply by 5/22. Transfer students with previous undergraduate degree not eligible for scholarship aid.

CONTACT

Anthony Gallonio, Director of Financial Aid
2 College Street, Providence, RI 02903-2784
(401) 454-6661

Roger Williams University

Bristol, Rhode Island — Federal Code: 003410
www.rwu.edu — CSS Code: 3729

4-year private university in large town.

Enrollment: 4,295 undergrads, 13% part-time. 997 full-time freshmen.

Selectivity: Admits over 75% of applicants.

BASIC COSTS (2013-2014)

Tuition and fees: $31,618.

Per-credit charge: $1,249.

Room and board: $13,690.

Additional info: Tuition at time of enrollment locked for 4 years.

FINANCIAL AID PICTURE (2012-2013)

Students with need: Out of 774 full-time freshmen who applied for aid, 622 were judged to have need. Of these, 619 received aid, and 59 had their full need met. Average financial aid package met 86% of need; average scholarship/grant was $12,615; average loan was $4,078. For part-time students, average financial aid package was $8,451.

Students without need: 148 full-time freshmen who did not demonstrate need for aid received scholarships/grants; average award was $11,051. No-need awards available for academics, leadership.

Cumulative student debt: 66% of graduating class had student loans; average debt was $38,550.

FINANCIAL AID PROCEDURES

Forms required: FAFSA. New students must complete CSS PROFILE by January 1.

Dates and Deadlines: Priority date 1/1; closing date 2/1. Applicants notified on a rolling basis; must reply within 2 week(s) of notification.

Transfers: Must reply by 5/1.

CONTACT

Tracy DaCosta, Assistant Vice President of Enrollment Management & Retention
1 Old Ferry Road, Bristol, RI 02809-2921
(401) 254-3100

Salve Regina University

Newport, Rhode Island — Federal Code: 003411
www.salve.edu — CSS Code: 3759

4-year private university and liberal arts college in large town, affiliated with Roman Catholic Church.

Enrollment: 2,020 undergrads, 2% part-time. 545 full-time freshmen.

Selectivity: Admits 50 to 75% of applicants.

BASIC COSTS (2012-2013)

Tuition and fees: $33,950.

Per-credit charge: $1,115.

Room and board: $11,950.

FINANCIAL AID PICTURE (2012-2013)

Students with need: Out of 502 full-time freshmen who applied for aid, 448 were judged to have need. Of these, 446 received aid, and 42 had their full need met. Average financial aid package met 70% of need; average scholarship/grant was $19,401; average loan was $3,314. For part-time students, average financial aid package was $4,404.

Students without need: 197 full-time freshmen who did not demonstrate need for aid received scholarships/grants; average award was $10,800. No-need awards available for academics, alumni affiliation, art, ROTC.

FINANCIAL AID PROCEDURES

Forms required: FAFSA, CSS PROFILE.

Dates and Deadlines: Priority date 3/1; no closing date. Applicants notified on a rolling basis starting 1/3; must reply by 5/1 or within 2 week(s) of notification.

Transfers: No deadline. Applicants notified on a rolling basis starting 3/1; must reply by 5/1 or within 2 week(s) of notification. Must provide financial aid transcripts from previous institutions attended.

CONTACT

Aida Mirante, Director of Financial Aid
100 Ochre Point Avenue, Newport, RI 02840-4192
(401) 341-2901

University of Rhode Island

Kingston, Rhode Island
www.uri.edu Federal Code: 003414

4-year public university in small town.
Enrollment: 13,149 undergrads, 10% part-time. 2,994 full-time freshmen.
Selectivity: Admits over 75% of applicants.

BASIC COSTS (2012-2013)

Tuition and fees: $12,450; out-of-state residents $28,016.
Per-credit charge: $453; out-of-state residents $1,102.
Room and board: $11,160.
Additional info: Tuition/fee waivers available for unemployed or children of unemployed.

FINANCIAL AID PICTURE (2012-2013)

Students with need: Out of 2,463 full-time freshmen who applied for aid, 2,012 were judged to have need. Of these, 1,842 received aid, and 1,288 had their full need met. Average financial aid package met 64% of need; average scholarship/grant was $9,665; average loan was $5,174. For part-time students, average financial aid package was $9,362.
Students without need: 190 full-time freshmen who did not demonstrate need for aid received scholarships/grants; average award was $5,476. No-need awards available for academics, alumni affiliation, art, athletics, music/drama, ROTC.
Scholarships offered: 11 full-time freshmen received athletic scholarships; average amount $10,318.
Cumulative student debt: 77% of graduating class had student loans; average debt was $30,387.

FINANCIAL AID PROCEDURES

Forms required: FAFSA.
Dates and Deadlines: Priority date 3/1; no closing date. Applicants notified on a rolling basis starting 3/15; must reply by 5/1.
Transfers: No deadline. Applicants notified on a rolling basis starting 4/1; must reply within 2 week(s) of notification.

CONTACT

Paul Langhammer, Senior Associate Director of Enrollment Services
Newman Hall, Kingston, RI 02881-1322
(401) 874-9500

South Carolina

Aiken Technical College

Aiken, South Carolina
www.atc.edu Federal Code: 010056

2-year public community and technical college in small city.
Enrollment: 2,828 undergrads, 68% part-time. 628 full-time freshmen.
Selectivity: Open admission; but selective for some programs.

BASIC COSTS (2012-2013)

Tuition and fees: $3,866; out-of-district residents $4,226; out-of-state residents $10,140.

FINANCIAL AID PICTURE (2012-2013)

Students with need: For part-time students, average financial aid package was $4,866.
Students without need: No-need awards available for academics, athletics, leadership, minority status, state/district residency.
Scholarships offered: Vernon Ford Scholarships: $1,000 annually; for candidates with minimum GPA of 3.0; 8 awarded annually. Presidential Scholarship: $10,000 annually; 10 awarded.

FINANCIAL AID PROCEDURES

Forms required: FAFSA.
Dates and Deadlines: Priority date 5/1; closing date 6/1. Applicants notified on a rolling basis starting 4/1; must reply within 2 week(s) of notification.
Transfers: Priority date 6/1. Applicants notified on a rolling basis; must reply within 2 week(s) of notification.

CONTACT

Amanda Chittum, Director of Financial Aid
PO Drawer 696, Aiken, SC 29802
(803) 593-9954 ext. 1261

Allen University

Columbia, South Carolina
www.allenuniversity.edu Federal Code: 003417

4-year private university and liberal arts college in large city, affiliated with African Methodist Episcopal Church.
Enrollment: 672 undergrads, 3% part-time. 121 full-time freshmen.
Selectivity: Admits less than 50% of applicants.

BASIC COSTS (2012-2013)

Tuition and fees: $12,340.
Per-credit charge: $460.
Room and board: $5,560.

FINANCIAL AID PICTURE

Students with need: Need-based aid available for full-time and part-time students.
Students without need: No-need awards available for academics, athletics, music/drama, ROTC.

FINANCIAL AID PROCEDURES

Forms required: FAFSA.
Dates and Deadlines: Priority date 4/15; closing date 7/20. Applicants notified on a rolling basis starting 4/1; must reply within 2 week(s) of notification.
Transfers: No deadline.

CONTACT

Shelline Warren, Financial Aid Director
1530 Harden Street, Columbia, SC 29204
(803) 376-5930

Anderson University

Anderson, South Carolina
www.andersonuniversity.edu Federal Code: 003418

4-year private university in large town, affiliated with Southern Baptist Convention.
Enrollment: 2,618 undergrads, 18% part-time. 554 full-time freshmen.
Selectivity: Admits 50 to 75% of applicants.

BASIC COSTS (2012-2013)

Tuition and fees: $21,730.
Room and board: $8,282.
Additional info: Tuition/fee waivers available for adults.

FINANCIAL AID PICTURE (2012-2013)
Students with need: Out of 520 full-time freshmen who applied for aid, 425 were judged to have need. Of these, 424 received aid, and 139 had their full need met. Average financial aid package met 78% of need; average scholarship/grant was $16,942; average loan was $4,308. For part-time students, average financial aid package was $5,776.
Students without need: 115 full-time freshmen who did not demonstrate need for aid received scholarships/grants; average award was $10,921. No-need awards available for academics, alumni affiliation, art, athletics, leadership, minority status, music/drama, religious affiliation, state/district residency.
Scholarships offered: 28 full-time freshmen received athletic scholarships; average amount $5,217.
Cumulative student debt: 73% of graduating class had student loans; average debt was $27,187.

FINANCIAL AID PROCEDURES
Forms required: FAFSA, state aid form.
Dates and Deadlines: Priority date 3/1; closing date 6/30. Applicants notified on a rolling basis starting 3/15; must reply within 2 week(s) of notification.
Transfers: No deadline. Applicants notified on a rolling basis. Transfers are awarded based on college GPA on a different merit scale than Firs-time-freshmen.

CONTACT
Michael Yohe, Director of Financial Aid
316 Boulevard, Anderson, SC 29621-4002
(864) 231-2070

Benedict College
Columbia, South Carolina
www.benedict.edu Federal Code: 003420

4-year private liberal arts college in large city, affiliated with American Baptist Churches in the USA.
Enrollment: 2,921 undergrads, 2% part-time. 737 full-time freshmen.
Selectivity: Admits over 75% of applicants.

BASIC COSTS (2012-2013)
Tuition and fees: $18,286.
Per-credit charge: $548.
Room and board: $8,104.

FINANCIAL AID PICTURE (2011-2012)
Students with need: 49% of average financial aid package awarded as scholarships/grants, 51% awarded as loans/jobs. Need-based aid available for part-time students.

FINANCIAL AID PROCEDURES
Forms required: FAFSA.
Dates and Deadlines: Priority date 4/15; no closing date. Applicants notified on a rolling basis starting 4/15.

CONTACT
Sul Black, Director of Financial Aid
1600 Harden Street, Columbia, SC 29204
(803) 253-5105

Bob Jones University
Greenville, South Carolina
www.bju.edu Federal Code: 003421

4-year private Bible and liberal arts college in small city, affiliated with nondenominational tradition.
Enrollment: 2,859 undergrads, 3% part-time. 695 full-time freshmen.
Selectivity: Admits 50 to 75% of applicants.

BASIC COSTS (2013-2014)
Tuition and fees: $13,430.
Per-credit charge: $641.
Room and board: $5,790.

FINANCIAL AID PICTURE (2012-2013)
Students with need: Out of 536 full-time freshmen who applied for aid, 481 were judged to have need. Of these, 461 received aid. Average financial aid package met 46% of need; average scholarship/grant was $6,500; average loan was $3,295. For part-time students, average financial aid package was $6,000.
Students without need: No-need awards available for state/district residency.

FINANCIAL AID PROCEDURES
Forms required: FAFSA.
Dates and Deadlines: Closing date 3/1. Applicants notified by 3/15.
Transfers: Applicants notified on a rolling basis.

CONTACT
Kevin Delp, Director of Financial Aid
1700 Wade Hampton Boulevard, Greenville, SC 29614
(864) 242-5100 ext. 3040

Central Carolina Technical College
Sumter, South Carolina
www.cctech.edu Federal Code: 003995

2-year public community and technical college in large town.
Enrollment: 4,277 undergrads.
Selectivity: Open admission; but selective for some programs.

BASIC COSTS (2012-2013)
Tuition and fees: $3,584; out-of-district residents $4,178; out-of-state residents $6,232.
Per-credit charge: $149; out-of-district residents $174; out-of-state residents $260.

FINANCIAL AID PICTURE
Students with need: Need-based aid available for full-time and part-time students. Work study available nights.

FINANCIAL AID PROCEDURES
Forms required: FAFSA.
Dates and Deadlines: Applicants notified on a rolling basis starting 4/11; must reply within 2 week(s) of notification.

CONTACT
Sarah Dowd, Director of Financial Aid
506 North Guignard Drive, Sumter, SC 29150-2499
(803) 778-7831

Charleston Southern University
Charleston, South Carolina
www.csuniv.edu Federal Code: 003419

4-year private university and liberal arts college in large city, affiliated with Southern Baptist Convention.
Enrollment: 2,763 undergrads.
Selectivity: Admits over 75% of applicants.

BASIC COSTS (2012-2013)
Tuition and fees: $21,400.
Per-credit charge: $470.
Room and board: $8,400.

FINANCIAL AID PICTURE

Students with need: Need-based aid available for full-time and part-time students. Work study available nights, weekends, and for part-time students.

Students without need: No-need awards available for academics, athletics, religious affiliation, ROTC.

FINANCIAL AID PROCEDURES

Forms required: FAFSA, state aid form.

Dates and Deadlines: Priority date 4/15; no closing date. Applicants notified on a rolling basis starting 3/1; must reply within 2 week(s) of notification.

CONTACT

Jenna Parish, Director of Financial Aid
9200 University Boulevard, Charleston, SC 29423-8087
(843) 863-7050

The Citadel

Charleston, South Carolina
www.citadel.edu Federal Code: 003423

4-year public military college in large city.
Enrollment: 2,555 undergrads, 5% part-time. 676 full-time freshmen.
Selectivity: Admits over 75% of applicants.

BASIC COSTS (2012-2013)

Tuition and fees: $11,772; out-of-state residents $30,025.
Per-credit charge: $410; out-of-state residents $743.
Room and board: $6,115.
Additional info: Freshmen pay $6,940 deposit and upperclassmen pay $2,874 deposit for uniforms, laundry, dry cleaning charges, infirmary fees, books, and supplies.

FINANCIAL AID PICTURE (2012-2013)

Students with need: Out of 574 full-time freshmen who applied for aid, 423 were judged to have need. Of these, 411 received aid, and 85 had their full need met. Average financial aid package met 54% of need; average scholarship/grant was $13,268; average loan was $3,372. For part-time students, average financial aid package was $6,329.

Students without need: 127 full-time freshmen who did not demonstrate need for aid received scholarships/grants; average award was $8,844. No-need awards available for academics, athletics, leadership, minority status, music/drama, ROTC, state/district residency.

Scholarships offered: 71 full-time freshmen received athletic scholarships; average amount $25,146.

Cumulative student debt: 52% of graduating class had student loans; average debt was $31,217.

FINANCIAL AID PROCEDURES

Forms required: FAFSA, institutional form.

Dates and Deadlines: Priority date 2/28; no closing date. Applicants notified on a rolling basis starting 4/1; must reply by 4/1 or within 2 week(s) of notification.

Transfers: No deadline. Applicants notified on a rolling basis starting 4/1; must reply within 2 week(s) of notification.

CONTACT

Henry Fuller, Director of Financial Aid
171 Moultrie Street, Charleston, SC 29409
(843) 953-5187

Claflin University

Orangeburg, South Carolina
www.claflin.edu Federal Code: 003424

4-year private liberal arts college in large town, affiliated with United Methodist Church.
Enrollment: 1,850 undergrads, 1% part-time. 440 full-time freshmen.
Selectivity: Admits 50 to 75% of applicants.

BASIC COSTS (2012-2013)

Tuition and fees: $14,308.
Per-credit charge: $582.
Room and board: $8,040.

FINANCIAL AID PICTURE (2012-2013)

Students with need: Out of 384 full-time freshmen who applied for aid, 354 were judged to have need. Of these, 319 received aid, and 31 had their full need met. Average financial aid package met 54% of need; average scholarship/grant was $12,184; average loan was $3,283. Need-based aid available for part-time students.

Students without need: 18 full-time freshmen who did not demonstrate need for aid received scholarships/grants; average award was $9,405.

Scholarships offered: 2 full-time freshmen received athletic scholarships; average amount $11,784.

Cumulative student debt: 90% of graduating class had student loans; average debt was $31,377.

FINANCIAL AID PROCEDURES

Forms required: FAFSA.

Dates and Deadlines: Closing date 4/15. Applicants notified on a rolling basis starting 5/3; must reply within 2 week(s) of notification.

Transfers: No deadline. Applicants notified on a rolling basis.

CONTACT

Terria Williams, Director of Financial Aid
400 Magnolia Street, Orangeburg, SC 29115
(803) 535-5334

Clemson University

Clemson, South Carolina
www.clemson.edu Federal Code: 003425

4-year public university and engineering college in large town.
Enrollment: 16,426 undergrads, 5% part-time. 3,435 full-time freshmen.
Selectivity: Admits 50 to 75% of applicants.

BASIC COSTS (2012-2013)

Tuition and fees: $12,774; out-of-state residents $29,700.
Per-credit charge: $530; out-of-state residents $1,264.
Room and board: $7,868.

FINANCIAL AID PICTURE

Students with need: Need-based aid available for full-time and part-time students. Work study available nights, weekends, and for part-time students.

Students without need: No-need awards available for academics, art, athletics, leadership, minority status, music/drama, ROTC, state/district residency.

FINANCIAL AID PROCEDURES

Forms required: FAFSA.

Dates and Deadlines: Priority date 4/1; no closing date. Applicants notified on a rolling basis starting 4/1; must reply within 3 week(s) of notification.

Transfers: Applicants notified on a rolling basis starting 5/1; must reply within 3 week(s) of notification. Transfer students must earn 12 semester hours before being considered for institutional scholarship.

CONTACT

Chuck Knepfle, Director of Student Financial Aid
105 Sikes Hall, Clemson, SC 29634-5124
(864) 656-2280

Coastal Carolina University

Conway, South Carolina
www.coastal.edu Federal Code: 003451

4-year public university in large town.
Enrollment: 8,466 undergrads, 7% part-time. 2,128 full-time freshmen.
Selectivity: Admits 50 to 75% of applicants.

BASIC COSTS (2012-2013)
Tuition and fees: $9,760; out-of-state residents $22,050.
Per-credit charge: $407; out-of-state residents $920.
Room and board: $7,700.

FINANCIAL AID PICTURE (2011-2012)
Students with need: Out of 1,948 full-time freshmen who applied for aid, 1,602 were judged to have need. Of these, 1,574 received aid, and 132 had their full need met. Average financial aid package met 48% of need; average scholarship/grant was $4,794; average loan was $7,987. For part-time students, average financial aid package was $5,176.
Students without need: 345 full-time freshmen who did not demonstrate need for aid received scholarships/grants; average award was $12,764. No-need awards available for academics, art, athletics, leadership, music/drama, ROTC, state/district residency.
Scholarships offered: 91 full-time freshmen received athletic scholarships; average amount $10,287.
Cumulative student debt: 72% of graduating class had student loans; average debt was $34,040.

FINANCIAL AID PROCEDURES
Forms required: FAFSA.
Dates and Deadlines: Priority date 3/1; no closing date. Applicants notified on a rolling basis starting 3/1; must reply by 5/15.
Transfers: No deadline. Applicants notified on a rolling basis starting 3/1; must reply within 4 week(s) of notification.

CONTACT
Dawn Hitchcock, Director of Financial Aid
PO Box 261954, Conway, SC 29528-6054
(843) 349-2313

Coker College

Hartsville, South Carolina
www.coker.edu Federal Code: 003427

4-year private liberal arts college in large town.
Enrollment: 1,136 undergrads, 12% part-time. 209 full-time freshmen.
Selectivity: Admits 50 to 75% of applicants.

BASIC COSTS (2012-2013)
Tuition and fees: $23,640.
Room and board: $7,285.
Additional info: Tuition/fee waivers available for adults.

FINANCIAL AID PICTURE (2011-2012)
Students with need: Out of 197 full-time freshmen who applied for aid, 184 were judged to have need. Of these, 184 received aid, and 49 had their full need met. Average financial aid package met 99% of need; average scholarship/grant was $6,489; average loan was $3,552. For part-time students, average financial aid package was $6,385.
Students without need: 19 full-time freshmen who did not demonstrate need for aid received scholarships/grants; average award was $5,375. No-need awards available for academics, alumni affiliation, art, athletics, leadership, music/drama.
Scholarships offered: ***Merit:*** Scholarships for Excellence, up to $17,000 per year, awarded to students showing potential for continued high performance and leadership. ***Athletic:*** 5 full-time freshmen received athletic scholarships; average amount $10,300.
Cumulative student debt: 89% of graduating class had student loans; average debt was $32,842.
Additional info: Endowed scholarship program for qualified applicants. June 1 deadline for filing South Carolina Tuition Grant forms.

FINANCIAL AID PROCEDURES
Forms required: FAFSA.
Dates and Deadlines: Priority date 4/1; closing date 6/1. Applicants notified on a rolling basis starting 3/1; must reply by 5/1 or within 3 week(s) of notification.
Transfers: No deadline.

CONTACT
Betty Williams, Director of Financial Aid
300 East College Avenue, Hartsville, SC 29550
(843) 383-8055

College of Charleston

Charleston, South Carolina
www.cofc.edu Federal Code: 003428

4-year public liberal arts college in large city.
Enrollment: 10,206 undergrads, 5% part-time. 2,330 full-time freshmen.
Selectivity: Admits 50 to 75% of applicants.

BASIC COSTS (2012-2013)
Tuition and fees: $9,918; out-of-state residents $25,304.
Per-credit charge: $413; out-of-state residents $1,054.
Room and board: $10,461.

FINANCIAL AID PICTURE (2011-2012)
Students with need: Out of 1,693 full-time freshmen who applied for aid, 1,217 were judged to have need. Of these, 1,154 received aid, and 243 had their full need met. Average financial aid package met 56% of need; average scholarship/grant was $3,476; average loan was $2,766. For part-time students, average financial aid package was $8,310.
Students without need: 501 full-time freshmen who did not demonstrate need for aid received scholarships/grants; average award was $10,364. No-need awards available for academics, alumni affiliation, art, athletics, music/drama.
Scholarships offered: ***Merit:*** Foundation Scholarships: from $1,000-$4,000 annually for up to 4 years; based on high school performance, test scores, and leadership qualities, no additional application required. ***Athletic:*** 36 full-time freshmen received athletic scholarships; average amount $22,227.
Cumulative student debt: 45% of graduating class had student loans; average debt was $26,024.

FINANCIAL AID PROCEDURES
Forms required: FAFSA.
Dates and Deadlines: Priority date 3/1; no closing date. Applicants notified on a rolling basis starting 4/10; must reply within 8 week(s) of notification.
Transfers: No aid available to transfer students who enroll for first time in summer school.

CONTACT
Donald Griggs, Director of Financial Assistance and Veterans Affairs
Office of Admissions and Adult Student Services, Charleston, SC 29424-0001
(843) 953-5540

Columbia College

Columbia, South Carolina
www.columbiasc.edu Federal Code: 003430

4-year private liberal arts college for women in large city, affiliated with United Methodist Church.

Enrollment: 1,081 undergrads, 23% part-time. 196 full-time freshmen.
Selectivity: Admits 50 to 75% of applicants.

BASIC COSTS (2013-2014)
Tuition and fees: $27,250.
Per-credit charge: $710.
Room and board: $6,978.

FINANCIAL AID PICTURE (2011-2012)
Students with need: Out of 185 full-time freshmen who applied for aid, 179 were judged to have need. Of these, 176 received aid, and 25 had their full need met. Average financial aid package met 68% of need; average scholarship/grant was $18,264; average loan was $2,914. For part-time students, average financial aid package was $6,209.
Students without need: No-need awards available for academics, alumni affiliation, art, athletics, leadership, music/drama.
Scholarships offered: Founders Scholarship: full tuition. Presidential Scholarships: $10,000 annually. Trustees Scholarships: $8,000 annually.
Cumulative student debt: 84% of graduating class had student loans; average debt was $28,699.

FINANCIAL AID PROCEDURES
Forms required: FAFSA.
Dates and Deadlines: Priority date 4/1; no closing date. Applicants notified on a rolling basis starting 3/15; must reply within 2 week(s) of notification.
Transfers: Priority date 4/15. Must meet institutional standards of satisfactory academic progress.

CONTACT
Donna Quick, Director of Financial Aid
1301 Columbia College Drive, Columbia, SC 29203
(803) 786-3612

Columbia International University
Columbia, South Carolina
www.ciu.edu Federal Code: 003429

4-year private university and Bible college in small city, affiliated with multidenominational/evangelical churches.
Enrollment: 503 undergrads, 3% part-time. 106 full-time freshmen.
Selectivity: Admits 50 to 75% of applicants.

BASIC COSTS (2012-2013)
Tuition and fees: $18,780.
Per-credit charge: $750.
Room and board: $6,890.
Additional info: Tuition/fee waivers available for minority students.

FINANCIAL AID PICTURE (2011-2012)
Students with need: Out of 91 full-time freshmen who applied for aid, 90 were judged to have need. Of these, 90 received aid, and 10 had their full need met. Average financial aid package met 71% of need; average scholarship/grant was $9,510; average loan was $3,484. For part-time students, average financial aid package was $9,540.
Students without need: 11 full-time freshmen who did not demonstrate need for aid received scholarships/grants; average award was $6,083. No-need awards available for academics, alumni affiliation, athletics, leadership, minority status, music/drama, state/district residency.
Cumulative student debt: 59% of graduating class had student loans; average debt was $25,638.
Additional info: Spouse scholarship program; special short quarter scholarships for missionaries on furlough.

FINANCIAL AID PROCEDURES
Forms required: FAFSA, state aid form, institutional form.
Dates and Deadlines: Priority date 4/15; no closing date. Applicants notified on a rolling basis starting 3/15.
Transfers: No deadline. Applicants notified on a rolling basis starting 3/15; must reply within 2 week(s) of notification. FAFSA must be processed by June 30 for state need-based aid. State aid requires 1-year residency prior to award in most cases. Non-need-based state aid requires graduation from state high school.

CONTACT
Keith Marion, VP Development & Operations
PO Box 3122, Columbia, SC 29203-3122
(803) 807-5036

Converse College
Spartanburg, South Carolina
www.converse.edu Federal Code: 003431

4-year private liberal arts and performing arts college for women in small city.
Enrollment: 687 undergrads, 11% part-time. 183 full-time freshmen.
Selectivity: Admits 50 to 75% of applicants.

BASIC COSTS (2012-2013)
Tuition and fees: $28,276.
Per-credit charge: $875.
Room and board: $8,854.

FINANCIAL AID PICTURE
Students with need: Need-based aid available for full-time and part-time students. Work study available nights.
Students without need: No-need awards available for academics, art, athletics, music/drama, ROTC, state/district residency.

FINANCIAL AID PROCEDURES
Forms required: FAFSA.
Dates and Deadlines: Priority date 3/15; no closing date. Applicants notified on a rolling basis starting 3/1; must reply by 5/1 or within 2 week(s) of notification.
Transfers: No deadline. Applicants notified on a rolling basis starting 3/1; must reply by 5/1 or within 2 week(s) of notification.

CONTACT
Margaret Collins, Director of Scholarships and Financial Assistance
580 East Main Street, Spartanburg, SC 29302-0006
(864) 596-9019

Denmark Technical College
Denmark, South Carolina
www.denmarktech.edu Federal Code: 005363

2-year public technical college in small town.
Enrollment: 2,003 undergrads.
Selectivity: Open admission.

BASIC COSTS (2012-2013)
Tuition and fees: $2,568; out-of-state residents $5,136.
Room and board: $3,366.

FINANCIAL AID PICTURE
Students with need: Need-based aid available for full-time and part-time students.

FINANCIAL AID PROCEDURES
Forms required: FAFSA.
Dates and Deadlines: Applicants notified on a rolling basis starting 6/1; must reply within 2 week(s) of notification.

CONTACT
Connie Williams, Director of Financial Aid
1126 Solomon Blatt Boulevard, Denmark, SC 29042
(803) 793-5161

Erskine College

Due West, South Carolina
www.erskine.edu Federal Code: 003432

4-year private liberal arts and seminary college in rural community, affiliated with Associate Reformed Presbyterian Church.
Enrollment: 553 undergrads.
Selectivity: Admits 50 to 75% of applicants.

BASIC COSTS (2012-2013)
Tuition and fees: $29,790.
Room and board: $9,625.

FINANCIAL AID PICTURE
Students with need: Need-based aid available for full-time and part-time students. Work study available nights, weekends, and for part-time students.
Students without need: No-need awards available for academics, alumni affiliation, athletics, leadership, minority status, music/drama, religious affiliation, state/district residency.
Additional info: Filing deadline 5/1 for institutional form, 6/30 for state form.

FINANCIAL AID PROCEDURES
Forms required: FAFSA, state aid form, institutional form.
Dates and Deadlines: Priority date 4/1; no closing date. Applicants notified on a rolling basis starting 12/15; must reply within 2 week(s) of notification.
Transfers: Closing date 5/1. South Carolina residents must have earned 24 hours in previous year to receive SC tuition grant and 30 hours plus 3.0 GPA to receive the Life Scholarship.

CONTACT
Becky Pressley, Director of Financial Aid
PO Box 338, Due West, SC 29639-0338
(864) 379-8832

Florence-Darlington Technical College

Florence, South Carolina
www.fdtc.edu Federal Code: 003990

2-year public community and technical college in small city.
Enrollment: 6,002 undergrads.
Selectivity: Open admission; but selective for some programs.

BASIC COSTS (2012-2013)
Tuition and fees: $3,766; out-of-district residents $4,028; out-of-state residents $5,862.

FINANCIAL AID PICTURE
Students with need: Need-based aid available for full-time and part-time students.
Students without need: No-need awards available for academics.

FINANCIAL AID PROCEDURES
Forms required: FAFSA.
Dates and Deadlines: Priority date 5/1; no closing date. Applicants notified on a rolling basis starting 7/1; must reply within 2 week(s) of notification.
Transfers: Priority date 4/1; no deadline.

CONTACT
Joseph Durant, Director of Financial Assistance
PO Box 100548, Florence, SC 29501-0548
(843) 661-8085

Forrest Junior College

Anderson, South Carolina
www.forrestcollege.edu Federal Code: 004924

2-year for-profit business college in large town.
Enrollment: 117 undergrads.
Selectivity: Open admission; but selective for some programs.

BASIC COSTS (2012-2013)
Tuition and fees: $12,975.
Per-credit charge: $245.

FINANCIAL AID PICTURE
Students with need: Need-based aid available for full-time and part-time students. Work study available nights, weekends, and for part-time students.
Students without need: This college awards aid only to students with need.

FINANCIAL AID PROCEDURES
Forms required: FAFSA.
Dates and Deadlines: Applicants notified on a rolling basis starting 4/30; must reply by 5/31 or within 4 week(s) of notification.
Transfers: No deadline. Applicants notified on a rolling basis; must reply within 3 week(s) of notification.

CONTACT
Liz Floyd, Finance and Records Administration Coordinator
601 East River Street, Anderson, SC 29624
(864) 225-7653 ext. 2209

Francis Marion University

Florence, South Carolina
www.fmarion.edu Federal Code: 009226

4-year public university and liberal arts college in small city.
Enrollment: 3,456 undergrads, 4% part-time. 814 full-time freshmen.
Selectivity: Admits 50 to 75% of applicants.

BASIC COSTS (2012-2013)
Tuition and fees: $9,066; out-of-state residents $17,774.
Per-credit charge: $445; out-of-state residents $891.
Room and board: $6,820.

FINANCIAL AID PICTURE (2011-2012)
Students with need: Out of 652 full-time freshmen who applied for aid, 615 were judged to have need. Of these, 615 received aid. For part-time students, average financial aid package was $3,387.
Students without need: 19 full-time freshmen who did not demonstrate need for aid received scholarships/grants; average award was $2,068. No-need awards available for academics, music/drama.
Scholarships offered: 4 full-time freshmen received athletic scholarships; average amount $2,524.

FINANCIAL AID PROCEDURES
Forms required: FAFSA.
Dates and Deadlines: Priority date 3/1; no closing date. Applicants notified on a rolling basis starting 1/30.
Transfers: Institutional scholarships available after 1 semester completed in residence.

CONTACT
Kim Ellisor, Director of Financial Assistance
PO Box 100547, Florence, SC 29502-0547
(843) 661-1190

Furman University

Greenville, South Carolina Federal Code: 003434
www.furman.edu CSS Code: 5222

4-year private liberal arts college in small city.
Enrollment: 2,731 undergrads, 4% part-time. 695 full-time freshmen.
Selectivity: Admits over 75% of applicants.

BASIC COSTS (2013-2014)

Tuition and fees: $43,164.
Room and board: $10,844.

FINANCIAL AID PICTURE (2012-2013)

Students with need: Out of 466 full-time freshmen who applied for aid, 283 were judged to have need. Of these, 282 received aid, and 81 had their full need met. Average financial aid package met 64% of need; average scholarship/grant was $21,093; average loan was $4,038. Need-based aid available for part-time students.
Students without need: 240 full-time freshmen who did not demonstrate need for aid received scholarships/grants; average award was $13,697. No-need awards available for academics, alumni affiliation, art, athletics, leadership, music/drama, religious affiliation, ROTC, state/district residency.
Scholarships offered: 59 full-time freshmen received athletic scholarships; average amount $43,246.
Cumulative student debt: 43% of graduating class had student loans; average debt was $26,661.
Additional info: 5-point comprehensive education financing plan includes financial aid packaging, money management counseling, debt management counseling, outside scholarship coordination, summer job-match program.

FINANCIAL AID PROCEDURES

Forms required: FAFSA, CSS PROFILE, state aid form, institutional form.
Dates and Deadlines: Closing date 1/15. Applicants notified by 4/1; must reply by 5/1 or within 2 week(s) of notification.
Transfers: Closing date 6/1. For South Carolina Tuition Grant, must have earned 24 credits in previous year. For Life Scholarship, must have 3.0 cumulative GPA and 30 credits earned.

CONTACT

Forrest Stuart, Assistant Vice President for Financial Aid
3300 Poinsett Highway, Greenville, SC 29613
(864) 294-2204

Greenville Technical College

Greenville, South Carolina
www.gvltec.edu Federal Code: 003991

2-year public community and technical college in large city.
Enrollment: 12,698 undergrads, 54% part-time. 1,749 full-time freshmen.
Selectivity: Open admission; but selective for some programs.

BASIC COSTS (2012-2013)

Tuition and fees: $3,866; out-of-district residents $4,190; out-of-state residents $7,910.

FINANCIAL AID PICTURE (2011-2012)

Students with need: 45% of average financial aid package awarded as scholarships/grants, 55% awarded as loans/jobs. Need-based aid available for part-time students. Work study available nights, weekends, and for part-time students.
Students without need: No-need awards available for academics, state/district residency.

FINANCIAL AID PROCEDURES

Forms required: FAFSA.
Dates and Deadlines: Priority date 5/1; no closing date. Applicants notified on a rolling basis starting 6/15; must reply within 2 week(s) of notification.
Transfers: No deadline. Applicants notified on a rolling basis starting 6/15; must reply within 2 week(s) of notification.

CONTACT

Janie Reid, Financial Aid Director
PO Box 5616, Greenville, SC 29606-5616
(864) 250-8128

Horry-Georgetown Technical College

Conway, South Carolina
www.hgtc.edu Federal Code: 004925

2-year public community and technical college in large town.
Enrollment: 7,685 undergrads.
Selectivity: Open admission; but selective for some programs.

BASIC COSTS (2012-2013)

Tuition and fees: $3,530; out-of-district residents $4,444; out-of-state residents $5,808.

FINANCIAL AID PICTURE

Students with need: Need-based aid available for full-time and part-time students.
Students without need: No-need awards available for academics, state/district residency.
Additional info: Participates in South Carolina lottery tuition assistance program. Full-time technical college students who are state residents receive assistance for tuition not covered by federal or need-based grants.

FINANCIAL AID PROCEDURES

Forms required: FAFSA.
Dates and Deadlines: Priority date 4/1; closing date 6/30. Applicants notified on a rolling basis starting 4/1.

CONTACT

Susan Thompson, Director of Financial Aid and Veterans Affairs
PO Box 261966, Conway, SC 29528-6066
(843) 349-5251

Lander University

Greenwood, South Carolina
www.lander.edu Federal Code: 003435

4-year public liberal arts and teachers college in large town.
Enrollment: 2,904 undergrads, 7% part-time. 567 full-time freshmen.
Selectivity: Admits less than 50% of applicants.

BASIC COSTS (2012-2013)

Tuition and fees: $9,792; out-of-state residents $18,552.
Per-credit charge: $408; out-of-state residents $773.
Room and board: $7,816.

FINANCIAL AID PICTURE

Students with need: Need-based aid available for full-time and part-time students. Work study available weekends and for part-time students.
Students without need: No-need awards available for academics, art, athletics, leadership, music/drama.

FINANCIAL AID PROCEDURES

Forms required: FAFSA.
Dates and Deadlines: Priority date 4/15; no closing date. Applicants notified on a rolling basis starting 4/15; must reply within 4 week(s) of notification.

CONTACT

Fred Hardin, Director of Financial Aid
Stanley Avenue, Greenwood, SC 29649-2099
(864) 388-8340

Limestone College

Gaffney, South Carolina
www.limestone.edu Federal Code: 003436

4-year private liberal arts college in large town.
Enrollment: 899 undergrads, 2% part-time. 245 full-time freshmen.
Selectivity: Admits 50 to 75% of applicants.

BASIC COSTS (2013-2014)

Tuition and fees: $22,080.
Per-credit charge: $920.
Room and board: $7,800.

FINANCIAL AID PICTURE (2012-2013)

Students with need: Average financial aid package met 63% of need; average scholarship/grant was $14,065; average loan was $3,306. For part-time students, average financial aid package was $7,103.
Students without need: No-need awards available for academics, art, athletics, job skills, leadership, music/drama, religious affiliation, ROTC, state/district residency.
Scholarships offered: Presidential Scholarship: full tuition; 1300 SAT, 3.5 GPA; 1 available. Academic Dean Scholarships: partial tuition; 3.0 GPA. Founders Scholarships: partial tuition; 2.75 GPA. McMillan Scholarships: female humanities & science majors, who are SC Hope, Life, or Palmetto-eligible; 3.0 GPA or above. R.S. Campbell Scholarship: SAT above 1100, GPA 3.25 or above; 1 available. Leadership Scholarship: partial tuition; based on evidence of student leadership. Drada Hoover Scholarship: SAT 1200 or higher; GPA 3.5; top 10% of graduating class. SAT scores exclusive of Writing.
Cumulative student debt: 91% of graduating class had student loans; average debt was $32,175.

FINANCIAL AID PROCEDURES

Forms required: FAFSA.
Dates and Deadlines: Priority date 2/1; no closing date. Applicants notified on a rolling basis starting 1/15; must reply within 3 week(s) of notification.
Transfers: Priority date 5/1; no deadline. Applicants notified on a rolling basis; must reply within 3 week(s) of notification.

CONTACT

Bobby Greer, Director of Financial Aid
1115 College Drive, Gaffney, SC 29340-3799
(800) 795-7151 ext. 8231

Medical University of South Carolina

Charleston, South Carolina
www.musc.edu Federal Code: 003438

Upper-division public university in small city.
Enrollment: 204 undergrads.

BASIC COSTS (2012-2013)

Additional info: Tuition and fees for BS in nursing for in-state $14,298 out-of-state $24,300 (plus fees); BS in cardiovascular perfusion, in-state $14,500, out-of-state $21,610. Tuition/fee waivers available for adults, minority students.

FINANCIAL AID PICTURE

Students with need: Need-based aid available for full-time and part-time students.
Students without need: No-need awards available for academics, alumni affiliation, minority status, state/district residency.

FINANCIAL AID PROCEDURES

Forms required: FAFSA, institutional form.
Dates and Deadlines: Closing date 3/10. Applicants notified on a rolling basis starting 4/21.

CONTACT

Cecile Kamath, Director, Student Financial Aid
41 Bee Street, Charleston, SC 29425-2030
(843) 792-2536

Midlands Technical College

Columbia, South Carolina
www.midlandstech.edu Federal Code: 003993

2-year public technical college in large city.
Enrollment: 11,408 undergrads, 63% part-time. 1,130 full-time freshmen.
Selectivity: Open admission; but selective for some programs.

BASIC COSTS (2012-2013)

Tuition and fees: $3,788; out-of-district residents $4,676; out-of-state residents $10,940.

FINANCIAL AID PICTURE

Students with need: Need-based aid available for full-time and part-time students.

FINANCIAL AID PROCEDURES

Forms required: FAFSA.
Dates and Deadlines: Priority date 4/15; no closing date. Applicants notified on a rolling basis; must reply within 2 week(s) of notification.

CONTACT

Angela Williams, Director of Student Financial Services
PO Box 2408, Columbia, SC 29202
(803) 738-7792

Morris College

Sumter, South Carolina
www.morris.edu Federal Code: 003439

4-year private liberal arts college in large town, affiliated with Baptist faith.
Enrollment: 874 undergrads, 1% part-time. 264 full-time freshmen.
Selectivity: Admits over 75% of applicants.

BASIC COSTS (2012-2013)

Tuition and fees: $10,840.
Per-credit charge: $438.
Room and board: $4,766.

FINANCIAL AID PICTURE (2012-2013)

Students with need: Average financial aid package met 54% of need; average scholarship/grant was $6,744; average loan was $3,328. For part-time students, average financial aid package was $3,574.
Students without need: This college awards aid only to students with need.
Scholarships offered: Presidential Scholarship: $750-$2,500; rank in the first quarter of high school graduating class; larger awards available to salutatorians ($2,000) and valedictorians ($2,500); awards renewable up to 4 years if student maintains B average and excellent citizenship record. Luns C. Richardson Endowed Scholarship: $4,500; freshman student who has completed college prep curriculum with GPA of 3.5 or better, has exceptional letters of recommendation from at least 2 classroom teachers and one guidance counselor, principal, or assistant principal, and plans to enroll as full-time student for 4 consecutive years.
Cumulative student debt: 98% of graduating class had student loans; average debt was $21,500.

FINANCIAL AID PROCEDURES

Forms required: FAFSA, institutional form.
Dates and Deadlines: Closing date 3/30. Applicants notified on a rolling basis starting 6/1; must reply within 2 week(s) of notification.
Transfers: Must reply within 2 week(s) of notification.

CONTACT
Sandra Gibson, Financial Aid Officer
100 West College Street, Sumter, SC 29150-3599
(803) 934-3238

Newberry College
Newberry, South Carolina
www.newberry.edu Federal Code: 003440

4-year private liberal arts college in large town, affiliated with Evangelical Lutheran Church in America.
Enrollment: 1,038 undergrads, 3% part-time. 280 full-time freshmen.
Selectivity: Admits 50 to 75% of applicants.

BASIC COSTS (2013-2014)
Tuition and fees: $23,800.
Per-credit charge: $525.
Room and board: $9,000.

FINANCIAL AID PICTURE (2011-2012)
Students with need: Out of 245 full-time freshmen who applied for aid, 227 were judged to have need. Of these, 226 received aid, and 36 had their full need met. Average financial aid package met 68% of need; average scholarship/grant was $17,870; average loan was $3,801. For part-time students, average financial aid package was $6,264.
Students without need: 26 full-time freshmen who did not demonstrate need for aid received scholarships/grants; average award was $10,655. No-need awards available for academics, alumni affiliation, athletics, leadership, music/drama, religious affiliation, ROTC, state/district residency.
Scholarships offered: 33 full-time freshmen received athletic scholarships; average amount $12,206.
Cumulative student debt: 83% of graduating class had student loans; average debt was $16,538.

FINANCIAL AID PROCEDURES
Forms required: FAFSA, state aid form, institutional form.
Dates and Deadlines: Priority date 3/15; no closing date. Applicants notified on a rolling basis starting 3/1; must reply by 5/1 or within 2 week(s) of notification.
Transfers: No deadline. Applicants notified on a rolling basis; must reply by 5/1 or within 2 week(s) of notification.

CONTACT
Danielle Bell, Interim Director of Financial Aid
2100 College Street, Newberry, SC 29108
(803) 321-5127

North Greenville University
Tigerville, South Carolina
www.ngu.edu Federal Code: 003441

4-year private liberal arts college in rural community, affiliated with Southern Baptist Convention.
Enrollment: 2,048 undergrads, 3% part-time. 521 full-time freshmen.
Selectivity: Admits 50 to 75% of applicants.

BASIC COSTS (2013-2014)
Tuition and fees: $14,772.
Per-credit charge: $295.
Room and board: $8,654.

FINANCIAL AID PICTURE
Students with need: Need-based aid available for full-time and part-time students.
Students without need: No-need awards available for academics, athletics, leadership, music/drama, religious affiliation, state/district residency.

FINANCIAL AID PROCEDURES
Forms required: FAFSA.
Dates and Deadlines: Priority date 6/1; closing date 6/30. Applicants notified on a rolling basis starting 8/1; must reply within 2 week(s) of notification.
Transfers: No deadline.

CONTACT
Mike Jordan, Director of Financial Aid
PO Box 1892, Tigerville, SC 29688-1892
(864) 977-7050

Orangeburg-Calhoun Technical College
Orangeburg, South Carolina
www.octech.edu Federal Code: 006815

2-year public community and technical college in large town.
Enrollment: 3,003 undergrads.
Selectivity: Open admission; but selective for some programs.

BASIC COSTS (2012-2013)
Tuition and fees: $3,650; out-of-district residents $4,514; out-of-state residents $6,218.

FINANCIAL AID PICTURE
Students with need: Need-based aid available for full-time and part-time students.
Students without need: This college awards aid only to students with need.
Scholarships offered: College Foundation Scholarship: full academic tuition; for high school valedictorians and salutatorians.

FINANCIAL AID PROCEDURES
Forms required: FAFSA, institutional form.
Dates and Deadlines: Priority date 6/4; no closing date. Applicants notified on a rolling basis starting 5/1; must reply within 2 week(s) of notification.
Transfers: Priority date 6/1. Financial aid transcripts required of mid-year transfers prior to disbursement of aid.

CONTACT
Bobbie Felder, Director of Institutional Research
3250 St. Matthews Road, Orangeburg, SC 29118-8222
(803) 535-1368

Piedmont Technical College
Greenwood, South Carolina
www.ptc.edu Federal Code: 003992

2-year public community and technical college in small city.
Enrollment: 5,535 undergrads, 54% part-time. 988 full-time freshmen.
Selectivity: Open admission; but selective for some programs.

BASIC COSTS (2012-2013)
Tuition and fees: $3,714; out-of-district residents $4,122; out-of-state residents $5,322.

FINANCIAL AID PICTURE (2011-2012)
Students with need: 69% of average financial aid package awarded as scholarships/grants, 31% awarded as loans/jobs. Need-based aid available for part-time students. Work study available nights.
Students without need: This college awards aid only to students with need.

FINANCIAL AID PROCEDURES
Forms required: FAFSA.
Dates and Deadlines: Priority date 5/1; no closing date. Applicants notified on a rolling basis starting 6/1; must reply within 2 week(s) of notification.

CONTACT
Missy Lutz, Director of Financial Aid
620 N. Emerald Road, Greenwood, SC 29648
(864) 941-8365

Presbyterian College
Clinton, South Carolina
www.presby.edu Federal Code: 003445

4-year private pharmacy and liberal arts college in small town, affiliated with Presbyterian Church (USA).
Enrollment: 1,130 undergrads, 1% part-time. 282 full-time freshmen.
Selectivity: Admits 50 to 75% of applicants.

BASIC COSTS (2012-2013)
Tuition and fees: $32,680.
Per-credit charge: $1,260.
Room and board: $8,750.

FINANCIAL AID PICTURE (2012-2013)
Students with need: Out of 262 full-time freshmen who applied for aid, 230 were judged to have need. Of these, 230 received aid, and 90 had their full need met. Average financial aid package met 90% of need; average scholarship/grant was $31,013; average loan was $3,068. For part-time students, average financial aid package was $12,114.
Students without need: 55 full-time freshmen who did not demonstrate need for aid received scholarships/grants; average award was $15,987. No-need awards available for academics, alumni affiliation, art, athletics, job skills, leadership, minority status, music/drama, religious affiliation, ROTC, state/district residency.
Scholarships offered: ***Merit:*** Academic and leadership scholarships, applications by December 5; number and amounts awarded vary; music awards based on audition. ***Athletic:*** 29 full-time freshmen received athletic scholarships; average amount $14,689.
Cumulative student debt: 48% of graduating class had student loans; average debt was $25,425.

FINANCIAL AID PROCEDURES
Forms required: FAFSA.
Dates and Deadlines: Priority date 3/15; closing date 6/30. Applicants notified by 3/1; must reply by 5/1.
Transfers: No deadline. Applicants notified on a rolling basis starting 5/1; must reply within 1 week(s) of notification.

CONTACT
Rebecca Pressley, Director of Financial Aid
503 South Broad Street, Clinton, SC 29325-2865
(864) 833-8290

South Carolina State University
Orangeburg, South Carolina
www.scsu.edu Federal Code: 003446

4-year public university in large town.
Enrollment: 3,230 undergrads.
Selectivity: Admits over 75% of applicants.

BASIC COSTS (2012-2013)
Tuition and fees: $9,258; out-of-state residents $18,170.
Per-credit charge: $386; out-of-state residents $757.
Room and board: $9,286.

FINANCIAL AID PICTURE
Students with need: Need-based aid available for full-time and part-time students.
Students without need: No-need awards available for academics, athletics, ROTC.

FINANCIAL AID PROCEDURES
Forms required: FAFSA.
Dates and Deadlines: Closing date 5/1. Applicants notified on a rolling basis starting 3/15; must reply by 7/1 or within 2 week(s) of notification.
Transfers: Must reply by 7/1 or within 2 week(s) of notification. Must provide documentation on amount of state aid received, and which semesters it was received, prior to transfer.

CONTACT
Sandra Davis, Director of Financial Aid
300 College Street NE, Orangeburg, SC 29117
(803) 536-7067

South University: Columbia
Columbia, South Carolina
www.southuniversity.edu Federal Code: 004922

4-year for-profit university in small city.
Enrollment: 1,124 undergrads.

BASIC COSTS (2012-2013)
Tuition and fees: $16,585.
Additional info: Tuition and fees are representative of most campus degree programs.

FINANCIAL AID PICTURE
Students with need: Need-based aid available for full-time and part-time students.
Students without need: This college awards aid only to students with need.

FINANCIAL AID PROCEDURES
Forms required: FAFSA.
Dates and Deadlines: Applicants notified on a rolling basis starting 5/30.

CONTACT
Walter Haversat, Financial Aid Director
9 Science Court, Columbia, SC 29203
(803) 799-9082

Spartanburg Community College
Spartanburg, South Carolina
www.sccsc.edu Federal Code: 003994

2-year public community and technical college in small city.
Enrollment: 5,226 undergrads, 46% part-time. 838 full-time freshmen.
Selectivity: Open admission; but selective for some programs.

BASIC COSTS (2012-2013)
Tuition and fees: $3,820; out-of-district residents $4,750; out-of-state residents $7,716.

FINANCIAL AID PICTURE (2011-2012)
Students with need: 94% of average financial aid package awarded as scholarships/grants, 6% awarded as loans/jobs. Need-based aid available for part-time students.
Students without need: No-need awards available for academics.
Additional info: Participates in South Carolina lottery tuition assistance program. Full-time technical college students who are state residents receive assistance for tuition not covered by federal or need-based grants.

FINANCIAL AID PROCEDURES
Forms required: FAFSA.
Dates and Deadlines: Priority date 2/28; closing date 5/1. Applicants notified on a rolling basis starting 5/1.

Transfers: No deadline. Applicants notified on a rolling basis starting 8/15.

CONTACT

Nancy Garmroth, Director of Financial Aid
Box 4386, Spartanburg, SC 29305-4386
(864) 592-4810

Spartanburg Methodist College

Spartanburg, South Carolina
www.smcsc.edu Federal Code: 003447

2-year private junior and liberal arts college in small city, affiliated with United Methodist Church.
Enrollment: 805 undergrads, 2% part-time. 459 full-time freshmen.
Selectivity: Admits 50 to 75% of applicants.

BASIC COSTS (2013-2014)

Tuition and fees: $15,785.
Per-credit charge: $402.
Room and board: $8,236.
Additional info: Tuition/fee waivers available for adults, unemployed or children of unemployed.

FINANCIAL AID PICTURE (2012-2013)

Students with need: Out of 459 full-time freshmen who applied for aid, 382 were judged to have need. Of these, 382 received aid, and 175 had their full need met. Average financial aid package met 77% of need; average scholarship/grant was $2,925; average loan was $2,465. For part-time students, average financial aid package was $2,500.
Students without need: 77 full-time freshmen who did not demonstrate need for aid received scholarships/grants; average award was $4,500. No-need awards available for academics, athletics, religious affiliation.
Scholarships offered: ***Merit:*** Milliken Scholars: $4,100. Camak Scholars: $3,500. Trustee Scholars: $3,000. Presidential Scholars: $2,400. ***Athletic:*** 89 full-time freshmen received athletic scholarships; average amount $2,800.
Cumulative student debt: 55% of graduating class had student loans; average debt was $6,000.

FINANCIAL AID PROCEDURES

Forms required: FAFSA, state aid form.
Dates and Deadlines: Priority date 6/30; closing date 8/22. Applicants notified on a rolling basis starting 3/1; must reply within 2 week(s) of notification.
Transfers: No deadline. Applicants notified on a rolling basis starting 3/1; must reply within 2 week(s) of notification. To be eligible for financial aid, full time students must pass the equivalent of 12 hours.

CONTACT

Debbie Sloan, Director of Financial Aid
1000 Powell Mill Road, Spartanburg, SC 29301-5899
(864) 587-4298

Technical College of the Lowcountry

Beaufort, South Carolina
www.tcl.edu Federal Code: 009910

2-year public community and technical college in small city.
Enrollment: 2,241 undergrads, 70% part-time. 173 full-time freshmen.
Selectivity: Open admission; but selective for some programs.

BASIC COSTS (2012-2013)

Tuition and fees: $3,772; out-of-state residents $8,212.

FINANCIAL AID PICTURE

Students with need: Need-based aid available for full-time and part-time students.
Students without need: This college awards aid only to students with need.
Additional info: State lottery aid may be available to South Carolina residents who take 6 credit hours or more.

FINANCIAL AID PROCEDURES

Forms required: FAFSA.

CONTACT

Cleo Martin, Director of Financial Aid
921 South Ribaut Road, Beaufort, SC 29901-1288
(843) 525-8337

Tri-County Technical College

Pendleton, South Carolina
www.tctc.edu Federal Code: 004926

2-year public community and technical college in small town.
Enrollment: 6,616 undergrads.
Selectivity: Open admission; but selective for some programs.

BASIC COSTS (2012-2013)

Tuition and fees: $3,648; out-of-district residents $4,752; out-of-state residents $8,124.

FINANCIAL AID PICTURE

Students with need: Need-based aid available for full-time and part-time students. Work study available nights.
Students without need: No-need awards available for academics, state/district residency.
Scholarships offered: General and departmental scholarships: some with special qualification criteria, such as student's career field or place of residency; more than 125 awarded.
Additional info: Deadline for application to institutional scholarships April 2.

FINANCIAL AID PROCEDURES

Forms required: FAFSA.
Dates and Deadlines: Priority date 4/1; closing date 7/30. Applicants notified on a rolling basis starting 6/15; must reply within 2 week(s) of notification.
Transfers: No deadline. Applicants notified on a rolling basis starting 6/1.

CONTACT

Sarah Dowd, Director of Financial Aid
PO Box 587, Pendleton, SC 29670
(864) 646-1650

Trident Technical College

Charleston, South Carolina
www.tridenttech.edu Federal Code: 004920

2-year public community and technical college in large city.
Enrollment: 15,791 undergrads, 53% part-time. 1,955 full-time freshmen.
Selectivity: Open admission; but selective for some programs.

BASIC COSTS (2012-2013)

Tuition and fees: $3,834; out-of-district residents $4,236; out-of-state residents $7,122.

FINANCIAL AID PICTURE (2011-2012)

Students with need: 52% of average financial aid package awarded as scholarships/grants, 48% awarded as loans/jobs. Need-based aid available for part-time students. Work study available nights, weekends, and for part-time students.
Students without need: No-need awards available for academics, alumni affiliation, state/district residency.

FINANCIAL AID PROCEDURES

Forms required: FAFSA.

Dates and Deadlines: Applicants notified on a rolling basis; must reply within 6 week(s) of notification.
Transfers: No deadline. Applicants notified on a rolling basis; must reply within 6 week(s) of notification.

CONTACT
Ellen Green, Director of Financial Aid/Veterans Assistance
PO.Box 118067, AM-M, Charleston, SC 29423-8067
(843) 574-6147

University of South Carolina: Aiken

Aiken, South Carolina
web.usca.edu/ Federal Code: 003449

4-year public university and liberal arts college in large town.
Enrollment: 2,876 undergrads, 16% part-time. 572 full-time freshmen.

BASIC COSTS (2012-2013)
Tuition and fees: $9,024; out-of-state residents $17,780.
Per-credit charge: $380; out-of-state residents $760.
Room and board: $6,780.

FINANCIAL AID PICTURE (2011-2012)
Students with need: Out of 562 full-time freshmen who applied for aid, 427 were judged to have need. Of these, 427 received aid, and 114 had their full need met. Average financial aid package met 75% of need; average scholarship/grant was $7,235; average loan was $3,188. For part-time students, average financial aid package was $8,039.
Students without need: 109 full-time freshmen who did not demonstrate need for aid received scholarships/grants; average award was $5,762. No-need awards available for academics, alumni affiliation, art, athletics, leadership, minority status, music/drama, state/district residency.
Scholarships offered: 25 full-time freshmen received athletic scholarships; average amount $3,747.
Cumulative student debt: 85% of graduating class had student loans; average debt was $22,677.
Additional info: Students must be enrolled at least half time and be able to present documentation which verifies eligibility to work in the U.S.

FINANCIAL AID PROCEDURES
Forms required: FAFSA.
Dates and Deadlines: Priority date 3/15; no closing date. Applicants notified on a rolling basis starting 4/20; must reply within 2 week(s) of notification.
Transfers: Financial aid transcripts from previous institutions required.

CONTACT
Linda Aubrey-Higgins, Director of Financial Aid
471 University Parkway, Aiken, SC 29801-6399
(803) 641-3476

University of South Carolina: Beaufort

Bluffton, South Carolina
www.uscb.edu Federal Code: 003450

4-year public university and liberal arts college in large town.
Enrollment: 1,739 undergrads, 20% part-time. 389 full-time freshmen.
Selectivity: Admits 50 to 75% of applicants.

BASIC COSTS (2012-2013)
Tuition and fees: $8,558; out-of-state residents $17,956.
Per-credit charge: $344; out-of-state residents $734.
Room and board: $6,910.

FINANCIAL AID PICTURE
Students with need: Need-based aid available for full-time and part-time students. Work study available nights, weekends, and for part-time students.
Students without need: No-need awards available for academics, art, athletics, leadership, religious affiliation, state/district residency.

FINANCIAL AID PROCEDURES
Forms required: FAFSA.
Dates and Deadlines: Priority date 3/1; no closing date. Applicants notified on a rolling basis starting 5/1; must reply within 2 week(s) of notification.
Transfers: No deadline. Applicants notified on a rolling basis starting 5/1.

CONTACT
Patricia Greene, Director and VA Coordinator of Financial Aid
One University Boulevard, Bluffton, SC 29909
(843) 521-3104

University of South Carolina: Columbia

Columbia, South Carolina
www.sc.edu Federal Code: 003448

4-year public university in small city.
Enrollment: 23,028 undergrads, 7% part-time. 4,500 full-time freshmen.
Selectivity: Admits 50 to 75% of applicants.

BASIC COSTS (2012-2013)
Tuition and fees: $10,488; out-of-state residents $27,644.
Per-credit charge: $421; out-of-state residents $1,136.
Room and board: $8,459.
Additional info: Health professions (pharmacy, health, nursing), law and medical professions have higher undergraduate and graduate fees.

FINANCIAL AID PICTURE (2012-2013)
Students with need: Out of 3,658 full-time freshmen who applied for aid, 2,285 were judged to have need. Of these, 2,285 received aid, and 691 had their full need met. Average financial aid package met 75% of need; average scholarship/grant was $4,860; average loan was $2,261. For part-time students, average financial aid package was $8,836.
Students without need: 1,816 full-time freshmen who did not demonstrate need for aid received scholarships/grants; average award was $5,304. No-need awards available for academics, alumni affiliation, art, athletics, job skills, leadership, minority status, music/drama, religious affiliation, ROTC, state/district residency.
Scholarships offered: 147 full-time freshmen received athletic scholarships; average amount $11,747.

FINANCIAL AID PROCEDURES
Forms required: FAFSA.
Dates and Deadlines: Priority date 4/1; no closing date. Applicants notified on a rolling basis starting 4/1.
Transfers: Applicants notified on a rolling basis starting 4/1.

CONTACT
Edgar Miller, Director of Financial Aid and Scholarships
Office of Undergraduate Admissions, Columbia, SC 29208
(803) 777-8134

University of South Carolina: Salkehatchie

Allendale, South Carolina
uscsalkehatchie.sc.edu Federal Code: 003454

2-year public branch campus college in rural community.
Enrollment: 1,155 undergrads.

BASIC COSTS (2012-2013)
Tuition and fees: $6,284; out-of-state residents $15,158.
Per-credit charge: $246; out-of-state residents $616.

FINANCIAL AID PICTURE
Students with need: Need-based aid available for full-time and part-time students. Work study available nights, weekends, and for part-time students.
Students without need: No-need awards available for academics.

FINANCIAL AID PROCEDURES
Forms required: FAFSA.
Dates and Deadlines: Priority date 4/30; no closing date. Applicants notified on a rolling basis starting 6/1.

CONTACT
Julie Hadwin, Director of Financial Aid
PO Box 617, Allendale, SC 29810
(803) 584-3446

University of South Carolina: Sumter
Sumter, South Carolina
www.uscsumter.edu Federal Code: 003426

2-year public branch campus college in small city.
Enrollment: 650 undergrads.

BASIC COSTS (2012-2013)
Tuition and fees: $6,334; out-of-state residents $15,208.
Per-credit charge: $246; out-of-state residents $616.

FINANCIAL AID PICTURE
Students with need: Need-based aid available for full-time and part-time students. Work study available nights, weekends, and for part-time students.
Students without need: This college awards aid only to students with need.

FINANCIAL AID PROCEDURES
Forms required: FAFSA.
Dates and Deadlines: Priority date 4/15; no closing date. Applicants notified on a rolling basis starting 4/16; must reply within 2 week(s) of notification.

CONTACT
Elizabeth White, Financial Aid Manager
200 Miller Road, Sumter, SC 29150-2498
(803) 938-3766

University of South Carolina: Union
Union, South Carolina
uscunion.sc.edu Federal Code: 004927

2-year public branch campus and liberal arts college in small town.
Enrollment: 492 undergrads.

BASIC COSTS (2012-2013)
Tuition and fees: $6,314; out-of-state residents $15,188.
Per-credit charge: $246; out-of-state residents $616.

FINANCIAL AID PICTURE
Students with need: Work study available nights, weekends, and for part-time students.
Students without need: This college awards aid only to students with need.

FINANCIAL AID PROCEDURES
Forms required: FAFSA.
Dates and Deadlines: Priority date 4/15; no closing date. Applicants notified on a rolling basis starting 7/15; must reply within 2 week(s) of notification.

CONTACT
Bobby Holcombe, Financial Aid Director
PO Drawer 729, Union, SC 29379
(864) 429-8728

University of South Carolina: Upstate
Spartanburg, South Carolina
www.uscupstate.edu Federal Code: 006951

4-year public university in small city.
Enrollment: 5,080 undergrads, 18% part-time. 751 full-time freshmen.
Selectivity: Admits 50 to 75% of applicants.

BASIC COSTS (2012-2013)
Tuition and fees: $9,722; out-of-state residents $19,444.
Per-credit charge: $403; out-of-state residents $815.
Room and board: $7,250.

FINANCIAL AID PICTURE (2011-2012)
Students with need: Out of 673 full-time freshmen who applied for aid, 553 were judged to have need. Of these, 553 received aid, and 101 had their full need met. Average financial aid package met 67% of need; average scholarship/grant was $4,819; average loan was $3,253. For part-time students, average financial aid package was $7,347.
Students without need: 27 full-time freshmen who did not demonstrate need for aid received scholarships/grants; average award was $4,442. No-need awards available for academics, athletics, minority status, ROTC, state/district residency.
Scholarships offered: 53 full-time freshmen received athletic scholarships; average amount $13,981.
Cumulative student debt: 69% of graduating class had student loans; average debt was $23,765.
Additional info: Out-of-state students who are recipients of financial aid may qualify for out-of-state fee waiver. Educational benefits available to veterans and children of deceased/disabled veterans.

FINANCIAL AID PROCEDURES
Forms required: FAFSA, institutional form.
Dates and Deadlines: Priority date 3/1; closing date 7/15. Applicants notified on a rolling basis starting 5/1; must reply within 2 week(s) of notification.
Transfers: Students eligible for financial assistance for total of 5 years or 10 full-time semesters at all post-secondary institutions attended for the bachelor's degree, and 5 full-time semesters of enrollment for associate's degree in nursing.

CONTACT
Allison Sullivan, Director of Financial Aid and Scholarships
800 University Way, Spartanburg, SC 29303
(864) 503-5974

Voorhees College
Denmark, South Carolina
www.voorhees.edu Federal Code: 003455

4-year private liberal arts college in small town, affiliated with Episcopal Church.
Enrollment: 650 undergrads.
Selectivity: Admits over 75% of applicants.

BASIC COSTS (2012-2013)
Tuition and fees: $10,780.
Room and board: $7,346.

FINANCIAL AID PICTURE
Students with need: Need-based aid available for full-time and part-time students. Work study available nights, weekends, and for part-time students.

FINANCIAL AID PROCEDURES
Forms required: FAFSA, institutional form.
Dates and Deadlines: Priority date 4/15; no closing date. Applicants notified on a rolling basis starting 3/1; must reply within 2 week(s) of notification.

CONTACT
Augusta Kitchen, Director of Student Financial Aid
213 Wiggins Road, Denmark, SC 29042
(803) 780-1159

Williamsburg Technical College

Kingstree, South Carolina
www.wiltech.edu Federal Code: 009322

2-year public community and technical college in small town.
Enrollment: 625 undergrads.
Selectivity: Open admission.

BASIC COSTS (2012-2013)
Tuition and fees: $3,540; out-of-district residents $3,660; out-of-state residents $6,840.

FINANCIAL AID PICTURE
Students with need: Need-based aid available for full-time and part-time students. Work study available nights, weekends, and for part-time students.
Students without need: No-need awards available for academics, leadership, minority status, state/district residency.
Additional info: Tuition waivers for children of war veterans.

FINANCIAL AID PROCEDURES
Forms required: FAFSA.
Dates and Deadlines: Closing date 4/15. Applicants notified on a rolling basis starting 7/1; must reply within 4 week(s) of notification.

CONTACT
Jean Boos, Director of Financial Aid
601 Martin Luther King Jr. Avenue, Kingstree, SC 29556-4197
(843) 355-4166

Winthrop University

Rock Hill, South Carolina
www.winthrop.edu Federal Code: 003456

4-year public university in small city.
Enrollment: 4,747 undergrads, 6% part-time. 969 full-time freshmen.
Selectivity: Admits 50 to 75% of applicants.

BASIC COSTS (2012-2013)
Tuition and fees: $13,266; out-of-state residents $24,716.
Per-credit charge: $543; out-of-state residents $1,020.
Room and board: $7,464.

FINANCIAL AID PICTURE (2011-2012)
Students with need: Out of 875 full-time freshmen who applied for aid, 738 were judged to have need. Of these, 736 received aid, and 167 had their full need met. Average financial aid package met 70% of need; average scholarship/grant was $10,154; average loan was $3,381. For part-time students, average financial aid package was $6,347.
Students without need: 95 full-time freshmen who did not demonstrate need for aid received scholarships/grants; average award was $6,212. No-need awards available for academics, art, athletics, leadership, music/drama.
Scholarships offered: 30 full-time freshmen received athletic scholarships; average amount $9,471.
Cumulative student debt: 70% of graduating class had student loans; average debt was $27,735.
Additional info: Academic scholarships from $1,500 to full tuition and board awarded to approximately one-third of entering freshman class each year.

FINANCIAL AID PROCEDURES
Forms required: FAFSA.
Dates and Deadlines: Priority date 3/15; no closing date. Applicants notified on a rolling basis starting 3/15; must reply within 2 week(s) of notification.
Transfers: Transfer students are not eligible for academic scholarship their first year.

CONTACT
Michelle Hare, Director, Office of Financial Aid
701 Oakland Avenue, Rock Hill, SC 29733
(803) 323-2189

Wofford College

Spartanburg, South Carolina
www.wofford.edu Federal Code: 003457

4-year private liberal arts college in small city, affiliated with United Methodist Church.
Enrollment: 1,568 undergrads, 2% part-time. 439 full-time freshmen.
Selectivity: Admits 50 to 75% of applicants.

BASIC COSTS (2012-2013)
Tuition and fees: $34,555.
Room and board: $9,920.

FINANCIAL AID PICTURE (2012-2013)
Students with need: Out of 360 full-time freshmen who applied for aid, 289 were judged to have need. Of these, 289 received aid, and 124 had their full need met. Average financial aid package met 82% of need; average scholarship/grant was $28,915; average loan was $3,330. For part-time students, average financial aid package was $16,433.
Students without need: 96 full-time freshmen who did not demonstrate need for aid received scholarships/grants; average award was $14,314. No-need awards available for academics, art, athletics, leadership, music/drama, ROTC.
Scholarships offered: 46 full-time freshmen received athletic scholarships; average amount $17,237.
Cumulative student debt: 50% of graduating class had student loans; average debt was $22,118.

FINANCIAL AID PROCEDURES
Forms required: FAFSA, institutional form.
Dates and Deadlines: Priority date 3/1; closing date 6/1. Applicants notified by 4/1; must reply by 5/1.

CONTACT
Carolyn Sparks, Director of Financial Aid
429 North Church Street, Spartanburg, SC 29303-3663
(864) 597-4160

York Technical College

Rock Hill, South Carolina
www.yorktech.edu Federal Code: 003996

2-year public community and technical college in large town.
Enrollment: 4,518 undergrads.
Selectivity: Open admission; but selective for some programs.

BASIC COSTS (2012-2013)
Tuition and fees: $3,712; out-of-district residents $4,060; out-of-state residents $8,392.

FINANCIAL AID PICTURE
Students with need: Need-based aid available for full-time and part-time students. Work study available nights.
Students without need: No-need awards available for academics, leadership, state/district residency.

FINANCIAL AID PROCEDURES
Forms required: FAFSA.

Dates and Deadlines: Priority date 6/1; no closing date. Applicants notified on a rolling basis starting 4/1; must reply within 2 week(s) of notification.
Transfers: No deadline. Applicants notified on a rolling basis starting 4/1; must reply within 2 week(s) of notification.

CONTACT
Angela Fowler, Director of Financial Aid
452 South Anderson Road, Rock Hill, SC 29730
(803) 327-8005

South Dakota

Augustana College
Sioux Falls, South Dakota
www.augie.edu Federal Code: 003458

4-year private liberal arts college in small city, affiliated with Evangelical Lutheran Church in America.
Enrollment: 1,709 undergrads, 3% part-time. 404 full-time freshmen.
Selectivity: Admits over 75% of applicants.

BASIC COSTS (2013-2014)
Tuition and fees: $28,630.
Per-credit charge: $420.
Room and board: $6,920.
Additional info: Tuition/fee waivers available for minority students.

FINANCIAL AID PICTURE (2012-2013)
Students with need: Out of 319 full-time freshmen who applied for aid, 260 were judged to have need. Of these, 260 received aid, and 64 had their full need met. Average financial aid package met 96% of need; average scholarship/grant was $20,145; average loan was $4,283. For part-time students, average financial aid package was $7,529.
Students without need: 138 full-time freshmen who did not demonstrate need for aid received scholarships/grants; average award was $14,693. No-need awards available for academics, alumni affiliation, art, athletics, leadership, minority status, music/drama, religious affiliation, ROTC, state/district residency.
Scholarships offered: ***Merit:*** Distinguished Scholars Scholarships: Trustees and Presidential Scholarships for students with a 27 ACT or above and 3.5 GPA and above; ProMusica scholarships, ProDramatis scholarships, ProArtis Scholarships; Fryxell Scholarships for journalism/English majors. ***Athletic:*** 57 full-time freshmen received athletic scholarships; average amount $9,650.
Cumulative student debt: 79% of graduating class had student loans; average debt was $34,878.

FINANCIAL AID PROCEDURES
Forms required: FAFSA.
Dates and Deadlines: Priority date 3/1; no closing date. Applicants notified on a rolling basis starting 4/1; must reply within 3 week(s) of notification.
Transfers: No deadline. Applicants notified on a rolling basis starting 4/1; must reply within 3 week(s) of notification.

CONTACT
Brenda Murtha, Director of Financial Aid
2001 South Summit Avenue, Sioux Falls, SD 57197-9990
(605) 274-5216

Black Hills State University
Spearfish, South Dakota
www.bhsu.edu Federal Code: 003459

4-year public liberal arts and teachers college in large town.
Enrollment: 3,181 undergrads.

BASIC COSTS (2012-2013)
Tuition and fees: $7,320; out-of-state residents $9,185.
Per-credit charge: $124; out-of-state residents $186.
Room and board: $5,641.
Additional info: Reciprocity agreements reduce tuition for some out-of-state students.

FINANCIAL AID PICTURE
Students with need: Need-based aid available for full-time and part-time students.
Students without need: This college awards aid only to students with need.

FINANCIAL AID PROCEDURES
Forms required: FAFSA.
Dates and Deadlines: Closing date 2/15. Applicants notified on a rolling basis starting 5/15; must reply within 3 week(s) of notification.

CONTACT
Deb Henriksen, Director of Financial Aid
1200 University Street Box 9502, Spearfish, SD 57799-9502
(605) 642-6581

Dakota State University
Madison, South Dakota
www.dsu.edu Federal Code: 003463

4-year public university in small town.
Enrollment: 1,728 undergrads, 31% part-time. 296 full-time freshmen.
Selectivity: Admits over 75% of applicants.

BASIC COSTS (2012-2013)
Tuition and fees: $7,950; out-of-state residents $9,815.
Per-credit charge: $124; out-of-state residents $186.
Room and board: $5,235.
Additional info: All degree-seeking undergraduates participate in the Wireless Mobile Computing Initiative and provided with a TabletPC. Students are assessed a fee each semester for these services.

FINANCIAL AID PICTURE (2011-2012)
Students with need: Out of 275 full-time freshmen who applied for aid, 228 were judged to have need. Of these, 227 received aid, and 28 had their full need met. Average financial aid package met 78% of need; average scholarship/grant was $4,453; average loan was $3,293. For part-time students, average financial aid package was $5,984.
Students without need: 26 full-time freshmen who did not demonstrate need for aid received scholarships/grants; average award was $2,394. No-need awards available for academics, alumni affiliation, art, athletics, leadership, minority status, music/drama, state/district residency.
Scholarships offered: 43 full-time freshmen received athletic scholarships; average amount $1,298.
Cumulative student debt: 79% of graduating class had student loans; average debt was $25,926.
Additional info: Application deadline for grants and scholarships 3/1. No deadline for loan and job applications.

FINANCIAL AID PROCEDURES
Forms required: FAFSA.
Dates and Deadlines: Priority date 3/1; no closing date. Applicants notified on a rolling basis starting 4/1; must reply within 2 week(s) of notification.
Transfers: Priority date 4/1; no deadline. Applicants notified on a rolling basis starting 4/1; must reply within 2 week(s) of notification.

CONTACT
Denise Grayson, Financial Aid Director
820 North Washington Avenue, Madison, SD 57042
(605) 256-5152

Globe University: Sioux Falls

Sioux Falls, South Dakota
www.globeuniversity.edu Federal Code: 004642

2-year for-profit career college in small city.
Enrollment: 195 undergrads.
Selectivity: Open admission.

BASIC COSTS (2012-2013)
Tuition and fees: $19,125.
Per-credit charge: $460.

FINANCIAL AID PICTURE
Students with need: Need-based aid available for full-time and part-time students.

FINANCIAL AID PROCEDURES
Forms required: FAFSA, institutional form.
Dates and Deadlines: Applicants notified on a rolling basis starting 7/1; must reply within 2 week(s) of notification.

CONTACT
Micah Hansen, Director of Financial Aid
5101 South Broadband Lane, Sioux Falls, SD 57108
(605) 977-0705

Kilian Community College

Sioux Falls, South Dakota
www.kilian.edu Federal Code: 015000

2-year private community college in small city.
Enrollment: 257 undergrads, 86% part-time. 12 full-time freshmen.
Selectivity: Open admission.

BASIC COSTS (2012-2013)
Tuition and fees: $8,490.
Per-credit charge: $275.

FINANCIAL AID PICTURE (2012-2013)
Students with need: Out of 12 full-time freshmen who applied for aid, 12 were judged to have need. Of these, 12 received aid. Average financial aid package met 33% of need; average scholarship/grant was $4,500; average loan was $3,500. Need-based aid available for part-time students.
Students without need: No-need awards available for academics, leadership.
Cumulative student debt: 85% of graduating class had student loans; average debt was $29,500.

FINANCIAL AID PROCEDURES
Forms required: FAFSA, institutional form.
Dates and Deadlines: Applicants notified on a rolling basis starting 7/1; must reply within 2 week(s) of notification.
Transfers: No deadline. Applicants notified on a rolling basis starting 7/1; must reply within 2 week(s) of notification.

CONTACT
Carolyn Halgerson, Director of Financial Aid
300 East 6th Street, Sioux Falls, SD 57103-7020
(605) 221-3105

Lake Area Technical Institute

Watertown, South Dakota
www.lakeareatech.edu Federal Code: 005309

2-year public technical college in large town.
Enrollment: 1,720 undergrads.
Selectivity: Open admission; but selective for some programs.

BASIC COSTS (2012-2013)
Tuition and fees: $6,300.

FINANCIAL AID PICTURE
Students with need: Need-based aid available for full-time and part-time students.
Students without need: This college awards aid only to students with need.

FINANCIAL AID PROCEDURES
Forms required: FAFSA.
Dates and Deadlines: Priority date 4/15; no closing date. Applicants notified on a rolling basis starting 5/1.
Transfers: Priority date 4/1.

CONTACT
Marlene Seeklander, Financial Aid Director
PO Box 730, Watertown, SD 57201
(605) 882-5284

Mitchell Technical Institute

Mitchell, South Dakota
www.mitchelltech.edu Federal Code: 008284

2-year public technical college in large town.
Enrollment: 1,037 undergrads, 16% part-time. 357 full-time freshmen.
Selectivity: Admits 50 to 75% of applicants.

BASIC COSTS (2012-2013)
Tuition and fees: $5,370; out-of-state residents $5,370.
Per-credit charge: $99; out-of-state residents $99.

FINANCIAL AID PICTURE (2011-2012)
Students with need: 49% of average financial aid package awarded as scholarships/grants, 51% awarded as loans/jobs. Need-based aid available for part-time students. Work study available nights.
Scholarships offered: Star Student program which awards $1,000 the first semester (and up to $3,000 total) to students with an ACT score of 24 or higher and a high school GPA of 3.0.

FINANCIAL AID PROCEDURES
Forms required: FAFSA.
Dates and Deadlines: Applicants notified on a rolling basis; must reply within 3 week(s) of notification.
Transfers: No deadline. Applicants notified on a rolling basis.

CONTACT
Morgan Huber, Financial Aid Coordinator
1800 E Spruce Street, Mitchell, SD 57301
(605) 995-3052

Mount Marty College

Yankton, South Dakota
www.mtmc.edu Federal Code: 003465

4-year private nursing and liberal arts college in large town, affiliated with Roman Catholic Church.
Enrollment: 714 undergrads, 24% part-time. 100 full-time freshmen.
Selectivity: Admits 50 to 75% of applicants.

BASIC COSTS (2013-2014)
Tuition and fees: $22,892.
Room and board: $6,646.

FINANCIAL AID PICTURE (2012-2013)
Students with need: Out of 100 full-time freshmen who applied for aid, 100 were judged to have need. Of these, 100 received aid, and 48 had their

full need met. Average financial aid package met 89% of need; average scholarship/grant was $6,129; average loan was $3,704. For part-time students, average financial aid package was $10,709.
Students without need: 4 full-time freshmen who did not demonstrate need for aid received scholarships/grants; average award was $11,400. No-need awards available for academics, athletics, leadership, music/drama, religious affiliation.
Scholarships offered: 2 full-time freshmen received athletic scholarships; average amount $4,000.
Additional info: Prestige scholarships application deadline 2/1.

FINANCIAL AID PROCEDURES
Forms required: FAFSA, institutional form.
Dates and Deadlines: Priority date 3/1; no closing date. Applicants notified on a rolling basis starting 3/15; must reply within 2 week(s) of notification.
Transfers: No deadline. Applicants notified on a rolling basis; must reply within 2 week(s) of notification.

CONTACT
Kenneth Kocer, Director of Financial Assistance
1105 West Eighth Street, Yankton, SD 57078
(605) 668-1589

National American University: Rapid City

Rapid City, South Dakota
www.national.edu Federal Code: 004057

4-year for-profit business and technical college in small city.
Enrollment: 1,999 undergrads.
Selectivity: Open admission; but selective for some programs.

FINANCIAL AID PICTURE
Students with need: Need-based aid available for full-time and part-time students. Work study available nights, weekends, and for part-time students.
Students without need: This college awards aid only to students with need.
Scholarships offered: Reduced tuition to military students and military dependents with a valid military ID card.

FINANCIAL AID PROCEDURES
Forms required: FAFSA, institutional form.
Dates and Deadlines: Applicants notified on a rolling basis; must reply within 4 week(s) of notification.

CONTACT
Cheryl Bullinger, Director of Financial Aid
5301 S. Hwy 16, Rapid City, SD 57701

Northern State University

Aberdeen, South Dakota
www.northern.edu Federal Code: 003466

4-year public university and liberal arts college in large town.
Enrollment: 1,769 undergrads, 20% part-time. 379 full-time freshmen.
Selectivity: Admits over 75% of applicants.

BASIC COSTS (2012-2013)
Tuition and fees: $7,269; out-of-state residents $9,134.
Per-credit charge: $124; out-of-state residents $186.
Room and board: $6,147.
Additional info: Reciprocity agreement for reduced tuition for Minnesota students.

FINANCIAL AID PICTURE (2012-2013)
Students with need: Need-based aid available for full-time and part-time students. Work study available nights, weekends, and for part-time students.
Students without need: No-need awards available for academics, art, athletics, leadership, minority status, music/drama.

FINANCIAL AID PROCEDURES
Forms required: FAFSA.
Dates and Deadlines: Priority date 3/1; no closing date. Applicants notified on a rolling basis starting 4/15; must reply within 2 week(s) of notification.
Transfers: Applicants notified by 4/15; must reply within 2 week(s) of notification. Financial aid transcript(s) required from all schools previously attended.

CONTACT
Sharon Kienow, Director of Student Financial Assistance
1200 South Jay Street, Aberdeen, SD 57401-7198
(605) 626-2640

Sisseton Wahpeton College

Sisseton, South Dakota
www.swc.tc Federal Code: 016080

2-year public technical college in large town.
Enrollment: 174 undergrads, 30% part-time. 49 full-time freshmen.
Selectivity: Open admission.

BASIC COSTS (2012-2013)
Tuition and fees: $3,790.
Per-credit charge: $110.
Additional info: Tuition rate shown is for Native American students. Non-Native American students pay a different rate.

FINANCIAL AID PICTURE (2011-2012)
Students with need: Out of 47 full-time freshmen who applied for aid, 47 were judged to have need. Of these, 45 received aid. For part-time students, average financial aid package was $2,375.
Students without need: 1 full-time freshmen who did not demonstrate need for aid received scholarships/grants; average award was $400.

FINANCIAL AID PROCEDURES
Forms required: FAFSA.
Dates and Deadlines: Priority date 12/15; no closing date. Applicants notified on a rolling basis.

CONTACT
Janel Many Lightnings, Director of Financial Aid
BIA 700, Box 689, Sisseton, SD 57262-0689
(605) 698-3966 ext. 1182

South Dakota School of Mines and Technology

Rapid City, South Dakota
www.sdsmt.edu Federal Code: 003470

4-year public university in small city.
Enrollment: 1,939 undergrads, 12% part-time. 443 full-time freshmen.
Selectivity: Admits over 75% of applicants.

BASIC COSTS (2012-2013)
Tuition and fees: $8,407; out-of-state residents $10,353.
Per-credit charge: $130; out-of-state residents $195.
Room and board: $5,888.
Additional info: Reciprocity agreement for reduced tuition for Minnesota students.

FINANCIAL AID PICTURE (2012-2013)
Students with need: Out of 427 full-time freshmen who applied for aid, 271 were judged to have need. Of these, 271 received aid, and 120 had their full need met. Average financial aid package met 81% of need; average

scholarship/grant was $4,115; average loan was $3,269. For part-time students, average financial aid package was $11,138.
Students without need: 116 full-time freshmen who did not demonstrate need for aid received scholarships/grants; average award was $2,799. No-need awards available for academics, athletics, leadership, ROTC.
Scholarships offered: ***Merit:*** Presidential Scholarship; $1,000 to $4,000; 5 awarded. Surbeck Scholars; $7,000; 2 awarded. All based on ACT/SAT, GPA, and class rank. Number of awards may vary from year to year depending on availability of funding. ***Athletic:*** 20 full-time freshmen received athletic scholarships; average amount $3,867.
Cumulative student debt: 60% of graduating class had student loans; average debt was $18,331.
Additional info: Closing date for scholarship applications 2/1.

FINANCIAL AID PROCEDURES
Forms required: FAFSA.
Dates and Deadlines: Applicants notified on a rolling basis starting 4/15; must reply within 3 week(s) of notification.

CONTACT
David Martin, Director of Financial Aid
501 East St. Joseph Street, Rapid City, SD 57701
(605) 394-2274

South Dakota State University

Brookings, South Dakota
www.sdstate.edu Federal Code: 003471

4-year public university in large town.
Enrollment: 10,043 undergrads, 15% part-time. 2,116 full-time freshmen.
Selectivity: Admits over 75% of applicants.

BASIC COSTS (2012-2013)
Tuition and fees: $7,404; out-of-state residents $9,350.
Per-credit charge: $130; out-of-state residents $195.
Room and board: $6,466.
Additional info: Reduced out-of-state tuition for Minnesota students.

FINANCIAL AID PICTURE (2012-2013)
Students with need: Out of 1,752 full-time freshmen who applied for aid, 1,462 were judged to have need. Of these, 1,462 received aid, and 1,238 had their full need met. Average financial aid package met 92% of need; average scholarship/grant was $4,876; average loan was $4,836. Need-based aid available for part-time students.
Students without need: 491 full-time freshmen who did not demonstrate need for aid received scholarships/grants; average award was $1,674. No-need awards available for academics, art, athletics, job skills, leadership, minority status, music/drama, ROTC, state/district residency.
Scholarships offered: ***Merit:*** Academic scholarships for first-year freshmen: $500-$7,000; based on academic performance in high school; 1,420 awarded. Minimum academic scholarship for new first-year students: $1,000; based on ACT 24+; renewable. ***Athletic:*** 138 full-time freshmen received athletic scholarships; average amount $7,354.
Cumulative student debt: 80% of graduating class had student loans; average debt was $22,735.

FINANCIAL AID PROCEDURES
Forms required: FAFSA.
Dates and Deadlines: Priority date 3/15; no closing date. Applicants notified on a rolling basis starting 3/30; must reply within 3 week(s) of notification.
Transfers: No deadline. Applicants notified on a rolling basis starting 4/1; must reply within 3 week(s) of notification.

CONTACT
Jay Larsen, Director of Financial Aid
Box 2201 SAD 200, Brookings, SD 57007-0649
(605) 688-4695

Southeast Technical Institute

Sioux Falls, South Dakota
www.southeasttech.edu Federal Code: 008285

2-year public technical college in small city.
Enrollment: 2,439 undergrads.
Selectivity: Open admission; but selective for some programs.

BASIC COSTS (2012-2013)
Tuition and fees: $5,130; out-of-state residents $5,130.
Per-credit charge: $99; out-of-state residents $99.
Additional info: Board plan not available. Cost of room only, $4,600. Mandatory laptop fee of $1,380 covers all required software and hardware needed, a Gorilla backpack and a 3 year warranty.

FINANCIAL AID PICTURE
Students with need: Need-based aid available for full-time and part-time students.
Students without need: This college awards aid only to students with need.

FINANCIAL AID PROCEDURES
Forms required: FAFSA.
Dates and Deadlines: Priority date 5/1; no closing date. Applicants notified on a rolling basis starting 5/1; must reply within 3 week(s) of notification.

CONTACT
Lynette Grabowska, Financial Aid Officer
2320 North Career Avenue, Sioux Falls, SD 57107
(605) 367-7867

University of Sioux Falls

Sioux Falls, South Dakota
www.usiouxfalls.edu Federal Code: 003469

4-year private university and liberal arts college in small city, affiliated with American Baptist Churches in the USA.
Enrollment: 1,156 undergrads, 14% part-time. 276 full-time freshmen.
Selectivity: Admits 50 to 75% of applicants.

BASIC COSTS (2013-2014)
Tuition and fees: $24,550.
Room and board: $6,900.
Additional info: Tuition/fee waivers available for adults.

FINANCIAL AID PICTURE
Students with need: Need-based aid available for full-time and part-time students. Work study available nights, weekends, and for part-time students.
Students without need: No-need awards available for academics, art, athletics, music/drama.

FINANCIAL AID PROCEDURES
Forms required: FAFSA.
Dates and Deadlines: Priority date 3/1; no closing date. Applicants notified on a rolling basis starting 3/1; must reply within 2 week(s) of notification.
Transfers: Applicants notified on a rolling basis; must reply within 2 week(s) of notification.

CONTACT
Laura Olson, Director of Financial Aid
1101 West 22nd Street, Sioux Falls, SD 57105-1699
(605) 331-6623

University of South Dakota

Vermillion, South Dakota
www.usd.edu Federal Code: 003474

4-year public university in large town.
Enrollment: 6,424 undergrads, 28% part-time. 1,127 full-time freshmen.
Selectivity: Admits over 75% of applicants.

BASIC COSTS (2012-2013)
Tuition and fees: $7,704; out-of-state residents $9,650.
Per-credit charge: $130; out-of-state residents $195.
Room and board: $6,264.
Additional info: Reciprocity agreement for reduced tuition for Minnesota students.

FINANCIAL AID PICTURE (2011-2012)
Students with need: Out of 1,015 full-time freshmen who applied for aid, 758 were judged to have need. Of these, 685 received aid, and 377 had their full need met. Average financial aid package met 74% of need; average scholarship/grant was $4,136; average loan was $3,588. For part-time students, average financial aid package was $6,114.
Students without need: 275 full-time freshmen who did not demonstrate need for aid received scholarships/grants; average award was $4,698. No-need awards available for academics, art, athletics, leadership, minority status, music/drama, ROTC.
Scholarships offered: 85 full-time freshmen received athletic scholarships; average amount $8,845.

FINANCIAL AID PROCEDURES
Forms required: FAFSA.
Dates and Deadlines: Priority date 3/15; no closing date. Applicants notified on a rolling basis starting 5/5.

CONTACT
Julie Pier, Director of Student Financial Aid
414 East Clark Street, Vermillion, SD 57069-2390
(605) 677-5446

Western Dakota Technical Institute

Rapid City, South Dakota
www.wdt.edu Federal Code: 010170

2-year public technical college in small city.
Enrollment: 939 undergrads, 17% part-time. 242 full-time freshmen.
Selectivity: Open admission; but selective for some programs.

BASIC COSTS (2012-2013)
Tuition and fees: $5,280; out-of-state residents $5,280.
Per-credit charge: $99; out-of-state residents $99.
Additional info: Total program cost can vary, depending on course of study.

FINANCIAL AID PICTURE (2011-2012)
Students with need: Need-based aid available for full-time and part-time students. Work study available nights, weekends, and for part-time students.

FINANCIAL AID PROCEDURES
Forms required: FAFSA.
Dates and Deadlines: Closing date 4/20. Applicants notified on a rolling basis starting 6/30; must reply within 2 week(s) of notification.

CONTACT
Starla Russell, Manager of Financial Aid
800 Mickelson Drive, Rapid City, SD 57703
(605) 718-2416

Tennessee

American Baptist College

Nashville, Tennessee
www.abcnash.edu Federal Code: 010460

4-year private Bible college in large city, affiliated with Baptist faith.
Enrollment: 108 undergrads, 23% part-time. 11 full-time freshmen.
Selectivity: Admits over 75% of applicants.

BASIC COSTS (2012-2013)
Tuition and fees: $11,324.
Per-credit charge: $362.
Additional info: Board plan not available. Cost of room only, $2,000.

FINANCIAL AID PICTURE
Students with need: Need-based aid available for full-time students.

FINANCIAL AID PROCEDURES
Forms required: FAFSA.
Dates and Deadlines: Priority date 5/1; no closing date. Applicants notified on a rolling basis; must reply within 2 week(s) of notification.
Transfers: Priority date 1/15; closing date 5/1. Applicants notified on a rolling basis starting 6/1; must reply by 7/1.

CONTACT
1800 Baptist World Center Drive, Nashville, TN 37207
(615) 687-6896 ext. 2227

Aquinas College

Nashville, Tennessee
www.aquinascollege.edu Federal Code: 003477

4-year private nursing and liberal arts college in very large city, affiliated with Roman Catholic Church.
Enrollment: 543 undergrads, 70% part-time. 19 full-time freshmen.
Selectivity: Admits 50 to 75% of applicants.

BASIC COSTS (2012-2013)
Tuition and fees: $19,800.
Per-credit charge: $640.

FINANCIAL AID PICTURE
Students with need: Need-based aid available for full-time and part-time students. Work study available nights.
Students without need: No-need awards available for academics, alumni affiliation, leadership, religious affiliation.

FINANCIAL AID PROCEDURES
Forms required: FAFSA.
Dates and Deadlines: Priority date 2/15; no closing date. Applicants notified on a rolling basis starting 2/15; must reply within 2 week(s) of notification.
Transfers: No deadline. Applicants notified on a rolling basis; must reply within 2 week(s) of notification.

CONTACT
Martha Martinez, Director of Financial Aid
4210 Harding Road, Nashville, TN 37205-2086
(615) 297-7545 ext. 442

Austin Peay State University

Clarksville, Tennessee
www.apsu.edu Federal Code: 003478

4-year public university and liberal arts college in small city.
Enrollment: 9,475 undergrads, 26% part-time. 1,274 full-time freshmen.

Selectivity: Admits over 75% of applicants.

BASIC COSTS (2012-2013)

Tuition and fees: $6,918; out-of-state residents $21,714.
Per-credit charge: $226; out-of-state residents $813.
Room and board: $7,380.

FINANCIAL AID PICTURE (2011-2012)

Students with need: For part-time students, average financial aid package was $7,281.
Students without need: 153 full-time freshmen who did not demonstrate need for aid received scholarships/grants; average award was $4,512. No-need awards available for academics, art, athletics, leadership, music/drama, ROTC, state/district residency.
Scholarships offered: 17 full-time freshmen received athletic scholarships; average amount $13,949.
Cumulative student debt: 59% of graduating class had student loans; average debt was $26,181.

FINANCIAL AID PROCEDURES

Forms required: FAFSA.
Dates and Deadlines: Priority date 2/11; no closing date. Applicants notified on a rolling basis starting 4/6.

CONTACT

Donna Price, Director of Financial Aid
PO Box 4548, Clarksville, TN 37044-4548
(931) 221-7907

Belmont University

Nashville, Tennessee
www.belmont.edu Federal Code: 003479

4-year private university in very large city, affiliated with interdenominational tradition.
Enrollment: 5,237 undergrads, 7% part-time. 1,254 full-time freshmen.
Selectivity: Admits over 75% of applicants.

BASIC COSTS (2012-2013)

Tuition and fees: $26,130.
Per-credit charge: $950.
Room and board: $9,670.

FINANCIAL AID PICTURE (2012-2013)

Students with need: Out of 1,001 full-time freshmen who applied for aid, 696 were judged to have need. Of these, 695 received aid, and 199 had their full need met. Average financial aid package met 64% of need; average scholarship/grant was $7,367; average loan was $3,595. Need-based aid available for part-time students.
Students without need: 153 full-time freshmen who did not demonstrate need for aid received scholarships/grants; average award was $6,828. No-need awards available for academics, art, athletics, leadership, music/drama, religious affiliation, state/district residency.
Scholarships offered: 22 full-time freshmen received athletic scholarships; average amount $20,216.
Cumulative student debt: 63% of graduating class had student loans; average debt was $33,515.

FINANCIAL AID PROCEDURES

Forms required: FAFSA.
Dates and Deadlines: Priority date 3/1; no closing date. Applicants notified on a rolling basis starting 3/15; must reply by 5/1 or within 2 week(s) of notification.
Transfers: Applicants notified on a rolling basis starting 3/1; must reply by 5/1 or within 2 week(s) of notification. Scholarships available.

CONTACT

Patricia Smedley, Director of Student Financial Services
1900 Belmont Boulevard, Nashville, TN 37212-3757
(615) 460-6403

Bethel University

McKenzie, Tennessee
www.bethelu.edu Federal Code: 003480

4-year private university and liberal arts college in small town, affiliated with Cumberland Presbyterian Church.
Enrollment: 4,900 undergrads.

BASIC COSTS (2012-2013)

Tuition and fees: $14,520.
Per-credit charge: $423.
Room and board: $8,364.

FINANCIAL AID PICTURE

Students with need: Need-based aid available for full-time and part-time students. Work study available nights, weekends, and for part-time students.
Students without need: No-need awards available for academics, athletics, music/drama, religious affiliation, state/district residency.

FINANCIAL AID PROCEDURES

Forms required: FAFSA, institutional form.
Dates and Deadlines: Priority date 3/3; closing date 6/30. Applicants notified on a rolling basis starting 3/1.
Transfers: Financial aid transcripts from previously attended institutions required.

CONTACT

Laura Bateman, Director of Financial Aid
325 Cherry Avenue, McKenzie, TN 38201
(731) 352-4021

Bryan University: Dayton

Dayton, Tennessee
www.bryan.edu Federal Code: 003536

4-year private liberal arts college in small town, affiliated with interdenominational tradition.
Enrollment: 1,375 undergrads.

BASIC COSTS (2012-2013)

Tuition and fees: $20,150.
Per-credit charge: $875.
Room and board: $5,950.
Additional info: Tuition/fee waivers available for adults, minority students, unemployed or children of unemployed.

FINANCIAL AID PICTURE

Students with need: Need-based aid available for full-time and part-time students. Work study available nights, weekends, and for part-time students.
Students without need: No-need awards available for academics, alumni affiliation, art, athletics, job skills, leadership, music/drama.

FINANCIAL AID PROCEDURES

Forms required: FAFSA.
Dates and Deadlines: Priority date 2/15; no closing date. Applicants notified on a rolling basis starting 1/1; must reply within 2 week(s) of notification.

CONTACT

David Haggard, Director of Financial Aid
PO Box 7000, Dayton, TN 37321-7000
(423) 775-7339

Carson-Newman University

Jefferson City, Tennessee
www.cn.edu Federal Code: 003481

4-year private liberal arts college in small town, affiliated with Southern Baptist Convention.

Enrollment: 1,623 undergrads, 4% part-time. 453 full-time freshmen.
Selectivity: Admits 50 to 75% of applicants.

BASIC COSTS (2012-2013)
Tuition and fees: $22,652.
Per-credit charge: $902.
Room and board: $6,406.
Additional info: Tuition/fee waivers available for adults, minority students.

FINANCIAL AID PICTURE
Students with need: Need-based aid available for full-time and part-time students. Work study available nights, weekends, and for part-time students.
Students without need: No-need awards available for academics, art, athletics, leadership, minority status, music/drama, religious affiliation, ROTC.

FINANCIAL AID PROCEDURES
Forms required: FAFSA, institutional form.
Dates and Deadlines: Priority date 4/1; no closing date. Applicants notified on a rolling basis starting 2/1; must reply within 2 week(s) of notification.

CONTACT
Danette Seale, Director of Financial Aid
1646 Russell Avenue, Jefferson City, TN 37760
(865) 471-3247

Chattanooga State Community College
Chattanooga, Tennessee
www.chattanoogastate.edu Federal Code: 003998

2-year public community and technical college in small city.
Enrollment: 8,317 undergrads, 48% part-time. 1,229 full-time freshmen.
Selectivity: Open admission; but selective for some programs.

BASIC COSTS (2012-2013)
Tuition and fees: $3,717; out-of-state residents $14,664.
Per-credit charge: $135; out-of-state residents $576.

FINANCIAL AID PICTURE
Students with need: Need-based aid available for full-time and part-time students. Work study available nights, weekends, and for part-time students.
Students without need: No-need awards available for state/district residency.

FINANCIAL AID PROCEDURES
Forms required: FAFSA.
Dates and Deadlines: Priority date 6/1; no closing date. Applicants notified on a rolling basis starting 4/1; must reply within 2 week(s) of notification.

CONTACT
Jeanne Hinchee, Director of Financial Aid
4501 Amnicola Highway, Chattanooga, TN 37406
(423) 697-4402

Christian Brothers University
Memphis, Tennessee
www.cbu.edu Federal Code: 003482

4-year private university in very large city, affiliated with Roman Catholic Church.
Enrollment: 1,224 undergrads, 12% part-time. 252 full-time freshmen.
Selectivity: Admits less than 50% of applicants.

BASIC COSTS (2012-2013)
Tuition and fees: $27,290.
Per-credit charge: $955.
Room and board: $6,550.
Additional info: Tuition/fee waivers available for adults.

FINANCIAL AID PICTURE
Students with need: Need-based aid available for full-time and part-time students.
Students without need: No-need awards available for academics, alumni affiliation, athletics, music/drama, state/district residency.
Additional info: ROTC scholarships available to qualified applicants.

FINANCIAL AID PROCEDURES
Forms required: FAFSA.
Dates and Deadlines: Priority date 2/15; no closing date. Applicants notified on a rolling basis starting 3/1; must reply within 2 week(s) of notification.

CONTACT
Jim Shannon, Dean of Student Financial Assistance
650 East Parkway South, Memphis, TN 38104-5519
(901) 321-3305

Cleveland State Community College
Cleveland, Tennessee
www.clevelandstatecc.edu Federal Code: 003999

2-year public community college in small city.
Enrollment: 2,778 undergrads, 38% part-time. 683 full-time freshmen.
Selectivity: Open admission; but selective for some programs.

BASIC COSTS (2012-2013)
Tuition and fees: $3,671; out-of-state residents $14,303.
Per-credit charge: $135; out-of-state residents $557.

FINANCIAL AID PICTURE (2012-2013)
Students with need: Out of 656 full-time freshmen who applied for aid, 553 were judged to have need. Of these, 530 received aid, and 173 had their full need met. Average financial aid package met 64% of need; average scholarship/grant was $2,790; average loan was $1,375. For part-time students, average financial aid package was $3,400.
Students without need: 130 full-time freshmen who did not demonstrate need for aid received scholarships/grants; average award was $868. No-need awards available for athletics, minority status.
Scholarships offered: 27 full-time freshmen received athletic scholarships; average amount $2,735.

FINANCIAL AID PROCEDURES
Forms required: FAFSA, institutional form.
Dates and Deadlines: Priority date 5/15; no closing date. Applicants notified on a rolling basis starting 7/1; must reply within 2 week(s) of notification.
Transfers: Closing date 7/27.

CONTACT
Brenda DiSorbo, Director of Financial Aid
3535 Adkisson Drive, Cleveland, TN 37320-3570
(423) 472-7141 ext. 215

Columbia State Community College
Columbia, Tennessee
www.columbiastate.edu Federal Code: 003483

2-year public community college in large town.
Enrollment: 4,518 undergrads.
Selectivity: Open admission; but selective for some programs.

BASIC COSTS (2012-2013)
Tuition and fees: $3,673; out-of-state residents $14,305.
Per-credit charge: $135; out-of-state residents $557.

FINANCIAL AID PICTURE
Students with need: Need-based aid available for full-time and part-time students.

Students without need: No-need awards available for academics, athletics, state/district residency.

FINANCIAL AID PROCEDURES

Forms required: FAFSA, institutional form.

Dates and Deadlines: Closing date 7/31. Applicants notified on a rolling basis starting 5/15; must reply within 2 week(s) of notification.

CONTACT

Brenda Burney, Director of Financial Assistance
1665 Hampshire Pike, Columbia, TN 38401
(931) 540-2583

Cumberland University

Lebanon, Tennessee
www.cumberland.edu Federal Code: 003485

4-year private university and liberal arts college in large town.
Enrollment: 1,167 undergrads, 9% part-time. 212 full-time freshmen.
Selectivity: Admits less than 50% of applicants.

BASIC COSTS (2013-2014)

Tuition and fees: $20,200.
Per-credit charge: $800.
Room and board: $8,000.

FINANCIAL AID PICTURE

Students with need: Need-based aid available for full-time and part-time students.

Students without need: No-need awards available for academics, art, athletics, music/drama.

FINANCIAL AID PROCEDURES

Forms required: FAFSA, institutional form.

Dates and Deadlines: Priority date 2/1; no closing date. Applicants notified on a rolling basis starting 5/1; must reply within 2 week(s) of notification.

Transfers: Priority date 2/15. Applicants notified on a rolling basis starting 5/1.

CONTACT

Beatrice LaChance, Financial Aid Director
1 Cumberland Square, Lebanon, TN 37087
(615) 444-2562 ext. 1222

Daymar Institute: Nashville

Nashville, Tennessee
www.daymarinstitute.edu Federal Code: 004934

2-year for-profit career college in very large city.
Enrollment: 400 undergrads.
Selectivity: Open admission; but selective for some programs.

BASIC COSTS (2012-2013)

Tuition and fees: $18,000.
Additional info: Program inclusive pricing, including tuition, books, and all fees.

FINANCIAL AID PICTURE

Students with need: Need-based aid available for full-time and part-time students. Work study available nights.

Students without need: This college awards aid only to students with need.

Additional info: Financial aid form for in-state applicants must be filed before 5/1.

FINANCIAL AID PROCEDURES

Forms required: FAFSA.

Dates and Deadlines: Applicants notified on a rolling basis.

Transfers: Students must notify Tennessee Student Assistance Corporation of institutional change before appropriate deadlines.

CONTACT

Janie Rager, Director of Financial Services
340 & 283 Plus Park at Pavilion Boulevard, Nashville, TN 37217
(615) 361-7555

Dyersburg State Community College

Dyersburg, Tennessee
www.dscc.edu Federal Code: 006835

2-year public community college in large town.
Enrollment: 2,723 undergrads, 42% part-time. 554 full-time freshmen.
Selectivity: Open admission; but selective for some programs.

BASIC COSTS (2012-2013)

Tuition and fees: $3,693; out-of-state residents $14,325.
Per-credit charge: $135; out-of-state residents $557.

FINANCIAL AID PICTURE

Students with need: Need-based aid available for full-time and part-time students. Work study available nights.

Students without need: No-need awards available for academics, alumni affiliation, athletics, job skills, leadership, minority status, music/drama, state/district residency.

FINANCIAL AID PROCEDURES

Forms required: FAFSA.

Dates and Deadlines: Priority date 3/1; no closing date. Applicants notified on a rolling basis starting 3/1; must reply within 2 week(s) of notification.

CONTACT

Sandra Rockett, Director of Financial Aid
1510 Lake Road, Dyersburg, TN 38024
(731) 286-3238

East Tennessee State University

Johnson City, Tennessee
www.etsu.edu Federal Code: 003487

4-year public university in small city.
Enrollment: 11,828 undergrads, 14% part-time. 2,038 full-time freshmen.
Selectivity: Admits over 75% of applicants.

BASIC COSTS (2012-2013)

Tuition and fees: $6,997; out-of-state residents $22,369.
Per-credit charge: $235; out-of-state residents $845.
Room and board: $6,304.

FINANCIAL AID PICTURE

Students with need: Need-based aid available for full-time and part-time students. Work study available nights, weekends, and for part-time students.

Students without need: No-need awards available for academics, alumni affiliation, art, athletics, leadership, minority status, music/drama, religious affiliation, ROTC, state/district residency.

Additional info: Housing costs payable by installment.

FINANCIAL AID PROCEDURES

Forms required: FAFSA.

Dates and Deadlines: Priority date 4/15; no closing date. Applicants notified on a rolling basis starting 4/15; must reply within 3 week(s) of notification.

CONTACT

Margaret Miller, Director of Financial Aid
ETSU Box 70731, Johnson City, TN 37614
(423) 439-4300

Fisk University

Nashville, Tennessee
www.fisk.edu Federal Code: 003490

4-year private liberal arts college in very large city, affiliated with United Church of Christ.
Enrollment: 580 undergrads, 4% part-time. 181 full-time freshmen.
Selectivity: Admits less than 50% of applicants.

BASIC COSTS (2013-2014)

Tuition and fees: $20,543.
Room and board: $10,023.

FINANCIAL AID PICTURE (2012-2013)

Students with need: Out of 181 full-time freshmen who applied for aid, 177 were judged to have need. Of these, 177 received aid, and 66 had their full need met. Average financial aid package met 85% of need; average scholarship/grant was $11,486; average loan was $2,904. For part-time students, average financial aid package was $7,397.
Students without need: This college awards aid only to students with need.
Cumulative student debt: 49% of graduating class had student loans; average debt was $6,147.

FINANCIAL AID PROCEDURES

Forms required: FAFSA.
Dates and Deadlines: Priority date 3/1; closing date 7/1. Applicants notified on a rolling basis starting 4/1; must reply within 2 week(s) of notification.

CONTACT

Mary Chambliss, Director of Financial Aid
1000 Seventeenth Avenue North, Nashville, TN 37208-3051
(615) 329-8585

Freed-Hardeman University

Henderson, Tennessee
www.fhu.edu Federal Code: 003492

4-year private university and liberal arts college in small town, affiliated with Church of Christ.
Enrollment: 1,328 undergrads.
Selectivity: Admits less than 50% of applicants.

BASIC COSTS (2012-2013)

Tuition and fees: $20,468.
Room and board: $7,296.
Additional info: Tuition/fee waivers available for minority students.

FINANCIAL AID PICTURE

Students with need: Need-based aid available for full-time and part-time students. Work study available nights, weekends, and for part-time students.
Students without need: No-need awards available for academics, art, athletics, leadership, minority status, music/drama.

FINANCIAL AID PROCEDURES

Forms required: FAFSA.
Dates and Deadlines: Priority date 2/1; no closing date. Applicants notified on a rolling basis starting 3/10; must reply within 4 week(s) of notification.

CONTACT

Molly Risley, Director of Financial Aid
158 East Main Street, Henderson, TN 38340
(731) 989-6662

Jackson State Community College

Jackson, Tennessee
www.jscc.edu Federal Code: 004937

2-year public community college in small city.
Enrollment: 3,726 undergrads. 764 full-time freshmen.
Selectivity: Open admission; but selective for some programs.

BASIC COSTS (2012-2013)

Tuition and fees: $3,679; out-of-state residents $14,311.
Per-credit charge: $135; out-of-state residents $557.
Additional info: Tuition/fee waivers available for adults, minority students.

FINANCIAL AID PICTURE

Students with need: Need-based aid available for full-time and part-time students. Work study available nights, weekends, and for part-time students.
Students without need: No-need awards available for academics, art, athletics, job skills, leadership, minority status, music/drama.

FINANCIAL AID PROCEDURES

Forms required: FAFSA, institutional form.
Dates and Deadlines: Priority date 3/15; no closing date. Applicants notified on a rolling basis starting 6/1; must reply within 2 week(s) of notification.
Transfers: No deadline. Applicants notified on a rolling basis.

CONTACT

Dewana Latimer, Director of Financial Aid
2046 North Parkway, Jackson, TN 38301-3797
(731) 425-2605

John A. Gupton College

Nashville, Tennessee
www.guptoncollege.edu Federal Code: 008859

2-year private school of mortuary science in large city.
Enrollment: 150 undergrads.
Selectivity: Open admission; but selective for some programs.

BASIC COSTS (2013-2014)

Tuition and fees: $9,260.
Per-credit charge: $290.
Room only: $3,600.

FINANCIAL AID PICTURE (2012-2013)

Students with need: Need-based aid available for part-time students.
Students without need: This college awards aid only to students with need.

FINANCIAL AID PROCEDURES

Forms required: FAFSA.
Dates and Deadlines: Applicants notified on a rolling basis; must reply within 2 week(s) of notification.
Transfers: No deadline. Applicants notified on a rolling basis starting 1/1; must reply within 2 week(s) of notification.

CONTACT

Rachel Johnson
1616 Church Street, Nashville, TN 37203-2920
(615) 327-3927

Johnson University

Knoxville, Tennessee
www.johnsonu.edu Federal Code: 003495

4-year private Bible and teachers college in large city, affiliated with Christian Church.

Enrollment: 777 undergrads, 4% part-time. 179 full-time freshmen.

BASIC COSTS (2012-2013)
Tuition and fees: $10,250.
Room and board: $5,550.
Additional info: Tuition/fee waivers available for minority students.

FINANCIAL AID PICTURE
Students with need: Need-based aid available for full-time and part-time students. Work study available nights, weekends, and for part-time students.
Students without need: No-need awards available for academics, leadership, minority status, music/drama, religious affiliation, state/district residency.

FINANCIAL AID PROCEDURES
Forms required: FAFSA, institutional form.
Dates and Deadlines: Closing date 3/1. Applicants notified on a rolling basis starting 4/30; must reply by 8/25 or within 2 week(s) of notification.
Transfers: No deadline.

CONTACT
Larry Rector, Financial Aid Director
7900 Johnson Drive, Knoxville, TN 37998-0001
(865) 251-2303

King College
Bristol, Tennessee
www.king.edu Federal Code: 003496

4-year private nursing and liberal arts college in large town, affiliated with Presbyterian Church (USA).
Enrollment: 1,866 undergrads, 2% part-time. 214 full-time freshmen.
Selectivity: Admits 50 to 75% of applicants.

BASIC COSTS (2012-2013)
Tuition and fees: $24,960.
Room and board: $8,180.

FINANCIAL AID PICTURE (2012-2013)
Students with need: Average financial aid package met 74% of need; average scholarship/grant was $18,066; average loan was $3,800. For part-time students, average financial aid package was $11,292.
Students without need: No-need awards available for academics, art, athletics, job skills, music/drama, state/district residency.
Cumulative student debt: 95% of graduating class had student loans; average debt was $28,946.

FINANCIAL AID PROCEDURES
Forms required: FAFSA.
Dates and Deadlines: Priority date 3/1; no closing date. Applicants notified on a rolling basis starting 3/1; must reply within 2 week(s) of notification.

CONTACT
John McCarroll, Financial Aid Director
1350 King College Road, Bristol, TN 37620-2699
(423) 652-4725

Lane College
Jackson, Tennessee
www.lanecollege.edu Federal Code: 003499

4-year private liberal arts college in small city, affiliated with Christian Methodist Episcopal Church.
Enrollment: 1,512 undergrads, 2% part-time. 325 full-time freshmen.
Selectivity: Admits less than 50% of applicants.

BASIC COSTS (2012-2013)
Tuition and fees: $8,560.
Room and board: $6,040.

FINANCIAL AID PICTURE
Students with need: Need-based aid available for full-time and part-time students.
Students without need: No-need awards available for academics, athletics, religious affiliation.

FINANCIAL AID PROCEDURES
Forms required: FAFSA.
Dates and Deadlines: Priority date 3/1; no closing date. Applicants notified on a rolling basis starting 3/31; must reply within 2 week(s) of notification.
Transfers: No deadline. Applicants notified on a rolling basis; must reply within 2 week(s) of notification.

CONTACT
Tony Calhoun, Director of Financial Aid
545 Lane Avenue, Jackson, TN 38301-4598
(731) 426-7537

Lee University
Cleveland, Tennessee
www.leeuniversity.edu Federal Code: 003500

4-year private university and liberal arts college in large town, affiliated with Church of God.
Enrollment: 4,217 undergrads, 9% part-time. 846 full-time freshmen.
Selectivity: Admits over 75% of applicants.

BASIC COSTS (2013-2014)
Tuition and fees: $13,750.
Per-credit charge: $550.
Room and board: $6,762.

FINANCIAL AID PICTURE (2012-2013)
Students with need: Out of 735 full-time freshmen who applied for aid, 568 were judged to have need. Of these, 564 received aid, and 170 had their full need met. Average financial aid package met 68% of need; average scholarship/grant was $10,814; average loan was $3,486. For part-time students, average financial aid package was $5,443.
Students without need: 179 full-time freshmen who did not demonstrate need for aid received scholarships/grants; average award was $9,913. No-need awards available for academics, alumni affiliation, athletics, leadership, minority status, music/drama, religious affiliation, state/district residency.
Scholarships offered: 35 full-time freshmen received athletic scholarships; average amount $8,520.
Cumulative student debt: 64% of graduating class had student loans; average debt was $27,882.

FINANCIAL AID PROCEDURES
Forms required: FAFSA.
Dates and Deadlines: Priority date 3/15; no closing date. Applicants notified on a rolling basis starting 2/1; must reply within 3 week(s) of notification.

CONTACT
Marian Huffman, Director of Student Financial Aid
1120 North Ocoee Street, Cleveland, TN 37320-3450
(423) 614-8304

LeMoyne-Owen College
Memphis, Tennessee
www.loc.edu Federal Code: 003501

4-year private liberal arts college in very large city, affiliated with United Church of Christ.
Enrollment: 1,078 undergrads, 12% part-time. 185 full-time freshmen.

Selectivity: Admits less than 50% of applicants.

BASIC COSTS (2012-2013)
Tuition and fees: $10,680.
Per-credit charge: $436.
Room and board: $4,852.

FINANCIAL AID PICTURE
Students with need: Need-based aid available for full-time and part-time students.
Students without need: No-need awards available for academics, athletics, music/drama.

FINANCIAL AID PROCEDURES
Forms required: FAFSA.
Dates and Deadlines: Priority date 4/15; no closing date. Applicants notified on a rolling basis starting 4/1.
Transfers: No deadline. Applicants notified on a rolling basis starting 4/1.

CONTACT
Phyllis Torry, Financial Aid Director
807 Walker Avenue, Memphis, TN 38126
(901) 435-1550

Lincoln Memorial University
Harrogate, Tennessee
www.lmunet.edu Federal Code: 003502

4-year private university and liberal arts college in small town.
Enrollment: 1,749 undergrads, 22% part-time. 312 full-time freshmen.
Selectivity: Admits 50 to 75% of applicants.

BASIC COSTS (2012-2013)
Tuition and fees: $18,740.
Per-credit charge: $760.
Room and board: $6,480.

FINANCIAL AID PICTURE (2011-2012)
Students with need: Out of 312 full-time freshmen who applied for aid, 288 were judged to have need. Of these, 288 received aid, and 26 had their full need met. Average financial aid package met 87% of need; average scholarship/grant was $4,200; average loan was $2,000. For part-time students, average financial aid package was $8,624.
Students without need: 2 full-time freshmen who did not demonstrate need for aid received scholarships/grants; average award was $1,500. No-need awards available for academics, alumni affiliation, athletics, music/drama, ROTC.
Scholarships offered: 6 full-time freshmen received athletic scholarships; average amount $2,350.
Cumulative student debt: 60% of graduating class had student loans; average debt was $22,439.

FINANCIAL AID PROCEDURES
Forms required: FAFSA.
Dates and Deadlines: Priority date 2/15; no closing date. Applicants notified on a rolling basis starting 3/15; must reply within 3 week(s) of notification.

CONTACT
Bryan Erslan, Director of Financial Aid
6965 Cumberland Gap Parkway, Harrogate, TN 37752-1901
(423) 869-6336

Lipscomb University
Nashville, Tennessee
www.lipscomb.edu Federal Code: 003486

4-year private university and liberal arts college in very large city, affiliated with Church of Christ.
Enrollment: 2,716 undergrads, 8% part-time. 670 full-time freshmen.
Selectivity: Admits 50 to 75% of applicants.

BASIC COSTS (2012-2013)
Tuition and fees: $24,654.
Per-credit charge: $960.
Room and board: $9,224.

FINANCIAL AID PICTURE (2012-2013)
Students with need: Out of 669 full-time freshmen who applied for aid, 451 were judged to have need. Of these, 451 received aid, and 104 had their full need met. Average financial aid package met 63% of need; average scholarship/grant was $4,744; average loan was $3,827. For part-time students, average financial aid package was $10,176.
Students without need: 218 full-time freshmen who did not demonstrate need for aid received scholarships/grants; average award was $10,406. No-need awards available for academics, art, athletics, leadership, minority status, music/drama, religious affiliation, state/district residency.
Scholarships offered: 25 full-time freshmen received athletic scholarships; average amount $15,243.
Cumulative student debt: 56% of graduating class had student loans; average debt was $15,155.

FINANCIAL AID PROCEDURES
Forms required: FAFSA.
Dates and Deadlines: Priority date 1/31; no closing date. Applicants notified on a rolling basis starting 1/31.

CONTACT
Karita Waters, Director of Financial Aid
One University Park Drive, Nashville, TN 37204-3951
(615) 966-1791

Martin Methodist College
Pulaski, Tennessee
www.martinmethodist.edu Federal Code: 003504

4-year private liberal arts college in small town, affiliated with United Methodist Church.
Enrollment: 1,027 undergrads, 7% part-time. 272 full-time freshmen.
Selectivity: Admits over 75% of applicants.

BASIC COSTS (2012-2013)
Tuition and fees: $21,548.
Per-credit charge: $865.
Room and board: $7,200.

FINANCIAL AID PICTURE
Students with need: Need-based aid available for full-time and part-time students. Work study available nights, weekends, and for part-time students.
Students without need: No-need awards available for academics, art, athletics, leadership, music/drama, religious affiliation, state/district residency.
Scholarships offered: Two full academic scholarships per year awarded through interview and essay competition.

FINANCIAL AID PROCEDURES
Forms required: FAFSA, institutional form.
Dates and Deadlines: Applicants notified on a rolling basis starting 3/1; must reply within 2 week(s) of notification.
Transfers: Closing date 9/13.

CONTACT
Emma Hlubb, Director of Financial Aid
433 West Madison, Pulaski, TN 38478-2799
(931) 363-9804

Maryville College
Maryville, Tennessee
www.maryvillecollege.edu Federal Code: 003505

4-year private liberal arts college in small city, affiliated with Presbyterian Church (USA).
Enrollment: 1,093 undergrads, 4% part-time. 313 full-time freshmen.
Selectivity: Admits 50 to 75% of applicants.

BASIC COSTS (2012-2013)
Tuition and fees: $30,522.
Room and board: $9,696.

FINANCIAL AID PICTURE (2012-2013)
Students with need: Out of 313 full-time freshmen who applied for aid, 281 were judged to have need. Of these, 281 received aid, and 54 had their full need met. Average financial aid package met 86% of need; average scholarship/grant was $25,510; average loan was $4,058. For part-time students, average financial aid package was $5,976.
Students without need: 32 full-time freshmen who did not demonstrate need for aid received scholarships/grants; average award was $18,877. No-need awards available for academics, alumni affiliation, art, leadership, minority status, music/drama, religious affiliation, state/district residency.

FINANCIAL AID PROCEDURES
Forms required: FAFSA.
Dates and Deadlines: Priority date 2/1; no closing date. Applicants notified on a rolling basis starting 3/12; must reply by 5/1 or within 4 week(s) of notification.

CONTACT
Richard Brand, Director of Financial Aid
502 East Lamar Alexander Parkway, Maryville, TN 37804-5907
(865) 981-8100

Memphis College of Art
Memphis, Tennessee
www.mca.edu Federal Code: 003507

4-year private visual arts college in very large city.
Enrollment: 346 undergrads, 9% part-time. 107 full-time freshmen.
Selectivity: Admits 50 to 75% of applicants.

BASIC COSTS (2012-2013)
Tuition and fees: $26,250.
Per-credit charge: $1,117.
Room and board: $8,500.

FINANCIAL AID PICTURE (2011-2012)
Students with need: Out of 106 full-time freshmen who applied for aid, 104 were judged to have need. Of these, 104 received aid, and 10 had their full need met. Average financial aid package met 69% of need; average scholarship/grant was $17,295; average loan was $3,539. For part-time students, average financial aid package was $9,678.
Students without need: 3 full-time freshmen who did not demonstrate need for aid received scholarships/grants; average award was $13,167. No-need awards available for academics, art.
Additional info: Students considered for institutional resources through admissions application process.

FINANCIAL AID PROCEDURES
Forms required: FAFSA.
Dates and Deadlines: Priority date 2/15; no closing date. Applicants notified on a rolling basis starting 3/15; must reply within 3 week(s) of notification.
Transfers: Applicants notified on a rolling basis; must reply within 3 week(s) of notification. Grants of $1,000 awarded to students who attended accredited junior or community college earning at least 60 credit hours.

CONTACT
Aaron White, Director of Financial Aid
1930 Poplar Avenue, Memphis, TN 38104-2764
(901) 272-5138

Middle Tennessee State University
Murfreesboro, Tennessee
www.mtsu.edu Federal Code: 003510

4-year public university in small city.
Enrollment: 22,121 undergrads, 17% part-time. 3,368 full-time freshmen.
Selectivity: Admits 50 to 75% of applicants.

BASIC COSTS (2012-2013)
Tuition and fees: $7,492; out-of-state residents $22,840.
Per-credit charge: $234; out-of-state residents $843.
Room and board: $7,737.

FINANCIAL AID PICTURE (2011-2012)
Students with need: Out of 3,350 full-time freshmen who applied for aid, 2,658 were judged to have need. Of these, 2,649 received aid, and 476 had their full need met. Average financial aid package met 67% of need; average scholarship/grant was $6,189; average loan was $3,046. For part-time students, average financial aid package was $5,731.
Students without need: 192 full-time freshmen who did not demonstrate need for aid received scholarships/grants; average award was $2,774. No-need awards available for academics, alumni affiliation, art, athletics, leadership, music/drama, ROTC, state/district residency.
Scholarships offered: 17 full-time freshmen received athletic scholarships; average amount $18,462.
Cumulative student debt: 59% of graduating class had student loans; average debt was $22,164.
Additional info: Deadline for scholarships 2/15.

FINANCIAL AID PROCEDURES
Forms required: FAFSA.
Dates and Deadlines: Priority date 3/1; no closing date. Applicants notified on a rolling basis starting 4/15; must reply within 2 week(s) of notification.

CONTACT
David Hutton, Director of Student Financial Aid
1301 East Main Street, Murfreesboro, TN 37132
(615) 898-2830

Miller-Motte Technical College: Clarksville
Clarksville, Tennessee
www.miller-motte.edu Federal Code: 026142

2-year for-profit business and health science college in small city.
Enrollment: 573 undergrads.
Selectivity: Open admission; but selective for some programs.

FINANCIAL AID PICTURE
Students with need: Need-based aid available for full-time and part-time students. Work study available nights, weekends, and for part-time students.
Students without need: This college awards aid only to students with need.

FINANCIAL AID PROCEDURES
Forms required: FAFSA, institutional form.
Dates and Deadlines: Applicants notified on a rolling basis.
Transfers: No deadline.

CONTACT
Debbie Stratman, Financial Aid Director
1820 Business Park Drive, Clarksville, TN 37040
(931) 553-0071

Milligan College
Milligan College, Tennessee
www.milligan.edu Federal Code: 003511

4-year private liberal arts college in small city, affiliated with Christian Church.
Enrollment: 910 undergrads, 5% part-time. 178 full-time freshmen.
Selectivity: Admits 50 to 75% of applicants.

BASIC COSTS (2012-2013)
Tuition and fees: $26,760.
Room and board: $5,850.

FINANCIAL AID PICTURE (2012-2013)
Students with need: Out of 173 full-time freshmen who applied for aid, 146 were judged to have need. Of these, 146 received aid, and 43 had their full need met. Average financial aid package met 79% of need; average scholarship/grant was $18,057; average loan was $3,377. For part-time students, average financial aid package was $6,003.
Students without need: 26 full-time freshmen who did not demonstrate need for aid received scholarships/grants; average award was $9,201. No-need awards available for academics, art, athletics, leadership, minority status, music/drama.
Scholarships offered: 27 full-time freshmen received athletic scholarships; average amount $9,017.
Cumulative student debt: 63% of graduating class had student loans; average debt was $27,687.

FINANCIAL AID PROCEDURES
Forms required: FAFSA.
Dates and Deadlines: Closing date 3/1. Applicants notified on a rolling basis starting 3/15; must reply within 2 week(s) of notification.

CONTACT
Diane Keasling, Coordinator of Financial Aid
Box 210, Milligan College, TN 37682
(800) 447-4880

Motlow State Community College
Lynchburg, Tennessee
www.mscc.edu Federal Code: 006836

2-year public community college in rural community.
Enrollment: 4,585 undergrads.
Selectivity: Open admission; but selective for some programs.

BASIC COSTS (2012-2013)
Tuition and fees: $3,678; out-of-state residents $14,310.
Per-credit charge: $135; out-of-state residents $557.

FINANCIAL AID PICTURE
Students with need: Need-based aid available for full-time and part-time students.
Students without need: No-need awards available for academics, alumni affiliation, art, athletics, leadership, music/drama.

FINANCIAL AID PROCEDURES
Forms required: FAFSA, institutional form.
Dates and Deadlines: Closing date 2/15. Applicants notified on a rolling basis starting 3/15.
Transfers: No deadline. Applicants notified on a rolling basis starting 3/15.

CONTACT
Joe Myers, Director of Financial Aid and Scholarships
Box 8500, Lynchburg, TN 37352-8500
(931) 393-1553

Nashville Auto-Diesel College
Nashville, Tennessee
www.nadcedu.com Federal Code: 007440

1-year for-profit technical college in large city.
Enrollment: 2,066 undergrads.

BASIC COSTS (2012-2013)
Additional info: Full program costs range from $26,798 to $32,398 for diploma programs; $33,398 to $34,898 for degree programs.

FINANCIAL AID PICTURE
Students with need: Need-based aid available for full-time students. Work study available nights, weekends, and for part-time students.
Students without need: This college awards aid only to students with need.

FINANCIAL AID PROCEDURES
Forms required: FAFSA, state aid form.
Dates and Deadlines: Applicants notified on a rolling basis.

CONTACT
Chris Biddle, Director of Financial Aid
1524 Gallatin Road, Nashville, TN 37206
(615) 650-8202

Nashville State Community College
Nashville, Tennessee
www.nscc.edu Federal Code: 007534

2-year public community and technical college in very large city.
Enrollment: 8,228 undergrads.
Selectivity: Open admission; but selective for some programs.

BASIC COSTS (2012-2013)
Tuition and fees: $3,627; out-of-state residents $14,259.
Per-credit charge: $135; out-of-state residents $567.

FINANCIAL AID PICTURE (2011-2012)
Students with need: 66% of average financial aid package awarded as scholarships/grants, 34% awarded as loans/jobs. Need-based aid available for part-time students. Work study available nights, weekends, and for part-time students.
Students without need: No-need awards available for academics, minority status.

FINANCIAL AID PROCEDURES
Forms required: FAFSA, institutional form.
Dates and Deadlines: Priority date 3/1; closing date 7/1. Applicants notified on a rolling basis starting 6/1; must reply within 2 week(s) of notification.

CONTACT
Josh Moran, Director of Financial Aid
120 White Bridge Road, Nashville, TN 37209-4515
(615) 353-3250

National College of Business and Technology: Bristol

Bristol, Tennessee
www.ncbt.edu Federal Code: 003726

2-year for-profit business college in large town.
Enrollment: 226 undergrads.
Selectivity: Open admission.

BASIC COSTS (2012-2013)
Tuition and fees: $14,310.
Per-credit charge: $317.

FINANCIAL AID PICTURE
Students with need: Need-based aid available for full-time and part-time students.
Students without need: This college awards aid only to students with need.

FINANCIAL AID PROCEDURES
Forms required: FAFSA.
Dates and Deadlines: Applicants notified on a rolling basis starting 9/1.

CONTACT
Pam Cotton, Director of Financial Aid Compliance and Auditing
1328 Highway 11W, Bristol, TN 37620

National College of Business and Technology: Nashville

Nashville, Tennessee
www.ncbt.edu Federal Code: 003726

2-year for-profit business and technical college in large city.
Enrollment: 155 undergrads.
Selectivity: Open admission.

BASIC COSTS (2012-2013)
Tuition and fees: $14,310.
Per-credit charge: $317.

FINANCIAL AID PICTURE
Students with need: Need-based aid available for full-time and part-time students.
Students without need: This college awards aid only to students with need.

FINANCIAL AID PROCEDURES
Forms required: FAFSA.

CONTACT
Pam Cotton, Director of Financial Aid Compliance and Auditing
1638 Bell Road, Nashville, TN 37211
(615) 333-3344

Northeast State Community College

Blountville, Tennessee
www.NortheastState.edu Federal Code: 005378

2-year public community and technical college in small city.
Enrollment: 6,478 undergrads.
Selectivity: Open admission; but selective for some programs.

BASIC COSTS (2012-2013)
Tuition and fees: $3,683; out-of-state residents $14,315.
Per-credit charge: $135; out-of-state residents $557.

FINANCIAL AID PICTURE
Students with need: Need-based aid available for full-time and part-time students. Work study available nights.
Students without need: No-need awards available for academics, alumni affiliation, art, job skills, leadership, minority status, music/drama, religious affiliation.

FINANCIAL AID PROCEDURES
Forms required: FAFSA.
Dates and Deadlines: Priority date 3/31; no closing date. Applicants notified on a rolling basis starting 3/1; must reply within 3 week(s) of notification.

CONTACT
Cruzita Lucero, Director of Financial Aid
Box 246, Blountville, TN 37617-0246
(423) 323-0252

Nossi College of Art

Madison, Tennessee
www.nossi.edu Federal Code: 017347

2-year for-profit visual arts and technical college in large town.
Enrollment: 311 undergrads.

BASIC COSTS (2012-2013)
Additional info: Tuition for first year (3 semesters) $14,200; required fees $700.

FINANCIAL AID PICTURE
Students with need: Need-based aid available for full-time and part-time students.

CONTACT
Mary Kidd, Financial Aid Director
907 Rivergate Parkway, Building E-6, Goodlettsville, TN 37072
(615) 851-1088

O'More College of Design

Franklin, Tennessee
www.omorecollege.edu Federal Code: 014663

4-year private visual arts college in large town.
Enrollment: 196 undergrads, 10% part-time. 34 full-time freshmen.
Selectivity: Admits 50 to 75% of applicants.

BASIC COSTS (2012-2013)
Tuition and fees: $25,000.

FINANCIAL AID PICTURE (2011-2012)
Students with need: Average financial aid package met 50% of need; average scholarship/grant was $8,300; average loan was $1,750. For part-time students, average financial aid package was $4,000.
Students without need: This college awards aid only to students with need.

FINANCIAL AID PROCEDURES
Forms required: FAFSA.
Dates and Deadlines: Closing date 4/8. Applicants notified on a rolling basis starting 3/1.
Transfers: No deadline. Applicants notified by 6/10.

CONTACT
Jerry Masterson, Financial Aid Director
423 South Margin Street, Franklin, TN 37064-0908
(615) 794-4254 ext. 238

Pellissippi State Community College

Knoxville, Tennessee
www.pstcc.edu Federal Code: 012693

2-year public community and technical college in small city.
Enrollment: 10,588 undergrads.
Selectivity: Open admission.

BASIC COSTS (2012-2013)
Tuition and fees: $3,720; out-of-state residents $14,352.
Per-credit charge: $135; out-of-state residents $557.

FINANCIAL AID PICTURE
Students with need: Need-based aid available for full-time and part-time students. Work study available nights, weekends, and for part-time students.
Students without need: No-need awards available for academics, art, minority status, music/drama.

FINANCIAL AID PROCEDURES
Forms required: FAFSA.
Dates and Deadlines: Priority date 5/1; no closing date. Applicants notified on a rolling basis starting 7/15; must reply within 2 week(s) of notification.

CONTACT
Richard Smelser, Director of Financial Aid
Box 22990, Knoxville, TN 37933-0990
(423) 694-6565

Remington College: Memphis

Memphis, Tennessee
www.remingtoncollege.edu/memphis

2-year private business and technical college in very large city.
Enrollment: 938 undergrads.

BASIC COSTS (2012-2013)
Additional info: Certificate program in pharmacy technician $15,995. Books and supplies included.

FINANCIAL AID PICTURE
Students with need: Need-based aid available for full-time and part-time students.
Students without need: This college awards aid only to students with need.

FINANCIAL AID PROCEDURES
Forms required: FAFSA, institutional form.
Dates and Deadlines: Applicants notified on a rolling basis; must reply within 2 week(s) of notification.

CONTACT
James Dunn, National Director of Financial Aid
2710 Nonconnah Boulevard, Memphis, TN 38132

Rhodes College

Memphis, Tennessee Federal Code: 003519
www.rhodes.edu CSS Code: 1730

4-year private liberal arts college in very large city, affiliated with Presbyterian Church (USA).
Enrollment: 1,887 undergrads. 554 full-time freshmen.
Selectivity: Admits 50 to 75% of applicants.

BASIC COSTS (2012-2013)
Tuition and fees: $38,092.
Room and board: $9,504.

FINANCIAL AID PICTURE (2012-2013)
Students with need: Out of 462 full-time freshmen who applied for aid, 309 were judged to have need. Of these, 309 received aid, and 149 had their full need met. Average financial aid package met 93% of need; average scholarship/grant was $23,691; average loan was $5,080.
Students without need: 214 full-time freshmen who did not demonstrate need for aid received scholarships/grants; average award was $16,832. No-need awards available for academics, art, minority status, music/drama, religious affiliation.
Cumulative student debt: 44% of graduating class had student loans; average debt was $16,831.
Additional info: Auditions required for theater and music achievement awards and art achievement awards. Interviews recommended for merit scholarships. Notification of admissions decision for Bellingrath Scholarship applicants by 3/15; must reply by 5/1.

FINANCIAL AID PROCEDURES
Forms required: FAFSA, CSS PROFILE.
Dates and Deadlines: Closing date 3/1. Must reply by 5/1.

CONTACT
Ashley Bianchi, Director of Financial Aid
2000 North Parkway, Memphis, TN 38112
(901) 843-3810

Roane State Community College

Harriman, Tennessee
www.roanestate.edu Federal Code: 009914

2-year public community and junior college in small town.
Enrollment: 5,106 undergrads, 51% part-time. 1,068 full-time freshmen.
Selectivity: Open admission; but selective for some programs.

BASIC COSTS (2012-2013)
Tuition and fees: $3,687; out-of-state residents $14,319.
Per-credit charge: $135; out-of-state residents $557.

FINANCIAL AID PICTURE (2011-2012)
Students with need: Out of 1,040 full-time freshmen who applied for aid, 890 were judged to have need. Of these, 871 received aid, and 58 had their full need met. Average financial aid package met 52% of need; average scholarship/grant was $4,881. Need-based aid available for part-time students.
Students without need: 33 full-time freshmen who did not demonstrate need for aid received scholarships/grants; average award was $7,308. No-need awards available for academics, art, athletics, leadership, music/drama, state/district residency.

FINANCIAL AID PROCEDURES
Forms required: FAFSA, institutional form.
Dates and Deadlines: Priority date 4/1; no closing date. Applicants notified on a rolling basis starting 5/1.

CONTACT
Tina Long, Director, Financial Aid
276 Patton Lane, Harriman, TN 37748
(865) 882-4545

Sewanee: The University of the South

Sewanee, Tennessee
www.sewanee.edu Federal Code: 003534

4-year private university in rural community, affiliated with Episcopal Church.
Enrollment: 1,450 undergrads. 453 full-time freshmen.
Selectivity: Admits 50 to 75% of applicants. GED not accepted.

BASIC COSTS (2012-2013)
Tuition and fees: $34,714.
Per-credit charge: $1,162.
Room and board: $9,916.

FINANCIAL AID PICTURE (2012-2013)
Students with need: Out of 167 full-time freshmen who applied for aid, 123 were judged to have need. Of these, 120 received aid, and 94 had their full need met. Average financial aid package met 95% of need; average scholarship/grant was $23,837; average loan was $8,424.
Students without need: 93 full-time freshmen who did not demonstrate need for aid received scholarships/grants; average award was $12,528. No-need awards available for academics, minority status, religious affiliation.
Scholarships offered: Benedict Scholars Program for exceptional freshmen; 3 full cost scholarships. Wilkins Scholarships for outstanding incoming freshmen; half tuition, 29 awarded.
Cumulative student debt: 42% of graduating class had student loans; average debt was $32,609.

FINANCIAL AID PROCEDURES
Forms required: FAFSA, institutional form.
Dates and Deadlines: Priority date 2/1; closing date 3/1. Must reply within 4 week(s) of notification.

CONTACT
Beth Cragar, Associate Dean of Admission for Financial Aid
Office of Admission, Sewanee, TN 37383-1000
(931) 598-1312

Southern Adventist University
Collegedale, Tennessee
www.southern.edu Federal Code: 003518

4-year private university and liberal arts college in small town, affiliated with Seventh-day Adventists.
Enrollment: 2,750 undergrads, 11% part-time. 557 full-time freshmen.
Selectivity: Admits over 75% of applicants.

BASIC COSTS (2013-2014)
Tuition and fees: $19,790.
Per-credit charge: $800.
Room and board: $5,900.

FINANCIAL AID PICTURE
Students with need: Need-based aid available for full-time and part-time students.
Students without need: No-need awards available for academics, alumni affiliation, art, athletics, leadership, music/drama.
Scholarships offered: Freshman scholarships; based on GPA, ACT/SAT, leadership positions held.

FINANCIAL AID PROCEDURES
Forms required: FAFSA.
Dates and Deadlines: Priority date 3/1; no closing date. Applicants notified on a rolling basis starting 2/15; must reply within 2 week(s) of notification.
Transfers: No deadline. Applicants notified on a rolling basis.

CONTACT
Paula Walter, Associate Vice President for Enrollment Services
PO Box 370, Collegedale, TN 37315-0370
(423) 236-2835

Southwest Tennessee Community College
Memphis, Tennessee
www.southwest.tn.edu Federal Code: 010439

2-year public community college in very large city.
Enrollment: 12,222 undergrads.
Selectivity: Open admission; but selective for some programs.

BASIC COSTS (2012-2013)
Tuition and fees: $3,717; out-of-state residents $14,349.
Per-credit charge: $135; out-of-state residents $557.
Additional info: Tuition/fee waivers available for minority students.

FINANCIAL AID PICTURE
Students with need: Need-based aid available for full-time and part-time students. Work study available nights, weekends, and for part-time students.
Students without need: No-need awards available for academics, athletics, minority status, music/drama, state/district residency.
Additional info: State grants available to eligible students who apply by 4/1.

FINANCIAL AID PROCEDURES
Forms required: FAFSA.
Dates and Deadlines: Priority date 3/15; no closing date. Applicants notified on a rolling basis starting 6/1; must reply within 4 week(s) of notification.
Transfers: Priority date 4/15.

CONTACT
Lechelle Davenport, Director Financial Aid
PO Box 780, Memphis, TN 38101-0780
(901) 333-5956

Tennessee State University
Nashville, Tennessee
www.tnstate.edu Federal Code: 003522

4-year public university in very large city.
Enrollment: 6,634 undergrads, 21% part-time. 1,017 full-time freshmen.
Selectivity: Admits 50 to 75% of applicants.

BASIC COSTS (2012-2013)
Tuition and fees: $6,702; out-of-state residents $19,944.
Per-credit charge: $287; out-of-state residents $809.
Room and board: $6,120.
Additional info: Tuition/fee waivers available for minority students.

FINANCIAL AID PICTURE (2011-2012)
Students with need: Need-based aid available for full-time students.
Students without need: No-need awards available for academics.

FINANCIAL AID PROCEDURES
Forms required: FAFSA.
Dates and Deadlines: Priority date 4/1; no closing date. Applicants notified on a rolling basis starting 4/15; must reply within 3 week(s) of notification.

CONTACT
Cynthia Brooks, Vice President of Finance/Accounting
3500 John A. Merritt Boulevard, Nashville, TN 37209-1561
(615) 963-5701

Tennessee Technological University
Cookeville, Tennessee
www.tntech.edu Federal Code: 003523

4-year public university in large town.
Enrollment: 9,957 undergrads.

Selectivity: Admits over 75% of applicants.

BASIC COSTS (2012-2013)

Tuition and fees: $6,996; out-of-state residents $21,864.
Per-credit charge: $228; out-of-state residents $818.
Room and board: $8,140.
Additional info: Tuition/fee waivers available for minority students.

FINANCIAL AID PICTURE

Students with need: Need-based aid available for full-time and part-time students. Work study available nights, weekends, and for part-time students.
Students without need: No-need awards available for academics, alumni affiliation, art, athletics, leadership, minority status, music/drama, ROTC, state/district residency.
Scholarships offered: Presidential Scholarship; $4,000 renewable annually. Awarded to National Merit Finalists.
Additional info: Tuition and/or fee waivers available for children of Tennessee public school teachers.

FINANCIAL AID PROCEDURES

Forms required: FAFSA.
Dates and Deadlines: Priority date 3/15; no closing date. Applicants notified on a rolling basis starting 3/15; must reply within 2 week(s) of notification.
Transfers: No deadline. Applicants notified on a rolling basis starting 6/1; must reply within 2 week(s) of notification.

CONTACT

Lester McKenzie, Director of Student Financial Aid
Office of Admissions, Cookeville, TN 38505-0001
(931) 372-3073

Tennessee Wesleyan College

Athens, Tennessee
www.twcnet.edu Federal Code: 003525

4-year private liberal arts and teachers college in large town, affiliated with United Methodist Church.
Enrollment: 1,100 undergrads, 7% part-time. 243 full-time freshmen.
Selectivity: Admits over 75% of applicants.

BASIC COSTS (2012-2013)

Tuition and fees: $21,200.
Room and board: $6,700.
Additional info: Tuition/fee waivers available for minority students.

FINANCIAL AID PICTURE (2011-2012)

Students with need: Out of 220 full-time freshmen who applied for aid, 192 were judged to have need. Of these, 186 received aid, and 33 had their full need met. Average financial aid package met 66% of need; average scholarship/grant was $13,790; average loan was $2,759. For part-time students, average financial aid package was $6,700.
Students without need: 21 full-time freshmen who did not demonstrate need for aid received scholarships/grants; average award was $9,847. No-need awards available for academics, alumni affiliation, athletics, minority status, music/drama, religious affiliation.
Scholarships offered: 28 full-time freshmen received athletic scholarships; average amount $8,386.
Cumulative student debt: 100% of graduating class had student loans; average debt was $27,011.

FINANCIAL AID PROCEDURES

Forms required: FAFSA, institutional form.
Dates and Deadlines: Priority date 2/15; no closing date. Applicants notified on a rolling basis starting 2/15; must reply within 2 week(s) of notification.

CONTACT

Bob Perry, Director of Financial Aid
204 East College Street, Athens, TN 37371-0040
(423) 746-5215

Trevecca Nazarene University

Nashville, Tennessee
www.trevecca.edu Federal Code: 003526

4-year private university and liberal arts college in very large city, affiliated with Church of the Nazarene.
Enrollment: 1,409 undergrads, 26% part-time. 234 full-time freshmen.

BASIC COSTS (2012-2013)

Tuition and fees: $21,290.
Room and board: $7,488.

FINANCIAL AID PICTURE

Students with need: Need-based aid available for full-time students.
Students without need: No-need awards available for academics, alumni affiliation, athletics, leadership, minority status, music/drama, religious affiliation.

FINANCIAL AID PROCEDURES

Forms required: FAFSA.
Dates and Deadlines: Priority date 3/1; closing date 8/1. Applicants notified on a rolling basis starting 3/1.

CONTACT

Eddie White, Director of Financial Aid
333 Murfreesboro Road, Nashville, TN 37210
(615) 248-1242

Tusculum College

Greeneville, Tennessee
www.tusculum.edu Federal Code: 003527

4-year private liberal arts college in large town, affiliated with Presbyterian Church (USA).
Enrollment: 1,980 undergrads.
Selectivity: Admits 50 to 75% of applicants.

BASIC COSTS (2013-2014)

Tuition and fees: $22,250.
Room and board: $8,500.

FINANCIAL AID PICTURE

Students with need: Need-based aid available for full-time and part-time students. Work study available nights, weekends, and for part-time students.
Students without need: No-need awards available for academics, athletics, leadership, religious affiliation, state/district residency.

FINANCIAL AID PROCEDURES

Forms required: FAFSA.
Dates and Deadlines: Closing date 2/15. Applicants notified on a rolling basis starting 3/1; must reply within 3 week(s) of notification.

CONTACT

Melina Verity, Director of Financial Aid
60 Shiloh Road, Greeneville, TN 37743
(423) 636-7376

Union University

Jackson, Tennessee
www.uu.edu Federal Code: 003528

4-year private university and liberal arts college in small city, affiliated with Southern Baptist Convention.
Enrollment: 2,520 undergrads, 12% part-time. 422 full-time freshmen.
Selectivity: Admits over 75% of applicants.

BASIC COSTS (2012-2013)
Tuition and fees: $25,650.
Per-credit charge: $845.
Room and board: $8,430.
Additional info: Tuition/fee waivers available for minority students.

FINANCIAL AID PICTURE (2012-2013)
Students with need: Out of 418 full-time freshmen who applied for aid, 356 were judged to have need. Of these, 356 received aid, and 91 had their full need met. Average financial aid package met 69% of need; average scholarship/grant was $6,693; average loan was $3,419. For part-time students, average financial aid package was $12,455.
Students without need: 81 full-time freshmen who did not demonstrate need for aid received scholarships/grants; average award was $11,054. No-need awards available for academics, alumni affiliation, art, athletics, job skills, leadership, minority status, music/drama, religious affiliation, state/district residency.
Scholarships offered: 48 full-time freshmen received athletic scholarships; average amount $8,675.
Cumulative student debt: 61% of graduating class had student loans; average debt was $26,936.

FINANCIAL AID PROCEDURES
Forms required: FAFSA, institutional form.
Dates and Deadlines: Closing date 2/1. Applicants notified on a rolling basis starting 3/1; must reply by 5/1 or within 2 week(s) of notification.

CONTACT
John Brandt, Director of Student Financial Planning
1050 Union University Drive, Jackson, TN 38305-3697
(731) 661-5015

University of Memphis
Memphis, Tennessee
www.memphis.edu Federal Code: 003509

4-year public university in very large city.
Enrollment: 16,741 undergrads, 24% part-time. 2,180 full-time freshmen.
Selectivity: Admits 50 to 75% of applicants.

BASIC COSTS (2012-2013)
Tuition and fees: $8,234; out-of-state residents $23,684.
Per-credit charge: $277; out-of-state residents $890.
Room and board: $6,860.
Additional info: Tuition/fee waivers available for adults, minority students.

FINANCIAL AID PICTURE (2012-2013)
Students with need: Out of 2,076 full-time freshmen who applied for aid, 1,684 were judged to have need. Of these, 1,576 received aid, and 363 had their full need met. Average financial aid package met 84% of need; average scholarship/grant was $6,678; average loan was $3,283. For part-time students, average financial aid package was $5,410.
Students without need: 381 full-time freshmen who did not demonstrate need for aid received scholarships/grants; average award was $7,927. No-need awards available for academics, alumni affiliation, art, athletics, leadership, minority status, music/drama, ROTC, state/district residency.
Scholarships offered: 61 full-time freshmen received athletic scholarships; average amount $12,564.
Cumulative student debt: 46% of graduating class had student loans; average debt was $28,746.

FINANCIAL AID PROCEDURES
Forms required: FAFSA.
Dates and Deadlines: Priority date 3/1; closing date 5/1. Applicants notified on a rolling basis starting 5/15; must reply by 8/1.

CONTACT
Richard Ritzman, Director of Student Financial Aid
101 Wilder Tower, Memphis, TN 38152
(901) 678-4825

University of Tennessee: Chattanooga
Chattanooga, Tennessee
www.utc.edu Federal Code: 003529

4-year public university in small city.
Enrollment: 10,015 undergrads, 11% part-time. 2,284 full-time freshmen.
Selectivity: Admits over 75% of applicants.

BASIC COSTS (2012-2013)
Tuition and fees: $7,212; out-of-state residents $21,558.
Per-credit charge: $238; out-of-state residents $836.
Room and board: $8,300.

FINANCIAL AID PICTURE
Students with need: Need-based aid available for full-time and part-time students. Work study available nights, weekends, and for part-time students.
Students without need: No-need awards available for academics, alumni affiliation, art, athletics, leadership, music/drama, religious affiliation, ROTC, state/district residency.

FINANCIAL AID PROCEDURES
Forms required: FAFSA.
Dates and Deadlines: Priority date 5/1; no closing date. Applicants notified on a rolling basis starting 3/15.
Transfers: Applicants notified on a rolling basis starting 3/1; must reply within 6 week(s) of notification.

CONTACT
Dianne Cox, Director of Financial Aid
615 McCallie Avenue, Chattanooga, TN 37403
(423) 425-4677

University of Tennessee: Knoxville
Knoxville, Tennessee
www.utk.edu Federal Code: 003530

4-year public university in large city.
Enrollment: 20,699 undergrads, 6% part-time. 4,197 full-time freshmen.
Selectivity: Admits 50 to 75% of applicants.

BASIC COSTS (2012-2013)
Tuition and fees: $9,092; out-of-state residents $27,282.
Per-credit charge: $326; out-of-state residents $1,085.
Room and board: $8,752.
Additional info: Out-of-state students pay additional required fees of $300.

FINANCIAL AID PICTURE (2012-2013)
Students with need: Out of 4,035 full-time freshmen who applied for aid, 2,562 were judged to have need. Of these, 2,561 received aid, and 694 had their full need met. Average financial aid package met 71% of need; average scholarship/grant was $10,391; average loan was $4,654. For part-time students, average financial aid package was $6,648.
Students without need: This college awards aid only to students with need.
Scholarships offered: 148 full-time freshmen received athletic scholarships; average amount $12,747.
Cumulative student debt: 49% of graduating class had student loans; average debt was $22,860.
Additional info: Application priority date for scholarships 2/1.

FINANCIAL AID PROCEDURES
Forms required: FAFSA.

Dates and Deadlines: Priority date 2/15; no closing date. Applicants notified on a rolling basis starting 3/15; must reply within 3 week(s) of notification.
Transfers: Priority date 4/1; no deadline. Applicants notified on a rolling basis starting 4/15; must reply within 3 week(s) of notification.

CONTACT
Jeff Gerkin, Director of Financial Aid
320 Student Services Building, Circle Park, Knoxville, TN 37996-0230
(865) 974-3131

University of Tennessee: Martin

Martin, Tennessee
www.utm.edu Federal Code: 003531

4-year public university in small town.
Enrollment: 6,703 undergrads, 9% part-time. 1,315 full-time freshmen.
Selectivity: Admits over 75% of applicants.

BASIC COSTS (2012-2013)
Tuition and fees: $7,049; out-of-state residents $20,205.
Per-credit charge: $249; out-of-state residents $798.
Room and board: $5,593.

FINANCIAL AID PICTURE (2012-2013)
Students with need: Out of 1,278 full-time freshmen who applied for aid, 1,031 were judged to have need. Of these, 1,024 received aid, and 276 had their full need met. Average financial aid package met 80% of need; average scholarship/grant was $6,516; average loan was $3,441. For part-time students, average financial aid package was $11,827.
Students without need: This college awards aid only to students with need.
Scholarships offered: 77 full-time freshmen received athletic scholarships; average amount $9,324.
Cumulative student debt: 57% of graduating class had student loans; average debt was $12,436.

FINANCIAL AID PROCEDURES
Forms required: FAFSA.
Dates and Deadlines: Priority date 2/15; no closing date. Applicants notified on a rolling basis starting 4/1; must reply within 2 week(s) of notification.

CONTACT
Sheryl Frazier, Director of Student Financial Assistance
200 Hall Moody Administration Building, Martin, TN 38238
(731) 881-7040

Vanderbilt University

Nashville, Tennessee Federal Code: 003535
www.vanderbilt.edu CSS Code: 1871

4-year private university in very large city.
Enrollment: 6,753 undergrads, 1% part-time. 1,608 full-time freshmen.
Selectivity: Admits less than 50% of applicants.

BASIC COSTS (2012-2013)
Tuition and fees: $42,794.
Per-credit charge: $1,712.
Room and board: $13,818.

FINANCIAL AID PICTURE (2012-2013)
Students with need: Out of 975 full-time freshmen who applied for aid, 824 were judged to have need. Of these, 821 received aid, and 821 had their full need met. Average financial aid package met 100% of need; average scholarship/grant was $39,892; average loan was $2,955.
Students without need: 126 full-time freshmen who did not demonstrate need for aid received scholarships/grants; average award was $20,968. No-need awards available for academics, athletics, leadership, music/drama, ROTC, state/district residency.
Scholarships offered: ***Merit:*** Scholarship programs; full-tuition plus summer stipends for study abroad, research or service projects; approximately 250 awarded. ***Athletic:*** 68 full-time freshmen received athletic scholarships; average amount $45,284.
Cumulative student debt: 34% of graduating class had student loans; average debt was $17,349.
Additional info: Financial aid packages awarded to incoming and returning undergraduate students are loan-free.

FINANCIAL AID PROCEDURES
Forms required: FAFSA, CSS PROFILE.
Dates and Deadlines: Closing date 2/5. Applicants notified by 4/1; must reply by 5/1.
Transfers: Priority date 4/15. Must reply within 2 week(s) of notification.

CONTACT
David Mohning, Director of Student Financial Aid
2305 West End Avenue, Nashville, TN 37203-1727
(615) 322-3591

Volunteer State Community College

Gallatin, Tennessee
www.volstate.edu Federal Code: 009912

2-year public community and junior college in small city.
Enrollment: 6,589 undergrads, 46% part-time. 1,167 full-time freshmen.
Selectivity: Open admission; but selective for some programs.

BASIC COSTS (2012-2013)
Tuition and fees: $3,673; out-of-state residents $14,305.
Per-credit charge: $135; out-of-state residents $557.
Additional info: Tuition/fee waivers available for minority students.

FINANCIAL AID PICTURE (2011-2012)
Students with need: Out of 1,099 full-time freshmen who applied for aid, 777 were judged to have need. Of these, 777 received aid, and 44 had their full need met. Average financial aid package met 50% of need; average scholarship/grant was $4,584; average loan was $2,518. For part-time students, average financial aid package was $4,522.
Students without need: 29 full-time freshmen who did not demonstrate need for aid received scholarships/grants; average award was $1,847. No-need awards available for academics, art, athletics, leadership, minority status, music/drama, state/district residency.
Scholarships offered: 5 full-time freshmen received athletic scholarships; average amount $7,958.

FINANCIAL AID PROCEDURES
Forms required: FAFSA, institutional form.
Dates and Deadlines: Priority date 4/15; no closing date. Applicants notified on a rolling basis; must reply within 2 week(s) of notification.
Transfers: No deadline. Applicants notified on a rolling basis; must reply within 2 week(s) of notification.

CONTACT
Sue Pedigo, Director of Financial Aid
1480 Nashville Pike, Gallatin, TN 37066-3188
(615) 452-8600 ext. 3456

Walters State Community College

Morristown, Tennessee
www.ws.edu Federal Code: 008863

2-year public culinary school and community college in small city.
Enrollment: 5,549 undergrads, 33% part-time. 1,325 full-time freshmen.

Selectivity: Open admission; but selective for some programs.

BASIC COSTS (2012-2013)
Tuition and fees: $3,681; out-of-state residents $14,313.
Per-credit charge: $135; out-of-state residents $557.
Additional info: Tuition/fee waivers available for minority students.

FINANCIAL AID PICTURE (2011-2012)
Students with need: 82% of average financial aid package awarded as scholarships/grants, 18% awarded as loans/jobs. Need-based aid available for part-time students.
Students without need: No-need awards available for academics, athletics, minority status, music/drama, state/district residency.

FINANCIAL AID PROCEDURES
Forms required: FAFSA.
Dates and Deadlines: Priority date 5/1; no closing date. Applicants notified on a rolling basis.
Transfers: No deadline. Applicants notified on a rolling basis.

CONTACT
Terri Stansberry, Director of Financial Aid
500 South Davy Crockett Parkway, Morristown, TN 37813-6899
(423) 585-6811

Watkins College of Art, Design & Film
Nashville, Tennessee
www.watkins.edu

4-year private visual arts college in very large city.
Enrollment: 269 full-time undergrads.
Selectivity: Admits over 75% of applicants.

BASIC COSTS (2013-2014)
Tuition and fees: $21,900.
Per-credit charge: $655.
Room only: $6,380.

FINANCIAL AID PICTURE
Students with need: Need-based aid available for full-time and part-time students. Work study available nights, weekends, and for part-time students.
Students without need: No-need awards available for academics, art, minority status.

FINANCIAL AID PROCEDURES
Forms required: FAFSA, institutional form.
Dates and Deadlines: Priority date 4/1; closing date 8/1. Applicants notified on a rolling basis starting 5/1; must reply within 2 week(s) of notification.

CONTACT
Regina Gilbert, Director of Financial Aid
2298 Rosa L. Parks Boulevard, Nashville, TN 37228
(615) 277-7420

Welch College
Nashville, Tennessee
www.welch.edu Federal Code: 030018

4-year private Bible and teachers college in very large city, affiliated with Free Will Baptists.
Enrollment: 260 undergrads, 22% part-time. 60 full-time freshmen.
Selectivity: Open admission.

BASIC COSTS (2013-2014)
Tuition and fees: $15,806.
Per-credit charge: $494.
Room and board: $6,642.

FINANCIAL AID PICTURE (2012-2013)
Students with need: Out of 60 full-time freshmen who applied for aid, 52 were judged to have need. Of these, 52 received aid, and 5 had their full need met. Average financial aid package met 53% of need; average scholarship/grant was $3,017; average loan was $1,690. For part-time students, average financial aid package was $3,421.
Students without need: No-need awards available for academics, alumni affiliation, art, music/drama.
Scholarships offered: Presidential Honors Scholarship: $1,000 per semester, renewable for 8 semesters; high school GPA 3.5+, and ACT 29+, must maintain college GPA 3.25; awarded to four students yearly.

FINANCIAL AID PROCEDURES
Forms required: FAFSA, institutional form.
Dates and Deadlines: Priority date 4/15; no closing date. Applicants notified on a rolling basis starting 7/1; must reply within 2 week(s) of notification.
Transfers: No deadline.

CONTACT
Angie Edgmon, Financial Aid Coordinator
3606 West End Avenue, Nashville, TN 37205-2403
(615) 844-5214

Williamson Christian College
Franklin, Tennessee
www.williamsoncc.edu Federal Code: 035315

4-year private liberal arts college in small city, affiliated with interdenominational tradition.
Enrollment: 83 undergrads, 8% part-time. 3 full-time freshmen.
Selectivity: Open admission; but selective for some programs.

BASIC COSTS (2012-2013)
Tuition and fees: $10,220.
Per-credit charge: $330.

FINANCIAL AID PICTURE
Students with need: Need-based aid available for full-time and part-time students.

FINANCIAL AID PROCEDURES
Forms required: FAFSA.
Dates and Deadlines: Applicants notified on a rolling basis starting 7/1; must reply within 2 week(s) of notification.
Transfers: No deadline. Applicants notified on a rolling basis starting 7/1; must reply within 2 week(s) of notification.

CONTACT
Becky Willenberg, Director of Financial Aid
274 Mallory Station Road, Franklin, TN 37067
(615) 771-7821

Texas

Abilene Christian University
Abilene, Texas
www.acu.edu Federal Code: 003537

4-year private university in small city, affiliated with Church of Christ.
Enrollment: 3,570 undergrads, 5% part-time. 864 full-time freshmen.
Selectivity: Admits less than 50% of applicants.

BASIC COSTS (2013-2014)
Tuition and fees: $28,350.

Per-credit charge: $950.
Room and board: $8,800.

FINANCIAL AID PICTURE (2011-2012)

Students with need: Out of 731 full-time freshmen who applied for aid, 604 were judged to have need. Of these, 604 received aid, and 138 had their full need met. Average financial aid package met 70% of need; average scholarship/grant was $14,412; average loan was $3,568. For part-time students, average financial aid package was $6,085.

Students without need: 255 full-time freshmen who did not demonstrate need for aid received scholarships/grants; average award was $2,866. No-need awards available for academics, art, athletics, leadership, minority status, music/drama, religious affiliation, state/district residency.

Scholarships offered: ***Merit:*** Presidential Scholarship: half or full tuition; based on interview, ACT or SAT scores. Academic Scholarship: $2,500-$10,000; based on ACT/SAT, class rank, and performance in high school courses. Transfer Scholarship: $1,500-$5,000; based on GPA. ***Athletic:*** 43 full-time freshmen received athletic scholarships; average amount $17,992.

Cumulative student debt: 69% of graduating class had student loans; average debt was $39,508.

Additional info: Early estimate service available.

FINANCIAL AID PROCEDURES

Forms required: FAFSA, institutional form.

Dates and Deadlines: Priority date 3/1; no closing date. Applicants notified on a rolling basis starting 4/1.

CONTACT

Ed Kerestly, Director of Student Financial Services
ACU Box 29000, Abilene, TX 79699
(325) 674-6850

Alvin Community College

Alvin, Texas
www.alvincollege.edu Federal Code: 003539

2-year public community and liberal arts college in large town.
Enrollment: 5,190 undergrads.
Selectivity: Open admission; but selective for some programs.

BASIC COSTS (2012-2013)

Tuition and fees: $2,168; out-of-district residents $3,428; out-of-state residents $4,808.

Per-credit charge: $42; out-of-district residents $84; out-of-state residents $130.

FINANCIAL AID PICTURE

Students with need: Need-based aid available for full-time and part-time students. Work study available nights, weekends, and for part-time students.

Students without need: This college awards aid only to students with need.

FINANCIAL AID PROCEDURES

Forms required: FAFSA.

Dates and Deadlines: Applicants notified on a rolling basis; must reply within 2 week(s) of notification.

CONTACT

Dora Sims, Director of Student Financial Aid and Placement
3110 Mustang Road, Alvin, TX 77511-4898
(281) 756-3524

Angelina College

Lufkin, Texas
www.angelina.edu Federal Code: 006661

2-year public community college in large town.
Enrollment: 5,443 undergrads, 61% part-time. 526 full-time freshmen.
Selectivity: Open admission; but selective for some programs.

BASIC COSTS (2013-2014)

Tuition and fees: $1,890; out-of-district residents $2,910; out-of-state residents $4,230.

Room and board: $5,850.

FINANCIAL AID PICTURE (2011-2012)

Students with need: Need-based aid available for full-time and part-time students. Work study available nights.

Students without need: No-need awards available for academics, art, athletics, job skills, leadership, music/drama, state/district residency.

Scholarships offered: Angelina Challenge Award: $750 per semester; available to graduating seniors from the six Angelina County high schools; students must receive less than $1,000 in other need-based aid.

FINANCIAL AID PROCEDURES

Forms required: FAFSA.

Dates and Deadlines: Priority date 7/15; no closing date. Applicants notified on a rolling basis starting 3/15.

Transfers: No deadline. Applicants notified on a rolling basis starting 4/1. Transfer students must provide the financial aid office with an official transcript from all colleges previously attended. All transfer credit will be used to calculate maximum time frame for Title IV funds and for completion pace.

CONTACT

Susan Jones, Director of Financial Aid
PO Box 1768, Lufkin, TX 75902-1768
(936) 633-5291

Angelo State University

San Angelo, Texas
www.angelo.edu Federal Code: 003541

4-year public university in small city.
Enrollment: 5,859 undergrads, 14% part-time. 1,243 full-time freshmen.
Selectivity: Admits over 75% of applicants.

BASIC COSTS (2012-2013)

Tuition and fees: $7,493; out-of-state residents $18,023.
Per-credit charge: $166; out-of-state residents $517.
Room and board: $8,026.

FINANCIAL AID PICTURE (2011-2012)

Students with need: Out of 1,160 full-time freshmen who applied for aid, 956 were judged to have need. Of these, 955 received aid, and 135 had their full need met. Average financial aid package met 75% of need; average scholarship/grant was $3,418; average loan was $3,357. For part-time students, average financial aid package was $7,967.

Students without need: 190 full-time freshmen who did not demonstrate need for aid received scholarships/grants; average award was $3,786. No-need awards available for academics, art, athletics, leadership, music/drama, ROTC, state/district residency.

Scholarships offered: 51 full-time freshmen received athletic scholarships; average amount $3,700.

Cumulative student debt: 57% of graduating class had student loans; average debt was $21,373.

FINANCIAL AID PROCEDURES

Forms required: FAFSA.

Dates and Deadlines: Priority date 4/1; no closing date. Applicants notified on a rolling basis starting 4/1; must reply within 4 week(s) of notification.

Transfers: Applicants notified on a rolling basis starting 4/1; must reply within 4 week(s) of notification.

CONTACT

Michelle Bennett, Financial Aid Director
ASU Station #11014, San Angelo, TX 76909-1014
(325) 942-2246

Arlington Baptist College

Arlington, Texas
www.arlingtonbaptistcollege.edu Federal Code: 014305

4-year private Bible and teachers college in very large city, affiliated with Baptist faith.
Enrollment: 236 undergrads, 15% part-time. 55 full-time freshmen.
Selectivity: Open admission.

BASIC COSTS (2012-2013)

Tuition and fees: $7,440.
Per-credit charge: $220.
Room and board: $4,800.

FINANCIAL AID PICTURE

Students with need: Need-based aid available for full-time and part-time students.
Students without need: This college awards aid only to students with need.

FINANCIAL AID PROCEDURES

Forms required: FAFSA.
Dates and Deadlines: Closing date 8/15. Applicants notified on a rolling basis starting 12/1; must reply by 8/15.
Transfers: Applicants notified by 12/1; must reply by 8/5.

CONTACT

Gerald Smith, Business Manager
3001 West Division Street, Arlington, TX 76012
(817) 461-8741 ext. 114

Austin College

Sherman, Texas
www.austincollege.edu Federal Code: 003543

4-year private liberal arts and teachers college in small city, affiliated with Presbyterian Church (USA).
Enrollment: 1,242 undergrads, 1% part-time. 308 full-time freshmen.
Selectivity: Admits 50 to 75% of applicants.

BASIC COSTS (2012-2013)

Tuition and fees: $32,850.
Room and board: $10,747.

FINANCIAL AID PICTURE (2012-2013)

Students with need: Out of 252 full-time freshmen who applied for aid, 205 were judged to have need. Of these, 205 received aid, and 205 had their full need met. Average financial aid package met 99% of need; average scholarship/grant was $23,205; average loan was $4,433. For part-time students, average financial aid package was $14,513.
Students without need: 99 full-time freshmen who did not demonstrate need for aid received scholarships/grants; average award was $15,139. No-need awards available for academics, alumni affiliation, art, leadership, music/drama, religious affiliation, state/district residency.

FINANCIAL AID PROCEDURES

Forms required: FAFSA.
Dates and Deadlines: Priority date 4/1; no closing date. Applicants notified on a rolling basis starting 3/1; must reply by 5/1.
Transfers: Applicants notified on a rolling basis starting 3/1; must reply by 5/1.

CONTACT

Laurie Coulter, Executive Director of Financial Aid
900 North Grand Avenue, Suite 6N, Sherman, TX 75090-4400
(903) 813-2900

Austin Community College

Austin, Texas
www.austincc.edu Federal Code: 012015

2-year public community college in very large city.
Enrollment: 43,315 undergrads. 2,228 full-time freshmen.
Selectivity: Open admission; but selective for some programs.

BASIC COSTS (2012-2013)

Tuition and fees: $2,340; out-of-district residents $7,200; out-of-state residents $9,720.

FINANCIAL AID PICTURE (2011-2012)

Students with need: Out of 1,481 full-time freshmen who applied for aid, 1,424 were judged to have need. Of these, 1,272 received aid. Need-based aid available for part-time students.

FINANCIAL AID PROCEDURES

Forms required: FAFSA, institutional form.
Dates and Deadlines: Closing date 4/1. Applicants notified on a rolling basis starting 6/1; must reply within 2 week(s) of notification.

CONTACT

Terry Bazan, Director, Financial Assistance
PO Box 15306, Austin, TX 78761-5306
(512) 223-7550

Baylor University

Waco, Texas
www.baylor.edu Federal Code: 003545

4-year private university in small city, affiliated with Baptist faith.
Enrollment: 12,820 undergrads, 2% part-time. 3,253 full-time freshmen.
Selectivity: Admits 50 to 75% of applicants.

BASIC COSTS (2013-2014)

Tuition and fees: $35,972.
Per-credit charge: $1,357.
Room and board: $10,748.
Additional info: Various options available for room and board. Reported cost includes unlimited meal plan. Other meal plans available based on less meals per week.

FINANCIAL AID PICTURE

Students with need: Need-based aid available for full-time and part-time students. Work study available nights, weekends, and for part-time students.
Students without need: No-need awards available for academics, alumni affiliation, art, athletics, job skills, leadership, music/drama, religious affiliation, ROTC.
Scholarships offered: Regent's Scholarship: full tuition; limited to National Merit finalists who list Baylor as first choice; unlimited number. President's Scholarship, Provost's Scholarship, Dean's Scholarship also available.

FINANCIAL AID PROCEDURES

Forms required: FAFSA.
Dates and Deadlines: Priority date 3/1; no closing date. Applicants notified on a rolling basis starting 3/1; must reply by 5/1 or within 2 week(s) of notification.
Transfers: No deadline. Applicants notified on a rolling basis starting 3/1; must reply by 5/1 or within 2 week(s) of notification. To be eligible for State Tuition Equalization, transfers must meet program guidelines, including overall 2.5 GPA and must have passed minimum of 12 hours in each semester attempted in the past year at previous institution. If transferring from a private school in Texas, must have been eligible at that school to have received Texas Tuition Equalization Grant.

CONTACT
Jackie Diaz, Assistant Vice President
One Bear Place #97056, Waco, TX 76798-7056
(800) 229-5678

Blinn College
Brenham, Texas
www.blinn.edu Federal Code: 003549

2-year public agricultural and community college in large town.
Enrollment: 17,874 undergrads, 44% part-time. 10,008 full-time freshmen.
Selectivity: Open admission; but selective for some programs.

BASIC COSTS (2012-2013)
Tuition and fees: $2,268; out-of-district residents $3,678; out-of-state residents $6,018.
Per-credit charge: $42; out-of-district residents $89; out-of-state residents $167.
Room and board: $5,750.

FINANCIAL AID PICTURE
Students with need: Need-based aid available for full-time and part-time students.

FINANCIAL AID PROCEDURES
Forms required: FAFSA, institutional form.
Dates and Deadlines: Priority date 6/1; no closing date. Applicants notified on a rolling basis starting 7/1.

CONTACT
Melanie Morgan, Director of Financial Aid
902 College Avenue, Brenham, TX 77833
(979) 830-4144

Brazosport College
Lake Jackson, Texas
www.brazosport.edu Federal Code: 007287

2-year public community college in large town.
Enrollment: 3,085 undergrads.
Selectivity: Open admission; but selective for some programs.

BASIC COSTS (2012-2013)
Tuition and fees: $2,295; out-of-district residents $3,315; out-of-state residents $4,725.
Per-credit charge: $59; out-of-district residents $93; out-of-state residents $140.

FINANCIAL AID PICTURE
Students with need: Need-based aid available for full-time and part-time students.
Students without need: No-need awards available for academics, art, job skills, leadership, music/drama, state/district residency.

FINANCIAL AID PROCEDURES
Forms required: FAFSA, institutional form.
Dates and Deadlines: Priority date 7/1; no closing date. Applicants notified on a rolling basis starting 5/1.

CONTACT
Kay Wright, Director of Financial Aid
500 College Drive, Lake Jackson, TX 77566
(979) 230-3377

Cedar Valley College
Lancaster, Texas
www.cedarvalleycollege.edu Federal Code: 014035

2-year public community college in large town.
Enrollment: 6,403 undergrads.
Selectivity: Open admission.

BASIC COSTS (2013-2014)
Tuition and fees: $1,560; out-of-district residents $2,910; out-of-state residents $4,590.
Per-credit charge: $52; out-of-district residents $97; out-of-state residents $153.

FINANCIAL AID PICTURE
Students with need: Need-based aid available for full-time students.

FINANCIAL AID PROCEDURES
Forms required: FAFSA.
Dates and Deadlines: Priority date 5/1; no closing date. Applicants notified on a rolling basis.

CONTACT
Cathy Adams, Director of Financial Aid
3030 North Dallas Avenue, Lancaster, TX 75134
(972) 587-2599

Central Texas College
Killeen, Texas
www.ctcd.edu Federal Code: 004003

2-year public community college in small city.
Enrollment: 17,268 undergrads, 83% part-time. 668 full-time freshmen.
Selectivity: Open admission; but selective for some programs.

BASIC COSTS (2012-2013)
Tuition and fees: $1,890; out-of-district residents $2,460; out-of-state residents $5,550.
Per-credit charge: $63; out-of-district residents $82; out-of-state residents $185.
Room and board: $3,800.

FINANCIAL AID PICTURE
Students with need: Need-based aid available for full-time and part-time students. Work study available nights, weekends, and for part-time students.
Students without need: This college awards aid only to students with need.

FINANCIAL AID PROCEDURES
Forms required: FAFSA, institutional form.
Dates and Deadlines: Closing date 6/1. Applicants notified on a rolling basis starting 3/1; must reply within 4 week(s) of notification.

CONTACT
Annabelle Smith, Director of Student Financial Aid
Box 1800, Killeen, TX 76540
(254) 526-1508

Cisco College
Cisco, Texas
www.cisco.edu Federal Code: 003553

2-year public community college in small town.
Enrollment: 3,261 undergrads, 51% part-time. 313 full-time freshmen.
Selectivity: Open admission.

BASIC COSTS (2013-2014)
Tuition and fees: $2,520; out-of-district residents $3,210; out-of-state residents $4,290.
Per-credit charge: $84; out-of-district residents $107; out-of-state residents $143.
Room and board: $3,877.
Additional info: In-state tuition per credit hour at Abilene campus is $122. Out of state tuition at Abilene campus is $158 per credit hour.

FINANCIAL AID PICTURE (2012-2013)
Students with need: 90% of average financial aid package awarded as scholarships/grants, 10% awarded as loans/jobs.
Students without need: No-need awards available for athletics, music/drama.
Additional info: Financial aid application deadline July 1 for Fall semester, November 1 for Spring semester.

FINANCIAL AID PROCEDURES
Forms required: FAFSA.
Dates and Deadlines: Applicants notified on a rolling basis starting 8/15.
Transfers: Transfer students must submit school code change on the FAFSA to have Student Aid Report sent to Cisco College. Students selected for verification must complete the verification process with college before financial aid can be awarded even if they have award letter from previous institution. Eligibility for financial assistance will be determined once the Student Aid Report is received.

CONTACT
Dianne Pharr, Director of Financial Aid
101 College Heights, Cisco, TX 76437
(254) 442-5151

Clarendon College
Clarendon, Texas
www.clarendoncollege.edu Federal Code: 003554

2-year public community college in rural community.
Enrollment: 1,250 undergrads.
Selectivity: Open admission; but selective for some programs.

BASIC COSTS (2012-2013)
Tuition and fees: $2,730; out-of-district residents $3,420; out-of-state residents $4,350.
Room and board: $4,176.

FINANCIAL AID PICTURE
Students with need: Need-based aid available for full-time and part-time students. Work study available nights, weekends, and for part-time students.
Students without need: No-need awards available for academics, art, athletics, leadership, music/drama, state/district residency.
Scholarships offered: Named and endowed scholarships available based on academic achievement, need, and/or other requirements as stipulated by the scholarship donor.

FINANCIAL AID PROCEDURES
Forms required: FAFSA, institutional form.
Dates and Deadlines: Priority date 8/1; no closing date. Applicants notified on a rolling basis starting 5/15; must reply by 8/15 or within 2 week(s) of notification.
Transfers: No deadline. Applicants notified on a rolling basis starting 11/15; must reply within 4 week(s) of notification.

CONTACT
Michele Copelin, Director of Financial Aid
PO Box 968, Clarendon, TX 79226
(806) 874-3571 ext. 112

Coastal Bend College
Beeville, Texas
www.coastalbend.edu Federal Code: 003546

2-year public community college in large town.
Enrollment: 2,346 undergrads.
Selectivity: Open admission; but selective for some programs.

BASIC COSTS (2012-2013)
Tuition and fees: $2,196; out-of-district residents $4,056; out-of-state residents $4,506.
Room and board: $4,655.

FINANCIAL AID PICTURE
Students with need: Need-based aid available for full-time and part-time students.
Students without need: No-need awards available for academics, leadership.

FINANCIAL AID PROCEDURES
Forms required: FAFSA, institutional form.
Dates and Deadlines: Priority date 4/1; no closing date. Applicants notified on a rolling basis starting 5/1; must reply within 2 week(s) of notification.
Transfers: No deadline. Applicants notified on a rolling basis.

CONTACT
Nora Morales, Director of Financial Aid
3800 Charco Road, Beeville, TX 78102
(361) 354-2238

The College of Saints John Fisher & Thomas More
Fort Worth, Texas
www.fishermore.edu Federal Code: 031894

4-year private liberal arts college in very large city, affiliated with Roman Catholic Church.
Enrollment: 21 undergrads. 13 full-time freshmen.
Selectivity: Admits less than 50% of applicants.

BASIC COSTS (2012-2013)
Tuition and fees: $12,800.
Per-credit charge: $500.
Additional info: Six meals a week provided by the school and is included in fees. Each unit of on-campus housing equipped with a kitchen. Cost of room only, $4,892.

FINANCIAL AID PICTURE (2012-2013)
Students with need: Out of 13 full-time freshmen who applied for aid, 13 were judged to have need. Of these, 13 received aid, and 1 had their full need met. Average financial aid package met 88% of need.
Students without need: This college awards aid only to students with need.
Additional info: The College no longer participates in US Department of Education Title IV funding which includes all loans, grants and work-study. The College no longer participates in any Texas State Aid programs, including loans, grants and work-study.

FINANCIAL AID PROCEDURES
Forms required: institutional form.
Dates and Deadlines: Closing date 6/22. Applicants notified on a rolling basis starting 1/1; must reply within 2 week(s) of notification.

CONTACT
Pete Capani, Director of Enrollment Management
3020 Lubbock Avenue, Fort Worth, TX 76109
(817) 923-8459 ext. 1

College of the Mainland

Texas City, Texas
www.com.edu Federal Code: 007096

2-year public community and technical college in large town.
Enrollment: 3,139 undergrads.
Selectivity: Open admission; but selective for some programs.

BASIC COSTS (2012-2013)

Tuition and fees: $1,773; out-of-district residents $2,973; out-of-state residents $3,873.

FINANCIAL AID PICTURE

Students with need: Need-based aid available for full-time and part-time students. Work study available nights, weekends, and for part-time students.
Students without need: This college awards aid only to students with need.

FINANCIAL AID PROCEDURES

Forms required: FAFSA, institutional form.
Dates and Deadlines: Applicants notified on a rolling basis.
Transfers: Priority date 8/1.

CONTACT

Carl Gordon, Director, Student Financial Services
1200 Amburn Road, Texas City, TX 77591
(409) 933-8274

Collin County Community College District

McKinney, Texas
www.collin.edu Federal Code: 016792

2-year public community college in large city.
Enrollment: 27,286 undergrads, 64% part-time. 2,949 full-time freshmen.
Selectivity: Open admission; but selective for some programs.

BASIC COSTS (2012-2013)

Tuition and fees: $1,234; out-of-district residents $2,254; out-of-state residents $3,904.
Per-credit charge: $36; out-of-district residents $70; out-of-state residents $121.

FINANCIAL AID PICTURE

Students with need: Need-based aid available for full-time and part-time students. Work study available nights, weekends, and for part-time students.
Students without need: No-need awards available for academics, art, athletics, job skills, leadership, minority status, music/drama, state/district residency.

FINANCIAL AID PROCEDURES

Forms required: FAFSA, institutional form.
Dates and Deadlines: Priority date 6/1; no closing date. Applicants notified on a rolling basis starting 5/1; must reply within 2 week(s) of notification.
Transfers: Applicants must have cumulative GPA of 2.0 and less than 90 transferable credit hours.

CONTACT

Debra Wilkison, Director of Financial Aid
2800 East Spring Creek Parkway, Plano, TX 75074
(972) 881-5760

Commonwealth Institute of Funeral Service

Houston, Texas
www.commonwealthinst.org Federal Code: 003556

2-year private school of mortuary science in very large city.
Enrollment: 224 undergrads.

BASIC COSTS (2012-2013)

Tuition and fees: $10,904.
Additional info: Reported tuition is for associate degree program. Includes cost of textbooks and clinical supplies.

FINANCIAL AID PICTURE

Students with need: Need-based aid available for full-time and part-time students.
Students without need: This college awards aid only to students with need.
Scholarships offered: Scholarship awards: $250-$500 based on funds available; recipients selected on academic achievement, leadership and professional promise, as well as any stipulations by the donor, by a committee of Commonwealth Institute graduate employers, alumni, and benefactors.

FINANCIAL AID PROCEDURES

Forms required: FAFSA.
Dates and Deadlines: Priority date 8/31; no closing date. Applicants notified on a rolling basis starting 7/12.

CONTACT

Jessika Jenkins, Director of Financial Aid
415 Barren Springs Drive, Houston, TX 77090-5913
(281) 873-0262

Concordia University Texas

Austin, Texas
www.concordia.edu Federal Code: 003557

4-year private university and liberal arts college in very large city, affiliated with Lutheran Church - Missouri Synod.
Enrollment: 1,533 undergrads, 21% part-time. 257 full-time freshmen.
Selectivity: Admits over 75% of applicants.

BASIC COSTS (2012-2013)

Tuition and fees: $25,980.
Room and board: $8,680.
Additional info: Tuition/fee waivers available for adults.

FINANCIAL AID PICTURE (2011-2012)

Students with need: Out of 238 full-time freshmen who applied for aid, 212 were judged to have need. Of these, 211 received aid, and 36 had their full need met. Average financial aid package met 74% of need; average scholarship/grant was $13,627; average loan was $3,969. For part-time students, average financial aid package was $7,185.
Students without need: 38 full-time freshmen who did not demonstrate need for aid received scholarships/grants; average award was $9,521. No-need awards available for academics, leadership, religious affiliation.
Cumulative student debt: 75% of graduating class had student loans; average debt was $22,787.

FINANCIAL AID PROCEDURES

Forms required: FAFSA.
Dates and Deadlines: Closing date 7/30. Applicants notified on a rolling basis starting 2/15.
Transfers: Financial aid transcripts from all previously attended trade/technical schools and colleges/universities required.

CONTACT
Russell Jeffrey, Director, Financial Services
11400 Concordia University Drive, Austin, TX 78726
(512) 313-4681

Criswell College

Dallas, Texas
www.criswell.edu

4-year private Bible and seminary college in very large city, affiliated with Southern Baptist Convention.
Enrollment: 244 undergrads.

BASIC COSTS (2012-2013)
Tuition and fees: $6,934.
Per-credit charge: $261.

FINANCIAL AID PICTURE
Students with need: Work study available nights.

FINANCIAL AID PROCEDURES
Forms required: FAFSA, institutional form.
Dates and Deadlines: Closing date 7/15. Applicants notified on a rolling basis.

CONTACT
Leigh Cooper, Director of Financial Aid
4010 Gaston Avenue, Dallas, TX 75246-1537
(214) 828-1345

Dallas Baptist University

Dallas, Texas
www.dbu.edu Federal Code: 003560

4-year private university in very large city, affiliated with Baptist faith.
Enrollment: 3,437 undergrads, 30% part-time. 489 full-time freshmen.
Selectivity: Admits less than 50% of applicants.

BASIC COSTS (2013-2014)
Tuition and fees: $22,350.
Per-credit charge: $735.
Room and board: $6,768.

FINANCIAL AID PICTURE (2012-2013)
Students with need: Out of 461 full-time freshmen who applied for aid, 355 were judged to have need. Of these, 351 received aid, and 193 had their full need met. Average financial aid package met 71% of need; average scholarship/grant was $3,634; average loan was $3,350. For part-time students, average financial aid package was $6,519.
Students without need: 98 full-time freshmen who did not demonstrate need for aid received scholarships/grants; average award was $7,724. No-need awards available for academics, athletics, job skills, leadership, music/drama, religious affiliation.
Scholarships offered: 27 full-time freshmen received athletic scholarships; average amount $14,604.
Cumulative student debt: 72% of graduating class had student loans; average debt was $18,943.

FINANCIAL AID PROCEDURES
Forms required: FAFSA, institutional form.
Dates and Deadlines: Priority date 3/6; closing date 5/1. Applicants notified on a rolling basis starting 2/1.
Transfers: Priority date 3/17; no deadline. Applicants notified on a rolling basis.

CONTACT
Lee Ferguson, Director of Financial Aid
3000 Mountain Creek Parkway, Dallas, TX 75211-9299
(214) 333-5363

Dallas Christian College

Dallas, Texas
www.dallas.edu Federal Code: 006941

4-year private Bible college in very large city, affiliated with nondenominational tradition.
Enrollment: 327 undergrads, 27% part-time. 48 full-time freshmen.
Selectivity: Admits less than 50% of applicants.

BASIC COSTS (2013-2014)
Tuition and fees: $13,820.
Per-credit charge: $434.
Room and board: $8,000.

FINANCIAL AID PICTURE
Students with need: Need-based aid available for full-time and part-time students.
Students without need: No-need awards available for leadership, music/drama.

FINANCIAL AID PROCEDURES
Forms required: FAFSA, institutional form.
Dates and Deadlines: Priority date 4/15; no closing date. Applicants notified on a rolling basis; must reply within 2 week(s) of notification.

CONTACT
Rebecca Akin-Sitka, Financial Aid Director
2700 Christian Parkway, Dallas, TX 75234-7299
(972) 241-3371 ext. 105

Del Mar College

Corpus Christi, Texas
www.delmar.edu Federal Code: 003563

2-year public community college in large city.
Enrollment: 11,022 undergrads.
Selectivity: Open admission; but selective for some programs.

BASIC COSTS (2012-2013)
Tuition and fees: $2,730; out-of-district residents $4,230; out-of-state residents $5,340.
Per-credit charge: $52; out-of-district residents $102; out-of-state residents $139.

FINANCIAL AID PICTURE
Students with need: Need-based aid available for full-time and part-time students. Work study available nights, weekends, and for part-time students.
Students without need: This college awards aid only to students with need.

FINANCIAL AID PROCEDURES
Forms required: FAFSA.
Dates and Deadlines: Priority date 5/1; no closing date. Applicants notified on a rolling basis starting 7/1; must reply within 2 week(s) of notification.

CONTACT
Enrique Garcia, Assistant Dean of Financial Aid and Retention Services
101 Baldwin Boulevard, Corpus Christi, TX 78404-3897
(361) 698-1293

DeVry University: Irving
Dallas, Texas
www.devry.edu Federal Code: 010139

4-year for-profit university in small city.
Enrollment: 926 undergrads, 64% part-time. 33 full-time freshmen.

BASIC COSTS (2012-2013)
Tuition and fees: $16,076.
Per-credit charge: $609.

FINANCIAL AID PICTURE
Students with need: Need-based aid available for full-time and part-time students.
Students without need: This college awards aid only to students with need.

CONTACT
Nga Phan, Director, Financial Aid
4800 Regent Boulevard, Dallas, TX 75063-2439
(972) 929-9740

East Texas Baptist University
Marshall, Texas
www.etbu.edu Federal Code: 003564

4-year private university and liberal arts college in large town, affiliated with Baptist faith.
Enrollment: 1,110 undergrads, 2% part-time. 329 full-time freshmen.
Selectivity: Admits 50 to 75% of applicants.

BASIC COSTS (2013-2014)
Tuition and fees: $22,590.
Per-credit charge: $723.
Room and board: $6,546.

FINANCIAL AID PICTURE (2011-2012)
Students with need: Out of 319 full-time freshmen who applied for aid, 291 were judged to have need. Of these, 291 received aid, and 34 had their full need met. Average financial aid package met 37% of need; average scholarship/grant was $6,066; average loan was $3,121. For part-time students, average financial aid package was $6,530.
Students without need: 38 full-time freshmen who did not demonstrate need for aid received scholarships/grants; average award was $7,542. No-need awards available for academics, alumni affiliation, leadership, music/drama, religious affiliation.
Scholarships offered: Presidential Scholarship: $10,000. Honor Scholarship: $8,500. Dean Scholarship: $7,000. Achievement Grant: $3,000, University Scholars: $1,000. Based on ACT/SAT (Critical Reading and Math) and recalculated high school GPA.
Cumulative student debt: 84% of graduating class had student loans; average debt was $23,458.

FINANCIAL AID PROCEDURES
Forms required: FAFSA, institutional form.
Dates and Deadlines: Priority date 6/1; no closing date. Applicants notified on a rolling basis starting 1/1.
Transfers: Applicants notified on a rolling basis starting 1/1.

CONTACT
Tommy Young, Director of Financial Aid
One Tiger Drive, Marshall, TX 75670-1498
(903) 923-2138

Eastfield College
Mesquite, Texas
www.efc.dcccd.edu Federal Code: 008510

2-year public community and liberal arts college in small city.
Enrollment: 14,307 undergrads.
Selectivity: Open admission.

BASIC COSTS (2012-2013)
Tuition and fees: $1,350; out-of-district residents $2,490; out-of-state residents $3,960.
Per-credit charge: $45; out-of-district residents $83; out-of-state residents $132.

FINANCIAL AID PICTURE
Students with need: Need-based aid available for full-time and part-time students. Work study available nights, weekends, and for part-time students.
Scholarships offered: Lecroy Scholars Program: $600 per semester; based on demonstrated church, community, or academic leadership and 3.0 GPA; requires enrollment in at least 12 credit hours; 5-10 awarded. Erin Tierney Kramp Encouragement Program: $600 per semester; based on demonstrated courage in the face of adversity, moral character, leadership, and high academic standards; requires enrollment in 8 hours for awarding semester, and maintenance of high academic standards; 2 awarded.

FINANCIAL AID PROCEDURES
Forms required: FAFSA, institutional form.
Dates and Deadlines: Priority date 5/1; no closing date. Applicants notified on a rolling basis starting 4/15.

CONTACT
Dana Mingo, Dean of Financial Aid
3737 Motley Drive, Mesquite, TX 75150
(972) 860-8385

El Centro College
Dallas, Texas
www.elcentrocollege.edu Federal Code: 004453

2-year public community college in very large city.
Enrollment: 9,078 undergrads, 76% part-time. 391 full-time freshmen.
Selectivity: Open admission; but selective for some programs.

BASIC COSTS (2012-2013)
Tuition and fees: $1,350; out-of-district residents $2,490; out-of-state residents $3,960.
Per-credit charge: $45; out-of-district residents $83; out-of-state residents $132.
Additional info: Tuition/fee waivers available for minority students, unemployed or children of unemployed.

FINANCIAL AID PICTURE
Students with need: Need-based aid available for full-time and part-time students.
Additional info: Interview required for financial aid applicants.

FINANCIAL AID PROCEDURES
Forms required: FAFSA.
Dates and Deadlines: Priority date 5/1; no closing date. Applicants notified on a rolling basis; must reply within 2 week(s) of notification.
Transfers: Financial aid transcript may be required from previous institutions attended.

CONTACT
Pamela Lucas, Director
801 Main Street, Dallas, TX 75202
(214) 860-2099

El Paso Community College

El Paso, Texas
www.epcc.edu Federal Code: 010387

2-year public community college in very large city.
Enrollment: 29,192 undergrads, 64% part-time. 2,929 full-time freshmen.
Selectivity: Open admission; but selective for some programs.

BASIC COSTS (2012-2013)
Tuition and fees: $2,430; out-of-state residents $4,530.
Per-credit charge: $71; out-of-state residents $141.
Additional info: Out-of-state student per-credit-hour rate is $200 for 1st credit hour, $282 for 2nd credit hour, $423 for 3rd credit hour. Each additional credit hour is $141.

FINANCIAL AID PICTURE
Students with need: Work study available nights, weekends, and for part-time students.
Students without need: No-need awards available for academics, athletics.

FINANCIAL AID PROCEDURES
Forms required: FAFSA, institutional form.
Dates and Deadlines: Priority date 5/1; no closing date. Applicants notified on a rolling basis starting 7/1; must reply within 2 week(s) of notification.

CONTACT
Linda Gonzalez-Hensgen, Director of Student Financial Services
Box 20500, El Paso, TX 79998
(915) 831-2566

Frank Phillips College

Borger, Texas
www.fpctx.edu Federal Code: 003568

2-year public community and junior college in large town.
Enrollment: 685 undergrads.
Selectivity: Open admission.

BASIC COSTS (2012-2013)
Tuition and fees: $2,526; out-of-district residents $3,216; out-of-state residents $3,398.
Room and board: $4,545.

FINANCIAL AID PICTURE
Students with need: Need-based aid available for full-time and part-time students. Work study available nights, weekends, and for part-time students.
Students without need: No-need awards available for academics, athletics, music/drama, state/district residency.
Additional info: Some Texas fire department and police department personnel, active duty military personnel, children of military missing in action may qualify for reduced or waived tuition. Out-of-state tuition waived for students living in Oklahoma counties adjacent to Texas.

FINANCIAL AID PROCEDURES
Forms required: FAFSA, institutional form.
Dates and Deadlines: Closing date 7/1. Applicants notified on a rolling basis; must reply within 2 week(s) of notification.
Transfers: No deadline. Applicants notified on a rolling basis.

CONTACT
Beverly Fields, Director of Financial Services
Box 5118, Borger, TX 79008-5118
(806) 457-4200 ext. 796

Galveston College

Galveston, Texas
www.gc.edu Federal Code: 004972

2-year public community college in small city.
Enrollment: 1,888 undergrads.
Selectivity: Open admission; but selective for some programs.

BASIC COSTS (2012-2013)
Tuition and fees: $1,900; out-of-district residents $2,260; out-of-state residents $4,150.
Per-credit charge: $37; out-of-district residents $49; out-of-state residents $112.

FINANCIAL AID PICTURE
Students with need: Need-based aid available for full-time and part-time students.
Students without need: This college awards aid only to students with need.

FINANCIAL AID PROCEDURES
Forms required: FAFSA.
Dates and Deadlines: Priority date 6/9; no closing date. Applicants notified on a rolling basis starting 6/1.

CONTACT
Ron Crumedy, Financial Aid Manager
4015 Avenue Q, Galveston, TX 77550-7447
(409) 944-1235

Grayson County College

Denison, Texas
www.grayson.edu Federal Code: 003570

2-year public community and technical college in large town.
Enrollment: 4,001 undergrads.
Selectivity: Open admission; but selective for some programs.

BASIC COSTS (2012-2013)
Tuition and fees: $1,800; out-of-district residents $2,850; out-of-state residents $4,320.
Per-credit charge: $60; out-of-district residents $95; out-of-state residents $215.
Room and board: $5,020.

FINANCIAL AID PICTURE
Students with need: Need-based aid available for full-time and part-time students.
Additional info: Short term loans available.

FINANCIAL AID PROCEDURES
Forms required: FAFSA.
Dates and Deadlines: Priority date 6/1; no closing date. Applicants notified on a rolling basis; must reply within 5 week(s) of notification.

CONTACT
Donna King, Director of Financial Aid
6101 Grayson Drive, Denison, TX 75020
(903) 463-8642

Hallmark College of Aeronautics

San Antonio, Texas
www.hallmarkcollege.edu Federal Code: 010509

2-year for-profit technical and career college in very large city.
Enrollment: 206 undergrads.

BASIC COSTS (2012-2013)
Tuition and fees: $30,502.
Additional info: Reported tuition is for the combined AAS Airframe Technology/AAS Powerplant Technology program. AAS Airframe Technology program is $19,630; AAS Powerplant Technology program is $19,932; Aviation Technician Diploma program is $27,784. Cost includes books, equipment and supplies. Security fee is $95. International students: 8% added to the total charge of the program.

FINANCIAL AID PICTURE
Students with need: Need-based aid available for full-time students.

FINANCIAL AID PROCEDURES
Forms required: FAFSA.
Dates and Deadlines: Applicants notified on a rolling basis.

CONTACT
Grace Calixto, Director of Financial Planning
8901 Wetmore Road, San Antonio, TX 78230-4229
(210) 690-9000 ext. 211

Hallmark College of Technology
San Antonio, Texas
www.hallmarkcollege.edu Federal Code: 010509

2-year for-profit technical and career college in very large city.
Enrollment: 336 undergrads.

BASIC COSTS (2012-2013)
Tuition and fees: $12,600.
Additional info: Reported cost is for the Accounting Certificate program. Medical Assistant Certificate and Healthcare Information Specialist (Billing/Coding) Certificate program is $13,400. AAS in Medical Assistant is $19,850. AAS in Information Systems Administration is $30,800. AAS in Nursing is $31,680 and the Bachelor of Science degree program is $55,000. All Allied Health programs have a $100 lab fee. Nursing program has a $4,800 program fee. International students: 8% added to the total charge of the program. Tuition includes books, equipment and supplies.

FINANCIAL AID PICTURE
Students with need: Need-based aid available for full-time students.

FINANCIAL AID PROCEDURES
Forms required: FAFSA.
Dates and Deadlines: Applicants notified on a rolling basis.

CONTACT
Grace Calixto, Director of Financial Planning
Hallmark College of Technology, San Antonio, TX 78230-1736
(210) 690-9000 ext. 211

Hardin-Simmons University
Abilene, Texas
www.hsutx.edu Federal Code: 003571

4-year private university in small city, affiliated with Baptist faith.
Enrollment: 1,788 undergrads, 9% part-time. 395 full-time freshmen.
Selectivity: Admits 50 to 75% of applicants.

BASIC COSTS (2013-2014)
Tuition and fees: $23,460.
Per-credit charge: $745.
Room and board: $6,792.
Additional info: Tuition rate will not increase while enrolled full-time during consecutive long semesters progressing toward a degree. Tuition at time of enrollment locked for 4 years.

FINANCIAL AID PICTURE (2012-2013)
Students with need: Out of 390 full-time freshmen who applied for aid, 297 were judged to have need. Of these, 297 received aid, and 93 had their full need met. Average financial aid package met 78% of need; average scholarship/grant was $7,200; average loan was $3,141. For part-time students, average financial aid package was $8,517.
Students without need: 96 full-time freshmen who did not demonstrate need for aid received scholarships/grants; average award was $11,150. No-need awards available for academics, alumni affiliation, art, music/drama, religious affiliation.
Cumulative student debt: 71% of graduating class had student loans; average debt was $40,972.

FINANCIAL AID PROCEDURES
Forms required: FAFSA.
Dates and Deadlines: Priority date 3/1; no closing date. Applicants notified on a rolling basis starting 2/1; must reply within 2 week(s) of notification.
Transfers: No deadline. Applicants notified on a rolling basis starting 2/1.

CONTACT
Bridget Moore, Director of Financial Aid & Scholarships
PO Box 16050, Abilene, TX 79698-0001
(325) 670-1206

Hill College
Hillsboro, Texas
www.hillcollege.edu Federal Code: 003573

2-year public community college in small town.
Enrollment: 4,380 undergrads, 66% part-time.
Selectivity: Open admission; but selective for some programs.

BASIC COSTS (2012-2013)
Tuition and fees: $2,070; out-of-district residents $2,760; out-of-state residents $3,160.
Room and board: $3,550.
Additional info: Johnson County residents pay $5 per credit hour differential, or $2,220 annual tuition.

FINANCIAL AID PICTURE
Students with need: Need-based aid available for full-time and part-time students.
Students without need: No-need awards available for academics, athletics, music/drama.

FINANCIAL AID PROCEDURES
Forms required: FAFSA, institutional form.
Dates and Deadlines: Closing date 7/1. Applicants notified on a rolling basis.

CONTACT
Susan Russell, Director of Student Financial Aid
112 Lamar Drive, Hillsboro, TX 76645
(254) 659-7600

Houston Baptist University
Houston, Texas
www.hbu.edu Federal Code: 003576

4-year private university and liberal arts college in very large city, affiliated with Baptist faith.
Enrollment: 2,041 undergrads, 8% part-time. 514 full-time freshmen.
Selectivity: Admits less than 50% of applicants.

BASIC COSTS (2013-2014)
Tuition and fees: $27,930.
Room and board: $6,500.

FINANCIAL AID PICTURE (2012-2013)

Students with need: Out of 441 full-time freshmen who applied for aid, 415 were judged to have need. Of these, 413 received aid, and 81 had their full need met. Average financial aid package met 72% of need; average scholarship/grant was $16,042; average loan was $4,599. For part-time students, average financial aid package was $15,109.

Students without need: 96 full-time freshmen who did not demonstrate need for aid received scholarships/grants; average award was $12,448. No-need awards available for academics, alumni affiliation, art, athletics, music/drama, religious affiliation, ROTC.

Scholarships offered: ***Merit:*** Endowed Academic Scholarship: full or three-quarters tuition for four years; limited number available; for new freshmen with 1300 SAT or 30 ACT. Founders Academic Scholarship: minimum 1250 SAT or 28 ACT required for freshmen, 3.75 GPA on 30 or more semester hours required for transfers. Presidential Academic Scholarship: $4,300 per year, renewable; 1175 SAT or 26 ACT required for freshmen, 3.5 GPA required for transfers. Legacy Grant: $2,700 per year; renewable; 1100 SAT or 24 ACT required for freshmen, 3.25 GPA required for transfers. All SAT scores are exclusive of Writing. Valedictorian Scholarship: $1,500 per year; renewable; for valedictorians from Texas high schools. Ministerial Dependents Grant: $4,300 per year; for dependent children of ordained/licensed Southern Baptist ministers and missionaries. Grants-In-Aid: awards vary; for students who contribute special abilities or services to the University; awarded in music, art, athletics and nursing. Church Matching Award: awards vary. ***Athletic:*** 45 full-time freshmen received athletic scholarships; average amount $20,857.

FINANCIAL AID PROCEDURES

Forms required: FAFSA.

Dates and Deadlines: Priority date 3/1; closing date 4/15. Applicants notified on a rolling basis starting 3/10.

CONTACT

Jene Gabbard, Senior Director of Financial Aid and Scholarships
7502 Fondren Road, Houston, TX 77074-3298
(281) 649-3471

Houston Community College System

Houston, Texas
www.hccs.edu Federal Code: 010422

2-year public community college in very large city.
Enrollment: 50,011 undergrads, 65% part-time. 3,990 full-time freshmen.
Selectivity: Open admission; but selective for some programs.

BASIC COSTS (2012-2013)

Tuition and fees: $2,025; out-of-district residents $4,185; out-of-state residents $4,680.

FINANCIAL AID PICTURE

Students with need: Need-based aid available for full-time and part-time students. Work study available nights, weekends, and for part-time students.

Additional info: Although financial aid applications can be submitted at any time during the academic year, FAFSA's received after priority filing date of April 15 will be considered for funding only after all on-time filers have been awarded and then only if funds are available.

FINANCIAL AID PROCEDURES

Forms required: FAFSA.

Dates and Deadlines: Priority date 4/15; closing date 6/30.

CONTACT

Boni Jacobs, Director of Financial Aid
PO Box 667517, MC 1136, Houston, TX 77266-7517
(713) 718-8490

Howard College

Big Spring, Texas
www.howardcollege.edu Federal Code: 003574

2-year public community college in large town.
Enrollment: 4,383 undergrads, 69% part-time. 412 full-time freshmen.
Selectivity: Open admission; but selective for some programs.

BASIC COSTS (2013-2014)

Tuition and fees: $2,222; out-of-district residents $3,242; out-of-state residents $4,752.
Per-credit charge: $57; out-of-district residents $89; out-of-state residents $138.
Room and board: $4,180.

FINANCIAL AID PICTURE (2012-2013)

Students with need: 73% of average financial aid package awarded as scholarships/grants, 27% awarded as loans/jobs. Need-based aid available for part-time students.

Students without need: No-need awards available for academics, art, athletics, leadership, music/drama.

FINANCIAL AID PROCEDURES

Forms required: FAFSA, institutional form.

Dates and Deadlines: Priority date 4/1; no closing date. Applicants notified on a rolling basis starting 7/15; must reply within 2 week(s) of notification.

CONTACT

Liz Adamson, Director of Financial Aid
1001 Birdwell Lane, Big Spring, TX 79720
(432) 264-5083

Howard Payne University

Brownwood, Texas
www.hputx.edu Federal Code: 003575

4-year private university and liberal arts college in large town, affiliated with Baptist faith.
Enrollment: 1,018 undergrads, 9% part-time. 280 full-time freshmen.
Selectivity: Admits 50 to 75% of applicants.

BASIC COSTS (2013-2014)

Tuition and fees: $23,200.
Room and board: $6,800.

FINANCIAL AID PICTURE (2011-2012)

Students with need: Out of 269 full-time freshmen who applied for aid, 240 were judged to have need. Of these, 240 received aid, and 44 had their full need met. Average financial aid package met 80% of need; average scholarship/grant was $12,917; average loan was $3,421. For part-time students, average financial aid package was $7,003.

Students without need: 38 full-time freshmen who did not demonstrate need for aid received scholarships/grants; average award was $8,257. No-need awards available for academics, alumni affiliation, art, athletics, leadership, music/drama, religious affiliation, state/district residency.

Scholarships offered: Merit-based scholarship available to all approved home school applicants, $5,000 annually ($20,000 over 4 years).

FINANCIAL AID PROCEDURES

Forms required: FAFSA, institutional form.

Dates and Deadlines: Priority date 3/15; no closing date. Applicants notified on a rolling basis starting 2/15; must reply within 2 week(s) of notification.

CONTACT

Glenda Huff, Director of Student Financial Aid
1000 Fisk Street, Brownwood, TX 76801-2794
(325) 649-8015

Huston-Tillotson University

Austin, Texas
www.htu.edu Federal Code: 003577

4-year private business and liberal arts college in very large city, affiliated with United Methodist Church and United Church of Christ.
Enrollment: 884 undergrads.
Selectivity: Admits 50 to 75% of applicants.

BASIC COSTS (2012-2013)
Tuition and fees: $13,054.
Per-credit charge: $368.
Room and board: $6,946.

FINANCIAL AID PICTURE
Students with need: Need-based aid available for full-time and part-time students. Work study available nights, weekends, and for part-time students.
Students without need: No-need awards available for academics, alumni affiliation, art, athletics, job skills, leadership, minority status, music/drama, religious affiliation, state/district residency.

FINANCIAL AID PROCEDURES
Forms required: FAFSA.
Dates and Deadlines: Priority date 3/15; no closing date. Applicants notified on a rolling basis starting 3/1.
Transfers: No deadline.

CONTACT
Antonio Holloway, Director of Financial Aid
900 Chicon Street, Austin, TX 78702-2795
(512) 505-3031

Jacksonville College

Jacksonville, Texas
www.jacksonville-college.edu Federal Code: 003579

2-year private junior and liberal arts college in large town, affiliated with Baptist faith.
Enrollment: 303 undergrads, 12% part-time. 127 full-time freshmen.
Selectivity: Open admission.

BASIC COSTS (2012-2013)
Tuition and fees: $7,200.
Per-credit charge: $210.
Room and board: $4,000.

FINANCIAL AID PICTURE
Students with need: Need-based aid available for full-time and part-time students.
Students without need: No-need awards available for academics, athletics, leadership, music/drama, religious affiliation, state/district residency.

FINANCIAL AID PROCEDURES
Forms required: FAFSA, state aid form, institutional form.
Dates and Deadlines: Priority date 8/1; no closing date. Applicants notified on a rolling basis.
Transfers: No deadline. Applicants notified on a rolling basis.

CONTACT
Paul Galyean, Financial Aid Officer
105 B.J. Albritton Drive, Jacksonville, TX 75766-4759
(903) 586-2518 ext. 7135

Jarvis Christian College

Hawkins, Texas
www.jarvis.edu Federal Code: 003637

4-year private liberal arts and teachers college in rural community, affiliated with Christian Church (Disciples of Christ).
Enrollment: 575 undergrads, 3% part-time. 175 full-time freshmen.
Selectivity: Open admission.

BASIC COSTS (2013-2014)
Tuition and fees: $11,369.
Room and board: $8,183.

FINANCIAL AID PICTURE (2012-2013)
Students with need: Average financial aid package met 87% of need; average scholarship/grant was $14,290; average loan was $3,460. For part-time students, average financial aid package was $10,017.
Students without need: This college awards aid only to students with need.
Cumulative student debt: 51% of graduating class had student loans; average debt was $35,547.
Additional info: High school transcript required for scholarship consideration.

FINANCIAL AID PROCEDURES
Forms required: FAFSA, state aid form.
Dates and Deadlines: Priority date 6/30; closing date 1/3. Applicants notified on a rolling basis starting 5/1; must reply by 5/30 or within 2 week(s) of notification.
Transfers: Priority date 4/15; no deadline. Applicants notified on a rolling basis starting 7/1; must reply within 2 week(s) of notification.

CONTACT
Alice Copeland, Director of Financial Aid
PO Box 1470, Hawkins, TX 75765-1470
(903) 730-4890

Kilgore College

Kilgore, Texas
www.kilgore.edu Federal Code: 003580

2-year public community college in large town.
Enrollment: 6,231 undergrads, 54% part-time. 908 full-time freshmen.
Selectivity: Open admission; but selective for some programs.

BASIC COSTS (2012-2013)
Tuition and fees: $1,710; out-of-district residents $3,720; out-of-state residents $5,160.
Per-credit charge: $29; out-of-district residents $96; out-of-state residents $144.
Room and board: $4,270.
Additional info: Tuition/fee waivers available for unemployed or children of unemployed.

FINANCIAL AID PICTURE
Students with need: Need-based aid available for full-time and part-time students.
Students without need: No-need awards available for academics, alumni affiliation, art, athletics, job skills, leadership, music/drama, state/district residency.
Scholarships offered: Presidential Scholarships: tuition, fees and books for 4 semesters; ACT 25 or top 10% of senior class; 20 available; renewable at 2.5 GPA.
Additional info: State of Texas grants and loans available for honor graduates with unmet needs and for non-traditional students.

FINANCIAL AID PROCEDURES
Forms required: FAFSA, state aid form, institutional form.

Dates and Deadlines: Priority date 6/1; closing date 7/15. Applicants notified on a rolling basis starting 3/1; must reply within 2 week(s) of notification.
Transfers: No deadline. Transfer students must submit financial aid transcript from previous school plus all appropriate internal aid forms and show proof of high school graduation or GED.

CONTACT
Annette Morgan, Director of Financial Aid
1100 Broadway, Kilgore, TX 75662-3299
(903) 983-8183

Lamar State College at Orange
Orange, Texas
www.lsco.edu Federal Code: 016748

2-year public junior and liberal arts college in small city.
Enrollment: 2,085 undergrads.
Selectivity: Open admission; but selective for some programs.

BASIC COSTS (2012-2013)
Tuition and fees: $3,880; out-of-state residents $14,410.
Per-credit charge: $94; out-of-state residents $445.

FINANCIAL AID PICTURE
Students with need: Need-based aid available for full-time and part-time students.
Students without need: This college awards aid only to students with need.

FINANCIAL AID PROCEDURES
Forms required: FAFSA, institutional form.
Dates and Deadlines: Priority date 4/1; no closing date. Applicants notified on a rolling basis starting 5/15; must reply within 2 week(s) of notification.

CONTACT
Kerry Olson, Director of Financial Aid
410 Front Street, Orange, TX 77630
(409) 882-3317

Lamar State College at Port Arthur
Port Arthur, Texas
www.lamarpa.edu Federal Code: 016666

2-year public community and technical college in small city.
Enrollment: 2,708 undergrads.
Selectivity: Open admission.

BASIC COSTS (2012-2013)
Tuition and fees: $5,052; out-of-state residents $15,523.

FINANCIAL AID PICTURE
Students with need: Need-based aid available for full-time and part-time students. Work study available nights.
Students without need: This college awards aid only to students with need.

FINANCIAL AID PROCEDURES
Forms required: FAFSA, institutional form.
Dates and Deadlines: Priority date 4/1; no closing date. Applicants notified on a rolling basis starting 4/15; must reply within 2 week(s) of notification.

CONTACT
Pedro Saldana, Director of Financial Aid
Box 310, Port Arthur, TX 77641-0310
(409) 984-6203

Lamar University
Beaumont, Texas
www.lamar.edu Federal Code: 003581

4-year public university in small city.
Enrollment: 9,454 undergrads, 26% part-time. 1,618 full-time freshmen.
Selectivity: Admits over 75% of applicants.

BASIC COSTS (2013-2014)
Tuition and fees: $9,011; out-of-state residents $21,041.
Per-credit charge: $208; out-of-state residents $609.
Room and board: $7,966.

FINANCIAL AID PICTURE
Students with need: Need-based aid available for full-time and part-time students.
Students without need: This college awards aid only to students with need.

FINANCIAL AID PROCEDURES
Forms required: FAFSA, institutional form.
Dates and Deadlines: Priority date 4/1; no closing date. Applicants notified on a rolling basis starting 4/1; must reply within 2 week(s) of notification.

CONTACT
Jill Rowley, Director of Financial Aid
Box 10009, Beaumont, TX 77705
(409) 880-8450

Lee College
Baytown, Texas
www.lee.edu Federal Code: 003583

2-year public community college in small city.
Enrollment: 6,046 undergrads.
Selectivity: Open admission; but selective for some programs.

BASIC COSTS (2012-2013)
Tuition and fees: $1,812; out-of-district residents $2,712; out-of-state residents $4,362.
Per-credit charge: $42; out-of-district residents $72; out-of-state residents $127.

FINANCIAL AID PICTURE
Students with need: Need-based aid available for full-time and part-time students.
Students without need: No-need awards available for academics, art, athletics, job skills, music/drama.

FINANCIAL AID PROCEDURES
Forms required: FAFSA.
Dates and Deadlines: Priority date 4/1; no closing date. Applicants notified on a rolling basis starting 6/1.

CONTACT
Sharon Mullins, Financial Aid Officer
Box 818, Baytown, TX 77522
(281) 425-6362

LeTourneau University
Longview, Texas
www.letu.edu Federal Code: 003584

4-year private university in small city, affiliated with nondenominational tradition.
Enrollment: 2,343 undergrads, 43% part-time. 321 full-time freshmen.

Selectivity: Admits less than 50% of applicants.

BASIC COSTS (2013-2014)
Tuition and fees: $25,740.
Room and board: $9,030.

FINANCIAL AID PICTURE
Students with need: Need-based aid available for full-time and part-time students. Work study available nights, weekends, and for part-time students.
Students without need: No-need awards available for academics, alumni affiliation, leadership, minority status, religious affiliation, state/district residency.
Scholarships offered: Freshmen scholarships: Honors Scholarship, $6,000 per year; Dean's Scholarship: $8,000 per year; Presidential: $9,000 per year; based on SAT and/or ACT scores and cumulative high school GPA.

FINANCIAL AID PROCEDURES
Forms required: FAFSA.
Dates and Deadlines: Priority date 2/1; no closing date. Applicants notified on a rolling basis starting 3/1; must reply within 2 week(s) of notification.

CONTACT
Tracy Watkins, Director of Financial Aid
PO Box 7001, Longview, TX 75607-7001
(903) 233-4350

Lone Star College System

The Woodlands, Texas
www.lonestar.edu/ Federal Code: 011145

2-year public community college in very large city.
Enrollment: 77,877 undergrads, 67% part-time. 5,095 full-time freshmen.
Selectivity: Open admission; but selective for some programs.

BASIC COSTS (2012-2013)
Tuition and fees: $1,744; out-of-district residents $3,844; out-of-state residents $4,294.
Per-credit charge: $40; out-of-district residents $110; out-of-state residents $125.

FINANCIAL AID PICTURE (2011-2012)
Students with need: Out of 3,407 full-time freshmen who applied for aid, 2,895 were judged to have need. Of these, 2,713 received aid, and 23 had their full need met. Average financial aid package met 62% of need. For part-time students, average financial aid package was $5,843.
Students without need: 15 full-time freshmen who did not demonstrate need for aid received scholarships/grants; average award was $14,971. No-need awards available for academics.

FINANCIAL AID PROCEDURES
Forms required: FAFSA.
Dates and Deadlines: Priority date 5/10; no closing date. Applicants notified on a rolling basis starting 4/1.

CONTACT
Carolyn Wade, Executive Director, Student Financial Aid
5000 Research Forest Drive, The Woodlands, TX 77381-4356

Lubbock Christian University

Lubbock, Texas
www.lcu.edu Federal Code: 003586

4-year private university and liberal arts college in small city, affiliated with Church of Christ.
Enrollment: 1,640 undergrads, 19% part-time. 322 full-time freshmen.
Selectivity: Admits over 75% of applicants.

BASIC COSTS (2012-2013)
Tuition and fees: $17,710.
Per-credit charge: $525.
Room and board: $5,400.

FINANCIAL AID PICTURE (2011-2012)
Students with need: Out of 244 full-time freshmen who applied for aid, 212 were judged to have need. Of these, 212 received aid, and 19 had their full need met. Average financial aid package met 68% of need; average scholarship/grant was $8,982; average loan was $3,437. For part-time students, average financial aid package was $5,931.
Students without need: 39 full-time freshmen who did not demonstrate need for aid received scholarships/grants; average award was $4,236. No-need awards available for academics, athletics, job skills, leadership, music/drama.
Scholarships offered: 18 full-time freshmen received athletic scholarships.

FINANCIAL AID PROCEDURES
Forms required: FAFSA, institutional form.
Dates and Deadlines: Priority date 6/1; no closing date. Applicants notified on a rolling basis starting 3/1.
Transfers: No deadline. Applicants notified on a rolling basis.

CONTACT
Amy Hardesty, Director, Financial Assistance
5601 19th Street, Lubbock, TX 79407-2099
(806) 720-7176

McLennan Community College

Waco, Texas
www.mclennan.edu Federal Code: 003590

2-year public community and junior college in small city.
Enrollment: 8,009 undergrads.
Selectivity: Open admission; but selective for some programs.

BASIC COSTS (2012-2013)
Tuition and fees: $3,450; out-of-district residents $3,990; out-of-state residents $5,700.
Per-credit charge: $106; out-of-district residents $124; out-of-state residents $181.

FINANCIAL AID PICTURE
Students with need: Need-based aid available for full-time and part-time students.
Students without need: No-need awards available for athletics.
Scholarships offered: Academic scholarship: awarded to individuals selected for Tartan scholar's program.

FINANCIAL AID PROCEDURES
Forms required: FAFSA.
Dates and Deadlines: Closing date 6/1. Applicants notified on a rolling basis starting 5/1.

CONTACT
James Kubacak, Director of Financial Aid
1400 College Drive, Waco, TX 76708
(254) 299-8698

McMurry University

Abilene, Texas
www.mcm.edu Federal Code: 003591

4-year private university and liberal arts college in small city, affiliated with United Methodist Church.
Enrollment: 1,292 undergrads, 11% part-time. 303 full-time freshmen.
Selectivity: Admits 50 to 75% of applicants.

BASIC COSTS (2013-2014)

Tuition and fees: $24,121.
Per-credit charge: $754.
Room and board: $7,771.
Additional info: Students pay a block tuition rate for 12 or more hours per semester for fall and spring semesters. Required fees (other than the $175 freshmen orientation fee) are included in tuition cost. The use of a tablet PC and school-related software is also included in tuition cost.

FINANCIAL AID PICTURE (2012-2013)

Students with need: Out of 283 full-time freshmen who applied for aid, 258 were judged to have need. Of these, 258 received aid, and 20 had their full need met. Average financial aid package met 82% of need; average scholarship/grant was $11,285; average loan was $3,697. For part-time students, average financial aid package was $6,462.
Students without need: 19 full-time freshmen who did not demonstrate need for aid received scholarships/grants; average award was $6,842. No-need awards available for academics, art, athletics, music/drama, religious affiliation.
Scholarships offered: 63 full-time freshmen received athletic scholarships; average amount $14,628.
Cumulative student debt: 82% of graduating class had student loans; average debt was $38,921.

FINANCIAL AID PROCEDURES

Forms required: FAFSA.
Dates and Deadlines: Priority date 3/15; no closing date. Applicants notified on a rolling basis starting 2/1; must reply within 3 week(s) of notification.
Transfers: No deadline. Applicants notified on a rolling basis starting 2/1; must reply by 6/30.

CONTACT

Rachel Atkins, Director of Financial Aid
South 14th and Sayles Boulevard, Abilene, TX 79697-0001
(325) 793-4713

Midland College

Midland, Texas
www.midland.edu Federal Code: 009797

2-year public community college in small city.
Enrollment: 5,554 undergrads.
Selectivity: Open admission; but selective for some programs.

BASIC COSTS (2012-2013)

Tuition and fees: $2,160; out-of-district residents $3,450; out-of-state residents $4,620.
Per-credit charge: $129; out-of-district residents $172; out-of-state residents $481.
Room and board: $4,489.

FINANCIAL AID PICTURE

Students with need: Need-based aid available for full-time and part-time students.
Students without need: No-need awards available for academics, athletics, minority status, music/drama, state/district residency.
Scholarships offered: Abell-Hangar Foundations Scholarships: varying amounts; renewable; available for full-time or part-time study to any Midland High, Midland Lee, or Greenwood High School graduate.

FINANCIAL AID PROCEDURES

Forms required: FAFSA.
Dates and Deadlines: Priority date 4/2; closing date 6/1. Applicants notified on a rolling basis starting 5/15; must reply within 2 week(s) of notification.
Transfers: No deadline.

CONTACT

Yolanda Ramos, Director of Financial Aid
3600 North Garfield, Midland, TX 79705
(432) 685-4733

Midwestern State University

Wichita Falls, Texas
www.mwsu.edu Federal Code: 003592

4-year public university and liberal arts college in small city.
Enrollment: 5,220 undergrads, 27% part-time. 623 full-time freshmen.
Selectivity: Admits over 75% of applicants.

BASIC COSTS (2012-2013)

Tuition and fees: $7,238; out-of-state residents $9,188.
Per-credit charge: $162; out-of-state residents $227.
Room and board: $6,350.

FINANCIAL AID PICTURE (2012-2013)

Students with need: Out of 545 full-time freshmen who applied for aid, 380 were judged to have need. Of these, 378 received aid, and 72 had their full need met. Average financial aid package met 74% of need; average scholarship/grant was $7,517; average loan was $5,330. For part-time students, average financial aid package was $5,759.
Students without need: 56 full-time freshmen who did not demonstrate need for aid received scholarships/grants; average award was $2,510. No-need awards available for academics, alumni affiliation, art, athletics, leadership, music/drama.
Scholarships offered: 36 full-time freshmen received athletic scholarships; average amount $4,639.
Cumulative student debt: 64% of graduating class had student loans; average debt was $22,891.

FINANCIAL AID PROCEDURES

Forms required: FAFSA, institutional form.
Dates and Deadlines: Priority date 3/1; no closing date. Applicants notified on a rolling basis starting 4/15; must reply within 4 week(s) of notification.
Transfers: No deadline. Applicants notified on a rolling basis starting 4/15; must reply within 4 week(s) of notification.

CONTACT

Kathy Pennartz, Director of Financial Aid
3410 Taft Boulevard, Wichita Falls, TX 76308-2099
(940) 397-4119

Mountain View College

Dallas, Texas
www.mvc.dcccd.edu Federal Code: 008503

2-year public community college in very large city.
Enrollment: 7,113 undergrads.
Selectivity: Open admission.

BASIC COSTS (2012-2013)

Tuition and fees: $1,350; out-of-district residents $2,490; out-of-state residents $3,960.
Per-credit charge: $45; out-of-district residents $83; out-of-state residents $132.
Additional info: Tuition/fee waivers available for adults.

FINANCIAL AID PICTURE

Students with need: Need-based aid available for full-time and part-time students. Work study available nights, weekends, and for part-time students.

FINANCIAL AID PROCEDURES

Forms required: FAFSA, institutional form.

Dates and Deadlines: Priority date 5/1; no closing date. Applicants notified on a rolling basis starting 6/1.

CONTACT

Pam Shuttlesworth, Director of Financial Aid
4849 West Illinois Avenue, Dallas, TX 75211-6599
(214) 860-8688

Navarro College

Corsicana, Texas
www.navarrocollege.edu Federal Code: 003593

2-year public community and junior college in large town.
Enrollment: 10,104 undergrads, 54% part-time. 1,397 full-time freshmen.
Selectivity: Open admission; but selective for some programs.

BASIC COSTS (2013-2014)

Tuition and fees: $1,668; out-of-district residents $2,688; out-of-state residents $4,008.
Room and board: $4,939.

FINANCIAL AID PICTURE (2011-2012)

Students with need: 62% of average financial aid package awarded as scholarships/grants, 38% awarded as loans/jobs.

FINANCIAL AID PROCEDURES

Forms required: FAFSA.
Dates and Deadlines: Priority date 6/1; no closing date. Applicants notified on a rolling basis starting 7/1; must reply within 2 week(s) of notification.

CONTACT

Krlstal Nicholson, Director of Financial Aid
3200 West Seventh Avenue, Corsicana, TX 75110
(903) 875-7362

North Central Texas College

Gainesville, Texas
www.nctc.edu Federal Code: 003558

2-year public community college in large city.
Enrollment: 10,234 undergrads.
Selectivity: Open admission; but selective for some programs.

BASIC COSTS (2012-2013)

Tuition and fees: $1,470; out-of-district residents $2,700; out-of-state residents $4,200.
Per-credit charge: $36; out-of-district residents $77; out-of-state residents $127.
Room and board: $3,338.

FINANCIAL AID PICTURE

Students with need: Need-based aid available for full-time and part-time students. Work study available nights.
Students without need: This college awards aid only to students with need.

FINANCIAL AID PROCEDURES

Forms required: FAFSA.
Dates and Deadlines: Priority date 5/1; closing date 6/1. Applicants notified on a rolling basis starting 6/1; must reply within 4 week(s) of notification.

CONTACT

Ashley Tatum, Director of Financial Aid
1525 West California Street, Gainesville, TX 76240

North Lake College

Irving, Texas
www.northlakecollege.edu Federal Code: 014036

2-year public community and liberal arts college in large city.
Enrollment: 8,773 undergrads.
Selectivity: Open admission.

BASIC COSTS (2012-2013)

Tuition and fees: $1,350; out-of-district residents $2,490; out-of-state residents $3,960.
Per-credit charge: $45; out-of-district residents $83; out-of-state residents $132.

FINANCIAL AID PICTURE

Students with need: Need-based aid available for full-time and part-time students. Work study available nights, weekends, and for part-time students.
Students without need: No-need awards available for academics, minority status, state/district residency.

FINANCIAL AID PROCEDURES

Forms required: FAFSA, state aid form.
Dates and Deadlines: Priority date 3/1; closing date 5/1. Applicants notified on a rolling basis starting 7/1.
Transfers: Priority date 2/1. Applicants notified on a rolling basis starting 8/1.

CONTACT

Paul Felix, Director of Financial Aid
5001 North MacArthur Boulevard, Irving, TX 75038-3899
(972) 273-3321

Northeast Texas Community College

Mount Pleasant, Texas
www.ntcc.edu Federal Code: 016396

2-year public community college in large town.
Enrollment: 2,573 undergrads, 38% part-time. 459 full-time freshmen.
Selectivity: Open admission; but selective for some programs.

BASIC COSTS (2012-2013)

Tuition and fees: $2,136; out-of-district residents $3,516; out-of-state residents $4,906.
Room and board: $5,500.

FINANCIAL AID PICTURE

Students with need: Need-based aid available for full-time and part-time students.

FINANCIAL AID PROCEDURES

Forms required: FAFSA, institutional form.
Dates and Deadlines: Priority date 6/1; no closing date. Applicants notified on a rolling basis starting 6/1.

CONTACT

Patricia Durst, Director of Financial Aid & Veterans Affairs
PO Box 1307, Mount Pleasant, TX 75456-1307
(903) 434-8132

Northwest Vista College

San Antonio, Texas
www.alamo.edu/nvc Federal Code: 033723

2-year public community college in very large city.
Enrollment: 16,141 undergrads.
Selectivity: Open admission.

BASIC COSTS (2012-2013)
Tuition and fees: $2,038; out-of-district residents $5,500; out-of-state residents $10,690.

FINANCIAL AID PICTURE
Students with need: Need-based aid available for full-time and part-time students. Work study available nights, weekends, and for part-time students.
Students without need: No-need awards available for academics, leadership.

FINANCIAL AID PROCEDURES
Forms required: FAFSA.
Dates and Deadlines: Priority date 4/1; no closing date. Applicants notified on a rolling basis starting 5/15; must reply within 2 week(s) of notification.

CONTACT
Noe Ortiz, Financial Aid Director
3535 North Ellison Drive, San Antonio, TX 78251-4217
(210) 486-4168

Northwood University: Texas
Cedar Hill, Texas
www.northwood.edu Federal Code: 013040

4-year private university and business college in large town.
Enrollment: 531 undergrads, 2% part-time. 172 full-time freshmen.
Selectivity: Admits 50 to 75% of applicants.

BASIC COSTS (2012-2013)
Tuition and fees: $20,996.
Per-credit charge: $776.
Room and board: $9,106.

FINANCIAL AID PICTURE (2012-2013)
Students with need: Out of 160 full-time freshmen who applied for aid, 147 were judged to have need. Of these, 147 received aid, and 25 had their full need met. Average financial aid package met 71% of need; average scholarship/grant was $8,209; average loan was $3,378. For part-time students, average financial aid package was $11,104.
Students without need: 9 full-time freshmen who did not demonstrate need for aid received scholarships/grants; average award was $9,056. No-need awards available for academics, athletics, leadership, minority status, state/district residency.
Scholarships offered: ***Merit:*** Academic Scholarships: $4,000-$10,000; based on test scores and GPA; unlimited number awarded. ***Athletic:*** 19 full-time freshmen received athletic scholarships; average amount $4,532.
Cumulative student debt: 81% of graduating class had student loans; average debt was $24,254.

FINANCIAL AID PROCEDURES
Forms required: FAFSA.
Dates and Deadlines: Priority date 2/1; no closing date. Applicants notified on a rolling basis starting 3/1.
Transfers: No deadline. Applicants notified on a rolling basis.

CONTACT
Dawn Shestko, Director of Financial Aid
1114 West FM 1382, Cedar Hill, TX 75104
(972) 293-5430

Odessa College
Odessa, Texas
www.odessa.edu Federal Code: 003596

2-year public community college in small city.
Enrollment: 3,796 undergrads.
Selectivity: Open admission; but selective for some programs.

BASIC COSTS (2012-2013)
Tuition and fees: $2,400; out-of-district residents $3,570; out-of-state residents $4,620.
Room and board: $4,850.

FINANCIAL AID PICTURE
Students with need: Need-based aid available for full-time and part-time students. Work study available nights.
Students without need: No-need awards available for academics, athletics, music/drama.

FINANCIAL AID PROCEDURES
Forms required: FAFSA.
Dates and Deadlines: Priority date 5/1; no closing date. Applicants notified on a rolling basis starting 6/1.

CONTACT
Dee Nesmith, Director of Student Financial Aid
201 West University, Odessa, TX 79764-7127
(432) 335-6429

Our Lady of the Lake University of San Antonio
San Antonio, Texas
www.ollusa.edu Federal Code: 003598

4-year private university in very large city, affiliated with Roman Catholic Church.
Enrollment: 1,486 undergrads.
Selectivity: Admits 50 to 75% of applicants.

BASIC COSTS (2013-2014)
Tuition and fees: $23,708.
Per-credit charge: $735.
Room and board: $7,436.

FINANCIAL AID PICTURE
Students with need: Need-based aid available for full-time and part-time students. Work study available nights, weekends, and for part-time students.
Students without need: No-need awards available for academics, alumni affiliation, art, athletics, leadership, music/drama.
Scholarships offered: General academic scholarship: $1,205 awarded yearly, renewable. Art/fine arts and music: 4 awarded yearly, renewable. Children of faculty/staff: 60 awarded yearly, renewable. All based on GPA scores and high school record.

FINANCIAL AID PROCEDURES
Forms required: FAFSA, institutional form.
Dates and Deadlines: Applicants notified on a rolling basis starting 3/1; must reply within 2 week(s) of notification.

CONTACT
Esmeralda Flores, Director of Financial Aid
411 Southwest 24th Street, San Antonio, TX 78207-4689
(210) 434-6711 ext. 2541

Palo Alto College
San Antonio, Texas
www.alamo.edu/pac Federal Code: 016615

2-year public community college in very large city.
Enrollment: 8,568 undergrads.
Selectivity: Open admission.

BASIC COSTS (2012-2013)
Tuition and fees: $2,038; out-of-district residents $5,500; out-of-state residents $10,690.

FINANCIAL AID PICTURE (2011-2012)
Students with need: 84% of average financial aid package awarded as scholarships/grants, 16% awarded as loans/jobs. Need-based aid available for part-time students.
Students without need: This college awards aid only to students with need.
Scholarships offered: Alamo Community College District Scholarship: $1,000; 50 awarded.

FINANCIAL AID PROCEDURES
Forms required: FAFSA, state aid form.
Dates and Deadlines: Priority date 4/1; closing date 5/1. Applicants notified on a rolling basis starting 5/31.

CONTACT
Shirley Leija, Director of Financial Aid
1400 West Villaret Blvd., San Antonio, TX 78224-2499
(210) 486-3600

Panola College

Carthage, Texas
www.panola.edu Federal Code: 003600

2-year public community and junior college in small town.
Enrollment: 2,580 undergrads, 54% part-time. 346 full-time freshmen.
Selectivity: Open admission; but selective for some programs.

BASIC COSTS (2012-2013)
Tuition and fees: $2,010; out-of-district residents $3,210; out-of-state residents $4,050.
Per-credit charge: $67; out-of-district residents $107; out-of-state residents $135.
Room and board: $4,800.

FINANCIAL AID PICTURE
Students with need: Need-based aid available for full-time and part-time students. Work study available nights, weekends, and for part-time students.
Students without need: No-need awards available for academics, alumni affiliation, art, athletics, leadership, music/drama.
Scholarships offered: Several departmental and organization-sponsored scholarships, Presidential scholarship, Dean's scholarship.

FINANCIAL AID PROCEDURES
Forms required: FAFSA, institutional form.
Dates and Deadlines: Priority date 6/1; no closing date. Applicants notified on a rolling basis starting 6/1.
Transfers: No deadline. Applicants notified on a rolling basis.

CONTACT
Denise Welch, Director of Financial Aid
1109 West Panola Street, Carthage, TX 75633
(903) 693-2039

Paris Junior College

Paris, Texas
www.parisjc.edu Federal Code: 003601

2-year public community and junior college in large town.
Enrollment: 5,522 undergrads.
Selectivity: Open admission; but selective for some programs.

BASIC COSTS (2012-2013)
Tuition and fees: $1,650; out-of-district residents $2,580; out-of-state residents $3,990.
Per-credit charge: $47; out-of-district residents $78; out-of-state residents $125.
Room and board: $4,976.

FINANCIAL AID PICTURE
Students with need: Need-based aid available for full-time and part-time students.
Students without need: No-need awards available for athletics, music/drama.

FINANCIAL AID PROCEDURES
Forms required: FAFSA.
Dates and Deadlines: Applicants notified on a rolling basis starting 6/1.

CONTACT
Linda Slawson, Director of Financial Aid
2400 Clarksville Street, Paris, TX 75460
(903) 782-0256

Prairie View A&M University

Prairie View, Texas
www.pvamu.edu Federal Code: 003630

4-year public university in small town.
Enrollment: 6,757 undergrads, 7% part-time. 1,529 full-time freshmen.
Selectivity: Admits less than 50% of applicants.

BASIC COSTS (2012-2013)
Tuition and fees: $7,738; out-of-state residents $18,268.
Room and board: $7,431.

FINANCIAL AID PICTURE (2012-2013)
Students with need: Out of 1,489 full-time freshmen who applied for aid, 1,340 were judged to have need. Of these, 992 received aid, and 9 had their full need met. Average financial aid package met 1% of need; average scholarship/grant was $4,120; average loan was $3,875. For part-time students, average financial aid package was $13,394.
Students without need: 36 full-time freshmen who did not demonstrate need for aid received scholarships/grants; average award was $2,510. No-need awards available for academics, athletics, ROTC.
Scholarships offered: 8 full-time freshmen received athletic scholarships; average amount $10,051.
Cumulative student debt: 76% of graduating class had student loans; average debt was $27,500.

FINANCIAL AID PROCEDURES
Forms required: FAFSA.
Dates and Deadlines: Closing date 3/15. Applicants notified by 6/1; must reply by 8/1.
Transfers: Closing date 3/1. Minimum 2.0 GPA from all colleges attended required to be considered for financial aid.

CONTACT
Kelvin Francois, Director of Financial Aid
PO Box 519, MS 1009, Prairie View, TX 77446-0519
(936) 261-1000

Ranger College

Ranger, Texas
www.rangercollege.edu Federal Code: 003603

2-year public junior college in rural community.
Enrollment: 760 undergrads.
Selectivity: Open admission; but selective for some programs.

BASIC COSTS (2012-2013)
Tuition and fees: $2,250; out-of-district residents $3,330; out-of-state residents $4,290.
Per-credit charge: $50; out-of-district residents $86; out-of-state residents $118.
Room and board: $3,752.

FINANCIAL AID PICTURE

Students with need: Need-based aid available for full-time and part-time students.

Students without need: This college awards aid only to students with need.

FINANCIAL AID PROCEDURES

Forms required: FAFSA.

Dates and Deadlines: Priority date 6/1; closing date 7/24. Applicants notified on a rolling basis; must reply within 2 week(s) of notification.

Transfers: Applicants notified on a rolling basis; must reply within 2 week(s) of notification.

CONTACT

Don Hilton, Financial Aid Director
1100 College Circle, Ranger, TX 76470
(254) 647-3234 ext. 117

Remington College: Houston

Houston, Texas
www.remingtoncollege.edu/houston
Federal Code: E00672

2-year private technical college in very large city.
Enrollment: 382 undergrads.
Selectivity: Open admission.

BASIC COSTS (2012-2013)

Additional info: Cost of diploma programs in Medical Assisting, Medical Billing and Coding, Pharmacy Technician: $15,995. Cost of diploma program in Electronic Technology, $19,995, Cosmetology, $21,700. Includes books, equipment, lab fees, and uniforms (if necessary).

FINANCIAL AID PICTURE

Students with need: Need-based aid available for full-time and part-time students. Work study available nights.

Students without need: No-need awards available for state/district residency.

FINANCIAL AID PROCEDURES

Forms required: FAFSA, institutional form.

Dates and Deadlines: Applicants notified on a rolling basis.

CONTACT

James Dunn, National Director of Financial Aid
3110 Hayes Road, Suite 380, Houston, TX 77082

Rice University

Houston, Texas
www.rice.edu
Federal Code: 003604
CSS Code: 6609

4-year private university in very large city.
Enrollment: 3,848 undergrads. 931 full-time freshmen.
Selectivity: Admits less than 50% of applicants.

BASIC COSTS (2012-2013)

Tuition and fees: $37,292.
Room and board: $12,600.

FINANCIAL AID PICTURE (2012-2013)

Students with need: Out of 621 full-time freshmen who applied for aid, 413 were judged to have need. Of these, 413 received aid, and 413 had their full need met. Average financial aid package met 100% of need; average scholarship/grant was $33,564; average loan was $1,340. Need-based aid available for part-time students.

Students without need: 149 full-time freshmen who did not demonstrate need for aid received scholarships/grants; average award was $12,033. No-need awards available for academics, art, athletics, leadership, minority status, music/drama, ROTC, state/district residency.

Scholarships offered: 61 full-time freshmen received athletic scholarships; average amount $44,255.

Cumulative student debt: 25% of graduating class had student loans; average debt was $18,133.

FINANCIAL AID PROCEDURES

Forms required: FAFSA, CSS PROFILE.

Dates and Deadlines: Priority date 3/1; no closing date. Applicants notified by 4/1; must reply by 5/1.

Transfers: Priority date 4/1.

CONTACT

Anne Walker, Director of Student Financial Services
6100 Main Street, Houston, TX 77251-1892
(713) 348-4958

Richland College

Dallas, Texas
www.rlc.dcccd.edu
Federal Code: 008504

2-year public community college in very large city.
Enrollment: 13,775 undergrads.
Selectivity: Open admission.

BASIC COSTS (2012-2013)

Tuition and fees: $1,350; out-of-district residents $2,490; out-of-state residents $3,960.
Per-credit charge: $45; out-of-district residents $83; out-of-state residents $132.

FINANCIAL AID PICTURE

Students with need: Need-based aid available for full-time and part-time students. Work study available nights.

Students without need: No-need awards available for art, leadership, music/drama.

FINANCIAL AID PROCEDURES

Forms required: FAFSA.

Dates and Deadlines: Priority date 5/11; no closing date. Applicants notified on a rolling basis starting 6/1; must reply within 2 week(s) of notification.

CONTACT

Sylvia Holmes, Director of Financial Aid
12800 Abrams Road, Dallas, TX 75243-2199
(972) 238-6188

St. Edward's University

Austin, Texas
www.stedwards.edu
Federal Code: 003621

4-year private university and liberal arts college in very large city, affiliated with Roman Catholic Church.
Enrollment: 4,224 undergrads, 18% part-time. 777 full-time freshmen.
Selectivity: Admits 50 to 75% of applicants.

BASIC COSTS (2013-2014)

Tuition and fees: $33,720.
Per-credit charge: $1,112.
Room and board: $10,954.

FINANCIAL AID PICTURE (2012-2013)

Students with need: Out of 622 full-time freshmen who applied for aid, 495 were judged to have need. Of these, 493 received aid, and 53 had their

full need met. Average financial aid package met 71% of need; average scholarship/grant was $16,713; average loan was $3,666. For part-time students, average financial aid package was $6,761.
Students without need: 50 full-time freshmen who did not demonstrate need for aid received scholarships/grants; average award was $11,198. No-need awards available for academics, athletics, leadership, music/drama.
Scholarships offered: ***Merit:*** President's Excellence Scholarship: $15,000 per year; minimum 1300 SAT; top 15% of class. Holy Cross Scholar Award: full tuition; minimum 1250 SAT; top 10% of class; for academic excellence, leadership ability and commitment to community service. Academic Scholar Award: $5,000-$15,000 per year; minimum 1100 SAT; top 25% of class. All SAT scores exclusive of Writing. ***Athletic:*** 42 full-time freshmen received athletic scholarships; average amount $14,553.
Cumulative student debt: 70% of graduating class had student loans; average debt was $34,314.

FINANCIAL AID PROCEDURES
Forms required: FAFSA.
Dates and Deadlines: Priority date 3/1; closing date 5/1. Applicants notified on a rolling basis starting 1/15; must reply by 5/1 or within 2 week(s) of notification.
Transfers: Closing date 7/15. Applicants notified on a rolling basis starting 2/1; must reply within 2 week(s) of notification.

CONTACT
Doris Constantine, Associate VP and Director of Student Financial Services
3001 South Congress Avenue, Austin, TX 78704-6489
(512) 448-8523

St. Mary's University
San Antonio, Texas
www.stmarytx.edu Federal Code: 003623

4-year private university and liberal arts college in very large city, affiliated with Roman Catholic Church.
Enrollment: 2,459 undergrads, 6% part-time. 584 full-time freshmen.
Selectivity: Admits less than 50% of applicants.

BASIC COSTS (2013-2014)
Tuition and fees: $25,188.
Per-credit charge: $755.
Room and board: $9,110.

FINANCIAL AID PICTURE
Students with need: Need-based aid available for full-time and part-time students. Work study available nights, weekends, and for part-time students.
Students without need: No-need awards available for academics, alumni affiliation, athletics, leadership, minority status, music/drama, ROTC, state/district residency.

FINANCIAL AID PROCEDURES
Forms required: FAFSA.
Dates and Deadlines: Priority date 3/31; no closing date. Applicants notified on a rolling basis starting 3/1; must reply by 5/1 or within 2 week(s) of notification.

CONTACT
David Krause, Director of Financial Assistance
One Camino Santa Maria, San Antonio, TX 78228-8503
(210) 436-3141

St. Philip's College
San Antonio, Texas
www.alamo.edu/spc Federal Code: 003608

2-year public community college in very large city.
Enrollment: 8,144 undergrads.
Selectivity: Open admission; but selective for some programs.

BASIC COSTS (2012-2013)
Tuition and fees: $2,038; out-of-district residents $5,500; out-of-state residents $10,690.

FINANCIAL AID PICTURE (2011-2012)
Students with need: 72% of average financial aid package awarded as scholarships/grants, 28% awarded as loans/jobs. Need-based aid available for part-time students. Work study available nights, weekends, and for part-time students.
Students without need: This college awards aid only to students with need.

FINANCIAL AID PROCEDURES
Forms required: FAFSA.

CONTACT
Diego Bernal, Director of Financial Aid
1801 Martin Luther King Drive, San Antonio, TX 78203
(210) 486-2275

Sam Houston State University
Huntsville, Texas
www.shsu.edu Federal Code: 003606

4-year public university in large town.
Enrollment: 15,611 undergrads, 17% part-time. 2,344 full-time freshmen.
Selectivity: Admits 50 to 75% of applicants.

BASIC COSTS (2012-2013)
Tuition and fees: $8,120; out-of-state residents $18,650.
Per-credit charge: $187; out-of-state residents $538.
Room and board: $8,092.

FINANCIAL AID PICTURE
Students with need: Need-based aid available for full-time and part-time students.
Students without need: No-need awards available for academics, alumni affiliation, art, athletics, job skills, leadership, music/drama, religious affiliation, ROTC, state/district residency.

FINANCIAL AID PROCEDURES
Forms required: FAFSA.
Dates and Deadlines: Priority date 4/1; no closing date. Applicants notified on a rolling basis starting 3/15; must reply within 4 week(s) of notification.
Transfers: No deadline. Applicants notified on a rolling basis starting 3/15; must reply within 4 week(s) of notification.

CONTACT
Lisa Tatom, Director of Financial Aid
Box 2418, Huntsville, TX 77341-2418
(936) 294-1774

San Antonio College
San Antonio, Texas
www.alamo.edu/sac Federal Code: 009163

2-year public community college in very large city.
Enrollment: 19,869 undergrads.
Selectivity: Open admission; but selective for some programs.

BASIC COSTS (2012-2013)
Tuition and fees: $2,038; out-of-district residents $5,500; out-of-state residents $10,690.

FINANCIAL AID PICTURE
Students with need: Need-based aid available for full-time and part-time students. Work study available nights, weekends, and for part-time students.

Students without need: This college awards aid only to students with need.

Additional info: Leveraging Educational Assistance Partnership (LEAP), public student incentive grant, towards excellence access and success grants (Texas and Texas II grants) available.

FINANCIAL AID PROCEDURES

Forms required: FAFSA.

Dates and Deadlines: Priority date 3/1; no closing date.

CONTACT

Carreon-Munoz Rose, Associate Director of Student Financial Services
1300 San Pedro Avenue, San Antonio, TX 78212-4299
(210) 486-0600

San Jacinto College

Pasadena, Texas
www.sanjac.edu

2-year public community and technical college in very large city.

Enrollment: 27,324 undergrads, 70% part-time. 2,779 full-time freshmen.

Selectivity: Open admission; but selective for some programs.

BASIC COSTS (2012-2013)

Tuition and fees: $1,850; out-of-district residents $3,080; out-of-state residents $4,580.

Per-credit charge: $43; out-of-district residents $84; out-of-state residents $134.

FINANCIAL AID PICTURE

Students with need: Need-based aid available for full-time and part-time students. Work study available nights, weekends, and for part-time students.

Students without need: This college awards aid only to students with need.

FINANCIAL AID PROCEDURES

Forms required: FAFSA, institutional form.

Dates and Deadlines: Priority date 7/1; no closing date. Applicants notified on a rolling basis starting 4/1; must reply within 4 week(s) of notification.

Transfers: Applicants notified on a rolling basis starting 4/1; must reply within 4 week(s) of notification.

CONTACT

Robert Merino, Director of Financial Aid
8060 Spencer Highway, Pasadena, TX 77505-5999
(281) 998-6150

Schreiner University

Kerrville, Texas
www.schreiner.edu Federal Code: 003610

4-year private liberal arts college in large town, affiliated with Presbyterian Church (USA).

Enrollment: 1,059 undergrads, 4% part-time. 265 full-time freshmen.

Selectivity: Admits 50 to 75% of applicants.

BASIC COSTS (2012-2013)

Tuition and fees: $21,540.

Per-credit charge: $894.

Room and board: $10,065.

FINANCIAL AID PICTURE (2011-2012)

Students with need: Out of 265 full-time freshmen who applied for aid, 221 were judged to have need. Of these, 221 received aid, and 27 had their full need met. Average financial aid package met 73% of need; average scholarship/grant was $14,885; average loan was $2,968. For part-time students, average financial aid package was $7,996.

Students without need: 33 full-time freshmen who did not demonstrate need for aid received scholarships/grants; average award was $7,575. No-need awards available for alumni affiliation, leadership, music/drama, religious affiliation.

Scholarships offered: Awards for students with exceptional academic achievement and leadership abilities; partial and full tuition; 3.5 GPA and 1100 SAT (exclusive of Writing) or 24 ACT.

Cumulative student debt: 36% of graduating class had student loans; average debt was $20,900.

FINANCIAL AID PROCEDURES

Forms required: FAFSA, state aid form.

Dates and Deadlines: Priority date 5/1; no closing date. Applicants notified on a rolling basis starting 2/13; must reply within 2 week(s) of notification.

Transfers: Priority date 4/15; no deadline.

CONTACT

Toni Bryant, Associate Dean of Admissions & Financial Aid
2100 Memorial Boulevard, Kerrville, TX 78028-5697
(830) 896-5411

South Plains College

Levelland, Texas
www.southplainscollege.edu Federal Code: 003611

2-year public community and junior college in large town.

Enrollment: 7,811 undergrads, 41% part-time. 1,139 full-time freshmen.

Selectivity: Open admission; but selective for some programs.

BASIC COSTS (2012-2013)

Tuition and fees: $2,463; out-of-district residents $3,122; out-of-state residents $3,602.

Room and board: $3,100.

FINANCIAL AID PICTURE

Students with need: Need-based aid available for full-time and part-time students.

Students without need: No-need awards available for academics, art, athletics, leadership, music/drama, state/district residency.

FINANCIAL AID PROCEDURES

Forms required: FAFSA.

Dates and Deadlines: Priority date 6/1; no closing date. Applicants notified on a rolling basis starting 6/30; must reply within 2 week(s) of notification.

CONTACT

Ronnie Watkins, Director of Financial Aid
1401 South College Avenue, Levelland, TX 79336
(806) 894-9611

South Texas College

McAllen, Texas
www.southtexascollege.edu Federal Code: 031034

2-year public community and technical college in very large city.

Enrollment: 30,055 undergrads, 65% part-time. 2,982 full-time freshmen.

Selectivity: Open admission; but selective for some programs.

BASIC COSTS (2012-2013)

Tuition and fees: $3,150; out-of-district residents $3,423; out-of-state residents $7,200.

FINANCIAL AID PICTURE (2011-2012)

Students with need: 99% of average financial aid package awarded as scholarships/grants, 1% awarded as loans/jobs. Need-based aid available for part-time students. Work study available nights, weekends, and for part-time students.

Students without need: No-need awards available for academics.

FINANCIAL AID PROCEDURES

Forms required: FAFSA.

Dates and Deadlines: Priority date 3/1; no closing date. Applicants notified on a rolling basis starting 4/15.

CONTACT

Miguel Carranza, Director of Financial Aid
3201 West Pecan Boulevard, McAllen, TX 78502
(956) 872-8375

Southern Methodist University

Dallas, Texas Federal Code: 003613
www.smu.edu CSS Code: 6660

4-year private university in large town, affiliated with United Methodist Church.

Enrollment: 6,175 undergrads, 3% part-time. 1,426 full-time freshmen.

Selectivity: Admits 50 to 75% of applicants. GED not accepted.

BASIC COSTS (2013-2014)

Tuition and fees: $43,800.

Per-credit charge: $1,624.

Room and board: $13,955.

FINANCIAL AID PICTURE (2011-2012)

Students with need: Out of 791 full-time freshmen who applied for aid, 608 were judged to have need. Of these, 605 received aid, and 216 had their full need met. Average financial aid package met 88% of need; average scholarship/grant was $20,189; average loan was $3,487. For part-time students, average financial aid package was $16,131.

Students without need: 453 full-time freshmen who did not demonstrate need for aid received scholarships/grants; average award was $15,674. No-need awards available for academics, alumni affiliation, art, athletics, leadership, music/drama.

Scholarships offered: 66 full-time freshmen received athletic scholarships; average amount $48,828.

Cumulative student debt: 30% of graduating class had student loans; average debt was $30,987.

FINANCIAL AID PROCEDURES

Forms required: FAFSA, CSS PROFILE.

Dates and Deadlines: Priority date 2/15; no closing date. Applicants notified on a rolling basis starting 4/1; must reply within 3 week(s) of notification.

Transfers: Priority date 4/1. Merit scholarships available for community college and senior institution honor transfers. Students entering without scholarship aid will receive need-based aid up to cost of tuition.

CONTACT

Marc Peterson, Executive Director of Enrollment Services
PO Box 750181, Dallas, TX 75275-0181
(214) 768-2068

Southwest Texas Junior College

Uvalde, Texas
www.swtjc.edu Federal Code: 003614

2-year public community and junior college in large town.

Enrollment: 3,858 undergrads.

Selectivity: Open admission.

BASIC COSTS (2012-2013)

Tuition and fees: $2,512; out-of-district residents $3,967; out-of-state residents $4,462.

Per-credit charge: $55; out-of-district residents $104; out-of-state residents $120.

Room and board: $3,600.

Additional info: Additional $13 per semester health fee for Uvalde campus students.

FINANCIAL AID PICTURE

Students with need: Need-based aid available for full-time and part-time students.

FINANCIAL AID PROCEDURES

Forms required: FAFSA.

Dates and Deadlines: Priority date 6/15; no closing date. Applicants notified on a rolling basis starting 5/1; must reply within 2 week(s) of notification.

Transfers: Financial aid application deadline for specific scholarships 4/1; priority deadline for grants 5/1.

CONTACT

Ana Almaraz, Director of Financial Aid
2401 Garner Field Road, Uvalde, TX 78801
(830) 278-4401

Southwestern Adventist University

Keene, Texas
www.swau.edu Federal Code: 003619

4-year private university and liberal arts college in small town, affiliated with Seventh-day Adventists.

Enrollment: 695 undergrads, 12% part-time. 117 full-time freshmen.

Selectivity: Admits less than 50% of applicants.

BASIC COSTS (2013-2014)

Tuition and fees: $18,640.

Per-credit charge: $760.

Room and board: $7,220.

FINANCIAL AID PICTURE (2011-2012)

Students with need: 42% of average financial aid package awarded as scholarships/grants, 58% awarded as loans/jobs. Need-based aid available for part-time students.

Students without need: No-need awards available for academics, leadership, music/drama.

FINANCIAL AID PROCEDURES

Forms required: FAFSA, institutional form.

Dates and Deadlines: Priority date 3/15; no closing date. Applicants notified on a rolling basis starting 4/15.

Transfers: No deadline. Applicants notified on a rolling basis.

CONTACT

Patricia Norwood, Assistant Vice President for Financial Administration, Student Finance
Box 567, Keene, TX 76059
(817) 202-6262

Southwestern Assemblies of God University

Waxahachie, Texas
www.sagu.edu Federal Code: 003616

4-year private university and Bible college in large town, affiliated with Assemblies of God.

Enrollment: 1,695 undergrads.

BASIC COSTS (2013-2014)

Tuition and fees: $16,630.

Per-credit charge: $525.

Room and board: $6,290.

FINANCIAL AID PICTURE

Students with need: Need-based aid available for full-time and part-time students.

FINANCIAL AID PROCEDURES

Forms required: FAFSA.

Dates and Deadlines: Priority date 3/1; no closing date. Applicants notified on a rolling basis starting 6/1; must reply within 2 week(s) of notification.

CONTACT

Jeff Francis, Senior Director of Financial Aid
1200 Sycamore Street, Waxahachie, TX 75165
(972) 825-4730

Southwestern Christian College

Terrell, Texas
www.swcc.edu Federal Code: 003618

4-year private Bible and liberal arts college in large town, affiliated with Church of Christ.

Enrollment: 204 undergrads.

Selectivity: Open admission.

BASIC COSTS (2012-2013)

Tuition and fees: $7,504.

Per-credit charge: $285.

Room and board: $4,757.

FINANCIAL AID PICTURE

Students with need: Need-based aid available for full-time and part-time students.

Students without need: No-need awards available for academics, athletics, music/drama.

FINANCIAL AID PROCEDURES

Forms required: FAFSA.

Dates and Deadlines: Closing date 6/1. Applicants notified on a rolling basis starting 7/15; must reply within 2 week(s) of notification.

CONTACT

Tonya Dean, Director of Financial Aid
Box 10, Terrell, TX 75160
(972) 524-3341 ext. 124

Southwestern University

Georgetown, Texas
www.southwestern.edu Federal Code: 003620

4-year private liberal arts and performing arts college in large town, affiliated with United Methodist Church.

Enrollment: 1,383 undergrads, 1% part-time. 357 full-time freshmen.

Selectivity: Admits 50 to 75% of applicants.

BASIC COSTS (2013-2014)

Tuition and fees: $35,240.

Per-credit charge: $1,470.

Room and board: $10,420.

FINANCIAL AID PICTURE (2012-2013)

Students with need: Average financial aid package met 92% of need; average scholarship/grant was $26,235; average loan was $4,053. For part-time students, average financial aid package was $9,049.

Students without need: No-need awards available for academics, alumni affiliation, art, leadership, minority status, music/drama, religious affiliation.

Scholarships offered: Academic Merit Scholarships: $2,000 to $22,000 per year. Brown Scholarships: full tuition, average room and average board. National Merit Finalist Awards: $2,000 per year. Fine Arts Scholarships: $3,500 to $10,000 per year; for students majoring in art, music or theater; based on talent, auditions or portfolio review. Music Performance Awards: up to $2,500; based on talent and awarded to non-fine arts majors who wish to participate in university ensemble. Dixon Scholarship: $5,000 per year or full tuition; awarded to high-achieving African-American, Hispanic, and Native American students. Beneficiary Grants: $6,000 per year; awarded to dependents of United Methodist clergy. Preministerial Scholarships: $3,000 per year; to students interested in full-time ministry careers.

Cumulative student debt: 57% of graduating class had student loans; average debt was $36,299.

FINANCIAL AID PROCEDURES

Forms required: FAFSA.

Dates and Deadlines: Priority date 3/1; no closing date. Applicants notified on a rolling basis starting 3/1; must reply by 5/1 or within 2 week(s) of notification.

Transfers: Closing date 5/15.

CONTACT

James Gaeta, Director of Financial Aid
PO Box 770, Georgetown, TX 78627-0770
(512) 863-1259

Stephen F. Austin State University

Nacogdoches, Texas
www.sfasu.edu Federal Code: 003624

4-year public university in large town.

Enrollment: 11,053 undergrads, 13% part-time. 2,407 full-time freshmen.

Selectivity: Admits 50 to 75% of applicants.

BASIC COSTS (2012-2013)

Tuition and fees: $7,928; out-of-state residents $18,457.

Per-credit charge: $192; out-of-state residents $543.

Room and board: $8,476.

FINANCIAL AID PICTURE (2011-2012)

Students with need: Out of 2,077 full-time freshmen who applied for aid, 1,730 were judged to have need. Of these, 1,730 received aid, and 142 had their full need met. Average financial aid package met 53% of need; average scholarship/grant was $7,120; average loan was $3,538. For part-time students, average financial aid package was $8,667.

Students without need: 187 full-time freshmen who did not demonstrate need for aid received scholarships/grants; average award was $4,735. No-need awards available for academics, alumni affiliation, art, athletics, leadership, music/drama, state/district residency.

Scholarships offered: ***Merit:*** Academic Excellence Scholarship Program: $3,000 per year; rank in top 10% of high school class or top quartile class with 1100 SAT (exclusive of Writing) or 24 ACT; renewable with 3.5 GPA. Dugas Honors Scholarship: $2,500 per semester; active member of School of Honors. University Scholars Program: $2,000 per semester; minimum 1220 SAT, 27 ACT, 3.0 GPA maintenance; up to 11 awarded. Student Foundation Association Leadership Scholarship: amounts vary; demonstrated leadership capabilities and academic achievement throughout high school career; 1 awarded. ***Athletic:*** 48 full-time freshmen received athletic scholarships; average amount $7,746.

Cumulative student debt: 71% of graduating class had student loans; average debt was $20,858.

Additional info: For students who qualify, Purple Promise tuition guarantee program covers the remaining balance of any tuition and mandatory fees not covered by other gift aid, for 15 hours per regular semester for up to 4 years.

FINANCIAL AID PROCEDURES

Forms required: FAFSA.

Dates and Deadlines: Priority date 4/1; no closing date. Applicants notified on a rolling basis starting 4/1.

CONTACT

Mike O'Rear, Director of Financial Aid
Box 13051, SFA Station, Nacogdoches, TX 75962-3051
(936) 468-2403

Sul Ross State University

Alpine, Texas
www.sulross.edu Federal Code: 003625

4-year public university in small town.
Enrollment: 1,236 undergrads, 19% part-time. 246 full-time freshmen.
Selectivity: Admits less than 50% of applicants.

BASIC COSTS (2012-2013)
Tuition and fees: $6,060; out-of-state residents $15,450.
Room and board: $7,000.

FINANCIAL AID PICTURE
Students with need: Need-based aid available for full-time and part-time students.

FINANCIAL AID PROCEDURES
Forms required: FAFSA, institutional form.
Dates and Deadlines: Priority date 3/1; closing date 4/1. Applicants notified on a rolling basis starting 5/1; must reply within 2 week(s) of notification.

CONTACT

Michael Corbett, Director Student Financial Assistance
PO Box C-2, Alpine, TX 79832
(432) 837-8055

Tarleton State University

Stephenville, Texas
www.tarleton.edu Federal Code: 003631

4-year public university in large town.
Enrollment: 8,914 undergrads, 21% part-time. 1,587 full-time freshmen.
Selectivity: Admits 50 to 75% of applicants.

BASIC COSTS (2012-2013)
Tuition and fees: $6,709; out-of-state residents $17,239.
Per-credit charge: $154; out-of-state residents $505.
Room and board: $7,747.

FINANCIAL AID PICTURE
Students with need: Need-based aid available for full-time and part-time students.
Students without need: No-need awards available for academics, alumni affiliation, art, athletics, leadership, music/drama, ROTC.
Additional info: Tuition guarantee program covers tuition and fees for qualified freshman.

FINANCIAL AID PROCEDURES
Forms required: FAFSA.
Dates and Deadlines: Priority date 4/1; no closing date. Applicants notified on a rolling basis starting 2/1.
Transfers: No deadline.

CONTACT

Betty Murray, Director, Student Financial Aid
Box T-0030, Stephenville, TX 76402
(254) 968-9070

Tarrant County College

Fort Worth, Texas
www.tccd.edu Federal Code: 003626

2-year public community college in very large city.
Enrollment: 51,363 undergrads. 17,293 full-time freshmen.
Selectivity: Open admission; but selective for some programs.

BASIC COSTS (2013-2014)
Tuition and fees: $1,650; out-of-district residents $2,580; out-of-state residents $6,150.
Per-credit charge: $55; out-of-district residents $86; out-of-state residents $205.

FINANCIAL AID PICTURE (2011-2012)
Students with need: 79% of average financial aid package awarded as scholarships/grants, 21% awarded as loans/jobs. Need-based aid available for part-time students.
Students without need: No-need awards available for academics.

FINANCIAL AID PROCEDURES
Forms required: FAFSA, institutional form.
Dates and Deadlines: Priority date 5/1; no closing date. Applicants notified on a rolling basis starting 5/1; must reply within 2 week(s) of notification.
Transfers: No deadline. Applicants notified on a rolling basis.

CONTACT

Samantha Stalnaker, District Director of Financial Aid
300 Trinity Campus Circle, Fort Worth, TX 76102-1964
(817) 515-4243

Temple College

Temple, Texas
www.templejc.edu Federal Code: 003627

2-year public community college in small city.
Enrollment: 5,094 undergrads, 63% part-time. 310 full-time freshmen.
Selectivity: Open admission; but selective for some programs.

BASIC COSTS (2012-2013)
Tuition and fees: $2,640; out-of-district residents $4,620; out-of-state residents $7,020.
Per-credit charge: $88; out-of-district residents $154; out-of-state residents $234.

FINANCIAL AID PICTURE
Students with need: Need-based aid available for full-time and part-time students. Work study available nights.
Students without need: This college awards aid only to students with need.

FINANCIAL AID PROCEDURES
Forms required: FAFSA.
Dates and Deadlines: Priority date 6/1; no closing date. Applicants notified on a rolling basis starting 5/1; must reply within 4 week(s) of notification.
Transfers: No deadline. Applicants notified on a rolling basis starting 5/1; must reply within 4 week(s) of notification.

CONTACT

Patricia Goodman, Director of Financial Aid
2600 South First Street, Temple, TX 76504-7435
(254) 298-8321

Texarkana College

Texarkana, Texas
www.texarkanacollege.edu Federal Code: 003628

2-year public community college in small city.
Enrollment: 3,957 undergrads.
Selectivity: Open admission.

BASIC COSTS (2012-2013)
Tuition and fees: $2,260; out-of-district residents $3,460; out-of-state residents $4,840.
Per-credit charge: $44; out-of-district residents $84; out-of-state residents $130.
Additional info: Arkansas and Oklahoma residents pay out-of-district rates.

FINANCIAL AID PICTURE (2011-2012)
Students with need: 99% of average financial aid package awarded as scholarships/grants, 1% awarded as loans/jobs. Need-based aid available for part-time students. Work study available nights, weekends, and for part-time students.
Students without need: No-need awards available for academics, athletics.
Scholarships offered: Rising Star Scholarship: Open scholarship for all high school graduates below a $75,000 household income.

FINANCIAL AID PROCEDURES
Forms required: FAFSA, institutional form.
Dates and Deadlines: Priority date 6/1; no closing date. Applicants notified on a rolling basis starting 3/1.
Transfers: Closing date 5/1. Applicants notified on a rolling basis.

CONTACT
Martin Hernandez, Director of Financial Aid
2500 North Robison Road, Texarkana, TX 75599
(903) 823-3163

Texas A&M International University

Laredo, Texas
www.tamiu.edu Federal Code: 009651

4-year public university in small city.
Enrollment: 6,384 undergrads.
Selectivity: Admits less than 50% of applicants.

BASIC COSTS (2012-2013)
Tuition and fees: $6,838; out-of-state residents $17,368.
Per-credit charge: $146; out-of-state residents $497.
Room and board: $7,313.

FINANCIAL AID PICTURE
Students with need: Need-based aid available for full-time and part-time students. Work study available nights.
Students without need: No-need awards available for academics.

FINANCIAL AID PROCEDURES
Forms required: FAFSA, institutional form.
Dates and Deadlines: Priority date 3/15; no closing date. Applicants notified on a rolling basis starting 4/15; must reply within 2 week(s) of notification.
Transfers: No deadline. Applicants notified on a rolling basis starting 11/30; must reply within 2 week(s) of notification.

CONTACT
Laura Elizondo, Director of Financial Aid
5201 University Boulevard, Laredo, TX 78041-1900
(956) 326-2225

Texas A&M University

College Station, Texas
www.tamu.edu Federal Code: 003632

4-year public university in small city.
Enrollment: 40,094 undergrads, 10% part-time. 7,174 full-time freshmen.
Selectivity: Admits 50 to 75% of applicants.

BASIC COSTS (2012-2013)
Tuition and fees: $8,506; out-of-state residents $25,036.
Per-credit charge: $177; out-of-state residents $728.
Room and board: $8,400.

FINANCIAL AID PICTURE
Students with need: Need-based aid available for full-time and part-time students. Work study available nights, weekends, and for part-time students.
Students without need: No-need awards available for academics, alumni affiliation, art, athletics, job skills, leadership, music/drama, religious affiliation, ROTC, state/district residency.
Scholarships offered: Texas residents: Regents scholarship, additional $5,000 annually for 4 years, first-generation students incomes <$40,000. Aggie Assurance, minimum scholarships, grants for Pell students, incomes <$30,000; incomes <$60,000 gift aid for tuition only. Students must maintain a 2.5 GPA.
Additional info: Short-term loans available.

FINANCIAL AID PROCEDURES
Forms required: FAFSA.
Dates and Deadlines: Priority date 3/1; no closing date. Applicants notified on a rolling basis starting 3/15.
Transfers: Must provide previous financial aid transcript.

CONTACT
Delisa Falks, Assistant Provost - Student Financial Aid
PO Box 30014, College Station, TX 77842-3014
(979) 845-3236

Texas A&M University-Baylor College of Dentistry

Dallas, Texas
www.bcd.tamhsc.edu Federal Code: 004948

Upper-division public health science college in very large city.
Enrollment: 61 undergrads.

BASIC COSTS (2012-2013)
Tuition and fees: $6,837; out-of-state residents $18,420.

FINANCIAL AID PICTURE (2011-2012)
Students with need: Average financial aid package for all full-time undergraduates was $9,750. 28% awarded as scholarships/grants, 72% awarded as loans/jobs. Need-based aid available for part-time students.
Students without need: No-need awards available for academics.

FINANCIAL AID PROCEDURES
Forms required: FAFSA, institutional form.
Dates and Deadlines: Priority date 3/15; no closing date. Applicants notified on a rolling basis starting 6/1; must reply within 2 week(s) of notification.

CONTACT
Kay Egbert, Director of Student Aid
PO Box 660677, Dallas, TX 75266-0677

Texas A&M University-Commerce

Commerce, Texas
www.tamuc.edu Federal Code: 003565

4-year public university in small town.
Enrollment: 6,768 undergrads, 51% part-time. 785 full-time freshmen.
Selectivity: Admits 50 to 75% of applicants.

BASIC COSTS (2012-2013)
Tuition and fees: $6,583; out-of-state residents $17,113.
Room and board: $7,770.

FINANCIAL AID PICTURE (2012-2013)
Students with need: Need-based aid available for full-time and part-time students.
Students without need: No-need awards available for academics, art, athletics, leadership, music/drama.
Additional info: Work-study also available for full-time students.

FINANCIAL AID PROCEDURES
Forms required: FAFSA.
Dates and Deadlines: Priority date 4/1; closing date 6/30. Applicants notified on a rolling basis starting 4/1; must reply within 2 week(s) of notification.

CONTACT
Maria Ramos, Director of Financial Aid
Box 3011, Commerce, TX 75429-3011
(903) 886-5091

Texas A&M University-Corpus Christi

Corpus Christi, Texas
www.tamucc.edu Federal Code: 011161

4-year public university in large city.
Enrollment: 8,731 undergrads, 21% part-time. 1,698 full-time freshmen.
Selectivity: Admits over 75% of applicants.

BASIC COSTS (2013-2014)
Tuition and fees: $7,778; out-of-state residents $18,398.
Per-credit charge: $167; out-of-state residents $521.
Room and board: $9,020.

FINANCIAL AID PICTURE (2012-2013)
Students with need: Out of 1,450 full-time freshmen who applied for aid, 1,158 were judged to have need. Of these, 1,112 received aid, and 100 had their full need met. Average financial aid package met 28% of need; average scholarship/grant was $3,227; average loan was $1,669. For part-time students, average financial aid package was $5,027.
Students without need: 75 full-time freshmen who did not demonstrate need for aid received scholarships/grants; average award was $1,095. No-need awards available for academics, art, athletics, leadership, music/drama, ROTC.
Scholarships offered: 42 full-time freshmen received athletic scholarships; average amount $2,840.
Cumulative student debt: 60% of graduating class had student loans; average debt was $16,000.

FINANCIAL AID PROCEDURES
Forms required: FAFSA.
Dates and Deadlines: Priority date 3/31; closing date 6/30. Applicants notified on a rolling basis starting 4/1; must reply within 2 week(s) of notification.
Transfers: No deadline. Applicants notified on a rolling basis starting 4/1; must reply within 2 week(s) of notification.

CONTACT
Jeannie Gage, Director, Financial Assistance
6300 Ocean Drive, Unit 5774, Corpus Christi, TX 78412-5774
(361) 825-2338

Texas A&M University-Galveston

Galveston, Texas
www.tamug.edu Federal Code: 003632

4-year public university and branch campus college in small city.
Enrollment: 1,905 undergrads, 8% part-time. 586 full-time freshmen.
Selectivity: Admits 50 to 75% of applicants.

BASIC COSTS (2012-2013)
Tuition and fees: $7,775; out-of-state residents $17,165.
Per-credit charge: $189; out-of-state residents $501.
Room and board: $7,926.

FINANCIAL AID PICTURE (2011-2012)
Students with need: Out of 403 full-time freshmen who applied for aid, 265 were judged to have need. Of these, 254 received aid, and 82 had their full need met. Average financial aid package met 72% of need; average scholarship/grant was $6,597; average loan was $6,671. For part-time students, average financial aid package was $10,294.
Students without need: 16 full-time freshmen who did not demonstrate need for aid received scholarships/grants; average award was $3,531. No-need awards available for academics, state/district residency.

FINANCIAL AID PROCEDURES
Forms required: FAFSA.
Dates and Deadlines: Priority date 4/1; no closing date. Applicants notified on a rolling basis starting 3/15; must reply within 3 week(s) of notification.

CONTACT
Cheryl Grefenstette-Moon, Executive Director of Enrollment Services
PO Box 1675, Galveston, TX 77553-1675
(409) 740-4500

Texas A&M University-Kingsville

Kingsville, Texas
www.tamuk.edu Federal Code: 003639

4-year public university in large town.
Enrollment: 5,435 undergrads, 12% part-time. 1,155 full-time freshmen.
Selectivity: Admits over 75% of applicants.

BASIC COSTS (2012-2013)
Tuition and fees: $6,940; out-of-state residents $17,470.
Room and board: $6,558.

FINANCIAL AID PICTURE (2011-2012)
Students with need: Out of 1,085 full-time freshmen who applied for aid, 971 were judged to have need. Of these, 941 received aid, and 39 had their full need met. Average financial aid package met 59% of need; average scholarship/grant was $7,688; average loan was $3,156. For part-time students, average financial aid package was $6,863.
Students without need: 49 full-time freshmen who did not demonstrate need for aid received scholarships/grants; average award was $3,576. No-need awards available for academics, alumni affiliation, art, athletics, job skills, leadership, music/drama, ROTC, state/district residency.
Scholarships offered: 48 full-time freshmen received athletic scholarships; average amount $5,342.
Cumulative student debt: 70% of graduating class had student loans; average debt was $21,902.

FINANCIAL AID PROCEDURES
Forms required: FAFSA.
Dates and Deadlines: Priority date 3/31; no closing date. Applicants notified on a rolling basis starting 5/1.

CONTACT
Ralph Perri, Director of Financial Aid
MSC 105, Kingsville, TX 78363-8201
(361) 593-3026

Texas A&M University-Texarkana

Texarkana, Texas
www.tamut.edu Federal Code: 031703

Upper-division public university in small city.
Enrollment: 1,401 undergrads.

BASIC COSTS (2012-2013)
Tuition and fees: $5,848; out-of-state residents $16,378.
Room and board: $7,190.

FINANCIAL AID PICTURE
Students with need: Need-based aid available for full-time and part-time students. Work study available nights, weekends, and for part-time students.
Students without need: No-need awards available for academics, leadership, state/district residency.

FINANCIAL AID PROCEDURES
Dates and Deadlines: Priority date 4/1; closing date 11/1.
Transfers: Applicants notified on a rolling basis; must reply within 10 week(s) of notification. Transfer students must have completed minimum of 54 semester hours of transferable college credit to apply for financial aid and notified applicants must reply within 45 days from date of award letter. Exceptions made on individual basis. April 1 financial aid deadline for scholarships.

CONTACT
Alyssa McClure, Director of Financial Aid
7101 University Avenue, Texarkana, TX 75505-5518
(903) 233-3060

Texas Christian University

Fort Worth, Texas
www.tcu.edu Federal Code: 003636

4-year private university in very large city, affiliated with Christian Church (Disciples of Christ).
Enrollment: 8,415 undergrads, 3% part-time. 1,854 full-time freshmen.
Selectivity: Admits less than 50% of applicants. GED not accepted.

BASIC COSTS (2012-2013)
Tuition and fees: $34,590.
Room and board: $10,650.
Additional info: Tuition/fee waivers available for adults, minority students.

FINANCIAL AID PICTURE (2012-2013)
Students with need: Out of 1,153 full-time freshmen who applied for aid, 746 were judged to have need. Of these, 735 received aid, and 228 had their full need met. Average financial aid package met 70% of need; average scholarship/grant was $18,555; average loan was $3,555. For part-time students, average financial aid package was $12,095.
Students without need: 491 full-time freshmen who did not demonstrate need for aid received scholarships/grants; average award was $13,166. No-need awards available for academics, alumni affiliation, art, minority status, music/drama, religious affiliation, ROTC, state/district residency.
Scholarships offered: 62 full-time freshmen received athletic scholarships; average amount $22,991.
Cumulative student debt: 41% of graduating class had student loans; average debt was $38,516.

FINANCIAL AID PROCEDURES
Forms required: FAFSA.
Dates and Deadlines: Closing date 5/1. Applicants notified on a rolling basis starting 3/15.
Transfers: Priority date 6/1. Applicants notified on a rolling basis starting 6/15.

CONTACT
Michael Scott, Director of Scholarships and Student Financial Aid
TCU Box 297013, Fort Worth, TX 76129
(817) 257-7858

Texas College

Tyler, Texas
www.texascollege.edu Federal Code: 003638

4-year private liberal arts college in small city, affiliated with Christian Methodist Episcopal Church.
Enrollment: 851 undergrads.
Selectivity: Open admission.

BASIC COSTS (2012-2013)
Tuition and fees: $9,682.
Room and board: $7,000.

FINANCIAL AID PICTURE
Students with need: Need-based aid available for full-time and part-time students.
Students without need: No-need awards available for academics, athletics, leadership, music/drama.

FINANCIAL AID PROCEDURES
Forms required: FAFSA, institutional form.
Dates and Deadlines: Priority date 6/1; no closing date. Applicants notified on a rolling basis starting 4/15.

CONTACT
Cecelia Jones, Director of Financial Aid
2404 North Grand Avenue, Tyler, TX 75712-4500
(903) 593-8311 ext. 2208

Texas Lutheran University

Seguin, Texas
www.tlu.edu Federal Code: 003641

4-year private university and liberal arts college in large town, affiliated with Evangelical Lutheran Church in America.
Enrollment: 1,269 undergrads, 2% part-time. 355 full-time freshmen.
Selectivity: Admits 50 to 75% of applicants.

BASIC COSTS (2013-2014)
Tuition and fees: $25,890.
Per-credit charge: $855.
Room and board: $8,180.

FINANCIAL AID PICTURE (2012-2013)
Students with need: Out of 337 full-time freshmen who applied for aid, 306 were judged to have need. Of these, 306 received aid, and 77 had their full need met. Average financial aid package met 83% of need; average scholarship/grant was $17,938; average loan was $4,089. For part-time students, average financial aid package was $7,590.
Students without need: 49 full-time freshmen who did not demonstrate need for aid received scholarships/grants; average award was $13,444. No-need awards available for academics, alumni affiliation, leadership, music/drama, religious affiliation.
Scholarships offered: National Merit Finalist Scholarship: full tuition; Pacesetter Award for College Excellence: up to $18,000 a year; Locus Aduro Award in Dramatic Media: up to $18,000 a year; Da capo Award in Music: up to $18,000 a year; TLU CHOICE Scholarship: difference between cost at TLU and University of Texas-Austin or Texas AM-College Station; Presidential Scholarship: up to $11,000 a year; Academic Excellence Award: up to $9,000 a year.

Cumulative student debt: 75% of graduating class had student loans; average debt was $37,145.

FINANCIAL AID PROCEDURES

Forms required: FAFSA.

Dates and Deadlines: Priority date 4/1; no closing date. Applicants notified on a rolling basis starting 3/1; must reply within 4 week(s) of notification.

Transfers: No deadline. Applicants notified on a rolling basis starting 3/1; must reply within 6 week(s) of notification.

CONTACT

Cathleen Wright, Director Financial Aid
1000 West Court Street, Seguin, TX 78155-5999
(830) 372-8075

Texas Southern University

Houston, Texas
www.tsu.edu Federal Code: 003642

4-year public university in very large city.
Enrollment: 7,021 undergrads, 16% part-time. 1,218 full-time freshmen.
Selectivity: Admits 50 to 75% of applicants.

BASIC COSTS (2012-2013)

Tuition and fees: $7,646; out-of-state residents $16,946.
Additional info: Tuition/fee waivers available for minority students.

FINANCIAL AID PICTURE (2011-2012)

Students with need: Need-based aid available for full-time and part-time students. Work study available nights, weekends, and for part-time students.
Students without need: This college awards aid only to students with need.

FINANCIAL AID PROCEDURES

Forms required: FAFSA.

Dates and Deadlines: Priority date 5/15; no closing date. Applicants notified on a rolling basis starting 6/1.

Transfers: Priority date 4/1; closing date 8/30.

CONTACT

Linda Ballard, Director of Financial Aid
3100 Cleburne Street, Houston, TX 77004
(713) 313-7071

Texas State Technical College: Harlingen

Harlingen, Texas
www.harlingen.tstc.edu Federal Code: 009225

2-year public technical college in small city.
Enrollment: 5,386 undergrads.
Selectivity: Open admission; but selective for some programs.

BASIC COSTS (2012-2013)

Tuition and fees: $4,065; out-of-state residents $9,000.
Room and board: $3,970.

FINANCIAL AID PICTURE

Students with need: Need-based aid available for full-time and part-time students.

FINANCIAL AID PROCEDURES

Forms required: FAFSA, institutional form.

Dates and Deadlines: Priority date 3/1; no closing date.

CONTACT

Mary Gallegos-Adams, Director of Financial Aid
1902 North Loop 499, Harlingen, TX 78550-3697
(956) 364-4337

Texas State Technical College: Waco

Waco, Texas
www.waco.tstc.edu Federal Code: 003634

2-year public technical college in small city.
Enrollment: 4,052 undergrads, 22% part-time. 916 full-time freshmen.
Selectivity: Open admission.

BASIC COSTS (2012-2013)

Tuition and fees: $4,200; out-of-state residents $9,000.
Room and board: $5,290.

FINANCIAL AID PICTURE

Students with need: Need-based aid available for full-time and part-time students.
Students without need: This college awards aid only to students with need.

FINANCIAL AID PROCEDURES

Forms required: FAFSA.

Dates and Deadlines: Priority date 6/1; no closing date. Applicants notified on a rolling basis starting 5/15.

Transfers: No deadline. Applicants notified on a rolling basis.

CONTACT

Jackie Adler, Director, Financial Aid
3801 Campus Drive, Waco, TX 76705
(254) 867-4814

Texas State Technical College: West Texas

Sweetwater, Texas
www.westtexas.tstc.edu Federal Code: 009932

2-year public technical college in large town.
Enrollment: 521 undergrads.
Selectivity: Open admission; but selective for some programs.

BASIC COSTS (2012-2013)

Tuition and fees: $4,200; out-of-state residents $9,000.
Room and board: $4,830.

FINANCIAL AID PICTURE

Students with need: Need-based aid available for full-time and part-time students. Work study available nights, weekends, and for part-time students.
Students without need: No-need awards available for academics, leadership.

FINANCIAL AID PROCEDURES

Forms required: FAFSA, institutional form.

Dates and Deadlines: Priority date 5/1; closing date 7/1. Applicants notified on a rolling basis starting 7/1.

Transfers: No deadline. Applicants notified on a rolling basis starting 7/1; must reply by 8/20.

CONTACT

Connie Chance, Director of Financial Aid
300 Homer K Taylor Drive, Sweetwater, TX 79556
(325) 235-7378

Texas State University: San Marcos

San Marcos, Texas
www.txstate.edu Federal Code: 003615

4-year public university in large town.
Enrollment: 29,458 undergrads, 18% part-time. 4,185 full-time freshmen.

Selectivity: Admits 50 to 75% of applicants.

BASIC COSTS (2012-2013)

Tuition and fees: $8,772; out-of-state residents $19,302.
Room and board: $7,070.

FINANCIAL AID PICTURE (2012-2013)

Students with need: Out of 3,704 full-time freshmen who applied for aid, 2,546 were judged to have need. Of these, 2,486 received aid, and 792 had their full need met. Average financial aid package met 72% of need; average scholarship/grant was $7,799; average loan was $5,247. For part-time students, average financial aid package was $9,242.
Students without need: 64 full-time freshmen who did not demonstrate need for aid received scholarships/grants; average award was $5,327. No-need awards available for academics, art, athletics, leadership, music/drama, ROTC, state/district residency.
Scholarships offered: ***Merit:*** Terry Foundation Scholarship: $12,500; 16 awarded. McCoy Scholarship of Excellence: $8,000; number awarded varies. McCoy Scholarship of Distinction: $5,000; number varies. University Scholars: $3,000; 8 awarded. Lone Star Scholarship: $2,500; 10 awarded. ***Athletic:*** 28 full-time freshmen received athletic scholarships; average amount $8,072.
Cumulative student debt: 62% of graduating class had student loans; average debt was $23,575.

FINANCIAL AID PROCEDURES

Forms required: FAFSA.
Dates and Deadlines: Priority date 4/1; no closing date. Applicants notified on a rolling basis starting 5/1; must reply within 3 week(s) of notification.

CONTACT

Christopher Murr, Director of Financial Aid & Scholarship Office
429 North Guadalupe Street, San Marcos, TX 78666-5709
(512) 245-2315

Texas Tech University

Lubbock, Texas
www.ttu.edu Federal Code: 003644

4-year public university in small city.
Enrollment: 26,276 undergrads, 10% part-time. 4,494 full-time freshmen.
Selectivity: Admits 50 to 75% of applicants.

BASIC COSTS (2012-2013)

Tuition and fees: $8,942; out-of-state residents $19,472.
Per-credit charge: $203; out-of-state residents $554.
Room and board: $8,275.

FINANCIAL AID PICTURE

Students with need: Need-based aid available for full-time and part-time students. Work study available nights, weekends, and for part-time students.
Students without need: No-need awards available for academics, art, athletics, job skills, leadership, music/drama, ROTC.
Scholarships offered: Presidential Scholarships: $6,000 per year, top 10% of high school graduating class and SAT 1400 or ACT 32; $4,000 per year, top 10% of high school class and SAT 1300 or ACT 29; $2,500 per year, top 10% of high school class and SAT 1250 or ACT 28; $5,000 per year, top 25%-11% of high school class and SAT 1500-1600 or ACT 34; $4,000 per year, top 25%-11% of high school class and SAT 1400-1500 or ACT 32-33; $3,000 per year, top 25%-11% of high school class and SAT 1300-1400 or ACT 29-31; $2,000 per year, top 25%-11% of high school class and SAT 1250-1300 or ACT 28; $2,000 per year, top 25% of high school class and SAT 1200-1250 or ACT 27. All are renewable for up to 4 years.
Additional info: Red Raider Guarantee program provides free tuition and mandatory fees for up to 15 credit hours per semester to new entering freshman who are Texas residents, enrolled full-time with family adjusted gross incomes that do not exceed $40,000. Eligible students who complete and submit the Free Application for Federal Student Aid (FAFSA) by required deadline are guaranteed to receive funds based on available state and federal allocations. Applications received after the deadline will be awarded based on available funding. Students may qualify for the program for up to eight (8) semesters of full-time enrollment.

FINANCIAL AID PROCEDURES

Forms required: FAFSA.
Dates and Deadlines: Closing date 3/15. Applicants notified on a rolling basis; must reply within 2 week(s) of notification.

CONTACT

Becky Wilson, Director of Financial Aid
Box 45005, Lubbock, TX 79409-5005
(806) 742-3681

Texas Tech University Health Sciences Center

Lubbock, Texas
www.ttuhsc.edu Federal Code: 010674

Upper-division public university in small city.
Enrollment: 1,305 undergrads, 9% part-time.

BASIC COSTS (2012-2013)

Tuition and fees: $7,533; out-of-state residents $18,063.
Additional info: Reported costs are for Allied Health Sciences and School of Nursing.

FINANCIAL AID PICTURE

Students with need: Need-based aid available for full-time and part-time students.
Students without need: No-need awards available for academics.

FINANCIAL AID PROCEDURES

Transfers: No deadline. Applicants notified on a rolling basis.

CONTACT

Marcus Wilson, Director, Financial Aid
3601 Fourth Street, Lubbock, TX 79430

Texas Wesleyan University

Fort Worth, Texas
www.txwes.edu Federal Code: 003645

4-year private university in large city, affiliated with United Methodist Church.
Enrollment: 1,517 undergrads, 19% part-time. 162 full-time freshmen.
Selectivity: Admits 50 to 75% of applicants.

BASIC COSTS (2013-2014)

Tuition and fees: $22,040.
Per-credit charge: $667.
Room and board: $7,846.

FINANCIAL AID PICTURE (2011-2012)

Students with need: Out of 141 full-time freshmen who applied for aid, 102 were judged to have need. Of these, 102 received aid, and 15 had their full need met. Average financial aid package met 63% of need; average scholarship/grant was $12,069; average loan was $3,100. For part-time students, average financial aid package was $8,432.
Students without need: This college awards aid only to students with need.
Scholarships offered: 8 full-time freshmen received athletic scholarships; average amount $6,129.

FINANCIAL AID PROCEDURES

Forms required: FAFSA.

Dates and Deadlines: Priority date 3/1; no closing date. Applicants notified on a rolling basis starting 3/1.

CONTACT

Laurie Rosenkrantz, Financial Aid Director
1201 Wesleyan Street, Fort Worth, TX 76105-1536
(817) 531-4420

Texas Woman's University

Denton, Texas
www.twu.edu Federal Code: 003646

4-year public university in small city.
Enrollment: 9,281 undergrads, 29% part-time. 1,135 full-time freshmen.
Selectivity: Admits over 75% of applicants.

BASIC COSTS (2013-2014)
Tuition and fees: $7,290; out-of-state residents $17,910.
Per-credit charge: $180; out-of-state residents $579.
Room and board: $7,119.

FINANCIAL AID PICTURE
Students with need: Need-based aid available for full-time and part-time students. Work study available nights, weekends, and for part-time students.
Scholarships offered: Chancellor's Endowed Scholarship: full tuition and fees, room and board; based on high school valedictorian status, extracurricular activities, SAT score; 2 awarded. Presidential Scholarship: full tuition and fees; awarded to valedictorian or salutatorian. Honors Scholarship: $1,500 annually up to 4 years; based on admission to honors program and SAT score. New Freshman Scholarship: $1,500 annually up to 4 years; based on SAT/ACT score, class rank and GPA. Transfer Student Scholarship: $1,500 annually up to 4 years; based on GPA, must have completed at least 12 credit hours. New Student Scholarship: $1,800 annually up to 4 years; based on high school rank, ACT/SAT score; 150 awarded.

FINANCIAL AID PROCEDURES
Forms required: FAFSA.
Dates and Deadlines: Priority date 4/1; no closing date. Must reply within 3 week(s) of notification.

CONTACT

Governor Jackson, Director of Financial Aid
Box 425589, Denton, TX 76204-5589
(940) 898-3064

Trinity University

San Antonio, Texas
www.trinity.edu Federal Code: 003647

4-year private university in very large city, affiliated with Presbyterian Church (USA).
Enrollment: 2,330 undergrads, 1% part-time. 596 full-time freshmen.
Selectivity: Admits 50 to 75% of applicants.

BASIC COSTS (2013-2014)
Tuition and fees: $35,262.
Per-credit charge: $1,423.
Room and board: $10,968.

FINANCIAL AID PICTURE (2012-2013)
Students with need: Out of 437 full-time freshmen who applied for aid, 338 were judged to have need. Of these, 337 received aid, and 125 had their full need met. Average financial aid package met 89% of need; average scholarship/grant was $23,064; average loan was $5,088. For part-time students, average financial aid package was $2,763.
Students without need: 209 full-time freshmen who did not demonstrate need for aid received scholarships/grants; average award was $14,255. No-need awards available for academics, leadership, music/drama.
Cumulative student debt: 46% of graduating class had student loans; average debt was $42,987.

FINANCIAL AID PROCEDURES
Forms required: FAFSA.
Dates and Deadlines: Priority date 2/15; closing date 4/1. Applicants notified by 4/1; must reply by 5/1 or within 3 week(s) of notification.
Transfers: Priority date 5/1; no deadline.

CONTACT

Glendi Gaddis, Director of Financial Aid
One Trinity Place, San Antonio, TX 78212-7200
(210) 999-8315

Trinity Valley Community College

Athens, Texas
www.tvcc.edu Federal Code: 003572

2-year public community college in large town.
Enrollment: 7,330 undergrads.
Selectivity: Open admission; but selective for some programs.

BASIC COSTS (2012-2013)
Tuition and fees: $2,100; out-of-district residents $3,540; out-of-state residents $4,380.
Per-credit charge: $30; out-of-district residents $78; out-of-state residents $106.
Room and board: $4,340.
Additional info: Tuition/fee waivers available for adults.

FINANCIAL AID PICTURE
Students with need: Need-based aid available for full-time and part-time students. Work study available nights, weekends, and for part-time students.
Students without need: No-need awards available for academics, athletics.

FINANCIAL AID PROCEDURES
Forms required: FAFSA, institutional form.
Dates and Deadlines: Closing date 7/1. Applicants notified on a rolling basis starting 7/1; must reply within 2 week(s) of notification.
Transfers: Students on suspension at previous institution ineligible to receive aid.

CONTACT

Julie Lively, Director, Student Financial Aid
100 Cardinal Drive, Athens, TX 75751
(903) 675-6233

Tyler Junior College

Tyler, Texas
www.tjc.edu Federal Code: 003648

2-year public community and junior college in small city.
Enrollment: 11,369 undergrads, 44% part-time. 2,316 full-time freshmen.
Selectivity: Open admission; but selective for some programs.

BASIC COSTS (2012-2013)
Tuition and fees: $2,262; out-of-district residents $3,642; out-of-state residents $4,242.
Per-credit charge: $30; out-of-district residents $76; out-of-state residents $96.
Room and board: $6,400.

FINANCIAL AID PICTURE
Students with need: Need-based aid available for full-time and part-time students.

FINANCIAL AID PROCEDURES

Dates and Deadlines: Priority date 6/1; no closing date. Applicants notified on a rolling basis starting 3/1; must reply within 2 week(s) of notification.

Transfers: Financial aid transcript required if student enrolled same year elsewhere.

CONTACT

Devon Wiggins, Director of Student Financial Aid and Scholarship
Box 9020, Tyler, TX 75711-9020
(903) 510-2385

University of Dallas

Irving, Texas
www.udallas.edu/index.html Federal Code: 003651

4-year private university and liberal arts college in small city, affiliated with Roman Catholic Church.

Enrollment: 1,353 undergrads, 2% part-time. 354 full-time freshmen.

Selectivity: Admits over 75% of applicants.

BASIC COSTS (2013-2014)

Tuition and fees: $33,010.

Per-credit charge: $1,300.

Room and board: $10,500.

FINANCIAL AID PICTURE

Students with need: Need-based aid available for full-time and part-time students.

Students without need: No-need awards available for academics, alumni affiliation, art, leadership, minority status, music/drama, religious affiliation, ROTC, state/district residency.

FINANCIAL AID PROCEDURES

Forms required: FAFSA.

Dates and Deadlines: Priority date 1/15; closing date 3/1. Applicants notified on a rolling basis starting 3/1; must reply by 5/1 or within 2 week(s) of notification.

Transfers: Priority date 4/1; closing date 7/15. Must reply by 5/1 or within 2 week(s) of notification.

CONTACT

Taryn Anderson, Director of Financial Aid
1845 East Northgate Drive, Irving, TX 75062-4736
(972) 721-5266

University of Houston

Houston, Texas
www.uh.edu Federal Code: 003652

4-year public university in very large city.

Enrollment: 31,367 undergrads, 26% part-time. 3,350 full-time freshmen.

Selectivity: Admits 50 to 75% of applicants.

BASIC COSTS (2012-2013)

Tuition and fees: $9,888; out-of-state residents $20,418.

Per-credit charge: $299; out-of-state residents $650.

Room and board: $8,753.

FINANCIAL AID PICTURE (2012-2013)

Students with need: Out of 2,648 full-time freshmen who applied for aid, 2,173 were judged to have need. Of these, 2,102 received aid, and 492 had their full need met. Average financial aid package met 76% of need; average scholarship/grant was $9,724; average loan was $5,295. For part-time students, average financial aid package was $10,737.

Students without need: 261 full-time freshmen who did not demonstrate need for aid received scholarships/grants; average award was $5,814. No-need awards available for academics, alumni affiliation, art, athletics, job skills, leadership, music/drama, ROTC, state/district residency.

Scholarships offered: 49 full-time freshmen received athletic scholarships; average amount $6,478.

Cumulative student debt: 47% of graduating class had student loans; average debt was $16,582.

Additional info: The Cougar Promise guarantees free tuition and mandatory fees to new in-state freshmen with family incomes at or below $45,000. Qualifying students will have tuition and fees guaranteed for up to four years as long as students continue to meet eligibility criteria and maintain at least a 2.5 GPA. Covers tuition and fees during the fall and spring semesters only. Eligibility is determined when a student fills out the FAFSA. Those who miss the April 1 deadline will be awarded based on the availability of funds.

FINANCIAL AID PROCEDURES

Forms required: FAFSA.

Dates and Deadlines: Priority date 4/1; no closing date. Applicants notified on a rolling basis starting 5/1.

Transfers: Applicants notified on a rolling basis starting 4/1; must reply by 7/1.

CONTACT

Sal Loria, Executive Director
Office of Admission, Houston, TX 77004
(713) 743-1010

University of Houston-Clear Lake

Houston, Texas
www.uhcl.edu Federal Code: 011711

Upper-division public university in very large city.

Enrollment: 4,689 undergrads, 54% part-time.

BASIC COSTS (2012-2013)

Tuition and fees: $6,514; out-of-state residents $18,364.

FINANCIAL AID PICTURE

Students with need: Need-based aid available for full-time and part-time students. Work study available nights, weekends, and for part-time students.

Students without need: No-need awards available for academics, leadership, state/district residency.

Scholarships offered: UCHL will begin accepting its first freshman class Fall 2014. Non-need, merit based scholarships will be available to entering freshmen.

Additional info: UHCL offers the automatic transfer scholarship to any first-time transfer student if their transfer GPA is 2.75 or above upon receiving all transcripts. No application necessary for the scholarship.

FINANCIAL AID PROCEDURES

Forms required: FAFSA.

Dates and Deadlines: Applicants notified on a rolling basis starting 6/4; must reply within 4 week(s) of notification.

Transfers: Priority date 3/15; no deadline. Applicants notified on a rolling basis starting 5/15; must reply within 4 week(s) of notification.

CONTACT

Billy Satterfield, Director of Student Financial Aid
2700 Bay Area Boulevard, Houston, TX 77058-1098
(281) 283-2481

University of Houston-Downtown

Houston, Texas
www.uhd.edu Federal Code: 003612

4-year public university in very large city.

Enrollment: 13,549 undergrads, 50% part-time. 1,157 full-time freshmen.

Selectivity: Admits over 75% of applicants.

BASIC COSTS (2012-2013)

Tuition and fees: $5,997; out-of-state residents $16,527.

Per-credit charge: $163; out-of-state residents $514.

Additional info: Tuition rates for College of Business courses that could count toward a Bachelor of Business Administration degree are an additional $2 per credit hour ($164.50 per hour for residents and $515.50 per hour for nonresident students).

FINANCIAL AID PICTURE

Students with need: Need-based aid available for full-time and part-time students. Work study available nights, weekends, and for part-time students.

Students without need: No-need awards available for academics, leadership.

FINANCIAL AID PROCEDURES

Forms required: FAFSA.

Dates and Deadlines: Priority date 4/1; no closing date. Applicants notified on a rolling basis starting 4/15; must reply within 4 week(s) of notification.

Transfers: No deadline. Applicants notified on a rolling basis starting 4/15; must reply within 4 week(s) of notification.

CONTACT

LaTasha Goudeau, Director of Scholarships and Financial Aid
One Main Street, Suite 350-S, Houston, TX 77002
(713) 221-8041

University of Houston-Victoria

Victoria, Texas
www.uhv.edu Federal Code: 013231

4-year public university in small city.

Enrollment: 2,651 undergrads.

Selectivity: Admits 50 to 75% of applicants.

BASIC COSTS (2012-2013)

Tuition and fees: $6,117; out-of-state residents $16,646.

Per-credit charge: $160; out-of-state residents $511.

FINANCIAL AID PICTURE

Students with need: Need-based aid available for full-time and part-time students. Work study available weekends and for part-time students.

Students without need: No-need awards available for academics, athletics, leadership, state/district residency.

Additional info: Short-term loans available at registration.

FINANCIAL AID PROCEDURES

Forms required: FAFSA, institutional form.

Dates and Deadlines: Closing date 3/15. Applicants notified on a rolling basis starting 3/30; must reply within 3 week(s) of notification.

Transfers: No deadline. Applicants notified on a rolling basis; must reply within 3 week(s) of notification.

CONTACT

Carolyn Mallory, Financial Aid Director
3007 North Ben Wilson, Victoria, TX 77901-4450
(361) 570-4131

University of Mary Hardin-Baylor

Belton, Texas
www.umhb.edu Federal Code: 003588

4-year private university in large town, affiliated with Baptist faith.

Enrollment: 2,921 undergrads, 9% part-time. 626 full-time freshmen.

Selectivity: Admits 50 to 75% of applicants.

BASIC COSTS (2013-2014)

Tuition and fees: $25,200.

Per-credit charge: $765.

Room and board: $6,750.

Additional info: Tuition/fee waivers available for minority students.

FINANCIAL AID PICTURE (2012-2013)

Students with need: Average financial aid package met 64% of need; average scholarship/grant was $13,838; average loan was $3,513. For part-time students, average financial aid package was $8,137.

Students without need: No-need awards available for academics, art, leadership, music/drama, religious affiliation, ROTC.

Cumulative student debt: 77% of graduating class had student loans; average debt was $37,890.

FINANCIAL AID PROCEDURES

Forms required: FAFSA.

Dates and Deadlines: Priority date 3/1; no closing date. Applicants notified on a rolling basis starting 2/1; must reply within 2 week(s) of notification.

Transfers: No deadline. Applicants notified on a rolling basis starting 11/1; must reply within 2 week(s) of notification.

CONTACT

Ron Brown, Director of Financial Aid
900 College Street, Belton, TX 76513
(254) 295-4517

University of North Texas

Denton, Texas
www.unt.edu Federal Code: 003594

4-year public university in small city.

Enrollment: 28,956 undergrads, 19% part-time. 4,171 full-time freshmen.

Selectivity: Admits 50 to 75% of applicants.

BASIC COSTS (2012-2013)

Tuition and fees: $8,717; out-of-state residents $19,247.

Per-credit charge: $216; out-of-state residents $567.

Room and board: $7,150.

FINANCIAL AID PICTURE (2012-2013)

Students with need: Out of 3,572 full-time freshmen who applied for aid, 2,704 were judged to have need. Of these, 2,665 received aid, and 605 had their full need met. Average financial aid package met 76% of need; average scholarship/grant was $7,989; average loan was $3,247. For part-time students, average financial aid package was $7,654.

Students without need: 691 full-time freshmen who did not demonstrate need for aid received scholarships/grants; average award was $4,051.

Scholarships offered: 21 full-time freshmen received athletic scholarships; average amount $11,391.

FINANCIAL AID PROCEDURES

Forms required: FAFSA.

Dates and Deadlines: Priority date 3/31; no closing date. Applicants notified on a rolling basis starting 4/1.

CONTACT

Zelma DeLeon, Director of Financial Aid
1401 West Prairie, Suite 309, Denton, TX 76203-5017
(940) 565-2302

University of St. Thomas

Houston, Texas
www.stthom.edu Federal Code: 003654

4-year private university and liberal arts college in very large city, affiliated with Roman Catholic Church.

Enrollment: 1,552 undergrads, 20% part-time. 265 full-time freshmen.
Selectivity: Admits over 75% of applicants.

BASIC COSTS (2013-2014)
Tuition and fees: $28,240.
Per-credit charge: $930.
Room and board: $8,250.

FINANCIAL AID PICTURE (2012-2013)
Students with need: Out of 201 full-time freshmen who applied for aid, 173 were judged to have need. Of these, 172 received aid, and 26 had their full need met. Average financial aid package met 72% of need; average scholarship/grant was $15,966; average loan was $3,343. For part-time students, average financial aid package was $6,790.
Students without need: 88 full-time freshmen who did not demonstrate need for aid received scholarships/grants; average award was $11,234. No-need awards available for academics, athletics, music/drama, religious affiliation, ROTC.
Scholarships offered: 6 full-time freshmen received athletic scholarships; average amount $2,667.
Cumulative student debt: 58% of graduating class had student loans; average debt was $33,936.

FINANCIAL AID PROCEDURES
Forms required: FAFSA.
Dates and Deadlines: Priority date 4/15; no closing date. Applicants notified on a rolling basis starting 2/15; must reply within 2 week(s) of notification.

CONTACT
Lynda McKendree, Dean of Scholarships and Financial Aid
3800 Montrose Boulevard, Houston, TX 77006-4626
(713) 942-3465

University of Texas at Arlington
Arlington, Texas
www.uta.edu Federal Code: 003656

4-year public university in large city.
Enrollment: 25,487 undergrads, 37% part-time. 2,413 full-time freshmen.
Selectivity: Admits 50 to 75% of applicants. GED not accepted.

BASIC COSTS (2012-2013)
Tuition and fees: $8,878; out-of-state residents $19,408.
Room and board: $7,708.

FINANCIAL AID PICTURE (2012-2013)
Students with need: Out of 1,949 full-time freshmen who applied for aid, 1,667 were judged to have need. Of these, 1,667 received aid, and 346 had their full need met. Average financial aid package met 76% of need; average scholarship/grant was $7,219; average loan was $3,286. For part-time students, average financial aid package was $10,606.
Students without need: 117 full-time freshmen who did not demonstrate need for aid received scholarships/grants; average award was $5,413. No-need awards available for academics, art, athletics, leadership, music/drama, ROTC.
Scholarships offered: ***Merit:*** Academic Scholarships: $1,000-$4,000 per year, renewable; based on minimum SAT 1050 (exclusive of Writing) or ACT 22, top 25% of high school class. ***Athletic:*** 2 full-time freshmen received athletic scholarships; average amount $5,150.
Cumulative student debt: 63% of graduating class had student loans; average debt was $22,137.
Additional info: Free tuition to eligible students whose household income is $65,000 or less through the Maverick Promise program.

FINANCIAL AID PROCEDURES
Forms required: FAFSA.
Dates and Deadlines: Priority date 4/15; no closing date. Applicants notified on a rolling basis starting 4/1; must reply within 3 week(s) of notification.
Transfers: Must reply within 3 week(s) of notification. To receive Texas grant or Texas B on Time loan, student must have either received Texas grant or completed associates degree at prior school.

CONTACT
Karen Krause, Director of Financial Aid
UTA Box 19088, Arlington, TX 76019
(817) 272-3561

University of Texas at Austin
Austin, Texas
www.utexas.edu Federal Code: 003658

4-year public university in very large city.
Enrollment: 39,215 undergrads, 6% part-time. 8,090 full-time freshmen.
Selectivity: Admits less than 50% of applicants.

BASIC COSTS (2012-2013)
Tuition and fees: $9,792; out-of-state residents $33,060.
Room and board: $10,946.

FINANCIAL AID PICTURE (2012-2013)
Students with need: Out of 6,126 full-time freshmen who applied for aid, 3,868 were judged to have need. Of these, 3,865 received aid, and 1,235 had their full need met. Average financial aid package met 78% of need; average scholarship/grant was $9,204; average loan was $3,601. Need-based aid available for part-time students.
Students without need: 111 full-time freshmen who did not demonstrate need for aid received scholarships/grants; average award was $6,031. No-need awards available for academics, art, athletics, leadership, music/drama, ROTC, state/district residency.
Cumulative student debt: 50% of graduating class had student loans; average debt was $26,097.

FINANCIAL AID PROCEDURES
Forms required: FAFSA, institutional form.
Dates and Deadlines: Priority date 3/31; no closing date. Applicants notified on a rolling basis starting 3/15; must reply by 5/1 or within 3 week(s) of notification.
Transfers: Limited number of scholarship funds available for transfer students.

CONTACT
Thomas Melecki, Director of Student Financial Services
PO Box 8058, Austin, TX 78713-8058
(512) 475-6282

University of Texas at Brownsville - Texas Southmost College
Brownsville, Texas
www.utb.edu Federal Code: 030646

4-year public university and community college in small city.
Enrollment: 10,751 undergrads.
Selectivity: Open admission; but selective for some programs.

BASIC COSTS (2012-2013)
Tuition and fees: $6,153; out-of-state residents $16,683.
Per-credit charge: $156; out-of-state residents $507.
Room and board: $6,602.

FINANCIAL AID PICTURE (2011-2012)
Students with need: 62% of average financial aid package awarded as scholarships/grants, 38% awarded as loans/jobs. Need-based aid available for part-time students. Work study available nights.

Students without need: No-need awards available for academics, alumni affiliation, art, athletics, minority status, music/drama, state/district residency.

FINANCIAL AID PROCEDURES

Forms required: FAFSA.

Dates and Deadlines: Priority date 3/1; closing date 8/15. Applicants notified by 5/1; must reply by 7/1 or within 12 week(s) of notification.

CONTACT

Mary Comerota, Director of Financial Aid
80 Fort Brown, Brownsville, TX 78520
(956) 882-8277

University of Texas at Dallas

Richardson, Texas
www.utdallas.edu Federal Code: 009741

4-year public university in very large city.
Enrollment: 11,749 undergrads, 20% part-time. 1,761 full-time freshmen.
Selectivity: Admits 50 to 75% of applicants.

BASIC COSTS (2012-2013)

Tuition and fees: $11,592; out-of-state residents $29,266.
Room and board: $9,050.
Additional info: Tuition and fees reflect the Guaranteed Tuition rate for incoming students enrolled for the first time during the Fall 2012 term. Tuition at time of enrollment locked for 4 years.

FINANCIAL AID PICTURE (2011-2012)

Students with need: Out of 1,230 full-time freshmen who applied for aid, 947 were judged to have need. Of these, 930 received aid, and 310 had their full need met. Average financial aid package met 77% of need; average scholarship/grant was $11,138; average loan was $3,284. For part-time students, average financial aid package was $6,941.

Students without need: 543 full-time freshmen who did not demonstrate need for aid received scholarships/grants; average award was $13,418. No-need awards available for academics.

Scholarships offered: Eugene McDermott Scholars Program Awards: full tuition and fees plus domestic and international travel costs for enhancement of scholar's education; based on being in top 10% of high school class, high scores on entrance exams, evidence of leadership abilities; 20 awarded. Academic Excellence Scholarships: based on SAT/ACT, class rank, high school GPA, AP/Honors work; Achievement level is $3,000/year, Distinction covers tuition/mandatory fees, Honors covers tuition/mandatory fees plus $3,000 stipend.

Cumulative student debt: 36% of graduating class had student loans; average debt was $17,516.

FINANCIAL AID PROCEDURES

Forms required: FAFSA.

Dates and Deadlines: Priority date 3/31; closing date 4/12. Applicants notified on a rolling basis starting 3/1; must reply within 2 week(s) of notification.

Transfers: Priority date 4/1. Applicants notified on a rolling basis; must reply within 2 week(s) of notification.

CONTACT

Beth Tolan, Director of Financial Aid
Admission and Enrollment Services, Richardson, TX 75080-3021
(972) 883-2941

University of Texas at El Paso

El Paso, Texas
www.utep.edu Federal Code: 003661

4-year public university in very large city.
Enrollment: 19,078 undergrads, 34% part-time. 2,689 full-time freshmen.
Selectivity: Admits over 75% of applicants.

BASIC COSTS (2012-2013)

Tuition and fees: $7,018; out-of-state residents $17,548.
Per-credit charge: $186; out-of-state residents $537.
Additional info: Optional a la carte meal plan available. Cost of room only, $4,725.

FINANCIAL AID PICTURE (2011-2012)

Students with need: Out of 2,507 full-time freshmen who applied for aid, 2,187 were judged to have need. Of these, 2,163 received aid, and 316 had their full need met. Average financial aid package met 79% of need; average scholarship/grant was $11,956; average loan was $4,156. For part-time students, average financial aid package was $10,584.

Students without need: 118 full-time freshmen who did not demonstrate need for aid received scholarships/grants; average award was $2,650. No-need awards available for academics, alumni affiliation, art, athletics, job skills, leadership, minority status, music/drama, religious affiliation, ROTC, state/district residency.

Scholarships offered: 24 full-time freshmen received athletic scholarships; average amount $7,573.

Cumulative student debt: 61% of graduating class had student loans; average debt was $21,123.

Additional info: Emergency loans available.

FINANCIAL AID PROCEDURES

Forms required: FAFSA, institutional form.

Dates and Deadlines: Closing date 3/15. Applicants notified by 6/30; must reply within 2 week(s) of notification.

Transfers: No deadline. Must reply within 2 week(s) of notification.

CONTACT

Raul Lerma, Director of Financial Aid
500 West University Avenue, El Paso, TX 79968-0510
(915) 747-5204

University of Texas at San Antonio

San Antonio, Texas
www.utsa.edu Federal Code: 010115

4-year public university in very large city.
Enrollment: 25,344 undergrads, 17% part-time. 4,901 full-time freshmen.
Selectivity: Admits 50 to 75% of applicants.

BASIC COSTS (2012-2013)

Tuition and fees: $8,419; out-of-state residents $18,949.
Per-credit charge: $198; out-of-state residents $549.
Room and board: $9,693.

FINANCIAL AID PICTURE (2011-2012)

Students with need: Out of 3,922 full-time freshmen who applied for aid, 3,074 were judged to have need. Of these, 3,024 received aid, and 709 had their full need met. Average financial aid package met 61% of need; average scholarship/grant was $7,557; average loan was $3,207. For part-time students, average financial aid package was $5,566.

Students without need: 609 full-time freshmen who did not demonstrate need for aid received scholarships/grants; average award was $1,518. No-need awards available for academics, alumni affiliation, art, athletics, job skills, leadership, music/drama, ROTC, state/district residency.

Scholarships offered: 105 full-time freshmen received athletic scholarships; average amount $8,557.

Cumulative student debt: 65% of graduating class had student loans; average debt was $25,140.

FINANCIAL AID PROCEDURES

Forms required: FAFSA, institutional form.

Dates and Deadlines: Priority date 3/15; no closing date. Applicants notified on a rolling basis starting 4/1; must reply within 4 week(s) of notification.

Transfers: No deadline. Applicants notified on a rolling basis starting 4/1; must reply within 4 week(s) of notification.

CONTACT

Lisa Blazer, Assistant Vice President of Financial Aid
One UTSA Circle, San Antonio, TX 78249-0617
(210) 458-7828

University of Texas at Tyler

Tyler, Texas
www.uttyler.edu Federal Code: 011163

4-year public university in small city.
Enrollment: 5,226 undergrads, 22% part-time. 625 full-time freshmen.
Selectivity: Admits over 75% of applicants.

BASIC COSTS (2012-2013)
Tuition and fees: $7,222; out-of-state residents $17,752.
Per-credit charge: $50; out-of-state residents $401.
Room and board: $8,979.

FINANCIAL AID PICTURE
Students with need: Need-based aid available for full-time and part-time students.
Students without need: No-need awards available for academics, art, music/drama.
Additional info: Apply early for all programs.

FINANCIAL AID PROCEDURES
Forms required: FAFSA, institutional form.
Dates and Deadlines: Priority date 4/1; no closing date. Applicants notified on a rolling basis starting 4/15; must reply within 2 week(s) of notification.

CONTACT

Marquita Hackett, Director of Student Financial Aid
3900 University Boulevard, Tyler, TX 75799
(903) 566-7180

University of Texas Health Science Center at Houston

Houston, Texas
www.uth.tmc.edu Federal Code: 013956

Upper-division public university and health science college in very large city.
Enrollment: 563 undergrads.

BASIC COSTS (2012-2013)
Tuition and fees: $6,985; out-of-state residents $23,995.
Additional info: Costs may vary by program.

FINANCIAL AID PICTURE
Students with need: Need-based aid available for full-time and part-time students.
Students without need: This college awards aid only to students with need.

FINANCIAL AID PROCEDURES
Forms required: FAFSA, institutional form.
Dates and Deadlines: Applicants notified on a rolling basis starting 6/1.

CONTACT

Wanda Williams, Director of Student Financial Aid
Box 20036, Houston, TX 77225
(713) 500-3860

University of Texas Medical Branch at Galveston

Galveston, Texas
www.utmb.edu Federal Code: 013976

Upper-division public health science and nursing college in large town.
Enrollment: 676 undergrads, 24% part-time.

BASIC COSTS (2012-2013)
Tuition and fees: $6,283; out-of-state residents $16,948.
Additional info: Costs reported are for undergraduate Allied Health Sciences program. Tuition and fees vary for other programs.

FINANCIAL AID PICTURE
Students with need: Need-based aid available for full-time and part-time students. Work study available nights, weekends, and for part-time students.
Students without need: No-need awards available for academics, minority status, state/district residency.

FINANCIAL AID PROCEDURES
Forms required: FAFSA.
Dates and Deadlines: Applicants notified on a rolling basis; must reply within 4 week(s) of notification.

CONTACT

Carol Cromie, Assistant Director of Enrollment Services for Financial Aid
301 University Boulevard, Galveston, TX 77555-1305
(409) 772-1215

University of Texas of the Permian Basin

Odessa, Texas
www.utpb.edu Federal Code: 009930

4-year public university in small city.
Enrollment: 2,704 undergrads, 26% part-time. 318 full-time freshmen.
Selectivity: Admits over 75% of applicants.

BASIC COSTS (2012-2013)
Tuition and fees: $6,458; out-of-state residents $16,988.
Per-credit charge: $168; out-of-state residents $519.

FINANCIAL AID PICTURE (2011-2012)
Students with need: Out of 273 full-time freshmen who applied for aid, 229 were judged to have need. Of these, 229 received aid, and 45 had their full need met. Average financial aid package met 80% of need; average scholarship/grant was $4,907; average loan was $2,727. For part-time students, average financial aid package was $7,002.
Students without need: 76 full-time freshmen who did not demonstrate need for aid received scholarships/grants; average award was $2,862. No-need awards available for academics, art, athletics, leadership, music/drama.
Scholarships offered: 6 full-time freshmen received athletic scholarships; average amount $3,291.
Cumulative student debt: 50% of graduating class had student loans; average debt was $14,629.

FINANCIAL AID PROCEDURES
Forms required: FAFSA.
Dates and Deadlines: Priority date 3/15; no closing date. Applicants notified on a rolling basis starting 3/15.

CONTACT

Joe Sanders, Director of Financial Aid
4901 East University, Odessa, TX 79762
(432) 552-2620

University of Texas-Pan American

Edinburg, Texas
www.utpa.edu Federal Code: 003599

4-year public university in small city.
Enrollment: 16,731 undergrads, 26% part-time. 2,870 full-time freshmen.
Selectivity: Admits 50 to 75% of applicants.

BASIC COSTS (2012-2013)
Tuition and fees: $6,124; out-of-state residents $16,654.
Per-credit charge: $174; out-of-state residents $525.
Room and board: $5,656.

FINANCIAL AID PICTURE (2011-2012)
Students with need: Out of 2,528 full-time freshmen who applied for aid, 2,405 were judged to have need. Of these, 2,405 received aid, and 137 had their full need met. Average financial aid package met 75% of need; average scholarship/grant was $10,577; average loan was $3,124. For part-time students, average financial aid package was $6,208.
Students without need: 62 full-time freshmen who did not demonstrate need for aid received scholarships/grants; average award was $3,673. No-need awards available for academics, alumni affiliation, art, athletics, leadership.
Scholarships offered: 14 full-time freshmen received athletic scholarships; average amount $7,191.
Cumulative student debt: 62% of graduating class had student loans; average debt was $15,257.

FINANCIAL AID PROCEDURES
Forms required: FAFSA.
Dates and Deadlines: Priority date 4/1; no closing date. Applicants notified on a rolling basis starting 3/15; must reply within 2 week(s) of notification.
Transfers: Priority date 3/1; no deadline. Applicants notified on a rolling basis; must reply within 2 week(s) of notification.

CONTACT
Elaine Rivera, Executive Director of Student Financial Services
1201 West University Drive, Edinburg, TX 78539-2999
(956) 665-2501

University of the Incarnate Word

San Antonio, Texas
www.uiw.edu Federal Code: 003578

4-year private university in very large city, affiliated with Roman Catholic Church.
Enrollment: 6,287 undergrads, 31% part-time. 1,023 full-time freshmen.
Selectivity: Admits over 75% of applicants.

BASIC COSTS (2013-2014)
Tuition and fees: $24,790.
Per-credit charge: $785.
Room and board: $10,410.

FINANCIAL AID PICTURE (2011-2012)
Students with need: Out of 925 full-time freshmen who applied for aid, 852 were judged to have need. Of these, 852 received aid, and 240 had their full need met. Average financial aid package met 70% of need; average scholarship/grant was $15,071; average loan was $3,235. For part-time students, average financial aid package was $6,766.
Students without need: 73 full-time freshmen who did not demonstrate need for aid received scholarships/grants; average award was $9,218. No-need awards available for academics, alumni affiliation, art, athletics, leadership, music/drama, religious affiliation, ROTC, state/district residency.
Scholarships offered: 6 full-time freshmen received athletic scholarships; average amount $1,033.

Additional info: Students encouraged to pursue outside scholarship programs.

FINANCIAL AID PROCEDURES
Forms required: FAFSA.
Dates and Deadlines: Priority date 4/1; no closing date. Applicants notified on a rolling basis starting 2/15; must reply within 2 week(s) of notification.

CONTACT
Amy Carcanagues, Director of Financial Assistance
4301 Broadway, San Antonio, TX 78209-6397
(210) 829-6008

Vernon College

Vernon, Texas
www.vernoncollege.edu Federal Code: 010060

2-year public community and junior college in large town.
Enrollment: 2,553 undergrads.
Selectivity: Open admission; but selective for some programs.

BASIC COSTS (2012-2013)
Tuition and fees: $2,580; out-of-district residents $3,840; out-of-state residents $5,940.
Room and board: $3,635.

FINANCIAL AID PICTURE
Students with need: Need-based aid available for full-time and part-time students. Work study available nights, weekends, and for part-time students.
Students without need: This college awards aid only to students with need.

FINANCIAL AID PROCEDURES
Forms required: FAFSA.
Dates and Deadlines: Priority date 7/1; no closing date. Applicants notified on a rolling basis starting 4/1.
Transfers: No deadline. Applicants notified on a rolling basis.

CONTACT
Melissa Elliott, Director of Financial Aid
4400 College Drive, Vernon, TX 76384-4092
(940) 552-6291

Vet Tech Institute of Houston

Houston, Texas
www.bradfordschools.com

2-year for-profit technical college in very large city.
Enrollment: 239 undergrads.

FINANCIAL AID PICTURE
Students with need: Need-based aid available for full-time students.

CONTACT
4669 Southwest Freeway, Houston, TX 77027

Wade College

Dallas, Texas
www.wadecollege.edu Federal Code: 010130

2-year for-profit business and career college in very large city.
Enrollment: 265 undergrads.
Selectivity: Open admission; but selective for some programs.

BASIC COSTS (2012-2013)
Tuition and fees: $11,725.

Additional info: Tuition includes textbooks, supplies, and the majority of fees. Tuition at time of enrollment locked for 2 years.

FINANCIAL AID PICTURE

Students with need: Need-based aid available for full-time and part-time students.

Students without need: This college awards aid only to students with need.

FINANCIAL AID PROCEDURES

Forms required: FAFSA.

Dates and Deadlines: Applicants notified on a rolling basis; must reply within 4 week(s) of notification.

CONTACT

Lisa Hoover, Director of Financial Services
Dallas Market Center, PO Box 421149, Dallas, TX 75342
(214) 637-3530

Wayland Baptist University

Plainview, Texas
www.wbu.edu Federal Code: 003663

4-year private university and liberal arts college in large town, affiliated with Southern Baptist Convention.

Enrollment: 1,255 undergrads, 19% part-time. 362 full-time freshmen.

Selectivity: Admits over 75% of applicants.

BASIC COSTS (2013-2014)

Tuition and fees: $14,630.

Per-credit charge: $455.

Room and board: $4,794.

FINANCIAL AID PICTURE (2012-2013)

Students with need: Out of 250 full-time freshmen who applied for aid, 221 were judged to have need. Of these, 220 received aid, and 15 had their full need met. Average financial aid package met 62% of need; average scholarship/grant was $9,244; average loan was $3,082. For part-time students, average financial aid package was $7,294.

Students without need: 41 full-time freshmen who did not demonstrate need for aid received scholarships/grants; average award was $6,407. No-need awards available for academics, alumni affiliation, art, athletics, leadership, music/drama.

Scholarships offered: 24 full-time freshmen received athletic scholarships; average amount $7,162.

Cumulative student debt: 82% of graduating class had student loans; average debt was $21,981.

FINANCIAL AID PROCEDURES

Forms required: FAFSA, institutional form.

Dates and Deadlines: Priority date 5/1; no closing date. Applicants notified on a rolling basis starting 1/1; must reply within 2 week(s) of notification.

Transfers: No deadline. Applicants notified on a rolling basis.

CONTACT

Karen LaQuey, Director of Financial Aid
1900 West Seventh Street, CMB #1294, Plainview, TX 79072
(806) 291-3520

Weatherford College

Weatherford, Texas
www.wc.edu Federal Code: 003664

2-year public community college in large town.

Enrollment: 1,864 full-time undergrads.

Selectivity: Open admission; but selective for some programs.

BASIC COSTS (2012-2013)

Tuition and fees: $2,130; out-of-district residents $3,210; out-of-state residents $4,860.

Room and board: $7,180.

FINANCIAL AID PICTURE

Students with need: Work study available nights, weekends, and for part-time students.

Students without need: This college awards aid only to students with need.

FINANCIAL AID PROCEDURES

Forms required: FAFSA.

Dates and Deadlines: Priority date 7/3; no closing date. Applicants notified on a rolling basis; must reply within 2 week(s) of notification.

CONTACT

Donnie Purvis, Director, Financial Aid
225 College Park Drive, Weatherford, TX 76086
(817) 598-6295

West Coast University: Dallas

Dallas, Texas
www.westcoastuniversity.edu Federal Code: 036983

2-year for-profit branch campus and nursing college in very large city.

Enrollment: 170 undergrads, 49% part-time. 2 full-time freshmen.

Selectivity: Open admission; but selective for some programs.

BASIC COSTS (2012-2013)

Tuition and fees: $24,600.

Per-credit charge: $1,360.

FINANCIAL AID PICTURE (2012-2013)

Students with need: 16% of average financial aid package awarded as scholarships/grants, 84% awarded as loans/jobs. Need-based aid available for part-time students. Work study available nights, weekends, and for part-time students.

Students without need: No-need awards available for academics.

FINANCIAL AID PROCEDURES

Forms required: FAFSA, institutional form.

Dates and Deadlines: Closing date 6/30. Applicants notified on a rolling basis.

CONTACT

Monita Saunders, Director of Financial Aid
8435 North Stemmons Freeway, Dallas, TX 75247
(214) 453-4533

West Texas A&M University

Canyon, Texas
www.wtamu.edu Federal Code: 003665

4-year public university in large town.

Enrollment: 6,535 undergrads, 20% part-time. 1,199 full-time freshmen.

Selectivity: Admits 50 to 75% of applicants.

BASIC COSTS (2012-2013)

Tuition and fees: $6,730; out-of-state residents $7,620.

Per-credit charge: $156; out-of-state residents $186.

Room and board: $6,912.

Additional info: All out-of-state students pay border state tuition rate (in-state cost plus $30 per semester credit hour), with the exception of international students.

FINANCIAL AID PICTURE

Students with need: Need-based aid available for full-time and part-time students. Work study available nights, weekends, and for part-time students.

Students without need: No-need awards available for academics, art, athletics, leadership, music/drama.

Additional info: Scholarship deadline February 1.

FINANCIAL AID PROCEDURES

Forms required: FAFSA.

Dates and Deadlines: Priority date 4/15; no closing date. Applicants notified on a rolling basis starting 3/1; must reply within 2 week(s) of notification.

Transfers: No deadline. Applicants notified on a rolling basis; must reply within 2 week(s) of notification. Must provide financial aid transcripts through last semester of attendance. All academic transcripts must be on file.

CONTACT

Jim Reed, Director of Financial Aid
2501 Fourth Avenue, WTAMU Box 60907, Canyon, TX 79016-0001
(806) 651-2055

Western Technical College

El Paso, Texas
www.westerntech.edu Federal Code: 014535

2-year for-profit technical college in very large city.
Enrollment: 691 undergrads.
Selectivity: Open admission; but selective for some programs.

BASIC COSTS (2013-2014)

Additional info: Tuition varies by program: Automotive technology, $26,480; Refrigeration/HVAC Technology, $26,480; Diesel Technology, $26,480; Advanced Welding Technology, $27.930; Medical/Clinical Assistant, $13,080. Registration fee $100.

FINANCIAL AID PICTURE (2012-2013)

Students with need: Need-based aid available for full-time and part-time students.

Students without need: This college awards aid only to students with need.

FINANCIAL AID PROCEDURES

Forms required: FAFSA.

Dates and Deadlines: Applicants notified on a rolling basis.

CONTACT

Danielle Picchi, Financial Aid Director
9624 Plaza Circle, El Paso, TX 79927
(915) 532-3737 ext. 8105

Western Texas College

Snyder, Texas
www.wtc.edu Federal Code: 009549

2-year public community and junior college in large town.
Enrollment: 2,178 undergrads.
Selectivity: Open admission; but selective for some programs.

BASIC COSTS (2013-2014)

Tuition and fees: $2,370; out-of-district residents $3,120; out-of-state residents $4,050.

Per-credit charge: $52; out-of-district residents $77; out-of-state residents $108.

Room and board: $5,100.

FINANCIAL AID PICTURE

Students with need: Need-based aid available for full-time and part-time students. Work study available nights, weekends, and for part-time students.

Students without need: No-need awards available for academics, art, athletics, leadership, music/drama, state/district residency.

FINANCIAL AID PROCEDURES

Forms required: FAFSA, institutional form.

Dates and Deadlines: Priority date 8/1; no closing date. Applicants notified on a rolling basis starting 5/1; must reply within 2 week(s) of notification.

Transfers: No deadline. Applicants notified on a rolling basis.

CONTACT

Greg Torres, Director of Student Financial Aid
6200 College Avenue, Snyder, TX 79549
(866) 270-6184

Wharton County Junior College

Wharton, Texas
www.wcjc.edu Federal Code: 003668

2-year public community and junior college in small town.
Enrollment: 7,407 undergrads, 61% part-time. 1,131 full-time freshmen.
Selectivity: Open admission; but selective for some programs.

BASIC COSTS (2012-2013)

Tuition and fees: $2,580; out-of-state residents $4,920.

Per-credit charge: $32; out-of-state residents $64.

Room and board: $3,900.

FINANCIAL AID PICTURE (2011-2012)

Students with need: 67% of average financial aid package awarded as scholarships/grants, 33% awarded as loans/jobs. Need-based aid available for part-time students.

Students without need: No-need awards available for academics, athletics, music/drama.

FINANCIAL AID PROCEDURES

Forms required: FAFSA, institutional form.

Dates and Deadlines: Closing date 6/1. Applicants notified on a rolling basis starting 3/1; must reply within 8 week(s) of notification.

CONTACT

Richard Hyde, Director of Financial Aid
911 Boling Highway, Wharton, TX 77488-0080
(979) 532-4560 ext. 6345

Wiley College

Marshall, Texas
www.wileyc.edu Federal Code: 003669

4-year private liberal arts college in large town, affiliated with United Methodist Church.
Enrollment: 1,401 undergrads.
Selectivity: Open admission; but selective for some programs.

BASIC COSTS (2012-2013)

Tuition and fees: $11,382.

Per-credit charge: $309.

Room and board: $6,352.

Additional info: Reported tuition includes cost of books.

FINANCIAL AID PICTURE

Students with need: Need-based aid available for full-time and part-time students.

Students without need: This college awards aid only to students with need.

FINANCIAL AID PROCEDURES

Forms required: FAFSA, institutional form.

Dates and Deadlines: Closing date 4/15. Applicants notified on a rolling basis.

CONTACT

Alan Jackson, Director of Financial Aid
711 Wiley Avenue, Marshall, TX 75670
(903) 927-3217

Utah

Brigham Young University

Provo, Utah
www.byu.edu Federal Code: 003670

4-year private university in small city, affiliated with Church of Jesus Christ of Latter-day Saints.
Enrollment: 31,060 undergrads, 9% part-time. 5,552 full-time freshmen.
Selectivity: Admits 50 to 75% of applicants. GED not accepted.

BASIC COSTS (2013-2014)
Tuition and fees: $4,850.
Room and board: $7,250.

FINANCIAL AID PICTURE (2011-2012)
Students with need: Out of 2,536 full-time freshmen who applied for aid, 1,820 were judged to have need. Of these, 1,669 received aid, and 36 had their full need met. Average financial aid package met 29% of need; average scholarship/grant was $4,515; average loan was $3,249. For part-time students, average financial aid package was $4,572.
Students without need: 1,851 full-time freshmen who did not demonstrate need for aid received scholarships/grants; average award was $3,641. No-need awards available for academics, art, athletics, leadership, minority status, music/drama, religious affiliation, ROTC, state/district residency.
Scholarships offered: 130 full-time freshmen received athletic scholarships; average amount $5,168.
Cumulative student debt: 31% of graduating class had student loans; average debt was $14,377.
Additional info: Students notified of scholarships on or about April 20.

FINANCIAL AID PROCEDURES
Forms required: FAFSA.
Dates and Deadlines: Priority date 4/15; no closing date. Applicants notified on a rolling basis starting 4/1.
Transfers: Must provide financial aid transcript.

CONTACT

Paul Conrad, Director of Financial Aid
A-153 ASB, Provo, UT 84602
(801) 422-4104

Broadview Entertainment Arts University

Salt Lake City, Utah
www.broadviewuniversity.edu Federal Code: 011166

2-year for-profit university and visual arts college in small city.
Enrollment: 118 undergrads.
Selectivity: Open admission.

BASIC COSTS (2012-2013)
Tuition and fees: $18,000.
Per-credit charge: $435.

FINANCIAL AID PICTURE
Students with need: Need-based aid available for full-time and part-time students.

FINANCIAL AID PROCEDURES
Forms required: FAFSA, institutional form.
Dates and Deadlines: Applicants notified on a rolling basis starting 7/1; must reply within 2 week(s) of notification.

CONTACT

Shelbie Malan, Director of Financial Aid
240 East Morris Avenue, Salt Lake City, UT 84115
(801) 300-4300

Broadview University: Layton

Layton, Utah
www.broadviewuniversity.edu Federal Code: 011166

2-year for-profit university and career college in small city.
Enrollment: 221 undergrads.
Selectivity: Open admission.

BASIC COSTS (2012-2013)
Tuition and fees: $18,000.
Per-credit charge: $435.

FINANCIAL AID PICTURE
Students with need: Need-based aid available for full-time and part-time students.

FINANCIAL AID PROCEDURES
Forms required: FAFSA, institutional form.
Dates and Deadlines: Applicants notified on a rolling basis starting 7/1; must reply within 2 week(s) of notification.

CONTACT

Lina Okazaki, Associate Director of Financial Aid
869 West Hill Field Road, Layton, UT 84041
(801) 660-6000

Broadview University: Orem

Orem, Utah
www.broadviewuniversity.edu Federal Code: 011166

4-year for-profit university and career college in small city.
Enrollment: 160 undergrads.
Selectivity: Open admission.

BASIC COSTS (2012-2013)
Tuition and fees: $18,000.
Per-credit charge: $435.
Additional info: Nursing: $590 per quarter hour.

FINANCIAL AID PICTURE
Students with need: Need-based aid available for full-time and part-time students.

FINANCIAL AID PROCEDURES
Forms required: FAFSA, institutional form.
Dates and Deadlines: Applicants notified on a rolling basis starting 7/1; must reply within 2 week(s) of notification.

CONTACT

Rachelle Rowan, Director of Financial Aid
898 North 1200 West, Orem, UT 84057
(801) 822-5800

Broadview University: West Jordan

West Jordan, Utah
www.broadviewuniversity.edu Federal Code: 011166

2-year for-profit technical and career college in small city.
Enrollment: 314 undergrads.
Selectivity: Open admission; but selective for some programs.

BASIC COSTS (2012-2013)

Tuition and fees: $18,000.
Per-credit charge: $435.
Additional info: Nursing program courses $590 per-credit-hour.

FINANCIAL AID PICTURE

Students with need: Need-based aid available for full-time and part-time students.

FINANCIAL AID PROCEDURES

Forms required: FAFSA, institutional form.
Dates and Deadlines: Applicants notified on a rolling basis starting 7/1; must reply within 2 week(s) of notification.

CONTACT

Kristi Snow, Director of Financial Aid
1902 West 7800 South, West Jordan, UT 84088
(801) 304-4224

Dixie State College

St. George, Utah
www.dixie.edu Federal Code: 003671

4-year public liberal arts college in small city.
Enrollment: 7,668 undergrads, 31% part-time. 1,561 full-time freshmen.
Selectivity: Open admission; but selective for some programs.

BASIC COSTS (2013-2014)

Tuition and fees: $4,508; out-of-state residents $11,742.
Per-credit charge: $145; out-of-state residents $463.
Room and board: $5,048.

FINANCIAL AID PICTURE (2011-2012)

Students with need: Out of 1,202 full-time freshmen who applied for aid, 1,096 were judged to have need. Of these, 1,063 received aid, and 27 had their full need met. Average financial aid package met 34% of need; average scholarship/grant was $5,096; average loan was $3,010. For part-time students, average financial aid package was $4,695.
Students without need: 275 full-time freshmen who did not demonstrate need for aid received scholarships/grants; average award was $2,252. No-need awards available for academics, alumni affiliation, art, athletics, leadership, minority status, music/drama, religious affiliation.
Scholarships offered: 17 full-time freshmen received athletic scholarships; average amount $4,056.
Cumulative student debt: 52% of graduating class had student loans; average debt was $22,412.

FINANCIAL AID PROCEDURES

Forms required: FAFSA.
Dates and Deadlines: Applicants notified on a rolling basis starting 3/1; must reply within 2 week(s) of notification.

CONTACT

JD Robertson, Director of Financial Aid
225 South 700 East, St. George, UT 84770-3876
(435) 652-7575

Independence University

Murray, Utah
www.independence.edu Federal Code: 014683

4-year for-profit business and health science college in very large city.
Enrollment: 611 undergrads.
Selectivity: Open admission.

BASIC COSTS (2012-2013)

Additional info: Cost of associate degree programs range from $22,500 - $47,615; bachelor's degree programs: $49,500; bachelor's completion programs: $25,000.

FINANCIAL AID PICTURE (2011-2012)

Students with need: 30% of average financial aid package awarded as scholarships/grants, 70% awarded as loans/jobs.
Students without need: This college awards aid only to students with need.
Additional info: Financial aid available for resident students only, not correspondence students.

FINANCIAL AID PROCEDURES

Forms required: FAFSA.
Dates and Deadlines: Closing date 7/23. Applicants notified on a rolling basis.
Transfers: No deadline. Applicants notified on a rolling basis.

CONTACT

Lana Moon, Director of Finance
4021 South 700 East, Suite 400, Murray, UT 84107

LDS Business College

Salt Lake City, Utah
www.ldsbc.edu Federal Code: 003672

2-year private business and junior college in large city, affiliated with Church of Jesus Christ of Latter-day Saints.
Enrollment: 2,191 undergrads, 27% part-time. 497 full-time freshmen.
Selectivity: Open admission; but selective for some programs.

BASIC COSTS (2012-2013)

Tuition and fees: $3,060.
Per-credit charge: $128.

FINANCIAL AID PICTURE

Students with need: Need-based aid available for full-time and part-time students.
Students without need: No-need awards available for academics, leadership.
Scholarships offered: Service scholarships; half-tuition for one semester; for Church of Jesus Christ of Latter-day Saints missionaries who have returned from mission within past year.

FINANCIAL AID PROCEDURES

Forms required: FAFSA.
Dates and Deadlines: Priority date 7/1; no closing date. Applicants notified on a rolling basis starting 3/1; must reply by 7/1 or within 3 week(s) of notification.
Transfers: No deadline. Applicants notified on a rolling basis starting 1/1.

CONTACT

Doug Horne, Financial Aid Administrator
95 North 300 West, Salt Lake City, UT 84101-3500
(801) 524-8110

Neumont University

South Jordan, Utah
www.neumont.edu Federal Code: 009948

4-year for-profit engineering and technical college in very large city.
Enrollment: 366 undergrads. 166 full-time freshmen.
Selectivity: Admits over 75% of applicants.

BASIC COSTS (2013-2014)

Tuition and fees: $23,100.
Per-credit charge: $495.
Room only: $4,950.
Additional info: One time laptop cost of $2,200.

FINANCIAL AID PICTURE

Students with need: Need-based aid available for full-time and part-time students.
Students without need: No-need awards available for academics, job skills, leadership, state/district residency.

FINANCIAL AID PROCEDURES

Forms required: FAFSA, institutional form.

CONTACT

Jeme Deviny, Director of Financial Services
10701 South River Front Parkway, Suite 300, South Jordan, UT 84095
(801) 302-2870

Salt Lake Community College

Salt Lake City, Utah
www.slcc.edu Federal Code: 005220

2-year public community and technical college in very large city.
Enrollment: 24,592 undergrads, 65% part-time. 1,309 full-time freshmen.
Selectivity: Open admission; but selective for some programs.

BASIC COSTS (2012-2013)

Tuition and fees: $3,170; out-of-state residents $10,012.
Per-credit charge: $115; out-of-state residents $401.
Additional info: Tuition/fee waivers available for adults, minority students.

FINANCIAL AID PICTURE

Students with need: Need-based aid available for full-time and part-time students. Work study available nights, weekends, and for part-time students.
Students without need: No-need awards available for academics, alumni affiliation, art, athletics, leadership, minority status, music/drama.

FINANCIAL AID PROCEDURES

Forms required: FAFSA, institutional form.
Dates and Deadlines: Priority date 5/1; no closing date. Applicants notified on a rolling basis starting 5/1; must reply within 4 week(s) of notification.

CONTACT

Cristi Millard, Director of Financial Aid
4600 South Redwood Road, Salt Lake City, UT 84130-0808
(801) 957-4410

Snow College

Ephraim, Utah
www.snow.edu Federal Code: 003679

2-year public junior college in small town.
Enrollment: 4,599 undergrads.
Selectivity: Open admission.

BASIC COSTS (2012-2013)

Tuition and fees: $3,086; out-of-state residents $10,230.
Per-credit charge: $119; out-of-state residents $434.
Additional info: Declining balance meal plan available. Room-only cost, $1,250. Tuition/fee waivers available for unemployed or children of unemployed.

FINANCIAL AID PICTURE (2012-2013)

Students with need: For part-time students, average financial aid package was $2,181.
Students without need: No-need awards available for academics, alumni affiliation, athletics, leadership, music/drama, state/district residency.

FINANCIAL AID PROCEDURES

Forms required: FAFSA, institutional form.
Dates and Deadlines: Priority date 3/1; closing date 6/1. Applicants notified on a rolling basis starting 8/1; must reply within 1 week(s) of notification.
Transfers: Priority date 3/15; closing date 6/15. Applicants notified on a rolling basis. F.A.T. required for mid-year transfers.

CONTACT

Jack Dalene, Director of Financial Aid
150 East College Avenue, Ephraim, UT 84627
(435) 283-7132

Southern Utah University

Cedar City, Utah
www.suu.edu Federal Code: 003678

4-year public university in large town.
Enrollment: 5,767 undergrads, 12% part-time. 1,192 full-time freshmen.
Selectivity: Admits 50 to 75% of applicants.

BASIC COSTS (2012-2013)

Tuition and fees: $5,576; out-of-state residents $16,984.
Room and board: $5,880.

FINANCIAL AID PICTURE (2011-2012)

Students with need: Out of 842 full-time freshmen who applied for aid, 720 were judged to have need. Of these, 715 received aid, and 65 had their full need met. Average financial aid package met 49% of need; average scholarship/grant was $7,936; average loan was $2,964. For part-time students, average financial aid package was $5,849.
Students without need: 265 full-time freshmen who did not demonstrate need for aid received scholarships/grants; average award was $4,083. No-need awards available for academics, alumni affiliation, art, athletics, job skills, leadership, minority status, music/drama, ROTC, state/district residency.
Scholarships offered: 57 full-time freshmen received athletic scholarships; average amount $8,631.
Cumulative student debt: 55% of graduating class had student loans; average debt was $13,478.

FINANCIAL AID PROCEDURES

Forms required: FAFSA.
Dates and Deadlines: Priority date 12/1; no closing date. Applicants notified on a rolling basis starting 11/1; must reply within 4 week(s) of notification.

CONTACT

Jan Carey-McDonald, Director of Financial Aid and Scholarships
351 West University Blvd, Cedar City, UT 84720
(435) 586-7735

University of Utah

Salt Lake City, Utah
www.utah.edu Federal Code: 003675

4-year public university in very large city.
Enrollment: 23,972 undergrads, 28% part-time. 3,079 full-time freshmen.

Selectivity: Admits over 75% of applicants.

BASIC COSTS (2012-2013)
Tuition and fees: $7,139; out-of-state residents $22,642.
Per-credit charge: $662; out-of-state residents $2,467.
Room and board: $7,155.

FINANCIAL AID PICTURE (2012-2013)
Students with need: Average financial aid package met 59% of need; average scholarship/grant was $7,065; average loan was $3,281. For part-time students, average financial aid package was $14,172.
Students without need: 235 full-time freshmen who did not demonstrate need for aid received scholarships/grants; average award was $6,945. No-need awards available for academics, alumni affiliation, art, athletics, leadership, minority status, music/drama, ROTC, state/district residency.
Scholarships offered: 6 full-time freshmen received athletic scholarships; average amount $18,708.
Cumulative student debt: 50% of graduating class had student loans; average debt was $20,796.

FINANCIAL AID PROCEDURES
Forms required: FAFSA, institutional form.
Dates and Deadlines: Priority date 4/1; no closing date. Applicants notified on a rolling basis starting 4/15; must reply within 6 week(s) of notification.
Transfers: No deadline. Applicants notified on a rolling basis starting 4/15; must reply within 6 week(s) of notification.

CONTACT
John Curl, Director of Financial Aid and Scholarship
201 South 1460 East, Room 250 S, Salt Lake City, UT 84112-9057
(801) 581-6211

Utah State University
Logan, Utah
www.usu.edu Federal Code: 003677

4-year public university in small city.
Enrollment: 21,129 undergrads, 27% part-time. 3,384 full-time freshmen.
Selectivity: Admits over 75% of applicants.

BASIC COSTS (2012-2013)
Tuition and fees: $5,931; out-of-state residents $17,076.
Per-credit charge: $440; out-of-state residents $1,417.
Room and board: $5,490.

FINANCIAL AID PICTURE (2012-2013)
Students with need: Out of 2,100 full-time freshmen who applied for aid, 1,756 were judged to have need. Of these, 1,718 received aid, and 261 had their full need met. Average financial aid package met 47% of need; average scholarship/grant was $7,295; average loan was $3,466. For part-time students, average financial aid package was $5,740.
Students without need: 210 full-time freshmen who did not demonstrate need for aid received scholarships/grants; average award was $1,876. No-need awards available for academics, alumni affiliation, art, athletics, leadership, minority status, music/drama, religious affiliation, ROTC, state/district residency.
Scholarships offered: 5 full-time freshmen received athletic scholarships; average amount $5,837.
Cumulative student debt: 47% of graduating class had student loans; average debt was $18,900.

FINANCIAL AID PROCEDURES
Forms required: FAFSA.
Dates and Deadlines: Applicants notified on a rolling basis starting 4/1; must reply within 4 week(s) of notification.
Transfers: No deadline. Applicants notified on a rolling basis starting 4/1; must reply within 4 week(s) of notification.

CONTACT
Steve Sharp, Director of Financial Aid
0160 Old Main Hill, Logan, UT 84322-0160
(435) 797-0173

Utah Valley University
Orem, Utah
www.uvu.edu Federal Code: 004027

4-year public university and technical college in small city.
Enrollment: 25,900 undergrads, 38% part-time. 2,841 full-time freshmen.
Selectivity: Open admission.

BASIC COSTS (2012-2013)
Tuition and fees: $4,786; out-of-state residents $13,518.

FINANCIAL AID PICTURE
Students with need: Need-based aid available for full-time and part-time students. Work study available nights, weekends, and for part-time students.
Students without need: No-need awards available for academics, alumni affiliation, art, athletics, job skills, leadership, minority status, music/drama, religious affiliation, ROTC, state/district residency.

FINANCIAL AID PROCEDURES
Forms required: FAFSA, institutional form.
Dates and Deadlines: Priority date 5/1; no closing date. Applicants notified on a rolling basis starting 5/15; must reply within 2 week(s) of notification.
Transfers: No deadline.

CONTACT
Michael Francis, Assistant Vice President for Finance and Controller
800 West University Parkway, Orem, UT 84058-5999
(801) 863-8442

Weber State University
Ogden, Utah
https://www.weber.edu Federal Code: 003680

4-year public university in small city.
Enrollment: 18,984 undergrads, 39% part-time. 1,939 full-time freshmen.
Selectivity: Open admission; but selective for some programs.

BASIC COSTS (2012-2013)
Tuition and fees: $4,775; out-of-state residents $12,893.
Additional info: Declining balance meal plan available. Cost of room only, $5,500.

FINANCIAL AID PICTURE
Students with need: Need-based aid available for full-time and part-time students. Work study available nights, weekends, and for part-time students.
Students without need: This college awards aid only to students with need.

FINANCIAL AID PROCEDURES
Forms required: FAFSA, institutional form.
Dates and Deadlines: Priority date 3/1; no closing date. Applicants notified on a rolling basis starting 3/15; must reply within 2 week(s) of notification.

CONTACT
Jeb Spencer, Director of Financial Aid
1137 University Circle, Ogden, UT 84408-1137
(801) 626-7569

Western Governors University

Salt Lake City, Utah
www.wgu.edu Federal Code: 033394

4-year private virtual university in very large city.
Enrollment: 31,353 undergrads. 45 full-time freshmen.
Selectivity: Open admission; but selective for some programs.

BASIC COSTS (2012-2013)

Tuition and fees: $5,925.
Additional info: Most programs cost $2,890 per six-month term. Students may complete an unlimited number of credit equivalency units in any term.

FINANCIAL AID PICTURE (2011-2012)

Students with need: Out of 45 full-time freshmen who applied for aid, 41 were judged to have need. Of these, 41 received aid, and 2 had their full need met. Average financial aid package met 45% of need; average scholarship/grant was $5,066.
Students without need: This college awards aid only to students with need.
Cumulative student debt: 73% of graduating class had student loans; average debt was $35,327.

FINANCIAL AID PROCEDURES

Forms required: FAFSA.
Dates and Deadlines: Applicants notified on a rolling basis.
Transfers: No deadline. Applicants notified on a rolling basis.

CONTACT

David Grow, Chief Financial Officer/Director of Financial Aid
4001 South 700 East, Salt Lake City, UT 84107
(877) 435-7948 ext. 3104

Westminster College

Salt Lake City, Utah
www.westminstercollege.edu Federal Code: 003681

4-year private liberal arts college in very large city.
Enrollment: 2,387 undergrads, 6% part-time. 495 full-time freshmen.
Selectivity: Admits 50 to 75% of applicants.

BASIC COSTS (2012-2013)

Tuition and fees: $28,210.
Per-credit charge: $1,155.
Room and board: $7,890.

FINANCIAL AID PICTURE (2012-2013)

Students with need: Out of 393 full-time freshmen who applied for aid, 331 were judged to have need. Of these, 331 received aid, and 74 had their full need met. Average financial aid package met 80% of need; average scholarship/grant was $18,070; average loan was $3,991. For part-time students, average financial aid package was $11,328.
Students without need: 135 full-time freshmen who did not demonstrate need for aid received scholarships/grants; average award was $12,539. No-need awards available for academics, alumni affiliation, art, athletics, minority status, music/drama, ROTC.
Scholarships offered: 11 full-time freshmen received athletic scholarships; average amount $7,889.
Cumulative student debt: 54% of graduating class had student loans; average debt was $28,323.

FINANCIAL AID PROCEDURES

Forms required: FAFSA.
Dates and Deadlines: Priority date 4/15; no closing date. Applicants notified on a rolling basis starting 3/1; must reply within 3 week(s) of notification.
Transfers: No deadline. Applicants notified on a rolling basis starting 5/1; must reply within 3 week(s) of notification. Full-time transfer students with 3.0 GPA eligible for work study, loans, scholarships and grants which range from $5,000-$10,000 per year.

CONTACT

Sean View, Director of Financial Aid
1840 South 1300 East, Salt Lake City, UT 84105
(801) 832-2500

Vermont

Bennington College

Bennington, Vermont Federal Code: 003682
www.bennington.edu CSS Code: 3080

4-year private liberal arts college in large town.
Enrollment: 688 undergrads, 1% part-time. 197 full-time freshmen.
Selectivity: Admits 50 to 75% of applicants.

BASIC COSTS (2012-2013)

Tuition and fees: $44,220.
Per-credit charge: $1,440.
Room and board: $12,770.

FINANCIAL AID PICTURE (2012-2013)

Students with need: Out of 154 full-time freshmen who applied for aid, 118 were judged to have need. Of these, 118 received aid, and 22 had their full need met. Average financial aid package met 82% of need; average scholarship/grant was $32,396; average loan was $3,103. For part-time students, average financial aid package was $17,197.
Students without need: 66 full-time freshmen who did not demonstrate need for aid received scholarships/grants; average award was $17,368. No-need awards available for academics.
Cumulative student debt: 68% of graduating class had student loans; average debt was $25,716.
Additional info: All applicants for undergraduate admission considered for scholarships based on quality of overall application.

FINANCIAL AID PROCEDURES

Forms required: FAFSA, institutional form. CSS PROFILE required of early decision applicants only.
Dates and Deadlines: Priority date 2/1; closing date 2/15. Applicants notified by 4/1; must reply by 5/1 or within 2 week(s) of notification.
Transfers: Priority date 3/15; closing date 8/1. Applicants notified on a rolling basis starting 5/1; must reply by 6/1 or within 2 week(s) of notification.

CONTACT

Meg Woolmington, Director of Financial Aid
One College Drive, Bennington, VT 05201-6003
(802) 440-4325

Burlington College

Burlington, Vermont
www.burlington.edu Federal Code: 012183

4-year private liberal arts college in small city.
Enrollment: 195 undergrads, 14% part-time. 36 full-time freshmen.
Selectivity: Admits over 75% of applicants.

BASIC COSTS (2013-2014)

Tuition and fees: $22,970.
Per-credit charge: $950.
Room only: $6,800.
Additional info: Tuition at time of enrollment locked for 4 years.

FINANCIAL AID PICTURE (2012-2013)
Students with need: Out of 33 full-time freshmen who applied for aid, 28 were judged to have need. Of these, 28 received aid. Average financial aid package met 53% of need; average scholarship/grant was $10,954; average loan was $4,711. For part-time students, average financial aid package was $9,434.
Students without need: No-need awards available for academics, leadership.
Cumulative student debt: 86% of graduating class had student loans; average debt was $39,107.

FINANCIAL AID PROCEDURES
Forms required: FAFSA.
Dates and Deadlines: Applicants notified on a rolling basis starting 2/15.
Transfers: No deadline. Applicants notified on a rolling basis starting 2/15.

CONTACT
Lindy Walsh, Director of Financial Aid
351 North Avenue, Burlington, VT 05401
(802) 862-9616 ext. 110

Castleton State College
Castleton, Vermont
www.castleton.edu Federal Code: 003683

4-year public liberal arts college in small town.
Enrollment: 2,017 undergrads, 6% part-time. 470 full-time freshmen.
Selectivity: Admits over 75% of applicants.

BASIC COSTS (2012-2013)
Tuition and fees: $9,864; out-of-state residents $22,464.
Per-credit charge: $372; out-of-state residents $897.
Room and board: $8,789.
Additional info: New England Board of Higher Education rate for students from other New England states: 150% of Vermont resident tuition. Available to degree candidates in academic areas not offered by educational institutions in their home states.

FINANCIAL AID PICTURE
Students with need: Need-based aid available for full-time and part-time students.
Students without need: No-need awards available for academics, alumni affiliation, music/drama, state/district residency.

FINANCIAL AID PROCEDURES
Forms required: FAFSA.
Dates and Deadlines: Priority date 4/1; no closing date. Applicants notified on a rolling basis starting 2/15; must reply by 5/1 or within 2 week(s) of notification.

CONTACT
Kathy O'Meara, Financial Aid Director
Seminary Street, Castleton, VT 05735
(802) 468-1286

Champlain College
Burlington, Vermont
www.champlain.edu Federal Code: 003684

4-year private liberal arts and career college in small city.
Enrollment: 2,711 undergrads, 18% part-time. 601 full-time freshmen.
Selectivity: Admits 50 to 75% of applicants.

BASIC COSTS (2013-2014)
Tuition and fees: $31,350.
Per-credit charge: $1,340.
Room and board: $13,500.

FINANCIAL AID PICTURE
Students with need: Need-based aid available for full-time and part-time students. Work study available nights, weekends, and for part-time students.
Students without need: No-need awards available for academics, leadership.

FINANCIAL AID PROCEDURES
Forms required: FAFSA.
Dates and Deadlines: Closing date 3/1. Applicants notified by 3/19; must reply by 5/1 or within 2 week(s) of notification.
Transfers: Closing date 5/1. Applicants notified on a rolling basis starting 5/1; must reply within 2 week(s) of notification.

CONTACT
Kristi Jovell, Director of Financial Aid
163 South Willard Street, Burlington, VT 05402-0670
(802) 860-2730

College of St. Joseph in Vermont
Rutland, Vermont
www.csj.edu Federal Code: 003685

4-year private liberal arts and teachers college in large town, affiliated with Roman Catholic Church.
Enrollment: 152 undergrads.

BASIC COSTS (2013-2014)
Tuition and fees: $21,200.
Per-credit charge: $280.
Room and board: $9,400.

FINANCIAL AID PICTURE
Students with need: Need-based aid available for full-time and part-time students. Work study available nights, weekends, and for part-time students.
Students without need: No-need awards available for academics, alumni affiliation.

FINANCIAL AID PROCEDURES
Forms required: FAFSA, institutional form.
Dates and Deadlines: Priority date 3/1; no closing date. Applicants notified on a rolling basis starting 3/1.
Transfers: No deadline. Applicants notified on a rolling basis starting 3/1.

CONTACT
Julie Rosmus, Financial Aid Director
71 Clement Road, Rutland, VT 05701-3899
(802) 773-5900 ext. 3262

Community College of Vermont
Montpelier, Vermont
www.ccv.edu Federal Code: 011167

2-year public community and liberal arts college in small town.
Enrollment: 4,684 undergrads.
Selectivity: Open admission.

BASIC COSTS (2012-2013)
Tuition and fees: $6,790; out-of-state residents $13,480.
Per-credit charge: $223; out-of-state residents $446.
Additional info: New England Board of Higher Education rate for students from other New England states: 150% of Vermont resident tuition. Available to degree candidates in academic areas not offered by educational institutions in their home states.

FINANCIAL AID PICTURE
Students with need: Need-based aid available for full-time and part-time students. Work study available nights, weekends, and for part-time students.

Students without need: This college awards aid only to students with need.

FINANCIAL AID PROCEDURES

Forms required: FAFSA, state aid form, institutional form.

Dates and Deadlines: Applicants notified on a rolling basis starting 9/1; must reply within 3 week(s) of notification.

CONTACT

Pam Chisholm, Associate Dean of Enrollment
PO Box 489, Montpelier, VT 05601
(802) 828-2800

Goddard College

Plainfield, Vermont
www.goddard.edu Federal Code: 003686

4-year private liberal arts college in rural community.
Enrollment: 232 undergrads. 7 full-time freshmen.
Selectivity: Admits over 75% of applicants.

BASIC COSTS (2012-2013)

Tuition and fees: $14,218.
Room and board: $1,392.
Additional info: Annualized tuition for Education BA with licensure and the Bachelor of Fine Arts in Creative Writing, $15,216. Tuition varies somewhat according to program and enrollment options, e.g. licensure or non-licensure for Education students.

FINANCIAL AID PICTURE (2011-2012)

Students with need: Average financial aid package met 41% of need; average scholarship/grant was $4,170; average loan was $3,094.
Students without need: No-need awards available for academics, art, job skills, leadership, music/drama, state/district residency.
Cumulative student debt: 74% of graduating class had student loans; average debt was $26,547.

FINANCIAL AID PROCEDURES

Forms required: FAFSA.
Dates and Deadlines: Applicants notified on a rolling basis starting 4/15; must reply within 4 week(s) of notification.
Transfers: No deadline. Applicants notified on a rolling basis starting 4/15; must reply within 4 week(s) of notification.

CONTACT

Beverly Jene, Director of Financial Aid
123 Pitkin Road, Plainfield, VT 05667
(800) 468-4888

Green Mountain College

Poultney, Vermont
www.greenmtn.edu Federal Code: 003687

4-year private liberal arts college in small town, affiliated with United Methodist Church.
Enrollment: 622 undergrads, 2% part-time. 180 full-time freshmen.
Selectivity: Admits 50 to 75% of applicants.

BASIC COSTS (2012-2013)

Tuition and fees: $30,718.
Per-credit charge: $987.
Room and board: $10,950.

FINANCIAL AID PICTURE (2012-2013)

Students with need: Out of 157 full-time freshmen who applied for aid, 146 were judged to have need. Of these, 146 received aid, and 8 had their full need met. Average financial aid package met 77% of need; average scholarship/grant was $25,144; average loan was $2,835. For part-time students, average financial aid package was $3,011.
Students without need: 29 full-time freshmen who did not demonstrate need for aid received scholarships/grants; average award was $14,454. No-need awards available for academics, alumni affiliation, art, leadership, music/drama, religious affiliation, state/district residency.
Cumulative student debt: 79% of graduating class had student loans; average debt was $42,269.
Additional info: Service/recognition awards available to all students, determined by their admission application and supplemental documentation.

FINANCIAL AID PROCEDURES

Forms required: FAFSA. CSS PROFILE is recommended to receive an earlier financial aid package.
Dates and Deadlines: Priority date 3/1; no closing date. Applicants notified on a rolling basis starting 11/1; must reply by 5/1 or within 3 week(s) of notification.
Transfers: No deadline. Applicants notified on a rolling basis; must reply by 5/1 or within 3 week(s) of notification.

CONTACT

Wendy Ellis, Director of Financial Aid
One Brennan Circle, Poultney, VT 05764
(802) 287-8210

Johnson State College

Johnson, Vermont
www.jsc.edu Federal Code: 003688

4-year public liberal arts college in small town.
Enrollment: 1,531 undergrads, 32% part-time. 236 full-time freshmen.
Selectivity: Admits over 75% of applicants.

BASIC COSTS (2012-2013)

Tuition and fees: $10,109; out-of-state residents $21,149.
Per-credit charge: $372; out-of-state residents $832.
Room and board: $8,786.
Additional info: New England Board of Higher Education rate for students from other New England states: 150% of Vermont resident tuition. Available to degree candidates in academic areas not offered by educational institutions in their home states.

FINANCIAL AID PICTURE (2012-2013)

Students with need: Out of 220 full-time freshmen who applied for aid, 184 were judged to have need. Of these, 184 received aid, and 18 had their full need met. Average financial aid package met 83% of need; average scholarship/grant was $9,207; average loan was $6,922. For part-time students, average financial aid package was $10,844.
Students without need: 27 full-time freshmen who did not demonstrate need for aid received scholarships/grants; average award was $6,817. No-need awards available for academics, alumni affiliation, art, leadership, music/drama, state/district residency.

FINANCIAL AID PROCEDURES

Forms required: FAFSA, state aid form.
Dates and Deadlines: Priority date 3/1; no closing date. Applicants notified on a rolling basis starting 4/1; must reply within 3 week(s) of notification.
Transfers: Financial aid transcripts from previously attended colleges required.

CONTACT

Lisa Cummings, Director of Financial Aid
337 College Hill, Johnson, VT 05656
(800) 635-2356

Landmark College

Putney, Vermont
www.landmark.edu Federal Code: 017157

2-year private liberal arts college in small town.
Enrollment: 472 undergrads. 110 full-time freshmen.
Selectivity: Admits over 75% of applicants.

BASIC COSTS (2013-2014)

Tuition and fees: $49,930.
Room and board: $10,300.

FINANCIAL AID PICTURE (2011-2012)

Students with need: Average financial aid package met 62% of need; average scholarship/grant was $20,089; average loan was $5,613. Need-based aid available for part-time students.
Students without need: No-need awards available for academics, art, leadership, minority status, music/drama.
Cumulative student debt: 47% of graduating class had student loans; average debt was $5,613.
Additional info: Students encouraged to apply to their state departments of vocational rehabilitation for additional financial assistance.

FINANCIAL AID PROCEDURES

Forms required: FAFSA.
Dates and Deadlines: Priority date 3/1; no closing date. Applicants notified on a rolling basis starting 3/15; must reply within 2 week(s) of notification.
Transfers: No deadline. Applicants notified on a rolling basis; must reply within 2 week(s) of notification.

CONTACT

Jennifer Desmarais, Director of Financial Aid
1 River Road South, Putney, VT 05346
(802) 387-6718

Lyndon State College

Lyndonville, Vermont
www.lyndonstate.edu Federal Code: 003689

4-year public liberal arts and teachers college in small town.
Enrollment: 1,374 undergrads, 6% part-time. 334 full-time freshmen.
Selectivity: Admits over 75% of applicants.

BASIC COSTS (2012-2013)

Tuition and fees: $9,864; out-of-state residents $20,136.
Room and board: $8,786.
Additional info: New England Board of Higher Education rate for students from other New England states: 150% of Vermont resident tuition. Available to degree candidates in academic areas not offered by educational institutions in their home states. Tuition/fee waivers available for unemployed or children of unemployed.

FINANCIAL AID PICTURE

Students with need: Need-based aid available for full-time and part-time students. Work study available nights, weekends, and for part-time students.
Students without need: No-need awards available for academics, leadership.

FINANCIAL AID PROCEDURES

Forms required: FAFSA.
Dates and Deadlines: Priority date 2/1; no closing date. Applicants notified on a rolling basis starting 4/1; must reply within 2 week(s) of notification.

CONTACT

Tanya Bradley, Director of Financial Aid
1001 College Road, Lyndonville, VT 05851
(802) 626-6218

Marlboro College

Marlboro, Vermont
www.marlboro.edu Federal Code: 003690

4-year private liberal arts college in rural community.
Enrollment: 238 undergrads, 1% part-time. 49 full-time freshmen.
Selectivity: Admits over 75% of applicants.

BASIC COSTS (2012-2013)

Tuition and fees: $37,640.
Per-credit charge: $1,210.
Room and board: $9,930.

FINANCIAL AID PICTURE (2012-2013)

Students with need: Out of 44 full-time freshmen who applied for aid, 40 were judged to have need. Of these, 40 received aid. Average financial aid package met 80% of need; average scholarship/grant was $24,667; average loan was $3,454. Need-based aid available for part-time students.
Students without need: 7 full-time freshmen who did not demonstrate need for aid received scholarships/grants; average award was $8,286. No-need awards available for academics, leadership.
Cumulative student debt: 71% of graduating class had student loans; average debt was $20,051.

FINANCIAL AID PROCEDURES

Forms required: FAFSA.
Dates and Deadlines: Closing date 3/1. Applicants notified on a rolling basis starting 3/15; must reply by 5/1 or within 2 week(s) of notification.

CONTACT

Cathy Fuller, Associate Director of Financial Aid
PO Box A, Marlboro, VT 05344-0300
(802) 258-9237

Middlebury College

Middlebury, Vermont Federal Code: 003691
www.middlebury.edu CSS Code: 3526

4-year private liberal arts college in small town.
Enrollment: 2,487 undergrads, 1% part-time. 598 full-time freshmen.
Selectivity: Admits less than 50% of applicants.

BASIC COSTS (2013-2014)

Tuition and fees: $45,314.
Room and board: $12,156.

FINANCIAL AID PICTURE (2012-2013)

Students with need: Out of 366 full-time freshmen who applied for aid, 266 were judged to have need. Of these, 266 received aid, and 254 had their full need met. Average financial aid package met 100% of need; average scholarship/grant was $36,277; average loan was $3,268. Need-based aid available for part-time students.
Students without need: This college awards aid only to students with need.
Cumulative student debt: 49% of graduating class had student loans; average debt was $17,246.
Additional info: Middlebury College maintains need-blind admissions policy and meets full demonstrated financial need of students who qualify for admission, to degree resources permit.

FINANCIAL AID PROCEDURES

Forms required: FAFSA, CSS PROFILE.
Dates and Deadlines: Priority date 11/15; closing date 2/1. Applicants notified by 4/1; must reply by 5/1.
Transfers: Closing date 3/1. Applicants notified by 4/10; must reply by 5/1.

CONTACT
Kim Downs, Director of Student Financial Services
The Emma Willard House, Middlebury, VT 05753-6002
(802) 443-5158

New England Culinary Institute

Montpelier, Vermont
www.neci.edu Federal Code: 015904

2-year for-profit culinary school in small town.
Enrollment: 445 undergrads. 63 full-time freshmen.

BASIC COSTS (2012-2013)
Tuition and fees: $26,425.
Room and board: $7,450.

FINANCIAL AID PICTURE (2011-2012)
Students with need: 46% of average financial aid package awarded as scholarships/grants, 54% awarded as loans/jobs. Work study available nights, weekends, and for part-time students.
Students without need: No-need awards available for academics, alumni affiliation, job skills.
Scholarships offered: Alumni Scholarship: $2,000 awarded to students recommended by an alumni.

FINANCIAL AID PROCEDURES
Forms required: FAFSA.
Dates and Deadlines: Applicants notified on a rolling basis.
Transfers: No deadline. Applicants notified on a rolling basis.

CONTACT
Nik Znamenskis, C.I.O.
56 College Street, Montpelier, VT 05602
(802) 225-3243

Norwich University

Northfield, Vermont
www.norwich.edu Federal Code: 003692

4-year private university and military college in small town.
Enrollment: 2,182 undergrads. 712 full-time freshmen.
Selectivity: Admits 50 to 75% of applicants.

BASIC COSTS (2012-2013)
Tuition and fees: $31,782.
Per-credit charge: $881.
Room and board: $10,976.
Additional info: Corps of Cadets freshmen students are charged $1,956 for Rooks Uniform for first two years.

FINANCIAL AID PICTURE (2012-2013)
Students with need: Average financial aid package met 79% of need; average scholarship/grant was $23,519; average loan was $4,525. For part-time students, average financial aid package was $14,539.
Students without need: No-need awards available for academics, ROTC.
Cumulative student debt: 78% of graduating class had student loans; average debt was $35,310.
Additional info: Winners of ROTC scholarships receive full room and board; must maintain 2.75 GPA. Renewable up to 4 years.

FINANCIAL AID PROCEDURES
Forms required: FAFSA.
Dates and Deadlines: Priority date 3/1; no closing date. Applicants notified on a rolling basis starting 11/15.

CONTACT
Tracey Mingo, Director of Financial Aid
158 Harmon Drive, Northfield, VT 05663
(802) 485-2015

Saint Michael's College

Colchester, Vermont
www.smcvt.edu Federal Code: 003694

4-year private liberal arts college in small city, affiliated with Roman Catholic Church.
Enrollment: 1,942 undergrads, 1% part-time. 544 full-time freshmen.
Selectivity: Admits over 75% of applicants.

BASIC COSTS (2012-2013)
Tuition and fees: $37,510.
Per-credit charge: $1,240.
Room and board: $9,350.

FINANCIAL AID PICTURE (2012-2013)
Students with need: Out of 471 full-time freshmen who applied for aid, 424 were judged to have need. Of these, 424 received aid, and 130 had their full need met. Average financial aid package met 82% of need; average scholarship/grant was $21,468; average loan was $4,922. Need-based aid available for part-time students.
Students without need: 107 full-time freshmen who did not demonstrate need for aid received scholarships/grants; average award was $12,993. No-need awards available for academics, art, athletics, ROTC.
Scholarships offered: 5 full-time freshmen received athletic scholarships; average amount $46,860.
Cumulative student debt: 71% of graduating class had student loans; average debt was $33,054.

FINANCIAL AID PROCEDURES
Forms required: FAFSA.
Dates and Deadlines: Closing date 2/15. Applicants notified on a rolling basis starting 4/1; must reply by 5/1 or within 2 week(s) of notification.
Transfers: Must reply within 2 week(s) of notification.

CONTACT
Daniel Couture, Director of Student Financial Services
One Winooski Park, Colchester, VT 05439
(802) 654-3244

Southern Vermont College

Bennington, Vermont
www.svc.edu Federal Code: 003693

4-year private liberal arts college in large town.
Enrollment: 532 undergrads.

BASIC COSTS (2012-2013)
Tuition and fees: $21,978.
Room and board: $9,941.

FINANCIAL AID PICTURE (2012-2013)
Students with need: Need-based aid available for full-time and part-time students. Work study available nights, weekends, and for part-time students.
Students without need: No-need awards available for academics, leadership.

FINANCIAL AID PROCEDURES
Forms required: FAFSA, state aid form.
Dates and Deadlines: Applicants notified on a rolling basis.

CONTACT
Joel Phelps, Assistant Dean of Financial Aid
982 Mansion Drive, Bennington, VT 05201-6002
(802) 447-6331

Sterling College
Craftsbury Common, Vermont
www.sterlingcollege.edu Federal Code: 014991

4-year private liberal arts college in rural community.
Enrollment: 94 undergrads, 13% part-time. 20 full-time freshmen.
Selectivity: Admits over 75% of applicants.

BASIC COSTS (2012-2013)
Tuition and fees: $28,760.
Room and board: $8,332.

FINANCIAL AID PICTURE (2011-2012)
Students with need: Out of 15 full-time freshmen who applied for aid, 15 were judged to have need. Of these, 15 received aid, and 1 had their full need met. Average financial aid package met 90% of need; average scholarship/grant was $19,137; average loan was $3,311. For part-time students, average financial aid package was $9,721.
Students without need: 5 full-time freshmen who did not demonstrate need for aid received scholarships/grants; average award was $1,500. No-need awards available for academics, leadership, state/district residency.
Scholarships offered: Gladys Brooks: up to $6,000; academic merit, resident of Northeast Kingdom of Vermont, leadership. Presidential Scholarship: up to $5,000, significant academic merit and achievement. Achievement Scholarships: up to $5,000; significant life achievement. Vermont Scholarship: up to $2,000 for Vermont residents. Service Scholarship: up to $5,000; significant service. Bounder Scholarship: $500; applicants who live west of the Mississippi or in the Deep South. SCA Award: $1,000; alumni of Student Conservation Association. Transfer Award: $1,000. Vermont Youth Conservation Corps Award: $1,000; awarded to alumni of VYCC. Scholarships also offered for service and volunteer commitments and experience; Work-Learning-Service Credit: $800/semester.
Cumulative student debt: 60% of graduating class had student loans; average debt was $39,724.

FINANCIAL AID PROCEDURES
Forms required: FAFSA, state aid form, institutional form.
Dates and Deadlines: Priority date 3/15; no closing date. Applicants notified on a rolling basis starting 2/1; must reply by 5/1 or within 3 week(s) of notification.
Transfers: Applicants notified on a rolling basis starting 2/1; must reply within 3 week(s) of notification.

CONTACT
Tim Patterson, Director of Admission and Financial Aid
PO Box 72, Craftsbury Common, VT 05827-0072
(800) 648-3591 ext. 3

University of Vermont
Burlington, Vermont
www.uvm.edu Federal Code: 003696

4-year public university in large town.
Enrollment: 10,192 undergrads, 4% part-time. 2,412 full-time freshmen.
Selectivity: Admits over 75% of applicants.

BASIC COSTS (2012-2013)
Tuition and fees: $15,284; out-of-state residents $35,612.
Per-credit charge: $556; out-of-state residents $1,403.
Room and board: $10,064.

FINANCIAL AID PICTURE (2011-2012)
Students with need: Out of 1,875 full-time freshmen who applied for aid, 1,483 were judged to have need. Of these, 1,467 received aid, and 166 had their full need met. Average financial aid package met 67% of need; average scholarship/grant was $15,554; average loan was $3,676. For part-time students, average financial aid package was $13,838.
Students without need: 641 full-time freshmen who did not demonstrate need for aid received scholarships/grants; average award was $6,995. No-need awards available for academics, art, athletics, ROTC.
Scholarships offered: 45 full-time freshmen received athletic scholarships; average amount $24,842.
Cumulative student debt: 59% of graduating class had student loans; average debt was $27,588.

FINANCIAL AID PROCEDURES
Forms required: FAFSA.
Dates and Deadlines: Priority date 2/10; no closing date. Applicants notified on a rolling basis starting 3/15; must reply within 4 week(s) of notification.
Transfers: Priority date 3/1; no deadline. Applicants notified on a rolling basis starting 3/15; must reply within 4 week(s) of notification. Merit scholarships are now available to transfer students.

CONTACT
Marie Johnson, Director Student Financial Services
194 South Prospect Street, Burlington, VT 05401-3596
(802) 656-5700

Vermont Technical College
Randolph Center, Vermont
www.vtc.edu Federal Code: 003698

4-year public nursing and technical college in small town.
Enrollment: 1,478 undergrads, 23% part-time. 215 full-time freshmen.
Selectivity: Admits 50 to 75% of applicants.

BASIC COSTS (2012-2013)
Tuition and fees: $12,024; out-of-state residents $22,128.
Room and board: $8,786.
Additional info: New England Board of Higher Education rate for students from other New England states: 150% of Vermont resident tuition. Available to degree candidates in academic areas not offered by educational institutions in their home states.

FINANCIAL AID PICTURE
Students with need: Need-based aid available for full-time and part-time students. Work study available nights, weekends, and for part-time students.
Students without need: No-need awards available for academics.

FINANCIAL AID PROCEDURES
Forms required: FAFSA.
Dates and Deadlines: Priority date 3/1; no closing date. Applicants notified on a rolling basis starting 3/15; must reply within 2 week(s) of notification.

CONTACT
Cathy McCullough, Director of Financial Aid
PO Box 500, Randolph Center, VT 05061-0500
(800) 965-8790

Virginia

Averett University

Danville, Virginia
www.averett.edu Federal Code: 003702

4-year private university and liberal arts college in small city, affiliated with Baptist General Association of Virginia (BGAV).
Enrollment: 886 undergrads, 2% part-time. 252 full-time freshmen.
Selectivity: Admits 50 to 75% of applicants.

BASIC COSTS (2013-2014)

Tuition and fees: $27,500.
Per-credit charge: $1,150.
Room and board: $8,500.

FINANCIAL AID PICTURE (2011-2012)

Students with need: Out of 228 full-time freshmen who applied for aid, 213 were judged to have need. Of these, 212 received aid, and 39 had their full need met. Average financial aid package met 72% of need; average scholarship/grant was $15,873; average loan was $3,595. For part-time students, average financial aid package was $6,459.
Students without need: 38 full-time freshmen who did not demonstrate need for aid received scholarships/grants. No-need awards available for academics, alumni affiliation, art, job skills, leadership, minority status, religious affiliation, state/district residency.
Scholarships offered: Founders Scholarship: $9,000; awarded to students for their quality academic preparation; renewable. Horizon Scholarship: $4,000; based on academic performance; renewable. Phi Theta Kappa Scholarship: $1,000; awarded to community college students who are members of Phi Theta Kappa; must be enrolled in a traditional program; renewable with a minimum cumulative grade point average of 3.0. Ministerial Tuition Discount: $400 (resident students), $200 (commuters); for full-time students who are children of ministers or students preparing for church-related vocations; renewable. Presidential scholarship $14,000. Deans Scholarship $12,000.

FINANCIAL AID PROCEDURES

Forms required: FAFSA, state aid form.
Dates and Deadlines: Priority date 4/1; no closing date. Applicants notified on a rolling basis starting 2/15; must reply within 2 week(s) of notification.
Transfers: No deadline. Applicants notified on a rolling basis starting 2/15; must reply within 2 week(s) of notification.

CONTACT

Carl Bradsher, Director of Student Financial Services
420 West Main Street, Danville, VA 24541
(434) 791-5890

Blue Ridge Community College

Weyers Cave, Virginia
www.brcc.edu Federal Code: 006819

2-year public community college in large town.
Enrollment: 4,694 undergrads.
Selectivity: Open admission; but selective for some programs.

BASIC COSTS (2012-2013)

Tuition and fees: $4,404; out-of-state residents $9,702.
Per-credit charge: $117; out-of-state residents $294.
Additional info: Out-of-state students pay an additional $465 capital outlay fee.

FINANCIAL AID PICTURE

Students with need: Need-based aid available for full-time and part-time students.
Students without need: No-need awards available for academics, job skills, leadership, minority status.

FINANCIAL AID PROCEDURES

Forms required: FAFSA, institutional form.
Dates and Deadlines: Priority date 5/1; no closing date. Applicants notified on a rolling basis starting 5/30; must reply within 2 week(s) of notification.

CONTACT

Robert Clemmer, Financial Aid Director
Box 80, Weyers Cave, VA 24486-9989
(540) 234-9261 ext. 2223

Bluefield College

Bluefield, Virginia
www.bluefield.edu Federal Code: 003703

4-year private liberal arts and teachers college in small town, affiliated with Baptist faith.
Enrollment: 806 undergrads, 5% part-time. 159 full-time freshmen.
Selectivity: Admits 50 to 75% of applicants.

BASIC COSTS (2012-2013)

Tuition and fees: $21,060.
Per-credit charge: $880.
Room and board: $7,640.

FINANCIAL AID PICTURE (2011-2012)

Students with need: Out of 144 full-time freshmen who applied for aid, 136 were judged to have need. Of these, 136 received aid, and 18 had their full need met. Average financial aid package met 66% of need; average scholarship/grant was $11,841; average loan was $3,029. For part-time students, average financial aid package was $4,959.
Students without need: 14 full-time freshmen who did not demonstrate need for aid received scholarships/grants; average award was $6,345. No-need awards available for academics, art, athletics, music/drama.
Scholarships offered: 18 full-time freshmen received athletic scholarships; average amount $6,383.
Cumulative student debt: 50% of graduating class had student loans; average debt was $27,225.

FINANCIAL AID PROCEDURES

Forms required: FAFSA, state aid form.
Dates and Deadlines: Priority date 6/1; no closing date. Applicants notified on a rolling basis starting 3/1; must reply within 3 week(s) of notification.
Transfers: No deadline. Applicants notified on a rolling basis starting 3/1; must reply within 3 week(s) of notification. Transfer students are not eligible to participate in the academic essay competition in which students competed for full-ride and half-ride scholarships.

CONTACT

Carly Kestner, Director of Financial Aid
3000 College Drive, Bluefield, VA 24605
(276) 326-4215

Bridgewater College

Bridgewater, Virginia
www.bridgewater.edu Federal Code: 003704

4-year private liberal arts college in small town, affiliated with Church of the Brethren.
Enrollment: 1,749 undergrads. 552 full-time freshmen.
Selectivity: Admits 50 to 75% of applicants.

BASIC COSTS (2013-2014)
Tuition and fees: $29,090.
Room and board: $10,790.

FINANCIAL AID PICTURE (2012-2013)
Students with need: Out of 515 full-time freshmen who applied for aid, 472 were judged to have need. Of these, 472 received aid, and 154 had their full need met. Average financial aid package met 85% of need; average scholarship/grant was $23,178; average loan was $3,727. For part-time students, average financial aid package was $6,497.
Students without need: 80 full-time freshmen who did not demonstrate need for aid received scholarships/grants; average award was $17,101. No-need awards available for academics, minority status, music/drama, religious affiliation.
Scholarships offered: Renewable academic scholarships are provided to freshmen based on high school grade point average and other criteria from the applicant's record.
Cumulative student debt: 78% of graduating class had student loans; average debt was $31,153.

FINANCIAL AID PROCEDURES
Forms required: FAFSA, state aid form.
Dates and Deadlines: Priority date 3/1; no closing date. Applicants notified on a rolling basis starting 3/21; must reply within 2 week(s) of notification.

CONTACT
Scott Morrison, Director of Financial Aid
402 East College Street, Bridgewater, VA 22812-1599
(540) 828-5377

Bryant & Stratton College: Richmond
Richmond, Virginia
www.bryantstratton.edu Federal Code: 010061

2-year for-profit career college in small city.
Enrollment: 938 undergrads.
Selectivity: Open admission; but selective for some programs.

BASIC COSTS (2012-2013)
Tuition and fees: $16,050.
Per-credit charge: $535.

FINANCIAL AID PICTURE
Students with need: Need-based aid available for full-time and part-time students. Work study available nights.
Students without need: This college awards aid only to students with need.

FINANCIAL AID PROCEDURES
Forms required: FAFSA.
Transfers: No deadline.

CONTACT
Dita Terry, Business Office Director
8141 Hull Street Road, Richmond, VA 23235
(804) 745-2444

Bryant & Stratton College: Virginia Beach
Virginia Beach, Virginia
www.bryantstratton.edu Federal Code: 002678

2-year for-profit business and junior college in large city.
Enrollment: 755 undergrads.
Selectivity: Open admission; but selective for some programs.

BASIC COSTS (2012-2013)
Tuition and fees: $16,050.
Per-credit charge: $535.

FINANCIAL AID PICTURE
Students with need: Need-based aid available for full-time and part-time students. Work study available nights.

FINANCIAL AID PROCEDURES
Forms required: FAFSA.
Dates and Deadlines: Applicants notified on a rolling basis.

CONTACT
Bethann Verbal, Director of Financial Aid
301 Centre Pointe Drive, Virginia Beach, VA 23462-4417
(757) 499-7900

Christendom College
Front Royal, Virginia
www.christendom.edu

4-year private liberal arts college in large town, affiliated with Roman Catholic Church.
Enrollment: 388 undergrads, 2% part-time. 104 full-time freshmen.
Selectivity: Admits over 75% of applicants.

BASIC COSTS (2012-2013)
Tuition and fees: $21,600.
Room and board: $7,970.

FINANCIAL AID PICTURE (2012-2013)
Students with need: Out of 84 full-time freshmen who applied for aid, 72 were judged to have need. Of these, 72 received aid, and 72 had their full need met. Average financial aid package met 90% of need; average scholarship/grant was $6,270; average loan was $6,540.
Students without need: 26 full-time freshmen who did not demonstrate need for aid received scholarships/grants; average award was $7,290. No-need awards available for academics, alumni affiliation.
Cumulative student debt: 60% of graduating class had student loans; average debt was $25,875.
Additional info: Christendom accepts no direct federal aid, nor does it participate in indirect programs of federal aid.

FINANCIAL AID PROCEDURES
Forms required: institutional form.
Dates and Deadlines: Priority date 4/1; closing date 6/1. Applicants notified on a rolling basis starting 2/1; must reply within 4 week(s) of notification.

CONTACT
Alisa Polk, Financial Aid Officer
134 Christendom Drive, Front Royal, VA 22630
(800) 877-5456

Christopher Newport University
Newport News, Virginia
www.cnu.edu Federal Code: 003706

4-year public university and liberal arts college in small city.
Enrollment: 5,036 undergrads, 2% part-time. 1,376 full-time freshmen.
Selectivity: Admits 50 to 75% of applicants.

BASIC COSTS (2012-2013)
Tuition and fees: $10,572; out-of-state residents $19,726.
Per-credit charge: $258; out-of-state residents $641.
Room and board: $9,728.
Additional info: Residential students pay annual $220 telecommunication fee. Out-of-state students pay annual $396 capital fee.

FINANCIAL AID PICTURE (2012-2013)

Students with need: Out of 1,180 full-time freshmen who applied for aid, 667 were judged to have need. Of these, 661 received aid, and 110 had their full need met. Average financial aid package met 69% of need; average scholarship/grant was $5,973; average loan was $3,312. For part-time students, average financial aid package was $6,660.

Students without need: 243 full-time freshmen who did not demonstrate need for aid received scholarships/grants; average award was $1,650. No-need awards available for academics, art, leadership, music/drama, ROTC, state/district residency.

Cumulative student debt: 55% of graduating class had student loans; average debt was $23,250.

FINANCIAL AID PROCEDURES

Forms required: FAFSA.

Dates and Deadlines: Priority date 3/1; no closing date. Applicants notified on a rolling basis starting 3/1; must reply within 3 week(s) of notification.

Transfers: No deadline. Applicants notified on a rolling basis starting 3/1; must reply within 3 week(s) of notification.

CONTACT

Lisa Raines, Dean of Enrollment Services and University Registrar
1 Avenue of the Arts, Newport News, VA 23606-3072
(757) 594-7170

College of William and Mary

Williamsburg, Virginia — Federal Code: 003705
www.wm.edu — CSS Code: 5115

4-year public university in large town.
Enrollment: 6,129 undergrads, 1% part-time. 1,465 full-time freshmen.
Selectivity: Admits less than 50% of applicants.

BASIC COSTS (2012-2013)

Tuition and fees: $13,570; out-of-state residents $36,753.
Per-credit charge: $300; out-of-district residents $1,000.
Room and board: $9,180.

FINANCIAL AID PICTURE

Students with need: Need-based aid available for full-time and part-time students.

Students without need: No-need awards available for academics, art, music/drama, ROTC.

FINANCIAL AID PROCEDURES

Forms required: FAFSA, CSS PROFILE.

Dates and Deadlines: Closing date 3/15. Applicants notified on a rolling basis starting 4/1; must reply by 5/1 or within 2 week(s) of notification.

CONTACT

Edward Irish, Director of Student Financial Aid
PO Box 8795, Williamsburg, VA 23187-8795
(757) 221-2420

Dabney S. Lancaster Community College

Clifton Forge, Virginia
www.dslcc.edu — Federal Code: 004996

2-year public community and technical college in small town.
Enrollment: 2,158 undergrads.
Selectivity: Open admission; but selective for some programs.

BASIC COSTS (2012-2013)

Tuition and fees: $3,810; out-of-state residents $9,108.
Per-credit charge: $117; out-of-state residents $294.
Additional info: Out-of-state students pay an additional $465 capital outlay fee.

FINANCIAL AID PICTURE

Students with need: Need-based aid available for full-time and part-time students.

Students without need: This college awards aid only to students with need.

FINANCIAL AID PROCEDURES

Forms required: FAFSA, institutional form.

Dates and Deadlines: Priority date 3/15; no closing date. Applicants notified on a rolling basis starting 4/15; must reply within 2 week(s) of notification.

CONTACT

Sandra Haverlack, Coordinator of Financial Aid and Veterans Affairs
Box 1000, Clifton Forge, VA 24422
(540) 863-2822

Danville Community College

Danville, Virginia
www.dcc.vccs.edu — Federal Code: 003758

2-year public community college in small city.
Enrollment: 4,420 undergrads.
Selectivity: Open admission; but selective for some programs.

BASIC COSTS (2012-2013)

Tuition and fees: $3,795; out-of-state residents $9,093.
Per-credit charge: $117; out-of-state residents $294.
Additional info: Out-of-state students pay an additional $465 capital outlay fee.

FINANCIAL AID PICTURE

Students with need: Need-based aid available for full-time and part-time students.

Students without need: This college awards aid only to students with need.

Scholarships offered: Educational Foundation Scholarship: $250 to $1,500; based on separate application; deadline mid-March prior to award year.

FINANCIAL AID PROCEDURES

Forms required: FAFSA.

Dates and Deadlines: Priority date 6/1; no closing date. Applicants notified on a rolling basis starting 5/1; must reply within 2 week(s) of notification.

Transfers: Limited aid available to transfer students admitted in spring semester.

CONTACT

Mary Gore, Assistant Coordinator of Financial Aid
1008 South Main Street, Danville, VA 24541
(434) 797-8439

DeVry University: Arlington

Arlington, Virginia
www.devry.edu

4-year for-profit university in very large city.
Enrollment: 540 undergrads, 52% part-time. 20 full-time freshmen.

BASIC COSTS (2012-2013)

Tuition and fees: $16,076.

FINANCIAL AID PICTURE

Students with need: Need-based aid available for full-time and part-time students.

Students without need: This college awards aid only to students with need.

FINANCIAL AID PROCEDURES

Forms required: FAFSA.

Dates and Deadlines: Applicants notified on a rolling basis.

CONTACT

Roberta McDevitt, Director of Student Finance
2450 Crystal Drive, Arlington, VA 22202
(703) 414-4000

Eastern Mennonite University

Harrisonburg, Virginia
www.emu.edu Federal Code: 003708

4-year private university and liberal arts college in large town, affiliated with Mennonite Church.
Enrollment: 1,118 undergrads, 5% part-time. 217 full-time freshmen.
Selectivity: Admits 50 to 75% of applicants.

BASIC COSTS (2012-2013)
Tuition and fees: $27,970.
Per-credit charge: $1,150.
Room and board: $9,100.

FINANCIAL AID PICTURE
Students with need: Need-based aid available for full-time and part-time students. Work study available nights, weekends, and for part-time students.
Students without need: No-need awards available for academics, alumni affiliation, art, leadership, religious affiliation, state/district residency.
Scholarships offered: President's Scholarship: GPA of 3.9 or higher. Academic Achievement Scholarship: minimum 3.2 GPA. University Grant: minimum 2.5 GPA; minimum SAT score of 920 (exclusive of Writing) or ACT score of 20 required for all scholarships. Amounts based on GPA and test scores; no limit on number of awards. Full-tuition scholarships available for 2 honors program applicants with highest test scores and GPA; half tuition scholarships available for next 10 candidates.

FINANCIAL AID PROCEDURES
Forms required: FAFSA, state aid form.
Dates and Deadlines: Priority date 3/1; no closing date. Applicants notified on a rolling basis starting 3/1; must reply within 4 week(s) of notification.
Transfers: No deadline. Applicants notified on a rolling basis starting 3/1; must reply within 4 week(s) of notification.

CONTACT

Michele Hensley, Director of Financial Assistance
1200 Park Road, Harrisonburg, VA 22802-2462
(540) 432-4137

Eastern Shore Community College

Melfa, Virginia
www.es.vccs.edu Federal Code: 003748

2-year public community college in rural community.
Enrollment: 989 undergrads.
Selectivity: Open admission; but selective for some programs.

BASIC COSTS (2012-2013)
Tuition and fees: $3,795; out-of-state residents $9,093.
Per-credit charge: $117; out-of-state residents $294.
Additional info: Out-of-state students pay an additional $465 capital outlay fee.

FINANCIAL AID PICTURE
Students with need: Need-based aid available for full-time and part-time students.
Students without need: This college awards aid only to students with need.
Additional info: ESCC is a member of the Servicemembers Opportunity Colleges program.

FINANCIAL AID PROCEDURES
Forms required: FAFSA.
Dates and Deadlines: Priority date 5/1; no closing date. Applicants notified on a rolling basis starting 6/1; must reply within 2 week(s) of notification.

CONTACT

P Smith, Chief Financial Aid Officer
29300 Lankford Highway, Melfa, VA 23410-9755
(757) 789-1732

ECPI University

Virginia Beach, Virginia
www.ecpi.edu Federal Code: 010198

4-year for-profit health science and technical college in very large city.
Enrollment: 10,763 undergrads.

BASIC COSTS (2012-2013)
Tuition and fees: $13,600.

FINANCIAL AID PICTURE
Students with need: Need-based aid available for full-time and part-time students. Work study available nights.
Students without need: No-need awards available for academics.

FINANCIAL AID PROCEDURES
Forms required: institutional form.
Dates and Deadlines: Applicants notified on a rolling basis.

CONTACT

Tammy Wyand, Director of Financial Aid
5555 Greenwich Road, Suite 300, Virginia Beach, VA 23462-6542
(757) 671-7171 ext. 311

Emory & Henry College

Emory, Virginia
www.ehc.edu Federal Code: 003709

4-year private liberal arts college in rural community, affiliated with United Methodist Church.
Enrollment: 875 undergrads, 3% part-time. 245 full-time freshmen.
Selectivity: Admits 50 to 75% of applicants.

BASIC COSTS (2012-2013)
Tuition and fees: $28,122.
Per-credit charge: $1,125.
Room and board: $9,426.

FINANCIAL AID PICTURE (2012-2013)
Students with need: Out of 227 full-time freshmen who applied for aid, 205 were judged to have need. Of these, 205 received aid, and 91 had their full need met. Average financial aid package met 90% of need; average scholarship/grant was $24,654; average loan was $3,540. For part-time students, average financial aid package was $10,330.
Students without need: 35 full-time freshmen who did not demonstrate need for aid received scholarships/grants; average award was $14,775. No-need awards available for academics, state/district residency.
Cumulative student debt: 79% of graduating class had student loans; average debt was $29,510.
Additional info: Virginia residents eligible for additional in-state tuition grants.

FINANCIAL AID PROCEDURES
Forms required: FAFSA, state aid form.

Dates and Deadlines: Priority date 4/1; no closing date. Applicants notified on a rolling basis starting 3/1; must reply within 2 week(s) of notification.
Transfers: Closing date 5/15. Applicants notified on a rolling basis starting 2/15; must reply by 6/15 or within 4 week(s) of notification. Financial aid based on academic credits accepted for transfer.

CONTACT
Scarlett Blevins, Director of Financial Aid and Student Services
PO Box 10, Emory, VA 24327
(276) 944-6115

Ferrum College

Ferrum, Virginia
www.ferrum.edu Federal Code: 003711

4-year private liberal arts college in rural community, affiliated with United Methodist Church.
Enrollment: 1,510 undergrads, 2% part-time. 577 full-time freshmen.
Selectivity: Admits over 75% of applicants.

BASIC COSTS (2012-2013)
Tuition and fees: $27,425.
Per-credit charge: $545.
Room and board: $9,130.

FINANCIAL AID PICTURE (2011-2012)
Students with need: Out of 543 full-time freshmen who applied for aid, 534 were judged to have need. Of these, 534 received aid, and 32 had their full need met. Average financial aid package met 37% of need; average scholarship/grant was $10,490; average loan was $2,858. For part-time students, average financial aid package was $7,127.
Students without need: 7 full-time freshmen who did not demonstrate need for aid received scholarships/grants; average award was $10,823. No-need awards available for academics, leadership, religious affiliation, state/district residency.
Scholarships offered: Ferrum Scholarship: $5,000-$10,000; high school GPA must be 3.0 or higher and SAT score must be 1500 or higher. Ferrum Merit Grant: $1,000-$7,000; high school GPA must be 2.0 or higher and SAT score must be in the range of 1050.
Cumulative student debt: 97% of graduating class had student loans; average debt was $24,788.

FINANCIAL AID PROCEDURES
Forms required: FAFSA, state aid form.
Dates and Deadlines: Priority date 3/1; no closing date. Applicants notified on a rolling basis starting 1/15.

CONTACT
Heather Hollandsworth, Director of Financial Aid
Spilman-Daniel House, 40 Stratton Lane, Ferrum, VA 24088
(540) 365-4282

George Mason University

Fairfax, Virginia
www.gmu.edu Federal Code: 003749

4-year public university in large town.
Enrollment: 20,067 undergrads, 19% part-time. 2,645 full-time freshmen.
Selectivity: Admits 50 to 75% of applicants.

BASIC COSTS (2012-2013)
Tuition and fees: $9,620; out-of-state residents $27,764.
Room and board: $9,250.

FINANCIAL AID PICTURE (2011-2012)
Students with need: Out of 2,160 full-time freshmen who applied for aid, 1,450 were judged to have need. Of these, 1,368 received aid, and 113 had their full need met. Average financial aid package met 62% of need; average scholarship/grant was $6,644; average loan was $3,273. For part-time students, average financial aid package was $6,703.
Students without need: 132 full-time freshmen who did not demonstrate need for aid received scholarships/grants; average award was $5,654. No-need awards available for academics, athletics, minority status, music/drama, ROTC, state/district residency.
Scholarships offered: 47 full-time freshmen received athletic scholarships; average amount $16,018.
Cumulative student debt: 57% of graduating class had student loans; average debt was $25,822.

FINANCIAL AID PROCEDURES
Forms required: FAFSA.
Dates and Deadlines: Priority date 3/1; no closing date. Applicants notified on a rolling basis starting 4/1; must reply within 3 week(s) of notification.

CONTACT
Heidi Granger, Director, Student Financial Aid
4400 University Drive, MSN 3A4, Fairfax, VA 22030-4444
(703) 993-2353

Germanna Community College

Locust Grove, Virginia
www.germanna.edu Federal Code: 008660

2-year public community college in rural community.
Enrollment: 7,520 undergrads.
Selectivity: Open admission; but selective for some programs.

BASIC COSTS (2012-2013)
Tuition and fees: $3,995; out-of-state residents $9,293.
Per-credit charge: $117; out-of-state residents $294.
Additional info: Out-of-state students pay additional $465 capital outlay fee.

FINANCIAL AID PICTURE
Students with need: Need-based aid available for full-time and part-time students.
Students without need: No-need awards available for academics.

FINANCIAL AID PROCEDURES
Forms required: FAFSA.
Dates and Deadlines: Priority date 4/1; no closing date. Applicants notified on a rolling basis starting 5/15; must reply within 2 week(s) of notification.

CONTACT
Michael Farris, Financial Aid Coordinator
2130 Germanna Highway, Locust Grove, VA 22508-2102
(540) 423-9124

Hampden-Sydney College

Hampden-Sydney, Virginia
www.hsc.edu Federal Code: 003713

4-year private liberal arts college for men in rural community, affiliated with Presbyterian Church (USA).
Enrollment: 1,080 undergrads. 342 full-time freshmen.
Selectivity: Admits 50 to 75% of applicants.

BASIC COSTS (2012-2013)
Tuition and fees: $35,570.
Room and board: $11,166.

FINANCIAL AID PICTURE (2012-2013)
Students with need: Out of 288 full-time freshmen who applied for aid, 226 were judged to have need. Of these, 226 received aid, and 38 had their full need met. Average financial aid package met 82% of need; average

scholarship/grant was $25,230; average loan was $4,318. Need-based aid available for part-time students.

Students without need: 119 full-time freshmen who did not demonstrate need for aid received scholarships/grants; average award was $13,708. No-need awards available for academics, leadership, minority status, music/drama, religious affiliation, ROTC, state/district residency.

Scholarships offered: Allan Scholarship: $30,000 annually. Venable Scholarship: $25,000 annually. Patrick Henry Scholarship: $20,000 annually. Achievement Awards: range from $2,000-$10,000 annually. All merit based.

Cumulative student debt: 55% of graduating class had student loans; average debt was $30,048.

FINANCIAL AID PROCEDURES

Forms required: FAFSA, state aid form.

Dates and Deadlines: Priority date 3/1; closing date 5/1. Must reply by 5/1 or within 2 week(s) of notification.

Transfers: No deadline. Applicants notified on a rolling basis; must reply within 2 week(s) of notification.

CONTACT

Zita Barree, Director of Financial Aid
Box 667, Hampden-Sydney, VA 23943
(434) 223-6119

Hampton University

Hampton, Virginia
www.hamptonu.edu Federal Code: 003714

4-year private university in small city.

Enrollment: 3,775 undergrads. 850 full-time freshmen.

Selectivity: Admits less than 50% of applicants.

BASIC COSTS (2012-2013)

Tuition and fees: $19,738.

Per-credit charge: $450.

Room and board: $8,790.

FINANCIAL AID PICTURE (2011-2012)

Students with need: Out of 563 full-time freshmen who applied for aid, 504 were judged to have need. Of these, 492 received aid, and 283 had their full need met. Average financial aid package met 58% of need; average scholarship/grant was $5,424; average loan was $4,500. For part-time students, average financial aid package was $3,571.

Students without need: 32 full-time freshmen who did not demonstrate need for aid received scholarships/grants; average award was $12,047. No-need awards available for academics, athletics, leadership, music/drama, ROTC.

Scholarships offered: 42 full-time freshmen received athletic scholarships; average amount $24,257.

FINANCIAL AID PROCEDURES

Forms required: FAFSA.

Dates and Deadlines: Applicants notified on a rolling basis starting 3/1; must reply within 2 week(s) of notification.

CONTACT

Martin Miles, Financial Aid Director
Office of Admissions, Hampton, VA 23668
(757) 727-5635

Hollins University

Roanoke, Virginia
www.hollins.edu Federal Code: 003715

4-year private university and liberal arts college for women in small city.

Enrollment: 607 undergrads, 3% part-time. 127 full-time freshmen.

Selectivity: Admits 50 to 75% of applicants.

BASIC COSTS (2013-2014)

Tuition and fees: $33,320.

Room and board: $11,660.

FINANCIAL AID PICTURE (2012-2013)

Students with need: Out of 114 full-time freshmen who applied for aid, 95 were judged to have need. Of these, 95 received aid, and 23 had their full need met. Average financial aid package met 84% of need; average scholarship/grant was $24,287; average loan was $3,889. For part-time students, average financial aid package was $12,379.

Students without need: 32 full-time freshmen who did not demonstrate need for aid received scholarships/grants; average award was $19,509. No-need awards available for academics, alumni affiliation, art, leadership, music/drama, state/district residency.

Scholarships offered: Scholar Awards: $5,000 full tuition; academic merit. Founder's Awards: $1,500-$7,000; organizational involvement. Creative Talent Awards: $1,500-$7,000; distinguished achievement or outstanding involvement in art, photography/film, creative writing, music, dance or theater.

Cumulative student debt: 77% of graduating class had student loans; average debt was $31,104.

FINANCIAL AID PROCEDURES

Forms required: FAFSA, state aid form.

Dates and Deadlines: Priority date 2/15; no closing date. Applicants notified on a rolling basis starting 3/1; must reply by 5/1.

Transfers: Priority date 7/1; closing date 7/15.

CONTACT

Mary Jean Corriss, Director of Scholarships and Financial Assistance
PO Box 9707, Roanoke, VA 24020-1707
(540) 362-6332

J. Sargeant Reynolds Community College

Richmond, Virginia
www.reynolds.edu Federal Code: 003759

2-year public community college in very large city.

Enrollment: 10,297 undergrads, 66% part-time. 1,097 full-time freshmen.

Selectivity: Open admission; but selective for some programs.

BASIC COSTS (2012-2013)

Tuition and fees: $4,053; out-of-state residents $9,351.

Per-credit charge: $119; out-of-state residents $296.

Additional info: Out-of-state students pay additional $465 capital outlay fee.

FINANCIAL AID PICTURE

Students with need: Need-based aid available for full-time and part-time students. Work study available nights, weekends, and for part-time students.

Students without need: No-need awards available for academics.

Scholarships offered: Local Board Scholarship: full tuition; high school students with minimum 3.0 GPA; 23 awarded. Eric and Jeanette Lipman Endowed Scholarship: based on academic excellence; number and amount awarded varies. Central Fidelity Bank Scholarship: $1,500; first-year students; minimum 2.5 cumulative GPA; 2 awarded.

FINANCIAL AID PROCEDURES

Forms required: FAFSA.

Dates and Deadlines: Priority date 4/15; no closing date. Applicants notified on a rolling basis starting 7/15; must reply within 2 week(s) of notification.

CONTACT

Kiesha Pope, Director of Financial Aid
Box 85622, Richmond, VA 23285-5622
(804) 523-5137

James Madison University
Harrisonburg, Virginia
www.jmu.edu Federal Code: 003721

4-year public university in large town.
Enrollment: 17,874 undergrads, 3% part-time. 4,323 full-time freshmen.
Selectivity: Admits 50 to 75% of applicants.

BASIC COSTS (2012-2013)
Tuition and fees: $8,808; out-of-state residents $22,796.
Per-credit charge: $154; out-of-state residents $580.
Room and board: $8,630.

FINANCIAL AID PICTURE (2012-2013)
Students with need: Average financial aid package met 41% of need; average scholarship/grant was $7,556; average loan was $3,624. For part-time students, average financial aid package was $8,368.
Students without need: No-need awards available for academics, alumni affiliation, art, athletics, leadership, minority status, music/drama, state/district residency.
Cumulative student debt: 54% of graduating class had student loans; average debt was $22,792.

FINANCIAL AID PROCEDURES
Forms required: FAFSA.
Dates and Deadlines: Closing date 3/1. Applicants notified on a rolling basis starting 4/1; must reply within 4 week(s) of notification.
Transfers: Applicants notified on a rolling basis starting 4/1; must reply within 4 week(s) of notification.

CONTACT
Lisa Turner, Director of Financial Aid and Scholarships
Sonner Hall, MSC 0101, Harrisonburg, VA 22807
(540) 568-7820

Jefferson College of Health Sciences
Roanoke, Virginia
www.jchs.edu Federal Code: 009893

4-year private health science and nursing college in small city.
Enrollment: 851 undergrads, 16% part-time. 75 full-time freshmen.
Selectivity: Admits less than 50% of applicants.

BASIC COSTS (2013-2014)
Tuition and fees: $22,400.
Per-credit charge: $650.
Additional info: Board plan not available. Cost of room only, $5,670.

FINANCIAL AID PICTURE (2011-2012)
Students with need: 53% of average financial aid package awarded as scholarships/grants, 47% awarded as loans/jobs. Need-based aid available for part-time students.
Students without need: No-need awards available for academics.

FINANCIAL AID PROCEDURES
Forms required: FAFSA, institutional form.
Dates and Deadlines: Applicants notified on a rolling basis; must reply within 2 week(s) of notification.

CONTACT
Deborah Johnson, Financial Aid Officer
101 Elm Avenue, SE, Roanoke, VA 24013-2222
(540) 985-8483

John Tyler Community College
Chester, Virginia
www.jtcc.edu Federal Code: 004004

2-year public community college in small city.
Enrollment: 6,508 undergrads, 59% part-time. 881 full-time freshmen.
Selectivity: Open admission; but selective for some programs.

BASIC COSTS (2012-2013)
Tuition and fees: $3,785; out-of-state residents $9,083.
Per-credit charge: $117; out-of-state residents $294.
Additional info: Out of state students pay additional $465 capital outlay fee.

FINANCIAL AID PICTURE
Students with need: Need-based aid available for full-time and part-time students. Work study available nights, weekends, and for part-time students.
Students without need: No-need awards available for academics, state/district residency.

FINANCIAL AID PROCEDURES
Forms required: FAFSA.
Dates and Deadlines: Priority date 5/15; closing date 7/15. Applicants notified on a rolling basis starting 6/15.

CONTACT
Fred Taylor, Vice President for Finance and Administration
13101 Jefferson Davis Highway, Chester, VA 23831-5316
(804) 706-5016

Liberty University
Lynchburg, Virginia
www.liberty.edu Federal Code: 010392

4-year private university in small city, affiliated with Baptist faith.
Enrollment: 11,507 undergrads, 3% part-time. 2,628 full-time freshmen.

BASIC COSTS (2013-2014)
Tuition and fees: $21,036.
Per-credit charge: $650.
Room and board: $7,976.

FINANCIAL AID PICTURE
Students with need: Need-based aid available for full-time and part-time students.
Students without need: No-need awards available for academics, alumni affiliation, athletics, leadership, music/drama, religious affiliation, ROTC, state/district residency.
Scholarships offered: Liberty Academic Achievement Scholarship: based on combination of high school grades and standardized test scores. Students may qualify for up to $6,000. Additional $3,500 could be applied if student is also accepted into the Honors Program.

FINANCIAL AID PROCEDURES
Forms required: FAFSA, state aid form.
Dates and Deadlines: Closing date 3/1. Applicants notified on a rolling basis starting 3/15; must reply within 3 week(s) of notification.
Transfers: Applicants notified on a rolling basis starting 3/15; must reply within 3 week(s) of notification.

CONTACT
Robert Ritz, Vice President of Student Financial Aid
1971 University Boulevard, Lynchburg, VA 24502
(434) 582-2270

Longwood University

Farmville, Virginia
www.longwood.edu Federal Code: 003719

4-year public university in small town.
Enrollment: 4,185 undergrads, 6% part-time. 1,043 full-time freshmen.
Selectivity: Admits over 75% of applicants.

BASIC COSTS (2012-2013)

Tuition and fees: $10,890; out-of-state residents $22,530.
Per-credit charge: $204; out-of-state residents $592.
Room and board: $9,120.
Additional info: Out of state students pay an additional $690 capital outlay fee.

FINANCIAL AID PICTURE (2011-2012)

Students with need: Out of 840 full-time freshmen who applied for aid, 576 were judged to have need. Of these, 564 received aid, and 279 had their full need met. Average financial aid package met 80% of need; average scholarship/grant was $6,387; average loan was $7,015. For part-time students, average financial aid package was $9,159.
Students without need: 26 full-time freshmen who did not demonstrate need for aid received scholarships/grants; average award was $3,252. No-need awards available for academics, alumni affiliation, art, athletics, leadership, music/drama, ROTC, state/district residency.
Scholarships offered: 33 full-time freshmen received athletic scholarships; average amount $11,172.
Cumulative student debt: 64% of graduating class had student loans; average debt was $26,439.

FINANCIAL AID PROCEDURES

Forms required: FAFSA.
Dates and Deadlines: Priority date 3/1; no closing date. Applicants notified on a rolling basis starting 4/1; must reply within 4 week(s) of notification.
Transfers: Closing date 3/1. Applicants notified by 4/1; must reply by 5/1.

CONTACT

Karen Schinabeck, Director of Financial Aid
201 High Street, Farmville, VA 23909-1898
(434) 395-2077

Lord Fairfax Community College

Middletown, Virginia
www.lfcc.edu Federal Code: 008659

2-year public community college in small town.
Enrollment: 6,196 undergrads.
Selectivity: Open admission; but selective for some programs.

BASIC COSTS (2012-2013)

Tuition and fees: $3,839; out-of-state residents $9,137.
Per-credit charge: $117; out-of-state residents $294.
Additional info: Out-of-state students pay an additional $465 capital outlay fee.

FINANCIAL AID PICTURE

Students with need: Need-based aid available for full-time and part-time students.
Students without need: This college awards aid only to students with need.

FINANCIAL AID PROCEDURES

Forms required: FAFSA.
Dates and Deadlines: Priority date 5/1; no closing date. Applicants notified on a rolling basis starting 6/1.

CONTACT

Aaron Whitacre, Director of Financial Aid
173 Skirmisher Lane, Middletown, VA 22645
(540) 868-7274

Lynchburg College

Lynchburg, Virginia
www.lynchburg.edu Federal Code: 003720

4-year private liberal arts college in small city, affiliated with Christian Church (Disciples of Christ).
Enrollment: 2,150 undergrads, 3% part-time. 517 full-time freshmen.
Selectivity: Admits 50 to 75% of applicants.

BASIC COSTS (2013-2014)

Tuition and fees: $33,565.
Per-credit charge: $450.
Room and board: $9,080.
Additional info: Tuition/fee waivers available for adults.

FINANCIAL AID PICTURE (2012-2013)

Students with need: Out of 484 full-time freshmen who applied for aid, 416 were judged to have need. Of these, 416 received aid, and 74 had their full need met. Average financial aid package met 82% of need; average scholarship/grant was $21,291; average loan was $3,607. For part-time students, average financial aid package was $6,706.
Students without need: 95 full-time freshmen who did not demonstrate need for aid received scholarships/grants; average award was $11,663. No-need awards available for academics, art, leadership, music/drama, state/district residency.
Cumulative student debt: 74% of graduating class had student loans; average debt was $33,353.

FINANCIAL AID PROCEDURES

Forms required: FAFSA, state aid form.
Dates and Deadlines: Priority date 3/1; no closing date. Applicants notified on a rolling basis starting 3/5; must reply within 2 week(s) of notification.
Transfers: Priority date 7/1; no deadline. Applicants notified on a rolling basis starting 3/5; must reply within 2 week(s) of notification.

CONTACT

Michelle Davis, Director of Financial Aid
1501 Lakeside Drive, Lynchburg, VA 24501-3199
(434) 544-8228

Mary Baldwin College

Staunton, Virginia
www.mbc.edu Federal Code: 003723

4-year private liberal arts college for women in large town, affiliated with Presbyterian Church (USA).
Enrollment: 1,391 undergrads, 29% part-time. 245 full-time freshmen.
Selectivity: Admits 50 to 75% of applicants.

BASIC COSTS (2012-2013)

Tuition and fees: $28,020.
Per-credit charge: $427.
Room and board: $8,180.

FINANCIAL AID PICTURE

Students with need: Need-based aid available for full-time and part-time students.
Students without need: No-need awards available for academics, leadership, state/district residency.

FINANCIAL AID PROCEDURES

Forms required: FAFSA, state aid form.

Dates and Deadlines: Priority date 3/1; no closing date. Applicants notified on a rolling basis starting 2/27; must reply by 5/1.
Transfers: No deadline. Applicants notified on a rolling basis starting 2/1; must reply by 5/1.

CONTACT
Andrew Modlin, Executive Director of Enrollment Management
Office of Admissions, Staunton, VA 24401
(540) 887-7022

Marymount University
Arlington, Virginia
www.marymount.edu Federal Code: 003724

4-year private university in small city, affiliated with Roman Catholic Church.
Enrollment: 2,439 undergrads, 11% part-time. 373 full-time freshmen.
Selectivity: Admits over 75% of applicants.

BASIC COSTS (2013-2014)
Tuition and fees: $26,430.
Per-credit charge: $850.
Room and board: $11,550.

FINANCIAL AID PICTURE
Students with need: Need-based aid available for full-time and part-time students.
Students without need: No-need awards available for academics, alumni affiliation, leadership, ROTC, state/district residency.
Scholarships offered: Freshman Academic Scholarship: Guaranteed for full-time freshman with cumulative high school GPA of 3.3 or better and combined SAT score (exclusive of Writing) of 1100 or higher; renewable for four years for students who maintain academic eligibility.

FINANCIAL AID PROCEDURES
Forms required: FAFSA.
Dates and Deadlines: Priority date 3/1; no closing date. Applicants notified on a rolling basis starting 3/15; must reply within 2 week(s) of notification.
Transfers: No deadline. Applicants notified on a rolling basis starting 3/15; must reply within 2 week(s) of notification. Academic scholarships available; apply by May 1.

CONTACT
Debbie Raines, Director of Financial Aid
2807 North Glebe Road, Arlington, VA 22207
(703) 284-1530

Mountain Empire Community College
Big Stone Gap, Virginia
www.mecc.edu Federal Code: 009629

2-year public community college in small town.
Enrollment: 3,089 undergrads.
Selectivity: Open admission; but selective for some programs.

BASIC COSTS (2012-2013)
Tuition and fees: $3,825; out-of-state residents $9,123.
Per-credit charge: $117; out-of-state residents $294.
Additional info: Out-of-state students pay additional $465 capital outlay fee.

FINANCIAL AID PICTURE
Students with need: Need-based aid available for full-time and part-time students.
Students without need: No-need awards available for academics, state/district residency.
Scholarships offered: Presidential Honor Scholarship: full tuition; for valedictorian or salutatorian. Dean's Academic Honor Award: $500-$1,000; for top 10 in graduating class.
Additional info: The college does not participate in loan programs. All financial aid is in form of grants, scholarships, or work study.

FINANCIAL AID PROCEDURES
Forms required: FAFSA.
Dates and Deadlines: Priority date 5/1; no closing date. Applicants notified on a rolling basis starting 1/1.

CONTACT
Kristy Hall, Director of Enrollment Services
3441 Mountain Empire Road, Big Stone Gap, VA 24219
(276) 523-2400

National College: Charlottesville
Charlottesville, Virginia
www.ncbt.edu Federal Code: 003726

2-year for-profit business college in small city.
Enrollment: 110 undergrads.
Selectivity: Open admission.

BASIC COSTS (2012-2013)
Tuition and fees: $14,310.
Per-credit charge: $317.

FINANCIAL AID PICTURE
Students with need: Need-based aid available for full-time and part-time students.
Students without need: This college awards aid only to students with need.

FINANCIAL AID PROCEDURES
Forms required: FAFSA.
Dates and Deadlines: Applicants notified on a rolling basis.

CONTACT
Pam Cotton, Director of Financial Aid Compliance and Auditing
PO Box 6400, Roanoke, VA 24017
(540) 986-1800

National College: Danville
Danville, Virginia
www.ncbt.edu Federal Code: 003726

2-year for-profit branch campus and business college in small city.
Enrollment: 191 undergrads.
Selectivity: Open admission.

BASIC COSTS (2012-2013)
Tuition and fees: $14,310.
Per-credit charge: $317.

FINANCIAL AID PICTURE
Students with need: Need-based aid available for full-time and part-time students.
Students without need: This college awards aid only to students with need.

FINANCIAL AID PROCEDURES
Forms required: FAFSA.
Dates and Deadlines: Applicants notified on a rolling basis starting 9/1.

CONTACT
Pam Cotton, Director of Financial Aid Compliance and Auditing
PO Box 6400, Roanoke, VA 24017
(540) 986-1800

National College: Harrisonburg

Harrisonburg, Virginia
www.national-college.edu Federal Code: 003726

2-year for-profit business college in large town.
Enrollment: 236 undergrads.
Selectivity: Open admission; but selective for some programs.

BASIC COSTS (2012-2013)
Tuition and fees: $14,310.
Per-credit charge: $317.

FINANCIAL AID PICTURE
Students with need: Need-based aid available for full-time and part-time students.
Students without need: This college awards aid only to students with need.

FINANCIAL AID PROCEDURES
Forms required: FAFSA.
Dates and Deadlines: Applicants notified on a rolling basis starting 9/1.

CONTACT
Pam Cotton, Director of Financial Aid Compliance and Auditing
PO Box 6400, Roanoke, VA 24017
(540) 986-1800

National College: Lynchburg

Lynchburg, Virginia
www.national-college.edu Federal Code: 010489

2-year for-profit business college in small city.
Enrollment: 251 undergrads.
Selectivity: Open admission.

BASIC COSTS (2012-2013)
Tuition and fees: $14,310.
Per-credit charge: $317.

FINANCIAL AID PICTURE
Students with need: Need-based aid available for full-time and part-time students.
Students without need: This college awards aid only to students with need.

FINANCIAL AID PROCEDURES
Forms required: FAFSA.
Dates and Deadlines: Applicants notified on a rolling basis starting 9/1.

CONTACT
Pam Cotton, Director of Financial Aid Compliance and Auditing
PO Box 6400, Roanoke, VA 24017
(540) 986-1000

National College: Martinsville

Martinsville, Virginia
www.national-college.edu Federal Code: 003726

2-year for-profit business and junior college in small city.
Enrollment: 220 undergrads.
Selectivity: Open admission.

BASIC COSTS (2012-2013)
Tuition and fees: $14,310.
Per-credit charge: $317.

FINANCIAL AID PICTURE
Students with need: Need-based aid available for full-time and part-time students.
Students without need: This college awards aid only to students with need.

FINANCIAL AID PROCEDURES
Forms required: FAFSA.
Dates and Deadlines: Applicants notified on a rolling basis.

CONTACT
Pam Cotton, Director of Financial Aid Compliance and Auditing
PO Box 6400, Roanoke, VA 24017
(540) 986-1800

National College: Salem

Roanoke, Virginia
www.national-college.edu Federal Code: 003726

4-year for-profit business college in large city.
Enrollment: 490 undergrads.
Selectivity: Open admission.

BASIC COSTS (2012-2013)
Tuition and fees: $14,310.
Per-credit charge: $317.

FINANCIAL AID PICTURE
Students with need: Need-based aid available for full-time and part-time students.
Students without need: This college awards aid only to students with need.

FINANCIAL AID PROCEDURES
Forms required: FAFSA.
Dates and Deadlines: Applicants notified on a rolling basis.

CONTACT
Pam Cotton, Director of Financial Aid Compliance and Auditing
PO Box 6400, Roanoke, VA 24017-0400
(540) 986-1800

New River Community College

Dublin, Virginia
www.nr.edu Federal Code: 005223

2-year public community college in rural community.
Enrollment: 5,083 undergrads.
Selectivity: Open admission.

BASIC COSTS (2012-2013)
Tuition and fees: $3,812; out-of-state residents $9,110.
Per-credit charge: $117; out-of-state residents $294.
Additional info: Out-of-state students pay additional $465 capital outlay fee.

FINANCIAL AID PICTURE
Students with need: Need-based aid available for full-time and part-time students.

FINANCIAL AID PROCEDURES
Forms required: FAFSA, institutional form.
Dates and Deadlines: Closing date 4/15. Applicants notified on a rolling basis starting 6/1.

CONTACT
Lori Nunn, Director of Financial Aid
Drawer 1127, Dublin, VA 24084
(540) 674-3615

Norfolk State University

Norfolk, Virginia
www.nsu.edu Federal Code: 003765

4-year public university in small city.
Enrollment: 6,312 undergrads, 18% part-time. 1,054 full-time freshmen.
Selectivity: Admits 50 to 75% of applicants.

BASIC COSTS (2012-2013)
Tuition and fees: $6,860; out-of-state residents $20,360.
Room and board: $8,130.

FINANCIAL AID PICTURE (2011-2012)
Students with need: 58% of average financial aid package awarded as scholarships/grants, 42% awarded as loans/jobs. Need-based aid available for part-time students.
Students without need: No-need awards available for academics, alumni affiliation, athletics, leadership, music/drama, ROTC, state/district residency.

FINANCIAL AID PROCEDURES
Forms required: FAFSA.
Dates and Deadlines: Priority date 5/31; no closing date. Applicants notified on a rolling basis starting 4/1; must reply within 2 week(s) of notification.

CONTACT
Kevin Burns, Director of Student Financial Services
700 Park Avenue, Norfolk, VA 23504
(757) 823-8381

Old Dominion University

Norfolk, Virginia
www.odu.edu Federal Code: 003728

4-year public university in large city.
Enrollment: 19,303 undergrads, 23% part-time. 2,668 full-time freshmen.
Selectivity: Admits 50 to 75% of applicants.

BASIC COSTS (2012-2013)
Tuition and fees: $8,450; out-of-state residents $23,330.
Per-credit charge: $273; out-of-state residents $769.
Room and board: $9,066.

FINANCIAL AID PICTURE (2012-2013)
Students with need: Out of 2,306 full-time freshmen who applied for aid, 1,744 were judged to have need. Of these, 1,636 received aid, and 249 had their full need met. Average financial aid package met 51% of need; average scholarship/grant was $7,761; average loan was $3,386. For part-time students, average financial aid package was $6,054.
Students without need: 180 full-time freshmen who did not demonstrate need for aid received scholarships/grants; average award was $1,868. No-need awards available for academics, alumni affiliation, art, athletics, leadership, music/drama, ROTC, state/district residency.
Scholarships offered: 86 full-time freshmen received athletic scholarships; average amount $17,885.
Cumulative student debt: 70% of graduating class had student loans; average debt was $25,585.

FINANCIAL AID PROCEDURES
Forms required: FAFSA.
Dates and Deadlines: Priority date 2/15; closing date 3/15. Applicants notified on a rolling basis starting 2/1; must reply within 2 week(s) of notification.
Transfers: Applicants notified on a rolling basis starting 3/1; must reply within 2 week(s) of notification.

CONTACT
Vera Riddick, Director of Financial Aid
5215 Hampton Boulevard, Norfolk, VA 23529
(757) 683-3683

Patrick Henry College

Purcellville, Virginia Federal Code: 039513
www.phc.edu CSS Code: 2804

4-year private liberal arts college in small town, affiliated with Christian Church.
Enrollment: 320 undergrads.

BASIC COSTS (2012-2013)
Tuition and fees: $24,352.
Room and board: $9,768.

FINANCIAL AID PICTURE
Students with need: Need-based aid available for full-time students.
Students without need: No-need awards available for academics, leadership, music/drama.

FINANCIAL AID PROCEDURES
Forms required: CSS/Financial aid profile required for students seeking need-based aid.
Dates and Deadlines: Priority date 3/15; closing date 6/15. Applicants notified on a rolling basis starting 3/1; must reply within 4 week(s) of notification.

CONTACT
Christine Guenard, Associate Director of Financial Aid
10 Patrick Henry Circle, Purcellville, VA 20132-3197
(540) 441-8142

Patrick Henry Community College

Martinsville, Virginia
www.ph.vccs.edu Federal Code: 003751

2-year public community college in large town.
Enrollment: 2,650 undergrads.
Selectivity: Open admission.

BASIC COSTS (2012-2013)
Tuition and fees: $3,804; out-of-state residents $9,102.
Per-credit charge: $117; out-of-state residents $294.
Additional info: Out-of-state students pay additional $465 capital outlay fee.

FINANCIAL AID PICTURE
Students with need: Need-based aid available for full-time and part-time students.

FINANCIAL AID PROCEDURES
Forms required: FAFSA.
Dates and Deadlines: Priority date 6/1; no closing date. Applicants notified on a rolling basis starting 6/15.

CONTACT
Cindy Keller, Financial Aid
645 Patriot Avenue, Martinsville, VA 24115-5311
(276) 656-0317

Paul D. Camp Community College

Franklin, Virginia
www.pdc.edu Federal Code: 009159

2-year public community college in small town.
Enrollment: 1,141 undergrads.
Selectivity: Open admission; but selective for some programs.

BASIC COSTS (2012-2013)
Tuition and fees: $3,800; out-of-state residents $9,098.
Per-credit charge: $117; out-of-state residents $294.

Additional info: Out-of-state students pay additional $465 capital outlay fee.

FINANCIAL AID PICTURE

Students with need: Need-based aid available for full-time and part-time students. Work study available nights, weekends, and for part-time students.

Students without need: This college awards aid only to students with need.

FINANCIAL AID PROCEDURES

Forms required: FAFSA.

Dates and Deadlines: Priority date 6/1; no closing date. Applicants notified on a rolling basis starting 8/1; must reply within 2 week(s) of notification.

CONTACT

Teresa Harrison, Financial Aid Coordinator
100 North College Drive, Franklin, VA 23851-0737
(757) 569-6715

Piedmont Virginia Community College

Charlottesville, Virginia
www.pvcc.edu Federal Code: 009928

2-year public community college in large town.
Enrollment: 3,912 undergrads, 73% part-time. 308 full-time freshmen.
Selectivity: Open admission; but selective for some programs.

BASIC COSTS (2012-2013)

Tuition and fees: $3,830; out-of-state residents $9,128.
Per-credit charge: $117; out-of-state residents $294.
Additional info: Out-of-state students pay additional $465 capital outlay fee.

FINANCIAL AID PICTURE

Students with need: Need-based aid available for full-time and part-time students. Work study available nights, weekends, and for part-time students.

Students without need: No-need awards available for academics.

FINANCIAL AID PROCEDURES

Forms required: FAFSA.

Dates and Deadlines: Applicants notified on a rolling basis starting 4/1.

Transfers: Must meet Satisfactory Academic Progress standards.

CONTACT

Carol Larson, Director of Financial Aid
501 College Drive, Charlottesville, VA 22902-7589
(434) 961-6545

Potomac College

Vienna, Virginia
www.potomac.edu Federal Code: 032183

4-year for-profit business college in large town.
Enrollment: 31 undergrads.
Selectivity: Open admission.

BASIC COSTS (2013-2014)

Tuition and fees: $12,760.

FINANCIAL AID PICTURE (2012-2013)

Students with need: Need-based aid available for full-time and part-time students.

FINANCIAL AID PROCEDURES

Forms required: FAFSA, institutional form.

Dates and Deadlines: Applicants notified on a rolling basis.

CONTACT

David Wilhelmi, Director of Financial Aid
2070 Chain Bridge Road, Vienna, VA 20170
(602) 734-4372

Radford University

Radford, Virginia
www.radford.edu Federal Code: 003732

4-year public university in large town.
Enrollment: 8,575 undergrads, 4% part-time. 2,052 full-time freshmen.
Selectivity: Admits over 75% of applicants.

BASIC COSTS (2012-2013)

Tuition and fees: $8,590; out-of-state residents $19,714.
Per-credit charge: $238; out-of-state residents $701.
Room and board: $7,881.

FINANCIAL AID PICTURE (2012-2013)

Students with need: Out of 1,614 full-time freshmen who applied for aid, 1,112 were judged to have need. Of these, 1,043 received aid, and 263 had their full need met. Average financial aid package met 81% of need; average scholarship/grant was $7,174; average loan was $3,255. For part-time students, average financial aid package was $6,726.

Students without need: 71 full-time freshmen who did not demonstrate need for aid received scholarships/grants; average award was $3,138. No-need awards available for academics, alumni affiliation, art, athletics, leadership, music/drama, ROTC, state/district residency.

Scholarships offered: ***Merit:*** Presidential Scholarship: $500 to $16,000; 3.5 GPA or higher; 1180 SAT combined critical reading and math sections or 26 ACT composite; 134 awarded. Academic Excellence Scholarship: $1,000 to $5,000; 3.5 GPA or higher; 1100 SAT combined on critical reading and math sections or 24 ACT composite; 145 awarded. ***Athletic:*** 31 full-time freshmen received athletic scholarships; average amount $13,083.

Cumulative student debt: 63% of graduating class had student loans; average debt was $25,241.

Additional info: Student's need and grades considered. Top consideration given to those with greatest need and who apply by deadline.

FINANCIAL AID PROCEDURES

Forms required: FAFSA.

Dates and Deadlines: Priority date 2/15; no closing date. Applicants notified on a rolling basis starting 4/15; must reply within 2 week(s) of notification.

CONTACT

Barbara Porter, Director of Financial Aid
115 Martin Hall, Radford, VA 24142
(540) 831-5408

Randolph College

Lynchburg, Virginia
www.randolphcollege.edu Federal Code: 003734

4-year private liberal arts college in small city, affiliated with United Methodist Church.
Enrollment: 607 undergrads, 1% part-time. 180 full-time freshmen.
Selectivity: Admits over 75% of applicants.

BASIC COSTS (2012-2013)

Tuition and fees: $31,541.
Per-credit charge: $1,245.
Room and board: $10,791.
Additional info: Tuition/fee waivers available for adults.

FINANCIAL AID PICTURE (2012-2013)

Students with need: Average financial aid package met 80% of need; average scholarship/grant was $22,650; average loan was $4,349. For part-time students, average financial aid package was $6,750.

Students without need: No-need awards available for academics, alumni affiliation, art, leadership, minority status, music/drama, religious affiliation, state/district residency.

Scholarships offered: Gottwald Scholarship: full tuition plus travel stipend; based on academic profile; approximately 3 awarded in each class. Presidential Scholars: $17,500; renewable annually; based on academic profile.
Cumulative student debt: 73% of graduating class had student loans; average debt was $33,737.

FINANCIAL AID PROCEDURES
Forms required: FAFSA.
Dates and Deadlines: Priority date 3/1; no closing date. Applicants notified on a rolling basis starting 3/1; must reply by 5/1 or within 2 week(s) of notification.
Transfers: Applicants notified on a rolling basis starting 3/1; must reply by 5/1 or within 2 week(s) of notification.

CONTACT
Kay Mattox, Director of Student Financial Services
2500 Rivermont Avenue, Lynchburg, VA 24503-1555
(434) 947-8128

Randolph-Macon College
Ashland, Virginia
www.rmc.edu Federal Code: 003733

4-year private liberal arts college in small town, affiliated with United Methodist Church.
Enrollment: 1,295 undergrads, 1% part-time. 409 full-time freshmen.
Selectivity: Admits 50 to 75% of applicants.

BASIC COSTS (2012-2013)
Tuition and fees: $33,525.
Room and board: $10,400.

FINANCIAL AID PICTURE (2012-2013)
Students with need: Out of 378 full-time freshmen who applied for aid, 316 were judged to have need. Of these, 316 received aid, and 68 had their full need met. Average financial aid package met 79% of need; average scholarship/grant was $21,759; average loan was $3,988. For part-time students, average financial aid package was $14,884.
Students without need: 92 full-time freshmen who did not demonstrate need for aid received scholarships/grants; average award was $15,275. No-need awards available for academics, alumni affiliation, minority status, religious affiliation, state/district residency.
Scholarships offered: Randolph-Macon College's academic scholarship; range from $12,500 to $20,000 per year based solely on the student's academic record and extra-curricular activities, renewable.
Cumulative student debt: 70% of graduating class had student loans; average debt was $31,112.

FINANCIAL AID PROCEDURES
Forms required: FAFSA, state aid form.
Dates and Deadlines: Priority date 3/1; closing date 2/15. Applicants notified by 3/15; must reply by 5/1 or within 2 week(s) of notification.
Transfers: Applicants notified by 3/15; must reply by 5/1 or within 2 week(s) of notification.

CONTACT
Mary Neal, Director of Financial Aid
PO Box 5005, Ashland, VA 23005-5505
(804) 752-7529

Rappahannock Community College
Glenns, Virginia
www.rappahannock.edu Federal Code: 009160

2-year public community college in rural community.
Enrollment: 1,813 undergrads.
Selectivity: Open admission; but selective for some programs.

BASIC COSTS (2012-2013)
Tuition and fees: $3,861; out-of-state residents $9,159.
Per-credit charge: $117; out-of-state residents $294.
Additional info: Out-of-state students pay additional $465 capital outlay fee.

FINANCIAL AID PICTURE (2011-2012)
Students with need: Need-based aid available for part-time students.

FINANCIAL AID PROCEDURES
Forms required: FAFSA, institutional form.
Dates and Deadlines: Priority date 4/15; no closing date. Applicants notified on a rolling basis starting 6/30.
Transfers: No deadline. Applicants notified on a rolling basis.

CONTACT
Carolyn Ward, Director of Financial Aid
12745 College Drive, Glenns, VA 23149-2616
(804) 758-6737

Regent University
Virginia Beach, Virginia
www.regent.edu Federal Code: 030913

4-year private university in large city, affiliated with interdenominational tradition.
Enrollment: 2,316 undergrads, 38% part-time. 202 full-time freshmen.
Selectivity: Admits over 75% of applicants.

BASIC COSTS (2013-2014)
Tuition and fees: $15,768.
Per-credit charge: $495.
Room only: $4,100.

FINANCIAL AID PICTURE (2012-2013)
Students with need: Out of 191 full-time freshmen who applied for aid, 175 were judged to have need. Of these, 175 received aid, and 15 had their full need met. Average financial aid package met 56% of need; average scholarship/grant was $8,368; average loan was $3,077. For part-time students, average financial aid package was $8,028.
Students without need: 23 full-time freshmen who did not demonstrate need for aid received scholarships/grants; average award was $5,521. No-need awards available for academics, alumni affiliation, leadership, ROTC.
Cumulative student debt: 67% of graduating class had student loans; average debt was $49,326.

FINANCIAL AID PROCEDURES
Forms required: FAFSA, state aid form, institutional form.
Dates and Deadlines: Priority date 3/15; no closing date. Applicants notified on a rolling basis starting 3/1; must reply within 2 week(s) of notification.
Transfers: Priority date 7/1; no deadline. Applicants notified on a rolling basis starting 3/15; must reply within 2 week(s) of notification. Must be able to determine number of transfer credits before full award package is offered. Student should submit all academic transcripts in a timely manner to ensure transfer articulation occurs in a timely manner.

CONTACT
Dotti Davidson, Director of Financial Aid
1000 Regent University Drive, Virginia Beach, VA 23464-9800
(757) 352-4125

Richard Bland College
Petersburg, Virginia
www.rbc.edu Federal Code: 003707

2-year public junior and liberal arts college in small city.
Enrollment: 1,248 undergrads.

BASIC COSTS (2012-2013)
Tuition and fees: $3,658; out-of-state residents $13,524.
Per-credit charge: $134; out-of-state residents $561.
Additional info: Board plan not available. Cost of room only, $9,670. Residential students pay an additional $726 per year.

FINANCIAL AID PICTURE
Students with need: Need-based aid available for full-time and part-time students.
Students without need: No-need awards available for academics.
Scholarships offered: Presidential Scholarships: average $1,000; for full-time first-time Virginia residents; based on minimum 3.5 high school GPA.

FINANCIAL AID PROCEDURES
Forms required: FAFSA, institutional form.
Dates and Deadlines: Closing date 4/1. Applicants notified by 6/1; must reply within 2 week(s) of notification.
Transfers: Priority date 4/15; no deadline. Applicants notified on a rolling basis starting 5/15; must reply within 2 week(s) of notification.

CONTACT
J. Tyler Hart, Coordinator of Financial Aid
11301 Johnson Road, Petersburg, VA 23805
(804) 862-6223

Roanoke College
Salem, Virginia
www.roanoke.edu Federal Code: 003736

4-year private liberal arts college in large town, affiliated with Evangelical Lutheran Church in America.
Enrollment: 2,010 undergrads, 2% part-time. 543 full-time freshmen.
Selectivity: Admits 50 to 75% of applicants.

BASIC COSTS (2013-2014)
Tuition and fees: $36,472.
Room and board: $11,524.
Additional info: Tuition/fee waivers available for adults.

FINANCIAL AID PICTURE (2012-2013)
Students with need: Out of 483 full-time freshmen who applied for aid, 418 were judged to have need. Of these, 418 received aid, and 88 had their full need met. Average financial aid package met 78% of need; average scholarship/grant was $24,168; average loan was $4,122. For part-time students, average financial aid package was $13,208.
Students without need: 117 full-time freshmen who did not demonstrate need for aid received scholarships/grants; average award was $13,196. No-need awards available for academics, minority status, music/drama, religious affiliation, state/district residency.
Scholarships offered: Roanoke College Scholars' Competition: William Beard Scholarship: up to 3 awarded; full tuition, room and board. David Bittle Scholarship: up to 12 awarded; full tuition. Christopher Baughman Scholarship: up to 50 awarded; $4,500 per year; added to previously awarded college scholarships. Julius Dreher Scholarship: up to 75 awarded; $1,500 per year added to previously awarded college scholarships. John Morehead Scholarship; $1,000 per year; added to previously awarded college scholarships. Davis Honors Scholarship: up to 35 awarded; $1,000 per year to Honors Program participants. Additional Roanoke College merit scholarships are available, up to $14,500 per year.
Cumulative student debt: 72% of graduating class had student loans; average debt was $33,004.

FINANCIAL AID PROCEDURES
Forms required: FAFSA, state aid form.
Dates and Deadlines: Priority date 3/1; no closing date. Applicants notified on a rolling basis starting 11/1; must reply within 2 week(s) of notification.
Transfers: No deadline. Applicants notified on a rolling basis starting 11/1; must reply within 2 week(s) of notification.

CONTACT
Thomas Blair, Director of Financial Aid
221 College Lane, Salem, VA 24153-3794
(540) 375-2235

St. Paul's College
Lawrenceville, Virginia
www.saintpauls.edu Federal Code: 003739

4-year private liberal arts college in small town, affiliated with Episcopal Church.
Enrollment: 410 undergrads.

BASIC COSTS (2012-2013)
Tuition and fees: $13,160.
Per-credit charge: $516.
Room and board: $6,640.
Additional info: Tuition/fee waivers available for minority students.

FINANCIAL AID PICTURE
Students with need: Work study available nights, weekends, and for part-time students.
Students without need: No-need awards available for academics, alumni affiliation, athletics.

FINANCIAL AID PROCEDURES
Forms required: FAFSA, state aid form.
Dates and Deadlines: Applicants notified on a rolling basis starting 1/15; must reply by 7/1 or within 4 week(s) of notification.
Transfers: No deadline. Applicants notified on a rolling basis; must reply within 2 week(s) of notification.

CONTACT
Karen Lyons, Assistant Director of Financial Aid
115 College Drive, Lawrenceville, VA 23868
(434) 848-6496

Shenandoah University
Winchester, Virginia
www.su.edu Federal Code: 003737

4-year private university in large town, affiliated with United Methodist Church.
Enrollment: 1,902 undergrads, 3% part-time. 457 full-time freshmen.
Selectivity: Admits over 75% of applicants.

BASIC COSTS (2012-2013)
Tuition and fees: $28,800.
Per-credit charge: $800.
Room and board: $9,240.

FINANCIAL AID PICTURE (2012-2013)
Students with need: Out of 389 full-time freshmen who applied for aid, 338 were judged to have need. Of these, 338 received aid, and 64 had their full need met. Average financial aid package met 71% of need; average scholarship/grant was $8,500; average loan was $3,500. Need-based aid available for part-time students.
Students without need: No-need awards available for academics, music/drama, religious affiliation, state/district residency.
Cumulative student debt: 85% of graduating class had student loans; average debt was $31,000.
Additional info: Emergency Grant Fund available for books, meals, tuition and fees.

FINANCIAL AID PROCEDURES
Forms required: FAFSA, state aid form.

Dates and Deadlines: Applicants notified on a rolling basis starting 3/15; must reply within 4 week(s) of notification.
Transfers: No deadline. Applicants notified on a rolling basis starting 3/15; must reply within 4 week(s) of notification.

CONTACT
Nancy Bragg, Director of Financial Aid
1460 University Drive, Winchester, VA 22601-5195
(540) 665-4538

Skyline College: Roanoke

Roanoke, Virginia
www.skyline.edu Federal Code: 017205

2-year for-profit technical college in small city.
Enrollment: 264 undergrads.

BASIC COSTS (2012-2013)
Tuition and fees: $13,600.

FINANCIAL AID PICTURE
Students with need: Need-based aid available for full-time and part-time students.

FINANCIAL AID PROCEDURES
Forms required: FAFSA.
Dates and Deadlines: Applicants notified on a rolling basis.

CONTACT
Walter Merchant, Director of Financial Aid
5234 Airport Road, Roanoke, VA 24012
(540) 563-8080

Southern Virginia University

Buena Vista, Virginia
www.svu.edu Federal Code: 003738

4-year private liberal arts college in small town, affiliated with Church of Jesus Christ of Latter-day Saints.
Enrollment: 725 undergrads, 2% part-time. 286 full-time freshmen.
Selectivity: Admits less than 50% of applicants.

BASIC COSTS (2013-2014)
Tuition and fees: $18,900.
Per-credit charge: $670.
Room and board: $6,800.

FINANCIAL AID PICTURE (2011-2012)
Students with need: Out of 242 full-time freshmen who applied for aid, 207 were judged to have need. Of these, 207 received aid, and 26 had their full need met. Average financial aid package met 59% of need; average scholarship/grant was $9,942; average loan was $3,041. For part-time students, average financial aid package was $5,836.
Students without need: 74 full-time freshmen who did not demonstrate need for aid received scholarships/grants; average award was $6,224. No-need awards available for academics, art, athletics, leadership, music/drama, ROTC.
Scholarships offered: 21 full-time freshmen received athletic scholarships; average amount $1,184.
Cumulative student debt: 86% of graduating class had student loans; average debt was $24,717.

FINANCIAL AID PROCEDURES
Forms required: FAFSA, state aid form.
Dates and Deadlines: Priority date 5/1; no closing date. Applicants notified on a rolling basis starting 3/1; must reply by 5/1 or within 3 week(s) of notification.
Transfers: No deadline. Applicants notified on a rolling basis starting 3/1.

CONTACT
John Brandt, Director of Financial Aid
One University Hill Drive, Buena Vista, VA 24416-3097
(540) 261-4351

Southside Virginia Community College

Alberta, Virginia
www.southside.edu Federal Code: 008661

2-year public community college in rural community.
Enrollment: 3,041 undergrads.
Selectivity: Open admission; but selective for some programs.

BASIC COSTS (2012-2013)
Tuition and fees: $3,810; out-of-state residents $9,108.
Per-credit charge: $117; out-of-state residents $294.
Additional info: Out-of-state students pay additional $465 capital outlay fee.

FINANCIAL AID PICTURE
Students with need: Need-based aid available for full-time and part-time students. Work study available nights.
Students without need: No-need awards available for academics.
Scholarships offered: Guaranteed Academic Merit Award: $1,500, for high school graduates within college's service area with 3.0 GPA who do not receive at least $1,500 in need-based aid.

FINANCIAL AID PROCEDURES
Forms required: FAFSA.
Dates and Deadlines: Priority date 6/1; closing date 8/1. Applicants notified on a rolling basis starting 6/15.
Transfers: State aid limited to in-state residents.

CONTACT
Sally Tharrington, Director of Financial Aid
109 Campus Drive, Alberta, VA 23821
(434) 736-2026

Southwest Virginia Community College

Richlands, Virginia
www.sw.edu Federal Code: 007260

2-year public community college in small town.
Enrollment: 2,061 undergrads, 41% part-time. 433 full-time freshmen.
Selectivity: Open admission; but selective for some programs.

BASIC COSTS (2012-2013)
Tuition and fees: $3,780; out-of-state residents $9,080.
Per-credit charge: $117; out-of-state residents $294.
Additional info: Out-of-state students pay an additional $465 capital outlay fee.

FINANCIAL AID PICTURE (2011-2012)
Students with need: Need-based aid available for part-time students.
Students without need: This college awards aid only to students with need.

FINANCIAL AID PROCEDURES
Forms required: FAFSA, institutional form.
Dates and Deadlines: Priority date 5/30; no closing date. Applicants notified on a rolling basis starting 7/1.

CONTACT
Virginia Stevens, Administrative and Office Specialist III, Financial Aid
PO Box SVCC, Richlands, VA 24641-1101
(276) 964-7290

Stratford University: Falls Church

Falls Church, Virginia
www.stratford.edu

4-year for-profit university and career college in small city.
Enrollment: 1,711 undergrads. 33 full-time freshmen.
Selectivity: Open admission.

BASIC COSTS (2012-2013)
Tuition and fees: $16,650.
Per-credit charge: $370.

FINANCIAL AID PICTURE (2011-2012)
Students with need: Out of 20 full-time freshmen who applied for aid, 20 were judged to have need. Of these, 20 received aid. Need-based aid available for part-time students.
Students without need: This college awards aid only to students with need.
Cumulative student debt: 50% of graduating class had student loans; average debt was $42,981.

FINANCIAL AID PROCEDURES
Forms required: FAFSA.
Dates and Deadlines: Applicants notified on a rolling basis starting 1/1.
Transfers: No deadline. Applicants notified on a rolling basis starting 1/1.

CONTACT
Carla Johnson, Financial Aid Director
7777 Leesburg Pike Suite 100S, Falls Church, VA 22043

Sweet Briar College

Sweet Briar, Virginia
www.sbc.edu Federal Code: 003742

4-year private liberal arts college for women in rural community.
Enrollment: 566 undergrads, 1% part-time. 194 full-time freshmen.
Selectivity: Admits over 75% of applicants.

BASIC COSTS (2013-2014)
Tuition and fees: $33,605.
Per-credit charge: $920.
Room and board: $11,800.
Additional info: Tuition/fee waivers available for adults.

FINANCIAL AID PICTURE (2011-2012)
Students with need: Out of 185 full-time freshmen who applied for aid, 160 were judged to have need. Of these, 160 received aid, and 29 had their full need met. Average financial aid package met 80% of need; average scholarship/grant was $22,129; average loan was $4,101. For part-time students, average financial aid package was $9,361.
Students without need: 34 full-time freshmen who did not demonstrate need for aid received scholarships/grants; average award was $11,883. No-need awards available for academics, art, leadership, music/drama, state/district residency.
Scholarships offered: Founders and Prothro Scholarships: up to $15,000. Commonwealth Scholarships: up to $13,000. Betty Bean Black Scholarships: up to $12,000. Sweet Briar Scholarships: up to $9,000; for students with special talents in specific area. All awards based on academic qualifications; renewable annually with specified GPA.
Cumulative student debt: 63% of graduating class had student loans; average debt was $23,596.

FINANCIAL AID PROCEDURES
Forms required: FAFSA.
Dates and Deadlines: Closing date 2/15. Applicants notified on a rolling basis starting 3/1; must reply by 5/1.
Transfers: Closing date 7/15.

CONTACT
Bobbi Carpenter, Director of Financial Aid
PO Box 1052, Sweet Briar, VA 24595-1502

Thomas Nelson Community College

Hampton, Virginia
www.tncc.edu Federal Code: 006871

2-year public community college in small city.
Enrollment: 10,942 undergrads.
Selectivity: Open admission; but selective for some programs.

BASIC COSTS (2012-2013)
Tuition and fees: $3,782; out-of-state residents $9,082.
Per-credit charge: $117; out-of-state residents $294.
Additional info: Out-of-state students pay additional $465 capital outlay fee.

FINANCIAL AID PICTURE (2011-2012)
Students with need: 59% of average financial aid package awarded as scholarships/grants, 41% awarded as loans/jobs. Need-based aid available for part-time students. Work study available nights.

FINANCIAL AID PROCEDURES
Forms required: FAFSA, institutional form.
Dates and Deadlines: Priority date 5/1; no closing date. Applicants notified on a rolling basis starting 6/1; must reply within 2 week(s) of notification.
Transfers: No deadline. Applicants notified on a rolling basis; must reply within 2 week(s) of notification.

CONTACT
Kathryn Anderson, Director of Financial Aid, Veterans Affairs, and Scholarships
PO Box 9407, Hampton, VA 23670
(757) 825-2848

Tidewater Community College

Norfolk, Virginia
www.tcc.edu Federal Code: 003712

2-year public community college in large city.
Enrollment: 27,226 undergrads.
Selectivity: Open admission; but selective for some programs.

BASIC COSTS (2012-2013)
Tuition and fees: $4,556; out-of-state residents $9,854.
Per-credit charge: $117; out-of-state residents $294.
Additional info: Out-of-state students pay additional $465 capital outlay fee.

FINANCIAL AID PICTURE
Students with need: Need-based aid available for full-time and part-time students.

FINANCIAL AID PROCEDURES
Forms required: FAFSA.
Dates and Deadlines: Priority date 4/1; no closing date. Applicants notified on a rolling basis starting 4/1.

CONTACT
Jennifer Harpham, Director of Financial Aid
1700 College Crescent, Virginia Beach, VA 23453
(757) 822-1360

University of Management and Technology

Arlington, Virginia
www.umtweb.edu Federal Code: 041103

4-year for-profit university in very large city.
Enrollment: 790 undergrads.
Selectivity: Open admission; but selective for some programs.

BASIC COSTS (2013-2014)

Tuition and fees: $11,700.
Per-credit charge: $390.

FINANCIAL AID PICTURE (2011-2012)

Students with need: 40% of average financial aid package awarded as scholarships/grants, 60% awarded as loans/jobs.

CONTACT

1901 Fort Myer Drive, Suite 700, Arlington, VA 22209-1609
(703) 516-0035

University of Mary Washington

Fredericksburg, Virginia
www.umw.edu Federal Code: 003746

4-year public university and teachers college in small city.
Enrollment: 4,378 undergrads, 12% part-time. 937 full-time freshmen.
Selectivity: Admits over 75% of applicants.

BASIC COSTS (2012-2013)

Tuition and fees: $9,246; out-of-state residents $21,560.
Per-credit charge: $329; out-of-state residents $841.
Room and board: $10,238.

FINANCIAL AID PICTURE (2012-2013)

Students with need: Out of 730 full-time freshmen who applied for aid, 415 were judged to have need. Of these, 370 received aid, and 55 had their full need met. Average financial aid package met 48% of need; average scholarship/grant was $7,800; average loan was $3,330. For part-time students, average financial aid package was $6,770.
Students without need: 102 full-time freshmen who did not demonstrate need for aid received scholarships/grants; average award was $2,840. No-need awards available for academics, alumni affiliation, art, leadership, music/drama, state/district residency.
Scholarships offered: Scholastic Excellence Awards: from $500 to $6,000. Eight Virginia residents will receive tuition, fees, room and board up to $10,000. Two non-Virginia awards: tuition, fees, room and board. All scholarships renewable.
Cumulative student debt: 45% of graduating class had student loans; average debt was $23,300.

FINANCIAL AID PROCEDURES

Forms required: FAFSA.
Dates and Deadlines: Closing date 3/1. Applicants notified on a rolling basis starting 4/5; must reply by 5/1 or within 2 week(s) of notification.
Transfers: Must reply by 5/15.

CONTACT

Debra Harber, Director of Financial Aid
1301 College Avenue, Fredericksburg, VA 22401-5300
(540) 654-2468

University of Richmond

University of Richmond, Virginia Federal Code: 003744
www.richmond.edu CSS Code: 5569

4-year private university and liberal arts college in small city.
Enrollment: 2,960 undergrads, 1% part-time. 781 full-time freshmen.
Selectivity: Admits less than 50% of applicants.

BASIC COSTS (2013-2014)

Tuition and fees: $45,320.
Per-credit charge: $2,266.
Room and board: $10,270.

FINANCIAL AID PICTURE (2012-2013)

Students with need: Out of 495 full-time freshmen who applied for aid, 309 were judged to have need. Of these, 309 received aid, and 291 had their full need met. Average financial aid package met 100% of need; average scholarship/grant was $35,334; average loan was $3,121. For part-time students, average financial aid package was $20,709.
Students without need: 75 full-time freshmen who did not demonstrate need for aid received scholarships/grants; average award was $40,071. No-need awards available for academics, art, athletics, leadership, music/drama, ROTC.
Scholarships offered: ***Merit:*** Richmond Scholars program: full tuition scholarships; up to 45 entering freshmen. Presidential Scholarships: up to $15,000. ***Athletic:*** 49 full-time freshmen received athletic scholarships; average amount $32,422.
Cumulative student debt: 43% of graduating class had student loans; average debt was $21,825.
Additional info: VA residents whose family income is $40,000 or less, qualify for need-based aid, and enter as first year student will receive grant assistance equal to full tuition, room and board. Early decision: Financial aid package estimated using historical data; applicant still required to submit all financial aid forms.

FINANCIAL AID PROCEDURES

Forms required: FAFSA, CSS PROFILE.
Dates and Deadlines: Closing date 2/15. Applicants notified by 4/1; must reply within 4 week(s) of notification.
Transfers: Applicants notified by 4/15; must reply within 4 week(s) of notification.

CONTACT

Cynthia Deffenbaugh, Director of Financial Aid
Brunet Memorial Hall: 28 Westhampton Way, University of Richmond, VA 23173
(804) 289-8438

University of Virginia

Charlottesville, Virginia
www.virginia.edu Federal Code: 003745

4-year public university in small city.
Enrollment: 14,640 undergrads, 3% part-time. 3,394 full-time freshmen.
Selectivity: Admits less than 50% of applicants.

BASIC COSTS (2012-2013)

Tuition and fees: $12,006; out-of-state residents $37,336.
Per-credit charge: $321; out-of-state residents $1,165.
Room and board: $9,419.

FINANCIAL AID PICTURE (2012-2013)

Students with need: Out of 2,387 full-time freshmen who applied for aid, 1,095 were judged to have need. Of these, 1,022 received aid, and 602 had their full need met. Average financial aid package met 87% of need; average scholarship/grant was $17,631; average loan was $5,791. For part-time students, average financial aid package was $12,672.

PART III: FINANCIAL AID COLLEGE BY COLLEGE

Students without need: 275 full-time freshmen who did not demonstrate need for aid received scholarships/grants; average award was $10,774. No-need awards available for academics, athletics, leadership, minority status, music/drama, state/district residency.
Scholarships offered: 109 full-time freshmen received athletic scholarships; average amount $19,116.
Cumulative student debt: 36% of graduating class had student loans; average debt was $21,591.

FINANCIAL AID PROCEDURES

Forms required: FAFSA, institutional form.
Dates and Deadlines: Priority date 3/1; no closing date. Must reply by 5/1.

CONTACT

Yvonne Hubbard, Director, Student Financial Services
Box 400160, Charlottesville, VA 22904-4160
(434) 982-6000

University of Virginia's College at Wise

Wise, Virginia
www.uvawise.edu Federal Code: 003747

4-year public liberal arts college in small town.
Enrollment: 1,618 undergrads, 7% part-time. 356 full-time freshmen.
Selectivity: Admits over 75% of applicants.

BASIC COSTS (2012-2013)

Tuition and fees: $8,228; out-of-state residents $21,843.
Per-credit charge: $190; out-of-state residents $770.
Room and board: $9,440.

FINANCIAL AID PICTURE (2012-2013)

Students with need: Out of 343 full-time freshmen who applied for aid, 289 were judged to have need. Of these, 289 received aid, and 126 had their full need met. Average financial aid package met 96% of need; average scholarship/grant was $6,933; average loan was $2,365. For part-time students, average financial aid package was $6,266.
Students without need: 33 full-time freshmen who did not demonstrate need for aid received scholarships/grants; average award was $3,879. No-need awards available for academics, alumni affiliation, art, athletics, job skills, leadership, music/drama, religious affiliation, state/district residency.
Scholarships offered: 7 full-time freshmen received athletic scholarships; average amount $1,493.
Cumulative student debt: 66% of graduating class had student loans; average debt was $7,076.

FINANCIAL AID PROCEDURES

Forms required: FAFSA.
Dates and Deadlines: Closing date 4/1. Applicants notified on a rolling basis starting 2/15; must reply within 4 week(s) of notification.
Transfers: Applicants notified on a rolling basis.

CONTACT

Rebecca Huffman, Director of Financial Aid
1 College Avenue, Wise, VA 24293-4412
(276) 328-0139

Virginia Commonwealth University

Richmond, Virginia
www.vcu.edu Federal Code: 003735

4-year public university in small city.
Enrollment: 22,178 undergrads, 11% part-time. 3,776 full-time freshmen.
Selectivity: Admits 50 to 75% of applicants.

BASIC COSTS (2012-2013)

Tuition and fees: $9,885; out-of-state residents $23,300.
Per-credit charge: $328; out-of-state residents $556.
Room and board: $8,748.

FINANCIAL AID PICTURE (2011-2012)

Students with need: Out of 2,955 full-time freshmen who applied for aid, 2,290 were judged to have need. Of these, 2,222 received aid, and 233 had their full need met. Average financial aid package met 59% of need; average scholarship/grant was $6,400; average loan was $3,533. For part-time students, average financial aid package was $5,676.
Students without need: 330 full-time freshmen who did not demonstrate need for aid received scholarships/grants; average award was $5,525. No-need awards available for academics, alumni affiliation, art, athletics, leadership, music/drama.
Scholarships offered: 22 full-time freshmen received athletic scholarships; average amount $11,997.
Cumulative student debt: 63% of graduating class had student loans; average debt was $28,889.

FINANCIAL AID PROCEDURES

Forms required: FAFSA.
Dates and Deadlines: Priority date 3/1; no closing date. Applicants notified on a rolling basis starting 4/1; must reply within 2 week(s) of notification.
Transfers: Applicants notified by 4/1.

CONTACT

Brenda Burke, Director of Financial Aid
Box 842526, Richmond, VA 23284-2526
(804) 828-6669

Virginia Intermont College

Bristol, Virginia
www.vic.edu Federal Code: 003752

4-year private liberal arts and teachers college in small city.
Enrollment: 457 undergrads, 5% part-time. 80 full-time freshmen.
Selectivity: Admits over 75% of applicants.

BASIC COSTS (2012-2013)

Tuition and fees: $24,642.
Per-credit charge: $292.
Room and board: $7,769.

FINANCIAL AID PICTURE (2012-2013)

Students with need: Out of 70 full-time freshmen who applied for aid, 65 were judged to have need. Of these, 64 received aid, and 10 had their full need met. Average financial aid package met 64% of need; average scholarship/grant was $16,355; average loan was $3,674. For part-time students, average financial aid package was $6,100.
Students without need: 7 full-time freshmen who did not demonstrate need for aid received scholarships/grants; average award was $10,091. No-need awards available for academics, art, athletics, music/drama, religious affiliation, state/district residency.
Scholarships offered: 11 full-time freshmen received athletic scholarships; average amount $13,704.
Cumulative student debt: 72% of graduating class had student loans; average debt was $18,335.

FINANCIAL AID PROCEDURES

Forms required: FAFSA, state aid form.
Dates and Deadlines: Closing date 2/15. Applicants notified on a rolling basis starting 3/1; must reply within 2 week(s) of notification.
Transfers: Priority date 2/15; no deadline. Applicants notified on a rolling basis starting 1/1; must reply within 3 week(s) of notification. Limited to certain number of units of state aid.

CONTACT
Denise Posey, Financial Aid Director
1013 Moore Street, Bristol, VA 24201
(276) 466-7870

Virginia Military Institute

Lexington, Virginia
www.vmi.edu Federal Code: 003753

4-year public liberal arts and military college in small town.
Enrollment: 1,664 undergrads. 453 full-time freshmen.
Selectivity: Admits less than 50% of applicants. GED not accepted.

BASIC COSTS (2012-2013)
Tuition and fees: $13,835; out-of-state residents $33,811.
Room and board: $7,733.

FINANCIAL AID PICTURE
Students with need: Need-based aid available for full-time students.
Students without need: No-need awards available for academics, alumni affiliation, athletics, leadership, music/drama, ROTC.
Scholarships offered: Institute Scholarship: up to $19,830; 10-12 awarded; for superior academic performance, demonstrated character and leadership, extracurricular activities, 3.7 high school GPA, minimum 1250 SAT (exclusive of Writing) or 27 ACT, rank in top 5% of class.

FINANCIAL AID PROCEDURES
Forms required: FAFSA, institutional form.
Dates and Deadlines: Closing date 3/1. Applicants notified on a rolling basis starting 3/1; must reply by 5/1.

CONTACT
Timothy Golden, Director of Financial Aid
VMI Office of Admissions, Lexington, VA 24450-9967
(540) 464-7208

Virginia Polytechnic Institute and State University

Blacksburg, Virginia
www.vt.edu Federal Code: 003754

4-year public university in large town.
Enrollment: 23,823 undergrads, 2% part-time. 5,216 full-time freshmen.
Selectivity: Admits 50 to 75% of applicants.

BASIC COSTS (2012-2013)
Tuition and fees: $10,923; out-of-state residents $25,311.
Per-credit charge: $383; out-of-state residents $982.
Room and board: $7,254.
Additional info: Funds for the Future program provides varying levels of tuition increase protection based on family income for both VA residents and non-VA residents. Tuition/fee waivers available for unemployed or children of unemployed.

FINANCIAL AID PICTURE (2011-2012)
Students with need: Out of 4,035 full-time freshmen who applied for aid, 2,363 were judged to have need. Of these, 2,219 received aid, and 361 had their full need met. Average financial aid package met 65% of need; average scholarship/grant was $7,178; average loan was $4,067. Need-based aid available for part-time students.
Students without need: 537 full-time freshmen who did not demonstrate need for aid received scholarships/grants; average award was $5,170. No-need awards available for academics, art, athletics, leadership, minority status, music/drama, ROTC, state/district residency.
Scholarships offered: 95 full-time freshmen received athletic scholarships; average amount $23,257.
Cumulative student debt: 54% of graduating class had student loans; average debt was $25,759.

FINANCIAL AID PROCEDURES
Forms required: FAFSA.
Dates and Deadlines: Closing date 3/1. Applicants notified by 4/1; must reply by 5/1 or within 4 week(s) of notification.
Transfers: Applicants notified by 4/1. Based on family EFC per FAFSA and available resources. Significant academic scholarships for graduates of Virginia Community College System.

CONTACT
Barry Simmons, Director of Financial Aid
965 Prices Fork Road, Blacksburg, VA 24061-0202
(540) 231-5179

Virginia State University

Petersburg, Virginia
www.vsu.edu Federal Code: 003764

4-year public university in large town.
Enrollment: 5,561 undergrads, 9% part-time. 1,241 full-time freshmen.
Selectivity: Admits over 75% of applicants.

BASIC COSTS (2012-2013)
Tuition and fees: $7,424; out-of-state residents $15,862.
Per-credit charge: $311; out-of-state residents $663.
Room and board: $9,680.
Additional info: Out-of-state students pay an additional required fee of $530.

FINANCIAL AID PICTURE
Students with need: Need-based aid available for full-time and part-time students. Work study available nights, weekends, and for part-time students.
Students without need: No-need awards available for academics, alumni affiliation, art, athletics, job skills, leadership, minority status, music/drama, religious affiliation, ROTC.
Scholarships offered: Presidential Scholarships, $7,000, 3.2 GPA, SAT 1100 or ACT 24. Provost's Scholarships, $3,500, 3.0 GPA, SAT 1000 (exclusive of writing) or ACT 21. Fine and Performing Arts Scholarships, $1,500, outstanding talent in music or fine arts, audition or portfolio may be required, recommendation required. Math, Science, and Technology Scholarships, $1,500, 3.0 GPA, above average ability in math, science, or technology, recommendation and essay required.
Additional info: Strongly recommend that students apply for scholarship assistance through federal, state, local and private agencies.

FINANCIAL AID PROCEDURES
Forms required: FAFSA, institutional form.
Dates and Deadlines: Priority date 3/31; closing date 5/1. Applicants notified on a rolling basis starting 3/1; must reply within 2 week(s) of notification.
Transfers: Priority date 3/1.

CONTACT
Myra Phillips, Director, Financial Aid
1 Hayden Drive, Petersburg, VA 23806
(804) 524-5990

Virginia Union University

Richmond, Virginia
www.vuu.edu Federal Code: 003766

4-year private university and liberal arts college in small city, affiliated with Baptist faith.
Enrollment: 1,359 undergrads, 3% part-time. 433 full-time freshmen.
Selectivity: Admits over 75% of applicants.

BASIC COSTS (2013-2014)
Tuition and fees: $14,930.
Per-credit charge: $422.
Room and board: $7,546.

FINANCIAL AID PICTURE (2012-2013)
Students with need: Out of 376 full-time freshmen who applied for aid, 358 were judged to have need. Of these, 355 received aid, and 16 had their full need met. Average financial aid package met 49% of need; average scholarship/grant was $8,305; average loan was $3,380. For part-time students, average financial aid package was $7,364.
Students without need: 17 full-time freshmen who did not demonstrate need for aid received scholarships/grants; average award was $4,741. No-need awards available for academics, athletics, ROTC, state/district residency.
Scholarships offered: 5 full-time freshmen received athletic scholarships; average amount $6,954.
Cumulative student debt: 98% of graduating class had student loans; average debt was $31,153.

FINANCIAL AID PROCEDURES
Forms required: FAFSA.
Dates and Deadlines: Priority date 4/27; no closing date. Applicants notified on a rolling basis starting 5/1; must reply within 2 week(s) of notification.
Transfers: No deadline. Student must submit a financial aid transcript from all prior schools attended before receiving aid.

CONTACT
Arcelia Jackson, Director of Financial Aid
1500 North Lombardy Street, Richmond, VA 23220
(804) 257-5882

Virginia Wesleyan College
Norfolk, Virginia
www.vwc.edu Federal Code: 003767

4-year private liberal arts college in large city, affiliated with United Methodist Church.
Enrollment: 1,385 undergrads, 8% part-time. 439 full-time freshmen.
Selectivity: Admits over 75% of applicants.

BASIC COSTS (2013-2014)
Tuition and fees: $32,182.
Per-credit charge: $1,314.
Room and board: $8,508.
Additional info: Tuition/fee waivers available for adults.

FINANCIAL AID PICTURE (2011-2012)
Students with need: Out of 435 full-time freshmen who applied for aid, 377 were judged to have need. Of these, 376 received aid, and 43 had their full need met. Average financial aid package met 70% of need; average scholarship/grant was $18,342; average loan was $6,241. For part-time students, average financial aid package was $4,487.
Students without need: 56 full-time freshmen who did not demonstrate need for aid received scholarships/grants; average award was $17,492. No-need awards available for academics, alumni affiliation, leadership, religious affiliation, ROTC, state/district residency.
Cumulative student debt: 85% of graduating class had student loans; average debt was $36,445.

FINANCIAL AID PROCEDURES
Forms required: FAFSA, state aid form.
Dates and Deadlines: Priority date 3/1; no closing date. Applicants notified on a rolling basis starting 2/15; must reply by 5/1 or within 2 week(s) of notification.
Transfers: No deadline. Applicants notified on a rolling basis starting 2/15; must reply by 5/1 or within 2 week(s) of notification. 4-semester maximum of special aid available for students who graduated with 3.0 GPA and earned an associate degree from local community college. Must enroll full time and maintain 2.5 GPA minimum.

CONTACT
Teresa Rhyne, Director of Financial Aid
1584 Wesleyan Drive, Norfolk, VA 23502-5599
(757) 455-3345

Virginia Western Community College
Roanoke, Virginia
www.virginiawestern.edu Federal Code: 003760

2-year public community college in small city.
Enrollment: 6,005 undergrads.
Selectivity: Open admission; but selective for some programs.

BASIC COSTS (2012-2013)
Tuition and fees: $4,053; out-of-state residents $9,351.
Per-credit charge: $117; out-of-state residents $294.
Additional info: Out-of-state students pay additional $465 capital outlay fee.

FINANCIAL AID PICTURE (2011-2012)
Students with need: 93% of average financial aid package awarded as scholarships/grants, 7% awarded as loans/jobs. Need-based aid available for part-time students.
Students without need: No-need awards available for academics, state/district residency.

FINANCIAL AID PROCEDURES
Forms required: FAFSA.
Dates and Deadlines: Applicants notified on a rolling basis starting 4/1.
Transfers: No deadline. Applicants notified on a rolling basis.

CONTACT
Chad Sartini, Financial Aid Officer
Box 14007, Roanoke, VA 24038
(540) 857-7331

Washington and Lee University
Lexington, Virginia Federal Code: 003768
www.wlu.edu CSS Code: 5887

4-year private university and liberal arts college in small town.
Enrollment: 1,837 undergrads. 479 full-time freshmen.
Selectivity: Admits less than 50% of applicants.

BASIC COSTS (2012-2013)
Tuition and fees: $43,362.
Per-credit charge: $1,515.
Room and board: $9,450.

FINANCIAL AID PICTURE (2012-2013)
Students with need: Out of 251 full-time freshmen who applied for aid, 214 were judged to have need. Of these, 214 received aid, and 214 had their full need met. Average financial aid package met 100% of need; average scholarship/grant was $39,120; average loan was $853. Need-based aid available for part-time students.
Students without need: 22 full-time freshmen who did not demonstrate need for aid received scholarships/grants; average award was $44,427. No-need awards available for academics.
Cumulative student debt: 31% of graduating class had student loans; average debt was $23,409.

FINANCIAL AID PROCEDURES
Forms required: FAFSA, CSS PROFILE.
Dates and Deadlines: Closing date 2/15. Applicants notified by 4/1; must reply by 5/1.

Transfers: Transfer students are awarded institutional funds only after commitments to enrolled students are met. Notification usually in late summer.

CONTACT

Jim Kaster, Director of Student Financial Aid
204 West Washington Street, Lexington, VA 24450-2116
(540) 458-8720

Wytheville Community College

Wytheville, Virginia
www.wcc.vccs.edu Federal Code: 003761

2-year public community college in small town.
Enrollment: 2,259 undergrads.
Selectivity: Open admission; but selective for some programs.

BASIC COSTS (2012-2013)

Tuition and fees: $3,810; out-of-state residents $9,108.
Per-credit charge: $117; out-of-state residents $294.
Additional info: Out-of-state students pay additional $465 capital outlay fee.

FINANCIAL AID PICTURE

Students with need: Need-based aid available for full-time and part-time students.
Students without need: This college awards aid only to students with need.

FINANCIAL AID PROCEDURES

Forms required: FAFSA, institutional form.
Dates and Deadlines: Priority date 4/1; no closing date. Applicants notified on a rolling basis starting 5/1; must reply within 4 week(s) of notification.

CONTACT

Mary Gallagher, Financial Aid Coordinator
1000 East Main Street, Wytheville, VA 24382
(540) 223-4703

Washington

Art Institute of Seattle

Seattle, Washington
www.ais.edu Federal Code: 016210

4-year for-profit culinary school and visual arts college in very large city.
Enrollment: 1,681 undergrads, 67% part-time.
Selectivity: Open admission; but selective for some programs.

BASIC COSTS (2013-2014)

Tuition and fees: $22,275.
Per-credit charge: $485.
Room and board: $8,664.

FINANCIAL AID PICTURE (2012-2013)

Students with need: 31% of average financial aid package awarded as scholarships/grants, 69% awarded as loans/jobs. Need-based aid available for part-time students. Work study available nights, weekends, and for part-time students.
Students without need: No-need awards available for academics, art.

FINANCIAL AID PROCEDURES

Forms required: FAFSA, state aid form.
Dates and Deadlines: Applicants notified on a rolling basis.

CONTACT

Angela Hedwall, Director of Student Financial Services
2323 Elliott Avenue, Seattle, WA 98121-1622
(206) 448-2501

Bastyr University

Kenmore, Washington
www.bastyr.edu Federal Code: 016059

Upper-division private university and health science college in small city.
Enrollment: 207 undergrads, 13% part-time.

BASIC COSTS (2013-2014)

Tuition and fees: $22,812.
Per-credit charge: $613.
Additional info: Board plan not available. Cost of room only, $6,975.

FINANCIAL AID PICTURE (2011-2012)

Students with need: Average financial aid package for all full-time undergraduates was $17,052; for part-time $15,205. 21% awarded as scholarships/grants, 79% awarded as loans/jobs. Work study available nights, weekends, and for part-time students.
Students without need: No-need awards available for academics, alumni affiliation, job skills, leadership.

FINANCIAL AID PROCEDURES

Forms required: FAFSA, institutional form.
Dates and Deadlines: Priority date 4/15; no closing date. Applicants notified on a rolling basis starting 2/1; must reply within 2 week(s) of notification.
Transfers: No deadline. Applicants notified on a rolling basis; must reply within 3 week(s) of notification.

CONTACT

Danette Carter, Director of Financial Aid
14500 Juanita Drive, NE, Kenmore, WA 98028
(425) 602-3080

Bates Technical College

Tacoma, Washington
www.bates.ctc.edu Federal Code: 012259

2-year public technical college in small city.
Enrollment: 1,755 undergrads, 12% part-time. 383 full-time freshmen.
Selectivity: Open admission.

BASIC COSTS (2012-2013)

Tuition and fees: $4,564; out-of-state residents $9,800.
Additional info: Cost of Books and Supplies varies, averages around $1,000 per program.

FINANCIAL AID PICTURE

Students with need: Need-based aid available for full-time and part-time students. Work study available nights.
Students without need: This college awards aid only to students with need.

FINANCIAL AID PROCEDURES

Forms required: FAFSA, institutional form.
Dates and Deadlines: Applicants notified on a rolling basis starting 9/7.
Transfers: No deadline. Applicants notified on a rolling basis.

CONTACT

Susan Neese, Financial Aid Officer
1101 South Yakima Avenue, Tacoma, WA 98405
(253) 680-7025

Bellevue College

Bellevue, Washington
www.bellevuecollege.edu Federal Code: 003769

2-year public community college in small city.
Enrollment: 14,156 undergrads.
Selectivity: Open admission; but selective for some programs.

BASIC COSTS (2012-2013)
Tuition and fees: $4,240; out-of-state residents $9,475.

FINANCIAL AID PICTURE
Students with need: Need-based aid available for full-time and part-time students. Work study available nights, weekends, and for part-time students.
Students without need: No-need awards available for academics, athletics.

FINANCIAL AID PROCEDURES
Forms required: FAFSA, institutional form.
Dates and Deadlines: Priority date 4/16; no closing date. Applicants notified on a rolling basis starting 8/1.

CONTACT
Sherri Ballantyne, Assistant Dean, Financial Aid
3000 Landerholm Circle SE, Bellevue, WA 98007-6484
(425) 564-2227

Bellingham Technical College

Bellingham, Washington
www.btc.ctc.edu Federal Code: 016227

2-year public technical college in small city.
Enrollment: 1,937 undergrads.
Selectivity: Open admission; but selective for some programs.

BASIC COSTS (2012-2013)
Tuition and fees: $3,806; out-of-state residents $9,193.
Per-credit charge: $81; out-of-state residents $201.

FINANCIAL AID PICTURE
Students with need: Need-based aid available for full-time and part-time students.
Students without need: This college awards aid only to students with need.

FINANCIAL AID PROCEDURES
Forms required: FAFSA.
Dates and Deadlines: Priority date 5/1; no closing date. Applicants notified on a rolling basis starting 7/1; must reply within 2 week(s) of notification.

CONTACT
Michael Fentress, Director of Financial Aid
3028 Lindbergh Avenue, Bellingham, WA 98225-1599
(360) 752-8351

Big Bend Community College

Moses Lake, Washington
www.bigbend.edu Federal Code: 003770

2-year public community college in large town.
Enrollment: 1,319 undergrads.
Selectivity: Open admission; but selective for some programs.

BASIC COSTS (2012-2013)
Tuition and fees: $4,150; out-of-state residents $9,385.
Additional info: Board plan not available. Cost of room only, $2,700. Tuition/fee waivers available for unemployed or children of unemployed.

FINANCIAL AID PICTURE
Students with need: Need-based aid available for full-time and part-time students. Work study available nights, weekends, and for part-time students.
Students without need: This college awards aid only to students with need.

FINANCIAL AID PROCEDURES
Forms required: FAFSA, institutional form.
Dates and Deadlines: Priority date 4/1; no closing date. Applicants notified on a rolling basis starting 5/15; must reply within 2 week(s) of notification.

CONTACT
Jille Shankar, Director of Financial Aid
7662 Chanute Street, Moses Lake, WA 98837-3299
(509) 793-2034

Cascadia Community College

Bothell, Washington
www.cascadia.edu Federal Code: 034835

2-year public community college in large town.
Enrollment: 1,712 undergrads, 44% part-time. 255 full-time freshmen.
Selectivity: Open admission.

BASIC COSTS (2012-2013)
Tuition and fees: $4,120; out-of-state residents $9,355.

FINANCIAL AID PICTURE (2011-2012)
Students with need: 78% of average financial aid package awarded as scholarships/grants, 22% awarded as loans/jobs. Work study available nights, weekends, and for part-time students.

FINANCIAL AID PROCEDURES
Forms required: FAFSA, institutional form.
Dates and Deadlines: Priority date 4/15; no closing date.

CONTACT
Sybil Smith, Director of Student Financial Services
18345 Campus Way, NE, Bothell, WA 98011
(425) 352-8860

Centralia College

Centralia, Washington
www.centralia.edu Federal Code: 003772

2-year public community college in large town.
Enrollment: 2,251 undergrads.
Selectivity: Open admission; but selective for some programs.

BASIC COSTS (2012-2013)
Tuition and fees: $4,335; out-of-state residents $4,735.
Additional info: Tuition/fee waivers available for unemployed or children of unemployed.

FINANCIAL AID PICTURE
Students with need: Need-based aid available for full-time and part-time students.
Students without need: No-need awards available for academics, alumni affiliation, art, athletics, leadership, minority status, music/drama.

FINANCIAL AID PROCEDURES
Forms required: FAFSA, institutional form.
Dates and Deadlines: Priority date 5/1; closing date 9/1. Applicants notified on a rolling basis starting 7/10; must reply within 2 week(s) of notification.

CONTACT
Tracy Dahl, Director of Financial Aid
600 Centralia College Boulevard, Centralia, WA 98531
(360) 736-9391 ext. 234

City University of Seattle

Bellevue, Washington
www.cityu.edu Federal Code: 013022

Upper-division private university in very large city.
Enrollment: 961 undergrads, 45% part-time. 29 full-time freshmen.
Selectivity: Open admission; but selective for some programs.

BASIC COSTS (2012-2013)
Tuition and fees: $17,550.

FINANCIAL AID PICTURE (2011-2012)
Students with need: 14% of average financial aid package awarded as scholarships/grants, 86% awarded as loans/jobs. Need-based aid available for part-time students.
Students without need: No-need awards available for academics, alumni affiliation, leadership, minority status, state/district residency.
Additional info: All degree programs approved for veteran's administration education benefits.

FINANCIAL AID PROCEDURES
Forms required: FAFSA.
Dates and Deadlines: Applicants notified on a rolling basis starting 5/1.

CONTACT
Jean Roberts, Director of Financial Aid
11900 NE First Street, Bellevue, WA 98005
(800) 426-5596

Clark College

Vancouver, Washington
www.clark.edu Federal Code: 003773

2-year public community college in small city.
Enrollment: 10,822 undergrads, 43% part-time. 1,118 full-time freshmen.
Selectivity: Open admission; but selective for some programs.

BASIC COSTS (2012-2013)
Tuition and fees: $4,154; out-of-state residents $9,389.
Additional info: Tuition/fee waivers available for unemployed or children of unemployed.

FINANCIAL AID PICTURE (2011-2012)
Students with need: 74% of average financial aid package awarded as scholarships/grants, 26% awarded as loans/jobs. Need-based aid available for part-time students. Work study available nights, weekends, and for part-time students.
Students without need: No-need awards available for academics, alumni affiliation, art, athletics, leadership, minority status, music/drama, state/district residency.
Scholarships offered: Clark College Foundation Scholarships; $500 to full tuition; recipients selected from those completing Clark's Foundation Standard Scholarship application form.

FINANCIAL AID PROCEDURES
Forms required: FAFSA, institutional form.
Dates and Deadlines: Applicants notified on a rolling basis starting 6/1; must reply within 2 week(s) of notification.

CONTACT
Karen Driscoll, Director of Financial Aid
Welcome Center, MS PUB002, Vancouver, WA 98663
(360) 992-2153

Clover Park Technical College

Lakewood, Washington
www.cptc.edu Federal Code: 015984

2-year public technical college in small city.
Enrollment: 1,558 undergrads, 19% part-time.
Selectivity: Open admission; but selective for some programs.

BASIC COSTS (2012-2013)
Tuition and fees: $3,968; out-of-state residents $9,204.

FINANCIAL AID PICTURE (2011-2012)
Students with need: 52% of average financial aid package awarded as scholarships/grants, 48% awarded as loans/jobs. Need-based aid available for part-time students. Work study available nights, weekends, and for part-time students.
Students without need: This college awards aid only to students with need.

FINANCIAL AID PROCEDURES
Forms required: FAFSA, institutional form.
Dates and Deadlines: Closing date 4/12. Applicants notified on a rolling basis starting 5/1.

CONTACT
Wendy Joseph, Financial Aid Director
4500 Steilacoom Boulevard, SW, Lakewood, WA 98499-4098
(253) 589-5660

Columbia Basin College

Pasco, Washington
www.columbiabasin.edu Federal Code: 003774

2-year public community college in small city.
Enrollment: 6,405 undergrads.
Selectivity: Open admission; but selective for some programs.

BASIC COSTS (2012-2013)
Tuition and fees: $4,395; out-of-state residents $9,630.
Additional info: Tuition/fee waivers available for unemployed or children of unemployed.

FINANCIAL AID PICTURE
Students with need: Need-based aid available for full-time and part-time students. Work study available nights, weekends, and for part-time students.
Students without need: No-need awards available for academics, athletics, state/district residency.

FINANCIAL AID PROCEDURES
Forms required: FAFSA, institutional form.
Dates and Deadlines: Closing date 4/15. Applicants notified on a rolling basis starting 6/15; must reply within 2 week(s) of notification.

CONTACT
Ceci Ratliff, Director of Student Financial Services
2600 North 20th Avenue, Pasco, WA 99301
(509) 542-4715

Cornish College of the Arts

Seattle, Washington
www.cornish.edu Federal Code: 012315

4-year private visual arts and performing arts college in very large city.
Enrollment: 788 undergrads, 3% part-time. 155 full-time freshmen.
Selectivity: Admits over 75% of applicants.

BASIC COSTS (2012-2013)
Tuition and fees: $32,380.
Per-credit charge: $1,335.
Room and board: $8,800.

FINANCIAL AID PICTURE
Students with need: Need-based aid available for full-time and part-time students. Work study available nights, weekends, and for part-time students.
Students without need: No-need awards available for academics, art, music/drama, state/district residency.

FINANCIAL AID PROCEDURES
Forms required: FAFSA.
Dates and Deadlines: Priority date 3/1; no closing date. Applicants notified on a rolling basis starting 3/15; must reply by 5/1 or within 2 week(s) of notification.
Transfers: No deadline. Applicants notified on a rolling basis; must reply by 2/15.

CONTACT
Monique Theriault, Director for Financial Aid
1000 Lenora Street, Seattle, WA 98121
(206) 726-5014

DeVry University: Federal Way
Federal Way, Washington
www.devry.edu

4-year for-profit university in large city.
Enrollment: 500 undergrads, 50% part-time. 8 full-time freshmen.

BASIC COSTS (2012-2013)
Tuition and fees: $16,156.
Per-credit charge: $609.

FINANCIAL AID PICTURE
Students with need: Need-based aid available for full-time and part-time students.
Students without need: This college awards aid only to students with need.

FINANCIAL AID PROCEDURES
Forms required: FAFSA.
Dates and Deadlines: Applicants notified on a rolling basis.

CONTACT
Scott Sand, Director of Financial Aid
3600 South 344th Way, Federal Way, WA 98001-9558
(253) 943-3060

DigiPen Institute of Technology
Redmond, Washington
www.digipen.edu Federal Code: 037243

4-year for-profit visual arts and engineering college in large town.
Enrollment: 950 undergrads. 131 full-time freshmen.
Selectivity: Admits less than 50% of applicants.

BASIC COSTS (2012-2013)
Tuition and fees: $24,910.
Per-credit charge: $825.
Additional info: Annual costs reported are average costs to U.S. students taking 16-22 credits per semester for two semesters. Average annual costs for International students taking 16-22 credits per semester: $28,160.

FINANCIAL AID PICTURE (2011-2012)
Students with need: Out of 7 full-time freshmen who applied for aid, 7 were judged to have need. Of these, 7 received aid. Need-based aid available for part-time students.
Students without need: 21 full-time freshmen who did not demonstrate need for aid received scholarships/grants; average award was $2,852. No-need awards available for academics, art, leadership, minority status.
Scholarships offered: Imagine America Scholarship: $1,000; based on financial need, GPA of 2.5 or greater, voluntary community service during the senior year; 7 awarded. First Scholarship: $5,000; based on essay and academic record; 2 awarded. Art scholarship: up to $10,000 for an incoming student who demonstrates considerable artistic talent. A limited number of scholarships offered to incoming students who have demonstrated academic achievements and are likely to make a positive impact in both the DigiPen community and their chosen field. Scholarships will be awarded in amounts of up to $10,000.
Cumulative student debt: 17% of graduating class had student loans; average debt was $47,500.
Additional info: Many aid programs are on a first-come, first-served basis.

FINANCIAL AID PROCEDURES
Forms required: FAFSA.
Dates and Deadlines: Priority date 4/15; no closing date. Applicants notified on a rolling basis starting 1/1; must reply within 2 week(s) of notification.
Transfers: No deadline. Applicants notified on a rolling basis starting 1/1; must reply within 2 week(s) of notification. Transfer students should meet with a financial aid administrator as soon as they are accepted. Must submit prior financial aid history to determine eligibility.

CONTACT
Kim King, Director of Financial Aid
9931 Willows Road NE, Redmond, WA 98052
(425) 629-5002

Eastern Washington University
Cheney, Washington
www.ewu.edu Federal Code: 003775

4-year public university in large town.
Enrollment: 11,336 undergrads, 16% part-time. 1,474 full-time freshmen.
Selectivity: Admits over 75% of applicants.

BASIC COSTS (2012-2013)
Tuition and fees: $7,933; out-of-state residents $18,678.
Per-credit charge: $246; out-of-state residents $604.
Room and board: $8,412.

FINANCIAL AID PICTURE (2011-2012)
Students with need: Out of 1,285 full-time freshmen who applied for aid, 991 were judged to have need. Of these, 970 received aid, and 264 had their full need met. Average financial aid package met 86% of need; average scholarship/grant was $7,455; average loan was $3,164. For part-time students, average financial aid package was $8,623.
Students without need: 159 full-time freshmen who did not demonstrate need for aid received scholarships/grants; average award was $3,007. No-need awards available for academics, alumni affiliation, art, athletics, job skills, music/drama, state/district residency.
Scholarships offered: ***Merit:*** Killin Scholarship; $3,500; three awards; for academic excellence, must have 3.7 GPA and 1100 SAT score (exclusive of Writing). Honors Scholarship; $2,500; 38 awards; for academic excellence. Presidential Scholarship; $2,000; 75 awards; based on GPA, SAT, early admission. ***Athletic:*** 34 full-time freshmen received athletic scholarships; average amount $8,895.
Cumulative student debt: 56% of graduating class had student loans; average debt was $23,604.
Additional info: The High Demand Scholarship program helps low income students pursue "high demand" careers.

FINANCIAL AID PROCEDURES
Forms required: FAFSA.

Dates and Deadlines: Priority date 2/15; no closing date. Applicants notified on a rolling basis starting 4/1; must reply within 4 week(s) of notification.
Transfers: No deadline. Applicants notified on a rolling basis. Educational Opportunity Grant (EOG); financially needy, placebound students with AA or junior status, $2,500 renewable, rolling priority, first-come, first-served at end of each month beginning April 1, ending September 30.

CONTACT
Bruce DeFrates, Director of Financial Aid
304 Sutton Hall, Cheney, WA 99004
(509) 359-2314

Everett Community College
Everett, Washington
www.everettcc.edu Federal Code: 003776

2-year public community college in small city.
Enrollment: 6,970 undergrads.
Selectivity: Open admission; but selective for some programs.

BASIC COSTS (2012-2013)
Tuition and fees: $4,229; out-of-state residents $9,464.

FINANCIAL AID PICTURE
Students with need: Need-based aid available for full-time and part-time students. Work study available nights, weekends, and for part-time students.
Students without need: No-need awards available for academics, alumni affiliation, art, athletics, job skills, leadership, minority status, music/drama, state/district residency.

FINANCIAL AID PROCEDURES
Forms required: FAFSA, institutional form.
Dates and Deadlines: Priority date 5/5; no closing date. Applicants notified on a rolling basis starting 4/15; must reply within 4 week(s) of notification.
Transfers: No deadline. Applicants notified on a rolling basis starting 6/15; must reply within 4 week(s) of notification.

CONTACT
Andrea Wilson, Director of Student Financial Services
2000 Tower Street, Everett, WA 98201-1352
(425) 388-9280

Evergreen State College
Olympia, Washington
www.evergreen.edu Federal Code: 008155

4-year public liberal arts college in small city.
Enrollment: 4,121 undergrads, 6% part-time. 537 full-time freshmen.
Selectivity: Admits over 75% of applicants.

BASIC COSTS (2012-2013)
Tuition and fees: $8,395; out-of-state residents $19,561.
Per-credit charge: $260; out-of-state residents $633.
Room and board: $9,240.
Additional info: Entering freshmen living in campus housing are required to choose a mandatory dining plan.

FINANCIAL AID PICTURE (2011-2012)
Students with need: Out of 425 full-time freshmen who applied for aid, 333 were judged to have need. Of these, 316 received aid, and 33 had their full need met. Average financial aid package met 84% of need; average scholarship/grant was $7,466; average loan was $3,149. For part-time students, average financial aid package was $3,905.
Students without need: 8 full-time freshmen who did not demonstrate need for aid received scholarships/grants; average award was $6,164. No-need awards available for academics, art, athletics, state/district residency.
Scholarships offered: 1 full-time freshmen received athletic scholarships; average amount $1,020.
Cumulative student debt: 48% of graduating class had student loans; average debt was $15,706.
Additional info: Application packets for all scholarships and tuition awards except the Merit Award (due by May 2) must be received by February 1. To meet priority deadline for required financial aid forms, official results of FAFSA must be received by March 1.

FINANCIAL AID PROCEDURES
Forms required: FAFSA, institutional form.
Dates and Deadlines: Priority date 3/1; no closing date. Applicants notified on a rolling basis starting 4/1; must reply within 6 week(s) of notification.

CONTACT
Tracy Hall, Director of Financial Aid
2700 Evergreen Parkway NW, Olympia, WA 98505
(360) 867-6205

Gonzaga University
Spokane, Washington
www.gonzaga.edu Federal Code: 003778

4-year private university and liberal arts college in large city, affiliated with Roman Catholic Church.
Enrollment: 4,829 undergrads, 1% part-time. 1,131 full-time freshmen.
Selectivity: Admits 50 to 75% of applicants. GED not accepted.

BASIC COSTS (2012-2013)
Tuition and fees: $33,652.
Per-credit charge: $885.
Room and board: $8,730.
Additional info: Tuition/fee waivers available for adults.

FINANCIAL AID PICTURE (2011-2012)
Students with need: Out of 986 full-time freshmen who applied for aid, 702 were judged to have need. Of these, 702 received aid, and 215 had their full need met. Average financial aid package met 83% of need; average scholarship/grant was $18,680; average loan was $4,365. For part-time students, average financial aid package was $17,428.
Students without need: 394 full-time freshmen who did not demonstrate need for aid received scholarships/grants; average award was $10,754. No-need awards available for academics, alumni affiliation, athletics, leadership, minority status, music/drama, ROTC.
Scholarships offered: ***Merit:*** All freshmen are considered for Academic Merit Scholarships: awards range from $3,000 to $10,000. ***Athletic:*** 40 full-time freshmen received athletic scholarships; average amount $26,818.
Cumulative student debt: 66% of graduating class had student loans; average debt was $29,776.

FINANCIAL AID PROCEDURES
Forms required: FAFSA.
Dates and Deadlines: Priority date 2/1; closing date 6/30. Applicants notified on a rolling basis starting 3/1; must reply by 5/1 or within 3 week(s) of notification.
Transfers: No deadline. Applicants notified on a rolling basis; must reply by 4/15 or within 3 week(s) of notification.

CONTACT
Jim White, Director of Financial Aid
502 East Boone Avenue, Spokane, WA 99258-0001
(509) 313-5816

Grays Harbor College

Aberdeen, Washington
www.ghc.edu Federal Code: 003779

2-year public community college in large town.
Enrollment: 1,450 full-time undergrads.
Selectivity: Open admission; but selective for some programs.

BASIC COSTS (2012-2013)
Tuition and fees: $4,381; out-of-state residents $9,616.
Additional info: Tuition/fee waivers available for adults, unemployed or children of unemployed.

FINANCIAL AID PICTURE
Students with need: Need-based aid available for full-time and part-time students. Work study available nights.
Students without need: No-need awards available for academics, art, athletics, music/drama.

FINANCIAL AID PROCEDURES
Forms required: FAFSA, institutional form.
Dates and Deadlines: Closing date 5/1. Applicants notified on a rolling basis starting 5/15.

CONTACT
Ben Beus, Director of Financial Aid
1620 Edward P Smith Drive, Aberdeen, WA 98520
(360) 538-4081

Green River Community College

Auburn, Washington
www.greenriver.edu Federal Code: 003780

2-year public community college in large town.
Enrollment: 8,309 undergrads.
Selectivity: Open admission; but selective for some programs.

BASIC COSTS (2012-2013)
Tuition and fees: $4,443; out-of-state residents $9,678.

FINANCIAL AID PICTURE
Students with need: Need-based aid available for full-time and part-time students.
Students without need: This college awards aid only to students with need.

FINANCIAL AID PROCEDURES
Forms required: FAFSA, institutional form.
Dates and Deadlines: Closing date 4/15. Applicants notified on a rolling basis starting 6/30; must reply within 2 week(s) of notification.

CONTACT
Mary Edington, Director of Financial Aid
12401 SE 320th Street, Auburn, WA 98092
(253) 833-9111 ext. 2440

Heritage University

Toppenish, Washington
www.heritage.edu Federal Code: 003777

4-year private liberal arts and teachers college in small town, affiliated with interdenominational tradition.
Enrollment: 861 undergrads, 24% part-time. 134 full-time freshmen.
Selectivity: Open admission.

BASIC COSTS (2013-2014)
Tuition and fees: $17,748.
Per-credit charge: $736.

FINANCIAL AID PICTURE (2011-2012)
Students with need: Out of 134 full-time freshmen who applied for aid, 131 were judged to have need. Of these, 131 received aid, and 3 had their full need met. Average financial aid package met 65% of need; average scholarship/grant was $13,065; average loan was $2,666. For part-time students, average financial aid package was $8,897.
Students without need: No-need awards available for academics, leadership, minority status.
Cumulative student debt: 86% of graduating class had student loans; average debt was $8,754.

FINANCIAL AID PROCEDURES
Forms required: FAFSA, institutional form.
Dates and Deadlines: Priority date 2/10; no closing date. Applicants notified on a rolling basis starting 3/1; must reply within 2 week(s) of notification.
Transfers: No deadline. Applicants notified on a rolling basis starting 3/1; must reply within 2 week(s) of notification. A request to the State is made to continue awarding State Need Grant funds to transfer students if they were receiving these funds at their previous institution.

CONTACT
Oscar Verduzco, Director of Financial Aid
3240 Fort Road, Toppenish, WA 98948-9599
(509) 865-8502

Highline Community College

Des Moines, Washington
www.highline.edu Federal Code: 003781

2-year public community college in small city.
Enrollment: 2,824 full-time undergrads.
Selectivity: Open admission; but selective for some programs.

BASIC COSTS (2012-2013)
Tuition and fees: $4,075; out-of-state residents $9,310.

FINANCIAL AID PICTURE
Students with need: Need-based aid available for full-time and part-time students.

FINANCIAL AID PROCEDURES
Forms required: FAFSA.
Dates and Deadlines: Priority date 6/1; no closing date. Applicants notified on a rolling basis starting 6/1.

CONTACT
Lorraine Odom, Director of Financial Aid
2400 South 240th Street, Des Moines, WA 98198-9800
(206) 878-3710

Lake Washington Institute of Technology

Kirkland, Washington
www.lwtech.edu Federal Code: 005373

2-year public technical college in large town.
Enrollment: 2,275 undergrads. 139 full-time freshmen.
Selectivity: Open admission; but selective for some programs.

BASIC COSTS (2012-2013)
Tuition and fees: $4,435; out-of-state residents $9,670.

FINANCIAL AID PICTURE (2012-2013)
Students with need: Need-based aid available for full-time and part-time students.

FINANCIAL AID PROCEDURES

Forms required: FAFSA, institutional form.

Dates and Deadlines: Closing date 4/15. Applicants notified on a rolling basis.

CONTACT

Bill Chaney, Director of Financial Aid
11605 132nd Avenue, NE, Kirkland, WA 98034
(425) 739-8119

Lower Columbia College

Longview, Washington
www.lowercolumbia.edu Federal Code: 003782

2-year public community college in small city.
Enrollment: 1,575 undergrads.
Selectivity: Open admission; but selective for some programs.

BASIC COSTS (2012-2013)

Tuition and fees: $4,275; out-of-state residents $9,785.
Additional info: Tuition/fee waivers available for adults, unemployed or children of unemployed.

FINANCIAL AID PICTURE (2011-2012)

Students with need: 57% of average financial aid package awarded as scholarships/grants, 43% awarded as loans/jobs. Need-based aid available for part-time students.

FINANCIAL AID PROCEDURES

Forms required: FAFSA, institutional form.
Dates and Deadlines: Priority date 5/1; no closing date. Applicants notified on a rolling basis starting 4/21; must reply within 2 week(s) of notification.
Transfers: State-need grant awards transfer with students if previously awarded at another WA institution; SEOG usually not available to transfer students. Student employment, loans, Pell Grant available.

CONTACT

Marisa Greear, Director of Financial Aid
1600 Maple Street, Longview, WA 98632-0310
(360) 442-2311

North Seattle Community College

Seattle, Washington
www.northseattle.edu Federal Code: 009704

2-year public community college in very large city.
Enrollment: 6,294 undergrads.
Selectivity: Open admission.

BASIC COSTS (2012-2013)

Tuition and fees: $4,173; out-of-state residents $9,408.
Additional info: Tuition/fee waivers available for adults, unemployed or children of unemployed.

FINANCIAL AID PICTURE

Students with need: Need-based aid available for full-time and part-time students. Work study available weekends and for part-time students.

FINANCIAL AID PROCEDURES

Forms required: FAFSA, institutional form.
Dates and Deadlines: Priority date 3/15; closing date 7/31. Applicants notified on a rolling basis starting 7/1; must reply within 2 week(s) of notification.

CONTACT

Bridget Doran, Director of Financial Aid
9600 College Way North, Seattle, WA 98103-3599
(206) 934-4706

Northwest College of Art & Design

Poulsbo, Washington
www.ncad.edu Federal Code: 026021

4-year for-profit visual arts college in small town.
Enrollment: 77 undergrads.
Selectivity: Admits over 75% of applicants.

BASIC COSTS (2012-2013)

Tuition and fees: $19,000.
Per-credit charge: $800.

FINANCIAL AID PICTURE

Students with need: Need-based aid available for full-time and part-time students.
Students without need: No-need awards available for academics, art, state/district residency.

FINANCIAL AID PROCEDURES

Forms required: FAFSA.
Dates and Deadlines: Priority date 3/1; closing date 6/1. Applicants notified on a rolling basis.

CONTACT

Julie Perigard, Financial Aid Officer
16301 Creative Drive NE, Poulsbo, WA 98370-8651
(360) 779-9993

Northwest Indian College

Bellingham, Washington
www.nwic.edu Federal Code: 021800

2-year public Tribal college in small town.
Enrollment: 701 undergrads.
Selectivity: Open admission.

BASIC COSTS (2012-2013)

Tuition and fees: $3,720; out-of-state residents $9,588.
Per-credit charge: $95; out-of-state residents $258.
Room and board: $4,050.
Additional info: Eligibility to pay resident costs based on tribal enrollment verification. Tuition/fee waivers available for minority students.

FINANCIAL AID PICTURE

Students with need: Need-based aid available for full-time and part-time students.
Students without need: No-need awards available for academics.

FINANCIAL AID PROCEDURES

Forms required: FAFSA, institutional form.
Dates and Deadlines: Applicants notified on a rolling basis.
Transfers: No deadline. Applicants notified on a rolling basis.

CONTACT

Karyl Jefferson, Vice President of Administration and Finance
2522 Kwina Road, Bellingham, WA 98226-9217
(360) 676-2772 ext. 4206

Northwest University

Kirkland, Washington
www.northwestu.edu Federal Code: 003783

4-year private university and liberal arts college in small city, affiliated with Assemblies of God.
Enrollment: 1,355 undergrads.

BASIC COSTS (2013-2014)
Tuition and fees: $25,934.
Per-credit charge: $1,060.
Room and board: $7,190.

FINANCIAL AID PICTURE
Students with need: Need-based aid available for full-time and part-time students. Work study available nights, weekends, and for part-time students.
Students without need: No-need awards available for academics, art, athletics, leadership, music/drama, religious affiliation.

FINANCIAL AID PROCEDURES
Forms required: FAFSA, institutional form.
Dates and Deadlines: Priority date 2/15; closing date 8/1. Applicants notified on a rolling basis starting 3/3; must reply within 4 week(s) of notification.
Transfers: No deadline. Applicants notified on a rolling basis starting 3/30; must reply within 4 week(s) of notification.

CONTACT
Roger Wilson, Director of Financial Aid
5520 108th Ave NE, Kirkland, WA 98083-0579
(425) 889-5210

Olympic College
Bremerton, Washington
www.olympic.edu Federal Code: 003784

2-year public community and liberal arts college in large town.
Enrollment: 8,260 undergrads.
Selectivity: Open admission; but selective for some programs.

BASIC COSTS (2012-2013)
Tuition and fees: $4,195; out-of-state residents $9,430.

FINANCIAL AID PICTURE
Students with need: Need-based aid available for full-time and part-time students. Work study available nights.
Students without need: No-need awards available for academics, state/district residency.
Additional info: Waivers available for select groups including Fallen Veterans, Children of Deceased or Disabled Law Enforcement Officers, and others.

FINANCIAL AID PROCEDURES
Forms required: FAFSA, institutional form.
Dates and Deadlines: Priority date 3/1; no closing date. Applicants notified on a rolling basis starting 6/1; must reply within 2 week(s) of notification.
Transfers: No deadline. Applicants notified on a rolling basis starting 1/2.

CONTACT
Heidi Townsend, Director Student Financial Services
1600 Chester Avenue, Bremerton, WA 98337-1699
(360) 475-7160

Pacific Lutheran University
Tacoma, Washington
www.plu.edu Federal Code: 003785

4-year private university in large city, affiliated with Evangelical Lutheran Church in America.
Enrollment: 3,111 undergrads, 4% part-time. 633 full-time freshmen.
Selectivity: Admits 50 to 75% of applicants.

BASIC COSTS (2012-2013)
Tuition and fees: $32,800.
Per-credit charge: $1,030.
Room and board: $9,620.

FINANCIAL AID PICTURE (2012-2013)
Students with need: Out of 585 full-time freshmen who applied for aid, 532 were judged to have need. Of these, 527 received aid, and 212 had their full need met. Average financial aid package met 92% of need; average scholarship/grant was $21,829; average loan was $7,688. For part-time students, average financial aid package was $16,473.
Students without need: 93 full-time freshmen who did not demonstrate need for aid received scholarships/grants; average award was $15,362. No-need awards available for academics, alumni affiliation, art, leadership, music/drama, religious affiliation, ROTC.
Cumulative student debt: 69% of graduating class had student loans; average debt was $29,649.

FINANCIAL AID PROCEDURES
Forms required: FAFSA.
Dates and Deadlines: Priority date 1/15; no closing date. Applicants notified on a rolling basis starting 3/1; must reply by 5/1 or within 3 week(s) of notification.
Transfers: Applicants notified on a rolling basis.

CONTACT
Kay Soltis, Director of Financial Aid
1010 South 122nd Street, Tacoma, WA 98447-0003
(253) 535-7134

Peninsula College
Port Angeles, Washington
www.pencol.edu Federal Code: 003786

2-year public community college in large town.
Enrollment: 1,283 undergrads.
Selectivity: Open admission; but selective for some programs.

BASIC COSTS (2012-2013)
Tuition and fees: $4,350; out-of-state residents $9,585.
Additional info: Tuition/fee waivers available for unemployed or children of unemployed.

FINANCIAL AID PICTURE
Students with need: Need-based aid available for full-time and part-time students.
Students without need: No-need awards available for academics, athletics, job skills.

FINANCIAL AID PROCEDURES
Forms required: FAFSA, institutional form.
Dates and Deadlines: Closing date 4/1. Applicants notified on a rolling basis starting 6/1; must reply within 2 week(s) of notification.

CONTACT
Krista Francis, Director of Financial Aid
1502 East Lauridsen Boulevard, Port Angeles, WA 98362
(360) 417-6390

Pierce College
Lakewood, Washington
www.pierce.ctc.edu Federal Code: 005000

2-year public community college in small city.
Enrollment: 7,511 undergrads.
Selectivity: Open admission; but selective for some programs.

BASIC COSTS (2012-2013)
Tuition and fees: $4,255; out-of-state residents $4,655.
Additional info: Tuition/fee waivers available for unemployed or children of unemployed.

FINANCIAL AID PICTURE
Students with need: Need-based aid available for full-time and part-time students.
Students without need: No-need awards available for academics, athletics, music/drama.

FINANCIAL AID PROCEDURES
Forms required: FAFSA, institutional form.
Dates and Deadlines: Closing date 5/1. Applicants notified on a rolling basis starting 4/15.

CONTACT
Mary Richards, Assistant Financial Aid Director
9401 Farwest Drive SW, Lakewood, WA 98498-1999
(253) 964-6544

Renton Technical College

Renton, Washington
www.RTC.edu Federal Code: 014001

2-year public technical college in large town.
Enrollment: 1,225 undergrads.
Selectivity: Open admission.

BASIC COSTS (2012-2013)
Tuition and fees: $5,735.

FINANCIAL AID PICTURE
Students with need: Need-based aid available for full-time and part-time students.
Students without need: This college awards aid only to students with need.

FINANCIAL AID PROCEDURES
Forms required: FAFSA, institutional form.
Dates and Deadlines: Priority date 5/1; closing date 7/1. Applicants notified on a rolling basis.

CONTACT
Debbie Solomon, Director of Financial Aid
3000 NE Fourth Street, Renton, WA 98056-4195
(425) 235-5841

Saint Martin's University

Lacey, Washington
www.stmartin.edu Federal Code: 003794

4-year private university in large town, affiliated with Roman Catholic Church.
Enrollment: 1,392 undergrads, 16% part-time. 180 full-time freshmen.
Selectivity: Admits over 75% of applicants.

BASIC COSTS (2013-2014)
Tuition and fees: $29,834.
Per-credit charge: $990.
Room and board: $9,660.

FINANCIAL AID PICTURE (2011-2012)
Students with need: Out of 180 full-time freshmen who applied for aid, 160 were judged to have need. Of these, 160 received aid, and 35 had their full need met. Average financial aid package met 79% of need; average scholarship/grant was $20,162; average loan was $3,245. For part-time students, average financial aid package was $10,523.
Students without need: 20 full-time freshmen who did not demonstrate need for aid received scholarships/grants; average award was $11,716. No-need awards available for academics, alumni affiliation, art, athletics, leadership, minority status, music/drama, religious affiliation, ROTC, state/district residency.
Scholarships offered: 18 full-time freshmen received athletic scholarships; average amount $5,218.
Cumulative student debt: 79% of graduating class had student loans; average debt was $34,235.

FINANCIAL AID PROCEDURES
Forms required: FAFSA.
Dates and Deadlines: Priority date 3/1; no closing date. Applicants notified on a rolling basis starting 2/15.

CONTACT
Isabelle Mora, Director, Office of Financial Aid
5000 Abbey Way SE, Lacey, WA 98503-7500
(360) 438-4397

Seattle Central Community College

Seattle, Washington
www.seattlecentral.edu Federal Code: 003787

2-year public community college in very large city.
Enrollment: 9,993 undergrads.
Selectivity: Open admission; but selective for some programs.

BASIC COSTS (2012-2013)
Tuition and fees: $4,249; out-of-state residents $9,484.
Additional info: Tuition/fee waivers available for unemployed or children of unemployed.

FINANCIAL AID PICTURE
Students with need: Need-based aid available for full-time and part-time students. Work study available nights, weekends, and for part-time students.
Students without need: This college awards aid only to students with need.
Additional info: Currently enrolled international students can apply for institutional scholarship in second year of study.

FINANCIAL AID PROCEDURES
Forms required: FAFSA, institutional form.
Dates and Deadlines: Closing date 7/27. Applicants notified on a rolling basis; must reply within 2 week(s) of notification.

CONTACT
Noel McBride, Assistant Dean, Financial Student Services
1701 Broadway, Seattle, WA 98122
(206) 587-3844

Seattle Pacific University

Seattle, Washington
www.spu.edu Federal Code: 003788

4-year private university in very large city, affiliated with Free Methodist Church of North America.
Enrollment: 3,231 undergrads, 4% part-time. 783 full-time freshmen.
Selectivity: Admits over 75% of applicants.

BASIC COSTS (2013-2014)
Tuition and fees: $33,813.
Per-credit charge: $929.
Room and board: $9,867.

FINANCIAL AID PICTURE (2012-2013)
Students with need: Out of 709 full-time freshmen who applied for aid, 608 were judged to have need. Of these, 607 received aid, and 32 had their full need met. Average financial aid package met 84% of need; average scholarship/grant was $22,155; average loan was $5,128. For part-time students, average financial aid package was $19,007.

Students without need: 150 full-time freshmen who did not demonstrate need for aid received scholarships/grants; average award was $19,215. No-need awards available for academics, alumni affiliation, art, athletics, leadership, minority status, music/drama, religious affiliation, ROTC.
Scholarships offered: 10 full-time freshmen received athletic scholarships; average amount $14,442.
Cumulative student debt: 67% of graduating class had student loans; average debt was $28,263.

FINANCIAL AID PROCEDURES
Forms required: FAFSA.
Dates and Deadlines: Priority date 2/1; no closing date. Applicants notified on a rolling basis starting 3/15; must reply by 5/1 or within 3 week(s) of notification.
Transfers: No deadline. Applicants notified on a rolling basis starting 3/13; must reply by 5/1 or within 4 week(s) of notification.

CONTACT
Jordan Grant, Director of Financial Aid
3307 Third Avenue West, Suite 115, Seattle, WA 98119-1997
(206) 281-2061

Shoreline Community College
Shoreline, Washington
www.shoreline.edu Federal Code: 003791

2-year public community college in small city.
Enrollment: 2,795 undergrads.
Selectivity: Open admission; but selective for some programs.

BASIC COSTS (2012-2013)
Tuition and fees: $4,410; out-of-state residents $9,645.

FINANCIAL AID PICTURE (2011-2012)
Students with need: 70% of average financial aid package awarded as scholarships/grants, 30% awarded as loans/jobs. Work study available nights, weekends, and for part-time students.
Additional info: Tuition and/or fee waiver for students with need on space-available basis.

FINANCIAL AID PROCEDURES
Forms required: FAFSA, institutional form.
Dates and Deadlines: Closing date 3/31. Applicants notified on a rolling basis starting 8/1; must reply within 3 week(s) of notification.

CONTACT
Ted Haase, Director of Financial Services
16101 Greenwood Avenue North, Seattle, WA 98133
(206) 546-4762

Skagit Valley College
Mount Vernon, Washington
www.skagit.edu Federal Code: 003792

2-year public community college in large town.
Enrollment: 5,464 undergrads.
Selectivity: Open admission; but selective for some programs.

BASIC COSTS (2012-2013)
Tuition and fees: $4,208; out-of-state residents $9,443.
Additional info: Board plan not available. Cost of room only: $3,960. Tuition/fee waivers available for unemployed or children of unemployed.

FINANCIAL AID PICTURE
Students with need: Need-based aid available for full-time and part-time students. Work study available nights, weekends, and for part-time students.
Students without need: This college awards aid only to students with need.

FINANCIAL AID PROCEDURES
Forms required: FAFSA, institutional form.
Dates and Deadlines: Priority date 5/1; no closing date. Applicants notified on a rolling basis starting 7/1; must reply within 2 week(s) of notification.

CONTACT
Steve Epperson, Financial Aid Director
2405 East College Way, Mount Vernon, WA 98273
(360) 416-7666

South Puget Sound Community College
Olympia, Washington
www.spscc.ctc.edu Federal Code: 005372

2-year public community college in small city.
Enrollment: 3,215 undergrads.
Selectivity: Open admission; but selective for some programs.

BASIC COSTS (2012-2013)
Tuition and fees: $4,200; out-of-state residents $9,438.

FINANCIAL AID PICTURE
Students with need: Need-based aid available for full-time and part-time students.
Students without need: No-need awards available for academics, athletics.

FINANCIAL AID PROCEDURES
Forms required: FAFSA, institutional form.
Dates and Deadlines: Priority date 5/1; closing date 6/27. Applicants notified on a rolling basis starting 7/10; must reply within 2 week(s) of notification.

CONTACT
Carla Idohl-Corwin, Dean of Student Financial Services
2011 Mottman Road, SW, Olympia, WA 98512-6218
(360) 596-5232

South Seattle Community College
Seattle, Washington
www.southseattle.edu Federal Code: 009706

2-year public community college in very large city.
Enrollment: 3,499 undergrads.
Selectivity: Open admission; but selective for some programs.

BASIC COSTS (2013-2014)
Tuition and fees: $4,485; out-of-state residents $10,065.
Additional info: Tuition/fee waivers available for unemployed or children of unemployed.

FINANCIAL AID PICTURE (2011-2012)
Students with need: Average financial aid package for all full-time undergraduates was $9,706. 95% awarded as scholarships/grants, 5% awarded as loans/jobs. Need-based aid available for part-time students.
Students without need: No-need awards available for academics, state/district residency.

FINANCIAL AID PROCEDURES
Forms required: FAFSA, institutional form.
Dates and Deadlines: Closing date 4/26. Applicants notified on a rolling basis starting 7/1.

CONTACT
Patricia Billings, Financial Aid Director
6000 16th Avenue, SW, Seattle, WA 98106-1499
(206) 934-5317

Tacoma Community College

Tacoma, Washington
www.tacomacc.edu Federal Code: 003796

2-year public community college in small city.
Enrollment: 4,126 undergrads.
Selectivity: Open admission; but selective for some programs.

BASIC COSTS (2012-2013)
Tuition and fees: $4,203; out-of-state residents $9,438.
Additional info: Tuition/fee waivers available for unemployed or children of unemployed.

FINANCIAL AID PICTURE (2011-2012)
Students with need: Need-based aid available for full-time and part-time students. Work study available nights, weekends, and for part-time students.
Students without need: This college awards aid only to students with need.

FINANCIAL AID PROCEDURES
Forms required: FAFSA, institutional form.
Dates and Deadlines: Priority date 3/26; no closing date. Applicants notified on a rolling basis starting 7/20; must reply within 4 week(s) of notification.

CONTACT
Kim Matison, Director, Financial Aid Services
6501 South 19th Street, Tacoma, WA 98466-9971
(253) 566-5080

Trinity Lutheran College

Everett, Washington
www.tlc.edu Federal Code: 013525

4-year private liberal arts college in small city, affiliated with Lutheran Church.
Enrollment: 176 undergrads, 7% part-time. 44 full-time freshmen.
Selectivity: Admits 50 to 75% of applicants.

BASIC COSTS (2012-2013)
Tuition and fees: $23,900.
Per-credit charge: $980.
Additional info: Lunch-only meal plan (5 days per week) for academic year, $1,000. Cost of room only, $5,884.

FINANCIAL AID PICTURE (2012-2013)
Students with need: Average financial aid package met 63% of need; average scholarship/grant was $12,578; average loan was $3,500. For part-time students, average financial aid package was $4,000.
Students without need: No-need awards available for academics, alumni affiliation, art, athletics, leadership, music/drama, religious affiliation.

FINANCIAL AID PROCEDURES
Forms required: FAFSA, institutional form.
Dates and Deadlines: Closing date 3/1. Applicants notified on a rolling basis starting 3/15; must reply within 2 week(s) of notification.
Transfers: No deadline. Applicants notified on a rolling basis starting 3/15; must reply within 2 week(s) of notification.

CONTACT
Shanna Pyzer, Director of Student Financial Aid
2802 Wetmore Avenue, Everett, WA 98201
(425) 249-4777

University of Puget Sound

Tacoma, Washington
www.pugetsound.edu Federal Code: 003797

4-year private university and liberal arts college in small city.
Enrollment: 2,577 undergrads, 1% part-time. 631 full-time freshmen.
Selectivity: Admits over 75% of applicants.

BASIC COSTS (2013-2014)
Tuition and fees: $41,868.
Per-credit charge: $1,313.
Room and board: $10,780.

FINANCIAL AID PICTURE (2012-2013)
Students with need: Out of 489 full-time freshmen who applied for aid, 385 were judged to have need. Of these, 385 received aid, and 75 had their full need met. Average financial aid package met 75% of need; average scholarship/grant was $23,431; average loan was $4,805. Need-based aid available for part-time students.
Students without need: 217 full-time freshmen who did not demonstrate need for aid received scholarships/grants; average award was $15,959. No-need awards available for academics, alumni affiliation, art, leadership, music/drama, religious affiliation.
Scholarships offered: Alumni, Faculty, Dean's, President's, Trustee Scholarships; all incoming freshman considered; $15,000 -$19,000; based on the student's overall admission application, including academic performance in high school and standardized test scores; no separate scholarship application required.
Cumulative student debt: 58% of graduating class had student loans; average debt was $28,923.

FINANCIAL AID PROCEDURES
Forms required: FAFSA. Students applying for Early Decision must complete the CSS PROFILE for notification of need-based financial aid eligibility.
Dates and Deadlines: Priority date 2/1; no closing date. Applicants notified on a rolling basis starting 3/15; must reply by 5/1 or within 2 week(s) of notification.
Transfers: Priority date 3/1; no deadline. Applicants notified on a rolling basis starting 3/15.

CONTACT
Maggie Mittuch, Associate Vice President of Student Financial Services
1500 North Warner Street, Tacoma, WA 98416-1062
(253) 879-3214

University of Washington

Seattle, Washington
www.washington.edu Federal Code: 003798

4-year public university in very large city.
Enrollment: 27,836 undergrads, 7% part-time. 5,978 full-time freshmen.
Selectivity: Admits 50 to 75% of applicants.

BASIC COSTS (2012-2013)
Tuition and fees: $12,428; out-of-state residents $29,983.
Room and board: $9,969.

FINANCIAL AID PICTURE (2012-2013)
Students with need: Out of 3,800 full-time freshmen who applied for aid, 2,300 were judged to have need. Of these, 2,300 received aid, and 524 had their full need met. Average financial aid package met 83% of need; average scholarship/grant was $13,500; average loan was $5,500. For part-time students, average financial aid package was $11,000.
Students without need: 125 full-time freshmen who did not demonstrate need for aid received scholarships/grants; average award was $7,100. No-need awards available for academics, alumni affiliation, art, athletics, leadership, music/drama, ROTC.

Scholarships offered: 40 full-time freshmen received athletic scholarships; average amount $9,600.
Cumulative student debt: 49% of graduating class had student loans; average debt was $20,800.
Additional info: Tuition not due until third week of term.

FINANCIAL AID PROCEDURES
Forms required: FAFSA.
Dates and Deadlines: Priority date 2/28; no closing date. Applicants notified on a rolling basis starting 4/1; must reply within 3 week(s) of notification.

CONTACT
Kay Lewis, Director of Student Financial Aid
1410 Northeast Campus Parkway, Box 355852, Seattle, WA 98195-5852
(206) 543-6101

University of Washington Bothell
Bothell, Washington
www.uwb.edu Federal Code: 003798

4-year public university in large town.
Enrollment: 3,618 undergrads, 16% part-time. 533 full-time freshmen.
Selectivity: Admits 50 to 75% of applicants.

BASIC COSTS (2012-2013)
Tuition and fees: $11,913; out-of-state residents $29,266.
Room and board: $9,969.

FINANCIAL AID PICTURE (2012-2013)
Students with need: Average financial aid package met 78% of need; average scholarship/grant was $14,200; average loan was $5,000. For part-time students, average financial aid package was $13,800.
Students without need: No-need awards available for academics.
Cumulative student debt: 51% of graduating class had student loans; average debt was $20,000.

FINANCIAL AID PROCEDURES
Forms required: FAFSA.
Dates and Deadlines: Priority date 2/28; no closing date. Applicants notified on a rolling basis starting 4/1; must reply within 3 week(s) of notification.

CONTACT
Danette Iyall, Assistant Director, Financial Aid
18115 Campus Way NE, Bothell, WA 98011-8246
(425) 352-5326

University of Washington Tacoma
Tacoma, Washington
www.tacoma.uw.edu Federal Code: 003798

4-year public university and branch campus college in small city.
Enrollment: 3,323 undergrads, 15% part-time. 326 full-time freshmen.
Selectivity: Admits over 75% of applicants.

BASIC COSTS (2012-2013)
Tuition and fees: $11,901; out-of-state residents $30,054.
Additional info: Board plan not available. Cost of room only, $9,969.

FINANCIAL AID PICTURE (2012-2013)
Students with need: Out of 260 full-time freshmen who applied for aid, 240 were judged to have need. Of these, 240 received aid, and 80 had their full need met. Average financial aid package met 78% of need; average scholarship/grant was $14,300; average loan was $5,000. For part-time students, average financial aid package was $13,000.
Students without need: 12 full-time freshmen who did not demonstrate need for aid received scholarships/grants; average award was $2,500. No-need awards available for academics.
Cumulative student debt: 62% of graduating class had student loans; average debt was $20,700.

FINANCIAL AID PROCEDURES
Forms required: FAFSA.
Dates and Deadlines: Priority date 2/28; no closing date. Applicants notified on a rolling basis starting 4/1; must reply within 3 week(s) of notification.
Transfers: Applicants notified on a rolling basis starting 11/15.

CONTACT
Shari King, Associate Director of Financial Aid and Veterans Affairs
Campus Box 358430, Tacoma, WA 98402-3100
(253) 692-4400

Walla Walla Community College
Walla Walla, Washington
www.wwcc.edu Federal Code: 005006

2-year public community and technical college in large town.
Enrollment: 4,907 undergrads.
Selectivity: Open admission; but selective for some programs.

BASIC COSTS (2012-2013)
Tuition and fees: $4,366; out-of-state residents $9,601.
Additional info: Tuition/fee waivers available for unemployed or children of unemployed.

FINANCIAL AID PICTURE
Students with need: Need-based aid available for full-time and part-time students. Work study available nights.
Students without need: No-need awards available for academics, athletics, leadership, music/drama.

FINANCIAL AID PROCEDURES
Forms required: FAFSA, institutional form.
Dates and Deadlines: Priority date 3/1; no closing date. Applicants notified on a rolling basis starting 6/1; must reply within 2 week(s) of notification.

CONTACT
Danielle Hodgen, Director of Financial Aid
500 Tausick Way, Walla Walla, WA 99362-9972
(509) 527-4301

Walla Walla University
College Place, Washington
www.wallawalla.edu Federal Code: 003799

4-year private university and liberal arts college in large town, affiliated with Seventh-day Adventists.
Enrollment: 1,653 undergrads, 5% part-time. 362 full-time freshmen.
Selectivity: Admits 50 to 75% of applicants.

BASIC COSTS (2013-2014)
Tuition and fees: $25,377.
Per-credit charge: $648.
Room and board: $5,970.

FINANCIAL AID PICTURE (2011-2012)
Students with need: Out of 296 full-time freshmen who applied for aid, 243 were judged to have need. Of these, 243 received aid, and 68 had their full need met. Average financial aid package met 92% of need; average scholarship/grant was $3,603; average loan was $2,465. For part-time students, average financial aid package was $15,930.
Students without need: 116 full-time freshmen who did not demonstrate need for aid received scholarships/grants; average award was $10,404. No-need awards available for academics, leadership, music/drama.

Cumulative student debt: 76% of graduating class had student loans; average debt was $35,367.

FINANCIAL AID PROCEDURES

Forms required: FAFSA, institutional form.

Dates and Deadlines: Priority date 4/30; no closing date. Applicants notified on a rolling basis starting 3/15.

CONTACT

Cassie Ragenovich, Director of Student Financial Services
204 South College Avenue, College Place, WA 99324-3000
(509) 527-2815

Washington State University

Pullman, Washington
www.wsu.edu Federal Code: 003800

4-year public university in large town.
Enrollment: 22,815 undergrads, 12% part-time. 4,401 full-time freshmen.
Selectivity: Admits over 75% of applicants.

BASIC COSTS (2012-2013)

Tuition and fees: $12,300; out-of-state residents $25,382.
Room and board: $9,848.

FINANCIAL AID PICTURE (2011-2012)

Students with need: Out of 3,569 full-time freshmen who applied for aid, 2,593 were judged to have need. Of these, 2,479 received aid, and 732 had their full need met. Average financial aid package met 92% of need; average scholarship/grant was $9,776; average loan was $3,494. For part-time students, average financial aid package was $12,809.

Students without need: 768 full-time freshmen who did not demonstrate need for aid received scholarships/grants; average award was $4,136. No-need awards available for academics, alumni affiliation, art, athletics, job skills, leadership, minority status, music/drama, religious affiliation, ROTC, state/district residency.

Scholarships offered: ***Merit:*** Regents Scholars Program: Distinguished Regents Scholars receive tuition and fees, Regents Scholars receive $4,000 per year; renewable; based on high school GPA, standardized test scores; community, civic, and co-curricular involvement; educator or tribal council recommendations; residency; 10 Distinguished Regents Scholar awards, number of Regents Scholar awards varies. University Achievement Award: $2,000 to $4,000; granted to Washington high school students who meet GPA and SAT/ACT requirements and apply for freshman admission to Pullman campus by January 31 priority date; renewable for one year. Cougar Academic Award: $4,000 or $9,000 per year, renewable for three years; out-of-state students; based on high school grades, standardized test scores. Lighty Leadership Award: full tuition for out-of-state students; based on academic achievement and community involvement; preference to applicants from Northern California; number varies. National Merit Scholarships: full tuition for up to four years for National Merit semifinalists who list Washington State University as their first choice and enroll fall semester after high school graduation; number varies. ***Athletic:*** 66 full-time freshmen received athletic scholarships; average amount $21,546.

Cumulative student debt: 57% of graduating class had student loans; average debt was $23,433.

FINANCIAL AID PROCEDURES

Forms required: FAFSA.

Dates and Deadlines: Priority date 2/15; no closing date. Applicants notified on a rolling basis starting 4/15.

Transfers: No deadline. Applicants notified on a rolling basis starting 4/15. Transfer Achievement Award offered to entering transfer students who have already earned their associate degree and are transferring to the Pullman campus. Must be residents of Washington, have a minimum grade point average of 3.0, and demonstrate financial need through the FAFSA. Award is valued at $2,500 and renewable for a second year.

CONTACT

Chio Flores, Director of Financial Aid and Scholarships
370 Lighty Student Services Bldg, Pullman, WA 99164-1067
(509) 335-9711

Wenatchee Valley College

Wenatchee, Washington
www.wvc.edu Federal Code: 003801

2-year public community college in large town.
Enrollment: 3,885 undergrads.
Selectivity: Open admission; but selective for some programs.

BASIC COSTS (2012-2013)

Tuition and fees: $4,105; out-of-state residents $9,340.
Additional info: Tuition/fee waivers available for adults, unemployed or children of unemployed.

FINANCIAL AID PICTURE

Students with need: Need-based aid available for full-time and part-time students.

Students without need: No-need awards available for academics, athletics.

FINANCIAL AID PROCEDURES

Forms required: FAFSA.

Dates and Deadlines: Closing date 3/1. Applicants notified by 7/2; must reply within 3 week(s) of notification.

Transfers: Priority date 3/1. Applicants notified on a rolling basis.

CONTACT

Kevin Berg, Financial Aid Director
1300 Fifth Street, Wenatchee, WA 98801-1799
(509) 682-6845

Western Washington University

Bellingham, Washington
www.wwu.edu Federal Code: 003802

4-year public university in small city.
Enrollment: 13,801 undergrads, 7% part-time. 2,660 full-time freshmen.
Selectivity: Admits over 75% of applicants.

BASIC COSTS (2012-2013)

Tuition and fees: $8,805; out-of-state residents $19,152.
Room and board: $9,372.
Additional info: Tuition/fee waivers available for adults, minority students.

FINANCIAL AID PICTURE (2012-2013)

Students with need: Out of 2,191 full-time freshmen who applied for aid, 1,410 were judged to have need. Of these, 1,348 received aid, and 271 had their full need met. Average financial aid package met 85% of need; average scholarship/grant was $8,828; average loan was $3,685. For part-time students, average financial aid package was $11,505.

Students without need: 56 full-time freshmen who did not demonstrate need for aid received scholarships/grants; average award was $1,923. No-need awards available for academics, alumni affiliation, art, athletics, job skills, leadership, minority status, music/drama, state/district residency.

Scholarships offered: 18 full-time freshmen received athletic scholarships; average amount $6,652.

Additional info: Short-term student loans ranging from $100 to $1,000 available on a quarterly basis.

FINANCIAL AID PROCEDURES

Forms required: FAFSA.

Dates and Deadlines: Priority date 2/15; no closing date. Applicants notified on a rolling basis starting 3/20; must reply within 3 week(s) of notification.

Transfers: No deadline. Applicants notified on a rolling basis starting 3/20; must reply within 3 week(s) of notification. Some state aid not available for out-of-state transfer students.

CONTACT
Clara Capron, Director of Financial Aid
516 High Street, Bellingham, WA 98225-9009
(360) 650-3470

Whatcom Community College
Bellingham, Washington
www.whatcom.ctc.edu Federal Code: 010364

2-year public community college in small city.
Enrollment: 5,000 undergrads.
Selectivity: Open admission; but selective for some programs.

BASIC COSTS (2012-2013)
Tuition and fees: $4,180; out-of-state residents $9,665.

FINANCIAL AID PICTURE
Students with need: Need-based aid available for full-time and part-time students. Work study available nights.
Students without need: No-need awards available for academics, athletics, state/district residency.

FINANCIAL AID PROCEDURES
Forms required: FAFSA, institutional form.
Dates and Deadlines: Closing date 4/1. Applicants notified on a rolling basis starting 7/1; must reply within 3 week(s) of notification.

CONTACT
Jack Wollens, Director of Financial Aid
237 West Kellogg Road, Bellingham, WA 98226
(360) 383-3010

Whitman College
Walla Walla, Washington Federal Code: 003803
www.whitman.edu CSS Code: 4951

4-year private liberal arts college in large town.
Enrollment: 1,525 undergrads, 1% part-time. 382 full-time freshmen.
Selectivity: Admits less than 50% of applicants.

BASIC COSTS (2013-2014)
Tuition and fees: $43,500.
Per-credit charge: $1,798.
Room and board: $10,900.

FINANCIAL AID PICTURE (2012-2013)
Students with need: Out of 245 full-time freshmen who applied for aid, 165 were judged to have need. Of these, 165 received aid, and 86 had their full need met. Average financial aid package met 93% of need; average scholarship/grant was $26,170; average loan was $4,308. For part-time students, average financial aid package was $31,467.
Students without need: 123 full-time freshmen who did not demonstrate need for aid received scholarships/grants; average award was $9,028. No-need awards available for academics, art, minority status.

FINANCIAL AID PROCEDURES
Forms required: FAFSA, CSS PROFILE.
Dates and Deadlines: Priority date 11/15; closing date 2/1. Applicants notified by 4/1; must reply by 5/1.
Transfers: Closing date 3/1. Applicants notified by 4/22; must reply by 5/15.

CONTACT
Tony Cabasco, Dean of Admission and Financial Aid
345 Boyer Avenue, Walla Walla, WA 99362-2046
(509) 527-5178

Whitworth University
Spokane, Washington
www.whitworth.edu Federal Code: 003804

4-year private university and liberal arts college in large city, affiliated with Presbyterian church.
Enrollment: 2,321 undergrads, 2% part-time. 631 full-time freshmen.
Selectivity: Admits 50 to 75% of applicants.

BASIC COSTS (2013-2014)
Tuition and fees: $36,012.
Per-credit charge: $1,472.
Room and board: $9,814.
Additional info: Tuition/fee waivers available for minority students.

FINANCIAL AID PICTURE (2012-2013)
Students with need: Out of 549 full-time freshmen who applied for aid, 462 were judged to have need. Of these, 460 received aid, and 93 had their full need met. Average financial aid package met 83% of need; average scholarship/grant was $21,734; average loan was $4,188. For part-time students, average financial aid package was $18,592.
Students without need: 156 full-time freshmen who did not demonstrate need for aid received scholarships/grants; average award was $16,155. No-need awards available for academics, art, minority status, music/drama, ROTC.
Cumulative student debt: 64% of graduating class had student loans; average debt was $23,636.

FINANCIAL AID PROCEDURES
Forms required: FAFSA.
Dates and Deadlines: Priority date 3/1; no closing date. Applicants notified on a rolling basis starting 3/15.
Transfers: Priority date 4/1; no deadline. Applicants notified on a rolling basis starting 3/1; must reply by 5/1.

CONTACT
Wendy Olson, Director of Financial Aid
300 West Hawthorne Road, Spokane, WA 99251-0002
(509) 777-3215

Yakima Valley Community College
Yakima, Washington
www.yvcc.edu Federal Code: 003805

2-year public community college in small city.
Enrollment: 4,534 undergrads.
Selectivity: Open admission; but selective for some programs.

BASIC COSTS (2013-2014)
Tuition and fees: $4,642; out-of-state residents $5,070.
Per-credit charge: $124.
Room and board: $9,492.
Additional info: Tuition/fee waivers available for unemployed or children of unemployed.

FINANCIAL AID PICTURE
Students with need: Need-based aid available for full-time and part-time students. Work study available nights, weekends, and for part-time students.
Students without need: No-need awards available for athletics.

FINANCIAL AID PROCEDURES
Forms required: FAFSA.

Dates and Deadlines: Closing date 4/15. Applicants notified on a rolling basis starting 8/1; must reply within 2 week(s) of notification.
Transfers: Priority date 4/15; no deadline. Applicants notified on a rolling basis starting 8/1; must reply within 2 week(s) of notification.

CONTACT
Janet Cantelon, Director, Office of Student Financial Aid
PO Box 22520, Yakima, WA 98907-2520
(509) 574-6855

West Virginia

Alderson-Broaddus College
Philippi, West Virginia
www.ab.edu Federal Code: 003806

4-year private liberal arts college in small town, affiliated with American Baptist Churches in the USA.
Enrollment: 812 undergrads, 4% part-time. 137 full-time freshmen.
Selectivity: Admits less than 50% of applicants.

BASIC COSTS (2013-2014)
Tuition and fees: $22,740.
Per-credit charge: $751.
Room and board: $7,236.

FINANCIAL AID PICTURE (2011-2012)
Students with need: Out of 137 full-time freshmen who applied for aid, 125 were judged to have need. Of these, 125 received aid, and 34 had their full need met. Average financial aid package met 84% of need; average scholarship/grant was $18,592; average loan was $3,797. For part-time students, average financial aid package was $6,844.
Students without need: 12 full-time freshmen who did not demonstrate need for aid received scholarships/grants; average award was $8,010. No-need awards available for academics, athletics, music/drama.
Scholarships offered: ***Merit:*** IMPACT Scholarship; $15,000; 25 ACT or 1150 SAT and 3.5 GPA required for consideration; 5 awards. ***Athletic:*** 7 full-time freshmen received athletic scholarships; average amount $12,000.

FINANCIAL AID PROCEDURES
Forms required: FAFSA, state aid form.
Dates and Deadlines: Priority date 3/1; no closing date. Applicants notified on a rolling basis starting 3/1; must reply within 2 week(s) of notification.

CONTACT
Amy King, Director of Financial Aid
101 College Hill Drive, Philippi, WV 26416
(304) 457-6354

American Public University System
Charles Town, West Virginia
www.apus.edu Federal Code: 038193

4-year for-profit virtual university in small town.
Enrollment: 89,175 undergrads.
Selectivity: Open admission.

BASIC COSTS (2013-2014)
Tuition and fees: $7,500.
Per-credit charge: $250.
Additional info: Required fees are $50 per course.

FINANCIAL AID PICTURE
Students with need: Need-based aid available for full-time and part-time students.
Additional info: Students should complete a Federal Student Aid Intent Form and register for classes at least 37 days prior to start to allow sufficient time for financial aid process.

FINANCIAL AID PROCEDURES
Forms required: FAFSA, institutional form.
Dates and Deadlines: Applicants notified on a rolling basis; must reply within 14 week(s) of notification.
Transfers: Must reply within 14 week(s) of notification. Students should ensure that financial aid is processed and confirmed at least 10-14 days prior to beginning a semester.

CONTACT
Gary Spoales, Associate Vice President, Financial Services
111 West Congress Street, Charles Town, WV 25414
(877) 777-9081

Appalachian Bible College
Mount Hope, West Virginia
www.abc.edu Federal Code: 007544

4-year private Bible college in large town, affiliated with nondenominational tradition.
Enrollment: 212 undergrads.
Selectivity: Admits 50 to 75% of applicants.

BASIC COSTS (2012-2013)
Tuition and fees: $12,680.
Room and board: $6,570.

FINANCIAL AID PICTURE
Students with need: Need-based aid available for full-time and part-time students.
Students without need: This college awards aid only to students with need.
Scholarships offered: Scholastic Achievement Scholarship; $1,500 per year; based on 26 ACT or 1180 SAT (exclusive of Writing).

FINANCIAL AID PROCEDURES
Forms required: FAFSA, state aid form, institutional form.
Dates and Deadlines: Closing date 6/15. Applicants notified on a rolling basis starting 6/15; must reply by 8/1 or within 4 week(s) of notification.

CONTACT
Deana Steinke, Director of Financial Aid
Director of Admissions, Mount Hope, WV 25880
(304) 877-6428 ext. 3247

Bethany College
Bethany, West Virginia
www.bethanywv.edu Federal Code: 003808

4-year private liberal arts college in rural community, affiliated with Christian Church (Disciples of Christ).
Enrollment: 805 undergrads. 266 full-time freshmen.
Selectivity: Admits less than 50% of applicants.

BASIC COSTS (2012-2013)
Tuition and fees: $24,780.
Per-credit charge: $675.
Room and board: $9,546.

FINANCIAL AID PICTURE
Students with need: Need-based aid available for full-time students. Work study available nights, weekends, and for part-time students.

Additional info: Scholarships available for travel program.

FINANCIAL AID PROCEDURES

Forms required: FAFSA, state aid form.
Dates and Deadlines: Priority date 3/1; no closing date. Applicants notified on a rolling basis starting 3/1; must reply within 2 week(s) of notification.
Transfers: No deadline.

CONTACT

Jason McClain, Director of Financial Aid
Office of Admission, Bethany, WV 26032-0428
(304) 829-7611

Blue Ridge Community and Technical College

Martinsburg, West Virginia
www.blueridgectc.edu Federal Code: 039573

2-year public community and technical college in small city.
Enrollment: 1,965 undergrads, 42% part-time. 288 full-time freshmen.
Selectivity: Open admission.

BASIC COSTS (2012-2013)

Tuition and fees: $3,120; out-of-state residents $5,616.
Per-credit charge: $130; out-of-state residents $234.

FINANCIAL AID PICTURE (2011-2012)

Students with need: Out of 270 full-time freshmen who applied for aid, 255 were judged to have need. Of these, 248 received aid, and 24 had their full need met. Average financial aid package met 63% of need; average scholarship/grant was $4,972; average loan was $2,922. For part-time students, average financial aid package was $7,436.26.
Students without need: 9 full-time freshmen who did not demonstrate need for aid received scholarships/grants.

FINANCIAL AID PROCEDURES

Forms required: FAFSA.
Dates and Deadlines: Closing date 4/15. Applicants notified on a rolling basis starting 6/10; must reply within 2 week(s) of notification.

CONTACT

Doris Glenn, Director of Financial Aid
13650 Apple Harvest Drive, Martinsburg, WV 25403
(304) 260-4380 ext. 2105

Bluefield State College

Bluefield, West Virginia
www.bluefieldstate.edu Federal Code: 003809

4-year public liberal arts and technical college in large town.
Enrollment: 1,935 undergrads, 18% part-time. 300 full-time freshmen.
Selectivity: Admits less than 50% of applicants.

BASIC COSTS (2012-2013)

Tuition and fees: $5,180; out-of-state residents $9,944.
Per-credit charge: $216; out-of-state residents $414.
Additional info: Tuition for students residing in border counties is $7,544.

FINANCIAL AID PICTURE (2012-2013)

Students with need: Out of 278 full-time freshmen who applied for aid, 234 were judged to have need. Of these, 234 received aid, and 19 had their full need met. Average financial aid package met 67% of need; average scholarship/grant was $3,721; average loan was $3,706. For part-time students, average financial aid package was $2,977.
Students without need: 32 full-time freshmen who did not demonstrate need for aid received scholarships/grants; average award was $1,108. No-need awards available for academics, alumni affiliation, art, athletics, job skills, leadership, minority status, state/district residency.
Scholarships offered: 28 full-time freshmen received athletic scholarships; average amount $1,426.
Cumulative student debt: 72% of graduating class had student loans; average debt was $24,999.

FINANCIAL AID PROCEDURES

Forms required: FAFSA, institutional form.
Dates and Deadlines: Priority date 3/1; no closing date. Applicants notified on a rolling basis starting 5/1.
Transfers: No deadline.

CONTACT

Tom Ilse, Director of Financial Aid
219 Rock Street, Bluefield, WV 24701
(304) 327-4020

Concord University

Athens, West Virginia
www.concord.edu Federal Code: 003810

4-year public university and liberal arts college in small town.
Enrollment: 2,365 undergrads, 6% part-time. 472 full-time freshmen.
Selectivity: Admits 50 to 75% of applicants.

BASIC COSTS (2012-2013)

Tuition and fees: $5,716; out-of-state residents $12,700.
Per-credit charge: $238; out-of-state residents $529.
Room and board: $7,596.

FINANCIAL AID PICTURE

Students with need: Need-based aid available for full-time and part-time students. Work study available nights, weekends, and for part-time students.
Students without need: No-need awards available for academics, alumni affiliation, art, athletics, job skills, leadership, minority status, music/drama, state/district residency.
Additional info: March 1 priority deadline for state forms. April 15 priority deadline for FAFSA.

FINANCIAL AID PROCEDURES

Forms required: FAFSA, state aid form, institutional form.
Dates and Deadlines: Closing date 4/15. Applicants notified on a rolling basis starting 5/1; must reply within 2 week(s) of notification.

CONTACT

Debra Turner, Director of Financial Aid
PO Box 1000, Athens, WV 24712-1000
(304) 384-6069

Davis and Elkins College

Elkins, West Virginia
www.dewv.edu Federal Code: 003811

4-year private liberal arts college in small town, affiliated with Presbyterian Church (USA).
Enrollment: 809 undergrads, 2% part-time. 228 full-time freshmen.
Selectivity: Admits over 75% of applicants.

BASIC COSTS (2012-2013)

Tuition and fees: $23,820.
Per-credit charge: $700.
Room and board: $8,350.

FINANCIAL AID PICTURE (2011-2012)

Students with need: Out of 185 full-time freshmen who applied for aid, 169 were judged to have need. Of these, 169 received aid, and 35 had their full need met. Average financial aid package met 84% of need; average scholarship/grant was $17,430; average loan was $3,411. For part-time students, average financial aid package was $9,612.

Students without need: 67 full-time freshmen who did not demonstrate need for aid received scholarships/grants; average award was $7,821. No-need awards available for academics, alumni affiliation, art, athletics, leadership, music/drama, religious affiliation, state/district residency.

Scholarships offered: ***Merit:*** Highlands Scholarship Program, $14,000 for residential students, $11,000 for commuter students, for freshmen students from surrounding seven counties with at least 2.5 GPA. ***Athletic:*** 18 full-time freshmen received athletic scholarships; average amount $9,421.

Cumulative student debt: 85% of graduating class had student loans; average debt was $37,122.

FINANCIAL AID PROCEDURES

Forms required: FAFSA.

Dates and Deadlines: Priority date 3/1; closing date 8/1. Applicants notified on a rolling basis; must reply by 8/30.

Transfers: Applicants notified on a rolling basis; must reply by 8/30.

CONTACT

Matthew Summers, Director of Financial Planning
100 Campus Drive, Elkins, WV 26241-3996
(304) 637-1990

Eastern West Virginia Community and Technical College

Moorefield, West Virginia
www.eastern.wvnet.edu

2-year public community and technical college in rural community.

Enrollment: 721 undergrads.

Selectivity: Open admission.

BASIC COSTS (2012-2013)

Tuition and fees: $2,424; out-of-state residents $6,816.

Per-credit charge: $101; out-of-state residents $284.

FINANCIAL AID PICTURE

Students with need: Need-based aid available for full-time and part-time students.

FINANCIAL AID PROCEDURES

Forms required: FAFSA, institutional form.

Dates and Deadlines: Priority date 6/1; no closing date. Applicants notified on a rolling basis; must reply within 2 week(s) of notification.

CONTACT

Amanda Sites, Director of Financial Aid
316 Eastern Drive, Moorefield, WV 26836
(304) 434-8000

Fairmont State University

Fairmont, West Virginia
www.fairmontstate.edu Federal Code: 003812

4-year public university in large town.

Enrollment: 4,036 undergrads, 12% part-time. 735 full-time freshmen.

Selectivity: Admits 50 to 75% of applicants.

BASIC COSTS (2012-2013)

Tuition and fees: $5,326; out-of-state residents $11,230.

Per-credit charge: $222; out-of-state residents $468.

Room and board: $7,369.

Additional info: Tuition/fee waivers available for adults, minority students.

FINANCIAL AID PICTURE (2011-2012)

Students with need: Out of 706 full-time freshmen who applied for aid, 547 were judged to have need. Of these, 535 received aid, and 58 had their full need met. Average financial aid package met 71% of need; average scholarship/grant was $6,181; average loan was $3,970. For part-time students, average financial aid package was $2,539.

Students without need: This college awards aid only to students with need.

Scholarships offered: 16 full-time freshmen received athletic scholarships; average amount $6,935.

Cumulative student debt: 71% of graduating class had student loans; average debt was $24,060.

FINANCIAL AID PROCEDURES

Forms required: FAFSA.

Dates and Deadlines: Closing date 3/1. Applicants notified on a rolling basis starting 4/1; must reply within 2 week(s) of notification.

Transfers: Academic transcripts required.

CONTACT

Cynthia Hudok, Director of Financial Aid and Scholarships
Office of Admissions, Fairmont, WV 26554-2470
(304) 367-4213

Glenville State College

Glenville, West Virginia
www.glenville.edu Federal Code: 003813

4-year public liberal arts and teachers college in rural community.

Enrollment: 1,511 undergrads, 21% part-time. 339 full-time freshmen.

Selectivity: Admits over 75% of applicants.

BASIC COSTS (2012-2013)

Tuition and fees: $5,860; out-of-state residents $13,824.

Per-credit charge: $244; out-of-state residents $576.

Room and board: $7,985.

Additional info: Tuition for students residing in border counties is $9,624.

FINANCIAL AID PICTURE

Students with need: Need-based aid available for full-time and part-time students. Work study available nights, weekends, and for part-time students.

Students without need: No-need awards available for academics, athletics, music/drama, state/district residency.

FINANCIAL AID PROCEDURES

Forms required: FAFSA.

Dates and Deadlines: Priority date 2/1; no closing date. Applicants notified on a rolling basis starting 3/1; must reply within 3 week(s) of notification.

CONTACT

Karen Lay, Director of Financial Aid
200 High Street, Glenville, WV 26351-1292
(304) 462-4103

Kanawha Valley Community and Technical College

South Charleston, West Virginia
www.kvctc.edu Federal Code: 040386

2-year public community and technical college in small town.

Enrollment: 1,502 undergrads.

Selectivity: Open admission; but selective for some programs.

BASIC COSTS (2012-2013)
Tuition and fees: $3,236; out-of-state residents $8,764.

FINANCIAL AID PICTURE (2012-2013)
Students with need: 8% of average financial aid package awarded as scholarships/grants, 92% awarded as loans/jobs. Work study available nights, weekends, and for part-time students.
Students without need: No-need awards available for academics, state/district residency.
Additional info: All students may apply for tuition waivers. Financial aid deadline enforced only if Federal financial aid is the only source of payment.

FINANCIAL AID PROCEDURES
Dates and Deadlines: Closing date 6/30.

CONTACT
Mary Blizzard, Director of Financial Aid
2001 Union Carbide Drive, South Charleston, WV 25303
(304) 205-6600

Marshall University
Huntington, West Virginia
www.marshall.edu Federal Code: 003815

4-year public university in small city.
Enrollment: 9,365 undergrads, 9% part-time. 1,900 full-time freshmen.
Selectivity: Admits over 75% of applicants.

BASIC COSTS (2012-2013)
Tuition and fees: $5,930; out-of-state residents $13,930.
Per-credit charge: $247; out-of-state residents $580.
Room and board: $9,125.
Additional info: Tuition for students residing in border counties is $10,240.

FINANCIAL AID PICTURE (2012-2013)
Students with need: Out of 1,819 full-time freshmen who applied for aid, 1,371 were judged to have need. Of these, 1,354 received aid, and 424 had their full need met. Average financial aid package met 50.7% of need; average scholarship/grant was $5,961; average loan was $5,928. For part-time students, average financial aid package was $4,519.
Students without need: 334 full-time freshmen who did not demonstrate need for aid received scholarships/grants; average award was $6,169. No-need awards available for academics, art, athletics, minority status, music/drama, ROTC, state/district residency.
Scholarships offered: ***Merit:*** Michael Perry Scholarship; $500 based on 3.2 GPA and 20 ACT score; $750 based on 3.5 GPA and 23 ACT, or 3.2 GPA and 25 ACT; one-year only. Presidential Scholarship; $1,250; 3.5 GPA and 25 ACT; renewable with 3.5 GPA. John Marshall Scholarship; tuition waiver plus $1,250 stipend; 3.5 GPA and 30 ACT; renewable yearly with 3.5 GPA. Yeager scholarship; full tuition and fees, full room and board, book allowance, stipend, personal computer for use during program, and $4,000 toward study abroad; 28 ACT/1260 SAT (exclusive of Writing). ***Athletic:*** 79 full-time freshmen received athletic scholarships; average amount $11,032.
Cumulative student debt: 62% of graduating class had student loans; average debt was $26,727.

FINANCIAL AID PROCEDURES
Forms required: FAFSA, state aid form.
Dates and Deadlines: Priority date 3/1; no closing date. Applicants notified on a rolling basis starting 5/1.
Transfers: Priority date 1/1.

CONTACT
Kathy Bialk, Director of Financial Aid
One John Marshall Drive, Huntington, WV 25755
(304) 696-3162

Mountain State College
Parkersburg, West Virginia
www.msc.edu Federal Code: 005008

2-year for-profit junior and career college in large town.
Enrollment: 162 undergrads.
Selectivity: Open admission.

BASIC COSTS (2012-2013)
Tuition and fees: $8,215.

FINANCIAL AID PICTURE
Students with need: Work study available nights, weekends, and for part-time students.

FINANCIAL AID PROCEDURES
Forms required: FAFSA.
Dates and Deadlines: Applicants notified on a rolling basis.

CONTACT
Faye Wagoner, Director of Student Financial Services
1508 Spring Street, Parkersburg, WV 26101-3993
(304) 485-5487

National College: Princeton
Princeton, West Virginia
www.national-college.edu Federal Code: 003726

2-year for-profit business college in small city.
Enrollment: 128 undergrads.
Selectivity: Open admission.

BASIC COSTS (2012-2013)
Tuition and fees: $14,310.
Per-credit charge: $317.

FINANCIAL AID PICTURE
Students with need: Need-based aid available for full-time and part-time students.
Students without need: This college awards aid only to students with need.

FINANCIAL AID PROCEDURES
Forms required: FAFSA.
Dates and Deadlines: Applicants notified on a rolling basis starting 9/1.

CONTACT
Pam Cotton, Director of Financial Aid Compliance and Auditing
421 Hilltop Drive, Princeton, WV 24739

Ohio Valley University
Vienna, West Virginia
www.ovu.edu Federal Code: 003819

4-year private university and liberal arts college in small city, affiliated with Church of Christ.
Enrollment: 414 undergrads, 7% part-time. 156 full-time freshmen.
Selectivity: Admits less than 50% of applicants.

BASIC COSTS (2012-2013)
Tuition and fees: $18,100.
Per-credit charge: $475.
Room and board: $7,126.

FINANCIAL AID PICTURE (2011-2012)
Students with need: Out of 145 full-time freshmen who applied for aid, 131 were judged to have need. Of these, 129 received aid, and 25 had their full need met. Average financial aid package met 66% of need; average

scholarship/grant was $11,113; average loan was $3,421. For part-time students, average financial aid package was $6,052.
Students without need: 18 full-time freshmen who did not demonstrate need for aid received scholarships/grants; average award was $5,158. No-need awards available for academics, alumni affiliation, athletics, job skills, leadership, music/drama.
Scholarships offered: 26 full-time freshmen received athletic scholarships; average amount $5,874.
Cumulative student debt: 75% of graduating class had student loans; average debt was $26,367.

FINANCIAL AID PROCEDURES
Forms required: FAFSA.
Dates and Deadlines: Priority date 2/15; no closing date. Applicants notified on a rolling basis starting 3/15; must reply within 4 week(s) of notification.
Transfers: No deadline. Applicants notified on a rolling basis starting 3/15; must reply within 4 week(s) of notification.

CONTACT
Dennis Cox, Director of Student Financial Services
One Campus View Drive, Vienna, WV 26105
(304) 865-6081

Potomac State College of West Virginia University
Keyser, West Virginia
www.potomacstatecollege.edu Federal Code: 003829

2-year public branch campus and junior college in small town.
Enrollment: 1,539 undergrads, 7% part-time. 721 full-time freshmen.
Selectivity: Open admission; but selective for out-of-state students.

BASIC COSTS (2012-2013)
Tuition and fees: $3,178; out-of-state residents $9,134.
Per-credit charge: $132; out-of-state residents $381.
Room and board: $7,289.
Additional info: Tuition for students residing in border counties is $5,438.

FINANCIAL AID PICTURE
Students with need: Need-based aid available for full-time and part-time students.
Students without need: No-need awards available for academics, athletics.

FINANCIAL AID PROCEDURES
Forms required: FAFSA.
Dates and Deadlines: Priority date 3/1; no closing date. Applicants notified on a rolling basis starting 3/15; must reply within 2 week(s) of notification.
Transfers: Applicants notified on a rolling basis starting 3/1; must reply within 3 week(s) of notification.

CONTACT
Harlan Shreve, Chief Business Officer
75 Arnold Street, Keyser, WV 26726
(304) 788-6820

Salem International University
Salem, West Virginia
www.salemu.edu Federal Code: 003820

4-year for-profit university and liberal arts college in rural community.
Enrollment: 633 undergrads. 232 full-time freshmen.

BASIC COSTS (2012-2013)
Tuition and fees: $15,000.
Room and board: $6,400.

FINANCIAL AID PICTURE (2012-2013)
Students with need: Need-based aid available for full-time and part-time students. Work study available nights, weekends, and for part-time students.
Students without need: No-need awards available for academics.
Scholarships offered: Scholarships; extensive amount awarded; based on high school GPA, standardized test scores. Breed-related awards; for students in equine career and industry management program. Awards for GED diploma recipients; based on academic excellence.

FINANCIAL AID PROCEDURES
Forms required: FAFSA.
Dates and Deadlines: Priority date 4/15; no closing date. Applicants notified on a rolling basis starting 2/15; must reply within 4 week(s) of notification.
Transfers: Priority date 3/1; closing date 4/15. Applicants notified on a rolling basis starting 3/1.

CONTACT
Marty Mehringer, Vice President for Financial Aid and Compliance
223 West Main Street, Salem, WV 26426

Shepherd University
Shepherdstown, West Virginia
www.shepherd.edu Federal Code: 003822

4-year public university in small town.
Enrollment: 3,852 undergrads, 10% part-time. 748 full-time freshmen.
Selectivity: Admits over 75% of applicants.

BASIC COSTS (2012-2013)
Tuition and fees: $5,834; out-of-state residents $15,136.
Per-credit charge: $243; out-of-state residents $631.
Room and board: $8,424.
Additional info: Tuition/fee waivers available for minority students.

FINANCIAL AID PICTURE (2012-2013)
Students with need: Out of 719 full-time freshmen who applied for aid, 482 were judged to have need. Of these, 474 received aid, and 119 had their full need met. Average financial aid package met 74% of need; average scholarship/grant was $4,992; average loan was $3,273. For part-time students, average financial aid package was $10,274.
Students without need: 188 full-time freshmen who did not demonstrate need for aid received scholarships/grants; average award was $9,945. No-need awards available for academics, art, athletics, job skills, leadership, minority status, music/drama, state/district residency.
Scholarships offered: 58 full-time freshmen received athletic scholarships; average amount $5,311.
Cumulative student debt: 69% of graduating class had student loans; average debt was $23,940.

FINANCIAL AID PROCEDURES
Forms required: FAFSA, state aid form.
Dates and Deadlines: Priority date 3/1; no closing date. Applicants notified on a rolling basis starting 3/15; must reply within 3 week(s) of notification.
Transfers: No deadline. Applicants notified on a rolling basis starting 11/1; must reply within 3 week(s) of notification.

CONTACT
Sandra Oerly-Bennett, Director of Financial Aid
PO Box 5000, Shepherdstown, WV 25443-5000
(304) 876-5470

Southern West Virginia Community and Technical College

Mount Gay, West Virginia
www.southernwv.edu Federal Code: 003816

2-year public community and technical college in small town.
Enrollment: 2,115 undergrads.
Selectivity: Open admission; but selective for some programs.

BASIC COSTS (2012-2013)
Tuition and fees: $2,740; out-of-state residents $4,322.

FINANCIAL AID PICTURE
Students with need: Need-based aid available for full-time and part-time students.

FINANCIAL AID PROCEDURES
Forms required: FAFSA.
Dates and Deadlines: Applicants notified on a rolling basis.

CONTACT
Cindy Powers, Financial Aid Director
PO Box 2900, Mount Gay, WV 25637
(304) 896-7382

University of Charleston

Charleston, West Virginia
www.ucwv.edu Federal Code: 003818

4-year private university in small city.
Enrollment: 1,016 undergrads, 2% part-time. 240 full-time freshmen.
Selectivity: Admits 50 to 75% of applicants.

BASIC COSTS (2012-2013)
Tuition and fees: $19,500.
Room and board: $9,000.

FINANCIAL AID PICTURE
Students with need: Need-based aid available for full-time and part-time students. Work study available nights, weekends, and for part-time students.
Students without need: No-need awards available for academics, alumni affiliation, art, athletics, leadership, music/drama, ROTC.
Additional info: All university tuition discounts (scholarships) are based on family or student need and talent. Higher need awards are given to middle and lower income students.

FINANCIAL AID PROCEDURES
Forms required: FAFSA, state aid form, institutional form.
Dates and Deadlines: Priority date 3/1; closing date 8/15. Applicants notified on a rolling basis starting 3/1; must reply by 5/1 or within 4 week(s) of notification.
Transfers: Applicants notified on a rolling basis starting 4/1; must reply by 5/1 or within 4 week(s) of notification.

CONTACT
Nina Morton, Director of Financial Aid
2300 MacCorkle Avenue, SE, Charleston, WV 25304
(304) 357-4947

Valley College

Martinsburg, West Virginia
www.valley.edu Federal Code: G26094

2-year for-profit career college in large town.
Enrollment: 57 undergrads.
Selectivity: Open admission.

BASIC COSTS (2013-2014)
Tuition and fees: $15,075.

FINANCIAL AID PICTURE
Students with need: Need-based aid available for full-time and part-time students.

FINANCIAL AID PROCEDURES
Forms required: FAFSA, institutional form.
Dates and Deadlines: Applicants notified on a rolling basis.
Transfers: No deadline. Applicants notified on a rolling basis.

CONTACT
Shari Cohen, Corporate Director of Financial Aid
287 Aikens Center, Martinsburg, WV 25404
(304) 263-0979

West Liberty University

West Liberty, West Virginia
www.westliberty.edu Federal Code: 003823

4-year public university in rural community.
Enrollment: 2,472 undergrads, 7% part-time. 517 full-time freshmen.
Selectivity: Admits 50 to 75% of applicants.

BASIC COSTS (2012-2013)
Tuition and fees: $5,930; out-of-state residents $13,540.
Per-credit charge: $247; out-of-state residents $564.
Room and board: $7,910.
Additional info: Tuition for students residing in border counties is $11,426.

FINANCIAL AID PICTURE
Students with need: Need-based aid available for full-time and part-time students. Work study available nights, weekends, and for part-time students.
Students without need: No-need awards available for academics, alumni affiliation, art, athletics, music/drama, state/district residency.
Additional info: Non-need based student employment available at food service, college union, bookstore, and tutoring office. Resident assistant and campus security jobs also available.

FINANCIAL AID PROCEDURES
Forms required: FAFSA.
Dates and Deadlines: Priority date 3/1; no closing date. Applicants notified on a rolling basis starting 3/1; must reply within 2 week(s) of notification.
Transfers: Financial aid transcript required from all previous colleges attended regardless of whether aid was received.

CONTACT
Katie Mills, Financial Aid Manager
208 University Drive, West Liberty, WV 26074
(304) 336-8016

West Virginia Junior College

Morgantown, West Virginia
www.wvjcmorgantown.edu Federal Code: 005007

2-year for-profit junior college in large town.
Enrollment: 205 undergrads.
Selectivity: Open admission.

BASIC COSTS (2012-2013)
Additional info: Estimated program costs: associate degree, $23,850 - $43,545; includes fees and supplies.

FINANCIAL AID PICTURE
Students with need: Need-based aid available for full-time and part-time students.

FINANCIAL AID PROCEDURES
Forms required: FAFSA.
Dates and Deadlines: Applicants notified on a rolling basis.

CONTACT
Patricia Callen, Executive Director
148 Willey Street, Morgantown, WV 26505

West Virginia Junior College: Bridgeport

Bridgeport, West Virginia
www.wvjc.edu

2-year for-profit health science and junior college in large town.
Enrollment: 250 undergrads.
Selectivity: Open admission; but selective for some programs.

BASIC COSTS (2012-2013)
Additional info: Cost of associate degree programs ranges from $20,850 to $23,904, including fees and supplies.

FINANCIAL AID PICTURE
Students with need: Need-based aid available for full-time and part-time students.

FINANCIAL AID PROCEDURES
Forms required: FAFSA, state aid form.

CONTACT
Frances Jenkins, Financial Aid Director
176 Thompson Drive, Bridgeport, WV 26330
(304) 842-4007 ext. 105

West Virginia Northern Community College

Wheeling, West Virginia
www.wvncc.edu Federal Code: 010920

2-year public community and technical college in large town.
Enrollment: 2,089 undergrads, 45% part-time. 275 full-time freshmen.
Selectivity: Open admission; but selective for some programs.

BASIC COSTS (2012-2013)
Tuition and fees: $2,546; out-of-state residents $8,106.
Per-credit charge: $106; out-of-state residents $338.
Additional info: Tuition for students residing in bordering counties is $5,698. Tuition/fee waivers available for adults.

FINANCIAL AID PICTURE (2012-2013)
Students with need: 74% of average financial aid package awarded as scholarships/grants, 26% awarded as loans/jobs. Need-based aid available for part-time students.

FINANCIAL AID PROCEDURES
Forms required: FAFSA, institutional form.
Dates and Deadlines: Priority date 3/15; no closing date. Applicants notified on a rolling basis starting 3/10.

CONTACT
Janet Fike, Vice President of Student Services/Director of Financial Aid
1704 Market Street, Wheeling, WV 26003
(304) 214-8844

West Virginia State University

Institute, West Virginia
www.wvstateu.edu Federal Code: 003826

4-year public liberal arts and teachers college in small town.
Enrollment: 2,589 undergrads.

BASIC COSTS (2012-2013)
Tuition and fees: $5,442; out-of-state residents $12,720.
Per-credit charge: $227; out-of-state residents $530.
Room and board: $7,159.
Additional info: Tuition for students residing in border counties is $9,928.

FINANCIAL AID PICTURE
Students with need: Need-based aid available for full-time and part-time students. Work study available nights, weekends, and for part-time students.
Students without need: No-need awards available for academics, athletics, ROTC, state/district residency.

FINANCIAL AID PROCEDURES
Forms required: FAFSA.
Dates and Deadlines: Priority date 3/1; closing date 6/15. Applicants notified on a rolling basis starting 2/15; must reply within 2 week(s) of notification.

CONTACT
JoAnn Ross, Director of Financial Aid
Campus Box 197, Institute, WV 25112-1000
(304) 204-4369

West Virginia University

Morgantown, West Virginia
www.wvu.edu Federal Code: 003827

4-year public university in small city.
Enrollment: 22,292 undergrads, 5% part-time. 5,106 full-time freshmen.
Selectivity: Admits over 75% of applicants.

BASIC COSTS (2012-2013)
Tuition and fees: $6,090; out-of-state residents $18,868.
Per-credit charge: $254; out-of-state residents $786.
Room and board: $8,782.

FINANCIAL AID PICTURE (2012-2013)
Students with need: Average financial aid package met 72% of need; average scholarship/grant was $4,561; average loan was $3,535. For part-time students, average financial aid package was $5,055.
Students without need: No-need awards available for academics, alumni affiliation, art, athletics, leadership, minority status, music/drama, state/district residency.

FINANCIAL AID PROCEDURES
Forms required: FAFSA, state aid form.
Dates and Deadlines: Closing date 3/1. Applicants notified on a rolling basis starting 4/15; must reply within 4 week(s) of notification.
Transfers: Applicants notified on a rolling basis starting 4/1; must reply within 4 week(s) of notification. Transfer scholarship available to those students who apply by 7/1 and transfer a minimum of 15 hours with 3.0 GPA.

CONTACT
Patricia Weimer, Interim Director of Financial Aid
Office of Admissions, Morgantown, WV 26506-6009
(800) 344-9881

West Virginia University at Parkersburg

Parkersburg, West Virginia
www.wvup.edu Federal Code: 003828

2-year public community college in large town.
Enrollment: 3,825 undergrads.
Selectivity: Open admission; but selective for some programs.

BASIC COSTS (2012-2013)

Tuition and fees: $2,496; out-of-state residents $8,856.
Per-credit charge: $104; out-of-state residents $369.
Additional info: Tuition for students residing in border counties is $4800.

FINANCIAL AID PICTURE

Students with need: Need-based aid available for full-time and part-time students. Work study available nights, weekends, and for part-time students.
Students without need: No-need awards available for academics, leadership, state/district residency.

FINANCIAL AID PROCEDURES

Forms required: FAFSA.
Dates and Deadlines: Priority date 3/1; no closing date. Applicants notified on a rolling basis; must reply within 2 week(s) of notification.

CONTACT

August Kafer, Director of Financial Aid
300 Campus Drive, Parkersburg, WV 26104-8647
(304) 424-8210

West Virginia University Institute of Technology

Montgomery, West Virginia
www.wvutech.edu Federal Code: 003825

4-year public engineering and liberal arts college in small town.
Enrollment: 987 undergrads, 15% part-time. 190 full-time freshmen.
Selectivity: Admits 50 to 75% of applicants.

BASIC COSTS (2012-2013)

Tuition and fees: $5,558; out-of-state residents $13,980.
Per-credit charge: $232; out-of-state residents $583.
Room and board: $8,414.

FINANCIAL AID PICTURE (2012-2013)

Students with need: Average financial aid package met 72% of need; average scholarship/grant was $5,099; average loan was $3,751. For part-time students, average financial aid package was $4,381.
Students without need: No-need awards available for academics, alumni affiliation, art, athletics, leadership, minority status, music/drama, state/district residency.
Scholarships offered: Students meeting our academic criteria will receive a scholarship/tuition waiver offer. These awards are renewable each year upon meeting the stated requirements.

FINANCIAL AID PROCEDURES

Forms required: FAFSA.
Dates and Deadlines: Closing date 3/1. Applicants notified on a rolling basis starting 3/21; must reply within 4 week(s) of notification.
Transfers: No deadline. Applicants notified on a rolling basis starting 3/21; must reply within 4 week(s) of notification.

CONTACT

Michael White, Director of Financial Aid Services
405 Fayette Pike, Montgomery, WV 25136-2436
(304) 442-3140

West Virginia Wesleyan College

Buckhannon, West Virginia
www.wvwc.edu Federal Code: 003830

4-year private liberal arts college in small town, affiliated with United Methodist Church.
Enrollment: 1,304 undergrads, 2% part-time. 404 full-time freshmen.
Selectivity: Admits over 75% of applicants.

BASIC COSTS (2012-2013)

Tuition and fees: $25,804.
Room and board: $7,510.

FINANCIAL AID PICTURE

Students with need: Need-based aid available for full-time and part-time students. Work study available nights, weekends, and for part-time students.
Students without need: No-need awards available for academics, alumni affiliation, art, athletics, leadership, music/drama, religious affiliation.
Cumulative student debt: 68% of graduating class had student loans; average debt was $25,655.

FINANCIAL AID PROCEDURES

Forms required: FAFSA.
Dates and Deadlines: Priority date 2/15; no closing date. Applicants notified on a rolling basis starting 3/1; must reply within 4 week(s) of notification.
Transfers: No deadline. Applicants notified on a rolling basis starting 3/15; must reply within 4 week(s) of notification. Financial aid transcripts required from all institutions previously attended.

CONTACT

Susan George, Director of Financial Aid
59 College Avenue, Buckhannon, WV 26201-2998
(304) 473-8080

Wheeling Jesuit University

Wheeling, West Virginia
www.wju.edu Federal Code: 003831

4-year private university and liberal arts college in small city, affiliated with Roman Catholic Church.
Enrollment: 1,034 undergrads, 12% part-time. 268 full-time freshmen.
Selectivity: Admits 50 to 75% of applicants.

BASIC COSTS (2013-2014)

Tuition and fees: $27,830.
Per-credit charge: $775.
Room and board: $5,140.

FINANCIAL AID PICTURE (2012-2013)

Students with need: Out of 241 full-time freshmen who applied for aid, 219 were judged to have need. Of these, 219 received aid, and 81 had their full need met. Average financial aid package met 97% of need; average scholarship/grant was $6,143; average loan was $4,275. For part-time students, average financial aid package was $6,764.
Students without need: 49 full-time freshmen who did not demonstrate need for aid received scholarships/grants; average award was $10,040. No-need awards available for academics, alumni affiliation, athletics, music/drama, religious affiliation.
Scholarships offered: 92 full-time freshmen received athletic scholarships; average amount $7,006.
Cumulative student debt: 79% of graduating class had student loans; average debt was $30,516.

FINANCIAL AID PROCEDURES

Forms required: FAFSA.
Dates and Deadlines: Applicants notified on a rolling basis starting 3/10; must reply within 2 week(s) of notification.

Transfers: No deadline. Applicants notified on a rolling basis starting 3/10; must reply within 2 week(s) of notification. Academic scholarships available to qualified transfer students.

CONTACT

Christie Tomczyk, Director of Financial Aid
316 Washington Avenue, Wheeling, WV 26003-6295
(304) 243-2304

Wisconsin

Alverno College

Milwaukee, Wisconsin
www.alverno.edu Federal Code: 003832

4-year private liberal arts college for women in very large city, affiliated with Roman Catholic Church.
Enrollment: 1,898 undergrads, 26% part-time. 191 full-time freshmen.
Selectivity: Admits 50 to 75% of applicants.

BASIC COSTS (2012-2013)
Tuition and fees: $22,126.
Per-credit charge: $899.
Room and board: $7,050.

FINANCIAL AID PICTURE (2012-2013)
Students with need: Out of 186 full-time freshmen who applied for aid, 181 were judged to have need. Of these, 181 received aid. For part-time students, average financial aid package was $9,090.
Students without need: 8 full-time freshmen who did not demonstrate need for aid received scholarships/grants; average award was $8,600. No-need awards available for academics, alumni affiliation.
Cumulative student debt: 92% of graduating class had student loans; average debt was $41,405.

FINANCIAL AID PROCEDURES
Forms required: FAFSA, institutional form.
Dates and Deadlines: Priority date 3/15; no closing date. Applicants notified on a rolling basis starting 3/15; must reply within 2 week(s) of notification.
Transfers: No deadline. Applicants notified on a rolling basis; must reply within 2 week(s) of notification. Transfer students are eligible for academic scholarships.

CONTACT

Dan Goyette, Director of Financial Aid
3400 South 43rd Street, Milwaukee, WI 53234-3922
(414) 382-6046

Beloit College

Beloit, Wisconsin
www.beloit.edu Federal Code: 003835

4-year private liberal arts college in large town.
Enrollment: 1,274 undergrads, 1% part-time. 311 full-time freshmen.
Selectivity: Admits 50 to 75% of applicants.

BASIC COSTS (2012-2013)
Tuition and fees: $38,474.
Per-credit charge: $1,194.
Room and board: $7,862.
Additional info: Tuition/fee waivers available for adults.

FINANCIAL AID PICTURE (2012-2013)
Students with need: Out of 255 full-time freshmen who applied for aid, 223 were judged to have need. Of these, 223 received aid, and 53 had their full need met. Average financial aid package met 87% of need; average scholarship/grant was $24,974; average loan was $3,256. For part-time students, average financial aid package was $18,956.
Students without need: 73 full-time freshmen who did not demonstrate need for aid received scholarships/grants; average award was $17,592. No-need awards available for academics, leadership, minority status, music/drama.
Scholarships offered: Presidential Scholarships: $13,000-$15,000 per year; campus interview required.
Cumulative student debt: 57% of graduating class had student loans; average debt was $27,981.

FINANCIAL AID PROCEDURES
Forms required: FAFSA, state aid form, institutional form.
Dates and Deadlines: Closing date 3/1. Applicants notified on a rolling basis starting 4/1; must reply by 5/1 or within 2 week(s) of notification.
Transfers: No deadline. Applicants notified on a rolling basis starting 4/1; must reply by 5/1 or within 2 week(s) of notification.

CONTACT

Jon Urish, Director of Student Financial Services
700 College Street, Beloit, WI 53511-5595
(608) 363-2663

Blackhawk Technical College

Janesville, Wisconsin
www.blackhawk.edu Federal Code: 005390

2-year public technical college in small city.
Enrollment: 2,967 undergrads, 56% part-time. 295 full-time freshmen.
Selectivity: Open admission; but selective for some programs.

BASIC COSTS (2012-2013)
Tuition and fees: $3,746; out-of-state residents $5,437.
Per-credit charge: $117; out-of-state residents $176.
Additional info: Material fees vary by program; minimum $4 per course. $10 per credit fee for online courses.

FINANCIAL AID PICTURE (2011-2012)
Students with need: 60% of average financial aid package awarded as scholarships/grants, 40% awarded as loans/jobs. Need-based aid available for part-time students. Work study available nights.

FINANCIAL AID PROCEDURES
Forms required: FAFSA.
Dates and Deadlines: Closing date 4/30. Applicants notified on a rolling basis starting 3/15.

CONTACT

Sue Ullrick, Financial Aid Officer
Box 5009, Janesville, WI 53547-5009
(608) 757-7664

Bryant & Stratton College: Milwaukee

Milwaukee, Wisconsin
www.bryantstratton.edu Federal Code: 005009

2-year for-profit business and junior college in very large city.
Enrollment: 905 full-time undergrads.

BASIC COSTS (2012-2013)
Tuition and fees: $16,050.
Per-credit charge: $535.
Additional info: Tuition and fees may vary by program.

FINANCIAL AID PICTURE

Students with need: Work study available nights.

Students without need: This college awards aid only to students with need.

FINANCIAL AID PROCEDURES

Forms required: FAFSA.

Dates and Deadlines: Closing date 9/22. Applicants notified on a rolling basis; must reply within 2 week(s) of notification.

CONTACT

Lois Trongard, Business Director
310 West Wisconsin Avenue, Suite 500, Milwaukee, WI 53203
(414) 276-5200

Cardinal Stritch University

Milwaukee, Wisconsin
www.stritch.edu Federal Code: 003837

4-year private university in very large city, affiliated with Roman Catholic Church.

Enrollment: 2,780 undergrads, 16% part-time. 158 full-time freshmen.

Selectivity: Admits less than 50% of applicants.

BASIC COSTS (2012-2013)

Tuition and fees: $24,005.

Per-credit charge: $740.

Room and board: $7,030.

FINANCIAL AID PICTURE (2011-2012)

Students with need: Out of 151 full-time freshmen who applied for aid, 147 were judged to have need. Of these, 147 received aid, and 15 had their full need met. Average financial aid package met 61% of need; average scholarship/grant was $14,184; average loan was $3,075. For part-time students, average financial aid package was $7,045.

Students without need: 9 full-time freshmen who did not demonstrate need for aid received scholarships/grants; average award was $11,194. No-need awards available for academics, art, athletics, music/drama.

Scholarships offered: 6 full-time freshmen received athletic scholarships; average amount $5,483.

Cumulative student debt: 89% of graduating class had student loans; average debt was $25,445.

FINANCIAL AID PROCEDURES

Forms required: FAFSA, institutional form.

Dates and Deadlines: Priority date 3/15; no closing date. Applicants notified on a rolling basis starting 3/1; must reply within 2 week(s) of notification.

CONTACT

Ben Baerbock, Director of Financial Aid
6801 North Yates Road, Box 516, Milwaukee, WI 53217-7516
(414) 410-4048

Carroll University

Waukesha, Wisconsin
www.carrollu.edu Federal Code: 003838

4-year private university and liberal arts college in small city, affiliated with Presbyterian Church (USA).

Enrollment: 3,148 undergrads, 11% part-time. 712 full-time freshmen.

Selectivity: Admits over 75% of applicants.

BASIC COSTS (2012-2013)

Tuition and fees: $26,475.

Per-credit charge: $325.

Room and board: $7,995.

FINANCIAL AID PICTURE

Students with need: Need-based aid available for full-time and part-time students. Work study available nights, weekends, and for part-time students.

Students without need: No-need awards available for academics, alumni affiliation, art, leadership, music/drama, ROTC.

FINANCIAL AID PROCEDURES

Forms required: FAFSA.

Dates and Deadlines: Applicants notified on a rolling basis starting 2/15; must reply by 5/1 or within 2 week(s) of notification.

Transfers: No deadline. Applicants notified on a rolling basis starting 2/15.

CONTACT

Dawn Scott, Director of Student Financial Services
100 North East Avenue, Waukesha, WI 53186-9988
(262) 524-7296

Carthage College

Kenosha, Wisconsin
www.carthage.edu Federal Code: 003839

4-year private liberal arts college in small city, affiliated with Evangelical Lutheran Church in America.

Enrollment: 2,531 undergrads.

BASIC COSTS (2012-2013)

Tuition and fees: $33,000.

Room and board: $9,000.

Additional info: Tuition/fee waivers available for minority students.

FINANCIAL AID PICTURE

Students with need: Need-based aid available for full-time and part-time students.

Students without need: No-need awards available for academics, alumni affiliation, art, leadership, minority status, music/drama, religious affiliation.

Scholarships offered: Lincoln Scholarship Program: range from 75% tuition to full tuition, room and board, renewable; separate scholarship application; 17 awarded. Math/Science Scholarship: three awarded; range from $17,000/year to full tuition, renewable; requires separate scholarship application, restricted to math and natural science majors. French/German Scholarship: four awarded; $17,000/year, renewable; requires separate scholarship application, restricted to French and German majors. Fine Arts Scholarships: $500-$10,000/year, renewable; requires separate audition/portfolio showing, open to majors and non majors in music and theater, and majors in studio art or graphic design. Tarble Scholarships: number awarded variable; up to $17,000 year, renewable; requires separate scholarship application, restricted to California residents.

FINANCIAL AID PROCEDURES

Forms required: FAFSA.

Dates and Deadlines: Priority date 2/15; no closing date. Applicants notified on a rolling basis starting 3/1.

Transfers: Priority date 3/1; no deadline. Applicants notified on a rolling basis starting 3/1.

CONTACT

Vatistas Vatistas, Director of Financial Aid
2001 Alford Park Drive, Kenosha, WI 53140-1994
(262) 551-6001

Chippewa Valley Technical College

Eau Claire, Wisconsin
www.cvtc.edu Federal Code: 005304

2-year public technical college in small city.

Enrollment: 6,085 undergrads, 57% part-time. 1,157 full-time freshmen.

Selectivity: Open admission; but selective for some programs.

BASIC COSTS (2012-2013)

Tuition and fees: $3,795; out-of-state residents $5,485.

Per-credit charge: $117; out-of-state residents $175.

Additional info: Material fees vary by program; minimum $4 per course. $10 per credit fee for online courses.

FINANCIAL AID PICTURE

Students with need: Need-based aid available for full-time and part-time students. Work study available nights, weekends, and for part-time students.

FINANCIAL AID PROCEDURES

Forms required: FAFSA.

Dates and Deadlines: Priority date 3/15; no closing date. Applicants notified on a rolling basis starting 4/30; must reply within 2 week(s) of notification.

CONTACT

Mary Gorud, Financial Aid Manager
620 West Clairemont Avenue, Eau Claire, WI 54701-6162
(715) 833-6252

College of Menominee Nation

Keshena, Wisconsin
www.menominee.edu Federal Code: 031251

2-year private community college in rural community.

Enrollment: 566 undergrads.

Selectivity: Open admission; but selective for some programs.

BASIC COSTS (2012-2013)

Tuition and fees: $7,670.

Per-credit charge: $250.

FINANCIAL AID PICTURE

Students with need: Need-based aid available for full-time and part-time students. Work study available nights.

Students without need: This college awards aid only to students with need.

FINANCIAL AID PROCEDURES

Forms required: FAFSA.

Dates and Deadlines: Applicants notified on a rolling basis.

Transfers: No deadline. Applicants notified on a rolling basis.

CONTACT

Nicole Fish, Financial Aid Director
N 172 State Highway 47/55, Keshena, WI 54135-1179
(715) 799-5600 ext. 3039

Columbia College of Nursing

Glendale, Wisconsin
www.ccon.edu Federal Code: 041594

4-year private nursing college in very large city.

Enrollment: 160 undergrads, 12% part-time.

BASIC COSTS (2012-2013)

Tuition and fees: $25,400.

Per-credit charge: $716.

FINANCIAL AID PICTURE (2012-2013)

Students with need: Average financial aid package for all full-time undergraduates was $15,400; for part-time $13,200. 64% awarded as scholarships/grants, 36% awarded as loans/jobs.

Students without need: No-need awards available for academics.

FINANCIAL AID PROCEDURES

Dates and Deadlines: Priority date 4/15; no closing date.

Transfers: No deadline. Applicants notified on a rolling basis starting 3/1; must reply by 6/1.

CONTACT

Wendy Hilvo, Financial Aid Director
4425 North Port Washington Road, Glendale, WI 53212-1099
(414) 326-2337

Concordia University Wisconsin

Mequon, Wisconsin
www.cuw.edu Federal Code: 003842

4-year private university and liberal arts college in large town, affiliated with Lutheran Church - Missouri Synod.

Enrollment: 4,326 undergrads, 34% part-time. 591 full-time freshmen.

Selectivity: Admits 50 to 75% of applicants.

BASIC COSTS (2012-2013)

Tuition and fees: $24,180.

Room and board: $9,050.

FINANCIAL AID PICTURE (2012-2013)

Students with need: Out of 564 full-time freshmen who applied for aid, 503 were judged to have need. Of these, 503 received aid, and 137 had their full need met. Average financial aid package met 79% of need; average scholarship/grant was $14,418; average loan was $5,342. For part-time students, average financial aid package was $6,599.

Students without need: 81 full-time freshmen who did not demonstrate need for aid received scholarships/grants; average award was $10,782. No-need awards available for academics, art, minority status, music/drama.

Cumulative student debt: 80% of graduating class had student loans; average debt was $31,927.

FINANCIAL AID PROCEDURES

Forms required: FAFSA.

Dates and Deadlines: Priority date 3/15; no closing date. Applicants notified on a rolling basis starting 2/1; must reply within 3 week(s) of notification.

CONTACT

Steve Taylor, Director of Financial Aid
12800 North Lake Shore Drive, Mequon, WI 53097
(262) 243-4392

Edgewood College

Madison, Wisconsin
www.edgewood.edu Federal Code: 003848

4-year private liberal arts college in small city, affiliated with Roman Catholic Church.

Enrollment: 1,932 undergrads, 14% part-time. 294 full-time freshmen.

Selectivity: Admits 50 to 75% of applicants.

BASIC COSTS (2012-2013)

Tuition and fees: $23,740.

Per-credit charge: $747.

Room and board: $8,476.

FINANCIAL AID PICTURE (2011-2012)

Students with need: Out of 263 full-time freshmen who applied for aid, 241 were judged to have need. Of these, 241 received aid, and 18 had their full need met. Average financial aid package met 77% of need; average scholarship/grant was $15,611; average loan was $3,619. For part-time students, average financial aid package was $8,906.

Students without need: 47 full-time freshmen who did not demonstrate need for aid received scholarships/grants; average award was $6,608. No-need awards available for academics, alumni affiliation, art, leadership, music/drama, religious affiliation.

Cumulative student debt: 75% of graduating class had student loans; average debt was $23,464.
Additional info: Auditions required for music scholarships, portfolios required for fine arts scholarships, essays required for a number of specialty institutional scholarships.

FINANCIAL AID PROCEDURES
Forms required: FAFSA.
Dates and Deadlines: Priority date 3/1; no closing date. Applicants notified on a rolling basis starting 3/15.
Transfers: No deadline. Applicants notified on a rolling basis starting 3/15; must reply by 5/1 or within 2 week(s) of notification.

CONTACT
Kari Gribble, Director of Edgewood Central and Financial Aid
1000 Edgewood College Drive, Madison, WI 53711-1997
(608) 663-4300

Fox Valley Technical College
Appleton, Wisconsin
www.fvtc.edu Federal Code: 009744

2-year public technical college in small city.
Enrollment: 7,796 undergrads, 62% part-time. 443 full-time freshmen.
Selectivity: Open admission; but selective for some programs.

BASIC COSTS (2012-2013)
Tuition and fees: $3,978; out-of-state residents $5,731.
Per-credit charge: $117; out-of-state residents $175.
Additional info: Material fees vary by program; minimum $4 per course. $10 per credit fee for online courses.

FINANCIAL AID PICTURE (2011-2012)
Students with need: 42% of average financial aid package awarded as scholarships/grants, 58% awarded as loans/jobs. Need-based aid available for part-time students. Work study available weekends and for part-time students.
Students without need: This college awards aid only to students with need.

FINANCIAL AID PROCEDURES
Forms required: FAFSA.
Dates and Deadlines: Priority date 4/15; no closing date. Applicants notified on a rolling basis.

CONTACT
1825 North Bluemound Drive, Appleton, WI 54912-2277
(920) 735-5650

Gateway Technical College
Kenosha, Wisconsin
www.gtc.edu Federal Code: 005389

2-year public technical college in small city.
Enrollment: 9,149 undergrads.
Selectivity: Open admission; but selective for some programs.

BASIC COSTS (2012-2013)
Tuition and fees: $3,850; out-of-state residents $5,540.
Per-credit charge: $117; out-of-state residents $175.
Additional info: Material fees vary by program; minimum $4 per course. $10 per credit fee for online courses.

FINANCIAL AID PICTURE
Students with need: Need-based aid available for full-time and part-time students.
Students without need: No-need awards available for state/district residency.

FINANCIAL AID PROCEDURES
Forms required: FAFSA, institutional form.
Dates and Deadlines: Priority date 7/1; no closing date. Applicants notified on a rolling basis starting 5/1; must reply within 2 week(s) of notification.

CONTACT
Janice Riutta, Director of Student Financial Aid
3520 30th Avenue, Kenosha, WI 53144-1690
(262) 564-3072

Globe University: Appleton
Grand Chute, Wisconsin
www.globeuniversity.edu Federal Code: 004642

2-year for-profit career college in small city.
Enrollment: 282 undergrads.
Selectivity: Open admission.

BASIC COSTS (2012-2013)
Tuition and fees: $19,125.
Per-credit charge: $460.

FINANCIAL AID PICTURE
Students with need: Need-based aid available for full-time and part-time students.

FINANCIAL AID PROCEDURES
Forms required: FAFSA, institutional form.
Dates and Deadlines: Applicants notified on a rolling basis starting 7/1; must reply within 2 week(s) of notification.

CONTACT
Melissa Crabb, Director of Financial Aid
5045 West Grande Market Drive, Grand Chute, WI 54913
(920) 364-1100

Globe University: Eau Claire
Eau Claire, Wisconsin
www.globeuniversity.edu Federal Code: 004642

2-year for-profit career college in small city.
Enrollment: 322 undergrads.
Selectivity: Open admission.

BASIC COSTS (2012-2013)
Tuition and fees: $19,125.
Per-credit charge: $460.

FINANCIAL AID PICTURE
Students with need: Need-based aid available for full-time and part-time students.

FINANCIAL AID PROCEDURES
Forms required: FAFSA, institutional form.
Dates and Deadlines: Applicants notified on a rolling basis starting 7/1; must reply within 2 week(s) of notification.

CONTACT
John Spaeth, Director of Financial Aid
4955 Bullis Farm Road, Eau Claire, WI 54701
(715) 855-6600

Globe University: Green Bay

Green Bay, Wisconsin
www.globeuniversity.edu Federal Code: 004642

4-year for-profit university and career college in small city.
Enrollment: 249 undergrads.
Selectivity: Open admission.

BASIC COSTS (2012-2013)
Tuition and fees: $19,125.
Per-credit charge: $460.

FINANCIAL AID PICTURE
Students with need: Need-based aid available for full-time and part-time students.

FINANCIAL AID PROCEDURES
Forms required: FAFSA, institutional form.
Dates and Deadlines: Applicants notified on a rolling basis starting 7/1; must reply within 2 week(s) of notification.

CONTACT
Kristin Thyrion, Director of Financial Aid
2620 Development Drive, Green Bay, WI 54311
(920) 264-1600

Globe University: La Crosse

Onalaska, Wisconsin
www.globeuniversity.edu Federal Code: 004642

2-year for-profit career college in large town.
Enrollment: 303 undergrads.
Selectivity: Open admission.

BASIC COSTS (2012-2013)
Tuition and fees: $19,125.
Per-credit charge: $460.

FINANCIAL AID PICTURE
Students with need: Need-based aid available for full-time and part-time students.

FINANCIAL AID PROCEDURES
Forms required: FAFSA, institutional form.
Dates and Deadlines: Applicants notified on a rolling basis starting 7/1; must reply within 2 week(s) of notification.

CONTACT
David Thom, Director of Financial Aid
2651 Midwest Drive, Onalaska, WI 54650
(608) 779-8600

Globe University: Madison East

Madison, Wisconsin
www.globeuniversity.edu Federal Code: 004642

2-year for-profit career college in small city.
Enrollment: 288 undergrads.
Selectivity: Open admission.

BASIC COSTS (2012-2013)
Tuition and fees: $19,125.
Per-credit charge: $460.

FINANCIAL AID PICTURE
Students with need: Need-based aid available for full-time and part-time students.

FINANCIAL AID PROCEDURES
Forms required: FAFSA, institutional form.
Dates and Deadlines: Applicants notified on a rolling basis starting 7/1; must reply within 2 week(s) of notification.

CONTACT
Bill Vache, Director of Financial Aid
4901 Eastpark Boulevard, Madison, WI 53718
(608) 216-9400

Globe University: Middleton

Middleton, Wisconsin
www.globeuniversity.edu Federal Code: 004642

2-year for-profit career college in large town.
Enrollment: 270 undergrads.
Selectivity: Open admission.

FINANCIAL AID PICTURE
Students with need: Need-based aid available for full-time and part-time students.

FINANCIAL AID PROCEDURES
Forms required: FAFSA, institutional form.
Dates and Deadlines: Applicants notified on a rolling basis starting 7/1; must reply within 2 week(s) of notification.

CONTACT
Bill Vache, Director of Financial Aid
1345 Deming Way, Middleton, WI 53562
(608) 830-6900

Globe University: Wausau

Rothschild, Wisconsin
www.globeuniversity.edu Federal Code: 004642

2-year for-profit career college in small town.
Enrollment: 266 undergrads.
Selectivity: Open admission.

BASIC COSTS (2012-2013)
Tuition and fees: $19,125.
Per-credit charge: $460.

FINANCIAL AID PICTURE
Students with need: Need-based aid available for full-time and part-time students.

FINANCIAL AID PROCEDURES
Forms required: FAFSA, institutional form.
Dates and Deadlines: Applicants notified on a rolling basis starting 7/1; must reply within 2 week(s) of notification.

CONTACT
Cheng Heu, Director of Financial Aid
1480 Country Road XX, Rothschild, WI 54474
(715) 301-1300

Herzing University: Madison

Madison, Wisconsin
www.herzing.edu/madison Federal Code: 009621

3-year for-profit business and career college in small city.
Enrollment: 665 undergrads.
Selectivity: Open admission; but selective for some programs.

BASIC COSTS (2012-2013)
Tuition and fees: $11,040.
Per-credit charge: $460.
Additional info: Reported annual tuition is representative. Actual costs vary by program with nursing programs somewhat more expensive.

FINANCIAL AID PICTURE
Students with need: Need-based aid available for full-time and part-time students.

FINANCIAL AID PROCEDURES
Forms required: FAFSA, institutional form.
Dates and Deadlines: Applicants notified on a rolling basis.

CONTACT
Beverly Faga, Director of Financial Services
5218 East Terrace Drive, Madison, WI 53718
(608) 249-6611

Lac Courte Oreilles Ojibwa Community College

Hayward, Wisconsin
www.lco.edu Federal Code: 017199

2-year public community college in small town.
Enrollment: 433 undergrads.
Selectivity: Open admission.

FINANCIAL AID PICTURE
Students with need: Need-based aid available for full-time students.

FINANCIAL AID PROCEDURES
Forms required: FAFSA.
Dates and Deadlines: Applicants notified on a rolling basis.

CONTACT
Diane McKnight, Financial Aid Director
13466 West Trepania Road, Hayward, WI 54843

Lakeland College

Sheboygan, Wisconsin
www.lakeland.edu Federal Code: 003854

4-year private liberal arts college in small city, affiliated with United Church of Christ.
Enrollment: 2,458 undergrads.

BASIC COSTS (2012-2013)
Tuition and fees: $21,242.
Room and board: $7,650.

FINANCIAL AID PICTURE
Students with need: Need-based aid available for full-time and part-time students. Work study available nights, weekends, and for part-time students.
Students without need: No-need awards available for academics, alumni affiliation, art, religious affiliation.
Scholarships offered: Trustees' Scholarship $11,000 minimum gpa of 3.5 and minimum ACT of 24. Presidential Scholarship $8,000 3.25 - 3.49 gpa and 21 or greater ACT. Dean's Scholarship $7,000 3.0 - 3.24 gpa and 21 or greater ACT. Faculty Scholarship $6,000 2.75 - 2.99 gpa and 19 or greater ACT.

FINANCIAL AID PROCEDURES
Forms required: FAFSA, institutional form.
Dates and Deadlines: Priority date 3/15; no closing date. Applicants notified on a rolling basis starting 2/15; must reply within 2 week(s) of notification.

CONTACT
Patty Taylor, Director of Financial Aid
Box 359, Sheboygan, WI 53082-0359
(920) 565-1297

Lakeshore Technical College

Cleveland, Wisconsin
www.gotoltc.edu Federal Code: 009194

2-year public technical college in rural community.
Enrollment: 2,184 undergrads, 62% part-time. 114 full-time freshmen.
Selectivity: Open admission; but selective for some programs.

BASIC COSTS (2012-2013)
Tuition and fees: $3,763; out-of-state residents $5,453.
Per-credit charge: $117; out-of-state residents $175.
Additional info: Material fees vary by program; minimum $4 per course. $10 per credit fee for online courses.

FINANCIAL AID PICTURE
Students with need: Need-based aid available for full-time and part-time students. Work study available nights.
Students without need: This college awards aid only to students with need.

FINANCIAL AID PROCEDURES
Forms required: FAFSA, institutional form.
Dates and Deadlines: Priority date 6/1; no closing date. Applicants notified on a rolling basis starting 6/1; must reply within 3 week(s) of notification.

CONTACT
Corey Givens-Novak, Financial Aid Manager
1290 North Avenue, Cleveland, WI 53015-9761
(920) 693-1118

Lawrence University

Appleton, Wisconsin
www.lawrence.edu Federal Code: 003856

4-year private music and liberal arts college in small city.
Enrollment: 1,471 undergrads, 2% part-time. 405 full-time freshmen.
Selectivity: Admits over 75% of applicants.

BASIC COSTS (2012-2013)
Tuition and fees: $40,023.
Room and board: $8,247.

FINANCIAL AID PICTURE (2012-2013)
Students with need: Out of 336 full-time freshmen who applied for aid, 278 were judged to have need. Of these, 278 received aid, and 102 had their full need met. Average financial aid package met 88% of need; average scholarship/grant was $26,494; average loan was $4,663. For part-time students, average financial aid package was $27,013.
Students without need: 117 full-time freshmen who did not demonstrate need for aid received scholarships/grants; average award was $17,324. No-need awards available for academics, alumni affiliation, leadership, minority status, music/drama.
Scholarships offered: Warch Scholarships: $15,000 per year. Trustee Scholarships: $12,000 per year. Presidential Scholarships: $9,000 per year. Alumni Scholarships: $7,000 per year. Conservatory Scholarships: $2,000-$12,000 per year.
Cumulative student debt: 65% of graduating class had student loans; average debt was $30,724.
Additional info: The first $1,000 (aggregate) of independently-sponsored scholarships received by a needy student will reduce student's loan or work-study commitment. Half of scholarships in excess of $1,000 will offset loan

or work-study and the other half will reduce institutional need-based grant funding.

FINANCIAL AID PROCEDURES
Forms required: FAFSA, institutional form. CSS PROFILE accepted as a required Supplemental Financial Aid form. Helpful if applying to other colleges that require PROFILE.
Dates and Deadlines: Priority date 3/1; no closing date. Applicants notified on a rolling basis starting 3/1; must reply by 5/1 or within 2 week(s) of notification.
Transfers: Priority date 4/1. Applicants notified on a rolling basis starting 5/23.

CONTACT
Ken Anselment, Dean of Admissions and Financial Aid
711 East Boldt Way SPC 29, Appleton, WI 54911-5699
(920) 832-6583

Maranatha Baptist Bible College
Watertown, Wisconsin
www.mbbc.edu Federal Code: 016394

4-year private Bible and liberal arts college in large town, affiliated with Baptist faith.
Enrollment: 775 undergrads, 11% part-time. 185 full-time freshmen.
Selectivity: Admits 50 to 75% of applicants.

BASIC COSTS (2012-2013)
Tuition and fees: $12,860.
Per-credit charge: $488.
Room and board: $6,480.

FINANCIAL AID PICTURE
Students with need: Need-based aid available for full-time and part-time students.
Students without need: No-need awards available for academics.

FINANCIAL AID PROCEDURES
Forms required: FAFSA.
Dates and Deadlines: Priority date 3/1; no closing date. Applicants notified on a rolling basis starting 2/1; must reply within 2 week(s) of notification.
Transfers: Financial aid transcript or equivalent required.

CONTACT
Randy Hibbs, Financial Aid Director
745 West Main Street, Watertown, WI 53094
(920) 206-2318

Marian University
Fond du Lac, Wisconsin
www.marianuniversity.edu Federal Code: 003861

4-year private university and liberal arts college in large town, affiliated with Roman Catholic Church.
Enrollment: 1,771 undergrads, 21% part-time. 321 full-time freshmen.
Selectivity: Admits over 75% of applicants.

BASIC COSTS (2012-2013)
Tuition and fees: $23,440.
Per-credit charge: $350.
Room and board: $6,140.

FINANCIAL AID PICTURE (2011-2012)
Students with need: Out of 315 full-time freshmen who applied for aid, 283 were judged to have need. Of these, 283 received aid, and 23 had their full need met. Average financial aid package met 71% of need; average scholarship/grant was $13,471; average loan was $5,205. For part-time students, average financial aid package was $5,334.
Students without need: 32 full-time freshmen who did not demonstrate need for aid received scholarships/grants; average award was $6,960. No-need awards available for academics.
Scholarships offered: Academic Achievement Award: $7,500; based on 3.5 GPA, 25 ACT, top 15% of class; 7 awarded. Presidential Scholarship: $5,000; based on 3.1 GPA, top 20% of class. Naber Leadership Scholarship: $3,000; based on 2.5 GPA, top 50% of class.

FINANCIAL AID PROCEDURES
Forms required: FAFSA, institutional form.
Dates and Deadlines: Priority date 3/1; no closing date. Applicants notified on a rolling basis starting 3/1; must reply within 4 week(s) of notification.
Transfers: No deadline. Applicants notified on a rolling basis; must reply within 4 week(s) of notification.

CONTACT
Pam Warren, Associate Director of Financial Aid
45 South National Avenue, Fond du Lac, WI 54935-4699
(920) 923-7614

Marquette University
Milwaukee, Wisconsin
www.marquette.edu Federal Code: 003863

4-year private university in very large city, affiliated with Roman Catholic Church.
Enrollment: 8,118 undergrads, 2% part-time. 1,927 full-time freshmen.
Selectivity: Admits 50 to 75% of applicants.

BASIC COSTS (2013-2014)
Tuition and fees: $34,640.
Per-credit charge: $995.
Room and board: $10,730.
Additional info: Antivirus software supplied to all students at no additional charge.

FINANCIAL AID PICTURE (2012-2013)
Students with need: Out of 1,570 full-time freshmen who applied for aid, 1,202 were judged to have need. Of these, 1,202 received aid, and 273 had their full need met. Average financial aid package met 73% of need; average scholarship/grant was $17,629; average loan was $4,153. For part-time students, average financial aid package was $8,785.
Students without need: 691 full-time freshmen who did not demonstrate need for aid received scholarships/grants; average award was $9,775. No-need awards available for academics, athletics, leadership, music/drama, ROTC.
Scholarships offered: 26 full-time freshmen received athletic scholarships; average amount $28,113.
Cumulative student debt: 65% of graduating class had student loans; average debt was $34,602.

FINANCIAL AID PROCEDURES
Forms required: FAFSA.
Dates and Deadlines: Priority date 2/1; no closing date. Applicants notified on a rolling basis starting 3/20; must reply by 5/1 or within 3 week(s) of notification.
Transfers: No deadline. Applicants notified on a rolling basis starting 3/15; must reply by 5/1 or within 3 week(s) of notification. Transfer scholarships available.

CONTACT
Susan Teerink, Director of Student Financial Aid
PO Box 1881, Milwaukee, WI 53201-1881
(414) 288-0200

Mid-State Technical College

Wisconsin Rapids, Wisconsin
www.mstc.edu Federal Code: 005380

2-year public technical college in large town.
Enrollment: 3,005 undergrads.
Selectivity: Open admission; but selective for some programs.

BASIC COSTS (2012-2013)
Tuition and fees: $3,745; out-of-state residents $5,435.
Per-credit charge: $117; out-of-state residents $175.
Additional info: Material fees vary by program; minimum $4 per course. $10 per credit fee for online courses.

FINANCIAL AID PICTURE
Students with need: Need-based aid available for full-time and part-time students. Work study available nights, weekends, and for part-time students.
Students without need: No-need awards available for academics, leadership.

FINANCIAL AID PROCEDURES
Forms required: FAFSA.
Dates and Deadlines: Priority date 4/15; no closing date. Applicants notified on a rolling basis starting 5/30; must reply within 2 week(s) of notification.
Transfers: No deadline.

CONTACT
Mary Jo Green, Financial Aid Supervisor
500 32nd Street North, Wisconsin Rapids, WI 54494
(715) 422-5501

Milwaukee Area Technical College

Milwaukee, Wisconsin
www.matc.edu Federal Code: 003866

2-year public junior and technical college in very large city.
Enrollment: 19,055 undergrads.
Selectivity: Open admission; but selective for some programs.

BASIC COSTS (2012-2013)
Tuition and fees: $3,998; out-of-state residents $5,748.
Per-credit charge: $117; out-of-state residents $175.
Additional info: Material fees vary by program; minimum $4 per course. $10 per credit fee for online courses. Tuition/fee waivers available for minority students.

FINANCIAL AID PICTURE
Students with need: Need-based aid available for full-time and part-time students.
Students without need: No-need awards available for academics.

FINANCIAL AID PROCEDURES
Forms required: FAFSA.
Dates and Deadlines: Priority date 3/15; no closing date. Applicants notified on a rolling basis starting 4/15.
Transfers: No deadline. Applicants notified on a rolling basis starting 4/15.

CONTACT
Jerry Manz, Director of Financial Aid
700 West State Street, Milwaukee, WI 53233-1443
(414) 297-8875

Milwaukee Institute of Art & Design

Milwaukee, Wisconsin
www.miad.edu Federal Code: 014203

4-year private visual arts college in very large city.
Enrollment: 668 undergrads, 2% part-time. 175 full-time freshmen.
Selectivity: Admits 50 to 75% of applicants.

BASIC COSTS (2012-2013)
Tuition and fees: $29,942.
Per-credit charge: $940.
Room and board: $8,650.

FINANCIAL AID PICTURE (2011-2012)
Students with need: Out of 175 full-time freshmen who applied for aid, 145 were judged to have need. Of these, 145 received aid, and 13 had their full need met. Average financial aid package met 63% of need; average scholarship/grant was $16,876; average loan was $4,025. For part-time students, average financial aid package was $8,376.
Students without need: 69 full-time freshmen who did not demonstrate need for aid received scholarships/grants; average award was $869. No-need awards available for academics, art.
Cumulative student debt: 98% of graduating class had student loans; average debt was $44,023.

FINANCIAL AID PROCEDURES
Forms required: FAFSA.
Dates and Deadlines: Priority date 2/15; no closing date. Applicants notified on a rolling basis starting 3/1; must reply by 5/1 or within 4 week(s) of notification.
Transfers: No deadline. Applicants notified on a rolling basis starting 4/1; must reply by 5/1 or within 2 week(s) of notification.

CONTACT
Carol Masse, Executive Director of Financial Aid
273 East Erie Street, Milwaukee, WI 53202
(414) 847-3270

Milwaukee School of Engineering

Milwaukee, Wisconsin
www.msoe.edu Federal Code: 003868

4-year private university in very large city.
Enrollment: 2,378 undergrads, 8% part-time. 438 full-time freshmen.
Selectivity: Admits 50 to 75% of applicants.

BASIC COSTS (2013-2014)
Tuition and fees: $33,330.
Per-credit charge: $570.
Room and board: $8,271.
Additional info: Tuition/fee waivers available for minority students.

FINANCIAL AID PICTURE (2011-2012)
Students with need: Out of 403 full-time freshmen who applied for aid, 369 were judged to have need. Of these, 369 received aid, and 38 had their full need met. Average financial aid package met 74% of need; average scholarship/grant was $21,207; average loan was $2,794. For part-time students, average financial aid package was $7,062.
Students without need: 63 full-time freshmen who did not demonstrate need for aid received scholarships/grants; average award was $12,170. No-need awards available for academics, ROTC.
Scholarships offered: Presidential Scholarship; full tuition; awarded to students with high academic standing; 8 awarded.
Cumulative student debt: 84% of graduating class had student loans; average debt was $38,038.

FINANCIAL AID PROCEDURES
Forms required: FAFSA.
Dates and Deadlines: Priority date 3/15; no closing date. Applicants notified on a rolling basis starting 3/1; must reply within 2 week(s) of notification.
Transfers: Applicants notified on a rolling basis.

CONTACT
Steven Midthun, Director, Financial Aid
1025 North Broadway, Milwaukee, WI 53202-3109
(414) 277-7223

Moraine Park Technical College

Fond du Lac, Wisconsin
www.morainepark.edu Federal Code: 005303

2-year public technical college in large town.
Enrollment: 3,337 undergrads, 69% part-time. 147 full-time freshmen.
Selectivity: Open admission; but selective for some programs.

BASIC COSTS (2012-2013)

Tuition and fees: $3,760; out-of-state residents $5,450.
Per-credit charge: $117; out-of-state residents $175.
Additional info: Material fees vary by program; minimum $4 per course. $10 per credit fee for online courses.

FINANCIAL AID PICTURE (2011-2012)

Students with need: 46% of average financial aid package awarded as scholarships/grants, 54% awarded as loans/jobs. Need-based aid available for part-time students. Work study available nights.
Students without need: No-need awards available for academics, job skills, leadership, minority status, state/district residency.

FINANCIAL AID PROCEDURES

Forms required: FAFSA, institutional form.
Dates and Deadlines: Priority date 5/1; no closing date. Applicants notified on a rolling basis starting 5/15; must reply within 2 week(s) of notification.
Transfers: Priority date 4/15; no deadline. Applicants notified on a rolling basis starting 5/15.

CONTACT

Julie Waldvogel, Financial Aid Associate
235 North National Avenue, Fond du Lac, WI 54935-1940

Mount Mary College

Milwaukee, Wisconsin
www.mtmary.edu Federal Code: 003869

4-year private liberal arts college for women in very large city, affiliated with Roman Catholic Church.
Enrollment: 916 undergrads, 21% part-time. 114 full-time freshmen.
Selectivity: Admits less than 50% of applicants.

BASIC COSTS (2013-2014)

Tuition and fees: $25,098.
Per-credit charge: $746.
Room and board: $7,738.

FINANCIAL AID PICTURE (2011-2012)

Students with need: Out of 114 full-time freshmen who applied for aid, 112 were judged to have need. Of these, 112 received aid, and 8 had their full need met. Average financial aid package met 76% of need; average scholarship/grant was $17,920; average loan was $3,345. For part-time students, average financial aid package was $6,400.
Students without need: 4 full-time freshmen who did not demonstrate need for aid received scholarships/grants; average award was $11,804. No-need awards available for academics, alumni affiliation, art, leadership, music/drama.
Cumulative student debt: 85% of graduating class had student loans; average debt was $25,313.

FINANCIAL AID PROCEDURES

Forms required: FAFSA.
Dates and Deadlines: Priority date 3/1; no closing date. Applicants notified on a rolling basis starting 3/1; must reply within 2 week(s) of notification.
Transfers: No deadline. Applicants notified on a rolling basis starting 3/1; must reply within 2 week(s) of notification.

CONTACT

Debra Duff, Director of Financial Aid
2900 North Menomonee River Parkway, Milwaukee, WI 53222-4597
(414) 256-1258

Nicolet Area Technical College

Rhinelander, Wisconsin
www.nicoletcollege.edu Federal Code: 008919

2-year public community and technical college in small town.
Selectivity: Open admission; but selective for some programs.

BASIC COSTS (2012-2013)

Tuition and fees: $3,745; out-of-state residents $5,435.
Per-credit charge: $117; out-of-state residents $175.
Additional info: Material fees vary by program; minimum $4 per course. $10 per credit fee for online courses.

FINANCIAL AID PICTURE

Students with need: Work study available nights, weekends, and for part-time students.

FINANCIAL AID PROCEDURES

Forms required: FAFSA, institutional form.
Dates and Deadlines: Priority date 4/1; no closing date. Applicants notified on a rolling basis starting 6/1; must reply within 2 week(s) of notification.

CONTACT

Jill Price, Director of Financial Aid
Box 518, Rhinelander, WI 54501
(715) 365-4423

Northcentral Technical College

Wausau, Wisconsin
www.ntc.edu Federal Code: 005387

2-year public community and technical college in small city.
Enrollment: 2,910 undergrads.
Selectivity: Open admission; but selective for some programs.

BASIC COSTS (2012-2013)

Tuition and fees: $3,851; out-of-state residents $5,541.
Per-credit charge: $117; out-of-state residents $175.
Additional info: Material fees vary by program; minimum $4 per course. $10 per credit fee for online courses.

FINANCIAL AID PICTURE

Students with need: Need-based aid available for full-time and part-time students: Work study available nights.

FINANCIAL AID PROCEDURES

Forms required: FAFSA.
Dates and Deadlines: Applicants notified on a rolling basis.
Transfers: No deadline.

CONTACT

May Lee, Director of Financial Aid
1000 West Campus Drive, Wausau, WI 54401
(715) 675-3331 ext. 5862

Northeast Wisconsin Technical College

Green Bay, Wisconsin
www.nwtc.edu Federal Code: 005301

2-year public community and technical college in small city.
Enrollment: 9,728 undergrads.

Selectivity: Open admission; but selective for some programs.

BASIC COSTS (2012-2013)
Tuition and fees: $3,827; out-of-state residents $5,518.
Per-credit charge: $117; out-of-state residents $175.
Additional info: Material fees vary by program; minimum $4 per course. $10 per credit fee for online courses.

FINANCIAL AID PICTURE
Students with need: Need-based aid available for full-time and part-time students. Work study available nights, weekends, and for part-time students.

FINANCIAL AID PROCEDURES
Forms required: FAFSA.
Dates and Deadlines: Priority date 4/15; no closing date. Applicants notified on a rolling basis starting 6/1; must reply within 2 week(s) of notification.
Transfers: No deadline. Applicants notified on a rolling basis starting 6/1; must reply within 2 week(s) of notification.

CONTACT
Emily Ysebaert, Financial Aid Director
2740 West Mason Street, Green Bay, WI 54307-9042
(920) 498-5444

Northland College
Ashland, Wisconsin
www.northland.edu Federal Code: 003875

4-year private liberal arts college in small town, affiliated with United Church of Christ.
Enrollment: 575 undergrads, 2% part-time. 182 full-time freshmen.
Selectivity: Admits 50 to 75% of applicants.

BASIC COSTS (2013-2014)
Tuition and fees: $29,990.
Per-credit charge: $600.
Room and board: $7,510.
Additional info: Tuition/fee waivers available for unemployed or children of unemployed.

FINANCIAL AID PICTURE (2012-2013)
Students with need: Out of 179 full-time freshmen who applied for aid, 164 were judged to have need. Of these, 164 received aid, and 28 had their full need met. Average financial aid package met 84% of need; average scholarship/grant was $22,229; average loan was $3,733. For part-time students, average financial aid package was $12,489.
Students without need: 17 full-time freshmen who did not demonstrate need for aid received scholarships/grants; average award was $17,527. No-need awards available for academics, alumni affiliation, art, job skills, leadership, minority status, music/drama, religious affiliation, state/district residency.
Cumulative student debt: 82% of graduating class had student loans; average debt was $24,374.

FINANCIAL AID PROCEDURES
Forms required: FAFSA.
Dates and Deadlines: Priority date 3/15; no closing date. Applicants notified on a rolling basis starting 3/1; must reply by 5/1 or within 4 week(s) of notification.
Transfers: No deadline.

CONTACT
Heather Shelly, Director of Financial Aid
1411 Ellis Avenue, Ashland, WI 54806-3999
(715) 682-1255

Northland International University
Dunbar, Wisconsin
www.ni.edu Federal Code: 038725

4-year private university and Bible college in rural community, affiliated with Baptist faith.
Enrollment: 487 undergrads.
Selectivity: Open admission.

BASIC COSTS (2012-2013)
Tuition and fees: $13,080.
Per-credit charge: $500.
Room and board: $5,990.

FINANCIAL AID PICTURE
Students with need: Need-based aid available for full-time and part-time students. Work study available nights, weekends, and for part-time students.
Students without need: No-need awards available for academics, job skills, state/district residency.

FINANCIAL AID PROCEDURES
Forms required: FAFSA, institutional form.
Dates and Deadlines: Priority date 6/1; closing date 12/1. Applicants notified on a rolling basis starting 1/1; must reply by 8/1.

CONTACT
Mandy McLain, Financial Aid Director
W10085 Pike Plains Road, Dunbar, WI 54119
(715) 324-6999 ext. 3150

Rasmussen College: Appleton
Appleton, Wisconsin
www.rasmussen.edu

4-year for-profit branch campus and career college in small city.
Enrollment: 313 undergrads.
Selectivity: Open admission; but selective for some programs.

BASIC COSTS (2012-2013)
Tuition and fees: $15,750.
Per-credit charge: $350.
Additional info: Full-time tuition varies according to program of study. Examples of per-credit-hour charges include Early Childhood Education ($310), Medical Lab Technician ($350), Professional Nursing, ($395), Information Systems Mgmt, Multimedia Technician ($350).

FINANCIAL AID PICTURE
Students with need: Need-based aid available for full-time and part-time students.

FINANCIAL AID PROCEDURES
Forms required: FAFSA, institutional form.
Dates and Deadlines: Applicants notified on a rolling basis.

CONTACT
Debora Murray, Director of Financial Aid
3500 East Destination Drive, Appleton, WI 54915

Rasmussen College: Green Bay
Green Bay, Wisconsin
www.rasmussen.edu

2-year for-profit technical college in small city.
Enrollment: 568 undergrads.
Selectivity: Open admission; but selective for some programs.

BASIC COSTS (2012-2013)
Tuition and fees: $15,750.
Per-credit charge: $350.
Additional info: Full-time tuition varies according to program of study. Examples of per-credit-hour charges include Early Childhood Education ($310), Medical Lab Technician ($350), Professional Nursing, ($395), Information Systems Mgmt, Multimedia Technician ($350).

FINANCIAL AID PICTURE
Students with need: Need-based aid available for full-time and part-time students.

FINANCIAL AID PROCEDURES
Forms required: FAFSA, institutional form.
Dates and Deadlines: Applicants notified on a rolling basis.

CONTACT
Debora Murray, Financial Aid Director
904 South Taylor Street, Suite 100, Green Bay, WI 54303-2349

Rasmussen College: Wausau

Wausau, Wisconsin
www.rasmussen.edu

2-year for-profit career college in large town.
Enrollment: 555 undergrads.
Selectivity: Open admission; but selective for some programs.

BASIC COSTS (2012-2013)
Tuition and fees: $15,750.
Per-credit charge: $350.
Additional info: Full-time tuition varies according to program of study. Examples of per-credit-hour charges include Early Childhood Education ($310), Medical Lab Technician ($350), Professional Nursing, ($395), Information Systems Mgmt, Multimedia Technician ($350).

FINANCIAL AID PICTURE
Students with need: Need-based aid available for full-time and part-time students.

FINANCIAL AID PROCEDURES
Forms required: FAFSA, institutional form.
Dates and Deadlines: Applicants notified on a rolling basis.

CONTACT
Debora Murray, Director of Financial Aid
1101 Westwood Drive, Wausau, WI 54401

Ripon College

Ripon, Wisconsin
www.ripon.edu Federal Code: 003884

4-year private liberal arts college in small town.
Enrollment: 904 undergrads. 249 full-time freshmen.
Selectivity: Admits over 75% of applicants.

BASIC COSTS (2012-2013)
Tuition and fees: $30,110.
Per-credit charge: $960.
Room and board: $8,545.

FINANCIAL AID PICTURE (2011-2012)
Students with need: Out of 235 full-time freshmen who applied for aid, 206 were judged to have need. Of these, 206 received aid, and 33 had their full need met. Average financial aid package met 86% of need; average scholarship/grant was $22,123; average loan was $4,161. Need-based aid available for part-time students.
Students without need: 38 full-time freshmen who did not demonstrate need for aid received scholarships/grants; average award was $14,704. No-need awards available for academics, alumni affiliation, art, leadership, minority status, music/drama, religious affiliation, ROTC, state/district residency.
Scholarships offered: Pickard Scholarship Competition; $16,000-$31,000 per year; based on 3.8 GPA, 28 ACT/1260 SAT; invitation only. Knop Scholars Program; full-tuition; for natural science or math major based on 3.8 GPA, top 5% of class, interview; invitation only; one awarded. All SAT scores exclusive of Writing. Rolling Academic Scholarships; $10,000 to $14,000 per year. Consideration given to those students who have academic and/or leadership achievements in their schools and communities. Army ROTC Scholarships; starting at $80,000. Diversity Scholarships; $20,000. Forensics Scholarships; $20,000; interview required. Art Scholarships; $20,000 maximum award; portfolio required. Theater Scholarships; up to $20,000; interview required. Music Scholarships; $20,000; audition required. Evans Achievement Awards; $24,000; not available to academic scholarship recipients. Boy/Girl State Scholarships; up to $16,000. Legacy Awards; $8,000. United Church of Christ Scholarships; $8,000; application required. National Latin Exam; $8,000. Alumni Award; $8,000; recommendation letter from alumnus required.
Cumulative student debt: 82% of graduating class had student loans; average debt was $32,511.

FINANCIAL AID PROCEDURES
Forms required: FAFSA.
Dates and Deadlines: Priority date 3/1; closing date 6/15. Applicants notified on a rolling basis starting 3/1; must reply within 2 week(s) of notification.
Transfers: No deadline. Applicants notified on a rolling basis starting 3/1; must reply within 2 week(s) of notification.

CONTACT
Office of Financial Aid
300 Seward Street, Ripon, WI 54971-0248
(920) 748-8301

St. Norbert College

De Pere, Wisconsin
www.snc.edu Federal Code: 003892

4-year private liberal arts college in large town, affiliated with Roman Catholic Church.
Enrollment: 2,189 undergrads, 2% part-time. 594 full-time freshmen.
Selectivity: Admits over 75% of applicants.

BASIC COSTS (2012-2013)
Tuition and fees: $30,675.
Per-credit charge: $943.
Room and board: $7,813.

FINANCIAL AID PICTURE (2011-2012)
Students with need: Out of 523 full-time freshmen who applied for aid, 441 were judged to have need. Of these, 441 received aid, and 112 had their full need met. Average financial aid package met 100% of need; average scholarship/grant was $21,146; average loan was $3,759. For part-time students, average financial aid package was $25,919.
Students without need: 145 full-time freshmen who did not demonstrate need for aid received scholarships/grants; average award was $10,291. No-need awards available for academics, art, leadership, minority status, music/drama, ROTC, state/district residency.
Cumulative student debt: 67% of graduating class had student loans; average debt was $31,331.

FINANCIAL AID PROCEDURES
Forms required: FAFSA.
Dates and Deadlines: Priority date 3/1; no closing date. Applicants notified on a rolling basis starting 3/15; must reply within 2 week(s) of notification.

CONTACT
Jeff Zahn, Director of Financial Aid
100 Grant Street, De Pere, WI 54115-2099
(800) 786-6721

Silver Lake College of the Holy Family

Manitowoc, Wisconsin
www.sl.edu Federal Code: 003850

4-year private liberal arts college in large town, affiliated with Roman Catholic Church.
Enrollment: 321 undergrads.

BASIC COSTS (2012-2013)
Tuition and fees: $22,470.
Per-credit charge: $740.
Room and board: $8,800.

FINANCIAL AID PICTURE
Students with need: Need-based aid available for full-time and part-time students. Work study available nights, weekends, and for part-time students.
Students without need: No-need awards available for academics, art, athletics, leadership, music/drama, state/district residency.

FINANCIAL AID PROCEDURES
Forms required: FAFSA.
Dates and Deadlines: Priority date 3/15; no closing date. Applicants notified on a rolling basis starting 3/15.
Transfers: No deadline. Applicants notified on a rolling basis starting 3/15. Transfer Merit Scholarships and Phi Theta Kappa Scholarships available, as well as other institutional scholarship and grant assistance.

CONTACT
Jodi Popp, Director of Student Financial Aid
2406 South Alverno Road, Manitowoc, WI 54220-9319
(920) 686-6122

Southwest Wisconsin Technical College

Fennimore, Wisconsin
www.swtc.edu Federal Code: 007699

2-year public technical college in rural community.
Enrollment: 3,434 undergrads.
Selectivity: Open admission; but selective for some programs.

BASIC COSTS (2012-2013)
Tuition and fees: $3,783; out-of-state residents $5,473.
Per-credit charge: $117; out-of-state residents $175.
Additional info: Material fees vary by program; minimum $4 per course. $10 per credit fee for online courses.

FINANCIAL AID PICTURE
Students with need: Work study available nights.

FINANCIAL AID PROCEDURES
Forms required: FAFSA, institutional form.
Dates and Deadlines: Priority date 4/15; no closing date. Applicants notified on a rolling basis starting 5/15; must reply within 4 week(s) of notification.

CONTACT
Joy Kite, Director of Financial Aid
1800 Bronson Boulevard, Fennimore, WI 53809
(608) 822-2319

University of Wisconsin-Baraboo/Sauk County

Baraboo, Wisconsin
www.baraboo.uwc.edu Federal Code: 003897

2-year public branch campus and liberal arts college in large town.
Enrollment: 597 undergrads.

BASIC COSTS (2012-2013)
Tuition and fees: $5,153; out-of-state residents $12,137.
Per-credit charge: $198; out-of-state residents $489.

FINANCIAL AID PICTURE
Students with need: Need-based aid available for full-time and part-time students. Work study available nights.
Students without need: This college awards aid only to students with need.
Scholarships offered: Campus scholarships; $250 to full tuition.

FINANCIAL AID PROCEDURES
Forms required: FAFSA, institutional form.
Dates and Deadlines: Priority date 4/15; no closing date. Applicants notified on a rolling basis starting 4/15; must reply within 3 week(s) of notification.
Transfers: Must reply within 3 week(s) of notification.

CONTACT
Marilyn Krump, Director of Student Financial Aid
1006 Connie Road, Baraboo, WI 53913-1098
(608) 263-7727

University of Wisconsin-Barron County

Rice Lake, Wisconsin
www.barron.uwc.edu Federal Code: 003897

2-year public branch campus and junior college in small town.
Enrollment: 631 undergrads.

BASIC COSTS (2012-2013)
Tuition and fees: $5,304; out-of-state residents $12,288.
Per-credit charge: $198; out-of-state residents $489.

FINANCIAL AID PICTURE
Students with need: Need-based aid available for full-time and part-time students.

FINANCIAL AID PROCEDURES
Forms required: FAFSA.
Dates and Deadlines: Priority date 4/15; no closing date. Applicants notified on a rolling basis starting 6/1.

CONTACT
William Trippett, Director of Student Financial Aid
1800 College Drive, Rice Lake, WI 54868

University of Wisconsin-Eau Claire

Eau Claire, Wisconsin
www.uwec.edu Federal Code: 003917

4-year public university in small city.
Enrollment: 10,269 undergrads, 7% part-time. 1,932 full-time freshmen.
Selectivity: Admits over 75% of applicants.

BASIC COSTS (2012-2013)
Tuition and fees: $8,685; out-of-state residents $16,258.
Per-credit charge: $307; out-of-state residents $622.
Room and board: $6,182.

FINANCIAL AID PICTURE (2011-2012)

Students with need: Out of 1,661 full-time freshmen who applied for aid, 1,077 were judged to have need. Of these, 1,057 received aid, and 291 had their full need met. Average financial aid package met 88% of need; average scholarship/grant was $5,646; average loan was $3,536. For part-time students, average financial aid package was $6,901.

Students without need: 109 full-time freshmen who did not demonstrate need for aid received scholarships/grants; average award was $1,327. No-need awards available for academics, art, leadership, minority status, music/drama, state/district residency.

Scholarships offered: Wisconsin Academic Excellence Scholars: $2,250; selected valedictorians. Mark of Excellence Award: $2,000; 25 awards. Chancellor's Award: $1,000; 35 awards. Diversity Scholar: up to $6,000 a year for 4 years; 5 awards. Blugold Fellowship: $1,000 scholarship and $1,200 research stipend; renewable; 20 awards. Freshman honor scholarship: ACT 28; top 5% of class; $1,000; 40-50 awards.

Cumulative student debt: 70% of graduating class had student loans; average debt was $23,825.

FINANCIAL AID PROCEDURES

Forms required: FAFSA.

Dates and Deadlines: Priority date 4/15; no closing date. Applicants notified on a rolling basis starting 4/15.

CONTACT

Kathleen Sahlhoff, Director of Financial Aid
111 Schofield Hall, Eau Claire, WI 54701
(715) 836-3373

University of Wisconsin-Fond du Lac

Fond du Lac, Wisconsin
www.fdl.uwc.edu Federal Code: 003897

2-year public junior college in large town.

Enrollment: 691 undergrads.

BASIC COSTS (2012-2013)

Tuition and fees: $5,133; out-of-state residents $12,117.

Per-credit charge: $198; out-of-state residents $489.

FINANCIAL AID PICTURE

Students with need: Need-based aid available for full-time and part-time students.

Students without need: No-need awards available for academics, leadership, music/drama.

FINANCIAL AID PROCEDURES

Forms required: FAFSA.

Dates and Deadlines: Priority date 4/15; no closing date. Applicants notified on a rolling basis starting 6/1; must reply within 2 week(s) of notification.

CONTACT

William Trippett, Director of Student Financial Aid
400 University Drive, Fond du Lac, WI 54935-2950
(608) 262-5928

University of Wisconsin-Fox Valley

Menasha, Wisconsin
www.uwfox.uwc.edu Federal Code: 011459

2-year public liberal arts college in small city.

Enrollment: 1,795 undergrads.

Selectivity: Admits over 75% of applicants.

BASIC COSTS (2012-2013)

Tuition and fees: $5,017; out-of-state residents $12,001.

Per-credit charge: $198; out-of-state residents $489.

FINANCIAL AID PICTURE

Students with need: Need-based aid available for full-time and part-time students. Work study available nights, weekends, and for part-time students.

Students without need: No-need awards available for academics, leadership.

FINANCIAL AID PROCEDURES

Forms required: FAFSA.

Dates and Deadlines: Priority date 4/15; no closing date. Applicants notified on a rolling basis starting 6/1; must reply within 3 week(s) of notification.

CONTACT

William Trippett, Director of Student Financial Aid
1478 Midway Road, Menasha, WI 54952-2850

University of Wisconsin-Green Bay

Green Bay, Wisconsin
www.uwgb.edu Federal Code: 003899

4-year public university and liberal arts college in small city.

Enrollment: 6,073 undergrads, 24% part-time. 894 full-time freshmen.

Selectivity: Admits 50 to 75% of applicants.

BASIC COSTS (2012-2013)

Tuition and fees: $7,610; out-of-state residents $15,183.

Per-credit charge: $262; out-of-state residents $578.

Room and board: $7,210.

FINANCIAL AID PICTURE (2012-2013)

Students with need: Out of 837 full-time freshmen who applied for aid, 662 were judged to have need. Of these, 638 received aid, and 207 had their full need met. Average financial aid package met 60% of need; average scholarship/grant was $6,696; average loan was $6,406. For part-time students, average financial aid package was $6,590.

Students without need: 73 full-time freshmen who did not demonstrate need for aid received scholarships/grants; average award was $2,865. No-need awards available for academics, art, athletics, leadership, minority status, music/drama.

Scholarships offered: 10 full-time freshmen received athletic scholarships; average amount $7,195.

Cumulative student debt: 70% of graduating class had student loans; average debt was $23,650.

Additional info: Auditions required for music and theater scholarships. Tuition waived for veterans and for children of Wisconsin soldiers or policemen who were slain in the line of duty.

FINANCIAL AID PROCEDURES

Forms required: FAFSA.

Dates and Deadlines: Priority date 4/1; no closing date. Applicants notified on a rolling basis starting 1/1; must reply within 3 week(s) of notification.

Transfers: Must reply within 3 week(s) of notification.

CONTACT

James Rohan, Director of Financial Aid and Student Employment
2420 Nicolet Drive, Green Bay, WI 54311-7001
(920) 465-2075

University of Wisconsin-La Crosse

La Crosse, Wisconsin
www.uwlax.edu Federal Code: 003919

4-year public university in small city.

Enrollment: 9,191 undergrads, 3% part-time. 1,973 full-time freshmen.

Selectivity: Admits 50 to 75% of applicants.

BASIC COSTS (2012-2013)

Tuition and fees: $8,755; out-of-state residents $16,328.

Per-credit charge: $316; out-of-state residents $632.
Room and board: $6,000.

FINANCIAL AID PICTURE (2011-2012)
Students with need: Out of 1,650 full-time freshmen who applied for aid, 1,027 were judged to have need. Of these, 1,015 received aid, and 172 had their full need met. Average financial aid package met 67% of need; average scholarship/grant was $5,634; average loan was $3,477. For part-time students, average financial aid package was $5,431.
Students without need: 60 full-time freshmen who did not demonstrate need for aid received scholarships/grants; average award was $1,729. No-need awards available for academics, alumni affiliation, art, leadership, minority status, music/drama, ROTC.
Cumulative student debt: 71% of graduating class had student loans; average debt was $24,863.

FINANCIAL AID PROCEDURES
Forms required: FAFSA.
Dates and Deadlines: Priority date 3/15; no closing date. Applicants notified on a rolling basis starting 4/1.

CONTACT
Louise Janke, Director of Financial Aid
1725 State Street, Cleary Center, La Crosse, WI 54601
(608) 785-8604

University of Wisconsin-Madison
Madison, Wisconsin
www.wisc.edu Federal Code: 003895

4-year public university in small city.
Enrollment: 29,118 undergrads, 4% part-time. 6,275 full-time freshmen.
Selectivity: Admits 50 to 75% of applicants.

BASIC COSTS (2012-2013)
Tuition and fees: $10,384; out-of-state residents $26,634.
Per-credit charge: $386; out-of-state residents $1,063.
Room and board: $8,080.

FINANCIAL AID PICTURE (2012-2013)
Students with need: Out of 4,175 full-time freshmen who applied for aid, 2,559 were judged to have need. Of these, 2,416 received aid, and 696 had their full need met. Average financial aid package met 70% of need; average scholarship/grant was $7,132; average loan was $4,689. For part-time students, average financial aid package was $9,946.
Students without need: 408 full-time freshmen who did not demonstrate need for aid received scholarships/grants; average award was $3,840. No-need awards available for academics, alumni affiliation, art, athletics, job skills, leadership, minority status, music/drama, ROTC, state/district residency.
Scholarships offered: 91 full-time freshmen received athletic scholarships; average amount $21,934.
Cumulative student debt: 49% of graduating class had student loans; average debt was $24,700.

FINANCIAL AID PROCEDURES
Forms required: FAFSA.
Dates and Deadlines: Applicants notified on a rolling basis starting 4/1; must reply within 3 week(s) of notification.

CONTACT
Susan Fischer, Director of Student Financial Aid
702 West Johnson Street, Suite 1101, Madison, WI 53715-1007
(608) 262-3060

University of Wisconsin-Manitowoc
Manitowoc, Wisconsin
www.manitowoc.uwc.edu Federal Code: 003897

2-year public branch campus and liberal arts college in large town.
Enrollment: 614 undergrads.

BASIC COSTS (2012-2013)
Tuition and fees: $5,305; out-of-state residents $12,289.
Per-credit charge: $198; out-of-state residents $489.

FINANCIAL AID PICTURE
Students with need: Need-based aid available for full-time and part-time students. Work study available nights.
Students without need: This college awards aid only to students with need.

FINANCIAL AID PROCEDURES
Forms required: FAFSA.
Dates and Deadlines: Priority date 3/1; no closing date. Applicants notified on a rolling basis starting 5/1; must reply within 2 week(s) of notification.
Transfers: Priority date 5/1; no deadline.

CONTACT
Marilyn Krump, Director of Student Financial Aid
705 Viebahn Street, Manitowoc, WI 54220-6699
(920) 683-4707

University of Wisconsin-Marathon County
Wausau, Wisconsin
www.uwmc.uwc.edu Federal Code: 003903

2-year public liberal arts college in small city.
Enrollment: 1,279 undergrads.

BASIC COSTS (2012-2013)
Tuition and fees: $5,096; out-of-state residents $12,080.
Per-credit charge: $198; out-of-state residents $489.
Room and board: $4,493.

FINANCIAL AID PICTURE
Students with need: Need-based aid available for full-time and part-time students. Work study available nights.
Students without need: This college awards aid only to students with need.

FINANCIAL AID PROCEDURES
Forms required: FAFSA, institutional form.
Dates and Deadlines: Priority date 4/15; no closing date. Applicants notified on a rolling basis starting 6/1; must reply within 3 week(s) of notification.

CONTACT
Bill Trippett, Director of Student Financial Aid
518 South Seventh Avenue, Wausau, WI 54401-5396
(715) 261-6235

University of Wisconsin-Marinette
Marinette, Wisconsin
www.marinette.uwc.edu Federal Code: 003897

2-year public branch campus and liberal arts college in large town.
Enrollment: 340 full-time undergrads.

BASIC COSTS (2012-2013)
Tuition and fees: $5,096; out-of-state residents $12,080.
Per-credit charge: $198; out-of-state residents $489.

FINANCIAL AID PICTURE

Students with need: Need-based aid available for full-time and part-time students. Work study available nights.

Students without need: This college awards aid only to students with need.

FINANCIAL AID PROCEDURES

Forms required: FAFSA.

Dates and Deadlines: Priority date 4/15; no closing date. Applicants notified on a rolling basis.

CONTACT

Bill Trippett, Director of Student Financial Aid
750 West Bay Shore Street, Marinette, WI 54143
(715) 735-4301

University of Wisconsin-Marshfield/ Wood County

Marshfield, Wisconsin
www.marshfield.uwc.edu Federal Code: 003897

2-year public branch campus college in large town.
Enrollment: 628 undergrads.

BASIC COSTS (2012-2013)

Tuition and fees: $5,356; out-of-state residents $12,340.
Per-credit charge: $198; out-of-state residents $489.

FINANCIAL AID PICTURE

Students with need: Need-based aid available for full-time and part-time students. Work study available nights, weekends, and for part-time students.

Students without need: This college awards aid only to students with need.

Scholarships offered: Special Entering Scholarships; $1,000; based on academic excellence; 2 awarded. Ken and Ardyce Helting Scholarship; $1,000; priority given to physically challenged or learning disabled; 1 awarded. Valedictorian, Salutatorian and National Merit Finalist and Semi-Finalists; $1,000, ACT of 25 or better. Greenhouse Scholarship; priority to students in Environmental Studies; 1 awarded. Patrice Ptacek Memorial Scholarship; 2 letters of recommendation; 1 awarded. Woman of the Future Scholarship; $1,000; must be full-time female freshman entering sophomore year, well-defined career goals other than nursing; 1 awarded.

FINANCIAL AID PROCEDURES

Forms required: FAFSA.

Dates and Deadlines: Closing date 4/15. Applicants notified on a rolling basis starting 5/15; must reply within 3 week(s) of notification.

CONTACT

William Trippett, Director of Student Financial Aid
2000 West Fifth Street, Marshfield, WI 54449
(715) 389-6500

University of Wisconsin-Milwaukee

Milwaukee, Wisconsin
www.uwm.edu Federal Code: 003896

4-year public university in very large city.
Enrollment: 22,685 undergrads, 14% part-time. 3,238 full-time freshmen.
Selectivity: Admits 50 to 75% of applicants.

BASIC COSTS (2012-2013)

Tuition and fees: $9,187; out-of-state residents $18,915.
Per-credit charge: $337; out-of-state residents $742.
Room and board: $7,935.

FINANCIAL AID PICTURE (2012-2013)

Students with need: Out of 2,818 full-time freshmen who applied for aid, 2,373 were judged to have need. Of these, 2,258 received aid, and 398 had their full need met. Average financial aid package met 39% of need; average scholarship/grant was $6,054; average loan was $3,688. For part-time students, average financial aid package was $7,261.

Students without need: 20 full-time freshmen who did not demonstrate need for aid received scholarships/grants; average award was $2,644. No-need awards available for academics, art, athletics, leadership, music/drama.

Scholarships offered: 18 full-time freshmen received athletic scholarships; average amount $7,705.

Cumulative student debt: 72% of graduating class had student loans; average debt was $32,371.

FINANCIAL AID PROCEDURES

Forms required: FAFSA.

Dates and Deadlines: Applicants notified on a rolling basis starting 3/10.

Transfers: No deadline. Applicants notified on a rolling basis.

CONTACT

Jane Hojan-Clark, Executive Director of Financial Aid
Box 749, Milwaukee, WI 53201
(414) 229-6300

University of Wisconsin-Oshkosh

Oshkosh, Wisconsin
www.uwosh.edu Federal Code: 003920

4-year public university in small city.
Enrollment: 10,771 undergrads, 13% part-time. 1,811 full-time freshmen.
Selectivity: Admits 50 to 75% of applicants.

BASIC COSTS (2012-2013)

Tuition and fees: $7,351; out-of-state residents $14,924.
Per-credit charge: $268; out-of-state residents $583.
Room and board: $6,452.

FINANCIAL AID PICTURE (2012-2013)

Students with need: Out of 1,567 full-time freshmen who applied for aid, 1,165 were judged to have need. Of these, 1,138 received aid, and 748 had their full need met. Average financial aid package met 38% of need; average scholarship/grant was $6,231; average loan was $2,140. For part-time students, average financial aid package was $6,929.

Students without need: 342 full-time freshmen who did not demonstrate need for aid received scholarships/grants; average award was $595. No-need awards available for academics, art, job skills, leadership, minority status, music/drama, ROTC, state/district residency.

Cumulative student debt: 66% of graduating class had student loans; average debt was $25,343.

FINANCIAL AID PROCEDURES

Forms required: FAFSA.

Dates and Deadlines: Priority date 3/15; no closing date. Applicants notified on a rolling basis starting 4/15; must reply within 2 week(s) of notification.

Transfers: Must send financial aid transcript to university.

CONTACT

Beatrice Contreras, Director of Financial Aid
800 Algoma Boulevard, Oshkosh, WI 54901-8602
(920) 424-3377

University of Wisconsin-Parkside

Kenosha, Wisconsin
www.uwp.edu Federal Code: 005015

4-year public university in small city.
Enrollment: 4,317 undergrads, 25% part-time. 675 full-time freshmen.

Selectivity: Admits 50 to 75% of applicants.

BASIC COSTS (2012-2013)

Tuition and fees: $7,293; out-of-state residents $14,866.

Per-credit charge: $262; out-of-state residents $578.

Room and board: $6,226.

Additional info: Minnesota reciprocity tuition: $282.67 per-credit-hour. Midwest Student Exchange Program tuition: $393.65 per-credit-hour.

FINANCIAL AID PICTURE (2011-2012)

Students with need: Out of 527 full-time freshmen who applied for aid, 442 were judged to have need. Of these, 417 received aid. Need-based aid available for part-time students.

Students without need: No-need awards available for academics, art, athletics, minority status, music/drama, state/district residency.

FINANCIAL AID PROCEDURES

Forms required: FAFSA.

Dates and Deadlines: Priority date 3/15; no closing date. Applicants notified on a rolling basis starting 4/1; must reply within 2 week(s) of notification.

CONTACT

Randall McCready, Director of Financial Aid
PO Box 2000, Kenosha, WI 53141-2000
(262) 595-2574

University of Wisconsin-Platteville

Platteville, Wisconsin
www.uwplatt.edu Federal Code: 003921

4-year public university in large town.

Enrollment: 7,563 undergrads, 8% part-time. 1,637 full-time freshmen.

Selectivity: Admits over 75% of applicants.

BASIC COSTS (2012-2013)

Tuition and fees: $7,457; out-of-state residents $15,030.

Per-credit charge: $267; out-of-state residents $583.

Room and board: $6,464.

FINANCIAL AID PICTURE

Students with need: Need-based aid available for full-time and part-time students. Work study available nights, weekends, and for part-time students.

Students without need: This college awards aid only to students with need.

FINANCIAL AID PROCEDURES

Forms required: FAFSA.

Dates and Deadlines: Priority date 3/15; no closing date. Applicants notified on a rolling basis starting 6/1; must reply within 2 week(s) of notification.

CONTACT

Sheila Trotter, Director of Financial Aid
One University Plaza, Platteville, WI 53818
(608) 342-1836

University of Wisconsin-Richland

Richland Center, Wisconsin
www.richland.uwc.edu Federal Code: 003897

2-year public liberal arts college in small town.

Enrollment: 519 undergrads.

BASIC COSTS (2012-2013)

Tuition and fees: $5,271; out-of-state residents $12,255.

Per-credit charge: $198; out-of-state residents $489.

FINANCIAL AID PICTURE (2012-2013)

Students with need: 71% of average financial aid package awarded as scholarships/grants, 29% awarded as loans/jobs. Need-based aid available for part-time students. Work study available nights, weekends, and for part-time students.

Students without need: This college awards aid only to students with need.

FINANCIAL AID PROCEDURES

Forms required: FAFSA.

Dates and Deadlines: Priority date 4/1; no closing date. Applicants notified on a rolling basis starting 5/15; must reply within 3 week(s) of notification.

CONTACT

William Trippett, Director of Student Financial Aid
1200 Highway 14 West, Richland Center, WI 53581
(608) 647-6186 ext. 3

University of Wisconsin-River Falls

River Falls, Wisconsin
www.uwrf.edu Federal Code: 003923

4-year public university and liberal arts college in large town.

Enrollment: 5,874 undergrads, 8% part-time. 1,096 full-time freshmen.

Selectivity: Admits 50 to 75% of applicants.

BASIC COSTS (2012-2013)

Tuition and fees: $7,700; out-of-state residents $15,273.

Per-credit charge: $262; out-of-state residents $578.

Room and board: $5,825.

Additional info: Minnesota reciprocity tuition: $283 per-credit-hour.

FINANCIAL AID PICTURE (2012-2013)

Students with need: Average financial aid package met 53% of need; average scholarship/grant was $4,416; average loan was $3,646. For part-time students, average financial aid package was $6,242.

Students without need: This college awards aid only to students with need.

Cumulative student debt: 74% of graduating class had student loans; average debt was $22,557.

FINANCIAL AID PROCEDURES

Forms required: FAFSA.

Dates and Deadlines: Priority date 3/15; no closing date. Applicants notified on a rolling basis starting 4/15.

Transfers: No deadline. Applicants notified on a rolling basis starting 4/1.

CONTACT

Barbara Stinson, Director of Financial Aid
410 South 3rd Street, River Falls, WI 54022-5001
(715) 425-3141

University of Wisconsin-Rock County

Janesville, Wisconsin
www.rock.uwc.edu Federal Code: 003897

2-year public branch campus and liberal arts college in small city.

Enrollment: 1,303 undergrads.

BASIC COSTS (2012-2013)

Tuition and fees: $5,098; out-of-state residents $12,082.

Per-credit charge: $198; out-of-state residents $489.

FINANCIAL AID PICTURE

Students with need: Need-based aid available for full-time and part-time students. Work study available nights, weekends, and for part-time students.

Students without need: This college awards aid only to students with need.

FINANCIAL AID PROCEDURES

Forms required: FAFSA, institutional form.

Dates and Deadlines: Closing date 3/15. Applicants notified on a rolling basis starting 6/1; must reply within 3 week(s) of notification.

CONTACT

William Trippet, Director of Student Financial Aid
2909 Kellogg Avenue, Janesville, WI 53546-5699
(608) 758-6565 ext. 200

University of Wisconsin-Sheboygan

Sheboygan, Wisconsin
www.sheboygan.uwc.edu Federal Code: 003897

2-year public community and junior college in small city.
Enrollment: 900 undergrads.

BASIC COSTS (2012-2013)
Tuition and fees: $5,061; out-of-state residents $12,045.
Per-credit charge: $198; out-of-state residents $489.

FINANCIAL AID PICTURE
Students with need: Need-based aid available for full-time and part-time students.
Students without need: No-need awards available for academics, leadership, music/drama.

FINANCIAL AID PROCEDURES
Forms required: FAFSA, institutional form.
Dates and Deadlines: Priority date 4/15; no closing date. Applicants notified on a rolling basis starting 6/1; must reply within 2 week(s) of notification.
Transfers: No deadline. Applicants notified on a rolling basis.

CONTACT

Mary Balde, Student Financial Aid Officer
One University Drive, Sheboygan, WI 53081
(920) 459-6633

University of Wisconsin-Stevens Point

Stevens Point, Wisconsin
www.uwsp.edu Federal Code: 003924

4-year public university in large town.
Enrollment: 9,118 undergrads, 5% part-time. 1,614 full-time freshmen.
Selectivity: Admits 50 to 75% of applicants.

BASIC COSTS (2012-2013)
Tuition and fees: $7,505; out-of-state residents $15,078.
Per-credit charge: $262; out-of-state residents $578.
Room and board: $6,338.

FINANCIAL AID PICTURE (2011-2012)
Students with need: Out of 1,417 full-time freshmen who applied for aid, 980 were judged to have need. Of these, 942 received aid, and 542 had their full need met. Average financial aid package met 73% of need; average scholarship/grant was $5,406; average loan was $3,960. For part-time students, average financial aid package was $7,119.
Students without need: 73 full-time freshmen who did not demonstrate need for aid received scholarships/grants; average award was $2,237. No-need awards available for academics, alumni affiliation, art, music/drama, ROTC.
Cumulative student debt: 75% of graduating class had student loans; average debt was $24,054.
Additional info: Tuition discounts offered to qualified residents from other states. Tuition waiver for state veterans.

FINANCIAL AID PROCEDURES
Forms required: FAFSA.
Dates and Deadlines: Priority date 3/15; closing date 5/1. Applicants notified on a rolling basis starting 3/1; must reply within 4 week(s) of notification.
Transfers: No deadline.

CONTACT

Paul Watson, Director of Financial Aid
Student Services Center, Stevens Point, WI 54481
(715) 346-4771

University of Wisconsin-Stout

Menomonie, Wisconsin
www.uwstout.edu Federal Code: 003915

4-year public university in large town.
Enrollment: 8,067 undergrads, 16% part-time. 1,455 full-time freshmen.
Selectivity: Admits over 75% of applicants.

BASIC COSTS (2012-2013)
Tuition and fees: $8,944; out-of-state residents $16,690.
Per-credit charge: $234; out-of-state residents $492.
Room and board: $6,054.
Additional info: Laptop computer included in the cost of tuition.

FINANCIAL AID PICTURE (2012-2013)
Students with need: Out of 1,247 full-time freshmen who applied for aid, 884 were judged to have need. Of these, 880 received aid, and 352 had their full need met. Average financial aid package met 81% of need; average scholarship/grant was $2,289; average loan was $3,759. For part-time students, average financial aid package was $8,833.
Students without need: 27 full-time freshmen who did not demonstrate need for aid received scholarships/grants; average award was $3,233. No-need awards available for academics.
Scholarships offered: Wisconsin Academic Excellence Scholarship: $2,250; selected by high school. National Merit Finalist Scholarship: $2,000; automatically awarded to NMSQT finalist. National Merit Semifinalist Scholarship: $1,000; automatically awarded to NMSQT semifinalist. Chancellor's Academic Honor Scholarship: $1,000; automatically awarded to top 5% of high school class with ACT of 25 who enroll by July 15.
Cumulative student debt: 68% of graduating class had student loans; average debt was $29,879.

FINANCIAL AID PROCEDURES
Forms required: FAFSA.
Dates and Deadlines: Priority date 3/15; no closing date. Applicants notified on a rolling basis starting 4/1; must reply within 4 week(s) of notification.

CONTACT

Beth Boisen, Director of Financial Aid
1 Clocktower Plaza, Menomonie, WI 54751
(715) 232-1363

University of Wisconsin-Superior

Superior, Wisconsin
www.uwsuper.edu Federal Code: 003925

4-year public university and liberal arts college in small city.
Enrollment: 2,460 undergrads, 18% part-time. 361 full-time freshmen.
Selectivity: Admits over 75% of applicants.

BASIC COSTS (2012-2013)
Tuition and fees: $7,904; out-of-state residents $15,477.
Per-credit charge: $272; out-of-state residents $588.
Room and board: $5,992.

FINANCIAL AID PICTURE (2012-2013)
Students with need: Out of 310 full-time freshmen who applied for aid, 248 were judged to have need. Of these, 241 received aid, and 60 had their

full need met. For part-time students, average financial aid package was $10,536.
Students without need: 11 full-time freshmen who did not demonstrate need for aid received scholarships/grants; average award was $2,685. No-need awards available for academics, alumni affiliation, art, leadership, minority status, music/drama, ROTC, state/district residency.
Cumulative student debt: 76% of graduating class had student loans; average debt was $26,486.
Additional info: Tuition Assistance Program (TAP) available to non-resident students on limited basis.

FINANCIAL AID PROCEDURES
Forms required: FAFSA.
Dates and Deadlines: Priority date 4/1; no closing date. Applicants notified on a rolling basis starting 4/1; must reply by 5/1 or within 4 week(s) of notification.
Transfers: No deadline. Applicants notified on a rolling basis starting 3/15; must reply by 5/1 or within 4 week(s) of notification.

CONTACT
Donna Dahlvang, Director of Financial Aid
Belknap and Catlin, Superior, WI 54880
(715) 394-8200

University of Wisconsin-Washington County

West Bend, Wisconsin
www.washington.uwc.edu Federal Code: 003897

2-year public branch campus and liberal arts college in large town.
Enrollment: 994 undergrads.

BASIC COSTS (2012-2013)
Tuition and fees: $5,077; out-of-state residents $12,061.
Per-credit charge: $198; out-of-state residents $489.

FINANCIAL AID PICTURE
Students with need: Need-based aid available for full-time and part-time students. Work study available weekends and for part-time students.
Students without need: No-need awards available for academics.

FINANCIAL AID PROCEDURES
Forms required: FAFSA.
Dates and Deadlines: Priority date 4/15; no closing date. Applicants notified on a rolling basis starting 4/30; must reply within 3 week(s) of notification.
Transfers: No deadline.

CONTACT
Maria Graciano, Director of Student Financial Aid
400 University Drive, West Bend, WI 53095
(262) 335-5207

University of Wisconsin-Waukesha

Waukesha, Wisconsin
www.waukesha.uwc.edu Federal Code: 003897

2-year public branch campus and junior college in small city.
Enrollment: 2,115 undergrads.

BASIC COSTS (2012-2013)
Tuition and fees: $5,082; out-of-state residents $12,066.
Per-credit charge: $198; out-of-state residents $489.

FINANCIAL AID PICTURE
Students with need: Need-based aid available for full-time and part-time students. Work study available nights, weekends, and for part-time students.
Students without need: No-need awards available for academics, alumni affiliation, art, leadership, minority status, music/drama, state/district residency.
Scholarships offered: University of Wisconsin-Waukesha Scholarship Program; numerous scholarships; amounts vary.

FINANCIAL AID PROCEDURES
Forms required: FAFSA.
Dates and Deadlines: Priority date 4/15; no closing date. Applicants notified on a rolling basis starting 5/15; must reply within 3 week(s) of notification.

CONTACT
Bill Trippett, Director of Student Financial Aid
1500 North University Drive, Waukesha, WI 53188
(262) 521-5210

University of Wisconsin-Whitewater

Whitewater, Wisconsin
www.uww.edu Federal Code: 003926

4-year public university in large town.
Enrollment: 10,441 undergrads, 6% part-time. 2,155 full-time freshmen.
Selectivity: Admits 50 to 75% of applicants.

BASIC COSTS (2012-2013)
Tuition and fees: $7,528; out-of-state residents $15,101.
Per-credit charge: $272; out-of-state residents $587.
Room and board: $5,736.
Additional info: Minnesota reciprocity tuition: $282.67 per-credit-hour.

FINANCIAL AID PICTURE
Students with need: Need-based aid available for full-time and part-time students. Work study available nights, weekends, and for part-time students.
Students without need: No-need awards available for academics, alumni affiliation, art, leadership, minority status, music/drama, ROTC, state/district residency.

FINANCIAL AID PROCEDURES
Forms required: FAFSA.
Dates and Deadlines: Priority date 3/15; no closing date. Applicants notified on a rolling basis starting 4/1; must reply within 3 week(s) of notification.
Transfers: No deadline. Applicants notified on a rolling basis starting 4/1; must reply within 3 week(s) of notification.

CONTACT
Carol Miller, Director of Financial Aid
800 West Main Street, Whitewater, WI 53190-1790
(262) 472-1130

Viterbo University

La Crosse, Wisconsin
www.viterbo.edu Federal Code: 003911

4-year private university in small city, affiliated with Roman Catholic Church.
Enrollment: 2,074 undergrads, 24% part-time. 304 full-time freshmen.
Selectivity: Admits 50 to 75% of applicants.

BASIC COSTS (2012-2013)
Tuition and fees: $22,670.
Room and board: $7,433.
Additional info: Tuition/fee waivers available for minority students.

FINANCIAL AID PICTURE
Students with need: Need-based aid available for full-time and part-time students. Work study available nights, weekends, and for part-time students.
Students without need: No-need awards available for academics, alumni affiliation, art, athletics, leadership, minority status, music/drama, ROTC.

Scholarships offered: Fine arts scholarships: up to $10,000 per year; for incoming full-time freshmen and transfer students talented in areas of art, music or theater. Dr. Scholl Scholarship: full, 4-year tuition; must enroll full-time and maintain 3.5 GPA, 1 awarded. Viterbo University Scholarship: $1,000-$8,000 per year; based on academic history; incoming freshmen and transfers automatically considered; renewable.

FINANCIAL AID PROCEDURES

Forms required: FAFSA, institutional form.

Dates and Deadlines: Priority date 3/15; no closing date. Applicants notified on a rolling basis starting 4/1; must reply within 3 week(s) of notification.

CONTACT

Terry Norman, Director of Financial Aid
900 Viterbo Drive, La Crosse, WI 54601-8804
(608) 796-3900

Waukesha County Technical College

Pewaukee, Wisconsin
www.wctc.edu Federal Code: 005294

2-year public technical college in large town.
Enrollment: 6,024 undergrads, 67% part-time. 329 full-time freshmen.
Selectivity: Open admission; but selective for some programs.

BASIC COSTS (2012-2013)

Tuition and fees: $3,780; out-of-state residents $5,470.
Per-credit charge: $117; out-of-state residents $175.
Additional info: Materials fees vary by program; minimum $4 per course. $10 per credit fee for online courses.

FINANCIAL AID PICTURE

Students with need: Need-based aid available for full-time students. Work study available nights.
Students without need: No-need awards available for academics.

FINANCIAL AID PROCEDURES

Forms required: FAFSA, institutional form.
Dates and Deadlines: Priority date 3/31; no closing date. Applicants notified on a rolling basis.

CONTACT

Tim Jacobson, Financial Aid Manager
800 Main Street, Pewaukee, WI 53072
(262) 691-5436

Western Technical College

La Crosse, Wisconsin
www.westerntc.edu Federal Code: 003840

2-year public community and technical college in small city.
Enrollment: 4,725 undergrads.
Selectivity: Open admission; but selective for some programs.

BASIC COSTS (2012-2013)

Tuition and fees: $3,977; out-of-state residents $5,667.
Per-credit charge: $117; out-of-state residents $175.
Room and board: $5,300.
Additional info: Material fees vary by program; minimum $4 per course. $10 per credit fee for online courses. Tuition/fee waivers available for unemployed or children of unemployed.

FINANCIAL AID PICTURE

Students with need: Need-based aid available for full-time and part-time students. Work study available nights, weekends, and for part-time students.

FINANCIAL AID PROCEDURES

Forms required: FAFSA, institutional form.
Dates and Deadlines: Priority date 3/1; no closing date. Applicants notified on a rolling basis starting 4/1.

CONTACT

Jerolyn Grandall, Student Financial Services Manager
PO Box 908, La Crosse, WI 54602-0908
(608) 785-9302

Wisconsin Indianhead Technical College

Shell Lake, Wisconsin
www.witc.edu Federal Code: 011824

2-year public technical college in small town.
Enrollment: 3,207 undergrads, 51% part-time. 319 full-time freshmen.
Selectivity: Open admission; but selective for some programs.

BASIC COSTS (2012-2013)

Tuition and fees: $3,876; out-of-state residents $5,566.
Per-credit charge: $117; out-of-state residents $175.
Additional info: Material fees vary by program; minimum $4 per course. $10 per credit fee for online courses.

FINANCIAL AID PICTURE (2011-2012)

Students with need: 50% of average financial aid package awarded as scholarships/grants, 50% awarded as loans/jobs. Need-based aid available for part-time students. Work study available nights, weekends, and for part-time students.
Students without need: This college awards aid only to students with need.

FINANCIAL AID PROCEDURES

Forms required: FAFSA.
Dates and Deadlines: Closing date 4/15. Applicants notified on a rolling basis starting 5/10; must reply by 9/1 or within 4 week(s) of notification.

CONTACT

Terry Klein, Director of Financial Aid
505 Pine Ridge Drive, Shell Lake, WI 54871
(715) 468-2815 ext. 2243

Wisconsin Lutheran College

Milwaukee, Wisconsin
www.wlc.edu Federal Code: 014658

4-year private liberal arts college in very large city, affiliated with Wisconsin Evangelical Lutheran Synod.
Enrollment: 1,009 undergrads.

BASIC COSTS (2012-2013)

Tuition and fees: $23,620.
Per-credit charge: $680.
Room and board: $8,530.

FINANCIAL AID PICTURE

Students with need: Need-based aid available for full-time and part-time students.
Students without need: No-need awards available for academics, art, leadership, music/drama, ROTC.

FINANCIAL AID PROCEDURES

Forms required: FAFSA, institutional form.
Dates and Deadlines: Priority date 3/1; no closing date. Applicants notified on a rolling basis starting 3/15; must reply within 2 week(s) of notification.
Transfers: Transfer scholarship and transfer grant available for qualifying students.

CONTACT
Linda Loeffel, Financial Aid Director
8800 West Bluemound Road, Milwaukee, WI 53226-4699
(414) 443-8856

Wyoming

Casper College

Casper, Wyoming
www.caspercollege.edu Federal Code: 003928

2-year public community college in small city.
Enrollment: 2,863 undergrads, 33% part-time. 632 full-time freshmen.
Selectivity: Open admission; but selective for some programs and for out-of-state students.

BASIC COSTS (2012-2013)
Tuition and fees: $2,232; out-of-state residents $5,832.
Per-credit charge: $75; out-of-state residents $225.
Room and board: $5,530.
Additional info: Western Undergraduate Exchange students pay $112 per credit-hour.

FINANCIAL AID PICTURE
Students with need: Need-based aid available for full-time and part-time students. Work study available nights, weekends, and for part-time students.
Students without need: No-need awards available for academics, art, athletics, leadership, music/drama, state/district residency.

FINANCIAL AID PROCEDURES
Forms required: FAFSA.
Dates and Deadlines: Priority date 3/15; no closing date. Applicants notified on a rolling basis starting 4/1.
Transfers: No deadline. Applicants notified on a rolling basis starting 4/1.

CONTACT
Darry Voigt, Executive Director Enrollment Services
125 College Drive, Casper, WY 82601
(307) 268-2510

Central Wyoming College

Riverton, Wyoming
www.cwc.edu Federal Code: 005018

2-year public community college in large town.
Enrollment: 1,248 undergrads, 43% part-time. 196 full-time freshmen.
Selectivity: Open admission; but selective for some programs.

BASIC COSTS (2012-2013)
Tuition and fees: $2,472; out-of-state residents $6,072.
Per-credit charge: $75; out-of-state residents $225.
Room and board: $5,694.
Additional info: Western Undergraduate Exchange students pay $112 per credit hour.

FINANCIAL AID PICTURE (2012-2013)
Students with need: Out of 161 full-time freshmen who applied for aid, 112 were judged to have need. Of these, 109 received aid. Need-based aid available for part-time students.
Students without need: No-need awards available for academics, alumni affiliation, art, athletics, leadership, minority status, music/drama, state/district residency.
Scholarships offered: Honors Scholarships: in-state tuition and general fees plus $300 book stipend; for graduating high school seniors with minimum 3.5 GPA or 25 ACT. Seniors Scholarships: in-state tuition; for graduating high school seniors with 3.0-3.49 GPA or 22 ACT. Full academic scholarships: in-state tuition, general fees, room and board, books and supplies; for Wyoming National Merit finalists.

FINANCIAL AID PROCEDURES
Forms required: FAFSA, institutional form.
Dates and Deadlines: Priority date 4/15; no closing date. Applicants notified on a rolling basis starting 5/1; must reply within 2 week(s) of notification.

CONTACT
Jacque Burns, Director of Financial Aid
2660 Peck Avenue, Riverton, WY 82501
(307) 855-2150

Eastern Wyoming College

Torrington, Wyoming
www.ewc.wy.edu Federal Code: 003929

2-year public community college in small town.
Enrollment: 786 undergrads, 38% part-time. 202 full-time freshmen.
Selectivity: Open admission.

BASIC COSTS (2012-2013)
Tuition and fees: $2,376; out-of-state residents $5,976.
Per-credit charge: $75; out-of-state residents $225.
Room and board: $4,880.

FINANCIAL AID PICTURE (2011-2012)
Students with need: Need-based aid available for full-time and part-time students. Work study available nights, weekends, and for part-time students.
Students without need: No-need awards available for academics, alumni affiliation, art, athletics, leadership, music/drama.
Additional info: Installment payment plan on room and board contracts offered.

FINANCIAL AID PROCEDURES
Forms required: FAFSA, institutional form.
Dates and Deadlines: Priority date 3/15; no closing date. Applicants notified on a rolling basis starting 1/1.

CONTACT
Molly Williams, Financial Aid DIrector
3200 West C Street, Torrington, WY 82240
(800) 658-3195 ext. 8325

Laramie County Community College

Cheyenne, Wyoming
www.lccc.wy.edu Federal Code: 009259

2-year public community college in small city.
Enrollment: 3,549 undergrads, 44% part-time. 349 full-time freshmen.
Selectivity: Open admission; but selective for some programs.

BASIC COSTS (2012-2013)
Tuition and fees: $2,640; out-of-state residents $6,240.
Per-credit charge: $75; out-of-state residents $225.
Room and board: $7,034.

FINANCIAL AID PICTURE (2011-2012)
Students with need: Out of 269 full-time freshmen who applied for aid, 133 were judged to have need. Of these, 68 received aid. Need-based aid available for part-time students.
Students without need: No-need awards available for academics, alumni affiliation, art, athletics, job skills, leadership, minority status, music/drama, religious affiliation, state/district residency.

Scholarships offered: 22 full-time freshmen received athletic scholarships; average amount $6,380.

FINANCIAL AID PROCEDURES

Forms required: FAFSA, institutional form.

Dates and Deadlines: Priority date 4/1; no closing date. Applicants notified on a rolling basis starting 4/1; must reply within 2 week(s) of notification.

Transfers: No deadline. Applicants notified on a rolling basis starting 4/1; must reply within 2 week(s) of notification.

CONTACT

Jennifer Almli, Director of Financial Aid
1400 East College Drive, Cheyenne, WY 82007-3299
(307) 778-1281

Northwest College

Powell, Wyoming
www.northwestcollege.edu Federal Code: 003931

2-year public community and junior college in small town.

Enrollment: 1,792 undergrads, 34% part-time. 422 full-time freshmen.

Selectivity: Open admission; but selective for some programs and for out-of-state students.

BASIC COSTS (2012-2013)

Tuition and fees: $2,436; out-of-state residents $6,036.

Per-credit charge: $75; out-of-state residents $225.

Room and board: $4,650.

Additional info: Western Undergraduate Exchange students pay $112 per credit-hour.

FINANCIAL AID PICTURE

Students with need: Need-based aid available for full-time and part-time students. Work study available nights, weekends, and for part-time students.

Students without need: No-need awards available for academics, alumni affiliation, art, athletics, leadership, music/drama, state/district residency.

FINANCIAL AID PROCEDURES

Forms required: FAFSA, institutional form.

Dates and Deadlines: Priority date 3/1; no closing date. Applicants notified on a rolling basis; must reply within 2 week(s) of notification.

CONTACT

Shaman Quinn, Financial Aid and Scholarships Director
Orendorff Building, Powell, WY 82435-1898
(307) 754-6158

Sheridan College

Sheridan, Wyoming
www.sheridan.edu Federal Code: 003930

2-year public community college in large town.

Enrollment: 2,060 undergrads, 35% part-time. 475 full-time freshmen.

Selectivity: Open admission; but selective for some programs.

BASIC COSTS (2012-2013)

Tuition and fees: $2,640; out-of-state residents $6,240.

Per-credit charge: $75; out-of-state residents $225.

Room and board: $5,186.

FINANCIAL AID PICTURE (2011-2012)

Students with need: 70% of average financial aid package awarded as scholarships/grants, 30% awarded as loans/jobs. Need-based aid available for part-time students. Work study available nights, weekends, and for part-time students.

Students without need: No-need awards available for academics, art, athletics, leadership, music/drama, state/district residency.

Scholarships offered: Merit scholarships; in-state tuition and fees; must have 25 ACT or 1120 SAT (exclusive of Writing); renewable.

FINANCIAL AID PROCEDURES

Forms required: FAFSA, institutional form.

Dates and Deadlines: Priority date 3/1; no closing date. Applicants notified on a rolling basis; must reply within 3 week(s) of notification.

CONTACT

Jennifer Smith, Director of Financial Aid
PO Box 1500, Sheridan, WY 82801-1500
(307) 674-6446 ext. 2100

University of Wyoming

Laramie, Wyoming
www.uwyo.edu Federal Code: 003932

4-year public university in large town.

Enrollment: 10,029 undergrads, 17% part-time. 1,531 full-time freshmen.

Selectivity: Admits over 75% of applicants.

BASIC COSTS (2012-2013)

Tuition and fees: $4,278; out-of-state residents $13,428.

Per-credit charge: $106; out-of-state residents $411.

Room and board: $9,084.

Additional info: International students must pay an additional $40 fee per semester.

FINANCIAL AID PICTURE (2011-2012)

Students with need: Out of 1,214 full-time freshmen who applied for aid, 771 were judged to have need. Of these, 757 received aid, and 198 had their full need met. Average financial aid package met 67% of need; average scholarship/grant was $4,660; average loan was $2,940. For part-time students, average financial aid package was $5,551.

Students without need: 176 full-time freshmen who did not demonstrate need for aid received scholarships/grants; average award was $1,936. No-need awards available for academics, alumni affiliation, art, athletics, leadership, minority status, music/drama, ROTC, state/district residency.

Scholarships offered: ***Merit:*** Western Heritage Scholarship: number awarded and packages vary. President's High School Honor Scholarship: covers undergraduate fees and tuition; number awarded varies. ***Athletic:*** 23 full-time freshmen received athletic scholarships; average amount $1,356.

Cumulative student debt: 47% of graduating class had student loans; average debt was $21,241.

FINANCIAL AID PROCEDURES

Forms required: FAFSA.

Dates and Deadlines: Priority date 3/1; no closing date. Applicants notified on a rolling basis starting 3/22; must reply within 3 week(s) of notification.

CONTACT

Joanna Carter, Director of Student Financial Aid
Dept 3435, Laramie, WY 82071
(307) 766-2116

Western Wyoming Community College

Rock Springs, Wyoming
www.wwcc.wy.edu Federal Code: 003933

2-year public community college in large town.

Enrollment: 2,927 undergrads, 56% part-time. 222 full-time freshmen.

Selectivity: Open admission; but selective for some programs.

BASIC COSTS (2012-2013)

Tuition and fees: $2,186; out-of-state residents $5,786.

Per-credit charge: $75; out-of-state residents $225.

Room and board: $4,184.

FINANCIAL AID PICTURE (2011-2012)

Students with need: 62% of average financial aid package awarded as scholarships/grants, 38% awarded as loans/jobs. Need-based aid available for part-time students.

Students without need: No-need awards available for academics, art, athletics, music/drama, state/district residency.

FINANCIAL AID PROCEDURES

Forms required: FAFSA.

Dates and Deadlines: Priority date 4/1; no closing date. Applicants notified on a rolling basis starting 2/15; must reply within 2 week(s) of notification.

CONTACT

Javier Flores, Financial Aid Director
Box 428, Rock Springs, WY 82902-0428
(307) 382-1643

WyoTech: Laramie

Laramie, Wyoming
www.wyotech.edu Federal Code: 009157

2-year for-profit technical college in large town.
Enrollment: 1,600 undergrads.
Selectivity: Open admission.

FINANCIAL AID PICTURE

Students with need: Need-based aid available for full-time and part-time students.

Students without need: This college awards aid only to students with need.

FINANCIAL AID PROCEDURES

Forms required: FAFSA.

Dates and Deadlines: Applicants notified on a rolling basis.

CONTACT

Thecla Woolcott, Director of Financial Services
4373 North Third Street, Laramie, WY 82072
(307) 742-3776

Part IV

Scholarship Lists

Academic scholarships

Alabama
Alabama State University
Amridge University
Athens State University
Auburn University at Montgomery
Bevill State Community College
Birmingham-Southern College
Bishop State Community College
Calhoun Community College
Central Alabama Community College
Chattahoochee Valley Community College
Enterprise State Community College
Faulkner State Community College
Faulkner University
Gadsden State Community College
George C. Wallace Community College at Dothan
George C. Wallace State Community College at Selma
Huntingdon College
Jacksonville State University
Jefferson Davis Community College
Jefferson State Community College
Judson College
Northeast Alabama Community College
Northwest-Shoals Community College
Oakwood University
Samford University
Selma University
Snead State Community College
Southeastern Bible College
Spring Hill College
Stillman College
Talladega College
Troy University
Tuskegee University
University of Alabama
University of Alabama
  Birmingham
  Huntsville
University of Mobile
University of Montevallo
University of North Alabama
University of South Alabama
University of West Alabama
Wallace State Community College at Hanceville

Alaska
Alaska Bible College
Alaska Pacific University
University of Alaska
  Anchorage
  Fairbanks
  Southeast

Arizona
Arizona Christian University
Arizona State University
Arizona Western College
DeVry University
  Phoenix
Dine College
Eastern Arizona College
Embry-Riddle Aeronautical University
  Prescott Campus
Grand Canyon University
Mesa Community College
Northern Arizona University
Northland Pioneer College
Pima Community College
Prescott College
Scottsdale Community College
South Mountain Community College
Southwest University of Visual Arts
University of Advancing Technology
University of Arizona
Yavapai College

Arkansas
Arkansas Northeastern College
Arkansas State University
Arkansas State University
  Beebe
  Mountain Home
Arkansas Tech University
Black River Technical College
Central Baptist College
Crowley's Ridge College
Ecclesia College
Harding University
Henderson State University
Hendrix College
John Brown University
Lyon College
Mid-South Community College
National Park Community College
North Arkansas College
Northwest Arkansas Community College
Ouachita Baptist University
Philander Smith College
Phillips Community College of the University of Arkansas
Rich Mountain Community College
Southeast Arkansas College
Southern Arkansas University
Southern Arkansas University Tech
University of Arkansas
University of Arkansas
  Community College at Batesville
  Community College at Hope
  Community College at Morrilton
  Fort Smith
  Little Rock
  Monticello
  Pine Bluff
University of Central Arkansas
University of the Ozarks
Williams Baptist College

California
Academy of Art University
Alliant International University
American Academy of Dramatic Arts: West
Art Institute of California
  Los Angeles
  Orange County
Azusa Pacific University
Bethesda University of California
Biola University
California Baptist University
California College of the Arts
California Institute of Integral Studies
California Institute of the Arts
California Lutheran University
California Maritime Academy
California Polytechnic State University: San Luis Obispo
California State Polytechnic University: Pomona
California State University
  Bakersfield
  Channel Islands
  Chico
  Dominguez Hills
  East Bay
  Fresno
  Fullerton
  Long Beach
  Monterey Bay
  Northridge
  San Marcos
  Stanislaus
Chaffey College
Chapman University
Claremont McKenna College
Cogswell Polytechnical College
College of the Canyons
College of the Desert
College of the Siskiyous
Columbia College
Concordia University
Deep Springs College
DeVry University
  Pomona
Dominican University of California
East Los Angeles College
El Camino College
Empire College
Fashion Institute of Design and Merchandising
  Los Angeles
  San Diego
  San Francisco
Fresno Pacific University
Glendale Community College
Golden Gate University
Golden West College
Harvey Mudd College
Holy Names University
Hope International University
Humboldt State University
Humphreys College
Imperial Valley College
La Sierra University
Life Pacific College
Loyola Marymount University
The Master's College
Mendocino College
Menlo College
Merced College
Mills College
Mount St. Mary's College
Mount San Jacinto College
Notre Dame de Namur University
Occidental College
Ohlone College
Otis College of Art and Design
Pacific States University
Pacific Union College
Patten University
Pepperdine University
Pitzer College
Point Loma Nazarene University
Riverside Community College
St. Mary's College of California
Samuel Merritt University
San Diego Christian College
San Diego State University
San Francisco Art Institute
San Francisco State University
San Joaquin Delta College
San Jose State University
Santa Clara University
Santa Rosa Junior College
School of Urban Missions: Oakland
Scripps College
Simpson University
Soka University of America
Sonoma State University
Southern California Institute of Architecture
Taft College
University of California
  Berkeley
  Davis
  Los Angeles
  Merced
  Riverside
  San Diego
  Santa Barbara
  Santa Cruz
University of La Verne
University of Redlands
University of San Diego
University of San Francisco
University of Southern California
University of the Pacific
University of the West
Vanguard University of Southern California
West Coast University: Los Angeles
West Coast University: Ontario
West Coast University: Orange County
Westmont College
Whittier College
William Jessup University
Woodbury University
Yuba Community College District

Colorado
Adams State College
Arapahoe Community College
Boulder College of Massage Therapy
Colorado Christian University
Colorado College
Colorado Heights University
Colorado Mesa University
Colorado Northwestern Community College
Colorado School of Mines
Colorado State University
Colorado State University
  Pueblo
Colorado Technical University
Community College of Aurora
Community College of Denver
DeVry University
  Westminster
Fort Lewis College
Front Range Community College
Johnson & Wales University
  Denver
Naropa University
Nazarene Bible College
Northeastern Junior College
Otero Junior College
Pueblo Community College
Red Rocks Community College
Regis University
Remington College
  Colorado Springs
Rocky Mountain College of Art & Design
Trinidad State Junior College
University of Colorado
  Boulder
  Colorado Springs
  Denver
University of Denver
University of Northern Colorado
Western State Colorado University
Westwood College
  Denver North

Connecticut
Albertus Magnus College
Central Connecticut State University
Eastern Connecticut State University
Fairfield University
Goodwin College
Housatonic Community College
Lincoln College of New England
Lyme Academy College of Fine Arts
Mitchell College
Norwalk Community College
Quinnipiac University
Sacred Heart University
Southern Connecticut State University
Trinity College
Tunxis Community College
University of Bridgeport
University of Connecticut
University of Hartford
University of Saint Joseph
Western Connecticut State University

Delaware
Delaware College of Art and Design
Delaware State University

Goldey-Beacom College
University of Delaware
Wesley College
Wilmington University

District of Columbia
American University
Catholic University of America
Gallaudet University
George Washington University
Howard University
Trinity Washington University

Florida
Ave Maria University
Baptist College of Florida
Barry University
Beacon College
Bethune-Cookman University
Brevard Community College
Broward College
Brown Mackie College
  Miami
Carlos Albizu University
Chipola College
Clearwater Christian College
College of Central Florida
Daytona State College
DeVry University
  Miramar
  Orlando
Eckerd College
Embry-Riddle Aeronautical University
Embry-Riddle Aeronautical University
  Worldwide Campus
Flagler College
Florida Agricultural and Mechanical University
Florida Atlantic University
Florida Christian College
Florida College
Florida Gateway College
Florida Gulf Coast University
Florida Institute of Technology
Florida International University
Florida Keys Community College
Florida Southern College
Florida State College at Jacksonville
Florida State University
Gulf Coast State College
Hillsborough Community College
Hobe Sound Bible College
Hodges University
Indian River State College
International Academy of Design and Technology: Tampa
Jacksonville University
Johnson & Wales University
  North Miami
Jones College
Jose Maria Vargas University
Lake-Sumter Community College
Lynn University
Miami Dade College
New College of Florida
North Florida Community College
Northwest Florida State College
Northwood University
  Florida
Nova Southeastern University
Palm Beach Atlantic University
Palm Beach State College
Pasco-Hernando Community College
Pensacola State College
Polk State College
Ringling College of Art and Design
Rollins College
Saint Leo University
St. Petersburg College
Saint Thomas University
Santa Fe College
Schiller International University
Seminole State College of Florida
South Florida Community College
Southeastern University
State College of Florida, Manatee-Sarasota
Stetson University
Tallahassee Community College
Trinity College of Florida
University of Central Florida
University of Florida
University of Miami
University of North Florida
University of South Florida
University of Tampa
University of West Florida
Warner University
Webber International University

Georgia
Abraham Baldwin Agricultural College
Agnes Scott College
Albany State University
Albany Technical College
Andrew College
Armstrong Atlantic State University
Athens Technical College
Berry College
Brenau University
Brewton-Parker College
Clark Atlanta University
Clayton State University
College of Coastal Georgia
Columbus State University
Covenant College
Dalton State College
Darton College
DeVry University
  Decatur
East Georgia College
Emmanuel College
Emory University
Fort Valley State University
Georgia College and State University
Georgia Highlands College
Georgia Institute of Technology
Georgia Regents University
Georgia Southern University
Georgia Southwestern State University
Georgia State University
Gordon College
Herzing University
  Atlanta
Kennesaw State University
LaGrange College
Life University
Mercer University
Middle Georgia State College
Morehouse College
Oglethorpe University
Oxford College of Emory University
Paine College
Piedmont College
Point University
Reinhardt University
Savannah College of Art and Design
Savannah State University
Savannah Technical College
Shorter University
South Georgia State College
Southern Polytechnic State University
Spelman College
Thomas University
Toccoa Falls College
Truett-McConnell College
University of Georgia
University of North Georgia
University of West Georgia
Valdosta State University
Wesleyan College
Wiregrass Georgia Technical College
Young Harris College

Hawaii
Brigham Young University-Hawaii
Chaminade University of Honolulu
Hawaii Pacific University
Hawaii Tokai International College
University of Hawaii
  Honolulu Community College
  Manoa
  West Oahu
  Windward Community College

Idaho
Boise Bible College
Boise State University
Brigham Young University-Idaho
College of Idaho
College of Western Idaho
Eastern Idaho Technical College
Idaho State University
Lewis-Clark State College
North Idaho College
Northwest Nazarene University
University of Idaho

Illinois
Augustana College
Aurora University
Benedictine University
Black Hawk College
Blackburn College
Blessing-Rieman College of Nursing
Bradley University
Carl Sandburg College
Chicago State University
College of DuPage
College of Lake County
Columbia College Chicago
Concordia University Chicago
Danville Area Community College
DePaul University
DeVry University
  Chicago
  Online
Dominican University
East-West University
Eastern Illinois University
Elgin Community College
Elmhurst College
Eureka College
Governors State University
Greenville College
Harper College
Harrington College of Design
Heartland Community College
Highland Community College
Illinois Central College
Illinois College
Illinois Eastern Community Colleges
  Frontier Community College
  Lincoln Trail College
  Olney Central College
  Wabash Valley College
Illinois Institute of Technology
Illinois State University
Illinois Valley Community College
Illinois Wesleyan University
Joliet Junior College
Judson University
Kaskaskia College
Kendall College
Kishwaukee College
Knox College
Lake Forest College
Lake Land College
Lewis University
Lexington College
Lincoln Christian University
Lincoln College
Lincoln Land Community College
Loyola University Chicago
MacCormac College
MacMurray College
McHenry County College
McKendree University
Millikin University
Monmouth College
Moody Bible Institute
Moraine Valley Community College
Morrison Institute of Technology
North Central College
North Park University
Northeastern Illinois University
Northern Illinois University
Northwestern College
Oakton Community College
Olivet Nazarene University
Parkland College
Principia College
Quincy University
Rend Lake College
Resurrection University
Richland Community College
Robert Morris University: Chicago
Rock Valley College
Rockford College
Roosevelt University
Rush University
St. Francis Medical Center College of Nursing
Saint Xavier University
Sauk Valley Community College
School of the Art Institute of Chicago
Shawnee Community College
Shimer College
South Suburban College of Cook County
Southeastern Illinois College
Southern Illinois University Carbondale
Southern Illinois University Edwardsville
Southwestern Illinois College
Spoon River College
Trinity Christian College
Trinity International University
Triton College
University of Chicago
University of Illinois
  Chicago
  Springfield
  Urbana-Champaign
University of St. Francis
VanderCook College of Music
Waubonsee Community College
Western Illinois University
Wheaton College

Indiana
Ancilla College
Anderson University
Ball State University
Bethel College
Butler University
Calumet College of St. Joseph
DePauw University
Earlham College
Franklin College
Goshen College
Grace College
Hanover College
Holy Cross College
Huntington University
Indiana Institute of Technology
Indiana State University
Indiana University
  Bloomington
  East
  Kokomo
  Northwest
  Purdue University Fort Wayne
  Purdue University Indianapolis
  South Bend
  Southeast
Indiana Wesleyan University
Manchester University
Marian University
Oakland City University
Purdue University
Purdue University
  Calumet
  North Central
Rose-Hulman Institute of Technology
Saint Joseph's College
St. Mary-of-the-Woods College

Saint Mary's College
Taylor University
Trine University
University of Evansville
University of Indianapolis
University of St. Francis
University of Southern Indiana
Valparaiso University
Vincennes University
Wabash College

Iowa
AIB College of Business
Allen College
Ashford University
Briar Cliff University
Buena Vista University
Central College
Clarke University
Coe College
Cornell College
Des Moines Area Community College
Dordt College
Drake University
Ellsworth Community College
Emmaus Bible College
Faith Baptist Bible College and Theological Seminary
Graceland University
Grand View University
Grinnell College
Hawkeye Community College
Iowa Central Community College
Iowa State University
Iowa Wesleyan College
Kaplan University
- Cedar Falls
- Cedar Rapids
- Davenport
- Mason City

Loras College
Luther College
Mercy College of Health Sciences
Morningside College
Mount Mercy University
North Iowa Area Community College
Northeast Iowa Community College
Northwestern College
St. Ambrose University
St. Luke's College
Simpson College
Southeastern Community College
Southwestern Community College
University of Dubuque
University of Iowa
University of Northern Iowa
Upper Iowa University
Vatterott College
- Des Moines

Waldorf College
Wartburg College
Western Iowa Tech Community College
William Penn University

Kansas
Allen County Community College
Baker University
Barclay College
Barton County Community College
Benedictine College
Bethel College
Butler Community College
Central Christian College of Kansas
Coffeyville Community College
Colby Community College
Cowley County Community College
Dodge City Community College
Donnelly College
Emporia State University
Fort Hays State University
Friends University
Garden City Community College
Hesston College
Highland Community College
Hutchinson Community College
Independence Community College
Johnson County Community College
Kansas City Kansas Community College
Kansas State University
Kansas Wesleyan University
Labette Community College
Manhattan Area Technical College
Manhattan Christian College
McPherson College
MidAmerica Nazarene University
Neosho County Community College
Newman University
North Central Kansas Technical College
Ottawa University
Pittsburg State University
Pratt Community College
Seward County Community College
Southwestern College
Sterling College
Tabor College
University of Kansas
University of Kansas Medical Center
University of St. Mary
Washburn University
Wichita State University

Kentucky
Asbury University
Ashland Community and Technical College
Beckfield College
Bellarmine University
Big Sandy Community and Technical College
Bluegrass Community and Technical College
Brescia University
Campbellsville University
Centre College
Clear Creek Baptist Bible College
Daymar College
- Bowling Green
- Owensboro

Eastern Kentucky University
Georgetown College
Hopkinsville Community College
Kentucky Christian University
Kentucky Mountain Bible College
Kentucky State University
Kentucky Wesleyan College
Maysville Community and Technical College
Mid-Continent University
Midway College
Morehead State University
Murray State University
National College
- Danville
- Florence
- Lexington
- Louisville
- Pikeville
- Richmond

Northern Kentucky University
Owensboro Community and Technical College
St. Catharine College
Somerset Community College
Southeast Kentucky Community and Technical College
Spalding University
Spencerian College
Spencerian College: Lexington
Sullivan College of Technology and Design
Thomas More College
Transylvania University
Union College
University of Kentucky
University of Louisville
University of the Cumberlands
Western Kentucky University

Louisiana
Baton Rouge Community College
Bossier Parish Community College
Centenary College of Louisiana
Delgado Community College
Dillard University
Grambling State University
Louisiana College
Louisiana State University
- Alexandria
- Health Sciences Center

Louisiana State University and Agricultural and Mechanical College
Louisiana Tech University
Loyola University New Orleans
McNeese State University
Nicholls State University
Northwestern State University
Our Lady of Holy Cross College
Remington College
- Baton Rouge

St. Joseph Seminary College
South Louisiana Community College
Southeastern Louisiana University
Southern University and Agricultural and Mechanical College
Tulane University
University of Louisiana at Monroe
University of New Orleans

Maine
Bowdoin College
Colby College
Eastern Maine Community College
Husson University
Maine College of Art
Maine Maritime Academy
New England School of Communications
Saint Joseph's College of Maine
Thomas College
Unity College
University of Maine
University of Maine
- Augusta
- Farmington
- Fort Kent
- Machias
- Presque Isle

University of Southern Maine
Washington County Community College
York County Community College

Maryland
Allegany College of Maryland
Bowie State University
Capitol College
Carroll Community College
Cecil College
Chesapeake College
College of Southern Maryland
Community College of Baltimore County
Coppin State University
Frederick Community College
Frostburg State University
Garrett College
Goucher College
Hood College
Johns Hopkins University
Johns Hopkins University: Peabody Conservatory of Music
Loyola University Maryland
Maryland Institute College of Art
McDaniel College
Montgomery College
Mount St. Mary's University
Notre Dame of Maryland University
Prince George's Community College
St. John's College
St. Mary's College of Maryland
Salisbury University
Stevenson University
Towson University
University of Maryland
- Baltimore County
- College Park
- Eastern Shore
- University College

Washington Adventist University
Washington College
Wor-Wic Community College

Massachusetts
American International College
Anna Maria College
Assumption College
Babson College
Bard College at Simon's Rock
Bay Path College
Bay State College
Becker College
Benjamin Franklin Institute of Technology
Bentley University
Berklee College of Music
Berkshire Community College
Boston Architectural College
Boston College
Boston University
Brandeis University
Bridgewater State University
Bristol Community College
Bunker Hill Community College
Cape Cod Community College
Clark University
College of the Holy Cross
Curry College
Dean College
Eastern Nazarene College
Elms College
Emerson College
Emmanuel College
Endicott College
Fisher College
Fitchburg State University
Framingham State University
Franklin W. Olin College of Engineering
Gordon College
Hampshire College
Hellenic College/Holy Cross
Holyoke Community College
Laboure College
Lasell College
Lesley University
Marian Court College
Massachusetts College of Art and Design
Massachusetts College of Liberal Arts
Massachusetts College of Pharmacy and Health Sciences
Massachusetts Maritime Academy
Merrimack College
Montserrat College of Art
Mount Holyoke College
Mount Wachusett Community College
New England Conservatory of Music
New England Institute of Art
Newbury College
Nichols College
North Shore Community College
Northeastern University
Northern Essex Community College
Northpoint Bible College
Pine Manor College
Quinsigamond Community College
Regis College
Salem State University
Simmons College
Smith College
Springfield College
Stonehill College
Suffolk University
Tufts University
University of Massachusetts
- Amherst
- Boston
- Dartmouth
- Lowell

Wentworth Institute of Technology
Western New England University
Wheaton College
Wheelock College

Worcester Polytechnic Institute
Worcester State University

Michigan
Adrian College
Albion College
Alma College
Alpena Community College
Andrews University
Aquinas College
Baker College
  Auburn Hills
  Cadillac
  Clinton Township
  Flint
  Jackson
  Muskegon
  Owosso
  Port Huron
Bay de Noc Community College
Calvin College
Cleary University
College for Creative Studies
Concordia University
Cornerstone University
Davenport University
Delta College
Eastern Michigan University
Ferris State University
Finlandia University
Glen Oaks Community College
Gogebic Community College
Grand Rapids Community College
Grand Valley State University
Great Lakes Christian College
Hillsdale College
Hope College
Jackson Community College
Kalamazoo College
Kalamazoo Valley Community College
Kellogg Community College
Kettering University
Kirtland Community College
Kuyper College
Lake Superior State University
Lansing Community College
Lawrence Technological University
Macomb Community College
Madonna University
Marygrove College
Michigan State University
Michigan Technological University
Mid Michigan Community College
Monroe County Community College
Montcalm Community College
Mott Community College
Northern Michigan University
Northwestern Michigan College
Northwood University
  Michigan
Oakland Community College
Oakland University
Olivet College
Robert B. Miller College
Rochester College
Sacred Heart Major Seminary
Saginaw Valley State University
Schoolcraft College
Siena Heights University
Southwestern Michigan College
Spring Arbor University
University of Detroit Mercy
University of Michigan
University of Michigan
  Dearborn
  Flint
Walsh College of Accountancy and Business Administration
Washtenaw Community College
Wayne State University
Western Michigan University

Minnesota
Art Institutes International Minnesota
Augsburg College
Bemidji State University
Bethany Lutheran College
Bethel University
Brown College
  Mendota Heights
Carleton College
College of St. Benedict
College of St. Scholastica
College of Visual Arts
Concordia College: Moorhead
Concordia University St. Paul
Crossroads College
Crown College
Dakota County Technical College
Dunwoody College of Technology
Fond du Lac Tribal and Community College
Gustavus Adolphus College
Hamline University
Itasca Community College
Lake Superior College
Le Cordon Bleu College of Culinary Arts
  Minneapolis-St. Paul
Macalester College
Martin Luther College
Metropolitan State University
Minneapolis College of Art and Design
Minnesota State College - Southeast Technical
Minnesota State Community and Technical College
Minnesota State University
  Mankato
  Moorhead
Normandale Community College
North Central University
North Hennepin Community College
Northland Community & Technical College
Northwest Technical College
Northwestern College
Oak Hills Christian College
Pine Technical College
Rainy River Community College
St. Catherine University
Saint Cloud State University
St. Cloud Technical and Community College
St. John's University
St. Mary's University of Minnesota
St. Olaf College
Southwest Minnesota State University
University of Minnesota
  Crookston
  Duluth
  Morris
  Rochester
  Twin Cities
University of St. Thomas
Winona State University

Mississippi
Alcorn State University
Belhaven University
Blue Mountain College
Coahoma Community College
Copiah-Lincoln Community College
Delta State University
East Mississippi Community College
Hinds Community College
Holmes Community College
Itawamba Community College
Jackson State University
Meridian Community College
Millsaps College
Mississippi College
Mississippi Delta Community College
Mississippi Gulf Coast Community College
Mississippi State University
Mississippi University for Women
Mississippi Valley State University
Pearl River Community College
Rust College
Tougaloo College
University of Mississippi
University of Mississippi Medical Center

Missouri
Avila University
Calvary Bible College and Theological Seminary
Central Bible College
Central Methodist University
Chamberlain College of Nursing
  St. Louis
College of the Ozarks
Columbia College
Conception Seminary College
Cottey College
Crowder College
Culver-Stockton College
DeVry University
  Kansas City
Drury University
East Central College
Evangel University
Fontbonne University
Goldfarb School of Nursing at Barnes-Jewish College
Hannibal-LaGrange University
Harris-Stowe State University
Jefferson College
Kansas City Art Institute
Lincoln University
Lindenwood University
Linn State Technical College
Maryville University of Saint Louis
Metropolitan Community College - Kansas City
Mineral Area College
Missouri Baptist University
Missouri Southern State University
Missouri State University
Missouri State University: West Plains
Missouri University of Science and Technology
Missouri Valley College
Missouri Western State University
Moberly Area Community College
North Central Missouri College
Northwest Missouri State University
Ozark Christian College
Park University
Research College of Nursing
Rockhurst University
St. Charles Community College
Saint Louis University
Southeast Missouri State University
Southwest Baptist University
State Fair Community College
Stephens College
Three Rivers Community College
Truman State University
University of Central Missouri
University of Missouri
  Columbia
  Kansas City
  St. Louis
Washington University in St. Louis
Webster University
Westminster College
William Jewell College
William Woods University

Montana
Carroll College
Chief Dull Knife College
Dawson Community College
Flathead Valley Community College
Little Big Horn College
Miles Community College
Montana State University
Montana State University
  Billings
  Great Falls College
  Northern
Montana Tech of the University of Montana
Rocky Mountain College
Stone Child College
University of Great Falls
University of Montana
University of Montana: Western

Nebraska
Bellevue University
BryanLGH College of Health Sciences
Central Community College
Chadron State College
Clarkson College
College of Saint Mary
Concordia University
Creative Center
Creighton University
Doane College
Grace University
Hastings College
Metropolitan Community College
Mid-Plains Community College
Nebraska Christian College
Nebraska Methodist College of Nursing and Allied Health
Nebraska Wesleyan University
Northeast Community College
Peru State College
Southeast Community College
Union College
University of Nebraska
  Kearney
  Lincoln
  Omaha
Wayne State College
Western Nebraska Community College
York College

Nevada
Roseman University of Health Sciences
Sierra Nevada College
Truckee Meadows Community College
University of Nevada
  Las Vegas
  Reno
Western Nevada College

New Hampshire
Colby-Sawyer College
Daniel Webster College
Franklin Pierce University
Hesser College
Keene State College
New England College
Plymouth State University
Rivier University
Saint Anselm College
Southern New Hampshire University
Thomas More College of Liberal Arts
University of New Hampshire
University of New Hampshire at Manchester

New Jersey
Berkeley College
Bloomfield College
Brookdale Community College
Burlington County College
Caldwell College
Centenary College
The College of New Jersey
College of St. Elizabeth
Cumberland County College
DeVry University
  North Brunswick
Drew University
Felician College
Georgian Court University
Kean University
Mercer County Community College
Monmouth University
Montclair State University
New Jersey Institute of Technology
Ocean County College
Passaic County Community College
Ramapo College of New Jersey
Raritan Valley Community College
Richard Stockton College of New Jersey

Rider University
Rowan University
Rutgers, The State University of New Jersey
Camden Campus
New Brunswick/Piscataway Campus
Newark Campus
Saint Peter's University
Salem Community College
Seton Hall University
Somerset Christian College
Stevens Institute of Technology
Union County College
Warren County Community College
William Paterson University of New Jersey

New Mexico
Central New Mexico Community College
Clovis Community College
Eastern New Mexico University
Institute of American Indian Arts
Luna Community College
Mesalands Community College
Navajo Technical College
New Mexico Highlands University
New Mexico Institute of Mining and Technology
New Mexico Junior College
New Mexico Military Institute
New Mexico State University
New Mexico State University
Alamogordo
Carlsbad
Northern New Mexico College
San Juan College
Santa Fe Community College
Santa Fe University of Art and Design
Southwest University of Visual Arts
Southwestern Indian Polytechnic Institute
University of New Mexico
University of the Southwest
Western New Mexico University

New York
Adelphi University
Adirondack Community College
Albany College of Pharmacy and Health Sciences
Alfred University
ASA Institute of Business and Computer Technology
Bard College
Briarcliffe College
Bryant & Stratton College
Albany
Syracuse
Canisius College
Cayuga Community College
Cazenovia College
City University of New York
Baruch College
Brooklyn College
City College
College of Staten Island
Hunter College
John Jay College of Criminal Justice
Medgar Evers College
Queens College
York College
Clarkson University
College of Mount St. Vincent
College of New Rochelle
College of Saint Rose
College of Westchester
Columbia University
School of General Studies
Concordia College
Cooper Union for the Advancement of Science and Art
Corning Community College
Culinary Institute of America
Daemen College
Davis College
Dominican College of Blauvelt
Dowling College
Dutchess Community College
D'Youville College
Eastman School of Music of the University of Rochester
Elmira College
Eugene Lang College The New School for Liberal Arts
Finger Lakes Community College
Five Towns College
Fordham University
Fulton-Montgomery Community College
Genesee Community College
Globe Institute of Technology
Hartwick College
Hilbert College
Hobart and William Smith Colleges
Hofstra University
Houghton College
Iona College
Ithaca College
Jamestown Business College
Jamestown Community College
Jefferson Community College
Jewish Theological Seminary of America
Keuka College
The King's College
Le Moyne College
LIM College
Long Island Business Institute
Long Island University
Brooklyn Campus
C. W. Post Campus
Manhattan College
Manhattan School of Music
Manhattanville College
Mannes College The New School for Music
Marist College
Marymount Manhattan College
Medaille College
Medaille College: Amherst
Mercy College
Mildred Elley
Mohawk Valley Community College
Molloy College
Monroe College
Monroe Community College
Mount Saint Mary College
Nassau Community College
Nazareth College
New York Institute of Technology
New York University
Niagara County Community College
Niagara University
Nyack College
Onondaga Community College
Pace University
Parsons The New School for Design
Paul Smith's College
Polytechnic Institute of New York University
Pratt Institute
Rensselaer Polytechnic Institute
Roberts Wesleyan College
Rochester Institute of Technology
The Sage Colleges
Saint Bonaventure University
St. Francis College
St. John Fisher College
St. John's University
St. Joseph's College New York: Suffolk Campus
St. Joseph's College, New York
St. Lawrence University
St. Thomas Aquinas College
Sarah Lawrence College
Schenectady County Community College
Siena College
Suffolk County Community College
SUNY
College at Brockport
College at Buffalo
College at Cortland
College at Fredonia
College at Geneseo
College at New Paltz
College at Old Westbury
College at Oneonta
College at Oswego
College at Plattsburgh
College at Potsdam
College at Purchase
College of Agriculture and Technology at Cobleskill
College of Agriculture and Technology at Morrisville
College of Environmental Science and Forestry
College of Technology at Alfred
College of Technology at Canton
Farmingdale State College
Institute of Technology at Utica/Rome
Maritime College
University at Albany
University at Binghamton
University at Buffalo
University at Stony Brook
Syracuse University
Technical Career Institutes
Tompkins Cortland Community College
Trocaire College
Union College
University of Rochester
Utica College
Vaughn College of Aeronautics and Technology
Villa Maria College of Buffalo
Wagner College
Webb Institute
Wells College
Westchester Community College
Yeshivat Mikdash Melech

North Carolina
Alamance Community College
Appalachian State University
Asheville-Buncombe Technical Community College
Barton College
Beaufort County Community College
Belmont Abbey College
Blue Ridge Community College
Brevard College
Brunswick Community College
Campbell University
Cape Fear Community College
Carolinas College of Health Sciences
Carteret Community College
Catawba College
Catawba Valley Community College
Central Carolina Community College
Central Piedmont Community College
Chowan University
Coastal Carolina Community College
College of the Albemarle
Davidson College
Davidson County Community College
Durham Technical Community College
East Carolina University
Elizabeth City State University
Elon University
Fayetteville State University
Forsyth Technical Community College
Gardner-Webb University
Gaston College
Greensboro College
Guilford College
Guilford Technical Community College
Haywood Community College
High Point University
Isothermal Community College
James Sprunt Community College
Johnson & Wales University
Charlotte
Johnson C. Smith University
Johnston Community College
Lees-McRae College
Lenoir Community College
Lenoir-Rhyne University
Livingstone College
Louisburg College
Mars Hill College
Martin Community College
McDowell Technical Community College
Meredith College
Methodist University
Mid-Atlantic Christian University
Montgomery Community College
Montreat College
Mount Olive College
Nash Community College
North Carolina Agricultural and Technical State University
North Carolina Central University
North Carolina State University
North Carolina Wesleyan College
Pfeiffer University
Pitt Community College
Queens University of Charlotte
Randolph Community College
Richmond Community College
Roanoke-Chowan Community College
Rowan-Cabarrus Community College
St. Andrews University
St. Augustine's University
Salem College
Sampson Community College
Sandhills Community College
Shaw University
Southeastern Community College
Stanly Community College
Surry Community College
University of North Carolina
Asheville
Chapel Hill
Charlotte
Greensboro
Pembroke
School of the Arts
Wilmington
Vance-Granville Community College
Wake Forest University
Wake Technical Community College
Warren Wilson College
Wayne Community College
Western Carolina University
Western Piedmont Community College
Wilkes Community College
William Peace University
Wilson Community College
Wingate University
Winston-Salem State University

North Dakota
Bismarck State College
Dakota College at Bottineau
Dickinson State University
Jamestown College
Lake Region State College
Mayville State University
Minot State University
North Dakota State College of Science
North Dakota State University
Trinity Bible College
University of Mary
University of North Dakota
Valley City State University
Williston State College

Ohio
Art Institute of Cincinnati
Ashland University
Aultman College of Nursing and Health Sciences
Baldwin Wallace University
Bluffton University
Bowling Green State University
Bowling Green State University: Firelands College
Brown Mackie College
Findlay

Bryant & Stratton College
Cleveland
Eastlake
Parma
Capital University
Case Western Reserve University
Cedarville University
Central Ohio Technical College
Central State University
Chatfield College
Cincinnati Christian University
Cincinnati State Technical and Community College
Cleveland Institute of Art
Cleveland Institute of Music
Cleveland State University
College of Mount St. Joseph
College of Wooster
Columbus College of Art and Design
Cuyahoga Community College
Metropolitan
Defiance College
Denison University
DeVry University
Columbus
Eastern Gateway Community College
Edison State Community College
ETI Technical College of Niles
Franciscan University of Steubenville
Franklin University
Hiram College
Hocking College
James A. Rhodes State College
John Carroll University
Kent State University
Kent State University
Ashtabula
East Liverpool
Geauga
Salem
Stark
Trumbull
Tuscarawas
Kenyon College
Kettering College
Lake Erie College
Lakeland Community College
Lorain County Community College
Lourdes University
Malone University
Marietta College
Marion Technical College
Mercy College of Ohio
Miami University
Hamilton
Oxford
Mount Carmel College of Nursing
Mount Vernon Nazarene University
Muskingum University
Northwest State Community College
Notre Dame College
Oberlin College
Ohio Christian University
Ohio Dominican University
Ohio Northern University
Ohio State University
Agricultural Technical Institute
Columbus Campus
Lima Campus
Mansfield Campus
Marion Campus
Newark Campus
Ohio University
Ohio University
Eastern Campus
Southern Campus at Ironton
Ohio Wesleyan University
Otterbein University
Owens Community College
Toledo
Pontifical College Josephinum
Rosedale Bible College
School of Advertising Art
Sinclair Community College
Southern State Community College
Stark State College of Technology
Terra State Community College
Tiffin University
Union Institute & University
University of Akron
University of Akron: Wayne College
University of Cincinnati
University of Cincinnati
Clermont College
Raymond Walters College
University of Dayton
University of Findlay
University of Mount Union
University of Northwestern Ohio
University of Rio Grande
University of Toledo
Ursuline College
Walsh University
Wilmington College
Wittenberg University
Wright State University
Wright State University: Lake Campus
Xavier University
Youngstown State University

Oklahoma

Cameron University
Carl Albert State College
Connors State College
East Central University
Langston University
Mid-America Christian University
Northeastern Oklahoma Agricultural and Mechanical College
Northeastern State University
Northwestern Oklahoma State University
Oklahoma Baptist University
Oklahoma Christian University
Oklahoma City Community College
Oklahoma City University
Oklahoma Panhandle State University
Oklahoma State University
Oklahoma State University
Oklahoma City
Oklahoma Wesleyan University
Oral Roberts University
Redlands Community College
Rogers State University
Rose State College
St. Gregory's University
Seminole State College
Southeastern Oklahoma State University
Southern Nazarene University
Southwestern Christian University
Southwestern Oklahoma State University
Tulsa Community College
University of Central Oklahoma
University of Oklahoma
University of Science and Arts of Oklahoma
University of Tulsa
Western Oklahoma State College

Oregon

Central Oregon Community College
Chemeketa Community College
Clackamas Community College
Clatsop Community College
Concordia University
Corban University
Eastern Oregon University
George Fox University
Lewis & Clark College
Linfield College
Linn-Benton Community College
Marylhurst University
Mt. Hood Community College
Multnomah University
New Hope Christian College
Northwest Christian University
Oregon College of Art & Craft
Oregon Institute of Technology
Oregon State University
Pacific Northwest College of Art
Pacific University
Portland State University
Southern Oregon University
Treasure Valley Community College
Umpqua Community College
University of Oregon
University of Portland
Warner Pacific College
Western Oregon University
Willamette University

Pennsylvania

Albright College
Allegheny College
Alvernia University
Arcadia University
Baptist Bible College of Pennsylvania
Bloomsburg University of Pennsylvania
Bryn Athyn College
Bryn Mawr College
Bucknell University
Bucks County Community College
Butler County Community College
Cabrini College
Cairn University
California University of Pennsylvania
Cambria-Rowe Business College
Cambria-Rowe Business College: Indiana
Carnegie Mellon University
Cedar Crest College
Central Penn College
Chatham University
Chestnut Hill College
Cheyney University of Pennsylvania
Clarion University of Pennsylvania
Community College of Allegheny County
Community College of Beaver County
Consolidated School of Business
Lancaster
York
Delaware County Community College
Delaware Valley College
DeSales University
DeVry University
Fort Washington
Dickinson College
Drexel University
Duquesne University
East Stroudsburg University of Pennsylvania
Eastern University
Edinboro University of Pennsylvania
Elizabethtown College
Gannon University
Geneva College
Gettysburg College
Grove City College
Gwynedd-Mercy College
Harcum College
Harrisburg Area Community College
Harrisburg University of Science and Technology
Holy Family University
Immaculata University
Indiana University of Pennsylvania
Juniata College
Keystone College
King's College
Kutztown University of Pennsylvania
La Roche College
La Salle University
Lackawanna College
Lafayette College
Lancaster Bible College
Laurel Technical Institute
Lebanon Valley College
Lehigh Carbon Community College
Lehigh University
Lincoln University
Lock Haven University of Pennsylvania
Lycoming College
Manor College
Mansfield University of Pennsylvania
Marywood University
Mercyhurst University
Messiah College
Millersville University of Pennsylvania
Misericordia University
Montgomery County Community College
Moore College of Art and Design
Moravian College
Mount Aloysius College
Muhlenberg College
Newport Business Institute: Lower Burrell
Northampton Community College
Peirce College
Penn State
Abington
Altoona
Beaver
Berks
Brandywine
DuBois
Erie, The Behrend College
Fayette, The Eberly Campus
Greater Allegheny
Harrisburg
Hazleton
Lehigh Valley
Mont Alto
New Kensington
Schuylkill
Shenango
University Park
Wilkes-Barre
Worthington Scranton
York
Pennsylvania Academy of the Fine Arts
Pennsylvania College of Technology
Pennsylvania Highlands Community College
Pennsylvania Institute of Technology
Philadelphia University
Point Park University
Robert Morris University
Rosemont College
St. Francis University
Saint Joseph's University
St. Vincent College
Seton Hill University
Shippensburg University of Pennsylvania
Slippery Rock University of Pennsylvania
Susquehanna University
Swarthmore College
Temple University
Thiel College
Thomas Jefferson University: College of Health Professions
Triangle Tech
DuBois
Pittsburgh
University of Pittsburgh
University of Pittsburgh
Bradford
Greensburg
Johnstown
Titusville
University of Scranton
University of the Arts
University of the Sciences in Philadelphia
Ursinus College
Valley Forge Christian College
Valley Forge Military Academy and College
Vet Tech Institute
Villanova University
Washington & Jefferson College
Waynesburg University
West Chester University of Pennsylvania
Westminster College
Westmoreland County Community College
Widener University
Wilkes University
Wilson College
York College of Pennsylvania

Puerto Rico
Inter American University of Puerto Rico
Aguadilla Campus
Arecibo Campus
Bayamon Campus
San German Campus
Pontifical Catholic University of Puerto Rico
Turabo University
Universidad del Este
Universidad Metropolitana
Universidad Pentecostal Mizpa
Universidad Politecnica de Puerto Rico
University of Puerto Rico
Bayamon University College
Cayey University College
Humacao
Mayaguez
Utuado
University of the Sacred Heart

Rhode Island
Bryant University
Johnson & Wales University
Providence
New England Institute of Technology
Providence College
Rhode Island College
Rhode Island School of Design
Roger Williams University
Salve Regina University
University of Rhode Island

South Carolina
Aiken Technical College
Allen University
Anderson University
Charleston Southern University
The Citadel
Clemson University
Coastal Carolina University
Coker College
College of Charleston
Columbia College
Columbia International University
Converse College
Erskine College
Florence-Darlington Technical College
Francis Marion University
Furman University
Greenville Technical College
Horry-Georgetown Technical College
Lander University
Limestone College
Medical University of South Carolina
Morris College
Newberry College
North Greenville University
Piedmont Technical College
Presbyterian College
South Carolina State University
Spartanburg Community College
Spartanburg Methodist College
Tri-County Technical College
Trident Technical College
University of South Carolina
Aiken
Beaufort
Columbia
Salkehatchie
Sumter
Union
Upstate
Williamsburg Technical College
Winthrop University
Wofford College
York Technical College

South Dakota
Augustana College
Black Hills State University
Dakota State University
Kilian Community College
Mount Marty College
Northern State University
South Dakota School of Mines and Technology
South Dakota State University
Southeast Technical Institute
University of Sioux Falls
University of South Dakota

Tennessee
Aquinas College
Austin Peay State University
Belmont University
Bethel University
Bryan University
Dayton
Carson-Newman University
Christian Brothers University
Columbia State Community College
Cumberland University
Dyersburg State Community College
East Tennessee State University
Fisk University
Freed-Hardeman University
Jackson State Community College
Johnson University
King College
Lane College
Lee University
LeMoyne-Owen College
Lincoln Memorial University
Lipscomb University
Martin Methodist College
Maryville College
Memphis College of Art
Middle Tennessee State University
Milligan College
Motlow State Community College
Nashville State Community College
National College of Business and Technology
Bristol
Nashville
Northeast State Community College
O'More College of Design
Pellissippi State Community College
Rhodes College
Roane State Community College
Sewanee: The University of the South
Southern Adventist University
Southwest Tennessee Community College
Tennessee State University
Tennessee Technological University
Tennessee Wesleyan College
Trevecca Nazarene University
Tusculum College
Union University
University of Memphis
University of Tennessee
Chattanooga
Knoxville
Martin
Vanderbilt University
Volunteer State Community College
Walters State Community College
Watkins College of Art, Design & Film
Welch College

Texas
Abilene Christian University
Alvin Community College
Amarillo College
Angelina College
Angelo State University
Arlington Baptist College
Austin College
Baylor University
Brazosport College
Brookhaven College
Central Texas College
Clarendon College
Coastal Bend College
College of the Mainland
Collin County Community College District
Commonwealth Institute of Funeral Service
Concordia University Texas
Dallas Baptist University
East Texas Baptist University
El Paso Community College
Frank Phillips College
Galveston College
Hardin-Simmons University
Hill College
Houston Baptist University
Howard College
Howard Payne University
Huston-Tillotson University
Jacksonville College
Jarvis Christian College
Kilgore College
Lee College
LeTourneau University
Lone Star College System
Lubbock Christian University
McMurry University
Midland College
Midwestern State University
North Central Texas College
North Lake College
Northwest Vista College
Northwood University
Texas
Odessa College
Our Lady of the Lake University of San Antonio
Palo Alto College
Panola College
Paul Quinn College
Prairie View A&M University
Rice University
St. Edward's University
St. Mary's University
Sam Houston State University
San Jacinto College
South Plains College
South Texas College
Southern Methodist University
Southwestern Adventist University
Southwestern Christian College
Southwestern University
Stephen F. Austin State University
Tarleton State University
Tarrant County College
Texarkana College
Texas A&M International University
Texas A&M University
Texas A&M University
Baylor College of Dentistry
Commerce
Corpus Christi
Galveston
Kingsville
Texarkana
Texas Christian University
Texas College
Texas Lutheran University
Texas Southern University
Texas State Technical College
Waco
West Texas
Texas State University: San Marcos
Texas Tech University
Texas Tech University Health Sciences Center
Texas Wesleyan University
Trinity University
Trinity Valley Community College
University of Dallas
University of Houston
University of Houston
Clear Lake
Downtown
Victoria
University of Mary Hardin-Baylor
University of St. Thomas
University of Texas
Arlington
Austin
Brownsville - Texas Southmost College
Dallas
El Paso
Medical Branch at Galveston
Pan American
the Permian Basin
San Antonio
Tyler
University of the Incarnate Word
Vernon College
Victoria College
Wayland Baptist University
West Coast University: Dallas
West Texas A&M University
Western Texas College
Wharton County Junior College

Utah
Brigham Young University
Dixie State College
LDS Business College
Neumont University
Salt Lake Community College
Snow College
Southern Utah University
University of Utah
Utah State University
Utah Valley University
Weber State University
Western Governors University
Westminster College

Vermont
Bennington College
Burlington College
Castleton State College
Champlain College
College of St. Joseph in Vermont
Goddard College
Green Mountain College
Johnson State College
Landmark College
Lyndon State College
Marlboro College
New England Culinary Institute
Norwich University
Saint Michael's College
Southern Vermont College
Sterling College
University of Vermont
Vermont Technical College

Virginia
Averett University
Blue Ridge Community College
Bluefield College
Bridgewater College
Bryant & Stratton College
Richmond
Central Virginia Community College
Christendom College
Christopher Newport University
College of William and Mary
DeVry University
Arlington
Eastern Mennonite University
ECPI University
Emory & Henry College
Ferrum College
George Mason University
Germanna Community College
Hampden-Sydney College
Hampton University
Hollins University
J. Sargeant Reynolds Community College
James Madison University
Jefferson College of Health Sciences
John Tyler Community College
Liberty University
Longwood University
Lynchburg College
Mary Baldwin College
Marymount University
Mountain Empire Community College

National College
Charlottesville
Danville
Harrisonburg
Lynchburg
Martinsville
Norfolk State University
Northern Virginia Community College
Old Dominion University
Patrick Henry College
Piedmont Virginia Community College
Radford University
Randolph College
Randolph-Macon College
Regent University
Richard Bland College
Roanoke College
St. Paul's College
Shenandoah University
Southern Virginia University
Southside Virginia Community College
Southwest Virginia Community College
Stratford University: Falls Church
Sweet Briar College
University of Mary Washington
University of Richmond
University of Virginia
University of Virginia's College at Wise
Virginia Commonwealth University
Virginia Intermont College
Virginia Military Institute
Virginia Polytechnic Institute and State University
Virginia State University
Virginia Union University
Virginia Wesleyan College
Virginia Western Community College
Washington and Lee University
Wytheville Community College

Washington
Art Institute of Seattle
Bastyr University
Bellevue College
Big Bend Community College
Centralia College
City University of Seattle
Clark College
Clover Park Technical College
Columbia Basin College
Cornish College of the Arts
DeVry University
Federal Way
DigiPen Institute of Technology
Eastern Washington University
Everett Community College
Evergreen State College
Gonzaga University
Grays Harbor College
Heritage University
Northwest College of Art & Design
Northwest Indian College
Northwest University
Olympic College
Pacific Lutheran University
Peninsula College
Pierce College
Saint Martin's University
Seattle Pacific University
Skagit Valley College
South Puget Sound Community College
South Seattle Community College
Tacoma Community College
Trinity Lutheran College
University of Puget Sound
University of Washington
University of Washington Bothell
University of Washington Tacoma
Walla Walla Community College
Walla Walla University
Washington State University
Wenatchee Valley College
Western Washington University
Whatcom Community College
Whitman College
Whitworth University

West Virginia
Alderson-Broaddus College
Bluefield State College
Concord University
Davis and Elkins College
Fairmont State University
Glenville State College
Kanawha Valley Community and Technical College
Marshall University
National College
Princeton
Ohio Valley University
Potomac State College of West Virginia University
Salem International University
Shepherd University
University of Charleston
West Liberty University
West Virginia State University
West Virginia University
West Virginia University at Parkersburg
West Virginia University Institute of Technology
West Virginia Wesleyan College
Wheeling Jesuit University

Wisconsin
Alverno College
Beloit College
Cardinal Stritch University
Carroll University
Carthage College
College of Menominee Nation
Columbia College of Nursing
Concordia University Wisconsin
Edgewood College
Lakeland College
Lakeshore Technical College
Lawrence University
Maranatha Baptist Bible College
Marian University
Marquette University
Mid-State Technical College
Milwaukee Area Technical College
Milwaukee Institute of Art & Design
Milwaukee School of Engineering
Moraine Park Technical College
Mount Mary College
Northland College
Northland International University
Ripon College
St. Norbert College
Silver Lake College of the Holy Family
University of Wisconsin
Baraboo/Sauk County
Eau Claire
Fond du Lac
Fox Valley
Green Bay
La Crosse
Madison
Marshfield/Wood County
Milwaukee
Oshkosh
Parkside
Richland
River Falls
Rock County
Sheboygan
Stevens Point
Stout
Superior
Washington County
Waukesha
Whitewater
Viterbo University
Waukesha County Technical College
Wisconsin Lutheran College

Wyoming
Casper College
Central Wyoming College
Eastern Wyoming College
Laramie County Community College
Northwest College
Sheridan College
University of Wyoming
Western Wyoming Community College

Art scholarships

Alabama
Alabama State University
Athens State University
Auburn University at Montgomery
Birmingham-Southern College
Chattahoochee Valley Community College
Enterprise State Community College
Faulkner State Community College
Gadsden State Community College
Jacksonville State University
Jefferson State Community College
Judson College
Northeast Alabama Community College
Northwest-Shoals Community College
Samford University
Selma University
Snead State Community College
Spring Hill College
Talladega College
Troy University
University of Alabama
University of Alabama
 Birmingham
 Huntsville
University of Montevallo
University of North Alabama
University of South Alabama
University of West Alabama

Alaska
Alaska Pacific University
University of Alaska
 Fairbanks

Arizona
Arizona State University
Arizona Western College
Eastern Arizona College
Glendale Community College
Grand Canyon University
Northern Arizona University
Northland Pioneer College
Pima Community College
University of Advancing Technology
University of Arizona

Arkansas
Arkansas Northeastern College
Arkansas State University
Harding University
Henderson State University
Hendrix College
John Brown University
Lyon College
Ouachita Baptist University
Southern Arkansas University
University of Arkansas
University of Arkansas
 Little Rock
 Pine Bluff
University of Central Arkansas
University of the Ozarks
Williams Baptist College

California
Academy of Art University
Art Institute of California
 Orange County
Biola University
California Baptist University
California College of the Arts
California Institute of Integral Studies
California Institute of the Arts
California Lutheran University
California Polytechnic State University: San Luis Obispo
California State University
 Bakersfield
 Chico
 Dominguez Hills
 Fresno
 Long Beach
 Stanislaus
Chapman University
College of the Canyons
College of the Desert
College of the Siskiyous
El Camino College
Irvine Valley College
La Sierra University
Loyola Marymount University
Marymount California University
The Master's College
Notre Dame de Namur University
Otis College of Art and Design
Pacific Union College
Pepperdine University
Point Loma Nazarene University
Riverside Community College
St. Mary's College of California
San Diego State University
San Francisco Art Institute
San Jose State University
Santa Rosa Junior College
Sonoma State University
University of California
 Riverside
 San Diego
 Santa Cruz
University of La Verne
University of Redlands
University of Southern California
Westmont College
Whittier College
William Jessup University

Colorado
Adams State College
Colorado Mesa University
Colorado State University
Colorado State University
 Pueblo
Fort Lewis College
Naropa University
Northeastern Junior College
Pueblo Community College
Rocky Mountain College of Art & Design
University of Colorado
 Boulder
University of Denver
University of Northern Colorado
Western State Colorado University

Connecticut
Albertus Magnus College
Fairfield University
Lyme Academy College of Fine Arts
Mitchell College
Sacred Heart University
University of Bridgeport
University of Connecticut
University of Hartford

Delaware
Delaware College of Art and Design
University of Delaware

District of Columbia
Gallaudet University
George Washington University
Howard University

Florida
Barry University
Chipola College
Digital Media Arts College
Eckerd College
Edison State College
Flagler College
Florida Agricultural and Mechanical University
Florida International University
Florida Keys Community College
Florida Southern College
Florida State College at Jacksonville
Hillsborough Community College
Jacksonville University
Miami Dade College
North Florida Community College
Palm Beach Atlantic University
Ringling College of Art and Design
Rollins College
St. Petersburg College
Santa Fe College
Seminole State College of Florida
State College of Florida, Manatee-Sarasota
Stetson University
Tallahassee Community College
University of Florida
University of South Florida
University of Tampa
University of West Florida
Warner University

Georgia
Albany State University
Andrew College
Armstrong Atlantic State University
Berry College
Brenau University
Clark Atlanta University
Columbus State University
Covenant College
Darton College
Emmanuel College
Emory University
Georgia College and State University
Georgia Highlands College
Georgia Southern University
Georgia State University
Kennesaw State University
LaGrange College
Mercer University
Middle Georgia State College
Morehouse College
Piedmont College
Reinhardt University
Savannah College of Art and Design
Shorter University
University of North Georgia
University of West Georgia
Valdosta State University
Wesleyan College
Young Harris College

Hawaii
Brigham Young University-Hawaii
Chaminade University of Honolulu
University of Hawaii
 Manoa

Idaho
Brigham Young University-Idaho
College of Idaho
Idaho State University
Lewis-Clark State College
North Idaho College
Northwest Nazarene University
University of Idaho

Illinois
American Academy of Art
Augustana College
Aurora University
Black Hawk College
Bradley University
Carl Sandburg College
College of DuPage
College of Lake County
Columbia College Chicago
Danville Area Community College
DePaul University
Dominican University
Eastern Illinois University
Elgin Community College
Elmhurst College
Eureka College
Greenville College
Harper College
Illinois College
Illinois State University
Illinois Valley Community College
Illinois Wesleyan University
Judson University
Knox College
Lake Forest College
Lewis University
Lincoln College
McKendree University
Millikin University
Monmouth College
Moraine Valley Community College
North Central College
North Park University
Northeastern Illinois University
Northern Illinois University
Oakton Community College
Olivet Nazarene University
Parkland College
Quincy University
Rend Lake College
Richland Community College
Robert Morris University: Chicago
School of the Art Institute of Chicago
Shawnee Community College
South Suburban College of Cook County
Southeastern Illinois College
Southern Illinois University Carbondale
Southern Illinois University Edwardsville
Spoon River College
University of Illinois
 Chicago
 Springfield
 Urbana-Champaign
University of St. Francis
Waubonsee Community College
Western Illinois University
Wheaton College

Indiana
Anderson University
Bethel College
Franklin College
Goshen College
Grace College
Hanover College
Huntington University
Indiana State University
Indiana University
 Bloomington
 Purdue University Fort Wayne
 Southeast
Indiana Wesleyan University
Marian University
Oakland City University
St. Mary-of-the-Woods College
Saint Mary's College
Taylor University
University of Evansville
University of Indianapolis
University of St. Francis
University of Southern Indiana
Valparaiso University
Vincennes University
Wabash College

Iowa
Ashford University
Briar Cliff University
Buena Vista University
Central College
Clarke University
Coe College
Cornell College
Dordt College
Drake University

Ellsworth Community College
Graceland University
Grand View University
Iowa Central Community College
Iowa State University
Iowa Wesleyan College
Kirkwood Community College
Luther College
Morningside College
Mount Mercy University
North Iowa Area Community College
Northwestern College
St. Ambrose University
Simpson College
Southeastern Community College
University of Iowa
University of Northern Iowa

Kansas
Allen County Community College
Baker University
Benedictine College
Bethel College
Butler Community College
Coffeyville Community College
Cowley County Community College
Emporia State University
Fort Hays State University
Friends University
Garden City Community College
Hesston College
Highland Community College
Kansas City Kansas Community College
Kansas State University
Kansas Wesleyan University
McPherson College
Neosho County Community College
Newman University
Pittsburg State University
Pratt Community College
Sterling College
University of Kansas
University of St. Mary
Washburn University
Wichita State University

Kentucky
Asbury University
Bellarmine University
Brescia University
Campbellsville University
Eastern Kentucky University
Georgetown College
Kentucky State University
Kentucky Wesleyan College
Midway College
Morehead State University
Murray State University
Northern Kentucky University
Sullivan College of Technology and Design
Thomas More College
Transylvania University
University of Kentucky
University of Louisville
Western Kentucky University

Louisiana
Centenary College of Louisiana
Dillard University
Grambling State University
Louisiana College
Louisiana Tech University
Loyola University New Orleans
McNeese State University
Northwestern State University
University of Louisiana at Monroe

Maine
Maine College of Art
University of Maine
University of Maine
 Machias
 Presque Isle
York County Community College

Maryland
Bowie State University
Carroll Community College
Chesapeake College
Goucher College
Maryland Institute College of Art
Montgomery College
Mount St. Mary's University
Notre Dame of Maryland University
Salisbury University
Stevenson University
Towson University
University of Maryland
 Baltimore County
 College Park
 Eastern Shore

Massachusetts
Bay State College
Boston Architectural College
Boston University
Bristol Community College
Cape Cod Community College
Dean College
Endicott College
Gordon College
Holyoke Community College
Lesley University
Massachusetts College of Art and Design
Massachusetts College of Liberal Arts
Montserrat College of Art
School of the Museum of Fine Arts
University of Massachusetts
 Amherst
 Lowell

Michigan
Adrian College
Albion College
Alma College
Alpena Community College
Aquinas College
Calvin College
College for Creative Studies
Concordia University
Eastern Michigan University
Ferris State University
Glen Oaks Community College
Gogebic Community College
Grand Valley State University
Hillsdale College
Hope College
Jackson Community College
Kalamazoo College
Kellogg Community College
Lawrence Technological University
Madonna University
Marygrove College
Michigan State University
Michigan Technological University
Mid Michigan Community College
Monroe County Community College
Mott Community College
Northern Michigan University
Northwestern Michigan College
Oakland University
Olivet College
Saginaw Valley State University
Siena Heights University
Southwestern Michigan College
Spring Arbor University
University of Michigan
University of Michigan
 Flint
Wayne State University
Western Michigan University

Minnesota
Bemidji State University
Bethany Lutheran College
Bethel University
College of St. Benedict
College of Visual Arts
Concordia College: Moorhead
Concordia University St. Paul
Gustavus Adolphus College
Hamline University
Minneapolis College of Art and Design
Minnesota State Community and Technical College
Minnesota State University
 Mankato
 Moorhead
Normandale Community College
North Hennepin Community College
Riverland Community College
Saint Cloud State University
St. John's University
St. Mary's University of Minnesota
St. Olaf College
Southwest Minnesota State University
University of Minnesota
 Duluth
 Twin Cities
Winona State University

Mississippi
Belhaven University
Blue Mountain College
Copiah-Lincoln Community College
Delta State University
East Mississippi Community College
Hinds Community College
Itawamba Community College
Meridian Community College
Millsaps College
Mississippi College
Mississippi State University
Tougaloo College
University of Mississippi

Missouri
Avila University
College of the Ozarks
Columbia College
Cottey College
Crowder College
Culver-Stockton College
Drury University
East Central College
Evangel University
Fontbonne University
Hannibal-LaGrange University
Harris-Stowe State University
Jefferson College
Kansas City Art Institute
Lincoln University
Lindenwood University
Maryville University of Saint Louis
Mineral Area College
Missouri Southern State University
Missouri State University
Missouri Western State University
Moberly Area Community College
Northwest Missouri State University
Park University
St. Charles Community College
Saint Louis University
Southeast Missouri State University
Southwest Baptist University
State Fair Community College
Truman State University
University of Central Missouri
University of Missouri
 Columbia
 Kansas City
 St. Louis
Webster University
William Woods University

Montana
Carroll College
Dawson Community College
Montana State University
Montana State University
 Billings
University of Great Falls
University of Montana: Western

Nebraska
Central Community College
Chadron State College
Concordia University
Creative Center
Creighton University
Doane College
Hastings College
Mid-Plains Community College
Nebraska Wesleyan University
Peru State College
University of Nebraska
 Kearney
 Lincoln
 Omaha
Wayne State College
Western Nebraska Community College

Nevada
Truckee Meadows Community College
University of Nevada
 Reno

New Hampshire
Colby-Sawyer College
Keene State College
New England College
Plymouth State University
University of New Hampshire

New Jersey
Caldwell College
Centenary College
The College of New Jersey
College of St. Elizabeth
Drew University
Georgian Court University
Kean University
Monmouth University
Montclair State University
Richard Stockton College of New Jersey
Rowan University
Rutgers, The State University of New Jersey
 Camden Campus
 New Brunswick/Piscataway Campus
 Newark Campus
Union County College

New Mexico
Eastern New Mexico University
Institute of American Indian Arts
New Mexico Highlands University
New Mexico Junior College
Santa Fe University of Art and Design
University of New Mexico
Western New Mexico University

New York
Adelphi University
Alfred University
Canisius College
City University of New York
 Brooklyn College
 City College
 College of Staten Island
College of New Rochelle
College of Saint Rose
Daemen College
Hartwick College
Hobart and William Smith Colleges
Hofstra University
Houghton College
Jamestown Community College
Long Island University
 Brooklyn Campus
 C. W. Post Campus
Manhattanville College
Marymount Manhattan College
Mohawk Valley Community College
Molloy College
Nazareth College

Parsons The New School for Design
Rensselaer Polytechnic Institute
Roberts Wesleyan College
Rochester Institute of Technology
St. John's University
Sarah Lawrence College
School of Visual Arts
Suffolk County Community College
SUNY
  College at Brockport
  College at Cortland
  College at Fredonia
  College at Geneseo
  College at New Paltz
  College at Plattsburgh
  College at Potsdam
  College at Purchase
  University at Binghamton
  University at Stony Brook
Syracuse University
University of Rochester
Villa Maria College of Buffalo

North Carolina
Appalachian State University
Barton College
Brevard College
College of the Albemarle
Davidson College
East Carolina University
Elon University
Greensboro College
High Point University
Louisburg College
Meredith College
Mount Olive College
North Carolina Central University
Queens University of Charlotte
St. Andrews University
St. Augustine's University
University of North Carolina
  Asheville
  Chapel Hill
  Greensboro
  Pembroke
  School of the Arts
  Wilmington
Wake Forest University
Warren Wilson College
Western Carolina University
Wilkes Community College
Wingate University

North Dakota
Dickinson State University
Jamestown College
Minot State University
North Dakota State University
Trinity Bible College
University of North Dakota

Ohio
Art Institute of Cincinnati
Ashland University
Baldwin Wallace University
Bluffton University
Bowling Green State University
Bowling Green State University: Firelands College
Capital University
Case Western Reserve University
Central State University
Cleveland Institute of Art
Cleveland State University
College of Mount St. Joseph
Columbus College of Art and Design
Cuyahoga Community College
  Metropolitan
Denison University
Edison State Community College
Heidelberg University
Kent State University
Kent State University
  Ashtabula
  East Liverpool
  Geauga
  Salem
  Stark
  Trumbull
  Tuscarawas
Kenyon College
Lake Erie College
Lakeland Community College
Lourdes University
Marietta College
Miami University
  Oxford
Muskingum University
Ohio Northern University
Ohio State University
  Agricultural Technical Institute
  Columbus Campus
  Lima Campus
  Mansfield Campus
  Marion Campus
  Newark Campus
Ohio University
Ohio Wesleyan University
Otterbein University
Pontifical College Josephinum
School of Advertising Art
Southern State Community College
University of Akron
University of Akron: Wayne College
University of Cincinnati
University of Dayton
University of Mount Union
University of Toledo
Ursuline College
Wittenberg University
Wright State University
Wright State University: Lake Campus
Xavier University

Oklahoma
Cameron University
Carl Albert State College
Northeastern State University
Northwestern Oklahoma State University
Oklahoma Baptist University
Oklahoma Christian University
Oklahoma City Community College
Oklahoma City University
Oklahoma Panhandle State University
Oklahoma State University
Oral Roberts University
Rogers State University
St. Gregory's University
Southeastern Oklahoma State University
Southwestern Oklahoma State University
Tulsa Community College
University of Central Oklahoma
University of Oklahoma
University of Science and Arts of Oklahoma
Western Oklahoma State College

Oregon
Art Institute of Portland
Clackamas Community College
Eastern Oregon University
George Fox University
Lane Community College
Linn-Benton Community College
New Hope Christian College
Oregon College of Art & Craft
Pacific Northwest College of Art
Pacific University
Portland State University
Southern Oregon University
Southwestern Oregon Community College
Western Oregon University

Pennsylvania
Albright College
Arcadia University
Bloomsburg University of Pennsylvania
Bucknell University
Bucks County Community College
Carnegie Mellon University
Cedar Crest College
Chatham University
Clarion University of Pennsylvania
DeSales University
Drexel University
East Stroudsburg University of Pennsylvania
Edinboro University of Pennsylvania
Elizabethtown College
Harrisburg Area Community College
Immaculata University
Indiana University of Pennsylvania
Juniata College
Keystone College
Kutztown University of Pennsylvania
Lehigh University
Lock Haven University of Pennsylvania
Lycoming College
Manor College
Mansfield University of Pennsylvania
Marywood University
Mercyhurst University
Messiah College
Moore College of Art and Design
Mount Aloysius College
Muhlenberg College
Northampton Community College
Oakbridge Academy of Arts
Pennsylvania Academy of the Fine Arts
Rosemont College
Saint Joseph's University
Seton Hill University
Slippery Rock University of Pennsylvania
Temple University
University of the Arts
Ursinus College
West Chester University of Pennsylvania

Puerto Rico
Colegio de Cinematografía, Artes y Televisión
Humacao Community College
University of Puerto Rico
  Mayaguez

Rhode Island
Rhode Island College
Rhode Island School of Design
Salve Regina University
University of Rhode Island

South Carolina
Anderson University
Clemson University
Coastal Carolina University
Coker College
College of Charleston
Columbia College
Converse College
Furman University
Lander University
Limestone College
Presbyterian College
University of South Carolina
  Aiken
  Beaufort
  Columbia
Winthrop University
Wofford College

South Dakota
Augustana College
Dakota State University
Northern State University
South Dakota State University
University of Sioux Falls
University of South Dakota

Tennessee
Austin Peay State University
Belmont University
Bryan University
  Dayton
Carson-Newman University
Cumberland University
East Tennessee State University
Freed-Hardeman University
Jackson State Community College
King College
Lipscomb University
Martin Methodist College
Maryville College
Memphis College of Art
Middle Tennessee State University
Milligan College
Motlow State Community College
Northeast State Community College
O'More College of Design
Pellissippi State Community College
Rhodes College
Roane State Community College
Southern Adventist University
Tennessee Technological University
Union University
University of Memphis
University of Tennessee
  Chattanooga
  Knoxville
  Martin
Volunteer State Community College
Watkins College of Art, Design & Film
Welch College

Texas
Abilene Christian University
Angelina College
Angelo State University
Austin College
Baylor University
Brazosport College
Clarendon College
College of the Mainland
Collin County Community College District
Galveston College
Hardin-Simmons University
Houston Baptist University
Howard College
Howard Payne University
Huston-Tillotson University
Kilgore College
Lee College
McMurry University
Midwestern State University
Our Lady of the Lake University of San Antonio
Panola College
Rice University
Richland College
Sam Houston State University
San Jacinto College
South Plains College
Southern Methodist University
Southwestern University
Stephen F. Austin State University
Tarleton State University
Temple College
Texas A&M University
Texas A&M University
  Commerce
  Corpus Christi
  Kingsville
Texas Christian University
Texas State University: San Marcos
Texas Tech University
University of Dallas
University of Houston
University of Mary Hardin-Baylor
University of Texas
  Arlington
  Austin
  Brownsville - Texas Southmost College
  El Paso
  Pan American
  the Permian Basin
  San Antonio

Tyler
University of the Incarnate Word
Victoria College
Wayland Baptist University
West Texas A&M University
Western Texas College

Utah
Brigham Young University
Dixie State College
Salt Lake Community College
Southern Utah University
University of Utah
Utah State University
Utah Valley University
Weber State University
Westminster College

Vermont
Goddard College
Green Mountain College
Johnson State College
Landmark College
Saint Michael's College
University of Vermont

Virginia
Averett University
Bluefield College
Christopher Newport University
College of William and Mary
Eastern Mennonite University
Hollins University
James Madison University
Longwood University
Lynchburg College
Old Dominion University
Radford University
Randolph College
Southern Virginia University
Sweet Briar College
University of Mary Washington
University of Richmond
University of Virginia's College at Wise
Virginia Commonwealth University
Virginia Intermont College
Virginia Polytechnic Institute and State University
Virginia State University

Washington
Art Institute of Seattle
Big Bend Community College
Centralia College
Clark College
Cornish College of the Arts
DigiPen Institute of Technology
Eastern Washington University
Everett Community College
Evergreen State College
Grays Harbor College
Northwest College of Art & Design
Northwest University
Pacific Lutheran University
Saint Martin's University
Seattle Pacific University
Trinity Lutheran College
University of Puget Sound
University of Washington
Washington State University
Western Washington University
Whitman College
Whitworth University

West Virginia
Bluefield State College
Concord University
Davis and Elkins College
Fairmont State University
Marshall University
Shepherd University
University of Charleston
West Liberty University
West Virginia University
West Virginia University Institute of Technology
West Virginia Wesleyan College

Wisconsin
Cardinal Stritch University
Carroll University
Carthage College
Concordia University Wisconsin
Edgewood College
Lakeland College
Milwaukee Institute of Art & Design
Mount Mary College
Northland College
Ripon College
St. Norbert College
Silver Lake College of the Holy Family
University of Wisconsin
Baraboo/Sauk County
Eau Claire
Green Bay
La Crosse
Madison
Manitowoc
Milwaukee
Oshkosh
Parkside
Richland
River Falls
Stevens Point
Superior
Waukesha
Whitewater
Viterbo University
Wisconsin Lutheran College

Wyoming
Casper College
Central Wyoming College
Eastern Wyoming College
Laramie County Community College
Northwest College
Sheridan College
University of Wyoming
Western Wyoming Community College

Athletic scholarships

Archery

Arizona
Dine College M,W

California
College of the Redwoods M

Kentucky
University of the Cumberlands M,W

Texas
Texas A&M University W

Badminton

California
Fresno City College M,W

New Jersey
New Jersey Institute of Technology M

Wisconsin
Milwaukee Area Technical College M

Baseball

Alabama
Alabama Agricultural and Mechanical University M
Alabama State University M
Auburn University M
Auburn University at Montgomery M
Central Alabama Community College M
Chattahoochee Valley Community College M
Enterprise State Community College M
Faulkner State Community College M
Gadsden State Community College M
George C. Wallace Community College at Dothan M
George C. Wallace State Community College at Selma M
Jacksonville State University M
Jefferson Davis Community College M
Lawson State Community College M
Lurleen B. Wallace Community College M
Marion Military Institute M
Miles College M
Samford University M
Selma University M
Shelton State Community College M
Snead State Community College M
Southern Union State Community College M
Spring Hill College M
Troy University M
Tuskegee University M
University of Alabama M
University of Alabama
Birmingham M
Huntsville M
University of Mobile M
University of Montevallo M
University of North Alabama M
University of South Alabama M
University of West Alabama M
Wallace State Community College at Hanceville M

Arizona
Arizona Christian University M
Arizona State University M
Arizona Western College M
Central Arizona College M
Chandler-Gilbert Community College M
Cochise College M
Eastern Arizona College M
GateWay Community College M
Glendale Community College M
Grand Canyon University M
Mesa Community College M
Paradise Valley Community College M
Pima Community College M
Scottsdale Community College M
South Mountain Community College M
University of Arizona M
Yavapai College M

Arkansas
Arkansas State University M
Arkansas Tech University M
Crowley's Ridge College M
Ecclesia College M
Harding University M
Henderson State University M
Lyon College M
North Arkansas College M
Ouachita Baptist University M
Southern Arkansas University M
University of Arkansas M
University of Arkansas
Fort Smith M
Little Rock M
Pine Bluff M
University of Central Arkansas M
Williams Baptist College M

California
Academy of Art University M
Azusa Pacific University M
Biola University M
California Baptist University M
California Polytechnic State University: San Luis Obispo M
California State Polytechnic University: Pomona M
California State University
Chico M
Dominguez Hills M
Fresno M
Fullerton M
Long Beach M
Los Angeles M
Monterey Bay M
Northridge M
Sacramento M
San Bernardino M
Stanislaus M
Concordia University M
Fresno City College M
Fresno Pacific University M
Grossmont College M
Holy Names University M
La Sierra University M
Loyola Marymount University M
The Master's College M
Menlo College M
Patten University M
Pepperdine University M
Point Loma Nazarene University M
St. Mary's College of California M
San Diego Christian College M
San Diego State University M
San Jose State University M
Santa Clara University M
Simpson University M
Sonoma State University M
Stanford University M
University of California
Berkeley M
Davis M
Irvine M
Los Angeles M
Riverside M
Santa Barbara M
University of San Diego M
University of San Francisco M
University of Southern California M
University of the Pacific M
Vanguard University of Southern California M
Westmont College M
Yuba Community College District M

Colorado
Colorado Christian University M
Colorado Mesa University M
Colorado Northwestern Community College M
Colorado School of Mines M
Colorado State University
Pueblo M
Lamar Community College M
Metropolitan State University of Denver M
Northeastern Junior College M
Otero Junior College M
Trinidad State Junior College M
University of Northern Colorado M

Connecticut
Central Connecticut State University M
Fairfield University M
Post University M
Quinnipiac University M
Sacred Heart University M
Southern Connecticut State University M
University of Bridgeport M
University of Connecticut M
University of Hartford M
University of New Haven M

Delaware
Delaware State University M
Delaware Technical and Community College
Owens M
University of Delaware M
Wilmington University M

District of Columbia
George Washington University M
Georgetown University M
Howard University M

Florida
Ave Maria University M
Barry University M
Bethune-Cookman University M
Brevard Community College M
Chipola College M
College of Central Florida M
Daytona State College M
Eckerd College M
Edward Waters College M
Embry-Riddle Aeronautical University M
Flagler College M
Florida Atlantic University M
Florida Gulf Coast University M
Florida Institute of Technology M
Florida Southern College M
Florida State College at Jacksonville M
Florida State University M
Gulf Coast State College M
Hillsborough Community College M
Indian River State College M
Jacksonville University M
Lake-Sumter Community College M
Lynn University M
Miami Dade College M
North Florida Community College M
Northwest Florida State College M
Northwood University
Florida M
Nova Southeastern University M
Palm Beach Atlantic University M
Palm Beach State College M
Pasco-Hernando Community College M
Pensacola State College M
Polk State College M
Rollins College M
Saint Johns River State College M
Saint Leo University M
St. Petersburg College M
Saint Thomas University M
Santa Fe College M
South Florida Community College M
Southeastern University M
State College of Florida, Manatee-Sarasota M
Stetson University M
Tallahassee Community College M
University of Central Florida M
University of Florida M
University of Miami M
University of North Florida M
University of South Florida M
University of Tampa M
University of West Florida M
Warner University M
Webber International University M

Georgia
Abraham Baldwin Agricultural College M
Albany State University M
Andrew College M
Armstrong Atlantic State University M
Brewton-Parker College M
Clark Atlanta University M
Columbus State University M
Darton College M
East Georgia College M
Emmanuel College M
Georgia College and State University M
Georgia Gwinnett College M
Georgia Highlands College M,W
Georgia Institute of Technology M
Georgia Perimeter College M
Georgia Southern University M
Georgia Southwestern State University M
Georgia State University M
Gordon College M
Kennesaw State University M
Mercer University M
Middle Georgia State College M
Morehouse College M
Paine College M
Point University M
Reinhardt University M
Savannah State University M
Shorter University M
Southern Polytechnic State University M
Thomas University M
Truett-McConnell College M
University of Georgia M
University of North Georgia M
University of West Georgia M
Valdosta State University M
Young Harris College M

Hawaii
Hawaii Pacific University M
University of Hawaii
Manoa M

Idaho
College of Idaho M
College of Southern Idaho M
Lewis-Clark State College M
Northwest Nazarene University M

Illinois
Black Hawk College M
Bradley University M
Carl Sandburg College M
Chicago State University M
College of Lake County M
Danville Area Community College M
Eastern Illinois University M
Elgin Community College M

Highland Community College M
Illinois Central College M
Illinois Eastern Community Colleges
- Lincoln Trail College M
- Olney Central College M
- Wabash Valley College M

Illinois Institute of Technology M
Illinois State University M
John A. Logan College M
John Wood Community College M
Judson University M
Kankakee Community College M
Kaskaskia College M
Kishwaukee College M
Lake Land College M
Lewis and Clark Community College M
Lewis University M
Lincoln College M
Lincoln Land Community College M
McHenry County College M
McKendree University M
Moraine Valley Community College M
Morton College M
Northwestern University M
Olivet Nazarene University M
Parkland College M
Quincy University M
Rend Lake College M
Robert Morris University: Chicago M
Saint Xavier University M
Sauk Valley Community College M
South Suburban College of Cook County M
Southeastern Illinois College M
Southern Illinois University Carbondale M
Southern Illinois University Edwardsville M
Southwestern Illinois College M
Spoon River College M
Trinity Christian College M
Trinity International University M
University of Illinois
- Chicago M
- Springfield M
- Urbana-Champaign M

University of St. Francis M
Western Illinois University M

Indiana

Ancilla College M
Ball State University M
Bethel College M
Butler University M
Calumet College of St. Joseph M
Goshen College M
Grace College M
Holy Cross College M
Huntington University M
Indiana Institute of Technology M
Indiana State University M
Indiana University
- Bloomington M
- Purdue University Fort Wayne M
- Southeast M

Indiana Wesleyan University M
Marian University M
Oakland City University M
Purdue University M
Purdue University
- North Central M

Saint Joseph's College M
Taylor University M
University of Evansville M
University of Indianapolis M
University of Notre Dame M
University of St. Francis M
University of Southern Indiana M
Valparaiso University M
Vincennes University M

Iowa

AIB College of Business M
Ashford University M
Briar Cliff University M
Clarke University M
Des Moines Area Community College M
Dordt College M
Ellsworth Community College M
Graceland University M
Grand View University M
Iowa Central Community College M
Iowa Lakes Community College M
Iowa Western Community College M
Kirkwood Community College M
Morningside College M
Mount Mercy University M
Muscatine Community College M
North Iowa Area Community College M
Northwestern College M
St. Ambrose University M
Southeastern Community College M
Southwestern Community College M
University of Iowa M
Waldorf College M
William Penn University M

Kansas

Allen County Community College M
Baker University M
Barton County Community College M
Benedictine College M
Brown Mackie College
- Salina M

Butler Community College M
Central Christian College of Kansas M
Cloud County Community College M
Coffeyville Community College M
Colby Community College M
Cowley County Community College M
Dodge City Community College M
Emporia State University M
Fort Scott Community College M
Friends University M
Garden City Community College M
Hesston College M
Highland Community College M
Hutchinson Community College M
Independence Community College M
Johnson County Community College M
Kansas City Kansas Community College M
Kansas State University M
Kansas Wesleyan University M
Labette Community College M
McPherson College M
MidAmerica Nazarene University M
Neosho County Community College M
Newman University M
Ottawa University M
Pittsburg State University M
Pratt Community College M
Seward County Community College M
Sterling College M
Tabor College M
University of Kansas M
University of St. Mary M
Washburn University M
Wichita State University M

Kentucky

Alice Lloyd College M
Asbury University M
Bellarmine University M
Brescia University M
Campbellsville University M
Eastern Kentucky University M
Georgetown College M
Kentucky State University M
Kentucky Wesleyan College M
Lindsey Wilson College M
Mid-Continent University M
Morehead State University M
Murray State University M
Northern Kentucky University M
St. Catharine College M
Union College M
University of Kentucky M
University of Louisville M
University of Pikeville M
University of the Cumberlands M
Western Kentucky University M

Louisiana

Bossier Parish Community College M
Delgado Community College M
Grambling State University M
Louisiana State University
- Eunice M
- Shreveport M

Louisiana State University and Agricultural and Mechanical College M
Louisiana Tech University M
Loyola University New Orleans M
McNeese State University M
Nicholls State University M
Northwestern State University M
Southeastern Louisiana University M
Southern University and Agricultural and Mechanical College M
Tulane University M
University of Louisiana at Lafayette M
University of Louisiana at Monroe M
University of New Orleans M

Maine

University of Maine M

Maryland

Anne Arundel Community College M
Chesapeake College M
College of Southern Maryland M
Community College of Baltimore County M
Coppin State University M
Garrett College M
Hagerstown Community College M
Harford Community College M
Mount St. Mary's University M
Towson University M
University of Maryland
- Baltimore County M
- College Park M
- Eastern Shore M

Washington Adventist University M

Massachusetts

American International College M
Boston College M
Dean College M
Merrimack College M
Northeastern University M
Stonehill College M
University of Massachusetts
- Amherst M
- Lowell M

Michigan

Aquinas College M
Central Michigan University M
Concordia University M
Davenport University M
Eastern Michigan University M
Glen Oaks Community College M
Hillsdale College M
Kalamazoo Valley Community College M
Kellogg Community College M
Lake Michigan College M
Lansing Community College M
Macomb Community College M
Madonna University M
Michigan State University M
Mott Community College M
Muskegon Community College M
Northwood University
- Michigan M

Oakland University M
Rochester College M
Saginaw Valley State University M
St. Clair County Community College M
Siena Heights University M
Spring Arbor University M
University of Michigan M
Wayne State University M
Western Michigan University M

Minnesota

Concordia University St. Paul M
Minnesota State University
- Mankato M

Saint Cloud State University M
Southwest Minnesota State University M
University of Minnesota
- Crookston M
- Duluth M
- Twin Cities M

Winona State University M

Mississippi

Alcorn State University M
Belhaven University M
Blue Mountain College M
Copiah-Lincoln Community College M
Delta State University M
East Mississippi Community College M
Hinds Community College M
Holmes Community College M
Itawamba Community College M
Jackson State University M
Meridian Community College M
Mississippi Gulf Coast Community College M
Mississippi State University M
Mississippi Valley State University M
Southwest Mississippi Community College M
University of Mississippi M
University of Southern Mississippi M

Missouri

Avila University M
Central Methodist University M
College of the Ozarks M
Crowder College M
Culver-Stockton College M
Drury University M
Evangel University M
Hannibal-LaGrange University M
Harris-Stowe State University M
Jefferson College M
Lincoln University M
Lindenwood University M
Metropolitan Community College - Kansas City M
Mineral Area College M
Missouri Baptist University M
Missouri Southern State University M
Missouri State University M
Missouri University of Science and Technology M
Missouri Valley College M
Missouri Western State University M
North Central Missouri College M
Northwest Missouri State University M
Park University M
Research College of Nursing M
Rockhurst University M
Saint Louis University M
Southeast Missouri State University M
Southwest Baptist University M
Three Rivers Community College M
University of Central Missouri M
University of Missouri
- Columbia M
- St. Louis M

William Jewell College M
William Woods University M

Montana

Miles Community College M
Montana State University
- Billings M

Nebraska

Bellevue University M
Concordia University M
Creighton University M
Doane College M
Hastings College M
Mid-Plains Community College M
Peru State College M

University of Nebraska
Kearney M
Lincoln M
Omaha M
Wayne State College M
Western Nebraska Community College M
York College M

Nevada
College of Southern Nevada M
University of Nevada
Las Vegas M
Reno M

New Hampshire
Franklin Pierce University M
Hesser College M
Southern New Hampshire University M

New Jersey
Bloomfield College M
Brookdale Community College M
Burlington County College M
Caldwell College M
Fairleigh Dickinson University
Metropolitan Campus M
Mercer County Community College M
Monmouth University M
New Jersey Institute of Technology M
Raritan Valley Community College M
Rider University M
Rutgers, The State University of New Jersey
New Brunswick/Piscataway Campus M
Saint Peter's University M
Salem Community College M
Seton Hall University M
Sussex County Community College M

New Mexico
Eastern New Mexico University M
New Mexico Highlands University M
New Mexico Junior College M
New Mexico Military Institute M
New Mexico State University M
University of New Mexico M
University of the Southwest M

New York
Adelphi University M
ASA Institute of Business and Computer Technology M
Canisius College M
City University of New York
Queens College M
College of Saint Rose M
Concordia College M
Dominican College of Blauvelt M
Dowling College M
Fordham University M
Genesee Community College M
Globe Institute of Technology M
Hofstra University M
Iona College M
Le Moyne College M
Long Island University
Brooklyn Campus M
C. W. Post Campus M
Manhattan College M
Marist College M
Mercy College M
Molloy College M
Monroe College M
Monroe Community College M
New York Institute of Technology M
Niagara University M
Nyack College M
Pace University M
Saint Bonaventure University M
St. John's University M
St. Thomas Aquinas College M
Siena College M
SUNY
University at Albany M
University at Binghamton M
University at Buffalo M
University at Stony Brook M
Wagner College M

North Carolina
Appalachian State University M
Barton College M
Belmont Abbey College M
Brevard College M
Campbell University M
Catawba College M
Chowan University M
Davidson College M
Duke University M
East Carolina University M
Elizabeth City State University M
Elon University M
Gardner-Webb University M
Guilford Technical Community College M
High Point University M
Lenoir Community College M
Lenoir-Rhyne University M
Louisburg College M
Mars Hill College M
Montreat College M
Mount Olive College M
North Carolina Agricultural and Technical State University M
North Carolina State University M
Pfeiffer University M
Pitt Community College M
St. Augustine's University M
Shaw University M
Southeastern Community College M
University of North Carolina
Asheville M
Chapel Hill M
Charlotte M
Greensboro M
Wilmington M
Wake Forest University M
Western Carolina University M
Wingate University M

North Dakota
Bismarck State College M
Dakota College at Bottineau M
Dickinson State University M
Jamestown College M
Mayville State University M
Minot State University M
North Dakota State University M
University of Mary M
University of North Dakota M
Valley City State University M
Williston State College M

Ohio
Ashland University M
Bowling Green State University M
Cedarville University M
Clark State Community College M
Kent State University M
Lake Erie College M
Lakeland Community College M
Lourdes University M
Malone University M
Miami University
Oxford M
Mount Vernon Nazarene University M
Notre Dame College M
Ohio Dominican University M
Ohio State University
Columbus Campus M
Ohio University M
Owens Community College
Toledo M
Shawnee State University M
Sinclair Community College M
Tiffin University M
University of Akron M
University of Cincinnati M
University of Dayton M
University of Findlay M
University of Rio Grande M
University of Toledo M
Walsh University M
Wright State University M
Xavier University M
Youngstown State University M

Oklahoma
Bacone College M
Cameron University M
Carl Albert State College M
Connors State College M
East Central University M
Eastern Oklahoma State College M
Mid-America Christian University M
Northeastern Oklahoma Agricultural and Mechanical College M
Northeastern State University M
Northern Oklahoma College M
Northwestern Oklahoma State University M
Oklahoma Baptist University M
Oklahoma Christian University M
Oklahoma City University M
Oklahoma Panhandle State University M
Oklahoma State University M
Oklahoma Wesleyan University M
Oral Roberts University M
Redlands Community College M
Rogers State University M
Rose State College M
St. Gregory's University M
Seminole State College M
Southeastern Oklahoma State University M
Southern Nazarene University M
Southwestern Oklahoma State University M
University of Central Oklahoma M
University of Oklahoma M
University of Science and Arts of Oklahoma M
Western Oklahoma State College M

Oregon
Chemeketa Community College M
Clackamas Community College M
Concordia University M
Corban University M
Lane Community College M
Linn-Benton Community College M
Mt. Hood Community College M
Oregon Institute of Technology M
Oregon State University M
Portland State University M
Southwestern Oregon Community College M
Treasure Valley Community College M
University of Oregon M
University of Portland M

Pennsylvania
Bloomsburg University of Pennsylvania M
California University of Pennsylvania M
Chestnut Hill College M
Clarion University of Pennsylvania M
East Stroudsburg University of Pennsylvania M
Gannon University M
Indiana University of Pennsylvania M
Kutztown University of Pennsylvania M
La Salle University M
Lackawanna College M
Lock Haven University of Pennsylvania M
Mansfield University of Pennsylvania M
Mercyhurst University M
Millersville University of Pennsylvania M
Penn State
University Park M
Philadelphia University M
Point Park University M
Saint Joseph's University M
Seton Hill University M
Shippensburg University of Pennsylvania M
Slippery Rock University of Pennsylvania M
Temple University M
University of Pittsburgh M
University of the Sciences in Philadelphia M
Villanova University M
West Chester University of Pennsylvania M

Puerto Rico
Inter American University of Puerto Rico
Aguadilla Campus M
Bayamon Campus M
Metropolitan Campus M
Ponce Campus M
San German Campus M
Turabo University M
Universidad del Este M
Universidad Metropolitana M
University of Puerto Rico
Carolina Regional College M
Cayey University College M
Humacao M
Mayaguez M
Utuado M

Rhode Island
Bryant University M
Community College of Rhode Island M
University of Rhode Island M

South Carolina
Anderson University M
Charleston Southern University M
The Citadel M
Claflin University M
Clemson University M
Coastal Carolina University M
Coker College M
College of Charleston M
Erskine College M
Francis Marion University M
Furman University M
Lander University M
Limestone College M
Morris College M
Newberry College M
North Greenville University M
Presbyterian College M
Spartanburg Methodist College M
University of South Carolina
Aiken M
Columbia M
Sumter M
Upstate M
Voorhees College M
Winthrop University M
Wofford College M

South Dakota
Augustana College M
Dakota State University M
Mount Marty College M
Northern State University M
South Dakota State University M
University of Sioux Falls M

Tennessee
Austin Peay State University M
Belmont University M
Bethel University M
Bryan University
Dayton M
Carson-Newman University M
Chattanooga State Community College M
Christian Brothers University M
Cleveland State Community College M
Columbia State Community College M
Cumberland University M
Dyersburg State Community College M
East Tennessee State University M
Freed-Hardeman University M
Jackson State Community College M
King College M
Lee University M
LeMoyne-Owen College M
Lincoln Memorial University M
Lipscomb University M
Martin Methodist College M
Middle Tennessee State University M

Milligan College M
Motlow State Community College M
Roane State Community College M
Southwest Tennessee Community College M
Tennessee Technological University M
Tennessee Wesleyan College M
Trevecca Nazarene University M
Tusculum College M
Union University M
University of Memphis M
University of Tennessee
Knoxville M
Martin M
Vanderbilt University M
Volunteer State Community College M
Walters State Community College M

Texas
Abilene Christian University M
Alvin Community College M
Angelina College M
Angelo State University M
Baylor University M
Blinn College M
Brookhaven College M
Clarendon College M
Dallas Baptist University M
El Paso Community College M
Frank Phillips College M
Galveston College M
Grayson County College M
Hill College M
Houston Baptist University M
Howard College M
Jarvis Christian College M
Lamar University M
Laredo Community College M
Lubbock Christian University M
McLennan Community College M
North Central Texas College M
Northeast Texas Community College M
Northwood University
Texas M
Odessa College M
Panola College M
Paris Junior College M
Prairie View A&M University M
Ranger College M
Rice University M
St. Edward's University M
St. Mary's University M
Sam Houston State University M
San Jacinto College M
Stephen F. Austin State University M
Tarleton State University M
Texas A&M University M
Texas A&M University
Corpus Christi M
Kingsville M
Texas Christian University M
Texas Southern University M
Texas State University: San Marcos M
Texas Tech University M
Texas Wesleyan University M
University of Houston M
University of Texas
Arlington M
Austin M
Pan American M
of the Permian Basin M
San Antonio M
University of the Incarnate Word M
Vernon College M
Wayland Baptist University M
Weatherford College M
West Texas A&M University M
Western Texas College M
Wharton County Junior College M
Wiley College M

Utah
Brigham Young University M
Dixie State College M
Salt Lake Community College M
University of Utah M
Utah Valley University M

Virginia
Bluefield College M
College of William and Mary M
George Mason University M
James Madison University M
Liberty University M
Longwood University M
Norfolk State University M
Old Dominion University M
Radford University M
University of Richmond M
University of Virginia M
University of Virginia's College at Wise M
Virginia Commonwealth University M
Virginia Intermont College M
Virginia Military Institute M
Virginia Polytechnic Institute and State University M
Virginia State University M

Washington
Big Bend Community College M
Centralia College M
Columbia Basin College M
Everett Community College M
Gonzaga University M
Grays Harbor College M
Green River Community College M
Lower Columbia College M
Olympic College M
Pierce College M
Saint Martin's University M
Shoreline Community College M
Skagit Valley College M
Spokane Community College M
Tacoma Community College M
University of Washington M
Walla Walla Community College M
Washington State University M
Yakima Valley Community College M

West Virginia
Alderson-Broaddus College M
Bluefield State College M
Concord University M
Davis and Elkins College M
Fairmont State University M
Marshall University M
Ohio Valley University M
Potomac State College of West Virginia University M
Salem International University M
Shepherd University M
University of Charleston M
West Liberty University M
West Virginia State University M
West Virginia University M
West Virginia University Institute of Technology M
West Virginia Wesleyan College M
Wheeling Jesuit University M

Wisconsin
Cardinal Stritch University M
Milwaukee Area Technical College M,W
University of Wisconsin
Milwaukee M
Parkside M
Viterbo University M

Basketball

Alabama
Alabama Agricultural and Mechanical University M,W
Alabama State University M,W
Auburn University M,W
Auburn University at Montgomery M,W
Chattahoochee Valley Community College M,W
Enterprise State Community College M,W
Faulkner State Community College M,W
Faulkner University M,W
Gadsden State Community College M,W
George C. Wallace State Community College at Selma M,W
Jacksonville State University M,W
Jefferson Davis Community College M
Judson College W
Lawson State Community College M,W
Lurleen B. Wallace Community College M,W
Marion Military Institute M
Miles College M,W
Samford University M,W
Shelton State Community College M,W
Snead State Community College M,W
Southern Union State Community College M,W
Spring Hill College M,W
Troy University M,W
Tuskegee University M,W
University of Alabama M,W
University of Alabama
Birmingham M,W
Huntsville M,W
University of Mobile M,W
University of Montevallo M,W
University of North Alabama M,W
University of South Alabama M,W
University of West Alabama M,W
Wallace State Community College at Hanceville M,W

Alaska
University of Alaska
Anchorage M,W
Fairbanks M,W

Arizona
Arizona Christian University M,W
Arizona State University M,W
Arizona Western College M,W
Central Arizona College M,W
Chandler-Gilbert Community College M,W
Cochise College M,W
Eastern Arizona College M,W
Glendale Community College M,W
Grand Canyon University M,W
Mesa Community College M,W
Northern Arizona University M,W
Pima Community College M,W
Scottsdale Community College M,W
South Mountain Community College M,W
University of Arizona M,W
Yavapai College M,W

Arkansas
Arkansas State University M,W
Arkansas Tech University M,W
Crowley's Ridge College M,W
Ecclesia College M,W
Harding University M,W
Henderson State University M,W
John Brown University M,W
Lyon College M,W
North Arkansas College M,W
Ouachita Baptist University M,W
Philander Smith College M,W
Southern Arkansas University M,W
University of Arkansas M,W
University of Arkansas
Fort Smith M,W
Little Rock M,W
Monticello M,W
Pine Bluff M,W
University of Central Arkansas M,W
Williams Baptist College M,W

California
Academy of Art University M,W
Azusa Pacific University M,W
Biola University M,W
California Baptist University M,W
California Polytechnic State University: San Luis Obispo M,W
California State Polytechnic University: Pomona M,W
California State University
Bakersfield M
Chico M,W
Dominguez Hills M,W
Fresno M,W
Fullerton M,W
Long Beach M,W
Los Angeles M,W
Monterey Bay M,W
Northridge M,W
Sacramento M,W
San Bernardino M,W
Stanislaus M,W
Concordia University M,W
Dominican University of California M,W
Fresno City College M,W
Fresno Pacific University M,W
Grossmont College M,W
Holy Names University M,W
Hope International University M,W
Humboldt State University M,W
La Sierra University M,W
Loyola Marymount University M,W
The Master's College M,W
Menlo College M,W
Notre Dame de Namur University M,W
Pepperdine University M,W
Point Loma Nazarene University M,W
St. Mary's College of California M,W
San Diego Christian College M,W
San Diego State University M,W
San Jose State University M,W
Santa Clara University M,W
Simpson University M,W
Sonoma State University M,W
Stanford University M,W
University of California
Berkeley M,W
Davis M,W
Irvine M,W
Los Angeles M,W
Riverside M,W
Santa Barbara M,W
University of San Diego M,W
University of San Francisco M,W
University of Southern California M,W
University of the Pacific M,W
Vanguard University of Southern California M,W
Westmont College M,W
William Jessup University M,W
Yuba Community College District M,W

Colorado
Adams State College M,W
Colorado Christian University M,W
Colorado Mesa University M,W
Colorado Northwestern Community College M,W
Colorado School of Mines M,W
Colorado State University M,W
Colorado State University
Pueblo M,W
Fort Lewis College M,W
Lamar Community College M,W
Metropolitan State University of Denver M,W
Northeastern Junior College M,W
Otero Junior College M,W
Trinidad State Junior College M,W
University of Colorado
Boulder M,W
Colorado Springs M,W
University of Denver M,W
University of Northern Colorado M,W
Western State Colorado University M,W

Connecticut
Central Connecticut State University M,W
Fairfield University M,W

Post University M,W
Quinnipiac University M,W
Sacred Heart University M,W
Southern Connecticut State University M,W
University of Bridgeport M,W
University of Connecticut M,W
University of Hartford M,W
University of New Haven M,W

Delaware
Delaware State University M,W
Delaware Technical and Community College
Stanton/Wilmington M,W
Goldey-Beacom College M,W
University of Delaware M,W
Wilmington University M,W

District of Columbia
American University M,W
George Washington University M,W
Georgetown University M,W
Howard University M,W
University of the District of Columbia M,W

Florida
Ave Maria University M,W
Barry University M,W
Bethune-Cookman University M,W
Brevard Community College M,W
Chipola College M,W
College of Central Florida M,W
Daytona State College M,W
Eckerd College M,W
Edward Waters College M,W
Embry-Riddle Aeronautical University M
Flagler College M,W
Florida Agricultural and Mechanical University M
Florida Atlantic University M,W
Florida College M
Florida Gulf Coast University M,W
Florida Institute of Technology M,W
Florida Southern College M,W
Florida State College at Jacksonville M,W
Florida State University M,W
Gulf Coast State College M,W
Hillsborough Community College M,W
Indian River State College M,W
Jacksonville University M,W
Lynn University M,W
Miami Dade College M,W
North Florida Community College W
Northwest Florida State College M,W
Nova Southeastern University M,W
Palm Beach Atlantic University M,W
Palm Beach State College M,W
Pasco-Hernando Community College M
Pensacola State College M,W
Polk State College M
Rollins College M,W
Saint Leo University M,W
St. Petersburg College M,W
Santa Fe College M,W
Southeastern University M,W
State College of Florida, Manatee-Sarasota M
Stetson University M,W
Tallahassee Community College M,W
University of Central Florida M,W
University of Florida M,W
University of Miami M,W
University of North Florida M,W
University of South Florida M,W
University of Tampa M,W
University of West Florida M,W
Warner University M,W
Webber International University M,W

Georgia
Albany State University M,W
Andrew College W
Armstrong Atlantic State University M,W
Brenau University W
Brewton-Parker College M,W
Clark Atlanta University M,W
Clayton State University M,W
College of Coastal Georgia M,W
Columbus State University M,W
Darton College W
East Georgia College M,W
Emmanuel College M,W
Fort Valley State University M,W
Georgia College and State University M,W
Georgia Highlands College M,W
Georgia Institute of Technology M,W
Georgia Perimeter College M,W
Georgia Southern University M,W
Georgia Southwestern State University M,W
Georgia State University M,W
Gordon College M
Kennesaw State University M,W
Mercer University M,W
Middle Georgia State College M,W
Morehouse College M
Paine College M,W
Point University M,W
Reinhardt University M,W
Savannah State University M,W
Shorter University M,W
Southern Polytechnic State University M,W
Truett-McConnell College M,W
University of Georgia M,W
University of North Georgia M,W
University of West Georgia M,W
Valdosta State University M,W
Young Harris College M,W

Hawaii
Brigham Young University-Hawaii M,W
Chaminade University of Honolulu M
Hawaii Pacific University M,W
University of Hawaii
Hilo M
Manoa M,W

Idaho
Boise State University M,W
College of Idaho M,W
College of Southern Idaho M,W
Idaho State University M,W
Lewis-Clark State College M,W
North Idaho College M,W
Northwest Nazarene University M,W
University of Idaho M,W

Illinois
Black Hawk College M,W
Bradley University M,W
Carl Sandburg College M,W
Chicago State University M,W
College of Lake County M,W
Danville Area Community College M,W
DePaul University M,W
Eastern Illinois University M,W
Elgin Community College M,W
Highland Community College M,W
Illinois Central College M,W
Illinois Eastern Community Colleges
Lincoln Trail College M,W
Olney Central College M,W
Wabash Valley College M,W
Illinois State University M,W
John A. Logan College M,W
John Wood Community College M,W
Judson University M,W
Kankakee Community College M,W
Kaskaskia College M,W
Kishwaukee College M,W
Lake Land College M,W
Lewis and Clark Community College M,W
Lewis University M,W
Lincoln College M,W
Lincoln Land Community College M,W
Loyola University Chicago M,W
McHenry County College M,W
McKendree University M,W
Moraine Valley Community College M,W
Morton College M,W
Northwestern University M,W
Olivet Nazarene University M,W
Parkland College M,W
Quincy University M,W
Rend Lake College M,W
Robert Morris University: Chicago M,W
Saint Xavier University M
Sauk Valley Community College M,W
Shawnee Community College M,W
South Suburban College of Cook County M,W
Southeastern Illinois College M,W
Southern Illinois University Carbondale M,W
Southern Illinois University Edwardsville M,W
Southwestern Illinois College M,W
Trinity Christian College M,W
Trinity International University M,W
University of Illinois
Chicago M,W
Springfield M,W
Urbana-Champaign M,W
University of St. Francis M,W
Waubonsee Community College M,W
Western Illinois University M,W

Indiana
Ancilla College M,W
Ball State University M,W
Bethel College M,W
Butler University M,W
Calumet College of St. Joseph M,W
Goshen College M,W
Grace College M,W
Holy Cross College M,W
Huntington University M,W
Indiana Institute of Technology M,W
Indiana State University M,W
Indiana University
Bloomington M,W
Northwest M,W
Purdue University Fort Wayne M,W
Purdue University Indianapolis M,W
South Bend M,W
Southeast M,W
Indiana Wesleyan University M,W
Marian University M,W
Oakland City University M,W
Purdue University M,W
Purdue University
Calumet M,W
North Central M
Saint Joseph's College M,W
St. Mary-of-the-Woods College W
Taylor University M,W
University of Evansville M,W
University of Indianapolis M,W
University of Notre Dame M,W
University of St. Francis M,W
University of Southern Indiana M,W
Valparaiso University M,W
Vincennes University M,W

Iowa
AIB College of Business M,W
Ashford University M,W
Briar Cliff University M,W
Clarke University M,W
Clinton Community College M
Des Moines Area Community College M,W
Dordt College M,W
Drake University M,W
Ellsworth Community College M,W
Graceland University M,W
Grand View University M,W
Iowa Central Community College M,W
Iowa Lakes Community College M,W
Iowa State University M,W
Iowa Western Community College M,W
Kirkwood Community College M,W
Marshalltown Community College M,W
Morningside College M,W
Mount Mercy University M,W
North Iowa Area Community College M,W
Northwestern College M,W
St. Ambrose University M,W
Southeastern Community College M,W
Southwestern Community College M,W
University of Iowa M,W
University of Northern Iowa M,W
Waldorf College M,W
William Penn University M,W

Kansas
Allen County Community College M,W
Baker University M,W
Barton County Community College M,W
Benedictine College M,W
Bethel College M,W
Brown Mackie College
Salina M,W
Butler Community College M,W
Central Christian College of Kansas M,W
Cloud County Community College M,W
Coffeyville Community College M,W
Colby Community College M,W
Cowley County Community College M,W
Dodge City Community College M,W
Emporia State University M,W
Fort Hays State University M,W
Fort Scott Community College M,W
Friends University M,W
Garden City Community College M,W
Hesston College M,W
Highland Community College M,W
Hutchinson Community College M,W
Independence Community College M,W
Johnson County Community College M,W
Kansas City Kansas Community College M,W
Kansas State University M,W
Kansas Wesleyan University M,W
Labette Community College M,W
McPherson College M,W
MidAmerica Nazarene University M,W
Neosho County Community College M,W
Newman University M,W
Northwest Kansas Technical College M,W
Ottawa University M,W
Pittsburg State University M,W
Pratt Community College M,W
Seward County Community College M,W
Southwestern College M,W
Sterling College M,W
Tabor College M,W
University of Kansas M,W
University of St. Mary M,W
Washburn University M,W
Wichita State University M,W

Kentucky
Alice Lloyd College M,W
Asbury University M,W
Bellarmine University M,W
Brescia University M,W
Campbellsville University M,W
Eastern Kentucky University M,W
Georgetown College M,W
Kentucky State University M,W
Kentucky Wesleyan College M,W
Lindsey Wilson College M,W
Mid-Continent University M,W
Midway College W
Morehead State University M,W
Murray State University M,W
Northern Kentucky University M,W
St. Catharine College M,W
Union College M,W
University of Kentucky M,W
University of Louisville M,W
University of Pikeville M,W
University of the Cumberlands M,W
Western Kentucky University M,W

Louisiana
Bossier Parish Community College M
Dillard University M,W
Grambling State University M,W
Louisiana State University

Eunice W
Shreveport M,W
Louisiana State University and Agricultural and Mechanical College M,W
Louisiana Tech University M,W
Loyola University New Orleans M,W
McNeese State University M,W
Nicholls State University M,W
Northwestern State University M,W
Southeastern Louisiana University M,W
Southern University
New Orleans M,W
Southern University and Agricultural and Mechanical College M,W
Tulane University M,W
University of Louisiana at Lafayette M,W
University of Louisiana at Monroe M,W
University of New Orleans M,W
Xavier University of Louisiana M,W

Maine
University of Maine M,W
University of Maine
Augusta M,W

Maryland
Allegany College of Maryland M,W
Anne Arundel Community College M,W
Bowie State University M,W
Chesapeake College M,W
College of Southern Maryland M,W
Community College of Baltimore County M,W
Coppin State University M,W
Garrett College M,W
Hagerstown Community College M,W
Harford Community College M,W
Howard Community College M,W
Loyola University Maryland M,W
Morgan State University M,W
Mount St. Mary's University M,W
Towson University M,W
University of Maryland
Baltimore County M,W
College Park M,W
Eastern Shore M,W
Washington Adventist University M,W

Massachusetts
American International College M,W
Assumption College M,W
Bentley University M,W
Boston College M,W
Boston University M,W
College of the Holy Cross M,W
Dean College M,W
Merrimack College M,W
Northeastern University M,W
Roxbury Community College M
Stonehill College M,W
University of Massachusetts
Amherst M,W
Lowell M,W

Michigan
Alpena Community College M,W
Aquinas College M,W
Central Michigan University M,W
Concordia University M,W
Cornerstone University M,W
Davenport University M,W
Delta College M,W
Eastern Michigan University M,W
Ferris State University M,W
Glen Oaks Community College M,W
Gogebic Community College M,W
Grand Valley State University M,W
Hillsdale College M,W
Kalamazoo Valley Community College M,W
Kellogg Community College M,W
Kirtland Community College M,W
Lake Michigan College M,W
Lake Superior State University M,W
Lansing Community College M,W
Macomb Community College M,W
Madonna University M,W
Michigan State University M,W
Michigan Technological University M,W
Mott Community College M,W
Muskegon Community College M,W
Northern Michigan University M,W
Northwood University
Michigan M,W
Oakland Community College M,W
Oakland University M,W
Rochester College M,W
Saginaw Valley State University M,W
St. Clair County Community College M,W
Siena Heights University M,W
Spring Arbor University M,W
University of Detroit Mercy M,W
University of Michigan M,W
University of Michigan
Dearborn M,W
Wayne State University M,W
Western Michigan University M,W

Minnesota
Bemidji State University M,W
Concordia University St. Paul M,W
Minnesota State University
Mankato M,W
Moorhead M,W
Saint Cloud State University M,W
Southwest Minnesota State University M,W
University of Minnesota
Crookston M,W
Duluth M,W
Twin Cities M,W
Winona State University M,W

Mississippi
Alcorn State University M,W
Belhaven University M,W
Blue Mountain College M,W
Coahoma Community College M,W
Copiah-Lincoln Community College M,W
Delta State University M,W
East Mississippi Community College M,W
Hinds Community College M,W
Holmes Community College M,W
Itawamba Community College M,W
Jackson State University M,W
Meridian Community College M,W
Mississippi Gulf Coast Community College M,W
Mississippi State University M,W
Mississippi Valley State University M,W
Southwest Mississippi Community College M,W
Tougaloo College M,W
University of Mississippi M,W
University of Southern Mississippi M,W

Missouri
Avila University M,W
Central Methodist University M,W
College of the Ozarks M,W
Columbia College M,W
Cottey College W
Crowder College W
Culver-Stockton College M,W
Drury University M,W
Evangel University M,W
Hannibal-LaGrange University M,W
Harris-Stowe State University M,W
Jefferson College W
Lincoln University M,W
Lindenwood University M,W
Maryville University of Saint Louis M,W
Metropolitan Community College - Kansas City M,W
Mineral Area College M,W
Missouri Baptist University M,W
Missouri Southern State University M,W
Missouri State University M,W
Missouri State University: West Plains M
Missouri University of Science and Technology M,W
Missouri Valley College M,W
Missouri Western State University M,W
Moberly Area Community College M,W
North Central Missouri College M,W
Northwest Missouri State University M,W
Park University M,W
Research College of Nursing M,W
Rockhurst University M,W
Saint Louis University M,W
Southeast Missouri State University M,W
Southwest Baptist University M,W
State Fair Community College M,W
Stephens College W
Three Rivers Community College M,W
Truman State University M,W
University of Central Missouri M,W
University of Missouri
Columbia M,W
Kansas City M,W
St. Louis M,W
William Jewell College M,W
William Woods University M,W

Montana
Carroll College M,W
Dawson Community College M,W
Miles Community College M,W
Montana State University M,W
Montana State University
Billings M,W
Northern M,W
Montana Tech of the University of Montana M,W
Rocky Mountain College W
University of Great Falls M,W
University of Montana M,W
University of Montana: Western M,W

Nebraska
Bellevue University M
Central Community College M
Chadron State College M,W
College of Saint Mary W
Concordia University M,W
Creighton University M,W
Doane College M,W
Hastings College M,W
Mid-Plains Community College M,W
Nebraska College of Technical Agriculture M,W
Northeast Community College M,W
Peru State College M,W
University of Nebraska
Kearney M,W
Lincoln M,W
Omaha M,W
Wayne State College M,W
Western Nebraska Community College M,W
York College M,W

Nevada
University of Nevada
Las Vegas M,W
Reno M,W

New Hampshire
Franklin Pierce University M,W
Hesser College M,W
Saint Anselm College M,W
Southern New Hampshire University M,W
University of New Hampshire M,W

New Jersey
Bloomfield College M,W
Brookdale Community College M,W
Burlington County College M,W
Caldwell College M,W
Essex County College M,W
Fairleigh Dickinson University
Metropolitan Campus M,W
Felician College M,W
Georgian Court University W
Mercer County Community College M,W
Monmouth University M,W
New Jersey Institute of Technology M,W
Raritan Valley Community College M,W
Rider University M,W
Rutgers, The State University of New Jersey
New Brunswick/Piscataway Campus M,W
Saint Peter's University M,W
Salem Community College M,W
Seton Hall University M,W
Union County College W

New Mexico
Eastern New Mexico University M,W
New Mexico Highlands University M,W
New Mexico Junior College M,W
New Mexico Military Institute M
New Mexico State University M,W
University of New Mexico M,W
University of the Southwest M,W
Western New Mexico University M,W

New York
Adelphi University M,W
ASA Institute of Business and Computer Technology M,W
Canisius College M,W
City University of New York
Queens College M,W
Colgate University M,W
College of Saint Rose M,W
Concordia College M,W
Daemen College M,W
Dominican College of Blauvelt M,W
Dowling College M,W
Fordham University M,W
Genesee Community College M,W
Globe Institute of Technology M,W
Hofstra University M,W
Iona College M,W
Le Moyne College M,W
Long Island University
Brooklyn Campus M,W
C. W. Post Campus M,W
Manhattan College M,W
Marist College M,W
Mercy College M,W
Molloy College M,W
Monroe College M
Monroe Community College M
New York Institute of Technology M,W
Niagara County Community College M,W
Niagara University M,W
Nyack College M,W
Pace University M,W
Roberts Wesleyan College M,W
Saint Bonaventure University M,W
St. Francis College M,W
St. John's University M,W
St. Thomas Aquinas College M,W
Siena College M,W
SUNY
College of Technology at Alfred M,W
University at Albany M,W
University at Binghamton M,W
University at Buffalo M,W
University at Stony Brook M,W
Syracuse University M,W
Wagner College M,W

North Carolina
Appalachian State University M,W
Barton College M,W
Belmont Abbey College M,W
Brevard College M,W
Campbell University M,W
Catawba College M,W
Chowan University M,W
Davidson College M,W
Duke University M,W
East Carolina University M,W
Elizabeth City State University M,W

Elon University M,W
Fayetteville State University M,W
Gardner-Webb University M,W
Guilford Technical Community College M,W
High Point University M,W
Johnson C. Smith University M,W
Lees-McRae College M,W
Lenoir Community College M,W
Lenoir-Rhyne University M,W
Livingstone College M,W
Louisburg College M,W
Mars Hill College M,W
Montreat College M,W
Mount Olive College M,W
North Carolina Agricultural and Technical State University M,W
North Carolina Central University M,W
North Carolina State University M,W
Pfeiffer University M,W
Queens University of Charlotte M,W
St. Andrews University M,W
St. Augustine's University M,W
Shaw University M,W
University of North Carolina
Asheville M,W
Chapel Hill M,W
Charlotte M,W
Greensboro M,W
Wilmington M,W
Wake Forest University M,W
Western Carolina University M,W
Wingate University M,W
Winston-Salem State University M,W

North Dakota

Bismarck State College M,W
Dakota College at Bottineau M,W
Dickinson State University M,W
Jamestown College M,W
Lake Region State College M,W
Mayville State University M,W
Minot State University M,W
North Dakota State College of Science M,W
North Dakota State University M,W
University of Mary M,W
University of North Dakota M,W
Valley City State University M,W
Williston State College M,W

Ohio

Ashland University M,W
Bowling Green State University M,W
Cedarville University M,W
Central State University M,W
Cincinnati State Technical and Community College M,W
Clark State Community College M,W
Cleveland State University M,W
Columbus State Community College M,W
Edison State Community College M,W
Kent State University M,W
Lake Erie College M,W
Lakeland Community College M,W
Lourdes University M,W
Malone University M,W
Miami University
Oxford M,W
Mount Vernon Nazarene University M,W
Notre Dame College M,W
Ohio Dominican University M,W
Ohio Mid-Western College M,W
Ohio State University
Columbus Campus M,W
Ohio University M,W
Owens Community College
Toledo M,W
Shawnee State University M,W
Sinclair Community College M,W
Southern State Community College M,W
Tiffin University M,W
University of Akron M,W
University of Cincinnati M,W
University of Dayton M,W
University of Findlay M,W
University of Rio Grande M,W
University of Toledo M,W
Ursuline College W
Walsh University M,W
Wright State University M,W
Xavier University M,W
Youngstown State University M,W

Oklahoma

Bacone College M,W
Cameron University M,W
Carl Albert State College M,W
Connors State College M,W
East Central University M,W
Eastern Oklahoma State College M,W
Langston University M,W
Mid-America Christian University M,W
Northeastern Oklahoma Agricultural and Mechanical College M,W
Northeastern State University M,W
Northern Oklahoma College M,W
Northwestern Oklahoma State University M,W
Oklahoma Baptist University M,W
Oklahoma Christian University M,W
Oklahoma City University M,W
Oklahoma Panhandle State University M,W
Oklahoma State University M,W
Oklahoma Wesleyan University M,W
Oral Roberts University M,W
Redlands Community College M,W
Rogers State University M,W
St. Gregory's University M,W
Seminole State College M,W
Southeastern Oklahoma State University M,W
Southern Nazarene University M,W
Southwestern Oklahoma State University M,W
University of Central Oklahoma M,W
University of Oklahoma M,W
University of Science and Arts of Oklahoma M,W
University of Tulsa M,W
Western Oklahoma State College M,W

Oregon

Chemeketa Community College M,W
Clackamas Community College M,W
Concordia University M,W
Corban University M,W
Eastern Oregon University M,W
Lane Community College M,W
Linn-Benton Community College M,W
Mt. Hood Community College M,W
Northwest Christian University M,W
Oregon Institute of Technology M,W
Oregon State University M,W
Portland Community College M,W
Portland State University M,W
Southern Oregon University M,W
Southwestern Oregon Community College M,W
Treasure Valley Community College M,W
University of Oregon M,W
University of Portland M,W
Warner Pacific College M,W

Pennsylvania

Bloomsburg University of Pennsylvania M,W
Bucknell University M,W
California University of Pennsylvania M,W
Carlow University W
Chestnut Hill College M,W
Cheyney University of Pennsylvania M,W
Clarion University of Pennsylvania M,W
Drexel University M,W
Duquesne University M,W
East Stroudsburg University of Pennsylvania M,W
Edinboro University of Pennsylvania M,W
Gannon University M,W
Harcum College M,W
Holy Family University M,W
Indiana University of Pennsylvania M,W
Kutztown University of Pennsylvania M,W
La Salle University M,W
Lackawanna College M,W
Lafayette College M,W
Lehigh University M,W
Lock Haven University of Pennsylvania M,W
Mansfield University of Pennsylvania M,W
Mercyhurst University M,W
Millersville University of Pennsylvania M,W
Penn State
University Park M,W
Philadelphia University M,W
Point Park University M,W
Robert Morris University M,W
St. Francis University M,W
Saint Joseph's University M,W
Seton Hill University M,W
Shippensburg University of Pennsylvania M,W
Slippery Rock University of Pennsylvania M,W
Temple University M,W
University of Pittsburgh M,W
University of Pittsburgh
Johnstown M,W
Titusville M,W
University of the Sciences in Philadelphia M,W
Valley Forge Military Academy and College M
Villanova University M,W
West Chester University of Pennsylvania M,W
Westminster College M,W

Puerto Rico

Bayamon Central University M,W
Inter American University of Puerto Rico
Aguadilla Campus M,W
Arecibo Campus M
Bayamon Campus M,W
Fajardo Campus M
Guayama Campus M,W
Metropolitan Campus M,W
Ponce Campus M,W
San German Campus M,W
Turabo University M,W
Universidad del Este M,W
Universidad Metropolitana M,W
University of Puerto Rico
Bayamon University College M,W
Carolina Regional College M,W
Cayey University College M,W
Humacao M,W
Mayaguez M,W
Ponce M,W
Utuado M
University of the Sacred Heart M

Rhode Island

Bryant University M,W
Community College of Rhode Island M,W
Providence College M,W
University of Rhode Island M,W

South Carolina

Aiken Technical College M
Allen University M,W
Anderson University M,W
Charleston Southern University M,W
The Citadel M
Claflin University M,W
Clemson University M,W
Coastal Carolina University M,W
Coker College M,W
College of Charleston M,W
Columbia College W
Converse College W
Erskine College M,W
Francis Marion University M,W
Furman University M,W
Lander University M,W
Limestone College M,W
Morris College M,W
Newberry College M,W
North Greenville University M,W
Presbyterian College M,W
South Carolina State University M,W
Spartanburg Methodist College M,W
University of South Carolina
Aiken M,W
Columbia M,W
Upstate M,W
Voorhees College M,W
Winthrop University M,W
Wofford College M,W

South Dakota

Augustana College M,W
Black Hills State University M,W
Dakota State University M,W
Mount Marty College M,W
Northern State University M,W
South Dakota School of Mines and Technology M,W
South Dakota State University M,W
University of Sioux Falls M,W
University of South Dakota M,W

Tennessee

Austin Peay State University M,W
Belmont University M,W
Bethel University M,W
Bryan University
Dayton M,W
Carson-Newman University M,W
Chattanooga State Community College M,W
Christian Brothers University M,W
Cleveland State Community College M,W
Columbia State Community College M,W
Cumberland University M,W
Dyersburg State Community College M,W
East Tennessee State University M,W
Freed-Hardeman University M,W
Jackson State Community College M,W
King College M,W
Lane College M,W
Lee University M,W
LeMoyne-Owen College M,W
Lincoln Memorial University M,W
Lipscomb University M,W
Martin Methodist College M,W
Middle Tennessee State University M,W
Milligan College M,W
Motlow State Community College M,W
Roane State Community College M,W
Southwest Tennessee Community College M,W
Tennessee State University M,W
Tennessee Technological University M,W
Tennessee Wesleyan College M,W
Trevecca Nazarene University M,W
Tusculum College M,W
Union University M,W
University of Memphis M,W
University of Tennessee
Chattanooga M,W
Knoxville M,W
Martin M,W
Vanderbilt University M,W
Volunteer State Community College M,W
Walters State Community College M,W

Texas

Abilene Christian University M,W
Angelina College M,W
Angelo State University M,W
Baylor University M,W
Blinn College M,W
Brookhaven College M
Clarendon College M,W
Collin County Community College District M,W
Dallas Baptist University M
Frank Phillips College M,W
Grayson County College M,W
Hill College M,W
Houston Baptist University M,W
Howard College M,W
Jacksonville College M,W
Jarvis Christian College M,W

Kilgore College M,W
Lamar University M,W
Lee College M
Lubbock Christian University M,W
McLennan Community College M,W
Midland College M,W
Midwestern State University M,W
Odessa College M,W
Panola College M,W
Paris Junior College M,W
Prairie View A&M University M,W
Ranger College M,W
Rice University M,W
St. Edward's University M,W
St. Mary's University M,W
Sam Houston State University M,W
San Jacinto College W
South Plains College M,W
Southern Methodist University M,W
Southwestern Assemblies of God University M,W
Stephen F. Austin State University M,W
Tarleton State University M,W
Temple College M,W
Texas A&M University M,W
Texas A&M University
- Commerce M,W
- Corpus Christi M,W
- Kingsville M,W

Texas Christian University M,W
Texas Southern University M,W
Texas State University: San Marcos M,W
Texas Tech University M,W
Texas Wesleyan University M,W
Texas Woman's University W
Trinity Valley Community College M,W
Tyler Junior College M,W
University of Houston M,W
University of North Texas M,W
University of St. Thomas M,W
University of Texas
- Arlington M,W
- Austin M,W
- Pan American M,W
- of the Permian Basin M,W
- San Antonio M,W

University of the Incarnate Word M,W
Wayland Baptist University M,W
Weatherford College M,W
West Texas A&M University M,W
Western Texas College M,W
Wiley College M,W

Utah
Brigham Young University M,W
Dixie State College M,W
Salt Lake Community College M,W
Snow College M,W
Southern Utah University M,W
University of Utah M,W
Utah State University M,W
Utah Valley University M,W
Weber State University M,W
Westminster College M,W

Vermont
Saint Michael's College M,W
University of Vermont M,W

Virginia
Bluefield College M,W
College of William and Mary M,W
George Mason University M,W
Hampton University M,W
James Madison University M,W
Liberty University M,W
Longwood University M,W
Norfolk State University M,W
Old Dominion University M,W
Radford University M,W
St. Paul's College M,W
University of Richmond M,W
University of Virginia M,W
University of Virginia's College at Wise M,W
Virginia Commonwealth University M,W
Virginia Intermont College M,W
Virginia Military Institute M
Virginia Polytechnic Institute and State University M,W
Virginia State University M,W
Virginia Union University M,W

Washington
Big Bend Community College M,W
Centralia College M,W
Clark College M,W
Columbia Basin College M,W
Eastern Washington University M,W
Everett Community College M,W
Evergreen State College M,W
Gonzaga University M,W
Grays Harbor College M,W
Green River Community College M,W
Highline Community College M,W
Lower Columbia College M,W
North Seattle Community College M,W
Northwest Indian College M,W
Northwest University M,W
Olympic College M,W
Peninsula College M,W
Pierce College M,W
Saint Martin's University M,W
Seattle Pacific University M,W
Seattle University M,W
Shoreline Community College M,W
Skagit Valley College M,W
Spokane Community College M,W
Tacoma Community College M,W
University of Washington M,W
Walla Walla Community College M,W
Washington State University M,W
Western Washington University M,W
Whatcom Community College M,W
Yakima Valley Community College M,W

West Virginia
Alderson-Broaddus College M,W
Bluefield State College M,W
Concord University M,W
Davis and Elkins College M,W
Fairmont State University M,W
Glenville State College M,W
Marshall University M,W
Ohio Valley University M,W
Potomac State College of West Virginia University M,W
Salem International University M,W
Shepherd University M,W
University of Charleston M,W
West Liberty University M,W
West Virginia State University M,W
West Virginia University M,W
West Virginia University Institute of Technology M,W
West Virginia Wesleyan College M,W
Wheeling Jesuit University M,W

Wisconsin
Cardinal Stritch University M,W
Marquette University M,W
Silver Lake College of the Holy Family M,W
University of Wisconsin
- Green Bay M,W
- Madison M,W
- Milwaukee M,W
- Parkside M,W

Viterbo University M,W

Wyoming
Casper College M,W
Central Wyoming College M,W
Eastern Wyoming College M,W
Laramie County Community College M
Northwest College M,W
Sheridan College M,W
University of Wyoming M,W
Western Wyoming Community College M,W

Bowling

Arkansas
Arkansas State University W
University of Arkansas
- Pine Bluff W

Connecticut
Sacred Heart University W

Delaware
Delaware State University W

Florida
Bethune-Cookman University W
Webber International University M,W

Illinois
McKendree University W
Robert Morris University: Chicago M,W

Indiana
Calumet College of St. Joseph M,W
Huntington University M,W
Indiana Institute of Technology M,W
Marian University M,W
Valparaiso University W
Vincennes University M,W

Iowa
AIB College of Business M,W
Clarke University M,W
Grand View University M,W
St. Ambrose University M,W

Kansas
Baker University W
Newman University M,W
Wichita State University M,W

Kentucky
Campbellsville University M,W
St. Catharine College M,W
University of Pikeville M,W

Louisiana
Southern University and Agricultural and Mechanical College W

Maryland
Bowie State University W
Coppin State University W
Morgan State University W

Michigan
Aquinas College M
Concordia University M,W
Davenport University M,W
Saginaw Valley State University M

Mississippi
Jackson State University W
Mississippi Valley State University M,W

Missouri
Missouri Baptist University M,W

Nebraska
University of Nebraska
- Lincoln W

New Jersey
Fairleigh Dickinson University
- Metropolitan Campus W

New York
Adelphi University W
Long Island University
- Brooklyn Campus W

North Carolina
Blue Ridge Community College M
Chowan University W
Elizabeth City State University W
Johnson C. Smith University W
Livingstone College M,W
North Carolina Central University M,W
St. Augustine's University W
Shaw University W

Ohio
Bowling Green State University M,W
Notre Dame College M,W
Ursuline College W

Pennsylvania
Cheyney University of Pennsylvania W

Tennessee
Bethel University M,W
Martin Methodist College M,W

Texas
Prairie View A&M University W
Stephen F. Austin State University W
Texas Southern University W

Virginia
Norfolk State University W

Wisconsin
Viterbo University M,W

Cheerleading

Alabama
Faulkner State Community College M,W
Shelton State Community College M,W
Southern Union State Community College M,W
Troy University M,W
Tuskegee University M,W
University of Alabama M,W
University of Alabama
- Huntsville M,W

University of Mobile W
University of North Alabama M,W
University of West Alabama M,W
Wallace State Community College at Hanceville M,W

Arizona
Arizona Western College M,W
Glendale Community College M,W

Arkansas
Arkansas Tech University M,W
John Brown University M,W
Lyon College M,W
North Arkansas College W
University of Arkansas M,W
University of Arkansas
- Fort Smith M,W
- Little Rock W
- Monticello M,W

University of Central Arkansas M,W
Williams Baptist College M,W

California
California Baptist University M,W
Concordia University M,W
Hope International University M,W
Menlo College M,W

Colorado
Adams State College M,W

Delaware
Delaware State University M,W
University of Delaware M,W

Florida
Pensacola State College M,W
University of Florida M,W
Warner University M,W
Webber International University M,W

Georgia
Brewton-Parker College M,W
Columbus State University M,W

Georgia Institute of Technology M,W
Gordon College W
Point University W
Reinhardt University M,W
Truett-McConnell College M,W
University of West Georgia M,W
Young Harris College M,W

Hawaii
Hawaii Pacific University M,W
University of Hawaii
Manoa M,W

Idaho
Boise State University M,W
North Idaho College M,W

Illinois
Danville Area Community College W
Judson University M,W
Kaskaskia College M,W
Lewis University W
McKendree University M,W
Northwestern University M,W
Olivet Nazarene University M,W
Rend Lake College W
Robert Morris University: Chicago M,W
University of St. Francis W

Indiana
Ancilla College M,W
Bethel College M,W
Grace College M,W
Indiana Institute of Technology M,W
Indiana Wesleyan University M,W
Marian University M,W
Oakland City University W
University of St. Francis M,W

Iowa
AIB College of Business M,W
Briar Cliff University W
Graceland University M,W
Grand View University W
Iowa Western Community College M,W
Kirkwood Community College W
Northwestern College M,W
St. Ambrose University M,W
Waldorf College W
William Penn University M,W

Kansas
Allen County Community College M,W
Baker University M,W
Barton County Community College M,W
Benedictine College M,W
Central Christian College of Kansas M,W
Cloud County Community College M,W
Coffeyville Community College M,W
Colby Community College M,W
Cowley County Community College M,W
Dodge City Community College M,W
Emporia State University M,W
Fort Scott Community College W
Friends University M,W
Garden City Community College M,W
Highland Community College M,W
Labette Community College M,W
McPherson College M,W
MidAmerica Nazarene University M,W
Neosho County Community College M,W
Newman University M,W
Northwest Kansas Technical College M,W
Ottawa University M,W
Pittsburg State University M,W
Pratt Community College M,W
Seward County Community College M,W
Southwestern College M,W
Tabor College M,W
University of St. Mary M,W
Washburn University M,W
Wichita State University M,W

Kentucky
Bellarmine University M,W
Campbellsville University M,W
Georgetown College W
Kentucky State University W
Murray State University W
St. Catharine College M,W
Union College M,W
University of Pikeville M,W
University of the Cumberlands M,W

Louisiana
Bossier Parish Community College M,W
McNeese State University M,W
University of Louisiana at Lafayette M,W
University of Louisiana at Monroe M,W

Maryland
Morgan State University W
University of Maryland
College Park W

Michigan
Concordia University M,W
Davenport University W
Northwood University
Michigan M,W
Siena Heights University M,W
University of Detroit Mercy M,W
Wayne State University M,W

Mississippi
Copiah-Lincoln Community College M,W
East Mississippi Community College M,W
Hinds Community College M,W
Itawamba Community College M,W
Mississippi Gulf Coast Community College M,W
Southwest Mississippi Community College M,W
University of Mississippi M,W

Missouri
Avila University W
Central Methodist University W
Culver-Stockton College M,W
Drury University W
Evangel University M,W
Hannibal-LaGrange University M,W
Harris-Stowe State University M,W
Lincoln University W
Maryville University of Saint Louis M,W
Missouri Baptist University M,W
Missouri Southern State University M,W
Missouri Valley College M,W
Moberly Area Community College M,W
Northwest Missouri State University M,W
Southeast Missouri State University M,W
University of Missouri
Kansas City M,W
William Jewell College M,W

Montana
Rocky Mountain College W

Nebraska
Concordia University W
Doane College W
Hastings College W
Peru State College W

Nevada
University of Nevada
Las Vegas M,W
Reno M,W

New Mexico
New Mexico Junior College M,W

New York
ASA Institute of Business and Computer Technology W
Hofstra University M,W
Nyack College M,W

North Carolina
Brevard College M,W
Elon University M,W
Gardner-Webb University M,W
Lenoir-Rhyne University M,W
Mars Hill College M,W
Methodist University M,W
Queens University of Charlotte M,W
St. Augustine's University W
University of North Carolina
Wilmington M,W

North Dakota
Williston State College M,W

Ohio
Ashland University W
Kent State University M,W
Notre Dame College W
Tiffin University M,W
University of Rio Grande M,W

Oklahoma
Bacone College M,W
Cameron University M,W
Carl Albert State College W
Connors State College M,W
Eastern Oklahoma State College M,W
Langston University M,W
Mid-America Christian University M,W
Northeastern Oklahoma Agricultural and Mechanical College M,W
Northwestern Oklahoma State University M,W
Oklahoma Christian University W
Oklahoma City University M,W
Oklahoma Panhandle State University M,W
Oral Roberts University M,W
Rogers State University M,W
St. Gregory's University M,W
Southeastern Oklahoma State University M,W
Southern Nazarene University M,W
Southwestern Oklahoma State University M,W
University of Oklahoma M,W
University of Science and Arts of Oklahoma M,W
University of Tulsa M,W
Western Oklahoma State College M,W

Oregon
Southwestern Oregon Community College M,W

Pennsylvania
Kutztown University of Pennsylvania W
Lackawanna College W
Penn State
University Park M,W
St. Francis University M,W
Seton Hill University M,W
Temple University M,W

Puerto Rico
Inter American University of Puerto Rico
Aguadilla Campus M,W
University of Puerto Rico
Carolina Regional College M,W
Cayey University College M,W
Humacao M,W

South Carolina
Anderson University W
Clemson University M,W
Limestone College M,W
Morris College M,W
Newberry College M,W
North Greenville University M,W
Presbyterian College M,W
Spartanburg Methodist College M,W
University of South Carolina
Columbia M,W

South Dakota
Northern State University W
University of Sioux Falls M,W

Tennessee
Bethel University M,W
Bryan University
Dayton W
Cumberland University M,W
Dyersburg State Community College M,W
Freed-Hardeman University W
King College M,W
Lee University M,W
Martin Methodist College W
Tennessee Technological University M,W
Tennessee Wesleyan College M,W
Tusculum College W
University of Memphis M,W
University of Tennessee
Martin W

Texas
Angelina College M,W
Baylor University W
Clarendon College M,W
East Texas Baptist University M,W
Houston Baptist University M,W
Howard College M,W
Jacksonville College M,W
Ranger College M,W
St. Edward's University M,W
San Jacinto College M,W
South Plains College M,W
Southern Methodist University M,W
Southwestern Assemblies of God University W
Tarleton State University M,W
Temple College M,W
Texas Southern University M,W
Texas Wesleyan University M,W
Tyler Junior College M,W
University of Texas
of the Permian Basin M,W
Wayland Baptist University M,W

Utah
Brigham Young University M,W
Snow College M,W
Southern Utah University M,W

Virginia
George Mason University M,W
Liberty University M,W
Old Dominion University W

Washington
University of Washington M,W
Walla Walla Community College W

West Virginia
Alderson-Broaddus College W
University of Charleston M,W

Wyoming
University of Wyoming M,W
Western Wyoming Community College M,W

Cricket

California
College of the Redwoods M

Cross-country

Alabama
Alabama Agricultural and Mechanical University M,W
Alabama State University M,W
Auburn University M,W
Jacksonville State University M,W
Miles College M,W
Samford University M,W
Spring Hill College M,W
Troy University M,W

University of Alabama M,W
University of Alabama
Birmingham W
Huntsville M,W
University of Mobile M,W
University of North Alabama M,W
University of South Alabama M,W
University of West Alabama M,W
Wallace State Community College at Hanceville M,W

Alaska
University of Alaska
Anchorage M,W
Fairbanks M,W

Arizona
Arizona Christian University M,W
Arizona State University M,W
Central Arizona College M,W
Dine College M,W
GateWay Community College M,W
Glendale Community College M,W
Grand Canyon University M,W
Mesa Community College M,W
Northern Arizona University M,W
Paradise Valley Community College M,W
Pima Community College M,W
Scottsdale Community College M,W
University of Arizona M,W
Yavapai College W

Arkansas
Arkansas State University M,W
Arkansas Tech University W
Harding University M,W
Henderson State University W
John Brown University M,W
Lyon College M,W
Ouachita Baptist University W
Southern Arkansas University M,W
University of Arkansas M,W
University of Arkansas
Fort Smith M,W
Little Rock M,W
Monticello W
Pine Bluff M,W
University of Central Arkansas M,W

California
Academy of Art University M,W
Azusa Pacific University M,W
Biola University M,W
California Baptist University M,W
California Polytechnic State University: San Luis Obispo M,W
California State Polytechnic University: Pomona M,W
California State University
Chico M,W
Dominguez Hills W
Fresno M,W
Fullerton M,W
Long Beach M,W
Los Angeles M,W
Monterey Bay M,W
Northridge M,W
Sacramento M,W
Stanislaus M,W
Concordia University M,W
Fresno City College M,W
Fresno Pacific University M,W
Holy Names University M,W
Hope International University M,W
Humboldt State University M,W
Loyola Marymount University M,W
The Master's College M,W
Menlo College M,W
Notre Dame de Namur University M,W
Pepperdine University M,W
Point Loma Nazarene University M,W
St. Mary's College of California M,W
San Diego Christian College M,W
San Diego State University W
San Jose State University M,W
Santa Clara University M,W
Santiago Canyon College M,W
Simpson University M,W
Soka University of America M,W
Stanford University M,W
University of California
Berkeley M,W
Davis M,W
Irvine M,W
Los Angeles M,W
Riverside M,W
Santa Barbara M,W
University of San Diego M,W
University of San Francisco M,W
University of Southern California W
University of the Pacific W
Vanguard University of Southern California M,W
Westmont College M,W
William Jessup University M,W

Colorado
Adams State College M,W
Colorado Christian University M,W
Colorado Mesa University W
Colorado School of Mines M,W
Colorado State University M,W
Colorado State University
Pueblo W
Fort Lewis College M,W
University of Colorado
Boulder M,W
Colorado Springs M,W
University of Northern Colorado W
Western State Colorado University M,W

Connecticut
Central Connecticut State University M,W
Fairfield University M,W
Post University M,W
Quinnipiac University M,W
Sacred Heart University M,W
Southern Connecticut State University M,W
University of Bridgeport M,W
University of Connecticut M,W
University of Hartford M,W
University of New Haven M,W

Delaware
Delaware State University M,W
Goldey-Beacom College M,W
Wilmington University M,W

District of Columbia
American University M,W
George Washington University M,W
Georgetown University M,W
Howard University M,W

Florida
Ave Maria University M,W
Bethune-Cookman University M,W
Chipola College W
Embry-Riddle Aeronautical University M,W
Flagler College M,W
Florida Atlantic University M,W
Florida Institute of Technology M,W
Florida Southern College M,W
Florida State University M,W
Jacksonville University M,W
Lynn University M,W
Nova Southeastern University M,W
Palm Beach Atlantic University W
Pasco-Hernando Community College W
Saint Leo University M,W
Saint Thomas University M,W
Southeastern University M,W
Stetson University M,W
University of Central Florida M,W
University of Florida M,W
University of Miami M,W
University of North Florida M,W
University of South Florida M,W
University of Tampa M,W
University of West Florida M,W
Warner University M,W
Webber International University M,W

Georgia
Albany State University M,W
Andrew College M,W
Brenau University W
Brewton-Parker College M,W
Clark Atlanta University M,W
Clayton State University M,W
Columbus State University M,W
Darton College M,W
Georgia College and State University M,W
Georgia Institute of Technology M,W
Georgia Southern University W
Georgia Southwestern State University W
Georgia State University M,W
Gordon College M,W
Kennesaw State University M,W
Mercer University M,W
Morehouse College M
Paine College M,W
Point University M,W
Reinhardt University M,W
Savannah State University M,W
Shorter University M,W
Truett-McConnell College M,W
University of Georgia M,W
University of West Georgia M,W
Valdosta State University M,W
Young Harris College M,W

Hawaii
Brigham Young University-Hawaii M,W
Chaminade University of Honolulu M,W
Hawaii Pacific University M,W
University of Hawaii
Hilo M,W
Manoa W

Idaho
Boise State University M,W
College of Idaho M,W
Idaho State University M,W
Lewis-Clark State College M,W
Northwest Nazarene University M,W
University of Idaho M,W

Illinois
Bradley University M,W
Chicago State University M,W
College of Lake County M,W
Danville Area Community College M,W
DePaul University M,W
Eastern Illinois University M,W
Illinois Central College M,W
Illinois Institute of Technology M,W
Illinois State University M,W
Judson University M,W
Kaskaskia College M,W
Lewis University M,W
Lincoln College M,W
Loyola University Chicago M,W
McKendree University M,W
Moraine Valley Community College M,W
Morton College M,W
Northwestern University W
Olivet Nazarene University M,W
Quincy University M,W
Rend Lake College M,W
Robert Morris University: Chicago M,W
Saint Xavier University M,W
Sauk Valley Community College M,W
Southern Illinois University Carbondale M,W
Southern Illinois University Edwardsville M,W
Spoon River College M,W
Trinity Christian College M,W
University of Illinois
Chicago M,W
Urbana-Champaign M,W
University of St. Francis M,W
Waubonsee Community College M,W
Western Illinois University M,W

Indiana
Ball State University W
Bethel College M,W
Butler University M,W
Calumet College of St. Joseph M,W
Goshen College M,W
Grace College M,W
Huntington University M,W
Indiana Institute of Technology M,W
Indiana State University M,W
Indiana University
Bloomington M,W
Purdue University Fort Wayne M,W
Purdue University Indianapolis M,W
Indiana Wesleyan University M,W
Marian University M,W
Oakland City University M,W
Purdue University M,W
Saint Joseph's College M,W
St. Mary-of-the-Woods College W
Taylor University M,W
University of Evansville M,W
University of Indianapolis M,W
University of Notre Dame M,W
University of St. Francis M,W
University of Southern Indiana M,W
Valparaiso University M,W
Vincennes University M,W

Iowa
Ashford University M,W
Briar Cliff University M,W
Clarke University M,W
Dordt College M,W
Drake University M,W
Ellsworth Community College M,W
Graceland University M,W
Grand View University M,W
Iowa State University M,W
Iowa Western Community College M,W
Morningside College M,W
Mount Mercy University M,W
North Iowa Area Community College M,W
Northwestern College M,W
St. Ambrose University M,W
Scott Community College M,W
University of Iowa M,W
University of Northern Iowa M,W
William Penn University M,W

Kansas
Allen County Community College M,W
Baker University M,W
Barton County Community College M,W
Benedictine College M,W
Bethel College M,W
Butler Community College M,W
Central Christian College of Kansas M,W
Cloud County Community College M,W
Coffeyville Community College M,W
Colby Community College M,W
Cowley County Community College M,W
Dodge City Community College M,W
Emporia State University M,W
Fort Hays State University M,W
Friends University M,W
Garden City Community College M,W
Hesston College M,W
Highland Community College M,W
Hutchinson Community College M,W
Johnson County Community College M,W
Kansas City Kansas Community College M,W
Kansas State University M,W
Kansas Wesleyan University M,W
McPherson College M,W
Neosho County Community College M,W
Newman University M,W
Ottawa University M,W
Pittsburg State University M,W
Pratt Community College M,W

Southwestern College M,W
Sterling College M,W
Tabor College M,W
University of Kansas M,W
University of St. Mary M,W
Wichita State University M,W

Kentucky
Asbury University M,W
Bellarmine University M,W
Brescia University M,W
Campbellsville University M,W
Eastern Kentucky University M,W
Georgetown College M,W
Kentucky State University M,W
Kentucky Wesleyan College M,W
Lindsey Wilson College M,W
Midway College W
Morehead State University M,W
Murray State University M,W
Northern Kentucky University M,W
St. Catharine College M,W
Union College M,W
University of Kentucky M,W
University of Louisville M,W
University of Pikeville M,W
University of the Cumberlands M,W
Western Kentucky University M,W

Louisiana
Dillard University M,W
Grambling State University M,W
Louisiana State University and Agricultural and Mechanical College M,W
Louisiana Tech University M,W
Loyola University New Orleans M,W
McNeese State University M,W
Nicholls State University M,W
Northwestern State University M,W
Southeastern Louisiana University M,W
Southern University
  New Orleans M,W
Southern University and Agricultural and Mechanical College M,W
Tulane University M,W
University of Louisiana at Lafayette M,W
University of Louisiana at Monroe M,W
University of New Orleans M,W
Xavier University of Louisiana M,W

Maine
University of Maine M,W

Maryland
Bowie State University M,W
Community College of Baltimore County W
Coppin State University M,W
Hagerstown Community College M,W
Harford Community College M,W
Loyola University Maryland M,W
Morgan State University M,W
Mount St. Mary's University M,W
Towson University W
University of Maryland
  Baltimore County M,W
  College Park W
  Eastern Shore M,W
Washington Adventist University M,W

Massachusetts
American International College M,W
Boston College M,W
Boston University M,W
Merrimack College M,W
Northeastern University M,W
Stonehill College M,W
University of Massachusetts
  Amherst M,W
  Lowell M,W

Michigan
Aquinas College M,W
Central Michigan University M,W
Cleary University M,W
Concordia University M,W
Cornerstone University M,W
Davenport University M,W
Eastern Michigan University M,W
Ferris State University M,W
Grand Valley State University M,W
Hillsdale College M,W
Kirtland Community College M,W
Lake Superior State University M,W
Lansing Community College M,W
Macomb Community College M,W
Madonna University M,W
Michigan State University M,W
Michigan Technological University M,W
Mott Community College M,W
Northern Michigan University W
Northwood University
  Michigan M,W
Oakland Community College M,W
Oakland University M,W
Saginaw Valley State University M,W
Siena Heights University M,W
Spring Arbor University M,W
University of Detroit Mercy M,W
University of Michigan M,W
Wayne State University M,W
Western Michigan University W

Minnesota
Concordia University St. Paul M,W
Minnesota State University
  Mankato M,W
  Moorhead M,W
Saint Cloud State University M,W
University of Minnesota
  Duluth M,W
  Twin Cities M,W
Winona State University M,W

Mississippi
Alcorn State University M,W
Belhaven University M,W
Blue Mountain College M,W
Delta State University W
Jackson State University M,W
Mississippi State University M,W
Mississippi Valley State University M,W
Tougaloo College M,W
University of Mississippi M,W
University of Southern Mississippi M,W

Missouri
Avila University M,W
Central Methodist University M,W
Columbia College M,W
Culver-Stockton College M,W
Drury University M,W
Evangel University M,W
Hannibal-LaGrange University M,W
Lincoln University W
Lindenwood University M,W
Maryville University of Saint Louis M,W
Metropolitan Community College - Kansas City W
Missouri Baptist University M,W
Missouri Southern State University M,W
Missouri State University M,W
Missouri University of Science and Technology M,W
Missouri Valley College M,W
Northwest Missouri State University M,W
Park University M,W
Saint Louis University M,W
Southeast Missouri State University M,W
Southwest Baptist University M,W
Stephens College W
Truman State University M,W
University of Central Missouri M,W
University of Missouri
  Columbia M,W
  Kansas City M,W
William Jewell College M,W
William Woods University M,W

Montana
Carroll College M,W
Flathead Valley Community College M,W
Montana State University M,W
Montana State University
  Billings M,W
Rocky Mountain College M,W
University of Great Falls M,W
University of Montana M,W

Nebraska
College of Saint Mary W
Concordia University M,W
Creighton University M,W
Doane College M,W
Hastings College M,W
Peru State College W
University of Nebraska
  Kearney M,W
  Lincoln M,W
Wayne State College M,W

Nevada
University of Nevada
  Las Vegas W
  Reno W

New Hampshire
Franklin Pierce University M,W
Saint Anselm College M,W
Southern New Hampshire University M,W
University of New Hampshire M,W

New Jersey
Bloomfield College M,W
Caldwell College W
Fairleigh Dickinson University
  Metropolitan Campus M,W
Felician College M,W
Georgian Court University W
Monmouth University M,W
Rider University M,W
Rutgers, The State University of New Jersey
  New Brunswick/Piscataway Campus M,W
Saint Peter's University M,W
Seton Hall University M,W

New Mexico
Eastern New Mexico University M,W
Navajo Technical College M,W
New Mexico Highlands University M,W
New Mexico Junior College M,W
New Mexico State University M,W
University of New Mexico M,W
University of the Southwest M,W

New York
Adelphi University M,W
Canisius College M,W
City University of New York
  Queens College M,W
Concordia College M,W
Daemen College M,W
Dominican College of Blauvelt W
Dowling College M,W
Fordham University M,W
Hofstra University M,W
Iona College M,W
Le Moyne College M,W
Long Island University
  Brooklyn Campus M,W
  C. W. Post Campus M,W
Manhattan College M,W
Marist College M,W
Mercy College M,W
Molloy College M,W
New York Institute of Technology M,W
Niagara University M,W
Nyack College M,W
Pace University M,W
Roberts Wesleyan College M,W
St. Francis College M,W
St. John's University W
St. Thomas Aquinas College M,W
Siena College M,W
SUNY
  University at Albany M,W
  University at Binghamton M,W
  University at Buffalo M,W
  University at Stony Brook M,W
Syracuse University M,W
Wagner College M,W

North Carolina
Appalachian State University M,W
Barton College M,W
Belmont Abbey College M,W
Brevard College M,W
Campbell University M,W
Catawba College M,W
Chowan University M,W
Davidson College M,W
East Carolina University M,W
Elon University M,W
Fayetteville State University M,W
Gardner-Webb University M,W
High Point University M,W
Johnson C. Smith University M,W
Lees-McRae College M,W
Lenoir-Rhyne University M,W
Livingstone College M,W
Mars Hill College M,W
Montreat College M,W
Mount Olive College M,W
North Carolina Agricultural and Technical State University M,W
North Carolina Central University M,W
North Carolina State University M,W
Pfeiffer University M,W
Queens University of Charlotte M,W
St. Andrews University M,W
St. Augustine's University M,W
Shaw University M,W
University of North Carolina
  Asheville M,W
  Chapel Hill M,W
  Charlotte M,W
  Greensboro M,W
  Wilmington M,W
Wake Forest University M,W
Western Carolina University M,W
Wingate University M,W
Winston-Salem State University M,W

North Dakota
Dickinson State University M,W
Jamestown College M,W
Minot State University M,W
North Dakota State University M,W
University of Mary M,W
University of North Dakota M,W
Valley City State University M,W

Ohio
Ashland University M,W
Bowling Green State University M,W
Cedarville University M,W
Central State University M,W
Cleveland State University W
Kent State University M,W
Lake Erie College M,W
Lourdes University M,W
Malone University M,W
Miami University
  Oxford M,W
Mount Vernon Nazarene University M,W
Notre Dame College M,W
Ohio Dominican University M,W
Ohio State University
  Columbus Campus M,W
Ohio University M,W
Shawnee State University M,W
Tiffin University M,W
University of Akron M,W
University of Cincinnati M,W
University of Dayton M,W

University of Findlay M,W
University of Rio Grande M,W
University of Toledo M,W
Ursuline College W
Walsh University M,W
Wright State University M,W
Xavier University M,W
Youngstown State University M,W

Oklahoma
Cameron University M
East Central University M,W
Langston University M,W
Northwestern Oklahoma State University M,W
Oklahoma Baptist University M,W
Oklahoma Christian University M,W
Oklahoma City University M,W
Oklahoma Panhandle State University M,W
Oklahoma State University M,W
Oklahoma Wesleyan University M,W
Oral Roberts University M,W
Rogers State University M,W
St. Gregory's University M,W
Southeastern Oklahoma State University W
Southern Nazarene University M,W
Southwestern Oklahoma State University W
University of Central Oklahoma M,W
University of Oklahoma M,W
University of Science and Arts of Oklahoma M,W
University of Tulsa M,W

Oregon
Clackamas Community College M,W
Concordia University M,W
Corban University M,W
Eastern Oregon University M,W
Lane Community College M,W
Mt. Hood Community College M,W
Northwest Christian University M,W
Oregon Institute of Technology M,W
Portland State University M,W
Southern Oregon University M,W
Southwestern Oregon Community College M,W
Treasure Valley Community College M,W
University of Oregon M,W
University of Portland M,W
Warner Pacific College M,W

Pennsylvania
Bloomsburg University of Pennsylvania M,W
Bucknell University W
California University of Pennsylvania M,W
Carlow University M
Chestnut Hill College M,W
Cheyney University of Pennsylvania M,W
Clarion University of Pennsylvania M,W
Duquesne University M,W
East Stroudsburg University of Pennsylvania M,W
Edinboro University of Pennsylvania M,W
Gannon University M,W
Holy Family University M,W
Indiana University of Pennsylvania M,W
Kutztown University of Pennsylvania M,W
La Salle University M,W
Lackawanna College M,W
Lehigh University M,W
Lock Haven University of Pennsylvania M,W
Mansfield University of Pennsylvania W
Mercyhurst University M,W
Millersville University of Pennsylvania M,W
Penn State
  University Park M,W
Philadelphia University M,W
Point Park University M,W
St. Francis University M,W
Saint Joseph's University M,W
Seton Hill University M,W
Shippensburg University of Pennsylvania M,W
Slippery Rock University of Pennsylvania M,W
Temple University M,W
University of Pittsburgh M,W
University of the Sciences in Philadelphia M,W
Villanova University M,W
West Chester University of Pennsylvania M,W
Westminster College W

Puerto Rico
Bayamon Central University M,W
Inter American University of Puerto Rico
  Aguadilla Campus M,W
  Bayamon Campus M,W
  Guayama Campus M,W
  Ponce Campus M,W
  San German Campus M,W
Turabo University M,W
Universidad del Este M,W
Universidad Metropolitana M,W
Universidad Politecnica de Puerto Rico M,W
University of Puerto Rico
  Carolina Regional College M,W
  Cayey University College M,W
  Humacao M,W
  Mayaguez M,W
  Ponce M,W
  Utuado M,W
University of the Sacred Heart M,W

Rhode Island
Bryant University M,W
Providence College M,W
University of Rhode Island M,W

South Carolina
Anderson University M,W
Charleston Southern University M,W
The Citadel M,W
Claflin University M,W
Clemson University M,W
Coastal Carolina University M,W
Coker College M,W
College of Charleston M,W
Converse College W
Erskine College M,W
Francis Marion University M,W
Furman University M,W
Limestone College M,W
Morris College M,W
Newberry College M,W
North Greenville University M,W
Presbyterian College M,W
South Carolina State University M,W
Spartanburg Methodist College M,W
University of South Carolina
  Aiken W
  Columbia W
  Upstate M,W
Voorhees College M,W
Winthrop University M,W
Wofford College M,W

South Dakota
Augustana College M,W
Black Hills State University M,W
Dakota State University M,W
Mount Marty College M,W
Northern State University M,W
South Dakota School of Mines and Technology M,W
South Dakota State University M,W
University of Sioux Falls M,W
University of South Dakota M,W

Tennessee
Austin Peay State University M,W
Belmont University M,W
Bethel University M,W
Bryan University
  Dayton M,W
Carson-Newman University M,W
Christian Brothers University M,W
Cumberland University M,W
East Tennessee State University M,W
King College M,W
Lee University M,W
LeMoyne-Owen College M
Lincoln Memorial University M,W
Lipscomb University M,W
Middle Tennessee State University M,W
Milligan College M,W
Tennessee Technological University M,W
Tennessee Wesleyan College M,W
Trevecca Nazarene University M,W
Tusculum College M,W
Union University M,W
University of Memphis M,W
University of Tennessee
  Chattanooga M,W
  Martin M,W
Vanderbilt University M,W

Texas
Abilene Christian University M,W
Angelo State University M,W
Baylor University M,W
Clarendon College M,W
Dallas Baptist University W
Houston Baptist University M,W
Lamar University M,W
Lubbock Christian University M,W
Midwestern State University W
Northwood University
  Texas M,W
Odessa College M,W
Prairie View A&M University M,W
Rice University M,W
Sam Houston State University M,W
South Plains College M,W
Southern Methodist University W
Stephen F. Austin State University M,W
Tarleton State University M,W
Texas A&M University M,W
Texas A&M University
  Commerce M,W
Texas Christian University M,W
Texas Southern University M,W
Texas State University: San Marcos M,W
Texas Tech University M,W
Texas Wesleyan University M,W
University of Houston M,W
University of North Texas M,W
University of Texas
  Austin M,W
  Pan American M,W
  of the Permian Basin M,W
  San Antonio M,W
University of the Incarnate Word M,W
Wayland Baptist University M,W
West Texas A&M University M,W
Western Texas College M,W

Utah
Brigham Young University M,W
Dixie State College M,W
Southern Utah University M,W
University of Utah W
Utah State University M,W
Utah Valley University M,W
Weber State University M,W
Westminster College M,W

Vermont
University of Vermont M,W

Virginia
Bluefield College M,W
College of William and Mary M,W
George Mason University M,W
Hampton University M,W
James Madison University W
Liberty University M,W
Longwood University M,W
Norfolk State University M,W
Radford University M,W
St. Paul's College M,W
University of Richmond M,W
University of Virginia M,W
University of Virginia's College at Wise M,W
Virginia Commonwealth University M,W
Virginia Military Institute M,W
Virginia Polytechnic Institute and State University M,W
Virginia State University M,W

Washington
Clark College M,W
Eastern Washington University M,W
Everett Community College M,W
Evergreen State College M,W
Gonzaga University M,W
Highline Community College M,W
Northwest University M,W
Saint Martin's University M,W
Seattle Pacific University M,W
Seattle University M,W
Spokane Community College M,W
University of Washington M,W
Washington State University M,W
Western Washington University M,W

West Virginia
Alderson-Broaddus College M,W
Bluefield State College M,W
Concord University M,W
Davis and Elkins College M,W
Fairmont State University M,W
Glenville State College M,W
Marshall University M,W
Ohio Valley University M,W
University of Charleston M,W
West Liberty University M,W
West Virginia University W
West Virginia Wesleyan College M,W
Wheeling Jesuit University M,W

Wisconsin
Cardinal Stritch University M,W
Marquette University M,W
Milwaukee Area Technical College M,W
Silver Lake College of the Holy Family M,W
University of Wisconsin
  Green Bay M,W
  Madison M,W
  Milwaukee M,W
  Parkside M,W
Viterbo University M,W

Wyoming
Sheridan College M,W
University of Wyoming M,W

Diving

Alabama
Auburn University M,W
University of Alabama M,W

Arizona
Arizona State University M,W
Northern Arizona University W
University of Arizona M,W

Arkansas
Ouachita Baptist University M,W
University of Arkansas W

California
California Baptist University M,W
California State University
  Fresno W
  Northridge M,W
College of the Redwoods M
San Diego State University W
San Jose State University W
Soka University of America M,W
Stanford University M,W
University of California
  Berkeley M,W
  Davis W
  Los Angeles M,W

University of San Diego W
University of Southern California M,W

Colorado
Colorado State University W
University of Denver M,W

Connecticut
Central Connecticut State University W
Fairfield University M,W
University of Connecticut M,W

District of Columbia
George Washington University M,W
Georgetown University M,W
Howard University M,W

Florida
Florida State University M,W
Indian River State College M,W
Nova Southeastern University M,W
University of Florida M,W
University of Miami M,W

Georgia
Georgia Institute of Technology M,W
Georgia Southern University W
University of Georgia M,W

Hawaii
University of Hawaii
Manoa M,W

Illinois
Illinois Institute of Technology M,W
Illinois State University W
Lincoln College M,W
Northwestern University M,W
Robert Morris University: Chicago W
Southern Illinois University Carbondale M,W
University of Illinois
Chicago M,W
Urbana-Champaign W
Western Illinois University M,W

Indiana
Ball State University M,W
Indiana University
Bloomington M,W
Purdue University Indianapolis M,W
Purdue University M,W
University of Evansville M,W
University of Notre Dame M,W
Valparaiso University M,W

Iowa
University of Iowa M,W

Kentucky
Asbury University M,W
University of Kentucky M,W
University of Louisville M,W
Western Kentucky University M,W

Maine
University of Maine M,W

Maryland
Loyola University Maryland M,W
Towson University M,W

Massachusetts
Boston College M,W
Boston University M,W
Northeastern University W
University of Massachusetts
Amherst M,W

Michigan
Eastern Michigan University M,W
Grand Valley State University M,W
Hillsdale College W
Michigan State University M,W
Northern Michigan University W
Oakland University M,W
University of Michigan M,W
Wayne State University M,W

Minnesota
Minnesota State University
Mankato M,W
Moorhead M
Saint Cloud State University M,W
University of Minnesota
Twin Cities M,W

Mississippi
Delta State University M,W

Missouri
Drury University M,W
Lindenwood University M,W
Saint Louis University M,W
University of Missouri
Columbia M,W

Nebraska
University of Nebraska
Kearney W
Lincoln W

Nevada
University of Nevada
Las Vegas M,W
Reno W

New Hampshire
University of New Hampshire W

New Jersey
Rider University M,W
Rutgers, The State University of New Jersey
New Brunswick/Piscataway Campus M,W
Saint Peter's University M,W

New Mexico
University of New Mexico W

New York
Fordham University M,W
Iona College M,W
Le Moyne College M,W
Marist College M,W
Niagara University M,W
Saint Bonaventure University M,W
St. Francis College M,W
Siena College W
SUNY
University at Binghamton M,W
University at Buffalo M,W
University at Stony Brook W

North Carolina
Davidson College M,W
East Carolina University M,W
University of North Carolina
Chapel Hill M,W
Wilmington M,W

North Dakota
University of North Dakota M,W

Ohio
Ashland University M,W
Cleveland State University M,W
Malone University M,W
Miami University
Oxford M,W
Notre Dame College M,W
Ohio University W
University of Akron W
University of Cincinnati M,W
University of Findlay M,W
University of Toledo W
Wright State University M,W

Oklahoma
Oklahoma Baptist University M,W

Pennsylvania
Clarion University of Pennsylvania M,W
Drexel University M,W
Gannon University M,W
La Salle University M,W
Lehigh University M,W
Penn State
University Park M,W
St. Francis University W
University of Pittsburgh M,W
Villanova University W
West Chester University of Pennsylvania M,W

Rhode Island
Bryant University M,W
University of Rhode Island W

South Carolina
Clemson University M,W
College of Charleston M,W
University of South Carolina
Columbia M,W

South Dakota
University of South Dakota M,W

Texas
Southern Methodist University M,W
Texas A&M University M,W
Texas Christian University M,W
University of Houston W
University of North Texas W
University of Texas
Austin M,W

Utah
Brigham Young University M,W
University of Utah M,W

Vermont
University of Vermont W

Virginia
George Mason University M,W
James Madison University W
Old Dominion University M,W
Radford University W
University of Richmond W
University of Virginia M,W
Virginia Military Institute M
Virginia Polytechnic Institute and State University M,W

West Virginia
West Virginia University M,W

Wisconsin
University of Wisconsin
Green Bay M,W
Milwaukee M,W

Wyoming
University of Wyoming M,W

Equestrian

California
California State University
Fresno W

Delaware
Delaware State University W

Georgia
University of Georgia W

Idaho
College of Southern Idaho M,W

Indiana
St. Mary-of-the-Woods College W

Kansas
Kansas State University W

Kentucky
Midway College W
Murray State University M,W

Massachusetts
Stonehill College W

Minnesota
University of Minnesota
Crookston W

Montana
University of Montana: Western M,W

Nebraska
Nebraska College of Technical Agriculture M,W

North Carolina
St. Andrews University M,W

Ohio
Tiffin University M,W

Oklahoma
Oklahoma Panhandle State University M,W
Oklahoma State University W

Oregon
Linn-Benton Community College M,W

Pennsylvania
Seton Hill University W

South Carolina
University of South Carolina
Columbia W

South Dakota
South Dakota State University W

Tennessee
University of Tennessee
Martin W

Texas
Baylor University W
Southern Methodist University W
Texas A&M University W
Texas Christian University W
West Texas A&M University W

Virginia
Virginia Intermont College M,W

Wyoming
Laramie County Community College M,W

Fencing

California
Stanford University M,W

Illinois
Northwestern University W

Indiana
University of Notre Dame M,W

Michigan
University of Detroit Mercy M,W
Wayne State University M,W

New Jersey
Fairleigh Dickinson University
Metropolitan Campus W
New Jersey Institute of Technology M,W
Rutgers, The State University of New Jersey
New Brunswick/Piscataway Campus M,W

New York
City University of New York
Queens College W
St. John's University M,W

Ohio
Cleveland State University M,W
Ohio State University
Columbus Campus M,W

Pennsylvania
Penn State
University Park M,W
Temple University W

Field Hockey

California
Stanford University W
University of California
Berkeley W
Davis W
University of the Pacific W

Connecticut
Fairfield University W
Quinnipiac University W
Sacred Heart University W
Southern Connecticut State University W
University of Connecticut W

Delaware
University of Delaware W

District of Columbia
American University W
Georgetown University W

Illinois
Northwestern University W
Robert Morris University: Chicago W

Indiana
Ball State University W

Iowa
University of Iowa W

Kentucky
Bellarmine University W
University of Louisville W

Maine
University of Maine W

Maryland
Towson University W
University of Maryland
College Park W

Massachusetts
American International College W
Boston College W
Boston University W
College of the Holy Cross W
Merrimack College W
Northeastern University W
Stonehill College W
University of Massachusetts
Lowell W

Michigan
Central Michigan University W
Michigan State University W
University of Michigan W

Missouri
Lindenwood University W
Missouri State University W
Saint Louis University W

New Hampshire
Franklin Pierce University W
Saint Anselm College W
University of New Hampshire W

New Jersey
Monmouth University W
Rider University W
Rutgers, The State University of New Jersey
New Brunswick/Piscataway Campus W

New York
Adelphi University W
Colgate University W
Hofstra University W
Long Island University
C. W. Post Campus W
Siena College W
SUNY
University at Albany W
Syracuse University W

North Carolina
Appalachian State University W
Davidson College W
Duke University W
University of North Carolina
Chapel Hill W
Wake Forest University W

Ohio
Kent State University W
Miami University
Oxford W
Ohio State University
Columbus Campus W
Ohio University W

Pennsylvania
Bloomsburg University of Pennsylvania W
Drexel University W
East Stroudsburg University of Pennsylvania W
Indiana University of Pennsylvania W
Kutztown University of Pennsylvania W
La Salle University W
Lafayette College W
Lehigh University W
Lock Haven University of Pennsylvania W
Mansfield University of Pennsylvania W
Mercyhurst University W
Millersville University of Pennsylvania W
Penn State
University Park W
Robert Morris University W
St. Francis University W
Saint Joseph's University W
Seton Hill University W
Shippensburg University of Pennsylvania W
Slippery Rock University of Pennsylvania W
Temple University W
Villanova University W
West Chester University of Pennsylvania W

Rhode Island
Bryant University W
Providence College W

South Carolina
Limestone College W

Vermont
University of Vermont W

Virginia
College of William and Mary W
James Madison University W
Longwood University W
Old Dominion University W
Radford University W
University of Richmond W
University of Virginia W
Virginia Commonwealth University W

Football (non-tackle)

Alabama
Faulkner University M

Illinois
Olivet Nazarene University M

Michigan
Southwestern Michigan College M,W

New York
SUNY
Institute of Technology at Utica/Rome M

Football (tackle)

Alabama
Alabama Agricultural and Mechanical University M
Alabama State University M
Auburn University M
Jacksonville State University M
Miles College M
Samford University M
Troy University M
Tuskegee University M
University of Alabama M
University of Alabama
Birmingham M
University of North Alabama M
University of West Alabama M

Arizona
Arizona State University M
Arizona Western College M
Eastern Arizona College M
Glendale Community College M
Mesa Community College M
Northern Arizona University M
Pima Community College M
Scottsdale Community College M
University of Arizona M

Arkansas
Arkansas State University M
Arkansas Tech University M
Harding University M
Henderson State University M
Ouachita Baptist University M
Southern Arkansas University M
University of Arkansas M
University of Arkansas
Monticello M
Pine Bluff M
University of Central Arkansas M

California
Azusa Pacific University M
California Polytechnic State University: San Luis Obispo M
California State University
Fresno M
Sacramento M
Fresno City College M
Grossmont College M
Humboldt State University M
Menlo College M
San Diego State University M
San Jose State University M
Stanford University M
University of California
Berkeley M
Davis M
Los Angeles M
University of Southern California M
Yuba Community College District M

Colorado
Adams State College M
Colorado Mesa University M
Colorado School of Mines M
Colorado State University M
Colorado State University
Pueblo M
Fort Lewis College M
University of Colorado
Boulder M
University of Northern Colorado M
Western State Colorado University M

Connecticut
Sacred Heart University M
Southern Connecticut State University M
University of Connecticut M
University of New Haven M

Delaware
Delaware State University M
University of Delaware M

District of Columbia
Georgetown University M
Howard University M

Florida
Ave Maria University M
Bethune-Cookman University M
Florida Agricultural and Mechanical University M
Florida Atlantic University M
Florida State University M
Southeastern University M
University of Central Florida M
University of Florida M
University of Miami M
University of South Florida M
Webber International University M

Georgia
Albany State University M
Clark Atlanta University M
Fort Valley State University M
Georgia Institute of Technology M
Georgia Military College M
Georgia Southern University M
Georgia State University M
Morehouse College M
Point University M
Reinhardt University M
Savannah State University M
Shorter University M
University of Georgia M
University of West Georgia M
Valdosta State University M

Hawaii
University of Hawaii
Manoa M

Idaho
Boise State University M
Idaho State University M
University of Idaho M

Illinois
Eastern Illinois University M
Illinois State University M
McKendree University M
Northwestern University M
Olivet Nazarene University M
Quincy University M
Robert Morris University: Chicago M
Saint Xavier University M
Southern Illinois University Carbondale M
Trinity International University M
University of Illinois
Urbana-Champaign M
University of St. Francis M
Western Illinois University M

Indiana
Ball State University M
Indiana State University M
Indiana University
Bloomington M
Marian University M
Purdue University M
Saint Joseph's College M
Taylor University M
University of Indianapolis M
University of Notre Dame M
University of St. Francis M

Iowa
Briar Cliff University M
Dordt College M
Ellsworth Community College M
Graceland University M
Grand View University M
Iowa Central Community College M
Iowa State University M
Iowa Western Community College M
Morningside College M
Northwestern College M
St. Ambrose University M
University of Iowa M
University of Northern Iowa M
Waldorf College M
William Penn University M

Kansas
Baker University M
Benedictine College M
Bethel College M
Butler Community College M
Coffeyville Community College M
Dodge City Community College M
Emporia State University M
Fort Hays State University M
Fort Scott Community College M
Friends University M
Garden City Community College M
Highland Community College M
Hutchinson Community College M
Independence Community College M
Kansas State University M
Kansas Wesleyan University M
McPherson College M
MidAmerica Nazarene University M
Ottawa University M
Pittsburg State University M
Southwestern College M
Sterling College M
Tabor College M
University of Kansas M
University of St. Mary M
Washburn University M

Kentucky
Campbellsville University M
Eastern Kentucky University M
Georgetown College M
Kentucky Christian University M
Kentucky State University M
Kentucky Wesleyan College M
Lindsey Wilson College M
Murray State University M
Union College M
University of Kentucky M
University of Louisville M
University of Pikeville M
University of the Cumberlands M
Western Kentucky University M

Louisiana
Grambling State University M
Louisiana State University and Agricultural and Mechanical College M
Louisiana Tech University M
McNeese State University M
Nicholls State University M
Northwestern State University M
Southeastern Louisiana University M
Southern University and Agricultural and Mechanical College M
Tulane University M
University of Louisiana at Lafayette M
University of Louisiana at Monroe M

Maine
University of Maine M

Maryland
Bowie State University M
Morgan State University M
Towson University M
University of Maryland
College Park M

Massachusetts
American International College M
Boston College M
Dean College M
Merrimack College M
Stonehill College M
University of Massachusetts
Amherst M

Michigan
Central Michigan University M
Concordia University M
Eastern Michigan University M
Ferris State University M
Grand Valley State University M
Hillsdale College M
Michigan State University M
Michigan Technological University M
Northern Michigan University M
Northwood University
Michigan M
Saginaw Valley State University M
Siena Heights University M
University of Michigan M
Wayne State University M
Western Michigan University M

Minnesota
Bemidji State University M
Concordia University St. Paul M
Minnesota State University
Mankato M
Moorhead M
Saint Cloud State University M
Southwest Minnesota State University M
University of Minnesota
Crookston M
Duluth M
Twin Cities M
Winona State University M

Mississippi
Alcorn State University M
Belhaven University M
Coahoma Community College M
Copiah-Lincoln Community College M
Delta State University M
East Mississippi Community College M
Hinds Community College M
Holmes Community College M
Itawamba Community College M
Jackson State University M
Mississippi Gulf Coast Community College M
Mississippi State University M
Mississippi Valley State University M
Southwest Mississippi Community College M
University of Mississippi M
University of Southern Mississippi M

Missouri
Avila University M
Central Methodist University M
Culver-Stockton College M
Evangel University M
Lincoln University M
Lindenwood University M
Missouri Southern State University M
Missouri State University M
Missouri University of Science and Technology M
Missouri Valley College M
Missouri Western State University M
Northwest Missouri State University M
Southeast Missouri State University M
Southwest Baptist University M
Truman State University M
University of Central Missouri M
University of Missouri
Columbia M
William Jewell College M

Montana
Carroll College M
Montana State University M
Montana State University
Northern M
Montana Tech of the University of Montana M
Rocky Mountain College M
University of Montana M
University of Montana: Western M

Nebraska
Chadron State College M
Concordia University M
Doane College M
Hastings College M
Peru State College M
University of Nebraska
Kearney M
Lincoln M
Wayne State College M

Nevada
University of Nevada
Las Vegas M
Reno M

New Hampshire
Saint Anselm College M
University of New Hampshire M

New Jersey
Monmouth University M
Rutgers, The State University of New Jersey
New Brunswick/Piscataway Campus M

New Mexico
Eastern New Mexico University M
New Mexico Highlands University M
New Mexico Military Institute M
New Mexico State University M
University of New Mexico M
Western New Mexico University M

New York
ASA Institute of Business and Computer Technology M
Hofstra University M
Long Island University
C. W. Post Campus M
SUNY
College of Technology at Alfred M
University at Albany M
University at Buffalo M
University at Stony Brook M
Syracuse University M
Wagner College M

North Carolina
Appalachian State University M
Brevard College M
Catawba College M
Chowan University M
Duke University M
East Carolina University M
Elizabeth City State University M
Elon University M
Fayetteville State University M
Gardner-Webb University M
Johnson C. Smith University M
Lenoir-Rhyne University M
Livingstone College M
Mars Hill College M
North Carolina Agricultural and Technical State University M
North Carolina Central University M
North Carolina State University M
St. Augustine's University M
Shaw University M
University of North Carolina
Chapel Hill M
Wake Forest University M
Western Carolina University M
Wingate University M
Winston-Salem State University M

North Dakota
Dakota College at Bottineau M
Dickinson State University M
Jamestown College M
Mayville State University M
Minot State University M
North Dakota State College of Science M
North Dakota State University M
University of Mary M
University of North Dakota M
Valley City State University M

Ohio
Ashland University M
Bowling Green State University M
Kent State University M
Lake Erie College M
Malone University M
Miami University
Oxford M
Notre Dame College M
Ohio Dominican University M
Ohio Mid-Western College M
Ohio State University
Columbus Campus M
Ohio University M
Tiffin University M
University of Akron M
University of Cincinnati M
University of Findlay M
University of Toledo M
Walsh University M
Youngstown State University M

Oklahoma
Bacone College M
East Central University M
Langston University M
Northeastern Oklahoma Agricultural and Mechanical College M
Northeastern State University M
Northwestern Oklahoma State University M
Oklahoma Baptist University M
Oklahoma Panhandle State University M
Oklahoma State University M
Southeastern Oklahoma State University M
Southwestern Oklahoma State University M
University of Central Oklahoma M
University of Oklahoma M
University of Tulsa M

Oregon
Eastern Oregon University M
Oregon State University M
Portland State University M
Southern Oregon University M
University of Oregon M

Pennsylvania
Bloomsburg University of Pennsylvania M
California University of Pennsylvania M
Cheyney University of Pennsylvania M
Clarion University of Pennsylvania M
Duquesne University M
East Stroudsburg University of Pennsylvania M
Edinboro University of Pennsylvania M
Gannon University M
Indiana University of Pennsylvania M
Kutztown University of Pennsylvania M
Lackawanna College M
Lehigh University M

Lock Haven University of Pennsylvania M
Mansfield University of Pennsylvania M
Mercyhurst University M
Millersville University of Pennsylvania M
Penn State
  University Park M
Robert Morris University M
St. Francis University M
Seton Hill University M
Shippensburg University of Pennsylvania M
Slippery Rock University of Pennsylvania M
Temple University M
University of Pittsburgh M
Valley Forge Military Academy and College M
Villanova University M
West Chester University of Pennsylvania M
Westminster College M

Rhode Island
Bryant University M
University of Rhode Island M

South Carolina
Charleston Southern University M
The Citadel M
Clemson University M
Coastal Carolina University M
Furman University M
Newberry College M
North Greenville University M
Presbyterian College M
South Carolina State University M
University of South Carolina
  Columbia M
Wofford College M

South Dakota
Augustana College M
Black Hills State University M
Dakota State University M
Northern State University M
South Dakota School of Mines and Technology M
South Dakota State University M
University of Sioux Falls M
University of South Dakota M

Tennessee
Austin Peay State University M
Bethel University M
Carson-Newman University M
Cumberland University M
Lane College M
Middle Tennessee State University M
Tennessee State University M
Tennessee Technological University M
Tusculum College M
University of Memphis M
University of Tennessee
  Chattanooga M
  Knoxville M
  Martin M
Vanderbilt University M

Texas
Abilene Christian University M
Angelo State University M
Baylor University M
Blinn College M
Kilgore College M
Midwestern State University M
Prairie View A&M University M
Rice University M
Sam Houston State University M
Southern Methodist University M
Southwestern Assemblies of God University M
Stephen F. Austin State University M
Tarleton State University M
Texas A&M University M
Texas A&M University
  Commerce M
  Kingsville M
Texas Christian University M
Texas Southern University M
Texas State University: San Marcos M
Texas Tech University M
Trinity Valley Community College M
Tyler Junior College M
University of Houston M
University of North Texas M
University of Texas
  Austin M
  San Antonio M
West Texas A&M University M

Utah
Brigham Young University M
Dixie State College M
Snow College M
Southern Utah University M
University of Utah M
Utah State University M
Weber State University M

Virginia
Bluefield College M
Hampton University M
James Madison University M
Liberty University M
Norfolk State University M
Old Dominion University M
University of Richmond M
University of Virginia M
University of Virginia's College at Wise M
Virginia Military Institute M
Virginia Polytechnic Institute and State University M
Virginia State University M
Virginia Union University M

Washington
Eastern Washington University M
University of Washington M
Washington State University M

West Virginia
Alderson-Broaddus College M
Concord University M
Fairmont State University M
Glenville State College M
Marshall University M
Shepherd University M
University of Charleston M
West Liberty University M
West Virginia State University M
West Virginia University M
West Virginia Wesleyan College M

Wisconsin
University of Wisconsin
  Madison M

Wyoming
University of Wyoming M

Golf

Alabama
Alabama State University M,W
Auburn University M,W
Central Alabama Community College M
Faulkner State Community College M,W
Faulkner University M,W
Jacksonville State University M,W
Samford University M,W
Spring Hill College M,W
Troy University M,W
University of Alabama M,W
University of Alabama
  Birmingham M,W
University of Mobile M,W
University of Montevallo M,W
University of North Alabama M
University of South Alabama M,W
Wallace State Community College at Hanceville M

Arizona
Arizona Christian University M,W
Arizona State University M,W
Chandler-Gilbert Community College M,W
Eastern Arizona College M
GateWay Community College M,W
Glendale Community College M
Grand Canyon University M,W
Mesa Community College M,W
Northern Arizona University W
Paradise Valley Community College M,W
Pima Community College M,W
Scottsdale Community College M
University of Arizona M,W

Arkansas
Arkansas State University M,W
Arkansas Tech University M,W
Harding University M,W
Henderson State University M,W
John Brown University M
Lyon College M,W
Ouachita Baptist University M,W
University of Arkansas M,W
University of Arkansas
  Fort Smith M,W
  Little Rock M,W
  Monticello M,W
  Pine Bluff M,W
University of Central Arkansas M,W

California
Academy of Art University M,W
Biola University M,W
California Baptist University M,W
California Polytechnic State University: San Luis Obispo M,W
California State University
  Bakersfield M
  Chico M,W
  Dominguez Hills M
  Fresno M,W
  Fullerton M,W
  Long Beach M,W
  Monterey Bay M,W
  Northridge M
  Sacramento M,W
  San Bernardino M
  Stanislaus M
Dominican University of California M,W
Fresno City College M,W
Holy Names University M
Loyola Marymount University M
The Master's College M
Menlo College M,W
Notre Dame de Namur University M
Pepperdine University M,W
Point Loma Nazarene University M
St. Mary's College of California M
San Diego State University M,W
San Jose State University M,W
Santa Clara University M,W
Santiago Canyon College M,W
Simpson University M,W
Sonoma State University M
Stanford University M,W
University of California
  Berkeley M,W
  Davis M,W
  Irvine M,W
  Los Angeles M,W
  Riverside M
  Santa Barbara M
University of San Diego M
University of San Francisco M,W
University of Southern California M,W
University of the Pacific M
William Jessup University M

Colorado
Adams State College M,W
Colorado Christian University M,W
Colorado Mesa University M,W
Colorado State University M,W
Colorado State University
  Pueblo M,W
Fort Lewis College M
Lamar Community College M
Trinidad State Junior College M
University of Colorado
  Boulder M,W
  Colorado Springs M
University of Denver M,W
University of Northern Colorado M,W

Connecticut
Central Connecticut State University M
Fairfield University M,W
Post University M
Quinnipiac University W
Sacred Heart University M,W
University of Connecticut M
University of Hartford M,W

Delaware
Goldey-Beacom College M
Wilmington University M

District of Columbia
George Washington University M
Georgetown University M,W

Florida
Ave Maria University M,W
Barry University M,W
Bethune-Cookman University M,W
Brevard Community College M
Daytona State College W
Eckerd College M,W
Embry-Riddle Aeronautical University M,W
Flagler College M,W
Florida Atlantic University M,W
Florida Gulf Coast University M,W
Florida Institute of Technology M,W
Florida Southern College M,W
Florida State University M,W
Jacksonville University M,W
Lynn University M,W
Northwood University
  Florida M,W
Nova Southeastern University M,W
Rollins College M,W
Saint Leo University M,W
Saint Thomas University M
Southeastern University M
Stetson University M,W
University of Central Florida M,W
University of Florida M,W
University of Miami W
University of North Florida M
University of South Florida M,W
University of Tampa M,W
University of West Florida M,W
Warner University M,W
Webber International University M,W

Georgia
Abraham Baldwin Agricultural College M
Andrew College M,W
Armstrong Atlantic State University M
Brewton-Parker College M,W
Clayton State University M
College of Coastal Georgia M,W
Columbus State University M,W
Darton College M
Georgia College and State University M
Georgia Institute of Technology M
Georgia Southern University M
Georgia Southwestern State University M
Georgia State University M,W
Kennesaw State University M,W
Mercer University M,W
Paine College M
Reinhardt University M
Shorter University M,W
Thomas University M,W
Truett-McConnell College M,W

University of Georgia M,W
University of North Georgia M,W
University of West Georgia M,W
Valdosta State University M
Young Harris College M,W

Hawaii
Chaminade University of Honolulu M,W
Hawaii Pacific University M
University of Hawaii
Hilo M
Manoa M,W

Idaho
Boise State University M,W
College of Idaho M,W
Idaho State University W
Lewis-Clark State College M,W
Northwest Nazarene University M
University of Idaho M,W

Illinois
Black Hawk College M
Bradley University M,W
Chicago State University M,W
College of Lake County M,W
Danville Area Community College M
DePaul University M
Eastern Illinois University M,W
Elgin Community College M
Highland Community College M
Illinois Central College M
Illinois State University M,W
John A. Logan College M,W
Judson University M,W
Kaskaskia College M,W
Kishwaukee College M,W
Lewis and Clark Community College M
Lewis University M,W
Lincoln College M,W
Loyola University Chicago M,W
McKendree University M,W
Moraine Valley Community College M
Northwestern University M,W
Olivet Nazarene University M
Parkland College M
Quincy University M,W
Rend Lake College M,W
Robert Morris University: Chicago M,W
Sauk Valley Community College M
Southern Illinois University Carbondale M,W
Southern Illinois University Edwardsville M,W
Spoon River College M,W
University of Illinois
Springfield M,W
Urbana-Champaign M,W
University of St. Francis M,W
Waubonsee Community College M
Western Illinois University M,W

Indiana
Ancilla College M,W
Ball State University M,W
Bethel College M,W
Butler University M,W
Calumet College of St. Joseph M,W
Goshen College M,W
Grace College M
Holy Cross College M,W
Huntington University M
Indiana Institute of Technology M,W
Indiana State University W
Indiana University
Bloomington M,W
Purdue University Fort Wayne M,W
Purdue University Indianapolis M,W
Indiana Wesleyan University M,W
Marian University M,W
Oakland City University M,W
Purdue University M,W
Purdue University
North Central M
Saint Joseph's College M,W
St. Mary-of-the-Woods College W
Taylor University M
University of Evansville M,W
University of Indianapolis M,W
University of Notre Dame M,W
University of St. Francis M,W
University of Southern Indiana M,W
Valparaiso University M,W
Vincennes University M

Iowa
AIB College of Business M,W
Ashford University M
Briar Cliff University M,W
Clarke University M,W
Dordt College M,W
Drake University M,W
Ellsworth Community College M,W
Graceland University M,W
Grand View University M,W
Iowa Central Community College M,W
Iowa Lakes Community College M,W
Iowa State University M,W
Iowa Western Community College M,W
Kirkwood Community College M
Marshalltown Community College M,W
Morningside College M,W
Mount Mercy University M,W
North Iowa Area Community College M,W
Northwestern College M,W
St. Ambrose University M,W
Southeastern Community College M,W
Southwestern Community College M
University of Iowa M,W
University of Northern Iowa M,W
Waldorf College M,W
William Penn University M,W

Kansas
Allen County Community College M
Baker University M,W
Barton County Community College M,W
Bethel College M,W
Central Christian College of Kansas M,W
Coffeyville Community College M,W
Colby Community College M,W
Dodge City Community College M,W
Friends University M
Garden City Community College M
Hutchinson Community College M
Johnson County Community College M
Kansas City Kansas Community College M
Kansas State University M,W
Kansas Wesleyan University M,W
Newman University M,W
Northwest Kansas Technical College M,W
Ottawa University M
Pittsburg State University M
Southwestern College M,W
Sterling College M,W
University of Kansas M,W
Washburn University M
Wichita State University M,W

Kentucky
Asbury University M,W
Bellarmine University M,W
Brescia University M,W
Campbellsville University M,W
Eastern Kentucky University M,W
Georgetown College M,W
Kentucky State University M
Kentucky Wesleyan College M,W
Lindsey Wilson College M,W
Morehead State University M
Murray State University M,W
Northern Kentucky University M,W
St. Catharine College M,W
Union College M,W
University of Kentucky M,W
University of Louisville M,W
University of Pikeville M,W
University of the Cumberlands M,W
Western Kentucky University M,W

Louisiana
Grambling State University M
Louisiana State University and Agricultural and Mechanical College M,W
Louisiana Tech University M
McNeese State University M,W
Nicholls State University M
Southeastern Louisiana University M
Southern University and Agricultural and Mechanical College M
University of Louisiana at Lafayette M
University of Louisiana at Monroe M
University of New Orleans M,W

Maryland
College of Southern Maryland M,W
Coppin State University W
Harford Community College M
Loyola University Maryland M
Towson University M,W
University of Maryland
College Park M,W

Massachusetts
Boston College M,W
Merrimack College W

Michigan
Aquinas College M,W
Cleary University M,W
Concordia University M,W
Cornerstone University M,W
Davenport University M,W
Eastern Michigan University M,W
Ferris State University M,W
Grand Valley State University M,W
Kalamazoo Valley Community College M
Kirtland Community College M,W
Lake Superior State University M,W
Madonna University M,W
Michigan State University M,W
Mott Community College M
Muskegon Community College M
Northern Michigan University M
Northwood University
Michigan M,W
Oakland Community College M
Oakland University M,W
Saginaw Valley State University M
Siena Heights University M,W
Spring Arbor University M,W
University of Detroit Mercy M,W
University of Michigan M,W
Wayne State University M
Western Michigan University W

Minnesota
Concordia University St. Paul M,W
Minnesota State University
Mankato M,W
Moorhead W
Saint Cloud State University M,W
Southwest Minnesota State University W
University of Minnesota
Crookston M,W
Twin Cities M,W
Winona State University M,W

Mississippi
Alcorn State University M,W
Belhaven University M,W
Blue Mountain College M,W
Copiah-Lincoln Community College M
Delta State University M
East Mississippi Community College M,W
Hinds Community College M
Itawamba Community College M
Jackson State University M,W
Meridian Community College M
Mississippi Gulf Coast Community College M
Mississippi State University M,W
Mississippi Valley State University M,W
University of Mississippi M,W
University of Southern Mississippi M,W

Missouri
Avila University M,W
Central Methodist University M,W
Columbia College M,W
Culver-Stockton College M,W
Drury University M,W
Evangel University M,W
Hannibal-LaGrange University M,W
Lincoln University M,W
Lindenwood University M,W
Maryville University of Saint Louis M,W
Missouri Baptist University M,W
Missouri Southern State University M
Missouri State University M,W
Missouri Valley College M,W
Missouri Western State University M
Northwest Missouri State University W
Park University W
Research College of Nursing M,W
Rockhurst University M,W
Southwest Baptist University M
Stephens College W
Truman State University W
University of Central Missouri M
University of Missouri
Columbia M,W
Kansas City M,W
St. Louis M,W
William Jewell College M,W
William Woods University M,W

Montana
Carroll College W
Miles Community College M,W
Montana State University W
Montana State University
Billings M,W
Northern W
Montana Tech of the University of Montana M,W
Rocky Mountain College M,W
University of Great Falls M,W
University of Montana W

Nebraska
Bellevue University M,W
Chadron State College W
College of Saint Mary W
Concordia University M,W
Creighton University M,W
Doane College M,W
Hastings College M,W
Mid-Plains Community College M
Peru State College W
University of Nebraska
Kearney M,W
Lincoln M,W
Omaha M,W
Wayne State College M,W

Nevada
University of Nevada
Las Vegas M,W
Reno M,W

New Hampshire
Franklin Pierce University M
Saint Anselm College M,W

New Jersey
Brookdale Community College M
Fairleigh Dickinson University
Metropolitan Campus M,W
Monmouth University M,W
Rider University M
Rutgers, The State University of New Jersey
New Brunswick/Piscataway Campus M,W
Saint Peter's University M
Salem Community College M
Seton Hall University M,W

New Mexico
New Mexico Junior College M
New Mexico Military Institute M

New Mexico State University M,W
University of New Mexico M,W
University of the Southwest M,W
Western New Mexico University M,W

New York
Adelphi University M
Canisius College M
Concordia College M
Daemen College M
Dominican College of Blauvelt M
Dowling College M
Hofstra University M,W
Iona College M
Le Moyne College M,W
Long Island University
  Brooklyn Campus M,W
Manhattan College M
Niagara University M
Nyack College M
Roberts Wesleyan College M
Saint Bonaventure University M
St. John's University M,W
St. Thomas Aquinas College M,W
Siena College M,W
SUNY
  University at Albany W
  University at Binghamton M
Wagner College M,W

North Carolina
Appalachian State University M,W
Barton College M
Belmont Abbey College M
Brevard College M
Campbell University M,W
Catawba College M,W
Chowan University M
Davidson College M
Duke University M,W
East Carolina University M,W
Elizabeth City State University M
Elon University M,W
Fayetteville State University M
Gardner-Webb University M,W
High Point University M,W
Johnson C. Smith University M
Johnston Community College M
Lees-McRae College M
Lenoir-Rhyne University M,W
Mars Hill College M
Montreat College M,W
Mount Olive College M
North Carolina Central University M,W
North Carolina State University M,W
Pfeiffer University M,W
Pitt Community College M
Queens University of Charlotte M,W
St. Andrews University M
St. Augustine's University M
University of North Carolina
  Chapel Hill M,W
  Charlotte M
  Greensboro M,W
  Wilmington M,W
Wake Forest University M,W
Western Carolina University M,W
Wingate University M,W

North Dakota
Dickinson State University M,W
Jamestown College M,W
Minot State University M,W
North Dakota State University W
University of Mary W
University of North Dakota M,W
Valley City State University M,W

Ohio
Ashland University M,W
Bowling Green State University M,W
Cedarville University M
Central State University M,W
Cleveland State University M,W
Kent State University M,W
Lake Erie College M,W
Lakeland Community College M
Lourdes University M,W
Malone University M,W
Miami University
  Oxford M
Mount Vernon Nazarene University M,W
Notre Dame College M,W
Ohio Dominican University M,W
Ohio State University
  Columbus Campus M,W
Ohio University M,W
Owens Community College
  Toledo M
Shawnee State University M
Tiffin University M,W
University of Akron M
University of Cincinnati M,W
University of Dayton M
University of Findlay M,W
University of Toledo M,W
Ursuline College W
Walsh University M,W
Wright State University M
Xavier University M,W
Youngstown State University M,W

Oklahoma
Bacone College M,W
Cameron University M,W
East Central University M,W
Mid-America Christian University M
Northeastern State University M,W
Northwestern Oklahoma State University M,W
Oklahoma Baptist University M,W
Oklahoma Christian University M
Oklahoma City University M,W
Oklahoma Panhandle State University M,W
Oklahoma State University M,W
Oklahoma Wesleyan University M
Oral Roberts University M,W
Redlands Community College W
Rogers State University M,W
St. Gregory's University W
Seminole State College M,W
Southeastern Oklahoma State University M
Southern Nazarene University M,W
Southwestern Oklahoma State University M,W
University of Central Oklahoma M,W
University of Oklahoma M,W
University of Tulsa M,W

Oregon
Concordia University M,W
Corban University M,W
Northwest Christian University M,W
Oregon State University M,W
Portland State University W
Southwestern Oregon Community College M,W
University of Oregon M,W
Warner Pacific College M,W

Pennsylvania
California University of Pennsylvania M,W
Chestnut Hill College M
Clarion University of Pennsylvania M
Drexel University M
Gannon University M,W
Holy Family University M
Indiana University of Pennsylvania M
Kutztown University of Pennsylvania W
La Salle University M,W
Lackawanna College M
Lehigh University M,W
Mercyhurst University M,W
Millersville University of Pennsylvania M
Penn State
  University Park M,W
Philadelphia University M
Robert Morris University M,W
St. Francis University M,W
Saint Joseph's University M
Seton Hill University W
Temple University M
University of the Sciences in Philadelphia M,W
West Chester University of Pennsylvania M,W

Rhode Island
Bryant University M
University of Rhode Island M

South Carolina
Anderson University M,W
Charleston Southern University M,W
The Citadel W
Clemson University M
Coastal Carolina University M,W
Coker College M,W
College of Charleston M,W
Columbia College W
Converse College W
Erskine College M,W
Francis Marion University M
Furman University M,W
Lander University M
Limestone College M,W
Newberry College M,W
North Greenville University M,W
Presbyterian College M,W
South Carolina State University M,W
Spartanburg Methodist College M,W
University of South Carolina
  Aiken M
  Columbia M,W
Winthrop University M,W
Wofford College M,W

South Dakota
Augustana College M,W
Mount Marty College M,W
Northern State University M,W
South Dakota School of Mines and Technology M,W
South Dakota State University M,W
University of Sioux Falls M,W

Tennessee
Austin Peay State University M,W
Belmont University M,W
Bethel University M,W
Bryan University
  Dayton M,W
Carson-Newman University M
Christian Brothers University M,W
Cumberland University M,W
East Tennessee State University M,W
King College M,W
Lee University M,W
LeMoyne-Owen College M,W
Lincoln Memorial University M,W
Lipscomb University M,W
Martin Methodist College M,W
Middle Tennessee State University M,W
Milligan College M
Tennessee Technological University M,W
Tennessee Wesleyan College M,W
Trevecca Nazarene University M,W
Tusculum College M,W
Union University M,W
University of Memphis M,W
University of Tennessee
  Chattanooga M,W
  Knoxville M,W
  Martin M
Vanderbilt University M,W
Walters State Community College M,W

Texas
Abilene Christian University M
Baylor University M,W
Dallas Baptist University W
Houston Baptist University M,W
Jacksonville College M,W
Lamar University M,W
Lubbock Christian University M,W
McLennan Community College M
Midland College M
Midwestern State University M,W
Northwood University
  Texas M,W
Odessa College M
Paris Junior College M
Prairie View A&M University M,W
Ranger College M,W
Rice University M
St. Edward's University M,W
St. Mary's University M
Sam Houston State University M,W
Southern Methodist University M,W
Stephen F. Austin State University M,W
Tarleton State University W
Texas A&M University M,W
Texas A&M University
  Commerce M
  Corpus Christi W
  Kingsville W
Texas Christian University M,W
Texas Southern University M,W
Texas State University: San Marcos M,W
Texas Tech University M,W
Texas Wesleyan University M,W
Tyler Junior College M,W
University of Houston M,W
University of North Texas M,W
University of St. Thomas M,W
University of Texas
  Austin M,W
  Brownsville - Texas Southmost College M,W
  Pan American M,W
  San Antonio M,W
University of the Incarnate Word M,W
Wayland Baptist University M,W
West Texas A&M University M,W
Western Texas College M,W

Utah
Brigham Young University M,W
Dixie State College M,W
Southern Utah University M,W
University of Utah M
Utah State University M
Utah Valley University M,W
Weber State University M,W
Westminster College M,W

Virginia
Bluefield College M
College of William and Mary M,W
George Mason University M
Hampton University M,W
James Madison University M,W
Liberty University M
Longwood University M,W
Old Dominion University M,W
Radford University M,W
St. Paul's College M
University of Richmond M,W
University of Virginia M,W
Virginia Commonwealth University M
Virginia Intermont College M
Virginia Polytechnic Institute and State University M
Virginia State University M,W
Virginia Union University M,W

Washington
Centralia College W
Columbia Basin College M,W
Eastern Washington University W
Gonzaga University M,W
Grays Harbor College M,W
Green River Community College M
Olympic College M,W
Saint Martin's University M,W
Seattle University M,W
Skagit Valley College M,W

Spokane Community College M,W
University of Washington M,W
Walla Walla Community College M,W
Washington State University M,W
Western Washington University M,W

West Virginia
Alderson-Broaddus College M,W
Bluefield State College M
Concord University M
Davis and Elkins College M
Fairmont State University M,W
Glenville State College M,W
Marshall University M,W
Ohio Valley University M,W
Salem International University M,W
University of Charleston M
West Liberty University M,W
West Virginia University Institute of Technology M
West Virginia Wesleyan College M,W
Wheeling Jesuit University M,W

Wisconsin
Silver Lake College of the Holy Family M,W
University of Wisconsin
Green Bay M,W
Madison M,W
Parkside M
Viterbo University M,W

Wyoming
Eastern Wyoming College M
University of Wyoming M,W

Gymnastics

Alabama
Auburn University W
University of Alabama W

Alaska
University of Alaska
Anchorage W

Arizona
Arizona State University W
University of Arizona W

Arkansas
University of Arkansas W

California
California State University
Sacramento W
San Jose State University W
Stanford University M,W
University of California
Berkeley M,W
Davis W
Los Angeles W
Santa Barbara W

Colorado
University of Denver W

Connecticut
Southern Connecticut State University W
University of Bridgeport W

District of Columbia
George Washington University W
Howard University M,W

Florida
University of Florida W

Georgia
University of Georgia W

Idaho
Boise State University W

Illinois
Illinois State University W
University of Illinois
Chicago M,W
Urbana-Champaign M,W

Indiana
Ball State University W

Iowa
Iowa State University W
University of Iowa M,W

Kansas
Fort Hays State University M

Kentucky
University of Kentucky W

Louisiana
Louisiana State University and Agricultural and Mechanical College W

Maryland
Towson University W
University of Maryland
College Park W
Washington Adventist University M,W

Michigan
Central Michigan University W
Eastern Michigan University W
Michigan State University W
University of Michigan M,W
Western Michigan University W

Minnesota
University of Minnesota
Twin Cities M,W

Missouri
Southeast Missouri State University W
University of Missouri
Columbia W

Nebraska
University of Nebraska
Lincoln M,W

New Hampshire
University of New Hampshire W

New Jersey
Rutgers, The State University of New Jersey
New Brunswick/Piscataway Campus W

North Carolina
North Carolina State University W
University of North Carolina
Chapel Hill W

Ohio
Bowling Green State University W
Kent State University W
Ohio State University
Columbus Campus M,W

Oklahoma
University of Oklahoma M,W

Oregon
Oregon State University W

Pennsylvania
Penn State
University Park M,W
Temple University M,W
University of Pittsburgh W
West Chester University of Pennsylvania W

Tennessee
Southern Adventist University M,W

Texas
Texas Woman's University W

Utah
Brigham Young University W
Southern Utah University W
University of Utah W
Utah State University W

Virginia
College of William and Mary M,W

Washington
Seattle Pacific University W
University of Washington W

West Virginia
Alderson-Broaddus College W
West Virginia University W

Ice hockey

Alabama
University of Alabama
Huntsville M

Alaska
University of Alaska
Anchorage M
Fairbanks M

Colorado
Colorado College M
University of Denver M

Connecticut
Quinnipiac University M,W
Sacred Heart University M,W
University of Connecticut M,W

Indiana
University of Notre Dame M

Maine
University of Maine M,W

Massachusetts
American International College M
Bentley University M
Boston College M,W
Boston University W
College of the Holy Cross M
Merrimack College M
Northeastern University M,W
University of Massachusetts
Amherst M
Lowell M

Michigan
Davenport University M,W
Ferris State University M
Lake Superior State University M
Michigan State University M
Michigan Technological University M
Northern Michigan University M
University of Michigan M
Wayne State University W
Western Michigan University M

Minnesota
Bemidji State University M,W
Minnesota State University
Mankato M,W
Saint Cloud State University M,W
University of Minnesota
Duluth M,W
Twin Cities M,W

Missouri
Lindenwood University W

Nebraska
University of Nebraska
Omaha M

New Hampshire
Franklin Pierce University M,W
University of New Hampshire M,W

New York
Canisius College M
Clarkson University M,W
Colgate University M,W
Monroe Community College M
Niagara University M
Rensselaer Polytechnic Institute M,W
St. Lawrence University M,W
Syracuse University W

North Dakota
Dakota College at Bottineau M
University of North Dakota M,W
Williston State College M

Ohio
Bowling Green State University M
Miami University
Oxford M
Ohio State University
Columbus Campus M,W

Pennsylvania
Mercyhurst University M,W
Penn State
University Park M,W
Robert Morris University M,W

Rhode Island
Providence College M,W

Vermont
University of Vermont M,W

Wisconsin
University of Wisconsin
Madison M,W

Judo

Puerto Rico
Inter American University of Puerto Rico
Aguadilla Campus M,W
Ponce Campus M,W
Turabo University W
Universidad Metropolitana M,W
Universidad Politecnica de Puerto Rico M,W
University of Puerto Rico
Humacao M,W

Lacrosse

California
California State University
Fresno W
Dominican University of California M
Notre Dame de Namur University M
St. Mary's College of California W
Stanford University W
University of California
Davis W

Colorado
Adams State College M,W
Colorado Mesa University M,W
Fort Lewis College W
University of Colorado
Boulder W
University of Denver M,W

Connecticut
Central Connecticut State University W
Fairfield University M,W
Post University M,W
Quinnipiac University M,W
Sacred Heart University M,W
Southern Connecticut State University W
University of Bridgeport W
University of Hartford M
University of New Haven W

Delaware
Delaware Technical and Community College
Dover M
University of Delaware M,W
Wilmington University W

District of Columbia
American University W
Georgetown University M,W

Florida
Florida Institute of Technology M
Florida Southern College M,W
Saint Leo University M,W
University of Florida W
University of Tampa M

Georgia
Kennesaw State University W
Point University M
Shorter University M,W
Young Harris College M,W

Illinois
Judson University M
McKendree University M
Northwestern University W
Robert Morris University: Chicago M,W

Indiana
Indiana Institute of Technology M,W
University of Notre Dame M,W

Iowa
St. Ambrose University M

Kentucky
Bellarmine University M
University of Louisville W
University of Pikeville W

Maryland
Anne Arundel Community College M,W
Community College of Baltimore County M,W
Harford Community College M,W
Howard Community College M,W
Johns Hopkins University M,W
Loyola University Maryland M,W
Mount St. Mary's University M,W
Towson University M,W
University of Maryland
College Park M,W

Massachusetts
American International College M,W
Boston College W
Boston University W
Dean College M,W
Merrimack College M,W
Stonehill College W
University of Massachusetts
Amherst M,W

Michigan
Davenport University M
Siena Heights University M,W
University of Detroit Mercy M,W
University of Michigan M,W

Minnesota
University of Minnesota
Duluth M

Missouri
Lindenwood University M,W
Missouri Baptist University M,W

New Hampshire
Franklin Pierce University M,W
Saint Anselm College M,W
Southern New Hampshire University M,W
University of New Hampshire W

New Jersey
Georgian Court University W
Monmouth University M,W
Rutgers, The State University of New Jersey
New Brunswick/Piscataway Campus
M,W

New York
Adelphi University M,W
Canisius College M,W
City University of New York
Queens College W
Colgate University M,W
College of Saint Rose M
Dominican College of Blauvelt M,W
Dowling College M,W
Hofstra University M,W
Iona College W
Le Moyne College M,W
Long Island University
Brooklyn Campus W
C. W. Post Campus M,W
Manhattan College M,W
Marist College M,W
Mercy College M,W
Molloy College M,W
Monroe Community College M
New York Institute of Technology M
Niagara University W
Nyack College W
Pace University M
Roberts Wesleyan College M,W
St. John's University M
St. Thomas Aquinas College W
Siena College M,W
SUNY
College of Technology at Alfred M
University at Albany M,W
University at Binghamton M,W
University at Stony Brook M,W
Syracuse University M,W
Wagner College M,W

North Carolina
Belmont Abbey College M,W
Catawba College M,W
Chowan University W
Davidson College W
Duke University M
Lees-McRae College M,W
Lenoir-Rhyne University M,W
Mars Hill College M
Pfeiffer University M,W
Queens University of Charlotte M,W
St. Andrews University M
University of North Carolina
Chapel Hill M,W
Wingate University M

Ohio
Lake Erie College M,W
Notre Dame College W
Ohio State University
Columbus Campus M,W
Tiffin University W
University of Cincinnati W
University of Findlay W
Ursuline College W
Walsh University M,W

Oklahoma
Oklahoma Baptist University W

Oregon
University of Oregon W

Pennsylvania
Bloomsburg University of Pennsylvania W
Bucknell University M,W
Chestnut Hill College M,W
Drexel University M,W
Duquesne University W
East Stroudsburg University of Pennsylvania W
Gannon University W
Holy Family University W
Indiana University of Pennsylvania W
Kutztown University of Pennsylvania W
La Salle University W
Lehigh University M,W
Lock Haven University of Pennsylvania W
Mercyhurst University M,W
Millersville University of Pennsylvania W
Penn State
University Park M,W
Philadelphia University W
Robert Morris University M,W
St. Francis University W
Saint Joseph's University M,W
Seton Hill University M,W
Shippensburg University of Pennsylvania W
Slippery Rock University of Pennsylvania W
Temple University W
West Chester University of Pennsylvania W

Rhode Island
Bryant University M,W

South Carolina
Coastal Carolina University W
Coker College M,W
Converse College W
Erskine College W
Furman University M,W
Limestone College M,W
Newberry College W
Presbyterian College W

Tennessee
Tennessee Wesleyan College M,W
Vanderbilt University W

Utah
Westminster College M,W

Vermont
University of Vermont M,W

Virginia
College of William and Mary W
George Mason University W
James Madison University W
Longwood University W
Old Dominion University W
University of Richmond M,W
University of Virginia M,W
Virginia Military Institute M
Virginia Polytechnic Institute and State
University W

West Virginia
Alderson-Broaddus College M,W
Shepherd University W
West Virginia Wesleyan College W
Wheeling Jesuit University M,W

Wisconsin
Marquette University M,W

Rifle

Alabama
Jacksonville State University M,W

Alaska
University of Alaska
Fairbanks M,W

Georgia
Columbus State University M,W
University of North Georgia M,W

Kentucky
Morehead State University M,W
Murray State University M,W
University of Kentucky M,W

Michigan
Hillsdale College M,W

Mississippi
University of Mississippi W

Nebraska
University of Nebraska
Lincoln W

Nevada
University of Nevada
Reno M,W

Ohio
Ohio State University
Columbus Campus M
University of Akron W

South Carolina
The Citadel M,W

Tennessee
Bethel University M,W
University of Memphis M,W
University of Tennessee
Martin M,W

Texas
Texas Christian University W

Virginia
Virginia Military Institute M,W

West Virginia
West Virginia University M,W

Rodeo

Alabama
Troy University M,W
University of West Alabama M,W

Arizona
Central Arizona College M,W
Cochise College M,W
Dine College M,W

Arkansas
Southern Arkansas University M,W
University of Arkansas
Monticello M,W

Colorado
Colorado Northwestern Community College
M,W
Northeastern Junior College M,W

Idaho
Boise State University M,W
College of Southern Idaho M,W

Kansas
Coffeyville Community College M,W
Colby Community College M
Dodge City Community College M,W
Fort Hays State University M
Fort Scott Community College M,W
Garden City Community College M,W
Northwest Kansas Technical College M,W
Pratt Community College M,W

Kentucky
Murray State University M,W

Louisiana
McNeese State University M,W

Mississippi
East Mississippi Community College M,W

Missouri
Missouri Valley College M,W
Northwest Missouri State University M,W

Montana
Dawson Community College M,W
Miles Community College M,W
Montana State University M,W
Montana State University
Northern M,W
University of Montana M
University of Montana: Western M,W

Nebraska
Chadron State College M,W
Nebraska College of Technical Agriculture M,W

New Mexico
Eastern New Mexico University M,W
Navajo Technical College M,W
New Mexico Junior College M,W

North Dakota
Dickinson State University M

Oklahoma
Bacone College M,W
Connors State College M,W
Eastern Oklahoma State College M,W
Northeastern Oklahoma Agricultural and Mechanical College M,W
Northwestern Oklahoma State University M,W
Oklahoma Panhandle State University M,W
Southeastern Oklahoma State University M,W
Southwestern Oklahoma State University M,W

Oregon
Eastern Oregon University M,W
Treasure Valley Community College M,W

Tennessee
University of Tennessee
Martin M,W

Texas
Clarendon College M,W
Hill College M,W
Howard College M,W
North Central Texas College M
Northeast Texas Community College M,W
Odessa College M,W
Panola College M,W
Ranger College M,W
Sam Houston State University M,W
South Plains College M,W
Tarleton State University M,W
Vernon College M,W
Weatherford College M,W
Western Texas College M,W
Wharton County Junior College M,W

Washington
Walla Walla Community College M,W

Wyoming
Casper College M,W
Central Wyoming College M,W
Eastern Wyoming College M,W
Laramie County Community College M,W
Northwest College M,W
Sheridan College M,W
University of Wyoming M,W

Rowing (crew)

California
California State University
Sacramento W
Humboldt State University W
Loyola Marymount University W
St. Mary's College of California W
San Diego State University W
Stanford University M,W
University of California
Berkeley M,W
Los Angeles M,W
University of San Diego W
University of Southern California W

Connecticut
Fairfield University M,W

Delaware
University of Delaware W

District of Columbia
George Washington University M,W
Georgetown University M,W

Florida
Ave Maria University W
Barry University W
Florida Institute of Technology M,W
Jacksonville University M,W
Nova Southeastern University W
Stetson University W
University of Central Florida W
University of Miami W
University of Tampa W

Indiana
Indiana University
Bloomington W
University of Notre Dame W

Iowa
University of Iowa W

Kansas
Kansas State University W
University of Kansas W

Kentucky
University of Louisville W

Massachusetts
Boston College W
Boston University M,W
Merrimack College W
Northeastern University M,W
University of Massachusetts
Amherst W

Michigan
Eastern Michigan University W
Michigan State University W
University of Michigan W

Nebraska
Creighton University W

New Jersey
Rutgers, The State University of New Jersey
New Brunswick/Piscataway Campus M,W

New York
Dowling College W
Fordham University W
Marist College W
SUNY
University at Buffalo W
Syracuse University M,W

North Carolina
Duke University W
University of North Carolina
Chapel Hill W

Oklahoma
Oklahoma City University M,W
University of Oklahoma W
University of Tulsa W

Pennsylvania
Drexel University M,W
Duquesne University W
Lehigh University W
Mercyhurst University M,W
Philadelphia University M,W
Robert Morris University W
Saint Joseph's University M,W
Temple University M,W

Rhode Island
University of Rhode Island W

South Carolina
Clemson University W

Tennessee
University of Tennessee
Knoxville W

Texas
Southern Methodist University W
University of Texas
Austin W

Virginia
George Mason University W
Old Dominion University W
University of Virginia W

Washington
Gonzaga University W
Seattle Pacific University W
University of Washington M,W
Washington State University W
Western Washington University M,W

West Virginia
University of Charleston W
West Virginia University W

Wisconsin
University of Wisconsin
Madison M,W

Rugby

California
University of California
Berkeley M

Connecticut
Quinnipiac University W

Illinois
Eastern Illinois University W

Michigan
Davenport University M,W

Pennsylvania
West Chester University of Pennsylvania W

Sailing

Georgia
Kennesaw State University M

Skiing

Alaska
University of Alaska
Anchorage M,W
Fairbanks M,W

Colorado
Colorado Mountain College M,W
University of Colorado
Boulder M,W
University of Denver M,W
Western State Colorado University M,W

Idaho
College of Idaho M,W

Michigan
Michigan Technological University M,W
Northern Michigan University M,W

Minnesota
Saint Cloud State University W
University of Minnesota
Twin Cities M,W

Montana
Montana State University W
Rocky Mountain College M,W

Nevada
Sierra Nevada College M,W

New Hampshire
Saint Anselm College M,W
University of New Hampshire M,W

New Mexico
University of New Mexico M,W

Tennessee
Carson-Newman University M,W

Utah
University of Utah M,W
Westminster College M,W

Vermont
University of Vermont M,W

Wisconsin
University of Wisconsin
Green Bay M,W

Soccer

Alabama
Auburn University W
Auburn University at Montgomery M,W
Judson College W
Samford University W
Spring Hill College M,W
Troy University W
University of Alabama W
University of Alabama
Birmingham M,W
Huntsville M,W
University of Mobile M,W
University of Montevallo M,W
University of North Alabama W
University of South Alabama W
University of West Alabama W
Wallace State Community College at Hanceville M

Arizona
Arizona Christian University M,W
Arizona State University W
Arizona Western College M
Chandler-Gilbert Community College M,W
Cochise College W
Embry-Riddle Aeronautical University
Prescott Campus M,W
GateWay Community College M
Glendale Community College M,W
Grand Canyon University M,W
Mesa Community College M,W
Northern Arizona University W
Paradise Valley Community College M,W
Pima Community College M,W
Scottsdale Community College M
South Mountain Community College M
University of Arizona W
Yavapai College M

Arkansas
Arkansas State University W
Crowley's Ridge College M
Harding University M,W
John Brown University M,W
Lyon College M,W
Ouachita Baptist University M,W
University of Arkansas W

University of Arkansas
Little Rock M,W
Pine Bluff W
University of Central Arkansas M,W
Williams Baptist College M

California
Academy of Art University M,W
Azusa Pacific University M,W
Bethesda University of California M
Biola University M,W
California Baptist University M,W
California Polytechnic State University: San Luis Obispo M,W
California State Polytechnic University: Pomona M,W
California State University
Bakersfield M,W
Chico M,W
Dominguez Hills M,W
Fresno W
Fullerton M,W
Los Angeles M,W
Monterey Bay M,W
Northridge M
Sacramento M,W
San Bernardino M,W
Stanislaus M,W
Concordia University M,W
Dominican University of California M,W
Fresno City College M,W
Fresno Pacific University M,W
Grossmont College W
Holy Names University M,W
Hope International University M,W
Humboldt State University M,W
Loyola Marymount University M,W
The Master's College M,W
Menlo College M,W
Notre Dame de Namur University M,W
Pepperdine University W
Point Loma Nazarene University M,W
St. Mary's College of California M,W
San Diego Christian College M,W
San Diego State University M,W
San Jose State University M,W
Santa Clara University M,W
Santiago Canyon College M,W
Simpson University M,W
Soka University of America M,W
Sonoma State University M,W
Stanford University M,W
University of California
Berkeley M,W
Davis M,W
Irvine M,W
Los Angeles M,W
Riverside M,W
Santa Barbara M,W
University of San Diego M,W
University of San Francisco M,W
University of Southern California W
University of the Pacific W
Vanguard University of Southern California M,W
Westmont College M,W
William Jessup University M,W
Yuba Community College District M,W

Colorado
Adams State College M,W
Colorado Christian University M,W
Colorado College W
Colorado Mesa University M,W
Colorado School of Mines M,W
Colorado State University
Pueblo M,W
Fort Lewis College M,W
Metropolitan State University of Denver M,W
Northeastern Junior College M,W
Otero Junior College M
Trinidad State Junior College M,W
University of Colorado
Boulder W
Colorado Springs M,W
University of Denver M,W
University of Northern Colorado W

Connecticut
Central Connecticut State University M,W
Fairfield University M,W
Post University M,W
Quinnipiac University M,W
Sacred Heart University M,W
Southern Connecticut State University M,W
University of Bridgeport M,W
University of Connecticut M,W
University of Hartford M,W
University of New Haven M,W

Delaware
Delaware State University W
Delaware Technical and Community College
Dover M
Stanton/Wilmington M
Goldey-Beacom College M,W
University of Delaware M,W
Wilmington University M,W

District of Columbia
American University M,W
George Washington University M,W
Georgetown University M,W
Howard University M

Florida
Ave Maria University M,W
Barry University M,W
Brevard Community College W
Eckerd College M,W
Embry-Riddle Aeronautical University M,W
Flagler College M,W
Florida Atlantic University M,W
Florida College M,W
Florida Institute of Technology M,W
Florida Southern College M,W
Florida State University W
Jacksonville University M,W
Lynn University M,W
Northwood University
Florida M,W
Nova Southeastern University M,W
Palm Beach Atlantic University M,W
Polk State College W
Rollins College M,W
Saint Leo University M,W
Saint Thomas University M,W
Southeastern University M,W
Stetson University M,W
University of Central Florida M,W
University of Florida W
University of Miami W
University of North Florida M,W
University of South Florida M,W
University of Tampa M,W
University of West Florida M,W
Warner University M,W
Webber International University M,W

Georgia
Abraham Baldwin Agricultural College W
Andrew College M,W
Brenau University W
Brewton-Parker College M,W
Clayton State University M,W
Columbus State University M,W
Darton College M,W
Emmanuel College M,W
Georgia College and State University W
Georgia Gwinnett College M,W
Georgia Military College M,W
Georgia Perimeter College M,W
Georgia Southern University M,W
Georgia Southwestern State University M,W
Georgia State University M,W
Gordon College M,W
Kennesaw State University W
Mercer University M,W
Middle Georgia State College M,W
Point University M,W
Reinhardt University M,W
Shorter University M,W
Southern Polytechnic State University M
Thomas University M,W
Truett-McConnell College M,W
University of Georgia W
University of North Georgia M,W
University of West Georgia W
Valdosta State University W
Young Harris College M,W

Hawaii
Brigham Young University-Hawaii M,W
Hawaii Pacific University M,W
University of Hawaii
Manoa W

Idaho
Boise State University W
College of Idaho M,W
Idaho State University W
Northwest Nazarene University W
University of Idaho W

Illinois
Bradley University M
College of Lake County M,W
Danville Area Community College M
DePaul University M,W
Eastern Illinois University M,W
Elgin Community College M,W
Illinois Central College M,W
Illinois Institute of Technology M,W
Illinois State University W
Judson University M,W
Kankakee Community College M
Kaskaskia College M,W
Kishwaukee College M
Lewis and Clark Community College M,W
Lewis University M,W
Lincoln College M,W
Lincoln Land Community College M
Loyola University Chicago M,W
McHenry County College M
McKendree University M,W
Moraine Valley Community College M,W
Morton College M
Northwestern University M,W
Olivet Nazarene University M,W
Parkland College M,W
Quincy University M,W
Robert Morris University: Chicago M,W
Saint Xavier University M,W
South Suburban College of Cook County M
Southern Illinois University Edwardsville M,W
Southwestern Illinois College M
Trinity Christian College M,W
Trinity International University M,W
University of Illinois
Chicago M
Springfield M,W
Urbana-Champaign W
University of St. Francis M,W
Waubonsee Community College M,W
Western Illinois University M,W

Indiana
Ancilla College M
Ball State University W
Bethel College M,W
Butler University M,W
Calumet College of St. Joseph M,W
Goshen College M,W
Grace College M,W
Holy Cross College M,W
Huntington University M,W
Indiana Institute of Technology M,W
Indiana State University W
Indiana University
Bloomington M,W
Purdue University Fort Wayne M,W
Purdue University Indianapolis M,W
Indiana Wesleyan University M,W
Marian University M,W
Oakland City University M,W
Purdue University W
Saint Joseph's College M,W
St. Mary-of-the-Woods College W
Taylor University M,W
University of Evansville M,W
University of Indianapolis M,W
University of Notre Dame M,W
University of St. Francis M,W
University of Southern Indiana M,W
Valparaiso University M,W

Iowa
AIB College of Business M,W
Ashford University M,W
Briar Cliff University M,W
Clarke University M,W
Dordt College M,W
Drake University M,W
Graceland University M,W
Grand View University M,W
Iowa Central Community College M,W
Iowa State University W
Iowa Western Community College M,W
Kirkwood Community College M
Morningside College M,W
Mount Mercy University M,W
North Iowa Area Community College M
Northwestern College M,W
St. Ambrose University M,W
Scott Community College M,W
University of Iowa W
University of Northern Iowa W
Waldorf College M,W
William Penn University M,W

Kansas
Allen County Community College M,W
Baker University M,W
Barton County Community College M,W
Benedictine College M,W
Bethel College M,W
Butler Community College W
Central Christian College of Kansas M,W
Cloud County Community College M,W
Coffeyville Community College M,W
Dodge City Community College M,W
Emporia State University W
Friends University M,W
Garden City Community College W
Hesston College M,W
Hutchinson Community College W
Johnson County Community College M
Kansas City Kansas Community College M
Kansas Wesleyan University M,W
MidAmerica Nazarene University M,W
Neosho County Community College M,W
Newman University M,W
Northwest Kansas Technical College M,W
Ottawa University M,W
Southwestern College M,W
Sterling College M,W
Tabor College M,W
University of Kansas W
University of St. Mary M,W
Washburn University W

Kentucky
Asbury University M,W
Bellarmine University M,W
Brescia University M,W
Campbellsville University M,W
Georgetown College M,W
Kentucky Wesleyan College M,W
Lindsey Wilson College M,W
Mid-Continent University M
Midway College W
Morehead State University W
Murray State University W

Northern Kentucky University M,W
St. Catharine College M,W
Union College M,W
University of Kentucky M,W
University of Louisville M,W
University of Pikeville M,W
University of the Cumberlands M,W

Louisiana

Louisiana College M
Louisiana State University
Shreveport M,W
Louisiana State University and Agricultural and Mechanical College W
McNeese State University W
Nicholls State University W
Northwestern State University W
Southeastern Louisiana University W
Southern University and Agricultural and Mechanical College W
University of Louisiana at Lafayette W
University of Louisiana at Monroe W

Maine

University of Maine M,W
University of Maine
Augusta M,W

Maryland

Anne Arundel Community College W
Chesapeake College M
College of Southern Maryland M,W
Community College of Baltimore County M,W
Hagerstown Community College M,W
Harford Community College M,W
Loyola University Maryland M,W
Mount St. Mary's University W
Towson University M,W
University of Maryland
College Park M,W
Eastern Shore M
Washington Adventist University M,W

Massachusetts

American International College W
Boston College M,W
Boston University M,W
College of the Holy Cross M,W
Dean College M,W
Merrimack College M,W
Northeastern University M,W
Stonehill College M,W
University of Massachusetts
Amherst M,W
Lowell M,W

Michigan

Aquinas College M,W
Central Michigan University W
Cleary University M,W
Concordia University M,W
Cornerstone University M,W
Davenport University M,W
Delta College W
Eastern Michigan University W
Ferris State University W
Grand Valley State University W
Kellogg Community College M
Madonna University M,W
Michigan State University M,W
Northern Michigan University W
Northwood University
Michigan M,W
Oakland University M,W
Rochester College M,W
Saginaw Valley State University M,W
Siena Heights University M,W
Southwestern Michigan College M,W
Spring Arbor University M,W
University of Detroit Mercy M,W
University of Michigan M,W
Western Michigan University M,W

Minnesota

Bemidji State University W
Concordia University St. Paul W
Minnesota State University
Mankato W
Moorhead W
Saint Cloud State University W
Southwest Minnesota State University W
University of Minnesota
Crookston W
Duluth W
Twin Cities W
Winona State University W

Mississippi

Alcorn State University W
Belhaven University M,W
Delta State University M,W
Hinds Community College M,W
Holmes Community College M
Jackson State University W
Meridian Community College M,W
Mississippi State University W
Southwest Mississippi Community College M,W
University of Mississippi W
University of Southern Mississippi W

Missouri

Avila University M,W
Central Methodist University M,W
Columbia College M,W
Culver-Stockton College M,W
Drury University M,W
East Central College M
Hannibal-LaGrange University M,W
Harris-Stowe State University M,W
Jefferson College M
Lindenwood University M,W
Maryville University of Saint Louis M,W
Metropolitan Community College - Kansas City M,W
Missouri Baptist University M,W
Missouri Southern State University M,W
Missouri State University M,W
Missouri University of Science and Technology M,W
Missouri Valley College M,W
Northwest Missouri State University W
Park University M,W
Research College of Nursing M,W
Rockhurst University M,W
Saint Louis University M,W
Southeast Missouri State University W
Southwest Baptist University M,W
Stephens College W
Truman State University M,W
University of Central Missouri W
University of Missouri
Columbia W
Kansas City M,W
St. Louis M,W
William Jewell College M,W
William Woods University M,W

Montana

Carroll College W
Montana State University
Billings M,W
Rocky Mountain College M,W
University of Great Falls W
University of Montana W

Nebraska

Bellevue University M,W
College of Saint Mary W
Concordia University M,W
Creighton University M,W
Doane College M,W
Hastings College M,W
University of Nebraska
Lincoln W
Omaha M,W
Wayne State College W
Western Nebraska Community College M,W
York College M,W

Nevada

University of Nevada
Las Vegas M,W
Reno W

New Hampshire

Franklin Pierce University M,W
Hesser College M,W
Saint Anselm College M,W
Southern New Hampshire University M,W
University of New Hampshire M,W

New Jersey

Bloomfield College M,W
Burlington County College M,W
Caldwell College M,W
Essex County College M
Fairleigh Dickinson University
Metropolitan Campus M,W
Felician College M,W
Georgian Court University W
Mercer County Community College M,W
Monmouth University M,W
New Jersey Institute of Technology M,W
Rider University M,W
Rutgers, The State University of New Jersey
New Brunswick/Piscataway Campus M,W
Saint Peter's University M,W
Salem Community College W
Seton Hall University M,W
Sussex County Community College W

New Mexico

Eastern New Mexico University M,W
New Mexico Highlands University W
University of New Mexico M,W
University of the Southwest M,W

New York

Adelphi University M,W
ASA Institute of Business and Computer Technology M
Bryant & Stratton College
Syracuse M,W
Canisius College M,W
City University of New York
Queens College M,W
Colgate University M,W
College of Saint Rose M,W
Concordia College M,W
Daemen College M,W
Dominican College of Blauvelt M,W
Dowling College M,W
Fordham University M,W
Globe Institute of Technology M
Hartwick College M
Hofstra University M,W
Iona College M,W
Le Moyne College M,W
Long Island University
Brooklyn Campus M,W
C. W. Post Campus M,W
Manhattan College M,W
Marist College M,W
Mercy College M,W
Molloy College M,W
Monroe Community College M,W
New York Institute of Technology M,W
Niagara University M,W
Nyack College M,W
Pace University W
Roberts Wesleyan College M,W
Saint Bonaventure University M,W
St. Francis College M
St. John's University M,W
St. Thomas Aquinas College M,W
Siena College M,W
SUNY
University at Albany M,W
University at Binghamton M,W
University at Buffalo M,W
University at Stony Brook M,W
Syracuse University M,W
Wagner College W

North Carolina

Appalachian State University M,W
Barton College M,W
Belmont Abbey College M,W
Brevard College M,W
Campbell University M,W
Catawba College M,W
Chowan University M,W
Davidson College M,W
Duke University M,W
East Carolina University W
Elon University M,W
Gardner-Webb University M,W
High Point University M,W
Lees-McRae College M,W
Lenoir-Rhyne University M,W
Louisburg College M,W
Mars Hill College M,W
Montreat College M,W
Mount Olive College M,W
North Carolina State University M,W
Pfeiffer University M,W
Queens University of Charlotte M,W
St. Andrews University M,W
University of North Carolina
Asheville M,W
Chapel Hill M,W
Charlotte M,W
Greensboro M,W
Pembroke W
Wilmington M,W
Wake Forest University M,W
Western Carolina University W
Wingate University M,W

North Dakota

Jamestown College M,W
North Dakota State University W
University of Mary M,W
University of North Dakota W

Ohio

Ashland University M,W
Bowling Green State University M,W
Bryant & Stratton College
Eastlake M
Cedarville University M,W
Cincinnati State Technical and Community College M,W
Cleveland State University M,W
Kent State University W
Lake Erie College M,W
Lakeland Community College M
Malone University M,W
Miami University
Oxford W
Mount Vernon Nazarene University M,W
Notre Dame College M,W
Ohio Dominican University M,W
Ohio Mid-Western College M,W
Ohio State University
Columbus Campus M,W
Ohio University W
Owens Community College
Toledo M,W
Shawnee State University M,W
Southern State Community College M
Tiffin University M,W
University of Akron M,W
University of Cincinnati M,W
University of Dayton M,W
University of Findlay M,W
University of Rio Grande M,W
University of Toledo W
Ursuline College W
Walsh University M,W
Wright State University M

Xavier University M,W
Youngstown State University W

Oklahoma
Bacone College M,W
East Central University W
Mid-America Christian University M,W
Northeastern Oklahoma Agricultural and Mechanical College M,W
Northeastern State University M,W
Northern Oklahoma College M,W
Northwestern Oklahoma State University W
Oklahoma Baptist University M,W
Oklahoma Christian University M,W
Oklahoma City University M,W
Oklahoma State University W
Oklahoma Wesleyan University M,W
Oral Roberts University M,W
Rogers State University M,W
St. Gregory's University M,W
Southern Nazarene University M,W
Southwestern Oklahoma State University M,W
University of Central Oklahoma W
University of Oklahoma W
University of Science and Arts of Oklahoma M,W
University of Tulsa M,W

Oregon
Concordia University M,W
Corban University M,W
Eastern Oregon University M,W
Lane Community College W
Northwest Christian University M,W
Oregon Institute of Technology W
Oregon State University M,W
Portland State University W
Southern Oregon University W
Southwestern Oregon Community College M,W
Treasure Valley Community College M,W
University of Oregon W
University of Portland M,W
Warner Pacific College M,W

Pennsylvania
Bloomsburg University of Pennsylvania M,W
Bucknell University M,W
California University of Pennsylvania M,W
Carlow University W
Chestnut Hill College M,W
Clarion University of Pennsylvania W
Drexel University M,W
Duquesne University M,W
East Stroudsburg University of Pennsylvania M,W
Edinboro University of Pennsylvania W
Gannon University M,W
Harcum College W
Holy Family University M,W
Indiana University of Pennsylvania W
Kutztown University of Pennsylvania W
La Salle University M,W
Lackawanna College W
Lafayette College M
Lehigh University M,W
Lock Haven University of Pennsylvania M,W
Mercyhurst University M,W
Millersville University of Pennsylvania M,W
Penn State
  University Park M,W
Philadelphia University M,W
Point Park University M,W
Robert Morris University M,W
St. Francis University M,W
Saint Joseph's University M,W
Seton Hill University M,W
Shippensburg University of Pennsylvania M,W
Slippery Rock University of Pennsylvania M,W
Temple University M,W
University of Pittsburgh M,W
Villanova University M,W
West Chester University of Pennsylvania M,W

Puerto Rico
Inter American University of Puerto Rico
  Aguadilla Campus M,W
  Bayamon Campus M
  Guayama Campus M
  Ponce Campus M,W
  San German Campus M
Turabo University M
Universidad Metropolitana M,W
Universidad Politecnica de Puerto Rico M
University of Puerto Rico
  Carolina Regional College M
  Cayey University College M,W
  Mayaguez M
  Utuado M

Rhode Island
Bryant University M,W
Community College of Rhode Island M,W
Providence College M,W
University of Rhode Island M,W

South Carolina
Anderson University M,W
Charleston Southern University M,W
The Citadel W
Clemson University M,W
Coastal Carolina University M,W
Coker College M,W
College of Charleston M,W
Columbia College W
Converse College W
Erskine College M,W
Francis Marion University M,W
Furman University M,W
Lander University M,W
Limestone College M,W
Newberry College M,W
North Greenville University M,W
Presbyterian College M,W
South Carolina State University W
Spartanburg Methodist College M,W
University of South Carolina
  Aiken M,W
  Columbia M,W
  Upstate M,W
Winthrop University M
Wofford College M,W

South Dakota
Augustana College W
Mount Marty College M,W
Northern State University W
South Dakota State University W
University of Sioux Falls M,W
University of South Dakota W

Tennessee
Austin Peay State University W
Belmont University M,W
Bethel University M,W
Bryan University
  Dayton M,W
Carson-Newman University M,W
Christian Brothers University M,W
Cumberland University M,W
East Tennessee State University M,W
Freed-Hardeman University M,W
King College M,W
Lee University M,W
Lincoln Memorial University M,W
Lipscomb University M,W
Martin Methodist College M,W
Middle Tennessee State University W
Milligan College M,W
Tennessee Technological University W
Tennessee Wesleyan College M,W
Trevecca Nazarene University M,W
Tusculum College M,W
Union University M,W
University of Memphis M,W
University of Tennessee
  Chattanooga W
  Knoxville W
  Martin W
Vanderbilt University W

Texas
Abilene Christian University W
Angelo State University W
Baylor University W
Brookhaven College W
Dallas Baptist University W
Hill College M,W
Houston Baptist University M,W
Lubbock Christian University M,W
Midwestern State University M,W
Northwood University
  Texas M,W
Paris Junior College M,W
Prairie View A&M University W
Ranger College M,W
Rice University W
St. Edward's University M,W
St. Mary's University M,W
Sam Houston State University W
Southern Methodist University M,W
Stephen F. Austin State University W
Texas A&M University W
Texas A&M University
  Commerce W
  Corpus Christi W
Texas Christian University W
Texas Southern University W
Texas State University: San Marcos W
Texas Tech University W
Texas Wesleyan University M,W
Texas Woman's University W
Tyler Junior College M
University of Houston W
University of North Texas W
University of St. Thomas M
University of Texas
  Austin W
  Brownsville - Texas Southmost College M,W
  of the Permian Basin M,W
  San Antonio W
University of the Incarnate Word M,W
Wayland Baptist University M,W
West Texas A&M University M,W
Western Texas College M,W

Utah
Brigham Young University W
Dixie State College M,W
Southern Utah University W
University of Utah W
Utah State University W
Utah Valley University W
Westminster College M,W

Vermont
University of Vermont M,W

Virginia
Bluefield College M,W
College of William and Mary M,W
George Mason University M,W
James Madison University M,W
Liberty University M,W
Longwood University M,W
Old Dominion University M,W
Radford University M,W
University of Richmond W
University of Virginia M,W
Virginia Commonwealth University M,W
Virginia Intermont College M,W
Virginia Military Institute M,W
Virginia Polytechnic Institute and State University M,W

Washington
Clark College M,W
Columbia Basin College M,W
Eastern Washington University W
Everett Community College M,W
Evergreen State College M,W
Gonzaga University M,W
Green River Community College M
Highline Community College M,W
Lower Columbia College W
Northwest University M,W
Olympic College M,W
Peninsula College M,W
Pierce College M
Saint Martin's University M,W
Seattle Pacific University M,W
Seattle University M,W
Shoreline Community College M,W
Skagit Valley College M,W
Spokane Community College W
Tacoma Community College M,W
Trinity Lutheran College M,W
University of Washington M,W
Walla Walla Community College M,W
Washington State University W
Western Washington University M,W
Whatcom Community College M,W
Yakima Valley Community College W

West Virginia
Alderson-Broaddus College M,W
Concord University W
Davis and Elkins College M,W
Marshall University M,W
Ohio Valley University M,W
Salem International University M,W
Shepherd University M,W
University of Charleston M,W
West Virginia University M,W
West Virginia Wesleyan College M,W
Wheeling Jesuit University M,W

Wisconsin
Cardinal Stritch University M,W
Marquette University M,W
Milwaukee Area Technical College M,W
University of Wisconsin
  Green Bay M,W
  Madison M,W
  Milwaukee M,W
  Parkside M,W
Viterbo University M,W

Wyoming
Central Wyoming College M,W
Laramie County Community College M,W
Northwest College M,W
University of Wyoming W
Western Wyoming Community College M,W

Softball

Alabama
Alabama State University W
Auburn University W
Central Alabama Community College W
Chattahoochee Valley Community College W
Enterprise State Community College W
Faulkner State Community College W
Faulkner University W
Gadsden State Community College W
George C. Wallace Community College at Dothan W
George C. Wallace State Community College at Selma W
Jacksonville State University W
Jefferson Davis Community College W
Judson College W
Lurleen B. Wallace Community College W
Marion Military Institute W
Miles College W
Samford University M,W
Shelton State Community College W
Snead State Community College W
Southern Union State Community College W
Spring Hill College W

Troy University W
Tuskegee University W
University of Alabama W
University of Alabama
- Birmingham W
- Huntsville W

University of Mobile W
University of North Alabama W
University of West Alabama W
Wallace State Community College at Hanceville W

Arizona

Arizona Christian University W
Arizona State University W
Arizona Western College W
Central Arizona College W
Chandler-Gilbert Community College W
Eastern Arizona College W
GateWay Community College W
Glendale Community College W
Grand Canyon University W
Mesa Community College W
Paradise Valley Community College W
Pima Community College W
Scottsdale Community College W
South Mountain Community College W
University of Arizona W

Arkansas

Arkansas Tech University W
Crowley's Ridge College W
Henderson State University W
Lyon College W
North Arkansas College W
Ouachita Baptist University W
Southern Arkansas University W
University of Arkansas W
University of Arkansas
- Monticello W
- Pine Bluff W

University of Central Arkansas W
Williams Baptist College W

California

Academy of Art University W
Azusa Pacific University W
Biola University W
California Baptist University W
California Polytechnic State University: San Luis Obispo W
California State University
- Bakersfield W
- Chico W
- Dominguez Hills W
- Fresno W
- Fullerton W
- Long Beach W
- Monterey Bay W
- Northridge W
- Sacramento W
- San Bernardino W
- Stanislaus W

Concordia University W
Dominican University of California W
Fresno City College W
Grossmont College W
Holy Names University W
Hope International University W
Humboldt State University W
La Sierra University W
Loyola Marymount University W
Menlo College W
Notre Dame de Namur University W
Patten University W
St. Mary's College of California W
San Diego State University W
San Jose State University W
Santa Clara University W
Sonoma State University W
Stanford University W
University of California
- Berkeley W
- Davis W
- Los Angeles W
- Riverside W
- Santa Barbara W

University of San Diego W
University of the Pacific W
Vanguard University of Southern California W
William Jessup University W
Yuba Community College District W

Colorado

Adams State College W
Colorado Mesa University W
Colorado Northwestern Community College W
Colorado School of Mines W
Colorado State University W
Colorado State University
- Pueblo W

Fort Lewis College W
Lamar Community College W
Northeastern Junior College W
Otero Junior College W
Trinidad State Junior College W
University of Colorado
- Colorado Springs W

University of Northern Colorado W

Connecticut

Central Connecticut State University W
Fairfield University W
Post University W
Quinnipiac University W
Sacred Heart University W
Southern Connecticut State University W
University of Bridgeport W
University of Connecticut W
University of New Haven W

Delaware

Delaware State University W
Delaware Technical and Community College
- Dover W
- Owens W
- Stanton/Wilmington W

Goldey-Beacom College W
University of Delaware W
Wilmington University W

District of Columbia

Georgetown University W

Florida

Ave Maria University W
Barry University W
Bethune-Cookman University W
Brevard Community College W
Chipola College W
College of Central Florida W
Daytona State College W
Eckerd College W
Edward Waters College W
Embry-Riddle Aeronautical University W
Flagler College W
Florida Atlantic University W
Florida Gulf Coast University W
Florida Institute of Technology W
Florida Southern College W
Florida State College at Jacksonville W
Florida State University W
Gulf Coast State College W
Hillsborough Community College W
Indian River State College W
Jacksonville University W
Lake-Sumter Community College W
Lynn University W
Miami Dade College W
North Florida Community College W
Northwest Florida State College W
Northwood University
- Florida W

Nova Southeastern University W
Palm Beach Atlantic University M,W
Palm Beach State College W
Pasco-Hernando Community College W
Pensacola State College W
Polk State College W
Rollins College W
Saint Johns River State College W
Saint Leo University W
St. Petersburg College W
Saint Thomas University W
Santa Fe College W
South Florida Community College W
Southeastern University W
State College of Florida, Manatee-Sarasota W
Stetson University W
Tallahassee Community College W
University of Central Florida W
University of Florida W
University of North Florida W
University of South Florida W
University of Tampa W
University of West Florida W
Warner University W
Webber International University W

Georgia

Abraham Baldwin Agricultural College W
Albany State University W
Andrew College W
Armstrong Atlantic State University W
Brenau University W
Brewton-Parker College W
Clark Atlanta University W
College of Coastal Georgia W
Columbus State University W
Darton College W
East Georgia College W
Emmanuel College W
Georgia College and State University W
Georgia Gwinnett College W
Georgia Highlands College M,W
Georgia Institute of Technology W
Georgia Perimeter College W
Georgia Southern University W
Georgia Southwestern State University W
Georgia State University W
Gordon College W
Kennesaw State University W
Mercer University W
Middle Georgia State College W
Paine College W
Point University W
Reinhardt University W
Shorter University W
South Georgia State College W
Thomas University W
Truett-McConnell College W
University of Georgia W
University of North Georgia W
University of West Georgia W
Valdosta State University W
Young Harris College W

Hawaii

Brigham Young University-Hawaii W
Chaminade University of Honolulu W
Hawaii Pacific University W
University of Hawaii
- Hilo W
- Manoa W

Idaho

Boise State University W
College of Idaho W
College of Southern Idaho M,W
Idaho State University W
North Idaho College W
Northwest Nazarene University W

Illinois

Black Hawk College W
Bradley University W
Carl Sandburg College W
College of Lake County W
Danville Area Community College W
DePaul University W
Eastern Illinois University W
Elgin Community College W
Highland Community College W
Illinois Central College W
Illinois Eastern Community Colleges
- Lincoln Trail College W
- Olney Central College W
- Wabash Valley College W

Illinois State University W
John A. Logan College W
John Wood Community College W
Judson University W
Kankakee Community College W
Kaskaskia College W
Kishwaukee College W
Lake Land College W
Lewis University W
Lincoln College W
Lincoln Land Community College W
Loyola University Chicago W
McHenry County College W
McKendree University W
Moraine Valley Community College W
Morton College W
Northwestern University W
Olivet Nazarene University W
Parkland College W
Quincy University W
Rend Lake College W
Robert Morris University: Chicago W
Saint Xavier University W
Sauk Valley Community College W
Shawnee Community College W
South Suburban College of Cook County W
Southeastern Illinois College W
Southern Illinois University Carbondale W
Southern Illinois University Edwardsville W
Southwestern Illinois College W
Spoon River College W
Trinity Christian College W
Trinity International University W
University of Illinois
- Chicago W
- Springfield W
- Urbana-Champaign W

University of St. Francis W
Waubonsee Community College W
Western Illinois University W

Indiana

Ancilla College W
Ball State University W
Bethel College W
Butler University W
Calumet College of St. Joseph W
Goshen College W
Grace College W
Huntington University W
Indiana Institute of Technology W
Indiana State University W
Indiana University
- Bloomington W
- Purdue University Fort Wayne W
- Purdue University Indianapolis W

Indiana Wesleyan University W
Marian University W
Oakland City University W
Purdue University W
Purdue University
- North Central W

Saint Joseph's College W
St. Mary-of-the-Woods College W
Taylor University W
University of Evansville W
University of Indianapolis W
University of Notre Dame W
University of St. Francis W
University of Southern Indiana W
Valparaiso University W

Iowa

AIB College of Business W
Ashford University W
Briar Cliff University W

Clarke University W
Dordt College W
Drake University W
Ellsworth Community College W
Graceland University W
Grand View University W
Iowa Central Community College W
Iowa Lakes Community College W
Iowa State University W
Iowa Western Community College W
Kirkwood Community College W
Marshalltown Community College W
Morningside College W
Mount Mercy University W
Muscatine Community College W
North Iowa Area Community College W
Northwestern College W
St. Ambrose University W
Southeastern Community College W
Southwestern Community College W
University of Iowa W
University of Northern Iowa W
Waldorf College W
William Penn University W

Kansas
Allen County Community College W
Baker University W
Barton County Community College W
Benedictine College W
Brown Mackie College
Salina W
Butler Community College W
Central Christian College of Kansas W
Cloud County Community College W
Coffeyville Community College W
Colby Community College W
Cowley County Community College W
Dodge City Community College W
Emporia State University W
Fort Hays State University W
Fort Scott Community College W
Friends University W
Garden City Community College W
Highland Community College W
Hutchinson Community College W
Independence Community College W
Johnson County Community College W
Kansas City Kansas Community College W
Kansas Wesleyan University W
Labette Community College W
McPherson College W
MidAmerica Nazarene University W
Neosho County Community College W
Newman University W
Ottawa University W
Pittsburg State University W
Pratt Community College W
Seward County Community College W
Southwestern College W
Sterling College W
Tabor College W
University of Kansas W
University of St. Mary W
Washburn University W
Wichita State University W

Kentucky
Asbury University W
Bellarmine University W
Brescia University W
Campbellsville University W
Eastern Kentucky University W
Georgetown College W
Kentucky State University W
Kentucky Wesleyan College W
Lindsey Wilson College W
Mid-Continent University W
Midway College W
Morehead State University W
Murray State University W
Northern Kentucky University W
St. Catharine College W
Union College W
University of Kentucky W
University of Louisville M
University of Pikeville W
University of the Cumberlands W
Western Kentucky University W

Louisiana
Bossier Parish Community College W
Louisiana State University
Eunice W
Louisiana State University and Agricultural and Mechanical College W
Louisiana Tech University W
McNeese State University W
Nicholls State University W
Northwestern State University W
Southeastern Louisiana University W
Southern University and Agricultural and Mechanical College W
University of Louisiana at Lafayette W
University of Louisiana at Monroe W

Maine
University of Maine W

Maryland
Bowie State University W
Chesapeake College W
College of Southern Maryland W
Community College of Baltimore County W
Coppin State University W
Garrett College W
Hagerstown Community College W
Harford Community College W
Morgan State University W
Mount St. Mary's University W
Towson University W
University of Maryland
College Park W
Eastern Shore W
Washington Adventist University W

Massachusetts
American International College W
Boston College W
Boston University W
Dean College W
Merrimack College W
Stonehill College W
University of Massachusetts
Amherst W
Lowell W

Michigan
Alpena Community College W
Aquinas College W
Central Michigan University W
Concordia University W
Cornerstone University W
Davenport University W
Delta College W
Eastern Michigan University W
Ferris State University W
Glen Oaks Community College W
Grand Valley State University W
Henry Ford Community College W
Hillsdale College W
Kalamazoo Valley Community College W
Kellogg Community College W
Lake Michigan College W
Lake Superior State University W
Lansing Community College W
Madonna University W
Michigan State University W
Mott Community College W
Muskegon Community College W
Northwood University
Michigan W
Oakland Community College W
Oakland University W
Rochester College W
Saginaw Valley State University W
St. Clair County Community College W
Siena Heights University W
Spring Arbor University W
University of Detroit Mercy W
University of Michigan W
University of Michigan
Dearborn W
Wayne State University W
Western Michigan University W

Minnesota
Bemidji State University W
Concordia University St. Paul W
Minnesota State University
Mankato W
Moorhead W
Saint Cloud State University W
Southwest Minnesota State University W
University of Minnesota
Crookston W
Duluth W
Twin Cities W
Winona State University W

Mississippi
Alcorn State University W
Belhaven University W
Blue Mountain College W
Copiah-Lincoln Community College W
Delta State University W
East Mississippi Community College W
Hinds Community College W
Holmes Community College W
Itawamba Community College W
Jackson State University W
Meridian Community College W
Mississippi Gulf Coast Community College W
Mississippi State University W
Mississippi Valley State University W
Southwest Mississippi Community College W
University of Mississippi W
University of Southern Mississippi W

Missouri
Avila University W
Central Methodist University W
Columbia College W
Cottey College W
Culver-Stockton College W
Drury University W
East Central College W
Evangel University W
Hannibal-LaGrange University W
Harris-Stowe State University W
Jefferson College W
Lincoln University W
Lindenwood University W
Maryville University of Saint Louis W
Metropolitan Community College - Kansas City W
Missouri Baptist University W
Missouri Southern State University W
Missouri State University W
Missouri University of Science and Technology W
Missouri Valley College W
Missouri Western State University W
North Central Missouri College W
Northwest Missouri State University W
Park University W
Research College of Nursing W
Rockhurst University W
Saint Louis University W
Southeast Missouri State University W
Southwest Baptist University W
Stephens College W
Three Rivers Community College W
Truman State University W
University of Central Missouri W
University of Missouri
Columbia W
Kansas City W
St. Louis W
William Jewell College W
William Woods University W

Montana
Montana State University
Billings W
University of Great Falls W

Nebraska
Bellevue University W
College of Saint Mary W
Concordia University W
Creighton University W
Doane College W
Hastings College W
Mid-Plains Community College W
Peru State College W
University of Nebraska
Kearney W
Lincoln W
Omaha W
Wayne State College W
Western Nebraska Community College W
York College W

Nevada
College of Southern Nevada W
University of Nevada
Las Vegas W
Reno W

New Hampshire
Franklin Pierce University W
Hesser College W
Saint Anselm College W
Southern New Hampshire University M,W

New Jersey
Bloomfield College W
Brookdale Community College W
Burlington County College W
Caldwell College W
Fairleigh Dickinson University
Metropolitan Campus W
Felician College W
Georgian Court University W
Mercer County Community College W
Monmouth University W
Raritan Valley Community College W
Rider University W
Rutgers, The State University of New Jersey
New Brunswick/Piscataway Campus W
Saint Peter's University W
Salem Community College W
Seton Hall University W

New Mexico
Eastern New Mexico University W
New Mexico Highlands University W
New Mexico State University W
University of New Mexico W
University of the Southwest W
Western New Mexico University W

New York
Adelphi University W
Canisius College W
City University of New York
Queens College W
Colgate University W
College of Saint Rose W
Concordia College W
Dominican College of Blauvelt W
Dowling College W
Fordham University W
Genesee Community College W
Hofstra University W
Iona College W
Le Moyne College W
Long Island University
Brooklyn Campus W
C. W. Post Campus W
Manhattan College W
Marist College W

Mercy College W
Molloy College W
New York Institute of Technology W
Niagara University W
Nyack College W
Pace University W
Saint Bonaventure University W
St. John's University W
St. Thomas Aquinas College W
Siena College W
SUNY
  University at Albany W
  University at Binghamton W
  University at Buffalo W
  University at Stony Brook W
Syracuse University W
Wagner College W

North Carolina
Appalachian State University W
Barton College W
Belmont Abbey College W
Brevard College W
Campbell University W
Catawba College W
Chowan University W
East Carolina University W
Elizabeth City State University W
Elon University W
Fayetteville State University W
Gardner-Webb University W
Johnson C. Smith University W
Lees-McRae College W
Lenoir-Rhyne University W
Louisburg College W
Mars Hill College W
Montreat College W
Mount Olive College W
North Carolina Central University W
North Carolina State University W
Pfeiffer University W
Pitt Community College W
Queens University of Charlotte W
St. Andrews University W
St. Augustine's University W
Shaw University W
University of North Carolina
  Chapel Hill W
  Charlotte W
  Greensboro W
  Wilmington W
Western Carolina University W
Wingate University W
Winston-Salem State University W

North Dakota
Dakota College at Bottineau W
Dickinson State University W
Jamestown College W
Mayville State University W
Minot State University W
North Dakota State University W
University of Mary W
University of North Dakota W
Valley City State University W
Williston State College W

Ohio
Ashland University W
Bowling Green State University W
Cedarville University W
Cleveland State University W
Kent State University W
Lake Erie College W
Lakeland Community College W
Lourdes University W
Malone University W
Miami University
  Oxford W
Mount Vernon Nazarene University W
Notre Dame College W
Ohio Dominican University W
Ohio University W
Owens Community College
  Toledo W
Shawnee State University W
Sinclair Community College W
Southern State Community College W
Tiffin University W
University of Akron W
University of Dayton W
University of Findlay W
University of Rio Grande W
University of Toledo W
Ursuline College W
Walsh University W
Wright State University W
Youngstown State University W

Oklahoma
Bacone College W
Cameron University W
Carl Albert State College W
Connors State College W
East Central University W
Eastern Oklahoma State College W
Mid-America Christian University W
Northeastern Oklahoma Agricultural and
  Mechanical College W
Northeastern State University W
Northern Oklahoma College M,W
Northwestern Oklahoma State University W
Oklahoma Baptist University W
Oklahoma Christian University W
Oklahoma City University W
Oklahoma Panhandle State University M,W
Oklahoma State University W
Oklahoma Wesleyan University W
Rogers State University W
Rose State College W
St. Gregory's University W
Seminole State College W
Southeastern Oklahoma State University W
Southern Nazarene University W
Southwestern Oklahoma State University W
University of Central Oklahoma W
University of Oklahoma W
University of Science and Arts of Oklahoma W
University of Tulsa W
Western Oklahoma State College W

Oregon
Clackamas Community College W
Concordia University W
Corban University W
Eastern Oregon University W
Mt. Hood Community College W
Northwest Christian University W
Oregon Institute of Technology W
Oregon State University W
Portland State University W
Southern Oregon University W
Southwestern Oregon Community College W
Treasure Valley Community College M,W
University of Oregon W

Pennsylvania
Bloomsburg University of Pennsylvania W
California University of Pennsylvania W
Carlow University W
Chestnut Hill College W
Clarion University of Pennsylvania W
Drexel University W
East Stroudsburg University of Pennsylvania W
Edinboro University of Pennsylvania W
Gannon University W
Holy Family University W
Indiana University of Pennsylvania W
Kutztown University of Pennsylvania W
La Salle University W
Lackawanna College W
Lehigh University W
Lock Haven University of Pennsylvania W
Mansfield University of Pennsylvania W
Mercyhurst University W
Millersville University of Pennsylvania W
Penn State
  University Park W
Philadelphia University W
Point Park University W
Robert Morris University W
St. Francis University W
Saint Joseph's University W
Seton Hill University W
Shippensburg University of Pennsylvania W
Slippery Rock University of Pennsylvania W
Temple University W
University of Pittsburgh W
University of the Sciences in Philadelphia W
Villanova University W
West Chester University of Pennsylvania W
Westminster College W

Puerto Rico
Inter American University of Puerto Rico
  Aguadilla Campus M,W
  Bayamon Campus M,W
  Guayama Campus M,W
  Ponce Campus M,W
Universidad del Este W
Universidad Metropolitana W
University of Puerto Rico
  Carolina Regional College W
  Cayey University College W
  Humacao W
  Mayaguez W
  Ponce M,W
  Utuado M

Rhode Island
Bryant University W
Community College of Rhode Island W
Providence College W
University of Rhode Island W

South Carolina
Aiken Technical College W
Anderson University W
Charleston Southern University W
Claflin University W
Coastal Carolina University W
Coker College W
Columbia College W
Erskine College W
Francis Marion University W
Furman University W
Lander University W
Limestone College W
Morris College W
Newberry College W
North Greenville University W
Presbyterian College W
South Carolina State University W
Spartanburg Methodist College W
University of South Carolina
  Aiken W
  Columbia W
  Upstate W
Voorhees College W
Winthrop University W

South Dakota
Augustana College W
Dakota State University W
Mount Marty College W
Northern State University W
South Dakota State University W
University of Sioux Falls W
University of South Dakota W

Tennessee
Austin Peay State University W
Belmont University W
Bethel University W
Bryan University
  Dayton W
Carson-Newman University W
Christian Brothers University W
Cleveland State Community College W
Columbia State Community College W
Cumberland University W
Dyersburg State Community College W
East Tennessee State University W
Freed-Hardeman University W
Jackson State Community College W
King College W
Lee University W
LeMoyne-Owen College W
Lincoln Memorial University W
Lipscomb University W
Martin Methodist College W
Middle Tennessee State University W
Milligan College W
Motlow State Community College W
Roane State Community College W
Southwest Tennessee Community College W
Tennessee Technological University W
Tennessee Wesleyan College W
Trevecca Nazarene University W
Tusculum College W
Union University W
University of Tennessee
  Chattanooga W
  Knoxville W
  Martin W
Volunteer State Community College W
Walters State Community College W

Texas
Abilene Christian University W
Alvin Community College W
Angelina College W
Angelo State University W
Baylor University W
Blinn College M
Clarendon College W
Frank Phillips College W
Galveston College W
Grayson County College W
Hill College W
Houston Baptist University W
Howard College W
Kilgore College W
Lubbock Christian University W
McLennan Community College W
Midland College W
Midwestern State University W
Northeast Texas Community College W
Northwood University
  Texas W
Odessa College W
Paris Junior College W
Prairie View A&M University W
Ranger College W
St. Edward's University W
Sam Houston State University W
Stephen F. Austin State University W
Tarleton State University W
Temple College W
Texas A&M University W
Texas A&M University
  Kingsville W
Texas Southern University W
Texas State University: San Marcos W
Texas Tech University W
Texas Wesleyan University W
Texas Woman's University W
University of Houston W
University of North Texas W
University of Texas
  Arlington W
  Austin W
  of the Permian Basin W
  San Antonio W
University of the Incarnate Word W
Vernon College W
Weatherford College W
Western Texas College W
Wiley College W

Utah
Brigham Young University W
Dixie State College W

Salt Lake Community College W
Snow College W
Southern Utah University W
University of Utah W
Utah State University W
Utah Valley University W

Virginia
Bluefield College W
George Mason University W
Hampton University W
James Madison University W
Liberty University W
Longwood University W
Norfolk State University W
Radford University W
St. Paul's College W
University of Virginia W
University of Virginia's College at Wise W
Virginia Intermont College W
Virginia Polytechnic Institute and State University W
Virginia State University W
Virginia Union University W

Washington
Big Bend Community College W
Centralia College W
Columbia Basin College W
Everett Community College W
Grays Harbor College W
Green River Community College W
Highline Community College W
Lower Columbia College W
Olympic College W
Pierce College W
Saint Martin's University W
Seattle University W
Shoreline Community College W
Skagit Valley College W
Spokane Community College W
University of Washington W
Walla Walla Community College W
Western Washington University W
Yakima Valley Community College W

West Virginia
Alderson-Broaddus College W
Bluefield State College W
Concord University W
Davis and Elkins College W
Fairmont State University W
Glenville State College W
Marshall University W
Ohio Valley University W
Potomac State College of West Virginia University W
Salem International University W
Shepherd University W
University of Charleston W
West Liberty University W
West Virginia State University W
West Virginia University Institute of Technology W
West Virginia Wesleyan College W
Wheeling Jesuit University W

Wisconsin
Cardinal Stritch University W
University of Wisconsin
Green Bay W
Madison W
Parkside W
Viterbo University W

Squash

New York
Fordham University M

Swimming

Alabama
Auburn University M,W
University of Alabama M,W

Alaska
University of Alaska
Fairbanks W

Arizona
Arizona State University M,W
Grand Canyon University M,W
Northern Arizona University W
University of Arizona M,W

Arkansas
Henderson State University M,W
Ouachita Baptist University M,W
University of Arkansas W
University of Arkansas
Little Rock M,W

California
Biola University M,W
California Baptist University M,W
California Polytechnic State University: San Luis Obispo M,W
California State University
Bakersfield M,W
Fresno W
Northridge M,W
San Bernardino M,W
Concordia University M,W
Fresno Pacific University M,W
Grossmont College M,W
Loyola Marymount University W
Pepperdine University W
San Diego State University W
San Jose State University W
Soka University of America M,W
Stanford University M,W
University of California
Berkeley M,W
Davis W
Los Angeles M,W
Santa Barbara M,W
University of San Diego W
University of Southern California M,W
University of the Pacific M,W
Vanguard University of Southern California M,W

Colorado
Adams State College W
Colorado Mesa University W
Colorado State University W
Metropolitan State University of Denver M,W
University of Denver M,W
University of Northern Colorado W

Connecticut
Central Connecticut State University W
Fairfield University M,W
Post University M,W
Sacred Heart University W
Southern Connecticut State University M,W
University of Bridgeport M,W
University of Connecticut M,W

Delaware
University of Delaware W

District of Columbia
George Washington University M,W
Georgetown University M,W
Howard University M,W

Florida
Daytona State College M,W
Florida Atlantic University M,W
Florida Institute of Technology M,W
Florida Southern College M,W
Florida State University M,W
Indian River State College M,W
Lynn University W
Nova Southeastern University M,W
Saint Leo University M,W
University of Florida M,W
University of Miami W
University of North Florida W
University of Tampa M,W

Georgia
Brenau University W
Darton College M,W
Georgia Institute of Technology M,W
Georgia Southern University W
University of Georgia M,W

Hawaii
University of Hawaii
Manoa M,W

Idaho
Boise State University W
College of Idaho M,W

Illinois
Eastern Illinois University M,W
Illinois Institute of Technology M,W
Illinois State University W
Lewis University M,W
Lincoln College M,W
Northwestern University M,W
Olivet Nazarene University M,W
Robert Morris University: Chicago W
Southern Illinois University Carbondale M,W
University of Illinois
Chicago M,W
Urbana-Champaign W
Western Illinois University M,W

Indiana
Ball State University M,W
Indiana University
Bloomington M,W
Purdue University Indianapolis M,W
Purdue University M,W
University of Evansville M,W
University of Indianapolis M,W
University of Notre Dame M,W
Valparaiso University M,W

Iowa
Iowa Central Community College M,W
Iowa State University W
Morningside College M,W
University of Iowa M,W
University of Northern Iowa W

Kansas
University of Kansas W

Kentucky
Asbury University M,W
Campbellsville University M,W
Lindsey Wilson College M,W
University of Kentucky M,W
University of Louisville M,W
University of the Cumberlands M,W
Western Kentucky University M,W

Louisiana
Louisiana State University and Agricultural and Mechanical College M,W
Tulane University W
University of Louisiana at Monroe M,W

Maine
University of Maine W

Maryland
Loyola University Maryland M,W
Mount St. Mary's University W
Towson University M,W

Massachusetts
Boston College M,W
Boston University M,W
Merrimack College W
Northeastern University W
University of Massachusetts
Amherst M,W
Lowell M,W

Michigan
Eastern Michigan University M,W
Grand Valley State University M,W
Hillsdale College W
Michigan State University M,W
Northern Michigan University W
Oakland University M,W
University of Michigan M,W
Wayne State University M,W

Minnesota
Minnesota State University
Mankato M,W
Saint Cloud State University M,W
University of Minnesota
Twin Cities M,W

Mississippi
Delta State University M,W

Missouri
Drury University M,W
Lindenwood University M,W
Missouri State University M,W
Missouri University of Science and Technology M
Saint Louis University M,W
Truman State University W
University of Missouri
Columbia M,W
William Jewell College M,W

Nebraska
College of Saint Mary W
University of Nebraska
Kearney W
Lincoln W
Omaha W

Nevada
University of Nevada
Las Vegas M,W
Reno W

New Hampshire
University of New Hampshire W

New Jersey
New Jersey Institute of Technology M,W
Rider University M,W
Rutgers, The State University of New Jersey
New Brunswick/Piscataway Campus M,W
Saint Peter's University M,W
Seton Hall University M,W

New Mexico
New Mexico State University W
University of New Mexico W

New York
Adelphi University M,W
Canisius College M,W
City University of New York
Queens College M,W
College of Saint Rose M,W
Fordham University M,W
Iona College M,W

Le Moyne College M,W
Long Island University
C. W. Post Campus W
Manhattan College M,W
Marist College M,W
Monroe Community College M,W
Niagara University M,W
Saint Bonaventure University M,W
St. Francis College M,W
Siena College W
SUNY
University at Binghamton M,W
University at Buffalo M,W
University at Stony Brook W
Wagner College W

North Carolina
Campbell University W
Catawba College M,W
Davidson College M,W
East Carolina University M,W
Gardner-Webb University M,W
Lenoir-Rhyne University M,W
Mars Hill College M,W
North Carolina Agricultural and Technical State University W
North Carolina State University M,W
Pfeiffer University M,W
Queens University of Charlotte M,W
University of North Carolina
Chapel Hill M,W
Wilmington M,W
Wingate University M,W

North Dakota
University of North Dakota M,W

Ohio
Ashland University M,W
Bowling Green State University W
Cleveland State University M,W
Lake Erie College M,W
Malone University M,W
Miami University
Oxford M,W
Notre Dame College M,W
Ohio State University
Columbus Campus M,W
Ohio University W
University of Akron W
University of Cincinnati M,W
University of Findlay M,W
University of Toledo W
Ursuline College W
Wright State University M,W
Xavier University M,W
Youngstown State University W

Oklahoma
Oklahoma Baptist University M,W

Oregon
Oregon State University W

Pennsylvania
Bloomsburg University of Pennsylvania M,W
Bucknell University M,W
California University of Pennsylvania W
Clarion University of Pennsylvania M,W
Drexel University M,W
Duquesne University W
East Stroudsburg University of Pennsylvania W
Edinboro University of Pennsylvania W
Gannon University M,W
Indiana University of Pennsylvania M,W
Kutztown University of Pennsylvania W
La Salle University M,W
Lehigh University M,W
Lock Haven University of Pennsylvania W
Mansfield University of Pennsylvania W
Millersville University of Pennsylvania W
Penn State
University Park M,W
St. Francis University W
Shippensburg University of Pennsylvania M,W
University of Pittsburgh M,W
Villanova University W
West Chester University of Pennsylvania M,W
Westminster College W

Puerto Rico
Bayamon Central University M,W
Inter American University of Puerto Rico
Bayamon Campus M,W
Ponce Campus M,W
Turabo University M,W
University of Puerto Rico
Cayey University College M
Humacao M,W
Mayaguez M,W
University of the Sacred Heart M,W

Rhode Island
Bryant University M,W
University of Rhode Island W

South Carolina
College of Charleston M,W
Converse College W
Limestone College M,W
University of South Carolina
Columbia M,W

South Dakota
Northern State University W
South Dakota State University M,W
University of South Dakota M,W

Tennessee
King College M,W
University of Tennessee
Knoxville M,W
Vanderbilt University W

Texas
Rice University W
Southern Methodist University M,W
Texas A&M University M,W
Texas Christian University M,W
University of Houston W
University of North Texas W
University of Texas
Austin M,W
of the Permian Basin M,W
University of the Incarnate Word M,W

Utah
Brigham Young University M,W
University of Utah M,W

Vermont
University of Vermont W

Virginia
George Mason University M,W
James Madison University W
Radford University W
University of Richmond W
University of Virginia M,W
Virginia Military Institute M
Virginia Polytechnic Institute and State University M,W

Washington
Seattle University M,W
Washington State University W

West Virginia
Alderson-Broaddus College M,W
Davis and Elkins College M,W
Fairmont State University M,W
Marshall University W
West Virginia University M,W
West Virginia Wesleyan College M,W
Wheeling Jesuit University M,W

Wisconsin
University of Wisconsin
Green Bay M,W
Madison M,W
Milwaukee M,W

Wyoming
University of Wyoming M,W

Synchronized swimming

Alabama
University of Alabama
Birmingham W

California
Stanford University W

New York
Canisius College W

Texas
University of the Incarnate Word W

Table tennis

Arizona
South Mountain Community College M,W

Puerto Rico
Inter American University of Puerto Rico
Aguadilla Campus M,W
Bayamon Campus M,W
Metropolitan Campus M,W
Ponce Campus M,W
Universidad Metropolitana M,W
Universidad Politecnica de Puerto Rico M,W
University of Puerto Rico
Cayey University College M,W
Humacao M,W
Mayaguez M,W
Ponce M,W
Utuado M

Texas
Texas Wesleyan University M,W

Tennis

Alabama
Alabama Agricultural and Mechanical University M,W
Alabama State University M,W
Auburn University M,W
Auburn University at Montgomery M,W
Faulkner State Community College M,W
Gadsden State Community College M,W
Jacksonville State University M,W
Judson College W
Marion Military Institute M,W
Samford University M,W
Snead State Community College W
Spring Hill College M,W
Troy University M,W
Tuskegee University M,W
University of Alabama M,W
University of Alabama
Birmingham M,W
Huntsville M,W
University of Mobile M,W
University of Montevallo W
University of North Alabama M,W
University of South Alabama M,W
University of West Alabama M,W
Wallace State Community College at Hanceville M,W

Arizona
Arizona Christian University M,W
Arizona State University W
Eastern Arizona College W
GateWay Community College M,W
Glendale Community College M,W
Grand Canyon University M,W
Northern Arizona University M,W
Paradise Valley Community College M,W
Pima Community College M,W
Scottsdale Community College M,W
South Mountain Community College M,W
University of Arizona M,W

Arkansas
Arkansas State University W
Arkansas Tech University W
Harding University M,W
Henderson State University W
John Brown University M,W
Ouachita Baptist University M,W
Southern Arkansas University W
University of Arkansas M,W
University of Arkansas
Fort Smith M,W
Little Rock M,W
Pine Bluff M,W
University of Central Arkansas W

California
Academy of Art University W
Azusa Pacific University M
Biola University M,W
California Polytechnic State University: San Luis Obispo M,W
California State Polytechnic University: Pomona M,W
California State University
Bakersfield W
Fresno M,W
Fullerton W
Long Beach W
Los Angeles M,W
Northridge W
Sacramento M,W
Concordia University M,W
Dominican University of California W
Fresno City College M,W
Fresno Pacific University M,W
Grossmont College M,W
Holy Names University W
Hope International University M,W
Loyola Marymount University M,W
The Master's College W
Notre Dame de Namur University W
Pepperdine University M,W
Point Loma Nazarene University M,W
St. Mary's College of California M,W
San Diego State University M,W
San Jose State University W
Santa Clara University M,W
Sonoma State University M,W
Stanford University M,W
University of California
Berkeley M,W
Davis M,W
Irvine M,W
Los Angeles M,W
Santa Barbara M,W
University of San Diego M,W
University of San Francisco M,W
University of Southern California M,W
University of the Pacific M,W
Vanguard University of Southern California M,W
Westmont College M,W

Colorado
Colorado Christian University M,W
Colorado Mesa University M,W
Colorado State University W
Colorado State University
Pueblo M,W

Metropolitan State University of Denver M,W
University of Colorado
Boulder W
University of Denver M,W
University of Northern Colorado M,W

Connecticut
Fairfield University M,W
Post University M,W
Quinnipiac University M,W
Sacred Heart University M,W
University of Connecticut M,W
University of Hartford M,W
University of New Haven W

Delaware
Delaware State University W
Goldey-Beacom College W

District of Columbia
George Washington University M,W
Georgetown University M,W
Howard University M,W

Florida
Ave Maria University M,W
Barry University M,W
Bethune-Cookman University M,W
Eckerd College M,W
Embry-Riddle Aeronautical University M,W
Flagler College M,W
Florida Atlantic University M,W
Florida Gulf Coast University M,W
Florida Institute of Technology M,W
Florida Southern College M,W
Florida State College at Jacksonville W
Florida State University M,W
Hillsborough Community College W
Jacksonville University M,W
Lynn University M,W
Northwood University
Florida M,W
Nova Southeastern University W
Palm Beach Atlantic University M,W
Rollins College M,W
Saint Leo University M,W
Saint Thomas University M,W
Southeastern University M,W
Stetson University M,W
University of Central Florida M,W
University of Florida M,W
University of Miami M,W
University of North Florida M,W
University of South Florida M,W
University of Tampa W
University of West Florida M,W
Warner University M,W
Webber International University M,W

Georgia
Abraham Baldwin Agricultural College M,W
Albany State University W
Armstrong Atlantic State University M,W
Brenau University W
Clark Atlanta University W
Clayton State University W
College of Coastal Georgia M,W
Columbus State University M,W
Emmanuel College M,W
Fort Valley State University M,W
Georgia College and State University M,W
Georgia Gwinnett College M,W
Georgia Institute of Technology M,W
Georgia Perimeter College M,W
Georgia Southern University M,W
Georgia Southwestern State University M,W
Georgia State University M,W
Gordon College W
Kennesaw State University M,W
Mercer University M,W
Morehouse College M
Reinhardt University M,W
Savannah State University W
Shorter University M,W
South Georgia State College W
University of Georgia M,W
University of North Georgia M,W
University of West Georgia W
Valdosta State University M,W
Young Harris College M,W

Hawaii
Brigham Young University-Hawaii M,W
Chaminade University of Honolulu M,W
Hawaii Pacific University M,W
University of Hawaii
Hilo M,W
Manoa M,W

Idaho
Boise State University M,W
College of Idaho W
Idaho State University M,W
Lewis-Clark State College M,W
University of Idaho M,W

Illinois
Bradley University M,W
Chicago State University M,W
College of Lake County M,W
DePaul University M,W
Eastern Illinois University M,W
Elgin Community College M,W
Illinois State University M,W
Judson University M,W
Kaskaskia College M,W
Lewis and Clark Community College M,W
Lewis University M,W
McHenry County College M,W
McKendree University M,W
Moraine Valley Community College M,W
Northwestern University M,W
Olivet Nazarene University M,W
Quincy University M,W
Rend Lake College W
Robert Morris University: Chicago W
Sauk Valley Community College M,W
Southern Illinois University Carbondale M,W
Southern Illinois University Edwardsville M,W
Southwestern Illinois College M,W
University of Illinois
Chicago M,W
Springfield M,W
Urbana-Champaign M,W
University of St. Francis M,W
Waubonsee Community College M,W
Western Illinois University M,W

Indiana
Ball State University M,W
Bethel College M,W
Butler University M,W
Calumet College of St. Joseph M,W
Goshen College M,W
Grace College M,W
Huntington University M,W
Indiana Institute of Technology M,W
Indiana University
Bloomington M,W
Purdue University Fort Wayne M,W
Purdue University Indianapolis M,W
Indiana Wesleyan University M,W
Marian University M,W
Oakland City University M,W
Purdue University M,W
Saint Joseph's College M,W
Taylor University M,W
University of Evansville W
University of Indianapolis M,W
University of Notre Dame M,W
University of St. Francis M,W
University of Southern Indiana M,W
Valparaiso University M,W
Vincennes University M

Iowa
Briar Cliff University M,W
Drake University M,W
Graceland University M,W
Grand View University M,W
Iowa State University W
Morningside College M,W
Northwestern College M,W
St. Ambrose University M,W
University of Iowa M,W
University of Northern Iowa W

Kansas
Baker University M,W
Barton County Community College M,W
Bethel College M,W
Central Christian College of Kansas M,W
Cowley County Community College M,W
Emporia State University M,W
Fort Hays State University W
Friends University M,W
Independence Community College M,W
Johnson County Community College M,W
Kansas State University W
Kansas Wesleyan University M,W
Labette Community College W
McPherson College M,W
Newman University M,W
Seward County Community College M,W
Southwestern College M,W
Tabor College M,W
University of Kansas W
Washburn University M,W
Wichita State University M,W

Kentucky
Asbury University M,W
Bellarmine University M,W
Brescia University M,W
Campbellsville University M,W
Eastern Kentucky University M,W
Georgetown College M,W
Kentucky Wesleyan College W
Lindsey Wilson College M,W
Midway College W
Morehead State University M,W
Murray State University M,W
Northern Kentucky University M,W
Union College M,W
University of Kentucky M,W
University of Louisville M,W
University of Pikeville M,W
University of the Cumberlands M,W
Western Kentucky University M,W

Louisiana
Dillard University M,W
Grambling State University M,W
Louisiana State University
Shreveport W
Louisiana State University and Agricultural and Mechanical College M,W
Louisiana Tech University W
McNeese State University W
Nicholls State University M,W
Northwestern State University W
Southeastern Louisiana University W
Southern University and Agricultural and Mechanical College W
Tulane University M,W
University of Louisiana at Lafayette M,W
University of New Orleans M,W
Xavier University of Louisiana M,W

Maryland
College of Southern Maryland M,W
Coppin State University M,W
Harford Community College M,W
Loyola University Maryland M,W
Morgan State University M,W
Mount St. Mary's University M,W
Towson University W
University of Maryland
College Park W
Eastern Shore M,W

Massachusetts
Boston College M,W
Boston University W
Merrimack College M,W
Stonehill College M,W
University of Massachusetts
Amherst W

Michigan
Aquinas College M,W
Davenport University M,W
Eastern Michigan University W
Ferris State University M,W
Grand Valley State University M,W
Hillsdale College W
Lake Superior State University M,W
Michigan State University M,W
Michigan Technological University M,W
Muskegon Community College W
Northwood University
Michigan M,W
Oakland Community College W
Oakland University W
Saginaw Valley State University W
Spring Arbor University M,W
University of Detroit Mercy W
University of Michigan M,W
Wayne State University M,W
Western Michigan University M,W

Minnesota
Bemidji State University W
Minnesota State University
Mankato M,W
Moorhead W
Saint Cloud State University M,W
Southwest Minnesota State University W
University of Minnesota
Crookston W
Duluth W
Twin Cities M,W
Winona State University W

Mississippi
Alcorn State University M,W
Belhaven University M,W
Copiah-Lincoln Community College M,W
Delta State University M,W
Hinds Community College M,W
Holmes Community College M,W
Jackson State University M,W
Meridian Community College M,W
Mississippi Gulf Coast Community College M,W
Mississippi State University M,W
Mississippi Valley State University M,W
Tougaloo College M,W
University of Mississippi M,W
University of Southern Mississippi M,W

Missouri
Drury University M,W
Evangel University M,W
Lincoln University W
Lindenwood University M,W
Maryville University of Saint Louis M,W
Missouri Baptist University M,W
Missouri Southern State University W
Missouri Valley College M,W
Missouri Western State University W
Northwest Missouri State University M,W
Research College of Nursing M,W
Rockhurst University M,W
Saint Louis University M,W
Southeast Missouri State University W
Southwest Baptist University M,W
Stephens College W
Truman State University W
University of Missouri
Columbia W
Kansas City M,W
St. Louis M,W
William Jewell College M,W

Montana
Montana State University M,W
Montana State University
Billings M,W
University of Montana M,W

Nebraska
Concordia University M,W
Creighton University M,W
Hastings College M,W
University of Nebraska
Kearney M,W
Lincoln M,W
Omaha M,W

Nevada
University of Nevada
Las Vegas M,W
Reno M,W

New Hampshire
Franklin Pierce University M,W
Saint Anselm College M,W
Southern New Hampshire University M,W

New Jersey
Bloomfield College M
Caldwell College M,W
Fairleigh Dickinson University
Metropolitan Campus M,W
Georgian Court University W
Monmouth University M,W
New Jersey Institute of Technology M,W
Rider University M,W
Rutgers, The State University of New Jersey
New Brunswick/Piscataway Campus M,W
Saint Peter's University M,W
Seton Hall University W

New Mexico
New Mexico Military Institute M
New Mexico State University M,W
University of New Mexico M,W
University of the Southwest M,W
Western New Mexico University M,W

New York
Adelphi University M,W
ASA Institute of Business and Computer Technology M,W
City University of New York
Queens College M,W
Concordia College M,W
Dowling College M,W
Fordham University M,W
Hofstra University M,W
Le Moyne College M,W
Long Island University
Brooklyn Campus W
C. W. Post Campus W
Manhattan College W
Marist College M,W
Mercy College M
Molloy College W
New York Institute of Technology M,W
Niagara University M,W
Saint Bonaventure University M,W
St. Francis College M,W
St. John's University M,W
Siena College M,W
SUNY
University at Albany W
University at Binghamton M,W
University at Buffalo M,W
University at Stony Brook M,W
Syracuse University W
Wagner College M,W

North Carolina
Appalachian State University M,W
Barton College M,W
Belmont Abbey College M,W
Brevard College M,W
Campbell University M,W
Catawba College M,W
Chowan University M,W
Davidson College M,W
Duke University M,W
East Carolina University M,W
Elizabeth City State University W
Elon University M,W
Fayetteville State University W
Gardner-Webb University M,W
High Point University M,W
Johnson C. Smith University M,W
Lees-McRae College M,W
Lenoir-Rhyne University M,W
Mars Hill College M,W
Mount Olive College M,W
North Carolina Agricultural and Technical State University W
North Carolina Central University M,W
North Carolina State University M,W
Pfeiffer University M,W
Queens University of Charlotte M,W
St. Andrews University W
St. Augustine's University M,W
Shaw University M,W
University of North Carolina
Asheville M,W
Chapel Hill M,W
Charlotte M,W
Greensboro M,W
Wilmington M,W
Wake Forest University M,W
Western Carolina University W
Wingate University M,W
Winston-Salem State University M,W

North Dakota
University of Mary W
University of North Dakota W

Ohio
Ashland University W
Bowling Green State University W
Cedarville University M,W
Central State University M,W
Cleveland State University M,W
Lake Erie College M,W
Malone University M,W
Miami University
Oxford W
Ohio Dominican University M,W
Ohio State University
Columbus Campus M,W
Shawnee State University W
Tiffin University M,W
University of Akron W
University of Cincinnati W
University of Dayton M,W
University of Findlay M,W
University of Toledo M,W
Ursuline College W
Walsh University M,W
Wright State University M,W
Xavier University M,W
Youngstown State University M,W

Oklahoma
Bacone College M,W
Cameron University M,W
East Central University M,W
Northeastern State University W
Oklahoma Baptist University M,W
Oklahoma Christian University M,W
Oklahoma State University M,W
Oklahoma Wesleyan University M,W
Oral Roberts University M,W
Seminole State College M,W
Southeastern Oklahoma State University M,W
Southern Nazarene University M,W
University of Central Oklahoma M,W
University of Oklahoma M,W
University of Tulsa M,W

Oregon
Portland State University W
Southern Oregon University W
Treasure Valley Community College M,W
University of Oregon M,W
University of Portland M,W

Pennsylvania
Bloomsburg University of Pennsylvania M,W
California University of Pennsylvania W
Carlow University W
Chestnut Hill College M,W
Clarion University of Pennsylvania W
Drexel University M,W
Duquesne University M,W
East Stroudsburg University of Pennsylvania W
Edinboro University of Pennsylvania M,W
Holy Family University W
Indiana University of Pennsylvania W
Kutztown University of Pennsylvania M,W
La Salle University M,W
Lehigh University M,W
Mercyhurst University M,W
Millersville University of Pennsylvania M,W
Penn State
University Park M,W
Philadelphia University M,W
Robert Morris University M,W
St. Francis University M,W
Saint Joseph's University M,W
Seton Hill University W
Shippensburg University of Pennsylvania W
Slippery Rock University of Pennsylvania W
Temple University M,W
University of Pittsburgh W
University of the Sciences in Philadelphia M,W
West Chester University of Pennsylvania M,W
Westminster College W

Puerto Rico
Inter American University of Puerto Rico
Aguadilla Campus M,W
Bayamon Campus M,W
Ponce Campus M,W
San German Campus M,W
Turabo University M,W
Universidad Metropolitana M,W
Universidad Politecnica de Puerto Rico M,W
University of Puerto Rico
Bayamon University College M,W
Carolina Regional College M,W
Cayey University College M,W
Humacao M,W
Mayaguez M,W
Ponce M,W
University of the Sacred Heart M

Rhode Island
Bryant University M,W
University of Rhode Island W

South Carolina
Anderson University M,W
Charleston Southern University M,W
The Citadel M
Clemson University M,W
Coastal Carolina University M,W
Coker College M,W
College of Charleston M,W
Columbia College W
Converse College W
Erskine College M,W
Francis Marion University M,W
Furman University M,W
Lander University M,W
Limestone College M,W
Newberry College M,W
North Greenville University M,W
Presbyterian College M,W
South Carolina State University M,W
Spartanburg Methodist College M,W
University of South Carolina
Aiken M,W
Columbia M,W
Upstate M,W
Winthrop University M,W
Wofford College M,W

South Dakota
Augustana College M,W
Mount Marty College W
Northern State University W
South Dakota State University M,W
University of Sioux Falls W

Tennessee
Austin Peay State University M,W
Belmont University M,W
Bethel University M,W
Carson-Newman University M,W
Christian Brothers University M,W
Cumberland University M,W
East Tennessee State University M,W
King College M,W
Lee University M,W
LeMoyne-Owen College M,W
Lincoln Memorial University M,W
Lipscomb University M,W
Martin Methodist College M,W
Middle Tennessee State University M,W
Milligan College M,W
Tennessee Technological University M
Tennessee Wesleyan College M,W
Tusculum College M,W
Union University M,W
University of Memphis M,W
University of Tennessee
Chattanooga M,W
Knoxville M,W
Martin W
Vanderbilt University M,W

Texas
Abilene Christian University M,W
Baylor University M,W
Collin County Community College District M,W
Dallas Baptist University W
Jacksonville College M,W
Lamar University M,W
Laredo Community College M,W
Lee College W
Midwestern State University M,W
North Central Texas College W
Prairie View A&M University M,W
Rice University M,W
St. Edward's University M,W
St. Mary's University M,W
Sam Houston State University M,W
Southern Methodist University M,W
Stephen F. Austin State University W
Tarleton State University W
Temple College M,W
Texas A&M University M,W
Texas A&M University
Corpus Christi M,W
Kingsville M,W
Texas Christian University M,W
Texas Southern University M,W
Texas State University: San Marcos W
Texas Tech University M,W
Tyler Junior College M,W
University of Houston W
University of North Texas W
University of Texas
Arlington M,W
Austin M,W
Pan American M,W
San Antonio M,W
University of the Incarnate Word M,W

Utah
Brigham Young University M,W
Dixie State College W
Southern Utah University M,W
University of Utah M,W

Utah State University M,W
Weber State University M,W

Virginia
Bluefield College M,W
College of William and Mary M,W
George Mason University M,W
Hampton University M,W
James Madison University M,W
Liberty University M,W
Longwood University M,W
Norfolk State University M,W
Old Dominion University M,W
Radford University M,W
St. Paul's College M,W
University of Richmond M,W
University of Virginia M,W
University of Virginia's College at Wise M,W
Virginia Commonwealth University M,W
Virginia Military Institute M
Virginia Polytechnic Institute and State University M,W
Virginia State University M,W
Virginia Union University M,W

Washington
Eastern Washington University M,W
Gonzaga University M,W
Green River Community College M,W
Seattle University M,W
Shoreline Community College M,W
Skagit Valley College M,W
Spokane Community College M,W
University of Washington M,W
Washington State University W

West Virginia
Alderson-Broaddus College W
Bluefield State College M,W
Concord University M,W
Davis and Elkins College M,W
Fairmont State University M,W
Marshall University W
Salem International University M
Shepherd University M,W
University of Charleston M,W
West Liberty University M,W
West Virginia University W
West Virginia Wesleyan College M,W

Wisconsin
Marquette University M,W
University of Wisconsin
- Green Bay M,W
- Madison M,W
- Milwaukee W

Wyoming
University of Wyoming W

Track and field

Alabama
Alabama Agricultural and Mechanical University M,W
Alabama State University M,W
Auburn University M,W
Miles College M,W
Samford University M,W
Spring Hill College M,W
Troy University M,W
Tuskegee University M,W
University of Alabama M,W
University of Alabama
- Birmingham W
- Huntsville M,W

University of South Alabama M,W
Wallace State Community College at Hanceville M,W

Arizona
Arizona Christian University M,W
Arizona State University M,W
Central Arizona College M,W
Glendale Community College M,W
Grand Canyon University M,W
Mesa Community College M,W
Northern Arizona University M,W
Paradise Valley Community College M,W
Pima Community College M,W
Scottsdale Community College M,W
University of Arizona M,W

Arkansas
Arkansas State University M,W
Harding University M,W
Southern Arkansas University M,W
University of Arkansas M,W
University of Arkansas
- Little Rock M,W
- Pine Bluff M,W

University of Central Arkansas M,W

California
Academy of Art University M,W
Azusa Pacific University M,W
Biola University M,W
California Baptist University M,W
California Polytechnic State University: San Luis Obispo M,W
California State Polytechnic University: Pomona M,W
California State University
- Bakersfield M,W
- Chico M,W
- Dominguez Hills W
- Fresno M,W
- Fullerton M,W
- Long Beach M,W
- Los Angeles M,W
- Northridge M,W
- Sacramento M,W
- Stanislaus M,W

Concordia University M,W
Fresno City College M,W
Fresno Pacific University M,W
Humboldt State University M,W
The Master's College M,W
Pepperdine University W
Point Loma Nazarene University M,W
St. Mary's College of California M,W
San Diego State University W
Santa Clara University M,W
Santiago Canyon College M,W
Soka University of America M,W
Sonoma State University W
Stanford University M,W
University of California
- Berkeley M,W
- Davis M,W
- Irvine M,W
- Los Angeles M,W
- Santa Barbara M,W

University of San Diego W
University of San Francisco M,W
University of Southern California M,W
Vanguard University of Southern California M,W
Westmont College M,W
William Jessup University M,W
Yuba Community College District M,W

Colorado
Adams State College M,W
Colorado Mesa University W
Colorado School of Mines M,W
Colorado State University M,W
Colorado State University
- Pueblo W

University of Colorado
- Boulder M,W
- Colorado Springs M,W

University of Northern Colorado M,W
Western State Colorado University M,W

Connecticut
Central Connecticut State University M,W
Quinnipiac University W
Sacred Heart University M,W
Southern Connecticut State University W
University of Connecticut M,W
University of New Haven M,W

Delaware
Delaware State University M,W
University of Delaware W

District of Columbia
American University M,W
Georgetown University M,W
Howard University M,W

Florida
Bethune-Cookman University M,W
Edward Waters College M
Embry-Riddle Aeronautical University M,W
Florida Agricultural and Mechanical University M,W
Florida Atlantic University W
Florida Institute of Technology M,W
Florida Southern College M,W
Florida State University M,W
Jacksonville University W
Nova Southeastern University M,W
University of Central Florida W
University of Florida M,W
University of Miami M,W
University of North Florida M,W
University of South Florida M,W
University of West Florida M,W
Warner University M,W
Webber International University M,W

Georgia
Albany State University M,W
Clark Atlanta University M,W
Columbus State University M,W
Fort Valley State University M,W
Georgia Institute of Technology M,W
Georgia Southern University W
Georgia State University M,W
Kennesaw State University M,W
Morehouse College M
Paine College M,W
Savannah State University M,W
Shorter University M,W
University of Georgia M,W

Hawaii
University of Hawaii
- Manoa W

Idaho
Boise State University M,W
College of Idaho M,W
Idaho State University M,W
Lewis-Clark State College M,W
Northwest Nazarene University M,W
University of Idaho M,W

Illinois
Bradley University M,W
Chicago State University M,W
DePaul University M,W
Eastern Illinois University M,W
Illinois State University M,W
Judson University M,W
Lewis University M,W
Lincoln College M,W
Loyola University Chicago M,W
McKendree University M,W
Olivet Nazarene University M,W
Rend Lake College M,W
Robert Morris University: Chicago W
Southern Illinois University Carbondale M,W
Southern Illinois University Edwardsville M,W
Trinity Christian College M,W
University of Illinois
- Chicago M,W
- Urbana-Champaign M,W

University of St. Francis M,W
Western Illinois University M,W

Indiana
Ball State University W
Bethel College M,W
Goshen College M,W
Grace College M,W
Huntington University M,W
Indiana Institute of Technology M,W
Indiana State University M,W
Indiana University
- Bloomington M,W
- Purdue University Fort Wayne W

Indiana Wesleyan University M,W
Marian University M,W
Purdue University M,W
Saint Joseph's College M,W
Taylor University M,W
University of Indianapolis M,W
University of Notre Dame M,W
University of St. Francis M,W
Valparaiso University M,W
Vincennes University M,W

Iowa
Ashford University M,W
Briar Cliff University M,W
Clarke University M,W
Dordt College M,W
Drake University M,W
Graceland University M,W
Iowa State University M,W
Iowa Western Community College M,W
Morningside College M,W
Mount Mercy University M,W
North Iowa Area Community College M,W
Northwestern College M,W
St. Ambrose University M,W
University of Iowa M,W
University of Northern Iowa M,W
William Penn University M,W

Kansas
Allen County Community College M,W
Baker University M,W
Barton County Community College M,W
Benedictine College M,W
Bethel College M,W
Butler Community College M,W
Cloud County Community College M,W
Coffeyville Community College M,W
Colby Community College M,W
Cowley County Community College M,W
Dodge City Community College M,W
Emporia State University M,W
Fort Hays State University M,W
Friends University M,W
Garden City Community College M,W
Highland Community College M,W
Hutchinson Community College M,W
Independence Community College M,W
Johnson County Community College M,W
Kansas City Kansas Community College M,W
Kansas State University M,W
Kansas Wesleyan University M,W
McPherson College M,W
Neosho County Community College M,W
Ottawa University M,W
Pittsburg State University M,W
Pratt Community College M,W
Southwestern College M,W
Sterling College M,W
Tabor College M,W
University of Kansas M,W
University of St. Mary M,W
Wichita State University M,W

Kentucky
Bellarmine University M,W
Brescia University M,W

Campbellsville University M,W
Eastern Kentucky University M,W
Kentucky State University M,W
Lindsey Wilson College M,W
Midway College W
Morehead State University M,W
Murray State University W
Northern Kentucky University M,W
St. Catharine College M,W
University of Kentucky M,W
University of Louisville M,W
University of Pikeville M,W
University of the Cumberlands M,W
Western Kentucky University M,W

Louisiana
Dillard University M,W
Grambling State University M,W
Louisiana State University and Agricultural and Mechanical College M,W
Louisiana Tech University M,W
McNeese State University M,W
Nicholls State University W
Northwestern State University M,W
Southeastern Louisiana University M,W
Southern University and Agricultural and Mechanical College M,W
Tulane University M,W
University of Louisiana at Lafayette M,W
University of Louisiana at Monroe M,W
University of New Orleans M,W

Maine
University of Maine M,W

Maryland
Bowie State University M,W
Community College of Baltimore County W
Coppin State University M,W
Hagerstown Community College M,W
Morgan State University M,W
Mount St. Mary's University M,W
Towson University W
University of Maryland
College Park M,W
Eastern Shore M,W
Washington Adventist University M,W

Massachusetts
American International College M,W
Boston College M,W
Boston University M,W
Merrimack College M,W
Northeastern University M,W
Stonehill College M,W
University of Massachusetts
Amherst M,W
Lowell M,W

Michigan
Aquinas College M,W
Central Michigan University M,W
Concordia University M,W
Cornerstone University M,W
Davenport University M,W
Eastern Michigan University M,W
Ferris State University M,W
Grand Valley State University M,W
Hillsdale College M,W
Lake Superior State University M,W
Macomb Community College M,W
Michigan State University M,W
Michigan Technological University M,W
Northern Michigan University W
Northwood University
Michigan M,W
Saginaw Valley State University M,W
Siena Heights University M,W
University of Detroit Mercy M,W
University of Michigan M,W
Western Michigan University W

Minnesota
Bemidji State University M,W
Concordia University St. Paul M,W
Minnesota State University
Mankato M,W
Moorhead M,W
Saint Cloud State University M,W
University of Minnesota
Duluth M,W
Twin Cities M,W
Winona State University W

Mississippi
Alcorn State University M,W
Hinds Community College M,W
Holmes Community College M
Jackson State University M,W
Mississippi State University M,W
Mississippi Valley State University M,W
University of Mississippi M,W
University of Southern Mississippi M,W

Missouri
Central Methodist University M,W
Culver-Stockton College M,W
Drury University M,W
Evangel University M,W
Hannibal-LaGrange University M,W
Lincoln University M,W
Lindenwood University M,W
Maryville University of Saint Louis M,W
Missouri Baptist University M,W
Missouri Southern State University M,W
Missouri State University M,W
Missouri University of Science and Technology M,W
Missouri Valley College M,W
Northwest Missouri State University M,W
Park University M,W
Saint Louis University M,W
Southeast Missouri State University M,W
Southwest Baptist University M,W
Truman State University M,W
University of Central Missouri M,W
University of Missouri
Columbia M,W
Kansas City M,W
William Jewell College M,W

Montana
Montana State University M,W
Montana State University
Billings M,W
Rocky Mountain College M,W
University of Montana M,W

Nebraska
Chadron State College M,W
Concordia University M,W
Doane College M,W
Hastings College M,W
University of Nebraska
Kearney M,W
Lincoln M,W
Wayne State College M,W

Nevada
University of Nevada
Las Vegas W
Reno W

New Hampshire
Franklin Pierce University M,W
University of New Hampshire M,W

New Jersey
Caldwell College W
Essex County College M,W
Fairleigh Dickinson University
Metropolitan Campus M,W
Felician College M,W
Georgian Court University W
Monmouth University M,W
Rider University M,W
Rutgers, The State University of New Jersey
New Brunswick/Piscataway Campus M,W
Saint Peter's University M,W

New Mexico
Eastern New Mexico University M,W
New Mexico Highlands University W
New Mexico Military Institute M
New Mexico State University W
University of New Mexico M,W
University of the Southwest M,W

New York
Adelphi University M,W
City University of New York
Queens College M,W
College of Saint Rose M,W
Dominican College of Blauvelt W
Fordham University M,W
Iona College M,W
Long Island University
Brooklyn Campus M,W
Manhattan College M,W
Marist College M,W
Mercy College M,W
Molloy College M,W
Niagara University W
Roberts Wesleyan College M,W
St. Francis College M,W
St. John's University W
St. Thomas Aquinas College M,W
SUNY
University at Albany M,W
University at Binghamton M,W
University at Buffalo M,W
University at Stony Brook M,W
Syracuse University M,W
Wagner College M,W

North Carolina
Appalachian State University M,W
Barton College M,W
Belmont Abbey College M,W
Brevard College M,W
Campbell University M,W
Davidson College M,W
East Carolina University M,W
Elon University W
Fayetteville State University W
Gardner-Webb University M,W
High Point University M,W
Johnson C. Smith University M,W
Lees-McRae College M,W
Lenoir-Rhyne University M,W
Livingstone College M,W
Mars Hill College M,W
Montreat College M,W
North Carolina Agricultural and Technical State University M,W
North Carolina Central University M,W
North Carolina State University M,W
Queens University of Charlotte M,W
St. Augustine's University M,W
Shaw University M,W
University of North Carolina
Asheville M,W
Chapel Hill M,W
Charlotte M,W
Wilmington M,W
Wake Forest University M,W
Western Carolina University M,W
Winston-Salem State University M,W

North Dakota
Dickinson State University M,W
Jamestown College M,W
Minot State University M,W
North Dakota State University M,W
University of Mary M,W
University of North Dakota M,W
Valley City State University M,W

Ohio
Ashland University M,W
Bowling Green State University W
Cedarville University M,W
Central State University M,W
Kent State University M,W
Lake Erie College M,W
Malone University M,W
Miami University
Oxford M,W
Notre Dame College M,W
Ohio Dominican University M,W
Ohio State University
Columbus Campus M,W
Ohio University W
Tiffin University M,W
University of Akron M,W
University of Cincinnati M,W
University of Dayton W
University of Findlay M,W
University of Rio Grande M,W
University of Toledo W
Ursuline College W
Walsh University M,W
Wright State University W
Xavier University M,W
Youngstown State University M,W

Oklahoma
Bacone College M,W
Langston University M,W
Oklahoma Baptist University M,W
Oklahoma Christian University M,W
Oklahoma State University M,W
Oklahoma Wesleyan University M,W
Oral Roberts University M,W
St. Gregory's University M,W
Southern Nazarene University M,W
University of Central Oklahoma M,W
University of Oklahoma M,W
University of Tulsa M,W

Oregon
Clackamas Community College M,W
Concordia University M,W
Eastern Oregon University M,W
Lane Community College M,W
Mt. Hood Community College M,W
Northwest Christian University M,W
Oregon Institute of Technology M,W
Portland State University M,W
Southern Oregon University M,W
Southwestern Oregon Community College M,W
Treasure Valley Community College M,W
University of Oregon M,W
University of Portland M,W
Warner Pacific College M,W

Pennsylvania
Bloomsburg University of Pennsylvania M,W
California University of Pennsylvania M,W
Cheyney University of Pennsylvania M,W
Clarion University of Pennsylvania M,W
Duquesne University M,W
East Stroudsburg University of Pennsylvania M,W
Edinboro University of Pennsylvania M,W
Harcum College M,W
Holy Family University M,W
Indiana University of Pennsylvania M,W
Kutztown University of Pennsylvania M,W
La Salle University M,W
Lehigh University M,W
Lock Haven University of Pennsylvania M,W
Millersville University of Pennsylvania M,W
Penn State
University Park M,W
Robert Morris University M,W
St. Francis University M,W
Saint Joseph's University M,W
Seton Hill University M,W
Shippensburg University of Pennsylvania M,W
Slippery Rock University of Pennsylvania M,W
Temple University M,W
University of Pittsburgh M,W
Villanova University M,W
West Chester University of Pennsylvania M,W

Puerto Rico
Bayamon Central University M,W
Inter American University of Puerto Rico
Aguadilla Campus M,W
Bayamon Campus M,W
Fajardo Campus M,W
Guayama Campus M,W
Metropolitan Campus M,W
Ponce Campus M,W
San German Campus M,W
Turabo University M,W
Universidad del Este M,W
Universidad Metropolitana M,W
Universidad Politecnica de Puerto Rico M,W
University of Puerto Rico
Bayamon University College M,W
Carolina Regional College M,W
Humacao M,W
Mayaguez M,W
Ponce M,W
Utuado M,W
University of the Sacred Heart M,W

Rhode Island
Bryant University M,W
Providence College M,W
University of Rhode Island M,W

South Carolina
Anderson University M,W
Charleston Southern University M,W
The Citadel M,W
Claflin University M,W
Clemson University M,W
Coastal Carolina University M,W
Converse College W
Furman University M,W
Limestone College M,W
Morris College M,W
North Greenville University M,W
South Carolina State University M,W
University of South Carolina
Columbia M,W
Upstate M,W
Voorhees College M,W
Winthrop University M,W
Wofford College M,W

South Dakota
Augustana College M,W
Black Hills State University M,W
Dakota State University M,W
Mount Marty College M,W
Northern State University M,W
South Dakota School of Mines and Technology M,W
South Dakota State University M,W
University of Sioux Falls M,W
University of South Dakota M,W

Tennessee
Austin Peay State University W
Belmont University M,W
Bethel University M,W
East Tennessee State University M,W
King College M,W
Lipscomb University M,W
Middle Tennessee State University M,W
Milligan College M,W
Tennessee Technological University W
University of Memphis M,W
University of Tennessee
Chattanooga M,W
Knoxville M,W
Vanderbilt University W

Texas
Abilene Christian University M,W
Angelo State University M,W
Baylor University M,W
Dallas Baptist University W
Houston Baptist University M,W
Lamar University M,W
Northwood University
Texas M,W
Prairie View A&M University M,W
Rice University M,W
Sam Houston State University M,W
South Plains College M,W
Stephen F. Austin State University M,W
Tarleton State University M,W
Texas A&M University M,W
Texas A&M University
Commerce M,W
Corpus Christi M,W
Kingsville M,W
Texas Christian University M,W
Texas Southern University M,W
Texas State University: San Marcos M,W
Texas Tech University M,W
Texas Wesleyan University M,W
University of Houston M,W
University of North Texas M,W
University of Texas
Austin M,W
Pan American M,W
San Antonio M,W
University of the Incarnate Word M,W
Wayland Baptist University M,W
Western Texas College M,W
Wiley College M,W

Utah
Brigham Young University M,W
Southern Utah University M,W
University of Utah W
Utah State University M,W
Utah Valley University M,W
Weber State University M,W
Westminster College M,W

Vermont
University of Vermont M,W

Virginia
College of William and Mary M,W
George Mason University M,W
Hampton University M,W
James Madison University W
Liberty University M,W
Norfolk State University M,W
Radford University M,W
St. Paul's College M,W
University of Richmond W
University of Virginia M,W
Virginia Commonwealth University M,W
Virginia Military Institute M,W
Virginia Polytechnic Institute and State University M,W
Virginia State University M,W
Virginia Union University M,W

Washington
Clark College M,W
Eastern Washington University M,W
Evergreen State College M,W
Highline Community College M,W
Northwest University M,W
Saint Martin's University M,W
Seattle Pacific University M,W
Seattle University M,W
Spokane Community College M,W
University of Washington M,W
Washington State University M,W
Western Washington University M,W

West Virginia
Alderson-Broaddus College M,W
Glenville State College M,W
Marshall University W
University of Charleston W
West Liberty University M,W
West Virginia State University M,W
West Virginia University W
West Virginia Wesleyan College M,W
Wheeling Jesuit University M,W

Wisconsin
Marquette University M,W
Milwaukee Area Technical College M,W
University of Wisconsin
Madison M,W
Milwaukee M,W
Parkside M,W

Wyoming
University of Wyoming M,W

Volleyball

Alabama
Alabama Agricultural and Mechanical University W
Alabama State University W
Auburn University W
Faulkner State Community College M,W
Faulkner University W
Gadsden State Community College W
Jacksonville State University W
Jefferson Davis Community College W
Judson College W
Lawson State Community College W
Miles College M,W
Samford University W
Southern Union State Community College W
Spring Hill College W
Troy University W
Tuskegee University W
University of Alabama W
University of Alabama
Birmingham W
Huntsville W
University of Mobile W
University of Montevallo W
University of North Alabama W
University of South Alabama W
University of West Alabama W
Wallace State Community College at Hanceville W

Alaska
University of Alaska
Anchorage W
Fairbanks W

Arizona
Arizona Christian University W
Arizona State University W
Arizona Western College W
Chandler-Gilbert Community College W
Eastern Arizona College W
Embry-Riddle Aeronautical University
Prescott Campus W
Glendale Community College W
Grand Canyon University M,W
Northern Arizona University W
Pima Community College W
Scottsdale Community College W
University of Arizona W
Yavapai College W

Arkansas
Arkansas State University W
Arkansas Tech University W
Crowley's Ridge College W
Harding University W
Henderson State University W
John Brown University W
Lyon College W
Ouachita Baptist University W
Southern Arkansas University W
University of Arkansas W
University of Arkansas
Fort Smith W
Little Rock W
Pine Bluff W
University of Central Arkansas W
Williams Baptist College W

California
Academy of Art University W
Azusa Pacific University W
Biola University W
California Baptist University M,W
California Polytechnic State University: San Luis Obispo W
California State Polytechnic University: Pomona W
California State University
Bakersfield W
Chico W
Dominguez Hills W
Fresno W
Fullerton W
Long Beach M,W
Los Angeles W
Monterey Bay W
Northridge M,W
Sacramento W
San Bernardino W
Stanislaus W
Concordia University M,W
Dominican University of California W
Fresno City College W
Fresno Pacific University W
Grossmont College M,W
Holy Names University M,W
Hope International University M,W
Humboldt State University W
Loyola Marymount University W
The Master's College W
Notre Dame de Namur University W
Pepperdine University M,W
Point Loma Nazarene University W
St. Mary's College of California W
San Diego Christian College W
San Diego State University W
San Jose State University W
Santa Clara University W
Simpson University W
Sonoma State University W
Stanford University M,W
University of California
Berkeley W
Davis W
Irvine M,W
Los Angeles W
Riverside W
Santa Barbara M,W
University of San Diego W
University of San Francisco W
University of Southern California M,W
University of the Pacific M,W
Vanguard University of Southern California W
Westmont College W
William Jessup University W
Yuba Community College District W

Colorado
Adams State College W
Colorado Christian University W
Colorado Mesa University W
Colorado Northwestern Community College W
Colorado School of Mines W
Colorado State University W
Colorado State University
Pueblo W
Fort Lewis College W
Lamar Community College W
Metropolitan State University of Denver W
Northeastern Junior College W
Otero Junior College W
Trinidad State Junior College W
University of Colorado
Boulder W
Colorado Springs W
University of Denver W
University of Northern Colorado W
Western State Colorado University W

Connecticut
Central Connecticut State University W
Fairfield University W

Post University W
Quinnipiac University W
Sacred Heart University M,W
Southern Connecticut State University W
University of Bridgeport W
University of Connecticut W
University of Hartford W
University of New Haven W

Delaware
Delaware State University W
Goldey-Beacom College W
University of Delaware W
Wilmington University W

District of Columbia
American University W
George Washington University W
Georgetown University W
Howard University W

Florida
Ave Maria University W
Barry University M,W
Bethune-Cookman University W
Brevard Community College W
College of Central Florida W
Eckerd College W
Embry-Riddle Aeronautical University W
Flagler College W
Florida Agricultural and Mechanical University W
Florida Atlantic University W
Florida College W
Florida Gulf Coast University W
Florida Institute of Technology W
Florida Southern College W
Florida State College at Jacksonville W
Florida State University W
Gulf Coast State College W
Hillsborough Community College W
Indian River State College W
Jacksonville University W
Lake-Sumter Community College W
Lynn University W
Miami Dade College W
Northwood University
  Florida W
Nova Southeastern University W
Palm Beach Atlantic University M,W
Palm Beach State College W
Pasco-Hernando Community College W
Pensacola State College W
Polk State College W
Rollins College W
Saint Johns River State College W
Saint Leo University W
St. Petersburg College W
Saint Thomas University W
South Florida Community College W
Southeastern University W
State College of Florida, Manatee-Sarasota W
Stetson University W
University of Central Florida W
University of Florida W
University of Miami W
University of North Florida W
University of South Florida W
University of Tampa W
University of West Florida W
Warner University M,W
Webber International University W

Georgia
Abraham Baldwin Agricultural College W
Albany State University W
Armstrong Atlantic State University W
Brenau University W
Brewton-Parker College W
Clark Atlanta University W
College of Coastal Georgia W
Fort Valley State University W
Georgia Institute of Technology W
Georgia Southern University W
Georgia State University W
Kennesaw State University W
Mercer University W
Paine College W
Savannah State University W
Shorter University W
Truett-McConnell College W
University of Georgia W
University of West Georgia W
Valdosta State University W

Hawaii
Brigham Young University-Hawaii W
Chaminade University of Honolulu W
Hawaii Pacific University W
University of Hawaii
  Hilo W
  Manoa M,W

Idaho
Boise State University W
College of Idaho W
College of Southern Idaho W
Idaho State University W
Lewis-Clark State College W
North Idaho College W
Northwest Nazarene University W
University of Idaho W

Illinois
Black Hawk College W
Bradley University W
Carl Sandburg College W
Chicago State University W
College of Lake County W
Danville Area Community College W
DePaul University W
Eastern Illinois University W
Elgin Community College W
Highland Community College W
Illinois Central College W
Illinois Institute of Technology W
Illinois State University W
John A. Logan College W
Judson University W
Kankakee Community College W
Kaskaskia College W
Kishwaukee College W
Lake Land College W
Lewis and Clark Community College W
Lewis University M,W
Lincoln College W
Loyola University Chicago M,W
McHenry County College W
McKendree University M,W
Moraine Valley Community College W
Morton College W
Northwestern University W
Olivet Nazarene University W
Parkland College W
Quincy University M,W
Rend Lake College W
Robert Morris University: Chicago M,W
Saint Xavier University W
Sauk Valley Community College W
Shawnee Community College W
South Suburban College of Cook County W
Southern Illinois University Carbondale W
Southern Illinois University Edwardsville W
Southwestern Illinois College W
Trinity Christian College W
Trinity International University W
University of Illinois
  Chicago W
  Springfield W
  Urbana-Champaign W
University of St. Francis W
Waubonsee Community College W
Western Illinois University W

Indiana
Ancilla College W
Ball State University M,W
Bethel College W
Butler University W
Calumet College of St. Joseph M,W
Goshen College W
Grace College W
Huntington University W
Indiana Institute of Technology W
Indiana State University W
Indiana University
  Bloomington W
  Purdue University Fort Wayne M,W
  Purdue University Indianapolis W
  Southeast W
Indiana Wesleyan University W
Marian University W
Oakland City University W
Purdue University W
Purdue University
  North Central W
Saint Joseph's College W
Taylor University W
University of Evansville W
University of Indianapolis W
University of Notre Dame W
University of St. Francis W
University of Southern Indiana W
Valparaiso University W
Vincennes University W

Iowa
AIB College of Business W
Ashford University W
Briar Cliff University W
Clarke University M,W
Clinton Community College W
Des Moines Area Community College W
Dordt College W
Drake University W
Ellsworth Community College W
Graceland University M,W
Grand View University M,W
Iowa Central Community College W
Iowa Lakes Community College W
Iowa State University W
Iowa Western Community College W
Kirkwood Community College W
Morningside College W
Mount Mercy University W
North Iowa Area Community College W
Northwestern College W
St. Ambrose University M,W
Southeastern Community College W
Southwestern Community College W
University of Iowa W
University of Northern Iowa W
Waldorf College W
William Penn University W

Kansas
Allen County Community College W
Baker University W
Barton County Community College W
Benedictine College W
Bethel College W
Butler Community College W
Central Christian College of Kansas W
Cloud County Community College W
Coffeyville Community College W
Colby Community College W
Cowley County Community College W
Dodge City Community College W
Emporia State University W
Fort Hays State University W
Fort Scott Community College W
Friends University W
Garden City Community College W
Hesston College W
Highland Community College W
Hutchinson Community College W
Independence Community College W
Johnson County Community College W
Kansas City Kansas Community College W
Kansas State University W
Kansas Wesleyan University W
Labette Community College W
McPherson College W
MidAmerica Nazarene University W
Neosho County Community College W
Newman University W
Ottawa University W
Pittsburg State University W
Pratt Community College W
Seward County Community College W
Southwestern College W
Sterling College W
Tabor College W
University of Kansas W
University of St. Mary W
Washburn University W
Wichita State University W

Kentucky
Asbury University W
Bellarmine University W
Brescia University W
Campbellsville University W
Eastern Kentucky University W
Georgetown College W
Kentucky State University W
Kentucky Wesleyan College W
Lindsey Wilson College W
Mid-Continent University W
Midway College W
Morehead State University W
Murray State University W
Northern Kentucky University W
St. Catharine College W
Union College W
University of Kentucky W
University of Louisville W
University of Pikeville W
University of the Cumberlands W
Western Kentucky University W

Louisiana
Dillard University W
Louisiana State University and Agricultural and Mechanical College W
Louisiana Tech University W
Loyola University New Orleans W
McNeese State University W
Nicholls State University W
Northwestern State University W
Southeastern Louisiana University W
Southern University and Agricultural and Mechanical College W
Tulane University W
University of Louisiana at Lafayette W
University of Louisiana at Monroe W
University of New Orleans W
Xavier University of Louisiana W

Maine
University of Maine W

Maryland
Bowie State University W
Chesapeake College W
College of Southern Maryland W
Community College of Baltimore County W
Coppin State University W
Garrett College W
Hagerstown Community College W
Harford Community College W
Loyola University Maryland W
Morgan State University W
Towson University W
University of Maryland
  College Park W
  Eastern Shore W

Massachusetts
American International College W
Boston College W
Merrimack College W
Northeastern University W
Stonehill College W

University of Massachusetts
Lowell W

Michigan
Alpena Community College W
Aquinas College W
Central Michigan University W
Concordia University W
Cornerstone University W
Davenport University W
Eastern Michigan University W
Ferris State University W
Grand Valley State University W
Hillsdale College W
Kalamazoo Valley Community College W
Kellogg Community College W
Lake Michigan College W
Lake Superior State University W
Lansing Community College W
Macomb Community College W
Madonna University W
Michigan State University W
Michigan Technological University W
Mott Community College W
Muskegon Community College W
Northern Michigan University W
Northwood University
Michigan W
Oakland Community College W
Oakland University W
Rochester College W
Saginaw Valley State University W
St. Clair County Community College W
Siena Heights University M,W
Spring Arbor University W
University of Michigan W
University of Michigan
Dearborn W
Wayne State University W
Western Michigan University W

Minnesota
Bemidji State University W
Concordia University St. Paul W
Minnesota State University
Mankato W
Moorhead W
Saint Cloud State University W
Southwest Minnesota State University W
University of Minnesota
Crookston W
Duluth W
Twin Cities W
Winona State University W

Mississippi
Alcorn State University W
Belhaven University W
Jackson State University W
Mississippi State University W
Mississippi Valley State University W
University of Mississippi W
University of Southern Mississippi W

Missouri
Avila University W
Central Methodist University W
College of the Ozarks W
Columbia College W
Cottey College W
Culver-Stockton College W
Drury University W
East Central College W
Evangel University W
Hannibal-LaGrange University M,W
Harris-Stowe State University W
Jefferson College W
Maryville University of Saint Louis W
Metropolitan Community College - Kansas City W
Mineral Area College W
Missouri Baptist University M,W
Missouri Southern State University W
Missouri State University W
Missouri State University: West Plains W
Missouri Valley College M,W
Missouri Western State University W
Northwest Missouri State University W
Park University M,W
Research College of Nursing W
Rockhurst University W
Saint Louis University W
Southeast Missouri State University W
Southwest Baptist University W
Stephens College W
Truman State University W
University of Central Missouri W
University of Missouri
Columbia W
Kansas City W
St. Louis W
William Jewell College W
William Woods University M,W

Montana
Carroll College W
Montana State University W
Montana State University
Billings W
Northern W
Montana Tech of the University of Montana W
Rocky Mountain College W
University of Great Falls W
University of Montana W
University of Montana: Western W

Nebraska
Bellevue University W
Central Community College W
Chadron State College W
College of Saint Mary W
Concordia University W
Creighton University W
Doane College W
Hastings College W
Mid-Plains Community College W
Nebraska College of Technical Agriculture W
Peru State College W
University of Nebraska
Kearney W
Lincoln W
Omaha W
Wayne State College W
Western Nebraska Community College W
York College W

Nevada
University of Nevada
Las Vegas W
Reno W

New Hampshire
Franklin Pierce University W
Hesser College M,W
Saint Anselm College W
University of New Hampshire W

New Jersey
Bloomfield College W
Caldwell College W
Fairleigh Dickinson University
Metropolitan Campus W
Georgian Court University W
New Jersey Institute of Technology M,W
Rider University W
Rutgers, The State University of New Jersey
New Brunswick/Piscataway Campus W
Newark Campus M
Saint Peter's University W
Seton Hall University W

New Mexico
Eastern New Mexico University W
New Mexico Highlands University W
New Mexico State University W
University of New Mexico W
University of the Southwest W
Western New Mexico University W

New York
Adelphi University W
Canisius College W
City University of New York
Queens College W
Colgate University W
College of Saint Rose W
Concordia College W
Daemen College W
Dominican College of Blauvelt W
Dowling College W
Fordham University W
Genesee Community College W
Globe Institute of Technology W
Hofstra University W
Iona College W
Le Moyne College W
Long Island University
Brooklyn Campus W
C. W. Post Campus W
Manhattan College W
Marist College W
Mercy College W
Molloy College W
New York Institute of Technology M
Niagara University W
Nyack College W
Pace University W
Roberts Wesleyan College W
St. Francis College W
St. John's University W
Siena College W
SUNY
University at Albany W
University at Binghamton W
University at Buffalo W
University at Stony Brook W
Syracuse University W

North Carolina
Appalachian State University W
Barton College M,W
Belmont Abbey College W
Brevard College W
Campbell University W
Catawba College W
Chowan University W
Davidson College W
Duke University W
East Carolina University M,W
Elizabeth City State University W
Elon University W
Fayetteville State University W
Gardner-Webb University W
Guilford Technical Community College W
High Point University W
Johnson C. Smith University W
Lees-McRae College M,W
Lenoir Community College W
Lenoir-Rhyne University W
Livingstone College W
Louisburg College W
Mars Hill College W
Montreat College W
Mount Olive College W
North Carolina Agricultural and Technical State University W
North Carolina Central University W
North Carolina State University W
Pfeiffer University W
Pitt Community College W
Queens University of Charlotte W
St. Andrews University W
St. Augustine's University W
Shaw University W
Southeastern Community College W
University of North Carolina
Asheville W
Chapel Hill W
Charlotte W
Greensboro W
Wilmington W
Wake Forest University W
Western Carolina University W
Wingate University W
Winston-Salem State University W

North Dakota
Bismarck State College W
Dakota College at Bottineau W
Dickinson State University W
Jamestown College W
Mayville State University W
Minot State University W
North Dakota State College of Science W
North Dakota State University W
University of Mary W
University of North Dakota W
Valley City State University W
Williston State College W

Ohio
Ashland University W
Bowling Green State University W
Cedarville University W
Central State University W
Clark State Community College W
Cleveland State University W
Edison State Community College W
Kent State University W
Lake Erie College W
Lakeland Community College W
Lourdes University M,W
Malone University W
Miami University
Oxford W
Mount Vernon Nazarene University W
Notre Dame College W
Ohio Dominican University W
Ohio State University
Columbus Campus M,W
Ohio University W
Owens Community College
Toledo W
Shawnee State University W
Sinclair Community College W
Southern State Community College W
Tiffin University W
University of Akron W
University of Cincinnati W
University of Dayton W
University of Findlay W
University of Rio Grande W
University of Toledo W
Ursuline College W
Walsh University W
Wright State University W
Xavier University W
Youngstown State University W

Oklahoma
Bacone College W
Cameron University W
East Central University W
Langston University W
Mid-America Christian University W
Northeastern Oklahoma Agricultural and Mechanical College W
Northwestern Oklahoma State University M,W
Oklahoma Baptist University W
Oklahoma City University W
Oklahoma Panhandle State University W
Oklahoma Wesleyan University W
Oral Roberts University W
Redlands Community College W
St. Gregory's University W
Seminole State College M,W
Southeastern Oklahoma State University W
Southern Nazarene University W
University of Central Oklahoma W
University of Oklahoma W
University of Tulsa W

Oregon
Chemeketa Community College W
Clackamas Community College W
Concordia University W

Corban University W
Eastern Oregon University W
Linn-Benton Community College W
Mt. Hood Community College W
Northwest Christian University W
Oregon Institute of Technology W
Oregon State University W
Portland State University W
Southern Oregon University W
Southwestern Oregon Community College W
Treasure Valley Community College W
University of Oregon W
University of Portland W
Warner Pacific College W

Pennsylvania
California University of Pennsylvania W
Carlow University W
Chestnut Hill College W
Cheyney University of Pennsylvania W
Duquesne University W
Edinboro University of Pennsylvania W
Gannon University W
Harcum College W
Holy Family University W
Indiana University of Pennsylvania W
Kutztown University of Pennsylvania W
La Salle University W
Lackawanna College W
Lehigh University W
Lock Haven University of Pennsylvania W
Mercyhurst University W
Millersville University of Pennsylvania W
Penn State
  University Park M,W
Philadelphia University W
Point Park University W
Robert Morris University W
St. Francis University M,W
Seton Hill University W
Shippensburg University of Pennsylvania W
Slippery Rock University of Pennsylvania W
Temple University W
University of Pittsburgh W
University of the Sciences in Philadelphia W
Villanova University W
West Chester University of Pennsylvania W
Westminster College W

Puerto Rico
Bayamon Central University M,W
Inter American University of Puerto Rico
  Aguadilla Campus M,W
  Bayamon Campus M,W
  Metropolitan Campus M,W
  Ponce Campus M,W
  San German Campus M,W
Turabo University M,W
Universidad del Este M,W
Universidad Metropolitana M,W
Universidad Politecnica de Puerto Rico M,W
University of Puerto Rico
  Bayamon University College M,W
  Carolina Regional College M,W
  Cayey University College M,W
  Humacao M,W
  Mayaguez M,W
  Ponce M,W
  Utuado M,W
University of the Sacred Heart M,W

Rhode Island
Bryant University W
Community College of Rhode Island W
University of Rhode Island W

South Carolina
Anderson University W
Charleston Southern University W
The Citadel W
Claflin University W
Clemson University W
Coastal Carolina University W
Coker College M,W
College of Charleston W
Columbia College W
Converse College W
Erskine College W
Francis Marion University W
Furman University W
Lander University W
Limestone College M,W
Morris College W
Newberry College W
North Greenville University W
Presbyterian College W
South Carolina State University W
Spartanburg Methodist College W
University of South Carolina
  Aiken W
  Columbia W
  Upstate W
Voorhees College W
Winthrop University W
Wofford College W

South Dakota
Augustana College W
Black Hills State University W
Dakota State University W
Mount Marty College W
Northern State University W
South Dakota School of Mines and Technology W
South Dakota State University W
University of Sioux Falls W

Tennessee
Austin Peay State University W
Belmont University W
Bethel University W
Bryan University
  Dayton W
Carson-Newman University W
Christian Brothers University W
Cumberland University W
East Tennessee State University W
Freed-Hardeman University W
King College W
Lane College W
Lee University W
LeMoyne-Owen College W
Lincoln Memorial University W
Lipscomb University W
Martin Methodist College W
Middle Tennessee State University W
Milligan College W
Tennessee Technological University W
Tennessee Wesleyan College W
Trevecca Nazarene University W
Tusculum College W
Union University W
University of Memphis W
University of Tennessee
  Chattanooga W
  Knoxville W
  Martin W

Texas
Abilene Christian University W
Angelo State University W
Baylor University W
Blinn College W
Brookhaven College W
Clarendon College W
Dallas Baptist University W
Frank Phillips College W
Galveston College W
Hill College W
Houston Baptist University W
Jarvis Christian College M,W
Lamar University W
Laredo Community College W
Lee College W
Lubbock Christian University W
Midwestern State University W
North Central Texas College W
Panola College W
Paris Junior College W
Prairie View A&M University W
Ranger College W
Rice University W
St. Edward's University W
St. Mary's University W
Sam Houston State University W
Southern Methodist University W
Southwestern Assemblies of God University W
Stephen F. Austin State University W
Tarleton State University W
Temple College W
Texas A&M University W
Texas A&M University
  Commerce W
  Corpus Christi W
  Kingsville W
Texas Christian University W
Texas Southern University W
Texas State University: San Marcos W
Texas Tech University M,W
Texas Wesleyan University W
Texas Woman's University W
Tyler Junior College W
University of Houston W
University of North Texas W
University of St. Thomas W
University of Texas
  Arlington W
  Austin W
  Brownsville - Texas Southmost College W
  Pan American W
  of the Permian Basin W
  San Antonio W
University of the Incarnate Word W
Vernon College W
Wayland Baptist University W
West Texas A&M University W
Western Texas College W
Wharton County Junior College W
Wiley College W

Utah
Brigham Young University M,W
Dixie State College W
Salt Lake Community College W
Snow College W
Southern Utah University W
University of Utah W
Utah State University W
Utah Valley University W
Weber State University W
Westminster College W

Virginia
Bluefield College W
College of William and Mary W
George Mason University M,W
Hampton University W
James Madison University W
Liberty University W
Norfolk State University W
Radford University W
St. Paul's College W
University of Virginia W
University of Virginia's College at Wise W
Virginia Commonwealth University W
Virginia Intermont College W
Virginia Polytechnic Institute and State University W
Virginia State University W
Virginia Union University W

Washington
Big Bend Community College W
Centralia College W
Clark College W
Columbia Basin College W
Eastern Washington University W
Everett Community College W
Evergreen State College W
Gonzaga University W
Grays Harbor College W
Green River Community College W
Highline Community College W
Lower Columbia College W
Northwest University W
Olympic College W
Pierce College W
Saint Martin's University W
Seattle University W
Shoreline Community College W
Skagit Valley College W
Spokane Community College W
Tacoma Community College W
University of Washington W
Walla Walla Community College W
Washington State University W
Western Washington University W
Whatcom Community College W
Yakima Valley Community College W

West Virginia
Alderson-Broaddus College M,W
Bluefield State College W
Concord University W
Davis and Elkins College W
Fairmont State University W
Glenville State College W
Marshall University W
Ohio Valley University W
Salem International University W
Shepherd University W
University of Charleston W
West Liberty University W
West Virginia University W
West Virginia University Institute of Technology W
West Virginia Wesleyan College W
Wheeling Jesuit University W

Wisconsin
Cardinal Stritch University M,W
Marquette University W
Milwaukee Area Technical College W
University of Wisconsin
  Green Bay W
  Madison W
  Milwaukee M,W
  Parkside W
Viterbo University W

Wyoming
Casper College W
Central Wyoming College W
Eastern Wyoming College W
Laramie County Community College W
Northwest College W
Sheridan College W
University of Wyoming W
Western Wyoming Community College W

Water polo

Arizona
Arizona State University W

California
California Baptist University M,W
California State University
  Bakersfield W
  Long Beach M,W
  Monterey Bay W
Concordia University M,W
Fresno Pacific University M,W
Grossmont College M,W
Loyola Marymount University M,W
Pepperdine University M
San Diego State University W
San Jose State University W
Santa Clara University M,W
Sonoma State University W

Stanford University M,W
University of California
Berkeley M,W
Davis M,W
Irvine M,W
University of Southern California M,W
University of the Pacific M,W

Colorado
Colorado State University W

District of Columbia
George Washington University M

Florida
Florida Atlantic University W

Hawaii
University of Hawaii
Manoa W

Indiana
Indiana University
Bloomington W

Maryland
University of Maryland
College Park W

Michigan
University of Michigan W

Missouri
Lindenwood University M,W

New York
City University of New York
Queens College M
Fordham University M
Hartwick College W
Iona College W
Marist College W
St. Francis College M,W
Siena College W
Wagner College W

Pennsylvania
Gannon University M,W
Mercyhurst University M,W

Puerto Rico
University of Puerto Rico
Mayaguez M

Virginia
Virginia Military Institute M,W

Weight lifting

New York
United States Merchant Marine Academy M,W

Puerto Rico
Inter American University of Puerto Rico
Aguadilla Campus M,W
Ponce Campus M,W
San German Campus M,W
Turabo University M,W
Universidad del Este M
Universidad Metropolitana M,W
University of Puerto Rico
Carolina Regional College M,W
Cayey University College M,W
Humacao M,W
Utuado M,W

Wrestling

Arizona
Arizona State University M
Embry-Riddle Aeronautical University
Prescott Campus M
Grand Canyon University M

Arkansas
Ouachita Baptist University M

California
California Baptist University M
California Polytechnic State University: San Luis Obispo M
California State University
Bakersfield M
Fresno City College M
Stanford University M
University of California
Los Angeles M,W

Colorado
Adams State College M
Colorado Mesa University M
Colorado School of Mines M
Colorado State University
Pueblo M
University of Northern Colorado M
Western State Colorado University M

Connecticut
Sacred Heart University M

District of Columbia
American University M
Howard University M

Georgia
Brewton-Parker College M
Darton College M
Shorter University M
Truett-McConnell College M

Idaho
Boise State University M
North Idaho College M

Illinois
City Colleges of Chicago
Wilbur Wright College M,W
Lincoln College M
McKendree University M
Northwestern University M
Rend Lake College M
Southern Illinois University Edwardsville M
University of Illinois
Urbana-Champaign M

Indiana
Calumet College of St. Joseph M
Indiana Institute of Technology M
Indiana University
Bloomington M
Purdue University M
University of Indianapolis M

Iowa
Briar Cliff University M
Ellsworth Community College M
Grand View University M
Iowa Central Community College M
Iowa State University M
Iowa Western Community College M
North Iowa Area Community College M
Northwestern College M
University of Iowa M
University of Northern Iowa M
Waldorf College M,W
William Penn University M

Kansas
Baker University M
Benedictine College M
Colby Community College M
Fort Hays State University M
Labette Community College M
Neosho County Community College M
Newman University M
Northwest Kansas Technical College M,W
Pratt Community College M

Kentucky
Campbellsville University M,W
Lindsey Wilson College M
University of the Cumberlands M,W

Maryland
University of Maryland
College Park M

Massachusetts
American International College M
Boston University M

Michigan
Central Michigan University M
Eastern Michigan University M
Michigan State University M
Muskegon Community College M
University of Michigan M

Minnesota
Minnesota State University
Mankato M
Moorhead M
Saint Cloud State University M
Southwest Minnesota State University M
University of Minnesota
Twin Cities M

Missouri
Hannibal-LaGrange University M
Lindenwood University M
Maryville University of Saint Louis M
Missouri Baptist University M,W
Missouri Valley College M,W
University of Central Missouri M
University of Missouri
Columbia M

Montana
Montana State University
Northern M
University of Great Falls M

Nebraska
Chadron State College M
Concordia University M
Hastings College M
University of Nebraska
Kearney M
Lincoln M
York College M

New Jersey
Rider University M
Rutgers, The State University of New Jersey
New Brunswick/Piscataway Campus M

New York
Hofstra University M
Niagara County Community College M
SUNY
University at Binghamton M
University at Buffalo M

North Carolina
Appalachian State University M
Belmont Abbey College M
Campbell University M
Davidson College M
Duke University M
Gardner-Webb University M
North Carolina State University M
University of North Carolina
Chapel Hill M

North Dakota
Dickinson State University M
Jamestown College M,W
North Dakota State University M
University of Mary M

Ohio
Ashland University M
Cleveland State University M
Kent State University M
Lake Erie College M
Notre Dame College M
Ohio Mid-Western College M
Ohio State University
Columbus Campus M
Ohio University M
Tiffin University M
University of Findlay M

Oklahoma
Bacone College M
Oklahoma City University M,W
Oklahoma State University M
University of Central Oklahoma M
University of Oklahoma M

Oregon
Clackamas Community College M
Oregon State University M
Southern Oregon University M
Southwestern Oregon Community College M

Pennsylvania
Bloomsburg University of Pennsylvania M
Bucknell University M
Clarion University of Pennsylvania M
Drexel University M
East Stroudsburg University of Pennsylvania M
Edinboro University of Pennsylvania M
Gannon University M
Kutztown University of Pennsylvania M
Lehigh University M
Lock Haven University of Pennsylvania M
Mercyhurst University M
Millersville University of Pennsylvania M
Penn State
University Park M
Seton Hill University M
Shippensburg University of Pennsylvania M
University of Pittsburgh M
University of Pittsburgh
Johnstown M

Puerto Rico
Inter American University of Puerto Rico
Bayamon Campus M
Ponce Campus M,W
Universidad Politecnica de Puerto Rico M
University of Puerto Rico
Bayamon University College M
Cayey University College M,W
Humacao M,W
Mayaguez M
University of the Sacred Heart M

South Carolina
Anderson University M
The Citadel M
Coker College M
Limestone College M
Newberry College M
Spartanburg Methodist College M

South Dakota
Augustana College M
Northern State University M
South Dakota State University M

Tennessee
Carson-Newman University M
Cumberland University M
King College M,W
University of Tennessee
Chattanooga M

Texas
Wayland Baptist University M,W

Utah
Utah Valley University M

Virginia
George Mason University W
Old Dominion University M

University of Virginia M
Virginia Military Institute M
Virginia Polytechnic Institute and State University M

Washington
Highline Community College M

West Virginia
Alderson-Broaddus College M
West Liberty University M
West Virginia University M

Wisconsin
University of Wisconsin
Madison M
Parkside M

Wyoming
Northwest College M
University of Wyoming M
Western Wyoming Community College M

Music/drama scholarships

Alabama
Alabama State University
Auburn University at Montgomery
Bevill State Community College
Birmingham-Southern College
Chattahoochee Valley Community College
Enterprise State Community College
Faulkner State Community College
Faulkner University
Gadsden State Community College
Huntingdon College
Jacksonville State University
Jefferson State Community College
Judson College
Northeast Alabama Community College
Northwest-Shoals Community College
Samford University
Selma University
Snead State Community College
Talladega College
Troy University
University of Alabama
University of Alabama
Birmingham
Huntsville
University of Mobile
University of Montevallo
University of North Alabama
University of South Alabama
University of West Alabama
Wallace State Community College at Hanceville

Alaska
Alaska Pacific University
University of Alaska
Fairbanks
Southeast

Arizona
Arizona Christian University
Arizona State University
Arizona Western College
Eastern Arizona College
Glendale Community College
Grand Canyon University
Northern Arizona University
Northland Pioneer College
Pima Community College
South Mountain Community College
University of Arizona

Arkansas
Arkansas Northeastern College
Arkansas State University
Arkansas State University
Beebe
Arkansas Tech University
Black River Technical College
Central Baptist College
Crowley's Ridge College
Ecclesia College
Harding University
Henderson State University
Hendrix College
John Brown University
Lyon College
National Park Community College
Northwest Arkansas Community College
Ouachita Baptist University
Philander Smith College
Phillips Community College of the University of Arkansas
Southern Arkansas University
University of Arkansas
University of Arkansas
Fort Smith
Little Rock
Monticello
Pine Bluff
University of Central Arkansas
University of the Ozarks
Williams Baptist College

California
American Academy of Dramatic Arts: West
American Jewish University
Azusa Pacific University
Bethesda University of California
Biola University
California Baptist University
California Institute of Integral Studies
California Institute of the Arts
California Lutheran University
California Polytechnic State University: San Luis Obispo
California State University
Bakersfield
Chico
Dominguez Hills
East Bay
Fresno
Long Beach
Stanislaus
Chapman University
College of the Canyons
College of the Desert
College of the Siskiyous
Concordia University
Dominican University of California
El Camino College
Fresno Pacific University
Holy Names University
Hope International University
Irvine Valley College
La Sierra University
Loyola Marymount University
Marymount California University
The Master's College
Mendocino College
Mills College
Mount St. Mary's College
Mount San Jacinto College
Notre Dame de Namur University
Occidental College
Pacific Union College
Pepperdine University
Point Loma Nazarene University
Riverside Community College
St. Mary's College of California
San Diego Christian College
San Diego State University
San Francisco Conservatory of Music
San Jose State University
Santa Clara University
Santa Rosa Junior College
Shasta Bible College and Graduate School
Simpson University
Sonoma State University
University of California
Riverside
San Diego
Santa Cruz
University of La Verne
University of Redlands
University of San Diego
University of Southern California
University of the Pacific
Vanguard University of Southern California
Westmont College
Whittier College
William Jessup University
Yuba Community College District

Colorado
Adams State College
Colorado Christian University
Colorado Mesa University
Colorado School of Mines
Colorado State University
Colorado State University
Pueblo
Community College of Aurora
Fort Lewis College
Naropa University
Northeastern Junior College
Pueblo Community College
Regis University
University of Colorado
Boulder
Denver
University of Denver
Western State Colorado University

Connecticut
Albertus Magnus College
Fairfield University
Sacred Heart University
University of Bridgeport
University of Connecticut
University of Hartford

Delaware
Delaware State University
University of Delaware

District of Columbia
American University
Catholic University of America
Gallaudet University
George Washington University
Howard University

Florida
Ave Maria University
Baptist College of Florida
Barry University
Bethune-Cookman University
Chipola College
Clearwater Christian College
College of Central Florida
Daytona State College
Eckerd College
Edison State College
Flagler College
Florida Agricultural and Mechanical University
Florida Atlantic University
Florida Christian College
Florida College
Florida Gateway College
Florida Gulf Coast University
Florida Institute of Technology
Florida International University
Florida Southern College
Florida State College at Jacksonville
Gulf Coast State College
Hillsborough Community College
Indian River State College
Jacksonville University
Lynn University
Miami Dade College
North Florida Community College
Nova Southeastern University
Palm Beach Atlantic University
Rollins College
St. Petersburg College
Santa Fe College
Seminole State College of Florida
South Florida Community College
Southeastern University
State College of Florida, Manatee-Sarasota
Stetson University
Tallahassee Community College
University of Florida
University of Miami
University of North Florida
University of South Florida
University of Tampa
University of West Florida
Warner University

Georgia
Agnes Scott College
Albany State University
Andrew College
Armstrong Atlantic State University
Berry College
Brenau University
Clark Atlanta University
Clayton State University
Columbus State University
Covenant College
Darton College
Emmanuel College
Emory University
Fort Valley State University
Georgia College and State University
Georgia Institute of Technology
Georgia Southern University
Georgia State University
Gordon College
Kennesaw State University
LaGrange College
Mercer University
Middle Georgia State College
Morehouse College
Oglethorpe University
Paine College
Piedmont College
Reinhardt University
Savannah College of Art and Design
Savannah State University
Shorter University
Spelman College
Toccoa Falls College
Truett-McConnell College
University of North Georgia
University of West Georgia
Valdosta State University
Wesleyan College
Young Harris College

Hawaii
Brigham Young University-Hawaii
Hawaii Pacific University
University of Hawaii
Manoa

Idaho
Boise Bible College
Boise State University
Brigham Young University-Idaho
College of Idaho
Idaho State University
Lewis-Clark State College
North Idaho College
Northwest Nazarene University
University of Idaho

Illinois
Augustana College
Aurora University
Benedictine University
Black Hawk College
Bradley University
Carl Sandburg College
College of DuPage
College of Lake County
Columbia College Chicago
Concordia University Chicago
Danville Area Community College
DePaul University
Eastern Illinois University
Elgin Community College
Elmhurst College
Eureka College
Harper College

Illinois Central College
Illinois College
Illinois State University
Illinois Valley Community College
Illinois Wesleyan University
Judson University
Kishwaukee College
Knox College
Lake Forest College
Lewis University
Lincoln College
Loyola University Chicago
McHenry County College
McKendree University
Millikin University
Monmouth College
Moody Bible Institute
Moraine Valley Community College
North Central College
North Park University
Northeastern Illinois University
Northern Illinois University
Northwestern University
Oakton Community College
Olivet Nazarene University
Parkland College
Quincy University
Rend Lake College
Richland Community College
Robert Morris University: Chicago
Rockford College
Roosevelt University
Saint Xavier University
Shawnee Community College
South Suburban College of Cook County
Southeastern Illinois College
Southern Illinois University Carbondale
Southern Illinois University Edwardsville
Spoon River College
Trinity Christian College
Trinity International University
University of Illinois
Chicago
Springfield
Urbana-Champaign
University of St. Francis
VanderCook College of Music
Waubonsee Community College
Western Illinois University
Wheaton College

Indiana

Anderson University
Ball State University
Bethel College
Butler University
DePauw University
Franklin College
Goshen College
Grace College
Hanover College
Huntington University
Indiana Institute of Technology
Indiana State University
Indiana University
Bloomington
Purdue University Fort Wayne
Southeast
Indiana Wesleyan University
Marian University
Oakland City University
Purdue University
Saint Joseph's College
St. Mary-of-the-Woods College
Saint Mary's College
Taylor University
Trine University
University of Evansville
University of Indianapolis
University of St. Francis
University of Southern Indiana
Valparaiso University
Vincennes University
Wabash College

Iowa

Ashford University
Briar Cliff University
Buena Vista University
Central College
Clarke University
Coe College
Cornell College
Dordt College
Drake University
Ellsworth Community College
Emmaus Bible College
Faith Baptist Bible College and Theological Seminary
Graceland University
Grand View University
Iowa Central Community College
Iowa State University
Iowa Wesleyan College
Iowa Western Community College
Kirkwood Community College
Loras College
Luther College
Morningside College
Mount Mercy University
Northwestern College
St. Ambrose University
Simpson College
Southwestern Community College
University of Dubuque
University of Iowa
University of Northern Iowa
Waldorf College
Wartburg College
Western Iowa Tech Community College
William Penn University

Kansas

Allen County Community College
Baker University
Barclay College
Benedictine College
Bethel College
Butler Community College
Central Christian College of Kansas
Coffeyville Community College
Colby Community College
Cowley County Community College
Dodge City Community College
Emporia State University
Fort Hays State University
Friends University
Garden City Community College
Hesston College
Highland Community College
Kansas City Kansas Community College
Kansas State University
Kansas Wesleyan University
McPherson College
MidAmerica Nazarene University
Neosho County Community College
Newman University
Ottawa University
Pittsburg State University
Pratt Community College
Southwestern College
Sterling College
Tabor College
University of Kansas
University of St. Mary
Washburn University
Wichita State University

Kentucky

Asbury University
Ashland Community and Technical College
Bellarmine University
Brescia University
Campbellsville University
Centre College
Eastern Kentucky University
Georgetown College
Kentucky Christian University
Kentucky Mountain Bible College
Kentucky State University
Kentucky Wesleyan College
Morehead State University
Murray State University
Northern Kentucky University
Thomas More College
Transylvania University
Union College
University of Kentucky
University of Louisville
University of the Cumberlands
Western Kentucky University

Louisiana

Bossier Parish Community College
Centenary College of Louisiana
Delgado Community College
Dillard University
Grambling State University
Louisiana College
Louisiana State University and Agricultural and Mechanical College
Louisiana Tech University
McNeese State University
Northwestern State University
Southeastern Louisiana University
Tulane University
University of Louisiana at Monroe
University of New Orleans

Maine

University of Maine
University of Maine
Augusta
Presque Isle
University of Southern Maine

Maryland

Bowie State University
Goucher College
Hood College
Johns Hopkins University: Peabody Conservatory of Music
Montgomery College
Mount St. Mary's University
Notre Dame of Maryland University
Salisbury University
Stevenson University
Towson University
University of Maryland
Baltimore County
Eastern Shore

Massachusetts

Anna Maria College
Berklee College of Music
Boston Conservatory
Boston University
Bristol Community College
Cape Cod Community College
College of the Holy Cross
Dean College
Emerson College
Endicott College
Gordon College
Holyoke Community College
Massachusetts College of Liberal Arts
Massachusetts Maritime Academy
New England Conservatory of Music
North Shore Community College
Northpoint Bible College
University of Massachusetts
Amherst
Lowell
Western New England University

Michigan

Adrian College
Albion College
Alma College
Alpena Community College
Andrews University
Aquinas College
Calvin College
Concordia University
Cornerstone University
Eastern Michigan University
Ferris State University
Gogebic Community College
Grand Valley State University
Great Lakes Christian College
Hillsdale College
Hope College
Jackson Community College
Kalamazoo College
Kellogg Community College
Macomb Community College
Madonna University
Marygrove College
Michigan State University
Michigan Technological University
Monroe County Community College
Mott Community College
Northern Michigan University
Northwestern Michigan College
Oakland University
Olivet College
Rochester College
Saginaw Valley State University
Schoolcraft College
Siena Heights University
Southwestern Michigan College
Spring Arbor University
University of Detroit Mercy
University of Michigan
University of Michigan
Flint
Wayne State University
Western Michigan University

Minnesota

Augsburg College
Bemidji State University
Bethany Lutheran College
Bethel University
College of St. Benedict
College of St. Scholastica
Concordia College: Moorhead
Concordia University St. Paul
Crossroads College
Crown College
Gustavus Adolphus College
Hamline University
Itasca Community College
Martin Luther College
Minnesota State Community and Technical College
Minnesota State University
Mankato
Moorhead
Normandale Community College
North Central University
Northwestern College
Riverland Community College
Saint Cloud State University
St. John's University
St. Mary's University of Minnesota
St. Olaf College
Southwest Minnesota State University
University of Minnesota
Crookston
Duluth
Twin Cities
University of St. Thomas
Winona State University

Mississippi

Belhaven University
Blue Mountain College
Copiah-Lincoln Community College
Delta State University
East Mississippi Community College
Hinds Community College

Itawamba Community College
Jackson State University
Meridian Community College
Millsaps College
Mississippi College
Mississippi Gulf Coast Community College
Mississippi State University
Mississippi University for Women
Pearl River Community College
Rust College
Tougaloo College
University of Mississippi

Missouri

Avila University
Calvary Bible College and Theological Seminary
Central Methodist University
College of the Ozarks
Columbia College
Cottey College
Crowder College
Culver-Stockton College
Drury University
East Central College
Evangel University
Fontbonne University
Hannibal-LaGrange University
Harris-Stowe State University
Jefferson College
Lincoln University
Lindenwood University
Mineral Area College
Missouri Baptist University
Missouri Southern State University
Missouri State University
Missouri University of Science and Technology
Missouri Western State University
Moberly Area Community College
Northwest Missouri State University
Park University
Rockhurst University
St. Charles Community College
Saint Louis University
Southeast Missouri State University
Southwest Baptist University
State Fair Community College
Stephens College
Truman State University
University of Central Missouri
University of Missouri
  Columbia
  Kansas City
  St. Louis
Webster University
Westminster College
William Jewell College
William Woods University

Montana

Carroll College
Dawson Community College
Montana State University
Montana State University
  Billings
University of Great Falls
University of Montana
University of Montana: Western

Nebraska

Central Community College
Chadron State College
Concordia University
Creighton University
Doane College
Grace University
Hastings College
Mid-Plains Community College
Nebraska Wesleyan University
Northeast Community College
Peru State College
University of Nebraska
  Kearney
  Lincoln
  Omaha
Wayne State College
Western Nebraska Community College
York College

Nevada

Truckee Meadows Community College
University of Nevada
  Las Vegas
  Reno

New Hampshire

Colby-Sawyer College
Franklin Pierce University
Keene State College
New England College
Plymouth State University
Saint Anselm College
University of New Hampshire

New Jersey

Caldwell College
Centenary College
The College of New Jersey
Drew University
Georgian Court University
Kean University
Montclair State University
New Jersey Institute of Technology
Richard Stockton College of New Jersey
Rider University
Rowan University
Rutgers, The State University of New Jersey
  Camden Campus
  New Brunswick/Piscataway Campus
  Newark Campus
Seton Hall University
Stevens Institute of Technology
William Paterson University of New Jersey

New Mexico

Eastern New Mexico University
New Mexico Highlands University
New Mexico Junior College
New Mexico State University
Santa Fe University of Art and Design
University of New Mexico
Western New Mexico University

New York

Adelphi University
Alfred University
Canisius College
City University of New York
  Brooklyn College
  City College
  College of Staten Island
  Queens College
College of New Rochelle
College of Saint Rose
Concordia College
Corning Community College
Eastman School of Music of the University of Rochester
Five Towns College
Hartwick College
Hobart and William Smith Colleges
Hofstra University
Houghton College
Ithaca College
Jamestown Community College
Juilliard School
Long Island University
  Brooklyn Campus
  C. W. Post Campus
Manhattan School of Music
Manhattanville College
Mannes College The New School for Music
Marist College
Molloy College
Monroe Community College
Nazareth College
Niagara University
Nyack College
Rensselaer Polytechnic Institute
Roberts Wesleyan College
The Sage Colleges
Saint Bonaventure University
St. John's University
Sarah Lawrence College
Skidmore College
Suffolk County Community College
SUNY
  College at Brockport
  College at Cortland
  College at Fredonia
  College at Geneseo
  College at New Paltz
  College at Oneonta
  College at Plattsburgh
  College at Potsdam
  College at Purchase
  University at Binghamton
  University at Buffalo
  University at Stony Brook
Syracuse University
University of Rochester
Villa Maria College of Buffalo
Wagner College

North Carolina

Appalachian State University
Barton College
Brevard College
Campbell University
Catawba College
Catawba Valley Community College
Chowan University
College of the Albemarle
Davidson College
East Carolina University
Elon University
Fayetteville State University
Gardner-Webb University
Greensboro College
High Point University
Isothermal Community College
Lees-McRae College
Lenoir-Rhyne University
Livingstone College
Louisburg College
Meredith College
Methodist University
Mid-Atlantic Christian University
Montreat College
Mount Olive College
North Carolina Central University
Pfeiffer University
Queens University of Charlotte
St. Augustine's University
Salem College
Shaw University
Southeastern Community College
University of North Carolina
  Asheville
  Chapel Hill
  Charlotte
  Greensboro
  Pembroke
  School of the Arts
  Wilmington
Wake Forest University
Western Carolina University
Wilkes Community College
William Peace University
Wingate University

North Dakota

Dakota College at Bottineau
Dickinson State University
Jamestown College
Lake Region State College
Mayville State University
Minot State University
North Dakota State College of Science
North Dakota State University
Trinity Bible College
University of Mary
University of North Dakota
Valley City State University
Williston State College

Ohio

Ashland University
Baldwin Wallace University
Bluffton University
Bowling Green State University
Bowling Green State University: Firelands College
Capital University
Case Western Reserve University
Cedarville University
Central State University
Cincinnati Christian University
Cleveland Institute of Music
Cleveland State University
College of Mount St. Joseph
College of Wooster
Cuyahoga Community College
  Metropolitan
Defiance College
Denison University
Hiram College
Kent State University
Kent State University
  Ashtabula
  East Liverpool
  Geauga
  Salem
  Stark
  Trumbull
  Tuscarawas
Kenyon College
Lake Erie College
Lakeland Community College
Malone University
Marietta College
Miami University
  Oxford
Mount Vernon Nazarene University
Muskingum University
Oberlin College
Ohio Northern University
Ohio State University
  Agricultural Technical Institute
  Columbus Campus
  Lima Campus
  Mansfield Campus
  Marion Campus
  Newark Campus
Ohio University
Ohio Wesleyan University
Otterbein University
Pontifical College Josephinum
Southern State Community College
Tiffin University
University of Akron
University of Akron: Wayne College
University of Cincinnati
University of Dayton
University of Findlay
University of Mount Union
University of Rio Grande
University of Toledo
Walsh University
Wittenberg University
Wright State University
Wright State University: Lake Campus
Xavier University

Oklahoma

Cameron University
Carl Albert State College
Mid-America Christian University
Northeastern Oklahoma Agricultural and Mechanical College
Northeastern State University
Northwestern Oklahoma State University
Oklahoma Baptist University

Oklahoma Christian University
Oklahoma City Community College
Oklahoma City University
Oklahoma Panhandle State University
Oklahoma State University
Oklahoma Wesleyan University
Oral Roberts University
Rogers State University
St. Gregory's University
Seminole State College
Southeastern Oklahoma State University
Southwestern Christian University
Southwestern Oklahoma State University
Tulsa Community College
University of Central Oklahoma
University of Oklahoma
University of Science and Arts of Oklahoma
University of Tulsa
Western Oklahoma State College

Oregon
Clackamas Community College
Concordia University
Corban University
Eastern Oregon University
George Fox University
Lane Community College
Linfield College
Linn-Benton Community College
New Hope Christian College
Northwest Christian University
Pacific University
Portland State University
Southern Oregon University
Southwestern Oregon Community College
Treasure Valley Community College
University of Oregon
University of Portland
Warner Pacific College
Western Oregon University
Willamette University

Pennsylvania
Albright College
Arcadia University
Baptist Bible College of Pennsylvania
Bloomsburg University of Pennsylvania
Bucknell University
Bucks County Community College
Cairn University
California University of Pennsylvania
Carnegie Mellon University
Cedar Crest College
Chatham University
Clarion University of Pennsylvania
Delaware Valley College
DeSales University
Drexel University
Duquesne University
East Stroudsburg University of Pennsylvania
Eastern University
Edinboro University of Pennsylvania
Elizabethtown College
Franklin & Marshall College
Gannon University
Geneva College
Harrisburg Area Community College
Immaculata University
Indiana University of Pennsylvania
Juniata College
Kutztown University of Pennsylvania
Lancaster Bible College
Lebanon Valley College
Lehigh University
Lincoln University
Lock Haven University of Pennsylvania
Lycoming College
Mansfield University of Pennsylvania
Marywood University
Mercyhurst University
Messiah College
Moravian College
Mount Aloysius College
Muhlenberg College
Northampton Community College
Point Park University
St. Francis University
Saint Joseph's University
Seton Hill University
Slippery Rock University of Pennsylvania
Susquehanna University
Temple University
Thiel College
University of the Arts
Ursinus College
Valley Forge Christian College
Valley Forge Military Academy and College
West Chester University of Pennsylvania
Widener University
Wilkes University
York College of Pennsylvania

Puerto Rico
Colegio de Cinematografía, Artes y Televisión
Humacao Community College
Pontifical Catholic University of Puerto Rico
Universidad Politecnica de Puerto Rico
University of Puerto Rico
 Aguadilla
 Humacao
 Mayaguez

Rhode Island
Providence College
Rhode Island College
University of Rhode Island

South Carolina
Allen University
Anderson University
The Citadel
Clemson University
Coastal Carolina University
Coker College
College of Charleston
Columbia College
Columbia International University
Converse College
Erskine College
Francis Marion University
Furman University
Lander University
Limestone College
Newberry College
North Greenville University
Presbyterian College
University of South Carolina
 Aiken
 Columbia
Winthrop University
Wofford College

South Dakota
Augustana College
Dakota State University
Mount Marty College
Northern State University
South Dakota State University
University of Sioux Falls
University of South Dakota

Tennessee
Austin Peay State University
Belmont University
Bethel University
Bryan University
 Dayton
Carson-Newman University
Christian Brothers University
Cumberland University
Dyersburg State Community College
East Tennessee State University
Fisk University
Freed-Hardeman University
Jackson State Community College
Johnson University
King College
Lee University
LeMoyne-Owen College
Lincoln Memorial University
Lipscomb University
Martin Methodist College
Maryville College
Middle Tennessee State University
Milligan College
Motlow State Community College
Northeast State Community College
Pellissippi State Community College
Rhodes College
Roane State Community College
Southern Adventist University
Southwest Tennessee Community College
Tennessee Technological University
Tennessee Wesleyan College
Trevecca Nazarene University
Union University
University of Memphis
University of Tennessee
 Chattanooga
 Knoxville
 Martin
Vanderbilt University
Volunteer State Community College
Walters State Community College
Welch College

Texas
Abilene Christian University
Angelina College
Angelo State University
Austin College
Baylor University
Brazosport College
Brookhaven College
Cisco College
Clarendon College
College of the Mainland
Collin County Community College District
Dallas Baptist University
Dallas Christian College
East Texas Baptist University
Frank Phillips College
Galveston College
Hardin-Simmons University
Hill College
Houston Baptist University
Howard College
Howard Payne University
Huston-Tillotson University
Jacksonville College
Kilgore College
Lee College
Lubbock Christian University
McMurry University
Midland College
Midwestern State University
Odessa College
Our Lady of the Lake University of San Antonio
Panola College
Paris Junior College
Paul Quinn College
Rice University
Richland College
St. Edward's University
St. Mary's University
Sam Houston State University
San Jacinto College
Schreiner University
South Plains College
Southern Methodist University
Southwestern Adventist University
Southwestern Christian College
Southwestern University
Stephen F. Austin State University
Tarleton State University
Temple College
Texas A&M University
Texas A&M University
 Commerce
 Corpus Christi
 Kingsville
Texas Christian University
Texas College
Texas Lutheran University
Texas State University: San Marcos
Texas Tech University
Texas Wesleyan University
Trinity University
University of Dallas
University of Houston
University of Mary Hardin-Baylor
University of St. Thomas
University of Texas
 Arlington
 Austin
 Brownsville - Texas Southmost College
 El Paso
 the Permian Basin
 San Antonio
 Tyler
University of the Incarnate Word
Vernon College
Victoria College
Wayland Baptist University
West Texas A&M University
Western Texas College
Wharton County Junior College

Utah
Brigham Young University
Dixie State College
Salt Lake Community College
Snow College
Southern Utah University
University of Utah
Utah State University
Utah Valley University
Weber State University
Westminster College

Vermont
Castleton State College
Goddard College
Green Mountain College
Johnson State College
Landmark College

Virginia
Bluefield College
Bridgewater College
Christopher Newport University
College of William and Mary
George Mason University
Hampden-Sydney College
Hampton University
Hollins University
James Madison University
Liberty University
Longwood University
Lynchburg College
Norfolk State University
Old Dominion University
Patrick Henry College
Radford University
Randolph College
Roanoke College
Shenandoah University
Southern Virginia University
Sweet Briar College
University of Mary Washington
University of Richmond
University of Virginia
University of Virginia's College at Wise
Virginia Commonwealth University
Virginia Intermont College
Virginia Military Institute
Virginia Polytechnic Institute and State University
Virginia State University

Washington
Big Bend Community College
Centralia College

Clark College
Cornish College of the Arts
Eastern Washington University
Everett Community College
Gonzaga University
Grays Harbor College
Northwest University
Pacific Lutheran University
Pierce College
Saint Martin's University
Seattle Pacific University
Trinity Lutheran College
University of Puget Sound
University of Washington
Walla Walla Community College
Walla Walla University
Washington State University
Western Washington University
Whitworth University

West Virginia
Alderson-Broaddus College
Concord University
Davis and Elkins College
Fairmont State University
Glenville State College
Marshall University
Ohio Valley University
Shepherd University
University of Charleston
West Liberty University
West Virginia University
West Virginia University Institute of Technology
West Virginia Wesleyan College
Wheeling Jesuit University

Wisconsin
Beloit College
Cardinal Stritch University
Carroll University
Carthage College
Concordia University Wisconsin
Edgewood College
Lawrence University
Marquette University
Mount Mary College
Northland College
Ripon College
St. Norbert College
Silver Lake College of the Holy Family
University of Wisconsin
- Baraboo/Sauk County
- Eau Claire
- Fond du Lac
- Green Bay
- La Crosse
- Madison
- Manitowoc
- Milwaukee
- Oshkosh
- Parkside
- Richland
- River Falls
- Rock County
- Sheboygan
- Stevens Point
- Superior
- Waukesha
- Whitewater

Viterbo University
Wisconsin Lutheran College

Wyoming
Casper College
Central Wyoming College
Eastern Wyoming College
Laramie County Community College
Northwest College
Sheridan College
University of Wyoming
Western Wyoming Community College

ROTC scholarships

Air Force ROTC

Alabama
Alabama State University
Auburn University
Auburn University at Montgomery
Birmingham-Southern College
Bishop State Community College
Faulkner University
Huntingdon College
Jefferson State Community College
Marion Military Institute
Miles College
Samford University
Shelton State Community College
Spring Hill College
Stillman College
Troy University
Tuskegee University
University of Alabama
University of Alabama
  Birmingham
University of Mobile
University of Montevallo
University of South Alabama
University of West Alabama

Alaska
Alaska Pacific University
University of Alaska
  Anchorage

Arizona
Arizona Christian University
Arizona State University
Coconino County Community College
DeVry University
  Phoenix
Embry-Riddle Aeronautical University
  Prescott Campus
Estrella Mountain Community College
GateWay Community College
Mesa Community College
Northern Arizona University
Phoenix College
Pima Community College
University of Arizona
Yavapai College

Arkansas
John Brown University
Northwest Arkansas Community College
University of Arkansas
University of Arkansas
  Fort Smith

California
Azusa Pacific University
Biola University
California Baptist University
California Institute of Technology
California Lutheran University
California Maritime Academy
California State University
  Dominguez Hills
  Fresno
  Los Angeles
  Northridge
  Sacramento
  San Bernardino
  San Marcos
Canada College
Chabot College
Chapman University
Claremont McKenna College
College of the Sequoias
Cuyamaca College
De Anza College
Foothill College
Fresno City College
Harvey Mudd College
Holy Names University
Irvine Valley College
Los Angeles City College
Los Angeles Mission College
Loyola Marymount University
The Master's College
Menlo College
MiraCosta College
Mission College
Mount San Antonio College
National University
Notre Dame de Namur University
Occidental College
Ohlone College
Pepperdine University
Pitzer College
Point Loma Nazarene University
Pomona College
Riverside Community College
Sacramento City College
St. Mary's College of California
Samuel Merritt University
San Diego Christian College
San Diego City College
San Diego State University
San Francisco State University
San Jose State University
Santa Clara University
Scripps College
Solano Community College
Sonoma State University
Stanford University
University of California
  Berkeley
  Davis
  Irvine
  Los Angeles
  Riverside
  Santa Cruz
University of Redlands
University of San Diego
University of San Francisco
University of Southern California
University of the Pacific
Vanguard University of Southern California
West Coast University: Orange County
West Valley College
Westmont College

Colorado
Arapahoe Community College
Colorado Christian University
Colorado School of Mines
Colorado State University
Metropolitan State University of Denver
Red Rocks Community College
Regis University
University of Colorado
  Boulder
  Denver
University of Denver
University of Northern Colorado

Connecticut
Capital Community College
Central Connecticut State University
Eastern Connecticut State University
Fairfield University
Quinnipiac University
Southern Connecticut State University
Tunxis Community College
University of Connecticut
University of Hartford
University of New Haven
Wesleyan University
Western Connecticut State University
Yale University

Delaware
Delaware State University
Delaware Technical and Community College
  Stanton/Wilmington
University of Delaware
Wilmington University

District of Columbia
American University
Catholic University of America
George Washington University
Georgetown University
Howard University
Trinity Washington University
University of the District of Columbia

Florida
Barry University
Bethune-Cookman University
Brevard Community College
Broward College
Clearwater Christian College
Daytona State College
Eckerd College
Embry-Riddle Aeronautical University
Florida Agricultural and Mechanical University
Florida Atlantic University
Florida College
Florida International University
Florida Southern College
Florida State University
Lynn University
Miami Dade College
Saint Leo University
Santa Fe College
Tallahassee Community College
University of Central Florida
University of Florida
University of Miami
University of South Florida
University of Tampa
University of West Florida
Valencia College

Georgia
Agnes Scott College
Clayton State University
Emory University
Georgia Institute of Technology
Georgia State University
Kennesaw State University
Morehouse College
Oglethorpe University
Southern Polytechnic State University
Spelman College
University of Georgia
University of West Georgia
Valdosta State University

Hawaii
Brigham Young University-Hawaii
Chaminade University of Honolulu
Hawaii Pacific University
University of Hawaii
  Honolulu Community College
  Manoa
  West Oahu

Idaho
Lewis-Clark State College
Northwest Nazarene University
University of Idaho

Illinois
Elmhurst College
Illinois Institute of Technology
John A. Logan College
Lewis University
Lincoln Land Community College
Loyola University Chicago
McKendree University
North Central College
North Park University
Northeastern Illinois University
Northwestern University
Parkland College
Saint Xavier University
Shawnee Community College
Shimer College
Southern Illinois University Carbondale
Southern Illinois University Edwardsville
Southwestern Illinois College
University of Chicago
University of Illinois
  Chicago
  Urbana-Champaign
Wheaton College

Indiana
Bethel College
Butler University
DePauw University
Holy Cross College
Indiana State University
Indiana University
  Bloomington
  Purdue University Indianapolis
  South Bend
  Southeast
Purdue University
Rose-Hulman Institute of Technology
St. Mary-of-the-Woods College
Saint Mary's College
Trine University
University of Notre Dame
Valparaiso University
Vincennes University

Iowa
Coe College
Drake University
Grand View University
Hawkeye Community College
Iowa State University
Iowa Western Community College
University of Iowa

Kansas
Baker University
Haskell Indian Nations University
Kansas State University
Manhattan Christian College
MidAmerica Nazarene University
University of Kansas
University of St. Mary
Washburn University

Kentucky
Asbury University
Bellarmine University
Centre College
Georgetown College
Kentucky State University
Midway College
Northern Kentucky University
Spalding University
Thomas More College
Transylvania University
University of Kentucky
University of Louisville
Western Kentucky University

Louisiana
Dillard University
Grambling State University
Louisiana State University and Agricultural and Mechanical College

Louisiana Tech University
Loyola University New Orleans
Northwestern State University
Our Lady of Holy Cross College
Our Lady of the Lake College
Southern University
    New Orleans
Southern University and Agricultural and Mechanical College
Tulane University
University of New Orleans
Xavier University of Louisiana

Maine
University of Maine
    Augusta
University of Southern Maine

Maryland
Anne Arundel Community College
Bowie State University
Goucher College
Johns Hopkins University
Loyola University Maryland
Prince George's Community College
Salisbury University
Stevenson University
Towson University
University of Maryland
    Baltimore County
    College Park

Massachusetts
American International College
Amherst College
Anna Maria College
Assumption College
Babson College
Bay Path College
Becker College
Bentley University
Boston College
Boston University
Brandeis University
Bridgewater State University
Clark University
College of the Holy Cross
Curry College
Eastern Nazarene College
Elms College
Emmanuel College
Harvard College
Holyoke Community College
Massachusetts College of Pharmacy and Health Sciences
Massachusetts Institute of Technology
Massachusetts Maritime Academy
Merrimack College
Middlesex Community College
Mount Holyoke College
Nichols College
Northeastern University
Pine Manor College
Quinsigamond Community College
Salem State University
Smith College
Springfield College
Tufts University
University of Massachusetts
    Amherst
    Boston
    Lowell
Wellesley College
Wentworth Institute of Technology
Western New England University
Westfield State University
Williams College
Worcester Polytechnic Institute
Worcester State University

Michigan
Central Michigan University
Concordia University
Eastern Michigan University
Finlandia University
Lansing Community College
Lawrence Technological University
Michigan State University
Michigan Technological University
Oakland University
Olivet College
Spring Arbor University
University of Michigan
University of Michigan
    Dearborn
Wayne State University

Minnesota
Anoka-Ramsey Community College
Augsburg College
Bethel University
Century College
College of St. Scholastica
Concordia College: Moorhead
Concordia University St. Paul
Hamline University
Inver Hills Community College
Macalester College
Minnesota State University
    Moorhead
North Central University
North Hennepin Community College
Northwestern College
St. Catherine University
University of Minnesota
    Crookston
    Duluth
    Twin Cities
University of St. Thomas

Mississippi
Belhaven University
East Mississippi Community College
Jackson State University
Millsaps College
Mississippi College
Mississippi State University
Mississippi University for Women
University of Mississippi
University of Southern Mississippi

Missouri
Central Bible College
Central Methodist University
Columbia College
Fontbonne University
Harris-Stowe State University
Lincoln University
Missouri University of Science and Technology
Saint Louis University
Southeast Missouri State University
Stephens College
University of Central Missouri
University of Missouri
    Columbia
    St. Louis
Washington University in St. Louis
Webster University
Westminster College
William Woods University

Montana
Montana State University

Nebraska
Bellevue University
Clarkson College
College of Saint Mary
Concordia University
Creighton University
Doane College
Grace University
Nebraska Wesleyan University
University of Nebraska
    Lincoln
    Medical Center
    Omaha
York College

Nevada
Nevada State College
University of Nevada
    Las Vegas

New Hampshire
Colby-Sawyer College
Daniel Webster College
Franklin Pierce University
Granite State College
Keene State College
New England College
Plymouth State University
Rivier University
University of New Hampshire
University of New Hampshire at Manchester

New Jersey
Brookdale Community College
The College of New Jersey
Fairleigh Dickinson University
    College at Florham
    Metropolitan Campus
Felician College
Kean University
Monmouth University
Montclair State University
New Jersey Institute of Technology
Princeton University
Ramapo College of New Jersey
Raritan Valley Community College
Rutgers, The State University of New Jersey
    Camden Campus
    New Brunswick/Piscataway Campus
    Newark Campus
Saint Peter's University
Stevens Institute of Technology
Union County College
William Paterson University of New Jersey

New Mexico
Central New Mexico Community College
Dona Ana Community College of New Mexico State University
New Mexico State University
New Mexico State University
    Alamogordo
University of New Mexico

New York
Adelphi University
Barnard College
Cazenovia College
Clarkson University
College of Mount St. Vincent
College of Saint Rose
Columbia University
Columbia University
    School of General Studies
Cornell University
Dowling College
Elmira College
Fordham University
Hamilton College
Hobart and William Smith Colleges
Hudson Valley Community College
Iona College
Ithaca College
Jewish Theological Seminary of America
Le Moyne College
Manhattan College
Maria College
Mercy College
Mesivta Torah Vodaath Seminary
Mohawk Valley Community College
Monroe Community College
Nazareth College
New York Institute of Technology
New York University
Onondaga Community College
Pace University
Polytechnic Institute of New York University
Rensselaer Polytechnic Institute
Roberts Wesleyan College
Rochester Institute of Technology
The Sage Colleges
St. Francis College
St. John Fisher College
St. Lawrence University
St. Thomas Aquinas College
Schenectady County Community College
Siena College
Skidmore College
SUNY
    College at Brockport
    College at Cortland
    College at Geneseo
    College at Old Westbury
    College at Oswego
    College at Potsdam
    College of Agriculture and Technology at Morrisville
    College of Environmental Science and Forestry
    College of Technology at Canton
    Farmingdale State College
    University at Albany
    University at Binghamton
    University at Stony Brook
Syracuse University
Union College
United States Merchant Marine Academy
University of Rochester
Utica College
Vaughn College of Aeronautics and Technology
Wells College

North Carolina
Belmont Abbey College
Bennett College for Women
Catawba Valley Community College
Davidson College
Duke University
East Carolina University
Elon University
Fayetteville State University
Gardner-Webb University
Greensboro College
High Point University
Johnson C. Smith University
Lenoir-Rhyne University
Meredith College
Methodist University
Mount Olive College
North Carolina Agricultural and Technical State University
North Carolina Central University
North Carolina State University
Randolph Community College
University of North Carolina
    Chapel Hill
    Charlotte
    Greensboro
    Pembroke
William Peace University
Wingate University

North Dakota
Mayville State University
North Dakota State University
University of North Dakota

Ohio
Baldwin Wallace University
Bowling Green State University
Capital University
Case Western Reserve University
Cedarville University
Central State University
Cleveland Institute of Art
Cleveland State University
College of Mount St. Joseph
Columbus State Community College
Cuyahoga Community College
    Metropolitan
Franciscan University of Steubenville

Heidelberg University
Hiram College
Hocking College
Kent State University
Kent State University
- Ashtabula
- East Liverpool
- Geauga
- Salem
- Stark
- Trumbull
- Tuscarawas

Lourdes University
Malone University
Miami University
- Hamilton
- Middletown
- Oxford

Mount Carmel College of Nursing
Ohio Christian University
Ohio Northern University
Ohio State University
- Agricultural Technical Institute
- Columbus Campus
- Lima Campus
- Mansfield Campus
- Marion Campus
- Newark Campus

Ohio University
Ohio University
- Lancaster Campus

Otterbein University
Owens Community College
- Toledo

Sinclair Community College
Tiffin University
University of Akron
University of Akron: Wayne College
University of Cincinnati
University of Cincinnati
- Raymond Walters College

University of Dayton
University of Findlay
University of Mount Union
University of Toledo
Wilberforce University
Wittenberg University
Wright State University
Xavier University
Youngstown State University

Oklahoma
Langston University
Northeastern Oklahoma Agricultural and Mechanical College
Oklahoma Baptist University
Oklahoma Christian University
Oklahoma City University
Oklahoma State University
Oral Roberts University
Rose State College
St. Gregory's University
Southern Nazarene University
University of Oklahoma
University of Tulsa

Oregon
Clackamas Community College
Concordia University
Corban University
George Fox University
Linfield College
Linn-Benton Community College
Oregon State University
Pacific University
Portland State University
University of Oregon
University of Portland
Warner Pacific College
Western Oregon University
Willamette University

Pennsylvania
Bloomsburg University of Pennsylvania
Bryn Athyn College
Bryn Mawr College
Cabrini College
Cairn University
Carlow University
Carnegie Mellon University
Chatham University
Drexel University
Duquesne University
East Stroudsburg University of Pennsylvania
Eastern University
Keystone College
King's College
La Roche College
La Salle University
Luzerne County Community College
Marywood University
Misericordia University
Penn State
- Abington
- Altoona
- Brandywine
- Hazleton
- New Kensington
- University Park
- Wilkes-Barre
- Worthington Scranton

Point Park University
Robert Morris University
Rosemont College
Saint Joseph's University
St. Vincent College
Swarthmore College
Temple University
Thomas Jefferson University: College of Health Professions
University of Pennsylvania
University of Pittsburgh
University of Pittsburgh
- Greensburg

University of Scranton
University of the Sciences in Philadelphia
Valley Forge Military Academy and College
Villanova University
Washington & Jefferson College
West Chester University of Pennsylvania
Widener University
Wilkes University

Puerto Rico
Bayamon Central University
Caribbean University
Inter American University of Puerto Rico
- Aguadilla Campus
- Bayamon Campus
- Fajardo Campus
- Metropolitan Campus
- San German Campus

Pontifical Catholic University of Puerto Rico
Universidad Metropolitana
Universidad Politecnica de Puerto Rico
University of Puerto Rico
- Mayaguez
- Rio Piedras

South Carolina
Anderson University
Benedict College
Charleston Southern University
The Citadel
Claflin University
Clemson University
College of Charleston
South Carolina State University
Tri-County Technical College
University of South Carolina
- Columbia
- Salkehatchie

Winthrop University

South Dakota
Augustana College
Dakota State University
South Dakota State University
University of Sioux Falls

Tennessee
Austin Peay State University
Belmont University
Carson-Newman University
Christian Brothers University
LeMoyne-Owen College
Lipscomb University
Middle Tennessee State University
Rhodes College
Southwest Tennessee Community College
Tennessee State University
Tennessee Technological University
Tennessee Wesleyan College
University of Memphis
University of Tennessee
- Knoxville

Vanderbilt University
Welch College

Texas
Angelo State University
Austin Community College
Baylor University
Concordia University Texas
Dallas Baptist University
Houston Baptist University
Houston Community College System
Lone Star College System
Lubbock Christian University
McLennan Community College
Midwestern State University
North Central Texas College
Our Lady of the Lake University of San Antonio
Rice University
St. Edward's University
St. Mary's University
San Antonio College
San Jacinto College
Southern Methodist University
Tarrant County College
Texas A&M University
Texas Christian University
Texas Lutheran University
Texas State University: San Marcos
Texas Tech University
Texas Wesleyan University
Texas Woman's University
Trinity University
University of Dallas
University of Houston
University of Houston
- Downtown
- Victoria

University of Mary Hardin-Baylor
University of North Texas
University of St. Thomas
University of Texas
- Arlington
- Austin
- Dallas
- El Paso
- San Antonio

University of the Incarnate Word
Wayland Baptist University
Weatherford College

Utah
Brigham Young University
LDS Business College
Salt Lake Community College
University of Utah
Utah State University
Utah Valley University
Weber State University
Westminster College

Vermont
Lyndon State College
Norwich University
Saint Michael's College

Virginia
George Mason University
James Madison University
Liberty University
Mary Baldwin College
Piedmont Virginia Community College
University of Virginia
Virginia Military Institute
Virginia Polytechnic Institute and State University

Washington
Clark College
Highline Community College
Saint Martin's University
Seattle Pacific University
Seattle University
South Puget Sound Community College
Spokane Community College
University of Washington
University of Washington Bothell
University of Washington Tacoma
Washington State University

West Virginia
Fairmont State University
Shepherd University
West Virginia University

Wisconsin
Alverno College
Carroll University
Carthage College
Edgewood College
Maranatha Baptist Bible College
Marquette University
Milwaukee School of Engineering
University of Wisconsin
- Madison
- Milwaukee
- Stout
- Superior
- Whitewater

Wisconsin Lutheran College

Wyoming
Laramie County Community College
University of Wyoming

Army ROTC

Alabama
Alabama Agricultural and Mechanical University
Alabama State University
Auburn University
Auburn University at Montgomery
Birmingham-Southern College
Bishop State Community College
Faulkner University
Gadsden State Community College
Huntingdon College
Jacksonville State University
Jefferson State Community College
Judson College
Marion Military Institute
Miles College
Samford University
Shelton State Community College
Spring Hill College
Stillman College
Talladega College
Troy University
Tuskegee University
University of Alabama

University of Alabama
- Birmingham
- Huntsville

University of Mobile
University of Montevallo
University of North Alabama
University of South Alabama

Alaska
University of Alaska
- Anchorage
- Fairbanks

Arizona
Arizona State University
Coconino County Community College
Embry-Riddle Aeronautical University
- Prescott Campus

GateWay Community College
Grand Canyon University
Mesa Community College
Northern Arizona University
Paradise Valley Community College
Phoenix College
Pima Community College
Southwest University of Visual Arts
University of Arizona
Yavapai College

Arkansas
Arkansas State University
Arkansas State University
- Beebe

Arkansas Tech University
Central Baptist College
College of the Ouachitas
Henderson State University
Hendrix College
John Brown University
Northwest Arkansas Community College
Ouachita Baptist University
University of Arkansas
University of Arkansas
- Fort Smith
- Little Rock
- Monticello
- Pine Bluff

University of Central Arkansas
Williams Baptist College

California
Azusa Pacific University
Biola University
California Baptist University
California Institute of Technology
California Lutheran University
California Polytechnic State University: San Luis Obispo
California State Polytechnic University: Pomona
California State University
- Dominguez Hills
- Fresno
- Fullerton
- Long Beach
- Los Angeles
- Northridge
- Sacramento
- San Bernardino
- San Marcos

Canada College
Chabot College
Chapman University
City College of San Francisco
Claremont McKenna College
De Anza College
Diablo Valley College
Foothill College
Fresno City College
Harvey Mudd College
Holy Names University
Hope International University
Los Angeles City College
Los Angeles Mission College
Loyola Marymount University
The Master's College
Menlo College
Mills College
MiraCosta College
National University
Occidental College
Pepperdine University
Pitzer College
Point Loma Nazarene University
Pomona College
Riverside Community College
Sacramento City College
St. Mary's College of California
Samuel Merritt University
San Diego Christian College
San Diego City College
San Diego State University
San Francisco State University
San Jose State University
Santa Clara University
Scripps College
Simpson University
Sonoma State University
Stanford University
University of California
- Berkeley
- Davis
- Irvine
- Los Angeles
- Riverside
- Santa Barbara
- Santa Cruz

University of La Verne
University of Redlands
University of San Diego
University of San Francisco
University of Southern California
Vanguard University of Southern California
West Valley College
Westmont College
Whittier College

Colorado
Arapahoe Community College
Colorado Christian University
Colorado College
Colorado School of Mines
Colorado State University
Colorado State University
- Pueblo

Colorado Technical University
Community College of Denver
Metropolitan State University of Denver
Red Rocks Community College
Regis University
University of Colorado
- Boulder
- Colorado Springs
- Denver

University of Denver
University of Northern Colorado

Connecticut
Capital Community College
Central Connecticut State University
Eastern Connecticut State University
Fairfield University
Quinnipiac University
Sacred Heart University
Southern Connecticut State University
Trinity College
Tunxis Community College
University of Bridgeport
University of Connecticut
University of Hartford
University of New Haven
Wesleyan University
Western Connecticut State University
Yale University

Delaware
Delaware State University
University of Delaware
Wesley College
Wilmington University

District of Columbia
American University
Catholic University of America
George Washington University
Georgetown University
Howard University
Trinity Washington University
University of the District of Columbia

Florida
Barry University
Bethune-Cookman University
Brevard Community College
Broward College
Clearwater Christian College
Daytona State College
Eckerd College
Embry-Riddle Aeronautical University
Florida Agricultural and Mechanical University
Florida Atlantic University
Florida College
Florida Institute of Technology
Florida International University
Florida Southern College
Florida State College at Jacksonville
Florida State University
Hillsborough Community College
Miami Dade College
Northwest Florida State College
Palm Beach Atlantic University
Pasco-Hernando Community College
Pensacola State College
Polk State College
Saint Leo University
Santa Fe College
Seminole State College of Florida
Southeastern University
Stetson University
Tallahassee Community College
University of Central Florida
University of Florida
University of Miami
University of North Florida
University of South Florida
University of Tampa
University of West Florida
Valencia College

Georgia
Agnes Scott College
Albany State University
Armstrong Atlantic State University
Clark Atlanta University
Clayton State University
Columbus State University
Covenant College
East Georgia College
Emory University
Fort Valley State University
Georgia College and State University
Georgia Gwinnett College
Georgia Institute of Technology
Georgia Military College
Georgia Regents University
Georgia Southern University
Georgia State University
Kennesaw State University
Mercer University
Middle Georgia State College
Morehouse College
Paine College
Savannah College of Art and Design
Savannah State University
Southern Polytechnic State University
Spelman College
University of Georgia
University of North Georgia

Hawaii
Brigham Young University-Hawaii
Chaminade University of Honolulu
Hawaii Pacific University
University of Hawaii
- Honolulu Community College
- Manoa
- West Oahu
- Windward Community College

Idaho
Boise State University
Brigham Young University-Idaho
College of Idaho
Idaho State University
Lewis-Clark State College
North Idaho College
Northwest Nazarene University
University of Idaho

Illinois
Aurora University
Benedictine University
Bradley University
Carl Sandburg College
Chicago State University
DePaul University
Eastern Illinois University
Elmhurst College
Illinois Institute of Technology
Illinois State University
Illinois Wesleyan University
John A. Logan College
Judson University
Kankakee Community College
Kishwaukee College
Lewis and Clark Community College
Lewis University
Lincoln Land Community College
Loyola University Chicago
McKendree University
Monmouth College
North Central College
North Park University
Northeastern Illinois University
Northern Illinois University
Northwestern University
Olivet Nazarene University
Parkland College
Robert Morris University: Chicago
Shawnee Community College
Shimer College
Southern Illinois University Carbondale
Southern Illinois University Edwardsville
Southwestern Illinois College
Spoon River College
University of Chicago
University of Illinois
- Chicago
- Urbana-Champaign

University of St. Francis
Waubonsee Community College
Western Illinois University
Wheaton College

Indiana
Ball State University
Bethel College
Butler University
DePauw University
Franklin College
Holy Cross College
Indiana Institute of Technology
Indiana State University
Indiana University
- Bloomington
- Kokomo
- Northwest
- Purdue University Fort Wayne
- Purdue University Indianapolis
- South Bend
- Southeast

Indiana Wesleyan University
Marian University
Purdue University
Rose-Hulman Institute of Technology

St. Mary-of-the-Woods College
Saint Mary's College
University of Evansville
University of Indianapolis
University of Notre Dame
University of Southern Indiana
Valparaiso University
Vincennes University

Iowa
Allen College
Briar Cliff University
Buena Vista University
Clarke University
Coe College
Drake University
Grand View University
Hawkeye Community College
Iowa State University
Iowa Western Community College
Loras College
Morningside College
University of Dubuque
University of Iowa
University of Northern Iowa

Kansas
Baker University
Benedictine College
Kansas State University
Manhattan Christian College
MidAmerica Nazarene University
Pittsburg State University
University of Kansas
University of St. Mary
Washburn University

Kentucky
Asbury University
Bellarmine University
Campbellsville University
Centre College
Eastern Kentucky University
Elizabethtown Community and Technical College
Georgetown College
Kentucky State University
Kentucky Wesleyan College
Midway College
Morehead State University
Murray State University
Northern Kentucky University
Spalding University
Thomas More College
Transylvania University
University of Kentucky
University of Louisville
University of Pikeville
University of the Cumberlands
Western Kentucky University

Louisiana
Dillard University
Grambling State University
Louisiana College
Louisiana State University
 Alexandria
 Shreveport
Louisiana State University and Agricultural and Mechanical College
Louisiana Tech University
Loyola University New Orleans
Northwestern State University
Our Lady of Holy Cross College
Our Lady of the Lake College
Southeastern Louisiana University
Southern University
 New Orleans
Southern University and Agricultural and Mechanical College
Tulane University
University of Louisiana at Lafayette
University of Louisiana at Monroe
University of New Orleans
Xavier University of Louisiana

Maine
Colby College
Eastern Maine Community College
Husson University
Maine Maritime Academy
New England School of Communications
Saint Joseph's College of Maine
University of Maine
University of Maine
 Augusta
University of New England
University of Southern Maine

Maryland
Allegany College of Maryland
Anne Arundel Community College
Bowie State University
Capitol College
Coppin State University
Goucher College
Hood College
Johns Hopkins University
Loyola University Maryland
Maryland Institute College of Art
McDaniel College
Morgan State University
Mount St. Mary's University
Notre Dame of Maryland University
Prince George's Community College
Salisbury University
Stevenson University
Towson University
University of Baltimore
University of Maryland
 Baltimore County
 College Park

Massachusetts
American International College
Amherst College
Assumption College
Babson College
Bay Path College
Becker College
Bentley University
Boston College
Boston University
Brandeis University
Bridgewater State University
Clark University
College of the Holy Cross
Curry College
Eastern Nazarene College
Elms College
Emmanuel College
Endicott College
Fisher College
Fitchburg State University
Gordon College
Hampshire College
Harvard College
Holyoke Community College
Massachusetts College of Pharmacy and Health Sciences
Massachusetts Institute of Technology
Massachusetts Maritime Academy
Middlesex Community College
Mount Holyoke College
Nichols College
Northeastern University
Pine Manor College
Quinsigamond Community College
Regis College
Roxbury Community College
Salem State University
Smith College
Springfield College
Stonehill College
Suffolk University
Tufts University
University of Massachusetts
 Amherst
 Boston
 Dartmouth
 Lowell
Wellesley College
Wentworth Institute of Technology
Western New England University
Westfield State University
Wheaton College
Worcester Polytechnic Institute
Worcester State University

Michigan
Adrian College
Alma College
Aquinas College
Calvin College
Central Michigan University
Concordia University
Eastern Michigan University
Ferris State University
Finlandia University
Hope College
Kalamazoo College
Kuyper College
Lansing Community College
Madonna University
Michigan State University
Michigan Technological University
Northern Michigan University
Siena Heights University
Spring Arbor University
University of Michigan
University of Michigan
 Dearborn
 Flint
Washtenaw Community College
Wayne State University
Western Michigan University

Minnesota
Anoka-Ramsey Community College
Augsburg College
Bethany Lutheran College
Bethel University
College of St. Benedict
Concordia College: Moorhead
Concordia University St. Paul
Crown College
Gustavus Adolphus College
Hamline University
Inver Hills Community College
Macalester College
Minnesota State University
 Mankato
 Moorhead
North Central University
North Hennepin Community College
Northwestern College
St. Catherine University
Saint Cloud State University
St. John's University
St. Mary's University of Minnesota
University of Minnesota
 Twin Cities
University of St. Thomas
Winona State University

Mississippi
Alcorn State University
Belhaven University
Delta State University
Hinds Community College
Jackson State University
Millsaps College
Mississippi College
Mississippi State University
Mississippi University for Women
Mississippi Valley State University
Tougaloo College
University of Mississippi
University of Southern Mississippi

Missouri
Avila University
Calvary Bible College and Theological Seminary
Central Bible College
Central Methodist University
College of the Ozarks
Columbia College
Drury University
Evangel University
Fontbonne University
Harris-Stowe State University
Lincoln University
Lindenwood University
Maryville University of Saint Louis
Missouri Baptist University
Missouri State University
Missouri University of Science and Technology
Missouri Valley College
Missouri Western State University
Northwest Missouri State University
Park University
Research College of Nursing
Rockhurst University
Saint Louis University
Southwest Baptist University
State Fair Community College
Stephens College
Truman State University
University of Central Missouri
University of Missouri
 Columbia
 Kansas City
 St. Louis
Washington University in St. Louis
Webster University
Wentworth Military Junior College
Westminster College
William Jewell College
William Woods University

Montana
Carroll College
Montana State University
Montana State University
 Billings
Rocky Mountain College
University of Montana

Nebraska
Bellevue University
BryanLGH College of Health Sciences
Chadron State College
Clarkson College
College of Saint Mary
Concordia University
Creighton University
Doane College
Nebraska Methodist College of Nursing and Allied Health
Nebraska Wesleyan University
University of Nebraska
 Kearney
 Lincoln
 Medical Center
 Omaha
Wayne State College
York College

Nevada
College of Southern Nevada
Truckee Meadows Community College
University of Nevada
 Las Vegas
 Reno

New Hampshire
Colby-Sawyer College
Daniel Webster College
Dartmouth College
Franklin Pierce University
Granite State College
New England College

Plymouth State University
Rivier University
Saint Anselm College
Southern New Hampshire University
University of New Hampshire
University of New Hampshire at Manchester

New Jersey
Bloomfield College
Brookdale Community College
Caldwell College
The College of New Jersey
Fairleigh Dickinson University
College at Florham
Metropolitan Campus
Felician College
Kean University
Middlesex County College
Monmouth University
Montclair State University
New Jersey Institute of Technology
Princeton University
Raritan Valley Community College
Rider University
Rowan University
Rutgers, The State University of New Jersey
Camden Campus
New Brunswick/Piscataway Campus
Newark Campus
Saint Peter's University
Seton Hall University
Stevens Institute of Technology

New Mexico
Central New Mexico Community College
Dona Ana Community College of New Mexico State University
New Mexico Military Institute
New Mexico State University
Santa Fe University of Art and Design
Southwest University of Visual Arts
University of New Mexico

New York
Adelphi University
Alfred University
Canisius College
Cazenovia College
City University of New York
Baruch College
Lehman College
Queens College
York College
Clarkson University
Colgate University
College of New Rochelle
College of Saint Rose
Columbia University
Columbia University
School of General Studies
Cornell University
Daemen College
Dowling College
D'Youville College
Elmira College
Erie Community College
Fordham University
Hamilton College
Herkimer County Community College
Hilbert College
Hobart and William Smith Colleges
Hofstra University
Houghton College
Hudson Valley Community College
Iona College
Ithaca College
Jewish Theological Seminary of America
The King's College
Le Moyne College
Long Island University
C. W. Post Campus
Manhattan College
Maria College
Marist College
Medaille College
Mercy College
Mohawk Valley Community College
Molloy College
Monroe College
Monroe Community College
Nazareth College
New York Institute of Technology
New York University
Niagara County Community College
Niagara University
Onondaga Community College
Orange County Community College
Pace University
Polytechnic Institute of New York University
Rensselaer Polytechnic Institute
Roberts Wesleyan College
Rochester Institute of Technology
The Sage Colleges
Saint Bonaventure University
St. Francis College
St. John Fisher College
St. John's University
St. Lawrence University
Siena College
Skidmore College
SUNY
College at Brockport
College at Buffalo
College at Cortland
College at Fredonia
College at Geneseo
College at Old Westbury
College at Oswego
College at Plattsburgh
College at Potsdam
College of Agriculture and Technology at Morrisville
College of Environmental Science and Forestry
College of Technology at Alfred
College of Technology at Canton
Farmingdale State College
Institute of Technology at Utica/Rome
Maritime College
University at Albany
University at Binghamton
University at Buffalo
University at Stony Brook
Upstate Medical University
Syracuse University
Talmudical Seminary Oholei Torah
Union College
United States Merchant Marine Academy
University of Rochester
Utica College
Vaughn College of Aeronautics and Technology
Wagner College
Wells College

North Carolina
Appalachian State University
Belmont Abbey College
Bennett College for Women
Campbell University
Catawba College
Davidson College
Duke University
East Carolina University
Elizabeth City State University
Elon University
Fayetteville State University
Gardner-Webb University
Greensboro College
High Point University
Johnson C. Smith University
Lenoir-Rhyne University
Livingstone College
Louisburg College
Meredith College
Methodist University
Mid-Atlantic Christian University
North Carolina Agricultural and Technical State University
North Carolina Central University
North Carolina State University
North Carolina Wesleyan College
Pfeiffer University
Pitt Community College
St. Augustine's University
Salem College
Shaw University
University of North Carolina
Chapel Hill
Charlotte
Greensboro
Pembroke
Wake Forest University
Wake Technical Community College
William Peace University
Wingate University
Winston-Salem State University

North Dakota
Mayville State University
North Dakota State University
University of North Dakota

Ohio
Baldwin Wallace University
Bowling Green State University
Capital University
Case Western Reserve University
Cedarville University
Central State University
Cincinnati State Technical and Community College
Cleveland Institute of Art
Cleveland State University
College of Mount St. Joseph
Columbus State Community College
Denison University
DeVry University
Columbus
Franciscan University of Steubenville
Franklin University
Heidelberg University
Hiram College
Hocking College
John Carroll University
Kent State University
Kent State University
Ashtabula
East Liverpool
Geauga
Salem
Stark
Trumbull
Tuscarawas
Lourdes University
Malone University
Miami University
Oxford
Mount Carmel College of Nursing
Notre Dame College
Ohio Dominican University
Ohio Northern University
Ohio State University
Agricultural Technical Institute
Columbus Campus
Lima Campus
Mansfield Campus
Marion Campus
Newark Campus
Ohio University
Ohio University
Lancaster Campus
Otterbein University
Owens Community College
Toledo
Sinclair Community College
Tiffin University
University of Akron
University of Akron: Wayne College
University of Cincinnati
University of Cincinnati
Clermont College
Raymond Walters College
University of Dayton
University of Findlay
University of Mount Union
University of Toledo
Ursuline College
Wilberforce University
Wittenberg University
Wright State University
Xavier University
Youngstown State University

Oklahoma
Cameron University
Langston University
Northeastern State University
Oklahoma Christian University
Oklahoma City University
Oklahoma State University
Southern Nazarene University
Southwestern Christian University
University of Central Oklahoma
University of Oklahoma

Oregon
Central Oregon Community College
Corban University
Eastern Oregon University
Lewis & Clark College
Linn-Benton Community College
Oregon Institute of Technology
Oregon State University
Pacific University
Portland State University
Southern Oregon University
University of Oregon
University of Portland
Western Oregon University
Willamette University

Pennsylvania
Arcadia University
Baptist Bible College of Pennsylvania
Bloomsburg University of Pennsylvania
Bryn Athyn College
Bucknell University
Cabrini College
California University of Pennsylvania
Carlow University
Carnegie Mellon University
Cedar Crest College
Chatham University
Cheyney University of Pennsylvania
Clarion University of Pennsylvania
Community College of Philadelphia
DeSales University
Dickinson College
Drexel University
Duquesne University
East Stroudsburg University of Pennsylvania
Eastern University
Edinboro University of Pennsylvania
Gannon University
Geneva College
Gettysburg College
Grove City College
Harrisburg Area Community College
Immaculata University
Indiana University of Pennsylvania
Keystone College
King's College
Kutztown University of Pennsylvania
La Roche College
La Salle University
Lackawanna College
Lafayette College
Lehigh Carbon Community College
Lehigh University
Lincoln University
Lock Haven University of Pennsylvania
Lycoming College

Mansfield University of Pennsylvania
Marywood University
Mercyhurst University
Millersville University of Pennsylvania
Misericordia University
Moravian College
Muhlenberg College
Neumann University
Penn State
  Abington
  Altoona
  Berks
  Brandywine
  Erie, The Behrend College
  Fayette, The Eberly Campus
  Harrisburg
  Hazleton
  Lehigh Valley
  Mont Alto
  University Park
  Wilkes-Barre
  Worthington Scranton
Pennsylvania College of Technology
Point Park University
Robert Morris University
Rosemont College
St. Francis University
Saint Joseph's University
St. Vincent College
Seton Hill University
Shippensburg University of Pennsylvania
Slippery Rock University of Pennsylvania
Susquehanna University
Swarthmore College
Temple University
University of Pennsylvania
University of Pittsburgh
University of Pittsburgh
  Bradford
  Greensburg
  Johnstown
University of Scranton
University of the Sciences in Philadelphia
Valley Forge Military Academy and College
Villanova University
Washington & Jefferson College
Waynesburg University
West Chester University of Pennsylvania
Westminster College
Widener University
Wilkes University
Wilson College
York College of Pennsylvania

Puerto Rico
American University of Puerto Rico
Bayamon Central University
Caribbean University
EDP University of Puerto Rico: Hato Rey
Inter American University of Puerto Rico
  Aguadilla Campus
  Arecibo Campus
  Bayamon Campus
  Guayama Campus
  Metropolitan Campus
  San German Campus
Pontifical Catholic University of Puerto Rico
Turabo University
Universidad del Este
Universidad Metropolitana
Universidad Politecnica de Puerto Rico
University of Puerto Rico
  Aguadilla
  Arecibo
  Bayamon University College
  Cayey University College
  Mayaguez
  Ponce
  Rio Piedras
  Utuado

Rhode Island
Brown University
Bryant University
Community College of Rhode Island
Johnson & Wales University
  Providence
Providence College
Rhode Island College
Roger Williams University
Salve Regina University
University of Rhode Island

South Carolina
Allen University
Anderson University
Benedict College
Charleston Southern University
The Citadel
Claflin University
Clemson University
Coastal Carolina University
Columbia College
Converse College
Francis Marion University
Furman University
Greenville Technical College
Lander University
Limestone College
Morris College
Newberry College
North Greenville University
Orangeburg-Calhoun Technical College
Presbyterian College
South Carolina State University
Spartanburg Methodist College
Tri-County Technical College
University of South Carolina
  Columbia
  Lancaster
  Salkehatchie
  Sumter
  Upstate
Voorhees College
Winthrop University
Wofford College

South Dakota
Augustana College
Black Hills State University
Mount Marty College
National American University
  Rapid City
South Dakota School of Mines and Technology
South Dakota State University
University of South Dakota

Tennessee
Austin Peay State University
Belmont University
Carson-Newman University
Christian Brothers University
Cumberland University
East Tennessee State University
Fisk University
Jackson State Community College
King College
LeMoyne-Owen College
Lincoln Memorial University
Lipscomb University
Middle Tennessee State University
Milligan College
Pellissippi State Community College
Rhodes College
Southwest Tennessee Community College
Tennessee Technological University
Tennessee Wesleyan College
Trevecca Nazarene University
Union University
University of Memphis
University of Tennessee
  Chattanooga
  Knoxville
  Martin
Vanderbilt University
Walters State Community College
Welch College

Texas
Alvin Community College
Angelina College
Austin Community College
Baylor University
Central Texas College
The College of Saints John Fisher & Thomas More
Collin County Community College District
Concordia University Texas
Dallas Baptist University
Del Mar College
El Centro College
El Paso Community College
Houston Baptist University
Houston Community College System
Huston-Tillotson University
Laredo Community College
Lone Star College System
Lubbock Christian University
Our Lady of the Lake University of San Antonio
Palo Alto College
Prairie View A&M University
Rice University
St. Edward's University
St. Mary's University
St. Philip's College
Sam Houston State University
San Antonio College
Southern Methodist University
Southwestern Assemblies of God University
Stephen F. Austin State University
Tarleton State University
Tarrant County College
Texas A&M International University
Texas A&M University
Texas A&M University
  Corpus Christi
  Kingsville
Texas Christian University
Texas Lutheran University
Texas Southern University
Texas State University: San Marcos
Texas Tech University
Texas Wesleyan University
Texas Woman's University
University of Dallas
University of Houston
University of Houston
  Downtown
University of Mary Hardin-Baylor
University of North Texas
University of St. Thomas
University of Texas
  Arlington
  Austin
  Brownsville - Texas Southmost College
  Dallas
  El Paso
  Pan American
  San Antonio
University of the Incarnate Word
Wayland Baptist University

Utah
Brigham Young University
Dixie State College
LDS Business College
Salt Lake Community College
Southern Utah University
University of Utah
Utah State University
Utah Valley University
Weber State University
Westminster College

Vermont
Castleton State College
Champlain College
Johnson State College
Lyndon State College
Middlebury College
Norwich University
Saint Michael's College
University of Vermont
Vermont Technical College

Virginia
Christopher Newport University
College of William and Mary
George Mason University
Hampden-Sydney College
Hampton University
James Madison University
John Tyler Community College
Liberty University
Longwood University
Mary Baldwin College
Marymount University
Norfolk State University
Old Dominion University
Piedmont Virginia Community College
Radford University
Randolph-Macon College
Regent University
Richard Bland College
St. Paul's College
Southern Virginia University
Southside Virginia Community College
Tidewater Community College
University of Mary Washington
University of Richmond
University of Virginia
University of Virginia's College at Wise
Virginia Commonwealth University
Virginia Military Institute
Virginia Polytechnic Institute and State University
Virginia State University
Virginia Union University
Virginia Wesleyan College
Washington and Lee University

Washington
Clark College
DeVry University
  Federal Way
Eastern Washington University
Gonzaga University
Highline Community College
Northwest University
Pacific Lutheran University
Pierce College
Saint Martin's University
Seattle Pacific University
Seattle University
Spokane Community College
University of Puget Sound
University of Washington
University of Washington Bothell
University of Washington Tacoma
Walla Walla University
Washington State University
Whitworth University

West Virginia
Fairmont State University
Glenville State College
Marshall University
University of Charleston
West Virginia State University
West Virginia University
West Virginia University Institute of Technology

Wisconsin
Alverno College
Carroll University
Carthage College
Edgewood College
Maranatha Baptist Bible College
Marquette University
Milwaukee School of Engineering
Mount Mary College
Ripon College
St. Norbert College

University of Wisconsin
- Eau Claire
- Green Bay
- La Crosse
- Madison
- Milwaukee
- Oshkosh
- Parkside
- Platteville
- River Falls
- Stevens Point
- Stout
- Whitewater

Viterbo University
Wisconsin Lutheran College

Wyoming
Laramie County Community College
University of Wyoming

Naval ROTC

Alabama
Auburn University
Stillman College
Tuskegee University

Arizona
Arizona State University
GateWay Community College
Mesa Community College
Pima Community College
University of Arizona

California
California Maritime Academy
California State University
- San Marcos

Contra Costa College
Diablo Valley College
Foothill College
Fullerton College
Los Angeles City College
Loyola Marymount University
MiraCosta College
Mission College
National University
Point Loma Nazarene University
Riverside Community College
Sacramento City College
Samuel Merritt University
San Diego Christian College
San Diego State University
Sonoma State University
Stanford University
University of California
- Berkeley
- Davis
- Los Angeles
- Santa Cruz

University of Redlands
University of San Diego
University of Southern California

Colorado
Regis University
University of Colorado
- Boulder

Connecticut
Capital Community College
Quinnipiac University
Tunxis Community College
Yale University

District of Columbia
Catholic University of America
George Washington University
Georgetown University
University of the District of Columbia

Florida
Clearwater Christian College
Embry-Riddle Aeronautical University
Florida Agricultural and Mechanical University
Florida State College at Jacksonville
Florida State University
Jacksonville University
Pasco-Hernando Community College
Tallahassee Community College
University of Florida
University of North Florida
University of South Florida
University of Tampa

Georgia
Armstrong Atlantic State University
Clark Atlanta University
Clayton State University
Emory University
Georgia Institute of Technology
Georgia State University
Morehouse College
Savannah State University
Southern Polytechnic State University
Spelman College

Hawaii
Brigham Young University-Hawaii
University of Hawaii
- Hawaii Community College

Idaho
Lewis-Clark State College
University of Idaho

Illinois
Illinois Institute of Technology
Lincoln Land Community College
Loyola University Chicago
Northwestern University
Parkland College
Shawnee Community College
Shimer College
University of Illinois
- Chicago
- Urbana-Champaign

Indiana
Indiana University
- South Bend

Purdue University
Saint Mary's College
University of Notre Dame

Iowa
Hawkeye Community College
Iowa State University

Kansas
University of Kansas
Washburn University

Louisiana
Dillard University
Louisiana State University and Agricultural and Mechanical College
Loyola University New Orleans
Our Lady of Holy Cross College
Southern University
- New Orleans

Southern University and Agricultural and Mechanical College
Tulane University
University of New Orleans
Xavier University of Louisiana

Maine
Husson University
Maine Maritime Academy
University of Maine
University of Maine
- Augusta

Maryland
University of Maryland
- College Park

Massachusetts
Boston College
Boston University
Clark University
College of the Holy Cross
Harvard College
Massachusetts College of Pharmacy and Health Sciences
Massachusetts Institute of Technology
Massachusetts Maritime Academy
Northeastern University
Tufts University
University of Massachusetts
- Boston

Worcester Polytechnic Institute
Worcester State University

Michigan
Eastern Michigan University
Finlandia University
University of Michigan
University of Michigan
- Dearborn

Wayne State University

Minnesota
Anoka-Ramsey Community College
Augsburg College
Macalester College
North Hennepin Community College
University of Minnesota
- Twin Cities

University of St. Thomas

Mississippi
East Mississippi Community College
Tougaloo College
University of Mississippi

Missouri
Columbia College
Lincoln University
Stephens College
University of Missouri
- Columbia

William Woods University

Nebraska
BryanLGH College of Health Sciences
University of Nebraska
- Lincoln

York College

New Hampshire
Rivier University

New Jersey
Montclair State University
Rutgers, The State University of New Jersey
- New Brunswick/Piscataway Campus
- Newark Campus

New Mexico
Central New Mexico Community College
University of New Mexico

New York
City University of New York
- Queens College

College of New Rochelle
College of Saint Rose
Columbia University
Columbia University
- School of General Studies

Cornell University
Eastman School of Music of the University of Rochester
Fordham University
Jewish Theological Seminary of America
Maria College
Mesivta Torah Vodaath Seminary
Molloy College
Monroe Community College
Rensselaer Polytechnic Institute
Rochester Institute of Technology
The Sage Colleges
St. John Fisher College
Siena College
SUNY
- College at Brockport
- Farmingdale State College
- Maritime College

Talmudical Seminary Oholei Torah
Union College
United States Merchant Marine Academy
University of Rochester

North Carolina
Belmont Abbey College
Duke University
North Carolina State University
University of North Carolina
- Chapel Hill

Ohio
Cleveland Institute of Art
Cuyahoga Community College
- Metropolitan

Kent State University
- Ashtabula
- East Liverpool
- Geauga
- Salem
- Stark
- Trumbull
- Tuscarawas

Miami University
- Hamilton
- Middletown
- Oxford

Mount Carmel College of Nursing
Ohio State University
- Agricultural Technical Institute
- Columbus Campus
- Lima Campus
- Mansfield Campus
- Marion Campus
- Newark Campus

Ohio University
- Lancaster Campus

University of Cincinnati
- Raymond Walters College

Oklahoma
University of Oklahoma

Oregon
Oregon State University
Western Oregon University

Pennsylvania
Carlow University
Carnegie Mellon University
Chatham University
Drexel University
Duquesne University
Penn State
- University Park

Saint Joseph's University
Swarthmore College
Temple University
Thomas Jefferson University: College of Health Professions
University of Pennsylvania
University of Pittsburgh
Villanova University
Widener University

Puerto Rico
Caribbean University
Inter American University of Puerto Rico
- Bayamon Campus
- Ponce Campus

Universidad Metropolitana

South Carolina
Allen University
The Citadel
University of South Carolina

Columbia
Salkehatchie

Tennessee
Belmont University
Christian Brothers University
Fisk University
Tennessee Wesleyan College
University of Memphis
Vanderbilt University

Texas
Houston Baptist University
Prairie View A&M University
Rice University
Texas A&M University
Texas A&M University
Galveston
University of Houston
University of Texas
Austin

Utah
University of Utah
Weber State University
Westminster College

Vermont
Lyndon State College
Norwich University

Virginia
Hampton University
Mary Baldwin College
New River Community College
Norfolk State University
Old Dominion University
Regent University
Tidewater Community College
University of Virginia
Virginia Military Institute
Virginia Polytechnic Institute and State University

Washington
Seattle Pacific University
Seattle University
Spokane Community College
University of Washington
University of Washington Bothell
University of Washington Tacoma
Washington State University

West Virginia
Everest Institute: Cross Lanes

Wisconsin
Edgewood College
Marquette University
Milwaukee School of Engineering
Mount Mary College
University of Wisconsin
Madison
Milwaukee
Wisconsin Lutheran College

Glossary

Accelerated program. A college program of study completed in less time than is usually required, most often by attending classes in summer or by taking extra courses during the regular academic terms.

Accreditation. A process that ensures that a college meets acceptable standards in its programs, facilities, and services. Only colleges that are accredited by an agency recognized by the U.S. Department of Education may distribute federal financial aid to their students. Every college described in this book is accredited by such an agency.

ACT. A college admission examination given at test centers on specified dates. Please visit the organization's website for further information.

Advanced placement. Admission or assignment of a first-year college student to an advanced course in a certain subject on the basis of evidence that he or she has already completed the equivalent of the college's course in that subject.

Advanced Placement Program (AP). An academic program of the College Board that provides high school students with the opportunity to study and learn at the college level. AP offers courses in 34 subjects, each culminating in a rigorous exam. High schools offer the courses and administer the exams to interested students. Most colleges and universities accept qualifying AP Exam scores for credit, advanced placement or both.

Agricultural college. A college or university that primarily trains students in the agricultural sciences and agribusiness operations.

American Opportunity Tax Credit. A federal income tax credit of as much as $2,500 per year, available for the first four years of college for each eligible student in a family. The amount of the credit is determined by income eligibility guidelines. See also *Lifetime Learning Tax Credit.*

AmeriCorps. A national network of community service programs for which people volunteer and from which they earn an education award that can used to pay for college or pay back student loans.

Articulation agreement. A formal agreement between two higher-education institutions, stating specific policies relating to transfer of credits and recognition of academic achievement in order to facilitate the successful transfer of students without duplication of course work.

Associate degree. A degree granted by a college or university upon completion of a two-year, full-time program of study or its part-time equivalent. In general, the associate of arts (A.A.) or associate of science (A.S.) program is similar to the first two years of a four-year college curriculum. The associate in applied science (A.A.S.) is awarded by many colleges on completion of technological or vocational programs of study.

Award letter. A means of notifying admitted students of the financial aid being offered by the college or university. The award letter provides information on the types and amounts of aid offered, as well as the students' responsibilities, and the conditions governing the awards. Usually the award letter gives students the opportunity to accept or decline the aid offered, and a deadline by which to respond.

Bachelor's degree. A degree received upon completion of a four- or five-year full-time program of study (or its part-time equivalent) at a college or university. The bachelor of arts (B.A.), bachelor of science (B.S.) and bachelor of fine arts (B.F.A.) are the most common such degrees. College catalogs describe the types of degrees awarded in each major.

Bible college. An undergraduate institution whose program, in addition to a general education in the liberal arts, includes a significant element of Bible study. Most Bible colleges seek to prepare their students for vocational or lay Christian ministry.

Branch campus. A part of a college, university or community college that is geographically separate from the main campus, has its own faculty and administration, and may have separate admissions requirements and degree programs.

Bursar. The college official responsible for handling billing and payments for tuition, fees, housing, etc.

Business college. A college that primarily prepares students to work in an office or entrepreneurial setting. The curriculum may focus on management, clerical positions, or both.

Campus. The physical location of a college or university. Includes classroom buildings, libraries, research facilities, dormitories, dining halls and administration buildings.

Campus-based programs. Federal financial aid programs that are administered directly by the college's financial aid office, which awards these funds to students using federal guidelines. Includes the Federal Supplemental Educational Opportunity Grant Program, Federal Perkins Loan Program and the Federal Work-Study Program.

Candidates' reply date. The date by which admitted students must accept or decline an offer of admission and (if any) the college's offer of financial aid. Most colleges and universities follow the College Board-sponsored Candidates' Reply Date Agreement (CRDA), under which they agree to not require a decision from applicants for admission in the fall semester before May 1. The purpose of this agreement is to give applicants time to hear from all the colleges to which they have applied before having to make a commitment to any of them.

Career college. Usually a for-profit two-year college that trains students for specific occupations. Also known as a vocational/technical school.

CB code. A four-digit College Board code number that students use to designate colleges or scholarship programs to receive their SAT score reports.

Certificate. An award for completing a particular program or course of study, sometimes given by two-year colleges or vocational or technical schools.

CLEP®. See *College-Level Examination Program.*

College. The generic term for an institution of higher education. Also a term used to designate divisions within a university.

College-Level Examination Program (CLEP). A program in which students receive college credit by earning a qualifying score in any of 33 examinations in business, composition and literature, world languages, history and social sciences, and science and mathematics. Sponsored by the College Board, exams are administered at over 1,700 test centers. Over 2,900 colleges and universities grant credit for passing a CLEP exam.

College Scholarship Service (CSS). A unit of the College Board that assists postsecondary institutions, state scholarship programs and private scholarship organizations in the equitable and efficient distribution of student financial aid funds, mainly through its stewardship of the CSS/Financial Aid PROFILE and the Institutional Methodology.

Community/junior college. A college offering two-year programs leading to an associate degree. Community colleges are public institutions, while junior colleges are privately operated on a not-for-profit basis. Most two-year colleges offer both vocational programs (also called "career" or "terminal" programs), as well as the first two years of a four-year program ("academic" or "transfer" programs). Students in the vocational program usually go directly into a career after graduation, while students in the academic program usually intend to transfer to a four-year institution or an upper-division college.

Comprehensive fee. If the college combines tuition, fees, room, and board expenses, that single figure is called a comprehensive fee.

Consortium. A group of colleges and universities that share a common geographic location. Consortiums of colleges in the same town often allow students at one institution to take classes at neighboring consortium colleges and use facilities such as libraries at the member colleges. Larger consortiums, at the state or regional level, may offer in-state tuition to out-of-state students.

Cooperative education (co-op). A program in which students alternate class attendance and employment in business, industry, or government. Co-op students are typically paid for their work and may receive academic credit for their participation in the program. Under a cooperative plan, five years are normally required for completion of a bachelor's degree, but graduates have the advantage of about a year's practical work experience in addition to their studies.

Core curriculum. A group of courses, usually in the liberal arts, designated by a college as one of the requirements for a degree. Some colleges have both core-curriculum requirements and general-education requirements.

Cost of attendance. A number of expenses, among them tuition and fees (including loan fees), books and supplies, and the student's living expenses while attending school. The cost of attendance is estimated by the school, within guidelines established by federal regulation. The cost of attendance is compared with the student's expected family contribution to determine the student's need for financial aid.

Coverdell Education Savings Account (ESA). A federal income-tax provision (formerly referred to as the Education IRA) that enables taxpayers to establish a college savings plan. A maximum of $2,000 may be contributed annually to the account, which earns interest and/or dividends on a tax-free basis.

Credit/placement by examination. Academic credit or placement out of introductory courses granted by a college to entering students who have demonstrated proficiency in college-level studies through examinations such as those administered by the College Board's AP and CLEP programs.

Credit Hour. The standard unit of measurement for a college course. Each credit hour requires one classroom hour per week. Most college courses are offered in one to five credit-hour increments. For financial aid purposes, students taking at least 12 credit hours of classes in a semester are considered to be attending the college full-time, and students taking at least six credit hours are considered half-time.

CSS code. A four-digit College Board number that students use to designate colleges or scholarship programs to receive their CSS/Financial Aid PROFILE information. If a college requires financial aid applicants to submit the PROFILE, its CSS code will appear in its description in Part III of this book. A complete list of all CSS codes can also be viewed on the PROFILE website.

CSS/Financial Aid PROFILE. A Web-based application service offered by the College Board and used by some colleges, universities, and private scholarship programs to award their private financial aid funds. Students complete the application online. The College Board processes and reports the application data to institutions. The PROFILE is not a federal form and may not be used to apply for federal student aid.

Culinary school. A vocational college that primarily prepares students to work as chefs or caterers.

Deferred admission. Postponing enrollment, usually for one year, after being accepted for admission by a college.

Degree. An award given by a college or university certifying that a student has completed a course of study. *See* bachelor's degree, associate degree, graduate degree. *See also* Certificate.

Dependent student. For federal financial aid purposes, such students are either under the age of 24, attend an undergraduate program, are not married, do not have children of their own, are not orphans or wards of the court, or veterans of the active-duty armed services. The term is used to define eligibility for certain financial aid programs, regardless of whether or not the student lives with a parent, receives financial support from a parent, or is claimed on a parent's tax return. If a student is defined as dependent, parental financial information must be supplied on the Free Application for Federal Student Aid (FAFSA) and on institutional aid applications.

Direct Loan Program. See *Federal Direct Loan Program.*

District. See *In-district tuition.*

Dual enrollment. The practice in which a student enrolls in college courses while still in high school, earning both high school and college credit for his or her work.

Early Action. A nonbinding early decision program in which a student can receive an admission decision from one or more colleges and universities earlier than the standard response date but is not required to accept the admission offer or to make a deposit before May 1. Compare to *Early Decision,* which is a binding program.

Early action single choice. An early action program in which the student may only apply early action to one college or university.

Early Decision. A binding program where students can receive an admission decision from one college or university before applications are due for regular admission. Participating students commit to enroll at the college if admitted and offered a satisfactory financial aid package.

Elective. A course, not required for one's chosen major or the college's core curriculum, that is selected to fulfill credit hours required for graduation.

Employer tuition assistance. Money that employers offer to employees or their dependents for use in paying education costs. Tuition assistance is considered an outside resource when colleges award financial aid.

Engineering college/institute/school. An institution of higher education that primarily prepares students for careers as licensed professional engineers or engineering technologists.

Expected family contribution (EFC). The total amount students and their families are expected to pay toward college costs from their income and assets for one academic year. The amount is derived from a need analysis of the family's overall financial circumstances. The *federal methodology* is used to determine a student's eligibility for federal and state student aid. Colleges and private aid programs may use a different methodology to determine eligibility for nonfederal financial aid. Frequently, these private institutions use the *institutional methodology.*

FAFSA. See *Free Application for Federal Student Aid.*

FAFSA on the Web. An electronic option for completing the Free Application for Federal Student Aid (www.fafsa.ed.gov).

Family Educational Rights and Privacy Act (FERPA). A federal law that protects the privacy of student education records. The law applies to all schools that receive funds under an applicable program of the U.S. Department of Education. FERPA gives parents certain rights with respect to their children's education records. These rights transfer to the student when he or she reaches the age of 18 or attends a school beyond the high school level.

Federal code number. A six-digit number that identifies a specific college to which students want their FAFSA information submitted. Each college's federal code appears in its profile in Part III of this book. Formerly known as the Title IV code.

Federal Direct Loan Program. A program whereby participating schools administer federal loans that students and parents borrow directly from the U.S. Department of Education. Direct loans include the subsidized and unsubsidized Federal Stafford Loan, PLUS Loan, and Loan Consolidation programs.

Federal methodology (FM). A need-analysis formula used by colleges and universities to determine students' financial need for the purpose of awarding federal financial aid. Most colleges also use this methodology to determine need for the purpose of awarding their own institutional funds, but some colleges use the *institutional methodology* for that. The federal methodology uses information submitted by students on the FAFSA to assess their ability to pay for college and calculate their expected family contribution.

Federal Parents' Loan for Undergraduate Students (PLUS). A program that permits parents of undergraduate students to borrow up to the full cost of education, less any other financial aid the student may have received.

Federal Pell Grant Program. A federally sponsored and administered program that provides need-based grants to undergraduate students. Congress annually sets the dollar range. Eligibility for Pell Grants is based on a student's expected family contribution, the total cost of attendance at the college, and whether the student is attending the college full time or part time.

Federal Perkins Loan Program. A federally funded campus-based program that provides low-interest student loans. The maximum amount of loan funds available to an individual for undergraduate study is $27,500. Repayment need not begin until completion of the student's education, and it may be deferred for limited periods of service in the military, Peace Corps or approved comparable organizations. The total debt may be forgiven by the federal government if the recipient enters a career of service as a public health nurse, law enforcement officer, public school teacher or social worker.

Federal Stafford Loan. A program that allows students to borrow money for educational expenses from banks and other lending institutions (and sometimes from the colleges themselves). Subsidized Stafford loans are offered by colleges based on need. The federal government pays the interest on subsidized loans while the borrower is in college, and repayment does not begin until completion of the student's education. Unsubsidized Stafford loans are non-need based; anyone may apply for one regardless of their ability to pay for college. The interest on unsubsidized loans begins accumulating immediately. For both programs, the amounts that may be borrowed depend on the student's year in school.

Federal student aid. A number of programs sponsored by the federal government that award students loans, grants or work-study jobs for the purpose of meeting their financial need. To receive any federal student aid, a student must demonstrate financial need by filing the Free Application for Federal Student Aid and meet certain other eligibility requirements.

Federal Supplemental Educational Opportunity Grant Program (SEOG). A federal campus-based program that provides need-based grants of up to $4,000 a year for undergraduate study. Each college is given a certain total amount of SEOG money each year to distribute among their financial aid applicants and determines the amount to which the student is entitled.

Federal Work-Study Program. A campus-based financial aid program that allows students to meet some of their financial need by working on- or off-campus while attending school. The wages earned are used to help pay the student's educational costs for the academic year. Job opportunities vary from campus to campus. The time commitment for a work-study job is usually between 10 and 15 hours each week.

Fee waiver. The waiver that significantly reduces the amount a student must pay for an application for admission, application for institutional financial aid, standardized tests or other college-related expenses. Fee waivers are most commonly awarded to low-income students, but are sometimes also awarded to students who are senior citizens or in the military. See also *Tuition and fee waiver.*

Financial aid. Money awarded to students to help them pay for college. Financial aid comes in the form of gifts (scholarships and grants) and self-help aid (loans and work-study opportunities). Most aid is awarded on the basis of financial need, but some awards are non-need based. Both need-based and non-need-based aid may or may not be offered on the additional basis of merit.

Financial aid application form. A form that collects information on the student, his or her income and assets, and (for dependent students) his or her parents' income and assets.

Financial aid award letter. See *Award letter.*

Financial aid package. The total financial aid offered to a student by a college, including all loans, grants, scholarships and work-study opportunities.

Financial Aid PROFILE. See *CSS/Financial Aid PROFILE.*

Financial need. The difference between the total cost of attending a college and a student's expected family contribution (EFC). Financial aid grants, loans and work-study will be offered by each college to fill all or a portion of the student's need.

529 Plan. See *Section 529 Plan.*

Fixed interest rate. An interest rate on a loan that is fixed for the lifetime of the loan. Compare to *Variable interest rate.*

For-profit college/university. A higher-education institution not supported by taxes and operated as a for-profit business, either as a publicly traded corporation or as a privately held company. Sometimes referred to as a "proprietary" college.

Free Application for Federal Student Aid (FAFSA). A form completed by all applicants for federal student aid. The FAFSA is available on the Web at www.fafsa.ed.gov. In many states, completion of the FAFSA is also sufficient to establish eligibility for state-sponsored aid programs. There is no charge for completing the FAFSA, and you can file it anytime after January 1 of the year for which you are seeking aid (e.g., after January 1, 2014, for the academic year 2014–2015).

Full need. A student's entire financial need at a college. A college that offers a financial aid package covering the complete difference between the cost of attendance and the expected family contribution is "meeting full need." See also *Gapping.*

Full-time status. Enrollment at a college or university for 12 or more credit hours per semester. Students must be enrolled full time to qualify for the maximum award available to them from federal grant programs.

Gapping. A practice by which a college does not meet the full financial need of an admitted student, leaving a gap that must be filled by the student's own financial resources, in addition to the student's expected family contribution.

General education requirements. Courses that give undergraduates a background in all major academic disciplines: natural sciences, social sciences, mathematics, literature, language and fine arts. Most colleges have general education requirements that students complete in their first and second years, giving students a chance to sample a wide range of courses before selecting a major. Some colleges refer to general education courses as the core curriculum; at others, a few courses within the general education requirements are core courses that all students must take.

Gift aid. Financial aid in the form of scholarships or grants that do not have to be repaid.

Grade point average (GPA) or ratio. A system used by many schools for evaluating the overall scholastic performance of students. Grade points are determined by first multiplying the number of hours given for a course by the numerical value of the grade and then dividing the sum of all grade points by the total number of hours carried. The most common system of numerical values for grades is A = 4, B = 3, C = 2, D = 1, and E or F = 0. Also called quality point average or ratio.

Graduate degree. A degree pursued after a student has earned a bachelor's degree. The master's degree, which requires one to three years of study, is usually the degree earned after the bachelor's. The doctoral degree requires further study. Professional degrees are also graduate degrees.

Grant. A financial aid award given to a student that does not have to be paid back. The terms "grant" and "scholarship" are often used interchangeably to refer to gift aid, but grants tend to be awarded solely on the basis of financial need, while scholarships may require the student to demonstrate merit.

Half-time status. Enrollment at a college or university for at least 6 credit hours per semester, but fewer than the 12 credit hours required to qualify as full time. Students must be enrolled at least half time to qualify for federal student aid loan programs.

Health sciences college. An institution of higher education that primarily prepares students to enter work in a clinic, hospital or private medical practice. For a complete description of health-related fields of study, see the *College Board Book of Majors.*

Independent student. For financial aid purposes, a student who is either age 24 or older, married, a veteran, an orphan, or has legal dependents. Independent students do not need to provide parental information to be considered for federal financial aid programs. However, private institutions may require independent students to provide parental information on their institutional forms in order to be considered for nonfederal sources of funding.

In-district tuition. The tuition charged by a community college or state university to residents of the district from which it draws tax support. Districts are usually individual counties or cities, but sometimes are larger.

Individual Retirement Account (IRA). A retirement account that earns tax-free income. Money withdrawn for college expenses is not charged the penalty that normally would be incurred for withdrawing IRA money before age 59½, but is taxed as regular income.

In-state tuition. The tuition that a public institution charges residents of its state. Some community colleges and state universities charge this rate to students who are not residents of their district, but who are residents of their state.

Institutional form. A financial aid application form custom-made by a particular college or university. Some institutional forms are designed to collect additional information on a family's finances beyond what is collected on the FAFSA, and are required of all financial aid applicants. Others serve specific purposes and are only required from certain students, for example early decision applicants or student athletes.

Institutional Methodology (IM). A need-analysis formula used by some colleges and universities to determine students' financial need and award their own institutional funds. Compared to the *federal methodology*, the IM takes into account a broader and deeper picture of family assets to determine a student's expected family contribution. Most colleges that use the IM collect this additional information through the CSS/Financial Aid PROFILE form, but some collect it using their own customized institutional forms.

International Baccalaureate (IB). A high school curriculum offered by some schools in the United States and other countries. Some colleges award credit for completion of this curriculum. Please visit the organization's website for further information.

Internship. Any short-term, supervised work, usually related to a student's major, for which academic credit is earned. The work can be full time or part time, on or off campus, paid or unpaid. Some majors require the student to complete an internship.

IRS Data Retrieval Tool. Accessible from FAFSA on the Web, this tool allows you or your parents to access the IRS tax return information needed to complete the FAFSA and to transfer the data directly onto your FAFSA online. It takes up to three weeks for IRS income information to be available if you filed your tax return electronically and eight weeks if you filed by mail. For many colleges, the IRS Data Retrieval process is the preferred means of completing your FAFSA. If you cannot use this process at the time you initially complete the FAFSA, check with your college(s) to determine how best to update your FAFSA information once your tax returns have been filed.

Junior college. See *Community/junior college.*

Liberal arts. The study of the humanities (literature, the arts and philosophy), history, foreign languages, social sciences, mathematics and natural sciences. Liberal arts study guides students in developing general knowledge and reasoning ability rather than specific skills.

Liberal arts college. A college that emphasizes the liberal arts in its core curriculum and academic offerings and does not offer vocation or professional programs.

Lifetime Learning Tax Credit. A federal income tax credit of as much as $2,000 per household annually; available to eligible taxpayers based on "out-of-pocket" tuition and fee expenditures, according to income eligibility guidelines. See also *American Opportunity Tax Credit.*

Major. The subject area in which students concentrate during their undergraduate study. At most colleges, students take one-third to one-half of their courses in the major; the rest of their course work is devoted to core requirements and electives.

Maritime college/institute/academy. An institution of higher education that prepares students to operate commercial shipping or fishing vessels. Upon graduation, students of most maritime academies are commissioned as officers in the United States Merchant Marine, and simultaneously commissioned as officers in the U.S. Navy Reserve.

Master Promissory Note (MPN). A special type of promissory note used to obtain a Federal Stafford loan. The MPN is designated for use as both a single-year and a multi-year note (for four-year and graduate/professional schools). Borrowers can sign a MPN once, the time they first borrow, and then receive additional loans during the same year or in subsequent years without signing an additional note.

Merit aid. Financial aid awarded on the basis of academic qualifications, artistic or athletic talent, leadership qualities, or similar qualities. Most merit aid comes in the form of scholarships. Merit aid may be non-need based, or the merit criteria may be in addition to a requirement that the student demonstrate financial need.

Military college/institute/academy. An institution of higher education that prepares students (who are called "cadets" while enrolled) to become active-duty officers in the armed services. The curriculum usually combines a study of the liberal arts, military science and engineering. Cadets usually participate in military training assignments during the summer term in addition to attending the college in the fall and spring semesters.

Minor. Course work that is not as extensive as that in a major but gives students some specialized knowledge of a second field.

NCAA. The National Collegiate Athletic Association. The largest collegiate athletic association, it oversees the most athletic scholarship money. The NCAA governs league play in 23 championship sports.

Need analysis. The process of analyzing the student's household and financial information to calculate an EFC and financial need. See also *Federal Methodology, Institutional Methodology.*

Need-analysis form. See *Financial aid application form.*

Need-based aid. Financial aid (scholarships, grants, loans or work-study opportunities) given to students who have demonstrated financial need, calculated by subtracting the student's expected family contribution from a college's total cost of attendance. The largest source of need-based aid is the federal government, but colleges, states and private foundations also award need-based aid to eligible students.

Need-blind admission. The policy of determining whether a student should be admitted to a college without regard to his or her financial need.

Non-need-based aid. Financial aid awarded without regard to the student's demonstrated ability to pay for college. Unsubsidized loans and scholarships awarded solely on the basis of merit are both non-need based. Some financial aid sponsors also offer non-need-based grants tied not to merit, but to other qualities, such as state of residence or participation in ROTC.

Nursing college. An institution of higher education that primarily prepares students to become registered nurses (RNs) or licensed practical nurses (LPNs).

Open admission. The college admissions policy of admitting high school graduates and other adults generally without regard to conventional academic qualifications, such as high school subjects, high school grades and admission test scores. Virtually all applicants with high school diplomas or their equivalent are accepted, although some programs of study may have additional requirements.

Origination fee. A fee charged to a borrower to cover the costs of processing a loan. The origination fee is usually a percentage of the total amount being borrowed. The origination fee for any loan will be disclosed in the promissory note for that loan.

Out-of-state tuition. The tuition a public college or university charges residents of other states.

Outside resources. Student financial aid granted by a source other than the college that the college must take into account when assembling an aid package. Examples of common outside resources include scholarships from private foundations, employer tuition assistance and veterans' educational benefits.

Parents' contribution. The amount a student's parents are expected to pay toward college costs from their income and assets. It is derived from need analysis of the parents' overall financial situation. The parents' contribution and the student's contribution together constitute the total expected family contribution (EFC).

Parents' Loan for Undergraduate Students. See *Federal Parents' Loan for Undergraduate Students.*

Part-time status. Enrollment at a college or university for 11 or fewer credit hours per semester.

Pell Grant. See *Federal Pell Grant Program.*

Perkins Loan. See *Federal Perkins Loan Program.*

PLUS loan. See *Federal Parents' Loan for Undergraduate Students.*

Prepaid tuition plan. See *Section 529 Plans.*

Portfolio. A collection of a student's work that demonstrates skills and accomplishments. Portfolios may be physical or electronic. There are academic portfolios that include student written papers and projects, and also portfolios that include created objects — art, photography, fashion illustrations, and more. Some scholarship programs request a portfolio.

Priority date. The date by which applications for financial aid must be received to be given the strongest possible consideration. The college will consider the financial need of applicants who make the priority date before any other applicants. Qualified applicants who do not make the priority date are considered on a first-come, first-served basis, and are only offered financial aid if (and to the extent to which) the college still has sufficient money left over after all the offers it has made. Can also refer to the priority date for admission applications, where, again, the college will make offers to the priority applicants first, and then consider subsequent applicants on a first-come, first-served basis, making offers only if there is still room in the incoming class.

Private college/university. An educational institution of higher education not supported by public taxes and operated on a not-for-profit basis. May be independent or affiliated with a religious denomination.

PROFILE. See *CSS/Financial Aid PROFILE.*

Promissory note. A binding legal document that a borrower signs to get a loan. By signing this note, a borrower promises to repay the loan, with interest, in specified installments. The promissory note also includes any information about origination fees, grace periods, deferment or cancellation provisions, and the borrower's rights and responsibilities with respect to that loan.

Proprietary college/university. See *For-profit college/university.*

PSAT/NMSQT® (Preliminary SAT/National Merit Scholarship Qualifying Test). A comprehensive program that helps schools put students on the path to college. The PSAT/NMSQT is administered by high schools to sophomores and juniors each year in October and serves as the qualifying test for scholarships awarded by the National Merit Scholarship Corporation.

Public college/university. An institution of higher education supported by public taxes.

Quarter. An academic calendar period of about 12 weeks. Four quarters make up an academic year, but at colleges using the quarter system, students make normal academic progress by attending three quarters each year. In some colleges, students can accelerate their progress by attending all four quarters in one or more years.

Reciprocity agreement: An agreement between neighboring states that allows residents to attend a public college in either state at the *in-state tuition* rate.

Regular admission. At colleges with early action or early decision plans, "regular" admission is the round of admission conducted in January or February, after the early admission rounds.

Renewal FAFSA. A simplified reapplication form for federal student aid. The Renewal FAFSA allows continuing students to update the prior year's FAFSA, rather than completing the entire FAFSA for each award year.

Reserve Officers Training Corps (ROTC). Programs conducted by certain colleges in cooperation with the United States Air Force, Army and Navy reserves. Participating students may receive a merit scholarship while they are in college, and will enter the reserves of their service branch as an officer upon graduation. Naval ROTC includes the Marine Corps. (The Coast Guard and Merchant Marine do not sponsor ROTC programs.) Local recruiting offices of the services themselves can supply detailed information about these programs, as can participating colleges.

Residency requirements. The minimum number of terms that a student must spend taking courses on campus (as opposed to independent study, transfer credits from other colleges or credit-by-examination) to be eligible for graduation. Can also refer to the minimum amount of time a student is required to have lived in-state in order to qualify for the in-state tuition rate at a public college or university.

Rolling admission. An admission procedure by which the college considers each student's application as soon as all the required credentials, such as school record and test scores, have been received. The college usually notifies an applicant of its decision without delay. At many colleges, rolling admission allows for early notification and works much like nonbinding early action programs.

Room and board. The cost of housing and meals for students who reside on campus and/or dine in college-operated meal halls.

Safety school. A college you'd like to attend that's also sure to accept you. Usually a public college in your state that is not selective in its admission criteria or practices open admissions.

SAR. See *Student Aid Report.*

SAT. A college entrance exam that tests critical reading, writing and mathematics skills, given on specified dates throughout the year at test centers in the United States and other countries. The SAT is used by most colleges and sponsors of financial aid programs.

Satisfactory academic progress. Standards set by a college or university to determine whether a student is meeting sufficient academic standards. The student must achieve these standards to continue to receive financial aid.

SAT Subject Tests. Admission tests in specific subjects given at test centers in the United States and other countries on specified dates throughout the year. The tests are used by colleges for help in both evaluating applicants for admission and determining course placement, and exemption of enrolled first-year students.

Scholarship. A type of financial aid that doesn't have to be repaid. Grants are often based on financial need. Scholarships may be based on need, on need combined with merit, or solely on the basis of merit or some other qualification, such as minority status.

School. In this book, used generically to refer interchangeably to colleges, universities and other institutions of higher education. At some universities, a "school" is a subdivision of the university — for example, the administrative unit that offers nursing courses may be called the "college of nursing" at one institution, and the "school of nursing" at another.

Section 529 Plans. State-sponsored college savings programs commonly referred to as "529 Plans" after the section of the Internal Revenue Code that provides the plan's tax breaks. There are two kinds: Section 529 college savings plans and Section 529 prepaid tuition plans.

Section 529 Prepaid Tuition Plan. State-sponsored plans through which parents can pay in advance for tuition at public institutions in their state of residence.

Self-help aid. Student financial aid, such as loans and work-study jobs, that requires repayment or employment.

Semester. A period of about 16 weeks. Colleges on a semester system offer two semesters of instruction a year; there may also be an additional summer session.

SEOG. See *Federal Supplemental Educational Opportunity Grant.*

Simplified needs test. In Federal Methodology need analysis, the simplified needs test excludes assets from the Expected Family Contribution calculation for low- to moderate-income families who file simplified tax returns (1040A, 1040EZ).

Stafford Loan. See *Federal Stafford Loan Program.*

Student Aid Report (SAR). A report produced by the U.S. Department of Education and sent to students in response to their having filed the Free Application for Federal Student Aid (FAFSA). The SAR contains information the student provided on the FAFSA as well as the federally calculated expected family contribution.

Student expense budget. A calculation of the annual cost of attending college that is used to determine your financial need. Student expense budgets usually include tuition and fees, books and supplies, room and board, personal expenses, and transportation. Sometimes additional expenses are included for students with special education needs, students who have a disability, or students who are married or have children.

Student's contribution. The amount you are expected to pay toward college costs from your income and assets. The amount is derived from a need analysis of your resources. Your contribution and your parents' contribution together compose the total expected family contribution.

Study abroad. Any arrangement by which a student completes part of the college program — typically the junior year but sometimes only a semester or a summer — by studying in another country. A college may operate a campus abroad, or it may have a cooperative agreement with some other U.S. college or an institution of the other country.

Subsidized loan. A loan awarded to a student on the basis of financial need. The federal government or the state awarding the loan pays the borrower's interest while they are in college at least half-time, thereby subsidizing the loan.

Supplemental Educational Opportunity Grant. See *Federal Supplemental Educational Opportunity Grant.*

Taxable income. Income earned from wages, salaries and tips, as well as from interest income, dividends, alimony, estates or trust income, business or farm profits, and rental or property income. Some scholarship awards must be reported as taxable income.

Teacher Education Assistance for College and Higher Education (TEACH) Grant. A federal grant program that provides up to $4,000 per year to students who intend to teach in a public or private elementary or secondary school serving students from low-income families. Recipients must teach in such a school for at least four academic years within eight years of completing the program of study for which they received the grant.

Teacher's college. A college that specializes in preparing students to teach in elementary or secondary schools. Most teacher's colleges offer a curriculum that combines a study of the liberal arts with the study of pedagogy.

Technical college/school. A college that offers a wide variety of vocational programs to students.

Terminal program. An education program designed to prepare students for immediate employment. These programs usually can be completed in fewer than four years beyond high school and are available in most community colleges and trade schools.

Title IV code. See *Federal code number.*

Transcript. A copy of a student's official academic record listing all courses taken and grades received.

Transfer program. An academic program in a community or junior college primarily for students who plan to continue their studies in a four-year college or university.

Transfer student. A student who has attended another college for any period, which may be defined by various colleges as any time from a single term up to three years. A transfer student may receive credit for all or some of the courses successfully completed before the transfer.

Trimester. An academic calendar period of about 15 weeks. Three trimesters make up one year. Students normally progress by attending two of the trimesters each year and in some colleges can accelerate their progress by attending all three trimesters in one or more years.

Tuition. The price of instruction at a college. Tuition may be charged per term or per credit hour.

Tuition and fee waiver. Some colleges reduce the tuition and/or fees for some categories of students, such as adults, senior citizens or children of alumni.

Two-year college. A college that offers only two years of undergraduate study. See *Community/junior college*; see also *Upper-division college.*

Undergraduate. A student in the freshman, sophomore, junior or senior year of study, as opposed to a graduate student who has earned an undergraduate degree and is pursuing a master's, doctoral or professional degree.

University. An institution of higher education that is divided into several colleges, schools or institutes.

Unmet need. The difference between a specific student's total available resources and the total cost for the student's attendance at a specific institution.

Unsubsidized loan. An education loan that is non-need based and therefore not subsidized by the federal government; the borrower is responsible for accrued interest throughout the life of the loan.

Upper-division college. A college that offers only the junior and senior years of study. Students must complete their freshman and sophomore years at other institutions before entering the upper-division institution to earn their bachelor's degree.

Variable interest rate. An interest rate that changes on an annual basis to better reflect market rates.

Virtual college/university. A degree-granting, accredited institution wherein all courses are delivered by distance learning, with no physical campus.

Work-study. An arrangement by which a student combines employment and college study. The employment may be an integral part of the academic program (as in cooperative education and internships) or simply a means of paying for college (as in the need-based *Federal Work-Study Program*).

Alphabetical Index of Colleges

Abilene Christian University (TX), 790
Academy College (MN), 466
Academy of Art University (CA), 171
Academy of Court Reporting: Columbus *see* Miami-Jacobs Career College: Columbus (OH)
Academy of Couture Art (CA), 171
Adams State College (CO), 226
Adelphi University (NY), 555
Adirondack Community College (NY), 556
Adrian College (MI), 445
Adventist University of Health Sciences (FL), 253
Agnes Scott College (GA), 276
AIB College of Business (IA), 354
Aiken Technical College (SC), 757
Aims Community College (CO), 226
Alabama Agricultural and Mechanical University (AL), 137
Alabama State University (AL), 137
Alamance Community College (NC), 608
Alaska Bible College (AK), 149
Alaska Pacific University (AK), 150
Albany College of Pharmacy and Health Sciences (NY), 556
Albany State University (GA), 277
Albany Technical College (GA), 277
Albertus Magnus College (CT), 240
Albion College (MI), 445
Albright College (PA), 697
Alcorn State University (MS), 489
Alderson-Broaddus College (WV), 872
Alexandria Technical and Community College (MN), 466
Alfred University (NY), 556
Alice Lloyd College (KY), 380
Allan Hancock College (CA), 171
Allegany College of Maryland (MD), 409
Allegheny College (PA), 697
Allen College (IA), 354
Allen County Community College (KS), 368
Allen University (SC), 757
Alliant International University (CA), 171
Alma College (MI), 446
Alpena Community College (MI), 446
Alvernia University (PA), 697
Alverno College (WI), 880
Alvin Community College (TX), 791
American Academy McAllister Institute of Funeral Service (NY), 557
American Academy of Art (IL), 303
American Academy of Dramatic Arts (NY), 557
American Baptist College (TN), 775
American International College (MA), 420
American Jewish University (CA), 172
American Public University System (WV), 872
American River College (CA), 172
American University (DC), 251
Amherst College (MA), 421
Amridge University (AL), 137
Ancilla College (IN), 337
Anderson University (IN), 337
Anderson University (SC), 757
Andrew College (GA), 277
Andrews University (MI), 446
Angelina College (TX), 791
Angelo State University (TX), 791
Anna Maria College (MA), 421
Anne Arundel Community College (MD), 409
Anoka Technical College (MN), 466
Anoka-Ramsey Community College (MN), 466
Antelope Valley College (CA), 172
Anthem College
    Aurora (CO), 227
    Phoenix (AZ), 151
Antioch University McGregor *see* Antioch University Midwest (OH)
Antioch University Midwest (OH), 642
Antioch University Santa Barbara (CA), 172
Antonelli Institute of Art and Photography (PA), 697
Appalachian Bible College (WV), 872
Appalachian State University (NC), 609
Aquinas College (MI), 446
Aquinas College (TN), 775
Arapahoe Community College (CO), 227
Arcadia University (PA), 698
Arizona Christian University (AZ), 152
Arizona State University (AZ), 152
Arizona Western College (AZ), 152
Arkansas Northeastern College (AR), 160
Arkansas State University (AR), 160
Arkansas State University
    Beebe (AR), 160
    Mountain Home (AR), 161
Arkansas Tech University (AR), 161
Arlington Baptist College (TX), 792
Armstrong Atlantic State University (GA), 277
Art Center College of Design (CA), 172
Art Center Design College *see* Southwest University of Visual Arts (AZ)
Art Center Design College *see* Southwest University of Visual Arts (NM)
Art Institute of California
    Hollywood (CA), 173
    Los Angeles (CA), 173
    Orange County (CA), 173
    San Diego (CA), 173
Art Institute of Charlotte (NC), 609
Art Institute of Cincinnati (OH), 642
Art Institute of Colorado (CO), 227
Art Institute of Phoenix (AZ), 152
Art Institute of Pittsburgh (PA), 698
Art Institute of Portland (OR), 687
Art Institute of Seattle (WA), 858
Art Institute of York (PA), 698
Art Institutes International Minnesota (MN), 467
ASA Institute of Business and Computer Technology (NY), 557
Asbury College *see* Asbury University (KY)
Asbury University (KY), 380
Ashford University (IA), 354
Ashland University (OH), 642
Asnuntuck Community College (CT), 240
Assumption College (MA), 421
Athens State University (AL), 137
Athens Technical College (GA), 277
Atlanta Christian College *see* Point University (GA)
Atlanta Metropolitan College (GA), 278
Atlanta Technical College (GA), 278
Atlantic Cape Community College (NJ), 536
Atlantic College *see* Atlantic University College (PR)
Atlantic University College (PR), 744
Auburn University (AL), 138
Auburn University at Montgomery (AL), 138
Augsburg College (MN), 467
Augustana College (IL), 303
Augustana College (SD), 771
Aultman College of Nursing and Health Sciences (OH), 642
Aurora University (IL), 303
Austin College (TX), 792
Austin Community College (TX), 792
Austin Peay State University (TN), 775
Ave Maria University (FL), 254
Averett University (VA), 838
Avila University (MO), 495
Azusa Pacific University (CA), 173
Babson College (MA), 421
Bacone College (OK), 676
Bainbridge College (GA), 278
Baker College of Auburn Hills (MI), 447
Baker College of Cadillac (MI), 447
Baker College of Clinton Township (MI), 447
Baker College of Muskegon (MI), 447
Baker College of Owosso (MI), 448
Baker College of Port Huron (MI), 448
Baker University (KS), 368
Baldwin Wallace University (OH), 643
Baldwin-Wallace College *see* Baldwin Wallace University (OH)
Ball State University (IN), 337
Baltimore City Community College (MD), 410
Baptist Bible College of Pennsylvania (PA), 698
Baptist College of Florida (FL), 254
Barclay College (KS), 368
Bard College (NY), 557
Bard College at Simon's Rock (MA), 422
Barnard College (NY), 558
Barnes-Jewish College of Nursing *see* Goldfarb School of Nursing at Barnes-Jewish College (MO)
Barry University (FL), 254
Barstow Community College (CA), 174
Barton College (NC), 609
Barton County Community College (KS), 369
Bastyr University (WA), 858
Bates College (ME), 402
Bates Technical College (WA), 858
Baton Rouge Community College (LA), 394
Bay de Noc Community College (MI), 448
Bay Mills Community College (MI), 448
Bay Path College (MA), 422
Bay State College (MA), 422
Bayamon Central University (PR), 744
Baylor University (TX), 792
Beacon College (FL), 254
Beaufort County Community College (NC), 609
Becker College (MA), 423
Beckfield College (KY), 380
Belhaven College *see* Belhaven University (MS)
Belhaven University (MS), 489
Bellarmine University (KY), 381
Bellevue College (WA), 859
Bellevue Community College *see* Bellevue College (WA)
Bellevue University (NE), 518
Bellingham Technical College (WA), 859
Belmont Abbey College (NC), 610
Belmont College (OH), 643
Belmont University (TN), 776
Beloit College (WI), 880
Bel-Rea Institute of Animal Technology (CO), 227
Bemidji State University (MN), 467
Benedict College (SC), 758
Benedictine College (KS), 369
Benedictine University (IL), 304
Benjamin Franklin Institute of Technology (MA), 423
Bennett College for Women (NC), 610
Bennington College (VT), 832
Bentley College *see* Bentley University (MA)
Bentley University (MA), 423
Berea College (KY), 381
Berkeley City College (CA), 174
Berkeley College (NJ), 536
Berklee College of Music (MA), 423
Berkshire Community College (MA), 424
Berry College (GA), 278
Bethany College (WV), 872
Bethany Lutheran College (MN), 467
Bethel College (IN), 337
Bethel College (KS), 369
Bethel University (MN), 468
Bethel University (TN), 776
Bethesda Christian University *see* Bethesda University of California (CA)
Bethesda University of California (CA), 174
Bethune-Cookman University (FL), 254
Beulah Heights University (GA), 279
Bevill State Community College (AL), 138
Big Bend Community College (WA), 859
Big Sandy Community and Technical College (KY), 381
Biola University (CA), 174
Birmingham-Southern College (AL), 138
Bismarck State College (ND), 636
Black Hawk College (IL), 304
Black Hills State University (SD), 771
Black River Technical College (AR), 161
Blackburn College (IL), 304
Blackfeet Community College (MT), 513
Blackhawk Technical College (WI), 880

Bladen Community College (NC), 610
Blessing-Rieman College of Nursing (IL), 305
Blinn College (TX), 793
Bloomfield College (NJ), 536
Bloomsburg University of Pennsylvania (PA), 699
Blue Mountain College (MS), 489
Blue Ridge Community and Technical College (WV), 873
Blue Ridge Community College (NC), 610
Blue Ridge Community College (VA), 838
Bluefield College (VA), 838
Bluefield State College (WV), 873
Bluegrass Community and Technical College (KY), 382
Bluffton University (OH), 643
Bob Jones University (SC), 758
Bohecker College ***see*** Fortis College: Ravenna (OH)
Boise Bible College (ID), 299
Boise State University (ID), 299
Bolivar Technical College (MO), 495
Boricua College (NY), 558
Bossier Parish Community College (LA), 394
Boston Architectural College (MA), 424
Boston College (MA), 424
Boston Conservatory (MA), 424
Boston University (MA), 425
Boulder College of Massage Therapy (CO), 227
Bowdoin College (ME), 402
Bowie State University (MD), 410
Bowling Green State University (OH), 643
Bowling Green State University Firelands College (OH), 644
Bradford School Pittsburgh (PA), 699
Bradford School of Business ***see*** Vet Tech Institute of Houston (TX)
Bradley Academy for the Visual Arts ***see*** Art Institute of York (PA)
Bradley University (IL), 305
Brandeis University (MA), 425
Brazosport College (TX), 793
Brenau University (GA), 279
Brescia University (KY), 382
Brevard College (NC), 611
Brevard Community College (FL), 255
Brewton-Parker College (GA), 279
Briar Cliff University (IA), 354
Briarcliffe College (NY), 558
Bridgewater College (VA), 838
Bridgewater State University (MA), 425
Brigham Young University (UT), 828
Brigham Young University-Hawaii (HI), 296
Brigham Young University-Idaho (ID), 300
Bristol Community College (MA), 425
Broadview Entertainment Arts University (UT), 828
Broadview University
  Boise (ID), 300
  Layton (UT), 828
  Orem (UT), 828
  West Jordan (UT), 829
Brookdale Community College (NJ), 537
Brookline College
  Albuquerque (NM), 548
  Phoenix (AZ), 152
  Tempe (AZ), 153
  Tucson (AZ), 153
Brookline College: Mesa ***see*** Brookline College: Tempe (AZ)
Brooks Institute (CA), 175
Broome Community College (NY), 558
Broward College (FL), 255
Broward Community College ***see*** Broward College (FL)
Brown Mackie College
  Cincinnati (OH), 644
  Findlay (OH), 644
  Miami (FL), 255
  North Canton (OH), 644
Brown University (RI), 754
Brunswick Community College (NC), 611
Bryan University Dayton (TN), 776
BryanLGH College of Health Sciences (NE), 518
Bryant & Stratton College
  Albany (NY), 558
  Cleveland (OH), 644
  Eastlake (OH), 645
  Milwaukee (WI), 880
  Parma (OH), 645
  Richmond (VA), 839
  Syracuse (NY), 559
  Syracuse North (NY), 559
  Virginia Beach (VA), 839
Bryant University (RI), 754
Bryn Athyn College (PA), 699
Bryn Mawr College (PA), 699
Bucknell University (PA), 699
Bucks County Community College (PA), 700
Buena Vista University (IA), 355
Bunker Hill Community College (MA), 426
Burlington College (VT), 832
Burlington County College (NJ), 537
Butler Community College (KS), 370
Butler County Community College (PA), 700
Butler University (IN), 338
Cabrillo College (CA), 175
Cabrini College (PA), 700
Cairn University (PA), 700
Caldwell College (NJ), 537
Caldwell Community College and Technical Institute (NC), 611
California Baptist University (CA), 175
California Christian College (CA), 175
California College of the Arts (CA), 176
California College San Diego (CA), 176
California Culinary Academy (CA), 176
California Design College ***see*** Art Institute of California: Hollywood (CA)
California Institute of Integral Studies (CA), 176
California Institute of Technology (CA), 177
California Institute of the Arts (CA), 177
California Lutheran University (CA), 177
California Maritime Academy (CA), 177
California Polytechnic State University San Luis Obispo (CA), 178
California School of Culinary Arts ***see*** Le Cordon Bleu College of Culinary Arts: Los Angeles (CA)
California State Polytechnic University Pomona (CA), 178
California State University
  Bakersfield (CA), 178
  Channel Islands (CA), 179
  Chico (CA), 179
  Dominguez Hills (CA), 179
  East Bay (CA), 179
  Fresno (CA), 180
  Fullerton (CA), 180
  Long Beach (CA), 180
  Los Angeles (CA), 181
  Monterey Bay (CA), 181
  Northridge (CA), 181
  Sacramento (CA), 181
  San Bernardino (CA), 182
  Stanislaus (CA), 182
California University of Management and Sciences (CA), 182
California University of Pennsylvania (PA), 701
Calumet College of St. Joseph (IN), 338
Calvary Bible College and Theological Seminary (MO), 495
Calvin College (MI), 449
Cambria-Rowe Business College (PA), 701
Cambria-Rowe Business College Indiana (PA), 701
Cambridge College ***see*** Anthem College: Aurora (CO)
Cambridge College (MA), 426
Camden County College (NJ), 538
Cameron University (OK), 677
Campbell University (NC), 611
Campbellsville University (KY), 382
Canisius College (NY), 559
Cankdeska Cikana Community College (ND), 637
Cape Cod Community College (MA), 426
Cape Fear Community College (NC), 612
Capella University (MN), 468
Capital Community College (CT), 240
Capital University (OH), 645
Cardinal Stritch University (WI), 881
Career Training Academy (PA), 701
Career Training Academy Monroeville (PA), 702
Caribbean University (PR), 745
Caritas Laboure College ***see*** Laboure College (MA)
Carl Albert State College (OK), 677
Carl Sandburg College (IL), 305
Carleton College (MN), 468
Carlos Albizu University (FL), 255
Carlow University (PA), 702
Carnegie Mellon University (PA), 702
Carolina Christian College (NC), 612
Carolinas College of Health Sciences (NC), 612
Carrington College California Emeryville (CA), 182
Carroll College (MT), 513
Carroll Community College (MD), 410
Carroll University (WI), 881
Carson-Newman College ***see*** Carson-Newman University (TN)
Carson-Newman University (TN), 776
Carteret Community College (NC), 612
Carthage College (WI), 881
Carver Bible College (GA), 279
Cascadia Community College (WA), 859
Case Western Reserve University (OH), 645
Casper College (WY), 899
Castleton State College (VT), 833
Catawba College (NC), 613
Catawba Valley Community College (NC), 613
Catholic University of America (DC), 251
Cayuga Community College (NY), 559
Cayuga County Community College ***see*** Cayuga Community College (NY)
Cazenovia College (NY), 560
Cecil College (MD), 410
Cedar Crest College (PA), 703
Cedar Valley College (TX), 793
Cedarville University (OH), 646
Centenary College (NJ), 538
Centenary College of Louisiana (LA), 394
Central Alabama Community College (AL), 139
Central Arizona College (AZ), 153
Central Baptist College (AR), 161
Central Carolina Community College (NC), 613
Central Carolina Technical College (SC), 758
Central Christian College of Kansas (KS), 370
Central College (IA), 355
Central Community College (NE), 519
Central Connecticut State University (CT), 240
Central Florida Community College ***see*** College of Central Florida (FL)
Central Georgia Technical College (GA), 280
Central Lakes College (MN), 468
Central Maine Community College (ME), 402
Central Maine Medical Center College of Nursing and Health Professions (ME), 403
Central Methodist University (MO), 495
Central Michigan University (MI), 449
Central Missouri State University ***see*** University of Central Missouri (MO)
Central New Mexico Community College (NM), 549
Central Ohio Technical College (OH), 646
Central Oregon Community College (OR), 687
Central Penn College (PA), 703
Central Pennsylvania College ***see*** Central Penn College (PA)
Central Piedmont Community College (NC), 613
Central State University (OH), 646
Central Texas College (TX), 793
Central Wyoming College (WY), 899
Centralia College (WA), 859
Centre College (KY), 382
Century College (MN), 469
Century Community and Technical College ***see*** Century College (MN)
Cerro Coso Community College (CA), 182
Chabot College (CA), 183
Chadron State College (NE), 519
Chaffey College (CA), 183
Chamberlain College of Nursing St. Louis (MO), 496
Chaminade University of Honolulu (HI), 296
Champlain College (VT), 833
Chandler-Gilbert Community College (AZ), 153
Chapman University (CA), 183
Charles Drew University of Medicine and Science (CA), 183
Charleston Southern University (SC), 758
Charter Oak State College (CT), 240
Chatfield College (OH), 646
Chatham University (PA), 703

Chattahoochee Technical College (GA), 280
Chattahoochee Valley Community College (AL), 139
Chattanooga State Community College (TN), 777
Chattanooga State Technical Community College *see* Chattanooga State Community College (TN)
Chemeketa Community College (OR), 687
Chesapeake College (MD), 410
Chestnut Hill College (PA), 703
Cheyney University of Pennsylvania (PA), 704
Chicago State University (IL), 305
Chief Dull Knife College (MT), 513
Chipola College (FL), 256
Chippewa Valley Technical College (WI), 881
Chowan University (NC), 614
Christendom College (VA), 839
Christian Brothers University (TN), 777
Christopher Newport University (VA), 839
Cincinnati Christian University (OH), 647
Cincinnati College of Mortuary Science (OH), 647
Cincinnati State Technical and Community College (OH), 647
Circleville Bible College *see* Ohio Christian University (OH)
Cisco College (TX), 793
Cisco Junior College *see* Cisco College (TX)
Citrus College (CA), 184
City College of San Francisco (CA), 184
City Colleges of Chicago
  Harold Washington College (IL), 306
  Harry S. Truman College (IL), 306
  Kennedy-King College (IL), 306
  Malcolm X College (IL), 306
  Olive-Harvey College (IL), 307
  Richard J. Daley College (IL), 307
  Wilbur Wright College (IL), 307
City University of New York
  Baruch College (NY), 560
  Borough of Manhattan Community College (NY), 560
  Bronx Community College (NY), 560
  Brooklyn College (NY), 561
  City College (NY), 561
  College of Staten Island (NY), 561
  CUNY Online (NY), 562
  Hostos Community College (NY), 562
  Hunter College (NY), 562
  John Jay College of Criminal Justice (NY), 562
  Kingsborough Community College (NY), 563
  LaGuardia Community College (NY), 563
  Lehman College (NY), 563
  Medgar Evers College (NY), 563
  New York City College of Technology (NY), 564
  Queens College (NY), 564
  Queensborough Community College (NY), 564
  York College (NY), 564
City University of Seattle (WA), 860
Clackamas Community College (OR), 687
Claflin University (SC), 759
Claremont McKenna College (CA), 184
Clarendon College (TX), 794
Clarion University of Pennsylvania (PA), 704
Clark Atlanta University (GA), 280
Clark College (WA), 860
Clark State Community College (OH), 647
Clark University (MA), 426
Clarke College *see* Clarke University (IA)
Clarke University (IA), 355
Clarkson College (NE), 519
Clarkson University (NY), 565
Clatsop Community College (OR), 688
Clayton State University (GA), 280
Clear Creek Baptist Bible College (KY), 383
Clearwater Christian College (FL), 256
Cleary University (MI), 449
Clemson University (SC), 759
Cleveland Community College (NC), 614
Cleveland Institute of Art (OH), 647
Cleveland Institute of Music (OH), 648
Cleveland State Community College (TN), 777
Cleveland State University (OH), 648
Clinton Community College (NY), 565
Cloud County Community College (KS), 370
Clover Park Technical College (WA), 860
Clovis Community College (NM), 549
Coahoma Community College (MS), 489
Coastal Bend College (TX), 794
Coastal Carolina Community College (NC), 614
Coastal Carolina University (SC), 760
Coastal Georgia Community College *see* College of Coastal Georgia (GA)
Coastline Community College (CA), 184
Cochise College (AZ), 153
Cochran School of Nursing (NY), 565
Coe College (IA), 356
Coffeyville Community College (KS), 370
Cogswell Polytechnical College (CA), 185
Coker College (SC), 760
Colby College (ME), 403
Colby Community College (KS), 370
Colby-Sawyer College (NH), 530
Colegio Pentecostal Mizpa *see* Universidad Pentecostal Mizpa (PR)
Coleman College *see* Coleman University (CA)
Coleman University (CA), 185
Coleman University San Marcos (CA), 185
Colgate University (NY), 565
College for Creative Studies (MI), 449
College of Business and Technology
  Cutler Bay (FL), 256
  Flagler (FL), 256
  Hialeah (FL), 257
  Kendall (FL), 257
College of Central Florida (FL), 257
College of Charleston (SC), 760
College of Coastal Georgia (GA), 280
College of DuPage (IL), 307
College of Idaho (ID), 300
College of Lake County (IL), 308
College of Marin (CA), 185
College of Menominee Nation (WI), 882
College of Mount St. Joseph (OH), 648
College of Mount St. Vincent (NY), 566
College of New Rochelle (NY), 566
College of Office Technology (IL), 308
College of Saint Mary (NE), 519
College of Saint Rose (NY), 566
College of San Mateo (CA), 186
College of Santa Fe *see* Santa Fe University of Art and Design (NM)
College of Southern Idaho (ID), 300
College of Southern Maryland (MD), 411
College of Southern Nevada (NV), 527
College of St. Benedict (MN), 469
College of St. Catherine *see* St. Catherine University (MN)
College of St. Elizabeth (NJ), 538
College of St. Joseph in Vermont (VT), 833
College of St. Mary Magdalen (NH), 530
College of St. Scholastica (MN), 469
College of the Albemarle (NC), 614
College of the Atlantic (ME), 403
College of the Canyons (CA), 186
College of the Desert (CA), 186
College of the Holy Cross (MA), 427
College of the Mainland (TX), 795
College of the Ouachitas (AR), 162
College of the Ozarks (MO), 496
College of the Redwoods (CA), 186
College of the Siskiyous (CA), 186
College of the Southwest *see* University of the Southwest (NM)
College of Visual Arts (MN), 470
College of Westchester (NY), 566
College of Western Idaho (ID), 301
College of William and Mary (VA), 840
College of Wooster (OH), 649
CollegeAmerica Denver (CO), 228
Collin County Community College District (TX), 795
Colorado Christian University (CO), 228
Colorado College (CO), 228
Colorado Heights University (CO), 228
Colorado Institute of Art *see* Art Institute of Colorado (CO)
Colorado Mesa University (CO), 228
Colorado Mountain College (CO), 229
Colorado Northwestern Community College (CO), 229
Colorado School of Healing Arts (CO), 229
Colorado School of Mines (CO), 229
Colorado School of Trades (CO), 230
Colorado State University (CO), 230
Colorado State University Pueblo (CO), 230
Colorado Technical University (CO), 230
Columbia Basin College (WA), 860
Columbia Centro Universitario
  Caguas (PR), 745
  Yauco (PR), 745
Columbia College (CA), 187
Columbia College (MO), 496
Columbia College (SC), 760
Columbia College Chicago (IL), 308
Columbia College of Nursing (WI), 882
Columbia International University (SC), 761
Columbia State Community College (TN), 777
Columbia Union College *see* Washington Adventist University (MD)
Columbia University (NY), 567
Columbia University School of General Studies (NY), 567
Columbia-Greene Community College (NY), 567
Columbus College of Art and Design (OH), 649
Columbus State Community College (OH), 649
Columbus State University (GA), 281
Columbus Technical College (GA), 281
Commonwealth Institute of Funeral Service (TX), 795
Community College of Allegheny County (PA), 704
Community College of Aurora (CO), 231
Community College of Baltimore County (MD), 411
Community College of Beaver County (PA), 704
Community College of Denver (CO), 231
Community College of Philadelphia (PA), 705
Community College of Rhode Island (RI), 754
Community College of Vermont (VT), 833
Conception Seminary College (MO), 497
Concord University (WV), 873
Concordia College (NY), 567
Concordia College Moorhead (MN), 470
Concordia University *see* Concordia University Chicago (IL)
Concordia University (CA), 187
Concordia University (MI), 450
Concordia University (NE), 520
Concordia University (OR), 688
Concordia University Chicago (IL), 308
Concordia University St. Paul (MN), 470
Concordia University Texas (TX), 795
Concordia University Wisconsin (WI), 882
Connecticut College (CT), 241
Connors State College (OK), 677
Conservatory of Music of Puerto Rico (PR), 745
Consolidated School of Business
  Lancaster (PA), 705
  York (PA), 705
Converse College (SC), 761
Cooking & Hospitality Institute of Chicago *see* Le Cordon Bleu College of Culinary Arts: Chicago (IL)
Cooper Union for the Advancement of Science and Art (NY), 568
Copiah-Lincoln Community College (MS), 490
Copper Mountain College (CA), 187
Coppin State University (MD), 411
Corban College *see* Corban University (OR)
Corban University (OR), 688
Cornell College (IA), 356
Cornell University (NY), 568
Cornerstone University (MI), 450
Corning Community College (NY), 568
Cornish College of the Arts (WA), 860
Cossatot Community College of the University of Arkansas (AR), 162
Cottey College (MO), 497
County College of Morris (NJ), 539
Covenant College (GA), 281
Cowley County Community College (KS), 371
Crafton Hills College (CA), 187
Creative Center (NE), 520
Creighton University (NE), 520
Criswell College (TX), 796
Crossroads College (MN), 471
Crowder College (MO), 497
Crowley's Ridge College (AR), 162
Crown College (MN), 471
Culinary Institute of America (NY), 568
Culver-Stockton College (MO), 497
Cumberland County College (NJ), 539
Cumberland University (TN), 778
Curry College (MA), 427

Curtis Institute of Music (PA), 705
Cuyahoga Community College Metropolitan (OH), 649
Cuyamaca College (CA), 188
Cypress College (CA), 188
D'Youville College (NY), 570
Dabney S. Lancaster Community College (VA), 840
Daemen College (NY), 569
Dakota College at Bottineau (ND), 637
Dakota County Technical College (MN), 471
Dakota State University (SD), 771
Dallas Baptist University (TX), 796
Dallas Christian College (TX), 796
Dalton State College (GA), 281
Daniel Webster College (NH), 530
Danville Area Community College (IL), 308
Danville Community College (VA), 840
Dartmouth College (NH), 530
Darton College (GA), 282
Davenport University (MI), 450
Davidson College (NC), 614
Davidson County Community College (NC), 615
Davis and Elkins College (WV), 873
Davis College (NY), 569
Davis College (OH), 650
Dawson Community College (MT), 514
Daymar College
    Bowling Green (KY), 383
    Chillicothe (OH), 650
    Owensboro (KY), 383
    Paducah (KY), 383
Daymar Institute Nashville (TN), 778
Daytona State College (FL), 257
De Anza College (CA), 188
Deaconess College of Nursing *see* Chamberlain College of Nursing: St. Louis (MO)
Dean College (MA), 427
Deep Springs College (NV), 188
Defiance College (OH), 650
DeKalb Technical College *see* Georgia Piedmont Technical College (GA)
Del Mar College (TX), 796
Delaware College of Art and Design (DE), 249
Delaware County Community College (PA), 706
Delaware State University (DE), 249
Delaware Technical and Community College
    Dover (DE), 249
    Owens (DE), 249
    Stanton/Wilmington (DE), 250
Delaware Valley College (PA), 706
Delgado Community College (LA), 395
Delta College (MI), 450
Delta State University (MS), 490
Denison University (OH), 650
Denmark Technical College (SC), 761
Denver School of Nursing (CO), 231
DePaul University (IL), 309
DePauw University (IN), 338
Des Moines Area Community College (IA), 356
DeSales University (PA), 706
DeVry College of New York *see* DeVry College of New York: Midtown Campus (NY)
DeVry College of New York Midtown Campus (NY), 569
DeVry University
    Arlington (VA), 840
    Chicago (IL), 309
    Columbus (OH), 651
    Decatur (GA), 282
    Federal Way (WA), 861
    Fort Washington (PA), 707
    Irving (TX), 797
    Kansas City (MO), 498
    Miramar (FL), 257
    North Brunswick (NJ), 539
    Orlando (FL), 258
    Phoenix (AZ), 154
    Pomona (CA), 188
    Westminster (CO), 231
DeVry University: Crystal City *see* DeVry University: Arlington (VA)
Diablo Valley College (CA), 189
Dickinson College (PA), 707
Dickinson State University (ND), 637
DigiPen Institute of Technology (WA), 861
Digital Media Arts College (FL), 258
Dillard University (LA), 395
Dine College (AZ), 154
Dixie State College (UT), 829
Doane College (NE), 521
Dodge City Community College (KS), 371
Dominican College of Blauvelt (NY), 569
Dominican University (IL), 309
Dominican University of California (CA), 189
Dona Ana Community College of New Mexico State University (NM), 549
Donnelly College (KS), 371
Dordt College (IA), 357
Douglas Education Center (PA), 707
Dowling College (NY), 570
Drake University (IA), 357
Draughons Junior College *see* Daymar College: Bowling Green (KY)
Drew University (NJ), 539
Drexel University (PA), 707
Drury University (MO), 498
DuBois Business College (PA), 707
Duke University (NC), 615
Dunwoody College of Technology (MN), 471
Duquesne University (PA), 708
Durham Technical Community College (NC), 615
Dutchess Community College (NY), 570
Dyersburg State Community College (TN), 778
Earlham College (IN), 339
East Arkansas Community College (AR), 162
East Carolina University (NC), 615
East Central College (MO), 498
East Central University (OK), 677
East Georgia College (GA), 282
East Los Angeles College (CA), 189
East Mississippi Community College (MS), 490
East Stroudsburg University of Pennsylvania (PA), 708
East Tennessee State University (TN), 778
East Texas Baptist University (TX), 797
Eastern Arizona College (AZ), 154
Eastern Connecticut State University (CT), 241
Eastern Gateway Community College (OH), 651
Eastern Idaho Technical College (ID), 301
Eastern Illinois University (IL), 310
Eastern Kentucky University (KY), 383
Eastern Maine Community College (ME), 404
Eastern Mennonite University (VA), 841
Eastern Michigan University (MI), 451
Eastern Nazarene College (MA), 428
Eastern New Mexico University (NM), 549
Eastern New Mexico University Roswell (NM), 550
Eastern Oklahoma State College (OK), 678
Eastern Oregon University (OR), 688
Eastern Shore Community College (VA), 841
Eastern Washington University (WA), 861
Eastern West Virginia Community and Technical College (WV), 874
Eastern Wyoming College (WY), 899
Eastfield College (TX), 797
Eastman School of Music of the University of Rochester (NY), 571
East-West University (IL), 310
Ecclesia College (AR), 163
Eckerd College (FL), 258
ECPI College of Technology: Virginia Beach *see* ECPI University (VA)
ECPI University (VA), 841
Edgecombe Community College (NC), 616
Edgewood College (WI), 882
EDIC College (PR), 745
Edinboro University of Pennsylvania (PA), 708
Edison College *see* Edison State College (FL)
Edison State College (FL), 258
Edison State Community College (OH), 651
EDP University of Puerto Rico
    Hato Rey (PR), 746
    San Sebastian (PR), 746
Edward Waters College (FL), 258
El Camino College (CA), 189
El Centro College (TX), 797
El Paso Community College (TX), 798
Elgin Community College (IL), 310
Elizabeth City State University (NC), 616
Elizabethtown College (PA), 708
Elizabethtown Community and Technical College (KY), 384
Ellsworth Community College (IA), 357
Elmhurst College (IL), 310
Elmira Business Institute (NY), 571
Elmira Business Institute Vestal (NY), 571
Elmira College (NY), 571
Elms College (MA), 428
Elon University (NC), 616
Embry-Riddle Aeronautical University (FL), 259
Embry-Riddle Aeronautical University
    Prescott Campus (AZ), 154
    Worldwide Campus (FL), 259
Emerson College (MA), 428
Emmanuel College (GA), 282
Emmanuel College (MA), 428
Emmaus Bible College (IA), 357
Emory & Henry College (VA), 841
Emory University (GA), 283
Empire College (CA), 190
Emporia State University (KS), 371
Endicott College (MA), 429
Enterprise State Community College (AL), 139
Enterprise-Ozark Community College *see* Enterprise State Community College (AL)
Erie Business Center (PA), 709
Erie Community College (NY), 572
Erskine College (SC), 762
Escuela de Artes Plasticas de Puerto Rico (PR), 746
Essex County College (NJ), 540
Estrella Mountain Community College (AZ), 155
ETI Technical College of Niles (OH), 651
Eugene Bible College *see* New Hope Christian College (OR)
Eugene Lang College The New School for Liberal Arts (NY), 572
Eureka College (IL), 311
Evangel University (MO), 498
Everest College
    Aurora (CO), 231
    Colorado Springs (CO), 232
    Las Vegas (NV), 527
Everett Community College (WA), 862
Evergreen State College (WA), 862
Excelsior College (NY), 572
Fairfield University (CT), 241
Fairmont State University (WV), 874
Faith Baptist Bible College and Theological Seminary (IA), 358
Fashion Institute of Technology (NY), 572
Faulkner State Community College (AL), 139
Faulkner University (AL), 140
Fayetteville State University (NC), 616
Fayetteville Technical Community College (NC), 617
Feather River College (CA), 190
Felician College (NJ), 540
Ferris State University (MI), 451
Ferrum College (VA), 842
Finger Lakes Community College (NY), 573
Finlandia University (MI), 451
Fisher College (MA), 429
Fisk University (TN), 779
Fitchburg State University (MA), 429
Five Towns College (NY), 573
Flagler College (FL), 259
Flathead Valley Community College (MT), 514
Florence-Darlington Technical College (SC), 762
Florida Agricultural and Mechanical University (FL), 259
Florida Atlantic University (FL), 260
Florida Christian College (FL), 260
Florida College (FL), 260
Florida College of Natural Health
    Bradenton (FL), 260
    Maitland (FL), 261
Florida Community College at Jacksonville *see* Florida State College at Jacksonville (FL)
Florida Gateway College (FL), 261
Florida Gulf Coast University (FL), 261
Florida Hospital College of Health Sciences *see* Adventist University of Health Sciences (FL)
Florida Institute of Technology (FL), 261
Florida International University (FL), 262
Florida Keys Community College (FL), 262
Florida National University (FL), 262
Florida Southern College (FL), 262

Florida State College at Jacksonville (FL), 263
Florida State University (FL), 263
Fond du Lac Tribal and Community College (MN), 472
Fontbonne University (MO), 499
Foothill College (CA), 190
Fordham University (NY), 573
Forrest Junior College (SC), 762
Forsyth Technical Community College (NC), 617
Fort Hays State University (KS), 372
Fort Lewis College (CO), 232
Fort Peck Community College (MT), 514
Fort Valley State University (GA), 283
Fortis College
  Centerville (OH), 652
  Ravenna (OH), 652
Fox Valley Technical College (WI), 883
Framingham State University (MA), 429
Francis Marion University (SC), 762
Franciscan University of Steubenville (OH), 652
Frank Phillips College (TX), 798
Franklin & Marshall College (PA), 709
Franklin College (IN), 339
Franklin Pierce University (NH), 531
Franklin University (OH), 652
Franklin W. Olin College of Engineering (MA), 430
Frederick Community College (MD), 411
Free Will Baptist Bible College ***see*** Welch College (TN)
Freed-Hardeman University (TN), 779
Fremont College Cerritos (CA), 190
Fresno City College (CA), 190
Fresno Pacific University (CA), 191
Friends University (KS), 372
Front Range Community College (CO), 232
Frostburg State University (MD), 412
Full Sail University (FL), 263
Fullerton College (CA), 191
Fulton-Montgomery Community College (NY), 573
Furman University (SC), 763
Gadsden State Community College (AL), 140
Gallaudet University (DC), 252
Gallipolis Career College (OH), 652
Galveston College (TX), 798
Gannon University (PA), 709
Garden City Community College (KS), 372
Gardner-Webb University (NC), 617
Garrett College (MD), 412
Gaston College (NC), 618
GateWay Community College (AZ), 155
Gateway Community College (CT), 242
Gateway Technical College (WI), 883
Genesee Community College (NY), 574
Geneva College (PA), 710
George Fox University (OR), 689
George Mason University (VA), 842
George Washington University (DC), 252
Georgetown College (KY), 384
Georgetown University (DC), 252
Georgia College and State University (GA), 283
Georgia Gwinnett College (GA), 284
Georgia Highlands College (GA), 284
Georgia Institute of Technology (GA), 284
Georgia Military College (GA), 284
Georgia Perimeter College (GA), 285
Georgia Piedmont Technical College (GA), 285
Georgia Regents University (GA), 285
Georgia Southern University (GA), 285
Georgia Southwestern State University (GA), 286
Georgia State University (GA), 286
Georgian Court University (NJ), 540
Germanna Community College (VA), 842
Gettysburg College (PA), 710
Glen Oaks Community College (MI), 451
Glendale Community College (AZ), 155
Glendale Community College (CA), 191
Glenville State College (WV), 874
Globe Institute of Technology (NY), 574
Globe University
  Appleton (WI), 883
  Eau Claire (WI), 883
  Green Bay (WI), 884
  La Crosse (WI), 884
  Madison East (WI), 884
  Middleton (WI), 884
  Minneapolis (MN), 472
  Sioux Falls (SD), 772
  Wausau (WI), 884
  Woodbury (MN), 472
Gloucester County College (NJ), 540
Goddard College (VT), 834
Gogebic Community College (MI), 452
Golden Gate University (CA), 191
Goldey-Beacom College (DE), 250
Goldfarb School of Nursing at Barnes-Jewish College (MO), 499
Gonzaga University (WA), 862
Goodwin College (CT), 242
Gordon College (GA), 286
Gordon College (MA), 430
Goshen College (IN), 339
Goucher College (MD), 412
Governors State University (IL), 311
Grace College (IN), 339
Grace University (NE), 521
Graceland University (IA), 358
Grambling State University (LA), 395
Grand Canyon University (AZ), 155
Grand Rapids Community College (MI), 452
Grand Valley State University (MI), 452
Grand View College ***see*** Grand View University (IA)
Grand View University (IA), 358
Granite State College (NH), 531
Grays Harbor College (WA), 863
Grayson County College (TX), 798
Great Basin College (NV), 527
Great Bay Community College (NH), 531
Great Falls College Montana State University (MT), 514
Great Lakes Christian College (MI), 452
Green Mountain College (VT), 834
Green River Community College (WA), 863
Greenfield Community College (MA), 430
Greensboro College (NC), 618
Greenville College (IL), 311
Greenville Technical College (SC), 763
Grinnell College (IA), 358
Grossmont College (CA), 192
Grove City College (PA), 710
Guilford College (NC), 618
Guilford Technical Community College (NC), 618
Gulf Coast State College (FL), 263
Gupton Jones College of Funeral Service (GA), 286
Gustavus Adolphus College (MN), 472
Gwinnett College (GA), 287
Gwinnett Technical College (GA), 287
Gwynedd-Mercy College (PA), 711
Hagerstown Community College (MD), 412
Halifax Community College (NC), 619
Hallmark College of Aeronautics (TX), 798
Hallmark College of Technology (TX), 799
Hamilton College (NY), 574
Hamline University (MN), 473
Hampden-Sydney College (VA), 842
Hampshire College (MA), 431
Hampton University (VA), 843
Hannibal-LaGrange College ***see*** Hannibal-LaGrange University (MO)
Hannibal-LaGrange University (MO), 499
Hanover College (IN), 340
Harcum College (PA), 711
Harding University (AR), 163
Hardin-Simmons University (TX), 799
Harford Community College (MD), 413
Harper College (IL), 311
Harrington College of Design (IL), 312
Harrisburg Area Community College (PA), 711
Harrisburg University of Science and Technology (PA), 711
Harrison College Indianapolis (IN), 340
Harris-Stowe State University (MO), 499
Hartwick College (NY), 574
Harvard College (MA), 431
Harvey Mudd College (CA), 192
Haskell Indian Nations University (KS), 373
Hastings College (NE), 521
Haverford College (PA), 712
Hawaii Pacific University (HI), 296
Hawkeye Community College (IA), 359
Haywood Community College (NC), 619
Hazard Community and Technical College (KY), 384
Heald College
  Concord (CA), 192
  Hayward (CA), 192
  Honolulu (HI), 296
  Rancho Cordova (CA), 193
  Roseville (CA), 193
  Salinas (CA), 193
  San Francisco (CA), 193
  San Jose (CA), 193
  Stockton (CA), 194
Heartland Community College (IL), 312
Heidelberg College ***see*** Heidelberg University (OH)
Heidelberg University (OH), 653
Helena College University of Montana (MT), 515
Helene Fuld College of Nursing (NY), 575
Hellenic College/Holy Cross (MA), 431
Henderson State University (AR), 163
Hendrix College (AR), 163
Henry Ford Community College (MI), 453
Heritage Christian University (AL), 140
Heritage University (WA), 863
Herkimer County Community College (NY), 575
Herzing University
  Atlanta (GA), 287
  Birmingham (AL), 140
  Kenner (LA), 395
  Madison (WI), 884
Hesser College (NH), 531
Hesston College (KS), 373
Hickey College (MO), 500
High Point University (NC), 619
Highland Community College (IL), 312
Highland Community College (KS), 373
Highline Community College (WA), 863
Hilbert College (NY), 575
Hill College (TX), 799
Hillsborough Community College (FL), 263
Hillsdale College (MI), 453
Hinds Community College (MS), 490
Hiram College (OH), 653
Hobart and William Smith Colleges (NY), 575
Hobe Sound Bible College (FL), 264
Hocking College (OH), 653
Hodges University (FL), 264
Hofstra University (NY), 576
Hollins University (VA), 843
Holmes Community College (MS), 491
Holy Apostles College and Seminary (CT), 242
Holy Cross College (IN), 340
Holy Family University (PA), 712
Holy Names University (CA), 194
Holyoke Community College (MA), 431
Hondros College (OH), 653
Hood College (MD), 413
Hope College (MI), 453
Hope International University (CA), 194
Hopkinsville Community College (KY), 384
Horry-Georgetown Technical College (SC), 763
Houghton College (NY), 576
Housatonic Community College (CT), 242
Houston Baptist University (TX), 799
Houston Community College System (TX), 800
Howard College (TX), 800
Howard Community College (MD), 413
Howard Payne University (TX), 800
Howard University (DC), 252
Hudson County Community College (NJ), 541
Huertas Junior College (PR), 746
Humacao Community College (PR), 746
Humboldt State University (CA), 194
Humphreys College (CA), 195
Huntingdon College (AL), 141
Huntington University (IN), 341
Hussian School of Art (PA), 712
Husson College ***see*** Husson University (ME)

Husson University (ME), 404
Huston-Tillotson University (TX), 801
Hutchinson Community College (KS), 373
ICM School of Business & Medical Careers *see* Kaplan Career Institute: Pittsburgh (PA)
Idaho State University (ID), 301
Ilisagvik College (AK), 150
Illinois Central College (IL), 312
Illinois College (IL), 313
Illinois Eastern Community Colleges
  Frontier Community College (IL), 313
  Lincoln Trail College (IL), 313
  Olney Central College (IL), 313
  Wabash Valley College (IL), 314
Illinois Institute of Art Chicago (IL), 314
Illinois Institute of Technology (IL), 314
Illinois State University (IL), 314
Illinois Valley Community College (IL), 315
Illinois Wesleyan University (IL), 315
Immaculata University (PA), 712
Imperial Valley College (CA), 195
Independence Community College (KS), 373
Independence University (UT), 829
Indian River State College (FL), 264
Indiana Business College: Indianapolis *see* Harrison College: Indianapolis (IN)
Indiana Institute of Technology (IN), 341
Indiana State University (IN), 341
Indiana University Bloomington (IN), 341
Indiana University East (IN), 342
Indiana University Kokomo (IN), 342
Indiana University Northwest (IN), 342
Indiana University of Pennsylvania (PA), 713
Indiana University South Bend (IN), 343
Indiana University Southeast (IN), 343
Indiana University-Purdue University Fort Wayne (IN), 343
Indiana University-Purdue University Indianapolis (IN), 344
Indiana Wesleyan University (IN), 344
Institute of American Indian Arts (NM), 550
Institute of Design and Construction (NY), 576
Institute of Production and Recording (MN), 473
IntelliTec College (CO), 233
IntelliTec College Grand Junction (CO), 233
Inter American University of Puerto Rico
  Aguadilla Campus (PR), 747
  Arecibo Campus (PR), 747
  Barranquitas Campus (PR), 747
  Bayamon Campus (PR), 747
  Guayama Campus (PR), 747
  Metropolitan Campus (PR), 748
  Ponce Campus (PR), 748
  San German Campus (PR), 748
International Academy of Design and Technology Tampa (FL), 264
International College *see* Hodges University (FL)
International College of Broadcasting (OH), 654
International Institute of the Americas: Albuquerque *see* Brookline College: Albuquerque (NM)
International Institute of the Americas: Phoenix *see* Brookline College: Phoenix (AZ)
International Institute of the Americas: Tucson *see* Brookline College: Tucson (AZ)
Inver Hills Community College (MN), 473
Iona College (NY), 577
Iowa Central Community College (IA), 359
Iowa Lakes Community College (IA), 359
Iowa State University (IA), 359
Iowa Wesleyan College (IA), 360
Iowa Western Community College (IA), 360
Irvine Valley College (CA), 195
Island Drafting and Technical Institute (NY), 577
Isothermal Community College (NC), 619
Itasca Community College (MN), 473
Itawamba Community College (MS), 491
Ithaca College (NY), 577
ITI Technical College (LA), 395
Ivy Tech Community College
  Bloomington (IN), 344
  Central Indiana (IN), 344
  Columbus (IN), 345
  East Central (IN), 345
  Kokomo (IN), 345
  Lafayette (IN), 345
  North Central (IN), 345
  Northeast (IN), 346
  Northwest (IN), 346
  Richmond (IN), 346
  South Central (IN), 346
  Southeast (IN), 346
  Southwest (IN), 347
  Wabash Valley (IN), 347
J. Sargeant Reynolds Community College (VA), 843
Jackson Community College (MI), 454
Jackson State Community College (TN), 779
Jackson State University (MS), 491
Jacksonville College (TX), 801
Jacksonville State University (AL), 141
Jacksonville University (FL), 264
James A. Rhodes State College (OH), 654
James Madison University (VA), 844
James Sprunt Community College (NC), 620
Jamestown Business College (NY), 577
Jamestown College (ND), 637
Jamestown Community College (NY), 578
Jarvis Christian College (TX), 801
Jefferson College (MO), 500
Jefferson College of Health Sciences (VA), 844
Jefferson Community College *see* Eastern Gateway Community College (OH)
Jefferson Community College (NY), 578
Jefferson Davis Community College (AL), 141
Jefferson State Community College (AL), 141
Jewish Theological Seminary of America (NY), 578
JNA Institute of Culinary Arts (PA), 713
John A. Gupton College (TN), 779
John A. Logan College (IL), 315
John Brown University (AR), 164
John Carroll University (OH), 654
John Tyler Community College (VA), 844
John Wesley College *see* Laurel University (NC)
John Wood Community College (IL), 315
Johns Hopkins University (MD), 413
Johns Hopkins University Peabody Conservatory of Music (MD), 414
Johnson & Wales University
  Denver (CO), 233
  North Miami (FL), 265
  Providence (RI), 755
Johnson Bible College *see* Johnson University (TN)
Johnson C. Smith University (NC), 620
Johnson County Community College (KS), 374
Johnson State College (VT), 834
Johnson University (TN), 779
Johnston Community College (NC), 620
Joliet Junior College (IL), 316
Jones College (FL), 265
Jones International University (CO), 233
Jose Maria Vargas University (FL), 265
Judson College (AL), 142
Judson University (IL), 316
Juilliard School (NY), 578
Juniata College (PA), 713
Kalamazoo College (MI), 454
Kalamazoo Valley Community College (MI), 454
Kanawha Valley Community and Technical College (WV), 874
Kankakee Community College (IL), 316
Kansas City Art Institute (MO), 500
Kansas City Kansas Community College (KS), 374
Kansas State University (KS), 374
Kansas Wesleyan University (KS), 374
Kaplan Career Institute
  Harrisburg (PA), 713
  Pittsburgh (PA), 714
Kaplan College
  Columbus (OH), 654
  Dayton (OH), 654
  Indianapolis (IN), 347
  Las Vegas (NV), 527
  Merrillville (IN), 347
  Riverside (CA), 195
Kaplan University
  Cedar Falls (IA), 360
  Cedar Rapids (IA), 360
  Davenport (IA), 361
  Des Moines (IA), 361
  Hagerstown (MD), 414
  Lincoln (NE), 521
  Omaha (NE), 522
Kaskaskia College (IL), 316
Kean University (NJ), 541
Keene State College (NH), 532
Keiser University (FL), 265
Kellogg Community College (MI), 454
Kendall College (IL), 317
Kennebec Valley Community College (ME), 404
Kennesaw State University (GA), 287
Kent State University (OH), 655
Kent State University
  Ashtabula (OH), 655
  East Liverpool (OH), 655
  Geauga (OH), 655
  Salem (OH), 656
  Stark (OH), 656
  Trumbull (OH), 656
  Tuscarawas (OH), 656
Kentucky Christian University (KY), 385
Kentucky Mountain Bible College (KY), 385
Kentucky State University (KY), 385
Kentucky Wesleyan College (KY), 385
Kenyon College (OH), 657
Kettering College (OH), 657
Kettering College of Medical Arts *see* Kettering College (OH)
Kettering University (MI), 455
Keuka College (NY), 579
Key College (FL), 265
Keystone College (PA), 714
Keystone Technical Institute (PA), 714
Kilgore College (TX), 801
Kilian Community College (SD), 772
King College (TN), 780
King's College (PA), 714
Kirkwood Community College (IA), 361
Kirtland Community College (MI), 455
Kishwaukee College (IL), 317
Klamath Community College (OR), 689
Knox College (IL), 317
Kutztown University of Pennsylvania (PA), 715
Kuyper College (MI), 455
La Roche College (PA), 715
La Salle University (PA), 715
La Sierra University (CA), 196
Labette Community College (KS), 375
Laboratory Institute of Merchandising *see* LIM College (NY)
Laboure College (MA), 431
Lac Courte Oreilles Ojibwa Community College (WI), 885
Lackawanna College (PA), 716
Lafayette College (PA), 716
LaGrange College (GA), 287
Laguna College of Art and Design (CA), 196
Lake Area Technical Institute (SD), 772
Lake City Community College *see* Florida Gateway College (FL)
Lake Erie College (OH), 657
Lake Forest College (IL), 317
Lake Land College (IL), 318
Lake Michigan College (MI), 455
Lake Region State College (ND), 638
Lake Superior College (MN), 474
Lake Superior State University (MI), 456
Lake Tahoe Community College (CA), 196
Lake Washington Institute of Technology (WA), 863
Lake Washington Technical College *see* Lake Washington Institute of Technology (WA)
Lakeland College (WI), 885
Lakeland Community College (OH), 658
Lakes Region Community College (NH), 532
Lakeshore Technical College (WI), 885
Lake-Sumter Community College (FL), 266
Lakeview College of Nursing (IL), 318
Lamar Community College (CO), 233
Lamar State College at Orange (TX), 802
Lamar State College at Port Arthur (TX), 802
Lamar University (TX), 802

Lancaster Bible College (PA), 716
Lander University (SC), 763
Landing School of Boatbuilding and Design (ME), 404
Landmark College (VT), 835
Lane College (TN), 780
Lane Community College (OR), 689
Langston University (OK), 678
Lansing Community College (MI), 456
Laramie County Community College (WY), 899
Las Positas College (CA), 196
Las Vegas College *see* Everest College: Las Vegas (NV)
Lasell College (MA), 432
Lassen College *see* Lassen Community College (CA)
Lassen Community College (CA), 197
Laurel Business Institute (PA), 716
Laurel University (NC), 620
Lawrence Technological University (MI), 456
Lawrence University (WI), 885
Lawson State Community College (AL), 142
LDS Business College (UT), 829
Le Cordon Bleu College of Culinary Arts
Chicago (IL), 318
Los Angeles (CA), 197
Le Moyne College (NY), 579
Lebanon College (NH), 532
Lebanon Valley College (PA), 717
Lee College (TX), 802
Lee University (TN), 780
Leech Lake Tribal College (MN), 474
Lees-McRae College (NC), 621
Lehigh Carbon Community College (PA), 717
Lehigh University (PA), 717
LeMoyne-Owen College (TN), 780
Lenoir Community College (NC), 621
Lenoir-Rhyne University (NC), 621
Lesley University (MA), 432
LeTourneau University (TX), 802
Lewis & Clark College (OR), 689
Lewis and Clark Community College (IL), 318
Lewis University (IL), 319
Lewis-Clark State College (ID), 301
Lexington College (IL), 319
Liberty University (VA), 844
Life Pacific College (CA), 197
LIFE Pacific College *see* Life Pacific College (CA)
Life University (GA), 288
LIM College (NY), 580
Limestone College (SC), 764
Lincoln Christian College and Seminary *see* Lincoln Christian University (IL)
Lincoln Christian University (IL), 319
Lincoln College (IL), 319
Lincoln College of New England (CT), 242
Lincoln College of Technology
Dayton (OH), 658
Florence (KY), 386
Tri-County (OH), 658
Lincoln Land Community College (IL), 320
Lincoln Memorial University (TN), 781
Lincoln University (CA), 197
Lincoln University (MO), 500
Lincoln University (PA), 718
Lindenwood University (MO), 501
Lindsey Wilson College (KY), 386
Linfield College (OR), 690
Linn State Technical College (MO), 501
Linn-Benton Community College (OR), 690
Lipscomb University (TN), 781
Little Big Horn College (MT), 515
Little Priest Tribal College (NE), 522
Livingstone College (NC), 621
Lock Haven University of Pennsylvania (PA), 718
Loma Linda University (CA), 198
Lone Star College System (TX), 803
Long Beach City College (CA), 198
Long Island Business Institute (NY), 580
Long Island University
Brooklyn Campus (NY), 580
C. W. Post Campus (NY), 580
Longwood University (VA), 845
Lorain County Community College (OH), 658
Loras College (IA), 361
Lord Fairfax Community College (VA), 845
Los Angeles City College (CA), 198
Los Angeles Harbor College (CA), 198
Los Angeles Mission College (CA), 198
Los Angeles Pierce College (CA), 199
Los Angeles Southwest College (CA), 199
Los Angeles Trade and Technical College (CA), 199
Los Angeles Valley College (CA), 199
Los Medanos College (CA), 199
Louisburg College (NC), 622
Louisiana College (LA), 396
Louisiana State University and Agricultural and Mechanical College (LA), 396
Louisiana State University at Alexandria (LA), 396
Louisiana State University at Eunice (LA), 396
Louisiana State University Health Sciences Center (LA), 396
Louisiana State University in Shreveport (LA), 397
Louisiana Tech University (LA), 397
Louisville Technical Institute *see* Sullivan College of Technology and Design (KY)
Lourdes College *see* Lourdes University (OH)
Lourdes University (OH), 658
Lower Columbia College (WA), 864
Loyola College in Maryland *see* Loyola University Maryland (MD)
Loyola Marymount University (CA), 200
Loyola University Chicago (IL), 320
Loyola University Maryland (MD), 414
Loyola University New Orleans (LA), 397
Loyola University of Chicago *see* Loyola University Chicago (IL)
Lubbock Christian University (TX), 803
Luna Community College (NM), 550
Lurleen B. Wallace Community College (AL), 142
Luther College (IA), 362
Luther Rice University (GA), 288
Luzerne County Community College (PA), 718
Lycoming College (PA), 718
Lyme Academy College of Fine Arts (CT), 243
Lynchburg College (VA), 845
Lyndon State College (VT), 835
Lynn University (FL), 266
Lyon College (AR), 164
Macalester College (MN), 474
MacMurray College (IL), 320
Macomb Community College (MI), 457
Madisonville Community College (KY), 386
Madonna University (MI), 457
Magdalen College *see* College of St. Mary Magdalen (NH)
Maharishi University of Management (IA), 362
Maine College of Art (ME), 404
Maine Maritime Academy (ME), 405
Malone University (OH), 659
Manatee Community College *see* State College of Florida, Manatee-Sarasota (FL)
Manchester Community College (CT), 243
Manchester Community College (NH), 532
Manchester University (IN), 347
Manhattan Area Technical College (KS), 375
Manhattan Christian College (KS), 375
Manhattan College (NY), 580
Manhattan School of Music (NY), 581
Manhattanville College (NY), 581
Mannes College The New School for Music (NY), 581
Manor College (PA), 719
Mansfield University of Pennsylvania (PA), 719
Maranatha Baptist Bible College (WI), 886
Maria College (NY), 582
Marian College *see* Marian University (IN)
Marian College of Fond du Lac *see* Marian University (WI)
Marian Court College (MA), 432
Marian University (IN), 348
Marian University (WI), 886
Marietta College (OH), 659
Marion Military Institute (AL), 142
Marion Technical College (OH), 659
Marist College (NY), 582
Marlboro College (VT), 835
Marquette University (WI), 886
Mars Hill College (NC), 622
Marshall University (WV), 875
Martin Community College (NC), 622
Martin Luther College (MN), 474
Martin Methodist College (TN), 781
Mary Baldwin College (VA), 845
Marygrove College (MI), 457
Maryland Institute College of Art (MD), 415
Marylhurst University (OR), 690
Marymount California University (CA), 200
Marymount College Palos Verdes California *see* Marymount California University (CA)
Marymount Manhattan College (NY), 582
Marymount University (VA), 846
Maryville College (TN), 782
Maryville University of Saint Louis (MO), 501
Marywood University (PA), 719
Massachusetts Bay Community College (MA), 433
Massachusetts College of Art and Design (MA), 433
Massachusetts College of Liberal Arts (MA), 433
Massachusetts College of Pharmacy and Health Sciences (MA), 433
Massachusetts Institute of Technology (MA), 434
Massachusetts Maritime Academy (MA), 434
Massasoit Community College (MA), 434
Mayland Community College (NC), 622
Maysville Community and Technical College (KY), 386
Mayville State University (ND), 638
McDaniel College (MD), 415
McDowell Technical Community College (NC), 622
McHenry County College (IL), 320
McKendree University (IL), 321
McLennan Community College (TX), 803
McMurry University (TX), 803
McNeese State University (LA), 397
McPherson College (KS), 375
Medaille College (NY), 582
Medaille College Amherst (NY), 583
Medcenter One College of Nursing *see* Sanford College of Nursing (ND)
Medical University of South Carolina (SC), 764
Memphis College of Art (TN), 782
Mendocino College (CA), 201
Menlo College (CA), 201
Mercer County Community College (NJ), 541
Mercer University (GA), 288
Mercy College (NY), 583
Mercy College of Health Sciences (IA), 362
Mercy College of Ohio (OH), 660
Mercyhurst College *see* Mercyhurst University (PA)
Mercyhurst University (PA), 719
Meredith College (NC), 623
Meridian Community College (MS), 491
Merrimack College (MA), 434
Merritt College (CA), 201
Mesa Community College (AZ), 155
Mesa State College *see* Colorado Mesa University (CO)
Mesabi Range Community and Technical College (MN), 475
Mesalands Community College (NM), 550
Messiah College (PA), 720
Methodist University (NC), 623
Metro Business College Jefferson City (MO), 502
Metropolitan Career Center Computer Technology Institute (PA), 720
Metropolitan College of New York (NY), 583
Metropolitan Community College (NE), 522
Metropolitan Community College - Kansas City (MO), 502
Metropolitan State College of Denver *see* Metropolitan State University of Denver (CO)
Metropolitan State University (MN), 475
Metropolitan State University of Denver (CO), 234
Miami Dade College (FL), 266
Miami University
Hamilton (OH), 660
Middletown (OH), 660
Oxford (OH), 660
Miami-Jacobs Career College
Columbus (OH), 661
Dayton (OH), 661
Michigan State University (MI), 457
Michigan Technological University (MI), 458
Mid Michigan Community College (MI), 458
Mid-America Christian University (OK), 678
MidAmerica Nazarene University (KS), 376
Mid-Atlantic Christian University (NC), 623
Mid-Continent University (KY), 387
Middle Georgia State College (GA), 288
Middle Tennessee State University (TN), 782

Middlebury College (VT), 835
Middlesex Community College (CT), 243
Middlesex Community College (MA), 435
Middlesex County College (NJ), 542
Midland College (TX), 804
Midlands Technical College (SC), 764
Mid-Plains Community College (NE), 522
Mid-South Community College (AR), 164
Midstate College (IL), 321
Mid-State Technical College (WI), 887
Midway College (KY), 387
Midwestern State University (TX), 804
Mildred Elley (NY), 583
Miles College (AL), 143
Miles Community College (MT), 515
Miller-Motte College Wilmington (NC), 624
Miller-Motte Technical College Clarksville (TN), 782
Millersville University of Pennsylvania (PA), 720
Milligan College (TN), 783
Millikin University (IL), 321
Mills College (CA), 201
Millsaps College (MS), 491
Milwaukee Area Technical College (WI), 887
Milwaukee Institute of Art & Design (WI), 887
Milwaukee School of Engineering (WI), 887
Mineral Area College (MO), 502
Minneapolis Business College (MN), 475
Minneapolis College of Art and Design (MN), 475
Minneapolis Community and Technical College (MN), 476
Minnesota School of Business
  Blaine (MN), 476
  Brooklyn Center (MN), 476
  Elk River (MN), 476
  Lakeville (MN), 476
  Moorhead (MN), 477
  Plymouth (MN), 477
  Richfield (MN), 477
  Rochester (MN), 477
  Shakopee (MN), 478
  St. Cloud (MN), 477
Minnesota State College - Southeast Technical (MN), 478
Minnesota State Community and Technical College (MN), 478
Minnesota State University Mankato (MN), 478
Minnesota State University Moorhead (MN), 479
Minnesota West Community and Technical College (MN), 479
Minot State University (ND), 638
Minot State University: Bottineau Campus ***see*** Dakota College at Bottineau (ND)
MiraCosta College (CA), 202
Misericordia University (PA), 721
Mississippi College (MS), 492
Mississippi Delta Community College (MS), 492
Mississippi Gulf Coast Community College (MS), 492
Mississippi State University (MS), 492
Mississippi University for Women (MS), 493
Missouri Baptist University (MO), 502
Missouri Southern State University (MO), 503
Missouri State University (MO), 503
Missouri State University West Plains (MO), 503
Missouri University of Science and Technology (MO), 503
Missouri Valley College (MO), 504
Missouri Western State University (MO), 504
Mitchell College (CT), 243
Mitchell Community College (NC), 624
Mitchell Technical Institute (SD), 772
Moberly Area Community College (MO), 504
Modesto Junior College (CA), 202
Mohave Community College (AZ), 156
Mohawk Valley Community College (NY), 584
Molloy College (NY), 584
Monmouth College (IL), 321
Monmouth University (NJ), 542
Monroe College (NY), 584
Monroe Community College (NY), 584
Monroe County Community College (MI), 458
Montana State University (MT), 515
Montana State University
  Billings (MT), 516
  Northern (MT), 516
Montana State University: Great Falls College of Technology ***see*** Great Falls College Montana State University (MT)
Montana Tech of the University of Montana (MT), 516
Montcalm Community College (MI), 458
Montclair State University (NJ), 542
Monterey Peninsula College (CA), 202
Montgomery College (MD), 415
Montgomery Community College (NC), 624
Montgomery County Community College (PA), 721
Montreat College (NC), 624
Montserrat College of Art (MA), 435
Moody Bible Institute (IL), 322
Moore College of Art and Design (PA), 721
Moraine Park Technical College (WI), 888
Moraine Valley Community College (IL), 322
Moravian College (PA), 721
Morehead State University (KY), 387
Morehouse College (GA), 289
Morgan Community College (CO), 234
Morgan State University (MD), 415
Morningside College (IA), 362
Morris College (SC), 764
Morrison Institute of Technology (IL), 322
Morrison University (NV), 527
Morton College (IL), 322
Motlow State Community College (TN), 783
Mott Community College (MI), 459
Mount Aloysius College (PA), 722
Mount Carmel College of Nursing (OH), 661
Mount Holyoke College (MA), 435
Mount Ida College (MA), 435
Mount Marty College (SD), 772
Mount Mary College (WI), 888
Mount Mercy College ***see*** Mount Mercy University (IA)
Mount Mercy University (IA), 363
Mount Olive College (NC), 624
Mount Saint Mary College (NY), 585
Mount San Antonio College (CA), 203
Mount San Jacinto College (CA), 203
Mount St. Mary's College (CA), 202
Mount St. Mary's University (MD), 415
Mount Union College ***see*** University of Mount Union (OH)
Mount Vernon Nazarene University (OH), 661
Mount Wachusett Community College (MA), 436
Mountain Empire Community College (VA), 846
Mountain State College (WV), 875
Mountain View College (TX), 804
Mt. Hood Community College (OR), 691
Mt. Sierra College (CA), 203
MTI College (CA), 203
Muhlenberg College (PA), 722
Multnomah University (OR), 691
Murray State University (KY), 387
Muskegon Community College (MI), 459
Muskingum College ***see*** Muskingum University (OH)
Muskingum University (OH), 662
Naropa University (CO), 234
Nash Community College (NC), 625
Nashua Community College (NH), 533
Nashville Auto-Diesel College (TN), 783
Nashville State Community College (TN), 783
Nassau Community College (NY), 585
National American University
  Kansas City (MO), 505
  Rapid City (SD), 773
National College
  Charlottesville (VA), 846
  Danville (KY), 388
  Danville (VA), 846
  Florence (KY), 388
  Harrisonburg (VA), 847
  Lexington (KY), 388
  Louisville (KY), 388
  Lynchburg (VA), 847
  Martinsville (VA), 847
  Pikeville (KY), 388
  Princeton (WV), 875
  Richmond (KY), 389
  Salem (VA), 847
National College of Business and Technology
  Bristol (TN), 784
  Nashville (TN), 784
National College of Business and Technology: Arecibo ***see*** National University College: Arecibo (PR)
National College of Business and Technology: Bayamon ***see*** National University College: Bayamon (PR)
National College of Business and Technology: Rio Grande ***see*** National University College: Rio Grande (PR)
National Park Community College (AR), 164
National University (CA), 203
National University College
  Arecibo (PR), 748
  Bayamon (PR), 749
  Ponce (PR), 749
  Rio Grande (PR), 749
National University of Health Sciences (IL), 323
Naugatuck Valley Community College (CT), 243
Navajo Technical College (NM), 551
Navarro College (TX), 805
Nazarene Bible College (CO), 234
Nazareth College (NY), 585
Nebraska Christian College (NE), 523
Nebraska College of Technical Agriculture (NE), 523
Nebraska Indian Community College (NE), 523
Nebraska Methodist College of Nursing and Allied Health (NE), 523
Nebraska Wesleyan University (NE), 524
Neosho County Community College (KS), 376
Neumann College ***see*** Neumann University (PA)
Neumann University (PA), 722
Neumont University (UT), 830
Nevada State College (NV), 528
New College of Florida (FL), 266
New England College (NH), 533
New England Conservatory of Music (MA), 436
New England Culinary Institute (VT), 836
New England Institute of Art (MA), 436
New England Institute of Technology (RI), 755
New England School of Communications (ME), 405
New Hampshire Community Technical College: Berlin ***see*** White Mountains Community College (NH)
New Hampshire Community Technical College: Claremont ***see*** River Valley Community College (NH)
New Hampshire Community Technical College: Laconia ***see*** Lakes Region Community College (NH)
New Hampshire Community Technical College: Manchester ***see*** Manchester Community College (NH)
New Hampshire Community Technical College: Nashua ***see*** Nashua Community College (NH)
New Hampshire Community Technical College: Stratham ***see*** Great Bay Community College (NH)
New Hampshire Technical Institute ***see*** NHTI-Concord's Community College (NH)
New Hope Christian College (OR), 691
New Jersey City University (NJ), 542
New Jersey Institute of Technology (NJ), 543
New Mexico Highlands University (NM), 551
New Mexico Institute of Mining and Technology (NM), 551
New Mexico Junior College (NM), 551
New Mexico Military Institute (NM), 552
New Mexico State University (NM), 552
New Mexico State University at Alamogordo (NM), 552
New Mexico State University at Carlsbad (NM), 552
New Mexico State University at Grants (NM), 553
New River Community College (VA), 847
New Saint Andrews College (ID), 302
New York Career Institute (NY), 586
New York Institute of Technology (NY), 586
New York School of Interior Design (NY), 586
New York University (NY), 586
Newberry College (SC), 765
Newbury College (MA), 436
Newman University (KS), 376
Newport Business Institute Lower Burrell (PA), 722
NHTI-Concord's Community College (NH), 533
Niagara County Community College (NY), 586
Niagara University (NY), 587
Nicholls State University (LA), 398
Nichols College (MA), 436
Nicolet Area Technical College (WI), 888
Norfolk State University (VA), 848
Normandale Community College (MN), 479
North Arkansas College (AR), 165
North Carolina Agricultural and Technical State University (NC), 625
North Carolina Central University (NC), 625
North Carolina School of the Arts ***see*** University of North Carolina School of the Arts (NC)
North Carolina State University (NC), 625

North Carolina Wesleyan College (NC), 626
North Central College (IL), 323
North Central Kansas Technical College (KS), 376
North Central Michigan College (MI), 459
North Central Missouri College (MO), 505
North Central State College (OH), 662
North Central Texas College (TX), 805
North Central University (MN), 479
North Country Community College (NY), 587
North Dakota State College of Science (ND), 639
North Dakota State University (ND), 639
North Florida Community College (FL), 267
North Georgia Technical College (GA), 289
North Greenville University (SC), 765
North Harris Montgomery Community College ***see*** Lone Star College System (TX)
North Hennepin Community College (MN), 480
North Idaho College (ID), 302
North Iowa Area Community College (IA), 363
North Lake College (TX), 805
North Park University (IL), 323
North Seattle Community College (WA), 864
North Shore Community College (MA), 437
Northampton Community College (PA), 723
Northcentral Technical College (WI), 888
Northcentral University (AZ), 156
Northeast Alabama Community College (AL), 143
Northeast Community College (NE), 524
Northeast Iowa Community College (IA), 363
Northeast State Community College (TN), 784
Northeast State Technical Community College ***see*** Northeast State Community College (TN)
Northeast Texas Community College (TX), 805
Northeast Wisconsin Technical College (WI), 888
Northeastern Illinois University (IL), 323
Northeastern Junior College (CO), 235
Northeastern Oklahoma Agricultural and Mechanical College (OK), 678
Northeastern State University (OK), 678
Northeastern University (MA), 437
Northern Arizona University (AZ), 156
Northern Essex Community College (MA), 437
Northern Illinois University (IL), 324
Northern Kentucky University (KY), 389
Northern Maine Community College (ME), 405
Northern Michigan University (MI), 459
Northern New Mexico College (NM), 553
Northern Oklahoma College (OK), 679
Northern State University (SD), 773
Northland Baptist Bible College ***see*** Northland International University (WI)
Northland College (WI), 889
Northland Community & Technical College (MN), 480
Northland International University (WI), 889
Northland Pioneer College (AZ), 156
Northpoint Bible College (MA), 437
Northwest Arkansas Community College (AR), 165
Northwest Christian University (OR), 691
Northwest College (WY), 900
Northwest College of Art & Design (WA), 864
Northwest Florida State College (FL), 267
Northwest Indian College (WA), 864
Northwest Iowa Community College (IA), 363
Northwest Missouri State University (MO), 505
Northwest Nazarene University (ID), 302
Northwest State Community College (OH), 662
Northwest Technical College (MN), 480
Northwest University (WA), 864
Northwest Vista College (TX), 805
Northwestern Business College ***see*** Northwestern College (IL)
Northwestern College (IA), 364
Northwestern College (IL), 324
Northwestern College (MN), 480
Northwestern Michigan College (MI), 460
Northwestern Oklahoma State University (OK), 679
Northwestern State University (LA), 398
Northwestern University (IL), 324
Northwest-Shoals Community College (AL), 143
Northwood University
  Florida (FL), 267
  Michigan (MI), 460
  Texas (TX), 806
Norwalk Community College (CT), 244
Norwich University (VT), 836
Nossi College of Art (TN), 784
Notre Dame College (OH), 662
Notre Dame de Namur University (CA), 204
Notre Dame of Maryland University (MD), 416
Nova Southeastern University (FL), 267
Nunez Community College (LA), 398
Nyack College (NY), 587
O'More College of Design (TN), 784
Oak Hills Christian College (MN), 481
Oakbridge Academy of Arts (PA), 723
Oakland City University (IN), 348
Oakland Community College (MI), 460
Oakland University (MI), 461
Oakton Community College (IL), 325
Oakwood University (AL), 143
Oberlin College (OH), 662
Occidental College (CA), 204
Ocean County College (NJ), 543
Odessa College (TX), 806
Oglethorpe University (GA), 289
Ohio Business College
  Sandusky (OH), 663
  Sheffield (OH), 663
Ohio Christian University (OH), 663
Ohio Dominican University (OH), 663
Ohio Institute of Photography and Technology ***see*** Kaplan College: Dayton (OH)
Ohio Northern University (OH), 664
Ohio State University
  Columbus Campus (OH), 664
  Lima Campus (OH), 664
  Mansfield Campus (OH), 665
  Marion Campus (OH), 665
  Newark Campus (OH), 665
Ohio State University Agricultural Technical Institute (OH), 664
Ohio University (OH), 666
Ohio University
  Chillicothe Campus (OH), 666
  Eastern Campus (OH), 666
  Lancaster Campus (OH), 666
  Southern Campus at Ironton (OH), 666
Ohio Valley College of Technology (OH), 667
Ohio Valley University (WV), 875
Ohio Wesleyan University (OH), 667
Ohlone College (CA), 204
Oklahoma Baptist University (OK), 679
Oklahoma Christian University (OK), 680
Oklahoma City Community College (OK), 680
Oklahoma City University (OK), 680
Oklahoma Panhandle State University (OK), 680
Oklahoma State University (OK), 681
Oklahoma State University Oklahoma City (OK), 681
Oklahoma State University Institute of Technology Okmulgee (OK), 681
Oklahoma Wesleyan University (OK), 681
Old Dominion University (VA), 848
Olivet College (MI), 461
Olivet Nazarene University (IL), 325
Olympic College (WA), 865
Onondaga Community College (NY), 588
Oral Roberts University (OK), 682
Orange Coast College (CA), 205
Orange County Community College (NY), 588
Orangeburg-Calhoun Technical College (SC), 765
Oregon College of Art & Craft (OR), 692
Oregon Health & Science University (OR), 692
Oregon Institute of Technology (OR), 692
Oregon State University (OR), 692
Otero Junior College (CO), 235
Otis College of Art and Design (CA), 205
Ottawa University (KS), 377
Otterbein College ***see*** Otterbein University (OH)
Otterbein University (OH), 667
Ouachita Baptist University (AR), 165
Ouachita Technical College ***see*** College of the Ouachitas (AR)
Our Lady of Holy Cross College (LA), 398
Our Lady of the Lake College (LA), 399
Our Lady of the Lake University of San Antonio (TX), 806
Owens Community College Toledo (OH), 667
Owensboro Community and Technical College (KY), 389
Oxford College of Emory University (GA), 289
Oxnard College (CA), 205
Ozark Christian College (MO), 505
Ozarka College (AR), 165
Ozarks Technical Community College (MO), 506
Pace University (NY), 588
Pacific Lutheran University (WA), 865
Pacific Northwest College of Art (OR), 692
Pacific Oaks College (CA), 205
Pacific States University (CA), 205
Pacific Union College (CA), 206
Pacific University (OR), 693
Paier College of Art (CT), 244
Paine College (GA), 289
Palm Beach Atlantic University (FL), 267
Palm Beach Community College ***see*** Palm Beach State College (FL)
Palm Beach State College (FL), 268
Palo Alto College (TX), 806
Palo Verde College (CA), 206
Palomar College (CA), 206
Panola College (TX), 807
Paradise Valley Community College (AZ), 157
Paris Junior College (TX), 807
Park University (MO), 506
Parkland College (IL), 325
Parks College: Aurora ***see*** Everest College: Aurora (CO)
Parsons The New School for Design (NY), 588
Pasco-Hernando Community College (FL), 268
Passaic County Community College (NJ), 543
Patricia Stevens College ***see*** Stevens Institute of Business & Arts (MO)
Patrick Henry College (VA), 848
Patrick Henry Community College (VA), 848
Patten University (CA), 206
Paul D. Camp Community College (VA), 848
Paul Smith's College (NY), 588
Peace College ***see*** William Peace University (NC)
Pearl River Community College (MS), 493
Peirce College (PA), 723
Pellissippi State Community College (TN), 785
Peninsula College (WA), 865
Penn Commercial Business and Technical School (PA), 723
Penn State Abington (PA), 724
Penn State Altoona (PA), 724
Penn State Beaver (PA), 724
Penn State Berks (PA), 724
Penn State Brandywine (PA), 725
Penn State DuBois (PA), 725
Penn State Erie, The Behrend College (PA), 725
Penn State Fayette, The Eberly Campus (PA), 726
Penn State Greater Allegheny (PA), 726
Penn State Harrisburg (PA), 726
Penn State Hazleton (PA), 726
Penn State Lehigh Valley (PA), 727
Penn State McKeesport ***see*** Penn State Greater Allegheny (PA)
Penn State Mont Alto (PA), 727
Penn State New Kensington (PA), 727
Penn State Schuylkill (PA), 727
Penn State Shenango (PA), 728
Penn State University Park (PA), 728
Penn State Wilkes-Barre (PA), 728
Penn State Worthington Scranton (PA), 729
Penn State York (PA), 729
Pennsylvania Academy of the Fine Arts (PA), 729
Pennsylvania College of Art and Design (PA), 729
Pennsylvania College of Technology (PA), 729
Pennsylvania Highlands Community College (PA), 730
Pennsylvania Institute of Technology (PA), 730
Pennsylvania School of Business (PA), 730
Pensacola Junior College ***see*** Pensacola State College (FL)
Pensacola State College (FL), 268
Pepperdine University (CA), 207
Peru State College (NE), 524
Pfeiffer University (NC), 626
Philadelphia Biblical University ***see*** Cairn University (PA)
Philadelphia University (PA), 730
Philander Smith College (AR), 166
Phillips Beth Israel School of Nursing (NY), 589
Phillips Community College of the University of Arkansas (AR), 166
Phoenix College (AZ), 157
Piedmont Baptist College ***see*** Piedmont International University (NC)

Piedmont College (GA), 290
Piedmont International University (NC), 626
Piedmont Technical College (SC), 765
Piedmont Virginia Community College (VA), 849
Pierce College (WA), 865
Pikes Peak Community College (CO), 235
Pikeville College *see* University of Pikeville (KY)
Pima Community College (AZ), 157
Pine Manor College (MA), 438
Pine Technical College (MN), 481
Pioneer Pacific College (OR), 693
Pitt Community College (NC), 627
Pittsburg State University (KS), 377
Pittsburgh Institute of Aeronautics (PA), 731
Pittsburgh Institute of Mortuary Science (PA), 731
Pitzer College (CA), 207
Platt College
    Aurora (CO), 235
    Los Angeles (CA), 207
    Oklahoma City Central (OK), 682
    Ontario (CA), 207
    San Diego (CA), 208
    Tulsa (OK), 682
Plymouth State University (NH), 533
Point Loma Nazarene University (CA), 208
Point Park University (PA), 731
Point University (GA), 290
Polk Community College *see* Polk State College (FL)
Polk State College (FL), 268
Polytechnic Institute of New York University (NY), 589
Pomona College (CA), 208
Pontifical Catholic University of Puerto Rico (PR), 749
Pontifical College Josephinum (OH), 668
Portland Community College (OR), 693
Portland State University (OR), 693
Post University (CT), 244
Potomac College (DC), 253
Potomac College (VA), 849
Potomac State College of West Virginia University (WV), 876
Prairie State College (IL), 325
Prairie View A&M University (TX), 807
Pratt Community College (KS), 377
Pratt Institute (NY), 589
Presbyterian College (SC), 766
Prescott College (AZ), 157
Prince George's Community College (MD), 416
Prince Institute of Professional Studies (AL), 143
Prince William Sound Community College (AK), 150
Princeton University (NJ), 543
Principia College (IL), 326
Professional Golfers Career College (CA), 208
Providence College (RI), 755
Pueblo Community College (CO), 235
Pulaski Technical College (AR), 166
Purdue University (IN), 348
Purdue University Calumet (IN), 349
Purdue University North Central (IN), 349
Queens University of Charlotte (NC), 627
Quincy University (IL), 326
Quinebaug Valley Community College (CT), 244
Quinnipiac University (CT), 245
Quinsigamond Community College (MA), 438
Radford University (VA), 849
Rainy River Community College (MN), 481
Ramapo College of New Jersey (NJ), 544
Randolph College (VA), 849
Randolph Community College (NC), 627
Randolph-Macon College (VA), 850
Randolph-Macon Woman's College *see* Randolph College (VA)
Ranger College (TX), 807
Ranken Technical College (MO), 506
Rappahannock Community College (VA), 850
Raritan Valley Community College (NJ), 544
Rasmussen College
    Appleton (WI), 889
    Aurora (IL), 326
    Bismarck (ND), 639
    Blaine (MN), 481
    Bloomington (MN), 481
    Brooklyn Park (MN), 482
    Eagan (MN), 482
    Fargo (ND), 639
    Fort Myers (FL), 269
    Green Bay (WI), 889
    Lake Elmo/Woodbury (MN), 482
    Mankato (MN), 482
    Mokena/Tinley Park (IL), 327
    Moorhead (MN), 483
    New Port Richey (FL), 269
    Ocala (FL), 269
    Rockford (IL), 327
    Romeoville/Joliet (IL), 327
    St. Cloud (MN), 483
    Tampa/Brandon (FL), 269
    Wausau (WI), 890
Red Rocks Community College (CO), 236
Redlands Community College (OK), 682
Redstone College (CO), 236
Reed College (OR), 694
Reedley College (CA), 208
Regent University (VA), 850
Regions University *see* Amridge University (AL)
Regis College (MA), 438
Regis University (CO), 236
Reinhardt College *see* Reinhardt University (GA)
Reinhardt University (GA), 290
Remington College
    Baton Rouge (LA), 399
    Colorado Springs (CO), 236
    Houston (TX), 808
    Lafayette (LA), 399
    Memphis (TN), 785
    Mobile (AL), 144
Rend Lake College (IL), 327
Rensselaer Polytechnic Institute (NY), 590
Renton Technical College (WA), 866
Research College of Nursing (MO), 506
Restaurant School at Walnut Hill College (PA), 731
Resurrection University (IL), 327
RETS College *see* Fortis College: Centerville (OH)
Rhode Island College (RI), 755
Rhode Island School of Design (RI), 756
Rhodes College (TN), 785
Rice University (TX), 808
Rich Mountain Community College (AR), 166
Richard Bland College (VA), 850
Richard Stockton College of New Jersey (NJ), 544
Richland College (TX), 808
Richland Community College (IL), 328
Richmond Community College (NC), 627
Rider University (NJ), 544
Ridgewater College (MN), 483
Ringling College of Art and Design (FL), 270
Rio Hondo College (CA), 209
Rio Salado College (AZ), 158
Ripon College (WI), 890
River Valley Community College (NH), 534
Riverland Community College (MN), 483
Riverside Community College (CA), 209
Rivier University (NH), 534
Roane State Community College (TN), 785
Roanoke Bible College *see* Mid-Atlantic Christian University (NC)
Roanoke College (VA), 851
Roanoke-Chowan Community College (NC), 627
Robert B. Miller College (MI), 461
Robert Morris College: Chicago *see* Robert Morris University: Chicago (IL)
Robert Morris University (PA), 731
Robert Morris University Chicago (IL), 328
Roberts Wesleyan College (NY), 590
Robeson Community College (NC), 628
Rochester College (MI), 461
Rochester Community and Technical College (MN), 483
Rochester Institute of Technology (NY), 590
Rock Valley College (IL), 328
Rockford Business College *see* Rockford Career College (IL)
Rockford Career College (IL), 328
Rockford College (IL), 329
Rockhurst University (MO), 507
Rockland Community College (NY), 591
Rocky Mountain College (MT), 516
Rocky Mountain College of Art & Design (CO), 237
Roger Williams University (RI), 756
Rogers State University (OK), 683
Rogue Community College (OR), 694
Rollins College (FL), 270
Roosevelt University (IL), 329
Rose State College (OK), 683
Rosedale Bible College (OH), 668
Rosedale Technical Institute (PA), 732
Rose-Hulman Institute of Technology (IN), 349
Roseman University of Health Sciences (NV), 528
Rosemont College (PA), 732
Rowan University (NJ), 545
Rowan-Cabarrus Community College (NC), 628
Roxbury Community College (MA), 438
Rush University (IL), 329
Rust College (MS), 493
Rutgers, The State University of New Jersey
    New Brunswick/Piscataway Campus (NJ), 545
    Newark Campus (NJ), 545
Sacramento City College (CA), 209
Sacred Heart Major Seminary (MI), 461
Sacred Heart University (CT), 245
Saddleback College (CA), 209
Saginaw Valley State University (MI), 462
Saint Anselm College (NH), 534
Saint Bonaventure University (NY), 591
Saint Cloud State University (MN), 484
Saint Johns River State College (FL), 270
Saint Joseph College *see* University of Saint Joseph (CT)
Saint Joseph's College (IN), 349
Saint Joseph's College of Maine (ME), 405
Saint Joseph's University (PA), 733
Saint Leo University (FL), 270
Saint Louis University (MO), 507
Saint Martin's University (WA), 866
Saint Mary's College (IN), 350
Saint Michael's College (VT), 836
Saint Peter's University (NJ), 546
Saint Xavier University (IL), 330
Salem College (NC), 629
Salem Community College (NJ), 546
Salem International University (WV), 876
Salem State University (MA), 439
Salisbury University (MD), 417
Salish Kootenai College (MT), 517
Salt Lake Community College (UT), 830
Salve Regina University (RI), 756
Sam Houston State University (TX), 809
Samford University (AL), 144
Sampson Community College (NC), 629
Samuel Merritt University (CA), 210
Samuel Stephen College *see* Daymar College: Chillicothe (OH)
San Antonio College (TX), 809
San Diego Christian College (CA), 210
San Diego City College (CA), 211
San Diego Miramar College (CA), 211
San Diego State University (CA), 211
San Francisco Art Institute (CA), 211
San Francisco Conservatory of Music (CA), 212
San Francisco State University (CA), 212
San Jacinto College (TX), 810
San Joaquin Delta College (CA), 212
San Joaquin Valley College (CA), 212
San Jose City College (CA), 213
San Jose State University (CA), 213
San Juan College (NM), 553
Sandhills Community College (NC), 629
Sanford College of Nursing (ND), 640
Sanford-Brown Institute Monroeville (PA), 733
Santa Barbara City College (CA), 213
Santa Clara University (CA), 213
Santa Fe College (FL), 271
Santa Fe Community College *see* Santa Fe College (FL)
Santa Fe Community College (NM), 554
Santa Fe University of Art and Design (NM), 554

Santa Monica College (CA), 214
Santa Rosa Junior College (CA), 214
Santiago Canyon College (CA), 214
Sarah Lawrence College (NY), 594
Sauk Valley Community College (IL), 330
Savannah College of Art and Design (GA), 291
Savannah Technical College (GA), 291
Schenectady County Community College (NY), 594
Schiller International University (FL), 271
School of Advertising Art (OH), 668
School of the Art Institute of Chicago (IL), 330
School of the Museum of Fine Arts (MA), 439
School of Urban Missions Oakland (CA), 214
School of Visual Arts (NY), 594
Schoolcraft College (MI), 462
Schreiner University (TX), 810
Scottsdale Community College (AZ), 158
Scripps College (CA), 214
Seattle Central Community College (WA), 866
Seattle Pacific University (WA), 866
Selma University (AL), 144
Seminole Community College *see* Seminole State College of Florida (FL)
Seminole State College (OK), 684
Seminole State College of Florida (FL), 271
Seton Hall University (NJ), 546
Seton Hill University (PA), 733
Sewanee The University of the South (TN), 785
Seward County Community College (KS), 377
Shasta Bible College and Graduate School (CA), 215
Shasta College (CA), 215
Shaw University (NC), 629
Shawnee Community College (IL), 330
Shawnee State University (OH), 668
Shelton State Community College (AL), 144
Shenandoah University (VA), 851
Shepherd University (WV), 876
Sheridan College (WY), 900
Shimer College (IL), 331
Shippensburg University of Pennsylvania (PA), 734
Shoreline Community College (WA), 867
Shorter College Rome *see* Shorter University (GA)
Shorter University (GA), 291
Siena College (NY), 595
Siena Heights University (MI), 463
Sierra College (CA), 215
Sierra Nevada College (NV), 528
Silver Lake College of the Holy Family (WI), 891
Simmons College (MA), 439
Simpson College (IA), 364
Simpson University (CA), 215
Sinclair Community College (OH), 668
Sisseton Wahpeton College (SD), 773
Sitting Bull College (ND), 640
Skagit Valley College (WA), 867
Skidmore College (NY), 595
Skyline College (CA), 216
Skyline College Roanoke (VA), 852
Slippery Rock University of Pennsylvania (PA), 734
Smith College (MA), 439
Snead State Community College (AL), 145
Snow College (UT), 830
Sojourner-Douglass College (MD), 417
Soka University of America (CA), 216
Somerset Christian College (NJ), 546
Somerset Community College (KY), 389
Sonoma State University (CA), 216
South Arkansas Community College (AR), 167
South Carolina State University (SC), 766
South Central College (MN), 486
South College (NC), 630
South Dakota School of Mines and Technology (SD), 773
South Dakota State University (SD), 774
South Florida Community College (FL), 272
South Georgia State College (GA), 291
South Louisiana Community College (LA), 399
South Mountain Community College (AZ), 158
South Piedmont Community College (NC), 630
South Plains College (TX), 810
South Puget Sound Community College (WA), 867
South Seattle Community College (WA), 867
South Suburban College of Cook County (IL), 331
South Texas College (TX), 810
South University
Columbia (SC), 766
Montgomery (AL), 145
Savannah (GA), 292
West Palm Beach (FL), 272
Southeast Arkansas College (AR), 167
Southeast Community College (NE), 524
Southeast Kentucky Community and Technical College (KY), 390
Southeast Missouri State University (MO), 508
Southeast Technical Institute (SD), 774
Southeastern Bible College (AL), 145
Southeastern College of the Assemblies of God *see* Southeastern University (FL)
Southeastern Community College (IA), 365
Southeastern Community College (NC), 630
Southeastern Illinois College (IL), 331
Southeastern Louisiana University (LA), 400
Southeastern Oklahoma State University (OK), 684
Southeastern Technical College (GA), 292
Southeastern University (FL), 272
Southern Adventist University (TN), 786
Southern Arkansas University (AR), 167
Southern Arkansas University Tech (AR), 167
Southern California Institute of Architecture (CA), 216
Southern Connecticut State University (CT), 245
Southern Illinois University Carbondale (IL), 331
Southern Illinois University Edwardsville (IL), 332
Southern Maine Community College (ME), 406
Southern Methodist University (TX), 811
Southern New Hampshire University (NH), 535
Southern Oregon University (OR), 694
Southern Polytechnic State University (GA), 292
Southern State Community College (OH), 669
Southern Union State Community College (AL), 145
Southern University and Agricultural and Mechanical College (LA), 400
Southern University at New Orleans (LA), 400
Southern Utah University (UT), 830
Southern Vermont College (VT), 836
Southern Virginia University (VA), 852
Southern West Virginia Community and Technical College (WV), 877
Southside Virginia Community College (VA), 852
Southwest Baptist University (MO), 508
Southwest Florida College (FL), 272
Southwest Georgia Technical College (GA), 292
Southwest Minnesota State University (MN), 486
Southwest Mississippi Community College (MS), 493
Southwest Tennessee Community College (TN), 786
Southwest Texas Junior College (TX), 811
Southwest University of Visual Arts (AZ), 158
Southwest University of Visual Arts (NM), 554
Southwest Virginia Community College (VA), 852
Southwest Wisconsin Technical College (WI), 891
Southwestern Adventist University (TX), 811
Southwestern Assemblies of God University (TX), 811
Southwestern Christian College (TX), 812
Southwestern Christian University (OK), 684
Southwestern College *see* Arizona Christian University (AZ)
Southwestern College (CA), 217
Southwestern College (KS), 377
Southwestern College: Florence *see* Lincoln College of Technology: Florence (KY)
Southwestern College: Tri-County *see* Lincoln College of Technology: Tri-County (OH)
Southwestern Community College (IA), 365
Southwestern Community College (NC), 630
Southwestern Illinois College (IL), 332
Southwestern Indian Polytechnic Institute (NM), 554
Southwestern Michigan College (MI), 463
Southwestern Oklahoma State University (OK), 684
Southwestern Oregon Community College (OR), 694
Southwestern University (TX), 812
Spalding University (KY), 390
Spartan College of Aeronautics and Technology (OK), 684
Spartanburg Community College (SC), 766
Spartanburg Methodist College (SC), 767
Spelman College (GA), 292
Spencerian College (KY), 390
Spencerian College Lexington (KY), 390
Spoon River College (IL), 332
Spring Arbor University (MI), 463
Spring Hill College (AL), 145
Springfield College (MA), 440
Springfield Technical Community College (MA), 440
St. Ambrose University (IA), 364
St. Andrews University (NC), 628
St. Augustine's University (NC), 628
St. Catharine College (KY), 389
St. Catherine University (MN), 484
St. Charles Borromeo Seminary - Overbrook (PA), 732
St. Charles Community College (MO), 507
St. Clair County Community College (MI), 462
St. Cloud Technical and Community College (MN), 484
St. Edward's University (TX), 808
St. Elizabeth College of Nursing (NY), 591
St. Francis College (NY), 592
St. Francis Medical Center College of Nursing (IL), 329
St. Francis University (PA), 732
St. Gregory's University (OK), 683
St. John Fisher College (NY), 592
St. John's College (IL), 330
St. John's College (MD), 416
St. John's College (NM), 553
St. John's University (MN), 484
St. John's University (NY), 592
St. Joseph Seminary College (LA), 399
St. Joseph's College New York Suffolk Campus (NY), 592
St. Joseph's College, New York (NY), 593
St. Joseph's College of Nursing (NY), 593
St. Lawrence University (NY), 593
St. Louis Christian College (MO), 507
St. Luke's College (IA), 364
St. Luke's College (MO), 508
St. Mary's College of California (CA), 210
St. Mary's College of Maryland (MD), 417
St. Mary's University (TX), 809
St. Mary's University of Minnesota (MN), 485
St. Mary-of-the-Woods College (IN), 350
St. Norbert College (WI), 890
St. Olaf College (MN), 485
St. Paul College (MN), 485
St. Paul's College (VA), 851
St. Petersburg College (FL), 271
St. Philip's College (TX), 809
St. Thomas Aquinas College (NY), 594
St. Vincent College (PA), 733
Stanford University (CA), 217
Stanly Community College (NC), 630
Stark State College of Technology (OH), 669
State College of Florida, Manatee-Sarasota (FL), 272
State Fair Community College (MO), 508
Stautzenberger College (OH), 669
Stautzenberger College Brecksville (OH), 669
Stephen F. Austin State University (TX), 812
Stephens College (MO), 509
Sterling College (KS), 378
Sterling College (VT), 837
Stetson University (FL), 273
Stevens Institute of Business & Arts (MO), 509
Stevens Institute of Technology (NJ), 547
Stevens-Henager College Boise (ID), 302
Stevenson University (MD), 417
Stillman College (AL), 146
Stone Child College (MT), 517
Stonehill College (MA), 440
Stratford University Falls Church (VA), 853
Suffolk County Community College (NY), 595
Suffolk University (MA), 441
Sul Ross State University (TX), 813
Sullivan College of Technology and Design (KY), 391
Sullivan County Community College (NY), 595
Sullivan University (KY), 391
SUNY College at Brockport (NY), 596
SUNY College at Buffalo (NY), 596
SUNY College at Cortland (NY), 596
SUNY College at Fredonia (NY), 596
SUNY College at Geneseo (NY), 597
SUNY College at New Paltz (NY), 597
SUNY College at Old Westbury (NY), 597
SUNY College at Oneonta (NY), 598
SUNY College at Oswego (NY), 598
SUNY College at Plattsburgh (NY), 598
SUNY College at Potsdam (NY), 598
SUNY College at Purchase (NY), 599

SUNY College of Agriculture and Technology at Cobleskill (NY), 599
SUNY College of Agriculture and Technology at Morrisville (NY), 599
SUNY College of Environmental Science and Forestry (NY), 600
SUNY College of Technology at Alfred (NY), 600
SUNY College of Technology at Canton (NY), 600
SUNY College of Technology at Delhi (NY), 601
SUNY Downstate Medical Center (NY), 601
SUNY Empire State College (NY), 601
SUNY Farmingdale State College (NY), 601
SUNY Institute of Technology at Utica/Rome (NY), 602
SUNY Maritime College (NY), 602
SUNY University at Albany (NY), 602
SUNY University at Binghamton (NY), 602
SUNY University at Buffalo (NY), 603
SUNY University at Stony Brook (NY), 603
SUNY Upstate Medical University (NY), 603
Surry Community College (NC), 631
Susquehanna University (PA), 734
Sussex County Community College (NJ), 547
Swarthmore College (PA), 735
Swedish Institute (NY), 604
Sweet Briar College (VA), 853
Syracuse University (NY), 604
Tabor College (KS), 378
Tacoma Community College (WA), 868
Taft College (CA), 217
Talladega College (AL), 146
Tallahassee Community College (FL), 273
Talmudical Yeshiva of Philadelphia (PA), 735
Tarleton State University (TX), 813
Tarrant County College (TX), 813
Taylor Business Institute (IL), 333
Taylor University (IN), 350
Technical Career Institutes (NY), 604
Technical College of the Lowcountry (SC), 767
Teikyo Loretto Heights University *see* Colorado Heights University (CO)
Temple College (TX), 813
Temple University (PA), 735
Tennessee State University (TN), 786
Tennessee Technological University (TN), 786
Tennessee Wesleyan College (TN), 787
Terra State Community College (OH), 669
Texarkana College (TX), 814
Texas A&M International University (TX), 814
Texas A&M University (TX), 814
Texas A&M University-Baylor College of Dentistry (TX), 814
Texas A&M University-Commerce (TX), 815
Texas A&M University-Corpus Christi (TX), 815
Texas A&M University-Galveston (TX), 815
Texas A&M University-Kingsville (TX), 815
Texas A&M University-Texarkana (TX), 816
Texas Christian University (TX), 816
Texas College (TX), 816
Texas County Technical Institute (MO), 509
Texas Lutheran University (TX), 816
Texas Southern University (TX), 817
Texas State Technical College
  Harlingen (TX), 817
  Waco (TX), 817
  West Texas (TX), 817
Texas State Technical College: Sweetwater *see* Texas State Technical College: West Texas (TX)
Texas State University San Marcos (TX), 817
Texas Tech University (TX), 818
Texas Tech University Health Sciences Center (TX), 818
Texas Wesleyan University (TX), 818
Texas Woman's University (TX), 819
Thaddeus Stevens College of Technology (PA), 736
The Citadel (SC), 759
The College of New Jersey (NJ), 538
The College of Saints John Fisher & Thomas More (TX), 794
The King's College (NY), 579
The King's College and Seminary *see* The King's University (CA)
The King's University (CA), 195
The Master's College (CA), 200
The Sage Colleges (NY), 591
Thiel College (PA), 736
Thomas Aquinas College (CA), 217
Thomas College (ME), 406
Thomas Edison State College (NJ), 547
Thomas Jefferson University College of Health Professions (PA), 736
Thomas More College (KY), 391
Thomas More College of Liberal Arts (NH), 535
Thomas Nelson Community College (VA), 853
Thomas University (GA), 293
Thompson Institute *see* Kaplan Career Institute: Harrisburg (PA)
Three Rivers Community College (CT), 246
Three Rivers Community College (MO), 509
Tidewater Community College (VA), 853
Tiffin University (OH), 670
Toccoa Falls College (GA), 293
Tohono O'odham Community College (AZ), 158
Tompkins Cortland Community College (NY), 604
Tougaloo College (MS), 494
Towson University (MD), 418
Transylvania University (KY), 391
Treasure Valley Community College (OR), 695
Trevecca Nazarene University (TN), 787
Triangle Tech
  Bethlehem (PA), 736
  DuBois (PA), 737
  Erie (PA), 737
  Greensburg (PA), 737
  Pittsburgh (PA), 737
  Sunbury (PA), 737
Tri-County Community College (NC), 631
Tri-County Technical College (SC), 767
Trident Technical College (SC), 767
Trident University International (CA), 218
Trine University (IN), 351
Trinidad State Junior College (CO), 237
Trinity Bible College (ND), 640
Trinity Christian College (IL), 333
Trinity College (CT), 246
Trinity College of Florida (FL), 273
Trinity College of Nursing & Health Sciences (IL), 333
Trinity International University (IL), 333
Trinity Lutheran College (WA), 868
Trinity University (TX), 819
Trinity Valley Community College (TX), 819
Trinity Washington University (DC), 253
Tri-State University *see* Trine University (IN)
Triton College (IL), 334
Trocaire College (NY), 605
Troy University (AL), 146
Truckee Meadows Community College (NV), 528
Truett-McConnell College (GA), 293
Truman State University (MO), 510
Trumbull Business College (OH), 670
Tufts University (MA), 441
TUI University *see* Trident University International (CA)
Tulane University (LA), 400
Tulsa Community College (OK), 685
Tulsa Welding School (OK), 685
Tunxis Community College (CT), 246
Turabo University (PR), 749
Tusculum College (TN), 787
Tuskegee University (AL), 146
Tyler Junior College (TX), 819
Ulster County Community College (NY), 605
Umpqua Community College (OR), 695
Union College (KY), 392
Union College (NE), 525
Union College (NY), 605
Union County College (NJ), 547
Union Institute & University (OH), 670
Union University (TN), 787
United States Air Force Academy (CO), 237
United States Coast Guard Academy (CT), 246
United States Merchant Marine Academy (NY), 605
United States Military Academy (NY), 606
United States Naval Academy (MD), 418
United Tribes Technical College (ND), 640
Unity College (ME), 406
Universal Technology College of Puerto Rico (PR), 750
Universidad Adventista de las Antillas (PR), 750
Universidad del Este (PR), 750
Universidad Metropolitana (PR), 750
Universidad Pentecostal Mizpa (PR), 751
Universidad Politecnica de Puerto Rico (PR), 751
University College of San Juan (PR), 751
University of Advancing Technology (AZ), 159
University of Akron (OH), 670
University of Akron Wayne College (OH), 671
University of Alabama (AL), 147
University of Alabama at Birmingham (AL), 147
University of Alabama in Huntsville (AL), 147
University of Alaska Anchorage (AK), 150
University of Alaska Fairbanks (AK), 151
University of Alaska Southeast (AK), 151
University of Arizona (AZ), 159
University of Arkansas (AR), 167
University of Arkansas
  Community College at Batesville (AR), 169
  Community College at Hope (AR), 169
  Community College at Morrilton (AR), 170
University of Arkansas at Fort Smith (AR), 168
University of Arkansas at Little Rock (AR), 168
University of Arkansas at Monticello (AR), 168
University of Arkansas at Pine Bluff (AR), 168
University of Arkansas for Medical Sciences (AR), 169
University of Baltimore (MD), 418
University of Bridgeport (CT), 247
University of California
  Berkeley (CA), 218
  Davis (CA), 218
  Irvine (CA), 218
  Los Angeles (CA), 219
  Merced (CA), 219
  Riverside (CA), 219
  San Diego (CA), 219
  Santa Barbara (CA), 220
  Santa Cruz (CA), 220
University of Central Arkansas (AR), 170
University of Central Florida (FL), 273
University of Central Missouri (MO), 510
University of Central Oklahoma (OK), 685
University of Charleston (WV), 877
University of Chicago (IL), 334
University of Cincinnati (OH), 671
University of Cincinnati
  Clermont College (OH), 671
  Raymond Walters College (OH), 671
University of Colorado Boulder (CO), 237
University of Colorado Colorado Springs (CO), 238
University of Colorado Denver (CO), 238
University of Connecticut (CT), 247
University of Dallas (TX), 820
University of Dayton (OH), 672
University of Delaware (DE), 250
University of Denver (CO), 238
University of Detroit Mercy (MI), 463
University of Dubuque (IA), 365
University of Evansville (IN), 351
University of Findlay (OH), 672
University of Florida (FL), 274
University of Georgia (GA), 293
University of Great Falls (MT), 517
University of Hartford (CT), 247
University of Hawaii
  Hawaii Community College (HI), 297
  Honolulu Community College (HI), 297
  Kapiolani Community College (HI), 298
  Kauai Community College (HI), 298
  Leeward Community College (HI), 298
  Maui College (HI), 298
  West Oahu (HI), 299
  Windward Community College (HI), 299
University of Hawaii at Hilo (HI), 297
University of Hawaii at Manoa (HI), 297
University of Houston (TX), 820
University of Houston-Clear Lake (TX), 820
University of Houston-Downtown (TX), 820
University of Houston-Victoria (TX), 821
University of Idaho (ID), 303
University of Illinois Springfield (IL), 335
University of Illinois at Chicago (IL), 334
University of Illinois at Urbana-Champaign (IL), 334
University of Indianapolis (IN), 351
University of Iowa (IA), 366
University of Judaism *see* American Jewish University (CA)
University of Kansas (KS), 378

University of Kansas Medical Center (KS), 379
University of Kentucky (KY), 392
University of La Verne (CA), 220
University of Louisiana at Lafayette (LA), 401
University of Louisiana at Monroe (LA), 401
University of Louisville (KY), 392
University of Maine (ME), 406
University of Maine at Augusta (ME), 407
University of Maine at Farmington (ME), 407
University of Maine at Fort Kent (ME), 407
University of Maine at Machias (ME), 408
University of Maine at Presque Isle (ME), 408
University of Management and Technology (VA), 854
University of Mary (ND), 640
University of Mary Hardin-Baylor (TX), 821
University of Mary Washington (VA), 854
University of Maryland
Baltimore (MD), 418
Baltimore County (MD), 418
College Park (MD), 419
Eastern Shore (MD), 419
University College (MD), 419
University of Massachusetts Amherst (MA), 441
University of Massachusetts Boston (MA), 441
University of Massachusetts Dartmouth (MA), 442
University of Massachusetts Lowell (MA), 442
University of Medicine and Dentistry of New Jersey
School of Health Related Professions (NJ), 547
School of Nursing (NJ), 548
University of Memphis (TN), 788
University of Miami (FL), 274
University of Michigan (MI), 464
University of Michigan
Dearborn (MI), 464
Flint (MI), 464
University of Minnesota
Crookston (MN), 486
Duluth (MN), 487
Morris (MN), 487
Rochester (MN), 487
Twin Cities (MN), 487
University of Mississippi (MS), 494
University of Mississippi Medical Center (MS), 494
University of Missouri
Columbia (MO), 510
Kansas City (MO), 511
St. Louis (MO), 511
University of Missouri: Rolla ***see*** Missouri University of Science and Technology (MO)
University of Mobile (AL), 148
University of Montana (MT), 517
University of Montana Western (MT), 518
University of Montana: Helena College of Technology ***see*** Helena College University of Montana (MT)
University of Montevallo (AL), 148
University of Mount Union (OH), 672
University of Nebraska - Kearney (NE), 525
University of Nebraska - Lincoln (NE), 525
University of Nebraska - Omaha (NE), 525
University of Nebraska Medical Center (NE), 526
University of Nevada
Las Vegas (NV), 529
Reno (NV), 529
University of New England (ME), 408
University of New Hampshire (NH), 535
University of New Hampshire at Manchester (NH), 535
University of New Haven (CT), 247
University of New Mexico (NM), 555
University of New Orleans (LA), 401
University of North Alabama (AL), 148
University of North Carolina at Asheville (NC), 631
University of North Carolina at Chapel Hill (NC), 631
University of North Carolina at Charlotte (NC), 632
University of North Carolina at Greensboro (NC), 632
University of North Carolina at Pembroke (NC), 632
University of North Carolina at Wilmington (NC), 633
University of North Carolina School of the Arts (NC), 633
University of North Dakota (ND), 641
University of North Florida (FL), 274
University of North Georgia (GA), 294
University of North Texas (TX), 821
University of Northern Colorado (CO), 239
University of Northern Iowa (IA), 366
University of Northwestern Ohio (OH), 673
University of Notre Dame (IN), 352
University of Oklahoma (OK), 685
University of Oregon (OR), 695
University of Pennsylvania (PA), 738
University of Phoenix Phoenix-Hohokam (AZ), 159
University of Pikeville (KY), 393
University of Pittsburgh (PA), 738
University of Pittsburgh at Bradford (PA), 738
University of Pittsburgh at Greensburg (PA), 739
University of Pittsburgh at Johnstown (PA), 739
University of Pittsburgh at Titusville (PA), 739
University of Portland (OR), 695
University of Puerto Rico
Aguadilla (PR), 751
Arecibo (PR), 751
Carolina Regional College (PR), 752
Cayey University College (PR), 752
Humacao (PR), 752
Mayaguez (PR), 752
Medical Sciences (PR), 753
Ponce (PR), 753
Rio Piedras (PR), 753
Utuado (PR), 753
University of Puget Sound (WA), 868
University of Redlands (CA), 221
University of Rhode Island (RI), 757
University of Richmond (VA), 854
University of Rio Grande (OH), 673
University of Rochester (NY), 606
University of Saint Joseph (CT), 248
University of San Diego (CA), 221
University of San Francisco (CA), 221
University of Science and Arts of Oklahoma (OK), 686
University of Scranton (PA), 740
University of Sioux Falls (SD), 774
University of South Alabama (AL), 149
University of South Carolina
Aiken (SC), 768
Beaufort (SC), 768
Columbia (SC), 768
Salkehatchie (SC), 768
Sumter (SC), 769
Union (SC), 769
Upstate (SC), 769
University of South Dakota (SD), 775
University of South Florida (FL), 275
University of Southern California (CA), 222
University of Southern Indiana (IN), 352
University of Southern Maine (ME), 408
University of Southern Mississippi (MS), 494
University of Southern Nevada ***see*** Roseman University of Health Sciences (NV)
University of St. Francis (IL), 335
University of St. Francis (IN), 352
University of St. Mary (KS), 379
University of St. Thomas (MN), 488
University of St. Thomas (TX), 821
University of Tampa (FL), 275
University of Tennessee
Chattanooga (TN), 788
Knoxville (TN), 788
Martin (TN), 789
University of Texas at Arlington (TX), 822
University of Texas at Austin (TX), 822
University of Texas at Brownsville - Texas Southmost College (TX), 822
University of Texas at Dallas (TX), 823
University of Texas at El Paso (TX), 823
University of Texas at San Antonio (TX), 823
University of Texas at Tyler (TX), 824
University of Texas Health Science Center at Houston (TX), 824
University of Texas Medical Branch at Galveston (TX), 824
University of Texas of the Permian Basin (TX), 824
University of Texas-Pan American (TX), 825
University of the Arts (PA), 740
University of the Cumberlands (KY), 393
University of the District of Columbia (DC), 253
University of the Incarnate Word (TX), 825
University of the Ozarks (AR), 170
University of the Pacific (CA), 222
University of the Sacred Heart (PR), 754
University of the Sciences in Philadelphia (PA), 740
University of the Southwest (NM), 555
University of the West (CA), 222
University of Toledo (OH), 673
University of Tulsa (OK), 686
University of Utah (UT), 830
University of Vermont (VT), 837
University of Virginia (VA), 854
University of Virginia's College at Wise (VA), 855
University of Washington (WA), 868
University of Washington Bothell (WA), 869
University of Washington Tacoma (WA), 869
University of West Alabama (AL), 149
University of West Florida (FL), 275
University of West Georgia (GA), 294
University of Wisconsin-Baraboo/Sauk County (WI), 891
University of Wisconsin-Barron County (WI), 891
University of Wisconsin-Eau Claire (WI), 891
University of Wisconsin-Fond du Lac (WI), 892
University of Wisconsin-Fox Valley (WI), 892
University of Wisconsin-Green Bay (WI), 892
University of Wisconsin-La Crosse (WI), 892
University of Wisconsin-Madison (WI), 893
University of Wisconsin-Manitowoc (WI), 893
University of Wisconsin-Marathon County (WI), 893
University of Wisconsin-Marinette (WI), 893
University of Wisconsin-Marshfield/Wood County (WI), 894
University of Wisconsin-Milwaukee (WI), 894
University of Wisconsin-Oshkosh (WI), 894
University of Wisconsin-Parkside (WI), 894
University of Wisconsin-Platteville (WI), 895
University of Wisconsin-Richland (WI), 895
University of Wisconsin-River Falls (WI), 895
University of Wisconsin-Rock County (WI), 895
University of Wisconsin-Sheboygan (WI), 896
University of Wisconsin-Stevens Point (WI), 896
University of Wisconsin-Stout (WI), 896
University of Wisconsin-Superior (WI), 896
University of Wisconsin-Washington County (WI), 897
University of Wisconsin-Waukesha (WI), 897
University of Wisconsin-Whitewater (WI), 897
University of Wyoming (WY), 900
Upper Iowa University (IA), 366
Urban College of Boston (MA), 442
Ursinus College (PA), 740
Ursuline College (OH), 673
Utah Career College ***see*** Broadview University: West Jordan (UT)
Utah State University (UT), 831
Utah Valley State College ***see*** Utah Valley University (UT)
Utah Valley University (UT), 831
Utica College (NY), 606
Valdosta State University (GA), 294
Valdosta Technical College ***see*** Wiregrass Georgia Technical College (GA)
Valencia College (FL), 275
Valencia Community College ***see*** Valencia College (FL)
Valley City State University (ND), 641
Valley College (WV), 877
Valley Forge Christian College (PA), 741
Valley Forge Military Academy and College (PA), 741
Valley Forge Military College ***see*** Valley Forge Military Academy and College (PA)
Valparaiso University (IN), 352
Vance-Granville Community College (NC), 633
Vanderbilt University (TN), 789
VanderCook College of Music (IL), 336
Vanguard University of Southern California (CA), 222
Vassar College (NY), 606
Vatterott College
Des Moines (IA), 367
Oklahoma City (OK), 686
St. Joseph (MO), 511
Vaughn College of Aeronautics and Technology (NY), 607
Ventura College (CA), 223
Vermilion Community College (MN), 488
Vermont Technical College (VT), 837
Vernon College (TX), 825
Vet Tech Institute (PA), 741
Vet Tech Institute of Houston (TX), 825
Victor Valley College (CA), 223
Villa Maria College of Buffalo (NY), 607
Villanova University (PA), 741

Vincennes University (IN), 353
Virginia College in Huntsville (AL), 149
Virginia Commonwealth University (VA), 855
Virginia Intermont College (VA), 855
Virginia Marti College of Art and Design (OH), 674
Virginia Military Institute (VA), 856
Virginia Polytechnic Institute and State University (VA), 856
Virginia State University (VA), 856
Virginia Union University (VA), 856
Virginia Wesleyan College (VA), 857
Virginia Western Community College (VA), 857
Vista Community College ***see*** Berkeley City College (CA)
Viterbo University (WI), 897
Volunteer State Community College (TN), 789
Voorhees College (SC), 769
Wabash College (IN), 353
Wade College (TX), 825
Wagner College (NY), 607
Wake Forest University (NC), 633
Wake Technical Community College (NC), 634
Walden University (MN), 488
Waldorf College (IA), 367
Walla Walla Community College (WA), 869
Walla Walla University (WA), 869
Wallace State Community College at Hanceville (AL), 149
Walsh College of Accountancy and Business Administration (MI), 464
Walsh University (OH), 674
Walters State Community College (TN), 789
Warner Pacific College (OR), 696
Warner Southern College ***see*** Warner University (FL)
Warner University (FL), 276
Warren County Community College (NJ), 548
Warren Wilson College (NC), 634
Wartburg College (IA), 367
Washburn University (KS), 379
Washington Adventist University (MD), 420
Washington & Jefferson College (PA), 742
Washington and Lee University (VA), 857
Washington College (MD), 420
Washington County Community College (ME), 409
Washington State University (WA), 870
Washington University in St. Louis (MO), 511
Watkins College of Art, Design & Film (TN), 790
Waubonsee Community College (IL), 336
Waukesha County Technical College (WI), 898
Wayland Baptist University (TX), 826
Wayne Community College (NC), 634
Wayne County Community College (MI), 465
Wayne State College (NE), 526
Wayne State University (MI), 465
Waynesburg University (PA), 742
Weatherford College (TX), 826
Webb Institute (NY), 607
Webber International University (FL), 276
Weber State University (UT), 831
Webster University (MO), 512
Welch College (TN), 790
Wellesley College (MA), 442
Wells College (NY), 608
Wenatchee Valley College (WA), 870
Wentworth Institute of Technology (MA), 443
Wesley College (DE), 250
Wesleyan College (GA), 295
Wesleyan University (CT), 248
West Chester University of Pennsylvania (PA), 742
West Coast University
  Dallas (TX), 826
  Los Angeles (CA), 223
  Ontario (CA), 223
  Orange County (CA), 223
West Georgia Technical College (GA), 295
West Hills College Coalinga (CA), 224
West Kentucky Community and Technical College (KY), 393
West Liberty State College ***see*** West Liberty University (WV)
West Liberty University (WV), 877
West Los Angeles College (CA), 224
West Shore Community College (MI), 465
West Suburban College of Nursing ***see*** Resurrection University (IL)
West Texas A&M University (TX), 826
West Valley College (CA), 224
West Virginia Junior College (WV), 877
West Virginia Junior College Bridgeport (WV), 878
West Virginia Northern Community College (WV), 878
West Virginia State Community and Technical College ***see*** Kanawha Valley Community and Technical College (WV)
West Virginia State University (WV), 878
West Virginia University (WV), 878
West Virginia University at Parkersburg (WV), 879
West Virginia University Institute of Technology (WV), 879
West Virginia Wesleyan College (WV), 879
Westark Community College ***see*** University of Arkansas at Fort Smith (AR)
Westchester Community College (NY), 608
Western Carolina University (NC), 635
Western Connecticut State University (CT), 248
Western Dakota Technical Institute (SD), 775
Western Governors University (UT), 832
Western Illinois University (IL), 336
Western International University (AZ), 159
Western Iowa Tech Community College (IA), 367
Western Kentucky University (KY), 393
Western Michigan University (MI), 465
Western Nebraska Community College (NE), 526
Western Nevada College (NV), 529
Western New England College ***see*** Western New England University (MA)
Western New England University (MA), 443
Western New Mexico University (NM), 555
Western Oklahoma State College (OK), 686
Western Oregon University (OR), 696
Western Piedmont Community College (NC), 635
Western School of Health and Business Careers: Monroeville ***see*** Sanford-Brown Institute: Monroeville (PA)
Western State College of Colorado ***see*** Western State Colorado University (CO)
Western State Colorado University (CO), 239
Western Technical College (TX), 827
Western Technical College (WI), 898
Western Texas College (TX), 827
Western Washington University (WA), 870
Western Wisconsin Technical College ***see*** Western Technical College (WI)
Western Wyoming Community College (WY), 900
Westfield State University (MA), 443
Westminster College (MO), 512
Westminster College (PA), 743
Westminster College (UT), 832
Westmont College (CA), 224
Westmoreland County Community College (PA), 743
Westwood College
  Denver North (CO), 239
  Denver South (CO), 239
Westwood College of Aviation Technology ***see*** Redstone College (CO)
Wharton County Junior College (TX), 827
Whatcom Community College (WA), 871
Wheaton College (IL), 336
Wheaton College (MA), 444
Wheeling Jesuit University (WV), 879
Wheelock College (MA), 444
White Mountains Community College (NH), 536
Whitman College (WA), 871
Whittier College (CA), 225
Whitworth University (WA), 871
Wichita State University (KS), 380
Widener University (PA), 743
Wilberforce University (OH), 674
Wiley College (TX), 827
Wilkes Community College (NC), 635
Wilkes University (PA), 743
Willamette University (OR), 696
William Jessup University (CA), 225
William Jewell College (MO), 512
William Paterson University of New Jersey (NJ), 548
William Peace University (NC), 635
William Penn University (IA), 368
William Rainey Harper College ***see*** Harper College (IL)
William Woods University (MO), 513
Williams Baptist College (AR), 170
Williams College (MA), 444
Williamsburg Technical College (SC), 770
Williamson Christian College (TN), 790
Williston State College (ND), 641
Wilmington College (OH), 674
Wilmington University (DE), 251
Wilson College (PA), 744
Wilson Community College (NC), 636
Wingate University (NC), 636
Winona State University (MN), 488
Winston-Salem Bible College ***see*** Carolina Christian College (NC)
Winston-Salem State University (NC), 636
Winthrop University (SC), 770
Wiregrass Georgia Technical College (GA), 295
Wisconsin Indianhead Technical College (WI), 898
Wisconsin Lutheran College (WI), 898
Wittenberg University (OH), 675
Wofford College (SC), 770
Woodbury University (CA), 225
Worcester Polytechnic Institute (MA), 444
Worcester State University (MA), 445
Wor-Wic Community College (MD), 420
Wright State University (OH), 675
Wright State University Lake Campus (OH), 675
WyoTech Laramie (WY), 901
Wytheville Community College (VA), 858
Xavier University (OH), 676
Xavier University of Louisiana (LA), 402
Yakima Valley Community College (WA), 871
Yale University (CT), 248
Yavapai College (AZ), 160
Yeshiva Ohr Elchonon Chabad/West Coast Talmudical Seminary (CA), 226
Yeshivat Mikdash Melech (NY), 608
York College (NE), 526
York College of Pennsylvania (PA), 744
York County Community College (ME), 409
York Technical College (SC), 770
Young Harris College (GA), 295
Youngstown State University (OH), 676
Yuba Community College District (CA), 226
Zane State College (OH), 676
Zion Bible College ***see*** Northpoint Bible College (MA)

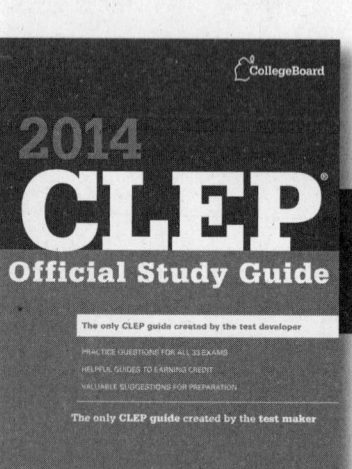

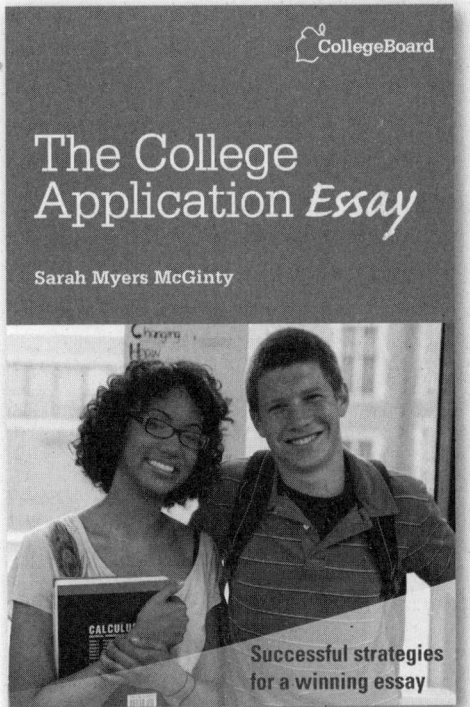

More College Planning Resources from the College Board

College Handbook 2014

The only guide listing all accredited universities, two-year and four-year colleges, and technical schools in the United States — more than 3,900 in total.

2,200 pages, paperback
ISBN: 978-1-4573-0018-9
$29.99

The Official SAT Study Guide™: Second Edition

The Official SAT Study Guide™ is the only book that features 10 official practice tests created by the test maker. The No. 1 best-selling guide is packed with valuable test-taking approaches and focused sets of practice questions — just like those on the actual SAT® — to help students get ready for the test.

998 pages, trade paper
ISBN: 978-0-87447-852-5
$21.99

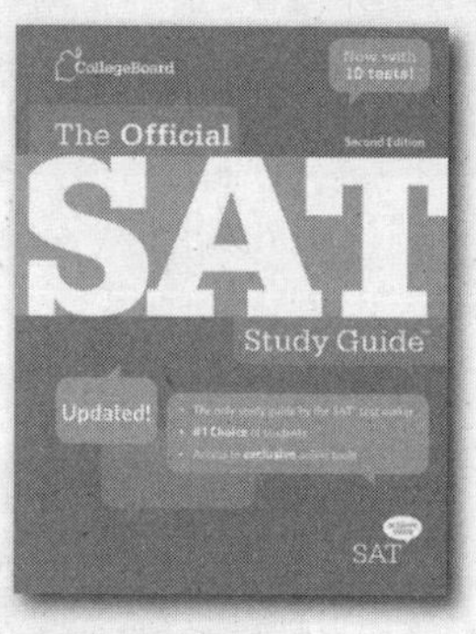

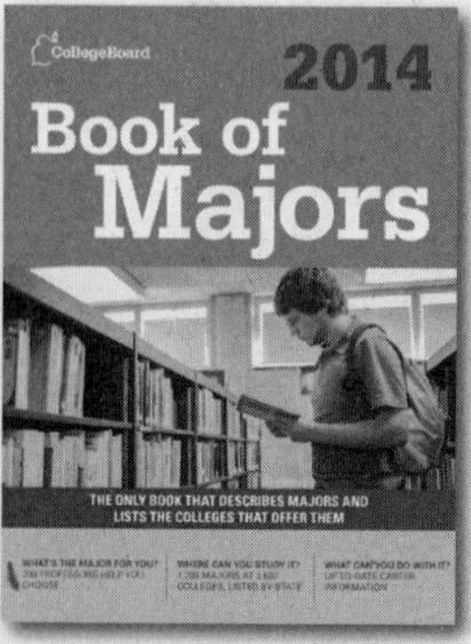

Book of Majors 2014

Explore in-depth descriptions of 200 majors, and see where over 1,100 majors are offered at colleges nationwide.

1,350 pages, paperback
ISBN: 978-1-4573-0022-6
$27.99

Get It Together for College, 2nd Edition

Take advantage of expert tips that help students stay on top of the college admission process.

240 pages, paperback
ISBN: 978-0-87447-974-4
$15.99

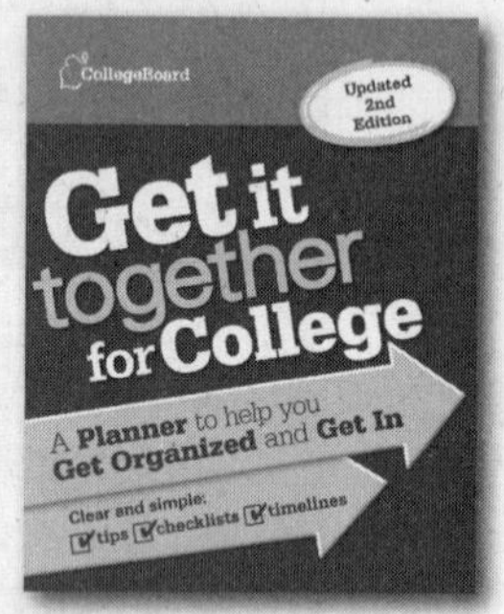

PAYING FOR COLLEGE

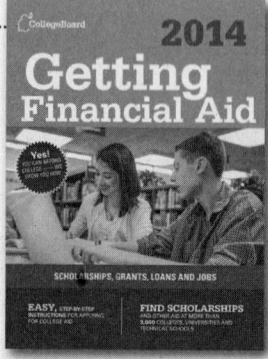

Getting Financial Aid 2014

A must-have book in today's economy, this is the perfect resource for families managing the high cost of college. This easy step-by-step guide shows why, when and how to apply for financial aid.

1,050 pages, paperback
978-1-4573-0019-6
$22.99

Scholarship Handbook 2014

The most complete and comprehensive guide to help families tap into the more than 1.7 million scholarships, internships and loans available to students each year.

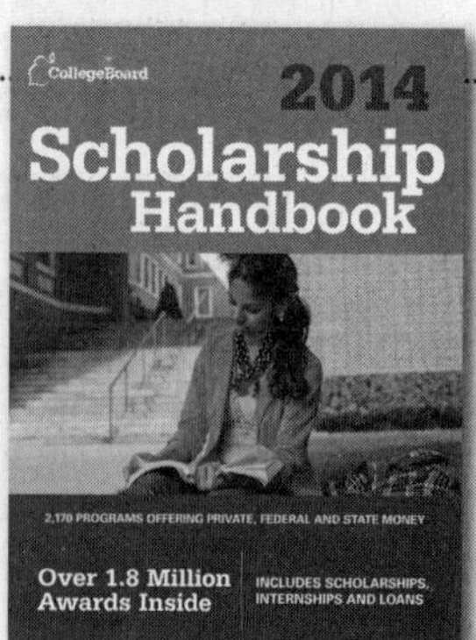

624 pages, paperback
ISBN: 978-1-4573-0020-2
$29.99

Available wherever books are sold. Distributed by Macmillan.

Visit the College Board on the Web: www.collegeboard.org.

13b-7693

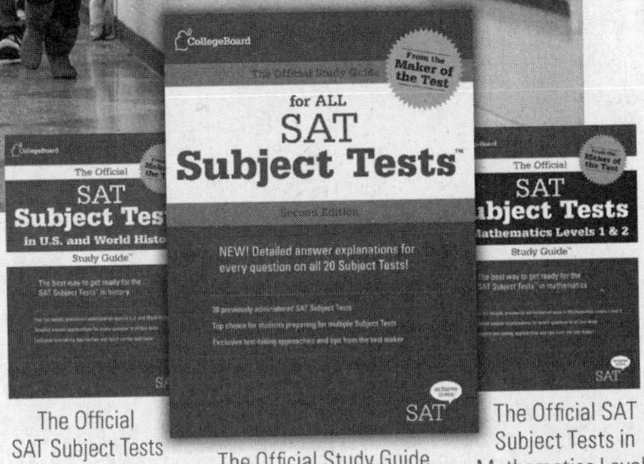